ANAGRAM
FINDER

EMILE

EEILM

jorse

egors

ADVERS

ADE RSTV

MURDER

AEDMRRU

ATOLL

ALLOT

ANAGRAM
FINDER

John Daintith

First published in 1993
by Bloomsbury Publishing Limited
2 Soho Square, London W1V 5DE

The moral right of the author has been asserted.

Copyright © Bloomsbury Publishing Ltd 1993.
This edition produced exclusively for Bookmart Limited 1993.

A copy of the CIP entry for this book is available from the British Library.

ISBN 0 7475 1586 7

Designed by ArtBar, London
Typeset by Market House Books Ltd, Aylesbury
Printed in Britain by Clays Ltd, St Ives plc

FOREWORD

This dictionary is intended to help crossword-puzzle solvers and other word-game enthusiasts to find anagrams quickly and easily.

It consists of lists of English words and phrases arranged into two-letter words, three-letter words, etc., up to words and phrases that have fifteen or more letters. Each word or phrase has been preceded by an anagram key, composed by taking the letters of the word or phrase and arranging them in alphabetical order. The entries themselves are also arranged in alphabetical order of anagram key.

The use of the book can best be illustrated by a simple example. Take the clue 'Ronny can get mixed up and fired'. The answer is an eight-letter word. The words 'mixed up' in the clue suggest that the answer may be an anagram of 'Ronny can'. Taking the letters of Ronny can and putting them in alphabetical order gives the key ACNNNORY. In the list of eight-letter words, this gives the correct solution – CANNONRY.

We have tried to include as many words and phrases as space permits, and we hope that the book will prove useful to everyone interested in crosswords.

JD
JANUARY, 1993

AB AB	CO CO	FI IF	JO JO	OW OW
AC AC	CP PC	FM FM	JP JP	OX OX
AD AD, DA	CQ QC	FO OF	KO KO	PR PR
AF FA	CV CV, VC	GI GI	KU UK	PS PS
AH AH, HA	CW WC	GO GO	LO LO	PT PT
AI AI	CY CY	GP GP	LP LP	PU UP
AL AL, LA	DE ED	GS GS	MO MO	PX PX
AM AM, MA	DI ID	HI HI	MP MP, PM	QT QT
AN AN	DJ DJ	HM H'M	MR MR	SU US
AP PA	DO DO	HO HO, OH	MS MS	SV VS
AS AS	DV VD	HP PH	MU UM	TV TV
AT AT, TA	EH EH, HE	HQ HQ	MY MY	
BC CB	EM ME	HS SH	NO NO, ON	
BE BE	EP PE	IM MI	NU UN	
BO BO	ER ER, RE	IN IN	OP OP	
BY BY	EW WE	IP PI	OR OR	
CD CD	EX EX	IQ IQ	OS SO	
CK KC	EY YE	IT IT, TI	OT TO	

AAB BAA	ADN AND, DAN, DNA	AHN HAN	ANO ONA	BDI BID
AAD ADA	ADO ADO	AHP HAP	ANP NAP, PAN	BDO BOD
AAH AHA	ADP PAD	AHS ASH, HAS	ANR RAN, RNA	BDU BUD, DUB
AAL À LA	ADS ADS, SAD	AHT HAT	ANT ANT, NAT, TAN	BEE BEE
AAS ASA	ADU AUD	AHW HAW	ANU UNA	BEG BEG
AAV AVA	ADV ADV	AHY HAY	ANV VAN	BEL BEL
ABB BAB	ADW WAD	AIL AIL	ANW WAN	BEN BEN
ABC ABC, CAB	ADY DAY	AIM AIM, MIA	ANY ANY, NAY	BES SEB
ABD BAD, DAB	AEG AGE	AIN IAN, INA	AOP OAP	BET BET
ABE ABE, BEA	AEH HAE	AIP IPA, PIA	AOR OAR	BEW WEB
ABF FAB	AEL ALE, LEA	AIR AIR, IRA, RIA	AOV OVA	BEY BYE
ABG BAG, GAB	AEM MAE	AIS ISA	APP PAP	BFI FBI, FIB
ABH BAH	AEN ENA	AIT ITA	APR PAR, RAP	BFO FOB
ABJ JAB	AEP APE, PEA	AIV VIA	APS ASP, PAS, SAP, SPA	BGI BIG
ABL LAB	AER EAR, ERA, RAE	AJM JAM	APT APT, PAT, PTA, TAP	BGO BOG, GOB
ABN BAN, NAB	AES SAE, SEA	AJN JAN	APW PAW	BGU BUG
ABO ABO, BOA	AET ATE, EAT, TEA	AJR JAR, RAJ	APY PAY, YAP	BHO HOB
ABR BAR, BRA, RAB	AEV EVA	AJW JAW	APZ ZAP	BHU HUB
ABT BAT, TAB	AEW AWE	AJY JAY	AQU QUA	BIJ JIB
ABY BAY	AEX AXE	AKO OAK	ART ART, RAT, TAR	BIL LIB
ACD CAD	AEY AYE, YEA	AKR ARK	ARW RAW, WAR	BIN BIN, NIB
ACE ACE	AFG FAG	AKS ASK	ARY RAY	BIR RIB
ACI CAI, CIA	AFL ALF	AKU AUK	ASS ASS	BIT BIT
ACM CAM, MAC	AFN FAN	AKY KAY, YAK	AST SAT	BJO JOB
ACN CAN	AFO OAF	AKZ ZAK	ASW SAW	BLO LOB
ACP CAP, CPA	AFR FAR, RAF	ALL ALL	ASY SAY	BMO MOB
ACR ARC, CAR	AFT AFT, FAT	ALN LAN	ATT TAT	BMU BUM
ACS SAC	AFX FAX	ALP LAP, PAL	ATV VAT	BNO NOB
ACT ACT, CAT	AFY FAY	ALS SAL	ATW WAT	BNU BUN, NUB
ACV VAC	AGG GAG	ALV VAL	ATX TAX	BOO BOO
ACW CAW	AGH HAG	ALW AWL, LAW, WAL	AWX WAX	BOP BOP
ADD ADD, DAD	AGJ JAG	ALX LAX	AWY WAY, YAW	BOR ORB, ROB
ADE EDA	AGL GAL, LAG	ALY LAY	BBC BBC	BOS SOB
ADF FAD	AGM AGM, MAG	AMM MAM	BBE EBB	BOW BOW
ADG GAD	AGN NAG	AMN MAN	BBI BIB	BOX BOX
ADH HAD	AGO AGO	AMP AMP, MAP, PAM	BBO BOB	BOY BOY, YOB
ADI AID, DAI, IDA	AGP GAP	AMR ARM, MAR, RAM	BBU BUB	BPU PUB
ADJ ADJ	AGR RAG	AMS MAS, SAM	BCO COB	BRU BUR, RUB
ADL LAD	AGS GAS, SAG	AMT MAT, TAM	BCU CUB	BSU BUS, SUB
ADM DAM, MAD	AGT TAG	AMW MAW	BDE BED, DEB	BTU BUT, TUB
	AGW WAG	AMX MAX		BUY BUY
	AGY GAY	AMY AMY, MAY, YAM		CDI CID
	AHH HAH	ANN ANN, NAN		CDL LCD
	AHL HAL			CDN CND
	AHM HAM			

2

CDO COD, DOC	DEH HE'D	DOU DUO	EHS HE'S, SHE	ERU RUE
CDS CDS	DEI DIE	DPS SDP	EHT HET, THE	ERV REV
CDU CUD	DEJ JED	DPU PUD	EHU HUE	ERX REX
CEE EEC	DEL DEL, LED	DRY DRY	EHW HEW	ERY RYE
CEG ECG, GCE	DEM DEM	DST DT'S, STD	EHX HEX	EST SET
CEI ICE	DEN DEN, END, NED	DSY SYD	EHY HEY	ESU SUE, USE
CES CSE, SEC	DEO DOE, ODE	DUV VDU	EIK IKE	ESW SEW
CET ECT, ETC	DEP DEP	EEF FEE	EIL ELI, LEI, LIE	ESX SEX
CEU CUE	DER RED	EEG GEE	EIP PIE	ESY YES
CGO COG	DES DES	EEK EEK	EIR IRE	ETV VET
CHI HIC	DET TED	EEL EEL, LEE	EIT TIE	ETW WET
CIN INC	DEU DUE	EEN NÉE	EIV VIE	ETX TEX
CIS CIS, SIC	DEW DEW, WED	EEP PEE	EJM JEM	ETY YET
CIT TIC	DEY DYE	EER ERE	EJO JOE	EVX VEX
CIV VIC	DEZ ZED	EES SEE	EJT JET	EWY YEW
CIY ICY	DGI DIG	EET TEE	EJW JEW	FFO OFF
CLM LCM	DGO DOG, GOD	EEV EVE	EKL ELK	FGI FIG
CLO COL	DGP GDP	EEW EWE, WEE	EKN KEN	FGO FOG
CLP PLC	DGU DUG	EEY EYE	EKY KEY	FGU FUG
CMS MSC	DHI HID	EFF EFF	ELM ELM, MEL	FHU UHF
CMU CUM	DHO DOH, HOD	EFI FIE	ELO LEO	FHV VHF
CMW CWM	DHP PHD	EFL ELF	ELT ELT, LET	FIN FIN
CNO CON, NCO	DIK KID	EFN FEN	ELW LEW	FIR FIR
COO COO	DIL LID	EFO FOE	EMN MEN	FIS IFS
COP COP	DIM DIM, MID	EFR REF	EMT MET	FIT FIT
COR ROC	DIN DIN	EFW FEW	EMU EMU	FIX FIX
COS COS	DIP DIP	EFY FEY	EMW MEW	FLU FLU
COT COT	DIR RID	EFZ FEZ	ENO EON, ONE	FLY FLY
COW COW	DIS IDS, SDI, SID	EGG EGG	ENP PEN	FNU FUN
COX COX	DIU IUD	EGK EKG, KEG	ENT NET, TEN	FOO OOF
COY COY	DIY DIY, YID	EGL GEL, LEG	ENW NEW	FOP FOP
CPS PCS	DJS DJS	EGM GEM, MEG	ENY NYE, YEN	FOR FOR, FRO
CPU CPU, CUP	DLO OLD	EGN GEN	ENZ ZEN	FOT OFT
CPV PVC	DLS LSD	EGO EGO	EOR ORE, O'ER, ROE	FOU UFO
CPW WPC	DMO MOD	EGP PEG	EOT TOE	FOX FOX
CQS QCS	DMU MUD	EGR ERG, REG	EOW OWE, WOE	FRU FUR
CRU CUR	DNO DON, NOD	EGT GET	EOZ ZOE	FRY FRY
CRV VCR	DNU DUN	EGV VEG	EPP PEP	GGI GIG
CRY CRY	DOO ODO	EHH HEH	EPR PER, REP	GHO HOG
CSV CVS, VCS	DOP POD	EHI HIE	EPS ESP	GHU HUG, UGH
CTU CUT, TUC	DOR ROD	EHL HEL	EPT PET	GIJ JIG
DDI DID	DOS DOS, SOD	EHM HEM	EPW PEW	GIL GIL
DDO ODD	DOT DOT, TOD	EHN HEN	EQS ESQ	GIN GIN
DDT DDT		EHO HOE	ERR ERR	GIP PIG
DDU DUD		EHP HEP		GIR RIG
DEE DEE		EHR HER		GIS GI'S
DEF FED				GIW WIG
				GJO JOG
				GJU JUG
				GLO LOG

GLU LUG	HOW HOW, WHO	IOU IOU	LUV LUV	OPW POW, WOP
GMU GUM, MUG	HOY HOY	IOV IVO	MMO MOM	OPX POX
GMY GYM	HPS PHS	IPP PIP	MMU MUM	ORS ROS
GNP GNP	HQS HQS	IPR RIP	MOO MOO	ORT ROT, TOR
GNU GNU, GUN	HSY SHY	IPS PIS, SIP	MOP MOP	ORU OUR
GOO GOO	HTU HUT	IPT PIT, TIP	MOR ROM	ORW ROW
GOP GOP	HTY THY	IPV VIP	MOS MOS	ORY ROY
GOT GOT, TOG	HUW HUW	IPX PIX	MOT MOT, TOM	OSS SOS
GOW WOG	HWY WHY	IPZ ZIP	MOW MOW	OST SOT
GPS GPS	IJM JIM	IQS IQS	MPS MPS, PMS	OSU SOU
GPU PUG	IKL ILK	IRS SIR	MRS MRS	OSW SOW
GPY GYP	IKM KIM	ISS SIS	MRU RUM	OSX SOX
GRU RUG	IKN INK, KIN	IST ITS, SIT	MSU SUM	OSY SOY
GSU GUS	IKP KIP	ISX SIX	NNU NUN	OTT TOT
GTU GUT, TUG	IKR IRK	ITT TIT	NOR NOR, RON	OTU OUT
GUV GUV	IKS SKI	ITV ITV	NOS SON	OTW TOW, TWO, WOT
GUY GUY	IKT KIT	ITW WIT	NOT NOT, TON	OTY TOY
HHU HUH	ILL ILL	IVV VIV	NOW NOW, OWN, WON	OUY YOU
HIM HIM	ILN NIL	IVY IVY	NPU PUN	OVW VOW
HIN HIN	ILO OIL	IVZ VIZ	NRU RUN, URN	OWW WOW
HIP HIP	ILP LIP	JNO JON	NSU SUN	PPS PPS
HIS HIS, HSI	ILT LIT	JOT JOT	NTT TNT	PPU PUP
HIT HIT	ILZ LIZ	JOY JOY	NTU NUT	PRU PRU
HMO HOM, OHM	IMP IMP	JPS JPS	OOT TOO	PRY PRY
HMU HUM	IMR RIM	JTU JUT	OOW WOO	PSU PUS, SUP
HNS NHS	IMS ISM, SIM	KOW WOK	OOZ ZOO	PSY SPY
HNT NTH	IMT TIM	KSY SKY	OPP POP	PTU PUT
HNU HUN	IMV VIM	LNY LYN	OPR PRO	PXY PYX
HOO HOO, OHO	IMX MIX	LOO LOO	OPS OPS, SOP	RTU RUT
HOP HOP	INN INN ·	LOP LOP	OPT OPT, POT, PTO, TOP	RTY TRY
HOS SOH	INO ION	LOS SOL		RWY WRY
HOT HOT	INP NIP, PIN	LOT LOT		STV TVS
	INS SIN	LOU LOU		STY STY
	INT NIT, TIN	LOW LOW, OWL		TTU TUT
	INV VIN	LOX LOX		
	INW WIN	LPS LPS		
	INX NIX	LPY PLY		
	INY YIN	LSY SLY		

AABR ARAB
AABS BAAS
AACR CARA
AADH ADAH
AADL ALDA
AADM ADAM
AADN DANA, NADA
AADT DATA
AAER AREA
AAFH HAAF
AAFR AFAR, AFRA
AAGG GAGA
AAGL GALA
AAGR AGRA, RAGA
AAGS SAGA
AAGZ GAZA
AAHH HA-HA
AAHM HAMA
AAHR HAAR
AAHS HASA
AAHY AYAH
AAIR ARIA
AAIS ASIA
AAJR AJAR
AAKR KARA
AALM ALMA, LAMA
AALN ALAN, ANAL, LANA
AALS ALAS
AALV ALVA, LAVA
AAMM MAMA, MA'AM
AAMR MARA
AAMY MAYA
AANN ANNA
AANS NASA, SAN'A
AANY ANYA
AANZ ZANA
AAPP PAPA
AAQU AQUA
AARS SARA
AART TARA
AARU AURA
AARZ ZARA
AATT TA-TA
AAWY AWAY
ABBE BABE
ABBL BLAB
ABBR BARB
ABBS BABS
ABBU BABU
ABBY ABBY, BABY
ABCK BACK
ABCR CRAB
ABCS ABCS, CABS, SCAB

ABCU CUBA
ABDE ABED, BADE, BEAD
ABDL BALD
ABDN BAND
ABDR BARD, BRAD, DRAB
ABDS DABS
ABDU BAUD, DAUB
ABDW BAWD
ABEK BAKE, BEAK
ABEL ABEL, ABLE, BALE, ELBA
ABEM BEAM
ABEN BANE, BEAN
ABER BARE, BEAR, BRAE
ABES BASE
ABET ABET, BEAT, BETA
ABEU AUBE, BEAU
ABFL FLAB
ABGI GABI
ABGN BANG
ABGR BRAG, GARB, GRAB
ABGS BAGS
ABGY GABY
ABHL BLAH
ABHS BASH
ABHT BATH
ABHU HABU
ABIL BAIL, BALI
ABIM IAMB
ABIN BINA
ABIS BIAS
ABIT BAIT
ABJM JAMB
ABJS JABS
ABKL BALK
ABKN BANK
ABKR BARK
ABKS BASK
ABKU BAKU
ABLL BALL
ABLM BALM, LAMB
ABLS LABS, SLAB
ABLW BAWL
ABLY ABLY
ABMO AMBO
ABMR BRAM
ABNR BARN, BRAN
ABNS BANS
ABNU BUNA
ABOR BOAR
ABOS ABOS, BOAS
ABOT BOAT
ABOZ BOAZ

ABRS BARS, BRAS
ABRT BART, BRAT
ABRY BRAY
ABSS BASS
ABST BAST, BATS, STAB, TABS
ABSW SWAB
ABSY BAYS
ABTU ABUT, TUBA
ACCD AC/DC
ACCT ACCT
ACCU UCCA
ACDH CHAD
ACDI ACID
ACDL CLAD
ACDO CODA
ACDR CARD
ACDS CADS
ACEF CAFE, FACE
ACEG CAGE
ACEH ACHE, EACH
ACEK CAKE
ACEL ALEC, LACE
ACEM ACME, CAME, MACE
ACEN ACNE, CAEN, CANE
ACEP CAPE, PACE
ACER ACRE, CARE, RACE
ACES ACES, CASE
ACEV CAVE
ACFL CALF
ACFT FACT
ACGR CRAG
ACGS SCAG
ACHK HACK
ACHM MACH
ACHP CHAP
ACHR ARCH, CHAR
ACHS CASH, CHAS
ACHT CATH, CHAT
ACHY CHAY
ACIL CALI
ACIM MICA
ACIN INCA
ACIP PICA
ACIR RICA
ACJK JACK
ACKL CALK, LACK
ACKP PACK
ACKR RACK
ACKS CASK, SACK
ACKT TACK
ACKZ ZACK
ACLL CALL
ACLM CALM, CLAM

ACLN CLAN
ACLO COAL, COLA
ACLP CLAP
ACLR CARL
ACLT TALC
ACLU CAUL
ACLW CLAW
ACLX CALX
ACLY CLAY, LACY
ACMO COMA
ACMP CAMP
ACMR CRAM, MARC
ACMS CAMS, MACS, SCAM
ACNS CANS, SCAN
ACNT CANT
ACNY CYAN
ACOR CORA
ACOT COAT, TACO
ACOX COAX, COXA
ACPR CARP, CRAP
ACPS CAPS
ACPT PACT
ACRS ARCS, CARS, SCAR
ACRT CART
ACRY CARY, RACY
ACRZ CZAR
ACSS CASS, SACS
ACST ACTS, CAST, CATS, SCAT
ACSV VACS
ACSW CAWS
ACTT TACT
ACTY TACY
ACVY CAVY
ADDE DEAD
ADDO DADO
ADDS DADS
ADDY ADDY, DYAD, D-DAY
ADEF DEAF, FADE
ADEG AGED
ADEH HADE, HEAD
ADEI AIDE, IDEA
ADEJ JADE
ADEL ALED, DALE, DEAL, LADE, LEAD
ADEM DAME, EDAM, MADE, MEAD
ADEN ADEN, DANE, DEAN, EDNA
ADEP APED
ADER DARE, DEAR, READ
ADET DATE
ADEU AUDE

ADEV DAVE
ADEW AWED, WADE
ADEX AXED
ADEZ ADZE, DAZE
ADFF DAFF
ADFS FADS
ADFT DAFT
ADGL GLAD
ADGO DAGO, GOAD
ADGR DRAG, GARD
ADGY G'DAY
ADHJ HADJ
ADHK DHAK
ADHN HAND
ADHO DOHA, HOAD
ADHP DAPH
ADHR HARD
ADHS DASH, SHAD
ADIL DIAL, LAID
ADIM AMID, MAID
ADIP PAID
ADIR ARID, RAID
ADIS AIDS, DAIS, SAID
ADIV AVID, VIDA
ADIW WADI
ADKN DANK
ADKR DARK
ADLN LAND
ADLO ALDO, LOAD
ADLR LARD
ADLS LADS
ADLU DUAL, LAUD
ADLY LADY
ADMN DAMN
ADMP DAMP
ADMR DRAM
ADMS DAMS
ADMU MAUD
ADNR DARN, RAND
ADNS SAND
ADNW DAWN, WAND
ADNY ANDY
ADOR DORA, ROAD
ADOS SODA
ADOT TOAD
ADOW WOAD
ADPS PADS
ADQU QUAD
ADRT DART, DRAT, TRAD
ADRW DRAW, WARD
ADRY DRAY, YARD
ADSW WADS
ADSY DAYS

ADUV VAUD
ADVY DAVY
AEES EASE
AEFK FAKE
AEFL FLEA, LEAF
AEFM FAME
AEFR FARE, FEAR, RAFE
AEFS SAFE
AEFT FATE, FEAT
AEFY FAYE
AEFZ FAZE
AEGG GAGE
AEGL GALE
AEGM GAME
AEGP GAPE, PAGE
AEGR AREG, GEAR, RAGE
AEGS AGES, SAGE
AEGT GATE
AEGU AGUE
AEGV GAVE
AEGW WAGE
AEGY GAYE
AEGZ GAZE
AEHK HAKE
AEHL HALE, HEAL, HELA, LEAH
AEHM AHEM, HAEM, HAME
AEHP HEAP
AEHR HARE, HEAR, HERA, RHEA
AEHT HATE, HEAT, THEA
AEHV HAVE
AEHY YEAH
AEHZ HAZE
AEIL ELIA
AEIN AINE
AEIR EIRA
AEJK JAKE
AEJL JAEL
AEJN JANE, JEAN
AEJP JAPE
AEKL KALE, LAKE, LEAK
AEKM MAKE
AEKN KANE
AEKP PEAK
AEKR RAKE
AEKS SAKE
AEKT KATE, TAKE, TEAK
AEKW WAKE, WEAK
AELL ELLA, LELA
AELM ELMA, LAME, MALE, MEAL

AELN ÉLAN, LANE, LEAN, LENA, NEAL
AELO ALOE
AELP LEAP, PALE, PEAL, PLEA
AELR EARL, REAL
AELS ELSA, LEAS, SALE, SEAL
AELT ET AL, LATE, LETA, TALE, TEAL
AELV VALE, VEAL
AELW WEAL
AELX ALEX, AXEL, AXLE
AELZ LAZE, ZEAL
AEMM EMMA
AEMN AMEN, MANE, MEAN, NAME
AEMR MARE, REAM
AEMS SAME, SEAM
AEMT MATE, MEAT, META, TAME, TEAM
AEMX EXAM
AEMZ MAZE
AENN ANNE
AENO AEON
AENP NAPE, PANE
AENR EARN, NEAR, RENA
AENS SANE, SEAN
AENT ANTE, NEAT
AENV EVAN, NAVE, NEVA, VANE
AENW ANEW, EWAN, WANE, WEAN
AENZ ZANE, ZENA
AEPR PARE, PEAR, RAPE, REAP
AEPS APES, APSE, PEAS
AEPT PATE, PEAT, PETA, TAPE
AEPV PAVE
AEPX APEX
AEPY PAYE
AERR RARE, REAR
AERS ARSE, EARS, ERAS, SEAR, SERA
AERT RATE, TARE, TEAR
AERV AVER, RAVE, VERA
AERW WEAR
AERY YEAR
AERZ EZRA, RAZE
AESS SEAS
AEST EAST, EATS, SATE, SEAT, SETA, TEAS
AESU ESAU
AESV SAVE, VASE

AESX AXES
AESY AYES, EASY, YEAS
AETT ETTA, TEAT
AEUV UVEA
AEVW WAVE
AFFG GAFF
AFFN NAFF
AFGL FLAG
AFGN FANG
AFGS FAGS
AFHL HALF
AFHT HAFT
AFIL FAIL
AFIN FAIN
AFIR FAIR
AFIT FIAT
AFIW WAIF
AFKL FLAK
AFLL FALL
AFLN FLAN
AFLO FOAL, LOAF, OLAF
AFLP FLAP
AFLT FLAT
AFLW FLAW
AFLX FLAX
AFLY FLAY
AFMO FOAM
AFMR FARM
AFNS FANS
AFNU FAUN
AFNW FAWN
AFOR AFRO, FORA
AFOS OAFS, SOFA
AFPR FRAP
AFRT FART, RAFT
AFRU FRAU
AFRY FRAY
AFST FAST, FATS
AFTW WAFT
AGGN GANG
AGGO AGOG
AGGS GAGS
AGHI HAIG
AGHN HANG
AGHS GASH, HAGS, SHAG
AGHT GHAT
AGIL GAIL
AGIM MAGI
AGIN GAIN, GINA, INGA
AGIO IAGO
AGIT GAIT
AGIZ GIZA
AGJO JAGO

AGJS JAGS
AGKW GAWK
AGLL GALL
AGLO GAOL, GOAL, OLGA
AGLS GALS, LAGS, SLAG
AGLY ALGY
AGMR GRAM
AGMS AGMS, MAGS
AGMY GAMY
AGNP PANG
AGNR GRAN, RANG
AGNS NAGS, SANG, SNAG
AGNT GNAT, TANG
AGNW GNAW
AGNY YANG
AGOS SAGO
AGOT GOAT, TOGA
AGOY YOGA
AGPS GAPS, GASP
AGPW GAWP
AGRS RAGS
AGRY GARY, GRAY
AGSS SAGS
AGST STAG, TAGS
AGSW SWAG, WAGS
AGSY GAYS
AHHS HASH, SHAH
AHHT HATH
AHIK HAIK
AHIL HAIL
AHIR HAIR
AHIV IVAH
AHJJ HAJJ
AHKL LAKH
AHKN ANKH, HANK, KHAN
AHKR HARK
AHKS HASK
AHKT KATH
AHKW HAWK
AHLL HALL
AHLM HALM
AHLO HALO
AHLR HARL
AHLS LASH
AHLT HALT, LATH
AHLU HAUL, HULA
AHMO HAMO, HOMA
AHMR HARM
AHMS HAMS, MASH, SHAM
AHMW WHAM
AHNO NOAH
AHNS HANS
AHNT TANH, THAN

AHNW HWAN
AHOR HOAR, HORA
AHOS SHOA
AHOT OATH
AHOW WHOA
AHOX HOAX
AHOY AHOY, HOYA
AHPR HARP
AHPS HASP
AHPT PATH
AHRS RASH
AHRT HART
AHRZ HARZ
AHSS SASH
AHST HAST, HATS, SHAT
AHSW SHAW, WASH
AHSY ASHY
AHTT THAT
AHTU UTAH
AHTW THAW, WHAT
AHYZ HAZY
AIIN IAIN
AIJL JAIL
AIKN AKIN
AIKR RIKA
AILL LILA
AILM ILMA, LIAM, LIMA, MAIL, MALI
AILN LAIN, LINA, NAIL
AILO IOLA
AILP PAIL
AILR LAIR, LIAR, LIRA, RAIL, RIAL
AILS ISLA, LIAS, LISA, SAIL
AILT ALIT, LITA, TAIL
AILV VIAL
AILW WAIL
AILX ALIX
AILZ LIZA
AIMM IMAM, MAIM, MIMA
AIMN MAIN, MINA
AIMR AMIR, IRMA, MAIR, MIRA
AIMS AIMS
AINN NINA
AINO IONA
AINP PAIN
AINR IRAN, RAIN, RANI, RINA
AINS ANIS, SIAN
AINT NITA, TINA
AINU AINU
AINV IVAN, VAIN, VINA
AINZ NAZI

AIOT IOTA
AIOW IOWA
AIPR PAIR
AIPS PISA
AIQR IRAQ
AIRS AIRS, SARI
AIRT RITA
AIRY AIRY
AISV AVIS, VISA
AISX AXIS
AITV VITA
AITW WAIT
AITX TAXI
AITZ ZITA
AIVV VIVA
AJMS JAMS
AJNO JOAN
AJNU JUAN
AJRS JARS
AJRU JURA
AJSW JAWS
AJSY JAYS
AJZZ JAZZ
AKLN LANK
AKLR KARL, LARK
AKLT TALK
AKLW WALK
AKMO AMOK
AKMR MARK
AKMS MASK
AKNP KNAP
AKNR NARK, RANK
AKNS SANK
AKNT TANK
AKNW WANK
AKNY YANK
AKOR OKRA
AKOS OAKS, SOAK
AKOY OKAY
AKPR PARK
AKRS ARKS
AKST TASK
AKSU AUKS, SKUA
AKSY YAKS
AKTY KATY
ALLM MALL
ALLO LOLA
ALLP PALL
ALLT TALL
ALLW WALL
ALLY ALLY
ALMM MALM
ALMO LOAM

ALMP LAMP, PALM
ALMR MARL
ALMS ALMS, SLAM
ALMT MALT
ALMU ALUM, MAUL
ALNO LOAN, NOLA
ALNP PLAN
ALNU ALUN, ULNA
ALNW LAWN
ALOP OPAL
ALOR LORA, ORAL
ALOS ALSO, LAOS
ALOT ALTO
ALOV OLAV, OVAL
ALOW AWOL
ALOZ ZOLA
ALPP LAPP, PALP
ALPS ALPS, LAPS, PALS, SLAP
ALPU PAUL
ALPW PAWL
ALPY PLAY
ALRS LARS
ALRY LYRA
ALSS LASS
ALST LAST, SALT, SLAT
ALSU SAUL
ALSV SLAV
ALSW AWLS, LAWS
ALSY ALYS, LAYS, SLAY
ALTW WALT
ALUW WAUL
ALWY YAWL
ALYZ LAZY
AMMS MAMS
AMNO MOAN, MONA
AMNX MANX
AMNY MANY, MYNA
AMOR OMAR, ROAM, ROMA
AMOS AMOS, SOMA
AMOT ATOM, MOAT
AMPR PRAM, RAMP
AMPS AMPS, MAPS, SPAM
AMPT TAMP
AMPU PUMA
AMPV VAMP
AMRS ARMS, MARS, RAMS
AMRT TRAM
AMRW WARM
AMRY ARMY, MARY, MYRA
AMSS MASS
AMST MAST, MATS
AMSW MAWS, SWAM
AMSX XMAS

AMSY MAYS, YAMS	ARTY ARTY, TRAY, TYRA	BDRU DRUB
AMTT MATT	ARTZ TZAR	BDSU BUDS
AMYZ MAZY	ARVY VARY	BEEF BEEF
ANNO ANON, NONA	ARWY AWRY, WARY	BEEH HEBE
ANOO OONA	ARXY X-RAY	BEEL ELBE
ANOR NORA, ORAN, ROAN,	ASSS SASS	BEEN EBEN
RONA	ASSW SAWS	BEER BEER
ANOT NATO	ASSY SAYS	BEES BEES
ANOV NOVA	ASTT TATS	BEET BEET
ANPS NAPS, PANS, SNAP,	ASTV VAST, VATS	BEGI GIBE
SPAN	ASTW SWAT	BEGY GYBE
ANPT PANT	ASTY STAY	BEHR HERB
ANPW PAWN	ASWY SWAY, WAYS, YAWS	BEHT BETH
ANRT RANT, TARN	ATTU TAUT	BEIJ JIBE
ANRW WARN	ATTW TWAT, WATT	BEIK BIKE
ANRY RYAN, YARN	AVWY WAVY	BEIL BILE
ANST ANTS, STAN, TANS	AWXY WAXY	BEIN BE IN
ANSU ANUS	BBES EBBS	BEIR BIER
ANSV VANS	BBIS BIBS	BEIT BITE
ANSW SAWN, SWAN	BBIY IBBY	BEIX IBEX
ANSY NAYS	BBLO BLOB	BEKO KOBE
ANTU AUNT, TUNA	BBLU BULB	BEKR BERK, KERB
ANTW WANT	BBMO BOMB	BELL BELL
ANUY YUAN	BBOO BOOB	BELO BOLE, LOBE
ANVY NAVY	BBOS BOBS	BELP PLEB
ANWY YAWN	BBOU BUBO	BELT BELT
ANYZ ZANY	BBSU BUBS	BELU BLUE
AOPS OAPS, SOAP	BCEK BECK	BELW BLEW
AOPT ATOP	BCEU CUBE	BENO BONE
AORR ROAR	BCIM ICBM	BENR BERN
AORS OARS, ROSA, SOAR	BCIR CRIB	BENS BENS
AORT ROTA, TARO	BCKU BUCK	BENT BENT
AORZ ZORA	BCLO BLOC	BEOO OBOE
AOST OATS	BCLU CLUB	BEOR BOER, BORE, ROBE
AOTU AUTO	BCMO COMB	BEOY OBEY
AOVW AVOW	BCOS COBS	BERT BERT, BRET
APPS PAPS	BCRU CURB	BERV VERB
APPU PUPA	BCSU CUBS	BERY BYRE
APRS PARS, RAPS, RASP, SPAR	BDEI BIDE	BESS BESS
APRT PART, PRAT, RAPT, TRAP	BDEL BLED	BEST BEST, BETS
APRW WARP, WRAP	BDEN BEND	BESW WEBS
APRY PRAY	BDEO BODE	BESY BYES
APSS ASPS, PASS, SAPS, SPAS	BDES BEDS, DEBS	BETU TUBE
APST PAST, PATS, SPAT, TAPS	BDET DEBT	BETY BYTE
APSW PAWS, SWAP, WASP	BDII IBID	BEUZ ZEBU
APSY SPAY, YAPS	BDIN BIND	BEVY BEVY
AQUY QUAY	BDIR BIRD	BFFI BIFF
ARST ARTS, RATS, STAR,	BDIS BIDS	BFFU BUFF
TARS, TSAR	BDLO BOLD	BFIS FIBS
ARSW WARS	BDMU DUMB	BFMU BUMF
ARSY RAYS	BDNO BOND	BFOS FOBS
ARTT TART	BDOS BODS	BGIL GLIB
ARTW WART	BDOY BODY, BOYD	BGIN BING

9

BGIO GOBI	BOOR BOOR	CEIL LICE
BGNU BUNG	BOOS BOOS	CEIM MICE
BGOO GOBO	BOOT BOOT	CEIN NICE
BGOS BOGS, GOBS	BOOZ BOZO	CEIP EPIC
BGRU GRUB	BOPS BOPS	CEIR CERI, ERIC, RICE
BGSU BUGS	BORS ORBS	CEIS ICES
BHOO HOBO	BORT BORT	CEIT CITE
BHOS BOSH, HOBS	BORW BROW	CEIV VICE
BHOT BOTH	BOSS BOSS, SOBS	CEKN NECK
BHSU BUSH, HUBS	BOSW BOWS	CEKO COKE
BIIS IBIS	BOSY BOYS, YOBS	CEKP PECK
BIJS JIBS	BOTU BOUT	CEKR RECK
BIKL BILK	BOTY TOBY	CELL CELL
BIKS IKBS	BOUY BUOY	CELM CLEM
BILL BILL	BPRU BURP	CELO CLEO
BILM LIMB	BPSU PUBS	CELU CLUE, LUCE
BILO BOIL	BRRU BURR	CELW CLEW
BILP BLIP	BRSU BURS, RUBS	CEMO COME
BIMR BRIM	BRTU BURT	CENO CONE, ONCE
BINS BINS, NIBS	BRUY BURY, RUBY	CENT CENT
BIOR BIRO	BSSU BUSS, SUBS	CEOP COPE, OPEC
BIRS RIBS	BSTU BUST, BUTS, STUB,	CEOR CORE
BIRT BRIT	TUBS	CEOV COVE
BIST BITS	BSUY BUSY, BUYS	CEPS SPEC
BJOS JOBS	BTTU BUTT	CEPU PUCE
BKLU BULK	BUZZ BUZZ	CERT CERT
BKNO KNOB	CCHI CHIC	CERU CURE, ECRU
BKNU BUNK	CCIN C-IN-C	CERW CREW
BKOO BOOK	CCKO COCK	CESS CSES, SECS
BKRU BURK	CDEE CEDE	CEST SECT
BKSU BUSK	CDEI DICE, ICED	CESU CUES
BLLO BOLL	CDEK DECK	CETU CUTE
BLLU BULL	CDEO CODE, COED	CFFU CUFF
BLOS LOBS, SLOB	CDEU CUED	CFIO COIF, FOCI
BLOT BLOT, BOLT	CDHI CHID	CFKU FUCK
BLOW BLOW, BOWL	CDIK DICK	CGHU CHUG
BLRU BLUR	CDIS DISC	CGLO CLOG
BLSU SLUB	CDKO DOCK	CGOS COGS
BMNU NUMB	CDKU DUCK	CHIK HICK
BMOO BOOM	CDLO CLOD, COLD	CHIN CHIN, INCH
BMOS MOBS	CDOR CORD	CHIP CHIP
BMOT TOMB	CDOS CODS, DOCS	CHIR RICH
BMOW WOMB	CDRU CURD	CHIT CHIT, ITCH
BMPU BUMP	CDSU SCUD	CHKO HOCK
BMSU BUMS	CDTU DUCT	CHLO LOCH
BNNO BONN	CEFH CHEF	CHMU CHUM, MUCH
BNOO BOON	CEFL CLEF	CHOP CHOP
BNOR BORN, BRNO	CEGS ECGS, GCES, GCSE	CHOS COSH
BNOS NOBS, SNOB	CEHK HECK	CHOU CHOU, OUCH
BNOY BONY	CEHO ECHO	CHOW CHOW
BNRU BURN	CEHR CHER	CHSU SUCH
BNRY BRYN	CEHT ETCH	CIKK KICK
BNSU BUNS, NUBS, SNUB	CEHW CHEW	CIKL LICK

CIKM MICK
CIKN NICK
CIKP PICK
CIKR RICK
CIKS SICK
CIKT TICK
CIKV VICK
CIKW WICK
CILO COIL, LOCI
CILP CLIP
CINO COIN, ICON
CINZ ZINC
CIOR COIR
CIPS SPIC
CIRU URIC
CISS CISS
CIST TICS
CITY CITY
CJKO JOCK
CKLO LOCK
CKLU LUCK
CKMO MOCK
CKMU MUCK
CKNO CONK
CKOO COOK
CKOR CORK, ROCK
CKOS SOCK
CKPU PUCK
CKRU RUCK
CKSU SUCK
CKTU TUCK
CKUY YUCK
CLLU CULL
CLMO COLM
CLMU CULM
CLOO COOL, LOCO
CLOP CLOP
CLOS COLS
CLOT CLOT, COLT
CLOW COWL
CLOY CLOY
CLRU CURL
CLTU CULT
CLUY LUCY
CMOR CORM
CMSU SCUM
CNNO CONN
CNOO COON
CNOR CORN
CNOS CONS, NCOS
CNOY CONY
CNSY SYNC
CNTU CUNT

COOP COOP
COOS COOS
COOT COOT
COPR CROP
COPS COPS
COPU COUP
COPY COPY
CORS ROCS
CORW CROW
COST COST, COTS
COSW COWS
COSY COSY
COYZ COZY
CPSU CUPS, CUSP
CPSW WPCS
CRSU CRUS, CURS
CRTU CURT
CRUX CRUX
CSSU CUSS
CSTU CUTS
CSTY CYST
DDEE DEED
DDEI DIED
DDEU DUDE
DDEY DYED, EDDY
DDJU JUDD
DDOO DODO
DDOS ODDS
DDOT TODD
DDSU DUDS
DEEF FEED
DEEG EDGE
DEEH HEED
DEEI EDIE
DEEL DELE
DEEM DEEM
DEEN EDEN, NEED
DEEP DEEP, PEED
DEER DEER, REED
DEES SEED
DEET TEED
DEEW WEED
DEEY EYED
DEFL FLED
DEFN FEND
DEFR FRED
DEFT DEFT
DEFU FEUD
DEFY DEFY
DEGL GELD
DEGO DOGE
DEGY EDGY
DEHI HIDE, HIED

DEHL HELD
DEHO HOED
DEHR HERD
DEHS SHED
DEHU HUED
DEHY HEDY, HYDE
DEIK DIKE
DEIL IDLE, LIED
DEIM DIME, IDEM
DEIN DINE, ENID
DEIP PIED
DEIR DIRE, RIDE
DEIS IDES, SIDE
DEIT DIET, EDIT, TIDE, TIED
DEIV DIVE, VIED
DEIW DEWI, WIDE
DEJN NEJD
DEJU JUDE
DEKS DESK
DEKU DUKE
DEKY DYKE
DELL DELL
DELN LEND
DELO DOLE, LODE
DELP PLED
DELS SLED
DELU DUEL
DELV VELD
DELW LEWD, WELD
DEMN MEND
DEMO DEMO, DOME, EDOM, MODE
DENO DONE, NODE
DENR NERD, REND
DENS DENS, ENDS, SEND
DENT DENT, TEND
DENU DUNE, NUDE
DENV VEND
DENW WEND
DENY DENY, DYNE
DEOP DOPE
DEOR DOER, REDO, RODE
DEOS DOES, DOSE, ODES
DEOT DOTE, TOED
DEOV DOVE
DEOW OWED
DEOZ DOZE
DEPS SPED
DEPU DUPE
DERS REDS
DERU RUDE, RUED
DERV DERV
DERW DREW

11

DERY DYER	**DIRT** DIRT	**DSTU** DUST, STUD
DESU DUES, SUED, USED	**DIRU** RUDI	**DSUV** VDUS
DESY DYES	**DISU** IUDS	**DTUY** DUTY
DESZ ZEDS	**DISY** YIDS	**EEEP** ÉPÉE
DETU DUET	**DITY** TIDY	**EEFL** FEEL, FLEE
DEWY DEWY	**DJOU** JUDO	**EEFR** FREE, REEF
DFFO DOFF	**DJOY** JODY	**EEFS** FEES
DFFU DUFF	**DJUY** JUDY	**EEFT** FEET, FETE
DFIN FIND	**DKNU** DUNK	**EEGH** GHEE
DFLO FOLD	**DKSU** DUSK	**EEGL** GLEE
DFNO FOND	**DKUU** KUDU	**EEGN** GENE
DFNU FUND	**DLLO** DOLL	**EEHL** HEEL
DFOO FOOD	**DLLU** DULL	**EEHR** HERE
DFOR FORD	**DLMO** MOLD	**EEHT** THEE
DGIL GILD	**DLOP** PLOD	**EEIR** EIRE, ERIE
DGIR GIRD, GRID	**DLOR** LORD	**EEIV** EVIE
DGIS DIGS	**DLOS** SOLD	**EEJP** JEEP
DGLO GOLD	**DLOT** DOLT, TOLD	**EEJR** JEER
DGNU DUNG	**DLOU** LOUD, LUDO	**EEKL** KEEL, LEEK
DGOO GOOD	**DLOW** WOLD	**EEKM** MEEK
DGOS DOGS, GODS	**DLOZ** LODZ	**EEKN** KEEN, KNEE
DGOU DOUG	**DLUY** DULY	**EEKP** KEEP, PEEK
DGRU DRUG	**DMOO** DOOM, MOOD	**EEKR** REEK
DGSU DUGS	**DMOS** MODS	**EEKS** SEEK
DHIN HIND	**DMPU** DUMP	**EEKW** WEEK
DHIS DISH	**DMRU** DRUM	**EELP** PEEL
DHLO HOLD	**DNOP** POND	**EELR** ERLE, LEER, REEL
DHOO HOOD	**DNOS** DONS, NODS	**EELS** EELS, ELSE, LEES
DHOS HODS, SHOD	**DNOU** UNDO	**EEMR** MERE
DHOW DHOW	**DNOW** DOWN	**EEMS** ESME, SEEM, SEME
DHTU THUD	**DNOZ** ZOND	**EEMT** MEET, METE, TEEM
DIIM MIDI	**DNSU** DUNS	**EENR** NE'ER, RENÉ
DIJO JODI	**DOOR** DOOR, ROOD	**EENS** SEEN
DIJU JUDI	**DOOT** TO-DO	**EENV** EVEN
DIKN KIND	**DOOW** WOOD	**EENW** EWEN
DIKR DIRK	**DOPR** DROP, PROD	**EEPP** PEEP
DIKS DISK, KIDS, SKID	**DOPS** PODS	**EEPR** PEER
DILL DILL	**DOQU** QUOD	**EEPS** SEEP
DILM MILD	**DORS** RODS	**EEPT** PETE
DILO IDOL, LIDO	**DORT** TROD	**EEPW** WEEP
DILS LIDS, SLID	**DORU** DOUR	**EERS** ERSE, SEER, SERE
DILW WILD	**DORW** WORD	**EERT** TREE
DILY IDLY	**DORY** DORY	**EERU** EURE
DIMN MIND	**DOSS** DOSS, SODS	**EERV** EVER, VEER, VERE
DINO DION	**DOST** DOTS, TODS	**EERW** EWER
DINR RIND	**DOSU** DUOS	**EESS** SEES
DINS DINS, SIND	**DOYZ** DOZY	**EEST** TEES
DINT DINT	**DPSU** PUDS, SPUD	**EESV** EVES
DINW WIND	**DRSU** SURD	**EESW** EWES
DIOV VOID	**DRTU** TURD	**EESX** EXES
DIPR DRIP	**DRUU** URDU	**EESY** EYES
DIPS DIPS	**DRUY** RUDY	**EETW** TWEE
DIQU QUID	**DSSU** SUDS	**EFFI** FIFE

EFFJ JEFF	EHKO HOKE	EILV EVIL, LEVI, LIVE, VEIL, VILE
EFHT HEFT	EHLL HELL	
EFIK EFIK	EHLM HELM	EILX ILEX
EFIL FILE, LIEF, LIFE	EHLO HOLE	EILY EILY
EFIN FINE	EHLP HELP	EIMM MIME
EFIR FIRE, RIFE	EHLR HERL	EIMN MIEN, MINE
EFIV FIVE	EHMO HOME	EIMR EMIR, MIRE, RIME
EFIW WIFE	EHMP HEMP	EIMS SEMI
EFLL FELL	EHMR HERM	EIMT EMIT, ITEM, MITE, TIME
EFLO FLOE	EHMS HEMS, MESH, SHEM	EINN NINE
EFLS SELF	EHMT THEM	EINP PINE
EFLT FELT, LEFT	EHMU HUME	EINR ERIN, REIN
EFLU FLUE, FUEL	EHNO HONE	EINS SINE
EFLW FLEW	EHNR HERN	EINT TINE
EFLX FLEX	EHNS HENS	EINV VEIN, VINE
EFMU FUME	EHNT HENT, THEN	EINW WINE
EFNR FERN	EHNW HEWN, WHEN	EINZ INEZ, ZEIN
EFNS FENS	EHOP HOPE	EIPP PIPE
EFOR FORE, FROE	EHOR HERO, HOER	EIPR PIER, RIPE
EFOS FOES	EHOS HOES, HOSE, SHOE	EIPS PIES
EFRS REFS, SERF	EHOT THEO	EIPW WIPE
EFRT FRET	EHOV HOVE	EIRS RISE, SIRE
EFSU FUSE	EHOW HOWE	EIRT RITE, TIER, TIRE
EFTW WEFT	EHPW PHEW	EIRV RIVE
EGGR GREG	EHPY HYPE	EIRW WEIR, WIRE
EGGS EGGS	EHRR HERR	EIST SITE, TIES
EGHU HUGE	EHRS HERS	EISV IVES, VISE
EGIN INGE	EHSS HESS	EISW WISE
EGIV GIVE	EHST HEST, SETH	EISZ SIZE
EGKS KEGS	EHSU HUES	EITX EXIT
EGLN GLEN	EHSW SHEW	EITY YETI
EGLO OGLE	EHTW WHET	EIVW VIEW
EGLS GELS, LEGS	EHTY THEY	EJKO JOKE
EGLU GLUE	EHUY HUEY	EJKR JERK
EGMR GERM	EHWW WHEW	EJLL JELL
EGMS GEMS	EHWY WHEY	EJLO JOEL
EGNO GONE	EIJV JIVE	EJNU JUNE
EGNT GENT	EIKK KIKE	EJOS JOSÉ
EGNU GENU	EIKL KIEL, LIKE	EJOV JOVE
EGNW GWEN	EIKM MIKE	EJOY JOEY
EGOR ERGO, GOER, GORE, OGRE	EIKN KINE	EJSS JESS
EGOS EGOS, GOES	EIKP PIKE	EJST JEST, JETS
EGPS PEGS	EIKR ERIK, KEIR, KERI	EJSW JEWS
EGRS ERGS	EIKT KITE	EJTU JUTE
EGRT GERT	EIKV KIEV	EKLP KELP
EGRU URGE	EILM EMIL, LIME, MILE	EKLS ELKS
EGRW GREW	EILN LIEN, LINE, NEIL	EKLU LUKE
EGRY GREY	EILP PILE	EKLY KYLE
EHHT HETH	EILR LIRE, RILE	EKMO MOKE
EHIK HIKE	EILS ILSE, ISLE, LEIS, LIES, LISE, SÍLE	EKNR KERN
EHIR HEIR, HIRE		EKNS KENS
EHIV HIVE	EILT TILE	EKNT KENT
	EILU LIEU	EKNU NUKE

EKNW KNEW	EMSS MESS	EPST PEST, PETS, STEP
EKOP POKE	EMST STEM	EPSW PEWS, SPEW
EKOW WOKE	EMSU EMUS, MUSE	EPSY ESPY
EKOY YOKE	EMSW MEWS	EPTW WEPT
EKPR PERK	EMTU MUTE	EPTY TYPE
EKPT KEPT	ENNO NEON, NONE	ERST REST
EKPU PUKE	ENOP NOPE, OPEN	ERSU RUSE, SUER, SURE,
EKRT TREK	ENOS ENOS, EONS, NOES,	USER
EKSW SKEW	NOSE, ONES	ERSV REVS
EKSY KEYS, SKYE	ENOT NOTE, TONE	ERSY RYES
ELLN NELL	ENOV OVEN	ERTU TRUE
ELLS SELL	ENOW OWEN	ERTY TYRE
ELLT TELL	ENOX OXEN	ERVY VERY
ELLW WELL	ENOZ ZONE	ESST SETS, TESS
ELLY LYLE, YELL	ENPS PENS	ESSU USES
ELMO MOLE	ENRT RENT, TERN	ESTT STET, TEST
ELMS ELMS	ENRU RUNE	ESTU SUET
ELMT MELT	ENRW WREN	ESTV VEST, VETS
ELMU MULE	ENST NEST, NETS, SENT,	ESTW STEW, WEST, WETS
ELMY YLEM	TENS	ESTZ ZEST
ELNO LEON, LONE, NOEL	ENSW NEWS, SEWN	ESUZ SUEZ
ELNS LENS	ENSY YENS	ESVY YVES
ELNT LENT	ENTT NETT, TENT	ESWY YEWS
ELOP LOPE, POLE	ENTU TUNE	ESXY SEXY
ELOR LORE, ROLE	ENTV VENT	ETTX TEXT
ELOS LEOS, LOSE, SLOE,	ENTW NEWT, WENT	ETTY ETTY
SOLE	ENTX NEXT	FFGU GUFF
ELOV LOVE, VOLE	ENVY ENVY	FFHU HUFF
ELPT PELT	EOOZ OOZE	FFII FIFI
ELPY YELP	EOPP POPE	FFIN NIFF
ELRU LURE, RULE	EOPR PORE, ROPE	FFIR RIFF
ELRY LYRE, RELY	EOPS PESO, POSE	FFIT TIFF
ELSS LESS	EOPT POET	FFIY IFFY
ELST LEST, LETS	EORS ORES, ROES, ROSE,	FFLU LUFF
ELSU SLUE	SORE	FFMU MUFF
ELSW SLEW	EORT ROTE, TORE	FFOT TOFF
ELTU LUTE	EORU ROUÉ	FFPU PUFF
ELTW WELT	EORV OVER, ROVE	FFRU RUFF
ELUY YULE	EORW WORE	FGIS FIGS
ELVY LEVY	EORY YORE	FGIT GIFT
EMMO MEMO	EORZ ZERO	FGLO FLOG, GOLF
EMNO OMEN	EOST TOES	FGLU GULF
EMNU MENU	EOSW WOES	FGOO GOOF
EMOP MOPE, POEM	EOTT TOTE	FGOR FROG
EMOR MORE	EOTV VETO, VOTE	FGOS FOGS
EMOS SOME	EOTY EYOT	FGOY FOGY
EMOT MOTE, TOME	EOVW WOVE	FHII HI-FI
EMOV MOVE	EOYZ OYEZ	FHIS FISH
EMOW MEOW	EPPR PREP	FHNO FOHN
EMPR PERM	EPRS REPS	FHOO HOOF
EMPT TEMP	EPRT PERT	FHOW HOWF
EMRT TERM	EPRU PERU, PRUE, PURE	FIIJ FIJI
EMRV MERV	EPRY PREY, PYRE	FIJU FUJI

FILL FILL	GGOR GROG	GNOP PONG
FILM FILM	GHHI HIGH	GNOS SNOG, SONG
FILO FOIL	GHHU HUGH	GNOW GOWN
FILP FLIP	GHIN NIGH	GNRU RUNG
FILT FLIT, LIFT	GHIS SIGH	GNSU GNUS, GUNS, SNUG,
FILW WILF	GHIW WHIG	SUNG
FIMR FIRM	GHNO HONG	GNWY GWYN
FINN FINN	GHNU HUNG	GOOT TOGO
FINO INFO	GHOS GOSH, HOGS	GORW GROW
FINS FINS	GHOU HUGO	GORY GORY, ORGY
FIOR IFOR	GHSU GUSH, HUGS	GOST TOGS
FIRS FIRS	GHTU THUG	GOSW WOGS
FIRT RIFT	GIJS JIGS	GOTU GOUT
FIST FIST, FITS, SIFT	GIKN KING	GPSU PUGS
FIZZ FIZZ	GILL GILL	GRSU RUGS
FKLO FOLK	GILN LING	GRTU TRUG
FKNU FUNK	GILR GIRL	GRUU GURU
FKOR FORK	GILT GILT	GSTU GUST, GUTS, TUGS
FLLU FULL	GIMP GIMP	GSUV GUVS
FLOO FOOL	GIMR GRIM	GSUY GUYS
FLOP FLOP	GINP PING	HHSU HUSH
FLOR ROLF	GINR GRIN, RING	HIKS SIKH
FLOT LOFT	GINS GINS, SIGN, SING	HILL HILL
FLOU FOUL	GINT TING	HILP PHIL
FLOW FLOW, FOWL, WOLF	GINW WING	HILT HILT
FLOY FLOY	GIOR GIRO, IGOR	HIMS SHIM
FLRU FURL	GIOY YOGI	HIMW WHIM
FLUX FLUX	GIPR GRIP, PRIG	HINS SHIN, SINH
FMOR FORM, FROM	GIPS PIGS	HINT HINT, THIN
FMUY FUMY	GIRS RIGS	HIOO OHIO
FNOT FONT	GIRT GIRT, GRIT	HIOP HOPI, IPOH
FOOP POOF	GIST GIST	HIPS HIPS, PISH, SHIP
FOOR ROOF	GISW SWIG, WIGS	HIPT PITH
FOOT FOOT	GITW TWIG	HIPW WHIP
FOOW WOOF	GJOS JOGS	HIRW WHIR
FOPR PROF	GJSU JUGS	HISS HISS
FOPS FOPS	GLLU GULL	HIST HIST, HITS, SHIT, THIS
FOPU POUF	GLMU GLUM	HISW WISH
FORT FORT	GLNO LONG	HITW WHIT, WITH
FORU FOUR	GLNU LUNG	HIWZ WHIZ
FOST SOFT	GLNY GLYN	HJNO JOHN
FOSU UFOS	GLOO LOGO	HJOS JOSH
FOXY FOXY	GLOS LOGS, SLOG	HKLO KOHL
FRSU FURS, SURF	GLOW GLOW	HKLU HULK
FRTU TURF	GLOY LOGY	HKNO HONK
FRUY FURY	GLPU GULP, PLUG	HKNU HUNK
FSSU FUSS	GLSU LUGS, SLUG	HKOO HOOK
FTTU TUFT	GLTU GLUT	HKSU HUSK
FUZZ FUZZ	GLUY UGLY	HLLU HULL
GGHO HOGG	GMOS SMOG	HLMO HOLM
GGIS GIGS	GMSU GUMS, MUGS, SMUG	HLOP HOLP
GGNO GONG	GMSY GYMS	HLOS HOLS
GGOO GO-GO	GNOO GOON, NO GO	HLOT HOLT, LOTH

HLOW HOWL
HLOY HOLY
HLRU HURL
HLSU LUSH
HLWY HWYL
HMNY HYMN
HMOO HOMO
HMOS HOMS, OHMS
HMOT MOTH, THOM
HMOW WHOM
HMOY HOMY
HMPU HUMP
HMSU HUMS, MUSH
HMTY MYTH
HNOP PHON
HNOR HORN
HNOS NOSH
HNOU HUON
HNSU SHUN
HNTU HUNT
HOOP HOOP, POOH
HOOS SHOO
HOOT HOOT, OTHO
HOPS HOPS, POSH, SHOP
HOPT PHOT
HOPW WHOP
HOPY HYPO
HORU HOUR
HOST HOST, HOTS, SHOT
HOSW SHOW
HOTU THOU
HPSU PUSH
HPTU PHUT
HRRU RUHR
HRSU RUSH
HRSY RHYS
HRTU HURT, RUTH, THRU
HSSU HUSS
HSTU HUTS, SHUT, THUS, TUSH
HSWY WHYS
HTUU HUTU
IIKW KIWI
IILL LILI
IIMM MIMI
IIMN MINI
IINS NISI
IIRS IRIS
IJLL JILL
IJLT JILT
IJNN JINN
IJNO JOIN
IJNX JINX

IKKN KINK
IKKR KIRK
IKLL KILL
IKLM MILK
IKLN KILN, LINK
IKLO KILO
IKLS SILK
IKLT KILT
IKMN MINK
IKMS SKIM
IKNO IKON, OINK
IKNP PINK
IKNR RINK
IKNS INKS, SINK, SKIN
IKNT KNIT
IKNW WINK
IKNY INKY
IKPS KIPS, SKIP, SPIK
IKRS KRIS, RISK
IKSS KISS, SKIS
IKST KITS, SKIT
ILLM MILL
ILLO LILO
ILLP PILL
ILLR RILL
ILLS ILLS, SILL
ILLT LILT, TILL
ILLW WILL
ILLY LILY
ILMN LIMN
ILMO MILO
ILMP LIMP
ILMS SLIM
ILMT MILT
ILMY LIMY
ILNO LION, LOIN
ILNT LINT
ILNZ LINZ
ILOO IOLO
ILOR LORI
ILOS LOIS, OILS, SILO, SOIL
ILOT TOIL
ILOV VIOL
ILOY OILY
ILPS LIPS, LISP, SLIP
ILST LIST, SILT, SLIT
ILTT TILT
ILTW WILT
ILWY WILY
IMMY IMMY
IMNT MINT
IMNX MINX
IMOT OMIT

IMPP PIMP
IMPR PRIM
IMPS IMPS
IMPW WIMP
IMRS RIMS
IMRT TRIM
IMRU MUIR
IMRY MIRY, RIMY
IMSS ISMS, MISS
IMST MIST
IMSW SWIM
IMTT MITT
INNS INNS
INOP PION
INOR IRON
INOS IONS
INOT INTO, TONI
INOV VINO
INOZ ZION
INPS NIPS, PINS, SNIP, SPIN
INPT PINT
INPY PINY
INQU QUIN
INRU RUIN
INSS SINS
INST NITS, TINS
INSW WINS
INTT TINT
INTU UNIT
INTW TWIN
INTY TINY
INWY WINY
IORT RIOT, TIRO, TRIO
IORV IVOR
IOST OTIS
IOSU IOUS
IPPS PIPS
IPQU QUIP
IPRS RIPS
IPRT TRIP
IPSS PISS, SIPS
IPST PITS, SPIT, TIPS
IPSV SPIV, VIPS
IPSW WISP
IPSZ ZIPS
IPTY PITY
IQTU QUIT
IQUZ QUIZ
IRSS SIRS
IRST STIR
IRTW WRIT
IRTX TRIX
IRWY WIRY

ISSY ISSY	LMPU LUMP, PLUM	MPPU PUMP
ISTT TITS	LMSU SLUM	MPRU RUMP
ISTU SUIT	LNNY LYNN	MPSU SUMP
ISTW WITS	LNOO LOON	MRSU RUMS
ISTZ ZITS	LNOR LORN	MSSU MUSS, SUMS
ITTW TWIT	LNOY LYON, ONLY	MSTU MUST, SMUT, STUM
IYZZ IZZY	LNUY LUNY	MSUW SWUM
IZZZ ZIZZ	LNXY LYNX	MTTU MUTT
JJUU JUJU	LOOP LOOP, POLO, POOL	NNOO NOON
JKNU JUNK	LOOS LOOS, OSLO, SOLO	NNOU NON-U, NOUN
JLOT JOLT	LOOT LOOT, TOOL	NNSU NUNS
JLOW JOWL	LOOW WOOL	NNWY WYNN
JLUY JULY	LOPP PLOP	NOOS SOON
JMPU JUMP	LOPS SLOP	NOOT ONTO
JNOU JUNO	LOPT PLOT	NOPR PORN
JOSS JOSS	LOPW PLOW	NOPU UPON
JOSY JOYS	LOPY PLOY, POLY	NOPY PONY
JRUY JURY	LORU LOUR	NORT TORN
JSTU JUST	LORY ORLY, ROLY	NORW WORN
KKOO KOOK	LOSS LOSS	NOSS SONS
KLOO LOOK	LOST LOST, LOTS, SLOT,	NOST SNOT, TONS
KLOY YOLK	STOL	NOSU NOUS, ONUS
KLRU LURK	LOSU SOUL	NOSW SNOW, SOWN
KLSU SULK	LOSW LOWS, OWLS, SLOW	NOSY NOSY
KMNO MONK	LOTU LOUT	NOTU UNTO
KMRU MURK	LOTV VOLT, VTOL	NOTW TOWN, WONT
KMSU MUSK	LOWY YOWL	NOTY TONY
KNOO NOOK	LPPU PULP	NOXY ONYX
KNOT KNOT	LPRU PURL	NPSU PUNS, SPUN
KNOW KNOW	LPSU PLUS	NPTU PUNT
KNPU PUNK	LRSU SLUR	NPUY PUNY
KNSU SUNK	LSTU LUST, SLUT	NRSU RUNS, URNS
KOOR ROOK	LSUV LUVS	NRTU RUNT, TURN
KOOT TOOK	LUUZ ZULU	NSSU SUNS
KOPR PORK	MMOS MOMS	NSTU NUTS, STUN
KOPY POKY	MMSU MUMS	OOPP POOP
KORW WORK	MNOO MONO, MOON	OOPR POOR
KOSW WOKS	MNOR MORN, NORM	OOPS OOPS
KRSU RUSK	MNOU MUON	OORT ROOT
KRTU KURT	MNOW MOWN	OOSS SO-SO
KSTU TUSK	MOOR MOOR, ROOM	OOST SOOT
LLLO LOLL	MOOS MOOS	OOSZ ZOOS
LLLU LULL	MOOT MOOT	OOTT OTTO, TOOT, TOTO
LLMO MOLL	MOOZ ZOOM	OOUZ OUZO
LLMU MULL	MOPP POMP	OOYY YOYO
LLNU NULL	MOPR PROM, ROMP	OOYZ OOZY
LLOP POLL	MOPS MOPS	OPPR PROP
LLOR ROLL	MORS ROMS	OPPS POPS
LLOT TOLL	MORT MORT	OPRS PROS
LLPU PULL	MORW WORM	OPRT PORT
LLUU LULU	MOSS MOSS	OPRU POUR
LMOO LOOM	MOST MOST, MOTS	OPRW PROW
LMOT MOLT	MOUV OVUM	OPRY ROPY

OPSS SOPS
OPST POST, POTS, SPOT, STOP, TOPS
OPSU OPUS, SOUP
OPSW POWS, SWOP, WOPS
OPSY POSY
OPTU POUT
ORRY RORY
ORSS ROSS
ORST ROTS, SORT, TORS
ORSU OURS, SOUR
ORSW ROWS
ORSY ROSY
ORTT TORT, TROT

ORTU ROUT, TOUR
ORTY TORY, TROY, TYRO
ORUX ROUX
ORUY YOUR
ORXY ORYX, ROXY
OSST SOTS, TOSS
OSSW SOWS
OSSY OSSY
OSTT TOTS
OSTU OUST
OSTW STOW, SWOT, TOWS, TWOS
OSTY TOYS
OSVW VOWS

OTTU TOUT
OYZZ OZZY
PPSU PUPS
PRRU PURR
PRSU SPUR
PRSY SPRY
PSST PSST
PSSU PUSS, SUPS
PTTU PUTT
RSSU RUSS
RSTU RUST, RUTS
SSSU SUSS
SUYZ SUZY
TTUU TUTU

AAABC ABACA	AADHI HAIDA	AAGLL ALGAL, GALLA
AAABQ AQABA	AADHL HADAL	AAGLN LAGAN
AAADN ADANA	AADIL ADLAI	AAGLR ALGAR
AAAGM AGAMA	AADIN AIDAN, DIANA,	AAGLS GALAS
AAALN ALANA	NADIA, NAIAD	AAGLV VAGAL
AAAMT AMATA	AADIR ADAIR	AAGMM GAMMA, MAGMA
AABCK ABACK	AADKR DAKAR	AAGMR GRAMA
AABCL CABAL	AADLS SALAD	AAGNP PAGAN
AABDE BAAED	AADLU DUALA	AAGOR AGORA
AABEM ABEAM, AMEBA	AADLV VALDA	AAGRS RAGAS
AABES ABASE	AADMM MADAM	AAGRZ ZARGA
AABET ABATE, BEATA	AADMN ADMAN, DAMAN	AAGSS SAGAS
AABFT ABAFT	AADMR DRAMA	AAGUV GUAVA
AABGR BRAGA	AADMS ADAMS	AAHHS HA-HAS
AABHI BAHAI, BAHIA	AADNP PANDA	AAHJR RAJAH
AABHS ABASH, SABAH	AADNV VANDA	AAHLL ALLAH, HALAL
AABLN ALBAN, BANAL,	AADNW WANDA	AAHLM HALMA, HAMAL
LABAN	AADPT ADAPT	AAHLP ALPHA
AABLS BALAS, BALSA,	AADPU PADUA	AAHLS LHASA
BASAL	AADRR RADAR	AAHLV ALVAH
AABMM MAMBA	AADRU AUDRA	AAHMO OMAHA
AABMR ABRAM	AADRW AWARD	AAHMR MARAH
AABMS SAMBA	AAEGL ALGAE, GALEA	AAHMZ HAMZA
AABNW BWANA	AAEGP AGAPE	AAHNS HANSA
AABRS ARABS, BASRA,	AAEGT AGATE	AAHPR APHRA
SABRA	AAEGV AGAVE	AAHPS PASHA
AABRT RABAT	AAEHK HAKEA	AAHRR HARAR
AACCD DACCA	AAEKP APEAK	AAHRS SARAH
AACCO CACAO	AAEKW AWAKE	AAHSU HAUSA
AACCR ACCRA	AAELP PALEA	AAHSW AWASH
AACEP APACE	AAELR AREAL	AAHSY AYAHS
AACER ARECA, CEARA	AAELT ALATE	AAHWZ AHWAZ
AACFI FACIA	AAELX ALEXA	AAIIL AALII
AACHS SACHA	AAEMZ AMAZE	AAIKS KASAI, SAKAI
AACIS ISAAC	AAENP PAEAN	AAIKZ IZAAK
AACKL ALACK	AAENR ARENA	AAILN ALAIN, ALINA, LIANA
AACLL CALLA	AAERS AREAS	AAILS AILSA, ALIAS
AACLN CANAL	AAERU AUREA	AAILT ALTAI
AACLR CARLA, CLARA	AAERW AWARE	AAILV AVAIL
AACMO MACAO	AAFFJ JAFFA	AAILX AXIAL
AACMW MACAW	AAFHI HAIFA	AAIMN ANIMA, MANIA
AACNN CANNA	AAFIM MAFIA	AAIMR MARIA
AACNZ ANZAC	AAFIN NAAFI	AAIMS AMIAS, MASAI
AACRT CARAT	AAFLT FATAL	AAIMZ ZAMIA
AADDX ADDAX	AAFNU FAUNA	AAINP APIAN
AADEG ADAGE	AAGHL GALAH	AAINR ARIAN, RAINA
AADEH AHEAD	AAGHN GHANA	AAINS ASIAN
AADEL ADELA	AAGHR HAGAR	AAINT ANITA, TANIA
AADFR DARAF, FARAD	AAGIN AGAIN	AAINV AVIAN
AADGG DAGGA	AAGIS SAIGA	AAIRS ARIAS, SARAI
AADGM MAGDA	AAGIT TAIGA	AAIRT ATRIA, TIARA
AADGN GANDA	AAGJN GANJA	AAIRV VARIA
AADGR GARDA	AAGKN KANGA	AAISS ASSAI

AAITW AWAIT
AAJLP JALAP
AAJNP JAPAN
AAKKY KAYAK
AAKLO KOALA
AAKLR KRAAL
AAKLT KALAT
AAKMR KARMA
AAKNZ KAZAN
AAKOS OSAKA
AAKPR PARKA
AAKRT KARAT
AALLM LLAMA
AALLN ALLAN
AALLV LAVAL
AALLY ALLAY
AALMO ALAMO
AALMP PALMA
AALMR ALARM, MALAR, MARLA
AALMS LAMAS
AALMT MALTA
AALMY MALAY
AALNN ANNAL
AALNS NASAL
AALNT NATAL
AALNU NUALA
AALNV NAVAL
AALNY NYALA
AALPP APPAL, PAPAL
AALPS SALPA
AALPU PAULA
AALPZ LA PAZ, PLAZA
AALRT ALTAR, RATAL
AALRU AURAL, LAURA
AALRV ALVAR, LARVA
AALRY ALARY
AALST ATLAS, SALTA
AALTY YALTA
AALUY AULAY
AAMMM MAMMA
AAMMN AMMAN
AAMMS MAMAS
AAMNN ANNAM, MANNA
AAMNS MASAN
AAMNT MANTA
AAMNY MAYAN
AAMOR AROMA
AAMOS SAMOA
AAMPR PARMA
AAMPT TAMPA
AAMRT MARTA, TAMAR
AAMRU MAURA

AAMSS AMASS, ASSAM
AAMSY AMYAS
AANNO ANONA
AANOR AARON
AANPP NAPPA
AANPT PATNA
AANRS SARAN
AANRV NAVAR, VARNA
AANRY ARYAN
AANST SATAN
AANSU SAUNA
AANSW ASWAN
AANTT TANTA
AANTY TANYA
AAORT AORTA
AAPPS PAPAS
AAPPU PAPUA
AAPPW PAPAW
AAPRS PARAS
AAPRT APART
AAPST PASTA
AAQRT QATAR
AARRS SARRA
AARRY ARRAY
AARST ASTRA
AARSU AURAS
AARTT ATTAR, TATAR, TATRA
AARTY TAYRA
AASSY ASSAY
AATZZ TAZZA
ABBCY CABBY
ABBEI ABBIE
ABBEK KEBAB
ABBEL BABEL
ABBEM BEMBA
ABBES BABES
ABBEY ABBEY
ABBGY GABBY
ABBIR RABBI
ABBLU BABUL, BUBAL
ABBNO NABOB
ABBOT ABBOT
ABBRS BARBS
ABBSU BABUS
ABBTY TABBY
ABCCY BACCY
ABCEH BEACH
ABCEI CEIBA
ABCEL CABLE, CALEB
ABCER BRACE, CABER
ABCHI CHIBA
ABCHT BATCH
ABCIN CABIN

ABCIO COBIA
ABCIR BARIC, RABIC
ABCIS BASIC
ABCJO JACOB
ABCKL BLACK
ABCKS BACKS
ABCLN BLANC
ABCNO BACON
ABCNU CUBAN
ABCOR CAROB, COBRA
ABCOV VOCAB
ABCRS CRABS
ABCRT BRACT
ABCSS SCABS
ABCSU SCUBA
ABDEG BADGE
ABDEI ABIDE
ABDEK BAKED
ABDEL BALED, BLADE
ABDEO ABODE, ADOBE
ABDER BARED, BEARD, BREAD, BREDA, DEBAR, DEBRA
ABDES BASED, BEADS
ABDET BATED
ABDEY BAYED, BEADY
ABDIL AD-LIB
ABDIR BRAID, RABID
ABDIU DUBAI
ABDLN BLAND
ABDLY BADLY
ABDNR BRAND, R AND B
ABDNS BANDS
ABDNY BANDY
ABDOR BOARD, BROAD
ABDRS BARDS, DRABS
ABDRY DARBY
ABDSU DAUBS
ABDSW BAWDS
ABDUY DAUBY
ABDWY BAWDY
ABDYY BY DAY
ABEEL ABELE
ABEFL FABLE
ABEGL BAGEL, GABLE
ABEGN BEGAN
ABEGR BARGE
ABEGS GABES
ABEGT BEGAT
ABEHO BOHEA
ABEHR HABER
ABEHS SHEBA
ABEHT BATHE

20

ABEIM I-BEAM
ABEIR BEIRA
ABEIS BASIE
ABEIZ BAIZE
ABEJZ JABEZ
ABEKL BLAKE, BLEAK
ABEKR BAKER, BRAKE,
   BREAK
ABEKS BEAKS
ABEKY BEAKY
ABELL BELLA, LABEL
ABELM AMBLE, BLAME,
   MABEL, MABLE, MELBA
ABELN BLANE
ABELR BALER, BLARE,
   BLEAR
ABELS BALES, BASEL,
   BLASE, SABLE
ABELT BLEAT, TABLE
ABELY BELAY
ABELZ BLAZE
ABEMR AMBER, BREAM
ABEMS BEAMS
ABEMY EMBAY, MAYBE
ABENO BEANO
ABENR ABNER
ABENS BANES, BEANS
ABEOV ABOVE
ABERR BARER
ABERS BASER, BEARS,
   BRAES, SABER, SABRE
ABERT BERTA
ABERV BRAVE
ABERY BARYE, BY EAR,
   YERBA
ABERZ BRAZE, ZEBRA
ABESS BASES
ABEST BASTE, BEAST,
   BEATS, BETAS, TABES
ABESU ABUSE, BEAUS
ABETU BEAUT
ABEUX BEAUX
ABFFN BANFF
ABFRY BY FAR
ABGGY BAGGY
ABGHN BHANG
ABGNO GABON
ABGNS BANGS
ABGRS GRABS
ABHIR BIHAR
ABHIS SAHIB
ABHIT HABIT
ABHMO ABOHM

ABHOR ABHOR
ABHRS BRASH
ABHST BATHS
ABIIL ALIBI
ABIIT TIBIA
ABIIZ IBIZA
ABIKT BATIK
ABILN ALBIN, BINAL, BLAIN
ABILR BLAIR, BRAIL, LIBRA
ABILS BAILS, BASIL
ABILY LIBYA
ABIMS IAMBS
ABIMT AMBIT
ABINR BAIRN, BRAIN, BRIAN
ABINS BASIN, SABIN
ABIOT BIOTA
ABIRR BRIAR
ABIRT BRITA
ABIRY BY AIR
ABISS BASIS
ABJMS JAMBS
ABJNO BANJO
ABJOT JABOT
ABKLN BLANK
ABKLS BALKS
ABKLU BAULK, KABUL
ABKNS BANKS
ABKRS BARKS
ABLLS BALLS
ABLLU BULLA
ABLLY BALLY
ABLMS BALMS, LAMBS
ABLMU ALBUM
ABLMY BALMY
ABLOP PABLO
ABLOR LOBAR
ABLOT BLOAT
ABLRW BRAWL
ABLSS SLABS
ABLST BLAST
ABLTU TUBAL
ABLWY BYLAW
ABLYY LAY-BY
ABMMO MAMBO
ABMRU BURMA, RUMBA,
   UMBRA
ABMRY AMBRY, BARMY
ABMTU BATUM
ABNNS BANNS
ABNOR BARON, BONAR
ABNOT BATON
ABNRS BARNS
ABNRU UNBAR, URBAN

ABNRW BRAWN
ABNRY BRYAN
ABNTU BANTU
ABOOT TABOO
ABORR ARBOR
ABORS BOARS
ABORT ABORT, TABOR
ABORV BRAVO
ABORX BORAX
ABOSS BASSO
ABOST BOAST, BOATS,
   SABOT
ABOTU ABOUT, U-BOAT
ABOUY BAYOU
ABQSU SQUAB
ABRRY BARRY
ABRSS BRASS
ABRST BRATS
ABRSU BURSA
ABRSY BRAYS
ABRXY BRAXY
ABSST STABS
ABSSW SWABS
ABSSY ABYSS
ABSTU TUBAS
ABTTY BATTY
ABWYY BYWAY
ACCDY CYCAD
ACCEH CACHE
ACCEM MECCA
ACCHO COACH
ACCHT CATCH
ACCIR CIRCA
ACCIT CACTI
ACCKL CLACK
ACCKR CRACK
ACCOO COCOA
ACCUY YUCCA
ACDDY CADDY
ACDEF FACED
ACDEG CADGE, CAGED
ACDEH ACHED
ACDEK CAKED
ACDEL CADEL, DECAL,
   LACED
ACDEN CANED, DANCE
ACDEP PACED
ACDER CADRE, CARED,
   CEDAR, RACED
ACDES CASED
ACDET ACTED, CADET
ACDEV CAVED
ACDEW CAWED

ACDEY DECAY	ACELV CALVE	ACHHT HATCH
ACDHO AD HOC	ACEMO CAMEO	ACHIL HALIC
ACDHR CHARD	ACEMR CREAM	ACHIM MICAH
ACDIR ACRID	ACEMS MACES	ACHIN CHAIN, CHINA
ACDIS ACIDS, ASDIC	ACENN NANCE	ACHIR CHAIR
ACDIT DICTA	ACENO CANOE, OCEAN	ACHIT AITCH, CHITA
ACDIZ CADIZ	ACENP PECAN	ACHKL CHALK
ACDLS SCALD	ACENR CANER, CARNE,	ACHKS HACKS, SHACK
ACDLU CLAUD, DUCAL	CRANE, NACRE, RANCE	ACHKW WHACK
ACDMO MADOC	ACENS CANES	ACHLO LOACH
ACDNY CANDY	ACENT ENACT	ACHLR LARCH
ACDOS CODAS	ACEOR OCREA	ACHLS CLASH
ACDOT OCTAD	ACEPR CAPER, CRAPE,	ACHLT LATCH
ACDRS CARDS	PACER, RECAP	ACHMO MACHO, MOCHA
ACDRY DARCY	ACEPS CAPES, PACES,	ACHMP CHAMP
ACDSS SCADS	SCAPE, SPACE	ACHMR CHARM, MARCH
ACDTU DUCAT	ACEPT EPACT	ACHMS CHASM
ACEEK ACKEE	ACERR RACER	ACHMT MATCH
ACEEP PEACE	ACERS ACRES, CARES,	ACHNR RANCH
ACEES CEASE	RACES, SCARE, SERAC	ACHNT CHANT
ACEFH CHAFE	ACERT CARET, CATER,	ACHNU NUCHA
ACEFL FECAL	CRATE, REACT, TRACE	ACHOP POACH
ACEFR FACER, FARCE	ACERV CARVE, CRAVE	ACHOR ORACH, ROACH
ACEFS CAFES, FACES	ACERY CAREY	ACHOS CHAOS
ACEFT FACET	ACERZ CRAZE	ACHOV HAVOC
ACEGL GLACÉ	ACESS CASES	ACHPR PARCH
ACEGR GRACE	ACEST CASTE	ACHPS CHAPS
ACEGS CAGES	ACESU CAUSE, SAUCE	ACHPT PATCH
ACEGY CAGEY	ACESV CAVES	ACHRS CHARS, CRASH
ACEHK HACEK	ACESY CASEY	ACHRT CHART
ACEHL CHELA, LEACH	ACETT TACET	ACHRY ARCHY, CHARY
ACEHN HANCE	ACETU ACUTE	ACHST CHATS
ACEHP CHEAP, PEACH	ACETX EXACT	ACHSW SCHWA
ACEHR REACH	ACETY TACEY	ACHTW WATCH
ACEHS ACHES, CHASE	ACETZ AZTEC	ACHTY CATHY, YACHT
ACEHT CHEAT, TEACH,	ACFFH CHAFF	ACIIL ILIAC
THECA	ACFHU CHUFA	ACIIS ASCII
ACEIL ALICE, CELIA, ILEAC	ACFIR FARCI	ACIKL ALICK
ACEIM AMICE	ACFKL FLACK	ACILL CILLA, LILAC
ACEIR ERICA	ACFLO FOCAL	ACILM CLAIM
ACEIV AVICE	ACFNR FRANC	ACILP PLICA
ACEKL ALECK	ACFNY FANCY	ACILS SALIC
ACEKR CRAKE, CREAK	ACFRS SCARF	ACILT TICAL
ACEKS CAKES	ACFRT CRAFT	ACILU LUCIA
ACELL CELLA	ACFRY FARCY	ACILV CAVIL
ACELM CAMEL, MACLE	ACFST FACTS	ACILX CALIX
ACELN ANCEL, CLEAN,	ACGIM GAMIC, MAGIC	ACIMN MANIC
LANCE	ACGIR CIGAR, CRAIG	ACINP PANIC
ACELP PLACE	ACGLN CLANG	ACINR CAIRN
ACELR CLARE, CLEAR,	ACGNO CONGA	ACINT ACTIN, ANTIC, CAN IT!
LACER	ACGOR CARGO	ACIOR CAIRO
ACELS LACES, SCALE	ACGOU GUACO	ACIOZ AZOIC
ACELT CLEAT, ECLAT	ACGRS CRAGS, SCRAG	ACIPR CAPRI

ACIPS ASPIC, SPICA	ACLXY CALYX	ADDER ADDER, DARED,
ACIRU AURIC, CURIA	ACMMO COMMA	DREAD, DREDA
ACIRV VICAR	ACMNO MACON	ADDET DATED
ACISU CAIUS	ACMOP CAMPO	ADDEV VEDDA
ACITT ATTIC, TACIT	ACMOR ARMCO, MARCO	ADDEW WADED
ACJKS JACKS	ACMOS COMAS	ADDEZ DAZED
ACJKY JACKY	ACMPR CRAMP	ADDFY FADDY
ACJNU CAJUN	ACMPS CAMPS, SCAMP	ADDGI GADID
ACKKN KNACK	ACMRS SCRAM	ADDIJ JIDDA
ACKLN CLANK	ACMRY CYMAR, MARCY	ADDIV DAVID
ACKLO CLOAK	ACMSS SCAMS	ADDMY MADDY
ACKLR CLARK	ACNNO ANCON, CANON,	ADDNO ADD-ON
ACKLS SLACK	CONAN	ADDNR R AND D
ACKLU CAULK	ACNNY CANNY, NANCY	ADDNY DANDY
ACKMS SMACK	ACNOP CAPON	ADDPY PADDY
ACKMU AMUCK	ACNOR ACORN	ADDRY DRYAD
ACKNR CRANK	ACNOT CANTO	ADEEL ADELE
ACKNS SNACK	ACNPU UNCAP	ADEEM EDEMA
ACKOR CROAK	ACNSS SCANS	ADEER EARED
ACKPS PACKS	ACNST CANTS, SCANT	ADEES AEDES, EASED
ACKQU QUACK	ACOPR COPRA	ADEEV EVADE
ACKRS RACKS	ACORS OSCAR	ADEFK FAKED
ACKRT TRACK	ACORT ACTOR, CROAT	ADEFM FAMED
ACKRW WRACK	ACOST ASCOT, COAST,	ADEFR FADER, FARED,
ACKSS CASKS, SACKS	COATS, COSTA, TACOS	FREDA
ACKST STACK, TACKS	ACOTT COTTA	ADEFT FATED
ACKTY TACKY	ACPPU CUPPA	ADEFX FAXED
ACKWY WACKY	ACPRS CARPS, CRAPS,	ADEFZ FAZED
ACLLO LOCAL	SCARP, SCRAP	ADEGG GAGED
ACLLS CALLS, SCALL	ACPST PACTS	ADEGL GLADE
ACLMO COMAL	ACPSU SCAUP	ADEGM GAMED, MADGE
ACLMP CLAMP	ACPTU CAPUT	ADEGP GAPED, PAGED
ACLMS CLAMS	ACRRU CRURA	ADEGR EDGAR, GERDA,
ACLMU CALUM	ACRRY CARRY	GRADE, RAGED
ACLNS CLANS	ACRSS CRASS, SCARS	ADEGS DEGAS
ACLOP COPAL	ACRST CARTS	ADEGT GATED
ACLOR CALOR, CARLO,	ACRSY CARYS, SCARY	ADEGW WADGE, WAGED
CAROL, CLARO, CORAL	ACRSZ CZARS	ADEGZ GAZED
ACLOS COALS	ACRTT TRACT	ADEHK KEDAH
ACLOT OCTAL	ACRTY TRACY	ADEHR HARED, HEARD
ACLOV VOCAL	ACRYZ CRAZY	ADEHS HADES, HEADS,
ACLOX COXAL	ACSST CASTS	SHADE
ACLOY COALY	ACSSU ASCUS	ADEHT DEATH, HATED
ACLOZ COLZA	ACSTY STACY	ADEHX HEXAD
ACLPS CLAPS, CLASP, SCALP	ACSUY SAUCY	ADEHY HEADY
ACLPU CULPA	ACTTY CATTY	ADEHZ HAZED
ACLRW CRAWL	ADDDE ADDED	ADEIL AILED, DELIA, IDEAL
ACLRY CARLY, CARYL,	ADDDY DADDY	ADEIM AIMED, AMIDE,
CLARY	ADDEF FADED	MEDIA
ACLSS CLASS	ADDEH HEDDA	ADEIN DIANE
ACLSU LUCAS	ADDEI ADDIE, AIDED	ADEIP A PIED
ACLSW CLAWS	ADDEJ JADED	ADEIR AIRED, REDIA
ACLSY SCALY	ADDEL ADDLE	

ADEIS AIDES, ASIDE, IDEAS, SADIE
ADEIU ADIEU
ADEIZ AZIDE
ADEJR JARED
ADEJS JADES
ADEJW JAWED
ADEKL KELDA
ADEKN KNEAD, NAKED
ADEKR DRAKE, RAKED
ADEKS ASKED
ADEKW WAKED
ADELL DELLA, LADLE
ADELM LAMED, MEDAL
ADELN ALDEN, ELAND, LADEN
ADELP PALED, PEDAL, PLEAD
ADELR ALDER, LADER
ADELS DALES, DEALS, LEADS
ADELT DEALT, DELTA
ADELV VELDA
ADELW WEALD
ADELY DELAY, LEADY
ADELZ LAZED, ZELDA
ADEMN ADMEN, AMEND, MANDE, MANED, MEDAN, NAMED
ADEMR AD REM, ARMED, DERMA, DREAM
ADEMS DAMES, MEADS
ADEMT MATED, TAMED
ADEMU MAUDE
ADENO ANODE
ADENR ANDRÉ, REDAN
ADENS ANDES, DEANS, SEDAN
ADENT ANTED, DANTE
ADENU DUANE
ADENV VENDA
ADENW WANED, WENDA
ADEOR ADORE, OARED
ADEPR DRAPE, PADRE, PARED, RAPED
ADEPS SPADE
ADEPT ADEPT, TAPED
ADEPV PAVED
ADEPW PAWED
ADERR DARER, DREAR
ADERS DARES, DEARS
ADERT DATER, RATED, TRADE, TREAD

ADERV RAVED
ADERW WADER
ADERY DEARY, READY
ADERZ RAZED
ADEST DATES, SATED, STEAD
ADESV SAVED
ADESW SAWED
ADESZ ADZES, DAZES
ADETX TAXED
ADEUX A DEUX
ADEVW WAVED
ADEWX WAXED
ADEWY YAWED
ADFFR DRAFF
ADFLO ADOLF
ADFRT DRAFT
ADFRU FRAUD
ADFRW DWARF
ADGIL ALGID, GILDA
ADGLN GLAND
ADGMO DOGMA
ADGNO GONAD
ADGNR GRAND
ADGOS DAGOS, GOADS
ADGOU GOUDA
ADGRS DRAGS
ADGRU GUARD
ADGUY GAUDY
ADHIJ HADJI, JIHAD
ADHIL HALID, HILDA
ADHIN DINAH
ADHIO IDAHO
ADHIP APHID
ADHJU JUDAH
ADHLU HULDA
ADHLY HYLDA
ADHNS HANDS
ADHNT HADN'T
ADHNY HANDY, HAYDN
ADHOR HOARD, RHODA
ADHRS HARDS, SHARD
ADHRY HARDY, HYDRA
ADHST HADST
ADHSU SADHU
ADHSY HYADS, SHADY
ADIIL ILIAD
ADIIN INDIA
ADIIR RADII
ADIKN DINKA
ADILN LINDA, NIDAL
ADILP PLAID
ADILR DRAIL, LAIRD

ADILS ALDIS, DIALS
ADILT TIDAL, TILDA
ADILU DULIA
ADILV VALID
ADILY DAILY, LYDIA
ADIMS MAIDS
ADIMT ADMIT
ADIMX ADMIX
ADINO DANIO
ADINR DINAR, DRAIN, NADIR
ADINV DIVAN, VIAND
ADIOP PODIA
ADIOR AROID, DORIA, RADIO
ADIOS ADIOS
ADIOU AUDIO
ADIOV AVOID
ADIOZ DIAZO
ADIPR RAPID
ADIPS SAPID
ADIPV VAPID
ADIRS RAIDS
ADIRT TRIAD
ADIRX RADIX
ADIRY DAIRY, DIARY
ADIST STAID
ADISW WADIS
ADISY DAISY
ADITU AUDIT
ADITV DAVIT
ADJOU OUJDA
ADJSU JUDAS
ADKLY ALKYD
ADKNR DRANK
ADKNY KANDY
ADKOV VODKA
ADKRS DARKS
ADKRY DARKY
ADLLO ALDOL
ADLLY DALLY
ADLMO MODAL
ADLMY MADLY
ADLNO DONAL, NODAL
ADLNS LANDS
ADLNY DYLAN, LYNDA
ADLOR ROALD
ADLOS LOADS
ADLOU ALOUD
ADLOW WALDO
ADLRW DRAWL
ADLRY DARYL
ADLSU ALDUS
ADLSY SADLY
ADLTU ADULT

ADLUY DYULA
ADMNO DAMON, MONAD, NOMAD
ADMNY MANDY
ADMOR RADOM
ADMRS DRAMS
ADMTU DATUM
ADNNO DONNA
ADNNY DANNY
ADNOR ADORN, DORAN, RADON
ADNRS DARNS
ADNRW DRAWN
ADNRY RANDY
ADNSS SANDS
ADNST STAND
ADNSU SUDAN
ADNSW DAWNS, WANDS
ADNSY SANDY
ADNTU DAUNT
ADOPT ADOPT
ADORS ROADS
ADOSS SODAS
ADOST TOADS
ADOTY TOADY, TODAY
ADQSU QUADS, SQUAD
ADRRU DURRA
ADRST DARTS
ADRSW DRAWS, SWARD, WARDS
ADRSY DRAYS, YARDS
ADRTY TARDY
ADUVZ VADUZ
AEEFZ FEAZE
AEEGL EAGLE
AEEGR AGREE, EAGER, EAGRE
AEEHV HEAVE
AEEIM AIMEE
AEELN ELENA
AEELS EASEL, LEASE
AEELT ELATE
AEELV LEAVE
AEEMN ENEMA
AEEMV MAEVE, MEAVE
AEENR RANEE
AEENT EATEN, ENATE
AEEPY PAYEE
AEERS EASER, ERASE
AEERT ARÊTE, EATER
AEEST TEASE
AEESV EAVES
AEEVW WEAVE

AEFFG GAFFE
AEFHS SHEAF
AEFIL ALFIE
AEFIR AFIRE, FERIA
AEFKL FLAKE
AEFKR FAKER, FREAK
AEFKS FAKES
AEFLM FLAME, FLEAM
AEFLR FARLE, FERAL, FLARE
AEFLS FALSE, FLEAS
AEFLT FETAL
AEFLY LEAFY
AEFMR FRAME
AEFOV FOVEA
AEFRR FARER
AEFRS FARES, FEARS, SAFER
AEFRT AFTER
AEFRW WAFER
AEFRY FAERY, FREYA
AEFSS SAFES
AEFST FATES, FEAST, FEATS
AEGGI AGGIE
AEGGR AGGER
AEGGS GAGES
AEGGU GAUGE
AEGHL HELGA
AEGHN HAGEN
AEGHU HAGUE
AEGIL AGILE, ALGIE
AEGIM IMAGE
AEGIN ANGIE
AEGIS AEGIS
AEGLL LEGAL
AEGLM GLEAM
AEGLN ANGEL, ANGLE, GLEAN
AEGLR ALGER, GLARE, LAGER, LARGE, REGAL
AEGLS GALES
AEGLT AGLET
AEGLV GAVEL, GÄVLE
AEGLY GAYLE
AEGLZ GLAZE
AEGMM GEMMA
AEGMN MANGE, MEGAN
AEGMO OMEGA
AEGMR MARGE
AEGMS GAMES
AEGMY GAMEY
AEGNO GENOA
AEGNR ANGER, RANGE
AEGNS AGNES, SENGA
AEGNT AGENT, TEGAN

AEGNV VEGAN
AEGPR GAPER, GRAPE
AEGPS GAPES, PAGES
AEGRS GEARS, RAGES, SARGE
AEGRT GRATE, GREAT, GRETA
AEGRU ARGUE, AUGER
AEGRV GRAVE
AEGRW WAGER
AEGRY GAYER
AEGRZ GAZER, GRAZE
AEGSS GASES, SAGES
AEGST GATES, STAGE
AEGSU AGUES, USAGE
AEGSW SWAGE, WAGES
AEGTU TAEGU
AEGUV VAGUE
AEGUZ GAUZE
AEHHT HEATH
AEHJZ HEJAZ
AEHKL HEKLA
AEHKS HAKES, SHAKE
AEHLR HALER
AEHLS LEASH, SHALE
AEHLT LATHE
AEHLV HALVE
AEHLW WHALE, WHEAL
AEHLZ HAZEL
AEHMN HE-MAN
AEHMR HAREM
AEHMS SHAME
AEHMT MEATH
AEHNN HENNA
AEHNS ASHEN, HANSE, SHANE, SHENA
AEHNT ETHAN, THANE, 'NEATH
AEHNV HAVEN
AEHNY HYENA
AEHOR HORAE
AEHOS HOSEA
AEHPR RAPHE
AEHPS HEAPS, PHASE, SHAPE
AEHRS ASHER, HARES, RHEAS, SHARE, SHEAR
AEHRT EARTH, HEART, HERAT
AEHRV HAVER, HAVRE
AEHRZ HAZER
AEHSS ASHES
AEHST HASTE, HATES

AEHSV HAVES, SHAVE
AEHSW HAWES, HAWSE
AEHSZ HAZES
AEHTT THETA
AEHTW WHEAT
AEHVY HEAVY
AEIIL AILIE
AEIJM JAMIE
AEIJN JANIE
AEIKL ALIKE
AEIKR ERIKA
AEIKT KATIE
AEIKZ KEZIA
AEILL ALLIE, LEILA, LELIA
AEILN ALIEN, ALINE, ANILE, ELAIN
AEILR ARIEL
AEILS AISLE, ELIAS
AEILT EILAT
AEILV ALIVE, ALVIE
AEILX AXILE
AEILZ ELIZA
AEIMM MAMIE
AEIMN AMINE, MAINE, MENAI
AEIMR MAIRE, MARIE, RAMIE
AEIMZ MAIZE
AEINN ANNIE, INANE
AEINR ARIEN, RAINE
AEINS AISNE, ANISE, SIENA
AEINT TINEA
AEINV NAIVE
AEINX XENIA
AEINZ AZINE
AEIPS SEPIA
AEIPT PIETA
AEIRS ARIES, ARISE, RAISE
AEIRT ARTIE, IRATE
AEIRZ ZAIRE
AEITV EVITA
AEIVW WAIVE
AEJMM JEMMA
AEJMR AJMER
AEJMS JAMES
AEJNN JENNA
AEJNS JEANS
AEJNT JANET
AEJNY JANEY, JAYNE
AEJPR JAPER
AEJPS JAPES
AEKLN ANKLE
AEKLR KAREL, LAKER

AEKLS LAKES, LEAKS, SLAKE
AEKLW KWELA
AEKLY LEAKY
AEKMR MAKER
AEKMS MAKES
AEKNO OAKEN
AEKNR KAREN
AEKNS SNAKE, SNEAK
AEKNT TAKEN
AEKNV KNAVE
AEKNW WAKEN
AEKNY KENYA
AEKOR KOREA
AEKOW AWOKE
AEKPR PERAK
AEKPS PEAKS, SPEAK
AEKPY PEAKY
AEKQU QUAKE
AEKRR RAKER
AEKRS ASKER, RAKES, SAKER
AEKRT TAKER
AEKRW WAKER, WREAK
AEKSS SAKES
AEKST SKATE, STAKE, STEAK, TAKES, TEAKS
AEKSW ASKEW, WAKES
AEKTW TWEAK
AELLN ALLEN
AELLP LAPEL
AELLY ALLEY
AELMM LEMMA
AELMP AMPLE, MAPLE
AELMR LAMER, REALM
AELMS MALES, MEALS, SALEM, SELMA
AELMT METAL
AELMV MELVA, VELMA
AELMY MEALY
AELMZ ZELMA
AELNO ALONE, ANOLE, LEONA
AELNP NEPAL, PANEL, PENAL, PLANE
AELNR LEARN, RENAL
AELNS ANSEL, LANES
AELNT LEANT
AELNV NAVEL, VENAL
AELOV OLAVE
AELOZ AZOLE
AELPP APPEL, APPLE
AELPR PALER, PEARL

AELPS LAPSE, LEAPS, PALES, PEALS, PLEAS, SALEP, SEPAL
AELPT LEAPT, PETAL, PLATE, PLEAT
AELQU EQUAL, QUALE
AELRS EARLS, LASER
AELRT ALERT, ALTER, ARTEL, LATER, RATEL
AELRU UREAL
AELRV LAVER, RAVEL, VELAR
AELRX RELAX
AELRY EARLY, LAYER, RELAY
AELSS SALES, SEALS
AELST LEAST, SETAL, SLATE, STALE, STEAL, TALES, TESLA
AELSV SALVE, SELVA, SLAVE, VALES
AELSW WEALS
AELSX AXLES
AELTV VALET
AELTX EXALT, LATEX
AELUV UVEAL, VALUE
AELVV VALVE
AEMMY MAMEY
AEMNO EAMON
AEMNR MARNE
AEMNS MANES, MANSE, MEANS, NAMES
AEMNT AMENT, MEANT
AEMRR REARM
AEMRS MARES, MASER, REAMS, SMEAR
AEMRT MATER, TAMER
AEMSS SEAMS
AEMST MATES, SATEM, STEAM, TEAMS
AEMSU AMUSE
AEMSX EXAMS
AEMSY SAMEY, SEAMY
AEMSZ MAZES
AEMTT MATTE
AEMTY MATEY, MEATY
AEMUV MAUVE
AENNP PANNE, PENNA
AENNS SENNA
AENNW ANWEN
AENNX ANNEX
AENOP PAEON
AENOS AEONS

26

AENOT ATONE, OATEN
AENOV NOVAE
AENOW OWENA
AENPP NAPPE
AENPS ASPEN, NAPES, PANES
AENPT PATEN
AENPZ PENZA
AENRR RERAN
AENRS NARES, SANER, SNARE
AENRV RAVEN, VERNA
AENRY YEARN
AENSS NESSA
AENST ANTES, NATES, NESTA
AENSV AVENS, NAVES, VANES
AENSW WANES
AENSZ SENZA
AENTT NETTA
AENWX WAXEN
AENWY WANEY, WAYNE
AEOPR OPERA
AEORS AROSE
AEORT ORATE
AEOSS OASES
AEOTV OVATE
AEOTZ AZOTE
AEPPR PAPER
AEPPU PUPAE
AEPRR PARER
AEPRS ASPER, PARSE, PEARS, PRASE, PRESA, RAPES, SPARE, SPEAR
AEPRT PATER, PETRA, PRATE, TAPER
AEPRY APERY, REPAY
AEPSS APSES, PASSÉ
AEPST PASTE, PATES, PEATS, SPATE, TAPES
AEPSU PAUSE
AEPTU TAUPE
AEPTY PEATY
AERRR RARER
AERRS REARS
AERRT TERRA
AERRV RAVER
AERRW RAWER
AERRZ RAZER
AERSS ARSES

AERST ASTER, RATES, RESAT, STARE, TARES, TEARS
AERSV SAVER
AERSW SAWER, SWEAR, WARES
AERSY SAYER, YEARS
AERTT TETRA, TREAT
AERTU URATE
AERTV AVERT, TRAVE
AERTW TAWER, WATER
AERTX EXTRA, TAXER
AERUZ AZURE
AERVV VARVE
AERVW WAVER
AERVY AVERY
AERWX WAXER
AERWY WEARY
AESSS ASSES
AESST ASSET, EASTS, SEATS, TESSA
AESSV SAVES, VASES
AESSY ESSAY
AESTT STATE, TASTE, TEATS, TESTA
AESTU SAUTÉ
AESTV STAVE, VESTA
AESTW SWEAT, WASTE
AESTX TAXES, TEXAS
AESTY AS YET, YEAST
AESUV SUAVE
AESVW WAVES
AFFGS GAFFS
AFFIX AFFIX
AFFLO OFFAL
AFFLU LUFFA
AFFQU QUAFF
AFFST STAFF
AFFTY TAFFY
AFGHU FAUGH
AFGLS FLAGS
AFGLU FUGAL
AFGNO FANGO
AFGNS FANGS
AFGRT GRAFT
AFHIT FAITH
AFHIZ HAFIZ
AFHLS FLASH
AFHRW WHARF
AFHST HAFTS, SHAFT
AFIKR FAKIR
AFILL FLAIL
AFILN FINAL

AFILP PILAF
AFILR FILAR, FLAIR, FRAIL
AFILS FAILS
AFINO FIONA
AFINT FAINT, FANTI
AFIOS SOFIA
AFIRR FRIAR
AFIRS FAIRS
AFIRY FAIRY
AFIST FIATS
AFISW WAIFS
AFKLN FLANK
AFKLS FLASK
AFKLY FLAKY
AFKNR FRANK
AFKRT KRAFT
AFLLO ALL OF
AFLLS FALLS
AFLMY FLAMY
AFLNS FLANS
AFLOO ALOOF
AFLOR FLORA
AFLOS FOALS, SOL-FA
AFLOT ALOFT, FLOAT
AFLOU AFOUL
AFLPS FLAPS
AFLST FLATS
AFLSW FLAWS
AFLTU FAULT
AFLUW AWFUL
AFLWY FLAWY
AFMOX OXFAM
AFMOY FOAMY
AFMRS FARMS
AFNNO FANON
AFNNY FANNY
AFNOR FARON
AFNRU FURAN
AFNSU FAUNS, SNAFU
AFNSW FAWNS
AFOOT AFOOT
AFORS AFROS, SOFAR
AFORY FORAY
AFOSS FOSSA, SOFAS
AFOST SOFTA
AFRST FARTS, RAFTS
AFRSW SWARF
AFSST FASTS
AFSUV FAVUS
AFTTY FATTY
AGGIN AGING
AGGLU GULAG
AGGNS GANGS

AGGOR AGGRO
AGGSY SAGGY
AGHHU HAUGH
AGHLU LAUGH
AGHNO HOGAN
AGHNS GNASH
AGHNW WHANG
AGHPR GRAPH
AGHRT GARTH
AGHSS SHAGS
AGHST GHATS
AGHTU AUGHT
AGIKN KIANG
AGILN ALGIN, ALIGN
AGILR ARGIL, GLAIR, GRAIL
AGILS SIGLA
AGILY GAILY
AGIMN GAMIN
AGIMO IMAGO
AGIMS AGISM, SIGMA
AGINP APING
AGINR GRAIN
AGINS GAINS
AGINT GIANT
AGINV GAVIN
AGINX AXING
AGIOS GOIAS
AGIRV VIRGA
AGIST AGIST, GAITS
AGISU GAIUS
AGJLU JUGAL
AGKWY GAWKY
AGLLO ALGOL
AGLLS GALLS
AGLMU MULGA
AGLNO ALONG
AGLNR GNARL
AGLNS GLANS, SLANG
AGLOR ALGOR, ARGOL,
  GORAL, LARGO
AGLOS GAOLS, GOALS,
  LAGOS
AGLOT GLOAT
AGLOW AGLOW
AGLRU GULAR
AGLRY GLARY, GYRAL
AGLSS GLASS, SLAGS
AGMMU GUMMA
AGMMY GAMMY
AGMNO AMONG, MANGO
AGMNY MANGY
AGMOR MARGO, MORAG
AGMRS GRAMS

AGMSU MAGUS
AGMTU GAMUT
AGNOR ARGON, GROAN,
  ORGAN
AGNOT TANGO, TONGA
AGNOU GUANO
AGNOW WAGON
AGNOY AGONY
AGNPS PANGS
AGNRS GRANS
AGNRT GRANT
AGNRY ANGRY, RANGY
AGNSS SNAGS
AGNST ANGST, GNATS
AGNSU ANGUS
AGNTU GAUNT
AGNTW TWANG
AGNTY TANGY
AGORT ARGOT, GROAT
AGOST GOATS, TOGAS
AGPRS GRASP, SPRAG
AGPSS GASPS
AGRRY GARRY
AGRSS GRASS
AGRSU SUGAR
AGRSY GRAYS
AGRUU AUGUR
AGRVY GRAVY
AGSST STAGS
AGSSU GAUSS
AGSSY GASSY
AGSTU GUSTA
AGSTY STAGY
AGSUV VAGUS
AGTTU GUTTA
AGUYZ GAUZY
AHHOO HOO-HA
AHHRS HARSH
AHHSS SHAHS
AHIIT HAITI
AHIJJ HAJJI
AHIJZ HIJAZ
AHIKK KHAKI
AHIKM HAKIM
AHIKU HAIKU
AHILL HILLA
AHILP PHIAL
AHILR HILAR
AHILS HAILS
AHILT LAHTI
AHIMR HIRAM
AHINO HANOI
AHINS HSIAN, SHANI

AHINT HAIN'T
AHIPS APHIS, APISH
AHIRS HAIRS, SHARI
AHIRU URIAH
AHIRY HAIRY
AHIST TISHA
AHJNO JONAH
AHJTU THUJA
AHKNS KHANS, SHANK
AHKNT THANK
AHKNY HANKY
AHKOS SHAKO
AHKRS SHARK
AHKSW HAWKS
AHKSY SHAKY
AHKTY KATHY
AHLLO HALLO, HOLLA
AHLLS HALLS, SHALL
AHLMU HAULM
AHLOR HORAL
AHLOS HALOS, SHOAL
AHLOT ATHOL, LOATH
AHLPR RALPH
AHLPS PLASH
AHLPY HAPLY, PHYLA
AHLSS SLASH
AHLST HALTS, LATHS, SHALT
AHLSU HAULS
AHLSW SHAWL
AHLSY SHALY
AHMMY HAMMY
AHMNO HAMON
AHMNU HUMAN, NAHUM
AHMNY HYMAN, MYNAH
AHMRS MARSH
AHMSS SHAMS, SMASH
AHMSW WHAMS
AHMTY MY HAT
AHNNO HONAN
AHNNU HUNAN
AHNOR NORAH, RHONA
AHNOS SHONA
AHNST HANTS, HASN'T,
   SHAN'T, SNATH
AHNSU SHAUN
AHNSW SHAWN
AHNTU HAUNT
AHNUW WUHAN
AHOOW WAHOO
AHOOY YAHOO
AHORS HORSA
AHORT THORA, TORAH
AHORY HOARY

AHORZ ZORAH
AHOST HOSTA, OATHS, SHOAT
AHOSX XHOSA
AHPPY HAPPY
AHPRS HARPS, SHARP
AHPRY HARPY
AHPSS HASPS
AHPST PATHS
AHQSU QUASH
AHRRY HARRY
AHRST HARTS, RASHT, TRASH
AHRSU SURAH
AHRTW WRATH
AHRTY THYRA
AHSST STASH
AHSSW SWASH
AHSTW SWATH, THAWS
AHSTY HASTY
AHSWY WASHY
AHTTY HATTY
AIILS AILIS
AIIMM MIAMI
AIINS SINAI
AIIPU PIAUI
AIIQR IRAQI
AIIVV VIVIA
AIJLS JAILS
AIJLU JULIA
AIJNS JANIS
AIJOU OUIJA
AIKMU UMIAK
AIKNR KARIN
AIKNT TAKIN
AIKOP OKAPI
AIKRT KRAIT
AIKRU KAURI
AILLL LILLA
AILLN NIALL
AILLV VILLA
AILLW WILLA
AILMN MILAN
AILMS ISLAM
AILMV VILMA
AILMW WILMA
AILNO ALOIN, ILONA
AILNP PLAIN
AILNS NAILS, SLAIN, SNAIL
AILNT LATIN
AILNV ALVIN, ANVIL, NIVAL
AILNW IN-LAW
AILNY INLAY

AILOV OLIVA, VIOLA
AILPP PIPAL
AILPR APRIL
AILPS PAILS
AILPT PLAIT
AILQU QUAIL
AILRS LAIRS, LIARS, LIRAS, RAILS, RIALS
AILRT TRAIL, TRIAL
AILRU LAURI
AILRV AVRIL, RIVAL, VIRAL
AILRY RIYAL
AILSS SAILS, SILAS, SISAL
AILST TAILS
AILSV ALVIS, VIALS
AILTV VITAL
AILTY ITALY, LAITY
AIMMS IMAMS
AIMMX MAXIM
AIMNN MINNA
AIMNO AMINO, NAOMI
AIMNR ARMIN, MARNI
AIMNS MAINS
AIMNT MATIN
AIMNZ MAINZ
AIMOR MAORI, MARIO, MOIRA
AIMOW MIAOW
AIMOX AXIOM
AIMRS AMIRS
AIMRT MARTI
AIMRZ MIZAR
AIMSS AMISS
AIMSV MAVIS
AIMSW SWAMI
AIMSY ISMAY
AIMTY AMITY
AINNO ANION
AINNP PINNA
AINNS ANNIS
AINOP PIANO
AINOR ON-AIR
AINOS SONIA
AINOT TONIA
AINOW OWAIN
AINOZ ANZIO
AINPR PIRAN
AINPS PAINS, SPAIN
AINPT INAPT, PAINT, PINTA
AINRS RAINS
AINRT TRAIN, TRINA
AINRV INVAR
AINRY RAINY

AINST SAINT, SATIN, STAIN
AINSV SAVIN
AINSW SWAIN
AINSZ NAZIS
AINTT TAINT, TITAN
AINTU UNIAT
AINTW TWAIN
AINUX AUXIN
AIOPT PATIO
AIORT RATIO
AIORY ORIYA
AIOSS OASIS
AIOST IOTAS
AIPPP PIPPA
AIPRS PAIRS, PARIS
AIPRT ATRIP, TAPIR
AIPRU PIURA
AIPSS APSIS
AIPST TAPIS
AIPTT PATTI
AIPZZ PIZZA
AIRRS ARRIS
AIRSS ARSIS, SARIS
AIRST ASTIR, SITAR, STAIR, STRIA, TARSI
AIRSY SYRIA
AIRSZ SIZAR
AIRTT TRAIT
AIRVX VARIX
AISSV SIVAS, VISAS
AISTV VISTA
AISTW WAIST
AISTX TAXIS
AISWZ SWAZI
AISXX X-AXIS
AISXY Y-AXIS
AISXZ Z-AXIS
AITTV VITTA
AJLRU JURAL
AJMMU JAMMU
AJMMY JAMMY
AJMOR MAJOR
AJNOS JASON, JONAS, SONJA
AJNOU ANJOU
AJNTU JAUNT, JUNTA
AJRTU JURAT
AJRUU JURUA
AJYZZ JAZZY
AKKLU KULAK
AKKOP KAPOK
AKKPU PUKKA
AKLLY ALKYL
AKLNP PLANK

AKLNY LANKY	ALLWY WALLY	ALRRU RURAL
AKLOP POLKA	ALLXY LAXLY	ALRRY LARRY
AKLOR KAROL	ALMMO MALMO	ALRSU SURAL, URALS
AKLRS LARKS	ALMNO MONAL	ALRTW TRAWL
AKLST STALK, TALKS	ALMNY MANLY	ALRWY RAWLY
AKLSW WALKS	ALMOR MOLAR, MORAL	ALSST LASTS, SALTS, SLATS
AKMOU OAKUM	ALMOY LOAMY	ALSSV SLAVS
AKMRS MARKS	ALMPS LAMPS, PALMS,	ALSTU TALUS, TULSA
AKMSS MASKS	PLASM, PSALM	ALSTY SALTY, SLATY
AKMUZ MUZAK	ALMPY AMPLY, PALMY	ALSUU USUAL
AKNOR KORAN, KRONA	ALMQU QUALM	ALSVY SYLVA
AKNOY KONYA	ALMRU MURAL	ALSWY YAWLS
AKNPR PRANK	ALMST SMALT	ALTTY LYTTA
AKNPS SPANK	ALMTY MALTY	ALTUV VAULT
AKNPU PUNKA	ALNNO NOLAN	ALTWZ WALTZ
AKNRS NARKS, RANKS	ALNNU ANNUL	ALUUV UVULA
AKNRY NARKY	ALNOP NOPAL	ALUVV VULVA
AKNST STANK, TANKS	ALNOR LORAN, LORNA	AMMMO MOMMA
AKNSU KANSU	ALNOS LOANS, SALON	AMMMY MAMMY
AKNSW SWANK	ALNOT TALON, TOLAN,	AMMOY MYOMA
AKNSY SNAKY, YANKS	TONAL	AMMRS SMARM
AKOOR KAROO	ALNOZ ZONAL	AMMSY SAMMY
AKOOZ KAZOO	ALNPS PLANS	AMMTY TAMMY
AKOPY YAPOK	ALNPT PLANT	AMNNU UNMAN
AKOSS SOAKS	ALNRS SNARL	AMNNY MANNY
AKOSY OKAYS	ALNRU LUNAR, ULNAR	AMNOR MANOR, MORNA,
AKOTY TOKAY	ALNST SLANT	NORMA, RAMON, ROMAN
AKPRS PARKS, SPARK	ALNSU ULNAS	AMNOS MASON, MOANS
AKPRY PARKY	ALNSW LAWNS	AMNOW WOMAN
AKPTU KAPUT	ALNTY LANTY	AMNOY MOYNA
AKPWY PAWKY	ALNUY UNLAY, YULAN	AMNOZ MONZA
AKQRU QUARK	ALNWY ALWYN, LAWNY,	AMNRU NAMUR
AKQUY QUAKY	WANLY	AMNRY MYRNA
AKRST KARST, STARK	ALNXY XYLAN	AMNSU MANUS
AKRSY SARKY	ALOOP PAOLO	AMNTY MAYN'T
AKSST TASKS	ALOPR PAROL, POLAR	AMNUY YUMAN
AKSSU SKUAS	ALOPS OPALS, SALOP	AMOPR PRO-AM
AKTUY YAKUT	ALORS LAROS, SOLAR	AMORU AMOUR
ALLLY ALLYL	ALORU RAOUL	AMORY MAYOR, MORAY,
ALLMO MOLAL	ALORV ORVAL, VOLAR	MOYRA
ALLMS MALLS, SMALL	ALORY ROYAL	AMOST ATOMS, MOATS,
ALLNO LLANO	ALOSS LASSO	STOMA
ALLOS SALOL	ALOST ALTOS	AMOTU OMUTA
ALLOT ALLOT, ATOLL	ALOSV OVALS, SALVO	AMPRS PRAMS, RAMPS
ALLOW ALLOW	ALOTT TOTAL	AMPRT TRAMP
ALLOY ALLOY, LOYAL	ALOTV LOVAT, VOLTA	AMPSS SPASM
ALLPS PALLS, SPALL	ALOVV VOLVA	AMPST STAMP
ALLPY PALLY	ALPPU PUPAL	AMPSU PUMAS
ALLRY RALLY	ALPPY APPLY	AMPSV VAMPS
ALLST STALL	ALPSS SLAPS	AMPSW SWAMP
ALLSW WALLS	ALPST SPLAT	AMRRY MARRY
ALLSY SALLY	ALPSY PALSY, PLAYS, SPLAY	AMRST SMART, TRAMS
ALLTY TALLY	ALPTY APTLY, PLATY	AMRSU RAMUS

AMRSW SWARM	AOPRT APORT, OP ART,	ASSTY STAYS
AMRTY MARTY, TRYMA	PRATO	ASTTW TWATS, WATTS
AMSST MASTS	AOPSS PSOAS, SOAPS	ASTTY TASTY
AMSTY MAYST	AOPSY SOAPY	ASVVY SAVVY
AMTTY MATTY	AOPTZ TOPAZ	ATTTY TATTY
ANNNY NANNY	AOQTU QUOTA	ATTWY WYATT
ANNOR RONNA	AORRS ROARS	BBBOY BOBBY
ANNOT ANTON	AORRW ARROW	BBCEU CUBEB
ANNOY ANNOY	AORRZ RAZOR	BBDEE EBBED
ANOOP POONA	AORSS SAROS	BBDOY DOBBY
ANOPR APRON, NO-PAR	AORST ROAST, ROTAS,	BBEII IBBIE
ANOPW POWAN	TAROS	BBEIL BIBLE
ANORS ARSON, ROANS,	AORTT TAROT	BBEIR BRIBE
SONAR	AORVY OVARY	BBEMO BOMBE
ANORT TRONA	AOSSY SAY-SO	BBEOP BEBOP
ANORW ROWAN	AOSTT STOAT, TOAST	BBEWY WEBBY
ANORY RAYON	AOSTU AUTOS	BBHMO H-BOMB
ANOSV NOVAS	AOSVY SAVOY	BBHOS HOBBS
ANOSX SAXON	APPPY PAPPY	BBHOY HOBBY
ANOSY SONYA	APPSU PUPAS	BBHUY HUBBY
ANOTT TANTO	APPSY SAPPY	BBILY LIBBY
ANOTX TAXON	APPYZ ZAPPY	BBISY SIBBY
ANOTY ATONY, TONYA	APRRY PARRY	BBITY TIBBY
ANOWY NO WAY	APRSS RASPS, SPARS	BBLOS BLOBS
ANPPY NAPPY	APRST PARTS, PRATS, SPRAT,	BBLOY LOBBY
ANPRW PRAWN	STRAP, TRAPS	BBLRU BLURB
ANPRY PYRAN	APRSU SUPRA	BBLSU BULBS
ANPSS SNAPS	APRSW WARPS, WRAPS	BBMOS BOMBS
ANPST PANTS	APRSY SPRAY	BBOOS BOOBS
ANPSU PUSAN	APRTY PARTY	BBOOY BOOBY
ANPSW PAWNS, SPAWN	APSST PASTS, SPATS	BBSUY BUSBY
ANPSY PANSY	APSSW SWAPS, WASPS	BBTUY TUBBY
ANPTU UNAPT	APSTY PASTY, PATSY	BCCIU CUBIC
ANPTY PANTY	APTTY PATTY	BCDEU CUBED
ANQRU QUR'AN	AQRTU QUART	BCEEH BEECH
ANQTU QUANT	AQSTU SQUAT	BCEHL BELCH
ANRST TARNS	AQSUW SQUAW	BCEHN BENCH
ANRSY YARNS	AQSUY QUAYS	BCEHO BOCHE
ANRUU NAURU	ARRTY TARRY	BCEIR BRICE
ANRUY UNARY	ARSST STARS, TRASS, TSARS	BCEKS BECKS
ANSSU SUSAN	ARSTT START, TARTS	BCEKY BECKY
ANSSW SWANS	ARSTU SURAT	BCEOY BOYCE
ANSTU AUNTS, TUNAS	ARSTW STRAW, WARTS	BCERU BRUCE
ANSTW WANTS	ARSTY SATYR, STRAY,	BCERY BRYCE
ANSTY NASTY, TANSY	TRAYS	BCESU CUBES
ANSUY UNSAY	ARSTZ TZARS	BCHIR BIRCH
ANSWY YAWNS	ARSUV VARUS	BCHIT BITCH
ANTTU TAUNT	ARSUY SAURY	BCHNU BUNCH
ANTTY NATTY	ARSXY X-RAYS	BCHOT BOTCH
ANTUV VAUNT	ARTTY RATTY	BCHTU BUTCH
ANTWY TAWNY	ARTWY WARTY	BCHUU BUCHU
ANVVY NAVVY	ASSSY SASSY	BCIKR BRICK
AOPPP POPPA	ASSTW SWATS	BCILM CLIMB

BCIOR BORIC

BCIPU PUBIC

BCIRS CRIBS

BCITU CUBIT

BCKLO BLOCK

BCKOR BROCK

BCKSU BUCKS

BCLOS BLOCS

BCLSU CLUBS

BCMOO COMBO

BCMOS COMBS

BCMRU CRUMB

BCRSU CURBS, SCRUB

BDDEI BIDED

BDDEO BODED

BDDIY BIDDY

BDDUY BUDDY

BDEEL BLEED

BDEEM EMBED

BDEER BREED

BDEGO BODGE

BDEGU BUDGE, DEBUG

BDEIJ JIBED

BDEIK BIKED

BDEIM IMBED

BDEIP BIPED

BDEIR BRIDE

BDEIS B-SIDE

BDEIT BIDET, DEBIT

BDELN BLEND

BDELO LOBED

BDEMO DEMOB

BDENO BONED

BDENS BENDS

BDEOO BOOED

BDEOR BORED, ROBED

BDEOW BOWED

BDEOX BOXED

BDERY DERBY

BDEST DEBTS

BDESU BUSED

BDETU DEBUT

BDFII BIFID

BDGIY DIGBY

BDIIR IRBID

BDILN BLIND

BDILU BUILD

BDINU IN BUD

BDIOP BIPOD

BDIOV BOVID

BDIRS BIRDS, DRIBS

BDLNO BLOND

BDLOO BLOOD

BDLOY DOLBY

BDNOS BONDS

BDNOU BOUND

BDNUU BUNDU

BDOOR BROOD, DOBRO

BDOSU DOUBS

BDOTU DOUBT

BEEFY BEEFY

BEEGI BEIGE

BEEGL GLEBE

BEEGR GREBE

BEEGT BEGET

BEEHP PHEBE

BEEHR HEBER

BEEIL BELIE

BEELL BELLE

BEELM BELEM

BEELP BLEEP

BEELR REBEL

BEELT BETEL

BEELV BEVEL

BEELZ BEZEL

BEEMR EMBER

BEENT BENET

BEEOS OBESE

BEERS BEERS

BEERT BERET

BEERV BREVE

BEERW WEBER

BEERY BEERY

BEEST BEETS, BESET

BEETT BETTE

BEFGO BEFOG

BEFIR BRIEF, FIBRE

BEFIT BEFIT

BEGIL BILGE

BEGIN BEGIN, BEING, BINGE

BEGIO BOGIE

BEGIR GIBER

BEGIS GIBES

BEGLO GLOBE

BEGLU BUGLE, BULGE

BEGMU BEGUM

BEGNU BEGUN

BEGOT BEGOT

BEGOY BOGEY

BEHOR HOREB

BEHRS HERBS

BEHRT BERTH

BEHRY HERBY

BEIJS JIBES

BEIKS BIKES

BEILL LIBEL

BEILR ERBIL

BEIMO BIOME

BEIMU IMBUE

BEINN BENIN

BEINR BRINE

BEIRR BRIER

BEIRS BIERS

BEIRT TRIBE

BEIST BITES

BEISV BEVIS, VIBES

BEITT TIBET

BEITZ ZIBET

BEJNY BENJY

BEKLO BLOKE

BEKOR BROKE

BEKRS BERKS, KERBS

BEKRU BURKE

BEKUZ UZBEK

BELLS BELLS

BELLY BELLY

BELMU UMBEL

BELNO NOBLE

BELOR ROBLE

BELOS BOLES, LOBES

BELOU BOULE

BELOW BELOW, BOWEL,
     ELBOW

BELPS PLEBS

BELRU BLUER, RUBLE

BELRY BERYL

BELSS BLESS

BELST BELTS, BLEST

BELSU BLUES

BELSY SELBY

BEMOR BROME

BEMOS BESOM

BEMOW EMBOW

BEMRU BRUME, UMBER

BEMSU SEBUM

BENNY BENNY

BENOR BORNE

BENOS BONES

BENOT T-BONE

BENOY EBONY

BENRT BRENT

BENRY BERNY

BENST BENTS

BEOOS OBOES

BEOOZ BOOZE

BEOPR PROBE

BEORR BORER

BEORS BOERS, BORES,
     ROBES, SOBER

BEORW BOWER
BEORX BOXER
BEOSU BOUSE
BEOSX BOXES
BEPSU PUBES
BERRY BERRY
BERST BREST
BERSU BURSE, REBUS
BERSV VERBS
BERSY BYRES
BERTT BRETT
BERTU BRUTE, REBUT,
    TUBER
BERUY BUYER
BESSU BUSES
BESSY BESSY
BESTU TUBES
BESTY BETSY, BYTES
BETTU BUTTE
BETTY BETTY
BFFIS BIFFS
BFFLU BLUFF
BFFSU BUFFS
BFLYY FLYBY
BGGOY BOGGY
BGGUY BUGGY
BGHIT BIGHT
BGHOU BOUGH
BGHRU BURGH
BGINO BINGO
BGINR BRING
BGIOT BIGOT
BGLUY BULGY
BGMOU GUMBO
BGNOO BONGO
BGNSU BUNGS
BGOOR BOGOR
BGOSU BOGUS
BGRSU GRUBS
BGRUY RUGBY
BHILU HUBLI
BHIRT BIRTH
BHLOO BOHOL
BHLSU BLUSH
BHMPU BUMPH
BHMRU RHUMB
BHMTU THUMB
BHOOS HOBOS
BHOOT BOOTH
BHORT BROTH, THROB
BHRSU BRUSH, SHRUB
BHSUY BUSHY
BIILN BLINI

BIIMN NIMBI
BIIOR ORIBI
BIISU SIBIU
BIJOU BIJOU
BIKLN BLINK
BIKNR BRINK
BIKRS BRISK
BIKRY KIRBY
BIKSY BIYSK
BILLR BRILL
BILLS BILLS
BILLY BILLY
BILMO LIMBO
BILMP BLIMP
BILMS LIMBS
BILOR BROIL
BILOS BOILS
BILPS BLIPS
BILSS BLISS
BILSY SIBYL, SYBIL
BILTU BUILT
BILTZ BLITZ
BINOR ROBIN
BINOS BISON
BINRU BRUIN, BURIN
BINRY BRINY
BIORS BIROS, BORIS
BIORT ORBIT
BIPSU PUBIS
BIQSU SQUIB
BIRST BRITS
BIRTT BRITT
BIRTU BRUIT
BITTY BITTY
BJMOU JUMBO
BJNOR BJORN
BKLSU BULKS
BKLUY BULKY
BKNOS KNOBS
BKNSU BUNKS
BKOOR BROOK
BKOOS BOOKS
BKOSY BOSKY
BKRSU BURKS
BLLOS BOLLS
BLLSU BULLS
BLLUY BULLY
BLMOO BLOOM
BLMPU PLUMB
BLNOW BLOWN
BLNOY NOBLY
BLNTU BLUNT
BLOSS SLOBS

BLOST BLOTS, BOLTS
BLOSU BOLUS
BLOSW BLOWS, BOWLS
BLOTY BY LOT
BLOWY BLOWY
BLRTU BLURT
BLRUY BURLY
BLTUY BUTYL
BMOOR BROOM
BMOOS BOOMS, BOSOM
BMOST TOMBS
BMOSW WOMBS
BMOTY BYTOM
BMOUX BUXOM
BMPSU BUMPS
BMPUY BUMPY
BNNOY BONNY
BNNUY BUNNY
BNOOR BORON
BNOOS BOONS, BOSON
BNORU BORNU, BOURN,
    BRUNO
BNORW BROWN
BNORX BRONX
BNORY BYRON, ROBYN
BNOSS SNOBS
BNOSU BONUS, BOSUN
BNRSU BURNS
BNRTU BRUNT, BURNT
BNSSU SNUBS
BOOPX PO BOX
BOORS BOORS
BOORT ROBOT
BOOST BOOST, BOOTS
BOOSZ BOZOS
BOOTY BOOTY
BOOWX OXBOW
BOOYZ BOOZY
BOPUW UP-BOW
BORRU BURRO
BORSW BROWS
BOSSY BOSSY
BOSTU BOUTS
BOSUY BUOYS
BPRSU BURPS
BRRSU BURRS
BRRUY BURRY
BRSTU BURST
BSSTU BUSTS, STUBS
BSTTU BUTTS
BSTUY BUSTY
BTTUY BUTTY
CCEHK CHECK

CCEHZ CZECH
CCEIL CECIL
CCEIR CERIC
CCELY CYCLE
CCEOS SECCO
CCESU CUSEC
CCHIK CHICK
CCHIN CINCH
CCHKO CHOCK
CCHKU CHUCK
CCHLU CULCH
CCHNO CONCH
CCHOU COUCH
CCHRU CURCH
CCIIT ICTIC
CCIIV CIVIC
CCIKL CLICK
CCIKR CRICK
CCILO COLIC
CCIMO COMIC
CCINO CONIC
CCINY CYNIC
CCIOS CISCO
CCKLO CLOCK
CCKLU CLUCK
CCKOR CROCK
CCKOS COCKS
CCKOY COCKY
CCORU OCCUR
CCOUZ CUZCO
CDDEE CEDED
CDDEI DICED
CDDEO CODED
CDDUY CUDDY
CDEEI DE-ICE
CDEER CEDER, CREED
CDEEU DEUCE, EDUCE
CDEHI CHIDE
CDEIM MEDIC
CDEIR CIDER, CRIED, DICER
CDEIT CITED, EDICT
CDEIV VEDIC
CDEIY DICEY
CDEKS DECKS
CDELO DOLCE
CDELU DULCE
CDELY CLYDE
CDEMO MEDOC
CDENS SCEND
CDENU DUNCE
CDEOO COOED
CDEOP COPED

CDEOR CODER, CORED, CREDO, DÉCOR
CDEOS CODES, COEDS
CDEOU COUDE
CDEOW COWED
CDEOX CODEX, COXED
CDEOY DECOY
CDERU CRUDE, CURED
CDERY CYDER, DECRY
CDETU EDUCT
CDHIL CHILD
CDHIT DITCH
CDHOR CHORD
CDHTU DUTCH
CDHUY DUCHY
CDIIN INDIC
CDIIO IODIC
CDIKS DICKS
CDIKY DICKY
CDILU LUCID
CDINY CINDY
CDIOR DORIC
CDIOS DISCO
CDIPU CUPID
CDISS DISCS
CDJOU JUDOC
CDKOS DOCKS
CDKSU DUCKS
CDKUY DUCKY
CDLOS CLODS, COLDS, SCOLD
CDLOU CLOUD, COULD
CDLWY CLWYD
CDMOR CD-ROM
CDNOO CODON
CDORS CORDS
CDORU DUROC
CDORW CROWD
CDRUY CURDY
CDSTU DUCTS
CEEEM EMCEE
CEEFN FENCE
CEEFS FECES
CEEHK CHEEK
CEEHL LEECH
CEEHN HENCE
CEEHP CHEEP
CEEHR CHEER
CEEIN NIECE
CEEIP PIECE
CEEJT EJECT
CEEKL CLEEK
CEEKR CREEK

CEELL CELLE
CEELR CREEL
CEELT ELECT
CEELX EXCEL
CEELY LYCÉE
CEEMR CREME
CEENP PENCE
CEENS CENSE, SCENE
CEEPR CREEP, CREPE, PERCE
CEERS CERES, SCREE
CEERT CRETE, ERECT
CEFHI CHIEF
CEFHS CHEFS
CEFHT FETCH
CEFIT FECIT
CEFKL FLECK
CEFLS CLEFS
CEFLT CLEFT
CEFOR FORCE
CEGIN GENIC
CEGKO GECKO
CEGNO CONGÉ
CEGSS GCSES
CEHIL CHILE
CEHIM CHIME
CEHIN CHINE, NICHE
CEHIR REICH
CEHIT ETHIC
CEHKO CHOKE
CEHKR KERCH
CEHKT KETCH
CEHLO CHLOE
CEHLW WELCH
CEHLY CHYLE
CEHMY CHYME
CEHNO ENOCH
CEHNT TENCH
CEHNW WENCH
CEHOP EPOCH
CEHOR CHORE, OCHRE
CEHOS CHOSE, SOCHE
CEHPR PERCH
CEHRT CHERT, RETCH
CEHRU RUCHE
CEHSS CHESS
CEHST CHEST
CEHSW CHEWS
CEHTU CHUTE
CEHTV VETCH
CEHTY TECHY
CEHWY CHEWY
CEIIR ICIER
CEIJU JUICE

CEILM CLIME
CEILN CLINE
CEILR RELIC
CEILS SLICE
CEILT TELIC
CEILU LUCIE
CEILV CLIVE
CEIMN MINCE
CEIMR CRIME
CEIMS MESIC
CEIMX CIMEX
CEINO ON ICE
CEINR NICER
CEINS SINCE
CEINV VINCE
CEINW WINCE
CEINZ ZENIC
CEIOV VOICE
CEIPR PRICE
CEIPS EPICS, SPICE
CEIPT TEPIC
CEIRR CRIER
CEIRS CRIES
CEIRT TRICE
CEIRU CURIE
CEIRX XERIC
CEISV VICES
CEITV CIVET, EVICT
CEITW TWICE
CEJOY JOYCE
CEKLR CLERK
CEKNS NECKS, SNECK
CEKNV V-NECK
CEKOS COKES
CEKPS PECKS, SPECK
CEKRW WRECK
CELLO CELLO
CELLS CELLS
CELNO CLONE
CELNU UNCLE
CELOS CLOSE, SOCLE
CELOV CLOVE
CELOY COLEY
CELPU CUPEL
CELRU CRUEL, LUCRE,
    ULCER
CELSU CLUES
CELSW CLEWS
CELTU CULET
CELUX CULEX
CEMOR COMER
CEMOT COMET
CEMRY MERCY

CENNO NONCE
CENOP PONCE
CENOR CRONE
CENOS CONES, SCONE
CENOT CENTO, CONTE
CENOU OUNCE
CENOV COVEN
CENOY CONEY
CENOZ COZEN
CENST CENTS, SCENT
CEOPS COPES, COPSE,
    SCOPE
CEOPU COUPÉ
CEORR CORER, CRORE
CEORS CORES, CORSE,
    SCORE
CEORT RECTO
CEORV COVER
CEORW COWER
CEORZ CROZE
CEOSV COVES
CEOSW COWES
CEOSX COXES
CEOTT OCTET
CEOTV COVET
CEOVY COVEY
CEPRT CREPT
CEPRY PERCY
CEPSS SPECS
CERRU RECUR
CERSS CRESS
CERST CERTS, CREST
CERSU CRUSE, CURES,
    CURSE
CERSW CREWS, SCREW
CERSY CERYS
CERTU CRUET, CURET,
    CUTER, ERUCT, TRUCE
CERUV CURVE
CESST SECTS
CESTU CETUS, SCUTE
CFFHU CHUFF
CFFIL CLIFF
CFFOS SCOFF
CFFSU CUFFS, SCUFF
CFHIL FILCH
CFHIN FINCH
CFHIT FITCH
CFHIU FICHU
CFIKL FLICK
CFIKU KUFIC
CFILO FOLIC
CFIOS COIFS

CFKLO FLOCK
CFKOR FROCK
CFKSU FUCKS
CFMOY COMFY
CFORT CROFT
CFOSU FOCUS
CFRSU SCURF
CFSUU FUCUS
CGHIN CHING
CGHLU GULCH
CGHOU COUGH
CGIIN ICING
CGILN CLING
CGILO LOGIC
CGINO COIGN
CGINU CUING
CGIOR CORGI
CGIOY YOGIC
CGIRU UGRIC
CGLNU CLUNG
CGLOS CLOGS
CGNOO COGON, CONGO
CHHIT HITCH
CHHIW WHICH
CHHNU HUNCH
CHHOO HOOCH
CHHTU HUTCH
CHIKN CHINK
CHIKO HOICK, KOCHI
CHIKS HICKS
CHIKT THICK
CHILL CHILL
CHILM MILCH
CHIMR CHIRM
CHIMT MITCH
CHIMU HUMIC
CHINP PINCH
CHINS CHINS
CHINW WINCH
CHIOR CHOIR
CHIOS SOCHI
CHIPR CHIRP
CHIPS CHIPS
CHIPT PITCH
CHIRR CHIRR
CHIRS CHRIS
CHIST CHITS, STICH
CHITW WITCH
CHITY ITCHY
CHIVY CHIVY, VICHY
CHKNU CHUNK
CHKOS HOCKS, SHOCK
CHKOY CHOKY

CHKSU SHUCK	CIKST STICK, TICKS	CKRSU RUCKS
CHKTU KUTCH	CIKSW WICKS	CKRTU TRUCK
CHLMU MULCH	CIKVY VICKY	CKSTU STUCK, TUCKS
CHLNU LUNCH	CILNO COLIN, NICOL	CKUYY YUCKY
CHLNY LYNCH	CILNT CLINT	CLLSU CULLS, SCULL
CHLOS LOCHS	CILOS COILS	CLMOU COLUM, LOCUM
CHLOT CLOTH	CILOT LOTIC	CLMPU CLUMP
CHLRU CHURL, LURCH	CILOW WILCO	CLMTU MULCT
CHMNU MUNCH	CILPS CLIPS	CLNOO COLON
CHMOO MOOCH	CILRU ULRIC	CLNOW CLOWN
CHMOP CHOMP	CILRY CYRIL, LYRIC	CLNUY CLUNY
CHMPU CHUMP	CILTY LYTIC	CLOOS COOLS
CHMSU CHUMS	CIMNU CUMIN, MUCIN	CLOST CLOTS, COLTS
CHNOT NOTCH	CIMOR MICRO	CLOSU LOCUS
CHNPU PUNCH	CIMOS OSMIC	CLOSW COWLS, SCOWL
CHNRU CHURN	CIMPR CRIMP	CLOTU CLOUT
CHOOP POOCH	CIMRS SCRIM	CLOYY COYLY
CHOPR PORCH	CIMSU MUSIC	CLRSU CURLS
CHOPS CHOPS	CINOS COINS, ICONS, SCION,	CLRUY CURLY
CHOPU POUCH	SONIC	CLSTU CULTS
CHORT TORCH	CINOT TONIC	CMOOP COMPO
CHOSU HOCUS	CINOV COVIN	CMOOS COSMO
CHOSW CHOWS	CINRU INCUR, RUNIC	CMORS CORMS
CHOTU TOUCH	CINSU INCUS	CMORU MUCRO
CHOUV VOUCH	CINTU CUTIN, TUNIC	CMPRU CRUMP
CHOUX CHOUX	CIOPT OPTIC, PICOT, TOPIC	CMRSU SCRUM
CHPSY PSYCH	CIORT TORIC	CMRYY CYMRY
CHRSU CRUSH	CIORU CURIO	CMSUU MUCUS
CHSUY CUSHY	CIOST STOIC	CNOOR CONOR, CROON
CIIKR RICKI	CIOTX TOXIC	CNOOS COONS
CIIKV VICKI	CIPRS CRISP, SCRIP	CNOPY PONCY
CIILT LICIT	CIPRY PRICY	CNORS CORNS, SCORN
CIILV CIVIL	CIPSS SPICS	CNORU CORNU
CIILY ICILY	CIPSY SPICY	CNORW CROWN
CIIMM MIMIC	CISSY CISSY	CNORY CORNY, CRONY
CIINO IONIC	CISTU CUTIS, ICTUS	CNOTU COUNT
CIINR RICIN	CJKOS JOCKS	CNOTY CYTON
CIINV VINIC	CJNOU JUNCO	CNSTU CUNTS
CIJUY JUICY	CKKNO KNOCK	CNSUU UNCUS
CIKKS KICKS	CKLNU CLUNK	CNTUU UNCUT
CIKLN CLINK	CKLOS LOCKS	COOPS COOPS, SCOOP
CIKLS LICKS, SLICK	CKLPU PLUCK	COOPT CO-OPT
CIKMS MICKS	CKLUY LUCKY	COOST COOTS, SCOOT
CIKMY MICKY	CKMOS MOCKS, SMOCK	COPRS CORPS, CROPS
CIKNS NICKS, SNICK	CKMUY MUCKY	COPRU CROUP
CIKNY NICKY	CKNOS CONKS	COPSU COUPS
CIKPR PRICK	CKOOR CROOK	COPUY COYPU
CIKPS PICKS	CKOOS COOKS	CORSS CROSS
CIKPY PICKY	CKORS CORKS, ROCKS	CORSU SCOUR
CIKQU QUICK	CKORY ROCKY	CORSW CROWS
CIKRS RICKS	CKOSS SOCKS	CORTU COURT
CIKRT TRICK	CKOST STOCK	CORWY COWRY
CIKRY RICKY	CKPSU PUCKS	COSST COSTS, SCOTS

COSTT SCOTT	DEEGH HEDGE	DEFLU FLUED
COSTU SCOUT	DEEGK KEDGE	DEFLY FYLDE
CPRTY CRYPT	DEEGL LEDGE	DEFMU FUMED
CPSSU CUSPS	DEEGO GEODE	DEFOX FOXED
CPTUU CUT UP	DEEGR EDGER, GREED	DEFPU FED UP
CRRUY CURRY	DEEGS EDGES, SEDGE	DEFSU FEUDS, FUSED
CRSTU CRUST	DEEGW WEDGE	DEGHY HEDGY
CRSUY CYRUS	DEEHW HEWED	DEGIL GELID, GLIDE
CSSTY CYSTS	DEEHX HEXED	DEGIM MIDGE
DDEEG EDGED	DEEIL ELIDE	DEGIN DEIGN
DDEEI EDDIE	DEEIR EIDER	DEGIO DOGIE, GEOID
DDEEN ENDED	DEEKN KNEED	DEGIR DIRGE, RIDGE
DDEES DEEDS	DEEKR DEREK	DEGIU GUIDE
DDEFY DYFED	DEEKY KEYED	DEGJU JUDGE
DDEGO DODGE	DEELR ELDER	DEGLO LODGE, OGLED
DDEIL IDLED	DEELU ELUDE	DEGLU GLUED
DDEIN DINED	DEELV DELVE	DEGLY LEDGY
DDEIO DIODE, DODIE	DEEMN EMEND	DEGNO OGDEN
DDEIR DRIED, REDID	DEEMT METED	DEGNU NUDGE
DDEIS SIDED	DEEMW MEWED	DEGOR GORED, RODGE
DDEIT TIDED	DEENO DONEE	DEGOS DOGES
DDEIV DIVED	DEENR ENDER	DEGRS DREGS
DDELO DOLED	DEENS DENSE, NEEDS	DEGRU URGED
DDEMO DOMED	DEENU ENDUE	DEGSY SEDGY
DDENY NEDDY	DEENY NEEDY	DEGUY GUYED
DDEOP DOPED	DEEOP EPODE	DEGWY WEDGY
DDEOR ODDER	DEEOR ERODE	DEHII HEIDI
DDEOS DOSED	DEEPS SPEED	DEHIK HIKED
DDEOT DOTED	DEERR ERRED	DEHIL DELHI
DDEOZ DOZED	DEERS REEDS	DEHIR HIDER, HIRED
DDEPU DUPED	DEERT DETER	DEHIS HIDES, SHIED
DDERU UDDER	DEERY REEDY	DEHIT EDITH
DDESU DUDES	DEESS SEEDS	DEHIV HIVED
DDETY TEDDY	DEEST STEED	DEHLO DHOLE
DDGIY GIDDY	DEESU SUEDE	DEHNO HONED
DDGOY DODGY	DEESW SEWED, SWEDE,	DEHOP HOPED
DDILO DILDO	WEEDS	DEHOR HEROD, HORDE
DDILY LIDDY	DEESX SEXED	DEHOS HOSED, SHOED
DDIMY MIDDY	DEESY SEEDY	DEHPT DEPTH
DDINU UNDID	DEETU ETUDE	DEHPY HYPED
DDIRU DRUID	DEETW TWEED	DEHRS HERDS, SHERD,
DDLOY ODDLY	DEEUX EXUDE	SHRED
DDMUY MUDDY	DEEVX VEXED	DEHSS SHEDS
DDNOY NODDY	DEEWY WEEDY	DEHSY SHYED
DDOOS DODOS	DEFGU FUDGE	DEIIM IMIDE
DDORY RODDY	DEFIL FIDEL, FIELD, FILED	DEIIV IVIED
DDOTY TODDY	DEFIN FIEND, FINED	DEIIX DIXIE
DDOWY DOWDY	DEFIR FIRED, FRIED	DEIJO JODIE
DDRUY RUDDY	DEFIT FETID	DEIJV JIVED
DEEFF EFFED	DEFIX FIXED	DEIKL LIKED
DEEFR DEFER, FREED	DEFIY DEIFY, EDIFY	DEIKN INKED
DEEFS FEEDS	DEFJL FJELD	DEIKR IRKED
DEEFT FETED	DEFLT DELFT	DEIKS DIKES, SKIED

37

DEILM LIMED
DEILN LINED
DEILO ODILE, OILED
DEILP PILED, PLIED
DEILR IDLER, RILED
DEILS SIDLE, SLIDE
DEILT TILDE, TILED
DEILV DEVIL, LIVED
DEILW WIELD
DEILY YIELD
DEIMM MIMED
DEIMN DENIM, MINED
DEIMR DIMER, MIRED
DEIMS DEISM, DIMES
DEIMT TIMED
DEIMX MIXED
DEINO DIONE
DEINP PINED
DEINR DINER, INDRE
DEINS DENIS, SNIDE
DEINU UDINE
DEINW EDWIN, WIDEN, WINED
DEINX INDEX, NIXED
DEIOV VIDEO
DEIOX OXIDE
DEIPP PIPED
DEIPR PRIDE, PRIED
DEIPS SPIED
DEIPT TEPID
DEIPW WIPED
DEIRR DIRER, DRIER, RIDER
DEIRS RIDES, SIRED
DEIRT TIRED, TRIED
DEIRV DIVER, DRIVE
DEIRW WEIRD, WIDER, WIRED, WRIED
DEISS SIDES
DEIST DEIST, DIETS, SITED, TIDES
DEISV DIVES
DEISW WIDES
DEISZ SIZED
DEITY DEITY
DEJKO JOKED
DEJOY JOYED
DEKKO DEKKO
DEKNU NUKED
DEKOP POKED
DEKOY YOKED
DEKPU PUKED
DEKRY DERYK
DEKSS DESKS

DEKSU DUKES
DEKSY DYKES
DELLS DELLS
DELLW DWELL
DELMO MODEL
DELNO ELDON, LODEN, OLDEN
DELOP LOPED, POLED
DELOR OLDER
DELOS DELOS, LODES, SOLED
DELOV LOVED
DELOW DOWEL, LOWED
DELOY YODEL
DELPU DUPLE
DELRU LURED, RULED
DELSS SLEDS
DELSU DUELS, DULSE, SLUED
DELSW WELDS
DELTW DWELT
DEMMO MODEM
DEMNO DEMON
DEMNS MENDS
DEMOO MOOED
DEMOP MOPED
DEMOR DROME
DEMOS DEMOS, DOMES, MODES
DEMOU ODEUM
DEMOV MOVED
DEMOW MOWED
DEMRU DEMUR
DEMSU MUSED, SEDUM
DEMTU MUTED
DENNY DENNY
DENOR DRONE
DENOS NODES, NOSED, SONDE
DENOT NOTED, TONED
DENOW ENDOW, OWNED
DENOY DOYEN
DENOZ DOZEN, ZONED
DENPS SPEND
DENPU UPEND
DENRS NERDS
DENRT TREND
DENRU UNDER
DENRY DERYN
DENST DENTS
DENSU DUNES, NUDES
DENSY DENYS
DENTU TUNED

DENUU UNDUE
DENWY EDWYN, WENDY
DEOOR RODEO
DEOOW WOOED
DEOOZ OOZED
DEOPR PEDRO, PORED, ROPED
DEOPS DOPES, POSED, SPODE
DEOPT DEPOT, OPTED
DEOPY DOPEY
DEORR ORDER
DEORS DOERS, DOSER
DEORT DOTER
DEORU UREDO
DEORV DROVE, ROVED
DEORW DOWER, ROWED
DEORZ DOZER
DEOSS DOSES
DEOSU DOUSE
DEOSV DOVES
DEOSW DOWSE, SOWED
DEOTT TOTED
DEOTV VOTED
DEOTW TOWED
DEOTY TOYED
DEOVW VOWED
DEOWW WOWED
DEPRU DRUPE, DUPER, PRUDE
DEPSU DUPES, PSEUD
DEPTY TYPED
DERRU RUDER
DERRY DERRY, DRYER
DERSS DRESS
DERSU DRUSE
DERSY DYERS
DERUX DUREX
DESTU DUETS
DETUV DUVET
DFFSU DUFFS
DFILU FLUID
DFINS FINDS
DFIOR FIORD
DFIRT DRIFT
DFJOR FJORD
DFLOO FLOOD, OF OLD
DFLOS FOLDS
DFLOY FLOYD
DFNOR FROND
DFNOU FOUND
DFNSU FUNDS
DFOOS FOODS

DFORS FORDS	DIKNY DINKY	DLOST DOLTS
DGGOO DOGGO	DIKRS DIRKS	DLOSW WOLDS
DGGOY DOGGY	DIKSS DISKS, SKIDS	DLOUW WOULD
DGHOU DOUGH	DILLR DRILL	DMMUY DUMMY
DGIIR RIGID	DILLY IDYLL	DMNOU MOUND
DGIIT DIGIT	DILMY DIMLY	DMOOS DOOMS, MOODS
DGILU GUILD	DILNY LINDY	DMOOY MOODY
DGINO DINGO, DOING, GONDI	DILOS IDOLS, LIDOS, SOLID	DMPSU DUMPS
	DILOY DOILY	DMPUY DUMPY
DGINR GRIND	DILRU LURID	DMRSU DRUMS
DGINY DINGY, DYING	DILRY DRILY	DMRUU DURUM
DGIOU GUIDO	DILSW WILDS	DNNOY DONNY
DGIRS GRIDS	DILSY DILYS	DNOOR DONOR, RONDO
DGIRY RIDGY	DIMNO MID-ON	DNOOS SNOOD
DGLOS GOLDS	DIMNS MINDS	DNOOT TONDO
DGLOY GODLY	DIMOU ODIUM	DNOPS PONDS
DGNUY DUNGY	DIMST MIDST	DNOPU POUND
DGOOR DROGO	DIMTU TUMID	DNORU ROUND
DGOOS GOODS	DINRS RINDS	DNORW DROWN
DGOOY GOODY	DINSU INDUS, NIDUS	DNOSU NODUS, SOUND
DGOPY PODGY	DINSW WINDS	DNOSW DOWNS
DGORU GOURD	DINWY WINDY	DNOSY SYNOD
DGPUY PUDGY	DIOOT OOTID	DNOUW WOUND
DGRSU DRUGS	DIOOV OVOID	DNOWY DOWNY
DHIIN HINDI	DIOOZ ZOOID	DOOPR DROOP
DHILP D PHIL	DIOPY PYOID	DOORS DOORS, ROODS
DHIMU HUMID	DIORS DORIS	DOORU DOURO, ODOUR
DHINS HINDS	DIORT DROIT	DOOST STOOD, TO-DOS
DHINU HINDU	DIOSV VOIDS	DOOSW WOODS
DHIOT DHOTI	DIOTT DITTO	DOOTU OUTDO
DHIRT THIRD	DIOTV DIVOT	DOOWY WOODY
DHISY DISHY	DIOWW WIDOW	DOPRS DROPS, PRODS
DHITW WIDTH	DIPRS DRIPS	DOPRU PROUD
DHLOS HOLDS	DIQSU SQUID	DORSS DROSS
DHNOO HONDO	DIRTU TRUDI	DORSU SUDOR
DHNOU HOUND	DIRTY DIRTY	DORSW SWORD, WORDS
DHOOS HOODS	DITTY DITTY	DORTU TUDOR
DHORY HYDRO	DIYZZ DIZZY	DORWY DOWRY, ROWDY, WORDY
DHOSW DHOWS	DKNRU DRUNK	
DHOWY HOWDY	DKNSU DUNKS	DOTTY DOTTY
DHRSU HURDS	DKOSU KUDOS	DPSSU SPUDS
DHSTU THUDS	DKSUY DUSKY	DRSSU SURDS
DIILP LIPID	DKUUZ KUDZU	DRSTU TURDS
DIILV LIVID	DLLOR DROLL	DRTUY TRUDY
DIIMO IDIOM	DLLOS DOLLS	DSSTU STUDS
DIIMT TIMID	DLLOY DOLLY, LLOYD	DSSUY SUDSY
DIIOT IDIOT	DLLUY DULLY	DSTUY DUSTY, STUDY
DIIRS IDRIS	DLMOS MOLDS	EEEGS GEESE
DIIVV VIVID	DLMOU MOULD	EEEIR EERIE
DIJNN DJINN	DLMOY MOLDY	EEELM MELEE
DIJNO DIJON	DLOOR DROOL	EEELV LEVEE
DIKNR DRINK	DLORS LORDS	EEEMS ESMEE
DIKNS KINDS	DLORW WORLD	EEENR RENÉE

EEEPS ÉPÉES	EEHRX HEXER	EELSV ELVES
EEEPT TEPEE	EEHSS HESSE	EELTU ELUTE
EEEPV PEEVE	EEHST SHEET, THESE	EELTX TELEX
EEEPW PEWEE	EEHSX HEXES	EEMMR EMMER
EEERV REEVE	EEHTT TEETH	EEMNS MESNE, SEMEN
EEFFI EFFIE	EEILL ELLIE	EEMNY ENEMY, YEMEN
EEFLR FLEER	EEILM ELEMI, EMILE	EEMOT EMOTE
EEFLT FLEET	EEILS ELISE, ELSÍE	EEMRS MERES
EEFRR FREER, REFER	EEILT ELITE	EEMRT METER, METRE
EEFRS REEFS	EEILV ELVIE	EEMRX REMEX
EEFRV FEVER	EEILX EXILE	EEMRY EMERY
EEFSS FESSE	EEIMM EMMIE	EEMST MEETS
EEFST FETES	EEINR ERNIE, IRENE, REINE,	EEMSU MEUSE
EEFSU FUSEE	RENIE	EENPR NEPER, PREEN
EEFSZ FEZES	EEINS SEINE	EENQU QUEEN
EEGGR EGGER	EEIPP EPPIE	EENRS SNEER
EEGHL HEGEL	EEIRS ISERE	EENRT ENTER, RENTE,
EEGHN HENGE	EEIRY EYRIE	TERNE, TREEN
EEGIL LIEGE	EEISS ESSIE, SEISE	EENRU ENURE
EEGIN GENIE	EEISV SIEVE	EENRV NERVE, NEVER
EEGIR EIGER	EEISZ SEIZE	EENRW NEWER, RENEW
EEGIS SIEGE	EEITT ETTIE	EENRY NYREE
EEGKR GREEK	EEJLW JEWEL	EENSS ESSEN, SENSE
EEGLR LEGER	EEJPS JEEPS	EENST TEENS, TENSE
EEGLS GLEES	EEJRS JEERS	EENSU ENSUE
EEGLT GLEET	EEJRZ JEREZ	EENSV EVENS, SEVEN
EEGLY ELEGY	EEJSS JESSE	EENTT TENET
EEGMR MERGE	EEKLN KNEEL	EENTV EVENT
EEGNR GENRE, GREEN	EEKLS KEELS, LEEKS, SLEEK	EENTW 'TWEEN
EEGNS GENES	EEKLV KEVEL	EENTY TEENY
EEGNT GENET	EEKNR KEREN	EENUV VENUE
EEGNV NEGEV	EEKNS KEENS, KNEES	EENWY WEENY
EEGRS SERGE	EEKOP PEKOE	EEOPT TOPEE
EEGRT EGRET, GREET	EEKOV EVOKE	EEORS EROSE
EEGRV VERGE	EEKPS KEEPS	EEOXY OXEYE
EEGST EGEST, GEEST	EEKRS ESKER	EEPPS PEEPS
EEHIN HENIE	EEKRY REEKY	EEPRS PEERS, PER SE, SPREE
EEHLL HELLE	EEKST SKEET	EEPRT PETER
EEHLN HELEN	EEKSW WEEKS	EEPRU PUREE, RUPEE
EEHLS HEELS	EELLN ELLEN	EEPST STEEP
EEHLT ETHEL	EELLV LEVEL	EEPSW SWEEP
EEHLV HELVE	EELMR ELMER, MERLE	EEPWY WEEPY
EEHLW WHEEL	EELNO NOELE	EEQRU QUEER
EEHMN HE-MEN	EELNW NEWEL	EEQUU QUEUE
EEHMT THEME	EELOP ELOPE	EERSS SEERS
EEHNS SHEEN	EELPR LEPER, REPEL	EERST ESTER, RESET,
EEHNT ETHNE	EELPS SLEEP	STEER, STERE, TERSE,
EEHPS SHEEP	EELPX EXPEL	TREES
EEHRS HERES, SHEER	EELRS LEERS, REELS	EERSU REUSE
EEHRT ETHER, THERE,	EELRV ELVER, LEVER,	EERSV SERVE, SEVER,
THREE	REVEL	VERSE
EEHRV HERVÉ	EELRY LEERY	EERSW EWERS, SEWER
EEHRW HEWER, WHERE	EELST SLEET, STEEL, STELE	EERSX REXES

EERTV EVERT, REVET
EERTX EXERT
EERUV REVUE
EERVV VERVE
EERVX VEXER
EERVY EVERY, VEERY
EESSX SEXES
EESTV STEVE
EESTW SWEET
EETTU TUTEE
EETTW TWEET
EFFGO GEOFF
EFFIR FIFER
EFFIS FIFES
EFFOR OFFER
EFFRU RUFFE
EFGIN FEIGN
EFGIR GRIEF
EFGOR FORGE, GOFER
EFGUU FUGUE
EFHIO HOFEI
EFHIT THIEF
EFHLS FLESH, SHELF
EFHRS FRESH
EFHTT THEFT
EFHTY HEFTY
EFIKN KNIFE
EFILN ELFIN
EFILR FILER, FLIER, LIFER,
   RIFLE
EFILS FILES, FLIES
EFILT FILET
EFILX FELIX
EFIMR FERMI
EFINR FINER, INFER
EFINS FINES
EFINT FEINT
EFIRR FIRER, FRIER
EFIRS FIRES, FRIES, FRISE,
   SERIF
EFIRT REFIT
EFIRV FIVER
EFIRX FIXER
EFIRY FIERY, REIFY
EFISV FIVES
EFISX FIXES
EFKLU FLUKE
EFLLS FELLS
EFLMU FLUME
EFLNO FELON
EFLOS FLOES
EFLRU FLEUR
EFLRY FLYER

EFLSU FLUES, FUELS, FUSEL
EFLSW FLEWS
EFLTU FLUTE
EFLTY LEFTY
EFMOR FORME
EFMRU FEMUR, FUMER
EFMSU FUMES
EFNNY FENNY
EFNOR FREON
EFNOT OFTEN
EFNRS FERNS
EFNRY FERNY
EFORT FETOR, FORTE
EFORY FOYER
EFORZ FROZE
EFOSS FOSSE
EFOSX FOXES
EFRRY FERRY, FRYER
EFRSS SERFS
EFRST FRETS
EFRUZ FURZE
EFSSU FUSES
EFSTU FETUS
EGGGR GREGG
EGGIU GIGUE
EGGLY LEGGY
EGGMY MEGGY
EGGNU GUNGE
EGGOP POGGE
EGGOR GORGE
EGGOU GOUGE
EGGPY PEGGY
EGHIL LEIGH
EGHIN HINGE, NEIGH
EGHIT EIGHT
EGHIW WEIGH
EGHNT GHENT, THEGN
EGHRU HUGER
EGIIN GENII
EGIJR REJIG
EGILN NIGEL
EGILR LIGER
EGILS GILES
EGILT GILET, LEGIT
EGILU GUILE
EGIMR GRIME
EGINR NIGER, REIGN
EGINS SINGE
EGINT TINGE
EGINV GIVEN
EGINW WINGE
EGINY EYING
EGIOV OGIVE

EGIPR GRIPE
EGIRT TIGER, TIGRE
EGIRV GIVER
EGISU GUISE
EGLMO GOLEM, GOMEL
EGLMU GLUME
EGLNN GLENN
EGLNS GLENS
EGLNU LUNGE
EGLOR OGLER
EGLOT LET GO
EGLOV GLOVE
EGLRU GLUER, GRUEL,
   LUGER
EGLSU GULES
EGLSY GYLES
EGLUY GLUEY
EGMNO GNOME
EGMRS GERMS
EGNOR GONER, NEGRO
EGNOS SEGNO
EGNOT GET ON
EGNPU UNPEG
EGNST GENTS
EGNSU GENUS, NEGUS
EGNTW GWENT
EGNUU ENUGU
EGOOS GOOSE
EGOOY GOOEY
EGOPR GROPE
EGORR ROGER
EGORS GOERS, GORES,
   GORSE, OGRES
EGORT ERGOT
EGORU ROGUE, ROUGE
EGORV GROVE
EGOSS GESSO
EGOUV VOGUE
EGPRU PURGE
EGPTU GETUP
EGPTY EGYPT
EGRRU URGER
EGRRY GERRY
EGRSU SURGE, URGES
EGRSY GREYS
EGSSU GUESS
EGSTU GUEST
EHHOP HOPEH
EHHPU HUPEH
EHIKR HIKER
EHIKS HIKES, SHEIK
EHIKT KEITH
EHILT ITHEL, LITHE

EHILU ELIHU
EHILW WHILE
EHILX HELIX
EHIMY HYMIE
EHINR HENRI, RHINE
EHINS HINES, SHINE
EHINT THINE
EHINW WHINE
EHIRR HIRER
EHIRS HEIRS, SHIER, SHIRE
EHIRT THEIR
EHISS SHIES
EHIST HEIST
EHISV HIVES, SHIVE
EHITT TITHE
EHITW WHITE, WITHE
EHJLO JEHOL
EHKLW WHELK
EHKMR KHMER
EHKOO HOOKE
EHLLO HELLO
EHLLS HELLS, SHELL
EHLMS HELMS
EHLMU HULME
EHLOS HOLES
EHLOT HELOT, HOTEL, THOLE
EHLOV HOVEL
EHLOW HOWEL, WHOLE
EHLOY HOLEY, HOYLE
EHLPS HELPS
EHLPW WHELP
EHLPY PHYLE
EHLSW WELSH
EHLTY ETHYL
EHLWY HYWEL
EHLXY HEXYL
EHMNY HYMEN
EHMOR HOMER, HORME
EHMOS HOMES, MOSHE
EHMOY HOMEY
EHMRT THERM
EHMRU RHEUM
EHMRY RHYME
EHMST METHS
EHMTY THYME
EHNNY HENNY
EHNOP PHONE
EHNOR HERON, RHONE
EHNOS SHONE
EHNOY HONEY
EHNRY HENRY
EHNSW SHEWN

EHNTT TENTH
EHOOY HOOEY
EHOPR HOPER
EHOPS HOPES
EHORS HORSE, SHORE
EHORT OTHER
EHORV HOVER
EHORW WHORE
EHOSS HOSES, SHOES
EHOST ETHOS, THOSE
EHOSU HOUSE
EHOSV SHOVE
EHOSW WHOSE
EHPRY HYPER
EHPSY HEPSY
EHPTU HET UP
EHRSU USHER
EHRSW SHREW
EHRSY SHYER
EHRTW THREW
EHRTZ HERTZ
EHSTW THEWS
EHTTY HETTY
EIILN LIE-IN
EIIMN IMINE
EIINT TIE-IN
EIIPX PIXIE
EIISV IVIES
EIJLU JULIE
EIJOS JOSIE
EIKKS KIKES
EIKLN INKLE, LIKEN
EIKLS LIKES
EIKLY KYLIE
EIKMS MIKES
EIKNO EIKON, KOINE
EIKNS SKEIN
EIKNV KEVIN
EIKPS PIKES, SPIKE
EIKRR KERRI
EIKRS SKIER
EIKRT TRIKE
EIKSS SKIES
EIKST KITES
EIKSV SKIVE
EIKTW KITWE
EILLL LILLE
EILLN NEILL
EILLO OLLIE
EILLS ELLIS, LIESL, LISLE
EILMN LIMEN
EILMP IMPEL
EILMR MILER

EILMS LIMES, MILES, SLIME, SMILE
EILMU ILEUM
EILMY EMILY, LIMEY
EILNN LINEN
EILNR LINER
EILNS LENIS, LIENS, LINES
EILNT INLET
EILNV ELVIN, LIVEN, NEVIL
EILOR LOIRE, OILER, ORIEL
EILOT ELIOT, TOILE
EILOU LOUIE
EILOV OLIVE, VOILE
EILPR PERIL, PLIER
EILPS PILES, SPIEL, SPILE
EILPX PIXEL
EILRT LITER, LITRE, TILER
EILRV LIVER, VILER
EILRY RILEY
EILSS ISLES
EILST ISLET, ISTLE, STILE, TILES
EILSU ILEUS, LIEUS
EILSV ELVIS, EVILS, LEVIS, LIVES, VEILS
EILSW LEWIS, WILES
EILSX LEXIS, SILEX
EILTT TITLE
EIMMR MIMER
EIMMS MIMES
EIMNR MINER
EIMNS MIENS, MINES, NIMES
EIMNV VIMEN
EIMOR MOIRE
EIMOV MOVIE
EIMOX OXIME
EIMPR PRIME
EIMPT TEMPI
EIMRS EMIRS, MIRES, MISER, REIMS
EIMRT MERIT, MITRE, REMIT, TIMER
EIMRX MIXER
EIMSS SEISM, SEMIS
EIMST ITEMS, MITES, SMITE, TIMES
EIMSX MIXES
EIMSY MYSIE
EINNR INNER, RENIN
EINNS NINES
EINNU ENNUI
EINNV VENIN
EINOP OPINE

EINOS EOSIN, NOISE
EINOT TIE-ON, TOE-IN
EINOV OVINE
EINPP PEPIN
EINPR RIPEN
EINPS PENIS, PINES, SNIPE,
  SPINE
EINPT INEPT
EINPY PINEY
EINRS REINS, RESIN, RINSE,
  RISEN, SERIN, SIREN
EINRT INERT, INTER, NITRE,
  TERNI, TRINE
EINRU INURE, URINE
EINRV RIVEN
EINRW ERWIN
EINSS SINES
EINST INSET, STEIN, TINES
EINSV VEINS, VINES
EINSW SINEW, SWINE, WINES
EINTU UNITE, UNTIE
EINTW TWINE
EINVX VIXEN
EINVY VEINY
EINWZ WINZE, WIZEN
EIOPS POISE
EIORS OSIER, ROSIE
EIORV VIREO
EIOSS OSSIE
EIOZZ OZZIE
EIPPR PIPER
EIPPS PIPES
EIPQU EQUIP, PIQUE
EIPRR PRIER, RIPER
EIPRS PIERS, PRISE, SPIRE
EIPRT TRIPE
EIPRV VIPER
EIPRW WIPER
EIPRZ PRIZE
EIPSS SPIES
EIPST PISTE, SPITE, STIPE
EIPSW SWIPE, WIPES
EIPTT PETIT
EIPTU TIE-UP
EIPTW PEWIT
EIPTY PIETY
EIPXY PYXIE
EIQRU QUIRE
EIQTU QUIET, QUITE
EIRRS RISER
EIRRT TERRI, TRIER
EIRRV RIVER
EIRRW WIRER, WRIER

EIRSS RISES, SIRES
EIRST RESIT, RITES, TIERS,
  TIRES, TRIES
EIRSW WEIRS, WIRES, WISER
EIRTT TITRE, TRITE
EIRTU UTERI
EIRTV RIVET
EIRTW WRITE
EISST SITES, STIES
EISSU ISSUE, SUSIE
EISSV VISES
EISSX SIXES
EISSZ SIZES
EISTU SUITE
EISTX EXIST, EXITS, SIXTE
EISTY YETIS
EISTZ ZEIST
EISVW VIEWS, WIVES
EITTW TWITE
EJKOR JOKER
EJKOS JOKES
EJKRS JERKS
EJKRY JERKY
EJLLO JELLO
EJLLY JELLY
EJLOP POLJE
EJLOU JOULE
EJLPU JULEP
EJLRU JUREL
EJLSU JULES
EJMMY JEMMY
EJNNY JENNY
EJNOY ENJOY
EJNSU JUNES
EJOSV JOVES
EJRRY JERRY
EJRWY JEWRY
EJSST JESTS
EJSSU JESUS
EJTTY JETTY
EKLLN KNELL
EKLLY KELLY
EKLNT KNELT
EKLOY YOKEL
EKLPS SKELP
EKMOS MOKES, SMOKE
EKNNY KENNY
EKNOR KRONE
EKNOT TOKEN
EKNOW WOKEN
EKOPR POKER
EKOPS POKES, SPOKE
EKOST STOKE

EKOSY YOKES
EKPRS PERKS
EKPRY PERKY
EKPSY PESKY
EKRRY KERRY
EKRST TREKS
EKSSW SKEWS
EKSUY SUKEY
ELLMS SMELL
ELLNY NELLY
ELLPS SPELL
ELLQU QUELL
ELLSW SWELL, WELLS
ELLSY YELLS
ELLTU TULLE
ELLTY TELLY
ELLWY WELLY
ELMMU LUMME
ELMMY LEMMY
ELMNO LEMON, MELON
ELMNU LUMEN
ELMNY EMLYN
ELMOR MOREL
ELMOS MOLES
ELMOT METOL, MOTEL
ELMOU OLEUM
ELMPU PLUME
ELMRU LEMUR
ELMRY MERYL
ELMST SMELT
ELMSU MULES
ELMSY MYLES
ELMUV VELUM
ELMUY MULEY
ELMXY XYLEM
ELNNY LENNY, LYNNE
ELNOR ENROL, LONER,
  LOREN, LORNE
ELNOT ELTON, LENTO
ELNOV NOVEL
ELNOW OLWEN
ELNPZ PLZEN
ELNWY ELWYN, NEWLY
ELOOP POOLE
ELOOS LOOSE
ELOPR LOPER, PROLE
ELOPS POLES, SLOPE
ELOPU LOUPE
ELORR ERROL
ELORS LOSER, ROLES
ELORV LOVER
ELORW LOWER, ROWEL
ELORY ELROY, LEROY

ELOSS LOESS, SLOES, SOLES
ELOST STOLE, TESOL
ELOSU LOUSE, SEOUL
ELOSV LOVES, SOLVE,
   VOLES
ELOTW OWLET, TOWEL
ELOTX EXTOL
ELOUV OVULE
ELOUZ OUZEL
ELOVW VOWEL
ELOVY LOVEY
ELPRU PULER
ELPRY REPLY
ELPST PELTS, SLEPT, SPELT
ELPSU PULSE
ELPSY SLYPE, YELPS
ELPTU LETUP
ELRRU LURER, RULER
ELRSU LURES, RULES
ELRSY LYRES, SLYER
ELRUX LUREX
ELSSW SLEWS
ELSTU LUTES
ELSTW WELTS
ELSTY STYLE
ELTTY LETTY
ELTUX EXULT
ELTWY WETLY
EMMOS MEMOS, SOMME
EMNOS MESON, OMENS
EMNOT MONTE
EMNOV VENOM
EMNOW WOMEN
EMNOY MONEY
EMNRU RUMEN
EMNSU MENUS
EMOOR ROMEO
EMOOS MOOSE
EMOOT ME-TOO
EMOPR MOPER, PROEM
EMOPS POEMS
EMOPT TEMPO
EMOPY MYOPE
EMORR ORMER
EMORS MORES
EMORT METRO
EMORV MOVER, VOMER
EMORW MOWER
EMOSS MOSES
EMOST MOTES, SMOTE,
   TOMES
EMOSU MOUSE
EMOSV MOVES

EMOSW MEOWS
EMOSY MOSEY
EMOTT MOTET, TOTEM
EMOZZ MEZZO
EMPRS SPERM
EMPST TEMPS
EMPSU SPUME
EMPTT TEMPT
EMPTY EMPTY
EMRRY MERRY
EMRST TERMS
EMRSU MUSER, SERUM
EMRSY EMRYS
EMRUX MUREX
EMSST STEMS
EMSSU MUSES
EMSSY MESSY
EMSTU MUTES
ENNOO NO ONE
ENNOT TENON, TONNE
ENNOX XENON
ENNOY YONNE
ENNPY PENNY
ENNWY WYNNE
ENOOS NOOSE
ENOOZ OZONE
ENOPR PRONE
ENOPY PEONY
ENORS NORSE, SEÑOR,
   SNORE
ENORT TENOR, TONER
ENORU ROUEN
ENORW OWNER
ENOSS NOSES
ENOST NOTES, ONSET,
   STONE, TONES
ENOSV OVENS
ENOSZ ZONES
ENOVW WOVEN
ENOVY ENVOY
ENPRU PRUNE
ENPST SPENT
ENQRU QUERN
ENRRU RERUN
ENRST RENTS, STERN,
   TERNS
ENRSU NURSE, RUNES
ENRSW WRENS
ENRSY NERYS
ENRTU TUNER
ENRTY ENTRY
ENRVY NERVY
ENSST NESTS

ENSSU NEUSS
ENSTT TENTS
ENSTU TUNES, UNSET
ENSTV VENTS
ENSTW NEWTS
ENSUV VENUS
ENSUX NEXUS, UNSEX
ENSWY NEWSY
EOORW WOOER
EOPPS POPES
EOPRS PORES, POSER,
   PROSE, ROPES, SPORE
EOPRT TOPER, TROPE
EOPRV PROVE
EOPRW POWER
EOPRY ROPEY
EOPSS PESOS, POSES, POSSE
EOPST ESTOP, POETS, STOPE
EOPSX POXES
EOPSY POESY, SEPOY
EOPXY EPOXY
EOQTU QUOTE, TOQUE
EORRR ERROR
EORRV ROVER
EORRW ROWER
EORSS ROSES, SORES
EORST STORE
EORSU ROUÉS, ROUSE
EORSV OVERS, SERVO,
   VERSO
EORSW SEROW, SOWER,
   SWORE, WORSE
EORSZ ZEROS
EORTT OTTER, TOTER
EORTU OUTER, OUTRÉ,
   ROUTE
EORTV OVERT, TROVE,
   VOTER
EORTW TOWER, WROTE
EORTY TOYER
EORVW VOWER
EORXX XEROX
EOSSU SOUSE
EOSTT SET-TO, TOTES
EOSTV STOVE, VOTES
EOSTY EYOTS
EPPRS PREPS
EPPRU UPPER
EPRRU PURER
EPRRY PERRY
EPRSS PRESS
EPRSU PURSE, SPRUE,
   SUPER

EPRSY PYRES	FFRSU RUFFS	FIRTU FRUIT
EPRTU ERUPT	FFSTU STUFF	FIRZZ FRIZZ
EPRTW TWERP	FGGOY FOGGY	FISST FISTS
EPRXY PYREX	FGGUY FUGGY	FISTW SWIFT
EPSST PESTS, STEPS	FGHIT FIGHT	FIYZZ FIZZY
EPSTU SET-UP, STUPE, UPSET	FGILN FLING	FKLNU FLUNK
EPSTW SWEPT	FGINO FINGO	FKLOS FOLKS
EPSTY TYPES	FGINU FUNGI	FKLUY FLUKY
EPSXY PYXES	FGIST GIFTS	FKNSU FUNKS
EPTTY PETTY	FGLNO FLONG	FKNUY FUNKY
EQRUY QUERY	FGLNU FLUNG	FKORS FORKS
EQSTU QUEST	FGLSU GULFS	FLLOY FOLLY
ERRSU SURER	FGOOR FORGO	FLLUY FULLY, LYULF
ERRTU TRUER	FGOOS GOOFS	FLNOW FLOWN
ERRTY RETRY, TERRY	FGOOY GOOFY	FLOOR FLOOR
ERRWY WRYER	FGORS FROGS	FLOOS FOOLS
ERSST RESTS, TRESS	FHIIS HI-FIS	FLOOW WOLOF
ERSSU RUSES, USERS	FHILT FILTH	FLOPS FLOPS
ERSTU TRUES	FHIRT FIRTH	FLORU FLOUR, FLUOR
ERSTW STREW, TREWS,	FHIST SHIFT	FLORY FLORY
WREST	FHISY FISHY	FLOSS FLOSS
ERSTY TYRES	FHLSU FLUSH	FLOST LOFTS
ERTTU UTTER	FHORT FORTH, FROTH	FLOSU FOULS
ESSTT TESTS	FIINS FINIS	FLOSW FOWLS
ESSTV VESTS	FIINX INFIX	FLOTU FLOUT
ESSTW STEWS	FIKRS FRISK	FLOTY LOFTY
ESTTX TEXTS	FILLR FRILL	FLTUY FLUTY
ESTTY TESTY	FILLY FILLY	FMORS FORMS
ESTUY SUETY	FILMS FILMS	FMORU FORUM
ESTYZ ZESTY	FILMU FILUM	FMPRU FRUMP
ETTTY TETTY	FILMY FILMY	FNNUY FUNNY
FFFLU FLUFF	FILNT FLINT	FNORS FRONS
FFGRU GRUFF	FILOO FOLIO	FNORT FRONT
FFHIT FIFTH	FILOR FORLI	FNORW FROWN
FFHIW WHIFF	FILOS FOILS	FNOST FONTS
FFHOU HOFUF	FILPS FLIPS	FNOTU FOUNT, FUTON
FFHUU HUFUF	FILRT FLIRT	FOOPR PROOF
FFHUY HUFFY	FILST LIFTS	FOOPS POOFS, SPOOF
FFIJY JIFFY	FILSU FUSIL	FOOPY POOFY
FFIKS SKIFF	FILTY FITLY	FOORS ROOFS
FFILO OLIFF	FIMOS FOISM	FOOST FOOTS
FFIMY MIFFY	FIMOT MOTIF	FOOSW WOOFS
FFINS SNIFF	FIMRS FIRMS	FOPRS PROFS
FFINY NIFFY	FIMTU MUFTI	FOPSU POUFS
FFIQU QUIFF	FINNY FINNY	FORST FORTS, FROST
FFIRS RIFFS	FINTU UNFIT	FORSU FOURS
FFIST STIFF, TIFFS	FINTY NIFTY	FORTY FORTY
FFITY FIFTY	FINUX UNFIX	FOSTY SOFTY
FFMSU MUFFS	FINUY UNIFY	FPRUY FRY-UP
FFNSU SNUFF	FIOST FOIST	FRRUY FURRY
FFOST TOFFS	FIRRY FIRRY	FRSTU TURFS
FFPSU PUFFS	FIRST FIRST, RIFTS	FRSUU RUFUS
FFPUY PUFFY	FIRTT FRITT	FRSUY SURFY

FRTUY TURFY	GILTU GUILT	GNOPS PONGS
FRUYZ FURZY	GILTZ GLITZ	GNOPY PONGY
FSSUY FUSSY	GIMNY MINGY	GNORW GROWN, WRONG
FSTTU TUFTS	GIMPY PIGMY	GNOSS SNOGS, SONGS
FSTUY FUSTY	GIMRY GRIMY	GNOST TONGS
FTTUY TUFTY	GINNY GINNY	GNOSW GOWNS
FUYZZ FUZZY	GINOP PINGO	GNOUY YOUNG
GGGLO GLOGG	GINOR GIRON, GROIN	GNRSU RUNGS
GGINO GOING	GINOT INGOT, TIGON	GNRTU GRUNT
GGIOT GIGOT	GINOW OWING	GNRUW WRUNG
GGIPY PIGGY	GINRS GRINS, RINGS	GNSSU SNUGS
GGMOY MOGGY	GINRU RUING, UNRIG	GNSTU STUNG
GGMUY MUGGY	GINRW WRING	GNSUW SWUNG
GGNOS GONGS	GINSS SIGNS	GOORS SORGO
GGOSY SOGGY	GINST STING, TINGS	GOOSY GOOSY
GHHIS HIGHS	GINSU SUING, USING	GOOTU OUTGO
GHHIT HIGHT, THIGH	GINSV V-SIGN	GOPRU GROUP
GHHOU HOUGH	GINSW SWING, WINGS	GOPRY PORGY
GHILT LIGHT	GINTY TYING	GORSS GROSS
GHIMT MIGHT	GINVY VYING	GORTU GROUT
GHINT NIGHT, THING	GINYZ ZINGY	GOSTU GUSTO
GHINY HYING	GIORR RIGOR	GOTUY GOUTY, GUYOT
GHIRT GIRTH, RIGHT	GIORV VIRGO	GPPUY GUPPY
GHISS SIGHS	GIOSY YOGIS	GPSYY GYPSY
GHIST SIGHT	GIPRS GRIPS, PRIGS, SPRIG	GRSTU TRUGS
GHISW WHIGS	GIPSY GIPSY	GRSUU GURUS
GHITT TIGHT	GIRST GRIST, GRITS	GSSTU GUSTS
GHITW WIGHT	GIRUU UIGUR	GSTUY GUSTY, GUTSY
GHLLY GHYLL	GISSW SWIGS	HHLSU SHLUH
GHLOU GHOUL, LOUGH	GISTW TWIGS	HHMPU HUMPH
GHLPY GLYPH	GJMUU JUGUM	HHSSU SHUSH
GHNOT THONG	GKNOO KONGO	HIILN NIHIL
GHORU ROUGH	GLLOY GOLLY	HIIRS IRISH
GHOST GHOST	GLLSU GULLS	HIKNT THINK
GHOSU SOUGH	GLLUY GULLY	HIKRS SHIRK
GHOTU OUGHT, TOUGH	GLMOO GLOOM	HIKSS SIKHS
GHRSU SHRUG	GLMOU MOGUL	HIKSW WHISK
GHSTU THUGS	GLNSU LUNGS, SLUNG	HILLS HILLS
GIILV VIGIL	GLOOS LOGOS	HILLY HILLY
GIINO INIGO	GLORW GROWL	HILMU HILUM
GIINP PIING	GLORY GLORY	HILOT THIOL
GIJNO GIJON, JINGO	GLOSS GLOSS, SLOGS	HILRS SHIRL
GIKNS KINGS	GLOUV VOGUL	HILRW WHIRL
GIKOR GORKI	GLPSU GULPS, PLUGS	HILST HILTS
GILLR GRILL	GLRUY LURGY	HILSU HILUS
GILLS GILLS	GLSSU SLUGS	HILSY SHILY
GILNO LINGO	GLSTU GLUTS	HILTT TILTH
GILNS SLING	GMMUY GUMMY	HIMRT MIRTH
GILNT GLINT	GMNOU MUNGO	HIMST SMITH
GILNY LYING	GMOOR GROOM	HIMSW WHIMS
GILOO IGLOO	GMPYY PYGMY	HINNT NINTH
GILRS GIRLS	GNOOS GOONS	HINNY HINNY
GILST GILTS	GNOPR PRONG	HINOR RHINO

HINSS SHINS	HMOPR MORPH	IIKKR RIKKI
HINST HINTS	HMOST MOTHS	IIKKV VIKKI
HINSY SHINY	HMOTU MOUTH	IIKNN KININ
HINWY WHINY	HMOTY MOTHY	IIKNR KIRIN
HIOPP HIPPO	HMPSU HUMPS	IIKSW KIWIS
HIORU HOURI	HMPTU THUMP	IILMT LIMIT
HIOST HOIST	HMPUY HUMPY	IILMU ILIUM
HIPPY HIPPY	HMRRY MYRRH	IILNN LININ
HIPSS SHIPS	HMRTU THRUM	IIMMN MINIM
HIPSW WHIPS	HMSTU MUSTH	IIMNS MINIS
HIPTY PITHY	HMSTY MYTHS	IIMRZ IZMIR
HIRRS SHIRR	HMSUU HUMUS	IIMST MITIS
HIRRW WHIRR	HMSUY MUSHY	IIMTZ IZMIT, MITZI
HIRST SHIRT	HNOOR HONOR	IINNO INION
HIRSW WHIRS	HNOOW NOHOW	IINRV IRVIN
HISST SHITS	HNORS HORNS, SHORN	IINRW IRWIN
HISSU SUSHI	HNORT NORTH, THORN	IINST SIT-IN
HISSW SWISH	HNORU HURON	IINTU INUIT
HISTW WHIST, WHITS	HNORY HORNY	IIPPT PIPIT
HISTX SIXTH	HNOSW SHOWN	IISTV VISIT
HISUW WUSIH	HNSTU HUNTS, SHUNT	IJKNS JINKS
HITWY WITHY	HOOPS HOOPS	IJMMY JIMMY
HIWZZ WHIZZ	HOOPT PHOTO	IJNNY JINNY
HKKOU HOKKU	HOOPW WHOOP	IJNOS JOINS
HKLSU HULKS	HOOST HOOTS, SHOOT,	IJNOT JOINT
HKMOU HOKUM	SOTHO	IJOST JOIST
HKNOS HONKS	HOOTT TOOTH	IKKNS KINKS, SKINK
HKNOY HONKY	HOPSS SHOPS	IKKNY KINKY
HKNSU HUNKS	HOPSY HYPOS, SOPHY	IKKOS KIOSK
HKOOS HOOKS, SHOOK	HOQTU QUOTH	IKKRS KIRKS
HKOOY HOOKY	HORRY HORRY	IKKRU KUKRI
HKSSU HUSKS	HORST HORST, SHORT	IKLLR KRILL
HKSUY HUSKY	HORSU HORUS, HOURS	IKLLS KILLS, SKILL
HLLOO HOLLO	HORSY HORSY	IKLMY MILKY
HLLOU HULLO	HORTT TROTH	IKLNS KILNS, LINKS, SLINK
HLLOY HOLLY	HORTW THROW, WORTH,	IKLOS KILOS
HLLSU HULLS	WROTH	IKLRS SKIRL
HLMPY LYMPH	HOSST HOSTS, SHOTS	IKLRU KURIL
HLOPR ROLPH	HOSSW SHOWS	IKLSS SILKS
HLOPX PHLOX	HOSTT SHOTT	IKLST KILTS
HLORW WHORL	HOSTU SHOUT, SOUTH	IKLSY SILKY
HLOSS SLOSH	HOSWY SHOWY	IKMNS MINSK
HLOST HOLST, SLOTH	HOTUY YOUTH	IKMPS SKIMP
HLOSW HOWLS	HPSTU PHUTS	IKMRS SMIRK
HLOTY HOTLY	HPSUY PUSHY	IKNOP PINKO
HLPSU PLUSH	HRRUY HURRY	IKNOS IKONS, OINKS
HLPSY SYLPH	HRSTU HURST, HURTS	IKNPR PRINK
HLSSU SLUSH	HRSUY RUSHY	IKNPS PINKS
HLSYY SHYLY	HRTTU TRUTH	IKNRS RINKS
HMNOT MONTH	HRUUU UHURU	IKNSS SINKS, SKINS
HMNPY NYMPH	HSSUY HUSSY	IKNST SKINT, STINK
HMNSY HYMNS	IIJNN JINNI	IKNSW WINKS
HMOOP OOMPH	IIKKN NIKKI	IKORV KIROV

IKPSS SKIPS, SPIKS	**ILSTT** STILT, TILTS	**INPST** PINTS
IKPSY SPIKY	**ILSTY** SILTY	**INPSY** SPINY
IKQRU QUIRK	**ILYZZ** LIZZY	**INPTU** INPUT
IKRSS RISKS	**IMMTY** TIMMY	**INPUZ** UNZIP
IKRST SKIRT, STIRK	**IMNOR** MINOR	**INQSU** QUINS
IKRSY RISKY	**IMNOS** SIMON	**INQTU** QUINT
IKRTU TURKI	**IMNST** MINTS	**INRSU** RUINS
IKSST SKITS	**IMNSU** IN SUM, MINUS	**INRTU** TURIN
IKTTY KITTY	**IMNTY** MINTY	**INSSU** NISUS, SINUS
ILLMS MILLS	**IMOPR** PRIMO	**INSTT** STINT, TINTS
ILLMY MILLY	**IMOPU** OPIUM	**INSTU** SUINT, TUNIS, UNITS
ILLOS LILOS	**IMOSS** MOSSI	**INSTW** TWINS
ILLPR PRILL	**IMOST** MOIST	**INTTY** NITTY
ILLPS PILLS, SPILL	**IMOSX** SIXMO	**INTUX** X-UNIT
ILLQU QUILL	**IMOTV** VOMIT	**INTUY** UNITY
ILLRS RILLS	**IMPPR** PRIMP	**IOPRR** PRIOR
ILLRT TRILL	**IMPPS** PIMPS	**IOPST** POSIT
ILLSS SILLS	**IMPRS** PRISM	**IOPSU** PIOUS
ILLST LILTS, STILL, TILLS	**IMPSW** WIMPS	**IOPTV** PIVOT
ILLSW SWILL, WILLS	**IMPUX** MIX-UP	**IOQTU** QUITO, QUOIT
ILLSY SILLY, SLILY	**IMPWY** WIMPY	**IORRS** ORRIS
ILLTW TWILL	**IMRST** TRIMS	**IORST** RIOTS, TIROS, TRIOS
ILLTY TILLY	**IMSST** MISTS	**IORSV** VISOR
ILLWY WILLY	**IMSSW** SWIMS	**IORVY** IVORY
ILMPY IMPLY	**IMSSY** MISSY	**IOSUX** SIOUX
ILMSY SLIMY	**IMSTT** MITTS	**IOTTW** TO WIT
ILNOR LORIN	**IMSTY** MISTY	**IPPYZ** ZIPPY
ILNOS LIONS, LOINS	**INNNO** NINON	**IPQSU** QUIPS
ILNPU LUPIN	**INNNY** NINNY	**IPRST** SPRIT, STRIP, TRIPS
ILNSY LYSIN	**INNOO** ONION	**IPRSY** SPIRY
ILNTU UNTIL	**INNOU** UNION	**IPRTW** TWIRP
ILNTY LINTY	**INNPU** UNPIN	**IPRVY** PRIVY
ILNVY VINYL	**INNPY** PINNY	**IPSST** SPITS
ILOOP POLIO	**INNQU** QUINN	**IPSSV** SPIVS
ILOPS SPOIL	**INNRU** INURN, RUN-IN	**IPSSW** WISPS
ILOPT PILOT	**INNSU** SUNNI	**IPSTU** SIT-UP
ILOPU POILU	**INNTY** TINNY	**IPSTY** TIPSY
ILOPX OXLIP	**INNVY** VINNY	**IPSTZ** SPITZ
ILORS LORIS	**INOOR** ORION	**IPSWY** WISPY
ILORT TRIOL	**INOPT** PINTO, PITON, POINT	**IPSXY** PYXIS
ILOSS SILOS, SOILS	**INOQU** QUOIN	**IQSTU** QUITS
ILOST TOILS	**INORS** IRONS, ROSIN	**IRSST** STIRS
ILOSU LOUIS	**INORT** INTRO	**IRSTW** WRIST, WRITS
ILOSV VIOLS	**INORY** IRONY	**IRSUV** VIRUS
ILPPU PUPIL	**INOSW** OSWIN	**IRTUV** VIRTU
ILPSS SLIPS	**INOSY** NOISY	**IRTYZ** RITZY
ILPST SPILT, SPLIT	**INOTW** IN TOW, IN TWO	**ISSSW** SWISS
ILPTU TULIP	**INOTX** TOXIN	**ISSSY** SISSY
ILQTU QUILT	**INPPU** PINUP	**ISSTU** SITUS, SUITS
ILRSW SWIRL	**INPPY** NIPPY	**ISTTU** TITUS
ILRTW TWIRL	**INPRT** PRINT	**ISTTW** TWIST, TWITS
ILSST LISTS, SLITS	**INPRU** UNRIP	**ISTUV** VITUS
ILSSY LYSIS	**INPSS** SNIPS, SPINS	**ISTXY** SIXTY

ITTTU TUTTI	KOPRY PORKY	LOPST PLOTS
ITTTY TITTY	KOPSV PSKOV	LOPSW PLOWS
ITTWX TWIXT	KORST STORK, TORSK	LOPSY PLOYS, POLYS
ITTWY WITTY	KORSW WORKS	LOPTU PLUTO, POULT
ITYZZ TIZZY	KRSSU RUSKS	LORRY LORRY
JJSUU JUJUS	KRTUU TURKU	LORTY TYROL
JKNSU JUNKS	KSSTU TUSKS	LORUX LUXOR
JLLOY JOLLY	LLLOY LOLLY	LOSST SLOTS
JLOST JOLTS	LLMOS MOLLS	LOSSU SOULS
JLOSW JOWLS	LLMOY MOLLY	LOSSY LOSSY
JMORU JORUM	LLMSU MULLS	LOSTU LOTUS, LOUTS
JMPSU JUMPS	LLOOR ROLLO	LOSTV VOLTS
JMPUY JUMPY	LLOPS POLLS	LOSUY LOUSY
JNOTU JUNTO	LLOPY POLLY	LOSWY YOWLS
JORRU JUROR	LLORS ROLLS	LOTTY LOTTY
JOSTU JOUST	LLORT TROLL	LOTYZ ZLOTY
KKLSU SKULK	LLORY ROLLY	LPPSU PULPS
KKNSU SKUNK	LLOST TOLLS	LPPUY PULPY
KKOOS KOOKS	LLOSY LYSOL, SOLLY	LPRSU SLURP
KKOOY KOOKY	LLOTY TOLLY, TOLYL	LPSUU LUPUS
KKRSU KURSK	LLOWY LOWLY	LRSSU SLURS
KLLNO KNOLL	LLOXY XYLOL	LRSUY SURLY
KLLSU SKULL	LLPSU PULLS	LRTUY TRULY
KLNOP PLONK	LLSTU STULL	LRWYY WRYLY
KLNPU PLUNK	LLSUY SULLY	LSSTU LUSTS, SLUTS
KLNRU KNURL	LLXYY XYLYL	LSTUY LUSTY
KLNSU SLUNK	LMOOS LOOMS	MMMOY MOMMY
KLOOS LOOKS	LMOOT MOLTO	MMMUY MUMMY
KLOSY YOLKS	LMOST MOLTS, SMOLT	MMOPY POMMY
KLOYY YOLKY	LMOSU MOSUL, SOLUM	MMOTY TOMMY
KLSSU SULKS	LMOTU MOULT	MMPSU MUMPS
KLSUY SULKY	LMPPU PLUMP	MMRUY RUMMY
KMNOS MONKS	LMPSU LUMPS, PLUMS,	MMTUY TUMMY
KMOOP MOKPO	SLUMP	MNOOR MORON
KMOST TOMSK	LMPUY LUMPY, PLUMY	MNOOS MOONS
KMOSY SMOKY	LMSSU SLUMS	MNOOY MOONY
KMRUY MURKY	LNNOY NYLON	MNORS MORNS, NORMS
KMSUY MUSKY	LNOOR ORLON	MNORU MOURN
KNNOW KNOWN	LNOOS LOONS	MNORY MYRON
KNOOR KROON	LNOOY LOONY	MNOTU MOUNT, NOTUM
KNOOS NOOKS, SNOOK	LNOPY PYLON	MNOTY MONTY
KNOST KNOTS	LNOUZ LUZON	MOOPR PROMO
KNOSW KNOWS	LNOWY OLWYN	MOORS MOORS, ROOMS
KNOSY YONKS	LOOOV OVOLO	MOORT MOTOR
KNOUY YUKON	LOOPR ORLOP	MOORY ROOMY
KNOWY WONKY	LOOPS LOOPS, POOLS,	MOOSS MOSSO
KNPSU PUNKS, SPUNK	SLOOP, SPOOL	MOOTT MOTTO
KNRTU TRUNK	LOOPY LOOPY	MOPPU MOP-UP
KNSTU STUNK	LOOSS SOLOS	MOPRS PROMS, ROMPS
KOOPS SPOOK	LOOST STOOL, TOOLS	MOPST STOMP
KOORS ROOKS	LOPPY POLYP	MORST STORM
KOOST STOOK	LOPRW PROWL	MORSW WORMS
KOOTY KYOTO, TOKYO	LOPSS SLOPS	MORTY MORTY

MORWY WORMY
MOSSY MOSSY
MOSUY MOUSY
MPPSU PUMPS
MPRSU RUMPS
MPRTU TRUMP
MPSSU SUMPS
MPSTU STUMP
MRSTU STRUM
MSSTU SMUTS
MSTTU MUTTS
MSTUY MUSTY
MUYZZ MUZZY
NNOSU NOUNS
NNOSY SONNY
NNRUY RUNNY
NNSUY SUNNY
NNTUY TUNNY
NOOPR PORNO
NOOPS SNOOP, SPOON
NOORS ORSON
NOOSW SWOON
NOOTW ON TOW
NOPTU PUT-ON, TON-UP,
   UPTON
NORST SNORT
NORSW SWORN
NORTU TORUN
NORTY TRY-ON
NOSSW SNOWS
NOSTU SNOUT, TONUS
NOSTW TOWNS
NOSTY STONY
NOSWY SNOWY
NPRSU SPURN
NPRUU RUN-UP
NPSTU PUNTS
NPSUU SUN-UP
NPTUY PUNTY

NRSTU RUNTS, TURNS
NRTUU U-TURN
NRTUY RUNTY
NSTTU STUNT
NTTUY NUTTY
OOPPS POOPS
OOPRS SOPOR, SPOOR
OOPRT TROOP
OOPST STOOP, TOPOS
OOPSW SWOOP
OOPTT POTTO
OORRT ROTOR
OORRU ORURO
OORST ROOST, ROOTS,
   TORSO
OOSTT TOOTS
OOSTY SOOTY
OOSYY YOYOS
OOWYZ WOOZY
OPPPU POP-UP
OPPPY POPPY
OPPRS PROPS
OPPSY POPSY, SOPPY
OPRST PORTS, SPORT, STROP
OPRSW PROWS
OPRSY PROSY
OPRUY ROUPY
OPRXY PROXY
OPSST POSTS, SPOTS, STOPS
OPSSU SOUPS
OPSSW SWOPS
OPSTU POUTS, SPOUT,
   STOUP
OPSTY TOPSY
OPSUY SOUPY
OPTTU PUTTO
OPTTY POTTY
OPTUZ TZU-PO
ORRSY SORRY

ORRTU TRURO
ORRWY WORRY
ORSST SORTS
ORSSU SORUS
ORSTT TORTS, TROTS
ORSTU ROUST, ROUTS,
   TORUS, TOURS
ORSTW WORST
ORSTY STORY, TYROS
ORSUY YOURS
ORTTU TROUT, TUTOR
OSSST STOSS
OSSTW SWOTS
OSTTU STOUT, TOUTS
OSUYZ SOYUZ
OTTTY TOTTY
PPPUY PUPPY
PRRSU PURRS
PRSSU SPURS
PRSTU SPURT, TURPS
PRSUU USURP
PRSUY SYRUP
PSSUY PUSSY
PSTTU PUTTS
PTTUY PUTTY
RSSTU TRUSS
RSTTU STRUT, TRUST
RSTTY TRYST
RSTUW WURST
RSTUY RUSTY
RSUUY USURY
RTTUY RUTTY
STTUU TUTUS
TTTUY TUTTY

AAABCN CABANA
AAABCS CASABA
AAABDN ABADAN
AAABHN HABANA
AAABIR ARABIA
AAABLM AMBALA
AAABLT BALATA
AAABNN ANNABA, BANANA
AAABNS ANABAS
AAABRZ BAZAAR
AAACCI ACACIA
AAACDI ACADIA
AAACDN CANADA
AAACEH ACHAEA
AAACGI AGACIA
AAACJN JACANA
AAACLP ALPACA
AAACMR MARACA
AAACNR ARCANA
AAACOX OAXACA
AAADLM ALMADA
AAADMN AMANDA
AAADMR ARMADA,
   DAMARA
AAADNP PANADA
AAAELZ AZALEA
AAAGHT AGATHA
AAAGLM MALAGA
AAAGLT GALATA
AAAGNN NAGANA
AAAGRU AARGAU
AAAHLM MAHALA
AAAHLS AL HASA
AAAHMR AMHARA
AAAHNV HAVANA
AAAHRS SAHARA
AAAILM AMALIA
AAAITX ATAXIA
AAAJMP PAJAMA
AAAKLM KAMALA
AAAKLS ALASKA
AAAKNR ANKARA, KANARA
AAALMS SALAAM
AAALMY MALAYA
AAALNN ALANNA
AAAMMN MANAMA
AAAMNN MANANA
AAAMNP PANAMA
AAAMRS ASMARA, SAMARA
AAAMRT TAMARA
AAAMRY AYMARA
AAANPR PARANA
AAAPPY PAPAYA

AAARRT ARARAT
AAARTV AVATAR
AABBBO BAOBAB
AABBCY ABBACY
AABBLL LABLAB
AABBLO BALBOA
AABBRR BARBRA
AABBST SABBAT
AABCIN BIANCA
AABCIR ARABIC
AABCIU CUIABA
AABCJO JACOBA
AABCLS CABALS
AABCMN CABMAN
AABCRS SCARAB
AABCSU ABACUS
AABDER ABRADE
AABDES ABASED
AABDET ABATED
AABDEU AUBADE
AABDIN IBADAN
AABDLL BALLAD
AABDLM LAMBDA
AABDOR ABOARD,
   ABROAD, BARODA
AABDRT TABARD
AABEGT TEABAG
AABELM AMABEL
AABELR ARABLE
AABELZ ABLAZE
AABEMO AMOEBA
AABEMS AMEBAS
AABERZ ZAREBA
AABFIN FABIAN
AABFIR BIAFRA
AABGGR RAGBAG
AABGGS GASBAG
AABGIM GAMBIA
AABGIN BAAING
AABGRT RATBAG
AABHKS KASBAH
AABHKZ ABKHAZ
AABIKR KARIBA
AABILL LABIAL
AABILN ALBINA
AABILU ABULIA
AABIMZ ZAMBIA
AABINS SABINA
AABIST ABATIS
AABISW SWABIA
AABKLN BALKAN
AABKMO BAMAKO
AABLMS BALSAM

AABLNY ALBANY
AABLOR ABORAL
AABLOV LAVABO
AABLSS BALSAS
AABLST BASALT
AABLTU ABLAUT
AABMMS MAMBAS
AABMNR BARMAN
AABMNT BANTAM, BATMAN
AABMRS SAMBAR
AABMRY AMBARY
AABMSS SAMBAS
AABNNY BANYAN
AABORR ARROBA
AABORT ABATOR, RABATO
AABRSS SABRAS
AABTTW ABWATT
AACCDI CICADA
AACCHH CHA-CHA
AACCHM CHACMA
AACCLO CLOACA
AACCLP CALPAC
AACCLR CALCAR
AACCMO MACACO
AACCNN CANCAN
AACDDU CAUDAD
AACDEF FACADE
AACDER ARCADE
AACDIR ACARID
AACDLU CAUDAL
AACDMP MADCAP
AACDNR CANARD
AACEFL FAECAL
AACEFR CARAFE
AACEHN AACHEN
AACEHP APACHE
AACEHT CHAETA
AACELP PALACE
AACELS ALSACE
AACELT ACETAL
AACELY CELAYA
AACEMO CAEOMA
AACEMR CAMERA
AACENP CANAPÉ
AACENR ARCANE
AACENT CATENA
AACERS CAESAR
AACETV CAVEAT, VACATE
AACFIL FACIAL
AACFIR AFRICA
AACFIS FASCIA
AACFLU FACULA, FAUCAL
AACFNR FRANCA

AACFNT CAFTAN
AACFRS FRACAS
AACFTT FAT CAT
AACGIM AGAMIC
AACGIR AGARIC
AACHIT ITHACA
AACHKW KWACHA
AACHLS CALASH
AACHNO CHAOAN
AACHTT ATTACH
AACIIL ALICIA
AACIIM AMICIA
AACILL LAICAL
AACILP APICAL
AACILR ALARIC, RACIAL
AACILS CALAIS
AACILT ALTAIC
AACIMN MANIAC
AACIMR MARCIA
AACINR ARNICA, CARINA,
    CRANIA
AACIPS CAPIAS
AACIRT CARITA
AACIRV CAVIAR
AACISS CASSIA
AACITT ATTICA
AACITX ATAXIC
AACJKL JACKAL
AACJOU ACAJOU
AACKRR ARRACK
AACKTT ATTACK
AACLLO CALLAO
AACLMT LACTAM
AACLMU MACULA
AACLNR CARNAL
AACLNS CANALS
AACLNT CANTAL
AACLNU LACUNA
AACLOR CAROLA
AACLPR CARPAL
AACLPS PASCAL
AACLPU PAUCAL
AACLRS LASCAR, RASCAL,
    SACRAL, SCALAR
AACLSU CASUAL, CAUSAL
AACLTU ACTUAL
AACMNR CARMAN
AACMNU CUMANA
AACMNY CAYMAN
AACMOT TACOMA
AACMRT TARMAC
AACMSS CAMASS
AACMSW MACAWS

AACNNO ANCONA
AACNPT CATNAP
AACNRY CANARY
AACNSV CANVAS
AACNTV VACANT
AACPPY PAPACY
AACPRS CASPAR
AACRST CARATS
AACRSU ACARUS
AACRTV CRAVAT
AADDIL LA-DI-DA
AADDIV DAVIDA
AADDOU AOUDAD
AADEGL GELADA
AADEGM DAMAGE
AADEGN AGENDA
AADEGS ADAGES
AADEHN HADEAN
AADEJU JUDAEA
AADEKW AWAKED
AADEMM MADAME
AADEMN MAENAD
AADEMZ AMAZED
AADENN ANDEAN, DEANNA
AADENR ANDREA
AADENT ADNATE
AADENV NEVADA
AADEOR ORADEA
AADEPR PARADE
AADFIR AFRAID
AADGIO ADAGIO
AADGIR AGADIR
AADGMR DAGMAR
AADGNU UGANDA
AADGOP PAGODA
AADHIL DAHLIA
AADHIN HAIDAN
AADHLR HARALD
AADHRZ ADZHAR, HAZARD
AADILR RADIAL
AADILS DALASI
AADIMN DAMIAN
AADIMT MATADI
AADINR ADRIAN, RADIAN
AADINS NAIADS
AADINT DANITA
AADINV DAVINA
AADIST STADIA
AADKMS DAMASK
AADKNU KADUNA
AADKOT DAKOTA
AADKPU PADAUK
AADLLS DALLAS

AADLMY MALADY
AADLNR RANALD, RANDAL
AADLNS SANDAL
AADLNU LANDAU, LUANDA
AADLNV VANDAL
AADLOP APODAL
AADLOU DOUALA
AADLRU RADULA
AADLSS SALADS
AADMMN MADMAN
AADMMR DAMMAR
AADMMS MADAMS
AADMNR ARMAND
AADMOU AMADOU
AADMRS DRAMAS, MADRAS
AADMRU MARAUD
AADMYY MAY DAY
AADNNR RANDAN
AADNPS PANDAS
AADNRS SANDRA
AADNRU ARNAUD
AADNRW RWANDA
AADNRZ ZANDRA
AADNTU DANUTA
AADNTW WANT AD
AADPYY PAYDAY
AADRSW AWARDS
AADRTU DATURA
AADRTY DATARY
AAEEGN AEGEAN
AAEENS AENEAS
AAEERT AERATE
AAEEST AT EASE
AAEFLM AFLAME
AAEFLR RAFAEL
AAEFNZ FAENZA
AAEGGR GARAGE
AAEGGV GAVAGE
AAEGLL LALAGE
AAEGLN ANGELA, ANLAGE,
    GALENA, LAGENA
AAEGLR ALEGAR, LAAGER
AAEGLV LAVAGE
AAEGMN MANAGE
AAEGNT AGNATE, AGNETA
AAEGRV RAVAGE
AAEGST AGATES
AAEGSV SAVAGE
AAEGTU GÂTEAU
AAEHLM HAEMAL, MEHALA
AAEHLT ALTHEA
AAEHMT HAMATE
AAEHNT ANTHEA

AAEHNY HYAENA	AAGGHI HAGGAI	AAHIIW HAWAII
AAEHRT EARTHA	AAGGQU QUAGGA	AAHILT HIATAL
AAEILM AMALIE, AMELIA	AAGGRS SAGGAR	AAHINN HAINAN
AAEILR AERIAL	AAGGRT RAGTAG	AAHIPR PARIAH
AAEILX ALEXIA	AAGHMR ARMAGH,	AAHIRS SHARIA
AAEIMN ANEMIA	GRAHAM	AAHJRR JARRAH
AAEINR ANEIRA, ARIANE	AAGHNP PAHANG	AAHJRS RAJAHS
AAEITV AVIATE	AAGHNR HANGAR	AAHKKZ KAZAKH
AAEKLN ALKANE	AAGHST AGHAST	AAHKNO HAAKON
AAEKLR KERALA	AAGILR ARGALI	AAHLLW WALLAH
AAEKNW AWAKEN	AAGILT GALATI	AAHLMT MALTHA
AAEKRT KARATE	AAGILV GAVIAL	AAHLNT ANHALT
AAELLP PAELLA	AAGIMN MAGIAN	AAHLPS ALPHAS
AAELMP PAMELA	AAGINN ANGINA	AAHLRS ASHLAR
AAELMT MALATE	AAGINR GRANIA	AAHLRT HARTAL
AAELNN ANNEAL	AAGINU GUIANA, IGUANA	AAHMNS SHAMAN
AAELNS SALENA	AAGINV VAGINA	AAHMRS MARSHA
AAELNT LANATE	AAGINW GAWAIN	AAHMRT MARTHA
AAELNV LAVENA	AAGJRU JAGUAR	AAHMST ASTHMA
AAELOR AREOLA	AAGKLU KALUGA	AAHNNS ANSHAN
AAELPP APPEAL	AAGKLY GALYAK	AAHNNT NATHAN
AAELPT PALATE	AAGKNS KANGAS	AAHNOV NAVAHO
AAELRV LARVAE	AAGLLN LALANG	AAHNPT PATHAN
AAEMNP APEMAN	AAGLLP PLAGAL	AAHNSS HASSAN
AAEMNS SEAMAN	AAGLMN MALANG	AAHNSU SHAUNA
AAENOP APNOEA	AAGLNO ANALOG, ANGOLA	AAHNTU UTAHAN
AAENPS PAEANS	AAGLNR RAGLAN	AAHNTV HAVANT
AAENPV PAVANE	AAGLRT TRAGAL	AAHPPR PARAPH
AAENRS ARENAS	AAGLST STALAG	AAHPTY APATHY
AAENRT RENATA	AAGLWY GALWAY	AAHRRR HARRAR
AAENST ANSATE	AAGLXY GALAXY	AAHRSS HARASS
AAENSU NAUSEA	AAGMMS GAMMAS	AAHRSU AARHUS
AAEPPR APPEAR	AAGMNR RAGMAN	AAHSSY SASHAY
AAERRT ERRATA	AAGMNS GASMAN	AAIKLL ALKALI
AAERWX EARWAX	AAGMRY MAGYAR,	AAIKLM KALMIA
AAESWY SEAWAY	MARGAY	AAIKNN ANNIKA
AAFFIR AFFAIR, RAFFIA	AAGNNO NAGANO	AAIKNR KARINA
AAFFJN JAFFNA	AAGNNY ANYANG	AAILLX AXILLA
AAFFRY AFFRAY	AAGNOR ANGORA, ARAGON	AAILMN ANIMAL, LAMINA,
AAFGHN AFGHAN	AAGNOY NAGOYA	MANILA
AAFIKS SIFAKA	AAGNPR PARANG	AAILMP IMPALA
AAFILV FLAVIA	AAGNPS PAGANS	AAILMS SALAMI
AAFINR FARINA	AAGNRY ANGARY	AAILMW MALAWI
AAFINS NAAFIS	AAGNUY GUYANA	AAILNR NARIAL
AAFIRS SAFARI	AAGPRS GASPAR	AAILNS NASIAL, SALINA
AAFITU AU FAIT	AAGRVY VAGARY	AAILNV ALVINA, LAVINA
AAFKNT KAFTAN	AAGSUV GUAVAS	AAILPS PALAIS
AAFLLL FALLAL	AAHHLL HALLAH	AAILPU APULIA
AAFLNU FAUNAL	AAHHLV HALVAH	AAILQU AQUILA
AAFLOT AFLOAT	AAHHNN HANNAH	AAILRT ALTAIR, LARIAT,
AAFNNT FAN-TAN	AAHHPT APHTHA	LATRIA
AAFNRR FARRAN	AAHHWW HAWHAW	AAILSS ASSAIL
AAFNSU FAUNAS	AAHIIS ISAIAH	

AAILSV SALIVA, SALVIA, VALAIS	AALMNP NAPALM	AANQTU QUANTA
AAILTU AU LAIT	AALMNU ALUMNA, MANUAL	AANRRT ARRANT
AAILTV LATVIA	AALMNY LAYMAN	AANRTT RATTAN, TARTAN
AAIMMR MARIAM	AALMOR AMORAL	AANRYZ RYAZAN
AAIMMS MIASMA	AALMOT AMATOL	AANSSU NASSAU, SAUNAS
AAIMMX MAXIMA	AALMPR PALMAR	AANSTV SAVANT
AAIMNR AIRMAN, ARMINA, MARIAN, MARINA	AALMPS LAMPAS, PLASMA	AANSTW TSWANA
AAIMNS MANIAS	AALMRS ALARMS	AANSTZ STANZA
AAIMNT AMINTA	AALMRT RATLAM	AANWYY ANYWAY
AAIMRS MARISA	AALMTY AMYTAL	AAOPST SAPOTA
AAIMRT AMRITA, MARITA	AALNNS ANNALS	AAORRU AURORA
AAINNT TAINAN	AALNNU ANNUAL	AAORST AORTAS
AAINOR ORIANA	AALNOT ALTONA, ATONAL	AAOTTV OTTAVA
AAINOX ANOXIA	AALNPR PLANAR	AAOTTW OTTAWA
AAINPP PAPAIN	AALNPT PLATAN	AAPPWW PAWPAW
AAINPR PARIAN	AALNRX LARNAX	AAPRST PATRAS
AAINPT PATINA, TAIPAN	AALNSS NASALS	AAPWXX PAXWAX
AAINRS SARINA	AALNST ASLANT	AAQRSU QUASAR
AAINRT TIRANA	AALOPY PAYOLA	AARRSY ARRAYS
AAINRU ANURIA	AALOVW AVOWAL	AARRTT TARTAR
AAINSS ASIANS	AALPSZ PLAZAS	AARSTT STRATA
AAINTT ATTAIN	AALRST ALTARS, ASTRAL, TARSAL	AARSTY ASTRAY
AAINTW TAIWAN	AALRSY SALARY	AARSWW WARSAW
AAIPRU AU PAIR	AALSSV VASSAL	AARTTT RAT-TAT
AAIPRY APIARY	AALSWY ALWAYS	AARTTY TATARY
AAIPZZ PIAZZA	AALWYY WAYLAY	AASSSY ASSAYS
AAIQRT QATARI	AAMNOR RAMONA	ABBBEL BABBLE
AAIRST ARISTA, SARITA, TIARAS	AAMNOS SAMOAN	ABBCOT BOBCAT
AAIRVY AVIARY	AAMNOZ AMAZON	ABBCRY CRABBY
AAIRWY AIRWAY	AAMNPS SAMPAN	ABBCSY SCABBY
AAITUY YAUTIA	AAMNST TASMAN	ABBDDE DABBED
AAJNNO JOANNA	AAMNSU MANAUS	ABBDEG GABBED
AAJPRU JAPURA	AAMNTX TAXMAN	ABBDEI BABIED
AAKKMR MARKKA	AAMOPR PARAMO	ABBDEJ JABBED
AAKKOP KAKAPO	AAMORS AROMAS	ABBDEL DABBLE
AAKKSY KAYAKS	AAMOSS SAMOSA	ABBDEN NABBED
AAKLMU MAKALU	AAMOTY TOYAMA	ABBDER BARBED, DABBER
AAKLOS KOALAS	AAMPPS PAMPAS	ABBDET TABBED
AAKLRS KRAALS	AAMQSU SQUAMA	ABBDEU BEDAUB
AAKLSU LUSAKA	AAMRSU ASARUM	ABBEGI GABBIE
AAKNOR ANORAK	AAMRSW ASWARM	ABBEGL GABBLE
AAKNSS KANSAS	AAMRSY RAMSAY	ABBEGR GABBER
AAKNSU KAUNAS	AAMRTU TRAUMA	ABBEIR BARBIE, RABBIE
AAKPRS PARKAS	AANNOR ANNORA	ABBEIS BABIES
AAKRST KARATS	AANNRU ANURAN	ABBEIU BAUBIE
AALLMS LLAMAS	AANNTT NATANT	ABBEJR JABBER
AALLPS PALLAS	AANORV NOVARA	ABBEKS KEBABS
AALLRV LARVAL	AANORX ROXANA	ABBELR BARBEL, RABBLE
AALMMM MAMMAL	AANOST SONATA	ABBELU BAUBLE
AALMMS LAMMAS	AANPPU PAPUAN	ABBERR BARBER
	AANPRT TARPAN	ABBERT BARBET
		ABBESS ABBESS
		ABBESY ABBEYS

ABBFLY FLABBY
ABBGOR GABBRO
ABBHSY SHABBY
ABBILO BILBAO
ABBIRS RABBIS
ABBIRT RABBIT
ABBLRU BULBAR
ABBMOO BAMBOO
ABBMOY BOMBAY
ABBNOO BABOON
ABBNOS NABOBS
ABBORS ABSORB
ABBOST ABBOTS
ABBRSU BUSBAR
ABCCLU BUCCAL
ABCDEK BACKED
ABCDEL CABLED
ABCDER BRACED
ABCDIR BARDIC
ABCDTU ABDUCT
ABCEEM BECAME
ABCEHL BLEACH
ABCEHR BREACH
ABCEHU HECUBA
ABCEIM AMEBIC
ABCEJT ABJECT
ABCEKR BACKER
ABCELS CABLES
ABCELT CABLET
ABCEMR CAMBER
ABCENO BEACON
ABCENU CUBANE
ABCERR BRACER
ABCERS BRACES, CABERS
ABCEST BE CAST
ABCFIR FABRIC
ABCGIT BIG CAT
ABCHLN BLANCH
ABCHNR BRANCH
ABCHOR BROACH
ABCHPU HUBCAP
ABCIIM IAMBIC
ABCILT BALTIC
ABCILU ABULIC
ABCINS CABINS
ABCISS BASICS
ABCISY BISCAY
ABCKLS BLACKS
ABCKPU BACKUP
ABCLMY CYMBAL
ABCLOT COBALT
ABCMOR CRAMBO
ABCMOT COMBAT, TOMBAC

ABCNOR CARBON, CORBAN
ABCORS CAROBS, COBRAS
ABCORX BOXCAR
ABCORY CARBOY
ABCOSV VOCABS
ABCSSU SCUBAS
ABDDEE BEADED
ABDDEI ABIDED
ABDDEN BANDED
ABDDER BADDER
ABDDEU DAUBED
ABDDHU BUDDHA
ABDEEH BEHEAD
ABDEEL BEADLE
ABDEEM BEAMED
ABDEES DEBASE, SEABED
ABDEET DEBATE
ABDEFL FABLED
ABDEGG BAGGED
ABDEGL GABLED
ABDEGN BANGED
ABDEGO BODEGA
ABDEGR BADGER, BARGED, GARBED
ABDEGS BADGES
ABDEHS BASHED
ABDEHT BATHED
ABDEIL BAILED, BALDIE
ABDEIR ABIDER, AIRBED
ABDEIS BIASED
ABDEIT BAITED
ABDEKL BALKED
ABDEKN BANKED
ABDEKR BARKED, BRAKED, ✓
   DEBARK
ABDEKS BASKED
ABDELM AMBLED,
   BEDLAM, BLAMED,
   LAMBED
ABDELO ALBEDO, DOABLE
ABDELR BLARED
ABDELS BLADES
ABDELT TABLED
ABDELW BAWLED
ABDELY DYABLE
ABDELZ BLAZED
ABDENN BANNED
ABDENP BEDPAN
ABDENR BRENDA
ABDENU DANUBE
ABDEOS ABODES
ABDEOT BOATED
ABDEPY PAYBED

ABDERR BARRED
ABDERS BEARDS
ABDERU DAUBER
ABDERV ADVERB, BRAVED
ABDERY BRAYED
ABDEST BASTED
ABDESU ABUSED
ABDETT BATTED
ABDFOR FORBAD
ABDHRY HARD BY
ABDIJM DJAMBI
ABDILR BRIDAL, RIBALD
ABDINT BANDIT
ABDIRS BRAIDS, DISBAR
ABDLLY BALDLY
ABDLNO BOLAND
ABDLRY DRABLY
ABDNOR ROBAND
ABDNOU ABOUND
ABDNRS BRANDS
ABDNRU DURBAN
ABDNRY BRANDY
ABDORS ADSORB, BOARDS, BROADS
ABDORY BYROAD
ABDOYY DAYBOY
ABDRRU DURBAR
ABDRSU ABSURD
ABEEGL BEAGLE
ABEEGR BARGEE
ABEEHV BEHAVE
ABEEIL BAILEE
ABEEKR BEAKER
ABEEKT BETAKE
ABEELN BALEEN, ENABLE
ABEENT BEATEN
ABEENU BEAUNE
ABEEOR AEROBE
ABEEOU EUBOEA
ABEERR BEARER
ABEERT BEATER, BERATE, REBATE
ABEERV BEAVER
ABEERW BEWARE
ABEFFL BAFFLE
ABEFHL BEHALF
ABEFLL BEFALL
ABEFLM FLAMBE
ABEFLR FABLER
ABEFLS FABLES
ABEFMR FERBAM
ABEFPR PREFAB
ABEGGR BEGGAR

ABEGIT GIBE AT
ABEGIU IBAGUE
ABEGLM GAMBLE
ABEGLN BANGLE, BENGAL
ABEGLR GARBLE
ABEGLS BAGELS, GABLES
ABEGLU BELUGA
ABEGMR BREGMA
ABEGNR BANGER, GRABEN
ABEGOR BORAGE
ABEGOZ GAZEBO
ABEGRS BARGES
ABEGRZ ZAGREB
ABEHIL HABILE
ABEHIT BETHIA
ABEHLR HERBAL
ABEHLU BEULAH
ABEHNT BETHAN
ABEHRT BATHER, BERTHA
ABEHSS BASHES
ABEIIR IBERIA
ABEIIT TIBIAE
ABEILL LABILE, LIABLE
ABEILN BLAINE
ABEILR BAILER
ABEILS ABSEIL, BLAISE,
   ISABEL
ABEILT ALBEIT, ALBITE
ABEILV VIABLE
ABEILW BEWAIL
ABEILY BAILEY
ABEINT BENITA, BINATE
ABEIRR BARRIE
ABEIRS BRAISE, RABIES,
   SERBIA
ABEISS BIASES
ABEJOR JERBOA
ABEJRU ABJURE
ABEKLR BALKER
ABEKLY KABYLE
ABEKMN EMBANK
ABEKMR EMBARK
ABEKNR BANKER
ABEKOU BOUAKE
ABEKRR BARKER
ABEKRS BAKERS, BRAKES,
   BREAKS
ABEKRY BAKERY
ABEKST BASKET
ABELLS LABELS
ABELLT BALLET
ABELMM EMBALM

ABELMR AMBLER, MARBLE,
   RAMBLE
ABELNU NEBULA, UNABLE
ABELOR BOREAL
ABELOT LOBATE, OBLATE
ABELPU PUEBLA
ABELRR BARREL
ABELRT ALBERT, BARTLE,
   LABRET
ABELRV VERBAL
ABELRW BAWLER, WARBLE
ABELRY BARELY, BARLEY,
   BLEARY
ABELRZ BLAZER
ABELSS SABLES
ABELST BLEATS, STABLE,
   TABLES
ABELSU SUABLE, USABLE
ABELSY BASELY
ABELSZ BLAZES
ABELTT BATTLE, TABLET
ABEMNO BEMOAN
ABEMNR BARMEN
ABEMNT BATMEN
ABENNR BANNER
ABENOR BORANE
ABENRR BARREN
ABENRT BANTER, BARNET
ABENRU URBANE
ABENRY BARNEY, NEARBY
ABENRZ BRAZEN
ABENST ABSENT
ABENTT BATTEN
ABENTU BUTANE
ABEORT BOATER, BORATE
ABEORZ BEZOAR
ABEOSS SASEBO
ABEPTU UPBEAT
ABEQRU BARQUE
ABEQSU BASQUE
ABERRT BARTER
ABERRV BRAVER
ABERRY BRAYER
ABERRZ BRAZER
ABERSS SABERS, SABRES
ABERST BAREST, BREAST
ABERSU ABUSER
ABERSV BRAVES
ABERSZ ZEBRAS
ABERTT BATTER
ABERTU AUBERT
ABERTY BETRAY
ABERUU BUREAU

ABERUY AUBREY
ABERZZ ZABRZE
ABESSS BASSES
ABESST BASEST, BASSET,
   BEASTS
ABESSU ABUSES
ABESTU BEAUTS
ABETTU BATTUE
ABETTY BEATTY
ABETUY BEAUTY
ABEUXY BAYEUX
ABFILU FIBULA
ABFISY BASIFY
ABGHTU HAGBUT
ABGIIL GALIBI
ABGIKN BAKING
ABGIKT KIT BAG
ABGILN BALING
ABGIMT GAMBIT
ABGIMY BIGAMY
ABGINO GABION, GOBIAN
ABGINR BARING
ABGINS BASING
ABGINU BANGUI
ABGINY BAYING
ABGLLO GLOBAL
ABGLMO GAMBOL
ABGOOT BOGOTA, TOBAGO
ABGRSU BURGAS
ABHIIR BIHARI
ABHINR HARBIN
ABHINS BANISH
ABHIOP PHOBIA
ABHISS SAHIBS
ABHIST HABITS
ABHLOP BHOPAL
ABHMSU AMBUSH
ABHNTU BHUTAN
ABHORT HOBART
ABHOST BATHOS
ABHOTX HATBOX
ABHOXY HAYBOX
ABHRSY BRASHY
ABIILS ALIBIS
ABIIST TIBIAS
ABIJRU JABIRU
ABIKMO AKIMBO
ABILMT TIMBAL
ABILMU LABIUM
ABILNO ALBINO, ALBION
ABILNR LIBRAN
ABILNY LIBYAN
ABILOR BAILOR

ABILRT TRIBAL	ABMNOY BONAMY	ACCERS SCARCE
ABILRU BURIAL	ABMNTU NUMBAT	ACCERU ACCRUE
ABILRZ BRAZIL	ABMOTV TAMBOV	ACCESS ACCESS
ABILVY VIABLY	ABMOTW WOMBAT	ACCESU ACCUSE
ABIMRU BARIUM, UMBRIA	ABMRSU RUMBAS	ACCGNO COGNAC
ABIMST AMBITS	ABNORR BARRON	ACCHNO CONCHA
ABIMSU IAMBUS	ABNORS BARONS	ACCHNY CHANCY
ABINOR ROBINA	ABNORY BARONY, BARYON	ACCHOU CACHOU
ABINOS BASION, BONSAI,	ABNOST BATONS	ACCHTY CATCHY
BOSNIA	ABNOTY BOTANY	ACCIIN ACINIC
ABINOT BONITA, OBTAIN	ABNRTU TURBAN	ACCILO CALICO
ABINRS BAIRNS, BRAINS	ABNRUU AUBURN	ACCILT LACTIC
ABINRU RUBINA	ABNRWY BRAWNY	ACCIMM MICMAC
ABINRY BINARY, BRAINY	ABOOST TABOOS	ACCINT CANTIC
ABINSS BASINS	ABORRU ARBOUR	ACCINY CYANIC
ABIORS ISOBAR	ABORRW BARROW	ACCIOS CAICOS
ABIOST TOBIAS	ABORSV BRASOV, BRAVOS	ACCIRT ARCTIC
ABIRSU AIRBUS	ABORTU RUBATO	ACCITT TACTIC
ABIRTZ TABRIZ	ABORTW TOWBAR	ACCKRS CRACKS
ABISSU BISSAU	ABORTY TORBAY	ACCLOU COUCAL
ABJNOS BANJOS	ABORUY YORUBA	ACCMOR CORMAC
ABJNPU PUNJAB	ABOSST BOASTS	ACCORW CRACOW
ABKLNS BLANKS	ABOSTU U-BOATS	ACCOST ACCOST
ABKLSU BAULKS	ABOSUY BAYOUS	ACCRUY CURACY
ABKLSY SKYLAB	ABOSWW BOWSAW	ACCSTU CACTUS
ABLLNO NO BALL	ABPRTU ABRUPT	ACCSUU CAUCUS
ABLLOT BALLOT	ABPSSY BYPASS	ACCSUY YUCCAS
ABLLTU ALL BUT	ABQSSU SQUABS	ACCTUU CUCUTA
ABLMOP APLOMB	ABRRSU BURSAR	ACDDEE DECADE
ABLMOR BROMAL	ABRSSY BRASSY	ACDDEG CADGED
ABLMRU BRUMAL,	ABRTUY BURYAT	ACDDEI CADDIE
LABRUM, LUMBAR,	ABSUWY SUBWAY	ACDDEN DANCED
UMBRAL	ABSWYY BYWAYS	ACDDER CARDED
ABLMRY MARBLY	ACCCIL CALCIC	ACDDEU ADDUCE
ABLMSU ALBUMS	ACCDEE ACCEDE	ACDDII DIACID
ABLNOZ BLAZON	ACCDEN DECCAN	ACDDIN CANDID
ABLNSU NABLUS	ACCDII ACIDIC	ACDDIR DARDIC, ID CARD
ABLOOR ROBALO	ACCDOR ACCORD	ACDDIS CADDIS
ABLORU LABOUR	ACCEHN CHANCE	ACDDIT ADDICT
ABLOST OBLAST	ACCEHS CACHES	ACDDIY DYADIC
ABLOTT TALBOT	ACCEHT CACHET	ACDDTU ADDUCT
ABLOTV ABVOLT	ACCEIN CANICE	ACDEEF DEFACE
ABLPRU BURLAP	ACCEIP ICE CAP, IPECAC	ACDEEN DECANE
ABLPYY BYPLAY	ACCEIT ACETIC	ACDEER DECARE
ABLRSU BURSAL	ACCEKL CACKLE	ACDEES CEASED
ABLRSW BRAWLS	ACCELN CANCEL	ACDEFH CHAFED
ABLRTU BRUTAL	ACCELR CERCAL	ACDEGR CADGER, GRACED
ABLSST BLASTS	ACCELS CALCES	ACDEGT GEDACT
ABLSTY STABLY	ACCEMS MECCAS	ACDEHK HACKED
ABLSWY BYLAWS	ACCEMU CAECUM	ACDEHR ARCHED, ECHARD
ABLSYY LAY-BYS	ACCENR CANCER	ACDEHS CASHED, CHASED
ABLTTY TYBALT	ACCENT ACCENT	ACDEHT DETACH
ABMNOW BOWMAN	ACCEPT ACCEPT	ACDEIM DECIMA

ACDEIV ADVICE
ACDEJK JACKED
ACDEKL CALKED, LACKED
ACDEKP PACKED
ACDEKR RACKED
ACDEKS SACKED
ACDEKT TACKED
ACDELL CADELL, CALLED
ACDELM CALMED
ACDELN CANDLE, DECLAN, LANCED
ACDELO COALED
ACDELP PLACED
ACDELR CRADLE
ACDELS DECALS, SCALED
ACDELU CAUDLE, CLAUDE
ACDELV CALVED
ACDELW CLAWED
ACDEMP CAMPED, DECAMP
ACDENN CANNED
ACDENO ACNODE, CANOED, DEACON
ACDENR CRANED, DANCER, NACRED
ACDENS ASCEND, DANCES
ACDENT CADENT, CANTED, DECANT
ACDEOT COATED
ACDEOX COAXED
ACDEPP CAPPED
ACDEPR CARPED, REDCAP
ACDEPS SPACED
ACDERS CADRES, CEDARS, SACRED, SCARED
ACDERT CARTED, CRATED, REDACT, TRACED
ACDERV CARVED, CRAVED
ACDERZ CRAZED
ACDEST CADETS
ACDESU CAUSED, SAUCED
ACDEUX CAUDEX
ACDHIR DIARCH
ACDHMR DRACHM
ACDHRS CHARDS
ACDIIM AMIDIC
ACDIJU JUDAIC
ACDILP PLACID
ACDINO ANODIC
ACDINR RANCID
ACDIOZ ZODIAC
ACDIPS CAPSID
ACDLNU UNCLAD
ACDLSS SCALDS

ACDLTY DACTYL
ACDMTU MUDCAT
ACDNNU DUNCAN
ACDNOR CONRAD, DACRON
ACDORS DORCAS
ACDORW COWARD
ACDSTU DUCATS
ACEEFF EFFACE
ACEEFN ENFACE
ACEEFR REFACE
ACEEFS FAECES
ACEEGI ICE AGE
ACEEGN ENCAGE
ACEEHN ACHENE
ACEEHT HECATE
ACEEIP APIECE
ACEEJT EJECTA
ACEELN ENLACE
ACEELR CEREAL
ACEELV CLEAVE
ACEEMN MENACE
ACEEMR RACEME
ACEEMZ ECZEMA
ACEENR CAREEN
ACEENS ENCASE, SÉANCE, SENECA
ACEENT CETANE, TENACE
ACEEPS ESCAPE, PEACES
ACEERR CAREER
ACEERS CREASE
ACEERT CERATE, CREATE, ECARTE
ACEFFT AFFECT
ACEFHR CHAFER
ACEFIL FACILE
ACEFIN FIANCÉ
ACEFIR FIACRE
ACEFIS FACIES
ACEFLU FECULA
ACEFNR FRANCE
ACEFRS FARCES
ACEFST FACETS
ACEFSU FAUCES
ACEFSY CASEFY
ACEFTU FAUCET
ACEGHN CHANGE
ACEGHR CHARGE
ACEGHU GAUCHE
ACEGIL GAELIC
ACEGIR CAGIER, GRACIE
ACEGLN GLANCE
ACEGLY LEGACY
ACEGNY AGENCY

ACEGOS SOCAGE
ACEGOW COWAGE
ACEGRS GRACES
ACEHIM HAEMIC
ACEHIR ARCHIE, CAHIER
ACEHIS CHAISE
ACEHKL HACKLE
ACEHKR HACKER
ACEHLP CHAPEL, PLEACH
ACEHLR RACHEL
ACEHLS LACHES
ACEHLT CHALET, THECAL, THECLA
ACEHMN MANCHE
ACEHMR MARCHE
ACEHMS SCHEMA
ACEHNS ENCASH
ACEHOR CHOREA, HORACE
ACEHPR EPARCH, PREACH
ACEHPT HEPCAT
ACEHPY PEACHY
ACEHRR ARCHER
ACEHRS ARCHES, CHASER, ESCHAR, SEARCH
ACEHRX EXARCH
ACEHSS CHASES, CHASSE
ACEHST CHASTE, CHEATS, SACHET
ACEHSW CASHEW
ACEIJK JACKIE
ACEIJN JANICE
ACEILM MALEIC, MALICE
ACEILN CELINA
ACEILP PLAICE
ACEILR CLAIRE, ÉCLAIR, LACIER
ACEIMN ANEMIC, CINEMA, ICEMAN
ACEIMO MACEIO
ACEIMR CRIMEA, MARCIE, MERCIA
ACEIMS CAMISE
ACEIMU AECIUM
ACEINN ANNICE, CANINE
ACEINS CASEIN
ACEINT ENATIC
ACEINV CAVE-IN
ACEINX AXENIC
ACEIPS APICES
ACEIQU CAIQUE
ACEIRR CARRIE, RACIER
ACEIRS CARIES
ACEIRU CURIAE

ACEISS CASSIE
ACEISV VESICA
ACEITV ACTIVE
ACEIVV VIVACE
ACEJKT JACKET
ACEJLO CAJOLE
ACEKLM MACKLE
ACEKLS ALECKS
ACEKLT TACKLE
ACEKLY LACKEY
ACEKNR CANKER
ACEKPR PACKER
ACEKPT PACKET
ACEKRR RACKER
ACEKRS CREAKS, SACKER
ACEKRT RACKET, TACKER
ACEKRY CREAKY
ACEKST CASKET
ACELLO LOCALE
ACELLR CALLER, CELLAR,
    RECALL
ACELMR CALMER,
    CARMEL, MARCEL
ACELMS CAMELS, MASCLE,
    MESCAL
ACELMT CAMLET
ACELMU ALMUCE, CAELUM
ACELNN CANNEL
ACELNR LANCER
ACELNS LANCES
ACELNT CANTLE, CENTAL,
    LANCET
ACELNU CUNEAL, LAUNCE,
    UNLACE
ACELOR CAROLE, COALER,
    ORACLE
ACELOS SOLACE
ACELOT LOCATE
ACELOV ALCOVE, COEVAL
ACELPR CARPEL, PARCEL,
    PLACER
ACELPS PLACES
ACELPT PLACET
ACELQU CALQUE, CLAQUE
ACELRR CARREL
ACELRS SCALER, SCLERA
ACELRT CARTEL, CLARET,
    RECTAL
ACELRW CLAWER
ACELSS SCALES
ACELST CASTLE, CLEATS
ACELSU CLAUSE
ACELSV CALVES

ACELTT CATTLE
ACELTY ACETYL
ACELYY CLAYEY
ACEMNP ENCAMP
ACEMNR CARMEN
ACEMNU ACUMEN
ACEMOP POMACE
ACEMOS CAMEOS
ACEMOT COMATE
ACEMPR CAMPER
ACEMRS CREAMS, SCREAM
ACEMRY CREAMY
ACEMTU ACETUM
ACENNS CANNES
ACENNU NUANCE
ACENNY ANNECY
ACENOR CORNEA
ACENOS CANOES, OCEANS
ACENOT OCTANE
ACENPR PRANCE
ACENPS PECANS
ACENRS CARNES, CASERN,
    CRANES
ACENRT CANTER, CARNET,
    CRETAN, NECTAR, RECANT,
    TRANCE
ACENRV CAVERN, CRAVEN
ACENST ASCENT, SECANT,
    STANCE
ACENSU USANCE
ACEOPS PASCOE
ACEOPT CAPOTE, TOE CAP
ACEOPW COWPEA
ACEORS COARSE
ACEORX COAXER
ACEOTV AVOCET, OCTAVE
ACEPPR CAPPER
ACEPRS CAPERS, ESCARP,
    PARSEC, RECAPS, SCRAPE,
    SPACER
ACEPRT CARPET
ACEPRU APERCU
ACEPSS SPACES
ACEPST ASPECT
ACEPTU TEACUP
ACEQSU CASQUE
ACERRS RACERS, SCARER
ACERRT CARTER, CRATER,
    TRACER
ACERRU CURARE
ACERRV CARVER
ACERSS CARESS, SCARES

ACERST CARETS, CASTER,
    CRATES, RECAST, TRACES
ACERSU SAUCER
ACERSY SCAREY
ACERSZ CRAZES
ACERTU CURATE
ACERTY TRACEY
ACESST CASTES
ACESSU CAUSES, SAUCES
ACESTU CUESTA
ACESTY STACEY
ACFFHY CHAFFY
ACFFLS SCLAFF
ACFGIN FACING
ACFILO AFL-CIO
ACFILS FISCAL
ACFINT IN FACT
ACFIOS FIASCO
ACFIPY PACIFY
ACFLNO FALCON, FLACON
ACFLRU FULCRA
ACFMOR CORFAM
ACFNOR FRANCO
ACFNRS FRANCS
ACFORT FACTOR
ACFRSS SCARFS
ACFRST CRAFTS
ACFRTY CRAFTY
ACGGIN CAGING
ACGGIO AGOGIC
ACGGRY CRAGGY
ACGHIN ACHING, ICHANG
ACGHOU GAUCHO
ACGHTU CAUGHT
ACGIKN CAKING
ACGILL GALLIC
ACGILN LACING
ACGILR GARLIC
ACGILS GLACIS
ACGILY CAGILY
ACGINN CANING
ACGINO AGONIC
ACGINP PACING
ACGINR CARING, RACING
ACGINS CASING
ACGINT ACTING
ACGINV CAVING
ACGINW CAWING
ACGIRS CIGARS
ACGIRT TRAGIC
ACGIUU IGUACU
ACGNOR GARÇON
ACGNOS CONGAS, GASCON

ACGORS CARGOS
ACGORU COUGAR
ACGTTU CATGUT
ACHHNU HAUNCH
ACHHTT THATCH
ACHIIS ISCHIA
ACHIJK HIJACK
ACHIKW HAWICK
ACHILO LOCHIA
ACHILP CALIPH
ACHINR INARCH, RANCHI
ACHINS CHAINS
ACHIPS PHASIC
ACHIPT HAPTIC
ACHIRS CHAIRS, CHARIS,
　RACHIS
ACHKKU CHUKKA
ACHKLS CHALKS
ACHKLY CHALKY
ACHKRU CHUKAR
ACHKSS SHACKS
ACHKSW WHACKS
ACHKTW THWACK
ACHLLO CHOLLA
ACHLNU LAUNCH, NUCHAL
ACHLOR CHORAL
ACHLRY ARCHLY
ACHMNU MANCHU
ACHMOR CHROMA
ACHMPS CHAMPS
ACHMRS CHARMS
ACHMSS CHASMS
ACHMSU SUMACH
ACHNOR ANCHOR
ACHNOS NACHOS
ACHNPU PAUNCH
ACHNST CHANTS, SNATCH,
　STANCH
ACHNTU NAUTCH
ACHNTY CHANTY
ACHOPR CARHOP
ACHORS SORCHA
ACHPTY PATCHY
ACHRST CHARTS, STARCH
ACHSSW SCHWAS
ACHSTW SWATCH
ACHSTY YACHTS
ACHTTY CHATTY
ACIILS SIALIC, SILICA
ACIILT ITALIC
ACIIRT TRICIA
ACIJQU JACQUI
ACIKLN CALKIN

ACIKMR KARMIC
ACIKNP INK-CAP
ACIKNS INK SAC
ACIKNT CATKIN
ACILLN CALL-IN, CLINAL
ACILLP PLICAL
ACILLS LILACS, SCILLA
ACILLY LACILY
ACILMO COLIMA
ACILMS CLAIMS
ACILMX CLIMAX
ACILNO ALNICO, COLINA,
　NICOLA, OILCAN
ACILNT TINCAL
ACILNU LUCIAN, LUCINA,
　UNCIAL
ACILNV CALVIN
ACILOR LORICA
ACILOS SOCIAL
ACILOT COITAL
ACILRT CITRAL, RICTAL
ACILRU ULRICA, URACIL,
　URALIC
ACILRY RACILY
ACILSV SLAVIC
ACIMNO ANOMIC, CAMION,
　MONICA
ACIMNT MANTIC
ACIMOR ROMAIC
ACIMOS MOSAIC
ACIMOT ATOMIC
ACIMPS SCAMPI
ACIMPT IMPACT
ACIMRS RACISM
ACIMRY MYRICA
ACIMST MASTIC
ACINNT TANNIC
ACINOS CASINO
ACINOT ACTION, ATONIC,
　CATION
ACINOX ANOXIC
ACINPS PANICS
ACINPT CATNIP
ACINRS CAIRNS
ACINRT CATRIN
ACINRU URANIC
ACINST ANTICS
ACINSU ACINUS
ACINTT INTACT
ACINTU TUNICA
ACINUV VICUÑA
ACIORS SCORIA
ACIORT AORTIC

ACIOST SCOTIA
ACIOSV OVISAC
ACIOTZ AZOTIC
ACIPRS PRISCA
ACIPRY PIRACY
ACIQTU ACQUIT
ACIRSS CRASIS
ACIRST CRISTA, RACIST
ACIRSV VICARS
ACIRTU URATIC
ACISSS CASSIS
ACISTT ATTICS, STATIC
ACITUY ACUITY
ACITVY CAVITY
ACKLOS CLOAKS
ACKLSS SLACKS
ACKMSS SMACKS
ACKNPU UNPACK
ACKNRS CRANKS
ACKNRY CRANKY
ACKNSS SNACKS
ACKORS CROAKS
ACKPSY SKYCAP
ACKQSU QUACKS
ACKRST TRACKS
ACKSST STACKS
ACLLMU CALLUM
ACLLMY CALMLY
ACLLNO CLONAL
ACLLOR COLLAR
ACLLOS LOCALS
ACLLOW CALLOW
ACLLPU CALL-UP
ACLLSU CALLUS
ACLMMY CLAMMY
ACLMOP COPALM
ACLMPS CLAMPS
ACLMTU TALCUM
ACLNOS CASLON
ACLNUY LUNACY
ACLOPU COPULA, CUPOLA
ACLORR CORRAL
ACLORS CARLOS, CAROLS,
　CORALS
ACLORU OCULAR
ACLOST COSTAL
ACLOSV VOCALS
ACLOTU TOLUCA
ACLPSS CLASPS, SCALPS
ACLRRU CRURAL
ACLRSW CRAWLS, SCRAWL
ACLSSY CLASSY
ACMMOS COMMAS

ACMNNO CONMAN
ACMNOO MONACO
ACMNOR MACRON
ACMNOS MASCON, SOCMAN
ACMNOW COWMAN
ACMOPS CAMPOS
ACMOST MASCOT
ACMOTT TOMCAT
ACMPRS CRAMPS
ACMPSS SCAMPS
ACMPSU CAMPUS
ACMRSU MARCUS, SACRUM
ACMSTU MUSCAT
ACMUUV VACUUM
ACNNNO CANNON
ACNNOS CANONS
ACNNOT CANNOT, CANTON
ACNNOY CANYON
ACNNRY CRANNY
ACNOOR CORONA, RACOON
ACNOPS CAPONS
ACNOPY CANOPY
ACNORS ACORNS
ACNORT CANTOR, CARTON
ACNORY CRAYON
ACNOST CANTOS
ACNOTT OCTANT
ACNOTU TOUCAN
ACNOTX CAXTON
ACNSTU CANTUS, TUSCAN
ACNSTY SCANTY
ACOOTV OCTAVO
ACOPRT CAPTOR
ACOPTW COWPAT
ACORRT CARROT, TROCAR
ACORSS ACROSS, OSCARS
ACORST ACTORS, CASTOR, CO-STAR, SCROTA
ACORTV CAVORT
ACORTX OXCART
ACORYZ CORYZA
ACOSST ASCOTS, COASTS
ACPPRY CRAPPY
ACPPSU CUPPAS
ACPRSS SCARPS, SCRAPS
ACPRSU CARPUS
ACPSTU CATSUP, UPCAST
ACRRWY WAR CRY
ACRSTT TRACTS
ACSTTY SCATTY
ADDDEG GADDED
ADDDEL ADDLED

ADDDEN ADDEND
ADDDEP PADDED
ADDDFY DAFYDD
ADDEEH HEADED
ADDEEN DEADEN
ADDEEV EVADED
ADDEGO GOADED
ADDEGR GADDER, GRADED
ADDEHN HANDED
ADDEHS DASHED, SHADED
ADDEIL DIALED, LADDIE
ADDEIM DIADEM, MADDIE
ADDEIR RAIDED
ADDELL LADLED
ADDELN DANDLE, LANDED
ADDELO LOADED
ADDELP PADDLE
ADDELR ALDRED, LADDER, LARDED, RADDLE
ADDELS SADDLE
ADDELU LAUDED
ADDELW DAWDLE, WADDLE
ADDELY DEADLY
ADDEMM DAMMED
ADDEMN DAMNED, DEMAND, MADDEN
ADDEMP DAMPED
ADDEMR MADDER
ADDENR DANDER, DARNED
ADDENS SADDEN, SANDED
ADDENW DAWNED
ADDEOR ADORED, DEODAR
ADDEOS DADOES
ADDEPP DAPPED
ADDEPR DRAPED
ADDERS ADDERS, DREADS, SADDER
ADDERT DARTED, TRADED
ADDERW EDWARD, WARDED
ADDGIN ADDING
ADDGIO GADOID
ADDGLU DUGALD
ADDGOO OGDOAD
ADDIMR MADRID
ADDIMY MIDDAY
ADDLNO DONALD
ADDNOS ADD-ONS
ADDNRU DURAND
ADDORS DORSAD
ADDORT DOTARD
ADDOST AT ODDS
ADDRSY DRYADS

ADEEFM DEFAME
ADEEFN DEAFEN
ADEEFR FEARED
ADEEFT DEFEAT
ADEEGG DEGAGE
ADEEGR AGREED, DRAGEE, GEARED
ADEEHI HAIDEE
ADEEHL HEALED
ADEEHP HEAPED
ADEEHR ADHERE, HEADER
ADEEHT HEATED
ADEEHV HEAVED
ADEEIL AEDILE
ADEEIT IDEATE
ADEEKL LEAKED
ADEEKP PEAKED
ADEELN LEADEN, LEANED
ADEELP LEAPED, PEALED
ADEELR DEALER, LEADER
ADEELS LEASED, SEALED
ADEELT ELATED
ADEELV LEAVED
ADEEMN DEMEAN
ADEEMO OEDEMA
ADEEMR REAMED, REMADE
ADEEMT TEAMED
ADEENN DEANNE, ENNEAD
ADEENR ANDRÉE, EARNED, ENDEAR, NEARED
ADEENT ANTEED
ADEENV EVADNE
ADEENW WEANED
ADEEPR REAPED
ADEEPS PESADE
ADEEPT PEDATE
ADEERR DEARER, READER, REARED, REREAD
ADEERS ERASED, RESEDA, SEARED
ADEERV EVADER
ADEERW DRAWEE
ADEERX EXEDRA
ADEEST SEATED, SEDATE, TEASED
ADEFGG FAGGED
ADEFGN FAG END, FANGED
ADEFIL AFIELD, FAILED
ADEFIN FADE-IN
ADEFIR FRIEDA
ADEFKL FLAKED
ADEFLM FLAMED
ADEFLO FOALED, LOAFED

ADEFLR ALFRED, FLARED
ADEFLU FEUDAL
ADEFLW FLAWED
ADEFLY FLAYED
ADEFMO FOAMED
ADEFMR FARMED, FRAMED
ADEFNN FANNED
ADEFNW FAWNED
ADEFOR FEDORA
ADEFRT DAFTER, FARTED,
RAFTED
ADEFRY DEFRAY, FRAYED
ADEFST FASTED
ADEFTW WAFTED
ADEGGG GAGGED
ADEGGJ JAGGED
ADEGGL LAGGED
ADEGGN GANGED, NAGGED
ADEGGR DAGGER, RAGGED
ADEGGS SAGGED
ADEGGT GADGET, TAGGED
ADEGGU GAUGED
ADEGGW WAGGED
ADEGHS GASHED
ADEGII EGIDIA
ADEGIN GAINED
ADEGIY ADYGEI
ADEGKW GAWKED
ADEGLL GALLED
ADEGLN ANGLED, DANGLE,
GLENDA
ADEGLO GAOLED, OLD AGE
ADEGLR GERALD, GLARED
ADEGLS GLADES
ADEGLZ GLAZED
ADEGMM GAMMED
ADEGNR DANGER,
GANDER, GARDEN, RANGED
ADEGNU AUGEND
ADEGNW GNAWED,
GWENDA
ADEGOR DOG-EAR
ADEGOS DAGOES, DOSAGE,
SEA DOG
ADEGOT DOTAGE
ADEGPP GAPPED
ADEGPS GASPED
ADEGPW GAWPED
ADEGRR GERARD,
GRADER, REGARD
ADEGRS GRADES
ADEGRT GRATED
ADEGRU ARGUED

ADEGRY GRAYED
ADEGRZ GRAZED
ADEGSS GASSED
ADEGST STAGED
ADEGSW WADGES
ADEHHS HASHED
ADEHIL HAILED, HALIDE
ADEHIR HARDIE
ADEHJS HADJES
ADEHJZ HEDJAZ
ADEHKR HARKED
ADEHKW HAWKED
ADEHLN HANDEL, HANDLE
ADEHLR HERALD
ADEHLS LASHED
ADEHLT HALTED
ADEHLU HAULED
ADEHLV HALVED
ADEHMM HAMMED
ADEHMR HARMED
ADEHMS MASHED, SHAMED
ADEHNO HEAD-ON
ADEHNP DAPHNE
ADEHNR HARDEN
ADEHNY HAYDEN
ADEHOX HOAXED
ADEHPR HARPED
ADEHPS PHASED, SHAPED
ADEHPT HEPTAD
ADEHRR HARDER
ADEHRS DASHER, SHARED
ADEHRT DEARTH, HATRED,
THREAD
ADEHSS DASHES, SHADES
ADEHST DEATHS
ADEHSV SHAVED
ADEHSW WASHED
ADEHSY HYADES
ADEHTW THAWED
ADEHYY HEYDAY
ADEIIM MAIDIE
ADEIJL JAILED
ADEILL ALLIED
ADEILM MAILED, MEDIAL
ADEILN DANIEL, DELIAN,
DENIAL, LEAD-IN, NAILED
ADEILP ALIPED, ELAPID,
PLEIAD
ADEILR DERAIL, RAILED,
RELAID
ADEILS IDEALS, LADIES,
SAILED

ADEILT DETAIL, DILATE,
TAILED
ADEILU AUDILE
ADEILW WAILED
ADEIMM MAIMED
ADEIMN DAMIEN, MAIDEN,
MEDIAN, MEDINA
ADEIMR ADMIRE
ADEIMU MAUDIE
ADEINN DIANNE, NADINE
ADEINO IDONEA
ADEINP PAINED
ADEINR RAINED
ADEINS SANDIE, SENDAI,
SINEAD
ADEINT DETAIN
ADEINV INVADE
ADEINW EDWINA
ADEIOT IODATE
ADEIPR DIAPER, PAIRED,
REPAID
ADEIRR RAIDER
ADEIRS RAISED
ADEIRT TIRADE
ADEIRV VARIED
ADEISS ASIDES, DAISES
ADEISU ADIEUS
ADEISV ADVISE, VISAED
ADEITV DATIVE
ADEITW WAITED
ADEITX TAXIED
ADEIUX ADIEUX
ADEIVW WAIVED
ADEJMM JAMMED
ADEJRR JARRED
ADEJRU ADJURE
ADEJUV DÉJÀ VU
ADEJZZ JAZZED
ADEKKY YAKKED
ADEKLN KENDAL
ADEKLR LARKED
ADEKLS SLAKED
ADEKLT TALKED
ADEKLW WALKED
ADEKMR MARKED
ADEKMS MASKED
ADEKNR DANKER,
DARKEN, KENDRA,
NARKED, RANKED
ADEKNS SNAKED
ADEKNW WANKED
ADEKNY YANKED
ADEKOS SOAKED

ADEKOY OKAYED
ADEKPR PARKED
ADEKQU QUAKED
ADEKRR DARKER
ADEKRS DRAKES
ADEKST SKATED, STAKED
ADELLP PALLED
ADELLR LADLER
ADELLS LADLES
ADELLU ALLUDE, ALUDEL
ADELLW WALLED
ADELMP PALMED
ADELMR DERMAL, MEDLAR
ADELMS DAMSEL, MEDALS
ADELMT MALTED
ADELMU MAULED
ADELNO LOANED
ADELNP PLANED
ADELNR DARNEL
ADELNS ELANDS, LANDES
ADELNT DENTAL
ADELNU UNLEAD
ADELOR LOADER, ORDEAL,
   RELOAD
ADELOS ALDOSE
ADELPP DAPPLE, LAPPED
ADELPR PEDLAR
ADELPS LAPSED, PEDALS
ADELPT PLATED
ADELPW DEWLAP
ADELPY PLAYED
ADELRR DARREL, LARDER
ADELRU ALURED, LAUDER
ADELRY DEARLY
ADELST DELTAS, LASTED,
   SALTED, SLATED, STALED
ADELSV SALVED, SLAVED
ADELSY DELAYS
ADELUV VALUED
ADELZZ DAZZLE
ADEMMN MADMEN
ADEMMR RAMMED
ADEMNN MANNED
ADEMNO DAEMON,
   MENADO, MOANED,
   MODENA
ADEMNP DAMPEN
ADEMNR REMAND
ADEMNS AMENDS, DESMAN
ADEMNT TANDEM
ADEMNU UNMADE
ADEMOP POMADE

ADEMOR RADOME,
   ROAMED
ADEMOT MOATED
ADEMOW MEADOW
ADEMPP MAPPED
ADEMPR DAMPER
ADEMPT TAMPED
ADEMPU MADE-UP
ADEMRR MARRED
ADEMRS DREAMS
ADEMRT DREAMT
ADEMRW WARMED
ADEMRY DREAMY
ADEMSS MASSED
ADEMSU AMUSED
ADEMTT MATTED
ADENNP PANNED
ADENNT TANNED
ADENNU DUENNA
ADENNW WANNED
ADENOS ANODES
ADENOT ATONED, DONATE
ADENPP APPEND, NAPPED
ADENPR PANDER, REPAND
ADENPT PANTED, PEDANT,
   PENTAD
ADENPW PAWNED
ADENPX EXPAND
ADENRR DARNER,
   DARREN, ERRAND
ADENRS SANDER, SNARED
ADENRT ARDENT, RANTED
ADENRU UNREAD
ADENRW ANDREW,
   WANDER, WARDEN,
   WARNED
ADENRY DENARY, YARNED
ADENSS SEDANS
ADENSU SUNDAE
ADENTT ATTEND
ADENTV ADVENT
ADENTW WANTED
ADENWY DWAYNE, YAWNED
ADEOPS SOAPED
ADEORR ROARED
ADEORS SOARED
ADEORW REDOWA
ADEOSS ODESSA
ADEOSV VADOSE
ADEOTT TO DATE
ADEOVW AVOWED
ADEPPR DAPPER, RAPPED
ADEPPS SAPPED

ADEPPT TAPPED
ADEPPY YAPPED
ADEPPZ ZAPPED
ADEPRR DRAPER
ADEPRS DRAPES, PADRES,
   PARSED, RASPED, SPADER,
   SPARED, SPREAD
ADEPRT DEPART, PARTED,
   PETARD, PRATED
ADEPRW WARPED
ADEPRY PRAYED
ADEPSS PASSED, SPADES
ADEPST ADEPTS, PASTED
ADEPSU PAUSED
ADEPSY SPAYED
ADEPTT PATTED
ADEPTU UPDATE
ADERRT DARTER, RETARD,
   TARRED, TRADER
ADERRW DRAWER,
   REWARD, WARDER,
   WARRED
ADERRY DREARY
ADERST STARED, TRADES,
   TREADS
ADERSW SEWARD, WADERS
ADERTT RATTED, TETRAD
ADERTV ADVERT
ADERTW WARTED
ADERUY AUDREY
ADERXY X-RAYED
ADESSS SASSED
ADESST STEADS
ADESSU DESSAU
ADESTT STATED, TASTED
ADESTV STAVED
ADESTW WASTED
ADESTY STAYED, STEADY
ADESWY SWAYED
ADETTT TATTED
ADFFOR AFFORD
ADFFRY DRAFFY
ADFGIN FADING
ADFGLY GADFLY
ADFIRT ADRIFT
ADFIRY FRIDAY
ADFLTY DAFTLY
ADFNOU AU FOND
ADFRRU DARFUR
ADFRST DRAFTS
ADFRSU FRAUDS
ADFRSW DWARFS
ADFRTY DRAFTY

ADGGOT DOG TAG
ADGGRY DRAGGY
ADGIIN AIDING
ADGILN LADING, LIGAND
ADGILO ALGOID
ADGIMY DIGAMY
ADGINO GANOID
ADGINR DARING, GRADIN,
   IN DRAG
ADGINT DATING
ADGINW WADING
ADGINY GDYNIA
ADGINZ DANZIG, DAZING
ADGIRV GRAVID
ADGLLO OLD LAG
ADGLLY GLADLY
ADGLNS GLANDS
ADGLOP LAPDOG
ADGLOU DOUGAL
ADGLOY DAYGLO
ADGLSY GLADYS
ADGMOS DOGMAS
ADGNOR DRAGON
ADGNOS GONADS
ADGNRS GRANDS
ADGRSU GRADUS, GUARDS
ADHHIT HADITH
ADHHLU HULDAH
ADHHOW HOWDAH
ADHHWY WHYDAH
ADHIJS HADJIS, JIHADS
ADHIKU HAIDUK
ADHILO HALOID
ADHILT ALDITH
ADHIMR DIRHAM
ADHINS DANISH, SANDHI
ADHIOR HAIRDO
ADHIPS APHIDS
ADHIRS RADISH
ADHIRY HYDRIA, RIYADH
ADHLOP ADOLPH
ADHLOR HAROLD
ADHLOT OLD HAT
ADHLRY HARDLY
ADHMNO HODMAN
ADHNNU UNHAND
ADHNOR HADRON,
   HARD-ON, RHONDA
ADHNOU HOUDAN
ADHNOY HAYDON
ADHNSY SHANDY
ADHORS HOARDS
ADHORW HOWARD

ADHOSW SHADOW
ADHPRU HARD UP, PURDAH
ADHRSS SHARDS
ADHRSY HYDRAS
ADHSSU SADHUS
ADIIKO AIKIDO
ADIILN INLAID
ADIILO ODILIA
ADIIMR MIDAIR
ADIINN INDIAN
ADIINV AVIDIN
ADIIPR DIAPIR
ADIJMS MASJID
ADIJNO ADJOIN
ADIKMO MIKADO
ADIKNP INKPAD, KIDNAP
ADIKTT DIKTAT
ADILLP PALLID
ADILMO AMIDOL
ADILMS DISMAL
ADILMY MILADY
ADILNN INLAND
ADILNO LADINO
ADILNR ALDRIN
ADILNS ISLAND
ADILNU UNLAID
ADILNW ALDWIN
ADILOS ISOLDA
ADILOZ OZALID
ADILPS PLAIDS
ADILRS LAIRDS
ADILRZ LIZARD
ADILST DISTAL
ADILVY AVIDLY
ADIMNO DOMAIN
ADIMOT DIATOM
ADIMRS DISARM
ADIMRU RADIUM
ADIMRY MYRIAD
ADIMSS SADISM
ADIMST AMIDST
ADIMSY DISMAY
ADIMWY MIDWAY
ADINOR DORIAN, INROAD,
   ORDAIN
ADINOX DIOXAN
ADINPT PANDIT
ADINPU UNPAID
ADINRS DINARS, DRAINS,
   NADIRS
ADINRU DURIAN
ADINRW INWARD
ADINSU UNSAID

ADINSV DIVANS, VIANDS
ADINTY DAINTY
ADIORS RADIOS
ADIORT ADROIT, DORITA
ADIPPU PAID-UP
ADIPRS RAPIDS, SPARID
ADIPSX SPADIX
ADIRRY AIR-DRY
ADIRST ASTRID, TRIADS
ADIRSU RADIUS
ADIRWZ WIZARD
ADISST SADIST
ADISTU AUDITS
ADISTV DAVITS
ADJKOU JUDOKA
ADJNOR JORDAN
ADJORR JARROD
ADJSTU ADJUST
ADKKNO KOKAND
ADKLRY DARKLY
ADLLOR DOLLAR
ADLMNO ALMOND,
   DOLMAN, OLD MAN
ADLMOS DOLMAS
ADLMPY DAMPLY
ADLMTU TALMUD
ADLNOP POLAND
ADLNOR ARNOLD,
   LARDON, ROLAND, RONALD
ADLNOT DALTON
ADLNOU UNLOAD
ADLNPU UPLAND
ADLNWY ALDWYN
ADLORS DORSAL
ADLOSS DOSSAL
ADLOSU ALDOUS
ADLOSW OSWALD
ADLRRY DARRYL
ADLRSW DRAWLS
ADLRWY DRAWLY
ADLSTU ADULTS
ADMNOR RANDOM
ADMNOS DAMSON,
   NOMADS
ADMNOY DYNAMO,
   MONDAY
ADMNPY DYMPNA
ADMNUY MAUNDY
ADMORR RAMROD
ADMORU MADURO
ADNNOU ADNOUN
ADNOPR PARDON
ADNOPT DOPANT

ADNORU AROUND
ADNORW ONWARD
ADNOTY DAYTON
ADNRST STRAND
ADNRTU TUNDRA
ADNSST STANDS
ADNSTY DYNAST
ADNSUY SUNDAY
ADOPRY PARODY
ADORRU ARDOUR
ADPRUW UPWARD
ADQSSU SQUADS
ADRSSW SWARDS
ADRTWY TAWDRY
AEEFIR FAERIE
AEEFLM FEMALE
AEEFRR FEARER
AEEGGN ENGAGÉ
AEEGGR REGGAE
AEEGIR ARIEGE
AEEGLL ALLEGE
AEEGLP PELAGE
AEEGLR GALERE, REGALE
AEEGLS EAGLES
AEEGLT EAGLET, LEGATE
AEEGLU LEAGUE
AEEGMN MANEGE,
   MÉNAGE
AEEGMR GRAEME, MEAGRE
AEEGMT GAMETE, METAGE
AEEGNN ENNAGE
AEEGNR ENRAGE, GENERA
AEEGNS SENEGA
AEEGNT NEGATE
AEEGNV AVENGE, GENEVA
AEEGOP APOGEE
AEEGOT GOATEE
AEEGRS GREASE
AEEGST EGESTA
AEEGSW SEWAGE
AEEHHW HEE-HAW
AEEHJN JEHANE
AEEHKT HEKATE
AEEHLN HELENA
AEEHLR HEALER
AEEHLX EXHALE
AEEHLY HEALEY
AEEHMR HAREEM
AEEHMU HEAUME
AEEHNN HEENAN
AEEHNP PEAHEN
AEEHNS SHEENA
AEEHNT ATHENE, ETHANE

AEEHNV HEAVEN
AEEHNX HEXANE
AEEHPR HEAPER
AEEHRR HEARER, REHEAR
AEEHRS HAERES, HEARSE
AEEHRT AETHER, HEATER,
   HEREAT, REHEAT
AEEHRV HEAVER
AEEHSV HEAVES, SHEAVE
AEEHTX THE AXE
AEEIJN JEANIE
AEEILN AILEEN, ELAINE
AEEIRS EASIER
AEEJNN JEANNE
AEEKLN ALKENE
AEEKLR LEAKER
AEEKMR REMAKE
AEEKNW WEAKEN
AEEKNY YANKEE
AEEKRT RETAKE
AEEKRU EUREKA
AEEKRW WEAKER
AEELLL ALLELE
AEELLM MALLEE
AEELLS SALLEE
AEELLV A LEVEL
AEELMN ENAMEL
AEELMP EMPALE
AEELNN LEANNE
AEELNR ARLEEN, ARLENE,
   LEANER
AEELNS SELENA
AEELNT LATEEN
AEELNV LEAVEN
AEELOT OLEATE
AEELPR LEAPER, REPEAL
AEELPS ASLEEP, ELAPSE,
   PLEASE, SAPELE
AEELRS LEASER, RESALE,
   SEALER
AEELRT ELATER, RELATE
AEELRV LEAVER, REVEAL
AEELSS EASELS, LEASES
AEELST TEASEL
AEELSV LEAVES, SLEAVE
AEELSW WEASEL
AEELTV VELATE
AEELWY LEEWAY
AEEMNR MEANER, RENAME
AEEMNS ENEMAS, SEAMEN
AEEMNX EXAMEN
AEEMPR AMPERE
AEEMRR REAMER

AEEMRS SEAMER
AEEMSS SESAME
AEEMTX TAXEME
AEENNT NEATEN
AEENNX ANNEXE
AEENQU QUEENA
AEENRR EARNER, NEARER
AEENRS RANEES, SERENA
AEENRT NEATER
AEENRV VERENA
AEENST SATEEN, SENATE
AEENSU UNEASE
AEENUV AVENUE
AEEPRR REAPER
AEEPRS PARSEE
AEEPRT REPEAT
AEEPST PESETA
AEEPSX APEXES
AEEPSY PAYEES
AEEQTU EQUATE
AEERRR REARER
AEERRS ERASER
AEERRT TEARER
AEERRW WEARER
AEERST ARÊTES, EASTER,
   EATERS, RESEAT, SEATER,
   TEASER, TERESA
AEERSU RESEAU, UREASE
AEERSV AVERSE
AEERVW WEAVER
AEESST TEASES
AEESSW SEESAW
AEESTT ESTATE
AEESVW WEAVES
AEFFGR GAFFER
AEFFGS GAFFES
AEFFIN AFFINE
AEFFIP PIAFFE
AEFFLR RAFFLE
AEFFLW WAFFLE
AEFFRZ ZAFFER
AEFGLN FLANGE
AEFGOR FORAGE
AEFHRS AFRESH
AEFHRT FATHER, HAFTER
AEFILL FAILLE
AEFILN FINALE
AEFILR FERIAL
AEFILT FETIAL
AEFIMN FAMINE
AEFINN FENIAN
AEFIRR FAIRER
AEFIRY AERIFY

AEFIST FIESTA	AEGGNR GANGER,	AEGLNT TANGLE
AEFITX FIXATE	GRANGE, NAGGER	AEGLNU LANGUE
AEFJNT FANJET	AEGGNS GANGES	AEGLNW WANGLE
AEFKLR FLAKER	AEGGNU GANGUE	AEGLOR GALORE, GAOLER
AEFKLS FLAKES	AEGGRT GARGET	AEGLOT LEGATO
AEFKRS FAKERS, FREAKS	AEGGRU GAUGER	AEGLOV LOVAGE
AEFKRY FREAKY	AEGGSU GAUGES	AEGLPU PLAGUE
AEFLLN FALLEN	AEGHIR HEGIRA	AEGLRR LARGER
AEFLLR FALLER	AEGHIS GEISHA	AEGLRS GLARES, LAGERS
AEFLMR FLAMER	AEGHIW AWEIGH	AEGLRT TERGAL
AEFLMS FLAMES	AEGHMN MEGHAN	AEGLRV GRAVEL
AEFLNX FLAXEN	AEGHMO HOMAGE,	AEGLRY ARGYLE
AEFLOR LOAFER	OHMAGE	AEGLRZ GLAZER
AEFLOT FOETAL	AEGHNO EOGHAN	AEGLSV GAVELS
AEFLOV FOVEAL	AEGHNR HANGER	AEGLSY SAGELY
AEFLRS FALSER, FLARES	AEGHRT GARETH, GATHER	AEGLSZ GLAZES
AEFLRT FALTER	AEGHSS GASHES	AEGMMR GRAMME
AEFLRU EARFUL, FERULA	AEGILN GENIAL, LINAGE	AEGMMS SMEGMA
AEFLRY FLAYER	AEGILS GISELA, SILAGE	AEGMNR ENGRAM,
AEFLST FESTAL	AEGILT LIGATE	GERMAN, MANGER
AEFLSY SAFELY	AEGILZ EL GIZA	AEGMNS GASMEN
AEFLTY FEALTY	AEGIMN ENIGMA, GAMINE	AEGMNT MAGNET
AEFMOR FEMORA	AEGIMP MAGPIE	AEGMOS OMEGAS
AEFMRR FARMER, FRAMER	AEGIMR GAMIER, MARGIE,	AEGMUY MAGUEY
AEFMRS FRAMES	MIRAGE	AEGMUZ ZEUGMA
AEFMRT FERMAT	AEGIMS AGEISM, IMAGES	AEGNNO NONAGE
AEFNNR FANNER	AEGINR EARING, GAINER,	AEGNNP PENANG
AEFNRR FARREN	REGAIN, REGINA	AEGNNT GANNET
AEFNRU FRAUEN	AEGINS EASING	AEGNOR GAENOR,
AEFNRW FAWNER	AEGINT EATING	ONAGER, ORANGE
AEFNST FASTEN	AEGINU GUINEA	AEGNRR GARNER, RANGER
AEFNSU UNSAFE	AEGIPP PIPAGE	AEGNRS ANGERS, RANGES
AEFNTT FATTEN	AEGIRT GAITER	AEGNRT ARGENT, GARNET
AEFNZZ FEZZAN	AEGIRW EARWIG	AEGNRV GRAVEN
AEFPPR FRAPPÉ	AEGIRZ GEZIRA	AEGNRW GNAWER
AEFRRS FRASER	AEGIST AGEIST	AEGNRY ANERGY
AEFRRT FRATER, RAFTER	AEGISV VISAGE	AEGNST AGENTS
AEFRRY RAREFY	AEGITU AUGITE	AEGNSV VEGANS
AEFRRZ FRAZER	AEGITY GAIETY	AEGOPT POTAGE
AEFRST AFTERS, FASTER,	AEGJLN JANGLE	AEGORT ORGEAT
STRAFE	AEGJLT JET LAG	AEGORU AERUGO
AEFRSW WAFERS	AEGJTU JUGATE	AEGOTU OUTAGE
AEFRTT FATTER	AEGKRW GAWKER	AEGOTW TOWAGE
AEFRTW WAFTER	AEGKST GASKET	AEGOVY VOYAGE
AEFSST FEASTS, SAFEST	AEGLLU ULLAGE	AEGPRS GASPER, GRAPES
AEFSTY SAFETY	AEGLLY GALLEY	AEGPRT PARGET
AEGGGL GAGGLE	AEGLMN MANGLE	AEGPRU PRAGUE
AEGGGR GAGGER	AEGLMS GLEAMS	AEGRRT GARRET, GARTER,
AEGGHL HAGGLE	AEGLMY GAMELY	GRATER
AEGGIM MAGGIE	AEGLNN GLENNA	AEGRRU ARGUER
AEGGIN AGEING	AEGLNO ANGELO	AEGRRV GRAVER
AEGGLR GARGLE	AEGLNR ANGLER, ERLANG	AEGRRY GRAYER
AEGGLW WAGGLE	AEGLNS ANGELS, ANGLES	AEGRRZ GRAZER

AEGRSS GASSER, SARGES
AEGRST GRATES, GREATS, STAGER
AEGRSU AUGERS, SAUGER
AEGRSV GRAVES
AEGRSW SWAGER, WAGERS
AEGRSY GREASY
AEGRSZ GRAZES
AEGRTT TARGET
AEGRTU TUAREG
AEGRTY GYRATE
AEGSSS GASSES
AEGSST STAGES
AEGSSU USAGES
AEGSTY GAYEST, STAGEY
AEHHLT HEALTH
AEHHRS REHASH
AEHHRT HEARTH
AEHHSS HASHES
AEHHST HEATHS, SHEATH
AEHHTY HEATHY
AEHIJL ELIJAH
AEHIJR HEJIRA
AEHIKN HANKIE
AEHIKZ KEZIAH
AEHILL LEILAH
AEHILM HIEMAL
AEHILN INHALE
AEHILP PHILAE
AEHILR HAILER
AEHILS ELISHA, ILESHA, SHEILA
AEHILT HALITE
AEHILW AWHILE
AEHIMN HAEMIN
AEHIMR HERMIA
AEHIMS MASHIE
AEHIMT HAMITE
AEHINR HERNIA
AEHINT AITHNE, IANTHE
AEHINW ANHWEI
AEHIRS ASHIER, SHERIA
AEHIRZ HAZIER
AEHIST HESTIA, SAITHE
AEHITT HATTIE
AEHJJS HAJJES
AEHKLT THEKLA
AEHKNR HANKER, HARKEN
AEHKNS SHAKEN
AEHKRS SHAKER
AEHKRW HAWKER
AEHKSS SHAKES
AEHLLL HALLEL

AEHLLS HELLAS
AEHLLT LETHAL
AEHLLY HALLEY
AEHLMP PELHAM
AEHLMR HARLEM
AEHLMT HAMLET, THELMA
AEHLNS HANSEL
AEHLOR LAHORE
AEHLOS HALOES
AEHLOT LOATHE
AEHLRS LASHER
AEHLRT HALTER, LATHER
AEHLRU HAULER
AEHLRW WHALER
AEHLRY HARLEY
AEHLSS HASSLE, LASHES
AEHLST HALEST, HASLET, LATHES
AEHLSV HALVES
AEHLSW WHALES
AEHLSY ASHLEY
AEHLSZ HAZELS
AEHLTW WEALTH
AEHLYY HAYLEY
AEHMMR HAMMER
AEHMMY MAYHEM
AEHMNR ARNHEM, HERMAN
AEHMNT ANTHEM, HAMNET, HETMAN
AEHMNU HUMANE
AEHMOT AT-HOME
AEHMPR HAMPER
AEHMRR HARMER
AEHMRS HAREMS, MASHER
AEHMSS MASHES
AEHMST THAMES
AEHNNS HANSEN
AEHNPP HAPPEN
AEHNPT HAPTEN
AEHNRT ANTHER, THENAR
AEHNRY HARNEY
AEHNST ATHENS, HASTEN, THANES
AEHNSV HAVENS, SHAVEN
AEHNSY HYENAS
AEHNTV HAVEN'T
AEHNTX XANTHE
AEHORS ASHORE, HOARSE
AEHORX HOAXER
AEHOSX HOAXES
AEHPRR HARPER

AEHPRS PHRASE, SERAPH, SHERPA
AEHPSS PHASES, SHAPES
AEHPST SPATHE
AEHRRS RASHER, SHARER
AEHRRT RATHER
AEHRSS RASHES, SHARES, SHEARS
AEHRST EARTHS, HEARST, HEARTS, SARTHE
AEHRSV SHAVER
AEHRSW HAWSER, WASHER
AEHRTT HATTER, THREAT
AEHRTW THAWER, WREATH
AEHRTY EARTHY, HEARTY
AEHRVW WHARVE
AEHRVY HARVEY
AEHSSS SASHES
AEHSSV SHAVES
AEHSSW WASHES
AEHSTW SWATHE
AEIILM EMILIA
AEIILS LIAISE
AEIIMS MAISIE
AEIINR EIRIAN
AEIIPT TAIPEI
AEIIRR AIRIER
AEIJKR RIJEKA
AEIJLR JAILER
AEIJMM JEMIMA
AEIJNN JANINE
AEIKLS ALSIKE
AEIKLT TALKIE
AEIKNR KIERAN
AEIKNS KINASE
AEIKNT INTAKE
AEIKRS KAISER
AEILLN LIENAL, LINEAL
AEILLR ALLIER
AEILLS ALLIES
AEILLT TELIAL
AEILMN MENIAL
AEILMP IMPALE
AEILMR MAILER, MARIEL
AEILMS MALISE
AEILNN LIANNE
AEILNP ALPINE, NEPALI, PINEAL
AEILNR ARLINE, LARINE, LINEAR, NAILER
AEILNS ALIENS, SALINE, SELINA
AEILNT ENTAIL, TINEAL

AEILNV ALVINE, ELVINA, VALINE, VEINAL, VENIAL
AEILNX XENIAL
AEILOS ELOISA
AEILPS ESPIAL, LIPASE
AEILPT APLITE
AEILRR RAILER
AEILRS ISRAEL, SAILER, SERIAL
AEILRT RETAIL, RETIAL
AEILRU AURIEL, LAURIE
AEILRV AVERIL, ELVIRA
AEILRW LAWRIE, WAILER
AEILRX RAILEX
AEILRZ LAZIER
AEILSS AISLES, ELISSA
AEILSV VALISE
AEILSX ALEXIS
AEILSY EASILY
AEIMMN AMMINE
AEIMMR MAIMER
AEIMNN IN NAME
AEIMNO ANOMIE
AEIMNR AIRMEN, ARMINE, MARINE, MARNIE, REMAIN
AEIMNS AMIENS
AEIMNT INMATE
AEIMNX MAXINE
AEIMRS ARMIES
AEIMRT MARTIE
AEIMST SAMITE
AEIMTT MATTIE
AEINNR NERINA
AEINNS INSANE, SIENNA
AEINNT INNATE
AEINNV VIENNA
AEINPR RAPINE
AEINRR RAINER
AEINRS ARISEN, ARSINE, SARNIE
AEINRT RATINE, RETAIN, RETINA
AEINRV RAVINE, VAINER
AEINRZ ZANIER
AEINSS SANIES
AEINST TISANE
AEINSV NAVIES
AEINTV NATIVE
AEINTY YENTAI
AEIOPR PEORIA
AEIOPT OPIATE
AEIOSV SAVOIE
AEIPPT PEPITA

AEIPRR RAPIER, REPAIR
AEIPRS ASPIRE, PARIES, PERSIA, PRAISE
AEIPRT PIRATE
AEIPTT PATTIE
AEIRRS RAISER, SIERRA
AEIRRT ARTIER
AEIRRV ARRIVE
AEIRRW WARIER
AEIRSS RAISES
AEIRST SATIRE
AEIRTT ATTIRE, RATITE
AEIRTW WAITER
AEIRVW WAIVER, WAVIER
AEIRVX XAVIER
AEIRWX WAXIER
AEISST SIESTA
AEISSU AUSSIE
AEISSZ ASSIZE
AEJMMR JAMMER
AEJMRT RAMJET
AEJMST JETSAM
AEJNNO JOANNE
AEJNOT TAEJON
AEJNST SEJANT
AEJNUU JUNEAU
AEJPRS JASPER
AEJPRY JAPERY
AEKLNR LANKER, RANKLE
AEKLNS ANKLES
AEKLNT ANKLET
AEKLNW KNAWEL
AEKLNY ALKYNE
AEKLPS SPLAKE
AEKLRR LARKER
AEKLRS SLAKER
AEKLRT TALKER
AEKLRW WALKER
AEKLSS KASSEL
AEKLST LASKET
AEKLTU AUKLET
AEKLWY WEAKLY
AEKMNR KERMAN
AEKMNU UNMAKE
AEKMPU MAKE-UP
AEKMRR MARKER, REMARK
AEKMRS MAKERS, MASKER
AEKMRT MARKET
AEKNNY KENYAN
AEKNOR KOREAN
AEKNOW AWOKEN
AEKNRR RANKER
AEKNRT TANKER

AEKNRW NEWARK, WANKER
AEKNSS SNAKES, SNEAKS
AEKNSV KNAVES
AEKNSY SNEAKY
AEKOPT TOPEKA
AEKORS ARKOSE, SOAKER
AEKPRR PARKER
AEKPTU TAKEUP, UPTAKE
AEKQRU QUAKER
AEKQSU QUAKES, SQUEAK
AEKRST SKATER, STRAKE, STREAK, TAKERS, TASKER
AEKSST SKATES, STAKES, STEAKS
AEKSTW TWEAKS
AEKWYY KEYWAY
AELLLU LUELLA
AELLMT MALLET
AELLMY LAMELY
AELLNS ANSELL
AELLPS LAPELS
AELLPT L-PLATE, PALLET, TELPAL
AELLPY PALELY
AELLRT TALLER
AELLRU ALLURE, LAUREL
AELLRY REALLY
AELLST STELLA
AELLSY ALLEYS
AELLTU LUTEAL
AELLTW WALLET
AELLTY LATELY
AELLVY VALLEY
AELMNS ANSELM, LE MANS, MANSEL
AELMNT LAMENT, MANTEL, MANTLE, MENTAL
AELMNU MANUEL
AELMNY LAYMEN, MANLEY, MEANLY, NAMELY
AELMOR MORALE
AELMOS SALOME
AELMPR PALMER
AELMPS MAPLES, SAMPLE
AELMPU AMPULE
AELMRS REALMS
AELMRT ARMLET
AELMRU MAULER
AELMRV MARVEL
AELMRY AYLMER
AELMST LAMEST, METALS
AELMSU SAMUEL

AELMSY MEASLY
AELMTU AMULET
AELMTY TAMELY
AELNNR LANNER
AELNOR LOANER
AELNOT ETALON, LEAN-TO
AELNPP PEN PAL
AELNPR PARNEL, PLANER,
    REPLAN
AELNPS NAPLES, PANELS,
    PLANES
AELNPT PLANET, PLATEN
AELNRT ANTLER, LEARNT,
    RENTAL
AELNRU LAUREN, NEURAL,
    UNREAL
AELNRV VERNAL
AELNRY NEARLY
AELNSU UNSEAL
AELNSV NAVELS
AELNSY SANELY
AELNTT LATENT, LATTEN,
    TALENT
AELNTU LUNATE
AELNTV LEVANT
AELNTY NEATLY
AELOPP ALEPPO
AELOPR PAROLE
AELOPS EL PASO
AELOPT PELOTA
AELOST OSTEAL
AELOSV LOAVES
AELOTZ ZEALOT
AELPPR LAPPER, RAPPEL
AELPPS APPLES
AELPPT LAPPET
AELPPU PAPULE
AELPQU PLAQUE
AELPRR PARREL
AELPRS LAPSER, PEARLS
AELPRT PALTER, PLATER
AELPRU PLEURA
AELPRY PARLEY, PEARLY, ~
    PLAYER, REPLAY
AELPSS LAPSES, SEPALS
AELPST PALEST, PASTEL,
    PETALS, PLATES, PLEATS,
    SEPTAL, STAPLE
AELPTU PETULA
AELQSU EQUALS, SQUEAL
AELRRY RARELY
AELRSS LASERS

AELRST ALERTS, LASTER,
    SALTER, SLATER, STALER,
    STELAR
AELRSV SALVER, SERVAL,
    SLAVER, VELARS
AELRSY LAYERS, RELAYS,
    SLAYER
AELRTT LATTER, RATTLE
AELRTV TRAVEL, VARLET
AELRTW WALTER
AELRTY LYRATE
AELRUV VALUER
AELRWY LAWYER
AELRYY YEARLY
AELRZZ RAZZLE
AELSSS LASSES
AELSST SLATES, TASSEL
AELSSV SALVES, SLAVES
AELSTT LATEST
AELSTU SALUTE
AELSTV VALETS, VESTAL
AELSUV VALUES
AELSUX SEXUAL
AELSVV VALVES
AELSYZ SLEAZY
AELTTT TATTLE
AELTTW WATTLE
AELTUX LUXATE
AELUUV UVULAE
AELUVV VULVAE
AEMMNR MERMAN
AEMMRR RAMMER
AEMMRY YAMMER
AEMNNO EAMONN
AEMNNP PENMAN
AEMNNR MANNER
AEMNOR MOANER
AEMNOY YEOMAN
AEMNPU PNEUMA
AEMNQU MANQUÉ
AEMNRT MARTEN
AEMNRU MANURE
AEMNST STAMEN
AEMNSU UNSEAM
AEMNSY YES-MAN
AEMNTX TAXMEN
AEMORR REMORA,
    ROAMER
AEMORS RAMOSE
AEMORX XEROMA
AEMPPR PAMPER
AEMPRT TAMPER
AEMPRV REVAMP

AEMQRU MARQUE
AEMQSU MASQUE
AEMRRR MARRER
AEMRRU ARMURE
AEMRRW WARMER
AEMRSS MASERS, SMEARS
AEMRST MASTER, STREAM,
    TAMERS
AEMRSU MASERU, MAUSER
AEMRSY RAMSEY, SMEARY
AEMRTT MATTER
AEMRTU MATURE
AEMSSS MASSES
AEMSSU ASSUME, SEAMUS,
    SEUMAS
AEMSSX XMASES
AEMSTT TAMEST
AEMSTU MEATUS
AEMSTY STEAMY
AEMSYZ ZYMASE
AEMTTU MUTATE
AENNOY ANYONE
AENNRS SENNAR
AENNRT TANNER
AENNRW WANNER
AENNST NANTES
AENNTT TENANT
AENOPW WEAPON
AENOPY PAEONY
AENORS REASON, SEÑORA
AENORT ATONER, ORNATE
AENORV VERONA
AENORW ROWENA
AENORX ROXANE
AENOSS SEASON
AENOTZ ZONATE
AENOWY ONE-WAY
AENPPR NAPPER
AENPRT ENTRAP, PARENT,
    TREPAN
AENPRW ENWRAP
AENPRZ PANZER
AENPTT PATENT, PATTEN
AENPTU PEANUT
AENRRS SNARER
AENRRT ERRANT, RANTER
AENRRW WARNER,
    WARREN
AENRRY RAYNER
AENRSS SNARES
AENRST ASTERN, STERNA
AENRSV RAVENS
AENRSW ANSWER

AENRSY SENARY
AENRTT NATTER
AENRTU NATURE
AENRTV TAVERN
AENRTW WANTER
AENRWY YAWNER
AENSST ASSENT, SANEST
AENSSU ANUSES
AENSTU AUSTEN, UNSEAT
AENSTY ANSTEY
AENSUV NAEVUS
AENSUY UNEASY
AENTTU ATTUNE, TAUTEN, TETUAN
AENTTX EXTANT
AEOPPS APPOSE
AEOPQU OPAQUE
AEOPRS OPERAS
AEOPRT PROTEA
AEOPTT TEAPOT
AEOPTY TEAPOY
AEORRR ROARER
AEORRS SOARER
AEORRU AURORE
AEORSS SEROSA
AEORSU AROUSE
AEORSZ AZORES
AEORTT ROTATE
AEORVW AVOWER
AEPPRR RAPPER
AEPPRS PAPERS, SAPPER
AEPPRT TAPPER
AEPPRU PAUPER
AEPPRY PAPERY, PREPAY, YAPPER
AEPPTT TAPPET
AEPPTU PUPATE
AEPRRS PARSER, RASPER, SPARER
AEPRRT PRATER
AEPRRU PARURE, UPREAR
AEPRRW PREWAR, WARPER
AEPRRY PRAYER
AEPRSS SPARES, SPARSE, SPEARS
AEPRST PATERS, REPAST, TAPERS
AEPRSU PAUSER
AEPRTT PATTER
AEPRUV RAVE-UP
AEPSSS PASSES
AEPSST PASTES, STAPES
AEPSSU PAUSES

AEQRSU SQUARE
AEQRUV QUAVER
AEQSUY QUEASY
AERRST ARREST, RAREST, RASTER, STARER
AERRSV RAVERS
AERRTT RATTER
AERRTY ARTERY
AERSST ASSERT, STARES
AERSSU ASSURE
AERSSV SAVERS
AERSSW WRASSE
AERSTT AT REST, STATER, TASTER, TREATS
AERSTV STARVE
AERSTW RAWEST, WASTER, WATERS
AERSTX EXTRAS
AERSTY ESTRAY, STAYER
AERSTZ ERSATZ
AERSUU AUREUS
AERSWY SAWYER, SWAYER
AERTTT TATTER
AERTTU TAUTER
AERTTY TREATY
AERTUU AUTEUR
AERTWY WATERY
AESSSS ASSESS, SASSES
AESSST ASSETS
AESSSY ESSAYS
AESSTT STATES, TASTES
AESSTV STAVES
AESSTW SWEATS, WASTES
AESTTT ATTEST
AESTTU ASTUTE, STATUE
AESTWY SWEATY
AESTYY YEASTY
AFFFOR FAR-OFF
AFFGUW GUFFAW
AFFIKR KAFFIR
AFFIMR AFFIRM
AFFIRT TARIFF
AFFLOY LAY-OFF
AFFLUX AFFLUX
AFFOPY PAYOFF
AFFSST STAFFS
AFGGIO FOGGIA
AFGGLY FLAGGY
AFGGOT FAGGOT
AFGIKN FAKING
AFGILN FINGAL
AFGINR FARING
AFGINX FAXING

AFGINZ FAZING
AFGISY GASIFY
AFGLNO FLAGON
AFGLNU FUNGAL
AFGLRU FRUGAL
AFGOTU FUGATO
AFGRST GRAFTS
AFGSTU GUSTAF
AFHIIR HAIRIF
AFHIKL KHALIF
AFHIMS FAMISH
AFHIOS OAFISH
AFHIST FAITHS
AFHLOO LOOFAH
AFHLSY FLASHY
AFHMOT FATHOM
AFHRSW WHARFS
AFHSST SHAFTS
AFIIJN FIJIAN
AFIILL FILIAL
AFIILN FINIAL
AFIKRS FAKIRS
AFILLS FLAILS
AFILMY FAMILY
AFILNO FINOLA
AFILNS FINALS
AFILNU FULANI
AFILNV FLAVIN
AFILNY FINLAY
AFILOR FOLIAR
AFILPS PILAFS
AFILRY FAIRLY
AFILRZ FRAZIL
AFILSY SALIFY
AFIMNY INFAMY
AFIMRY RAMIFY
AFIMSS MASSIF
AFINNO FANION
AFINNT INFANT
AFINRU UNFAIR
AFINST FAINTS
AFINSU FUSAIN
AFIRRS FRIARS
AFIRRY FRIARY
AFIRTY RATIFY
AFKLNS FLANKS
AFKLSS FLASKS
AFLLOR FLORAL
AFLLOW FALLOW
AFLLTY FLATLY
AFLLUW LAWFUL
AFLMNU MANFUL
AFLMOR FORMAL

AFLMRU ARMFUL, FULMAR	AGHTTU TAUGHT	AGINWX WAXING
AFLMYY MAYFLY	AGIILN AILING, NILGAI	AGINWY YAWING
AFLNOT FONTAL	AGIIMN AIMING	AGIORU GIAOUR
AFLNTU FLAUNT	AGIINR AIRING	AGIORV VIRAGO
AFLOST FLOATS	AGIJNW JAWING	AGIOTU AGOUTI
AFLOTY FLOATY	AGIJSW JIGSAW	AGIRST GRATIS
AFLRTU ARTFUL	AGIKMN MAKING	AGIRTU GUITAR
AFLSTU FAULTS, FLATUS	AGIKNN ANKING	AGJLMO LOGJAM
AFLSWY SAWFLY	AGIKNR RAKING	AGJNOR JARGON
AFLTUY FAULTY	AGIKNS ASKING, GASKIN	AGKLNO KALONG
AFMORT FORMAT	AGIKNT TAKING	AGKNOR ANGKOR
AFMOSU FAMOUS	AGIKNW WAKING	AGKNRU KURGAN
AFNNRY FRANNY	AGILLU LIGULA	AGKORT GO-KART
AFNSSU SNAFUS	AGILMM GIMMAL	AGLLNO GALLON
AFORRW FARROW	AGILMN LAMING, MALIGN	AGLLOP GALLOP
AFORSY FORAYS	AGILMO GLIOMA	AGLLRY ARGYLL
AFORTU FAR-OUT	AGILNP PALING	AGLNNO LONGAN
AFORUV FAVOUR	AGILNS SIGNAL	AGLNOO LAGOON
AGGGIN GAGING	AGILNU LINGUA	AGLNOS SLOGAN
AGGHIS HAGGIS	AGILNY GAINLY, LAYING	AGLNOU LANUGO
AGGHSY SHAGGY	AGILNZ LAZING	AGLNOY LOYANG
AGGILO LOGGIA	AGILOR GLORIA	AGLNRU LANGUR
AGGIMN GAMING	AGILOT GALIOT	AGLNSY SLANGY
AGGINP GAPING, PAGING	AGILOV OGIVAL	AGLNTY TANGLY
AGGINR RAGING	AGILRY GLAIRY	AGLNUU UNGUAL, UNGULA
AGGINW WAGING	AGIMNN NAMING	AGLORS LARGOS
AGGINZ GAZING	AGIMNR ARMING, INGRAM,	AGLOSS GLOSSA
AGGIWW WIGWAG	MARGIN	AGLOST GLOATS
AGGIZZ ZIGZAG	AGIMNT MATING, TAMING	AGLPUY PLAGUY
AGGLSY SLAGGY	AGIMST STIGMA	AGLRUV VULGAR
AGGLWY WAGGLY	AGIMWW WIGWAM	AGLSSY GLASSY
AGGMOT MAGGOT	AGINNW AWNING, WANING	AGLSUV VALGUS
AGGNSY SNAGGY	AGINOR ORIGAN	AGMMNO GAMMON
AGGQUY QUAGGY	AGINOS SAIGON	AGMMNU MAGNUM
AGHILT ALIGHT	AGINPR PARING, RAPING	AGMNNU GUNMAN
AGHINN HANG IN	AGINPT TAPING	AGMNOR MORGAN
AGHINR HARING	AGINPV PAVING	AGMNOS MANGOS
AGHINS HSIANG	AGINPW PAWING	AGMNSU MAGNUS
AGHINT HATING	AGINPY PAYING	AGMOOY OOGAMY
AGHINV HAVING	AGINRR RARING	AGMORS ORGASM
AGHINZ HAZING	AGINRS GRAINS	AGMORT MARGOT
AGHIRS GARISH	AGINRT RATING	AGMOYZ ZYGOMA
AGHIRT ARIGHT	AGINRU AIRGUN, UGRIAN	AGMPUZ GAZUMP
AGHKRU GURKHA	AGINRV INGVAR, RAVING	AGNNOT TONGAN
AGHLLU GULLAH	AGINRY GRAINY	AGNNRY GRANNY
AGHLOS GALOSH	AGINRZ RAZING	AGNNTU ANTUNG
AGHLSU LAUGHS	AGINSS ASSIGN	AGNOQU QUANGO
AGHNOO OONAGH	AGINST GIANTS, SATING	AGNORS GROANS,
AGHNPU HANG-UP	AGINSV SAVING	ORGANS, SARONG
AGHNTU NAUGHT	AGINSW SAWING	AGNORY GAYNOR
AGHNUV VAUGHN	AGINSY SAYING	AGNOST TANGOS, TSONGA
AGHOQU QUAHOG	AGINTX TAXING	AGNOSW WAGONS
AGHPRS GRAPHS	AGINVW WAVING	AGNOTU NOUGAT

AGNPRS SPRANG	AHINSU HUSAIN	AHMRSY MARSHY
AGNPRU NAGPUR	AHINSV VANISH	AHMRTW WARMTH
AGNRST GRANTS	AHINSW WASHIN	AHMSSU SHAMUS
AGNRTY GANTRY	AHINTT TANITH, TIN HAT	AHNNSY SHANNY
AGNSTW TWANGS	AHIOPS SOPHIA	AHNOOR HONORA
AGNTWY TWANGY	AHIORT HOT AIR	AHNOPR ORPHAN
AGORST ARGOTS, GROATS	AHIPRS PARISH	AHNORS SHARON, SHORAN
AGORSY ARGOSY	AHIPRU RUPIAH	AHNOSX XHOSAN
AGORTU RAGOUT	AHIRRS HARRIS, SIRRAH	AHNOWY ANYHOW
AGOSTU OUTGAS	AHIRST THIRSA, TRISHA	AHNSTU HAUNTS
AGOTTU TAUTOG	AHIRSV RAVISH	AHNSTY SHANTY
AGRSSU SUGARS	AHIRSZ SHIRAZ	AHOORY HOORAY
AGRSSY GRASSY	AHIRTW WRAITH	AHOPST PASHTO, PATHOS,
AGRSTU TRAGUS	AHIRTZ THIRZA, TIRZAH	POTASH
AGRSUY SUGARY	AHISTU HIATUS	AHOPTT TOP HAT
AGRUUY AUGURY	AHISTV VASHTI	AHORRW HARROW
AGSTUU AUGUST	AHJMOT JOTHAM	AHORRY HORARY
AGSTUV GUSTAV	AHJOSU JOSHUA	AHORTT THROAT
AHHIMS HAMISH	AHKLNU KHULNA	AHORTU AUTHOR
AHHKOO HOOKAH	AHKMOW MOHAWK	AHORTX THORAX
AHHOOR HOORAH	AHKNOW HANKOW	AHPRSS SHARPS
AHHORT HATHOR	AHKNPU PUNKAH	AHQSSU SQUASH
AHHORW HOWRAH	AHKNRS SHRANK	AHRRTU ARTHUR
AHHPPU HUPPAH	AHKNSS SHANKS	AHRRUY HURRAY
AHHRRU HURRAH	AHKNST THANKS	AHRSSU HUSSAR
AHHRST THRASH	AHKRSS SHARKS	AHRSTY TRASHY
AHHUZZ HUZZAH	AHLLMU MULLAH	AHRTTW THWART
AHIILT AILITH, LITHIA	AHLLOO HALLOO	AHSSTU TUSSAH
AHIITT TAHITI	AHLLOS HALLOS	AHSSTW SWATHS
AHIJJS HAJJIS	AHLLOW HALLOW	AIIKLS LIKASI
AHIJNS JHANSI	AHLLRT THRALL	AIILLN LILIAN
AHIJOS JOSIAH	AHLLUX HALLUX	AIILLS LILIAS
AHIKMO KOHIMA	AHLMNY HAMLYN, HYMNAL	AIILNS IN SAIL
AHIKMS HAKIMS	AHLMOS SHALOM	AIILOV OLIVIA
AHIKRS RAKISH	AHLNSU UNLASH	AIILRY AIRILY
AHILLL LILLAH	AHLOOP HOOP-LA	AIILSV SILVIA
AHILLZ ZILLAH	AHLORT HARLOT	AIIMMN MINIMA
AHILMP IMPHAL	AHLORW HARLOW	AIIMMR MIRIAM
AHILNR RHINAL	AHLOSS SHOALS	AIIMNR MAIRIN
AHILNU INHAUL	AHLOSY SHOALY	AIIMNS SIMIAN
AHILNY HYALIN	AHLPSS SPLASH	AIIMNT INTIMA
AHILPS PALISH, PHIALS	AHLPSU LASH-UP	AIIMPR IMPAIR
AHILRY HILARY	AHLPSY PLASHY	AIINNN NINIAN
AHILST LATISH	AHLRSY RASHLY	AIINNO IONIAN
AHILSV LAVISH	AHLSSW SHAWLS	AIINNZ ZINNIA
AHILTW WITHAL	AHMMSY SHAMMY	AIINRS RAISIN
AHILYZ HAZILY	AHMNOS HANSOM	AIINST ISATIN
AHIMNT HIT MAN	AHMNPY NYMPHA	AIINVV VIVIAN
AHIMOR MOHAIR	AHMNSU HUMANS	AIIPTW WAPITI
AHIMPS MISHAP	AHMNSY MYNAHS	AIIRST ISTRIA
AHINPT HATPIN	AHMOST THOMAS	AIIRTV TRIVIA
AHINRU UNHAIR	AHMOTU MAHOUT	AIJJNU UJJAIN
AHINSS SHANSI	AHMOWY HAYMOW	AIJLNU JULIAN

AIJLOV JOVIAL
AIJOSS JOSIAS
AIJPRU JAIPUR
AIJRSV JARVIS
AIKLNO KAOLIN
AIKLNW WALK-IN
AIKLSU SALUKI
AIKMNR KIRMAN
AIKMOP MAIKOP
AIKMSU KUMASI
AIKNNP NAPKIN
AIKNPR PARKIN
AIKNRV NARVIK
AIKORT TROIKA
AIKTUW KUWAIT
AILLMU ALLIUM
AILLOT LOLITA
AILLPR PILLAR
AILLSV VILLAS
AILLSW WALLIS
AILLTW AT WILL
AILLYZ LAZILY
AILMNO OILMAN
AILMNR MARLIN
AILMNU ALUMNI
AILMNV MALVIN
AILMNY MAINLY
AILMOP LIPOMA
AILMOS SOMALI
AILMPR PRIMAL
AILMRT MITRAL, RAMTIL
AILMSS MISSAL
AILMSX SMILAX
AILMSY MISLAY
AILMTU LATIUM, ULTIMA
AILMUV VALIUM
AILMYZ MAZILY
AILNOS ALISON
AILNOT TALION
AILNPS PLAINS, SPINAL
AILNPT PLAINT, PLIANT
AILNRT TRINAL
AILNRU URINAL
AILNSS SNAILS
AILNST LATINS
AILNSU INSULA
AILNSV ANVILS, SILVAN
AILNSW IN-LAWS
AILNSY INLAYS
AILNTY LITANY
AILNVY VAINLY
AILNWY AYLWIN
AILNYZ ZANILY

AILORS SAILOR
AILORT RIALTO, TAILOR
AILORU AURIOL
AILOSU LOUISA
AILOSV VIOLAS
AILOSX OXALIS
AILOTX OXTAIL
AILPPS PIPALS
AILPRS APRILS, SPIRAL
AILPST PLAITS, SPITAL
AILQSU QUAILS
AILRRW WIRRAL
AILRST TRAILS, TRIALS
AILRSV RIVALS
AILRSY RIYALS
AILRTU RITUAL
AILRWY WARILY
AILSTV VITALS
AILSUV VISUAL
AILSVY SYLVIA
AILTXY LAXITY
AILVWY WAVILY
AILWXY WAXILY
AIMMOS MAOISM, MIMOSA
AIMMSX MAXIMS
AIMNNO AMNION, MINOAN
AIMNOR MARION
AIMNOS SIMONA
AIMNPT PITMAN
AIMNRT MARTIN
AIMNRV MARVIN
AIMNST MANTIS, MATINS,
     TAMSIN
AIMNSU ANIMUS
AIMNSY YASMIN
AIMNSZ NAZISM
AIMOPY MYOPIA
AIMOST MAOIST, TAOISM
AIMOSW MIAOWS
AIMOSX AXIOMS
AIMPRT ARMPIT, IMPART
AIMPSS PASSIM
AIMQSU MAQUIS
AIMRSU MARIUS
AIMRTU ATRIUM
AIMRTX MATRIX
AIMSSW SWAMIS
AIMSTU AUTISM
AINNNT TANNIN
AINNOS NASION
AINNOT ANOINT, NATION
AINNPW IN PAWN
AINNST TSINAN

AINOPS PIANOS
AINORS ROSINA
AINORT RATION
AINOSU SIOUAN
AINPRS SPRAIN
AINPST PAINTS, PINTAS,
     PTISAN
AINPSV SPAVIN
AINQRT QINTAR
AINQTU QUAINT
AINRST INSTAR, STRAIN,
     TRAINS
AINRSY SYRIAN
AINRTU IN A RUT, NUTRIA
AINRYZ ZYRIAN
AINSST SAINTS, STAINS
AINSSW SWAINS
AINSTT TITANS
AINSTU AUSTIN
AINSTY SANITY, SATINY
AINTVY VANITY
AIOORS ARIOSO
AIOPRT PORTIA
AIOPST PATIOS, PATOIS
AIOPTU UTOPIA
AIORSS ORISSA
AIORST AORIST, ARTOIS,
     RATIOS, ROSITA
AIOSTT TAOIST
AIOSYZ ZOYSIA
AIPPRY PAPYRI
AIPPST PAPIST
AIPRST RAPIST, TAPIRS
AIPRSW RIPSAW
AIPRSX PRAXIS
AIPRTY PARITY
AIPRUY PYURIA
AIPSTW PITSAW
AIPSZZ PIZZAS
AIRRTY RARITY
AIRSST SITARS, STAIRS
AIRSSU RUSSIA
AIRSTT ARTIST, STRAIT,
     TRAITS
AIRSTV TRAVIS
AIRSTY STYRIA
AIRTTY YTTRIA
AISSST ASSIST, STASIS
AISSTV VISTAS
AISSTW WAISTS
AISTUW WATUSI
AJKORT RAJKOT
AJLOPY JALOPY

AJMORS MAJORS
AJNORT TROJAN
AJNSTU JAUNTS, JUNTAS
AJNTUY JAUNTY
AJPRTU RAJPUT
AKLLNY LANKLY
AKLMOY KOLYMA
AKLNOW WALK-ON
AKLNOX KLAXON
AKLNPS PLANKS
AKLNRY RANKLY
AKLOPS POLKAS
AKLOSV SLOVAK
AKLPUW WALK-UP
AKLSST STALKS
AKLSTY STALKY
AKMNSU UNMASK
AKMPRU MARKUP
AKNORU KORUNA
AKNPRS PRANKS
AKNPRU KANPUR
AKNPSS SPANKS
AKNSSW SWANKS
AKNSWY SWANKY
AKOTVY VOTYAK
AKPRSS SPARKS
AKQRSU QUARKS
AKQSUW SQUAWK
ALLMOS SLALOM
ALLMOW MALLOW
ALLMSS SMALLS
ALLNOP POLLAN
ALLNUU LUNULA
ALLOOP APOLLO
ALLOPR PALLOR
ALLOPW WALLOP
ALLORY ORALLY
ALLOST ATOLLS
ALLOSW SALLOW
ALLOSY ALLOYS
ALLOTW TALLOW
ALLOWW WALLOW
ALLPRU PLURAL
ALLQSU SQUALL
ALLSST STALLS
ALLSTY LASTLY
ALLUVV VULVAL
ALMMUY AMYLUM
ALMNOR NORMAL
ALMNOS SALMON
ALMNRY MARLYN
ALMNTU MULTAN
ALMORS MOLARS, MORALS

ALMORT MORTAL
ALMORU MORULA
ALMORY MALORY
ALMOST ALMOST, SMALTO
ALMPSS PSALMS
ALMQSU QUALMS
ALMRSU MURALS
ALMRWY WARMLY
ALMSUY ASYLUM
ALMTUU MUTUAL, UMLAUT
ALNNOU NOUNAL
ALNOOS ALONSO, SALOON
ALNOOZ ALONZO
ALNOSS SALONS
ALNOST TALONS
ALNOTV VOLANT
ALNOTY LAYTON
ALNPST PLANTS
ALNRSS SNARLS
ALNRSY SNARLY
ALNRUY URANYL
ALNRXY LARYNX
ALNSST SLANTS
ALNSTU SULTAN
ALNSVY SYLVAN
ALNTUW WALNUT
ALOOPS SALOOP
ALOPPR POPLAR
ALOPPT LAP-TOP
ALOPRT PATROL, PORTAL
ALOPST POSTAL
ALOQTU LOQUAT
ALORSV SALVOR
ALORSY ROYALS
ALORTY TAYLOR
ALORUV LOUVAR, OVULAR,
   VALOUR
ALOSSS LASSOS
ALOSSV SALVOS
ALOSTT TOTALS
ALOTUW OUTLAW
ALOTUY LAYOUT, OUTLAY
ALPPSU SLAP-UP
ALPRSU PULSAR
ALPRSW SPRAWL
ALPRTY PALTRY, PARTLY
ALPSSU LAPSUS
ALRSTW TRAWLS
ALRSTY STYLAR
ALRSUU URSULA
ALRSUW WALRUS
ALRTTY RATTLY, TARTLY
ALRUUV UVULAR

ALSSTU SALTUS
ALSTUV VAULTS
ALSTUY SALYUT
ALSTVY VASTLY
ALSUUV UVULAS
ALSUVV VULVAS
ALTTUY TAUTLY
AMMMNO MAMMON
AMMMOS MOMMAS
AMMORT MARMOT
AMMOSU OMASUM
AMMOXY MYXOMA
AMMPUW WAMPUM
AMMRSY SMARMY
AMMSTU SUMMAT
AMNNOR NORMAN
AMNOOR MAROON,
   ROMANO
AMNOPT TAMPON
AMNORR MARRON
AMNORS MANORS,
   RANSOM, ROMANS
AMNORT MATRON
AMNORY MORNAY,
   ROMANY
AMNOSS MASONS, SAMSON
AMNOTU AMOUNT,
   OUTMAN
AMNPTY TYMPAN
AMNRTU ANTRUM
AMNRTY MARTYN
AMNRVY MARVYN
AMNSSU SAMSUN
AMNTTU MUTANT
AMNTUU AUTUMN
AMOOTT TOMATO
AMOPRS PRO-AMS
AMORRT MORTAR
AMORRU ARMOUR
AMORRW MARROW
AMORSS MORASS
AMORST STROMA
AMORSU AMOURS
AMORSY MAYORS
AMPRRU RAMPUR
AMPRST TRAMPS
AMPRUW WARM-UP
AMPSSS SPASMS
AMPSST STAMPS
AMPSSW SWAMPS
AMPSWY SWAMPY
AMRRTY MARTYR
AMRRUY MURRAY

AMRSSW SWARMS	AOPPPS POPPAS	BBBINO BOBBIN
AMRSTU STRUMA	AOPPRT POP ART	BBBLUY BUBBLY
ANNNUY YUNNAN	AOPRRT PARROT, RAPTOR	BBCDEU CUBBED
ANNOPZ POZNAN	AOPRRU UPROAR	BBCELO COBBLE
ANNORT NATRON	AOPRST PASTOR	BBCEOR COBBER
ANNOST SONANT	AOPRUV VAPOUR	BBCEOW COBWEB
ANNOSW WONSAN	AOPTUY PAYOUT	BBCHUY CHUBBY
ANNOTW WANTON	AOQRTU QUARTO	BBCLUY CLUBBY
ANNOTY ANTONY, TANNOY	AOQSTU QUOTAS	BBDDEI DIBBED
ANNPSU UNSNAP	AORRST ROSTRA	BBDDEU DUBBED
ANNRTY TRANNY	AORRSW ARROWS	BBDEEI DEBBIE
ANNSTU SUNTAN	AORRSY ROSARY	BBDEEW WEBBED
ANNTTU NUTANT	AORRSZ RAZORS	BBDEFI FIBBED
ANOOPS NO SOAP	AORRTY ROTARY	BBDEFO FOBBED
ANOOPX A POX ON	AORRWY YARROW	BBDEGI GIBBED
ANOORS SONORA	AORSST ASSORT, ROASTS	BBDEGU BEDBUG
ANOORT RATOON	AORSTT STATOR, TAROTS	BBDEIJ JIBBED
ANOPRS APRONS, PARSON	AORSTX STORAX	BBDEIL DIBBLE
ANOPRT PARTON, PATRON,	AORSUU AUROUS	BBDEIR DIBBER, RIBBED
TARPON	AORSUV SAVOUR	BBDEIY BIDE BY
ANOPUY YAUPON	AORSVY SAVORY	BBDEJO JOBBED
ANORRW NARROW	AORTVY VOTARY	BBDELO LOBBED
ANORRY RAYNOR	AOSSTT STOATS, TOASTS	BBDEMO BOMBED, MOBBED
ANORSW ROWANS	AOSSVY SAVOYS	BBDEOO BOOBED
ANORTT ATTORN	AOSTWW SWATOW	BBDEOR ROBBED
ANORTU OUTRAN	AOTUWY WAY-OUT	BBDEOS SOBBED
ANORTY NOTARY	AOTWWY TWO-WAY	BBDERU RUBBED
ANORWY NORWAY	APPPSU PAPPUS	BBDESU SUBBED
ANOSST SANTOS	APRRSY SPARRY	BBDETU TUBBED
ANOSSX SAXONS	APRSST SPRATS, STRAPS	BBDINO DOBBIN
ANOSXY SAXONY	APRSSY SPRAYS	BBDINU DUBBIN
ANPPSY SNAPPY	APRSTY PASTRY	BBEELP PEBBLE
ANPRSW PRAWNS	AQRRUY QUARRY	BBEFIR FIBBER
ANPRTY PANTRY	AQRSTU QUARTS	BBEGIN EBBING
ANPRUW UNWRAP	AQRTUZ QUARTZ	BBEGIR GIBBER
ANRSTU SATURN	AQSSTU SQUATS	BBEGIT GIBBET
ANRSUU URANUS	AQSSUW SQUAWS	BBEGLO GOBBLE
ANRSUY SUNRAY	ARRSTY STARRY	BBEGOT GOBBET
ANRSYZ SYZRAN	ARSSTT STARTS	BBEHLO HOBBLE
ANRTTU TRUANT	ARSSTU TARSUS	BBEHLU HUBBLE
ANRTTY TYRANT	ARSSTW STRAWS	BBEHOS HOBBES
ANRUWY RUNWAY,	ARSSTY SATYRS, STRAYS	BBEIIM IMBIBE
UNWARY	ARSTTU STUART	BBEIIS SIBBIE
ANSTTU TAUNTS, TUTSAN	ARSTUU TAURUS	BBEIJR JIBBER
ANSTUV VAUNTS	ARSTUX SURTAX	BBEILN NIBBLE
ANSTWY WYSTAN	ARSTWY STRAWY	BBEILR LIBBER
ANSTXY SYNTAX	ARSTXY STYRAX	BBEILS BIBLES
ANSYZZ SNAZZY	ASSTTU STATUS	BBEIOR ROBBIE
ANVVYY VYVYAN	BBBDEO BOBBED	BBEIRR BRIBER
AOOPTT POTATO	BBBEIO BOBBIE	BBEJOR JOBBER
AOOPTW PAOTOW	BBBELO BOBBLE	BBELMU BUMBLE
AOORRT ORATOR	BBBELU BUBBLE	BBELNO NOBBLE
AOOTTT TATTOO	BBBHUU HUBBUB	BBELNU NUBBLE

BBELOW WOBBLE
BBELPY PEBBLY, PLEBBY
BBELRU BURBLE, LUBBER,
   RUBBLE
BBEMNU BENUMB
BBEMOR BOMBER, MOBBER
BBEORR ROBBER
BBEORS SOBBER
BBERRU RUBBER
BBGINO GIBBON
BBGRUY GRUBBY
BBHMOS H-BOMBS
BBHNOO HOBNOB
BBIIIO IBIBIO
BBIKOS SKIBOB
BBILLU BULBIL
BBINOR RIBBON, ROBBIN
BBLLUU BULBUL
BBLNUY NUBBLY
BBLOWY BY-BLOW,
   WOBBLY
BBLRSU BLURBS
BBLRUY RUBBLY
BBNNOO BONBON
BBNSUY SNUBBY
BBORTU BURBOT
BBOSUY BUS BOY
BBRSUU SUBURB
BBSTUY STUBBY
BCDEEK BEDECK
BCDEIO BODICE
BCDEKU BUCKED
BCDEMO COMBED
BCDERU CURBED
BCDIOU CUBOID
BCEEHR BREECH
BCEEKT BECKET
BCEEMO BECOME
BCEEQU QUEBEC
BCEHLN BLENCH
BCEHOR BROCHE
BCEHRU CHERUB
BCEIKR BICKER
BCEIOX ICEBOX
BCEIPS BICEPS
BCEIRS SCRIBE
BCEIRT TERBIC
BCEIST BISECT
BCEJOT OBJECT
BCEKLU BUCKLE, LUBECK
BCEKNO BECKON
BCEKTU BUCKET
BCELNO EN BLOC

BCELOR CORBEL
BCELOU BOUCLE
BCEMOR COMBER
BCEMRU CUMBER
BCENOU BOUNCE
BCEOTT OBTECT
BCGINU CUBING
BCHIOP PHOBIC
BCHITY BITCHY
BCHLOT BLOTCH
BCHMOU BOCHUM
BCHNRU BRUNCH
BCHNUY BUNCHY
BCHOOR BROOCH
BCHOTY BOTCHY
BCIILM LIMBIC
BCIINO BIONIC, NIOBIC
BCIINU INCUBI
BCIIOP BIOPIC
BCIIOT BIOTIC
BCILMS CLIMBS
BCILPU PUBLIC
BCIMOR BROMIC
BCIMSU CUBISM
BCINOR BICORN
BCIORS SORBIC
BCIRRU RUBRIC
BCISTU CUBIST, CUBITS
BCKLOS BLOCKS
BCMOOS COMBOS
BCMORY CORYMB
BCMRSU CRUMBS
BCMRUY CRUMBY
BCNOOR BRONCO
BCNOTU COBNUT
BCNOUY BOUNCY
BCOOWY COWBOY
BCRSSU SCRUBS
BDDDEE BEDDED
BDDDEU BUDDED
BDDEER BEDDER
BDDEGU BUDGED
BDDEIN BIDDEN
BDDELU BUDDLE
BDDENO BONDED
BDDERU REDBUD
BDDIOR DO BIRD
BDDISU DISBUD
BDEEEF BEEFED
BDEEGG BEGGED
BDEEHL BEHELD
BDEEIL BELIED, EDIBLE
BDEEIS BESIDE

BDEEIT BETIDE
BDEELN BLENDE
BDEELT BELTED
BDEEOY OBEYED
BDEEST BESTED
BDEETT BETTED
BDEFFI BIFFED
BDEFFU BUFFED
BDEFIR FIBRED
BDEGGO BOGGED
BDEGGU BUGGED
BDEGIN BIG END
BDEGIR BRIDGE
BDEGLU BULGED
BDEGNU BUNGED
BDEGTU BUDGET
BDEHIN BEHIND
BDEHLO BEHOLD
BDEHOT HOTBED
BDEHSU BUSHED
BDEIIR BIRDIE, BRIDIE
BDEIKL BILKED
BDEILL BILLED
BDEILO BOILED, BOLIDE
BDEILR BRIDLE
BDEIMU IMBUED
BDEINN BINNED
BDEINR BINDER, INBRED,
   REBIND
BDEINT IN DEBT
BDEIOR BORIDE
BDEIOS BODIES
BDEIPS BIPEDS
BDEIRS DEBRIS
BDEIRU BURIED
BDEIRV VERBID
BDEIST BIDETS, DEBITS
BDEISU BUSIED
BDEKLU BULKED
BDEKNU BUNKED, DEBUNK
BDEKOO BOOKED
BDEKSU BUSKED
BDELNO BLONDE
BDELNS BLENDS
BDELNU BUNDLE
BDELOR BOLDER
BDELOT BOLTED
BDELOU DOUBLE
BDELOW BOWLED
BDEMMU BUMMED
BDEMNU NUMBED
BDEMOO BOOMED
BDEMOY EMBODY

BDEMPU BUMPED	BEEEMS BESEEM	BEFFTU BUFFET
BDEMRU DUMBER	BEEERZ BREEZE	BEFILM FIMBLE
BDENNU UNBEND	BEEFIL BELIEF	BEFILO FOIBLE
BDENOY BEYOND	BEEFLL BEFELL	BEFIRS FIBRES
BDENRU BURDEN, BURNED	BEEFLY FEEBLY	BEFLMU FUMBLE
BDENSU SUNBED	BEEFOR BEFORE	BEFLOO BEFOOL
BDEOOT BOOTED	BEEFRT BEREFT	BEFLOU BEFOUL
BDEOOZ BOOZED	BEEGLS GLEBES	BEFLRY BELFRY
BDEOPP BOPPED	BEEGNO BEGONE	BEGGII BIGGIE
BDEOPR PROBED	BEEGNR BERGEN	BEGGIR BIGGER
BDEORR BORDER	BEEGRS GREBES	BEGGLO BOGGLE
BDEORS DESORB	BEEGRT EGBERT	BEGGRU BUGGER
BDEORT DEBTOR	BEEGRU BURGEE	BEGILO OBLIGE
BDEOSS BOSSED	BEEHIR HERBIE	BEGILR GERBIL
BDEOUY BUOYED	BEEHLT BETHEL	BEGILS BILGES
BDEPRU BURPED	BEEHOP PHOEBE	BEGINN BENIGN
BDERRU BURRED	BEEHOV BEHOVE	BEGINO BIOGEN
BDESSU BUSSED	BEEHRW HEBREW	BEGINR BERING
BDESTU BUSTED, DEBUTS	BEEHRY HEREBY	BEGINS BEINGS, BINGES
BDESUU SUBDUE	BEEHST BEHEST	BEGIOS BOGIES
BDETTU BUTTED	BEEILR BELIER	BEGIOU BOUGIE
BDEUZZ BUZZED	BEEILZ BELIZE	BEGLNO BELONG
BDFIOR FORBID	BEEINR BERNIE	BEGLNU BLUNGE, BUNGLE
BDGIIN BIDING	BEEIRT BERTIE	BEGLOS GLOBES
BDGIIR BRIGID	BEEISS BESSIE	BEGLOT GOBLET
BDGINO BODING	BEEISV BEVIES	BEGLRU BUGLER, BURGLE
BDHIRY HYBRID	BEEISW BE WISE	BEGLSU BUGLES, BULGES
BDIILO LIBIDO	BEEISX IBEXES	BEGMSU BEGUMS
BDIIMR MIDRIB	BEEKRU REBUKE	BEGNOY BYGONE
BDIITT TIDBIT	BEELLS BELLES	BEGOPX PEG BOX
BDIKNO BODKIN	BEELMM EMBLEM	BEGORU BROGUE
BDILNS BLINDS	BEELNS BELSEN	BEGOSY BOGEYS
BDILNU DUBLIN	BEELPS BLEEPS	BEGRRU BURGER
BDILOY BODILY	BEELRS REBELS	BEGRSU BRUGES
BDILSU BUILDS	BEELRT TREBLE	BEHILS ISHBEL
BDIMOR MORBID	BEELSV BEVELS	BEHILT BLITHE
BDINNU UNBIND	BEEMMR MEMBER	BEHINT HENBIT
BDIOTU OUTBID	BEEMNR BREMEN	BEHKOR RHEBOK
BDIRTU TURBID	BEEMRS EMBERS	BEHKRY KHYBER
BDLLOY BOLDLY	BEEMSU BEMUSE	BEHLMU HUMBLE
BDLMUY DUMBLY	BEENNT BENNET	BEHLSU BUSHEL
BDLNOY BLODYN	BEENOR ENROBE	BEHLTY BLYTHE
BDLOOS BLOODS	BEENRU REUBEN	BEHMOR HOMBRE
BDLOOY BLOODY, OLD BOY	BEENTU BUTENE	BEHMRU HUMBER
BDLOUY DOUBLY	BEEOOT BOOTEE	BEHNOR HEBRON
BDNOOY NOBODY	BEEOPP PEEPBO	BEHOOS HOBOES
BDNOSU BOUNDS	BEEORY OBEYER	BEHORT BOTHER
BDOORS BROODS	BEERRW BREWER	BEHRST BERTHS
BDOORY BROODY	BEERST BERETS	BEHRTU HUBERT
BDORWY BYWORD	BEERTT BETTER	BEHSSU BUSHES
BDOSTU DOUBTS	BEERTV BREVET	BEIILL BILLIE
BEEEFL FEEBLE	BEERYZ BREEZY	BEIISS IBISES
BEEELT BEETLE	BEFFRU BUFFER, REBUFF	BEIKLR BILKER

BEIKOO BOOKIE	BELNOS NOBLES	BEORVV BOVVER
BEILLS LIBELS	BELNOZ BENZOL	BEORWY BOWERY,
BEILLT BILLET	BELNTU UNBELT	BOWYER
BEILMN NIMBLE	BELNYZ BENZYL	BEOSSS BOSSES, OBSESS
BEILMO MOBILE	BELOOR BOLERO	BEOSTU OBTUSE
BEILMR LIMBER	BELOPU PUEBLO	BEOSTW BESTOW
BEILMW WIMBLE	BELORT BOLTER	BEPRSU SUPERB
BEILMY BLIMEY	BELORU ROUBLE	BERSTU BRUTES, BUSTER,
BEILNR BERLIN	BELORW BLOWER, BOWLER	TUBERS
BEILNU NUBILE	BELOSU BLOUSE, BOULES,	BERSUX EXURBS
BEILNY BY-LINE	OBELUS	BERSUY BUYERS
BEILOR BOILER	BELOSW BOWELS, ELBOWS	BERTTU BUTTER
BEILOS ISOBEL	BELOTT BOTTLE	BERTWY WYBERT
BEIMOV B-MOVIE	BELRRU BURLER	BERUZZ BUZZER
BEIMOZ ZOMBIE	BELRSU RUBLES	BESSTU SUBSET
BEIMRT TIMBER, TIMBRE	BELRSY BERYLS	BESTTU BUTTES
BEIMRU ERBIUM, IMBRUE	BELRTU BUTLER	BESUZZ BUZZES
BEINNO BENONI, BONNIE	BELRTY TREBLY	BFFIIN BIFFIN
BEINOR BONIER	BELRUY BURLEY	BFFINO BOFFIN
BEINOT BENITO	BELSTU BLUEST, BUSTLE,	BFFLSU BLUFFS
BEINOV BOVINE	SUBLET, SUBTLE	BFGOOW FOGBOW
BEINRU BRUNEI	BELTUU TUBULE	BFIILR FIBRIL
BEINTT BITTEN	BEMNOT ENTOMB	BFIINR FIBRIN
BEIORS RIBOSE	BEMNOW BOWMEN,	BFINOW BOWFIN
BEIOTW BOW TIE	ENWOMB	BFLOOT BOTOLF
BEIQSU BISQUE	BEMNRU NUMBER	BFLOTU BOTULF
BEIRRU BURIER	BEMORS SOMBRE	BFLOTY BOTFLY
BEIRRY BRIERY	BEMORY EMBRYO	BFLSYY FLYBYS
BEIRST BESTIR, BISTRE,	BEMOSS BESOMS, EMBOSS	BGGIIW BIGWIG
TRIBES	BEMPRU BUMPER	BGHIIL GHIBLI
BEIRSU BRUISE, BUSIER,	BENNOT BONNET	BGHILT BLIGHT
RUBIES	BENNTU UNBENT	BGHIRT BRIGHT
BEIRTT BITTER	BENOOR BORNEO, OBERON	BGHIST BIGHTS
BEIRTU BEIRUT	BENORR REBORN	BGHMUU HUMBUG
BEJJUU JUJUBE	BENORT BRETON	BGHOSU BOUGHS
BEJLMU JUMBLE	BENORZ BONZER, BRONZE	BGHOTU BOUGHT
BEKLOS BLOKES	BENOST T-BONES	BGHRSU BURGHS
BEKNOR BROKEN	BENOTY BETONY	BGIIJN JIBING
BEKNRU BUNKER	BENRRU BURNER	BGIIKN BIKING
BEKOOT BETOOK	BENRTU BURNET	BGIINT BITING
BEKORR BROKER	BEOORR OREBRO	BGIIRT BIRGIT, BRIGIT
BEKOST BOSKET	BEOORZ BOOZER	BGILLY GLIBLY
BEKRSU BUSKER	BEOPRR PROBER	BGILNO GLOBIN, GOBLIN
BELLOU BOULLE, LOBULE	BEOPRS PROBES	BGINNO BONING
BELLOW BELLOW	BEORRS BORERS, RESORB	BGINOO BOOING
BELLTU BULLET	BEORRT ROBERT	BGINOR BORING, ROBING
BELMMU MUMBLE	BEORST OSBERT, SORBET,	BGINOS BINGOS
BELMNY EMBLYN	STROBE	BGINOW BOWING
BELMOY EMBOLY	BEORSU BOURSE	BGINOX BOXING
BELMRU LUMBER, RUMBLE	BEORSW BOWERS, BROWSE	BGINSU BUSING
BELMTU TUMBLE	BEORSX BOXERS	BGINTU TUBING
BELNNY BLENNY	BEORTV OBVERT	BGINUY BUYING
BELNOR NOBLER	BEORTY BY ROTE	BGIOPT BIG TOP

BGIOST BIGOTS	BIOORZ BORZOI	BOTUUY BUYOUT
BGLNOO OBLONG	BIOOST OBOIST	BPSTUU BUST-UP
BGMOSU GUMBOS	BIOPSY BIOPSY	BRSSTU BURSTS
BGNOOS BONGOS	BIORST BISTRO, ORBITS	BSSSUY BYSSUS
BHIKOS KIBOSH	BIOSTU SUBITO	CCCDIO COCCID
BHILSU BLUISH	BIOTTW TWO-BIT	CCCILY CYCLIC
BHIOPS BISHOP	BIQSSU SQUIBS	CCCOSU COCCUS
BHIOSY BOYISH	BIRTTU TURBIT	CCCOXY COCCYX
BHIRST BIRTHS	BJLOOT JOB LOT	CCDEIR CEDRIC, CERDIC
BHIRSU HUBRIS	BKMNUU BUNKUM	CCDEKO COCKED
BHIRSY HYBRIS	BKNPUU BUNK-UP	CCDELY CYCLED
BHLMUY HUMBLY	BKOORS BROOKS	CCDEOT DECOCT
BHLOSY BOLSHY	BKORTU TOBRUK	CCEEHR CRÈCHE
BHMSTU THUMBS	BLLORY BROLLY	CCEEIL CECILE
BHOOOO BOOHOO	BLMNUY NUMBLY	CCEEOR COERCE
BHOOPS PHOBOS	BLMOOS BLOOMS	CCEHIL CHICLE, CLICHÉ
BHOOST BOOTHS	BLMOSY SYMBOL	CCEHIO CHOICE, ECHOIC
BHORST THROBS	BLMRUY RUMBLY	CCEHIT HECTIC
BHRSSU SHRUBS	BLNOOS BOLSON	CCEHKS CHECKS
BIIIKN BIKINI	BLNOTU UNBOLT	CCEHKY CHECKY
BIINOT BIOTIN	BLOOTT BLOTTO	CCEHLN CLENCH
BIIORV VIBRIO	BLOPUW BLOW-UP	CCEHLO CLOCHE
BIISTV VIBIST	BLOWYZ BLOWZY	CCEHOS COSECH
BIITTT TITBIT	BLRRUY BLURRY	CCEIIL CILICE, ICICLE
BIKLNS BLINKS	BLSTUY SUBTLY	CCEILR CIRCLE, CLERIC
BIKLNU IN BULK	BMNOOT BON MOT	CCEILT CELTIC
BIKNSU BUSKIN	BMOORS BROOMS	CCEILY CECILY, CICELY
BILLNO BILLON	BMOOSS BOSOMS	CCEINS SCENIC
BILLNU LUBLIN	BMOOSY BOSOMY	CCEIOR CICERO
BILLOW BILLOW	BMOOTT BOTTOM	CCEIPT PECTIC
BILLOY BILLY-O	BMOOTY TOMBOY	CCEIRS CERCIS
BILMNY NIMBLY	BNNORU UNBORN	CCEIRT CRETIC
BILMOS LIMBOS	BNOORS OSBORN	CCEKLO COCKLE
BILMPS BLIMPS	BNOOST BOSTON	CCELSY CYCLES
BILMSU LIMBUS	BNORSU BOURNS, SUBORN	CCENOS SCONCE
BILNOS LISBON	BNORSW BROWNS	CCEORS SOCCER
BILNOY BONILY	BNORTU BURTON	CCERSU CERCUS
BILNTZ BLINTZ	BNORYY BRYONY	CCHHII CHICHI
BILOOT LOBITO	BNORYZ BRONZY	CCHHRU CHURCH
BILOTW BLOW IT!	BNOSSU BOSUNS	CCHIKS CHICKS
BILRTY TRILBY	BNOSUW SUNBOW	CCHILN CLINCH
BILRUW WILBUR	BNOTTU BUTTON	CCHILY CHICLY
BILSSY SIBYLS	BNOTUY BOUNTY	CCHINO COCHIN
BILSUY BUSILY	BOOOTT TO BOOT	CCHIOR CHORIC
BIMNSU NIMBUS	BOOPTY POTBOY	CCHIPU HICCUP
BIMSTU SUBMIT	BOORRW BORROW	CCHKOS CHOCKS
BINNOR INBORN	BOORST ROBOTS	CCHKSU CHUCKS
BINNOU BUNION	BOOSST BOOSTS	CCHLTU CLUTCH
BINOOT BONITO	BOOWWW BOWWOW	CCHNOY CONCHY
BINORS ROBINS	BORRSU BURROS	CCHNRU CRUNCH
BINORT BRITON	BORRUW BURROW	CCHORS SCORCH
BINORY BRIONY	BORSTU ROBUST	CCHORT CROTCH
BINOSS BISONS	BORTTU TURBOT	CCHORU CROUCH

CCHOST SCOTCH
CCHRTU CRUTCH
CCHSTU SCUTCH
CCIILN CLINIC
CCIILT CLITIC
CCIINO ICONIC
CCIINP PICNIC
CCIINZ ZINCIC
CCIIRT CITRIC, CRITIC
CCIISV CIVICS
CCIKLS CLICKS
CCIKRS CRICKS
CCILNO CLONIC
CCILTU CULTIC
CCIMOS COMICS, COSMIC
CCIMRY CYMRIC
CCINOS CONICS
CCINSY CYNICS
CCIOPT COPTIC
CCIPRU CUPRIC
CCIRSU CIRCUS
CCISTY CYSTIC
CCKLOO O'CLOCK
CCKLOS CLOCKS
CCKLSU CLUCKS
CCKOOU CUCKOO
CCKOPU COCK-UP
CCKORS CROCKS
CCLOTU OCCULT
CCNOOO COCOON
CCNORU CONCUR
CCOOOR ROCOCO
CCOPUY OCCUPY
CCORSU CROCUS
CCOSTU STUCCO
CCSSUU CUSCUS
CDDEEI DECIDE, DE-ICED
CDDEEK DECKED
CDDEEO DECODE
CDDEEU DEDUCE, DEUCED
CDDEHI CHIDED
CDDEIU CUDDIE
CDDEKO DOCKED
CDDEKU DUCKED
CDDELO CODDLE
CDDELU CUDDLE
CDDEOR CORDED
CDDETU DEDUCT
CDDLOY CLODDY
CDDLUY CUDDLY
CDEEER DECREE, RECEDE
CDEEES SECEDE
CDEEEX EXCEED

CDEEFN FENCED
CDEEFT DEFECT
CDEEHO ECHOED
CDEEHT ETCHED
CDEEHW CHEWED
CDEEIL DECILE
CDEEIP PIECED
CDEEIR DE-ICER
CDEEIT DECEIT
CDEEIV DEVICE
CDEEJT DEJECT
CDEEKL DECKLE
CDEEKN NECKED
CDEEKO DECOKE
CDEEKP PECKED
CDEEKR RECKED
CDEENO ENCODE
CDEENT DECENT
CDEERS CREEDS, SCREED
CDEERU REDUCE
CDEERW CREWED
CDEESU SEDUCE
CDEETT DETECT
CDEFFU CUFFED
CDEFII DEIFIC
CDEFKU FUCKED
CDEFNU FECUND
CDEFOR FORCED
CDEGGO COGGED
CDEGIN CEDING
CDEGIO GEODIC
CDEGLU CUDGEL
CDEGOR CODGER
CDEHIM CHIMED
CDEHIN INCHED
CDEHIR CHIDER, HERDIC
CDEHIT ITCHED
CDEHIU HEIDUC
CDEHKO CHOKED, HOCKED
CDEHNR DRENCH
CDEHOS COSHED
CDEHOU DOUCHE
CDEIIK DICKIE
CDEIIR DICIER
CDEIJU JUICED
CDEIKK KICKED
CDEIKL LICKED
CDEIKM MEDICK
CDEIKN NICKED
CDEIKP PICKED
CDEIKR DICKER, RICKED
CDEIKS SICKED
CDEIKT TICKED

CDEIKW WICKED
CDEILO COILED, DOCILE
CDEILS SLICED
CDEILT DELICT
CDEILU DULCIE
CDEIMN MINCED
CDEIMO MEDICO
CDEIMR DERMIC
CDEIMS MEDICS
CDEINO COINED
CDEINR CINDER
CDEINU INDUCE
CDEINW WINCED
CDEIOP COPIED
CDEIOR DORICE
CDEIOV VOICED
CDEIPR PRICED
CDEIPS SPICED
CDEIPT DEPICT
CDEIRS CIDERS
CDEIRT CREDIT, DIRECT
CDEIRV CERVID
CDEIRY DRY ICE
CDEIST EDICTS
CDEKLO LOCKED
CDEKMO MOCKED
CDEKMU MUCKED
CDEKNO CONKED
CDEKOO COOKED
CDEKOP POCKED
CDEKOR CORKED,
   DOCKER, ROCKED
CDEKOS SOCKED
CDEKOT DOCKET
CDEKRU DUCKER, RUCKED
CDEKRY DERYCK
CDEKSU SUCKED
CDEKTU TUCKED
CDELLU CULLED
CDELOO COOLED
CDELOR COLDER
CDELOS CLOSED
CDELOY CLOYED
CDELRU CURDLE, CURLED
CDELTU DULCET
CDEMOO COMEDO
CDEMOY COMEDY
CDENNO CONNED
CDENOS SECOND
CDENOT DOCENT
CDENSU DUNCES, SECUND
CDEOOP COOPED
CDEOPP COPPED

80

CDEORR RECORD
CDEORS CREDOS, DÉCORS, SCORED
CDEORW CROWED
CDEOSU ESCUDO
CDEOSY DECOYS
CDEPPU CUPPED
CDERRU CRUDER
CDERSU CURSED
CDERSY CYDERS, DESCRY
CDERUV CURVED
CDESSU CUSSED
CDFINU FUNDIC
CDFIOU FUCOID
CDFIOY CODIFY
CDGIIN DICING
CDGINO CODING
CDHIOR ORCHID, RHODIC
CDHIRY HYDRIC
CDHORS CHORDS
CDIIIM IMIDIC
CDIIIR IRIDIC
CDIINT INDICT
CDIIOY IDIOCY
CDIISV VISCID
CDIKNO DICKON
CDIMOU MUCOID
CDIMOY CYMOID
CDIMSU MUSCID
CDIMTU DICTUM
CDINOO CONOID
CDINOR NORDIC
CDINSY SYNDIC
CDINTU INDUCT
CDIOSS DISCOS
CDIPSU CUPIDS, CUSPID
CDISSU DISCUS
CDJNOU JOCUND
CDLLOY COLDLY
CDLOSS SCOLDS
CDLOSU CLOUDS
CDLOUY CLOUDY
CDMNOO CONDOM, MOD CON
CDMORS CD-ROMS
CDNOOR CONDOR, CORDON
CDOORT DOCTOR
CDORSW CROWDS
CEEEFL FLEECE
CEEEGR GREECE
CEEEHS CHEESE
CEEENO EOCENE

CEEFFO COFFEE
CEEFFT EFFECT
CEEFHL FLECHE
CEEFIL FELICE
CEEFIR FIERCE, RECIFE
CEEFLY FLEECY
CEEFNN FENNEC
CEEFNR FENCER
CEEFNS FENCES
CEEFSU FESCUE
CEEHIR CHERIE
CEEHIS SEICHE
CEEHKL HECKLE
CEEHKS CHEEKS
CEEHKY CHEEKY
CEEHLR LECHER
CEEHLY LYCHEE
CEEHMS SCHEME
CEEHNT THENCE
CEEHNW WHENCE
CEEHOR COHERE, REECHO
CEEHOS ECHOES
CEEHPS CHEEPS, SPEECH
CEEHQU CHEQUE
CEEHRS CHEERS
CEEHRT ETCHER
CEEHRU EUCHRE
CEEHRW CHEWER
CEEHRY CHEERY
CEEHSW ESCHEW
CEEHSY CHEESY
CEEIKL KIELCE
CEEILN CELINE
CEEILS SIECLE
CEEIMN ICEMEN
CEEIMT EMETIC
CEEINS NIECES
CEEINT ENTICE
CEEINU EUNICE
CEEINV EVINCE, VENICE
CEEIPR PIECER, PIERCE, RECIPE
CEEIPS PIECES, SPECIE
CEEIRS CERISE
CEEIRT RECITE, TIERCE
CEEIRU ECURIE
CEEISS ECESIS
CEEISX EXCISE
CEEITX EXCITE
CEEJRT REJECT
CEEKNR NECKER
CEEKPR PECKER
CEEKRS CREEKS

CEELMO CLEOME
CEELNR CRENEL
CEELOR CREOLE
CEELOU COULEE
CEELOV VELOCE
CEELRS CREELS
CEELRT TERCEL
CEELRV CLEVER
CEELRW CREWEL
CEELRY CELERY
CEELST SELECT
CEELSY LYCÉES
CEEMNT CEMENT
CEEMNY CYMENE
CEEMRR MERCER
CEEMRT CERMET
CEENOR ENCORE
CEENPT PECTEN
CEENRS CENSER, SCREEN
CEENRT CENTER, CENTRE, RECENT, TENREC
CEENSS SCENES
CEEPRS CREEPS
CEEPRT RECEPT
CEEPRY CREEPY
CEEPTX EXCEPT, EXPECT
CEEPTY ECTYPE
CEERSS RECESS
CEERST RESECT, SECRET
CEERSU CEREUS, CERUSE, CREUSE, RESCUE, SECURE
CEERTT TERCET
CEESSX EXCESS
CEESUX EXCUSE
CEFFIO OFFICE
CEFFOR COFFER
CEFHIS CHIEFS
CEFHLT FLETCH
CEFHNR FRENCH
CEFIKL FICKLE
CEFINT INFECT
CEFINU UNICEF
CEFIRR FERRIC
CEFKLS FLECKS
CEFKRU FUCKER
CEFLOS FO'C'SLE
CEFLST CLEFTS
CEFNOR CONFER
CEFORR FORCER
CEFORS FORCES, FRESCO
CEFRUW CURFEW
CEGGPU EGGCUP
CEGHIO CHIGOE

CEGINR CRINGE
CEGKOS GECKOS
CEGLRY CLERGY
CEGNOR CONGER
CEGNOS CONGÉS
CEGNOT COGENT
CEGNTY CYGNET
CEGORR GROCER
CEHHIT HI-TECH
CEHIIR RICHIE
CEHIKY HICKEY
CEHILN LICHEN
CEHILS CHILES, CHISEL
CEHIMS CHIMES
CEHINP PENCHI
CEHINR ENRICH
CEHINS CHINES, INCHES,
  NICHES
CEHINT ETHNIC
CEHIOR COHEIR, HEROIC
CEHIPR CIPHER
CEHIQU QUICHE
CEHIRR RICHER
CEHIRS RICHES
CEHIRT THRICE
CEHIST ETHICS, ITCHES
CEHISV CHIVES
CEHITT THETIC
CEHKLU HUCKLE
CEHKOR CHOKER, HOCKER
CEHKOS CHOKES
CEHKOY HOCKEY
CEHKST SKETCH
CEHLOR CHOLER
CEHLOT CLOTHE
CEHLPS SCHLEP
CEHLRY CHERYL
CEHMOR CHROME
CEHNOS CHOSEN
CEHNOU COHUNE
CEHNQU QUENCH
CEHNRT TRENCH
CEHNRW WRENCH
CEHNST STENCH
CEHNUU EUNUCH
CEHOOS CHOOSE
CEHORS CHORES
CEHORT HECTOR, ROCHET,
  TROCHE
CEHOSS COSHES
CEHOTU TOUCHÉ
CEHPRY CYPHER
CEHPSY PSYCHE

CEHRRY CHERRY
CEHRTW WRETCH
CEHRTY CHERTY
CEHSST CHESTS
CEHSTU CHUTES, TUSCHE
CEHSTY CHESTY, SCYTHE
CEHTTY TETCHY
CEIIKV VICKIE
CEIILT ELICIT
CEIILX EXILIC
CEIINR IRENIC
CEIINS INCISE
CEIINT INCITE
CEIISS CISSIE
CEIIST CITIES, ICIEST
CEIISV CIVIES
CEIJNT INJECT
CEIJSU JUICES
CEIKKR KICKER
CEIKLN NICKEL
CEIKLP PICKLE
CEIKLR LICKER
CEIKLS SICKLE
CEIKLT KELTIC, TICKLE
CEIKMY MICKEY
CEIKNR NICKER
CEIKNS SICKEN
CEIKOO COOKIE
CEIKOS KOSICE
CEIKPR PICKER
CEIKPT PICKET
CEIKRS SICKER
CEIKRT TICKER
CEIKRW WICKER
CEIKRY CRIKEY
CEIKTT TICKET
CEIKTW WICKET
CEILLO COLLIE
CEILMS CLIMES
CEILNO CINEOL, NICOLE
CEILNP PENCIL
CEILNS CLINES
CEILNT CLIENT, LENTIC
CEILNU LUCIEN, NUCLEI
CEILNY NICELY
CEILOO COOLIE
CEILOP POLICE
CEILOR COILER, RECOIL
CEILPS SPLICE
CEILPV PELVIC
CEILQU CLIQUE
CEILRS RELICS, SLICER
CEILRT RELICT

CEILSS SLICES
CEILSU SLUICE
CEILSV CLEVIS
CEIMNO INCOME
CEIMNR MINCER
CEIMOX MEXICO
CEIMPU PUMICE
CEIMRS CRIMES
CEIMRT METRIC
CEIMRU CERIUM
CEIMSU MISCUE
CEINNO CONNIE
CEINOR COINER, ORCEIN
CEINOS CONIES, COSINE,
  OSCINE
CEINOT NOETIC, NOTICE
CEINOV NOVICE
CEINPR PINCER, PRINCE
CEINPT INCEPT, PECTIN
CEINQU CINQUE, QUINCE
CEINRT CRETIN
CEINRW WINCER
CEINST INCEST, INSECT,
  NICEST
CEINSU INCUSE
CEINSW WINCES
CEINTY NICETY
CEINWY WINCEY
CEIOOZ EOZOIC
CEIOPR COPIER
CEIOPS COPIES
CEIOPT POETIC
CEIORS COSIER
CEIORT EROTIC
CEIORV VOICER
CEIORW COWRIE
CEIORZ COZIER
CEIOSS COSIES
CEIOSV VOICES
CEIOTX EXOTIC
CEIPPT PEPTIC
CEIPRS CRIPES, PRÉCIS,
  PRICES, SPICER
CEIPRY PRICEY
CEIPSS PISCES, SPICES
CEIPST SEPTIC
CEIPTU CUP TIE
CEIQRU CIRQUE
CEIRRS CRIERS
CEIRSS CRISES
CEIRST STERIC, TRICES
CEIRSU CRUISE
CEIRTU URETIC

CEIRVX CERVIX
CEISTV CIVETS
CEJKOY JOCKEY
CEJNOU JOUNCE
CEJOOS JOCOSE
CEKKOP KOPECK
CEKLOR LOCKER
CEKLOT LOCKET
CEKLRS CLERKS
CEKLSU SUCKLE
CEKMOR MOCKER
CEKMRU MUCKER
CEKNOR CONKER, RECKON
CEKNSV V-NECKS
CEKOOR COOKER
CEKOPT POCKET
CEKORR CORKER, ROCKER
CEKORT ROCKET
CEKOST SOCKET
CEKPRU PUCKER
CEKPSS SPECKS
CEKRSU SUCKER
CEKRSW WRECKS
CEKRTU TUCKER
CELLOS CELLOS
CELLOT COLLET
CELLOU LOCULE
CELLOY COLLEY
CELLRU CULLER
CELLTU CULLET
CELMOO COELOM
CELMOP COMPEL
CELMOR CORMEL
CELMOY COMELY
CELMSU MUSCLE
CELMUY LYCEUM
CELNOR CORNEL
CELNOS CLONES
CELNOV CLOVEN
CELNOY CEYLON
CELNSU UNCLES
CELNTU LUCENT
CELOOR COOLER
CELOOT OCELOT
CELOPU COUPLE
CELORS CLOSER, CRESOL
CELORT LECTOR
CELORU COLURE
CELORV CLOVER, VELCRO
CELOSS CLOSES
CELOST CLOSET
CELOSU COLEUS
CELOSV CLOVES

CELOSX SCOLEX
CELOSY COLEYS
CELPUU CUPULE
CELRRU CURLER
CELRSU ULCERS
CELRTU CUTLER
CELRUW CURLEW
CELTTU CUTLET
CELTUY CUTELY
CEMNNO CONMEN, NEM
    CON
CEMNOO COME ON!
CEMNOW COWMEN
CEMNTU CENTUM
CEMOOS COMOSE
CEMORS COMERS
CEMOST COMETS
CEMOSY CYMOSE
CEMOTU TEMUCO
CEMRTU RECTUM
CENNOS NONCES
CENOPS PONCES
CENOPU POUNCE
CENOPY PONCEY
CENORR CORNER
CENORS CENSOR, CRONES
CENORT CORNET
CENORY CORNEY
CENOSS SCONES
CENOSU OUNCES, UNESCO
CENOSV COVENS
CENOSY CONEYS
CENOVX CONVEX
CENOVY CONVEY
CENSST SCENTS
CENSSU CENSUS
CENSTY ENCYST
CEOOPR COOPER
CEOOTY COYOTE, OOCYTE
CEOPPR COPPER
CEOPRS CORPSE
CEOPRU RECOUP
CEOPSS COPSES
CEOPSU COUPÉS
CEOQTU COQUET
CEORRS CORERS, CRORES,
    SCORER
CEORRT RECTOR
CEORRW CROWER
CEORSS CORSES, CROSSE,
    SCORES
CEORST CORSET, ESCORT,
    RECTOS, SCOTER, SECTOR

CEORSU CEROUS, COURSE,
    SOURCE
CEORSV COVERS
CEORSW ESCROW
CEORTT COTTER
CEORTV COVERT, VECTOR
CEORTX CORTEX
CEOSST COSSET
CEOSSU SCOUSE
CEOSTT OCTETS
CEOSVY COVEYS
CEPRSU SPRUCE
CERSST CRESTS
CERSSU CRUSES, CURSES
CERSSW SCREWS
CERSTU CRUETS, RECTUS,
    TRUCES
CERSUV CURVES
CERSUX CRUXES
CERSWY SCREWY
CERTTU CUTTER
CERTUV CURVET
CESSSU CUSSES
CESTTU CUTEST
CFFILS CLIFFS
CFFINO COFFIN
CFFOSS SCOFFS
CFFOTU CUTOFF
CFFRSU SCRUFF
CFFSSU SCUFFS
CFGINU FUNGIC
CFHILN FLINCH
CFHILT FLITCH
CFHLSY FLYSCH
CFHOUU FU-CHOU
CFIILM FILMIC
CFIINN FINNIC
CFIIST FISTIC
CFIITY CITIFY
CFIKLS FLICKS
CFILOR FROLIC
CFIMOR FORMIC
CFIMOT COMFIT
CFISTU FUSTIC
CFKLOS FLOCKS
CFKLOY FLOCKY
CFKORS FROCKS
CFKPUU FUCK-UP
CFORST CROFTS
CFRSUY SCURFY
CGGLOY CLOGGY
CGHHOU CHOUGH
CGHILT GLITCH

CGHIOT GOTHIC	CHIRST CHRIST	CIKNYZ ZINCKY
CGHORU GROUCH	CHIRUZ ZURICH	CIKPPU PICK-UP
CGHOSU COUGHS	CHISST SCHIST	CIKPRS PRICKS
CGIINT CITING	CHISTT STITCH	CIKRST STRICK, TRICKS
CGILNY CLINGY	CHISTW SWITCH	CIKRTU TURKIC
CGIMNO COMING, GNOMIC	CHITTW TWITCH	CIKRTY TRICKY
CGINOO COOING	CHITTY TITCHY	CIKSST STICKS
CGINOP COPING	CHJNOU CHONJU	CIKSTY STICKY
CGINOR CORING	CHKNSU CHUNKS	CILLSU CULLIS
CGINOW COWING	CHKNUY CHUNKY	CILNOP CLIP-ON
CGINOX COXING	CHKOSS SHOCKS	CILNOU UNCOIL
CGINRU CURING	CHKSSU SHUCKS	CILOPU OILCUP
CGINRY CRYING	CHLMOO MOLOCH	CILOPY POLICY
CGIORS CORGIS	CHLOOS SCHOOL	CILOSY COSILY
CGLLOY GLYCOL	CHLORS SCHORL	CILOYZ COZILY
CGLNOU UNCLOG	CHLOST CLOTHS	CILRSY LYRICS
CGNOOU CONGOU	CHLOSU SLOUCH	CILSUU LUCIUS
CGNSUY CYGNUS	CHLRSU CHURLS	CIMMOS COMMIS
CHHOOS COHOSH	CHMMUY CHUMMY	CIMMOT COMMIT
CHIILL CHILLI	CHMOOS SMOOCH	CIMNOR MICRON
CHIILT LITCHI, LITHIC	CHMPSU CHUMPS	CIMNOU CONIUM
CHIINT CHITIN	CHMSTU SMUTCH	CIMNRU CRINUM
CHIKKO HICKOK	CHNOOP PONCHO	CIMOOS COSIMO
CHIKNO IN HOCK	CHNPUY PUNCHY	CIMOPY MYOPIC
CHIKNS CHINKS	CHNRSU CHURNS	CIMORS MICROS
CHIKOS HOICKS	CHOORT COHORT	CIMORU CORIUM
CHIKRS KIRSCH	CHOOSY CHOOSY	CIMOST SITCOM
CHIKST KITSCH	CHOPPY CHOPPY	CIMOTY COMITY
CHILLS CHILLS	CHOPUY POUCHY	CIMPRS SCRIMP
CHILLY CHILLY	CHORSU CHORUS	CIMRUU CURIUM
CHILMO HOLMIC	CHOSUU SUCHOU	CIMSTY MYSTIC
CHILOR ORCHIL	CHOTUY TOUCHY	CINNOU NUNCIO
CHILRY RICHLY	CHPSTU PUTSCH	CINOPT PONTIC
CHIMNU MUNICH	CHSSSU SCHUSS	CINORT CITRON
CHIMOR HORMIC	CHSWYZ SCHWYZ	CINORZ ZIRCON
CHIMRS CHRISM, SMIRCH	CIIIRT IRITIC	CINOSS SCIONS
CHIMSS SCHISM	CIILMU CILIUM	CINOST TOCSIN, TONICS
CHIMTY THYMIC	CIILSY SICILY	CINOSU COUSIN
CHINNO INCHON	CIIMMS MIMICS	CINQUY QUINCY
CHINOP PHONIC	CIIMOT MIOTIC	CINSTU TUNICS
CHINOT CHITON	CIIMTV VICTIM	CIOOPT OCTOPI
CHINRU URCHIN	CIINOR IRONIC	CIOPRT TROPIC
CHINST SNITCH	CIINOT TICINO	CIOPST OPTICS, TOPICS
CHINTZ CHINTZ	CIINRT CITRIN, NITRIC	CIORSU CURIOS
CHIOPT PHOTIC	CIIRSS CRISIS	CIORTT TRICOT
CHIORS CHOIRS, ORCHIS	CIIRTV VITRIC	CIORTV VICTOR
CHIORT THORIC	CIKLSS SLICKS	CIOSST STOICS
CHIOST SOTHIC	CIKLSY SICKLY	CIOSTU COITUS
CHIPPY CHIPPY	CIKNOT ON TICK	CIPRSS CRISPS
CHIPRS CHIRPS	CIKNPU UNPICK	CIPRST SCRIPT
CHIPRY CHIRPY	CIKNPY PYKNIC	CIPRSY CRISPY
CHIPSY PHYSIC	CIKNSS SNICKS	CIRRSU CIRRUS
CHIPTY PITCHY	CIKNTU TUCK-IN	CIRSTT STRICT

CIRSTU CITRUS, CURTIS, RICTUS, RUSTIC
CIRTTY YTTRIC
CKKNOS KNOCKS
CKLNOU UNLOCK
CKLOPU LOCKUP
CKLPSU PLUCKS
CKLPUY PLUCKY
CKMOPU MOCK-UP
CKMOSS SMOCKS
CKNORU UNCORK
CKNTUU UNTUCK
CKOORS CROOKS
CKOSST STOCKS
CKOSTY STOCKY
CKRSTU STRUCK, TRUCKS
CKRSUU RUCKUS
CLLOOY COOLLY
CLLORS SCROLL
CLMNOU COLUMN
CLMOPY COMPLY
CLMOSU LOCUMS
CLMPSU CLUMPS
CLMPUY CLUMPY
CLMSUY CLUMSY, MUSCLY
CLNOOS COLONS
CLNOOY COLONY
CLNOSU CLONUS, CONSUL
CLNOSW CLOWNS
CLNRUU UNCURL
CLOORU COLOUR
CLOSSW SCOWLS
CLOSTU CLOUTS, LOCUST
CLOSTY COSTLY
CLPSTU SCULPT
CLRTUY CURTLY
CLSSUU SULCUS
CMMNOO COMMON
CMMRUY CRUMMY
CMMSUY SCUMMY
CMNOSY SYNCOM
CMOOOR COMORO
CMOOSS COSMOS
CMOOSW MOSCOW
CMOSTU CUSTOM
CMOSUU MUCOUS
CMPRSU SCRUMP
CMRSSU SCRUMS
CMSTUU SCUTUM
CNNOOR CONNOR
CNOOPU COUPON
CNOORT CROTON
CNOOST NOSTOC, ONCOST

CNOOTT COTTON
CNOOTY TYCOON
CNOOVY CONVOY
CNORSS SCORNS
CNORSW CROWNS
CNOSTU COUNTS, TUCSON
CNOTUY COUNTY
COOPRS SCROOP
COOPSS SCOOPS
COOPTU COP-OUT
COOPWX COWPOX
COPRSU CORPUS, CROUPS
COPSUY COYPUS
CORRSU CURSOR
CORSTU COURTS
CORTUY OUTCRY
COSSTU SCOUTS
COTTUU CUTOUT
CPRSTY CRYPTS
CPRSUY CYPRUS
CPSTUU CUTUPS
CRRSUY SCURRY
CRSSTU CRUSTS
CRSTUY CRUSTY, CURTSY
CRSUVY SCURVY
CSUYZZ SCUZZY
DDDEEI EDDIED
DDDEEW WEDDED
DDDEGO DODGED
DDDEIK KIDDED
DDDEIL DIDDLE, LIDDED
DDDEIR RIDDED
DDDELO DODDLE
DDDEMU MUDDED
DDDENO NODDED
DDDEOP PODDED
DDDEOR DODDER
DDDEOS SODDED
DDEEEH HEEDED
DDEEEM DEEMED
DDEEEN NEEDED
DDEEES SEEDED
DDEEEW WEEDED
DDEEFI DEFIED
DDEEFN DEFEND, FENDED
DDEEFU FEUDED
DDEEGH HEDGED
DDEEGL GELDED
DDEEGR DREDGE
DDEEGW WEDGED
DDEEHL HEDDLE
DDEEHR HERDED
DDEEIL ELIDED

DDEEIN DENIED, INDEED, NEDDIE
DDEEIR DERIDE
DDEEIS EDDIES
DDEEIT DIETED, EDITED, TEDDIE
DDEELM MEDDLE
DDEELP PEDDLE
DDEELR ELDRED
DDEELU DELUDE, DUELED, ELUDED
DDEELV DELVED
DDEELW WELDED
DDEEMN MENDED
DDEEMO DÉMODÉ
DDEENN DENNED
DDEENP DEPEND
DDEENR REDDEN
DDEENT DENTED, TENDED
DDEENU DENUDE, DUDEEN, DUNDEE, ENDUED
DDEENV VENDED
DDEENW WENDED
DDEEOR ERODED
DDEERR REDDER
DDEERT TEDDER
DDEEUX EXUDED
DDEFFO DOFFED
DDEFGU FUDGED
DDEFIL FIDDLE
DDEFLO FOLDED
DDEFLU FUDDLE
DDEFNU FUNDED
DDEFOR FODDER, FORDED
DDEFRY FREDDY
DDEGGO DOGGED
DDEGIL GILDED, GLIDED
DDEGIR GIRDED, RIDGED
DDEGIU GUIDED
DDEGJU JUDGED
DDEGLO LODGED
DDEGMO DODGEM
DDEGNU NUDGED
DDEGOR DODGER
DDEGOS DODGES
DDEGRU DRUDGE
DDEHIN HIDDEN
DDEHIS DISHED
DDEHLU HUDDLE
DDEHNO HODDEN
DDEHOO HOODED
DDEIIK KIDDIE
DDEIIO IODIDE

DDEIIV DIVIDE	DDHINO HODDIN	DEEGHR HEDGER
DDEIKR KIDDER	DDHOSY SHODDY	DEEGHS HEDGES
DDEILM MIDDLE	DDIIKK DIK-DIK	DEEGIR EDGIER
DDEILP PIDDLE	DDILNR DIRNDL	DEEGLL GELLED
DDEILR RIDDLE	DDILOS DILDOS	DEEGLN LEGEND
DDEILS SIDLED	DDILTY TIDDLY	DEEGLP PLEDGE
DDEIMM DIMMED	DDIOOS DO-SI-DO	DEEGLR LEDGER
DDEIMN MIDDEN, MINDED	DDIOPY DIPODY	DEEGLS LEDGES, SLEDGE
DDEIMS DESMID	DDIORS SORDID	DEEGLU DELUGE
DDEINN DINNED	DDIOTU OUTDID	DEEGMM GEMMED
DDEINR RIDDEN	DDIOTY ODDITY	DEEGMR MERGED
DDEINW WINDED	DDIRSU DRUIDS	DEEGNO ON EDGE
DDEIOV DEVOID, VOIDED	DDLPUY PUDDLY	DEEGNR GENDER
DDEIPP DIPPED	DDMMUU DUMDUM	DEEGNU DENGUE
DDEIPR PRIDED	DDNOOS ODDS-ON	DEEGRV VERGED
DDEIRR RIDDER	DEEEFR FEEDER, REEFED	DEEGRY GREEDY, GREYED
DDEITY TIDYED	DEEEGR DEGREE	DEEGSW WEDGES
DDEJRU JUDDER	DEEEHL HEELED	DEEGSZ SZEGED
DDEKNU DUNKED	DEEEHR HEEDER	DEEHLP HELPED
DDELLO DOLLED	DEEEJR JEERED	DEEHLY HEDLEY
DDELLU DULLED	DEEEKL KEELED	DEEHMM HEMMED
DDELMO MOLDED	DEEEKN KEENED	DEEHMS MESHED
DDELMU MUDDLE	DEEEKP PEEKED	DEEHRR HERDER
DDELNO NODDLE	DEEEKR REEKED	DEEHRT THREE-D
DDELOO DOODLE	DEEELN NEEDLE	DEEHSW SHEWED
DDELOR LORDED	DEEELP PEELED	DEEILN ELINED, LEIDEN
DDELOT TODDLE	DEEELR LEERED, REELED	DEEILR RELIED
DDELPU PUDDLE	DEEELT DELETE	DEEILS DIESEL, SEDILE
DDELRU RUDDLE	DEEEMR REDEEM	DEEILV LEVIED, VEILED
DDELUY DUDLEY	DEEEMS SEEMED	DEEILX EXILED
DDEMNO EDMOND	DEEEMT TEEMED	DEEILY EYELID
DDEMNU EDMUND	DEEENP DEEPEN	DEEIMP IMPEDE
DDEMOO DOOMED	DEEENV VENDEE	DEEIMS DEMISE
DDEMPU DUMPED	DEEEPP PEEPED	DEEINN DENNIE, INDENE
DDENNO DONNED	DEEEPR DEEPER, PEERED	DEEINR DENIER, NEREID,
DDENNU DUNNED	DEEEPS SEEPED	REINED
DDENOR DRONED	DEEEPV PEEVED	DEEINS DENISE
DDENOS SODDEN	DEEERS SEEDER	DEEINV ENDIVE, ENVIED,
DDENOW DOWNED	DEEERV VEERED	VEINED
DDENOY DYNODE	DEEERW WEEDER	DEEIPP DIEPPE
DDENSU SUDDEN	DEEFGL FLEDGE	DEEIPS ESPIED
DDEOOS DODOES	DEEFIL DEFILE	DEEIRS DESIRE, RESIDE
DDEOOW WOODED	DEEFIN DEFINE	DEEIRT DIETER
DDEORW WORDED	DEEFIR DEFIER	DEEIRU UREIDE
DDEOSS DOSSED	DEEFLL FELLED	DEEIRV DERIVE
DDEOST ODDEST	DEEFLU FUELED	DEEIRW DEWIER
DDEOSU DOUSED	DEEFLX FLEXED	DEEISS SEISED
DDEOSW DOWSED	DEEFNR FENDER	DEEISV DEVISE, SIEVED
DDEOTT DOTTED	DEEFRT RED EFT	DEEISZ SEIZED
DDERRU RUDDER	DEEFSU DEFUSE	DEEITX EXITED
DDERSU UDDERS	DEEFZZ FEZZED	DEEITY TIE-DYE
DDESTU DUSTED	DEEGGL LEGGED	DEEIVW VIEWED
DDFILY FIDDLY	DEEGGP PEGGED	DEEJKR JERKED

DEEJLL JELLED
DEEJRU DE JURE
DEEJST JESTED
DEEJTT JETTED
DEEKNN KENNED
DEEKOV EVOKED
DEEKPR PERKED
DEEKSW SKEWED
DEELLW WELLED
DEELLY YELLED
DEELMT MELTED
DEELMY MEDLEY
DEELNR LENDER
DEELNU ELUNED
DEELNW DELWEN, WEDELN
DEELOP ELOPED
DEELPT PELTED
DEELPY DEEPLY, YELPED
DEELRS ELDERS
DEELRU ELUDER
DEELRV DELVER
DEELRW WELDER
DEELST ELDEST
DEELSW SLEWED
DEELTU TELEDU
DEELUX DE LUXE
DEEMNR MENDER
DEEMOT DEMOTE
DEEMOW MEOWED
DEEMPR PERMED
DEEMPT TEMPED
DEEMRT TERMED
DEEMRU DEMURE
DEEMRY REMEDY
DEEMSS MESSED
DEENNP PENNED
DEENNT NEEDN'T
DEENOP OPENED
DEENOR DOREEN, REDONE
DEENOS ODENSE
DEENOT DENOTE
DEENPX EXPEND
DEENRR RENDER
DEENRS DENSER, SENDER
DEENRT RENTED, TENDER
DEENRU ENDURE
DEENRV DENVER, NERVED
DEENSS SENSED
DEENST NESTED, TENSED
DEENSU ENSUED
DEENSW SWEDEN
DEENTT DETENT, NETTED
DEENTV VENTED

DEENTX DENTEX, EXTEND
DEEOPS DEPOSE
DEEORT TEREDO
DEEORZ ZEROED
DEEOTT ODETTE
DEEOTV DEVOTE, VETOED
DEEPPP PEPPED
DEEPRU PUREED
DEEPRY PREYED
DEEPSS SPEEDS
DEEPSW SPEWED
DEEPSY SPEEDY
DEEPTT PETTED
DEEPTU DEPUTE
DEEQUU QUEUED
DEERST DESERT, RESTED
DEERSU REUSED
DEERSV SERVED, VERSED
DEERTX DEXTER
DEERVV REVVED
DEESST STEEDS
DEESSW SWEDES
DEESTT DETEST, TESTED
DEESTV VESTED
DEESTW STEWED, TWEEDS
DEETTV VETTED
DEETTW WETTED
DEETWY TWEEDY
DEFFHU HUFFED
DEFFIM MIFFED
DEFFIR DIFFER
DEFFLU DUFFEL, LUFFED
DEFFMU MUFFED
DEFFNO OFFEND
DEFFOR DOFFER
DEFFPU PUFFED
DEFFRU DUFFER
DEFGGO FOGGED
DEFGIR FRIDGE
DEFGIT FIDGET, GIFTED
DEFGOO GOOFED
DEFGOR FORGED
DEFHIS FISHED
DEFHOO HOOFED
DEFIKN KNIFED
DEFILL FILLED
DEFILM FILMED
DEFILO FOILED
DEFILR RIFLED
DEFILS FIELDS
DEFILT LIFTED
DEFIMR FIRMED
DEFINN FINNED

DEFINR FINDER, FRIEND,
    REDFIN
DEFINS FIENDS
DEFIOO FOODIE
DEFIOT FOETID
DEFIRV FERVID
DEFIST SIFTED
DEFITT FITTED
DEFIZZ FIZZED
DEFKNU FUNKED
DEFKOR FORKED
DEFLNO ENFOLD, FONDLE
DEFLOO FOOLED
DEFLOR FOLDER
DEFLOT LOFTED
DEFLOU FOULED
DEFLOW FLOWED, WOLFED
DEFLRU FURLED
DEFLTU FLUTED
DEFLTY DEFTLY
DEFMOR DEFORM, FORMED
DEFNOR FONDER
DEFNOU FONDUE
DEFNRU REFUND
DEFOOR ROOFED
DEFRRU FURRED
DEFRSU SURFED
DEFRTU TURFED
DEFSSU FUSSED
DEFTTU TUFTED
DEFUZZ FUZZED
DEGGHO HOGGED
DEGGHU HUGGED
DEGGIJ JIGGED
DEGGIN EDGING
DEGGIP PIGGED
DEGGIR DIGGER, RIGGED
DEGGIU DUGGIE
DEGGIW WIGGED
DEGGJO JOGGED
DEGGJU JUGGED
DEGGLO DOGLEG, LOGGED
DEGGLU LUGGED
DEGGMU MUGGED
DEGGOR DOGGER, GORGED
DEGGOT TOGGED
DEGGOU GOUGED
DEGGPU PUGGED
DEGGRU GRUDGE, RUGGED
DEGGRY DREGGY
DEGGTU TUGGED
DEGHIN HINGED
DEGHIS SIGHED

DEGHIW HEDWIG
DEGHSU GUSHED
DEGILL GILLED
DEGILN DINGLE
DEGILO GOLDIE
DEGILR GILDER, GIRDLE,
    GLIDER
DEGILS GLIDES
DEGILY EDGILY
DEGIMS MIDGES
DEGIMT MIDGET
DEGINN ENDING
DEGINO GIDEON
DEGINP PINGED
DEGINR RINGED
DEGINS DESIGN, SIGNED,
    SINGED
DEGINT TINGED
DEGINW WINGED
DEGINY DYEING
DEGIOS DOGIES
DEGIOU DOUGIE
DEGIPR GRIPED
DEGIRR GIRDER
DEGIRS DIRGES, RIDGES
DEGIRU GUIDER
DEGIST DIGEST
DEGISU GUIDES
DEGITW WIDGET
DEGJRU JUDGER
DEGJSU JUDGES
DEGLLU GULLED
DEGLNO GOLDEN, LONGED
DEGLNU GULDEN, LUNGED
DEGLOR LODGER
DEGLOS LODGES
DEGLOV GLOVED
DEGLOW GLOWED
DEGLPU GULPED
DEGLSU SLUDGE
DEGMMU GUMMED
DEGMSU SMUDGE
DEGNNU GUNNED
DEGNOP PONGED
DEGNRU GERUND, NUDGER
DEGNSU NUDGES
DEGOPR GROPED
DEGORR RODGER
DEGORU DROGUE, ROUGED
DEGOST STODGE
DEGPPY GYPPED
DEGPRU PURGED
DEGRSU SURGED

DEGRTU TRUDGE
DEGSTU GUSTED
DEGTTU GUTTED
DEHHSU HUSHED
DEHILP DELPHI
DEHILS SHIELD
DEHILW WHILED
DEHINO HOIDEN, HONIED
DEHINR HINDER
DEHINT HINTED
DEHINW WHINED
DEHIOS HESIOD
DEHIPP HIPPED
DEHIRT DITHER
DEHISS DISHES, HISSED
DEHISW WISHED
DEHIUY YEHUDI
DEHJOS JOSHED
DEHKNO HONKED
DEHKOO HOOKED
DEHLLU HULLED
DEHLNO HOLDEN
DEHLOR HOLDER
DEHLOW HOWLED
DEHLPU UPHELD
DEHLRU HURDLE, HURLED
DEHLTY DELYTH
DEHMMU HUMMED
DEHMNY HYMNED
DEHMOT METHOD
DEHMPU HUMPED
DEHMRY RHYMED
DEHNOP PHONED
DEHNOR DEHORN, HORNED
DEHNOS NOSHED
DEHNOY HOYDEN
DEHNTU HUNTED
DEHOOP HOOPED
DEHOOS SHOOED
DEHOOT HOOTED
DEHOPP HOPPED
DEHORS HORDES, SHORED
DEHORT RED-HOT
DEHOST HOSTED
DEHOSU HOUSED
DEHOSV SHOVED
DEHOSW SHOWED
DEHPST DEPTHS
DEHPSU PUSHED
DEHRSS SHERDS, SHREDS
DEHRSU RUSHED
DEHRSW SHREWD
DEHRTY RHEYDT

DEIIKR KEDIRI
DEIINO IODINE
DEIINS INSIDE
DEIINT TINEID
DEIINV DIVINE
DEIIOS IODISE
DEIIOZ IODIZE
DEIIPT PITIED
DEIIRT TIDIER
DEIISS DIESIS
DEIISX DEIXIS
DEIJLT JILTED
DEIJNO JOINED
DEIJNX JINXED
DEIKLL KILLED
DEIKLM MILKED
DEIKLN KINDLE, LINKED
DEIKLO KELOID
DEIKLT KILTED
DEIKNO OINKED
DEIKNP PINKED
DEIKNR KINDER
DEIKNW WINKED
DEIKNY KIDNEY
DEIKPP KIPPED
DEIKPS SPIKED
DEIKRS RISKED
DEIKRU DUIKER
DEIKSS KISSED
DEIKSV SKIVED
DEIKTT KITTED
DEILLM MILLED
DEILLT TILLED
DEILLW WILLED
DEILMN LIMNED, MINDEL
DEILMO MELOID
DEILMP DIMPLE, LIMPED
DEILMR MILDER
DEILMS MISLED, SMILED
DEILMW MILDEW
DEILNN LINDEN
DEILNO DOLINE, INDOLE,
    LEONID
DEILNT DENTIL
DEILNZ DENZIL
DEILOP DIPLOE, DIPOLE,
    POLDIE
DEILOS ISOLDE, SOILED
DEILOT TOILED
DEILPS DISPEL, LISPED
DEILPX DIPLEX
DEILRS SIDLER
DEILRV DRIVEL

DEILRW WILDER
DEILSS SLIDES
DEILST IDLEST, LISTED, SILTED, TILDES
DEILSV DEVILS
DEILSY YIELDS
DEILTT TILTED, TITLED
DEILTU DILUTE
DEILTW WILTED
DEILWY DEWILY, WIDELY, WIELDY
DEIMMR DIMMER, RIMMED
DEIMMU MEDIUM
DEIMNP IMPEND
DEIMNR MINDER, REMIND
DEIMNS DENIMS
DEIMNT MINTED
DEIMOR DORMIE
DEIMOT DO TIME
DEIMPP PIMPED
DEIMPR PRIMED
DEIMPU MUD PIE
DEIMRS DERMIS
DEIMSS MISSED
DEIMST DEMIST, MISTED
DEIMTU TEDIUM
DEINNO DIONNE
DEINNP PINNED
DEINNR DINNER
DEINNS DENNIS, SINNED
DEINNT DENTIN, INDENT, INTEND, TINNED
DEINNW ENWIND
DEINOP OPINED
DEINOR INDORE, IRONED
DEINOS NO-SIDE, ONSIDE, SIDE-ON
DEINPP NIPPED
DEINPS SNIPED
DEINRS DINERS, RINSED, SNIDER
DEINRT TINDER
DEINRU INURED, RUINED
DEINRV DRIVEN, VERDIN
DEINRW REWIND, WINDER
DEINSU UNDIES
DEINSY SIDNEY
DEINTT TINTED
DEINTU DUNITE, UNITED, UNTIED
DEINTW TWINED
DEIOOR OROIDE
DEIOOV OVIEDO

DEIOPR DOPIER, PERIOD
DEIOPS POISED
DEIORR DORRIE
DEIORS DORIES
DEIORT EDITOR, RIOTED, TRIODE
DEIORV VOIDER
DEIORW WEIRDO
DEIORZ DOZIER
DEIOSV VIDEOS
DEIOSX OXIDES
DEIOTT DOTTIE
DEIPPP PIPPED
DEIPPR DIPPER, RIPPED
DEIPPS SIPPED
DEIPPT TIPPED
DEIPPZ ZIPPED
DEIPQU PIQUED
DEIPRS PRIDES, PRISED, SPIDER
DEIPRZ PRIZED
DEIPSS PISSED
DEIPST SPITED
DEIPSU UPSIDE
DEIPSV VESPID
DEIPSW SWIPED
DEIPTT PITTED
DEIRRS DERRIS, DRIERS, RIDERS
DEIRRV DRIVER
DEIRST DIREST, DRIEST, STRIDE
DEIRSU DISEUR
DEIRSV DIVERS, DRIVES
DEIRTU TRUDIE
DEIRTV DIVERT
DEISST DEISTS, DESIST
DEISSU DISUSE, ISSUED
DEISTU DUTIES, SUITED
DEISTV DIVEST
DEISTW WIDEST
DEJKNU JUNKED
DEJLOT JOLTED
DEJMPU JUMPED
DEJOTT JOTTED
DEJTTU JUTTED
DEKLOO LOOKED
DEKLRU LURKED
DEKLSU SULKED
DEKMOS SMOKED
DEKNOY DONKEY
DEKNOZ ZONKED
DEKNRU DUNKER

DEKOOR ROOKED
DEKORW WORKED
DEKOST STOKED
DELLLO LOLLED
DELLLU LULLED
DELLMU MULLED
DELLOP POLLED
DELLOR ROLLED
DELLOT TOLLED
DELLOU DUELLO
DELLPU PULLED
DELLRU DULLER
DELLWY LEWDLY
DELMNO DOLMEN
DELMOO LOOMED
DELMOR MOLDER
DELMOS MODELS, SELDOM
DELMOT MCLTED
DELMOU MODULE
DELMOY MELODY
DELMPU LUMPED, PLUMED
DELNOO NOODLE
DELNOR RONDEL
DELNOU LOUDEN, NODULE
DELNRU RUNDLE
DELNWY DELWYN
DELOOP LOOPED, POODLE, POOLED
DELOOS LOOSED, OODLES
DELOOT LOOTED, TOOLED
DELOPP LOPPED
DELOPR POLDER
DELOPS SLOPED
DELOPW PLOWED
DELOPY DEPLOY
DELORS SOLDER
DELORT RETOLD
DELORU LOUDER, LOURED
DELOST OLDEST
DELOSU LOUSED
DELOSV SOLVED
DELOSW SLOWED
DELOSY YODELS
DELOTT DOTTLE, LOTTED
DELOWY YOWLED
DELOYY DOYLEY
DELPPU PULPED
DELPRU PURLED
DELPSU PULSED
DELPTU DUPLET
DELPUX DUPLEX
DELRUY RUDELY
DELSTU LUSTED

DELSTY STYLED
DEMMOS MODEMS
DEMMSU SUMMED
DEMNOO MOONED
DEMNOR MODERN
DEMNOS DEMONS, ESMOND
DEMOOR MOORED,
　ROOMED
DEMOOT MOOTED
DEMOOZ ZOOMED
DEMOPP MOPPED
DEMOPR ROMPED
DEMOPS MOPEDS
DEMORR DORMER
DEMORT DERMOT
DEMORW WORMED
DEMOST MODEST
DEMPPU PUMPED
DEMPRU DUMPER
DEMRRU MURDER
DEMRSU DEMURS
DEMSSU MUSSED
DENNOT TENDON
DENNOU UNDONE
DENNPU PUNNED
DENNRU DUNNER
DENNSU SUNNED
DENOOS DO ONE'S,
　NODOSE
DENOOW WOODEN
DENOPR PERNOD, PONDER
DENORS DRONES, SNORED
DENORT RODENT
DENORU UNDOER
DENORV VENDOR
DENORW DOWNER,
　WONDER
DENORY RODNEY, YONDER
DENOST OSTEND, STONED
DENOSW SNOWED
DENOSY DOYENS
DENOSZ DOZENS
DENOTW WONTED
DENPRU PRUNED
DENPSU SEND-UP
DENPTU PUNTED
DENRST TRENDS
DENRSU NURSED, SUNDER
DENRTU TURNED
DENRTY TRENDY
DENSUU UNUSED
DENSUW SUNDEW
DENSYY SYDNEY

DENTTU NUTTED
DEOOPP POOPED
DEOORS RODEOS
DEOORT ROOTED
DEOORV OVERDO
DEOOTT TOOTED
DEOPPP POPPED
DEOPPS SOPPED
DEOPPT TOPPED
DEOPRT DEPORT, DE TROP,
　PORTED
DEOPRU POURED
DEOPRV PROVED
DEOPRW POWDER
DEOPST DEPOTS, DESPOT,
　POSTED
DEOPTT POTTED
DEOPTU POUTED
DEOQTU QUOTED
DEORRS ORDERS
DEORRU ORDURE
DEORRV DROVER
DEORRW REWORD
DEORSS DOSSER
DEORST SORTED, STORED,
　STRODE
DEORSU DOUSER, ROUSED,
　SOURED
DEORSV DROVES
DEORSW DOWSER,
　DROWSE
DEORTT DOTTER, ROTTED
DEORTU DETOUR, ROUTED,
　TOURED
DEORUV DEVOUR
DEOSST TOSSED
DEOSSU SOUSED
DEOSTU OUSTED
DEOSTW STOWED
DEOSUX EXODUS
DEOTTT TOTTED
DEOTTU TOUTED
DEOTUV DEVOUT
DEOTUX TUXEDO
DEPPPU PUPPED
DEPPSU SUPPED
DEPPTU TUPPED
DEPRRU PURRED
DEPRSU PRUDES, PURSED
DEPRUY DUPERY
DEPSSU PSEUDS
DEPSUY PSEUDY
DEPTTU PUTTED

DEPTUY DEPUTY
DERRSY DRYERS
DERSSU DURESS
DERSSY DRESSY
DERSTU DUSTER, RUDEST,
　RUSTED
DERTTU RUTTED
DESSSU SUSSED
DESTUV DUVETS
DFFIMO MID-OFF
DFGGOO FOGDOG
DFGIIR FRIGID
DFIINY NIDIFY
DFIIRT TRIFID
DFIKNO KIND OF
DFILOR FLORID
DFILSU FLUIDS
DFIMOY MODIFY
DFIORS FIORDS
DFIRST DRIFTS
DFIRTY DRIFTY
DFJORS FJORDS
DFLNOU UNFOLD
DFLNOY FONDLY
DFLOOS FLOODS
DFLORU RUDOLF
DFNORS FRONDS
DFNSUU FUNDUS
DGGNOU DUGONG,
　GUNDOG
DGHIIN HIDING
DGHINY DINGHY
DGHITW DWIGHT
DGHOOT HOT DOG
DGHOUY DOUGHY
DGIILN IDLING
DGIINN DINING
DGIINO INDIGO
DGIINP PIDGIN
DGIINR INGRID, RIDING
DGIINS SIDING
DGIINT TIDING
DGIINV DIVING
DGIIST DIGITS
DGIJOU JUDOGI
DGILNO DOLING
DGILOT DIGLOT
DGILSU GUILDS
DGIMTU MIDGUT
DGINOP DOPING, PONGID
DGINOS DOINGS, DOSING
DGINOT DOTING, TIN GOD
DGINOU GUIDON

DGINOW GODWIN	DIINRS INDRIS	DLLOOP DOLLOP
DGINOZ DOZING	DIIOST IDIOTS	DLLORY DROLLY, LORDLY
DGINPU DUPING	DIJNNS DJINNS	DLLOUW LUDLOW
DGINRS GRINDS	DIKLNY KINDLY	DLLOUY LOUDLY
DGINRU DURING	DIKMNU DINKUM	DLMOSU MOULDS
DGINRY DRYING	DIKNNU UNKIND	DLMOUY MOULDY
DGIOTW GODWIT	DIKNRS DRINKS	DLNNOO LONDON
DGIRTU TURGID	DILLMY MILDLY	DLNNOY LYNDON
DGLOOY GOODLY	DILLNO DILLON	DLNOOS SOLD ON
DGLSUY SLUDGY	DILLRS DRILLS	DLNOTU UNTOLD
DGMSUY SMUDGY	DILLSY IDYLLS	DLNUUY UNDULY
DGNOOR DRONGO,	DILLWY WILDLY	DLOOPZ PODZOL
GORDON, GRODNO	DILMOR MILORD	DLOORU DOLOUR
DGNOOS GODSON	DILMPY DIMPLY	DLORSW WORLDS
DGNORU GROUND	DILNNU DUNLIN	DLORUY DOURLY
DGNOSU SUN GOD	DILNTU INDULT	DMNOOS OSMOND
DGOOPT TOP DOG	DILOSS SOLIDS	DMNOSU MOUNDS,
DGORSU GOURDS	DILOST STOLID	OSMUND
DGOSTY STODGY	DILOXY XYLOID	DMOOSY SODOMY
DGOTUU DUGOUT	DILOYZ DOZILY	DMORSU DORSUM
DHIINS SINDHI	DIMMSU DIM SUM	DMRTUU UDMURT
DHIIPS HISPID	DIMNOO DOMINO	DNOORS DONORS, RONDOS
DHIISW WIDISH	DIMNSU NUDISM	DNOPSU POUNDS
DHIJTU JUDITH	DIMOPU PODIUM	DNORSU ROUNDS
DHILOS OLDISH	DIMOSU SODIUM	DNORTU ROTUND
DHIMOS MODISH	DIMOSW WISDOM	DNOSSU SOUNDS
DHINOO HINDOO	DIMSST MIDSTS	DNOSSY SYNODS
DHINSU HINDUS	DINNUW UNWIND	DNOSUW WOUNDS
DHIORR HORRID	DINOOR INDOOR	DNRSUY SUNDRY
DHIOST DHOTIS	DINOPU UNIPOD	DOOOOV VOODOO
DHIOSV DOVISH	DINOSW DISOWN	DOOPRU UROPOD
DHIRST THIRDS	DINOSY SIDONY	DOOPRY DROOPY
DHISTW WIDTHS	DINOWW WINDOW	DOORSU ODOURS
DHLOPU HOLDUP, UPHOLD	DINPTU PUNDIT	DOPRSY DROPSY
DHLOSU SHOULD	DINPUW UPWIND	DORRTY DRY ROT
DHLTUU DULUTH	DINSTU DUSTIN, NUDIST	DORSSW SWORDS
DHNOSU HOUNDS, HUDSON	DINTUY NUDITY, UNTIDY	DORSSY DROSSY
DHOOOO HOODOO	DIOOPS ISOPOD	DORSTU STROUD
DHOORT HOT ROD	DIOORT TOROID	DORSWY DROWSY
DHORSU SHROUD	DIOOSU IODOUS, ODIOUS	DPSTUU DUSTUP
DIILMP LIMPID	DIOOSV OVOIDS	DRSTUY STURDY
DIILOP LIPOID	DIOOTX TOXOID	EEEEGG GEE-GEE
DIILOS SOLIDI	DIOPRT TORPID, TRIPOD	EEEEPT TEEPEE
DIILPS LIPIDS	DIORRT TORRID	EEEEWW WEE-WEE
DIILQU LIQUID	DIOSTT DITTOS	EEEFFT EFFETE
DIILST DISTIL	DIOSTU STUDIO	EEEFLR FEELER
DIILTY TIDILY	DIOSWW WIDOWS	EEEFRR REEFER
DIIMNU INDIUM	DIPPRY DRIPPY	EEEFRZ FREEZE
DIIMOS IDIOMS, IODISM	DIPRTU PUTRID	EEEGMR EMERGE
DIIMOU OIDIUM	DIPSTU STUPID	EEEGNO EOGENE
DIIMTW DIMWIT	DIQSSU SQUIDS	EEEGNR RENEGE
DIIMTY DIMITY	DJNNOO DONJON	EEEGNU EUGENE
DIINOX DIOXIN	DKNRSU DRUNKS	EEEGRZ GEEZER

EEEHLN HELENE
EEEHLR HEELER
EEEHNT ETHENE
EEEHST SEETHE
EEEHTT TEETHE
EEEHWZ WHEEZE
EEEILN EILEEN
EEEJRR JEERER
EEEKLY KEELEY
EEEKMR MEEKER
EEEKNR KEENER
EEEKNT KETENE
EEEKPR KEEPER
EEEKRS SEEKER
EEELMS MELEES
EEELNV ELEVEN
EEELPR PEELER
EEELRR REELER
EEELSS LESSEE
EEELSV LEVEES, SLEEVE
EEELSY ELYSEE
EEELTY EYELET
EEEMMS SEMEME
EEEMRS SEEMER
EEEMRT MEETER
EEEMST ESTEEM
EEENRS SERENE
EEENRT ENTRÉE, RETENE
EEENRV VENEER
EEENSZ SNEEZE
EEEOPP EPOPEE
EEEPPR PEEPER
EEEPRW WEEPER
EEEPST TEPEES
EEERRV REVERE
EEERSV REEVES, SEVERE
EEERTT TEETER, TERETE
EEERVW WEEVER
EEESTT SETTEE
EEESTV STEEVE
EEFFOT TOFFEE
EEFFSU EFFUSE
EEFGIR FERGIE
EEFGRU REFUGE
EEFHIR HEIFER
EEFHOR HEREOF
EEFHRT HEFTER
EEFILN FELINE
EEFILR RELIEF
EEFINR REFINE
EEFIRZ FRIEZE
EEFLLO FELLOE
EEFLLR FELLER

EEFLNN FENNEL
EEFLNS FLENSE
EEFLRT REFLET
EEFLRU FERULE, REFUEL
EEFLRX REFLEX
EEFLRY FREELY
EEFLST FLEETS
EEFLSX FLEXES
EEFLTT FETTLE
EEFLUY EYEFUL
EEFPRR PREFER
EEFPTY TEPEFY
EEFRRT FERRET
EEFRST FESTER, FREEST
EEFRSU REFUSE
EEFRTT FETTER
EEFRTU REFUTE
EEFSZZ FEZZES
EEGGIM MEGGIE
EEGGIR REGGIE
EEGGLP PEG LEG
EEGGOR GEORGE
EEGILS LIEGES
EEGILT ELEGIT
EEGIMR ÉMIGRÉ, REGIME
EEGINN ENGINE
EEGINP PEEING
EEGINS GENIES, SEEING
EEGINT TEEING
EEGINW WEEING
EEGINY EYEING
EEGIRS SERGEI
EEGIRT GERTIE
EEGIRV GRIEVE
EEGISS SIEGES
EEGLMU LEGUME
EEGLNT GENTLE
EEGLRS LEGERS
EEGLRT GRETEL, REGLET
EEGLTY GLEETY
EEGMNO GENOME
EEGMNR GERMEN
EEGMNT TEGMEN
EEGMRR MERGER
EEGNOP PONGEE
EEGNRS GENRES, GREENS
EEGNRT REGENT
EEGNRY ENERGY
EEGNTW TEGWEN
EEGRRT REGRET
EEGRRV VERGER
EEGRRY GREYER
EEGRSS EGRESS

EEGRST EGRETS
EEGRSV VERGES
EEGRSY GEYSER
EEGRTT GETTER
EEHIMP PHEMIE
EEHINN HENNIE
EEHINR HEREIN, INHERE
EEHINT EITHNE, THEINE
EEHIPS HEPSIE
EEHIRT EITHER
EEHITV THIEVE
EEHKLS SHEKEL
EEHLLN HELLEN
EEHLLR HELLER
EEHLLS HELLES
EEHLMT HELMET
EEHLNY HENLEY
EEHLPR HELPER
EEHLSV HELVES, SHELVE
EEHLSW WHEELS
EEHMMR HEMMER
EEHMNP HEMPEN
EEHMNS ENMESH
EEHMRS HERMES
EEHMSS MESHES
EEHMST THEMES
EEHMUX EXHUME
EEHNOR HEREON
EEHNOX HEXONE
EEHNPS SPHENE
EEHNPW NEPHEW
EEHNRR HERREN
EEHNRT NETHER
EEHNTY ETHYNE
EEHORR HERERO
EEHORS HEROES
EEHORT HERETO
EEHORW HOWE'ER
EEHOSX HEXOSE
EEHOTW TOWHEE
EEHPRS HERPES, SPHERE
EEHPSY HEPSEY
EEHRST ESTHER, HESTER,
   THREES
EEHRSW HEWERS
EEHRSY HERESY
EEHRTT TETHER
EEHRTW WETHER
EEHRVY HERVEY
EEHSST SHEETS, THESES
EEHWYY WHEYEY
EEHWYZ WHEEZY
EEIJNN JENNIE

EEIJSS JESSIE
EEIKLL KELLIE
EEIKLP KELPIE
EEIKRR KERRIE
EEILLN NELLIE
EEILLS LESLIE, LIESEL
EEILMR MERIEL
EEILNN LENNIE
EEILNO LEONIE
EEILNR LIERNE, RELINE
EEILNS ENSILE, SENILE
EEILNW EILWEN
EEILOS ELOISE
EEILPS ELSPIE
EEILPT PELITE
EEILRS RESILE
EEILRV EVILER, LEVIER,
    RELIVE, REVILE, VEILER
EEILRY EERILY
EEILSV LEVIES
EEILSX EXILES, ILEXES
EEILTT LETTIE
EEILVW WEEVIL
EEIMNR ERMINE
EEIMNY YEMENI
EEIMPR EMPIRE
EEIMRS MISERE, REMISE
EEIMRT MÉTIER
EEIMSS EMESIS
EEIMST SEMITE
EEINNP PINENE
EEINNV VIENNE
EEINPR REPINE
EEINQU EQUINE
EEINRS NEREIS, SEREIN,
    SERINE
EEINRT ENTIRE
EEINRV ENVIER, NIEVRE,
    VENIRE
EEINSS NESSIE, SEINES
EEINSV ENVIES
EEINTT NETTIE
EEINTX EXTINE
EEIORS SOIREE
EEIPPY YIPPEE
EEIPRR PIERRE
EEIPRS ESPIER
EEIPRX EXPIRE
EEIPTT PETITE
EEIPTW PEEWIT
EEIRRT RETIRE
EEIRRW REWIRE
EEIRSS SEISER, SERIES

EEIRSV REVISE
EEIRSX SEXIER
EEIRSY EYRIES
EEIRSZ SEIZER
EEIRVV REVIVE
EEIRVW REVIEW, VIEWER
EEISST TESSIE
EEISSV SIEVES
EEISTV STEVIE
EEJJNU JEJUNE
EEJKRR JERKER
EEJLNO JOLEEN, JOLENE
EEJLSW JEWELS
EEJMOR JEROME
EEJMRY JEREMY
EEJNNT JENNET
EEJRST JESTER
EEJRSY JERSEY
EEJSSW JEWESS
EEJSTT JET SET
EEKLMN KENELM
EEKLMY MEEKLY
EEKLNN KENNEL
EEKLNR KERNEL
EEKLNY KEENLY
EEKLTT KETTLE
EEKLWY WEEKLY
EEKMNS MEKNES
EEKMRS KERMES
EEKNOT KETONE
EEKORV EVOKER, REVOKE
EEKOST KETOSE
EEKPPU UPKEEP
EEKPRU PERUKE
EEKRST KESTER
EEKRSW SKEWER
EEKRSY KERSEY
EELLMU LEMUEL
EELLNO NOELLE
EELLOV O LEVEL
EELLPT PELLET
EELLRS SELLER
EELLRT RETELL, TELLER
EELLRY ELLERY, YELLER
EELLSV LEVELS
EELLSY LESLEY
EELMNY EMELYN
EELMPT PELMET, TEMPLE
EELMRT MELTER
EELMRW MEWLER
EELMRY MERELY
EELMSY SEEMLY
EELMTT METTLE

EELNNT LENTEN
EELNOR LENORE, LOREEN
EELNOV ELEVON
EELNPS SPLEEN
EELNRT RELENT
EELNSS LENSES, LESSEN
EELNST NESTLE
EELNTT NETTLE
EELNUV VENULE
EELNVY EVELYN, EVENLY
EELNXY XYLENE
EELOPP PEOPLE
EELOPR ELOPER
EELORS OR ELSE
EELORZ LOZERE
EELOVV EVOLVE
EELPPU PEEPUL
EELPRS LEPERS
EELPRT PELTER, PETREL
EELPRY YELPER
EELPST PESTLE
EELPSV PELVES
EELPSY SLEEPY
EELQSU SEQUEL
EELRSS LESSER
EELRST LESTER
EELRSV LEVERS
EELRTT LETTER
EELRTW WELTER
EELRUV VELURE
EELSST STEELS
EELSSV SELVES, VESSEL
EELSTT SETTLE
EELSTV SVELTE
EELSTY SLEETY, STEELY
EELSWY WESLEY
EELTVV VELVET
EELTVW TWELVE
EEMNOR MOREEN
EEMNOY YEOMEN
EEMNSS MENSES
EEMNSY YES-MEN
EEMNYZ ENZYME
EEMOPT METOPE
EEMORT EMOTER,
    METEOR, REMOTE
EEMORV REMOVE
EEMPRS SEMPRE
EEMPRT TEMPER
EEMPTX EXEMPT
EEMRST METERS, METRES
EEMRSU RÉSUMÉ
EEMRTU MEERUT

EEMSSS MESSES	EEOSTV VETOES	EFFILP PIFFLE
EEMSTU MUSTEE	EEPPPR PEPPER	EFFILR RIFFLE
EENNOR NOREEN	EEPPST STEPPE	EFFLMU MUFFLE
EENNOV EVONNE	EEPRRY PREYER	EFFLRU RUFFLE
EENNRS RENNES	EEPRSS SPREES	EFFLUX EFFLUX
EENNRT RENNET, TENNER	EEPRST PESTER, PETERS,	EFFNOO ONE-OFF
EENNSU UNSEEN	PRESET	EFFORS OFFERS
EENNUV UNEVEN	EEPRSU PERUSE, PUREES,	EFFORT EFFORT
EENOPR OPENER, REOPEN,	RUPEES	EFFOST OFFSET, SET-OFF
REPONE	EEPRSV VESPER	EFFPRU PUFFER
EENOPT POTEEN	EEPRSW SPEWER	EFFRSU SUFFER
EENOSV VENOSE	EEPRTT PETTER	EFFTTU TUFFET
EENOTV VENETO	EEPRTU REPUTE	EFGINR FINGER, FRINGE
EENOTW TOWNEE	EEPRTW PEWTER	EFGINT FETING
EENOVZ EVZONE	EEPRTX EXPERT	EFGIOS FOGIES
EENPRT REPENT	EEPSSW SWEEPS	EFGIRU FIGURE
EENPRY PYRENE	EEPSTT SEPTET	EFGLNU ENGULF
EENQSU QUEENS	EEPTTU PUTTEE	EFGLOR GOLFER
EENQUY QUEENY	EEQRSU QUEERS	EFGOOR FOREGO
EENRRT RENTER	EEQSUU QUEUES	EFGORR FORGER
EENRSS SNEERS	EERRST RESTER	EFGORS FORGES, GOFERS
EENRST ERNEST, NESTER,	EERRSV REVERS, SERVER	EFGORT FORGET
RESENT, TENSER	EERRTT TERRET	EFGRSU FERGUS
EENRSU ENSURE	EERRTU URETER	EFGSUU FUGUES
EENRSV NERVES	EERRTV REVERT	EFHILS ELFISH
EENRTT TENTER	EERSST STEERS	EFHIRS FISHER
EENRTU NEUTER, TENURE,	EERSSV SERVES, SEVRES,	EFHISS FISHES
TUREEN	VERSES	EFHIST FETISH
EENRTV VENTER	EERSSW SEWERS	EFHLSY FLESHY
EENRTX EXTERN	EERSTT SETTER, STREET,	EFHRRU FUHRER
EENRVY VENERY	TESTER	EFHSTT THEFTS
EENSSS SENSES	EERSTU RETUSE	EFIINT FINITE
EENSST TENSES	EERSTV REVEST	EFIKNR KNIFER
EENSSV SEVENS	EERSTW WESTER	EFIKNU FUKIEN
EENSTT TENETS	EERSTX EXSERT	EFILLR FILLER, REFILL
EENSTV EVENTS, STEVEN	EERSUV REVUES	EFILLT FILLET
EENSTW NEWEST	EERSVW SWERVE	EFILNY FINELY
EENSUV VENUES	EERTTT TETTER	EFILOS FILOSE
EENSWY SWEENY	EERTTW WETTER	EFILPP FIPPLE
EENSYZ SNEEZY	EERTUY TUYERE	EFILPR PILFER
EENTTX EXTENT	EERTVV VERVET	EFILRR RIFLER
EENTUX EXEUNT	EERTVX VERTEX	EFILRS FLIERS, LIFERS,
EEOPRS REPOSE	EESSTT SESTET, TESTES	RIFLES
EEOPRU EUROPE	EESSTW SWEETS	EFILRT FILTER, LIFTER,
EEOPST TOPEES	EESTTU SUTTEE	TRIFLE
EEOPSX EXPOSÉ	EESTTW TWEETS	EFILRU IREFUL
EEOPTU TOUPEE	EESTTX SEXTET	EFILST FILETS, ITSELF,
EEORST STEREO	EETTVY YVETTE	STIFLE
EEORSV SOEVER	EFFFFO EFF OFF	EFILSU FUSILE
EEORSZ ZEROES	EFFGIN EFFING	EFILTU FUTILE
EEORTV VETOER	EFFGIR GRIFFE	EFILWY WIFELY
EEORUV OEUVRE	EFFGIY EFFIGY	EFILZZ FIZZLE
EEOSST SETOSE	EFFGOR GOFFER	EFIMRR FIRMER

EFINRY FINERY
EFINST FEINTS, FINEST, INFEST
EFINSU INFUSE
EFIORX FOXIER
EFIOST SOFTIE
EFIPRX PREFIX
EFIRRS FRIERS
EFIRSS SERIFS
EFIRST REFITS, SIFTER, STRIFE
EFIRSU FURIES
EFIRSV FIVERS
EFIRSX FIXERS
EFIRTT FITTER, TITFER
EFIRVY VERIFY
EFIRZZ FIZZER
EFISTY FEISTY
EFKLSU FLUKES
EFKLUY FLUKEY
EFKNRU FUNKER
EFLLOW FELLOW
EFLLRU FULLER
EFLMSY MYSELF
EFLNNU FUNNEL
EFLNOS FELONS
EFLNOT TEFLON
EFLNOY FELONY
EFLNTU FLUENT
EFLOOT FOOTLE
EFLOOZ FOOZLE
EFLORT FLORET, LOFTER
EFLORU FOULER
EFLORW FLOWER, FOWLER
EFLORX FLEXOR
EFLOUW WOEFUL
EFLPRU PURFLE
EFLRRU FURLER
EFLRSY FLYERS
EFLRTU FLUTER
EFLRUU RUEFUL
EFLRUX REFLUX
EFLSTU FLUTES
EFLSUU USEFUL
EFMNOT FOMENT
EFMORR FORMER, REFORM
EFMRSU FEMURS
EFMTUY TUMEFY
EFNORS FRESNO
EFNORZ FROZEN
EFNOST SEFTON, SOFTEN
EFNRUZ FRUNZE
EFNRYZ FRENZY

EFOORT FOETOR, FOOTER
EFOORW WOOFER
EFORRT TREFOR
EFORRU FURORE
EFORST FOREST, FORTES, FOSTER, SOFTER
EFORSY FOYERS
EFOSTU FOETUS
EFRRSU SURFER
EFRRSY FRYERS
EFRRTU ERFURT
EFRSSU FUSSER
EFRTTU TUFTER
EFRTUU FUTURE
EFSSSU FUSSES
EGGGIL GIGGLE
EGGGLO GOGGLE
EGGGNO EGGNOG
EGGHIL HIGGLE
EGGHOR HOGGER
EGGHRU HUGGER
EGGIJL JIGGLE
EGGIJR JIGGER
EGGILN NIGGLE
EGGILW WIGGLE
EGGINR GINGER, NIGGER
EGGIRR RIGGER
EGGJLO JOGGLE
EGGJLU JUGGLE
EGGJOR JOGGER
EGGLOR LOGGER
EGGLOT TOGGLE
EGGLRU GURGLE, LUGGER
EGGMRU MUGGER
EGGNTU NUGGET
EGGORR GORGER, GREGOR
EGGORS GORGES
EGGORU GOUGER
EGGOSU GOUGES
EGGRTU TUGGER
EGHHIR HIGHER
EGHHIT EIGHTH, HEIGHT
EGHHIU HUGHIE
EGHHSU HUGHES
EGHIIN HIEING
EGHILS SLEIGH
EGHINO HOEING
EGHINR HINGER
EGHINS HINGES, NEIGHS
EGHINT GETHIN
EGHINW HEWING, WHINGE
EGHINX HEXING
EGHIOT HOGTIE

EGHIRS SIGHER
EGHIST EIGHTS
EGHITW WEIGHT
EGHITY EIGHTY
EGHLMP PHLEGM
EGHLNT LENGTH
EGHLUY HUGELY
EGHMMO MEGOHM
EGHNOU ENOUGH
EGHNRU HUNGER
EGHNST THEGNS
EGHOPR GOPHER
EGHOTT GHETTO
EGHRSU GUSHER
EGHSTU HUGEST
EGIILL GILLIE
EGIILR GIRLIE
EGIIMN GEMINI
EGIINT IGNITE
EGIJLN JINGLE
EGIJRS REJIGS
EGIKNP PEKING
EGIKNY KEYING
EGILLR GRILLE
EGILLU LIGULE
EGILMN MINGLE
EGILMP MEGILP
EGILMT GIMLET
EGILNO LEGION
EGILNR LINGER
EGILNS GLENIS, SINGLE
EGILNT TINGLE
EGILOR LOGIER
EGILPT PIGLET
EGILRS GRILSE
EGILRU UGLIER
EGILRZ GRIZEL
EGILST LEGIST
EGIMNO IMOGEN
EGIMNT METING
EGIMNW MEWING
EGIMOS EGOISM
EGIMPU GUIMPE
EGINNS ENSIGN
EGINOP PIGEON
EGINOR IGNORE, REGION
EGINOS SOIGNÉ
EGINOT TOEING
EGINOW WIGEON
EGINRR ERRING, RINGER
EGINRS REIGNS, RESIGN, SIGNER, SINGER
EGINRW WINGER

EGINSS GNEISS, SINGES
EGINST INGEST, SIGNET
EGINSU GENIUS
EGINSW SEWING, SWINGE, WINGES
EGINSX SEXING
EGINTW TWINGE
EGINVX VEXING
EGIOOR GOOIER
EGIORR GORIER
EGIORS ORGIES, SERGIO
EGIORT GOITRE
EGIOST EGOIST
EGIPRR GRIPER
EGIPRS GRIPES
EGIRRT TRIGER
EGIRST TIGERS
EGIRTV GRIVET
EGISSU GUISES, GUSSIE
EGJLNU JUNGLE
EGKMNO MEKONG
EGKRRU KRUGER
EGLLTU GULLET
EGLNNU GUNNEL
EGLNOR LONGER
EGLNOU LOUNGE
EGLNPU PLUNGE
EGLNRU LUNGER
EGLNSU LUNGES
EGLNSY GLENYS
EGLNTU GLUTEN
EGLNTY GENTLY
EGLOPR PROLEG
EGLOPS GOSPEL
EGLORU REGULO
EGLORV GLOVER, GROVEL
EGLORW GLOWER
EGLOSV GLOVES
EGLOUY EULOGY
EGLPRU GULPER
EGLUZZ GUZZLE
EGMNNU GUNMEN
EGMNOR MONGER
EGMNOS GNOMES
EGMNTU NUTMEG
EGMORU MORGUE
EGMRTU TERGUM
EGNNOO NONEGO
EGNNOU GUENON
EGNNRU GUNNER
EGNOOR OREGON
EGNOPS SPONGE
EGNORS GONERS

EGNORV GOVERN
EGNORY ERYNGO, GROYNE
EGNOTU TONGUE
EGNOXY OXYGEN
EGNPPU PENGPU
EGNRTU GUNTER, URGENT
EGNRTY GENTRY
EGNRWY GERWYN
EGOORV GROOVE
EGOOST STOOGE
EGOPRR GROPER
EGOPRS GROPES
EGORRV GROVER
EGORRW GROWER
EGORSS OGRESS
EGORSU GROUSE, ROGUES, RUGOSE
EGORSV GROVES
EGORSY GYROSE
EGOSSV VOSGES
EGOSUV VOGUES
EGOSYZ ZYGOSE
EGOTYZ ZYGOTE
EGPRRU PURGER
EGPRSU PURGES, SPURGE
EGPSTU GETUPS
EGRRSU SURGER
EGRSSU SURGES
EGRTTU GUTTER
EGSSTU GUESTS, GUSSET
EHHIKS SHEIKH
EHHIRT HITHER
EHHNPY HYPHEN
EHHRST THRESH
EHIIJM HIMEJI
EHIIPP HIPPIE
EHIIST SHIITE
EHIJSW JEWISH
EHIKRS HIKERS, SHRIEK, SHRIKE
EHILLL HILLEL
EHILLR HILLER
EHILMU HELIUM
EHILOR HOLIER
EHILOS HELIOS, ISOHEL
EHILOT EOLITH
EHILRS RELISH
EHILRT HITLER, LITHER
EHIMNR MENHIR
EHIMNT HIT MEN
EHIMNU INHUME
EHIMOR HOMIER
EHIMRT HERMIT

EHIMST THEISM
EHINOR HEROIN, ON HIRE
EHINOT HOTIEN
EHINRS SHINER, SHRINE
EHINRT HINTER
EHINRW WHINER
EHINSS SHENSI
EHINSW NEWISH, WHINES
EHINTW WHITEN
EHINTZ ZENITH
EHIOPS SOPHIE
EHIOPT OPHITE
EHIORS HOSIER
EHIORT HERIOT
EHIOST HOSTIE
EHIOTT HOTTIE
EHIPPR HIPPER
EHIPRS PERISH, RESHIP
EHIRRS SHERRI
EHIRSS HISSER, SHIRES
EHIRST THEIRS
EHIRSV SHIVER, SHRIVE
EHIRSW WISHER
EHIRTT HITTER, TITHER
EHIRTU RUTHIE
EHIRTV THRIVE
EHIRTW WHITER, WITHER, WRITHE
EHIRTZ ZITHER
EHISSS HISSES
EHISST SHIEST, THESIS
EHISSW WISHES
EHISTT THEIST, TITHES
EHISTW WHITES
EHJOOR JOHORE
EHJOPS JOSEPH
EHJORT JETHRO
EHJOSS JOSHES
EHKLSW WHELKS
EHKNOR HONKER
EHKOOR HOOKER
EHKORS KOSHER
EHKRSU HUSKER
EHLLOR HOLLER
EHLLOS HELLOS
EHLLOW HOWELL
EHLLRU HULLER
EHLLSS SHELLS
EHLLSY SHELLY
EHLMMU HUMMEL
EHLMOO MOHOLE
EHLMOP PHLOEM
EHLMOS HOLMES

EHLMOY HOMELY	EHOSSU HOUSES	EIIRTX TRIXIE
EHLMTY METHYL	EHOSSV SHOVES	EIIRVZ VIZIER
EHLNOP HOLPEN, PHENOL	EHPRSU PUSHER	EIISSS SISSIE
EHLNPY PHENYL	EHPRSY SYPHER	EIJKNR JERKIN
EHLOPP HOPPLE	EHPRYZ ZEPHYR	EIJKNU JUNKIE
EHLORW HOWLER	EHPSSU PUSHES	EIJLRT JILTER
EHLOST HOSTEL, HOTELS	EHRRSU RUSHER	EIJLSU JULIES
EHLOSU HOUSEL	EHRRSY SHERRY	EIJLTU JULIET
EHLOSV HOVELS, SHOVEL	EHRRTU HURTER	EIJNNO ENJOIN
EHLOTW HOWLET	EHRRWY WHERRY	EIJNOR JOINER, REJOIN
EHLPSW WHELPS	EHRSSU RHESUS, RUSHES,	EIJNRU INJURE
EHLRRU HURLER	USHERS	EIJNSX JINXES
EHLRSY SHERYL	EHRSSW SHREWS	EIJRSU JURIES
EHLRTU HURTLE, LUTHER	EHRSTY THYRSE	EIJRTT JITTER
EHLRUY HURLEY	EHSSTU TUSHES	EIJSTU JESUIT
EHLSSU LUSHES	EHSSTY SHYEST	EIKLLR KILLER
EHLSTU HUSTLE, SLEUTH	EIIKNP PINKIE	EIKLLY LIKELY
EHLUXY HUXLEY	EIIKNR INKIER	EIKLMR MILKER
EHMMRU HUMMER	EIILLL LILLIE	EIKLNS SILKEN
EHMNOR HERMON	EIILLM MILLIE	EIKLNT TINKLE
EHMNSY HYMENS	EIILLS LILIES	EIKLNU UNLIKE
EHMORT MOTHER	EIILLW WILLIE	EIKLNV KELVIN
EHMRST THERMS	EIILMR LIMIER	EIKLNW WELKIN, WINKLE
EHMRSY RHYMES	EIILMS SIMILE	EIKLRT KILTER
EHMRUY RHEUMY	EIILMU MILIEU	EIKMOS ESKIMO
EHMSSU MUSHES	EIILNN IN LINE	EIKMST KISMET
EHNOPS PHONES	EIILNR INLIER	EIKNOV INVOKE
EHNOPY PHONEY	EIILNS LIE-INS	EIKNPR PINKER
EHNORS HERONS	EIILNU IN LIEU	EIKNRS SINKER
EHNORT HORNET, THRONE	EIILNV LIVE-IN	EIKNRT TINKER
EHNOST HONEST	EIILOR OILIER	EIKNRW WINKER
EHNRTU HUNTER	EIILRV VIRILE	EIKNSS SKEINS
EHNSTT TENTHS	EIILRW WILIER	EIKNSV KNIVES
EHOOOP HOOPOE	EIILRX ELIXIR	EIKNTT KITTEN
FHOOPR HOOPER	EIILZZ LIZZIE	EIKOOR ROOKIE
EHOOPY PHOOEY	EIIMNN MINNIE	EIKOPR POKIER
EHOORT HOOTER	EIINNT INTINE	EIKPPR KIPPER
EHOORV HOOVER	EIINNV VINNIE	EIKPSS SPIKES
EHOOST SOOTHE	EIINNW WINNIE	EIKRRS RISKER
EHOOSV HOOVES	EIINOS IONISE	EIKRSS KISSER, KRISES,
EHOPPR HOPPER	EIINOZ IONIZE	SKIERS
EHOPRS POSHER	EIINPR PINIER	EIKRST STRIKE, TRIKES
EHOPRT POTHER	EIINPT PINITE, TIEPIN	EIKRSV SKIVER
EHOPRU UPHROE	EIINRT TINIER	EIKSSS KISSES
EHORSS SHORES	EIINRV IRVINE	EILLMR MILLER
EHORST OTHERS, THROES	EIINSS SEISIN	EILLMT MILLET
EHORSV SHOVER	EIINST TIE-INS	EILLNO LIONEL, NIELLO
EHORSW SHOWER,	EIINTV INVITE	EILLNT LENTIL, LINTEL
WHORES	EIINVV VIVIEN	EILLOT ELLIOT
EHORTT HOTTER	EIIPST PITIES	EILLPU PILULE
EHORTV THROVE	EIIPSX PIXIES	EILLRT RILLET, TILLER
EHORTX EXHORT	EIIRRW WIRIER	EILLRW WILLER
EHORTY THEORY	EIIRSS IRISES	EILLSU ILL-USE

97

EILLTT LITTLE
EILLTW WILLET
EILLVY EVILLY, LIVELY,
   VILELY
EILMNO OILMEN
EILMNR LIMNER, MERLIN
EILMNS SIMNEL
EILMNV MELVIN
EILMNY MYELIN
EILMOS MOLISE
EILMOT MOTILE
EILMPP PIMPLE
EILMPR LIMPER
EILMPS SIMPLE
EILMPT LIMPET
EILMPU PILEUM
EILMPW WIMPLE
EILMRS MILERS, SMILER
EILMRT MILTER
EILMRU MURIEL
EILMRW WILMER
EILMSS SMILES
EILMSU MUESLI
EILMSY LIMEYS
EILMTU TELIUM
EILMTY TIMELY
EILNNO LONNIE, ONLINE
EILNNT LINNET
EILNOR ELINOR
EILNOS INSOLE, LESION
EILNPP NIPPLE
EILNPS SPINEL, SPLINE
EILNPT PINTLE
EILNPU LINEUP, LUPINE
EILNRS LINERS
EILNRT LINTER
EILNST ENLIST, INLETS,
   LISTEN, SILENT, TINSEL
EILNSV SNIVEL
EILNSY LYSINE
EILNTY LENITY
EILNUV UNLIVE, UNVEIL
EILOOR ORIOLE
EILOOT OOLITE
EILOPS PILOSE
EILOPT POLITE
EILORT LOIRET, LOITER,
   TOILER
EILORV OLIVER
EILOSU LOUISE
EILOSV OLIVES
EILOSX ISOLEX
EILOTT LOTTIE, TOILET

EILOTV OLIVET, VIOLET
EILPPR RIPPLE
EILPPT TIPPLE
EILPPU PILEUP
EILPRS LISPER, PERILS,
   PERLIS, PLIERS
EILPRT TRIPLE
EILPSS PLISSE, SPIELS
EILPST STIPEL
EILPSU PILEUS
EILPSV PELVIS
EILPSX PIXELS
EILRST LITERS, LITRES,
   TILERS
EILRSV LIVERS, SILVER,
   SLIVER
EILRSY RILEYS
EILRTT LITTER, TILTER
EILRTU RUTILE
EILRVY LIVERY, VERILY
EILSST ISLETS, STILES
EILSSY SISLEY
EILSTT TITLES
EILSTU ISEULT
EILSTV VILEST
EILSVW SWIVEL
EILSVY SYLVIE
EILSWY WISELY
EILSXY SEXILY
EILSZZ SIZZLE
EILTTT TITTLE
EILTVY LEVITY
EIMMNU IMMUNE
EIMMOR MEMOIR
EIMMRS SIMMER
EIMMRU IMMURE
EIMNOR MERINO
EIMNOS EONISM, MONIES,
   SIMEON, SIMONE
EIMNPT PITMEN
EIMNRS MERSIN, MINERS
EIMNRT MINTER
EIMNRU MURINE
EIMNRV MERVIN, VERMIN
EIMNSX MINXES
EIMNTT MITTEN
EIMNTU MINUET, MINUTE
EIMNTY ENMITY
EIMNZZ MIZZEN
EIMOPS IMPOSE
EIMORS ISOMER, RIMOSE
EIMOST SOMITE
EIMOSV MOVIES

EIMOTV MOTIVE
EIMOTY MOIETY
EIMPRR PRIMER
EIMPRS PRIMES, SIMPER
EIMPRT PERMIT
EIMPRU IMPURE, UMPIRE
EIMPTU IMPUTE
EIMRRT TRIMER
EIMRSS MISERS, REMISS
EIMRST MERITS, MISTER,
   MITRES, SMITER, TIMERS
EIMRSV VERISM, VERMIS
EIMRSX MIXERS
EIMRSY MISERY
EIMSSS MISSES
EIMSST TMESIS
EIMSSU MISUSE
EIMSSX SEXISM
EIMSTY STYMIE
EINNNR RENNIN
EINNOO IONONE
EINNOR RONNIE
EINNOT INTONE
EINNPR PINNER
EINNPT TENPIN
EINNRS SINNER
EINNRT INTERN
EINNRW WINNER
EINNST SENNIT, TENNIS
EINNTT INTENT
EINNTU IN TUNE
EINNTV INVENT
EINNTY NINETY
EINOPR ORPINE
EINOPS PONIES
EINOPT POINTE
EINORR IRONER
EINORS NOSIER, SENIOR
EINORT NORITE, ORIENT
EINORV RENVOI
EINOSS ENOSIS, NOESIS,
   NOISES, OSSEIN
EINOSW NOWISE
EINPPR NIPPER
EINPPS PEPSIN
EINPRS SNIPER
EINPRU PUNIER, PURINE,
   UNRIPE
EINPRY PINERY
EINPSS SNIPES, SPINES
EINPST INSTEP, SPINET
EINPSU SUPINE
EINQSU SEQUIN

EINQUU UNIQUE
EINRRS RINSER
EINRRU RUINER
EINRSS RESINS, RINSES,
  SIRENS
EINRST INSERT, SINTER
EINRSU INSURE, URSINE
EINRTU TRIUNE, UNITER
EINRTV INVERT
EINRTW TWINER, WINTER
EINRVY VINERY
EINSST INSETS, STEINS
EINSSW SINEWS, SWINES
EINSTV INVEST
EINSTZ ZENIST
EINSUW UNWISE
EINSUX UNISEX
EINSVX VIXENS
EINSWY SINEWY
EINTTY ENTITY
EIOORZ OOZIER
EIOOST OTIOSE
EIOPRR ROPIER
EIOPSS POSIES
EIOPST POSTIE
EIOPTT TIPTOE
EIORRS ROSIER
EIORRT RIOTER
EIORSS OSIERS
EIORST SORTIE, TORIES,
  TRIOSE
EIOSTV SOVIET
EIOTVV VOTIVE
EIPPRR RIPPER
EIPPRS PIPERS, SIPPER
EIPPRT TIPPER
EIPPRZ ZIPPER
EIPPST SIPPET
EIPPTT TIPPET
EIPPUY YUPPIE
EIPQSU PIQUES
EIPQTU PIQUET
EIPRRS SPRIER
EIPRSS PRISES, SPIRES
EIPRST ESPRIT, PRIEST,
  RIPEST, SPRITE, STRIPE
EIPRSU EPIRUS, UPRISE
EIPRSV VIPERS
EIPRSZ PRIZES
EIPRTV PRIVET
EIPRTY PYRITE
EIPRXY EXPIRY

EIPSSS PISSES, SEPSIS,
  SPEISS
EIPSST STIPES
EIPSSW SWIPES
EIPSTU TIE-UPS
EIPSTW PEWITS
EIQRSU QUIRES, RISQUÉ,
  SQUIRE
EIQRUV QUIVER
EIQTUY EQUITY
EIRRSS RISERS
EIRRST TRIERS
EIRRSV RIVERS
EIRRTW WRITER
EIRSST RESIST, RESITS,
  SISTER
EIRSSU ISSUER
EIRSTT SITTER
EIRSTV RIVETS, STRIVE,
  VERIST
EIRSTW WRIEST
EIRTTT TITTER
EIRTTV TRIVET
EIRTUV VIRTUE
EIRTVY VERITY
EISSSU ISSUES
EISSTT TESTIS
EISSTU SUITES, TISSUE
EISSTW WISEST
EISSTX SEXIST
EJKNTU JUNKET
EJKOPS SKOPJE
EJKORS JOKERS
EJLOST JOSTLE
EJLOSU JOULES
EJLPSU JULEPS
EJMPRU JUMPER
EJNOTT JETTON
EJOPRT PROJET
EJORTT JOTTER
EJRTTU JUTTER
EKLLNS KNELLS
EKLLSY SKELLY
EKLMMU KÜMMEL
EKLMOW WELKOM
EKLOOR LOOKER
EKLOSY YOKELS
EKLOWY LOW-KEY
EKLRRU LURKER
EKLRSU SULKER
EKMNOY MONKEY
EKMOOP MOPOKE
EKMORS SMOKER

EKMOSS SMOKES
EKMSTU MUSKET
EKNNOT KENTON, NEKTON
EKNNSU SUNKEN
EKNOPS SPOKEN
EKNORR KRONER
EKNORW KNOWER
EKNOST TOKENS
EKNOUY UNYOKE
EKOORT RETOOK
EKOPRR PORKER
EKOPRS POKERS
EKOPSS SPOKES
EKORRW REWORK,
  WORKER
EKORRY YORKER
EKORST STOKER, STROKE
EKOSST STOKES
EKRSTU TUSKER
EKRTUY TURKEY
ELLLOR LOLLER
ELLLOV LOVELL
ELLLOW LOWELL
ELLMOW MELLOW
ELLMRU MULLER
ELLMSS SMELLS
ELLMSY SMELLY
ELLMTU MULLET
ELLMUV VELLUM
ELLNOP POLLEN
ELLNOW NOWELL
ELLNOY LONELY
ELLNSU SULLEN
ELLNUW UNWELL
ELLOPX POLLEX
ELLORR ORRELL, ROLLER
ELLOSY SOLELY
ELLOVY LOVELY, VOLLEY
ELLOWY YELLOW
ELLPSS SPELLS
ELLPTU PULLET
ELLPUY PULLEY
ELLSSW SWELLS
ELMMOP POMMEL
ELMMOS MOSLEM
ELMMPU PUMMEL
ELMNOR MERLON
ELMNOS LEMONS,
  MELONS, SOLEMN
ELMNOT LOMENT, MELTON,
  MOLTEN
ELMNOY LEMONY
ELMNPU LUMPEN, PLENUM

ELMNVY MELVYN	ELOPRX PLEXOR	EMNOPY EPONYM
ELMOPY EMPLOY	ELOPSS SLOPES	EMNORS SERMON
ELMORS MORSEL	ELOPTU TUPELO	EMNORT MENTOR, MERTON
ELMOST MOLEST, MOTELS	ELORRS SORREL	EMNOSY MONEYS
ELMOTT MOTTLE	ELORSS LESSOR, LOSERS	EMNOTY ETYMON
ELMOTY MOTLEY	ELORST OSTLER, STEROL	EMNOXY EXONYM
ELMOUV VOLUME	ELORSV LOVERS, SOLVER	EMNRVY MERVYN
ELMPPU PEPLUM	ELORSW SLOWER	EMNTUY TYUMEN
ELMPRU RUMPLE	ELORSY SORELY	EMOORR ROOMER
ELMPSU PLUMES	ELORTV REVOLT	EMOORS MOROSE, ROMEOS
ELMRSU LEMURS	ELORTW TROWEL	EMOORT MOOTER
ELMRTY MYRTLE, TERMLY	ELORUV LOUVRE, VELOUR	EMOOSS OSMOSE
ELMSST SMELTS	ELORVW WOLVER	EMOPPT MOPPET
ELMSSU MUSSEL	ELORVY OVERLY	EMOPRT PRO TEM, TROMPE
ELMTUU MUTULE	ELORWY YOWLER	EMOPST TEMPOS
ELMTUY MUTELY	ELOSSS LOSSES	EMOQSU MOSQUE
ELMUZZ MUZZLE	ELOSST STOLES	EMORRT TERMOR, TREMOR
ELNNOS NELSON	ELOSTU SOLUTE, TOUSLE	EMORRW WORMER
ELNNOX LENNOX	ELOSTW LOWEST, OWLETS,	EMORST METROS
ELNNRU RUNNEL	TOWELS	EMORSU MOUSER
ELNNTU TUNNEL	ELOSVW VOWELS, WOLVES	EMORSV MOVERS
ELNOOS LOOSEN	ELOSVY LOVEYS	EMORSW MOWERS
ELNOOY LOONEY	ELOSXY XYLOSE	EMORSY MYSORE
ELNOPT LEPTON	ELOTTU OUTLET	EMOSSU MOUSSE
ELNOPY OPENLY, POLEYN	ELOTUV VOLUTE	EMOSTT MOTETS, TOTEMS
ELNORS LONERS	ELOTWY OWELTY	EMOSZZ MEZZOS
ELNOSS LESSON	ELPPRU PURPLE	EMPRSS SPERMS
ELNOST STOLEN, TELSON	ELPPSU SUPPLE	EMPSSU MESS-UP
ELNOSU ENSOUL	ELPRRU PURLER	EMPSTU SEPTUM
ELNOSV NOVELS, SLOVEN	ELPRTY PELTRY, PERTLY	EMRSSU SERUMS
ELNOUZ ZONULE	ELPRUY PURELY	EMRSTU MUSTER, STUMER
ELNOZZ NOZZLE	ELPSSU PLUSES, PULSES	EMRTTU MUTTER
ELNPTU PENULT	ELPSTU LETUPS	EMSSTY SYSTEM
ELNPTY PENTYL, PLENTY	ELPSUX PLEXUS	ENNNOP PENNON
ELNSSU UNLESS	ELPUZZ PUZZLE	ENNORU NEURON
ELNSWY SELWYN	ELRRSU RULERS	ENNORV VERNON
ELNSXY LYNXES	ELRSSU RUSSEL	ENNORW RENOWN
ELNSYY LYNSEY	ELRSTU LUSTRE, RESULT,	ENNOST SONNET, TENONS,
ELNTTU NUTLET	RUSTLE, ULSTER	TONNES
ELNTTY NETTLY	ELRSTY STYLER	ENNOTW NEWTON
ELNUZZ NUZZLE	ELRSUY SURELY	ENNOVY YVONNE
ELOOPR LOOPER	ELRTTU TURTLE	ENNPTU PUNNET
ELOORS LOOSER	ELRTTY TETRYL	ENNRRU RUNNER
ELOORT LOOTER, RETOOL,	ELSSTU TUSSLE	ENOOPR OPERON
TOOLER	ELSSTY SLYEST, STYLES	ENOORS SOONER
ELOOSS LOOSES	ELSTTY STYLET	ENOORT ENROOT
ELOOTT TOOTLE	EMMMRU MUMMER	ENOOSS NOOSES
ELOPPP POPPLE	EMMNOT MOMENT	ENOOSZ SNOOZE
ELOPPR LOPPER, PROPEL	EMMORY MEMORY	ENOPRR PERRON
ELOPPT TOPPLE	EMMRRU RUMMER	ENOPRS PERSON
ELOPRS PROLES, SLOPER	EMMRSU SUMMER	ENOPRV PROVEN
ELOPRT PETROL	EMMSUU MUSEUM	ENOPRY PYRONE
ELOPRV PLOVER	EMNNOT MENTON	ENOPTT POTENT

ENORRS SNORER
ENORRY ORNERY
ENORSS SEÑORS, SENSOR, SNORES
ENORST STONER, TENORS, TENSOR
ENORSW OWNERS, WORSEN
ENORTT ROTTEN
ENORTY TYRONE
ENOSST STONES
ENOSTX SEXTON
ENOSUV VENOUS
ENOSVY ENVOYS
ENOTTU TENUTO, TEUTON
ENPPTU PENT UP
ENPRRU PRUNER
ENPRSU PRUNES
ENPRTU PUNTER
ENPRUY PENURY
ENPSTU UNSTEP
ENPTUU TUNE-UP
ENPTUW UNWEPT
ENRRSU RERUNS
ENRRTU RETURN, TURNER
ENRSST STERNS
ENRSSU NURSES
ENRSTU TUNERS, UNREST
ENRSTW STREWN
ENRSTY SENTRY
ENRSUU UNSURE
ENRTTU NUTTER
ENRTUU UNTRUE
ENRVWY WYVERN
ENSSTU SUNSET
ENTTWY TWENTY
EOOPPR POOPER
EOOPPS OPPOSE
EOOPRR POORER
EOORRT ROOTER, TORERO
EOORST TOROSE
EOORSW WOOERS
EOORTT TOOTER
EOOSTW SOWETO
EOPPPR POPPER
EOPPPT POPPET
EOPPRR PROPER
EOPPRT TOPPER
EOPPRY POPERY, PYROPE
EOPRRT PORTER, REPORT
EOPRRU POURER
EOPRSS POSERS, PROSES, SPORES

EOPRST POSTER, PRESTO, TROPES
EOPRSU POSEUR
EOPRSW POWERS
EOPRSY OSPREY
EOPRTT POTTER
EOPRTU POUTER, TROUPE
EOPRTX EXPORT
EOPRTY POETRY
EOPSSS POSSES
EOPSST POSSET
EOPSSU OPUSES, SPOUSE
EOPSTX SEXPOT
EOQRTU ROQUET, TORQUE
EOQSTU QUOTES
EORRRS ERRORS
EORRRT TERROR
EORRRY ORRERY
EORRST RESORT, ROSTER, SORTER
EORRSU ROUSER, SOURER
EORRSV ROVERS
EORRSW ROWERS
EORRTT RETORT, ROTTER
EORRTU ROUTER, TOURER
EORRTV TREVOR, TROVER
EORRZZ ROZZER
EORSST STORES, TOSSER
EORSSU SEROUS
EORSSV SERVOS, VERSOS
EORSSW SOWERS
EORSTT OTTERS
EORSTU OUSTER, ROUTES
EORSTV STOVER, STROVE, TROVES, VOTERS
EORSTW TOWERS
EORSTY OYSTER, STOREY
EORSTZ ZOSTER
EORTTT TOTTER
EORTTX EXTORT
EORTVX VORTEX
EORUVY VOYEUR
EOSSST TOSSES
EOSSTV STOVES
EOSTTU OUTSET
EPPPRY PREPPY
EPPPTU PUPPET
EPPRSU SUPPER, UPPERS
EPRRSU PURSER
EPRRTU RUPERT
EPRSSU PURSES
EPRSTU PUREST
EPRSTW TWERPS

EPRSUU PURSUE
EPRTTU PUTTER
EPRTTY PRETTY
EPRUVY PURVEY
EPSSSU PUSSES
EPSSTU SET-UPS, UPSETS
EQRTWY QWERTY
EQSSTU QUESTS
ERRSUU USURER
ERRSUY SURREY
ERRTTU TURRET
ERSSST STRESS
ERSSTU RUSSET, SUREST
ERSSTY TRESSY
ERSSUV VERSUS
ERSTTU TRUEST
ERSTUU SUTURE, UTERUS
ERSTUV TURVES
ERSTUY SURETY
ERSTVY VESTRY
ERSTWY WRYEST
ERSTXY XYSTER
ERSUVY SURVEY
ERTTUX URTEXT
ESSTUX SEXTUS
FFFLUY FLUFFY
FFGINO OFFING
FFHIST FIFTHS
FFHISW WHIFFS
FFHIWY WHIFFY
FFIINT TIFFIN
FFIKSS SKIFFS
FFILLU FULFIL
FFILTU FITFUL
FFIMNU MUFFIN
FFINPU PUFFIN
FFINSS SNIFFS
FFINSY SNIFFY
FFIOPR RIP-OFF
FFIOPT TIP-OFF
FFIOST SOFFIT
FFIQSU QUIFFS
FFISST STIFFS
FFISUX SUFFIX
FFLRUY RUFFLY
FFNORU RUN OFF
FFNSUY SNUFFY
FFOPTU PUT-OFF
FFRRUU FURFUR
FFSTUY STUFFY
FGGIIZ FIZGIG
FGGINU FUGING
FGGORY FROGGY

FGHILT FLIGHT	FILNSU SINFUL	FOORST SORT OF
FGHIRT FRIGHT	FILNTY FLINTY	FOOTUX OUTFOX
FGHIST FIGHTS	FILNUX INFLUX	FORRUW FURROW
FGHOTU FOUGHT	FILOOS FOLIOS	FORSST FROSTS
FGIILN FILING	FILORV FRIVOL	FORSTY FROSTY
FGIINN FINING	FILOSS FOSSIL	FORSUU RUFOUS
FGIINR FIRING	FILOXY FOXILY	FORWYZ FROWZY
FGIINX FIXING	FILPTU UPLIFT	FPRSUY FRY-UPS
FGILNY FLYING	FILRST FLIRTS	GGGILY GIGGLY
FGILUY UGLIFY	FIMNOR INFORM	GGGORY GROGGY
FGIMNU FUMING	FIMOST MOTIFS	GGHNOU GUNG-HO
FGINOX FOXING	FIMSTU MUFTIS	GGIINP PIGGIN
FGINRY FRINGY, FRYING	FINORX FORNIX	GGIINV GIVING
FGINSU FUSING	FINOSU FUSION	GGIIRR GRIGRI
FGKNUU KUNG FU	FINOTY NOTIFY	GGIJLY JIGGLY
FGNSUU FUNGUS	FIOOTT FOOT IT	GGIKNO GINKGO
FGOORT FORGOT	FIOPRT PROFIT	GGILNO OGLING
FHIINS FINISH	FIORST FORTIS	GGILNU GLUING
FHILTY FILTHY	FIOSSY OSSIFY	GGILOO GIGOLO
FHIRST FIRTHS, SHRIFT	FIOTTU OUTFIT	GGILWY WIGGLY
FHIRTT THRIFT	FIPRUY PURIFY	GGINNO NOGGIN
FHISST SHIFTS	FIPTYY TYPIFY	GGINOR GORING, GRINGO
FHISTU SHUFTI	FIRSST FIRSTS	GGINRU URGING
FHISTY SHIFTY	FIRSTU FRUITS	GGINUY GUYING
FHNSUU FUSHUN	FIRTUY FRUITY	GGITWY TWIGGY
FHORST FROTHS	FIRYZZ FRIZZY	GGLLOO LOGLOG
FHORTU FOURTH	FISSTW SWIFTS	GGLOOO GOOGOL
FHORTY FROTHY	FJLOUY JOYFUL	GGLOOY GOOGLY
FHSTUY SHUFTY	FKLNUY FLUNKY	GGMOSY SMOGGY
FIIKNR FIRKIN	FKLOSY FOLKSY	GGNOOR GORGON
FIILLN FILL-IN	FLLOOW FOLLOW	GGRRUU GRUGRU
FIILLP FILLIP	FLLOUY FOULLY	GHHILY HIGHLY
FIILRU FRIULI	FLMOOS FOLSOM	GHHIST THIGHS
FIILST TIFLIS	FLMORY FORMYL	GHHOTU THOUGH
FIILVY VILIFY	FLNRUU UNFURL	GHIIKN HIKING
FIIMNR INFIRM	FLOORS FLOORS	GHIINR HIRING
FIIMNY MINIFY	FLOOYZ FLOOZY	GHIINV HIVING
FIIMST MISFIT	FLOPPY FLOPPY	GHIKNT KNIGHT
FIINOR FIORIN	FLOPTU POTFUL	GHILPT PLIGHT
FIITXY FIXITY	FLOPUU FOUL-UP	GHILST LIGHTS, SLIGHT
FIIVVY VIVIFY	FLORUY FLOURY	GHIMNO HOMING
FIJLOR FRIJOL	FLOSSY FLOSSY	GHIMTY MIGHTY
FIKRSS FRISKS	FLOSTY SOFTLY	GHINNO HONING
FIKRSY FRISKY	FLRRUY FLURRY	GHINOP HOPING
FILLRS FRILLS	FMORSU FORUMS	GHINOS HOSING
FILLRY FRILLY	FMPRSU FRUMPS	GHINPY HYPING
FILLUW WILFUL	FMPRUY FRUMPY	GHINST NIGHTS, THINGS
FILMOU FOLIUM	FNNRUU FUN RUN	GHINSY SHYING
FILMRY FIRMLY	FNORST FRONTS	GHIOPZ PHIZOG
FILMSY FLIMSY	FNORSW FROWNS	GHIRST GIRTHS, RIGHTS
FILNOR FLORIN	FNOSTU FOUNTS, FUTONS	GHIRTW WRIGHT
FILNOW INFLOW	FOOPRS PROOFS	GHISST SIGHTS
FILNST FLINTS	FOOPSS SPOOFS	GHISTT TIGHTS

GHISTW WIGHTS
GHLLSY GHYLLS
GHLOPU PLOUGH
GHLOSU GHOULS, LOUGHS,
   SLOUGH
GHNORT THRONG
GHNOST THONGS
GHNOSU SHOGUN
GHNOTU HOGNUT, NOUGHT
GHNRUY HUNGRY
GHNSUY GUNSHY
GHORTU TROUGH
GHORTW GROWTH
GHOSST GHOSTS
GHOSSU SOUGHS
GHOSTU SOUGHT
GHRSSU SHRUGS
GIIJNV JIVING
GIIKLN LIKING
GIIKNN INKING
GIIKNR IRKING
GIIKNS SKIING
GIIKNV VIKING
GIILMN LIMING
GIILNN LIGNIN, LINING
GIILNO OILING
GIILNP PILING
GIILNR RILING
GIILNT TILING
GIILNV LIVING
GIILOR OILRIG
GIILRV VIRGIL
GIILSV VIGILS
GIIMMN MIMING
GIIMNN MINING
GIIMNR MIRING
GIIMNT TIMING
GIIMNX MIXING
GIINNN INNING
GIINNP PINING
GIINNS SINING
GIINNW WINING
GIINNX NIXING
GIINOR ORIGIN
GIINPP PIPING
GIINPW WIPING
GIINRS RISING, SIRING
GIINRT TIRING
GIINRV IRVING, VIRGIN
GIINRW WIRING
GIINST SITING
GIINSZ SIZING
GIIRST TIGRIS

GIJKNO JOKING
GIJLNY JINGLY
GIJNOY JOYING
GIKLNY KINGLY
GIKNNU NUKING
GIKNOP POKING
GIKNOY YOKING
GIKNPU PUKING
GILLRS GRILLS
GILMRY GRIMLY
GILMWY GWILYM, GWYLIM
GILNOO LOGION
GILNOP LOPING, POLING
GILNOS LOSING, SOLING
GILNOV LOVING
GILNOW LOWING
GILNPY PLYING
GILNRU LURING, RULING
GILNSS SLINGS
GILNST GLINTS
GILNSU SLUING
GILNSY GLINYS, GLYNIS,
   SINGLY
GILNTY TINGLY
GILOOS IGLOOS
GILORY GILROY, GORILY
GILRSY GRISLY
GILTUY GUILTY
GILTYZ GLITZY
GIMNNO MIGNON
GIMNOO MOOING
GIMNOP MOPING
GIMNOV MOVING
GIMNOW MOWING
GIMNPU IMPUGN
GIMNSU MUSING
GIMNTU MUTING
GIMOSY YOGISM
GIMOTU GOMUTI
GINNOO GONION
GINNOP NINGPO
GINNOS NOSING
GINNOT NOTING, TONING
GINNOW OWNING
GINNOZ ZONING
GINNTU TUNING
GINOOS ISOGON
GINOOW WOOING
GINOOZ OOZING
GINOPR PORING, ROPING
GINOPS POSING
GINOPT OPTING

GINORS GRISON, GROINS,
   SIGNOR
GINORV ROVING
GINORW ROWING
GINOSS GNOSIS
GINOST INGOTS
GINOSW SOWING
GINOTT TOTING
GINOTU OUTING
GINOTV VOTING
GINOTW TOWING
GINOTY TOYING
GINOVW VOWING
GINOWW WOWING
GINPRS SPRING
GINPRY PRYING
GINPSU PIGNUS
GINPSY SPYING
GINPTU PIGNUT
GINPTY TYPING
GINRST STRING
GINRTY TRYING
GINRWY WRYING
GINSST STINGS
GINSSV V-SIGNS
GINSSW SWINGS
GINSTY STINGY
GINSUU UNGUIS
GIOPSS GOSSIP
GIOPST SPIGOT
GIORRU RIGOUR
GIORSV VIRGOS
GIORTU RIG-OUT
GIORUV VIGOUR
GIOSTU GIUSTO
GIPRSS SPRIGS
GIPSTY PIGSTY
GIRSST GRISTS
GIRTTY GRITTY
GJLNUY JUNGLY
GJNRUU GURJUN
GLLMUY GLUMLY
GLLOOP GOLLOP
GLMNOO MONGOL
GLMOOY GLOOMY
GLMOSU MOGULS
GLMSUY SMUGLY
GLNOOO OOLONG
GLNPUU UNPLUG
GLNSUY SNUGLY
GLOOOY OOLOGY
GLOOPR PROLOG
GLOOSW GO-SLOW

GLOPTU PUTLOG	HILOPS POLISH	HLSSUY SLUSHY
GLORSW GROWLS	HILOSW OWLISH	HMNOST MONTHS
GLOSSY GLOSSY	HILRSW WHIRLS	HMNPSY NYMPHS
GMNNOO GNOMON	HILSTW WHILST	HMOOST SMOOTH
GMOOPR POGROM	HIMMSU HUMISM	HMORUU HUMOUR
GMOORS GROOMS	HIMNOY HOMINY	HMORUZ HORMUZ
GMPRUY GRUMPY	HIMPRS SHRIMP	HMOSTU MOUTHS
GMPSUY GYPSUM	HIMSST SMITHS	HMOSTY MYTHOS
GNNOOS ON SONG	HIMSTY SMITHY	HMPSTU THUMPS
GNNSUU UNSUNG	HIMSWY WHIMSY	HMPTUY HUMPTY
GNOORT TROGON	HINNST NINTHS	HMSTUY THYMUS
GNOPPU OPPUGN, POPGUN	HINNSY SHINNY	HNNOOP PHONON
GNOPRS PRONGS	HINNWY WHINNY	HNOOPT PHOTON
GNOPSY SPONGY	HINOPS SIPHON	HNOORT THORON
GNORST STRONG	HINOST SHINTO	HNOORU HONOUR
GNORSW WRONGS	HINPSU PUNISH, UNSHIP	HNOPSU NOSH-UP
GNORUV GUVNOR	HINPSX SPHINX	HNOPSY SYPHON
GNORYZ GROZNY	HINRSU INRUSH	HNOPTY PHYTON, PYTHON
GNPRSU SPRUNG	HIOPPS POPISH	HNORST NORTHS, THORNS
GNRSTU GRUNTS, STRUNG	HIOPST PITHOS	HNORSU ONRUSH
GNRTUU GUNTUR	HIOPSY PHYSIO	HNORTW THROWN
GNSTUU TUNGUS	HIORSU HOURIS	HNORTY RHYTON, THORNY
GOOPST STOP-GO	HIOSST HOISTS	HNOSTU HUSTON
GOORTT GROTTO	HIPPSU UPPISH	HNSSTU SHUNTS
GOORVY GROOVY	HIPPWY WHIPPY	HOOPST PHOTOS
GOPRSU GROUPS	HIPRST THRIPS	HOOPSW WHOOPS
GORRTU TURGOR	HIQSSU SQUISH	HOOPTT HOTPOT
GORSTU GROUTS	HIRSST SHIRTS	HOORRR HORROR
GORTTU ROTGUT	HIRSTT THIRST, T-SHIRT	HOOSST SHOOTS
GORTTY GROTTY	HIRSTY IRTYSH, SHIRTY	HOOSSW SWOOSH
GSYYYZ SYZYGY	HIRTTY THIRTY	HOOTTY TOOTHY
HHMRTY RHYTHM	HISSTX SIXTHS	HOPPSU HOPPUS
HHNOSU HONSHU	HISTTY SHITTY	HOPRTY TROPHY
HHOOSW WHOOSH	HJNNOY JOHNNY	HOPSTU TOPHUS, UPSHOT
HHPSUU HUSH-UP	HJNOST ST JOHN	HORSST SHORTS
HHRSTU THRUSH	HKNOOU UNHOOK	HORSTT TROTHS
HIILLT LILITH	HKNRSU SHRUNK	HORSTW THROWS
HIILPP PHILIP	HKOOPU HOOKUP	HORSTY SHORTY
HIIMPS IMPISH	HKSUUY KYUSHU	HORTWY WORTHY
HIIMST MISHIT	HLLOOW HOLLOW	HOSSTU SHOUTS
HIINTW WITHIN	HLLOSU HULLOS	HOSTUY YOUTHS
HIKNRS SHRINK	HLLOWY WHOLLY	HPPSUU PUSH-UP
HIKSSW WHISKS	HLLPUY LYULPH	HPSTUY TYPHUS
HIKSWY WHISKY	HLMOTY THYMOL	HRSTTU THRUST, TRUTHS
HILLOY HOLILY	HLMPUY PHYLUM	IIIMNR RIMINI
HILLPU UPHILL	HLNOUY UNHOLY	IIIRST IRITIS
HILLRS SHRILL	HLNSUU LU-SHUN	IIKKMS SIKKIM
HILLRT THRILL	HLOOST SHOLTO, THOLOS	IIKNPP PIPKIN
HILMOS HOLISM	HLOPSS SPLOSH	IIKNSS SISKIN
HILMOY HOMILY	HLORSW WHORLS	IIKPST SKIP IT!
HILMSU MULISH	HLORUY HOURLY	IILLOY GILILY
HILNPT PLINTH	HLOSST SLOTHS	IILLSW WILLIS
HILNTY THINLY	HLOSSY SLOSHY	IILMMU MILIUM

IILMST LIMITS	IKNSST STINKS	ILPPSU PUPILS, SLIP-UP
IILNNU INULIN	IKQRSU QUIRKS	ILPPSY SLIPPY
IILNOV VIOLIN	IKQRUY QUIRKY	ILPPTU PULPIT
IILNST INSTIL	IKRSST SKIRTS	ILPSST SPLITS
IILPST PISTIL	IKRSTY KIRSTY	ILPSTU TULIPS
IILRWY WIRILY	IKSVVY SKIVVY	ILPTTU UPTILT
IILTTW TWILIT	ILLMPY LIMPLY	ILQSTU QUILTS
IIMMNS MINIMS	ILLMSY SLIMLY	ILRSSW SWIRLS
IIMMNU MINIUM	ILLNOS LLINOS	ILRSTW TWIRLS
IIMNNO MINION	ILLNPU PULL-IN	ILRSTY LYRIST
IIMOSS MIOSIS	ILLOPW PILLOW	ILRSWY SWIRLY
IIMSSS MISSIS	ILLOWW WILLOW	ILRTWY TWIRLY
IINNOP PINION	ILLPSS SPILLS	ILSSTT STILTS
IINNTU INNUIT	ILLQSU QUILLS, SQUILL	IMMMOS MOMISM
IINORS ROISIN	ILLRST TRILLS	IMMNOS MONISM, NOMISM
IINOSV VISION	ILLSST STILLS	IMMOOS SIMOOM
IINPPP PIPPIN	ILLSSW SWILLS	IMMOSU OSMIUM
IINPTX PINXIT	ILLSTY STILLY	IMMSTU MUTISM, SUMMIT
IINSST INSIST, SIT-INS	ILLSUV VILLUS	IMNNOW MINNOW
IINSTU IN SITU, INUITS	ILMMSU MUSLIM	IMNOOR MORION
IINTTU INTUIT	ILMNOT MILTON	IMNOOT MOTION
IINTTW NITWIT	ILMNOU MOULIN	IMNORS MINORS
IIOSTT OTITIS	ILMNSU MUSLIN	IMNOST INMOST, MONIST
IIPPST PIPITS	ILMOSS LISSOM	IMNOSY MYOSIN, SIMONY
IIPRST SPIRIT	ILMOTW WILMOT	IMNTUY MUTINY
IIRSSU SIRIUS	ILMPPY PIMPLY	IMOPRS PORISM
IISSTV VISITS	ILMPRY PRIMLY	IMOPRT IMPORT
IJLSUU JULIUS	ILMPSY SIMPLY	IMOPST IMPOST
IJNORU JUNIOR	ILMRTY TRIMLY	IMORRR MIRROR
IJNOST JOINTS	ILMSTU LITMUS	IMORRS MORRIS
IJNRUY INJURY	ILMTUU TUMULI	IMOSTU OSTIUM
IJNSTU JUSTIN	ILNOOT LOTION	IMPRSS PRISMS
IJOSST JOISTS	ILNOPP POPLIN	IMPRSU PRIMUS, PURISM
IJRSTU JURIST	ILNOPS SLIP-ON	IMPSUX MIX-UPS
IKKKRU KIRKUK	ILNOPT PONTIL	IMQRSU SQUIRM
IKKOSS KIOSKS	ILNOQU QUINOL	IMRSTU TRUISM
IKKRSU KUKRIS	ILNOST TONSIL	IMSSSU MISSUS
IKKUUY KIKUYU	ILNOSY NOSILY	INNOOS ONIONS
IKLLSS SKILLS	ILNPRU PURLIN	INNOOT NOTION
IKLNOO LOOK-IN	ILNPST SPLINT	INNOPP NIPPON
IKLNPU LINKUP	ILNPSU LUPINS	INNOSU UNIONS, UNISON
IKLNSY SLINKY	ILNSTU INSULT, SUNLIT	INNOWW WINNOW
IKLNTY TINKLY	ILNSVY VINYLS	INNSSU SUNNIS
IKLOPY POKILY	ILOOYZ OOZILY	INOOPS POISON
IKLSSU SUSLIK	ILOPRX PROLIX	INOOPT OPTION, POTION
IKMNOO KIMONO	ILOPRY ROPILY	INOORS ORISON
IKMPSY SKIMPY	ILOPSS SPOILS	INOOTT IN TOTO
IKMRSS SMIRKS	ILOPST PILOTS, PISTOL,	INOPRS PRISON
IKMSSU KUMISS	POSTIL, SPOILT	INOPST PISTON, POINTS
IKNNOT TONKIN	ILOPTY POLITY	INOPTT TIN-POT
IKNNSY SKINNY	ILOQRU LIQUOR	INORRS NORRIS
IKNNTU UNKNIT	ILORSY ROSILY	INORST INTROS
IKNOPS PINKOS	ILPPRY RIPPLY	INORSY ROSINY

INORTT TRITON	KLLSSU SKULLS	LRUUXY LUXURY
INORTU TURION	KLNNUU KUNLUN	LSSTUY STYLUS
INOSTX TOXINS	KNOORR KRONOR	MMNOOR MORMON
INOSUV VINOUS	KNOTTY KNOTTY	MMNOSU SUMMON
INPPSU PINUPS	KNPSUY SPUNKY	MMOOPP POMPOM
INPPSY SNIPPY	KNRSTU TRUNKS	MMOOTT MOTMOT,
INPRST PRINTS, SPRINT	KOOPSS SPOOKS	TOM-TOM
INPRTU TURNIP	KOOPSY SPOOKY	MMRRUU MURMUR
INQSTU SQUINT	KOORVV KOVROV	MNOOPP POMPON
INQSUY QUINSY	KOOSTV VOSTOK	MNOORS MORONS
INRSXY SYRINX	KOOTWW KOWTOW	MNOORU UNMOOR
INRTWY WINTRY	KORSST STORKS	MNOOTU MOUTON
INSSTT STINTS	LLLOOP LOLLOP	MNOOTW MOTOWN
IOPPTT TIP-TOP	LLNOOR ROLL-ON	MNOSTU MOUNTS
IOPRRS PRIORS	LLNOPU PULL-ON	MNOTTU MUTTON
IOPRRY PRIORY	LLNORU UNROLL	MNSTTU MUSTN'T
IOPRST TRIPOS	LLOOWY WOOLLY	MOOPRS PROMOS
IOPSST PTOSIS	LLOPUX POLLUX	MOORRW MORROW
IOPSSY PYOSIS	LLORST STROLL, TROLLS	MOORST MOTORS
IOPSTV PIVOTS	LLOSWY SLOWLY	MOOSSU OSMOUS
IOQSTU QUOITS	LLOTUY TOLUYL	MOOSTT MOTTOS
IORSSV VISORS	LMMOUX LUMMOX	MOPPRT PROMPT
IORSTU SUITOR	LMMPUY PLUMMY	MOPSSU POSSUM
IOTTUW OUTWIT	LMMSUY SLUMMY	MOQRUU QUORUM
IPPPSU PUPPIS	LMOORU ORMOLU	MORRUU RUMOUR
IPPSSU PISS-UP	LMOSTU MOULTS	MORSST STORMS
IPPTUY UPPITY	LMOSTY MOSTLY	MORSTY STORMY
IPRRTU IRRUPT	LMPRUY RUMPLY	MORTUU TUMOUR
IPRSST STIRPS, STRIPS	LMPSSU SLUMPS	MOSTTU UTMOST
IPRSSY PRISSY	LMTTUU TUMULT	MPRSTU TRUMPS
IPRSTU PURIST	LNNOSY NYLONS	MPRSUU RUMPUS
IPRSTW TWIRPS	LNOOPY POLONY	MPSSTU STUMPS
IPRSTY STRIPY	LNOOST STOLON	MPSTUU SPUTUM
IPRTUY PURITY	LNOOTU TOULON	MPSTUY STUMPY
IPSSTU SIT-UPS	LNOPSY PYLONS	MSTTUY SMUTTY
IPSTTY TYPIST	LNOPTU PLUTON	NNOORT NORTON
IPTTTU TITTUP	LNORSY ROSLYN	NNOOWW NOW NOW!
IQRSTU SQUIRT	LNRUUY UNRULY	NNORTU TURN-ON
IRSSTW WRISTS	LOOPRY POORLY	NOOPRT PRONTO, PROTON
IRSTWY WRISTY	LOOPSS SLOOPS, SPOOLS	NOOPSS SNOOPS, SPOONS
ISSSTU SUSS IT, TUSSIS	LOOSST STOOLS	NOOPST SPOT-ON
ISSTTW TWISTS	LOOVVX VOLVOX	NOOPSY SNOOPY
ISTTWY TWISTY	LOPPRY PROPYL	NOOSSW SWOONS
JLNOOY JOLYON	LOPPSY POLYPS, SLOPPY	NOOSTY SNOOTY
JLSTUY JUSTLY	LOPRSW PROWLS	NOOSYZ SNOOZY
JNOORU JOURNO	LOPRTY PORTLY	NOPSTU PUT-ONS, UNSTOP
JNSTUU UNJUST	LOPTWY TWO-PLY	NOPTUW UPTOWN
JOOSUY JOYOUS	LORSUY SOURLY	NORSST SNORTS
JORRSU JURORS	LORTTY TROTYL	NORTUU OUTRUN
JOSSTU JUST SO	LPPSUY SUPPLY	NOSSTU SNOUTS
KKLMUU MUKLUK	LPRSYY SPRYLY	NOSTTY SNOTTY
KKNSSU SKUNKS	LRRSUY SLURRY	NPRSUU RUN-UPS
KLLNOS KNOLLS	LRSTUY SULTRY	NPRTUU TURN-UP, UPTURN

NRSTUU U-TURNS	OORRST ROTORS	ORTTUY TRY-OUT
NSSTTU STUNTS	OORRSW SORROW	PRRSUY SPURRY
OOOPRT OPORTO	OORSST ROOSTS, TORSOS	PRSSTU SPURTS
OOPPRT TROPPO	OORSTV ROSTOV	PRSUYY SYRUPY
OOPPVX VOX POP	OPRSST SPORTS, STROPS	RSSTTU STRUTS, TRUSTS
OOPRRT TORPOR	OPRSTU SPROUT, STUPOR	RSSTTY TRYSTS
OOPRSS SPOORS	OPRSTY SPORTY	RSTTUY TRUSTY
OOPRST TROOPS	OPSSTU SPOUTS, STOUPS,	TTTTUU TUT-TUT
OOPRSU POROUS	TOSS-UP	
OOPRTU UPROOT	OPSTTY SPOTTY	
OOPSSW SWOOPS	OPTTUU OUTPUT	
OOPWWW POWWOW	ORSTTU TROUTS, TUTORS	

AAAABLM ALABAMA
AAAADMW ADAMAWA
AAAALMT ALMA-ATA
AAAABBCL CABBALA
AAAABBMR BAMBARA
AAAABBRR BARBARA
AAAABCMR CARAMBA
AAAABCOR CARABAO
AAAABDFR ABFARAD
AAAABDGN BAGANDA
AAAABFIN FABIANA
AAAABFLL FALBALA
AAAABHMR ABRAHAM
AAAABHMS BAHAMAS
AAAABILN ALBANIA
AAAABILX ABAXIAL
AAAABINR ARABIAN
AAAABIPR PARAIBA
AAAABIRV BAVARIA
AAAABKLR KARBALA
AAAABLMR MALABAR
AAAABNNS BANANAS
AAAABNPR PAN-ARAB
AAAABORR ARAROBA
AAAABRSZ BAZAARS
AAAACCIS ACACIAS
AAAACCLM MALACCA
AAAACCLR CARACAL
AAAACCRS CARACAS,
   CASCARA
AAAACDIN ACADIAN
AAAACDIR ARCADIA
AAAACDLU ACAUDAL
AAAACDMM MACADAM
AAAACEHN ACHAEAN
AAAACENP PANACEA
AAAACHLZ CHALAZA
AAAACIJM JAMAICA
AAAACIMR ARAMAIC
AAAACINT CATANIA
AAAACJMR JACAMAR
AAAACJRU ARACAJU
AAAACLLV CAVALLA
AAAACLMN ALMANAC
AAAACLNT CANTALA,
   CATALAN
AAAACLPS ALPACAS
AAAACLPT CATALPA
AAAACLRZ ALCAZAR
AAAACMRS MARACAS,
   MARASCA, MASCARA
AAAACMRY MARACAY
AAAACNRV CARAVAN

AAAACNST CANASTA
AAAACNTT CANTATA
AAAACRWY CARAWAY
AAAACSST CASSATA
AAAACSSV CASSAVA
AAAADFRY FARADAY
AAAADGNR GRANADA
AAAADHMN HAMADAN
AAAADHWY HADAWAY
AAAADILX ADAXIAL
AAAADIMN ADAMINA
AAAADINR ADRIANA
AAAADKNN KANNADA
AAAADMNN ADAMNAN
AAAADMNR RAMADAN
AAAADMNT ADAMANT
AAAADMRS ARMADAS
AAAAEFLR RAFAELA
AAAAEGLT GALATEA
AAAAEGNP PANGAEA
AAAAEHLT ALTHAEA
AAAAEIMN ANAEMIA
AAAAENST ANATASE
AAAAERWY AREAWAY
AAAAFFLL ALFALFA
AAAAFIRT RATAFIA
AAAAFRSS AS FAR AS
AAAAFRWY FARAWAY
AAAAGHIP APHAGIA
AAAAGHPR AGRAPHA
AAAAGINR NIAGARA
AAAAGKNT KATANGA
AAAAGLMM AMALGAM
AAAAGLNS LASAGNA
AAAAGLOS ALAGOAS
AAAAGMNR ANAGRAM
AAAAGMNU MANAGUA
AAAAHHKL HALAKAH
AAAAHHLM MAHALAH
AAAAHHLV HALAVAH
AAAAHILM MAHALIA
AAAAHIPS APHASIA
AAAAHIRZ AZARIAH
AAAAHMMT MAHATMA
AAAAHMRT MARATHA
AAAAHNRS SAHARAN
AAAAHNRY HARYANA
AAAAHNST NATASHA
AAAAHOPR ARAPAHO
AAAAHPPR HARAPPA
AAAAILMR MALARIA
AAAAILNT NATALIA
AAAAILPS APLASIA

AAAAILPT PATIALA
AAAAIMNT AMANITA
AAAAINNR ARIANNA
AAAAINTT TATIANA
AAAAIPRX APRAXIA
AAAAIPSS ASPASIA
AAAAIQRU AQUARIA
AAAAJMPS PAJAMAS
AAAAKLMP KAMPALA
AAAAKLNS ALASKAN
AAAAKLSS KASSALA
AAAAKMOY OKAYAMA
AAAAKMRS MAKASAR
AAAAKRSW SARAWAK
AAAALLPT PALATAL
AAAALMNY MALAYAN
AAAALMRS MARSALA
AAAALMSS SALAAMS
AAAALMTY MALATYA
AAAALNNT LANTANA
AAAALNTT ATLANTA
AAAALRRY ARRAYAL
AAAAMNPS PANAMAS
AAAAMRTU TAMARAU
AAAANNRS SARANNA
AAAANNSV SAVANNA
AAAAPPSY PAPAYAS
AAAARRST TARRASA
AAAARSTV AVATARS
AAAARTTT RAT-A-TAT
AAAARTTU TUATARA
AABBCEG CABBAGE
AABBEMN MBABANE
AABBERT BARBATE
AABBGGR GRAB BAG
AABBHST SABBATH
AABBMRU RUM BABA
AABBNRT BRABANT
AABBNRY BARNABY
AABBRRY BARBARY
AABBSSU BABASSU
AABBSTY BABY-SAT
AABCCET BACCATE
AABCDIR CARABID
AABCEFR FACEBAR
AABCELN BALANCE
AABCELP CAPABLE
AABCELT ACTABLE
AABCEMR MACABRE
AABCERT ABREACT,
   CABARET
AABCFKT FATBACK
AABCHNR BARCHAN

AABCILM CAMBIAL
AABCIMR CAMBRAI
AABCIMS CABIMAS
AABCIOP COPAIBA
AABCITX TAXICAB
AABCKNR CAB RANK
AABCKRR BARRACK
AABCKSW BACKSAW
AABCLPY CAPABLY
AABCLRY BARCLAY
AABCORT ACROBAT
AABCOST TABASCO
AABCOTT CATBOAT
AABCRSS SCARABS
AABDDER ABRADED
AABDDGH BAGHDAD
AABDDHN DAB HAND
AABDEFL FADABLE
AABDEGN BANDAGE
AABDEHS ABASHED
AABDEIS DIABASE
AABDELL BALLADE
AABDELR ALBREDA
AABDELT DATABLE
AABDELW WADABLE
AABDENU BANDEAU
AABDERR ABRADER
AABDFYZ FYZABAD
AABDGHN HANDBAG
AABDGLY BAG LADY
AABDGMO GAMBADO
AABDGNS SANDBAG
AABDGNU BUGANDA
AABDHIO OBADIAH
AABDHNT HATBAND
AABDIJN ABIDJAN
AABDIMR BARMAID
AABDINT TABANID
AABDIOT BIODATA
AABDJOZ BADAJOZ
AABDLLS BALLADS
AABDLRW BRADAWL
AABDMNR ARMBAND
AABDNNO ABANDON
AABDNNR BRANDAN
AABDNRR BARNARD
AABDNRS SANDBAR
AABDORV BRAVADO
AABDRRW DRAWBAR
AABDRST BASTARD
AABDSTU DATA BUS
AABEELT EATABLE
AABEEMO AMOEBAE

AABEFFL AFFABLE
AABEFGL FLEABAG
AABEGGG BAGGAGE
AABEGGR GARBAGE
AABEGLR ALGEBRA
AABEGRR BARRAGE
AABEGSS BAGASSE
AABEGST TEABAGS
AABEIKN IKEBANA
AABEILM AMIABLE
AABEILT LABIATE
AABEIRS AIRBASE
AABEKLT TAKABLE
AABELLM MABELLA
AABELLN BALNEAL
AABELLS SALABLE
AABELMN NAMABLE
AABELMT TAMABLE
AABELNN ANNABEL
AABELNO ABALONE
AABELPR PARABLE
AABELPY PAYABLE
AABELRT ALBERTA,
   RATABLE
AABELSV SAVABLE
AABELTU TABLEAU
AABELTX TAXABLE
AABEMOS AMOEBAS
AABEMST MASBATE
AABENTY ABEYANT
AABERST ABREAST
AABFFLY AFFABLY
AABFINS FABIANS
AABGGRS RAGBAGS
AABGGSS GASBAGS
AABGIIL ABIGAIL
AABGILM MAILBAG
AABGIMN GAMBIAN
AABGINR BARGAIN
AABGINS ABASING
AABGINT ABATING
AABGLOR AALBORG
AABGRST RATBAGS
AABHIMS BAHAISM
AABHINR BAHRAIN
AABHIST BAHAIST
AABHITT HABITAT, TABITHA
AABHKRU BUKHARA
AABHLTY BATHYAL
AABHMNR BRAHMAN
AABHMTT BATH MAT
AABHSUU BAUHAUS
AABIILN ALBINIA

AABIILS BASILIA
AABIILX BIAXIAL
AABIIMN NAMIBIA
AABIKNS BANKSIA
AABILLR BARILLA
AABILLS BASILLA, LABIALS
AABILMY AMIABLY
AABILRS BASILAR
AABIMMR MARIMBA
AABIMNZ ZAMBIAN
AABINOU OUABAIN
AABINRS SABRINA
AABINST ABSTAIN, BASTIAN
AABINSW SWABIAN
AABIRST ARABIST
AABIRSV BRAVAIS
AABKNRT TANBARK
AABKOOZ BAZOOKA
AABLLST BALLAST
AABLLWY WALLABY
AABLMOS ABSALOM
AABLMSS BALSAMS
AABLMSY ABYSMAL
AABLNOT BALATON
AABLNRU BARNAUL
AABLNTT BLATANT
AABLORT ABLATOR
AABLOTW AT A BLOW
AABLRTU TABULAR
AABLRTY RATABLY
AABLSSY ABYSSAL
AABLTTU ABUTTAL
AABMMOS MOMBASA
AABMNOT BOATMAN
AABMNOY AMBOYNA,
   BAYAMON
AABMNST BANTAMS,
   BATSMAN
AABMORU MARABOU
AABNNOZ BONANZA
AABNNSY BANYANS
AABORRS RASBORA
AABQSUU SUB-AQUA
AABRRUV BRAVURA
AABSSSY SASSABY
AABSTUX SAXTUBA
AACCDEN CANDACE
AACCDES CASCADE
AACCDIR CARDIAC
AACCDIS CICADAS
AACCDOR CARADOC
AACCEST SACCATE
AACCHHS CHA-CHAS

AACCHIR ARCHAIC
AACCHMP CHAMPAC
AACCIJO AJACCIO
AACCILM ACCLAIM
AACCILU ACICULA
AACCIOR CARIOCA
AACCITT ATACTIC
AACCLLO CLOACAL
AACCLLT CATCALL
AACCLRU ACCRUAL,
   CARACUL
AACCNNS CANCANS
AACCNVY VACANCY
AACCORU CURACAO
AACCOTT TOCCATA
AACCRSS CARCASS
AACDDEL DECADAL
AACDDIN CANDIDA
AACDEFS FACADES
AACDEHL CHALDEA
AACDEHR CHARADE
AACDEHT CATHEAD
AACDELN CANDELA,
   DECANAL
AACDELR CALDERA
AACDEMY ACADEMY
AACDENV ADVANCE
AACDENZ CADENZA
AACDERS ARCADES
AACDERV CADAVER
AACDERY DAY-CARE
AACDETU CAUDATE
AACDETV VACATED
AACDFIR FARADIC
AACDGOR CARADOG
AACDHMR DRACHMA
AACDIJU JUDAICA
AACDILR RADICAL
AACDILU CLAUDIA
AACDINT ANTACID
AACDINV VANADIC
AACDIOR ACAROID
AACDIRR RICARDA
AACDIRS ASCARID
AACDJKW JACKDAW
AACDLNO ACNODAL
AACDLNS SCANDAL
AACDLPR PLACARD
AACDNRS CANARDS
AACDOOV AVOCADO
AACDRSZ CZARDAS
AACEEGR ACREAGE
AACEEHR EARACHE

AACEEKT TEACAKE
AACEEPT AT PEACE
AACEERT ACERATE
AACEESS CASEASE
AACEEST CASEATE
AACEETT ACETATE
AACEFLT FALCATE
AACEFRR CARFARE
AACEFRS CARAFES
AACEGKP PACKAGE
AACEGNR CARNAGE
AACEGRT CARTAGE
AACEHLR RACHAEL
AACEHNP PANACHE
AACEHPU CHAPEAU
AACEHRT TRACHEA
AACEHTT ATTACHÉ
AACEHTU CHÂTEAU
AACEHWY EACH WAY
AACEIMN ANAEMIC
AACEIMR AMERICA
AACEINO OCEANIA
AACEIPP CAP-A-PIE
AACEIRV AVARICE
AACEKNP PANCAKE
AACEKNS ASKANCE
AACEKOT OATCAKE
AACELLN CANELLA
AACELLP CAPELLA,
   LAPLACE
AACELLT LACTEAL
AACELLW WALLACE
AACELMN MANACLE
AACELMR CAMERAL,
   CARAMEL, CARMELA
AACELNU LACUNAE
AACELNV VALANCE
AACELPR CARPALE
AACELPS PALACES,
   PASCALE
AACELPT PLACATE
AACELRV CARAVEL
AACELST LACTASE
AACELTT LACTATE
AACELTV CLAVATE
AACEMMR MACRAMÉ
AACEMNV CAVEMAN
AACEMQU MACAQUE
AACEMRS CAMERAS
AACENPS CANAPÉS
AACENRS SARACEN
AACENTY CYANATE
AACEPRS PESCARA

AACEPRT RATE-CAP
AACERRT RAT RACE
AACERST CASERTA,
   CAT'S-EAR
AACERSU CAESURA
AACERTU ARCUATE
AACESTV CAVEATS
AACETTU ACTUATE
AACFILS FACIALS, FASCIAL
AACFINR AFRICAN
AACFINT FANATIC
AACFISS FASCIAS
AACFLLY FALLACY
AACFLRU FACULAR
AACFLTU FACTUAL
AACFNST CAFTANS
AACFSTT FAT CATS
AACGIIL GALICIA
AACGILL GLACIAL
AACGILM MAGICAL
AACGLOS COAL GAS
AACGLRY CALGARY
AACGNOU GUANACO
AACHHKR CHARKHA
AACHHLL CHALLAH
AACHIKL HALAKIC
AACHIKR KARACHI
AACHILM MALACHI
AACHILR RACHIAL
AACHIMN MAHICAN
AACHIMR AMHARIC
AACHIMS CHIASMA
AACHINS SANCHIA
AACHINT ITHACAN
AACHIPS CHIAPAS
AACHIRT CITHARA
AACHKRY HAYRACK
AACHKSW HACKSAW
AACHLLN LACHLAN
AACHLMS CHASMAL
AACHLMY MALACHY
AACHLPP CHAPPAL
AACHLPS PASCHAL
AACHNOP PANOCHA
AACHNPX PANCHAX
AACHNRY ANARCHY
AACHNSU ANCHUSA
AACHRRT CATARRH
AACHRWY ARCHWAY
AACHRYZ ZACHARY
AACIINT ACTINIA
AACIIST ASIATIC
AACIJLP JALAPIC

AACIJNT JACINTA
AACIKLL ALKALIC
AACIKLR CLARKIA
AACILLM CAMILLA
AACILLS CALLAIS
AACILNR ACRILAN,
  CRANIAL
AACILNT ACTINAL
AACILNU LUCIANA
AACILOS ASOCIAL
AACILOX COAXIAL
AACILPT CAPITAL
AACIMNS MANIACS
AACINOR OCARINA
AACINPS CASPIAN
AACINPT CAPTAIN
AACINRZ CZARINA
AACINST SATANIC
AACINTV VATICAN
AACIOPT TAPIOCA
AACIORT CROATIA
AACIORV CRAIOVA
AACIOTV OCTAVIA
AACIPRX APRAXIC
AACIQTU AQUATIC
AACISTT ASTATIC
AACJKLS JACKALS
AACJKMN MAN JACK
AACJKRT JACK TAR
AACJKSS JACKASS
AACJMOR MAJORCA
AACJOST JOCASTA
AACKLTW CATWALK
AACKNRS RANSACK
AACKPRR CAR PARK
AACKSTT ATTACKS
AACLLNT CALLANT
AACLLSU CLAUSAL
AACLMNT CLAMANT
AACLMRU MACULAR
AACLMSU CALAMUS
AACLNNO ANCONAL
AACLNNU CANNULA
AACLNPY CLAYPAN
AACLNRU LACUNAR
AACLNSU LACUNAS
AACLOPR CAPORAL
AACLORT COAL TAR
AACLOST COASTAL
AACLOTT CATTALO
AACLPSU SCAPULA
AACLPTY PLAY-ACT

AACLRSS RASCALS,
  SCALARS
AACLRVY CALVARY,
  CAVALRY
AACLSTU LUCASTA
AACLSUX LASCAUX
AACLTTU TACTUAL
AACMNNO MONACAN
AACMNRU ARCANUM
AACMNTX MANX CAT
AACMORS SARCOMA
AACMRRT TRAMCAR
AACMRSS SARCASM
AACMRST TARMACS
AACNNOZ CANZONA
AACNOST SACATON
AACNPST CAPSTAN,
  CATNAPS
AACNSSV CANVASS
AACNTUY YUCATAN
AACOPPR APOCARP
AACPSTW CAT'S PAW
AACRSTV CRAVATS
AACRTTT ATTRACT
AACRTUY ACTUARY
AACTUWY CUTAWAY
AADDDEN ADDENDA
AADDEFI DEAF-AID
AADDEGM DAMAGED
AADDEIL ALIDADE
AADDELR ALDREDA
AADDENP DEADPAN
AADDEPR PARADED
AADDEPT ADAPTED
AADDERW AWARDED
AADDGNR GRANDAD
AADDHKR KHADDAR
AADDIMS DADAISM
AADDIST DADAIST
AADDLNO DONALDA
AADDNVV DVANDVA
AADEELT DEALATE
AADEERT AERATED
AADEERW AWARDEE
AADEFHO AHEAD OF
AADEFHT FATHEAD
AADEFLR ALFREDA
AADEGGR AGGRADE,
  GARAGED
AADEGHO GO-AHEAD
AADEGMN MANAGED
AADEGMR DAMAGER
AADEGMS DAMAGES

AADEGNS AGENDAS
AADEGRT GRADATE
AADEGRV RAVAGED
AADEGRY YARDAGE
AADEGSV SAVAGED
AADEHLN HALDANE
AADEHMN HEADMAN
AADEHMS ASHAMED
AADEHRW WARHEAD
AADEHWY HEADWAY
AADEILN ADELINA
AADEILV AVAILED, VEDALIA
AADEIMR MADEIRA
AADEINR ARANEID,
  ARIADNE
AADEINS NAIADES
AADEINZ IN A DAZE
AADEIRT RADIATE
AADEITW AWAITED
AADEJNU JUDAEAN
AADELLY ALLAYED
AADELMO À LA MODE
AADELMR ALARMED
AADELNR ADRENAL
AADELRW RAW DEAL
AADELRY ALREADY
AADELTU ADULATE
AADEMMN MAN-MADE
AADEMNO ADENOMA
AADEMNS MAENADS
AADEMNT MANDATE
AADEMNY NAME DAY
AADEMSS AMASSED
AADENNT ANDANTE
AADENRS ANDREAS
AADENRV VERANDA
AADEPRR PARADER
AADEPRS PARADES
AADEPRT ADAPTER
AADEPSS PASSADE
AADERRW AWARDER
AADERRY ARRAYED
AADERSY DARESAY
AADESSY ASSAYED
AADFGLY FLAG DAY
AADGGHR HAGGARD
AADGGLR LAGGARD
AADGIMM DIGAMMA
AADGIMR DIAGRAM
AADGIOS ADAGIOS
AADGIPR PADRAIG
AADGLLW GADWALL
AADGLNO GONADAL

AADGLNR GARLAND	AADLNSS SANDALS	AAEFRRW WARFARE
AADGLNT LANDTAG	AADLNSU LANDAUS	AAEFRST FAR EAST
AADGLNU LUGANDA	AADLNSV VANDALS	AAEGGNO ANAGOGE
AADGLRU GRADUAL	AADLOPY PAYLOAD	AAEGGOP APAGOGE
AADGMNR GRANDMA	AADLPPU APPLAUD	AAEGGRS GARAGES
AADGNNU UGANDAN	AADLRRU RADULAR	AAEGHLU HAULAGE
AADGNPR GRANDPA	AADMNNO MADONNA	AAEGHMR GRAHAME
AADGOPR PODAGRA	AADMNOR MADRONA,	AAEGILR ALGERIA,
AADGOPS PAGODAS	MONARDA, ROADMAN	REGALIA
AADHHMS MASHHAD	AADMNRS MANSARD	AAEGISS ASSEGAI
AADHHNR DHAHRAN	AADMNRY MAYNARD	AAEGITT AGITATE
AADHILS DAHLIAS	AADMORT MATADOR	AAEGKNT TANKAGE
AADHINP DAPHNIA	AADMRRY YARDARM	AAEGKOS SOAKAGE
AADHINR HADRIAN	AADMRZZ MAZZARD	AAEGLLR ALLEGRA
AADHLRY HALYARD	AADMSYY MAY DAYS	AAEGLLT TALLAGE
AADHMNO DAHOMAN	AADNOPR PANDORA	AAEGLMN GAMELAN
AADHNPR HARDPAN	AADNORR ANDORRA	AAEGLMT GAMETAL
AADHNRS HANSARD	AADNRVW VANWARD	AAEGLNS LASAGNE
AADHNSW HANDSAW	AADNSTW WANT ADS	AAEGLRR REALGAR
AADHOSS SODA ASH	AADOPRX PARADOX	AAEGLSV SALVAGE
AADHRRV HARVARD	AADORTX ROAD TAX	AAEGMNR MANAGER
AADHRSZ HAZARDS	AADORWY ROADWAY	AAEGMNT MAGENTA,
AADHRWY HAYWARD	AADQRTU QUADRAT	MAGNATE
AADHSWY WASHDAY	AADRWWY WAYWARD	AAEGMPR RAMPAGE
AADIINN INDIANA	AAEEFGL LEAFAGE	AAEGMRW WAR GAME
AADIINO DIANOIA	AAEEFLT TEALEAF	AAEGMSS MASSAGE
AADIINV DAVINIA	AAEEGKL LEAKAGE	AAEGNNT TANNAGE
AADIIRR AIR RAID	AAEEGLT GALEATE	AAEGNPT PAGEANT
AADIISV ADIVASI	AAEEGMT AGAMETE	AAEGNPW PAWNAGE
AADILMR ADMIRAL	AAEEGNO NEOGAEA	AAEGNRR ARRANGE
AADILMT MATILDA	AAEEGRV AVERAGE	AAEGNRT TANAGER
AADILNP PALADIN	AAEEHLT ALETHEA	AAEGNSU GUANASE
AADILPS APSIDAL	AAEEHRT HETAERA	AAEGNTV VANTAGE
AADILRS RADIALS	AAEELLP PALE ALE	AAEGPRW WARPAGE
AADILTV DATIVAL	AAEELMT MALEATE	AAEGPSS PASSAGE
AADILWY WAYLAID	AAEELNS SEA-LANE	AAEGQUY QUAYAGE
AADIMNR MIRANDA	AAEELRZ ELEAZAR	AAEGRRV RAVAGER
AADIMOR DIORAMA	AAEEMNT EMANATE,	AAEGRST TEAR GAS
AADIMRS DAMARIS	MANATEE	AAEGRSV RAVAGES
AADIMRU MADURAI	AAEEPPS APPEASE	AAEGRTT REGATTA
AADINRT RADIANT	AAEERSW SEAWARE	AAEGSSU ASSUAGE,
AADIORS ISADORA	AAEERTU AUREATE	SAUSAGE
AADKLNO OAKLAND	AAEERTX EXARATE	AAEGSSV SAVAGES
AADKNOT DAKOTAN	AAEFFGR AGRAFFE	AAEGSTW WASTAGE
AADKNRT TANKARD	AAEFFIR AFFAIRE	AAEGTTW WATTAGE
AADKRWW AWKWARD	AAEFFNR FANFARE	AAEGTUX GÂTEAUX
AADLLMR MALLARD	AAEFFTT TAFFETA	AAEGTWY GATEWAY,
AADLLMS SMALL AD	AAEFGLN FALANGE	GETAWAY
AADLLNP LAPLAND	AAEFGTW WAFTAGE	AAEHHIL HIALEAH
AADLLNR RANDALL	AAEFLPR EARFLAP	AAEHHLM MEHALAH
AADLNOR RONALDA	AAEFMRT FERMATA	AAEHILM MEHALIA
AADLNOY YOLANDA	AAEFNST SANTA FE	AAEHIMN ANAHEIM
AADLNRY LANYARD	AAEFRRR FERRARA	AAEHIRT HETAIRA

AAEHKLN ELKANAH
AAEHKMY MAKE HAY
AAEHKNT KHANATE
AAEHLLL ALLHEAL
AAEHLPR RAPHAEL
AAEHLPX HEXAPLA
AAEHLRT TREHALA
AAEHNPR HANAPER
AAEHNPS SAPHENA
AAEHNSY HYAENAS
AAEHRSY HEARSAY
AAEHSTT HASTATE
AAEIKLS AS ALIKE
AAEIKMT TAKE AIM
AAEILLU EULALIA
AAEILMN MELANIA
AAEILMP PAMELIA
AAEILMR ALMERIA
AAEILMS MALAISE
AAEILNN ALANINE
AAEILNR AIRLANE,
　LARAINE
AAEILNT NATALIE
AAEILOT AETOLIA
AAEILRS AERIALS
AAEILRU AURELIA
AAEILRV VALERIA
AAEILSS ALIASES
AAEIMMT IMAMATE
AAEIMNR ARMENIA
AAEIMNS AMNESIA
AAEIMNT AMENTIA,
　ANIMATE
AAEIMPY PYAEMIA
AAEIMRU URAEMIA
AAEINNO AEONIAN
AAEINST ENTASIA
AAEIPRR PAREIRA
AAEIPRS SPIRAEA
AAEIPTT APATITE
AAEIRSU EURASIA
AAEIRTT ARIETTA
AAEIRTV VARIATE
AAEISTT SATIATE
AAEJNTT JANETTA
AAEKKRY KAYAKER
AAEKLNT ALKANET
AAEKMRR EARMARK
AAEKMRS SEAMARK
AAEKMWY MAKE WAY
AAEKPRT PARTAKE
AAEKSTT AT STAKE
AAELLLM LAMELLA

AAELLPT PATELLA
AAELLRS ALL EARS
AAELLRT LATERAL
AAELLSV SAVE-ALL
AAELLSW SEAWALL
AAELMNS ANSELMA
AAELMNU ALUMNAE,
　MANUELA
AAELMOT OATMEAL
AAELMPT PALMATE
AAELMST MALTASE
AAELMSY AMYLASE
AAELNNP ANNAPLE
AAELNRS ARSENAL
AAELNST SEALANT
AAELNSY ANALYSE
AAELORR AREOLAR
AAELORU AUREOLA
AAELOTX OXALATE
AAELPPR APPAREL
AAELPPS APPEALS
AAELPPT PALPATE
AAELPRT APTERAL
AAELPRV PALAVER
AAELPST PALATES
AAELPTT TAPETAL
AAELPTU PLATEAU
AAELPTY APETALY
AAELRTT ARLETTA
AAELSST ATLASES
AAELSUX ASEXUAL
AAELTVV VALVATE
AAEMMMR MAREMMA
AAEMNPP PAMPEAN
AAEMRSS AMASSER
AAEMRST ARTEMAS
AAEMRTU AMATEUR
AAENNNT ANTENNA
AAENNRV RAVENNA
AAENNST ANNATES
AAENNTT TANNATE
AAENPST ANAPEST,
　PEASANT
AAENPSV PAVANES
AAENRRT NARRATE
AAENRRV NAVARRE
AAENRTU TAUREAN
AAENRUW UNAWARE
AAENSSV VANESSA
AAENSSW SWANSEA
AAENSTV AVESTAN
AAEORRT AERATOR
AAEORRU AURORAE

AAEPPRT PARAPET
AAERRRS ARREARS
AAERSSY ASSAYER
AAESSWY SEAWAYS
AAFFINS SAFFIAN
AAFFIRS AFFAIRS
AAFFRSY AFFRAYS
AAFGHNS AFGHANS
AAFGLMN FLAGMAN
AAFGORR FARRAGO
AAFHILX HALIFAX
AAFHINS ISFAHAN
AAFHLMO HALF A MO
AAFHLWY HALFWAY
AAFHNST FATSHAN
AAFIILR FILARIA
AAFILNT FANTAIL
AAFIMRY MAYFAIR
AAFINNT INFANTA
AAFIPRT PARFAIT
AAFIRSS SAFARIS
AAFIRWY FAIRWAY
AAFKNST KAFTANS
AAFLLTY FATALLY
AAFLWYY FLYAWAY
AAFNSTT FANTAST
AAFNSTY FANTASY
AAFPSUX FAUX PAS
AAGGIUZ GAGAUZI
AAGGIZZ ZAGAZIG
AAGGNWY GANGWAY
AAGHILR ALIGARH
AAGHITU GAUHATI
AAGHKRS KASHGAR
AAGHMNN HANGMAN
AAGHNNY HANYANG
AAGHNRS HANGARS
AAGHNUV VAUGHAN
AAGIINO GOIANIA
AAGIINT NIIGATA
AAGIKNW AWAKING
AAGILMY MYALGIA
AAGILNN ANGINAL,
　ANGLIAN
AAGILNP PAGINAL
AAGILNV VAGINAL
AAGILTW WAGTAIL
AAGIMNO ANGIOMA
AAGIMNS SIAMANG
AAGIMNZ AMAZING
AAGINRR ARRAIGN
AAGINRS SANGRIA
AAGINRU GUARANI

AAGINST AGAINST	AAHLNPX PHALANX	AAILNOT LAOTIAN
AAGINSU IGUANAS	AAHLNRW NARWHAL	AAILNOV VALONIA
AAGINSV VAGINAS	AAHLNTU NAHUATL	AAILNPT PLATINA
AAGINSY GAINSAY	AAHLPRS PHRASAL	AAILNRU LAURINA
AAGINTU ANTIGUA	AAHLPST ASPHALT	AAILNRY LANIARY
AAGIOTT AGITATO	AAHMNNU HANUMAN	AAILNSV SILVANA
AAGJRSU JAGUARS	AAHMNSS SHAMANS	AAILNTV LATVIAN, VALIANT
AAGJRTU GUJARAT	AAHMOPR AMPHORA	AAILNWY WAYLAIN
AAGKMSS GAS MASK	AAHMRTU MATHURA	AAILORS ROSALIA,
AAGKNRS ANGARSK	AAHNNOS HOSANNA	SOLARIA
AAGLLNT GALLANT	AAHNPST PATHANS	AAILORV VARIOLA
AAGLNNO ANGOLAN	AAHNRTX ANTHRAX	AAILOSY ALOYSIA
AAGLNOR GRANOLA	AAHNRTY RHATANY	AAILPRT PARTIAL, PATRIAL
AAGLNOY ANALOGY	AAHPRTW WARPATH	AAILPST SPATIAL
AAGLNRU ANGULAR	AAHPTWY PATHWAY	AAILRRV ARRIVAL
AAGLRUU AUGURAL	AAHRSTY ASHTRAY	AAILRSS LARISSA
AAGMMRR GRAMMAR	AAHRTTW ATHWART	AAILRST LARIATS
AAGMNOR ROMAGNA	AAIILMR AIRMAIL	AAILRTV TRAVAIL
AAGMNRT TANGRAM	AAIILNT ITALIAN	AAILRWY RAILWAY
AAGMOPY APOGAMY	AAIILNV LAVINIA	AAILSSW WASSAIL
AAGMRUX MARGAUX	AAIILOS ALOISIA	AAILSTU LUSATIA
AAGNOPR PARAGON	AAIILPT TILAPIA	AAIMMNO AMMONIA
AAGNORS ANGORAS	AAIINNR IRANIAN	AAIMMSS MIASMAS
AAGNORZ ORGANZA	AAIINTT TITANIA	AAIMNOS ANOSMIA
AAGNRRY GRANARY	AAIINVV VIVIANA	AAIMNOT ANIMATO
AAGNRTV VAGRANT	AAIJLNU JULIANA	AAIMNRS MARINAS
AAGOPSS SAPSAGO	AAIJNTU JUANITA	AAIMNRT MARTIAN,
AAGORSU SAGUARO	AAIKLLS ALKALIS	MARTINA, TAMARIN
AAGSTUU AUGUSTA	AAIKMNN MANAKIN	AAIMNRU RUMANIA
AAHHKKL KHALKHA	AAIKNNT KANTIAN	AAIMNRX MARXIAN
AAHHNPT NAPHTHA	AAIKNOW OKINAWA	AAIMNST STAMINA
AAHHOPR PHARAOH	AAIKNRT KATRINA	AAIMORV MORAVIA
AAHIINT HAITIAN	AAIKPPR PAPRIKA	AAIMRSS MARISSA
AAHIJNR HARIJAN	AAILLMM MAMILLA	AAIMRSU MASURIA,
AAHIKRU HAURAKI	AAILLMX MAXILLA	SAMURAI
AAHILTT TALITHA	AAILLNV VANILLA	AAIMSTV ATAVISM
AAHIMNO MAHONIA	AAILLPP PAPILLA	AAINNOT ANTONIA
AAHIMRT MARATHI	AAILLUV ALLUVIA	AAINNRU URANIAN
AAHINNU HUAI-NAN	AAILMMN MAILMAN	AAINNRV NIRVANA
AAHINOP APHONIA	AAILMMS LAMAISM,	AAINORV OVARIAN
AAHINOR HONIARA	MIASMAL	AAINORZ ARIZONA
AAHINPR PIRANHA	AAILMMX MAXIMAL	AAINRST ARTISAN,
AAHINST ASHANTI	AAILMNR LAMINAR	TSARINA
AAHIORT HORATIA	AAILMNS ANIMALS	AAINRSU SAURIAN
AAHIPRS PARIAHS	AAILMNV MALVINA	AAINRTV VARIANT
AAHIPTY HYPATIA	AAILMOS SOMALIA	AAINRTY NAYARIT
AAHJNNO JOHANNA	AAILMPR PALMIRA	AAINRTZ TZARINA
AAHKKSS KHAKASS	AAILMPS IMPALAS	AAINSVY VISAYAN
AAHKMSY YASHMAK	AAILMRT MARITAL,	AAINTTT ATTAINT
AAHLLSW WALLAHS	MARTIAL	AAINTUY TAIYUAN
AAHLLWY HALLWAY	AAILMST LAMAIST	AAIOPRR PAIR-OAR
AAHLMRS MARSHAL	AAILNOP PIANOLA	AAIORTV AVIATOR
AAHLMRU HAMULAR	AAILNOS SINALOA	AAIPPTT PIT-A-PAT

AAIPRSU AU PAIRS
AAIPRTT PARTITA
AAIPSZZ PIAZZAS
AAIQSSU QUASSIA
AAIQTUV AQUAVIT
AAIRSSS SASSARI
AAIRSSY ASSYRIA
AAIRSTU AUSTRIA
AAIRSWY AIRWAYS
AAISTTV ATAVIST
AAITWXY TAXIWAY
AAJKLWY JAYWALK
AAJMPSY PYJAMAS
AAJNNSU SAN JUAN
AAJNRUY JANUARY
AAKKLRU KARAKUL
AAKLMNW WALKMAN
AAKMNUU MANUKAU
AAKMRUZ MAZURKA
AAKNNTU NUNATAK
AAKNORS ANORAKS
AAKNOSU ANOUSKA
AAKNRSS SARANSK
AAKPRWY PARKWAY
AAKRTUY AUTARKY
AALLLNS LALLANS
AALLMPU AMPULLA
AALLNPU PLANULA
AALLNSY NASALLY
AALLRST ALL-STAR
AALLRUY AURALLY
AALMMMS MAMMALS
AALMMNO AMMONAL
AALMNOS SALAMON
AALMNOY ANOMALY
AALMNSU MANUALS
AALMORY MAYORAL
AALMPRY PALMYRA
AALNNRU ANNULAR
AALNNSU ANNUALS
AALNORS ALSO-RAN
AALNPRT PLANTAR
AALNPST SALTPAN
AALNQTU QUANTAL
AALNRTU NATURAL
AALNSTT SALTANT
AALNSTU SULTANA
AALNSTY ANALYST
AALOPRS PARASOL
AALOPTV POLTAVA
AALORRU AURORAL
AALORSU AROUSAL
AALOSVW AVOWALS

AALPPSU UPPSALA
AALPSTU SPATULA
AALRSTT STRATAL
AALRSTU AUSTRAL
AALRSTY ASTYLAR
AALRSUZ LAZARUS
AALSSSV VASSALS
AALSSTU ASSAULT
AAMMMRY MAMMARY
AAMMNNX MANXMAN
AAMNNOT MONTANA
AAMNORS OARSMAN
AAMNOSZ AMAZONS
AAMNOTY ANATOMY
AAMNPRT RAMPANT
AAMNPSS SAMPANS
AAMNPTY TYMPANA
AAMORSV SAMOVAR
AAMORTY AMATORY
AAMOSSS SAMOSAS
AAMOTTU AUTOMAT
AAMPRRT RAMPART
AAMRSTU SUMATRA,
    TRAUMAS
AAMRTWY TRAMWAY
AAMSSTU SATSUMA
AANNORS ROSANNA
AANNORX ROXANNA
AANNOTT ANNATTO
AANNRUU NAURUAN
AANNSSU SUSANNA
AANNSUZ SUZANNA
AANORTT TARANTO
AANOSST SONATAS
AANPRST SPARTAN
AANPRUU URUAPAN
AANPSST PASSANT
AANQRTU QUARTAN
AANRRTW WARRANT
AANRSTT TARTANS
AANRUWY RUNAWAY
AANSSTV SAVANTS
AANSSTZ STANZAS
AANSTTT STATANT
AAOPRRT PRO RATA
AAOQSSU OQUASSA
AAORRSU AURORAS
AAORSTV OSTRAVA,
    SARATOV
AAOTTUY TATOUAY
AAPPSWW PAWPAWS
AAPRRTT RAT TRAP
AAQRSSU QUASARS

AARRSTT TARTARS
AARSSTT STRATAS
ABBBDEL BABBLED,
    BLABBED
ABBBELR BABBLER,
    BLABBER
ABBBITT BABBITT
ABBCDER CRABBED
ABBCEIS CABBIES
ABBCELS SCABBLE
ABBCRYY CRYBABY
ABBDDEL DABBLED
ABBDDET BAD DEBT
ABBDEGL GABBLED
ABBDEGR GRABBED
ABBDELR DABBLER,
    DRABBLE
ABBDERR DRABBER
ABBDEST STABBED
ABBDESW SWABBED
ABBDGIN DABBING
ABBDINR RIBBAND
ABBDMOR BOMBARD
ABBDNOX BANDBOX
ABBEETT BABETTE
ABBEGLR GABBLER,
    GRABBLE
ABBEGNU BUGBANE
ABBEGRR GRABBER
ABBEGRU BUGBEAR
ABBEHMO HOBBEMA
ABBEIST TABBIES
ABBELLR BARBELL
ABBELMR BRAMBLE
ABBELRR RABBLER
ABBELRS RABBLES
ABBELRU BARBULE
ABBELSU BAUBLES
ABBERRS BARBERS
ABBERST STABBER
ABBERSW SWABBER
ABBESSU SUBBASE
ABBGGIN GABBING
ABBGIJN JABBING
ABBGINN NABBING
ABBGINT TABBING
ABBGINY BABYING
ABBGOOU BUGABOO
ABBHISY BABYISH
ABBHRRU RHUBARB
ABBHTTU BATHTUB
ABBILOT BOBTAIL
ABBIMNO BAMBINO

ABBIRST RABBITS	ABCEIOR AEROBIC	ABCINOR NICOBAR
ABBISTY BABY-SIT	ABCEIRS ASCRIBE	ABCIORU CARIBOU
ABBKLOU BLAUBOK	ABCEISS ABSCISE, SCABIES	ABCIOUV BIVOUAC
ABBMOOS BAMBOOS	ABCEKLN BLACKEN	ABCKLLY BLACKLY
ABBMOST BOMBAST	ABCEKLR BLACKER	ABCKMRU BUCKRAM
ABBMOTU BUMBOAT	ABCEKNR BRACKEN	ABCKNNO BANNOCK
ABBNOOS BABOONS	ABCEKRS BACKERS	ABCKOTU OUTBACK
ABBOSTY BOBSTAY	ABCEKRT BRACKET	ABCKPSU BACKUPS
ABBQSUY SQUABBY	ABCEKST SETBACK	ABCKSUW BUCKSAW
ABBSSSU SUBBASS	ABCELLU BULLACE	ABCLLOX CALL BOX
ABCCEER REBECCA	ABCELMO CEMBALO	ABCLLOY CALLBOY
ABCCEIR ACERBIC,	ABCELMR CLAMBER	ABCLMNU CLUBMAN
BRECCIA	ABCELOP PLACEBO	ABCLMOU COLUMBA
ABCCILU CUBICAL	ABCELOV VOCABLE	ABCLMSY CYMBALS
ABCCIMR CAMBRIC	ABCELRU CURABLE	ABCLMUU BACULUM
ABCCIOR BORACIC	ABCELRY CYBALER	ABCLNOY BALCONY
ABCCKTU CUTBACK	ABCELSU BASCULE	ABCLRUY CURABLY
ABCCOOT TOBACCO	ABCEMRS CAMBERS	ABCMNRW CWMBRAN
ABCDEEH BEACHED	ABCENOS BEACONS	ABCMOST COMBATS
ABCDEEL DÉBÂCLE	ABCENOW COWBANE	ABCNORS CARBONS
ABCDEHU DEBAUCH	ABCENOZ CABEZON	ABCORRW CROWBAR
ABCDEIK DIEBACK	ABCENRU UNBRACE	ABCORSX BOXCARS
ABCDEIR CARBIDE	ABCEOOS CABOOSE	ABCORSY CARBOYS
ABCDEKL BLACKED	ABCESSS ABSCESS	ABDDEER BEARDED
ABCDEMP CAMP BED	ABCFIKN FINBACK	ABDDEES DEBASED
ABCDEOR BAR CODE,	ABCFILO BIFOCAL	ABDDEET DEBATED
BROCADE	ABCFIRS FABRICS	ABDDEIN BANDIED
ABCDERU CUDBEAR	ABCFKLY FLYBACK	ABDDEIR BRAIDED
ABCDHIO ICHABOD	ABCGHKO HOGBACK	ABDDELR BLADDER
ABCDIIS DIBASIC	ABCGIKN BACKING	ABDDENR BRANDED
ABCDIRT CATBIRD	ABCGILN CABLING	ABDDEOR BOARDED,
ABCDISU SUBACID	ABCGINR BRACING	ROADBED
ABCDNOS ABSCOND	ABCGIST BIG CATS	ABDDEST BADDEST
ABCDOOR CORDOBA	ABCGKLO BACKLOG	ABDDINS DISBAND
ABCEEHS BEACHES	ABCHHII HIBACHI	ABDDLLO ODDBALL
ABCEEMR EMBRACE	ABCHILS CHABLIS	ABDEEFG FEEDBAG
ABCEENR CARBENE	ABCHILU BALUCHI	ABDEEFL FEEL BAD
ABCEENS ABSENCE	ABCHIOT COHABIT	ABDEEHV BEHAVED
ABCEERR CEREBRA	ABCHKTU HACKBUT	ABDEEIL BEDELIA
ABCEESU BECAUSE	ABCHPSU HUBCAPS	ABDEEIR BEADIER
ABCEGIR RIB CAGE	ABCIILL BACILLI	ABDEELL LABELED
ABCEGOS BOSCAGE	ABCIILN ALBINIC	ABDEELN ENABLED
ABCEHIR HEBRAIC	ABCIILS BASILIC	ABDEELS BEADLES
ABCEHLN BLANCHE	ABCIILT ALBITIC	ABDEELT BELATED,
ABCEHMR CHAMBER	ABCIIMN MINICAB	BLEATED
ABCEHST BATCHES	ABCIIMS IAMBICS	ABDEELY BELAYED
ABCEILL ICEBALL	ABCIJNO JACOBIN	ABDEERS DEBASER
ABCEILM ALEMBIC	ABCIKSY SICKBAY	ABDEERT BERATED,
ABCEILR ALBERIC, CALIBRE	ABCILRS SCRIBAL	DEBATER
ABCEILT CITABLE	ABCILTU CUBITAL	ABDEEST DEBATES
ABCEIMO AMOEBIC	ABCIMMU CAMBIUM	ABDEETT ABETTED
ABCEINR CARBINE	ABCIMOR COIMBRA	ABDEFFL BAFFLED
ABCEINT CABINET	ABCIMST CAMBIST	ABDEFLT FLAT-BED

ABDEFOR FORBADE	ABDENPS BEDPANS	ABEEERV BEREAVE
ABDEGGR BRAGGED	ABDENRR BERNARD	ABEEGHR HERBAGE
ABDEGHI BIGHEAD	ABDENSS BADNESS	ABEEGLS BEAGLES
ABDEGIL BIG DEAL	ABDEORR BOARDER,	ABEEGLT GETABLE
ABDEGIN BEADING	BROADER	ABEEGRS BARGEES
ABDEGIR ABRIDGE,	ABDEORT ABORTED	ABEEGRU AUBERGE
BRIGADE	ABDEOST BOASTED	ABEEGRW BREWAGE
ABDEGLM GAMBLED	ABDEPSY PAYBEDS	ABEEHKR REBEKAH
ABDEGLR GARBLED	ABDERSV ADVERBS	ABEEHNN HENBANE
ABDEGNO BONDAGE,	ABDERUY DAUBERY	ABEEHNS BANSHEE,
DOGBANE	ABDETTU ABUTTED	HAS-BEEN
ABDEGRS BADGERS	ABDFIIR BID FAIR	ABEEHNT BENEATH
ABDEHIL HIDABLE	ABDFMOR BAD FORM	ABEEHRT BREATHE
ABDEHIT HABITED	ABDGIIN ABIDING	ABEEHTY EYEBATH
ABDEHLR HALBERD	ABDGILN BALDING	ABEEINT BETAINE
ABDEHOR DEBORAH	ABDGINN BANDING	ABEEITT BEATTIE
ABDEHOW BOWHEAD	ABDGINR BRIGAND	ABEEKLR BLEAKER
ABDEHRT BREADTH	ABDGINU DAUBING	ABEEKNT BETAKEN
ABDEILN BELINDA	ABDGINW WINDBAG	ABEEKPS BESPEAK
ABDEILP PIEBALD	ABDGNNU BANDUNG	ABEEKRR BREAKER
ABDEILR BEDRAIL	ABDHMTU MUD BATH	ABEEKRS BEAKERS
ABDEILS DISABLE	ABDHNSU HUSBAND	ABEELLM MABELLE
ABDEILU AUDIBLE	ABDHOSW BAD SHOW	ABEELLY EYEBALL
ABDEILY BEADILY	ABDILNW BALDWIN	ABEELNR ENABLER
ABDEINR BANDIER,	ABDILOO DIABOLO	ABEELNT TENABLE
BRAINED	ABDILOR LABROID	ABEELNU NEBULAE
ABDEIRR BRAIDER	ABDILOT TABLOID	ABEELOR EARLOBE
ABDEIRS AIRBEDS,	ABDILUY AUDIBLY	ABEELQU EQUABLE
BRAISED, SEABIRD	ABDILWY BAWDILY	ABEELRT BLEATER,
ABDEIRT TRIBADE	ABDINOR INBOARD	RETABLE
ABDEIRW BAWDIER	ABDINOT BANTOID	ABEEMRS BESMEAR
ABDEISS BIASSED	ABDINST BANDITS	ABEENOU EUBOEAN
ABDEJRU ABJURED	ABDIPRU UPBRAID	ABEENRS BENARES
ABDEKLU BAULKED	ABDIRSU SUBARID	ABEENRV VERBENA
ABDELMR MARBLED,	ABDJORU DOBRUJA	ABEERRS BEARERS
RAMBLED	ABDKNOU DO A BUNK	ABEERRT REBATER
ABDELMS BEDLAMS	ABDKOOY DAYBOOK	ABEERST BEATERS,
ABDELNR BLANDER	ABDLLNY BLANDLY	REBATES
ABDELOT BLOATED	ABDLLOR BOLLARD	ABEERSV BEAVERS
ABDELOW DOWABLE	ABDLMOR LOMBARD	ABEESWX BEESWAX
ABDELPU DUPABLE	ABDLORY BROADLY	ABEFFLR BAFFLER
ABDELRU DURABLE	ABDLRUY DURABLY	ABEFFLS BAFFLES
ABDELRW BRAWLED,	ABDLSUU SUBDUAL	ABEFFOT OFFBEAT
WARBLED	ABDNNOR BRANDON	ABEFILN FINABLE
ABDELRY BRADLEY,	ABDNOSS DONBASS	ABEFILR FRIABLE
DRYABLE	ABDNOSX SANDBOX	ABEFILU FIBULAE
ABDELST BLASTED,	ABDNOYY ANYBODY	ABEFILX FIXABLE
STABLED	ABDNSTY STANDBY	ABEFITY BEATIFY
ABDELTT BATTLED	ABDOOWY BAYWOOD	ABEFLLU BALEFUL
ABDEMNO ABDOMEN	ABDOSYY DAYBOYS	ABEFLLY FLYABLE
ABDEMRU BERMUDA	ABDRSTU BUSTARD	ABEFLNT FAN BELT
ABDENNR BRENDAN	ABDRUZZ BUZZARD	ABEFLNU BANEFUL
ABDENOR BROADEN	ABEEEFT BEEF TEA	ABEFORR FORBEAR

ABEFPRS PREFABS	ABEIIRS SIBERIA	ABEKLNT BLANKET
ABEGGIM BIG GAME	ABEIJNS BASENJI	ABEKNRS BANKERS
ABEGGIR BAGGIER	ABEIKLL LIKABLE	ABEKRRS BARKERS
ABEGGMO GAMBOGE	ABEIKLS SKIABLE	ABEKSST BASKETS
ABEGGRR BRAGGER	ABEIKNR BIKANER,	ABELLNT NETBALL
ABEGGRS BEGGARS	BREAK-IN	ABELLOS LOSABLE
ABEGGRY BEGGARY	ABEIKNT BEATNIK	ABELLOV LOVABLE
ABEGHMR MAGHREB	ABEILLN LINABLE	ABELLRU RUBELLA,
ABEGHNS SHEBANG	ABEILLO LOBELIA	RULABLE
ABEGHRU BEAR HUG	ABEILLP PLIABLE	ABELLST BALLETS
ABEGILN BELGIAN,	ABEILLR BRAILLE, LIBERAL	ABELLSY SYBELLA
BENGALI	ABEILLS SIBELLA	ABELLTU BULLATE
ABEGILR GABRIEL	ABEILLV LIVABLE	ABELLUW BLUE LAW
ABEGILV GIVABLE	ABEILMN MINABLE	ABELMNT LAMBENT
ABEGIMN BEAMING, BIG	ABEILMR BALMIER,	ABELMNU ALBUMEN
NAME	MIRABEL	ABELMOV MOVABLE
ABEGIMR GAMBIER	ABEILMT LIMBATE,	ABELMRR MARBLER,
ABEGINO BEGONIA	TIMBALE	RAMBLER
ABEGINR BEARING	ABEILMX MIXABLE	ABELMRS MARBLES,
ABEGINT BEATING	ABEILNP BIPLANE	RAMBLES
ABEGIPP BAGPIPE	ABEILNS LESBIAN	ABELMRT LAMBERT
ABEGLMR GAMBLER,	ABEILRT LIBRATE, TRIABLE	ABELMRY BRAMLEY
GAMBREL	ABEILST BESTIAL, STABILE	ABELMTU MUTABLE
ABEGLNS BANGLES	ABEILSY BAILEYS	ABELNNO LEBANON
ABEGLOT GLOBATE	ABEILSZ SIZABLE	ABELNOT NOTABLE
ABEGLRR GARBLER	ABEILVV BIVALVE	ABELNOY BALONEY
ABEGMOR BERGAMO,	ABEIMNT AMBIENT	ABELNRU NEBULAR
EMBARGO	ABEIMRR BARMIER	ABELNRY BLARNEY
ABEGMRU UMBRAGE	ABEIMZZ ZAMBEZI	ABELNSU NEBULAS
ABEGNOS NOSEBAG	ABEINOZ ZENOBIA	ABELNTU TUNABLE
ABEGNRS BANGERS	ABEINRS SERBIAN	ABELOPT POTABLE
ABEGOPY PAGEBOY	ABEINRW WINE BAR	ABELORS ROSABEL
ABEGORX GEARBOX	ABEINSS BASSEIN	ABELORT BLOATER
ABEGOSZ GAZEBOS	ABEINST ANTIBES	ABELORU RUBEOLA
ABEGOTT TOTE BAG	ABEINTT BETTINA, TIBETAN	ABELOSV ABSOLVE
ABEGOUY BUOYAGE	ABEIOTV OBVIATE	ABELOTV VOTABLE
ABEHILR HIRABLE	ABEIPST BAPTISE	ABELQUY EQUABLY
ABEHIMO BOHEMIA	ABEIPTZ BAPTIZE	ABELRRS BARRELS
ABEHIRS BEARISH	ABEIRRR BARRIER	ABELRRW BRAWLER,
ABEHITU HABITUÉ	ABEIRRT ARBITER, RAREBIT	WARBLER
ABEHKRU HAUBERK	ABEIRRZ BIZARRE, BRAZIER	ABELRSZ BLAZERS
ABEHLMS SHAMBLE	ABEIRSS BRASSIE	ABELRTT BARTLET
ABEHLRS HERBALS	ABEIRTT BATTIER, BIRETTA	ABELRVY BRAVELY
ABEHLRT BLATHER	ABEIRTV VIBRATE	ABELSST STABLES
ABEHNRY ABHENRY	ABEIRTX BEATRIX	ABELSTT BATTLES
ABEHNTY BETHANY	ABEIRUX EXURBIA	ABELSTY BEASTLY
ABEHRRS BRASHER	ABEISTT BATISTE	ABELTWY BELTWAY
ABEHRST BATHERS	ABEISUV ABUSIVE	ABEMNOT BOATMEN
ABEHRTY BREATHY	ABEITUX BAUXITE	ABEMNST BATSMEN, BEST
ABEIILR LIBERIA	ABEJLUY BLUE JAY	MAN
ABEIILS BASILIE	ABEJNOW JAWBONE	ABEMNSU SUNBEAM
ABEIINR IBERIAN	ABEJRRU ABJURER	ABEMORS AMBROSE
ABEIINT BAINITE	ABEKLLY BLEAKLY	ABEMORT BROMATE

ABEMRRT BERTRAM
ABEMSSY EMBASSY
ABENNRS BANNERS
ABENNRW BRANWEN
ABENORT BARONET
ABENORU AUBERON
ABENOTY BAYONET
ABENOWX BONE WAX
ABENQTU BANQUET
ABENRST BARENTS
ABENRSY BARNEYS
ABENSTT BATTENS, TEST
  BAN
ABENTUZ BAUTZEN
ABEOOTV OBOVATE
ABEOPRS SAPROBE
ABEOPRT PROBATE
ABEOQRU BAROQUE
ABEORRT ROBERTA
ABEORST BAROTSE,
  BOASTER, BOATERS
ABEORTT ABETTOR,
  TABORET
ABEPRTY TYPEBAR
ABEQRSU BARQUES
ABERRTT BARRETT
ABERRVY BRAVERY
ABERSSS BRASSES
ABERSSU SURBASE
ABERSTT BATTERS
ABERSTV BRAVEST
ABERSTY BARYTES
ABERTTU ABUTTER
ABERTTY BATTERY
ABERUUX BUREAUX
ABESSST BASSETS
ABESSSY ABYSSES
ABFFIIL BAILIFF
ABFFLOU BUFFALO
ABFHIST BATFISH
ABFHLSU BASHFUL
ABFIILR BIFILAR
ABFIIMR FIMBRIA
ABFILRU FIBULAR
ABFILSU FIBULAS
ABFIMOR FIBROMA
ABFLOTY FLYBOAT
ABGGGIN BAGGING
ABGGILY BAGGILY
ABGGINN BANGING
ABGGINR BARGING,
  GARBING
ABGHINS BASHING

ABGHINT BATHING
ABGHLRU BURGHAL
ABGHMRU HAMBURG
ABGIILN BAILING
ABGIINS BIASING
ABGIINT BAITING
ABGIKLN BALKING
ABGIKLT TALK BIG
ABGIKNN BANKING
ABGIKNR BARKING,
  BRAKING
ABGIKNS BASKING
ABGIKST KIT BAGS
ABGILMN AMBLING,
  BLAMING, LAMBING
ABGILMS GIMBALS
ABGILNR BLARING
ABGILNT TABLING
ABGILNW BAWLING
ABGILNZ BLAZING
ABGIMST GAMBITS
ABGINNN BANNING
ABGINOT BOATING
ABGINRR BARRING
ABGINRV BRAVING
ABGINRY BRAYING
ABGINST BASTING
ABGINSU ABUSING
ABGINTT BATTING
ABGINTW BATWING
ABGKKNO BANGKOK
ABGKORW WORKBAG
ABGLMOS GAMBOLS
ABGLMOU LUMBAGO
ABGLNOO BOLOGNA
ABGLRRU BURGLAR
ABGMORW BAGWORM
ABGNOPR PROBANG
ABGNOTU GUNBOAT
ABGOPST POSTBAG
ABHHIPT HIPBATH
ABHHOOP POOH-BAH
ABHHSUY HUSHABY
ABHIINT INHABIT
ABHIKRS BASHKIR
ABHILNO HOBNAIL
ABHILOS ABOLISH
ABHILTU HALIBUT
ABHINOS SIOBHAN
ABHINRS BAS-RHIN
ABHINST ABSINTH
ABHIOPS PHOBIAS
ABHIORS BOARISH

ABHIOST ISOBATH
ABHISTU HABITUS
ABHLRSY BRASHLY
ABHMNSU BUSHMAN
ABHOOST BASOTHO
ABHORRU HARBOUR
ABHOTUY HAUTBOY
ABHSTUW WASHTUB
ABIILLS SIBILLA
ABIILMU BULIMIA
ABIILOV BOLIVIA
ABIILRY BILIARY
ABIILTY ABILITY
ABIINOR NAIROBI
ABIIOSS ABIOSIS
ABIJNPU PUNJABI
ABIJPRU BIJAPUR
ABIKLLM KIMBALL
ABILLMY BALMILY
ABILLNP PINBALL
ABILLSW SAWBILL
ABILLSY SIBYLLA,
  SYBILLA, SYLLABI
ABILLWX WAXBILL
ABILLWY WAYBILL
ABILMNU ALBUMIN
ABILMOX MAILBOX
ABILNOS ALBINOS
ABILOPR BIPOLAR, PARBOIL
ABILORT ORBITAL
ABILORV BOLIVAR
ABILRRY LIBRARY
ABILRSU BURIALS
ABIMNRU UMBRIAN
ABIMOSS BIOMASS
ABIMPST BAPTISM
ABINNOS BOSNIAN
ABINORT TABORIN
ABINORW RAINBOW
ABINOST BASTION
ABINRTV VIBRANT
ABIORSS ISOBARS
ABIORTV VIBRATO
ABIORUX ROUBAIX
ABIPRTT BIT PART
ABIPSTT BAPTIST
ABIRUZZ ABRUZZI
ABISSST BASSIST
ABKLLNY BLANKLY
ABKLRUW BULWARK
ABKNRSY BRYANSK
ABLLLUY LULLABY
ABLLNOO BALLOON

ABLLNOS NO BALLS	ACCDHIL CHALCID	ACCERSU ACCUSER
ABLLORR ROLL BAR	ACCDINS SCANDIC	ACCFIIP PACIFIC
ABLLORU LOBULAR	ACCDIOT OCTADIC	ACCFILY CALCIFY
ABLLOST BALLOTS	ACCDORS ACCORDS	ACCGHIO CHICAGO
ABLLOTY TALLBOY	ACCEELN CENACLE	ACCGNOS COGNACS
ABLLPSU BALLS-UP	ACCEERT ACCRETE	ACCHINO CHICANO
ABLMOOT TOMBOLA	ACCEFLU FELUCCA	ACCHIOT CHAOTIC
ABLMOVY MOVABLY	ACCEHIL CALICHE,	ACCHIOU ACOUCHI
ABLMSTU STAMBUL	CHALICE	ACCHKNO HANCOCK
ABLMTUY MUTABLY	ACCEHIN CHICANE	ACCHKOY HAYCOCK
ABLNOOZ BOLZANO	ACCEHLN CHANCEL	ACCHLNO CONCHAL
ABLNOSZ BLAZONS	ACCEHLO COCHLEA	ACCHNUY CHAUNCY
ABLNOTU BUTANOL	ACCEHNR CHANCRE	ACCHOTW CHOCTAW
ABLNOTY NOTABLY	ACCEHNS CHANCES	ACCHRST SCRATCH
ABLOPYY PLAYBOY	ACCEHOS COACHES	ACCIINT ACTINIC
ABLORST BORSTAL	ACCEHRT CATCHER	ACCIIST ASCITIC, SCIATIC
ABLORSU LABOURS	ACCEHST CACHETS,	ACCIKRR CARRICK
ABLOSTX SALTBOX	CATCHES	ACCIKRS CARSICK
ABLRTUU TUBULAR	ACCEHTU CATECHU	ACCIKRT CRACK IT
ABMORTU TAMBOUR	ACCEIIL CECILIA	ACCILLU CALCULI
ABMOSTW WOMBATS	ACCEIKP ICE PACK, PACK	ACCILMO COMICAL
ABNOORZ BORAZON	ICE	ACCILMU CALCIUM
ABNOOSS BASSOON	ACCEILN CALCINE	ACCILNO CONICAL,
ABNORUY YORUBAN	ACCEILO COELIAC	LACONIC
ABNOTUY BOUYANT,	ACCEILR CLARICE	ACCILNU CLUNIAC
BUOYANT	ACCEILT CALCITE	ACCILNY CYNICAL
ABNRSTU TURBANS	ACCEIMR CERAMIC,	ACCILOR CALORIC
ABOOPSX SOAPBOX	RACEMIC	ACCILOS CALICOS
ABOOTTU ABOUT TO	ACCEINO COCAINE,	ACCILOV VOCALIC
ABOOTTW TOWBOAT	OCEANIC	ACCILRU CRUCIAL
ABORRSU ARBOURS	ACCEINV VACCINE	ACCILRY ACRYLIC
ABORRSW BARROWS	ACCEIPR CAPRICE	ACCILSS CLASSIC
ABORSSU SUB ROSA	ACCEIPS ICE CAPS	ACCILST CLASTIC
ABRRSSU BURSARS	ACCEIPV PECCAVI	ACCIORS CORSICA
ABRRSUY BURSARY	ACCEIST ASCETIC	ACCISTT TACTICS
ABRRTUY TURBARY	ACCEKLR CACKLER,	ACCISTU CAUSTIC
ABRSTUU ARBUTUS	CRACKLE	ACCKOSS CASSOCK
ABSSUWY SUBWAYS	ACCEKLS CACKLES	ACCKPRU CRACKUP
ACCCILY ACYCLIC	ACCEKOP PEACOCK	ACCKTTU CUTTACK
ACCDDEE ACCEDED	ACCEKOS SEACOCK	ACCMOOY COCOYAM
ACCDEEN CADENCE	ACCEKPU CUP CAKE	ACCMOPT COMPACT
ACCDEER ACCEDER	ACCEKRR CRACKER	ACCMRUU CURCUMA
ACCDEHN CHANCED	ACCELLY CALYCLE	ACCNOOR RACCOON
ACCDEHO COACHED	ACCELNO CONCEAL	ACCNOTT CONTACT
ACCDEIN CANDICE	ACCELOR CORACLE	ACCNOTU ACCOUNT
ACCDEKL CACKLED,	ACCELSU SACCULE	ACCOPTY COPYCAT
CLACKED	ACCELSY CALYCES	ACCOQSU SQUACCO
ACCDEKO COCKADE	ACCENOV CONCAVE	ACDDDEI CADDIED
ACCDEKR CRACKED	ACCENPT PECCANT	ACDDDEU ADDUCED
ACCDENY CADENCY	ACCENRS CANCERS	ACDDEEF DEFACED
ACCDERU ACCRUED	ACCENST ACCENTS	ACDDEES DECADES
ACCDESU ACCUSED	ACCEPRY PECCARY	ACDDEEY DECAYED
ACCDFIL FLACCID	ACCERRS SCARCER	ACDDEHR CHEDDAR

ACDDEIN CANDIED
ACDDEIS CADDIES
ACDDEIU DECIDUA
ACDDELO CLADODE
ACDDELR CRADLED
ACDDELS SCALDED
ACDDEOP DECAPOD
ACDDHIS CADDISH
ACDDHKO HADDOCK
ACDDIRS DISCARD, ID
　　CARDS
ACDDIRY DRYADIC
ACDDIST ADDICTS
ACDDKOP PADDOCK
ACDEEES DECEASE
ACDEEFF EFFACED
ACDEEFR DEFACER,
　　REFACED
ACDEEHL LEACHED
ACDEEHR ARDECHE,
　　REACHED
ACDEEHT CHEATED
ACDEEIR DECIARE
ACDEEJT DEJECTA
ACDEEKR CREAKED
ACDEELL CADELLE
ACDEELN CLEANED
ACDEELR CLEARED,
　　CREEDAL, DECLARE
ACDEELS DESCALE
ACDEELV CLEAVED
ACDEEMN MENACED
ACDEEMR CREAMED
ACDEENS ENCASED
ACDEENT ENACTED
ACDEENV VENDACE
ACDEEPR CAPERED,
　　RECAPED
ACDEEPS ESCAPED
ACDEERS CREASED
ACDEERT CATERED,
　　CERATED, CREATED,
　　REACTED
ACDEETU EDUCATE
ACDEETX EXACTED
ACDEFFH CHAFFED
ACDEFIN FANCIED
ACDEFOP PO-FACED
ACDEFOT DE FACTO
ACDEFRT CRAFTED
ACDEGHN CHANGED
ACDEGHR CHARGED
ACDEGKO DOCKAGE

ACDEGLN CLANGED,
　　GLANCED
ACDEGNO DECAGON
ACDEGNU UNCAGED
ACDEGOR CORDAGE
ACDEGRS CADGERS
ACDEHHT HATCHED
ACDEHIN CHAINED,
　　ECHIDNA
ACDEHIP EDAPHIC
ACDEHIR CHAIRED
ACDEHIX HEXACID
ACDEHKL CHALKED
ACDEHKS SHACKED
ACDEHKW WHACKED
ACDEHLS CLASHED
ACDEHLT LATCHED
ACDEHMP CHAMPED
ACDEHMR CHARMED,
　　MARCHED
ACDEHMT MATCHED
ACDEHNR ENDARCH
ACDEHNT CHANTED
ACDEHOP POACHED
ACDEHOT CATHODE
ACDEHPP CHAPPED
ACDEHPR PARCHED
ACDEHPT PATCHED
ACDEHRR CHARRED
ACDEHRS CRASHED
ACDEHRT CHARTED
ACDEHTT CHATTED
ACDEHTW WATCHED
ACDEILL CEDILLA
ACDEILM CLAIMED,
　　DECIMAL, DECLAIM,
　　MEDICAL
ACDEILN ICELAND
ACDEILR DECRIAL,
　　RADICEL, RADICLE
ACDEILT CITADEL,
　　DELTAIC, DIALECT, EDICTAL
ACDEILV CAVILED
ACDEIMY MEDIACY
ACDEINS CANDIES
ACDEINY CYANIDE
ACDEIPR PERACID
ACDEIRR CARRIED
ACDEIRS RADICES,
　　SIDECAR
ACDEIST DIE-CAST
ACDEISV ADVICES
ACDEITT DICTATE

ACDEITY EDACITY
ACDEJLO CAJOLED
ACDEKLN CLANKED
ACDEKLO CLOAKED
ACDEKLS SLACKED
ACDEKLT TACKLED
ACDEKLU CAULKED
ACDEKMS SMACKED
ACDEKNR CRANKED
ACDEKNS SNACKED
ACDEKOR CROAKED
ACDEKQU QUACKED
ACDEKRT TRACKED
ACDEKST STACKED
ACDELMM CLAMMED
ACDELMP CLAMPED
ACDELNO CELADON
ACDELNR CANDLER
ACDELNS CALENDS,
　　CANDLES
ACDELOP PEDOCAL
ACDELOR CAROLED
ACDELOS SOLACED
ACDELOT LOCATED
ACDELPP CLAPPED
ACDELPS CLASPED,
　　SCALPED
ACDELRS CRADLES
ACDELRW CRAWLED
ACDELSS CLASSED,
　　DECLASS
ACDELST CASTLED
ACDELWW DEWCLAW
ACDEMMR CRAMMED
ACDEMNO MACEDON
ACDEMOR COMRADE
ACDEMPR CRAMPED
ACDENNS SCANNED
ACDENOS DEACONS
ACDENOT TACNODE
ACDENPR PRANCED
ACDENPT PANDECT
ACDENRS DANCERS
ACDENRT TANCRED
ACDENRY ARDENCY
ACDENST DESCANT
ACDEORR CORRADE
ACDEORT ART DECO,
　　CORDATE, REDCOAT
ACDEORU ECUADOR
ACDEOST COASTED
ACDEOUV COUVADE
ACDEPPR CRAPPED

ACDEPRS SCRAPED	ACDKLOP PADLOCK	ACEEMNR MENACER
ACDEQSU CASQUED	ACDKMPU MUDPACK	ACEEMNS MENACES
ACDERRS SCARRED	ACDLLOR COLLARD	ACEEMNV CAVEMEN
ACDERSU CRUSADE	ACDLNOR CALDRON	ACEEMNY MYCENAE
ACDERTT DETRACT	ACDLORW COLD WAR	ACEEMRR CREAMER
ACDERTU TRADUCE	ACDLSTY DACTYLS	ACEEMRT CREMATE
ACDESTT SCATTED	ACDMMNO COMMAND	ACEENNP PENANCE
ACDFIIY ACIDIFY	ACDMOOW CAMWOOD	ACEENNT CANTEEN
ACDGGIN CADGING	ACDNOOR CARDOON	ACEENNY CAYENNE
ACDGHLO CLODAGH	ACDNORU CANDOUR	ACEENOT ACETONE
ACDGINN DANCING	ACDORST COSTARD	ACEENRT CRENATE
ACDGINR CARDING	ACDORSW COWARDS	ACEENSS SÉANCES
ACDGKLO DAGLOCK	ACDRSTU CUSTARD	ACEENTU CUNEATE
ACDGORT DOGCART	ACEEEPS ESCAPEE	ACEEORS ACEROSE
ACDHIIL CHILIAD	ACEEEUV EVACUEE	ACEEORT OCREATE
ACDHIIS HASIDIC	ACEEFFR EFFACER	ACEEOSS CASEOSE
ACDHIRR RICHARD	ACEEFIN FAIENCE	ACEEPRS ESCAPER
ACDHIRY DIARCHY	ACEEFPR PREFACE	ACEEPSS ESCAPES
ACDHLOR CHORDAL	ACEEGIL ELEGIAC	ACEEPST PECTASE
ACDHMRS DRACHMS	ACEEGIS ICE AGES	ACEEPTT PECTATE
ACDHNOW COWHAND	ACEEHHT CHEETAH	ACEERRS CAREERS
ACDHOPR POCHARD	ACEEHIV ACHIEVE	ACEERRT CATERER,
ACDHORR ORCHARD	ACEEHLR LEACHER	RETRACE, TERRACE
ACDHRYY DYARCHY	ACEEHLT CHELATE	ACEERSS CREASES
ACDIIIN INDICIA	ACEEHMT MACHETE	ACEERTX EXCRETA
ACDIINN INDICAN	ACEEHNN ENHANCE	ACEESTU EUSTACE
ACDIIRT TRIACID, TRIADIC	ACEEHNP CHEAPEN	ACEESTY CAT'S EYE
ACDIITY ACIDITY	ACEEHPR CHEAPER	ACEFFFO FACE-OFF
ACDILMO DOMICAL	ACEEHPS PEACHES	ACEFFHR CHAFFER
ACDILNO NODICAL	ACEEHRR REACHER	ACEFHMR CHAMFER
ACDILNU LUCINDA	ACEEHRS REACHES	ACEFIIL FELICIA
ACDILOP PLACOID	ACEEHRT CHEATER,	ACEFILL ICEFALL
ACDILOR CORDIAL	HECTARE, TEACHER	ACEFILM MALEFIC
ACDILOT COTIDAL	ACEEILP CALIPEE	ACEFINN FINANCE
ACDILTW WILDCAT	ACEEILT ELEATIC	ACEFINR FANCIER,
ACDIMMU CADMIUM	ACEEINU EUCAINE	FRANCIE
ACDIMNO MONADIC,	ACEEKNP KNEECAP	ACEFINS FANCIES,
NOMADIC	ACEELLN NACELLE	FASCINE, FIANCÉS
ACDIMNY DYNAMIC	ACEELMP EMPLACE	ACEFITY ACETIFY
ACDINSU SUDANIC	ACEELNR CARLEEN,	ACEFLRU CAREFUL
ACDIOPR PARODIC,	CARLENE, CLEANER	ACEFNRS FRANCES
PICADOR	ACEELNS CLEANSE,	ACEFNRU FURNACE
ACDIORR CORRIDA,	SCALENE	ACEFOTU OUTFACE
RICARDO	ACEELNV ENCLAVE,	ACEFRRT REFRACT
ACDIORS SARCOID	VALENCE	ACEFRRU FARCEUR
ACDIORT CAROTID	ACEELPR PERCALE,	ACEFRSU SURFACE
ACDIOSZ ZODIACS	REPLACE	ACEFRTU FURCATE
ACDIOXY OXYACID	ACEELRR CLEARER	ACEFSTU FAUCETS
ACDIPRY PICARDY	ACEELRS CEREALS	ACEGHNR CHANGER
ACDIQRU QUADRIC	ACEELRT TREACLE	ACEGHNS CHANGES
ACDIRST DRASTIC	ACEELRV CLEAVER	ACEGHOU GOUACHE
ACDITUV VIADUCT	ACEELST CELESTA	ACEGHRR CHARGER
ACDJNTU ADJUNCT	ACEELVX EXCLAVE	ACEGHRS CHARGES

ACEGILN ANGELIC, GALENIC
ACEGILP PELAGIC
ACEGILR GLACIER, GRACILE
ACEGIMR GRIMACE
ACEGINO COINAGE
ACEGINR ANERGIC, GRECIAN
ACEGINS CEASING
ACEGIST CAGIEST
ACEGKLO LOCKAGE
ACEGKLR GRACKLE
ACEGKOR CORKAGE
ACEGLLO COLLAGE
ACEGLNO CONGEAL
ACEGLNR CLANGER
ACEGLNS GLANCES
ACEGLOU CAGOULE
ACEGNOR ACROGEN
ACEGNOT COGNATE
ACEGORS CARGOES, CORSAGE, SOCAGER
ACEGORU COURAGE
ACEGOTT COTTAGE
ACEHHLT HATCHEL
ACEHHRT HATCHER
ACEHHRU HACHURE
ACEHHST HATCHES
ACEHHTT HATCHET
ACEHILL HELICAL
ACEHILM MICHAEL
ACEHILN CHILEAN
ACEHILR CHARLIE
ACEHILT ETHICAL
ACEHIMN MACHINE
ACEHIMP IMPEACH
ACEHIMR CHIMERA
ACEHINN ENCHAIN
ACEHINR ARCHINE
ACEHINT TEACH-IN
ACEHINY HYAENIC
ACEHIPT HEPATIC
ACEHIRR CHARIER
ACEHIRS CASHIER
ACEHIRT RHAETIC
ACEHIRV ARCHIVE
ACEHISS CHAISES
ACEHIST AITCHES
ACEHITT CHATTIE
ACEHKLR HACKLER
ACEHKLS HACKLES, SHACKLE

ACEHKNY HACKNEY
ACEHKRS HACKERS
ACEHKRW WHACKER
ACEHLLS SHELLAC
ACEHLLT HELLCAT
ACEHLMY ALCHEMY
ACEHLNN CHANNEL
ACEHLNO CHALONE
ACEHLNR CHARNEL
ACEHLOP EPOCHAL
ACEHLOR CHOLERA, CHORALE, CHOREAL
ACEHLPS CHAPELS
ACEHLPT CHAPLET
ACEHLPY CHEAPLY
ACEHLRS CHARLES, CLASHER, LARCHES
ACEHLRY CHARLEY
ACEHLSS CLASHES
ACEHLST CHALETS, LATCHES, SATCHEL
ACEHLTT CHATTEL, LATCHET
ACEHMRR CHARMER, MARCHER
ACEHMRS MARCHES, MESARCH
ACEHMRT REMATCH
ACEHMST MATCHES
ACEHMTY ECTHYMA
ACEHNNT ENCHANT
ACEHNRR RANCHER
ACEHNRS RANCHES
ACEHNRT CHANTER
ACEHNST CHASTEN
ACEHOOT OOTHECA
ACEHOPR POACHER
ACEHORS ROACHES
ACEHOTY CHAYOTE
ACEHPRT CHAPTER, PATCHER
ACEHPRY EPARCHY
ACEHPST PATCHES
ACEHQUU QUECHUA
ACEHRRS ARCHERS
ACEHRRT CHARTER
ACEHRRX XERARCH
ACEHRRY ARCHERY
ACEHRSS CHASERS, CRASHES
ACEHRST CHASTER
ACEHRTT CHATTER, RATCHET

ACEHRTW WATCHER
ACEHSST SACHETS
ACEHSSW CASHEWS
ACEHSTW WATCHES
ACEIILS LAICISE
ACEIILT CILIATE
ACEIILZ LAICIZE
ACEIJSS JESSICA
ACEIKPX PICKAXE
ACEIKRT TACKIER
ACEIKSS SEASICK
ACEILLL ALLELIC
ACEILLM CAMILLE
ACEILLX LEXICAL
ACEILMN MELANIC
ACEILMR CLAIMER, MIRACLE, RECLAIM
ACEILMT CLIMATE
ACEILMX EXCLAIM
ACEILNP CAPELIN, IN PLACE, PANICLE, PELICAN
ACEILNR CARLINE
ACEILNS SANICLE
ACEILNU CAULINE
ACEILOR CALORIE, CARIOLE, CORALIE
ACEILOT ALOETIC
ACEILPR REPLICA
ACEILPS SPECIAL
ACEILPT PLICATE
ACEILRR CLARRIE
ACEILRS ÉCLAIRS, SCALIER
ACEILRT ARTICLE, RECITAL
ACEILRU AURICLE
ACEILRV CLAVIER, VALERIC
ACEILST CASTILE, ELASTIC, LACIEST
ACEILSV VESICAL
ACEILTT LATTICE, TACTILE
ACEIMNO ENCOMIA
ACEIMNR CARMINE, CRIMEAN
ACEIMNS CINEMAS
ACEIMNT NEMATIC
ACEIMNX MEXICAN
ACEIMPY PYAEMIC
ACEIMRU MAURICE, URAEMIC
ACEIMST SEMATIC
ACEIMSU CAESIUM
ACEINNP PINNACE
ACEINNR CANNIER
ACEINNS CANINES

ACEINNT ANCIENT
ACEINNY CYANINE
ACEINOT ACONITE
ACEINRS ARSENIC
ACEINRT CERTAIN
ACEINST ANSTICE
ACEINSV CAVE-INS
ACEINTT TETANIC
ACEINTV VENATIC
ACEINTX INEXACT
ACEINTY CYANITE
ACEINTZ ZINCATE
ACEINVZ VICENZA
ACEIOPT ECTOPIA
ACEIORT EROTICA
ACEIOTX EXOTICA
ACEIPPR CRAPPIE, EPICARP
ACEIPRT PARETIC, PICRATE
ACEIPSS CAPSISE
ACEIPST ASEPTIC, SPICATE
ACEIPSU AUSPICE
ACEIPSZ CAPSIZE
ACEIPTV CAPTIVE
ACEIQRU ACQUIRE
ACEIQSU CAIQUES
ACEIRRR CARRIER
ACEIRRS CARRIES,
   SCARIER
ACEIRRT CIRRATE, ERRATIC
ACEIRRW AIRCREW
ACEIRRZ CRAZIER
ACEIRST RACIEST, STEARIC
ACEIRSU SAUCIER
ACEIRSV VISCERA
ACEIRTT CATTIER, CITRATE
ACEISST ASCITES
ACEJKST JACKETS
ACEJNOT JACONET
ACEJQSU JACQUES
ACEJRTT TRAJECT
ACEKLNS SLACKEN
ACEKLPT PLACKET
ACEKLRS SLACKER
ACEKLRT TACKLER
ACEKLRU CAULKER
ACEKLST TACKLES
ACEKLSY LACKEYS
ACEKMRS SMACKER
ACEKNRS CANKERS
ACEKORR CROAKER
ACEKPPR PREPACK
ACEKPRS PACKERS
ACEKPST PACKETS

ACEKRRT TRACKER
ACEKRST RACKETS,
   STACKER
ACEKRTY RACKETY
ACEKSST CASKETS
ACELLMO CALOMEL
ACELLNY CLEANLY
ACELLOR OCELLAR
ACELLOS LOCALES
ACELLOT COLLATE
ACELLPS SCALPEL
ACELLPY CLYPEAL
ACELLRS CALLERS,
   CELLARS, RECALLS
ACELLRU CURE-ALL
ACELLRY CLEARLY
ACELMOT CAMELOT
ACELMOU LEUCOMA
ACELMPR CLAMPER
ACELMST CALMEST
ACELNNU UNCLEAN
ACELNNY LYNCEAN
ACELNOP NO-PLACE
ACELNOR CORNEAL
ACELNOT LACTONE
ACELNPS SPANCEL
ACELNPU CLEANUP
ACELNRS LANCERS
ACELNRT CENTRAL
ACELNRU NUCLEAR,
   UNCLEAR
ACELNRY LARCENY
ACELNST LANCETS
ACELNSU CENSUAL
ACELNTY LATENCY
ACELNVY VALENCY
ACELOPT POLECAT
ACELOQU COEQUAL
ACELORS ESCOLAR,
   ORACLES, SOLACER
ACELORT LOCATER
ACELOSS SOLACES
ACELOST LACTOSE,
   TALCOSE
ACELOSV ALCOVES,
   COEVALS
ACELOTT CALOTTE
ACELOTY ACOLYTE
ACELOUV VACUOLE
ACELPPR CLAPPER
ACELPRS CLASPER,
   PARCELS, SCALPER
ACELPRY PRELACY

ACELPSU CAPSULE
ACELPSY CYPSELA
ACELPTY ECTYPAL
ACELQRU LACQUER
ACELQSU CLAQUES
ACELRRW CRAWLER
ACELRST CARTELS,
   SCARLET
ACELRSU SECULAR
ACELRTT CLATTER
ACELRTY TREACLY
ACELSSS CLASSES
ACELSST CASTLES
ACELSSU CLAUSES
ACELSTU SULCATE
ACELSUU ACULEUS
ACELSUX EXCUSAL
ACELSXY CALYXES
ACELTTU LUCETTA
ACELTUY ACUTELY
ACELTXY EXACTLY
ACEMMRR CRAMMER
ACEMNOR CAMERON,
   ROMANCE
ACEMOPR COMPARE
ACEMORU MORCEAU
ACEMPRS CAMPERS,
   SCAMPER
ACEMRSS SCREAMS
ACENNOS SONANCE
ACENNOT CONNATE
ACENNOZ CANZONE
ACENNRS SCANNER
ACENNRY CANNERY
ACENNST NASCENT
ACENNSU NUANCES
ACENNTY TENANCY
ACENOOR CORONAE
ACENORS COARSEN
ACENORT ENACTOR, NOT
   CARE
ACENOST OCTANES
ACENOSZ COSENZA
ACENOTV CENTAVO
ACENPRR PRANCER
ACENPTY PATENCY
ACENRRY ERRANCY
ACENRST CANTERS,
   TRANCES
ACENRSV CAVERNS
ACENRTU CENTAUR
ACENRTY NECTARY

ACENSST ASCENTS,
  STANCES
ACENSTU NUTCASE
ACEOOPP APOCOPE
ACEOPSS SCAPOSE
ACEOPST TOE CAPS
ACEOPTZ ZAPOTEC
ACEORRS COARSER
ACEORRT ACROTER,
  CREATOR, REACTOR
ACEORST COASTER
ACEORSU CAROUSE
ACEORTV OVERACT
ACEORTW EAT CROW
ACEORTX EXACTOR
ACEOSSU CASEOUS
ACEOSTT COSTATE
ACEOSTU ACETOUS
ACEOSTV OCTAVES
ACEOSTY TEA COSY
ACEOTTV CAVETTO
ACEOTUU AUTOCUE
ACEPRRS SCARPER,
  SCRAPER
ACEPRSS SCRAPES
ACEPRST CARPETS,
  PRECAST, SPECTRA
ACEPRTU CAPTURE
ACEPSST ASPECTS
ACEPSTU CUSPATE,
  TEACUPS
ACEQRTU RACQUET
ACEQSSU CASQUES
ACERRST CARTERS,
  CRATERS, TRACERS
ACERRSV CARVERS
ACERRTT RETRACT
ACERRTY TRACERY
ACERRUV VERRUCA
ACERSST ACTRESS,
  CASTERS
ACERSSU SAUCERS,
  SUCRASE
ACERSSV SCARVES
ACERSTT SCATTER
ACERSTU CURATES
ACERSTY SECTARY
ACERTTX EXTRACT
ACERTTY CATTERY
ACERTUY CAUTERY
ACESSTY ECSTASY
ACESTTU SCUTATE
ACESTTY TESTACY

ACFFILT AFFLICT
ACFFIRT TRAFFIC
ACFFLTU FACTFUL
ACFFOST CAST-OFF
ACFGHIN CHAFING
ACFGINS FACINGS
ACFHIST CATFISH
ACFHISU FUCHSIA
ACFHLNU FLAUNCH,
  FUNCHAL
ACFILNO FOLACIN
ACFILNY FANCILY
ACFILRY CLARIFY
ACFILSS FISCALS
ACFIMOR FORMICA
ACFIMRU FUMARIC
ACFIMSS FASCISM
ACFINNY INFANCY
ACFINOT FACTION
ACFINRS FRANCIS
ACFINRT FRANTIC,
  INFARCT, INFRACT
ACFINRY CARNIFY
ACFIOSS FIASCOS
ACFIRSY SCARIFY
ACFISST FASCIST
ACFKLLU FUCK ALL
ACFLNOS FALCONS
ACFLRUU FURCULA
ACFLTTU TACTFUL
ACFLTUY FACULTY
ACFOQRT Q-FACTOR
ACFORST FACTORS
ACFORTY FACTORY
ACFRSTU FRACTUS
ACGGINR GRACING
ACGGRSY SCRAGGY
ACGHIKN HACKING
ACGHINR ARCHING,
  CHAGRIN
ACGHINS CASHING,
  CHASING
ACGHINT GNATHIC
ACGHINW CHINWAG
ACGHIPR GRAPHIC
ACGHOSU GAUCHOS
ACGIITU AUGITIC
ACGIJKN JACKING
ACGIKLN CALKING,
  LACKING
ACGIKNP PACKING
ACGIKNR RACKING
ACGIKNS SACKING

ACGIKNT TACKING
ACGIKRR GARRICK
ACGILLN CALLING
ACGILLO LOGICAL
ACGILMN CALMING
ACGILMY MYALGIC
ACGILNN LANCING
ACGILNO COALING
ACGILNP PLACING
ACGILNR CARLING
ACGILNS SCALING
ACGILNT CATLING
ACGILNV CALVING
ACGILNW CLAWING
ACGIMNO COAMING
ACGIMNP CAMPING
ACGINNN CANNING
ACGINNR CRANING
ACGINNT CANTING
ACGINOR ORGANIC
ACGINOT COATING,
  COTINGA
ACGINOX COAXING
ACGINPP CAPPING
ACGINPR CARPING
ACGINPS SPACING
ACGINRS SCARING
ACGINRT CARTING,
  CRATING, TRACING
ACGINRV CARVING,
  CRAVING
ACGINSS CASINGS
ACGINST CASTING
ACGINSU CAUSING,
  SAUCING
ACGIORT ARGOTIC
ACGIRST GASTRIC
ACGLNOR CLANGOR
ACGNOOT OCTAGON
ACGNORS GARÇONS
ACGNOSY GASCONY
ACGORSU COUGARS
ACHHIRW HARWICH
ACHHSUV CHUVASH
ACHIILS ISCHIAL
ACHIIMT HAMITIC
ACHIINT CHIANTI
ACHIITW WICHITA
ACHIJKS HIJACKS
ACHIJMO JOACHIM
ACHIJNT JACINTH
ACHIKLN NALCHIK
ACHILLO LOCHIAL

ACHILLP PHALLIC
ACHILLS CHALLIS
ACHILLT THALLIC
ACHILMR RICHMAL
ACHILNO NICHOLA
ACHILPS CALIPHS
ACHILRY CHARILY
ACHIMNO MOHICAN
ACHIMOS CHAMOIS
ACHINNU UNCHAIN
ACHINOP APHONIC
ACHINPS SPINACH
ACHINTX XANTHIC
ACHINTY CYNTHIA
ACHIOPT APHOTIC
ACHIORT CHARIOT,
    HARICOT
ACHIPST SPATHIC
ACHIQRU CHARQUI
ACHIRTU HAIRCUT
ACHIRTY CHARITY
ACHISSS CHASSIS
ACHISTT CATTISH
ACHITTW WATCH IT!
ACHKMMO HAMMOCK
ACHKOPS HOPSACK
ACHKOSS HASSOCK
ACHKSTW THWACKS
ACHLLOO ALCOHOL
ACHLLOR CHLORAL
ACHLNOW LANCHOW
ACHLNOY HALCYON
ACHLNTU UNLATCH
ACHLORS SCHOLAR
ACHLORT TROCHAL
ACHMNOR MONARCH
ACHMOPR CAMPHOR
ACHMOST STOMACH
ACHNNOS CHANSON
ACHNORS ANCHORS
ACHNOTY TACHYON
ACHNOVY ANCHOVY
ACHNPUY PAUNCHY
ACHNRTY CHANTRY
ACHNRUY RAUNCHY
ACHNSTU CANTHUS,
    STAUNCH
ACHNSTY SNATCHY
ACHOOST CAHOOTS
ACHOPRS CARHOPS
ACHOPRT TOPARCH
ACHOPRY CHARPOY
ACHRSTY STARCHY

ACIIKRS AIRSICK
ACIILMS ISLAMIC, LAICISM
ACIILNS SALICIN
ACIILNT CAITLIN
ACIILNV VICINAL
ACIILPT APLITIC
ACIILRY CILIARY
ACIILSS LIASSIC
ACIILST ITALICS
ACIIMRS CASIMIR
ACIINNO ANIONIC
ACIINOS NICOSIA
ACIINOV AVIONIC
ACIINPS PISCINA
ACIINTT TITANIC
ACIIPRT PIRATIC
ACIJLOS JALISCO
ACIJUZZ JACUZZI
ACIKLOR AIRLOCK
ACIKLTY TACKILY
ACIKNPY PANICKY
ACIKNST CATKINS
ACIKNTT TINTACK
ACIKPRT PATRICK
ACIKPSX SIX-PACK
ACIKPSY SICK PAY
ACIKRST KARSTIC
ACIKRWW WARWICK
ACIKUWZ ZWICKAU
ACILLLU LUCILLA
ACILLMS MISCALL
ACILLNS CALL-INS
ACILLRY LYRICAL
ACILMNO LIMACON
ACILMPS PSALMIC
ACILMSU MUSICAL
ACILNNY CANNILY
ACILNOR CLARINO,
    CLARION
ACILNOS NICOLAS,
    OILCANS
ACILNPY PLIANCY
ACILNTU LUNATIC
ACILOOR AIR-COOL
ACILOPT CAPITOL,
    OPTICAL, TOPICAL
ACILOSS SOCIALS
ACILOST STOICAL
ACILOTV VOLTAIC
ACILPST PLASTIC
ACILPTY TYPICAL
ACILRSS CRISSAL
ACILRTU CURTAIL

ACILRTY CLARITY
ACILRYZ CRAZILY
ACILSSS CLASSIS
ACILSUV CLAVIUS
ACILSUY SAUCILY
ACILTTY CATTILY, TACITLY
ACILTUV VICTUAL
ACIMMNO AMMONIC
ACIMNOP CAMPION
ACIMNOR MINORCA
ACIMNOS MASONIC
ACIMNRU CRANIUM
ACIMNTT CATMINT
ACIMOPT APOMICT,
    TAMPICO
ACIMOSS MOSAICS
ACIMOST SOMATIC
ACIMPRY PRIMACY
ACIMPST IMPACTS
ACIMSST MISCAST
ACINNOR CORINNA
ACINNOT ACTINON,
    CONTAIN
ACINNST STANNIC
ACINOPT CAPTION
ACINOQU COQUINA
ACINORR CARRION
ACINORS SARONIC
ACINOSS CAISSON,
    CASINOS, CASSINO
ACINOST ACTIONS
ACINOTU AUCTION,
    CAUTION
ACINOUV IN VACUO
ACINPRY CYPRIAN
ACINQTU QUANTIC
ACINRTU CURTAIN
ACINSUV VICUÑAS
ACIOPRS PROSAIC
ACIOPRT APRICOT, PAROTIC
ACIOPTY OPACITY
ACIORRS CORSAIR
ACIORSU CARIOUS,
    CURIOSA
ACIORTT RIOT ACT
ACIPRSY PISCARY
ACIPRVY PRIVACY
ACIPSST SPASTIC
ACIPTUY PAUCITY
ACIQRTU QUARTIC
ACIRSST RACISTS
ACIRSSU CUIRASS
ACIRSTY SATYRIC

ACISSTT STATICS
ACISSTU CASUIST
ACISTTU CATSUIT
ACITUVY VACUITY
ACJKKSY SKYJACK
ACJKLOW LOCKJAW
ACJKNOS JACKSON
ACJKOPT JACKPOT
ACJLORU JOCULAR
ACJMNTU MUNTJAC
ACJPTUU CAJUPUT
ACKKLMU KALMUCK
ACKLLOP POLLACK
ACKLLSY SLACKLY
ACKLNOU UNCLOAK
ACKLOOR OARLOCK
ACKLORW WARLOCK
ACKMOTT MATTOCK
ACKPSSY SKYCAPS
ACLLLOY LOCALLY
ACLLMMO MALCOLM
ACLLOOR COROLLA
ACLLOPS SCALLOP
ACLLORS COLLARS
ACLLORU LOCULAR
ACLLOSU CALLOUS
ACLLOVY VOCALLY
ACLLRYY ACRYLYL
ACLMNUY CALUMNY
ACLMORU CLAMOUR
ACLNOOR CORONAL
ACLNOOT COOLANT
ACLNOOV VOLCANO
ACLNORT CARLTON
ACLNORU CORNUAL
ACLNORY CAROLYN
ACLNOTY CLAYTON
ACLNPSU UNCLASP
ACLOOPR CAR POOL
ACLOPRT CALTROP
ACLOPRU COPULAR
ACLOPSU CUPOLAS,
   SCOPULA
ACLOPSY CALYPSO
ACLORRS CORRALS
ACLORSU CAROLUS,
   OSCULAR
ACLORWW WROCLAW
ACLPRTY CRYPTAL
ACLRSSW SCRAWLS
ACLRSSY CRASSLY
ACLRSTU CRUSTAL
ACLRSTY CRYSTAL

ACLRSWY SCRAWLY
ACLSSTU CUTLASS
ACMNOPR CRAMPON
ACMNOPY COMPANY
ACMNORY ACRONYM
ACMNSTU SANCTUM
ACMNTUU TUCUMAN
ACMOOPT POTOMAC
ACMOOST SCOTOMA
ACMOPSS COMPASS
ACMOSST MASCOTS
ACMOSTT TOMCATS
ACMQTUU CUMQUAT
ACMSUUV VACUUMS
ACNNNOS CANNONS
ACNNNUY UNCANNY
ACNNORY CANONRY
ACNNOST CANTONS
ACNNOSY CANYONS
ACNOORS CORONAS,
   RACOONS
ACNOORT CARTOON
ACNOPSU CANOPUS
ACNOPSW SNOWCAP
ACNORRU RANCOUR
ACNORRY CARRY-ON
ACNORST CANTORS,
   CARTONS
ACNORSY CRAYONS
ACNOSTU CONATUS,
   TOUCANS
ACNPRSY SYNCARP
ACNRRTU CURRANT
ACNRSWY SCRAWNY
ACNRTUY TRUANCY
ACNSSTU SANCTUS
ACNSTUY TUSCANY
ACOOPRR CORPORA
ACOOPTT TOPCOAT
ACOORTU TOURACO
ACOPPRR PROCARP
ACOPRRT CARPORT
ACOPRST CAPTORS
ACOPSTW COWPATS
ACORRST CARROTS
ACORRTT TRACTOR
ACORRTU CURATOR
ACORRTY CARROTY
ACORSST CASTORS,
   CO-STARS
ACORSSU SARCOUS
ACORSTU SURCOAT
ACORSTX OXCARTS

ACORSUU RAUCOUS
ACOSTTU OUTCAST
ACOSUUV VACUOUS
ACPPRSY SCRAPPY
ADDDEEN DEAD END
ADDDEER DREADED
ADDDEIS DADDIES
ADDDELN DANDLED
ADDDELP PADDLED
ADDDELS SADDLED
ADDDELW DAWDLED,
   WADDLED
ADDEEEY DEADEYE
ADDEEFM DEFAMED
ADDEEGR DEGRADE
ADDEEHR ADHERED,
   REDHEAD
ADDEEIR READIED
ADDEEKN KNEADED
ADDEELP PEDALED,
   PLEADED
ADDEELR ELDREDA, RED
   DEAL
ADDEELY DELAYED
ADDEEMN AMENDED
ADDEEMR DREAMED
ADDEEST SEDATED
ADDEFRT DRAFTED
ADDEFRU DEFRAUD
ADDEFRW DWARFED
ADDEGGR DRAGGED
ADDEGHO GODHEAD
ADDEGJU ADJUDGE
ADDEGLN DANGLED,
   GLADDEN
ADDEGLR GLADDER
ADDEGRU GUARDED
ADDEHIO HODEIDA
ADDEHIR DIEHARD
ADDEHLN HANDLED
ADDEHOR HOARDED
ADDEILL DALLIED, DIALLED
ADDEILS LADDIES
ADDEILT DILATED
ADDEIMR ADMIRED
ADDEIMS DIADEMS
ADDEINO ADENOID
ADDEINR DANDIER,
   DRAINED
ADDEINS DANDIES
ADDEINU UNAIDED
ADDEINV INVADED
ADDEIOR RADIOED

ADDEIOT TOADIED
ADDEIOV AVOIDED
ADDEIPS PADDIES
ADDEISV ADVISED
ADDEITU AUDITED
ADDEJRU ADJURED
ADDELLU ALLUDED
ADDELNR DANDLER
ADDELPP DAPPLED
ADDELPR PADDLER
ADDELPS PADDLES
ADDELRS LADDERS,
SADDLER
ADDELRW DAWDLER,
DRAWLED, WADDLER
ADDELSS SADDLES
ADDELST STADDLE
ADDELSW SWADDLE,
WADDLES
ADDELTW TWADDLE
ADDELYZ DAZEDLY
ADDELZZ DAZZLED
ADDEMNS DEMANDS
ADDEMST MADDEST
ADDENOR ADORNED
ADDENOT DONATED
ADDENOU DUODENA
ADDENPU PUDENDA
ADDENRS DANDERS
ADDENTU DAUNTED
ADDEOPT ADOPTED
ADDEPTU UPDATED
ADDERSS ADDRESS
ADDERTT DRATTED
ADDESST SADDEST
ADDFHIS FADDISH
ADDFIMS FADDISM
ADDFINY DANDIFY
ADDFIST FADDIST
ADDGGIN GADDING
ADDGINP PADDING
ADDGINW WADDING
ADDGMNO GODDAMN
ADDGOOY GOOD DAY
ADDGOSY DOG DAYS
ADDHITY HYDATID
ADDHLNO OLD HAND
ADDHNOR RHONDDA
ADDIINS DISDAIN
ADDIKTY KATYDID
ADDILMN MIDLAND
ADDILMO OLD MAID
ADDIMNO DIAMOND

ADDINOR ANDROID,
DORINDA
ADDLLOY OLD LADY
ADDLLRU DULLARD
ADDLNRY DRY LAND
ADDLOSY LAY ODDS
ADEEESW SEAWEED
ADEEFKR FREAKED
ADEEFLR ELFREDA,
FEDERAL
ADEEFLT DEFLATE
ADEEFMR DEFAMER
ADEEFRT DRAFTEE
ADEEFST DEFEATS,
FEASTED
ADEEGGH EGGHEAD
ADEEGGN ENGAGED
ADEEGLL ALLEGED
ADEEGLM GLEAMED
ADEEGLN GLEANED
ADEEGLU LEAGUED
ADEEGLY GLAD EYE
ADEEGMN END GAME
ADEEGNR ANGERED,
DERANGE, EN GARDE,
ENRAGED, GRANDEE,
GRENADE
ADEEGNT NEGATED
ADEEGNV AVENGED
ADEEGOT GOATEED
ADEEGRS GREASED
ADEEGRW RAGWEED,
WAGERED
ADEEHIR HEADIER
ADEEHLX EXHALED
ADEEHMN HEADMEN
ADEEHNS DASHEEN
ADEEHRS HEADERS,
SHEARED
ADEEHRT EARTHED
ADEEHST HEADSET
ADEEHSY HAYSEED
ADEEIJT JADEITE
ADEEILM LIMEADE
ADEEILN ADELINE,
DELAINE
ADEEIMT MEDIATE
ADEEINN ADENINE
ADEEINS ANISEED
ADEEIRR READIER
ADEEIRS DEARIES, READIES
ADEEIRW WEARIED
ADEEISS DISEASE, SEASIDE

ADEEITV DEVIATE
ADEEKNP KNEEPAD
ADEEKNR KNEADER
ADEEKNS SNEAKED
ADEEKNW WAKENED
ADEEKRW WREAKED
ADEEKTW TWEAKED
ADEEKWY WEEKDAY
ADEELLS ALLSEED
ADEELMR EMERALD
ADEELMT METALED
ADEELMZ DEMELZA
ADEELNP PANELED
ADEELNR DARLENE,
LEANDER, LEARNED
ADEELNT AL DENTE
ADEELNW ALEDWEN, NEW
DEAL
ADEELNZ ZEELAND
ADEELPR PLEADER
ADEELPS ELAPSED,
PLEASED
ADEELPT PLEATED
ADEELQU EQUALED
ADEELRS DEALERS,
LEADERS
ADEELRT ALERTED,
ALTERED, RELATED,
TREADLE
ADEELRV RAVELED
ADEELRW LEEWARD
ADEELRX RELAXED
ADEELRY DELAYER,
LAYERED, RELAYED
ADEELTX EXALTED
ADEELUV DEVALUE
ADEEMNR AMENDER,
MEANDER, RENAMED
ADEEMRR DREAMER,
REARMED
ADEEMRS SMEARED
ADEEMRT RED MEAT
ADEEMST STEAMED
ADEEMWY MAYWEED
ADEENNX ANNEXED
ADEENRY DEANERY,
YEARNED
ADEENST EAST END
ADEENTT DANETTE,
DENTATE
ADEEPPR PAPERED
ADEEPRS SPEARED

ADEEPRT PREDATE, RED TAPE, TAPERED
ADEEPRV DEPRAVE, PERVADE
ADEEQTU EQUATED
ADEERRS READERS
ADEERRT RETREAD, TREADER
ADEERRV AVERRED, EVERARD
ADEERST DEAREST
ADEERSV ADVERSE
ADEERTT TREATED
ADEERTV AVERTED
ADEERTW WATERED
ADEERVW WAVERED
ADEESSY ESSAYED
ADEESTU SAUTÉED
ADEESTW SWEATED
ADEFFIX AFFIXED
ADEFFLR RAFFLED
ADEFFLW WAFFLED
ADEFFST STAFFED
ADEFGGL FLAGGED
ADEFGLR RED FLAG
ADEFGNS FAG ENDS
ADEFGOR FORAGED
ADEFGRT GRAFTED
ADEFHLS FLASHED
ADEFHST SHAFTED
ADEFIIL FIDELIA
ADEFILL FLAILED
ADEFILR ELFRIDA
ADEFINT DEFIANT, FAINTED
ADEFITX FIXATED
ADEFKLN FLANKED
ADEFKNR FRANKED
ADEFLOT FLOATED
ADEFLPP FLAPPED
ADEFLTU DEFAULT, FAULTED
ADEFMNR MANFRED
ADEFOOR FEODORA
ADEFOOS SEAFOOD
ADEFORS FEDORAS
ADEFORY FORAYED
ADEFOTU FADEOUT
ADEFRRT DRAFTER, REDRAFT
ADEFRST STRAFED
ADEFSTT DAFTEST
ADEGGHL HAGGLED
ADEGGHS SHAGGED

ADEGGLR DRAGGLE, GARGLED
ADEGGLS SLAGGED
ADEGGLW WAGGLED
ADEGGNS SNAGGED
ADEGGRS DAGGERS
ADEGGST GADGETS
ADEGGTY GADGETY
ADEGHIN HEADING
ADEGHLU LAUGHED
ADEGHNS GNASHED
ADEGILN ALIGNED, DEALING, LEADING
ADEGINR READING
ADEGINV EVADING
ADEGINW WINDAGE
ADEGIRU GAUDIER
ADEGJLN JANGLED
ADEGLLU ULLAGED
ADEGLMN MANGLED
ADEGLNN ENGLAND
ADEGLNO DONEGAL
ADEGLNR DANGLER, GNARLED
ADEGLNS SLANGED
ADEGLNT TANGLED
ADEGLNW WANGLED
ADEGLOT GLOATED
ADEGLPU PLAGUED
ADEGLSS GLASSED
ADEGMNU AGENDUM
ADEGNNU DUNNAGE
ADEGNOR GROANED
ADEGNOS SONDAGE
ADEGNOT TANGOED
ADEGNOV DOGVANE
ADEGNPU UNPAGED
ADEGNRR GRANDER
ADEGNRS DANGERS, GANDERS, GARDENS
ADEGNRT DRAGNET, GRANTED
ADEGNTW TWANGED
ADEGNUW UNWAGED
ADEGORW DOWAGER, WORDAGE
ADEGOSS DOSAGES, SEA DOGS
ADEGOST DOTAGES
ADEGOVY VOYAGED
ADEGPRS GRASPED
ADEGPRU UPGRADE
ADEGRRR GERRARD

ADEGRRS REGARDS
ADEGRRU GUARDER
ADEGRSS GRASSED
ADEGRSU SUGARED
ADEGRTY GYRATED, TRAGEDY
ADEGRUU AUGURED
ADEGRUY GAUDERY
ADEGSSU DEGAUSS
ADEHHOP HOPHEAD
ADEHHOT HOTHEAD
ADEHILL DELILAH
ADEHILN HIELAND, INHALED
ADEHILY HEADILY
ADEHIMO HAEMOID
ADEHINP HEADPIN, PINHEAD
ADEHINR HANDIER
ADEHIPR RAPHIDE
ADEHIPS DIPHASE
ADEHIPT PITHEAD
ADEHIRR HARDIER, HARRIED
ADEHIRS SHADIER
ADEHIRW RAWHIDE
ADEHKNT THANKED
ADEHLLM ALDHELM
ADEHLMN HELMAND
ADEHLNR HANDLER
ADEHLNS HANDLES, HANDSEL
ADEHLOP ADOLPHE
ADEHLOT LOATHED
ADEHLRS HERALDS
ADEHLSS HASSLED, SLASHED
ADEHLTY DEATHLY
ADEHMMS SHAMMED
ADEHMNP HAMPDEN
ADEHMOY DAHOMEY
ADEHMSS SMASHED
ADEHNRU UNHEARD
ADEHNST HANDSET
ADEHNTU HAUNTED
ADEHOPX HEXAPOD
ADEHORR HOARDER
ADEHOTW TOWHEAD
ADEHPRS PHRASED
ADEHQSU QUASHED
ADEHRST HARDEST, THREADS, TRASHED

ADEHRTY HYDRATE,
  THREADY
ADEHSST STASHED
ADEHSTW SWATHED
ADEIILS DAILIES, LIAISED,
  SEDILIA
ADEIIMN DIAMINE
ADEIINZ DIAZINE
ADEIIRS DAIRIES, DIARIES
ADEIISS DAISIES
ADEIJSU JUDAISE
ADEIJUZ JUDAIZE
ADEIKLM LIKE MAD
ADEIKLR KILDARE
ADEIKRS DARKIES
ADEILLR DIALLER, RALLIED
ADEILLS SALLIED
ADEILLT TALLIED
ADEILLY IDEALLY
ADEILMM DILEMMA
ADEILMN MELINDA
ADEILMP IMPALED,
  IMPLEAD
ADEILMS MISDEAL,
  MISLEAD
ADEILNN ANNELID,
  LINDANE
ADEILNR IRELAND
ADEILNS DENIALS,
  LEAD-INS
ADEILNT TAIL END
ADEILNU ALIUNDE
ADEILOP OEDIPAL
ADEILOR DARIOLE
ADEILOZ DIAZOLE
ADEILPP APPLIED
ADEILPR LIP-READ
ADEILPS PALSIED
ADEILPT PLAITED, TALIPED
ADEILQU QUAILED
ADEILRT TRAILED
ADEILRU UREDIAL
ADEILRV RIVALED
ADEILRY READILY
ADEILST DETAILS
ADEILSV DEVISAL
ADEILSY DIALYSE
ADEIMMR MERMAID
ADEIMNS MAIDENS,
  MEDIANS
ADEIMNT MEDIANT
ADEIMOW MIAOWED

ADEIMRR ADMIRER,
  MARRIED
ADEIMRS MISREAD,
  SIDEARM
ADEIMRY MIDYEAR
ADEIMTU IDEATUM
ADEIMTY DAYTIME
ADEINOR ANEROID
ADEINOS ANODISE
ADEINOV NAEVOID
ADEINOZ ANODIZE
ADEINPT PAINTED
ADEINRR DRAINER,
  RANDIER
ADEINRS SANDIER,
  SARDINE
ADEINRT DETRAIN,
  TRADE-IN, TRAINED
ADEINRU URANIDE
ADEINRV INVADER
ADEINST INSTEAD,
  SAINTED, STAINED
ADEINTT TAINTED
ADEINTV DEVIANT
ADEIOPS ADIPOSE
ADEIORV AVOIDER
ADEIOST TOADIES
ADEIOSX OXIDASE
ADEIOTX OXIDATE
ADEIPPR PREPAID
ADEIPRR PARRIED
ADEIPRS ASPIRED,
  DESPAIR, DIAPERS, PRAISED
ADEIPRT PARTIED,
  PERDITA, PIRATED
ADEIRRS RAIDERS
ADEIRRT TARDIER, TARRIED
ADEIRRV ARRIVED
ADEIRST ASTRIDE,
  DIASTER, DISRATE, TIRADES
ADEIRSV ADVISER
ADEIRTT ATTIRED
ADEIRTY DIETARY
ADEISTV DATIVES, VISTAED
ADEISTW WAISTED
ADEISWY WAYSIDE
ADEITUZ DEUTZIA
ADEITWY TIDEWAY
ADEJMOR MAJORED
ADEJNTU JAUNTED
ADEJRRU ADJURER
ADEJSSU JUDASES
ADEKLLN KENDALL

ADEKLNR RANKLED
ADEKLNS KALENDS
ADEKLNY NAKEDLY
ADEKLST STALKED
ADEKMNR DENMARK
ADEKNPS SPANKED
ADEKNST DANKEST
ADEKNSW SWANKED
ADEKPRS SPARKED
ADEKRST DARKEST
ADELLMU MEDULLA
ADELLOW ALLOWED
ADELLOY ALLOYED
ADELLRR DARRELL
ADELLRU ALLURED
ADELLST STALLED
ADELMMS SLAMMED
ADELMNR MANDREL
ADELMNT MANTLED
ADELMOR EARLDOM
ADELMPS SAMPLED
ADELMRS MEDLARS
ADELMSS DAMSELS
ADELNNP PLANNED
ADELNOR LEONARD
ADELNOY YOLANDE
ADELNPT PLANTED
ADELNRS SLANDER,
  SNARLED
ADELNRU LAUNDER
ADELNST SLANTED
ADELNUU ULAN-UDE
ADELOPR LEOPARD,
  PAROLED
ADELOPS DEPOSAL
ADELOPT TADPOLE
ADELORS ORDEALS
ADELORT LEOTARD
ADELOSS LASSOED
ADELOTT TOTALED
ADELOVY LOVEDAY
ADELPPS SLAPPED
ADELPRS PEDLARS
ADELPST STAPLED
ADELPSW DEWLAPS
ADELPSY SPLAYED
ADELPTY ADEPTLY
ADELRRS LARDERS
ADELRRU RUDERAL
ADELRRW DRAWLER
ADELRTT RATTLED
ADELRTW TRAWLED
ADELRTX DEXTRAL

ADELSTT SLATTED
ADELSTU SALUTED
ADELTTT TATTLED
ADELTUV VAULTED
ADELTWZ WALTZED
ADEMNNU MUNDANE,
UNNAMED
ADEMNOR ROADMEN
ADEMNOS DAEMONS
ADEMNOZ MENDOZA
ADEMNRS REMANDS
ADEMNRU MANURED,
MAUNDER, UNARMED
ADEMNSS MADNESS
ADEMNST TANDEMS
ADEMORS MODERAS
ADEMOSW MEADOWS
ADEMOSY SAMOYED,
SOMEDAY
ADEMPRS DAMPERS
ADEMPRT TRAMPED
ADEMPST DAMPEST,
STAMPED
ADEMPSW SWAMPED
ADEMRRU EARDRUM
ADEMRST SMARTED
ADEMRSW SWARMED
ADEMRTU MATURED
ADEMSSU ASSUMED
ADENNOY ANNOYED,
ANODYNE
ADENNPS SPANNED
ADENNPT PENDANT
ADENNSU DUENNAS
ADENNSW SWANNED
ADENOPR OPERAND,
PADRONE, PANDORE
ADENOPT NOTEPAD
ADENORR RED ROAN
ADENORU RONDEAU
ADENOUY YAOUNDE
ADENPPS SNAPPED
ADENPST PEDANTS
ADENPSW SPAWNED
ADENRRS ERRANDS
ADENRRY REYNARD
ADENRSS SANDERS
ADENRST STANDER
ADENRSU ASUNDER,
DANSEUR
ADENRSW WARDENS
ADENRTU DAUNTER
ADENRTV VERDANT

ADENRTX DEXTRAN
ADENRUY UNREADY
ADENSSS SADNESS
ADENSSU SUNDAES
ADENSTV ADVENTS
ADENSWY ENDWAYS
ADENTTU ATTUNED,
TAUNTED
ADENTUV VAUNTED
ADEOPST PODESTA
ADEORRW ARROWED
ADEORST ROASTED,
TORSADE
ADEORSU AROUSED
ADEORTT ROTATED
ADEORTU READOUT
ADEORTY YEAR DOT
ADEORYZ ZEDOARY
ADEOSTT TOASTED
ADEOTTU OUTDATE
ADEPPRT TRAPPED
ADEPPRW WRAPPED
ADEPPSW SWAPPED
ADEPRRS DRAPERS,
SPARRED
ADEPRRY DRAPERY
ADEPRSS SPREADS
ADEPRST PETARDS
ADEPRSY SPRAYED
ADEPRTU UPDATER
ADEPSTU UPDATES
ADEQRSU SQUARED
ADERRST STARRED,
TRADERS
ADERRSW DRAWERS,
REWARDS, WARDERS
ADERSSU ASSURED
ADERSTT STARTED
ADERSTV STARVED
ADERSTW STEWARD
ADERSTY STRAYED
ADERSUY DASYURE
ADERSVW DWARVES
ADESTTU STATUED
ADESTTW SWATTED
ADESTUY TUESDAY
ADFFHNO OFFHAND
ADFFIST DISTAFF
ADFFLOO OFF-LOAD
ADFHLNU HANDFUL
ADFHOOS SHADOOF
ADFIINO IN AID OF
ADFILLU FLUIDAL

ADFILNN FINLAND
ADFILOR FLORIDA
ADFILOT DO A FLIT
ADFIMNY DAMNIFY
ADFIRSY FRIDAYS
ADFLMPU MUDFLAP
ADFLMTU MUDFLAT
ADFLNOP PLAFOND
ADFLNSY SAND FLY
ADFLORU FOULARD
ADFNNOT FONDANT
ADFOOPT FOOTPAD
ADFORRW FORWARD,
FROWARD
ADFPRTU UPDRAFT
ADGGHNO HANGDOG
ADGGINO GOADING
ADGGINR GRADING,
NIGGARD
ADGGOST DOG TAGS
ADGHILO HIDALGO
ADGHINN HANDING
ADGHINR HARDING
ADGHINS DASHING,
SHADING
ADGHIPR DIGRAPH
ADGHNNU HANDGUN
ADGHOOR ROAD HOG
ADGHRTU DRAUGHT
ADGIILN DIALING, GLIADIN
ADGIILT DIGITAL
ADGIINR RAIDING
ADGILLN LADLING
ADGILNN LANDING
ADGILNO LOADING
ADGILNR DARLING,
LARDING
ADGILNS LADINGS
ADGILNU LANGUID,
LAUDING
ADGILUY GAUDILY
ADGIMMN DAMMING
ADGIMNN DAMNING
ADGIMNP DAMPING
ADGINNR DARNING
ADGINNS SANDING
ADGINNW DAWNING
ADGINOR ADORING
ADGINPP DAPPING
ADGINPR DRAPING
ADGINRT DARTING,
TRADING

ADGINRW DRAWING, WARDING
ADGINWY GWYNIAD
ADGIRZZ GIZZARD
ADGKNOZ DZONGKA
ADGLLOS OLD LAGS
ADGLNOO GONDOLA
ADGLNOY DAYLONG
ADGLNRY GRANDLY
ADGLOOV VOLOGDA
ADGLOPS LAPDOGS
ADGLORY GAYLORD
ADGLOSU DOUGLAS
ADGLSWY GWLADYS
ADGMOOR MOGADOR
ADGNOOR DRAGOON, GADROON
ADGNORS DRAGONS
ADGNORU AGROUND, DURANGO
ADGNRRU GURNARD
ADHHMOS SHAHDOM
ADHHOSW HOWDAHS
ADHIIMS HASIDIM
ADHIKTZ TADZHIK
ADHILMO HALIDOM
ADHILNY HANDILY
ADHILOP HAPLOID
ADHILOY HOLIDAY, HYALOID
ADHILRY HARDILY
ADHILSY SHADILY
ADHIMPS DAMPISH, PHASMID
ADHINPU DAUPHIN
ADHIORS HAIRDOS
ADHLLLO HOLDALL
ADHLLNO HOLLAND
ADHLNOW HOWLAND
ADHMMNO HAMMOND
ADHMNOO MANHOOD
ADHMNPY DYMPHNA
ADHMNWY WYNDHAM
ADHNNOS HANDS-ON
ADHNORS HARD-ONS
ADHNOTU HANDOUT
ADHNOVZ ZHDANOV
ADHNPSU HANDS UP
ADHNRTU HARD NUT
ADHNRTY HYDRANT
ADHOPRT HARDTOP
ADHOSSW SHADOWS
ADHOSWY SHADOWY

ADIIJNU JUNDIAI
ADIILMS MISLAID
ADIILNO LIANOID
ADIILNV INVALID
ADIILOS SIALOID
ADIINNS INDIANS
ADIINOS SIDONIA
ADIIORS ISIDORA
ADIIRST DIARIST
ADIIRTY ARIDITY
ADIITVY AVIDITY
ADIJMSU JUDAISM
ADIJNOT ADJOINT
ADIJSTU JUDAIST
ADIKMNN MANKIND
ADIKMOS MIKADOS
ADIKNPS INKPADS, SKIDPAN
ADILLMM MILLDAM
ADILLRW WILLARD
ADILLVY VALIDLY
ADILMNU MAUDLIN
ADILMOP DIPLOMA
ADILMOY AMYLOID
ADILMSU DUALISM
ADILNOR LORINDA, ORDINAL
ADILNRU DIURNAL
ADILNSS ISLANDS
ADILNSU SUNDIAL
ADILNSY LINDSAY
ADILOPR DIPOLAR
ADILORT DILATOR
ADILOUV OLDUVAI
ADILPRY PYRALID, RAPIDLY
ADILPST PLASTID
ADILPSY DISPLAY
ADILPTU PLAUDIT
ADILPVY VAPIDLY
ADILQSU SQUALID
ADILRSZ LIZARDS
ADILRTY TARDILY
ADILSTU DUALIST
ADILSTY STAIDLY
ADILTUY DUALITY
ADIMNOS DOMAINS, MADISON
ADIMORR MIRADOR
ADIMOST MASTOID
ADIMPRY PYRAMID
ADIMRSY MYRIADS
ADIMSST DISMAST
ADIMSTU STADIUM

ADINNOP DIPNOAN
ADINNOR ANDIRON
ADINNRS INNARDS
ADINNRW INDRAWN
ADINNST STAND-IN
ADINOPR PONIARD
ADINORS INROADS, SADIRON
ADINOTX OXIDANT
ADINPST PANDITS, SANDPIT
ADINRSW INWARDS
ADINSTT DISTANT
ADINTTY DITTANY
ADIOOSW WOODSIA
ADIOPRR AIRDROP
ADIOPRT PAROTID
ADIORST ASTROID
ADIORTU AUDITOR
ADIOSUV VAUDOIS
ADIOSVW DISAVOW
ADIPRTY PAY DIRT
ADIPRUU UDAIPUR
ADIRSSU SARDIUS
ADIRSTY SATYRID
ADIRSUY DYSURIA
ADIRSWZ WIZARDS
ADISSST SADISTS
ADJLNTU JUTLAND
ADJNNOU DON JUAN
ADJNORU ADJOURN
ADKORWY WORKDAY
ADLLLOR LOLLARD
ADLLMOY MODALLY
ADLLNOW LOWLAND
ADLLOPR POLLARD
ADLLORS DOLLARS
ADLMNOS ALMONDS
ADLMNUU ALUNDUM
ADLMORU MODULAR
ADLNOOR ORLANDO
ADLNOPU POUNDAL
ADLNORU NODULAR
ADLNORW ROWLAND
ADLNOSY SYNODAL
ADLNPSU UPLANDS
ADLNRUY LAUNDRY
ADLNTWY TYNWALD
ADLOPRU POULARD
ADLORRW WARLORD
ADLORUY OUR LADY
ADLOSSW SOD'S LAW
ADLRSTY DRY-SALT
ADMMNSU SUMMAND

ADMNOOR DOORMAN
ADMNOOW WOODMAN
ADMNOQU QUONDAM
ADMNORS RANDOMS
ADMNORT DORMANT,
 MORDANT
ADMNORY RAYMOND
ADMNOSS DAMSONS
ADMNOSU OSMUNDA
ADMNOSY DYNAMOS,
 MONDAYS
ADMNRUY RAYMUND
ADMNSTU DUSTMAN
ADMOORT DOORMAT
ADMOORY DAYROOM
ADMOPPU POPADUM
ADMOPST POTSDAM
ADMORRS RAMRODS
ADMORST STARDOM,
 TSARDOM
ADMORTW MADWORT
ADMRSTU DURMAST,
 MUSTARD
ADNNOOV DONOVAN
ADNNOOY NOONDAY
ADNNSTU DUNSTAN
ADNOORT DONATOR,
 TORNADO
ADNOOSS SO-AND-SO
ADNOPRS PARDONS
ADNORSW ONWARDS
ADNORTU ROTUNDA
ADNOSTU ASTOUND
ADNPPUU UP-AND-UP
ADNPSTU DUSTPAN,
 STAND-UP
ADNRSST STRANDS
ADNSSUY SUNDAYS
ADNSTYY DYNASTY
ADOOPSW SAPWOOD
ADOORWY DOORWAY
ADORSTW TOWARDS
ADORSUU ARDUOUS
ADORTUW OUTWARD
ADPRSUW UPWARDS
ADSSTUW SAWDUST
AEEEGLT LEGATEE
AEEEGNT TEENAGE
AEEEGPR PEERAGE
AEEEGPS SEEPAGE
AEEEGRT ETAGERE
AEEEILN ALIENEE
AEEELNR RAELENE

AEEELRS RELEASE
AEEEELTV ELEVATE
AEEFHRT FEATHER
AEEFILR LEAFIER
AEEFIRS FREESIA
AEEFLLN FENELLA
AEEFLLT LEAFLET
AEEFLMS FEMALES
AEEFLRT REFLATE
AEEFLRW WELFARE
AEEFLSU EASEFUL
AEEFMNR FREEMAN
AEEFORS FAEROES
AEEFOTV FOVEATE
AEEFRRT FERRATE
AEEFRST FEASTER
AEEFRTU FEATURE
AEEFRTX TAX-FREE
AEEFRWY FREEWAY
AEEGGLM GAME LEG
AEEGGLT GATE-LEG
AEEGGNR ENGAGER
AEEGHNW WHANGEE
AEEGILL GALILEE
AEEGILM MILEAGE
AEEGILN LINEAGE
AEEGILP EPIGEAL
AEEGILW WEIGELA
AEEGINU EUGENIA
AEEGISS AEGISES
AEEGLLZ GAZELLE
AEEGLMN MÉLANGE
AEEGLMT MELTAGE
AEEGLNR ENLARGE,
 GENERAL, GLEANER
AEEGLNS SENEGAL
AEEGLNT ELEGANT
AEEGLNU EUGLENA
AEEGLNV EVANGEL
AEEGLOR AEROGEL
AEEGLRY EAGERLY
AEEGLSS AGELESS, SEA
 LEGS
AEEGLST EAGLETS,
 LEGATES
AEEGLSU LEAGUES
AEEGLSV SELVAGE
AEEGLTV VEGETAL
AEEGMMT GEMMATE,
 TAGMEME
AEEGMNR GERMANE
AEEGMNS MÉNAGES
AEEGMSS MESSAGE

AEEGNNV GENEVAN
AEEGNPP GENAPPE
AEEGNRT GRANTEE,
 REAGENT
AEEGNRV AVENGER,
 ENGRAVE, GENEVRA
AEEGNTT TENTAGE
AEEGNTV VENTAGE
AEEGOPS APOGEES
AEEGORV OVERAGE
AEEGOST GOATEES
AEEGPRS PRESAGE
AEEGRRS GREASER
AEEGRRT GREATER,
 REGRATE
AEEGRRW WAGERER
AEEGRSV GERVASE,
 GREAVES
AEEGSTT GESTATE
AEEGTTZ GAZETTE
AEEHHNT HEATHEN
AEEHHRT HEATHER
AEEHHST SHEATHE
AEEHIRV HEAVIER
AEEHISV HEAVIES
AEEHKNR HEARKEN
AEEHLPT HEELTAP
AEEHLRS HEALERS
AEEHLRT HALTERE,
 LEATHER
AEEHLRV LE HAVRE
AEEHLSS LEASHES
AEEHLSY EYELASH
AEEHLTT ATHLETE
AEEHMNT METHANE
AEEHNPS PEAHENS
AEEHNPT HAPTENE,
 HEPTANE
AEEHNRT EARTHEN,
 HEARTEN, TEHERAN
AEEHNSV HEAVENS
AEEHNSW SHAWNEE
AEEHNTW WHEATEN
AEEHPRS RESHAPE
AEEHPRT PREHEAT
AEEHPTT PET HATE
AEEHPUV UPHEAVE
AEEHRRS SHEARER
AEEHRRS HEARSES
AEEHRST HEATERS,
 THERESA
AEEHRSW WHEREAS

AEEHRTT THEATRE,
THEREAT
AEEHRTW WEATHER,
WHEREAT, WREATHE
AEEHSSV SHEAVES
AEEHSTT THE EAST
AEEHSWY EYEWASH
AEEIJNN JEANNIE
AEEIKLP APELIKE
AEEIKLR LEAKIER
AEEIKPR PEAKIER
AEEILLU EULALIE
AEEILMN MELANIE
AEEILMR MEALIER
AEEILMS SEA MILE
AEEILMT ELAMITE
AEEILNT LINEATE
AEEILNV AVELINE, EVELINA
AEEILPR PEARLIE
AEEILPT PILEATE
AEEILRR EARLIER
AEEILRS REALISE
AEEILRT ATELIER
AEEILRV VALERIE
AEEILRZ REALIZE
AEEILTV ELATIVE
AEEIMNT ETAMINE,
MATINÉE
AEEIMNX EXAMINE
AEEIMRS SEAMIER,
SERIEMA
AEEIMRT EMIRATE,
MEATIER
AEEIMSS SIAMESE
AEEINRT ARENITE,
RETINAE, TRAINEE
AEEINST ETESIAN
AEEINTV NAIVETE,
VENETIA
AEEINVW INWEAVE
AEEIPRR PEREIRA
AEEIPTX EXPIATE
AEEIRRT ERITREA
AEEIRRW WEARIER
AEEIRST SERIATE
AEEIRSZ ZAIRESE
AEEIRTT ITERATE
AEEISST EASIEST
AEEISVV EVASIVE
AEEIUVX EXUVIAE
AEEJNTT JANETTE
AEEJRSW JEW'S-EAR
AEEKKNO KOKANEE

AEEKMRS REMAKES
AEEKMRT MEERKAT
AEEKNNN NANKEEN
AEEKNRS SNEAKER
AEEKNRT RETAKEN
AEEKNRW WAKENER
AEEKNSY YANKEES
AEEKPRS SPEAKER
AEEKRRT RETAKER
AEEKRRW WREAKER
AEEKRST RETAKES
AEEKSTW WEAKEST
AEELLST ESTELLA
AEELLSV A LEVELS
AEELLWY WALLEYE
AEELMNP EMPANEL
AEELMNR MARLENE
AEELMNU EMANUEL
AEELMNV VELAMEN
AEELMNY AMYLENE
AEELMPR EMPALER
AEELMPX EXAMPLE
AEELMSS MEASLES
AEELMST MALTESE
AEELMTU EMULATE
AEELNNP ENPLANE
AEELNOR ELEANOR
AEELNRR LEARNER
AEELNRT ETERNAL,
TELERAN
AEELNRU LAUREEN
AEELNRV LAVERNE
AEELNRW RENEWAL
AEELNST LEANEST
AEELNSV ENSLAVE,
LEAVENS
AEELOPX POLEAXE
AEELORU AUREOLE
AEELPRR PEARLER
AEELPRS PLEASER,
RELAPSE
AEELPRT PLEATER,
PRELATE
AEELPTT PALETTE, PELTATE
AEELPTU EPAULET
AEELQSU SEQUELA
AEELRRT RELATER
AEELRRX RELAXER
AEELRSS SEALERS
AEELRST STEALER
AEELRSV SEVERAL
AEELRSY SEALERY
AEELRTT ARLETTE

AEELRTX EXALTER
AEELRUV REVALUE
AEELSST TEASELS
AEELSSW WEASELS
AEELSTT SEATTLE
AEELTTY LAYETTE
AEELTVW WAVELET
AEEMMPY EMPYEMA
AEEMMRT AMMETER,
METAMER
AEEMNNO ANEMONE
AEEMNNP PEN NAME
AEEMNNY MAYENNE
AEEMNPT PET NAME
AEEMNRU MAUREEN
AEEMNSS EN MASSE
AEEMNST MEANEST
AEEMORT EROTEMA
AEEMOSW AWESOME
AEEMPRT TAMPERE,
TEMPERA
AEEMPTU AMPUTEE
AEEMQRU MARQUEE
AEEMRRS REAMERS,
SMEARER
AEEMRST STEAMER
AEEMRSU MEASURE
AEENNOT NEONATE
AEENNPT PENNATE,
PENTANE
AEENNRS ENSNARE
AEENNSX ANNEXES
AEENNTT ANNETTE,
NANETTE
AEENOPU EUPNOEA
AEENPSX EXPANSE
AEENRRS EARNERS
AEENRRT TERRANE
AEENRRV RAVENER
AEENRRY YEARNER
AEENRST EARNEST,
EASTERN, NEAREST
AEENRTT ENTREAT,
TERNATE
AEENRTV NERVATE,
VETERAN
AEENRVY YEREVAN
AEENRWY NEW YEAR
AEENSST SENATES,
SENSATE
AEENSTT NEATEST
AEENSUV AVENUES
AEENVWW NEW WAVE

AEEOPRT OPERATE
AEEORST ROSEATE
AEEORVW OVERAWE
AEEPPRR PAPERER,
  PREPARE
AEEPRRS REAPERS,
  SPEARER
AEEPRRT TAPERER
AEEPRSS ASPERSE,
  PARSEES
AEEPRST REPEATS
AEEPRTX EX PARTE
AEEPRTZ TRAPEZE
AEEPSST PESETAS
AEEPSTT SEPTATE
AEERRSS ERASERS
AEERRST SERRATE
AEERRSU ERASURE
AEERRSW SWEARER
AEERRTT RETREAT,
  TREATER
AEERRTW WATERER
AEERRVW WAVERER
AEERSST EASTERS,
  TEASERS, TESSERA
AEERSTT ESTREAT,
  RESTATE
AEERSTU AUSTERE
AEERSTW SWEATER
AEERSVW WEAVERS
AEESSSW SEESAWS
AEESSTT ESTATES
AEESTTT TESTATE
AEFFGIL FIG LEAF
AEFFGIR GIRAFFE
AEFFGRS GAFFERS
AEFFIST TAFFIES
AEFFISX AFFIXES
AEFFKOP OFF-PEAK
AEFFKOR RAKE-OFF
AEFFKOT TAKEOFF
AEFFLLY FLYLEAF
AEFFLNS SNAFFLE
AEFFLRR RAFFLER
AEFFLRS RAFFLES
AEFFLRU FEARFUL
AEFFLSW WAFFLES
AEFFLTU FATEFUL
AEFFMRU EARMUFF
AEFFOVW WAVEOFF
AEFFQRU QUAFFER
AEFFRST STAFFER
AEFGGLR FLAGGER

AEFGIKN KAIFENG
AEFGILN FINAGLE
AEFGILO FOLIAGE
AEFGILR FRAGILE
AEFGINR FEARING
AEFGINU FUEGIAN
AEFGIRT FRIGATE
AEFGITU FATIGUE
AEFGLNR FLANGER
AEFGLNS FLANGES
AEFGLOT FLOTAGE
AEFGLOW FLOWAGE
AEFGNOR FAR GONE
AEFGNRT ENGRAFT
AEFGOOT FOOTAGE
AEFGORR FORAGER
AEFGORS FORAGES
AEFGORV FORGAVE
AEFGRRT GRAFTER
AEFGRSU FEARGUS
AEFHLRS FLASHER
AEFHLSS FLASHES
AEFHLTU HATEFUL
AEFHRRT FARTHER
AEFHRST FATHERS
AEFIILT FILIATE
AEFIIRS FAIRIES
AEFIKLR FLAKIER
AEFIKNR FRANKIE
AEFILLM FAMILLE
AEFILMN INFLAME
AEFILNS FINALES
AEFILNT INFLATE
AEFILOT FOLIATE
AEFILPT FLEAPIT
AEFILRR FRAILER
AEFILRU FAILURE
AEFILRV FAVRILE
AEFILSS FALSIES
AEFIMNR FIREMAN
AEFIMNS FAMINES
AEFIMOR FOAMIER
AEFIMRR FIREARM
AEFINNR FRANNIE
AEFINNS FANNIES
AEFINNT INFANTE
AEFINNZ FANZINE
AEFINPR FIREPAN
AEFINRR REFRAIN
AEFINRT FAINTER, FINE ART
AEFINTX ANTEFIX
AEFIQRU AQUIFER
AEFIRRR FARRIER

AEFIRST FAIREST
AEFIRSX FAIR SEX
AEFIRTT FATTIER
AEFISST FIESTAS
AEFISTT FATTIES
AEFKLNR FLANKER
AEFKLRT FARTLEK
AEFKLST FLASKET
AEFKLUW WAKEFUL
AEFKNRR FRANKER
AEFKORS FORSAKE
AEFLLNN FLANNEL
AEFLLSY FALSELY
AEFLLTT FLATLET
AEFLMOR FEMORAL
AEFLNOV FLAVONE
AEFLNRU FLANEUR,
  FUNERAL
AEFLNTT FLATTEN
AEFLOOV FOVEOLA
AEFLOPW PEAFOWL
AEFLORS LOAFERS,
  SAFROLE
AEFLORT FLOATER
AEFLPPR FLAPPER
AEFLPRS FELSPAR
AEFLPRU FLARE-UP
AEFLPRY PALFREY
AEFLRSU REFUSAL
AEFLRTT FLATTER
AEFLRTU TEARFUL
AEFLRZZ FRAZZLE
AEFLSST FALSEST
AEFMNOR FORAMEN,
  FOREMAN
AEFMNRU FRAENUM
AEFMORR FOREARM
AEFMORT FORMATE
AEFMPRU FRAME-UP
AEFMRRS FARMERS
AEFNOPR PROFANE
AEFNRSS FARNESS
AEFNSST FATNESS
AEFOPRW FOREPAW
AEFORRY FORAYER
AEFORSW FORESAW
AEFPPRS FRAPPÉS
AEFRRST RAFTERS,
  STRAFER
AEFRSTW FRETSAW
AEFSSTT FASTEST
AEFSTTT FATTEST
AEGGGLU LUGGAGE

AEGGHLR HAGGLER
AEGGINR GEARING
AEGGIOR GEORGIA
AEGGIOS ISAGOGE
AEGGIRS SAGGIER
AEGGJRY JAGGERY
AEGGLRR GARGLER
AEGGLRS GARGLES
AEGGLRY GREYLAG
AEGGLSW WAGGLES
AEGGNRS GANGERS,
    GRANGES, NAGGERS
AEGGRSS AGGRESS
AEGGRST STAGGER,
    TAGGERS
AEGGRSW SWAGGER
AEGGRTY GARGETY
AEGHHIT HIGH TEA
AEGHHLS SHELAGH
AEGHIKL HAGLIKE
AEGHILN HEALING
AEGHILR RALEIGH
AEGHINP HEAPING
AEGHINR HEARING
AEGHINT GAHNITE,
    HEATING
AEGHINV HEAVING
AEGHISS GEISHAS
AEGHLNO HALOGEN
AEGHLRU LAUGHER
AEGHMNN HANGMEN
AEGHNOX HEXAGON
AEGHNRS HANGERS
AEGHNSS GNASHES
AEGHOST HOSTAGE
AEGHRST GATHERS
AEGIIMN IMAGINE
AEGIINR NIGERIA
AEGIKLN LEAKING,
    LINKAGE
AEGIKNP PEAKING
AEGIKPR GARPIKE
AEGIKRW GAWKIER
AEGILLL ILLEGAL
AEGILLN GILLEAN
AEGILLP PILLAGE
AEGILLT TILLAGE
AEGILLV VILLAGE
AEGILLY AGILELY
AEGILMR GREMIAL
AEGILMT TIME LAG
AEGILNN LEANING
AEGILNP LEAPING, PEALING

AEGILNR ENGRAIL,
    REALIGN
AEGILNS LEASING,
    SEALING
AEGILNT GELATIN, GENITAL
AEGILNV LEAVING
AEGILOS SOILAGE
AEGILOU EULOGIA
AEGILRS ALGIERS
AEGILRZ GLAZIER
AEGIMNN MEANING
AEGIMNR GERMAIN,
    MANGIER, REAMING
AEGIMNS ENIGMAS
AEGIMNT MINTAGE,
    TEAMING
AEGIMPR EPIGRAM
AEGIMPS MAGPIES
AEGIMRR ARMIGER
AEGIMRS GISARME,
    MIRAGES
AEGIMRT MIGRATE,
    RAGTIME
AEGIMRY IMAGERY
AEGIMST GAMIEST,
    SIGMATE
AEGINNR EARNING,
    ENGRAIN, GRAINNE,
    NEARING
AEGINNT ANTEING,
    ANTIGEN, GENTIAN
AEGINNU ANGUINE,
    GUANINE, GUINEAN
AEGINNV ANGEVIN
AEGINNW WEANING
AEGINOR IRON AGE
AEGINOS AGONIES,
    AGONISE
AEGINOZ AGONIZE
AEGINPP GENIPAP
AEGINPR REAPING
AEGINRR ANGRIER,
    EARRING, GRAINER,
    REARING
AEGINRS ERASING,
    GAINERS, REGINAS,
    SEARING, SERINGA
AEGINRT GERAINT,
    GRANITE, INGRATE,
    TANGIER, TEARING
AEGINRV GINEVRA,
    VINEGAR
AEGINRW WEARING

AEGINST EASTING,
    INGESTA, SEATING,
    TEASING
AEGINSU GUINEAS
AEGINTV VINTAGE
AEGINVW WEAVING
AEGIPRU PERUGIA
AEGIRRZ GRAZIER
AEGIRSS GASSIER
AEGIRST GAITERS, SEAGIRT
AEGIRSV GERVAIS
AEGIRSW EARWIGS
AEGIRTV VIRGATE
AEGIRUZ GAUZIER
AEGISST AGEISTS
AEGISSV VISAGES
AEGJLNR JANGLER
AEGKRSW GAWKERS
AEGKSST GASKETS
AEGLLLY LEGALLY
AEGLLNO GALLEON
AEGLLOR ALLEGRO
AEGLLRY ALLERGY,
    GALLERY, LARGELY,
    REGALLY
AEGLLSU SEAGULL,
    SULLAGE
AEGLLSY GALLEYS
AEGLLTU GLUTEAL
AEGLMNR MANGLER
AEGLMNS MANGLES
AEGLMPU PLUMAGE
AEGLNOT TANGELO
AEGLNPR GRAPNEL
AEGLNPS SPANGLE
AEGLNRS LANGRES
AEGLNRT TANGLER
AEGLNRU GRANULE
AEGLNRW WANGLER,
    WRANGLE
AEGLNST TANGLES
AEGLNSU ANGELUS
AEGLNSW WANGLES
AEGLNTT GANTLET
AEGLNUW GUNWALE
AEGLOPR PERGOLA
AEGLORS GAOLERS
AEGLORT GLOATER,
    LEGATOR
AEGLORV VORLAGE
AEGLOTV VOLTAGE
AEGLPPR GRAPPLE

AEGLPRU EARPLUG,	AEGOPST GESTAPO,	AEHINOT HIONATE
GRAUPEL, PLAGUER	POSTAGE	AEHINPR HEPARIN
AEGLPSU PLAGUES	AEGOPTT POTTAGE	AEHINPS IN PHASE,
AEGLRRU REGULAR	AEGORST STORAGE	PHINEAS
AEGLRSS LARGESS	AEGORTU OUTRAGE	AEHINRS HERNIAS
AEGLRST LARGEST	AEGORVY VOYAGER	AEHINRT HAIRNET
AEGLRSV VERGLAS	AEGOSSU GASEOUS	AEHINSS HESSIAN
AEGLRTU TEGULAR	AEGOSTW STOWAGE	AEHIORR HOARIER
AEGLRTY GREATLY	AEGOSVY VOYAGES	AEHIPPR HAPPIER
AEGLRVY GRAVELY	AEGOTTV GAVOTTE	AEHIPPT EPITAPH
AEGLSSS GLASSES	AEGOTTW GET A TOW	AEHIPRS HARPIES
AEGLSTT GESTALT	AEGPRRS GRASPER	AEHIPSS APHESIS
AEGLTUV VULGATE	AEGPSTU UPSTAGE	AEHIRRR HARRIER
AEGLUUY GUAYULE	AEGRRST GARRETS,	AEHIRRT HARRIET
AEGLUVY VAGUELY	GARTERS, GRATERS	AEHIRST HASTIER
AEGMMRS GRAMMES	AEGRRTT GARRETT	AEHIRWY HAYWIRE
AEGMMRU RUMMAGE	AEGRRUV GRAVURE	AEHISST ASHIEST
AEGMNNO AGNOMEN	AEGRSSS GRASSES	AEHISTT ATHEIST
AEGMNOS MANGOES	AEGRSTT TARGETS	AEHISTZ HAZIEST
AEGMNOT MAGNETO,	AEGRSTV GRAVEST	AEHJOPS JOSEPHA
MEGATON, MONTAGE	AEGRSTY GRAYEST	AEHKLOY HOYLAKE
AEGMNRS GERMANS,	AEGSTUV GUSTAVE	AEHKPSU SHAKE-UP
MANGERS	AEGTTTU GUTTATE	AEHKRSS SHAKERS
AEGMNRT GARMENT	AEHHILS SHEILAH	AEHKRSW HAWKERS
AEGMNRY GERMANY	AEHHJOV JEHOVAH	AEHKRTU KETURAH
AEGMNST MAGNETS	AEHHJPT JAPHETH	AEHLLUV HELLUVA
AEGMNTU AUGMENT,	AEHHLST HEALTHS	AEHLMNO MANHOLE
MUTAGEN	AEHHLTY HEALTHY	AEHLMOR ARMHOLE
AEGMOOR MOORAGE	AEHHMSY HEYSHAM	AEHLMRT THERMAL
AEGMOXY EXOGAMY	AEHHRRS HARSHER	AEHLMRU HUMERAL
AEGMRRY MARGERY	AEHHRST HEARTHS	AEHLMST HAMLETS
AEGNNOR ARGONNE,	AEHHSST SHEATHS	AEHLNOT ETHANOL
GARONNE	AEHIIRR HAIRIER	AEHLNRT ENTHRAL
AEGNNOT TONNAGE	AEHIKLT HATLIKE	AEHLNSU UNLEASH
AEGNNRT REGNANT	AEHIKNS HANKIES	AEHLOPT TAPHOLE
AEGNNST GANNETS	AEHIKRS SHAKIER	AEHLORT LOATHER
AEGNNTT TANGENT	AEHILMN HAMELIN	AEHLOSS ASSHOLE
AEGNOOR OREGANO	AEHILMO HEMIOLA	AEHLPRS SPHERAL
AEGNORR GROANER	AEHILNR HERNIAL,	AEHLPSS HAPLESS
AEGNORS ORANGES	INHALER	AEHLPSY SHAPELY
AEGNORT NEGATOR	AEHILNY HYALINE	AEHLRSS SLASHER
AEGNORW WAGONER	AEHILOP OPHELIA	AEHLRST HALTERS,
AEGNOSY NOSEGAY	AEHILPR HARELIP	HARSLET
AEGNPRT TREPANG	AEHILPT HAPLITE	AEHLRSW WHALERS
AEGNRRS RANGERS	AEHILRU HAULIER	AEHLRTY EARTHLY,
AEGNRRT GRANTER	AEHILSS SHEILAS	HARTLEY, LATHERY
AEGNRST GARNETS,	AEHILTY HYALITE	AEHLSSS HASSLES,
STRANGE	AEHILVY HEAVILY	SLASHES
AEGNSSY GAYNESS	AEHIMNS HSIA-MEN	AEHLSST HATLESS
AEGNTYZ YANGTZE	AEHIMPR EPHRAIM	AEHLSTT STEALTH
AEGOORT ROOTAGE	AEHIMRS MISHEAR	AEHLTWY WEALTHY
AEGOPRS GO SPARE	AEHIMSS MESSIAH	AEHMMRS HAMMERS,
AEGOPRT PORTAGE	AEHIMST ATHEISM	SHAMMER

AEHMNNR HERMANN	AEIIKNT KAINITE	AEILLUV ELUVIAL
AEHMNST ANTHEMS	AEIILNN ANILINE	AEILLVY VIYELLA
AEHMOPT APOTHEM	AEIILNR AIRLINE	AEILMMN MAILMEN
AEHMPRS HAMPERS	AEIILNS AINSLIE	AEILMMS MELISMA
AEHMPTY EMPATHY	AEIILRS ISRAELI	AEILMNN LINEMAN,
AEHMRSS MARSHES,	AEIILSS SILESIA	MELANIN
SMASHER	AEIILTT LETITIA	AEILMNP IMPANEL
AEHMRST HAMSTER	AEIIMTT IMITATE	AEILMNR MANLIER,
AEHMSSS SMASHES	AEIINNR ANEIRIN	MARLINE, MINERAL
AEHMTTW MATTHEW	AEIINNS ASININE	AEILMNS MALINES,
AEHNNPY HA'PENNY	AEIINRR RAINIER	MENIALS, SEMINAL
AEHNOPT PHAETON,	AEIINRT INERTIA	AEILMNT AILMENT,
PHONATE	AEIIPRR PRAIRIE	ALIMENT
AEHNORS HOARSEN	AEIIRRV RIVIERA	AEILMNV MELVINA
AEHNORT ANOTHER	AEIIRST AIRIEST	AEILMNY EL MINYA
AEHNORV HANOVER	AEIITTV VITIATE	AEILMOR MELIORA,
AEHNOSX HEXOSAN	AEIJLNV JAVELIN	MORELIA
AEHNPRS SHARPEN	AEIJLRS JAILERS	AEILMPR IMPALER,
AEHNPRT PANTHER	AEIJMMR JAMMIER	PALMIER
AEHNRSS HARNESS	AEIJMNS JASMINE	AEILMRS REALISM
AEHNRST ANTHERS	AEIJRZZ JAZZIER	AEILMRT MARLITE
AEHNRTU HAUNTER,	AEIKLMN MALINKE,	AEILMSS AIMLESS, MELISSA
UNEARTH	MANLIKE	AEILMTY MEATILY
AEHNRTX NARTHEX	AEIKLNR LANKIER	AEILNNY INANELY
AEHOORT TOHEROA	AEIKLOT KEITLOA	AEILNNZ LIZANNE
AEHOPST TEASHOP	AEIKLRW WARLIKE	AEILNOP OPALINE
AEHORRS HOARSER	AEIKLST TALKIES	AEILNOR AILERON,
AEHORST EARSHOT	AEIKLSW WALKIES	ALIENOR, LORAINE
AEHORSX HOAXERS	AEIKLUZ ZULEIKA	AEILNOS ANISOLE, SEA
AEHORTX OXHEART	AEIKLWX WAXLIKE	LION
AEHOSTT HOT SEAT	AEIKMNP PIKEMAN	AEILNOT ELATION, TOENAIL
AEHPPRS PERHAPS	AEIKMNR RAMEKIN	AEILNPR PLAINER, PRALINE
AEHPRRS SHARPER	AEIKMST MISTAKE	AEILNPS SPANIEL
AEHPRSS PHRASES,	AEIKNRR NARKIER	AEILNPT PANTILE
SERAPHS, SHERPAS	AEIKNRT KATRINE, KERATIN	AEILNPU PAULINE
AEHPRTY THERAPY	AEIKNRU UKRAINE	AEILNPX EXPLAIN
AEHPSTT THE PAST	AEIKNST INTAKES	AEILNRT LATRINE,
AEHRRSS RASHERS,	AEIKNSY KYANISE	RATLINE, RELIANT,
SHARERS	AEIKNYZ KYANIZE	RETINAL
AEHRRTU URETHRA	AEIKPRR PARKIER	AEILNRV RAVELIN
AEHRSST RASHEST	AEIKPRW PAWKIER	AEILNRX RELAXIN
AEHRSSV SHAVERS	AEIKRRS SARKIER	AEILNRY INLAYER
AEHRSSW HAWSERS,	AEIKRSS KAISERS	AEILNST ELASTIN, SALIENT
WASHERS	AEIKRSY KAYSERI	AEILNSY AINSLEY, ELYSIAN
AEHRSTT HATTERS,	AEILLMT ALL-TIME	AEILNTU ALUNITE
SHATTER, THREATS	AEILLNR RALLINE	AEILNVY NAIVELY
AEHRSTV HARVEST	AEILLPR PALLIER	AEILOPR PELORIA
AEHRSTW WREATHS	AEILLRR RALLIER	AEILORS ROSALIE
AEHRSVW WHARVES	AEILLRS RALLIES, SALLIER	AEILORV VARIOLE
AEHRSWY WASHERY	AEILLRT LITERAL, TALLIER	AEILOST ISOLATE
AEHRTUU HAUTEUR	AEILLSS SALLIES	AEILOTV VIOLATE
AEHSSST STASHES	AEILLST TALLIES	AEILPPR APPLIER
AEHSTUX EXHAUST	AEILLSW WALLIES	AEILPRV PREVAIL

AEILPST TALIPES
AEILPSY PAISLEY
AEILQTU LIQUATE, TEQUILA
AEILRRT RETRIAL, TRAILER
AEILRSS AIRLESS, SERIALS
AEILRST REALIST, SALTIER,
   SALTIRE
AEILRSV REVISAL
AEILRTT TERTIAL
AEILRTU URALITE
AEILRTY IRATELY, REALITY
AEILRVV REVIVAL
AEILRVY VIRELAY
AEILRWY WEARILY
AEILSST SET SAIL
AEILSSV VALISES
AEILSTZ LAZIEST
AEILTVV TEL AVIV
AEILUVX EXUVIAL
AEIMMMS MAMMIES
AEIMMRT MARMITE
AEIMNNT MANNITE
AEIMNOR MORAINE,
   ROMAINE
AEIMNPR PERMIAN
AEIMNRR MARINER
AEIMNRS MARINES,
   REMAINS, SEMINAR
AEIMNRT MARTINE,
   MINARET, RAIMENT
AEIMNRV MINERVA
AEIMNSS MESSINA,
   SAMISEN
AEIMNST INMATES
AEIMNTV VIETNAM
AEIMNTY AMENITY
AEIMOOP IPOMOEA
AEIMOPR EMPORIA
AEIMORR ARMOIRE
AEIMOST ATOMISE
AEIMOTZ ATOMIZE
AEIMPRS IMPRESA
AEIMPRT PRIMATE
AEIMPRV VAMPIRE
AEIMPSS IMPASSE
AEIMPST IMPASTE,
   PASTIME, SEPTIMA
AEIMRRR MARRIER
AEIMRST MAESTRI
AEIMRTW WARTIME
AEIMSST SEA MIST
AEIMSSV MASSIVE
AEIMSTZ MESTIZA

AEINNNS NANNIES
AEINNOT ANTOINE
AEINNPR PANNIER
AEINNPT PINNATE
AEINNRT ENTRAIN
AEINNRU ANEURIN
AEINOPR OPEN-AIR
AEINOPZ APIEZON
AEINORS ERASION
AEINOSV EVASION
AEINOXZ OXAZINE
AEINPPS NAPPIES
AEINPRS PERSIAN
AEINPRT PAINTER,
   PERTAIN, PETRINA
AEINPSS PANSIES
AEINPST PANTIES, SAPIENT
AEINPTT PATIENT
AEINPTU PETUNIA
AEINQTU ANTIQUE,
   QUINATE
AEINRRS SIERRAN
AEINRRT TERRAIN,
   TRAINER
AEINRSS NERISSA, SARNIES
AEINRST NASTIER,
   RETINAS, RETSINA,
   STAINER, STEARIN
AEINRSV RAVINES
AEINRTT ITERANT,
   NATTIER, NITRATE,
   TERTIAN
AEINRTU TAURINE,
   URANITE, URINATE
AEINRTW TINWARE
AEINRVV VERVAIN
AEINSST ENTASIS, SESTINA
AEINSSV VINASSE
AEINSTT INSTATE, SATINET
AEINSTU SINUATE
AEINSTV NATIVES, VAINEST
AEINSTW IN A STEW
AEINSTZ ZANIEST
AEINSVV NAVVIES
AEINSWY ANYWISE
AEINTVY NAIVETY
AEINTXY ANXIETY
AEIOPRS SOAPIER
AEIOPST OPIATES
AEIOQSU SEQUOIA
AEIORSV OVARIES
AEIOSST OSSETIA
AEIPPPS PAPPIES

AEIPPRS APPRISE, SAPPIER
AEIPPRZ ZAPPIER
AEIPRRS ASPIRER,
   PARRIES, PRAISER,
   RAPIERS, REPAIRS
AEIPRSS PARESIS, PRAISES
AEIPRST PARTIES, PASTIER,
   PIASTRE, PIRATES, TRAIPSE
AEIPRSU PIRAEUS, UPRAISE
AEIPRTT PARTITE
AEIPRTV PRIVATE
AEIPRTW WIRETAP
AEIPRXY PYREXIA
AEIPSSS ASEPSIS
AEIPSST PASTIES
AEIPSSV PASSIVE
AEIPSTT PATTIES
AEIPSTU IAPETUS
AEIPTXY EPITAXY
AEIRRRV ARRIVER
AEIRRSS RAISERS, SIERRAS
AEIRRST TARSIER
AEIRRTT RATTIER
AEIRRTU ETRURIA
AEIRSSS SASSIER
AEIRSST SATIRES
AEIRSTT ARTIEST, ARTISTE,
   STRIATE, TASTIER   *ATTIRES*
AEIRSTW WAITERS,
   WARIEST
AEIRSVW WAIVERS
AEIRTTT TATTIER, TITRATE
AEIRTUZ AZURITE
AEIRTVY VARIETY
AEISSSS ASSISES
AEISSST SIESTAS
AEISSSU AUSSIES
AEISSSZ ASSIZES
AEISSUX AUXESIS
AEISTTU SITUATE
AEISTTV STATIVE
AEISTTY SATIETY
AEISTVW WAVIEST
AEISTWX WAXIEST
AEITTTV VITTATE
AEJJLNU JEJUNAL
AEJLOSU JEALOUS
AEJMSTY MAJESTY
AEJNOSS SAN JOSE
AEKLNST ANKLETS,
   LANKEST
AEKLOST SKATOLE
AEKLPPT PEP TALK

AEKLPRS SPARKLE	AELLSVY VALLEYS	AELNRTV VENTRAL
AEKLRST STALKER,	AELLTUU ULULATE	AELNRUV UNRAVEL,
TALKERS	AELLUVV VALVULE	VENULAR
AEKLRSW WALKERS	AELMMOY MYELOMA	AELNSSU SENSUAL
AEKMNRU UNMAKER	AELMMRT TRAMMEL	AELNSSX LAXNESS
AEKMRRS MARKERS,	AELMMST STAMMEL	AELNSTT TALENTS
REMARKS	AELMMSY MALMSEY	AELNSTY STANLEY
AEKMRST MARKETS	AELMNOR ALMONER	AELOORS AEROSOL,
AEKNOPS SPOKANE	AELMNOT TELAMON	ROSEOLA
AEKNPPR KNAPPER	AELMNPR LAMPERN	AELOPRS PAROLES,
AEKNPRS SPANKER	AELMNRU NUMERAL	REPOSAL
AEKNRRS RANKERS	AELMNST LAMENTS,	AELOPRT PROLATE
AEKNRST TANKERS	MANTLES	AELOPRV OVERLAP
AEKNRSW WANKERS	AELMOPR PALERMO	AELOPST APOSTLE,
AEKNRVY KNAVERY	AELMOPU AMPOULE	PELOTAS
AEKOTTU OUT-TAKE,	AELMOPY MAYPOLE	AELOPSX EXPOSAL
TAKEOUT	AELMORV REMOVAL	AELORRT REALTOR,
AEKPSSY PASSKEY	AELMOST MALTOSE	RELATOR
AEKPSTU TAKEUPS,	AELMOSY AMYLOSE	AELORSS LASSOER
UPTAKES	AELMPRS SAMPLER	AELORTT LORETTA
AEKQRSU QUAKERS	AELMPRT TRAMPLE	AELORTV LEVATOR
AEKQSSU SQUEAKS	AELMPRY LAMPREY	AELORUU ROULEAU
AEKQSUY SQUEAKY	AELMPSS SAMPLES	AELORVY OVERLAY
AEKRRST STARKER	AELMPTU PLUMATE	AELOSSV SALVOES
AEKRSST STREAKS	AELMRSS ARMLESS	AELOSTV SOLVATE
AEKRSTY STREAKY	AELMRSU SERUMAL	AELOSTZ ZEALOTS
AELLLOU LOUELLA	AELMRSV MARVELS	AELOSUZ ZEALOUS
AELLMNS MANSELL	AELMRTU RELATUM	AELOTTU TOLUATE
AELLMNU LUMENAL	AELMSTU AMULETS	AELOTUV OVULATE
AELLMRS SMALLER	AELNNPR PLANNER	AELOTVV VOLVATE
AELLMST MALLETS	AELNNRT LANTERN	AELPPRS SLAPPER
AELLMSU MALLEUS	AELNNRU UNLEARN	AELPPSU APPULSE
AELLMWX MAXWELL	AELNNTU ANNULET	AELPQSU PLAQUES
AELLNOV NOVELLA	AELNOOR LEONORA	AELPRST PLASTER,
AELLNPR PARNELL	AELNOPU APOLUNE	PSALTER, STAPLER
AELLNPY PENALLY	AELNORS ORLEANS,	AELPRSU PERUSAL
AELLNVY VENALLY	SALERNO	AELPRSY PARLEYS,
AELLORS ROSELLA	AELNORV VERONAL	PARSLEY, PLAYERS,
AELLORV ALL OVER,	AELNOST LEAN-TOS	REPLAYS
OVERALL	AELNPPS PEN PALS	AELPRTT PLATTER,
AELLPRU PLEURAL	AELNPPY PLAYPEN	PRATTLE
AELLPST L-PLATES,	AELNPRT PLANTER	AELPRTY PTERYLA
PALLETS	AELNPRY PLENARY	AELPSSS SAPLESS
AELLPTY PLAYLET	AELNPST PLANETS	AELPSST PASTELS, STAPLES
AELLQUY EQUALLY	AELNPTX EXPLANT	AELPSSU PAS SEUL
AELLRRU ALLURER	AELNPTY APLENTY,	AELPSTU PULSATE
AELLRST STELLAR	PENALTY	AELQRRU QUARREL
AELLRSU LAURELS	AELNQUU UNEQUAL	AELQSSU SQUEALS
AELLRTY ALERTLY	AELNRRS SNARLER	AELQTUZ QUETZAL
AELLRVY RAVELLY	AELNRST ANTLERS,	AELRRSU SURREAL
AELLSSW LAWLESS	RENTALS, SALTERN,	AELRRTW TRAWLER
AELLSTT TALLEST	STERNAL	AELRSST ARTLESS
AELLSTW WALLETS	AELNRTU NEUTRAL	

AELRSSV SALVERS, SLAVERS
AELRSSY SLAYERS
AELRSTT RATTLES, STARLET, STARTLE, TELSTAR
AELRSTU SALUTER
AELRSTV TRAVELS, VARLETS, VESTRAL
AELRSTW WASTREL
AELRSUV VALUERS
AELRSVY SLAVERY
AELRSWY LAWYERS
AELRSZZ RAZZLES
AELRTTT TATTLER
AELRTUV VAULTER
AELRTWZ WALTZER
AELSSST TASSELS
AELSSTT STALEST
AELSSTU SALUTES
AELSTTW WATTLES
AELSTTY STATELY
AELSTWZ WALTZES
AELSUVY SUAVELY
AELTTUX TEXTUAL
AEMMNOT MOMENTA
AEMMRST STAMMER
AEMNNOS MANNOSE
AEMNNOT MONTANE
AEMNNRS MANNERS
AEMNNRT REMNANT
AEMNNTU UNMEANT
AEMNOPR MANROPE
AEMNORS MOANERS, OARSMEN
AEMNORU ENAMOUR, NEUROMA
AEMNORV OVERMAN
AEMNPTU PUTAMEN
AEMNPTY PAYMENT
AEMNRRU MANURER
AEMNRST MARTENS, SMARTEN
AEMNRSU SURNAME
AEMNSST STAMENS
AEMNSTY AMNESTY
AEMOORT TEAROOM
AEMOORW WOOMERA
AEMOOST OSTEOMA
AEMOOSV VAMOOSE
AEMOPST PETSAMO
AEMORRS ROAMERS
AEMORRV OVERARM

AEMORST MAESTRO
AEMORTU EURATOM
AEMOSWY SOMEWAY
AEMPRRT TRAMPER
AEMPRST STAMPER
AEMPTTT ATTEMPT
AEMPTTU TAPETUM
AEMQSSU MASQUES
AEMRRRY REMARRY
AEMRRST ARMREST, SMARTER
AEMRRTU ERRATUM
AEMRSST MASTERS, STREAMS
AEMRSSU ASSUMER, ERASMUS, MASSEUR
AEMRSTT MATTERS, SMATTER
AEMRSTU ARTEMUS
AEMRSTW WARMEST
AEMRSTY MASTERY
AENNNPT PENNANT
AENNORS ROSANNE, ROSEANN
AENNORX ROXANNE
AENNOTU TONNEAU
AENNPRS SPANNER
AENNRST TANNERS
AENNRTT ENTRANT
AENNRTY TANNERY
AENNSSU SUSANNE
AENNSSW WANNESS
AENNSTT TENANTS
AENNSTW WANNEST
AENNSUZ SUZANNE
AENOPPR PROPANE
AENOPRS PERSONA
AENOPRT OPERANT, PRONATE, PROTEAN
AENOPSW WEAPONS
AENORRV OVERRAN
AENORSS REASONS, SEÑORAS
AENORST ONE-STAR, SENATOR, TREASON
AENORSY REYNOSA
AENORVY AVEYRON
AENOSSS SEASONS
AENOSTU SOUTANE
AENPPRS SNAPPER
AENPRRT PARTNER
AENPRRW PRAWNER

AENPRST PARENTS, PASTERN
AENPRSW SPAWNER
AENPRSZ PANZERS
AENPRTT PATTERN, REPTANT
AENPRTW ANTWERP
AENPRUV PARVENU
AENPSST APTNESS
AENPSSY SYNAPSE
AENPSTT PATENTS, PATTENS
AENPSTU PEANUTS
AENRRST RANTERS
AENRRSW WARRENS
AENRRTY TERNARY
AENRSSW ANSWERS, RAWNESS
AENRSTU NATURES, SAUNTER
AENRSTV SERVANT, TAVERNS, VERSANT
AENRSUW UNSWEAR
AENRTTU TAUNTER
AENRTUV VAUNTER
AENSTTU TETANUS
AENSTTX SEXTANT
AEOOPPS PAPOOSE
AEOPPPS PAPPOSE
AEOPPRV APPROVE
AEOPRST ESPARTO, SEAPORT
AEOPRVY OVERPAY
AEOPSTT TEAPOTS
AEOPSTZ TOPAZES
AEOQRTU EQUATOR, QUORATE
AEOQSUU AQUEOUS
AEORRST ROASTER
AEORRSU AROUSER
AEORSTT ROSETTA, TOASTER
AEORSVW OVERSAW
AEORTUW OUTWEAR
AEORTVX OVERTAX
AEPPRRT TRAPPER
AEPPRRW WRAPPER
AEPPRSS SAPPERS
AEPPRSU PAUPERS
AEPPRSW SWAPPER
AEPPSTT TAPPETS
AEPPSTU PASTE-UP
AEPQRTU PARQUET

AEPRRSS PARSERS,	AFFNOSW SAWN-OFF	AFILLNY FINALLY
SPARSER	AFGGGIN FAGGING	AFILLPT PITFALL
AEPRRSY PRAYERS,	AFGGOST FAGGOTS	AFILLUV FLUVIAL
SPRAYER	AFGHHIS HAGFISH	AFILLUW WAILFUL
AEPRRTU RAPTURE,	AFGHIRS GARFISH	AFILMOR ALIFORM
RUPERTA	AFGHRTU FRAUGHT	AFILMPY AMPLIFY
AEPRSST REPASTS	AFGIILN FAILING	AFILNOR FLORIAN
AEPRSSY PESSARY	AFGIINR FAIRING	AFILNPU PAINFUL
AEPRSTT PATTERS,	AFGIKLN FLAKING	AFILNTY FAINTLY
SPATTER	AFGILLN FALLING	AFILORW AIRFLOW
AEPRSTU PASTURE	AFGILMN FLAMING	AFILOTX FOXTAIL
AEPRSUV RAVE-UPS	AFGILNO FOALING,	AFILQUY QUALIFY
AEQRRSU SQUARER	LOAFING	AFILRTY FRAILTY
AEQRRTU QUARTER	AFGILNR FLARING	AFILSSY SALSIFY
AEQRRSSU SQUARES	AFGILNT FATLING	AFILSTU FISTULA
AEQRSTU T-SQUARE	AFGILNU GAINFUL	AFILSTY FALSITY
AEQRSUV QUAVERS	AFGILNW FLAWING	AFILTTY FATTILY
AEQRTTU QUARTET	AFGILNY ANGLIFY, FLAYING	AFIMOOS MAFIOSO
AEQRUVY QUAVERY	AFGILRU FIGURAL	AFIMSSS MASSIFS
AERRSST ARRESTS	AFGIMNO FOAMING	AFIMSUV FAUVISM
AERRSSU ASSURER	AFGIMNR FARMING,	AFINNST INFANTS
AERRSTT STARTER	FRAMING	AFINORS INSOFAR
AERRSTV STARVER,	AFGIMNY MAGNIFY	AFINRTU UT INFRA
TRAVERS	AFGINNN FANNING	AFINSTU FUSTIAN
AERRSTY STRAYER	AFGINNW FAWNING	AFISSTY SATISFY
AERSSTT TASTERS	AFGINRT FARTING,	AFISTUV FAUVIST
AERSSTW WASTERS	RAFTING	AFITTUY FATUITY
AERSSTY STAYERS	AFGINRY FRAYING	AFKKOUU FUKUOKA
AERSTTT STRETTA,	AFGINST FASTING	AFKLNRY FRANKLY
TATTERS	AFGINTW WAFTING	AFKRRTU FRAKTUR
AERSTTU STATURE	AFGIRTY GRATIFY	AFLLOOY ALOOFLY
AERSTTW STEWART,	AFGKORT KOFTGAR	AFLLOTU FALLOUT,
SWATTER	AFGLLLY GALLFLY	OUTFALL
AERSTUY ESTUARY	AFGLLUY FALL GUY	AFLLPUY PLAYFUL
AESSTTU STATUES	AFGLMOP FOG LAMP	AFLLUWY AWFULLY
AESSTUY EUSTASY	AFGLNOS FLAGONS	AFLMORU FORMULA
AESTTTU STATUTE,	AFGMNOR FROGMAN	AFLMORW WOLFRAM
TAUTEST	AFHIIRS FAIRISH	AFLMOST FLOTSAM
AFFGSUW GUFFAWS	AFHIKLS KHALIFS	AFLMRSU ARMFULS,
AFFHINU IN A HUFF	AFHILTW HALF-WIT	FULMARS
AFFHIRS RAFFISH	AFHIMNU HAFNIUM	AFLNOOS ALFONSO
AFFHLLY FLY HALF	AFHINOS FASHION	AFLNORT FRONTAL
AFFHLUU AL HUFUF	AFHIORS OARFISH	AFLORUV FLAVOUR
AFFIKRS KAFFIRS	AFHISSW SAWFISH	AFLPRTY FLYTRAP
AFFILSY FALSIFY	AFHISTT FATTISH	AFLPSTY FLYPAST
AFFIMST MASTIFF	AFHKORY HAYFORK	AFMNOOT FOOTMAN
AFFINRU FUNFAIR, RUFFIAN	AFHLMRU HARMFUL	AFMNORT FORMANT
AFFINTY TIFFANY	AFHLOOS LOOFAHS	AFMNWYY MYFANWY
AFFIRST TARIFFS	AFHMOST FATHOMS	AFMOORS FORMOSA
AFFLOPY PLAY-OFF	AFHORTW WHAT FOR	AFMORST FORMATS
AFFLOSY LAY-OFFS	AFIILRT AIRLIFT	AFMOSTU SFUMATO
AFFNORS SAFFRON	AFIINRS FRISIAN	AFOORST OF A SORT
AFFNORT AFFRONT	AFIKNNU IN A FUNK	AFOOTWY FOOTWAY

AFORSUV FAVOURS
AFORUWY FOUR-WAY
AFOSTUU FATUOUS
AGGGGIN GAGGING
AGGGIJN JAGGING
AGGGILN LAGGING
AGGGINN GANGING,
 NAGGING
AGGGINR RAGGING
AGGGINS SAGGING
AGGGINT TAGGING
AGGGINU GAUGING
AGGGINW WAGGING
AGGHHIS HAGGISH
AGGHIMN GINGHAM
AGGHINN HANGING
AGGHINS GASHING
AGGHISW WAGGISH
AGGIINN GAINING
AGGIINV GINGIVA
AGGIKNW GAWKING
AGGILLN GALLING
AGGILNN ANGLING
AGGILNO GAOLING
AGGILNR GLARING
AGGILNZ GLAZING
AGGILOS LOGGIAS
AGGINNR RANGING
AGGINNW GNAWING
AGGINPP GAPPING
AGGINPS GASPING
AGGINPW GAWPING
AGGINRT GRATING
AGGINRU ARGUING
AGGINRY GRAYING
AGGINRZ GRAZING
AGGINSS GASSING
AGGINST STAGING
AGGISZZ ZIGZAGS
AGGKNOT GANGTOK
AGGLOSW GLASGOW
AGGMORR GROGRAM
AGGMOST MAGGOTS
AGGMOTY MAGGOTY
AGHHINS HASHING
AGHHIWY HIGHWAY
AGHHNOW HWANG HO
AGHHORT HOGARTH
AGHHOSW HOGWASH
AGHHTUY HAUGHTY
AGHIILN HAILING
AGHIKNN KHINGAN
AGHIKNR HARKING

AGHIKNS SHAKING
AGHIKNW HAWKING
AGHILNS LASHING
AGHILNT ALTHING,
 HALTING
AGHILNU HAULING
AGHILNV HALVING
AGHILNW WHALING
AGHILOT GOLIATH
AGHILRS LARGISH
AGHILRT ALRIGHT
AGHIMMN HAMMING
AGHIMNR HARMING
AGHIMNS MASHING,
 SHAMING
AGHINOX HOAXING
AGHINPR HARPING
AGHINPS PHASING,
 SHAPING
AGHINRS GARNISH,
 SHARING
AGHINSU ANGUISH
AGHINSV SHAVING
AGHINSW WASHING
AGHINTT AT NIGHT
AGHINTW THAWING
AGHJMNO MAH-JONG
AGHKOSW GOSHAWK
AGHLMPU GALUMPH
AGHLOSU GOULASH
AGHLSTY GHASTLY
AGHMNNU HUNGNAM
AGHMRTU MURTAGH
AGHNOTU HANGOUT
AGHNPSU HANG-UPS
AGHNRUY HUNGARY
AGHNTUY NAUGHTY
AGHORTW WARTHOG
AGHRTUU THURGAU
AGIIJLN JAILING
AGIIKNS KIANGSI
AGIILLN GILLIAN
AGIILMN MAILING
AGIILNN NAILING
AGIILNR RAILING
AGIILNS AISLING, SAILING
AGIILNT TAILING
AGIILNW WAILING
AGIILPT PIGTAIL
AGIILRU LIGURIA
AGIILTY AGILITY
AGIIMMN MAIMING
AGIIMMS IMAGISM

AGIIMOR ORIGAMI
AGIIMST IMAGIST
AGIINNP PAINING
AGIINNR INGRAIN, RAINING
AGIINPR PAIRING
AGIINRS AIRINGS, ARISING,
 RAISING
AGIINSV VISAING
AGIINTW WAITING
AGIINTX TAXIING
AGIINVW WAIVING
AGIJMMN JAMMING
AGIJNNU JUNGIAN
AGIJNRR JARRING
AGIJNZZ JAZZING
AGIJSSW JIGSAWS
AGIKKNY YAKKING
AGIKLNR LARKING
AGIKLNS SLAKING
AGIKLNT TALKING
AGIKLNW WALKING
AGIKMNR MARKING
AGIKMNS MAKINGS,
 MASKING
AGIKNNN NANKING
AGIKNNR NARKING,
 RANKING
AGIKNNS SNAKING
AGIKNNW WANKING
AGIKNNY YANKING
AGIKNOS SOAKING
AGIKNOY OKAYING
AGIKNPR PARKING
AGIKNQU QUAKING
AGIKNRT KARTING
AGIKNST SKATING,
 STAKING, TAKINGS
AGIKNSU KIANGSU
AGILLMU GALLIUM
AGILLNP PALLING
AGILLNU LINGUAL
AGILLNW WALLING
AGILLNY ALLYING
AGILLOR GORILLA
AGILLRU LIGULAR
AGILLSU LUGSAIL
AGILMNP PALMING
AGILMNT MALTING
AGILMNU MAULING
AGILMNY MANGILY
AGILNNO LOANING
AGILNNP PLANING

AGILNNS LANSING,
  LINSANG
AGILNPP LAPPING
AGILNPS LAPSING,
  PALINGS, SAPLING
AGILNPT PLATING
AGILNPW LAPWING
AGILNPY PLAYING
AGILNRY ANGRILY,
  RANGILY
AGILNSS SIGNALS
AGILNST LASTING,
  SALTING, SLATING,
  STALING
AGILNSV SALVING,
  SLAVING
AGILNSY SLAYING
AGILNUV VALUING
AGILOPT GALIPOT
AGILORS GIRASOL
AGILORW AIRGLOW,
  GWALIOR
AGILSTY STAGILY
AGIMMNR RAMMING
AGIMNNN MANNING
AGIMNNO MOANING
AGIMNOR ROAMING
AGIMNPP MAPPING
AGIMNPT TAMPING
AGIMNRR MARRING
AGIMNRS MARGINS
AGIMNRT MIGRANT
AGIMNRW WARMING
AGIMNSS MASSING
AGIMNSU AMUSING
AGIMNTT MATTING
AGIMORU GOURAMI
AGIMOSY ISOGAMY
AGIMSST STIGMAS
AGIMSWW WIGWAMS
AGINNNN NANNING
AGINNNP PANNING
AGINNNT TANNING
AGINNNW WANNING
AGINNOT ATONING
AGINNOV AVIGNON
AGINNPP NAPPING
AGINNPT PANTING
AGINNPW PAWNING
AGINNRS SNARING
AGINNRT RANTING
AGINNRW WARNING
AGINNRY YARNING

AGINNSW AWNINGS
AGINNTW WANTING
AGINNWY YAWNING
AGINOOP POGONIA
AGINOPS SOAPING
AGINOPT PAOTING
AGINORR ROARING
AGINORS SIGNORA,
  SOARING
AGINORV VIRGOAN
AGINOST AGONIST
AGINOVW AVOWING
AGINPPR RAPPING
AGINPPS SAPPING
AGINPPT TAPPING
AGINPPY YAPPING
AGINPPZ ZAPPING
AGINPRS PARINGS,
  PARSING, RASPING,
  SPARING
AGINPRT GIN TRAP,
  PARTING, PRATING
AGINPRW WARPING
AGINPRY PRAYING
AGINPSS PASSING
AGINPST PASTING
AGINPSU PAUSING
AGINPSV PAVINGS
AGINPSY SPAYING
AGINPTT PATTING
AGINRRT TARRING
AGINRRW WARRING
AGINRST GASTRIN,
  RATINGS, STARING
AGINRSU AIRGUNS
AGINRSV RAVINGS
AGINRSY SYRINGA
AGINRTT RATTING
AGINRVY VARYING
AGINRXY X-RAYING
AGINSSS SASSING
AGINSSV SAVINGS
AGINSSY SAYINGS
AGINSTT STATING, TASTING
AGINSTV STAVING
AGINSTW WASTING
AGINSTY STAYING,
  STYGIAN
AGINSWY SWAYING
AGINTTT TATTING
AGINWWX WAXWING
AGIORSV VIRAGOS
AGIRSTU GUITARS

AGIRTVY GRAVITY
AGJKNUW KWANGJU
AGJLMOS LOGJAMS
AGJLRUU JUGULAR
AGJNORS JARGONS
AGKORST GO-KARTS
AGLLNOO GALLOON
AGLLNOS GALLONS
AGLLNTU GALLNUT,
  NUTGALL
AGLLOPS GALLOPS
AGLLOSS GLOSSAL
AGLLOSU GALLOUS
AGLLOSW GALLOWS
AGLLOTT GLOTTAL
AGLMORU GLAMOUR
AGLNOOS LAGOONS
AGLNOOW OWN GOAL
AGLNOPS GOSPLAN
AGLNORU LANGUOR
AGLNOSS SLOGANS
AGLNPSY SPANGLY
AGLNRUU UNGULAR
AGLOOPY APOLOGY
AGMMNSU MAGNUMS
AGMNORU ORGANUM
AGMNOTU MONTAGU
AGMNSTU MUSTANG
AGMNSTY GYMNAST
AGMNSYY SYNGAMY
AGMOPRR PROGRAM
AGMORRW RAGWORM
AGMORSS ORGASMS
AGMPRSU GRAMPUS
AGNNNOO NONAGON
AGNNNTU NANTUNG
AGNNOOP GO NAP ON
AGNNOOR ORGANON,
  RANGOON
AGNOQSU QUANGOS
AGNORRT GRANTOR
AGNORSS SARONGS
AGNOSTU NOUGATS
AGOPPST STOPGAP
AGORRTW RAGWORT
AGORRTY GYRATOR
AGORSTU RAGOUTS
AGOSUYZ AZYGOUS
AGRUUUY URUGUAY
AHHHISS HASHISH
AHHIKSW HAWKISH
AHHKOOS HOOKAHS
AHHKSTY SHAKHTY

AHHLRSY HARSHLY	AHKKORV KHARKOV	AHORRSW HARROWS
AHHOPRT HAP'ORTH	AHKLTUY HAKLUYT	AHORSTT THROATS
AHHORTW HAWORTH	AHKMORR MARKHOR	AHORSTU AUTHORS
AHIIKNT HAITINK	AHKNPSU PUNKAHS	AHORTTY THROATY
AHIILSW SWAHILI	AHKNRTY KATHRYN	AHOSTUW OUTWASH,
AHIINPR HAIRPIN	AHLLMSU MULLAHS	WASHOUT
AHIINRT THIN AIR	AHLLOPS SHALLOP	AHPRRTY PHRATRY
AHIIPRS AIRSHIP	AHLLOST SHALLOT	AHQSSUY SQUASHY
AHIKLSY SHAKILY	AHLLOSW SHALLOW	AHRRSUY HURRAYS
AHIKMNS KHAMSIN	AHLLOTY LOATHLY,	AHRSSSU HUSSARS
AHIKMRS KASHMIR	TALLYHO	AHRSTWY SWARTHY
AHIKMSW MAWKISH	AHLLPSU PHALLUS	AHRTUWY THRUWAY
AHIKNOS KHOISAN	AHLLPYY APHYLLY	AIIILMT MILITIA
AHIKNRS KRISHNA	AHLLRST THRALLS	AIIILNT INITIAL
AHIKNSV KNAVISH	AHLLSTU THALLUS	AIIJLLN JILLIAN
AHIKNSW HAWKINS	AHLMNPY NYMPHAL	AIIKLNN KALININ
AHIKOSU HOKUSAI	AHLMNSY HYMNALS	AIIKMMS SKIMMIA
AHILLNT ANTHILL	AHLMNUY HUMANLY	AIIKMNN MANIKIN
AHILLRY HILLARY	AHLMORU HUMORAL	AIIKSTU KUTAISI
AHILLST TALLISH	AHLMOSW OHM'S LAW	AIIKTUW KUWAITI
AHILNPS PLANISH	AHLMSUU HAMULUS	AIILLLN LILLIAN
AHILORY HOARILY	AHLNOPR ALPHORN	AIILLLS LILLIAS
AHILPPY HAPPILY	AHLNORT ALTHORN	AIILLMN LIMINAL
AHILSSV SLAVISH	AHLORST HARLOTS	AIILLMW WILLIAM
AHILSTY HASTILY	AHLOTUU OUTHAUL	AIILLNV VILLAIN
AHILTTZ HAZLITT	AHLPRSY SHARPLY	AIILMMN MINIMAL
AHIMMRS RAMMISH	AHLPSSU LASH-UPS	AIILMNT INTIMAL
AHIMNNS MANNISH	AHLPSSY SPLASHY	AIILMRS SIMILAR
AHIMNNU INHUMAN	AHMMMOT MAMMOTH	AIILMRY MILIARY
AHIMPSS MISHAPS	AHMNNTU MANHUNT	AIILNNS AISLINN
AHIMRST MITHRAS	AHMNOPT HAMPTON,	AIILNOS LIAISON
AHIMTUZ AZIMUTH	PHANTOM	AIILNOV LIVONIA
AHIMTVZ MITZVAH	AHMNORU MANHOUR	AIILNPT PINTAIL
AHINNTX XANTHIN	AHMNORY HARMONY	AIILNRY RAINILY
AHINOOR HONORIA	AHMNOSS HANSOMS	AIILNTY ANILITY
AHINOTZ HOATZIN	AHMNOSU HOUSMAN	AIILORV RAVIOLI
AHINPRS HARPINS	AHMNOSW SHOWMAN	AIILOTT OTTILIA
AHINPSS SPANISH	AHMOOPS SHAMPOO	AIILQSU SILIQUA
AHINPST HATPINS	AHMOSTU MAHOUTS	AIILRTV TRIVIAL
AHINRST TARNISH	AHMPSSU SMASH-UP	AIIMMNS ANIMISM
AHINRSV VARNISH	AHNNNOS SHANNON	AIIMMNX MAXIMIN,
AHINSTT TIN HATS	AHNNOTY ANTHONY	MINIMAX
AHIOORT HORATIO	AHNOOPR HARPOON	AIIMNPS PIANISM
AHIORRT HARRIOT	AHNOPRS ORPHANS	AIIMNPT TIMPANI
AHIPRST HARPIST	AHNORRS SHARRON	AIIMNRT MARTINI
AHIPRSW WARSHIP	AHNORSX SAXHORN	AIIMNSS SIMIANS
AHIPSSW WASPISH	AHNOTTW WHATNOT	AIIMNST ANIMIST
AHIPSWW WHIPSAW	AHNPPUY UNHAPPY	AIIMNTV VITAMIN
AHIPSWY SHIPWAY	AHNPRXY PHARYNX	AIIMSSY MYIASIS
AHIRRSS SIRRAHS	AHOORSY HOORAYS	AIINNTY INANITY
AHIRSTT RATTISH	AHOPRTY ATROPHY	AIINPRS ASPIRIN
AHIRSTW WRAITHS	AHOPSTT TOP HATS	AIINPST PIANIST
AHISTTW WHATSIT	AHOPTTW TOWPATH	AIINRSS RAISINS

AIINRST ISTRIAN	AILMPSY MISPLAY	AIMNOPT MAINTOP
AIINRSY RAISINY	AILMRST MISTRAL	AIMNOTU TINAMOU
AIINRTV VITRAIN	AILMRSU SIMULAR	AIMNPRU MANIPUR
AIINSTU TUNISIA	AILMSSS MISSALS	AIMNRRU MURRAIN
AIIOOTV VOIOTIA	AILNNOT ANTLION	AIMNRST MARTINS
AIIOPRR A PRIORI	AILNORT ON TRIAL	AIMNRSU SURINAM
AIIORTV VITORIA	AILNOUV LOUVAIN	AIMNRTV VARMINT
AIIPSTW WAPITIS	AILNPST PLAINTS	AIMNRUU URANIUM
AIISSVV VIS-À-VIS	AILNPSX SALPINX	AIMNSTT MATTINS
AIJJMMS JIMJAMS	AILNPTU NUPTIAL	AIMNSTU TSUNAMI
AIJLTTU JULITTA	AILNPTY INAPTLY, PTYALIN	AIMOPRX PROXIMA
AIJLYZZ JAZZILY	AILNQTU QUINTAL	AIMOPST IMPASTO
AIJNORT JANITOR	AILNRSU INSULAR,	AIMORST AMORIST
AIJNSTU JUSTINA	URINALS	AIMOSST MAOISTS
AIKLLNY LANKILY	AILNSTY NASTILY, SAINTLY	AIMOSTT ATOMIST
AIKLMMN MILKMAN	AILNTTY NATTILY	AIMPRRY PRIMARY
AIKLMNN LINKMAN	AILOPRS POLARIS	AIMPRST ARMPITS
AIKLNSY SNAKILY	AILOPST APOSTIL, TOPSAIL	AIMQRSU MARQUIS
AIKLOST SIALKOT	AILOPSY SOAPILY	AIMRSTX MARXIST
AIKLPWY PAWKILY	AILOPTT TALIPOT	AIMSSTT STATISM
AIKLQUY QUAKILY	AILOPTV PIVOTAL	AINNOOT ANTONIO
AIKLSSY SKYSAIL	AILOQTU ALIQUOT	AINNOOX OXONIAN
AIKMNNS KINSMAN	AILORSS SAILORS	AINNOPS SAPONIN
AIKNNPS NAPKINS	AILORST TAILORS	AINNOST NATIONS
AIKORST TROIKAS	AILORUX UXORIAL	AINNQTU QUINTAN
AILLMOP PALM OIL	AILORVY OLIVARY	AINNRTU URINANT
AILLMPU PALLIUM	AILOSSU SAO LUIS	AINNSTT INSTANT
AILLMSW SAWMILL	AILPPSY PAYSLIP, SAPPILY	AINNTUY ANNUITY
AILLNNO LANOLIN	AILPRSS SPIRALS	AINOORT ONTARIO,
AILLNNT TALLINN	AILPRSU SPIRULA	ORATION
AILLNOS ALLISON	AILPSTU PAULIST	AINOOTV OVATION
AILLNPY PLAINLY	AILPSTY PASTILY	AINOOVV IVANOVO
AILLNST INSTALL	AILPSWY SLIPWAY, WASPILY	AINOPPT APPOINT
AILLORZ ZORILLA	AILQTUY QUALITY	AINOPSS PASSION
AILLPRS PILLARS	AILRRVY RIVALRY	AINOPTU OPUNTIA,
AILLPRU PILULAR	AILRSTT STARLIT	UTOPIAN
AILLPUV PLUVIAL	AILRSTU RITUALS	AINORST RATIONS
AILLQSU SQUILLA	AILRSTY TRYSAIL	AINORTU RAINOUT
AILLSTY SALTILY	AILRTTU TITULAR	AINOSTT STATION
AILLTVY VITALLY	AILRTTY RATTILY	AINOSUX ANXIOUS
AILMMOR IMMORAL	AILRTUV VIRTUAL	AINOSVY SYNOVIA
AILMNNO NOMINAL	AILSTTW SALT WIT	AINPPRS PARSNIP
AILMNOY ALIMONY	AILSTTY TASTILY	AINPQTU PIQUANT
AILMNPS PLASMIN	AILSTUV VISTULA	AINPRSS SPRAINS
AILMNPT IMPLANT	AILSTUW LAWSUIT	AINPRST SPIRANT
AILMNRS MARLINS	AILTTTY TATTILY	AINPRTU PURITAN
AILMNRY MARILYN	AIMMMUX MAXIMUM	AINQRTU TARQUIN
AILMOOV MOVIOLA	AIMMORZ MIZORAM	AINQRUY QUINARY
AILMOPT OPTIMAL	AIMMOST ATOMISM	AINRRTY TRINARY
AILMOPY OLYMPIA	AIMMRSX MARXISM	AINRRUY URINARY
AILMOST SOMITAL	AIMMSUX MAXIMUS	AINRSST STRAINS
AILMPRU PRIMULA	AIMNNOS MANSION	AINRSSU RUSSIAN
AILMPST PALMIST	AIMNOPR RAMPION	AINRSTT TRANSIT, TRISTAN

AINRSTU NUTRIAS	AKORWWX WAXWORK	ALNORUZ ZONULAR
AINRTTT TITRANT	AKQSSUW SQUAWKS	ALNPRSU SNARL-UP
AINRTUY UNITARY	ALLLOYY LOYALLY	ALNSSTU SULTANS
AINSSTU SUSTAIN	ALLMNOY ALLONYM	ALNSTUW WALNUTS
AIOORRS ROSARIO	ALLMNPU PULLMAN	ALNSUUU UNUSUAL
AIOPRRT AIRPORT	ALLMORY MALLORY,	ALOOPRW POOR LAW
AIOPRTT PATRIOT	MORALLY	ALOPPRS POPLARS
AIOPRTY TOPIARY	ALLMOSS SLALOMS	ALOPPRU POPULAR
AIOPRUV PAVIOUR	ALLMOSW MALLOWS	ALOPRRU PARLOUR
AIOPSTU UTOPIAS	ALLNOOW WALLOON	ALOPRST PATROLS,
AIORRRW WARRIOR	ALLNOYZ ZONALLY	PORTALS
AIORRTT TRAITOR	ALLNTUU ULULANT	ALOPRSU PARLOUS
AIORSTV TRAVOIS	ALLOOTX AXOLOTL	ALOPSSU SPOUSAL
AIORSUV SAVIOUR,	ALLOPRY PAYROLL	ALOPSTT SALTPOT
VARIOUS	ALLOPSW WALLOPS	ALOPTUY OUTPLAY
AIOSSTT TAOISTS	ALLOPTX POLL TAX	ALOQRRU RORQUAL
AIPPSST PAPISTS	ALLORWY ROLLWAY	ALOQRSU SQUALOR
AIPRRTU TRIPURA	ALLORYY ROYALLY	ALOQSTU LOQUATS
AIPRSST RAPISTS	ALLOSSW SALLOWS	ALORRST ROSTRAL
AIPRSSU PRUSSIA	ALLOSWW SWALLOW,	ALORTWW AWLWORT
AIPRSSW RIPSAWS	WALLOWS	ALORTYY ROYALTY
AIPZZZZ PIZZAZZ	ALLOTTY TOTALLY	ALOSTTU OUTLAST
AIRSSTT ARTISTS, STRAITS,	ALLOTYY LOYALTY	ALOSTUW OUTLAWS
TSARIST	ALLPRSU PLURALS	ALOSTUY LAYOUTS,
AIRSTVY VARSITY	ALLQSSU SQUALLS	OUTLAYS
AISSTTT STATIST	ALLQSUY SQUALLY	ALOSTXY OXYSALT
AISTTVY VASTITY	ALLRSTU LUSTRAL	ALPRSSU PULSARS
AISTUVY SUAVITY	ALLSUUY USUALLY	ALPRSSW SPRAWLS
AJLLMOR JAM ROLL	ALMNNUY UNMANLY	ALPRSWY SPRAWLY
AJLNORU JOURNAL	ALMNOOP LAMPOON	ALRSTUU SUTURAL
AJMNRUY JURYMAN	ALMNOPS PLASMON	ALRSUUV UVULARS
AJNORST TROJANS	ALMNORU UNMORAL	AMMNRUY NUMMARY
AKKLRSY SKYLARK	ALMNOSS SALMONS	AMMORST MARMOTS
AKKSTUY YAKUTSK	ALMNOSU SOLANUM	AMMRSUY SUMMARY
AKLLNOW KNOW-ALL	ALMNOWY WOMANLY	AMNNORS NORMANS
AKLMNOO KOLOMNA	ALMNPSU SUNLAMP	AMNNOSW SNOWMAN
AKLNOSW WALK-ONS	ALMNSUU ALUMNUS	AMNNOTY ANTONYM
AKLNOSX KLAXONS	ALMORRU MORULAR	AMNOOPP POMPANO
AKLOPUV VOLAPUK	ALMORST MORTALS	AMNOORS MAROONS
AKLOTTU OUTTALK	ALMOTTU MULATTO	AMNOOTT OTTOMAN
AKLOTUW WALKOUT	ALMRSTY SMARTLY	AMNOOTY TOO MANY
AKLPSUW WALK-UPS	ALMRTUU TUMULAR	AMNOPRY PARONYM
AKLRSTY STARKLY	ALMSSUY ALYSSUM,	AMNOPSS SAMPSON
AKLUUWZ KWAZULU	ASYLUMS	AMNOPST POSTMAN,
AKMNORU RUN AMOK	ALMSTUU UMLAUTS	TAMPONS
AKMNORW WORKMAN	ALNNRSU UNSNARL	AMNOPTU PANTOUM
AKMORST OSTMARK	ALNNSUU ANNULUS	AMNORSS RAMSONS,
AKMPRSU MARKUPS	ALNOOPT PLATOON	RANSOMS
AKMQTUU KUMQUAT	ALNOORT ORTOLAN	AMNORST MATRONS,
AKMRSTU MUSKRAT	ALNOOSS SALOONS	TRANSOM
AKNORTU OUTRANK	ALNOPPY PANOPLY	AMNORSY MASONRY
AKOOPRT PARTOOK	ALNOPYY POLYNYA	AMNOSTU AMOUNTS
AKORRTW ARTWORK	ALNORSY ROSALYN	AMNQTUU QUANTUM

AMNRTTU TANTRUM
AMNSTTU MUTANTS
AMNSTUU AUTUMNS
AMOOORS AMOROSO
AMOOPRT TAPROOM
AMOORSU AMOROUS
AMOPSTT TOPMAST
AMORRST MORTARS
AMORRSW MARROWS
AMORRUY ARMOURY
AMPRSUW WARM-UPS
AMRRSTY MARTYRS
AMRRTYY MARTYRY
AMRSTTU STRATUM
ANNRTYY TYRANNY
ANNSSTU SUNTANS
ANOOPRS SOPRANO
ANOPRRS SPORRAN
ANOPRSS PARSONS
ANOPRST PATRONS
ANORRSW NARROWS
ANORSUU ANUROUS,
   URANOUS
ANPRSTU SUNTRAP,
   UNSTRAP
ANRSSTU SUNSTAR
ANRSTTU TRUANTS
ANRSTTY TYRANTS
ANRSUWY RUNWAYS
AOOPPRS APROPOS,
   SAPPORO
AOOPRTT TAPROOT
AOORRST ORATORS
AOORRTT ROTATOR
AOORRTY ORATORY
AOOSTTT TATTOOS
AOPPRRT RAPPORT
AOPPRTU UP TO PAR
AOPRRST PARROTS
AOPRRSW SPARROW
AOPRRTY PORTRAY
AOPRSST PASTORS
AOPRSTW POSTWAR
AOPRSUV VAPOURS
AOPSTUY AUTOPSY,
   PAYOUTS
AOQRSTU QUARTOS
AOQRTUY TORQUAY
AORSSUY OSSUARY
AORSTTW AT WORST,
   TWO-STAR
AORSUVY SAVOURY
AOSTTUY OUTSTAY

APPRRUU PURPURA
APPRSUY PAPYRUS
APRSSSU SURPASS
APRSTTU UPSTART
APRSTUU UT SUPRA
ARSSTTU STRATUS
BBBDELU BUBBLED
BBBEIOS BOBBIES
BBBELOS BOBBLES
BBBELRU BLUBBER,
   BUBBLER
BBBELSU BUBBLES
BBBEORY BOBBERY
BBBGINO BOBBING
BBBINOS BOBBINS
BBCCIKO BIBCOCK
BBCDEIR CRIBBED
BBCDELO COBBLED
BBCDELU CLUBBED
BBCELOR CLOBBER,
   COBBLER
BBCEORS COBBERS
BBCEOSW COBWEBS
BBCGINU CUBBING
BBCINOU BUBONIC
BBCKLOU LUBBOCK
BBCRSUY SCRUBBY
BBDDEIL DIBBLED
BBDEEIT EBB TIDE
BBDEGLO GOBBLED
BBDEGRU GRUBBED
BBDEGSU BEDBUGS
BBDEHLO HOBBLED
BBDEIIM IMBIBED
BBDEILN NIBBLED
BBDEILO LOBBIED
BBDEILR DIBBLER, DRIBBLE
BBDEILS DIBBLES
BBDELMU BUMBLED
BBDELNO NOBBLED
BBDELOS BOBSLED
BBDELOW WOBBLED
BBDELRU BURBLED
BBDENSU SNUBBED
BBDERRU DRUBBER
BBDESTU STUBBED
BBDGIIN DIBBING
BBDGINU DUBBING
BBEEENT ENTEBBE
BBEELPS PEBBLES
BBEESTT BEST BET
BBEESUY BUSY BEE
BBEESYY BYE-BYES

BBEFILR FRIBBLE
BBEFIRS FIBBERS
BBEGILR GLIBBER, GRIBBLE
BBEGINW WEBBING
BBEGIST GIBBETS
BBEGLOR GOBBLER
BBEGLOS GOBBLES
BBEGOST GOBBETS
BBEGRRU GRUBBER
BBEHIOS HOBBIES
BBEHISU HUBBIES
BBEHLOR HOBBLER
BBEIIMR IMBIBER
BBEILNR NIBBLER
BBEILNS NIBBLES
BBEILOS BILBOES, LOBBIES
BBEILOT BIBELOT
BBEILQU QUIBBLE
BBEILRS LIBBERS
BBEIOOS BOOBIES
BBEIRRY BRIBERY
BBEIRTU TUBBIER
BBEISSU BUSBIES
BBEJORS JOBBERS
BBEJORY JOBBERY
BBEKLOS BLESBOK
BBELLOY BELLBOY
BBELMRU BUMBLER
BBELNOR NOBBLER
BBELORS SLOBBER
BBELORW WOBBLER
BBELORY LOBBYER
BBELOSW WOBBLES
BBELRRU BURBLER
BBELSTU STUBBLE
BBEMORS BOMBERS
BBENRSU SNUBBER
BBEORRS ROBBERS
BBEORRY ROBBERY
BBERRSU RUBBERS
BBERRUY RUBBERY
BBFGIIN FIBBING
BBFGINO FOBBING
BBGGIIN GIBBING
BBGIIJN JIBBING
BBGIINR RIBBING
BBGIJNO JOBBING
BBGILNO LOBBING
BBGIMNO BOMBING,
   MOBBING
BBGINOO BOOBING
BBGINOR ROBBING

BBGINOS GIBBONS,
  SOBBING
BBGINRU RUBBING
BBGINSU SUBBING
BBGINTU TUBBING
BBGIOSU GIBBOUS
BBHIMOS HOBBISM
BBHIOST HOBBIST
BBHIRSU RUBBISH
BBHRSUY SHRUBBY
BBIKOSS SKIBOBS
BBIKTUZ KIBBUTZ
BBINORS RIBBONS
BBKLNOY KNOBBLY
BBLOSUU BULBOUS
BBLSTUY STUBBLY
BBNNOOS BONBONS
BBNOORU BOURBON
BBOSSUY BUS BOYS
BBRSSUU SUBURBS
BCCEILO ECBOLIC
BCCEILU CUBICLE
BCCEILY BICYCLE
BCCIIMR CIMBRIC
BCCILOU BUCOLIC
BCCINOO OBCONIC
BCCISUU SUCCUBI
BCCMOOX COXCOMB
BCCMSUU SUCCUMB
BCCNOOR CORNCOB
BCDEEHL BELCHED
BCDEEIL DECIBEL
BCDEHIR BIRCHED
BCDEHIT BITCHED
BCDEHNU BUNCHED
BCDEHOT BOTCHED
BCDEHOU DEBOUCH
BCDEIIO BIOCIDE
BCDEIKS SICKBED
BCDEILM CLIMBED
BCDEIOS BODICES
BCDEKLO BLOCKED
BCDEKLU BUCKLED
BCDEKOR BEDROCK
BCDENOU BOUNCED
BCDIIRU RUBIDIC
BCDINOW COWBIND
BCDIORW COWBIRD
BCDKORU BURDOCK
BCDSTUU SUBDUCT
BCEEEHS BEECHES,
  BESEECH
BCEEELS CELEBES

BCEEGIR ICEBERG
BCEEHIT HEBETIC
BCEEHLS BELCHES
BCEEHNR BENCHER
BCEEHNS BENCHES
BCEEHOU BOUCHEE
BCEEINR BERNICE
BCEEKUY BUCKEYE
BCEENOS OBSCENE
BCEHIOR BRIOCHE
BCEHIRS BIRCHES
BCEHIST BITCHES
BCEHITW BEWITCH
BCEHNSU BUNCHES
BCEHORT BOTCHER
BCEHORW COWHERB
BCEHRSU CHERUBS
BCEHRTU BUTCHER
BCEILMO EMBOLIC
BCEILMR CLIMBER
BCEILOR BRICOLE,
  CORBEIL
BCEIMNO COMBINE
BCEIMOR MICROBE
BCEINOZ BENZOIC
BCEINRU BRUCINE
BCEIRRS SCRIBER
BCEIRSS SCRIBES
BCEJOST OBJECTS
BCEJSTU SUBJECT
BCEKLRU BUCKLER
BCEKLSU BUCKLES
BCEKORT BROCKET
BCEKORU ROEBUCK
BCEKSTU BUCKETS
BCELLOW COWBELL
BCELMRU CRUMBLE
BCELMSU SCUMBLE
BCELORS CORBELS
BCEMORS COMBERS
BCENORU BOUNCER
BCENOSU BOUNCES
BCEOORT OCTOBER
BCEORSU OBSCURE
BCFSSUU SUBFUSC
BCGIKNU BUCKING
BCGIMNO COMBING
BCGINRU CURBING
BCHIKOU CHIBOUK
BCHIMOR RHOMBIC
BCHINOR BRONCHI
BCHIOPR PIBROCH
BCHIOPS PHOBICS

BCHLOTY BLOTCHY
BCHOPTU BOTCH-UP
BCHORST BORSCHT
BCIINOS BIONICS
BCIIOPS BIOPICS
BCIIOPT BIOPTIC
BCIISTU BISCUIT
BCILMPU PLUMBIC
BCINORU RUBICON
BCINORY BYRONIC
BCINSUU INCUBUS
BCIORST STROBIC
BCIRRSU RUBRICS
BCIRTUY BUTYRIC
BCKLLOU BULLOCK
BCKOTTU BUTTOCK
BCLMOOO COLOMBO
BCLMOOU COULOMB
BCLMRUY CRUMBLY
BCLOOSU COLOBUS
BCMOOTU COMB-OUT
BCMOSTU COMBUST
BCNOORS BRONCOS
BCOOSWY COWBOYS
BCOOTTY BOYCOTT
BDDEEES SEEDBED
BDDEEEW BEDEWED
BDDEEIS BEDSIDE
BDDEEIT BETIDED, DEBITED
BDDEELN BLENDED
BDDEFOR BEDFORD
BDDEGIN BEDDING
BDDEILN BLINDED
BDDEISU BUDDIES
BDDELNU BUNDLED
BDDELOO BLOODED
BDDELOU DOUBLED
BDDENOU BOUNDED
BDDEOOR BROODED
BDDEOTU DOUBTED
BDDESUU SUBDUED
BDDGIIN BIDDING
BDDGINU BUDDING
BDDGIOR BIRD DOG
BDEEELP BLEEPED
BDEEELR BLEEDER
BDEEELT BEETLED
BDEEELV BEVELED
BDEEERR BREEDER
BDEEERT RED BEET
BDEEFIR DEBRIEF
BDEEGUY BUG-EYED
BDEEHRT BERTHED

BDEEILL LIBELED
BDEEILV BEDEVIL
BDEEIMT BEDTIME
BDEEINR INBREED
BDEEIRS DERBIES
BDEEISS BESIDES
BDEEKRU REBUKED
BDEELNR BLENDER
BDEELOV BELOVED
BDEELOW ELBOWED
BDEELRT TREBLED
BDEELSS BLESSED
BDEEMSU BEMUSED
BDEENPR PREBEND
BDEEORS BEDSORE,
   SOBERED
BDEEOTW WEB-TOED
BDEERUW BURWEED
BDEFFLU BLUFFED
BDEFLMU FUMBLED
BDEGGLO BOGGLED
BDEGILO OBLIGED
BDEGINN BENDING
BDEGINS BIG ENDS
BDEGIOT BIGOTED
BDEGIRT BRIDGET
BDEGLNU BUNGLED
BDEGLRU BURGLED
BDEGOOY GOODBYE
BDEGSTU BUDGETS
BDEHINS BEHINDS
BDEHLMU HUMBLED
BDEHLSU BLUSHED
BDEHMTU THUMBED
BDEHOST HOTBEDS
BDEHRSU BRUSHED
BDEIIRS BIRDIES
BDEIKLN BLINKED
BDEILLR ILL-BRED
BDEILLU BULLIED
BDEILNR BRINDLE
BDEILOR BROILED
BDEILRT DRIBLET
BDEILRU BUILDER,
   REBUILD
BDEILTZ BLITZED
BDEIMOR BROMIDE
BDEINOU BEDOUIN
BDEINRS BINDERS
BDEINRY BINDERY
BDEINTW TWIN BED
BDEIORS DISROBE
BDEIORT ORBITED

BDEIORV OVERBID
BDEIOSY DISOBEY
BDEIOWY WIDE BOY
BDEIRST BESTRID
BDEIRSU BRUISED
BDEIRTU BRUITED
BDEISSU SUBSIDE
BDEISTU SUBEDIT
BDEITUY DUBIETY
BDEJLMU JUMBLED
BDEKNOO BOOKEND
BDEKOOR BROOKED
BDELMMU MUMBLED
BDELMOO BLOOMED
BDELMPU PLUMBED
BDELMRU RUMBLED
BDELMTU TUMBLED
BDELNOR BLONDER
BDELNOS BLONDES
BDELNOW BLODWEN
BDELNRU BLUNDER,
   BUNDLER
BDELNSU BUNDLES
BDELNTU BLUNTED
BDELORU BOULDER,
   DOUBLER
BDELOST BOLDEST
BDELOSU DOUBLES
BDELOTT BLOTTED,
   BOTTLED
BDELOTU DOUBLET
BDELOUW WOULD-BE
BDELRRU BLURRED
BDELRTU BLURTED
BDELSTU BUSTLED
BDEMOOR BEDROOM,
   BOREDOM
BDEMSTU DUMBEST
BDENNOU BOUNDEN,
   UNBONED
BDENORU BOUNDER,
   REBOUND
BDENORW BROWNED
BDENORY BONE-DRY
BDENORZ BRONZED
BDENOUW UNBOWED
BDENRSU BURDENS
BDENSSU SUNBEDS
BDENSTU SUBTEND
BDEOORR BROODER
BDEOOST BOOSTED
BDEOPST BEDPOST
BDEORRS BORDERS

BDEORRU BORDURE
BDEORST DEBTORS
BDEORSU ROSEBUD
BDEORSW BROWSED
BDEORTU DOUBTER,
   OBTRUDE, REDOUBT
BDFIIOR FIBROID
BDGGINU BUDGING
BDGHIIR BRIGHID
BDGIINN BINDING
BDGIIOO GOBIOID
BDGILOO GLOBOID
BDGINNO BONDING
BDGLLOU BULLDOG
BDHIRSY HYBRIDS
BDHOOOY BOYHOOD
BDIILOR OILBIRD
BDIILOS LIBIDOS
BDIISTT TIDBITS
BDIKNOS BODKINS
BDILLNY BLINDLY
BDILPUU BUILDUP,
   UPBUILD
BDINNOU INBOUND
BDINOOR BRIDOON
BDINOTU IN DOUBT
BDINRSU SUNBIRD
BDINRUU BURUNDI
BDINSTU DUSTBIN
BDIOOOV OBOVOID
BDIOORU BOUDOIR
BDIOSUU DUBIOUS
BDIRSTU DISTURB
BDISSUY SUBSIDY
BDLOOOT OLD BOOT
BDLOOOX OXBLOOD
BDLOOSY OLD BOYS
BDLORWY BLOW-DRY
BDNNOUU UNBOUND
BDNOORU BOURDON
BDNOOWW DOWN-BOW
BDNORUW RUBDOWN
BDOOOWX BOXWOOD
BDORSWY BYWORDS
BEEEFIR BEEFIER, FREEBIE
BEEEFLR FEEBLER
BEEEGIS BESIEGE
BEEEHIV BEEHIVE
BEEEHNS SHEBEEN
BEEEILN BEELINE
BEEEILV BELIEVE
BEEEJLW BEJEWEL
BEEEJLZ JEZEBEL

BEEEKLL BELLEEK
BEEEELPR BLEEPER
BEEEELPS PEEBLES
BEEEELST BEETLES
BEEEMRS BERSEEM
BEEENNZ BENZENE
BEEENRS BERNESE
BEEENTW BETWEEN
BEEFGIN BEEFING
BEEFILR FEBRILE
BEEFILS BELIEFS
BEEFINT BENEFIT
BEEFIRS FRISBEE
BEEFLOR FROEBEL
BEEFLTY BEETFLY
BEEGILL LEGIBLE
BEEGILO OBLIGEE
BEEGILU BEGUILE
BEEGINR BIGENER
BEEGJRS ESBJERG
BEEHLLT BETHELL
BEEHLRT BLETHER
BEEHLST BETHELS
BEEHRRT HERBERT
BEEHRST SHERBET
BEEHRSW HEBREWS
BEEHRTY THEREBY
BEEHRWY WHEREBY
BEEIJLU JUBILEE
BEEILLS BELLIES
BEEILOS OBELISE
BEEILOZ OBELIZE
BEEIMST BETIMES
BEEINNZ BENZINE
BEEINOS EBONISE
BEEINOT EBONITE
BEEINOZ EBONIZE
BEEINRZ ZEBRINE
BEEIQUZ BEZIQUE
BEEIRRS BERRIES
BEEIRRV BREVIER
BEEIRST BISERTE
BEEIRTZ BIZERTE
BEEKNOT BETOKEN
BEEKOPS BESPOKE
BEEKRRS BERSERK
BEEKRRU REBUKER
BEEKRSU REBUKES
BEELMMS EMBLEMS
BEELMRT TREMBLE
BEELMSS BLESS ME!
BEELMWY WEMBLEY
BEELNNO ENNOBLE

BEELNOR BORNEEL
BEELNTY BENTLEY
BEELNUX BENELUX
BEELOTY EYEBOLT
BEELRST TREBLES
BEELRVY BEVERLY
BEEMMRS MEMBERS
BEEMNRU E NUMBER
BEEMRSU BURMESE
BEENNRR BRENNER
BEENNTT BENNETT
BEENORR ENROBER
BEENOST BONESET
BEEOOST BOOTEES
BEEORSV OBSERVE,
 OBVERSE, VERBOSE
BEEORWY EYEBROW
BEEQSTU BEQUEST
BEERRWY BREWERY
BEERSSU REBUSES
BEERSTT BETTERS
BEERSTW BESTREW
BEERTTU BURETTE
BEFFLRU BLUFFER
BEFFOST BEST-OFF
BEFFRSU BUFFERS,
 REBUFFS
BEFFSTU BUFFETS
BEFGIIL FILIBEG
BEFGIRU FIREBUG
BEFILOS FOIBLES
BEFILRT FILBERT
BEFILSU FUSIBLE
BEFINOR BONFIRE
BEFIORX FIREBOX
BEFIRVY VERBIFY
BEFITUX TUBIFEX
BEFLMRU FUMBLER
BEFLMSU FUMBLES
BEFLORT BELFORT
BEFLRTU FULBERT
BEFOORR FORBORE
BEFOOTW WEBFOOT
BEGGGIN BEGGING
BEGGIIS BIGGIES
BEGGIOR BOGGIER
BEGGIST BIGGEST
BEGGISU BUGGIES
BEGGRSU BUGGERS
BEGGRUY BUGGERY
BEGHRRU BURGHER
BEGIIMT BIG TIME
BEGIKNR KERBING

BEGILLY LEGIBLY
BEGILMU BELGIUM
BEGILNO GOBELIN,
 IGNOBLE
BEGILNT BELTING
BEGILNU BLUEING
BEGILNY BELYING
BEGILOR OBLIGER
BEGILRS GERBILS
BEGILRT GILBERT
BEGILRU BULGIER
BEGILST GIBLETS
BEGINOY OBEYING
BEGINRW BREWING
BEGINSS BIGNESS
BEGINST BESTING
BEGINTT BETTING
BEGKMOS GEMSBOK
BEGLLOU GLOBULE
BEGLMRU GRUMBLE
BEGLMUU BLUE GUM
BEGLNRU BLUNGER,
 BUNGLER
BEGLNSU BUNGLES
BEGLOOS GLOBOSE
BEGLOOT BOOTLEG
BEGLOST GOBLETS
BEGLOUY BEYOGLU
BEGLRSU BUGLERS
BEGNOOS BONGOES
BEGNORU BURGEON
BEGNOSY BYGONES
BEGORSU BROGUES
BEGRRSU BURGERS
BEGRSSU BURGESS
BEHIITX EXHIBIT
BEHIKLO HOBLIKE
BEHIKNT BETHINK
BEHILMS BLEMISH
BEHILMT THIMBLE
BEHILOS BOLSHIE
BEHILRT HILBERT
BEHILST LISBETH
BEHILTZ LIZBETH
BEHIMOR BIOHERM
BEHINOP HIPBONE
BEHIOTW HOWBEIT
BEHIRRT REBIRTH
BEHIRSU BUSHIER,
 BUSHIRE
BEHKKOO KOKOBEH
BEHKNOO HOBOKEN
BEHLLOX HELLBOX

151

BEHLMRU HUMBLER
BEHLORT BROTHEL
BEHLRSU BLUSHER
BEHLSSU BLUSHES,
    BUSHELS
BEHMOTT THE TOMB
BEHMRTU HUMBERT
BEHNOST BENTHOS
BEHNPRU HEPBURN
BEHNRTU BURTHEN
BEHOPRT POTHERB
BEHORRT BROTHER
BEHORTT BETROTH
BEHOSTY THE BOYS
BEHRRSU BRUSHER
BEHRSSU BRUSHES
BEIILLS BILLIES
BEIILRS RISIBLE
BEIILSV VISIBLE
BEIINOT NIOBITE
BEIINST STIBINE
BEIIOTT BIOTITE
BEIIRTT BITTIER
BEIKLNR BLINKER
BEIKLOS OBELISK
BEIKLRU BULKIER
BEIKRRS BRISKER
BEIKRST BRISKET
BEIKSTV VITEBSK
BEILLST BILLETS
BEILLSU BULLIES
BEILMNR NIMBLER
BEILMOR EMBROIL
BEILMOS MOBILES
BEILMRT TIMBREL
BEILMRU UMBRIEL
BEILMSU SUBLIME
BEILNOW BOWLINE
BEILNSY BY-LINES
BEILOPY EPIBOLY
BEILOQU OBLIQUE
BEILORR BROILER
BEILORS BOILERS
BEILORW BLOWIER
BEILRRU BURLIER
BEILRST BLISTER, BRISTLE
BEILRTT BRITTLE
BEILRTU REBUILT
BEILRTW WILBERT
BEILRTY LIBERTY
BEILSTW BLEWITS
BEILSTZ BLITZES
BEILTTU BLUETIT

BEIMMRR BRIMMER
BEIMNOR BROMINE
BEIMNTU BITUMEN
BEIMOSV B-MOVIES
BEIMOSZ ZOMBIES
BEIMPRU BUMPIER
BEIMRST TIMBERS,
    TIMBRES
BEIMRTU IMBRUTE,
    TERBIUM
BEINNOR BONNIER
BEINNOZ BENZOIN
BEINNSU BUNNIES
BEINOOT EOBIONT
BEINORT BORNITE
BEINORW BROWNIE
BEINOST BONIEST
BEINRSU SUBERIN
BEINRTT BITTERN
BEINRTU TRIBUNE,
    TURBINE
BEIOOPT BIOTOPE
BEIOORZ BOOZIER
BEIOPTY BIOTYPE
BEIORSS BOSSIER
BEIOSTW BOW TIES
BEIOSTY OBESITY
BEIRRSU BRUISER
BEIRSSU BRUISES
BEIRSTT BITTERS
BEIRSTU BUSTIER
BEIRTTU TRIBUTE
BEIRTVY BREVITY
BEISSTU BUSIEST
BEISTTU BUTTIES
BEITTWX BETWIXT
BEJJSUU JUJUBES
BEJKOUX JUKEBOX
BEJLMRU JUMBLER
BEJLMSU JUMBLES
BEJLOSS JOBLESS
BEKLNOZ KOBLENZ
BEKLOOT BOOKLET
BEKLSUY BLUE-SKY,
    SKY-BLUE
BEKNORS BONKERS
BEKNRSU BUNKERS
BEKORRS BROKERS
BEKRSSU BUSKERS
BELLOSU SOLUBLE
BELLOSW BELLOWS
BELLOUV VOLUBLE
BELLSTU BULLETS

BELMMRU MUMBLER
BELMNOU NELUMBO
BELMOOR BLOOMER
BELMOPR PROBLEM
BELMOSU EMBOLUS
BELMPRU PLUMBER
BELMRRU RUMBLER
BELMRSU RUMBLES,
    SLUMBER
BELMRTU TUMBLER,
    TUMBREL
BELMRTY TREMBLY
BELMSTU STUMBLE,
    TUMBLES
BELNOOY BOLONEY
BELNOST NOBLEST
BELNOYZ BENZOYL
BELNSTU SUNBELT
BELOOPR BLOOPER
BELOORS BOLEROS
BELOOVY BYELOVO
BELORST BOLSTER,
    LOBSTER
BELORSU ROUBLES
BELORSW BLOWERS,
    BOWLERS
BELORSY SOBERLY
BELORTT BLOTTER
BELORTU TROUBLE
BELOSSU BLOUSES
BELOSTT BOTTLES
BELOSTU BOLETUS
BELRSTU BLUSTER,
    BUSTLER, BUTLERS,
    SUBTLER
BELRTUY BUTLERY
BELSSTU BUSTLES
BEMNRSU NUMBERS
BEMORST MOBSTER
BEMORSY EMBRYOS
BEMPRSU BUMPERS
BEMSSUU SUBSUME
BENNORW BRONWEN,
    NEWBORN
BENNOST BONNETS
BENOORS OSBORNE
BENORRT NORBERT
BENORRW BROWNER
BENORSZ BRONZES
BENORTY RENT BOY
BENOSSU BONUSES
BENRRSU BURNERS
BEOOPSX PO BOXES

BEOOPUZ BOOZE-UP	BGIIMNU IMBUING	BHIMOPR BIMORPH
BEOORSS SORBOSE	BGIINNN BINNING	BHIMSTU BISMUTH
BEOORST BOOSTER	BGIJNOY BY JINGO	BHINRSU BURNISH
BEOORSZ BOOZERS	BGIKLNU BULKING	BHIOORS BOORISH
BEOPRRV PROVERB	BGIKNNU BUNKING	BHIOPSS BISHOPS
BEOQTUU BOUQUET	BGIKNOO BOOKING	BHIRSTU BRUTISH
BEORRSW BROWSER	BGIKNSU BUSKING	BHISTTU BUSHTIT
BEORSST SORBETS	BGILMOU GUMBOIL	BHLOOPT BOTOLPH
BEPRRTU PERTURB	BGILMRU LIMBURG	BHLRSUU BULRUSH
BEPRTUY PUBERTY	BGILNOS GOBLINS	BHMORSU RHOMBUS
BEPSTUY SUBTYPE	BGILNOT BILTONG,	BHOOSTW BOWSHOT
BEQRSUU BRUSQUE	BOLTING	BHPRSUU BRUSH-UP
BERRSTU BURSTER	BGILNOW BLOWING,	BIIIKNS BIKINIS
BERSSTU BUSTERS	BOWLING	BIIILTZ TBILIZI
BERSTTY BETTRYS	BGILNOY IGNOBLY	BIILLNO BILLION
BERSTUV SUBVERT	BGILOOR OBLIGOR	BIILNTU BUILT-IN
BERSUZZ BUZZERS	BGILOOY BIOLOGY	BIILOSU BILIOUS
BERTTUY BUTTERY	BGILRTU TILBURG	BIILRSY RISIBLY
BESSSTU SUBSETS	BGIMMNU BUMMING	BIILSVY VISIBLY
BFFGIIN BIFFING	BGIMNNU NUMBING	BIIMNOU NIOBIUM
BFFGINU BUFFING	BGIMNOO BOOMING	BIIMNSU MINIBUS
BFFINOS BOFFINS	BGIMNPU BUMPING	BIISTTT TITBITS
BFFLLUY BLUFFLY	BGINNRU BURNING	BIJNOSU SUBJOIN
BFFNOOU BUFFOON	BGINNTU BUNTING	BIKLLUY BULKILY
BFGIORT FROG-BIT	BGINOOT BOOTING	BIKLRSY BRISKLY
BFHIRSU FURBISH	BGINOOZ BOOZING	BIKMNPU BUMPKIN
BFIINOR FIBROIN	BGINOPP BOPPING	BIKNRSY RYBINSK
BFILMRU BRIMFUL	BGINOPR PROBING	BILLNOU BULLION
BFIORSU FIBROUS	BGINOSS BOSSING	BILLOPX PILLBOX
BFKLOOY FLYBOOK	BGINOUY BUOYING	BILLOSW BILLOWS
BFLLOWY BLOWFLY,	BGINPRU BURPING	BILLOWY BILLOWY
FLYBLOW	BGINRRU BURRING	BILLRWY WRYBILL
BFOOOTY FOOTBOY	BGINRUY BURYING	BILMNOO IN BLOOM
BGGGINO BOGGING	BGINSSU BUSSING	BILMNOR NOMBRIL
BGGGINU BUGGING	BGINSTU BUSTING	BILMNRU MILBURN
BGGIISW BIGWIGS	BGINSUY BUSYING	BILMPUY BUMPILY
BGGILNU BULGING	BGINTTU BUTTING	BILNOTU BOTULIN
BGGINNU BUNGING	BGINUZZ BUZZING	BILOOYZ BOOZILY
BGHHIOY HIGHBOY	BGIOPST BIG TOPS	BILOSSU SUBSOIL
BGHILST BLIGHTS	BGIORTY BIGOTRY	BILOSSY BOSSILY
BGHINOR BIGHORN	BGJOTUY TOBY JUG	BILPTUU BUILT-UP
BGHINSU BUSHING	BGKLOOO LOGBOOK	BILRSTY BRISTLY
BGHINTY BY NIGHT	BGLNOOS OBLONGS	BIMMORS BROMISM
BGHIOST BIG SHOT	BGLNOOW LONGBOW	BIMNOSU OMNIBUS
BGHIPSU BUSHPIG	BGLOSSU BUGLOSS	BINNOSU BUNIONS
BGHMORU HOMBURG	BGMOOTU GUMBOOT	BINOOSU NIOBOUS
BGHMSUU HUMBUGS	BHIIINT INHIBIT	BINORST BRITONS
BGHOOOS OSHOGBO	BHIIRST BRITISH	BINRTUY BUTYRIN
BGHOORU BOROUGH	BHIKOOS BOOKISH	BIOORSZ BORZOIS
BGIIKLN BILKING	BHILLSU BULLISH	BIOOSST OBOISTS
BGIILLN BILLING	BHILOTU HOLIBUT	BIOOSUV OBVIOUS
BGIILNO BOILING	BHILPSU PUBLISH	BIOPRTY PROBITY
BGIILNS SIBLING	BHIMOOS HOBOISM	BIORRTU BURRITO

BIORRTW RIBWORT
BIORSST BISTROS
BIORSTT BISTORT
BIORSUU RUBIOUS
BISSSTU SUBSIST
BJLOOST JOB LOTS
BJNOORU BONJOUR
BJORUXY JURY BOX
BKNOOTW BOWKNOT
BKNPSUU BUNK-UPS
BKOORWX WORKBOX
BLLNTUY BLUNTLY
BLLOUVY VOLUBLY
BLMOOOT TOMBOLO
BLMOOSS BLOSSOM
BLMOSSY SYMBOLS
BLNOORW LOWBORN
BLOOQUY OBLOQUY
BLOORWW LOWBROW
BLOOTUW BLOWOUT
BLOPSTU SUBPLOT
BLOPSUW BLOW-UPS
BMNOOSU UNBOSOM
BMOOORX BOXROOM
BMOOSTT BOTTOMS
BMOOSTY TOMBOYS
BMORSUU BRUMOUS
BNNORWY BRONWYN
BNNRSUU SUNBURN
BNORSTU BURTONS
BNORSUU BURNOUS
BNORTUU BURNOUT
BNOSTTU BUTTONS
BOOPRTT BOTTROP
BOOPSTX POSTBOX
BOPSSTU BUS STOP
BORRSUW BURROWS
BORSTTU TURBOTS
BOSTUUY BUYOUTS
BPSSTUU BUST-UPS
CCCDIOO COCCOID
CCCEHIO CHOC-ICE
CCCNOOT CONCOCT
CCCOOSU COCCOUS
CCDEEHK CHECKED
CCDEENO CONCEDE
CCDEENY DECENCY
CCDEEOR COERCED
CCDEESU SUCCEED
CCDEHIL CLICHÉD
CCDEHKO CHOCKED
CCDEHKU CHUCKED
CCDEHOU COUCHED

CCDEHRY CEDRYCH
CCDEIIL ICICLED
CCDEIIT DEICTIC
CCDEIKL CLICKED
CCDEIKR CRICKED
CCDEILO ICE-COLD
CCDEILR CIRCLED
CCDEIMO COMEDIC
CCDEIOS CODICES
CCDEKLO CLOCKED
CCDEKLU CLUCKED
CCDELOU OCCLUDE
CCDENOU CONDUCE
CCDHIIL CICHLID
CCDIILO CODICIL
CCDIILU CULICID
CCDIIOR CRICOID
CCDILOY CYCLOID
CCDKLOU CUCKOLD
CCDNOOR CONCORD
CCDNOTU CONDUCT
CCEEHHN CHECHEN
CCEEHOR ECORCHE
CCEEHRS CRÈCHES,
   SCREECH
CCEEIIL CECILIE
CCEEILN LICENCE
CCEEINR ECCRINE
CCEEINS SCIENCE
CCEEIRV CREVICE
CCEELRU LUCRECE
CCEELRY RECYCLE
CCEERSY SECRECY
CCEFNOT CONFECT
CCEGNOY COGENCY
CCEHIKN CHECK-IN,
   CHICKEN
CCEHILS CLICHÉS
CCEHINT TECHNIC
CCEHIOR CHOICER
CCEHIOS CHOICES
CCEHKLU CHUCKLE
CCEHKPU CHECKUP
CCEHLOS CLOCHES
CCEHNOS CONCHES
CCEHORT CROCHET
CCEHORU COUCHER
CCEHOSU COUCHES
CCEIIKP ICE PICK
CCEIILS ICICLES
CCEIIRT ICTERIC
CCEIKLR CLICKER
CCEIKOR COCKIER

CCEIKRT CRICKET
CCEILRR CIRCLER
CCEILRS CIRCLES, CLERICS
CCEILRT CIRCLET
CCEILTU CUTICLE
CCEIMST SMECTIC
CCEINOR CORNICE,
   CROCEIN
CCEINOS CONCISE
CCEINOT CONCEIT
CCEINRT CENTRIC
CCEIOPP COPPICE
CCEIOPT ECTOPIC
CCEIORT ORECTIC
CCEIPST SCEPTIC
CCEKLOS COCKLES
CCEKNOY COCKNEY
CCEKOPT PETCOCK
CCEKORT CROCKET
CCELLOT COLLECT
CCELNOY CYCLONE
CCEMNOO COMECON
CCENNOR CONCERN
CCENNOT CONNECT
CCENOPT CONCEPT
CCENORT CONCERT
CCENOSS SCONCES
CCEOOTT COCOTTE
CCEORRT CORRECT
CCERTUW CREW CUT
CCESSSU SUCCESS
CCFIRUY CRUCIFY
CCFLOSU FLOCCUS
CCGHINO GNOCCHI
CCGIKNO COCKING
CCGILNY CYCLING
CCHHIKU CHUKCHI
CCHIIST STICHIC
CCHILOR CHLORIC
CCHIMOR CHROMIC
CCHINOR CHRONIC
CCHIORY CHICORY
CCHIPSU HICCUPS
CCHIPSY PSYCHIC
CCHKMSU SCHMUCK
CCHNRSU SCRUNCH
CCHNRUY CRUNCHY
CCIIILS SILICIC
CCIILNS CLINICS
CCIILOT COLITIC
CCIINPS PICNICS
CCIIRST CRITICS
CCIIRTU CIRCUIT

CCIKLOW COWLICK	CDDKORY DRY DOCK	CDEENOZ COZENED
CCIKLOY COLICKY	CDEEEFL FLEECED	CDEENRT CENTRED,
CCIKOPT COCKPIT	CDEEEFN DEFENCE	CREDENT, RED CENT
CCILNOO COLONIC	CDEEEHK CHEEKED	CDEENST DESCENT,
CCILNOU COUNCIL	CDEEEHP CHEEPED	SCENTED
CCILOOP PICCOLO	CDEEEHR CHEERED	CDEEOPR PROCEED
CCILSTY CYCLIST	CDEEEIV DECEIVE	CDEEORV COVERED
CCIMOTY MYCOTIC	CDEEEJT EJECTED	CDEEORW COWERED
CCINOTV CONVICT	CDEEELT ELECTED	CDEEORY DECOYER
CCIOORS SIROCCO	CDEEEPR PRECEDE	CDEEOST CESTODE
CCIOPTU OCCIPUT	CDEEERR DECREER	CDEEOTV COVETED
CCIPRTY CRYPTIC	CDEEERS DECREES,	CDEERRU REDUCER
CCKOOSU CUCKOOS	SECEDER	CDEERSS SCREEDS
CCKOPSU COCK-UPS	CDEEERT ERECTED	CDEERST CRESTED
CCLOPSY CYCLOPS	CDEEFHT FETCHED	CDEERSU RESCUED,
CCMOOOR MOROCCO	CDEEFII EDIFICE	SECURED, SEDUCER
CCNOOOS COCOONS	CDEEFKL FLECKED	CDEERSW SCREWED
CCNOOPU PUCCOON	CDEEFLT DEFLECT	CDEESUX EXCUSED
CCNOOTU COCONUT	CDEEFOR DEFORCE	CDEFFHU CHUFFED
CCNOSSU CONCUSS	CDEEFST DEFECTS	CDEFFOS SCOFFED
CCORSUU SUCCOUR	CDEEHIS DEHISCE	CDEFFSU SCUFFED
CCSSSUU SUCCUSS	CDEEHKL HECKLED	CDEFHIL FILCHED
CDDDEEI DECIDED	CDEEHLW WELCHED	CDEFIIT DEFICIT
CDDDEEO DECODED	CDEEHMS SCHEMED	CDEFIKL FLICKED
CDDDEEU DEDUCED	CDEEHNW WENCHED	CDEFINO CONFIDE
CDDDELO CODDLED	CDEEHOR COHERED	CDEFIRR FREDRIC
CDDDELU CUDDLED	CDEEHPR PERCHED	CDEFKLO FLOCKED
CDDDESU SCUDDED	CDEEHRT RETCHED	CDEFKOR DEFROCK
CDDEEER DECREED,	CDEEHST CHESTED	CDEFNTU DEFUNCT
RECEDED	CDEEIIT EIDETIC	CDEFOSU FOCUSED
CDDEEES SECEDED	CDEEILN DECLINE	CDEGGHU CHUGGED
CDDEEII DEICIDE	CDEEILP PEDICEL, PEDICLE	CDEGGLO CLOGGED
CDDEEIR DECIDER,	CDEEIMN ENDEMIC	CDEGHOU COUGHED
DECRIED	CDEEINO CODEINE	CDEGIIN DE-ICING
CDDEENO ENCODED	CDEEINT ENTICED	CDEGIKN DECKING
CDDEENS DESCEND	CDEEINV EVINCED	CDEGINR CRINGED
CDDEEOY DECOYED	CDEEIOS DIOCESE	CDEGLSU CUDGELS
CDDEERU REDUCED	CDEEIOV DEVOICE	CDEGORS CODGERS
CDDEESU SEDUCED	CDEEIPR PIERCED	CDEHHIT HITCHED
CDDEEUW CUDWEED	CDEEIRR DECRIER	CDEHHNU HUNCHED
CDDEHIN CHIDDEN	CDEEIRT RECITED	CDEHIIV CHIVIED
CDDEHIT DITCHED	CDEEISV DEVICES	CDEHIKN CHINKED
CDDEILM MIDDLE C	CDEEISX EXCISED	CDEHILL CHILLED
CDDEINU INDUCED	CDEEITV EVICTED	CDEHILP DELPHIC
CDDELOS SCOLDED	CDEEITX EXCITED	CDEHINO HEDONIC
CDDELOU CLOUDED	CDEEKLR CLERKED	CDEHINP PINCHED
CDDELRU CURDLED	CDEEKNR REDNECK	CDEHINW WINCHED
CDDEORW CROWDED	CDEEKNV V-NECKED	CDEHIOW COWHIDE
CDDIIOS DISCOID	CDEEKRW WRECKED	CDEHIPP CHIPPED
CDDIIOY DIDICOY	CDEELPU DECUPLE	CDEHIPR CHIRPED
CDDIIRU DRUIDIC	CDEELSU SECLUDE	CDEHIPT PITCHED
CDDIKOP PIDDOCK	CDEELUX EXCLUDE	CDEHIRT DITCHER
CDDIORS DISCORD	CDEENOR ENCODER	CDEHIST DITCHES

CDEHISU DUCHIES	CDEILPU CLUPEID	CDELOTT CLOTTED
CDEHKOS SHOCKED	CDEILSU SLUICED	CDELOTU CLOUTED
CDEHKSU SHUCKED	CDEILTU DUCTILE	CDELRUY CRUDELY
CDEHKUY HEYDUCK	CDEIMNO DEMONIC	CDEMMNO COMMEND
CDEHLMU MULCHED	CDEIMOR DORMICE	CDEMMOO COMMODE
CDEHLNU LUNCHED	CDEIMOS MEDICOS	CDEMNNO CONDEMN
CDEHLNY LYNCHED	CDEIMOT DEMOTIC	CDEMORU DECORUM
CDEHLOT CLOTHED	CDEIMPR CRIMPED	CDENNOO CONDONE
CDEHLRU LURCHED	CDEIMSU DECIMUS	CDENNOT CONTEND
CDEHMMU CHUMMED	CDEINOT CTENOID,	CDENOOR CROONED
CDEHMNU MUNCHED	DEONTIC, D-NOTICE,	CDENOOS SECONDO
CDEHMOO MOOCHED	NOTICED	CDENOPU POUNCED
CDEHMOP CHOMPED	CDEINRS CINDERS,	CDENORS SCORNED
CDEHNOT NOTCHED	DISCERN, RESCIND	CDENORU CRUNODE
CDEHNPU PUNCHED	CDEINRU INDUCER	CDENORW CROWNED
CDEHNRU CHURNED	CDEINRY CINDERY	CDENOSS SECONDS
CDEHOPP CHOPPED	CDEINSX EXSCIND	CDENOTU COUNTED
CDEHOPU POUCHED	CDEIOPR PERCOID	CDEOOPP COPEPOD
CDEHORW CHOWDER,	CDEIOPZ ZIP CODE	CDEOOPS SCOOPED
COWHERD	CDEIORT CORDITE	CDEOOPT CO-OPTED
CDEHOSU DOUCHES	CDEIORV DIVORCE	CDEOORR CORRODE
CDEHOSW COWSHED	CDEIOST CESTOID	CDEOORT COTE-D'OR
CDEHOTU TOUCHED	CDEIPRS CRISPED	CDEOOST SCOOTED
CDEHOUV VOUCHED	CDEIPRT PREDICT	CDEOPPR CROPPED
CDEHPSY PSYCHED	CDEIRRU CURRIED	CDEOPRU PRODUCE
CDEHRSU CRUSHED	CDEIRST CREDITS	CDEORRS RECORDS
CDEHSSU DUCHESS	CDEIRSU CRUISED	CDEORSS CROSSED
CDEHSTY SCYTHED	CDEIRTV VERDICT	CDEORSU COURSED,
CDEIIKR DICKIER	CDEISST DISSECT	SCOURED
CDEIIKS DICKIES	CDEISSY ECDYSIS	CDEORTU COURTED
CDEIINR DINERIC	CDEKKNO KNOCKED	CDEOSTU SCOUTED
CDEIINS INCISED	CDEKLOW WEDLOCK	CDEPRSU SPRUCED
CDEIINT IDENTIC, INCITED	CDEKLPU PLUCKED	CDERSTU CRUDEST
CDEIIST DEISTIC, DICIEST	CDEKLSU SUCKLED	CDFHIOS CODFISH
CDEIISU SUICIDE	CDEKOOR CROOKED	CDFIILU FLUIDIC
CDEIJST DISJECT	CDEKORS DOCKERS	CDGHIIN CHIDING
CDEIKLN CLINKED	CDEKOST DOCKETS,	CDGIKNO DOCKING
CDEIKLP PICKLED	STOCKED	CDGIKNU DUCKING
CDEIKLS SLICKED	CDEKRTU TRUCKED	CDGILNO CODLING,
CDEIKLT TICKLED	CDELLOU COLLUDE	LINGCOD
CDEIKNS DICKENS,	CDELLSU SCULLED	CDGINNO CONDIGN
SNICKED	CDELMPU CLUMPED	CDGINOR CORDING
CDEIKPR PRICKED	CDELMSU MUSCLED	CDHIIST DISTICH
CDEIKRR DERRICK	CDELMTU MULCTED	CDHILOS COLDISH
CDEIKRT TRICKED	CDELNOO CONDOLE	CDHIOOR CHOROID,
CDEIKSU DUCKIES	CDELNOW CLOWNED	OCHROID
CDEILLO COLLIDE	CDELNOY CONDYLE	CDHIORS ORCHIDS
CDEILMO MELODIC	CDELNWY CLEDWYN	CDHIPTY DIPTYCH
CDEILNU INCLUDE,	CDELOPP CLOPPED	CDHMORU MURDOCH
NUCLIDE	CDELOPU COUPLED	CDIIIOT IDIOTIC
CDEILOP POLICED	CDELORS SCOLDER	CDIILLY IDYLLIC
CDEILPP CLIPPED	CDELOST COLDEST	CDIILNY DICLINY
CDEILPS SPLICED	CDELOSW SCOWLED	CDIIMNO DOMINIC

CDIINOR CRINOID
CDIINOT DICTION
CDIINOV VIDICON
CDIIORS CIRSOID
CDIIOSS CISSOID
CDIIOSV VISCOID
CDIKLNO OLD NICK
CDIKNOR DORNICK
CDILLOO COLLOID
CDILLUY LUCIDLY
CDILOUV LUDOVIC
CDIMMOU MODICUM
CDIMOOS COSMOID
CDIMSTU DICTUMS
CDINOSY SYNODIC
CDINOTU CONDUIT,
   NOCTUID
CDIOPRR RIPCORD
CDIOSTY CYSTOID
CDIOTUV OVIDUCT
CDIRSUY DYSURIC
CDIRTUY CRUDITY
CDISSSU DISCUSS
CDLNOTU COULDN'T
CDLOOPY LYCOPOD
CDLOSTU COULDST
CDMNOOS CONDOMS,
   MOD CONS
CDNOORS CONDORS,
   CORDONS
CDOOOPT OCTOPOD
CDOORST DOCTORS
CDOOTUW WOODCUT
CDOPRTU PRODUCT
CDOSTUY CUSTODY
CEEEFLS FLEECES
CEEEHLS LEECHES
CEEEHPR CHEEPER
CEEEHSS CHEESES
CEEEINP EPICENE
CEEEIRV RECEIVE
CEEEKNW EWE-NECK
CEEELRT RE-ELECT
CEEELST CELESTE
CEEENNO NEOCENE
CEEENRT TERENCE
CEEENSS ESSENCE
CEEEPRR CREEPER
CEEERRT ERECTER
CEEERST SECRETE
CEEERTX EXCRETE
CEEETUX EXECUTE
CEEFFNO OFFENCE

CEEFFST EFFECTS
CEEFHRT FETCHER
CEEFIRR FIERCER
CEEFKLR FRECKLE
CEEFLRT REFLECT
CEEFNOR ENFORCE
CEEFNRS FENCERS
CEEFPRT PERFECT,
   PREFECT
CEEGINR GENERIC
CEEGINT GENETIC
CEEGINU EUGENIC
CEEGKOS GECKOES
CEEGLLO COLLEGE
CEEGLNT NEGLECT
CEEGLOU ECLOGUE
CEEGNRY REGENCY
CEEGORT CORTEGE
CEEHILM MICHELE
CEEHILS HELICES
CEEHILV VEHICLE
CEEHIMR CHIMERE
CEEHIMS CHEMISE
CEEHINS CHINESE
CEEHIOR CHEERIO
CEEHIRT ETHERIC, HERETIC
CEEHIRW CHEWIER
CEEHKLR HECKLER
CEEHKNP HENPECK
CEEHKST KETCHES
CEEHLNO ECHELON
CEEHLRS LECHERS
CEEHLRY LECHERY
CEEHLSY LYCHEES
CEEHMRS SCHEMER
CEEHMSS SCHEMES
CEEHNRW WENCHER
CEEHNST TENCHES
CEEHNSW WENCHES
CEEHOPS EPOCHES
CEEHORT TROCHEE
CEEHPRR PERCHER
CEEHPRS PERCHES
CEEHPSU CEPHEUS
CEEHQRU CHEQUER
CEEHQSU CHEQUES
CEEHRST CHESTER,
   ETCHERS
CEEHSTV VETCHES
CEEIIPR EPEIRIC
CEEIJOR REJOICE
CEEIKNT NECKTIE
CEEILLM MICELLE

CEEILNR RECLINE
CEEILNS LICENSE,
   SELENIC, SILENCE
CEEILNU LEUCINE
CEEILPS ECLIPSE
CEEILRT RETICLE
CEEILST SECTILE
CEEILSV VESICLE
CEEILTT LETTICE
CEEILTU LEUCITE
CEEIMNO MIOCENE
CEEIMNT CENTIME
CEEIMRS MERCIES
CEEIMST EMETICS
CEEINNS INCENSE
CEEINNW CEINWEN
CEEINRS SINCERE
CEEINRT ENTERIC, ENTICER
CEEINRV CERVINE
CEEIOPT PICOTEE
CEEIORT COTERIE
CEEIORV REVOICE
CEEIPRR PIERCER
CEEIPRS PRECISE, RECIPES
CEEIPRT RECEIPT
CEEIPRU EPICURE
CEEIPSS SPECIES
CEEIPST PECTISE
CEEIPTZ PECTIZE
CEEIRRT RECITER
CEEIRSV SERVICE
CEEIRTX EXCITER
CEEJORT EJECTOR
CEEJRST REJECTS
CEEKLNT NECKLET
CEEKLPS SPECKLE
CEEKOSY SOCKEYE
CEEKPRS PECKERS
CEEKRRW WRECKER
CEELLLU CELLULE
CEELLNO COLLEEN
CEELMNT CLEMENT
CEELMOW WELCOME
CEELNOS ENCLOSE
CEELNRT LECTERN
CEELNRU LUCERNE
CEELORS CREOLES
CEELORT ELECTOR
CEELOTT COLETTE
CEELRSU RECLUSE
CEELRTU LECTURE
CEELRTY ERECTLY

CEELTTU LETTUCE,	CEFIKLR FLICKER	CEGOORS SCROOGE
LUCETTE	CEFILNT INFLECT	CEGOOTY CETOOGY
CEEMNRU CERUMEN	CEFILNU FUNICLE	CEGORRS GROCERS
CEEMOPR COMPEER,	CEFILOR LEOFRIC	CEGORRY GROCERY
COMPERE	CEFILRU LUCIFER	CEGORSU SCOURGE
CEEMOPT COMPETE	CEFIMOR COMFIER	CEHHIRS CHERISH
CEENNOU ENOUNCE	CEFINNO CONFINE	CEHHIRT HITCHER
CEENNOV CONVENE	CEFINOR CONIFER	CEHHIST HITCHES
CEENNRT CENTNER	CEFINTU FINE-CUT	CEHHITU HUTCHIE
CEENOOT ECOTONE	CEFIPSY SPECIFY	CEHHNSU HUNCHES
CEENORS ENCORES,	CEFIRTY CERTIFY, RECTIFY	CEHHSTU HUTCHES
NECROSE	CEFKLOT FETLOCK	CEHIILS CHILIES
CEENORZ COZENER	CEFKRSU FUCKERS	CEHIINR HIRCINE
CEENPRS SPENCER	CEFLNOU FLOUNCE	CEHIINT ICHNITE
CEENPRT PER CENT	CEFLNUY FLUENCY	CEHIIRT ITCHIER
CEENRSS SCREENS	CEFLOSS FO'C'SLES	CEHIJOR JERICHO
CEENRST CENTERS,	CEFMORY COMFREY	CEHIKNT KITCHEN,
CENTRES	CEFNOSS CONFESS	THICKEN
CEENRSU CENSURE	CEFNOSU CONFUSE	CEHIKPS PECKISH
CEENRSY SCENERY	CEFNOTU CONFUTE	CEHIKRR HERRICK
CEEOPTY ECOTYPE	CEFOPRS FORCEPS	CEHIKRT THICKER
CEEORRT ERECTOR	CEFORRT CROFTER	CEHIKRW WHICKER
CEEORRV COVERER,	CEFORSS FRESCOS	CEHIKTT THICKET
RECOVER	CEFORSU FOCUSER	CEHILNO CHOLINE,
CEEORRZ CORREZE	CEFOSSU FOCUSES	HELICON
CEEORTV COVETER	CEFRSUW CURFEWS	CEHILRV CHERVIL
CEEPPRT PERCEPT,	CEGGHIR CHIGGER	CEHILSS CHISELS
PRECEPT	CEGGIOR GEORGIC	CEHILTY ETHYLIC, TECHILY
CEEPPRU PREPUCE	CEGGPSU EGGCUPS	CEHIMNY CHIMNEY
CEEPRSS PRECESS	CEGHINO ECHOING	CEHIMOR HOMERIC
CEEPRST RESPECT,	CEGHINT ETCHING	CEHIMOS ECHOISM
SCEPTRE, SPECTRE	CEGHINW CHEWING	CEHIMRT THERMIC
CEEPRTX EXCERPT	CEGHLSU GULCHES	CEHIMRU RHEUMIC
CEERRSU RESCUER,	CEGHNTU CHENGTU	CEHIMST CHEMIST
SECURER	CEGIILN CEILING	CEHINOP PHOCINE
CEERRSW SCREWER	CEGIILW GLIWICE	CEHINPR PHRENIC
CEERRUV RECURVE	CEGIINP PIECING	CEHINPS PINCHES, SPHENIC
CEERSST CRESSET,	CEGIKNN NECKING	CEHINRW WINCHER
SECRETS	CEGIKNP PECKING	CEHINST STHENIC
CEERSSU RESCUES	CEGIKNR RECKING	CEHINSU ECHINUS
CEESSUX EXCUSES	CEGILNR CLINGER,	CEHINSW WINCHES
CEFFIOR OFFICER	CRINGLE	CEHIOPS HOSPICE
CEFFIOS OFFICES	CEGILNY GLYCINE	CEHIOPT POTICHE
CEFFISU SUFFICE	CEGINOS COGNISE	CEHIORS HEROICS
CEFFLSU SCUFFLE	CEGINOZ COGNIZE	CEHIOTV CHEVIOT
CEFFORS COFFERS,	CEGINRW CREWING	CEHIPPR CHIPPER
SCOFFER	CEGLNOO COLOGNE	CEHIPRR CHIRPER
CEFGINN FENCING	CEGLOOY ECOLOGY	CEHIPRS CIPHERS
CEFHILR FILCHER	CEGLOSU GLUCOSE	CEHIPRT PITCHER
CEFHILY CHIEFLY	CEGNORY CRYOGEN	CEHIPST PITCHES
CEFHINS FINCHES	CEGNOST CONGEST	CEHIQSU QUICHES
CEFIILT FICTILE	CEGNRUY URGENCY	CEHIRST RICHEST
CEFIIOR ORIFICE	CEGNSTY CYGNETS	CEHIRSU CUSHIER

CEHISTW WITCHES	CEIILNN INCLINE	CEIKPRT PRICKET
CEHKKRU CHUKKER	CEIILPP CLIPPIE	CEIKPST PICKETS, SKEPTIC
CEHKLMO HEMLOCK	CEIILPT PELITIC	CEIKQRU QUICKER
CEHKNOY HOCKNEY	CEIIMMT MIMETIC	CEIKRRT TRICKER
CEHKORS CHOKERS,	CEIIMOT MEIOTIC	CEIKRST RICKETS,
SHOCKER	CEIIMPR EMPIRIC	STICKER, TICKERS
CEHKPTU KETCHUP	CEIIMSS SEISMIC	CEIKRTY RICKETY
CEHKRSU SHUCKER	CEIIMST SEMITIC	CEIKRUY YUCKIER
CEHKSTY SKETCHY	CEIIMTT TITMICE	CEIKSST SICKEST
CEHLMWY WYCH-ELM	CEIINNO CONIINE	CEIKSTT TICKETS
CEHLNRU LUNCHER	CEIINNR CINERIN	CEIKSTW WICKETS
CEHLNRY LYNCHER	CEIINOS EOSINIC	CEILLLU LUCILLE
CEHLNSU LUNCHES	CEIINOV INVOICE	CEILLOR COLLIER
CEHLORT CHORTLE	CEIINPS PISCINE	CEILLOS COLLIES
CEHLOST CLOTHES	CEIINRS IRENICS, SERICIN	CEILLST CELLIST
CEHLQSU SQUELCH	CEIINRT CITRINE, CRINITE,	CEILMOP COMPILE,
CEHLRRU LURCHER	INCITER, NERITIC	POLEMIC
CEHLRSU LURCHES	CEIINSS ICINESS	CEILMPR CRIMPLE
CEHMNRU MUNCHER	CEIINSU CUISINE	CEILNNU NUCLEIN
CEHMOOR MOOCHER	CEIINTZ CITIZEN, ZINCITE	CEILNOS INCLOSE
CEHMOOW HOW COME?	CEIIOPZ EPIZOIC	CEILNOT LECTION
CEHNOOP HENCOOP	CEIIPRR PRICIER	CEILNOX LEXICON
CEHNORV CHEVRON	CEIIPRS SPICIER	CEILNPS SPLENIC
CEHNOST NOTCHES	CEIIPRT PICRITE	CEILNST CLIENTS, STENCIL
CEHNPRU PUNCHER	CEIIRST ERISTIC	CEILNTU TUNICLE
CEHNPSU PUNCHES	CEIISSS CISSIES	CEILOOS COOLIES
CEHNSUU EUNUCHS	CEIISVV CIVVIES	CEILOSS OSSICLE
CEHNTUY CHUTNEY	CEIITUV UVEITIC	CEILPPR CLIPPER, CRIPPLE
CEHOOPS POOCHES	CEIJSTU JUSTICE	CEILPRS SPLICER
CEHOORS CHOOSER	CEIKKNR KENRICK	CEILPSS SPLICES
CEHOORT CHEROOT	CEIKKSW KESWICK	CEILPSU SPICULE
CEHOPPR CHOPPER	CEIKLNR CLINKER,	CEILQSU CLIQUES
CEHOPRS PORCHES	CRINKLE	CEILQUY CLIQUEY
CEHOPSU POUCHES	CEIKLNS NICKELS	CEILRRU CURLIER
CEHORST TORCHES	CEIKLPR PICKLER, PRICKLE	CEILRTU UTRICLE
CEHORSZ SCHERZO	CEIKLPS PICKLES	CEILSSU CELSIUS, SLUICES
CEHORTU RETOUCH,	CEIKLRS SLICKER	CEIMNOS COSMINE,
TOUCHER	CEIKLRT TICKLER, TRICKLE	INCOMES
CEHORTW WOTCHER	CEIKLRU LUCKIER	CEIMNRS MINCERS
CEHORUV VOUCHER	CEIKLRW LERWICK	CEIMOPT METOPIC
CEHOSTU TOUCHES	CEIKLSS SICKLES	CEIMOTT TOTEMIC
CEHPRSY CYPHERS	CEIKLST STICKLE, TICKLES	CEIMOTV VICOMTE
CEHPSSY PSYCHES	CEIKMRU MUCKIER	CEIMPRR CRIMPER
CEHRSSU CRUSHES	CEIKMSY MICKEYS	CEIMRST METRICS
CEHRSTT STRETCH	CEIKNOT KENOTIC,	CEINNOR CORINNE
CEHRTTU UTRECHT	KETONIC	CEINNOV CONNIVE
CEHSSTY SCYTHES	CEIKNQU QUICKEN	CEINNTV VINCENT
CEIIJRU JUICIER	CEIKNRS SNICKER	CEINOOT COONTIE
CEIIKNR ICE RINK	CEIKOOS COOKIES	CEINOOZ NEOZOIC
CEIIKNT KINETIC	CEIKORR ROCKIER	CEINOPR PORCINE
CEIIKPR PICKIER	CEIKORS ROCKIES	CEINOPT ENTOPIC,
CEIIKQU QUICKIE	CEIKPRR PRICKER	NEPOTIC
CEIILLS SILICLE	CEIKPRS PICKERS	CEINORR CORNIER

CEINORS COINERS,
  CRONIES
CEINORV CORVINE
CEINOSS CESSION, COSINES
CEINOST NOTICES,
  SECTION
CEINOSV NOVICES
CEINOTT TONETIC
CEINOTX EXCITON
CEINOUV UNVOICE
CEINPRS PINCERS, PRINCES
CEINPST INSPECT
CEINQSU QUINCES
CEINRST CISTERN, CRETINS
CEINRUV INCURVE
CEINSST INSECTS
CEINSTY CYSTINE
CEINTTX EXTINCT
CEIOPRS COPIERS
CEIOPST POETICS
CEIOPSU PICEOUS
CEIORRS CROSIER
CEIORRU COURIER
CEIORRZ CROZIER
CEIORSW COWRIES
CEIORTV EVICTOR
CEIORTX EXCITOR,
  XEROTIC
CEIORVY VICEROY
CEIOSST COSIEST, OSSETIC
CEIOSSV VISCOSE
CEIOSTV COSTIVE
CEIOSTX COEXIST
CEIOSTY SOCIETY
CEIOSTZ COZIEST
CEIPRST TRICEPS
CEIPRSY SPICERY
CEIPRTU CUPRITE, PICTURE
CEIPRTY PYRETIC
CEIPSST CESSPIT
CEIPSTU CUP TIES
CEIQRSU CIRQUES
CEIRRRU CURRIER
CEIRRSU CRUISER,
  CURRIES
CEIRRTT CRITTER
CEIRRTU RECRUIT
CEIRRTX RECTRIX
CEIRSSU CRUISES
CEIRSTT TRISECT
CEIRSTU ICTERUS
CEIRSUV CURSIVE
CEIRTTX TECTRIX

CEJKOSY JOCKEYS
CEJLNOY JOCELYN
CEJNORU CONJURE
CEJOPRT PROJECT
CEKKLNU KNUCKLE
CEKKNOR KNOCKER
CEKKOPS KOPECKS
CEKLORS LOCKERS
CEKLOST LOCKETS
CEKLPRU PLUCKER
CEKLRSU SUCKLER
CEKLRTU TRUCKLE
CEKMORS MOCKERS
CEKMORY MOCKERY
CEKNOOV CONVOKE
CEKNORS CONKERS
CEKNRWY WRYNECK
CEKOOPR PRECOOK
CEKOORS COOKERS
CEKOORY COOKERY
CEKOPST POCKETS
CEKORRS CORKERS,
  ROCKERS
CEKORRY ROCKERY
CEKORST RESTOCK,
  ROCKETS, STOCKER
CEKOSST SOCKETS
CEKPRSU PUCKERS
CEKRRTU TRUCKER
CEKRSSU SUCKERS
CELLNOO COLONEL
CELLOSU OCELLUS
CELLOSY CLOSELY
CELLRSU SCULLER
CELLRUY CRUELLY
CELMNOO MONOCLE
CELMOPX COMPLEX
CELMPRU CRUMPLE
CELMSSU MUSCLES
CELMTUU CUMULET
CELNNOU NUCLEON
CELNOOS CONSOLE
CELNOSU COUNSEL,
  UNCLOSE
CELNOTU NOCTULE
CELNSUU NUCLEUS
CELOORS COOLERS,
  CREOSOL
CELOOST COOLEST,
  OCELOTS
CELOPRU COUPLER
CELOPSU CLOSE-UP,
  COUPLES

CELOPTU COUPLET,
  OCTUPLE
CELORSU CLOSURE
CELORSW SCOWLER
CELORTU CLOTURE,
  COULTER
CELOSST CLOSEST,
  CLOSETS
CELPRSU SCRUPLE
CELPSUY CLYPEUS
CELRRSU CURLERS
CELRSTU CLUSTER,
  CUTLERS
CELRSUW CURLEWS
CELRTTU CLUTTER
CELRTUU CULTURE
CELRTUV CULVERT
CELRTUY CRUELTY,
  CUTLERY
CELSTTU CUTLETS,
  SCUTTLE
CEMMNOT COMMENT
CEMMNOU COMMUNE
CEMMOTU COMMUTE
CEMMRSU SCUMMER
CEMNNOT CONTEMN
CEMNOOY ECONOMY
CEMNOSU CONSUME
CEMNRTU CENTRUM
CEMOOPS COMPOSE
CEMOOPT COMPOTE
CEMOOTU OUTCOME
CEMOPTU COMPUTE
CEMOSTU COSTUME
CEMPRTU CRUMPET
CEMRRUY MERCURY
CEMRSTU RECTUMS
CENNOOT CONNOTE
CENNOST CONSENT
CENNOTT CONTENT
CENNOTV CONVENT
CENOORR CORONER,
  CROONER
CENOORT CORONET
CENOPSU POUNCES
CENOPSY SYNCOPE
CENOPTY POTENCY
CENOQRU CONQUER
CENORRS CORNERS,
  SCORNER
CENORSS CENSORS
CENORST CORNETS

CENORTU CORNUTE, COUNTER, RECOUNT, TROUNCE
CENORTV CONVERT
CENORUV UNCOVER
CENOSSY COYNESS
CENOSTT CONTEST
CENOSTU CONTUSE
CENOTTX CONTEXT
CENRRTU CURRENT
CENRSTU ENCRUST
CENRSUW UNSCREW
CENRTUY CENTURY
CEOOPRS COOPERS, SCOOPER
CEOORST SCOOTER
CEOOSTY COYOTES
CEOPPRR CROPPER
CEOPPRS COPPERS
CEOPPRY COPPERY
CEOPRRS SCORPER
CEOPRRU PROCURE
CEOPRSS CORPSES, PROCESS
CEOPRTT PROTECT
CEOPRUV COVER-UP
CEOQRTU CROQUET
CEORRSS CROSSER, SCORERS
CEORRST RECTORS
CEORRSU COURSER, SCOURER
CEORRSY SORCERY
CEORRTY RECTORY
CEORSSS CROSSES
CEORSST CORSETS, ESCORTS, SECTORS
CEORSSU COURSES, SOURCES, SUCROSE
CEORSTU SCOUTER
CEORSTV COVERTS, VECTORS
CEORTUU COUTURE
CEOSSSU SCOUSES
CEPPRRU CRUPPER
CEPPRSU SCUPPER
CEPRSSU PERCUSS, SPRUCES
CEPRSSY CYPRESS
CEPSSTU SUSPECT
CERSTTU CUTTERS
CERSTUY CURTESY
CFFGINU CUFFING

CFFHINO CHIFFON
CFFIKKO KICKOFF
CFFINOS COFFINS
CFFOSTU CUTOFFS
CFFRSSU SCRUFFS
CFFRSUY SCRUFFY
CFGIKNU FUCKING
CFGINOR FORCING
CFHINSU FUCHSIN
CFHIOSW COWFISH
CFHOOOW FOOCHOW
CFIIKNY FINICKY
CFIILNT INFLICT
CFIINOT FICTION
CFILNOT CLIFTON
CFILORS FROLICS
CFILORU FLUORIC
CFIMNOR CONFIRM
CFIMOST COMFITS
CFIORSY SCORIFY
CFKNORU UNFROCK
CFKOTTU FUTTOCK
CFKPSUU FUCK-UPS
CFLMRUU FULCRUM
CFLORWY CRY WOLF
CFMNOOR CONFORM
CFMOORT COMFORT
CFOSSUU FUSCOUS
CGGGINO COGGING
CGHIIMN CHIMING
CGHIINN INCHING
CGHIINT ITCHING
CGHIKNO CHOKING, HOCKING
CGHIKNU KUCHING
CGHILNU CHILUNG
CGHILPY GLYPHIC
CGHINNO CHIGNON
CGHINOS COSHING
CGHINRU RUCHING
CGHORUY GROUCHY
CGIIJNU JUICING
CGIIKKN KICKING
CGIIKLN LICKING
CGIIKMM GIMMICK
CGIIKNN NICKING
CGIIKNP PICKING
CGIIKNR RICKING
CGIIKNS SICKING
CGIIKNT TICKING
CGIIKNW WICKING
CGIILNO COILING
CGIILNS SLICING

CGIIMNN MINCING
CGIINNO COINING
CGIINNW WINCING
CGIINOV VOICING
CGIINPR PRICING
CGIINPS SPICING
CGIKLNO LOCKING
CGIKMNO MOCKING
CGIKMNU MUCKING
CGIKNNO CONKING
CGIKNOO COOKING
CGIKNOR CORKING, ROCKING
CGIKNOS SOCKING
CGIKNPU KINGCUP
CGIKNRU RUCKING
CGIKNSU SUCKING
CGIKNTU TUCKING
CGILLNU CULLING
CGILNOO COOLING
CGILNOS CLOSING
CGILNOW COWLING
CGILNOY CLOYING
CGILNRU CURLING
CGILORW COWGIRL
CGILOTT GLOTTIC
CGILPTY GLYPTIC
CGIMNOS COMINGS
CGINNNO CONNING
CGINNNU CUNNING
CGINNOS CONSIGN
CGINOPP COPPING
CGINOPS COPINGS
CGINOPY COPYING
CGINORS SCORING
CGINORW CROWING
CGINOST COSTING, GNOSTIC
CGINOSU CONGIUS
CGINPPU CUPPING
CGINRSU CURSING
CGINRUV CURVING
CGINSSU CUSSING
CGINTTU CUTTING
CGIOTYZ ZYGOTIC
CGKLNOU GUNLOCK
CHHOSUU HSU-CHOU
CHIILST LITCHIS
CHIIMSU ISCHIUM
CHIINOT THIONIC
CHIIOPT OPHITIC
CHIIPST PICTISH
CHIIPSW IPSWICH

CHIKLLO HILLOCK	CIILNOP CIPOLIN	CILSTTU CULTIST
CHIKLTY THICKLY	CIILNOS SILICON	CIMNOOR MORONIC,
CHIKNOO CHINOOK	CIILNOT NILOTIC	OMICRON
CHIKORY HICKORY	CIILNUV UNCIVIL	CIMNORS CRIMSON,
CHIKPSU PUCKISH	CIILOOT OOLITIC	MICRONS
CHIKSTY KITSCHY	CIILOPT POLITIC	CIMOOST OSMOTIC
CHILLMU CHILLUM	CIILOST COLITIS, SOLICIT	CIMOSST SITCOMS
CHILNSY LYCHNIS	CIILPSY SPICILY	CIMOSSY MYCOSIS
CHILOOS COOLISH	CIIMMRY MIMICRY	CIMOTYZ ZYMOTIC
CHILOST COLTISH	CIIMOTT MITOTIC	CIMPRSY SCRIMPY
CHILPSY SYLPHIC	CIIMRST TRISMIC	CIMRSSU CRISSUM
CHIMRUU URUMCHI	CIIMSTV VICTIMS	CIMSSTY MYSTICS
CHIMSSS SCHISMS	CIINORS INCISOR	CINNORU UNICORN
CHIMSTY TYCHISM	CIINPRS CRISPIN	CINNOSU NUNCIOS
CHINOOR CHORION	CIINQTU QUINTIC	CINNOTU UNCTION
CHINOPS PHONICS	CIIOSUV VICIOUS	CINNSUU UNCINUS
CHINORS CORNISH	CIIPRTY PYRITIC	CINOOOR ORINOCO
CHINORT CORINTH	CIJMORW JIM CROW	CINOOPS OPSONIC
CHINORW NORWICH	CIJNNOO CONJOIN	CINORRT TRICORN
CHINOSU CUSHION	CIKLLOP PILLOCK	CINORSS INCROSS
CHINOTU IN TOUCH	CIKLLOR ROLLICK	CINORST CISTRON,
CHINQSU SQUINCH	CIKLLSY SLICKLY	CITRONS
CHINRSU URCHINS	CIKLLUY LUCKILY	CINORTU RUCTION
CHINTYZ CHINTZY	CIKLMOS MISKOLC	CINORTY TYRONIC
CHIOORS ISOCHOR	CIKLMUY MUCKILY	CINOSST CONSIST, TOCSINS
CHIOPRT TROPHIC	CIKLNRY CRINKLY	CINOSSU COUSINS
CHIORST OSTRICH	CIKLPRY PRICKLY	CINOSTU SUCTION
CHIPRRU CHIRRUP	CIKLQUY QUICKLY	CIOOPRS SCORPIO
CHIPRRY PYRRHIC	CIKLRTY TRICKLY	CIOOPRT PORTICO
CHIPSSY PHYSICS	CIKMORR RIMROCK	CIOOPSU COPIOUS
CHIRRSU CURRISH	CIKNOST STICK-ON	CIOOQTU COQUITO
CHIRSSY CHRISSY	CIKNSTU UNSTICK	CIOPRST TROPICS
CHIRSTY CHRISTY	CIKPPSU PICK-UPS	CIOPRTY CYPRIOT
CHKMMOU HUMMOCK	CIKPSTU STICK-UP	CIOPSTY COPYIST
CHLMORY CHROMYL	CIKRSTY TRICKSY	CIORSSS SCISSOR
CHLOOSS SCHOOLS	CILLNNO LINCOLN	CIORSTV VICTORS
CHLOSUY SLOUCHY	CILLOOR CRIOLLO	CIORSUU CURIOUS
CHMOSUY CHYMOUS	CILMNOP COMPLIN	CIORTVY VICTORY
CHMSTUY SMUTCHY	CILMOOS LOCOISM	CIOSSSY SYCOSIS
CHNNOOR CHRONON	CILMOPY OLYMPIC	CIOSSUV VISCOUS
CHNOOPS PONCHOS	CILMSTU CULTISM	CIPRSST SCRIPTS
CHNORSY SYNCHRO	CILNNOT CLINTON	CIPRTTY TRYPTIC
CHNOTUU UNCOUTH	CILNOOR ORCINOL	CIPSTTY STYPTIC
CHNPPUU PUNCH-UP	CILNOTU LINOCUT	CIRSSTU RUSTICS
CHOOOSW SOOCHOW	CILNPSU SCULPIN	CKKLNUY KNUCKLY
CHOORST COHORTS	CILNSTU LINCTUS	CKKNNOO KNOCK-ON
CHOORWZ CHORZOW	CILOOPT COPILOT	CKKNOPU KNOCK-UP
CIIILLT ILLICIT	CILOORU COULOIR	CKLNOTU LOCKNUT
CIIINPT INCIPIT	CILOOSS COLOSSI	CKLNOUW LUCKNOW
CIIINST SINITIC	CILOPSW COWSLIP	CKLNUUY UNLUCKY
CIIJLUY JUICILY	CILOSTU OCULIST	CKLOORW ROWLOCK
CIIKKLL KILLICK	CILPRSY CRISPLY	CKLOOTU LOCKOUT
CIILLVY CIVILLY	CILPRTU CULPRIT	CKLOPSU LOCKUPS

CKLOPTU POTLUCK	CORRSSU CURSORS	DDEEINW WIDENED
CKMOPSU MOCK-UPS	CORRSUY CURSORY	DDEEINX INDEXED
CKNOOOR ROCKOON	COSTTUU CUTOUTS	DDEEIOV VIDEOED
CKNSTUU UNSTUCK	DDDDEIL DIDDLED	DDEEIPS DEPSIDE
CKOOOTU COOKOUT	DDDEEGR DREDGED	DDEEIRR DEIRDRE,
CKOORST ROSTOCK	DDDEEIR DERIDED	DERIDER
CKORTUW CUTWORK	DDDEELM MEDDLED	DDEEIRS DESIRED,
CKOSSTU TUSSOCK	DDDEELP PEDDLED	RESIDED
CKPSTUU STUCK-UP	DDDEELS SLEDDED	DDEEIRV DERIVED
CLLMOSU MOLLUSC	DDDEELU DELUDED	DDEEISV DEVISED
CLLOOPS SCOLLOP	DDDEENU DENUDED	DDEELLU DUELLED
CLLORSS SCROLLS	DDDEFIL FIDDLED	DDEELLW DWELLED
CLMNOSU COLUMNS	DDDEFLU FUDDLED	DDEELMO MODELED
CLMOSUU OSCULUM	DDDEGRU DRUDGED	DDEELMR MEDDLER
CLMPRUY CRUMPLY	DDDEHLU HUDDLED	DDEELOY YODELED
CLMSUUU CUMULUS	DDDEHTU THUDDED	DDEELPR PEDDLER
CLNOORT CONTROL	DDDEIIV DIVIDED	DDEELRS SLEDDER
CLNOOSS CONSOLS	DDDEIKS SKIDDED	DDEELRU DELUDER
CLNOSSU CONSULS	DDDEILP PIDDLED	DDEEMOT DEMOTED
CLNOSTU CONSULT	DDDEILR RIDDLED	DDEENOT DENOTED
CLOORSU COLOURS	DDDEIMU MUDDIED	DDEENOW ENDOWED
CLORSSY CROSSLY	DDDEIOV VEDDOID	DDEENPU UPENDED
CLORTUY COURTLY	DDDELMU MUDDLED	DDEENRS DRESDEN
CLOSSTU LOCUSTS	DDDELOO DOODLED	DDEENRU DENUDER,
CMMNOOS COMMONS	DDDELOP PLODDED	ENDURED
CMNOOPY COMPONY	DDDELOS DODDLES	DDEEOPS DEPOSED
CMOOPRT COMPORT	DDDELOT TODDLED	DDEEORR ORDERED
CMOOPST COMPOST	DDDELPU PUDDLED	DDEEOTV DEVOTED
CMOORSU CORMOUS	DDDEOPR PRODDED	DDEEPTU DEPUTED
CMORSTU SCROTUM	DDDEORY DODDERY	DDEERSS DRESSED
CMORTUW CUTWORM	DDDESTU STUDDED	DDEERST REDDEST
CMOSSTU CUSTOMS	DDEEELN NEEDLED	DDEERTU DETRUDE
CMPRSUY SCRUMPY	DDEEELT DELETED	DDEERYY DRY-EYED
CNNORTU NOCTURN	DDEEEMN EMENDED	DDEFILR FIDDLER
CNOOPPR POPCORN	DDEEEPS SPEEDED	DDEFILS FIDDLES
CNOOPSU COUPONS,	DDEEERR RED DEER	DDEFIRT DRIFTED
SOUPÇON	DDEEFII DEIFIED, EDIFIED	DDEFLNO FONDLED
CNOORST CONSORT	DDEEFIL DEFILED, FIELDED	DDEFLOO FLOODED
CNOORTT CONTORT	DDEEFIN DEFINED	DDEFLSU FUDDLES
CNOORTU CONTOUR,	DDEEFIR FREDDIE	DDEFNOR FRONDED
CROUTON	DDEEFSU DEFUSED	DDEFNOU FOUNDED
CNOOSTY TYCOONS	DDEEGIN DEIGNED	DDEGGRU DRUGGED,
CNOOSVY CONVOYS	DDEEGLP PLEDGED	GRUDGED
CNOOTTY COTTONY	DDEEGLS SLEDGED	DDEGIIR GIDDIER
CNORSSU UNCROSS	DDEEGLU DELUGED	DDEGILR GIRDLED,
CNORTUY COUNTRY	DDEEGRR DREDGER	GRIDDLE
COOPRRT PROCTOR	DDEEHRS SHEDDER	DDEGIMO DEMIGOD
COOPRTU OUTCROP	DDEEIIT TIE-DIED	DDEGINW WEDDING
COOPSTU COP-OUTS,	DDEEILV DEVILED	DDEGINY EDDYING
OCTOPUS	DDEEILW WIELDED	DDEGIOR DODGIER
COOSTTY OTOCYST	DDEEILY YIELDED	DDEGMOS DODGEMS
COPRRTU CORRUPT	DDEEIMP IMPEDED	DDEGMSU SMUDGED
COPRSUU CUPROUS	DDEEIMS MISDEED	DDEGNOS GODSEND

DDEGNOU DUDGEON
DDEGNWY GWYNEDD
DDEGORS DODGERS
DDEGOSS GODDESS
DDEGRRU DRUDGER
DDEGRSU DRUDGES
DDEGRTU TRUDGED
DDEHIRS REDDISH
DDEHIRY HYDRIDE
DDEHLRU HUDDLER,
 HURDLED
DDEHLSU HUDDLES
DDEHNOU HOUNDED
DDEHNRU HUNDRED
DDEHRSU SHUDDER
DDEIIKS KIDDIES
DDEIINV DIVINED
DDEIIOX DIOXIDE
DDEIIRT DIRTIED
DDEIIRV DIVIDER
DDEIISV DIVIDES
DDEIKLN KINDLED
DDEIKNR KINDRED
DDEIKRS KIDDERS
DDEILLR DRILLED
DDEILMR MILDRED
DDEILNW DWINDLE
DDEILOS DILDOES
DDEILOT DELTOID
DDEILRR RIDDLER
DDEILRS RIDDLES
DDEILRT TIDDLER
DDEILTU DILUTED, LUDDITE
DDEILTW TWIDDLE
DDEILTY LYDDITE
DDEIMNS MIDDENS
DDEIMOR DERMOID
DDEIMOS DESMOID
DDEIMRU MUDDIER
DDEINOT DENTOID
DDEINST DISTEND
DDEIOOR DO-OR-DIE
DDEIORV OVERDID
DDEIORW DOWDIER
DDEIOST TODDIES
DDEIOWW WIDOWED
DDEIPPR DRIPPED
DDEIRRU RUDDIER
DDEISSU DISUSED
DDEISTU STUDIED
DDEKMOU DUKEDOM
DDELMOU MOULDED
DDELMRU MUDDLER

DDELMSU MUDDLES
DDELNOS NODDLES
DDELOOR DOODLER,
 DROOLED
DDELOOS DOODLES
DDELOPR PLODDER
DDELORT TODDLER
DDELPRU PUDDLER
DDELPSU PUDDLES
DDEMMRU DRUMMED
DDEMNOS DESMOND
DDEMNOT ODDMENT
DDENOPS DESPOND
DDENOPU POUNDED
DDENORT TRODDEN
DDENORU REDOUND,
 ROUNDED, UNDERDO
DDENORW DROWNED
DDENOSS ODDNESS
DDENOSU SOUNDED
DDENOUW WOUNDED
DDEOOPR DROOPED
DDEOORW REDWOOD
DDEOOWY DYEWOOD
DDEOPPR DROPPED
DDEOPRR PRODDER
DDEOPRW DEWDROP
DDEORSW DROWSED
DDERRSU RUDDERS
DDGGINO DODGING
DDGHOOO GODHOOD
DDGIIKN KIDDING
DDGIILY GIDDILY
DDGIINR RIDDING
DDGIMNU MUDDING
DDGINNO NODDING
DDGINOP PODDING
DDGINOS SODDING
DDGINPU PUDDING
DDGOOOW DOGWOOD
DDHIISY YIDDISH
DDHIORY HYDROID
DDHORSY DRY-SHOD
DDIILOP DIPLOID
DDILMUY MUDDILY
DDILNRS DIRNDLS
DDILOWY DOWDILY
DDILRUY RUDDILY
DDILTWY TWIDDLY
DDIMOOS DODOISM
DDIPRRY DRIP-DRY
DEEEFRS FEEDERS
DEEEFRV FEVERED

DEEEGMR EMERGED
DEEEGNR GREENED,
 RENEGED
DEEEGRS DEGREES
DEEEGRT DETERGE,
 GREETED
DEEEHLW WHEEDLE,
 WHEELED
DEEEHRS HEREDES,
 SHEERED
DEEEHST SEETHED
DEEEHWZ WHEEZED
DEEEILT LEE TIDE
DEEEINR NEEDIER
DEEEIPY PIE-EYED
DEEEIRR REEDIER
DEEEIRS DESIREE, SEEDIER
DEEEIRW WEEDIER
DEEEISV DEVISEE
DEEEKLN KNEELED
DEEEKLS SLEEKED
DEEEKNW WEEKEND
DEEELLV LEVELED
DEEELNS NEEDLES
DEEELPT DEPLETE
DEEELRV LEVERED,
 REVELED
DEEELST SLEETED,
 STEELED
DEEELTX TELEXED
DEEEMNS DEMESNE
DEEEMRS EMERSED
DEEEMRT METERED
DEEENPR PREENED
DEEENQU QUEENED
DEEENRS SNEERED
DEEENRT ENTERED
DEEENRW RENEWED
DEEENSZ SNEEZED
DEEENTT DÉTENTE
DEEEORR ROE DEER
DEEEOTV DEVOTEE
DEEEPRS SPEEDER
DEEEPST DEEPEST,
 STEEPED
DEEEQRU QUEERED
DEEERRV REVERED
DEEERST STEERED
DEEERSV DESERVE,
 SEVERED
DEEERTX EXERTED
DEEETTV VEDETTE
DEEETTW TWEETED

DEEFFOR OFFERED
DEEFGIN FEEDING,
   FEIGNED
DEEFHLS FLESHED
DEEFHLU HEEDFUL
DEEFIIR DEIFIER, EDIFIER
DEEFILR DEFILER, FIELDER
DEEFILS DEFILES
DEEFILT FILETED
DEEFINR DEFINER, REFINED
DEEFINT FEINTED
DEEFIRR FERRIED
DEEFKLR KREFELD
DEEFLLU FUELLED
DEEFLLW WELL-FED
DEEFLNU NEEDFUL
DEEFLOT FEEDLOT
DEEFMOR FREEDOM
DEEFNRS FENDERS
DEEFPRY DEEP FRY
DEEFRSU REFUSED
DEEFRTT FRETTED
DEEFRTU REFUTED
DEEGHIN HEEDING,
   NEIGHED
DEEGHIW WEIGHED
DEEGHOW HOGWEED
DEEGILS LEG SIDE
DEEGIMN DEEMING
DEEGINN NEEDING
DEEGINR ENERGID,
   REEDING, REIGNED
DEEGINS SEEDING
DEEGINW WEEDING
DEEGIOR GEORDIE
DEEGIPW PIGWEED
DEEGIRV DIVERGE,
   GRIEVED
DEEGIST EDGIEST
DEEGLNS LEGENDS
DEEGLOY GOLDEYE
DEEGLPR PLEDGER
DEEGLPS PLEDGES
DEEGLPT PLEDGET
DEEGLRS LEDGERS
DEEGLSS SLEDGES
DEEGLSU DELUGES
DEEGNRS GENDERS
DEEGOSY GEODESY
DEEGSSU GUESSED
DEEGSTU GUESTED
DEEHITV THIEVED
DEEHLLS SHELLED

DEEHLSV SHELVED
DEEHLSW WELSHED
DEEHMUX EXHUMED
DEEHNOY HONEYED
DEEHNRT DRENTHE
DEEHORV HOVERED
DEEHRSU USHERED
DEEHTTW WHETTED
DEEIINS SINE DIE
DEEIIRW WEIRDIE
DEEIIST DEITIES
DEEIJLL JELLIED
DEEIJMM JEMMIED
DEEIKLN LIKENED
DEEIKMW MIDWEEK
DEEILMO MELODIE
DEEILNR RELINED
DEEILNS LINSEED
DEEILNU EILUNED
DEEILNV LIVENED
DEEILNY DYELINE
DEEILPR REPLIED
DEEILRV DELIVER,
   EVERILD, RELIVED,
   REVILED
DEEILRW WIELDER
DEEILRY YIELDER
DEEILSS DIESELS
DEEILSY EYELIDS, SEEDILY
DEEILTU DILUTEE
DEEILWY WEEDILY
DEEIMNO DOMINEE
DEEIMPR IMPEDER, PER
   DIEM
DEEIMPT EMPTIED
DEEIMRT DEMERIT,
   DIMETER, MERITED
DEEIMTT EMITTED
DEEINNS DENISEN
DEEINNT DENTINE
DEEINNZ DENIZEN
DEEINPR DNIEPER,
   REPINED, RIPENED
DEEINRS DENIERS,
   NEREIDS
DEEINRW WIDENER
DEEINRX INDEXER
DEEINST DESTINE
DEEINSV ENDIVES
DEEINSW WISENED
DEEINSX INDEXES
DEEINTT DINETTE
DEEINTU DETINUE

DEEINTV EVIDENT
DEEINWZ WIZENED
DEEIOPS EPISODE
DEEIOPT EPIDOTE
DEEIPPT PEPTIDE
DEEIPRS DEPISER,
   PERSEID, PRESIDE
DEEIPRV DEPRIVE
DEEIPRX EXPIRED
DEEIPSS DESPISE
DEEIPST DESPITE
DEEIQRU QUERIED
DEEIRRS DESIRER,
   RESIDER, SERRIED
DEEIRRT RETIRED
DEEIRRV DERIVER
DEEIRRW REWIRED,
   WEIRDER
DEEIRSS DESIRES
DEEIRSU RESIDUE
DEEIRSV DEVISER,
   DIVERSE, REVISED
DEEIRTU ERUDITE
DEEIRTV RIVETED
DEEIRVV REVIVED
DEEISSU DISEUSE
DEEISTW DEWIEST
DEEISTX EXISTED
DEEJNOY ENJOYED
DEEKKRT TREKKED
DEEKNNY KENNEDY
DEEKORV REVOKED
DEEKPUY KEYED UP
DEELLMS SMELLED
DEELLNW WENDELL
DEELLPS SPELLED
DEELLQU QUELLED
DEELLRU DUELLER
DEELLRW DWELLER
DEELLRY ELDERLY
DEELLSW SWELLED
DEELMOR REMODEL
DEELMPU DEPLUME
DEELMST SMELTED
DEELMSY MEDLEYS
DEELNRS LENDERS,
   SLENDER
DEELNSS ENDLESS
DEELNST NESTLED
DEELNSY DENSELY
DEELNTT NETTLED
DEELOPP PEOPLED
DEELOPR DEPLORE

DEELOPV DEVELOP
DEELOPX EXPLODE
DEELORU URODELE
DEELORW LOWERED
DEELOSU DELOUSE
DEELOTW TOWELED
DEELOVV DEVOLVE,
    EVOLVED
DEELPRU PRELUDE
DEELRSW WELDERS
DEELSTT SETTLED
DEELTUX EXULTED
DEELVXY VEXEDLY
DEEMMST STEMMED
DEEMNOY MONEYED
DEEMNRS MENDERS
DEEMORV REMOVED
DEEMORX EXODERM
DEEMOSY MOSEYED
DEEMPTT TEMPTED
DEEMRRU DEMURER
DEEMRSU RESUMED
DEENNPT PENDENT
DEENOPS SPONDEE
DEENOPT PENTODE
DEENORS ENDORSE
DEENORT ERODENT
DEENORW ENDOWER
DEENPPR PERPEND
DEENPRS SPENDER
DEENPRT PRETEND
DEENRSS REDNESS,
    SENDERS
DEENRST TENDERS
DEENRSU END USER,
    ENSURED
DEENRTU DENTURE
DEENSST DENSEST
DEENSTW WEST END
DEEOPPY POP-EYED
DEEOPRS DEPOSER,
    REPOSED
DEEOPRW POWERED
DEEOPSX EXPOSED
DEEORRR ORDERER,
    REORDER
DEEORRS REREDOS
DEEORST OERSTED
DEEORTT DORETTE,
    TETRODE
DEEORTW TOWERED
DEEORUV OVERDUE
DEEORXX XEROXED

DEEPPST STEPPED
DEEPRSS DEPRESS,
    PRESSED
DEEPRSU PERUSED
DEEPRTU ERUPTED,
    REPUTED
DEEQSTU QUESTED
DEERRSS DRESSER,
    REDRESS
DEERRSV REDVERS
DEERRUV VERDURE
DEERSSS DRESSES
DEERSST DESERTS,
    DESSERT
DEERSTW STREWED,
    WRESTED
DEERSVW SWERVED
DEERTTU UTTERED
DEERTUX EXTRUDE
DEESSTU SUDETES
DEFFFLU FLUFFED
DEFFILR RIFFLED
DEFFINS SNIFFED
DEFFIOS OFFSIDE
DEFFISU DIFFUSE
DEFFLMU MUFFLED
DEFFLRU RUFFLED
DEFFNOS SEND-OFF
DEFFNSU SNUFFED
DEFFRSU DUFFERS
DEFFSTU STUFFED
DEFGGLO FLOGGED
DEFGINN FENDING
DEFGINR FRINGED
DEFGINU FEUDING
DEFGINY DEFYING
DEFGIOR FIREDOG
DEFGIRS FRIDGES
DEFGIRU FIGURED
DEFGIST FIDGETS
DEFGITY FIDGETY
DEFGORY GODFREY
DEFHIRS REDFISH
DEFHIST SHIFTED
DEFHLSU FLUSHED
DEFHORT FROTHED
DEFIILN INFIDEL, INFIELD
DEFIIMS FIDEISM
DEFIIMW MIDWIFE
DEFIINU UNIFIED
DEFIIST FIDEIST
DEFIKRS FRISKED
DEFILLR FRILLED

DEFILPP FLIPPED
DEFILRT FLIRTED, TRIFLED
DEFILRU DIREFUL
DEFILRW WILFRED
DEFILST STIFLED
DEFILTT FLITTED
DEFILXY FIXEDLY
DEFIMOR DEIFORM
DEFINRS FRIENDS
DEFINRW WINFRED
DEFINSU INFUSED
DEFIOOS FOODIES
DEFIOST FOISTED
DEFIPRY PERFIDY
DEFIRRT DRIFTER
DEFIRTU FRUITED
DEFIRZZ FRIZZED
DEFKLNU FLUNKED
DEFLLOU DOLEFUL
DEFLNOR FONDLER
DEFLNOT TENFOLD
DEFLOOR FLOODER,
    FLOORED
DEFLOPP FLOPPED
DEFLORS FOLDERS
DEFLORU FLOURED
DEFLOSS FLOSSED
DEFLOTU FLOUTED
DEFMORS SERFDOM
DEFNORT FRONTED
DEFNORU FOUNDER
DEFNORW FROWNED
DEFNOST FONDEST
DEFNOSU FONDUES
DEFNRSU REFUNDS
DEFOOPR PROOFED
DEFORST DEFROST,
    FROSTED
DEGGGIL GIGGLED
DEGGGLO GOGGLED
DEGGHIN HEDGING
DEGGIJL JIGGLED
DEGGILN GELDING,
    NIGGLED
DEGGILW WIGGLED
DEGGINS EDGINGS
DEGGINW WEDGING
DEGGIOS DOGGIES
DEGGIRS DIGGERS
DEGGISW SWIGGED
DEGGITW TWIGGED
DEGGJLO JOGGLED
DEGGJLU JUGGLED

166

DEGGLOS DOGLEGS, SLOGGED
DEGGLPU PLUGGED
DEGGLRU GURGLED
DEGGLSU SLUGGED
DEGGNOO DOGGONE
DEGGNOS SNOGGED
DEGGNOU GUDGEON
DEGGORY DOGGERY
DEGGRRU GRUDGER
DEGGRSU GRUDGES
DEGGRTU DRUGGET
DEGHILT DELIGHT, LIGHTED
DEGHINR HERDING
DEGHINW WHINGED
DEGHIRT RIGHTED
DEGHIST SIGHTED
DEGHOST GHOSTED
DEGHOSU SOUGHED
DEGIILN ELIDING
DEGIINR DINGIER
DEGIINT DIETING, EDITING, IGNITED
DEGIISU EGIDIUS
DEGIJLN JINGLED
DEGIKLO GODLIKE
DEGILLR GRILLED
DEGILMN MINGLED
DEGILNN LENDING
DEGILNO GLENOID, ON-GLIDE
DEGILNS DINGLES, SINGLED
DEGILNT GLINTED, TINGLED
DEGILNU DUELING, ELUDING, INDULGE
DEGILNV DELVING
DEGILNW WELDING
DEGILOR GLORIED, GODLIER
DEGILRR GIRDLER
DEGILRS GIRDLES, GLIDERS
DEGILRU GUILDER
DEGILUV DIVULGE
DEGIMNN MENDING
DEGIMST MIDGETS
DEGINNN DENNING
DEGINNP PENDING
DEGINNR GRINNED, RENDING
DEGINNS ENDINGS, SENDING

DEGINNT DENTING, TENDING
DEGINNU ENDUING
DEGINNV VENDING
DEGINNW WENDING
DEGINNY DENYING
DEGINOR ERODING, GIRONDE, IGNORED, NEGROID, REDOING
DEGINOS DINGOES
DEGINOW WIDGEON
DEGINRR GRINDER
DEGINRW REDWING
DEGINSS DESIGNS
DEGINUX EXUDING
DEGIOOS GOODIES
DEGIOPR PODGIER
DEGIPPR GRIPPED
DEGIPRU PUDGIER
DEGIRRS GIRDERS
DEGIRSS DIGRESS
DEGIRTT GRITTED
DEGISST DIGESTS
DEGLNOU LOUNGED
DEGLNPU PLUNGED
DEGLNSU GULDENS
DEGLOPR PLEDGOR
DEGLOPS SPLODGE
DEGLORS LODGERS
DEGLORW GROWLED
DEGLOSS GLOSSED, GODLESS
DEGLTTU GLUTTED
DEGLUZZ GUZZLED
DEGMOOR GROOMED
DEGMSSU SMUDGES
DEGNNOU DUNGEON
DEGNOPS SPONGED
DEGNORU UNDERGO
DEGNORW WRONGED
DEGNRSU GERUNDS
DEGNRTU GRUNTED, TRUDGEN
DEGOORV GROOVED
DEGOPRU GROUPED
DEGORSS GROSSED
DEGORSU GROUSED
DEGRRTU TRUDGER
DEGRSTU TRUDGES
DEHHSSU SHUSHED
DEHIIRS DISHIER
DEHIKRS SHIRKED
DEHIKSW WHISKED

DEHILRW WHIRLED
DEHILSS SHIELDS
DEHIMOP HEMIPOD
DEHIMOR HEIRDOM
DEHIMOT ETHMOID
DEHINNS SHINNED
DEHINNT THINNED
DEHINOR HORDEIN
DEHINPT IN-DEPTH
DEHINRX HENDRIX
DEHINSW WENDISH
DEHIORT THEROID
DEHIOST HOISTED
DEHIOSU HIDEOUS
DEHIPPS SHIPPED
DEHIPPW WHIPPED
DEHIRRU HURRIED
DEHIRRW WHIRRED
DEHIRSV DERVISH
DEHIRTV THRIVED
DEHIRTW WRITHED
DEHISSW SWEDISH, SWISHED
DEHISTT SHITTED
DEHIWZZ WHIZZED
DEHJNOO JOHN DOE
DEHLMNO DENHOLM
DEHLNOS SHELDON
DEHLOOT TOEHOLD
DEHLORS HOLDERS
DEHLORW WHORLED
DEHLOSS SLOSHED
DEHLRRU HURDLER
DEHLRSU HURDLES
DEHLRTU HURTLED
DEHLSTU HUSTLED
DEHMOST METHODS
DEHMOTU MOUTHED
DEHMPTU THUMPED
DEHNNSU SHUNNED
DEHNOOW HOEDOWN
DEHNORU HOUNDER
DEHNOSY HOYDENS
DEHNOTZ DOZENTH
DEHNRTU THUNDER
DEHNSTU SHUNTED
DEHOOPW WHOOPED
DEHOOST SOOTHED
DEHOOWY HEYWOOD
DEHOPPS SHOPPED
DEHOPPW WHOPPED
DEHOQTU QUOTHED
DEHORST SHORTED

DEHOSTU SHOUTED
DEHPPUY HYPED UP
DEIIKLS DISLIKE
DEIIKNR DINKIER
DEIILMP IMPLIED
DEIILMT DELIMIT, LIMITED
DEIILOS DOILIES, IDOLISE
DEIILOZ IDOLIZE
DEIINOS IONISED, SIDONIE
DEIINOT EDITION
DEIINOZ IONIZED
DEIINRS INSIDER
DEIINRT NITRIDE
DEIINRU URIDINE
DEIINRV DIVINER, DRIVE-IN
DEIINRW WINDIER
DEIINSS INSIDES
DEIINTV INVITED
DEIIORS IODISER, ISIDORE
DEIIORT DIORITE
DEIIORZ IODIZER
DEIIOSX OXIDISE
DEIIOXZ OXIDIZE
DEIIPRT RIPTIDE
DEIIRRT DIRTIER
DEIIRZZ DIZZIER
DEIISTT DITTIES, TIDIEST
DEIISTV VISITED
DEIJLLO JOLLIED
DEIJNOR JOINDER
DEIJNOT JOINTED
DEIJNRU INJURED
DEIJORY JOYRIDE
DEIKLLS SKILLED
DEIKLNR KINDLER
DEIKLNT TINKLED
DEIKLNW WINKLED
DEIKLOR RODLIKE
DEIKMMS SKIMMED
DEIKMPS SKIMPED
DEIKMRS SMIRKED
DEIKNNS SKINNED
DEIKNOS DOESKIN,
  SEKONDI
DEIKNOV INVOKED
DEIKNRR DRINKER
DEIKNRS REDSKIN
DEIKNST KINDEST
DEIKNSY KIDNEYS
DEIKNTT KNITTED
DEIKPPS SKIPPED
DEIKRST SKIRTED
DEIKRSU DUSKIER

DEIKSVY SKYDIVE
DEILLOS DOLLIES
DEILLPS SPILLED
DEILLRR DRILLER
DEILLRT TRILLED
DEILLST STILLED
DEILLSU SULLIED
DEILLSW SWILLED
DEILMMS SLIMMED
DEILMOP IMPLODE
DEILMOR MOLDIER
DEILMOT OLDTIME
DEILMOY MYELOID
DEILMPP PIMPLED
DEILMPS DIMPLES
DEILMST MILDEST
DEILMWY MILDEWY
DEILNNS LINDENS
DEILNOO EIDOLON
DEILNOW LIE-DOWN
DEILNPS SPINDLE
DEILNRT TENDRIL
DEILNSW SWINDLE
DEILNSY LINDSEY, SNIDELY
DEILNTU DILUENT
DEILOPR LEPORID
DEILOPS DESPOIL, SPOILED
DEILOPT PILOTED
DEILOPU EUPLOID
DEILORS SOLDIER
DEILOTW LOW TIDE
DEILPPR RIPPLED
DEILPPS SLIPPED
DEILPRT TRIPLED
DEILPTY TEPIDLY
DEILQTU QUILTED
DEILRRV L-DRIVER
DEILRSW SWIRLED
DEILRTU DILUTER
DEILRTW TWIRLED
DEILRTY TIREDLY
DEILRVY DEVILRY
DEILRWY WEIRDLY
DEILRZZ DRIZZLE
DEILSTT SLITTED, STILTED
DEILSTW WILDEST
DEILSZZ SIZZLED
DEIMMRS DIMMERS
DEIMMRT MIDTERM,
  TRIMMED
DEIMMRU IMMURED
DEIMMST DIMMEST

DEIMMSU DUMMIES,
  MEDIUMS
DEIMNPS MENDIPS
DEIMNRS MINDERS
DEIMNSS DIMNESS
DEIMNTU MINUTED
DEIMOOR MOIDORE,
  MOODIER
DEIMOPS IMPOSED
DEIMOST MODISTE
DEIMOTT OMITTED
DEIMOTV VOMITED
DEIMPRU DUMPIER,
  UMPIRED
DEIMPSU MUD PIES
DEIMPTU IMPUTED
DEIMPUX MIXED UP
DEIMRUU UREDIUM
DEIMSSU MISUSED
DEIMSTW MIDWEST
DEIMSTY STYMIED
DEINNOT INTONED
DEINNRS DINNERS
DEINNST INDENTS
DEINNTU DUNNITE
DEINNTW TWINNED
DEINOPT POINTED
DEINORS INDORSE,
  ROSINED
DEINORU DOURINE
DEINORW DOWNIER
DEINPPS SNIPPED
DEINPRT PRINTED
DEINPST STIPEND
DEINRSU INSURED
DEINRTT TRIDENT
DEINRTU INTRUDE,
  TURDINE, UNTRIED
DEINRTX DEXTRIN
DEINSST DISSENT, SNIDEST
DEINSTT DENTIST, STINTED
DEINSTY DENSITY, DESTINY
DEIOORW WOODIER
DEIOOST OSTEOID
DEIOPRS PERIODS
DEIOPRT DIOPTRE,
  PERIDOT
DEIOPRV PROVIDE
DEIOPSS DISPOSE
DEIOPST DEPOSIT,
  DOPIEST, POSITED, TOPSIDE
DEIOPTT TIPTOED
DEIOPTV PIVOTED

DEIORRW ROWDIER,
WORDIER, WORRIED
DEIORSS DOSSIER
DEIORST EDITORS,
STEROID, STORIED
DEIORSV DEVISOR,
DEVOIRS
DEIORSW DOWRIES,
WEIRDOS
DEIORTT DETROIT, DOTTIER
DEIORTU OUTRIDE
DEIORWW WIDOWER
DEIOSTU OUTSIDE,
TEDIOUS
DEIOSTZ DOZIEST
DEIOSUV DEVIOUS
DEIPPQU QUIPPED
DEIPPRS DIPPERS
DEIPPRT TRIPPED
DEIPRSS SPIDERS
DEIPRST STRIPED
DEIPRSY SPIDERY
DEIPSTU DISPUTE
DEIQTTU QUITTED
DEIQUZZ QUIZZED
DEIRRST STIRRED
DEIRRSV DRIVERS
DEIRSST STRIDES
DEIRSTU DUSTIER
DEISSTU STUDIES
DEISTTW TWISTED
DEITTTW TWITTED
DEJLOST JOSTLED
DEJOSTU JOUSTED
DEKKLSU SKULKED
DEKLNOP PLONKED
DEKNNRU DRUNKEN
DEKNOST DONETSK
DEKNOSY DONKEYS
DEKNOTT KNOTTED
DEKNRRU DRUNKER
DEKOOPS SPOOKED
DEKOPST DESKTOP
DEKORST STROKED
DELLOOP LEOPOLD
DELLOPR REDPOLL
DELLORR DROLLER
DELLORT TROLLED
DELLSTU DULLEST
DELMMSU SLUMMED
DELMNOS DOLMENS
DELMORS SMOLDER

DELMORU MOULDER,
REMOULD
DELMOSU MODULES
DELMOTT MOTTLED
DELMOTU MOULTED
DELMOUV VOLUMED
DELMPPU PLUMPED
DELMPRU RUMPLED
DELMPSU SLUMPED
DELMUZZ MUZZLED
DELNOOS NOODLES
DELNORU ROUNDEL
DELNORY REYNOLD
DELNOSU NODULES
DELNOTW LETDOWN
DELNPRU PLUNDER
DELNRTU TRUNDLE
DELNUZZ NUZZLED
DELOOPS POODLES
DELOORS DOLORES
DELOOTT TOOTLED
DELOPPP PLOPPED
DELOPPS SLOPPED
DELOPPT TOPPLED
DELOPRT DROPLET
DELOPRW PROWLED
DELOPTT PLOTTED
DELORRY ORDERLY
DELORST OLDSTER
DELORSU LOURDES
DELOSTT SLOTTED
DELOSTU LOUDEST,
TOUSLED
DELOSYY DOYLEYS
DELOSZZ SOZZLED
DELPRSU SLURPED
DELPUZZ PUZZLED
DELRRSU SLURRED
DELRSTU RUSTLED,
STRUDEL
DELSSTU TUSSLED
DEMMRRU DRUMMER
DEMNOOR DOORMEN
DEMNORS MODERNS
DEMNORT MORDENT
DEMNORU MOURNED
DEMNOST ENDMOST
DEMNOTU DEMOUNT,
MOUNTED
DEMNOUV UNMOVED
DEMNSTU DUSTMEN
DEMOOPP POPEDOM
DEMOORT MOTORED

DEMOPST STOMPED
DEMORRS DORMERS
DEMORST STORMED
DEMOSTY MODESTY
DEMPRSU DUMPERS
DEMPRTU TRUMPED
DEMPSTU STUMPED
DEMRRSU MURDERS
DENNOST TENDONS
DENNSTU DUNNEST,
STUNNED
DENOOPS SNOOPED,
SPOONED
DENOOSW SWOONED
DENOOSZ SNOOZED
DENOOTU DUOTONE,
OUTDONE
DENOPPR PROPEND
DENOPRS RESPOND
DENOPRT PORTEND
DENOPRU POUNDER
DENOPUX EXPOUND
DENORRU RONDURE,
ROUNDER
DENORRW DROWNER
DENORST RODENTS,
SNORTED
DENORSU RESOUND,
SOUNDER
DENORSV VENDORS
DENORSW DOWNERS,
WONDERS
DENORUW WOUNDER
DENPRSU SPURNED
DENPRTU PRUDENT
DENPSSU SEND-UPS,
SUSPEND
DENRSSU UNDRESS
DENRSSY DRYNESS
DENSTTU STUDENT,
STUNTED
DENTUVY DUVETYN
DEOOPPS OPPOSED
DEOOPRT TORPEDO,
TROOPED
DEOOPST STOOPED
DEOOPSW SWOOPED
DEOORRT REDROOT
DEOORST ROOSTED
DEOORTU OUTRODE
DEOPPPR PROPPED
DEOPPRR DROPPER
DEOPPST STOPPED

DEOPPSW SWOPPED
DEOPRRU PROUDER
DEOPRST SPORTED
DEOPRSW POWDERS
DEOPRWY POWDERY
DEOPSST DESPOTS
DEOPSTT SPOTTED
DEOPSTU SPOUTED
DEORRSV DROVERS
DEORSSS DOSSERS
DEORSSW DOWSERS
DEORSTU DETOURS
DEORSTW WORSTED
DEORSTY DESTROY
DEORTTT TROTTED
DEORTTU TUTORED
DEOSSYY ODYSSEY
DEOSTTW SWOTTED
DEOSTUX TUXEDOS
DEPRRSU SPURRED
DEPRRUY PRUDERY
DEPRSTU SPURTED
DEPRSUU PURSUED,
   USURPED
DERSSTU DUSTERS,
   TRUSSED
DERSTTU TRUSTED
DERSTUU SUTURED
DFFGINO DOFFING
DFFIIMR MIDRIFF
DFGGINU FUDGING
DFGHIOS DOGFISH
DFGIINN FINDING
DFGIINY DIGNIFY
DFGILNO FOLDING
DFGINNU FUNDING
DFGINOR FORDING
DFGINOU FUNGOID
DFGLOOY OLD FOGY
DFHILSU DISHFUL
DFHIMSU MUDFISH
DFIILRW WILFRID
DFIINRW WINFRID
DFILMNU MINDFUL
DFILNOO IN FLOOD
DFILNOP PINFOLD
DFILOSX SIXFOLD
DFILTUU DUTIFUL
DFLOOTU FOLDOUT
DFLOOTW TWOFOLD
DFNORUY FOUNDRY
DFNORWY WYNFORD
DGGGIIN DIGGING

DGGGINO DOGGING
DGGIILN GILDING, GLIDING
DGGIINR GIRDING, RIDGING
DGGIINU GUIDING
DGGIJNU JUDGING
DGGILNO LODGING
DGGINNU NUDGING
DGGIORY DIGGORY
DGGNOSU GUNDOGS
DGHIINS DISHING, HIDINGS,
   SHINDIG
DGHIKNO HODGKIN
DGHILNO HOLDING
DGHINTU HINDGUT
DGHIOOS GOODISH
DGHOOST HOT DOGS
DGHORTU DROUGHT
DGHOTUY DOUGHTY
DGIILNS SIDLING, SLIDING
DGIILNW WILDING
DGIILNY DINGILY
DGIILRY RIGIDLY
DGIIMMN DIMMING
DGIIMNN MINDING
DGIIMNS SMIDGIN
DGIIMOS SIGMOID
DGIINNN DINNING
DGIINNW WINDING
DGIINOV VOIDING
DGIINPP DIPPING
DGIINPR PRIDING
DGIINPS PIDGINS
DGIINPU PINGUID
DGIINRV DRIVING
DGIINSS SIDINGS
DGIINST TIDINGS
DGIINTY DIGNITY, TIDYING
DGIKMNO KINGDOM
DGIKNNU DUNKING
DGILLNO DOLLING
DGILLNU DULLING
DGILMNO MOLDING
DGILNOR LORDING
DGILNOW GOLDWIN
DGILOPY PODGILY
DGILPUY PUDGILY
DGIMNOO DOOMING
DGIMNPU DUMPING
DGIMNSU SIGMUND
DGINNNO DONNING
DGINNNU DUNNING
DGINNOR DRONING
DGINNOU UNDOING

DGINNOW DOWNING
DGINNUY UNDYING
DGINORW WORDING
DGINOSS DOSSING
DGINOST TIN GODS
DGINOSU DOUSING
DGINOSW DOWSING
DGINOTT DOTTING
DGINSTU DUSTING
DGIOORR RODRIGO
DGIOPRY PRODIGY
DGIQSUY SQUIDGY
DGISSTU DISGUST
DGLNOUY UNGODLY
DGLNOWY GOLDWYN
DGLOOOW LOGWOOD
DGLOPSY SPLODGY
DGMOPRU GUMDROP
DGNORSU GROUNDS
DGNOSSU SUN GODS
DGOOPST TOP DOGS
DGOORTT DOGTROT
DGOSTUU DUGOUTS
DHIILOT LITHOID
DHIIMNO HOMINID
DHIINOU HOUDINI
DHIINRU HIRUDIN
DHIIOPX XIPHOID
DHIIORZ RHIZOID
DHIIOST HISTOID
DHIKRSU KURDISH
DHILLOS DOLLISH
DHILMUY HUMIDLY
DHILNOP DOLPHIN
DHILOST DOLTISH
DHILPSY SYLPHID
DHIMOPR DIMORPH
DHIMORU HUMIDOR,
   RHODIUM
DHINNOS DONNISH
DHINORS DRONISH
DHIOPTY TYPHOID
DHIORTY THYROID
DHIPRSU PRUDISH
DHIPRSY SYRPHID
DHJOPRU JODHPUR
DHKORSY DROSHKY
DHLMOOU HOODLUM
DHLOOPR RODOLPH
DHLOPRU RUDOLPH
DHLOPSU HOLDUPS
DHMMRUU HUMDRUM
DHOOOOS HOODOOS

DHOORST HOT RODS
DHOORTY DOROTHY
DHOPRSU PUSHROD
DHORSSU SHROUDS
DIIIMRU IRIDIUM
DIIINPS INSIPID
DIIJNOS DISJOIN
DIIKKNS KIDSKIN
DIIKNRU KIRUNDI
DIILLVY LIVIDLY
DIILMTY TIMIDLY
DIILNWY WINDILY
DIILQSU LIQUIDS
DIILRSU SILURID
DIILRTY DIRTILY
DIILVVY VIVIDLY
DIILYZZ DIZZILY
DIIMNOR MIDIRON
DIIMSSS DISMISS
DIIMSTW DIMWITS
DIIOPRS SPIROID
DIIORSV DIVISOR
DIJOSTU JUDOIST
DIKKNRU DUNKIRK
DIKORSW SKID ROW
DILLOSY SOLIDLY
DILLPSY PSYLLID
DILLRUY LURIDLY
DILMNRU DRUMLIN
DILMOOY MOODILY
DILNOPT DIPLONT
DILNOXY INDOXYL
DILNPSY SPINDLY
DILOPVV PLOVDIV
DILORWY ROWDILY,
    WORDILY
DILOSSU DULOSIS, SOLIDUS
DILOSTY STYLOID
DILRYZZ DRIZZLY
DIMMOST MIDMOST
DIMNOPU IMPOUND
DIMNORV MORDVIN
DIMOPSU PODIUMS
DIMRTUU TRIDUUM
DINOORS INDOORS,
    SORDINO
DINORSW WINDSOR
DINORWW WINDROW
DINOSTW SIT-DOWN
DINOSWW WINDOWS
DINPRSY SPIN-DRY
DINPSTU PUNDITS
DINSSTU NUDISTS

DIOORTT RIDOTTO
DIOPRST DISPORT, TRIPODS
DIOPRTY TRIPODY
DIORRST STRIDOR
DIORSTT DISTORT
DIOSSTU STUDIOS
DIPRSTU DISRUPT
DKLOOPS PODOLSK
DLLOOPS DOLLOPS
DLLORWY WORLDLY
DLMOSUU MODULUS
DLNOOWW LOW-DOWN
DLNORUY ROUNDLY
DLNOSUY SOUNDLY
DLNOTUW WOULDN'T
DLOOPPY POLYPOD
DLOOPWY PLYWOOD
DLOORRU OUR LORD
DLOOSTU OUTSOLD
DLOPRUY PROUDLY
DNNORUW RUN-DOWN
DNNOSUU UNSOUND
DNNOSUW SUNDOWN
DNNOUUW UNWOUND
DNOORTU OROTUND
DNOOTUW NUTWOOD
DNOPRUU ROUNDUP
DNOPTUW PUT-DOWN
DNOPUUW WOUND-UP
DOOORSU ODOROUS
DOOORTU OUTDOOR
DOOORWW WOODROW
DOOPRSY PROSODY
DOOPRTU DROPOUT
DPSSTUU DUSTUPS
EEEEFRR REFEREE
EEEEGGS GEE-GEES
EEEEGTX EXEGETE
EEEELNV EVELEEN
EEEEPST TEEPEES
EEEFGRU REFUGEE
EEEFLRS FEELERS
EEEFLRT FLEETER
EEEFMNR FREEMEN
EEEFORS FORESEE
EEEFRRS REEFERS
EEEFRRZ FREEZER
EEEGILS ELEGIES, ELEGISE
EEEGILZ ELEGIZE
EEEGINP EPIGENE
EEEGINU EUGENIE
EEEGIPR PERIGEE
EEEGLNT GENTEEL

EEEGNNO NEOGENE
EEEGNOS GENOESE
EEEGNPR EPERGNE
EEEGNRR GREENER,
    RENEGER
EEEGNRV REVENGE
EEEGRRT GREETER
EEEGRSZ GEEZERS
EEEGRUX EXERGUE
EEEHILW WHEELIE
EEEHLLN HELLENE
EEEHLNR HEERLEN
EEEHLRW WHEELER
EEEHRRS SHEERER
EEEHRST THÉRÈSE
EEEHRWZ WHEEZER
EEEHSTT ESTHETE
EEEHSWZ WHEEZES
EEEIKLL EEL-LIKE
EEEIKLZ EZEKIEL
EEEILMN EMELINE
EEEILNV EVELINE
EEEILRR LEERIER
EEEILRV RELIEVE
EEEILVY EVIL EYE
EEEIMNS ENEMIES
EEEIMNT EMETINE
EEEIMPR EPIMERE
EEEIMRT EREMITE
EEEINQU QUEENIE
EEEINRS ESERINE
EEEINRW WEENIER
EEEINST STEENIE
EEEIPST EPEEIST
EEEIRRV REVERIE
EEEISTW SWEETIE
EEEKLNX KLEENEX
EEEKLRS SLEEKER
EEEKMST MEEKEST
EEEKNPT KEEPNET
EEEKNST KEENEST
EEEKPRS KEEPERS
EEEKRSS SEEKERS
EEELLST ESTELLE
EEELMNT ELEMENT
EEELNNO NOELEEN
EEELNSV ELEVENS
EEELPRS SLEEPER
EEELPRT REPLETE
EEELPST STEEPLE
EEELRTV LEVERET
EEELSSS LESSEES
EEELSSV SLEEVES

EEELSSY EYELESS
EEELSTX TELEXES
EEELSTY EYELETS
EEEMNSS NEMESES
EEEMRTX EXTREME
EEENNPT PENTENE
EEENNTT ENTENTE
EEENPRR PREENER
EEENPRT TERPENE
EEENPST STEEPEN
EEENPSX EXPENSE
EEENRRS SNEERER
EEENRRT ENTERER,
RE-ENTER, TERRENE
EEENRRW RENEWER
EEENRST ENTRÉES
EEENRSV VENEERS
EEENRSZ SNEEZER
EEENRUV REVENUE,
UNREEVE
EEENSSZ SNEEZES
EEENSTW SWEETEN
EEEORSV OVERSEE
EEEORSY EYESORE
EEEPPRS PEEPERS
EEEPRSS PEERESS
EEEPRST STEEPER
EEEPRSW SWEEPER
EEEQRRU QUEERER
EEEQSUZ SQUEEZE
EEERRRV REVERER
EEERRST STEERER
EEERRSV RESERVE,
REVERSE
EEERSTV EVEREST
EEERSTW SWEETER
EEERTTW TWEETER
EEESSTT SETTEES
EEFFFNO ENFEOFF
EEFFINT FIFTEEN
EEFFJRY JEFFERY, JEFFREY
EEFFORR OFFERER
EEFFOST TOFFEES
EEFGILN FEELING, FLEEING
EEFGINR FEIGNER,
FREEING, REEFING
EEFGLLU GLEEFUL
EEFGLOR FORELEG
EEFGRSU REFUGES
EEFHIRS HEIFERS
EEFHIRT HEFTIER
EEFHISY FISH-EYE
EEFHITZ HEIFETZ

EEFHLRS FLESHER,
HERSELF
EEFHLSS FLESHES
EEFHNRS FRESHEN
EEFHORT THEREOF
EEFHORW WHEREOF
EEFHRRS FRESHER,
REFRESH
EEFHRST FRESHET
EEFIIRR FIERIER, REIFIER
EEFIJNR JENIFER
EEFILLX FLEXILE
EEFILNO OLEFINE
EEFILNS FELINES
EEFILOS FIESOLE
EEFILRS RELIEFS
EEFILRT FERTILE
EEFILST FELSITE, LEFTIES
EEFIMNR FIREMEN
EEFINRR REFINER
EEFINSS FINESSE
EEFIRRS FERRIES
EEFIRRT FERRITE, FIRTREE
EEFIRSZ FRIEZES
EEFISTV FESTIVE
EEFLLRS FELLERS
EEFLLRU FUELLER
EEFLNOS ONESELF
EEFLNRS FLENSER,
FRESNEL
EEFLRRU FERRULE
EEFLRUX FLEXURE
EEFMNOR FOREMEN
EEFMNRT FERMENT
EEFMOTT MOFETTE
EEFMPRU PERFUME
EEFNRRY FERNERY
EEFNRTV FERVENT
EEFNSSW FEWNESS
EEFNSSY FEYNESS
EEFORRV FOREVER
EEFOTTU FOUETTE
EEFPRSU PERFUSE
EEFRRST FERRETS
EEFRRSU REFUSER
EEFRRTU REFUTER
EEFRRTY FERRETY
EEFRSTT FETTERS
EEFSSTU FETUSES
EEGGILR LEGGIER
EEGGIOR GEORGIE
EEGGLNO GEELONG
EEGGLPS PEG LEGS

EEGGNOR ENGORGE
EEGGNST NEST EGG
EEGHILN HEELING
EEGHINY HYGIENE
EEGHIRW WEIGHER
EEGHMNU HEGUMEN
EEGHNRY GREYHEN
EEGIJNR JEERING
EEGIKLN KEELING
EEGIKNN KEENING,
KNEEING
EEGIKNP KEEPING,
PEEKING
EEGIKNR REEKING
EEGIKNS SEEKING
EEGILLS GISELLE
EEGILNP PEELING
EEGILNR LEERING,
REELING
EEGILNT GENTILE
EEGILRV VELIGER
EEGILST ELEGIST
EEGIMNR REGIMEN
EEGIMNS SEEMING
EEGIMNT MEETING,
TEEMING
EEGIMRS ÉMIGRÉS,
REGIMES
EEGINNS ENGINES
EEGINNU GENUINE,
INGENUE
EEGINNV EVENING
EEGINOP EPIGONE
EEGINPP PEEPING
EEGINPR PEERING
EEGINPS SEEPING
EEGINPV PEEVING
EEGINPW WEEPING
EEGINRS GREISEN
EEGINRT INTEGER
EEGINRV VEERING
EEGINSS GENESIS
EEGINTT GINETTE
EEGINTX EXIGENT
EEGIPRS SERGIPE
EEGIRRV GRIEVER
EEGISTV VESTIGE
EEGISTW GET WISE
EEGKNRU GERENUK
EEGLLSS LEGLESS
EEGLMMU GEMMULE
EEGLMSU LEGUMES
EEGLNOU EUGENOL

EEGLNOZ LOZENGE
EEGMNST SEGMENT
EEGMRRS MERGERS
EEGMRTU GUM TREE
EEGNORS NEGROES
EEGNPUX EXPUNGE
EEGNRSS NEGRESS
EEGNRST REGENTS
EEGOPRT PROTÉGÉ
EEGRRSS REGRESS
EEGRRST REGRETS
EEGRRSV VERGERS
EEGRRUY GRUYÈRE
EEGRSSU GUESSER
EEGRSSY GEYSERS
EEGRSTU GESTURE
EEGRSTY GREYEST
EEGSSSU GUESSES
EEHHRTW WHETHER
EEHIKLO HOELIKE
EEHILMN HEMLINE
EEHILOS HELOISE
EEHINOR HEROINE
EEHINOS HESIONE
EEHINRR ERRHINE
EEHINRT NEITHER,
   THEREIN
EEHINRW WHEREIN
EEHIPRT PRITHEE
EEHIPSV PEEVISH
EEHIPTT EPITHET
EEHIRSS HEIRESS
EEHIRST HEISTER
EEHISST HESSITE
EEHISTV THIEVES
EEHKLOY KEYHOLE
EEHKLSS SHEKELS
EEHKNNT KENNETH
EEHLLMP PHELLEM
EEHLLRY HELLERY
EEHLLSY SHELLEY
EEHLMST HELMETS
EEHLNUW HEULWEN
EEHLOSY HOLY SEE
EEHLPRT TELPHER
EEHLPST ELSPETH
EEHLRST SHELTER
EEHLRSV SHELVER
EEHLRSW WELSHER
EEHLSSV SHELVES
EEHMNOP PHONEME
EEHMNRY MYNHEER
EEHMORT THEOREM

EEHMRUX EXHUMER
EEHNNRY HENNERY
EEHNOPT POTHEEN
EEHNORT THEREON
EEHNORW NOWHERE,
   WHEREON
EEHNPST STEPHEN
EEHNPSW NEPHEWS
EEHNSTU ENTHUSE
EEHNSTV SEVENTH
EEHOOPW WHOOPEE
EEHOPRT THE ROPE
EEHOPRU EUPHROE
EEHOPST HEPTOSE
EEHORRV HOVERER
EEHORST HERE'S TO
EEHORSU REHOUSE
EEHORTT THERETO
EEHORTW WHERETO
EEHORVW HOWEVER,
   WHOEVER
EEHOSTY EYESHOT
EEHPRSS SPHERES
EEHRRST THREE R'S
EEHRSTT TETHERS
EEHRTTW WHETTER
EEHSTTW THE WEST
EEHSTUY SHUT-EYE
EEIIMST ITEMISE
EEIIMTZ ITEMIZE
EEIIPST PIETIES
EEIIRRV RIVIERE
EEIJKRR JERKIER
EEIJLLS JELLIES
EEIJMMS JEMMIES
EEIJNNS JENNIES
EEIJSTT JETTIES
EEIKMNP PIKEMEN
EEIKNPY PINKEYE
EEIKNRT KERNITE
EEIKPRR PERKIER
EEIKPRS PESKIER
EEIKTTT TEKTITE
EEILLNO LEOLINE
EEILLNS NELLIES
EEILLNV NEVILLE
EEILLOR LORELEI
EEILLPS ELLIPSE
EEILLRV EVILLER
EEILLST TELLIES
EEILLSV SEVILLE
EEILLSW WELLIES
EEILMNN LINEMEN

EEILMRV VERMEIL
EEILNNO LEONINE,
   NOELINE
EEILNNT LENIENT
EEILNNV ENLIVEN
EEILNPS PENSILE
EEILNRV LIVENER
EEILNST SETLINE, TENSILE
EEILNTT ENTITLE, LINETTE
EEILNTV VEINLET
EEILOPT PETIOLE
EEILORV OVERLIE
EEILOTZ ZEOLITE
EEILPRR REPLIER
EEILPRS REPLIES, SPIELER
EEILPRT PERLITE, REPTILE
EEILPRU PUERILE
EEILPST EPISTLE
EEILRRV REVILER
EEILRST LEISTER, STERILE
EEILRSU LEISURE
EEILRSV SERVILE
EEILSSS SESSILE
EEILSST TELESIS
EEILSSU ELEUSIS
EEILSTT LISETTE
EEILSTV EVILEST
EEILSTX SEXTILE
EEILSUV ELUSIVE
EEILSVW WEEVILS
EEILTTX TEXTILE
EEILVWY WEEVILY
EEIMMNS IMMENSE
EEIMMRS IMMERSE
EEIMNNO NOMINEE
EEIMNNT EMINENT
EEIMNOT ONETIME
EEIMNRS ERMINES
EEIMNSS MEISSEN,
   NEMESIS, SIEMENS
EEIMOPS EPISOME
EEIMOPT EPITOME
EEIMOTV EMOTIVE
EEIMPRR PREMIER
EEIMPRS EMPIRES,
   EPIMERS, PREMISE,
   SPIREME
EEIMPRT EMPTIER
EEIMPST EMPTIES, SEPTIME
EEIMQRU REQUIEM
EEIMRRR MERRIER
EEIMRRT TRIREME
EEIMRSS MESSIER

EEIMRST MÉTIERS
EEIMRTT EMITTER, TERMITE
EEINNPS PENNIES
EEINNRV INNERVE, NERVINE
EEINNST INTENSE
EEINNTT NINETTE
EEINNTW ENTWINE
EEINOPR PIONEER
EEINOPS PEONIES
EEINORT ORIENTE
EEINPRR RIPENER
EEINPRS EREPSIN
EEINPSS PENISES
EEINPSV PENSIVE, VESPINE
EEINQRU ENQUIRE
EEINQTU QUIETEN
EEINRRT RENTIER, TERRINE
EEINRRV NERVIER, VERNIER
EEINRST ENTRIES
EEINRSV INVERSE
EEINRTU RETINUE, REUNITE, UTERINE
EEINSTV TENSIVE
EEINSTX SIXTEEN
EEINSTY SYENITE
EEIORSS SOIREES
EEIORSV EROSIVE
EEIPPST PEPTISE
EEIPPTT PIPETTE
EEIPPTZ PEPTIZE
EEIPQRU PERIQUE
EEIPRRS REPRISE, RESPIRE
EEIPRRX EXPIRER
EEIPRST RESPITE
EEIPRTT PETTIER
EEIPRVW PREVIEW
EEIPRZZ PREZZIE
EEIPSTW PEEWITS
EEIQRRU REQUIRE
EEIQRSU ESQUIRE, QUERIES
EEIQRTU QUIETER, REQUITE
EEIRRRT RETIRER, TERRIER
EEIRRSV REVISER
EEIRRTV RIVETER
EEIRRTW REWRITE
EEIRRVV REVIVER
EEIRSSU REISSUE
EEIRSTT TESTIER, TRIESTE

EEIRSTV RESTIVE
EEIRSUZ SEIZURE
EEIRSVW REVIEWS, VIEWERS
EEIRTVV VETIVER
EEISSTX SEXIEST
EEJNORY ENJOYER
EEJNOSS JONESES
EEJOSTT JOSETTE
EEJPRRU PERJURE
EEJRSST JESTERS
EEJRSSY JERSEYS
EEKKRRT TREKKER
EEKLLSY SLEEKLY
EEKLLUU UKULELE
EEKLNNS KENNELS
EEKLNOS KEELSON
EEKLNRS KERNELS
EEKLRST KESTREL
EEKLSTT KETTLES
EEKNOTY KEYNOTE
EEKNSTU NETSUKE
EEKORRV REVOKER
EEKRSSW SKEWERS
EELLMOS MOSELLE
EELLNOV NOVELLE
EELLORV VELLORE
EELLOSV O LEVELS
EELLPRS SPELLER
EELLPST PELLETS
EELLQRU QUELLER
EELLRSS SELLERS
EELLRST TELLERS
EELLSTW WELL-SET
EELMORW EELWORM
EELMPST PELMETS, TEMPLES
EELMRST SMELTER
EELNOPR PERONEL
EELNOPV ENVELOP
EELNOSV SLOVENE
EELNOTT NOTELET
EELNOTU TOLUENE
EELNPSS SPLEENS
EELNQUY QUEENLY
EELNRST NESTLER
EELNSTT NETTLES
EELNSTY TENSELY
EELNTTU LUNETTE
EELNTTY LYNETTE
EELOPPS PEOPLES
EELOPRS LEPROSE
EELOPRX EXPLORE

EELOPTU EELPOUT
EELORSV RESOLVE
EELORTT LORETTE
EELORVV EVOLVER, REVOLVE
EELOSTT TELEOST
EELOTUV EVOLUTE
EELPPRX PERPLEX
EELPRST PETRELS, SPELTER
EELPRSU REPULSE
EELPRTZ PRETZEL
EELPRVY REPLEVY
EELPSST PESTLES
EELPSTY STEEPLY
EELQRUY QUEERLY
EELQSSU SEQUELS
EELRRVY REVELRY
EELRSTT LETTERS, SETTLER, STERLET, TRESTLE
EELRSTW SWELTER, WRESTLE
EELRSTY RESTYLE, TERSELY
EELRSTZ SELTZER
EELSSSU USELESS
EELSSSV VESSELS
EELSSSX SEXLESS
EELSSTT SETTLES
EELSTVW TWELVES
EELSTWY SWEETLY
EELTVVY VELVETY
EEMMNOT MEMENTO
EEMMRST STEMMER
EEMNNOV ENVENOM
EEMNOOS SOMEONE
EEMNOOY MOONEYE
EEMNPTU UMPTEEN
EEMNSYZ ENZYMES
EEMOPRR EMPEROR
EEMOPRW EMPOWER
EEMORRS REMORSE
EEMORRT REMOTER
EEMORRV REMOVER
EEMORST METEORS
EEMORSV REMOVES
EEMPPRT PREEMPT
EEMPRSS EMPRESS
EEMPRST TEMPERS
EEMPRSU PRESUME, SUPREME
EEMPRTT TEMPTER

EEMPRTU PERMUTE
EEMPSTT TEMPEST
EEMRSSU RÉSUMÉS
EENNORT ENTERON,
  TENONER
EENNOSS ESSONNE,
  ONENESS
EENNOTY NEOTENY
EENNPTU NEPTUNE
EENNRST TENNERS
EENNRUV UNNERVE
EENNSSW NEWNESS
EENOPPR PROPENE
EENOPPT PEPTONE
EENOPRS OPENERS
EENOPST ONE-STEP,
  PENTOSE
EENOPTY NEOTYPE
EENORTU EN ROUTE
EENPRST PRESENT,
  SERPENT
EENPRTV PREVENT
EENQSTU SEQUENT
EENRRST RENTERS,
  STERNER
EENRRSU ENSURER
EENRRTY RE-ENTRY
EENRRUV NERVURE
EENRSTU TUREENS
EENRSTW WESTERN
EENRSTY STYRENE
EENRTUV VENTURE
EENSSTT TENSEST
EENSSTW WETNESS
EENSSUX NEXUSES
EENSTTX EXTENTS
EENSTVY SEVENTY
EEOPRRS REPOSER
EEOPRRV REPROVE
EEOPRSX EXPOSER
EEOPSST POETESS
EEOPSSU ESPOUSE
EEOPSSX EXPOSÉS
EEOPSTU TOUPEES
EEOPSTY EYESPOT
EEORRST RESTORE
EEORRTV EVERTOR
EEORRTW REWROTE
EEORSST STEREOS
EEORSTT ROSETTE
EEORSTV OVERSET
EEORSUV OVERUSE
EEORSVW OVERSEW

EEORSXX XEROXES
EEPPPRS PEPPERS
EEPPPRY PEPPERY
EEPPRST STEPPER
EEPPRSX PERSPEX
EEPPSST STEPPES
EEPPSUW UPSWEEP
EEPRRSS REPRESS
EEPRRSU PERUSER
EEPRRTV PERVERT
EEPRSSS PRESSES
EEPRSSV VESPERS
EEPRSSX EXPRESS
EEPRSTT PRETEST
EEPRSTX EXPERTS
EEPRTTX PRETEXT
EEPSSTT SEPTETS
EEPSTTY TYPESET
EEQRRUY EQUERRY
EEQRSTU QUESTER,
  REQUEST
EERRSSV SERVERS
EERRSTW STREWER,
  WRESTER
EERRSVW SWERVER
EERRSVY SERVERY
EERRTTU UTTERER
EERSSST TRESSES
EERSSTT SETTERS,
  STREETS, TESTERS
EERSSVW SWERVES
EERSTTU TRUSTEE
EERSTUV VESTURE
EERTTUX TEXTURE
EESSTTX SEXTETS
EESTTTW WETTEST
EESTTUZ SUZETTE
EFFGRRU GRUFFER
EFFHILW WHIFFLE
EFFHIRS SHERIFF
EFFHIRU HUFFIER
EFFHIRW WHIFFER
EFFHLSU SHUFFLE
EFFIIST FIFTIES
EFFIKLS SKIFFLE
EFFILNS SNIFFLE
EFFILRR RIFFLER
EFFILRY FIREFLY
EFFINRS SNIFFER
EFFINST STIFFEN
EFFIORT FORFEIT
EFFIORX FOXFIRE
EFFIPRU PUFFIER

EFFIRST STIFFER
EFFLLOW WELL-OFF
EFFLMRU MUFFLER
EFFLNSU SNUFFLE
EFFLOSU SOUFFLÉ
EFFLRRU RUFFLER
EFFLRSU RUFFLES
EFFLRTU FRETFUL,
  TRUFFLE
EFFNOOS ONE-OFFS
EFFNRSU SNUFFER
EFFOPRR PROFFER
EFFORST EFFORTS
EFFRSTU STUFFER
EFFSSUU SUFFUSE
EFGGIOR FOGGIER
EFGGIRU FUGGIER
EFGGLOR FLOGGER
EFGHIRT FIGHTER, FREIGHT
EFGILLN FELLING
EFGILMN FLEMING
EFGILNR FLINGER
EFGILNT FELTING
EFGILNU FUELING
EFGILNX FLEXING
EFGIMNT FIGMENT
EFGINNP PFENNIG
EFGINOR FOREIGN
EFGINRS FINGERS, FRINGES
EFGINRU GUNFIRE
EFGIOOR GOOFIER
EFGIORV FORGIVE
EFGIRRU FIGURER
EFGIRSU FIGURES
EFGLNTU FULGENT
EFGLORS GOLFERS
EFGMNOR FROGMEN
EFGNOOR FORGONE
EFGOORR FORGOER
EFGORRS FORGERS
EFGORRY FORGERY
EFGORTU FOREGUT
EFHIIRS FISHIER
EFHIJSW JEWFISH
EFHILMS FLEMISH,
  HIMSELF
EFHILSS SELFISH
EFHILTY HEFTILY
EFHINST FISHNET
EFHIORR FOR HIRE
EFHIRST SHIFTER
EFHIRSY FISHERY
EFHLLPU HELPFUL

EFHLLSY FLESHLY
EFHLOOX FOXHOLE
EFHLOPU HOPEFUL
EFHLRSU FLUSHER
EFHLRSY FRESHLY
EFHLSSU FLUSHES
EFHLSTY THYSELF
EFHLTTW TWELFTH
EFHRRTU FURTHER
EFHRTTU THE TURF
EFIILLS FILLIES
EFIILMR FILMIER
EFIILMS MISFILE
EFIILSS FISSILE
EFIIMRR RIM-FIRE
EFIIMRS MISFIRE
EFIINRT NIFTIER
EFIINRU UNIFIER
EFIIRZZ FIZZIER
EFIJLLY JELLIFY
EFIJLOT JETFOIL
EFIKLNU LIKE FUN
EFIKLOX FOXLIKE
EFIKNRU FUNKIER
EFIKRRS FRISKER
EFIKRST FRISKET
EFILLOS FOLLIES
EFILLOW LOW LIFE
EFILLRS REFILLS
EFILLST FILLETS
EFILMST FILMSET, LEFTISM
EFILNOX FLEXION
EFILOOS FOLIOSE
EFILOPR PROFILE, PRO-LIFE
EFILORR FLORRIE
EFILORT LOFTIER, TREFOIL
EFILOSS FLOSSIE
EFILPPR FLIPPER
EFILQUY LIQUEFY
EFILRRT FLIRTER, TRIFLER
EFILRRY RIFLERY
EFILRST FILTERS, STIFLER,
   TRIFLES
EFILRTT FLITTER
EFILRVV FLIVVER
EFILRZZ FRIZZLE
EFILSTT LEFTIST
EFIMMRU FERMIUM
EFIMNOR FERMION
EFIMNTT FITMENT
EFIMRST FIRMEST
EFIMRTY METRIFY
EFINNOR INFERNO

EFINNRU FUNNIER
EFINRST SNIFTER
EFINRSU INFUSER
EFINRUY REUNIFY
EFINSST FITNESS
EFIOOPR POOFIER
EFIOOST FOOTSIE
EFIORRT ROTIFER
EFIORRU FOURIER
EFIORST FORTIES
EFIOSST SOFTIES
EFIOSTX FOXIEST
EFIPRTY PETRIFY
EFIRRRU FURRIER
EFIRRSU FRISEUR
EFIRRTT FRITTER
EFIRRTU FRUITER
EFIRRTY TERRIFY
EFIRRZZ FRIZZER
EFIRSST SIFTERS
EFIRSSU FISSURE, FUSSIER
EFIRSTT FITTERS, TITFERS
EFIRSTU FUSTIER, SURFEIT
EFIRSTW SWIFTER
EFIRSVY VERSIFY
EFIRTUV FURTIVE
EFIRTUX FIXTURE
EFIRUZZ FUZZIER
EFISTTT FITTEST
EFISTTY TESTIFY
EFKLMNO MENFOLK
EFKLNUY FLUNKEY
EFLLOSW FELLOWS
EFLLSTU FULLEST
EFLMOSU FULSOME
EFLMSUU MUSEFUL
EFLNNSU FUNNELS
EFLNORU FLEURON
EFLNORY FELONRY
EFLNSSU FULNESS
EFLNTUU TUNEFUL
EFLOORY FOOLERY
EFLOORZ FOOZLER
EFLORSU OURSELF
EFLORSW FLOWERS
EFLORTU FLOUTER
EFLORTW FELWORT
EFLORVY FLYOVER,
   OVERFLY
EFLORWY FLOWERY
EFLOSTU FOULEST
EFLRSTU FLUSTER,
   RESTFUL

EFLRTTU FLUTTER
EFLSTUZ ZESTFUL
EFMNOOT FOOTMEN
EFMNORT FREMONT
EFMOPRR PERFORM
EFMORRS REFORMS
EFNOOST FESTOON
EFNORRU FORERUN
EFNORRW FROWNER
EFNORTU FORTUNE
EFNORTW FORWENT
EFNRSSU FURNESS
EFOOPRR REPROOF
EFOOPRS SPOOFER
EFOOPRT FORETOP
EFOORSW WOOFERS
EFOPPRY FOPPERY
EFOPRSS PROFESS
EFOPRSU PROFUSE
EFORRSU FERROUS
EFORRTY TORREFY
EFORRUV FERVOUR
EFORSST FORESTS
EFOSSTT SOFTEST
EFPRTUY PUTREFY
EFPSTUY STUPEFY
EFRRSSU SURFERS
EFRSTUU FUTURES
EGGGILN LEGGING
EGGGILR GIGGLER
EGGGILS GIGGLES
EGGGINP PEGGING
EGGGLOS GOGGLES
EGGIIPR PIGGIER
EGGIIPS PIGGIES
EGGIJLS JIGGLES
EGGIJRS JIGGERS
EGGILLN GELLING
EGGILNR NIGGLER
EGGILNS SNIGGLE
EGGILNU GLUEING
EGGILRW WIGGLER,
   WRIGGLE
EGGILSW WIGGLES
EGGIMMN GEMMING
EGGIMNR MERGING
EGGIMOS MOGGIES
EGGIMRU MUGGIER
EGGINNS GINSENG
EGGINRS NIGGERS,
   SNIGGER
EGGINRV VERGING

EGGINRY GINGERY, GREYING	EGHISTW WEIGHTS	EGILLNY YELLING
EGGINTT GETTING	EGHITWY WEIGHTY	EGILLRR GRILLER
EGGIORS SOGGIER	EGHLLOU LUGHOLE	EGILLRS GRILLES
EGGIPRY PIGGERY	EGHLNOR LEGHORN	EGILLSU GULLIES
EGGIRRT TRIGGER	EGHLNST LENGTHS	EGILMMN LEMMING
EGGIRSW SWIGGER	EGHLNTY LENGTHY	EGILMMR GLIMMER
EGGJLOR JOGGLER	EGHMORS GERSHOM	EGILMNR GREMLIN
EGGJLOS JOGGLES	EGHMOSU GUMSHOE	EGILMNT MELTING
EGGJLRU JUGGLER	EGHNOOS HOGNOSE	EGILMNU LEGUMIN
EGGLLOR EGG ROLL	EGHNORU ROUGHEN	EGILMOS LIMOGES
EGGLMSU SMUGGLE	EGHNOTU TOUGHEN	EGILMOV MOGILEV
EGGLNSU SNUGGLE	EGHNRTU GUNTHER	EGILMPS GLIMPSE
EGGLOOY GEOLOGY	EGHNSUY HUYGENS	EGILMST GIMLETS
EGGLORS LOGGERS, SLOGGER	EGHNTWY GWYNETH	EGILNOP ELOPING
EGGLOST TOGGLES	EGHOPRS GOPHERS	EGILNOS LEGIONS, LINGOES
EGGLRSU LUGGERS	EGHORRU ROUGHER	EGILNOT LENTIGO
EGGMRSU MUGGERS, SMUGGER	EGHORTU TOUGHER	EGILNPS SPIGNEL
EGGNSTU NUGGETS	EGHORTZ HERTZOG	EGILNPT PELTING
EGGNTUY NUGGETY	EGHOSTT GHETTOS	EGILNPY YELPING
EGGORRY GREGORY	EGHRSSU GUSHERS	EGILNRS SLINGER
EGGSSTU SUGGEST	EGHRTUY THEURGY	EGILNRT RINGLET, TINGLER
EGHHHIO HEIGH-HO	EGIILLS GILLIES	EGILNRY RELYING
EGHHIST EIGHTHS, HEIGHTS, HIGHEST	EGIILNT LIGNITE	EGILNSS SINGLES
EGHIILL GHILLIE	EGIILNV VEILING	EGILNST GLISTEN, SINGLET
EGHIINT NIGHTIE	EGIILNX EXILING	EGILNSW SLEWING, SWINGLE
EGHIINV INVEIGH	EGIILPZ LEIPZIG	EGILNTT LETTING
EGHIKLO HOGLIKE	EGIIMNP IMPINGE	EGILNTW WINGLET
EGHIKNR GHERKIN	EGIIMNR MINGIER	EGILNVY LEVYING
EGHILNP HELPING	EGIIMPS PIGMIES	EGILORR GROLIER
EGHILNS ENGLISH, SHINGLE	EGIIMRR GRIMIER	EGILORS GLORIES
EGHILNT LIGHTEN	EGIINNR REINING	EGILOST LOGIEST
EGHILRT LIGHTER	EGIINNV VEINING	EGILPST PIGLETS
EGHILSS SLEIGHS	EGIINRT IGNITER	EGILRST GRISTLE
EGHILST SLEIGHT	EGIINSV SIEVING	EGILRSU LURGIES
EGHIMMN HEMMING	EGIINSZ SEIZING	EGILRTT GLITTER
EGHIMNS MESHING	EGIINTX EXITING	EGILRUV VIRGULE
EGHINNU UNHINGE	EGIINVW VIEWING	EGILRZZ GRIZZEL, GRIZZLE
EGHINOS SHOEING	EGIIPRW PERIWIG	EGILSTU UGLIEST
EGHINRR HERRING	EGIIPSS GIPSIES	EGIMMRR GRIMMER
EGHINST HENGIST	EGIJKNR JERKING	EGIMMRU GUMMIER
EGHINSW SHEWING	EGIJLLN JELLING	EGIMMTU GUMMITE
EGHINTT TIGHTEN	EGIJLNR JINGLER	EGIMNOW MEOWING
EGHIORS OGREISH	EGIJLNS JINGLES	EGIMNPR PERMING
EGHIOTV EIGHTVO	EGIJNST JESTING	EGIMNPT PIGMENT, TEMPING
EGHIRRT RIGHTER	EGIJNTT JETTING	EGIMNRT TERMING
EGHIRST SIGHTER	EGIKNNN KENNING	EGIMNSS MESSING
EGHIRSY GREYISH	EGIKNOV EVOKING	EGIMOST EGOTISM
EGHIRTT TIGHTER	EGIKNPR PERKING	EGIMPSY PYGMIES
	EGIKNRY KEY RING	EGINNNP PENNING
	EGIKNSW SKEWING	EGINNOP OPENING
	EGILLNS SELLING	
	EGILLNT TELLING	
	EGILLNW WELLING	

EGINNPU PENGUIN
EGINNRR GRINNER
EGINNRT RENTING,
   RINGENT
EGINNRV NERVING
EGINNSS ENSIGNS,
   SENSING
EGINNST NESTING,
   TENSING
EGINNSU ENSUING
EGINNTT NETTING
EGINNTV VENTING
EGINNVY ENVYING
EGINOPR PERIGON,
   PONGIER
EGINOPS PIGEONS
EGINORR IGNORER
EGINORS REGIONS,
   SIGNORE
EGINORT GENITOR,
   NEGRITO
EGINORZ ZEROING
EGINOSU IGNEOUS
EGINOSY ISOGENY
EGINOTV VETOING
EGINOUV IN VOGUE
EGINPPP PEPPING
EGINPRS SPRINGE
EGINPRY PREYING
EGINPSW SPEWING
EGINPSY ESPYING
EGINPTT PETTING
EGINPYY EPIGYNY
EGINQUU QUEUING
EGINRRS RINGERS
EGINRRW WRINGER
EGINRSS INGRESS
EGINRST RESTING,
   STINGER
EGINRSU REUSING
EGINRSV SERVING
EGINRSW SWINGER,
   WINGERS
EGINRSY SYRINGE
EGINRTT GITTERN
EGINRVV REVVING
EGINSST SIGNETS
EGINSTT SETTING, TESTING
EGINSTV VESTING
EGINSTW STEWING,
   TWINGES, WESTING
EGINTTV VETTING
EGINTTW WETTING

EGIOOST GOOIEST
EGIOPRS SERPIGO
EGIOPRT EGO TRIP
EGIOPRU GROUPIE
EGIORST GORIEST
EGIORTV VERTIGO
EGIOSST EGOISTS
EGIOSTT EGOTIST
EGIPPRR GRIPPER
EGIPRRS GRIPERS
EGIPRUU GUIPURE
EGIPSSY GYPSIES
EGIRSST TIGRESS
EGIRSSU SERGIUS
EGIRSTU GUSTIER,
   GUTSIER
EGIRTTU TURGITE
EGISUWY WISE GUY
EGJLNSU JUNGLES
EGKLORW LEGWORK
EGLLLPU LEG-PULL
EGLLOUY YULE LOG
EGLLSTU GULLETS
EGLMMRU GLUMMER
EGLMNOR MONGREL
EGLMOOR LEGROOM
EGLNNSU GUNNELS
EGLNORU LOUNGER
EGLNOST LONGEST
EGLNOSU LOUNGES
EGLNPRU PLUNGER
EGLOORS REGOSOL
EGLOPSS GOSPELS
EGLORRW GROWLER
EGLORSS GLOSSER
EGLORSU REGULOS
EGLPRSU SPLURGE
EGLRSUU REGULUS
EGLRUZZ GUZZLER
EGLSSTU GUTLESS
EGLSTUU GLUTEUS
EGMMORT GROMMET
EGMNOYZ ZYMOGEN
EGMNSTU NUTMEGS
EGMOORR GROOMER
EGMORSU MORGUES
EGMORTU GOURMET
EGNNORT RÖNTGEN
EGNNPTU PUNGENT
EGNNRSU GUNNERS
EGNNRUY GUNNERY
EGNNSTU STEN GUN
EGNNTUU UNGUENT

EGNOORY OROGENY
EGNOPRS SPONGER
EGNOPRY PROGENY,
   PYROGEN
EGNOPSS SPONGES
EGNORRW WRONGER
EGNORSS ENGROSS
EGNORSU SURGEON
EGNORSY GROYNES
EGNORUY YOUNGER
EGNOSTU TONGUES
EGNRRTU GRUNTER
EGNRSYY SYNERGY
EGOORSV GROOVES
EGOOSST STOOGES
EGOPRRU GROUPER,
   REGROUP
EGORRSS GROSSER
EGORRSU GROUSER
EGORRSW GROWERS
EGORRTU GROUTER
EGORRUY ROGUERY
EGORSSS GROSSES
EGORSSU GROUSES
EGORTUW OUTGREW
EGPRSUU UPSURGE
EGRRSUY SURGERY
EGRSTTU GUTTERS
EGSSSTU GUSSETS
EHHHOTU HUHEHOT
EHHIKSS SHEIKHS
EHHILLS HELLISH
EHHIRTT THITHER
EHHIRTW WHITHER
EHHMPTU THE HUMP
EHHNPSY HYPHENS
EHIIIKT HEITIKI
EHIIKLP HIPLIKE
EHIILLR HILLIER
EHIINRS SHINIER
EHIINRT INHERIT
EHIIPPS HIPPIES
EHIIPRT PITHIER
EHIISST SHIITES
EHIITTT HITTITE
EHIJNNO JOHNNIE
EHIKLNU HUNLIKE
EHIKLTU HUTLIKE
EHIKNOS HONKIES
EHIKNRT RETHINK
EHIKNST KENTISH
EHIKOOS HOOKIES
EHIKRRS SHIRKER

EHIKRSS SHRIEKS, SHRIKES
EHIKRSU HUSKIER
EHIKRSW WHISKER
EHIKSSU HUSKIES
EHIKSVZ IZHEVSK
EHIKSWY WHISKEY
EHILLNO HELLION
EHILLRY HILLERY
EHILLTY LITHELY
EHILNOP PINHOLE
EHILNOT HOT LINE,
　NEOLITH
EHILOPT HOPLITE
EHILOST HOLIEST,
　HOSTILE, THE SOIL
EHILPRT PHILTRE
EHILPSS HIPLESS
EHILRRW WHIRLER
EHILRST SLITHER
EHILRSV SHRIVEL
EHILRSY SHIRLEY
EHILSTT LITHEST, THISTLE
EHILSTW WHISTLE
EHILTTW WHITTLE
EHIMMPS MEMPHIS
EHIMMRS SHIMMER
EHIMNRU INHUMER,
　RHENIUM
EHIMNTY THYMINE
EHIMORS HEROISM,
　MOREISH
EHIMORZ RHIZOME
EHIMOST HOMIEST
EHIMPRW WHIMPER
EHIMRST HERMITS
EHIMRSU MUSHIER
EHIMRTT THERMIT
EHINNOP PHONE-IN
EHINNRT THINNER
EHINOPR PHONIER
EHINOPX PHOENIX
EHINORR HORNIER
EHINORS INSHORE
EHINOST HISTONE
EHINOSU HEINOUS,
　IN-HOUSE
EHINRSS SHRINES
EHINRSW WHINERS
EHINSSU HUSSEIN
EHINSTZ ZENITHS
EHIOPRS ROSE HIP
EHIORRS HORSIER
EHIORRT HERITOR

EHIORSS HOSIERS
EHIORST HOISTER, SHORTIE
EHIORSW SHOWIER
EHIORSY HOSIERY
EHIORTT THORITE
EHIOSTY ISOHYET
EHIPPRS SHIPPER
EHIPPRW WHIPPER
EHIPPST HIPPEST
EHIPPTW WHIPPET
EHIPRST HIPSTER
EHIPRSU PUSHIER
EHIPRSW WHISPER
EHIPSTT PETTISH
EHIRRSV SHRIVER
EHIRRTW WHERRIT,
　WRITHER
EHIRSSV SHIVERS
EHIRSSW SWISHER
EHIRSTU HIRSUTE
EHIRSTW WITHERS
EHIRSTZ ZITHERS
EHIRSVY SHIVERY
EHISSSU HUSSIES
EHISSSW SWISHES
EHISSTT THEISTS
EHISSTU HUSSITE
EHISTTW WETTISH,
　WHITEST
EHISWZZ WHIZZES
EHKNORS KHERSON
EHKNRSU HUNKERS
EHKOORS HOOKERS
EHLLORS HOLLERS
EHLMNOT MENTHOL
EHLOOPT POTHOLE
EHLOOST LESOTHO
EHLOPPR HOPPLER
EHLOPSX PHLOXES
EHLORST HOLSTER,
　HOSTLER
EHLORSW HOWLERS
EHLORTY HELOTRY,
　THORLEY
EHLOSST HOSTELS
EHLOSSV SHOVELS
EHLPRSU PLUSHER
EHLRSTU HUSTLER
EHLSSTU SLEUTHS
EHLSTTU SHUTTLE
EHMNOOR HORMONE,
　MOORHEN
EHMNORU HOME RUN

EHMNOSW SHOWMEN
EHMNPTY NYMPHET
EHMNTTU HUTMENT
EHMOOSW SOMEHOW
EHMORST MOTHERS,
　SMOTHER, THERMOS
EHMORTU MOUTHER
EHMPRTU THUMPER
EHMRSUU HUMERUS
EHNNOPR NEPHRON
EHNNORW RHONWEN
EHNNRSU SHUNNER
EHNOORS ONSHORE
EHNOPSY PHONEYS
EHNOPUY EUPHONY
EHNORRY HERONRY
EHNORST HORNETS,
　SHORTEN, THRONES
EHNORSU UNHORSE
EHNOSST HOTNESS
EHNOSTT SHOTTEN
EHNOSTY HONESTY
EHNRSTU HUNTERS,
　SHUNTER
EHNSSSY SHYNESS
EHOOPRW WHOOPER
EHOOPTY OOPHYTE
EHOORST HOOTERS,
　SHOOTER, SOOTHER
EHOORSV HOOVERS
EHOOSST SESOTHO
EHOPPRS HOPPERS,
　SHOPPER
EHOPPRT PROPHET
EHOPPRW WHOPPER
EHOPRRY ORPHREY
EHOPRST STROPHE
EHOPSST POSHEST
EHOPSTT THE TOPS
EHORRST SHORTER
EHORRTW THROWER
EHORSSW SHOWERS
EHORSTU SHOUTER,
　SOUTHER
EHORSWY SHOWERY
EHOSSST HOSTESS
EHOSTTT HOTTEST
EHPRSSU PUSHERS
EHPRSYZ ZEPHYRS
EHPRTTU TURPETH
EHRSSTY SHYSTER
EHRSTTU SHUTTER
EHRSTTW STREWTH

EIIILST ILEITIS	EIINNQU QUININE	EIKLLNW INKWELL
EIIJMMS JIMMIES	EIINNRT TINNIER	EIKLLRS KILLERS
EIIKKNR KINKIER	EIINORS IONISER, IRONIES,	EIKLLST SKILLET
EIIKLMR MILKIER	NOISIER	EIKLMMN MILKMEN
EIIKLNW KWEILIN	EIINORT NITEROI	EIKLMNR KREMLIN
EIIKLRS SILKIER	EIINORZ IONIZER	EIKLMRS MILKERS
EIIKNPS PINKIES	EIINPPR NIPPIER	EIKLNRU URNLIKE
EIIKNST INKIEST	EIINPRS INSPIRE	EIKLNRW WRINKLE
EIIKPRS SPIKIER	EIINPST PINIEST, TIEPINS	EIKLNST TINKLES
EIIKRRS RISKIER	EIINQRU INQUIRE	EIKLNSV KELVINS
EIIKSTT KITTIES	EIINQTU INQUIET	EIKLNSW WINKLES
EIILLMN MILLINE	EIINRTT NITRITE	EIKLNSY SKYLINE
EIILLNV VILLEIN	EIINRTV INVITER, VITRINE	EIKLNTW TWINKLE
EIILLRS SILLIER	EIINRTW WRITE-IN	EIKLOPS SKI POLE
EIILLSS SILLIES	EIINSTT TINIEST	EIKLPRY PERKILY
EIILLSW WILLIES	EIINSTU UNITIES	EIKLPST LIPETSK
EIILMPR IMPERIL	EIINTUV UNITIVE	EIKLRST KILTERS
EIILMRS SLIMIER	EIIORSV IVORIES	EIKLRSU SULKIER
EIILMRT LEITRIM, LIMITER	EIIOSTZ ZOISITE	EIKLSTT SKITTLE
EIILMSS MISSILE, SIMILES	EIIPPRZ ZIPPIER	EIKMMRS SKIMMER
EIILMST ELITISM, LIMIEST	EIIPRRV PRIVIER	EIKMNNS KINSMEN
EIILMSU MILIEUS	EIIPRST TIPSIER	EIKMORS IRKSOME,
EIILMUX MILIEUX	EIIPRSV PRIVIES	SMOKIER
EIILNOS ELISION, ISOLINE,	EIIPRSW WISPIER	EIKMOSS ESKIMOS
LIONISE	EIIQUVV QUI VIVE	EIKMRRS SMIRKER
EIILNOV OLIVINE	EIIRSSS SISSIER	EIKMRRU MURKIER
EIILNOZ LIONIZE	EIIRSST TRISSIE	EIKMRSU MUSKIER
EIILNRT NITRILE	EIIRSTW WIRIEST	EIKNNOR EINKORN
EIILNTU INUTILE	EIIRSVZ VIZIERS	EIKNNRS SKINNER
EIILORV OLIVIER	EIIRTTW WITTIER	EIKNOPS PINKOES
EIILOST OILIEST	EIISSSS SISSIES	EIKNORV INVOKER
EIILOTT OTTILIE	EIISSTX SIXTIES	EIKNORW WONKIER
EIILRSX ELIXIRS	EIISTTT TITTIES	EIKNOSS KENOSIS
EIILSTT ELITIST	EIISTUV UVEITIS	EIKNPRR PRINKER
EIILSTU UTILISE	EIISTZZ TIZZIES	EIKNPST PINKEST
EIILSTW WILIEST	EIJKLRY JERKILY	EIKNRSS SINKERS
EIILTUZ UTILIZE	EIJKNRS JERKINS	EIKNRST KIRSTEN,
EIIMMSS MIMESIS	EIJKNSU JUNKIES	KRISTEN, STINKER,
EIIMMST MISTIME	EIJLLOR JOLLIER	TINKERS
EIIMNOR MEIRION	EIJMPRU JUMPIER	EIKNRSW WINKERS
EIIMNPR PRIMINE	EIJNORS JOINERS	EIKNRTT KNITTER, TRINKET
EIIMNRT INTERIM, TERMINI	EIJNORT JOINTER	EIKNSTT KITTENS
EIIMNRV MINIVER	EIJNORY JOINERY	EIKNTUZ KUNZITE
EIIMNTV MINIVET	EIJNPRU JUNIPER	EIKOORS ROOKIES
EIIMOPP POMPEII	EIJNRRU INJURER	EIKOPPR PORK PIE
EIIMOSS MEIOSIS	EIJNSTU JUSTINE	EIKOPRR PORKIER
EIIMPSW WIMPIES	EIJPRTU JUPITER	EIKOPST POKIEST
EIIMPTY IMPIETY	EIJRSTT JITTERS	EIKOSST KETOSIS
EIIMSSS MISSIES	EIJRTTY JITTERY	EIKPPRS KIPPERS, SKIPPER
EIIMSSV MISSIVE	EIJSSTU JESUITS	EIKPPST SKIPPET
EIINNNP NINEPIN	EIJSSUV JUSSIVE	EIKRRST SKIRRET, STRIKER
EIINNNS NINNIES	EIKKOOR KOOKIER	EIKRSSS KISSERS
EIINNPS PINNIES	EIKKOPS KOPEISK	EIKRSST STRIKES

EIKRSSV SKIVERS
EIKRSTT SKITTER
EILLLOS LOLLIES
EILLLOW OIL WELL
EILLMNU MULLEIN
EILLMOT MELILOT
EILLMOU MOUILLE
EILLMRS MILLERS
EILLMTU MULLITE
EILLNSS ILLNESS
EILLNST LENTILS, LINTELS
EILLORV ORVILLE
EILLORW LOWLIER
EILLOTT ELLIOTT
EILLPPP PEP PILL
EILLPRS SPILLER
EILLRST STILLER, TILLERS,
    TRELLIS
EILLRSW SWILLER
EILMMRS SLIMMER
EILMNRY MERILYN
EILMOPR IMPLORE
EILMPPS PIMPLES
EILMPRS PRELIMS, SIMPLER
EILMPRU LUMPIER
EILMPST LIMPEST, LIMPETS
EILMPSU IMPULSE
EILMPSW WIMPLES
EILMPSX SIMPLEX
EILMPTY EMPTILY
EILMQSU QUILMES
EILMRRY MERRILY
EILMRSS RIMLESS
EILMRSU MISRULE
EILMRSY MISERLY
EILMSSY MESSILY
EILMSUY ELYSIUM
EILMUUV ELUVIUM
EILNNPU PINNULE
EILNNST LINNETS
EILNOOR LOONIER
EILNOOS LOONIES
EILNOPR PROLINE
EILNOPS EPSILON
EILNORT RETINOL
EILNOSS INSOLES,
    LESIONS, LIONESS
EILNOSU ELUSION
EILNOTU LINE-OUT,
    OUTLINE
EILNOTV VIOLENT
EILNOTW TOWLINE
EILNOVV INVOLVE

EILNPPS NIPPLES
EILNPRS PILSNER
EILNPSU LINEUPS, SPINULE
EILNPTY INEPTLY
EILNPUV VULPINE
EILNRTY INERTLY
EILNRVY NERVILY
EILNSSS SINLESS
EILNSST SILENTS
EILNSTU UTENSIL
EILOOST OSTIOLE
EILOPRS SPOILER
EILOPST PLOESTI
EILOPSU PILEOUS
EILOPSV PLOSIVE
EILOPTX EXPLOIT
EILORRS LORRIES
EILORSS RISSOLE
EILORSU LOUSIER
EILORSW LOW-RISE
EILORTT TRIOLET
EILORTU OUTLIER
EILOSTT LITOTES, TOILETS
EILOSTV VIOLETS
EILOTUV OUTLIVE
EILPPRR RIPPLER
EILPPRS RIPPLES, SLIPPER
EILPPRT RIPPLET, TIPPLER
EILPPRU PULPIER
EILPPST STIPPLE, TIPPLES
EILPPSU PILEUPS
EILPPSW SWIPPLE
EILPRTT TRIPLET
EILPRTX TRIPLEX
EILPRUU PURLIEU
EILPSTT SPITTLE
EILPSTU STIPULE
EILPTTY PETTILY
EILQRTU QUILTER
EILQRUU LIQUEUR
EILQTUY QUIETLY
EILRRSU SURLIER
EILRRTW TWIRLER
EILRSSV SILVERS, SLIVERS
EILRSTT LITTERS, SLITTER
EILRSVY SILVERY
EILRSZZ SIZZLER
EILRTTY TRITELY
EILRTUV RIVULET
EILSSTW WITLESS
EILSSTY STYLISE
EILSSVW SWIVELS
EILSTTY TESTILY

EILSTVY SYLVITE
EILSTYZ STYLIZE
EILSWZZ SWIZZLE
EIMMMOS MOMMIES
EIMMMSU MUMMIES
EIMMOPS POMMIES
EIMMORS MEMOIRS
EIMMPRR PRIMMER
EIMMPRU PREMIUM
EIMMRRT TRIMMER
EIMMRSW SWIMMER
EIMMSTU TUMMIES
EIMNNOT MENTION
EIMNOOS NOISOME
EIMNOOT EMOTION
EIMNOPT PIMENTO
EIMNOQU MONIQUE
EIMNORR MERRION
EIMNOST MOISTEN
EIMNOSW WINSOME
EIMNOTU MOUNTIE
EIMNPTU PINETUM
EIMNRST MINSTER
EIMNSSU MINUSES
EIMNSTT MITTENS,
    SMITTEN
EIMNSTU MINUETS,
    MINUTES
EIMNUZZ MUEZZIN
EIMOORR ROOMIER
EIMOPRS IMPOSER,
    PROMISE
EIMOPRV IMPROVE
EIMORRW WORMIER
EIMORSS MOSSIER
EIMORST MORTISE,
    TRISOME
EIMORSU MOUSIER
EIMORSV VERISMO
EIMORTT OMITTER
EIMORTV VOMITER
EIMOSTV MOTIVES
EIMOSTZ MESTIZO
EIMOTTW TWO-TIME
EIMPRRS PRIMERS
EIMPRSS IMPRESS,
    PREMISS, SIMPERS
EIMPRST IMPREST, PERMITS
EIMPRSU UMPIRES
EIMPRTU IMPUTER
EIMPSTU IMPETUS
EIMRSST MISTERS

EIMRSSU MISUSER, SURMISE
EIMRSTT METRIST
EIMRSTU MUSTIER
EIMRTUX MIXTURE
EIMRUZZ MUZZIER
EIMSSSU MISUSES
EINNOPS PENSION
EINNOPT PONTINE
EINNOQU QUINONE
EINNORT INTONER
EINNORU REUNION
EINNORV ENVIRON
EINNOST TENSION
EINNOSV VENISON
EINNOTT TONTINE
EINNPRS SPINNER
EINNPST TENPINS
EINNPSY SPINNEY
EINNQTU QUENTIN
EINNRRU RUNNIER
EINNRSS SINNERS
EINNRST INTERNS
EINNRSU SUNNIER
EINNRSW WINNERS
EINNRTV VINTNER
EINNSTU TUNNIES
EINOOPZ EPIZOON
EINOORS EROSION
EINOOST ISOTONE
EINOOSZ OZONISE
EINOOZZ OZONIZE
EINOPRT POINTER, PROTEIN
EINOPSS IN POSSE, SPINOSE
EINOQUX EQUINOX
EINORSS SENIORS
EINORST IN STORE, STONIER
EINORSV VERSION
EINORSW SNOWIER
EINORTT TRITONE
EINORTU ROUTINE
EINOSSS SESSION
EINOSST NOSIEST
EINOSUV ENVIOUS, NIVEOUS
EINPPRS NIPPERS
EINPPST SNIPPET
EINPRRT PRINTER, REPRINT
EINPRSS SNIPERS
EINPSST INSTEPS, SPINETS
EINPSTU PUNIEST

EINPTTY TINTYPE
EINQRUY ENQUIRY
EINQSSU SEQUINS
EINQSTU INQUEST
EINQTTU QUINTET
EINQTUU UNQUIET
EINRRSU INSURER
EINRSST INSERTS
EINRSSU SUNRISE
EINRSTT STINTER
EINRSTV STRIVEN
EINRSTW WINTERS
EINRTTU NUTTIER
EINRTTW WRITTEN
EINSSSU SINUSES
EINSSSY SYNESIS
EINSSTW WITNESS
EINSSUW SUNWISE
EINSTTW TWIN SET
EINTTUY TENUITY
EIOOPST ISOTOPE
EIOORST SOOTIER
EIOORWZ WOOZIER
EIOOSTT TOOTSIE
EIOOSTZ OOZIEST
EIOPPPS POPPIES
EIOPPRS SOPPIER
EIOPRRS PROSIER
EIOPRST REPOSIT, RIPOSTE, ROPIEST
EIOPRSX PROXIES
EIOPRTT POTTIER
EIOPSST POSTIES
EIOPSTT POTTIES, TIPTOES
EIOPSTU PITEOUS
EIORRRS SORRIER
EIORRRW WORRIER
EIORRST RIOTERS, ROISTER
EIORRSW WORRIES
EIORSST ROSIEST, SORITES, SORTIES, STORIES
EIORSSU SERIOUS
EIORSSX XEROSIS
EIOSSTU OUTSISE
EIOSSTV SOVIETS
EIOSTUZ OUTSIZE
EIPPPSU PUPPIES
EIPPRRT TRIPPER
EIPPRST TIPPERS
EIPPRSZ ZIPPERS
EIPPRTT TRIPPET
EIPPSUY YUPPIES
EIPRRST STRIPER

EIPRRSU UPRISER
EIPRRUV UPRIVER
EIPRSST PERSIST, PRIESTS, SPRIEST, SPRITES, STRIPES
EIPRSTT SPITTER, TIPSTER
EIPRSTY PYRITES, STRIPEY
EIPRSUU EURIPUS
EIPRTUW WRITE-UP
EIPRUVW PURVIEW
EIPSSSU PUSSIES
EIQRSSU SQUIRES
EIQRSTU QUERIST
EIQRSUV QUIVERS
EIQRTTU QUITTER
EIQRUVY QUIVERY
EIQRUZZ QUIZZER
EIQSTUU QUIETUS
EIQSUZZ QUIZZES
EIRRRST STIRRER
EIRRSTU RUSTIER
EIRRSTV STRIVER
EIRRSTW WRITERS
EIRSSST SISTERS
EIRSSTT SITTERS
EIRSSUV VIRUSES
EIRSTTT TITTERS
EIRSTTU TERTIUS
EIRSTTV TRIVETS
EIRSTTW TWISTER
EIRSTUV VIRTUES
EIRSUVV SURVIVE
EIRTTTW TWITTER
EISSSTU TISSUES
EISSSTX SEXISTS
EISSTUV TUSSIVE
EISTTUW WET SUIT
EJJMNUU JEJUNUM
EJKNSTU JUNKETS
EJLORST JOSTLER
EJLOSSY JOYLESS
EJMPRSU JUMPERS
EJNORUY JOURNEY
EJOORVY OVERJOY
EJOPRTT JETPORT
EJORSTT JOTTERS
EJORSTU JOUSTER
EJPRRUY PERJURY
EKKLRSU SKULKER
EKLNORS SNORKEL
EKLOORS LOOKERS
EKLOOTW WET-LOOK
EKMNORW WORKMEN
EKMNOSY MONKEYS

EKMNPTU UNKEMPT	ELMSSSU MUSSELS	ELRRSTU RUSTLER
EKMNRTU TURKMEN	ELMSUZZ MUZZLES	ELRRTTU TURTLER
EKMORSS SMOKERS	ELNNRSU RUNNELS	ELRSSTU LUSTRES,
EKMSSTU MUSKETS	ELNNSTU TUNNELS	RESULTS
EKNOORS SNOOKER	ELNOORZ LORENZO	ELRSTTU TURTLES
EKNORSY ORKNEYS,	ELNOOSU UNLOOSE	ELRTTUY UTTERLY
YONKERS	ELNOPRU PLEURON	ELRTUUV VULTURE
EKNORTT KNOTTER	ELNOPTU OPULENT	ELSSSTU TUSSLES
EKNORTW NETWORK	ELNORSY ROSELYN	ELSSSUY ULYSSES
EKNORUY YUKONER	ELNORTY ELYTRON	EMMMRSU MUMMERS
EKNRTUY TURNKEY	ELNOSSS LESSONS	EMMMRUY MUMMERY
EKOOPRV PROVOKE	ELNOSSW LOWNESS	EMMNOOR MONOMER
EKOORRY ROOKERY	ELNOSTV SOLVENT	EMMNOST MOMENTS
EKOORST STOOKER	ELNOSZZ NOZZLES	EMMNOTU OMENTUM
EKOPRRS PORKERS	ELNOTVY NOVELTY	EMMNOTY METONYM
EKORRSW WORKERS	ELNRSTY STERNLY	EMMOOTY MYOTOME
EKORSST STOKERS,	ELNSSSU SUNLESS	EMMRSSU SUMMERS
STROKES	ELNSSSY SLYNESS	EMMRSTU RUMMEST
EKORSWX EX-WORKS	ELOORST LOOTERS	EMMRSUY SUMMERY
EKRSSTU TUSKERS	ELOORTT ROOTLET,	EMMSSUU MUSEUMS
EKRSTUY TURKEYS	TOOTLER	EMNNOOW NEW MOON
ELLMOOR MORELLO	ELOOSST LOOSEST	EMNNOSW SNOWMEN
ELLMPUU PLUMULE	ELOOSTT TOOTLES	EMNOOST MOONSET
ELLMSTU MULLETS	ELOOSTU OUTSOLE	EMNOPST POSTMEN
ELLNOOW WOOLLEN	ELOPRRW PROWLER	EMNOPSU SPUMONE
ELLNOSW SWOLLEN	ELOPRRY PYRROLE	EMNOPYY EPONYMY
ELLNSTU NULL SET	ELOPRSU LEPROUS,	EMNORRU MOURNER
ELLOOSY LOOSELY	PELORUS, SPORULE	EMNORSS SERMONS
ELLOPTU POLLUTE	ELOPRSV PLOVERS	EMNORST MENTORS,
ELLORRS ROLLERS	ELOPRSY LEPROSY	MONSTER
ELLORTY TROLLEY	ELOPRTT PLOTTER	EMNORTT TORMENT
ELLOSTU OUTSELL,	ELOPRTY PROTYLE	EMNORTU MOUNTER,
SELL-OUT	ELOPSST TOPLESS	REMOUNT
ELLOSVY VOLLEYS	ELORSSS LESSORS	EMNORTV VERMONT
ELLOSWY YELLOWS	ELORSST OSTLERS	EMNOSST STEMSON
ELLPSTU PULLETS	ELORSSV SOLVERS	EMNRSTU MUNSTER,
ELLPSUY PULLEYS	ELORSTT SLOTTER	STERNUM
ELLRSSU RUSSELL	ELORSTV REVOLTS	EMOOPRS OOSPERM
ELMMOPS POMMELS	ELORSTW TROWELS	EMOOPRT PROMOTE
ELMMORT TROMMEL	ELORSUV LOUVRES,	EMOORRS ROOMERS
ELMMOSS MOSLEMS	VELOURS	EMOOSTT MOTTOES
ELMMPTU PLUMMET	ELORTTY LOTTERY	EMOOSTW TWOSOME
ELMMRSU SLUMMER	ELORTVY OVERTLY	EMOPPST MOPPETS
ELMOORS MORELOS	ELOSSTU LOTUSES	EMOPRRS ROMPERS
ELMOORT TREMOLO	ELOSSTW SLOWEST	EMOPRST STOMPER
ELMOPRY POLYMER	ELOSSTY SYSTOLE	EMOPRSU SUPREMO
ELMORSS MORSELS	ELOSTTU OUTLETS	EMOQSSU MOSQUES
ELMORTU MOULTER	ELOSTUU LUTEOUS	EMORRST TREMORS
ELMOSUU EMULOUS	ELPPRSU PURPLES,	EMORSSU MOUSERS
ELMOSUV VOLUMES	SUPPLER	EMORSUY SEYMOUR
ELMPPRU PLUMPER	ELPRUZZ PUZZLER	EMOSSSU MOUSSES
ELMRSTY MYRTLES	ELPSTUU PUSTULE	EMPRSTU STUMPER
ELMRUZZ MUZZLER	ELPSUZZ PUZZLES	EMPRTTU TRUMPET

EMPSSSU MESS-UPS
EMRRUUZ ERZURUM
EMRSSTU MUSTERS
EMRSTYY MYSTERY
EMSSSTY SYSTEMS
ENNNOPS PENNONS
ENNNRUY NUNNERY
ENNORTT TRENTON
ENNORTU NEUTRON
ENNOSST SONNETS
ENNOTWW NEW TOWN
ENNPSTU PUNNETS
ENNRRSU RUNNERS
ENNRSTU STUNNER
ENOOPRS SNOOPER
ENOORRT TORREON
ENOORSU ONEROUS
ENOORSZ SNOOZER
ENOOSSZ SNOOZES
ENOOTTW TWO-TONE
ENOOTXY OXYTONE
ENOPRSS PERSONS
ENOPRST POSTERN,
  PRESTON
ENOPRTT PORTENT
ENOPRTY ENTROPY
ENOPSST STEPSON
ENOQTUU UNQUOTE
ENORRSS SNORERS
ENORRST SNORTER
ENORRTT TORRENT
ENORRUV OVERRUN
ENORSSS SENSORS
ENORSSY SENSORY
ENORSTT STENTOR
ENORSTU TONSURE
ENORSUV NERVOUS
ENORTUY TOURNEY
ENOSSTT STETSON
ENOSSTX SEXTONS
ENOSTUU TENUOUS
ENPRRSU SPURNER
ENPRSTU PUNSTER,
  PUNTERS
ENRRSTU RETURNS,
  TURNERS
ENRRSUY NURSERY
ENRRTUU NURTURE
ENRRTUY TURNERY
ENRSSWY WRYNESS
ENRSTTU ENTRUST
ENRSVWY WYVERNS
ENSSSTU SUNSETS

EOOOPRS OOSPORE
EOOPPRS OPPOSER,
  POOPERS, PROPOSE
EOOPPRV POPOVER
EOOPRRS SPOORER
EOOPRRT TROOPER
EOOPRST POOREST,
  STOOPER
EOOPRTV OVERTOP
EOOPRTW TOWROPE
EOORRST ROOSTER
EOOSSSU OSSEOUS
EOOTTUV OUTVOTE
EOPPPRS POPPERS
EOPPPST POPPETS
EOPPRRS PROSPER
EOPPRSS OPPRESS
EOPPRST STOPPER,
  TOPPERS
EOPPRSU PURPOSE
EOPPSSU SUPPOSE
EOPRRSS PRESSOR
EOPRRST PORTERS,
  REPORTS, SPORTER
EOPRRTU TROUPER
EOPRSST POSTERS,
  PRESTOS
EOPRSSU POSEURS
EOPRSSW PROWESS
EOPRSSY OSPREYS
EOPRSTT POTTERS,
  PROTEST, SPOTTER
EOPRSTU PETROUS,
  POSTURE, SPOUTER,
  TROUPES
EOPRSTX EXPORTS
EOPRTTY POTTERY
EOPRTVY POVERTY
EOPSSSS POSSESS
EOPSSST POSSETS
EOPSSSU SPOUSES
EOPSSTX SEXPOTS
EOPSTTW TWO-STEP
EOQRSTU TORQUES
EORRRST TERRORS
EORRSST RESORTS,
  ROSTERS
EORRSTT RETORTS,
  ROTTERS, STERTOR
EORRSTU TROUSER
EORRSZZ ROZZERS
EORRTTT TROTTER
EORRTTU TORTURE

EORSSTU OESTRUS,
  OUSTERS, SOUREST
EORSSTY OYSTERS,
  STOREYS
EORSTTT STRETTO
EORSTTU STOUTER
EORSUVY VOYEURS
EORTTTY TOTTERY
EPPPSTU PUPPETS
EPPRRUU PURPURE
EPPRSSU PRESS-UP,
  SUPPERS
EPRRSSU PURSERS
EPRRSUU PURSUER,
  USURPER
EPRRTUU RUPTURE
EPRSTTU PUTTERS,
  SPUTTER
ERRSSTU TRUSSER
ERRSSUU USURERS
ERRSSUY SURREYS
ERRSTTU TRUSTER,
  TURRETS
ERRSTTY TRYSTER
ERSSSTU TRUSSES
ERSSTUU SUTURES
ERSSUVY SURVEYS
ERSTTTU STUTTER
FFFILOT LIFT-OFF
FFGHINU HUFFING
FFGIINR GRIFFIN
FFGILNU LUFFING
FFGIMNU MUFFING
FFGINOR GRIFFON
FFGINOS OFFINGS
FFGINPU PUFFING
FFGLRUY GRUFFLY
FFHHISU HUFFISH
FFHILSY FLY-FISH
FFHILUY HUFFILY
FFHOOSW SHOW-OFF
FFHOSTU SHUT-OFF
FFILPUY PUFFILY
FFILSTY STIFFLY
FFIMNSU MUFFINS
FFINOOT FINFOOT
FFINOPS SPIN-OFF
FFINOPT PONTIFF
FFINPSU PUFFINS
FFINSTU SNUFF IT
FFIOPRS RIP-OFFS
FFIOPST TIP-OFFS
FFIORTY FORTIFY

FFIQSUY SQUIFFY	FGINSSU FUSSING	FILRSTY FIRSTLY
FFJMOPU JUMP-OFF	FGINUZZ FUZZING	FILSSUY FUSSILY
FFKLORU FORKFUL	FGIOORT GO FOR IT	FILSTTU FLUTIST
FFLNSUY SNUFFLY	FGIORTW FIGWORT	FILSTUW WISTFUL
FFNORSU RUN-OFFS	FGLNOOR FOR LONG	FILSTWY SWIFTLY
FFNORTU TURN-OFF	FGLNORU FURLONG	FILUYZZ FUZZILY
FFOPSTU PUT-OFFS	FGLNOSU SONGFUL	FIMMMUY MUMMIFY
FGGGINO FOGGING	FGNORWY GWYNFOR	FIMNORU UNIFORM
FGGHIIS FISHGIG	FGNOSUU FUNGOUS	FIMOORV OVIFORM
FGGILNO GOLFING	FHIINNS FINNISH	FIMORTY MORTIFY
FGGILOY FOGGILY	FHIINPS PINFISH	FIMSTYY MYSTIFY
FGGINOO GOOFING	FHIKLOS FOLKISH	FINOPSU SOUPFIN
FGGINOR FORGING	FHILOOS FOOLISH	FINORSS FRISSON
FGHHIOS HOGFISH	FHILOSW WOLFISH	FIOORSU FURIOSO
FGHIINS FISHING	FHILSUW WISHFUL	FIOPRST PROFITS
FGHIIPS PIGFISH	FHINRSU FURNISH	FIOPSTX POSTFIX
FGHILST FLIGHTS	FHINSSU SUNFISH	FIORSUU FURIOUS
FGHILTY FLIGHTY	FHIOPPS FOPPISH	FIORTYZ FITZROY
FGHIOSY FOGYISH	FHIORRY HORRIFY	FIOSTTU OUTFITS
FGHIRST FRIGHTS	FHIRSST SHRIFTS	FIRRSTY STIR-FRY
FGHNOOR FOGHORN	FHIRSTT THRIFTS	FKLNOOR NORFOLK
FGIIKNN KNIFING	FHIRTTY THRIFTY	FKOOORS FORSOOK
FGIILLN FILLING	FHLRTUU HURTFUL	FLLOSUU SOULFUL
FGIILMN FILMING	FHNOTUX FOXHUNT	FLLSTUU LUSTFUL
FGIILNO FOILING	FHOOOTT HOTFOOT	FLMMOUX FLUMMOX
FGIILNR RIFLING	FHORSTU FOURTHS	FLMNOOU MOUFLON
FGIILNS FILINGS	FIIKLST SKI LIFT	FLMOOOT TOMFOOL
FGIILNT LIFTING	FIILLMY FILMILY	FLMOORU ROOMFUL
FGIILNY LIGNIFY	FIILLNS FILL-INS	FLNOORR FORLORN
FGIIMNR FIRMING	FIILLPS FILLIPS	FLOOTUW OUTFLOW
FGIINNN FINNING	FIILNOT TINFOIL	FLOPSTU POTFULS
FGIINNS FININGS	FIILNTY NIFTILY	FLOPSUU FOUL-UPS
FGIINST SIFTING	FIILPTU PITIFUL	FLOSUUV FULVOUS
FGIINSY SIGNIFY	FIIMSST MISFITS	FMOOPRR PRO-FORM
FGIINTT FITTING	FIINOSS FISSION	FMRSTUU FRUSTUM
FGIINZZ FIZZING	FIINRTY NITRIFY	FNNRSUU FUN RUNS
FGIKNNU FUNKING	FIIOPST POSITIF	FNOOOTT FOOT-TON
FGIKNOR FORKING	FIIRTVY VITRIFY	FNOORSU SUNROOF
FGILNOO FOOLING	FIJLLOY JOLLIFY	FNOPRTU UPFRONT
FGILNOT LOFTING	FIJSTUY JUSTIFY	FNORSTY Y-FRONTS
FGILNOU FOULING	FIKKLNO KINFOLK	FOOOPRT ROOFTOP
FGILNOW FLOWING,	FIKLLSU SKILFUL	FOORSST OF SORTS
FOWLING, WOLFING	FIKLNSU SKINFUL	FOORTTX FOXTROT
FGILNRU FURLING	FILLMOY MOLLIFY	FOPSSTU FUSSPOT
FGILNTU FLUTING	FILLNUY NULLIFY	FORRSUW FURROWS
FGILOOY GOOFILY	FILLOTY LOFTILY	FORRUWY FURROWY
FGILORY GLORIFY	FILNNUY FUNNILY	FORSTWY FROWSTY
FGIMNOR FORMING	FILNORS FLORINS	GGGHINO HOGGING
FGINOOR ROOFING	FILNOSW INFLOWS	GGGHINU HUGGING
FGINOOT FOOTING	FILNOUX FLUXION	GGGIIJN JIGGING
FGINRRU FURRING	FILORST FLORIST	GGGIINP PIGGING
FGINRSU SURFING	FILORTU FLORUIT	GGGIINR RIGGING
FGINRTU TURFING	FILOSSS FOSSILS	GGGIINW WIGGING

GGGIJNO JOGGING	GHHINSU HUSHING	GHINRSU RUSHING
GGGIJNU JUGGING	GHHLOOY HOOGHLY	GHINRTU HURTING
GGGILNO LOGGING	GHHORTU THROUGH	GHIOPSZ PHIZOGS
GGGILNU LUGGING	GHHOTTU THOUGHT	GHIORSU ROGUISH
GGGIMNU MUGGING	GHIIKRZ KIRGHIZ	GHIPRTU UPRIGHT
GGGINNO NOGGING	GHIILNW WHILING	GHIPTTU UPTIGHT
GGGINOR GORGING	GHIILRS GIRLISH	GHLMOOO HOMOLOG
GGGINOT TOGGING	GHIINNS HSINING, SHINING	GHLOPSU PLOUGHS
GGGINOU GOUGING	GHIINNT HINTING	GHLORUY ROUGHLY
GGGINPU PUGGING	GHIINNW WHINING	GHLOSSU SLOUGHS
GGGINTU TUGGING	GHIINSS HISSING	GHLOSTY GHOSTLY
GGHHIOS HOGGISH	GHIINST INSIGHT	GHLOSUY SLOUGHY
GGHIINN HINGING	GHIINSW WISHING	GHLOTUY TOUGHLY
GGHIINS SIGHING	GHIINTT HITTING, TITHING	GHMORSU SORGHUM
GGHIIPS PIGGISH	GHIINTW WHITING	GHMOSTU MUGSHOT
GGHINSU GUSHING	GHIJNOS JOSHING	GHNOPRY GRYPHON
GGIIILN GINGILI	GHIKLNU HULKING	GHNORST THRONGS
GGIINNO INGOING	GHIKNNO HONKING	GHNOSSU SHOGUNS
GGIINNP PINGING	GHIKNOO HOOKING	GHNOSTU GUNSHOT,
GGIINNR RINGING	GHIKNST KNIGHTS	NOUGHTS, SHOTGUN
GGIINNS SIGNING, SINGING	GHILLNU HULLING	GHNOTTU OUGHTN'T
GGIINNT TINGING	GHILLTY LIGHTLY	GHORSTU TROUGHS
GGIINNW WINGING	GHILNOS LONGISH	GHORSTW GROWTHS
GGIINPR GRIPING	GHILNOW HOWLING	GHORTUW WROUGHT
GGILLNU GULLING	GHILNRU HURLING	GHORTUY YOGHURT
GGILMUY MUGGILY	GHILNSY SHINGLY	GIIJLNT JILTING
GGILNNO LONGING	GHILNTY NIGHTLY	GIIJNNO JOINING
GGILNNU LUNGING	GHILPST PLIGHTS	GIIJNNX JINXING
GGILNOS GOSLING	GHILRTY RIGHTLY	GIIKLLN KILLING
GGILNOW GLOWING	GHILSST SLIGHTS	GIIKLMN MILKING
GGILNPU GULPING	GHILSTY SIGHTLY	GIIKLNN INKLING, LINKING
GGILOOS GIGOLOS	GHILTTY TIGHTLY	GIIKLNS LIKINGS
GGILOSY SOGGILY	GHIMMNU HUMMING	GIIKNNO OINKING
GGILRWY WRIGGLY	GHIMNNY HYMNING	GIIKNNP KINGPIN, PINK
GGIMMNU GUMMING	GHIMNOS GNOMISH	GIN, PINKING
GGIMNSU MUGGINS	GHIMNPU HUMPING	GIIKNNS SINKING
GGINNNU GUNNING	GHIMNRY RHYMING	GIIKNNW WINKING
GGINNOO ONGOING	GHIMNTT MIGHTN'T	GIIKNPP KIPPING
GGINNOP PONGING	GHINNOP PHONING	GIIKNPS PIGSKIN, SPIKING
GGINNOS NOGGINS	GHINNOS NOSHING	GIIKNRS RISKING
GGINOPR GROPING	GHINNOT NOTHING	GIIKNSS KISSING
GGINORS GRINGOS	GHINNTU HUNTING	GIIKNSV SKIVING, VIKINGS
GGINORU ROUGING	GHINOOS SHOOING	GIIKNTT KITTING
GGINORW GROWING	GHINOOT HOOTING	GIILLMN MILLING
GGINPPY GYPPING	GHINOPP HOPPING	GIILLNT LILTING, TILLING
GGINPRU PURGING	GHINORS SHORING	GIILLNW WILLING
GGINRST G-STRING	GHINOST HOSTING	GIILMNN LIMNING
GGINRSU SURGING	GHINOSU HOUSING	GIILMNP LIMPING
GGINSTU GUSTING	GHINOSV SHOVING	GIILMNS SMILING
GGINTTU GUTTING	GHINOSW SHOWING	GIILMPR PILGRIM
GGIPRSY SPRIGGY	GHINOTT TONIGHT	GIILNNS LININGS
GGNOORS GORGONS	GHINOTU HOUTING	GIILNNY LYING-IN
GHHIKSY SKY-HIGH	GHINPSU PUSHING	GIILNOR LIGROIN

GIILNOS SOILING	GIJMNPU JUMPING	GILSTUY GUSTILY
GIILNOT TOILING	GIJNOTT JOTTING	GIMMMNU MUMMING
GIILNPS LISPING	GIJNTTU JUTTING	GIMMNSU SUMMING
GIILNST LISTING, SILTING	GIKLNOO LOOKING	GIMNNOO MOONING
GIILNSV LIVINGS	GIKLNRU LURKING	GIMNNOR MORNING
GIILNTT TILTING	GIKLNSU SULKING	GIMNOOR MOORING,
GIILNTW WILTING	GIKMNNU KUNMING	ROOMING
GIILORS OILRIGS	GIKMNOS SMOKING	GIMNOOT MOOTING
GIIMMNR RIMMING	GIKNNOO KONGONI	GIMNOOZ ZOOMING
GIIMNNT MINTING	GIKNNOW KNOWING	GIMNOPP MOPPING
GIIMNPP PIMPING	GIKNOOR ROOKING	GIMNOPR ROMPING
GIIMNPR PRIMING	GIKNORW WORKING	GIMNORW WORMING
GIIMNSS MISSING	GIKNOST STOKING	GIMNOSU MOUSING
GIIMNST MISTING, SMITING	GIKNOWY YINGKOW	GIMNOWY WYOMING
GIINNNP PINNING	GILLLNO LOLLING	GIMNPPU PUMPING
GIINNNS INNINGS, SINNING	GILLLNU LULLING	GIMNSSU MUSSING
GIINNNT TINNING	GILLMNU MULLING	GINNNPU PUNNING
GIINNNW WINNING	GILLNOP POLLING	GINNNRU RUNNING
GIINNOP OPINING	GILLNOR ROLLING	GINNNSU SUNNING
GIINNOR IRONING	GILLNOT TOLLING	GINNOPS SPONGIN
GIINNPP NIPPING	GILLNPU PULLING	GINNORS SNORING
GIINNPS SNIPING	GILMNOO LOOMING	GINNORW INGROWN
GIINNRS RINSING	GILMNOT MOLTING	GINNORY GIRONNY
GIINNRU INURING, RUINING	GILMNPU LUMPING,	GINNOST STONING
GIINNSW INSWING	PLUMING	GINNOSW SNOWING
GIINNTT TINTING	GILMPSY GYMSLIP	GINNPRU PRUNING
GIINNTU UNITING	GILNNSU UNSLING	GINNPTU PUNTING
GIINNTW TWINING	GILNOOP LOOPING,	GINNRSU NURSING
GIINOPR PIG IRON	POOLING	GINNRTU TURNING
GIINOPS POISING	GILNOOS LOOSING	GINNTTU NUTTING
GIINORS ORIGINS	GILNOOT LOOTING,	GINNTUW WING NUT
GIINORT RIOTING	TOOLING	GINNTUY UNTYING
GIINPPP PIPPING	GILNOPP LOPPING	GINOORT ROOTING
GIINPPR RIPPING	GILNOPS SLOPING	GINOOTT TOOTING
GIINPPS SIPPING	GILNOPW PLOWING	GINOOTW OWING TO
GIINPPT TIPPING	GILNORU LOURING	GINOPPP POPPING
GIINPPZ ZIPPING	GILNOSS LOSINGS	GINOPPS SOPPING
GIINPQU PIQUING	GILNOSU LOUSING	GINOPPT TOPPING
GIINPRS PRISING	GILNOSV SOLVING	GINOPRT PORTING
GIINPRZ PRIZING	GILNOSW SLOWING	GINOPRU IN-GROUP,
GIINPSS PISSING	GILNOTT LOTTING	POURING
GIINPST SPITING	GILNOWY YOWLING	GINOPRV PROVING
GIINPSW SWIPING	GILNPPU PULPING	GINOPST POSTING,
GIINPTT PITTING	GILNPRU PURLING	STOPING
GIINPTY PITYING	GILNPSU PULSING	GINOPTT POTTING
GIINRSS RISINGS	GILNRSU RULINGS	GINOPTU POUTING
GIINRSV VIRGINS	GILNSTU LUSTING	GINOQTU QUOTING
GIINRTW WRITING	GILNSTY STYLING	GINORSS SIGNORS
GIINSSU ISSUING	GILORTY TRILOGY	GINORST SORTING,
GIINSTT SITTING	GILOSTT GLOTTIS	STORING
GIINSTU SUITING	GILRSTY GRISTLY	GINORSU ROUSING,
GIJKNNU JUNKING	GILRTUY LITURGY	SOURING
GIJLNOT JOLTING	GILRYZZ GRIZZLY	GINORTT ROTTING

187

GINORTU ROUTING, TOURING	GNORSUV GUVNORS	HINOOST IN SOOTH
GINOSST TOSSING	GOORSTT GROTTOS	HINOPSS SIPHONS
GINOSSU SOUSING	GOORTUW OUTGROW	HINORSU NOURISH
GINOSTU OUSTING, OUTINGS	HHINNSU HUNNISH	HINORTT IN TROTH
	HHIORSW WHORISH	HINORTW THROW-IN
GINOSTW STOWING	HHMRSTY RHYTHMS	HINRSTU RUNTISH
GINOTTT TOTTING	HIIKNPS KINSHIP, PINKISH	HINSTUW WHITSUN
GINOTTU TOUTING	HIILLPP PHILLIP	HIOPRSW WORSHIP
GINPPPU PUPPING	HIILLPS PHILLIS	HIOPSST SOPHIST
GINPPSU SUPPING	HIILMTU LITHIUM	HIOPSSY PHYSIOS
GINPPTU TUPPING	HIILPTY PITHILY	HIORSTY HISTORY
GINPRRU PURRING	HIILSTT HIT LIST	HIOSSTT SOTTISH
GINPRSS SPRINGS	HIIMNSX MINXISH	HIOTTUW WITHOUT
GINPRSU PURSING	HIIMPSW WIMPISH	HIQSSUY SQUISHY
GINPRSY SPRINGY	HIINSSW SWINISH	HIRSSTT THIRSTS, T-SHIRTS
GINPSUW UPSWING	HIINSTW SWITHIN	HIRSTTU RUTTISH
GINPTTU PUTTING	HIKKOSU SHIKOKU	HIRSTTY THIRSTY
GINRSST STRINGS	HIKLSUY HUSKILY	HKKLOOZ KOLKHOZ
GINRSTU RUSTING	HIKMNOS MONKISH	HKNOOOS SHOOK ON
GINRSTY STRINGY	HIKMSUU SUKHUMI	HKNOOWW KNOW-HOW
GINRTTU RUTTING	HIKNNTU UNTHINK	HKOOOPT POTHOOK
GINSSSU SUSSING	HIKNOPS HOPKINS	HKOOPSU HOOKUPS
GIOPRRU PRURIGO	HIKNRSS SHRINKS	HKOOSVZ SOVKHOZ
GIOPSSS GOSSIPS	HIKRSTU TURKISH	HKORSWY WORKSHY
GIOPSST SPIGOTS	HILLPSY PHYLLIS	HLLOOSW HOLLOWS
GIOPSSY GOSSIPY	HILLRST THRILLS	HLMNOTY MONTHLY
GIORSTU RIG-OUTS	HILLRSY SHRILLY	HLORSTY SHORTLY
GIOSSYZ ZYGOSIS	HILMMOU HOLMIUM	HLPRSUU SULPHUR
GJOORTT JOG TROT	HILMPSU LUMPISH	HMMNOOY HOMONYM
GLMNOOS MONGOLS	HILMSUY MUSHILY	HMOOOST MOSOTHO
GLMOOYY MYOLOGY	HILMTUU THULIUM	HMOOSUU HOUMOUS
GLMORUW LUGWORM	HILNORY HORNILY	HMORSUU HUMOURS
GLNNOOR LORGNON	HILNOTY THIONYL	HNOOPTY TYPHOON
GLNNOOT LONG TON	HILNPST PLINTHS	HNOORSU HONOURS
GLNOOPR PROLONG	HILOOTT OTOLITH	HNOOSTU HOUSTON
GLNOOPY POLYGON	HILORSY HORSILY	HNOPSSY SYPHONS
GLNORWY WRONGLY	HILORTU UROLITH	HNOPSTY PYTHONS
GLNOSUW SUNGLOW	HILOSTU LOUTISH	HNRTTUU UNTRUTH
GLNOTTU GLUTTON	HILOSWY SHOWILY	HOOPSTT HOTPOTS, HOT SPOT, POTSHOT
GLOOORY OROLOGY	HILOTWW WHITLOW	
GLOOOTY OTOLOGY	HILPSUY PUSHILY	HOORRRS HORRORS
GLOOOYZ ZOOLOGY	HILSSTY STYLISH	HOPRSTU HOTSPUR
GLOORUY UROLOGY	HILSTTY THISTLY	HOPRTUW UPTHROW
GLOOSSW GO-SLOWS	HIMOORS MOORISH	HOPSTTU SHOT PUT
GLORSSY GROSSLY	HIMOPSS SOPHISM	HOPSTUY TYPHOUS
GMMPUUW MUGWUMP	HIMORTU THORIUM	HOSTTUU SHUTOUT
GMOOPRS POGROMS	HIMOTTY TIMOTHY	HPPSSUU PUSH-UPS
GMORSUU GRUMOUS	HIMPRSS SHRIMPS	HRSSTTU THRUSTS
GMORTUW MUGWORT	HIMPRTU TRIUMPH	HRSSTUY THYRSUS
GMRUYYZ ZYMURGY	HIMSSSU HUSSISM	IIJNSUU SINUIJU
GNOPPSU POPGUNS	HIMSSTU ISTHMUS	IIKKLNY KINKILY
GNOPRUW GROWN-UP	HINNOOT HONITON	IIKLLMY MILKILY
	HINOORZ HORIZON	IIKLLSY SILKILY

IIKLMNP LIMPKIN	IIORSTV VISITOR	ILMSTUY MUSTILY
IIKLNOS OILSKIN	IIOSTTT TITOIST	ILMUYZZ MUZZILY
IIKLPSY SPIKILY	IIPRSST SPIRITS	ILNNSUY SUNNILY
IIKLRSY RISKILY	IIPRTVY PRIVITY	ILNOOPS PLOSION
IIKNRST KRISTIN	IJJSTUU JUJITSU	ILNOORV LIVORNO
IILLLLW ILL WILL	IJKLLOY KILLJOY	ILNOOST LOTIONS
IILLMNO MILLION	IJKMPSU SKI JUMP	ILNOPRU PURLOIN
IILLMSY SLIMILY	IJLLLOY JOLLILY	ILNOPSS SLIP-ONS
IILLNOP PILLION	IJLLOTY JOLLITY	ILNOPSU UPSILON
IILLNOZ ZILLION	IJLMPUY JUMPILY	ILNORST NOSTRIL
IILMSTU STIMULI	IJLNOQU JONQUIL	ILNOSST TONSILS
IILMSTY MISTILY	IJLNOTY JOINTLY	ILNOSTT STILTON
IILNNSU INSULIN	IJNORSU JUNIORS	ILNOSTY STONILY
IILNNTY TINNILY	IJRSSTU JURISTS	ILNOSWY SNOWILY
IILNORS SIRLOIN	IKKRSTU IRKUTSK	ILNPSST SPLINTS
IILNOSV VIOLINS	IKLLSUY SULKILY	ILNSSTU INSULTS
IILNOSY NOISILY	IKLMNRU MILK RUN	ILNTTUY NUTTILY
IILNPPY NIPPILY	IKLMOPS MILKSOP	ILOOPST TOPSOIL
IILNSUV VILNIUS	IKLMOSY SMOKILY	ILOOSST SOLOIST
IILOPRT TRIPOLI	IKLMRUY MURKILY	ILOOSTY SOOTILY
IILORTV VITRIOL	IKLNOOT KILOTON	ILOOWYZ WOOZILY
IILOSTV VIOLIST	IKLNPSU LINKUPS	ILOPPSY SOPPILY
IILPRVY PRIVILY	IKLNRWY WRINKLY	ILOPRSY PROSILY
IILPSST PISTILS	IKMNOOS KIMONOS	ILOPSST PISTOLS
IILPSTY TIPSILY	IKMNPPU PUMPKIN	ILOPSTT SPOTLIT
IILPSWY WISPILY	IKMOOST MISTOOK	ILOPSUY PIOUSLY
IILTTUY UTILITY	IKNOPRW PINWORK	ILOQRTU TORQUIL
IILTTWY WITTILY	IKNORTW TINWORK	ILORRSY SORRILY
IIMMMNU MINIMUM	IKNPSTU SPUTNIK	ILOSSTY TYLOSIS
IIMMNSU MINIMUS	IKORSTY YORKIST	ILPPSSU SLIP-UPS
IIMNNOS MINIONS	ILLMNOU MULLION	ILPPSTU PULPITS
IIMNOSS MISSION	ILLMNRU MILLRUN	ILRSTUY RUSTILY
IIMNOSZ ZIONISM	ILLMPUY LUMPILY	ILRTTUY RUTTILY
IIMNPRT IMPRINT	ILLMSUU LIMULUS	ILSSTTY STYLIST
IIMOPSU IMPIOUS	ILLNPSU PULL-INS	IMMOPTU OPTIMUM
IIMOSST MITOSIS	ILLNPUU LUPULIN	IMMSSTU SUMMITS
IIMOSSU SIMIOUS	ILLNTUY NULLITY	IMNNOSW MINNOWS
IIMOSTT TITOISM	ILLOPRY PILLORY	IMNOORT MONITOR
IIMRTTU TRITIUM	ILLOPSW PILLOWS	IMNOOST MOTIONS
IINNOOP OPINION	ILLOSUV VILLOUS	IMNOOSU OMINOUS
IINNOPS PINIONS	ILLOSUY LOUSILY	IMNOOSY ISONOMY
IINNORS IN IRONS	ILLOSWW WILLOWS	IMNOPRW PINWORM
IINNQTU QUINTIN	ILLOTUW WILL OUT	IMOOSSS OSMOSIS
IINORST IRONIST	ILLOWWY WILLOWY	IMOOSSU OSMIOUS
IINORTT INTROIT	ILLRSUY SURLILY	IMOPRST IMPORTS,
IINORTV IN VITRO	ILLSTUY LUSTILY	TROPISM
IINOSSV VISIONS	ILMMSSU MUSLIMS	IMOPRTU PROTIUM
IINOSTZ ZIONIST	ILMNOOT MOONLIT	IMORRRS MIRRORS
IINOTTU TUITION	ILMNOOY MOONILY	IMORSTU TOURISM
IINPPPS PIPPINS	ILMOOPP LIMPOPO	IMORSTY TORYISM
IINQRUY INQUIRY	ILMOORY ROOMILY	IMOSSYZ ZYMOSIS
IINRTTY TRINITY	ILMORTU TURMOIL	IMOSTUV VOMITUS
IINSTTW NITWITS	ILMOSTY MOISTLY	IMQRSSU SQUIRMS

IMQRSUY SQUIRMY	IPRSSTU PURISTS	MOOOTYZ ZOOTOMY
IMRSSTU TRISMUS,	IPRSTUU PURSUIT	MOOPPSU POMPOUS
TRUISMS	IPSSSTY STYPSIS	MOOPSSU OPOSSUM
IMRTTUY YTTRIUM	IPSSTTY TYPISTS	MOOPSTT TOPMOST
INNNOOR NON-IRON	IQRSSTU SQUIRTS	MOORRSW MORROWS
INNOOPS OPSONIN	JNOORSU JOURNOS,	MOOSTTU OUTMOST
INNOOST NOTIONS	SOJOURN	MOPPRST PROMPTS
INNOSTU NONSUIT	KLNOOOW KOWLOON	MOPSSSU POSSUMS
INNOSTW WINSTON	KLOOOTU LOOKOUT,	MOPSSUU SPUMOUS
INOOPRT PORTION	OUTLOOK	MOQRSUU QUORUMS
INOOPSS POISONS	KNNNOUW UNKNOWN	MORRSTU ROSTRUM
INOOPST OPTIONS,	KNNOOTW NOT KNOW	MORRSUU RUMOURS
POTIONS	KNOOPTT TOPKNOT	MORSTUU TUMOURS
INOORSS ORISONS	KNOOSSS KNOSSOS	NNOOOPT PONTOON
INOORST ISOTRON,	KNOPRTY KRYPTON	NNOOPRS NON-PROS
NITROSO, TORSION	KOOPRTW WORKTOP	NNOOPRU PRONOUN
INOORTT TORTONI	KOORTUW OUTWORK,	NNOOPSS SPONSON
INOOSUX NOXIOUS	WORKOUT	NNOOPST NONSTOP
INOPPST TOPSPIN	LLMOOPR ROLLMOP	NNORSTU TURN-ONS
INOPPTY PIT PONY	LLNOORS ROLL-ONS	NOOOORTT TORONTO
INOPRSS PRISONS	LLOOPRT ROLL-TOP,	NOOPRSS SPONSOR
INOPSST PISTONS	TROLLOP	NOOPRST PROTONS
INOPSSU SPINOUS	LLOPTUU PULLOUT	NOORSTY ROYSTON
INORSTU NITROUS	LLORSST STROLLS	NOORTUW OUTWORN,
INORSUU RUINOUS,	LMMPSUU LUMP SUM	WORN-OUT
URINOUS	LMNOOOS SOLOMON	NOPPTUU PUT-UPON
INORTTY TRY IT ON	LMOPSUY OLYMPUS	NOPSSTU SUNSPOT
INOSSUU SINUOUS	LMSTTUU TUMULTS	NORTTUU TURNOUT
INPRSST SPRINTS	LMSTUUU TUMULUS	NPRSTUU TURN-UPS,
INPRSTU TURNIPS	LNNOPSU NONPLUS	UPTURNS
INPRSTY TRYPSIN	LNORSSY ROSSLYN	NRSSTUU UNTRUSS
INQSSTU SQUINTS	LOPPSUY POLYPUS	OOPPSVX VOX POPS
INQSTUY SQUINTY	LOPRSUY PYLORUS	OOPRSSU SOURSOP
INRSTTU INTRUST	LOPRTUY POULTRY	OOPRSTV PROVOST
IOOPRRT PRIOR TO	LOPSSTY STYLOPS	OOPRTTU OUTPORT
IOOPRSV PROVISO	LOSTTUY STOUTLY	OOPRTUU OUTPOUR
IOOPSTY ISOTOPY	LPRSSUU SURPLUS	OOPSTTU OUTPOST
IOORSSS SOROSIS	MMNOORS MORMONS	OOPSWWW POWWOWS
IOORSTT RISOTTO	MMNOSSU SUMMONS	OORRSSW SORROWS
IOORSTU RIOTOUS	MMOOPPS POMPOMS	OORSTTU SORT-OUT
IOOSSST OSTOSIS	MMOOSTT TOM-TOMS	OPPRRTU PURPORT
IOPPPRT PIT PROP	MMOPSTY SYMPTOM	OPPRSTU SUPPORT
IOPRSSY PYROSIS	MMRRSUU MURMURS	OPPRSTY STROPPY
IOPRSTT PROTIST	MNNOOOS MONSOON	OPRSSTU SPROUTS,
IOQRTTU QUITTOR	MNNOSYY SYNONYM	STUPORS
IORSSTU SUITORS	MNOOPTY TOPONYM	OPSSSTU TOSS-UPS
IORSTTU TOURIST	MNOPRTU NO-TRUMP	OPSTTUU OUTPUTS
IPPSSSU PISS-UPS	MNORSTU NOSTRUM	
IPRRSTU STIRRUP	MNOTTUY MUTTONY	

AAAABENN ANABAENA	AAACDOTV ADVOCAAT	AAAERTWY TEARAWAY
AAAACCRR CARACARA	AAACEHNR ARCHAEAN	AAAFGLNO FANAGALO
AAAACNRS ANASARCA	AAACELRT À LA CARTE	AAAFHHRT HAFTARAH
AAAADTVV AVADAVAT	AAACELST CATALASE	AAAFHILN HALAFIAN
AAAAGLRT AGARTALA	AAACENNP PANACEAN	AAAFINST FANTASIA
AAAAHJMR MAHARAJA	AAACENPS PANACEAS	AAAFINUV AVIFAUNA
AAAAIMPR ARAPAIMA	AAACGLSW SCALAWAG	AAAGGLLN GALANGAL
AAAAIRTX ATARAXIA	AAACGMNP CAMPAGNA	AAAGHINN GHANAIAN
AAAAKKNT KATAKANA	AAACGMNR ARMAGNAC	AAAGHINR HIRAGANA
AAAAKMWY WAKAYAMA	AAACHLLZ CHALAZAL	AAAGHIPR AGRAPHIA
AAAAKNRW ARAWAKAN	AAACIJMN JAMAICAN	AAAGIKNS NAGASAKI
AAAAKNWZ KANAZAWA	AAACILMN MANIACAL	AAAGINRR AGRARIAN
AAAANNST SANTA ANA	AAACILRV CALVARIA	AAAGJMNR JAMNAGAR
AAABBILT ABBATIAL	AAACILSY CALISAYA	AAAGLMMS AMALGAMS
AAABBNRS BARNABAS	AAACIMNP CAMPANIA	AAAGLMSY MALAGASY
AAABCCRT BACCARAT	AAACINTV CAVATINA	AAAGLNRW WARANGAL
AAABÇHLS CALABASH	AAACKMRT TAMARACK	AAAGLRST ASTRAGAL
AAABCILR CALABRIA	AAACLLTX TLAXCALA	AAAGMMRY GAMMA RAY
AAABCINT ANABATIC	AAACLMNS ALMANACS	AAAGMNNN NAMANGAN
AAABCNRU CARNAUBA	AAACLRTZ ALCATRAZ	AAAGMNRS ANAGRAMS
AAABCPRY CAPYBARA	AAACNOSV CASANOVA	AAAGMNRT RAMAT GAN
AAABDEST DATABASE	AAACNRSV CARAVANS	AAAGORZZ ZARAGOZA
AAABDFIZ FAIZABAD	AAACNSTT CANTATAS	AAAGPRUY PARAGUAY
AAABDLNO BADALONA	AAACRSWY CARAWAYS	AAAHHITW HIAWATHA
AAABDNNN BANDANNA	AAACSTWY CASTAWAY	AAAHHTWY HATHAWAY
AAABDNRS SARABAND	AAADELMS SALAAMED	AAAHIINW HAWAIIAN
AAABDNRT ABRADANT	AAADELRW A RAW DEAL	AAAHIKLR KALAHARI
AAABEHNR HABANERA	AAADENTV VANADATE	AAAHIMNR MAHARANI
AAABEHRT BARATHEA	AAADGGHH HAGGADAH	AAAHINNY HINAYANA
AAABELLR ARABELLA	AAADGHNR ANGHARAD	AAAHJLMT TAJ MAHAL
AAABGNST BATANGAS	AAADGLMY AMYGDALA	AAAHKNSW WAKASHAN
AAABGRTU RUTABAGA	AAADGLNN NAGALAND	AAAHMMST MAHATMAS
AAABHIKZ ABKHAZIA	AAADHHSS HADASSAH	AAAHMNOR MARANHAO
AAABHIMN BAHAMIAN	AAADHKNR KANDAHAR	AAAHMNRT AMARANTH
AAABHLMR ALHAMBRA	AAADHRTZ AT HAZARD	AAAHMNST SAMANTHA
AAABHPRT BHATPARA	AAADILMT DALMATIA	AAAHNNSV SAVANNAH
AAABILNN ALBANIAN	AAADILRS ALASDAIR	AAAHNOPR ANAPHORA
AAABINRV BAVARIAN	AAADILRU ADULARIA	AAAHNPPR HARAPPAN
AAABINSS ANABASIS	AAADIMNY ADYNAMIA	AAAIINPR APIARIAN
AAABLLRT BALLARAT	AAADJKRT DJAKARTA	AAAIKKSW KAWASAKI
AAABLOPR PARABOLA	AAADKRRV AARDVARK	AAAILLMR MALARIAL
AAABRSUY SURABAYA	AAADLMNY MANDALAY	AAAILLPT PALATIAL
AAACCEPR CARAPACE	AAADLNRS SAARLAND	AAAILMSV MALVASIA
AAACCISU CAUCASIA	AAADMNTU TAMANDUA	AAAILMSY MALAYSIA
AAACCRTT CATARACT	AAAEGNPP APPANAGE	AAAILNNS ANNALISA
AAACDEIM ACADEMIA	AAAEHLPR RAPHAELA	AAAILNOT ANATOLIA
AAACDENR DRACAENA	AAAEHMNT ANATHEMA	AAAILNST ALSATIAN
AAACDIMM MACADMIA	AAAEHNPS ANAPHASE	AAAILRST ALASTAIR
AAACDINN CANADIAN	AAAEKTWY TAKEAWAY	AAAIMNOR MARIANAO
AAACDINR ARCADIAN	AAAELMMN ANALEMMA	AAAIMNRT ARAMINTA
AAACDNNO ANACONDA	AAAELNPT PANATELA	AAAIMNST TASMANIA
AAACDNPR PANDA CAR	AAAENPRV PARAVANE	AAAIMRTV AMRAVATI
AAACDNRS SANDARAC	AAAENPST ANAPAEST	AAAINNTZ TANZANIA

AAAINOPR PARANOIA
AAAINRSV VARANASI
AAAINRTT TATARIAN
AAAIPSSV PIASSAVA
AAAIRRSV RARA AVIS
AAAKKMRU KAMAKURA
AAAKKORT KRAKATOA
AAAKLWWY WALKAWAY
AAAKNRSS ARKANSAS
AAALLPRX PARALLAX
AAALLPST PALATALS
AAALMNTZ MAZATLAN
AAALNRTT TARLATAN
AAAMNOPR PANORAMA
AAAMNOSZ AMAZONAS
AAAMOTTU AUTOMATA
AAANNSSV SAVANNAS
AAANOPRZ PARAZOAN
AAANQTUU AQUANAUT
AAAPQRTU PARAQUAT
AABBCDRS SCABBARD
AABBCEGS CABBAGES
AABBCEKR BAREBACK
AABBCINR BARBICAN
AABBCIRR BARBARIC
AABBCIST SABBATIC
AABBDHIU ABU DHABI
AABBDORS BARBADOS
AABBEELR BEARABLE
AABBEELT BEATABLE
AABBEILL BAILABLE
AABBELLM BLAMABLE
AABBELLS BASEBALL
AABBELRY BEARABLY
AABBGGRS GRAB BAGS
AABBIILL BILABIAL
AABBIRSU BABIRUSA
AABBKLTY BABY TALK
AABCCEHK BACKACHE
AABCCELR CABLE CAR
AABCCHKT BACKCHAT
AABCCINN CANNABIC
AABCCKKP BACKPACK
AABCCKLP BLACKCAP
AABCCMOT CATACOMB
AABCDEIN ABIDANCE
AABCDEIT ABDICATE
AABCDEKT BACKDATE
AABCDELN BALANCED
AABCDHKN BACKHAND
AABCDHKR HARDBACK
AABCDIIS DIABASIC
AABCDIKL LAID-BACK

AABCDIMO CAMBODIA
AABCDKRW BACKWARD,
    DRAWBACK
AABCDKRY BACKYARD
AABCEEFL FACEABLE
AABCEENY ABEYANCE
AABCEERT ACERBATE
AABCEGOT CABOTAGE
AABCEHLS CASHABLE
AABCEILM AMICABLE
AABCEILR BALEARIC
AABCEIRT BACTERIA
AABCEJNO JACOBEAN
AABCEKLM CLAMBAKE
AABCEKLP PACKABLE
AABCEKST BACK SEAT
AABCELLL CALLABLE
AABCELLP PLACABLE
AABCELLS SCALABLE
AABCELNR BALANCER,
    BARNACLE
AABCELNS BALANCES
AABCELOR ALBACORE
AABCELRT BRACTEAL
AABCELSU CAUSABLE
AABCELWY CABLEWAY
AABCEMRV VAMBRACE
AABCENRR CANBERRA
AABCEPRS SPACE-BAR
AABCERST CABARETS
AABCESSU ABACUSES
AABCFHKL HALFBACK
AABCFIIL BIFACIAL
AABCFKST FASTBACK
AABCGIMO CAMBOGIA
AABCHILR BRACHIAL
AABCHINR BRANCHIA
AABCHKLS BACKLASH
AABCHKSW BACKWASH
AABCHMRY CHAMBRAY
AABCHRRT BAR CHART
AABCIILR BIRACIAL
AABCIILS BASILICA
AABCIJNO JACOBIAN,
    JACOBINA
AABCIKLT TAILBACK
AABCILLR CABRILLA
AABCILMS BALSAMIC
AABCILMY AMICABLY
AABCILNN CANNIBAL
AABCILNO ANABOLIC
AABCIMNR CAMBRIAN
AABCINNN CANNABIN

AABCINNR CINNABAR
AABCINNS CANNABIS
AABCINRT BACTRIAN
AABCIRSS BRASSICA
AABCISSS ABSCISSA
AABCKKLT BACK TALK
AABCKLPY PLAYBACK
AABCKLRT BLACK ART
AABCKNPS SNAPBACK
AABCKNRS CAB RANKS,
    SNACK BAR
AABCKRRS BARRACKS
AABCKSTY BACKSTAY
AABCKSWY SWAY-BACK
AABCLLSY SCALABLY
AABCLNTY BLATANCY
AABCLOOR COOLABAR
AABCOORS SOROCABA
AABCORST ACROBATS
AABCRSTT ABSTRACT
AABDDEET DEAD BEAT
AABDDEGN BANDAGED
AABDDEHN HEADBAND
AABDDHNS DAB HANDS
AABDDLNS BADLANDS
AABDEELR READABLE
AABDEELT DATEABLE
AABDEELV EVADABLE
AABDEGIN BADINAGE
AABDEGLR GRADABLE
AABDEGNS BANDAGES
AABDEHKR HARDBAKE
AABDEKRY DAYBREAK
AABDELLS BALLADES,
    SABADELL
AABDELLU LAUDABLE
AABDELMN DAMNABLE
AABDELOR ADORABLE
AABDELPR DRAPABLE
AABDELRT TRADABLE
AABDELRW DRAWABLE
AABDELRY READABLY
AABDENOS A BAD NOSE
AABDENTU UNABATED
AABDENVW WAVE BAND
AABDEORS SEABOARD
AABDFHIT BAD FAITH
AABDFHLN FAHLBAND
AABDGHNS HANDBAGS
AABDGHOT GODTHAAB
AABDGINR ABRADING
AABDGNOV VAGABOND
AABDGNSS SANDBAGS

AABDGORR GARBOARD
AABDGOTU GADABOUT
AABDHLLN HANDBALL
AABDHLLR HARDBALL
AABDHNST HATBANDS
AABDHRUY BURAYDAH
AABDHRYZ BY HAZARD
AABDIILR BIRADIAL
AABDIILS BASIDIAL
AABDIMRS BARMAIDS
AABDINNR RAINBAND
AABDINNU DANUBIAN
AABDIOST BIODATAS
AABDKNNS SANDBANK
AABDLLRY BALLADRY
AABDLLUY LAUDABLY
AABDLMNU LABDANUM
AABDLMNY DAMNABLY
AABDLMRU ADUMBRAL
AABDLOOT BOATLOAD
AABDLOPR LAPBOARD
AABDLORR LABRADOR,
LARBOARD
AABDLRSV SVALBARD
AABDLRSW BRADAWLS
AABDMNNS BANDSMAN
AABDMNRS ARMBANDS
AABDNNTU ABUNDANT
AABDNRRY BARNYARD
AABDNRSS SANDBARS
AABDORWY BROADWAY
AABDRRSS BRASSARD
AABDRSST BASTARDS
AABDRSTY BASTARDY
AABEEFLN FLEABANE
AABEEGKR BREAKAGE
AABEEGNT ABNEGATE
AABEEHLL HEALABLE
AABEEHLR HEARABLE
AABEEHLT HATEABLE
AABEEHMR HARAMBEE
AABEEKRT TEA BREAK
AABEELLS LEASABLE,
SALEABLE, SEALABLE
AABEELMN AMENABLE
AABEELMT MATABELE,
TAMEABLE
AABEELPR REAPABLE
AABEELRS ERASABLE
AABEELRT TEARABLE
AABEELRW WEARABLE
AABEEMPR ABAMPERE
AABEENOR ANAEROBE

AABEERST BASE RATE
AABEFGLS FLEABAGS
AABEFHKL HALFBEAK
AABEFLMR FARMABLE,
FRAMABLE
AABEFLMU FLAMBEAU
AABEGGGS BAGGAGES
AABEGILN GAINABLE
AABEGLLL GLABELLA
AABEGLLM BALL GAME
AABEGLNW GNAWABLE
AABEGLRU ARGUABLE
AABEGMNY MANGABEY
AABEGNOR BARONAGE
AABEGORT ABROGATE
AABEGOST SABOTAGE
AABEGRRS BARRAGES
AABEHIMS MAEBASHI
AABEHKLS SHAKABLE
AABEHLMS SHAMABLE
AABEHLPS SHAPABLE
AABEHLPT ALPHABET
AABEHLRS SHARABLE
AABEHLSV SHAVABLE
AABEHLSW WASHABLE
AABEIKRR AIRBRAKE
AABEILLM MAILABLE
AABEILLS ISABELLA,
SAILABLE
AABEILMN LIMA BEAN
AABEILRS RAISABLE
AABEILRV VARIABLE
AABEILST SATIABLE
AABEILTV ABLATIVE
AABEIRSS AIRBASES
AABEIRSV ABRASIVE
AABEISUV BEAUVAIS
AABEKLLS SLAKABLE
AABEKLLT TALKABLE
AABEKLLW WALKABLE
AABEKNRS NEBRASKA
AABEKNRT BANK RATE
AABEKOTU ABEOKUTA
AABELLMT MEATBALL
AABELLNO LOANABLE
AABELLOV ABOVE ALL
AABELLPP PALPABLE
AABELLPS LAPSABLE
AABELLPY PLAYABLE
AABELLSV SALVABLE
AABELLSY SALEABLY
AABELLUV VALUABLE
AABELMPP MAPPABLE

AABELMST BLASTEMA,
LAMBASTE
AABELMTT TABLEMAT
AABELMTU AMBULATE
AABELNOT ATONABLE
AABELNPS ANABLEPS
AABELORR ARBOREAL
AABELOVW AVOWABLE
AABELPPT TAPPABLE
AABELPRS PARABLES,
PARSABLE, SPARABLE
AABELPSS PASSABLE
AABELRTY BETRAYAL
AABELSTT STATABLE,
TASTABLE
AABELSTU TABLEAUS
AABELSTW WASTABLE
AABELSWY SWAYABLE
AABELTTU TABULATE
AABELTUX TABLEAUX
AABENOSY SOYA BEAN
AABENRRT ABERRANT
AABENRST RATSBANE
AABENSTU ANTABUSE
AABFLOTT FALTBOAT,
FLATBOAT
AABGGGNN GANG-BANG
AABGGRRT BRAGGART
AABGHKRS SHAGBARK
AABGHPRR BAR GRAPH
AABGILMS MAILBAGS
AABGILRU BULGARIA
AABGINRS BARGAINS
AABGLMNU GALBANUM
AABGLNPS SLAP-BANG
AABGLRUW WALBURGA
AABGLRUY ARGUABLY
AABGMORR BAROGRAM
AABHHORU BROUHAHA
AABHIINR BAHRAINI
AABHIINU BAUHINIA
AABHILLR HAIRBALL
AABHILLN HANNIBAL
AABHILTU HABITUAL
AABHIMNR BRAHMANI
AABHINTT HABITANT
AABHISTT HABITATS
AABHKKKU HABAKKUK
AABHMNRS BRAHMANS
AABHMSTT BATH MATS
AABHNOTU AUTOBAHN
AABHRSST BRASS HAT
AABIILRS BRASILIA

AABIIMNN NAMIBIAN	AACCDHRS CASH CARD	AACDEINR RADIANCE
AABIKLNU KINABALU	AACCDOVY ADVOCACY	AACDEJNT ADJACENT
AABILMNS BAILSMAN	AACCEENT CETACEAN	AACDEKTT ATTACKED
AABILNNU BIANNUAL	AACCEFKP FACE PACK	AACDELMN MANACLED
AABILNOR BARONIAL	AACCEFLO COALFACE	AACDELNR CALENDAR,
AABILNOT ABLATION	AACCEHIX CACHEXIA	LANDRACE
AABILNRU BINAURAL	AACCEIRR CERCARIA	AACDELNV VALANCED
AABILNTY BANALITY	AACCEKRS SACK RACE	AACDELPT PLACATED
AABILRRT ARBITRAL	AACCELOR CARACOLE	AACDENPT TAP DANCE
AABILRSY BASILARY	AACCELTY CALYCATE	AACDENRV ADVANCER
AABILRVY VARIABLY	AACCENTU ACUTANCE	AACDENRW WAR DANCE
AABILSTY SATIABLY	AACCERTU ACCURATE	AACDENSV ADVANCES
AABIMMRS MARIMBAS	AACCFILR FARCICAL	AACDENSZ CADENZAS
AABIMNOT MANITOBA	AACCGILT GALACTIC	AACDEOTV ADVOCATE
AABIMORS AMBROSIA	AACCHHRT CARTHACH	AACDEQUY ADEQUACY
AABINNPR BRAINPAN	AACCHINR ANARCHIC,	AACDERST CADASTER
AABINORS ABRASION	CHARACIN	AACDERSV CADAVERS
AABINRTZ BARTIZAN	AACCHISV VISCACHA	AACDETTU ACTUATED
AABINRZZ ZANZIBAR	AACCHLLT CATCH-ALL	AACDFIST ACID-FAST
AABIORTT ABATTOIR	AACCHLOR CHARCOAL	AACDGGHI HAGGADIC
AABIOSSY BIO-ASSAY	AACCHLOT CACHALOT	AACDGINR CARANGID,
AABISTUZ ZAIBATSU	AACCHMNO COACHMAN	CARDIGAN
AABJLPRU JABALPUR	AACCIINV VACCINIA	AACDHHKR HARDHACK
AABKLLPR BALL PARK	AACCIIST SCIATICA	AACDHHRS HARD CASH
AABKOOSZ BAZOOKAS	AACCILNU CULIACAN	AACDHINP HANDICAP
AABKOPRS SOAPBARK	AACCILNV VACCINAL	AACDHINR ARACHNID
AABLLMOR BALMORAL	AACCILRU ACICULAR	AACDHKRT HARD TACK
AABLLPPY PALPABLY	AACCILTT TACTICAL	AACDHLNP HANDCLAP
AABLLSTU BLASTULA	AACCIPTY CAPACITY	AACDHLRY CHARLADY
AABLLSVY SALVABLY	AACCLLST CATCALLS	AACDHMRS DRACHMAS
AABLMNOR ABNORMAL	AACCLOPU ACAPULCO	AACDHNRT HANDCART
AABLMNTU AMBULANT	AACCLTTU CALCUTTA	AACDIINR ACID RAIN
AABLOTUY LAYABOUT	AACCOPRS ASCOCARP	AACDIINS ASCIDIAN
AABLOUWY BULAWAYO	AACCOSTT STACCATO,	AACDIIRT ADRIATIC
AABLPSSY PASSABLY	TOCCATAS	AACDILLP PALLADIC
AABLSTTU ABUTTALS	AACCSSUU CAUCASUS	AACDILMT DALMATIC
AABMMOSU ABOMASUM	AACDDENV ADVANCED	AACDILMU CALADIUM
AABMMOSY MAMA'S BOY	AACDDETY TEA CADDY	AACDILNO DIACONAL
AABMNRTU RAMBUTAN	AACDDINR RADICAND	AACDILNR CARDINAL,
AABMORSU MARABOUS	AACDEEHH HEADACHE	CLARINDA
AABNNOSZ BONANZAS	AACDEEHR HEADRACE	AACDILNU DULCIANA
AABNOSTW BOTSWANA	AACDEELS ESCALADE	AACDILOZ ZODIACAL
AABORRRT BARRATOR	AACDEEOR AREA CODE	AACDILRS RADICALS
AABORSTT BAROSTAT	AACDEEPS ESCAPADE	AACDIMNY ADYNAMIC
AABRRRTY BARRATRY	AACDEGKP PACKAGED	AACDIMRT DRAMATIC
AACCCHHU CACHUCHA	AACDEHHY HEADACHY	AACDIOTU AUTACOID
AACCCLOO COCA-COLA	AACDEHIN HACIENDA	AACDIRTY CARYATID
AACCCRUY ACCURACY	AACDEHLP CEPHALAD	AACDITUY AUDACITY
AACCDDES CASCADED	AACDEHMR DRACHMAE	AACDJKSW JACKDAWS
AACCDEFR FACE CARD	AACDEHRS CHARADES	AACDJQRU JACQUARD
AACCDEIM ACADEMIC	AACDEHRT CATHEDRA	AACDKLNU AUCKLAND
AACCDELO ACCOLADE	AACDEHTT ATTACHED	AACDLLUY CAUDALLY
AACCDESS CASCADES	AACDEIMN MAENADIC	AACDLNSS SCANDALS

AACDLOSV CALVADOS
AACDLPRS PLACARDS
AACDMMOR CARDAMOM
AACDMSSU DAMASCUS
AACDNSST SAND-CAST
AACDOOSV AVOCADOS
AACDQRSU SQUAD CAR
AACEEFIT FACETIAE
AACEEFLP PALEFACE
AACEEGLV CLEAVAGE
AACEEGPS SPACE-AGE
AACEEHLR HERACLEA
AACEEIMT EMACIATE
AACEEINN ENCAENIA
AACEEIRT ACIERATE
AACEEKST TEACAKES
AACEELRT LACERATE
AACEELST ESCALATE
AACEELTU ACULEATE
AACEEMRT MACERATE
AACEEMST CASEMATE
AACEENNT CATENANE
AACEENRS CESAREAN
AACEENTT CATENATE
AACEEPSS SEASCAPE
AACEERTV ACERVATE
AACEETUV EVACUATE
AACEETVX EXCAVATE
AACEFFIN AFFIANCE
AACEFIST FASCIATE
AACEFRTT ARTEFACT
AACEGHRT CARTHAGE
AACEGILN ANGELICA
AACEGILT GLACIATE
AACEGINR CANAIGRE
AACEGIRR CARRIAGE
AACEGIRV VICARAGE
AACEGKPR PACKAGER
AACEGKPS PACKAGES
AACEGMUY CAMAGUEY
AACEHILL HELIACAL
AACEHILM MICHAELA
AACEHILN ACHENIAL
AACEHIMR CHIMAERA
AACEHIMT HAEMATIC
AACEHIPT HEPATICA
AACEHIRS ARCHAISE
AACEHIRZ ARCHAIZE
AACEHLRT TRACHEAL
AACEHLRX EXARCHAL
AACEHMRS MARCHESA
AACEHMST SCHEMATA
AACEHRST TRACHEAS

AACEHRTT ATTACHER
AACEHSTT ATTACHÉS
AACEIKMT KAMACITE
AACEILLM CAMELLIA
AACEILLN ALLIANCE,
   CANAILLE
AACEILMN CALAMINE
AACEILMT CALAMITE
AACEILNS CANALISE
AACEILNT ALICANTE,
   ANALCITE
AACEILNV VALENCIA,
   VALIANCE
AACEILNZ CANALIZE
AACEILOP ALOPECIA
AACEILRT TAILRACE
AACEILRV CAVALIER
AACEIMNR AMERICAN,
   CINERAMA, IN CAMERA
AACEIMNS AMNESIAC
AACEIMTT CATAMITE
AACEINNO OCEANIAN
AACEINPZ PIACENZA
AACEINRS CANARIES
AACEINRT CARINATE,
   CRANIATE
AACEINRV VARIANCE
AACEINST ESTANCIA
AACEIPPS PAPACIES
AACEIPRS AIRSPACE
AACEIPTT APATETIC,
   CAPITATE
AACEISTU EUSTACIA
AACEITTV ACTIVATE
AACEKKLW CAKEWALK
AACEKLST SALT CAKE
AACEKNPS PANCAKES
AACEKOST OATCAKES
AACEKRTT ATTACKER
AACELLLR ALL CLEAR
AACELLMR MARCELLA
AACELLOT ALLOCATE
AACELMNS MANACLES
AACELMPT PLACE MAT
AACELMPU MEA CULPA
AACELMRS CARAMELS
AACELNPR PARLANCE
AACELNPT PLACENTA
AACELNPY ANYPLACE
AACELNRT LACERANT
AACELNST ANALECTS
AACELNSV VALANCES
AACELRWY CLEARWAY

AACELSTY CATALYSE
AACELTTY CATTLEYA
AACEMNPS SPACEMAN
AACEMRRS ARMS RACE
AACEMRSS MASSACRE
AACENPRS PANCREAS
AACENPSU SAUCEPAN
AACENRSS SARACENS
AACENRTT REACTANT
AACENRTY CATENARY
AACENSSV CANVASES
AACENTUV EVACUANT
AACEORTV CAVEATOR
AACEOSST SEACOAST
AACERRTU ARCATURE
AACERSSU CAESURAS
AACERSTT CASTRATE
AACERTTT TRACTATE
AACESUWY CAUSEWAY
AACFHMST CAMSHAFT
AACFILLY FACIALLY
AACFINRS AFRICANS
AACFINST FANATICS
AACFIOPR A FAIR COP
AACFIRRT AIRCRAFT
AACFIRTT ARTIFACT
AACFJKLP FLAPJACK
AACFMNNY FANCY MAN
AACGGINO ANAGOGIC
AACGGIOP APAGOGIC
AACGHHNS CHANGSHA
AACGHNNN NANCHANG
AACGHOPZ GAZPACHO
AACGIILN GALICIAN
AACGIILR CAGLIARI
AACGIIMN MAGICIAN
AACGILNN ANGLICAN
AACGILNV GALVANIC
AACGILOU GUAIACOL
AACGILOX COXALGIA
AACGIMNN MANGANIC
AACGIMNP CAMPAIGN
AACGIMOP APOGAMIC
AACGIMRR MARGARIC
AACGIMUU GUAIACUM
AACGINTV VACATING
AACGISTY SAGACITY
AACGLMOU GLAUCOMA
AACGLORS CALOR GAS
AACGNRVY VAGRANCY
AACHHKNU CHANUKAH
AACHHTWY HATCHWAY
AACHILMS CHIASMAL

AACHILMT THALAMIC
AACHILNP CHAPLAIN
AACHILOU COAHUILA
AACHILPS CALIPASH
AACHILRV ARCHIVAL
AACHIMNN CHAINMAN,
  CHINAMAN
AACHIMNR CHAIRMAN,
  CHARMIAN
AACHIMRR ARMCHAIR
AACHIMRS ARCHAISM,
  CHARISMA
AACHINSW CHAIN SAW
AACHIPTT CHAPATTI
AACHIRSS CHARISSA
AACHIRST ARCHAIST
AACHKSSW HACKSAWS
AACHKSTY HAYSTACK
AACHLMNO MONACHAL
AACHLPRT LAP-CHART
AACHLSTU CALATHUS
AACHMNTW WATCHMAN
AACHMORT ACHROMAT,
  TRACHOMA
AACHMPRY PHARMACY
AACHNORT AT ANCHOR
AACHNRST TRASHCAN
AACHNSTU ACANTHUS
AACHOPPR APPROACH
AACHRSWY ARCHWAYS
AACHRTUY AUTARCHY
AACIILRV VICARIAL
AACIIPRT PATRICIA
AACIJLMO MAJOLICA
AACIJNOP JAPONICA
AACIKRTU AUTARKIC
AACILLMR LACRIMAL
AACILLRY RACIALLY
AACILMNT CALAMINT,
  CLAIMANT
AACILMTY CALAMITY
AACILNOR CAROLINA
AACILNRV CARNIVAL
AACILNTT ATLANTIC,
  TANTALIC
AACILNTU NAUTICAL
AACILNTY ANALYTIC
AACILOTT COAT-TAIL,
  TAILCOAT
AACILPRU PIACULAR
AACILPST APLASTIC,
  CAPITALS
AACILPTY ATYPICAL

AACILRSS CLARISSA
AACILRTY ALACRITY
AACILRUU AURICULA
AACILSTT STATICAL
AACILSTY SALACITY
AACIMMNO AMMONIAC
AACIMMRS MARASMIC
AACIMNOR MACARONI
AACIMNPS CAMPINAS
AACIMORT AROMATIC
AACINORS OCARINAS
AACINORT CATRIONA,
  RAINCOAT
AACINOTV OCTAVIAN,
  VACATION
AACINPST CAPTAINS
AACINQTU ACQUAINT
AACINRSZ CZARINAS
AACINSTZ STANZAIC
AACIPRTY RAPACITY
AACIQSTU AQUATICS
AACIRRTT TARTARIC
AACJKRST JACK TARS
AACJKSTY JACKSTAY
AACKKNPS KNAPSACK
AACKLSTW CATWALKS
AACKPRRS CAR PARKS
AACLLRRY CARRYALL
AACLLRSY RASCALLY
AACLLSUY CASUALLY,
  CAUSALLY
AACLLTUY ACTUALLY
AACLMNNS CLANSMAN
AACLMRRU MACRURAL
AACLNNOT CANTONAL
AACLNNOW CANON LAW
AACLNOPR COPLANAR
AACLNORU LA CORUNA
AACLNTVY VACANTLY
AACLORRU ORACULAR
AACLORSU CAROUSAL
AACLORTT CARLOTTA
AACLORUV VACUOLAR
AACLPPRT CLAPTRAP
AACLPRSU CAPSULAR,
  SCAPULAR
AACLPRTY CALYPTRA
AACLPSSU SCAPULAS
AACLPTTU CATAPULT
AACLRSUV VASCULAR
AACLSTTY CATALYST
AACLSTUY CASUALTY
AACMNOOR MACAROON

AACMNPRY RAMPANCY
AACMNRRU MACRURAN
AACMNSTX MANX CATS
AACNPSST CAPSTANS
AACNRSTT TRANSACT
AACOPRSU ACARPOUS
AACOPSTV POSTCAVA
AACORRTV VARACTOR
AACORSTT CASTRATO
AACORTTU ACTUATOR,
  AUTOCRAT
AACPSSTW CAT'S PAWS
AACSTUWY CUTAWAYS
AADDEEHT DEAD HEAT
AADDEEIL ADELAIDE
AADDEFIS DEAF-AIDS
AADDEFLL DEADFALL
AADDEHLN HEADLAND
AADDEHMN HANDMADE
AADDEHRW HEADWARD
AADDEHRZ HAZARDED
AADDEIRT RADIATED
AADDEMNT MANDATED
AADDEMRY DAYDREAM
AADDGHLN GLAD HAND
AADDGNRS GRANDADS
AADDHHIL LAH-DI-DAH
AADDLLNY LANDLADY
AADDLNRW LANDWARD
AADDNRST STANDARD
AADDOTYY DAY-TO-DAY
AADEEGHR HEADGEAR
AADEEGHT GET AHEAD
AADEEGMN ENDAMAGE
AADEEGRV AVERAGED
AADEEILR AIREDALE
AADEEIRT ERADIATE
AADEEKNW AWAKENED
AADEELNN ANNEALED
AADEELPP APPEALED
AADEELRW DELAWARE
AADEEMNT EMANATED
AADEEMRR DEMERARA
AADEENTT ANTEDATE
AADEEPPR APPEARED
AADEEPPS APPEASED
AADEEQTU ADEQUATE
AADEFHLT FLATHEAD
AADEFHST FATHEADS,
  HEADFAST
AADEFILR FAIRLEAD
AADEFIRS FARADISE
AADEFIRZ FARADIZE

AADEFLLR FALDERAL,
  LEAF-LARD
AADEFLRY DEFRAYAL
AADEGILL DIALLAGE,
  LEGAL AID
AADEGILT GLADIATE
AADEGINR DRAINAGE,
  GARDENIA
AADEGITT AGITATED
AADEGKRS DARK AGES
AADEGLMN MAGDALEN
AADEGLMY AMYGDALE
AADEGLSV SALVAGED
AADEGMPR RAMPAGED
AADEGMSS MASSAGED
AADEGNRR ARRANGED
AADEGNST DAGESTAN
AADEGPRT TRADE GAP
AADEGRRT RAG TRADE
AADEGRTU GRADUATE
AADEGSSU ASSUAGED
AADEHILN NAILHEAD
AADEHILR HEADRAIL,
  RAILHEAD
AADEHILS HEADSAIL
AADEHIWY HIDEAWAY
AADEHKOT HAKODATE
AADEHLNR ANHEDRAL
AADEHMNS HEADSMAN
AADEHMST MASTHEAD
AADEHRRW HARDWARE
AADEHRSS HARASSED
AADEHRSW WARHEADS
AADEHSSY SASHAYED
AADEHSWY HEADWAYS
AADEIIMV VIA MEDIA
AADEIKLP KLAIPEDA
AADEILLN DANIELLA
AADEILMN MADELINA
AADEILMS MALADIES
AADEILPR PRAEDIAL
AADEILPS PALISADE
AADEILRS SALARIED
AADEILSS ASSAILED
AADEILTV VALIDATE
AADEIMNR MARINADE
AADEIMNT ANIMATED,
  DIAMANTE
AADEIMST ADAMSITE,
  DIASTEMA
AADEINNR ADRIANNE
AADEINTT ATTAINED
AADEIPRS PARADISE

AADEIPSU DIAPAUSE
AADEIPTV ADAPTIVE
AADEISST DIASTASE
AADEISTT SATIATED
AADEJNNP JAPANNED
AADEKMNR MANDRAKE
AADELLPP APPALLED
AADELMNR ALDERMAN
AADELMNS DALESMAN,
  LEADSMAN
AADELNSY ANALYSED
AADELPPT PALPATED
AADELRSW RAW DEALS
AADEMNST MANDATES
AADEMNSY NAME DAYS
AADEMRRU MARAUDER
AADENNST ANDANTES
AADENRRT NARRATED
AADENRSV VERANDAS
AADEPRST ADAPTERS
AADEQRTU QUADRATE
AADERRRW REARWARD
AADERSSW SEAWARDS
AADERSTW EASTWARD
AADFGLSY FLAG DAYS
AADFGNNO FANDANGO
AADFHMNR FARMHAND
AADFHNST HANDFAST
AADFIMRS FARADISM
AADFKLLN FALKLAND
AADFLLLN LANDFALL
AADFLMNR FARMLAND
AADFLORW AARDWOLF
AADFLOTX TOADFLAX
AADFLOWY FOLDAWAY
AADFMRRY FARMYARD
AADGGIMN DAMAGING
AADGGLNN GANGLAND
AADGGLRS GLAD RAGS,
  LAGGARDS
AADGGRST STAGGARD
AADGHINN GANDHIAN
AADGHIPR DIAGRAPH
AADGIINS GAINSAID
AADGILLR GALLIARD
AADGILMR MADRIGAL
AADGILNO DIAGONAL
AADGIMPR PARADIGM
AADGIMRS DIAGRAMS
AADGINPR PARADING
AADGINPT ADAPTING
AADGINRU GUARDIAN
AADGINRW AWARDING

AADGLMNR GRAND MAL
AADGLNRS GARLANDS
AADGLOPR PODAGRAL
AADGMNOR DRAGOMAN,
  GARAMOND
AADGMNRS GRANDMAS
AADGNPRS GRANDPAS
AADGNRTU GUARDANT
AADGNRUV VANGUARD
AADHILLR HALLIARD
AADHILNR HANDRAIL
AADHILNT THAILAND
AADHILNU LUDHIANA
AADHILRV HAVILDAR
AADHINNZ ANDIZHAN
AADHINRR HARRIDAN
AADHLPSS SLAPDASH
AADHLRSY HALYARDS
AADHMNNY HANDYMAN
AADHMNRU DAMANHUR
AADHSSWY WASHDAYS
AADIIMRT DIARMAIT
AADIINRS SARDINIA
AADIIRRS AIR RAIDS
AADIKLLO ALKALOID
AADIKORT TAKORADI
AADILLLO ALLODIAL
AADILLRY RADIALLY
AADILMNN MAINLAND
AADILMOV MOLDAVIA
AADILMRS ADMIRALS
AADILNPR PRANDIAL
AADILNPS PALADINS
AADILNRU LAURINDA
AADILNTT DILATANT
AADILORR RAILROAD
AADILPRY LAPIDARY
AADILRST DIASTRAL
AADIMNNR MANDARIN
AADIMNOT MANATOID
AADIMNRT TAMARIND
AADIMNRY DAIRYMAN
AADIMNUV VANADIUM
AADIMSTZ SAMIZDAT
AADINOPR PARANOID
AADINOPS DIAPASON
AADINPRS SPANIARD
AADIOPRS DIASPORA
AADIORRT RADIATOR
AADIRRSY DISARRAY
AADJNTTU ADJUTANT
AADJNTUV ADJUVANT
AADJRTZZ TRAD JAZZ

AADKLMNR LANDMARK	AAEEKMRT TEA-MAKER	AAEGILNR ALGERIAN,
AADKLNPR PARKLAND	AAEEKNRS KANARESE	GERANIAL
AADKMNTU KATMANDU	AAEEKNRW REAWAKEN	AAEGILNT AGENTIAL,
AADKNRST TANKARDS	AAEEKPRT PARAKEET	ALGINATE
AADKORWY WORKADAY	AAEEKPTW TAKE A PEW	AAEGILSX GALAXIES
AADLLMRS MALLARDS	AAEEKQSU SEAQUAKE	AAEGILTT TAILGATE
AADLLMSS SMALL ADS	AAEELLMR AMARELLE	AAEGIMNO EGOMANIA
AADLMNOR MANDORLA	AAEELMMT METAMALE	AAEGIMNS MAGNESIA
AADLMNRY MARYLAND	AAEELMNU EMANUELA	AAEGIMNT AGMINATE
AADLMNSS LANDMASS	AAEELNNR ANNEALER	AAEGIMNZ MAGAZINE
AADLMNUU LAUDANUM	AAEELNOR ELEANORA	AAEGIMRR MARRIAGE
AADLNOPR PARLANDO	AAEELNPS SEAPLANE,	AAEGINPS PAGANISE
AADLNRSY LANYARDS	SPELAEAN	AAEGINPT PAGINATE
AADLOPSY PAYLOADS	AAEELPPR APPEALER	AAEGINPZ PAGANIZE
AADLORST LOADSTAR	AAEELPRY LEAP YEAR	AAEGINRT AERATING
AADLORSV SALVADOR	AAEELRTU LAUREATE	AAEGINTV NAVIGATE,
AADLORTU ADULATOR	AAEELTUV EVALUATE	VAGINATE
AADMMNSU MANDAMUS	AAEEMMTT TEAM-MATE	AAEGIRSV VAGARIES
AADMNNOS MADONNAS	AAEEMNRT MAN-EATER	AAEGIRTX EX GRATIA
AADMNRSS MANSARDS	AAEEMSSS ASSAMESE	AAEGISSS ASSEGAIS
AADMORST MATADORS	AAEENNRZ NAZARENE	AAEGIVWY GIVEAWAY
AADMRRSY YARDARMS	AAEENRST ARSENATE,	AAEGKTTT KATTEGAT
AADNNORR ANDORRAN	NEAR EAST, SERENATA	AAEGLLMN MAGELLAN
AADNNPSU PANDANUS	AAEENRTT ANTEATER	AAEGLLPR PELLAGRA
AADNOPSS SANDSOAP	AAEENSTU NAUSEATE	AAEGLLSS GALLEASS
AADNOSUV VANADOUS	AAEEPPRR REAPPEAR	AAEGLNOU ANALOGUE
AADNOSWY NOWADAYS	AAEEPRST SEPARATE	AAEGLNTU ANGULATE
AADNPRST SAND TRAP	AAEERSTT STEARATE	AAEGLRST AGRESTAL
AADNPSTT STAND PAT	AAEFFILS FAIL-SAFE	AAEGLRSV SALVAGER
AADNQRTU QUADRANT	AAEFFNRS FANFARES	AAEGLSSV LAS VEGAS
AADNQRUY QUANDARY	AAEFGHRW WHARFAGE	AAEGLSVY SAVAGELY
AADOPPRR PARADROP	AAEFGIMR FAIR GAME	AAEGMNRS MANAGERS,
AADORSVY SAVOYARD	AAEFGLOT FLOATAGE	SEMARANG
AADRSTUY SATURDAY	AAEFILTY FAYALITE	AAEGMNRV GRAVAMEN
AAEEFLNW A NEW LEAF	AAEFIMRR AIRFRAME	AAEGMNST MAGNATES
AAEEFRRS SEAFARER	AAEFINNT FAINEANT	AAEGMORR AEROGRAM
AAEEGILN ALIENAGE	AAEFLMTT FLATMATE	AAEGMPRR RAMPAGER
AAEEGKLS LEAKAGES	AAEFLPSY PLAY SAFE	AAEGMRRT MARGARET
AAEEGMPR AMPERAGE	AAEFLRTW FLATWARE	AAEGMRSS MASSAGER
AAEEGNNO NEOGAEAN	AAEFRRWY WAYFARER	AAEGMRSW WAR GAMES
AAEEGNRS SANGAREE	AAEGGIOT AGIOTAGE	AAEGMRTU AGERATUM
AAEEGRRY GREY AREA	AAEGGLNU LANGUAGE	AAEGMSSS MASSAGES
AAEEGRSV AVERAGES	AAEGGLNY LAY AN EGG	AAEGMTTW MEGAWATT
AAEEGRTW WATERAGE	AAEGGNRY GARGANEY	AAEGNOOR NO-GO AREA
AAEEHHRR HEAR! HEAR!	AAEGGOPR PARAGOGE	AAEGNOOT NOTOGAEA
AAEEHIMR HAEREMAI	AAEGHIRS HARGEISA	AAEGNPST PAGEANTS
AAEEHRTW AWEATHER,	AAEGHLNP PHALANGE	AAEGNRRR ARRANGER
WHEATEAR	AAEGHLPS SLAGHEAP	AAEGNSTT STAGNATE
AAEEHTVW HEAT WAVE	AAEGHMRX HEXAGRAM	AAEGORRT ARROGATE
AAEEILNT ALIENATE	AAEGHNRU HARANGUE	AAEGORTT AEGROTAT
AAEEJNPS JAPANESE	AAEGILLM GAMALIEL	AAEGPSSS PASSAGES
AAEEJNSV JAVANESE	AAEGILLN GALILEAN	AAEGRSSU ASSUAGER
AAEEKMNS NAMESAKE	AAEGILNN ANGELINA	AAEGRSTT REGATTAS

AAEGRSTZ STARGAZE
AAEGRSVY SAVAGERY
AAEGSSSU SAUSAGES
AAEGSTWY GATEWAYS
AAEHHRST HEAT RASH
AAEHILNP APHELIAN
AAEHIMNT HAEMATIN
AAEHINNT ATHENIAN
AAEHINPT APHANITE
AAEHINRT RHAETIAN
AAEHINST ASTHENIA
AAEHKLST ALKAHEST
AAEHKMRY HAYMAKER
AAEHLMSY SEALYHAM
AAEHLNTX EXHALANT
AAEHLPRX HEXAPLAR
AAEHLPUV UPHEAVAL
AAEHMNSS MANASSEH
AAEHMOPR AMPHORAE
AAEHMORT ATHEROMA
AAEHNPST PHEASANT
AAEHNRTZ NAZARETH
AAEHNTTX XANTHATE
AAEHNTVX TAX HAVEN
AAEHPRSW PESHAWAR
AAEHRRSS HARASSER
AAEHRSTT HATTERAS
AAEHRSTU ARETHUSA
AAEIILTT LAETITIA
AAEIIPRS APIARIES
AAEIIRSV AVIARIES
AAEIJMNS JAMESINA
AAEIKKMZ KAMIKAZE
AAEIKLLN ALKALINE
AAEIKLLS ALKALIES,
  ALKALISE
AAEIKLLZ ALKALIZE
AAEIKLMS MAKE SAIL
AAEIKLNR KARELIAN
AAEILLLU ALLELUIA
AAEILLNT ALLANITE
AAEILLPT PALLIATE
AAEILLRT ARILLATE
AAEILLRY AERIALLY
AAEILMNT LAMINATE
AAEILMRT MATERIAL
AAEILMSS MALAISES
AAEILNPR AIRPLANE
AAEILNPT PALATINE
AAEILNRR LARRAINE
AAEILNRS AIRLANES
AAEILNRU AURELIAN,
  LAURAINE

AAEILNRV VALERIAN
AAEILNSS NASALISE
AAEILNSZ NASALIZE
AAEILNTT LATINATE
AAEILPRT PARIETAL
AAEILPRX PREAXIAL
AAEILPST STAPELIA
AAEILPSZ LA SPEZIA
AAEILRRT ARTERIAL
AAEILRSS ASSAILER,
  SALARIES
AAEILRTV VARIETAL
AAEILSTV SALIVATE
AAEILTVX LAXATIVE
AAEIMMNR MARIAMNE
AAEIMNNR ARMENIAN,
  MARIANNE
AAEIMNPR PEARMAIN
AAEIMNRT MARINATE
AAEIMNST TAMASINE
AAEIMOTX TOXAEMIA
AAEIMOTZ AZOTEMIA
AAEIMPRT PIA MATER
AAEIMRTT MARIETTA
AAEINORT AERATION
AAEINORX ANOREXIA
AAEINRST ARTESIAN
AAEINRSU EURASIAN
AAEINRSY ARYANISE
AAEINRYZ ARYANIZE
AAEINSTT ASTATINE, IN A
  STATE
AAEINSTW IN A SWEAT
AAEINTTT TITANATE
AAEIPPRS APPRAISE
AAEIPQRU AREQUIPA
AAEIPRST ASPIRATE,
  PARASITE
AAEIPRTZ TRAPEZIA
AAEIRSTT ARISTATE
AAEIRSVW AIRWAVES
AAEIRTTZ ZARATITE
AAEJORSV SARAJEVO
AAEKKRSY KAYAKERS
AAEKLMRY MALARKEY
AAEKLNNT KELANTAN
AAEKNPRT PARTAKEN
AAEKPRRT PARTAKER
AAELLLMR LAMELLAR
AAELLLPR PARALLEL
AAELLORV ALVEOLAR
AAELLPRT PATELLAR
AAELLPST PATELLAS

AAELLRST LATERALS
AAELLSSW SEAWALLS
AAELLTTV VALLETTA
AAELLWYY ALLEYWAY
AAELMMNO MELANOMA
AAELMNRT MATERNAL
AAELMNSS SALESMAN
AAELMNST TALESMAN
AAELMPTY PLAYMATE
AAELMRSY LAMASERY
AAELMRTT MALTREAT
AAELNNOT NEONATAL
AAELNNSU LAUSANNE
AAELNNTU ANNULATE
AAELNOSS SEASONAL
AAELNPRT PARENTAL,
  PATERNAL, PRENATAL
AAELNPRW WARPLANE
AAELNPST PLEASANT
AAELNRSS ARSENALS
AAELNRST ASTERNAL
AAELNRSY ANALYSER
AAELNRTX RELAXANT
AAELNSSY ANALYSES
AAELOPRS PSORALEA
AAELORTY ALEATORY
AAELPPSU APPLAUSE
AAELPRSV PALAVERS
AAELPRSY PARALYSE
AAELPRUV PAR VALUE
AAELRTTU LAURETTA
AAELRWYY WAYLAYER
AAELSSTX SALES TAX
AAEMMNRT ARMAMENT
AAEMNORT EMANATOR
AAEMNOTZ METAZOAN
AAEMNPRS PARMESAN
AAEMNPRT PARAMENT
AAEMNRST SANTAREM
AAEMNRTW WATERMAN
AAEMNSSS MANASSES
AAEMORTT TERATOMA
AAEMOTTU AUTOMATE
AAEMPTTU AMPUTATE
AAEMQSTU SQUAMATE
AAEMRRTU ARMATURE
AAEMRSTU AMATEURS
AAEMRTTU MATURATE
AAENNNST ANTENNAS
AAENNORS ROSEANNA
AAENNOTT ANNOTATE
AAENORTU AERONAUT
AAENPPRT APPARENT

AAENPSST PEASANTS
AAENRSUW UNAWARES
AAEOPSTT APOSTATE
AAEORSTT AEROSTAT
AAEPPRST PARAPETS
AAEPPSTT APPESTAT
AAEPRTTY TEA PARTY
AAEPRTXY TAXPAYER
AAERRTTT TARTRATE
AAERRTTW WATER RAT
AAERSSTV VASTERAS
AAERSTTU SATURATE
AAERTWWY WATERWAY
AAFFGILS GAFFSAIL
AAFFILRT TAFFRAIL
AAFFINPR PARAFFIN
AAFFLSTU AFFLATUS
AAFFMNST STAFFMAN
AAFFMORR FROM AFAR
AAFGLLNU LANGLAUF
AAFGLNRT FLAGRANT
AAFGNRRT FRAGRANT
AAFHLMST HALF-MAST
AAFHLSTY LAYSHAFT
AAFHQRRU FARQUHAR
AAFHRSUU HAUSFRAU
AAFIILLM FAMILIAL
AAFIILLR FILARIAL
AAFIILMR FAMILIAR
AAFIKLLY ALKALIFY
AAFILLNR RAINFALL
AAFILMST FATALISM
AAFILSTT FATALIST
AAFILTTY FATALITY
AAFINNOV FAVONIAN
AAFINNST INFANTAS
AAFINRRW WARFARIN
AAFINSTU FAUSTIAN,
    FAUSTINA
AAFIRSWY FAIRWAYS
AAFLSTWY FLATWAYS
AAFMNORW MAN-OF-WAR
AAGGGINR GARAGING
AAGGILLN GANGLIAL
AAGGIMNN MANAGING
AAGGINRV RAVAGING
AAGGINSV SAVAGING
AAGGNORT TAGANROG
AAGGNSWY GANGWAYS
AAGHHINS SHANGHAI
AAGHHINW HWANG HAI
AAGHHNUU HUANG HUA
AAGHILNN HANGNAIL

AAGHKMNY GYMKHANA
AAGHLNPY ANAGLYPH
AAGHMNOY HOGMANAY,
    MAHOGANY
AAGHMRSS MARSH GAS
AAGHNNST TANGSHAN
AAGIILMN IMAGINAL
AAGIILNV AVAILING
AAGIINNU IGUANIAN
AAGIINTW AWAITING
AAGIJRTU GUJARATI
AAGIKLNO KAOLIANG
AAGIKNNW KINGWANA
AAGILLNY ALLAYING
AAGILMNO MAGNOLIA
AAGILMNR ALARMING,
    MARGINAL
AAGILNOY LIAOYANG
AAGILNRR LARRIGAN
AAGILOOP APOLOGIA
AAGILSTT SAGITTAL
AAGILSTW WAGTAILS
AAGIMNNN MANGANIN
AAGIMNPR GRAMPIAN
AAGIMNPS PAGANISM
AAGIMNSS AMASSING
AAGIMPTU PATAGIUM
AAGIMSTT STIGMATA
AAGINNST SIANGTAN
AAGINOST SANTIAGO
AAGINPRU PAGURIAN
AAGINPST PAGANIST
AAGINRRS SRINAGAR
AAGINRRY ARRAYING
AAGINSST ASSIGNAT
AAGINSSY ASSAYING
AAGIORTT AGITATOR
AAGIRSTV GRAVITAS
AAGKMSSS GAS MASKS
AAGKNOOR KANGAROO
AAGLLMOY ALLOGAMY
AAGLLNST GALLANTS
AAGLLOPY POLYGALA
AAGLLOWY GALLOWAY
AAGLMNSS GLASSMAN
AAGLNQUU AQUALUNG
AAGLNRRU GRANULAR
AAGLRSTU GASTRULA
AAGMNORT MARTAGON
AAGMOTUY AUTOGAMY
AAGNNSTT STAGNANT
AAGNOPRS PARAGONS
AAGNOPRT TRAGOPAN

AAGNORRT ARROGANT,
    TARRAGON
AAGNRSTV VAGRANTS
AAGNRTUY GUARANTY
AAGORSSS SARGASSO
AAGRSSTU SASTRUGA
AAHHKKNU HANUKKAH
AAHHNSSU SHUSHANA
AAHHOPRS PHARAOHS
AAHIIKRR HARA-KIRI,
    HARIKARI
AAHIILRT HAIRTAIL
AAHIINPS HISPANIA
AAHIINTT TAHITIAN
AAHIKLNS SAKHALIN
AAHIKNSS KINSHASA
AAHILNNT INHALANT
AAHILNOT HALATION
AAHIMNRR HARRIMAN
AAHIMSTT MATTHIAS
AAHINORT HORATIAN
AAHINPRS PIRANHAS
AAHINPRT PARTHIAN
AAHIPPRS SAPPHIRA
AAHIPSXY ASPHYXIA
AAHITWWY AWAY WITH
AAHJNNOT JONATHAN
AAHKLLMR HALLMARK
AAHKLMOO OKLAHOMA
AAHKMOOY YOKOHAMA
AAHKMOTW TOMAHAWK
AAHKMSSY YASHMAKS
AAHKRSTV HRVATSKA
AAHLLLTU TALLULAH
AAHLLMRS MARSHALL
AAHLLOPT ALLOPATH
AAHLLSWY HALLWAYS
AAHLMRSS MARSHALS
AAHLMSTU THALAMUS
AAHMNORT MARATHON
AAHMNOTX XANTHOMA
AAHMNPST PHANTASM
AAHMOPRS AMPHORAS
AAHNNOSS HOSANNAS
AAHNNSSU SUSANNAH
AAHNPSTY PHANTASY
AAHNRTTY HANRATTY
AAHPRSTW WARPATHS
AAHPSTWY PATHWAYS
AAHRSSTY ASHTRAYS
AAIIILMR MILIARIA
AAIIILMS ISMAILIA
AAIIJJPP JIPIJAPA

AAIILMNS MAINSAIL
AAIILNRZ ALIZARIN
AAIILNST ITALIANS
AAIILNUX UNIAXIAL
AAIILRST ALISTAIR
AAIILRTX TRIAXIAL
AAIIMNNT MAINTAIN
AAIIMNPX PANMIXIA
AAIIMNRS ARIANISM
AAIINOTV AVIATION
AAIINPRR RIPARIAN
AAIINPRS PARISIAN
AAIINRST INTARSIA
AAIIORRT AIR-TO-AIR
AAIIPRST APIARIST
AAIIRTVX AVIATRIX
AAIKLNRS SRI LANKA
AAIKLOSV SLOVAKIA
AAIKMRST TAMARISK
AAIKNNTT ANTITANK
AAIKNPST PAKISTAN
AAIKNRTX TAXI RANK
AAIKSSTW SWASTIKA
AAILLLUV ALLUVIAL
AAILLMNT MANTILLA
AAILLMOR AMARILLO
AAILLMRX MAXILLAR
AAILLRXY AXILLARY
AAILMMRS ALARMISM
AAILMNOR MANORIAL,
  MORAINAL
AAILMNOS SOMALIAN
AAILMNST STAMINAL,
  TALISMAN
AAILMORR ARMORIAL
AAILMRST ALARMIST
AAILMTTU ULTIMATA
AAILNNOT NATIONAL
AAILNNPT PLANTAIN
AAILNNST ANNALIST
AAILNOPP APPOLINA
AAILNOPS PIANOLAS
AAILNOPT TALAPOIN
AAILNORS ORINASAL
AAILNORT NOTARIAL,
  RATIONAL
AAILNOSV SLAVONIA
AAILNOTV LAVATION
AAILNOTX LAXATION
AAILNQTU ALIQUANT
AAILNSSY ANALYSIS
AAILNSTT ATLÀNTIS
AAILNSTU LUSATIAN

AAILNSTY NASALITY
AAILORRS RASORIAL
AAILORRV VARIOLAR
AAILPPRU PUPARIAL
AAILPRST PATRIALS
AAILRRSV ARRIVALS
AAILRSVY SALIVARY
AAILRSWY RAILWAYS
AAILSSTY STAYSAIL
AAIMMNST MAINMAST
AAIMMRSU SAMARIUM
AAIMNNRU RUMANIAN
AAIMNORT ANIMATOR
AAIMNORV MORAVIAN
AAIMNORW AIRWOMAN
AAIMNPRZ MARZIPAN
AAIMNRRT TRIMARAN
AAIMNRST MARTIANS
AAIMNRSU MASURIAN
AAIMNSST MANTISSA,
  SATANISM
AAIMNSTY MAINSTAY
AAIMOPRS MARIPOSA
AAIMPRST PASTRAMI
AAIMQRUU AQUARIUM
AAIMRRST AMRITSAR
AAIMRRSU SAMURAIS
AAINNNOT ANTONINA
AAINNOST SONATINA
AAINNOTT NATATION
AAINNRSV NIRVANAS
AAINNSST NAISSANT
AAINOPRV PAR AVION
AAINORRS ROSARIAN
AAINORRT ROTARIAN
AAINOTTX TAXATION
AAINPRST ASPIRANT,
  PARTISAN
AAINPRTW WAR PAINT
AAINQRTU QUATRAIN
AAINQTTU AQUATINT
AAINRSST ARTISANS,
  TSARINAS
AAINRSSY ASSYRIAN
AAINRSTU AUSTRIAN
AAINRSTV VARIANTS
AAINRSTY SANITARY
AAINRSTZ TZARINAS
AAINSSSS ASSASSIN
AAINSSTT SATANIST
AAIORSTV AVIATORS
AAIQRSTU AQUARIST
AAIQRSUU AQUARIUS

AAIRSSTU ASTURIAS
AAIRSTWY STAIRWAY
AAJMMORR MARJORAM
AAKLMNSW WALKMANS
AAKMMNRS MARKSMAN
AAKMOSSU MOUSSAKA
AAKMRSUZ MAZURKAS
AAKPRSWY PARKWAYS
AALLLLMP PALL MALL
AALLMNTY TALLYMAN
AALLMNUY MANUALLY
AALLMPRU AMPULLAR
AALLNNUY ANNUALLY
AALLNOTY ATONALLY
AALLNPRU PLANULAR
AALLOORW WALLAROO
AALLORWY ROLLAWAY
AALLPRST PLASTRAL
AALLRUVV VALVULAR
AALMNOPP PAMPLONA
AALMNORT MATRONAL
AALMNORU MONAURAL
AALMNORW ROMAN LAW
AALMNOWY LAYWOMAN
AALMNTTU TANTALUM
AALMNTUU AUTUMNAL
AALMOSTT STOMATAL
AALNNOST SONANTAL
AALNOPRT PATRONAL
AALNORSS ALSO-RANS
AALNPSST SALTPANS
AALNPTWX WAXPLANT
AALNRSTU NATURALS
AALNSSTU SULTANAS
AALNSSTY ANALYSTS
AALNSTTU TANTALUS
AALOOPSU SAO PAULO
AALOPPRV APPROVAL
AALOPRSS PARASOLS
AALOPRST PASTORAL
AALORTUV VALUATOR
AALORTVY LAVATORY
AALPRSTU SPATULAR
AALPSSTU SPATULAS
AALRSTTW STALWART
AALRSTUY SALUTARY
AALSSSTU ASSAULTS
AAMMNNOT MAN-TO-MAN
AAMMRSSU MARASMUS
AAMNRSTU SUMATRAN
AAMNRSTW STRAW MAN
AAMOPRRU PARAMOUR
AAMORSSV SAMOVARS

AAMOSTTU AUTOMATS
AAMPRRST RAMPARTS
AAMSSSTU SATSUMAS
AANNOSST ASSONANT
AANNRSTY STANNARY
AANOOSSS AS SOON AS
AANORRRT NARRATOR
AANRRSTW WARRANTS
AANRRTWY WARRANTY
AANRSTTU SATURANT
AANRSUWY RUNAWAYS
AAOPSSTY APOSTASY
AAOSTWWY STOWAWAY
AAPRRSTT RAT TRAPS
AARRSSTW STAR WARS
AARSTTUY STATUARY
ABBBEILR BRIBABLE
ABBBELRS BABBLERS
ABBBELUY BLUE BABY
ABBBGILN BABBLING,
   BLABBING
ABBBHSUY BUSHBABY
ABBCCKMO BACKCOMB
ABBCEERU BARBECUE
ABBCEGIR CRIBBAGE
ABBCEIKT BACKBITE
ABBCEILR BARBICEL
ABBCEIRR CRABBIER
ABBCEIRS SCABBIER
ABBCEKNO BACKBONE
ABBCEKNU BUCKBEAN
ABBCELRS SCRABBLE
ABBCGINR CRABBING
ABBCGIOR GABBROIC
ABBCIILL BIBLICAL
ABBCIKRT BRICKBAT
ABBCILSY SCABBILY
ABBCINOY CABIN BOY
ABBCKLOX BLACK BOX
ABBDDEEU BEDAUBED
ABBDDEIL AD-LIBBED,
   BIDDABLE
ABBDDEST BAD DEBTS
ABBDDLOO BAD BLOOD
ABBDEEER BEEBREAD
ABBDEEJR JABBERED
ABBDEILR AD-LIBBER
ABBDEINR BREAD BIN
ABBDEIRT RABBITED
ABBDELRS DABBLERS
ABBDEORS ABSORBED
ABBDERST DRABBEST
ABBDGILN DABBLING

ABBDHIRT BIRDBATH
ABBDHOOY BABYHOOD
ABBDOORX BOXBOARD
ABBEEJRR JABBERER
ABBEELVW EBBW VALE
ABBEESSS ABBESSES
ABBEFILR FLABBIER
ABBEGLRR GRABBLER
ABBEGRSU BUGBEARS
ABBEHIRS SHABBIER
ABBEHORT BATHROBE
ABBEILLO BOILABLE
ABBEILNU BUBALINE
ABBEILOT BILOBATE
ABBEIMWZ ZIMBABWE
ABBEINRS BRISBANE
ABBEIRRT RABBITER
ABBEKLOO BOOKABLE
ABBELMRS BRAMBLES
ABBELOPR PROBABLE
ABBELORU BELABOUR
ABBELQSU SQUABBLE
ABBENORY NABOBERY
ABBEORRS ABSORBER
ABBEORTW BROWBEAT
ABBERRRY BARBERRY
ABBERRYY BAYBERRY
ABBERSST STABBERS
ABBFILLY FLABBILY
ABBGGILN GABBLING
ABBGGINR GRABBING
ABBGHRSU HABSBURG
ABBGINST STABBING
ABBGINSW SWABBING
ABBGOOSU BUGABOOS
ABBHILSY SHABBILY
ABBHRRSU RHUBARBS
ABBHSTTU BATHTUBS
ABBILLSU SILLABUB
ABBILOST BOBTAILS
ABBIRRTY RABBITRY
ABBIRSUU SUBURBIA
ABBKKNOO BANKBOOK
ABBLLSUY SYLLABUB
ABBLOPRY PROBABLY
ABBMMOOT ATOM BOMB
ABBNRSUU SUBURBAN
ABCCDHIK DABCHICK
ABCCEELP PECCABLE
ABCCEIKL BLACK ICE
ABCCEILY CELIBACY
ABCCEKMO COMEBACK
ABCCHISU BACCHIUS

ABCCHNOO CABOCHON
ABCCIKKK KICKBACK
ABCCILOR CARBOLIC
ABCCILOT COBALTIC
ABCCINOR CARBONIC
ABCCIORS ASCORBIC
ABCCKLLO BALLCOCK
ABCCKSTU CUTBACKS
ABCCOOST TOBACCOS
ABCDDEOR BROCADED
ABCDDETU ABDUCTED
ABCDEEFK FEEDBACK
ABCDEEHL BLEACHED
ABCDEEHR BREACHED
ABCDEELM BECALMED
ABCDEELS DÉBÂCLES
ABCDEELU EDUCABLE
ABCDEEMR EMBRACED
ABCDEFLO BOLDFACE
ABCDEGIR BIRDCAGE
ABCDEHLN BLANCHED
ABCDEHNR BRANCHED
ABCDEHOR BROACHED
ABCDEIIT DIABETIC
ABCDEIKS BACKSIDE
ABCDEILR CALIBRED
ABCDEIRS ASCRIBED
ABCDEKLO BLOCKADE
ABCDEKNN NECKBAND
ABCDEKNU UNBACKED
ABCDELOO CABOODLE
ABCDEMNU DUMB-CANE
ABCDEMOT COMBATED
ABCDEMPS CAMP BEDS
ABCDENTU ABDUCENT
ABCDEORS BAR CODES
ABCDIILO BIOCIDAL,
   DIABOLIC
ABCDIIRT TRIBADIC
ABCDIKLS BACKSLID
ABCDKOOR BACK DOOR
ABCDKOPR BACKDROP
ABCDOPRU CUPBOARD
ABCDORUY OBDURACY
ABCEEEFK BEEFCAKE
ABCEEHLM BECHAMEL
ABCEEHLR BLEACHER
ABCEEHLW CHEWABLE
ABCEEHRS BREACHES
ABCEEILT CELIBATE
ABCEEIMN AMBIENCE
ABCEEIRT BEATRICE
ABCEEKLY BLACK EYE

ABCEELOV EVOCABLE
ABCEELRR CEREBRAL
ABCEELRT BRACELET
ABCEEMRR EMBRACER
ABCEEMRS EMBRACES
ABCEENSS ABSENCES
ABCEFIIT BEATIFIC
ABCEFIKR BACKFIRE,
     FIREBACK
ABCEFINO BONIFACE
ABCEFLSS BASS CLEF
ABCEGHIN BEACHING
ABCEGIRS RIB CAGES
ABCEGKLL BLACKLEG
ABCEGKLO BLOCKAGE
ABCEGKRY GREYBACK
ABCEHITT BATHETIC
ABCEHLOR BACHELOR
ABCEHLSU CHASUBLE
ABCEHMOT HECATOMB
ABCEHMRS CHAMBERS
ABCEHNRS BRANCHES
ABCEHOOT COHOBATE
ABCEHORR BROACHER
ABCEHORU BAROUCHE
ABCEIJOT JACOBITE
ABCEIKKL KICKABLE
ABCEIKLP PICKABLE
ABCEIKLT BLACK-TIE
ABCEIKWZ ZWIEBACK
ABCEILLR CLARIBEL
ABCEILNN BINNACLE
ABCEILOR CABRIOLE
ABCEILOS SOCIABLE
ABCEILRS CALIBRES
ABCEINRS BRISANCE,
     CARBINES
ABCEINRT BACTERIN
ABCEINST CABINETS
ABCEINTU INCUBATE
ABCEIORS AEROBICS
ABCEIORT BORACITE
ABCEIRSW CRABWISE
ABCEIRTT BRATTICE
ABCEIRTY ACERBITY
ABCEJKLT JET-BLACK
ABCEJLTY ABJECTLY
ABCEKKSW SKEWBACK
ABCEKLLO LOCKABLE
ABCEKLMO MOCKABLE
ABCEKLOO COOKABLE
ABCEKLSS BACKLESS
ABCEKLST BLACKEST

ABCEKOOS BOOKCASE
ABCEKRST BRACKETS
ABCEKSST SETBACKS
ABCELLMP CAMPBELL
ABCELLPU CULPABLE
ABCELMNY LAMBENCY
ABCELMRS SCRAMBLE
ABCELNUU NUBECULA
ABCELOOT BOOTLACE
ABCELOPS PLACEBOS
ABCELOST OBSTACLE
ABCEMORT COMBATER
ABCENNOS BESANCON
ABCEOOSS CABOOSES
ABCERRTU CARBURET
ABCERTUU CUBATURE
ABCESTUU SUBACUTE
ABCFHOTW FOB WATCH
ABCFIKLL BACKFILL
ABCFILOS BIFOCALS
ABCFKLLU FULLBACK
ABCFKLLY BLACKFLY
ABCGIKLN BLACKING
ABCGIKNS BACKINGS
ABCGILNO LOG CABIN
ABCGKLOS BACKLOGS
ABCHIKLS BLACKISH
ABCHIKRS BRACKISH
ABCHIMOR CHORIAMB
ABCHIMRU BRACHIUM
ABCHINOR BRONCHIA
ABCHIRRT TRIBRACH
ABCHKMPU HUMPBACK
ABCHKOOP CHAPBOOK
ABCHKOOS CASH-BOOK
ABCHLLUU CLUBHAUL
ABCHMOTX MATCHBOX
ABCIIKRR AIRBRICK
ABCIIMNR CIMBRIAN
ABCIIMNS MINICABS
ABCIIORS ISOBARIC
ABCIIRST TRIBASIC
ABCIIRTU CURITIBA
ABCIISTY BASICITY
ABCIKLST BACKLIST
ABCIKNPS BACKSPIN
ABCIKSSY SICKBAYS
ABCILLSU BACILLUS
ABCILLSY SYLLABIC
ABCILMOO COLOMBIA
ABCILMOU COLUMBIA
ABCILNPU PUBLICAN
ABCILOSY SOCIABLY

ABCILRRU RUBRICAL
ABCIMNRU CUMBRIAN
ABCINRVY VIBRANCY
ABCIOPRS SAPROBIC
ABCIORSU CARIBOUS
ABCIOSSU SCABIOUS
ABCIOSUV BIVOUACS
ABCJKOOT JACKBOOT
ABCKKOOR BOOKRACK
ABCKLOPT BLACKTOP
ABCKLOTU BLACKOUT
ABCKNNOS BANNOCKS
ABCKOORU BUCKAROO
ABCKOPST BACKSTOP
ABCLLPUY CULPABLY
ABCLNORY CARBONYL
ABCLPRUW PUB-CRAWL
ABCLSSSU SUBCLASS
ABCMOORT MOBOCRAT
ABCNOUYY BUOYANCY
ABCORRSS CROSSBAR
ABCORRSW CROWBARS
ABCORRTU TURBOCAR
ABCORSSU SCABROUS
ABCRSTTU SUBTRACT
ABDDEEEH BEHEADED
ABDDEEGR BADGERED
ABDDEEHT DEATHBED
ABDDEEKR DEBARKED
ABDDEERR DEBARRED
ABDDEEST BEDSTEAD
ABDDEGIR ABRIDGED
ABDDEHMO HEBDOMAD
ABDDEILS DISABLED
ABDDEILU BUDDLEIA
ABDDEINS SIDEBAND
ABDDELRS BLADDERS
ABDDENOU ABOUNDED
ABDDILMO LAMBDOID
ABDDILRY LADYBIRD
ABDDLLOS ODDBALLS
ABDEEEFL FEEDABLE
ABDEEEIW BIDE A WEE
ABDEEEKR BAEDEKER
ABDEEERV BEAVERED,
     BEREAVED
ABDEEFGS FEEDBAGS
ABDEEGGR BEGGARED
ABDEEGLR BELGRADE
ABDEEHLS SHEDABLE
ABDEEHNO BONEHEAD
ABDEEILN DENIABLE
ABDEEILS ABSEILED

ABDEEILW BEWAILED
ABDEEIST BEADIEST, DIABETES
ABDEEKMR EMBARKED
ABDEELLL LABELLED
ABDEELLW WELDABLE
ABDEELMM EMBALMED
ABDEELMN MENDABLE
ABDEELNS SENDABLE
ABDEELOR LEEBOARD
ABDEELPT BEDPLATE
ABDEELZZ BEDAZZLE
ABDEEMNO BEMOANED
ABDEEMNS BEAM-ENDS
ABDEENRT BANTERED
ABDEENRZ BRAZENED
ABDEENST ABSENTED
ABDEENTT BATTENED
ABDEERRT BARTERED
ABDEERST DEBATERS
ABDEERTT BATTERED
ABDEERTW WATERBED
ABDEERTY BETRAYED
ABDEESTT BEAD TEST
ABDEFILN FINDABLE
ABDEFINO BONA FIDE
ABDEFLLO FOLDABLE
ABDEFLOR FORDABLE
ABDEGHIS BIGHEADS
ABDEGILN BLINDAGE
ABDEGILU GUIDABLE
ABDEGIMX MIXED BAG
ABDEGINR BEARDING
ABDEGINS BEADINGS, DEBASING
ABDEGINT DEBATING
ABDEGIRR ABRIDGER
ABDEGLMO GAMBOLED
ABDEGOPR PEGBOARD
ABDEHINS BANISHED
ABDEHITU HABITUDE
ABDEHKLU BULKHEAD
ABDEHLLN HANDBELL
ABDEHLLO HOLDABLE
ABDEHLLU BULLHEAD
ABDEHLMS SHAMBLED
ABDEHLOT THEOBALD
ABDEHLRS HALBERDS
ABDEHMSU AMBUSHED
ABDEHNRR BERNHARD
ABDEHNSU DUSHANBE
ABDEHORR ABHORRED
ABDEHRST BREADTHS

ABDEIIRT DIATRIBE
ABDEILLS SLIDABLE
ABDEILMN MANDIBLE
ABDEILNO BODLEIAN
ABDEILNW WINDABLE
ABDEILOV VOIDABLE
ABDEILPS PIEBALDS
ABDEILRV DRIVABLE
ABDEILTU DUTIABLE
ABDEIMOO AMOEBOID
ABDEIMOR AMBEROID
ABDEINNR ENDBRAIN
ABDEINOR DEBONAIR
ABDEINOT OBTAINED
ABDEINRS BRANDIES
ABDEINST BANDIEST
ABDEINSU UNBIASED
ABDEIOTV OBVIATED
ABDEIPST BAPTISED
ABDEIPTZ BAPTIZED
ABDEIRSS SEABIRDS
ABDEIRTV VIBRATED
ABDEISSU DISABUSE
ABDEISTW BAWDIEST
ABDEKLSW SKEWBALD
ABDEKNSU SUNBAKED
ABDEKORY KEYBOARD
ABDELLOT BALLOTED
ABDELNOR OBERLAND
ABDELNOZ BLAZONED
ABDELNRY BENADRYL
ABDELNSS BALDNESS
ABDELNST BLANDEST
ABDELORU LABOURED
ABDELOSV ABSOLVED
ABDELOSW DOWSABEL
ABDEMNNS BANDSMEN
ABDEMNOS ABDOMENS
ABDEMRTU DRUMBEAT
ABDENNOS NOSEBAND
ABDENNPY BAD PENNY
ABDENNRW BRAND-NEW
ABDENORW RAW-BONED
ABDENOTW DOWNBEAT
ABDENRRT BERTRAND
ABDENRRU UNBARRED
ABDENRSS DRABNESS
ABDENRTU BREADNUT, TURBANED
ABDEOPRT PROBATED
ABDEORRS BOARDERS
ABDEORRW DRAWBORE, WARDROBE

ABDEORST BROADEST
ABDEORSW SOWBREAD
ABDEORTU OBDURATE
ABDEORUX BORDEAUX
ABDEPSSY BYPASSED
ABDEPSTU BUDAPEST
ABDERSTW BEDSTRAW
ABDERTUW DRAWTUBE
ABDESTTU TASTE BUD
ABDFFLOY BADLY-OFF
ABDFLOOT FOLDBOAT
ABDGGGOY DOGGY BAG
ABDGHINR HANGBIRD
ABDGIINR BRAIDING
ABDGILOR GAOLBIRD
ABDGINNR BRANDING
ABDGINNY BANDYING
ABDGINOR BOARDING
ABDGINSW WINDBAGS
ABDHILLN HANDBILL
ABDHILNS BLANDISH
ABDHINRS BRANDISH
ABDHIRTY BIRTHDAY
ABDHKNOO HANDBOOK
ABDHLOPR BARDOLPH
ABDHLORW BLOWHARD
ABDHMOTU BAD-MOUTH
ABDHMSTU MUD BATHS
ABDHNSSU HUSBANDS
ABDIIJLR JAILBIRD
ABDIILLR BILLIARD
ABDIIMNR MIDBRAIN
ABDIIMSU BASIDIUM
ABDIINOS OBSIDIAN
ABDIIRTY RABIDITY
ABDILORW WILD BOAR
ABDILOST TABLOIDS
ABDILRRY RIBALDRY
ABDILRZZ BLIZZARD
ABDINOTY ANTIBODY
ABDINRTY BANDITRY
ABDJMOOR DOORJAMB
ABDLLORS BOLLARDS
ABDLMORY LOMBARDY
ABDLRSUY ABSURDLY
ABDNORUY BOUNDARY
ABDNSSTY STANDBYS
ABDOORTU OUTBOARD
ABDOOSSW BASSWOOD
ABDRSUZZ BUZZARDS
ABEEEERT BEE-EATER
ABEEEFRS FREE-BASE
ABEEEGRV BEVERAGE

ABEEEHTT HEBETATE
ABEEEELLR REELABLE
ABEEEENST ABSENTEE
ABEEFILN FINEABLE
ABEEFILR AFEBRILE,
   FIREABLE
ABEEFILS FEASIBLE
ABEEFILT FLEABITE
ABEEFLLL FELLABLE
ABEEFLLN BEFALLEN
ABEEFORR FOREBEAR
ABEEGIRV VERBIAGE
ABEEGMRT BERGAMET
ABEEGNOS GABONESE
ABEEGTTU BAGUETTE
ABEEHINT THEBAINE
ABEEHIRS HEBRAISE
ABEEHIRZ HEBRAIZE
ABEEHLLL HEELBALL
ABEEHLLP HELPABLE
ABEEHLLR HAREBELL
ABEEHNNS HENBANES
ABEEHNSS BANSHEES,
   HAS-BEENS
ABEEHORS RHEOBASE
ABEEHQTU BEQUEATH
ABEEHRRT BREATHER
ABEEIKLT BAKELITE
ABEEIKRS BAKERIES
ABEEILLR RELIABLE
ABEEILLS ISABELLE
ABEEILLV LEVIABLE
ABEEILNP PLEBEIAN
ABEEILNS BALINESE,
   BASELINE
ABEEILNV ENVIABLE
ABEEILPX EXPIABLE
ABEEILRR BLEARIER
ABEEILRT LIBERATE
ABEEILRW BEWAILER
ABEEILSS SEISABLE,
   SISEABLE
ABEEILSZ SEIZABLE,
   SIZEABLE
ABEEISTU BEAUTIES
ABEEJMOR JAMBOREE
ABEEKLST BLEAKEST
ABEEKOOP PEEKABOO
ABEEKRRS BREAKERS
ABEELLLR LABELLER
ABEELLLT TELLABLE
ABEELLMT MELTABLE
ABEELLRY REELABLY

ABEELLSY EYEBALLS
ABEELMMR EMBALMER
ABEELMNO BONE MEAL
ABEELMPR PREAMBLE
ABEELMSS ASSEMBLE
ABEELMTT EMBATTLE
ABEELNOP BEANPOLE
ABEELNRT RENTABLE
ABEELOPR OPERABLE
ABEELORS EARLOBES
ABEELORX EXORABLE
ABEELRSU REUSABLE
ABEELRSV SERVABLE
ABEELSSS BASELESS
ABEELSSU SUBLEASE
ABEELSTT SEAT BELT,
   TESTABLE
ABEELTTW WETTABLE
ABEEMMNR MEMBRANE
ABEEMNST BASEMENT
ABEENNOT NOTA BENE
ABEENNTU UNBEATEN
ABEENORS SEABORNE
ABEENOTZ BENZOATE
ABEENRRT BANTERER
ABEENRSS BARENESS
ABEENRST ABSENTER
ABEENSSS BASENESS
ABEEOORV OVERBEAR
ABEERRRT BARTERER
ABEERRTT BARRETTE,
   BATTERER
ABEERRTV VERTEBRA
ABEERRTY BETRAYER,
   TEABERRY
ABEFHILS FISHABLE
ABEFILLL FALLIBLE
ABEFILLO FOILABLE
ABEFILLR FIREBALL
ABEFILLT LIFTABLE
ABEFILOT LIFEBOAT
ABEFILSY FEASIBLY
ABEFILTT FITTABLE
ABEFIORT FIREBOAT
ABEFIRRT FIREBRAT
ABEFITUY BEAUTIFY
ABEFLLMU BLAMEFUL
ABEFLLRU FURLABLE
ABEFLMOR FORMABLE
ABEFLNST FAN BELTS
ABEFLRSU SURFABLE
ABEFOORT BAREFOOT
ABEFORRS FORBEARS

ABEFRRUY FEBRUARY
ABEGGHLU HUGGABLE
ABEGGILN BEAGLING
ABEGGIST BAGGIEST
ABEGGLRY BEGGARLY
ABEGHIMR MAGHREBI
ABEGHINV BEHAVING
ABEGHINZ BENGHAZI
ABEGHRSU BEAR HUGS
ABEGIJTU BIJUGATE
ABEGIKNR BREAKING
ABEGIKNT BETAKING
ABEGILLN LABELING
ABEGILNN ENABLING
ABEGILNS SINGABLE
ABEGILNT BLEATING,
   TANGIBLE
ABEGILNY BELAYING
ABEGILOT OBLIGATE
ABEGILRT GILBERTA
ABEGIMNS BIG NAMES
ABEGINRS BEARINGS
ABEGINRT BERATING
ABEGINRW BEWARING
ABEGINST BEATINGS
ABEGINTT ABETTING
ABEGIPPS BAGPIPES
ABEGKORS GROSBEAK
ABEGLMRS GAMBLERS
ABEGLORW GROWABLE
ABEGLRSS GARBLESS
ABEGMNOY BOGEYMAN
ABEGMRSU UMBRAGES
ABEGNOOR GABORONE
ABEGNOSS NOSEBAGS
ABEGNSTU SUBAGENT
ABEGOSTT TOTE BAGS
ABEGSSTU SUBSTAGE
ABEHHIPZ HEPZIBAH
ABEHIINR HIBERNIA
ABEHILNR HIBERNAL
ABEHILPS SHIPABLE
ABEHILTT TITHABLE
ABEHIMMS MEMSAHIB
ABEHIMNO BOHEMIAN
ABEHIMRS HEBRAISM
ABEHINST ABSINTHE
ABEHIRST HEBRAIST
ABEHISTU HABITUÉS
ABEHLMSS SHAMBLES
ABEHMNOR HORNBEAM
ABEHMOOR REHOBOAM
ABEHMSSU AMBUSHES

ABEHNSTU SUNBATHE
ABEHORRR ABHORRER
ABEHRSST BRASHEST
ABEIILMT IMITABLE
ABEIILNN BIENNIAL
ABEIILNR BILINEAR,
  LIBERIAN
ABEIILNV INVIABLE
ABEIILPT PITIABLE
ABEIILST SIBILATE
ABEIILTV VITIABLE
ABEIINRR BRAINIER
ABEIINRS SIBERIAN
ABEIJLTU JUBILATE
ABEIJMNN BENJAMIN
ABEIKLLN LINKABLE
ABEIKLNS SINKABLE
ABEIKLSS KISSABLE
ABEIKNRS BEARSKIN,
  BREAK-INS
ABEIKNST BEATNIKS
ABEILLLM MILLABLE
ABEILLLT TILLABLE
ABEILLLW WILLABLE
ABEILLOS ISOLABLE
ABEILLOV VIOLABLE
ABEILLRS LIBERALS
ABEILLRY BAREILLY,
  BLEARILY, RELIABLY
ABEILLST BASTILLE,
  LISTABLE
ABEILMNT BAILMENT
ABEILMST BALMIEST
ABEILNNW WINNABLE
ABEILNPS BIPLANES
ABEILNPT PINTABLE
ABEILNRS RINSABLE
ABEILNRU RUINABLE
ABEILNSS LESBIANS
ABEILNTV BIVALENT
ABEILNVY ENVIABLY
ABEILPPR RIPPABLE
ABEILPPT TIPPABLE
ABEILPRT PARTIBLE
ABEILPSS PASSIBLE
ABEILPST EPIBLAST
ABEILRYY BIYEARLY
ABEILSSU ISSUABLE
ABEILSTU SUITABLE
ABEILSUX BISEXUAL
ABEILSVV BIVALVES
ABEIMRST BARMIEST

ABEIMRTV AMBIVERT,
  VERBATIM
ABEIMSSU IAMBUSES
ABEINORR AIRBORNE
ABEINORS BARONIES
ABEINORT BARITONE,
  OBTAINER
ABEINOST BOTANISE,
  OBEISANT
ABEINOTZ BOTANIZE
ABEINRRW BRAWNIER
ABEINRST BANISTER
ABEINRSU URBANISE
ABEINRSW WINE BARS
ABEINRTU BRAUNITE
ABEINRUZ URBANIZE
ABEINSST BASSINET
ABEINTTU INTUBATE
ABEIORTV ABORTIVE
ABEIPRRS SPARERIB
ABEIRRRS BARRIERS
ABEIRRSS BRASSIER
ABEIRRST ARBITERS
ABEIRRSZ BRAZIERS
ABEIRRVY BREVIARY
ABEIRSSU AIRBUSES
ABEIRSTT BIRETTAS
ABEIRSTY BESTIARY,
  SYBARITE
ABEIRTTY YTTERBIA
ABEISTTT BATTIEST
ABEJLMPU JUMPABLE
ABEJLSUY BLUE JAYS
ABEJMOOR JEROBOAM
ABEJNOSW JAWBONES
ABEKLMOS ABELMOSK,
  SMOKABLE
ABEKLNOW KNOWABLE
ABEKLNST BLANKETS
ABEKLORW WORKABLE
ABEKNNOT BANK NOTE
ABEKOORY YEARBOOK
ABEKORTU OUTBREAK
ABEKRSTY BASKETRY
ABELLLMU LABELLUM
ABELLLSY SYLLABLE
ABELLMRU UMBRELLA
ABELLNOT BALLONET
ABELLOSV SOLVABLE
ABELLRVY VERBALLY
ABELLSUW BLUE LAWS
ABELMNNO NOBLEMAN
ABELMNOP BELMOPAN

ABELMNOZ EMBLAZON
ABELMNTU NEMBUTAL
ABELMOSV MOVABLES
ABELMRRS RAMBLERS
ABELMSSY ASSEMBLY
ABELNORU BLUE ROAN
ABELNOST NOTABLES,
  STONABLE
ABELNPRU PRUNABLE
ABELNRTU TURNABLE
ABELNRUY URBANELY
ABELNRYZ BRAZENLY
ABELNSTU UNSTABLE
ABELNSTY ABSENTLY
ABELNSUU UNUSABLE
ABELNUVY NAVY BLUE
ABELOPRT PORTABLE
ABELOPRV PROVABLE
ABELOPRY OPERABLY
ABELOQTU QUOTABLE
ABELORRU LABOURER,
  RUBEOLAR
ABELORST BLOATERS,
  SORTABLE, STORABLE
ABELORSV ABSOLVER
ABELOSTU ABSOLUTE
ABELOSTW BESTOWAL
ABELOVWW BLOW-WAVE
ABELRRSW BRAWLERS,
  WARBLERS
ABELRSTU BALUSTER
ABELRTTT BARTLETT
ABELRTTU REBUTTAL
ABELSTUU SUBULATE
ABELSTWY BELTWAYS
ABELTTUU TUBULATE
ABEMMNOO MOONBEAM
ABEMNOTU UMBONATE
ABEMNPRU PENUMBRA
ABEMNSSU SUNBEAMS
ABEMNTTU ABUTMENT
ABENNOTU BUTANONE
ABENOPSU SUBPOENA
ABENORSS BARONESS
ABENORST BARONETS
ABENORTT BETATRON
ABENORTV BEVATRON
ABENOSSW SAWBONES
ABENOSTY BAYONETS
ABENQSTU BANQUETS
ABENRTTU BRUNETTA
ABENSSTT TEST BANS
ABEOPPRY PAPERBOY

ABEOPRST PROBATES
ABEORSST BOASTERS
ABEORSTT ABETTORS
ABEORSTU SABOTEUR
ABEORTUV OUTBRAVE
ABEOSSST ASBESTOS
ABEOSTWX SWEATBOX
ABEPRSSY PASSERBY
ABEPSSSY BYPASSES
ABERRWXY WAXBERRY
ABERSSTU ABSTRUSE
ABERTTUY BUTYRATE
ABFFGILN BAFFLING
ABFFIILS BAILIFFS
ABFFLLPU PUFFBALL
ABFFLOST BLAST-OFF
ABFFLOSU BUFFALOS
ABFFNOTU BOUFFANT
ABFGLLLO GOLF BALL
ABFGORUU FAUBOURG
ABFHIORS BOARFISH
ABFIILMR FIMBRIAL
ABFIILRR FIBRILAR
ABFILSTU FABULIST
ABFIRTTU FRUIT BAT
ABFLLOOT FOOTBALL
ABFLLORU FOUR-BALL
ABFLLOST SOFTBALL
ABFLOSTU BOASTFUL
ABFLOSUU FABULOUS
ABFNORTU TURBOFAN
ABFORSTU SURFBOAT
ABGGGINR BRAGGING
ABGGILMN GAMBLING
ABGGILNR GARBLING
ABGGNOOT TOBOGGAN
ABGGRSUU AUGSBURG
ABGHHILL HIGHBALL
ABGHINWZ WHIZ-BANG
ABGHMORU BROUGHAM
ABGHPRSU HAPSBURG
ABGIIMST BIGAMIST
ABGIINNO BIGNONIA
ABGIINNR BRAINING
ABGIINRS BRAISING
ABGIINSS BIASSING
ABGIIRTT BIRGITTA,
　BRIGITTA
ABGIJNRU ABJURING
ABGIKLNU BAULKING
ABGILMNR MARBLING,
　RAMBLING

ABGILNRW BRAWLING,
　WARBLING
ABGILNST BLASTING,
　STABLING
ABGILNTT BATTLING
ABGILNTY TANGIBLY
ABGIMOSU BIGAMOUS
ABGINORT ABORTING
ABGINOST BOASTING
ABGINTTU ABUTTING
ABGKORSW WORKBAGS
ABGLLLOY GLOBALLY
ABGLLORU GLOBULAR
ABGLMOPU PLUMBAGO
ABGLNOOT LONGBOAT
ABGLNOUW BUNGALOW
ABGLORSU GLABROUS
ABGLRRSU BURGLARS
ABGLRRUY BURGLARY
ABGLRSUZ SALZBURG
ABGNORSU OSNABURG
ABGNOSTU GUNBOATS
ABGOPSST POSTBAGS
ABHHIPST HIPBATHS
ABHIKLLW HAWKBILL
ABHIKLOR KOHLRABI
ABHILNOS HOBNAILS
ABHILNOT BIATHLON
ABHILOPS BASOPHIL
ABHILSTU HALIBUTS
ABHIMNOR MORBIHAN
ABHIOSTU HAUTBOIS
ABHIRRSU AIRBRUSH
ABHKOOOT BOAT HOOK
ABHLLMOT MOTHBALL
ABHLLOOY BALLYHOO
ABHLOSWW WASHBOWL
ABHLSSTU SALTBUSH
ABHMNSUU SUBHUMAN
ABHMOORT BATHROOM
ABHOORST TARBOOSH
ABHOOSTW SHOWBOAT
ABHORRSU HARBOURS
ABHOSTUY HAUTBOYS
ABHRSTTU BATHURST
ABIIINOT AB INITIO
ABIIKLSS BASILISK
ABIILLMR MILLIBAR
ABIILLTY LABILITY
ABIILMNO BINOMIAL
ABIILMNS ALBINISM
ABIILNOT LIBATION
ABIILNOV BOLIVIAN

ABIILNRZ BRAZILIN
ABIILNST SIBILANT
ABIILPTY PITIABLY
ABIIMNOT AMBITION
ABIIRSSV VIBRISSA
ABIJLNTU JUBILANT
ABIKLMNS LAMBSKIN
ABIKNORR IRONBARK
ABILLLPY PLAYBILL
ABILLSWY WAYBILLS
ABILMNOU OLIBANUM
ABILMOPS BIOPLASM
ABILNOOT BOLTONIA,
　OBLATION
ABILNOTU ABLUTION,
　ABUTILON
ABILNRTU TRIBUNAL
ABILNRWY BRAWNILY
ABILNSTU ISTANBUL
ABILORST STROBILA
ABILRSSY BRASSILY
ABILSTUY SUITABLY
ABIMNOSU BIMANOUS
ABIMORSU BIRAMOUS
ABIMPSST BAPTISMS
ABINOORT ABORTION
ABINORSW RAINBOWS
ABINOSST BASTIONS
ABINOSTT BOTANIST
ABINRTTY BRITTANY
ABINRTUY URBANITY
ABIOPRSU BIPAROUS
ABIORRTV VIBRATOR
ABIORSTV VIBRATOS
ABIORTUY OBITUARY
ABIPRSTT BIT PARTS
ABIPRSUU UBI SUPRA
ABIPSSTT BAPTISTS
ABIRRSTU AIRBURST
ABISSSST BASSISTS
ABKKMOOR BOOKMARK
ABKLLNOR BANKROLL
ABKLRSUW BULWARKS
ABKNPRTU BANKRUPT
ABKOOPSS PASSBOOK
ABLLMOOR BALLROOM
ABLLMOPW BLOWLAMP
ABLLNOOS BALLOONS
ABLLNOSW SNOWBALL
ABLLORRS ROLL BARS
ABLLOSTY TALLBOYS
ABLLPSSU BALLS-UPS
ABLLRTUY BRUTALLY

ABLLSSUY SYLLABUS	ACCEEHMP CAMPECHE	ACCEKLNR CRACKNEL
ABLMNRUU LABURNUM	ACCEEILR CELERIAC	ACCEKLRS CACKLERS
ABLNORYZ BLAZONRY	ACCEEILS ECCLESIA	ACCEKOPS PEACOCKS
ABLOORTY OBLATORY	ACCEEIMR ICE CREAM	ACCEKPSU CUP CAKES
ABLOPRVY PROVABLY	ACCEEKLN NECKLACE	ACCEKRRS CRACKERS
ABLOPSYY PLAYBOYS	ACCEELNR CLARENCE	ACCELMNY CYCLAMEN
ABLORSST BORSTALS	ACCEELOS COALESCE	ACCELNOV CONCLAVE
ABLORSSU SUBSOLAR	ACCEENNS NASCENCE	ACCELNRU CARUNCLE
ABLOSSUU SABULOUS	ACCEENST ACESCENT	ACCELNTU CLEAN-CUT
ABLOSTTU SUBTOTAL	ACCEESSS ACCESSES	ACCELORS CORACLES
ABLPRTUY ABRUPTLY	ACCEFFIY EFFICACY	ACCELRSY SCARCELY
ABMORSTU TAMBOURS	ACCEFILS FASCICLE	ACCELRTU CLEAR-CUT
ABNOORYZ BRYOZOAN	ACCEGKMO GAMECOCK	ACCENOPT CONCEPTA
ABNOOSSS BASSOONS	ACCEHIKP CHICKPEA	ACCENORT ACCENTOR
ABNORTUU RUN-ABOUT	ACCEHILM ALCHEMIC,	ACCENOST COSECANT
ABNOSSUU AUBUSSON	CHEMICAL	ACCENOTT CONCETTA
ABOPRSST TOP BRASS	ACCEHILP CEPHALIC	ACCEOPRT ACCEPTOR
ACCCENPY PECCANCY	ACCEHILS CHALICES	ACCEORST ECTOSARC
ACCCFIIL CALCIFIC	ACCEHIMN MECHANIC	ACCERSST SCARCEST
ACCCIILT CALCITIC	ACCEHINO ANECHOIC	ACCERSSU ACCUSERS
ACCDDEOR ACCORDED	ACCEHINR ACRE-INCH,	ACCESSTU CACTUSES
ACCDDIII DIACIDIC	CHANCIER, CHICANER	ACCESSUU CAUCUSES
ACCDDIIT DIDACTIC	ACCEHINT CATECHIN	ACCFHKLO HALF COCK
ACCDEELN CANCELED	ACCEHIRT CATCHIER	ACCFHLTY CATCHFLY
ACCDEENS CADENCES	ACCEHKPY PAYCHECK	ACCFLNOO CONFOCAL
ACCDEENT ACCENTED	ACCEHLNS CHANCELS	ACCGHINN CHANCING
ACCDEEPT ACCEPTED	ACCEHLOR COCHLEAR	ACCGHINO COACHING
ACCDEESS ACCESSED	ACCEHLOT CATECHOL	ACCGHINT CATCHING
ACCDEGIN ACCEDING	ACCEHMNO COACHMEN,	ACCGIKLN CACKLING,
ACCDEILY DELICACY	COMANCHE	CLACKING
ACCDEINO DECANOIC	ACCEHNNO CHACONNE	ACCGIKMR GIMCRACK
ACCDEINT ACCIDENT	ACCEHNOR ENCROACH	ACCGIKNR CRACKING
ACCDEIRT ACCREDIT	ACCEHNRY CHANCERY	ACCGILOX COXALGIC
ACCDEKLR CRACKLED	ACCEHNUY CHAUNCEY	ACCGINRU ACCRUING
ACCDEKOS COCKADES	ACCEHOPT CACHEPOT	ACCGINSU ACCUSING
ACCDELSU CUL-DE-SAC	ACCEIKPS ICE PACKS	ACCHHITT CHITCHAT
ACCDELSY CYCLADES	ACCEILLR CLERICAL	ACCHIIMS CHIASMIC
ACCDEORR ACCORDER	ACCEILLU CAULICLE	ACCHIIST CHIASTIC
ACCDEOST ACCOSTED	ACCEILLV CLAVICLE	ACCHILNY CHANCILY
ACCDERSU ACCURSED	ACCEILNT CANTICLE	ACCHILOT CATHOLIC
ACCDESUU CADUCEUS	ACCEILNY CALYCINE	ACCHILOY CHICLAYO
ACCDHIIR DIARCHIC	ACCEILRV CERVICAL	ACCHILTY CATCHILY
ACCDHIOT CATHODIC	ACCEIMRS CERAMICS	ACCHIMOR ACHROMIC
ACCDHIRY DYARCHIC	ACCEINRT ACENTRIC,	ACCHINNO CINCHONA
ACCDHPTU DUTCH CAP	NEARCTIC	ACCHINOS CHICANOS
ACCDIIOT ACIDOTIC	ACCEINSV VACCINES	ACCHINPU CAPUCHIN
ACCDILTY DACTYLIC	ACCEIOTV COACTIVE	ACCHIORT THORACIC,
ACCDINOR CANCROID,	ACCEIPRS CAPRICES	TROCHAIC
DRACONIC	ACCEIPRT PRACTICE	ACCHKLOR CHARLOCK
ACCDIOOR CORACOID	ACCEIRTU CRUCIATE	ACCHKOSY HAYCOCKS
ACCDITUY CADUCITY	ACCEISST ASCETICS	ACCHNOTU COUCHANT
ACCDOSUU CADUCOUS	ACCEISTT ECSTATIC	ACCHOPRS CASH CROP
ACCEEHLO COCHLEAE	ACCEKKOR ROCK CAKE	ACCHORTY OCTARCHY

ACCHORVY CRY HAVOC
ACCHRSTY SCRATCHY
ACCIILLN CLINICAL
ACCIILMT CLIMATIC
ACCIILRT CRITICAL
ACCIINOT ACONITIC, CATIONIC
ACCIINTY CYANITIC
ACCIIRTX CICATRIX
ACCIKKNN NICKNACK
ACCIKKRR RICKRACK
ACCIKKTT TICKTACK
ACCIKLLS SICK CALL
ACCIKLOT COCKTAIL
ACCILMUU ACICULUM
ACCILNOT LACTONIC
ACCILNOV VOLCANIC
ACCILORT CORTICAL
ACCILRRU CIRCULAR
ACCILRSY ACRYLICS
ACCILSSS CLASSICS
ACCILTUU CUTICULA
ACCIMNOS MOCCASIN
ACCIMORU COUMARIC
ACCIMPSU CAPSICUM
ACCINOOS OCCASION
ACCINOOT COACTION
ACCINORT NARCOTIC
ACCINORV CAVICORN
ACCINOTY CYANOTIC
ACCIOPST SPICCATO
ACCIORST ACROSTIC, SOCRATIC
ACCIORSY ISOCRACY
ACCIOSTU ACOUSTIC
ACCIRRTT TRICTRAC
ACCIRSTY SCARCITY
ACCKKRSU RUCKSACK
ACCKOOOT COCKATOO
ACCKOPRT CRACKPOT
ACCKORST STOCKCAR
ACCKOSSS CASSOCKS
ACCKPRSU CRACKUPS
ACCLLOSU OCCLUSAL
ACCLLSUU CALCULUS
ACCMNOOR MOROCCAN
ACCMOPST COMPACTS
ACCMOSTU ACCUSTOM
ACCNOORS RACCOONS
ACCNOPTU OCCUPANT
ACCNORTT CONTRACT
ACCNORTU ACCUTRON
ACCNOSTT CONTACTS

ACCNOSTU ACCOUNTS
ACCOPSTY COPYCATS
ACCORRTY CARRYCOT
ACDDDEIT ADDICTED
ACDDDEKU DEAD DUCK
ACDDEEES DECEASED
ACDDEEFR RED-FACED
ACDDEEHT DETACHED
ACDDEEIT DEDICATE
ACDDEELR DECLARED
ACDDEELS DESCALED
ACDDEEMP DECAMPED
ACDDEENS ASCENDED
ACDDEENT DECADENT, DECANTED
ACDDEETU EDUCATED
ACDDEHKN DECKHAND
ACDDEIIL DEICIDAL
ACDDEIIM MEDICAID
ACDDEILU DECIDUAL
ACDDEINR RIDDANCE
ACDDEITT DICTATED
ACDDEKLO DEADLOCK
ACDDENTU ADDUCENT
ACDDERSU CRUSADED
ACDDERTU TRADUCED
ACDDGINU ADDUCING
ACDDGINY CADDYING
ACDDHIRY HYDRACID
ACDDHKOS SHADDOCK
ACDDIIOR CARDIOID
ACDDILNY CANDIDLY
ACDDIRSS DISCARDS
ACDDKLNO DOCKLAND
ACDDKOPS PADDOCKS
ACDDKORY DOCKYARD
ACDDORTU ADDUCTOR
ACDEEEFT DEFECATE
ACDEEENR CAREENED
ACDEEENT ANTECEDE
ACDEEERR CAREERED
ACDEEERS DECREASE
ACDEEESS SEEDCASE
ACDEEFFT AFFECTED
ACDEEFIN DEFIANCE
ACDEEFPR PREFACED
ACDEEGLY DELEGACY
ACDEEHIV ACHIEVED
ACDEEHMR DEMARCHE
ACDEEHNN ENHANCED
ACDEEHPR PREACHED
ACDEEHRS SEARCHED
ACDEEHRT DETACHER

ACDEEILT DELICATE
ACDEEIMR MEDICARE
ACDEEIMT DECIMATE, MEDICATE
ACDEEINN ENNEADIC
ACDEEINU AUDIENCE
ACDEEINV DEVIANCE
ACDEEKPT TAPE DECK
ACDEELLR RECALLED
ACDEELNR CALENDER
ACDEELNS CLEANSED
ACDEELPR PARCELED, REPLACED
ACDEELRR DECLARER
ACDEELRT DECRETAL
ACDEELSS DECLASSE
ACDEEMNP ENCAMPED
ACDEEMRS SCREAMED
ACDEEMRT CREMATED
ACDEENOT ANECDOTE
ACDEENRS ASCENDER
ACDEENRT CANTERED, DECANTER, RECANTED
ACDEENRZ CREDENZA
ACDEEORT DECORATE
ACDEEPPR RECAPPED
ACDEEPRT CARPETED
ACDEERRT RETRACED
ACDEERSS CARESSED
ACDEFGIN DEFACING
ACDEFIIP PACIFIED
ACDEFILN CANFIELD
ACDEFILR FILECARD
ACDEFINN FINANCED
ACDEFIRR FREDRICA
ACDEFOTU OUTFACED
ACDEFOTW TWOFACED
ACDEFRSU SURFACED
ACDEFRTU FURCATED
ACDEGGRS SCRAGGED
ACDEGIMR GRIMACED
ACDEGINU GUIDANCE
ACDEGINY DECAYING
ACDEGIRS DISGRACE
ACDEHHNU HAUNCHED
ACDEHHTT THATCHED
ACDEHIJK HIJACKED
ACDEHILL HELLADIC
ACDEHILR HERALDIC
ACDEHIMN MACHINED
ACDEHINR RICHENDA
ACDEHIRT TRACHEID
ACDEHKLO HEADLOCK

ACDEHKLS SHACKLED
ACDEHKRU ARCHDUKE
ACDEHKSS CASH DESK
ACDEHKTW THWACKED
ACDEHLNR CHANDLER
ACDEHLNU LAUNCHED
ACDEHNOR ANCHORED
ACDEHNST SNATCHED,
  STANCHED
ACDEHORR HARD-CORE
ACDEHORT CHORDATE
ACDEHOST CATHODES
ACDEHOTT COT DEATH
ACDEHPST DESPATCH
ACDEHRRS CHRESARD
ACDEHRST STARCHED
ACDEIILN ALCIDINE
ACDEIINR ACRIDINE
ACDEIINS SCIAENID
ACDEIINT ACTINIDE,
  INDICATE
ACDEIJNU JAUNDICE
ACDEIKNP PANICKED
ACDEILLM MEDALLIC
ACDEILLS CEDILLAS
ACDEILLV CAVILLED
ACDEILMS DECIMALS,
  MEDICALS
ACDEILMX CLIMAXED
ACDEILNP PANICLED
ACDEILNU CLAUDINE
ACDEILOR CORDELIA
ACDEILPS DISPLACE
ACDEILRT ARTICLED
ACDEILST CITADELS,
  DIALECTS
ACDEILSY ECDYSIAL
ACDEIMNO COMEDIAN,
  DAEMONIC, DEMONIAC
ACDEIMNP PANDEMIC
ACDEIMOR MORDECAI
ACDEIMPT IMPACTED
ACDEIMRT TIMECARD
ACDEINNR CRANNIED
ACDEINOS DIOCESAN
ACDEINOT CATENOID
ACDEINOV VOIDANCE
ACDEINPT PEDANTIC
ACDEINRT DICENTRA
ACDEINSS ACIDNESS
ACDEINST DISTANCE
ACDEINTU INCUDATE
ACDEIOPS DIASCOPE

ACDEIORT CERATOID
ACDEIOSU EDACIOUS
ACDEIPSS CAPSISED
ACDEIPSZ CAPSIZED
ACDEIQRU ACQUIRED
ACDEIRSS CRESSIDA,
  SIDECARS
ACDEIRTT TETRACID
ACDEISTT ACID TEST,
  DICTATES
ACDEKLMU LAME DUCK
ACDEKNPU UNPACKED
ACDEKOST STOCKADE
ACDELLOR CAROLLED,
  COLLARED
ACDELLOS SO-CALLED
ACDELLOT COLLATED
ACDELMOS DAMOCLES
ACDELNOO CANOODLE
ACDELNOR COLANDER
ACDELNPU UNPLACED
ACDELNRY DRY-CLEAN
ACDELRSW SCRAWLED
ACDELRSY SACREDLY
ACDEMMRS SCRAMMED
ACDEMNOR ROMANCED
ACDEMOPR COMPARED
ACDEMORS COMRADES
ACDEMORT DEMOCRAT
ACDEMUUV VACUUMED
ACDENNNO CANNONED
ACDENNOR ORDNANCE
ACDENOPR ENDOCARP
ACDENORY CRAYONED,
  DEACONRY
ACDENRTU UNDERACT
ACDENRVY VERDANCY
ACDENSST DESCANTS
ACDEORRT REDACTOR
ACDEORST REDCOATS,
  SACRED TO
ACDEORSU CAROUSED
ACDEORTU EDUCATOR
ACDEORTV CAVORTED
ACDEPPRS SCRAPPED
ACDEPRTU CAPTURED
ACDEQTUU AQUEDUCT
ACDERRSU CRUSADER
ACDERRTU TRADUCER
ACDERSSU CRUSADES
ACDERSTT TEST CARD
ACDFFHNU HANDCUFF
ACDFFILR RADCLIFF

ACDFFIRT DIFFRACT
ACDFFLOS SCAFFOLD
ACDFGOOT ACT OF GOD
ACDFIILU FIDUCIAL
ACDFILOU FUCOIDAL
ACDGHOTW DOGWATCH,
  WATCHDOG
ACDGILNR CRADLING
ACDGILNS SCALDING
ACDGIMOT DOGMATIC
ACDGORST DOGCARTS
ACDHILPR PILCHARD
ACDHINOR HADRONIC
ACDHINSW SANDWICH
ACDHIPST DISPATCH
ACDHIQRU CHARQUID
ACDHKLRU HARD LUCK
ACDHKORS ROCK DASH
ACDHLNOR CHALDRON
ACDHMNTU DUTCHMAN
ACDHNOSW CASH DOWN,
  COWHANDS
ACDHOOTW WOODCHAT
ACDHOPRY HARD COPY
ACDHORRS ORCHARDS
ACDIIILN INDICIAL
ACDIIJLU JUDICIAL
ACDIILMS DISCLAIM
ACDIILNO CONIDIAL
ACDIILSU SUICIDAL
ACDIILTY DIALYTIC
ACDIIMNO DOMINICA
ACDIIMOR DIORAMIC
ACDIIMOT DIATOMIC
ACDIIMSU ASCIDIUM
ACDIINNT INDICANT
ACDIINOT ACTINOID,
  DIATONIC
ACDIIOSS ACIDOSIS
ACDIIOSX OXIDASIC
ACDIIRST CARDITIS
ACDIIRTY ACRIDITY
ACDIISST SADISTIC
ACDILLOT CLOTILDA
ACDILLPY PLACIDLY
ACDILMTU TALMUDIC
ACDILNOO CONOIDAL
ACDILNOR IRONCLAD
ACDILNOT DALTONIC
ACDILNSY SYNDICAL
ACDILNUU NUDICAUL
ACDILORS CORDIALS
ACDILOUV OVIDUCAL

ACDILSTW WILDCATS
ACDILSUU CLAUDIUS
ACDIMNOO CODOMAIN, MONOACID
ACDIMNSU SCANDIUM
ACDIMNSY DYNAMICS
ACDINOPS SPONDAIC
ACDINORS SARDONIC
ACDINORT TORNADIC
ACDINSTY DYNASTIC
ACDIOPRS PICADORS, SPORADIC
ACDIORTT DICTATOR
ACDIOSTX DOXASTIC
ACDIRSTT DISTRACT
ACDISTUV VIADUCTS
ACDJNSTU ADJUNCTS
ACDKLOPS PADLOCKS
ACDKMPSU MUDPACKS
ACDLNOPS COLD SNAP
ACDLNORS CALDRONS
ACDLNORU CAULDRON, COURLAND
ACDLNORY CONDYLAR
ACDLNOST SCOTLAND
ACDLOOOR COLORADO
ACDLOORT DOCTORAL
ACDLORWY COWARDLY
ACDMMNOO COMMANDO
ACDMMNOS COMMANDS
ACDMNORY DORMANCY, MORDANCY
ACDNOORT ACRODONT
ACDNOORV CORDOVAN
ACDNOSTW DOWNCAST
ACDOORST OSTRACOD
ACDOPRST POSTCARD
ACDRSSTU CUSTARDS
ACDRSTTU DUSTCART
ACEEEFRR CAREFREE
ACEEEGLN ELEGANCE
ACEEEIPR EARPIECE
ACEEEKPV KEEP CAVE
ACEEELMR CAMELEER
ACEEENSV EVANESCE
ACEEEPSS ESCAPEES
ACEEERRT RECREATE
ACEEERTX EXECRATE
ACEEESUV EVACUEES
ACEEFFIN CAFFEINE
ACEEFHWY WHEYFACE
ACEEFLPU PEACEFUL
ACEEFLSS FACELESS

ACEEFPRR PREFACER
ACEEFPRS PREFACES
ACEEFPTY TYPEFACE
ACEEFRSU FARCEUSE
ACEEGHNX EXCHANGE
ACEEGHRR RECHARGE
ACEEGILS LEGACIES
ACEEGIMY MAGIC EYE
ACEEGINS AGENCIES
ACEEGINT AGENETIC
ACEEGKRW WRECKAGE
ACEEGNOZ COZENAGE
ACEEGNSV SCAVENGE
ACEEGORV COVERAGE
ACEEHHST CHEETAHS
ACEEHINS EISENACH
ACEEHINT ECHINATE
ACEEHIPT PETECHIA
ACEEHIRT HETAERIC
ACEEHIRV ACHIEVER
ACEEHLNR CHARLENE
ACEEHLNT CATHLEEN
ACEEHLOS SHOELACE
ACEEHLRS HERACLES
ACEEHLSW ESCHEWAL
ACEEHMNP CAMPHENE
ACEEHMNR MENARCHE
ACEEHMRS CASHMERE, MARCHESE
ACEEHMST MACHETES
ACEEHNNR ENHANCER
ACEEHNRT CHARENTE
ACEEHPRR PREACHER
ACEEHPST CHEAPEST
ACEEHRRS RESEARCH, SEARCHER
ACEEHRSS SEARCHES
ACEEHRST HECTARES, TEACHERS
ACEEHRTT CATHETER
ACEEHRTY CYTHEREA
ACEEHSTT TEA CHEST
ACEEIKRR CREAKIER
ACEEIKST ICE SKATE
ACEEILNR RELIANCE
ACEEILNS SALIENCE
ACEEILPS ESPECIAL
ACEEIMRR CREAMIER
ACEEINNR NARCEINE
ACEEINPS SAPIENCE
ACEEINPT PATIENCE
ACEEINRS INCREASE

ACEEINRT CENTIARE, CREATINE
ACEEINST CINEASTE
ACEEINTV ENACTIVE
ACEEINTX EXITANCE
ACEEIRSU CAUSERIE
ACEEIRSW WISEACRE
ACEEIRTV CREATIVE, REACTIVE
ACEEIRTW ICE WATER, WATER ICE
ACEEISTV VESICATE
ACEEKLMR MACKEREL
ACEEKNPS KNEECAPS
ACEELLMR MARCELLE
ACEELLNS NACELLES
ACEELLNT LANCELET
ACEELLRR CELLARER
ACEELLRT CELLARET
ACEELNOR CAERLEON
ACEELNPT PENTACLE
ACEELNRS CLEANERS, CLEANSER
ACEELNRU CERULEAN, LAURENCE
ACEELNRW LAWRENCE
ACEELNST CLEANEST
ACEELNSU NUCLEASE
ACEELNSV ENCLAVES
ACEELNTT TENTACLE
ACEELNTU NUCLEATE
ACEELOPS ESCALOPE, OPALESCE
ACEELORT RELOCATE
ACEELPRR REPLACER
ACEELPRV PERCEVAL
ACEELPTU PECULATE
ACEELRSS CARELESS
ACEELRST CLEAREST
ACEELRSV CLEAVERS
ACEELRTU ULCERATE
ACEELRTV CERVELAT
ACEELRTX EXCRETAL
ACEELSTT TELECAST
ACEEMNPS SPACEMEN
ACEEMNST CASEMENT
ACEEMORS RACEMOSE
ACEEMORV OVERCAME
ACEEMRRS CREAMERS, SCREAMER
ACEEMRRY CREAMERY
ACEENNPS PENANCES
ACEENNPZ PENZANCE

ACEENNRT ENTRANCE
ACEENNST CANTEENS
ACEENORT CAROTENE
ACEENOST NOTECASE
ACEENPRR PARCENER
ACEENRRT RECANTER,
RECREANT
ACEENRTT ENTR'ACTE
ACEEPSTT SPECTATE
ACEERRSS CARESSER
ACEERRST TERRACES
ACEERRSU ECRASEUR
ACEERRTU CREATURE
ACEERRUV VERRUCAE
ACEERSSS CARESSES
ACEERSST CERASTES
ACEERSSV CREVASSE
ACEESSTT CASSETTE,
TEST CASE
ACEESSTY CAT'S EYES
ACEFFGIN EFFACING
ACEFFHRU CHAUFFER
ACEFFILT FACE-LIFT
ACEFFLRS SCLAFFER
ACEFGINR REFACING
ACEFGLNO LONG FACE
ACEFGLRU GRACEFUL
ACEFHIKS FISHCAKE
ACEFHISV CAVEFISH
ACEFHORU FAROUCHE
ACEFIIPR PACIFIER
ACEFIIRT ARTIFICE
ACEFILLY FACILELY
ACEFILOP EPIFOCAL
ACEFILOS FOCALISE
ACEFILOZ FOCALIZE
ACEFIMPR CAMPFIRE
ACEFINNR FRANCINE
ACEFINNS FINANCES
ACEFINRS FANCIERS
ACEFINST FANCIEST
ACEFIORR AIRFORCE
ACEFIOSS FIASCOES
ACEFIRRT CRAFTIER
ACEFLLOV CALF LOVE
ACEFLMNO FLAMENCO
ACEFLNOR FALCONER
ACEFLNOT CONFLATE,
FALCONET
ACEFLNRY CRANE FLY
ACEFLORS ALFRESCO
ACEFMNNY FANCY MEN
ACEFNORV CONFERVA

ACEFNRSU FURNACES
ACEFOOPT FOOTPACE
ACEFOORT ACRE-FOOT,
FOOTRACE
ACEFORST FORECAST
ACEFRRSU SURFACER
ACEFRRTU FRACTURE
ACEFRSSU SURFACES
ACEGGILN CAGELING
ACEGGIRR CRAGGIER
ACEGHHNT CHANGTEH
ACEGHIIT CHIGETAI
ACEGHIKN CHEKIANG
ACEGHILN LEACHING
ACEGHINR REACHING
ACEGHINT CHEATING,
TEACHING
ACEGHLTY LYCHGATE
ACEGHOSU GOUACHES
ACEGHRRS CHARGERS
ACEGIKNR CREAKING
ACEGILLR ALLERGIC
ACEGILMU MUCILAGE
ACEGILNN CLEANING
ACEGILNR CLEARING
ACEGILNV CLEAVING
ACEGILNW LACEWING
ACEGILRS GLACIERS
ACEGIMMT TAGMEMIC
ACEGIMNN MENACING
ACEGIMNR CREAMING,
GERMANIC
ACEGIMNT MAGNETIC
ACEGIMRR GRIMACER
ACEGIMRS GRAECISM,
GRIMACES
ACEGINNO CANOEING
ACEGINNS ENCASING
ACEGINNT ENACTING
ACEGINOS COINAGES
ACEGINPR CAPERING
ACEGINPS ESCAPING
ACEGINRS CREASING
ACEGINRT ARGENTIC,
CATERING, CREATING,
REACTING
ACEGINSS CAGINESS
ACEGINTX EXACTING
ACEGIOTT COGITATE
ACEGIPRT PRICE TAG
ACEGLLNO COLLAGEN
ACEGLLOS COLLAGES
ACEGLNRS CLANGERS

ACEGLOSU CAGOULES
ACEGMNOY GEOMANCY
ACEGNNOY CYANOGEN
ACEGNNTY TANGENCY
ACEGNOST COGNATES
ACEGORSS CORSAGES
ACEGORTT COTTAGER
ACEGORTY CATEGORY
ACEGOSTT COTTAGES
ACEHHIRR HIERARCH
ACEHHIRT THE CHAIR
ACEHHMNN HENCHMAN
ACEHHNRT ETHNARCH
ACEHHNSU HAUNCHES
ACEHHPRT HEPTARCH
ACEHHRTT THATCHER
ACEHHRTY HATCHERY,
THEARCHY
ACEHHSTT HATCHETS,
THATCHES
ACEHIIRT HIERATIC
ACEHIJKR HIJACKER
ACEHIKLR CHALKIER
ACEHILLS ACHILLES
ACEHILNP CEPHALIN
ACEHILPR PARHELIC
ACEHILRS CHARLIES
ACEHILTT ATHLETIC
ACEHIMNR CHAIRMEN
ACEHIMNS MACHINES
ACEHIMPT EMPATHIC,
EMPHATIC
ACEHIMRS CHIMERAS
ACEHIMTT THEMATIC
ACEHINOT INCHOATE
ACEHINOX HEXANOIC
ACEHINST ASTHENIC,
CHANTIES, TEACH-INS
ACEHIPRS SERAPHIC
ACEHIPRT PATCHIER,
PHREATIC, PIE CHART
ACEHIPST PASTICHE
ACEHIPTT PATHETIC
ACEHIPTW WHITECAP
ACEHIRSS CASHIERS
ACEHIRST CHARIEST
ACEHIRSU EUCHARIS
ACEHIRSV ARCHIVES
ACEHIRTT CHATTIER
ACEHISST CHASTISE
ACEHISTX CATHEXIS
ACEHKLOV HAVELOCK
ACEHKLRS SHACKLER

ACEHKLSS SHACKLES	ACEHRRST CHARTERS,	ACEILMRT METRICAL
ACEHKLTY LATCHKEY	STARCHER	ACEILMST CLEMATIS,
ACEHKMPU MUCKHEAP	ACEHRRTT TETRARCH	CLIMATES
ACEHKNSY HACKNEYS	ACEHRSST STARCHES	ACEILMSU MUSICALE
ACEHKORV HAVOCKER	ACEHRSSU CHASSEUR	ACEILMSX CLIMAXES
ACEHKRTW THWACKER	ACEHRSTT RATCHETS	ACEILNNP PINNACLE
ACEHLLOO COALHOLE	ACEHRTTY TRACHYTE	ACEILNOR ACROLEIN,
ACEHLLST HELLCATS	ACEHSSTT CHASTEST	CAROLINE, CORNELIA
ACEHLNNS CHANNELS	ACEHSSTW SWATCHES	ACEILNPS PELICANS
ACEHLNOU EULACHON	ACEIILMN LIMACINE	ACEILNRT CLARINET
ACEHLNOY HALCYONE	ACEIILMX MEXICALI	ACEILNSS LACINESS
ACEHLNPT PLANCHET	ACEIILST SILICATE	ACEILOPR CAPRIOLE
ACEHLNRU LAUNCHER	ACEIIMTU MAIEUTIC	ACEILOPT POETICAL
ACEHLNSU LAUNCHES	ACEIINRT ANTI-ICER,	ACEILORS CALORIES
ACEHLOOT OOTHECAL	ARENITIC, IN A TRICE	ACEILORT LORICATE
ACEHLORS CHORALES	ACEIINTV INACTIVE	ACEILOST SOCIETAL
ACEHLORT CHLORATE,	ACEIIPRS PIRACIES	ACEILOSV VOCALISE
TROCHLEA	ACEIIRRT CRITERIA	ACEILOTV LOCATIVE
ACEHLOTT TEA CLOTH	ACEIISTV CAVITIES	ACEILOVZ VOCALIZE
ACEHLPST CHAPLETS	ACEIJMST MAJESTIC	ACEILPPY PIPECLAY
ACEHLSSS CASHLESS	ACEIKKLS SACKLIKE	ACEILPRS CALIPERS,
ACEHLSST SATCHELS	ACEIKLLY CLAYLIKE	REPLICAS, SPIRACLE
ACEHLSTT CHATTELS	ACEIKLRY CREAKILY	ACEILPRT PARTICLE,
ACEHLSTY CHASTELY	ACEIKMNN NICKNAME	PRELATIC
ACEHMNRT MERCHANT	ACEIKMRV MAVERICK	ACEILPRU PECULIAR
ACEHMNSS CHESSMAN	ACEIKNPS CAPESKIN	ACEILPRV PERCIVAL
ACEHMNTW WATCHMEN	ACEIKNRR CRANKIER	ACEILPSS SLIPCASE,
ACEHMORT CHROMATE	ACEIKOTW KATOWICE	SPECIALS
ACEHMRRS CHARMERS,	ACEIKPPR PIPE RACK	ACEILPXY EPICALYX
MARCHERS	ACEIKPSX PICKAXES	ACEILRSS CLASSIER
ACEHMSTU MUSTACHE	ACEIKSTT TACKIEST	ACEILRST ARTICLES,
ACEHNNPT PENCHANT	ACEILLMR MICELLAR,	RECITALS
ACEHNOPR CHAPERON	MILLRACE	ACEILRSU AURICLES
ACEHNOPT CENOTAPH	ACEILLMT METALLIC	ACEILRSV VISCERAL
ACEHNPSU PAUNCHES	ACEILLMY MYCELIAL	ACEILRTT TRACTILE
ACEHNQUU QUECHUAN	ACEILLNT CLIENTAL	ACEILRTU LUCRETIA
ACEHNRRS RANCHERS	ACEILLOP CALLIOPE	ACEILRTV VERTICAL
ACEHNRSS ARCHNESS	ACEILLOR ROCAILLE	ACEILRTY LITERACY
ACEHNRST SNATCHER,	ACEILLOS LOCALISE	ACEILRUZ LUCREZIA
STANCHER	ACEILLOT TEOCALLI	ACEILSST SCALIEST
ACEHNSST SNATCHES	ACEILLOZ LOCALIZE	ACEILSTT LATTICES
ACEHNSTU UNCHASTE	ACEILLPR CALLIPER	ACEILTVY ACTIVELY
ACEHNSWZ SZECHWAN	ACEILLPS ALLSPICE	ACEIMMNP PEMMICAN
ACEHOPRR REPROACH	ACEILLRS CARLISLE	ACEIMMRS RACEMISM
ACEHOPRS POACHERS	ACEILLRV CAVILLER	ACEIMNRU MANICURE
ACEHORRV OVERARCH	ACEILMMO CAMOMILE	ACEIMNST SEMANTIC
ACEHORST THORACES	ACEILMMR CLAMMIER	ACEIMNSY SYCAMINE
ACEHORTT THEOCRAT	ACEILMNO COALMINE	ACEIMOTX TOXAEMIC
ACEHORTU OUTREACH	ACEILMNP MANCIPLE	ACEIMOTZ AZOTEMIC,
ACEHOSSW SHOWCASE	ACEILMNS MESCALIN	METAZOIC
ACEHOSTU SOUTACHE	ACEILMOS CAMISOLE	ACEIMPSS ESCAPISM
ACEHPRST CHAPTERS	ACEILMPS MISPLACE	ACEIMPST CAMPSITE
ACEHPRSU PURCHASE	ACEILMRS MIRACLES	ACEIMRRW WAR CRIME

ACEIMRST CERAMIST,
    MATRICES
ACEIMRTU MURICATE
ACEINNOS CANONISE
ACEINNOZ CANONIZE
ACEINNPS PINNACES
ACEINNRS CRANNIES
ACEINNST ANCIENTS,
    CANNIEST, INSTANCE
ACEINNSU NUISANCE
ACEINNTU UNCINATE
ACEINOPR APOCRINE,
    PROCAINE
ACEINOPS CANOPIES,
    CAPONISE
ACEINOPZ CAPONIZE
ACEINORS SCENARIO
ACEINORT CREATION,
    REACTION
ACEINORV VERONICA
ACEINOST CANOEIST
ACEINOTT TACONITE
ACEINOTV CONATIVE
ACEINOTX EXACTION
ACEINPTT PITTANCE
ACEINRRY CINERARY
ACEINRSS RACINESS
ACEINRST CANISTER,
    CISTERNA, SCANTIER
ACEINRTT INTERACT
ACEINRTV NAVICERT
ACEINRVY VICENARY
ACEINSSU ISSUANCE
ACEINSTV VESICANT
ACEINTTU TUNICATE
ACEINTTX EXCITANT
ACEINTTY TENACITY
ACEIOPRT OPERATIC
ACEIORSV VARICOSE
ACEIOTVV VOCATIVE
ACEIOVVV VIVA VOCE
ACEIPPRR CRAPPIER,
    PERICARP
ACEIPRRS PERISARC
ACEIPRST CRISPATE,
    PRACTISE
ACEIPRTY APYRETIC
ACEIPSST ESCAPIST
ACEIPSSU AUSPICES
ACEIPSTV CAPTIVES
ACEIQRRU ACQUIRER
ACEIRRRS CARRIERS
ACEIRRSU CURARISE

ACEIRRSW AIRCREWS,
    AIRSCREW, WAR CRIES
ACEIRRUZ CURARIZE
ACEIRSST SCARIEST
ACEIRSTT CRISTATE,
    SCATTIER
ACEIRSTU SURICATE
ACEIRSTZ CRAZIEST
ACEIRTTU URTICATE
ACEIRTTV TRACTIVE
ACEIRTUV CURATIVE
ACEIRTVY VERACITY
ACEISSTU SAUCIEST,
    SUITCASE
ACEISTTT CATTIEST
ACEISTTU EUSTATIC
ACEJLORY CAJOLERY
ACEKKMRU MUCKRAKE
ACEKLSST SLACKEST
ACEKMRSS SMACKERS
ACEKNORT ONE-TRACK
ACEKNPRU UNPACKER
ACEKNRRT RACK-RENT
ACEKORSW CASEWORK
ACEKQRUY QUACKERY
ACELLLRU CELLULAR
ACELLNOT LANCELOT
ACELLNRU NUCELLAR
ACELLOPS COLLAPSE
ACELLORV OVERCALL
ACELLOSW COLESLAW
ACELLPSS SCALPELS
ACELLRSU CURE-ALLS
ACELLRTY RECTALLY
ACELLSSU CALLUSES
ACELMNNS CLANSMEN
ACELMNSS CALMNESS
ACELMNSU UNCLE SAM
ACELMORS SCLEROMA
ACELMORY CLAYMORE
ACELMSTU MUSCATEL
ACELNOOT ECOTONAL
ACELNORT CARLETON
ACELNOSU LACUNOSE
ACELNOTV COVALENT
ACELNRVY CRAVENLY
ACELNSSU SCALENUS
ACELOPPU POPULACE
ACELOPRT PECTORAL
ACELOPST POLECATS
ACELOPTU COPULATE
ACELOQSU COEQUALS
ACELORSS LACROSSE

ACELORST SECTORAL
ACELORSU CAROUSEL
ACELORSY COARSELY
ACELORTU CLEAROUT
ACELOSTU OSCULATE
ACELOSTY ACOLYTES
ACELPPRS CLAPPERS
ACELPRSS SCALPERS
ACELPRST SPECTRAL
ACELPRSU SPECULAR
ACELPSSU CAPSULES
ACELPTUU CUPULATE
ACELRRSW CRAWLERS,
    SCRAWLER
ACELRSTT CLATTERS,
    SCARLETT
ACELRTTU CULTRATE
ACELRTTY CLATTERY
ACELSSTT TACTLESS
ACELSUUV VAUCLUSE
ACEMMOTY MYCETOMA
ACEMMRRS CRAMMERS
ACEMNOOR CAMEROON
ACEMNORS ROMANCES
ACEMNRUY NUMERACY
ACEMOOST COMATOSE
ACEMOPRR COMPARER
ACEMOPRS COMPARES,
    MESOCARP
ACEMORRT CREMATOR
ACEMORSY SYCAMORE
ACEMPSSU CAMPUSES
ACENNNOU ANNOUNCE
ACENNOSS CANONESS
ACENNOTT COTENANT
ACENNOTV COVENANT
ACENNOTZ CANZONET
ACENNRSS SCANNERS
ACENOPST CAPSTONE,
    OPENCAST
ACENORRT TORRANCE
ACENORRW CAREWORN
ACENORST ANCESTOR
ACENORSU NACREOUS
ACENORTU COURANTE
ACENORTY ENACTORY
ACENOSTV CENTAVOS
ACENPTTU PUNCTATE
ACENRSTT TRANSECT
ACENRSTU CENTAURS,
    ETRUSCAN, RECUSANT
ACENRSTY ANCESTRY
ACENRTTU TRUNCATE

ACENRTUY CENTAURY
ACENSSTU NUTCASES
ACENSSTW NEWSCAST
ACEOOPSU POACEOUS
ACEOORTV EVOCATOR,
OVERCOAT
ACEOPPRS COPPERAS
ACEORRST CREATORS,
REACTORS
ACEORRTT RETROACT
ACEORRTU EUROCRAT
ACEORSST COARSEST,
COASTERS
ACEORSTV OVERCAST
ACEOSSUY SOY SAUCE
ACEOSTTU OUTCASTE
ACEOSTUU AUTOCUES
ACEPRRSS SCRAPERS
ACEPRSTU CAPTURES
ACEPSTTY TYPECAST
ACEQRSTU RACQUETS
ACERRSUV VERRUCAS
ACERRUVZ VERACRUZ
ACERSSUY SYRACUSE
ACERSTTX EXTRACTS
ACERSTTY CYTASTER
ACERTTUW CUTWATER
ACFFGHIN CHAFFING
ACFFIILO OFFICIAL
ACFFILNU FANCIFUL
ACFGIIPR CAPRIFIG
ACFGINNY FANCYING
ACFGINRT CRAFTING
ACFGITUY FUGACITY
ACFHHINW HAWFINCH
ACFHIJKS JACKFISH
ACFHILNO FALCHION
ACFHILOS COALFISH
ACFHIRSW CRAWFISH
ACFHIRSY CRAYFISH
ACFHISSU FUCHSIAS
ACFHLOSW CASH FLOW
ACFHLTUW WATCHFUL
ACFHORRT RH FACTOR
ACFIILTY FACILITY
ACFIIMPS PACIFISM
ACFIIPST PACIFIST
ACFIKLNS CALFSKIN
ACFILLSY FISCALLY
ACFILNOR FORNICAL
ACFILNPU CUP FINAL
ACFILORT TRIFOCAL
ACFILRTY CRAFTILY

ACFILSSY CLASSIFY
ACFIMNRU FRANCIUM
ACFINORT FRACTION
ACFINOST FACTIONS
ACFINSTY SANCTIFY
ACFIOPRY FAIR COPY
ACFIOSTU FACTIOUS
ACFISSST FASCISTS
ACFKLLOR ROCKFALL
ACFKOORR ROOF RACK
ACFLLMRU CRAM-FULL
ACFLMNOO MOONCALF
ACFLNORY FALCONRY
ACFLOOPS FOOLSCAP
ACFLORSU SCROFULA
ACFMOTTU FACTOTUM
ACFOOSTT CAT'S-FOOT
ACGGHINN CHANGING
ACGGHINR CHARGING
ACGGIINT GIGANTIC
ACGGIIOS ISAGOGIC
ACGGILNN CLANGING,
GLANCING
ACGGLNOU GLUCAGON
ACGGLRSY SCRAGGLY
ACGHHIJK HIGHJACK
ACGHHINT HATCHING
ACGHHNOW HANGCHOW
ACGHIIMN MICHIGAN
ACGHIINN CHAINING
ACGHIINR CHAIRING
ACGHIKLN CHALKING
ACGHIKNS SHACKING
ACGHIKNW WHACKING
ACGHILNS CLASHING
ACGHILNT LATCHING
ACGHILOR OLIGARCH
ACGHIMNP CHAMPING
ACGHIMNR CHARMING,
MARCHING
ACGHIMNT MATCHING
ACGHINNT CHANTING
ACGHINOP POACHING
ACGHINPP CHAPPING
ACGHINPR PARCHING
ACGHINPT NIGHTCAP,
PATCHING
ACGHINRR CHARRING
ACGHINRS CRASHING
ACGHINRT CHARTING
ACGHINST SCATHING
ACGHINTT CHATTING
ACGHINTU TAICHUNG

ACGHINTW WATCHING
ACGHINTY YACHTING
ACGHIPRS GRAPHICS
ACGHNRYY GYNARCHY
ACGIILMN CLAIMING
ACGIILNO LOGICIAN
ACGIILNV CAVILING
ACGIINRT GRANITIC
ACGIJLNO CAJOLING
ACGIKLNN CLANKING
ACGIKLNO CLOAKING
ACGIKLNS SLACKING
ACGIKLNT TACKLING
ACGIKLNU CAULKING
ACGIKLRY GARLICKY
ACGIKMNS SMACKING
ACGIKNNR CRANKING
ACGIKNNS SNACKING
ACGIKNOR CROAKING
ACGIKNQU QUACKING
ACGIKNRT TRACKING
ACGIKNST STACKING
ACGILLLR CALL GIRL
ACGILLNS CALLINGS
ACGILMMN CLAMMING
ACGILMNP CLAMPING
ACGILNOR CAROLING
ACGILNOS SOLACING
ACGILNOT LOCATING
ACGILNPP CLAPPING
ACGILNPS CLASPING,
SCALPING
ACGILNRW CRAWLING
ACGILNSS CLASSING
ACGILRSU SURGICAL
ACGIMMNR CRAMMING
ACGIMNPR CRAMPING
ACGIMNSY SYNGAMIC
ACGIMORS ORGASMIC
ACGINNNS SCANNING
ACGINNPR PRANCING
ACGINOST AGNOSTIC,
COASTING, COATINGS
ACGINPPR CRAPPING
ACGINPRS SCRAPING
ACGINRRS SCARRING
ACGINRRY CARRYING
ACGINRST TRACINGS
ACGINRSV CARVINGS,
CRAVINGS
ACGINSST CASTINGS
ACGINSTT SCATTING
ACGIORSU GRACIOUS

ACGJKLPU JACK PLUG
ACGJLNOU CONJUGAL
ACGLMOUU COAGULUM
ACGLOSUU GLAUCOUS
ACGLSSTU CUT GLASS
ACGNNOOT CONTANGO
ACGNOOST OCTAGONS
ACGNORST CONGRATS
ACHHILPT PHTHALIC
ACHHINTW WHINCHAT
ACHHINTY HYACINTH
ACHHIORT HATHORIC
ACHHIPPR HIPPARCH
ACHHLNOR RHONCHAL
ACHHNTTU NUTHATCH
ACHHOSTW CHAT SHOW
ACHHPTUZ CHUTZPAH
ACHHSTTU SUCH THAT
ACHIILMS CHILIASM
ACHIILPT HAPLITIC
ACHIILST CHILIAST
ACHIINPS HISPANIC
ACHIINRT TRICHINA
ACHIKKSW KICKSHAW
ACHIKOOW KIAOCHOW
ACHIKRSW RICKSHAW
ACHIKRTT HAT TRICK
ACHILLTY CITY HALL
ACHILMRS CHRISMAL
ACHILMTY MYTHICAL
ACHILNNS CLANNISH
ACHILNOS NICHOLAS
ACHILORT ACROLITH
ACHILPSY PHYSICAL
ACHILPTY PATCHILY
ACHILRVY CHIVALRY
ACHILTTY CHATTILY
ACHIMMOS MACHISMO
ACHIMMST MISMATCH
ACHIMNOP CHAMPION
ACHIMNOR HARMONIC
ACHIMNSU INASMUCH
ACHIMPSS SCAMPISH
ACHIMRST CHARTISM
ACHIMSSU CHIASMUS
ACHINOTZ HOACTZIN
ACHIOPRT ATROPHIC
ACHIORST CHARIOTS,
   HARICOTS
ACHIPRRT PHRATRIC
ACHIRRTY TRIARCHY
ACHIRSTT CHARTIST
ACHIRSTU HAIRCUTS

ACHISTTY CHASTITY
ACHKKORW HACKWORK
ACHKMMOS HAMMOCKS
ACHKMORS SHAMROCK
ACHKOSSS HASSOCKS
ACHLLNWY LYNCH LAW
ACHLLOOS ALCOHOLS
ACHLMSTZ SCHMALTZ
ACHLNORT CHARLTON
ACHLORSS SCHOLARS
ACHLRSTY CHRYSTAL
ACHMNORS MONARCHS,
   ROMANSCH
ACHMNORY MONARCHY
ACHMOSST STOMACHS
ACHMOSTY STOMACHY
ACHNOPRU UP-ANCHOR
ACHNPPSS SCHNAPPS
ACHNRSYY SYNARCHY
ACHOORTU COAUTHOR
ACHOPRTY TOPARCHY
ACHPRSTU PUSHCART
ACIIILMN INIMICAL
ACIIILNS SICILIAN
ACIIILNV CIVILIAN
ACIIINST ISATINIC, SINAITIC
ACIIKLNO KAOLINIC
ACIIKNNN CANNIKIN
ACIIKNPT PACK IT IN
ACIILLNV VANILLIC
ACIILLTV VILLATIC
ACIILLVW CIVIL LAW
ACIILMNR CRIMINAL
ACIILNPT PLATINIC
ACIILNRS SINCLAIR
ACIILRTU URALITIC
ACIILRVW CIVIL WAR
ACIILSST SILASTIC
ACIIMNNT MANNITIC
ACIIMNOS SIMONIAC
ACIIMNOT AMNIOTIC
ACIIMNST ACTINISM
ACIIMNSU MUSICIAN
ACIIMNTU ACTINIUM
ACIIMNTY INTIMACY
ACIIMOST IOTACISM
ACIIMOTT AMITOTIC
ACIIMPRV VAMPIRIC
ACIIMRST SCIMITAR
ACIIMSTV ACTIVISM
ACIIMTUV VIATICUM
ACIINNOT INACTION
ACIINNQU CINQUAIN

ACIINNRV NIRVANIC
ACIINOPT OPTICIAN
ACIINORZ ZIRCONIA
ACIINOSV AVIONICS
ACIINOTT CITATION
ACIINPRS CRISPIAN
ACIINRSS NARCISSI
ACIINRTU URANITIC
ACIIORST AORISTIC
ACIIORTV VICTORIA
ACIIRSST TRIASSIC
ACIIRSTT ARTISTIC
ACIISTTU AUTISTIC
ACIISTTV ACTIVIST
ACIITTVY ACTIVITY
ACIITVVY VIVACITY
ACIJKKPS SKIPJACK
ACIJRSSU JURASSIC
ACIJSUZZ JACUZZIS
ACIKLLST SALTLICK
ACIKLORS AIRLOCKS
ACIKLORY CROAKILY
ACIKNNPR CRANKPIN
ACIKNSTT TINTACKS
ACIKPSSX SIX-PACKS
ACILLLOP POLLICAL
ACILLMMY CLAMMILY
ACILLMOS LOCALISM
ACILLMSU CAMILLUS
ACILLNOO COLONIAL
ACILLNOR CARILLON
ACILLNOS SCALLION
ACILLORT CLITORAL
ACILLOST CALLISTO,
   LOCALIST
ACILLOSY SOCIALLY
ACILLOTY LOCALITY
ACILMNOP COMPLAIN
ACILMOPR PROCLAIM
ACILMOSV VOCALISM
ACILMSSS CLASSISM
ACILMSSU MUSICALS
ACILMSTY MYSTICAL
ACILNOOT LOCATION
ACILNOPS SALPICON
ACILNOPT PLATONIC
ACILNORS CLARIONS
ACILNORT CONTRAIL
ACILNOSU UNSOCIAL
ACILNOSV SLAVONIC
ACILNOUV UNIVOCAL
ACILNRSU CISLUNAR

ACILNRUY CULINARY, URANYLIC
ACILNSTU LUNATICS, SULTANIC
ACILNSTY SCANTILY
ACILOPRT TROPICAL
ACILORTV VORTICAL
ACILOSTV VOCALIST
ACILOTVY VOCALITY
ACILPSST PLASTICS
ACILRSTU RUSTICAL
ACILRTUV CULTIVAR
ACILSSST CLASSIST
ACILSTTY SCATTILY
ACILSTUV VICTUALS
ACILSTVY SYLVATIC
ACIMMTUY CYMATIUM
ACIMNNNO CINNAMON
ACIMNNOR MINORCAN
ACIMNOOR ACROMION
ACIMNORT ROMANTIC
ACIMNORU COUMARIN
ACIMNORY ACRIMONY
ACIMNOST MONASTIC
ACIMNPTY TYMPANIC
ACIMNRSU CRANIUMS
ACIMOSST MASSICOT
ACIMOSTT STOMATIC
ACIMRRSY MISCARRY
ACINNOOT CONATION
ACINNOSS SCANSION
ACINNOST CANONIST, SANCTION
ACINNOSU ASUNCION
ACINNOTU CONTINUA
ACINOOTV VOCATION
ACINOPPT PANOPTIC
ACINOPST CAPTIONS
ACINORSS NARCOSIS
ACINORST CAST-IRON
ACINORTT TRACTION
ACINOSSS CAISSONS
ACINOSSY CYANOSIS
ACINOSTT OSCITANT
ACINOSTU AUCTIONS, CAUTIONS
ACINOSTW WAINSCOT
ACINOSWX COXSWAIN
ACINOTTX TOXICANT
ACINPQUY PIQUANCY
ACINPSTY SYNAPTIC
ACINRSTU CURTAINS
ACINRTTU TACITURN

ACINSTTY SANCTITY
ACIOOPST SCOTOPIA
ACIOOPTX COTOPAXI
ACIOPRST APRICOTS
ACIOPSST POTASSIC
ACIOPSSU SPACIOUS
ACIOPSTU CAPTIOUS
ACIORRSS CORSAIRS
ACIORRSU SCARIOUS
ACIORSTT RIOT ACTS
ACIORTTY ATROCITY
ACIORTVY VORACITY
ACIOSTUU CAUTIOUS
ACIOSTUV OCTAVIUS
ACIPSSST SPASTICS
ACIRSSTY SACRISTY
ACISSSTU CASUISTS
ACISSTTU CATSUITS
ACJKOPST JACKPOTS
ACKKMOPR POCKMARK
ACKLLPSU SKULLCAP
ACKLOOPW WOOLPACK
ACKLOORS OARLOCKS
ACKLOOSW WOOLSACK
ACKLORST ROCK SALT
ACKLORSW WARLOCKS
ACKMNOST STOCKMAN
ACLLLLOR ROLL CALL
ACLLOORT COLLATOR
ACLLOOSS COLOSSAL
ACLLOPSS SCALLOPS
ACLLRTUU CULTURAL
ACLMMNOU COMMUNAL
ACLMNORU COLUMNAR
ACLMORSU CLAMOURS
ACLMRSUU MUSCULAR
ACLMSTUU CUSTUMAL
ACLMSUUV VASCULUM
ACLNOORT COLORANT
ACLNOOST COOLANTS
ACLNOOSV VOLCANOS
ACLNORSU CONSULAR
ACLNORTU CALUTRON
ACLNOSTU OSCULANT
ACLNPTUU PUNCTUAL
ACLOOPRR CORPORAL
ACLOOPRS CAR POOLS
ACLOOPRT COALPORT
ACLOPRRW PROWL CAR
ACLOPRXY XYLOCARP
ACLOPSSY CALYPSOS
ACLOSSTU OUTCLASS
ACLRSSTY CRYSTALS

ACMMNOSY SCAMMONY
ACMNOOPR MONOCARP
ACMNOORT MONOCRAT
ACMNOPRS CRAMPONS
ACMNORSY ACRONYMS
ACMNOSST SCOTSMAN
ACMNSSTU SANCTUMS
ACMOORRT MOTORCAR
ACMORSTW WORM CAST
ACMORSTY COSTMARY
ACMQSTUU CUMQUATS
ACNNNORY CANNONRY
ACNNORST SCRANTON
ACNNOSTT CONSTANT
ACNOORRY CORONARY
ACNOORST CARTOONS
ACNORRTY CONTRARY
ACNORSTT CONTRAST
ACNORTTU TURNCOAT
ACNPRSYY SYNCARPY
ACNRRSTU CURRANTS
ACOOPSTT TOPCOATS
ACOPRRST CARPORTS
ACOPRRTT PROTRACT
ACOPRTUY PAY COURT
ACORRSTT TRACTORS
ACORRSTU CURATORS
ACORRTUY CARRYOUT
ACORRTUZ RAZOR-CUT
ACORSSTU SURCOATS
ACORSSUW CURASSOW
ACORSTTY CRYOSTAT
ACOSSTTU OUTCASTS
ACRRSTUU ARCTURUS
ADDDEEEN DEADENED
ADDDEEGR DEGRADED
ADDDEELR LADDERED
ADDDEEMN DEMANDED, MADDENED
ADDDEENS DEAD ENDS, SADDENED
ADDDEGJU ADJUDGED
ADDDELSW SWADDLED
ADDDEMNU ADDENDUM
ADDDEOOW DEAD WOOD
ADDEEEFN DEAFENED
ADDEEEFT DEFEATED
ADDEEEMN DEMEANED
ADDEEENR DEADENER, ENDEARED
ADDEEFHN HANDFEED
ADDEEFLT DEFLATED
ADDEEFRY DEFRAYED

ADDEEGNR DERANGED, GARDENED
ADDEEGOR DOG-EARED
ADDEEGRR DEGRADER, REGARDED
ADDEEHIL ADELHEID
ADDEEHLR HERALDED
ADDEEHLY ALDEHYDE
ADDEEHNR HARDENED
ADDEEHRS REDHEADS
ADDEEHRT THREADED
ADDEEILN DEADLINE
ADDEEILP DEEP-LAID
ADDEEILR DEADLIER, DERAILED
ADDEEILT DETAILED
ADDEEIMT MEDIATED
ADDEEINT DETAINED
ADDEEISS DISEASED
ADDEEIST STEADIED
ADDEEITV DEVIATED
ADDEEKNR DARKENED
ADDEELLP PEDALLED
ADDEELOR RELOADED
ADDEELUV DEVALUED
ADDEEMNP DAMPENED
ADDEEMNR DEMANDER, REDEMAND, REMANDED
ADDEENPP APPENDED
ADDEENPR PANDERED
ADDEENPX EXPANDED
ADDEENRW WANDERED
ADDEENSS DEADNESS
ADDEENTT ATTENDED
ADDEENTU DENUDATE
ADDEEPRT DEPARTED, PREDATED
ADDEEPRV DEPRAVED, PERVADED
ADDEERRT RETARDED
ADDEERRW REWARDED
ADDEERTV ADVERTED
ADDEFFOR AFFORDED
ADDEFILY FIELD DAY
ADDEFLRU DREADFUL
ADDEFORW WORD-DEAF
ADDEGGLR DRAGGLED
ADDEGINR DREADING
ADDEGLST GLADDEST
ADDEGPRU UPGRADED
ADDEHIIJ JEDIDIAH
ADDEHILR DIHEDRAL
ADDEHINW HEADWIND

ADDEHIRS DIEHARDS
ADDEHMRU DRUMHEAD
ADDEHNNU UNHANDED
ADDEHORW HEADWORD
ADDEHOSW SHADOWED
ADDEHRTY HYDRATED
ADDEHSTU THADDEUS
ADDEIITV ADDITIVE
ADDEIJNO ADJOINED
ADDEIKNP KIDNAPED
ADDEIMOS SODAMIDE
ADDEIMRS DISARMED
ADDEIMSY DISMAYED
ADDEIMTT ADMITTED
ADDEINOR ORDAINED
ADDEINOS ADENOIDS
ADDEINST DANDIEST
ADDEIOPR PARODIED
ADDEIORS ROADSIDE
ADDEISSU DISSUADE
ADDEJSTU ADJUSTED
ADDELNOU DUODENAL, UNLOADED
ADDELNSU UNSADDLE
ADDELOOR EL DORADO
ADDELRSS SADDLERS
ADDELRST STRADDLE
ADDELRSW DAWDLERS
ADDELRSY SADDLERY
ADDELRTW TWADDLER
ADDEMNPU UNDAMPED
ADDENNSU SAND DUNE
ADDENOPR PARDONED
ADDENRST STRANDED
ADDENRYY YARN-DYED
ADDEOTTU OUTDATED
ADDFFILO DAFFODIL
ADDFFNRU DANDRUFF
ADDGILNN DANDLING
ADDGILNP PADDLING
ADDGILNS SADDLING
ADDGILNW DAWDLING, WADDLING
ADDGLORU OLD GUARD
ADDGMRUU MUDGUARD
ADDHHLNO HANDHOLD
ADDHIKRS HARD DISK
ADDHINSY DANDYISH
ADDHLNOS OLD HANDS
ADDHOORW HARDWOOD
ADDIIMRU DIARMUID
ADDIINOT ADDITION
ADDIINRT TRINIDAD

ADDILMNS MIDLANDS
ADDILMOS OLD MAIDS
ADDIMNOS DIAMONDS
ADDIMNSY DANDYISM
ADDINNOR ORDINAND
ADDINORS ANDROIDS
ADDINRWW WINDWARD
ADDIORRT DIRT ROAD
ADDKNRRU DRUNKARD
ADDLLNOR LANDLORD
ADDLLRSU DULLARDS
ADDLNOOW DOWNLOAD, WOODLAND
ADDMOOSY DOOMSDAY
ADDNORWW DOWNWARD
ADEEEFRT DEFEATER, FEDERATE
ADEEEGLT DELEGATE
ADEEEGNR RENEGADE
ADEEEGUW AGUEWEED
ADEEEHSY EYESHADE
ADEEEINT DETAINEE
ADEEEKNW WEAKENED
ADEEELMN ENAMELED
ADEEELNV LEAVENED
ADEEELPR REPEALED
ADEEELRS RELEASED
ADEEELRV REVEALED
ADEEELSW WEASELED
ADEEELTV ELEVATED
ADEEENRS SERENADE
ADEEENTT EDENTATE
ADEEEPRS RAPESEED
ADEEEPRT REPEATED
ADEEESSW SEESAWED
ADEEFHNR FREEHAND
ADEEFHOR FOREHEAD
ADEEFHRT FATHERED
ADEEFILN ENFILADE
ADEEFIRR RAREFIED
ADEEFLMS SELF-MADE
ADEEFLOR FREELOAD
ADEEFLPR PEDALFER
ADEEFLRT FALTERED, REFLATED
ADEEFLSS FADELESS
ADEEFLSX FLAXSEED
ADEEFMNR FREEDMAN
ADEEFMTU DEAF-MUTE
ADEEFNOT TONE-DEAF
ADEEFNSS DEAFNESS
ADEEFNST FASTENED
ADEEFNTT FATTENED

ADEEFRRY DEFRAYER
ADEEFRST DRAFTEES
ADEEFRTU FEATURED
ADEEGGHS EGGHEADS
ADEEGHRT GATHERED
ADEEGINN ENGADINE
ADEEGINR REGAINED
ADEEGIRS DISAGREE
ADEEGLLN GLENDALE
ADEEGLNR ENLARGED
ADEEGLRV GRAVELED
ADEEGMNR GENDARME
ADEEGMNS END GAMES
ADEEGMNY GANYMEDE
ADEEGNNR ENDANGER
ADEEGNRR GARDENER,
    GARNERED
ADEEGNRS GRANDEES,
    GRENADES
ADEEGNRU DUNGAREE,
    UNDERAGE
ADEEGNRV ENGRAVED
ADEEGORT DEROGATE
ADEEGPRS PRESAGED
ADEEGRSS DEGASSER,
    DRESSAGE
ADEEGRTT TARGETED
ADEEGSWY EDGEWAYS
ADEEHHRS REHASHED
ADEEHHST SHEATHED
ADEEHIKL HEADLIKE
ADEEHIKZ ZEDEKIAH
ADEEHILN HEADLINE
ADEEHIST HEADIEST
ADEEHISV ADHESIVE
ADEEHKNR HANKERED,
    HARKENED
ADEEHKWW HAWKWEED
ADEEHKWY HAWK-EYED
ADEEHLLW WELLHEAD
ADEEHLRT LATHERED
ADEEHLSS HEADLESS
ADEEHLTY HEATEDLY
ADEEHMMO HOMEMADE
ADEEHMMR HAMMERED
ADEEHMNN MENHADEN
ADEEHMPR HAMPERED
ADEEHMST STEMHEAD
ADEEHNPP HAPPENED
ADEEHNRR HARDENER
ADEEHNRT ADHERENT
ADEEHNST HASTENED
ADEEHORV OVERHEAD

ADEEHRRT THREADER
ADEEHRRW HEREWARD
ADEEHRST HEADREST
ADEEHRTW WREATHED
ADEEHSST HEADSETS
ADEEIILS IDEALISE
ADEEIILZ IDEALIZE
ADEEIITV IDEATIVE
ADEEIJMR JEREMIAD
ADEEILLN DANIELLE
ADEEILMN ENDEMIAL,
    MADELINE
ADEEILMR REMEDIAL
ADEEILMT LEAD TIME
ADEEILMV MEDIEVAL
ADEEILNT DATELINE,
    ENTAILED
ADEEILPS PLEIADES
ADEEILPT DEPILATE
ADEEILRS REALISED,
    SIDEREAL
ADEEILRT ELATERID,
    RETAILED
ADEEILRZ REALIZED
ADEEIMNR REMAINED
ADEEIMNT DEMENTIA
ADEEIMNX EXAMINED
ADEEIMRT DIAMETER
ADEEIMTT MEDITATE
ADEEINNR ADRIENNE
ADEEINNS ANDESINE
ADEEINPT NEAP TIDE
ADEEINRS ARSENIDE,
    NEARSIDE
ADEEINRT DETAINER,
    RETAINED
ADEEINST ANDESITE
ADEEIPRR REPAIRED
ADEEIPRS AIRSPEED
ADEEIPTX EXPIATED
ADEEIRRR DREARIER
ADEEIRST READIEST,
    STEADIER
ADEEISSS DISEASES
ADEEISST EAST SIDE
ADEEISTV SEDATIVE
ADEEKMRR REMARKED
ADEEKMRT MARKETED
ADEEKNPW KNAPWEED
ADEEKNRR DARKENER
ADEEKQSU SQUEAKED
ADEEKRST STREAKED
ADEEKSWY WEEKDAYS

ADEELLLP LAPELLED
ADEELLMT METALLED
ADEELLNP PANELLED
ADEELLPR PREDELLA
ADEELLPS SEPALLED
ADEELLQU EQUALLED
ADEELLRV RAVELLED
ADEELLRW WELL-READ
ADEELLWY WALLEYED
ADEELMMR MAL DE MER
ADEELMNO LEMONADE
ADEELMNR ALDERMEN
ADEELMNT LAMENTED
ADEELMRS DEMERSAL,
    EMERALDS
ADEELMRV MARVELED
ADEELMTU EMULATED
ADEELNOR OLEANDER
ADEELNPT ENDPLATE
ADEELNRV LAVENDER
ADEELNRY ALDERNEY
ADEELNSV ENSLAVED
ADEELNSW NEW DEALS
ADEELNTT TALENTED
ADEELOPR LOP-EARED
ADEELOPX POLEAXED
ADEELOST DESOLATE
ADEELPPT LAPPETED
ADEELPRS RELAPSED
ADEELPRY PARLEYED,
    REPLAYED
ADEELPST PEDESTAL
ADEELQSU SQUEALED
ADEELRRT RED ALERT,
    TREADLER
ADEELRST TREADLES
ADEELRSV SLAVERED
ADEELRTV TRAVELED
ADEELRUV REVALUED
ADEELSST TASSELED
ADEELSTY SEDATELY
ADEEMMRY YAMMERED
ADEEMMSS MESDAMES
ADEEMNNR MANNERED
ADEEMNOT NEMATODE
ADEEMNPR DAMPENER
ADEEMNSS SEEDSMAN
ADEEMORT MODERATE
ADEEMPPR PAMPERED
ADEEMPRT TAMPERED
ADEEMPRV REVAMPED
ADEEMPST STAMPEDE
ADEEMRRS DREAMERS

ADEEMRST MASTERED,
STREAMED
ADEEMRSU MADURESE,
MEASURED
ADEEMRTT MATTERED
ADEEMRTW WET DREAM
ADEENNRS ARDENNES,
ENSNARED
ADEENNRU UNEARNED
ADEENOPW WEAPONED
ADEENORS REASONED
ADEENORY AERODYNE
ADEENOSS SEASONED
ADEENOTT DETONATE
ADEENPPR ENDPAPER
ADEENPRR PANDERER
ADEENPRX EXPANDER
ADEENPTT PATENTED
ADEENRRW WANDERER
ADEENRSS DEARNESS
ADEENRSU UNDERSEA
ADEENRSW ANSWERED
ADEENRTT NATTERED
ADEENRTU DENATURE
ADEENSST ASSENTED
ADEENSSU SUDANESE
ADEENSTU UNSEATED
ADEENTTU TAUTENED
ADEENTTV VENDETTA
ADEEOPRT OPERATED
ADEEORVW OVERAWED
ADEEPPRR PREPARED
ADEEPRRS SPREADER
ADEEPRRV DEPRAVER,
PERVADER
ADEEPRST PEDERAST
ADEEPRSU PERSUADE
ADEEPRTT PATTERED
ADEEPRTU DEPURATE
ADEEPSWY SPEEDWAY
ADEEQRUV QUAVERED
ADEERRRT RETARDER
ADEERRRW REWARDER
ADEERRST ARRESTED,
RETREADS, SERRATED
ADEERSST ASSERTED,
DEARESTS
ADEERSTT RESTATED
ADEERTTT TATTERED
ADEERVYY EVERYDAY
ADEESSSS ASSESSED
ADEESTTT ATTESTED
ADEFFGUW GUFFAWED

ADEFFIMR AFFIRMED
ADEFFLNS SNAFFLED
ADEFFORT TRADE-OFF
ADEFGILR GARFIELD
ADEFGILS GADFLIES
ADEFGIMN DEFAMING
ADEFGIRT DRIFTAGE
ADEFGITU FATIGUED
ADEFGLLO GOLD LEAF
ADEFGLOT GATEFOLD
ADEFGLRS RED FLAGS
ADEFHILS DEALFISH
ADEFHILT HATFIELD
ADEFHIMS FAMISHED
ADEFHLNT LEFT-HAND
ADEFHMOT FATHOMED
ADEFHNOR FOREHAND
ADEFIILN FINIALED
ADEFIILR AIRFIELD
ADEFIIMR RAMIFIED
ADEFIIRT RATIFIED
ADEFIKRR FREDRIKA
ADEFILLT ILL-FATED
ADEFILMN INFLAMED
ADEFILNT INFLATED
ADEFILOT FOLIATED
ADEFILRW WILFREDA
ADEFIMPR FIREDAMP
ADEFINRR INFRARED
ADEFINRU FREUDIAN
ADEFINRW FINE-DRAW
ADEFIRRT DRAFTIER
ADEFLLMO OLD FLAME
ADEFLNOR FORELAND
ADEFLNRS FLANDERS
ADEFLNTU FLAUNTED
ADEFLORT DEFLATOR
ADEFLORU FOUR-DEAL
ADEFLPRS FELDSPAR
ADEFLRTW LEFTWARD
ADEFLRZZ FRAZZLED
ADEFLSTU DEFAULTS
ADEFNNOR FERNANDO
ADEFNOPR PROFANED
ADEFNSST DAFTNESS
ADEFORRW FARROWED
ADEFORRY FOREYARD
ADEFORUV FAVOURED
ADEFOSTU FADEOUTS
ADEGGIRR DRAGGIER
ADEGGJLY JAGGEDLY
ADEGGLRY RAGGEDLY
ADEGGMOY DEMAGOGY

ADEGGOPY PEDAGOGY
ADEGGRTY GADGETRY
ADEGHHOS HOGSHEAD
ADEGHILT ALIGHTED,
GILTHEAD
ADEGHINR ADHERING
ADEGHINS HEADINGS,
SHEADING
ADEGHLNO HEADLONG
ADEGHORT GOATHERD
ADEGHRTU DAUGHTER
ADEGIILP DIPLEGIA
ADEGIIMN IMAGINED
ADEGIITT DIGITATE
ADEGIKNN KNEADING
ADEGILLP PILLAGED
ADEGILMN MALIGNED
ADEGILNP PEDALING,
PLEADING
ADEGILNR DRAGLINE,
REGINALD
ADEGILNS DEALINGS,
SIGNALED
ADEGILNY DELAYING
ADEGILOU DIALOGUE
ADEGILRS GRISELDA
ADEGILSS GLISSADE
ADEGIMNN AMENDING
ADEGIMNR DREAMING
ADEGIMOR IDEOGRAM
ADEGIMRT MIGRATED
ADEGINOR ORGANDIE
ADEGINOS AGONISED,
DIAGNOSE, SAN DIEGO
ADEGINOZ AGONIZED
ADEGINRS READINGS
ADEGINRT GRADIENT, RED
GIANT, TREADING
ADEGINRY READYING
ADEGINSS ASSIGNED
ADEGINST SEDATING
ADEGISTU GAUDIEST
ADEGLLNU GLANDULE
ADEGLLOP GALLOPED
ADEGLNPS SPANGLED
ADEGLNRS GLANDERS
ADEGLNRW WRANGLED
ADEGLNSS GLADNESS
ADEGLPPR GRAPPLED
ADEGMMRU RUMMAGED
ADEGMNOY ENDOGAMY
ADEGMPUZ GAZUMPED
ADEGNNOR ANDROGEN

ADEGNOPU POUNDAGE
ADEGNORT DRAGONET
ADEGNRRU GRANDEUR
ADEGNRST DRAGNETS,
   GRANDEST
ADEGOPRR DRAGROPE
ADEGORSW DOWAGERS
ADEGORTU OUTRAGED
ADEGPRRU UPGRADER
ADEGPSTU UPSTAGED
ADEHHIPS HEADSHIP
ADEHHLOY HOLYHEAD
ADEHHNTU HEADHUNT
ADEHHOST HOTHEADS
ADEHHRST THRASHED
ADEHIKLN HANDLIKE
ADEHIKNS SKINHEAD
ADEHILLM HEIMDALL
ADEHILNP DELPHIAN
ADEHILNR HARD LINE
ADEHILRY HYDER ALI
ADEHILSV LAVISHED
ADEHIMRS MISHEARD
ADEHINOP DIAPHONE
ADEHINOS ADHESION
ADEHINPS DEANSHIP,
   PINHEADS
ADEHINPU DAUPHINE
ADEHINRS SHERIDAN
ADEHINSS SHANDIES
ADEHINST HANDIEST
ADEHINSV VANISHED
ADEHIORS HERODIAS,
   RHODESIA
ADEHIPRS SEPHARDI
ADEHIPST PITHEADS
ADEHIRSS RADISHES
ADEHIRST HARDIEST
ADEHIRSV RAVISHED
ADEHIRSW RAWHIDES
ADEHISST SHADIEST
ADEHKNRS REDSHANK
ADEHKORW HEADWORK
ADEHLLOW HALLOWED
ADEHLLRS HARD SELL
ADEHLMNO HOMELAND
ADEHLNRS HANDLERS
ADEHLNSS HANDLESS
ADEHLOPS ASPHODEL
ADEHLPSS SPLASHED
ADEHLRRY HERALDRY
ADEHMMMO MOHAMMED
ADEHMNNY HANDYMEN

ADEHMNOS HANDSOME
ADEHMNRS HERDSMAN
ADEHMOOR HEADROOM
ADEHMORW HOMEWARD
ADEHMOST HEADMOST
ADEHMOSU MADHOUSE
ADEHNOPR ORPHANED
ADEHNORV HANDOVER,
   OVERHAND
ADEHNOSS SANDSHOE
ADEHNPRS SHARP END
ADEHNRSS HARDNESS
ADEHNRTU UNTHREAD
ADEHNSSU SUNSHADE
ADEHNSUW UNWASHED
ADEHOORT DOROTHEA,
   THEODORA
ADEHOPXY HEXAPODY
ADEHORRW HARROWED
ADEHORSW SHADOWER
ADEHORTU AUTHORED
ADEHORTW DEATH ROW
ADEHPSUW WASHED-UP
ADEHQSSU SQUASHED
ADEHRSTY HYDRATES
ADEHRTTW THWARTED
ADEIILMS IDEALISM
ADEIILST IDEALIST
ADEIILTV DILATIVE
ADEIILTY IDEALITY
ADEIIMNN INDAMINE
ADEIIMNR MERIDIAN
ADEIIMPR IMPAIRED
ADEIIMRS SEMIARID
ADEIIMTT IMITATED
ADEIINOT IDEATION
ADEIINRT DAINTIER
ADEIINST ADENITIS,
   DAINTIES
ADEIIPRS PRESIDIA
ADEIITTV VITIATED
ADEIJRSU JUDAISER
ADEIJRUZ JUDAIZER
ADEIKLLO KELOIDAL
ADEIKLLY LADYLIKE
ADEIKLSW SIDEWALK
ADEIKMRT TIDEMARK
ADEIKORT KERATOID
ADEILLMY MEDIALLY
ADEILLOR ARILLODE
ADEILLRV RIVALLED
ADEILLSW SIDEWALL
ADEILMMS DILEMMAS

ADEILMNN LANDMINE
ADEILMNO MELANOID
ADEILMNY MAIDENLY
ADEILMOX ALDOXIME
ADEILMPS MISPLEAD
ADEILMRY DREAMILY
ADEILMSV MALDIVES
ADEILNNR INLANDER
ADEILNNT DENTINAL
ADEILNOP PALINODE
ADEILNRS ISLANDER
ADEILNST TAIL ENDS
ADEILNTV DIVALENT
ADEILOPS SEPALOID
ADEILOPT PETALOID
ADEILORT IDOLATER,
   TAILORED
ADEILORV OVERLAID
ADEILORX EXORDIAL
ADEILOST DIASTOLE,
   ISOLATED, SODALITE
ADEILOSV VAL-D'OISE
ADEILOTT DATOLITE
ADEILOTV DOVETAIL,
   VIOLATED
ADEILPPP PEDIPALP
ADEILPRS SPIRALED
ADEILPRT DIPTERAL
ADEILPRU EPIDURAL
ADEILRRY DREARILY
ADEILRSU RESIDUAL
ADEILRSY DIALYSER
ADEILRTT DETRITAL
ADEILSTY DIASTYLE,
   STEADILY
ADEILSXY DYSLEXIA
ADEILTTU ALTITUDE,
   LATITUDE
ADEIMMRS MERMAIDS
ADEIMNNT IN TANDEM
ADEIMNOT DOMINATE
ADEIMNRY DAIRYMEN
ADEIMNSS MAN-SISED,
   SIDESMAN
ADEIMNSZ MAN-SIZED
ADEIMNTY DYNAMITE
ADEIMORT MEDIATOR
ADEIMOSS SESAMOID
ADEIMPRT IMPARTED
ADEIMRRS ADMIRERS,
   DISARMER, MARRIEDS
ADEIMRSS SIDEARMS
ADEIMRXY READY-MIX

221

ADEIMSTY DAYTIMES	ADEJOPRY JEOPARDY	ADEMNPSS DAMPNESS
ADEINNOT ANOINTED,	ADEJRSTU READJUST	ADEMNRRU UNDERARM
ANTINODE	ADEKLMRY MARKEDLY	ADEMOORT MODERATO
ADEINNOV DEVONIAN	ADEKLPRS SPARKLED	ADEMOOSV VAMOOSED
ADEINNRZ RENDZINA	ADEKMNRU UNMARKED	ADEMOPRY PYODERMA
ADEINNTU INUNDATE	ADEKMNSU UNMASKED	ADEMORRU ARMOURED
ADEINORR ORDAINER	ADEKNNSS DANKNESS	ADEMRRSU EARDRUMS
ADEINORT ORDINATE,	ADEKNPTU TANKED UP	ADEMRRTY MARTYRED
RATIONED	ADEKNRSS DARKNESS	ADENNOSY ANODYNES
ADEINOST SEDATION	ADEKQSUW SQUAWKED	ADENNPST PENDANTS
ADEINOTT ANTIDOTE	ADELLNNU ANNULLED	ADENOORW WANDEROO
ADEINOTV DONATIVE	ADELLOPW WALLOPED	ADENOPRR PARDONER
ADEINPPX APPENDIX	ADELLOTT ALLOTTED,	ADENOPST NOTEPADS
ADEINPRS SPRAINED	TOTALLED	ADENOPSY DYSPNOEA
ADEINPRT DIPTERAN	ADELLOWW WALLOWED	ADENORRW NARROWED
ADEINPSS IN SPADES	ADELLQSU SQUALLED	ADENORTW DANEWORT
ADEINRRS SERRANID	ADELMOPS MALPOSED	ADENPPTU UNTAPPED
ADEINRSS SARDINES	ADELMORS EARLDOMS	ADENPRTY PEDANTRY
ADEINRST RANDIEST,	ADELMOTU MODULATE	ADENPRUY UNDERPAY
STRAINED	ADELMPRT TRAMPLED	ADENQRSU SQUANDER
ADEINRSV INVADERS	ADELMRRU DEMURRAL	ADENRRWY WARDENRY
ADEINRTU URINATED	ADELMSSY MASSEDLY	ADENRSTU TRANSUDE
ADEINRVY VINEYARD	ADELNORS SOLANDER	ADENSTUY UNSTEADY
ADEINSST SANDIEST	ADELNORU UNLOADER	ADEOORRT TOREADOR
ADEINSSV AVIDNESS	ADELNORV OVERLAND	ADEOOTTT TATTOOED
ADEINSTV DEVIANTS	ADELNPRS SPANDREL	ADEOPPRV APPROVED
ADEIOPRS DIASPORE,	ADELNRSS SLANDERS	ADEOPRRS EARDROPS
PARODIES	ADELNRTY ARDENTLY	ADEOPRRT PARROTED,
ADEIOPRV OVERPAID	ADELNRUY UNDERLAY	PREDATOR, TEARDROP
ADEIOPST DIOPTASE	ADELNTUU UNDULATE	ADEOPRTT TETRAPOD
ADEIOPTV ADOPTIVE	ADELNUUV UNVALUED	ADEOPSTT POSTDATE
ADEIORST ASTEROID	ADELOORV OVERLOAD	ADEOPTTU UP-TO-DATE
ADEIORTT TERATOID	ADELOPRS LEOPARDS	ADEORRST ROADSTER
ADEIORTV DEVIATOR	ADELOPST TADPOLES	ADEORRVW OVERDRAW
ADEIPPRS APPRISED	ADELOPTY PETALODY	ADEORSST ASSORTED
ADEIPRST TRAIPSED	ADELORST LEOTARDS,	ADEORSTT ROAD TEST
ADEIPRSY PRISE DAY	LODESTAR	ADEORSTU READOUTS
ADEIPRYZ PRIZE DAY	ADELORTW LEADWORT	ADEORSTX EXTRADOS
ADEIPTTU APTITUDE	ADELOTUV OVULATED	ADEORSUV SAVOURED
ADEIQRRU QUARRIED	ADELOTUW OUTLAWED	ADEPPRST STRAPPED
ADEIRRWW WIREDRAW	ADELPRSW SPRAWLED	ADEPRSTU PASTURED
ADEIRSST DISASTER	ADELPRTT PRATTLED	ADEQSTTU SQUATTED
ADEIRSSV ADVISERS	ADELPSTT SPLATTED	ADERRSSW WARDRESS
ADEIRSTT STRIATED,	ADELPSTU PULSATED	ADERRSTT REDSTART
TARDIEST	ADELRSTT STARTLED	ADERSSTW STEWARDS
ADEIRTUV DURATIVE	ADELRTUY ADULTERY	ADERSTWW WESTWARD
ADEIRVWY DRIVEWAY	ADEMNNNU UNMANNED	ADESSTUY TUESDAYS
ADEISSST ASSISTED	ADEMNOOR MAROONED	ADFFHNOS HANDS-OFF
ADEISSTT DISTASTE	ADEMNOPR NAMEDROP,	ADFFISST DISTAFFS
ADEISSWY SIDEWAYS	POMANDER	ADFFOOST FAST FOOD
ADEISTTU SITUATED	ADEMNORS RANSOMED	ADFFORST STAFFORD
ADEISTWY TIDEWAYS	ADEMNORY RAYMONDE	ADFGIINR INFRA DIG
ADEITTTU ATTITUDE	ADEMNOTU AMOUNTED	ADFGINRT DRAFTING

ADFGINRW DWARFING
ADFGLOUW GOD-AWFUL
ADFHIOST TOADFISH
ADFHIRSW DWARFISH
ADFHLNSU HANDFULS
ADFHLOST HOLDFAST
ADFHORRT HARTFORD
ADFIILRW WILFRIDA
ADFIIRST FIRST AID
ADFILLNW WINDFALL
ADFILMNO MANIFOLD
ADFILNOR FLORINDA
ADFIMRSW DWARFISM
ADFIRSTY FIRST-DAY
ADFKNOOR KORDOFAN
ADFLLNOU ALL FOUND
ADFLLNOW DOWNFALL
ADFLMNOR LANDFORM
ADFLMSTU MUDFLATS
ADFMORST STAMFORD
ADFNNOST FONDANTS
ADFNOORT TO-AND-FRO
ADFNOORZ FORZANDO
ADFNORST STANFORD
ADFOOPST FOOTPADS
ADFORRSW FORWARDS
ADGGGINR DRAGGING
ADGGILNN DANGLING
ADGGINRS NIGGARDS
ADGGINRU GUARDING
ADGGLRSU SLUGGARD
ADGHHILN HIGHLAND
ADGHHIOR HIGH ROAD
ADGHILNN HANDLING
ADGHILTY DAYLIGHT
ADGHINOR HOARDING
ADGHINPR HANDGRIP
ADGHINSS SHADINGS
ADGHIPRS DIGRAPHS
ADGHLNNO LONGHAND
ADGHNNSU HANDGUNS
ADGHOORS ROAD HOGS
ADGHRSTU DRAUGHTS
ADGHRTUY DRAUGHTY
ADGIILLN DIALLING
ADGIILLO GLADIOLI
ADGIILNO GONIDIAL
ADGIILNT DILATING
ADGIILPY PYGIDIAL
ADGIIMNR ADMIRING
ADGIIMST DIGAMIST
ADGIINNR DRAINING
ADGIINNV INVADING

ADGIINOR RADIOING
ADGIINOV AVOIDING
ADGIINSV ADVISING
ADGIINTU AUDITING
ADGIJNRU ADJURING
ADGILLNU ALLUDING
ADGILLNW WINDGALL
ADGILLNY DALLYING
ADGILMOR MARIGOLD
ADGILNNS LANDINGS
ADGILNOS LOADINGS
ADGILNRS DARLINGS
ADGILNRW DRAWLING
ADGILNRY DARINGLY
ADGILNZZ DAZZLING
ADGILOOS SOLIDAGO
ADGILOPR PRODIGAL
ADGILOST DOG'S-TAIL
ADGIMOSU DIGAMOUS
ADGINNOR ADORNING
ADGINNOT DONATING
ADGINNST STANDING
ADGINNTU DAUNTING
ADGINOOR RIGADOON
ADGINOPT ADOPTING
ADGINORR RING ROAD
ADGINOTY TOADYING
ADGINPTU UPDATING
ADGINRSW DRAWINGS
ADGINRTT DRATTING
ADGIORTT TITOGRAD
ADGIRSZZ GIZZARDS
ADGLNOOS GONDOLAS
ADGMNOOR ONDOGRAM
ADGMNORU GOURMAND
ADGNNOQU QUANDONG
ADGNNORS GRANDSON
ADGNNRYY GYNANDRY
ADGNOORS DRAGOONS
ADHHINPW WHIP HAND
ADHHIPRS HARDSHIP
ADHHNRTY HYDRANTH
ADHIILLP PHILLIDA
ADHIILLR HILLIARD
ADHIIMSS HASIDISM
ADHIINOP OPHIDIAN
ADHIKKOO HOKKAIDO
ADHILLOT THALLOID
ADHILLOY HOLLIDAY
ADHILLPY PHYLLIDA
ADHILNOR RHODINAL
ADHILOOW HAILWOOD
ADHILOPS SHIPLOAD

ADHILOSY HOLIDAYS
ADHILPSY LADYSHIP
ADHIMNOS ADMONISH
ADHIMNOU HUMANOID
ADHIMOPP AMPHIPOD
ADHINOPY DIAPHONY
ADHINPSU DAUPHINS
ADHINSST STANDISH
ADHINSTU DIANTHUS
ADHIPRSW WARDSHIP
ADHIPRSY SHIPYARD
ADHIRTWW WITHDRAW
ADHLLLOS HOLDALLS
ADHLLNOS HOLLANDS
ADHLMNOO HANDLOOM
ADHLMORT THRALDOM
ADHLNOPR RANDOLPH
ADHLNOUW DOWNHAUL
ADHLOPSU ADOLPHUS
ADHNNORU HONDURAN
ADHNOPRU HARD UPON
ADHNORSU HONDURAS
ADHNOSTU HANDOUTS,
    THOUSAND
ADHNOSWW DOWNWASH
ADHNRSTU HARD NUTS
ADHNRSTY HYDRANTS
ADHOOPRS HOSPODAR
ADHOORSW ROADSHOW
ADHOPRST HARDTOPS
ADHOPRSY RHAPSODY
ADHORRTY HYDRATOR
ADHORSTY SHORT-DAY
ADHRSTUY THURSDAY
ADIIINRV VIRIDIAN
ADIIIQRU DAIQUIRI
ADIIKLMM MILKMAID
ADIIKLST TAILSKID
ADIILLMR MILLIARD
ADIILLOP LIPOIDAL
ADIILLUV DILUVIAL
ADIILMRV VLADIMIR
ADIILNOT DILATION
ADIILNSU INDUSIAL
ADIILNSV INVALIDS
ADIILNSW WINDSAIL
ADIILNTW TAILWIND
ADIILNTY DAINTILY
ADIILOPP DIPLOPIA
ADIILSSY DIALYSIS
ADIILTVY VALIDITY
ADIIMRST TRIADISM
ADIINOOT IODATION

ADIINOSY DIONYSIA
ADIINOTU AUDITION
ADIINRST DISTRAIN
ADIIPRTY RAPIDITY
ADIIPSTY SAPIDITY
ADIIPTVY VAPIDITY
ADIIRSST DIARISTS
ADIIRSTT DISTRAIT
ADIKNNST INKSTAND
ADIKNPSS SKIDPANS
ADILLLPY PALLIDLY
ADILLMNR MANDRILL
ADILLMOU ALLODIUM
ADILLMSY DISMALLY
ADILLNPS LANDSLIP
ADILLOSW DISALLOW
ADILLOSY DISLOYAL
ADILLRSU DRUSILLA
ADILMNNO MANDOLIN
ADILMOPS DIPLOMAS
ADILMOPT DIPLOMAT
ADILMOPY OLYMPIAD
ADILMOTY MODALITY
ADILNNOR LONDRINA
ADILNNSU DISANNUL
ADILNOOR DOORNAIL
ADILNORS ORDINALS,
   ROSALIND
ADILNOTY NODALITY
ADILNRWY INWARDLY
ADILNSSU SUNDIALS
ADILNSSW WINDLASS
ADILOOPR POLAROID
ADILOORT TOROIDAL
ADILOPRS SLIP ROAD
ADILOPRT DIOPTRAL,
   TRIPODAL
ADILOPSS DISPOSAL
ADILORSY SOLIDARY
ADILORTY ADROITLY,
   DILATORY, IDOLATRY
ADILOSTW WILD OATS
ADILPSSY DISPLAYS
ADILPSTU PLAUDITS
ADILRTWY TAWDRILY
ADIMMNOS MONADISM,
   NOMADISM
ADIMMNSY DYNAMISM
ADIMMNOT DOMINANT
ADIMNSTY DYNAMIST
ADIMOPRY MYRIAPOD
ADIMOSST MASTOIDS
ADIMOSTY TOADYISM

ADIMPRSY PYRAMIDS
ADIMSSTU STADIUMS
ADINNNTU INUNDANT
ADINNOOT DONATION
ADINNORS ANDIRONS
ADINNSST STAND-INS
ADINOOPS ISOPODAN
ADINOOPT ADOPTION
ADINOORT TANDOORI
ADINOOTT DOTATION
ADINOPRR RAINDROP
ADINOPRS PONIARDS
ADINORRY ORDINARY
ADINORST INTRADOS
ADINORSU DINOSAUR
ADINORTU DURATION
ADINPSST SANDPITS
ADIOOPRT PAROTOID
ADIOOPSS APODOSIS
ADIOPPST POSTPAID
ADIOPRST PARODIST, PORT
   SAID
ADIOPRTY PODIATRY
ADIORSTU AUDITORS
ADIORSVY ADVISORY
ADIORTUY AUDITORY
ADIRRWYZ WIZARDRY
ADJKNRUY JUNKYARD
ADJNNOSU DON JUANS
ADKLOOPT POLKA DOT
ADKLOORW WOODLARK,
   WORKLOAD
ADKMNORW MARKDOWN
ADKMOORR DARKROOM
ADKOORRW ROADWORK
ADKORSWY WORKDAYS
ADKRSSWY SKYWARDS
ADLLLORY LOLLARDY
ADLLNORU ALL-ROUND
ADLLNOSW LOWLANDS
ADLLNUUZ ZULULAND
ADLLOPRS POLLARDS
ADLMNOOR MOORLAND
ADLMNOOW OLD WOMAN
ADLMNORY RANDOMLY
ADLMOPSY PSALMODY
ADLNNTUU UNDULANT
ADLNOORW LOANWORD
ADLNOPWY DOWNPLAY
ADLOOPRU UROPODAL
ADLOPRWY WORDPLAY
ADLORRSW WARLORDS
ADLORSTW LAST WORD

ADMMNORU OMDURMAN
ADMNNORY MONANDRY,
   NORMANDY
ADMNOORS ROSAMOND
ADMNOOST MASTODON
ADMNOOSW WOODSMAN
ADMNORRU ROUND-ARM
ADMNORSU ROSAMUND
ADMNORSW SANDWORM
ADMOOPPP POPPADOM
ADMOORRW WARDROOM
ADMOORST DOORMATS
ADMOORSY DAYROOMS
ADMOPPSU POPADUMS
ADNNORTY DYNATRON
ADNOOQRU QUADROON
ADNOORST TORNADOS
ADNOOSSS SO-AND-SOS
ADNOQRSU SQUADRON
ADNORSTU ROTUNDAS
ADNORSTW SANDWORT
ADNORSXY SARDONYX
ADNORTUW UNTOWARD
ADNOSTTU OUTSTAND
ADNPPSUU UP-AND-UPS
ADNPSSTU DUSTPANS
ADNRSSUW SUNWARDS
ADOOPRRT TRAPDOOR
ADOOPRSU SAUROPOD
ADOORSWY DOORWAYS
ADOPRSSW PASSWORD
ADOPSSSU SOAPSUDS
ADORSTUW OUTWARDS
ADORSTUY SUDATORY
ADRSSTTU STARDUST
AEEEFORS FAEROESE
AEEEGGLU LEE GAUGE
AEEEGLLS LEGALESE
AEEEGLRT REGELATE,
   RELEGATE
AEEEGLRV LEVERAGE
AEEEGLST LEGATEES
AEEEGNPR PEA GREEN
AEEEGNRT GENERATE,
   GREEN TEA, TEENAGER
AEEEGPRS PEERAGES
AEEEGRST STEERAGE
AEEEGRSW SEWERAGE
AEEEGTTV VEGETATE
AEEEHLRT ETHEREAL
AEEEHMPR EPHEMERA
AEEEHRRS REHEARSE
AEEEHRRT REHEATER

AEEEHSTT AESTHETE
AEEEIMNX EXAMINEE
AEEEJNTT JEANETTE
AEEEKKPS KEEPSAKE
AEEEKNRW WEAKENER
AEEEELLPP APPELLEE
AEEEELLSV SEA LEVEL
AEEEELNPS NEPALESE
AEEEELNRV VENEREAL
AEEEELNST SELENATE
AEEEELPRR REPEALER
AEEEELRRS RELEASER
AEEEELRRV REVEALER
AEEEELRSS RELEASES
AEEEELRTX AXLETREE
AEEEMMRT METAMERE
AEEEMNST EASEMENT
AEEEMPRT PERMEATE
AEEENPTT PATENTEE
AEEENRTV ENERVATE,
    VENERATE
AEEEPPRS PRAESEPE
AEEEPRRT REPARTEE,
    REPEATER
AEEEPSTW SWEET PEA
AEEERSST ESTERASE
AEEFFLLR FREE-FALL
AEEFFLTT FLAT FEET
AEEFFNRT AFFERENT
AEEFGILN FINE GAEL
AEEFGILR FILAGREE
AEEFGIRR FERRIAGE
AEEFGLSU FUSELAGE
AEEFHLLS SELFHEAL
AEEFHRST FEATHERS
AEEFHRTY FEATHERY
AEEFHRVY HAY FEVER
AEEFILNR FLANERIE
AEEFILST FETIALES,
    LEAFIEST
AEEFINST STEFANIE
AEEFIRRR RAREFIER
AEEFIRSS FREESIAS
AEEFISST SAFETIES
AEEFKOPR FOREPEAK
AEEFLLRW FAREWELL
AEEFLLST LEAFLETS
AEEFLMSS SELFSAME
AEEFLNRU FUNEREAL
AEEFLORV OVERLEAF
AEEFLRRR REFERRAL
AEEFLRRT FALTERER
AEEFLRSS FEARLESS

AEEFMNOR FORENAME
AEEFMORS FEARSOME
AEEFNRST FASTENER,
    FENESTRA
AEEFNRTT FATTENER
AEEFNSSS SAFENESS
AEEFPRSS FREE PASS
AEEFRSTU FEATURES
AEEFRSWY FREEWAYS
AEEGGIRV AGGRIEVE
AEEGGKOR OAK EGGER
AEEGGNNR GANGRENE
AEEGHHLS SHEELAGH
AEEGHILN HEGELIAN
AEEGHIRT HERITAGE
AEEGHMPR GRAPHEME
AEEGHNRS SHAGREEN
AEEGHRRT GATHERER
AEEGILLS LEGALISE
AEEGILLZ LEGALIZE
AEEGILMS MILEAGES
AEEGILNN ANGELINE
AEEGILNR ALGERINE
AEEGILNS ENSILAGE,
    LINEAGES
AEEGILNT GELATINE,
    LEGATINE
AEEGILTV LEVIGATE
AEEGIMNR GERMAINE
AEEGIMNT GEMINATE
AEEGIMRT EMIGRATE
AEEGINPR PERIGEAN
AEEGINRR REGAINER
AEEGINSS AGENESIS,
    ASSIGNEE
AEEGINSU GUIANESE
AEEGINSV ENVISAGE
AEEGINTV AGENTIVE,
    NEGATIVE
AEEGIPQU EQUIPAGE
AEEGIRRS GREASIER
AEEGIRTT AIGRETTE
AEEGLLNR ALLERGEN
AEEGLLSZ GAZELLES
AEEGLMNS MÉLANGES
AEEGLMOS MESOGLEA
AEEGLMRT TELEGRAM
AEEGLMRY MEAGRELY
AEEGLNNO ANGELENO
AEEGLNNT ENTANGLE
AEEGLNOT ELONGATE
AEEGLNRR ENLARGER
AEEGLNRS GENERALS

AEEGLNRT REGENTAL
AEEGLNSY ANGLESEY
AEEGLORT ALTER EGO
AEEGLRSS EELGRASS,
    LARGESSE
AEEGLRTU REGULATE
AEEGLRUX EXERGUAL
AEEGLSSV SELVAGES
AEEGLSSY EYEGLASS
AEEGLTTU TUTELAGE
AEEGMNSS GAMENESS
AEEGMRST GAMESTER
AEEGMSSS MESSAGES
AEEGMSSU MESSUAGE
AEEGNNNO ENNEAGON
AEEGNOST STONE AGE
AEEGNRRV ENGRAVER
AEEGNRST ESTRANGE,
    REAGENTS, SERGEANT
AEEGNRSV AVENGERS
AEEGNRUV AUVERGNE
AEEGNSUY GUYANESE
AEEGPRRS PRESAGER
AEEGPRSS PRESAGES
AEEGRRRT REGRATER
AEEGRRSS GREASERS
AEEGRSTT GREATEST
AEEGSTTZ GAZETTES
AEEHHIKZ HEZEKIAH
AEEHHIMN NEHEMIAH
AEEHHLNZ HAZELHEN
AEEHHNST HEATHENS
AEEHHRSS REHASHES
AEEHHRTY HEATHERY
AEEHIJMR JEREMIAH
AEEHIKLR HARELIKE
AEEHILTV HELVETIA
AEEHIMPU EUPHEMIA
AEEHIPRS HESPERIA,
    PHARISEE
AEEHIRRT EARTHIER,
    HEARTIER
AEEHIRST THERESIA
AEEHISTT HESITATE
AEEHISTV HEAVIEST
AEEHKLNT KATHLEEN
AEEHKNRR HANKERER,
    HARKENER
AEEHLLRT HEAR TELL
AEEHLLSS SEASHELL
AEEHLMNY HYMENEAL
AEEHLMPT HELPMATE
AEEHLNOT ANETHOLE

225

AEEHLNPT ELEPHANT
AEEHLNSS HALENESS
AEEHLNVY HEAVENLY
AEEHLOSU ALEHOUSE
AEEHLRTY LEATHERY
AEEHLSST HEATLESS
AEEHLSTT ATHLETES
AEEHLTTY ETHYLATE
AEEHMMRR HAMMERER
AEEHMPRR HAMPERER
AEEHMPSS EMPHASES
AEEHMRTY ERYTHEMA
AEEHNNTX XANTHENE
AEEHNOPR EARPHONE
AEEHNRST HASTENER
AEEHNRTT THREATEN
AEEHNRTU URETHANE
AEEHNRTW ENWREATH
AEEHNRWY ANYWHERE
AEEHNSTW ENSWATHE
AEEHORRV OVERHEAR
AEEHORSS SEAHORSE,
    SEASHORE
AEEHORTV OVERHEAT
AEEHOSTU TEAHOUSE
AEEHPRRS REPHRASE
AEEHRSTT THEATRES
AEEHRTVW WHATEVER
AEEHSTVY HEAVY-SET
AEEIJMNR JERMAINE
AEEIJMRS JEREMIAS
AEEIJNNN JEANNINE
AEEIKLMU LEUKEMIA
AEEIKLST LEAKIEST
AEEIKLVW WAVELIKE
AEEIKNRS SNEAKIER
AEEIKNRT ANKERITE
AEEIKNTW KEEWATIN
AEEIKPST PEAKIEST
AEEILMMN MELAMINE
AEEILMNS MILANESE
AEEILMNT MELANITE
AEEILMRT MATERIEL,
    REAL-TIME
AEEILMSS SEA MILES
AEEILMST MEALIEST
AEEILNPS PENALISE
AEEILNPT PETALINE
AEEILNPZ PENALIZE
AEEILNRT ELATERIN,
    ENTAILER, TREENAIL
AEEILNSV VASELINE
AEEILORT AEROLITE

AEEILOTT ETIOLATE
AEEILPPP APPLE PIE
AEEILPRR PEARLIER
AEEILPRS ESPALIER
AEEILPRT PEARLITE
AEEILQSU EQUALISE
AEEILQUZ EQUALIZE
AEEILRRS REALISER
AEEILRRT RETAILER
AEEILRRZ REALIZER
AEEILRST EARLIEST
AEEILRSV VELARISE
AEEILRSZ SLEAZIER
AEEILRTT LATERITE,
    LITERATE
AEEILRTV RELATIVE
AEEILRVW LIVEWARE,
    REVIEWAL
AEEILRVZ VELARIZE
AEEILTTV LEVITATE
AEEIMMNT MEANTIME
AEEIMNRT ANTIMERE
AEEIMNRX EXAMINER
AEEIMNSS MESSENIA
AEEIMNST MATINÉES
AEEIMORV AVIEMORE
AEEIMRST EMIRATES,
    STEAMIER
AEEIMRTT MARIETTE
AEEIMSST SEAMIEST
AEEIMSTT ESTIMATE,
    MEATIEST
AEEINNRS ANSERINE
AEEINNTV VENETIAN
AEEINOPS PAEONIES
AEEINPRT APERIENT
AEEINRRT RETAINER
AEEINRSS ASNIERES
AEEINRST ARSENITE,
    RESINATE, TERESINA,
    TRAINEES
AEEINRSU UNEASIER
AEEINSSS EASINESS
AEEINSTT ANISETTE,
    TETANISE
AEEINTTZ TETANIZE
AEEIPPSU EUPEPSIA
AEEIPPTT APPETITE
AEEIPRRR REPAIRER
AEEIQRSU QUEASIER
AEEIRRST ARTERIES
AEEIRSTT TREATIES,
    TREATISE

AEEIRSTW AS IT WERE,
    SWEATIER, WEARIEST
AEEIRSVV AVERSIVE
AEEIRTTZ TREATIZE
AEEISTTT STEATITE
AEEITUVX EXUVIATE
AEEKLLST SKELETAL
AEEKLMRT TELEMARK
AEEKLSSW WAKELESS
AEEKLSTY EYESTALK
AEEKMRRR REMARKER
AEEKMRRT MARKETER
AEEKNPSW NEWSPEAK
AEEKNRSS SNEAKERS
AEEKNSSW WEAKNESS
AEEKORST KERATOSE
AEEKORTV OVERTAKE,
    TAKEOVER
AEEKPRSS SPEAKERS
AEEKQRSU SQUEAKER
AEEKRRST STREAKER
AEELLLTT TELLTALE
AEELLMNW MEAN WELL
AEELLNOT LET ALONE
AEELLOTT ALLOTTEE
AEELLPPY ALLEPPEY
AEELLPTT PLATELET
AEELLPTY TELEPLAY
AEELLRRV RAVELLER
AEELLSTT STELLATE
AEELLSWY WEASELLY
AEELMMNU EMMANUEL
AEELMNRT LAMENTER
AEELMNSS LAMENESS,
    MALENESS, NAMELESS,
    SALESMEN
AEELMPRX EXEMPLAR
AEELMPRY EMPYREAL
AEELMPSX EXAMPLES
AEELMPTT PALMETTE,
    TEMPLATE
AEELMSSS SEAMLESS
AEELNNRT LANNERET
AEELNNSS LEANNESS
AEELNOOR ELEONORA
AEELNOPR PERONEAL
AEELNOPT ANTELOPE
AEELNORS ROSALEEN
AEELNPSS PALENESS
AEELNQSU SQUALENE
AEELNRRS LEARNERS
AEELNRSS REALNESS
AEELNRSV ENSLAVER

AEELNRSW RENEWALS
AEELNRTV LEVANTER,
   RELEVANT
AEELNRTX EXTERNAL
AEELNSST LATENESS
AEELNSWY WESLEYAN
AEELNTUV EVENTUAL
AEELORST OLEASTER
AEELORSU AUREOLES
AEELORTT TOLERATE
AEELORTV ELEVATOR
AEELOTTT TEETOTAL
AEELOTTW TEA TOWEL
AEELPRRS RELAPSER
AEELPRRT PALTERER
AEELPRRY PARLEYER
AEELPRSS RELAPSES
AEELPRST PRELATES
AEELPRSU PLEASURE
AEELPRSV VESPERAL
AEELPSTT PALETTES
AEELPSTU EPAULETS
AEELPTTU PAULETTE
AEELQRSU SQUEALER
AEELRRSV REVERSAL,
   SLAVERER
AEELRRTU URETERAL
AEELRSST TESSERAL
AEELRSTT LETRASET
AEELRSTY EASTERLY
AEELRTTU LAURETTE
AEELSTTY LAYETTES
AEEMMRRY YAMMERER
AEEMMRST AMMETERS
AEEMMSST MESSMATE
AEEMNNOS ANEMONES
AEEMNNPS PEN NAMES
AEEMNNSS MEANNESS
AEEMNPRT PERMEANT
AEEMNPRY EMPYREAN
AEEMNPST PET NAMES
AEEMNPTV PAVEMENT
AEEMNRSW MENSWEAR
AEEMNRTU NUMERATE
AEEMNRTV AVERMENT
AEEMNRUV MANEUVER
AEEMNRVY EVERYMAN
AEEMNSSS SAMENESS
AEEMNSST TAMENESS
AEEMPPRR PAMPERER
AEEMPRRT TAMPERER
AEEMPRRV REVAMPER
AEEMPSTU AMPUTEES

AEEMPSTW SWAP MEET
AEEMQRRU REMARQUE
AEEMQRSU MARQUEES
AEEMQTTU MAQUETTE
AEEMRRST STREAMER
AEEMRRSU MEASURER
AEEMRSST MASSETER,
   STEAMERS
AEEMRSSU MEASURES
AEEMRSTT TEAMSTER
AEENNORS ROSEANNE
AEENNPRY PYRENEAN
AEENNRRS ENSNARER
AEENNRSS NEARNESS
AEENNRTV REVENANT
AEENNSSS SANENESS
AEENNSST NEATNESS
AEENOPRU EUROPEAN
AEENORRS REASONER
AEENORSS SEASONER
AEENORST RESONATE
AEENORTV RENOVATE
AEENORVW OVENWARE
AEENRRSS RARENESS
AEENRRTV TAVERNER
AEENRSTV VETERANS
AEENRTTV ANTEVERT
AEENRTTY ENTREATY
AEENSVWW NEW WAVES
AEEOPRRT PERORATE
AEEOPRSW SEA POWER
AEEOPRTT OPERETTA
AEEORRTV OVERRATE
AEEORSSV OVERSEAS
AEEPPRTU PERPETUA
AEEPRRRT PARTERRE
AEEPRRSS ASPERSER
AEEPRRTU APERTURE
AEEPRSTZ TRAPEZES
AEEQRRUV QUAVERER
AEERRRST ARRESTER
AEERRSST ASSERTER
AEERRSSU ERASURES,
   REASSURE
AEERRSTT RETREATS
AEERRSTU TREASURE
AEERRSTV TRAVERSE
AEERRSVW WAVERERS
AEERSSTW SWEATERS
AEFFGIIL EFFIGIAL
AEFFGILS FIG LEAFS
AEFFGIRS GIRAFFES
AEFFGOST OFFSTAGE

AEFFGRSU SUFFRAGE
AEFFHILL HALF-LIFE
AEFFIMRR AFFIRMER,
   REAFFIRM
AEFFKORS RAKE-OFFS
AEFFKOST TAKEOFFS
AEFFLNSS SNAFFLES
AEFFLNTU AFFLUENT
AEFFLORU FOUR-LEAF
AEFFMRSU EARMUFFS
AEFFORST AFFOREST
AEFGIIRS GASIFIER
AEFGIKNR FREAKING
AEFGILNR FINAGLER
AEFGIMTU FUMIGATE
AEFGINST FEASTING
AEFGIORS FOIE GRAS
AEFGIRST FRIGATES
AEFGIRTU FIGURATE,
   FRUITAGE
AEFGISTU FATIGUES
AEFGLLOP FLAGPOLE
AEFGLLPU FULL-PAGE
AEFGLMNU FUGLEMAN
AEFGLOOR FLOORAGE
AEFGLOPR LEAPFROG
AEFGLRTU GRATEFUL
AEFGMNRT FRAGMENT
AEFGNORT FRONTAGE
AEFGOORT FOOTGEAR
AEFGRRST GRAFTERS
AEFHIKRS FREAKISH
AEFHIKSW WEAKFISH
AEFHILMT HALF TIME
AEFHILRS FLASHIER
AEFHLMRT HALF TERM
AEFHLMSU SHAMEFUL
AEFHLNOT HALF NOTE,
   HALFTONE
AEFHLRSS FLASHERS
AEFHLRTY FATHERLY
AEFHLSST FLASHEST
AEFHLSTU HASTEFUL
AEFHMNRS FRESHMAN
AEFHMORT FATHOMER
AEFHRSTT FARTHEST
AEFIILLN NAIL FILE
AEFIILMS FAMILIES
AEFIILNS FINALISE
AEFIILNZ FINALIZE
AEFIIMNS INFAMIES
AEFIINRS FRIESIAN
AEFIIPRT APERITIF

AEFIIRRS FRIARIES
AEFIIRRT RATIFIER
AEFIITVX FIXATIVE
AEFIKLMO FOAMLIKE
AEFIKLST FLAKIEST
AEFIKLTY FLY A KITE
AEFILLOT FELLATIO
AEFILMNR INFLAMER,
   RIFLEMAN
AEFILMNT FILAMENT
AEFILMUY EL FAIYUM
AEFILNNR INFERNAL
AEFILNPS LIFESPAN
AEFILNRT INFLATER
AEFILNRU FRAULEIN
AEFILOOR AEROFOIL
AEFILORS FORESAIL
AEFILPRX PREFIXAL
AEFILPST FLEAPITS
AEFILRST FRAILEST
AEFILRSU FAILURES
AEFILRTT FILTRATE
AEFILRTU FAULTIER,
   FILATURE
AEFILSTV FESTIVAL
AEFILTUU FAUTEUIL
AEFIMNST MANIFEST
AEFIMOST FOAMIEST
AEFIMRRS FIREARMS
AEFIMRRW FIRMWARE
AEFINNSZ FANZINES
AEFINOPR PINAFORE
AEFINORS FARINOSE
AEFINOTT FETATION
AEFINRRS REFRAINS
AEFINRRU UNFAIRER
AEFINRSS FAIRNESS
AEFINRST FINE ARTS
AEFINSTT FAINTEST
AEFIPRRT FIRETRAP
AEFIRRRS FARRIERS
AEFIRRRY FARRIERY
AEFIRSTV FIVE-STAR
AEFISTTT FATTIEST
AEFKLLOT FOLKTALE
AEFKNORS FORSAKEN
AEFKNRST FRANKEST
AEFKORRS FORSAKER
AEFLLNNS FLANNELS
AEFLLRUX FLEXURAL
AEFLLSSW FLAWLESS
AEFLLSTT FLATLETS

AEFLMORU FORMULAE,
   FUMAROLE
AEFLMOTU FLAMEOUT
AEFLNORS FARNESOL
AEFLNRSU FUNERALS
AEFLNRTU FLAUNTER
AEFLNSST FLATNESS
AEFLOORV FOVEOLAR
AEFLOPRY FOREPLAY
AEFLOPSW PEAFOWLS
AEFLORST FLOATERS,
   FORESTAL
AEFLORTT FLORETTA
AEFLORTW FLEAWORT
AEFLOSTT FALSETTO
AEFLPPRY FLYPAPER
AEFLPRSU FLARE-UPS
AEFLPRSY PALFREYS
AEFLRSSU REFUSALS
AEFLRTTU AFLUTTER
AEFLRTTY FLATTERY
AEFLSTTT FLATTEST
AEFLSTTU TASTEFUL
AEFLSTUW WASTEFUL
AEFMNORW MEN-OF-WAR
AEFMNRRY FERRYMAN
AEFMORRS FOREARMS
AEFMORST FOREMAST
AEFMORVW WAVEFORM
AEFMPRSU FRAME-UPS
AEFNNSTU UNFASTEN
AEFNOPRR PROFANER
AEFNORRW FOREWARN
AEFNORST SEAFRONT
AEFNRRST TRANSFER
AEFNRRUY FUNERARY
AEFNSSST FASTNESS
AEFOORTW FOOTWEAR
AEFOPRRT FOREPART
AEFOPTUU POT-AU-FEU
AEFORRSW FORSWEAR
AEFORRUV FAVOURER
AEFORSTW SOFTWARE
AEFORSTY FORESTAY
AEFRSSTW FRETSAWS
AEGGGINN ENGAGING
AEGGHIRS SHAGGIER
AEGGHNNY HENG-YANG
AEGGHOPY GEOPHAGY
AEGGHORU ROUGHAGE
AEGGILLN ALLEGING
AEGGILLR GRILLAGE
AEGGILMN GLEAMING

AEGGILNN GLEANING
AEGGILNU LEAGUING
AEGGINNR ANGERING,
   ENRAGING
AEGGINNT NEGATING
AEGGINNV AVENGING
AEGGINOR GEORGIAN,
   GEORGINA
AEGGINOS SEAGOING
AEGGINRS GREASING
AEGGINRW WAGERING
AEGGIOPR ARPEGGIO
AEGGISST SAGGIEST
AEGGLNPT EGGPLANT
AEGGLORY GARGOYLE
AEGGLRST STRAGGLE
AEGGMMSU MUG'S GAME
AEGGMORT MORTGAGE
AEGGNRST GANGSTER
AEGGOPRU AGE GROUP
AEGGRSST STAGGERS
AEGHHISS HIGH SEAS
AEGHILLT LIGHT ALE
AEGHILMT MEGALITH
AEGHILNX EXHALING
AEGHILRT LITHARGE
AEGHINRS HEARINGS,
   SHEARING
AEGHINRT EARTHING,
   INGATHER
AEGHINRV HAVERING
AEGHINRY HARINGEY
AEGHINTT GNATHITE
AEGHIPPR EPIGRAPH
AEGHIPRT GRAPHITE
AEGHLOSS GALOSHES
AEGHLRTU LAUGHTER
AEGHLRTY LETHARGY
AEGHNNOR HANGER-ON
AEGHNNSY SHENYANG
AEGHNOPT HEPTAGON,
   PATHOGEN
AEGHNORV HANGOVER,
   OVERHANG
AEGHNOSX HEXAGONS
AEGHOPPR PROPHAGE
AEGHOPPY APOPHYGE
AEGHORST SHORTAGE
AEGHOSST HOSTAGES
AEGIILLU AIGUILLE
AEGIILMR REMIGIAL
AEGIILTT LITIGATE
AEGIILTV LIGATIVE

AEGIIMNR IMAGINER, MIGRAINE
AEGIIMTT MITIGATE
AEGIINNR ARGININE, NIGERIAN
AEGIIRRT IRRIGATE
AEGIKLNS LINKAGES
AEGIKLNW WEAKLING
AEGIKMNR REMAKING
AEGIKNNS SNEAKING
AEGIKNNW WAKENING
AEGIKNPS SPEAKING
AEGIKNRT RETAKING
AEGIKNRW WREAKING
AEGIKNTW TWEAKING
AEGIKNWY KWEIYANG
AEGIKSTW GAWKIEST
AEGILLMS LEGALISM
AEGILLMU GULIELMA
AEGILLNO GOAL LINE
AEGILLNY GENIALLY
AEGILLPR PILLAGER
AEGILLPS SPILLAGE
AEGILLRV VILLAGER
AEGILLST LEGALIST
AEGILLSV VILLAGES
AEGILLTU LIGULATE
AEGILLTY LEGALITY
AEGILMNR GERMINAL, MALIGNER, MALINGER
AEGILMNS GALENISM
AEGILMNT LIGAMENT, METALING, TEGMINAL
AEGILMST TIME LAGS
AEGILNNP PANELING
AEGILNNR LEARNING
AEGILNNS LEANINGS
AEGILNNT GANTLINE
AEGILNNW WEANLING
AEGILNNY YEANLING
AEGILNOR GERANIOL, REGIONAL
AEGILNOS GASOLINE
AEGILNOT GELATION, LEGATION
AEGILNPS ELAPSING, PLEASING
AEGILNPT PLEATING
AEGILNQU EQUALING
AEGILNRT ALERTING, ALTERING, INTEGRAL, RELATING, TRIANGLE
AEGILNRV RAVELING

AEGILNRX RELAXING
AEGILNRY LAYERING, RELAYING, YEARLING
AEGILNSS GLASSINE
AEGILNST GALENIST, GENITALS, STEALING
AEGILNSV LEAVINGS
AEGILNTX EXALTING
AEGILOPS SPOILAGE
AEGILOPT PILOTAGE
AEGILORS GASOLIER, SERAGLIO
AEGILPPS SLIPPAGE
AEGILRSS GLASSIER
AEGILRSY GREASILY
AEGILRSZ GLAZIERS
AEGILRTU LIGATURE
AEGILRTY REGALITY
AEGILRVW LAWGIVER
AEGILRYZ GLAZIERY
AEGIMNNR RENAMING
AEGIMNNS MEANINGS
AEGIMNRR REARMING
AEGIMNRS SMEARING
AEGIMNRT EMIGRANT
AEGIMNRU GERANIUM
AEGIMNSS GAMINESS
AEGIMNST MANGIEST, STEAMING
AEGIMPRS EPIGRAMS
AEGIMQRU QUAGMIRE
AEGIMRST STERIGMA
AEGIMSSU MISUSAGE
AEGINNNX ANNEXING
AEGINNOS ANGINOSE
AEGINNOT NEGATION
AEGINNRS EARNINGS, GRANNIES
AEGINNRV RAVENING
AEGINNRY YEARNING
AEGINNST ANTIGENS, GENTIANS
AEGINNSU SANGUINE
AEGINORS ORGANISE
AEGINORZ ORGANIZE
AEGINOTV GO NATIVE
AEGINPPR PAPERING
AEGINPRS SPEARING
AEGINPRT TAPERING
AEGINPRY REPAYING
AEGINPTY EGYPTIAN
AEGINQTU EQUATING
AEGINRRS EARRINGS

AEGINRRV AVERRING
AEGINRSS ASSIGNER
AEGINRST ANGRIEST, GANISTER, GANTRIES, INGRATES
AEGINRSW SWEARING
AEGINRTT TREATING
AEGINRTV AVERTING, VINTAGER
AEGINRTW WATERING
AEGINRVW WAVERING
AEGINRVY VINEGARY
AEGINRWY WEARYING
AEGINSST GIANTESS
AEGINSSY ESSAYING
AEGINSTT TANGIEST
AEGINSTU SAUTÉING
AEGINSTV VINTAGES
AEGINSTW SWEATING
AEGIORSV VIRAGOES
AEGIOSTX GEOTAXIS
AEGIRRSS GRASSIER
AEGIRSST SEAGIRTS
AEGIRSUU AUGURIES
AEGISSST GASSIEST
AEGISTUZ GAUZIEST
AEGLLNOS GALLEONS
AEGLLOPR GALLOPER
AEGLLORY ALLEGORY
AEGLLOTT TOLLGATE
AEGLLRVY GRAVELLY
AEGLLSSU SEAGULLS
AEGLMNNO MANGONEL
AEGLMNTU GUNMETAL
AEGLMOTV MEGAVOLT
AEGLNNOR ALGERNON
AEGLNNPT PLANGENT
AEGLNNTU UNTANGLE
AEGLNORS SELANGOR
AEGLNORY YEARLONG
AEGLNOVW LONG WAVE
AEGLNPRS GRAPNELS
AEGLNPSS SPANGLES
AEGLNRRW WRANGLER
AEGLNRST STRANGLE
AEGLNRSU GRANULES
AEGLNRSW WRANGLES
AEGLNRSY LARYNGES
AEGLNSUW GUNWALES
AEGLNTTU GAUNTLET
AEGLNTUU UNGULATE
AEGLOOOZ ZOOGLOEA
AEGLOOPU APOLOGUE

AEGLOORY AEROLOGY
AEGLOPRS PERGOLAS
AEGLOPRY PLAYGOER
AEGLOSTV VOLTAGES
AEGLPPRR GRAPPLER
AEGLPRSU EARPLUGS
AEGLRRSU REGULARS
AEGLRSTU GESTURAL
AEGLSSTT GESTALTS
AEGMMNOR GAMMONER
AEGMMRRU RUMMAGER
AEGMMRSU RUMMAGES
AEGMNNOT MAGNETON
AEGMNORV MANGROVE
AEGMNOST MAGNETOS,
   MEGATONS, MONTAGES
AEGMNOTU MONTAGUE
AEGMNOXY XENOGAMY
AEGMNRST GARMENTS
AEGMNRTU ARGUMENT
AEGMOPRW GAPEWORM
AEGMORRW WORM GEAR
AEGMORSS GOSSAMER
AEGMPRUZ GAZUMPER
AEGNNOPT PENTAGON
AEGNNOST TONNAGES
AEGNNPRT PREGNANT
AEGNNSTT TANGENTS
AEGNORRY ORANGERY
AEGNORST ESTRAGON
AEGNORSX SEX ORGAN
AEGNOSSY NOSEGAYS
AEGNPPRU GUNPAPER
AEGNRRST STRANGER
AEGOPPST STOPPAGE
AEGOPSST GESTAPOS
AEGOPSTT GATEPOST
AEGORRTT GARROTTE
AEGORSTU GOAT'S-RUE,
  OUTRAGES
AEGORSVY VOYAGERS
AEGORTTU TUTORAGE
AEGOSTTV GAVOTTES
AEGRRSSY RYEGRASS
AEGRSTTY STRATEGY
AEHHHJPT JEPHTHAH
AEHHINPR HA-ERH-PIN
AEHHINPS PHINEHAS
AEHHRRST THRASHER
AEHHRSST HARSHEST
AEHIIKLR HAIRLIKE
AEHIILNR HAIRLINE
AEHIIMNT THIAMINE

AEHIINTZ THIAZINE
AEHIIOPT ETHIOPIA
AEHIIRST HAIRIEST
AEHIJNOV JEHOVIAN
AEHIKKLW HAWKLIKE
AEHIKLLO HALO-LIKE
AEHIKMNR KHMERIAN
AEHIKSST SHAKIEST
AEHILMSW LIMEWASH
AEHILNOP APHELION
AEHILNOT IOLANTHE
AEHILNRS INHALERS
AEHILNTX ANTHELIX
AEHILNTZ ZENITHAL
AEHILOTZ THIAZOLE
AEHILRSS HAIRLESS
AEHILRSU HAULIERS
AEHILRSV LAVISHER,
  SHRIEVAL
AEHILRTY EARTHILY,
  HEARTILY
AEHIMMNN MANNHEIM
AEHIMMSS SHAMMIES
AEHIMNNU INHUMANE
AEHIMNOR HOMERIAN
AEHIMNSU HUMANISE
AEHIMNUZ HUMANIZE
AEHIMOTT TIMOTHEA
AEHIMPRS SAMPHIRE,
  SERAPHIM
AEHIMPSS EMPHASIS,
  MISSHAPE
AEHIMPST SHIPMATE
AEHIMSSS MESSIAHS
AEHINNTX XANTHEIN,
  XANTHINE
AEHINORT ANTIHERO
AEHINPPY EPIPHANY
AEHINPRT PERIANTH
AEHINPST THESPIAN
AEHINRST HAIRNETS
AEHINRSV VANISHER
AEHINRTZ HERTZIAN
AEHINSSS HESSIANS
AEHINSST ANTHESIS,
  SHANTIES
AEHINSSZ HAZINESS
AEHINSTT HESITANT
AEHINTTW WHITE ANT
AEHINTWY IN THE WAY
AEHIOPRS APHORISE
AEHIOPRU EUPHORIA
AEHIOPRZ APHORIZE

AEHIORST HOARIEST
AEHIORTU THIOUREA
AEHIPPRS SAPPHIRE
AEHIPPST EPITAPHS,
  HAPPIEST
AEHIPRSS PARISHES
AEHIRRRS HARRIERS
AEHIRRST TRASHIER
AEHIRRSV RAVISHER
AEHIRRSY AYRSHIRE
AEHIRSTY HYSTERIA
AEHISSTT ATHEISTS,
  HASTIEST
AEHISSTU HIATUSES
AEHJNNOS JOHANNES
AEHJPRSW JEW'S HARP
AEHKLOOY HOLYOAKE
AEHKNSTT TASHKENT
AEHKOSTU SHAKEOUT
AEHKPSSU SHAKE-UPS
AEHLLLTY LETHALLY
AEHLLMTY METHYLAL
AEHLLNRT HARTNELL
AEHLLORW HALLOWER
AEHLMMNS HELMSMAN
AEHLMNNP HELPMANN
AEHLMNOS MANHOLES
AEHLMNOT METHANOL
AEHLMNUY HUMANELY
AEHLMORS ARMHOLES
AEHLMPPT PAMPHLET
AEHLMRSS HARMLESS
AEHLMRST THERMALS
AEHLNOPS ALPHONSE
AEHLNPRS SHRAPNEL
AEHLNPTY ENTHALPY
AEHLNRTU LUTHERAN
AEHLNTUZ HAZELNUT
AEHLOPRT PLETHORA
AEHLOPTT HOTPLATE
AEHLORSY HOARSELY
AEHLORUV OVERHAUL
AEHLOSSS ASSHOLES
AEHLPRSS SPLASHER
AEHLPSST PATHLESS
AEHLPSTU SULPHATE
AEHLRRTU URETHRAL
AEHLSSTY THESSALY
AEHLSTTY STEALTHY
AEHMNORS HORSEMAN
AEHMNOSU HOUSEMAN
AEHMOPRT METAPHOR
AEHMOSTW SOMEWHAT

AEHMPPTU HEAT PUMP
AEHMRSSS SMASHERS
AEHMRSST HAMSTERS
AEHMSTTY AMETHYST
AEHNNOPT PANTHEON
AEHNNPSU UNSHAPEN
AEHNNSUV UNSHAVEN
AEHNOPPY PAY PHONE
AEHNOPRT HAPTERON
AEHNOPST PHAETONS
AEHNORST SHERATON
AEHNOSTV HAVE-NOTS
AEHNPRST PANTHERS
AEHNPRTY HEN PARTY,
TRYPHENA
AEHNRSSS RASHNESS
AEHNRTTU EARTHNUT
AEHNSTUW UNSWATHE
AEHOPPRS PROPHASE
AEHOPSTU PHASE-OUT
AEHOPSTW TWO-PHASE
AEHOPTVY TOP-HEAVY
AEHORRRW HARROWER
AEHORRSW WARHORSE
AEHORSST EARSHOTS,
HOARSEST
AEHORSSW SAWHORSE
AEHORSTT RHEOSTAT
AEHORSTU SHARE-OUT
AEHORSTX THORAXES
AEHORTTW HOT WATER
AEHPRSST SHARPEST,
SHARP-SET
AEHPRSUX HARUSPEX
AEHPRSUY EUPHRASY
AEHQRSSU SQUASHER
AEHQSSSU SQUASHES
AEHRRSTU URETHRAS
AEHRRTTW THWARTER
AEHRSSTV HARVESTS
AEHSSTUX EXHAUSTS
AEIIINTT INITIATE
AEIILLTV ILLATIVE
AEIILMNN MAIN LINE
AEIILMNS ALIENISM
AEIILMPR IMPERIAL
AEIILMTT MILITATE
AEIILNPR PLEIN-AIR
AEIILNQU AQUILINE
AEIILNRR AIRLINER
AEIILNRS AIRLINES
AEIILNRT INERTIAL

AEIILNST ALIENIST,
LATINISE, LITANIES,
TALIESIN
AEIILNTZ LATINIZE
AEIILPPT TAIL PIPE
AEIILRSS ISRAELIS
AEIILRTT LITERATI
AEIILSTV VITALISE
AEIILTVZ VITALIZE
AEIIMMRT MARITIME
AEIIMMSX MAXIMISE
AEIIMMXZ MAXIMIZE
AEIIMNTT INTIMATE
AEIIMNTU MINUTIAE
AEIIMPRR IMPAIRER
AEIIMRST SERIATIM
AEIINNRS SIRENIAN
AEIINRSS AIRINESS
AEIINRST RAINIEST
AEIINRTZ TRIAZINE
AEIINSST SANITISE
AEIINSTZ SANITIZE
AEIINSVV INVASIVE
AEIINTTT TITANITE
AEIIPRRS PRAIRIES
AEIIPRZZ PIZZERIA
AEIIPSST EPITASIS
AEIIRRST RARITIES
AEIIRRSV RIVIERAS
AEIIRRTT IRRITATE
AEIIRSST SATIRISE
AEIIRSTW WISTERIA
AEIIRSTZ SATIRIZE
AEIITTTV TITIVATE
AEIJLNNU JULIANNE
AEIJLNSV JAVELINS
AEIJLOPS JALOPIES
AEIJLOSU JALOUSIE
AEIJMMST JAMMIEST
AEIJMNSS JASMINES
AEIJMORR MARJORIE
AEIJNRTU JAUNTIER
AEIJORST JAROSITE
AEIJSTZZ JAZZIEST
AEIKLLLW WALL-LIKE
AEIKLNPS SKI PLANE
AEIKLNSS SEALSKIN
AEIKLNST LANKIEST
AEIKLNSY SNEAKILY
AEIKLRST STARLIKE
AEIKMNOS ESKIMOAN
AEIKMNRS RAMEKINS
AEIKMNST MISTAKEN

AEIKMSST MISTAKES
AEIKNRST NARKIEST,
TRANSKEI
AEIKNRSW SWANKIER
AEIKNRTW KNITWEAR
AEIKPRSS APRES-SKI
AEIKPRST PARKIEST
AEIKPSST PISS-TAKE
AEIKPSTW PAWKIEST
AEIKRSST ASTERISK,
SARKIEST
AEIKRSTW WATER-SKI
AEILLLMS ALLELISM
AEILLLNY LINEALLY
AEILLMNY MENIALLY
AEILLNPS SPLENIAL
AEILLNST ANTILLES
AEILLNUV LAEVULIN
AEILLOSS LOESSIAL
AEILLOTV VOLATILE
AEILLPRS PIS ALLER
AEILLPST PALLIEST,
PASTILLE
AEILLRRY RAILLERY
AEILLRST LITERALS
AEILLRSY SERIALLY
AEILLRTT ILL-TREAT
AEILLSST TAILLESS
AEILLSUV ALLUSIVE
AEILLSYZ SLEAZILY
AEILLTUZ LAZULITE
AEILMMNS MELANISM
AEILMMOR MEMORIAL
AEILMMOT IMMOLATE
AEILMMRT TRILEMMA
AEILMNNS LINESMAN
AEILMNOS SEMOLINA
AEILMNRS MINERALS
AEILMNRT TERMINAL,
TRAMLINE
AEILMNST AILMENTS,
MANLIEST, MELANIST
AEILMOPR PROEMIAL
AEILMORS MORALISE
AEILMORZ MORALIZE
AEILMPRV PRIMEVAL
AEILMPST PALMIEST
AEILMPTT PETIT MAL
AEILMPTY PLAYTIME
AEILMRSY MISLAYER
AEILMSTT SMALTITE
AEILMSTU SIMULATE
AEILMSTY STEAMILY

AEILMTTU MUTILATE,
  ULTIMATE
AEILNNRT INTERNAL
AEILNNSY INSANELY
AEILNNTY INNATELY
AEILNOPP APPOLINE
AEILNORR LORRAINE
AEILNORS AILERONS,
  ROSALINE
AEILNORT ORIENTAL,
  RELATION
AEILNORV OVERLAIN
AEILNOSS SEA LIONS
AEILNOST INSOLATE,
  TOENAILS
AEILNOSV SLOVENIA
AEILNOSX SILOXANE
AEILNPRS PRALINES
AEILNPRT TRIPLANE
AEILNPSS PAINLESS,
  SPANIELS
AEILNPST PANTILES,
  PLAINEST
AEILNPTT TINPLATE
AEILNRSS RAINLESS
AEILNRST ENTRAILS,
  LATRINES
AEILNRTU TENURIAL
AEILNRTV INTERVAL
AEILNRTY INTERLAY
AEILNSST SALIENTS
AEILNSSZ LAZINESS
AEILNSTU INSULATE
AEILNSUY UNEASILY
AEILNTVY VENALITY
AEILNUVV UNIVALVE
AEILOPPT OPPILATE
AEILOPRS POLARISE
AEILOPRZ POLARIZE
AEILOPST SPOLIATE
AEILORSS SOLARISE
AEILORSV VALORISE
AEILORSZ SOLARIZE
AEILORTZ TRIAZOLE
AEILORVZ VALORIZE
AEILOSTT TOTALISE
AEILOTTV VIOLETTA
AEILOTTZ TOTALIZE
AEILPPQU APPLIQUÉ
AEILPPST SPLIT PEA
AEILPRRS REPRISAL
AEILPRRT PALTRIER
AEILPRST PILASTER

AEILPRTV LIVETRAP
AEILPRXY PYREXIAL
AEILPSUV PLAUSIVE
AEILQRTU QUARTILE,
  REQUITAL
AEILQSUY QUEASILY
AEILQTUY EQUALITY
AEILRRST RETRIALS,
  TRAILERS
AEILRRSU RURALISE
AEILRRTY LITERARY
AEILRRUZ RURALIZE
AEILRSST REALISTS
AEILRSVV REVIVALS
AEILRTUZ LAZURITE
AEILSSTT SALTIEST
AEILSTWY SWEATILY
AEILSTYY YEASTILY
AEIMMNNT IMMANENT
AEIMMNOT AMMONITE
AEIMMRRS SMARMIER
AEIMMRTU IMMATURE
AEIMNNNR INNER MAN
AEIMNNOT NOMINATE
AEIMNOPT PTOMAINE
AEIMNORS MORAINES,
  ROMANIES
AEIMNORW AIRWOMEN
AEIMNOSW WOMANISE
AEIMNOTZ MONAZITE
AEIMNOWZ WOMANIZE
AEIMNRRS MARINERS
AEIMNRSS NEAR MISS,
  SEMINARS
AEIMNRST MINARETS
AEIMNRSY SEMINARY
AEIMNRTT MARTINET
AEIMNRTU RUMINATE
AEIMNRTY TYRAMINE
AEIMNSST MANTISES
AEIMORST AMORTISE,
  ATOMISER
AEIMORTZ AMORTIZE,
  ATOMIZER
AEIMOTTV MOTIVATE
AEIMPRRT IMPARTER
AEIMPRST PRIMATES
AEIMPRSV VAMPIRES
AEIMPRTT PART-TIME
AEIMPSSS IMPASSES
AEIMPSST PASTIMES
AEIMQRSU MARQUISE
AEIMRSST ASTERISM

AEIMRSSY EMISSARY
AEIMRSTT MISTREAT,
  TERATISM
AEIMRSTX MATRIXES
AEIMSSST SEA MISTS
AEIMSSTT MISSTATE
AEINNOPV PAVONINE
AEINNORT ANOINTER
AEINNOST ESTONIAN
AEINNOTT INTONATE
AEINNOTV INNOVATE,
  VENATION
AEINNPRS PANNIERS
AEINNRST TRANNIES
AEINNSSV VAINNESS
AEINNSSZ ZANINESS
AEINNSTT STANNITE
AEINNSUV VENUSIAN
AEINOPRT ATROPINE
AEINOPST SAPONITE
AEINOQTU EQUATION
AEINORRT ANTERIOR
AEINORRW IRONWARE
AEINORST NOTARIES,
  NOTARISE, SEÑORITA
AEINORSV AVERSION
AEINORTU TOURAINE
AEINORTZ NOTARIZE
AEINOSSV EVASIONS
AEINOTVX VEXATION
AEINPPPS PANPIPES
AEINPPRS SNAPPIER
AEINPRRT TERRAPIN
AEINPRST PAINTERS,
  PANTRIES, PINASTER
AEINPRTT TRIPTANE
AEINPRUV PERUVIAN
AEINPSST STEAPSIN
AEINPSTT PATIENTS
AEINPSTU PETUNIAS,
  SUPINATE
AEINPSTY EPINASTY
AEINQSTU ANTIQUES,
  QUANTISE
AEINQTTU EQUITANT
AEINQTUZ QUANTIZE
AEINRRST RESTRAIN,
  STRAINER, TERRAINS,
  TRAINERS
AEINRSST ARTINESS
AEINRSSU ANURESIS
AEINRSSW WARINESS

AEINRSTT NITRATES,
   STRAITEN, TRAIN SET
AEINRSUZ SUZERAIN
AEINRSZZ SNAZZIER
AEINSSTT NASTIEST
AEINSSVW WAVINESS
AEINSSWX WAXINESS
AEINSTTT NATTIEST
AEINSUVV VESUVIAN
AEINTTUU AUTUNITE
AEIOPPST APPOSITE
AEIOPRRT PRETORIA,
   PRIORATE
AEIOPRSV VAPORISE
AEIOPRTX EXPIATOR
AEIOPRVZ VAPORIZE
AEIOPSST SOAPIEST
AEIOPTTV OPTATIVE
AEIOQSSU SEQUOIAS
AEIORRSS ROSARIES
AEIORRUV AU REVOIR
AEIORSSV SAVORIES
AEIORSTV VOTARIES
AEIORTTV ROTATIVE
AEIPPSST SAPPIEST
AEIPPSTZ ZAPPIEST
AEIPQRTU PRATIQUE
AEIPRRSU UPRAISER
AEIPRSST PASTRIES,
   PIASTRES
AEIPRSTV PRIVATES
AEIPRSTW WIRETAPS
AEIPRSTY ASPERITY
AEIPRSVY VESPIARY
AEIPRTVY VARITYPE
AEIPSSTT PASTIEST
AEIPTTUV PUTATIVE
AEIQRRRU QUARRIER
AEIQRRSU QUARRIES
AEIRRRST STARRIER
AEIRRTTY TERTIARY
AEIRSSST ASSISTER
AEIRSSTT ARTISTES
AEIRSSTW WAITRESS
AEIRSTTT RATTIEST
AEISSSST SASSIEST
AEISSSTY ESSAYIST
AEISSTTT TASTIEST
AEISTTTT TATTIEST
AEJLOSUY JEALOUSY
AEJMNSSY JESSAMYN
AEKKMNOO KAKEMONO
AEKLMORS LARKSOME

AEKLMRUW LUKEWARM
AEKLNNSS LANKNESS
AEKLNOSY ANKYLOSE
AEKLOPRW ROPEWALK
AEKLORVW WALKOVER
AEKLPPST PEP TALKS
AEKLPRRS SPARKLER
AEKLPRSS SPARKLES
AEKLRSST STALKERS
AEKMMNRS MARKSMEN
AEKMNRSU UNMASKER
AEKMORTW TEAMWORK
AEKMPRTU UP-MARKET
AEKNNRSS RANKNESS
AEKNOOTY KOOTENAY
AEKOSTTU OUT-TAKES,
   TAKEOUTS
AEKOSTVW TAKE VOWS
AEKPSSSY PASSKEYS
AEKQRSUW SQUAWKER
AEKRRSST STARKERS
AEKRSSTT STARKEST
AELLMNTY MENTALLY
AELLMORT MARTELLO
AELLMSST SMALLEST
AELLNOPV VOLPLANE
AELLNOSV NOVELLAS
AELLNPRU PRUNELLA
AELLNSST TALLNESS
AELLNTUU LUNULATE
AELLOPRW WALLOPER
AELLOPRY ROLE PLAY
AELLORSV OVERALLS
AELLORWW WALLOWER
AELLOSUV ALVEOLUS
AELLPPSU SELL A PUP
AELLQRSU SQUALLER
AELLRTTY LATTERLY
AELLSSTY TASSELLY
AELLSUXY SEXUALLY
AELMMORW MEALWORM
AELMMRST TRAMMELS
AELMNNOT NONMETAL
AELMNNRY MANNERLY
AELMNOPS NEOPLASM,
   PLEONASM
AELMNORS ALMONERS
AELMNORT MONTREAL
AELMNOSU MELANOUS
AELMNOWY LAYWOMEN
AELMNOYY YEOMANLY
AELMNRSU MENSURAL,
   NUMERALS

AELMOORS SALEROOM
AELMOPRR PREMOLAR
AELMOPRT TEMPORAL
AELMOPSU AMPOULES
AELMOPSY MAYPOLES
AELMOPTT PALMETTO
AELMORSU RAMULOSE
AELMORSV REMOVALS
AELMORTU EMULATOR
AELMOSSS MOLASSES
AELMPRRT TRAMPLER
AELMPRSS SAMPLERS
AELMPRSY LAMPREYS
AELMRSTT MALTSTER
AELMRSTY MASTERLY
AELMRTUY MATURELY
AELNNOOP NAPOLEON
AELNNOPP OPEN-PLAN
AELNNOSU ANNULOSE
AELNNPRS PLANNERS
AELNNRST LANTERNS
AELNOPRS PERSONAL
AELNORTT TOLERANT
AELNORTY ORNATELY
AELNOSSV OVALNESS
AELNPPSY PLAYPENS
AELNPRST PLANTERS
AELNPRSU PURSLANE,
   SUPERNAL
AELNPTTU PETULANT
AELNPTTY PATENTLY
AELNRSTT SLATTERN
AELNRSTU NEUTRALS
AELNRSXY LARYNXES
AELNSSST SALTNESS
AELNTTUX EXULTANT
AELOORRS ROSEOLAR
AELOORSS AEROSOLS
AELOORTW WATERLOO
AELOORTZ ZOOLATER
AELOPPRS PROLAPSE,
   SAPROPEL
AELOPPTU POPULATE
AELOPPXY APOPLEXY
AELOPQUY OPAQUELY
AELOPRRV REPROVAL
AELOPRST PETROSAL,
   POLE STAR
AELOPRSV OVERLAPS
AELOPRVY OVERPLAY
AELOPRYZ PYRAZOLE
AELOPSSS SOAPLESS
AELOPSST APOSTLES

AELOPSSU ESPOUSAL
AELORRST REALTORS
AELORSVY OVERLAYS
AELORTWW LOW WATER
AELORTYZ ZEALOTRY
AELOSTUY AUTOLYSE
AELPRRSW SPRAWLER
AELPRRTT PRATTLER
AELPRSST PLASTERS,
   PSALTERS, STAPLERS
AELPRSSU PERUSALS
AELPRSSY SPARSELY
AELPRSTT PLATTERS,
   SPLATTER
AELPRSTY PSALTERY
AELQRRSU QUARRELS
AELQRSUY SQUARELY
AELRRSTT STARTLER
AELRRSTW TRAWLERS
AELRSSST STARLESS
AELRSSTT STARLETS
AELRSSTW WASTRELS
AELRSSUW WALRUSES
AELRSTTT TATTLERS
AELRSTTU LUSTRATE
AELRSTUV VAULTERS,
   VESTURAL
AELRTTUX TEXTURAL
AELRTTUY TUTELARY
AELSTTUY ASTUTELY
AEMMNRTU RAMENTUM
AEMMOORT ROOMMATE
AEMMORST MARMOSET
AEMMRSST STAMMERS
AEMNNORS NORSEMAN
AEMNNORT ORNAMENT
AEMNNORW MORWENNA
AEMNNPRU PER ANNUM
AEMNNRST REMNANTS
AEMNOORT ANTEROOM
AEMNOPRW MANPOWER
AEMNORRS RANSOMER
AEMNORST ONSTREAM
AEMNORTY MONETARY
AEMNORYY YEOMANRY
AEMNOSTU SEAMOUNT
AEMNPRSS PRESSMAN
AEMNPRSU SUPERMAN
AEMNPSTY PAYMENTS
AEMNRRUY NUMERARY
AEMNRSSU SURNAMES
AEMNRSSW WARMNESS
AEMNRSTW STRAW MEN

AEMNRSUY ANEURYSM
AEMOORST TEAROOMS
AEMOORTT AMORETTO
AEMOOSST MAESTOSO
AEMOOSTT TOMATOES
AEMOOSTU AUTOSOME
AEMOPRTW TAPEWORM
AEMORRRU ARMOURER
AEMORRST REARMOST
AEMORRSY ROSEMARY
AEMORSSS MORASSES
AEMORSST MAESTROS
AEMORSSY MAYORESS
AEMORTTU TAUTOMER
AEMOTTZZ MOZZETTA
AEMPRRSY SPERMARY
AEMPRSTU UPSTREAM
AEMPSTTT ATTEMPTS
AEMQRSSU MARQUESS
AEMRSSSU MASSEURS
AEMRSSTT MATTRESS,
   SMARTEST
AENNNPST PENNANTS
AENNOPST PENTOSAN
AENNORST RESONANT
AENNORSU UNREASON
AENNPRSS SPANNERS
AENNRSTT ENTRANTS
AENNRSWY SWANNERY
AENNRTTY TENANTRY
AENOOPST TEASPOON
AENOPRSS PERSONAS
AENOPRTT PATENTOR
AENOPRWY WEAPONRY
AENORRST ANTRORSE
AENORSST ASSENTOR,
   SENATORS
AENORSUV RAVENOUS
AENORTTY ATTORNEY
AENOSSUU NAUSEOUS
AENPPRSS SNAPPERS
AENPRRST PARTNERS
AENPRSST PASTERNS,
   RAPTNESS
AENPRSTT PATTERNS,
   TRANSEPT
AENPRSUV PARVENUS
AENQRRTU QUARTERN
AENRRRTY ERRANTRY
AENRSSTT TARTNESS
AENRSSTU SAUNTERS
AENRSSTV SERVANTS
AENRSTWY STERNWAY

AENRTWYY ENTRYWAY
AENSSSTV VASTNESS
AENSSTTU TAUTNESS
AENSSTTX SEXTANTS
AEOOPPSS PAPOOSES
AEOOPRRT OPERATOR
AEOOPSTT POTATOES
AEOORRST SORORATE
AEOORTTT TATTOOER
AEOPRRUV VAPOURER
AEOPRRVW WRAPOVER
AEOPRSST SEAPORTS
AEOPRSSV OVERPASS,
   PASSOVER
AEOPRSTT PROSTATE
AEOPRSTU APTEROUS
AEOPTTUY AUTOTYPE
AEOQRTTU TORQUATE
AEORRSST ASSORTER,
   ROASTERS
AEORRTZZ TERRAZZO
AEORSSSS ASSESSOR
AEORSSTT TOASTERS
AEORSSTV VOTARESS
AEORSTTT TESTATOR
AEORSTTU OUTSTARE
AEORSTVY OVERSTAY
AEPPRRST TRAPPERS
AEPPRRSW WRAPPERS
AEPPSSTU PASTE-UPS
AEPRRSSY SPRAYERS
AEPRRSTU RAPTURES
AEPRSSST SPARSEST,
   TRESPASS
AEPRSSTT SPATTERS
AEPRSSTU PASTURES
AEPRSTTY TAPESTRY
AEPRSTUX SUPERTAX
AEQRRSTU QUARTERS
AEQRSSTU SQUAREST,
   T-SQUARES
AEQRSTTU QUARTETS,
   SQUATTER
AERRSSTT STARTERS
AERRSTUY TREASURY
AERSSTTU STATURES
AERSSTTW SWATTERS
AERSTTVY TRAVESTY
AERTTUXY TEXTUARY
AESSSTTU STATUSES
AESSTTTU STATUTES
AFFFFIRR RIFFRAFF
AFFGIINX AFFIXING

AFFGIIRT GRAFFITI
AFFGILNR RAFFLING
AFFGILNW WAFFLING
AFFGINST STAFFING
AFFGIORT GRAFFITO
AFFGLNRU FAR-FLUNG
AFFHILLS FALLFISH
AFFHILST FLATFISH
AFFHILTU FAITHFUL
AFFHIMRS FISH FARM
AFFIINTY AFFINITY
AFFILLMM FLIMFLAM
AFFILSUX SUFFIXAL
AFFIMSST MASTIFFS
AFFINOSU AFFUSION
AFFINRSU FUNFAIRS,
   RUFFIANS
AFFIPSTT TIPSTAFF
AFFLLOOT FOOTFALL
AFFLOOTT FLATFOOT
AFFLOPSY PLAY-OFFS
AFFNORST AFFRONTS
AFFNRRUU FURFURAN
AFGGGILN FLAGGING
AFGGINOR FORAGING
AFGGINRT GRAFTING
AFGHILNS FLASHING
AFGHILNT FANLIGHT
AFGHILPS FLAGSHIP
AFGHINRT FARTHING
AFGHINST SHAFTING
AFGHLNSU FLASHGUN
AFGIILLN FLAILING
AFGIILNS FAILINGS
AFGIINNT FAINTING
AFGIINRS FAIRINGS
AFGIKLNN FLANKING
AFGIKNNR FRANKING
AFGIKORT KOFTGARI
AFGILMNO FLAMINGO
AFGILNOT FLOATING
AFGILNOW FOWLIANG
AFGILNPP FLAPPING
AFGILNTT FLATTING
AFGILNTU FAULTING
AFGIMNTU FUMIGANT
AFGIMORS GASIFORM
AFGINORY FORAYING
AFGINRST STRAFING
AFGINRTU FIGURANT
AFGIPRTW GIFT-WRAP
AFGJNRUU JUNGFRAU
AFGLLRUY FRUGALLY

AFGLLSUY FALL GUYS
AFGLMOPS FOG LAMPS
AFGNOORS FOR A SONG
AFGORTUW TUG-OF-WAR
AFHIILSS SAILFISH
AFHIILST FISHTAIL
AFHIINST FAINTISH
AFHIKLPS HIP FLASK
AFHIKNRS FRANKISH
AFHILLSY FLASHILY
AFHILOSY OAFISHLY
AFHILSTT FLATTISH
AFHILSTW HALF-WITS
AFHINOSS FASHIONS
AFHIRSST STARFISH
AFHKLNTU THANKFUL
AFHKORSY HAYFORKS
AFHLMNOO HALF MOON
AFHLRTUW WRATHFUL
AFHOOPTT FOOTPATH
AFIILLNU UNFILIAL
AFIILMNS FINALISM
AFIILNRU FRIULIAN
AFIILNST FINALIST
AFIILNTY FINALITY
AFIILRST AIRLIFTS
AFIINNOS SAINFOIN,
   SINFONIA
AFIINOTX FIXATION
AFIKLNNR FRANKLIN
AFIKMNNR FINNMARK
AFILLLOT FLOTILLA
AFILLPST PITFALLS
AFILLTUY FAULTILY
AFILMNOR FORMALIN,
   INFORMAL
AFILMNOS FOILSMAN
AFILMRST FILM STAR
AFILNPPT FLIPPANT
AFILNPST FLAT SPIN
AFILNRUY UNFAIRLY
AFILSTTU FLAUTIST
AFIMMNOY AMMONIFY
AFIMNOPR NAPIFORM
AFIMNOSU INFAMOUS
AFIMORRV VARIFORM
AFINNOOP ON PAIN OF
AFINNOTU FOUNTAIN
AFINNRTY INFANTRY
AFINOPSY SAPONIFY
AFINORUV IN FAVOUR
AFINQTUY QUANTIFY
AFINRSTX TRANSFIX

AFIRSTTY STRATIFY
AFKLNOTU OUTFLANK
AFKLOSWY FOLKWAYS
AFKMOORT FOOTMARK
AFLLLORY FLORALLY
AFLLLUWY LAWFULLY
AFLLMNUY MANFULLY
AFLLMORY FORMALLY
AFLLMRSY SMALL FRY
AFLLNOSW SNOWFALL
AFLLNUUW UNLAWFUL
AFLLOOTW FOOTWALL
AFLLOPUY FOUL PLAY
AFLLOSTU FALLOUTS,
   OUTFALLS
AFLLRTUY ARTFULLY
AFLMNOPR PLANFORM
AFLMOPRT PLATFORM
AFLMORSU FORMULAS
AFLMORTW FLATWORM
AFLMOSUY FAMOUSLY
AFLORSUV FLAVOURS
AFLPSSTY FLYPASTS
AFMNNORT FRONT MAN
AFMOOPRR PRO FORMA
AFMOORTZ FROM A TO Z
AFMORTUY FUMATORY
AFOOPSST SOFT SOAP
AFORRSTU FOUR-STAR
AFPPPTUY PUPPY FAT
AGGGHILN HAGGLING
AGGGHINS SHAGGING
AGGGILNN GANGLING
AGGGILNR GARGLING
AGGGILNS SLAGGING
AGGGILNW WAGGLING
AGGGINNS SNAGGING
AGGHILNU LAUGHING
AGGHILST GASLIGHT
AGGHILSY SHAGGILY
AGGHINNS GNASHING,
   HANGINGS
AGGHISTT GASTIGHT
AGGIILNN ALIGNING
AGGIILNV GINGIVAL
AGGIINNR GRAINING
AGGIJLNN JANGLING
AGGILMNN MANGLING
AGGILMNO GLOAMING
AGGILNNO GANGLION
AGGILNNS SLANGING
AGGILNNT TANGLING
AGGILNNW WANGLING*

AGGILNOT GLOATING
AGGILNPU PLAGUING
AGGILNPY GAPINGLY
AGGILNRY GRAYLING
AGGILNSS GLASSING
AGGINNOR GROANING
AGGINNOT TANGOING
AGGINNRT GRANTING
AGGINNTW TWANGING
AGGINOVY VOYAGING
AGGINPRS GRASPING
AGGINRSS GRASSING
AGGINRST GRATINGS
AGGINRSU SUGARING
AGGINRTY GYRATING
AGGINRUU AUGURING
AGGINSST STAGINGS
AGGLLOOY ALGOLOGY
AGGLMOOR LOGOGRAM
AGGLOORY AGROLOGY
AGGLRSTY STRAGGLY
AGGNUWZZ ZUGZWANG
AGHHIILT HIGHTAIL
AGHHIMSS HIGH MASS
AGHHINOP HAIPHONG
AGHHISWY HIGHWAYS
AGHHLOTU ALTHOUGH
AGHIILNN INHALING
AGHIINST TSINGHAI
AGHIIPRR HAIRGRIP
AGHIIRTT AIRTIGHT
AGHIJNRT NIGHTJAR
AGHIKLRU GURKHALI
AGHIKNNT THANKING
AGHILLRT ALL RIGHT
AGHILMTY ALMIGHTY
AGHILNOO HOOLIGAN
AGHILNOT LOATHING
AGHILNRS RINGHALS
AGHILNSS HASSLING,
    LASHINGS, SLASHING
AGHILNSU LANGUISH
AGHILOST GOLIATHS
AGHILRSY GARISHLY
AGHIMMNS SHAMMING
AGHIMNSS SMASHING
AGHINNOT GNATHION
AGHINNTU HAUNTING
AGHINNTY ANYTHING
AGHINPRS HARPINGS,
    PHRASING
AGHINQSU QUASHING
AGHINRRY HARRYING

AGHINRST TRASHING
AGHINSST HASTINGS,
    STASHING
AGHINSSV SHAVINGS
AGHINSTW SWATHING
AGHIPRRT TRIGRAPH
AGHIRSTT STRAIGHT
AGHLLNOU LONG-HAUL
AGHLMOOR HOLOGRAM
AGHMMOOY HOMOGAMY
AGHMNPSU SPHAGNUM
AGHMOPRY MYOGRAPH
AGHNNSTU SHANTUNG
AGHNOSTU HANGOUTS
AGHNTTUU UNTAUGHT
AGHORSTW WARTHOGS
AGIIIKMR KIRIGAMI
AGIIILNS LIAISING
AGIIINNS INSIGNIA
AGIIINRV VIRGINIA
AGIILMNP IMPALING
AGIILNNO LIAONING
AGIILNNU INGUINAL
AGIILNOR ORIGINAL
AGIILNOT INTAGLIO,
    LIGATION
AGIILNOX GLOXINIA
AGIILNPT PLAITING
AGIILNQU QUAILING
AGIILNRS RAILINGS
AGIILNRT TRAILING
AGIILNRU LIGURIAN
AGIILNRV RIVALING,
    VIRGINAL
AGIILNSS SAILINGS
AGIILNST TAILINGS
AGIILNTT LITIGANT
AGIILNTV VIGILANT
AGIILORU OLIGURIA
AGIILPST PIGTAILS
AGIIMNOW MIAOWING
AGIINNPT PAINTING
AGIINNRT TRAINING
AGIINNST STAINING
AGIINNTT TAINTING
AGIINORT RIGATONI
AGIINPRS ASPIRING,
    PRAISING
AGIINPRT PIRATING
AGIINRRV ARRIVING
AGIINRTT ATTIRING
AGIINRUU UIGURIAN
AGIINSTU IGNATIUS

AGIJLNPY JAPINGLY
AGIJMNOR MAJORING
AGIJNNTU JAUNTING
AGIKLMOR KILOGRAM
AGIKLNNP PLANKING
AGIKLNNR RANKLING
AGIKLNST STALKING
AGIKMNRS MARKINGS
AGIKNNPS SPANKING
AGIKNNSW SWANKING
AGIKNOST GOATSKIN
AGIKNPRS SPARKING
AGILLMNY MALIGNLY
AGILLMSU GAULLISM
AGILLNOW ALLOWING
AGILLNOY ALLOYING
AGILLNRU ALLURING
AGILLNRY RALLYING
AGILLNST STALLING
AGILLNSY SALLYING,
    SIGNALLY, SLANGILY
AGILLNTY TALLYING
AGILLOPT GALLIPOT
AGILLORS GORILLAS
AGILLPUY PLAGUILY
AGILLSSU LUGSAILS
AGILLSTU GAULLIST
AGILMMNS SLAMMING
AGILMNNT MANTLING
AGILMNOO MONGOLIA
AGILMNPS SAMPLING
AGILMORS ALGORISM
AGILNNNP PLANNING
AGILNNOP PANGOLIN
AGILNNPT PLANTING
AGILNNRS SNARLING
AGILNNST SLANTING
AGILNNUY UNGAINLY
AGILNOOO OOGONIAL
AGILNOPR PAROLING
AGILNORT TRIGONAL
AGILNOSS LASSOING
AGILNOTT TOTALING
AGILNOTU LIAOTUNG
AGILNOTW WAGON-LIT
AGILNPPS SLAPPING
AGILNPPY APPLYING
AGILNPRS SPARLING
AGILNPSS SAPLINGS
AGILNPST STAPLING
AGILNPSW LAPWINGS
AGILNPSY SPLAYING
AGILNRST STARLING

AGILNRSU SINGULAR	AGINPPSW SWAPPING	AGOPPSST STOPGAPS
AGILNRTT RATTLING	AGINPRRS SPARRING	AGORRTYY GYRATORY
AGILNRTW TRAWLING	AGINPRRY PARRYING	AGSSTUUU AUGUSTUS
AGILNSTU SALUTING	AGINPRSS RASPINGS	AGSSTUUV GUSTAVUS
AGILNTTT TATTLING	AGINPRST GIN TRAPS,	AHHILPSW WHIPLASH
AGILNTUV VAULTING	PARTINGS	AHHIMMSS MISHMASH
AGILNTWZ WALTZING	AGINPRSY SPRAYING	AHHIPRSS SHARPISH
AGILNTXY TAXINGLY	AGINPRTY PARTYING	AHHLNOPT NAPHTHOL
AGILOOPY APIOLOGY	AGINPSST PASTINGS	AHHLNPTY NAPHTHYL
AGILOOXY AXIOLOGY	AGINQRSU SQUARING	AHHMPRRU HARRUMPH
AGILSYYZ SYZYGIAL	AGINRRST STARRING	AHHNORTW HAWTHORN
AGIMMOSY MISOGAMY	AGINRRTY TARRYING	AHIIKMRS KASHMIRI
AGIMNNRU MANURING	AGINRSST STAR SIGN	AHIILLPP PHILLIPA
AGIMNORS ORGANISM	AGINRSSU ASSURING	AHIILPPP PHILIPPA
AGIMNORY AGRIMONY	AGINRSTT STARTING	AHIILRTY HILARITY
AGIMNPPS MAPPINGS	AGINRSTV STARVING	AHIIMNOT HIMATION
AGIMNPRT TRAMPING	AGINRSTY STINGRAY,	AHIIMNRS IRISHMAN
AGIMNPST STAMPING	STRAYING	AHIIMNST ISTHMIAN
AGIMNPSW SWAMPING	AGINSTTW SWATTING	AHIINPRS HAIRPINS
AGIMNRRY MARRYING	AGINSTUU AUGUSTIN	AHIIPRSS AIRSHIPS
AGIMNRST MIGRANTS,	AGIOORTU AUTOGIRO	AHIKLRSY RAKISHLY
SMARTING	AGIOPPRT AGITPROP	AHIKNPRS PRANKISH
AGIMNRSW SWARMING	AGIRTTUY GRATUITY	AHIKOSUZ SHIZUOKA
AGIMNRTU MATURING	AGJLRSUU JUGULARS	AHILLMSS SMALLISH
AGIMNSSU ASSUMING	AGKLOORV GORLOVKA	AHILLMTU THALLIUM
AGIMORRT MIGRATOR	AGKORSSW GASWORKS	AHILLNST ANTHILLS
AGINNNOY ANNOYING	AGLLRUVY VULGARLY	AHILLSVY LAVISHLY
AGINNNPS SPANNING	AGLMOPYY POLYGAMY	AHILMNOT HAMILTON
AGINNNSW SWANNING	AGLNOOSW OWN GOALS	AHILMOST MAILSHOT
AGINNOPT POIGNANT	AGLNOSWY LONGWAYS	AHILMQSU QUALMISH
AGINNORT IGNORANT	AGLNSSSU SUNGLASS	AHILNOPS SIPHONAL
AGINNPPS SNAPPING	AGLOOPST GOALPOST	AHILNORT HORNTAIL
AGINNPSW SPAWNING,	AGLOPRTU PORTUGAL	AHILOORT LOTHARIO
WINGSPAN	AGLORSSY GLOSSARY	AHILOPSS ALPHOSIS,
AGINNRSW WARNINGS	AGLOSUVY YUGOSLAV	HAPLOSIS
AGINNTTU ATTUNING,	AGLPSSSY SPYGLASS	AHILOPST HOSPITAL
TAUNTING	AGLRTTUU GUTTURAL	AHILRSTY TRASHILY
AGINNTUV VAUNTING	AGLSTUUY AUGUSTLY	AHIMMNSU HUMANISM
AGINOORT ROGATION	AGMMNOOR MONOGRAM	AHIMNOST THOMASIN
AGINORRS GARRISON	AGMMNOOY MONOGAMY	AHIMNOSW WOMANISH
AGINORRW ARROWING	AGMMORSY MYOGRAMS	AHIMNSTU HUMANIST
AGINORSS ASSIGNOR,	AGMNOORY AGRONOMY	AHIMNTUY HUMANITY
SIGNORAS	AGMNORST ANGSTROM	AHIMOOSY YAHOOISM
AGINORST ORGANIST,	AGMNSSTU MUSTANGS	AHIMOPRS APHORISM
ROASTING	AGMNSSTY GYMNASTS	AHIMORRW HAIRWORM
AGINORSU AROUSING	AGMOOOSU OOGAMOUS	AHIMSSTU TSUSHIMA
AGINORTT ROTATING	AGMOOTVY VAGOTOMY	AHIMSTUZ AZIMUTHS
AGINORTV GRAVITON	AGMOPRRS PROGRAMS	AHINNNOR RHIANNON
AGINORTY GYRATION	AGNNOSSW SWANSONG	AHINNOPT ANTIPHON
AGINOSTT TANGOIST,	AGNOPRST PART-SONG	AHINORRS HARRISON
TOASTING, TSINGTAO	AGNORTUY NUGATORY	AHINOSST ASTONISH
AGINPPRT TRAPPING	AGNPRSUY SPRAY GUN	AHINPPSS SNAPPISH
AGINPPRW WRAPPING	AGOORRTY ROGATORY	AHINQSUV VANQUISH

AHIOOPPT PHOTOPIA
AHIOPRST APHORIST
AHIPRSST HARPISTS
AHIPRSSW WARSHIPS
AHIQRSSU SQUARISH
AHISSTTW WHATSITS
AHKLLOOY HOLLY OAK
AHKLOPRU KOLHAPUR
AHKLOPST SHOPTALK,
   TALK SHOP
AHKLOSTW TALK SHOW
AHKMORTU KHARTOUM
AHKNOTUY THANKYOU
AHLLNOOS SHALLOON
AHLLNOTW TOWN HALL
AHLLOSST SHALLOTS
AHLLOSSW SHALLOWS
AHLLOSTU THALLOUS
AHLMMOPY LYMPHOMA
AHLMNOOR HORMONAL
AHLMOOPS OMPHALOS
AHLMOPTY POLYMATH
AHLNOOPS ALPHONSO
AHLOPRSU SHOLAPUR
AHLORRTY HARLOTRY
AHMMMOST MAMMOTHS
AHMNNNSTU HUNTSMAN,
   MANHUNTS
AHMNOPST PHANTOMS
AHMNORSU MANHOURS
AHMOOPPT PHOTOMAP
AHMOOPSS SHAMPOOS
AHMOORSW WASHROOM
AHMPSSSU SMASH-UPS
AHMPSTYY SYMPATHY
AHMQSSUU MUSQUASH
AHNOOPRS HARPOONS
AHNOORRY HONORARY
AHNOPPSW PAWNSHOP
AHNOPPSY PANSOPHY
AHNOPSST SNAPSHOT
AHNOSTTW WHATNOTS
AHNOSTUX XANTHOUS
AHNRSTTU THURSTAN
AHOOSSTY SOOTHSAY
AHOOSTTW SAWTOOTH
AHOPSTTW TOWPATHS
AHOPSTUW SOUTHPAW
AHORTTUW WATT-HOUR
AHOSSTUW WASHOUTS
AHRSTUWY THRUWAYS
AIIILMST MILITIAS
AIIILNST INITIALS

AIIKLNOR IRAKLION
AIIKMNNS MANIKINS
AIIKNNNP PANNIKIN
AIIKNRST KRISTINA
AIILLMRY MILLIARY
AIILLNNV VANILLIN
AIILLNSV VILLAINS
AIILLNVY VILLAINY
AIILLWWW WILLIWAW
AIILMNPS ALPINISM
AIILMNPT PALMITIN
AIILMNST LATINISM
AIILMNTT MILITANT
AIILMRST MISTRIAL
AIILMRTY LIMITARY,
   MILITARY
AIILMSTV VITALISM
AIILNNOV LIVONIAN
AIILNOPT OIL PAINT
AIILNOPV PAVILION
AIILNOSS LIAISONS
AIILNOSV VISIONAL
AIILNPST ALPINIST,
   TAILSPIN
AIILNRSU SILURIAN
AIILNSTT LATINIST
AIILNSTY SALINITY
AIILNTTY LATINITY
AIILSTTV VITALIST
AIILTTVY VITALITY
AIIMNNOS INSOMNIA
AIIMNPSS SINAPISM
AIIMNRST MARTINIS
AIIMNSST ANIMISTS
AIIMNSTT TITANISM
AIIMNSTU UNIATISM
AIIMNSTV NATIVISM,
   VITAMINS
AIIMNTTU TITANIUM
AIIMOPSX APOMIXIS
AIIMORTT IMITATOR
AIIMOSST AMITOSIS
AIIMPPRS PRIAPISM
AIIMPRTY IMPARITY
AIIMRUVV VIVARIUM
AIIMSSTT MASTITIS
AIINNOSV INVASION
AIINNOTV NIVATION
AIINNSTU TUNISIAN
AIINNSTV VINNITSA
AIINNSTY INSANITY
AIINPRSS ASPIRINS
AIINPSST PIANISTS

AIINRRTT IRRITANT
AIINSTTV NATIVIST,
   VISITANT
AIINTTVY NATIVITY
AIIORSTV OVARITIS
AIIORTTV VITIATOR
AIIPRRST AIRSTRIP
AIIRSSTT SATIRIST,
   SITARIST
AIJKKNOU KINKAJOU
AIJKLMNU JUNK MAIL
AIJLLOVY JOVIALLY
AIJLNTUY JAUNTILY
AIJMORTY MAJORITY
AIJNOPPY POPINJAY
AIJNORST JANITORS
AIKLLSTY STALKILY
AIKLMWYY MILKY WAY
AIKLNSWY SWANKILY
AIKLOTTW KILOWATT
AIKMRSTZ SITZMARK
AIKNNOOS NAINSOOK
AIKNNSSW SWANSKIN
AIKNRSST SANSKRIT
AILLLNOO LINALOOL
AILLLOST SALTILLO
AILLLPSU LAPILLUS
AILLMOSS LIMASSOL
AILLMOSY LOYALISM
AILLMOTY MOLALITY
AILLMRTY MYRTILLA
AILLMRUY ARUM LILY
AILLMSSW SAWMILLS
AILLMUUV ALLUVIUM
AILLNOPP PAPILLON
AILLNOST STALLION
AILLNOSU ALLUSION
AILLNPTY PLIANTLY
AILLORSY SAILORLY
AILLORTT LITTORAL,
   TORTILLA
AILLOSTY LOYALIST
AILLPRTY PALTRILY
AILLPSWY SPILLWAY
AILLRTUY RITUALLY
AILLSUVY VISUALLY
AILMMNOO MONOMIAL
AILMMORS MORALISM
AILMMORT IMMORTAL
AILMMSTU SUMMITAL
AILMNNOT MANNITOL
AILMNOOP PALOMINO
AILMNOOR MONORAIL

AILMNOPY OLYMPIAN
AILMNPST IMPLANTS
AILMNPTU PLATINUM
AILMNRUY LUMINARY
AILMNSTU SIMULANT
AILMOPRX PROXIMAL
AILMORST MORALIST
AILMORSU SOLARIUM
AILMORSY ROYALISM
AILMORTY MORALITY
AILMOSTV VOLTAISM
AILMPPSY MISAPPLY
AILMPRSU PRIMULAS
AILMPSST PALMISTS,
   PSALMIST
AILMPSTY PTYALISM
AILMRRSU RURALISM
AILMRSTU ALTRUISM,
   MURALIST, ULTRAISM
AILNNOOT NOTIONAL
AILNNOSW SON-IN-LAW
AILNNOSY LYONNAIS
AILNNOTU LUNATION
AILNNSTU INSULANT
AILNOOPT OPTIONAL
AILNOPRU UNIPOLAR
AILNOPTY PONYTAIL
AILNOSUV AVULSION
AILNOSVY SYNOVIAL
AILNOTTY TONALITY
AILNOTUX LUXATION
AILNPPSY SNAPPILY
AILNPSTU NUPTIALS
AILNPSUU NAUPLIUS
AILNQRTU TRANQUIL
AILNQTUY QUAINTLY
AILNRRTU TRIAL RUN
AILNSSUV SILVANUS
AILNSTTU LUTANIST
AILNSTUU NAUTILUS
AILNSYZZ SNAZZILY
AILOORST ISOLATOR,
   OSTIOLAR
AILOORTV VIOLATOR
AILOPRTU TROUPIAL
AILOPRTY POLARITY
AILOPRUY POLYURIA
AILORSTY ROYALIST,
   SOLITARY
AILORTTU TUTORIAL
AILORTUV OUTRIVAL
AILOSSUY ALOYSIUS
AILOTTTY TOTALITY

AILPPSSY PAYSLIPS
AILPRSTU STIPULAR
AILPSSWY SLIPWAYS
AILPSTUY PLAYSUIT
AILRRSTU RURALIST
AILRRSTY STARRILY
AILRRTUY RURALITY
AILRSTTU ALTRUIST,
   ULTRAIST
AILRSUVV SURVIVAL
AILSSTUW LAWSUITS
AIMMMNOU AMMONIUM
AIMMMSUX MAXIMUMS
AIMMNORT MORTMAIN
AIMNNOSS MANSIONS
AIMNNOTU MOUNTAIN
AIMNNOTY ANTIMONY,
   ANTINOMY
AIMNNRTU RUMINANT
AIMNOORV MONROVIA
AIMNOOTY MYOTONIA
AIMNOQRU MAROQUIN
AIMNORTU MINOTAUR
AIMNORTY MINATORY
AIMNOTTU MUTATION
AIMNRRSU MURRAINS
AIMNRSTT TRANSMIT
AIMNRSTU NATURISM
AIMNRSTV VARMINTS
AIMOPRSS PROSAISM
AIMOPSSY SYMPOSIA
AIMORRUV VARIORUM
AIMORSTY RAMOSITY
AIMPPRUU PUPARIUM
AIMRRSTT TRISTRAM
AIMRSSTX MARXISTS
AIMRTTUY MATURITY
AINNNOST SANTONIN
AINNOOTT NOTATION
AINNOOTV NOVATION
AINNOOTZ ZONATION
AINNOTTU NUTATION
AINNRSTU NURISTAN
AINNSSTT INSTANTS
AINNSTTY NYSTATIN
AINOOPTT POTATION
AINOORST ORATIONS
AINOORTT ROTATION
AINOOSTT OSTINATO
AINOOSTV OVATIONS
AINOPPTU PUPATION
AINOPSSS PASSIONS
AINORSST ARSONIST

AINOSSTT STATIONS
AINOSTTU TITANOUS
AINPPRSS PARSNIPS
AINPRSSU PRUSSIAN
AINPRSTU PURITANS
AINPSSSY SYNAPSIS
AINPSSTU PUISSANT
AINQTTUY QUANTITY
AINRSSTT TRANSITS
AINRSTTU NATURIST
AIOOORRT ORATORIO
AIOPRRST AIRPORTS
AIOPRRTT PORTRAIT
AIOPRSST PROTASIS
AIOPRSTT PATRIOTS
AIORRRSW WARRIORS
AIORRSTT TRAITORS
AIORRSTV VARISTOR
AIORSSUV SAVIOURS
AIORSTTV VOTARIST
AIOSSSTY ISOSTASY
AIPPRSTT TRAPPIST
AIPPRSTY PAPISTRY
AIPRSSTU UPSTAIRS
AIRRSTTY ARTISTRY
AJLNORSU JOURNALS
AJORRTUY JURATORY
AKKLRSSY SKYLARKS
AKKORSTW TASKWORK
AKLLNOSW KNOW-ALLS
AKLNNOPT PLANKTON
AKLOSTUW WALKOUTS
AKLPRRSU LARKSPUR
AKMMNRSU MURMANSK
AKMMOOTU KUMAMOTO
AKMNORTU TURKOMAN
AKMOORST KOSTROMA
AKMOPRST POSTMARK
AKMQSTUU KUMQUATS
AKOPRRTW PART WORK
AKORSWWX WAXWORKS
ALLLPRUY LYALLPUR
ALLMNORY NORMALLY
ALLMNPSU PULLMANS
ALLMOPSX SMALLPOX
ALLMORTY MORTALLY
ALLMTUUY MUTUALLY
ALLNOOPS PLANOSOL
ALLOPRSY PAYROLLS
ALLOSSWW SWALLOWS
ALMMNRUU NUMMULAR
ALMNOOPS LAMPOONS
ALMNORTY MATRONLY

ALMNPSSU SUNLAMPS	ANOPRRSS SPORRANS	BBEEIIRR BERIBERI
ALMOOPRY PLAYROOM	ANOPRTTU TRAPUNTO	BBEEILPR PLEBBIER
ALMOORTU ALUMROOT	ANPRSSTU SUNTRAPS	BBEELLLU BLUEBELL
ALMOPPST LAMPPOST	ANPRSTUU PURSUANT	BBEFILRR FRIBBLER
ALMOSTTU MULATTOS,	AOOOPRTZ PROTOZOA	BBEGIIST GIBBSITE
SUM TOTAL	AOOPPRSY APOSPORY	BBEGILNP PEBBLING
ALNNOTWY WANTONLY	AOOPRSTT TAPROOTS	BBEGILST GLIBBEST
ALNOOPST PLATOONS	AOOPRSTW SOAPWORT	BBEGIRRU GRUBBIER
ALNOOPYZ POLYZOAN	AOOPRSUV VAPOROUS	BBEHIOTW BOBWHITE
ALNOPPTT POT PLANT	AOORRTTY ROTATORY	BBEILORW WOBBLIER
ALNOPRST PLASTRON	AOORSSUV SAVOROUS	BBEILQRU QUIBBLER
ALNORRWY NARROWLY	AOPPRSST PASSPORT	BBEILQSU QUIBBLES
ALNPPSTU SUPPLANT	AOPRRSSW SPARROWS	BBEILRRY BILBERRY
ALNPRSSU SNARL-UPS	AOPRSTTY PYROSTAT	BBEIMMOT TIME BOMB
ALNSSUVY SYLVANUS	AOPTTUYY AUTOTYPY	BBEIMOST BOMBSITE
ALOOPPRS PROPOSAL	AORRSTTW STARWORT	BBEIRSTU STUBBIER
ALOOPRSW POOR LAWS	APRSSTTU UPSTARTS	BBEISTTU TUBBIEST
ALOORSUV VALOROUS	BBBCEOWY COBWEBBY	BBEKLOOU BLUE BOOK
ALOORTYZ ZOOLATRY	BBBEILRU BUBBLIER	BBEKNOOT BONTEBOK
ALOPPRYY POLYPARY	BBBEINOT BOBBINET	BBELLOSY BELLBOYS
ALOPPTUY PLAY UP TO	BBBGILNU BUBBLING	BBELORSY SLOBBERY
ALOPRRSU PARLOURS	BBBINOPY BOBBY PIN	BBENORSY SNOBBERY
ALOPRSTU POSTURAL,	BBCDERSU SCRUBBED	BBEORRXY BOXBERRY
PULSATOR	BBCDIMOY BOMBYCID	BBERRRUY BURBERRY
ALOPSSTT LAST POST	BBCEHIRU CHUBBIER	BBGGILNO GOBBLING
ALOPSTUU PATULOUS	BBCEILRS SCRIBBLE	BBGGINRU GRUBBING
ALORSTTW SALTWORT	BBCELORS COBBLERS	BBGHILNO HOBBLING
ALORTUWY OUTLAWRY	BBCERRSU SCRUBBER	BBGIIIMN IMBIBING
ALOSTTUZ ZLATOUST	BBCGIINR CRIBBING	BBGIILNN NIBBLING
ALPPSTUY PLATYPUS	BBCGILNO COBBLING	BBGILMNU BUMBLING
ALPRSTUU PUSTULAR	BBCGILNU CLUBBING	BBGILNNO NOBBLING
AMMNOORT MOTORMAN	BBCHKSUU BUSHBUCK	BBGILNOW WOBBLING
AMMNPTUY TYMPANUM	BBCKLOOU BOOK CLUB	BBGILNOY LOBBYING
AMMNOSTW TOWNSMAN	BBDDEEMO DEMOBBED	BBGILNRU BURBLING
AMMNOSTY ANTONYMS	BBDDEILR DRIBBLED	BBGILRUY GRUBBILY
AMMNSTTU STUNT MAN	BBDDEIRY BY-BIDDER	BBGINNSU SNUBBING
AMNOOSTT OTTOMANS	BBDEEGIR GIBBERED	BBGINRSU RUBBINGS
AMNOOTUY AUTONOMY	BBDEEIST EBB TIDES	BBGINSTU STUBBING
AMNOOTXY TAXONOMY	BBDEEMNU BENUMBED	BBHINOSS SNOBBISH
AMNORSST TRANSOMS	BBDEHORT THROBBED	BBHIOSTY HOBBYIST
AMNOTTUY TAUTONYM	BBDEILLR BELLBIRD	BBHIRSUY RUBBISHY
AMNRSTTU TANTRUMS	BBDEILQU QUIBBLED	BBHRSSUU SUBSHRUB
AMOORRTY MORATORY	BBDEILRR DRIBBLER	BBIKLNOO BOBOLINK
AMOORTWY MOTORWAY	BBDEILRS DRIBBLES	BBILMOSY LOBBYISM
AMOOTTUY AUTOTOMY	BBDEILRU BLUEBIRD	BBILOSTY LOBBYIST
AMOPRSXY PAROXYSM	BBDEIMOV DIVE-BOMB	BBILOSUU BIBULOUS
AMOQSSUU SQUAMOUS	BBDELLMU DUMBBELL	BBILSTUY STUBBILY
AMORRTUY MORTUARY	BBDELSTU STUBBLED	BBLLOUYY BULLYBOY
AMORSTTU OUTSMART	BBDGIILN DIBBLING	BBNORSTU STUBBORN
ANNOORST SONORANT	BBDGINRU DRUBBING	BCCCIILY BICYCLIC
ANNOSSTU STANNOUS	BBDLOOWY BODY BLOW	BCCDEILY BICYCLED
ANOOPRRT PRONATOR	BBDOSUYY BUSYBODY	BCCEEIRR CEREBRIC
ANOOPRSS SOPRANOS	BBEEHTYY BY THE BYE	BCCEHIRU CHERUBIC

BCCEIILO LIBECCIO
BCCEILOY BIOCYCLE
BCCEILRU CRUCIBLE
BCCEILSU CUBICLES
BCCEILSY BICYCLES
BCCEMRUU CUCUMBER
BCCIISTU CUBISTIC
BCCILMOU COLUMBIC
BCCILOOR BROCCOLI
BCCIRTUU CUCURBIT
BCCMOOSX COXCOMBS
BCCNOORS CORNCOBS
BCCSSUUU SUCCUBUS
BCDDEEEK BEDECKED
BCDEEEMR DECEMBER
BCDEEENR DEBRECEN
BCDEEHLN BLENCHED
BCDEEIKN BENEDICK
BCDEEIKR BICKERED
BCDEEILR CREDIBLE
BCDEEILS DECIBELS
BCDEEILU EDUCIBLE
BCDEEINT BENEDICT
BCDEEIRS DESCRIBE
BCDEEIST BISECTED
BCDEEJOT OBJECTED
BCDEEKNO BECKONED
BCDEEKRU REEDBUCK
BCDEEKTU BUCKETED
BCDEEMRU CUMBERED
BCDEIIRR RICEBIRD
BCDEIKRR REDBRICK
BCDEIKSS SICKBEDS
BCDEILRY CREDIBLY
BCDEIMNO COMBINED
BCDEINOU ICEBOUND
BCDELMRU CRUMBLED
BCDEORSU OBSCURED
BCDIIPSU BICUSPID
BCDILMOY MOLYBDIC
BCDILORU COLUBRID
BCDINRUU RUBICUND
BCEEEFIN BENEFICE
BCEEEHRS BREECHES
BCEEEINR BERENICE
BCEEERSU BERCEUSE
BCEEFLTU CLUBFEET
BCEEGIRS ICEBERGS
BCEEHHNT THE BENCH
BCEEHHSU BUCHSHEE
BCEEHKSU BUCKSHEE
BCEEHLNR BLENCHER
BCEEHNTU BEECHNUT

BCEEIILM IMBECILE
BCEEIKRR BICKERER
BCEEIOSX ICEBOXES
BCEEKNOR BECKONER
BCEELRTU TUBERCLE
BCEEMNRU ENCUMBER
BCEEMRRU CEREBRUM
BCEERTVY BREVETCY
BCEFFIIR FEBRIFIC
BCEFILOR FORCIBLE
BCEGHILN BELCHING
BCEGIMNO BECOMING
BCEHHIRT THE BIRCH
BCEHIIRT BITCHIER
BCEHILPU BLUE CHIP
BCEHIMOT CHIMBOTE
BCEHIMRS BESMIRCH
BCEHIORS BRIOCHES
BCEHIORT BOTCHIER
BCEHIRST BRITCHES
BCEHLOST BLOTCHES
BCEHNRSU BRUNCHES
BCEHOORS BROOCHES
BCEHORRU BROCHURE
BCEHORST BOTCHERS
BCEHRSTU BUTCHERS
BCEHRTTU CUTHBERT
BCEHRTUY BUTCHERY
BCEIIKLN ICEBLINK
BCEIILMS MISCIBLE
BCEIILOP EPIBOLIC
BCEIINRS INSCRIBE
BCEILMRS CLIMBERS
BCEILPRU REPUBLIC
BCEIMNOR COMBINER
BCEIMNOS COMBINES
BCEIMORS MICROBES
BCEINORU BOUNCIER
BCEINOVX BICONVEX
BCEIOOPS BIOSCOPE
BCEIOOVX VOICE BOX
BCEIORST BISECTOR
BCEJNOOT NO OBJECT
BCEJOORT OBJECTOR
BCEJSSTU SUBJECTS
BCEKLLNU BULLNECK
BCEKLNUU UNBUCKLE
BCEKLRSU BUCKLERS
BCEKORSU ROEBUCKS
BCELLOSW COWBELLS
BCELMRSU CRUMBLES
BCENORSU BOUNCERS
BCEOORST OCTOBERS

BCEOORTU CUBE ROOT
BCEORRWY COWBERRY
BCFGLLOU GOLF CLUB
BCFIIMOR MORBIFIC
BCFIIORT FIBROTIC
BCFILORY FORCIBLY
BCFIMORU CUBIFORM
BCFLOOTU CLUBFOOT
BCGHIINR BIRCHING
BCGHIINT BITCHING
BCGHINNU BUNCHING
BCGHINOT BOTCHING
BCGIIKST BIG STICK
BCGIILMN CLIMBING
BCGIKLNO BLOCKING
BCGIKLNU BUCKLING
BCGINNOU BOUNCING
BCHIILTY BITCHILY
BCHIISSU HIBISCUS
BCHILOTY BOTCHILY
BCHIOORY CHOIRBOY
BCHKNORU BUCKHORN
BCHKOSTU BUCKSHOT
BCHNOORS BRONCHOS
BCHNORSU BRONCHUS
BCHOPSTU BOTCH-UPS
BCIIIOTT BIOTITIC
BCIILOTY BIOLYTIC
BCIIMNOO BIONOMIC
BCIIMORU CIBORIUM
BCIINORV VIBRONIC
BCIIOPTY BIOTYPIC
BCIISSTU BISCUITS,
    CUBISIST
BCIKKNSU BUCKSKIN
BCIKOSTT BITSTOCK
BCILLPUY PUBLICLY
BCILMOSY SYMBOLIC
BCILNOUY BOUNCILY
BCILOORU BICOLOUR
BCINORSU RUBICONS
BCINOSSU SUBSONIC
BCINOSTU SUBTONIC
BCIOOPSY BIOSCOPY
BCIOORST ROBOTICS
BCKKOOOO COOKBOOK
BCKLLOOS BOLLOCKS
BCKLLOSU BULLOCKS
BCKOOOPY COPYBOOK
BCKOSTTU BUTTOCKS
BCLMOSUU COLUMBUS
BCOOORTW CROWBOOT
BCOORSSW CROSSBOW

BCOOSTTY BOYCOTTS
BCOOSTUY BOY SCOUT
BCORSTTU OBSTRUCT
BDDDEEEM EMBEDDED
BDDDEEIM IMBEDDED
BDDEEESS SEEDBEDS
BDDEEGGU DEBUGGED
BDDEEGTU BUDGETED
BDDEEIMM BEDIMMED
BDDEEIMO EMBODIED
BDDEEINT INDEBTED
BDDEEINW BINDWEED
BDDEEIRS BIRDSEED
BDDEEISS BEDSIDES
BDDEEKNU DEBUNKED
BDDEENRU BURDENED
BDDEEORR BORDERED
BDDEINNU UNBIDDEN
BDDEINOU UNBODIED
BDDEINRU UNDERBID
BDDEIORS DISROBED
BDDEISSU SUBSIDED
BDDELOOR BLOOD RED
BDDEORTU OBTRUDED
BDDEOTYY TEDDY BOY
BDDGIORS BIRD DOGS
BDDGOOSY DOGSBODY
BDDHIIRY DIHYBRID
BDDHIMSU BUDDHISM
BDDHISTU BUDDHIST
BDEEEGIS BESIEGED
BDEEEHTU HEBETUDE
BDEEEILV BELIEVED
BDEEELLR REBELLED
BDEEELLV BEVELLED
BDEEELRS BLEEDERS
BDEEERTT BETTERED
BDEEFFRU BUFFERED,
　　REBUFFED
BDEEFFTU BUFFETED
BDEEFINR BEFRIEND
BDEEFITT BEFITTED
BDEEFOOR FOREBODE
BDEEFOOW BEEFWOOD
BDEEGGIW BEWIGGED
BDEEGGRU BEGRUDGE,
　　BUGGERED
BDEEGILN BLEEDING
BDEEGILU BEGUILED
BDEEGINR BREEDING
BDEEGLNO BELONGED
BDEEHIRS HEBRIDES
BDEEHLNO BEHOLDEN

BDEEHLOR BEHOLDER
BDEEHMOR HOMEBRED
BDEEHORT BOTHERED
BDEEIILL ELIDIBLE
BDEEIILN INEDIBLE
BDEEILLL LIBELLED
BDEEILLT BILLETED
BDEEILNN BED LINEN
BDEEILNO BONE-IDLE
BDEEILNR RENDIBLE
BDEEILNV VENDIBLE
BDEEILRW BEWILDER
BDEEIMST BEDTIMES
BDEEINOT OBEDIENT
BDEEIRRV RIVERBED
BDEEIRST BESTRIDE
BDEEIRSY BIRD'S-EYE
BDEEKNRU DEBUNKER
BDEELLOW BELLOWED
BDEELLRW WELL-BRED
BDEELMNO EMBOLDEN
BDEELMRT TREMBLED
BDEELMRU LUMBERED
BDEELNNO ENNOBLED
BDEELNRS BLENDERS
BDEELORU REDOUBLE
BDEELOSV BELOVEDS
BDEEMNOT ENTOMBED
BDEEMNRU NUMBERED
BDEEMOSS EMBOSSED
BDEENPRS PREBENDS
BDEEORRR BORDERER
BDEEORSS BEDSORES
BDEEORST BESTRODE
BDEEORSV OBSERVED
BDEEORTU OUTBREED
BDEEOSSS OBSESSED
BDEEOSSY BOSS-EYED
BDEEOSTT BESOTTED
BDEEOSTW BESTOWED
BDEEPRRU PUREBRED
BDEERRWY DEWBERRY
BDEERTTU BUTTERED,
　　REBUTTED
BDEGHILT BLIGHTED
BDEGIINT BETIDING,
　　DEBITING
BDEGILNN BLENDING
BDEGIORX OXBRIDGE
BDEGLMRU GRUMBLED
BDEGLNOU BLUDGEON
BDEGOOSY GOODBYES
BDEGORRY DOGBERRY

BDEHLORT BERTHOLD
BDEHLSUV BUSHVELD
BDEHMOOY HOMEBODY
BDEHOOOO BOOHOOED
BDEIIKLR BIRDLIKE
BDEIIKRT DIRT BIKE
BDEIILMR BIRDLIME
BDEIILNY INEDIBLY
BDEIILTY DEBILITY
BDEILLMU BDELLIUM
BDEILLOW BILLOWED
BDEILNRS BLINDERS
BDEILNRU UNBRIDLE
BDEILORV LOVEBIRD
BDEILOSS BODILESS
BDEILRRY LYREBIRD
BDEILRST BRISTLED,
　　DRIBLETS
BDEILRSU BUILDERS
BDEIMORS BROMIDES
BDEIMORY EMBRYOID
BDEINOOS NOBODIES
BDEINOOW WOODBINE
BDEINORV OVENBIRD
BDEINOSU BEDOUINS
BDEINSTW TWIN BEDS
BDEIOORR BROODIER
BDEIORRS DISROBER
BDEIORSV OVERBIDS
BDEIOSUX SUBOXIDE
BDEIOSWY WIDE BOYS
BDEIRSSU DISBURSE,
　　SUBSIDER
BDEKNOOS BOOKENDS
BDELLOOR BORDELLO,
　　DOORBELL
BDELLOUZ BULLDOZE
BDELMSTU STUMBLED
BDELNNOW END-BLOWN
BDELNOOW NEW BLOOD
BDELNOSS BOLDNESS
BDELNOST BLONDEST
BDELNOTU UNBOLTED
BDELNRSU BLUNDERS
BDELORSU BOULDERS
BDELORTU TROUBLED
BDELORUU DOUBLURE
BDELOSTU DOUBLETS
BDEMNSSU DUMBNESS
BDEMOORS BEDROOMS
BDEMOOSY SOMEBODY
BDEMSSUU SUBSUMED
BDENNOTU DUBONNET

BDENNRUU UNBURDEN	BDIOORSU BOUDOIRS	BEEGINNR BEGINNER
BDENOOTW BENTWOOD	BDKNOOOR DOORKNOB	BEEGINSW BEESWING
BDENORSU BOUNDERS,	BDKOOORW WORDBOOK	BEEGLNOR GRENOBLE
REBOUNDS, SUBORNED	BDKOORWY BODYWORK	BEEGMRSU SUBMERGE
BDENOTTU BUTTONED	BDKOOSTU STUDBOOK	BEEGNOTT BEGOTTEN
BDENRUUY UNDERBUY	BDLNOOOU DOUBLOON	BEEHIKLR HERBLIKE
BDEOORRS BROODERS	BDLOSTUW DUSTBOWL	BEEHILMN BLENHEIM
BDEOORRW BORROWED	BDNOOPTU POTBOUND	BEEHIMOT BOEHMITE
BDEOPSST BEDPOSTS	BDNOOSUX SOUNDBOX	BEEHLLNT HELL-BENT
BDEORRSU SUBORDER	BDNOOTUU OUTBOUND	BEEHLOOR BOREHOLE
BDEORRTU OBTRUDER	BDNORSUW RUBDOWNS	BEEHMORW HOME BREW
BDEORRUW BURROWED	BDORUWZZ BUZZWORD	BEEHNRRT BRETHREN
BDEORSTU DOUBTERS,	BEEEEFLN ENFEEBLE	BEEHRSST SHERBETS
REDOUBTS	BEEEENRT TEREBENE	BEEIILNZ ZIBELINE
BDFFIPRU PUFFBIRD	BEEEENRZ EBENEZER	BEEIJLSU JUBILEES
BDFGNOOU FOGBOUND	BEEEFIRS FREEBIES	BEEIKLWY BIWEEKLY
BDFIIITY BIFIDITY	BEEEFIST BEEFIEST	BEEILLLR LIBELLER
BDFILLLO BILLFOLD	BEEEFLST FEEBLEST	BEEILLNO LOBELINE
BDFILNOO BLOODFIN	BEEEGIRS BESIEGER	BEEILLTT BELITTLE
BDFIRRSU SURFBIRD	BEEEGNRR BERENGER	BEEILMPR PERIBLEM
BDFLOTUU DOUBTFUL	BEEEGRTT BEGETTER	BEEILNNO BENNE OIL
BDGGIINR BRIDGING	BEEEHISV BEEHIVES	BEEILNRY BERYLINE
BDGIIKNR KINGBIRD	BEEEHNOY HONEYBEE	BEEILNSS SENSIBLE
BDGIILNN BLINDING	BEEEHNSS SHEBEENS	BEEILNST STILBENE,
BDGIILNU BUILDING	BEEEILLL LIBELLEE	TENSIBLE
BDGIINNS BINDINGS	BEEEILNS BEELINES	BEEILNSU NEBULISE
BDGILNNU BUNDLING	BEEEILRV BELIEVER	BEEILNUZ NEBULIZE
BDGILNOO BLOODING	BEEEJLSZ JEZEBELS	BEEILRRT TERRIBLE
BDGILNOU DOUBLING	BEEEKLRY BERKELEY	BEEILRTU RUBELITE
BDGINNOU BOUNDING	BEEELMNS ENSEMBLE	BEEILRYZ BREEZILY
BDGINOOR BROODING	BEEELMRS RESEMBLE	BEEIMRTT EMBITTER
BDGINORS SONGBIRD	BEEELMZZ EMBEZZLE	BEEIRSSU SUBERISE
BDGINOTU DOUBTING	BEEELPRS BLEEPERS	BEEIRSUZ SUBERIZE
BDGINSUU SUBDUING	BEEELRVY BEVERLEY	BEEIRTVY EVERY BIT
BDGIRSUU DUISBURG	BEEEMMRR REMEMBER	BEEKNOPS BESPOKEN
BDGKOOOO GOOD BOOK	BEEFFRTU BUFFETER	BEELLORW BELLOWER
BDGLLOSU BULLDOGS	BEEFILLT LIFE BELT	BEELLSUY BULL'S-EYE
BDGNRUUY BURGUNDY	BEEFILLX FLEXIBLE	BEELMNNO NOBLEMEN
BDHIMOOR RHOMBOID	BEEFILNU UNBELIEF	BEELMRRT TREMBLER
BDHLMOTU HUMBOLDT	BEEFILRS BELFRIES	BEELMRRU LUMBERER
BDHMOSUW DUMB SHOW	BEEFINST BENEFITS	BEELMRST TREMBLES
BDIIIORV VIBRIOID	BEEFIRSS FRISBEES	BEELNNOR ENNOBLER
BDIIJOTU DJIBOUTI	BEEFLORU BEFOULER	BEELNOSS BONELESS
BDIIMRUU RUBIDIUM	BEEFNORR FREEBORN	BEELNSSU BLUENESS
BDILLOOY BLOODILY	BEEFOORT FREEBOOT	BEELOOST OBSOLETE
BDILMORY MORBIDLY	BEEGHILW BIG WHEEL	BEELRTUU TRUE-BLUE
BDILNPRU PURBLIND	BEEGHLTU THE BULGE	BEELSSTU TUBELESS
BDILOORY BROODILY	BEEGIILL ELIGIBLE	BEEMNORV NOVEMBER
BDILPSUU BUILDUPS	BEEGIILX EXIGIBLE	BEEMNRSU E NUMBERS
BDIMNORU MORIBUND	BEEGILNP BLEEPING	BEEMORRY RYE-BROME
BDINNRUW WINDBURN	BEEGILNT BEETLING	BEEMORSS EMBOSSER
BDINORSW SNOWBIRD	BEEGILNV BEVELING	BEENORTV VERBOTEN
BDINSSTU DUSTBINS	BEEGILRU BEGUILER	BEENRSTW BESTREWN

BEENRTTU BRUNETTE
BEEOOORRT ROOT BEER
BEEOORRV OVERBORE
BEEOORTT BEETROOT
BEEORRSV OBSERVER
BEEORSSU SUBEROSE
BEEORSTU TUBEROSE
BEEORSTW BESTOWER
BEEORSWY EYEBROWS
BEEQSSTU BEQUESTS
BEERRTTU REBUTTER
BEERSSUV SUBSERVE
BEESTTTU TEST TUBE
BEFGIINR BRIEFING
BEFGILNU FUNGIBLE
BEFGIRRU FREIBURG
BEFGIRSU FIREBUGS
BEFHILSU BLUEFISH
BEFHINOS BONEFISH
BEFILLMU BLUE FILM
BEFILLXY FLEXIBLY
BEFILMOR FORELIMB
BEFILOUY LIFE BUOY
BEFINORS BONFIRES
BEFLLLUY BELLYFUL
BEFLORUW FURBELOW
BEFNOORR FORBORNE
BEGGIINN BEGINING
BEGGINOR INGEBORG
BEGGIOST BOGGIEST
BEGGOORT GOTEBORG
BEGHILRT BLIGHTER
BEGHINRT BERTHING,
   BRIGHTEN
BEGHLNOU BUNGHOLE
BEGHOSTU BESOUGHT
BEGHRRSU BURGHERS
BEGIILLN LIBELING
BEGIIMRT BIG-TIMER
BEGIIRTT BRIGITTE
BEGIKNRU REBUKING
BEGILLLU BLUEGILL,
   GULLIBLE
BEGILNNY BENIGNLY
BEGILNOW ELBOWING
BEGILNRT TREBLING
BEGILNSS BLESSING,
   GLIBNESS
BEGILSTU BULGIEST
BEGINNOR RINGBONE
BEGINORS SOBERING
BEGLLOSU GLOBULES
BEGLMRRU GRUMBLER

BEGLMRSU GRUMBLES
BEGLMSUU BLUE GUMS
BEGLNOOU BOULOGNE
BEGLNRSU BUNGLERS
BEGLNRUU LUNEBURG
BEGNORRU ORENBURG
BEGNSSUU SUBGENUS
BEHIISTX EXHIBITS
BEHIKOSS KIBOSHES
BEHIKPSU PUSHBIKE
BEHILLOS SHOEBILL
BEHILLTY BLITHELY
BEHILMRW WHIMBREL
BEHILMST THIMBLES
BEHILNPY BIPHENYL
BEHILORR HORRIBLE
BEHILORS BOLSHIER
BEHILRTU THURIBLE
BEHIMNOO BONHOMIE
BEHINNOS SHINBONE
BEHINOSW WISHBONE
BEHISSTU BUSHIEST
BEHLLOOT BOLTHOLE
BEHLLOOW BLOWHOLE
BEHLMSTU HUMBLEST
BEHLORST BROTHELS
BEHLRSSU BLUSHERS
BEHMNOTU ON THE BUM
BEHNOOPX PHONE BOX
BEHNRSTU BURTHENS
BEHOORSX HORSEBOX
BEHOOSUY HOUSEBOY
BEHORRST BROTHERS
BEHORSSU ROSEBUSH
BEIILMMO IMMOBILE
BEIILMOS MOBILISE
BEIILMOZ MOBILIZE
BEIILNNR BIN-LINER
BEIILRST TRILBIES
BEIILRSX EX LIBRIS
BEIILRTT LIBRETTI
BEIILSTT STILBITE
BEIINSTT STIBNITE
BEIIOPSS BIOPSIES
BEIISTTT BITTIEST
BEIKLMOT TOMBLIKE
BEIKLMOW WOMBLIKE
BEIKLMRY KIMBERLY
BEIKLNRS BLINKERS
BEIKLOSS OBELISKS
BEIKLOTY KILOBYTE
BEIKLSTU BULKIEST
BEIKNOST STEINBOK

BEIKNRRY INKBERRY
BEIKOORT BROOKITE
BEIKRSST BRISKEST
BEILLMSS LIMBLESS
BEILLNTU BULLETIN
BEILLORS BROLLIES
BEILMMOS EMBOLISM
BEILMNOU NOBELIUM
BEILMNRU UNLIMBER
BEILMNST NIMBLEST
BEILMRST TIMBRELS
BEILNNTU BUNTLINE
BEILNSSY SENSIBLY
BEILOPPW BLOWPIPE
BEILOPSS POSSIBLE
BEILOQSU OBLIQUES
BEILORRS BROILERS
BEILORTT LIBRETTO
BEILORWZ BLOWZIER
BEILOSTW BLOWIEST
BEILRRTY TERRIBLY
BEILRSST BLISTERS,
   BRISTLES
BEILRSTU BURLIEST
BEILRTTY BITTERLY
BEILSTTU SUBTITLE
BEIMNORY IN EMBRYO
BEIMNSSU NIMBUSES
BEIMOORS RIBOSOME
BEIMORTY BIOMETRY
BEIMPSTU BUMPIEST
BEINNOSS BONINESS
BEINNOST BONNIEST
BEINOQRU QUIBERON
BEINORSW BROWNIES
BEINOSTU BOUNTIES
BEINRSTT BITTERNS
BEINRSTU TRIBUNES,
   TURBINES
BEINSSSU BUSINESS
BEIOOSTZ BOOZIEST
BEIOQTUU BOUTIQUE
BEIORSTY SOBRIETY
BEIOSSST BOSSIEST
BEIRRSSU BRUISERS
BEIRSTTU TRIBUTES
BEISSTTU BUSTIEST
BEJJMOTU JUMBO JET
BEJORTTU TURBOJET
BEKLNORY BROKENLY
BEKLOORU RULEBOOK
BEKLOOST BOOKLETS
BEKNNORU UNBROKEN

BEKNOOOT NOTEBOOK
BEKOOORV OVERBOOK
BEKOOTTX TEXTBOOK
BELLLLPU BELLPULL
BELLOPTY POTBELLY
BELLORTW BELLWORT
BELLOSWX SWELL BOX
BELMNOOU BLUE MOON
BELMOORS BLOOMERS
BELMOORY BLOOMERY
BELMOPRS PROBLEMS
BELMORSY SOMBRELY
BELMPRSU PLUMBERS
BELMPRUY PLUMBERY
BELMRRUY MULBERRY
BELMRSTU STUMBLER,
   TUMBLERS, TUMBRELS
BELMSSTU STUMBLES
BELNOSUU NEBULOUS
BELNSSTU SUNBELTS
BELOOOSX LOOSEBOX
BELOOPRS BLOOPERS
BELOOPRT BOLTROPE
BELOOSST BOOTLESS
BELOOTUV OBVOLUTE
BELORRTU TROUBLER
BELORSST BOLSTERS,
   LOBSTERS
BELORSTT BLOTTERS
BELORSTU TROUBLES
BELOSSUY BLESS YOU!
BELOSTUY OBTUSELY
BELPRSUY SUPERBLY
BELRSSSU BRUSSELS
BELRSTUY BLUSTERY
BELSSTTU SUBTLEST
BELSTTUY SUBTLETY
BEMNNSSU NUMBNESS
BEMNOORT TROMBONE
BEMNOORW NEW BROOM
BEMNOOXY MONEYBOX
BEMOORRS SOMBRERO
BEMORSST MOBSTERS
BENNOORS SORBONNE
BENOORSU BURNOOSE
BENORRSU SUBORNER
BENORRTU TRUEBORN
BENORSTW BROWNEST
BENORSTY RENT BOYS
BENSSSUY BUSYNESS
BEOOPSUZ BOOZE-UPS
BEOORRRW BORROWER
BEOORSST BOOSTERS

BEOPRRSV PROVERBS
BEOPRSSX PRESS BOX
BEOQSTUU BOUQUETS
BEORRRUW BURROWER
BEORSTUU TUBEROUS
BERSSTTU BUTTRESS
BFFGILNU BLUFFING
BFFHORSU BRUSH-OFF
BFFLLOUY BULLY-OFF
BFFLMOPU OFF PLUMB
BFFLOTUU OUTBLUFF
BFFNOOSU BUFFOONS
BFFNOSUX SNUFFBOX
BFGILMNU FUMBLING
BFGIORRU FRIBOURG
BFGLLORU BULLFROG
BFHIILLS BILLFISH
BFHILOST FISHBOLT
BFHILOSW BLOWFISH,
   FISHBOWL
BFHIMNSU NUMBFISH
BFIIORSS FIBROSIS
BFILLSSU BLISSFUL
BFIMORTU TUBIFORM
BFLLNOWY FLYBLOWN
BFLOORSU SUBFLOOR
BGGGILNO BOGGLING
BGGIILNO OBLIGING
BGGIILNY GIBINGLY
BGGILNNU BUNGLING
BGGILNRU BURGLING
BGHHINOR HIGHBORN
BGHHIORW HIGHBROW
BGHHIOSY HIGHBOYS
BGHIIKNT THINK BIG
BGHILMNU HUMBLING
BGHILNSU BLUSHING
BGHIMNTU THUMBING
BGHINORT BRIGHTON
BGHINRSU BRUSHING
BGHIOSST BIG SHOTS
BGHMORSU HOMBURGS
BGHOORSU BOROUGHS
BGIIKLNN BLINKING
BGIILNOR BROILING
BGIILNRS BRISLING
BGIILNSS SIBLINGS
BGIILNTY BITINGLY
BGIILNTZ BLITZING
BGIINORT ORBITING
BGIINRSU BRUISING
BGIINRTU BRUITING
BGIJLMNU JUMBLING

BGIKLNOT KINGBOLT
BGIKNOOR BROOKING
BGIKNOOS BOOKINGS
BGILLLUY GULLIBLY
BGILLNOU GLOBULIN
BGILLNRU BULLRING
BGILLNUY BULLYING
BGILMMNU MUMBLING
BGILMNOO BLOOMING
BGILMNPU PLUMBING
BGILMNRU RUMBLING
BGILMNTU TUMBLING
BGILMOSU GUMBOILS
BGILMOTU GUMBOTIL
BGILNNTU BLUNTING
BGILNORT RINGBOLT
BGILNORY BORINGLY
BGILNOTT BLOTTING,
   BOTTLING
BGILNRRU BLURRING
BGILNRTU BLURTING
BGILNSTU BUSTLING
BGINNORW BROWNING
BGINNORZ BRONZING
BGINOOST BOOSTING
BGINORSW BROWSING
BGINRSTU BURSTING
BGJOSTUY TOBY JUGS
BGKLOOOS LOGBOOKS
BGKNOOOS SONGBOOK
BGLNOOSW LONGBOWS
BGLOORYY BRYOLOGY
BGMNOOOR GOMBROON
BGMOOSTU GUMBOOTS
BGOPRSUU SUBGROUP
BGRRUUWZ WURZBURG
BHIILMPS BLIMPISH
BHIIOPRT PROHIBIT
BHIKLLOO BILLHOOK
BHILLNOR HORNBILL
BHILLSTU BULLSHIT
BHILORRY HORRIBLY
BHILOSYY BOYISHLY
BHIMNORT THROMBIN
BHINORSW BROWNISH
BHINORTU THONBURI
BHJLLNOU JOHN BULL
BHKNOOOR HORNBOOK
BHKOOOPS BOOKSHOP
BHLLNORU BULLHORN
BHMNTTUU THUMBNUT
BHMORSTU THROMBUS
BHMPSTUU THUMBS UP

245

BHOOSSTW BOWSHOTS
BHPRSSUU BRUSH-UPS
BIIKNOUV BUKOVINI
BIILLNOS BILLIONS
BIILMOTY MOBILITY
BIILNOOV OBLIVION
BIILNOTY NOBILITY
BIILNTUY NUBILITY
BIILOSSY BIOLYSIS
BIIMMOSZ ZOMBIISM
BIIQTUUY UBIQUITY
BIIRSSTU BURSITIS
BIKMNPSU BUMPKINS
BIKMTTUU TIMBUKTU
BIKOOUUZ BOUZOUKI
BILLNOOU BOUILLON,
     BOULLION
BILLOWYZ BLOWZILY
BILMMPSU PLUMBISM
BILMOSTU BOTULISM
BILNNOOY LOONY BIN
BILOORST SORBITOL
BILOPSSY POSSIBLY
BIMNORSY BYRONISM
BIMNOSTY SYMBIONT
BIMNRUUV VIBURNUM
BIMOORST ROBOTISM
BIOOPSTT POST-OBIT
BIOPRSTW BOWSPRIT
BIORRSTU BURRITOS
BIORSTUY BISTOURY
BJOPPTUU PUT-UP JOB
BKKOOORW WORKBOOK
BKLNOORY BROOKLYN
BKMOOORW BOOKWORM
BLLLLOOY LOBLOLLY
BLLMOORW BOLLWORM
BLMOOOTY LOBOTOMY
BLMOOSSS BLOSSOMS
BLMOPSUU PLUMBOUS
BLOORSWW LOWBROWS
BLOOSTUW BLOWOUTS
BLOPSSTU SUBPLOTS
BLORSTUY ROBUSTLY
BLOSTUUU TUBULOUS
BMNOOSST BONS MOTS
BMOOORSX BOXROOMS
BMOORSSU SOMBROUS
BMOORSTU MOTORBUS
BMOORTTY BOTTOMRY
BNNORTUW NUT-BROWN
BNNOTTUU UNBUTTON
BNNRSTUU SUNBURNT

BNOOOSUY SONOBUOY
BNORSTUU BURNOUTS
BNRSSTUU SUNBURST
BOOPRSSU BOSPORUS
BOORSSTY SOB STORY
BOPSSSTU BUS STOPS
BORSTTUU OUTBURST
CCCEEILT ECLECTIC
CCCEGOSY COCCYGES
CCCEHIOS CHOC-ICES
CCCEILNY ENCYCLIC
CCCIINSU SUCCINIC
CCCILNOY CYCLONIC
CCCINSTU SUCCINCT
CCCKOORW COCKCROW
CCDDEENO CONCEDED
CCDDENOU CONDUCED
CCDEEENR CREDENCE
CCDEEHLN CLENCHED
CCDEEIOP CODPIECE
CCDEEKOY COCKEYED
CCDEELRY RECYCLED
CCDEHILN CLINCHED
CCDEHIPU HICCUPED
CCDEHKLU CHUCKLED
CCDEHLTU CLUTCHED
CCDEHNRU CRUNCHED
CCDEHORS SCORCHED
CCDEHORU CROUCHED
CCDEHOST SCOTCHED
CCDEIINO COINCIDE
CCDEINOT OCCIDENT
CCDEIOPU OCCUPIED
CCDELNOU CONCLUDE
CCDENOOO COCOONED
CCDENORU CONDUCER
CCDEORRU OCCURRED
CCDEOSTU STUCCOED
CCDHIILO CICHLOID
CCDHIIOR DICHROIC
CCDHINOO CONCHOID
CCDIILOS CODICILS
CCDIINOS SCINCOID
CCDIIORT DICROTIC
CCDKLOOR OLD CROCK
CCDKLOSU CUCKOLDS
CCDKOOOW WOODCOCK
CCDLOSTU COLD CUTS
CCEEELMN CLEMENCE
CCEEHKRS CHECKERS
CCEEHLNS CLENCHES
CCEEHRSY SCREECHY
CCEEILNR ENCIRCLE

CCEEILNS LICENCES
CCEEILNT ELENCTIC
CCEEILPY EPICYCLE
CCEEILRT ELECTRIC
CCEEIMNU ECUMENIC
CCEEINOR CICERONE
CCEEINOV CONCEIVE
CCEEINSS SCIENCES
CCEEIORV COERCIVE
CCEEIRSV CERVICES,
     CREVICES
CCEEITTU EUTECTIC
CCEEKLOR COCKEREL
CCEEKNRW CREW NECK
CCEELMNY CLEMENCY
CCEEMMNO COMMENCE
CCEEMMOR COMMERCE
CCEENNOS ENSCONCE
CCEENORT CONCRETE
CCEENRST CRESCENT
CCEFIIPS SPECIFIC
CCEFIRRU CRUCIFER
CCEFLLOU FLOCCULE
CCEFLOOS FLOCCOSE
CCEGHIKN CHECKING
CCEGILRY GLYCERIC
CCEGINOR COERCING
CCEHHRSU CHURCHES
CCEHIIMS ISCHEMIC
CCEHIKNS CHECK-INS,
     CHICKENS
CCEHILNR CLINCHER
CCEHILNS CLINCHES
CCEHILOR CHOLERIC
CCEHILOY CHOICELY
CCEHINOR CORNICHE
CCEHINOZ ZECCHINO
CCEHINST TECHNICS
CCEHIORT RICOCHET
CCEHIOST CHOICEST
CCEHKLRU CHUCKLER
CCEHKLSU CHUCKLES
CCEHKOTU CHECKOUT
CCEHKPSU CHECKUPS
CCEHLMOR CROMLECH
CCEHLNNU UNCLENCH
CCEHLSTU CLUTCHES
CCEHORRS SCORCHER
CCEHORSS SCORCHES
CCEHORST CROTCHES
CCEHORTT CROTCHET
CCEHRSTU CRUTCHES
CCEIIKLN NICKELIC

CCEIIKPS ICE PICKS	CCGIIKLN CLICKING	CDDEEETT DETECTED
CCEIILNT ENCLITIC	CCGIIKNR CRICKING	CDDEEGLU CUDGELED
CCEIILOR LICORICE	CCGIILNR CIRCLING	CDDEEHIT CHEDDITE
CCEIILPT ECLIPTIC	CCGIKLNO CLOCKING	CDDEEHNR DRENCHED
CCEIILST SCILICET	CCGIKLNU CLUCKING	CDDEEIKR DICKERED
CCEIILTU LEUCITIC	CCGILLOY GLYCOLIC	CDDEEILN DECLINED
CCEIKOST COCKIEST	CCGILOSU GLUCOSIC	CDDEEIPT DEPICTED
CCEIKRST CRICKETS	CCHHIITY ICHTHYIC	CDDEEIRS DESCRIED
CCEILNUY UNICYCLE	CCHHINOU CHIN-CHOU	CDDEEIRT CREDITED,
CCEILRRU CURRICLE	CCHHNRUU UNCHURCH	DIRECTED
CCEILRST CIRCLETS	CCHHOOPP CHOP-CHOP	CDDEEKOT DOCKETED
CCEILRSY CRESYLIC	CCHHOOWW	CDDEEKUW DUCKWEED
CCEILRTY TRICYCLE	CHOW-CHOW	CDDEELSU SECLUDED
CCEILRUU CURLICUE	CCHIINUZ ZUCCHINI	CDDEELUX EXCLUDED
CCEILSTU CUTICLES	CCHIIORT ORCHITIC	CDDEELUY DEUCEDLY
CCEIMNOO ECONOMIC	CCHILMOW MILCH COW	CDDEENOS SECONDED
CCEIMOST COSMETIC	CCHIPSSY PSYCHICS	CDDEEORR RECORDED
CCEIMRRU MERCURIC	CCHKMSSU SCHMUCKS	CDDEERUV DECURVED
CCEINNOV CONVINCE	CCIILLRY CYRILLIC	CDDEFIIO CODIFIED
CCEINOOR COERCION	CCIIMNSY CYNICISM	CDDEFINO CONFIDED
CCEINOOZ CENOZOIC	CCIINORZ ZIRCONIC	CDDEGIIN DECIDING
CCEINORS CORNICES	CCIIRSTU CIRCUITS	CDDEGINO DECODING
CCEINORT NECROTIC	CCIIRTUY CIRCUITY	CDDEGINU DEDUCING
CCEINOST CONCEITS	CCIKKLOP PICKLOCK	CDDEIINT INDICTED
CCEINOTT TECTONIC	CCIKKOTT TICKTOCK	CDDEIKOS DOCKSIDE
CCEINPRT PRECINCT	CCIKLOSW COWLICKS	CDDEILLO COLLIDED
CCEINRTU CINCTURE	CCIKOPST COCKPITS	CDDEILMS MIDDLE CS
CCEINSZZ SZCZECIN	CCILNOSU COUNCILS	CDDEILNU INCLUDED
CCEIOORT CROCOITE	CCILOOPS PICCOLOS	CDDEILRU CUDDLIER
CCEIOPRU OCCUPIER	CCILORUU CURCULIO	CDDEINTU INDUCTED
CCEIOPTY ECOTYPIC	CCILOSSY CYCLOSIS	CDDEIORV DIVORCED
CCEIORST CORTICES	CCILSSTY CYCLISTS	CDDELLOU COLLUDED
CCEIPRTU CUT-PRICE	CCINOPSY SYNCOPIC	CDDELLOW COLD-WELD
CCEIPSST SCEPTICS	CCINORSY CRYONICS	CDDELNOO CONDOLED
CCEIRSSU CIRCUSES	CCINOSTV CONVICTS	CDDENNOO CONDONED
CCEKNOSY COCKNEYS	CCIOOPST SCOTOPIC	CDDENOOR CORDONED
CCEKORRY CROCKERY	CCIOORSS SIROCCOS	CDDEOORR CORRODED
CCEKORSU COCKSURE	CCIOOTXY OXYTOCIC	CDDEOORT DOCTORED
CCELLOST COLLECTS	CCJNNOTU CONJUNCT	CDDEOPRU PRODUCED
CCELNOSY CYCLONES	CCKMOOOR MOORCOCK	CDDGHILO GODCHILD
CCENNORS CONCERNS	CCKNORTU TURNCOCK	CDDGILNO CODDLING
CCENOORT CONCERTO	CCKOOPST STOPCOCK	CDDGILNU CUDDLING
CCENOPST CONCEPTS	CCKOPRSU COCKSPUR	CDDGINSU SCUDDING
CCENORST CONCERTS	CCNOOSTU COCONUTS	CDDHILOS CLODDISH
CCENRRUY CURRENCY	CCOOSSUU COUSCOUS	CDDIISTY DYTISCID
CCEORSSU CROCUSES	CCOOTTUU TUCOTUCO	CDDIORSS DISCORDS
CCERSTUW CREW CUTS	CCORSSTU CROSSCUT	CDDKORSY DRY DOCKS
CCFFHKOU CHUCK OFF	CDDDEETU DEDUCTED	CDDOOORW CORDWOOD
CCFIIRUX CRUCIFIX	CDDEEEEX EXCEEDED	CDEEEERX EXCEEDER
CCFILNOT CONFLICT	CDDEEEFT DEFECTED	CDEEEFFT EFFECTED
CCGHIKNO CHOCKING	CDDEEEIV DECEIVED	CDEEEFNS DEFENCES
CCGHIKNU CHUCKING	CDDEEEJT DEJECTED	CDEEEHNS ENSCHEDE
CCGHINOU COUCHING	CDDEEEPR PRECEDED	CDEEEHOR REECHOED

CDEEEHSW ESCHEWED
CDEEEINV EVIDENCE
CDEEEIRV DECEIVER,
   RECEIVED
CDEEEJRT REJECTED
CDEEELLX EXCELLED
CDEEELST SELECTED
CDEEEMNT CEMENTED
CDEEEMRS MERCEDES
CDEEENRS SCREENED
CDEEENRT CENTERED
CDEEEPTX EXCEPTED,
   EXPECTED
CDEEERSS RECESSED
CDEEERST SECRETED
CDEEERTT DETECTER
CDEEERTX EXCRETED
CDEEETUX EXECUTED
CDEEFFOR FORCE-FED
CDEEFIIS EDIFICES
CDEEFIIT FETICIDE
CDEEFINT INFECTED
CDEEFIRR FREDERIC
CDEEFKLR FRECKLED
CDEEFKOR FOREDECK
CDEEFLOT COLD FEET
CDEEFNOR ENFORCED
CDEEFORT DEFECTOR
CDEEGIIR REGICIDE
CDEEGINO GENOCIDE
CDEEGINR RECEDING
CDEEGINS SECEDING
CDEEGIOS GEODESIC
CDEEGIOT GEODETIC
CDEEHILS CHISELED
CDEEHINR ENRICHED
CDEEHIPR CIPHERED,
   DECIPHER
CDEEHKST SKETCHED
CDEEHLSU SCHEDULE
CDEEHNQU QUENCHED
CDEEHNRR DRENCHER
CDEEHNRW WRENCHED
CDEEHORT HECTORED
CDEEHPRY CYPHERED
CDEEHRTW WRETCHED
CDEEIILT ELICITED
CDEEIIMN MEDICINE
CDEEIIMP EPIDEMIC
CDEEIINT INDICTEE
CDEEIIRT DIERETIC
CDEEIISV DECISIVE
CDEEIITT DIETETIC

CDEEIJNT INJECTED
CDEEIJOR REJOICED
CDEEIKLN NICKELED
CDEEIKNS SICKENED
CDEEIKPT PICKETED
CDEEIKTT TICKETED
CDEEILNP PENCILED
CDEEILNR DECLINER,
   RECLINED
CDEEILNS DECLINES,
   LICENSED, SILENCED
CDEEILNT DENTICLE
CDEEILOR RECOILED
CDEEILPS ECLIPSED
CDEEILRT DERELICT
CDEEIMNR ENDERMIC
CDEEIMOR MEDIOCRE
CDEEIMOS COMEDIES
CDEEINNS INCENSED
CDEEINNT INDECENT
CDEEINRW CERIDWEN
CDEEIORV DIVORCÉE
CDEEIOSS DIOCESES
CDEEIPRT DECREPIT,
   DEPICTER
CDEEIPRU PEDICURE
CDEEIRRS DESCRIER
CDEEIRRT REDIRECT
CDEEIRST DISCREET,
   DISCRETE
CDEEIRSV SERVICED
CDEEITUV EDUCTIVE
CDEEJKOY JOCKEYED
CDEEKLPS SPECKLED
CDEEKNOR RECKONED
CDEEKNRS REDNECKS
CDEEKOPT POCKETED
CDEEKORT ROCKETED
CDEEKORW ROCKWEED
CDEEKPRU PUCKERED
CDEEKRTU TUCKERED
CDEELMOW WELCOMED
CDEELNOS ENCLOSED
CDEELNPU PEDUNCLE
CDEELNTY DECENTLY
CDEELOOW LOCOWEED
CDEELOST CLOSETED
CDEELPRU PRECLUDE
CDEELRTU LECTURED
CDEELRUX EXCLUDER
CDEEMOPR COMPERED
CDEEMOPT COMPETED
CDEEMORT ECTODERM

CDEENNOS CONDENSE
CDEENNOU DENOUNCE
CDEENNOV CONVENED
CDEENNTY TENDENCY
CDEENORR CORNERED
CDEENORS CENSORED,
   SECONDER, SEEDCORN
CDEENOSY ECDYSONE
CDEENOTX COEXTEND
CDEENOVY CONVEYED
CDEENPRU PRUDENCE
CDEENRSU CENSURED
CDEENSST DESCENTS
CDEEOOTV DOVECOTE
CDEEOPRS PROCEEDS
CDEEOPRU RECOUPED
CDEEORRR RECORDER
CDEEORST CORSETED,
   ESCORTED
CDEEORTT DETECTOR
CDEERRRU RECURRED
CDEERSSU SEDUCERS
CDEFFISU SUFFICED
CDEFFLSU SCUFFLED
CDEFHILN FLINCHED
CDEFIIIL FILICIDE
CDEFIIIT CITIFIED
CDEFIIOR CODIFIER
CDEFIIST DEFICITS
CDEFIKRR FREDRICK
CDEFINNO CONFINED
CDEFINOR CONFIDER
CDEFLNOU FLOUNCED
CDEFNORU UNFORCED
CDEFNOSU CONFUSED
CDEFNOTU CONFUTED
CDEFOSSU FOCUSSED
CDEGHORU GROUCHED
CDEGIILO GOIDELIC
CDEGINNO ENCODING
CDEGINOY DECOYING
CDEGINRU REDUCING
CDEGINRY DECRYING
CDEGINSU SEDUCING
CDEGINSY DYSGENIC
CDEGORSU SCOURGED
CDEHIILO HELICOID
CDEHIIMO HOMICIDE
CDEHIINO ECHINOID
CDEHIIOS HESIODIC
CDEHIKOT HOCKTIDE
CDEHIKRW HERDWICK
CDEHILNR CHILDREN

CDEHILOR CHLORIDE
CDEHILRT ELDRITCH
CDEHIMRS SMIRCHED
CDEHINOS HEDONICS
CDEHINST SNITCHED
CDEHIOSW COWHIDES
CDEHISTT STITCHED
CDEHISTW SWITCHED
CDEHITTW TWITCHED
CDEHKLSU SHELDUCK
CDEHLOOS SCHOOLED
CDEHLORT CHORTLED
CDEHLOSU SLOUCHED
CDEHMOOS SMOOCHED
CDEHNOOP CHENOPOD
CDEHORSU CHORUSED
CDEHORSW COWHERDS
CDEHOSSW COWSHEDS
CDEIIILS SILICIDE
CDEIIIMT MITICIDE
CDEIIIOS IDIOCIES
CDEIIKKS SIDEKICK
CDEIIKMM MIMICKED
CDEIIKST DICKIEST
CDEIILMO DOMICILE
CDEIILNN INCLINED
CDEIILNO INDOCILE
CDEIILOT IDIOLECT
CDEIILPS DISCIPLE
CDEIILRU RIDICULE
CDEIIMRT DIMETRIC
CDEIINNT INCIDENT
CDEIINOS DECISION
CDEIINOV INVOICED
CDEIINRT INDIRECT
CDEIINTY CYTIDINE
CDEIIOPR PERIODIC
CDEIIOPS EPISODIC
CDEIIOPT EPIDOTIC
CDEIIRTU DIURETIC
CDEIISSU SUICIDES
CDEIKLNR CRINKLED
CDEIKLPR PRICKLED
CDEIKLRT TRICKLED
CDEIKLWY WICKEDLY
CDEIKNOS SOCKED IN
CDEIKNPU UNPICKED
CDEIKORR RODERICK
CDEIKOST DIESTOCK
CDEIKRRS DERRICKS
CDEILLOU CELULOID,
    LODICULE
CDEILLPU PELLUCID

CDEILMOP COMPILED,
    COMPLIED
CDEILMOY MYCELOID
CDEILMRU DULCIMER
CDEILNOS INCLOSED
CDEILNRY CYLINDER
CDEILOOW WOODLICE
CDEILOPU CLUPEOID
CDEILORS SCLEROID
CDEILORU CLOUDIER
CDEILOSS DISCLOSE
CDEILPPR CRIPPLED
CDEILRTY DIRECTLY
CDEILSTU DUCTILES
CDEILSXY DYSLEXIC
CDEIMOST DOMESTIC
CDEIMPRS SCRIMPED
CDEINNOU UNCOINED
CDEINNOV CONNIVED
CDEINORS CONSIDER
CDEINORT CENTROID,
    DOCTRINE
CDEINOST D-NOTICES
CDEINOTU EDUCTION
CDEINOUV UNVOICED
CDEINPRU UNPRICED
CDEINRRU INCURRED
CDEINSTY SYNDETIC
CDEIOPST DESPOTIC
CDEIOPSZ ZIP CODES
CDEIOPTY COPY-EDIT
CDEIORRT CREDITOR,
    DIRECTOR
CDEIORRV DIVORCER
CDEIORSV DISCOVER,
    DIVORCES
CDEIPRST SCRIPTED
CDEIPRTU PICTURED
CDEIRRSU SCURRIED
CDEIRSTU CRUDITÉS,
    CURTSIED
CDEIRSTV VERDICTS
CDEISSSU DISCUSES
CDEJNORU CONJURED
CDEKKLNU KNUCKLED
CDEKLMOR CLERKDOM
CDEKLNOU UNLOCKED
CDEKLRTU TRUCKLED
CDEKNOOV CONVOKED
CDEKNORU UNCORKED
CDELLORS SCROLLED
CDELLOTU CLOUDLET
CDELMNOU COLUMNED

CDELMPRU CRUMPLED
CDELNOOR CONDOLER
CDELNOOS CONSOLED
CDELNOSS COLDNESS
CDELNOSY SECONDLY
CDELOORS COLD SORE
CDELOORU COLOURED,
    DECOLOUR
CDELORSS CORDLESS
CDELPRSU SCRUPLED
CDELRSUY CURSEDLY
CDELRTUU CULTURED
CDELSSUY CUSSEDLY
CDELSTTU SCUTTLED
CDEMMNOU COMMUNED
CDEMMOOS COMMODES
CDEMMOTU COMMUTED
CDEMNOOW COMEDOWN
CDEMNOSU CONSUMED
CDEMNOTU DOCUMENT
CDEMOOPS COMPOSED
CDEMOPTU COMPUTED
CDEMPRSU SCRUMPED
CDENNOOR CONDONER
CDENNOOT CONNOTED
CDENOORT CREODONT
CDENOOVY CONVOYED
CDENORTU TROUNCED
CDENOSTU CONTUSED
CDENRTUU UNDERCUT
CDEOOPST POSTCODE
CDEOORRR CORRODER
CDEOORSU DECOROUS
CDEOPRRU PROCURED,
    PRODUCER
CDEORRSS RED CROSS
CDERSTTU DESTRUCT
CDFFILOR CLIFFORD
CDFHILOS COLD FISH
CDFIILMS DISC FILM
CDFIILSU FLUIDICS
CDFNNOOU CONFOUND
CDGHIINT DITCHING
CDGHINOR CHORDING
CDGIINNU INDUCING
CDGIKLNU DUCKLING
CDGILNOS SCOLDING
CDGILNOU CLOUDING
CDGILNRU CURDLING
CDGINORW CROWDING
CDHHIILS CHILDISH
CDHIINNW CHINDWIN

CDHIIORT HIDROTIC, TRICHOID
CDHIIOSZ SCHIZOID
CDHILOOP CHILOPOD
CDHIOORT TROCHOID
CDHIOPRW WHIPCORD
CDHLOOPY COPYHOLD
CDHOORRU UROCHORD
CDIIIORT DIORITIC
CDIIKMNO DOMINICK
CDIIKPST DIPSTICK
CDIILOPP DIPLOPIC
CDIILOTY DOCILITY
CDIILTUY LUCIDITY
CDIIMNOU CONIDIUM
CDIINPRY CYPRINID
CDIINSTT DISTINCT
CDIIOPRT DIOPTRIC
CDIIORSU SCIUROID
CDIIPTUY CUPIDITY
CDIIRSTT DISTRICT
CDIJNSTU DISJUNCT
CDIKLPUY LUCKY DIP
CDIKNOSW WINDSOCK
CDILLOUY CLOUDILY
CDILOOPZ PODZOLIC
CDILOORT LORDOTIC
CDILOOTY COTYLOID
CDIMOORT MICRODOT
CDINNQUU QUIDNUNC
CDINORTU INDUCTOR
CDINOSTU CONDUITS, DISCOUNT
CDIOOPRS PROSODIC
CDIOORRR CORRIDOR
CDIOPRRS RIPCORDS
CDIOPRSU CUSPIDOR
CDKOOORW CORKWOOD
CDLOOSTW COTSWOLD
CDMNOOPU COMPOUND
CDMNORUU CORUNDUM
CDNNOOOT CONODONT
CDOORRUY CORDUROY
CDOOSTUW WOODCUTS
CDOPRSTU PRODUCTS
CEEEEIPY EYEPIECE
CEEEFFRT EFFECTER
CEEEFNOR CONFEREE
CEEEGITX EXEGETIC
CEEEGMNR MERGENCE
CEEEHIKR CHEEKIER
CEEEHIRR CHEERIER
CEEEHIST ICE SHEET

CEEEHKOR CHEROKEE
CEEEHNNY CHEYENNE
CEEEHPSS SPEECHES
CEEEHRSW ESCHEWER
CEEEIJTV EJECTIVE
CEEEILNS LICENSEE
CEEEILRT ERECTILE
CEEEILTV CLEVEITE, ELECTIVE
CEEEIMNN EMINENCE
CEEEINOP ONE-PIECE
CEEEIPRR CREEPIER
CEEEIPRV PERCEIVE
CEEEIPST SET PIECE
CEEEIRRV RECEIVER
CEEEIRSX EXERCISE
CEEEJRRT REJECTER
CEEELRTT ELECTRET
CEEEMNRT CEMENTER, CEREMENT
CEEEMORT ECTOMERE
CEEEMRTY CEMETERY
CEEEMSUX EXCUSE ME!
CEEENNST SENTENCE
CEEENNSV CEVENNES
CEEENPRS PRESENCE
CEEENPRT PRETENCE
CEEENQSU SEQUENCE
CEEENRRS SCREENER
CEEENRRT TERRENCE
CEEENSSS ESSENCES
CEEEPRRS CREEPERS
CEEERRTX EXCRETER
CEEERSSS RECESSES
CEEERTUX EXECUTER
CEEESSSX EXCESSES
CEEFFINT IN EFFECT
CEEFFNOS OFFENCES
CEEFFORT EFFECTOR
CEEFGILN FLEECING
CEEFHIKR KERCHIEF
CEEFHLRT FLETCHER
CEEFHLRU CHEERFUL
CEEFIKKR FREE KICK
CEEFILRY FIERCELY
CEEFINRT FRENETIC
CEEFIRRU FIRE-CURE
CEEFIRST FIERCEST
CEEFKLRS FRECKLES
CEEFKLSS FECKLESS
CEEFLNOR FLORENCE
CEEFLNTU FECULENT
CEEFLRUU FLUE-CURE

CEEFNORR CONFRÈRE, ENFORCER
CEEFNRVY FERVENCY
CEEFOPRR PERFORCE
CEEFORSS FRESCOES
CEEFORST SCOT-FREE
CEEFPRST PREFECTS
CEEGHIKN CHEEKING
CEEGHINP CHEEPING
CEEGHINR CHEERING
CEEGHLOW COGWHEEL
CEEGHNRT GRETCHEN
CEEGIJNT EJECTING
CEEGILNT ELECTING
CEEGILOT ECLOGITE
CEEGINPR CREEPING
CEEGINRT ERECTING
CEEGINST GENETICS
CEEGINSU EUGENICS
CEEGINXY EXIGENCY
CEEGIORX EXOERGIC
CEEGLLMR GERM CELL
CEEGLLOS COLLEGES
CEEGMNOY CYMOGENE
CEEGNNOR CONGENER
CEEGNORV CONVERGE
CEEGORST CORTEGES
CEEHHLRS HERSCHEL
CEEHHMNN HENCHMEN
CEEHIIST ETHICISE
CEEHIITZ ETHICIZE
CEEHIKLY CHEEKILY
CEEHILLM MICHELLE
CEEHILLN CHENILLE, HELLENIC
CEEHILRW CLERIHEW
CEEHILRY CHEERILY
CEEHILSV VEHICLES
CEEHILTV HELVETIC
CEEHIMRT HERMETIC
CEEHIMSS CHEMISES
CEEHINPR ENCIPHER
CEEHINPT PHENETIC
CEEHINRR ENRICHER
CEEHINTT ENTHETIC
CEEHIOSV COHESIVE
CEEHIPRT HERPETIC
CEEHIRRS CHERRIES
CEEHIRST CHESTIER, HERETICS
CEEHIRTT TETCHIER
CEEHISTW CHEWIEST
CEEHKLRS HECKLERS

CEEHKRST SKETCHER
CEEHKSST SKETCHES
CEEHLLOR ROCHELLE
CEEHLNOO HOLOCENE
CEEHLNOS ECHELONS
CEEHLNSU ELENCHUS
CEEHLRSU HERCULES
CEEHMRSS SCHEMERS
CEEHNNRT ENTRENCH
CEEHNORT COHERENT
CEEHNQRU QUENCHER
CEEHNRRT RETRENCH,
    TRENCHER
CEEHNRST TRENCHES
CEEHNRSW WRENCHES
CEEHNSST STENCHES
CEEHOPRY CORYPHEE
CEEHORRT TORCHERE
CEEHORST THE SCORE,
    TROCHEES
CEEHQRSU CHEQUERS
CEEHRSTW WRETCHES
CEEIIKLV VICELIKE
CEEIIMNP MINCE PIE
CEEIIMRT EREMITIC
CEEIINST NICETIES
CEEIINVV EVINCIVE
CEEIJNOT EJECTION
CEEIJORR REJOICER
CEEIJRUV VERJUICE
CEEIKLNN NECKLINE
CEEIKLPR PICKEREL
CEEIKNRS SICKENER
CEEIKNST NECKTIES
CEEIKPRT PICKETER
CEEILLLP PELLICLE
CEEILLNT LENTICEL
CEEILMNT MELICENT
CEEILMOR COMELIER
CEEILMPS SEMPLICE
CEEILNNU LUCIENNE
CEEILNNY LENIENCY
CEEILNOP PLIOCENE
CEEILNOT ELECTION
CEEILNOV VIOLENCE
CEEILNRR RECLINER
CEEILNRS LICENSER,
    SILENCER
CEEILNSS SILENCES
CEEILORR RECOILER
CEEILPRS ECLIPSER
CEEILPRY CREEPILY
CEEILPSS ECLIPSES

CEEILQSU LIQUESCE
CEEILRST SCLERITE
CEEILRSV VERSICLE
CEEILRTU RETICULE
CEEILRTY CELERITY
CEEILSSV VESICLES
CEEILSTT TESTICLE
CEEIMMPY EMPYEMIC
CEEIMMRS MESMERIC
CEEIMNPS SPECIMEN
CEEIMNST CENTIMES,
    TENESMIC
CEEIMORT CORE TIME,
    METEORIC
CEEINNPZ PINCE-NEZ
CEEINNSS NICENESS
CEEINNST NESCIENT
CEEINOPU EUPNOEIC
CEEINORT ERECTION,
    NEOTERIC
CEEINORX EXOCRINE
CEEINOTV EVECTION
CEEINPRT TERPENIC
CEEINPSX SIXPENCE
CEEINQRU QUERCINE
CEEINRST SECRETIN
CEEINRSU INSECURE,
    SINECURE
CEEINRTT RETICENT
CEEINRTU ENURETIC
CEEINSSX IN EXCESS
CEEINSTY CYSTEINE
CEEIOPPS EPISCOPE
CEEIOPTW TWO-PIECE
CEEIORST COTERIES,
    ESOTERIC
CEEIORSX EXORCISE
CEEIORTX EXOTERIC
CEEIORXZ EXORCIZE
CEEIPPTU EUPEPTIC
CEEIPRST RECEIPTS
CEEIPRSU EPICURES
CEEIRRST RECITERS
CEEIRRSW SCREWIER
CEEIRSSV SERVICES
CEEIRSTV VERTICES
CEEIRSVX CERVIXES
CEEKLNST NECKLETS
CEEKLPSS SPECKLES
CEEKLRSS RECKLESS
CEEKNORR RECKONER
CEEKOPRX OXPECKER
CEEKRRSW WRECKERS

CEELLMOU MOLECULE
CEELLNOS COLLEENS
CEELLRVY CLEVERLY
CEELLSSU CLUELESS
CEELMOPT COMPLETE
CEELMORW WELCOMER
CEELMOSW WELCOMES
CEELMRTU ELECTRUM
CEELNOPU OPULENCE
CEELNORS ENCLOSER
CEELNORT ELECTRON
CEELNRST LECTERNS
CEELNRTY RECENTLY
CEELNSTU ESCULENT
CEELORST CORSELET,
    ELECTORS, SELECTOR
CEELORTV COVERLET
CEELOSST CLOSE-SET
CEELRRTU LECTURER
CEELRSSU RECLUSES
CEELRSTU LECTURES
CEELRSTY SECRETLY
CEELRSUY SECURELY
CEELSTTU LETTUCES
CEEMMNTU CEMENTUM
CEEMNORW NEWCOMER
CEEMNORY CEREMONY
CEEMNOYZ COENZYME
CEEMOORV OVERCOME
CEEMOPRS COMPEERS,
    COMPERES
CEENNOOS NOSECONE
CEENNORS ON-SCREEN
CEENNORT CRETONNE
CEENNORU RENOUNCE
CEENNORV CONVENER
CEENOORV ONCE-OVER
CEENOPRV PROVENCE
CEENOPTW TWOPENCE
CEENORSV CONSERVE,
    CONVERSE
CEENORTT CORNETTE
CEENORVY CONVEYER
CEENPPTU TUPPENCE
CEENRSSU CENSURES
CEENSSSU CENSUSES
CEENSSTU CUTENESS
CEEOORST CREOSOTE
CEEOPRRT RECEPTOR
CEEOPRTY CEROTYPE
CEEOQTTU COQUETTE
CEEORRRS SORCERER

CEEORRSU RECOURSE,
   RESOURCE
CEEORRVY RECOVERY
CEEORSSY CROSS-EYE
CEEORTTV CORVETTE
CEEORTUX EXECUTOR
CEEOSSTX TO EXCESS
CEEPPRST PRECEPTS
CEEPRSST RESPECTS,
   SCEPTRES, SPECTRES
CEEPRSTX EXCERPTS
CEERRSSU RESCUERS
CEERRSTU REST CURE
CEERSSTU SECUREST
CEERSSTW SETSCREW
CEFFIORS OFFICERS
CEFFIORU COIFFEUR,
   COIFFURE
CEFFIRSU SUFFICER
CEFFLORU FORCEFUL
CEFFLSSU SCUFFLES
CEFGHINT FETCHING
CEFGIKLN FLECKING
CEFHIIMS MISCHIEF
CEFHILNR FLINCHER
CEFIILNO OLEFINIC
CEFIILST FELSITIC
CEFIILTY FELICITY
CEFIIORS ORIFICES
CEFIIRRT TERRIFIC
CEFIKLRY FLICKERY
CEFILLLO FOLLICLE
CEFILMRU MERCIFUL
CEFILNOT FLECTION
CEFILOUV VOICEFUL
CEFIMOST COMFIEST
CEFINNOS CONFINES
CEFINORS CONIFERS,
   FORENSIC
CEFINORT INFECTOR
CEFINOTT CONFETTI
CEFIORTY FEROCITY
CEFKLOOR FORELOCK
CEFKLOST FETLOCKS
CEFKLPSY FLYSPECK
CEFLNOSU FLOUNCES
CEFLNRUU FURUNCLE
CEFNORTU CONFUTER
CEFORRST CROFTERS
CEFORSTU FRUCTOSE
CEGGHIRS CHIGGERS
CEGGLNOY GLYCOGEN
CEGHHHIT HIGH TECH

CEGHIINY HYGIENIC
CEGHIKLN HECKLING
CEGHILNW WELCHING
CEGHILST GLITCHES
CEGHIMNS SCHEMING
CEGHINNW WENCHING
CEGHINOR COHERING
CEGHINPR PERCHING
CEGHINRT RETCHING
CEGHINST ETCHINGS
CEGHIRTU THEURGIC
CEGHMRUY CHEMURGY
CEGHNORS GROSCHEN
CEGHORSU GROUCHES
CEGIILNS CEILINGS
CEGIINNT ENTICING
CEGIINNV EVINCING
CEGIINPR PIERCING
CEGIINRT NEGRITIC,
   RECITING
CEGIINSS GNEISSIC
CEGIINSX EXCISING
CEGIINTV EVICTING
CEGIINTX EXCITING
CEGIIOST EGOISTIC
CEGIKLNR CLERKING
CEGIKNRW WRECKING
CEGILNRY GLYCERIN
CEGILNTU CULTIGEN
CEGIMNOY MYOGENIC
CEGINNOZ COZENING
CEGINNRT CENTRING
CEGINNST SCENTING
CEGINOOP GEOPONIC
CEGINOOR OROGENIC
CEGINOPY PYOGENIC
CEGINORV COVERING
CEGINORW COWERING
CEGINOTV COVETING,
   VIETCONG
CEGINOXY OXYGENIC
CEGINRST CRESTING
CEGINRSU RESCUING,
   SECURING
CEGINRSW SCREWING
CEGINRSY SYNERGIC
CEGINSUX EXCUSING
CEGLLOOU COLLOGUE
CEGLLORY GLYCEROL
CEGLLRYY GLYCERYL
CEGLNOTY COGENTLY
CEGMNNOO COGNOMEN
CEGNNPUY PUNGENCY

CEGNOOTY GONOCYTE
CEGNORSS CONGRESS
CEGNORSU SCROUNGE
CEGOORSS SCROOGES
CEGORRSU SCOURGER
CEGORSSU SCOURGES
CEHIILLR CHILLIER
CEHIILLS CHILLIES
CEHIILMO HEMIOLIC
CEHIILNN LICHENIN
CEHIILNT LECITHIN
CEHIILOT EOLITHIC
CEHIIMOS ISOCHEIM
CEHIIMPT MEPHITIC
CEHIIMRT HERMITIC
CEHIIOPT ETHIOPIC
CEHIIPPS CHIPPIES
CEHIIPRR CHIRPIER
CEHIIRSS CHRISSIE
CEHIIRST CHRISTIE
CEHIIRTT TITCHIER,
   TRICHITE
CEHIISTT ETHICIST,
   ITCHIEST, THEISTIC
CEHIKLNY HINCKLEY
CEHIKLSU SUCHLIKE
CEHIKMNT CHIMKENT
CEHIKMOS HOMESICK
CEHIKNRU CHUNKIER
CEHIKNST KITCHENS
CEHIKOWW KWEICHOW
CEHIKRSW WHICKERS
CEHIKSTT THICKEST,
   THICKETS, THICKSET
CEHILLMT MITCHELL
CEHILLRS SCHILLER
CEHILMTY METHYLIC
CEHILNOP PHENOLIC,
   PINOCHLE
CEHILNOR CHLORINE
CEHILNSS CHINLESS
CEHILORT CHLORITE,
   CLOTHIER
CEHILOSU CHOISEUL
CEHILPTY PHYLETIC
CEHILSTY CHESTILY
CEHILTTY TETCHILY
CEHIMMRU CHUMMIER
CEHIMNOP PHONEMIC
CEHIMNOR NICHROME
CEHIMNOW CHOW MEIN
CEHIMNSY CHIMNEYS

CEHIMORT CHROMITE,
   TRICHOME
CEHIMRRS SMIRCHER
CEHIMSST CHEMISTS
CEHINNRT INTRENCH
CEHINOOS COHESION
CEHINOPT PHONETIC
CEHINOPU EUPHONIC
CEHINPRU PUNCHIER
CEHINRSS RICHNESS
CEHINRST CHRISTEN
CEHINRSW SCHWERIN
CEHINRTU RUTHENIC
CEHINSST SNITCHES
CEHIOORS CHOOSIER
CEHIOPPR CHOPPIER
CEHIOPRU EUPHORIC
CEHIOPSS HOSPICES
CEHIOPST POSTICHE
CEHIOPTU EUPHOTIC
CEHIORRT RHETORIC,
   TORCHIER
CEHIORTU TOUCHIER
CEHIPRSS SPHERICS
CEHIPRST PITCHERS
CEHIRSTT STITCHER
CEHIRSTW SWITCHER
CEHIRSTY HYSTERIC
CEHIRTTW TWITCHER
CEHIRTWY WITCHERY
CEHISSTT STITCHES
CEHISSTU CUSHIEST
CEHISSTW SWITCHES
CEHISTTW TWITCHES
CEHKKRSU CHUKKERS
CEHKLMOS HEMLOCKS
CEHKNPUY KEYPUNCH
CEHKORSS SHOCKERS
CEHKRSTU HUCKSTER
CEHLNNOU LUNCHEON
CEHLNOTU UNCLOTHE
CEHLORST CHORTLES
CEHLORSU SLOUCHER
CEHLQSUY SQUELCHY
CEHMNSSU MUCHNESS
CEHMORUV OVERMUCH
CEHNNOPU PUNCHEON
CEHNNOSU NONESUCH
CEHNOORS SCHOONER
CEHNORSV CHEVRONS
CEHNSTTU CHESTNUT
CEHOOORZ ZOOCHORE
CEHOORST CHEROOTS

CEHOORSU OCHREOUS
CEHOPPRS CHOPPERS
CEHOPPRY PROPHECY
CEHOPSUY CHOP SUEY
CEHORSSU CHORUSES
CEHORSSZ SCHERZOS
CEHORSUV VOUCHERS
CEHPSSTU PUTSCHES
CEHRSTTY STRETCHY
CEIIILSV CIVILISE
CEIIILVZ CIVILIZE
CEIIINSV INCISIVE
CEIIJSTU JESUITIC,
   JUICIEST
CEIIKLMR LIMERICK
CEIIKLRS SICKLIER
CEIIKMMR MIMICKER
CEIIKNRS ICE RINKS
CEIIKNST KINETICS
CEIIKPST PICKIEST
CEIIKQSU QUICKIES
CEIIKRRT TRICKIER
CEIIKRST STICKIER
CEIIKSST EKISTICS
CEIILMNT LIMNETIC
CEIILMNY MYELINIC
CEIILNNR INCLINER
CEIILNNS INCLINES
CEIILNOP PICOLINE
CEIILNOS ISOCLINE,
   SILICONE
CEIILOPS POLICIES
CEIILORT ELICITOR
CEIILOTZ ZEOLITIC
CEIILPPS CLIPPIES
CEIILPRT PERLITIC
CEIILPSS ECLIPSIS
CEIILPTX EXPLICIT
CEIILPTY PYELITIC
CEIILRTV VERTICIL
CEIILSSS SCISSILE
CEIIMOPT EPITOMIC
CEIIMORS ISOMERIC
CEIIMOST COMITIES,
   SEMIOTIC
CEIIMRST MERISTIC
CEIIMRTT TERMITIC
CEIIMSST SEMITICS
CEIINNOT NICOTINE
CEIINORS RECISION,
   SORICINE
CEIINOSV INVOICES
CEIINOSX EXCISION

CEIINOTV EVICTION
CEIINRSU INCISURE,
   SCIURINE
CEIINRTU NEURITIC
CEIINSST CITISENS
CEIINSTU CUTINISE
CEIINSTY SYENITIC
CEIINSTZ CITIZENS
CEIINTUZ CUTINIZE
CEIIOPRT PERIOTIC
CEIIOSTT OSTEITIC
CEIIPRRS CRISPIER
CEIIPRST PRICIEST
CEIIPSST SPICIEST
CEIIQRTU CRITIQUE
CEIIRSTV VERISTIC
CEIISTVV VIVISECT
CEIJLNOS JOSCELIN
CEIJNORT INJECTOR
CEIJSSTU JUSTICES
CEIKKNRS KNICKERS
CEIKLNRS CLINKERS,
   CRINKLES
CEIKLOSV LOVESICK
CEIKLPRS PRICKLES
CEIKLPRU PLUCKIER
CEIKLRSS SLICKERS
CEIKLRST STICKLER,
   STRICKLE
CEIKLSST SLICKEST
CEIKLSTU LUCKIEST
CEIKMPPU PICK-ME-UP
CEIKMSTU MUCKIEST
CEIKNNOT NEKTONIC
CEIKNRSS SNICKERS
CEIKNRST STRICKEN
CEIKNSSS SICKNESS
CEIKORST ROCKIEST,
   STOCKIER
CEIKPSST SKEPTICS
CEIKQSTU QUICKEST,
   QUICKSET
CEIKRRTY TRICKERY
CEIKRSST STICKERS
CEIKSTUY YUCKIEST
CEILLLOY ICE LOLLY
CEILLOQU COQUILLE
CEILLORS COLLIERS
CEILLORY COLLIERY
CEILLRTU TELLURIC
CEILLSST CELLISTS
CEILMMUY MYCELIUM
CEILMNOP COMPLINE

CEILMOPR COMPILER,
   COMPLIER
CEILMOPS POLEMICS
CEILMOSS SOLECISM
CEILMOSU COLISEUM
CEILMRSU CLUMSIER
CEILNNOT NON LICET
CEILNNSY SYNCLINE
CEILNOOS COLONIES,
   COLONISE, ECLOSION
CEILNOOZ COLONIZE
CEILNORV IN CLOVER
CEILNOST TELSONIC
CEILNOSX LEXICONS
CEILNPRY PRINCELY
CEILNRUV CULVERIN
CEILNSST STENCILS
CEILOPPS POPSICLE
CEILOPRT PETROLIC
CEILOPTU POULTICE
CEILOPTY EPICOTYL
CEILORST CLOISTER,
   COSTLIER
CEILORTY CRYOLITE
CEILOSST SOLECIST,
   SOLSTICE
CEILOSSU COULISSE
CEILOTVY VELOCITY
CEILPPRS CLIPPERS,
   CRIPPLES
CEILPRSS SPLICERS
CEILPRSU SURPLICE
CEILRSTU CURLIEST
CEIMMNNO MNEMONIC
CEIMMNOU ENCOMIUM,
   MECONIUM
CEIMMORT RECOMMIT
CEIMMRRU CRUMMIER
CEIMNNOY NEOMYCIN
CEIMNOPT PENTOMIC
CEIMNOPY EPONYMIC
CEIMNORS SERMONIC
CEIMNORT INTERCOM
CEIMNSSU MENISCUS
CEIMOOSZ MESOZOIC
CEIMOPRS COMPRISE
CEIMORSX EXORCISM
CEIMRRTU TURMERIC
CEIMSSTY SYSTEMIC
CEINNNOT INNOCENT
CEINNORU NEURONIC
CEINNORV CONNIVER
CEINNOTU CONTINUE

CEINOOTZ ENTOZOIC,
   ENZOOTIC
CEINOPRS CONSPIRE
CEINOPRT INCEPTOR
CEINOPRV PROVINCE
CEINORSS NECROSIS
CEINORST CORNIEST
CEINORSU COINSURE
CEINORSW IN ESCROW
CEINORTT CONTRITE
CEINORTU NEUROTIC
CEINORTV CONTRIVE
CEINOSSS CESSIONS,
   COSINESS
CEINOSST SECTIONS
CEINOSSZ COZINESS
CEINOSTT STENOTIC
CEINOSTU COUNTIES
CEINOSTY CYTOSINE
CEINOTTU TEUTONIC
CEINPRSS PRINCESS
CEINRSST CISTERNS
CEINRSTT CENTRIST
CEINRTTU TINCTURE
CEIOOTXX EXOTOXIC
CEIOPRRU CROUPIER
CEIOPRSU PRECIOUS
CEIOPSSU SPECIOUS
CEIORRSS CROSIERS
CEIORRSZ CROZIERS
CEIORRTU COURTIER
CEIORSTU CITREOUS,
   OUTCRIES
CEIORSTV VORTICES
CEIORSTX EXORCIST
CEIORSVY VICEROYS
CEIORTTU TOREUTIC
CEIPRRST RESCRIPT
CEIPRSTU PICTURES,
   PIECRUST
CEIPSSST CESSPITS
CEIRRRUY CURRIERY
CEIRRSSU CRUISERS
CEIRRSTT CRITTERS,
   RESTRICT, STRICTER
CEIRRSTU CRUSTIER,
   RECRUITS
CEIRSSTU CITRUSES,
   CURTSIES
CEIRSTUY SECURITY
CEJLOOSY JOCOSELY
CEJNORRU CONJURER
CEJNRTUU JUNCTURE

CEJOPRST PROJECTS
CEKKLNSU KNUCKLES
CEKKNORS KNOCKERS
CEKKNTUY KENTUCKY
CEKLLSSU LUCKLESS
CEKLNOOP POLO NECK
CEKMNOST STOCKMEN
CEKNOORV CONVOKER
CEKNOPST PENSTOCK
CEKOOORV OVERCOOK
CEKOORRS ROCKROSE
CEKOORRW CO-WORKER
CEKOPRST SPROCKET
CEKORRTY ROCKETRY
CEKRRSTU TRUCKERS
CEKRSSUU RUCKUSES
CELLNOOS COLONELS
CELLNSUU NUCELLUS
CELLRSSU SCULLERS
CELLRSUY SCULLERY
CELMNOOS MONOCLES
CELMNOTU UNCLE TOM
CELMPRTU PLECTRUM
CELMPSUU SPECULUM
CELNOORS CONSOLER
CELNOOSS CONSOLES,
   COOLNESS
CELNOPUU UNCOUPLE
CELNORWY CLOWNERY
CELNOSUV CONVULSE
CELNOSVY SOLVENCY
CELNOVXY CONVEXLY
CELOOPSS CESSPOOL
CELOPSSU CLOSE-UPS
CELOPSTU COUPLETS
CELORSST CROSSLET
CELORSSU CLOSURES,
   SCLEROUS
CELORSUU ULCEROUS
CELORTVY COVERTLY
CELOSTTU CULOTTES
CELPRSSU SCRUPLES
CELPRSUY SPRUCELY
CELRSSTU CLUSTERS
CELRSTUU CULTURES
CELRSTUV CULVERTS
CELRSTUY CLUSTERY
CELSSTTU SCUTTLES
CEMMNOOR COMMONER
CEMMNOOS CONSOMMÉ
CEMMNOST COMMENTS
CEMMNOSU COMMUNES
CEMMORTU COMMUTER

CEMNOOTY MONOCYTE	CEPPRTUU UPPERCUT	CGHILNNU LUNCHING
CEMNOPTT CONTEMPT	CEPRSTUU CUTPURSE	CGHILNNY LYNCHING
CEMNORSU CONSUMER	CEPSSSTU SUSPECTS	CGHILNOT CLOTHING
CEMOOPRS COMPOSER	CERSSUUX EXCURSUS	CGHILNRU LURCHING
CEMOOPST COMPOTES	CFFGINOS SCOFFING	CGHIMMNU CHUMMING
CEMOOSTU OUTCOMES	CFFGINSU SCUFFING	CGHIMNNU MUNCHING
CEMOPRSS COMPRESS	CFFIKKOS KICKOFFS	CGHIMNOO MOOCHING
CEMOPRTU COMPUTER	CFFIKLNU CUFF LINK	CGHIMNOP CHOMPING
CEMORSTU CUSTOMER	CFFIRTUY FRUCTIFY	CGHIMPSY SPHYGMIC
CEMOSSTU COSTUMES	CFGHIILN FILCHING	CGHINNOS CHIGNONS
CEMPRSTU CRUMPETS,	CFGIIKLN FLICKING	CGHINNOT NOTCHING
SPECTRUM	CFGIKLNO FLOCKING	CGHINNPU PUNCHING
CEMRSSTU SET SCRUM	CFGIKNOR FROCKING	CGHINNRU CHURNING
CENNOOPR CORN PONE	CFGINOSU FOCUSING	CGHINOPP CHOPPING
CENNORTU NOCTURNE	CFHIINOO FINOCHIO	CGHINOTU TOUCHING
CENNOSTT CONTENTS	CFHIIORR HORRIFIC	CGHINOUV VOUCHING
CENNOSTV CONVENTS	CFHIKORS ROCKFISH	CGHINPSY PSYCHING
CENOORRS CORONERS,	CFIIILSY SILICIFY	CGHINRSU CRUSHING
CROONERS	CFIILMNU FULMINIC	CGHINSTY SCYTHING
CENOORST CORONETS	CFIILOPR PROLIFIC	CGHNOOSU SOUCHONG
CENOORSU CORNEOUS	CFIINORT FRICTION	CGIIILNT LIGNITIC
CENOORVY CONVEYOR	CFIINOST FICTIONS	CGIIINNS INCISING
CENOQSTU CONQUEST	CFIKLSTU STICKFUL	CGIIINNT INCITING
CENORSTU CONSTRUE,	CFIMNORU UNCIFORM	CGIIKLNN CLINKING
COUNTERS, RECOUNTS	CFINNOTU FUNCTION	CGIIKLNP PICKLING
CENORSTV CONVERTS	CFKKLOOR FOLK-ROCK	CGIIKLNS LICKINGS,
CENORSUU CERNUOUS,	CFLMRSUU FULCRUMS	SLICKING
COENURUS	CFLNORSU SCORNFUL	CGIIKLNT TICKLING
CENORSUY CYNOSURE	CFMOORST COMFORTS	CGIIKMMS GIMMICKS
CENORTUY COURTNEY	CFNNOORT CONFRONT	CGIIKMMY GIMMICKY
CENORTVY COVENTRY	CFOOORTW CROWFOOT	CGIIKNNS SNICKING
CENOSSTT CONTESTS	CFOOPSTY SOFT COPY	CGIIKNPR PRICKING
CENOSSTU COUNTESS	CFRSTUUU USUFRUCT	CGIIKNPS PICKINGS
CENOSTTX CONTEXTS	CGGGHINU CHUGGING	CGIIKNRT TRICKING
CENPRTUU PUNCTURE	CGGGILNO CLOGGING	CGIIKNST STICKING
CENRRSTU CURRENTS	CGGHINOU COUGHING	CGIIKPST PIGSTICK
CENRSSTU CURTNESS	CGGIILNN CLINGING	CGIILMOS LOGICISM
CEOOOPST OTOSCOPE	CGGIINNR CRINGING	CGIILNOP POLICING
CEOOPRRV OVERCROP	CGHHIINT HITCHING	CGIILNPP CLIPPING
CEOORSST SCOOTERS	CGHHINNU HUNCHING	CGIILNPS SPLICING
CEOOSTUV COVETOUS	CGHIIKNN CHINKING	CGIILNSU SLUICING
CEOPPRRS CROPPERS	CGHIILLN CHILLING	CGIILOST LOGISTIC
CEOPPRST PROSPECT	CGHIINNP PINCHING	CGIIMNNO INCOMING
CEOPRRRU PROCURER	CGHIINNW WINCHING	CGIIMNPR CRIMPING
CEOPRSTW SCREW TOP	CGHIINPP CHIPPING	CGIINNOT NOTICING
CEOPRSUU CUPREOUS	CGHIINPR CHIRPING	CGIINOOS ISOGONIC
CEOPRSUV COVER-UPS	CGHIINPT PITCHING	CGIINPRS CRISPING
CEOQRTUY COQUETRY	CGHIINTW WITCHING	CGIINRSU CRUISING
CEORRSSU SCOURERS	CGHIINVY CHIVYING	CGIKKNNO KNOCKING
CEORRSTY CORSETRY	CGHIJNNO CHONGJIN	CGIKLNOR ROCKLING
CEORSSST CROSSEST	CGHIKNOS SHOCKING	CGIKLNPU PLUCKING
CEORSTUY COURTESY	CGHIKNSU SHUCKING	CGIKLNSU SUCKLING
CEPPRSSU SCUPPERS	CGHILMNU MULCHING	CGIKMNOS SMOCKING

CGIKNOOR CROOKING	CHIILNNP LINCHPIN	CIIKLSTY STICKILY
CGIKNOST STOCKING	CHIILOPT HOPLITIC	CIIKNPPR PINPRICK
CGIKNRTU TRUCKING	CHIILOST HOLISTIC	CIIKNPST STICKPIN
CGILLNSU SCULLING	CHIILPRY CHIRPILY	CIILLMTU TILLICUM
CGILMNOO MONGOLIC	CHIILQSU CLIQUISH	CIILLNOP POLLINIC
CGILMNPU CLUMPING	CHIINORT ORNITHIC	CIILMNOT MILTONIC
CGILMNSU MUSCLING	CHIIORST HISTORIC,	CIILMOPY IMPOLICY
CGILMNTU MULCTING	ORCHITIS	CIILMRSY LYRICISM
CGILMNUU CINGULUM,	CHIIRSTT TRISTICH	CIILOOPT POLITICO
GLUCINUM	CHIKLLOS HILLOCKS	CIILOPST COLPITIS,
CGILMOOY MYOLOGIC	CHIKMNPU CHIPMUNK	POLITICS
CGILNNOW CLOWNING	CHIKOPTY KYPHOTIC	CIILORST CLITORIS
CGILNOPP CLOPPING	CHILLOOT OILCLOTH	CIILRSTY LYRICIST
CGILNOPU COUPLING	CHILMMUY CHUMMILY	CIIMNOST MONISTIC,
CGILNOSW COWLINGS,	CHILMOSU SCHOLIUM	NOMISTIC
SCOWLING	CHILMPSU CLUMPISH	CIIMORST TRISOMIC
CGILNOTT CLOTTING	CHILNOSW CLOWNISH	CIIMOSST STOICISM
CGILNOTU CLOUTING	CHILOOOZ HOLOZOIC	CIIMRTTU TRITICUM
CGILOORU UROLOGIC	CHILOPPY CHOPPILY	CIINNSTT INSTINCT
CGILPSTY GLYPTICS	CHILOTUY TOUCHILY	CIINOOST ISOTONIC
CGIMNNOO GNOMONIC,	CHIMMORU CHROMIUM	CIINOPSU OPINICUS
ONCOMING	CHIMNOSU INSOMUCH	CIINORSS INCISORS
CGIMNOPU UPCOMING	CHIMNOSY CHYMOSIN	CIINOSSS SCISSION
CGINNOOR CROONING	CHINOPTY HYPNOTIC,	CIINOTTY TONICITY
CGINNOPU POUNCING	PYTHONIC, TYPHONIC	CIINPSTU SINCIPUT
CGINNORS SCORNING	CHINOSSU CUSHIONS	CIIOOPST ISOTOPIC
CGINNORW CROWNING	CHINOSTZ SCHIZONT	CIIOQTUX QUIXOTIC
CGINNOTU COUNTING	CHINOSUY CUSHIONY	CIIOTTXY TOXICITY
CGINOOPS SCOOPING	CHIOOPPT PHOTOPIC	CIIPRRTU PRURITIC
CGINOOPT COOPTING	CHIOOPTY OOPHYTIC	CIIPRSTU PURISTIC
CGINOOST SCOOTING	CHIOPRST STROPHIC	CIIRSTTU TRUISTIC
CGINOPPR CROPPING	CHIOSSTT SCOTTISH	CIISSTTY CYSTITIS
CGINORSS CROSSING	CHIPRRUY CHIRRUPY	CIJKOSTY JOYSTICK
CGINORSU COURSING,	CHIPRTTY TRIPTYCH	CIJNNOOT CONJOINT
SCOURING	CHIRRSSU SCIRRHUS	CIJNNOTU JUNCTION
CGINORTU COURTING	CHKMMOSU HUMMOCKS	CIJOOSTY JOCOSITY
CGINOSTU SCOUTING	CHKMMOUY HUMMOCKY	CIKLLOPS PILLOCKS
CGINPRSU SPRUCING	CHLNOOOP COLOPHON	CIKLLPUY PLUCKILY
CGINRRUY CURRYING	CHLOORSU CHLOROUS	CIKLNOST LINSTOCK
CGINSTTU CUTTINGS,	CHMNORRU CRUMHORN	CIKLOSTY STOCKILY
TUNGSTIC	CHMOORSU CHROMOUS	CIKMOORS SICKROOM
CGINSTUU TUNGUSIC	CHNOOPTT TOP-NOTCH	CIKNNOOS COONSKIN
CGKNOSTU GUNSTOCK	CHNPPSUU PUNCH-UPS	CIKNNOST NONSTICK
CGLMOOYY MYCOLOGY	CHORSTTU SHORT CUT	CIKOSSTT STOCKIST
CGLNOOOY ONCOLOGY	CIIILMPT IMPLICIT	CIKPSSTU STICK-UPS
CGLOOOTY TOCOLOGY	CIIILTVY CIVILITY	CILLMSUY CLUMSILY
CGLOOTYY CYTOLOGY	CIIINNOS INCISION	CILLNOSU SCULLION
CHHIIPST PHTHISIC	CIIINNOT COIN IT IN	CILLOOOT OCOTILLO
CHHILRSU CHURLISH	CIIINTVY VICINITY	CILMNOPU PULMONIC
CHHIMRTY RHYTHMIC	CIIJRSTU JURISTIC	CILMNOUU INOCULUM
CHHNORSU RHONCHUS	CIIKLLOS OIL SLICK	CILMNUUV VINCULUM
CHHOOPTT HOTCHPOT	CIIKLPST LIPSTICK	CILMPSUU SPICULUM
CHIIKLST TICKLISH	CIIKLRTY TRICKILY	CILNOOST COLONIST

CILNOOTU LOCUTION
CILNOPTU PLUTONIC
CILNOSTU LINOCUTS
CILOOPST COPILOTS
CILOOPYZ POLYZOIC
CILOPRRY PYRROLIC
CILOPRUY POLYURIC
CILOPSSW COWSLIPS
CILOSSTU OCULISTS
CILOSSTY SYSTOLIC
CILOSSUU LUSCIOUS
CILPRSTU CULPRITS
CILPSSTU SCULPSIT
CILRSTTY STRICTLY
CILRSTUY CRUSTILY
CILRSUVY SCURVILY
CIMNOOTY MYOTONIC
CIMNORSS CRIMSONS
CIMNOSTU MISCOUNT
CIMNOSUU MUCINOUS
CIMNOSUY SYCONIUM
CIMOOOTZ ZOOTOMIC
CIMOSTUU MUTICOUS
CIMOSTUY MUCOSITY
CINNOOTU CONTINUO
CINNOOTX NONTOXIC
CINNOOVY IN CONVOY
CINNORSU UNICORNS
CINNOSTY SYNTONIC
CINNQUUX QUINCUNX
CINOOOPT COOPTION
CINOOPRS SCORPION
CINOOTXY OXYTOCIN
CINOPSTY SYNOPTIC
CINOSTUV VISCOUNT
CINRSTTU INSTRUCT
CINRSTUY SCRUTINY
CIOOOPRS OOSPORIC
CIOOOTXZ ZOOTOXIC
CIOOPRSS SCORPIOS
CIOOPRST PORTICOS
CIOPRSSU SCORPIUS
CIOPSSTY COPYISTS
CIORSSSS SCISSORS
CIOTTTUU CUT IT OUT
CIPRRUVY PYRRUVIC
CIPSSTTY STYPTICS
CKKNOOTU KNOCKOUT
CKKNOPSU KNOCK-UPS
CKLOORSW ROWLOCKS
CKLOOSTU LOCKOUTS
CKLOPSTU POTLUCKS
CKMMORUW MUCKWORM

CKNOOSTT STOCKTON
CKOOOSTU COOKOUTS
CKOOPSTT STOCKPOT
CKOSSSTU TUSSOCKS
CKOSSTUY TUSSOCKY
CLLMOSSU MOLLUSCS
CLLOOPSS SCOLLOPS
CLLOOQUY COLLOQUY
CLLOSUUY CULOUSLY
CLMMNOOY COMMONLY
CLMOOOTY COLOTOMY
CLMOSUUU CUMULOUS
CLNOORST CONTROLS
CLOOOPRT PROTOCOL
CLOOSSSU COLOSSUS
CLOPRSSY CROSSPLY
CLOPRSTU SCULPTOR
CLOPSSTU COST-PLUS
CMMNNOOU UNCOMMON
CMORSSTU SCROTUMS
CNOOOORT OCTOROON
CNOORRTY CRYOTRON
CNOORSST CONSORTS
CNOORSTU CONTOURS,
    CROUTONS
CNOSTUUU UNCTUOUS
COOOOPRRT ROOT CROP
COOPRRST PROCTORS
COOPRSTU OUTCROPS
COOPRSUU CROUPOUS
COOPRSUY UROSCOPY
COORSSTU OUTCROSS
DDDDEEOR DODDERED
DDDEEEFN DEFENDED
DDDEEENP DEPENDED
DDDEEENR REDDENED
DDDEEHRS SHREDDED
DDDEEJRU JUDDERED
DDDEEORR DODDERER
DDDEIINV DIVIDEND
DDDEILNW DWINDLED
DDDEILTW TWIDDLED
DDDEINOR DENDROID
DDDGIILN DIDDLING
DDEEEEMR REDEEMED
DDEEEENP DEEPENED
DDEEEFLX DEFLEXED
DDEEEFNR DEFENDER,
    FENDERED
DDEEEFRR DEFERRED
DDEEEHLW WHEEDLED
DDEEEIMR REMEDIED
DDEEEIWY WIDE-EYED

DDEEEELPT DEPLETED
DDEEEEMNT DEMENTED
DDEEENPX EXPENDED
DDEEENRR RENDERED
DDEEENRT TENDERED
DDEEENSU UNSEEDED
DDEEENTX EXTENDED
DDEEERRT DETERRED
DDEEERST DESERTED
DDEEERSV DESERVED
DDEEESTT DETESTED
DDEEEWYY DEWY-EYED
DDEEFFIR DIFFERED
DDEEFFNO OFFENDED
DDEEFGIT FIDGETED
DDEEFLNO ENFOLDED
DDEEFMOR DEFORMED
DDEEFNRU REFUNDED
DDEEGINS DESIGNED
DDEEGIRV DIVERGED
DDEEGIST DIGESTED
DDEEGOPS GODSPEED
DDEEGOTW TWO-EDGED
DDEEGRRS DREDGERS
DDEEHILS SHIELDED
DDEEHINR HINDERED
DDEEHIRT DITHERED
DDEEHRRS SHREDDER
DDEEIINT INEDITED
DDEEILLV DEVILLED
DDEEILMW MILDEWED
DDEEILRV DRIVELED
DDEEILWY WILD-EYED
DDEEIMNR REMINDED
DDEEIMSS MISDEEDS
DDEEIMST DEMISTED
DDEEINNT INDENTED,
    INTENDED
DDEEINOS ONE-SIDED
DDEEINRT DENDRITE
DDEEINST DESTINED
DDEEIPRS PRESIDED
DDEEIPRV DEPRIVED
DDEEIPSS DESPISED
DDEEIRTV DIVERTED
DDEEISST DESISTED
DDEEISTV DIVESTED
DDEELLMO MODELLED
DDEELLOP DEED POLL
DDEELLOY YODELLED
DDEELMOR MOLDERED
DDEELMRS MEDDLERS
DDEELOPR DEPLORED

DDEELOPX EXPLODED	DDEHIORS SHODDIER	DDEOPRSW DEWDROPS
DDEELOPY DEPLOYED	DDEHNRSU HUNDREDS	DDFGIILN FIDDLING
DDEELORS SOLDERED	DDEHOOSW WOODSHED	DDFGILNU FUDDLING
DDEELOSU DELOUSED	DDEHORSU SHROUDED	DDGGINNO DINGDONG
DDEELOVV DEVOLVED	DDEHRSSU SHUDDERS	DDGGINRU DRUDGING
DDEELPRS PEDDLERS	DDEHRSUY SHUDDERY	DDGHILNU HUDDLING
DDEEMNOR ENDODERM	DDEIIKLS DISLIKED	DDGHINTU THUDDING
DDEEMRRU DEMURRED,	DDEIILNR DIELDRIN	DDGIIINO INDIGOID
MURDERED	DDEIILOS IDOLISED	DDGIIINV DIVIDING
DDEENOPR PONDERED	DDEIILOZ IDOLIZED	DDGIIKNS SKIDDING
DDEENOPW PONDWEED	DDEIIOPS DIOPSIDE	DDGIILMN MIDDLING
DDEENORS ENDORSED	DDEIIOST ODDITIES	DDGIILNP PIDDLING
DDEENORW WONDERED	DDEIIOSX DIOXIDES,	DDGIILNR RIDDLING
DDEENRSU SUNDERED	OXIDISED	DDGILMNU MUDDLING
DDEEOPRT DEPORTED	DDEIIOXZ OXIDIZED	DDGILNOO DOODLING
DDEEOPRW POWDERED	DDEIIRSV DIVIDERS	DDGILNOP PLODDING
DDEEORRW REWORDED	DDEIIRUV REDUVIID	DDGILNOT TODDLING
DDEEORUV DEVOURED	DDEIKNRS KINDREDS	DDGILNPU PUDDLING
DDEERTUX EXTRUDED	DDEILMOP IMPLODED	DDGIMNUY MUDDYING
DDEFFISU DIFFUSED	DDEILNPS SPLENDID	DDGINOPR PRODDING
DDEFIILM MIDFIELD	DDEILNRU UNRIDDLE	DDGINPSU PUDDINGS
DDEFIIMO MODIFIED	DDEILNSW SWINDLED	DDGINSTU STUDDING
DDEFLNOU UNFOLDED	DDEILOPS LOP-SIDED	DDGLOSTU GOLD DUST
DDEGGINR DREDGING	DDEILRST TIDDLERS	DDGOOORW GOOD WORD
DDEGGLOY DOGGEDLY	DDEILRTW TWIDDLER	DDGOOOSW DOGWOODS
DDEGGNOO DOGGONED	DDEILRZZ DRIZZLED	DDGOORSY DRY GOODS
DDEGHINS SHEDDING	DDEILSTU LUDDITES	DDHILOSY SHODDILY
DDEGIINR DERIDING	DDEILSTW TWIDDLES	DDIIIIVV DIVI-DIVI
DDEGIIST GIDDIEST	DDEIMOSU MEDUSOID	DDIIMMUY DIDYMIUM
DDEGILMN MEDDLING	DDEIMSTU MUDDIEST	DDIIMRSU DRUIDISM
DDEGILNP PEDDLING	DDEINORS INDORSED	DDIIQTUY QUIDDITY
DDEGILNS SLEDDING	DDEINOSW DISENDOW,	DDILOOPP DIPLOPOD
DDEGILNU DELUDING,	DISOWNED	DDILORSY SORDIDLY
INDULGED	DDEINRST STRIDDEN	DDIMOSUY DIDYMOUS
DDEGILOS DISLODGE	DDEINRTU INTRUDED	DDINNOWW DOWNWIND
DDEGILRS GRIDDLES	DDEIOPRS DROPSIED	DDINOOOT ODONTOID
DDEGILUV DIVULGED	DDEIOPRV PROVIDED	DDINOOWW WOODWIND
DDEGIMOS DEMIGODS	DDEIOPSS DISPOSED	DDLLOORW OLD WORLD
DDEGINNU DENUDING	DDEIORRS DISORDER	DDLMORSU DOLDRUMS
DDEGINSW WEDDINGS	DDEIOSTW DOWDIEST,	DDMNORTU DORTMUND
DDEGIORT DOG-TIRED	TWO-SIDED	DEEEEFRR REFEREED
DDEGIOST DODGIEST	DDEIPSTU DISPUTED	DEEEEGKR KEDGEREE
DDEGIOSV GIVE ODDS	DDEIRSTU RUDDIEST	DEEEEKNP KNEE-DEEP
DDEGNOOR DORDOGNE	DDEKMOSU DUKEDOMS	DEEEEMRR REDEEMER
DDEGNORU GROUNDED,	DDELNRTU TRUNDLED	DEEEEMST ESTEEMED
UNDERDOG	DDELNSUY SUDDENLY	DEEEENPR DEEPENER
DDEGNOSS GODSENDS	DDELOPRS PLODDERS	DEEEENRV VENEERED
DDEGOOOR DO-GOODER	DDELORST TODDLERS	DEEEERTT TEETERED
DDEGOOWW WEDGWOOD	DDEMNOST ODDMENTS	DEEEFIIX IDEE FIXE
DDEGRRUY DRUDGERY	DDEMNOUU DUODENUM	DEEEFIRW FIREWEED
DDEHIISS SIDE DISH	DDEMNPUU PUDENDUM	DEEEFLRU REFUELED
DDEHILNY HIDDENLY	DDEMOOTU OUTMODED	DEEEFNRT DEFERENT
DDEHINOR DIHEDRON	DDEOORSW REDWOODS	

DEEEFRRR DEFERRER, REFERRED
DEEEFRRT FERRETED
DEEEFRST FESTERED
DEEEFRTT FETTERED
DEEEGIPR PEDIGREE
DEEEGIRR GREEDIER
DEEEGNNR ENGENDER
DEEEGNRV REVENGED
DEEEHLMT HELMETED
DEEEHLRT ETHELRED
DEEEHLRW WHEEDLER
DEEEHLSS HEEDLESS
DEEEHMNS ENMESHED
DEEEHRTT TETHERED
DEEEILRV RELIEVED
DEEEILST LEE TIDES
DEEEIMRS REMEDIES
DEEEINRR REINDEER
DEEEINST NEEDIEST
DEEEINTV EVENTIDE
DEEEIPRS SPEEDIER
DEEEIPTX EXPEDITE
DEEEIRSS DIERESES
DEEEIRST REEDIEST
DEEEIRVW REVIEWED
DEEEISST SEEDIEST, TEESSIDE
DEEEISTW WEEDIEST
DEEEJLLW JEWELLED
DEEEKLNN KENNELED
DEEEKNSW WEEKENDS
DEEEKOPW POKEWEED
DEEEKRSW SKEWERED
DEEELLLV LEVELLED
DEEELLPR REPELLED
DEEELLPX EXPELLED
DEEELLRV REVELLED
DEEELNRT RELENTED
DEEELNSS LESSENED, NEEDLESS
DEEELOSY SLOE-EYED
DEEELRTT LETTERED
DEEELSSS SEEDLESS
DEEEMNSS DEMESNES, SEEDSMEN
DEEEMPRT TEMPERED
DEEEMPTX EXEMPTED
DEEEMRST DEEMSTER
DEEENNRT ENTENDRE
DEEENOPR REOPENED
DEEENOPY OPEN-EYED
DEEENORS ENDORSEE

DEEENPRT REPENTED, REPETEND
DEEENPRX EXPENDER
DEEENPSS DEEPNESS
DEEENRRR RENDERER
DEEENRRT TENDERER
DEEENRRV REVEREND
DEEENRST RESENTED
DEEENRTU NEUTERED
DEEENRTX EXTENDER
DEEENRUV REVENUED
DEEENSTT DÉTENTES
DEEEOPRT DEPORTEE
DEEEOSTV DEVOTEES
DEEEPPPR PEPPERED
DEEEPRST PESTERED
DEEEQSUZ SQUEEZED
DEEERRST DESERTER
DEEERRSV DESERVER, RESERVED, REVERSED
DEEERRTV REVERTED
DEEERSTT DETESTER
DEEFFNOR OFFENDER
DEEFFRSU SUFFERED
DEEFGINR FINGERED
DEEFGLNU ENGULFED
DEEFGLUW GULFWEED
DEEFHLOR FREEHOLD
DEEFHORR HEREFORD
DEEFIINT DEFINITE
DEEFIIRS FIRESIDE
DEEFIIRV VERIFIED
DEEFILLR REFILLED
DEEFILLT FILLETED
DEEFILNX INFLEXED
DEEFILPR PILFERED
DEEFILRS DEFILERS, FIELDERS
DEEFILRT FILTERED
DEEFINRR INFERRED
DEEFINRW WINEFRED
DEEFINRZ FRENZIED
DEEFINST INFESTED
DEEFIORS FORESIDE
DEEFIPRX PREFIXED
DEEFIRTT REFITTED
DEEFLNNU FUNNELED
DEEFLNOR ENFOLDER
DEEFLORW DEFLOWER, FLOWERED
DEEFMNOT FOMENTED
DEEFMORR DEFORMER, REFORMED

DEEFMPRU PERFUMED
DEEFNOST SOFTENED
DEEFNRRU REFUNDER
DEEFNSST DEFTNESS
DEEFORST DEFOREST, FORESTED, FOSTERED
DEEFORUY FOUR-EYED
DEEFRTUY DUTY-FREE
DEEGGHHO HEDGEHOG
DEEGGIJR JIGGERED, REJIGGED
DEEGGINR GINGERED
DEEGGLOR DOGGEREL
DEEGHHOP HEDGEHOP
DEEGHITW WEIGHTED
DEEGHNRU HUNGERED
DEEGHOPS SHEEPDOG
DEEGHORW HEDGEROW
DEEGIINN INDIGENE
DEEGILNN NEEDLING
DEEGILNP IN PLEDGE
DEEGILNR LINGERED, REEDLING
DEEGILNS SEEDLING
DEEGILNT DELETING
DEEGILRY GREEDILY
DEEGILSS LEG SIDES
DEEGIMNN EMENDING
DEEGINPS SPEEDING
DEEGINRS DESIGNER, REDESIGN, RESIGNED
DEEGINSS EDGINESS
DEEGINST INGESTED
DEEGIORS GEORDIES
DEEGIRST DIGESTER
DEEGJPRU PREJUDGE
DEEGLNRY LEGENDRY
DEEGLORV GROVELED
DEEGLORW GLOWERED
DEEGNNOY ENDOGENY
DEEGNORV GOVERNED
DEEGNPUX EXPUNGED
DEEGOTUW GOUTWEED
DEEGRRTU GERTRUDE
DEEGRSTU GESTURED
DEEGRTTU GUTTERED
DEEHHPRS SHEPHERD
DEEHHRST THRESHED
DEEHIKRS SHRIEKED
DEEHILNP DELPHINE
DEEHILRS RELISHED, SHIELDER
DEEHILSS HIDELESS

DEEHILSV DISHEVEL
DEEHIMOP HEMIPODE
DEEHIMRT MEREDITH
DEEHINRR HINDERER
DEEHINTW WHITENED
DEEHIOTX ETHOXIDE
DEEHIPPS SHEEPDIP
DEEHIPRS PERISHED
DEEHIRRT DITHERER
DEEHIRSV SHIVERED
DEEHIRTW WITHERED
DEEHIRTY HEREDITY
DEEHKNOS KEESHOND
DEEHLLOR HOLLERED
DEEHLOSV SHOVELED
DEEHMNRS HERDSMEN
DEEHMORT MOTHERED
DEEHNORT DETHRONE
DEEHNOWY HONEYDEW
DEEHNSTU ENTHUSED
DEEHOORT THEODORE
DEEHOORV HOOVERED
DEEHORSU REHOUSED
DEEHORSW SHOWERED
DEEHORTX EXHORTED
DEEHRRSW SHREWDER
DEEIILNS SIDELINE
DEEIILRV LIVERIED
DEEIIMST ITEMISED
DEEIIMTZ ITEMIZED
DEEIIPRU PRIE-DIEU
DEEIIRSS DIERESIS
DEEIIRST SIDERITE
DEEIIRSV DERISIVE
DEEIISSS DISSEISE
DEEIJNNO ENJOINED
DEEIJNOR REJOINED
DEEIKLLR KILLDEER
DEEIKLMO DOMELIKE
DEEIKLMW MILKWEED
DEEIKLNN ENKINDLE
DEEIKLNR REKINDLE
DEEIKNPS SKIN-DEEP
DEEIKNRS DEERSKIN
DEEIKNRT TINKERED
DEEIKSTT DISKETTE
DEEILLMN MEDELLIN
DEEILLMP IMPELLED
DEEILLST LET SLIDE
DEEILLVY VEILEDLY
DEEILMNU DEMILUNE
DEEILMOS MELODIES,
    MELODISE

DEEILMOZ MELODIZE
DEEILNOT DELETION
DEEILNRU UNDERLIE
DEEILNSS IDLENESS
DEEILNST ENLISTED,
    LISTENED
DEEILNSV SNIVELED
DEEILNTT ENTITLED
DEEILNUV UNVEILED
DEEILOPT LEPIDOTE
DEEILORT DOLERITE,
    LOITERED
DEEILORV EVILDOER
DEEILPRX DIPLEXER
DEEILPSY SPEEDILY
DEEILRSU LEISURED
DEEILRSV SILVERED
DEEILRSW WIELDERS
DEEILRTT LITTERED
DEEILRVY DELIVERY
DEEILSUV DELUSIVE
DEEILSVW SWIVELED
DEEILTUY YULETIDE
DEEIMMNS ENDEMISM
DEEIMMOS SEMIDOME
DEEIMMRS IMMERSED,
    SIMMERED
DEEIMNOR DOMINEER
DEEIMNOS DEMONISE
DEEIMNOZ DEMONIZE
DEEIMNPT PEDIMENT
DEEIMNRR REMINDER
DEEIMNST SEDIMENT
DEEIMNSY MIND'S EYE
DEEIMPRR PERIDERM
DEEIMPRS SIMPERED
DEEIMRST DEMERITS,
    DEMISTER
DEEIMRTT REMITTED
DEEINNRT INDENTER,
    INTENDER, INTERNED
DEEINNSS DENISENS
DEEINNST DESINENT
DEEINNSZ DENIZENS
DEEINNTV INVENTED
DEEINNTW ENTWINED
DEEINOPW WIDE-OPEN
DEEINOSV NOSEDIVE
DEEINPSS DISPENSE
DEEINQRU ENQUIRED
DEEINQSU SEQUINED
DEEINRRT INTERRED,
    TRENDIER

DEEINRRW REWINDER
DEEINRST DNIESTER,
    INSERTED, RESIDENT,
    TRENDIES
DEEINRSX INDEXERS
DEEINRTU RETINUED,
    REUNITED
DEEINRTV INVERTED
DEEINRTW WINTERED
DEEINSSW DEWINESS,
    WIDENESS
DEEINSTT INSETTED
DEEINSTV INVESTED
DEEINSTY TYNESIDE
DEEIOPRX PEROXIDE
DEEIOPSS EPISODES
DEEIORRV OVERRIDE
DEEIORSV OVERSIDE
DEEIPPQU EQUIPPED
DEEIPRRS PRESIDER,
    RESPIRED
DEEIPRRV DEPRIVER
DEEIPRSS DISPERSE
DEEIPSST SIDESTEP
DEEIPSTU DEPUTIES,
    DEPUTISE
DEEIPTUZ DEPUTIZE
DEEIQRRU REQUIRED
DEEIQRTU REQUITED
DEEIQRUV QUIVERED
DEEIQTUU QUIETUDE
DEEIRRSS DRESSIER
DEEIRRTV DIVERTER
DEEIRSST RESISTED
DEEIRSSU REISSUED,
    RESIDUES
DEEIRSSV DISSEVER
DEEIRSTW WEIRDEST
DEEIRTTT TITTERED
DEEJPRRU PERJURED
DEEKMNOY MONKEYED
DEEKNOTW KNOTWEED
DEEKORRW REWORKED
DEELLMOR MODELLER
DEELLMOW MELLOWED
DEELLNOR ENROLLED
DEELLNOW WELL-DONE
DEELLORY YODELLER
DEELLOTW TOWELLED
DEELLOTX EXTOLLED
DEELLOVY VOLLEYED
DEELLOWY YELLOWED
DEELMMPU PUMMELED

DEELMNOO MELODEON
DEELMOPY EMPLOYED
DEELMOST MOLESTED
DEELMRUY DEMURELY
DEELNNTU TUNNELED
DEELNOOS LOOSE END,
  LOOSENED
DEELNORT REDOLENT,
  RONDELET
DEELNRTU UNDERLET
DEELNRTY TENDERLY
DEELNSSW LEWDNESS
DEELNWWY NEWLYWED
DEELOPRR DEPLORER
DEELOPRX EXPLODER,
  EXPLORED
DEELOPRY REDEPLOY
DEELORRS SOLDERER
DEELORSV RESOLVED
DEELORTT DOTTEREL
DEELORTV REVOLTED
DEELORVV REVOLVED
DEELPRRU PRELUDER
DEELPRSU PRELUDES,
  REPULSED
DEELPRTU DRUPELET
DEELPSUX DUPLEXES
DEELRSTU RESULTED
DEELRSTW WRESTLED
DEEMMORS MESODERM
DEEMMRSU SUMMERED
DEEMNOOS ENDOSOME,
  MOONSEED
DEEMNOQU QUEENDOM
DEEMNORT ENTODERM
DEEMOORT ODOMETER
DEEMORSW WORMSEED
DEEMPRST DEMPSTER
DEEMPRSU PRESUMED
DEEMPRTU PERMUTED
DEEMRRRU DEMURRER,
  MURDERER
DEEMRSTU DEMUREST,
  MUSTERED
DEEMRTTU MUTTERED
DEENNOPT DEPONENT
DEENNOPU UNOPENED
DEENNORW RENOWNED
DEENNRUV UNNERVED
DEENNSSU NUDENESS
DEENOORV OVERDONE
DEENOPRR PONDERER
DEENOPSS SPONDEES

DEENORRS ENDORSER
DEENORRW WONDERER
DEENORSW WORSENED
DEENORTU DEUTERON
DEENPRSS SPENDERS
DEENPSTU TENSED UP
DEENRRTU RETURNED
DEENRSSU END USERS,
  RUDENESS
DEENRSTU DENTURES,
  UNDERSET
DEENRSUV UNVERSED
DEENRTUV VENTURED
DEEOOORRV OVERRODE
DEEOOORSV OVERDOSE
DEEOPRRT REPORTED
DEEOPRRV REPROVED
DEEOPRRW POWDERER
DEEOPRTT POTTERED
DEEOPRTX EXPORTED
DEEOPSSU ESPOUSED
DEEORRST RESORTED,
  RESTORED
DEEORRTT RETORTED
DEEORRUV DEVOURER
DEEORRVW OVERDREW
DEEORSTX DEXTROSE
DEEORSTY STOREYED
DEEORTTT TOTTERED
DEEORTTX EXTORTED
DEEORTUV DEVOUTER
DEEPRTTU PUTTERED
DEEPRUVY PURVEYED
DEERRSSS DRESSERS
DEERRTTU TURRETED
DEERSSST DESSERTS,
  STRESSED
DEERSUVY SURVEYED
DEFFGILO OFF-GLIDE
DEFFHLSU SHUFFLED
DEFFILNS SNIFFLED
DEFFILOV FIVEFOLD
DEFFIRSU DIFFUSER
DEFFLNSU SNUFFLED
DEFFNOSS SEND-OFFS
DEFFSSUU SUFFUSED
DEFFSTUY DYESTUFF
DEFGIILN DEFILING,
  FIELDING
DEFGIINN DEFINING
DEFGIINY DEIFYING,
  EDIFYING
DEFGIIST DIGESTIF

DEFGINSU DEFUSING
DEFGIORS FIREDOGS
DEFGJORU FORJUDGE
DEFGLOOS GOOD SELF
DEFHIINS FIENDISH,
  FINISHED
DEFHLOOS SELFHOOD
DEFHORRT HERTFORD
DEFIIILV VILIFIED
DEFIILLO OILFIELD
DEFIILLW WILDLIFE
DEFIILNS INFIDELS
DEFIILOR OIL-FIRED
DEFIILPS FLIP SIDE
DEFIILRW WILDFIRE
DEFIILSU FLUIDISE
DEFIILTY FIDELITY
DEFIILUZ FLUIDIZE
DEFIIMOR MODIFIER
DEFIIMRS MISFIRED
DEFIINOT NOTIFIED
DEFIINRW WINIFRED
DEFIINTY IDENTIFY
DEFIIOSS OSSIFIED
DEFIIPRU PURIFIED
DEFIIPSS FISSIPED
DEFIIPTY TYPIFIED
DEFILNNO NINEFOLD
DEFILNRU UNRIFLED,
  URNFIELD
DEFILNRY FRIENDLY
DEFILOPR PROFILED
DEFILORU FLUORIDE
DEFILOTU OUTFIELD
DEFILPRU PRIDEFUL
DEFILPTU UPLIFTED
DEFILRRU FLURRIED
DEFILRVY FERVIDLY
DEFILRZZ FRIZZLED
DEFIMNOR INFORMED
DEFIMOPR PEDIFORM
DEFIMRRU DRUMFIRE
DEFINORW FOREWIND
DEFIOORW FIREWOOD
DEFIOPRT PROFITED
DEFIRRST DRIFTERS
DEFLLOOW FOLLOWED
DEFLNORU FLOUNDER,
  UNFOLDER
DEFLNRUU UNFURLED
DEFLOORT FORETOLD
DEFMNORU UNFORMED
DEFMOOOR FOREDOOM

DEFNNOSS FONDNESS
DEFNOOPS SPOON-FED
DEFNORRU FRONDEUR
DEFNORSU FOUNDERS
DEFNRRUU UNDERFUR
DEFOORRW FOREWORD
DEFOOTUX OUTFOXED
DEFORRUW FURROWED
DEGGHRSU SHRUGGED
DEGGIINN DEIGNING
DEGGILNP PLEDGING
DEGGILNS GELDINGS,
   SLEDGING
DEGGILNU DELUGING
DEGGILOO LIE DOGGO
DEGGILRW WRIGGLED
DEGGIORS DISGORGE
DEGGLMSU SMUGGLED
DEGGLNSU SNUGGLED
DEGGLORY GORGEDLY
DEGGLRUY RUGGEDLY
DEGGRSTU DRUGGETS
DEGHHIIT HIGH TIDE
DEGHHILV HIGHVELD
DEGHIINS DINGHIES
DEGHIKNT KNIGHTED
DEGHILPT PLIGHTED
DEGHILRT RED LIGHT
DEGHILST DELIGHTS,
   SLIGHTED
DEGHINNU UNHINGED
DEGHLOPU PLOUGHED
DEGHLOSU SLOUGHED
DEGHNORT THRONGED
DEGHNORY HYDROGEN
DEGHOOSU DOGHOUSE
DEGIIIST DIGITISE
DEGIIITZ DIGITIZE
DEGIILNT DILIGENT
DEGIILNV DEVILING
DEGIILNW WIELDING
DEGIILNY YIELDING
DEGIILTY GELIDITY
DEGIIMNP IMPEDING,
   IMPINGED
DEGIIMSU MISGUIDE
DEGIINNT INDIGENT
DEGIINNW WIDENING
DEGIINNX INDEXING
DEGIINOV VIDEOING
DEGIINRS DESIRING,
   RESIDING, RINGSIDE
DEGIINRV DERIVING

DEGIINST DINGIEST
DEGIINSV DEVISING
DEGIINTY TIE-DYING
DEGIISSU DISGUISE
DEGIJMSU MISJUDGE
DEGIKLOV KID-GLOVE
DEGIKNRY RING-DYKE
DEGILLNU DUELLING
DEGILLNW DWELLING
DEGILMNO GOLDMINE,
   MODELING
DEGILMPS GLIMPSED
DEGILNOS SIDELONG
DEGILNOY YODELING
DEGILNRU INDULGER
DEGILOOR GOODLIER
DEGILOOY IDEOLOGY
DEGILOST GODLIEST
DEGILRSU GUILDERS,
   SLUDGIER
DEGILRUV DIVULGER
DEGILRZZ GRIZZLED
DEGIMNOT DEMOTING
DEGIMNPU IMPUGNED
DEGINNNU UNENDING
DEGINNOT DENOTING
DEGINNOW ENDOWING
DEGINNPS SPENDING
DEGINNPU UPENDING
DEGINNRU ENDURING
DEGINOPS DEPOSING
DEGINORR ORDERING
DEGINORV RINGDOVE
DEGINOSW WIDGEONS
DEGINOTV DEVOTING
DEGINPTU DEPUTING
DEGINRRS GRINDERS
DEGINRRY GRINDERY
DEGINRSS DRESSING
DEGINRSY SYRINGED
DEGIOPRR PORRIDGE
DEGIOPSS GOSSIPED
DEGIOPST PODGIEST
DEGIORST STODGIER
DEGIPSTU PUDGIEST
DEGJMNTU JUDGMENT
DEGLMNOT LODGMENT
DEGLOOPY PEDOLOGY
DEGLOOUU DUOLOGUE
DEGLOPSS SPLODGES
DEGLPRSU SPLURGED
DEGNNOSU DUNGEONS
DEGNOOSS GOODNESS

DEHHILTW WITHHELD
DEHIILLS HILLSIDE
DEHIILSV DEVILISH
DEHIIMST DITHEISM
DEHIINNS SHINNIED
DEHIINNW WHINNIED
DEHIISST DISHIEST
DEHIISTT DITHEIST
DEHIJMNO DEMIJOHN
DEHIKLOO HOODLIKE
DEHIKMOS SHEIKDOM
DEHILLRT THRILLED
DEHILMOS DEMOLISH
DEHILNOY HONIEDLY
DEHILNPY DIPHENYL
DEHILOPS POLISHED
DEHILOTY HOLYTIDE
DEHILPSU SULPHIDE
DEHILSTW WHISTLED
DEHILTTW WHITTLED
DEHIMNOS HEDONISM
DEHINOPS SIPHONED,
   SPHENOID
DEHINOST HEDONIST
DEHINPSU PUNISHED
DEHINSUW UNWISHED
DEHIOPRS SPHEROID
DEHIOSSW SIDESHOW
DEHIQSSU SQUISHED
DEHIRTWW WITHDREW
DEHKLNOU ELKHOUND
DEHLLOOW HOLLOWED
DEHLLOPY PHYLLODE
DEHLMORY HYDROMEL
DEHLNTUY HUNTEDLY
DEHLOORV HOLDOVER
DEHLOOSS HOODLESS
DEHLOOST TOEHOLDS
DEHLOPRU UPHOLDER
DEHLOPSS SPLOSHED
DEHLORSU SHOULDER
DEHLRRSU HURDLERS
DEHLRSWY SHREWDLY
DEHLSTTU SHUTTLED
DEHMMRTU THRUMMED
DEHMOORW WHOREDOM
DEHMOOST SMOOTHED
DEHMORUU HUMOURED
DEHNOORU HONOURED
DEHNOPSY SYPHONED
DEHNORSU ENSHROUD,
   UNHORSED
DEHNORTY THRENODY

DEHNOSSW SNOWSHED
DEHNRSTU THUNDERS
DEHNRTUY THUNDERY
DEHOOPRT THEROPOD
DEHOORTU OUT-HEROD
DEHOPRST POTSHERD
DEIIINSV DIVINISE
DEIIINVZ DIVINIZE
DEIIISVV DIVISIVE
DEIIKLNR KINDLIER
DEIIKLSS DISLIKES
DEIIKMOS ESKIMOID
DEIIKNST DINKIEST
DEIIKNSV SKIN-DIVE
DEIIKSVV SKIVVIED
DEIILLMT ILL-TIMED
DEIILMRU DELIRIUM
DEIILNNU INDULINE
DEIILNOS LIONISED
DEIILNOT TOLIDINE
DEIILNOZ LIONIZED
DEIILNVY DIVINELY
DEIILNXY XYLIDINE
DEIILORS IDOLISER
DEIILORZ IDOLIZER
DEIILPSS SIDESLIP
DEIILSTU UTILISED
DEIILTUZ UTILIZED
DEIIMMRS DIMERISM
DEIIMMST MISTIMED
DEIIMNRT DIRIMENT
DEIIMNTU MUTINIED
DEIIMPRU PERIDIUM
DEIIMSVW MIDWIVES
DEIINNOP PINIONED
DEIINNPP PINNIPED
DEIINORS DERISION,
   RESINOID
DEIINOST EDITIONS,
   SEDITION
DEIINPPW WINDPIPE
DEIINPRS INSPIRED
DEIINPRT INTREPID
DEIINPRY PYRIDINE
DEIINQRU INQUIRED
DEIINRSS INSIDERS
DEIINRST DISINTER
DEIINRSV DIVINERS,
   DRIVE-INS
DEIINSST INSISTED,
   TIDINESS
DEIINSTU DISUNITE
DEIINSTW WINDIEST

DEIINTTU INTUITED
DEIINTTY IDENTITY
DEIIOPRS PRESIDIO
DEIIORSX OXIDISER
DEIIORTX TRIOXIDE
DEIIORXZ OXIDIZER
DEIIPRST RIPTIDES,
   SPIRITED
DEIIPTTY TEPIDITY
DEIIQSTU DISQUIET
DEIIRSSU DIURESIS
DEIIRSTT DIRTIEST
DEIISTZZ DIZZIEST
DEIJORRY JOYRIDER
DEIJORSY JOYRIDES
DEIKKLNO KLONDIKE
DEIKLNRW WRINKLED
DEIKLNTW TWINKLED
DEIKMNOO KIMONOED
DEIKNNRU UNKINDER
DEIKNNSS KINDNESS
DEIKNRRS DRINKERS
DEIKNRSS REDSKINS
DEIKRSVY SKYDIVER
DEIKSSTU DUSKIEST
DEILLOPW PILLOWED
DEILLORR LORDLIER
DEILLSTU DUELLIST
DEILMNSS MILDNESS,
   MINDLESS
DEILMOOT DOLOMITE
DEILMOPR IMPLORED
DEILMORT OLD-TIMER
DEILMORU LEMUROID,
   MOULDIER
DEILMOST MELODIST,
   MOLDIEST
DEILMOSU EMULSOID
DEILMOTV DEMIVOLT
DEILMPTU MULTIPED
DEILNNOT INDOLENT
DEILNOOS SOLENOID
DEILNOSU DELUSION
DEILNOSW LIE-DOWNS
DEILNOTU OUTLINED
DEILNOVV INVOLVED
DEILNPSS SPINDLES
DEILNPST SPLIT END
DEILNRST TENDRILS
DEILNRSW SWINDLER
DEILNRTY TRENDILY
DEILNSSW SWINDLES,
   WILDNESS

DEILNSTU INSULTED,
   UNLISTED
DEILNTTU UNTITLED
DEILNTUY UNITEDLY
DEILNUWY UNWIELDY
DEILOOPW WOODPILE
DEILORSS SOLDIERS
DEILORSY SOLDIERY
DEILORTY ELYTROID
DEILOSSV DISSOLVE
DEILOSTU SOLITUDE
DEILOSTW LOW TIDES
DEILOTUV OUTLIVED
DEILPPST STIPPLED
DEILPPSU SUPPLIED
DEILPRSU SERPULID
DEILRRSV L-DRIVERS
DEILRSSY DRESSILY
DEILSSTY STYLISED
DEILSTUY SEDULITY
DEILSTWW WILD WEST
DEILSTYZ STYLIZED
DEIMMNOS DEMONISM
DEIMMOST IMMODEST
DEIMNOOS DOMINOES
DEIMNOOT DEMOTION,
   MOTIONED
DEIMNOOX MONOXIDE
DEIMNOPT PIEDMONT
DEIMNOST DEMONIST
DEIMNOTW DOWNTIME
DEIMNPSS MISSPEND
DEIMNPTU IMPUDENT
DEIMNRTU RUDIMENT
DEIMOOST MOODIEST,
   SODOMITE
DEIMOPRS PROMISED
DEIMOPRT IMPORTED
DEIMOPRV IMPROVED
DEIMORRR MIRRORED
DEIMORSU DIMEROUS,
   SOREDIUM
DEIMORUX EXORDIUM
DEIMOSTT DEMOTIST
DEIMOTTW TWO-TIMED
DEIMPSTU DUMPIEST
DEIMQRSU SQUIRMED
DEIMRSSU SURMISED
DEIMRSUU RESIDUUM
DEINNNOU INNUENDO
DEINNOWW WINNOWED
DEINNPRU UNDERPIN
DEINNRSU IN SUNDER

DEINNRTV   TV DINNER
DEINNRUW   UNWINDER
DEINOOPS   POISONED
DEINOOPW   PINEWOOD
DEINOOTV   DEVOTION
DEINOPPW   DOWNPIPE
DEINOPRY   PYRENOID
DEINOPSS   DOPINESS
DEINORSU   SOURDINE
DEINORSW   DISOWNER
DEINORVW   OVERWIND
DEINOSSZ   DOZINESS
DEINOSTW   DOWNIEST
DEINPPUZ   UNZIPPED
DEINPRST   SPRINTED
DEINPSST   STIPENDS
DEINPTTU   INPUTTED
DEINQSTU   SQUINTED
DEINRRTU   INTRUDER
DEINRSSU   SUNDRIES
DEINRSTT   STRIDENT,
    TRIDENTS
DEINSSST   DISSENTS
DEINSSSY   SYNDESIS
DEINSTUU   UNSUITED
DEIOORTV   OVERDO IT
DEIOOSTW   WOODIEST
DEIOPRRV   PROVIDER
DEIOPRSS   DISPOSER
DEIOPRST   RIPOSTED
DEIOPRSV   DISPROVE
DEIOPSST   DEPOSITS
DEIOPTUW   WIPED OUT
DEIORRSY   DERISORY
DEIORRTU   OUTRIDER
DEIORSSS   DOSSIERS
DEIORSST   STEROIDS
DEIORSSU   DESIROUS
DEIORSTU   OUTSIDER
DEIORSTW   ROWDIEST,
    WORDIEST
DEIORSWW   WIDOWERS
DEIOSSTU   OUTSIDES
DEIOSTTT   DOTTIEST
DEIPPRST   STRIPPED
DEIPRSTU   DISPUTER,
    STUPIDER
DEIPSSTU   DISPUTES
DEIQRSTU   SQUIRTED
DEIRRSTU   STURDIER
DEIRSSST   DISTRESS
DEIRSTTU   DETRITUS
DEIRSUVV   SURVIVED

DEISSTTU   DUSTIEST
DEISTTTU   DUETTIST
DEJMPPUU   JUMPED-UP
DEKKORSW   DESKWORK
DEKNRSTU   DRUNKEST
DEKOOPRV   PROVOKED
DEKOOTWW   KOWTOWED
DEKOPRUW   WORKED UP
DELLLOOP   LOLLOPED
DELLNOPU   UNPOLLED
DELLNORU   UNROLLED
DELLNSSU   DULLNESS
DELLOOTW   WELL-TO-DO
DELLOPTU   POLLUTED
DELLORRY   DROLLERY
DELLORST   DROLLEST,
    STROLLED
DELMNOOW   OLD WOMEN
DELMNOTW   MELTDOWN
DELMNPUU   PENDULUM
DELMORSU   REMOULDS,
    SMOULDER
DELMOSTY   MODESTLY
DELNNOOR   LONDONER
DELNOOSU   UNLOOSED
DELNOOWY   WOODENLY
DELNORSU   ROUNDELS
DELNORWW   NEW WORLD
DELNOSSU   LOUDNESS
DELNOSTW   LETDOWNS
DELOORRV   OVERLORD
DELOORSV   OVERSOLD
DELOPRST   DROPLETS
DELOPSTU   POSTLUDE
DELOPSTW   SPOT-WELD
DELORSST   OLDSTERS
DELORSSW   WORDLESS
DELORSUY   DELUSORY
DELOSSUU   SEDULOUS
DELOTUVY   DEVOUTLY
DELRSSTU   STRUDELS
DEMMNOSU   SUMMONED
DEMMRRSU   DRUMMERS
DEMMRRUU   MURMURED
DEMMRSTU   STRUMMED
DEMNNOOT   EDMONTON
DEMNOOSW   WOODSMEN
DEMNORSY   SYNDROME
DEMNOSTU   MUDSTONE
DEMOOPRR   PRODROME
DEMOOPRT   PROMOTED
DEMOORSU   DORMOUSE
DEMOPPRT   PROMPTED

DEMORRUU   RUMOURED
DENNOORW   NO WONDER
DENNOSTY   SYNDETON
DENNOTUW   UNWONTED
DENOOOTW   WOODNOTE
DENOORRS   ENDORSOR
DENOORTX   NEXT-DOOR
DENORRSU   ROUNDERS
DENORSSU   DOURNESS
DENORSTU   ROUNDEST
DENORSTY   DRY-STONE
DENORTUW   UNDERTOW
DENPRTUU   UPTURNED
DENRRTUU   NURTURED
DENSSTTU   STUDENTS
DEOOORSW   ROSEWOOD
DEOOPPRS   PROPOSED
DEOOPPRT   PTEROPOD
DEOOPRST   DOORSTEP
DEOOPRTU   UPROOTED
DEOORRSW   SORROWED
DEOOTTUV   OUTVOTED
DEOPPRRS   DROPPERS
DEOPPRSU   PURPOSED
DEOPPSSU   SUPPOSED
DEOPRRTU   PROTRUDE
DEOPRSST   TOP-DRESS
DEOPRSTU   POSTURED,
    PROUDEST, SPROUTED
DEORRTTU   TORTURED
DEOSSSYY   ODYSSEYS
DEPRRTUU   RUPTURED
DERSTTTU   STRUTTED
DFFIIMRS   MIDRIFFS
DFFLOORU   FOURFOLD
DFFOORUW   WOODRUFF
DFGGHIOT   DOGFIGHT
DFGHILOS   GOLDFISH
DFGIILRY   FRIGIDLY
DFGIINNS   FINDINGS
DFGIINRT   DRIFTING
DFGILNNO   FONDLING
DFGILNOO   FLOODING
DFGINNOU   FOUNDING
DFHIIMUY   HUMIDIFY
DFHILSSU   DISHFULS
DFHIMRSU   DRUMFISH
DFHLOOOT   FOOTHOLD
DFHNOOUX   FOXHOUND
DFIILMTU   MULTIFID
DFIILOSY   SOLIDIFY
DFIILTUY   FLUIDITY
DFILLOOT   FLOODLIT

DFILLORY FLORIDLY
DFILLOWW WILDFOWL
DFIMOOOR IODOFORM
DFIOOPRS DISPROOF
DFJKNOOU JUNK FOOD
DFNOOPRU PROFOUND
DFOOOSTW SOFTWOOD
DGGGIINS DIGGINGS
DGGGINRU DRUGGING,
   GRUDGING
DGGIILNR GIRDLING
DGGIINNR GRINDING
DGGILNOS LODGINGS
DGGIMNSU SMUDGING
DGGINRTU TRUDGING
DGGIRSTU DRUGGIST
DGHIIINN IN HIDING
DGHIIMNT MIDNIGHT
DGHIINSS SHINDIGS
DGHILLNU DUNGHILL
DGHILNOS HOLDINGS
DGHILNRU HURDLING
DGHILOOR GIRLHOOD
DGHINNOU HOUNDING
DGHLORSU GOLD RUSH
DGHNOTUU DOUGHNUT
DGHOOOSW GOOD SHOW
DGHOOOTT DOGTOOTH
DGHORRUY ROUGH-DRY
DGHORSTU DROUGHTS
DGHORTUY DROUGHTY
DGIIINNV DIVINING
DGIIIRTY RIGIDITY
DGIIKLNN KINDLING
DGIIKNNR DRINKING
DGIILLNR DRILLING
DGIILLOU LIGULOID
DGIILNTU DILUTING
DGIIMNOU GONIDIUM
DGIIMPUY PYGIDIUM
DGIINORR GRIDIRON
DGIINORT DIGITRON
DGIINPPR DRIPPING
DGIINRTY DIRTYING
DGIKMNOS KINGDOMS
DGIKNOOW KINGWOOD
DGILLOOW GOODWILL
DGILMNOS MOLDINGS
DGILMNOU MOULDING
DGILMNPU DUMPLING
DGILMSUY SMUDGILY
DGILNOOR DROOLING
DGILNOOY INDOLOGY

DGILNOTY DOTINGLY
DGILOSTY STODGILY
DGILRTUY TURGIDLY
DGIMMNRU DRUMMING
DGINNOPU POUNDING
DGINNORU ROUNDING
DGINNORW DROWNING
DGINNOSU SOUNDING
DGINNOUW WOUNDING
DGINOOPR DROOPING
DGINOOPS GOSPODIN
DGINOOTU OUTDOING
DGINOPPR DROPPING
DGINORSW DROWSING
DGINSTUY STUDYING
DGLOOOXY DOXOLOGY
DGMOPRSU GUMDROPS
DGNOOORV NOVGOROD
DGOORSTT DOGTROTS
DHHILOTW WITHHOLD
DHIIIMNS DIMINISH
DHIIKWZZ WHIZZ KID
DHIIMNOO HOMINOID
DHIIMNSU HINDUISM
DHIIMOST ISTHMOID
DHIIMTUY HUMIDITY
DHIIORSS HIDROSIS
DHIJOPRU JODHPURI
DHIKNOOW HOODWINK
DHILLNOW DOWNHILL
DHILLOPY PHYLLOID
DHILMOPY LYMPHOID
DHILMOSY MODISHLY
DHILNOPS DOLPHINS
DHILOPRS LORDSHIP
DHILOPSS SLIPSHOD
DHILORRY HORRIDLY
DHIMNOST HINDMOST
DHINORSU ROUNDISH
DHINOTUW WHODUNIT
DHIOOPRZ RHIZOPOD
DHIORSTY THYROIDS,
   THYRSOID
DHJOPRSU JODHPURS
DHKMNOOO MONKHOOD
DHLMOOSU HOODLUMS
DHLNOSTU SHOULDN'T
DHMNOOOT HOMODONT
DHNOOSWW SHOWDOWN
DHNOSTUW SHUTDOWN
DHOOORTX ORTHODOX
DHOORSUW WOODRUSH
DIIILLQU ILLIQUID

DIIIMTTY TIMIDITY
DIIINOSV DIVISION
DIIINTVY DIVINITY
DIIIPRST DISPIRIT
DIIIRTVY VIRIDITY
DIIJNOST DISJOINT
DIILLMNW WINDMILL
DIILLMPY LIMPIDLY
DIILLSTY IDYLLIST
DIILNOTU DILUTION
DIILNTUY UNTIDILY
DIILOPRT TRIPLOID
DIILOPSS DIPLOSIS
DIILOSTY SOLIDITY
DIIMMNOU DOMINIUM
DIIMNNOO DOMINION
DIIMNOPT MIDPOINT
DIIMNSUU INDUSIUM
DIIMOPRS PRISMOID
DIIMPUXY PYXIDIUM
DIIMTTUY TUMIDITY
DIINNOSU DISUNION
DIINOOPS IODOPSIN
DIINOSSU SINUSOID
DIINSTUY DISUNITY
DIIORSST SISTROID
DIIORSSV DIVISORS
DIKLNNUY UNKINDLY
DILLMNOP MILLPOND
DILLOORS DOORSILL
DILLOSTY STOLIDLY
DILMOOSU MODIOLUS
DILOOPPY POLYPOID
DILOOPRY DROOPILY
DILOORSS LORDOSIS
DILOOSUY ODIOUSLY
DILOPRTY TORPIDLY
DILORRTY TORRIDLY
DILORSWY DROWSILY
DILPSTUY STUPIDLY
DILRSTUY STURDILY
DIMNOSTU DISMOUNT
DIMORSWY ROWDYISM
DINOOORW IRONWOOD
DINOOSTY NODOSITY
DINOSSTW SIT-DOWNS
DINRSTUY INDUSTRY
DIOSSTUU STUDIOUS
DIRSSTTU DISTRUST
DKOOORWW WOODWORK
DKORSTUW STUDWORK
DLNOOSWW SLOWDOWN
DLOOOORS DOLOROSO

DLOOORSU DOLOROUS
DLOOPPUW PULPWOOD, WOOD PULP
DLOOPPYY POLYPODY
DMMNRUUY DUMMY RUN
DMOOORWW WOODWORM, WORMWOOD
DNNOOTWW DOWNTOWN
DNNORSUW RUNDOWNS
DNNORTUW DOWNTURN
DNOOPPRU PROPOUND
DNOOPRSW SNOWDROP
DNOOPRUW DOWNPOUR
DNOORSUW WONDROUS
DNOPRSUU ROUNDUPS
DNOPSTUW PUT-DOWNS
DNORRSUU SURROUND
DOOOPRST DOORPOST, DOORSTOP
DOOORSTU OUTDOORS
DOOPRRTW DROPWORT
DOOPRSTU DROPOUTS
EEEEFRRS REFEREES
EEEEGQSU SQUEEGEE
EEEEGSSX EXEGESES
EEEEHTTY EYETEETH
EEEELLPX EXPELLEE
EEEENRRV VENEERER
EEEFFINT TENEFIFE
EEEFFNOR FREEFONE
EEEFFNRT EFFERENT
EEEFFORT FOREFEET
EEEFFRVW FEVERFEW
EEEFGRSU REFUGEES
EEEFILPR LIFE PEER
EEEFINRR FREE REIN
EEEFLRSX REFLEXES
EEEFLSTT FLEETEST
EEEFNORS FORESEEN
EEEFNRRT REFERENT, RENT-FREE, TREE FERN
EEEFNRUZ UNFREEZE
EEEFORRS FORESEER
EEEFPRUZ FREEZE-UP
EEEFRRRR REFERRER
EEEFRRRT FERRETER
EEEFRRSZ FREEZERS
EEEFRRTT FETTERER
EEEGGILN NEGLIGEE
EEEGHINT EIGHTEEN
EEEGINNR ENGINEER
EEEGINRS ENERGISE
EEEGINRZ ENERGIZE

EEEGIPRS PERIGEES
EEEGISSX EXEGESIS
EEEGISTV EGESTIVE
EEEGLNRT GREENLET
EEEGMNRT EMERGENT
EEEGMORT GEOMETER
EEEGNRRV REVENGER
EEEGNRRY GREENERY
EEEGNRST GREENEST
EEEGOPRT PROTEGEE
EEEHILSW HELEWISE, WHEELIES
EEEHIRSS HERESIES
EEEHIRST ETHERISE
EEEHIRTZ ETHERIZE
EEEHITWY WHITE-EYE
EEEHLLNS HELLENES
EEEHLLSS HEELLESS
EEEHLMPT HELPMEET
EEEHLNTV ELEVENTH
EEEHLNTY ETHYLENE
EEEHLOPP PEEPHOLE
EEEHLORS LEE SHORE
EEEHMNTV VEHEMENT
EEEHNNPT NEPENTHE
EEEHNNQU HENEQUEN
EEEHNPRS ENSPHERE
EEEHNRVW WHENEVER
EEEHORST SHOETREE
EEEHRRVW WHEREVER
EEEHRSST SHEEREST
EEEHSSTT ESTHETES
EEEIKLSW WEEKLIES
EEEIKNPS PEKINESE
EEEILLRV REVEILLE
EEEILMMN EMMELINE
EEEILNRT TREELINE
EEEILNRY EYELINER
EEEILNST SELENITE
EEEILPRS SLEEPIER
EEEILRRV RELIEVER
EEEILRST LEERIEST, STEELIER
EEEILSTV TELEVISE
EEEIMNRU MEUNIERE
EEEIMPRR PREMIERE
EEEIMRRS MISERERE
EEEIMRSZ MEZIERES
EEEINNNT NINETEEN
EEEINNRT INTERNEE, RETINENE
EEEINNSV VIENNESE
EEEINPRT PINETREE

EEEINRSS EERINESS
EEEINRST ETERNISE
EEEINRTZ ETERNIZE
EEEINSTW WEENIEST
EEEINTUX EUXENITE
EEEIPRRV REPRIEVE
EEEIQSUX EXEQUIES
EEEIRRSV REVERIES
EEEIRRTV RETRIEVE
EEEIRRVW REVIEWER
EEEIRTVX EXERTIVE
EEEISSTW SWEETIES
EEEJKKNR KNEE-JERK
EEEJLLRW JEWELLER
EEEKLSST SLEEKEST
EEEKMNSS MEEKNESS
EEEKNNSS KEENNESS
EEEKNORS KEROSENE
EEEKNSTV KESTEVEN
EEELLLRV LEVELLER
EEELLNOR ENROLLEE
EEELLPRR REPELLER
EEELLPRX EXPELLER
EEELLRRV REVELLER
EEELMNST ELEMENTS
EEELMOPY EMPLOYEE
EEELMOTT OMELETTE
EEELMRTU MULETEER
EEELNOPP PENELOPE
EEELNOPV ENVELOPE
EEELNRSW NEWSREEL
EEELNRSY SERENELY
EEELNRTY TERYLENE
EEELOPPR REPEOPLE
EEELPRSS PEERLESS, SLEEPERS
EEELPSST STEEPLES
EEELPTTY TELETYPE
EEELRRTT LETTERER
EEELRSST TREELESS
EEELRSTT RESETTLE
EEELRSTV LEVERETS
EEELRSVY SEVERELY
EEELTTTX TELETEXT
EEEMMRUZ MEZEREUM
EEEMNNTT TENEMENT
EEEMNORZ MEZEREON
EEEMORRV EVERMORE
EEEMPRRT TEMPERER
EEEMRSST SEMESTER
EEEMRSTX EXTREMES
EEENNOPR NEOPRENE
EEENNSSV EVENNESS

EEENNSTT ENTENTES
EEENORSV OVERSEEN,
  VERONESE
EEENORVY EVERYONE
EEENPPRS PREPENSE
EEENPRRT REPENTER
EEENPRSY PYRENEES
EEENPSSX EXPENSES
EEENRRTV REVERENT
EEEORRSV OVERSEER
EEEORRSX XEROSERE
EEEORSSY EYESORES
EEEPRRST PESTERER
EEEPRRSV PERVERSE,
  PRESERVE
EEEPRRTW PEWTERER
EEEPRSSW SWEEPERS
EEEPSSTT STEEPEST
EEEQRSTU QUEEREST
EEEQRSUZ SQUEEZER
EEEQSSUZ SQUEEZES
EEERRRSV RESERVER,
  REVERSER
EEERRRTV REVERTER
EEERRSSV RESERVES,
  REVERSES
EEERRSTT RESETTER
EEERSTTW TWEETERS
EEERSTVX VERTEXES
EEERSTWZ TWEEZERS
EEESSTTW SWEETEST
EEFFGIIS EFFIGIES
EEFFGORY GEOFFREY
EEFFISUV EFFUSIVE
EEFFLNTU EFFLUENT
EEFFRRSU SUFFERER
EEFGIILR FILIGREE
EEFGILNS FEELINGS
EEFGILNT FLEETING
EEFGINRR FINGERER
EEFGINRZ FREEZING
EEFGLNRY GREENFLY
EEFGLNUV VENGEFUL
EEFGLORS FORELEGS
EEFGNOOR FOREGONE
EEFGOORR FOREGOER
EEFHILLR HELLFIRE
EEFHILRS FLESHIER
EEFHIRSV FEVERISH
EEFHIRTY ETHERIFY
EEFHISST FETISHES
EEFHISTT HEFTIEST
EEFHLLPS SELF-HELP

EEFHLLWY FLYWHEEL
EEFHLSTY FLYSHEET
EEFHMNRS FRESHMEN
EEFHRSST FRESHEST
EEFIIKLL LIFELIKE
EEFIILLN LIFELINE
EEFIILMT LIFETIME
EEFIILSS LIFE-SISE
EEFIILSZ LIFE-SIZE
EEFIIMNN FEMININE
EEFIIMNS FEMINISE
EEFIIMNZ FEMINIZE
EEFIIRRV VERIFIER
EEFIIRST FIERIEST
EEFIJNNR JENNIFER
EEFIKNNP PENKNIFE
EEFILLRW FREE WILL
EEFILLSS LIFELESS
EEFILMST FISTMELE
EEFILNOS FELONIES
EEFILPRR PILFERER
EEFILRTU TRUE-LIFE
EEFIMORT FORETIME
EEFINNSS FINENESS
EEFINNTU FINE-TUNE
EEFINRRR INFERRER
EEFINRRY REFINERY
EEFINRSS RIFENESS
EEFINRST INFESTER
EEFIPRSX PREFIXES
EEFIRRST FIRTREES
EEFIRRSU SUREFIRE
EEFIRSTT FRISETTE
EEFIRSTY ESTERIFY
EEFKNORT REEF KNOT
EEFLLLNU FLUELLEN
EEFLLORT FORETELL,
  TOLL-FREE
EEFLLRSU SELF-RULE
EEFLLSSS SELFLESS
EEFLMSSU FUMELESS
EEFLNORU FLUORENE
EEFLNTUV EVENTFUL
EEFLORRW FLOWERER
EEFLORTT FLORETTE
EEFLORTV LEFTOVER
EEFLORVW OVERFLEW
EEFLORWW WEREWOLF
EEFLRRSU FERRULES
EEFLRSST FRETLESS
EEFMNORT FOMENTER
EEFMNRRY FERRYMEN
EEFMORRR REFORMER

EEFMPRRU PERFUMER
EEFMPRSU PERFUMES
EEFNORST SOFTENER
EEFNORTU FOURTEEN
EEFNORTW FOREWENT,
  FREETOWN
EEFNQRTU FREQUENT
EEFNRTTU UNFETTER
EEFOORRT ROOFTREE
EEFOPRRT FREE PORT
EEFOPRST FREEPOST,
  POST-FREE
EEFORRST FORESTER,
  FOSTERER, REFOREST
EEFORRSU FERREOUS
EEFORRTY FERETORY
EEFORSUY FOUREYES
EEFOSSTT FOSSETTE
EEFOSSTU FOETUSES
EEGGHLLS EGGSHELL
EEGGHNOR HONEGGER
EEGGILST LEGGIEST
EEGGIMNR EMERGING
EEGGIMRT EGG TIMER
EEGGINNR GREENING,
  RENEGING
EEGGINRT GREETING
EEGGNSST NEST EGGS
EEGGORTT GO-GETTER
EEGHHIKN KNEE-HIGH
EEGHHINT HEIGHTEN
EEGHIIST EIGHTIES
EEGHIKLY KEIGHLEY
EEGHILNW WHEELING
EEGHILRS SLEIGHER
EEGHINRS GREENISH,
  SHEERING
EEGHINST SEETHING,
  SHEETING
EEGHINTT TEETHING
EEGHINWZ WHEEZING
EEGHIOTT GOETHITE
EEGHIRTW WEIGHTER
EEGHISST SIGHTSEE
EEGHISTY EYESIGHT
EEGHLNNT LENGTHEN
EEGHMNOY HEGEMONY
EEGHNOPS PHOSGENE
EEGHNSSU HUGENESS
EEGHOPTY GEOPHYTE
EEGHORTT TOGETHER
EEGHOSTT GHETTOES
EEGIILNR LINGERIE

EEGIILNV INVEIGLE	EEGIPRST PRESTIGE	EEHINNRT INHERENT
EEGIINTV GENITIVE	EEGIRRST REGISTER	EEHINORT HEREINTO
EEGIJMNN NIJMEGEN	EEGIRSTT GRISETTE	EEHINPRT NEPHRITE,
EEGIKLNN KNEELING	EEGISSTV VESTIGES	TREPHINE
EEGIKLNS SLEEKING	EEGLNOPY POLYGENE	EEHINRTT THIRTEEN
EEGILLNV LEVELING	EEGLNOSZ LOZENGES	EEHINRTW WHITENER
EEGILNPS PEELINGS,	EEGLNOTY TELEGONY	EEHIORRT EITHER-OR
SLEEPING	EEGLOOST TOGOLESE	EEHIORST ISOTHERE,
EEGILNRR LINGERER	EEGMNOST GEMSTONE	THEORIES, THEORISE
EEGILNRU REGULINE	EEGMNSST SEGMENTS	EEHIORTZ THEORIZE
EEGILNRV LEVERING,	EEGMORSU GRUESOME	EEHIPPST PSEPHITE
REVELING	EEGMORTY GEOMETRY	EEHIPPTY EPIPHYTE
EEGILNST GENTILES,	EEGMRSTU GUM TREES	EEHIPRRS PERISHER
SLEETING, STEELING	EEGNNORT ROENTGEN	EEHIPRTT TEPHRITE
EEGILNSV SLEEVING	EEGNNOSV EVENSONG	EEHIPSTT EPITHETS
EEGILNTX TELEXING	EEGNOPTY GENOTYPE	EEHIRRSV SHIVERER
EEGILOPU EPILOGUE	EEGNORSU GENEROUS	EEHIRRTW WITHERER
EEGILOSU EULOGIES,	EEGNOTYZ ZYGOTENE	EEHIRSTT TEE SHIRT
EULOGISE	EEGNPRUX EXPUNGER	EEHIRTVY THIEVERY
EEGILOUZ EULOGIZE	EEGNRSSY GREYNESS	EEHKLOSY KEYHOLES
EEGILRTV VERLIGTE	EEGNRSUY GUERNSEY	EEHKLOWY HOLY WEEK
EEGIMNNS MENINGES	EEGOPRST PROTÉGÉS	EEHLLMSS HELMLESS
EEGIMNRS REGIMENS	EEGOPRSU SUPEREGO	EEHLLPSS HELPLESS
EEGIMNRT METERING,	EEGORRRU GUERRERO	EEHLMMNS HELMSMEN
REGIMENT	EEGRRSTU GESTURER	EEHLMORU HOME RULE
EEGIMNRU MERINGUE	EEGRSSTU GESTURES	EEHLMOSS HOMELESS
EEGIMNST MEETINGS	EEHHIPSS SHEEPISH	EEHLNOSW HENSLOWE
EEGINNPR PREENING	EEHHIRST THIS HERE	EEHLOPSS HOPELESS
EEGINNQU QUEENING	EEHHIRTW HEREWITH	EEHLOPST HEELPOST,
EEGINNRS SNEERING	EEHHLLLO HELLHOLE	PESTHOLE
EEGINNRT ENTERING	EEHHLMOP HOME HELP	EEHLORSV SHOVELER
EEGINNRW RENEWING	EEHHLSTW THE WELSH	EEHLPRSU SPHERULE
EEGINNRY ENGINERY	EEHHNOSU HEN HOUSE	EEHLPRTY THREE-PLY
EEGINNSU INGENUES,	EEHHRRST THRESHER	EEHLRSST SHELTERS
UNSEEING	EEHHRSST THRESHES	EEHLRSSW WELSHERS
EEGINNSV EVENINGS	EEHIIKLV HIVELIKE	EEHMMOPR MORPHEME
EEGINNSZ SNEEZING	EEHIILTV HELVETII	EEHMMORT OHMMETER
EEGINORR ERIGERON	EEHIILTW WHITE LIE	EEHMNOPS PHONEMES
EEGINOST EGESTION	EEHIITTW WHITE-TIE	EEHMNORS HORSEMEN
EEGINPRU PUREEING	EEHIKLMO HOMELIKE	EEHMNOSU HOUSEMEN
EEGINPST STEEPING	EEHIKRRS SHRIEKER	EEHMORST REST HOME,
EEGINPSW SWEEPING	EEHILMNS HEMLINES	THEOREMS
EEGINQRU QUEERING	EEHILMOR HOMELIER	EEHMORVW WHOMEVER
EEGINRRS RESIGNER	EEHILNPW PINWHEEL	EEHNNOOT ETHONONE
EEGINRRV REVERING	EEHILORT HOTELIER	EEHNNORT ENTHRONE
EEGINRST INTEGERS,	EEHILRSS HEIRLESS,	EEHNOORS ONE-HORSE
STEERING	RELISHES	EEHNOPRU HEREUPON
EEGINRSU SEIGNEUR	EEHILWYZ WHEEZILY	EEHNOPTY NEOPHYTE
EEGINRSV SEVERING	EEHIMNOR HERMIONE	EEHNORST HORTENSE,
EEGINRTX EXERTING	EEHIMNRT THEREMIN	THE NORSE
EEGINSSU GENIUSES	EEHIMRST ERETHISM	EEHNORTU HEREUNTO
EEGINTTV VIGNETTE	EEHIMRTT THERMITE	EEHNSSTV SEVENTHS
EEGINTTW TWEETING	EEHINNRS ENSHRINE	EEHOOPRS OOSPHERE

EEHOOPSW WHOOPEES
EEHOORSV OVERSHOE
EEHOOTTY EYETOOTH
EEHOPPSW PEEPSHOW
EEHORRSV HOVERERS
EEHORRTX EXHORTER
EEHPRSSU HESPERUS
EEIIKLLR LIKELIER
EEIIKLSW LIKEWISE
EEIILLRV LIVELIER
EEIILMNT ILMENITE,
MELINITE
EEIILMRT TIMELIER
EEIILNPP PIPELINE
EEIILNTV LENITIVE
EEIILRSV LIVERIES
EEIILRVW LIVE WIRE
EEIILSTW LEWISITE
EEIIMMTT MIMETITE
EEIIMOST MOIETIES
EEIIMRSS MISERIES
EEIIMSSV EMISSIVE
EEIINNST NINETIES
EEIINNVV VIVIENNE
EEIINPPR PIPERINE
EEIINPRV VIPERINE
EEIINRRV RIVERINE
EEIINRSS IN SERIES
EEIINRTT RETINITE
EEIINSSV INESSIVE
EEIINSTT ENTITIES
EEIIOPTZ EPIZOITE
EEIIQSTU EQUITIES
EEIIRSTV VERITIES
EEIJKRST JERKIEST
EEIJLNNU JULIENNE
EEIJLNRT JETLINER
EEIJLNUV JUVENILE
EEIJLTTU JULIETTE
EEIJNNOR ENJOINER
EEIKLNSS LIKENESS
EEIKLORT LORIKEET
EEIKLPST SPIKELET
EEIKMOTX KETOXIME
EEIKNRRT TINKERER
EEIKPRST PERKIEST
EEIKPSST PESKIEST
EEILLLMV MELVILLE
EEILLMPR IMPELLER
EEILLMRS SMELLIER
EEILLNOR LONELIER
EEILLORV LOVELIER
EEILLOSV LOVELIES

EEILLPSS ELLIPSES
EEILLPSY SLEEPILY
EEILLSTT STELLITE
EEILLSTV EVILLEST
EEILMNNO LIMONENE
EEILMNNS LINESMEN
EEILMNST MELISENT
EEILMNSU SELENIUM
EEILMSST TIMELESS
EEILMSUV EMULSIVE
EEILNNST SENTINEL
EEILNOPR LEPORINE
EEILNORS ROSELINE
EEILNPPZ ZEPPELIN
EEILNPRU PERILUNE
EEILNPRV REPLEVIN
EEILNRST ENLISTER,
LEINSTER, LISTENER
EEILNRTY ENTIRELY,
LIENTERY
EEILNSSV EVILNESS,
VILENESS
EEILNSVY YVELINES
EEILORRT LOITERER
EEILOSVW VOWELISE
EEILOTTT TOILETTE
EEILOTTV VIOLETTE
EEILOVWZ VOWELIZE
EEILPPSY EPILEPSY
EEILPRST EPISTLER,
REPTILES
EEILPSST EPISTLES
EEILPSSV PELVISES
EEILPSTY EPISTYLE
EEILRRSV REVILERS,
SILVERER, SLIVERER
EEILRSST TIRELESS
EEILRSSW WIRELESS
EEILSSVW VIEWLESS
EEILSTTX TEXTILES
EEIMMORS MEMORIES,
MEMORISE
EEIMMORZ MEMORIZE
EEIMMOST SOMETIME
EEIMMRST MERISTEM
EEIMNNOS NOMINEES
EEIMNORS EMERSION
EEIMNORV VOMERINE
EEIMNOST MONETISE,
SEMITONE
EEIMNOTZ MONETIZE,
TIME ZONE, ZONETIME
EEIMNPRS SPERMINE

EEIMNPRU PERINEUM
EEIMNRTU MUTINEER
EEIMOPRS REIMPOSE
EEIMORST TIRESOME
EEIMORTV OVERTIME
EEIMPRRS PREMIERS,
SIMPERER
EEIMPRSS PREMISES
EEIMPSTT EMPTIEST
EEIMQRSU REQUIEMS
EEIMQSTU MESQUITE
EEIMRRST MERRIEST,
TRIREMES
EEIMRRTT REMITTER,
TRIMETER
EEIMRSTT TERMITES
EEIMRSTU EMERITUS
EEIMRTTY TEMERITY
EEIMSSST MESSIEST
EEINNNPS PENNINES
EEINNPTT PENITENT
EEINNSTT SENTIENT
EEINOPRS ISOPRENE,
PIONEERS
EEINORST SEROTINE
EEINORSV EVERSION
EEINORTT TENORITE
EEINORTX EXERTION
EEINOSTT TEOSINTE
EEINPRSS RIPENESS
EEINPRTX INEXPERT
EEINQRRU ENQUIRER
EEINRRST INSERTER,
RENTIERS
EEINRRSU REINSURE
EEINRRTU REUNITER
EEINRRTV INVERTER
EEINRRTW WINTERER
EEINRRTX INTERREX
EEINRSST SENTRIES
EEINRSSU ENURESIS
EEINRSTT INSETTER,
INTEREST
EEINRSTU ESURIENT,
RETINUES
EEINRSTV NERVIEST,
REINVEST
EEINRSTX INTERSEX
EEINRSTY SERENITY
EEINRSUV UNIVERSE
EEINRTTY ENTIRETY,
ETERNITY
EEINSSSW WISENESS

EEINSSSX SEXINESS
EEINSSTX SIXTEENS
EEINSTTW TWENTIES
EEINSTTX EXISTENT
EEIOPRRT PORTIERE
EEIOPRRV OVERRIPE
EEIORRRS ORRERIES
EEIORRTV OVERTIRE
EEIORRTX EXTERIOR
EEIORSSV OVERSISE
EEIORSVZ OVERSIZE
EEIORVVW OVERVIEW
EEIORVWW WIRE-WOVE
EEIPPQRU EQUIPPER
EEIPPRRS PERSPIRE
EEIPPRST PEPTISER
EEIPPRTZ PEPTIZER
EEIPPSTT PIPETTES
EEIPRRSS REPRISES
EEIPRRTT PRETTIER
EEIPRSST RESPITES
EEIPRSTX PREEXIST
EEIPRSVW PREVIEWS
EEIPRSZZ PREZZIES
EEIPRTUV ERUPTIVE
EEIPSSTW STEPWISE
EEIPSTTT PETTIEST
EEIQRRRU REQUIRER
EEIQRRTU REQUITER
EEIQRRUV QUIVERER
EEIQSTTU QUIETEST
EEIRRRST TERRIERS
EEIRRSST RESISTER
EEIRRSSU REISSUER
EEIRRSSV REVISERS
EEIRRSTV RIVETERS
EEIRRSTW REWRITES
EEIRRTTT TITTERER
EEIRSSSU REISSUES
EEIRSSTU SURETIES
EEIRSSTV VESTRIES
EEIRSSUZ SEIZURES
EEIRSTVY SEVERITY
EEISSTTT TESTIEST
EEJKNRTU JUNKETER
EEJLPSTU PULSEJET
EEJPRRRU PERJURER
EEKLLSUU UKULELES
EEKLNNNU UNKENNEL
EEKLNOST SKELETON
EEKLRSST KESTRELS
EEKMNOYY KEY MONEY
EEKMOORV KEMEROVO

EEKNOSTY KEYNOTES,
   KEYSTONE
EELLLLMP PELL-MELL
EELLLNWY LLEWELYN
EELLMNOY MELLONEY
EELLMORW MELLOWER
EELLNORR ENROLLER
EELLNPRU PRUNELLE
EELLNRSU SULLENER
EELLNSTU ENTELLUS
EELLOPTV TOP-LEVEL
EELLORSV OVERSELL
EELLORTX EXTOLLER
EELLORVY VOLLEYER
EELLOSSV LOVELESS
EELMMPUX EXEMPLUM
EELMNOOS LONESOME
EELMNSUY UNSEEMLY
EELMOPRY EMPLOYER,
   RE-EMPLOY
EELMORST MOLESTER
EELMORTY REMOTELY
EELMOTVW TWELVEMO
EELMRRTU MURRELET
EELMRSST TERMLESS
EELMRSTY SMELTERY
EELNNRTU TUNNELER
EELNNTTY LYNNETTE
EELNNUVY UNEVENLY
EELNOORS LOOSENER
EELNOPPU UNPEOPLE
EELNOQTU ELOQUENT
EELNORST ENTRESOL
EELNOSST TONELESS
EELNOSTT NOTELETS
EELNSSTU TUNELESS
EELNSTTU UNSETTLE
EELOPPST ESTOPPEL
EELOPRRX EXPLORER
EELORRSV RESOLVER
EELORRTV REVOLTER
EELORRUV OVERRULE
EELORRVV REVOLVER
EELORSSV RESOLVES
EELORSTU RESOLUTE
EELORSTY TYROLESE
EELORTTU ROULETTE
EELORTUV REVOLUTE,
   TRUELOVE
EELPPSTU SEPTUPLE
EELPRRSU REPULSER
EELPRSSU REPULSES
EELPRSTZ PRETZELS

EELPRTXY EXPERTLY
EELPSTUX SEXTUPLE
EELRRSTW WRESTLER
EELRSSST RESTLESS
EELRSSTT SETTLERS,
   TRESTLES
EELRSSTU STREUSEL
EELRSTWY WESTERLY
EEMMNOST MEMENTOS
EEMMNOTV MOVEMENT
EEMNNORS NORSEMEN
EEMNOOPT TONE POEM
EEMNPRSS PRESSMEN
EEMNPRSU SUPERMEN
EEMNPRTU ERUMPENT
EEMNRSTU MUENSTER
EEMNSSTU MUTENESS,
   TENESMUS
EEMNSTTV VESTMENT
EEMOORRT OROMETER
EEMOORRV MOREOVER
EEMOPRRS EMPERORS,
   PREMORSE
EEMOQRSU MORESQUE
EEMOQTTU MOQUETTE
EEMORRSV REMOVERS
EEMORSST SOMERSET
EEMORSTT REMOTEST
EEMPRRSU PRESUMER
EEMPRSTT TEMPTERS
EEMPSSTT TEMPESTS
EEMRRTTU MUTTERER
EENNNOSS NONSENSE
EENNNOTV NON-EVENT
EENNOOOT ONE-TO-ONE
EENNOORT ROTENONE
EENNOPSS OPENNESS
EENNOPTX EXPONENT
EENNORTT RONNETTE
EENOORST OESTRONE
EENOORTV OVERTONE
EENOPRSS RESPONSE
EENOPRTT ENTREPOT
EENOPRTU PURE TONE
EENOPRXY PYROXENE
EENORSSS SORENESS
EENORSSU NEUROSES
EENORSTX EXTENSOR
EENPRSST PERTNESS,
   PRESENTS, SERPENTS
EENPRSSU PURENESS
EENPSSSU SUSPENSE
EENPSTTU PETUNTSE

EENRRRTU RETURNER
EENRRTUV VENTURER
EENRSSSU SURENESS
EENRSSTT STERNEST
EENRSSTU TRUENESS
EENRSSTW WESTERNS
EENRSTUV VENTURES
EENRSTUW WET NURSE
EEOOPRST PROTEOSE
EEOOPRSX EXOSPORE
EEOORRVV ROVE-OVER
EEOPRRRT REPORTER
EEOPRRRV REPROVER
EEOPRRTT POTTERER
EEOPRRTX EXPORTER,
    RE-EXPORT
EEOPRSSS ESPRESSO
EEOPRSSU ESPOUSER,
    REPOUSSE
EEOPRSTV OVERSTEP
EEOPRSUX EXPOSURE
EEOPSSTW SWEETSOP
EEORRRST RESORTER,
    RESTORER, RETRORSE
EEORRRTT RETORTER
EEORRSTX EXTRORSE
EEORRTTT TOTTERER
EEORRTTX EXTORTER
EEORRTUV OVERTURE
EEORSSTT ROSETTES
EEORSSTV ESTOVERS
EEORSTVX VORTEXES
EEORTTTZ TERZETTO
EEPRRSSU PRESSURE
EEPRRSTV PERVERTS
EEPRSSUX SUPERSEX
EEPRSTTU UPSETTER
EEPRSTTX PRETEXTS
EEQRSSTU REQUESTS
EERRSSTU TRESSURE
EERSSSST STRESSES
EERSSTTU TRUSTEES
EERSSTUU UTERUSES
EERSTTUX TEXTURES
EFFFILRU FLUFFIER
EFFGINOR OFFERING
EFFGRSTU GRUFFEST
EFFHIILS FILEFISH
EFFHIIRW WHIFFIER
EFFHIISW FISHWIFE
EFFHIITT FIFTIETH
EFFHIOTW OFF-WHITE
EFFHIRSS SHERIFFS

EFFHISTU HUFFIEST
EFFHLRSU SHUFFLER
EFFHLSSU SHUFFLES
EFFHOORS OFFSHORE
EFFILNRS SNIFFLER
EFFILNSS SNIFFLES
EFFINOSU EFFUSION
EFFIORST FORFEITS
EFFIORTW WRITE-OFF
EFFIPSTU PUFFIEST
EFFIRSTU STUFFIER
EFFISSTT STIFFEST
EFFISSUX SUFFIXES
EFFLMRSU MUFFLERS
EFFLNRSU SNUFFLER
EFFLNSSU SNUFFLES
EFFLOSSU SOUFFLÉS
EFFLRSTU TRUFFLES
EFFNRSSU SNUFFERS
EFFOOORT FOREFOOT
EFFOORSW WORSE-OFF
EFGGIINN FEIGNING
EFGGIOST FOGGIEST
EFGGISTU FUGGIEST
EFGHHIIL HIGH LIFE
EFGHILNS FLESHING
EFGHINRT FRIGHTEN
EFGHIRST FIGHTERS
EFGIILNT FILETING
EFGIILRU UGLIFIER
EFGIINNR INFRINGE,
    REFINING
EFGIINNT FEINTING
EFGIINRU FIGURINE
EFGIITUV FUGITIVE
EFGILLNO LIFELONG,
    LONG-LIFE
EFGILLNU FUELLING
EFGILLUU GUILEFUL
EFGILNOR FLORIGEN
EFGILNTT FETTLING
EFGILNTW LEFT WING
EFGILPRU FIRE-PLUG
EFGIMNST FIGMENTS
EFGIMRUU REFUGIUM
EFGINNPS PFENNIGS
EFGINORV FORGIVEN
EFGINORW FOREWING
EFGINRRY FERRYING
EFGINRSU REFUSING
EFGINRTT FRETTING
EFGINRTU REFUTING
EFGINRTY GENTRIFY

EFGIOOST GOOFIEST
EFGIOPTT PETTIFOG
EFGIORRV FORGIVER
EFGIORTT FORGET IT!
EFGLOOVX FOXGLOVE
EFGNSSUU FUNGUSES
EFHIILRT FILTHIER
EFHIILST TILEFISH
EFHIINRS FINISHER,
    REFINISH
EFHIINSS FINISHES
EFHIIPPS PIPEFISH
EFHIIRST SHIFTIER
EFHIISST FISHIEST
EFHIKLOO HOOFLIKE
EFHIKSTY SHIFT KEY
EFHILTWY WHITEFLY
EFHINSST FISHNETS
EFHIORRT FROTHIER
EFHIORSS ROSEFISH
EFHIORTT FORTIETH
EFHIRRTU THURIFER
EFHLNORS HORNFELS
EFHLOOSS HOOFLESS
EFHLOOSX FOXHOLES
EFHLOPST FLESHPOT
EFHLOPSU HOPEFULS
EFHLORSY HORSEFLY
EFHLOSUU HOUSEFUL
EFHLOSUY HOUSEFLY
EFHLSTTW TWELFTHS
EFHRSTTU FURTHEST
EFIIILRV VILIFIER
EFIIINNT INFINITE
EFIIIRVV VIVIFIER
EFIIKRRS FRISKIER
EFIILLRR FRILLIER
EFIILMRS FLIMSIER
EFIILMST FILMIEST
EFIILNOU IN LIEU OF
EFIILNRT FLINTIER
EFIILNTY FELINITY,
    FINITELY
EFIILRSU FUSILIER
EFIIMMNS FEMINISM
EFIIMNST FEMINIST
EFIIMRSS MISFIRES
EFIINNNS SINN FEIN
EFIINORR INFERIOR
EFIINORT NOTIFIER
EFIINPSV FIVEPINS
EFIINPSX SPINIFEX
EFIINRRT FERRITIN

EFIINSTT NIFTIEST
EFIINSUV INFUSIVE
EFIIORSS OSSIFIER
EFIIPRRU PURIFIER
EFIIPRST SPITFIRE
EFIIPRTY TYPIFIER
EFIIRRTU FRUITIER
EFIIRRZZ FRIZZIER
EFIIRVVY REVIVIFY
EFIISTVW FIVE WITS
EFIISTZZ FIZZIEST
EFIJLOST JETFOILS
EFIKLLOW WOLFLIKE
EFIKLORW LIFE WORK
EFIKLRSU SURFLIKE
EFIKLRUY LIKE FURY
EFIKNORS FORESKIN
EFIKNSTU FUNKIEST
EFIKORRW FIREWORK
EFILLLSW SELF-WILL
EFILLMTU FULL-TIME
EFILLSTY STELLIFY
EFILMSUY EMULSIFY
EFILNNTU INFLUENT
EFILNORU FLUORINE
EFILNSUX INFLUXES
EFILOOSZ FLOOZIES
EFILOPPR FLOPPIER
EFILOPRS PROFILES
EFILORST TREFOILS
EFILOSTT LOFTIEST
EFILPPRS FLIPPERS
EFILPPST FLIPPEST
EFILPRTU UPLIFTER
EFILPSTU SPITEFUL
EFILPSTY SELF-PITY
EFILRRSU FLURRIES
EFILRRZZ FRIZZLER
EFILSSTT LEFTISTS
EFIMNORR INFORMER,
    RENIFORM
EFIMNORS ENSIFORM
EFIMNRSS FIRMNESS
EFIMNSTT FITMENTS
EFIMORST SETIFORM
EFIMPRRU FRUMPIER
EFIMRSTU FREMITUS
EFINNORS INFERNOS
EFINNPSU FINESPUN
EFINNSTU FUNNIEST
EFINOPTX PONTIFEX
EFINORRT FRONTIER
EFINOSSX FOXINESS

EFINRSST SNIFTERS
EFIOOPST POOFIEST
EFIOOSST FOOTSIES
EFIOPRRT PROFITER
EFIORRST FROSTIER
EFIORRTT RETROFIT
EFIORRWZ FROWZIER
EFIPPRRY FRIPPERY
EFIPRSUX SUPERFIX
EFIPRTTY PRETTIFY
EFIRRRSU FURRIERS
EFIRRRUY FURRIERY
EFIRRSTT FRITTERS
EFIRRSTU FURRIEST
EFIRSSSU FISSURES
EFIRSTUX FIXTURES
EFISSSTU FUSSIEST
EFISSTTU FUSTIEST
EFISSTTW SWIFTEST
EFISTUZZ FUZZIEST
EFKLLOOR FOLKLORE
EFKLNSUY FLUNKEYS
EFKNOORW FOREKNOW
EFKORRTW FRETWORK
EFLLLLUW FULL WELL
EFLLNOOW LONE WOLF
EFLLNSSU FULLNESS
EFLLNTUY FLUENTLY
EFLLOORW FOLLOWER
EFLLOSST SOFT SELL
EFLLOUWY WOEFULLY
EFLLRUUY RUEFULLY
EFLLSUUY USEFULLY
EFLMMRUY FLUMMERY
EFLMNRUU FRENULUM
EFLMORRY FORMERLY
EFLMORSS FORMLESS
EFLNORTT FRONTLET
EFLNOSSU FOULNESS
EFLNOSTY STONEFLY
EFLOORSS ROOFLESS
EFLOORVW OVERFLOW
EFLOPRUW POWERFUL
EFLOPSTW FOWL PEST
EFLORSUY YOURSELF
EFLORSVY FLYOVERS
EFLOSUUX FLEXUOUS
EFLRSTTU FLUTTERS
EFLRSTUU FRUSTULE
EFLRTTUY FLUTTERY
EFMNNORT FRONT MEN
EFMNORTY FROMENTY
EFMNRTUY FRUMENTY

EFMOORST FOREMOST
EFMOORSU FOURSOME
EFNNOOOR FORENOON
EFNOOOTT FOOTNOTE
EFNOOSST FESTOONS
EFNORSTU FORTUNES
EFNOSSST SOFTNESS
EFOOOPRT FOOTROPE
EFOOORST FOOTSORE
EFOOPRRS REPROOFS
EFOOPSTT FOOTSTEP
EFOORRSW FORSWORE
EFOORSTT FOOTREST
EFORRRUW FURROWER
EFORRSST FORTRESS
EFORRSTY FORESTRY
EGGGILNS LEGGINGS
EGGGIORR GROGGIER
EGGHIINN NEIGHING
EGGHIINW WEIGHING
EGGHIRWY WHIGGERY
EGGHRTUY THUGGERY
EGGIINNR REIGNING
EGGIINNS SINGEING
EGGIINRV GRIEVING
EGGIIPST PIGGIEST
EGGILNRS NIGGLERS,
    SNIGGLER
EGGILNRY GINGERLY
EGGILOOS GOOGLIES
EGGILQSU SQUIGGLE
EGGILRRW WRIGGLER
EGGILRSW WRIGGLES
EGGIMSTU MUGGIEST
EGGINORR GORGERIN
EGGINRSS SNIGGERS
EGGINSSU GUESSING
EGGINSTU GUESTING
EGGIOSST SOGGIEST
EGGIPRRS SPRIGGER
EGGIPRRY PRIGGERY
EGGIRRST TRIGGERS
EGGJLRSU JUGGLERS
EGGJLRUY JUGGLERY
EGGLLORS EGG ROLLS
EGGLMOOY GEMOLOGY
EGGLMRSU SMUGGLER
EGGLORSS SLOGGERS
EGGLRSTU STRUGGLE
EGGMSSTU SMUGGEST
EGGNOOSY GEOGNOSY
EGGNRSUY SNUGGERY
EGGOORSU GORGEOUS

EGHHIIMT HIGH TIME
EGHHIIRS HIGH-RISE
EGHHINSS HIGHNESS
EGHHIPRU HIGHER-UP
EGHHIPTY TYPE-HIGH
EGHHORUW ROUGH-HEW
EGHIILNR HIRELING
EGHIILNS SHIELING
EGHIIMRT MIGHTIER
EGHIINTV THIEVING
EGHIKNRS GHERKINS
EGHILLNS SHELLING
EGHILLNW WELL-NIGH
EGHILNOT LEIGHTON
EGHILNPS HELPINGS
EGHILNRS SHINGLER
EGHILNSS SHINGLES
EGHILNSV SHELVING
EGHILNSW WELSHING
EGHILPRT PLIGHTER
EGHILRST LIGHTERS,
SLIGHTER
EGHILSTT LIGHTEST
EGHIMNUX EXHUMING
EGHINORV HOVERING
EGHINOST HISTOGEN
EGHINRRS HERRINGS
EGHINRRU HUNGRIER
EGHINRSU USHERING
EGHINTTW WHETTING
EGHIOTUW OUTWEIGH
EGHISTTT TIGHTEST
EGHLLNUW WELL-HUNG
EGHLLOPU PLUGHOLE
EGHLLOSU LUGHOLES
EGHLOOOR HOROLOGE
EGHLOORY RHEOLOGY
EGHLOOTY ETHOLOGY,
THEOLOGY
EGHLOPRU PLOUGHER
EGHMNOOY HOMOGENY
EGHMOSSU GUMSHOES
EGHNNTWY GWYNNETH
EGHNORUV HUNG OVER,
OVERHUNG
EGHNOTUU HUGUENOT
EGHNRSTT STRENGTH
EGHOOOSW HOOSEGOW
EGHORRTW REGROWTH
EGHORSTU ROUGHEST
EGHOSTTU TOUGHEST
EGIIKLNN LIKENING
EGIIKLNR KINGLIER

EGIIKLNW WINGLIKE
EGIIKNSS KING-SISE
EGIIKNSZ KING-SIZE
EGIILNNR RELINING
EGIILNNV LIVENING
EGIILNOR RELIGION
EGIILNRS RIESLING
EGIILNRV RELIVING,
REVILING
EGIILRRS GRISLIER
EGIILRTU GUILTIER
EGIILRTZ GLITZIER
EGIIMNPR IMPINGER
EGIIMNRT MERITING
EGIIMNST MINGIEST
EGIIMNTT EMITTING
EGIIMOPT IMPETIGO
EGIIMRST GRIMIEST
EGIINNPR REPINING,
RIPENING
EGIINNPW WINNIPEG
EGIINOPR PEIGNOIR
EGIINPRX EXPIRING
EGIINRRT RETIRING
EGIINRRW REWIRING
EGIINRST STINGIER
EGIINRSV REVISING
EGIINRTU INTRIGUE
EGIINRTV RIVETING
EGIINRVV REVIVING
EGIINSTX EXISTING
EGIIPRSW PERIWIGS
EGIIPSST PIGSTIES
EGIIRRTT GRITTIER
EGIITUXY EXIGUITY
EGIJMMNY JEMMYING
EGIJNNOY ENJOYING
EGIKKNRT TREKKING
EGIKLNSY KINGSLEY
EGIKNORV REVOKING
EGIKNRSY KEY RINGS
EGILLMNS SMELLING
EGILLNOR NEGRILLO
EGILLNOV LIVELONG
EGILLNPS SPELLING
EGILLNQU QUELLING
EGILLNSW SWELLING
EGILLNTU GLUTELIN
EGILMMNS LEMMINGS
EGILMMRS GLIMMERS
EGILMNRS GREMLINS
EGILMNST SMELTING
EGILMOOR GLOOMIER

EGILMPRS GLIMPSER
EGILMPSS GLIMPSES
EGILNNOS SOLINGEN
EGILNNST NESTLING
EGILNNTT NETTLING
EGILNOPP PEOPLING
EGILNORW LOWERING
EGILNOSU LIGNEOUS
EGILNOTW TOWELING
EGILNOVV EVOLVING
EGILNPRY REPLYING
EGILNRST RINGLETS,
STERLING
EGILNSST SINGLETS
EGILNSSU UGLINESS
EGILNSSW WINGLESS
EGILNSTT LETTINGS,
SETTLING
EGILNTUX EXULTING
EGILNVXY VEXINGLY
EGILOOSU ISOLOGUE
EGILOOTY ETIOLOGY
EGILORSS GLOSSIER
EGILOSTU EULOGIST
EGILRRZZ GRIZZLER
EGILRSTT GLITTERS
EGILRTTY GLITTERY
EGIMMNST STEMMING
EGIMMRST GRIMMEST
EGIMMSTU GUMMIEST
EGIMNORS NEGROISM
EGIMNORV REMOVING
EGIMNOSY MOSEYING
EGIMNPRU IMPUGNER
EGIMNPST PIGMENTS
EGIMNPTT TEMPTING
EGIMNPTY EMPTYING
EGIMNRSS GRIMNESS
EGIMNRSU RESUMING
EGIMORST ERGOTISM
EGIMPRRU GRUMPIER
EGINNOPS OPENINGS
EGINNORT NITROGEN
EGINNPSU PENGUINS
EGINNRRU UNERRING
EGINNRSU ENSURING
EGINOPRS REPOSING,
SPONGIER
EGINOPRW POWERING
EGINOPST PONGIEST
EGINOPSX EXPOSING
EGINORRY IRON-GREY
EGINORSS GORINESS

EGINORTW TOWERING	EGLNPRSU PLUNGERS	EHIIKNSV KISHINEV
EGINORVW WINGOVER	EGLNRTUY URGENTLY	EHIIKSSW WHISKIES
EGINORXX XEROXING	EGLOOPRU PROLOGUE	EHIILLST HILLIEST
EGINPPST STEPPING	EGLOOPTY LOGOTYPE	EHIILMOS HOMILIES
EGINPRRS SPRINGER	EGLOORSY SEROLOGY	EHIILRSV LIVERISH
EGINPRSS PRESSING	EGLOOSXY SEXOLOGY	EHIIMNRS IRISHMEN
EGINPRSU PERUSING	EGLORRSW GROWLERS	EHIIMNTV VIETMINH
EGINPRTU ERUPTING	EGLPRSSU SPLURGES	EHIIMPST MEPHITIS
EGINPRYY PERIGYNY	EGLRSUZZ GUZZLERS	EHIIMSST SMITHIES
EGINQRUY QUERYING	EGMNNOOY MONOGENY	EHIIMSSW WHIMSIES
EGINQSTU QUESTING	EGMNOOOS MONGOOSE	EHIINNOT THIONINE
EGINRRST STRINGER	EGMNSSSU SMUGNESS	EHIINNSW WHINNIES
EGINRRSW WRINGERS	EGMORSTU GOURMETS	EHIINSST SHINIEST
EGINRSST STINGERS	EGNNOOTY ONTOGENY	EHIINSVX VIXENISH
EGINRSSV SERVINGS	EGNNORST RÖNTGENS	EHIIPSTT PITHIEST
EGINRSSW SWINGERS	EGNNSSSU SNUGNESS	EHIIRRST SHIRTIER
EGINRSSY SYRINGES	EGNNSSTU STEN GUNS	EHIIRSTT SHITTIER,
EGINRSTW STREWING,	EGNNSTTU TUNGSTEN	THIRTIES
WRESTING	EGNNSTUU UNGUENTS	EHIISTTX SIXTIETH
EGINRSVW SWERVING	EGNOOOPR GONOPORE	EHIJNNOS JOHNNIES
EGINRTTU UTTERING	EGNOORRV GOVERNOR	EHIKKLOO HOOKLIKE
EGINSSTT SETTINGS	EGNOOTUX OXTONGUE	EHIKKLSU HUSKLIKE
EGINSTTW WETTINGS	EGNOPPRU OPPUGNER	EHIKLMPU HUMPLIKE
EGIOORRV GROOVIER	EGNOPRSS SPONGERS	EHIKLNOR HORNLIKE
EGIOPRSS GOSSIPER	EGNORRST STRONGER	EHIKLNOS SINKHOLE
EGIOPRST EGO TRIPS	EGNORSST SONGSTER	EHIKLOOP HOOPLIKE
EGIOPRSU GROUPIES	EGNORSSU SURGEONS	EHIKLOSY YOKELISH
EGIORRTT GROTTIER	EGNORSTU STURGEON	EHIKNRRS SHRINKER
EGIORSST STRIGOSE	EGNOSTUY YOUNGEST	EHIKRRSS SHIRKERS
EGIORSUV GRIEVOUS	EGOOPRRU PROROGUE	EHIKRSSW WHISKERS
EGIOSSTT EGOTISTS	EGOORRVW OVERGROW	EHIKRSWY WHISKERY
EGIOSUUX EXIGUOUS	EGOORSTT GROTTOES	EHIKSSTU HUSKIEST
EGIRRSTY REGISTRY	EGOPRRSS PROGRESS	EHILLLMO MOLEHILL
EGISSTTU GUSTIEST,	EGOPSSUY GYPSEOUS	EHILLPTY PHYLLITE
GUTSIEST	EGORSSST GROSSEST	EHILLRRS SHRILLER
EGISSUWY WISE GUYS	EGPRSSUU UPSURGES	EHILLRRT THRILLER
EGLLLPSU LEG-PULLS	EHHIIPRS HEIRSHIP	EHILMNOP PHILEMON
EGLLMORW GROMWELL	EHHIIRST THE IRISH	EHILMOOR HEIRLOOM
EGLLOOPR GOLLOPER	EHHIISTV THIEVISH	EHILMOST HELOTISM
EGLLOSUY YULE LOGS	EHHILMNT HELMINTH	EHILMPSY SYMPHILE
EGLMMSTU GLUMMEST	EHHIORTT HITHERTO	EHILNOSS HOLINESS
EGLMNOOY MENOLOGY	EHHIOTTW WHITE-HOT	EHILNOST HOLSTEIN, HOT
EGLMNORS MONGRELS	EHHIRSSW SHREWISH	LINES
EGLMNORT LONG-TERM	EHHMPRUY HUMPHREY	EHILNOTX XENOLITH
EGLMNSSU GLUMNESS	EHHNOORS SHOEHORN	EHILOOPZ ZOOPHILE
EGLMORSS GORMLESS	EHHNORTT THE NORTH	EHILOPRS POLISHER
EGLNNOOR LONGERON	EHHOOSSW WHOOSHES	EHILOPRT HELIPORT
EGLNOOOY OENOLOGY	EHHOOSTU HOTHOUSE	EHILOPSS POLISHES
EGLNOOPY PENOLOGY	EHHOPRTW HEPWORTH	EHILOPST ISOPLETH
EGLNOORV OVERLONG	EHHOSTTU THE SOUTH	EHILORTY RHYOLITE
EGLNORSU LOUNGERS	EHHRSSTU THRUSHES	EHILPRST PHILTRES
EGLNORUU LONGUEUR	EHIIKLNS HELSINKI	EHILPSTU SULPHITE
	EHIIKLPW WHIPLIKE	EHILRSSU SLUSHIER

EHILRSTW WHISTLER
EHILRSTY SLITHERY
EHILRTTW WHITTLER
EHILSSTT THISTLES
EHILSSTW WHISTLES
EHIMMRSY SHIMMERY
EHIMNOPR MORPHINE
EHIMNORT THERMION
EHIMNOSS HOMINESS
EHIMNOTT MONTEITH
EHIMNPST SHIPMENT
EHIMNRRU MURRHINE
EHIMOOST SMOOTHIE
EHIMORST ISOTHERM
EHIMORSZ RHIZOMES
EHIMPRRS SHRIMPER
EHIMPRSW WHIMPERS
EHIMPSUU EUPHUISM
EHIMRSTY SMITHERY
EHIMSSTU MUSHIEST
EHINNOPS PHONE-INS
EHINNOTW NONWHITE
EHINNSST THINNESS
EHINNSSU SUNSHINE
EHINNSTT THINNEST
EHINOOPS ISOPHONE
EHINOPPR HORNPIPE
EHINOPST PHONIEST
EHINORRT THORNIER
EHINORST HORNIEST
EHINORTY IN THEORY
EHINOSTU OUTSHINE
EHINPRSU PUNISHER
EHINPSSX SPHINXES
EHIOORTT TOOTHIER
EHIOPRSS ROSE HIPS
EHIOPRST TROPHIES
EHIORRTW IORWERTH,
    WORTHIER
EHIORSST HORSIEST,
    SHORTIES
EHIORSTT THEORIST
EHIORSTW WORTHIES
EHIORTWZ HOWITZER
EHIOSSTW SHOWIEST
EHIOTTUW WHITEOUT
EHIPPRSS SHIPPERS
EHIPPSTW WHIPPETS
EHIPQSUY PHYSIQUE
EHIPRSST HIPSTERS
EHIPRSSW WHISPERS
EHIPSSTU PUSHIEST
EHIPSTUU EUPHUIST

EHISSSTW SWISHEST
EHKLNOOT KNOTHOLE
EHKLOOSS HOOKLESS
EHKMMNOR MON-KHMER
EHKMOORW HOMEWORK
EHKNNRSU SHRUNKEN
EHKNOOOS HOOKNOSE
EHLLLSSU HULL-LESS
EHLLMOPY PHYLLOME
EHLLNSTU NUTSHELL
EHLLOOOP LOOPHOLE
EHLLOORW HOLLOWER
EHLLOPST TOP-SHELL
EHLMOORW WORMHOLE
EHLMORTY MOTHERLY
EHLMOSUU MULHOUSE
EHLNOPSU SULPHONE
EHLNORSS HORNLESS
EHLNOSTY HONESTLY, ON
    THE SLY
EHLNSSSU LUSHNESS
EHLOOPRT PORTHOLE,
    POTHOLER
EHLOOPST POTHOLES
EHLOOPTY HOLOTYPE
EHLOPSSS SPLOSHES
EHLORSST HOLSTERS,
    HOSTLERS
EHLORSTY HOSTELRY
EHLORTTT THROTTLE
EHLPSSTU PLUSHEST
EHLRSSTU HUSTLERS,
    RUTHLESS
EHLSSTTU SHUTTLES
EHMMOOPR ROMP HOME
EHMMRRTU THRUMMER
EHMNNSTU HUNTSMEN
EHMNOORS HORMONES,
    MOORHENS
EHMNOOST SMOOTHEN
EHMNOOTW HOMETOWN
EHMNOPSU HOMESPUN
EHMNORSU HOME RUNS
EHMNPSTY NYMPHETS
EHMOORST SMOOTHER
EHMOPRSU MORPHEUS
EHMORSTY SMOTHERY
EHMORTUV VERMOUTH
EHNNOPRT PENN'ORTH
EHNNORRT NORTHERN
EHNNORSY HENRYSON
EHNOOPPS OPEN SHOP
EHNOORRU HONOURER

EHNOORTW HONEWORT
EHNOORVZ VORONEZH
EHNOOSSW SNOWSHOE
EHNOOSTU OUTSHONE
EHNORSSU ONRUSHES
EHNORSTU SOUTHERN
EHNOSTUU NUTHOUSE
EHNRSSTU HUNTRESS,
    SHUNTERS
EHOOPRTY ORTHOEPY
EHOOPSTT PHOTOSET
EHOOPSTU HOUSETOP
EHOOPTYZ ZOOPHYTE
EHOORRUZ ZERO HOUR
EHOORSST SHOOTERS
EHOORSTV OVERSHOT
EHOORSUW ROW HOUSE
EHOOSTUU OUTHOUSE
EHOPPRSS SHOPPERS
EHOPPRST PROPHETS
EHOPPRSW WHOPPERS
EHOPPRSY PROPHESY
EHOPRSST STROPHES
EHOPRSUV PUSHOVER
EHORSSTT SHORTEST
EHRRSTTU THRUSTER
EHRSSSTY SHYSTERS
EHRSSTTU SHUTTERS
EIIIMMNS MINIMISE
EIIIMMNZ MINIMIZE
EIIJNRSU INJURIES
EIIKKNST KINKIEST
EIIKLLMN LIMEKILN
EIIKLMST MILKIEST
EIIKLNRS SLINKIER
EIIKLSST SILKIEST
EIIKMPRS SKIMPIER
EIIKNNRS SKINNIER
EIIKNNSS INKINESS
EIIKNNSW WINESKIN
EIIKNRST KRISTINE
EIIKPSST SPIKIEST
EIIKQRRU QUIRKIER
EIIKRSST RISKIEST
EIIKSSVV SKIVVIES
EIILLMNR MILLINER
EIILLNST NIELLIST
EIILLNSV VILLEINS
EIILLNTV VITELLIN
EIILLPSS ELLIPSIS
EIILLSST SILLIEST
EIILMMOT IMMOTILE
EIILMNNS LENINISM

EIILMNNT LINIMENT
EIILMNOT LIMONITE
EIILMNSS LIMINESS
EIILMOPT IMPOLITE
EIILMSSS MISSILES
EIILMSST SLIMIEST
EIILMSTY MYELITIS
EIILNNST LENINIST
EIILNORS LIONISER
EIILNORZ LIONIZER
EIILNOSS ELISIONS,
　　OILINESS
EIILNQTU QUINTILE
EIILNSSW WILINESS
EIILNSTY SENILITY
EIILNTUV VITULINE
EIILOPST PISOLITE,
　　POLITIES
EIILOTVV VOLITIVE
EIILPPRS SLIPPIER
EIILPSST PITILESS
EIILPSTY PYELITIS
EIILRSTU UTILISER
EIILRTUZ UTILIZER
EIILSSTT ELITISTS
EIIMMNNT IMMINENT
EIIMMNSU IMMUNISE
EIIMMNUZ IMMUNIZE
EIIMMPRU IMPERIUM
EIIMMSSS SEISMISM
EIIMNOPT PIMIENTO
EIIMNOSS EMISSION
EIIMNRST INTERIMS,
　　MINISTER
EIIMNRTT INTERMIT
EIIMNRTX INTERMIX
EIIMNSTU MUTINIES
EIIMOPRX MIREPOIX
EIIMOPST OPTIMISE
EIIMOPSZ EPIZOISM
EIIMOPTZ OPTIMIZE
EIIMOTVV VOMITIVE
EIIMQSTU QUIETISM
EIIMRSTT METRITIS
EIIMSSSV MISSIVES
EIIMSSTT SEMITIST
EIINNNPS NINEPINS
EIINNOSU UNIONISE
EIINNOSV ENVISION
EIINNOUZ UNIONIZE
EIINNSTT TIENTSIN,
　　TINNIEST
EIINOPTT PETITION

EIINORRT INTERIOR
EIINORSS IONISERS
EIINORSV REVISION
EIINORSZ IONIZERS
EIINOSST NOISIEST
EIINPPST NIPPIEST
EIINPRRS INSPIRER
EIINPRST PRISTINE
EIINPSST PINT-SISE
EIINPSTZ PINT-SIZE
EIINPTUV PUNITIVE
EIINQRRU INQUIRER
EIINQTUY EQUINITY,
　　INEQUITY
EIINRRTW WINTRIER
EIINRSST INSISTER,
　　SINISTER
EIINRSSW WIRINESS
EIINRSTU NEURITIS
EIINRSTW WRITE-INS
EIIOPRRS PRIORIES
EIIOPSTV POSITIVE
EIIOSSTT OSTEITIS
EIIPPSTZ ZIPPIEST
EIIPRRSS PRISSIER
EIIPRRST STRIPIER
EIIPRRTW TRIPWIRE
EIIPRSTV PRIVIEST
EIIPSSTT TIPSIEST
EIIPSSTW WISPIEST
EIIQSTTU QUIETIST
EIIRSTTW TWISTIER
EIISSSST SISSIEST
EIISTTTW WITTIEST
EIJKORRS SKIJORER
EIJLLOST JOLLIEST
EIJMPSTU JUMPIEST
EIJNORTU JOINTURE
EIJNOSTT JETTISON
EIJNPRSU JUNIPERS
EIKKLNNY KILKENNY
EIKKLSTU TUSKLIKE
EIKKOOST KOOKIEST
EIKLLNSW INKWELLS
EIKLLNTW WELL-KNIT
EIKLLNUY UNLIKELY
EIKLLORV OVERKILL
EIKLLSST SKILLETS
EIKLMNOS MOLESKIN
EIKLMORW WORMLIKE
EIKLNPRS SPRINKLE
EIKLNRSW WRINKLES
EIKLNRTW TWINKLER

EIKLNSSS SKINLESS
EIKLNSSY SKYLINES
EIKLOORT ROOTLIKE
EIKLOPSS SKI POLES
EIKLSSTT SKITTLES
EIKLSSTU SULKIEST
EIKMMRSS SKIMMERS
EIKMNOST TOKENISM
EIKMORTW TIMEWORK
EIKMOSST SMOKIEST
EIKMPSST SKEPTISM
EIKMRSTU MURKIEST
EIKMSSTU MUSKIEST
EIKNOPSS POKINESS
EIKNORTT KNOTTIER
EIKNOSTW WONKIEST
EIKNPRSU SPUNKIER
EIKNPRTU TURNPIKE
EIKNRSST STINKERS
EIKNRSTT KNITTERS,
　　TRINKETS
EIKOOPRS SPOOKIER
EIKOPPRS PORK PIES
EIKOPRST PORKIEST
EIKORRWW WIREWORK
EIKPPRSS SKIPPERS
EIKRRSST STRIKERS
EILLLOSW OIL WELLS
EILLMNOU LINOLEUM
EILLMPSS MISSPELL
EILLMPTU MULTIPLE
EILLMUVX VEXILLUM
EILLNOTU LUTEOLIN
EILLNSTY SILENTLY,
　　TINSELLY
EILLNSVY SNIVELLY
EILLOORW WOOLLIER
EILLOOSW WOOLLIES
EILLOPTY POLITELY
EILLOSTW LOWLIEST
EILLPPPS PEP PILLS
EILLSSST LISTLESS
EILLSSTT STILLEST
EILMMNOU MOULMEIN
EILMMPRU PLUMMIER
EILMMRSS SLIMMERS
EILMMSST SLIMMEST
EILMNOSU EMULSION
EILMNOTY MYLONITE
EILMNPSS LIMPNESS
EILMNRRY MERRILYN
EILMNRST MINSTREL
EILMNSSS SLIMNESS

EILMNTUY MINUTELY,	EILPPSSU SUPPLIES	EIMOORST MOTORISE,
UNTIMELY	EILPPSTU PULPIEST	ROOMIEST
EILMOOST TOILSOME	EILPRSTT SPLITTER,	EIMOORTZ MOTORIZE
EILMOPRR IMPLORER	TRIPLETS	EIMOPPRR IMPROPER
EILMOPST MILEPOST	EILPRSTY PRIESTLY	EIMOPRRS PRIMROSE,
EILMPSST MISSPELT,	EILPRSUU PURLIEUS	PROMISER
SIMPLEST	EILPRSUY PLEURISY	EIMOPRRT IMPORTER,
EILMPSSU IMPULSES	EILPRTTY PRETTILY	REIMPORT
EILMPSTU LUMPIEST	EILQRRSU SQUIRREL	EIMOPRRV IMPROVER
EILMTTUU LUTETIUM	EILQRSUU LIQUEURS	EIMOPRSS PROMISES
EILNNOST INSOLENT	EILRRSTU SULTRIER	EIMOPRUU EUROPIUM
EILNNOSW SNOWLINE	EILRRSTW TWIRLERS	EIMOQSTU MISQUOTE
EILNNPTY IN PLENTY	EILRSSTU SURLIEST	EIMORRST MORTISER,
EILNNTTY INTENTLY	EILRSSTY SISTERLY,	STORMIER
EILNOOST LOONIEST,	STYLISER	EIMORRWW WIREWORM
OILSTONE	EILRSSZZ SIZZLERS	EIMORSST MORTISES
EILNOPRT INTERPOL	EILRSTTW WRISTLET	EIMORSTU MOISTURE
EILNOPTY LINOTYPE	EILRSTUV RIVULETS	EIMORSTW WORMIEST
EILNORTT TROTLINE	EILRSTYZ STYLIZER	EIMORSTY ISOMETRY
EILNORTV IN REVOLT	EILRSUUX LUXURIES	EIMORTTW TWO-TIMER
EILNORVV INVOLVER	EIMMNNTU MUNIMENT	EIMOSSST MOSSIEST
EILNOSTU OUTLINES	EIMMNORS MISNOMER	EIMOSSTU MOUSIEST
EILNOSTV NOVELIST	EIMMOPRU EMPORIUM	EIMOSSTZ MESTIZOS
EILNOTUV INVOLUTE	EIMMORRT MORTIMER	EIMOSTTT TOTEMIST
EILNPRST SPLINTER	EIMMOSTT TOTEMISM	EIMOSTTU TITMOUSE
EILNPSSU SPLENIUS	EIMMPRST PRIMMEST	EIMPRSSU PRIMUSES
EILNPSUY SUPINELY	EIMMPRSU PREMIUMS	EIMPRSTU STUMPIER
EILNQUUY UNIQUELY	EIMMRRST TRIMMERS	EIMPSSTU SEPTIMUS
EILNRSTU INSULTER	EIMMRSSW SWIMMERS	EIMQRRSU SQUIRMER
EILNRSUU URSULINE	EIMMRSTT TRIMMEST	EIMQSTUY MYSTIQUE
EILNRTUV VIRULENT	EIMNNOOT NOONTIME	EIMRRSSU SURMISER
EILNSSTU UTENSILS	EIMNNOPY PIN MONEY	EIMRSSST MISTRESS
EILNSTTU LUTENIST	EIMNNOST MENTIONS	EIMRSSSU SURMISES
EILOOPRR POORLIER	EIMNNOTT OINTMENT	EIMRSTTU SMUTTIER
EILOORST OESTRIOL	EIMNOORS MOONRISE	EIMRSTUX MIXTURES
EILOORWW WIRE WOOL	EIMNOORT MOTIONER	EIMSSTTU MUSTIEST
EILOPPRS SLOPPIER	EIMNOORV OMNIVORE	EIMSTUZZ MUZZIEST
EILOPRRT PORTLIER	EIMNOOST EMOTIONS	EINNOPSS PENSIONS
EILOPRSS SPOILERS	EIMNOPRT ORPIMENT	EINNORSU REUNIONS
EILOPRSU PERILOUS	EIMNOPST NEPOTISM,	EINNORSV ENVIRONS
EILOPRTW PILEWORT	PIMENTOS	EINNORTU NEUTRINO
EILOPSSV PLOSIVES	EIMNOPTT IMPOTENT	EINNORTV INVENTOR
EILOPSTX EXPLOITS	EIMNORSU MONSIEUR	EINNORWW WINNOWER
EILORRTU ULTERIOR	EIMNORTW TIMEWORN	EINNOSSS NOSINESS
EILORSSS RISSOLES	EIMNORTY ENORMITY	EINNOSST TENSIONS
EILORTTY TOILETRY	EIMNOSTU MOUNTIES	EINNPRSS SPINNERS
EILOSSTU LOUSIEST	EIMNPRSS PRIMNESS	EINNPSSU PUNINESS
EILOSTTT STILETTO	EIMNPSST MISSPENT	EINNPSSY SPINNEYS
EILPPRSS SLIPPERS	EIMNRSST MINSTERS,	EINNPSXY SIXPENNY
EILPPRST STIPPLER,	TRIMNESS	EINNRSTU RUNNIEST
TIPPLERS	EIMNRSTU TERMINUS	EINNRSTV VINTNERS
EILPPRSU SUPPLIER	EIMNRSTY ENTRYISM	EINNRTTU NUTRIENT
EILPPRSY SLIPPERY	EIMNSUZZ MUEZZINS	EINNSSTU SUNNIEST

EINOOPRS POISONER
EINOOPSS OPSONISE
EINOOPSZ OPSONIZE
EINOOPTT ON TIPTOE
EINOORST SNOOTIER
EINOORSZ OZONISER
EINOORZZ OZONIZER
EINOOSSZ OOZINESS
EINOOTXX EXOTOXIN
EINOPRRS PRISONER
EINOPRSS ROPINESS
EINOPRST POINTERS,
    PROTEINS
EINOPRSU PRUINOSE
EINOPRTU ERUPTION
EINOPSTT NEPOTIST, STEP
    ON IT
EINOPSWX SWINEPOX
EINOQSTU QUESTION
EINOQTTU QUOTIENT
EINORRST INTRORSE
EINORSSS ROSINESS
EINORSSU NEUROSIS,
    RESINOUS
EINORSSV VERSIONS
EINORSTT SNOTTIER
EINORSTU ROUTINES
EINORSTV INVESTOR
EINORSUV SOUVENIR
EINORTTU RITENUTO
EINOSSSS SESSIONS
EINOSSST STENOSIS
EINOSSTT STONIEST
EINOSSTW SNOWIEST
EINOSTVY VENOSITY
EINPPSST SNIPPETS
EINPRRST PRINTERS,
    REPRINTS, SPRINTER
EINPRRTU PRURIENT
EINPRSST SPINSTER
EINQRSTU SQUINTER
EINQSSTU INQUESTS
EINQSTTU QUINTETS
EINRRSSU INSURERS
EINRSSSU SUNRISES
EINSSTTW TWIN SETS
EINSTTTU NUTTIEST
EIOOPPRS PORPOISE
EIOOPPST OPPOSITE
EIOOPSST ISOTOPES
EIOORSTT TORTOISE
EIOOSSTT SOOTIEST,
    TOOTSIES

EIOOSTWZ WOOZIEST
EIOPPRTW PIPEWORT
EIOPPSST SOPPIEST
EIOPRRSS PRIORESS
EIOPRRST SPORTIER
EIOPRRSU SUPERIOR
EIOPRSST PROSIEST,
    RIPOSTES, TRIPOSES
EIOPRSTT SPOTTIER
EIOPRSTV SPORTIVE
EIOPRSUV PERVIOUS,
    PREVIOUS, VIPEROUS
EIOPSTTT POTTIEST
EIORRRSW WORRIERS
EIORRSST RESISTOR,
    SORRIEST
EIORRSTV SERVITOR
EIORRSVY REVISORY
EIORSSTY SEROSITY
EIORSTUV VITREOUS
EIPPRRST STRIPPER,
    TRIPPERS
EIPQRSTU QUIPSTER
EIPRRSSU SURPRISE
EIPRSSTT TIPSTERS
EIPRSTUW WRITE-UPS
EIQRRSTU SQUIRTER
EIQRSTTU QUITTERS
EIRRRSST STIRRERS
EIRRSTTU TRUSTIER
EIRSSTTU RUSTIEST,
    TRUSTIES
EIRSSTTW TWISTERS
EIRSTTTW TWITTERS
EIRTTTWY TWITTERY
EISSTTUW WET SUITS
EISSUUVV VESUVIUS
EJMOSTTU MOT JUSTE
EJNORSUY JOURNEYS
EJNSSSTU JUSTNESS
EKKNSTUZ KUZNETSK
EKLMNOSS SMOLENSK
EKLNOOOR LOOKER-ON,
    ONLOOKER
EKLNORSS SNORKELS
EKLOOORV OVERLOOK
EKMRSTUY MUSKETRY
EKNNOPSU UNSPOKEN
EKNOOPRW OPENWORK
EKNORSTW NETWORKS
EKNRSTUY TURNKEYS
EKOOORTV OVERTOOK
EKOORRVW OVERWORK

EKOORTWW KOWTOWER
EKOPRSTU UPSTROKE
ELLLMOWY MELLOWLY
ELLLNSUY SULLENLY
ELLMNOSY SOLEMNLY
ELLNOORV LOVELORN
ELLNOOSW WOOLLENS
ELLNORRT RENT-ROLL
ELLNORWW WELL-WORN
ELLNOSVY SLOVENLY
ELLNOUVY UNLOVELY
ELLNSSTU NULL SETS
ELLOPRST POLLSTER
ELLOPRTU POLLUTER
ELLOPRUV PULLOVER
ELLORRST STROLLER
ELLORSTY TROLLEYS
ELLOSSSU SOULLESS
ELLOSSTU SELL-OUTS
ELMNOOSS MOONLESS
ELMNOOSZ ZOOM LENS
ELMNUUZZ UNMUZZLE
ELMOORST TREMOLOS
ELMOORSY MOROSELY
ELMOOSSY LYSOSOME
ELMOPRSY POLYMERS
ELMOPSYY POLYSEMY
ELMOSTUU TUMULOSE
ELMOSYYZ LYSOZYME
ELMPPSTU PLUMPEST
ELNNOOSU UNLOOSEN
ELNOOSTZ SOLONETZ
ELNOPRVY PROVENLY
ELNOPSTU PLEUSTON
ELNOPTTY POTENTLY
ELNORSTU TURNSOLE
ELNORTTY ROTTENLY
ELNOSSSW SLOWNESS
ELNOSSTV SOLVENTS
ELNPRTUU PURULENT
ELOORSST ROOTLESS
ELOOSTUU TOULOUSE
ELOPPRRY PROPERLY
ELOPRRSW PROWLERS
ELOPRSTY PROSTYLE
ELOPSSST SPOTLESS
ELORSTUY UROSTYLE
ELPPSSTU SUPPLEST
ELPRSTTU SPLUTTER
ELPRSUZZ PUZZLERS
ELPSSTUU PUSTULES
ELRRSSTU RUSTLERS
ELRSTUUV VULTURES

ELSSSTUY STYLUSES
EMMMNOTU MOMENTUM
EMMNNOTU MONUMENT
EMMNOOOS MONOSOME
EMMNOORS MEN'S ROOM
EMMNOORT MOTORMEN
EMMNOOSY MONOSEMY
EMMNOTTU TOMENTUM
EMMNOTYY METONYMY
EMMRRRUU MURMURER
EMMRRSTU STRUMMER
EMMRSTYY SYMMETRY
EMNNOOOT MONOTONE
EMNNOOSW NEW MOONS
EMNNOSTW TOWNSMEN
EMNNSTTU STUNT MEN
EMNOOPTY MONOTYPE
EMNOORSU ENORMOUS
EMNOORSW NEWSROOM
EMNOOSUV VENOMOUS
EMNOOTTY TENOTOMY
EMNORRSU MOURNERS
EMNORSST MONSTERS
EMNORSTT TORMENTS
EMNORSTU REMOUNTS
EMNORSUU NUMEROUS
EMNOSUUY EUONYMUS
EMNOSUVY EVONYMUS
EMNRSSTU STERNUMS
EMOOPRRT PROMOTER
EMOOPRSZ ZOOSPERM
EMOORRST REST ROOM
EMOORTYZ ZOOMETRY
EMOOSSTW TWOSOMES
EMOPPRRT PROMPTER
EMOPRSSU SPERMOUS,
SUPREMOS
EMPRRTUY TRUMPERY
EMPRSTTU STRUMPET,
TRUMPETS
ENNOOOTZ ENTOZOON
ENNOOPPT OPPONENT
ENNOORTV NONVOTER
ENNOPRUV UNPROVEN
ENNOPTWY TWOPENNY
ENNORSST STERNSON
ENNORSTU NEUTRONS
ENNOSTWW NEW TOWNS
ENNPPTUY TUPPENNY
ENNPRRUU RUNNER-UP
ENNRSSTU STUNNERS
ENOOPPST POSTPONE

ENOOPRSS POORNESS,
SNOOPERS
ENOOPSTT POTSTONE
ENOPRSTT PORTENTS
ENOPSSSY SYNOPSES
ENORRSST SNORTERS
ENORRSTT TORRENTS
ENORRTUV OVERTURN,
TURNOVER
ENORSSSU SOURNESS
ENORSSTU TONSURES
ENORSTUY TOURNEYS
ENOSSSTT STETSONS
ENOSSSUU SENSUOUS
ENPRSSSY SPRYNESS
ENPRSSTU PUNSTERS
ENRRRTUU NURTURER
EOOOPRSZ ZOOSPORE
EOOORRST ROSE-ROOT
EOOPPRRS PROPOSER
EOOPPRSV POPOVERS
EOOPPTTY TOPOTYPE
EOOPRRST TROOPERS
EOOPRRTU UPROOTER
EOOPRSTV STOPOVER
EOOPRSTW TOWROPES
EOORRRSW SORROWER
EOORRSST ROOSTERS
EOORSSTU OESTROUS
EOPPRRTY PROPERTY
EOPPRSST STOPPERS
EOPPRSSU PURPOSES,
SUPPOSER
EOPRRSTU POSTURER,
TROUPERS
EOPRRUVY PURVEYOR
EOPRSSTT PROTESTS,
SPOTTERS
EOPRSSTU POSTURES,
SPOUTERS
EOPSSTTW TWO-STEPS
EORRRTTU TORTURER
EORRSSTU TROUSERS
EORRSTTT TROTTERS
EORRSTTU TORTURES
EORRSUVY SURVEYOR
EOSSTTTU STOUTEST
EPPPRTUY PUPPETRY
EPPRSSSU PRESS-UPS,
SUPPRESS
EPRRSSUU PURSUERS,
USURPERS
EPRRSTUU RUPTURES

EPRSSTTU SPUTTERS
ERRSTTTU STRUTTER
ERSSTTTU STUTTERS
FFFGILNU FLUFFING
FFFILOST LIFT-OFFS
FFGHIIRT GRIFFITH
FFGHIORS FROGFISH
FFGHIRSU GRUFFISH
FFGIILNP PIFFLING
FFGIILNR RIFFLING
FFGIINNS SNIFFING
FFGIINRS GRIFFINS
FFGILMNU MUFFLING
FFGILNRU RUFFLING
FFGINNSU SNUFFING
FFGINSTU STUFFING
FFHILOSW WOLFFISH
FFHOOOST OFFSHOOT
FFHOOSSW SHOW-OFFS
FFHOSTTU HOT STUFF
FFIILMOR FILIFORM
FFIKLORT FORK-LIFT
FFILLOPP FLIP-FLOP
FFILLTUY FITFULLY
FFILRTUU FRUITFUL
FFILRTUY FRUIT FLY
FFILSTUY STUFFILY
FFIMORSU FUSIFORM
FFINOPRT OFFPRINT
FFINOPSS SPIN-OFFS
FFINOPST PONTIFFS
FFNORSTU TURN-OFFS
FFOORRUU FROUFROU
FFOORSTW WORST-OFF
FGGGIINR FRIGGING
FGGGILNO FLOGGING
FGGHIINT FIGHTING
FGGIILNN FLINGING
FGGIINNR FRINGING
FGGIINRU FIGURING
FGGINOOR FORGOING
FGGINORS FORGINGS
FGHIIKNS KINGFISH
FGHIILNT IN-FLIGHT
FGHIINST SHIFTING
FGHILNSU FLUSHING,
LUNGFISH
FGHILRTU RIGHTFUL
FGHINORT FROTHING
FGHIOTTU OUTFIGHT
FGHLORUU FURLOUGH
FGHNOORS FOGHORNS
FGIIKNRS FRISKING

FGIILLNS FILLINGS
FGIILNPP FLIPPING
FGIILNRT FLIRTING,
   TRIFLING
FGIILNST STIFLING
FGIILNTT FLITTING
FGIINNSU INFUSING
FGIINNUY UNIFYING
FGIINOST FOISTING
FGIINRTU FRUITING
FGIINRZZ FRIZZING
FGIINSST SIFTINGS
FGIINSTT FITTINGS
FGIKLNNU FLUNKING
FGILMNUY FUMINGLY
FGILNNTU GUNFLINT
FGILNOOR FLOORING
FGILNOOT FOOTLING
FGILNOPP FLOPPING
FGILNORU FLOURING
FGILNOSS FLOSSING
FGILNOTU FLOUTING
FGILNPRU PURFLING
FGINNORT FRONTING
FGINNORW FROWNING
FGINOOPR PROOFING
FGINORST FROSTING
FGLLMOOU GLOOMFUL
FGLNORSU FURLONGS
FGLNORUW WRONGFUL
FGLOOOST FOOTSLOG
FHHIKOOS FISH-HOOK
FHHLOSTU HOT FLUSH
FHIIKLMS MILKFISH
FHIIKNSS FISHSKIN
FHIILLTY FILTHILY
FHIILMNT THIN-FILM
FHIILNOS LIONFISH
FHIILSTY SHIFTILY
FHIKLSWY FLYWHISK
FHIKMNOS MONKFISH
FHILLOOT FOOTHILL
FHILLORT HILLFORT
FHILMPSU LUMPFISH
FHILMRTU MIRTHFUL
FHILOPST SHOPLIFT
FHILORSU FLOURISH
FHILORTY FROTHILY
FHIMNOOS MOONFISH
FHIMPRSU FRUMPISH
FHIOOPTT PHOTOFIT
FHLLOSTU SLOTHFUL
FHLMOTUU MOUTHFUL

FHLOTUUY YOUTHFUL
FHLRTTUU TRUTHFUL
FHNOSTUX FOXHUNTS
FHOOORST FORSOOTH
FIIILNOP FILIPINO
FIIINNOX INFIXION
FIIINNTY INFINITY
FIIKLRSY FRISKILY
FIIKLSST SKI LIFTS
FIILLMSY FLIMSILY
FIILMOPR PILIFORM
FIILMPSY SIMPLIFY
FIILTTUY FUTILITY
FIIMOPRS PISIFORM
FIINNOSU INFUSION
FIINORTU FRUITION
FIKKLNOS KINSFOLK
FILLLUWY WILFULLY
FILLNSUY SINFULLY
FILLOPPY FLOPPILY
FILORSST FLORISTS
FILORSTY FROSTILY
FILSSTTU FLUTISTS
FILSTTUY STULTIFY
FIMNORSU UNIFORMS
FIMOPRRY PYRIFORM
FIMORTUY FUMITORY
FIMRSTUU FUTURISM
FINORSSS FRISSONS
FIORTTUY FORTUITY
FIRSTTUU FUTURIST
FIRTTUUY FUTURITY
FJLLOUYY JOYFULLY
FKMOORRW FORMWORK
FKNOORTX FORT KNOX
FKOOORTW FOOTWORK
FLLMNOOU FULL MOON
FLLNOOOW FOLLOW-ON
FLLOOPUW FOLLOW-UP
FLLOPSTU FULL STOP
FLMNORUU MOURNFUL
FLNOOPSU SPOONFUL
FLOOSTUW OUTFLOWS
FLOPRSTU SPORTFUL
FLRSTTUU TRUSTFUL
FNOOORTW FOOTWORN
FNOORRSW FORSWORN
FNOORSSU SUNROOFS
FOOOPRST ROOFTOPS
FOOPSSTT SOFT SPOT
FOORSTTX FOXTROTS
FOPSSSTU FUSSPOTS
GGGGIILN GIGGLING

GGGGILNO GOGGLING
GGGIIJLN JIGGLING
GGGIILNN NIGGLING
GGGIILNW WIGGLING
GGGIINSW SWIGGING,
   WIGGINGS
GGGIINTW TWIGGING
GGGIJLNO JOGGLING
GGGIJLNU JUGGLING
GGGILNOS SLOGGING
GGGILNPU PLUGGING
GGGILNRU GURGLING
GGGILNSU SLUGGING
GGGILORY GROGGILY
GGGIMNSU MUGGINGS
GGGINNOS SNOGGING
GGHHIISW WHIGGISH
GGHIILNT LIGHTING
GGHIINNW WHINGING
GGHIINRT RIGHTING
GGHIINST SIGHTING
GGHIIPRS PRIGGISH
GGHILSSU SLUGGISH
GGHINORU ROUGHING
GGHINOST GHOSTING
GGHINOSU SOUGHING
GGHKNNOO HONG KONG
GGIIINNT IGNITING
GGIIJLNN JINGLING
GGIILLNR GRILLING
GGIILMNN MINGLING
GGIILNNS GIN SLING,
   SINGLING, SLINGING
GGIILNNT GLINTING,
   TINGLING
GGIIMPRS PRIGGISM
GGIINNNR GRINNING
GGIINNOR IGNORING
GGIINNRW WRINGING
GGIINNSS SIGNINGS
GGIINNST STINGING
GGIINNSW SWINGING
GGIINPPR GRIPPING
GGIINRTT GRITTING
GGILLOOW GOLLIWOG
GGILNNOS LONGINGS
GGILNNOU LOUNGING
GGILNNPU PLUNGING
GGILNORW GROWLING
GGILNORY GLORYING
GGILNOSS GLOSSING,
   GOSLINGS
GGILNRUY URGINGLY

GGILNTTU GLUTTING
GGILNUZZ GUZZLING
GGILQSUY SQUIGGLY
GGIMNOOR GROOMING
GGINNOOS GOINGS-ON
GGINNOPP PING-PONG
GGINNOPS SPONGING
GGINNORW WRONGING
GGINNOSS SINGSONG
GGINNRTU GRUNTING
GGINOOTU OUTGOING
GGINOPRU GROUPING
GGINORSS GROSSING
GGINORSU GROUSING
GGINRSST G-STRINGS
GHHIJMPU HIGH JUMP
GHHILOSU GHOULISH
GHHINSSU SHUSHING
GHHIOPST HIGH SPOT
GHHOORTU THOROUGH
GHHOSTTU THOUGHTS
GHIIKNNS HSINKING
GHIIKNNT THINKING
GHIIKNPS KINGSHIP
GHIIKNRS SHIRKING
GHIIKNSW WHISKING
GHIILLNS SHILLING
GHIILMTY MIGHTILY
GHIILNRW WHIRLING
GHIILTTW TWILIGHT
GHIIMRST RIGHTISM
GHIINNNS SHINNING
GHIINNNT THINNING
GHIINOST HOISTING
GHIINPPS SHIPPING
GHIINPPW WHIPPING
GHIINRRS SHIRRING
GHIINRRW WHIRRING
GHIINRST SHIRTING
GHIINRTV THRIVING
GHIINRTW WRITHING
GHIINSST INSIGHTS
GHIINSSW SWISHING
GHIINSTT SHITTING
GHIINSTW WHITINGS
GHIINWZZ WHIZZING
GHIIRSTT RIGHTIST
GHIKLNTY KNIGHTLY
GHIKLSTY SKYLIGHT
GHILLSTY SLIGHTLY
GHILNOPS LONGSHIP
GHILNOSS SLOSHING
GHILNOTW NIGHT OWL

GHILNRTU HURTLING
GHILNRUY HUNGRILY
GHILNSTU HUSTLING,
   SUNLIGHT
GHILOPRS SHOPGIRL
GHILORSW SHOWGIRL
GHILPRTY TRIGLYPH
GHIMNOTU MOUTHING
GHIMNPTU THUMPING
GHIMNSTU GUNSMITH
GHINNNSU SHUNNING
GHINNORT NORTHING
GHINNSTU SHUNTING
GHINOOPW WHOOPING
GHINOOST SHOOTING,
   SOOTHING
GHINOPPS SHOPPING
GHINOPPW WHOPPING
GHINOQTU QUOTHING
GHINORST SHORTING
GHINORTW INGROWTH,
   THROWING
GHINOSSU HOUSINGS
GHINOSSW SHOWINGS
GHINOSTU SHOUTING,
   SOUTHING
GHINOSUY YOUNGISH
GHINRRUY HURRYING
GHINSSTU HUSTINGS
GHINSTTU SHUTTING
GHIORTTU OUTRIGHT
GHLMOOOY HOMOLOGY
GHLNNOOR LONGHORN
GHLNOOST LONG SHOT
GHLOOORY HOROLOGY
GHLORTUU TURLOUGH
GHMNOOOY HOMOGONY
GHMOSSTU MUGSHOTS
GHNNOPUU HUNG UP ON
GHNOPRSY GRYPHONS
GHNOSSTU GUNSHOTS,
   SHOTGUNS
GHOPRTUW UPGROWTH
GIIILMNT LIMITING
GIIILOTV VITILIGO
GIIINNOT IGNITION
GIIINNOZ IONIZING
GIIINNTV INVITING
GIIINSTV VISITING
GIIJMNOS JINGOISM
GIIJNNOT JOINTING
GIIJNNRU INJURING
GIIJNOST JINGOIST

GIIKLLNS KILLINGS
GIIKLNNS SLINKING
GIIKLNNT TINKLING
GIIKLNNW WINKLING
GIIKMMNS SKIMMING
GIIKMNPS SKIMPING
GIIKMNRS SMIRKING
GIIKNNNS SKINNING
GIIKNNOV INVOKING
GIIKNNPS KINGPINS, PINK
   GINS
GIIKNNST STINKING
GIIKNNTT KNITTING
GIIKNPPS SKIPPING
GIIKNPSS PIGSKINS
GIIKNRST SKIRTING,
   STRIKING
GIILLNPS SPILLING
GIILLNRT TRILLING
GIILLNST STILLING
GIILLNSW SWILLING
GIILLPSW PIGSWILL
GIILLTUY GUILTILY
GIILMMNS SLIMMING
GIILMNPY IMPLYING
GIILMPRS PILGRIMS
GIILMPSU PUGILISM
GIILNNSY LYINGS-IN
GIILNOPS SPOILING
GIILNOPT PILOTING
GIILNPPR RIPPLING
GIILNPPS SLIPPING
GIILNPRT TRIPLING
GIILNQSU QUISLING
GIILNQTU QUILTING
GIILNRST STIRLING
GIILNRSW SWIRLING
GIILNRTW TWIRLING
GIILNSTT SLITTING
GIILNSTU LINGUIST
GIILNSTY STINGILY
GIILNSZZ SIZZLING
GIILPSTU PUGILIST
GIILRTTY GRITTILY
GIIMMNRT TRIMMING
GIIMMNRU IMMURING
GIIMMNSW SWIMMING
GIIMNNOY IGNOMINY
GIIMNNTU MINUTING
GIIMNOPS IMPOSING
GIIMNOTT OMITTING
GIIMNOTV VOMITING
GIIMNPRU UMPIRING

GIIMNPTU IMPUTING	GILMNPPU PLUMPING	GINNOPTU GUNPOINT
GIIMNSSU MISUSING	GILMNPRU RUMPLING	GINNORST SNORTING
GIIMORRS RIGORISM	GILMNPSU SLUMPING	GINNPRSU SPURNING
GIINNNOT INTONING	GILMNSUY MUSINGLY	GINNRSTU TURNINGS,
GIINNNPS SPINNING	GILMNUZZ MUZZLING	UNSTRING
GIINNNSW WINNINGS	GILMOOSY MISOLOGY	GINNSTTU STUNTING
GIINNNTW TWINNING	GILMPRUY GRUMPILY	GINNSTUW WING NUTS
GIINNOPT POINTING	GILMPSSY GYMSLIPS	GINOOPPS OPPOSING
GIINNORS ROSINING	GILNNRSU NURSLING	GINOOPRT TROOPING
GIINNORT IGNITRON	GILNNUZZ NUZZLING	GINOOPST STOOPING
GIINNPPS SNIPPING	GILNOOSY SINOLOGY	GINOOPSW SWOOPING
GIINNPRT PRINTING	GILNOOTT TOOTLING	GINOORST ROOSTING
GIINNRSU INSURING	GILNOPPP PLOPPING	GINOPPPR PROPPING
GIINNRTU UNTIRING	GILNOPPS SLOPPING	GINOPPST STOPPING,
GIINNSTT STINTING	GILNOPPT TOPPLING	TOPPINGS
GIINOPST POSITING	GILNOPRW PROWLING	GINOPPSW SWOPPING
GIINOPTV PIVOTING	GILNOPSY SPONGILY	GINOPRST SPORTING
GIINORUV IN VIGOUR	GILNOPTT PLOTTING	GINOPRSU IN-GROUPS
GIINPPQU QUIPPING	GILNOSTT SLOTTING	GINOPSST POSTINGS,
GIINPPRT TRIPPING	GILNOSTU LONG SUIT,	SIGNPOST
GIINPRSU UPRISING	TOUSLING	GINOPSTT SPOTTING
GIINPSTT SPITTING	GILNOTUY OUTLYING	GINOPSTU SPOUTING
GIINQTTU QUITTING	GILNPRSU SLURPING	GINORRWY WORRYING
GIINQUZZ QUIZZING	GILNPUZZ PUZZLING	GINORSTW WORSTING
GIINRRST STIRRING	GILNRRSU SLURRING	GINORTTT TROTTING
GIINRSTW WRITINGS	GILNRSTU RUSTLING	GINORTTU TUTORING
GIINSSTT SITTINGS	GILNSSTU TUSSLING	GINOSTTW SWOTTING
GIINSTTW TWISTING	GILOOOST OOLOGIST	GINOSTUW OUTSWING
GIINTTTW TWITTING	GILOORSU GLORIOUS	GINPRRSU SPURRING
GIIORRST RIGORIST	GILOORVY VIROLOGY	GINPRSTU SPURTING
GIJKLNOY JOKINGLY	GILOOSSS ISOGLOSS	GINPRSUU PURSUING,
GIJLLNOY JOLLYING	GILOOSTY SITOLOGY	USURPING
GIJLNOST JOSTLING	GIMMNRUY GIN RUMMY	GINPSSUW UPSWINGS
GIJNOSTT JOTTINGS	GIMMOSSU GUMMOSIS	GINRSSTU TRUSSING
GIJNOSTU JOUSTING	GIMNNORS MORNINGS	GINRSTTU TRUSTING
GIKKLNSU SKULKING	GIMNNORU MOURNING	GINRSTUU SUTURING
GIKLNNOP PLONKING	GIMNNOTU MOUNTING	GIOOORSV VIGOROSO
GIKNNOST KINGSTON	GIMNOOOU OOGONIUM	GIOORRSU RIGOROUS
GIKNNOTT KNOTTING	GIMNOORS MOORINGS	GIOORSTU GOITROUS
GIKNOOPS SPOOKING	GIMNOORT MOTORING	GIOORSUV VIGOROUS
GIKNORST STROKING	GIMNOPST STOMPING	GIORSTUY RUGOSITY
GIKNORSW WORKINGS	GIMNOPTU GUMPTION	GJLMNOPU LONG JUMP
GILLMOOY GLOOMILY	GIMNORRW RINGWORM	GLLOOPTY POLYGLOT
GILLNORT TROLLING	GIMNORST STORMING	GLMNOOOY MONOLOGY,
GILLNOVY LOVINGLY	GIMNOSYY MISOGYNY	NOMOLOGY
GILLNOWY LOW-LYING	GIMNPRTU TRUMPING	GLMNORUW LUNGWORM
GILLNRUY LURINGLY	GIMNPSTU STUMPING	GLMOOOPY POMOLOGY
GILLNSUY SULLYING	GIMNSTYY STYMYING	GLMOORWW
GILLOSSY GLOSSILY	GINNNSTU STUNNING	GLOW-WORM
GILMMNSU SLUMMING	GINNOOPS SNOOPING,	GLMOOYYZ ZYMOLOGY
GILMNOPY MOPINGLY	SPOONING	GLMORSUW LUGWORMS
GILMNOTU MOULTING	GINNOOSW SWOONING	GLNNOOST LONG TONS
GILMNOVY MOVINGLY	GINNOOSZ SNOOZING	GLNOOOSY NOSOLOGY

GLNOOOTY ONTOLOGY
GLNOOPSY POLYGONS
GLNOPYYY POLYGYNY
GLNORSTY STRONGLY
GLNORTUW LUNGWORT
GLNOSTTU GLUTTONS
GLNOTTUY GLUTTONY
GLOOOPSY POSOLOGY
GLOOOPTY TOPOLOGY
GLOOPTYY LOGOTYPY,
   TYPOLOGY
GMMNOTUY TOMMY GUN
GMMPSUUW MUGWUMPS
GMNNOOYY MONOGYNY
GNOOOTTW GO TO TOWN
GNOORTUW OUTGROWN
GNOPPUUY YOUNG PUP
GNOPRSUW GROWN-UPS
GNPRSTUU STRUNG-UP
GOOPRTUU OUT-GROUP
HHHHSSUU HUSH-HUSH
HHIIOORT HIROHITO
HHIIPSST PHTHISIS
HHKKSSUU KHUSKHUS
HHOOOOPP POOH-POOH
HHOOPPRS PHOSPHOR
HHORRSUU RUSH HOUR
HIIILMNS NIHILISM
HIIILNST NIHILIST
HIIILNTY NIHILITY
HIIINRST RHINITIS
HIIKMRSS SKIRMISH
HIIKSSTT SKITTISH
HIILMOST HOMILIST
HIILMPSY IMPISHLY
HIILMTUY HUMILITY
HIILOPST PISOLITH
HIILPSSY SYPHILIS
HIILSSTT HIT LISTS
HIIMNSTT TINSMITH
HIIMOPSS PHIMOSIS
HIIMORTU HIRI MOTU
HIIMORTZ ZHITOMIR
HIISSSSY SISSYISH
HIKNOOOR KOHINOOR
HIKOOPSS SPOOKISH
HIKOPSSY KYPHOSIS
HILLLOSU SOLIHULL
HILLMSUY MULISHLY
HILLOSWY OWLISHLY
HILMNOOT MONOLITH
HILNORTY THORNILY
HILOOTTY TOOTHILY

HILORSUU URUSHIOL
HILORTWY HOLY WRIT,
   WORTHILY
HILOSTWW WHITLOWS
HILPPRSU PURPLISH
HILSSTTU SLUTTISH
HIMOOPRS ISOMORPH
HIMOPRRT TRIMORPH
HIMOPRSW SHIPWORM
HIMOPRWW WHIPWORM
HIMOPSSS SOPHISMS
HIMORSTU HUMORIST
HIMPRSTU TRIUMPHS
HINNSSUY SUNSHINY
HINOORSZ HORIZONS
HINOPRTW WINTHROP
HINOPSSY HYPNOSIS
HINOPSTW TOWNSHIP
HINORSTW THROW-INS
HIOORTWZ HOROWITZ
HIOPRSSW WORSHIPS
HIOPRSUZ RHIZOPUS
HIOPSSST SOPHISTS
HIPPPSUY PUPPYISH
HKMOOORW HOOKWORM
HKOOPRSW WORKSHOP
HLLLOOWY HOLLOWLY
HLLMNOOU MONOHULL
HLLNOOUU HONOLULU
HLLPPSUU PUSH-PULL
HLMOOSTY SMOOTHLY
HLMOPTUY PLYMOUTH
HLNOOSUW HOUNSLOW
HMMNOOSY HOMONYMS
HMMOORSU MUSHROOM
HMNOOOST MOON SHOT
HMNOPSYY SYMPHONY
HMOOORSW SHOWROOM
HMOORSUU HUMOROUS
HNNOORTT THORNTON
HNOOOSTT NOT SO HOT
HNOOPRST POST HORN
HNOOPSTY TYPHOONS
HNOORRTW HORNWORT
HNORSTTU THURSTON
HNORTUWY UNWORTHY
HNRSTTUU UNTRUTHS
HOOOSTTU OUTSHOOT,
   SHOOT-OUT
HOOPSSTT HOT SPOTS,
   POTSHOTS
HOPPRRYY PORPHYRY
HPRSTTUU UPTHRUST

IIILLNOS ILLINOIS
IIILMRSV VIRILISM
IIILMUVX LIXIVIUM
IIILRTVY VIRILITY
IIINPRST INSPIRIT
IIINQTUY INIQUITY
IIJJSTUU JIUJITSU
IIKLLNSY SLINKILY
IIKLMPSY SKIMPILY
IIKLNOSS OILSKINS
IIKLQRUY QUIRKILY
IILLMNOS MILLIONS
IILLMRTU TRILLIUM
IILLMUUV ILLUVIUM
IILLNOPS PILLIONS
IILLNORT TRILLION
IILLNOSU ILLUSION
IILLNOSZ ZILLIONS
IILMMPSS SIMPLISM
IILMNOSU LIMOUSIN
IILMOTTY MOTILITY
IILNOOST INOSITOL
IILNOOTV VOLITION
IILNORSS SIRLOINS
IILNPPSY SNIPPILY
IILNRTWY WINTRILY
IILPRSSY PRISSILY
IILSTUUV UVULITIS
IILSTUVV VULVITIS
IIMMMNSU MINIMUMS
IIMMNTUY IMMUNITY
IIMMOPST OPTIMISM
IIMMOPSU OPIUMISM
IIMMSTTU MITTIMUS
IIMNNOOT MONITION
IIMNNOSU UNIONISM
IIMNNOTU MUNITION
IIMNOOSS OMISSION
IIMNOPRS IMPRISON
IIMNORTY MINORITY
IIMNOSSS MISSIONS
IIMNOSST SIMONIST
IIMNPRST IMPRINTS,
   MISPRINT
IIMNPTUY IMPUNITY
IIMNRSTY MINISTRY
IIMOPSTT OPTIMIST
IIMORSSU MISSOURI
IIMORSTY RIMOSITY
IIMOTTVY MOTIVITY
IIMPRTUY IMPURITY
IIMSSTUW SWIMSUIT
IINNNOSU IN UNISON

IINNOOPS OPINIONS	ILNOSTTY SNOTTILY	IORSSTTU TOURISTS
IINNOPPT PINPOINT	ILNPSUUV PULVINUS	IORSSUUU USURIOUS
IINNOSTU UNIONIST	ILOOPPRS PROPOLIS	IORSTTUY TOURISTY
IINNSTTU TINNITUS	ILOOSSST SOLOISTS	IORSTUUV VIRTUOUS
IINOOPST POSITION	ILOPPSTU POPULIST	IPRRSSTU STIRRUPS
IINOSSTZ ZIONISTS	ILOPRSTY SPORTILY	IPRRSTUU PRURITUS
IINOSTVY VINOSITY	ILOPSTTY SPOTTILY	IPRSSTUU PURSUITS
IINRTTUY TRIUNITY	ILOPSUUV PLUVIOUS	JLOOSUYY JOYOUSLY
IIOOPSTV OVIPOSIT	ILOQRTUU LOQUITUR	JNNOORRU NONJUROR
IIOOQRSU IROQUOIS	ILRSTTUY TRUSTILY	JNOORSSU SOJOURNS
IIOOSTTY OTIOSITY	ILSSSTTY STYLISTS	KLLMNSUU NUMSKULL
IIOPRRTY PRIORITY	IMMNOORS MORONISM	KLMMOOOS KOMSOMOL
IIORSSTV VISITORS	IMNNOSUU NUMINOUS	KLNORSTY KLYSTRON
IIORSTUV VIRTUOSI	IMNOORST MONITORS	KLOOOSTU LOOKOUTS,
IJKLLOSY KILLJOYS	IMNOORTY MONITORY	OUTLOOKS
IJKMPSSU SKI JUMPS	IMNOSTUU MUTINOUS	KLOOPRSW SLOPWORK
IJLLORTU TRUJILLO	IMOOPRRS PROMISOR	KMOOORRW WORKROOM
IJMPSTUU JUMPSUIT	IMOOPRST IMPOSTOR	KNNNOSUW UNKNOWNS
IKKLNORW LINKWORK	IMOOQSTU MOSQUITO	KNOOPSTT TOPKNOTS
IKKLNOSY KOLINSKY	IMOORSTT MOTORIST	KOOPRSTW WORKTOPS
IKLLOOTV KILOVOLT	IMOORSTU TIMOROUS	KOORSTUW OUTWORKS,
IKLMNRSU MILK RUNS	IMOORTVY VOMITORY	WORKOUTS
IKLMOPSS MILKSOPS	IMOOSSTY MYOSOTIS	LLMOOPRS ROLLMOPS
IKLMORSW SILKWORM	IMRSSTTU MISTRUST	LLOOPRST TROLLOPS
IKLMORTW MILKWORT	INNNNOOU NONUNION	LLOOPRYY ROLY-POLY
IKLNOPST SLIPKNOT	INNNORTU TRUNNION	LLOPSTUU PULLOUTS
IKLNOTTY KNOTTILY	INNOOPSS SPONSION	LLOSUUVV VOLVULUS
IKLNPSUY SPUNKILY	INNOORST NOTORNIS	LMMPSSUU LUMP SUMS
IKLOOPSY SPOOKILY	INOOOSSZ ZOONOSIS	LMNOOOPY MONOPOLY
IKMNPPSU PUMPKINS	INOOOTXZ ZOOTOXIN	LMOOPRTU PULMOTOR
IKNOOPRT PINKROOT	INOOPRST PORTIONS,	LMOORSWW SLOWWORM
IKNOORRW IRONWORK	POSITRON, SORPTION	LMOOTXYY XYLOTOMY
IKORSSTU KURTOSIS	INOOPSTT SPITTOON	LMOPPRTY PROMPTLY
ILLLMOPS PLIMSOLL	INOOPTTU OUTPOINT	LNOOOPRT POLTROON
ILLLOOPP LOLLIPOP	INOORSTY SONORITY	LOOPPSUU POPULOUS
ILLLOOWY WOOLLILY	INOPRTTU PRINTOUT	LOOPPSUY POLYPOUS
ILLMNOSU MULLIONS	INOPSSSY SYNOPSIS	LORSSTUU LUSTROUS
ILLMOSSY LISSOMLY	INORSSUV SUN VISOR	MMOOPPRU PUMP ROOM
ILLMPTUY MULTIPLY	INPPRRUU PURPURIN	MMOORTTY TOMMYROT
ILLOPPSY SLOPPILY	INPRRSTU SURPRINT	MMOPSSTY SYMPTOMS
ILLORSUY ILLUSORY	IOOPRSSV PROVISOS	MNNOOOSS MONSOONS
ILLRSTUY SULTRILY	IOOPRSTY ISOTROPY,	MNNOOOTY MONOTONY
ILMNOOPU POLONIUM	POROSITY	MNNOSSYY SYNONYMS
ILMNOSUU LUMINOUS	IOORRSTY SORORITY	MNNOSYYY SYNONYMY
ILMOPPSU POPULISM	IOORSSTT RISOTTOS	MNOOORTW MOONWORT
ILMORSTY STORMILY	IOORSSUV VOUSSOIR	MNOOORXY OXYMORON
ILMSSTUU STIMULUS	IOORSTTU TORTIOUS	MNOOPTYY TOPONYMY
ILMSTTUY SMUTTILY	IOORSTUV VIRTUOSO	MNORSSTU NOSTRUMS
ILNOOSTU SOLUTION	IOORSUUX UXORIOUS	MNORSTUU SURMOUNT
ILNOOSTY SNOOTILY	IOPPPRST PIT PROPS	MOOOORRTW MOORWORT,
ILNOOTUV VOLUTION	IOPRSSUU SPURIOUS	TOMORROW
ILNORSST NOSTRILS	IOPRSTTU OUTSTRIP	MOOPSSSU OPOSSUMS
ILNORSTY NITROSYL	IORRSUVV SURVIVOR	MOORSTUU TUMOROUS

MORRSSTU	ROSTRUMS
NNOOOPST	PONTOONS
NNOOPRSU	PRONOUNS
NNOORTUU	RUN OUT ON
NOOORSSU	SONOROUS

NOOPRSSS	SPONSORS
NOPSSSTU	SUNSPOTS
NORSTTUU	TURNOUTS
OOPRSSTV	PROVOSTS
OOPSSTTU	OUTPOSTS

OORSTTUU	TORTUOUS
OPPRSSTU	SUPPORTS
OPRSSSUU	SOURPUSS

AAAABCLLV BALACLAVA
AAAABDHLL ALLAHABAD
AAAABGNRU GUANABARA
AAAABIKLL BALALAIKA
AAAABILMN ALABAMIAN
AAAABKLLV BALAKLAVA
AAAACCHMT TACAMAHAC
AAAACDJNR JACARANDA
AAAACHSUY AYAHUASCA
AAAACINRU ARAUCANIA
AAAACIRRU ARAUCARIA
AAAACLMNS SALAMANCA
AAAACMNRT CATAMARAN
AAAADGKNR KARAGANDA
AAAADILLM DALAI LAMA
AAAAEHKLL HALEAKALA
AAAAGIKMS AMAGASAKI
AAAAHHJMR MAHARAJAH
AAAAHJMRS MAHARAJAS
AAAAILNPS ANAPLASIA
AAAAINSST ANASTASIA
AAAALLMMY MALAYALAM
AAAAMPRTT PARAMATTA
AAABBDINR BARBADIAN
AAABBINRR BARBARIAN
AAABCCHLN BACCHANAL
AAABCCHNR CHARABANC
AAABCCITT CATABATIC
AAABCDIIT ADIABATIC
AAABCDRRU BARRACUDA
AAABCELTV VACATABLE
AAABCEMRT CARBAMATE
AAABCIKTT KATABATIC
AAABCILNT ABACTINAL
AAABCIMOR MARACAIBO
AAABCISST CATABASIS
AAABCLNOT CANAL BOAT
AAABDDEHM
  AHMEDABAD
AAABDDMOR
  MORADABAD
AAABDELNR ALDEBARAN
AAABDELPT ADAPTABLE
AAABDELRW AWARDABLE
AAABDESST DATABASES
AAABDHHKS ASHKHABAD
AAABDILLS SABADILLA
AAABDILMS ISLAMABAD
AAABDINNT ANABANTID
AAABDLLOR ALL ABOARD!
AAABDNNNS BANDANNAS
AAABDNRSS SARABANDS
AAABEEMNO AMOEBAEAN

AAABEHLLV HAVE A BALL
AAABEILLV AVAILABLE
AAABEKRWY BREAKAWAY
AAABELLNN ANNABELLA
AAABELLPT PALATABLE
AAABELRST ALABASTER
AAABELSSY ASSAYABLE
AAABGHNRV BHAVNAGAR
AAABGLORR ALGARROBA
AAABGMNOZ
  ZAMBOANGA
AAABGRSTU RUTABAGAS
AAABHIRTY BHARATIYA
AAABHLRST BALTHASAR
AAABHLRTZ BALTHAZAR
AAABILLVY AVAILABLY
AAABLLPTY PALATABLY
AAABLOPRS PARABOLAS
AAABLPRST PARABLAST
AAACCCHHH
  CHA-CHA-CHA
AAACCDELV CAVALCADE
AAACCELLN CALCANEAL
AAACCEPRS CARAPACES
AAACCESTZ ZACATECAS
AAACCGIMU GUM ACACIA
AAACCIRTT ATARACTIC
AAACCLMNO
  CALAMANCO
AAACCRSTT CATARACTS
AAACDEHRS A HARD
  CASE
AAACDEHRZ AZEDARACH
AAACDNNOS ANACONDAS
AAACDNPRS PANDA CARS
AAACDNRSS CASSANDRA
AAACEENRS CAESAREAN
AAACEGNRT CARTAGENA
AAACEGORT ARCTOGAEA
AAACEHLNV AVALANCHE
AAACEIMNR AMERICANA
AAACEIMNT CATAMENIA
AAACEINNT CANAANITE
AAACELNRV CANAVERAL
AAACEMMNR
  CAMERAMAN
AAACENRTT AT A CANTER
AAACFILNT FANATICAL
AAACGILSU CAUSALGIA
AAACGINRU NICARAGUA
AAACGLSSW SCALAWAGS
AAACHHIRZ ZACHARIAH
AAACHIRSZ ZACHARIAS

AAACHKKMT KAMCHATKA
AAACHLNRT CHARLATAN
AAACHLRRT CATARRHAL
AAACIIRSS ACARIASIS
AAACILLNN ANACLINAL
AAACILNOT CATALONIA
AAACILNPT APLANATIC
AAACILRTU ACTUARIAL
AAACINOPR PARANOIAC
AAACINOTT CATATONIA
AAACINRSU CASUARINA
AAACLMNPU CAMPANULA
AAACLMPST CATAPLASM
AAACMRTUX TARAXACUM
AAACNOSSV CASANOVAS
AAACSSTWY CASTAWAYS
AAADDHMRY
  HAMADRYAD
AAADDLSSY SALAD DAYS
AAADEGLMN MAGDALENA
AAADEGNTV ADVANTAGE
AAADELMMR
  MARMALADE
AAADELNRX ALEXANDRA
AAADEMNSU AD
  NAUSEAM
AAADHHPRZ HAPHAZARD
AAADHIILR HAIDAR ALI
AAADHMRSY HAMADRYAS
AAADILLNP PALLADIAN
AAADILMNT DALMATIAN
AAADILNSU ANDALUSIA
AAADJJPRU DJAJAPURA
AAADKMNRS
  SAMARKAND
AAADLMNTY ADAMANTLY
AAADLNNSY ANALYSAND,
  NYASALAND
AAADMNRTY MANDATARY
AAAEELQRU EQUAL-AREA
AAAEGGRTV AGGRAVATE
AAAEGILNS ANALGESIA
AAAEGLMNU MALAGUENA
AAAEGLMTU GUATEMALA
AAAEGLSSV VASSALAGE
AAAEGMNNT MANGANATE
AAAEGMRRT MARGARETA
AAAEHHLMR HALMAHERA
AAAEHLNNT NATHANAEL
AAAEHMMOT
  HAEMATOMA
AAAEHMNST ANATHEMAS
AAAEIMNOX ANOXAEMIA

AAAEIMPRS SAPRAEMIA
AAAEKSTWY TAKEAWAYS
AAAELMMRT ALMA MATER
AAAELNNTT ANTENATAL,
   ATLANTEAN
AAAELNPQU AQUAPLANE
AAAELNPST PANATELAS
AAAELNTTT TANTALATE
AAAENPSST ANAPAESTS
AAAERSTWY TEARAWAYS
AAAFGLRRT TRAFALGAR
AAAFIILLR ALFILARIA
AAAFIKNRS AFRIKAANS
AAAFILNUV AVIFAUNAL
AAAFINORS AFRO-ASIAN
AAAFLORST SOLFATARA
AAAFRSSSS SASSAFRAS
AAAGGLOPS GALAPAGOS
AAAGHPPRR PARAGRAPH
AAAGILMNS SALAAMING
AAAGIMRRT MARGARITA
AAAGINNRV VARANGIAN
AAAGINOPT PATAGONIA
AAAGINSST AS AGAINST
AAAGMMRSY GAMMA
   RAYS
AAAGPRSSU ASPARAGUS
AAAHHHPRT HAPHTARAH
AAAHIKRTW KATHIAWAR
AAAHILMSY HIMALAYAS
AAAHIMNRS MAHARANIS
AAAHINRRT ANARTHRIA
AAAHJNRST RAJASTHAN
AAAHKNRST ASTRAKHAN
AAAHLLOTY AYATOLLAH
AAAHLNNTU NAHUATLAN
AAAHLNOPR ANAPHORAL
AAAHMMSTU
   HAMAMATSU
AAAHMNNTT MANHATTAN
AAAHMNRTT HARMATTAN
AAAHTTUYY AYUTTHAYA
AAAIILMNR LAMINARIA
AAAIINRST SANITARIA
AAAIJMNRU MARIJUANA
AAAIKLLNT ANTALKALI
AAAILMMMN MAMMALIAN
AAAILMNSY MALAYSIAN
AAAILNNOT ANATOLIAN
AAAILNNPR PLANARIAN
AAAILNSST ALSATIANS,
   ASSAILANT
AAAILPPRS APPRAISAL

AAAILRSTU AUSTRALIA
AAAIMNNOZ AMAZONIAN
AAAIMNNST TASMANIAN
AAAIMNORT INAMORATA
AAAIMNRST SAMARITAN
AAAINNNTZ TANZANIAN
AAAINORST SANATORIA
AAAINPSTV VANASPATI
AAAIPPRZZ PAPARAZZI
AAAIPRSTX PARATAXIS
AAAKKMORR
   KARAKORAM
AAAKLSWWY
   WALKAWAYS
AAAKMSTTU TAKAMATSU
AAAKRRSTU SURAKARTA
AAALLMPSS LAS PALMAS
AAALMPPRS PARAPLASM
AAALNPSTY ANAPLASTY
AAALNRSTV TRANSVAAL
AAALNRTTU TARANTULA
AAALOOPPS APPALOOSA
AAAMMMNRST
   MAN-AT-ARMS
AAAMMSTUY MATSUYAMA
AAAMNOPRS PANORAMAS
AAANNNPRU ANNAPURNA
AAAOPPRZZ PAPARAZZO
AAAPPRSTU APPARATUS
AABBCCIRR BRIC-A-BRAC
AABBCDEIL ABDICABLE
AABBCDKOR BACKBOARD
AABBCDRSS SCABBARDS
AABBCEHLL BEACH BALL
AABBCEINR CARIBBEAN
AABBCINRS BARBICANS
AABBCKLLL BLACKBALL
AABBDEELT DEBATABLE
AABBDENOR BROAD
   BEAN
AABBDEORS BASEBOARD
AABBDNRSS BRASS BAND
AABBEEKLR BREAKABLE
AABBEELRT REBATABLE
AABBEHHST BATHSHEBA
AABBEHILT HABITABLE
AABBEIILT BILABIATE
AABBEINRT RABBINATE
AABBEIRRS BARBARISE
AABBEIRRZ BARBARIZE
AABBEKMMO MAKE A
   BOMB
AABBELLSS BASEBALLS

AABBELLTU TABULABLE
AABBHILTY HABITABLY
AABBIILLS BILABIALS
AABBIMRRS BARBARISM
AABBIRRTY BARBARITY
AABBORRSU BARBAROUS
AABCCEHKS BACKACHES
AABCCEKPS BACKSPACE
AABCCELRS CABLE CARS
AABCCHHKT HATCHBACK
AABCCHKKU HUCKABACK
AABCCILOT CATABOLIC
AABCCIORT ACROBATIC
AABCCJKKL BLACKJACK
AABCCKKPS BACKPACKS
AABCCKKRT BACKTRACK
AABCCMOST CATACOMBS
AABCDDEIT ABDICATED
AABCDDEKT BACKDATED
AABCDDORR CARDBOARD
AABCDEEFR BAREFACED
AABCDEEHH BEACHHEAD
AABCDEHKL BLACKHEAD
AABCDEILL CABLE-LAID
AABCDEIRR BARRICADE
AABCDEKLL BLACK LEAD
AABCDEKLP BACKPEDAL
AABCDEKRR BARRACKED
AABCDENNR BARN
   DANCE
AABCDENNU ABUNDANCE
AABCDENPS SPACEBAND
AABCDHILR ARCHIBALD
AABCDHKNS BACKHANDS
AABCDHKRS HARDBACKS
AABCDIORS SCARABOID
AABCDIORT ABDICATOR
AABCDKLMP BLACKDAMP
AABCDKRSW
   BACKWARDS, DRAWBACKS
AABCDKRSY BACKYARDS
AABCDLOPR CLAPBOARD
AABCDNOOR
   CARBONADO
AABCDORST BROADCAST
AABCEEELP PEACEABLE
AABCEEHLR REACHABLE
AABCEEHLT TEACHABLE
AABCEEHRW
   BEACHWEAR
AABCEEKLS LEASEBACK
AABCEELLN CLEANABLE
AABCEELLR LACERABLE

287

AABCEELPS ESCAPABLE
AABCEELPY PEACEABLY
AABCEELRT TRACEABLE
AABCEELTX EXACTABLE
AABCEENRR ABERRANCE
AABCEERTT BRACTEATE
AABCEFIRT FABRICATE
AABCEFOSU FABACEOUS
AABCEGILR ALGEBRAIC
AABCEGKST BACKSTAGE
AABCEGLMR CABLEGRAM
AABCEGPRT CARPETBAG
AABCEHHLT HATCHABLE
AABCEHIRT BRACHIATE
AABCEHITZ CHABAZITE
AABCEHLPT PATCHABLE
AABCEHLRT CHARTABLE
AABCEILLM CLAIMABLE
AABCEILMN IMBALANCE
AABCEILNP INCAPABLE
AABCEILNT CANTABILE
AABCEILRT BACTERIAL,
   CALIBRATE
AABCEINOR ANAEROBIC
AABCEIORT AEROBATIC
AABCEJKMR AMBERJACK
AABCEKLMS CLAMBAKES
AABCEKLRT TRACKABLE
AABCEKPPR PAPERBACK
AABCEKRTW BACKWATER
AABCEKSST BACK SEATS
AABCELLOR CABALLERO
AABCELLOT LOCATABLE
AABCELMNU AMBULANCE
AABCELNNU UNBALANCE
AABCELNOR BARCELONA
AABCELNRS BARNACLES
AABCELOOS CALABOOSE
AABCELORR BARCAROLE
AABCELORZ CARBAZOLE
AABCELPPR CRAB APPLE
AABCELPRS SCRAPABLE
AABCELRTT TRACTABLE
AABCELRTU TRABECULA
AABCENORT CARBONATE
AABCFHKLS FLASHBACK,
   HALFBACKS
AABCGILNN BALANCING
AABCHHIRT BATH CHAIR
AABCHILNR BRANCHIAL
AABCHRRST BAR CHARTS
AABCIILNS BASILICAN
AABCIILSS BASILICAS

AABCIKLLM BLACKMAIL
AABCIKLLT BLACKTAIL
AABCIKLST TAILBACKS
AABCILLRY BACILLARY
AABCILLSY ASYLLABIC,
   BASICALLY
AABCILNNS CANNIBALS
AABCILNOT BOTANICAL
AABCILNPY INCAPABLY
AABCILOPR PARABOLIC
AABCINNOR CARBANION
AABCKLLMP LAMP-BLACK
AABCKLMSS BLACK MASS
AABCKLPSY PLAYBACKS
AABCKNRSS SNACK BARS
AABCKORRZ RAZORBACK
AABCMNOTT COMBATANT
AABCRSSTT ABSTRACTS
AABDDEEST DEADBEATS
AABDDEGLS SADDLEBAG
AABDDEHNS HEADBANDS
AABDDEHOR HEADBOARD
AABDDEHRY HYDERABAD
AABDDENNO ABANDONED
AABDDHORR
   HARDBOARD
AABDDHORS DASHBOARD
AABDDNNST BANDSTAND
AABDDORRT DARTBOARD
AABDEELLP PLEADABLE
AABDEELMN AMENDABLE
AABDEEMNO
   ENDAMOEBA
AABDEERTT TRABEATED
AABDEFHKL HALF-BAKED
AABDEFLOR BROADLEAF
AABDEGILS BAG LADIES
AABDEGINO GABIONADE
AABDEGINR BARGAINED,
   GABARDINE
AABDEGLRU GUARDABLE
AABDEGORT ABROGATED
AABDEGOST SABOTAGED
AABDEHKNR HANDBRAKE
AABDEHLNR HANDLEBAR
AABDEHLSY ABASHEDLY
AABDEHNSU UNABASHED
AABDEILLT DILATABLE
AABDEILMR ADMIRABLE
AABDEILNN LENINABAD
AABDEILNR DRAINABLE
AABDEILNV INVADABLE
AABDEILOV AVOIDABLE

AABDEILRV ADVERBIAL
AABDEILSV ADVISABLE
AABDEINNR BERNADINA
AABDEINST ABSTAINED
AABDELLNT TABLELAND
AABDELLST BALLASTED
AABDELMST LAMBASTED
AABDELTTU TABULATED
AABDELTWY TWAYBLADE
AABDEMNNR BRAND
   NAME
AABDEMORT DREAMBOAT
AABDEMRTU ADUMBRATE
AABDENNPY A BAD PENNY
AABDENSTW SWEATBAND
AABDENSVW WAVE
   BANDS
AABDEORSS SEABOARDS
AABDEORST ADSORBATE
AABDESSTU DATA BUSES
AABDFHLOR HALF BOARD
AABDFILOT BIT OF A LAD
AABDFKNRT BANK DRAFT
AABDGGINN BANDAGING
AABDGIILR GARIBALDI
AABDGNNOW
   BANDWAGON
AABDGNOSV VAGABONDS
AABDGOSTU GADABOUTS
AABDHLRSU HASDRUBAL
AABDHORSW
   WASHBOARD
AABDIJNOR JABORANDI
AABDIKORV KIROVABAD
AABDILMNO ABDOMINAL
AABDILMRY ADMIRABLY
AABDILORS SAILBOARD
AABDILORT BROADTAIL,
   TAILBOARD
AABDILSSU DISABUSAL
AABDINOST BASTINADO
AABDINSTW WAISTBAND
AABDKLORW
   BOARDWALK
AABDKNNSS SANDBANKS
AABDLLORW WALLBOARD
AABDLNSST SANDBLAST
AABDLNTWY WANT BADLY
AABDLORRS LABRADORS
AABDLORUY LABOUR DAY
AABDNRRSY BARNYARDS
AABDORRST STARBOARD
AABEEEGLR AGREEABLE

AABEEGGLU GAUGEABLE
AABEEGKRS BREAKAGES
AABEEGLLN GLEANABLE
AABEEGLLT BAGATELLE
AABEEGLRY AGREEABLY
AABEEGRRT GREAT BEAR
AABEEHLLX EXHALABLE
AABEEHRTT HEARTBEAT
AABEEIILLN ALIENABLE
AABEEINRS BEARNAISE
AABEEKLPS SPEAKABLE
AABEEKRST TEA BREAKS
AABEELLLM MALLEABLE
AABEELLNN ANNABELLE
AABEELLNR LEARNABLE
AABEELLPS PLEASABLE
AABEELLRS RESALABLE
AABEELLRT ALTERABLE,
   RELATABLE
AABEELLRX RELAXABLE
AABEELMST BASE METAL
AABEELNTU UNEATABLE
AABEELORT ELABORATE
AABEELPRR REPARABLE
AABEELPRS SEPARABLE
AABEELPRY REPAYABLE
AABEELQTU EQUATABLE
AABEELRTT TREATABLE
AABEELRTW TABLEWARE
AABEELRTY BETA LYRAE
AABEELTTX BATTLEAXE
AABEEMNOT ENTAMOEBA
AABEEMNST ABASEMENT
AABEEMNTT ABATEMENT
AABEEQRSU ARABESQUE
AABEERSST BASE RATES
AABEFGILT FATIGABLE
AABEFKLNR FRANKABLE
AABEFKRST BREAKFAST
AABEFLLMM FLAMMABLE
AABEFLLOT FLOATABLE
AABEGGLUY GAUGEABLY
AABEGHLLU LAUGHABLE
AABEGILLR GABRIELLA
AABEGILNV NAVIGABLE
AABEGILRV BELGRAVIA
AABEGINRR BARGAINER
AABEGIRRT ARBITRAGE
AABEGIRRU BIGARREAU
AABEGLLLR GLABELLAR
AABEGLLMS BALL GAMES
AABEGLMNP PALEMBANG
AABEGLNOR BANGALORE

AABEGLNRT GRANTABLE
AABEGLPRS GRASPABLE
AABEGNORT ABNEGATOR
AABEHILRR HERBARIAL
AABEHITTU HABITUATE
AABEHLMSS SMASHABLE
AABEHLOTW WHALEBOAT
AABEHLPST ALPHABETS
AABEHLSTW SWATHABLE
AABEIILLS LABIALISE
AABEIILLZ LABIALIZE
AABEIIMNR BAIN-MARIE
AABEIIRTU AUBRIETIA
AABEIJKLR JAILBREAK
AABEIKLNS BALKANISE
AABEIKLNZ BALKANIZE
AABEIKNRR KARABINER
AABEIKRRS AIRBRAKES
AABEILLMN LAMINABLE
AABEILLMR MIRABELLA
AABEILLNR BALLERINA
AABEILLRT BILATERAL
AABEILLSW WALLABIES
AABEILMNS LIMA BEANS
AABEILNOT ANABOLITE
AABEILNRT ALBERTINA,
   TRAINABLE
AABEILNST STAINABLE
AABEILPST BASIPETAL
AABEILRSV VARIABLES
AABEIMNOT ABOMINATE
AABEIMNZZ ZAMBEZIAN
AABEINORS ARABINOSE
AABEINRST ABSTAINER
AABEINRVW BRAINWAVE
AABEINSST SEBASTIAN
AABEIRRTT ARBITRATE
AABEIRSSV ABRASIVES
AABEKMNRS BRAKESMAN
AABELLLOW ALLOWABLE
AABELLMST MEATBALLS
AABELLNPT PLANTABLE
AABELLOPR PAROLABLE
AABELLORS ROSABELLA
AABELLPPR PALPEBRAL
AABELLSUV VALUABLES
AABELMSSU ASSUMABLE
AABELMSTT TABLEMATS
AABELNPPS SNAPPABLE
AABELOPRR POLAR BEAR
AABELORST ASTROLABE
AABELORTT ROTATABLE
AABELPRRY REPARABLY

AABELPRSY SEPARABLY
AABELRSSU ASSURABLE
AABELRSTU SATURABLE
AABELRSTY BETRAYALS
AABELRTTU TABLATURE
AABEMOSTT STEAMBOAT
AABEMRRSS EMBARRASS
AABENOSSY SOYA BEANS
AABEOPPRT APPROBATE
AABERSTUX BEAUX-ARTS
AABFIIMNS FABIANISM
AABFORTTU FART ABOUT
AABGGGNNS
   GANG-BANGS
AABGGIMNO GAMBOGIAN
AABGGRRST BRAGGARTS
AABGHLLUY LAUGHABLY
AABGHLPRU BHAGALPUR
AABGHOPRR BAROGRAPH
AABGHPRRS BAR GRAPHS
AABGIINWY IN A BIG WAY
AABGILNRU BULGARIAN
AABGILNVY NAVIGABLY
AABGILRRT GIBRALTAR
AABGINNOR BORN-AGAIN
AABGOORRT ABROGATOR
AABGORTVY GRAVY BOAT
AABHIILRZ BILHARZIA
AABHIIMNP AMPHIBIAN
AABHIMMRU HAMMURABI
AABHINRSW BRAINWASH
AABHINSSW WASHBASIN
AABHRSSST BRASS HATS
AABIILLMS LABIALISM
AABIILLTY LABIALITY
AABIILNRR LIBRARIAN
AABIILNRZ BRAZILIAN
AABIINNRT BRITANNIA
AABIINOSS ANABIOSIS
AABIINRZZ ZANZIBARI
AABIINSSY ABYSSINIA
AABILLORS ISALLOBAR
AABILMNOS ANABOLISM
AABILMNRU MANUBRIAL
AABILMOPY AMBLYOPIA
AABILMORS AMBROSIAL
AABILMPST BAPTISMAL
AABILNOTT BATTALION
AABILRRSU BURSARIAL
AABIMNORS AMBROSINA
AABIMORSU SIMAROUBA
AABINORSS ABRASIONS
AABINORTT BOAT TRAIN

AABINOSTW BOATSWAIN
AABIORSTT ABATTOIRS
AABIRRRTY ARBITRARY
AABJJLLNU LJUBLJANA
AABKLOTUW WALKABOUT
AABKRSSSY SASSY BARK
AABLLLOWY ALLOWABLY
AABLLNTTY BLATANTLY
AABLLRSTU BLASTULAR
AABLLRSYY SYLLABARY
AABLMNORY MYROBALAN
AABLNOORS SALOON BAR
AABLNORTU ULAN BATOR
AABLORSST ALBATROSS
AABLORTTU TABULATOR
AABLOSTUY LAYABOUTS
AABMMOSSY MAMA'S
  BOYS
AABMNNOTU
  MONTAUBAN
AABNNSTTU BANTUSTAN
AABRSSTTU SUBSTRATA
AACCCLOOS COCA-COLAS
AACCDDINY CANDIDACY
AACCDEFRS FACE CARDS
AACCDEILM ACCLAIMED
AACCDEIMS ACADEMICS
AACCDEJNY ADJACENCY
AACCDELLT CATCALLED
AACCDELOS ACCOLADES
AACCDELPR PLACE CARD
AACCDGINS CASCADING
AACCDHLRU ARCHDUCAL
AACCDHRSS CASH CARDS
AACCDIILM MALIC ACID
AACCDIINR CIRCADIAN
AACCDIOSU CAUCASOID
AACCDNORT ACCORDANT
AACCEELNR CLEARANCE
AACCEENRT REACTANCE
AACCEENST CETACEANS
AACCEFKPS FACE PACKS
AACCEFLOS COALFACES
AACCEFNRS FRANCESCA
AACCEHJKP CHEAP-JACK
AACCEHRRT CHARACTER
AACCEHSUZ ZACCHAEUS
AACCEIILN CAECILIAN
AACCEILNT ANALECTIC
AACCEILRR CERCARIAL
AACCEILTU ACICULATE
AACCEINRS SARACENIC
AACCEINRY CYRENAICA

AACCEINSV VACANCIES
AACCEINTV VACCINATE
AACCEKNRS CRANKCASE
AACCEKRRT RACETRACK
AACCEKRSS SACK RACES
AACCELLTU CALCULATE
AACCELMTY CYCLAMATE
AACCELNSU CALCANEUS
AACCELNTU ACCENTUAL
AACCELSTU SACCULATE
AACCENPTT ACCEPTANT
AACCEORTT COARCTATE
AACCEPRTU CUT A CAPER
AACCERSSS CARCASSES
AACCFINRS FRANCISCA
AACCHILMO MAILCOACH
AACCHIMNO MICHOACAN
AACCHINRS SACCHARIN
AACCHIPRR ARCHICARP
AACCHIRTT CATHARTIC
AACCHIRTU AUTARCHIC
AACCHLORS CHARCOALS
AACCIILNT ANACLITIC
AACCIILNV VACCINIAL
AACCIINPS CAPSAICIN
AACCIINTT TACTICIAN
AACCIIRSS CIRCASSIA
AACCILLSS CLASSICAL
AACCILMNU CACUMINAL
AACCILNNO CANONICAL
AACCILNRU CANICULAR
AACCILPRT PRACTICAL
AACCILTTY CATALYTIC
AACCIMNOR CARCINOMA,
  MACARONIC
AACCINOTT CATATONIC
AACCINPTY CAPTAINCY
AACCINRTT ANTARCTIC
AACCIOPRT CAPACITOR
AACCIOPSU CAPACIOUS
AACCIORST COSTA RICA
AACCIRSST SARCASTIC
AACCKMNRS
  CRACKSMAN
AACCKRRTT CART TRACK
AACCLMORY CYCLORAMA
AACCLMSTY CATACLYSM
AACCMNOPY
  ACCOMPANY
AACCOPRRS SARCOCARP
AACCORTUY AUTOCRACY
AACDDEERT A DEAD CERT

AACDDEHMR DEAD
  MARCH
AACDDEINT CANDIDATE
AACDDELOP DECAPODAL
AACDDELPR PLACARDED
AACDDEOTV ADVOCATED
AACDDGNOT
  CAT-AND-DOG
AACDDIIST DADAISTIC
AACDEEFLT DEFALCATE
AACDEEHHR HEADREACH
AACDEEHHS HEADACHES
AACDEEIMT ACETAMIDE,
  EMACIATED
AACDEEIRT ERADICATE
AACDEELRS ESCALADER
AACDEELRT LACERATED
AACDEELST ESCALATED
AACDEEMNS DAMASCENE
AACDEEMRT
  DEMARCATE, MACERATED
AACDEEORS AREA CODES
AACDEEPSS ESCAPADES
AACDEETUV EVACUATED
AACDEETUX EXCAUDATE
AACDEETVX EXCAVATED
AACDEFFIN AFFIANCED
AACDEFHRS HEADSCARF
AACDEGLNO DECAGONAL
AACDEHILN ENCHILADA
AACDEHINS HACIENDAS
AACDEHLRT CATHEDRAL
AACDEILLN DALLIANCE
AACDEILLT DIALECTAL
AACDEILNO LAODICEAN
AACDEILNS CANALISED
AACDEILNZ CANALIZED
AACDEILTU ACIDULATE
AACDEIMNY CYANAMIDE
AACDEIMPR PARAMEDIC
AACDEINOT DIACONATE
AACDEINOV AVOIDANCE
AACDEINPT CAPTAINED
AACDEINRS RADIANCES
AACDEINRT ERADICANT
AACDEITTV ACTIVATED
AACDEJKMP JAM-PACKED
AACDEKMRT TARMACKED
AACDEKNRS RANSACKED
AACDELLNU CALENDULA
AACDELLOT ALLOCATED
AACDELMNS CANDLEMAS
AACDELNOT ANECDOTAL

AACDELNPS LANDSCAPE	AACEEFLUV FACE VALUE	AACEGLOTU CATALOGUE,
AACDELNRS CALENDARS	AACEEFRRT AFTERCARE	COAGULATE
AACDELNRT DECLARANT	AACEEFRSV FACE-SAVER	AACEGNORR ARROGANCE
AACDELPTY PLAY-ACTED	AACEEGHNS SEA CHANGE	AACEGNRSU SUGARCANE
AACDEMRSS MASSACRED	AACEEGLLR CELLARAGE	AACEGOPST SCAPEGOAT
AACDENNNO	AACEEGLSV CLEAVAGES	AACEGORTT GREATCOAT
CANNONADE	AACEEGNRR CARRAGEEN	AACEHHIRZ ZECHARIAH
AACDENNST ASCENDANT	AACEEHHRT HEARTACHE	AACEHIIMS ISCHAEMIA
AACDENOTU COADUNATE	AACEEHLNR HERACLEAN	AACEHILLO ECHOLALIA
AACDENPRT TAP DANCER	AACEEJLTU EJACULATE	AACEHILMR CAMELHAIR
AACDENPST TAP DANCES	AACEEKMPR PACEMAKER	AACEHILMT MALACHITE
AACDENRSW WAR	AACEEKRRT CARETAKER	AACEHILNS SELACHIAN
DANCES	AACEELNPS PLEASANCE	AACEHILNT CHATELAIN
AACDENSSV CANVASSED	AACEELNPT PLACENTAE	AACEHILNU ACHEULIAN
AACDEOSTV ADVOCATES	AACEELNST ELASTANCE	AACEHILPR EPARCHIAL
AACDERSTT CASTRATED	AACEELRTT ALTERCATE	AACEHILPT CALIPHATE
AACDERTTT ATTRACTED	AACEELTTY ACETYLATE	AACEHIMNO HEOMANIAC
AACDFHNRT HANDCRAFT	AACEEMMNR	AACEHIMNR CHARMAINE
AACDGIMNW MAGIC	CAMERAMEN	AACEHIMNT MACHINATE
WAND	AACEEMNNY MYCENAEAN	AACEHINNT ACANTHINE
AACDGINNV ADVANCING	AACEEMRRT MACERATER	AACEHINRT CATHARINE
AACDGINRS CARDIGANS	AACEENRSS CESAREANS	AACEHINRW CHINAWARE
AACDHIILL CHILIADAL	AACEEOPRS AEROSPACE	AACEHINST HANSEATIC
AACDHIILS DICHASIAL	AACEEPRSS CASSAREEP	AACEHIPTT APATHETIC
AACDHINOR ARACHNOID	AACEEPSSS SEASCAPES	AACEHIRRS ARCHAISER
AACDHINOT ACANTHOID	AACEERSTT ESTATE CAR	AACEHIRRZ ARCHAIZER
AACDHINPS HANDICAPS	AACEFFIRT AFFRICATE	AACEHIRSY EASY CHAIR
AACDHLNPS HANDCLAPS,	AACEFGLNR FLAGRANCE	AACEHKMOR
HANDCLASP	AACEFGNRR FRAGRANCE	HACKAMORE
AACDHLNPU LAUNCH PAD	AACEFGORT FACTORAGE	AACEHKMRR
AACDHLNRS CRASH-LAND	AACEFGOSU FAGACEOUS	MARRAKECH
AACDHNRST HANDCARTS	AACEFHLST HALF-CASTE	AACEHKRSV HAVERSACK
AACDHPRRS CARDSHARP	AACEFILLS FALLACIES	AACEHLRSU ARCHELAUS
AACDIIMNO AMINO ACID	AACEFINST FASCINATE	AACEHLRTT CLATHRATE
AACDIINNR CNIDARIAN	AACEFRSTT ARTEFACTS	AACEHMNRU HUMAN
AACDIISST DIASTASIC	AACEGHLNR ARCHANGEL	RACE
AACDIISTT DIASTATIC	AACEGHMNP CHAMPAGNE	AACEHNSSS SASSENACH
AACDILLRY RADICALLY	AACEGHNOR	AACEHPPRS SCRAP HEAP
AACDILNRS CARDINALS	ANCHORAGE	AACEHPRTU PARACHUTE
AACDILNTY DILATANCY	AACEGHRST GATECRASH	AACEHRSST CATHARSES
AACDILORT CAROTIDAL	AACEGILLN ANGELICAL,	AACEIILNT LACINIATE
AACDIMRST DRAMATICS	ENGLACIAL, GALENICAL	AACEIINRR CINERARIA
AACDINNOR DRACONIAN	AACEGILNS ANALGESIC	AACEIIRTV VICARIATE
AACDINOTU CAUDATION	AACEGILRS ALGECIRAS	AACEILLMS CAMELLIAS
AACDIOSUU AUDACIOUS	AACEGILRT CARTILAGE	AACEILLNS ALLIANCES
AACDIQRTU QUADRATIC	AACEGIMNO EGOMANIAC	AACEILLRV VARICELLA
AACDIRSTY CARYATIDS	AACEGIRRS CARRIAGES	AACEILLTV VACILLATE
AACDJNTUY ADJUTANCY	AACEGIRSV VICARAGES	AACEILMNN ALEMANNIC
AACDQRSSU SQUAD CARS	AACEGISTT CASTIGATE	AACEILMNP CAMPANILE
AACEEFINN FAINEANCE	AACEGKPRS PACKAGERS	AACEILMPS ECLAMPSIA
AACEEFIRT CAFETERIA	AACEGLOST GALACTOSE	AACEILMRT CARMELITA
AACEEFLPS PALEFACES	AACEGLOSU COAGULASE	AACEILMTV CALMATIVE
AACEEFLPT FACEPLATE		AACEILNNR CARNELIAN

AACEILNNT LANCINATE
AACEILNPP APPLIANCE
AACEILNPT ANALEPTIC
AACEILNRS ARSENICAL
AACEILNRT LACERTIAN,
NECTARIAL
AACEILNRU LAURENCIA
AACEILPTU APICULATE
AACEILRSV CALVARIES,
CAVALIERS
AACEILSTU ACTUALISE
AACEILTUZ ACTUALIZE
AACEIMNOX ANOXAEMIC
AACEIMNRS AMERICANS
AACEIMNSS AMNESIACS
AACEIMNTU ACUMINATE
AACEIMPRS SAPRAEMIC
AACEIMRST MARCASITE
AACEIMSTT MASTICATE
AACEINNRT INCARNATE
AACEINOST CASEATION
AACEINPST ANAPESTIC
AACEINRST ASCERTAIN,
CARTESIAN, SECTARIAN
AACEINRSV VARIANCES
AACEIOSST ASSOCIATE
AACEIPPRT PER CAPITA
AACEIPTTV CAPTIVATE
AACEIRSST STAIRCASE
AACEIRSTU ACTUARIES
AACEISTUV CAUSATIVE
AACEJKLPP APPLEJACK
AACEJKSSS JACKASSES
AACEJQTTU JACQUETTA
AACEKLPRT PLATE RACK
AACEKLPSW SPACEWALK
AACEKNRRS RANSACKER
AACEKPPTY PAY PACKET
AACEKRSTT ATTACKERS
AACELLLRU ACELLULAR
AACELLLUV VALLECULA
AACELLNOR OLECRANAL
AACELLNOW ALLOWANCE
AACELLNPT PLACENTAL
AACELMNTT CATTLEMAN
AACELMPST PLACE MATS
AACELMSST CLASSMATE
AACELNNTU CANNULATE
AACELNPST PLACENTAS
AACELNRST ANCESTRAL,
LANCASTER
AACELOPRT ACROPETAL,
CLEOPATRA

AACELORST ESCALATOR
AACELOTUV AUTOCLAVE,
VACUOLATE
AACELPPRT APPLE CART
AACELPSTU CAPSULATE
AACELPSTY CATALEPSY
AACELPTXY CATAPLEXY
AACELRRTU CREATURAL
AACELRSTY CATALYSER
AACELRSWY CLEARWAYS
AACELRTUW CATERWAUL
AACEMNNOR
CONNEMARA
AACEMNPRT MERCAPTAN
AACEMNRST SACRAMENT
AACEMRRSS ARMS
RACES, MASSACRER
AACEMRSSS MASSACRES
AACENNNOY ANNOYANCE
AACENNOSS ASSONANCE
AACENOPTZ ZAPOTECAN
AACENPRRY PARCENARY
AACENPSSU SAUCEPANS
AACENRSSU ASSURANCE
AACENRSSV CANVASSER
AACENRTTU CAUTERANT
AACENSSSV CANVASSES
AACENSSTT CASTANETS
AACEOOPPT APOCOPATE
AACEORTUV EVACUATOR
AACEORTVX EXCAVATOR
AACEOSTUX TAXACEOUS
AACESSUWY CAUSEWAYS
AACFGLNRY FLAGRANCY
AACFHJKST JACKSHAFT
AACFHMSST CAMSHAFTS
AACFIILNN FINANCIAL
AACFILNOT FACTIONAL
AACFILORT FACTORIAL
AACFINSTT FANTASTIC
AACFIRSTT ARTIFACTS
AACFJKLPS FLAPJACKS
AACFLLTUY FACTUALLY
AACFLOPSW SCAPA FLOW
AACFLRRTU FRACTURAL
AACFMNRST CRAFTSMAN
AACGGHINN CHAIN GANG
AACGGIKNP PACKAGING
AACGGIOPR PARAGOGIC
AACGHHIRY HAGIARCHY
AACGHIKUW KAWAGUCHI
AACGHIMNP CHAMPAIGN
AACGHINTT ATTACHING

AACGHMORT
TACHOGRAM
AACGHOPRR ARCOGRAPH
AACGIIMNS MAGICIANS
AACGIKNTT ATTACKING
AACGILLMY MAGICALLY
AACGILLOS SCAGLIOLA
AACGILMNN MANACLING
AACGILNNS ANGLICANS
AACGILNPT PLACATING
AACGIMNPS CAMPAIGNS
AACGIMPRT PRAGMATIC
AACGINTTU ACTUATING
AACGIOSSU SAGACIOUS
AACGLLSWY SCALLYWAG
AACGLNOOT OCTAGONAL
AACGLNOTU COAGULANT
AACGLOORY ACAROLOGY
AACGMORRT
CARTOGRAM
AACGNNSTY STAGNANCY
AACHHHIUU CHIHUAHUA
AACHHINTY HYACINTHA
AACHHSTWY HATCHWAYS
AACHIILMN CHAIN MAIL
AACHIILPT ALIPHATIC
AACHIINRT CARINTHIA
AACHIIPRS PHARISAIC
AACHIIRRV CHARIVARI
AACHILNPS CHAPLAINS
AACHILOPR PAROCHIAL
AACHILOPT CHIPOLATA
AACHILPST ASPHALTIC
AACHILSST THALASSIC
AACHIMNOR HARMONICA
AACHIMNRS ANARCHISM
AACHIMNRU MANCHURIA
AACHIMRRS ARMCHAIRS
AACHIMRRT MATRIARCH
AACHIMRSS ARCHAISMS
AACHIMSTT ASTHMATIC
AACHINRST ANARCHIST
AACHINSSW CHAIN SAWS
AACHIPRRT PATRIARCH
AACHIRSST CATHARSIS
AACHKMMRT
MATCHMARK
AACHKSSTY HAYSTACKS
AACHLLMRY LACHRYMAL
AACHLLPTY CATAPHYLL
AACHLLRTW WALLCHART
AACHLMNOR
MONARCHAL

AACHLMRSY MARSHALCY
AACHLOPVY PLAY HAVOC
AACHMNORW
　CHARWOMAN
AACHMNSTY YACHTSMAN
AACHMPRST MARCH-PAST
AACHNOSTU ACANTHOUS
AACHNOTTY CHATOYANT
AACHNRSST TRASHCANS
AACHOPPRY APOCRYPHA
AACIILLRT ALTRICIAL
AACIILMRS RACIALISM
AACIILMST LAMAISTIC
AACIILNPT ANCIPITAL
AACIILNSS ANACLISIS
AACIILNST CASTILIAN
AACIILPRT PIRATICAL
AACIILRST RACIALIST,
　SATIRICAL
AACIIMOTX AXIOMATIC
AACIINNOP POINCIANA
AACIINNOT NICOTIANA
AACIINPRT PATRICIAN
AACIIPRST PARASITIC
AACIIRRTU URTICARIA
AACIISTTV ATAVISTIC
AACIJNOPS JAPONICAS
AACIKMNNY KANAMYCIN
AACILLNOT ALLANTOIC
AACILLNRY ANCILLARY
AACILLNTU LUNATICAL
AACILLNTV VACILLANT
AACILLPRY CAPILLARY
AACILMMNO AMMONICAL
AACILMNST CLAIMANTS
AACILMRSU SIMULACRA
AACILNNUV VULCANIAN
AACILNOPT PLACATION
AACILNOTT LACTATION
AACILNOTY CLAYTONIA
AACILNPPT APPLICANT
AACILNRST CARNALIST
AACILNRSV CARNIVALS
AACILNRTY CARNALITY
AACILNRUV NAVICULAR
AACILNSTY ANALYTICS
AACILORTU AUCTORIAL
AACILOSSU SALACIOUS
AACILOSTT COAT TAILS,
　TAILCOATS
AACILPRTU CAPITULAR
AACILPRTY PARALYTIC
AACILQTTU ACQUITTAL

AACILRRTU ARTICULAR
AACILRRUU AURICULAR
AACILRSTY RASCALITY
AACILSSTY CATALYSIS
AACILSTUY CAUSALITY
AACILTTUY ACTUALITY
AACIMNNNU MANCUNIAN
AACIMNOPR PANORAMIC
AACIMNOST ANOSMATIC
AACIMORTU AMAUROTIC
AACIMOTTU AUTOMATIC
AACIMRRSU SACRARIUM
AACIMRTTU TRAUMATIC
AACINNORT CARNATION
AACINNOST SANTONICA
AACINOOTV AVOCATION
AACINOPRS CAPARISON
AACINORST RAINCOATS
AACINORTU ARCUATION
AACINOSST CASSATION
AACINOSTU CAUSATION
AACINOSTV VACATIONS
AACINOTTU ACTUATION
AACINRRTU ARCTURIAN
AACINRSST SACRISTAN
AACINRSSU ANACRUSIS
AACIOPRSU RAPACIOUS
AACIORTTV ACTIVATOR
AACIOSTTW WAISTCOAT
AACKKNPSS KNAPSACKS
AACLLOPRS COLLAPSAR
AACLLRRSY CARRYALLS
AACLNOPTU CANTALOUP
AACLNRUUV AVUNCULAR
AACLOPRRR PARLOR CAR
AACLOPRRT PATROL CAR
AACLOPRTU PORTULACA
AACLOPRTY PLACATORY
AACLORSSU CAROUSALS
AACLPSTTU CATAPULTS
AACLRRTUY CARTULARY
AACLSSTTY CATALYSTS
AACMNOORS
　MACAROONS
AACMNOTTU CATAMOUNT
AACNNOSTT CONSTANTA
AACNORTUU AU
　COURANT
AACNRSTUY SANCTUARY
AACNRSTUZ SANTA CRUZ
AACORRSTT CASTRATOR
AACORRSTU TUSCARORA
AACORRTTT ATTRACTOR

AACORSSWY CASSOWARY
AACORSTTU AUTOCRATS
AADDDGNRY
　GRANDADDY
AADDEEFHT FATHEADED
AADDEEHST DEAD HEATS
AADDEEMRY
　READY-MADE
AADDEENRV VERANDAED
AADDEENTT ANTEDATED
AADDEGLNR GARLANDED
AADDEGRTU GRADUATED
AADDEHHRS HARDHEADS
AADDEHLNS HEADLANDS
AADDEHNST HEADSTAND
AADDEHOST A DEAD
　SHOT
AADDEHRSW
　HEADWARDS
AADDEILNO ADENOIDAL
AADDEILTV VALIDATED
AADDEIMNW WAD
　MEDANI
AADDEINRT ANDRADITE
AADDEINRW EDWARDIAN
AADDEKRST STARK DEAD
AADDELLNS SANDALLED
AADDELMNR DREAMLAND
AADDELPPU APPLAUDED
AADDELRST ASTRADDLE
AADDEMNNT
　DEMANDANT
AADDEMNOR
　ANDROMEDA
AADDEMRSY DAYDREAMS
AADDEMRYY DAYDREAMY
AADDEORST ROADSTEAD
AADDHLNNO AN OLD
　HAND
AADDHNNST HANDSTAND
AADDIIMRY DAIRYMAID
AADDIINRV DRAVIDIAN
AADDILNNO DONALDINA
AADDIRRWY IRRAWADDY
AADDLNRSW LANDWARDS
AADDLRSTY DASTARDLY
AADDMRSTT DARMSTADT
AADDNRSST STANDARDS
AADEEGHMT MEGADEATH
AADEEGLMN MAGDALENE
AADEEGNOR ORANGEADE
AADEEGNPP APPENDAGE

AADEEGNRT GREAT
DANE, TEAGARDEN
AADEEHPRS SPEARHEAD
AADEEHRTT DEATH RATE
AADEEIKWW WIDE-AWAKE
AADEEILMV MEDIAEVAL
AADEEIILNT ALIENATED
AADEEIIMNT DEAMINATE
AADEEKMRR EARMARKED
AADEEELMRS ESMERALDA
AADEELNNR LEND AN EAR
AADEELNPS ESPLANADE
AADEELNRX ALEXANDER
AADEELRRY LAY READER
AADEELTUV DEVALUATE,
EVALUATED
AADEEMNRT TRADE
NAME
AADEEMRSU ADMEASURE
AADEENSTU NAUSEATED
AADEEPRST PAEDERAST,
SEPARATED
AADEERRTT RETARDATE
AADEESTTV DEVASTATE
AADEFFILR FAR AFIELD
AADEFGLNN FANDANGLE
AADEFGRSU SAFEGUARD
AADEFILNT FAN-TAILED
AADEFIORS AFORESAID
AADEFIRRS FARADISER
AADEFIRRZ FARADIZER
AADEFLNOR FARANDOLE
AADEFMPRT AFTERDAMP
AADEFMRST FARMSTEAD
AADEFSSTT STEADFAST
AADEGHNRU
HARANGUED
AADEGHNRY HYDRANGEA
AADEGHNST STAGEHAND
AADEGILRT TALIGRADE
AADEGILTT TAILGATED
AADEGIMNT DIAMAGNET
AADEGINRR ARRAIGNED
AADEGINRS GARDENIAS
AADEGINRT TRAGEDIAN
AADEGINTV NAVIGATED
AADEGIPRS DISPARAGE
AADEGLNNT LAND AGENT
AADEGNRRT REGARDANT
AADEGNSTT STAGNATED
AADEGORRT ARROGATED
AADEGPRST TRADE GAPS
AADEGRRRU REARGUARD

AADEGRRVY GRAVEYARD
AADEGRSTU GRADUATES
AADEHHKNS HANDSHAKE
AADEHILRS RAILHEADS
AADEHIMOT HAEMATOID
AADEHIORR DIARRHOEA
AADEHIPRT APARTHEID,
HIT PARADE
AADEHIRST STAIRHEAD
AADEHISWY HIDEAWAYS
AADEHKMST DEATH MASK
AADEHLLST HEADSTALL
AADEHLMNN
MANHANDLE
AADEHLMPS LAMPSHADE
AADEHLMRS MARSHALED
AADEHLMSY ASHAMEDLY
AADEHLNNP PANHANDLE
AADEHLNRT HEARTLAND
AADEHLPST ASPHALTED
AADEHMNSU
UNASHAMED
AADEHMPST HAMPSTEAD
AADEHMSST MASTHEADS
AADEHORRW
ARROWHEAD
AADEHPRTT DEATH TRAP
AADEHRRTW EARTHWARD
AADEHRSTT HEAD START
AADEIIPRS PRAESIDIA
AADEIIRRT IRRADIATE
AADEIIRTV RADIATIVE
AADEIKKVY KADIYEVKA
AADEILLPT PALLIATED
AADEILMNN ALMANDINE
AADEILMNS LADIES' MAN
AADEILMNT LAMINATED
AADEILMRT DIAMETRAL
AADEILNNN ANNELIDAN
AADEILNNR ADRENALIN
AADEILNOT DEALATION
AADEILNSV VANDALISE
AADEILNVZ VANDALIZE
AADEILPSS PALISADES
AADEILPST STAPEDIAL
AADEILRTV TRAVAILED
AADEILSTV SALIVATED
AADEILTVW TIDAL WAVE
AADEIMMNR DRAMAMINE
AADEIMMSS MASS MEDIA
AADEIMNRS MARINADES
AADEIMNRT MARINATED

AADEIMNSW ADAM'S
WINE
AADEIMRST DRAMATISE
AADEIMRTZ DRAMATIZE
AADEINPRT PINTADERA
AADEINRST STERADIAN
AADEINRTT ATTAINDER
AADEIPPRS APPRAISED,
DISAPPEAR
AADEIPRSS PARADISES
AADEIPRST ASPIRATED,
DISPARATE
AADEJKLWY JAYWALKED
AADEKMMRU
MARMADUKE
AADEKMNRS MANDRAKES
AADEKMRRT TRADEMARK
AADELLNOT LANOLATED
AADELLNPR LAPLANDER
AADELLNTU LANDAULET
AADELMMOR
MELODRAMA
AADELMNRS MALANDERS
AADELMORV AD
VALOREM
AADELNSTW WASTELAND
AADELPPRU APPLAUDER
AADELPRSY PARALYSED
AADELPRTW DRAWPLATE
AADELRTTY LATTER-DAY
AADELSSTU ASSAULTED
AADEMMNOR
MEMORANDA
AADEMMRST
AMSTERDAM
AADEMNPRS AMPERSAND
AADEMNRST TRADESMAN
AADEMOTTU AUTOMATED
AADEMPTTU AMPUTATED
AADEMRRSU MARAUDERS
AADEMRRTU DURA
MATER
AADENNOTT ANNOTATED
AADENNPPT APPENDANT
AADENNRST SANTANDER
AADENNTTT ATTENDANT
AADENPPRS SANDPAPER
AADENPRTU PANDURATE
AADENRRTT RETARDANT
AADENRRTW
WARRANTED
AADEOPRSX PARADOXES

AADEORSTW SODA
WATER
AADEORSTX ROAD TAXES
AADERRRSW REARWARDS
AADERRSVY ADVERSARY
AADERSSTW EASTWARDS
AADERSTTU SATURATED
AADFFIITV AFFIDAVIT
AADFGHRRT HARD GRAFT
AADFGNNOS FANDANGOS
AADFHMNRS FARMHANDS
AADFILNRY FAIRYLAND
AADFIMNRY MAN FRIDAY
AADFIMRRY DAIRY FARM
AADFLLLNS LANDFALLS
AADFMNRST DRAFTSMAN
AADFMRRSY FARMYARDS
AADGGHIST HAGGADIST
AADGGHLRY HAGGARDLY
AADGHIMPR DIAPHRAGM
AADGHINRZ HAZARDING
AADGHIPSY DYSPHAGIA
AADGIINRT RADIATING
AADGILMNY AMYGDALIN
AADGILMRS MADRIGALS
AADGILNOS DIAGONALS
AADGILORT GLADIATOR
AADGILRRU GUARDRAIL
AADGIMMNO GAMMADION
AADGIMNNT MANDATING
AADGIMNRU MARAUDING
AADGIMORR RADIOGRAM
AADGIMPRS PARADIGMS
AADGIMRRS MARDI GRAS
AADGINORT GRADATION
AADGINRSU GUARDIANS
AADGINRUZ DZUNGARIA
AADGLLNRU GLANDULAR
AADGLLRUY GRADUALLY
AADGLMNRS GRAND
SLAM
AADGLNOOW
WAGONLOAD
AADGLNRSS GRASSLAND
AADGMNORS
DRAGOMANS
AADGMNRSU
GUARDSMAN
AADGNRSUV GUARD'S
VAN, VANGUARDS
AADGORRTU GRADUATOR
AADHILLNO HOLLANDIA
AADHILLRS HALLIARDS

AADHILLSS ALLIS SHAD
AADHILNRS HANDRAILS
AADHINRRS HARRIDANS
AADHIPSSY DYSPHASIA
AADHNSSTW WASHSTAND
AADHORRSU HADROSAUR
AADHORSUZ HAZARDOUS
AADIILLNP PLAIN-LAID
AADIILMNV MALDIVIAN
AADIILSUV VISUAL AID
AADIINNRS SARDINIAN
AADIINORT RADIATION
AADIINRRT IRRADIANT
AADIISSST DIASTASIS
AADIJNNOR JORDANIAN
AADILLMOR ARMADILLO
AADILLMPU PALLADIUM
AADILLNOT ALLANTOID
AADILLOPS SAPODILLA
AADILLPRY RADIAL-PLY
AADILMNNO ADNOMINAL
AADILMNOV MOLDAVIAN
AADILMNSV VANDALISM
AADILMNTU TAMIL NADU
AADILMORT MALADROIT
AADILMPRY PYRAMIDAL
AADILMRTY ADMIRALTY
AADILNNOT ANTINODAL
AADILNOPT ANTIPODAL
AADILNORS ROSALINDA
AADILNOTU ADULATION,
LAUDATION
AADILNRTY RADIANTLY
AADILNSWZ SWAZILAND
AADILORRS RAILROADS
AADILOSVW DISAVOWAL
AADILPSSY DYSPLASIA
AADIMNNOT DAMNATION
AADIMNNRS MANDARINS
AADIMNRST TAMARINDS
AADIMRSTT DRAMATIST
AADINNNOT ANDANTINO
AADINOORT ADORATION
AADINPRSS SPANIARDS
AADINSSTY SAINT'S DAY
AADIORRST RADIATORS
AADJNSTTU ADJUTANTS
AADKLMNRS LANDMARKS
AADKLRWWY
AWKWARDLY
AADKNORRS KRASNODAR
AADLLNORU ALL-AROUND
AADLLOPSU PALLADOUS

AADLMNPSW
SWAMPLAND
AADLORSST LOADSTARS
AADLORTUY ADULATORY,
LAUDATORY
AADMMNOOR
MONODRAMA
AADMNORTY
DAMNATORY, MANDATORY
AADNNORSU ANANDROUS
AADNPRSST SAND TRAPS
AADNQRSTU QUADRANTS
AADRSSTUY SATURDAYS
AAEEEHLRT AETHEREAL
AAEEELSTV TEALEAVES
AAEEFHRTT AFTERHEAT
AAEEFKPRT AFTERPEAK
AAEEFLOTV FAVEOLATE
AAEEGGGRT AGGREGATE
AAEEGINTV EVAGINATE
AAEEGIRTV VARIEGATE
AAEEGKNST KATANGESE
AAEEGLMNT MENTAL AGE
AAEEGLSVW WAGE SLAVE
AAEEGMNNS MANGANESE
AAEEGMNST STAGE NAME
AAEEGNORS ARAGONESE
AAEEGNPRT PARENTAGE
AAEEGNRRR REARRANGE
AAEEGNRTU GUARANTEE
AAEEGPRUV AVERAGE UP
AAEEGRRSY GREY AREAS
AAEEHIMNT HAEMATEIN
AAEEHIMTT HAEMATITE
AAEEHISST AESTHESIA
AAEEHKMST MAKE HASTE
AAEEHLRRS REHEARSAL
AAEEHMNTU ATHENAEUM
AAEEHMNTX EXANTHEMA
AAEEHMPST METAPHASE
AAEEHRRRT RARE EARTH
AAEEHSTVW HEAT WAVES
AAEEIKLMP MAKE A PILE
AAEEIKLMU LEUKAEMIA
AAEEILLMN EL ALAMEIN
AAEEILLST ILL AT EASE
AAEEILLTV ALLEVIATE
AAEEILMNS MELANESIA
AAEEILRTT RETALIATE
AAEEIMNRT REANIMATE
AAEEIMNTV EMANATIVE
AAEEIMNTX EXANIMATE
AAEEINSTW TAIWANESE

AAEEIPTTX EXPATIATE
AAEEISTTV AESTIVATE
AAEEKKMVY MAKEYEVKA
AAEEKMNSS NAMESAKES
AAEEKPRST PARAKEETS
AAEEKPSSY SPEAKEASY
AAEELLOTV ALVEOLATE
AAEELLPPT APPELLATE
AAEELLPTT PATELLATE
AAEELLQRU AQUARELLE
AAEELLRWW

     WELL-AWARE

AAEELMMNU

     EMMANUELA

AAEELMMRT METAMERAL
AAEELMNPT NAMEPLATE
AAEELMSST MATELASSE
AAEELMSTT STALEMATE
AAEELNOPR AEROPLANE
AAEELNPSS SEAPLANES
AAEELNRTT ALTERNATE
AAEELPPSX SEX APPEAL
AAEELPRSY LEAP YEARS
AAEELRRTT RETREATAL
AAEELRSTU LAUREATES
AAEEMMNTZ AMAZEMENT
AAEEMNRST MAN-EATERS
AAEEMPRRT PARAMETER
AAEENRRTW WARRANTEE
AAEENRSSW AWARENESS
AAEENRSTT ANTEATERS
AAEENTTTU ATTENUATE
AAEEOPRSU AEROPAUSE
AAEEOPRTV EVAPORATE
AAEEPRRTY RATEPAYER
AAEEPRSST SEPARATES
AAEERRTTW WATER RATE
AAEFFIILT AFFILIATE
AAEFFILRS RAFFLESIA
AAEFGHMNR

     FERMANAGH

AAEFGINRS SEAFARING
AAEFGIRSX SAXIFRAGE
AAEFGLLLR FLAGELLAR
AAEFGLRVW FLAG-WAVER
AAEFGORRS FARRAGOES
AAEFHLPRT FLARE PATH
AAEFHMRTT AFTERMATH
AAEFIKNRR AFRIKANER
AAEFILMRR FIRE ALARM
AAEFILNTX ANTEFIXAL
AAEFILRTY FAIRY-TALE
AAEFIMMNR MAINFRAME

AAEFINNRS SAFRANINE
AAEFINSST FANTASIES,

     FANTASISE

AAEFINSTZ FANTASIZE
AAEFINTTU INFATUATE
AAEFKLLST LEAFSTALK
AAEFLLLRY FALLALERY
AAEFLLRTW WATERFALL
AAEFLMSTT FLATMATES
AAEFLNRRT FRATERNAL
AAEFLORTZ FORTALEZA
AAEFRRSWY WAYFARERS
AAEGGILLN GALINGALE
AAEGGILNW GALWEGIAN
AAEGGINOR GEORGIANA
AAEGGINRU RAIN GAUGE
AAEGGINRV AVERAGING
AAEGGLLNO GALLONAGE
AAEGGLNSU LANGUAGES
AAEGHIILM HEMIALGIA
AAEGHLNOX HEXAGONAL
AAEGHLNPR PHALANGER
AAEGHLNPS PHALANGES
AAEGHLPSS SLAGHEAPS
AAEGHMRSX

     HEXAGRAMS

AAEGHNOPR ORPHANAGE
AAEGHNRRU HARANGUER
AAEGHNRSU HARANGUES
AAEGHORRT HARROGATE
AAEGIILQU AQUILEGIA
AAEGIKNNW AWAKENING
AAEGILMRT METRALGIA
AAEGILNNN ANNEALING
AAEGILNNT GALANTINE
AAEGILNOS ANALOGIES,

     ANALOGISE

AAEGILNOZ ANALOGIZE
AAEGILNPP APPEALING
AAEGILNRU NEURALGIA
AAEGILNSV GALVANISE
AAEGILNVZ GALVANIZE
AAEGILSTT TAILGATES
AAEGIMMNS MISMANAGE
AAEGIMNNS MAGNESIAN
AAEGIMNNT EMANATING,

     MANGANITE, MAN-EATING

AAEGIMNRR MARGARINE
AAEGIMNRT MARGINATE
AAEGIMNSZ MAGAZINES
AAEGIMRRS MARRIAGES
AAEGIMRRT MARGARITE
AAEGINNRT ARGENTINA

AAEGINORT ARAGONITE
AAEGINPPR APPEARING
AAEGINPPS APPEASING
AAEGINPRS PAGANISER
AAEGINPRZ PAGANIZER
AAEGINPTZ GAZIANTEP
AAEGINRRR ARRAIGNER
AAEGINRRS GRANARIES
AAEGINRSY GAINSAYER
AAEGIRTTV GRAVITATE
AAEGISTTT SAGITTATE
AAEGISVWY GIVEAWAYS
AAEGKKRRS SKAGERRAK
AAEGLLMPS PLASMAGEL
AAEGLLNRY LARYNGEAL
AAEGLMNOR

     MANGALORE

AAEGLNOSU ANALOGUES
AAEGLNRTU GRANULATE
AAEGLRSSW GLASSWARE
AAEGMNNOR

     ORANGEMAN

AAEGMNORT

     MATRONAGE

AAEGMNPRT PENTAGRAM
AAEGMNRTT TERMAGANT
AAEGMRRTT TETRAGRAM
AAEGMRSTT STRATAGEM
AAEGNNOOT NOTOGAEAN
AAEGNOORS NO-GO

     AREAS

AAEGNOPRS PARSONAGE
AAEGNOPRT PATRONAGE
AAEGNPRTY PAGEANTRY
AAEGNRSTV STAVANGER
AAEGNRTTU GREAT-AUNT
AAEGOPPRT PROPAGATE
AAEGPRSTU PASTURAGE
AAEGRRSTZ STARGAZER
AAEHHINPZ ZEPHANIAH
AAEHHLNOT HALOTHANE
AAEHIKNRT KATHARINE
AAEHIKNSZ ASHKENAZI
AAEHILNNT NATHANIEL
AAEHILNTV LEVIATHAN
AAEHIMNOT THEOMANIA
AAEHINPRS SERAPHINA
AAEHINPRT PARTHENIA
AAEHINRSV HAVERSIAN
AAEHJLLLU HALLELUJA
AAEHLLNOP ALLOPHANE
AAEHLMSSY SEALYHAMS
AAEHLNPSX PHALANXES

AAEHLNPSY SYNALEPHA
AAEHLNSTT ATHELSTAN
AAEHLOPPR PHALAROPE
AAEHLPSUV UPHEAVALS
AAEHMOSTT HAEMOSTAT
AAEHMRSTU SHAMATEUR
AAEHNPSST PHEASANTS
AAEHNSTVX TAX HAVENS
AAEHRRSTT EARTHSTAR
AAEIIKNRT AIR-INTAKE
AAEIILMNS ANIMALISE
AAEIILMNZ ANIMALIZE
AAEIILMRT LATIMERIA
AAEIILNRT INTER ALIA
AAEIILPTX EPITAXIAL
AAEIIMNNT INANIMATE
AAEIIMRST ARTEMISIA
AAEIINQTU AQUITAINE
AAEIINSST TAENIASIS
AAEIJNRSU JANUARIES
AAEIKLNNN LENINAKAN
AAEIKLTTV TALKATIVE
AAEIKMNRR RAINMAKER
AAEIKNPST TAKE PAINS
AAEIKRSTU AUTARKIES
AAEILLLSU ALLELUIAS
AAEILLMMT MAMILLATE
AAEILLNPS SAILPLANE
AAEILLNPT TAILPLANE
AAEILLNTV ÉLAN VITAL
AAEILLPSS PAILLASSE,
  PALLIASSE
AAEILMNOS ANOMALIES
AAEILMNST LAMINATES
AAEILMNSZ MANIZALES
AAEILMNTU ALUMINATE
AAEILMPRV PRIMAEVAL
AAEILMPTT PALMITATE
AAEILMRST MATERIALS
AAEILNNTV VALENTINA
AAEILNORT ALIENATOR,
  RATIONALE
AAEILNPRS AIRPLANES
AAEILNPRT PERINATAL
AAEILNRTU LAURENTIA
AAEILNSTT TANTALISE
AAEILNTTT TANTALITE
AAEILNTTZ TANTALIZE
AAEILORTV VARIOLATE
AAEILPPTT PALPITATE
AAEILPRTZ TRAPEZIAL
AAEILRSSW WASSAILER
AAEILRSTU ESTUARIAL

AAEILSSSV VASSALISE
AAEILSSVZ VASSALIZE
AAEILSTVX LAXATIVES
AAEIMMNOT AMMONIATE
AAEIMNNOT EMANATION
AAEIMNNSS ANAMNESIS
AAEIMNOPR POMERANIA
AAEIMNOST ANATOMIES,
  ANATOMISE
AAEIMNOTZ AMAZONITE,
  ANATOMIZE
AAEIMNPRR REPAIRMAN
AAEIMNPRS PEARMAINS
AAEIMNRTW WATER MAIN
AAEIMNSTT STAMINATE
AAEIMOPRT AMETROPIA
AAEIMORST AROMATISE
AAEIMORTZ AROMATIZE
AAEIMRRST AIRSTREAM
AAEINNRSW RAW SIENNA
AAEINPPRT APPERTAIN
AAEINPRST SEPTARIAN
AAEINQTTU ANTIQUATE
AAEINRRRS IN ARREARS
AAEINRRTV NARRATIVE
AAEINRRTW RAINWATER
AAEIPPRRS APPRAISER
AAEIPRSST ASPIRATES,
  PARASITES
AAEIRRSTT TARTARISE
AAEIRRTTZ TARTARIZE
AAEISSSUV ASSUASIVE
AAEJKLRWY JAYWALKER
AAEKLLSST SALES TALK
AAEKMRRTW
  WATERMARK
AAELLLMOR MALLEOLAR
AAELLLPRS PARALLELS
AAELLLRTY LATERALLY
AAELLNPPT APPELLANT
AAELLORSV ALVEOLARS
AAELLPPRW WALLPAPER
AAELLSUXY ASEXUALLY
AAELLSWYY ALLEYWAYS
AAELMMORR
  MARMOREAL
AAELMMPST METAPLASM
AAELMNOSU MAUSOLEAN
AAELMNRSU EL MANSURA
AAELMPSTY PLAYMATES
AAELNPRTY PLANETARY
AAELNRSTT TRANSLATE
AAELNRTUU AU NATUREL

AAELNSTTU SULTANATE
AAELOPRST PASTORALE
AAELOPSSU ASEPALOUS
AAELOPSTU APETALOUS
AAELORRSY SOLAR YEAR
AAELORSTV SALVATORE
AAELORTTZ LAZARETTO
AAELORTUV EVALUATOR
AAELPPRST STAR-APPLE
AAELPRRSY PARALYSER
AAELPRSSY PARALYSES
AAELPSTTU SPATULATE
AAELRRSTV TRAVERSAL
AAELRSSTU ASSAULTER,
  SALERATUS
AAELRSTTW SALTWATER
AAELSSTWY LEASTWAYS
AAEMMNRST
  ARMAMENTS,
  MEN-AT-ARMS
AAEMNORTY EMANATORY
AAEMNPRTT APARTMENT
AAEMNSSTT STATESMAN
AAEMPRSTY PAYMASTER
AAEMRRSTU ARMATURES
AAENNPSST EN PASSANT
AAENNTTTU ATTENUANT
AAENPRSTY PEASANTRY
AAENRRRTW WARRANTER
AAENSTTTT ATTESTANT
AAEOOPPRS SOAP OPERA
AAEOPRRST SEPARATOR
AAEOPRSTT PASTORATE
AAEOPSSTT APOSTATES
AAEPPRRST SPARE PART
AAEPRSTXY TAXPAYERS
AAERRSTTU SATURATER
AAERRSTTW WATER RATS
AAERSTWWY WATERWAYS
AAFFFGLST FLAGSTAFF
AAFFGNRSU SUFFRAGAN
AAFGILMNS FALANGISM
AAFGILNRS FRANGLAIS
AAFGILNST FALANGIST
AAFGINRWY WAYFARING
AAFGORTTU AUTOGRAFT
AAFIILMRS FAMILIARS
AAFILLNOP FALLOPIAN
AAFILLNRS RAINFALLS
AAFILMMNY FAMILY MAN
AAFILMNOR FORAMINAL
AAFILNNOU FIONNUALA
AAFILNOOV OF NO AVAIL

AAFILNOTX AFLATOXIN
AAFILORUW RAUWOLFIA
AAFILSSTT FATALISTS
AAFIOTTTU TOUT A FAIT
AAFKLOOST ASK A LOT OF
AAFLORSWY FOR ALWAYS
AAFMOPRRT APART FROM
AAFMORRTW
     MARROWFAT
AAGGIINTT AGITATING
AAGGILNSV SALVAGING
AAGGIMNPR RAMPAGING
AAGGIMNSS MASSAGING
AAGGINNRR ARRANGING
AAGGINSSU ASSUAGING
AAGGKLNNP GANGPLANK
AAGHIKMNY HAYMAKING
AAGHIKMOS KAGOSHIMA
AAGHILNNS HANGNAILS
AAGHILNRS SHANGRI-LA
AAGHIMOOP OMOPHAGIA
AAGHINNRU HUNGARIAN
AAGHINRSS HARASSING
AAGHINSSY SASHAYING
AAGHKMNSY
     GYMKHANAS
AAGHLLOPR ALLOGRAPH
AAGHOPRTU AUTOGRAPH
AAGIIKNNS KISANGANI
AAGIILNSS ASSAILING
AAGIIMNNT ANIMATING
AAGIIMNRY IMAGINARY
AAGIINNTT ATTAINING
AAGIINOTT AGITATION
AAGIINSTT SATIATING
AAGIJNNNP JAPANNING
AAGIKNPRT PARTAKING
AAGILLNTV GALLIVANT
AAGILLORT ALLIGATOR
AAGILMNNO AGNOMINAL
AAGILMNNS SIGNALMAN
AAGILMNNT MALIGNANT
AAGILMNOS MAGNOLIAS
AAGILMNSV GALVANISM
AAGILMNYZ AMAZINGLY
AAGILMRST MAGISTRAL
AAGILNNSY ANALYSING
AAGILNOST ANALOGIST,
     NOSTALGIA
AAGILNPPT PALPATING
AAGILNRUU INAUGURAL
AAGILNRUV VULGARIAN
AAGILNWYY WAYLAYING

AAGILOOPS APOLOGIAS
AAGILQUUY GUAYAQUIL
AAGIMMMST MAGMATISM
AAGIMNOSY ANISOGAMY
AAGIMNPRT PTARMIGAN
AAGINNRRT NARRATING
AAGINOOTV VAGOTONIA
AAGINORTV NAVIGATOR
AAGINSTUU AUGUSTINA
AAGIORSTT AGITATORS
AAGKMORYY
     KARYOGAMY
AAGKNOORS
     KANGAROOS
AAGLLLNTY GALLANTLY
AAGLLNRTY GALLANTRY
AAGLMMMOY
     MAMMALOGY
AAGLMNORU
     GRANULOMA
AAGLNNNOO
     NONAGONAL
AAGLNOOSU ANALOGOUS
AAGLNQSUU AQUALUNGS
AAGLRRSTU GASTRULAR
AAGMNNOSU
     MANGANOUS
AAGMOOPSU
     APOGAMOUS
AAGMRSSSU SARGASSUM
AAGNNNOTY NANNY
     GOAT
AAGNNORTU
     ORANG-UTAN
AAGNORRTU GUARANTOR
AAGNORSTU ANGOSTURA
AAGNRUUUY URUGUAYAN
AAGOORRRT ARROGATOR
AAGPRSTTY STAG PARTY
AAHHNNSSU SHUSHANNA
AAHIILNSW SWAHILIAN
AAHIILNTU LITHUANIA
AAHILMNOT MALATHION
AAHILMTUZ AZIMUTHAL
AAHILNNST INHALANTS
AAHILNORT INHALATOR
AAHILNSTU AILANTHUS
AAHILORTU AUTHORIAL
AAHILPSXY ASPHYXIAL
AAHIMMNSS SHAMANISM
AAHIMNOST THOMASINA
AAHIMNSST SHAMANIST
AAHIMNSTU AMIANTHUS

AAHINOORR HONORARIA
AAHINOPRT PARATHION
AAHINORRV HARROVIAN
AAHINPTTY ANTIPATHY
AAHINRRTU ARTHURINA
AAHIOPPSS APOPHASIS
AAHJNRTUV THANJAVUR
AAHKLLMRS HALLMARKS
AAHKLMNOO
     OKLAHOMAN
AAHKMOSTW
     TOMAHAWKS
AAHLLMOSW
     HALLOWMAS
AAHLLOPTY ALLOPATHY
AAHLLSTTT HALLSTATT
AAHLMNNTU LANTHANUM
AAHLMPSTU ASPHALTUM
AAHLPPPSY SLAPHAPPY
AAHMNORST MARATHONS
AAHMNPSST PHANTASMS
AAHMOPPRR PARAMORPH
AAHNNOOTZ ANTHOZOAN
AAHNNOSTU ANANTHOUS
AAHNOTTXY ANTHOTAXY
AAHORTWWY
     THROWAWAY
AAIIKNNRU UKRAINIAN
AAIIKNPST PAKISTANI
AAIILMMNS ANIMALISM
AAIILMNSS MAINSAILS
AAIILMNST ANIMALIST
AAIILMNTY ANIMALITY
AAIILMPRT IMPARTIAL,
     PRIMATIAL
AAIILNOSU LOUISIANA
AAIILRUXY AUXILIARY
AAIIMMNST ANIMATISM
AAIIMMNOT ANIMATION
AAIIMNRTU MAURITIAN
AAIIMORST TIMISOARA
AAIIMPPRR PRIMIPARA
AAIINNRTU UNITARIAN
AAIINNRTV INVARIANT
AAIINOPRT TOPIARIAN
AAIINORTV VARIATION
AAIINOSTT SATIATION
AAIINPRSS PARISIANS
AAIJNRSSY JANISSARY
AAIKLLOSS ALKALOSIS
AAIKLNOSV SLOVAKIAN
AAIKNNOPT PONTIANAK
AAIKNRSTX TAXI RANKS

AAIKSSSTW SWASTIKAS
AAILLLNOT LALLATION
AAILLMMRY MAMILLARY
AAILLMMXY MAXIMALLY
AAILLMNST MANTILLAS
AAILLMOPP PAPILLOMA
AAILLMRSY AMARYLLIS
AAILLMRTY MARITALLY
AAILLMRXY MAXILLARY
AAILLNOOP APOLLONIA
AAILLNOPT ALTIPLANO
AAILLNOST ALLANTOIS
AAILLNOTV VALLATION
AAILLNPRU NULLIPARA
AAILLNTVY VALIANTLY
AAILLOPRT PALLIATOR
AAILLPPRY PAPILLARY
AAILLPRTY PARTIALLY
AAILLPSTY SPATIALLY
AAILMNNPS PLAINSMAN
AAILMNOPT PALMATION
AAILMNORT LAMINATOR
AAILMNOST ATONALISM
AAILMNSST TALISMANS
AAILMNTTU MATUTINAL
AAILMORTY AMORALITY
AAILMPRSU MARSUPIAL
AAILMPRTU MULTIPARA
AAILMRSST ALARMISTS
AAILNNOPT PLANATION
AAILNNOST NATIONALS
AAILNNOSV SLAVONIAN
AAILNNPQU PALANQUIN
AAILNNPRU UNIPLANAR
AAILNNPST PLANTAINS
AAILNNSST ANNALISTS
AAILNOOTV OVATIONAL
AAILNOPPT PALPATION
AAILNOPSS PASSIONAL
AAILNOPUW PAULOWNIA
AAILNOSTT SALTATION
AAILNOSTV SALVATION
AAILNOTTY ATONALITY
AAILNOTUV VALUATION
AAILNPRTU TARPAULIN
AAILNPSTU SAINT PAUL
AAILNSSST STANISLAS
AAILOPRRT RAPTORIAL
AAILOPSTX POSTAXIAL
AAILORRST SARTORIAL
AAILPRSSY PARALYSIS
AAIMMNNOO MONOMANIA
AAIMMNRST MARTINMAS

AAIMMNNSST MAINMASTS
AAIMNNORS SAN MARINO
AAIMNOPRY PYROMANIA
AAIMNOSTT ANATOMIST
AAIMNPRSZ MARZIPANS
AAIMNRRST TRIMARANS
AAIMNRSTT TARANTISM
AAIMNSSTY MAINSTAYS
AAIMOORRT MORATORIA
AAIMORSSU AMAUROSIS
AAIMQRSUU AQUARIUMS
AAINNNTTU ANNUITANT
AAINNORRT NARRATION
AAINNPRSY SPIN A YARN
AAINNRSTU SATURNIAN
AAINORRST ROTARIANS
AAINPRSST ASPIRANTS,
   PARTISANS
AAINPSTXY ANAPTYXIS
AAINQRSTU QUATRAINS
AAINQRTUY ANTIQUARY
AAINQSTTU AQUATINTS
AAINSSSSS ASSASSINS
AAINSSSTT ASSISTANT,
   SATANISTS
AAIOPPRRT APPARITOR,
   PRO PATRIA
AAIOPRRST ASPIRATOR
AAIORRTTT TRATTORIA
AAIPPRSSU PARI PASSU
AAJMORRSU URSA MAJOR
AAKLLLMST SMALL TALK
AAKNOOSST SASKATOON
AALLLMMSS SMALL SLAM
AALLLMOPS ALLOPLASM
AALLMMRSS SMALL ARMS
AALLMOPSS PLASMASOL
AALLNNOPY POLLYANNA
AALLNRTUY NATURALLY
AALLORSVY YAROSLAVL
AALLPRTWY PARTY WALL
AALMNOOSU
   ANOMALOUS
AALMNOPRT PATROLMAN
AALMNPRTY RAMPANTLY
AALMOOSTU AUTOSOMAL
AALMOQSSU SQUAMOSAL
AALMORTYY MAYORALTY
AALNNRTUU UNNATURAL
AALNOPSTT POSTNATAL
AALNOSTTU TANTALOUS
AALNPRTWY LAWN PARTY
AALOPRRTY PORTRAYAL

AALOPRSST PASTORALS
AALRSSTTW LAST STRAW,
   STALWARTS
AAMMOORST
   MATAMOROS
AAMNNOTUY ANY
   AMOUNT
AAMNOOTTU
   AUTOMATON
AAMNOPRTU PARAMOUNT
AAMOPRRSU PARAMOURS
AANNOORTT ANNOTATOR
AANORRRST NARRATORS
AANORRRTW
   WARRANTOR
AANORSTTU ASTRONAUT
AANPRSSSU PARNASSUS
AAORRSTTU TARTAROUS
AAOSSTWWY
   STOWAWAYS
ABBBCELLU CLUBBABLE
ABBBDEELR BLABBERED
ABBCCEHKN BACKBENCH
ABBCCKKLU BLACKBUCK
ABBCDEERU BARBECUED
ABBCDELRS SCRABBLED
ABBCDELRY CRABBEDLY
ABBCDIKLR BLACKBIRD
ABBCDKORU BUCKBOARD
ABBCEEIRS CARIBBEES
ABBCEERSU BARBECUES
ABBCEIKRT BACKBITER
ABBCEIRST CRABBIEST
ABBCEIRSY CRYBABIES
ABBCEISST SCABBIEST
ABBCEKLLT BLACK BELT
ABBCEKLLU BLUE-BLACK
ABBCEKLNO BONEBLACK
ABBCEKNOS BACKBONES
ABBCELRRS SCRABBLER
ABBCILPRU PUBLIC BAR
ABBCIMOST BOMBASTIC
ABBCINOSY CABIN BOYS
ABBCKLOOT BOOTBLACK
ABBCLMOOU
   ABCOULOMB
ABBDDEMOR
   BOMBARDED
ABBDEELRU BLUEBEARD
ABBDEGINU BEDAUBING
ABBDEILOT BOBTAILED
ABBDEILTU DUBITABLE
ABBDEINRS BREAD BINS

ABBDEIRTT RABBITTED
ABBDELOTU DOUBTABLE
ABBDELQSU SQUABBLED
ABBDELSUU SUBDUABLE
ABBDGIILN AD-LIBBING
ABBDHLOOT BLOODBATH
ABBDILLOR BILLBOARD,
   BROADBILL
ABBDKLNOO BLOOD BANK
ABBDMNOOR
   BOMBARDON
ABBEEHTTY BABY TEETH
ABBEEJRRS JABBERERS
ABBEEKLRU REBUKABLE
ABBEELMOT BE TO BLAME
ABBEELOPR PROBEABLE
ABBEENORS BARE BONES
ABBEENRRY BANEBERRY
ABBEERRRY BEARBERRY
ABBEFILST FLABBIEST
ABBEGIJNR JABBERING
ABBEGILLO OBLIGABLE
ABBEHINOS HOBBESIAN
ABBEHISST SHABBIEST
ABBEHORST BATHROBES
ABBEILMSU ABU SIMBEL
ABBEIMNOZ BOMBAZINE
ABBEINORT BARBITONE
ABBEKLOOR BROOKABLE
ABBELLMPU PLUMBABLE
ABBELMOOZ BAMBOOZLE
ABBELOPRS PROBABLES
ABBELOSTY STABLE BOY
ABBELQRSU SQUABBLER
ABBELQSSU SQUABBLES
ABBENORST ABSORBENT
ABBFHLLSU FLASHBULB
ABBGIINRT RABBITING
ABBGILMNR BRAMBLING
ABBGILOOT OBBLIGATO
ABBGINORS ABSORBING
ABBHOOTTY BABY TOOTH
ABBILLSSU SILLABUBS
ABBJMRUUU BUJUMBURA
ABBKKNOOS BANKBOOKS
ABBLLSSUY SYLLABUBS
ABBMMOOST ATOM
   BOMBS
ABBOOPRTY BOOBY TRAP
ABBOORRWY BARROW
   BOY
ABCCCEFIO BECCAFICO
ABCCCKKLO BLACKCOCK

ABCCEEHKL CHECKABLE
ABCCEENRU BUCCANEER
ABCCEIIST SCABIETIC
ABCCEINOV BICONCAVE
ABCCEKMOS COMEBACKS
ABCCELNRU CARBUNCLE
ABCCEMNRU
   CUMBRANCE
ABCCEMNTU ACCUMBENT
ABCCFIINO FIBONACCI
ABCCFIMOR BACCIFORM
ABCCGHLTU CLUTCH BAG
ABCCHHKNU HUNCHBACK
ABCCHKLOT BACKCLOTH
ABCCIKKKS KICKBACKS
ABCCIKRST CRABSTICK
ABCCILORU CORBICULA
ABCCIRSTU SUBARCTIC
ABCCKLLOS BALLCOCKS
ABCCKORSS BACKCROSS
ABCCMOORY
   MOBOCRACY
ABCDDEEHU DEBAUCHED
ABCDDEEIL DECIDABLE
ABCDDEFLO BOLDFACED
ABCDDEKLO BLOCKADED
ABCDDENOS ABSCONDED
ABCDDKORU
   DUCKBOARD
ABCDEEEHU DEBAUCHEE
ABCDEEHRU DEBAUCHER
ABCDEEHSU DEBAUCHES
ABCDEEILM MEDICABLE
ABCDEEINT BENEDICTA
ABCDEEKLN BLACKENED
ABCDEEKRT BRACKETED
ABCDEELMR CLAMBERED
ABCDEFIKR BACKFIRED
ABCDEHIOT COHABITED
ABCDEHKLO BLOCKHEAD
ABCDEIIST DIABETICS
ABCDEIJLU JUDICABLE
ABCDEIKLS BACKSLIDE
ABCDEIKRU RUDBECKIA
ABCDEIKSS BACKSIDES
ABCDEILMY MEDICABLY
ABCDEINTU INCUBATED
ABCDEIORT BACTEROID
ABCDEKLOR BLOCKADER
ABCDEKLOS BLOCKADES
ABCDEKNNS NECKBANDS
ABCDELLOS SCOLDABLE
ABCDELMRS SCRAMBLED

ABCDELOOS CABOODLES
ABCDEMOTT COMBATTED
ABCDENORR CORN
   BREAD
ABCDENORS ABSCONDER
ABCDENOSU
   CASEBOUND, SUBDEACON
ABCDEOORT OBCORDATE
ABCDGINOR BROCADING
ABCDGINTU ABDUCTING
ABCDHINRS DISBRANCH
ABCDHIOPR CHIPBOARD
ABCDHNRTU DUTCH
   BARN
ABCDIKRRY BRICKYARD
ABCDILMOR LOMBARDIC
ABCDILOPR CLIPBOARD
ABCDINOOT BANDICOOT
ABCDINOTU ABDUCTION
ABCDKLNOU CLOUDBANK
ABCDKLOOR ROADBLOCK
ABCDKOORR
   CORKBOARD
ABCDKOORS BACK
   DOORS
ABCDKOOSW
   BACKWOODS
ABCDKOPRS BACKDROPS
ABCDLNRSU SCRUBLAND
ABCDNOOXX BOX AND
   COX
ABCDOPRSU CUPBOARDS
ABCEEELRT CELEBRATE,
   ERECTABLE
ABCEEELRX EXECRABLE
ABCEEFFOR COFFEE BAR
ABCEEFIRS BRIEFCASE
ABCEEFLOR FORCEABLE
ABCEEFOSU BECAUSE OF
ABCEEGKNR GREENBACK
ABCEEHKLO CHOKEABLE
ABCEEHLLY BELLYACHE
ABCEEHLRS BLEACHERS
ABCEEILLS SLICEABLE
ABCEEILPR PIERCABLE
ABCEEILRT RECITABLE
ABCEEILST CELIBATES
ABCEEILSX EXCISABLE
ABCEEILTX EXCITABLE
ABCEEIMNS AMBIENCES
ABCEEINOS OBEISANCE
ABCEEINRR CARBINEER
ABCEEKKNR BREAKNECK

ABCEEKLSY BLACK EYES
ABCEEKPSW SWEEPBACK
ABCEELMNS SEMBLANCE
ABCEELNRT CELEBRANT
ABCEELNST ALBESCENT
ABCEELOPS PLACEBOES
ABCEELORT BRACTEOLE
ABCEELORV REVOCABLE
ABCEELRST BRACELETS
ABCEELRSU RESCUABLE,
SECURABLE
ABCEELRXY EXECRABLY
ABCEELSUX EXCUSABLE
ABCEEMMRT CAMEMBERT
ABCEEMORR EMBRACEOR
ABCEEMORT EMBROCATE
ABCEEMRRY EMBRACERY
ABCEENRTY CYBERNATE
ABCEENSTT TABESCENT
ABCEEOSSU SEBACEOUS
ABCEEPRRU CUPBEARER
ABCEESSSS ABSCESSES
ABCEFFHNO OFFENBACH
ABCEFHLSU FLASHCUBE
ABCEFIRTU BIFURCATE
ABCEFLOSU FOCUSABLE
ABCEFLSSS BASS CLEFS
ABCEFOSTU OBFUSCATE
ABCEGHILN BLEACHING
ABCEGHINR BREACHING
ABCEGIMNR EMBRACING
ABCEGKLLS BLACKLEGS
ABCEGKLOS BLOCKAGES
ABCEHINNO BONE CHINA
ABCEHINOT AITCHBONE
ABCEHKLLO BLACK HOLE
ABCEHKLOS SHOCKABLE
ABCEHKMNR BENCH
MARK
ABCEHKORS HORSEBACK
ABCEHKRRY HACKBERRY
ABCEHKTUW BUCKWHEAT
ABCEHLORS BACHELORS
ABCEHLOTU TOUCHABLE
ABCEHLSSU CHASUBLES
ABCEHOQRU QUEBRACHO
ABCEHRSTU BUCHAREST
ABCEIILNS SIBILANCE
ABCEIILRS IRASCIBLE
ABCEIIMRT IMBRICATE
ABCEIJLNU JUBILANCE
ABCEIJNOT ABJECTION
ABCEIJOST JACOBITES

ABCEILLOS OBELISCAL
ABCEILMOT METABOLIC
ABCEILMST BLASTEMIC
ABCEILNOS BALCONIES
ABCEILNOV INVOCABLE
ABCEILNRU BINUCLEAR,
INCURABLE
ABCEILNVY BIVALENCY
ABCEILORS CARBOLISE
ABCEILORT CABRIOLET
ABCEILORZ CARBOLIZE
ABCEILOTT COBALTITE
ABCEILRTU LUBRICATE
ABCEILRUX EXCALIBUR
ABCEILSTU BISULCATE
ABCEIMOTV COMBATIVE
ABCEIMRTU BACTERIUM
ABCEINORS CARBONISE
ABCEINORZ CARBONIZE
ABCEIRRSU CARBURISE
ABCEIRRTU RUBRICATE
ABCEIRRUZ CARBURIZE
ABCEJNSTU SUBJACENT
ABCEKLNSS BLACKNESS
ABCEKLPRU PARBUCKLE
ABCEKOOSS BOOKCASES
ABCEKPSTW
BACKSWEPT, SWEPT-BACK
ABCEKRTUW WATERBUCK
ABCELLOSX CALL BOXES
ABCELLRSW SCREWBALL
ABCELMRRS SCRAMBLER
ABCELMRSS SCRAMBLES
ABCELNOST CONSTABLE
ABCELNOTU COUNTABLE
ABCELOOST BOOTLACES
ABCELORVY REVOCABLY
ABCELOSST OBSTACLES
ABCELOSTT ECTOBLAST
ABCELRTTY BATTLE CRY
ABCELRTUU LUCUBRATE
ABCELSUXY EXCUSABLY
ABCEMORSS CROSSBEAM
ABCENORTY BARONETCY
ABCENRRRY CRANBERRY
ABCENSSTU SUBSTANCE
ABCEOOPRS BAROSCOPE
ABCEOPRRY REPROBACY
ABCFHIKLS BLACKFISH
ABCFKLLSU FULLBACKS
ABCGGIKPY PIGGYBACK
ABCGHIKST BACKSIGHT
ABCGHILNN BLANCHING

ABCGHINNR BRANCHING
ABCGHINOR BROACHING
ABCGIINRS ASCRIBING
ABCGILNOS LOG CABINS
ABCGILNRY BRACINGLY
ABCGIMNOT COMBATING
ABCHIILLN CHILBLAIN
ABCHIIOST ISOBATHIC
ABCHILMOS SHAMBOLIC
ABCHILNOR BRONCHIAL
ABCHKMPSU HUMPBACKS
ABCHKMTTU THUMBTACK
ABCHKNORT THORNBACK
ABCHKORTW
THROWBACK
ABCHLLNPU PUNCH BALL
ABCHLRWYZ WALBRZYCH
ABCIIIKLW BAILIWICK
ABCIIILPT BICIPITAL
ABCIIKNRS BRAINSICK
ABCIILLMU UMBILICAL
ABCIILLST BALLISTIC
ABCIILMOR MICROBIAL
ABCIILRSY IRASCIBLY
ABCIINNRT BRITANNIC
ABCIINRRU RUBRICIAN
ABCIIOSTT BIOSTATIC
ABCIIRSTY SYBARITIC
ABCIKLLST BLACKLIST
ABCILLMRU LUMBRICAL
ABCILLORU BILOCULAR
ABCILMNOO COLOMBIAN
ABCILMNOU COLUMBIAN,
COLUMBINA
ABCILMOPY AMBLYOPIC
ABCILMSTY CYMBALIST
ABCILMSUX SUBCLIMAX
ABCILNNOU CONNUBIAL
ABCILNORU BINOCULAR
ABCILNPSU PUBLICANS
ABCILNRTU LUBRICANT
ABCILNRUY INCURABLY
ABCILOPSY POLYBASIC
ABCILORRU ORBICULAR
ABCILOSSU SUBSOCIAL
ABCIMNOOS MONOBASIC
ABCIMOSTU SUBATOMIC
ABCIMRSTY CAMBISTRY
ABCINORTU INCUBATOR
ABCINOSTY OBSTINACY
ABCIOPRRT PORTACRIB
ABCJKOOST JACKBOOTS
ABCKLLLOP BLACKPOLL

ABCKLOPST BLACK SPOT
ABCKLOSTU BLACKOUTS
ABCKNORSU OSNABRUCK
ABCKOOPRS SCRAPBOOK
ABCLMNNOT MONT
   BLANC
ABCLOORRU COLOUR
   BAR
ABCLOOSTU COBALTOUS
ABCLPRSUW PUB-CRAWLS
ABCMOSSUU SUBMUCOSA
ABCNOORSU CARBONOUS
ABCNORSTU OBSCURANT
ABCORRSSS CROSSBARS
ABDDDEINS DISBANDED
ABDDEEHIJ JIB-HEADED
ABDDEEHST DEATHBEDS
ABDDEELNY NEED BADLY
ABDDEENOR BROADENED
ABDDEEPRS BEDSPREAD
ABDDEERTY TEDDY BEAR
ABDDEESST BEDSTEADS
ABDDEHNSU HUSBANDED
ABDDEIILV DIVIDABLE
ABDDEILNT BLIND DATE
ABDDEIORS BROADSIDE,
   SIDEBOARD
ABDDEIPRU UPBRAIDED
ABDDEIRRS DISBARRED
ABDDEISSU DISABUSED
ABDDELOSW SADDLEBOW
ABDDGORUY
   BODYGUARD
ABDDHINTW BANDWIDTH
ABDDHNORU
   HARDBOUND
ABDDILNNS SAND-BLIND
ABDDILRSY LADYBIRDS
ABDDJMNOO ODD-JOB
   MAN
ABDEEEFRS FREE-BASED
ABDEEEGLL DELEGABLE
ABDEEELLY EYEBALLED
ABDEEELMN EMENDABLE
ABDEEEMRS BESMEARED
ABDEEFHLR HALF-BREED
ABDEEFIIT BEATIFIED
ABDEEFILN DEFINABLE
ABDEEFORR FREEBOARD
ABDEEGGLR BEDRAGGLE
ABDEEGHIN BEHEADING
ABDEEGINR GABERDINE
ABDEEGJLU JUDGEABLE

ABDEEGLLO LODGEABLE
ABDEEGMOR
   EMBARGOED
ABDEEGRRY GREYBEARD
ABDEEGRSY SAGE DERBY
ABDEEHINR HEBRIDEAN
ABDEEHLRT BLATHERED
ABDEEHNOS BONEHEADS
ABDEEIILR DIABLERIE
ABDEEILLW WIELDABLE
ABDEEILLY YIELDABLE
ABDEEILMS DEMISABLE
ABDEEILNR BREADLINE
ABDEEILNS DISENABLE
ABDEEILRS DESIRABLE
ABDEEILRT LIBERATED
ABDEEILRV DERIVABLE
ABDEEILSV DEVISABLE
ABDEEINNR BERNADINE
ABDEEINSS BEADINESS
ABDEEINSW WIESBADEN
ABDEEINTT BIDENTATE
ABDEEINTU BUTADIENE
ABDEEITTU BEATITUDE
ABDEEKLNT BLANKETED
ABDEELLTY BELATEDLY
ABDEELMSS ASSEMBLED
ABDEELMTT EMBATTLED
ABDEELNOR BANDEROLE,
   BANDOLEER
ABDEELNOT DENOTABLE
ABDEELNPR PREBENDAL
ABDEELNPS SPENDABLE
ABDEELNRU ENDURABLE
ABDEELNST STEEL BAND
ABDEELOPS DEPOSABLE
ABDEELRSS BEARDLESS
ABDEELSSU SUBLEASED
ABDEEMNOU BEAU
   MONDE
ABDEEMNRT DEBARMENT
ABDEENOTY BAYONETED
ABDEENQTU BANQUETED
ABDEENRRT BARTENDER
ABDEENTTU DEBUTANTE
ABDEEOPST SPEEDBOAT
ABDEERRST REDBREAST
ABDEFFGLU DUFFEL BAG
ABDEFIISX BASIFIXED
ABDEFINOS BONA FIDES
ABDEFINRR FIREBRAND
ABDEFLLOO FLOODABLE
ABDEFORTY AFTERBODY

ABDEGGINR BADGERING
ABDEGGMRU
   MAGDEBURG
ABDEGIINU BIGUANIDE
ABDEGIIRR BRIGADIER
ABDEGIKNR DEBARKING
ABDEGILOT OBLIGATED
ABDEGINRR DEBARRING
ABDEGNOTU ON A
   BUDGET
ABDEGNSTU BUNDESTAG
ABDEGRTUY BUDGETARY
ABDEHIINT INHABITED
ABDEHILNO HOBNAILED
ABDEHILOS ABOLISHED
ABDEHKLSU BULKHEADS
ABDEHLOOT BLOOD HEAT
ABDEHLOTW DEATHBLOW
ABDEHNRSU HUSBANDER
ABDEHNSTU SUNBATHED
ABDEHORRU HARBOURED
ABDEIILNU INAUDIBLE
ABDEIILNV DIVINABLE
ABDEIILOS DIABOLISE
ABDEIILOZ DIABOLIZE
ABDEIIRST DIATRIBES
ABDEIKLNR DRINKABLE
ABDEIKMRS DISEMBARK
ABDEIKNRW WINDBREAK
ABDEILLLO LABELLOID
ABDEILLLR DRILLABLE
ABDEILMNS MANDIBLES
ABDEILMOR BROMELIAD
ABDEILOPR PARBOILED
ABDEILORV OLIVE DRAB
ABDEILRRY EARLY BIRD
ABDEILRSY DESIRABLY
ABDEINOST BOTANISED
ABDEINOTZ BOTANIZED
ABDEINSSW BAWDINESS
ABDEIPRRU UPBRAIDER
ABDEIRRTW WATER BIRD
ABDEJORTT OBJET D'ART
ABDEKLSSW SKEWBALDS
ABDEKNORW
   BREAKDOWN
ABDEKORRW
   WORDBREAK
ABDEKORSY KEYBOARDS
ABDELLMOU MOULDABLE
ABDELLNOO BALLOONED
ABDELMOTY MOLYBDATE
ABDELNNSS BLANDNESS

ABDELNOST ENDOBLAST
ABDELNOSU SOUNDABLE
ABDELNOUW
　WOUNDABLE
ABDELOOPS PASO DOBLE
ABDELORTX EXTRABOLD
ABDELORUV BOULEVARD
ABDEMRSTU DRUMBEATS
ABDENORSS BROADNESS
ABDENORST ADSORBENT
ABDENOSSX SANDBOXES
ABDENOSTU EASTBOUND
ABDENRRST ST BERNARD
ABDENRSTU BUNDESRAT
ABDENRSTY BYSTANDER
ABDEOORRT BREADROOT
ABDEOORRV OVERBOARD
ABDEOORWZ
　ZEBRAWOOD
ABDEORRSW
　WARDROBES
ABDEORTUV OUTBRAVED
ABDESSTTU TASTE BUDS
ABDFHORSU SHUFBOARD
ABDFIIKOR FABRIKOID
ABDFIIRRR FRIARBIRD
ABDFLLORU FULL BOARD
ABDFOOORT FOOTBOARD
ABDFORRSU SURFBOARD
ABDGGGOSY DOGGY
　BAGS
ABDGGIINR ABRIDGING
ABDGIILNS DISABLING
ABDGIILNY ABIDINGLY
ABDGILNNR BRANDLING
ABDGILORS GAOLBIRDS
ABDGINNOU ABOUNDING
ABDGINORS SIGNBOARD
ABDGINOXY BOXING DAY
ABDGLOPRU PLUGBOARD
ABDHIINNR HINDBRAIN
ABDHILLNS HANDBILLS
ABDHIMRTY DITHYRAMB
ABDHIOPRS SHIPBOARD
ABDHIRSTY BIRTHDAYS
ABDHKNOOS HANDBOOKS
ABDHLORSW
　BLOWHARDS
ABDHNOORU
　BOARHOUND
ABDHNRSUY HUSBANDRY
ABDHOOSWX
　SHADOW-BOX

ABDIIILLN LIBIDINAL
ABDIIJLRS JAILBIRDS
ABDIILLRS BILLIARDS
ABDIILMOS DIABOLISM
ABDIILNUY INAUDIBLY
ABDIILOST DIABOLIST,
　IDIOBLAST
ABDIIMRST TRIBADISM
ABDILLMOR MILLBOARD
ABDILORSW WILD BOARS
ABDILRSZZ BLIZZARDS
ABDIMNNOT BADMINTON
ABDIMPQSU DAMP SQUIB
ABDINOWWY BAY
　WINDOW
ABDINRSTW WRISTBAND
ABDIRSTUY ABSURDITY
ABDJMOPRU BROAD JUMP
ABDKLNORW WORLD
　BANK
ABDKNOOST BOOKSTAND
ABDLMOOOR
　BROADLOOM
ABDMMNOSU
　OMBUDSMAN
ABDMOOORR
　BOARDROOM
ABDNNOSTY ON
　STAND-BY
ABEEEEFRT BEEFEATER
ABEEEERSZ SEA BREEZE
ABEEEFKST BEEFSTEAK
ABEEEFLRR REFERABLE
ABEEEFLRZ FREEZABLE
ABEEEGLNR GENERABLE
ABEEEGLNS BENGALESE
ABEEEGLRU BELEAGUER
ABEEEGLTV VEGETABLE
ABEEEGNNR GREEN BEAN
ABEEEGRSV BEVERAGES
ABEEEHLMT MEHETABEL
ABEEEHLSW WHEELBASE
ABEEEKNRV BREAKEVEN
ABEEELMPR PERMEABLE
ABEEELNRT ENTERABLE
ABEEELNRV VENERABLE
ABEEELNRW RENEWABLE
ABEEELRRV REVERABLE
ABEEELRST STEERABLE
ABEEELRSV SEVERABLE
ABEEENSST ABSENTEES
ABEEERRTV VERTEBRAE
ABEEERTUX EXUBERATE

ABEEFFILN INEFFABLE
ABEEFGLOR FORGEABLE
ABEEFIKRR FIREBREAK
ABEEFILNR INFERABLE,
　REFINABLE
ABEEFILRS BAS-RELIEF
ABEEFILST FLEABITES
ABEEFLRSU REFUSABLE
ABEEFLRTU REFUTABLE
ABEEFLSSU SELF-ABUSE
ABEEFORRR FORBEARER
ABEEFORRS FOREBEARS
ABEEGGLOR GORGEABLE
ABEEGHILW WEIGHABLE
ABEEGHNOR HABERGEON
ABEEGHRTU HAGBUTEER
ABEEGILLR GABRIELLE
ABEEGILLV GIVE A BELL
ABEEGILNN BENGALINE
ABEEGINRU AUBERGINE
ABEEGINRV BEAVERING,
　BEREAVING
ABEEGKORR BROKERAGE
ABEEGLLRU REGULABLE
ABEEGLNPR PREGNABLE
ABEEGLOPR BARGE
　POLE, PORBEAGLE
ABEEGLSSU GUESSABLE
ABEEGMORS EMBARGOES
ABEEGNORZ BRONZE AGE
ABEEGORSX GEARBOXES
ABEEGRSTU SUGAR BEET
ABEEHILMT MEHITABEL
ABEEHILRT HERITABLE
ABEEHILST ELISABETH
ABEEHILTZ ELIZABETH
ABEEHIMSV MISBEHAVE
ABEEHINRT HIBERNATE
ABEEHIRRS HEBRAISER
ABEEHIRRZ HEBRAIZER
ABEEHKORS BRAKE SHOE
ABEEHLLRS HAREBELLS
ABEEHLMPS BLASPHEME
ABEEHLNOW
　WHALEBONE
ABEEHNSTU BHUTANESE
ABEEHRSTT HARTBEEST
ABEEIINRT INEBRIATE
ABEEIKLRZ ZEBRA-LIKE
ABEEIKNST SNAKEBITE
ABEEILLMR MIRABELLE
ABEEILLRV RELIVABLE
ABEEILMPT EMPTIABLE

ABEEILMRS MISERABLE
ABEEILMST ESTIMABLE
ABEEILMTT TIMETABLE
ABEEILNPS PLEBEIANS
ABEEILNRT ALBERTINE
ABEEILNSS BASELINES
ABEEILNTW TABLE WINE
ABEEILQTU EQUITABLE
ABEEILRRW REWIRABLE
ABEEILRST BEASTLIER,
    BLEARIEST
ABEEILRSV REVISABLE,
    VERBALISE
ABEEILRTT ALBERTITE,
    BEAR TITLE
ABEEILRTV AVERTIBLE,
    VERITABLE
ABEEILRVV REVIVABLE
ABEEILRVZ VERBALIZE
ABEEIMSSS EMBASSIES
ABEEIPSTT A BIT STEEP
ABEEIRRSS BRASSERIE,
    BRASSIERE
ABEEIRRST BISERRATE
ABEEIRSTT BATTERIES
ABEEJLLNY JELLY BEAN
ABEEJLNOY ENJOYABLE
ABEEJLNSU BLUE JEANS
ABEEJMORS JAMBOREES
ABEEKLNNO ANKLEBONE
ABEEKLNSS BLEAKNESS
ABEEKLORV REVOKABLE
ABEELLLPS SPELLABLE
ABEELLMRS SMALL BEER
ABEELLMSS BLAMELESS
ABEELLMTU UMBELLATE
ABEELLORS ROSABELLE
ABEELLORT TOLERABLE
ABEELLORW LOWERABLE
ABEELLOVV EVOLVABLE
ABEELMMOR
    MEMORABLE
ABEELMMRS EMBALMERS
ABEELMNRU NUMERABLE
ABEELMORV REMOVABLE
ABEELMOSV MOVEABLES
ABEELMPRS PREAMBLES
ABEELMPTT TEMPTABLE
ABEELMRSS ASSEMBLER
ABEELMRSU RESUMABLE
ABEELNNTU UNTENABLE
ABEELOPSX EXPOSABLE
ABEELPRSU SUPERABLE

ABEELPRTU REPUTABLE
ABEELRRTV VERTEBRAL
ABEELRSVW SWERVABLE
ABEELRTTU UTTERABLE
ABEELSSSU SUBLEASES
ABEELSSTT SEAT BELTS
ABEEMMNRS
    MEMBRANES
ABEEMMNTY EMBAYMENT
ABEEMNSST BASEMENTS
ABEEMORRT BAROMETER
ABEEMRRSU EMBRASURE
ABEEMRSTU A BUM STEER
ABEENQTTU BANQUETTE
ABEENRSSV BRAVENESS
ABEENRTUX EXUBERANT
ABEEOPRRT PERBORATE,
    REPROBATE
ABEEOPRSW POWER
    BASE
ABEEOSTUU BEAUTEOUS
ABEEPRSTT BESPATTER
ABEERRSTT BARRETTES
ABEERRSTY BETRAYERS
ABEFFILNY INEFFABLY
ABEFFLOSU BUFFALOES
ABEFGILLN BEFALLING
ABEFGILNR FRANGIBLE
ABEFGLOOR GABLE ROOF
ABEFIILNU UNIFIABLE
ABEFIILOT BIFOLIATE
ABEFIIMRT FIMBRIATE
ABEFILLRS FIREBALLS
ABEFILOST LIFEBOATS
ABEFILTUU BEAUTIFUL
ABEFIMORS FRAMBOISE
ABEFINORR FOREBRAIN
ABEFLLLMU FLABELLUM
ABEFLLLUY BALEFULLY
ABEFLLNUY BANEFULLY
ABEFLNOSW WOLFSBANE
ABEFOORST BEAR'S-FOOT
ABEFRTTTU BUTTERFAT
ABEGGGINR BEGGARING
ABEGGINSS BAGGINESS
ABEGGLLRU BUGGER ALL
ABEGGNOPS SPONGE BAG
ABEGHHILT HIGH TABLE
ABEGHILST SIGHTABLE
ABEGHINRR HARBINGER
ABEGHINRT BREATHING
ABEGHMRRU
    HAMBURGER

ABEGHRSSU SAGEBRUSH
ABEGIILLT LITIGABLE
ABEGIILMT MITIGABLE
ABEGIILNS ABSEILING
ABEGIILNT IGNITABLE
ABEGIILNW BEWAILING
ABEGIILRR IRRIGABLE
ABEGIINOR ABORIGINE
ABEGIKMNR EMBARKING
ABEGILLLN LABELLING
ABEGILMMN EMBALMING
ABEGIMNNO BEMOANING
ABEGIMRRS AMBERGRIS
ABEGINNNT BENIGNANT
ABEGINNOW WINNEBAGO
ABEGINNRT BANTERING
ABEGINNRZ BRAZENING
ABEGINNST ABSENTING
ABEGINNTT BATTENING
ABEGINRRT BARTERING
ABEGINRTT BATTERING
ABEGINRTY BETRAYING
ABEGJORTU OBJURGATE
ABEGJSTUU SUBJUGATE
ABEGKRSTU GRUBSTAKE
ABEGLNORU LOUNGE BAR
ABEGLRSSU BLUEGRASS
ABEGMNOOR
    BOOMERANG
ABEGMNOSY
    MONEYBAGS
ABEGORSTU SUBROGATE
ABEHHHIPZ HEPHZIBAH
ABEHIINNR HIBERNIAN
ABEHIITTW WHITEBAIT
ABEHIKLNT THINKABLE
ABEHILMOP AMPHIBOLE
ABEHILORS ABOLISHER
ABEHILRST HERBALIST
ABEHILRSY BEARISHLY
ABEHILRTY BREATHILY,
    HERITABLY
ABEHILSST ESTABLISH
ABEHIMMSS MEMSAHIBS
ABEHIMNOS BOHEMIANS
ABEHIMRRU HERBARIUM
ABEHIOPRU EUPHORBIA
ABEHIORUV BEHAVIOUR
ABEHIRRTT BIRTHRATE
ABEHLMPSY BLASPHEMY
ABEHLNNSU SHUNNABLE
ABEHLOPRY HYPERBOLA
ABEHLORTT BETROTHAL

ABEHNORRT ABHORRENT
ABEHNRRTU HEARTBURN
ABEHNRSSS BRASHNESS
ABEHNRSTU SUNBATHER
ABEHOOSTU BOATHOUSE,
　HOUSEBOAT
ABEHORRRU HARBOURER
ABEHQRSUU HARQUEBUS
ABEIIILST ABILITIES
ABEIILLLR ILLIBERAL
ABEIILLMT LIMITABLE
ABEIILNRZ BRAZILEIN
ABEIILRRS LIBRARIES
ABEIILRRT IRRITABLE
ABEIILRTV VIBRATILE
ABEIILSST STABILISE
ABEIILSTV VISITABLE
ABEIILSTZ STABILIZE
ABEIINNPT BIPINNATE
ABEIINNRT INEBRIANT
ABEIINRST BRAINIEST
ABEIIPRTT BIPARTITE
ABEIIRTVV VIBRATIVE
ABEIJLNRU INJURABLE
ABEIKLNTT KNITTABLE
ABEIKNORW WAKE-ROBIN
ABEIKNRSS BEARSKINS
ABEILLLNT LIBELLANT
ABEILLLRY LIBERALLY
ABEILLLSU LULLABIES,
　SULLIABLE
ABEILLPSU PLAUSIBLE
ABEILLRTX BELLATRIX
ABEILLSTY BESTIALLY
ABEILMMOV IMMOVABLE
ABEILMMSW SWIMMABLE
ABEILMMTU IMMUTABLE
ABEILMNSS BALMINESS
ABEILMOPS IMPOSABLE
ABEILMORT BALTIMORE
ABEILMOSX MAILBOXES
ABEILMPTU IMPUTABLE
ABEILMRSV VERBALISM
ABEILMRSY MISERABLY
ABEILMSTU SUBLIMATE
ABEILNPRT PRINTABLE
ABEILNPST PINTABLES
ABEILNPSU SUBALPINE
ABEILNRSS BRAINLESS
ABEILNRSU INSURABLE
ABEILORRT LIBERATOR
ABEILORTT TRILOBATE
ABEILORTU LABOURITE

ABEILQTUY EQUITABLY
ABEILRRST STIRRABLE
ABEILRRYZ BIZARRELY
ABEILRSTU BRUTALISE
ABEILRSTV VERBALIST
ABEILRTUZ BRUTALIZE
ABEILRTVY VERITABLY
ABEILRVVY REVIVABLY
ABEILSSUX BISEXUALS
ABEILSTTW TWISTABLE
ABEILSUVY ABUSIVELY
ABEIMNORS AMBROSINE
ABEIMNORT BROMINATE
ABEIMNRST TRIBESMAN
ABEIMNRSU SUBMARINE
ABEIMNSTU SEMI-BANTU
ABEINNSTT ABSTINENT
ABEINNTYZ BYZANTINE
ABEINORST BARITONES
ABEINOSTT OBSTINATE
ABEINRSST BANISTERS
ABEINRSTW BRAWNIEST
ABEINRTTU TRIBUNATE,
　TURBINATE
ABEINSSST BASSINETS
ABEINSSTT BATTINESS
ABEIOPRTV PROBATIVE
ABEIPRRSS SPARERIBS
ABEIRRRST BARRISTER
ABEIRRSST ARBITRESS
ABEIRRSSU BURSARIES
ABEIRSSST BRASSIEST
ABEIRSSTY SYBARITES
ABEIRTTTU ATTRIBUTE
ABEJLNOYY ENJOYABLY
ABEJMOORS JEROBOAMS
ABEKKMOOR
　BOOKMAKER
ABEKLNNSS BLANKNESS
ABEKLOOPT BOOKPLATE
ABEKLORTW WORKTABLE
ABEKLORVY REVOKABLY
ABEKNNOST BANK NOTES
ABEKOORSY YEARBOOKS
ABEKORSTU OUTBREAKS
ABELLLSSY SYLLABLES
ABELLMRSU UMBRELLAS
ABELLORTY TOLERABLY
ABELLORUY ROYAL BLUE
ABELLOSWY BOYLE'S
　LAW
ABELMMNRU
　LUMBERMAN

ABELMMORY
　MEMORABLY
ABELMNOTU MOUNTABLE
ABELMNPRU PENUMBRAL
ABELMNRUY NUMERABLY
ABELMNSTU SUBMENTAL
ABELMORVY REMOVABLY
ABELNNORV NONVERBAL
ABELNOOTW AT ONE
　BLOW
ABELNOSTT ENTOBLAST
ABELNOSYZ LAZYBONES
ABELNRSTU SUBALTERN
ABELNRTTU TURNTABLE
ABELOOPPS OPPOSABLE
ABELOPPST STOPPABLE
ABELOPSTT SPOTTABLE
ABELORRSU LABOURERS
ABELORTTX RATTLEBOX
ABELOSTTY STYLOBATE
ABELPRTUY REPUTABLY
ABELRSTTU REBUTTALS,
　TRUSTABLE
ABEMMNOOS
　MOONBEAMS
ABEMNPRSU PENUMBRAS
ABEMNSTTU ABUTMENTS
ABEMOOPRR
　BROOMRAPE
ABEMOPRTY AMBROTYPE
ABEMORRTU ARBORETUM
ABENNSTTU SUBTENANT
ABENOPSSU SUBPOENAS
ABENORSTV OBSERVANT
ABEOOPRTW POWERBOAT
ABEOOPSSX SOAPBOXES
ABEOORRSU ARBOREOUS
ABEOPPRSY PAPERBOYS
ABEOPRRSY SOAPBERRY
ABEORSSTU SABOTEURS
ABEPRRRSY RASPBERRY
ABEPRSSSY PASSERSBY
ABERSSTTU SUBSTRATE
ABERTTTUW WATER BUTT
ABFGLLLOS GOLF BALLS
ABFHLLSUY BASHFULLY
ABFIILOTT BIT OF TAIL
ABFIIORSU BIFARIOUS
ABFILLSYY SYLLABIFY
ABFILMSUY SUBFAMILY
ABFIRSTTU FRUIT BATS
ABFLLOOST FOOTBALLS
ABGGIKNPY PIGGYBANK

ABGGILMNO GAMBOLING
ABGGNOOST TOBOGGANS
ABGHHILLS HIGHBALLS
ABGHIINNS BANISHING
ABGHILMNS SHAMBLING
ABGHIMNSU AMBUSHING
ABGHINORR ABHORRING
ABGHIOPRY BIOGRAPHY
ABGHMORSU
   BROUGHAMS
ABGIILLNU BILINGUAL
ABGIIMSST BIGAMISTS
ABGIIMTUY AMBIGUITY
ABGIINNOT OBTAINING
ABGIINOTV OBVIATING
ABGIINPTZ BAPTIZING
ABGIINRTV VIBRATING
ABGILLMOS GLOBALISM
ABGILLNOT BALLOTING
ABGILLOST GLOBALIST
ABGILLOTY BILLY GOAT
ABGILNNOZ BLAZONING
ABGILNORU LABOURING
ABGILNOSV ABSOLVING
ABGILNOSX SIGNAL BOX
ABGILOORT OBLIGATOR
ABGIMOSUU AMBIGUOUS
ABGINNRRU UNBARRING
ABGINOPRT PROBATING
ABGINPSSY BYPASSING
ABGLMNOOS
   BOOMSLANG
ABGLNOOST LONGBOATS
ABGLNOSUW
   BUNGALOWS
ABHHIIRUV BAHUVRIHI
ABHHILOTT BATHOLITH
ABHHIRRSU HAIRBRUSH
ABHIKLLSW HAWKSBILL
ABHIKMRRT BIRTHMARK
ABHILMNTU THUMBNAIL
ABHILMSTU BISMUTHAL
ABHILNOOT HALOBIONT
ABHILNRSU NAILBRUSH
ABHILNRTY LABYRINTH
ABHIOOOPZ ZOOPHOBIA
ABHKOOOST BOAT HOOKS
ABHLLMOST MOTHBALLS
ABHLLMSTU ALL THUMBS
ABHLPRSUY SUBPHYLAR
ABHMOORST BATHROOMS
ABIIILLTY LIABILITY
ABIIILNTY INABILITY

ABIIILTVY VIABILITY
ABIIJMMUY MBUJIMAYI
ABIIKLSSS BASILISKS
ABIILLMRS MILLIBARS
ABIILLNRT BRILLIANT
ABIILMNOS BINOMIALS
ABIILMRST TRIBALISM
ABIILNOOT ABOLITION
ABIILNORT LIBRATION
ABIILNORY NOBILIARY
ABIILNOST LIBATIONS
ABIILNSST SIBILANTS
ABIILRRTY IRRITABLY
ABIILRSSV VIBRISSAL
ABIILRSTT TRIBALIST
ABIILSTTY STABILITY
ABIILSTUY SUABILITY,
   USABILITY
ABIIMNOST AMBITIONS
ABIIMORSS ISOBARISM
ABIIMOSTU AMBITIOUS
ABIINOOTV OBVIATION
ABIINORTV VIBRATION
ABIKLMNSS LAMBSKINS
ABIKLOSTY BIALYSTOK
ABILLMSSY SYLLABISM
ABILLNOPT BALLPOINT
ABILLOPRX PILLAR BOX
ABILLORRZ RAZORBILL
ABILLPSUY PLAUSIBLY
ABILMMOVY IMMOVABLY
ABILMMTUY IMMUTABLY
ABILMOORS RIBOSOMAL
ABILMORSU LABOURISM
ABILMSTTU SUBMITTAL
ABILNOOST OBLATIONS
ABILNOSTU ABLUTIONS
ABILNRSTU TRIBUNALS
ABILNRTVY VIBRANTLY
ABILOORSU LABORIOUS
ABILORRTY LIBRATORY
ABILORSTU LABOURIST
ABILRSSUY SALISBURY
ABILRTTUY BRUTALITY
ABIMMNRUU MANUBRIUM
ABIMNTUYZ BYZANTIUM
ABIMORSSU AMBROSIUS
ABINNOTVV BON VIVANT
ABINOOPRT PROBATION
ABINOORST ABORTIONS
ABINOSSTT BOTANISTS
ABINRRTUY TRIBUNARY
ABIOORRRT BRIARROOT

ABIORRSTV VIBRATORS
ABIRRTTUY TRIBUTARY
ABKKMOORS
   BOOKMARKS
ABKLLNORS BANKROLLS
ABKLLOOST BOOKSTALL
ABKNPRSTU BANKRUPTS
ABKOOPSSS PASSBOOKS
ABLLMOORS BALLROOMS
ABLLMOPSW BLOWLAMPS
ABLLNOSSW SNOWBALLS
ABLMNORSU SUBNORMAL
ABLMNRSUU LABURNUMS
ABLNOTUYY BUOYANTLY
ABLNRSUUY SUBLUNARY
ABLOOPPSY OPPOSABLY
ABLORTTUU TUBULATOR
ABLOSSTTU SUBTOTALS
ABMNORRST BARNSTORM
ABMOOOORTT MOTORBOAT
ABNNSTUUY BUNYA NUTS
ABNORSTUU RUN-ABOUTS
ABNORTTUU
   ABOUT-TURN, TURNABOUT
ABOOPRSTT BOOTSTRAP
ACCCCEHIT CACHECTIC
ACCCDEEEN ACCEDENCE
ACCCDEEIN ACCIDENCE
ACCCDIIMU MUCIC ACID
ACCCEEENS ACESCENCE
ACCCEGLOY COCCYGEAL
ACCCEHIOT CACOETHIC
ACCCEIIRT CICATRICE
ACCCEILLO CALCICOLE
ACCCHKOOR
   COCKROACH
ACCCHOPRT CATCH CROP
ACCCIILLY ALICYCLIC
ACCCIILMT CLIMACTIC
ACCCIIOPR CAPRICCIO
ACCCNOPUY OCCUPANCY
ACCDDEEEN DECADENCE
ACCDDEILS DISCALCED
ACCDDIIST DIDACTICS
ACCDDIORS DISACCORD
ACCDEEHIK CHICKADEE
ACCDEEIST DESICCATE
ACCDEELLN CANCELLED
ACCDEELNO CONCEALED
ACCDEELOS COALESCED
ACCDEFIIL CALCIFIED
ACCDEFILS FASCICLED
ACCDEFILY DECALCIFY

ACCDEHIKR DECKCHAIR
ACCDEHKOT COCKED HAT
ACCDEHRST SCRATCHED
ACCDEIILN ICELANDIC
ACCDEIILT DIALECTIC
ACCDEINOT ANECDOTIC
ACCDEINST ACCIDENTS,
DESICCANT
ACCDEIORW COWARDICE
ACCDEKOSS CASSOCKED
ACCDELMOR COLD
CREAM
ACCDELSSU CUL-DE-SACS
ACCDEMNOO
CACODEMON
ACCDEMOPT COMPACTED
ACCDEMORY
DEMOCRACY
ACCDENOTT CONTACTED
ACCDENOTU ACCOUNTED
ACCDENPSU DUNCE'S
CAP
ACCDEORRS SCORECARD
ACCDEORSW SACRED
COW
ACCDFILLY FLACCIDLY
ACCDGINOR ACCORDING
ACCDHHRUY
ARCHDUCHY
ACCDHINOR CHANCROID
ACCDHNPRU CARDPUNCH
ACCDHORTW
CATCHWORD
ACCDHPSTU DUTCH CAPS
ACCDIIINT DIACTINIC
ACCDIIIRT DIACRITIC
ACCDIIOPT APODICTIC
ACCDILLOY CYCLOIDAL
ACCDILSTY DACTYLICS
ACCDINOOR ACCORDION
ACCDKNORW
CRACKDOWN
ACCDNOORT CONCORDAT
ACCDORRTU COURT
CARD
ACCEEGLMY MEGACYCLE
ACCEEHILR CHELICERA
ACCEEHIST CATECHISE
ACCEEHITY HAECCEITY
ACCEEHITZ CATECHIZE
ACCEEHKMT CHECKMATE
ACCEEHLOT COCHLEATE
ACCEEHNPR PERCHANCE

ACCEEHOST CACOETHES
ACCEEIMRS ICE CREAMS
ACCEEIPRS PECCARIES
ACCEEIQSU ACQUIESCE
ACCEEIRTV ACCRETIVE
ACCEEISTX EXSICCATE
ACCEEKLNS NECKLACES
ACCEELLNR CANCELLER
ACCEELNPR PRECANCEL
ACCEELPST SPECTACLE
ACCEENNST CANESCENT
ACCEEORSU CERACEOUS
ACCEFGILU CALCIFUGE
ACCEFHLOT FACECLOTH
ACCEFIIRS SACRIFICE
ACCEFILSU FASCICULE
ACCEFNORS FRANCESCO
ACCEGILNN CANCELING
ACCEGINNT ACCENTING
ACCEGINOR ACROGENIC
ACCEGINPT ACCEPTING
ACCEGINSS ACCESSING
ACCEGIOTT GEOTACTIC
ACCEGKMOS
GAMECOCKS
ACCEHHIRT THEARCHIC
ACCEHIKNR RAIN CHECK
ACCEHIKPS CHICKPEAS
ACCEHILLO ECHOLALIC
ACCEHILMS CHEMICALS
ACCEHILNO COCHINEAL
ACCEHILNT TECHNICAL
ACCEHILOT CHICALOTE
ACCEHIMNS MECHANICS,
MISCHANCE
ACCEHIMST CATECHISM,
SCHEMATIC
ACCEHINRY CHICANERY
ACCEHINST CHANCIEST
ACCEHIRTT ARCHITECT
ACCEHISTT CATCHIEST,
CATECHIST
ACCEHKPSY PAYCHECKS
ACCEHLOOT CHOCOLATE
ACCEHMNTT CATCHMENT
ACCEHORTU CARTOUCHE
ACCEHORTY THEOCRACY
ACCEHRRST SCRATCHER
ACCEHRSST SCRATCHES
ACCEIILMN CALCIMINE
ACCEIIMNT CINEMATIC
ACCEIINOS COCAINISE
ACCEIINOZ COCAINIZE

ACCEIINRT CIRCINATE
ACCEIIPRT ACCIPITER
ACCEIIRST CICATRISE
ACCEIIRTZ CICATRIZE
ACCEIISTV SICCATIVE
ACCEIKLOT COCKATIEL
ACCEIKRSW WISECRACK
ACCEILLSV CLAVICLES
ACCEILMPT ECLAMPTIC
ACCEILNST CANTICLES
ACCEILNTU INCULCATE
ACCEILOPR PRECOCIAL
ACCEILPST SCEPTICAL
ACCEILRTU CIRCULATE
ACCEIMOSU MICACEOUS
ACCEINORT ACCRETION
ACCEINOSS ACCESSION
ACCEINSTU ENCAUSTIC,
SUCCINATE
ACCEIORTT CORTICATE
ACCEIPRST PRACTICES
ACCEISSTT ECSTATICS
ACCEKKORS ROCK CAKES
ACCEKMNRS CRACKSMEN
ACCEKNORR CORNCRAKE
ACCELLLOS CLOSE CALL
ACCELLOOT COLLOCATE
ACCELLTUU CUCULLATE
ACCELNOSV CONCLAVES
ACCELNOVY COVALENCY
ACCEMNRTU ACCRUMENT
ACCEMOPRT COMPACTER
ACCEMORTY MACROCYTE
ACCEMPRSU CREAMCUPS
ACCENNOST CONSTANCE
ACCENNOTY COTENANCY
ACCENOORS COENOSARC
ACCENORSU CANCEROUS
ACCENRSUY RECUSANCY
ACCEORRSW
SCARECROW
ACCEORSSY ACCESSORY
ACCEORSTU CORUSCATE
ACCFFHHIN CHAFFINCH
ACCFIILOR CALORIFIC
ACCFIISST FASCISTIC
ACCFINNOU CONFUCIAN
ACCFINORS FRANCISCO
ACCFKOORT FROCK COAT
ACCGHHNNU
CHANGCHUN
ACCGHHNOW
CHANGCHOW

ACCGHINRY GYNARCHIC
ACCGIKLNR CRACKLING
ACCGINOST ACCOSTING
ACCHHMNRU

   CHURCHMAN

ACCHIILRV CHIVALRIC
ACCHILLOO ALCOHOLIC
ACCHILLOT LACCOLITH
ACCHILORT HOLARCTIC
ACCHILOST CATHOLICS
ACCHILPSY PSYCHICAL
ACCHIMOPR CAMPHORIC
ACCHIMORT CHROMATIC
ACCHIMOST STOMACHIC
ACCHIRTTY TRACHYTIC
ACCHKLOST SACKCLOTH
ACCHKOOOP

   COCK-A-HOOP

ACCHKOORW

   COACHWORK

ACCHLOORT

   COLCOTHAR, OCHLOCRAT

ACCHLOOSW

   SLOWCOACH

ACCHLOOTY CHOCOLATY
ACCHNOOPY CACOPHONY
ACCHNORSU CHANCROUS
ACCHOPRSS CASH CROPS
ACCIIILNN CLINICIAN
ACCIILLVY CIVICALLY
ACCIILNOR CONCILIAR
ACCIILOPT OCCIPITAL
ACCIILRTU CIRCUITAL
ACCIILTVY ACCLIVITY
ACCIIMNOS COCAINISM
ACCIINRTY INTRICACY
ACCIIORST ISOCRATIC
ACCIIOSTT ISOTACTIC
ACCIISSTU CASUISTIC
ACCIKKNNS NICKNACKS
ACCIKLOST COCKTAILS
ACCILLMOY COMICALLY
ACCILLNOY CONICALLY
ACCILLNYY CYNICALLY
ACCILLRUY CRUCIALLY
ACCILNORV CLAVICORN
ACCILNOTU NOCTILUCA
ACCILRRSU CIRCULARS
ACCILRRUU CURRICULA
ACCILRTUU CUTICULAR
ACCIMNORY ACRONYMIC
ACCIMNOSS MOCCASINS
ACCIMNOSY SCIOMANCY

ACCIMORSY COSMIC RAY
ACCIMORTY TIMOCRACY
ACCIMPSSU CAPSICUMS
ACCINNOTT IN CONTACT
ACCINOOSS OCCASIONS
ACCINOPRR CAPRICORN
ACCINORST NARCOTICS
ACCINOSTY OSCITANCY
ACCINOTVY CONCAVITY
ACCINSTTY SYNTACTIC
ACCIOPRTT CATOPTRIC
ACCIORSST ACROSTICS
ACCIOSSTU ACOUSTICS
ACCKKRSSU RUCKSACKS
ACCKOOOST COCKATOOS
ACCKOPRST CRACKPOTS
ACCKORSST STOCKCARS
ACCLLOSUU CALCULOUS
ACCLMOPTY COMPACTLY
ACCMMOORS

   MACROCOSM

ACCMNOORY

   MONOCRACY,
   NOMOCRACY

ACCMNOTUY

   CONTUMACY

ACCMORSTY MACROCYST
ACCNNOOTU

   NO-ACCOUNT

ACCNNOSTY CONSTANCY
ACCNOORTT CONTACTOR
ACCNOPSTU OCCUPANTS
ACCNORSTT CONTRACTS
ACCOPRSTY CYSTOCARP
ACCORRSTY CARRYCOTS
ACDDDEEIT DEDICATED
ACDDDEIRS DISCARDED
ACDDDEKSU DEAD DUCKS
ACDDEEEFT DEFECATED
ACDDEEEIT DEDICATEE
ACDDEEERS DECREASED
ACDDEEILM DECLAIMED
ACDDEEIMT DECIMATED,

   MEDICATED

ACDDEEORT DECORATED
ACDDEERTT DETRACTED
ACDDEFIII ACIDIFIED
ACDDEGIRS DISGRACED
ACDDEGNOO

   DODECAGON

ACDDEHIRR HARD CIDER
ACDDEHKNS DECKHANDS

ACDDEHNRU DUDE

   RANCH

ACDDEIINT INDICATED
ACDDEIITV ADDICTIVE
ACDDEIJNU JAUNDICED
ACDDEILPS DISPLACED
ACDDEINRS RIDDANCES
ACDDEINRX CARD INDEX
ACDDEINST DISTANCED
ACDDEIORT DEDICATOR
ACDDEIPRY RICE PADDY
ACDDEIRRS DISCARDER
ACDDEKLOP PADLOCKED
ACDDEKLOS DEADLOCKS
ACDDEKOST STOCKADED
ACDDELNOO CANOODLED
ACDDEMMNO

   COMMANDED

ACDDHHNSU DACHSHUND
ACDDIILOS DISCOIDAL
ACDDIINOT ADDICTION
ACDDINOTU ADDUCTION
ACDDKORSY DOCKYARDS
ACDDLNORW

   COLD-DRAWN

ACDEEEHIP HEADPIECE
ACDEEEHNP CHEAPENED
ACDEEEHNR ADHERENCE
ACDEEELRY CLEAR-EYED
ACDEEEPRT DEPRECATE
ACDEEERRT RECREATED
ACDEEERSS DECREASES
ACDEEERST DESECRATE
ACDEEERTU RE-EDUCATE
ACDEEERTX EXECRATED
ACDEEFIRR FREDERICA
ACDEEFKRT AFTERDECK
ACDEEFNOP OPEN-FACED
ACDEEFNTU FECUNDATE
ACDEEFORT DEFECATOR
ACDEEFRRT REFRACTED
ACDEEGHNX EXCHANGED
ACDEEGHRR RECHARGED
ACDEEGLNO CONGEALED
ACDEEGLOU DECALOGUE
ACDEEGNSV SCAVENGED
ACDEEGOPU DECOUPAGE
ACDEEHIMP IMPEACHED
ACDEEHINN ENCHAINED
ACDEEHIRS CASHIERED
ACDEEHKNY HACKNEYED
ACDEEHLLN CHANDELLE
ACDEEHLNN CHANNELED

ACDEEHLPT CHAPLETED
ACDEEHNNT ENCHANTED
ACDEEHNST CHASTENED
ACDEEHPSY SPEECH DAY
ACDEEHRRT CHARTERED
ACDEEHRTT CHATTERED
ACDEEIJTV ADJECTIVE
ACDEEIKST ICE-SKATED
ACDEEILMR DECLAIMER,
RECLAIMED
ACDEEILMX EXCLAIMED
ACDEEILNN CELANDINE,
DECENNIAL
ACDEEILNR ICELANDER
ACDEEILNT DECLINATE
ACDEEILNU EUCLIDEAN
ACDEEILTU ELUCIDATE
ACDEEILTY ACETYLIDE
ACDEEIMNO MACEDOINE
ACDEEIMNP IMPEDANCE
ACDEEINRS INCREASED
ACDEEINSU AUDIENCES
ACDEEIOPR ADIPOCERE
ACDEEIPRT PREDICATE
ACDEEITUV EDUCATIVE
ACDEEKKNR KNACKERED
ACDEEKLNS SLACKENED
ACDEEKPPR PREPACKED
ACDEEKPST TAPE DECKS
ACDEELLOT DECOLLATE,
OCELLATED
ACDEELLPR PARCELLED
ACDEELLTW WELL-ACTED
ACDEELNRS CALENDERS
ACDEELORT RELOCATED
ACDEELPTU PECULATED
ACDEELQRU LACQUERED
ACDEELRTT CLATTERED
ACDEELRTU ULCERATED
ACDEELSTY DECASTYLE
ACDEELTTU CLAUDETTE
ACDEEMPRS SCAMPERED
ACDEENNRT ENTRANCED
ACDEENNRU ENDURANCE
ACDEENORS COARSENED
ACDEENOSS DEACONESS
ACDEENOST ANECDOTES
ACDEENRST DECANTERS,
DESCANTER
ACDEENRTU UNCREATED
ACDEEOPRR CROP-EARED
ACDEEORTV OVERACTED
ACDEEPRRS SCARPERED

ACDEEPRRT RED CARPET
ACDEEPSTT SPECTATED
ACDEERRTT RETRACTED
ACDEERSTT SCATTERED
ACDEERSTU REDUCTASE
ACDEERTTX EXTRACTED
ACDEESSTU DECUSSATE
ACDEFFILR RADCLIFFE
ACDEFFILT AFFLICTED
ACDEFFIST DISAFFECT
ACDEFFLLU FULL-FACED
ACDEFFMOR COFFERDAM
ACDEFHINR ARCHFIEND
ACDEFIIIL EDIFICIAL
ACDEFIIIR ACIDIFIER
ACDEFIILR CLARIFIED
ACDEFIILT FETICIDAL
ACDEFIIRS SCARIFIED
ACDEFILLO COALFIELD
ACDEFINRT INFARCTED
ACDEFKLNO FOLK DANCE
ACDEFLMOR COLD FRAME
ACDEFLNOT CONFLATED
ACDEFMNOO
MOON-FACED
ACDEFRRTU FRACTURED
ACDEGGIMO DEMAGOGIC
ACDEGGIOP PEDAGOGIC
ACDEGHINR CHAGRINED
ACDEGHINT DETACHING
ACDEGHIRS DISCHARGE
ACDEGHNRU
UNCHARGED
ACDEGIILR REGICIDAL
ACDEGILNO GENOCIDAL
ACDEGILNR DECLARING
ACDEGILNS DESCALING
ACDEGILOO LOGAOEDIC
ACDEGIMNP DECAMPING
ACDEGINNS ASCENDING
ACDEGINNT DECANTING
ACDEGINOY GYNAECOID
ACDEGINTU EDUCATING
ACDEGIOTT COGITATED
ACDEGIRRS DISGRACER
ACDEGIRRT CARTRIDGE
ACDEGLNOU LANGUEDOC
ACDEGNNOU
UNDECAGON
ACDEHHIKT THICKHEAD
ACDEHHORX HEXACHORD
ACDEHIITT DIATHETIC
ACDEHINNR HINDRANCE

ACDEHINSV CAVENDISH
ACDEHIOPX HEXAPODIC
ACDEHIPRS SEPHARDIC
ACDEHIPRT DIRT CHEAP
ACDEHIRSV CRASH-DIVE
ACDEHISST CHASTISED
ACDEHKMPU CHEMPADUK
ACDEHKOST HEADSTOCK
ACDEHKPST SKETCHPAD
ACDEHKRSU ARCHDUKES
ACDEHKSSS CASH DESKS
ACDEHLNOR CHLORDANE
ACDEHLNOT DECATHLON
ACDEHLNRS CHANDLERS
ACDEHLNRY CHANDLERY
ACDEHLRSU SCHEDULAR
ACDEHMNTU UNMATCHED
ACDEHMOST STOMACHED
ACDEHMPRY PACHYDERM
ACDEHNRTU UNCHARTED
ACDEHNRUY HUE AND
CRY
ACDEHNSTU STAUNCHED,
UNSCATHED
ACDEHNTUW
UNWATCHED
ACDEHOOPT CHAETOPOD
ACDEHORRS HARD CORES
ACDEHORRV HARDCOVER
ACDEHORSS CROSSHEAD
ACDEHOSTT COT DEATHS
ACDEHPRSU PURCHASED
ACDEIIINT DIETICIAN
ACDEIILMN ADMINICLE,
MEDICINAL
ACDEIILNT IDENTICAL
ACDEIILNX INDEXICAL
ACDEIILRV LARVICIDE,
VERIDICAL
ACDEIILTW TWICE-LAID
ACDEIIMMY IMMEDIACY
ACDEIIMNR AMERINDIC
ACDEIIMRT DIAMETRIC,
MATRICIDE
ACDEIINOT DIANOETIC
ACDEIINTV VINDICATE
ACDEIIOPR APERIODIC
ACDEIIPRR PARRICIDE
ACDEIIPRT PATRICIDE
ACDEIKMNN NICKNAMED
ACDEIKRST SIDETRACK
ACDEILLMS MISCALLED

ACDEILLMY DECIMALLY,
  MEDICALLY
ACDEILLOS LOCALISED
ACDEILLOZ LOCALIZED
ACDEILMPS MISPLACED
ACDEILNVY DIVALENCY
ACDEILOPT PETALODIC
ACDEILOST DISLOCATE
ACDEILPRS DISPLACER
ACDEILPRU PEDICULAR
ACDEILPTU DUPLICATE
ACDEILRTU CURTAILED
ACDEILTUV VICTUALED
ACDEIMNNO DOMINANCE
ACDEIMNNT MENDICANT
ACDEIMNOP COMPENDIA
ACDEIMNOS COMEDIANS
ACDEIMNPS PANDEMICS
ACDEIMNRU MANICURED
ACDEIMNSU MUSCADINE
ACDEIMNTY MENDACITY
ACDEIMORT DECIMATOR
ACDEINNOR ORDINANCE
ACDEINNOS CANONISED
ACDEINNOT CONTAINED
ACDEINNOZ CANONIZED
ACDEINNST INSTANCED
ACDEINORR CORIANDER
ACDEINORS DINOCERAS
ACDEINORT REDACTION
ACDEINOTU AUCTIONED,
  CAUTIONED, EDUCATION
ACDEINOTV ADVECTION
ACDEINPRT PREDICANT
ACDEINRTU CURTAINED
ACDEINSST DISTANCES
ACDEINSTY ASYNDETIC,
  SYNDICATE
ACDEIPRST PRACTISED
ACDEIPSTU CUSPIDATE
ACDEIQTTU ACQUITTED
ACDEIRTTX DIRECT TAX
ACDEISSTT ACID TESTS
ACDEJKKSY SKYJACKED
ACDEKLMSU LAME DUCKS
ACDEKOPTU PACKED-OUT
ACDEKOSST STOCKADES
ACDELLOPS COLLAPSED,
  SCALLOPED
ACDELLORR CORRALLED
ACDELMOPR PLACODERM
ACDELMORU
  CLAMOURED

ACDELMORY COMRADELY
ACDELNNOO COLONNADE
ACDELNNOR CLARENDON
ACDELNNTU CANDLENUT
ACDELNNUU UNDULANCE
ACDELNOOW
  LANCEWOOD
ACDELNORS COLANDERS
ACDELNRUY UNDERCLAY
ACDELOPTU COPULATED,
  CUPOLATED
ACDELOSTW COLD SWEAT
ACDEMMMNO
  COMMENDAM
ACDEMMNOR
  COMMANDER
ACDEMNOPR
  COMPANDER
ACDEMOORR
  ACRODROME
ACDEMOORT
  MOTORCADE
ACDEMORST DEMOCRATS
ACDENNNOU
  ANNOUNCED
ACDENNRST TRANSCEND
ACDENOOTT COTTONADE
ACDENORSY SECONDARY
ACDENORTU UNDERCOAT
ACDENRTTU TRUNCATED
ACDEOORRT DECORATOR
ACDEOORTT DOCTORATE
ACDEOPSTU SPACED OUT
ACDEOPTTU COUP D'ÉTAT
ACDEORRST CO-STARRED
ACDEORRTT DETRACTOR
ACDEORSTU CERATODUS,
  EDUCATORS
ACDEORSUU RUDACEOUS
ACDEORTUY EDUCATORY
ACDEORTUZ COTE
  D'AZUR
ACDEQSTUU AQUEDUCTS
ACDERRSSU CRUSADERS
ACDERRSTU TRADUCERS
ACDERSSTT TEST CARDS
ACDESSTUY CASE STUDY
ACDFFHNSU HANDCUFFS
ACDFFLOSS SCAFFOLDS
ACDFGOOST ACTS OF
  GOD
ACDFHILSS SCALDFISH
ACDFIIILL FILICIDAL

ACDFIIRUY FIDUCIARY
ACDFINNOT CONFIDANT
ACDFNTTUY CANDYTUFT
ACDFOORTW
  WOODCRAFT
ACDGHIIPR DIGRAPHIC
ACDGHIMOY DICHOGAMY
ACDGHIPSY DYSPHAGIC
ACDGHOSTW
  WATCHDOGS
ACDGIILNO GADOLINIC
ACDGIINNR DINING CAR
ACDGIINTT DICTATING
ACDGIIRST DIGASTRIC
ACDGIMOST DOGMATICS
ACDGINRSU CRUSADING
ACDGINRTU TRADUCING
ACDGLLOOR DOG COLLAR
ACDHIILMO HOMICIDAL
ACDHIILOP ACIDOPHIL
ACDHIILST DISTICHAL
ACDHIIMSU DICHASIUM
ACDHIINNO INDOCHINA
ACDHIINOP DIAPHONIC
ACDHIKPRT PITCH-DARK
ACDHILNOO CONHOIDAL
ACDHILPRS PILCHARDS
ACDHILRUY HYDRAULIC
ACDHILSTT LAST-DITCH
ACDHIMORT CHROMATID
ACDHIOPRS RHAPSODIC
ACDHIORYZ HYDRAZOIC
ACDHIPSSY DYSPHASIC
ACDHLOOSY DAY SCHOOL
ACDHMNOOR
  CHONDROMA
ACDHMOOTW
  MATCHWOOD
ACDHOOPPS SCAPHOPOD
ACDHORTWW
  WATCHWORD
ACDIIILMT MITICIDAL
ACDIIIMOT IDIOMATIC
ACDIIJLRU JURIDICAL
ACDIIJRUY JUDICIARY
ACDIILMNO DOMINICAL
ACDIILMSX DISCLIMAX
ACDIILOST DIASTOLIC
ACDIILPTY PLACIDITY
ACDIILSTU DUALISTIC
ACDIIMNNO DOMINICAN
ACDIIMNTY DYNAMITIC
ACDIIMRTY MYDRIATIC

ACDIINORT INDICATOR
ACDIINOTT DICTATION
ACDIINRTY RANCIDITY
ACDIIOPRT DIATROPIC
ACDIJORTU JUDICATOR
ACDIKKLRY KIRKCALDY
ACDIKNQSU QUICKSAND
ACDIKRRTT DIRT TRACK
ACDIKRSTY YARDSTICK
ACDILLLOO COLLOIDAL
ACDILLOOR CORALLOID
ACDILLORY CORDIALLY
ACDILMOPS PSALMODIC
ACDILMOPY DIPLOMACY
ACDILMOTU COMATULID
ACDILNOOR COORDINAL
ACDILNORT DOCTRINAL
ACDILOPRS DROPSICAL
ACDILORSY CORYDALIS
ACDILOSTU CUSTODIAL
ACDILOSUU ACIDULOUS
ACDILRTTY TRIDACTYL
ACDIMOPSS SPASMODIC
ACDIMORRU MACRUROID
ACDIMORTY MORDACITY
ACDINOOPT ACTINOPOD
ACDINOSTU CUSTODIAN
ACDIORSTT DICTATORS
ACDJOORTU COADJUTOR
ACDKLORTU TRUCKLOAD
ACDKMNNOO
   MONADNOCK
ACDKORSTY STOCKYARD
ACDLMNOOY
   CONDYLOMA
ACDLMNOPW
   CLAMPDOWN
ACDLNOPSS COLD SNAPS
ACDLNORSU CAULDRONS
ACDLNSTYY SYNDACTYL
ACDLORSUW WAR
   CLOUDS
ACDMMNOOS
   COMMANDOS
ACDMOOSUV
   MUSCOVADO
ACDMPRRTU TRUMP
   CARD
ACDNOOORRT CORRODANT
ACDOPRSST POSTCARDS
ACDORRTUY COURTYARD
ACDRSSTTU DUSTCARTS
ACEEEFIRS CEASE-FIRE

ACEEEFLNR FREELANCE
ACEEEGHPR REPECHAGE
ACEEEGNNV VENGEANCE
ACEEEILMP PIECEMEAL
ACEEEIMPT PEACETIME
ACEEEIPPP PEACE PIPE
ACEEEIPRS EARPIECES
ACEEEKRRT RACKETEER
ACEEELNRV RELEVANCE
ACEEELNTU ENUCLEATE
ACEEELNTY ACETYLENE
ACEEELSSS CEASELESS
ACEEEMNNR REMANENCE
ACEEEMNPR PERMEANCE
ACEEENPPT APPETENCE
ACEEENRSV SEVERANCE
ACEEERSTT ETCETERAS
ACEEFFHRU RECHAUFFE
ACEEFFITV AFFECTIVE
ACEEFFLNU AFFLUENCE
ACEEFFLTU EFFECTUAL
ACEEFFNRY FANCY-FREE
ACEEFHLNP HALFPENCE
ACEEFHMRR CHAMFERER
ACEEFHORR FOREREACH
ACEEFIIRT ACETIFIER
ACEEFILPR FIREPLACE
ACEEFINNR REFINANCE
ACEEFINRT INTERFACE
ACEEFIRSS FRICASSEE
ACEEFKOPR POKER FACE
ACEEFLOTV VOLTE-FACE
ACEEFMORT FORCEMEAT
ACEEFPSTY TYPEFACES
ACEEFRRSU RESURFACE
ACEEGHIRU GAUCHERIE
ACEEGHLLN CHALLENGE
ACEEGHNRX EXCHANGER
ACEEGHNSX EXCHANGES
ACEEGILRS SACRILEGE
ACEEGILRV VICEGERAL,
   VICEREGAL
ACEEGIMSY MAGIC EYES
ACEEGINNR CAREENING
ACEEGINRR CAREERING
ACEEGINRV GRIEVANCE
ACEEGIRTT CIGARETTE
ACEEGKRWY
   GREYWACKE
ACEEGLLOU COLLEAGUE
ACEEGLNRT RECTANGLE
ACEEGLRSS GRACELESS

ACEEGMNOR
   GEOMANCER
ACEEGNORU ENCOURAGE
ACEEGNRSV SCAVENGER
ACEEGNRSY SERGEANCY
ACEEGOOPR COOPERAGE
ACEEGRTTU CURETTAGE
ACEEHHORT EACH OTHER
ACEEHHTUX HEXATEUCH
ACEEHIIPR HAIRPIECE
ACEEHILMS ALCHEMISE
ACEEHILMZ ALCHEMIZE
ACEEHILPT PETECHIAL
ACEEHILRT HERETICAL
ACEEHILRV CHEVALIER
ACEEHIMNS MECHANISE
ACEEHIMNZ MECHANIZE
ACEEHIMPR IMPEACHER
ACEEHINNV ENHANCIVE
ACEEHINPT PHENACITE
ACEEHINRT CATHERINE
ACEEHISTT AESTHETIC
ACEEHLMNO CHAMELEON
ACEEHLMOO HAEMOCOEL
ACEEHLMPV CHAMPLEVE
ACEEHLNRU HERCULEAN
ACEEHLNRW WALCHEREN
ACEEHLNSS SENESCHAL
ACEEHLNTU NEUCHATEL
ACEEHLOSS SHOELACES
ACEEHLRTW CARTWHEEL
ACEEHMMRT
   MACHMETER
ACEEHMNRY ARCHENEMY
ACEEHMOTY HAEMOCYTE
ACEEHMRSU CHARMEUSE
ACEEHNNRT ENCHANTER
ACEEHNPSS CHEAPNESS
ACEEHNPTY PACHYTENE
ACEEHNRST CHASTENER
ACEEHNRTT ENTRECHAT
ACEEHNSTU CHANTEUSE
ACEEHORRS RACEHORSE
ACEEHORRV OVERREACH
ACEEHOSTU THEACEOUS
ACEEHPRRS PREACHERS
ACEEHPRTY ARCHETYPE
ACEEHRRTT CHATTERER
ACEEHRRTY TREACHERY
ACEEHRSTT CATHETERS
ACEEHSSTT TEA CHESTS
ACEEIILPT TAILPIECE
ACEEIKLSV SICK LEAVE

ACEEIKRST CREAKIEST,
ICE-SKATER
ACEEIKSST ICE SKATES
ACEEILLST CELESTIAL
ACEEILMNS MESCALINE
ACEEILMNT CLEMENTIA
ACEEILMRT CARMELITE
ACEEILMRX EXCLAIMER
ACEEILNPR PERCALINE
ACEEILNRS LARCENIES
ACEEILNRT INTERLACE,
RECLINATE
ACEEILNST CELESTINA
ACEEILNSV VALENCIES
ACEEILPRS PERICLASE
ACEEILPRT REPLICATE
ACEEILPTX EXPLICATE
ACEEIMMNN IMMANENCE
ACEEIMMNT MINCEMEAT
ACEEIMMRT METAMERIC
ACEEIMNPR MEPACRINE
ACEEIMNSX EXCISEMAN
ACEEIMPRT IMPRECATE
ACEEIMPST SPACE-TIME
ACEEIMRRS CAREERISM
ACEEIMRSS CASSIMERE
ACEEIMRST CREAMIEST,
MISCREATE
ACEEINNRS CANNERIES
ACEEINNRT NECTARINE
ACEEINNST INSECTEAN,
TENANCIES
ACEEINNTU ENUNCIATE
ACEEINPRU EPICUREAN
ACEEINPTT PECTINATE
ACEEINRRS INCREASER
ACEEINRSS INCREASES
ACEEIORTX EXCORIATE
ACEEIOSST TEA COSIES
ACEEIOTVV EVOCATIVE
ACEEIPPRR RICE PAPER
ACEEIPRTT CREPITATE
ACEEIRRST CAREERIST
ACEEIRSTT CATTERIES
ACEEIRSTU CAUTERISE
ACEEIRSTW WATER ICES
ACEEIRSVV VICE VERSA
ACEEIRTTX EXTRICATE
ACEEIRTUZ CAUTERIZE
ACEEISSST ECSTASIES
ACEEKLMRS MACKERELS
ACEELLLSU CELLULASE
ACEELLORT ELECTORAL

ACEELMNPT PLACEMENT
ACEELMOPS SOMEPLACE
ACEELMORT LATECOMER
ACEELNNRU CANNELURE
ACEELNNSS CLEANNESS
ACEELNORT TOLERANCE
ACEELNPTU PETULANCE
ACEELNRSS CLEANSERS,
CLEARNESS
ACEELNRTU CALENTURE,
CRENULATE
ACEELNRVY RELEVANCY
ACEELNSTT TENTACLES
ACEELOOSU OLEACEOUS
ACEELOPRT PERCOLATE
ACEELOPSS ESCALOPES
ACEELORRT CORRELATE
ACEELORSS CASSEROLE
ACEELORSW LOWER
CASE
ACEELORTT LECTORATE
ACEELORTU URCEOLATE
ACEELPSSS SPACELESS
ACEELPSTU SPECULATE
ACEELPTUX EXCULPATE
ACEELQRRU LACQUERER
ACEELRTUY ELECTUARY
ACEELSSTT TELECASTS
ACEEMMOOT
AMMOCOETE
ACEEMNNTT ENACTMENT
ACEEMNRRY MERCENARY
ACEEMORTT OCTAMETER
ACEEMPRRS SCAMPERER
ACEEMRRTU MERCURATE
ACEENNOPR CAN OPENER
ACEENNORS RESONANCE
ACEENNOST CANTONESE
ACEENNRST ENTRANCES,
RENASCENT
ACEENNRTY CENTENARY
ACEENPRRT CARPENTER
ACEENPTTX EXPECTANT
ACEENRRST RECREANTS
ACEENRSSY NECESSARY
ACEENRTTU UTTERANCE
ACEENSSTU ACUTENESS
ACEENSSTX EXACTNESS
ACEENTTUX EXECUTANT
ACEEOOPRT COOPERATE
ACEEOPRRT PROCREATE
ACEEORRRT RE-CREATOR
ACEEORRTT RECTORATE

ACEEORRTV OVERREACT
ACEEOSSTU SETACEOUS
ACEEPPRSU UPPER CASE
ACEEPRRTU RECAPTURE
ACEERRSTT SCATTERER,
STREETCAR
ACEERRSTU CREATURES
ACEERRSTY SECRETARY
ACEERSSST ACTRESSES
ACEERSSSV CREVASSES
ACEERSSTT TESSERACT
ACEERSSTU SECATEURS
ACEESSSTT CASSETTES,
TEST CASES
ACEFFGINT AFFECTING
ACEFFHRUU CHAUFFEUR
ACEFFIIOT OFFICIATE
ACEFFILST FACE-LIFTS
ACEFFINOT AFFECTION
ACEFFIORT FORFICATE
ACEFFOSTU SUFFOCATE
ACEFGINPR PREFACING
ACEFGLNOS LONG FACES
ACEFHIINT CHIEFTAIN
ACEFHIKLT THICKLEAF
ACEFHIKSS FISHCAKES
ACEFHINRS FRANCHISE
ACEFHIPRY PREACHIFY
ACEFHMNNR FRENCHMAN
ACEFHOSUV VOUCHSAFE
ACEFIILMS FACSIMILE
ACEFIILRR CLARIFIER
ACEFIINNR FINANCIER
ACEFIIPRS PACIFIERS
ACEFIIRRS SCARIFIER
ACEFIIRRT ARTIFICER
ACEFIIRST ARTIFICES
ACEFIIRTV FRICATIVE
ACEFIITTV FACTITIVE
ACEFIJKKN JACK KNIFE
ACEFIKRTU FRUITCAKE
ACEFILNNO FALCONINE
ACEFILORT FORTALICE
ACEFILSTU FACULTIES
ACEFIMPRS CAMPFIRES
ACEFINNSS FANCINESS
ACEFINORT FORNICATE
ACEFINSTU INFUSCATE
ACEFIORRS AIRFORCES
ACEFIORST FACTORIES,
FACTORISE
ACEFIORTZ FACTORIZE
ACEFIOSTU FACETIOUS

ACEFIRSTT CRAFTIEST
ACEFKORST TASK FORCE
ACEFLLLSU FULL-SCALE
ACEFLLRUY CAREFULLY
ACEFLNORS FALCONERS
ACEFLNORV CONFERVAL
ACEFLTTUU FLUCTUATE
ACEFMNRST CRAFTSMEN
ACEFOORST FOOTRACES
ACEFORRRT REFRACTOR
ACEFORRRU CARREFOUR
ACEFORSST FORECASTS
ACEFRRSTU FRACTURES
ACEGGIRRS SCRAGGIER
ACEGGIRST CRAGGIEST
ACEGHHPTU HUGH CAPET
ACEGHIINV ACHIEVING
ACEGHILRT LETHARGIC
ACEGHINNN ENHANCING
ACEGHINPR PREACHING
ACEGHINRS SEARCHING
ACEGHLSTY LYCHGATES
ACEGHMNOS
  CHEONGSAM
ACEGHMORT
  HECTOGRAM
ACEGHOPRY CREOPHAGY
ACEGHOPTY PHAGOCYTE
ACEGHRRSU SURCHARGE
ACEGIILLS GALLICISE
ACEGIILLZ GALLICIZE
ACEGIILNS ANGLICISE
ACEGIILNT GENITALIC
ACEGIILNV VIGILANCE
ACEGIILNZ ANGLICIZE
ACEGIIMNT ENIGMATIC
ACEGIINNT ANTIGENIC
ACEGIIRRT GERIATRIC
ACEGILLLO COLLEGIAL
ACEGILLNO COLLEGIAN
ACEGILLNR RECALLING
ACEGILLOT COLLIGATE
ACEGILNNO CONGENIAL
ACEGILNNS CLEANSING
ACEGILNPR PARCELING,
  REPLACING
ACEGILNRS CLEARINGS
ACEGILNRU NEURALGIC
ACEGILNRW CLEARWING
ACEGILNTU CINGULATE
ACEGILOOR AEROLOGIC
ACEGILRTU CURTILAGE,
  GRATICULE

ACEGIMMNR ENGRAMMIC
ACEGIMMRS SCRIMMAGE
ACEGIMMST TAGMEMICS
ACEGIMNNP ENCAMPING
ACEGIMNOT GEOMANTIC
ACEGIMNRS SCREAMING
ACEGIMNRT CENTIGRAM,
  CREMATING
ACEGIMNST MAGNETICS
ACEGIMNTU MUTAGENIC
ACEGIMTUZ ZEUGMATIC
ACEGINNOR IGNORANCE
ACEGINNRT CANTERING,
  RECANTING
ACEGINNSU UNCEASING
ACEGINPPR RECAPPING
ACEGINPRT CARPETING
ACEGINPRY PANEGYRIC
ACEGINRRT RETRACING
ACEGINRSS CARESSING
ACEGINRST RECASTING
ACEGIOPRR PAREGORIC
ACEGIOSTT GEOSTATIC
ACEGIPRST PRICE TAGS
ACEGIRSTT STRATEGIC
ACEGJNOTU CONJUGATE
ACEGLMNRY CLERGYMAN
ACEGLNNPY PLANGENCY
ACEGMMNOO
  COMMONAGE
ACEGMMRSU
  SCRUMMAGE
ACEGNNOTT COTANGENT
ACEGNNPRY PREGNANCY
ACEGORRTU CORRUGATE
ACEGORSTT COTTAGERS
ACEHHILPS CHELASHIP
ACEHHIRRY HIERARCHY
ACEHHISTX HEXASTICH
ACEHHLWYZ
  WYCH-HAZEL
ACEHHMNTT HATCHMENT
ACEHHNRTY ETHNARCHY
ACEHHOOTT TOOTHACHE
ACEHHPRTY HEPTARCHY
ACEHHRSTT THATCHERS
ACEHHSSTY HESYCHAST
ACEHIINOP PHOENICIA
ACEHIINPP EPIPHANIC
ACEHIIPPT EPITAPHIC
ACEHIIRST CHARITIES
ACEHIISTT ATHEISTIC
ACEHIJKRS HIJACKERS

ACEHIKLST CHALKIEST
ACEHIKORT ARTICHOKE
ACEHIKRST HEARTSICK
ACEHILLLY HELICALLY
ACEHILLTY ETHICALLY
ACEHILMMO CHAMOMILE
ACEHILMST ALCHEMIST
ACEHILNNO CHELONIAN
ACEHILNOO HOLOCAINE
ACEHILNOR ENCHORIAL
ACEHILNOT CHELATION
ACEHILNTU UNETHICAL
ACEHILNTY THYLACINE
ACEHILPRS SPHERICAL
ACEHILRUV VEHICULAR
ACEHILSTT ATHLETICS
ACEHIMMNS MECHANISM
ACEHIMNRY MACHINERY
ACEHIMNST MECHANIST
ACEHIMRTU RHEUMATIC
ACEHINNRY HERCYNIAN
ACEHINORT ANCHORITE,
  ANTECHOIR
ACEHINORX CHRONAXIE
ACEHINOSV ANCHOVIES
ACEHINPST CATHEPSIN
ACEHINRRU HURRICANE,
  RAUNCHIER
ACEHINRSS CHARINESS
ACEHINRSU SEA URCHIN
ACEHINRTT IN THE CART
ACEHINSST CAITHNESS
ACEHINSTY HESITANCY
ACEHINTTU AUTHENTIC
ACEHIPPSS SPACESHIP
ACEHIPRST PIE CHARTS
ACEHIPSST PASTICHES
ACEHIPSTT PATCHIEST
ACEHIPSTW WHITECAPS
ACEHIRRST STARCHIER
ACEHIRSTT THEATRICS
ACEHIRSTU EUCHARIST
ACEHISTTT CHATTIEST
ACEHKLNSU UNSHACKLE
ACEHKLSTY LATCHKEYS
ACEHKMPSU MUCKHEAPS
ACEHKNORT ON THE
  RACK
ACEHKOPRS PACKHORSE
ACEHKORST SHORTCAKE
ACEHLLLOR CHLORELLA
ACEHLLOOS COALHOLES
ACEHLMOST MOSCHATEL

ACEHLMSST MATCHLESS
ACEHLNPTY PHLYCTENA
ACEHLOOSU COALHOUSE
ACEHLOPSW SHOWPLACE
ACEHLORRT TROCHLEAR
ACEHLORSU HOUSECARL
ACEHLORTT CHARLOTTE
ACEHLOSTT TEA CLOTHS
ACEHLTTYY TACHYLYTE
ACEHMNOPY
    CYMOPHANE
ACEHMNORW
    CHARWOMEN
ACEHMNPRT PARCHMENT
ACEHMNRST MERCHANTS
ACEHMNSTY YACHTSMEN
ACEHMNTTU HUMECTANT
ACEHMOSTT CHEMOSTAT
ACEHMOSTU MOUSTACHE
ACEHMPRTY CHAMPERTY
ACEHMSSTU MUSTACHES
ACEHMSTTT TEST MATCH
ACEHNNPST PENCHANTS
ACEHNNRTT TRENCHANT
ACEHNOOTT ON THE
    COAT
ACEHNOPRS CHAPERONS
ACEHNOPST CENOTAPHS
ACEHNORSS ANCHORESS
ACEHNOSTT STONECHAT
ACEHNPRTY PENTARCHY
ACEHNRSTU STAUNCHER
ACEHNRSUZ SCHNAUZER
ACEHOOSTU HOUSECOAT
ACEHOPRRS SHARECROP
ACEHORRST CARTHORSE,
    ORCHESTRA
ACEHORSTY THEOCRASY
ACEHOSSSW SHOWCASES
ACEHPRRSU PURCHASER
ACEHPRSSU PURCHASES
ACEHPSTTY PETTY CASH
ACEHRRTTY TETRARCHY
ACEIIILST ITALICISE
ACEIIILTZ ITALICIZE
ACEIIKLST EKISTICAL
ACEIIKMNT KINEMATIC
ACEIILLOT CILIOLATE
ACEIILMPR EMPIRICAL
ACEIILMPT IMPLICATE
ACEIILNNT ANTICLINE
ACEIILNNV VICENNIAL
ACEIILNPR CIRALPINE

ACEIILNST INELASTIC,
    SCIENTIAL
ACEIILOSS SOCIALISE
ACEIILOST SOCIALITE
ACEIILOSZ SOCIALIZE
ACEIILPRT PEARLITIC
ACEIILRST ERISTICAL,
    REALISTIC
ACEIILRTT LATERITIC
ACEIILSST SILICATES
ACEIILSTV CALVITIES
ACEIIMMNR CIMMERIAN
ACEIIMMRU AMERICIUM
ACEIIMNRT ANTIMERIC
ACEIIMNSS MESSIANIC
ACEIIMRST ARMISTICE
ACEIINNTV VINCENTIA
ACEIINPRS PRECISIAN
ACEIINPST EPINASTIC
ACEIINRTT INTRICATE
ACEIINTTT NICTITATE
ACEIIPSTT EPISTATIC
ACEIIRSTV VARISCITE
ACEIISTTT STEATITIC
ACEIJKNPS JACKSNIPE
ACEIJMSST MAJESTICS
ACEIKLPST SKEPTICAL
ACEIKMNNS NICKNAMES
ACEIKMRSV MAVERICKS
ACEIKNRST CRANKIEST
ACEIKNSST TACKINESS
ACEIKNSSW WACKINESS
ACEIKOPRT AIRPOCKET
ACEIKOPSS SKIASCOPE
ACEIKPPRS PIPE RACKS
ACEIKPRRT PERITRACK
ACEIKRSTW WATER-SICK
ACEILLLXY LEXICALLY
ACEILLMOP POLEMICAL
ACEILLMOT COLLIMATE,
    LOCAL TIME
ACEILLMSY MESICALLY
ACEILLNOR COLLINEAR,
    CORALLINE
ACEILLORS LOCALISER
ACEILLORZ LOCALIZER
ACEILLOST OSCILLATE
ACEILLOTV COLLATIVE
ACEILLPSY SPECIALLY
ACEILLRSV CAVILLERS
ACEILLRXY XERICALLY
ACEILMMST CLAMMIEST
ACEILMNNU LUMINANCE

ACEILMNOP POLICEMAN
ACEILMNOS COALMINES
ACEILMNRU NUMERICAL
ACEILMNSU CALUMNIES,
    MASCULINE
ACEILMNTU CULMINATE
ACEILMOPT PTOLEMAIC
ACEILMOSS CAMISOLES,
    COSEISMAL
ACEILMOSV SEMIVOCAL
ACEILMRRU MERCURIAL
ACEILNNOR CORNELIAN
ACEILNNOT OCTENNIAL
ACEILNNPS PINNACLES
ACEILNOPR PORCELAIN
ACEILNORS CENSORIAL
ACEILNOST COASTLINE,
    SECTIONAL
ACEILNOSV VOLCANISE
ACEILNOTU INOCULATE
ACEILNOVZ VOLCANIZE
ACEILNPTU INCULPATE
ACEILNRST CLARINETS,
    LARCENIST
ACEILNRTU CENTURIAL
ACEILNRTY CERTAINLY
ACEILNSSS SCALINESS
ACEILNSUV VULCANISE
ACEILNTUV VULCANITE
ACEILNUVZ VULCANIZE
ACEILOPPS EPISCOPAL
ACEILOPST SCAPOLITE
ACEILOQUV EQUIVOCAL
ACEILORRT RECTORIAL
ACEILORST SECTORIAL
ACEILORSV VOCALISER
ACEILORTV VECTORIAL
ACEILORVZ VOCALIZER
ACEILOTVY COEVALITY
ACEILPPPR PAPER CLIP
ACEILPRST PARTICLES
ACEILPSSS SLIPCASES
ACEILPSTU EUPLASTIC,
    SPICULATE
ACEILPSTY SPECIALTY
ACEILRSUV VESICULAR
ACEILRTUV LUCRATIVE
ACEILSSST CLASSIEST
ACEILTTUV CULTIVATE
ACEIMMNNY IMMANENCY
ACEIMNOPS COMPANIES
ACEIMNORT CREMATION
ACEIMNOST ENCOMIAST

ACEIMNOTX INCOME TAX
ACEIMNPTU PNEUMATIC
ACEIMNRST MISCREANT
ACEIMNRSU MANICURES,
MUSCARINE
ACEIMNSST SEMANTICS
ACEIMNTYZ ENZYMATIC
ACEIMORVW MICROWAVE
ACEIMOSTU AUTOECISM
ACEIMPRST SPERMATIC
ACEIMPSST CAMPSITES
ACEIMRRSW WAR CRIMES
ACEINNNRU UNCANNIER
ACEINNNSS CANNINESS
ACEINNOOV NOVOCAINE
ACEINNORT CONTAINER,
CRENATION
ACEINNOSS ASCENSION
ACEINNRSU INSURANCE
ACEINNRTU RUNCINATE,
UNCERTAIN
ACEINNSST INCESSANT,
INSTANCES
ACEINNSSU NUISANCES
ACEINOOST ISOOCTANE
ACEINOOTV EVOCATION
ACEINOPRT RECAPTION
ACEINOPSU PINACEOUS
ACEINORRV CARNIVORE
ACEINORSS SCENARIOS
ACEINORST CREATIONS,
NARCOTISE, REACTIONS
ACEINORTT CARNOTITE
ACEINORTU COINTREAU
ACEINORTZ NARCOTIZE
ACEINOSST CANOEISTS,
CESSATION
ACEINOSTU TENACIOUS
ACEINOSUV VINACEOUS
ACEINOTTY TO A NICETY
ACEINPRTT CREPITANT
ACEINPRUY PECUNIARY
ACEINPSSU PUISSANCE
ACEINPSTT PITTANCES
ACEINQTTU QUITTANCE
ACEINRRSW SCRAWNIER
ACEINRSST CANISTERS,
SCENARIST
ACEINRSSZ CRAZINESS
ACEINRTTY CERTAINTY
ACEINRTUV INCURVATE
ACEINSSSU SAUCINESS

ACEINSSTT CATTINESS,
SCANTIEST, TACITNESS
ACEINSTTY INTESTACY
ACEIOPRRS ACROSPIRE
ACEIOPRTV PROACTIVE
ACEIOPTTT PETTICOAT
ACEIORRSV CORRASIVE
ACEIORSST OSTRACISE
ACEIORSTZ OSTRACIZE
ACEIORSUV VERACIOUS
ACEIOSTUV VITACEOUS
ACEIOSTVV VOCATIVES
ACEIOSVVV VIVA VOCES
ACEIPPRRS SCRAPPIER
ACEIPPRST CRAPPIEST
ACEIPSSST ESCAPISTS
ACEIPSSTU SPACESUIT
ACEIQRTTU ACQUITTER
ACEIQSTUY SEQUACITY
ACEIRSSSU CUIRASSES
ACEIRSTTU RUSTICATE
ACEIRSTUV CURATIVES
ACEISSSTU SUITCASES
ACEISSTTT SCATTIEST
ACEISTTTY CITY-STATE
ACEJKKRSY SKYJACKER
ACEJKLMST JACKSMELT
ACEJLMSUU MAJUSCULE
ACEJLNQUY JACQUELYN
ACEKKMRRU
MUCKRAKER
ACEKLLMMU MALLEMUCK
ACEKLNSSS SLACKNESS
ACEKLOPRW WORKPLACE
ACEKLRSST TRACKLESS
ACEKNNTTU NANTUCKET
ACEKNORSU CANKEROUS
ACEKOPRRT RETROPACK
ACEKPRSSU SAPSUCKER
ACEKRSTUW AWESTRUCK
ACELLLMOU COLUMELLA
ACELLLORS SOLAR CELL
ACELLMORU MOLECULAR
ACELLMRSU MARCELLUS
ACELLNORU NUCLEOLAR
ACELLNOTU LAUNCELOT
ACELLNRTY CENTRALLY
ACELLOPRS SCALLOPER
ACELLOPSS COLLAPSES
ACELLOQUY COEQUALLY
ACELLORSS SCLEROSAL
ACELLORSV COVERALLS
ACELLRSTU SCUTELLAR

ACELLSSSS CLASSLESS
ACELMMNOS
COMMENSAL
ACELMMNSU
MUSCLEMAN
ACELMNTUU TENACULUM
ACELMOPST ECTOPLASM
ACELMORSY CLAYMORES
ACELMOSUU ULMACEOUS
ACELMSSTU MUSCATELS
ACELNNOOR OLECRANON
ACELNOOSV VOLCANOES
ACELNOPRV PROVENCAL
ACELNORSU LARCENOUS
ACELNORTU NUCLEATOR,
RECOUNTAL
ACELNOSTU CONSULATE
ACELNOSTY CLAYSTONE
ACELNRTTU RELUCTANT
ACELOOPRR CORPORALE,
CORPOREAL
ACELOORTW
WATER-COOL
ACELOOSTT COELOSTAT
ACELOPRRU OPERCULAR
ACELOPRTU PECULATOR
ACELOPSTU SCOPULATE
ACELORSSU CAROUSELS
ACELOSSTU CASSOULET,
LOST CAUSE
ACELPPRRU CURLPAPER
ACELSSSTU CUTLASSES
ACEMMOTTU
COMMUTATE
ACEMNOOPS MOONSCAPE
ACEMNOPSS ENCOMPASS
ACEMNORTU MUCRONATE
ACEMOOPSU POMACEOUS
ACEMOORSU
MORACEOUS
ACEMOPSSS COMPASSES
ACEMORRSU SOUR
CREAM
ACEMORRTY CREMATORY
ACEMORSSY SYCAMORES
ACEMOSSUU MUSACEOUS
ACEMOSTVY VASECTOMY
ACEMPRSUY SUPREMACY
ACENNNORU
ANNOUNCER
ACENNOSTV COVENANTS
ACENNSSST SCANTNESS

ACENOPRRT COPARTNER,
   PROCREANT
ACENOPSTW TOWNSCAPE
ACENOPSTY SYNCOPATE
ACENOPTYY CYANOTYPE
ACENORRTU RACONTEUR
ACENORSST ANCESTORS
ACENORSTU COURTESAN
ACENORSUV CAVERNOUS
ACENORTUY COURTENAY
ACENORUVV VANCOUVER
ACENOSTUU CUTANEOUS
ACENPRRTY CARPENTRY
ACENPRSUU PURSUANCE
ACENPTTUU PUNCTUATE
ACENRSSSS CRASSNESS
ACENRSSTU RECUSANTS
ACENRSTUU CENTAURUS
ACEOOPRRT CORPORATE
ACEOOPRSS ASCOSPORE
ACEOORSSU ROSACEOUS
ACEOORSTV OVERCOATS
ACEOPPRST SPACEPORT
ACEOPRSTT SPECTATOR
ACEORRRTT RETRACTOR
ACEORRRVY CARRY-OVER
ACEORRSTU CRATEROUS,
   EUROCRATS
ACEORRTTX EXTRACTOR
ACEORSTTY ASTROCYTE
ACEORSTUU RUTACEOUS
ACEOSSTTU OUTCASTES
ACERRTUUV CURVATURE
ACFFIILOS OFFICIALS
ACFFIINOT OFFICIANT
ACFFIIORY OFFICIARY
ACFGHMORR
   FROGMARCH
ACFGIIMNO MAGNIFICO
ACFGIINNN FINANCING
ACFGIINPY PACIFYING
ACFGINORT FACTORING
ACFGINOTU OUTFACING
ACFGINRSU SURFACING
ACFGIOSUU FUGACIOUS
ACFGLNORY GYRFALCON
ACFHIILRT CHAIR LIFT
ACFHKORST ROCKSHAFT
ACFHLMRSU SCRUMHALF
ACFHLNORW HALF
   CROWN
ACFHLORTW FLOWCHART
ACFHORRST RH FACTORS

ACFIILNOT FICTIONAL
ACFIIMNOR ACINIFORM
ACFIIOPRV VAPORIFIC
ACFIIPSST PACIFISTS
ACFIJKRTU JACKFRUIT
ACFIKNRSS SCARFSKIN
ACFILMORU FORMULAIC,
   FUMAROLIC
ACFILNNOR FRANCOLIN
ACFILNOOT OLFACTION
ACFILNPPY FLIPPANCY
ACFILNPSU CUP FINALS
ACFILNRUU FUNICULAR
ACFIMORRY FORMICARY
ACFINORRT INFRACTOR
ACFINORST FRACTIONS
ACFINORTU FURCATION
ACFIOOPST IPSO FACTO
ACFIORSTU FRACTIOUS
ACFJKORST JACK FROST
ACFKLLORS ROCKFALLS
ACFKMRRTU TRUCK FARM
ACFKNORWY
   FANCYWORK
ACFKOORRS ROOF RACKS
ACFLLTTUY TACTFULLY
ACFLMNOOR CONFORMAL
ACFLNTTUU FLUCTUANT
ACFLOORTY OLFACTORY
ACGGGINRS SCRAGGING
ACGGIIMNR GRIMACING
ACGGIIOSS ISAGOGICS
ACGGILRSY SCRAGGILY
ACGHHHIIR HIGH CHAIR
ACGHHILSS HIGH-CLASS
ACGHHINOT HOATCHING
ACGHHINTT THATCHING
ACGHIIJKN HIJACKING
ACGHIIKNN CHINKIANG
ACGHIIMNN MACHINING
ACGHIIPRT GRAPHITIC
ACGHIKLNS SHACKLING
ACGHIKNSW WHACKINGS
ACGHIKNTW THWACKING
ACGHILNNU LAUNCHING
ACGHILORY OLIGARCHY
ACGHIMOOP OMOPHAGIC
ACGHINNOR ANCHORING
ACGHINNST SNATCHING,
   STANCHING
ACGHINPST NIGHTCAPS
ACGHINRST STARCHING
ACGHINSTY YACHTINGS

ACGHLMOOY
   LOGOMACHY
ACGHMOPRY
   CYMOGRAPH
ACGHORSTU ROUGHCAST
ACGIIIMST IMAGISTIC
ACGIIKNNP PANICKING
ACGIILLLO ILLOGICAL
ACGIILLMS GALLICISM
ACGIILLNV CAVILLING
ACGIILLOR CIGARILLO
ACGIILMNS ANGLICISM
ACGIILMNX CLIMAXING
ACGIILNOS GASOLINIC,
   LOGICIANS
ACGIILNRT ARTICLING
ACGIIMNPT IMPACTING
ACGIIMSTT STIGMATIC
ACGIINNOR INORGANIC
ACGIINOST AGONISTIC
ACGIINPSZ CAPSIZING
ACGIINQRU ACQUIRING
ACGIIORST ORGIASTIC
ACGIIRSTT GASTRITIC
ACGIKNNPU UNPACKING
ACGILLLOY LOGICALLY
ACGILLLRS CALL GIRLS
ACGILLNOR CAROLLING,
   COLLARING
ACGILLNOT COLLATING
ACGILLOOO OOLOGICAL
ACGILLOST COLLAGIST
ACGILNNST SCANTLING
ACGILNOST NOSTALGIC
ACGILNOXY COAXINGLY
ACGILNRSW SCRAWLING
ACGILNRSY SCARINGLY
ACGIMMNRS SCRAMMING
ACGIMNNOR ROMANCING
ACGIMNOOR AGRONOMIC
ACGIMNOPR COMPARING
ACGIMNORR CAIRNGORM
ACGIMNOTU CONTAGIUM
ACGIMNSTY GYMNASTIC,
   NYSTAGMIC
ACGIMNUUV VACUUMING
ACGIMOTYZ ZYGOMATIC
ACGINNNNO CANNONING
ACGINNOOT COGNATION,
   CONTAGION
ACGINNOPY POIGNANCY
ACGINNORY CRAYONING
ACGINNOTZ COGNIZANT

ACGINORSU CAROUSING
ACGINORTV CAVORTING
ACGINOSST AGNOSTICS
ACGINPPRS SCRAPPING
ACGINPRSS SCRAPINGS
ACGINPRTU CAPTURING
ACGINPTUY PUGNACITY
ACGIOORTT COGITATOR
ACGJNNOTU CONJUGANT
ACGLOOPRY CARPOLOGY
ACGLOOSTY SCATOLOGY
ACGMOPRTY CRYPTOGAM
ACGORRSUY SURROGACY
ACHHILORT HAIRCLOTH
ACHHINNOT CHTHONIAN
ACHHINSTY HYACINTHS
ACHHIPRSU PUSHCHAIR
ACHHLOSTU SLOUCH HAT
ACHHLOSTW WASHCLOTH
ACHHOSSTW CHAT
    SHOWS
ACHIILMSW WHIMSICAL
ACHIIMNST MACHINIST
ACHIINPSY PHYSICIAN
ACHIINRST CHRISTIAN,
    CHRISTINA
ACHIIOPST PISTACHIO
ACHIIPRSV VICARSHIP
ACHIIRRTT ARTHRITIC
ACHIIRSTV ARCHIVIST
ACHIKLPTU CHALK IT UP
ACHIKRSSW RICKSHAWS
ACHIKRSTT HAT TRICKS
ACHILLMSU MUSIC HALL
ACHILLOST SAILCLOTH
ACHILLSTY CITY HALLS
ACHILMPTY ITCHY PALM,
    LYMPHATIC
ACHILNORT ANTICHLOR
ACHILNRUY RAUNCHILY
ACHILNSTY SNATCHILY
ACHILOPTU PATCHOULI
ACHILORTV ARCHIVOLT
ACHILOSST SCHOLIAST
ACHILPSSY PHYSICALS
ACHILRSSY CHRYSALIS
ACHILRSTY STARCHILY
ACHIMMNOS MONACHISM
ACHIMMOSS MASOCHISM
ACHIMNOPS CHAMPIONS
ACHIMNORS HARMONICS
ACHIMNORT CHROMATIN
ACHIMOOTX HOMOTAXIC

ACHIMORST RHOTACISM
ACHIMOSST MASOCHIST
ACHIMOSTU MUSTACHIO
ACHIMRSST CHRISTMAS
ACHIMRSSW SCRIMSHAW
ACHINNOST STANCHION
ACHINNOTW CHINATOWN
ACHINOPPS PANSOPHIC
ACHINPRST CHINSTRAP
ACHIOOPST SOCIOPATH
ACHIOPPRS HIPPOCRAS
ACHIORSTT RHOTACIST
ACHIPRSUY HARUSPICY
ACHKLNOOS SOLONCHAK
ACHKMORTU
    TOUCHMARK
ACHKOPRTW PATCHWORK
ACHKORRXY ROCK
    HYRAX
ACHLLORSY SCHOLARLY
ACHLMSTYZ SCHMALTZY
ACHLNSTUY STAUNCHLY
ACHLOOSTU HOLOCAUST
ACHNOPSTY SYCOPHANT
ACHOPSTTW STOPWATCH
ACHORSSST TROSSACHS
ACHORTTTU CUTTHROAT
ACHPRSSTU PUSHCARTS
ACIIILNOT CILIATION
ACIIILNSV CIVILIANS
ACIIIMNST ANIMISTIC
ACIIIMNTV VITAMINIC
ACIIINPST PIANISTIC
ACIIJRSTU JUSTICIAR
ACIIKMNRT MINITRACK
ACIILLNOS COLLINSIA,
    ISOCLINAL
ACIILLNST SCINTILLA
ACIILLOPT POLITICAL
ACIILLPRS PRISCILLA
ACIILMNPU MUNICIPAL
ACIILMNRS CRIMINALS
ACIILMNSV CALVINISM
ACIILMNTY MILITANCY
ACIILMOSS SOCIALISM
ACIILMOSU MALICIOUS
ACIILMQTU QUITCLAIM
ACIILNNOT CLINTONIA
ACIILNOOT COALITION
ACIILNOPT PLICATION
ACIILNOVV CONVIVIAL
ACIILNOVY INVIOLACY
ACIILNPPR PRINCIPAL

ACIILNRSU INCISURAL
ACIILNSTV CALVINIST
ACIILOPRT PICTORIAL
ACIILORST SORITICAL
ACIILORTZ TRIAZOLIC
ACIILOSST SOCIALIST
ACIILOSTY SOCIALITY
ACIILQUZZ QUIZZICAL
ACIILRSVW CIVIL WARS
ACIILTTTY TACTILITY
ACIIMMNOT AMMONITIC
ACIIMNNOS INSOMNIAC
ACIIMNNOT ANTIMONIC,
    ANTINOMIC
ACIIMNOPT IMPACTION
ACIIMNORT MORTICIAN
ACIIMNSSU MUSICIANS
ACIIMOPST SIMPATICO
ACIIMORTT TRIATOMIC
ACIIMOSST MOSAICIST
ACIIMOSTT ATOMISTIC
ACIIMOTTY ATOMICITY
ACIIMPRST PRISMATIC
ACIIMPSSS SIC PASSIM
ACIIMRSST SCIMITARS
ACIINNOTU INCAUTION
ACIINOPST OPTICIANS
ACIINORTV VICTORIAN
ACIINOSTT CITATIONS
ACIINOTTX ANTITOXIC
ACIINOTTY ATONICITY
ACIIOPRST PSORIATIC
ACIIOPRTT PATRIOTIC
ACIIOPTZZ PIZZICATO
ACIIORSSV VARICOSIS
ACIIORSTY CARIOSITY
ACIIORSUV VICARIOUS
ACIIOSSTT ISOSTATIC
ACIIOSUVV VIVACIOUS
ACIIPRSTT PATRISTIC
ACIIPTTVY CAPTIVITY
ACIISSTTT STATISTIC
ACIISSTTV ACTIVISTS
ACIJKNNOU UNION JACK
ACIKKNNOT ANTIKNOCK
ACIKLLSST SALTLICKS
ACIKLMSTU MAULSTICK
ACIKLOSTT TAILSTOCK
ACIKLPSST SLAPSTICK
ACIKOPSSY SKIASCOPY
ACIKRSTTU TRACKSUIT
ACILLLOUV COLLUVIAL
ACILLLRYY LYRICALLY

ACILLMSUY MUSICALLY
ACILLNNSY SYNCLINAL
ACILLNOOS COLONIALS
ACILLNOOT COLLATION
ACILLNORS CARILLONS
ACILLNOSS SCALLIONS
ACILLOPTY OPTICALLY,
　TOPICALLY
ACILLORST CLOISTRAL
ACILLORYZ ZIRCALLOY
ACILLOSTY CALLOSITY,
　STOICALLY
ACILLOTXY TOXICALLY
ACILLPTYY TYPICALLY
ACILMMOTT COMMITTAL
ACILMNNTU CULMINANT
ACILMNOPT COMPLAINT,
　COMPLIANT
ACILMNOSV VOLCANISM
ACILMNSUU UNMUSICAL
ACILMOPRS COMPRISAL
ACILMPTUU CAPITULUM
ACILNNNUY UNCANNILY
ACILNNOTU CONTINUAL
ACILNNQTU CLINQUANT
ACILNOOST LOCATIONS
ACILNOPRT PROLACTIN
ACILNORST CONTRAILS
ACILNOSTT CLINOSTAT
ACILNOSTU SUCTIONAL,
　SULCATION
ACILNPTUY UNTYPICAL
ACILNRSWY SCRAWNILY
ACILOOPRS ACROPOLIS
ACILOOPST APOSTOLIC
ACILOORST CASTOR OIL
ACILOQTUY LOQUACITY
ACILORRSU CURSORIAL
ACILORSSU OSSICULAR
ACILORSTU SUCTORIAL
ACILOSSTV VOCALISTS
ACILOTTUY AUTOLYTIC
ACILPPRSY SCRAPPILY
ACILPSTTY STYPTICAL
ACILRRTUU UTRICULAR
ACILSSTTY SYSTALTIC
ACIMMNOOT MONATOMIC
ACIMMORSS COMMISSAR
ACIMNNOOP COMPANION
ACIMNOOST ONOMASTIC
ACIMNOOTU AUTONOMIC
ACIMNOOTX TAXONOMIC
ACIMNOPRY PARONYMIC

ACIMNORST NARCOTISM,
　ROMANTICS
ACIMNOSUU ACUMINOUS
ACIMOOTTU AUTOTOMIC
ACIMOPSSY SYMPOSIAC
ACIMORSST OSTRACISM
ACIMORSTT STROMATIC
ACIMPRSTY SYMPATRIC
ACIMRSTTU STRUMATIC
ACINNORST CONSTRAIN,
　TRANSONIC
ACINNOSST SANCTIONS
ACINOORRS CORRASION
ACINOORST CONSORTIA
ACINOOSTV VOCATIONS
ACINORSST CROISSANT
ACINORSTY CRAYONIST
ACINOSSTW WAINSCOTS
ACINOSTTU SCUTATION
ACINRSSSU NARCISSUS
ACIOOPRSU PAROICOUS
ACIOOPRSZ SAPROZOIC
ACIOORSTU ATROCIOUS
ACIOORSUV VORACIOUS
ACIOOSTUU AUTOICOUS
ACIOOTTUX AUTOTOXIC
ACIOPRSSY CARYOPSIS
ACIOPRSTT PROSTATIC
ACIOPTTUY AUTOTYPIC
ACIRSSTUY CASUISTRY
ACJKOPRST JOCKSTRAP
ACJLLORUY JOCULARLY
ACKKMOPRS POCKMARKS
ACKLLNRTU TRUNK CALL
ACKLLPSSU SKULLCAPS
ACKLMOOOR
　CLOAKROOM
ACKLNOPRT ROCK PLANT
ACKLNORST CORNSTALK
ACKLORSST CROSS TALK
ACKLORSSW CROSSWALK
ACLLLLORS ROLL CALLS
ACLLLOSUY CALLOUSLY
ACLLMNOSU MOLLUSCAN
ACLLOORRY COROLLARY
ACLLOORST COLOSTRAL
ACLMMNOOW
　COMMON-LAW
ACLMNOORU
　MONOCULAR
ACLMOORSS CLASSROOM
ACLMOORSU
　CLAMOROUS

ACLMOPSTY CYTOPLASM
ACLNNORTU NOCTURNAL
ACLNOORTT CONTRALTO
ACLOOOORRT CORALROOT
ACLOOPRRS CORPORALS
ACLOPPRYY POLYCARPY
ACLOPRRSW PROWL
　CARS
ACLOPRSUU CRAPULOUS
ACLOPRTTU PLUTOCRAT
ACLOPSTTY CYTOPLAST
ACLORSUUY RAUCOUSLY
ACLOSUUVY VACUOUSLY
ACMNOORRT
　CORMORANT
ACMNOOSTU
　COSMONAUT
ACMNOPRYY
　PYROMANCY
ACMOORRST
　MOTORCARS
ACMORRSUU
　MACRUROUS
ACMORSSTW WORM
　CASTS
ACMORSTUY CUSTOMARY
ACNNNOOST CONSONANT
ACNNOSSTT CONSTANTS
ACNOOPRST CORPOSANT
ACNOORRSU
　RANCOROUS
ACNORSSTT CONTRASTS
ACNORSTTU TURNCOATS
ACNORSTTY CONTRASTY
ACOOPPRRS SPOROCARP
ACOORSSTU AUTOCROSS
ACOPRRSST SPORTS CAR
ACOSSTTTY STATOCYST
ADDDEEEHR RED-HEADED
ADDDEEFRU DEFRAUDED
ADDDEEGLN GLADDENED
ADDDEEHNR
　RED-HANDED
ADDDEEKLS SKEDADDLE
ADDDEERSS ADDRESSED
ADDDEFIIN DANDIFIED
ADDDEGLOP DOG PADDLE
ADDDEIINS DISDAINED
ADDDEISSU DISSUADED
ADDDELNSU UNSADDLED
ADDDELRST STRADDLED
ADDEEEFRT FEDERATED
ADDEEEGLT DELEGATED

ADDEEEGRY DEGREE-DAY
ADDEEEMNR MEANDERED
ADDEEENRS SERENADED
ADDEEERRT RETREADED
ADDEEERSS ADDRESSEE
ADDEEFHIX FIXED-HEAD
ADDEEFILN ENFILADED
ADDEEFLTU DEFAULTED
ADDEEFNNT DEFENDANT
ADDEEFNSS FADEDNESS
ADDEEFRRU DEFRAUDER
ADDEEGHIP PIGHEADED
ADDEEGILM MIDDLE AGE
ADDEEGINN DEADENING
ADDEEGIRS DISAGREED
ADDEEGLNR
    GLADDENER, GLANDERED
ADDEEGNSW SAND
    WEDGE
ADDEEGORT DEROGATED
ADDEEHHOT HOTHEADED
ADDEEHILN HEADLINED
ADDEEHRSS HEADDRESS
ADDEEHRTY DEHYDRATE
ADDEEIILS IDEALISED
ADDEEIILZ IDEALIZED
ADDEEILNS DEADLINES
ADDEEILRV DAREDEVIL
ADDEEILST DEADLIEST
ADDEEIMTT MEDITATED
ADDEEINRT DETRAINED
ADDEEIPRR DRAPERIED
ADDEEIPRS DESPAIRED
ADDEELNRS SLANDERED
ADDEELNRU LAUNDERED
ADDEELOST DESOLATED
ADDEEMNOS
    DESDEMONA
ADDEEMNRU
    MAUNDERED
ADDEEMNST DAMNEDEST
ADDEEMORT MODERATED
ADDEEMPST STAMPEDED
ADDEENNPT DEPENDANT
ADDEENOST STONE-DEAD
ADDEENOTT DETONATED
ADDEENSST DATEDNESS
ADDEENSWY WEDNESDAY
ADDEEOPRS DESPERADO
ADDEEPRSU PERSUADED
ADDEEPSUX PAS DE DEUX
ADDEERRSS ADDRESSER,
    READDRESS

ADDEERSSS ADDRESSES
ADDEFFHNO OFFHANDED
ADDEFFLOO OFF-LOADED
ADDEFIIPT PEDATIFID
ADDEFILSY FIELD DAYS
ADDEFINNR FERDINAND
ADDEFINSS FADDINESS
ADDEFORRW
    FORWARDED
ADDEGGINR DEGRADING
ADDEGGOOT
    DOG-EAT-DOG
ADDEGHILR HILDEGARD
ADDEGHILT DEADLIGHT
ADDEGHINR HAG-RIDDEN
ADDEGILNR LADDERING
ADDEGIMNN
    DEMANDING, MADDENING
ADDEGINNS SADDENING
ADDEGINOS DIAGNOSED
ADDEGIRRS DISREGARD
ADDEGLLMO GOLD
    MEDAL
ADDEGLRUY GUARDEDLY
ADDEGNOOR
    DRAGOONED,
    GADROONED
ADDEGNORW
    DOWNGRADE
ADDEGNRUU
    UNGUARDED
ADDEHHOTY HYDATHODE
ADDEHILOY HOLIDAYED
ADDEHINRY ANHYDRIDE
ADDEHINSW HEADWINDS
ADDEHINSY HENDIADYS
ADDEHNNRU
    UNDERHAND
ADDEHNORS
    HARD-NOSED
ADDEHNORU
    ROUNDHEAD
ADDEHNOTW
    TWO-HANDED
ADDEHORSW
    HEADWORDS
ADDEHTTUY DEATH DUTY
ADDEIIIMT DIMIDIATE
ADDEIILNV INVALIDED
ADDEIILNX DIXIELAND
ADDEIIMNS DESMIDIAN
ADDEIINNR RED INDIAN
ADDEIISTV ADDITIVES

ADDEIKNPP KIDNAPPED
ADDEILLNS LANDSLIDE
ADDEILMMN MIDDLEMAN
ADDEILNNO DANDELION
ADDEILNSY DEADLY SIN
ADDEILPSY DISPLAYED
ADDEILSVY ADVISEDLY
ADDEIMNOT DEMANTOID,
    DOMINATED
ADDEIMNSY MANY-SIDED
ADDEIMNTY DYNAMITED
ADDEIMORT DERMATOID
ADDEIMSST DISMASTED
ADDEINNTU INUNDATED
ADDEINPRU UNDERPAID
ADDEINRTT DITTANDER
ADDEINRTW TRADE WIND
ADDEINSUV UNADVISED
ADDEIOSVW DISAVOWED
ADDEIRSSU DISSUADER
ADDEIRSSW SIDEWARDS
ADDEJNORU ADJOURNED
ADDELLOPR POLLARDED
ADDELMOTU MODULATED
ADDELNTUU UNDULATED
ADDELRRST STRADDLER
ADDEMORRY
    DROMEDARY
ADDENNRTU REDUNDANT
ADDENNSSU SAND DUNES
ADDENNTUU UNDAUNTED
ADDENOORT DEODORANT
ADDENOPTU UNADOPTED
ADDENORUY DUODENARY
ADDENOSTU ASTOUNDED
ADDEOPSTT POSTDATED
ADDEPPRSU SUPPERADD
ADDEPQRUU QUADRUPED
ADDFFILOS DAFFODILS
ADDFHILSY FADDISHLY
ADDFIIQRU QUADRIFID
ADDGGIJNU ADJUDGING
ADDGHNORU
    DRAGHOUND
ADDGILNSW SWADDLING
ADDGMRSUU
    MUDGUARDS
ADDHHIOOR HARDIHOOD
ADDHIKNRR HARD DRINK
ADDHIKRSS HARD DISKS
ADDHNNOSW HANDS
    DOWN

ADDHOORSW
  HARDWOODS
ADDIINOST ADDITIONS
ADDINORSU DIANDROUS
ADDIOPRTY ODD PARITY
ADDIORRST DIRT ROADS
ADDKNRRSU DRUNKARDS
ADDLLNORS LANDLORDS
ADDLNNOOP PONDOLAND
ADDMNOOTU ODD MAN
  OUT
ADDNNOPUW
  UP-AND-DOWN
ADDNORSWW
  DOWNWARDS
ADEEEEGLY EAGLE-EYED
ADEEEFHRT FEATHERED
ADEEEFLLT LEAFLETED
ADEEEFNRR REFERENDA
ADEEEFRRT FREE TRADE
ADEEEGHNR GREENHEAD
ADEEEGLRT RELEGATED
ADEEEGLST DELEGATES
ADEEEGNRS RENEGADES
ADEEEGNRT GENERATED
ADEEEGTTV VEGETATED
ADEEEHHRT HEATHERED
ADEEEHKNR HEARKENED
ADEEEHLST STEELHEAD
ADEEEHNRT HEARTENED
ADEEEHPRT PREHEATED
ADEEEHRRS REHEARSED
ADEEEHRTW WEATHERED
ADEEEILMN MADELEINE
ADEEEILNT DELINEATE
ADEEEINRS DEANERIES
ADEEEINST DETAINEES
ADEEEIRSS DIAERESES
ADEEEKKNW
  WEAK-KNEED
ADEEELLMN ENAMELLED
ADEEELLNS LEND-LEASE
ADEEELMNP EMPANELED
ADEEELNRZ ZEELANDER
ADEEELPRR REPLEADER
ADEEEMNRR MEANDERER
ADEEEMPRT PERMEATED
ADEEENRRS SERENADER
ADEEENRSS SERENADES
ADEEENRST EAST ENDER
ADEEENRTT ENTREATED
ADEEENRTV ENERVATED,
  VENERATED

ADEEEPRST DESPERATE
ADEEERRTT RETREATED
ADEEERTWW
  WATERWEED
ADEEFFILR FIELDFARE
ADEEFFLOT FLOAT-FEED
ADEEFGINN DEAFENING
ADEEFGINT DEFEATING
ADEEFHORS FOREHEADS
ADEEFIKRR FREDERIKA
ADEEFILNS ENFILADES
ADEEFILOT DEFOLIATE
ADEEFILSU FEUDALISE
ADEEFILUZ FEUDALIZE
ADEEFIMST DEFEATISM
ADEEFINRR REFRAINED
ADEEFISTT DEFEATIST
ADEEFLLNN FLANNELED
ADEEFLLST STALL-FEED
ADEEFLNTT FLATTENED
ADEEFLRTT FLATTERED
ADEEFLRTU DEFAULTER
ADEEFMNOR FORENAMED
ADEEFMORR FOREARMED
ADEEFMSTU DEAF-MUTES
ADEEFNOST STONE-DEAF
ADEEGGINS DISENGAGE
ADEEGGIRV AGGRIEVED
ADEEGGLNO GOLDEN AGE
ADEEGGMOU
  DEMAGOGUE
ADEEGGOPU PEDAGOGUE
ADEEGGRST STAGGERED
ADEEGGRSW
  SWAGGERED
ADEEGILLR GALLERIED
ADEEGILLS LEGALISED
ADEEGILLZ LEGALIZED
ADEEGILNR GERALDINE,
  REALIGNED
ADEEGILNW WIDE-ANGLE
ADEEGIMNN DEMEANING
ADEEGIMRT EMIGRATED
ADEEGINNR ENDEARING,
  GRENADINE
ADEEGINRR GRENADIER
ADEEGINRT DENIGRATE
ADEEGINST DESIGNATE
ADEEGINSV ENVISAGED
ADEEGINTV NEGATIVED
ADEEGIRST TRAGEDIES
ADEEGIUVW WAVEGUIDE
ADEEGLLLY ALLEGEDLY

ADEEGLLRV GRAVELLED
ADEEGLNNR GREENLAND
ADEEGLNNT ENTANGLED
ADEEGLNOT ELONGATED
ADEEGLNRY ENRAGEDLY,
  LEGENDARY
ADEEGLOOW
  EAGLEWOOD
ADEEGLRTU REGULATED
ADEEGMNRR
  GERMANDER
ADEEGMNRS GENDARMES
ADEEGMNTU
  AUGMENTED
ADEEGMRRU
  DEMURRAGE
ADEEGNNRS GREENSAND
ADEEGNRRS GARDENERS
ADEEGNRST ESTRANGED
ADEEGNRSU DUNGAREES
ADEEGORRZ RAZOR EDGE
ADEEGRRSS DEERGRASS
ADEEHIISV HEAVISIDE
ADEEHIKLT DEATHLIKE
ADEEHILNR HEADLINER
ADEEHILNS HEADLINES
ADEEHILNT ETHELINDA
ADEEHILTW WHITE DEAL,
  WHITE LEAD
ADEEHIMNV MIDHEAVEN
ADEEHINRT HERNIATED
ADEEHINSS HEADINESS
ADEEHIRRV RIVERHEAD
ADEEHISSV ADHESIVES
ADEEHISTT HESITATED
ADEEHLLOS LEASEHOLD
ADEEHLNSU UNLEASHED
ADEEHLOSU HEAD LOUSE
ADEEHLSST DEATHLESS
ADEEHMNOT
  METHADONE
ADEEHMOST HOMESTEAD
ADEEHNOST HEADSTONE
ADEEHNPPR APPREHEND
ADEEHNPRS SHARPENED
ADEEHNRSS HARNESSED
ADEEHNRST ADHERENTS
ADEEHNRTU UNEARTHED
ADEEHORRV OVERHEARD
ADEEHORSV OVERHEADS
ADEEHOSWY EYE
  SHADOW
ADEEHPRRS REPHRASED

ADEEHPRSY SHARP-EYED
ADEEHRSST HEADRESTS
ADEEHRSTT SHATTERED
ADEEHRSTV HARVESTED
ADEEHRSTW WATERSHED
ADEEHSTUX EXHAUSTED
ADEEIILRS IDEALISER
ADEEIILRZ IDEALIZER
ADEEIIMMT IMMEDIATE
ADEEIIMST MEDIATISE
ADEEIIMTV MEDIATIVE
ADEEIIMTZ MEDIATIZE
ADEEIIRSS DIAERESIS
ADEEIJMRS JEREMIADS
ADEEIKLMR DREAMLIKE
ADEEILMNN MENDELIAN
ADEEILMNS LADIES' MEN,
  MÉLISANDE
ADEEILMPR EPIDERMAL,
  IMPLEADER
ADEEILMRS MISDEALER,
  MISLEADER
ADEEILMST LEAD TIMES
ADEEILNPS PENALISED
ADEEILNPX EXPLAINED
ADEEILNPZ PENALIZED
ADEEILNST DATELINES
ADEEILOTT ETIOLATED
ADEEILPRR LIP-READER
ADEEILPRS PEARLISED
ADEEILPRV PREVAILED
ADEEILPRZ PEARLIZED
ADEEILPSS DISPLEASE
ADEEILQSU EQUALISED
ADEEILQUZ EQUALIZED
ADEEILTTV LEVITATED
ADEEIMNNO MENADIONE
ADEEIMNOU EUDEMONIA
ADEEIMNRR REMAINDER
ADEEIMNRT MINARETED
ADEEIMPPR PIPE DREAM
ADEEIMRRR REMARRIED
ADEEIMRST DIAMETERS
ADEEIMSST DEMITASSE
ADEEIMSTT ESTIMATED
ADEEINNOS ADENOSINE
ADEEINNRT ENTRAINED
ADEEINPRT PERTAINED
ADEEINPST NEAP TIDES
ADEEINRSS READINESS
ADEEINRST RESINATED
ADEEINRTT DENITRATE
ADEEINRUW UNWEARIED

ADEEINTVV ADVENTIVE
ADEEIOPRT PERIODATE
ADEEIOPTV VIDEOTAPE
ADEEIPPST PEPTIDASE
ADEEIPRRS DRAPERIES
ADEEIPRTU REPUDIATE
ADEEIRRST DREARIEST
ADEEIRSTV ADVERTISE
ADEEIRSTW WATERSIDE
ADEEIRTTW TIDEWATER
ADEEIRTTX EXTRADITE
ADEEISSTT STATESIDE,
  STEADIEST
ADEEISSTV SEDATIVES
ADEEITUVX EXUDATIVE
ADEEKNNSS NAKEDNESS
ADEEKNRTU UNDERTAKE
ADEELLMRV MARVELLED
ADEELLNRY LEARNEDLY
ADEELLPSY PLEASEDLY
ADEELLRTV TRAVELLED
ADEELLRXY RELAXEDLY
ADEELLTXY EXALTEDLY
ADEELMRSS DREAMLESS
ADEELNNRU UNLEARNED
ADEELNORS OLEANDERS
ADEELNORV OVERLADEN
ADEELNOST ENDOSTEAL
ADEELNRRS SLANDERER
ADEELNRRU LAUNDERER
ADEELNRSU UNDERSEAL
ADEELNRTU UNRELATED
ADEELNRUV UNRAVELED
ADEELORST DESOLATER
ADEELORTT TOLERATED
ADEELPRST PLASTERED
ADEELPSST PEDESTALS
ADEELQRRU QUARRELED
ADEELRRST RED ALERTS
ADEELRRTT RED RATTLE
ADEELRRTU ADULTERER
ADEELRSTY STEELYARD
ADEELRSVY ADVERSELY
ADEEMMNNT
  AMENDMENT
ADEEMMORT
  DERMATOME
ADEEMMOXY
  MYXOEDEMA
ADEEMMRST STAMMERED
ADEEMNOPR PROMENADE
ADEEMNORT EMENDATOR

ADEEMNORU
  DEMEANOUR,
  ENAMOURED
ADEEMNRRU
  MAUNDERER
ADEEMNRST
  SMARTENED, TRADESMEN
ADEEMNRTY DYNAMETER
ADEEMOORR
  AERODROME
ADEEMOPRR MADREPORE
ADEEMORRX
  XERODERMA
ADEEMORST MODERATES
ADEEMORTT TREMATODE
ADEEMOSTU EDEMATOUS
ADEEMPRST STAMPEDER
ADEEMPSST STAMPEDES
ADEEMPSTU DESPUMATE,
  STEAMED-UP
ADEEMPTTT ATTEMPTED
ADEEMRSTW WET
  DREAMS
ADEENNPRT TREPANNED
ADEENORST RESONATED
ADEENORTV RENOVATED
ADEENORUV ENDEAVOUR
ADEENORVY
  OVEN-READY
ADEENPPRT ENTRAPPED
ADEENPRRT PARTNERED
ADEENPRTT PATTERNED
ADEENRRSW WANDERERS
ADEENRRTU UNDERRATE
ADEENRRUW
  UNDERWEAR
ADEENRSTU SAUNTERED
ADEENRSTY SEDENTARY
ADEENRTTU UNTREATED
ADEENRTUV ADVENTURE
ADEENSTTV VENDETTAS
ADEEOPRSV EAVESDROP
ADEEORRTV OVERRATED,
  OVERTRADE
ADEEORTVX OVERTAXED
ADEEPPRSS APPRESSED
ADEEPPRST SPEED TRAP
ADEEPRRSU PERSUADER
ADEEPRRTU DEPARTURE
ADEEPRSST PEDERASTS
ADEEPRSTT SPATTERED
ADEEPRSTU DEPASTURE
ADEEPRSTY PEDERASTY

ADEEPSSWY SPEEDWAYS
ADEEQRRTU QUARTERED
ADEERRSSU REASSURED
ADEERRSTU TREASURED
ADEERRSTV TRAVERSED
ADEERSTYY YESTERDAY
ADEFFIILS FALSIFIED
ADEFFNORT AFFRONTED
ADEFFORST TRADE-OFFS
ADEFGHORT GODFATHER
ADEFGIIMN MAGNIFIED
ADEFGIIRT GRATIFIED
ADEFGILNT DEFLATING
ADEFGILRU LIFEGUARD
ADEFGIMTU FUMIGATED
ADEFGINRY DEFRAYING
ADEFGIRRU FIREGUARD
ADEFGLOOT FLOODGATE
ADEFGLRRU REGARDFUL
ADEFHIMST HAM-FISTED
ADEFHINOS FASHIONED
ADEFHINRT THREADFIN
ADEFHIPSS SPADEFISH
ADEFHIRST HEADFIRST
ADEFHLOOS FALSEHOOD
ADEFHNORS FOREHANDS
ADEFHNORU
　UNHEARD-OF
ADEFIILMP AMPLIFIED
ADEFIILNS FINALISED
ADEFIILNZ FINALIZED
ADEFIILQU QUALIFIED
ADEFIILRS AIRFIELDS
ADEFIILRT AIRLIFTED
ADEFIIPRR RAPID-FIRE
ADEFIISST SATISFIED
ADEFIKNRW DRAWKNIFE
ADEFILLSU FUSILLADE
ADEFILMNS FIELDSMAN
ADEFILMSU FEUDALISM
ADEFILNOT DEFLATION,
　DEFOLIANT
ADEFILNRS FRIESLAND
ADEFILNSS SAND FLIES
ADEFILNTY DEFIANTLY
ADEFILORT FLORIATED
ADEFILSTU FEUDALIST
ADEFILTUY FEUDALITY
ADEFIMORS ASIDE FROM
ADEFINOST INSTEAD OF
ADEFIRSTT DRAFTIEST
ADEFIRSTX FIXED STAR
ADEFLLMOS OLD FLAMES

ADEFLLMOU LEAF MOULD
ADEFLLMSY DAMSELFLY
ADEFLMMOR
　MALFORMED
ADEFLOPST SOFT-PEDAL
ADEFLORUV FLAVOURED
ADEFLORWY DAYFLOWER
ADEFLRSTW LEFTWARDS
ADEFMNNTU FUNDAMENT
ADEFMNRST DRAFTSMEN
ADEFMOORR
　DOORFRAME
ADEFMORTT FORMATTED
ADEFOOPRR PROOFREAD
ADEFOOTTU OUT-OF-DATE
ADEFORRRW
　FORWARDER
ADEFORRTV OVERDRAFT
ADEFORRTW AFTERWORD
ADEFORTUY FEUDATORY
ADEGGGIZZ ZIGZAGGED
ADEGGHHIR HIGH-GRADE
ADEGGINNR GARDENING
ADEGGINRR REGARDING
ADEGGINUW WIND
　GAUGE
ADEGGIRST DRAGGIEST
ADEGGLORY GARGOYLED
ADEGGLRST STRAGGLED
ADEGGMORT
　MORTGAGED
ADEGGNORU
　GROUNDAGE
ADEGHHILT HEADLIGHT
ADEGHHOSS HOGSHEADS
ADEGHILNR HERALDING
ADEGHINNR HARDENING
ADEGHINRS GARNISHED
ADEGHINRT THREADING
ADEGHINSU ANGUISHED
ADEGHIRST SIGHT-READ
ADEGHLLNO HELGOLAND
ADEGHLMPU GALUMPHED
ADEGHLORS GASHOLDER
ADEGHMORU HOME
　GUARD
ADEGHNOPR HOP
　GARDEN
ADEGHNOUZ GAZEHOUND
ADEGHORST GOATHERDS
ADEGHRRTU DRAUGHTER
ADEGHRSTU DAUGHTERS

ADEGIILNR DERAILING,
　GRINDELIA
ADEGIILNT DETAILING
ADEGIILOS DIALOGISE
ADEGIILOZ DIALOGIZE
ADEGIILPT PIGTAILED
ADEGIILTT LITIGATED
ADEGIIMNT MEDIATING
ADEGIIMTT MITIGATED
ADEGIINNR INGRAINED
ADEGIINNT DETAINING
ADEGIINNU GUANIDINE
ADEGIINTV DEVIATING
ADEGIIRRT IRRIGATED
ADEGIKNNR DARKENING
ADEGILLNP PEDALLING
ADEGILLNS SIGNALLED
ADEGILNNR LENINGRAD
ADEGILNOR GIRANDOLE,
　RELOADING
ADEGILNOS ALONGSIDE
ADEGILNPS PLEADINGS
ADEGILNRU GERUNDIAL
ADEGILNUV DEVALUING
ADEGILNVY EVADINGLY
ADEGILORU DIALOGUER
ADEGILOSU DIALOGUES
ADEGILRSS GLISSADER
ADEGIMNNP DAMPENING
ADEGIMNNR REMANDING
ADEGIMNTU MAGNITUDE
ADEGIMORS IDEOGRAMS
ADEGIMOST DOGMATISE
ADEGIMOTZ DOGMATIZE
ADEGINNPP APPENDING
ADEGINNPR PANDERING
ADEGINNPX EXPANDING
ADEGINNRT INTEGRAND
ADEGINNRW WANDERING
ADEGINNTT ATTENDING
ADEGINORR RIO GRANDE
ADEGINORS GRANDIOSE,
　ORGANISED
ADEGINORZ ORGANIZED
ADEGINOSS DIAGNOSES
ADEGINPRS SPREADING
ADEGINPRT DEPARTING,
　PREDATING
ADEGINPRV DEPRAVING,
　PERVADING
ADEGINRRT RETARDING
ADEGINRRW REWARDING

ADEGINRST GRADIENTS,
    RED GIANTS
ADEGINRTV ADVERTING
ADEGINSSU GAUDINESS
ADEGINSTT DIGESTANT
ADEGINSTY STEADYING
ADEGIPRRT PARTRIDGE
ADEGIRTTU GRATITUDE
ADEGLLOPT GOLD PLATE
ADEGLNNTU UNTANGLED
ADEGLNRST STRANGLED
ADEGLOOPY PAEDOLOGY
ADEGLORST OLD STAGER
ADEGMNRSU
    GUARDSMEN
ADEGMOPRR
    PROGRAMED
ADEGNNOPR PENDRAGON
ADEGNNORW
    DOWNRANGE
ADEGNNRSS GRANDNESS
ADEGNOOOS A GOOD
    NOSE
ADEGNOORS
    GOOSANDER
ADEGNOPRT GODPARENT
ADEGNORSS DRAGONESS
ADEGNORSU DANGEROUS
ADEGNOSTW
    DOWNSTAGE
ADEGOORST STAGE DOOR
ADEGORRTT GARROTTED
ADEHHIPSS HEADSHIPS
ADEHHISTW DEATH WISH
ADEHIILRS HAIR SLIDE
ADEHIISST DIATHESIS
ADEHIKNPS HANDSPIKE
ADEHIKNRT IN THE DARK
ADEHIKNSS SKINHEADS
ADEHILLMR HEIMDALLR
ADEHILMNS MISHANDLE
ADEHILMOT ETHMOIDAL
ADEHILNNR RHINELAND
ADEHILNPR PHILANDER
ADEHILNRR HARD-LINER
ADEHILNRS HARD LINES
ADEHILRRT TRIHEDRAL
ADEHILRST HERALDIST
ADEHIMNOR RHODAMINE
ADEHIMNSU HUMANISED
ADEHIMNUZ HUMANIZED
ADEHIMOSU HOUSEMAID
ADEHIMPTW WHITEDAMP

ADEHIMRTY DIATHERMY
ADEHINNSS HANDINESS
ADEHINOPU AUDIPHONE
ADEHINORS RHODESIAN
ADEHINOSS ADHESIONS
ADEHINRSS HARDINESS
ADEHINRST TARNISHED
ADEHINRSV VARNISHED
ADEHINRTY ANHYDRITE
ADEHINRYZ HYDRAZINE
ADEHINSSS SHADINESS
ADEHIOOST THEODOSIA
ADEHIOPRT ATROPHIED
ADEHIORSW SHADOWIER
ADEHIPRST THERAPSID
ADEHIRRTT THIRD-RATE
ADEHIRSTW DISHWATER
ADEHKNOSW
    SHAKEDOWN
ADEHKORRS DARK HORSE
ADEHLLNOR HOLLANDER
ADEHLLOSW SHALLOWED
ADEHLLOTT DEATH TOLL
ADEHLMNOS HOMELANDS
ADEHMOOPS
    SHAMPOOED
ADEHMORSW
    HOMEWARDS
ADEHMOSSU MADHOUSES
ADEHNOOPR HARPOONED
ADEHNOPRS HORNED ASP
ADEHNORSV HANDOVERS
ADEHNOSSS SANDSHOES
ADEHNPPRU UPPER HAND
ADEHNSSSU SUNSHADES
ADEHOORSU ROADHOUSE
ADEHOORTW
    HEARTWOOD
ADEHOOSTT STATEHOOD
ADEHOPPPY POPPYHEAD
ADEHOSTUW
    WASHED-OUT
ADEHTUVYY HEAVY-DUTY
ADEIIILNT INITIALED
ADEIIINTT DIETITIAN,
    INITIATED
ADEIILMNN MAINLINED
ADEIILMOZ IMIDAZOLE
ADEIILMTT MILITATED
ADEIILNRT DELIRIANT
ADEIILNST DISENTAIL
ADEIILORT EDITORIAL
ADEIILQTU LIQUIDATE

ADEIILSST IDEALISTS
ADEIIMMSX MAXIMISED
ADEIIMMXZ MAXIMIZED
ADEIIMNOT MEDIATION
ADEIIMNRS MERIDIANS
ADEIIMNRT AD INTERIM
ADEIIMNTT INTIMATED
ADEIIMOTT DIATOMITE
ADEIIMSSV ADMISSIVE,
    MISADVISE
ADEIINNOS INDONESIA
ADEIINOTV DEVIATION
ADEIINPPR DRAINPIPE
ADEIINSST SANITISED
ADEIINSTT DAINTIEST
ADEIINSTZ SANITIZED
ADEIIOSTZ DIAZOTISE
ADEIIOTVX OXIDATIVE
ADEIIOTZZ DIAZOTIZE
ADEIIPRRS DISREPAIR
ADEIIPRSS DISPRAISE
ADEIIPSST DISSIPATE
ADEIIRRTT IRRITATED
ADEIIRSST SATIRISED
ADEIIRSTZ SATIRIZED
ADEIITTTV TITIVATED
ADEIKMORS KAISERDOM
ADEIKMRST TIDEMARKS
ADEIKNPPR KIDNAPPER
ADEIKNPRS SPIKENARD
ADEILLMNO MEDALLION
ADEILLMOT METALLOID
ADEILLMRT TREADMILL
ADEILLMST MEDALLIST
ADEILLNST INSTALLED
ADEILLPRS SPIRALLED
ADEILLPRU PRELUDIAL
ADEILLQRU QUADRILLE
ADEILMMOT IMMOLATED
ADEILMNNS LANDMINES
ADEILMNPT IMPLANTED
ADEILMNST DISMANTLE
ADEILMNTU DENTALIUM
ADEILMOPT DIPLOMATE
ADEILMOPY POLYAMIDE
ADEILMORR MAIL ORDER
ADEILMORS MORALISED
ADEILMORZ MORALIZED
ADEILMOTV MOLDAVITE
ADEILMPTU AMPLITUDE
ADEILMSTU SIMULATED
ADEILMTTU MUTILATED
ADEILNNRU UNDERLAIN

ADEILNOPP PANOPLIED
ADEILNOPT PLANETOID
ADEILNOPU ANEUPLOID
ADEILNRRT INTERLARD
ADEILNRSS ISLANDERS
ADEILNRSU LAUNDRIES
ADEILNRTU UITLANDER
ADEILNSSV VALIDNESS
ADEILNSTU INSULATED
ADEILOPRS POLARISED
ADEILOPRT DEPILATOR
ADEILOPRZ POLARIZED
ADEILOQSU ODALISQUE
ADEILORST IDOLATERS
ADEILOSTV DOVETAILS
ADEILPPRY REPLY-PAID
ADEILPRSS DISPERSAL
ADEILPRSU EPIDURALS
ADEILPRSY DISPLAYER
ADEILPTTU PLATITUDE
ADEILRTTU RUTILATED
ADEILSSTU LASSITUDE
ADEILSTTU ALTITUDES,
    LATITUDES
ADEIMNNOT NOMINATED
ADEIMNOPT ADEMPTION
ADEIMNORS RANDOMISE
ADEIMNORZ RANDOMIZE
ADEIMNOST STAMINODE
ADEIMNOSW WOMANISED
ADEIMNOWZ WOMANIZED
ADEIMNPRR REPRIMAND
ADEIMNPRS SPIDERMAN
ADEIMNRRU UNMARRIED
ADEIMNRSU NURSEMAID
ADEIMNRTU RUMINATED
ADEIMNRTY DYNAMITER
ADEIMORST AMORTISED,
    MEDIATORS
ADEIMORTT MEDITATOR
ADEIMORTZ AMORTIZED
ADEIMOTTV MOTIVATED
ADEIMPRST SPERMATID
ADEIMRTUX ADMIXTURE
ADEIMRTXY TAXIDERMY
ADEIMSSTT MISSTATED
ADEINNNTT INTENDANT
ADEINNOTT DENTATION
ADEINNOTV INNOVATED
ADEINNRSS RANDINESS
ADEINNSSS SANDINESS
ADEINOOTX EXODONTIA
ADEINOPPT APPOINTED

ADEINOPRR PREORDAIN
ADEINOPRT PREDATION
ADEINOPST ANTIPODES
ADEINORST NOTARISED
ADEINORTY ARYTENOID
ADEINORTZ NOTARIZED
ADEINOSTT ANTIDOTES,
    STATIONED
ADEINOTUX EXUDATION
ADEINPPRS SANDPIPER
ADEINPPST STANDPIPE
ADEINPRSS RAPIDNESS
ADEINPSSV VAPIDNESS
ADEINRSST TARDINESS
ADEINRSVY VINEYARDS
ADEINSSST STAIDNESS
ADEINSSTU SUSTAINED
ADEINSSTY DYNASTIES
ADEIOPRSV VAPORISED
ADEIOPRTZ TRAPEZOID
ADEIOPRVZ VAPORIZED
ADEIORSST ASTEROIDS
ADEIORSVW DISAVOWER
ADEIORTVY DEVIATORY
ADEIPPSSY DYSPEPSIA
ADEIPRSSY PRISE DAYS
ADEIPRSYZ PRIZE DAYS
ADEIPRTVY DEPRAVITY
ADEIPSTTU APTITUDES
ADEIRRSUY RESIDUARY
ADEIRSSST DISASTERS
ADEIRSTVY ADVERSITY
ADEIRSVWY DRIVEWAYS
ADEISTTTU ATTITUDES
ADEJLNRTU JUTLANDER
ADEKKLRSY SKYLARKED
ADEKLOTTU OUTTALKED
ADEKNORTU OUTRANKED
ADEKOPRSW SPADEWORK
ADELLLOWY ALLOWEDLY
ADELLMRUY MEDULLARY
ADELLNORW LOWLANDER
ADELLNOUY UNALLOYED
ADELLOPRT PATROLLED
ADELLORRT TALL ORDER
ADELLOSWW
    SWALLOWED
ADELMNNUY MUNDANELY
ADELMNOOP LAMPOONED
ADELMNOPS ENDOPLASM
ADELMORST OLD MASTER
ADELNNORW
    LANDOWNER

ADELNOOPR APELDOORN
ADELNOOST LOADSTONE
ADELNOPSY DYSPNOEAL
ADELNORRV LAND ROVER
ADELNORSU UNLOADERS
ADELNORUY ROUNDELAY
ADELNPRUY UNDERPLAY
ADELNRSSU LAUNDRESS
ADELNRSUY UNDERLAYS
ADELNSSTU DAUNTLESS
ADELOOPRT DOORPLATE
ADELOORSV OVERLOADS
ADELOPPRS PROLAPSED
ADELOPPTU POPULATED
ADELOPTUY OUTPLAYED,
    PLAYED-OUT
ADELORSST LODESTARS
ADELOSTTU OUTLASTED
ADELPQRUU QUADRUPLE
ADELRSSUY ASSUREDLY
ADEMMORST
    MASTERDOM
ADEMNNORT ADORNMENT
ADEMNOPRS POMANDERS
ADEMNORSU
    MEANDROUS
ADEMNRRSU SNARE
    DRUM
ADEMNSSUU UNASSUMED
ADEMOORRT
    MODERATOR
ADEMOORST
    ASTRODOME, MODERATOS
ADEMORRTT ROTTERDAM
ADENNNSTU SUNTANNED
ADENNOPSS SENNA PODS
ADENNOSST SANDSTONE
ADENNOSTY ASYNDETON
ADENNSSTW NEWSSTAND
ADENOORST TORNADOES
ADENOORTT DETONATOR
ADENOOSTT TOADSTONE
ADENOPRRS PARDONERS
ADENOPRTV DAVENPORT
ADENORRVW
    OVERDRAWN
ADENOTTWY WYANDOTTE
ADENPRSSU UNDERPASS
ADEOORRST TOREADORS
ADEOPRRST PREDATORS,
    TEARDROPS
ADEOPRRTU DEPURATOR

ADEOPRRTW TOP
  DRAWER
ADEOPRRTY PORTRAYED,
  PREDATORY
ADEOPRSTU OUTSPREAD
ADEOPRTTY TETRAPODY
ADEORRSST ROADSTERS
ADEORRSWW
  SWEARWORD
ADEORSSTT ROAD TESTS
ADEORSTTU OUTSTARED
ADEOSTTUY OUTSTAYED
ADEPPPRUW WRAPPED
  UP
ADEPRSSSU SURPASSED
ADERSSTWW
  WESTWARDS
ADFFGINOR AFFORDING
ADFFIIMRS DISAFFIRM
ADFGHIOOT GOOD FAITH
ADFGINORS SANGFROID
ADFGLNORY DRAGONFLY
ADFHINRST FIRSTHAND
ADFHLOORY FOOLHARDY
ADFILLNSW WINDFALLS
ADFILMNOS MANIFOLDS
ADFILRSTY FIRST LADY
ADFIORSUV DISFAVOUR
ADFLLNOSW DOWNFALLS
ADFLLOOST FALDSTOOL
ADFLORRWY FORWARDLY
ADFMOOPST FOOD STAMP
ADFNOORSZ SFORZANDO
ADGGILNRY NIGGARDLY
ADGGINPRU UPGRADING
ADGGLOORV
  VOLGOGRAD
ADGGLRSSU SLUGGARDS
ADGHHILNS HIGHLANDS
ADGHHINRT RIGHT-HAND
ADGHHIORS HIGH ROADS
ADGHIIMNS GANDHIISM
ADGHILLLU GUILDHALL
ADGHILNSY DASHINGLY
ADGHILSTY DAYLIGHTS
ADGHINNNU UNHANDING
ADGHINORS DRAGONISH,
  HOARDINGS
ADGHINOSW SHADOWING
ADGHINRTU INDRAUGHT
ADGHIRRTW RIGHTWARD
ADGHLOPUY PLAY DOUGH

ADGHNOOPR
  ONDOGRAPH
ADGHNOSTU STAGHOUND
ADGIIILNT DIGITALIN
ADGIIILST DIGITALIS
ADGIIJNNO ADJOINING
ADGIIKNNP KIDNAPING
ADGIILMOS DIALOGISM
ADGIILOST DIALOGIST
ADGIIMNRS DISARMING
ADGIIMNSY DISMAYING
ADGIIMNTT ADMITTING
ADGIINNNT INDIGNANT
ADGIINNOR ORDAINING
ADGIINOSS DIAGNOSIS
ADGIINRTY DIGNITARY
ADGIIRTVY GRAVIDITY
ADGIJNSTU ADJUSTING
ADGILLNUY LANGUIDLY
ADGILLOSU GLADIOLUS
ADGILMNSU GUILDSMAN
ADGILMORS MARIGOLDS
ADGILNNOU UNLOADING
ADGILNOSS GLISSANDO
ADGILOORY RADIOLOGY
ADGILOOUY AUDIOLOGY
ADGILOPRS PRODIGALS
ADGIMMOST DOGMATISM
ADGIMOSTT DOGMATIST
ADGINNOOU IGUANODON
ADGINNOPR PARDONING
ADGINOORS GRANDIOSO
ADGINOPRY PARODYING
ADGINORRS RING ROADS
ADGINPRRX GRAND PRIX
ADGJNRRUY GRAND JURY
ADGMNORSU
  GOURMANDS
ADGMOORRU
  GUARDROOM
ADGNNORSS GRANDSONS
ADGOOPRST GASTROPOD
ADHHIPRSS HARDSHIPS
ADHHNOORU
  HOARHOUND
ADHHNORST SHORTHAND
ADHIILORZ RHIZOIDAL
ADHIIMPSS AMIDSHIPS
ADHIIOPSU APHIDIOUS
ADHIIOPTY IDIOPATHY
ADHIIPSSY DIAPHYSIS
ADHIKMNNU HUMANKIND
ADHIKNORW HANDIWORK

ADHILMNPY NYMPHALID
ADHILOPTY TYPHOIDAL
ADHILPSSY LADYSHIPS
ADHIMNOSU HUMANOIDS
ADHIMNOTU ANTHODIUM
ADHIMSTYY DYSTHYMIA
ADHINNOTY HYDANTOIN
ADHINNRTU HIT-AND-RUN
ADHINNSTU HINDUSTAN
ADHINOOST SAINTHOOD
ADHINOPSY DYSPHONIA
ADHINORTY HYDRATION
ADHINRTWW WITHDRAWN
ADHINSTTW WITHSTAND
ADHIOPRSY DYSPHORIA
ADHIPRSSY SHIPYARDS
ADHIRSSTY HYDRASTIS
ADHLLMORT THRALLDOM
ADHLMNOOS
  HANDLOOMS
ADHMNOOOW
  WOMANHOOD
ADHNORRTW
  NORTHWARD
ADHNORSUY ANHYDROUS
ADHNOSSTU THOUSANDS
ADHOOPRRT ARTHROPOD
ADHOORSSW
  ROADSHOWS
ADHORSTUW
  SOUTHWARD
ADHRSSTUY THURSDAYS
ADIIIKNNN INDIAN INK
ADIIINOSZ ISONIAZID
ADIIIQRSU DAIQUIRIS
ADIIKLMMS MILKMAIDS
ADIILLNTU LUNITIDAL
ADIILLNVY INVALIDLY
ADIILMSSS DISMISSAL
ADIILNOPT PLATINOID
ADIILNOTU NAUTILOID
ADIILNSTW TAILWINDS
ADIILOORV VARIOLOID
ADIIMNOSS ADMISSION
ADIIMNOUZ DIAZONIUM
ADIIMRSSY MYDRIASIS
ADIINOOTX OXIDATION
ADIINOQTU QUOTIDIAN
ADIINORTT TRADITION
ADIINOSST SOI-DISANT
ADIINOSTU AUDITIONS
ADIINRSTT DISTRAINT
ADIINRSTU SATURNIID

ADIIPRSTY DISPARITY
ADIISSTUY ASSIDUITY
ADIJNOOVV VOJVODINA
ADIKMNNOW
    WOMANKIND
ADIKNNSST INKSTANDS
ADIKNRSTU KURDISTAN
ADILLMNRS MANDRILLS
ADILLNPSS LANDSLIPS
ADILLNRUY DIURNALLY
ADILLQSUY SQUALIDLY
ADILMMSTU TALMUDISM
ADILMNNOS MANDOLINS
ADILMNOOS SALMONOID
ADILMNOST DALTONISM
ADILMNRUU DURALUMIN
ADILMOPST DIPLOMATS
ADILMOPSY OLYMPIADS,
    SYMPODIAL
ADILMSTTU TALMUDIST
ADILNOORS DOORNAILS
ADILNORTW ANTIWORLD
ADILNSTTY DISTANTLY
ADILOOPRS POLAROIDS
ADILOPRSS SLIP ROADS
ADILOPRSV DISPROVAL
ADILOPRXY PYRIDOXAL
ADILORSTW SWORDTAIL
ADIMNOORT DOMINATOR
ADIMNOSTY STAMINODY
ADINNOOST DONATIONS
ADINNOOSW SNOWDONIA
ADINNORTU INUNDATOR
ADINNOSST DISSONANT
ADINOOPST ADOPTIONS
ADINOORST TANDOORIS
ADINOOSTW SATINWOOD
ADINOPRRS RAINDROPS
ADINORSSU DINOSAURS
ADINPSTTU DISPUTANT
ADIOPRSST PARODISTS
ADIOSSSUU ASSIDUOUS
ADJMMOOOR
    MAJORDOMO
ADJMMORRU DRUM
    MAJOR
ADKLOOPST POLKA DOTS
ADKLOORSW
    WORKLOADS
ADKMNORSW
    MARKDOWNS
ADKMOORRS
    DARKROOMS

ADKNORRTU TRUNK
    ROAD
ADKNORSTT KRONSTADT
ADKOORRSW ROAD
    WORKS
ADLMNORTY MORDANTLY
ADLMOOPRR
    PRODROMAL
ADLMOORTU MODULATOR
ADLNOORSW
    LOANWORDS
ADLNOPRYY POLYANDRY
ADLNORTUU UNDULATOR
ADLOOOSTT TOADSTOOL
ADLOPRSWY SWORDPLAY
ADLORSUUY ARDUOUSLY
ADLORTUWY OUTWARDLY
ADLPQRUUY QUADRUPLY
ADMMNOOPW MOP AND
    MOW
ADMMORRTY
    MARTYRDOM
ADMNNORSU
    ROUNDSMAN
ADMNOORTY
    DYNAMOTOR
ADMNOOSST MASTODONS
ADMNORSST SANDSTORM
ADMNORSSW
    SWORDSMAN
ADMOOPPRU
    POMPADOUR
ADMOORRSW
    WARDROOMS
ADNNORRUU
    RUN-AROUND
ADNNOSSWW
    SWAN'S-DOWN
ADNOOTTUU
    OUT-AND-OUT
ADNOPRRTY PROTANDRY
ADNOPSTTU STAND UP TO
ADNOQRSSU SQUADRONS
ADOOOORRWW
    ARROWWOOD
ADOOPRRST TRAPDOORS
ADOPRSSSW PASSWORDS
ADOPSSSUY SOAPSUDSY
AEEEETTTT TÊTE-À-TÊTE
AEEEFGNRR FREE-RANGE
AEEEFGNRT FREE AGENT
AEEEFHRRT HEREAFTER
AEEEFIRRT FIRE-EATER

AEEEGGGNR GREENGAGE
AEEEGGRST EASTER
    EGG, SEGREGATE
AEEEGHLRW GEARWHEEL
AEEEGHTTX GET THE AXE
AEEEGIMNR MENAGERIE
AEEEGLRRV GEAR LEVER
AEEEGMNNP EMPENNAGE
AEEEGMNRT AGREEMENT
AEEEGNRSS EAGERNESS
AEEEGNRST TEENAGERS
AEEEGRTTZ GAZETTEER
AEEEHHSTV THE HEAVES
AEEEHKNRR HEARKENER
AEEEHLMPR EPHEMERAL
AEEEHLSSY EYELASHES
AEEEHMRTX HEXAMETER
AEEEHRRRS REHEARSER
AEEEHRRTW WEATHERER
AEEEHSSTT AESTHETES
AEEEILNNS ANNELIESE
AEEEILRTT ELATERITE
AEEEIMNRX RE-EXAMINE
AEEEIPPRT PAPETERIE
AEEEIRRTT REITERATE
AEEEJNNTT JEANNETTE
AEEEKKPSS KEEPSAKES
AEEEKLTTT TEAKETTLE
AEEEKMRRT MARKETEER
AEEEKRSWX WEAKER
    SEX
AEEELLMNR ENAMELLER
AEEELLMNT ELEMENTAL
AEEELNPRT PLANE TREE
AEEELNUVZ VENEZUELA
AEEELPSSY YES PLEASE
AEEEMNNRT NEMERTEAN
AEEEMNRTU ENUMERATE
AEEEMORRT AEROMETER
AEEEMPRTT TEMPERATE
AEEEMRRTT ETRAMETER
AEEEMRTVW WAVEMETER
AEEEMSTTW SWEETMEAT
AEEENNPRT PERENNATE
AEEENOPRW WEAPONEER
AEEENORTX EXONERATE
AEEENPRTT PENETRATE
AEEENPSTT PATENTEES
AEEENRRST EASTERNER
AEEENRRTW TREENWARE
AEEENTTUV EVENTUATE
AEEENTTUX EXTENUATE

AEEEPRRST REPARTEES, REPEATERS
AEEEPSSTW SWEET PEAS
AEEFFILRT AFTERLIFE
AEEFGILPR PILFERAGE
AEEFGINPY FEE-PAYING
AEEFGINRS FAR-SEEING
AEEFGLLOT FLAGEOLET
AEEFGLORW FLOWERAGE
AEEFGLSSU FUSELAGES
AEEFGORST FOSTERAGE
AEEFHIKPT KEEP FAITH
AEEFHLRTT HEARTFELT
AEEFHOSSU SAFE HOUSE
AEEFIKLLM FLAMELIKE
AEEFILLMN EN FAMILLE
AEEFILMPR RELIEF MAP
AEEFILNRT INTERLEAF
AEEFILNSS LEAFINESS
AEEFILOTX EXFOLIATE
AEEFILRSV LIFE-SAVER
AEEFINRRR REFRAINER
AEEFIRRTW FIREWATER
AEEFLLOOS LOOSE-LEAF
AEEFLLRSW FAREWELLS
AEEFLLSVY FLYLEAVES
AEEFLMNRT FREMANTLE
AEEFLNORW ON WELFARE
AEEFLNRST FENESTRAL
AEEFLNRTT FLATTENER
AEEFLNSSS FALSENESS
AEEFLOOTV FOVEOLATE
AEEFLRRRS REFERRALS
AEEFLRRTT FLATTERER
AEEFMNORS FORENAMES, FREEMASON
AEEFMPTTT TEMPT FATE
AEEFNRSST FASTENERS
AEEFNSTTY SAFETY NET
AEEFOPRRT PERFORATE
AEEFORSTT FORETASTE
AEEGGILNR GINGER ALE
AEEGGINRR GREGARINE
AEEGGIRUW WIRE-GAUGE
AEEGGLNOY GENEALOGY
AEEGGMORT MORTGAGEE
AEEGGNRSU GREASE GUN
AEEGGRRST STAGGERER
AEEGGRRSW SWAGGERER
AEEGHIMRT HERMITAGE
AEEGHLPRT TELEGRAPH

AEEGHMNOP MEGAPHONE
AEEGHMNOT ON THE GAME
AEEGHMRTW WHEAT GERM
AEEGHMRTZ MEGAHERTZ
AEEGHOSTU GATEHOUSE
AEEGIKNNW WEAKENING
AEEGILLRS ALLERGIES, GALLERIES
AEEGILLRT TREILLAGE
AEEGILLST LEGISLATE
AEEGILMNN ENAMELING
AEEGILNNT EGLANTINE, INELEGANT
AEEGILNNV LEAVENING
AEEGILNPR REPEALING
AEEGILNQU ANGELIQUE
AEEGILNRS RELEASING
AEEGILNRV REVEALING
AEEGILNST ANGLESITE
AEEGILNSW WEASELING
AEEGILNTV ELEVATING
AEEGILPTT TITLE PAGE
AEEGILRTU GAULEITER
AEEGILUVY IVY LEAGUE
AEEGIMNNV GIVEN NAME
AEEGIMNRS GERMANISE
AEEGIMNRT GERMANITE, GERMINATE
AEEGIMNRZ GERMANIZE
AEEGIMNST MAGNESITE, MAGNETISE
AEEGIMNTT MAGNETITE
AEEGIMNTZ MAGNETIZE
AEEGIMOST ISOGAMETE
AEEGIMPTT PEGMATITE
AEEGINNRT ARGENTINE, TANGERINE
AEEGINOPS ESPIONAGE
AEEGINOTT NEGOTIATE
AEEGINPRT REPEATING
AEEGINPRV GRAPEVINE
AEEGINRTT ARGENTITE, INTEGRATE
AEEGINSSW SEESAWING
AEEGINSTV NEGATIVES
AEEGIORTV GIVE EAR TO
AEEGIRSST GREASIEST
AEEGLLNOR ORGANELLE
AEEGLLNRY GENERALLY
AEEGLLNTY ELEGANTLY

AEEGLMNNT GENTLEMAN
AEEGLMNST SEGMENTAL
AEEGLMORT ALGOMETER, GLOMERATE
AEEGLMRRW LEG-WARMER
AEEGLMRST TELEGRAMS
AEEGLNNRT ENTANGLER
AEEGLNRSS LARGENESS
AEEGLORST ALTER EGOS
AEEGLORVZ OVERGLAZE
AEEGMNRRS MERGANSER
AEEGMOPRS MEGASPORE
AEEGMORST GASOMETER
AEEGNNSTW NEWSAGENT
AEEGNOPRS PERSONAGE
AEEGNORRT GENERATOR
AEEGNORTU ENTOURAGE
AEEGNOTTW WAGONETTE
AEEGNOTXY OXYGENATE
AEEGNPRSS PASSENGER
AEEGNRRST ESTRANGER
AEEGNRRSV ENGRAVERS
AEEGNRSST GREATNESS, SERGEANTS
AEEGNRSSV GRAVENESS
AEEGNSSUV VAGUENESS
AEEGOPPST ESTOPPAGE
AEEGOPRRT PORTERAGE, REPORTAGE
AEEGPRTUX EXPURGATE
AEEGRSTTY GREY-STATE
AEEHHIKLT HEATHLIKE
AEEHHILRT HEALTHIER
AEEHHIMST HASHEMITE
AEEHHITTW WHITE HEAT
AEEHHLMTT AT THE HELM
AEEHHLOSW HAWSEHOLE
AEEHHNNPT NAPHTHENE
AEEHHNPTY HYPHENATE
AEEHHNSTU UNSHEATHE
AEEHIKNRT KATHERINE
AEEHILLNN HELLENIAN
AEEHILMNW MEANWHILE
AEEHILNSS SINHALESE
AEEHILNTV HELVETIAN
AEEHILPRS SHAPELIER
AEEHILRRT EARTHLIER
AEEHILRTW WEALTHIER
AEEHIMNST MAINSHEET
AEEHIMPSS EMPHASISE
AEEHIMPST EMPATHISE
AEEHIMPSZ EMPHASIZE

AEEHIMPTZ EMPATHIZE	AEEHMNNOP	AEEILLPTT PAILLETTE
AEEHIMRST HETAERISM	PHENOMENA	AEEILLSTT SATELLITE
AEEHIMTTW WHITE MEAT	AEEHMNOTT MOTH-EATEN	AEEILLTVW WAVELLITE
AEEHINNPZ PHENAZINE	AEEHMOPRS SEMAPHORE	AEEILLTVX VEXILLATE
AEEHINPRS HESPERIAN	AEEHMORST HEARTSOME	AEEILMNNT LINEAMENT
AEEHINPST STEPHANIE	AEEHMPRST PETERSHAM	AEEILMNRY MINELAYER
AEEHINRSV HAVERSINE	AEEHNNOTW ON THE	AEEILMNSS MESSALINE
AEEHINRTT HENRIETTA	WANE	AEEILMORT MELIORATE
AEEHINRTU EUTHERIAN	AEEHNOOPR AEROPHONE	AEEILMPST TIME-LAPSE
AEEHINSSV HEAVINESS	AEEHNOPRS EARPHONES	AEEILMRST SALIMETER
AEEHIPPSW HAWSEPIPE	AEEHNOPTX TOXAPHENE	AEEILMRTT ALTIMETER
AEEHIPRSS APHERESIS,	AEEHNPRRS SHARPENER	AEEILMRTU ELATERIUM
PHARISEES	AEEHNRRSS HARNESSER	AEEILMRTW LIMEWATER
AEEHIPRST THERAPIES	AEEHNRSSS HARNESSES	AEEILMTUV EMULATIVE
AEEHIRRST EARTHRISE	AEEHORSSS SEAHORSES	AEEILNNPP PENEPLAIN
AEEHIRRTT HARRIETTE	AEEHORSUW	AEEILNNPR PERENNIAL
AEEHIRSTT EARTHIEST,	WAREHOUSE	AEEILNNSX SEXENNIAL
HEARTIEST, HESITATER,	AEEHOSSTU TEAHOUSES	AEEILNNTV LEVANTINE,
HETAERIST	AEEHPRSTU EUPHRATES,	VALENTINE
AEEHKLPSW SHEEPWALK	SUPERHEAT	AEEILNOTV ELEVATION
AEEHKMMOR	AEEHRRSTT SHATTERER,	AEEILNPPP PINEAPPLE
HOMEMAKER	THREE-STAR	AEEILNPRX EXPLAINER
AEEHKMORS SHOEMAKER	AEEHRRSTV HARVESTER	AEEILNPST PALESTINE,
AEEHKMPRT THEME PARK	AEEHRSTUX EXHAUSTER	PENALTIES
AEEHKMRTT THE MARKET	AEEIILLOP AEOLIPILE	AEEILNPSX EXPANSILE
AEEHLLMOW	AEEIILMNT ELIMINATE	AEEILNRSS EARLINESS
WHOLEMEAL	AEEIILRSS SERIALISE	AEEILNRSV VERNALISE
AEEHLLNOW	AEEIILRST ISRAELITE,	AEEILNRTW WATERLINE
HALLOWE'EN	REALITIES	AEEILNRVZ VERNALIZE
AEEHLLOSW WHOLESALE	AEEIILRSZ SERIALIZE	AEEILNSST ESSENTIAL
AEEHLLSSS SEASHELLS	AEEIIMNST AMENITIES	AEEILNTTV VENTILATE
AEEHLMMNT EMMENTHAL	AEEIINNTV VIENTIANE	AEEILOPTT PETIOLATE
AEEHLMPST HELPMATES	AEEIINRTT ITINERATE	AEEILORRT ARTERIOLE
AEEHLMRSY HAMERSLEY	AEEIINSTV NAIVETIES	AEEILPPPS APPLE PIES
AEEHLMSSS SHAMELESS	AEEIINSTX ANXIETIES	AEEILPRRV PREVAILER
AEEHLMTTY METHYLATE	AEEIIRSTV VARIETIES	AEEILPRST PEARLIEST
AEEHLNOPS ANOPHELES	AEEIIRTTV ITERATIVE	AEEILQRSU EQUALISER
AEEHLNOPT PHENOLATE	AEEIJMNSS JESSAMINE	AEEILQRUZ EQUALIZER
AEEHLNOSW HALESOWEN	AEEIJMSST MAJESTIES	AEEILRRST RETAILERS
AEEHLNPST ELEPHANTS	AEEIKLLPT PETAL-LIKE	AEEILRRTT AIRLETTER
AEEHLNSSV HAVENLESS	AEEIKLMUW MILWAUKEE	AEEILRRTV RETRIEVAL
AEEHLOPST TELOPHASE	AEEIKLNSS LEAKINESS	AEEILRSTV RELATIVES,
AEEHLORST TREHALOSE	AEEIKMNSY YANKEEISM	VERSATILE
AEEHLORTW WATERHOLE	AEEIKNRSV KNAVERIES	AEEILRTTU ELUTRIATE
AEEHLOSSU ALEHOUSES	AEEIKNSST SNEAKIEST	AEEILSSTZ SLEAZIEST
AEEHLPSSS SHAPELESS	AEEIKQRSU SQUEAKIER	AEEILSVVY EVASIVELY
AEEHLPTTY TELEPATHY	AEEIKRRST STREAKIER	AEEIMMNST MEANTIMES
AEEHLRSST HEARTLESS	AEEILLMNT METALLINE	AEEIMNNZZ MEZZANINE
AEEHLSTXY HEXASTYLE	AEEILLMRS MARSEILLE	AEEIMNRSX EXAMINERS
AEEHMMORT	AEEILLMST METALLISE	AEEIMNRTT TERMINATE
HAMMERTOE	AEEILLMTZ METALLIZE	AEEIMNSSS SEAMINESS
AEEHMMPSY EMPHYSEMA	AEEILLNOT LINEOLATE,	AEEIMNSST AMNESTIES,
	LINOLEATE	MEATINESS

AEEIMNSTT ESTAMINET	AEEIRSSTU ESTUARIES	AEELPPRTU PERPETUAL
AEEIMORRS ROSEMARIE	AEEIRSSTV ASSERTIVE	AEELPRRST PLASTERER
AEEIMORSW WEARISOME	AEEISSTTW SWEATIEST	AEELPRRTU PRELATURE
AEEIMPRRT PRIME RATE	AEEJLMRSU JERUSALEM	AEELPRSSU PLEASURES
AEEIMPRTT IMPETRATE	AEEJMORTT MAJORETTE	AEELPRSTT SALTPETRE
AEEIMRSTT TASIMETER	AEEJMRSTT JET STREAM	AEELQRSSU SQUEALERS
AEEIMRSTV TIMESAVER	AEEKKOPRT KAPOK TREE	AEELRRSSV REVERSALS
AEEIMRTTX TAXIMETER	AEEKLLPSW SLEEPWALK	AEELRRSTU SERRULATE
AEEIMSSTT ESTIMATES,	AEEKLSTTW SWEET TALK	AEELRSSTW WATERLESS
STEAMIEST	AEEKMMRRY MAKE	AEELRSTUY AUSTERELY
AEEINNNPS APENNINES	MERRY	AEELRSTVY SEVERALTY
AEEINNRST IN EARNEST,	AEEKMRRST MARKETERS	AEELSSSTT STATELESS,
TANNERIES	AEEKMRSTY MASTER KEY	TASTELESS
AEEINNRTT ENTERTAIN	AEEKNORTV OVERTAKEN	AEEMMNORT
AEEINNRTV INNERVATE	AEEKORSTV TAKEOVERS	MANOMETER
AEEINNSST INSENSATE	AEEKQRSSU SQUEAKERS	AEEMMNSTU
AEEINNSSV NAIVENESS	AEEKRRSST STREAKERS	AMUSEMENT
AEEINOPPT APPOINTEE	AEELLLSTT TELLTALES	AEEMMORTT ATMOMETER
AEEINOPRT PERITONEA	AEELLMNTW	AEEMMPRUY
AEEINORTT ORIENTATE	WELL-MEANT	EMPYREUMA
AEEINPPST PEPSINATE	AEELLNPPZ APPENZELL	AEEMMRRST STAMMERER
AEEINPRSS PASSERINE	AEELLNPTX EXPELLANT	AEEMNNORT NANOMETER
AEEINPRST SPARTEINE	AEELLNRTY ENTERALLY,	AEEMNNOTT ATONEMENT
AEEINPSVX EXPANSIVE	ETERNALLY	AEEMNNPRT PERMANENT
AEEINRRST RETAINERS	AEELLOPST SELLOTAPE	AEEMNOPRT TREPONEMA
AEEINRRTT REITERANT	AEELLOSUV LAEVULOSE	AEEMNOPSU MENOPAUSE
AEEINRRTV VERATRINE	AEELLPSTT PLATELETS	AEEMNOPYZ APOENZYME
AEEINRSSW WEARINESS	AEELLRRTV TRAVELLER	AEEMNORTW
AEEINRSTT REINSTATE	AEELLRSVY SEVERALLY	WORM-EATEN
AEEINRSTU ESTUARINE	AEELLRTTU TELLURATE	AEEMNORUV
AEEINRSTV INVERTASE	AEELLSSUV VALUELESS	MANOEUVRE
AEEINRSTY EYESTRAIN	AEELLSSVV VALVELESS	AEEMNPRTY REPAYMENT
AEEINSSTU UNEASIEST	AEELMMRRT TRAMMELER	AEEMNPSTV PAVEMENTS
AEEINSTTT ENSTATITE,	AEELMMTXY METAXYLEM	AEEMNRSST MARE'S
INTESTATE	AEELMORST ELASTOMER	NEST, STEERSMAN
AEEINSTTU AUSTENITE	AEELMPRXY EXEMPLARY	AEEMNRSUV MANEUVERS
AEEINTTTV ATTENTIVE,	AEELMPSTT TEMPLATES	AEEMNRTTT TREATMENT
TENTATIVE	AEELMRSST SEMESTRAL	AEEMNSSTT MEANS TEST,
AEEIOPRTV EVAPORITE,	AEELMRTTW MELTWATER	STATESMEN
OPERATIVE	AEELNNNTU ANTENNULE	AEEMNSSTY MATEYNESS
AEEIPPRST APPETISER	AEELNOPST ANTELOPES	AEEMNSTTT STATEMENT,
AEEIPPRSU PAUPERISE	AEELNPRTV PREVALENT	TESTAMENT
AEEIPPRTW WATER PIPE	AEELNRSST ALERTNESS	AEEMOPRRT PERMEATOR
AEEIPPRTZ APPETIZER	AEELNRSTX EXTERNALS	AEEMOPSSU MESOPAUSE
AEEIPPRUZ PAUPERIZE	AEELNRSTY EARNESTLY	AEEMORRTT ROTAMETER
AEEIPPSTT APPETITES	AEELNRTTV TERVALENT	AEEMORRTY AEROMETRY
AEEIPRRTV PRIVATEER	AEELNSSST STALENESS	AEEMPRRTU PREMATURE
AEEIPRSSS PESSARIES	AEELNSSWY WESLEYANS	AEEMPRTTT ATTEMPTER
AEEIPRSSV ASPERSIVE	AEELORRTV REVELATOR	AEEMPSSTW SWAP MEETS
AEEIPRSVV PERVASIVE	AEELORSTV ELEVATORS	AEEMRRSST STREAMERS
AEEIPRTTX EXTIRPATE	AEELORTVW WATER VOLE	AEEMRRSTT SMATTERER
AEEIQSSTU QUEASIEST	AEELOSTTW TEA TOWELS	AEEMRSSTT SMEAR TEST,
AEEIRSSTT TREATISES	AEELPPRRU PUERPERAL	TEAMSTERS

AEEMRSSTY EASY TERMS
AEEMRTTTW WATTMETER
AEENNPRTT PENETRANT,
   REPENTANT
AEENNRRTT RE-ENTRANT
AEENOPPRT NOTEPAPER
AEENOPRST ESPERANTO,
   PERSONATE
AEENOPTTT POTENTATE
AEENOQRSU SQUARE ONE
AEENORRTV ENERVATOR,
   VENERATOR
AEENORSTW STONEWARE
AEENPPRRT ENTRAPPER
AEENPPRSW NEWSPAPER
AEENPRRTU ENRAPTURE
AEENPRSSS SPARENESS
AEENPRSTT AT PRESENT
AEENPRSTY SEPTENARY
AEENRRSTU SAUNTERER
AEENRSSTU SAUTERNES
AEENSSSUV SUAVENESS
AEEOOPRTZ AZEOTROPE
AEEOPPRSU PEA SOUPER
AEEOPRSSW SEA POWERS
AEEOPRSTT OPERETTAS,
   POETASTER
AEEOQRRTU QUERETARO
AEEORRSTW ROSEWATER
AEEORSTTV OVERSTATE
AEEORSTTW TWO-SEATER
AEEPRRRST PARTERRES
AEEPRRSTU APERTURES
AEEPRRSTY SPARE TYRE
AEEQRSSTU SETSQUARE
AEEQRTUUX EXEQUATUR
AEERRRSSU REASSURER
AEERRRSTU TREASURER
AEERRRSTV TRAVERSER
AEERRSSTU TREASURES
AEERRSSTV TRAVERSES
AEERRTTVX EXTRAVERT
AEESTTTTU STATUETTE
AEFFFLTUW LUFTWAFFE
AEFFGRSSU SUFFRAGES
AEFFHMOPT OFF THE MAP
AEFFIILRS FALSIFIER
AEFFIKPST PIKESTAFF
AEFFILLUV EFFLUVIAL
AEFFINORS RAFFINOSE
AEFFIRTUX AFFIXTURE
AEFFKMNOU MAKE FUN
   OF

AEFFLLRUY FEARFULLY
AEFFLLTUY FATEFULLY
AEFFLORSW SAFFLOWER
AEFFMORST OFF STREAM
AEFGHILNS ANGELFISH
AEFGHILST SAFELIGHT
AEFGHILTW WHITE FLAG
AEFGHINRT FATHERING
AEFGHORRT FORGATHER
AEFGIIMNR MAGNIFIER
AEFGIINNR FINE-GRAIN
AEFGIIRRT GRATIFIER
AEFGILMOR GALEIFORM
AEFGILNRT FALTERING,
   REFLATING
AEFGILRUY LAY FIGURE
AEFGINNST FASTENING
AEFGINNTT FATTENING
AEFGINRTU FEATURING
AEFGIORSS OSSIFRAGE
AEFGIRSTT GAS FITTER
AEFGLLLMU FLAGELLUM
AEFGLLOPS FLAGPOLES
AEFGLNOST FLAGSTONE
AEFGLORTW AFTERGLOW
AEFGMNRST FRAGMENTS
AEFGNOPRT FRONT-PAGE
AEFGNORST FRONTAGES
AEFHHISST SHEATFISH
AEFHHLLTU HEALTHFUL
AEFHHLOTW HEATHFOWL
AEFHIKMST MAKESHIFT
AEFHILLSV HALF-LIVES
AEFHILPST FISHPLATE
AEFHILSST FAITHLESS,
   FLASHIEST
AEFHIMNRS FISHERMAN
AEFHINORS FASHIONER
AEFHINRTW WAFER-THIN
AEFHKNORS FORESHANK
AEFHLLSVY FLY HALVES
AEFHLLTUY HATEFULLY
AEFHLNNPY HALFPENNY
AEFHLNOST HALF NOTES,
   HALFTONES
AEFHLORSV FLASHOVER
AEFHMORSU FARMHOUSE
AEFHORRTU OUR FATHER
AEFIIKLRY FAIRY-LIKE
AEFIILLNS NAIL FILES
AEFIILMNS SEMIFINAL
AEFIILMPR AMPLIFIER
AEFIILNNT INFANTILE

AEFIILQRU QUALIFIER
AEFIILRST FRAILTIES
AEFIILSST FALSITIES
AEFIINRSS FRIESIANS
AEFIINRTU INFURIATE
AEFIIPRST APERITIFS
AEFIIRSST SATISFIER
AEFIISTVX FIXATIVES
AEFIKLNSS FLAKINESS
AEFILLNOX FLEXIONAL
AEFILLOOT FOLIOLATE
AEFILMMNY FAMILY MEN
AEFILMNST FILAMENTS
AEFILMNTU FULMINATE
AEFILMORS FORMALISE
AEFILMORZ FORMALIZE
AEFILNNUZ INFLUENZA
AEFILNORT REFLATION
AEFILNPSS LIFESPANS
AEFILORRT ROTIFERAL
AEFILSSTV FESTIVALS
AEFILSTTU FAULTIEST
AEFIMMNRT FIRMAMENT
AEFIMNOSS FOAMINESS
AEFIMNOST MANIFESTO
AEFIMNRST FIRST NAME
AEFIMNSST MANIFESTS
AEFIMORTV FORMATIVE
AEFINNSST FAINTNESS
AEFINOOTT FOETATION
AEFINOPRR PORIFERAN
AEFINOPRS PINAFORES
AEFINORSS SANFORISE
AEFINORSU NEFARIOUS
AEFINORSZ SANFORIZE
AEFINPSTY SAFETY PIN
AEFINRSSS SANS SERIF
AEFINRSTU UNFAIREST
AEFINSSTT FATTINESS
AEFIORTUV FAVOURITE
AEFIPRRST FIRETRAPS
AEFIRRSTT FIRST-RATE
AEFKLLOST FOLKTALES
AEFKLLUWY WAKEFULLY
AEFKLNOSW SNOWFLAKE
AEFKMORRW
   FRAMEWORK
AEFKNNRSS FRANKNESS
AEFKNOPTU POKE FUN AT
AEFLLNTTU FLATULENT
AEFLLORST FORESTALL
AEFLLRTUY TEARFULLY
AEFLLSSTU FAULTLESS

AEFLMORTU FORMULATE
AEFLMORWY
  MAYFLOWER
AEFLMRSTU MASTERFUL
AEFLNOOSS ALOOFNESS
AEFLNOPRY PROFANELY
AEFLNSSUW AWFULNESS
AEFLOOPTT FOOTPLATE
AEFLORRUV FLAVOURER
AEFLORTWW WATERFOWL
AEFLPRRUY PRAYERFUL
AEFMNOORW
  FOREWOMAN
AEFNNOORT AFTERNOON
AEFNORSST SEAFRONTS
AEFNORTTU FORTUNATE
AEFNRRSST TRANSFERS
AEFNRRSTU TRANSFUER
AEFNRSSTU TRANSFUSE
AEFOOPRRW
  WEARPROOF
AEFOPRRTY PREFATORY
AEFRRSTTU FRUSTRATE
AEGGGIRWW
  WIGWAGGER
AEGGGIRZZ ZIGZAGGER
AEGGHINRT GATHERING
AEGGHIRTZ GIGAHERTZ
AEGGHISST SHAGGIEST
AEGGHOPRR ERGOGRAPH
AEGGHOPRY GEOGRAPHY
AEGGIINNR REGAINING
AEGGIINPU GUINEA PIG
AEGGILNNR ENLARGING
AEGGILNNS GLEANINGS
AEGGILNRV GRAVELING
AEGGINNRR GARNERING
AEGGINNRV ENGRAVING
AEGGINORR GREGORIAN
AEGGINOSY EASYGOING
AEGGINPRS PRESAGING
AEGGINPRT PARGETING
AEGGINRTT TARGETING
AEGGIOPRS ARPEGGIOS
AEGGLNNOR
  LONG-RANGE
AEGGLNPST EGGPLANTS
AEGGLNRRY GLENGARRY
AEGGLORSY GARGOYLES
AEGGLRRST STRAGGLER
AEGGMORST MORTGAGES
AEGGNNRTU TRENGGANU
AEGGNOSUY SYNAGOGUE

AEGGNPRSS PRESSGANG
AEGGNRSST GANGSTERS
AEGGOPRSU AGE
  GROUPS
AEGGORRSS AGGRESSOR
AEGHHINRS REHASHING
AEGHHINST SHEATHING
AEGHHIRTU HAUGHTIER
AEGHHIRTW HIGH WATER
AEGHHRRTU HEARTHRUG
AEGHIILNS GHISLAINE
AEGHIKNNR HANKERING,
  HARKENING
AEGHIKNRS SHRINKAGE
AEGHILLNY HEALINGLY
AEGHILMST MEGALITHS
AEGHILNRS SHEARLING
AEGHILNRT EARTHLING,
  LATHERING
AEGHILRST GHASTLIER
AEGHILRSV GRAVELISH
AEGHILRTY LIGHT YEAR
AEGHIMMNR HAMMERING
AEGHIMNPR HAMPERING
AEGHIMNRT NIGHTMARE
AEGHIMNWY HEMINGWAY
AEGHIMORR HIEROGRAM
AEGHIMPPR EPIPHRAGM
AEGHINNPP HAPPENING
AEGHINNRT NEAR THING
AEGHINNST HASTENING
AEGHINOPS SIPHONAGE
AEGHINRRS GARNISHER
AEGHINRSS GARNISHES
AEGHINRTU NAUGHTIER
AEGHINRTW NIGHTWEAR,
  WREATHING
AEGHIORWY GO HAYWIRE
AEGHIPPRY EPIGRAPHY
AEGHIPRRS SERIGRAPH
AEGHIPSTT SPAGHETTI
AEGHLOOPR OLEOGRAPH
AEGHLORTT LARGHETTO
AEGHLRSTU SLAUGHTER
AEGHMNOPR
  NEPHOGRAM
AEGHNNORS
  HANGERS-ON
AEGHNOORR
  GONORRHEA
AEGHNOPST HEPTAGONS
AEGHNORSV
  HANGOVERS, OVERHANGS

AEGHOPRST GRAPESHOT
AEGHOPSSU ESOPHAGUS
AEGHORSST SHORTAGES
AEGIILLRS GRISAILLE
AEGIILLRT ARGILLITE
AEGIILMSV VIGESIMAL
AEGIILNNT ENTAILING
AEGIILNRT RETAILING
AEGIILNRZ REALIZING
AEGIILNSS SIGNALISE
AEGIILNSZ SIGNALIZE
AEGIILNTV GENITIVAL,
  VIGILANTE
AEGIILNTY GENIALITY
AEGIILSTV VESTIGIAL
AEGIIMMRT IMMIGRATE
AEGIIMNNR REMAINING
AEGIIMNNX EXAMINING
AEGIIMNRS MIGRAINES
AEGIINNRT RETAINING
AEGIINORT ORIGINATE
AEGIINOTT GONIATITE
AEGIINPRR REPAIRING
AEGIINPTX EXPIATING
AEGIINRTT GRANITITE
AEGIINSTT INSTIGATE
AEGIJNORS JARGONISE
AEGIJNORZ JARGONIZE
AEGIJNTUU UNIJUGATE
AEGIKKMNR KINGMAKER
AEGIKLNSW WEAKLINGS
AEGIKMNRR REMARKING
AEGIKMNRT MARKETING
AEGIKNQSU SQUEAKING
AEGIKNRST STREAKING
AEGIKNSSW GAWKINESS
AEGILLLLY ILLEGALLY
AEGILLLNU GALLINULE
AEGILLMNT METALLING
AEGILLMRU MALGRE LUI
AEGILLNNP PANELLING
AEGILLNNW GWENLLIAN
AEGILLNOS GOAL LINES
AEGILLNOT NO-TILLAGE
AEGILLNQU EQUALLING
AEGILLNRS SIGNALLER
AEGILLNRV GRANVILLE,
  RAVELLING
AEGILLNTU LINGULATE
AEGILLNTY GENITALLY
AEGILLPPU PUPILLAGE
AEGILLPRS PILLAGERS
AEGILLRRU GUERRILLA

AEGILLRSS SALESGIRL
AEGILLRST ALLERGIST
AEGILLRSV VILLAGERS
AEGILMNNS SIGNALMEN
AEGILMNNT ALIGNMENT,
  LAMENTING
AEGILMNRV MARVELING
AEGILMNST LIGAMENTS
AEGILMNTU EMULATING,
  GLUTAMINE
AEGILMORR RIGMAROLE
AEGILMORS GLAMORISE
AEGILMORZ GLAMORIZE
AEGILNNSV ENSLAVING
AEGILNOPX POLEAXING
AEGILNORU NEUROGLIA
AEGILNORY LEGIONARY
AEGILNOST LEGATIONS
AEGILNPRS RELAPSING
AEGILNPRY PARLEYING,
  REPLAYING
AEGILNQSU SQUEALING
AEGILNRST TRIANGLES
AEGILNRSV SLAVERING
AEGILNRSY SYRINGEAL,
  YEARLINGS
AEGILNRTU GRANULITE
AEGILNRTV TRAVELING
AEGILNRTY TEARINGLY
AEGILNRUV REVALUING
AEGILNRWY WEARINGLY
AEGILNSSW WINEGLASS
AEGILNSTY TEASINGLY
AEGILOOPS APOLOGIES,
  APOLOGISE
AEGILOOPZ APOLOGIZE
AEGILOOTY AETIOLOGY
AEGILORSS SERAGLIOS
AEGILORSU GLAIREOUS
AEGILORTV LEVIGATOR
AEGILPPSS SLIPPAGES
AEGILRRRU IRREGULAR
AEGILRRTW WRIT LARGE
AEGILRSTU LIGATURES
AEGILRSUV VULGARISE
AEGILRTUV VIRGULATE
AEGILRUVZ VULGARIZE
AEGILSSST GLASSIEST
AEGIMMNOT GEMMATION
AEGIMMNRS GERMANISM
AEGIMMNRU GERMANIUM
AEGIMMNRY YAMMERING
AEGIMMNST MAGNETISM

AEGIMMNSU MAGNESIUM
AEGIMNNNU UNMEANING
AEGIMNNOR OMNIRANGE
AEGIMNNRT GERMINANT
AEGIMNNSS MANGINESS
AEGIMNORS ORANGEISM
AEGIMNORT MORGANITE
AEGIMNPPR PAMPERING
AEGIMNPRT TAMPERING
AEGIMNPRV REVAMPING
AEGIMNRST EMIGRANTS,
  MASTERING, STREAMING
AEGIMNRSU GERANIUMS,
  MEASURING
AEGIMNRTT MATTERING
AEGIMQRSU QUAGMIRES
AEGIMRSTY MAGISTERY
AEGINNNRS ENSNARING
AEGINNORS REASONING
AEGINNORW NORWEGIAN
AEGINNORZ ORGANZINE
AEGINNOSS SEASONING
AEGINNOST NEGATIONS
AEGINNOSU GUANOSINE
AEGINNOTT NEGOTIANT
AEGINNPPR PERPIGNAN
AEGINNPRT PARENTING
AEGINNPTT PATENTING
AEGINNRSS RANGINESS
AEGINNRSW ANSWERING
AEGINNRSY YEARNINGS
AEGINNRTT INTEGRANT,
  NATTERING
AEGINNSST ASSENTING
AEGINNSTU UNSEATING
AEGINNTTU TAUTENING
AEGINOPRS SINGAPORE
AEGINOPRT OPERATING
AEGINORRS ORGANISER
AEGINORRV GRANIVORE
AEGINORRZ ORGANIZER
AEGINORVW OVERAWING
AEGINOSTT GESTATION
AEGINPPRR PREPARING
AEGINPPRY PREPAYING
AEGINPRTT PATTERING
AEGINPSTY EGYPTIANS
AEGINQRUV QUAVERING
AEGINRRST ARRESTING
AEGINRRTU GARNITURE
AEGINRSST ASSERTING
AEGINRSTT RESTATING
AEGINRSTU SIGNATURE

AEGINSSSS ASSESSING,
  GASSINESS
AEGINSSST STAGINESS
AEGINSSUZ GAUZINESS
AEGINSTTT ATTESTING
AEGINSTUU AUGUSTINE
AEGIPRTUV PURGATIVE
AEGIRRRST REGISTRAR
AEGIRSSST GRASSIEST
AEGLLNOPW ALPENGLOW
AEGLLNOST GALLSTONE
AEGLLOOOZ ZOOGLOEAL
AEGLLOSTT TOLLGATES
AEGLLRRUY REGULARLY
AEGLMNOOY
  ANEMOLOGY
AEGLMNORW
  ANGLEWORM
AEGLMORTY ALGOMETRY
AEGLNOSTU LANGOUSTE
AEGLNRRST STRANGLER
AEGLNRRSW WRANGLERS
AEGLNRSST STRANGLES
AEGLNRSTY STRANGELY
AEGLNSTTU GAUNTLETS
AEGLOPPRU PROPAGULE
AEGLOPRSY PLAYGOERS
AEGLORRTU REGULATOR
AEGLORTTY TETRALOGY
AEGMMOPRR
  PROGRAMME
AEGMNNORT
  MAGNETRON
AEGMNORRW
  WARMONGER
AEGMNORSU
  GERMANOUS
AEGMNORSV
  MANGROVES
AEGMNORTU
  AUGMENTOR
AEGMNOTTU
  MANGETOUT
AEGMNRSTU ARGUMENTS
AEGMOOSUX
  EXOGAMOUS
AEGMOPRRR
  PROGRAMER
AEGMORRSW WORM
  GEARS
AEGMORSTY GASOMETRY
AEGMPRSSU GRAMPUSES
AEGNNOPST PENTAGONS

AEGNNPRTU REPUGNANT
AEGNNSSTU GAUNTNESS
AEGNORSSX SEX ORGANS
AEGNORSTU ARGENTOUS
AEGNRRSST STRANGERS
AEGNRRSTT STRANGEST
AEGNRSSTU ASSURGENT
AEGOPPSST STOPPAGES
AEGOPSSTT GATEPOSTS
AEGORRRTT GARROTTER
AEGORRSTT GARROTTES
AEGORRSTU SURROGATE
AEGORSTTY GESTATORY
AEGPRRRUY PRAYER RUG
AEHHHITTY HIT THE HAY
AEHHHOOTU
    HU-HO-HAO-T'E
AEHHILLTW WHITEHALL
AEHHILLTY HEALTHILY
AEHHILNPT PHTHALEIN
AEHHILOPT THEOPHILA
AEHHIMPRS HAMPSHIRE
AEHHIORRS HORSEHAIR
AEHHIPPSS SHIPSHAPE
AEHHISTWW WHITEWASH
AEHHLNTUY UNHEALTHY
AEHHLOPTY HALOPHYTE
AEHHMOOPT HOMEOPATH
AEHHNORTW
    HAWTHORNE
AEHHNRSSS HARSHNESS
AEHHOPPST PHOSPHATE
AEHIILMTU HUMILIATE
AEHIILNRS HAIRLINES
AEHIIMNRT HERMITIAN
AEHIIMNST HISTAMINE
AEHIIMRST HETAIRISM
AEHIIMRTY HIMYARITE
AEHIINOPT ETHIOPIAN
AEHIINRSS HAIRINESS
AEHIIPSTT HEPATITIS
AEHIKKLMS MILK SHAKE
AEHIKLMNU HUMAN-LIKE
AEHIKMOTT MAKE IT HOT
AEHIKNOST SHAKE ON IT
AEHIKNSSS SHAKINESS
AEHILLNRT ALLETHRIN
AEHILLNSV NASHVILLE
AEHILLPTY PHILATELY
AEHILLTTY LETHALITY
AEHILLTWW WHITEWALL
AEHILLTWY WEALTHILY
AEHILMNOP PHILOMENA

AEHILNNOT ANTHELION
AEHILNOOZ HELIOZOAN
AEHILNOPR PARHELION
AEHILNOST HAILSTONE
AEHILNPRS PLANISHER
AEHILNQRU HARLEQUIN
AEHILORST HORSETAIL,
    ISOTHERAL
AEHILOSTT HELIOSTAT
AEHILPRSS SPLASHIER
AEHILRSTY HAIRSTYLE
AEHIMNNOT ANTHEMION
AEHIMNORS HARMONIES,
    HARMONISE
AEHIMNORZ HARMONIZE
AEHIMNOST THOMASINE
AEHIMNPSS MISSHAPEN
AEHIMNPST PANTHEISM
AEHIMNRSU HUMANISER
AEHIMNRUZ HUMANIZER
AEHIMPSST SHIPMATES,
    STEAMSHIP
AEHIMQSSU SQUEAMISH
AEHINNRSS IN HARNESS
AEHINNRTU RUTHENIAN
AEHINORSS HOARINESS
AEHINORST HORTENSIA
AEHINORTT ANORTHITE
AEHINPPSS HAPPINESS
AEHINPSSS APISHNESS
AEHINPSST THESPIANS
AEHINPSSY SISYPHEAN
AEHINPSTT PANTHEIST
AEHINRRST TARNISHER
AEHINRRSV VARNISHER
AEHINRRTU ARTHURINE
AEHINRSSV VARNISHES
AEHINSSST HASTINESS
AEHINSSSW WASHINESS
AEHINSTTW WHITE ANTS
AEHIORRTT THROATIER
AEHIORSTU AUTHORISE
AEHIORSTX RHEOTAXIS
AEHIORTTV HORTATIVE
AEHIORTUZ AUTHORIZE
AEHIPPRSS SAPPHIRES
AEHIPRSTT THERAPIST
AEHIQRSSU SQUASHIER
AEHIRRSTW SWARTHIER
AEHIRSSTT TRASHIEST
AEHJLLNOS HALL-JONES
AEHJPRSSW JEW'S HARPS
AEHKLNSST THANKLESS

AEHKLRRSU KARLSRUHE
AEHKORRTW
    EARTHWORK
AEHKOSSTU SHAKEOUTS
AEHLLLNPU ALEPH-NULL
AEHLLNOOP ALLOPHONE
AEHLLORSW SHALLOWER
AEHLLPSSU PHALLUSES
AEHLLPSSY HAPLESSLY
AEHLMOOST LOATHSOME
AEHLMOSSU ALMS-HOUSE
AEHLMPPST PAMPHLETS
AEHLNRTUY UNEARTHLY
AEHLOPPSY POLYPHASE
AEHLOPRSY HORSEPLAY
AEHLOPSTT HOTPLATES
AEHLOPSUY PLAYHOUSE
AEHLORSUV OVERHAULS
AEHLPRRSU SPHERULAR
AEHLPSSTU SULPHATES
AEHMMOORT
    HARMOTOME
AEHMNNRTU
    MANHUNTER
AEHMNNSSU HUMANNESS
AEHMNRRWY
    WHERRYMAN
AEHMOOPRS SHAMPOOER
AEHMOPRST METAPHORS
AEHMORRTW
    EARTHWORM,
    HEARTWORM
AEHMORTWW
    WHEATWORM
AEHMPPSTU HEAT PUMPS
AEHMSSTTY AMETHYSTS
AEHNNOPRT PARTHENON
AEHNNOPST PANTHEONS
AEHNNRSSU UNHARNESS
AEHNOOPRR HARPOONER
AEHNOOPSX SAXOPHONE
AEHNOPPSY PAY PHONES
AEHNOPRTU NEUROPATH
AEHNOPRWY PHONEY
    WAR
AEHNOPSSU SAPHENOUS
AEHNOPSTY PANTY HOSE
AEHNORSTT NORTHEAST
AEHNPRSSS SHARPNESS
AEHNPRSXY PHARYNXES
AEHOOPRRY PYORRHOEA
AEHOOPSTT OSTEOPATH
AEHOOSSTU OAST HOUSE

AEHOPSSTT POSTHASTE
AEHOPSSTU PHASE-OUTS
AEHOPSSTW SWEATSHOP
AEHOPTTUY AUTOPHYTE
AEHORRSSW WARHORSES
AEHORSSTT RHEOSTATS
AEHORSSTU AUTHORESS
AEHORSTTW HOT WATERS
AEHORSTVW SHORT WAVE
AEHORSTWY SEAWORTHY
AEHOSSTTU SOUTHEAST
AEHRSSTUU THESAURUS
AEIIILNRT INITIALER
AEIIILNTW LIE IN WAIT
AEIIIMTTV IMITATIVE
AEIIINNST INANITIES
AEIIINSTT INITIATES
AEIIJLNUV JUVENILIA
AEIIKKTTW KITTIWAKE
AEIIKLLNS SILKALINE
AEIIKLNOT KAOLINITE
AEIIKRSTT KERATITIS
AEIILLMNN MILLENNIA
AEIILLTTT TITILLATE
AEIILMNNS MAIN LINES
AEIILMNNT ELIMINANT
AEIILMNSU ALUMINISE
AEIILMNUZ ALUMINIZE
AEIILMOSV MALVOISIE
AEIILMRSS SERIALISM
AEIILMRTT LITERATIM
AEIILNNOT LINEATION
AEIILNNRT TRIENNIAL
AEIILNOTV INVIOLATE
AEIILNPRT REPTILIAN
AEIILNPST PLATINISE
AEIILNPTV PLAINTIVE
AEIILNPTZ PLATINIZE
AEIILNRRS AIRLINERS
AEIILNRRT TRILINEAR
AEIILNRST LATINISER
AEIILNRTY LINEARITY
AEIILNRTZ LATINIZER
AEIILNSTW WAISTLINE
AEIILNTVY VENIALITY
AEIILORST SOLITAIRE
AEIILORTV VARIOLITE
AEIILOSTV ISOLATIVE
AEIILOTVV VIOLATIVE
AEIILPPST TAIL PIPES
AEIILQSTU QUALITIES
AEIILRRST TRISERIAL
AEIILRRSV RIVALRIES

AEIILRSTU RITUALISE
AEIILRSTV VITALISER
AEIILRTUZ RITUALIZE
AEIILRTVZ VITALIZER
AEIILSSUV VISUALISE
AEIILSUVZ VISUALIZE
AEIIMMRSX MAXIMISER
AEIIMMRXZ MAXIMIZER
AEIIMNNRT NITRAMINE
AEIIMNPST IMPATIENS
AEIIMNPTT IMPATIENT
AEIIMNRTU MINIATURE
AEIIMNSTT INTIMATES
AEIIMPRRS PRIMARIES
AEIIMPSSV IMPASSIVE
AEIINNNTV ANTIVENIN
AEIINNPTT IN-PATIENT
AEIINNRSS RAININESS
AEIINNRSV NIVERNAIS
AEIINNRTT ITINERANT
AEIINNRTU URANINITE
AEIINNSTU ANNUITIES,
    INSINUATE
AEIINOPTX EXPIATION
AEIINORTT ITERATION
AEIINOTTV NOVITIATE
AEIINRRTY ITINERARY
AEIINRTUV URINATIVE
AEIIPRSTV PRIVATISE
AEIIPRTTV PARTITIVE
AEIIPRTVV PRIVATIVE
AEIIPRTVZ PRIVATIZE
AEIIPSSST EPISTASIS
AEIIPSSTX EPISTAXIS
AEIIPSTTT STIPITATE
AEIIRRSST SATIRISER
AEIIRRSTT ARTERITIS
AEIIRRSTV ARRIVISTE
AEIIRRSTZ SATIRIZER
AEIIRSSTV VARSITIES
AEIIRTTTV ATTRITIVE
AEIJKKRVY REYKJAVIK
AEIJMNNSS JANSENISM
AEIJNNSST JANSENIST
AEIJNSTTU JAUNTIEST
AEIKKLLOO LOOK-ALIKE
AEIKKNNSS SNAKESKIN
AEIKLLNRY KILLARNEY
AEIKLMNOW WOMAN-LIKE
AEIKLNNSS LANKINESS
AEIKLNORT OIL TANKER
AEIKLNOVY NIKOLAYEV
AEIKLNPSS SKI PLANES

AEIKLRSTY STREAKILY
AEIKMQRSU QUAKERISM
AEIKNNPRS SPINNAKER
AEIKNNSSS SNAKINESS
AEIKNORTU KETONURIA
AEIKNPSSW PAWKINESS
AEIKNQSSU QUAKINESS
AEIKNSSTW SWANKIEST
AEIKORSST KERATOSIS
AEIKPPQSU PIPSQUEAK
AEIKPRSTY STRIKE PAY
AEIKPSSST PISS-TAKES
AEIKRSSST ASTERISKS
AEILLLRTY LITERALLY
AEILLMMST SMALL-TIME
AEILLMNRY MILLENARY
AEILLMRTW WATERMILL
AEILLMSSY AIMLESSLY
AEILLMSTT METALLIST
AEILLNOPT POLLINATE
AEILLNPRY PLENARILY
AEILLNPST PANELLIST
AEILLNRST INSTALLER,
    REINSTALL
AEILLNRTU TELLURIAN
AEILLOPPT PAPILLOTE,
    POPLITEAL
AEILLOSTY LOYALTIES
AEILLPRSU PLURALISE
AEILLPRUZ PLURALIZE
AEILLPSSS SALES SLIP
AEILLPSST PASTILLES
AEILLPSTU PULSATILE
AEILLQRSU SQUALLIER
AEILLRRTY ARTILLERY
AEILLRSTW STAIRWELL
AEILLRTWY WATER LILY
AEILLRVXY VEXILLARY
AEILMMNPS PELMANISM
AEILMMNST MENTALISM
AEILMMORS MEMORIALS
AEILMNNOT MELATONIN
AEILMNNSS MANLINESS
AEILMNOOT EMOTIONAL
AEILMNOPR PROLAMINE
AEILMNORS NORMALISE
AEILMNORT MENTORIAL
AEILMNORZ NORMALIZE
AEILMNOSS LOAMINESS,
    MELANOSIS
AEILMNOTU EMULATION
AEILMNPRT IMPLANTER

AEILMNRST TERMINALS,
 TRAMLINES
AEILMNRSU SEMILUNAR
AEILMNRVY LIVERYMAN
AEILMNSST MALTINESS
AEILMNTTY MENTALITY
AEILMORRS MORALISER
AEILMORRZ MORALIZER
AEILMOSTU MOUSETAIL
AEILMPRST PRELATISM
AEILMRSTY SALIMETRY
AEILMRTTY ALTIMETRY
AEILMSSVY MASSIVELY
AEILMSTTU STIMULATE
AEILMSTUU MUTUALISE
AEILMTUUZ MUTUALIZE
AEILNNOPR NONPAREIL
AEILNNOST TENSIONAL
AEILNNOSV SLOVENIAN
AEILNNOSY LYONNAISE
AEILNNPSS PLAINNESS
AEILNNPSU PENINSULA
AEILNNTUV UNIVALENT
AEILNOOPS POLONAISE
AEILNOORS EROSIONAL
AEILNOPPR PIPERONAL
AEILNOPST SEAL-POINT
AEILNOPSY POLYNESIA
AEILNOPTT PELTATION,
 POTENTIAL
AEILNORST ORIENTALS,
 RELATIONS, SEROTINAL,
 TENSORIAL
AEILNORSV VERSIONAL
AEILNORTT NATROLITE
AEILNOSSS SESSIONAL
AEILNPRTY INTERPLAY,
 PAINTERLY, PARTY LINE
AEILNPSTY SAPIENTLY
AEILNPTTY PATIENTLY
AEILNPTUV PULVINATE
AEILNRSTT STERILANT
AEILNRSTV INTERVALS
AEILNRSUV UNIVERSAL
AEILNRTTV TRIVALENT
AEILNRTUV AVIRULENT
AEILNRTUY UNREALITY
AEILNSSST SALTINESS,
 SLATINESS, STAINLESS
AEILNSSTW SLANTWISE
AEILNSTVY SYLVANITE
AEILNSUUX UNISEXUAL
AEILOPRRS POLARISER

AEILOPRRZ POLARIZER
AEILOPRST SAPROLITE
AEILORSTT TOTALISER
AEILORSTY ROYALTIES
AEILORTTV LEVITATOR
AEILORTTZ TOTALIZER
AEILPPRTU PREPUTIAL
AEILPPSST SPLIT PEAS
AEILPPSUV APPULSIVE
AEILPRRSS REPRISALS
AEILPRSST PILASTERS
AEILPRSTT PALTRIEST,
 PRELATIST
AEILPRTVY PRIVATELY
AEILPSSVY PASSIVELY
AEILPSTTU STIPULATE
AEILPSTUV PULSATIVE
AEILQRRUY RELIQUARY
AEILRSSTY LAY SISTER
AEILRTUUX LUXURIATE
AEILSTUXY SEXUALITY
AEIMMNNRS MANNERISM
AEIMMNOPT PANTOMIME
AEIMMRSST SMARMIEST
AEIMMRSSU SUMMARIES,
 SUMMARISE
AEIMMRSUZ SUMMARIZE
AEIMNNNQU MANNEQUIN
AEIMNNOPU PNEUMONIA
AEIMNNOST MINNESOTA
AEIMNNRST MANNERIST
AEIMNOPRT PROTAMINE
AEIMNORST STEAM IRON
AEIMNORSW WOMANISER
AEIMNORTV NORMATIVE
AEIMNORWZ WOMANIZER
AEIMNPRST SPEARMINT
AEIMNRSTT MARTINETS
AEIMNRSTU ANTISERUM
AEIMNRTTY MATERNITY
AEIMOPRTX PROXIMATE
AEIMORRSU ARMOURIES
AEIMORSST ATOMISERS
AEIMORSTT ESTIMATOR
AEIMORSTV MOVIE STAR
AEIMORSTZ ATOMIZERS
AEIMORTTU AUTOTIMER
AEIMPPRSU PAUPERISM
AEIMPRSTU SEPTARIUM
AEIMPRTUZ TRAPEZIUM
AEIMQRSSU MARQUISES
AEIMRRRTU TERRARIUM
AEIMRSTTY TASIMETRY

AEINNNOTW NEWTONIAN
AEINNNPTU NEPTUNIAN
AEINNOPSX EXPANSION
AEINNORTV VERNATION
AEINNOSST SENSATION
AEINNOTTT ATTENTION,
 TENTATION
AEINNPPSS NAPPINESS
AEINNPSST INAPTNESS
AEINNRSTT INSTANTER,
 TRANSIENT
AEINNRSTU SATURNINE
AEINNRSTY TYRANNIES,
 TYRANNISE
AEINNRTYZ TYRANNIZE
AEINNSSST NASTINESS
AEINNSSTT NATTINESS
AEINOOPRT OPERATION
AEINOOPSU IONOPAUSE
AEINOPPRT APPOINTER,
 REAPPOINT
AEINOPRSS ASPERSION
AEINOPRST PATRONISE
AEINOPRSY AEPYORNIS
AEINOPRTZ PATRONIZE
AEINOPSSS SOAPINESS
AEINOQRTU INQUORATE,
 ORTANIQUE
AEINOQSTU EQUATIONS
AEINOQTTU TOTAQUINE
AEINORRST SERRATION
AEINORSST ASSERTION,
 SEÑORITAS
AEINORSSU ARSENIOUS
AEINORSSV AVERSIONS
AEINORSTT STATIONER
AEINOSTVX VEXATIONS
AEINPPSSS SAPPINESS
AEINPPSST SNAPPIEST
AEINPRRST TERRAPINS,
 TRANSPIRE
AEINPRTTY PATERNITY
AEINPSSST PASTINESS
AEINPSSSW WASPINESS
AEINRRSST STRAINERS
AEINRRSTT RESTRAINT
AEINRSSTT RATTINESS,
 RESISTANT, TRAIN SETS
AEINRSSTU SUSTAINER
AEINRSSUZ SUZERAINS
AEINRSTTT IN TATTERS
AEINSSSTT TASTINESS
AEINSSTTT TATTINESS

AEINSSTZZ SNAZZIEST
AEIOORRST ORATORIES
AEIOPRRSV VAPORISER
AEIOPRRVZ VAPORIZER
AEIOPRTTV PORTATIVE
AEIOPRTXY EXPIATORY
AEIOPSSTU AUTOPSIES
AEIORTUVV UVAROVITE
AEIOSTUVX VEXATIOUS
AEIPRRTVY VARITYPER
AEIPRSSTU PRUSSIATE
AEIPRSTUZ TRAPEZIUS
AEIQRTTUZ QUARTZITE
AEIRRSSTT STARRIEST
AEIRRTTTU TRITURATE
AEIRSSTTU TESSITURA
AEIRSTTTX TESTATRIX
AEIRSTTUY AUSTERITY
AEISSSSTY ESSAYISTS
AEJLLOSUY JEALOUSLY
AEJMPRTUW WATER JUMP
AEJOPSTUX JUXTAPOSE
AEKKLRRSY SKYLARKER
AEKLMOORT
   TOOL-MAKER
AEKLMORTW
   METALWORK
AEKLORSVW WALKOVERS
AEKLPRRSS SPARKLERS
AEKMNOORR
   MOONRAKER
AEKMNOPSS SPOKESMAN
AEKMNOPTW KEPT
   WOMAN
AEKMOORSY
   KARYOSOME
AEKMPRRSS PRESSMARK
AEKNOORST SNAKEROOT
AEKNOOTTU TAKE OUT
   ON
AEKNPRRST PRANKSTER
AEKNRSSST STARKNESS
AEKNRSTTU TURKESTAN
AEKOPPRRW PAPERWORK
AEKOPRTYY KARYOTYPE
AEKORRWWX
   WAXWORKER
AEKQRSSUW SQUAWKERS
AELLLMOSU MALLEOLUS
AELLLPTUU PULLULATE
AELLLRSTU STELLULAR
AELLLSSWY LAWLESSLY
AELLMNOTT ALLOTMENT

AELLMNSSS SMALLNESS
AELLMOPRY PERMALLOY
AELLMORTY ALLOMETRY
AELLNNOTW ALLENTOWN
AELLNOSTW STONEWALL
AELLNQUUY UNEQUALLY
AELLNRTUY NEUTRALLY
AELLOOPRT ALLOTROPE
AELLOOPRT ALLOTROPE
AELLOPRRT PATROLLER
AELLOPRSY ROLE PLAYS
AELLOPSTX POLL TAXES
AELLOPTUV POLE VAULT
AELLORSWW
   SWALLOWER
AELLOSUYZ ZEALOUSLY
AELLRSSTY ARTLESSLY
AELMMORST MAELSTROM
AELMMOSUU
   MAUSOLEUM
AELMNNNTU ANNULMENT
AELMNNOOP MONOPLANE
AELMNOOPR LAMPOONER
AELMNOORT MONOLATER
AELMNOORY MONOLAYER
AELMNOPRT PATROLMEN
AELMNOPSS PLEONASMS
AELMNOPTU PULMONATE
AELMNORST MESTRANOL
AELMNORWW
   LAWNMOWER
AELMNRSTU MENSTRUAL
AELMNRTTU TREMULANT
AELMOORSS
   SALEROOMS, SALESROOM
AELMOOSTT LOOM-STATE
AELMOPSTT PALMETTOS
AELMOSTTU MULATTOES
AELMRSSTT MALTSTERS
AELNOOSSW LOW
   SEASON
AELNOPRSS PERSONALS
AELNOPRSY LAYPERSON
AELNOPSTY NEOPLASTY
AELNORSTU SOLUTREAN
AELNOTUVV
   VOL-AU-VENT
AELNRRUVY VULNERARY
AELNRSSTT SLATTERNS
AELNRSTTU RESULTANT
AELNSSSUU USUALNESS
AELOOPRTW WATER POLO
AELOORRTT TOLERATOR
AELOPPRSS PROLAPSES

AELOPRSTU SPORULATE
AELOPSSSU ESPOUSALS
AELOPSTTU POSTULATE
AELPPRTUW WUPPERTAL
AELPRRSTT PRATTLERS
AELPRSSST STRAPLESS
AELPSTTUU PUSTULATE
AELQRRTUY QUARTERLY
AEMMNORTY
   MANOMETRY,
   MOMENTARY
AEMMOORST
   ROOMMATES
AEMMORSST MARMOSETS
AEMMORTTY ATMOMETRY
AEMMRSTYY ASYMMETRY
AEMNNOORS ROMAN
   NOSE
AEMNNORST ORNAMENTS
AEMNNORTT REMONTANT
AEMNOOPRT PROTONEMA
AEMNOORST ANTEROOMS
AEMNORRSS RANSOMERS
AEMNORRTU NUMERATOR
AEMNORSTY MONASTERY
AEMNPRTUY PRYTANEUM
AEMNRSSST SMARTNESS
AEMNRSTTU TRANSMUTE
AEMNRSTVY VESTRYMAN
AEMOORSTT STATEROOM
AEMOPRRTY TEMPORARY
AEMOPRSTU MOUSETRAP
AEMOPRSTW
   TAPEWORMS
AEMOPSTTY ASYMPTOTE
AEMORRRSU
   ARMOURERS
AEMQRRTUY MARQUETRY
AENNORRST RESNATRON
AENNPSSTU UNAPTNESS
AENNRSTTU TRANSEUNT
AENOOPSST SOAPSTONE,
   TEASPOONS
AENOORRST RESONATOR
AENOORRTV RENOVATOR
AENOPPRRT EN RAPPORT
AENOPRSST PATRONESS,
   TRANSPOSE
AENOPRSUV SUPERNOVA
AENORRTWW
   WATERWORN
AENORSSTU ANOESTRUS
AENORSTTY ATTORNEYS

AENPRSSTT TRANSEPTS	AFGILLNUY GAINFULLY	AFINNOSTU FOUNTAINS
AENQSSSTU SQUATNESS	AFGILMNOS FLAMINGOS	AFINOOPRR RAINPROOF
AENRSTWYY ENTRYWAYS	AFGILNNTU FLAUNTING	AFINOPRTY PROFANITY
AEOOPRRST OPERATORS	AFGILNNWY FAWNINGLY	AFIORTTTT TIT FOR TAT
AEOOPRTTV VAPORETTO	AFGILRTUY FRUGALITY	AFIOSTTUU FATUITOUS
AEOPRRRTY PORTRAYER	AFGIMORTU FUMIGATOR	AFKLOOSTT FOOTSTALK
AEOPRRSTT PROSTRATE	AFGINNOPR PROFANING	AFLLLPUYY PLAYFULLY
AEOPRRSTW SPEARWORT	AFGINNPRY FRYING PAN	AFLLNORTY FRONTALLY
AEOPRSSSV PASSOVERS	AFGINORRW FARROWING	AFLLNOSSW SNOWFALLS
AEOPRSSTT PROSTATES	AFGINORUV FAVOURING	AFLLOOSTT FOOTSTALL
AEOQRRSSU SQUARROSE	AFGINSTTU FUNGISTAT	AFLMOPRST PLATFORMS
AEORSSSSS ASSESSORS	AFGNNOOSU	AFLMORRUY FORMULARY
AEORSSTTT TESTATORS	SON-OF-A-GUN	AFLOOPSTY SPLAYFOOT
AEORSSTUU TROUSSEAU	AFGNOPRSW FROGSPAWN	AFLOORSUV FLAVOROUS
AEPPRSSUY PAPYRUSES	AFGORSTUW	AFLOPRRSU FLUORSPAR
AEPPRSTUU SUPPURATE	TUGS-OF-WAR	AFLOSTUUY FATUOUSLY
AEPQRRTUY PARQUETRY	AFHHLRTTU HALF-TRUTH	AFMNORRST TRANSFORM
AEPRRSSTU SUPERSTAR	AFHIILNTU HIFALUTIN	AFMOORSTY STYROFOAM
AEQRSSTTU SQUATTERS	AFHIKLOTT OF THAT ILK	AGGHHILSY HAGGISHLY
AEQSSTTTU SQUATTEST	AFHIKLPSS HIP FLASKS	AGGHIILNT ALIGHTING
AERRSSTUU SUSURRATE	AFHIKMSUU FUKUSHIMA	AGGHILOOY HAGIOLOGY
AFFGGINUW GUFFAWING	AFHIORSTY FORSYTHIA	AGGHILSST GASLIGHTS
AFFGIIMNR AFFIRMING	AFHLLMRUY HARMFULLY	AGGHILSWY WAGGISHLY
AFFGILNNS SNAFFLING	AFHLLORST SHORTFALL	AGGIIIMNN IMAGINING
AFFGIORST SGRAFFITO	AFHLMNOOS HALF	AGGIILLNP PILLAGING
AFFHILRSY RAFFISHLY	MOONS	AGGIILMNN MALIGNING
AFFHILSTU FAITHFULS	AFHOOPSTT FOOTPATHS	AGGIILNNS SIGNALING
AFFHIMRSS FISH FARMS	AFHOORRST HOARFROST	AGGIILNNT TINGALING
AFFIILNPT PLAINTIFF	AFIIILNOT FILIATION	AGGIILNVW LAWGIVING
AFFILNRUY RUFFIANLY	AFIILNNOT INFLATION	AGGIIMNRT MIGRATING
AFFLLOOST FOOTFALLS	AFIILNOOT FOLIATION	AGGIIMNST GIGANTISM
AFFLOOTTU FOOT FAULT	AFIILNSST FINALISTS	AGGIINNOZ AGONIZING
AFFMNNRUY FUNNY FARM	AFIILORRT TRIFORIAL	AGGIINNSS ASSIGNING
AFGGGINOT FAGGOTING	AFIIMNRRY INFIRMARY	AGGILLNOP GALLOPING
AFGGIINTU FATIGUING	AFIINOSTX FIXATIONS	AGGILLNRY GLARINGLY
AFGHHILLT HALF-LIGHT	AFIIOORRT A FORTIORI	AGGILNNOS GANGLIONS
AFGHILLNT NIGHTFALL	AFIKLLMOT MILK FLOAT	AGGILNNPS SPANGLING
AFGHILNST FANLIGHTS	AFILLLOST FLOTILLAS	AGGILNNRW WRANGLING
AFGHILPSS FLAGSHIPS	AFILLNOUX FLUXIONAL	AGGILNOOY ANGIOLOGY
AFGHILSTT LIGHT-FAST	AFILLNPUY PAINFULLY	AGGILNPPR GRAPPLING
AFGHIMNOT FATHOMING	AFILLOOPR APRIL FOOL	AGGILNPSY GASPINGLY
AFGHINRST FARTHINGS	AFILMMORS FORMALISM	AGGILNRTY GRATINGLY
AFGHLNSSU FLASHGUNS	AFILMNNTU FULMINANT	AGGIMMNRU
AFGHMOORT	AFILMOPRS SALPIFORM	RUMMAGING
HOMOGRAFT	AFILMORST FORMALIST	AGGIMNPUZ GAZUMPING
AFGIILMNN INFLAMING	AFILMORTY FORMALITY	AGGINNOOR GORGONIAN
AFGIILNNT INFLATING	AFILMRSST FILM STARS	AGGINORRS GROSGRAIN
AFGIILNNU UNFAILING	AFILNOOTT FLOTATION	AGGINORTU OUTRAGING
AFGIILRTY FRAGILITY	AFILNPSST FLAT SPINS	AGGINPSTU UPSTAGING
AFGIIMNRY RAMIFYING	AFILOORSS FOSSORIAL	AGGKNNTUW
AFGIINRTY RATIFYING	AFILSSTTU FLAUTISTS	KWANGTUNG
AFGIKNORS FORSAKING	AFIMNNORT INFORMANT	AGGMOORRT
AFGIKNRST SKIN GRAFT	AFIMNOORT FORMATION	MORTGAGOR

AGGMOSTYY
  MYSTAGOGY
AGGNNOPYY PYONGYANG
AGHHIKNTW NIGHTHAWK
AGHHILTUY HAUGHTILY
AGHHINRST THRASHING
AGHHLOOPR HOLOGRAPH
AGHHMOOPR
  HOMOGRAPH
AGHIILLTT TAILLIGHT
AGHIILNSV LAVISHING
AGHIIMMMN IMMINGHAM
AGHIINNSV VANISHING
AGHIINRSV RAVISHING
AGHIINRTU THURINGIA
AGHIIPRRS HAIRGRIPS
AGHIKNOSU KAOHSIUNG
AGHILLNOW HALLOWING
AGHILLNSY LASHINGLY
AGHILLNTY HALTINGLY
AGHILLORY HOLY GRAIL
AGHILMORT ALGORITHM,
  LOGARITHM
AGHILNOOS HOOLIGANS
AGHILNORT GRANOLITH
AGHILNOTW ALONG WITH
AGHILNPSS SPLASHING
AGHILNPTY PLAYTHING
AGHILNTUY NAUGHTILY
AGHILRSTT STARLIGHT
AGHIMNRST HAMSTRING
AGHIMOPRY AMPHIGORY
AGHIMORST HISTOGRAM
AGHINNOPR ORPHANING
AGHINORRW HARROWING
AGHINPSUW WASHING-UP
AGHINQSSU SQUASHING
AGHINRTTW THWARTING
AGHIRSSTT STRAIGHTS
AGHKMOPRY
  KYMOGRAPH
AGHKOPRRU GORAKHPUR
AGHLLOOPY HAPLOLOGY
AGHLMNOPU
  PLOUGHMAN
AGHLMOOPR
  LAGOMORPH
AGHLMOORS
  HOLOGRAMS
AGHLMOOTU
  GOALMOUTH
AGHLNOOTY ANTHOLOGY
AGHLNOSTU ONSLAUGHT

AGHLOOPTY PATHOLOGY
AGHLOPPRY POLYGRAPH
AGHLOPRXY XYLOGRAPH
AGHLORSSU HOURGLASS
AGHMNOOPR
  MONOGRAPH,
  NOMOGRAPH, PHONOGRAM
AGHMNOOPY
  MONOPHAGY
AGHMNPSSU SPHAGNUMS
AGHMNRSTU
  HAMSTRUNG
AGHMOOPRT
  PHOTOGRAM
AGHMOPRYY
  MYOGRAPHY
AGHNNSTUU HSUAN
  T'UNG
AGHNOPSSU SPHAGNOUS
AGHOOPRRY
  OROGRAPHY
AGHOOPRYZ ZOOGRAPHY
AGIIIMNPR IMPAIRING
AGIIIMNTT IMITATING
AGIIINNRV VIRGINIAN
AGIIINSTV VAGINITIS
AGIIINTTV VITIATING
AGIIKLMNR GRIMALKIN
AGIIKMNST MISTAKING
AGIILLLOP GALLIPOLI
AGIILLMMR MILLIGRAM
AGIILLNOR GORILLIAN
AGIILLNRV RIVALLING
AGIILLNWY WAILINGLY
AGIILMNSY MISLAYING
AGIILMNTY MALIGNITY
AGIILNORS ORIGINALS
AGIILNORT TAILORING
AGIILNOST INTAGLIOS,
  ISOLATING
AGIILNOTV VIOLATING
AGIILNPRS SPIRALING
AGIILNRSV VIRGINALS
AGIILNSSS ISINGLASS
AGIILNSTT LITIGANTS
AGIILORTT LITIGATOR
AGIILOTTT TOGLIATTI
AGIIMMNRT IMMIGRANT
AGIIMNNRT INMIGRANT
AGIIMNORT MIGRATION
AGIIMNOST SIGMATION
AGIIMNPRT IMPARTING
AGIIMORTT MITIGATOR

AGIINNNOT ANOINTING
AGIINNORS SIGNORINA
AGIINNORT RATIONING
AGIINNPRS SPRAINING
AGIINNPSS IN PASSING
AGIINNPST PAINTINGS
AGIINNRST STRAINING,
  TRAININGS
AGIINNRTU URINATING
AGIINOORT IGNORATIO
AGIINPPRS APPRISING
AGIINPRST TRAIPSING
AGIINSSST ASSISTING
AGIINSTTU SITUATING
AGIIORRRT IRRIGATOR
AGIIRSSTT GASTRITIS
AGIIRSTTU GUITARIST
AGIKLMORS KILOGRAMS
AGIKLNOSY SOAKINGLY
AGIKLNOTT TALKING-TO
AGIKLNPRS SPARKLING
AGIKMNNSU UNMASKING
AGIKNNPSS SPANKINGS
AGIKNOSST GOATSKINS
AGIKNQSUW SQUAWKING
AGILLNNNU ANNULLING
AGILLNOPW WALLOPING
AGILLNOTT ALLOTTING,
  TOTALLING
AGILLNOWW WALLOWING
AGILLNQSU SQUALLING
AGILLNSTY LASTINGLY
AGILMNNOO MONGOLIAN
AGILMNNOY MOANINGLY
AGILMNPRT TRAMPLING
AGILMNSUY AMUSINGLY
AGILMRSUV VULGARISM
AGILNNOPS PLAINSONG
AGILNNOQU ALGONQUIN
AGILNNRSY SNARINGLY
AGILNNRTY RANTINGLY
AGILNNWYY YAWNINGLY
AGILNORSY SOARINGLY
AGILNORVY VAINGLORY
AGILNOTUV OVULATING
AGILNOTUW OUTLAWING
AGILNOTUY OUTLAYING
AGILNPRSW SPRAWLING
AGILNPRSY RASPINGLY,
  SPARINGLY
AGILNPRTT PRATTLING
AGILNPRTY PRATINGLY
AGILNPSTT SPLATTING

AGILNPSTU PULSATING
AGILNPSUY PAUSINGLY
AGILNRSST STARLINGS
AGILNRSSU SINGULARS
AGILNRSTT STARTLING
AGILNRVYY VARYINGLY
AGILNSWYY SWAYINGLY
AGILOOPST APOLOGIST
AGILOPRUY UROPYGIAL
AGILRRTUY GARRULITY
AGILRTUVY VULGARITY
AGIMMNSUY GYMNASIUM
AGIMNNOOR MAROONING
AGIMNNORS RANSOMING
AGIMNNOTU AMOUNTING
AGIMNNOVV MOVING VAN
AGIMNOOSV VAMOOSING
AGIMNORSS ORGANISMS
AGIMNORSU IGNORAMUS
AGIMNRRTY MARTYRING
AGIMOOSSU ISOGAMOUS
AGIMORRTY MIGRATORY
AGINNORRW NARROWING
AGINNPRSU UNSPARING
AGINNPSSW WINGSPANS
AGINNSTUU TUNGUSIAN
AGINOOPSS POISON GAS
AGINOOTTT TATTOOING
AGINOPPRV APPROVING
AGINOPRRT PARROTING
AGINOPRTU PURGATION
AGINORRSS GARRISONS
AGINORSST ASSORTING,
  ORGANISTS, ROASTINGS
AGINORSTY GYRATIONS,
  SIGNATORY
AGINORSUV SAVOURING
AGINPPRST STRAPPING,
  TRAPPINGS
AGINPPRSW WRAPPINGS
AGINPRSTU PASTURING
AGINQRRUY QUARRYING
AGINQSTTU SQUATTING
AGINRSSST STAR SIGNS
AGINRSSTY STINGRAYS
AGIOPRRSY SPIROGYRA
AGIQRSSTU GRASSQUIT
AGJKNORRU KURRAJONG
AGKLLNOOO A LONG
  LOOK
AGKLORSSW GLASSWORK
AGKLPPRSU SPARK PLUG
AGKNORSST KNOTGRASS

AGLLNOOPY POLYGONAL
AGLMOORSU
  GLAMOROUS
AGLOOPSST GOALPOSTS
AGLOORSTY ASTROLOGY
AGLOOTTUY TAUTOLOGY
AGLOPPRUY PLAYGROUP
AGLORRSUU GARRULOUS
AGLORSSTW GLASSWORT
AGMMNOORS
  GROOMSMAN,
  MONOGRAMS
AGMMOSTUU
  GUMMATOUS
AGMNORRST
  STRONGARM
AGMNSSTUY NYSTAGMUS
AGNNOSSSW
  SWANSONGS
AGNOPRSST PART-SONGS
AGNPRSSUY SPRAY GUNS
AGNRRSTUY STRANGURY
AGOPRRTUY PURGATORY
AGORSTTUY GUSTATORY
AGRSTTTTU STUTTGART
AHHIIMORS HIROSHIMA
AHHIIRRST HAIR SHIRT
AHHLORSTU SHORT-HAUL
AHHMOSTUW
  MOUTHWASH
AHHNORRST HARTSHORN
AHHNORSTW
  HAWTHORNS
AHHOPPRUY HAPPY HOUR
AHIIILSST LITHIASIS
AHIIILLPPP PHILLIPPA
AHIILLTWW WITH A WILL
AHIILOOPZ ZOOPHILIA
AHIILORSU HILARIOUS
AHIILOSST HALITOSIS
AHIILRSTT SHIRTTAIL
AHIINORST HISTORIAN
AHIIPRSSZ SIZARSHIP
AHIIRRSTT ARTHRITIS
AHIKKNNTT THINK TANK
AHIKKNRSS SHARKSKIN
AHIKLMSWY MAWKISHLY
AHIKLNSVY KNAVISHLY
AHILLPSSY SPLASHILY
AHILLPSTW WHIPSTALL
AHILLSSVY SLAVISHLY
AHILMNNSY MANNISHLY
AHILMOPSY SYPHILOMA

AHILMORST HAILSTORM
AHILMOSST MAILSHOTS
AHILMPRTU TRIUMPHAL
AHILNPPUY UNHAPPILY
AHILOPPTY HIPPOLYTA
AHILOPSST HOSPITALS
AHILORSTW SHOW TRIAL
AHILORTTY THROATILY
AHILOSTTT STATOLITH
AHILPSSWY WASPISHLY
AHILQSSUY SQUASHILY
AHILRSTWY SWARTHILY
AHIMMNORU HARMONIUM
AHIMMOPRS AMORPHISM
AHIMNNORY INHARMONY
AHIMNORST HARMONIST
AHIMNPSTY SYMPATHIN
AHIMNRTUU ANTHURIUM
AHIMNSSTU HUMANISTS
AHIMOOSTX HOMOTAXIS
AHIMOPRSS APHORISMS
AHIMOPRSY MAYORSHIP
AHIMOPSUX AMPHIOXUS
AHINNOOPT PHONATION
AHINNOPTY ANTIPHONY
AHINOOPRS SOPHRONIA
AHINOOSTU HOUSTONIA
AHINPRSST TRANSSHIP
AHIOPPSSY APOPHYSIS
AHIOPRSUV VAPOURISH
AHIORRTWY AIRWORTHY
AHIORTTUY AUTHORITY
AHKLOOPYY PLAY HOOKY
AHKLOSSTW TALK SHOWS
AHKNOSTUY THANKYOUS
AHKORSTUW
  SOUTHWARK
AHLLLOSWY SHALLOWLY
AHLLMOOPR ALLOMORPH
AHLLNOSTW TOWN HALLS
AHLLOPSUY APHYLLOUS
AHLMOOOPR
  HOMOPOLAR
AHLMOOPSY HOMOPLASY
AHLMOPSTY POLYMATHS
AHLNOPSSU ALPHONSUS
AHMOOPRSU
  AMORPHOUS
AHMOORSSW
  WASHROOMS
AHMOPRTTU MOUTHPART
AHNNNOOTY
  HOOTNANNY

AHNOOPRTY PHONATORY
AHNOPPSSW PAWNSHOPS
AHNOPSSST SNAPSHOTS
AHNORRTTY THYRATRON
AHOOOPTTT HOT POTATO
AHOOPRRTX PROTHORAX
AHOOPSTTT PHOTOSTAT
AHOORRTTY HORTATORY
AHOPSSTUW SOUTHPAWS
AIIILLNTY INITIALLY
AIIILMNST LAMINITIS
AIIIMNOTT IMITATION
AIIINNNOT INANITION
AIIINNSTY ASININITY
AIIINORTT INITIATOR
AIIINOTTV VITIATION
AIIJLOTVY JOVIALITY
AIIKNNNPS PANNIKINS
AIIILLMMNY MINIMALLY
AIIILLMRSY SIMILARLY
AIIILLNSTY SAINTLILY
AIIILLPRRS SPIRILLAR
AIIILLRTVY TRIVIALLY
AIIILMMNUU ALUMINIUM
AIIILMNORT TRINOMIAL
AIIILMNSST STALINISM
AIIILMNSTT MILITANTS
AIIILMOSST ALTISSIMO
AIIILMPRRY PRIMARILY
AIIILMRSST MISTRIALS
AIIILMRSTU RITUALISM
AIIILNOOST ISOLATION
AIIILNOOTV VIOLATION
AIIILNOPST OIL PAINTS
AIIILNOPSV PAVILIONS
AIIILNOQTU LIQUATION
AIIILNORTT INTROITAL
AIIILNOSTT SILTATION
AIIILNOTTU TUITIONAL
AIIILNPSST TAILSPINS
AIIILNRSST SINISTRAL
AIIILNSSTT STALINIST
AIIILPRSST SPRITSAIL
AIIILPRSTU SPIRITUAL
AIIILRSTTU RITUALIST
AIIIMMPRSV VAMPIRISM
AIIIMNNTUY UNANIMITY
AIIIMNOPRS PROSIMIAN
AIIIMNOPSS IMPASSION
AIIIMNOSTY ANIMOSITY
AIIIMNPSTT TIMPANIST
AIIIMORSTT IMITATORS
AIIIMPSSSV PASSIVISM

AIIIMRSTUU MAURITIUS
AIIIMRSUVV VIVARIUMS
AIIINNNOPT PINNATION
AIIINNORTT NITRATION
AIIINNORTU RUINATION,
   URINATION
AIIINNOSSV INVASIONS
AIIINNOTTX ANTITOXIN
AIIINNRSTT IN TRANSIT
AIIINOOQRU IROQUOIAN
AIIINOPRTT PARTITION
AIIINOPRTV PRIVATION
AIIINORSTT STRIATION
AIIINORSVY VISIONARY
AIIINORTTT ATTRITION,
   TITRATION
AIIINOSTTU SITUATION
AIIINQTTUY ANTIQUITY
AIIINRRSTT IRRITANTS
AIIIOPRRTY APRIORITY
AIIIOPRSSS PSORIASIS
AIIIOPRSTT PAROTITIS,
   TOPIARIST
AIIIORRRTT IRRITATOR
AIIIORTTTV TITIVATOR
AIIIPPRRST PARTI PRIS
AIIIPRRSST AIRSTRIPS
AIIIPRTTUY PITUITARY
AIIIPSSSTV PASSIVIST
AIIIPSSTVY PASSIVITY
AIJMORSTU MAJOR SUIT
AIJNOPPSY POPINJAYS
AIKLNOSSY ANKYLOSIS
AIKLOSTTW KILOWATTS
AIKMNNOSW KINSWOMAN
AIKNOPRTW PAINTWORK
AILLMMORY IMMORALLY
AILLMNNOY NOMINALLY
AILLMPRSU PLURALISM
AILLMSUUV ALLUVIUMS
AILLNQRST TONSILLAR
AILLNORSU LUNISOLAR
AILLNOSST STALLIONS
AILLNOSSU ALLUSIONS
AILLNOTUU ULULATION
AILLORSTT LITTORALS,
   TORTILLAS
AILLOSSTY LOYALISTS
AILLPPRUY PUPILLARY
AILLPRSTU PLURALIST
AILLPRTUY PLURALITY
AILLPSSWY SPILLWAYS
AILLRTUVY VIRTUALLY

AILMMOORT IMMOLATOR
AILMMORST IMMORTALS
AILMMRSUY SUMMARILY
AILMMTTUU ULTIMATUM
AILMNNOTY ANTIMONYL
AILMNOOPS PALOMINOS
AILMNOORS MONORAILS
AILMNOPSY AMYLOPSIN,
   OLYMPIANS
AILMNORST MORTAL SIN
AILMNORTY NORMALITY
AILMNOSUU ALUMINOUS
AILMNSTTU STIMULANT
AILMORSST MORALISTS
AILMORSSU SOLARIUMS
AILMORSTU SIMULATOR
AILMORTTU MUTILATOR
AILMORTTY MORTALITY
AILMOSSTY ATMOLYSIS
AILMPRSTY PALMISTRY
AILMPSSST PSALMISTS
AILMTTUUY MUTUALITY
AILNNOSSW SONS-IN-LAW
AILNNSTTY INSTANTLY
AILNOORST TONSORIAL,
   TORSIONAL
AILNOOSTV SOLVATION
AILNOOTUV OVULATION
AILNOPSTU PLATINOUS,
   PULSATION
AILNOPSTY PONYTAILS
AILNORSTU INSULATOR
AILNOSTUY AUTOLYSIN
AILNOSUXY ANXIOUSLY
AILNPPSTU SUPPLIANT
AILNPQTUY PIQUANTLY
AILNRRSTU TRIAL RUNS
AILNRTUUX LUXURIANT
AILNSSTTU LUTANISTS
AILOORSTV VIOLATORS
AILOORSUV VARIOLOUS
AILORRSUV RIVALROUS
AILORSSTY ROYALISTS
AILORSTTU TUTORIALS
AILORSUVY VARIOUSLY
AILOSSTUY AUTOLYSIS
AILRSSTTU ALTRUISTS
AILRSSUVV SURVIVALS
AIMMMMNOS
   MAMMONISM
AIMMMNOST MAMMONIST
AIMMNORTY MATRIMONY
AIMMNOSTU SUMMATION

AIMMPRSUU MARSUPIUM
AIMNNOORT NOMINATOR
AIMNNOPST POINTSMAN
AIMNNOSTU MOUNTAINS
AIMNNOSUU UNANIMOUS
AIMNNOTYY ANONYMITY
AIMNNRSTU RUMINANTS
AIMNOPRSY PARSIMONY
AIMNOPRTT IMPORTANT
AIMNOPRTY PATRIMONY
AIMNORRST RAINSTORM
AIMNORRTU RUMINATOR
AIMNORSUU UNIRAMOUS
AIMNOSTTU MUTATIONS
AIMNPSTTY TYMPANIST
AIMNRSSTU SATURNISM
AIMOPSSTU POTASSIUM
AINNOOPRS SOPRANINO
AINNOOPRT PRONATION
AINNOORTV INNOVATOR
AINNOOSTT NOTATIONS
AINNORSTT STRONTIAN
AINOOPPRT APPOINTOR,
   APPORTION
AINOOPSTT POTATIONS
AINOOQTTU QUOTATION
AINOORSTT ROTATIONS
AINOOTTUX AUTOTOXIN
AINOPRSTU PUT ON AIRS,
   SUPINATOR
AINOPRSUU UNIPAROUS
AINORSSST ARSONISTS
AINRSSTTU NATURISTS
AIOOORRST ORATORIOS
AIOOPRSUV APIVOROUS,
   OVIPAROUS
AIOOSTTTT TATTOOIST
AIOPRRSTT PORTRAITS
AIORRSSTU SARTORIUS
AIPPRSSTT TRAPPISTS
AJMMNNOPU
   PANMUNJOM
AJMPRSTTU JUMP-START
AKKRSTVYY SYKTYVKAR
AKLNOOTUW WALK OUT
   ON
AKLNOSUVY ULYANOVSK
AKLOPRRRY LORRY PARK
AKLORSSTW SALTWORKS
AKLPRRSSU LARKSPURS
AKMOPRSST POSTMARKS
AKNNORSYY SYNKARYON
AKOPRRSTW PART WORKS

ALLMOOSSY LYSOSOMAL
ALLNOOPTY POLYTONAL
ALLNOPTTU POLLUTANT
ALLNSUUUY UNUSUALLY
ALLOOPRTY ALLOTROPY
ALLOPPRUY POPULARLY
ALLOPRSTW STRAW POLL
ALLORSTTY TALL STORY
ALMNOORTY MONOLATRY
ALMNOPRUY PULMONARY
ALMOOPRSY PLAYROOMS
ALMOORSUY AMOROUSLY
ALMOPPSST LAMPPOSTS
ALNOPPRUU UNPOPULAR
ALNOPPSTT POT PLANTS
ALNOPSTTU POSTULANT
ALNORTUVY VOLUNTARY
ALNPSTTUU PUSTULANT
ALOOPPRSS PROPOSALS
ALOOPRSTV STAVROPOL
ALOOPSTYZ ZOOPLASTY
ALOPRSTUY PULSATORY
AMMNPSTUY TYMPANUMS
AMMOOSTTU
   MATSUMOTO
AMNNOOSUY
   ANONYMOUS
AMNOORSTY
   ASTRONOMY
AMNOPRSST SPORTSMAN
AMNOTTUYY TAUTONYMY
AMOOORSTV
   VASOMOTOR
AMOORRRWW
   ARROWWORM
AMOORSTWY
   MOTORWAYS
AMOPRSSXY PAROXYSMS
AMPRSTUUY SUMPTUARY
ANNOOPRSU NONPAROUS
ANNORSTUY TYRANNOUS
ANOOOPRSZ SPOROZOAN
ANOOOPRTZ PROTOZOAN
ANOPRRSTT TRANSPORT
ANORSUUVY UNSAVOURY
ANRRSSTUU SUSURRANT
AOOOORRRTW
   ARROWROOT
AOOOORRTTV ROTOVATOR
AOOPRRSTT PROTOSTAR
AOPPRSSST PASSPORTS
AOPRRSTUU RAPTUROUS
AOQSSTTUU STATUS QUO

AORRRTWWY
   WORRYWART
AORSTTTUY STATUTORY
BBBDEELRU BLUBBERED
BBBDEHNOO HOBNOBBED
BBBEEELMU BUMBLEBEE
BBBEEELUZ BEELZEBUB
BBBEGLMUU BUBBLE
   GUM
BBBEILSTU BUBBLIEST
BBBINOPSY BOBBY PINS
BBCDEELOR CLOBBERED
BBCDEILRS SCRIBBLED
BBCEHISTU CHUBBIEST
BBCEHLOUY CUBBYHOLE
BBCEILRRS SCRIBBLER
BBCEILRSS SCRIBBLES
BBCEIRRSU SCRUBBIER
BBCEIRSSU SUBSCRIBE
BBCERRSSU SCRUBBERS
BBCGINRSU SCRUBBING
BBCIIILOT BIBLIOTIC
BBCKLOOSU BOOK CLUBS
BBDDEELOU DOUBLE BED
BBDEELORS SLOBBERED
BBDEGIMNO DEMOBBING
BBDEHIRSU RUBBISHED
BBDEILRSU BLUEBIRDS
BBDEIORRW BOWERBIRD
BBDELLMSU DUMBBELLS
BBDELLOOU BLUE BLOOD
BBDGIILNR DRIBBLING
BBDGINRSU DRUBBINGS
BBDLOOSWY BODY
   BLOWS
BBEEEEINR BEBEERINE
BBEEEHLMU HUMBLEBEE
BBEEEINRR BERBERINE
BBEEFLLUY BULLY BEEF
BBEEILPST PLEBBIEST
BBEEIORRS ROBBERIES
BBEEIRRSU RUBBERISE
BBEEIRRUZ RUBBERIZE
BBEELLLSU BLUEBELLS
BBEELORRS SLOBBERER
BBEELRRUY BLUEBERRY
BBEGGIINR GIBBERING
BBEGHIIRS GIBBERISH
BBEGHILOS BOBSLEIGH
BBEGIRSTU GRUBBIEST
BBEHKOOTY BY THE
   BOOK
BBEHLLMOS BOMBSHELL

BBEHRRSUY SHRUBBERY
BBEIKLNOR KNOBBLIER
BBEIKSTUZ KIBBUTZES
BBEILOSTW WOBBLIEST
BBEILQRSU QUIBBLERS
BBEIMMOST TIME BOMBS
BBEIMOSST BOMBSITES
BBEINSSTU TUBBINESS
BBEISSTTU STUBBIEST
BBEKLOOSU BLUE BOOKS
BBEMNORUX BOX
 NUMBER
BBERRTTUU BUTTERBUR
BBFMOOOPR BOMBPROOF
BBGGINOPU GO PUBBING
BBGHILLTU LIGHT BULB
BBGHILNOO HOBGOBLIN
BBGHIMOST BOMBSIGHT
BBGHINORT THROBBING
BBGIILNQU QUIBBLING
BBGILNOSY SOBBINGLY
BBIIILNRU BILIRUBIN
BBIIKMTUZ KIBBUTZIM
BBIKMNOST STINK-BOMB
BBLLOSUYY BULLYBOYS
BCCCKMOOS
 COCKSCOMB
BCCDEHKOY BODYCHECK
BCCDEMSUU SUCCUMBED
BCCEEILOR COERCIBLE
BCCEHIKNP PINCHBECK
BCCEILRSU CRUCIBLES
BCCEINNOU CONCUBINE
BCCEKLORU COCKLEBUR
BCCEKOSTU STOCK CUBE
BCCEMRSUU
 CUCUMBERS, SUCCUMBER
BCCGIILNY BICYCLING
BCCIILSTY BICYCLIST
BCCIOOPRS BROSCOPIC
BCCIORSTU SCORBUTIC
BCCMOORXY
 COXCOMBRY
BCCMORRUY
 CURRYCOMB
BCCOSSTUU CUB SCOUTS
BCDDEEHOU DEBOUCHED
BCDDEEILU DEDUCIBLE
BCDDEEIRS DESCRIBED
BCDDIIKRY DICKYBIRD
BCDEEEEHS BESEECHED
BCDEEEINO OBEDIENCE
BCDEEEMRS DECEMBERS

BCDEEGIKN BEDECKING
BCDEEHIIR HERBICIDE
BCDEEHITW BEWITCHED
BCDEEHRTU BUTCHERED
BCDEEILRU REDUCIBLE
BCDEEILSU SEDUCIBLE
BCDEEIORR CEREBROID
BCDEEIRRS DESCRIBER
BCDEEJSTU SUBJECTED
BCDEEMNTU DECUMBENT
BCDEIILNU INDUCIBLE
BCDEIINRS INSCRIBED
BCDEIJSUU SUB JUDICE
BCDEIKORR BRODERICK
BCDEIKRRS REDBRICKS
BCDEKLNUU UNBUCKLED
BCDEOOTTY BOYCOTTED
BCDEORRSS CROSSBRED
BCDGOSYZZ BYDGOSZCZ
BCDHKNOUU
 BUCKHOUND
BCDILMNOW
 CLIMB-DOWN
BCDIMOORS SCOMBROID
BCDKLOOOW
 WOODBLOCK
BCDKNOOOS
 BOONDOCKS
BCDKNOORU
 ROCKBOUND
BCDOPRTUY BY-PRODUCT
BCEEEFINS BENEFICES
BCEEEGHIS BIG CHEESE
BCEEEHKNO CHEEKBONE
BCEEELQRU BECQUEREL
BCEEGHINR BREECHING
BCEEGIINR BIGENERIC
BCEEHKTTU BUCKTEETH
BCEEHORTT BROCHETTE
BCEEIIJTV BIJECTIVE
BCEEIILMS IMBECILES
BCEEIILNV EVINCIBLE
BCEEIJOTV OBJECTIVE
BCEEILLOS BELLICOSE
BCEEILRTY CELEBRITY
BCEEINOOT COENOBITE
BCEEIOQSU QUEBECOIS
BCEEIPRRS PRESCRIBE
BCEEJNORT JOB CENTRE
BCEEJOSTX SEX OBJECT
BCEELNOSY OBSCENELY
BCEELOOSS OBSOLESCE
BCEEMNRTU RECUMBENT

BCEEMRRSU CEREBRUMS
BCEENPSTU PUBESCENT
BCEENRSTU RUBESCENT
BCEFFIOOX BOX OFFICE
BCEFFIOOY OFFICE BOY
BCEFIIKRR FIREBRICK
BCEFIIRTY FEBRICITY
BCEFIJOTY OBJECTIFY
BCEGHILNN BLENCHING
BCEGHORRU
 CHERBOURG
BCEGIIKNR BICKERING
BCEGIINST BISECTING
BCEGIJNOT OBJECTING
BCEGIKNNO BECKONING
BCEGIKNTU BUCKETING
BCEGIMNRU CUMBERING
BCEHIILPT PHLEBITIC
BCEHIISTT BITCHIEST
BCEHILORT BLOTCHIER
BCEHILPSU BLUE CHIPS
BCEHIMORS CHEMISORB
BCEHIOSTT BOTCHIEST
BCEHKNORW
 WORKBENCH
BCEHLOSUU CLUBHOUSE
BCEHMNOOY
 HONEYCOMB
BCEHORRSU BROCHURES
BCEIIJNOT BIJECTION
BCEIILPSU PUBLICISE
BCEIILPUZ PUBLICIZE
BCEIIMORT BIOMETRIC
BCEIINOST BISECTION
BCEIINRRS INSCRIBER
BCEIIRSTX BISECTRIX
BCEIJLOPU JOE PUBLIC
BCEIJNOOT OBJECTION
BCEILLMRU CRIBELLUM
BCEILMNOU COLUMBINE
BCEILMORY COR BLIMEY
BCEILMOTU COLUMBITE
BCEILMRRU CRUMBLIER
BCEILNOOT BOLECTION
BCEILNORU COLUBRINE
BCEILPRSU REPUBLICS
BCEIMNNTU INCUMBENT
BCEIMNORY EMBRYONIC
BCEINORRW BROWN RICE
BCEINOSTU BOUNCIEST
BCEINOSTY OBSCENITY
BCEINSSUU INCUBUSES
BCEIOPRRS PROSCRIBE

BCEIORSTT OBSTETRIC
BCEJOORST OBJECTORS
BCEKLOOTV BLOCK VOTE
BCELMOOTY LOBECTOMY
BCELORSUY OBSCURELY
BCEMOORSY CORYMBOSE
BCENOORTY CON BY
    ROTE
BCEOORSTU CUBE ROOTS
BCEORRRWY
    CROWBERRY
BCEORSTUX SUBCORTEX
BCEPRTTUU BUTTERCUP
BCFGLLOSU GOLF CLUBS
BCFHILLNU BULLFINCH
BCGHILNTU NIGHTCLUB
BCGIIMNNO COMBINING
BCGILMNRU CRUMBLING
BCGINORSU OBSCURING
BCHIIMSTU BISMUTHIC
BCHIIOPRS BISHOPRIC
BCHIIRSTU HUBRISTIC
BCHIIRSTY HYBRISTIC
BCHILLOTY BLOTCHILY
BCHILOOPY LYOPHOBIC
BCHINORTY BRYTHONIC
BCHIOORSY CHOIRBOYS
BCHKNORTU BUCKTHORN
BCHKOOTTU BUCKTOOTH
BCHLNOPUW PUNCH
    BOWL
BCHLOOOSY SCHOOLBOY
BCHMOOOTT
    TOOTHCOMB
BCIIIMRST BRITICISM
BCIILMSUU UMBILICUS
BCIILPSTU PUBLICIST
BCIILPTUY PUBLICITY
BCIILRTUY LUBRICITY
BCIIMNOOS BIONOMICS
BCIIMOSTY SYMBIOTIC
BCIISSSTU CUBISISTS
BCIKKORRW BRICKWORK
BCIKNNRSU INNSBRUCK
BCIKNRSUW BRUNSWICK
BCILLORSS CROSSBILL
BCILMMOOU COLUMBIUM
BCILMNOPU PLUMBICON
BCILORSUU LUBRICOUS
BCILPRSTU STRIP CLUB
BCIMNOOOS SONIC BOOM
BCIOOPRSS PROBOSCIS
BCIORSTUY OBSCURITY

BCIPRSSTU SUBSCRIPT
BCKOOOPSY COPYBOOKS
BCMNOOORR
    BROOMCORN
BCMOORSTU
    COMBUSTOR
BCOORSSSW
    CROSSBOWS
BCOOSSTUY BOY SCOUTS
BDDDEEINR BEDRIDDEN
BDDEEEFIR DEBRIEFED
BDDEEEILV BEDEVILED
BDDEEFOOR FOREBODED
BDDEEGGRU BEGRUDGED
BDDEEGIMN EMBEDDING
BDDEEIOSY DISOBEYED
BDDEEISTU SUBEDITED
BDDEELNRU BLUNDERED
BDDEELORU REDOUBLED
BDDEENORU REBOUNDED
BDDEENRRU UNDERBRED
BDDEENSTU SUBTENDED
BDDEFINOR FORBIDDEN
BDDEFIORR FORBIDDER
BDDEFLOOU BLOOD FEUD
BDDEGIIMN IMBEDDING
BDDEGLOOU DOODLEBUG
BDDEHINOU HIDEBOUND
BDDEHLOOS BLOODSHED
BDDEIIMOR DIBROMIDE
BDDEIISUV SUBDIVIDE
BDDEILNRU UNBRIDLED
BDDEILORW BLOW-DRIED
BDDEIMOSY DISEMBODY
BDDEINRSU DISBURDEN
BDDEIRSSU DISBURSED
BDDEIRSTU DISTURBED
BDDELLOUZ BULLDOZED
BDDELSUUY SUBDUEDLY
BDDENNOUU
    UNBOUNDED
BDDENORUY UNDERBODY
BDDENOTUU UNDOUBTED
BDDEOSTYY TEDDY BOYS
BDDFILLNO BLINDFOLD
BDDFMNOUU
    DUMBFOUND
BDDHISSTU BUDDHISTS
BDDILLORY DOLLY BIRD
BDDINNOUW WINDBOUND
BDEEEEFLN ENFEEBLED
BDEEEELRV BELVEDERE
BDEEEFILL BIELEFELD

BDEEEFINT BENEFITED
BDEEEGLUW BUGLEWEED
BDEEEHLRT BLETHERED
BDEEEIOTW WOE BETIDE
BDEEEKNOT BETOKENED
BDEEELMRS RESEMBLED
BDEEELMZZ EMBEZZLED
BDEEELNOS NOSEBLEED
BDEEELOSU SEE DOUBLE
BDEEEMMNT
    EMBEDMENT
BDEEENRTU DEBENTURE
BDEEERSTW BESTREWED
BDEEFIILS DISBELIEF
BDEEFLLOW BEDFELLOW
BDEEFLORW FLOWERBED
BDEEFLOTT BOTTLE-FED
BDEEFOORR FOREBODER
BDEEFOOTW
    WEB-FOOTED
BDEEGGLOW
    BOW-LEGGED
BDEEGHINT BENIGHTED
BDEEGMRSU SUBMERGED
BDEEGNORU BURGEONED
BDEEHIITX EXHIBITED
BDEEHILMS BLEMISHED
BDEEHLORS BEHOLDERS
BDEEHNRTU BURTHENED
BDEEHORTT BETROTHED
BDEEIILLN INDELIBLE
BDEEIILRS DERISIBLE
BDEEIINNZ BENZIDINE
BDEEIKLNR BLINKERED
BDEEILLTT BELITTLED
BDEEILMOR EMBROILED
BDEEILMSS DISSEMBLE
BDEEILNNO NONEDIBLE
BDEEILRST BLISTERED
BDEEIMMRS DISMEMBER
BDEEIMORR EMBROIDER
BDEEINRRT INTERBRED
BDEEIORSY DISOBEYER
BDEEIPRSW SPIDERWEB
BDEEIRRST BESTIRRED
BDEEIRRSV RIVERBEDS
BDEEIRSTT BED-SITTER
BDEEKNRSU DEBUNKERS
BDEEKOORW
    BROOKWEED
BDEELLSSY BLESSEDLY
BDEELMRSU SLUMBERED
BDEELNRRU BLUNDERER

BDEELNSSU UNBLESSED
BDEELORST BOLSTERED
BDEELRSTU BLUSTERED
BDEEMMOOS
    EMBOSOMED
BDEEORSTY OYSTER BED
BDEEORVYY EVERYBODY
BDEEPRRSU PUREBREDS
BDEEPRRTU PERTURBED
BDEERSTUV SUBVERTED
BDEFFLORU OLD BUFFER
BDEFHIRSU FURBISHED
BDEFIILRR RIFLEBIRD
BDEFILLOO LIFEBLOOD
BDEFINORY BOYFRIEND
BDEFLOSTU SELF-DOUBT
BDEGGGINU DEBUGGING
BDEGGINTU BUDGETING
BDEGGNUUY DUNE
    BUGGY
BDEGHILNO BEHOLDING
BDEGHINRU EDINBURGH
BDEGIIILR DIRIGIBLE
BDEGIILOS DISOBLIGE
BDEGIINNR REBINDING
BDEGIIPPR BIG DIPPER
BDEGIKNNU DEBUNKING
BDEGIMNOY EMBODYING
BDEGINNNU UNBENDING
BDEGINNRU BURDENING
BDEGINORR BORDERING
BDEGINORT TONBRIDGE
BDEGLNORU OLDENBURG
BDEGLNOSU BLUDGEONS
BDEHIIINT INHIBITED
BDEHIIRSY HYBRIDISE
BDEHIIRYZ HYBRIDIZE
BDEHILPSU PUBLISHED
BDEHINRSU BURNISHED
BDEHIORSU BIRDHOUSE
BDEIIILSV DIVISIBLE
BDEIIILTY EDIBILITY
BDEIIJNOS INSIDE JOB
BDEIIKRST DIRT BIKES
BDEIILLNY INDELIBLY
BDEIILMOS MOBILISED
BDEIILMOZ MOBILIZED
BDEIILNNO BLENNIOID
BDEIISSSU SUBSIDIES,
    SUBSIDISE
BDEIISSUZ SUBSIDIZE
BDEIJNOSU SUBJOINED
BDEILLNPS SPELLBIND

BDEILMOOR DORMOBILE
BDEILNNSS BLINDNESS
BDEILOQTU QUODLIBET
BDEILORSV LOVEBIRDS
BDEILORSW BLOW-DRIES
BDEILORUV OVERBUILD
BDEILPRUU UPBUILDER
BDEILRRSY LYREBIRDS
BDEILSTTU SUBTITLED
BDEIMSTTU SUBMITTED
BDEINNORW WIND-BORNE
BDEINORTX TINDERBOX
BDEIOORST BROODIEST
BDEIORSTU SUBEDITOR
BDEIPRSTU BUPRESTID
BDEIRRSSU DISBURSER
BDEIRRSTU DISTURBER
BDEISSSTU SUBSISTED
BDELLOORS BORDELLOS,
    DOORBELLS
BDELLOOSS BLOODLESS
BDELLORUZ BULLDOZER
BDELLRRUY BLURREDLY
BDELMNPUU UNPLUMBED
BDELMOOSS BLOSSOMED
BDELMRTUY TUMBLE-DRY
BDELNNOSS BLONDNESS
BDELNOOTU DOUBLETON
BDELNOSSU BOUNDLESS
BDELOOPTY BLOOD TYPE
BDELOOSUY BODY LOUSE
BDELOSSTU DOUBTLESS
BDEMMNOSU
    OMBUDSMEN
BDEMNOOSU
    UNBOSOMED
BDENNOSSU SNUB-NOSED
BDENNRSUU SUNBURNED
BDENOSTUW
    WESTBOUND
BDEOOOORRW
    WOODBORER
BDFHIILNS BLINDFISH
BDFHNOOOU
    HOOFBOUND
BDFILLLOS BILLFOLDS
BDFIOORST BIRD'S-FOOT
BDGIILNSU BUILDINGS
BDGIINNNU UNBINDING
BDGIINORS DISROBING
BDGIINSSU SUBSIDING
BDGINORSS SONGBIRDS
BDGINORTU OBTRUDING

BDHIIMRSY HYBRIDISM
BDHIIRTYY HYBRIDITY
BDHIMOORS RHOMBOIDS
BDHLOOOST BLOODSHOT
BDHMOSSUW DUMB
    SHOWS
BDHOORSUW
    BRUSHWOOD
BDIIMORTY MORBIDITY
BDIIRTTUY TURBIDITY
BDIKNORUV DUBROVNIK
BDILLORSW SWORDBILL
BDILNNOSW SNOW-BLIND
BDILNNOWW
    WINDBLOWN
BDILNOPST BLIND SPOT
BDILOSUUY DUBIOUSLY
BDINNOORU IRONBOUND
BDINNRTUW WINDBURNT
BDINOOWWW BOW
    WINDOW
BDINOOWWX WINDOW
    BOX
BDKNOOORS
    DOORKNOBS
BDKOOSSTU STUDBOOKS
BDLLOOSTU BLOOD LUST
BDLMOOORW
    BLOODWORM
BDLMOOSUY MOLYBDOUS
BDLNOOOSU DOUBLOONS
BDLOOOORT BLOODROOT
BDLOSSTUW DUSTBOWLS
BDNNOOSUW
    SNOWBOUND
BDORSUWZZ BUZZWORDS
BEEEEEKPR BEEKEEPER
BEEEEFLNR ENFEEBLER
BEEEFINSS BEEFINESS
BEEEGGRUZ ZEEBRUGGE
BEEEGLNOS BOLEGNESE
BEEEGLNRT GREEN BELT
BEEEGNOOW
    WOEBEGONE
BEEEGNOTW
    GO-BETWEEN
BEEEHHLMT BETHLEHEM
BEEEHLLOR HELLEBORE
BEEEHLRTT ETHELBERT
BEEEHNOSY HONEYBEES
BEEEILMNT BELEMNITE
BEEEILRSV BELIEVERS,
    EVERSIBLE

BEEEIMRSV SEMIBREVE
BEEEINORT BÊTE-NOIRE
BEEEINRSS BEERINESS
BEEELMNSS ENSEMBLES
BEEELMRRS RESEMBLER
BEEELMRZZ EMBEZZLER
BEEELPRTU BLUE PETER
BEEELSSSU SUBLESSEE
BEEEMPRST SEPTEMBER
BEEFFGIRU FEBRIFUGE
BEEFFORTT BETTER OFF
BEEFFOSTW WEB OFFSET
BEEFIILMS MISBELIEF
BEEFILLST LIFE BELTS
BEEFIORSX FIREBOXES
BEEGGIINS BESIEGING
BEEGGINTT BEGETTING
BEEGHILSW BIG WHEELS
BEEGHIRTY EYEBRIGHT
BEEGIILLL ILLEGIBLE
BEEGIILNV BELIEVING
BEEGILLNR REBELLING
BEEGILLNV BEVELLING
BEEGILLNW WELLBEING
BEEGILNRS INSELBERG
BEEGINNRS BEGINNERS
BEEGINRTT BETTERING
BEEGINSST BEESTINGS
BEEGINSTT BESETTING
BEEGKORRS GO BERSERK
BEEGMNRRU NUREMBERG
BEEGMRRSU MERSEBURG
BEEGMSTUY BE MY GUEST
BEEGRSSSU BURGESSES
BEEHILLMS EMBELLISH
BEEHILMRS BLEMISHER
BEEHILMSS BLEMISHES
BEEHINRTT TEREBINTH
BEEHIOPRS BIOSPHERE
BEEHIORRV HERBIVORE
BEEHLLRSU BUSHELLER
BEEHLOORS BOREHOLES
BEEHLOPRY HYPERBOLE
BEEHLOTTT THE BOTTLE
BEEHNOOPX XENOPHOBE
BEEIIKNRZ BEREZNIKI
BEEIILNRT LIBERTINE
BEEIILRST LIBERTIES
BEEIINRTY INEBRIETY
BEEIKLMRU BERKELIUM
BEEIKLMRY KIMBERLEY

BEEILLNOR REBELLION
BEEILLNTU EBULLIENT
BEEILLRTT BELITTLER
BEEILMORR EMBROILER
BEEILNOPX EXPONIBLE
BEEILNRSU NEBULISER
BEEILNRUZ NEBULIZER
BEEILORTT BRIOLETTE
BEEILOTTU OUBLIETTE
BEEILPRTU ERUPTIBLE
BEEILRRSV VERS LIBRE
BEEILSTUV VESTIBULE
BEEIMNRST TENEBRISM, TRIBESMEN
BEEIMRRSU REIMBURSE
BEEINNOTT BENTONITE
BEEINNRTU INNER TUBE
BEEINRSTT TENEBRIST
BEEINRTTU BUTTERINE
BEEIOQSSU OBSEQUIES
BEEIOSSSV OBSESSIVE
BEEIQRTTU BRIQUETTE
BEEIRTTTY YTTERBITE
BEEJKOSUX JUKEBOXES
BEEKNORST KERBSTONE
BEEKOPRRY POKEBERRY
BEELLLMUU UMBELLULE
BEELLORSU RESOLUBLE
BEELLSSUY BULL'S-EYES
BEELMMNRU LUMBERMEN
BEELMNORU MELBOURNE
BEELMOORT BOLOMETER
BEELMRRSU SLUMBERER
BEELNNOSS NOBLENESS
BEELNOSTU BLUESTONE
BEELORRST BOLSTERER
BEELORSVY VERBOSELY
BEELORTTX LETTERBOX
BEELQRSUU BURLESQUE
BEELRRSTU BLUSTERER
BEEMMNOTW EMBOWMENT
BEEMNNORU NUMBER ONE
BEEMNNRTU NUMBER TEN
BEEMNORSV NOVEMBERS
BEENOORRV OVERBORNE
BEENOQSTU OBSEQUENT
BEENORRST RESORBENT
BEENORSSS SOBERNESS
BEENORSTU TENEBROUS

BEENRSTTU BRUNETTES
BEEOORSTT BEETROOTS
BEEORRSSV OBSERVERS
BEEORSTTU SOUBRETTE
BEEPRRSTY PRESBYTER
BEEQRSTUY BY REQUEST
BEERRSTUV SUBVERTER
BEESSTTTU TEST TUBES
BEFFGINRU BUFFERING, REBUFFING
BEFFGINTU BUFFETING
BEFFHINTU IN THE BUFF
BEFFIILLR FIBREFILL
BEFFLNSSU BLUFFNESS
BEFGIINTT BEFITTING
BEFHIRRSU FURBISHER, REFURBISH
BEFHKLOOS BOOKSHELF
BEFIILNSU INFUSIBLE
BEFIILRTY FEBRILITY
BEFILLMSU BLUE FILMS
BEFILLOSW BLOWFLIES
BEFILOSUY LIFE BUOYS
BEFIORSTT FROSTBITE
BEFLLLOPY BELLY FLOP
BEFLRTTUY BUTTERFLY
BEFNNNOUY FUNNY BONE
BEGGGINRU BUGGERING
BEGGGLOOX GOGGLE BOX
BEGGHMRUU HUMBUGGER
BEGGIILNU BEGUILING
BEGGIINNN BEGINNING
BEGGILNNO BELONGING
BEGGINOSS BOGGINESS
BEGHHINOT THIGHBONE
BEGHHOTTU BETHOUGHT
BEGHIINTW BEGIN WITH
BEGHILRST BLIGHTERS
BEGHINORT BOTHERING
BEGHINORU NEIGHBOUR
BEGHLNOSU BUNGHOLES
BEGIILLLN LIBELLING
BEGIILLLY ILLEGIBLY
BEGIILLNT BILLETING
BEGIIMRST BIG-TIMERS
BEGIINNTY BENIGNITY
BEGIJRTTU JITTERBUG
BEGILLNOW BELLOWING
BEGILMNRT TREMBLING
BEGILMNRU LUMBERING
BEGILNNNO ENNOBLING

345

BEGILNSSS BLESSINGS
BEGILNSSU BULGINESS
BEGIMNNOT ENTOMBING
BEGIMNNRU NUMBERING
BEGIMNOSS EMBOSSING
BEGINORSU SUBREGION
BEGINORSV OBSERVING
BEGINOSSS OBSESSING
BEGINOSTW BESTOWING
BEGINRTTU BUTTERING,
   REBUTTING
BEGIOORSU BOURGEOIS
BEGLMRRSU GRUMBLERS
BEHIIINRT INHIBITER
BEHIILPRT PHILIBERT
BEHIILPST PHLEBITIS
BEHIIMNOY YOHIMBINE
BEHIIORTX EXHIBITOR
BEHIIRRST BRITISHER
BEHIKLOSV BOLSHEVIK
BEHIKPSSU PUSHBIKES
BEHIKSUVY KUIBYSHEV
BEHILNOOT ON THE BOIL
BEHILOSST BOLSHIEST
BEHILPRSU PUBLISHER,
   REPUBLISH
BEHINNOSS SHINBONES
BEHINOSSW WISHBONES
BEHINRRSU BURNISHER
BEHINSSSU BUSHINESS
BEHKNOOOP PHONE
   BOOK
BEHKNOSUU BUNKHOUSE
BEHLLOOST BOLTHOLES
BEHLLOOSW BLOWHOLES
BEHLORRTY BROTHERLY
BEHLRSSUU BULRUSHES
BEHMORSSU RHOMBUSES
BEHNORSTU BUHRSTONE
BEHOOPTTU PHOTOTUBE
BEHOOSSUY HOUSEBOYS
BEHOPRTYY BRYOPHYTE
BEIIILNSV INVISIBLE
BEIILLNSY SIBYLLINE
BEIILMOSS OMISSIBLE
BEIILNNRS BIN-LINERS
BEIILNRTT LITTERBIN
BEIILORTT TRILOBITE
BEIILSSTU SUBTILISE
BEIILSTUZ SUBTILIZE
BEIIMNSSU MINIBUSES
BEIINNRSS BRININESS
BEIINSSTT BITTINESS

BEIKLMOOR BROOKLIME
BEIKLNSSU BULKINESS
BEIKLOORT ROBOT-LIKE
BEIKLOSTY KILOBYTES
BEIKMOORT MOTORBIKE
BEIKNRSSS BRISKNESS
BEILLLOSU LIBELLOUS
BEILLMNPU PLUMB LINE
BEILLMRUY BERYLLIUM
BEILLMSUY SUBLIMELY
BEILLNOSU INSOLUBLE
BEILLNSTU BULLETINS
BEILLOPSX PILLBOXES
BEILMMOSS EMBOLISMS
BEILMNOSW WOMEN'S LIB
BEILMOSSY SYMBOLISE
BEILMOSYZ SYMBOLIZE
BEILNORTU IN TROUBLE
BEILNPRTU BLUEPRINT
BEILNRSSU BURLINESS
BEILOOPRT POTBOILER
BEILOPPSW BLOWPIPES
BEILOPSSS POSSIBLES
BEILORSSU SUBSOILER
BEILORSTT LIBRETTOS
BEILOSTWZ BLOWZIEST
BEILSSTTU SUBTITLES
BEIMMNORR MERBROMIN
BEIMNOORS BROMEOSIN
BEIMNORST BRIMSTONE
BEIMNOSSU OMNIBUSES
BEIMNPSSU BUMPINESS
BEIMOORST BIOSTROME
BEIMRSTTU SUBMITTER
BEIMRTTUY YTTERBIUM
BEINOOPRT OBREPTION
BEINOORSV OBVERSION
BEINOOSSS OBSESSION
BEINOOSSZ BOOZINESS
BEINOSSSS BOSSINESS
BEINRTTTU BITTERNUT
BEIOOPRRU POURBOIRE
BEIOPTTTU PITOT TUBE
BEIOQRSTU SOBRIQUET
BEIOQSTUU BOUTIQUES
BEIORSTUV OBTRUSIVE
BEIORSTVY VERBOSITY
BEIRSSSTU SUBSISTER
BEJJMOSTU JUMBO JETS
BEJORSTTU TURBOJETS
BEJORSUXY JURY BOXES
BEKKNOOOT BOOK
   TOKEN

BEKLOORSU RULEBOOKS
BEKLOOSTY STYLEBOOK
BEKNNNOUW
   UNBEKNOWN
BEKNOOOST NOTEBOOKS
BEKOOSTTX TEXTBOOKS
BELMOOORW
   ELBOWROOM
BELMOPSUU PLUMBEOUS
BELNNSSTU BLUNTNESS
BELNOORVW
   OVERBLOWN
BELNRTTUU TURBULENT
BELORSSSU SUBLESSOR
BELQRSUUY BRUSQUELY
BEMNOORST TROMBONES
BEMNOORSW NEW
   BROOMS
BEMNOOSTT TOMBSTONE
BEMNORTUU
   OUTNUMBER
BEMNOSSUX BUXOMNESS
BEMOORRSS SOMBREROS
BENOOSTUU BOUNTEOUS
BENORRSWY
   SNOWBERRY
BENORSSUU BURNOUSES
BENORSTTU OBSTRUENT
BENORSTXY SENTRY BOX
BENRTTTUU BUTTERNUT
BEOORRRSW
   BORROWERS
BFFHORSSU BRUSH-OFFS
BFFIIMORR FIBRIFORM
BFFLLOSUY BULLY-OFFS
BFGHILLTU BULLFIGHT
BFGLLORSU BULLFROGS
BFIILMORR LIBRIFORM
BFIINORSU FIBRINOUS
BFILNOTUU BOUNTIFUL
BFIMORRSU BURSIFORM
BFINORRST FIRSTBORN
BFLLLNOUW FULL-BLOWN
BFMMOOORR
   BROMOFORM
BFOORTUWY
   TWO-BY-FOUR
BGGHIILNT BLIGHTING
BGGILLNUY BULGINGLY
BGGILMNRU GRUMBLING
BGHHIORSW HIGHBROWS
BGHINOOOO BOOHOOING
BGHLOOPUY PLOUGHBOY

BGHMOOOOS
  OGBOMOSHO
BGIILLNOW BILLOWING
BGIILLNOY BOILINGLY
BGIILMOOR IMBROGLIO
BGIILNRST BRISTLING
BGIILOOST BIOLOGIST
BGIKNOPRS SPRINGBOK
BGILLNRSU BULLRINGS
BGILMNOOY MYOGLOBIN
BGILMNRSU RUMBLINGS
BGILMNSTU STUMBLING
BGILNNRUY BURNINGLY
BGILNOPRY PROBINGLY
BGILNORTU TROUBLING
BGILOORTY TRIBOLOGY
BGILOOSTY GLOBOSITY
BGILORSUU LOUISBURG
BGIMNSSUU SUBSUMING
BGINNORSU SUBORNING
BGINNORTU BINTURONG
BGINNOTTU BUTTONING
BGINOORRW BORROWING
BGINORRUW BURROWING
BGINORSTW BOWSTRING
BGKNOOOSS SONGBOOKS
BGLMOOSYY SYMBOLOGY
BGNOORSTX STRONGBOX
BHIIINORT INHIBITOR
BHIILLLLY HILLBILLY
BHIILLNOT BILLIONTH
BHIIMORUZ RHIZOBIUM
BHIKLLOOS BILLHOOKS
BHILLLSUY BULLISHLY
BHILLNORS HORNBILLS
BHILLNORT THORNBILL
BHILMNOTY BIMONTHLY
BHILOORSY BOORISHLY
BHILRSTUY BRUTISHLY
BHIMOOSTY TOMBOYISH
BHIOORRTT BIRTHROOT
BHIORRTTW BIRTHWORT
BHKOOOPSS BOOKSHOPS
BHKORRSUW
  BRUSHWORK
BHLLNORSU BULLHORNS
BHLLOOOTT TOLLBOOTH
BHLMPSUUY SUBPHYLUM
BIIILNSVY INVISIBLY
BIILMSTUY SUBLIMITY
BIILOOSUV OBLIVIOUS
BIILOQTUY OBLIQUITY
BIIMNOOST BIONOMIST

BIIMOPRTY IMPROBITY
BIIMOSSSY SYMBIOSIS
BIISSTTYY ITSY-BITSY
BIKLNNOSW SNOWBLINK
BILLNOOPS SPOONBILL
BILLNOOSU BOUILLONS
BILLNORST STILLBORN
BILMMOSSY SYMBOLISM
BILMNOOSS IN BLOSSOM
BILMOSSTY SYMBOLIST
BILNNOOSY LOONY BINS
BILNOSTUU BOTULINUS
BILOOPRTU POLITBURO
BILOOSUVY OBVIOUSLY
BILORSSTU STROBILUS
BIMOPSTUU BUMPTIOUS
BINOOOSUX OBNOXIOUS
BINOORSTU OBTRUSION
BIOPRSSTW BOWSPRITS
BJOPPSTUU PUT-UP JOBS
BKKOOORSW
  WORKBOOKS
BKLLMNSUU NUMBSKULL
BKMOOORSW
  BOOKWORMS
BKOOORSTY STORYBOOK
BLOORSTUU TROUBLOUS
BOOPPRRTU TURBOPROP
BORSSTTUU OUTBURSTS
CCCDENOOT CONCOCTED
CCCEEINRT ECCENTRIC
CCCEIILPY EPICYCLIC
CCCENOORT CONCOCTER
CCCHHIKOT HITCHCOCK
CCCHIKNOP PINCHCOCK
CCCHILMOU COLCHICUM
CCCHILOOT COCCOLITH
CCCIILRTY TRICYCLIC
CCDDEEESU SUCCEEDED
CCDDEIINO COINCIDED
CCDDEKLOU CUCKOLDED
CCDDELNOU CONCLUDED
CCDDENOTU CONDUCTED
CCDEEEHKR CHECKERED
CCDEEEHRS SCREECHED
CCDEEEINS DECENCIES
CCDEEERSU SUCCEEDER
CCDEEHIKW CHICKWEED
CCDEEHKNU UNCHECKED
CCDEEHORT CROCHETED
CCDEEIINN INCIDENCE
CCDEEILNR ENCIRCLED
CCDEEILOW COLICWEED

CCDEEINNY INDECENCY
CCDEEINOT CONCEITED
CCDEEINOV CONCEIVED
CCDEEIOPS CODPIECES
CCDEELLOT COLLECTED
CCDEEMMNO
  COMMENCED
CCDEENNOR CONCERNED
CCDEENNOS ENSCONCED
CCDEENNOT CONNECTED
CCDEENORS CRESCENDO
CCDEENORT
  CONCERTED, CONCRETED
CCDEEORRT CORRECTED
CCDEFIIRU CRUCIFIED
CCDEGINNO CONCEDING
CCDEHNRSU SCRUNCHED
CCDEIIKNP PICNICKED
CCDEILOOR CROCODILE
CCDEILSTY DYSLECTIC
CCDEINNOV CONVINCED
CCDEINOOT DECOCTION
CCDEINOTV CONVICTED
CCDEINOUV CONDUCIVE
CCDEKLOOR OLD COCKER
CCDELNOTU OCCLUDENT
CCDENORRU
  CONCURRED
CCDENOSSU CONCUSSED
CCDEORSUU SUCCOURED
CCDGINNOU CONDUCING
CCDHIILOR CHLORIDIC
CCDHIIMOR DICHROMIC
CCDHKOOUW
  WOODCHUCK
CCDKOOOSW
  WOODCOCKS
CCDNOORTU
  CONDUCTOR
CCEEEFLNU FECULENCE
CCEEEHHRR RECHERCHÉ
CCEEEHNOR COHERENCE
CCEEEHRRS SCREECHER
CCEEEHRSS SCREECHES
CCEEEIKNP NECKPIECE
CCEEEINNS NESCIENCE
CCEEEINRT RETICENCE
CCEEELORT RECTOCELE
CCEEFILLY LIFE CYCLE
CCEEGINOR CONCIERGE
CCEEHIKOY ICE HOCKEY
CCEEHILMY HEMICYCLE
CCEEHKORV OVERCHECK

CCEEHLORT CERECLOTH
CCEEHORRT CROCHETER
CCEEHOTTU COUCHETTE
CCEEIIPPR PRECIPICE
CCEEIKRRT CRICKETER
CCEEILNOR RECONCILE
CCEEILOST SCOLECITE
CCEEILPRY PERICYCLE
CCEEILRST ELECTRICS
CCEEIMORT ECTOMERIC
CCEEINNNO INNOCENCE
CCEEINORS CICERONES
CCEEKLORS COCKERELS
CCEEKNRSW CREW
     NECKS
CCEELLORT RECOLLECT
CCEELOSTY CYSTOCELE
CCEELOTUY LEUCOCYTE
CCEENNORT CONCENTRE
CCEENOOTY COENOCYTE
CCEENRSST CRESCENTS
CCEESSSSU SUCCESSES
CCEFFIIIL FELICIFIC
CCEFIIPSS SPECIFICS
CCEFIIRRU CRUCIFIER
CCEFKNOYY COCKNEYFY
CCEGGHOST SCOTCH EGG
CCEGHHNOW
     CHENGCHOW
CCEGHILNN CLENCHING
CCEGHIMRU CHEMURGIC
CCEGILNRY RECYCLING
CCEHHNRTU THE CRUNCH
CCEHIILRS SCHLIERIC
CCEHIKLST CHECKLIST
CCEHILNOR CHRONICLE
CCEHILNRS CLINCHERS
CCEHINRRU CRUNCHIER
CCEHIORST RICOCHETS
CCEHKLNOT NECKCLOTH
CCEHKMOOR
     CHECKROOM
CCEHKOORS COCKHORSE
CCEHKOPST SPOT CHECK
CCEHKOSTU CHECKOUTS
CCEHLMORS CROMLECHS
CCEHNOSTU SCUTCHEON
CCEHORRSS SCORCHERS
CCEHORSTT CROTCHETS
CCEHORTTY CROTCHETY
CCEIIIPRT EPICRITIC
CCEIIIRST CRITICISE
CCEIIIRTZ CRITICIZE

CCEIIKNPR PICNICKER
CCEIILNOT NICCOLITE
CCEIILRST SCLERITIC
CCEIILSTT CELTICIST
CCEIINSTY CYSTEINIC
CCEIKLLOY KILOCYCLE
CCEIKLOSW CLOCKWISE
CCEIKNOSS COCKINESS
CCEILNNOU NUCLEONIC
CCEILNOSY CONCISELY
CCEILNOTY CYCLONITE
CCEILORST SCLEROTIC
CCEILOSUV OCCLUSIVE
CCEILRSTY TRICYCLES
CCEILRSUU CURLICUES
CCEIMNOOS ECONOMICS
CCEIMORTY MICROCYTE
CCEIMOSST COSMETICS
CCEINNORV CONVINCER
CCEINOOSS CONSOCIES
CCEINORRT INCORRECT
CCEINOSTT TECTONICS
CCEINPRST PRECINCTS
CCEINRSTU CINCTURES
CCEINRSTY SYNCRETIC
CCEINSSTY SYNECTICS
CCEIOORST CREOSOTIC
CCEIOPRST COST PRICE
CCEIOPRSU OCCUPIERS
CCEIOPRTY PRECOCITY
CCEKORRSW
     CORKSCREW
CCELLNOOY COLONELCY
CCELLOORT COLLECTOR
CCELMOOTY COLECTOMY
CCELNSTUU SUCCULENT
CCELOPRSU CORPUSCLE
CCELOPSSY CYCLOPSES
CCELORRTY CORRECTLY
CCENNNORU
     UNCONCERN
CCENNOORT CONNECTOR
CCENOORST CONCERTOS
CCENOORSU CONCOURSE
CCENOORTV CONVECTOR
CCENORRTU OCCURRENT
CCENORSTU SUCCENTOR
CCEOOPRSY CRYOSCOPE
CCEOOPRTT ECTOPROCT
CCEOORRRT CORRECTOR
CCEOPPRUY PREOCCUPY
CCEORRSUU SUCCOURER
CCEORSSSU SUCCESSOR

CCFGHIKOT COCKFIGHT
CCFHKLLOU CHOCK-FULL
CCFIILOOR COLORIFIC
CCFILNOST CONFLICTS
CCFIMORRU CRUCIFORM
CCFKOOOST COCKSFOOT
CCFLLOSUU FLOCCULUS
CCGHIILNN CLINCHING
CCGHIINPU HICCUPING
CCGHIKLNU CHUCKLING
CCGHILNTU CLUTCHING
CCGHILOOP CHOPLOGIC
CCGHINNRU CRUNCHING
CCGHINORS SCORCHING
CCGHINORU CROUCHING
CCGHINOST SCOTCHING
CCGINNOOO COCOONING
CCGINOPUY OCCUPYING
CCGINORRU OCCURRING
CCHHOOPST HOPSCOTCH
CCHIIIRTT TRICHITIC
CCHIILORT CHLORITIC
CCHIIMOPR MICROCHIP
CCHIIMORT TRICHOMIC
CCHIINOOR CHORIONIC
CCHIINSUZ ZUCCHINIS
CCHIIOORS ISOCHORIC
CCHIIORRT CIRRHOTIC,
     TRICHROIC
CCHIKOPST CHOPSTICK
CCHILMOSW MILCH COWS
CCHILNRUY CRUNCHILY
CCHILOORT CHLOROTIC
CCHINRSTY STRYCHNIC
CCHIOPSTY PSYCHOTIC
CCHLNOOTY COLOCYNTH
CCIIILNOP PICOLINIC
CCIIILNRT TRICLINIC
CCIIIMRST CRITICISM
CCIIINNOT NICOTINIC
CCIILNOTY CLONICITY
CCIILOOST SCOLIOTIC
CCIILOPRT PROCLITIC
CCIINNOOS CONCISION
CCIIORRTT TRICROTIC
CCIIRRTUY CIRCUITRY
CCILMOSTU OCCULTISM
CCILNOOSU OCCLUSION
CCILOOORT COLICROOT
CCILOSTTU OCCULTIST
CCIMMOORS MICROCOSM
CCIMNOOTY MONOCYTIC
CCIMOOPRY MICROCOPY

CCINOOSSU CONSCIOUS
CCINOPRST CONSCRIPT
CCINORSTT CONSTRICT
CCIOOOPST OTOSCOPIC
CCIOOPRSU UROSCOPIC
CCIOOSTTY OTOCYSTIC
CCKKLOORW

    CLOCKWORK

CCKNORSTU TURNCOCKS
CCKOOPPPY POPPYCOCK
CCKOOPSST STOPCOCKS
CCLNOORTY CYCLOTRON
CCNORSTTU CONSTRUCT
CCOOPRSYY CRYOSCOPY
CDDDEEENS DESCENDED
CDDDEEILY DECIDEDLY
CDDDEEINU UNDECIDED
CDDEEEFLT DEFLECTED
CDDEEEIPY PIECE-DYED
CDDEEENRS DESCENDER
CDDEEEOPR PROCEEDED
CDDEEFKOR DEFROCKED
CDDEEGLLU CUDGELLED
CDDEEHLSU SCHEDULED
CDDEEINRS DISCERNED,

    RESCINDED

CDDEEIPRT PREDICTED
CDDEEISST DISSECTED
CDDEEITUV DEDUCTIVE
CDDEELNPU PEDUNCLED
CDDEELPRU PRECLUDED
CDDEEMMNO

    COMMENDED

CDDEEMNNO

    CONDEMNED

CDDEEMNRU

    CREDENDUM

CDDEENNOS CONDENSED
CDDEENNOT CONTENDED
CDDEENNOU

    DENOUNCED

CDDEGINTU DEDUCTING
CDDEHORRT DORDRECHT
CDDEIILMO DOMICILED
CDDEIILRU RIDICULED
CDDEIINRT DENDRITIC
CDDEIIOSV VIDEODISC
CDDEIIRST DISCREDIT
CDDEILOSS DISCLOSED
CDDEILSTU CUDDLIEST
CDDEIMOOU DUODECIMO
CDDEINOTU DEDUCTION
CDDEIOSUU DECIDUOUS

CDDEISSSU DISCUSSED
CDDHHILOO CHILDHOOD
CDDHIIORY HYDRIODIC
CDDIIILOP DIPLOIDIC
CDDILNOOY CONDYLOID
CDEEEEFNR DEFERENCE
CDEEEELRT RE-ELECTED
CDEEEFFOR FORCE-FEED
CDEEEFITV DEFECTIVE
CDEEEFLRT REFLECTED
CDEEEFPRT PERFECTED
CDEEEGINR DECREEING
CDEEEGINX EXCEEDING
CDEEEGLNT NEGLECTED
CDEEEHKNP HENPECKED
CDEEEHQRU CHEQUERED
CDEEEIMRT DECIMETRE
CDEEEINNS DESINENCE
CDEEEINPT CENTIPEDE
CDEEEINRS RESIDENCE
CDEEEINRT INTERCEDE
CDEEEINUV UNDECEIVE
CDEEEIPRV PERCEIVED
CDEEEIPTV DECEPTIVE
CDEEEIRSV DECEIVERS
CDEEEIRSX EXERCISED
CDEEEIRTV DECRETIVE
CDEEEITTV DETECTIVE
CDEEELLOT DÉCOLLETÉ
CDEEELNOR REDOLENCE
CDEEELORT ELECTRODE
CDEEEMNRT DECREMENT
CDEEENNST SENTENCED
CDEEENPRT PRECEDENT
CDEEEOPRR PROCEEDER
CDEEEORRT RETROCEDE
CDEEEORRV RE-COVERED
CDEEEPRST RESPECTED
CDEEFGINT DEFECTING
CDEEFIINT DEFICIENT
CDEEFIIOT FOETICIDE
CDEEFIIPS SPECIFIED
CDEEFIIRT CERTIFIED,

    RECTIFIED

CDEEFIKLR FLICKERED
CDEEFIKRR FREDERICK
CDEEFILNT INFLECTED
CDEEFILTU DECEITFUL
CDEEFINOT DEFECTION
CDEEFLORT DEFLECTOR
CDEEFNORR CONFERRED
CDEEFNOSS CONFESSED
CDEEFORST DEFECTORS

CDEEGIILN DILIGENCE
CDEEGIIMR GERMICIDE
CDEEGIINN INDIGENCE
CDEEGIINT DIGENETIC
CDEEGIINV DECEIVING
CDEEGIIRS REGICIDES
CDEEGILRY GLYCERIDE
CDEEGINOR ENDOERGIC
CDEEGINPR PRECEDING
CDEEGINTT DETECTING
CDEEGLLRU CUDGELLER
CDEEGNORV CONVERGED
CDEEGNOST CONGESTED
CDEEHHIRS CHERISHED
CDEEHIKNT THICKENED
CDEEHIKRW WHICKERED
CDEEHILLS CHISELLED
CDEEHIMRS REMSCHEID
CDEEHINST DEHISCENT
CDEEHKOSU DECKHOUSE
CDEEHLORY HYDROCELE
CDEEHLPPS SCHLEPPED
CDEEHLQSU SQUELCHED
CDEEHLSSU SCHEDULES
CDEEHORTU RETOUCHED
CDEEHRSTT STRETCHED
CDEEHSSSU DUCHESSES
CDEEIILTV VIDELICET
CDEEIIMNS MEDICINES
CDEEIIMPS EPIDEMICS
CDEEIIMRV VERMICIDE
CDEEIIPRR CIRRIPEDE
CDEEIIPST PESTICIDE
CDEEIIPTV DEPICTIVE
CDEEIIRTV DIRECTIVE
CDEEIISTT DIETETICS
CDEEIJNOT DEJECTION
CDEEIJPRU PREJUDICE
CDEEIKLLN NICKELLED
CDEEIKNQU QUICKENED
CDEEIKNRS SNICKERED
CDEEIKSST STICKSEED
CDEEIKSTW STICKWEED
CDEEILLNP PENCILLED
CDEEILNNO INDOLENCE
CDEEILNPR RED-PENCIL
CDEEILNST STENCILED
CDEEILORS CREOLISED
CDEEILORZ CREOLIZED
CDEEILRST DERELICTS
CDEEILTXY EXCITEDLY
CDEEIMNOU EUDEMONIC
CDEEIMNPU IMPUDENCE

CDEEINNOR ENDOCRINE
CDEEINNSU SECUNDINE
CDEEINOPT DECEPTION
CDEEINORT RECONDITE
CDEEINOST SECTIONED
CDEEINOTT DETECTION
CDEEINPST INSPECTED
CDEEINRRS DISCERNER,
RESCINDER
CDEEINRST STRIDENCE
CDEEINRSY RESIDENCY
CDEEIORSV DIVORCÉES
CDEEIORSX EXORCISED
CDEEIORXZ EXORCIZED
CDEEIOSTX COEXISTED
CDEEIPRSU PEDICURES
CDEEIPRTU DEPICTURE
CDEEIRRTU RECRUITED
CDEEIRSTT TRISECTED
CDEEIRTTU CERTITUDE,
RECTITUDE
CDEEISTUV SEDUCTIVE
CDEEJOPRT PROJECTED
CDEEKLNOW
LOW-NECKED
CDEEKOOPR PRECOOKED
CDEEKORST RESTOCKED
CDEELLMOP COMPELLED
CDEELLNRU CULLENDER
CDEELLOST COLD STEEL
CDEELMNTU DEMULCENT
CDEELMOPT COMPLETED
CDEELNOSU COUNSELED
CDEELORSS SCLEROSED
CDEELRSTU CLUSTERED
CDEELRTTU CLUTTERED
CDEEMMNOR
RECOMMEND
CDEEMMNOT
COMMENTED
CDEEMNNOR
CONDEMNER
CDEEMOOPS DECOMPOSE
CDEEMOORS MORSE
CODE
CDEENNORS CONDENSER
CDEENNORT CONTENDER
CDEENNORU
DENOUNCER, RENOUNCED
CDEENNOST CONSENTED
CDEENNOTT CONTENTED
CDEENOOPS ENDOSCOPE

CDEENOQRU
CONQUERED
CDEENORSS SECONDERS
CDEENORSV
CONSERVED, CONVERSED
CDEENORTU
COUNTERED, RECOUNTED
CDEENORTV CONVERTED
CDEENORUV UNCOVERED
CDEENOSTT CONTESTED
CDEENRRTU DECURRENT
CDEENRSTU ENCRUSTED
CDEENRSUU UNSECURED
CDEENRSUW
UNSCREWED
CDEEOORST CREOSOTED
CDEEOOSTV DOVECOTES
CDEEOPRRR PRERECORD
CDEEOPRRU
PROCEDURE, REPRODUCE
CDEEOPRSS PROCESSED
CDEEOPRTT PROTECTED
CDEEORRRS RECORDERS
CDEEORRTY DECRETORY
CDEEORSSY CROSS-EYED
CDEEORSTT DETECTORS
CDEEOSSTT COSSETTED
CDEEPPRSU SCUPPERED
CDEEPSSTU SUSPECTED
CDEFFIORU COIFFURED
CDEFGIINU FUNGICIDE
CDEFIIIST FIDEISTIC
CDEFIILNT INFLICTED
CDEFIINST DISINFECT
CDEFIKLOR FROLICKED
CDEFILNOR CORNFIELD
CDEFIMNOR CONFIRMED
CDEFINNOT CONFIDENT
CDEFINTUY FECUNDITY
CDEFKNORU UNFROCKED
CDEFMNOOR
CONFORMED
CDEFMOORT COMFORTED
CDEGGILNU CUDGELING
CDEGHINNR DRENCHING
CDEGIIKNR DICKERING
CDEGIILNN DECLINING
CDEGIINPT DEPICTING
CDEGIINRT CREDITING,
DIRECTING
CDEGIKNOT DOCKETING
CDEGILNSU SECLUDING
CDEGILNUX EXCLUDING

CDEGILOSU GLUCOSIDE
CDEGILOSY GLYCOSIDE
CDEGINNOS CONSIGNED,
SECONDING
CDEGINORR RECORDING
CDEGINRSY DESCRYING
CDEGINSSY DYSGENICS
CDEGLORST GOLDCREST
CDEGNORSU SCROUNGED
CDEHIIKLL CHILDLIKE
CDEHIILNO LICHENOID
CDEHIIMOS HOMICIDES
CDEHIIORT DICHROITE
CDEHIKLLO HILLOCKED
CDEHILLOV LOVECHILD
CDEHILLSS CHILDLESS
CDEHILOOR CHOLEROID
CDEHILORS CHLORIDES
CDEHILPST STEPCHILD
CDEHINORT CHONDRITE
CDEHINOSU CUSHIONED
CDEHIOORT THEODORIC
CDEHIORRS CIRRHOSED
CDEHIORTW DOWITCHER
CDEHKLSSU SHELDUCKS
CDEHLNORU CHONDRULE
CDEHNOOTT THECODONT
CDEHNOTUU UNTOUCHED
CDEHNOTUV DUTCH
OVEN
CDEHOOOPS HODOSCOPE
CDEIIILSV CIVILISED
CDEIIILVZ CIVILIZED
CDEIIIRST SIDERITIC
CDEIIKKSS SIDEKICKS
CDEIIKMTW MID-WICKET
CDEIILLNO CELLOIDIN,
DECILLION
CDEIILMOS DOMICILES
CDEIILMTU MULTICIDE
CDEIILNTU INDUCTILE
CDEIILORT DOLERITIC
CDEIILOST IDIOLECTS,
SOLICITED
CDEIILOSU DELICIOUS
CDEIILPSS DISCIPLES
CDEIILRRU RIDICULER
CDEIILTVY DECLIVITY
CDEIIMNOS MENISCOID
CDEIIMNTU CTENIDIUM
CDEIIMRST MISDIRECT
CDEIINNST INCIDENTS
CDEIINOPT DEPICTION

CDEIINORT CRETINOID,
DIRECTION
CDEIINOSS DECISIONS
CDEIINRTT INTERDICT
CDEIINTUV INDUCTIVE
CDEIIOOSU DIOECIOUS
CDEIIORST SIDEROTIC
CDEIIORUX UXORICIDE
CDEIIORVV DIVORCIVE
CDEIIRRTX DIRECTRIX
CDEIIRSTU CRUDITIES,
DIURETICS
CDEIJNNOO CONJOINED
CDEIKNSTY STICKY END
CDEILLLOU CELLULOID
CDEILMRSU DULCIMERS
CDEILNNOU CLOUD NINE
CDEILNOOS COLONISED
CDEILNOOZ COLONIZED
CDEILNRSY CYLINDERS
CDEILORSS DISCLOSER
CDEILOSTU CLOUDIEST
CDEILOTTW TWICE-TOLD
CDEILRTUY CREDULITY
CDEIMMNOO INCOMMODE
CDEIMMOTT COMMITTED
CDEIMNNOT CONDIMENT
CDEIMNOPR PRINCEDOM
CDEIMNORS CRIMSONED
CDEIMNORU INDECORUM
CDEIMNOSU NICODEMUS
CDEIMOPRS COMPRISED
CDEIMOSST DOMESTICS
CDEINNOTU CONTINUED,
UNNOTICED
CDEINOOTX ENDOTOXIC
CDEINOPRS CONSPIRED
CDEINORST DOCTRINES
CDEINORTU INTRODUCE,
REDUCTION
CDEINORTV CONTRIVED
CDEINOSST CONSISTED
CDEINOSTU SEDUCTION
CDEINRSSU CURDINESS
CDEINRSTY STRIDENCY
CDEIOPRRT PREDICTOR
CDEIORRST CREDITORS,
DIRECTORS
CDEIORRTY DIRECTORY
CDEIORSST DISSECTOR
CDEIORSSU DISCOURSE
CDEIORSTV DISCOVERT
CDEIORSVY DISCOVERY

CDEIPPSTY DYSPEPTIC
CDEKLOORY CROOKEDLY
CDELLOOPS SCOLLOPED
CDELLOSSU CLOUDLESS
CDELMNORU LEMON
CURD
CDELMOOWY LOW
COMEDY
CDELNOORT DECONTROL
CDELNOOST STONE-COLD
CDELNOOSW
CLOSEDOWN
CDELNOOTY COTYLEDON
CDELNOPUU UNCOUPLED
CDELNORSU SCOUNDREL
CDELNOSTU CONSULTED
CDELNOSUV CONVULSED
CDELOORSS COLD SORES
CDELOORSU COLOUREDS
CDELOORUV OVERCLOUD
CDELORSUU CREDULOUS
CDEMMOOOR
COMMODORE
CDEMNOORW
DOWNCOMER
CDEMNOOSW
COMEDOWNS
CDEMNOSTU DOCUMENTS
CDEMOOPRT COMPORTED
CDEMOOPST COMPOSTED
CDENNORUW
UNCROWNED
CDENNOTUU UNCOUNTED
CDENOOPSY ENDOSCOPY
CDENOORST CONSORTED
CDENOORTT CONTORTED
CDENOORTU CONTOURED
CDENORSTU CONSTRUED
CDENPRTUU PUNCTURED
CDEOOPRRT PROCTORED
CDEOOPSST POSTCODES
CDEOORRVW
OVERCROWD
CDEOORSWW
WOODSCREW
CDEOPRRSU PRODUCERS
CDEOPRRTU CORRUPTED
CDFFIILTU DIFFICULT
CDFGHILNO GOLDFINCH
CDFGIINNO CONFIDING
CDFGIINOY CODIFYING
CDFHINORY CHONDRIFY
CDFIIMOST DISCOMFIT

CDFIIORSU SUDORIFIC
CDFIMOORR CORDIFORM
CDFLNOORT COLD FRONT
CDGIIINNT INDICTING
CDGIIINOT INDIGOTIC
CDGIILLNO COLLIDING
CDGIILNNU INCLUDING
CDGIILOTT DIGLOTTIC
CDGIINNTU INDUCTING
CDGIINORV DIVORCING
CDGIKLNSU DUCKLINGS
CDGILLNOU COLLUDING
CDGILNNOO CONDOLING
CDGILNNOY CONDIGNLY
CDGILNOSS SCOLDINGS
CDGINNNOO CONDONING
CDGINNOOR CORDONING
CDGINOORR CORRODING
CDGINOORT DOCTORING
CDGINOPRU PRODUCING
CDHHIILTW WITH CHILD
CDHHIIOTY ICHTHYOID
CDHHILOST DISHCLOTH
CDHIIINOT CHITINOID
CDHIIMORS DICHROISM
CDHIIORRS SCIRRHOID
CDHIIPSTW DIPSWITCH
CDHIIRRTY TRIHYDRIC
CDHIMOOTY DICHOTOMY
CDHIMSTYY DYSTHYMIC
CDHINOPSY DYSPHONIC
CDHIOOPRY CHIROPODY
CDHIOOPSZ SCHIZOPOD
CDHIOPRSY DYSPHORIC
CDHLLOOOS OLD SCHOOL
CDHMNOOOR
MONOCHORD
CDHNOOORT
NOTOCHORD
CDHNOOTUW
TOUCHDOWN
CDHOOORTW
TORCHWOOD
CDHOOOTUW
TOUCHWOOD
CDIIILMNS DICLINISM
CDIIISTVY VISCIDITY
CDIIJOSUU JUDICIOUS
CDIIKPSST DIPSTICKS
CDIILMOOT DOLOMITIC
CDIILNOSU DICLINOUS
CDIILPTUY DUPLICITY
CDIILTTUY DUCTILITY

CDIIMNPUY PYCNIDIUM
CDIIMORST DICROTISM
CDIINNOOT CONDITION
CDIINNOTU INDUCTION
CDIINOPRY CYPRINOID
CDIIOOPRS SCORPIOID
CDIIORRTT TORTRICID
CDIIPRSTU TRICUSPID
CDIIRSSTT DISTRICTS
CDIJNOTUY JOCUNDITY
CDIKLPSUY LUCKY DIPS
CDIKMRSTU DRUMSTICK
CDIKNOSSW WINDSOCKS
CDILLNOOO COLLODION
CDILOORSU DISCOLOUR
CDILORSUU LUDICROUS
CDIMMNOOS DISCOMMON
CDIMMOOTY COMMODITY
CDIMNOORT MICRODONT
CDIMNOORU DORONICUM
CDIMNORSY SYNDROMIC
CDINORSSW CROSSWIND
CDINOSSTU DISCOUNTS
CDINOSTUY IN CUSTODY
CDIOORRRS CORRIDORS
CDIOPRSSU CUSPIDORS
CDKKNNOOW
   KNOCKDOWN
CDMNNORUU
   CONUNDRUM
CDMNOOPSU
   COMPOUNDS
CDNNOOTUW
   COUNTDOWN
CDOORRSSW
   CROSSWORD
CEEEEFFNR EFFERENCE
CEEEEFNRR REFERENCE
CEEEEGMNR EMERGENCE
CEEEEHILP HEELPIECE
CEEEEHMNV VEHEMENCE
CEEEEIPSY EYEPIECES
CEEEENRRV REVERENCE
CEEEFFITV EFFECTIVE
CEEEFFLNU EFFLUENCE
CEEEFINNR INFERENCE
CEEEFNORR FERROCENE,
   RE-ENFORCE
CEEEFNQRU FREQUENCE
CEEEFPRRT PERFECTER
CEEEGILNT TELEGENIC
CEEEGINRS REGENCIES
CEEEGINRT ENERGETIC

CEEEGISTX EXEGETICS
CEEEGLNOR CONGER EEL
CEEEGLNRT NEGLECTER
CEEEGMNRY EMERGENCY
CEEEHIKST CHEEKIEST
CEEEHILST SCHEELITE
CEEEHINNR INHERENCE
CEEEHIRST CHEERIEST
CEEEHISST ICE SHEETS
CEEEHLNTY ENTELECHY
CEEEHLRSS CHEERLESS
CEEEHOPRS ECOSPHERE
CEEEHQRUX EXCHEQUER
CEEEHRTTV CHEVRETTE
CEEEIIMPT TIMEPIECE
CEEEIINRV VICEREINE
CEEEIJRTV REJECTIVE
CEEEILLNT CLIENTELE
CEEEILNSS LICENSEES
CEEEILNST CELESTINE
CEEEILRST LEICESTER
CEEEILSTT CELESTITE
CEEEILSTV SELECTIVE
CEEEIMNNS EMINENCES
CEEEIMNTT CEMENTITE
CEEEIMRRS MERCERISE
CEEEIMRRZ MERCERIZE
CEEEINNPT PENITENCE
CEEEINNSS IN ESSENCE
CEEEINNST SENTIENCE
CEEEINPRT EPICENTRE
CEEEINRSU ESURIENCE
CEEEINSTX EXISTENCE
CEEEIPRRV PERCEIVER
CEEEIPRST CREEPIEST
CEEEIPRTV RECEPTIVE
CEEEIPSST SET PIECES
CEEEIPTVX EXCEPTIVE
CEEEIRRSV RECEIVERS
CEEEIRRSX EXERCISER
CEEEIRSSV RECESSIVE
CEEEIRSSX EXERCISES
CEEEIRSTV SECRETIVE
CEEEIRTVX EXCRETIVE
CEEEISSVX EXCESSIVE
CEEEITUVX EXECUTIVE
CEEEKORRT ROCKETEER
CEEELLNTX EXCELLENT
CEEELNOQU ELOQUENCE
CEEELOPST TELESCOPE
CEEEMNRRT RECREMENT
CEEEMNRTX EXCREMENT

CEEENNSST SENESCENT,
   SENTENCES
CEEENORTT ENTRECOTE
CEEENPRSS PRESENCES
CEEENPRST PRETENCES
CEEENQRSU SEQUENCER
CEEENQSSU SEQUENCES
CEEENRSST ERECTNESS
CEEEORRRV RECOVERER
CEEEPRRST RESPECTER
CEEEPRRTX EXCERPTER
CEEEPRSTU PERSECUTE
CEEFFFORT FOR EFFECT
CEEFFGINT EFFECTING
CEEFFIINT EFFICIENT
CEEFFOOPT COFFEEPOT
CEEFGLNTU GENUFLECT
CEEFHHNRT THE FRENCH
CEEFHIKRS KERCHIEFS
CEEFHIPSY SPEECHIFY
CEEFHITTY ITCHY FEET
CEEFHMNNR FRENCHMEN
CEEFIINTV INFECTIVE
CEEFIIPRS SPECIFIER
CEEFIIRRT RECTIFIER
CEEFIKKRS FREE KICKS
CEEFILNNU INFLUENCE
CEEFILRTY ELECTRIFY
CEEFIMPRT IMPERFECT
CEEFINORR REINFORCE
CEEFINORT REFECTION
CEEFINTTU FETTUCINE
CEEFIRRST FIRECREST
CEEFLOORS FORECLOSE
CEEFLORRT REFLECTOR
CEEFLORSU FLUORESCE
CEEFLPRTY PERFECTLY
CEEFNORRR CONFERRER
CEEFNORRS CONFRÈRES
CEEFNQRUY FREQUENCY
CEEFNRSTU RUFESCENT
CEEFORRTY REFECTORY
CEEFORSTW CROW'S
   FEET
CEEGHIMNO HEGEMONIC
CEEGHINOR RE-ECHOING
CEEGHINRW GREENWICH
CEEGHINSW ESCHEWING
CEEGHLOSW
   COGWHEELS
CEEGIINRV RECEIVING
CEEGIJNRT REJECTING
CEEGILLNX EXCELLING

CEEGILNOO OLIGOCENE
CEEGILNOT TELEGONIC
CEEGILNRY GLYCERINE
CEEGILNST SELECTING
CEEGIMNNT CEMENTING
CEEGIMORT GEOMETRIC
CEEGINNOS CONSIGNEE
CEEGINNRS SCREENING
CEEGINNRT CENTERING
CEEGINNST IGNESCENT
CEEGINOOT OOGENETIC
CEEGINORS CONGERIES,
　RECOGNISE
CEEGINORZ RECOGNIZE
CEEGINPTX EXCEPTING,
　EXPECTING
CEEGINRSS RECESSING
CEEGINRST SECRETING
CEEGINRTX EXCRETING
CEEGINTUX EXECUTING
CEEGIORRS GROCERIES
CEEGKNOOS GOOSENECK
CEEGLLMRS GERM CELLS
CEEGLMNRY CLERGYMEN
CEEGLNOOS CONGOLESE
CEEGORTTU COURGETTE
CEEHHIRRS CHERISHER
CEEHHIRVW WHICHEVER
CEEHHOPST HOPE CHEST
CEEHIILLN HELICLINE
CEEHIIPTT EPITHETIC
CEEHIKNNT IN THE NECK
CEEHIKNRT KITCHENER,
　THICKENER
CEEHIKPPR PIKEPERCH
CEEHIKRST SKETCHIER
CEEHILLRS CHISELLER
CEEHILNRS SCHLIEREN
CEEHILNTY ETHYLENIC
CEEHILPRT TELPHERIC
CEEHILRSW CLERIHEWS
CEEHILSTT TELESTICH
CEEHINQTU TECHNIQUE
CEEHINRVY EVERY INCH
CEEHINSST TECHINESS
CEEHINSTU EUTHENICS
CEEHIOPSW SHOWPIECE
CEEHISSTT CHESTIEST,
　ESTHETICS
CEEHISTTT TETCHIEST
CEEHKRSST SKETCHERS
CEEHLORSU LECHEROUS
CEEHLPRSU SEPULCHRE

CEEHLQRSU SQUELCHER
CEEHMNORZ CHERNOZEM
CEEHNOPRR PERCHERON
CEEHNRRST TRENCHERS
CEEHOPTTY ECTOPHYTE
CEEHORRTU RETOUCHER
CEEHRRSTT STRETCHER
CEEHRSSTT STRETCHES
CEEIIJNTV INJECTIVE
CEEIILNPR PERICLINE
CEEIILNRT LIENTERIC
CEEIILPPT EPILEPTIC
CEEIIMMNN IMMINENCE
CEEIIMNPS EPICENISM,
　MINCE PIES
CEEIIMNRS REMINISCE
CEEIIMPRS IMPRECISE
CEEIIMPST EPISTEMIC
CEEIIMRST METRICISE
CEEIIMRTZ METRICIZE
CEEIINNOR EIRENICON
CEEIINNRS INSINCERE
CEEIINNRT ENCRINITE
CEEIINNTV INCENTIVE
CEEIINPRT RECIPIENT
CEEIINPTV INCEPTIVE
CEEIINPTX EXCIPIENT
CEEIINRSV IN SERVICE
CEEIINTVV INVECTIVE
CEEIIOPST POETICISE
CEEIIOPTZ POETICIZE
CEEIIOSST SOCIETIES
CEEIJNORT REJECTION
CEEIJNRTT INTERJECT
CEEIKLNNS NECKLINES
CEEIKMORS MOCKERIES
CEEIKOPRW PIECEWORK,
　WORKPIECE
CEEIKORRS ROCKERIES
CEEILLNPR PENCILLER
CEEILLNTT INTELLECT
CEEILMNNT INCLEMENT
CEEILMNOP POLICEMEN
CEEILMNPR CRIMPLENE
CEEILMNSU LUMINESCE
CEEILMOST COMELIEST
CEEILMRSS MERCILESS
CEEILNNOS INSOLENCE
CEEILNORT CENTRIOLE
CEEILNOST ELECTIONS,
　SELECTION
CEEILNOTT NICOLETTE
CEEILNPST SPLENETIC

CEEILNRSS SILENCERS
CEEILNRSY SINCERELY
CEEILNRTV VENTRICLE
CEEILNRUV VIRULENCE
CEEILORSX EXCELSIOR
CEEILOSSS ISOSCELES
CEEILOSSV VOICELESS
CEEILPRSS PRICELESS
CEEILPRSY PRECISELY
CEEILRSTU CRUELTIES,
　RETICULES
CEEILRSTW CREWELIST
CEEILRSUV RECLUSIVE
CEEILSSTT TESTICLES
CEEILSSUV SECLUSIVE
CEEILSUVX EXCLUSIVE
CEEIMMOTT COMMITTEE
CEEIMNNRT INCREMENT
CEEIMNOOS ECONOMIES,
　ECONOMISE
CEEIMNOOZ ECONOMIZE
CEEIMNOPT IMPOTENCE
CEEIMNORR MEROCRINE
CEEIMNPSS SPECIMENS
CEEIMNSTU INTUMESCE
CEEINNORS RECENSION
CEEINOPRS PRECONISE
CEEINOPRT RECEPTION
CEEINOPRZ PRECONIZE
CEEINOPTX EXCEPTION
CEEINORSS RECESSION
CEEINORST ERECTIONS,
　RESECTION, SECRETION
CEEINORSU CINEREOUS
CEEINORTX EXCRETION
CEEINOSSS SECESSION
CEEINOSTX EXSECTION
CEEINOTUX EXECUTION
CEEINPRRU PRURIENCE
CEEINPRST PRESCIENT
CEEINPRTT INTERCEPT
CEEINPSSX SIXPENCES
CEEINQRTU QUERCETIN
CEEINQSTU QUIESCENT
CEEINRSSU SINECURES
CEEINRSTT INTERSECT
CEEINRSTU CENTURIES
CEEINRSTV VIRESCENT
CEEINSSTY NECESSITY
CEEIOORTZ OZOCERITE
CEEIOORVV VOICE-OVER
CEEIOPPRS PERISCOPE
CEEIORRST RECTORIES

CEEIORRSX EXORCISER
CEEIORRSSU SERICEOUS
CEEIPRSST TRICEPSES
CEEIRRRTU RECRUITER
CEEIRSSTU CERUSSITE
CEEIRSSTW SCREWIEST
CEEIRSUVX EXCURSIVE
CEEIRTUXX EXECUTRIX
CEELLLOSU CELLULOSE
CEELLMNTY CLEMENTLY
CEELLMOPR COMPELLER
CEELLMOSU MOLECULES
CEELLORTU COURTELLE
CEELMMNSU MUSCLEMEN
CEELMNOUW
     UNWELCOME
CEELMOPRT COMPLETER
CEELMOPSX COMPLEXES
CEELNORST ELECTRONS
CEELNORSU ENCLOSURE
CEELNOSSS CLOSENESS
CEELNPRUU PURULENCE
CEELNSSST SCENTLESS
CEELOPSTY TELESCOPY
CEELORSSS SCLEROSES
CEELORSST CORSELETS,
     SELECTORS
CEELORSSV COVERLESS
CEELORSTV COVERLETS
CEELRRSTU LECTURERS
CEEMMNORT
     COMMENTER
CEEMNNORT CONTEMNER
CEEMNOPTT COMPETENT
CEEMNORSW
     NEWCOMERS
CEEMNSTTU TUMESCENT
CEEMOOPRS RECOMPOSE
CEEMORRTY CRYOMETER
CEEMOSSTY ECOSYSTEM
CEENNOOSS NOSECONES
CEENNORRU RENOUNCER
CEENNORST CONSENTER
CEENNORSV CONVENERS
CEENNORTU ENCOUNTER
CEENOOPST COPESTONE
CEENOORSV
     ONCE-OVERS
CEENOORTV COVER NOTE
CEENOPRRT PRECENTOR
CEENOPSTT PENTECOST
CEENOPSTW TWOPENCES

CEENORRSV CONSERVER,
     CONVERSER
CEENORRTV CONVERTER,
     RECONVERT
CEENORSSV CONSERVES
CEENORSTT CONTESTER
CEENORSTW SWEET
     CORN
CEENORSVY CONVEYERS
CEENPPSTU TUPPENCES
CEENRRRTU RECURRENT
CEENRRTUX EXCURRENT
CEEOOORRS OVERSCORE
CEEOPPRRT PRECEPTOR
CEEOPRRSS REPROCESS
CEEOPRSSS PROCESSES
CEEOPRSTT TOP-SECRET
CEEOPRSTU PROSECUTE
CEEOQRTTU CROQUETTE
CEEOQSTTU COQUETTES
CEEORRRSS SORCERERS
CEEORRRSS SORCERESS
CEEORRSST CROSSTREE
CEEORRSSU RESOURCES
CEEORRSTW WORCESTER
CEEORRSTY SECRETORY
CEEORRSUV VERRUCOSE
CEEORRTUV COVERTURE
CEEORRTXY EXCRETORY
CEEORSTTV CORVETTES
CEEORSTUX EXECUTORS
CEEORTUXY EXECUTORY
CEEPRSSSY CYPRESSES
CEEPRSSTU SUSPECTER
CEERRRSTU RESURRECT
CEERRSSTU REST CURES
CEFFHINRY FRENCHIFY
CEFFIIOOX EX OFFICIO
CEFFIORSU COIFFEURS,
     COIFFURES
CEFFIRRSU SCRUFFIER
CEFGIINNT INFECTING
CEFGINNOR ENFORCING
CEFHIILSS FISH SLICE
CEFHIIMSS MISCHIEFS
CEFHIKRSW WRECKFISH
CEFHILMOR CHELIFORM
CEFHKOORS FORESHOCK
CEFHPRRSU SURFPERCH
CEFIILNRT INFLICTER
CEFIILNRU LUCIFERIN
CEFIINNOT INFECTION
CEFIIORRS SCORIFIER

CEFIKLORR FROLICKER
CEFILLLOS FOLLICLES
CEFILNORT INFLECTOR
CEFIMNORU CUNEIFORM
CEFINORSS FORENSICS
CEFINORTU CONFITURE
CEFIOORSU FEROCIOUS
CEFIORRSS CROSSFIRE
CEFKLOORS FORELOCKS
CEFKLOPTU POCKETFUL
CEFKOORRW
     WORKFORCE
CEFLNNOTU CONFLUENT
CEFMNOORR
     CONFORMER
CEFMOORRT COMFORTER
CEFNOORSS CONFESSOR
CEFOORRTU FORECOURT
CEGHIILNS CHISELING
CEGHIINNR ENRICHING
CEGHIINPR CIPHERING
CEGHIKNST SKETCHING
CEGHILLOU GUILLOCHE
CEGHILMTU GEMUTLICH
CEGHILNTV VETCHLING
CEGHILOOT ETHOLOGIC
CEGHINNQU QUENCHING
CEGHINNRW WRENCHING
CEGHINORT HECTORING
CEGHINPRY CYPHERING
CEGHIOPTY GEOPHYTIC
CEGHIORRU GROUCHIER
CEGHKNORU
     ROUGHNECK
CEGHMNOOR
     CHROMOGEN
CEGIIILNT ELICITING
CEGIIJNNT INJECTING
CEGIIJNOR REJOICING
CEGIIKLNN NICKELING
CEGIIKNNS SICKENING
CEGIIKNPT PICKETING
CEGIIKNTT TICKETING
CEGIILNNP PENCILING
CEGIILNNR RECLINING
CEGIILNNS LICENSING,
     SILENCING
CEGIILNOR RECOILING
CEGIILNPS ECLIPSING
CEGIINNNS INCENSING
CEGIINOTV COGNITIVE
CEGIINRSV SERVICING
CEGIIOSTT EGOTISTIC

CEGIJKNOY JOCKEYING
CEGIKNNOR RECKONING
CEGIKNOPT POCKETING
CEGIKNORT ROCKETING
CEGIKNPRU PUCKERING
CEGIKNRTU TUCKERING
CEGILLMOU COLLEGIUM
CEGILMMNO COMMINGLE
CEGILMNOW WELCOMING
CEGILNNOS ENCLOSING
CEGILNOST CLOSETING
CEGILNRSU SURCINGLE
CEGILNRTU LECTURING
CEGILOORS SEROLOGIC
CEGILOOST ECOLOGIST
CEGIMNNOO MONOGENIC
CEGIMNOOR ERGONOMIC
CEGIMNOPR COMPERING
CEGIMNOPT COMPETING
CEGIMNOUY GYNOECIUM
CEGIMNOYZ ZYMOGENIC
CEGINNNOV CONVENING
CEGINNOOT ONTOGENIC
CEGINNORR CORNERING
CEGINNORS CENSORING
CEGINNOVY CONVEYING
CEGINNRSU CENSURING
CEGINOOPS GEOPONICS
CEGINOPRU RECOUPING
CEGINOPRY PYROGENIC
CEGINOPTY GENOTYPIC
CEGINORST ESCORTING
CEGINORSV COVERINGS
CEGINRRRU RECURRING
CEGIOOPRT GEOTROPIC
CEGLNOORY NECROLOGY
CEGMNNOOS
  COGNOMENS
CEGNNORTU CONGRUENT
CEGNORRSU SCROUNGER
CEGNORSUY SURGEONCY
CEGOOPRSY GYROSCOPE
CEHHHIIKT HITCHHIKE
CEHHIIMST HEMISTICH
CEHHIMSTT HEMSTITCH
CEHHOOPSU CHOPHOUSE
CEHIIKLTW WITCHLIKE
CEHIIKORS HICKORIES
CEHIILLST CHILLIEST
CEHIILMOT HOMILETIC
CEHIILNOT NEOLITHIC
CEHIIMSTY MYTHICISE
CEHIIMTYZ MYTHICIZE

CEHIINNOT ON THIN ICE
CEHIINPRT NEPHRITIC,
  PHRENITIC
CEHIINRST CHRISTINE
CEHIINRTZ CHINTZIER
CEHIINSST ITCHINESS
CEHIINTWZ ZINC WHITE
CEHIIPPTY EPIPHYTIC
CEHIIPRST CHIRPIEST
CEHIIPRTT TEPHRITIC
CEHIIRSTU HEURISTIC
CEHIISTTT TITCHIEST
CEHIKLPRS CLERKSHIP
CEHIKLSTY SKETCHILY
CEHIKNSST THICKNESS
CEHIKNSTU CHUNKIEST
CEHIKOPPT HIP POCKET
CEHIKPRSW SHIPWRECK
CEHILNNPU PUNCH LINE
CEHILNOOR HOLOCRINE
CEHILNOSU LICHENOUS
CEHILNOTU TOUCHLINE
CEHILNSTZ SCHNITZEL
CEHILORST CLOTHIERS
CEHIMMOPR MORPHEMIC
CEHIMMORS MICROMESH
CEHIMMSTU CHUMMIEST
CEHIMNNOU ICHNEUMON
CEHIMNOPS PHONEMICS
CEHIMRSTY CHEMISTRY
CEHINOPRT NEPHROTIC
CEHINOPST PHONETICS
CEHINOPTY NEOPHYTIC
CEHINPRST SPHINCTER
CEHINPSTU PUNCHIEST
CEHINSSSU CUSHINESS
CEHINSTTY SYNTHETIC
CEHIOOPRT ORTHOEPIC
CEHIOOSST CHOOSIEST
CEHIOPPRT PROPHETIC
CEHIOPPST CHOPPIEST
CEHIOPRRT CHIROPTER
CEHIOPRTT PROTHETIC
CEHIOPRTU EUTROPHIC
CEHIOPRTY HYPOCRITE
CEHIORRST CHORISTER
CEHIORSST OSTRICHES
CEHIOSSST SCHISTOSE
CEHIOSTTU TOUCHIEST
CEHIPRRRU CHIRRUPER
CEHIRSSTY HYSTERICS
CEHKOOOSU
  COOKHOUSE

CEHKRSSTU HUCKSTERS
CEHLLOOPT PHOTOCELL
CEHLOOPRS PRESCHOOL
CEHMOOPRT ECTOMORPH
CEHMOORRU
  UROCHROME
CEHNNORTU TRUNCHEON
CEHNOOPPY PHENOCOPY
CEHNOORSS SCHOONERS
CEHNSSTTU CHESTNUTS
CEHOOOPRS HOROSCOPE
CEHOPRTYY CRYOPHYTE
CEHOPSSSY PSYCHOSES
CEHOPTTUY TOUCH-TYPE
CEIIILRSV CIVILISER
CEIIILRVZ CIVILIZER
CEIIIMSTV VICTIMISE
CEIIIMTVZ VICTIMIZE
CEIIINNPT INCIPIENT
CEIIIPRSS EPICRISIS
CEIIJNNOT INJECTION
CEIIJNSSU JUICINESS
CEIIJNSTU INJUSTICE
CEIIKLMQU QUICKLIME
CEIIKLMRS LIMERICKS
CEIIKLMST KELTICISM
CEIIKLNRR CRINKLIER
CEIIKLPRR PRICKLIER
CEIIKLSST SICKLIEST
CEIIKLSTT KELTICIST
CEIIKNPRT NITPICKER
CEIIKNPSS PICKINESS
CEIIKRSTT TRICKIEST
CEIIKSSTT STICKIEST
CEIILLMNT MILLICENT
CEIILMNSU MINISCULE
CEIILNNOR CRINOLINE
CEIILNPPR PRINCIPLE
CEIILNSUV INCLUSIVE
CEIILOQRU LIQUORICE
CEIILOSSU SILICEOUS
CEIILPRST LIST PRICE
CEIILPRTU PLEURITIC
CEIILRSST SCLERITIS
CEIILSTTY SECTILITY
CEIIMNOST SEMITONIC
CEIIMNRST CRETINISM
CEIIMNSST SCIENTISM
CEIIMORST EROTICISM,
  ISOMETRIC
CEIIMOSST SEMIOTICS
CEIIMOSTX EXOTICISM
CEIIMPRSU EPICURISM

CEIIMRRTT TRIMETRIC
CEIINNOPT INCEPTION
CEIINNORT INCRETION
CEIINNRTY INNER CITY
CEIINOPRS PRECISION
CEIINORRT CRITERION
CEIINORTT TRICOTINE
CEIINORTV VICTORINE
CEIINOSSX EXCISIONS
CEIINOSTV EVICTIONS
CEIINPRSS PRICINESS
CEIINPSSS SPICINESS
CEIINRSTX EXTRINSIC
CEIINRSTY CITISENRY, SINCERITY
CEIINRSUV INCURSIVE
CEIINRTTY INTERCITY
CEIINRTYZ CITIZENRY
CEIINSSTT SCIENTIST
CEIIOOPTZ EPIZOOTIC
CEIIORSST ISOSTERIC
CEIIORSTV VICTORIES
CEIIPRSST CRISPIEST
CEIIPSTTY SEPTICITY
CEIIQRSTU CRITIQUES
CEIJNNOOR CONJOINER
CEIJNORTT INTROJECT
CEIKLNORT INTERLOCK
CEIKLNOST CLOSE-KNIT
CEIKLNOSU NICKELOUS
CEIKLNSSS SLICKNESS
CEIKLNSSU LUCKINESS
CEIKLOPST STOCKPILE
CEIKLOSTV LIVESTOCK
CEIKLPSTU PLUCKIEST
CEIKLRSST STICKLERS
CEIKMNSSU MUCKINESS
CEIKMPPSU PICK-ME-UPS
CEIKNORSS ROCKINESS
CEIKNOSTT STOCKINET
CEIKNQSSU QUICKNESS
CEIKORRTV OVERTRICK
CEIKOSSTT STOCKIEST
CEIKPQSTU QUICKSTEP
CEIKRRSTT TRICKSTER
CEILLLMTU CLITELLUM
CEILLNOOR COLOR LINE
CEILLNOUV INVOLUCEL
CEILLOPTU POLLUCITE
CEILLOSUV COLLUSIVE
CEILLPSTY SYLLEPTIC
CEILMNNOO MONOCLINE
CEILMNOOS SEMICOLON

CEILMNOTU MONTICULE
CEILMNSSU LEMNISCUS
CEILMNSUU MINUSCULE
CEILMOPRS COMPILERS
CEILMOPRY MICROPYLE, POLYMERIC
CEILMOSSS SOLECISMS
CEILMRTUU RETICULUM
CEILMSSTU CLUMSIEST
CEILNNOOS CLOISONNÉ
CEILNOOPS SCOPOLINE
CEILNOORS COLONISER
CEILNOORZ COLONIZER
CEILNOOTU ELOCUTION
CEILNOPRV PIN CLOVER
CEILNORSU CORNELIUS, INCLOSURE, RECLUSION
CEILNORUV INVOLUCRE
CEILNOSSU SECLUSION
CEILNOSUX EXCLUSION
CEILNRSSU CURLINESS
CEILNRUVY VIRULENCY
CEILOOPRT COPROLITE
CEILOPPRT PROLEPTIC
CEILOPPSS POPSICLES
CEILOPSTU POULTICES
CEILORRTU COURTLIER
CEILORSSS SCLEROSIS
CEILORSST CLOISTERS
CEILOSSST SOLSTICES
CEILOSSTT COSTLIEST
CEILPRSSU SURPLICES
CEILRSUVY CURSIVELY
CEIMMNNOS MNEMONICS
CEIMMNOOR MONOMERIC
CEIMMNOSU COMMUNISE, ENCOMIUMS
CEIMMNOTU COMMINUTE
CEIMMNOUZ COMMUNIZE
CEIMMOORS MICROSOME
CEIMMOORT MICROTOME
CEIMMORTT COMMITTER
CEIMMRSTU CRUMMIEST
CEIMNNOPU PNEUMONIC
CEIMNOORT MICROTONE
CEIMNOOST ECONOMIST
CEIMNORST INTERCOMS
CEIMNORTT METRIC TON
CEIMOOPRR POROMERIC
CEIMOOPST COMPOSITE
CEIMOORTZ ZOOMETRIC
CEIMOOSTX EXOSMOTIC
CEIMOPRST PRIME COST

CEIMOPSUU PUMICEOUS
CEIMORSSX EXORCISMS
CEIMORSTU COSTUMIER
CEIMOSSTU CUSTOMISE
CEIMOSTUV MUSCOVITE
CEIMOSTUZ CUSTOMIZE
CEINNNOTT CONTINENT
CEINNNOTV CONNIVENT
CEINNOPRT PRINCETON
CEINNORTU CENTURION, CONTINUER
CEINNRRTU INCURRENT
CEINOORST CORTISONE
CEINOOSSW SOSNOWIEC
CEINOPPRU PORCUPINE
CEINOPRRT INTERCROP
CEINOPRST INSPECTOR
CEINOPRSV PROVINCES
CEINOPRXY PYROXENIC
CEINORRTW TOWN CRIER
CEINORSTT CORNETIST
CEINORSTU COUNTRIES, CRETINOUS, NEUROTICS
CEINORSUX EXCURSION
CEINOSTUV CONTUSIVE
CEINOTVXY CONVEXITY
CEINPRSSS CRISPNESS
CEINRSSTT CENTRISTS
CEINRSTTU TINCTURES
CEIOOPRSS COREOPSIS
CEIOOPRST PORTICOES
CEIOORRSV CORROSIVE
CEIOPRRSU CROUPIERS
CEIORRSTT TRISECTOR
CEIORRSTU COURTIERS
CEIORRTUU COUTURIER
CEIORSSSW CROSSWISE
CEIORSSTX EXORCISTS
CEIORSTTU TOREUTICS
CEIPPRRST PRESCRIPT
CEIPRRSTU SCRIPTURE
CEIPRSSTU PIECRUSTS
CEIRRSTTU STRICTURE
CEIRSSTTT STRICTEST
CEIRSSTTU CRUSTIEST
CEJNORRSU CONJURERS
CEJNRSTUU JUNCTURES
CEJOOPRRT PROJECTOR
CEKKORSTY SKYROCKET
CEKLNOOPS POLO NECKS
CEKLNORTW TOWN CLERK

CEKOORRSW CO-WORKERS
CEKOORSTV OVERSTOCK
CEKOPRSST SPROCKETS
CELLMSTUU SCUTELLUM
CELLNOSUU NUCLEOLUS
CELLOOPTY COLLOTYPE
CELMNOTUY CONTUMELY
CELMOOPRY COPOLYMER
CELMOOTUY LEUCOTOMY
CELMOPRUU OPERCULUM
CELMPRSTU PLECTRUMS
CELNOOSTU CONSOLUTE
CELNOOTUV CONVOLUTE
CELNOPRTU CORPULENT
CELNORSTU CONSULTER
CELNOSSTU COUNTLESS
CELNRRTUY CURRENTLY
CELNRTTUU TRUCULENT
CELOOPRSU SUPERCOOL
CELORSSUU SURCULOSE
CELPRSTUU SCULPTURE
CEMMNOORS COMMONERS
CEMMORSTU COMMUTERS
CEMNNOOPT COMPONENT
CEMNOOOQU MONOCOQUE
CEMNOORTY NECROTOMY
CEMNORSSU CONSUMERS
CEMNORTUY EMUNCTORY
CEMOOPRSS COMPOSERS
CEMOOPRSU COMPOSURE
CEMOPRSTU COMPUTERS
CEMORRSUU MERCUROUS
CEMORRSWW SCREWWORM
CEMORRTYY CRYOMETRY
CEMORSSTU CUSTOMERS
CENNOOPPY OPPONENCY
CENNOOPRU PRONOUNCE
CENNORSTU NOCTURNES
CENNOSSSU CONSENSUS
CENOOPRST STONECROP
CENOOQRRU CONQUEROR
CENOORRST CONSORTER

CENOQSSTU CONQUESTS
CENORRSTU CONSTRUER
CENORSSSS CROSSNESS
CENORSSTW CROW'S NEST
CENORSSUY CYNOSURES
CENORSTXY XENOCRYST
CENPRRTUU PUNCTURER
CENPRSTUU PUNCTURES
CEOOOSTTV SOTTO VOCE
CEOOPRRSS PROCESSOR
CEOOPRRST PROSECTOR
CEOOPRRTT PROTECTOR
CEOOPRSTY SPOROCYTE
CEOOPSSTU OCTOPUSES
CEOORRSSU SORCEROUS
CEOORRSSV CROSSOVER
CEOORSTUU COURTEOUS
CEOPPRSST PROSPECTS
CEOPRRRSU PRECURSOR, PROCURERS
CEOPRRRTU CORRUPTER
CEOPRRSSU PERCUSSOR
CEOPRSSTW SCREW TOPS
CEPPRSTUU UPPERCUTS
CEPRSSTUU CUTPURSES
CERRSTTUU STRUCTURE
CFFGIINSU SUFFICING
CFFGILNSU SCUFFLING
CFFIIOOSU OFFICIOUS
CFFIKLNSU CUFF LINKS
CFFLOOORU OFF COLOUR
CFGHIILNN FLINCHING
CFGHIILNS CLINGFISH
CFGIILLMN CLINGFILM
CFGIINNNO CONFINING
CFGILNNOU FLOUNCING
CFGILNORY FORCINGLY
CFGINNOSU CONFUSING
CFGINNOTU CONFUTING
CFGINOSSU FOCUSSING
CFHIIKSST FISH STICK
CFHIINOOR HONORIFIC
CFHIKOPRT PITCHFORK
CFHIKOSST STOCKFISH
CFHMNOOTU NOT MUCH OF
CFHOOSTTU SOFT TOUCH
CFIIKKLNS SKIN FLICK
CFIILMMOR MICROFILM
CFIILORST FLORISTIC
CFIIOOPRS SOPORIFIC
CFIIOPRRT TRPORIFIC

CFIKLLNOT FLINTLOCK
CFIKLLOOR FOLKLORIC
CFIKLMOST FILM STOCK
CFILNSUUU FUNICULUS
CFIMORSTU SCUTIFORM
CFINNOOSU CONFUSION
CFINNOSTU FUNCTIONS
CFLLOORUU COLOURFUL
CFLNOORRU CORNFLOUR
CFLOOOSTT COLTSFOOT
CFOOORSTW CROW'S FOOT
CFORSTUUU FRUCTUOUS
CGGHIKNNU CHUNGKING
CGGHINORU GROUCHING
CGGINORSU SCOURGING
CGHHIORTU HIGH COURT
CGHIILLNS SCHILLING
CGHIIMNRS SMIRCHING
CGHIIMOST GOTHICISM
CGHIINNST SNITCHING
CGHIINPPS CHIPPINGS
CGHIINSTT STITCHING
CGHIINSTW SWITCHING
CGHIINTTW TWITCHING
CGHILNOOS SCHOOLING
CGHILNOOY ICHNOLOGY
CGHILNORT CHORTLING
CGHILNOSU SLOUCHING
CGHILOOOR HOROLOGIC
CGHILORUY GROUCHILY
CGHIMNOOS SMOOCHING
CGHINORSU CHORUSING
CGHIOPRTY COPYRIGHT
CGHKLOTUU TOUGH LUCK
CGHLLNOOT LONGCLOTH
CGHLOOORY CHOROLOGY
CGHLOOPYY PHYCOLOGY
CGIIKMMN MIMICKING
CGIIILNNN INCLINING
CGIIINNOV INVOICING
CGIIKLNNR CRINKLING
CGIIKLNPR PRICKLING
CGIIKLNRT TRICKLING
CGIIKMMRY GIMMICKRY
CGIIKNNPU UNPICKING
CGIILMNNY MINCINGLY
CGIILMNOP COMPILING
CGIILNNOS INCLOSING
CGIILNNWY WINCINGLY
CGIILNPPR CRIPPLING

CGIILNPPS CLIPPINGS
CGIILOSST GLOSSITIC,
　LOGISTICS
CGIILRSTU LITURGICS
CGIIMNPRS SCRIMPING
CGIINNNOV CONNIVING
CGIINNOOT COGNITION,
　INCOGNITO
CGIINNRRU INCURRING
CGIINPRTU PICTURING
CGIJNNORU CONJURING
CGIKKLNNU KNUCKLING
CGIKLMNOY MOCKINGLY
CGIKLNNOU UNLOCKING
CGIKLNRTU TRUCKLING
CGIKLNSSU SUCKLINGS
CGIKNNOOV CONVOKING
CGIKNNORU UNCORKING
CGIKNOSST STOCKINGS
CGIKOOPST POGO STICK
CGILLNORS SCROLLING
CGILLNOYY CLOYINGLY
CGILMNOOO MONOLOGIC
CGILMNOPY COMPLYING
CGILMNPRU CRUMPLING
CGILMOOYZ ZYMOLOGIC
CGILNNNUY CUNNINGLY
CGILNNOOR LONGICORN
CGILNNOOS CONSOLING
CGILNOOOY ICONOLOGY
CGILNOORU COLOURING
CGILNOPSU COUPLINGS
CGILNOPUV LOVING CUP
CGILNPRSU SCRUPLING
CGILNSTTU SCUTTLING
CGILNTTUY CUTTINGLY
CGILOOOPT TOPOLOGIC
CGILOOOSY SOCIOLOGY
CGIMMNNOU
　COMMUNING
CGIMMNOTU COMMUTING
CGIMNNOSU CONSUMING
CGIMNOOPS COMPOSING
CGIMNOPTU COMPUTING
CGIMNPRSU SCRUMPING
CGINNNOOT CONNOTING
CGINNOORS CONSIGNOR
CGINNOOTT COTTON GIN
CGINNOOVY CONVOYING
CGINNORTU TROUNCING
CGINNOSTU CONTUSING
CGINOPRRU PROCURING
CGINORSSS CROSSINGS

CGINORSSU SCOURINGS
CGINORTUY CONGRUITY
CGINRRSUY SCURRYING
CGINRSTUY CURTSYING
CGLMOOOSY
　COSMOLOGY
CGMNOOOSY
　COSMOGONY
CGNNOOTTU GUN
　COTTON
CGNOORSUU
　CONGRUOUS
CHHHIIMNO HO CHI MINH
CHHIMRSTY RHYTHMICS
CHHINTTUW WITCH-HUNT
CHHKLLOOY HOLLYHOCK
CHIIILPPP PHILIPPIC
CHIILLOPY LYOPHILIC
CHIILLPTY PHYLLITIC
CHIILNNPS LINCHPINS
CHIILOOPZ ZOOPHILIC
CHIILOOTT OTOLITHIC
CHIILORTU UROLITHIC
CHIILORTY RHYOLITIC
CHIILPSTU SULPHITIC
CHIILPTTY TYPHLITIC
CHIINOSTU CHITINOUS
CHIIOPSST SOPHISTIC
CHIIORRSS CIRRHOSIS
CHIIORSST TRICHOSIS
CHIIPSSTY PHYSICIST
CHIKLMOST LOCKSMITH
CHIKLPSUY PUCKISHLY
CHIKMNPSU CHIPMUNKS
CHIKOOPTT TOOTHPICK
CHIKOPSTW WHIPSTOCK
CHILLMOPY PHYLLOMIC
CHILLNOOT LOINCLOTH
CHILLOSTY COLTISHLY
CHILLOSUY SLOUCHILY
CHILMOOTY HOMOLYTIC
CHILOOPTY HOLOTYPIC
CHILOORSS CHLOROSIS
CHILORTUY ULOTRICHY
CHILOSTTY CYSTOLITH
CHIMMNOOY HOMONYMIC
CHIMNOOST MONOSTICH
CHIMNOPSY SYMPHONIC
CHIOOPRTT ORTHOPTIC
CHIOOPTYZ ZOOPHYTIC
CHIOPRSTU COURTSHIP
CHIOPRSYY HYPOCRISY
CHIOPSSSY PSYCHOSIS

CHIORRSSU SCIRRHOUS
CHIPRSTTY TRIPTYCHS
CHKLMOOST STOCKHOLM
CHLNOTUUY UNCOUTHLY
CHLOPPTYY POLYPTYCH
CHOOOPPTY PHOTOCOPY
CHOOOPRSY HOROSCOPY
CHORSSTTU SHORT CUTS
CIIILLLTY ILLICITLY
CIIILLSTV CIVIL LIST
CIIILMOPT IMPOLITIC
CIIILORTV VITRIOLIC
CIIILOSSS SILICOSIS
CIIIMSTTW WITTICISM
CIIINNOSS INCISIONS
CIIINNRST INTRINSIC
CIIINOSTZ ZIONISTIC
CIIJLNOPT CLIP JOINT
CIIKLLOSS OIL SLICKS
CIIKLPSST LIPSTICKS
CIIKNPPRS PINPRICKS
CIIKNPSST STICKPINS
CIILLNOOS COLLISION
CIILLNOOT COTILLION,
　OCTILLION
CIILLOPTY LIPOLYTIC
CIILMPRSY SCRIMPILY
CIILMRSSY LYRICISMS
CIILNNOSU INCLUSION
CIILNOPTU PUNCTILIO,
　UNPOLITIC
CIILOOPST POLITICOS
CIILOORST SOLICITOR
CIILOOSSS SCOLIOSIS
CIILOPRTY PYROLITIC
CIILOSUVY VICIOUSLY
CIILRSSTY LYRICISTS
CIILSSTTY STYLISTIC
CIIMMSSTY MYSTICISM
CIIMNORUZ ZIRCONIUM
CIIMOOSST ISOSMOTIC
CIIMORSTV VORTICISM
CIINNNOTU INUNCTION
CIINNORSU INCURSION
CIINNOSSW WISCONSIN
CIINNSSTT INSTINCTS
CIINOOPRT INOTROPIC
CIINOPSSU SUSPICION
CIINORSUU INCURIOUS
CIINOSTVY SYNOVITIC
CIIOOPRST ISOTROPIC
CIIOOSSTX TOXICOSIS
CIIOPRSTT TROPISTIC

CIIORSTTU TOURISTIC
CIIORSTTV VORTICIST
CIIORSTUV VIRTUOSIC
CIIORSTUY CURIOSITY
CIIOSSTVY VISCOSITY
CIIRSTTUY RUSTICITY
CIJKOSSST JOSS STICK
CIJKOSSTY JOYSTICKS
CIJNNOSTU JUNCTIONS
CIJNNOTTU T-JUNCTION
CIKKOOSSU KOSCIUSKO
CIKLLNUUY UNLUCKILY
CIKLNORSS CROSS-LINK
CIKLOOPST POLO STICK
CIKLOORSU COKULORIS
CIKLORSTW WRISTLOCK
CIKMOORSS SICKROOMS
CIKOSSSTT STOCKISTS
CILLMORUY COLLYRIUM
CILLMOUUV COLLUVIUM
CILLNOOSU COLLUSION
CILLNOSSU SCULLIONS
CILLOOOTY COYOTILLO
CILMNOSTU COLUMNIST
CILMOOPSY POLYSOMIC
CILMOSSUU SOUL MUSIC
CILMOTYYZ ZYMOLYTIC
CILNOORUU UNICOLOUR
CILNOOSST COLONISTS
CILNOOSTU LOCUTIONS
CILNOSTYY CYTOLYSIN
CILOOPSUY COPIOUSLY
CILOORRTU TRICOLOUR
CILOORSTU COLOURIST
CILOPPTYY POLYTYPIC
CILORRSUY CURSORILY
CILORSUUY CURIOUSLY
CILOSSTYY CYTOLYSIS
CILRSTTUU CULTURIST
CIMMMNOSU
　　COMMUNISM
CIMMNNOOU
　　COMMUNION
CIMMNOOOS MONOSOMIC
CIMMNOOOT COMMOTION
CIMMNOSTU COMMUNIST
CIMMNOTUY COMMUNITY
CIMMOORTY MICROTOMY
CIMNNOOOT MONOTONIC
CIMNNOSYY SYNONYMIC
CIMNNOTUU CONTINUUM
CIMNOOPTY MONOTYPIC,
　　TOPONYMIC

CIMNOSSTU MISCOUNTS
CIMNSTUYY SYNCYTIUM
CINNOOSTU CONTINUOS,
　　CONTUSION
CINNOOSUU INNOCUOUS
CINOOOORRS CORROSION
CINOOPRSS SCORPIONS
CINOPRRTU INCORRUPT
CINOSSTUV VISCOUNTS
CIOOOPRSZ ZOOSPORIC
CIOOPSSTU POSTICOUS
CKKNOOSTU KNOCKOUTS
CKLLNOORR ROCK 'N'
　　ROLL
CKMOOORST
　　STOCKROOM
CKNOORRWW
　　CROWNWORK
CKOOORSTT ROOTSTOCK
CKOOPSSTT STOCKPOTS
CKOPRSTTU TRUCK STOP
CLMOOOORT
　　LOCOMOTOR
CLMOOOSTY COLOSTOMY
CLMOORSTU COLOSTRUM
CLNOOPRSU PROCONSUL
CLOOOPRST PROTOCOLS
CLOPRRTUY CORRUPTLY
CLOPRSSTU SCULPTORS
CMNOOORST
　　COSMOTRON
CMOOOORRTU
　　COURTROOM
CMOOORSST MOTOCROSS
CMOOOSTTY COSTOTOMY
CMOOSTTYY CYSTOTOMY
CNNNOOTUU COUNT
　　NOUN
CNOPRTUUY UP-COUNTRY
COOOOPRRST ROOT CROPS
COOPRSSTY SPOROCYST
COORRSSTW
　　CROSSWORT
DDDEEHRSU SHUDDERED
DDDEEINST DISTENDED
DDDEENORU
　　REDOUNDED
DDDEEORRS DODDERERS
DDDEGILOS DISLODGED
DDDEGINOR DODDERING
DDDEIINSV DIVIDENDS
DDDEIINUV UNDIVIDED
DDDEIIPRR DRIP-DRIED

DDEEEEKNW
　　WEEKENDED
DDEEEFIPR DEEP FRIED
DDEEEFNRS DEFENDERS
DDEEEFNRU UNDERFEED
DDEEEGIPR PEDIGREED
DDEEEILRV DELIVERED
DDEEEILTT TITLE DEED
DDEEEINRX DEXEDRINE
DDEEEIPTX EXPEDITED
DDEEEIRTU DEUTERIDE
DDEEELMOR REMODELED
DDEEELOPV DEVELOPED
DDEEENNOP OPEN-ENDED
DDEEENNPT DEPENDENT
DDEEENPRT PRETENDED
DDEEEPRSS DEPRESSED
DDEEERRSS REDRESSED
DDEEERSWY
　　DYER'S-WEED
DDEEESTUU DESUETUDE
DDEEFGINN DEFENDING
DDEEFGLNU UNFLEDGED
DDEEFNORU FOUNDERED
DDEEFORST DEFROSTED
DDEEGGGLO DOGLEGGED
DDEEGGILT GILT-EDGED
DDEEGHILT DELIGHTED
DDEEGINNP DEPENDING
DDEEGINNR REDDENING
DDEEGIRSS DIGRESSED
DDEEGJPRU PREJUDGED
DDEEHIINT HIDDENITE
DDEEHNORT DETHRONED
DDEEHNORU
　　DEERHOUND
DDEEHNRTU THUNDERED
DDEEHRRSS SHREDDERS
DDEEIILMT DELIMITED
DDEEIILNS SIDELINED
DDEEIIOSX DEOXIDISE
DDEEIIOXZ DEOXIDIZE
DDEEIKLNR REKINDLED
DDEEILLPS DISPELLED
DDEEILLRV DRIVELLED
DDEEILMMN MIDDLEMEN
DDEEILMSX MIDDLESEX
DDEEILOPS DESPOILED
DDEEILORS SOLDIERED
DDEEIMMNO DEMIMONDE
DDEEINNST INTENDEDS
DDEEINORW EIDERDOWN
DDEEINOSV NOSEDIVED

DDEEINPSS DISPENSED
DDEEINRST DISTENDER
DDEEINRSU UNDERSIDE,
   UNDESIRED
DDEEINSST DISSENTED
DDEEIOORS DEODORISE
DDEEIOORZ DEODORIZE
DDEEIOPST DEPOSITED
DDEEIORRS SIDE ORDER
DDEEIPRSS DISPERSED
DDEEIPSTU DEPUTISED
DDEEIPTUZ DEPUTIZED
DDEEIRSSS SIDE-DRESS
DDEELLOPS DEED POLLS,
   DEEDS POLL
DDEELMORS SMOLDERED
DDEELMORU
   MOULDERED, REMOULDED
DDEELNPRU PLUNDERED
DDEELOTVY DEVOTEDLY
DDEEMOPUY PUY DE
   DOME
DDEENNORU
   UNDERDONE
DDEENOPRS RESPONDED
DDEENOPRT PORTENDED
DDEENOPUX EXPOUNDED
DDEENORSU RESOUNDED
DDEENOSTY EDDYSTONE
DDEENPSSU SUSPENDED
DDEENRSSU UNDRESSED
DDEEOOPRT TORPEDOED
DDEEOORSV OVERDOSED
DDEEORSTY DESTROYED
DDEFFIINT DIFFIDENT
DDEFGIIIN DIGNIFIED
DDEFGILLO GOLDFIELD
DDEFILOOT FLOOD TIDE
DDEFNNOUU UNFOUNDED
DDEGGIORS DISGORGED
DDEGHINRS SHREDDING
DDEGIIIST DIGITISED
DDEGIIITZ DIGITIZED
DDEGIIMSU MISGUIDED
DDEGIINSS GIDDINESS
DDEGIISSU DISGUISED
DDEGIJMSU MISJUDGED
DDEGIJNRU JUDDERING
DDEGINORR DERRING-DO
DDEGINRRU UNDERGIRD
DDEGIOOSS GOOD-SISED
DDEGIOOSZ GOOD-SIZED
DDEGISSTU DISGUSTED

DDEGLNOOR
   GOLDENROD
DDEGNORSU
   UNDERDOGS
DDEGOOORS
   DO-GOODERS
DDEHHNRTU HUNDREDTH
DDEHIOSST SHODDIEST
DDEHOOSSW
   WOODSHEDS
DDEIIKNSV SKIN-DIVED
DDEIIKRSV DISK DRIVE
DDEIILLST DISTILLED
DDEIIMSSS DISMISSED
DDEIIMTTW DIM-WITTED
DDEIINPRS SPIN-DRIED
DDEIINSST DISSIDENT
DDEIINSTU DISUNITED
DDEILMNOW
   LOW-MINDED
DDEILNRRU UNRIDDLER
DDEILORWW WORLDWIDE
DDEILOSSV DISSOLVED
DDEIMNOPU IMPOUNDED
DDEIMNSSU MUDDINESS
DDEINORTU OUTRIDDEN
DDEINOSSW DOWDINESS
DDEINRSSU RUDDINESS
DDEINSTUU UNSTUDIED
DDEIOPRST DISPORTED
DDEIOPRSV DISPROVED
DDEIORRSS DISORDERS
DDEIORSTT DISTORTED
DDEIPRSTU DISRUPTED
DDELNORSU UNDERSOLD
DDEMNOOTU ODD MEN
   OUT
DDEMNOSUU
   DUODENUMS
DDENNORUU
   UNROUNDED
DDENOOPRS DROPSONDE
DDENOORSW DO
   WONDERS
DDEOPRRTU PROTRUDED
DDFIOORTW DRIFTWOOD
DDGGINNOS DINGDONGS
DDGIILNNW DWINDLING
DDGIILNTW TWIDDLING
DDGOOORSW GOOD
   WORDS
DDHIOOOWW
   WIDOWHOOD

DEEEEKNRW WEEKENDER
DEEEEMRRS REDEEMERS
DEEEENPST STEEPENED
DEEEFGIKN KNIFE-EDGE
DEEEFHNRS FRESHENED
DEEEFHRRS REFRESHED
DEEEFINSV DEFENSIVE
DEEEFLLRU REFUELLED
DEEEFMNRT DEFERMENT,
   FERMENTED
DEEEFPRRR PREFERRED
DEEEFRRYZ FREEZE-DRY
DEEEGIMNR REDEEMING
DEEEGINNP DEEPENING
DEEEGINRS ENERGISED
DEEEGINRZ ENERGIZED
DEEEGIPRS PEDIGREES
DEEEGIRST GREEDIEST
DEEEGKLNT KENTLEDGE
DEEEGLNOY GOLDENEYE
DEEEGMNST SEGMENTED
DEEEGNRTT DETERGENT
DEEEGRRSS REGRESSED
DEEEGRRTT REGRETTED
DEEEHIMPR EPHEMERID
DEEEHINPR EPHEDRINE
DEEEHLRST SHELTERED
DEEEHNPRR REPREHEND
DEEEHNRRU HEREUNDER
DEEEHORSW
   HORSEWEED
DEEEILLMP MILLEPEDE
DEEEILNNV ENLIVENED
DEEEILPTV DEPLETIVE
DEEEILRRV DELIVERER,
   REDELIVER
DEEEILSSW EDELWEISS
DEEEILSTV TELEVISED
DEEEIMNRT DETERMINE
DEEEIMPRR PREMIERED
DEEEIMSST DISESTEEM
DEEEINNSS NEEDINESS
DEEEINOPR PIONEERED
DEEEINPTX EXPEDIENT
DEEEINQTU QUIETENED
DEEEINRSS REEDINESS
DEEEINRST TENDERISE
DEEEINRTZ TENDERIZE
DEEEINSSS SEEDINESS
DEEEINSSW WEEDINESS
DEEEIPRRV REPRIEVED
DEEEIPRTX EXPEDITER
DEEEIPRVW PREVIEWED

DEEEIPSST SPEEDIEST
DEEEIRRTV RETRIEVED
DEEEIRSTV DETERSIVE
DEEEIRUZZ ZUIDER ZEE
DEEEKLLNN KENNELLED
DEEEELLPSW SPEEDWELL
DEEEELNOPV ENVELOPED
DEEEELNRWY RENEWEDLY
DEEEELOPRV DEVELOPER,
    REDEVELOP
DEEEELPPRX PERPLEXED
DEEEELRSTT RESETTLED
DEEEELRSTW SWELTERED
DEEEEMNRTT DETERMENT
DEEEMOPRW
    EMPOWERED
DEEEMPPRT PRE-EMPTED
DEEENNRST ENTENDRES
DEEENNSSS DENSENESS
DEEENPRRT PRETENDER
DEEENPRST PRESENTED
DEEENPRTV PREVENTED
DEEENRRSV REVERENDS
DEEENRRTT DETERRENT
DEEENRSTT TENDEREST
DEEENSSVX VEXEDNESS
DEEEOPRST DEPORTEES
DEEEORRSS REREDOSES
DEEEORSTV STEVEDORE
DEEEORSVX OVERSEXED
DEEEPPPRR RED PEPPER
DEEEPRRSS REPRESSED
DEEEPRRSV PRESERVED
DEEEPRRTV PERVERTED
DEEEPRSST SPEEDSTER
DEEEPRSSU SUPERSEDE
DEEEPRSSX EXPRESSED
DEEEQRSTU REQUESTED
DEEERRRSS REDRESSER
DEEERRSST DESERTERS
DEEFFINRT DIFFERENT
DEEFFINST STIFFENED
DEEFFIORT FORFEITED
DEEFFNORS OFFENDERS
DEEFFOPRR PROFFERED
DEEFGHIRT FREIGHTED
DEEFGIIRS SIEGFRIED
DEEFGINNU UNFEIGNED
DEEFGINRR DEFERRING
DEEFGJORU FOREJUDGE
DEEFGLNNO DOG FENNEL
DEEFHLLUY HEEDFULLY
DEEFHLOPS SHEEPFOLD

DEEFHLORS FREEHOLDS
DEEFHLORT THREEFOLD
DEEFHRRTU FURTHERED
DEEFIILMN MINEFIELD
DEEFIILNR INFIELDER
DEEFIILQU LIQUEFIED
DEEFIINNS DEFINIENS
DEEFIIPRS PERFIDIES
DEEFIIPRT PETRIFIED
DEEFIIRRT TERRIFIED
DEEFIIRSS FIRESIDES
DEEFIISTT TESTIFIED
DEEFILMNS FIELDSMEN
DEEFILRSV SELF-DRIVE
DEEFILSTT FIELD-TEST
DEEFINNPR PEN FRIEND
DEEFINNRU UNREFINED
DEEFINNTU FINE-TUNED
DEEFIPRTU PUTREFIED
DEEFIPSTU STUPEFIED
DEEFIRRTT FRITTERED
DEEFIRSTU SURFEITED
DEEFLLNNU FUNNELLED
DEEFLLNUY NEEDFULLY
DEEFLNOSV SEVENFOLD
DEEFLNRTU UNDERFELT
DEEFLORRW FREE
    WORLD
DEEFLRSTU FLUSTERED
DEEFLRTTU FLUTTERED
DEEFMOPRR PERFORMED
DEEFNOOPS SPOON-FEED
DEEFNOOST FESTOONED
DEEFOPRSS PROFESSED
DEEFORRST DEFROSTER
DEEFRSTUY DUTY-FREES
DEEGGGILN LEGGINGED
DEEGGHHOS HEDGEHOGS
DEEGGINRS SNIGGERED
DEEGGIRRT TRIGGERED
DEEGGSSTU SUGGESTED
DEEGHHIPS HIGH-SPEED
DEEGHIINV INVEIGHED
DEEGHILNT LIGHTENED
DEEGHILNW WHEEDLING
DEEGHILRT DELIGHTER
DEEGHINTT TIGHTENED
DEEGHINUW UNWEIGHED
DEEGHNORU
    ROUGHENED
DEEGHNOTU TOUGHENED
DEEGHOPSS SHEEPDOGS

DEEGHORSW
    HEDGEROWS
DEEGIILNU GUIDELINE
DEEGIILNV INVEIGLED
DEEGIINSS DIGENESIS
DEEGIINTY TIE-DYEING
DEEGIISTV DIGESTIVE
DEEGILLOR LIEGE LORD
DEEGILMMR GLIMMERED
DEEGILNPT DEPLETING
DEEGILNSS SEEDLINGS
DEEGILNST GLISTENED
DEEGILOOU IDEOLOGUE
DEEGILOPR RIDGEPOLE
DEEGILOSU EULOGISED
DEEGILOUZ EULOGIZED
DEEGILRTT GLITTERED
DEEGIMNRY REMEDYING
DEEGIMORT GEOMETRID
DEEGINNPX EXPENDING
DEEGINNRR RENDERING
DEEGINNRT TENDERING
DEEGINNTX EXTENDING
DEEGINRRR DERRINGER
DEEGINRRT DETERRING
DEEGINRSS DESIGNERS
DEEGINRST DESERTING
DEEGINRSV DESERVING
DEEGINRTU NEGRITUDE
DEEGINRTV DIVERGENT
DEEGINRUV GERUNDIVE
DEEGINSTT DETESTING
DEEGIOSST GEODESIST
DEEGIPRST PREDIGEST
DEEGIRRSS DIGRESSER
DEEGIRRUU DE RIGUEUR
DEEGJMNTU JUDGEMENT
DEEGJPRRU PREJUDGER
DEEGKLNOW
    KNOWLEDGE
DEEGKOPRW POWDER
    KEG
DEEGLLORV GROVELLED
DEEGLNNOU GUENDOLEN
DEEGLNNOW
    GWENDOLEN
DEEGNNORU
    UNDERGONE
DEEGNNSSU DUNGENESS
DEEGNOORW
    GREENWOOD
DEEGNORRU
    UNDERGOER

DEEGNORSS ENGROSSED
DEEGOPRRU REGROUPED
DEEHHINST IN THE SHED
DEEHHIORS HORSEHIDE
DEEHHPRSS SHEPHERDS
DEEHIINRT INHERITED
DEEHIKRSW WHISKERED
DEEHILLRV HELLDIVER
DEEHILORU HIERODULE
DEEHILPRS ELDERSHIP
DEEHILRST SLITHERED
DEEHILRSV SHRIVELED
DEEHIMMRS SHIMMERED
DEEHIMOST METHODISE
DEEHIMOTX METHOXIDE
DEEHIMOTZ METHODIZE
DEEHIMPRW WHIMPERED
DEEHINNOV EINDHOVEN
DEEHINNRS ENSHRINED
DEEHINNTU IN THE NUDE
DEEHINOPX PHENOXIDE
DEEHINORT DINOTHERE
DEEHINPRT TREPHINED
DEEHINRSW SWINEHERD
DEEHIORST THEORISED
DEEHIORTZ THEORIZED
DEEHIOSTU TIED HOUSE
DEEHIPPSS SHEEPDIPS
DEEHIPRSW WHISPERED
DEEHIRSSV DERVISHES
DEEHLLOSV SHOVELLED
DEEHLNOYY HONEYEDLY
DEEHLORST HOLSTERED
DEEHMNNOT ON THE
    MEND
DEEHMOORT
    HODOMETER
DEEHMORST SMOTHERED
DEEHNNORT ENTHRONED
DEEHNOPTY ENDOPHYTE
DEEHNORRT DETHRONER
DEEHNORST SHORTENED
DEEHNRRTU THUNDERER
DEEHOORTX HETERODOX
DEEHOPSTU DEEP SOUTH
DEEHRSSTW SHREWDEST
DEEHRSTTU SHUTTERED
DEEHSSTTU DUSTSHEET
DEEIIINPR PIERIDINE
DEEIILLMP MILLIPEDE
DEEIILMPR IMPERILED
DEEIILNSS SIDELINES
DEEIIMPRS EPIDERMIS

DEEIINSST DENSITIES,
    DESTINIES
DEEIIPSSW SIDESWIPE
DEEIIRRSV RIVERSIDE
DEEIIRTVV DIVERTIVE
DEEIISSSU SIDE ISSUE
DEEIJNORR REJOINDER
DEEIKLNNR ENKINDLER
DEEIKNSTW STINKWEED
DEEIKPPRS SKIPPERED
DEEIKRSTT SKITTERED
DEEIKSSTT DISKETTES
DEEILLLNW WELL-LINED
DEEILLLOW WELL-OILED
DEEILLMNO ILL-OMENED
DEEILLMTW WELL-TIMED
DEEILLNSV SNIVELLED
DEEILLPRS DISPELLER
DEEILLRRV DRIVELLER
DEEILLRSU SLIDE RULE
DEEILLRTU TELLURIDE
DEEILLRTW WELL-TRIED
DEEILLSVW SWIVELLED
DEEILMMNS MENDELISM
DEEILMNTV DEVILMENT
DEEILMORS MELODISER
DEEILMORZ MELODIZER
DEEILMRTY MERITEDLY
DEEILNNRU UNDERLINE
DEEILNOPT DEPLETION,
    DIPLOTENE
DEEILNOST DELETIONS
DEEILNPTU PLENITUDE
DEEILNRRU UNDERLIER
DEEILNRTU INTERLUDE
DEEILNTVY EVIDENTLY
DEEILOPRS DESPOILER
DEEILOPTX EXPLOITED
DEEILORRS ORDERLIES
DEEILORSV EVILDOERS
DEEILRRSS RIDERLESS
DEEILRSVY DIVERSELY
DEEILRTUY ERUDITELY
DEEIMMORS MEMORISED
DEEIMMORZ MEMORIZED
DEEIMNNOT MENTIONED
DEEIMNNRU UNDERMINE
DEEIMNORS MODERNISE
DEEIMNORZ MODERNIZE
DEEIMNOSS DES MOINES
DEEIMNOST MOISTENED
DEEIMNPST PEDIMENTS
DEEIMNRRS REMINDERS

DEEIMNRTT DETRIMENT
DEEIMNSST SEDIMENTS
DEEIMOORT METEOROID
DEEIMORST DOSIMETER
DEEIMPRSS IMPRESSED
DEEIMPRST DISTEMPER
DEEIMPRTT PERMITTED
DEEIMRTUU DEUTERIUM
DEEINNOPS PENSIONED
DEEINNORT INTERNODE
DEEINNOTT DETENTION
DEEINNRTU INDENTURE
DEEINNSSS SNIDENESS
DEEINOPTX PENTOXIDE
DEEINORST DESERTION
DEEINORSW ROSINWEED
DEEINOSSV NOSEDIVES
DEEINPRRT REPRINTED
DEEINPRSS DISPENSER
DEEINPRST PRESIDENT
DEEINRRSU REINSURED
DEEINRSST DISSENTER,
    RESIDENTS, TIREDNESS
DEEINRSSW WEIRDNESS
DEEINRSTT TRENDIEST
DEEINSSTW WITNESSED
DEEIOPRVW POWER DIVE
DEEIORRRV OVERRIDER
DEEIORRVV OVERDRIVE
DEEIORSSV OVERSISED
DEEIORSVZ OVERSIZED
DEEIORTTX TETROXIDE
DEEIPPRRS PERSPIRED
DEEIPRRSS DISPERSER
DEEIPRSST PERSISTED
DEEIPRSTU DISREPUTE
DEEIPSSST SIDESTEPS
DEEIRSSST DRESSIEST
DEEIRSTUV SERVITUDE
DEEIRTTTW TWITTERED
DEEIRTTXY DEXTERITY
DEEISTTTU DESTITUTE
DEEJNORUY JOURNEYED
DEEJOORVY OVERJOYED
DEEKNOORS SNOOKERED
DEEKNORTW
    NETWORKED
DEELLMMPU PUMMELLED
DEELLMOOR ROLE MODEL
DEELLNNTU TUNNELLED
DEELLNRSU UNDERSELL
DEELLNSSY ENDLESSLY
DEELLOPPR PROPELLED

DEELMMPTU PLUMMETED
DEELMOORV VELODROME
DEELNOOSS LOOSE ENDS
DEELNOOST LODESTONE
DEELNPRRU PLUNDERER
DEELNSTTU UNSETTLED
DEELNSWWY
  NEWLYWEDS
DEELOPRSY REPOSEDLY
DEELORRUV OVERRULED
DEELPRTUY REPUTEDLY
DEEMNNOTW
  ENDOWMENT
DEEMNNRUY
  RUNNYMEDE
DEEMNOORT
  ONDOMETER
DEEMNOPRS ENDOSPERM
DEEMNOPSU SPODUMENE
DEEMNORTT TORMENTED
DEEMNORTU
  REMOUNTED
DEEMNOSTU ENDOSTEUM
DEEMOORST ODOMETERS
DEEMPRTTU TRUMPETED
DEEMRRRSU MURDERERS
DEEMRRSSU MURDERESS
DEENNORTU UNDERTONE
DEENNRTUW
  UNDERWENT
DEENOOPRS ENDOSPORE
DEENOPRRS RESPONDER
DEENOPRRV PROVENDER
DEENOPRSV OVERSPEND
DEENOPRUX EXPOUNDER
DEENPRSSU SUSPENDER
DEENRRRSU SURRENDER
DEENRSTTU ENTRUSTED
DEENRSTUW
  WET-NURSED
DEENRSTYY DYSENTERY
DEEOOOPRST TORPEDOES
DEEOORSSV OVERDOSES
DEEOPPRRS PROSPERED
DEEOPPRSS OPPRESSED
DEEOPPRST STOPPERED
DEEOPRRSS DEPRESSOR
DEEOPSSSS POSSESSED
DEEORRSSV OVERDRESS
DEEORRSTX DEXTRORSE
DEEORRSTY DESTROYER
DEEORSTUX DEXTEROUS
DEEOSTTUV DEVOUTEST

DEEPRRSSU PRESSURED
DEEPRSTTU SPUTTERED
DEERSTTTU STUTTERED
DEFFGIINR DIFFERING
DEFFGINNO OFFENDING
DEFFIIORT FORTIFIED
DEFFIISUV DIFFUSIVE
DEFFILLLU FULFILLED
DEFFILSUY DIFFUSELY
DEFFLNRUU UNRUFFLED
DEFGGIINT FIDGETING
DEFGGILLN FLEDGLING
DEFGHILOT EIGHTFOLD
DEFGHIOSS DOGFISHES
DEFGIIINS SIGNIFIED
DEFGIILOR GLORIFIED
DEFGIINNR INFRINGED
DEFGIIRSU DISFIGURE
DEFGILNNO ENFOLDING
DEFGIMNOR DEFORMING
DEFGINNRU REFUNDING
DEFHIILSV DEVILFISH
DEFHIIORR HORRIFIED
DEFHINRSU FURNISHED
DEFHLOOOW
  WHOLEFOOD
DEFHOOOTT HOTFOOTED
DEFIIIRTV VITRIFIED
DEFIIJSTU JUSTIFIED
DEFIILLMO MOLLIFIED
DEFIILLNU NULLIFIED
DEFIILLOS OILFIELDS
DEFIILLRR FIRE DRILL
DEFIILMSU SEMIFLUID
DEFIILPRT FIELD TRIP
DEFIILRSU FLUIDISER
DEFIILRSW WILDFIRES
DEFIILRUZ FLUIDIZER
DEFIIMMMU MUMMIFIED
DEFIIMNNY INDEMNIFY
DEFIIMORS MODIFIERS
DEFIIMORT MORTIFIED
DEFIIMRWY MIDWIFERY
DEFIIMSTY MYSTIFIED
DEFIINNRW WINNIFRED
DEFIINRTY DENITRIFY
DEFIINSST DISINFEST
DEFIIRRST STIR-FRIED
DEFIIRSVY DIVERSIFY
DEFIIRTVY DEVITRIFY
DEFIKLORW FIELDWORK
DEFILLRUY DIREFULLY
DEFILMNRU REMINDFUL

DEFILMSUY DEMULSIFY
DEFILNOSW SNOWFIELD
DEFIMNORT DENTIFORM
DEFIMNORU UNIFORMED
DEFIMORTY DEFORMITY
DEFIMSTYY DEMYSTIFY
DEFINORSU FOUNDRIES
DEFIORSST DISFOREST
DEFIORTTU FORTITUDE
DEFIOTTTU OUTFITTED
DEFLLLOUY DOLEFULLY
DEFLLNOUW
  WELL-FOUND
DEFLLRSSU FULL DRESS
DEFLMMOUX
  FLUMMOXED
DEFLNORSU FLOUNDERS
DEFLNORUW
  WONDERFUL
DEFNOORTU UNDERFOOT
DEFOORRSW
  FOREWORDS
DEGGIILNR RIDGELING
DEGGIILRU GIRL GUIDE
DEGGIINNS DESIGNING
DEGGIINRV DIVERGING
DEGGIINST DIGESTING
DEGGIORRS DISGORGER
DEGGLRSTU STRUGGLED
DEGHHIIST HIGH TIDES
DEGHHINOT HIGH-TONED
DEGHIILNS SHIELDING
DEGHIILST SIDELIGHT
DEGHIINNR HINDERING
DEGHIINRT DITHERING
DEGHIJPSU JUDGESHIP
DEGHILMSU GUMSHIELD
DEGHILRST RED LIGHTS
DEGHIMNRU HUMDINGER
DEGHINSTU UNSIGHTED
DEGHIORTU DOUGHTIER
DEGHMOORT
  GODMOTHER
DEGHNNRUU
  UNDERHUNG
DEGHNORUY
  GREYHOUND
DEGHOOSSU DOGHOUSES
DEGIIIMRS SEMIRIGID
DEGIIINST DIGNITIES
DEGIIIRST DIGITISER
DEGIIIRTZ DIGITIZER
DEGIILLNV DEVILLING

DEGIILNOV EVILDOING
DEGIILNRV DRIVELING
DEGIIMNNP IMPENDING
DEGIIMNNR REMINDING
DEGIIMNST DEMISTING
DEGIIMRSU MISGUIDER
DEGIINNNT INDENTING,
    INTENDING
DEGIINNSS DINGINESS
DEGIINOST DIGESTION
DEGIINPRS PRESIDING
DEGIINPRV DEPRIVING
DEGIINPSS DESPISING
DEGIINRTU INTRIGUED
DEGIINRTV DIVERTING
DEGIINSST DESISTING
DEGIINSTU DISTINGUÉ
DEGIINSTV DIVESTING
DEGIIOPRS PRODIGIES
DEGIIQRSU SQUIDGIER
DEGIIRRSV VERDIGRIS
DEGIIRSSU DISGUISER
DEGIISSSU DISGUISES
DEGIJMRSU MISJUDGER
DEGIKLOSV KID GLOVES
DEGILLMNO MODELLING
DEGILLNOV LONG-LIVED
DEGILLNOY YODELLING
DEGILLNSW DWELLINGS
DEGILMNOR
    GOLD-MINER, MOLDERING
DEGILMNOS GOLDMINES
DEGILNNRU UNDERLING
DEGILNNTU INDULGENT
DEGILNOOR GONDOLIER
DEGILNOPR DEPLORING
DEGILNOPX EXPLODING
DEGILNOPY DEPLOYING
DEGILNORS SOLDERING
DEGILNOSS GODLINESS
DEGILNOSU DELOUSING
DEGILNOTU LONGITUDE
DEGILNOVV DEVOLVING
DEGILOOST GOODLIEST
DEGILOSTT GLOTTIDES
DEGILSSTU SLUDGIEST
DEGIMNRRU DEMURRING,
    MURDERING
DEGINNOPR PONDERING
DEGINNORS ENDORSING
DEGINNORW WONDERING
DEGINNRSU SUNDERING
DEGINNRUW UNDERWING

DEGINOORV OVERDOING
DEGINOPRT DEPORTING
DEGINOPRW POWDERING
DEGINOPSS PODGINESS
DEGINORRW REWORDING
DEGINORUV DEVOURING
DEGINPSSU PUDGINESS
DEGINRSSS DRESSINGS
DEGINRTUX EXTRUDING
DEGIOPRTY PTERYGOID
DEGIOPSTU GUIDEPOST
DEGIOSSTT STODGIEST
DEGJMNSTU JUDGMENTS
DEGLLOSSY GODLESSLY
DEGLNNOWY
    GWENDOLYN
DEGLNOOPR PROLONGED
DEGLNORSU GROUNDSEL
DEGLOOSUU DUOLOGUES
DEGNOORRW
    WRONGDOER
DEGNOPRUW
    GUNPOWDER
DEGOOPRRU
    PROROGUED
DEGORRSTU DRUGSTORE
DEHHIINOS HOIDENISH
DEHHIKMOS SHEIKHDOM
DEHHILNOS HOLINSHED
DEHHINOSY HOYDENISH
DEHHIOPPS PHOSPHIDE
DEHHLLNOU HELLHOUND
DEHHLOOSU HOUSEHOLD
DEHHLORST THRESHOLD
DEHHNOORU
    HOREHOUND
DEHIIINST HISTIDINE
DEHIILLSS HILLSIDES
DEHIILRSS DISRELISH
DEHIIMNTY THYMIDINE
DEHIINNRU HIRUNDINE
DEHIINOOP IDIOPHONE
DEHIISTWW WIDTHWISE
DEHIJMNOS DEMIJOHNS
DEHIKKOOZ KOZHIKODE
DEHILOORT RHODOLITE
DEHILORSW WILD HORSE
DEHILOSTW DISH TOWEL
DEHILOSUY HIDEOUSLY
DEHILPSSU SULPHIDES
DEHILRRUY HURRIEDLY
DEHIMMOST METHODISM
DEHIMNOOT IN THE MOOD

DEHIMNORT TRONDHEIM
DEHIMNSSU HUMIDNESS
DEHIMOSTT METHODIST
DEHIMPRTU TRIUMPHED
DEHINOORT RHODONITE
DEHINORRT TRIHEDRON
DEHINORSU NOURISHED
DEHINOSST DISHONEST,
    HEDONISTS
DEHINRRUU UNHURRIED
DEHIOOTWW
    HOWTOWDIE, WHITEWOOD
DEHIOPRSS SPHEROIDS
DEHIOPRSW WORSHIPED
DEHIOSSSW SIDESHOWS
DEHKLOOST STOKEHOLD
DEHKNOOOS
    HOOK-NOSED
DEHLMNOPY ENDOLYMPH
DEHLOORSV HOLDOVERS
DEHLOPRSU UPHOLDERS
DEHLORSSU SHOULDERS
DEHLORSYY HYDROLYSE
DEHLORTTT THROTTLED
DEHLORTYY HYDROLYTE
DEHMNOOPR
    ENDOMORPH
DEHMOORTY
    HODOMETRY
DEHNNOOPS SPHENODON
DEHNNOSUW
    NEWSHOUND
DEHNORSTU UNDERSHOT
DEHOORSTU HERODOTUS
DEHOOSSSU DOSSHOUSE
DEHOPRSST POTSHERDS
DEHORSSTU STUDHORSE
DEIIIKNTT IDENTIKIT
DEIIILQSU LIQUIDISE
DEIIILQUZ LIQUIDIZE
DEIIIMMNS MINIMISED
DEIIIMMNZ MINIMIZED
DEIIINNQU QUINIDINE
DEIIINSSS DISSEISIN
DEIIKLNST KINDLIEST
DEIIKNRSV SKIN DIVER
DEIILLNST INSTILLED
DEIILLOPR PILLORIED
DEIILLOPS ELLIPSOID
DEIILLRST DISTILLER
DEIILMNTU UNLIMITED
DEIILMOSS SEMISOLID
DEIILMRSU DELIRIUMS

DEIILNPRS SPINDLIER
DEIILNSSV LIVIDNESS
DEIILOPRT REPTILOID
DEIILORSU DELIRIOUS
DEIILPSSS SIDESLIPS
DEIILSUVV DIVULSIVE
DEIIMMNSU IMMUNISED
DEIIMMNUZ IMMUNIZED
DEIIMNNOS DIMENSION
DEIIMNNTY INDEMNITY
DEIIMNOQU DOMINIQUE
DEIIMNPRT IMPRINTED
DEIIMNRSS MINIDRESS
DEIIMNRTW MIDWINTER
DEIIMOPST OPTIMISED
DEIIMOPTZ OPTIMIZED
DEIIMPRSU PRESIDIUM
DEIINNNOT INDENTION
DEIINNORT RENDITION
DEIINNOSU UNIONISED
DEIINNOTT DENTITION
DEIINNOTV VENDITION
DEIINNOUZ UNIONIZED
DEIINNSSW WINDINESS
DEIINOPRT PERDITION
DEIINOPSS INDISPOSE
DEIINORSS IRONSIDES
DEIINORSV DIVERSION
DEIINORTT DETRITION
DEIINORTU ERUDITION
DEIINPPSW WINDPIPES
DEIINRSST DIRTINESS
DEIINSSVV VIVIDNESS
DEIINSSZZ DIZZINESS
DEIIORSSS DISSEISOR,
    SIDEROSIS
DEIIOSSTU SEDITIOUS
DEIIRSTVY DIVERSITY
DEIJORRSY JOYRIDERS
DEIKLLNSU UNSKILLED
DEIKLNPRS SPRINKLED
DEIKNNSTU UNKINDEST
DEIKNSSSU DUSKINESS
DEIKRSSVY SKYDIVERS
DEILLMNOU MULLIONED
DEILLORRW WORLDLIER
DEILLORST LORDLIEST
DEILLORSY SOLDIERLY
DEILLSSTU DUELLISTS
DEILLSTTY STILTEDLY
DEILMNOSS MOLDINESS
DEILMOOST DOLOMITES
DEILMOOSU MELODIOUS

DEILMORST OLD-TIMERS
DEILMOSTU MOULDIEST
DEILMTTUU MULTITUDE
DEILNOPRU PURLOINED
DEILNOPTY POINTEDLY
DEILNORSU UNDERSOIL
DEILNOSSS SOLIDNESS
DEILNOSSU DELUSIONS
DEILNPSST SPLIT ENDS
DEILNRSSU LURIDNESS
DEILNRSSW SWINDLERS
DEILORRWY WORRIEDLY
DEILORSSV DISSOLVER
DEILOSSTU DISSOLUTE
DEILOSTUY TEDIOUSLY
DEILOSUVY DEVIOUSLY
DEILPTUXY DUPLEXITY
DEILSTTWY TWISTEDLY
DEIMMMRSU MIDSUMMER
DEIMMNORS MODERNISM
DEIMMNOUY NEODYMIUM
DEIMMOSTY IMMODESTY
DEIMNOORT MONITORED
DEIMNOOSS MOODINESS
DEIMNOOST DEMOTIONS
DEIMNOOSX MONOXIDES
DEIMNOPRU IMPOUNDER
DEIMNORST MODERNIST
DEIMNORTY MODERNITY
DEIMNPRTU IMPRUDENT
DEIMNPSSU DUMPINESS
DEIMNRSTU RUDIMENTS
DEIMOOORT IDEOMOTOR
DEIMOORST MOTORISED
DEIMOORTY IODOMETRY
DEIMOORTZ MOTORIZED
DEIMOOSST SODOMITES
DEIMOPSST DESPOTISM
DEIMOQSTU MISQUOTED
DEIMORSTY DOSIMETRY
DEINNNOSU INNUENDOS
DEINNOOTX ENDOTOXIN
DEINNOSTU TENDINOUS
DEINNRSTV TV DINNERS
DEINNRSUU UNINSURED
DEINNRTTU UNDERTINT
DEINOOPRT PORTIONED
DEINOOPSW PINEWOODS
DEINOOSSW WOODINESS
DEINOOSTV DEVOTIONS
DEINOPRST DRIPSTONE
DEINOPRTV PROVIDENT

DEINORRWW
    WINDROWER
DEINORSSW ROWDINESS,
    WORDINESS
DEINORSTU DETRUSION
DEINOSSTT DOTTINESS
DEINPRRSY SPIN-DRYER
DEINPRSTU UNSTRIPED
DEINPSTWW WINDSWEPT
DEINRRSTU INTRUDERS
DEINRSTTU INTRUSTED
DEINRSTTY DENTISTRY
DEIOOPRST DEPOSITOR
DEIOOPRTX PROTOXIDE
DEIOPRRSV PROVIDERS
DEIOPRSTU DIPTEROUS
DEIORRSTT DISTORTER
DEIORRSTU OUTRIDERS
DEIORSSTU DIOESTRUS,
    OUTSIDERS
DEIOTTTUW OUTWITTED
DEIPRRSSU SURPRISED
DEIPRRSTU DISRUPTER
DEIPRTTUU TURPITUDE
DEIPSSTTU STUPIDEST
DEIRSSTTU STURDIEST
DEJNOORSU SOJOURNED
DEKLNNRUY DRUNKENLY
DEKNOORTU UNDERTOOK
DELLNORSS DROLLNESS
DELMNOSTW
    MELTDOWNS
DELMNPSUU PENDULUMS
DELNOPRSU SPLENDOUR
DELNOPRTU UNDERPLOT
DELNOPSUU PENDULOUS
DELNOSSSU SOUNDLESS
DELNPRTUY PRUDENTLY
DELOOOSUW
    WOODLOUSE
DELOORRSV OVERLORDS
DELOORSSU ODOURLESS
DELORSTUY DESULTORY
DEMMNOSSU
    SUMMONSED
DEMNNORSU
    ROUNDSMEN
DEMNOPSUY PSEUDONYM
DEMNORSSW
    SWORDSMEN
DEMNORSSY SYNDROMES
DEMNORSTU UNDERMOST

DEMORRSUU
  MURDEROUS
DENNOOSTU DO ONE'S
  NUT
DENNORSSU ROUNDNESS
DENNORSUW
  SUNDOWNER
DENNOSSSU SOUNDNESS
DENOOPPST POSTPONED
DENOOPPSU UNOPPOSED
DENOOPRSS SPONSORED
DENOOPRSU PONDEROUS
DENOPPRRU UNDERPROP
DENOPPSTU UNSTOPPED
DENOPRSSU PROUDNESS
DENOPSTTU UNSPOTTED
DENORTTUU UNTUTORED
DEOOPRSST DOORSTEPS
DEOPPRRTU PURPORTED
DEOPPRSTU SUPPORTED
DEORRSUUV VERDUROUS
DEPRSSSTU PRESS-STUD
DETTTTTUU TUT-TUTTED
DFFFOOSTU FOODSTUFF
DFFGIINSU DIFFUSING
DFFIINOSU DIFFUSION
DFGGHIOST DOGFIGHTS
DFGIIIRTY FRIGIDITY
DFGIIMNOY MODIFYING
DFGILNNOU FOUNDLING,
  UNFOLDING
DFHILOORY HYDROFOIL
DFHIORSSW SWORDFISH
DFHLNOOUW
  WOLFHOUND
DFHLNSSUU SLUSH FUND
DFHLOOOST FOOTHOLDS
DFHNOOSUX FOXHOUNDS
DFIILORTY FLORIDITY
DFIINPRST SPINDRIFT
DFIKOOPRS SKIDPROOF
DFILLMOTU MULTIFOLD
DFILLTUUY DUTIFULLY
DFILMNNUU UNMINDFUL
DFINORSTW SNOWDRIFT
DFNOOOPTU FOOT-POUND
DFNOOORRT FRONT
  DOOR
DFNRSTTUU TRUST FUND
DFOOOSSTW
  SOFTWOODS
DGGHINOOT GOODNIGHT
DGGIILLNY GLIDINGLY

DGGIILNNU INDULGING
DGGIILNUV DIVULGING
DGGIILNUY GUIDINGLY
DGGIJLNUY JUDGINGLY
DGGINNORU GROUNDING
DGGIRSSTU DRUGGISTS
DGHHIINST HINDSIGHT
DGHHINOPT DIPHTHONG
DGHHOORSU
  ROUGHSHOD
DGHIIMNST MIDNIGHTS
DGHILMOST GOLDSMITH
DGHILNOPU UPHOLDING
DGHILOPRT DROPLIGHT
DGHIMOPSY SPHYGMOID
DGHINORSU SHROUDING
DGHINORTW DOWNRIGHT
DGHLOORYY HYDROLOGY
DGHNOSTUU
  DOUGHNUTS
DGIIIKLNS DISLIKING
DGIIILNOZ IDOLIZING
DGIIINNRT NITRIDING
DGIIINNTY INDIGNITY
DGIIINOTX DIGITOXIN
DGIIINOXZ OXIDIZING
DGIIJNORY JOYRIDING
DGIIKNSVY SKYDIVING
DGIILLOOR GORILLOID
DGIILMNOP IMPLODING
DGIILNNSW SWINDLING
DGIILNNWY WINDINGLY
DGIILNRZZ DRIZZLING
DGIIMNORS GIRONDISM
DGIIMNSSU SIGISMUND
DGIINNNUW UNWINDING
DGIINNORS INDORSING
DGIINNOSW DISOWNING
DGIINNRTU INTRUDING
DGIINOPRV PROVIDING
DGIINOPSS DISPOSING
DGIINORRS GRIDIRONS
DGIINORST GIRONDIST
DGIINORTU OUTRIDING
DGIINPSTU DISPUTING
DGIIRTTUY TURGIDITY
DGILLNORW WORLDLING
DGILMNOOO MONGOLOID
DGILMNOSU MOULDINGS
DGILMNPSU DUMPLINGS
DGILNNRTU TRUNDLING
DGINNOPSU POUNDINGS
DGINNOSSU SOUNDINGS

DGINNOSWW
  DOWNSWING
DGINOPPRS DROPPINGS
DGKLOOOOS GOOD
  LOOKS
DGNNORTUU
  GROUNDNUT
DHHIKNSUU HINDU KUSH
DHIIIPSTY HISPIDITY
DHIIKSWZZ WHIZZ KIDS
DHIILNRWW WHIRLWIND
DHIILOPSY SYPHILOID
DHIIMNOOS HINDOOISM
DHIINOPTY TYPHOIDIN
DHILLOSTY DOLTISHLY
DHILNNOSY DONNISHLY
DHILOPRSS LORDSHIPS
DHILPRSUY PRUDISHLY
DHIMOOOOS HOODOOISM
DHINOOPRS DONORSHIP,
  RHODOPSIN
DHINOORSU DISHONOUR
DHINOPRUW WHIP-ROUND
DHINOSTUW WHODUNITS
DHIOOSTTW WITHSTOOD
DHKMNOOOS
  MONKSHOOD
DHKNORUYY
  HUNKY-DORY
DHLLOOOWY
  HOLLYWOOD
DHLMOOTUU
  LOUDMOUTH
DHLNOOOTU HOLD OUT
  ON
DHNOORTWW
  DOWNTHROW
DHNOOSSWW
  SHOWDOWNS
DHNOOSTUW
  SOUTHDOWN
DHNOSSTUW
  SHUTDOWNS
DHOOOORTXY
  ORTHODOXY
DHOOPPPUY PUPPYHOOD
DHOPRSTYY DYSTROPHY
DIIILMPTY LIMPIDITY
DIIILNPSY INSIPIDLY
DIIILQTUY LIQUIDITY
DIIINOSSU INSIDIOUS
DIIINOSSV DIVISIONS
DIIINOSUV INVIDIOUS

DIILLMNOO MODILLION
DIILLMNSW WINDMILLS
DIILNOSTU DILUTIONS
DIILNOSUV DIVULSION
DIILOSTTY STOLIDITY
DIIMNNOOS DOMINIONS
DIIMNOPST MIDPOINTS
DIIMOORTY IRIDOTOMY
DIIMORSSY DIMISSORY
DIINNOOQU QUINONOID
DIINOSSUY DIONYSIUS
DIIOPRTTY TORPIDITY
DIIORRTTY TORRIDITY
DIIPRTTUY PUTRIDITY
DIIPSTTUY STUPIDITY
DIKNOOSTW STINKWOOD
DIKORRTWY DIRTY WORK
DILLMNOPS MILLPONDS
DILLOOPPY POLYPLOID
DILOOPTUW TULIPWOOD
DIMMOPSUY SYMPODIUM
DIMNORSTW WINDSTORM
DIMOOOOSV VOODOOISM
DIMOORRTY DORMITORY
DINOOPRTW WOODPRINT
DINOPRRTU ROUND-TRIP
DINOPTTUY POINT DUTY
DINORTTUY ROTUNDITY
DIOOOOSTV VOODOOIST
DIOOPRSST PROSODIST
DJLLNRUUU JULLUNDUR
DKORSTUWY
   WORK-STUDY
DLLNORUWY
   UNWORLDLY
DLNOOSSWW
   SLOWDOWNS
DMMNRSUUY DUMMY
  RUNS
DMNOORRUW
   ROUNDWORM
DMORSSTTU DUST STORM
DNNORRTUU
   TURNROUND
DNNORSTUW
   DOWNTURNS
DNOOPRSSW
   SNOWDROPS
DNOOPRSUW
   DOWNPOURS
DNOOPSSTU SOUNDPOST
DNOOPSTUW
   DOWNSPOUT

DNOORTUWW
   WOUNDWORT
DNORRSSUU SURROUNDS
EEEEELRTY EYELETEER
EEEEFHLRW FREEWHEEL
EEEEFHRST FREESHEET
EEEEFRRSV FREE VERSE
EEEEGINVV GENEVIEVE
EEEEGNRRV EVERGREEN
EEEEGQSSU SQUEEGEES
EEEEHLRSW ELSEWHERE
EEEEKLNSX KLEENEXES
EEEELLMRS ELLESMERE
EEEELMRTT TELEMETER
EEEELNOPT ELEOPTENE
EEEELNSSV ELEVENSES
EEEELNTVV VELVETEEN
EEEENNSST TENNESSEE
EEEENNSTV SEVENTEEN
EEEENOPRY EYE-OPENER
EEEENPRST PRESENTEE
EEEENRSTW SWEETENER
EEEEPRRSV PERSEVERE
EEEEPRSSS PEERESSES
EEEFGKNRU FENUGREEK
EEEFHNOPR FREEPHONE
EEEFHNRRS FRESHENER
EEEFHORRT THEREFORE
EEEFHORRW WHEREFORE
EEEFHORST FORESHEET
EEEFHORSU FREE HOUSE
EEEFHRRRS REFRESHER
EEEFILPRS LIFE PEERS
EEEFILRRV FREE-LIVER
EEEFILRVX REFLEXIVE
EEEFINRRT INTERFERE
EEEFLNSST FLEETNESS
EEEFLRSTY FREESTYLE
EEEFLRTTU FLEURETTE
EEEFMNRRT FERMENTER
EEEFNORST FREESTONE
EEEFNRRST TREE FERNS
EEEGGILNS NEGLIGEES
EEEGGORTT GEORGETTE
EEEGHILNT GEHLENITE
EEEGHLRSS SHEERLEGS
EEEGIISSS EISEGESIS
EEEGIJNNT JET ENGINE
EEEGIKNPS PEKINGESE
EEEGIMNST ESTEEMING
EEEGINNRS ENGINEERS
EEEGINNRV VENEERING
EEEGINPRR PEREGRINE

EEEGINRRS ENERGISER
EEEGINRRZ ENERGIZER
EEEGINRTT TEETERING
EEEGINRUV GUINEVERE
EEEGIRSTY GEYSERITE
EEEGLLNTY GENTEELLY
EEEGLMNNT GENTLEMEN
EEEGLNSTX GENTLE SEX
EEEGMNNRU
   ENERGUMEN
EEEGMNRSS MESSENGER
EEEGMORRT ERGOMETER
EEEGNNRSS GREENNESS
EEEGRRRTT REGRETTER
EEEHILLNS HELLENISE
EEEHILLNZ HELLENIZE
EEEHILNNP NEPHELINE
EEEHIMPRS EPHEMERIS
EEEHIMPSU EUPHEMISE
EEEHIMPUZ EUPHEMIZE
EEEHIMSTT TIME SHEET
EEEHINRTT HENRIETTE
EEEHIRRST ETHERISER
EEEHIRRTZ ETHERIZER
EEEHIRSSS HEIRESSES
EEEHKLOSU HOUSELEEK
EEEHLMNTY METHYLENE
EEEHLNOPT PHENETOLE,
   TELEPHONE
EEEHLNSTV ELEVENTHS
EEEHLOPPS PEEPHOLES
EEEHLOPPT THE PEOPLE
EEEHLORSS LEE SHORES
EEEHLRRST SHELTERER
EEEHMMNTY
   ENTHYMEME
EEEHMNOPR EPHEMERON
EEEHMORRT RHEOMETER
EEEHMORST THREESOME
EEEHMORSW
   SOMEWHERE
EEEHNRSSS SHEERNESS
EEEHNSSTW NEWSSHEET
EEEHOPRSX EXOSPHERE
EEEHORSST SHOETREES
EEEHRSTTU USHERETTE
EEEIIKRST KIESERITE
EEEIKNNPR INNKEEPER
EEEIKNPSS PEKINESES
EEEILNNRV ENLIVENER
EEEILPRTV REPLETIVE
EEEILPSST SLEEPIEST
EEEILPTVX EXPLETIVE

EEEILRSTX EXSERTILE
EEEILSSTT STEELIEST
EEEIMMRSS MESMERISE
EEEIMMRSZ MESMERIZE
EEEIMORTT METEORITE
EEEIMPRRS PREMIERES
EEEIMPRRT PERIMETER
EEEINNNST NINETEENS
EEEINNRST ERNESTINE,
   INTERNEES
EEEINNRTV INTERVENE
EEEINPRRS RESERPINE
EEEINPRST PINETREES
EEEINPSSW WEEPINESS
EEEINPSVX EXPENSIVE
EEEINRRST RE-ENTRIES
EEEINRRTW WERNERITE
EEEINRTTV RETENTIVE
EEEINSSTV SEVENTIES
EEEINSTVX EXTENSIVE
EEEIPRRRV REPRIEVER
EEEIPRRSV REPRIEVES
EEEIPRRTT PRETERITE
EEEIPRSTX EXPERTISE
EEEIQRRSU EQUERRIES
EEEIQTTTU ETIQUETTE
EEEIRRRTV RETRIEVER
EEEIRRSSV SERVERIES
EEEIRRSVW REVIEWERS
EEEIRRTVV REVERTIVE
EEEIRSTTV SERVIETTE
EEEJLLRSW JEWELLERS
EEEJLLRWY JEWELLERY
EEEJRSTTT JET-SETTER
EEEKLNSSS SLEEKNESS
EEEKMRSTU MUSKETEER
EEEKNOSTY SYNOEKETE
EEELLLRSV LEVELLERS
EEELLNPRT REPELLENT
EEELLPSSS SLEEPLESS
EEELMNOPT ELOPEMENT
EEELMNRTV REVELMENT
EEELMOPSY EMPLOYEES
EEELMOSTT OMELETTES
EEELMRSTU MULETEERS
EEELMRTTY TELEMETRY
EEELMRTXY EXTREMELY
EEELNOPSV ENVELOPES
EEELNOPTT LEPTOTENE
EEELNOTTV NOVELETTE
EEELNRSSV NERVELESS
EEELNRSSW NEWSREELS
EEELNSSSS SENSELESS

EEELOPRSV OVERSLEEP
EEEMMNPRS PER
   MENSEM
EEEMNNSTT TENEMENTS
EEEMNORRV NEVERMORE
EEEMNOXYZ EXOENZYME
EEEMNRSST STEERSMEN
EEEMNRSTT ENTREMETS
EEEMNRSTY MESENTERY
EEEMNRTTV REVETMENT
EEEMOPRTX EXTEMPORE
EEEMPRSSS EMPRESSES
EEEMRSSST SEMESTERS
EEENNORST SONNETEER
EEENNSSST TENSENESS
EEENPRRST PRESENTER,
   REPRESENT
EEENPRRTV PREVENTER
EEENPRSUV SUPERVENE
EEENPSSST STEEPNESS
EEENQRSSU QUEERNESS
EEENRRSTW WESTERNER
EEENRRSUV UNRESERVE
EEENRSSST TERSENESS
EEENSSSTW SWEETNESS
EEEOPSSST POETESSES
EEEORRSSV OVERSEERS
EEEPPPRTU PUPPETEER
EEEPRRRSS REPRESSER
EEEPRRRSV PRESERVER
EEEPRRRTV PERVERTER
EEEPRRSSV PRESERVES
EEEPRRSSX EXPRESSER
EEEPRRSTT PRESETTER
EEEPRSSSX EXPRESSES
EEEQRRSTU REQUESTER
EEEQRSSTU SEQUESTER
EEEQRSSUZ SQUEEZERS
EEFFFKLRU KERFUFFLE
EEFFGLNTU EFFULGENT
EEFFHILLS SHELF LIFE
EEFFHINTT FIFTEENTH
EEFFHLRSU RESHUFFLE
EEFFIILRS FIREFLIES
EEFFINOSV OFFENSIVE
EEFFINRST STIFFENER
EEFFIORRT FORFEITER
EEFFJNORS JEFFERSON
EEFFLNSTU EFFLUENTS
EEFFOPRRR PROFFERER
EEFFORSTT OFF-STREET
EEFFRRSSU SUFFERERS
EEFGHIRRT FREIGHTER

EEFGILLNY FEELINGLY
EEFGILNNU UNFEELING
EEFGILNRU REFUELING
EEFGIMRUV VERMIFUGE
EEFGINORR FOREIGNER
EEFGINRRR REFERRING
EEFGINRRT FERRETING
EEFGINRST FESTERING
EEFGINRTT FETTERING
EEFGIORRS FORGERIES
EEFGIPRRU PREFIGURE
EEFGLLLUY GLEEFULLY
EEFGLNRTU REFULGENT
EEFGLRRTU REGRETFUL
EEFGORRTT FORGETTER
EEFHIIRSS FISHERIES
EEFHIJLSW JEWELFISH
EEFHILLRS SHELLFIRE
EEFHILSST FLESHIEST
EEFHIMNRS FISHERMEN
EEFHINSST HEFTINESS
EEFHIOSUW HOUSEWIFE
EEFHLLSWY FLYWHEELS
EEFHLORUW
   FOUR-WHEEL
EEFHLSSTY FLYSHEETS
EEFHMORRT THE FORMER
EEFHNRSSS FRESHNESS
EEFHOORRS FORESHORE
EEFHOORTT TO THE FORE
EEFHRRRTU FURTHERER
EEFIILLNS LIFELINES
EEFIILMST LIFETIMES
EEFIILMTX FLEXITIME
EEFIILNRT INFERTILE,
   INTERFILE
EEFIILQRU LIQUEFIER
EEFIILRST FERTILISE
EEFIILRTZ FERTILIZE
EEFIIMRRT METRIFIER
EEFIINRST FINISTERE
EEFIIPRRT PETRIFIER
EEFIIRRRT TERRIFIER
EEFIIRRSV VERSIFIER
EEFIIRSTT TESTIFIRE
EEFILLLOS FILOSELLE
EEFILLSTY LIFESTYLE
EEFILMPXY EXEMPLIFY
EEFILNTUW WULFENITE
EEFILOORS FOOLERIES
EEFILPRRS PILFERERS
EEFINORST FIRESTONE
EEFINPRSU SUPERFINE

EEFINRSTU INTERFUSE
EEFIOPRRT PROFITEER
EEFIOPRRW FIREPOWER
EEFIORRRT RETROFIRE
EEFIPRRTU PUTREFIER
EEFIPRSTU STUPEFIER
EEFIPRSUV PERFUSIVE
EEFIRRRTT FRITTERER
EEFIRRRTU FRUITERER
EEFIRRSTU SURFEITER
EEFKNOORT FORETOKEN
EEFKNORST REEF KNOTS
EEFLLNPSU SPLEENFUL
EEFLMRTUX FLUXMETER
EEFLNRSTU RESENTFUL
EEFLNRTVY FERVENTLY
EEFLOPRSU REPOSEFUL
EEFLORRTX RETROFLEX
EEFLORSTV LEFTOVERS
EEFLRRTTU FLUTTERER
EEFLSSTTY TSETSE FLY
EEFLTTYZZ TZETZE FLY
EEFMNOORW
    FOREWOMEN
EEFMOPRRR PERFORMER
EEFMORRRS REFORMERS
EEFMPRRUY PERFUMERY
EEFOPRRST FREE PORTS
EEFOPRRTY FERROTYPE
EEFORRSST FORESTERS
EEFORRTVW FEVERWORT
EEGGHLLSS EGGSHELLS
EEGGIILNT GELIGNITE
EEGGIIPRS PIGGERIES
EEGGILNNR GREENLING
EEGGILNNT NEGLIGENT
EEGGILNSS LEGGINESS
EEGGILOOS GEOLOGISE
EEGGILOOZ GEOLOGIZE
EEGGIMRST EGG TIMERS
EEGGINNRV REVENGING
EEGGINRST GREETINGS
EEGGIORSU EGREGIOUS
EEGGORSTT GO-GETTERS
EEGGRSSTU SUGGESTER
EEGHHIITT EIGHTIETH
EEGHHILLV HIGH-LEVEL
EEGHIIKLN HINGELIKE
EEGHIINRV INVEIGHER
EEGHIKNTW WEEKNIGHT
EEGHILNNT ENLIGHTEN
EEGHILNOR RHIGOLENE
EEGHILNRT LENGTHIER

EEGHILNSS HINGELESS
EEGHIMNNS ENMESHING
EEGHINRTT TETHERING,
    TIGHTENER
EEGHIORVW OVERWEIGH
EEGHIRSST SIGHTSEER
EEGHLLNOP PHELLOGEN
EEGHMNOST THEME
    SONG
EEGHMNOSU
    HEGUMENOS
EEGHNNORR
    GREENHORN
EEGHNNOTY ETHNOGENY
EEGHNORTU TOUGHENER
EEGHRTTTU THE GUTTER
EEGIILNRV INVEIGLER,
    RELIEVING
EEGIILORS RELIGIOSE
EEGIILPRV PRIVILEGE
EEGIINRVW REVIEWING
EEGIINSTV GENITIVES,
    INGESTIVE
EEGIISTTZ ZEITGEIST
EEGIJLLNW JEWELLING
EEGIJLNRY JEERINGLY
EEGIKLNNN KENNELING
EEGIKLNRY REEKINGLY
EEGIKNNRT KENTIGERN
EEGIKNRSW SKEWERING
EEGILLLNV LEVELLING
EEGILLNPR REPELLING
EEGILLNPX EXPELLING
EEGILLNRT RETELLING
EEGILLNRV GRENVILLE,
    REVELLING
EEGILLNRY LEERINGLY
EEGILLSSU GUILELESS
EEGILMMSU GELSEMIUM
EEGILMNSY SEEMINGLY
EEGILNNRT RELENTING
EEGILNNSS LESSENING
EEGILNNUY GENUINELY
EEGILNOOS NEOLOGISE
EEGILNOOZ NEOLOGIZE
EEGILNPWY WEEPINGLY
EEGILNRRS LINGERERS
EEGILNRTT LETTERING
EEGILNRVY VEERINGLY
EEGILOPSU EPILOGUES
EEGILORST SORTILEGE
EEGIMNPRT TEMPERING
EEGIMNPTX EXEMPTING

EEGIMNRST REGIMENTS
EEGIMNRSU MERINGUES
EEGINNOPR REOPENING
EEGINNPRT REPENTING
EEGINNRST RESENTING
EEGINNRTU NEUTERING
EEGINOOSS OOGENESIS
EEGINOPRY EPIROGENY
EEGINOPSU EPIGENOUS
EEGINORSV SOVEREIGN
EEGINORVY ROVING EYE
EEGINOSXY OXYGENISE
EEGINOXYZ OXYGENIZE
EEGINPPPR PEPPERING
EEGINPRST PESTERING
EEGINPSSW SWEEPINGS
EEGINQSUZ SQUEEZING
EEGINRRSV RESERVING,
    REVERSING
EEGINRRTV REVERTING
EEGINRSSU SEIGNEURS
EEGINRSTT RESETTING
EEGINRSTW WESTERING
EEGINSTTV VIGNETTES
EEGIORRSU ROGUERIES
EEGIPRSST PRESTIGES
EEGIRRSST REGISTERS
EEGIRRSSU SURGERIES
EEGIRSSST TIGRESSES
EEGLLMORU GLOMERULE
EEGLLOOTY TELEOLOGY
EEGLLOPRS GOSPELLER
EEGLLORRV GROVELLER
EEGLMNNOU
    MELUNGEON
EEGLNORTT LORGNETTE
EEGMNOORR
    GREENROOM
EEGNNORST ROENTGENS
EEGNOORST OESTROGEN
EEGNOORSU EROGENOUS
EEGNOOSUX EXOGENOUS
EEGNORRSS ENGROSSER
EEGNORSSV GOVERNESS
EEGNRRSTU RESURGENT
EEGOOPSST GOOSESTEP
EEGOPRSSU SUPEREGOS
EEGOQRSTU GROTESQUE
EEGORRRSS REGRESSOR
EEHHHLNOO HOHENLOHE
EEHHINOPT THIOPHENE
EEHHINOSS SHOESHINE
EEHHIOPTW WHITE HOPE

EEHHIORTT THIO-ETHER
EEHHIRSST THE SHIRES
EEHHIRTTW THEREWITH
EEHHIRTWW WHEREWITH
EEHHLMOPS HOME HELPS
EEHHNOPPS PHOSPHENE
EEHHNOSSU HEN HOUSES
EEHHOORSS HORSESHOE
EEHHRRSST THRESHERS
EEHIIKRSS ESKISEHIR
EEHIILSTW WHITE LIES
EEHIINNTT NINETIETH
EEHIIRTTW WITHERITE
EEHIJNOPS JOSEPHINE
EEHIKLNOY HONEY-LIKE
EEHIKLORS HORSELIKE
EEHIKNPSS SHEEPSKIN
EEHILLLMW MILLWHEEL
EEHILLMNS HELLENISM
EEHILLNST HELLENIST
EEHILMOST HOMELIEST
EEHILNNOO HOLE IN ONE
EEHILNOPX XENOPHILE
EEHILNORS SHORELINE
EEHILNOSU HOUSELINE
EEHILNPRS REPLENISH
EEHILNPSS SPLEENISH
EEHILNPSW PINWHEELS
EEHILNSST LITHENESS
EEHILOPTY HELIOTYPE
EEHILORST HOTELIERS
EEHILPSST SLIPSHEET
EEHILPSVY PEEVISHLY
EEHILRSTW ERSTWHILE
EEHILSTUV HELVETIUS
EEHIMMOOV HOME MOVIE
EEHIMMPSU EUPHEMISM
EEHIMOPRT HEMITROPE
EEHIMPRRW WHIMPERER
EEHIMPSTU EUPHEMIST
EEHINNORT THREONINE
EEHINOPSU EUPHONISE
EEHINOPSX PHOENIXES
EEHINOPUZ EUPHONIZE
EEHINORTT THEREINTO
EEHINOSST HESSONITE
EEHINPRST TREPHINES
EEHINSSTW WHITENESS
EEHINSTTU EUTHENIST
EEHINSTTX SIXTEENTH
EEHINTTTW TWENTIETH
EEHIORRST THEORISER
EEHIORRTZ THEORIZER

EEHIORSST HETEROSIS
EEHIORSTW OTHERWISE
EEHIPPRRY PERIPHERY
EEHIPRRSS PERISHERS
EEHIPRRSW WHISPERER
EEHIRRSST HERITRESS
EEHIRRTTY ERYTHRITE
EEHIRSSTT TEE SHIRTS
EEHKLOOST STOKEHOLE
EEHKLORWW

   WHEELWORK

EEHLLLNVY HELVELLYN
EEHLLORST HOSTELLER
EEHLMOOSW

   WHOLESOME

EEHLMORVW

   OVERWHELM

EEHLMORWW WORM

   WHEEL

EEHLNOOTW WHOLE

   NOTE

EEHLNOPTY POLYTHENE,

   TELEPHONY

EEHLNOSSW WHOLENESS
EEHLOPPTU UP THE POLE
EEHLORSSS HORSELESS,

   SHORELESS

EEHLOSSSU HOUSELESS
EEHMMOPRS

   MORPHEMES

EEHMNOOPR

   PHEROMONE

EEHMNORTY HETERONYM
EEHMNOSSY HOMEYNESS
EEHMNPTTU UMPTEENTH
EEHMOPSTY MESOPHYTE
EEHMORRTY RHEOMETRY
EEHMORSST REST

   HOMES, THERMOSES

EEHMRRSTY RHYMESTER
EEHMRSSUU HUMERUSES
EEHMSSTTY THE SYSTEM
EEHNOOPSU OPEN HOUSE
EEHNOPPTY PHENOTYPE
EEHNOPRTU THEREUPON
EEHNOPRUW

   WHEREUPON

EEHNOPSTU PENTHOUSE
EEHNOPSTY NEOPHYTES
EEHNOPTTY ENTOPHYTE
EEHNORRST SHORTENER
EEHNORSST OTHERNESS
EEHNOSTTW WHETSTONE

EEHNPPRSU PEN PUSHER
EEHNSSSTY SYNTHESES
EEHOORSSV OVERSHOES
EEHOORSVW

   HOWSOEVER, WHOSOEVER

EEHOPRSTY HEY PRESTO
EEHOPRTXY XEROPHYTE
EEHORRTVW

   OVERTHREW

EEHORSTTY SET THEORY
EEHOSSSST HOSTESSES
EEIIIMPST IMPIETIES
EEIIKKMSS SIKKIMESE
EEIIKLLST LIKELIEST
EEIIKNNTZ ZINKENITE
EEIILLMRT MILLERITE
EEIILLMTW WILLEMITE
EEIILLNTV VITELLINE
EEIILLSTV LIVELIEST
EEIILMSTT TIMELIEST
EEIILNNRT INTERLINE
EEIILNORT TRIOELEIN
EEIILNOTV OLIVENITE
EEIILNPPS PIPELINES
EEIILNRST RESILIENT
EEIILOPST SEPIOLITE
EEIILRSST STERILISE
EEIILRSTU REUTILISE,

   TUILERIES

EEIILRSTZ STERILIZE
EEIILRSVW LIVE WIRES
EEIILRTUZ REUTILIZE
EEIIMMPRT PRIME TIME
EEIIMMRST EREMITISM
EEIIMOPST EPITOMISE
EEIIMOPTZ EPITOMIZE
EEIIMORSS ISOMERISE
EEIIMORSZ ISOMERIZE
EEIIMRSSV REMISSIVE
EEIINNNPT PENNINITE
EEIINNSTT INTESTINE
EEIINNSTV INTENSIVE
EEIINNTVV INVENTIVE
EEIINQRSU ENQUIRIES
EEIINRRVV VIVERRINE
EEIINRSTT ENTERITIS
EEIINRSVV INVERSIVE
EEIINRTVW INTERVIEW
EEIINSSST SENSITISE
EEIINSSTV SENSITIVE
EEIINSSTZ SENSITIZE
EEIIOPQSU EQUIPOISE
EEIIOSSTV SOVIETISE

EEIIOSTVZ SOVIETIZE
EEIIQRSTU REQUISITE
EEIIQSTUX EXQUISITE
EEIJKNRSS JERKINESS
EEIJLNSUV JUVENILES
EEIJPRRSU PERJURIES
EEIKLMORT KILOMETRE
EEIKLRTWY TRIWEEKLY
EEIKNNPSV PENKNIVES
EEIKNPRSS PERKINESS
EEIKOORRS ROOKERIES
EEILLMNOT EMOLLIENT
EEILLMNPT IMPELLENT
EEILLMOPR MILLEPORE
EEILLMSST SMELLIEST
EEILLNNTY LENIENTLY
EEILLNOST LONELIEST
EEILLNRSV SNIVELLER
EEILLNSSS ILLNESSES
EEILLOPTU PETIOLULE
EEILLORTT TITLE ROLE
EEILLOSTV LOVELIEST
EEILLRSST TRELLISES
EEILLRSTU TELLURISE
EEILLRSUY LEISURELY
EEILLRSVY SERVILELY
EEILLRTTU TELLURITE
EEILLRTUZ TELLURIZE
EEILLSUVY ELUSIVELY
EEILMMNPT IMPLEMENT
EEILMMNSY IMMENSELY
EEILMMORS SOMMELIER
EEILMMORT MILOMETER
EEILMNNTY EMINENTLY
EEILMNOSS SOLEMNISE
EEILMNOST LIMESTONE,
  MILESTONE
EEILMNOSZ SOLEMNIZE
EEILMNPPR PIMPERNEL
EEILMNRVY LIVERYMEN
EEILMNSTU MUSTELINE
EEILMORTT TREMOLITE
EEILMOSTT MISTLETOE
EEILMOSVW SEMIVOWEL
EEILMOTVY EMOTIVELY
EEILMRSST MERITLESS
EEILMRSTY LYSIMETER
EEILNNOPT LEPONTINE
EEILNNPSS PENNILESS
EEILNNSST SENTINELS
EEILNNSTY INTENSELY
EEILNOORS OLEORESIN

EEILNOPRT INTERLOPE,
  REPLETION, TERPINEOL
EEILNORVW WOLVERINE
EEILNOSSS NOISELESS
EEILNOSSU SELENIOUS
EEILNOSTV NOVELTIES
EEILNPPSZ ZEPPELINS
EEILNPSSS SPINELESS
EEILNPSTT PESTILENT
EEILNPSVY PENSIVELY
EEILNRSST LISTENERS
EEILNRSVY INVERSELY
EEILOPRTX EXPLOITER
EEILOPSST POLITESSE
EEILOPSVX EXPLOSIVE
EEILORRST LOITERERS
EEILORSTT LOTTERIES
EEILPRSTX TRIPLEXES
EEILPRSTY PERISTYLE
EEILPRSUV PRELUSIVE,
  PULVERISE, REPULSIVE
EEILPRUVZ PULVERIZE
EEILPSUVX EXPULSIVE
EEILRSSTV SILVESTER
EEILRSTVY RESTIVELY
EEILRSUVV REVULSIVE
EEIMMMRSS MESMERISM
EEIMMNRRT MERRIMENT
EEIMMORRS MEMORISER
EEIMMORRZ MEMORIZER
EEIMMOSST SOMETIMES
EEIMMRSST MESMERIST
EEIMMRSTW SWIMMERET
EEIMMRSTX EXTREMISM
EEIMNNORT MENTIONER
EEIMNNRTT INTERMENT
EEIMNNSTT SENTIMENT
EEIMNOOTV MOVIETONE
EEIMNOPTX EXEMPTION
EEIMNORSS SERMONISE
EEIMNORST MOISTENER
EEIMNORSZ SERMONIZE
EEIMNOSST SEMITONES
EEIMNOSTX SIXTEENMO
EEIMNOSTZ TIME ZONES
EEIMNPQTU EQUIPMENT
EEIMNPRSS PRIMENESS
EEIMNPSST EMPTINESS
EEIMNRRSS MERRINESS
EEIMNRSTU MUTINEERS
EEIMNSSSS MESSINESS
EEIMOOPRS MEIOSPORE
EEIMOORTZ MEROZOITE

EEIMOPRST PERISTOME,
  TEMPORISE
EEIMOPRTZ TEMPORIZE
EEIMPPRRS PERISPERM
EEIMPRRSS IMPRESSER
EEIMPRRTT PERMITTER
EEIMPRRTY PERIMETRY
EEIMPRSSS IMPRESSES
EEIMPSSTU IMPETUSES
EEIMQSTUU EQUISETUM
EEIMRRSTT TRIMESTER
EEIMRSSSU MESSIEURS
EEIMRSSTY MYSTERIES
EEIMRSTTX EXTREMIST
EEIMRTTXY EXTREMITY
EEINNNRSU NUNNERIES
EEINNOPPS NIPPONESE
EEINNOPRS PENSIONER
EEINNOPRT TIN OPENER
EEINNORTT RETENTION
EEINNOSTV VEINSTONE
EEINNOSTX EXTENSION
EEINNPRST SPINNERET
EEINNPRTT PERTINENT
EEINNPSST INEPTNESS
EEINNPSTT PENITENTS
EEINNPSWY PENNY-WISE
EEINNRSST INERTNESS
EEINNRSSV INVERNESS,
  NERVINESS
EEINNSSSW NEWSINESS
EEINOPPST PEPTONISE,
  PIPESTONE
EEINOPPTZ PEPTONIZE
EEINOPRST INTERPOSE
EEINOQRUV VÉRONIQUE
EEINOQSUX EQUINOXES
EEINORRSV REVERSION
EEINORSTX EXERTIONS,
  EXSERTION
EEINORTVW INTERWOVE
EEINOSSTV OSTENSIVE
EEINPRRRT REPRINTER
EEINPRRTT INTERPRET
EEINPRSSW WINEPRESS
EEINPSSTT PETTINESS
EEINQRSTU IN REQUEST
EEINQSSTU QUIETNESS
EEINRRRSU REINSURER
EEINRRSSU NURSERIES
EEINRSSSY SYNERESIS
EEINRSSTT INTERESTS,
  TRITENESS

EEINRSSTW WITNESSER
EEINRSSUV UNIVERSES
EEINSSSTT TESTINESS
EEINSSSTW WITNESSES
EEINSTTXY EXTENSITY
EEIOPPSTV STOVEPIPE
EEIOPRSTT POTTERIES
EEIOPRSTV POVERTIES
EEIOPRTTU PIROUETTE
EEIOQQUUV EQUIVOQUE
EEIORRRST ROISTERER,
   TERRORISE
EEIORRRSV RESERVOIR
EEIORRRTZ TERRORIZE
EEIORRSTX EXTERIORS
EEIORRTVW OVERWRITE
EEIORSSUV OVERISSUE
EEIORSVVW OVERVIEWS
EEIORTTVX EXTORTIVE
EEIPRRSST PERSISTER
EEIPRSSST PRIESTESS
EEIPRSSUV SUPERVISE
EEIPRSTTT PRETTIEST
EEIPRTTWY TYPEWRITE
EEIQSSTUU QUIETUSES
EEIRRSSST RESISTERS
EEIRRSSTV RESERVIST
EEIRRTTTW TWITTERER
EEIRSTUVX EXTRUSIVE
EEJMNNOTY ENJOYMENT
EEJMPQUUU QUEUE-JUMP
EEJNOQSUU JUNOESQUE
EEJNORRUY JOURNEYER
EEJPRRRSU PERJURERS
EEKKORSTY KEYSTROKE
EEKLMOSSS SMOKELESS
EEKLNOSST SKELETONS
EEKLNPRSU SPELUNKER
EEKLORSTW STEELWORK
EEKMNOPTW KEPT
   WOMEN
EEKNOSSTY KEYSTONES
EELLLLNWY LLEWELLYN
EELLMNOOS LEMON SOLE
EELLMOSTW MELLOWEST
EELLNNRTU TUNNELLER
EELLNSSTU SULLENEST
EELLOOSTW STEEL WOOL
EELLOPPRR PROPELLER
EELLORRTW TROWELLER
EELLSSSTY STYLELESS
EELLSSSUY USELESSLY

EELMMNOTU
   EMOLUMENT
EELMNNORT ENROLMENT
EELMNOSSY MONEYLESS
EELMNOTTX EXTOLMENT
EELMOOPST LEPTOSOME
EELMOOPTT TOTEM POLE
EELMOPRSY EMPLOYERS
EELMOPRTU PETROLEUM
EELMORSST MOLESTERS
EELMORTTV VOLTMETER
EELMORTUV VOLUMETER
EELMPRSUY SUPREMELY
EELNNOOUV NUEVO LEON
EELNNOPRS PERSONNEL
EELNNRSTU TUNNELERS
EELNOOSSS LOOSENESS
EELNOPSTU PLENTEOUS
EELNORSTV RESOLVENT
EELNORTUV VOLUNTEER
EELNOSSST STONELESS
EELNPRSTY PRESENTLY
EELNRSTTU NET RESULT
EELOPRRSX EXPLORERS
EELOPRRTU POULTERER
EELOPRSSW POWERLESS
EELOPRSTV OVERSLEPT
EELOPRSTY POLYESTER,
   PROSELYTE
EELORRSUV REVELROUS
EELORRSVV REVOLVERS
EELORSSUV OURSELVES
EELORSTUV TRUELOVES
EELPPSTTU SEPTUPLET
EELPRSSXY EXPRESSLY
EELPRSTUU SEPULTURE
EELPSTTUX SEXTUPLET
EELRRSSTW WRESTLERS
EELRSSTTU UTTERLESS
EELRSSTVY SYLVESTER
EEMMNOORT
   METRONOME,
   MONOMETER, MONOTREME
EEMMNOSTV
   MOVEMENTS
EEMMOORST
   OSMOMETER
EEMMORTYZ
   ZYMOMETER
EEMNOOPST TONE POEMS
EEMNOORTT TONOMETER
EEMNORRTV VERMONTER
EEMNORRTY MONTERREY

EEMNSSTTV VESTMENTS
EEMOOOSTT OSTEOTOME
EEMOOPRTT OPTOMETER
EEMOPPRRT PRE-EMPTOR
EEMOPRRTY PYROMETER
EEMPRRTTU TRUMPETER
EEMPRSSTT TEMPTRESS
EEMRRSTTU MUTTERERS
EENNNOSTV NON-EVENTS
EENNOOSTU NEOTENOUS
EENNOPRSS PRONENESS
EENNOPSTX EXPONENTS
EENNORSTU ENTRE NOUS
EENNRSSST STERNNESS
EENOOPPSS POPE'S NOSE
EENOORRSU ERRONEOUS
EENOORSTV OVERTONES
EENOPPRTT PREPOTENT
EENOPRRSS RESPONSER
EENOPRSSS RESPONSES
EENOPSTTY STENOTYPE
EENOQRSTU ON REQUEST
EENORTTTU NEUTRETTO
EENRRSTUV VENTURERS
EENRSSTUW WET NURSES
EEOOPRRVW
   OVERPOWER
EEOPPPPRT PEPPER POT
EEOPPRSSU SUPERPOSE
EEOPRRRST REPORTERS
EEOPRRRTY REPERTORY
EEOPRRSTT PROTESTER
EEOPRRSTX EXPORTERS
EEOPRSSSS ESPRESSOS,
   REPOSSESS
EEOPRSSSW PROWESSES
EEOPRSSUX EXPOSURES
EEORRRSST RESTORERS
EEORRSSTU RETROUSSÉ
EEORRSTUV OVERTURES
EEORRTTVX EXTROVERT
EEORSSTUW
   SOU'WESTER
EEPRRSSST PRESTRESS
EEPRRSSSU PRESSURES
EEPRRSTTU SPUTTERER
EERRSTTTU STUTTERER
EFFFILSTU FLUFFIEST
EFFFLORTU EFFORTFUL
EFFGINORS OFFERINGS
EFFGINRSU SUFFERING
EFFGLORTU FORGETFUL
EFFGNRSSU GRUFFNESS

EFFHIIKNS   FISH KNIFE
EFFHIISTT   FIFTIETHS
EFFHIISTW   WHIFFIEST
EFFHIKSWW   SKEW-WHIFF
EFFHILRSY   FLY-FISHER
EFFHINSSU   HUFFINESS
EFFHLRSSU   SHUFFLERS
EFFIIMNSS   MIFFINESS
EFFIIORRT   FORTIFIER
EFFIIQRSU   SQUIFFIER
EFFILLLRU   FULFILLER
EFFILMUUV   EFFLUVIUM
EFFILNRSS   SNIFFLERS
EFFILORRS   FLOS FERRI
EFFINOOSS   NOISES OFF
EFFINOSSU   EFFUSIONS
EFFINPSSU   PUFFINESS
EFFINSSST   STIFFNESS
EFFIOOPRR   FIREPROOF
EFFIORSTW   WRITE-OFFS
EFFIORTVY   FORTY-FIVE
EFFISSTTU   STUFFIEST
EFFISSUUV   SUFFUSIVE
EFFLLRTUY   FRETFULLY
EFFNOORRT   FOREFRONT
EFFOORRTY   OFFERTORY
EFGGIINNR   FINGERING
EFGGILNNU   ENGULFING
EFGGILOOS   SOLFEGGIO
EFGGINOOR   FOREGOING
EFGGINOSS   FOGGINESS
EFGHHIILR   HIGH-FLIER
EFGHIILNT   NIGHTLIFE
EFGHIILRT   FIRELIGHT,
    FLIGHTIER
EFGHIINRT   INFIGHTER
EFGHILNSS   FLESHINGS
EFGHILPRT   PREFLIGHT
EFGHILTWY   FLYWEIGHT
EFGHIORST   FORESIGHT,
    GIFT HORSE
EFGHOOSTT   GET SHOT OF
EFGHOSTTU   GET SHUT OF
EFGIIINRS   SIGNIFIER
EFGIILLNR   REFILLING
EFGIILLNT   FILLETING
EFGIILNPR   PILFERING
EFGIILNRT   FILTERING
EFGIILORR   GLORIFIER
EFGIINNRR   INFERRING,
    INFRINGER
EFGIINNST   INFESTING
EFGIINPRT   FINGERTIP

EFGIINPRX   PREFIXING
EFGIINRSU   FIGURINES
EFGIINRTT   REFITTING
EFGIINRVY   VERIFYING
EFGIISTUV   FUGITIVES
EFGILNNNU   FUNNELING
EFGILNORW   FLOWERING
EFGILPRSU   FIRE-PLUGS
EFGILRTUU   FULGURITE
EFGIMNNOT   FOMENTING
EFGIMNORR   REFORMING
EFGIMNPRU   PERFUMING
EFGINNOST   SOFTENING
EFGINOOSS   GOOFINESS
EFGINORST   FOSTERING
EFGLOOSVX   FOXGLOVES
EFGLOOTUV
    TUG-OF-LOVE
EFGNOORTT   FORGOTTEN
EFGOOOOST   GOOSEFOOT
EFHHIISTW   WHITEFISH
EFHHILLSS   SHELLFISH
EFHHNOOOT   ON THE
    HOOF
EFHIILSTT   FILTHIEST
EFHIIMSST   FETISHISM
EFHIINPSS   SNIPEFISH
EFHIINSSS   FISHINESS
EFHIIRRTT   THRIFTIER
EFHIISSTT   FETISHIST,
    SHIFTIEST
EFHIJLLSY   JELLYFISH
EFHIKSSTY   SHIFT KEYS
EFHILLSSW   SWELLFISH
EFHILLSSY   SELFISHLY
EFHILNSSU   UNSELFISH
EFHILSSST   SHIFTLESS
EFHIMOPRZ   PFORZHEIM
EFHINOOTT   FINE-TOOTH
EFHINORRT   FIRETHORN
EFHINOSST   STONEFISH
EFHINRRSU   FURNISHER
EFHIORSTT   FORTIETHS,
    FROTHIEST
EFHLLLPUY   HELPFULLY
EFHLLOPUY   HOPEFULLY
EFHLLOSUU   FULL HOUSE
EFHLOOPSU   FLOPHOUSE
EFHLOPSST   FLESHPOTS
EFHMNOORT   HOME
    FRONT
EFHNORTUX   FOXHUNTER
EFHOOORTT   FORETOOTH

EFIIJRSTU   JUSTIFIER
EFIIKRSST   FRISKIEST
EFIILLLST   STILL LIFE
EFIILLMOR   MOLLIFIER
EFIILLNRU   NULLIFIER
EFIILLRST   FILLISTER,
    FRILLIEST
EFIILMNSS   FILMINESS
EFIILMSST   FLIMSIEST
EFIILNSTT   FLINTIEST
EFIILOSSS   FOSSILISE
EFIILOSSZ   FOSSILIZE
EFIILPRTT   FILTER TIP
EFIILRTTY   FERTILITY
EFIIMNSST   FEMINISTS
EFIIMORRT   MORTIFIER
EFIIMRSTY   MYSTIFIER
EFIINNNOT   NON-FINITE
EFIINNPRT   FINE PRINT
EFIINNSST   NIFTINESS
EFIINNSTY   INTENSIFY
EFIINOPST   IN SPITE OF
EFIINORRS   FIRE IRONS,
    INFERIORS
EFIINSSZZ   FIZZINESS
EFIIPRRSU   PURIFIERS
EFIIPRSST   SPITFIRES
EFIIRSTTU   FRUITIEST
EFIIRSTZZ   FRIZZIEST
EFIISTTVY   FESTIVITY
EFIKLNSSU   FLUKINESS
EFIKNORSS   FORESKINS
EFIKORRSW   FIREWORKS
EFILLMOPU   FILOPLUME
EFILLNPTU   PLENTIFUL
EFILLORRV   FRIVOLLER
EFILMNOSY   SOLEMNIFY
EFILMOPRX   PLEXIFORM
EFILNNOOS   NO FLIES ON
EFILNNORT   FRONT LINE
EFILNOORS   SOLFERINO
EFILNOOSU   FELONIOUS
EFILNOOTU   OUT OF LINE
EFILNOSST   LOFTINESS
EFILOPPST   FLOPPIEST
EFILORSTY   LIFE STORY
EFILQRUUV   QUIVERFUL
EFILRSSTU   FRUITLESS
EFILRTUVY   FURTIVELY
EFIMMORRS   REFORMISM
EFIMMORRV   VERMIFORM
EFIMNORRS   INFORMERS
EFIMNORST   IN TERMS OF

EFIMORRRS SERRIFORM
EFIMORRST FIRESTORM,
　REFORMIST, RESTIFORM
EFIMPRSTU FRUMPIEST
EFINNNSSU FUNNINESS
EFINNSSTU UNFITNESS
EFINOPRSU PERFUSION
EFINOPRSY PERSONIFY
EFINORRST FRONTIERS
EFINRRSSU FURRINESS
EFINRRTUU FURNITURE
EFINRSSTU TURFINESS
EFINSSSSU FUSSINESS
EFINSSSTU FUSTINESS
EFINSSSTW SWIFTNESS
EFINSSUZZ FUZZINESS
EFIOORSTX SIX-FOOTER
EFIOORSUV OVIFEROUS
EFIOPRTTU PETIT FOUR
EFIORRSTW FROWSTIER
EFIORSSTT FROSTIEST
EFIORSTWZ FROWZIEST
EFIORTTTU OUTFITTER
EFKLMNOOW
　WOMENFOLK
EFKNOOPRS SPOKEN FOR
EFKORRSTW FRETWORKS
EFLLMOSUY FULSOMELY
EFLLNOOSW LONE WOLFS
EFLLNTUUY TUNEFULLY
EFLLOORSW FOLLOWERS
EFLLRSTUY RESTFULLY
EFLLSTUYZ ZESTFULLY
EFLNOORVW
　OVERFLOWN
EFLNOPRTU PROFLUENT
EFLNORSUW SUNFLOWER
EFLOOOOST FOOTLOOSE
EFLOOPRTW FLOWERPOT
EFLOORSVW OVERFLOWS
EFLOOSTTW LOWESTOFT
EFLOPRSUY PROFUSELY
EFLORRRTU TERRORFUL
EFLRSSSTU STRESSFUL
EFMOORSSU FOURSOMES
EFNOOOSTT FOOTNOTES
EFNOOTTUU OUT OF TUNE
EFOOOPRRV OVERPROOF
EFOOPRRSS PROFESSOR
EFOOPSSTT FOOTSTEPS
EFOOQRRTU ROQUEFORT
EGGGIIJNR REJIGGING
EGGGIINNR GINGERING

EGGGIORST GROGGIEST
EGGHIINTW WEIGHTING
EGGHINNRU HUNGERING
EGGIILNNR LINGERING
EGGIINNRS RESIGNING
EGGIINNST INGESTING
EGGIINNSW SWINGEING
EGGILLNRU GRUELLING
EGGILNORV GROVELING
EGGILNORW GLOWERING
EGGILOOST GEOLOGIST
EGGILQRSU SQUIGGLER
EGGILQSSU SQUIGGLES
EGGIMNNOR MONGERING
EGGIMNSSU MUGGINESS,
　MUGGINSES
EGGINNNOR GRONINGEN
EGGINNORV GOVERNING
EGGINNOTT GOTTINGEN
EGGINNPTU TUNING PEG
EGGINNPUX EXPUNGING
EGGINNRTU GINGER NUT
EGGINOORV GOING-OVER
EGGINOSSS SOGGINESS
EGGINRSTU GESTURING
EGGINRTTU GUTTERING
EGGIORRTU OUTRIGGER
EGGJLMNUY JUNGLE GYM
EGGLMRSSU SMUGGLERS
EGGLRRSTU STRUGGLER
EGGLRSSTU STRUGGLES
EGHHHIORS HIGH HORSE
EGHHIIORS HIROSHIGE
EGHHIIRSS HIGH-RISES
EGHHINRST THRESHING
EGHHIPRSU HIGHER-UPS
EGHHNORUW
　ROUGH-HEWN
EGHHORTTU RETHOUGHT
EGHIIKNRS SHRIEKING
EGHIILLMT LIMELIGHT
EGHIILNRS HIRELINGS,
　RELISHING
EGHIILTWY WEIGHTILY
EGHIIMNTT NIGHTTIME
EGHIIMSTT MIGHTIEST
EGHIINNTW WHITENING
EGHIINPRS PERISHING
EGHIINRSV SHIVERING
EGHIINRTW WITHERING
EGHIINSTY HYGIENIST
EGHILLNOR HOLLERING
EGHILLNTY LENGTHILY

EGHILNNOT NEON LIGHT
EGHILNOSV SHOVELING
EGHILNSST LIGHTNESS
EGHILOORY HIEROLOGY
EGHILORST GHOSTLIER
EGHILRTVY VERY LIGHT
EGHILSSST SIGHTLESS
EGHILSSTT SLIGHTEST
EGHIMNORT MOTHERING
EGHIMNOST SOMETHING
EGHIMPPSU PEMPHIGUS
EGHINNSTU ENTHUSING
EGHINOORV HOOVERING
EGHINORSU REHOUSING
EGHINORSW SHOWERING
EGHINORTV OVERNIGHT
EGHINORTX EXHORTING
EGHINOSTY HISTOGENY
EGHINPRSY SYPHERING
EGHINRSST RIGHTNESS
EGHINRSTU HUNGRIEST,
　SURE THING
EGHINSSTT TIGHTNESS
EGHIOPRTT TIGHTROPE
EGHIORSTU RIGHTEOUS
EGHIORSTV OVERSIGHT
EGHIRSTTU THEURGIST
EGHLLOORY GLORY HOLE
EGHLLOPSU PLUGHOLES
EGHLMNOPU
　PLOUGHMEN
EGHLNOOPY
　NEPHOLOGY, PHENOLOGY
EGHLNOORS LONGSHORE
EGHLNOOTY ETHNOLOGY
EGHLNOPYY PHYLOGENY
EGHMNOORW
　HOMEGROWN
EGHNOOOPR
　GONOPHORE
EGHNOOPRY GYNOPHORE
EGHNORSSU ROUGHNESS
EGHNOSSTU TOUGHNESS
EGHNRSSTT STRENGTHS
EGHOPTYYZ ZYGOPHYTE
EGIIIMNTZ ITEMIZING
EGIIJNNNO ENJOINING
EGIIJNNOR REJOINING
EGIIKLNST KINGLIEST
EGIIKLNSV KING'S EVIL
EGIIKNNRT TINKERING
EGIIKRSTZ SITZKREIG
EGIILLMNP IMPELLING

EGIILNNST ENLISTING,
   LISTENING
EGIILNNSV SNIVELING
EGIILNNTT ENTITLING
EGIILNNUV UNVEILING
EGIILNORS RELIGIONS
EGIILNORT LOITERING
EGIILNOST GILSONITE
EGIILNRSV SILVERING
EGIILNRTT LITTERING
EGIILNSVW SWIVELING
EGIILNTTY GENTILITY
EGIILOPST EPILOGIST
EGIILORST TRILOGIES
EGIILORSU RELIGIOUS
EGIILRRST GRISTLIER
EGIILRSST GRISLIEST
EGIILRSTU LITURGIES
EGIILSTTU GUILTIEST
EGIILSTTZ GLITZIEST
EGIIMMNRS IMMERSING,
   SIMMERING
EGIIMNPRS SIMPERING
EGIIMNRSS GRIMINESS
EGIIMNRTT REMITTING
EGIINNNRT INTERNING
EGIINNNTV INVENTING
EGIINNNTW ENTWINING
EGIINNORS NIGROSINE
EGIINNOST INGESTION
EGIINNOSU INGENIOUS
EGIINNQRU ENQUIRING
EGIINNRRT INTERRING
EGIINNRST INSERTING
EGIINNRSW INSWINGER
EGIINNRTU REUNITING
EGIINNRTV INVERTING
EGIINNRTW WINTERING
EGIINNSTT INSETTING
EGIINNSTV INVESTING
EGIINNTUY INGENUITY
EGIINPPQU EQUIPPING
EGIINPRRS RESPIRING,
   SPRINGIER
EGIINQRRU REQUIRING
EGIINQRTU REQUITING
EGIINQRUV QUIVERING
EGIINRRST STRINGIER
EGIINRRTU INTRIGUER
EGIINRRTW REWRITING
EGIINRSST RESISTING
EGIINRSSU REISSUING
EGIINRSTT RESITTING

EGIINRSTU INTRIGUES
EGIINRTTT TITTERING
EGIINRTTY INTEGRITY
EGIINSSTT STINGIEST
EGIIRSTTT GRITTIEST
EGIJKLNRY JERKINGLY
EGIJKNNTU JUNKETING
EGIJLNSTY JESTINGLY
EGIJNPRRU PERJURING
EGIKLNNOO INGLENOOK
EGIKMNNOY MONKEYING
EGIKNORRW REWORKING
EGILLLNTY TELLINGLY
EGILLMNOW MELLOWING
EGILLMNTY MELTINGLY
EGILLMOTU GUILLEMOT
EGILLNNOR ENROLLING
EGILLNOTT ILL-GOTTEN
EGILLNOTW TOWELLING
EGILLNOTX EXTOLLING
EGILLNOUU LONGUEUIL
EGILLNOVY VOLLEYING
EGILLNOWY YELLOWING
EGILLNPSS SPELLINGS
EGILLNSSW SWELLINGS
EGILLOSSY SYLLOGISE
EGILLOSYZ SYLLOGIZE
EGILLSSTU GUILTLESS
EGILMMNPU PUMMELING
EGILMNOOS NEOLOGISM
EGILMNOPY EMPLOYING
EGILMNOST MOLESTING
EGILMOOST GLOOMIEST
EGILNNNTU TUNNELING
EGILNNOOS LOOSENING
EGILNNOST SINGLETON
EGILNNRSU NURSELING
EGILNNSST NESTLINGS
EGILNNSUY ENSUINGLY
EGILNNVYY ENVYINGLY
EGILNOOST NEOLOGIST
EGILNOOSU SINOLOGUE
EGILNOPRX EXPLORING
EGILNORSV RESOLVING
EGILNORTV REVOLTING
EGILNORVV REVOLVING
EGILNORVY OVERLYING
EGILNOTVY LONGEVITY
EGILNPRSU REPULSING
EGILNRSTU RESULTING
EGILNRSTW WRESTLING
EGILNSSTT SETTLINGS
EGILNSTTY TESTINGLY

EGILOSSST GLOSSIEST
EGILOSSTT GLOTTISES
EGILOSSTU EULOGISTS
EGIMMNRSU SUMMERING
EGIMMNSSU GUMMINESS
EGIMNORST GERMISTON
EGIMNORSV MISGOVERN
EGIMNPRSU PRESUMING
EGIMNPRTU PERMUTING
EGIMNRSSY SYNERGISM
EGIMNRSTU MUSTERING
EGIMNRTTU MUTTERING
EGIMPRSTU GRUMPIEST
EGINNNRRU RERUNNING
EGINNNRUV UNNERVING
EGINNORSW WORSENING
EGINNOSUU INGENUOUS
EGINNRRTU RETURNING
EGINNRSTT STRINGENT
EGINNRSTU INSURGENT
EGINNRTUV VENTURING
EGINOOSSS GOOSINESS
EGINOOSSU ISOGENOUS
EGINOPRRR PORRINGER
EGINOPRRT REPORTING
EGINOPRRV REPROVING
EGINOPRST PROGESTIN
EGINOPRTT POTTERING
EGINOPRTX EXPORTING
EGINOPSST SPONGIEST
EGINOPSSU ESPOUSING
EGINOPSUY EPIGYNOUS
EGINORRST RESORTING,
   RESTORING
EGINORRTT RETORTING
EGINORSTU GERONTIUS
EGINORTTT TOTTERING
EGINORTTX EXTORTING
EGINOSSTU GOUTINESS
EGINPRSSS PRESSINGS
EGINPRTTU PUTTERING
EGINPRUVY PURVEYING
EGINPSTTU UPSETTING
EGINPSTWW SWEPTWING
EGINRSSST STRESSING
EGINRSSTY SYNERGIST
EGINRSUVY SURVEYING
EGINSSSTU GUSTINESS
EGINSTTTU TUNGSTITE
EGIOORSTV GROOVIEST
EGIORSTTT GROTTIEST
EGKORSSUW
   GUESSWORK

EGLMNOOOU
MONOLOGUE
EGLMOORTY METROLOGY
EGLMOOTYY ETYMOLOGY
EGLNNOSUU SUN LOUNGE
EGLNNPTUY PUNGENTLY
EGLNOOPRR PROLONGER
EGLNOORUY NEUROLOGY
EGLNOOSUV LONGEVOUS
EGLNORSTY STRONGYLE
EGLNORSUU LONGUEURS
EGLNOSTUU GLUTENOUS
EGLOOOSTY OSTEOLOGY
EGLOOPRSU PROLOGUES
EGLOOPRTY PETROLOGY
EGMNOOOSS
MONGOOSES
EGMOORSTU
GUESTROOM
EGNNNRRUU
GUNRUNNER
EGNNORSSW
WRONGNESS
EGNOOPRSS PROGNOSES
EGNOORRSV GOVERNORS
EGNOORRVW
OVERGROWN
EGNOORSUU
UROGENOUS
EGNORSSSS GROSSNESS
EGNORSSST SONGSTERS
EGNORSSTT STRONGEST
EGNORSSTU STURGEONS
EGNORSTUY YOUNGSTER
EGOOPRSYZ ZYGOSPORE
EHHIINSTT IN THE SHIT
EHHIIRTTT THIRTIETH
EHHILLLSY HELLISHLY
EHHILMOOP HOMOPHILE
EHHINOPPS PHOSPHINE
EHHIOPPST PHOSPHITE
EHHIOPRSW HORSEWHIP
EHHIORSST HORSESHIT
EHHIORTTT THITHERTO
EHHLOOPTY HOLOPHYTE
EHHMNNOPP PHNOM
PENH
EHHMNOOOP
HOMOPHONE
EHHMNOSUY HUSH
MONEY
EHHMORTTU HOME
TRUTH

EHHMRTUYY EURHYTHMY
EHHNOORSS SHOEHORNS
EHHOOPSTY THEOSOPHY
EHHOOSSTU HOTHOUSES
EHIIKNSTT KITTENISH
EHIILLTWY LILY-WHITE
EHIILMRST HITLERISM
EHIILRSTW WILTSHIRE
EHIINNORT ORNITHINE
EHIINNSSS SHININESS
EHIINORRT INHERITOR
EHIINPPRW WHIPPER-IN
EHIINPRST NEPHRITIS,
PHRENITIS
EHIINPSST PITHINESS
EHIIORSST HISTORIES
EHIIPPSSY EPIPHYSIS
EHIIQRSSU SQUISHIER
EHIIRRSTT THIRSTIER
EHIIRSSTT SHIRTIEST
EHIIRSSTW IRISH STEW
EHIIRSTTZ ZITHERIST
EHIISSTTT SHITTIEST
EHIISSTTX SIXTIETHS
EHIKLLPSY SYLPHLIKE
EHIKLORTZ KILOHERTZ
EHIKNSSSU HUSKINESS
EHIKPRSSU SPIKE-RUSH
EHILLLMOS MOLEHILLS
EHILLOSTY HOSTILELY
EHILLOSWY YELLOWISH
EHILLRRST THRILLERS
EHILLRSST SHRILLEST
EHILMNOST MONTHLIES
EHILMOORS HEIRLOOMS
EHILMPPRY PERILYMPH
EHILMRSST MIRTHLESS
EHILMRSTU LUTHERISM
EHILMRSUV HILVERSUM
EHILNOOPT LITHOPONE,
PHONOLITE
EHILNOSST HOLSTEINS
EHILNOSUY HEINOUSLY
EHILOPPTY HIPPOLYTE
EHILOPRST HELIPORTS
EHILOPRXY XEROPHILY
EHILPSTTY PETTISHLY
EHILRSTTW WHITTLERS
EHILSSSTU SLUSHIEST
EHIMNNOOS MOONSHINE
EHIMNOPUU EUPHONIUM
EHIMNORST HORSEMINT
EHIMNPSST SHIPMENTS

EHIMNPSSU HUMPINESS
EHIMNRTUU RUTHENIUM
EHIMNSSSU MUSHINESS
EHIMOOSST SMOOTHIES
EHIMOPPRR PERIMORPH
EHIMORSST ISOTHERMS
EHIMORSTT SHORT TIME
EHIMPRRTU TRIUMPHER
EHIMRRSTY ERYTHRISM
EHIMSSSTU ISTHMUSES
EHINNOPSS PHONINESS
EHINNORSS HORNINESS
EHINNOSST THONINESS
EHINNOSTW NONWHITES,
WHINSTONE
EHINNSSTU NISSEN HUT
EHINOPPRS HORNPIPES
EHINOPRSS NEPHROSIS
EHINOPRSW OWNERSHIP,
SHIPOWNER
EHINOPSTU IN THE SOUP
EHINOPSTY HYPNOTISE
EHINOPTYZ HYPNOTIZE
EHINORRSU NOURISHER
EHINORSSS HORSINESS
EHINORSTT THORNIEST
EHINORTXY THYROXINE
EHINOSSSW SHOWINESS
EHINOSTWW
SNOW-WHITE
EHINPRRTY PYRETHRIN
EHINPSSSU PUSHINESS
EHINRSSSU RUSHINESS
EHINSSSTY SYNTHESIS
EHIOOPRTW POOR WHITE
EHIOOSTTT TOOTHIEST
EHIOPRSST PROTHESIS,
SOPHISTER
EHIORSSTT THEORISTS
EHIORSTTW WORTHIEST
EHIORSTWZ HOWITZERS
EHIPQSSUY PHYSIQUES
EHIRSSSTU RUSSETISH
EHKNPRRSU PRESHRUNK
EHKOORRSW
WORKHORSE
EHKOORSUW
HOUSEWORK,
WORKHOUSE
EHLLMOPSY MESOPHYLL
EHLLNSSTU NUTSHELLS
EHLLOOOPS LOOPHOLES
EHLLOOSTU TOLLHOUSE

EHLLOOSTW HOLLOWEST	EHOOPPTTY PHOTOTYPE	EIILNPSST SPLENITIS
EHLMOORSW	EHOOPRRTT ORTHOPTER	EIILNPSTY PENSILITY
WORMHOLES	EHOOPRRTV HOVERPORT	EIILNSTTY TENSILITY
EHLNOOPPY POLYPHONE	EHOOPSSTU HOUSETOPS	EIILOQSSU SILIQUOSE
EHLNOOPRT NORTH POLE	EHOORRTVW	EIILPPSST SLIPPIEST
EHLNOOPXY XYLOPHONE	OVERTHROW	EIILPRTUY PUERILITY
EHLNOOSTY HOLYSTONE	EHOORSSUW ROW	EIILRSTTY STERILITY
EHLNORRTY NORTHERLY	HOUSES	EIILRSTVY SERVILITY
EHLNPSSSU PLUSHNESS	EHOOSSTUU OUTHOUSES	EIILSSSTY SESSILITY
EHLOOPRST PORTHOLES,	EHOPRSTXY EXSTROPHY	EIIMMNORS IMMERSION
POTHOLERS	EHORRSTTW THROWSTER	EIIMMNOSS MISONEISM
EHLOOPSTU SOUTH POLE	EHOSSTTUW SOUTHWEST	EIIMMNRSU IMMUNISER
EHLOOSSTT TOOTHLESS	EHRRSSTTU THRUSTERS	EIIMMNRUZ IMMUNIZER
EHLOPRSTU UPHOLSTER	EIIILMMTT TIME LIMIT	EIIMMNSTY IMMENSITY
EHLORRTTT THROTTLER	EIIILNNQU INQUILINE	EIIMMORSS ISOMERISM
EHLORSSTW WORTHLESS	EIIILSTTU UTILITIES	EIIMMOSTV EMOTIVISM
EHLORSTTT THROTTLES	EIIIMMNRS MINIMISER	EIIMMPSSS PESSIMISM
EHLORSTUY SOUTHERLY	EIIIMMNRZ MINIMIZER	EIIMMPSUY EPIMYSIUM
EHLPRSTUU SULPHURET	EIIIMPRTV PRIMITIVE	EIIMNNRTU TRIENNIUM
EHMMOOPRS	EIIINQRSU INQUIRIES	EIIMNORSS MISSIONER,
MESOMORPH	EIIINRSTT RETINITIS,	REMISSION
EHMNNOOOY	TRINITIES	EIIMNOSSS EMISSIONS
HONEYMOON	EIIINTTUV INTUITIVE	EIIMNOSST MISONEIST
EHMNOOSTW	EIIJMSSTU JESUITISM	EIIMNOSUV VIMINEOUS
HOMETOWNS	EIIKKNNSS KINKINESS	EIIMNPRRT IMPRINTER
EHMOOOPRS	EIIKLLORT KILOLITRE	EIIMNRSST MINISTERS
SOPHOMORE	EIIKLMNSS MILKINESS	EIIMNSSST MISTINESS
EHMOOORSU	EIIKLNNRT INTERLINK	EIIMOPRSU IMPERIOUS
HOUSEROOM	EIIKLNSSS SILKINESS	EIIMOPRSV IMPROVISE
EHMOOOSTT TOOTHSOME	EIIKLNSST SLINKIEST	EIIMOPSTT EPITOMIST
EHMOOSSTT SMOOTHEST	EIIKMPSST SKIMPIEST	EIIMOSSTV SOVIETISM
EHMORRSTT SHORT-TERM	EIIKNNSST SKINNIEST	EIIMPSSST PESSIMIST
EHMPRRTUY PYRETHRUM	EIIKNPSSS SPIKINESS	EIINNNOST INTENSION
EHNNOORST HORNSTONE	EIIKNRSSS RISKINESS	EIINNNOTT INTENTION
EHNNOOTTW ON THE	EIIKQRSTU QUIRKIEST	EIINNNOTV INVENTION
TOWN	EIILLMNRS MILLINERS	EIINNNSST TINNINESS
EHNNOPRST PENN'ORTHS	EIILLMNRY MILLINERY	EIINNORST INSERTION
EHNOOPPSS OPEN SHOPS	EIILLMSST LIMITLESS	EIINNORSV INVERSION
EHNOOPPTY PHONOTYPE	EIILLNRST INSTILLER	EIINNOSSS NOISINESS
EHNOORSSW	EIILLNSSS SILLINESS	EIINNPPSS NIPPINESS
SNOWSHOER	EIILLNSTU NULLITIES	EIINNPSSS SPININESS
EHNOOSSSW	EIILLOPRS PILLORIES	EIINNRSTT INTERNIST
SNOWSHOES	EIILMMORS MELIORISM	EIINNSSTT INSISTENT
EHNOOSTUW TOWN	EIILMNORV VERMILION	EIINNSTTY INTENSITY
HOUSE	EIILMNOSU LIMOUSINE	EIINOPPST PIT PONIES
EHNOOTTTT HOTTENTOT	EIILMNSSS SLIMINESS	EIINOPRSV PREVISION
EHNOPRTTU POTHUNTER	EIILMOPSV IMPLOSIVE	EIINOPSTT PETITIONS
EHNORRTTU TRUE NORTH	EIILMOTTV LEITMOTIV	EIINOPTVW VIEWPOINT
EHNORSSST SHORTNESS	EIILMPRSU PUERILISM	EIINORRST INTERIORS
EHNORSTTW NORTHWEST	EIILMPSUV IMPULSIVE	EIINORSSV REVISIONS
EHNOSSTUU NUTHOUSES	EIILMRSST LISTERISM	EIINORSTY SENIORITY
EHOOOPRSU POORHOUSE	EIILMRSSY MISSILERY	EIINPPRST PINSTRIPE
EHOOORSTV OVERSHOOT	EIILNNOQU QUINOLINE	EIINPSSST TIPSINESS

EIINPSSSW WISPINESS
EIINRSTTW WINTRIEST
EIINRSTUV INTRUSIVE
EIINRTTUV NUTRITIVE
EIINSSSSY SYNISESIS
EIINSSSYZ SYNIZESIS
EIINSSTTW WITTINESS
EIINSTTTU INSTITUTE
EIIOPSSTV POSITIVES
EIIOSSTTV SOVIETIST
EIIPRRSTW TRIPWIRES
EIIPRRTUV IRRUPTIVE
EIIPRSSST PRISSIEST
EIIPRSSTT STRIPIEST
EIIQSSTTU QUIETISTS
EIISSTTTW TWISTIEST
EIJLLNOSS JOLLINESS
EIJLMNPTU MINT JULEP
EIJMNPSSU JUMPINESS
EIJNORSST JOINTRESS
EIKKNOOSS KOOKINESS
EIKLLNOVX KNOXVILLE
EIKLMNOSS MOLESKINS
EIKLNPRRS SPRINKLER
EIKLNPRSS SPRINKLES
EIKLNSSSU SULKINESS
EIKMNOSSS SMOKINESS
EIKMNRSSU MURKINESS
EIKMNSSSU MUSKINESS
EIKNOPRSS PORKINESS
EIKNOSTTT KNOTTIEST
EIKNPRSTU TURNPIKES
EIKNPSSTU SPUNKIEST
EIKOOPSST SPOOKIEST
EIKORRSTV OVERSKIRT
EIKORRSWW WIREWORKS
EIKRRSTWY SKYWRITER
EILLMNOST MILLSTONE
EILLMNSSU SENSILLUM
EILLMOOPT MELITOPOL
EILLMPSTU MULTIPLES
EILLMPTTU MULTIPLET
EILLMPTUX MULTIPLEX
EILLMRTUU TELLURIUM
EILLNOPRU NULLIPORE
EILLNORTU TELLURION
EILLNOSSW LOWLINESS
EILLNOSTY STONE-LILY
EILLNOTVY VIOLENTLY
EILLNSSST STILLNESS
EILLOOPRV LIVERPOOL
EILLOOSTW WOOLLIEST
EILLOPRSV OVERSPILL

EILLOPRTY PELLITORY
EILLOPRWW WILLPOWER
EILLOSTTY STYLOLITE
EILLPSSSY SYLLEPSIS
EILLSSTWY WITLESSLY
EILMMNTUU NUMMULITE
EILMMPSTU PLUMMIEST
EILMNOPST SIMPLETON
EILMNOPSU ON IMPULSE
EILMNORTT TORMENTIL
EILMNORTU MONTREUIL
EILMNOSSU EMULSIONS
EILMNOSTY SOLEMNITY
EILMNOSWY WINSOMELY
EILMNPSSU LUMPINESS
EILMNRSST MINSTRELS
EILMOOSTY ILEOSTOMY
EILNNOOSS LOONINESS
EILNNOSTV INSOLVENT
EILNOOPSS SLIPNOOSE
EILNOOPSX EXPLOSION
EILNOOTUV EVOLUTION
EILNOPRRU PURLOINER
EILNOPRSU PRELUSION,
  REPULSION
EILNOPRTY LINOTYPER
EILNOPSST POINTLESS
EILNOPSSU SPINULOSE
EILNOPSUX EXPULSION
EILNORSTY STORY LINE
EILNORSUV REVULSION
EILNORTUY ROUTINELY
EILNOSSSU LOUSINESS
EILNOSSTV NOVELISTS
EILNOSUVY ENVIOUSLY
EILNPPSSU PULPINESS
EILNPQTUU QUINTUPLE
EILNPRSST SPLINTERS
EILNPRSTY SPLINTERY
EILNRSSSU SURLINESS
EILNRSTTU TURNSTILE
EILNRTUUV VULTURINE
EILNSSSTU LUSTINESS
EILOOPRST POORLIEST
EILOPPRSS PROLEPSIS
EILOPPRTY PROPYLITE
EILOPPSST SLOPPIEST
EILOPRSTT PORTLIEST
EILOPRSTU POULTRIES
EILOPSSTY STYLOPISE
EILOPSTTT TEST PILOT
EILOPSTUY PITEOUSLY
EILOPSTYZ STYLOPIZE

EILORRTVW LIVERWORT
EILORSSUY SERIOUSLY
EILOSSTTT STILETTOS
EILPPRSSU SUPPLIERS
EILQRRSSU SQUIRRELS
EILRSSTTU SULTRIEST
EILRSSTTW WRISTLETS
EIMMNNSTU MUNIMENTS
EIMMNOPRS PERSIMMON
EIMMNORRS MORRIS MEN
EIMMNORSS MISNOMERS
EIMMOPRSU EMPORIUMS
EIMNNOOSS MOONINESS
EIMNNOOTZ MONZONITE
EIMNNOPRT PROMINENT
EIMNNORST INNERMOST
EIMNNOSTT OINTMENTS
EIMNNPTUU NEPTUNIUM
EIMNNRTTU NUTRIMENT
EIMNOORRT REMONTOIR
EIMNOORSS ROOMINESS
EIMNOPRTU IMPORTUNE
EIMNORSST MONITRESS
EIMNORSSU SENSORIUM
EIMNORSUV VERMINOUS
EIMNOSSSS MOSSINESS
EIMNOSSST MOISTNESS
EIMNOSSSU MOUSINESS
EIMNOSTTY TESTIMONY
EIMNOTTZZ MEZZOTINT
EIMNSSSTU MUSTINESS
EIMNSSUZZ MUZZINESS
EIMOOPRTV PROMOTIVE
EIMOORRSW WORRISOME
EIMOORSSU ISOMEROUS
EIMOOSSSX EXOSMOSIS
EIMOPRRSS PRIMROSES
EIMOPRRST IMPORTERS,
  MISREPORT
EIMOPRSTU IMPOSTURE
EIMOPSTUU IMPETUOUS
EIMORRRST TERRORISM
EIMORRSTU TRIMEROUS
EIMORRSWW
  WIREWORMS
EIMORRTTW MITREWORT
EIMORSSTT STORMIEST
EIMORSTTW TWO-TIMERS
EIMORSUVY VOYEURISM
EIMPRSTUY SUPREMITY
EIMPSSTTU STUMPIEST
EIMQSSTUY MYSTIQUES
EIMSSTTTU SMUTTIEST

EINNNOTTY NONENTITY
EINNNSSSU SUNNINESS
EINNOOPST ON POINTES
EINNOORST IRONSTONE,
　SEROTONIN
EINNORSTV INVENTORS
EINNORTVY INVENTORY
EINNOSSST STONINESS
EINNOSSSW SNOWINESS
EINNPRSTW NEWSPRINT
EINNRSSTU RUNTINESS
EINNRSTTU NUTRIENTS
EINNRTTUW UNWRITTEN
EINNSSTTU NUTTINESS
EINOOPRSS POISONERS
EINOORRST RETORSION
EINOORRTT RETORTION
EINOORSST ROOTINESS
EINOORTTX EXTORTION
EINOORTTY NOTORIETY
EINOOSSST SOOTINESS
EINOOSSTT SNOOTIEST
EINOOSSWZ WOOZINESS
EINOPPSSS SOPPINESS
EINOPRRSS PRISONERS
EINOPRRTV OVERPRINT
EINOPRSSS PROSINESS
EINOPRSTU ERUPTIONS
EINOPRSUU PENURIOUS
EINOPSSSU PIOUSNESS
EINOPSSTT POTTINESS
EINOQSSTU QUESTIONS
EINOQSTTU QUOTIENTS
EINORRSSS SORRINESS
EINORRTTV INTROVERT
EINORSSUV SOUVENIRS
EINORSTUX EXTRUSION
EINOSSTTT SNOTTIEST
EINPRRSST SPRINTERS
EINPRRTTU INTERRUPT
EINPRSSST SPINSTERS
EINRSSSTU RUSTINESS
EINRSSTTU RUTTINESS
EIOOPPRSS PORPOISES
EIOOPPSST OPPOSITES
EIOOPRRST POSTERIOR
EIOOPRSTX EXPOSITOR
EIOORSSTT TORTOISES
EIOORSTTT TROOSTITE
EIOOSSSTX EXOSTOSIS
EIOOSSTTV OVOTESTIS
EIOPPRRST STROPPIER
EIOPPRRTY PROPRIETY

EIOPPRSUV PURPOSIVE
EIOPRRSSU SUPERIORS
EIOPRSSTT SPORTIEST
EIOPRSTTU PROUSTITE
EIOPRSTTY POSTERITY
EIOPSSTTT SPOTTIEST
EIOQRSTUU TURQUOISE
EIORRRSTT TERRORIST
EIORRRTTY TERRITORY
EIORRSSST RESISTORS
EIORRSSTV SERVITORS
EIPPRRSST STRIPPERS
EIPRRRSSU SURPRISER
EIPRRSSSU SURPRISES
EIPRSSSTU PERTUSSIS
EIQRRSSTU SQUIRTERS
EIRSSTTTU TRUSTIEST
EJLLLLORY JELLY ROLL
EJLLOSSYY JOYLESSLY
EJNOORRSU SOJOURNER
EKKOOPRRW
　POKERWORK
EKLLNNOWW
　WELL-KNOWN
EKLMMNOSU
　MUSKMELON
EKLNOOORS ONLOOKERS
EKMNNOORS
　NONSMOKER
EKMNNOTUY MONKEY
　NUT
EKNOOPSTU OUTSPOKEN
EKNOORSTW
　STONEWORK
EKNORSSTU SUNSTROKE
EKOORRTUW
　OUTWORKER
EKOORSTTW
　TWO-STROKE
EKOPRRSSW PRESSWORK
ELLMORSTU ROSTELLUM
ELLNOPTUY OPULENTLY
ELLOPRSST POLLSTERS
ELLOPRSUV PULLOVERS
ELLORRSST STROLLERS
ELLORSTUU TELLUROUS
ELMNNOOST SOMNOLENT
ELMNPPSSU PLUMPNESS
ELMOOOPRW POWER
　LOOM
ELMOORSTW
　LOWERMOST
ELMORSTUU TREMULOUS

ELMORTUVY VOLUMETRY
ELMSSTUUU TUMULUSES
ELNOOOPRV PROVOLONE
ELNOORSUY ONEROUSLY
ELNORSUVY NERVOUSLY
ELNOSTUUY TENUOUSLY
ELOOORSTZ ZOOSTEROL
ELOORSTUW LOUSEWORT
ELOPPPUVY PUPPY LOVE
ELOPPRSUY PURPOSELY
ELOQRSUUU QUERULOUS
ELPRSSSUU SURPLUSES
ELPRSSTTU SPLUTTERS
EMMMNOSTU
　MOMENTUMS
EMMNNOSTU
　MONUMENTS
EMMNOOOST
　MONOSTOME
EMMNOORSS MEN'S
　ROOMS
EMMNOOSTU
　MOMENTOUS
EMMNOSSSU
　SUMMONSES
EMMNRSTUU
　MENSTRUUM
EMMOORSTY
　OSMOMETRY
EMNNOOOST
　MOONSTONE
EMNOOPRTY MONOTYPER
EMNOOPSUY
　EPONYMOUS
EMNOOORTT TORMENTOR
EMNOORSSW
　NEWSROOMS
EMNOORTTY TONOMETRY
EMNOORTUY
　NEUROTOMY
EMNOORTWY
　MONEYWORT
EMNOPRSST SPORTSMEN
EMNORSSTT STERNMOST
EMOOORRST
　STOREROOM
EMOOOSTTY OSTEOTOMY
EMOOPRRSS PRESSROOM
EMOOPRRST PROMOTERS
EMOOPRTTY OPTOMETRY
EMOORRSST REST ROOMS
EMOORRSTU
　TREMOROUS

EMOORSTTU OUTERMOST
EMOPPRSTU UPPERMOST
EMOPRRTUV OVERTRUMP
EMOPRRTYY PYROMETRY
EMPRSSTTU STRUMPETS
ENNOOPPRT PROPONENT
ENNOOPPST OPPONENTS
ENNOPRTWY
    PENNYWORT
ENNORRTUU OUTRUNNER
ENNORSTTU TURNSTONE
ENNPRRSUU
    RUNNERS-UP, RUNNER-UPS
ENOOPPRST POSTPONER
ENOOPPRSU ON PURPOSE
ENOOPPRTU OPPORTUNE
ENOORSTTW STONEWORT
ENOOSSTTU SOSTENUTO
ENOPRSSSU SUSPENSOR
ENOPRSSTT STERNPOST
ENOPSTTYY STENOTYPY
ENORRSTUV TURNOVERS
ENORSSTUU STRENUOUS
ENOSSSTTU STOUTNESS
EOOOPRRTU EUROPOORT
EOOPPRRSS OPPRESSOR,
    PROPOSERS
EOOPPRTTY PROTOTYPE
EOOPRSSSS POSSESSOR
EOOPRSSTV STOPOVERS
EOPPRRSTU SUPPORTER
EOPPRSSST STOP PRESS
EOPRRSUVY PURVEYORS
EORRRSTTU TORTURERS
EORRSSUVY SURVEYORS
FFFOOPTUU OUT OF PUFF
FFGHILNSU SHUFFLING
FFGHILRTU FRIGHTFUL
FFGIILLNU IN FULL FIG
FFGIILNNS SNIFFLING
FFGILNNSU SNUFFLING
FFGILNOXY FLYING FOX
FFGIMNORU FUNGIFORM
FFGINOPRS OFFSPRING
FFGINSSUU SUFFUSING
FFHOOOSST OFFSHOOTS
FFIINOSUX SUFFIXION
FFILLOPPS FLIP-FLOPS
FFINOSSUU SUFFUSION
FFIORSTTU SOFT FRUIT
FFLOOOOPR FOOLPROOF
FFLOOOPRY POORLY OFF
FFNOPSTUU UP TO SNUFF

FGGGILNOS FLOGGINGS
FGGIINORV FORGIVING
FGHHILNOW HIGH-FLOWN
FGHHIOSTW SHOW FIGHT
FGHIIINNS FINISHING
FGHIILLTY FLIGHTILY
FGHILOPTT TOP-FLIGHT
FGHINORTT FORTNIGHT
FGHLORSUU FURLOUGHS
FGHMOORTU
    FROGMOUTH
FGHOOTTUU OUTFOUGHT
FGIIILNVY VILIFYING
FGIIIMNRS MISFIRING
FGIILMNOR LIGNIFORM
FGIILNOPR PROFILING
FGIILNPTU UPLIFTING
FGIILNRST FIRSTLING
FGIILNRZZ FRIZZLING
FGIIMNNOR INFORMING
FGIINNOTY NOTIFYING
FGIINOPRT PROFITING
FGIINOSSY OSSIFYING
FGIINPRUY PURIFYING
FGIINPTYY TYPIFYING
FGIKLLNOS GOLF LINKS
FGILLNOOW FOLLOWING
FGILLNOWY FLOWINGLY
FGILNNRUU UNFURLING
FGILNRRUY FLURRYING
FGINOOTUX OUTFOXING
FGINORRUW FURROWING
FGLLNORUW
    FULL-GROWN
FGLORSUUU FULGUROUS
FHHIORTTW FORTHWITH
FHIIIKLLS KILLIFISH
FHIILRTTY THRIFTILY
FHIKLSSWY FLYWHISKS
FHIKNRSTU TRUNKFISH
FHILLOOST FOOTHILLS
FHILLOOSY FOOLISHLY
FHIMORSTX SIXTH FORM
FHLLRTUUY HURTFULLY
FHLMORUUU
    HUMOURFUL
FHLMOSTUU MOUTHFULS
FHLOOOPRS SHOP FLOOR
FHLOOORSW FLOOR
    SHOW
FHMOOOPRT MOTHPROOF
FIIILSSTY FISSILITY
FIIIMNRTY INFIRMITY

FIIKLNNST SKINFLINT
FIILLMORV VILLIFORM
FIILLMOTU MULTIFOIL
FIILMORTU TRIFOLIUM
FIILMPRST FILMSTRIP
FIILORTVY FRIVOLITY
FIIMMNORS MISINFORM
FIIMNOSSU FUSIONISM
FIIMOPRST STIPIFORM
FIIMORRTU TRIFORIUM
FIIMORRTV VITRIFORM
FIINNOSSU INFUSIONS
FIINOSSTU FUSIONIST
FIKLLLSUY SKILFULLY
FIKLLNSUU UNSKILFUL
FILLLMORU FLOURMILL
FILLSTUWY WISTFULLY
FILMMORSU FORMULISM
FILMMORTU MULTIFORM
FILMNORUY UNIFORMLY
FILMORSTU FORMULIST
FILMORSTY STYLIFORM
FILMORUVV VULVIFORM
FILOOOPRT PORTFOLIO
FILOORSSU FLUOROSIS
FILOORSUV FRIVOLOUS
FILORSUUY FURIOUSLY
FILOSSTUU FISTULOUS
FINOOPRSU PROFUSION
FINOOPRTT FOOTPRINT
FIOPRSSTT FIRST POST
FIRSSTTUU FUTURISTS
FKOORRSTW FROSTWORK
FLLLOSUUY SOULFULLY
FLLLSTUUY LUSTFULLY
FLLMNOOSU FULL MOONS
FLLNOORRY FORLORNLY
FLLOOPSUW FOLLOW-UPS
FLLOPSSTU FULL STOPS
FLNOOPSSU SPOONFULS,
    SPOONSFUL
FLOOOOSTT FOOTSTOOL
FLOORRSUW
    SORROWFUL
FLOPRSSUU PLUS FOURS
FMNOOORRT FRONT
    ROOM
FOOPRRSTU RUSTPROOF
FOOPSSSTT SOFT SPOTS
FOOPSSTUY PUSSYFOOT
GGGHINRSU SHRUGGING
GGGIILNRW WRIGGLING
GGGILMNSU SMUGGLING

GGGILNNSU SNUGGLING	GHIILLNSS SHILLINGS	GHLLOOOPY HOPLOLOGY
GGHHHIILT HIGHLIGHT	GHIILLRSY GIRLISHLY	GHLMOOTYY
GGHHILOSY HOGGISHLY	GHIILNNWY WHININGLY	MYTHOLOGY
GGHIIILRW WHIRLIGIG	GHIILNOPS POLISHING	GHLNOOOPY PHONOLOGY
GGHIIKNNT KNIGHTING	GHIILNOST NIGHT SOIL	GHLNOOSST LONG SHOTS
GGHIILNNT LIGHTNING	GHIILNSTW WHISTLING	GHNNOOPRR
GGHIILNPT PLIGHTING	GHIILNTTW WHITTLING	PRONGHORN
GGHIILNST SLIGHTING	GHIINNNSY SHINNYING	GHNOOSTTW GHOST
GGHIILPSY PIGGISHLY	GHIINNNWY WHINNYING	TOWN
GGHIINNNU UNHINGING	GHIINNOPS SIPHONING	GHOORTTUW
GGHIINRTW RIGHT WING	GHIINNPSU PUNISHING	OUTGROWTH
GGHIINSST SIGHTINGS	GHIINOPPT PIPING HOT	GHOPRTUUW
GGHILNNOT NIGHTLONG	GHIINPPSW WHIPPINGS	WROUGHT-UP
GGHILNOPU PLOUGHING	GHIINQSSU SQUISHING	GIIILNNOZ LIONIZING
GGHILNOSU SLOUGHING	GHIIRSSTT RIGHTISTS	GIIILNTUZ UTILIZING
GGHILNSUY GUSHINGLY	GHIKLSSTY SKYLIGHTS	GIIILOSTU LITIGIOUS
GGHILOOPR LOGOGRIPH	GHILLNOOW HOLLOWING	GIIIMMNST MISTIMING
GGHINNORT THRONGING	GHILLNOWY HOWLINGLY	GIIINNNOP PINIONING
GGHINNOTW NIGHTGOWN	GHILLOOPY PHILOLOGY	GIIINNPRS INSPIRING
GGIIMMNNP IMPINGING	GHILLOOTY LITHOLOGY	GIIINNQRU INQUIRING
GGIIIMNSV MISGIVING	GHILMNOOT MOONLIGHT	GIIINNSST INSISTING
GGIILMNPS GLIMPSING	GHILNOOPT POTHOLING	GIIINNTTU INTUITING
GGIILNNSS GIN SLINGS	GHILNOORY RHINOLOGY	GIIINPRST SPIRITING
GGIILNNSY SINGINGLY	GHILNOPSS LONGSHIPS,	GIIINRTVY VIRGINITY
GGIILNPRY GRIPINGLY	SPLOSHING	GIIJKNORS SKIJORING
GGIILNRZZ GRIZZLING	GHILNOSST SLINGSHOT	GIIKLLLNY KILLINGLY
GGIIMNNPU IMPUGNING	GHILNOSTW NIGHT OWLS	GIIKLNNOP LINKOPING
GGIINNORW INGROWING	GHILNPSUY PUSHINGLY	GIIKLNNRW WRINKLING
GGIINNPRS SPRINGING	GHILNRSUY RUSHINGLY	GIIKLNNTW TWINKLING
GGIINNRST STRINGING	GHILNSTTU SHUTTLING	GIIKMMNSS SKIMMINGS
GGIINNRSY SYRINGING	GHILNSTUY UNSIGHTLY	GIIKNSVVY SKIVVYING
GGIINNSWW SWING-WING	GHILOOOPY OPHIOLOGY	GIILLLNWY WILLINGLY
GGIINOPSS GOSSIPING	GHILOOSTY HISTOLOGY	GIILLMNPY LIMPINGLY
GGILLNNOY LONGINGLY	GHILOPSTT SPOTLIGHT,	GIILLMNSY SMILINGLY
GGILLNOWY GLOWINGLY	STOPLIGHT	GIILLMRST GRISTMILL
GGILLNPUY GULPINGLY	GHILORSSW SHOWGIRLS	GIILLNNUW UNWILLING
GGILLOOSW GOLLIWOGS	GHILORSUY ROGUISHLY	GIILLNOPW PILLOWING
GGILNOPRY GROPINGLY	GHILOSTTU LIGHTS-OUT	GIILLNPSY LISPINGLY
GGILNPRSU SPLURGING	GHILPRSTY SPRIGHTLY	GIILMNOPR IMPLORING
GGINNOSSS SINGSONGS	GHILPRTUY UPRIGHTLY	GIILMRSTU LITURGISM
GGINOOSTU OUTGOINGS	GHIMMNRTU THRUMMING	GIILNNOTU OUTLINING
GGINOPRSU GROUPINGS	GHIMNOOST SMOOTHING	GIILNNOVV INVOLVING
GHHIIJKNS HIGH JINKS	GHIMNORUU HUMOURING	GIILNNSTU INSULTING
GHHIILPST LIGHTSHIP	GHIMNSSTU GUNSMITHS	GIILNOTUV OUTLIVING
GHHIIINOPT HIGH POINT	GHIMOOPSS GOMPHOSIS	GIILNPPST STIPPLING
GHHIJMPSU HIGH JUMPS	GHINNOORU HONOURING	GIILNPRST SPLIT RING,
GHHILRSTU RUSHLIGHT	GHINNOPSY SYPHONING	STRIPLING
GHHIOPSST HIGH SPOTS	GHINNORSU ONRUSHING,	GIILNPRSY SPRINGILY
GHHLOOSTY HOLY GHOST	UNHORSING	GIILNPSTT SPLITTING
GHIIKNNRS SHRINKING	GHINOOSST SHOOTINGS	GIILNPTYY PITYINGLY
GHIIKNSTT SKIN-TIGHT	GHINOTUWY WITH YOUNG	GIILNQSSU QUISLINGS
GHIIKNTTT TIGHTKNIT	GHINRSTTU THRUSTING	GIILNRSTY STRINGILY
GHIILLNRT THRILLING	GHJLNNOOS LONG JOHNS	GIILNSSTU LINGUISTS

GIILNSTYZ STYLIZING
GIILOSSST GLOSSITIS
GIILPSSTU PUGILISTS
GIILRSTTU LITURGIST
GIIMMNRST TRIMMINGS
GIIMNNOOT MOTIONING
GIIMNNTUY MUTINYING
GIIMNOPRS PROMISING
GIIMNOPRT IMPORTING
GIIMNOPRV IMPROVING
GIIMNORRR MIRRORING
GIIMNOTTW TWO-TIMING
GIIMNQRSU SQUIRMING
GIIMNRSSU SURMISING
GIINNNOWW WINNOWING
GIINNOOPS POISONING
GIINNPPUZ UNZIPPING
GIINNPRST PRINTINGS,
    SPRINTING
GIINNPTTU INPUTTING
GIINNQSTU SQUINTING
GIINNTTUW UNWITTING
GIINOPRST RIPOSTING
GIINPPRST STRIPPING
GIINPRSSU UPRISINGS
GIINQRSTU SQUIRTING
GIINRSUVV SURVIVING
GIJKNNOOP JONKOPING
GIKLLNRUY LURKINGLY
GIKLNNOOO ONLOOKING
GIKLNNOWY KNOWINGLY
GIKLNOOOY KONIOLOGY
GIKNNNOUW UNKNOWING
GIKNNOSTW KINGSTOWN
GIKNOOPRV PROVOKING
GIKNOOTWW
    KOWTOWING
GILLLLNOY LOLLINGLY
GILLLLNUY LULLINGLY
GILLLNOOP LOLLOPING
GILLLNORY ROLLINGLY
GILLMNOOY LIMNOLOGY
GILLMOORR GRILLROOM
GILLMOSSY SYLLOGISM
GILLNNORU UNROLLING
GILLNOPSY SLOPINGLY
GILLNOPTU POLLUTING
GILLNORST STROLLING
GILLOOOPY OLIGOPOLY
GILMMNOOS MONGOLISM
GILMNNOTY LYMINGTON
GILMNOPRY ROMPINGLY
GILMOOSTY MYOLOGIST

GILNNOOSU UNLOOSING
GILNNRSSU NURSLINGS
GILNOPTUY POUTINGLY
GILNOSTUU GLUTINOUS
GILNPPSUY SUPPLYING
GILNSSTUU SINGULTUS
GILOOORST OROLOGIST
GILOOOSSU ISOLOGOUS
GILOOOSTT OTOLOGIST
GILOOOSTZ ZOOLOGIST
GILOORSTU UROLOGIST
GIMMNNOSU SUMMONING
GIMMNPSUU SUMMING-UP
GIMMNRRUU MURMURING
GIMMNRSTU STRUMMING
GIMNNOORS MONSIGNOR
GIMNOOPRT PROMOTING
GIMNOPPRT PROMPTING
GIMOPRUUY UROPYGIUM
GINNOSUUU UNGUINOUS
GINNRRTUU NURTURING
GINOOPPRS PROPOSING
GINOOPRSS PROGNOSIS
GINOOPRTU UPROOTING
GINOORRSW SORROWING
GINOORSTU TRIGONOUS
GINOOTTUV OUTVOTING
GINOPPRSU PURPOSING
GINOPPSSU SUPPOSING
GINOPRSTU POSTURING,
    SPROUTING
GINOPSSST SIGNPOSTS
GINORRTTU TORTURING
GINPRRTUU RUPTURING
GINRSTTTU STRUTTING
GIOPRSTWY GIPSYWORT
GLLOOPSTY POLYGLOTS
GLMNOOPUY
    POLYGONUM
GLMOORSWW
    GLOW-WORMS
GLNOOOSTY NOSTOLOGY
GLOOOPRTY TROPOLOGY
GMMNOSTUY TOMMY
    GUNS
GMNOORSSW
    MOSS-GROWN
GNOOOPRSY SPOROGONY
GNOOPRTYY PROTOGYNY
GNORSTTUU
    STRUNG-OUT
HHILNNSUY HUNNISHLY
HHLMOOPYY HOMOPHYLY

HHMNOOOPY
    HOMOPHONY
HHNOORRST SHORTHORN
HHORRSSUU RUSH
    HOURS
HIIILNSST NIHILISTS
HIILLMNOT MILLIONTH
HIILLOOOP HOI POLLOI
HIILNSSWY SWINISHLY
HIILOSTTY HOSTILITY
HIILPSTTY TYPHLITIS
HIILRSTTY THIRSTILY
HIIMOPSTU HOSPITIUM
HIIMORSST HIT-OR-MISS
HIKLMOOTT MILK TOOTH
HIKNNORST STINKHORN
HILLLMTUU MULTIHULL
HILLOOPRW WHIRLPOOL
HILLSSTYY STYLISHLY
HILMNOOST MONOLITHS
HILMOOSSY HOMOLYSIS
HILMOOTTY LITHOTOMY
HILOOPTXY TOXOPHILY
HILORSSTT SHORT LIST
HIMNOPSTY HYPNOTISM
HIMOOPRSS MORPHOSIS
HIMOORTYZ RHIZOTOMY
HIMORSSTU HUMORISTS
HIMPSSSYY SYMPHYSIS
HINOPPRRY PORPHYRIN
HINOPRSUU ONUPHRIUS
HINOPSSTW TOWNSHIPS
HINOPSTTY HYPNOTIST
HIOOPPRST TROOPSHIP
HIOPRSSTY SOPHISTRY
HIORRSTTY THYRISTOR
HKKNNOOTY
    HONKY-TONK
HKMOOORSW
    HOOKWORMS
HKOOPRSSW
    WORKSHOPS
HLLNOOORR HONOR
    ROLL
HLLPRSUUY SULPHURYL
HLMOOPPRY POLYMORPH
HLNOOPPYY POLYPHONY
HLNOORSTU SOLOTHURN
HMMOORSSU
    MUSHROOMS
HMNNOOOPY
    MONOPHONY

HMNOOOSST MOON
SHOTS
HMOOOPRSY
HOMOSPORY
HMOOORSSW
SHOWROOMS
HNOOPPTYY PHONOTYPY
HNOOPRSST POST HORNS
HNOOPRTTY PHYTOTRON
HOOOORTTTW
TOOTHWORT
HOOOSSTTU SHOOT-OUTS
IIIKLLNPS SPILLIKIN
IIIKMNRST MINISKIRT
IIILNOSTV VIOLINIST
IIILNTTUY INUTILITY
IIINNOTTU INTUITION
IIINPRSSU NISI PRIUS
IIINSSSTU SINUSITIS
IIJNORSUU INJURIOUS
IIKLLMPST SPILT MILK
IIKNNNOOS ONIONSKIN
IILLMNOPU POLLINIUM
IILLMPRSU SPIRILLUM
IILLNNNOO NONILLION
IILLNORST TRILLIONS
IILLNOSSU ILLUSIONS
IILLOPSSY LIPOLYSIS
IILLOSTVY VILLOSITY
IILMMMSSU MUSLIMISM
IILMNOOPS IMPLOSION
IILMNOPSU IMPULSION
IILMOPSSS SOLIPSISM
IILMOPSUY IMPIOUSLY
IILNOOPST POSTILION
IILOPRTXY PROLIXITY
IILOPSSST SOLIPSIST
IILOSTVVZ SLIVOVITZ
IIMNNOSTU MUNITIONS
IIMNOOSSS OMISSIONS
IIMNORSTU MINOR SUIT,
ROUTINISM
IIMNPRSST MISPRINTS
IIMOPRTXY PROXIMITY
IIMOPSSTT OPTIMISTS
IIMOQSTUX QUIXOTISM
IIMORSTTU TUTIORISM
IINNOORST INTORSION
IINNOPPST PINPOINTS

IINNORSTU INTRUSION
IINNORTTU NUTRITION
IINNOSSTU UNIONISTS
IINOOPRSV PROVISION
IINOOPSST POSITIONS
IINOOPSVY POISON IVY
IINOORSTT SORTITION
IINOPRRTU IRRUPTION
IINOPSSTY SPINOSITY
IINORSTTU ROUTINIST
IINOSSTUY SINUOSITY
IINOSSTVY SYNOVITIS
IIOOPRSST SPIRITOSO
IIOPSTTTU SPIT IT OUT!
IIORSTTTU TUTIORIST
IJMNOORTW JOINTWORM
IJMPSSTUU JUMPSUITS
IKLMORSSW SILKWORMS
IKLNOPSST SLIPKNOTS
IKNOORRSW IRONWORKS
IKORSSTTU OUTSKIRTS
ILLLMOPSS PLIMSOLLS
ILLLOOPPS LOLLIPOPS
ILLLPSUUV PULVILLUS
ILLNOOPTU POLLUTION
ILLNOPVYY POLYVINYL
ILLOOQSUY SOLILOQUY
ILLOORSSW SLOW LORIS
ILLOQRTUW QUILLWORT
ILLORSSSW SWISS ROLL
ILMNOOSUY OMINOUSLY
ILMNOPTUU PLUTONIUM
ILMNOPXYY POLYMYXIN
ILMOSSYYZ ZYMOLYSIS
ILNOOPRSU PROLUSION
ILNOOSSTU SOLUTIONS
ILNOOSUXY NOXIOUSLY
ILNOPRXYY PYROXYLIN
ILNORSUUY RUINOUSLY
ILNOSSUUY SINUOUSLY
ILOOPPRSY ISOPROPYL
ILOORSTUY RIOTOUSLY
ILOPPSSTU POPULISTS
ILOPRSSYY PYROLYSIS
ILORSUUUX LUXURIOUS
IMMMNOORS
MORMONISM
IMMOPPRTU IMPROMPTU
IMMOPSSUY SYMPOSIUM

IMNNOOPTW TOPMINNOW
IMNOOOPRT PROMOTION
IMNOOOPTT MOOT POINT
IMNORSTTU STRONTIUM
IMOOOSTTZ ZOOTOMIST
IMOOPPSTY POMPOSITY
IMOOPRSST IMPOSTORS
IMOOQSSTU MOSQUITOS
IMOORSSTT MOTORISTS
IMORSUVXY MYXOVIRUS
INNOOSSUU UNISONOUS
INOOOPSSU POISONOUS
INOOORSTU NOTORIOUS
INOOPPTTU PUT OPTION
INOOPRSST POSITRONS
INOOPSSTT SPITTOONS
INOPRSTTU PRINTOUTS
INORSSSUV SUN VISORS
INRSTTTUU UNIT TRUST
IOOPPRRTU POTPOURRI
IOOPPRSST PROPTOSIS
IOOPRRSVY PROVISORY
IOORSSTUV VIRTUOSOS
IORRSSUVV SURVIVORS
KLLMNSSUU NUMSKULLS
KMOOORRSW
WORKROOMS
LMOOPPSUY POMPOUSLY
LMOORSSWW
SLOWWORMS
LNOOOOPRST POLTROONS
LOOPRRSUY PROLUSORY
LORSTUUUV VULTUROUS
MMOOPPRSU PUMP
ROOMS
MNNOOOPSY
MONOPSONY
MNOORSSTU
MONSTROUS
MNOORSSTW
SNOWSTORM
MOOOORRSTW
TOMORROWS
MOPSSTUUU SUMPTUOUS
NOOOPPSSU SOUP SPOON
OOPRSSTUU STUPOROUS
OOPRTTTUY PUTTYROOT

AAAAABCCRS ASARABACCA
AAAAABBDDIS ADDIS ABABA
AAAAABCCLNS CASABLANCA
AAAAABCLLSV BALACLAVAS
AAAAABCNNTU CABANATUAN
AAAAABGKORY
  KABARAGOYA
AAAAABHJRSY RAJYA SABHA
AAAAABIKLLS BALALAIKAS
AAAACDGMNS
  MADAGASCAN
AAAACDGMRS
  MADAGASCAR
AAAACGMNRT MAGNA
  CARTA
AAAACHILPP APPALACHIA
AAAACILPST CATAPLASIA
AAAACINNRU ARAUCANIAN
AAAACLNRST SANTA CLARA
AAAACMNRST CATAMARANS
AAAADFNRWY FAR AND
  AWAY
AAAADIJVWY VIJAYAWADA
AAAADILLMS DALAI LAMAS
AAAAEGLMMT
  AMALGAMATE
AAAAGGGGWW WAGGA
  WAGGA
AAAAGMSSSU
  MASSASAUGA
AAAAGNPRUY PARAGUAYAN
AAAAIMNNNP PANAMANIAN
AAAAIMNRST SANTA MARIA
AAAAKKKLPR KARA-KALPAK
AAAALMNRSZ SALMANAZAR
AAAAMNRSTT SANTA MARTA
AAABBCCHMO
  COCHABAMBA
AAABBCILST SABBATICAL
AAABBEIRSS BESSARABIA
AAABBINRRS BARBARIANS
AAABCCHLNS BACCHANALS
AAABCCHNRS CHARABANCS
AAABCCKNSV CANVASBACK
AAABCDEIRS SCARABAEID
AAABCDELNR CANDELABRA
AAABCDRRSU BARRACUDAS
AAABCEGGGR BAGGAGE
  CAR
AAABCEGGNR GARBAGE
  CAN
AAABCEHLSS CALABASHES
AAABCEHLTT ATTACHABLE
AAABCELLLR CLARABELLA
AAABCERSSU SCARABAEUS
AAABCIILST BASILICATA
AAABCIKLMR BLACK MARIA
AAABCIKRSS CASSIA BARK
AAABCINNRT CANTABRIAN

AAABCLLMRU AMBULACRAL
AAABCLNOST CANAL BOATS
AAABDEEGLM
  DAMAGEABLE
AAABDEHLRZ HAZARDABLE
AAABDEORVW ABOVE
  AWARD
AAABDMNRRU
  BARRAMUNDA
AAABDMORSS
  AMBASSADOR
AAABEEGLMN
  MANAGEABLE
AAABEELLPP APPEALABLE
AAABEELMNS ABLE SEAMAN
AAABEELPPS APPEASABLE
AAABEGLMNY
  MANAGEABLY
AAABEIJNRZ AZERBAIJAN
AAABEILLMR MARIABELLA
AAABEILLSS ASSAILABLE
AAABEILNTT ATTAINABLE
AAABEKRSWY BREAKAWAYS
AAABELLNSY ANALYSABLE
AAABELNRRT NARRATABLE
AAABELRSTW BASALTWARE
AAABHIOPQU AQUAPHOBIA
AAABIKLNPP BALIKPAPAN
AAABIKNNNS BANANA SKIN
AAABILLNOS LABIONASAL
AAABILRSTV BRATISLAVA
AAABIMNPRS PAN-ARABISM
AAACCDELSV CAVALCADES
AAACCEHRSS SACCHARASE
AAACCEHRST SACCHARATE
AAACCEIPTT CAPACITATE
AAACCENRUV CUERNAVACA
AAACCILLNT CATACLINAL
AAACCILLRS CASCARILLA
AAACCINRTT ANTARCTICA
AAACCIPRTT PARATACTIC
AAACDEIMMS MACADAMISE
AAACDEIMMZ MACADAMIZE
AAACDEKNPY PANCAKE DAY
AAACDELMNR
  CALAMANDER
AAACDELMRS SALAD
  CREAM
AAACDGIILR CARDIALGIA
AAACDHINNR ARACHNIDAN
AAACDILNOP PIÑA COLADA
AAACDILRTY CARYATIDAL
AAACEEENPPR APPEARANCE
AAACEEENRSS CAESAREANS
AAACEFLQTU CATAFALQUE
AAACEGNORT
  ARCTOGAEAN
AAACEHLNSV AVALANCHES
AAACEILMNT CATAMENIAL

AAACEINNRT CATENARIAN
AAACEINPST ANAPAESTIC,
  SEA CAPTAIN
AAACEINRRS SARRACENIA
AAACEJKNPS JACKANAPES
AAACELLNPT APLACENTAL
AAACELMPRT METACARPAL
AAACGHNRTT TRAGACANTH
AAACGILLMY AGAMICALLY
AAACGILLNO ANALOGICAL
AAACGINNRU NICARAGUAN
AAACHINPRT CARPATHIAN
AAACHLNOTU TALCAHUANO
AAACHLNRST CHARLATANS
AAACHNPRTY PYRACANTHA
AAACIINNPR INCAPARINA
AAACIIRSSS ASCARIASIS
AAACIKLMNP PACK ANIMAL
AAACIKLMNR LAMARCKIAN
AAACILLMNY MANIACALLY
AAACILLRTU URAL-ALTAIC
AAACILMMNO AMMONIACAL
AAACILMNOT ANATOMICAL
AAACILNPST ANAPLASTIC
AAACILNRSS CARNASSIAL
AAACILNRST SCARLATINA
AAACINOPRS PARANOIACS
AAACISSSTT CATASTASIS
AAACLMNRVY CAVALRYMAN
AAACLNSSTU SANTA CLAUS
AAACNORSSU ANASARCOUS
AAADEELLNV AVELLANEDA
AAADEELNRW
  DELAWAREAN
AAADEFIOST ASAFOETIDA
AAADEGGRTV AGGRAVATED
AAADEGHMNR
  AHMEDNAGAR
AAADEGLMTY AMYGDALATE
AAADEGNRTV AVANT-GARDE
AAADEGNSTV ADVANTAGES
AAADEHLPRT HARD PALATE
AAADEILNRX ALEXANDRIA
AAADEIMNNT ADAMANTINE
AAADELMNRS SALAMANDER
AAADELMPPS ADAM'S
  APPLE
AAADELNPQU AQUAPLANED
AAADGIILLR GAILLARDIA
AAADGILLNR GRANADILLA
AAADGINNPT GIANT PANDA
AAADGLLNOR ALLARGANDO
AAADGNOPPR PROPAGANDA
AAADHHMRTU
  HADHRAMAUT
AAADHMMMNU
  MUHAMMADAN
AAADIILNPR LAPIDARIAN
AAADILMNST DALMATIANS

AAADILMORR   RADIO ALARM
AAADILNOPS   DIAPASONAL
AAADINOPTT   ADAPTATION
AAADLNQRTU   QUADRANTAL
AAADORSTTU   AUTOSTRADA
AAAEEGGLRS   GARAGE SALE
AAAEFLLMRS   FALSE ALARM
AAAEFLMNST   MALFEASANT
AAAEGHIOPR   AEROPHAGIA
AAAEGHLLNP   PHALANGEAL
AAAEGILMNR   MANAGERIAL
AAAEGILNST   EAST ANGLIA
AAAEGILPPR   PARAPLEGIA
AAAEGINPRS   ASPARAGINE
AAAEGLMTXY   METAGALAXY
AAAEGMRRTT   MARGARETTA
AAAEGNNTTT   AT A TANGENT
AAAEGPSSWY   PASSAGEWAY
AAAEHHLSSV   HAVE A SLASH
AAAEHIMRTU   HAEMATURIA
AAAEHINSTU   EUTHANASIA
AAAEHKNOTT   TAKE AN OATH
AAAEHPPRRS   PARAPHRASE
AAAEIILNTT   ITALIANATE
AAAEILLPST   PALATALISE
AAAEILLPTZ   PALATALIZE
AAAEILMPST   METAPLASIA
AAAEILMRTU   TULARAEMIA
AAAEILNPRT   PLANETARIA
AAAEILNPTT   PALATINATE
AAAEIMNPRS   PARAMNESIA
AAAEIMNQRU   AQUAMARINE
AAAEINNRTV   TANANARIVE
AAAELLNRTT   TARANTELLA
AAAELMMRST   ALMA
    MATERS
AAAELNPQSU   AQUAPLANES
AAAFFIILNN   FIANNA FAIL
AAAFIKPRRS   SAFARI PARK
AAAGGILLNO   ALGOLAGNIA
AAAGGILRST   GASTRALGIA
AAAGGNNRTU
    GARGANTUAN
AAAGHILRRT   ARTHRALGIA
AAAGHIMNOP   PHAGOMANIA
AAAGHNPSTU   AGAPANTHUS
AAAGHPPRRS   PARAGRAPHS
AAAGIILMNR   MARGINALIA
AAAGIKNNTY   TANGANYIKA
AAAGIMMNRR
    GRAMMARIAN
AAAGIMNSTT   ANASTIGMAT
AAAGIMRRST   MARGARITAS
AAAGJJKORT   JOGJAKARTA
AAAGJLNRUW   GUJRANWALA
AAAGJNOTUU   GUANAJUATO
AAAGLNRSTU   NATURAL GAS
AAAGLRSSTU   ASTRAGALUS

AAAGMNNOTU
    GUANTANAMO
AAAHLLOSTY   AYATOLLAHS
AAAHLMNPST   PHANTASMAL
AAAHNPRRSU   SAHARANPUR
AAAIIMNRTU   MAURITANIA
AAAIINNRST   SANITARIAN
AAAILLLPTY   PALATIALLY
AAAILLMNNZ   MANZANILLA
AAAILLMRTW   MARTIAL LAW
AAAILLNOTV   LAVATIONAL
AAAILLORTV   LAVATORIAL
AAAILMPSTU   TAMAULIPAS
AAAILMRRTT   MARTIAL ART
AAAILNNOTT   NATATIONAL
AAAILNOTTX   TAXATIONAL
AAAILNRSTU   AUSTRALIAN,
    SATURNALIA
AAAILNSSST   ASSAILANTS
AAAILOPRSV   VALPARAISO
AAAILPPRSS   APPRAISALS
AAAIMNORST   INAMORATAS
AAAIMNRSST   SAMARITANS
AAAIPPRRSX   PARAPRAXIS
AAALMNOPRR
    PARANORMAL
AAALNNOSST   ASSONANTAL
AAALNRSTTU   TARANTULAS
AAAMRTZZZZ   RAZZMATAZZ
AABBBELORS   ABSORBABLE
AABBCDKLOR   BLACKBOARD
AABBCEEHLL   BLEACHABLE
AABBCEHLLS   BEACH BALLS
AABBCEILRS   ASCRIBABLE
AABBCELMOT   COMBATABLE
AABBCENORS   ABSORBANCE
AABBCIILNR   RABBINICAL
AABBCIJKRT   JACKRABBIT
AABBDDEENN
    BADEN-BADEN
AABBDDEORR
    BREADBOARD
AABBDEGILR   ABRIDGABLE
AABBDEIRRS   BARBARISED
AABBDEIRRZ   BARBARIZED
AABBDELORS   ADSORBABLE
AABBDENORS   BROAD
    BEANS
AABBDEOORV
    ABOVEBOARD
AABBDNRSSS   BRASS BANDS
AABBEEIRTV   ABBREVIATE
AABBEELLRT   BARBELLATE
AABBEELNRU   UNBEARABLE
AABBEELNTU   UNBEATABLE
AABBEILMNO   ABOMINABLE
AABBEILNOT   OBTAINABLE
AABBEILRRT   ARBITRABLE
AABBEKLLST   BASKETBALL

AABBELLOSV   ABSOLVABLE
AABBELNRUY   UNBEARABLY
AABBILMNOY   ABOMINABLY
AABBIMRRSS   BARBARISMS
AABBMMNPYY
    NAMBY-PAMBY
AABBNNUUYY
    BUNYA-BUNYA
AABCCDELOR   ACCORDABLE
AABCCEELPT   ACCEPTABLE
AABCCEHHIR   BEACHCHAIR
AABCCEKKPR   BACKPACKER
AABCCEKPSS   BACKSPACES
AABCCELLLU   CALCULABLE
AABCCELOST   ACCOSTABLE
AABCCELPTY   ACCEPTABLY
AABCCGIKLM   BLACK MAGIC
AABCCHHKST   HATCHBACKS
AABCCIINRT   BACITRACIN
AABCCIKNRR   CRACKBRAIN
AABCCILNSS   CABIN CLASS
AABCCIORST   ACROBATICS
AABCCJKKLS   BLACKJACKS
AABCDDEELU   ADDUCEABLE
AABCDDEHKN
    BACKHANDED
AABCDDEIRR   BARRICADED
AABCDDEKLS   SADDLEBACK
AABCDEEEFL   DEFACEABLE
AABCDEEHHS   BEACHHEADS
AABCDEEHLT   DETACHABLE
AABCDEEILR   ERADICABLE
AABCDEELLR   DECLARABLE
AABCDEFIRT   FABRICATED
AABCDEHKLS   BLACKHEADS
AABCDEHKLT   BLACK DEATH
AABCDEHKNR
    BACKHANDER
AABCDEIITV   ABDICATIVE
AABCDEILRT   CALIBRATED
AABCDEIRRR   BARRICADER
AABCDEIRRS   BARRICADES
AABCDELNNU   UNBALANCED
AABCDELORS   SCALEBOARD
AABCDELORT   CARBOLATED
AABCDENNRS   BARN
    DANCES
AABCDENORT   CARBONATED
AABCDERSTT   ABSTRACTED
AABCDGIINT   ABDICATING
AABCDGIKNT   BACKDATING
AABCDGKLRU   BLACKGUARD
AABCDHKLOR   CHALKBOARD
AABCDHMORT
    MATCHBOARD
AABCDIILLO   DIABOLICAL
AABCDIINOT   ABDICATION
AABCDILMMS   LAMBDACISM

      385

AABCDKLRWY
BACKWARDLY
AABCDNNORT
CONTRABAND
AABCDORSST BROADCASTS
AABCEEEFFL EFFACEABLE
AABCEEEMRR MACEBEARER
AABCEEEERTT EBRACTEATE
AABCEEEERTX EXACERBATE
AABCEEEGHLN CHANGEABLE
AABCEEGHLR CHARGEABLE
AABCEEHILV ACHIEVABLE
AABCEEHLMP PEACH MELBA
AABCEEHLNS ENCASHABLE
AABCEEHLRS SEARCHABLE
AABCEEHLTY CHALYBEATE
AABCEEIRTU EUBACTERIA
AABCEEKLSS LEASEBACKS
AABCEELLLR RECALLABLE
AABCEELLNS CLEANSABLE
AABCEELNRT TABERNACLE
AABCEESTTU SUBACETATE
AABCEFLORT FACTORABLE
AABCEGHLNY CHANGEABLY
AABCEGIRRR CARRIER BAG
AABCEGLLOU COAGULABLE
AABCEGLMNN
BLANCMANGE
AABCEHILMN MACHINABLE
AABCEHILRT CHARITABLE
AABCEHINRT BRANCHIATE
AABCEHKLRT BLACKHEART
AABCEHKLSS BACKLASHES
AABCEHLNST STANCHABLE
AABCEHRRTT TETRABRACH
AABCEIINTU BEAUTICIAN
AABCEILLMP IMPLACABLE
AABCEILLPP APPLICABLE
AABCEILMNS IMBALANCES
AABCEILMST MASTICABLE
AABCEILNOT ACTIONABLE
AABCEILOSS ASSOCIABLE
AABCEILOTT CATABOLITE
AABCEILQRU ACQUIRABLE
AABCEINORT ABREACTION
AABCEIORST AEROBATICS
AABCEIRSTT TETRABASIC
AABCEKKLNS BLACKSNAKE
AABCEKPPRS PAPERBACKS
AABCEKRSTW BACKWATERS
AABCELMNSU AMBULANCES
AABCELMOPR COMPARABLE
AABCELMTUU ACETABULUM
AABCELNOTU OUTBALANCE
AABCELOOSS CALABOOSES
AABCELPPRS CRAB APPLES
AABCELRRTU TRABECULAR
AABCERRTUU BUREAUCRAT
AABCFHKLSS FLASHBACKS

AABCFIORRT FABRICATOR
AABCGIKNRR BARRACKING
AABCGILLSU SUBGLACIAL
AABCGKMMNO
BACKGAMMON
AABCGLRRTU CAT BURGLAR
AABCHHIMPR AMPHIBRACH
AABCHHIRST BATH CHAIRS
AABCHHPSTY BATHYSCAPH
AABCHILRTY CHARITABLY
AABCHINOTT COHABITANT
AABCHIOOPR ACROPHOBIA
AABCHKLPSS SPLASHBACK
AABCHNRRUY
BRACHYURAN
AABCIILLMY IAMBICALLY
AABCIILNOT ANABOLITIC
AABCIILPTY CAPABILITY
AABCIILTTY ACTABILITY
AABCIIOPRT PARABIOTIC
AABCIKRSST BACKSTAIRS
AABCILMOPR PROCAMBIAL
AABCILMOST CATABOLISM
AABCILNNUU INCUNABULA
AABCILNSUV SUBCLAVIAN
AABCILORRT CALIBRATOR
AABCILRRUV VIBRACULAR
AABCIQSTUU SUBAQUATIC
AABCKLMOOR
BLACKAMOOR
AABCKRSSST BRASS TACKS
AABCLLNNNO CANNONBALL
AABCLMMRUU
AMBULACRUM
AABCLMOPRY COMPARABLY
AABCLORUVY VOCABULARY
AABCMNOSTT COMBATANTS
AABCNORSST CONTRABASS
AABDDDEEHL BALDHEADED
AABDDEEEHR BAREHEADED
AABDDEEGLR DEGRADABLE
AABDDEELMN
DEMANDABLE
AABDDEGGNS
SANDBAGGED
AABDDEGLSS SADDLEBAGS
AABDDEHLMO
HEBDOMADAL
AABDDEHLRS BALDERDASH
AABDDEHORS
HEADBOARDS
AABDDEILRY DAILY BREAD
AABDDEMRTU
ADUMBRATED
AABDDHORSS DASHBOARDS
AABDDNNSST BANDSTANDS
AABDDORRST DARTBOARDS
AABDEEELMS SEALED-BEAM
AABDEEFLRY DEFRAYABLE

AABDEEGLRR REGARDABLE
AABDEEHLLN HANDLEABLE
AABDEEHRRT THREADBARE
AABDEEILNT DETAINABLE
AABDEELNPX EXPANDABLE
AABDEELNRU UNREADABLE
AABDEELORT ELABORATED
AABDEELPRS SPREADABLE
AABDEELRRW REWARDABLE
AABDEFFLOR AFFORDABLE
AABDEGGGNN
GANG-BANGED
AABDEGGNRS
SANDBAGGER
AABDEGGORU BROAD
GAUGE
AABDEGHLNS BANGLADESH
AABDEGINRS GABARDINES
AABDEGORST GOATSBEARD
AABDEHITTU HABITUATED
AABDEHKNRS HANDBRAKES
AABDEHLLNR HANDBALLER
AABDEHLNRS HANDLEBARS
AABDEIKNUZ ADZUKI BEAN
AABDEILLNR BANDERILLA
AABDEILLSY DIALYSABLE
AABDEILRSV ADVERBIALS
AABDEIMNOT ABOMINATED
AABDEINNRR BERNARDINA
AABDEIQRTU BIQUADRATE
AABDEIRRTT ARBITRATED
AABDEIRSST BASTARDISE
AABDEIRSTZ BASTARDIZE
AABDEJLSTU ADJUSTABLE
AABDEKLNRU DARK
NEBULA
AABDEKORST SKATEBOARD
AABDELLNNO BELLADONNA
AABDELLNST TABLELANDS
AABDELNOPR PARDONABLE
AABDELNRUY UNREADABLY
AABDELRSTU BALUSTRADE
AABDEMNNNO ONE-MAN
BAND
AABDEMNNRS BRAND
NAMES
AABDEMNRST BANDMASTER
AABDEMORST DREAMBOATS
AABDENSSTW SWEATBANDS
AABDEOPPRR PAPERBOARD
AABDEOPRST PASTEBOARD
AABDFHIINT IN BAD FAITH
AABDFHLORS FLASHBOARD
AABDFKNRST BANK DRAFTS
AABDGIILNW LAW-ABIDING
AABDGIKNOS BAKING SODA
AABDGINNNO ABANDONING
AABDGNNOSW
BANDWAGONS

AABDHLORRU HARD
  LABOUR
AABDHMNNSU
  HUSBANDMAN
AABDHNORRW
  HANDBARROW
AABDIIKRRY DIYARBAKIR
AABDIINNRR BRAIN DRAIN
AABDIJOORU OUIJA BOARD
AABDILOOPR PARABOLOID
AABDILORSS SAILBOARDS
AABDILORST TAILBOARDS
AABDINSSTW WAISTBANDS
AABDKLORSW
  BOARDWALKS
AABDLNNTUY ABUNDANTLY
AABDLNOPRY PARDONABLY
AABDLNOSTU BASUTOLAND
AABDLORSUY LABOUR DAYS
AABDORRSTW
  STRAWBOARD
AABEEEELLPR REPEALABLE
AABEEEELLRV REVEALABLE
AABEEEELMNS ABLE SEAMEN
AABEEEELPRT REPEATABLE
AABEEEELRRT TALEBEARER
AABEEFHORT FEATHER BOA
AABEEFILRR RAREFIABLE
AABEEFLLLT FLABELLATE
AABEEFLNTT FATTENABLE
AABEEGHLRT GATHERABLE
AABEEGILNR REGAINABLE
AABEEGIMNS SENEGAMBIA
AABEEGINRR BERENGARIA
AABEEGLMSS ASSEMBLAGE
AABEEGNORT BARONETAGE
AABEEHKRRT HEARTBREAK
AABEEHRSTT HEARTBEATS
AABEEILLRZ REALIZABLE
AABEEILMNX EXAMINABLE
AABEEILNRT RETAINABLE
AABEEILPRR REPAIRABLE
AABEEJKRRW JAWBREAKER
AABEEKLMRR REMARKABLE
AABEEKLMRT MARKETABLE
AABEEKLRRW
  LAW-BREAKER
AABEEKRRTW BREAKWATER
AABEELLMNT LAMENTABLE
AABEELLNSU UNSEALABLE
AABEELLPRR PALLBEARER
AABEELMRSU MEASURABLE
AABEELMSST BASE METALS
AABEELMSTT METASTABLE
AABEELNORS REASONABLE
AABEELNOSS SEASONABLE
AABEELNPTT PATENTABLE
AABEELNRSW ANSWERABLE
AABEELOPRV EVAPORABLE

AABEELPPRT PALPEBRATE
AABEELPPRY PREPAYABLE
AABEELRTTW WATER TABLE
AABEELSSSS ASSESSABLE
AABEELSTTT ATTESTABLE
AABEELSTTX BATTLEAXES
AABEEQRSSU ARABESQUES
AABEFGIILS GASIFIABLE
AABEFGKLNR KLANGFARBE
AABEFHIKRT BREAK FAITH
AABEFHLMOT FATHOMABLE
AABEFIILLS SALIFIABLE
AABEFIILRT RATIFIABLE
AABEFILLNT INFLATABLE
AABEFINRRT AFTERBRAIN
AABEFKRSST BREAKFASTS
AABEFLORUV FAVOURABLE
AABEGHORRU
  HARBOURAGE
AABEGIILMN IMAGINABLE
AABEGILNSS ASSIGNABLE
AABEGILRST ALGEBRAIST
AABEGINNOT ABNEGATION
AABEGLOPPR PROPAGABLE
AABEHIILTT HABILITATE
AABEHIOOPR AEROPHOBIA
AABEHKLNSU UNSHAKABLE
AABEIILNRV INVARIABLE
AABEIILNST BANALITIES,
  INSATIABLE
AABEIILPRT BIPARIETAL
AABEIILSST ASSIBILATE
AABEIIMOSS AMOEBIASIS
AABEIINNST IN ABSENTIA
AABEIIRRTT ABIRRITATE
AABEIJKLRS JAILBREAKS
AABEIJLOSU BEAUJOLAIS
AABEIKLMST MISTAKABLE
AABEILLMPP IMPALPABLE
AABEILLNRS BALLERINAS
AABEILLNUV INVALUABLE
AABEILLORV LABIOVELAR
AABEILLRYZ REALIZABLY
AABEILMMRU BARIUM MEAL
AABEILMNTU ALBUMINATE
AABEILMNTV AMBIVALENT
AABEILMPSS IMPASSABLE
AABEILNNTU BIANNULATE
AABEILOPRS PARABOLISE
AABEILOPRZ PARABOLIZE
AABEILRSTU TABULARISE
AABEILRSVY ABRASIVELY
AABEILRTTT TITRATABLE
AABEILRTUZ TABULARIZE
AABEIMPRTV VAMPIRE BAT
AABEINORRT ABERRATION
AABEINORTT TRABEATION
AABEINRSST ABSTAINERS
AABEINRSVW BRAINWAVES

AABEIRRTTT BITARTRATE
AABEKLMRRY REMARKABLY
AABEKLMRTY MARKETABLY
AABEKNNRRU RUN A
  BANKER
AABEKRSSTT BASKET-STAR
AABELLLNNU ANNULLABLE
AABELLMNTY LAMENTABLY
AABELLNPUY UNPLAYABLE
AABELMPRRU PREAMBULAR
AABELMRSUY MEASURABLY
AABELNORSY REASONABLY
AABELNOSSY SEASONABLY
AABELNRSWY ANSWERABLY
AABELOORRT ELABORATOR
AABELOPRRS POLAR BEARS
AABELOPRUV VAPOURABLE
AABELSTTTU STATUTABLE
AABEMOSSTT STEAMBOATS
AABEMRSTTU MASTURBATE
AABFFIILTY AFFABILITY
AABFLMNOTY FLAMBOYANT
AABFLORUVY FAVOURABLY
AABGGIINNR BARGAINING
AABGGILNRZ GLAZING-BAR
AABGGINORT ABROGATING
AABGGINOST SABOTAGING
AABGHILOOP ALGOPHOBIA
AABGIILNOR ABORIGINAL
AABGIINNST ABSTAINING
AABGILLNST BALLASTING
AABGILMNST LAMBASTING
AABGILNTTU TABULATING
AABGINNOTW ANGWANTIBO
AABGINOORT ABROGATION
AABGIRSSTU BASS GUITAR
AABGORSTVY GRAVY BOATS
AABHIIMNPS AMPHIBIANS
AABHIINNTT INHABITANT
AABHIINOTT HABITATION
AABHIKLLRU RUB' AL KHALI
AABHILLTUY HABITUALLY
AABHIMMNRS BRAHMANISM
AABHIMRTVZ BAR MITZVAH
AABHINSSSW WASHBASINS
AABHKKORSV KHABAROVSK
AABHLLLOOU HULLABALOO
AABIIILMTY AMIABILITY
AABIIILLNOT LIBATIONAL
AABIIILLSTY SALABILITY
AABIIILMTTY TAMABILITY
AABIIILNRRS LIBRARIANS
AABIIILNRVY INVARIABLY
AABIIILNSTY INSATIABLY
AABIIILRTTY RATABILITY
AABIIILTTXY TAXABILITY
AABIIINNSSY ABYSSINIAN
AABIIINPRST BIPARTISAN
AABIIINRRTT ABIRRITANT

AABIIOPRSS PARABIOSIS
AABIJNORTU ABJURATION
AABIKLMSTY MISTAKABLY
AABILLRUVV BIVALVULAR
AABILMNOTU AMBULATION
AABILMRSST STRABISMAL
AABILNOORT ABORTIONAL
AABILNOSTT BATTALIONS
AABILNOTTU TABULATION
AABILOPRST PARABOLIST
AABIMNOORT ABOMINATOR
AABINNORTY ANTIBARYON
AABINORSTT BOAT TRAINS
AABINOSSTW BOATSWAINS
AABIORRRTT ARBITRATOR
AABKKOORRU
   KOOKABURRA
AABKLOSTUW WALKABOUTS
AABLLMNORY ABNORMALLY
AABLMORTUY AMBULATORY
AABLNOORSS SALOON BARS
AABLOORRTY LABORATORY
AABLOSSTTT STATOBLAST
AABNOORRTW NARROW
   BOAT
AABORRRSTU BARRATROUS
AACCCDEIIT ACETIC ACID
AACCCDENOR
   ACCORDANCE
AACCCDIILT LACTIC ACID
AACCCEENPT ACCEPTANCE
AACCCEILTT CATALECTIC
AACCCEIORT CACCIATORE
AACCCEOSTU CACTACEOUS
AACCCINRUY INACCURACY
AACCDDEHKN
   CACK-HANDED
AACCDEGHRR CHARGE
   CARD
AACCDEHIRS SACCHARIDE
AACCDEHNOR
   ARCHDEACON
AACCDEIIPR EPICARDIAC
AACCDEILNT ACCIDENTAL
AACCDEINTV VACCINATED
AACCDELLTU CALCULATED
AACCDELNOR CLADOCERAN
AACCDELPRS PLACE CARDS
AACCDELRST CAT'S CRADLE
AACCDENNSY ASCENDANCY
AACCDERSTY SCAREDY CAT
AACCDGIILR CARDIALGIC
AACCDHIORS SACCHAROID
AACCDHPRST SCRATCHPAD
AACCDIISTU DIACAUSTIC
AACCEEELRT ACCELERATE
AACCEEFFOT FACE-TO-FACE
AACCEEGPRS SCAPEGRACE

AACCEEKMRS MAKE
   SCARCE
AACCEELLNT CANCELLATE
AACCEELNRS CLEARANCES
AACCEELNRT ACCELERANT
AACCEENTTU ACCENTUATE
AACCEEORTV COACERVATE
AACCEFPRST SPACECRAFT
AACCEGHOST STAGECOACH
AACCEHILMN MECHANICAL
AACCEHIMNN MAIN CHANCE
AACCEHINNT CACHINNATE
AACCEHINRS SACCHARINE
AACCEHINRT CHAIN-REACT
AACCEHLNOT COELACANTH
AACCEHMNNO
   COMANCHEAN
AACCEHORSS SACCHAROSE
AACCEHRRST CHARACTERS
AACCEIIPST CAPACITIES
AACCEIIPTV CAPACITIVE
AACCEILPTT CATALEPTIC
AACCEINNOT CANONICATE
AACCEINORV COVARIANCE
AACCEINPRT PANCREATIC
AACCEINRTT CANTATRICE
AACCEINRTU INACCURATE
AACCEIRRTU CARICATURE
AACCEISTUV ACCUSATIVE
AACCEKOPPT COP A PACKET
AACCEKRRST RACETRACKS
AACCELMSTY CYCLAMATES
AACCELMTUU ACCUMULATE
AACCELORSU CALCAREOUS
AACCELRTUY ACCURATELY
AACCENRSTU CRUSTACEAN
AACCFGILLU CALCIFUGAL
AACCFHIRSY SACCHARIFY
AACCFILLRY FARCICALLY
AACCFILRSU FASCICULAR
AACCFINNRS FRANCISCAN
AACCGHIORY HAGIOCRACY
AACCGHOPRY
   CACOGRAPHY
AACCGIILMN ACCLAIMING
AACCGILLNT CATCALLING
AACCHIIRST ARCHAISTIC
AACCHILNPY CHAPLAINCY
AACCHIMORT ACHROMATIC
AACCHKLLUW
   CHUCKWALLA
AACCHLNORY
   ACRONYCHAL
AACCHNORST CAST
   ANCHOR
AACCHNOTYY CHATOYANCY
AACCIILORS SACROILIAC
AACCIILPRT ACCIPITRAL
AACCIINPTY INCAPACITY

AACCIINSTT TACTICIANS
AACCILLRUV CLAVICULAR
AACCILLTTY TACTICALLY
AACCILMMUY IMMACULACY
AACCILNNOT CLACTONIAN
AACCILNOOS OCCASIONAL
AACCILPRST PRACTICALS
AACCINORST COSTA RICAN
AACCINOSTU ACCUSATION,
   ANACOUSTIC
AACCINPTTY ANAPTYCTIC
AACCINRSTU ANACRUSTIC
AACCIOPRST CAPACITORS
AACCIORTTU AUTOCRATIC
AACCKLLMOR ALARM
   CLOCK
AACCKRRSTT CART TRACKS
AACCLLORTU CALCULATOR
AACCLMSSTY CATACLYSMS
AACCLNOTTU CONTACTUAL
AACCLNRRUU
   CARUNCULAR
AACCMNORTY
   CARTOMANCY
AACCNNOTTU ACCOUNTANT
AACCNORSST SACROSANCT
AACDDEEHLR DECAHEDRAL
AACDDEEIMP AIDE-DE-CAMP
AACDDEEIRT ERADICATED
AACDDEEIST TEA CADDIES
AACDDEEMRT DEMARCATED
AACDDEIJTU ADJUDICATE
AACDDEINST CANDIDATES
AACDDEKLPS PACKSADDLE
AACDDELNPS LANDSCAPED
AACDDIKNOR ADIRONDACK
AACDEEEFNS DEFEASANCE
AACDEEEHNX HEXADECANE
AACDEEELST DE-ESCALATE
AACDEEFHMS SHAMEFACED
AACDEEFHNR
   FACE-HARDEN
AACDEEGNOT ANECDOTAGE
AACDEEHNRS
   CASE-HARDEN
AACDEEHRTX EX CATHEDRA
AACDEEIINT TAENIACIDE
AACDEEINRT DERACINATE
AACDEEINRV CADAVERINE
AACDEEIPTT DECAPITATE
AACDEEITTV DEACTIVATE
AACDEEJLTU EJACULATED
AACDEENNTT ATTENDANCE
AACDEEPPRT RATE-CAPPED
AACDEFINRU FRICANDEAU
AACDEFINST FASCINATED
AACDEFLORT DEFALCATOR
AACDEFPSTY PASTY-FACED

AACDEGHHNR CHARGE
   HAND
AACDEGIMNP CAMPAIGNED
AACDEGISTT CASTIGATED
AACDEGLOTU
   CATALOGUED, COAGULATED
AACDEHHTTW DEATHWATCH
AACDEHILNR HERACLIDAN
AACDEHILNS ENCHILADAS
AACDEHILRS CHARLADIES
AACDEHILRT TRACHEIDAL
AACDEHINRS SEDAN CHAIR
AACDEHJKLT JACK THE LAD
AACDEHKPRT PACKTHREAD
AACDEHLMTY CHLAMYDATE
AACDEHLNNS CLEAN HANDS
AACDEHLORT OCTAHEDRAL
AACDEHLRST CATHEDRALS
AACDEHNTTU UNATTACHED
AACDEHOPPR APPROACHED
AACDEHPRTU PARACHUTED
AACDEIINRR IRRADIANCE
AACDEIIPRT PAEDIATRIC
AACDEIIRTV DIVARICATE
AACDEIJLTV ADJECTIVAL
AACDEIKPRS SICK PARADE
AACDEILLTV VACILLATED
AACDEILMNO DEMONIACAL
AACDEILMNR ALDERMANIC
AACDEILNNO CALEDONIAN
AACDEILNOR ANDROECIAL
AACDEILNSS SCANDALISE
AACDEILNSZ SCANDALIZE
AACDEIMNNO MACEDONIAN
AACDEIMNTT ADMITTANCE
AACDEIMPRS PARAMEDICS
AACDEIMSTT MASTICATED
AACDEINNRT INCARNATED
AACDEINORU ECUADORIAN
AACDEINOTV VACATIONED
AACDEINQTU ACQUAINTED
AACDEINQUY INADEQUACY
AACDEINRTX TAXI DANCER
AACDEIORRT ERADICATOR
AACDEIOSST ASSOCIATED
AACDEIPTTV CAPTIVATED
AACDELMRSU CLEAR AS
   MUD
AACDELNOPR ENDOCARPAL
AACDELNPSS LANDSCAPES
AACDELNSST SANDCASTLE
AACDELORST SACERDOTAL
AACDELPTTU CATAPULTED
AACDEMORRT
   DEMARCATOR
AACDEMRRST MASTER
   CARD
AACDENNNOS
   CANNONADES

AACDENNSST ASCENDANTS
AACDENPRST TAP DANCERS
AACDENRSTT TRANSACTED
AACDEOPRRS RADARSCOPE
AACDEORSUV CADAVEROUS
AACDFHINRT HANDICRAFT
AACDFIINOO AFICIONADO
AACDGHHINR CHANDIGARH
AACDGHNORR DRAG
   ANCHOR
AACDGILNPR PLACARDING
AACDGIMNSW MAGIC
   WANDS
AACDGIMORR CARDIOGRAM
AACDGINNPT TAP DANCING
AACDGINOTV ADVOCATING
AACDGNNOPW CAP AND
   GOWN
AACDGORSTU
   COASTGUARD
AACDHINORT ANTHRACOID
AACDHLNPSU LAUNCH PADS
AACDHPRRSS CARDSHARPS
AACDIIILMR MIRACIDIAL
AACDIILLRV LARVICIDAL
AACDIILMRS RADICALISM
AACDIILMRT MATRICIDAL
AACDIILPRR PARRICIDAL
AACDIILPRT PATRICIDAL
AACDIILSTT DIASTALTIC
AACDIIMNOS AMINO ACIDS
AACDILMNNO CALAMONDIN
AACDILMORY MYOCARDIAL
AACDINOOTV ADVOCATION
AACDIQRSTU QUADRATICS
AACDJNOTTU COADJUTANT
AACDLNOSSU SCANDALOUS
AACDLOSTUY ADACTYLOUS
AACDMMNNOT
   COMMANDANT
AACDNOORST
   OSTRACODAN
AACDOORTVY ADVOCATORY
AACEEEHKPS CHESAPEAKE
AACEEEKMPR PEACEMAKER
AACEEELMNP ELECAMPANE
AACEEELNOP PALAEOCENE
AACEEFIRST CAFETERIAS
AACEEFLSUV FACE VALUES
AACEEFRSSV FACE-SAVERS
AACEEGHNSS SEA CHANGES
AACEEGILLN ALLEGIANCE
AACEEGKPPR PREPACKAGE
AACEEGKPTT GET A PACKET
AACEEGLLRS LARGE-SCALE
AACEEGNOST ACT ONE'S
   AGE
AACEEHIKLN HAECKELIAN
AACEEHILNT CHATELAINE

AACEEHINNP PHENACAINE
AACEEHKPST CHEAPSKATE
AACEEHLMNR
   MENARCHEAL
AACEEHMNRY
   AERENCHYMA
AACEEHNNPT ANTHRACENE
AACEEHPPRS PAPER CHASE
AACEEILMRS CARAMELISE
AACEEILMRZ CARAMELIZE
AACEEILPRT ALTARPIECE
AACEEILRTV CALAVERITE,
   LACERATIVE
AACEEIMNPT EMANCIPATE
AACEEIMRTV MACERATIVE
AACEEIMSST SIAMESE CAT
AACEEIPPRT APPRECIATE
AACEEIRTTV REACTIVATE
AACEEITUVV EVACUATIVE
AACEEKMPRS PACEMAKERS
AACEEKRRST CARETAKERS
AACEELLNOT LANCEOLATE
AACEELLNST CLEAN SLATE
AACEELLORT REALLOCATE
AACEELLPRT CARPELLATE
AACEELMSTU EMASCULATE
AACEELNTTU CATENULATE
AACEELOPRT CAPREOLATE
AACEELOPSU PALEACEOUS
AACEENORSU ARENACEOUS
AACEENPRSS PANCREASES
AACEEPRSTW WATERSCAPE
AACEERSSTT ESTATE CARS
AACEERSSTV STAVESACRE
AACEFFIRST AFFRICATES
AACEFGHNOR FOR A
   CHANGE
AACEFGINSV FACE-SAVING
AACEFGLMOU
   CAMOUFLAGE
AACEFGNRRS FRAGRANCES
AACEFGRSTT STAGECRAFT
AACEFHLLNP CHAPFALLEN
AACEFHLSST HALF-CASTES
AACEFIILTT FACILITATE
AACEFIIMPR PRIMA FACIE
AACEFIINST FANATICISE
AACEFIINTZ FANATICIZE
AACEFLMORT MALEFACTOR
AACEFRRTTW WATERCRAFT
AACEFRSTTT STATECRAFT
AACEGHLNRS ARCHANGELS
AACEGHMOPR
   MACROPHAGE
AACEGHNORS
   ANCHORAGES
AACEGHNORT COAT
   HANGER
AACEGILLPR PREGLACIAL

AACEGILNRT LACERATING
AACEGILNSS ANALGESICS
AACEGILNST ESCALATING
AACEGILPPR PARAPLEGIC
AACEGILRST CARTILAGES
AACEGIMNPR CAMPAIGNER
AACEGIMNRT MACERATING
AACEGINTUV EVACUATING
AACEGINTVX EXCAVATING
AACEGLMORY
   ACROMEGALY
AACEGLORTU CATALOGUER
AACEGLOSTU CATALOGUES
AACEGMNRTY
   TERMAGANCY
AACEGOPSST SCAPEGOATS
AACEGORSTT GREATCOATS
AACEHHILRR HIERARCHAL
AACEHHKLMS HAMSHACKLE
AACEHHMNTT HATCHET
   MAN
AACEHIIMNT HAEMATINIC
AACEHIIMTT HAEMATITIC
AACEHIKLMR LIKE A CHARM
AACEHILMMS MICHAELMAS
AACEHILNPT CHAINPLATE
AACEHILNRS LANCASHIRE
AACEHILOPT APOTHECIAL
AACEHILPST CALIPHATES
AACEHILRTT THEATRICAL
AACEHIMMPR AMPHIMACER
AACEHIMPRS PHARMACIES
AACEHIMPRT AMPHEATRIC
AACEHIMRTU HAEMATURIC
AACEHINNOU OUANANICHE
AACEHINRRT CATARRHINE
AACEHINRTT ANTHRACITE
AACEHINSTU EUSTACHIAN
AACEHIOPRX ECHOPRAXIA
AACEHIRRTV ARCHITRAVE
AACEHIRSSY EASY CHAIRS
AACEHIRSTU AUTARCHIES
AACEHJKMMR
   JACKHAMMER
AACEHKLMRS RAMSHACKLE
AACEHKMMRT
   MATCHMAKER
AACEHKMRTW
   WATCHMAKER
AACEHKRSSV HAVERSACKS
AACEHLOPSU ACEPHALOUS
AACEHLPRTY ARCHETYPAL
AACEHMNPRY
   PARENCHYMA
AACEHMNRRT
   CARMARTHEN
AACEHMNRTY
   ATHERMANCY
AACEHMNTTT ATTACHMENT

AACEHMOPRT CAMPHORATE
AACEHOPPRS APPROACHES
AACEHOPRTY APOTHECARY
AACEHPPRSS SCRAP HEAPS
AACEHPRSTU PARACHUTES
AACEIILMST CALAMITIES
AACEIILPST CAPITALISE
AACEIILPTZ CAPITALIZE
AACEIIMNOT EMACIATION
AACEIINNRV INVARIANCE
AACEIINORT ACIERATION
AACEIINPTT ANTICIPATE
AACEIINTTV INACTIVATE
AACEIIOPSS CASSIOPEIA
AACEIIPRTT PATRICIATE
AACEIIPTTV CAPITATIVE
AACEILLMNU ANIMALCULE
AACEILLMNY ANEMICALLY
AACEILLNRT CARNALLITE
AACEILLNTT CANTILLATE
AACEILLOSU ALLIACEOUS
AACEILLRRV VARICELLAR
AACEILLSTY SALICYLATE
AACEILMMTU IMMACULATE
AACEILMNPS CAMPANILES
AACEILMNRT RECLAIMANT
AACEILMNRU UNICAMERAL
AACEILMNSU MAIN CLAUSE
AACEILMNTU CALUMNIATE
AACEILMRTU TULARAEMIC
AACEILNNRS CARNELIANS
AACEILNORT CREATIONAL,
   LACERATION, REACTIONAL
AACEILNOST ESCALATION
AACEILNPPS APPLIANCES
AACEILNPPS SNAIL'S PACE
AACEILNPTU PANICULATE
AACEILOOPZ PALAEOZOIC
AACEILPRRS PERISARCAL
AACEILPTTU CAPITULATE
AACEILRTTU ARTICULATE
AACEILRTUU AURICULATE
AACEILSSTU CASUALTIES
AACEILSTTT STALACTITE
AACEIMMPRU PARAMECIUM
AACEIMNNRU UN-AMERICAN
AACEIMNNST ANAMNESTIC
AACEIMNORT MACERATION
AACEIMNORU OCEANARIUM
AACEIMOPST APOSEMATIC
AACEIMORRT CREMATORIA
AACEIMPRRT PARAMETRIC
AACEIMSTTT METASTATIC
AACEINNNTU ANNUNCIATE
AACEINNOTT CATENATION
AACEINNPRT PANCREATIN
AACEINORTU AERONAUTIC
AACEINORTV VACATIONER
AACEINOTUV EVACUATION

AACEINOTVX EXCAVATION
AACEINPRST PERSIAN CAT
AACEINPRTY AT ANY PRICE
AACEINRSST INCRASSATE
AACEINSSST ASSISTANCE
AACEIORSTT AEROSTATIC
AACEIOSSST ASSOCIATES
AACEIRSSST STAIRCASES
AACEIRTTTV ATTRACTIVE
AACEJKNRTT NATTERJACK
AACEJLORTU EJACULATOR
AACEKKMRST MAKE
   TRACKS
AACEKLMRST SMART ALECK
AACEKLPRST PLATE RACKS
AACEKLRRTY TRACKLAYER
AACEKPPSTY PAY PACKETS
AACELLLMSS SMALL-SCALE
AACELLLORT COLLATERAL
AACELLLRST SALTCELLAR
AACELLLRUV VALLECULAR
AACELLNOSW ALLOWANCES
AACELLPRRY CARPELLARY
AACELLPSST CAST A SPELL
AACELMNRVY CAVALRYMEN
AACELMOPSU PALMACEOUS
AACELMOSUV MALVACEOUS
AACELMOSUY
   AMYLACEOUS
AACELMPRST CAMPESTRAL
AACELMSSST CLASSMATES
AACELNNOTV COVENANTAL
AACELNOPTU CANTALOUPE
AACELNOTTV OCTAVALENT
AACELNRRUV VERNACULAR
AACELNRTTU TENTACULAR
AACELNSSSU CASUALNESS
AACELNTUUV AVUNCULATE
AACELOPPSY APOCALYPSE
AACELORSST ESCALATORS
AACELORSUU LAURACEOUS
AACELPPRST APPLE CARTS
AACELPRTTY CALYPTRATE
AACELSTTUU AUSCULTATE
AACEMNOPSW
   SPACEWOMAN
AACEMNORST
   SACRAMENTO
AACEMNRSST SACRAMENTS
AACEMPRSTU METACARPUS
AACENNNOSY ANNOYANCES
AACENNSSTV VACANTNESS
AACENOTTUZ UTO-AZTECAN
AACENRRSTU EARN A
   CRUST
AACENRSSSU ASSURANCES
AACENRSSSV CANVASSERS
AACEORRTTT TERRACOTTA
AACEORSTVX EXCAVATORS

AACEPPPRRS SCRAP PAPER
AACFFIJMRT TRAFFIC JAM
AACFGILNRT FLAT RACING
AACFHKNRST CRANKSHAFT
AACFHLNORW HALF A
   CROWN
AACFIIILRT ARTIFICIAL
AACFIILNOR CALIFORNIA
AACFIILSTT FATALISTIC
AACFIIMNST FANATICISM
AACFIINOST FASCIATION
AACFILLOSU FALLACIOUS
AACFILMSTU FACTUALISM
AACFILNORT FRACTIONAL
AACFILORST SOLFATARIC
AACFILSTTU FACTUALIST
AACFINNNOR FRANCONIAN
AACFLNNOTU NONFACTUAL
AACFMNNOWY FANCY
   WOMAN
AACFMOORST COAT OF
   ARMS
AACFNRSTTU SURFACTANT
AACFRRTTYY ARTY-CRAFTY
AACGGHINNS CHAIN GANGS
AACGGIILOS SIALAGOGIC
AACGGILLNO ALGOLAGNIC
AACGGILRST GASTRALGIC
AACGHHOPRT TACHOGRAPH
AACGHILNPY ANAGLYPHIC
AACGHILRRT ARTHRALGIC
AACGHIOPRS SARCOPHAGI
AACGHMOPRR
   MACROGRAPH
AACGIILLST GLACIALIST
AACGIILNNZ CANALIZING
AACGIILNOT GLACIATION
AACGIIMSTT ASTIGMATIC
AACGIINNPT CAPTAINING
AACGIINPST PAGANISTIC
AACGIINTTV ACTIVATING
AACGIKMNRT TARMACKING
AACGIKMORY KARYOGAMIC
AACGIKNNRS RANSACKING
AACGILLNOT ALLOCATING
AACGILLRTY TRAGICALLY
AACGILMNNY MALIGNANCY
AACGILNORS COR ANGLAIS
AACGILNPTY PLAY-ACTING
AACGIMNORT MORGANATIC
AACGIMNRSS MASSACRING
AACGIMPRST PRAGMATICS
AACGIMRSTY MAGISTRACY
AACGINNSSV CANVASSING
AACGINRSTT CASTRATING
AACGINRTTT ATTRACTING
AACGIORSTT CASTIGATOR
AACGLLMOOY
   MALACOLOGY

AACGLLSSWY SCALLYWAGS
AACGLNORTU OCTANGULAR
AACHHHISUU CHIHUAHUAS
AACHIINRST CHRISTIANA
AACHILLOPT ALLOPATHIC
AACHILNNPT PLAINCHANT
AACHILOPST CHIPOLATAS
AACHILPRSU HARUSPICAL
AACHIMMNRS RACHMANISM
AACHIMNNRU MANCHURIAN
AACHIMNOPR ANAMORPHIC
AACHIMNORS
   ANACHORISM, HARMONICAS,
   MARASCHINO
AACHIMNORT ACHROMATIN,
   MACHINATOR
AACHIMNORW
   CHAIRWOMAN
AACHIMPRST PHARMACIST
AACHIMRRST MATRIARCHS
AACHIMRRTY MATRIARCHY
AACHIMRSTT MAASTRICHT
AACHIMSSTT ASTHMATICS
AACHINRSST ANARCHISTS
AACHINRSTU CARTHUSIAN
AACHIPRRST PATRIARCHS
AACHIPRRTY PATRIARCHY
AACHIPRSTY PARASTICHY
AACHLLRSTW WALLCHARTS
AACHLMOPRS ARCHOPLASM
AACHLNNNOT NONCHALANT
AACHLOPPRY APOCRYPHAL
AACHMOOPRT
   APOCHROMAT
AACHMORTUY
   TAUROMACHY
AACHMPRSST MARCH-PASTS
AACHPRSTTW WATCHSTRAP
AACIILLNNT ANTICLINAL
AACIILLOPT APOLITICAL
AACIILMNOS SIMONIACAL
AACIILMNST TALISMANIC
AACIILMNTX ANTICLIMAX
AACIILMPST CAPITALISM
AACIILNNOR CAROLINIAN
AACIILNNST ANNALISTIC
AACIILNORS SALICORNIA
AACIILNOST ANTISOCIAL
AACIILPPST PAPISTICAL
AACIILPSTT CAPITALIST
AACIILRRTU URTICARIAL
AACIILRSST RACIALISTS
AACIIMNNRT MARTINICAN
AACIIMSSTT ASTATICISM
AACIINNPTT ANTICIPANT
AACIINOPTT CAPITATION
AACIINOTTV ACTIVATION,
   CAVITATION
AACIINPRST PATRICIANS

AACIINSTTT ANTISTATIC
AACIIORSUV AVARICIOUS
AACIKLMMRS LAMARCKISM
AACILLMNTY MANTICALLY
AACILLMORT MATRILOCAL
AACILLMOTY ATOMICALLY,
   LAY CLAIM TO
AACILLNOOT ALLOCATION
AACILLNTUY NAUTICALLY
AACILLOOPR COPROLALIA
AACILLOPRT ALLOPATRIC,
   PATRILOCAL
AACILLORTV VACILLATOR
AACILLPTYY ATYPICALLY
AACILLRWXY WAX LYRICAL
AACILLTVWY CAVITY WALL
AACILMNOTU MACULATION
AACILMORRT LACRIMATOR
AACILMORSU MARLACIOUS
AACILMOSTU CALAMITOUS
AACILNNRTY TYRANNICAL
AACILNOOTV VOCATIONAL
AACILNOPTY NYCTALOPIA
AACILNORSS SCANSORIAL
AACILNORTT TRACTIONAL
AACILNPPST APPLICANTS
AACILOORRT ORATORICAL
AACILOPPRT APPLICATOR
AACILOPRTT OPTICAL ART
AACILORRTU CURATORIAL
AACILORSTU ALACRITOUS
AACILPRRSU SPIRACULAR
AACILPRRTU PARTICULAR
AACILPRSTT PLASTIC ART
AACILPRSTY PARALYTICS
AACILQSTTU ACQUITTALS
AACIMMNNOO
   MONOMANIAC
AACIMNNNSU MANCUNIANS
AACIMNOPRY PYROMANIAC
AACIMORSTT MASTICATOR
AACIMOSTTU AUTOMATICS
AACINNOOTZ ACTINOZOAN
AACINNORST CARNATIONS
AACINNOSTT CONSTANTIA
AACINOOPTT COAPTATION
AACINOOSTV AVOCATIONS,
   NOVA SCOTIA
AACINOPRSS CAPARISONS
AACINORSTT CASTRATION
AACINORTTT ATTRACTION
AACINORTUY CAUTIONARY
AACINRSSST SACRISTANS
AACIOOPPRT APOTROPAIC
AACIOPRTTV CAPTIVATOR
AACIORRSTT ARISTOCRAT
AACIOSSTTW WAISTCOATS
AACJLMRSUU MAJUSCULAR

AACLMNNOSW
CLANSWOMAN
AACLNOPSTU CANTALOUPS
AACLOORRTU COLORATURA
AACLOPRRRS PARLOR CARS
AACLOPRRST PATROL CARS
AACMOOPRRT
COMPARATOR
AACNNNOSTT CONSTANTAN
AACNORRSTT TRANSACTOR
AACOOPPRSU APOCARPOUS
AACORRSTTT STRATOCRAT
AADDDEEHHR
HARDHEADED
AADDDEEMRY
DAYDREAMED
AADDDGRSUY SUGAR
DADDY
AADDEEHHST
DEATH'S-HEAD
AADDEEHIMN MAIDENHEAD
AADDEEIRST DESIDERATA
AADDEEMRRY
DAYDREAMER
AADDEESTTV DEVASTATED
AADDEFINRW FAR AND WIDE
AADDEGHNOR
DRAGONHEAD
AADDEGIPRS DISPARAGED
AADDEGIRRT TARDIGRADE
AADDEGMNOR
ARMAGEDDON
AADDEHIMNN HANDMAIDEN
AADDEHLMNN
MANHANDLED
AADDEHLMOT THE OLD
ADAM
AADDEHLNNP PANHANDLED
AADDEHQSTU DEATH
SQUAD
AADDEIILPT DILAPIDATE
AADDEIIRRT IRRADIATED
AADDEILLNS LANDLADIES
AADDEILMRR RED ADMIRAL
AADDEILNSV VANDALISED
AADDEILNVZ VANDALIZED
AADDEILORR RAILROADED
AADDEIMRST DRAMATISED
AADDEIMRTZ DRAMATIZED
AADDEINRSW EDWARDIANS
AADDELMNRS
DREAMLANDS
AADDELMRSS MALADDRESS
AADDGILMOY AMYGDALOID
AADDGNNRST GRANDSTAND
AADDHNNSST HANDSTANDS
AADDIILNOT ADDITIONAL
AADDIIMRSY DAIRYMAIDS
AADDILLLOV VALLADOLID

AADDINORRT RITARDANDO
AADDLNOOSW
SANDALWOOD
AADEEEPPRR REAPPEARED
AADEEFGHOR FORGE
AHEAD
AADEEFGLRT DEFLAGRATE
AADEEFHRRZ HAZARD-FREE
AADEEGGGRT AGGREGATED
AADEEGIRTV VARIEGATED
AADEEGNPPS APPENDAGES
AADEEGNRRR
REARRANGED
AADEEGNRST GREAT
DANES, TEAGARDENS
AADEEGNRTU GUARANTEED
AADEEHHLRX HEXAHEDRAL
AADEEHHMMR
HAMMERHEAD
AADEEHLNVY HEAVY-LADEN
AADEEHLTWY LEAD THE
WAY
AADEEHMRST
HEADMASTER, HEADSTREAM
AADEEHNRVW
HEAVENWARD
AADEEHPPRS PEAR-SHAPED
AADEEHPRSS SPEARHEADS
AADEEHQRSU HEADSQUARE
AADEEHRSTT DEATH RATES
AADEEHRSTW HEADWATERS
AADEEILLTV ALLEVIATED
AADEEILMNT DELAMINATE
AADEEILNNR ADRENALINE
AADEEILNST DESALINATE
AADEEILRTT RETALIATED
AADEEIMMNN MAIDEN
NAME
AADEEIMNRT REANIMATED
AADEEIMPRT PREADAMITE
AADEEINQTU INADEQUATE
AADEEIPTTX EXPATIATED
AADEEIRSTT ASTERIATED
AADEEKKKOT TAKE A
DEKKO
AADEELLLMT LAMELLATED
AADEELLLPR PARALLELED
AADEELLPPR APPARELLED
AADEELMNRV
VAL-DE-MARNE
AADEELMRTT MALTREATED
AADEELMSTT STALEMATED
AADEELNNWZ NEW
ZEALAND
AADEELNPSS ESPLANADES
AADEELNRTT ALTERNATED
AADEELQTUY ADEQUATELY
AADEELRRSY LAY READERS
AADEELRSTV SLAVE TRADE

AADEELRTTU ADULTERATE
AADEEMNRST TRADE
NAMES
AADEEMQRSU
MASQUERADE
AADEEMQSTU DESQUAMATE
AADEENTTTU ATTENUATED
AADEEOPRTV EVAPORATED
AADEEPPRWX WAXED
PAPER
AADEEPRSST PAEDERASTS
AADEEPRSTY PAEDERASTY
AADEERRTTW TREAD
WATER
AADEFFIILT AFFILIATED
AADEFFNORT FORE AND AFT
AADEFGRSSU SAFEGUARDS
AADEFHHIOR HEAD OF HAIR
AADEFHLNRT FATHERLAND
AADEFIKNRR AFRIKANDER
AADEFIMNOT DEFAMATION
AADEFINSST FANTASISED
AADEFINSTZ FANTASIZED
AADEFINTTU INFATUATED
AADEFLLMNO AN OLD
FLAME
AADEFMORTY DEFAMATORY
AADEFMRSST FARMSTEADS
AADEFRRSTW AFTERWARDS
AADEGGINRS AGGRANDISE
AADEGGINRZ AGGRANDIZE
AADEGGNOOR
DRAGOONAGE
AADEGGOSSU SAUSAGE
DOG
AADEGHHINS SHANGHAIED
AADEGHIINR HEARING AID
AADEGHNRSY
HYDRANGEAS
AADEGHNSST STAGEHANDS
AADEGILMNY AMYGDALINE
AADEGILNSV GALVANISED
AADEGILNVZ GALVANIZED
AADEGILRST SALTIGRADE
AADEGIMMNS MISMANAGED
AADEGIMRST SMARAGDITE
AADEGINNTT ANTEDATING
AADEGINRRS DISARRANGE
AADEGINRST TRAGEDIANS
AADEGIPRRS DISPARAGER
AADEGIRTTV GRAVITATED
AADEGLNNST LAND AGENTS
AADEGLNQRU
QUADRANGLE
AADEGLNRTU GRANULATED
AADEGLNSTW SWEAT
GLAND
AADEGMRRTU
DRAMATURGE

AADEGNOPRR GRAND
OPERA
AADEGOPPRT PROPAGATED
AADEGRRRSU REARGUARDS
AADEGRRSVY GRAVEYARDS
AADEHHKNSS
HANDSHAKES, SHAKE HANDS
AADEHIIMNR MAIDENHAIR
AADEHILNNT LANTHANIDE
AADEHILORR DIARRHOEAL
AADEHIPRST HIT PARADES
AADEHKLLMR HALLMARKED
AADEHKMSST DEATH MASKS
AADEHLLMRS MARSHALLED
AADEHLMPSS LAMPSHADES
AADEHLNNPR PANHANDLER
AADEHLNNPS PANHANDLES
AADEHMMMNO
MOHAMMEDAN
AADEHORRSW
ARROWHEADS
AADEHPRSTT DEATH TRAPS
AADEHRRSTW
EARTHWARDS
AADEIILNNR DAIL EIRANN
AADEIILNOT IDEATIONAL
AADEIILNTV INVALIDATE
AADEIILPRS LAPIDARIES
AADEIIMNNR AMERINDIAN
AADEIIMNNT MAINTAINED
AADEIINNST EAST INDIAN
AADEIINNTV VANADINITE
AADEIINORT ERADIATION
AADEIINTTV ADVENTITIA
AADEIIRRTT TRIRADIATE
AADEILMNRV VINA DEL MAR
AADEILMNTY ANIMATEDLY
AADEILMORT TAILOR-MADE
AADEILMRTX TAXIDERMAL
AADEILNSTT TANTALISED
AADEILNSTU ANDALUSITE
AADEILNTTZ TANTALIZED
AADEILORST ASTEROIDAL
AADEILPPTT PALPITATED
AADEILSTVW TIDAL WAVES
AADEIMNRTV ANIMADVERT
AADEIMRRST DRAMATISER
AADEIMRRTZ DRAMATIZER
AADEINNOPT ANTIPODEAN
AADEINPQSU PASQUINADE
AADEINQRSU QUANDARIES
AADEINQTTU ANTIQUATED
AADEINRSTT ANTITRADES
AADEIOPQRU RADIOPAQUE
AADEKLMORW
MEADOWLARK
AADEKMRRST TRADEMARKS
AADELLORSV EL SALVADOR

AADELMMORS
MELODRAMAS
AADELMNSSS LANDMASSES
AADELMOOST STOMODAEAL
AADELMOPRR
MADREPORAL
AADELNRSTT TRANSLATED
AADELNRTTU ADULTERANT
AADELNRTUY DAY-NEUTRAL
AADELNSSTW WASTELANDS
AADELRSTWY EASTWARDLY
AADEMNPRSS AMPERSANDS
AADENNRTTU DENATURANT
AADENNSTTT ATTENDANTS
AADENRSTTU TRANSUDATE
AADEORSTTV DEVASTATOR
AADEQRRTUU QUADRATURE
AADEQRRTUY QUARTER
DAY
AADFFIISTV AFFIDAVITS
AADFILNRSY FAIRYLANDS
AADFILRSTU FRUIT SALAD
AADFIMNRSY MAN FRIDAYS
AADFIMRRSY DAIRY FARMS
AADFNORRTU FART AROUND
AADGGILNNR GARLANDING
AADGGINRTU GRADUATING
AADGHIMPRS DIAPHRAGMS
AADGHINSWY WASHING DAY
AADGHIOPRR RADIOGRAPH
AADGIILNTV VALIDATING
AADGIINNRT GRANT-IN-AID
AADGIJNORU JAGUARONDI
AADGILLNOY DIAGONALLY
AADGILMRSU GRADUALISM
AADGILNOOT ODONTALGIA
AADGILNPPU APPLAUDING
AADGILORST GLADIATORS
AADGILPSUV DAUGAVPILS
AADGILRRSU GUARDRAILS
AADGILRSTU GRADUALIST
AADGIMORRS RADIOGRAMS
AADGINNOPR GRAND PIANO
AADGINORST GRADATIONS
AADGINORTU GRADUATION
AADGLMNRSS GRAND
SLAMS
AADGMRRTUY
DRAMATURGY
AADGMRSSTU MUSTARD
GAS
AADGNNOPRS
SNAPDRAGON
AADGNRSSUV GUARD'S
VANS
AADHIILPSY DIAPHYSIAL
AADHIIOPRS APHRODISIA
AADHILRTWW WITHDRAWAL
AADHINOPSU DIAPHANOUS

AADHNSSSTW WASHSTANDS
AADIILLNST TILLANDSIA
AADIILMMOT OMMATIDIAL
AADIILNOTT DILATATION
AADIILNOTV VALIDATION
AADIILNPRW RAWALPINDI
AADIILQRUV QUADRIVIAL
AADIILSSST DIASTALSIS
AADIILSSUV VISUAL AIDS
AADIIMNOPS DIPSOMANIA
AADIIMNORT ADMIRATION
AADIINORST RADIATIONS
AADIINORTX X-RADIATION
AADIIORRRT IRRADIATOR
AADIIPRSST ASPIDISTRA
AADIJNORTU ADJURATION
AADILLMNOS SOMALILAND
AADILLMORS ARMADILLOS
AADILNORTU DURATIONAL
AADILORSTU AUSTRALOID
AADILORTVY VALIDATORY
AADILOSSVW DISAVOWALS
AADIMNNOPR PRIMA DONNA
AADIMNOPRY MYRIAPODAN
AADIMOPPRU PARAPODIUM
AADIMRSSTT DRAMATISTS
AADINSSSTY SAINT'S DAYS
AADIOOPSSY OOPS-A-DAISY
AADJMNNPRU PANJANDRUM
AADJORRTUY ADJURATORY
AADLMNNNOS
NO-MAN'S-LAND
AADLMNNRUY
LAUNDRYMAN
AADLMNPSUY PALM SUNDAY
AADMNOORSU
ANADROMOUS
AADNOOPPSW
SAPPANWOOD
AAEEEFLMMT METAFEMALE
AAEEEGGMMT
MEGAGAMETE
AAEEEGGRTX EXAGGERATE
AAEEEGLNOP PALAEOGENE
AAEEEHRSST HEARTSEASE
AAEEELMNRW
ENAMELWARE
AAEEELNPRS PARASELENE
AAEEELRSTT REAL ESTATE
AAEEEMNNOS SEA
ANEMONE
AAEEEPRSTX EXASPERATE
AAEEERSSTV ASSEVERATE
AAEEFGIMRT AFTERIMAGE
AAEEFGINTU TAENIAFUGE
AAEEFGLLLT FLAGELLATE
AAEEFHRSTV AFTERSHAVE
AAEEFKLMRT FLEA MARKET
AAEEFNRRST FAR EASTERN

AAEEFRSTTT AFTERTASTE
AAEEGGGRST AGGREGATES
AAEEGGHMOU
　HAEMAGOGUE
AAEEGHLLRT ALL THE RAGE
AAEEGHLNOT HALOGENATE
AAEEGHRRSV HARGREAVES
AAEEGILLTT TAGLIATELE
AAEEGILNNV EVANGELINA
AAEEGIMNRT EMARGINATE
AAEEGIMSSX SEXAGESIMA
AAEEGINRTV VEGETARIAN
AAEEGIRSSV SAVAGERIES
AAEEGLMNPS PLASMAGENE
AAEEGLMNST MENTAL AGES
AAEEGLSSVW WAGE SLAVES
AAEEGMMNNT
　MANAGEMENT
AAEEGMMORR
　AEROGRAMME
AAEEGMNRSS
　MANAGERESS
AAEEGMNRST EAST
　GERMAN
AAEEGMNRTV RAVAGEMENT
AAEEGMNSST STAGE NAMES
AAEEGNPRRR PREARRANGE
AAEEGNRRRR
　REARRANGER
AAEEGNRSTU GUARANTEES
AAEEGNRSXY SEXAGENARY
AAEEGNSSSV SAVAGENESS
AAEEGQRRTU QUARTERAGE
AAEEHHRSST HEAT RASHES
AAEEHILRTX EXHILARATE
AAEEHINSST ANESTHESIA
AAEEHKMOSU MAKE A
　HOUSE
AAEEHKQRTU EARTHQUAKE
AAEEHLNTTT LATENT HEAT
AAEEHLNTVX HEXAVALENT
AAEEHLRRSS REHEARSALS
AAEEHMNRTW
　WEATHERMAN
AAEEHMPRST METAPHRASE
AAEEHPTVWY PAVE THE
　WAY
AAEEHRRRST RARE EARTHS
AAEEHRRSTW SHEARWATER
AAEEHRTVWY HEAVY
　WATER
AAEEIKLMNS SEAMANLIKE
AAEEILLNST LATEEN SAIL
AAEEILLRTT ALLITERATE
AAEEILMNNS MELANESIAN
AAEEILMORT AMELIORATE
AAEEILMRSS LAMASERIES
AAEEILNPRT PENETRALIA
AAEEILRTTV ALTERATIVE

AAEEILTUVV EVALUATIVE
AAEEINPPRV PAPAVERINE
AAEEIPPRRS REAPPRAISE
AAEEIPRRTT REPATRIATE
AAEEIPRRTV REPARATIVE
AAEEIPRSTT TEA PARTIES
AAEEIPRSTV SEPARATIVE
AAEEIPRTTX EXPATRIATE
AAEEKKWWYY WAKEY
　WAKEY
AAEEKNQRSU NEAR
　SQUEAK
AAEELLPRTY PLATELAYER
AAEELMNPST NAMEPLATES
AAEELMQRSU SQUARE
　MEAL
AAEELMRRTT MALTREATER
AAEELMSSTT STALEMATES
AAEELNOPRS AEROPLANES
AAEELNPRRT PARENTERAL
AAEELNPRST PLEASANTER
AAEELPRSTY SEPARATELY
AAEELSSSTX SALES TAXES
AAEEMMNRRT
　REARMAMENT
AAEEMNNSSU
　AMANUENSES
AAEEMPRRST PARAMETERS
AAEEPPRSTW WASTE PAPER
AAEERRSTTW WATER RATES
AAEFFHRSTT AFTERSHAFT
AAEFFIILST AFFILIATES
AAEFFILORV LOVE AFFAIR
AAEFGIISTT FASTIGIATE
AAEFGLLLNT FLAGELLANT
AAEFGLLNRU LANGLAUFER
AAEFGLMNRT FRAGMENTAL
AAEFHLPRST FLARE PATHS
AAEFHMRSTT AFTERMATHS
AAEFIILSTT FATALITIES
AAEFIKNRRS AFRIKANERS
AAEFILLNRX FRAXINELLA
AAEFILMMNY FAMILY NAME
AAEFILMRRS FIRE ALARMS
AAEFILRSTY FAIRY TALES
AAEFIMMNRS MAINFRAMES
AAEFIMRRRT TERRA FIRMA
AAEFINPRST AFTERPAINS
AAEFKLMOOT MAKE A LOT
　OF
AAEFLLNSTU FUSTANELLA
AAEFLLRSTW WATERFALLS
AAEFLMPSTY SAFETY LAMP
AAEFLOPSTT SOFT PALATE
AAEFLORTZZ TO A FRAZZLE
AAEFLRSSTT FALSE START
AAEGGGLNUV LUGGAGE
　VAN
AAEGGILNSW GLASWEGIAN

AAEGGILOSU SIALAGOGUE
AAEGGINRSU RAIN GAUGES
AAEGHILLSS GALASHIELS
AAEGHILNPR NEPHRALGIA
AAEGHILORT HAGIOLATER
AAEGHILRTU GAULTHERIA
AAEGHINNNS SHENANIGAN
AAEGHLNOPT HEPTAGONAL
AAEGHLNPRY PHARYNGEAL
AAEGHLNRUX HEXANGULAR
AAEGHMNOPR
　ANEMOGRAPH,
　PHANEROGAM
AAEGHNOPRS ORPHANAGES
AAEGHOPRRY
　AEROGRAPHY, AREOGRAPHY
AAEGHPPPRR GRAPH PAPER
AAEGIILNNT ALIENATING
AAEGIILPRS PLAGIARISE
AAEGIILPRZ PLAGIARIZE
AAEGIINNTV INVAGINATE
AAEGIINRTT INGRATIATE
AAEGIKMNRR EARMARKING
AAEGIKNNSW AWAKENINGS
AAEGILLNOT ALLEGATION
AAEGILLORT LEGATORIAL
AAEGILMNRT MARTINGALE
AAEGILMSTT STALAGMITE
AAEGILNNTT TANGENTIAL
AAEGILNRSV GALVANISER
AAEGILNRVZ GALVANIZER
AAEGILNSWX SEALING WAX
AAEGILNTUV EVALUATING
AAEGILPRTY APTERYGIAL
AAEGIMMNRS MISMANAGER
AAEGIMRRTU MARGUERITA
AAEGIMRSTT MAGISTRATE
AAEGINNOST ANTAGONISE
AAEGINNOTZ ANTAGONIZE
AAEGINNSTU NAUSEATING
AAEGINPRST SEPARATING
AAEGINRSTU GUARANTIES
AAEGINRTTV GRAVETTIAN
AAEGINRTUU INAUGURATE
AAEGIORRTV ARROGATIVE
AAEGIRRTTV GRAVITATER
AAEGKLMRSS
　GLASS-MAKER
AAEGLLPSST PLATE GLASS
AAEGLNNOPT PENTAGONAL
AAEGLNORTT TETRAGONAL
AAEGMNPRST PENTAGRAMS
AAEGMNRSTT TERMAGANTS
AAEGMOPRSU
　RAMPAGEOUS
AAEGMRSSTT STRATAGEMS
AAEGNNNOTT ON A
　TANGENT
AAEGNOPRSS PARSONAGES

AAEGRRSSTZ STARGAZERS
AAEHHINOPT THEOPHANIA
AAEHHJLLLU HALLELUJAH
AAEHHKMNRS
KERMANSHAH
AAEHIILMNS LEISHMANIA
AAEHIILNNT ANNIHILATE
AAEHIIMNNT AMIANTHINE
AAEHIKRRST HAIRSTREAK
AAEHILLOPT PALAEOLITH
AAEHILNOTX EXHALATION
AAEHILNRTX EXHILARANT
AAEHILNSST THESSALIAN
AAEHILNSTV LEVIATHANS
AAEHILPSTT ASPHALTITE
AAEHILPSTW WESTPHALIA
AAEHIMNPSS SEAMANSHIP
AAEHIMNSTY MYASTHENIA
AAEHIMOSST HAEMATOSIS
AAEHIMPRST AMPHIASTER
AAEHIMRSTU AMATEURISH
AAEHINNORV HANOVERIAN
AAEHINOPST ASTHENOPIA
AAEHINPSST PHANTASIES
AAEHIPSTXY ASPHYXIATE
AAEHKLRSST SALT SHAKER
AAEHLLMRRS MARSHALLER
AAEHMNRSST HARASSMENT
AAEHMNRSTV HARVESTMAN
AAEHMORTTX METATHORAX
AAEHMOSTTY
STAY-AT-HOME
AAEHMPRSTT METAPHRAST
AAEHMRSSTU SHAMATEURS
AAEHOPPSTY APOPHYSATE
AAEHRRTTTU ARTHURETTA
AAEIILLPTV PALLIATIVE
AAEIILMMRT IMMATERIAL
AAEIILMNRS SEMINARIAL
AAEIILMSST ASSIMILATE
AAEIILNNOT ALIENATION
AAEIILNPST SAPIENTIAL
AAEIILNSTV INSALIVATE
AAEIIMNNNR RIEMANNIAN
AAEIIMNNRS SEMINARIAN
AAEIIMNNRT MAINTAINER
AAEIIPPRSV APPRAISIVE
AAEIIPRSST PARASITISE
AAEIIPRSTZ PARASITIZE
AAEIKMRSST SAMARSKITE
AAEIKNNRST TRANSKEIAN
AAEILLLLNV VILLANELLA
AAEILLLNPR IN PARALLEL
AAEILLMPRX PREMAXILLA
AAEILLMRTY MATERIALLY
AAEILLNORT RELATIONAL
AAEILLNPSS SAILPLANES
AAEILLNRTU UNILATERAL
AAEILLORTV ALLEVIATOR

AAEILLPSSS PAILLASSES,
PALLIASSES
AAEILLRRTT TRILATERAL
AAEILMNNSU SEMIANNUAL
AAEILMNORT AMELIORANT
AAEILMNPRT PARLIAMENT
AAEILMNPTU MANIPULATE
AAEILMNRTY ALIMENTARY
AAEILMNSST ASSAILMENT
AAEILMPRRT PREMARITAL
AAEILNNOPT NEAPOLITAN
AAEILNNOTV VENATIONAL
AAEILNNRTU LAURENTIAN
AAEILNOORT AREOLATION
AAEILNOQTU EQUATIONAL
AAEILNORST RATIONALES,
SENATORIAL
AAEILNORTT ALTERATION
AAEILNORTU LAUREATION
AAEILNORTX RELAXATION
AAEILNOTTX EXALTATION
AAEILNOTUV EVALUATION
AAEILNRSTT TANTALISER
AAEILNRSTU NATURALISE
AAEILNRTTZ TANTALIZER
AAEILNRTUZ NATURALIZE
AAEILOQRTU EQUATORIAL
AAEILORRTT RETALIATOR
AAEILORSTV LAVATORIES
AAEILSTUXY ASEXUALITY
AAEIMMNRST MAINSTREAM
AAEIMMPRTU AT A PREMIUM
AAEIMMRSTU AMATEURISM
AAEIMNNOPR POMERANIAN
AAEIMNNOST EMANATIONS
AAEIMNNOSY MAYONNAISE
AAEIMNNSSU AMANUENSIS
AAEIMNNTTT ATTAINMENT
AAEIMNOORT EROTOMANIA
AAEIMNORST ANATOMISER
AAEIMNORTZ ANATOMIZER
AAEIMNRSTW WATER MAINS
AAEIMNRTTT ANTIMATTER
AAEIMPRSST SEPARATISM
AAEIMQRSTU MARQUISATE
AAEIMRSTTU TRAUMATISE
AAEIMRTTUV MATURATIVE
AAEIMRTTUZ TRAUMATIZE
AAEIMSSSTT METASTASIS
AAEINNNOTX ANNEXATION
AAEINNOSTU NAUSEATION
AAEINNOTTV ANNOTATIVE
AAEINNQRTU QUARANTINE
AAEINOPRRT REPARATION
AAEINOPRST SEPARATION
AAEINOPSST PASSIONATE
AAEINRRSTV NARRATIVES
AAEINRRSTW WARRANTIES
AAEIOPRTTX EXPATIATOR

AAEIOPSSST APOSTASIES
AAEIOPSSTT APOSTATISE
AAEIOPSTTZ APOSTATIZE
AAEIORSTTV AESTIVATOR
AAEIPRRSTX SEPARATRIX
AAEIPRSSTT SEPARATIST
AAEJKLRSWY JAYWALKERS
AAEKKOSTTT TAKE TO TASK
AAEKMRRSTW
WATERMARKS
AAEKMRSSTT TASKMASTER
AAEKRRSTUU SAUERKRAUT
AAELLLMNOS SALMONELLA
AAELLLORST SALTARELLO
AAELLMNRTY MATERNALLY
AAELLMORTT MARTELLATO
AAELLMORZZ MOZZARELLA
AAELLNOPRS SOLAR PANEL
AAELLNPRTY PATERNALLY,
PRENATALLY
AAELLNPSTY PLEASANTLY
AAELLPPRSW WALLPAPERS
AAELLRSTTT TATTERSALL
AAELMNNORT ORNAMENTAL
AAELMNOPSU MENOPAUSAL
AAELMNORVV REMOVAL
VAN
AAELMNOSSW
SALESWOMAN
AAELMNRSUY ANEURYSMAL
AAELMRRTUX EXTRAMURAL
AAELNNPSTU UNPLEASANT
AAELNORRTT ALTERNATOR
AAELNPPRTY APPARENTLY
AAELNPRRSU SUPRARENAL
AAELNPRSTT TRANSEPTAL
AAELNPRSTY PLEASANTRY
AAELNRSTUV TRANSVALUE
AAELNSSTTU SULTANATES,
TANTALUSES
AAELOOPSTT APOSTOLATE
AAELORRSSY SOLAR YEARS
AAELPRRTTT RATTLETRAP
AAELSTTTUW STATUTE LAW
AAEMNNORTT
TRAMONTANE
AAEMNNRSTV MANSERVANT
AAEMNOOSST
ANASTOMOSE
AAEMNPRSTT APARTMENTS
AAEMPRSSTT PAST MASTER
AAEMPRSSTY PAYMASTERS
AAEMRSSTTU METATARSUS
AAENORTTTU ATTENUATOR
AAENORTUUV ART
NOUVEAU
AAENQRRTUY QUATERNARY
AAENRRSTTU RESTAURANT
AAEOOPPRSS SOAP OPERAS

AAEOOPRRTV EVAPORATOR
AAEOPRRSST SEPARATORS
AAEPPRRSST SPARE PARTS
AAEQRRSTUW
    QUARTERSAW
AAFFFGLSST FLAGSTAFFS
AAFFGIMNRU RAGAMUFFIN
AAFGGILNVW FLAG-WAVING
AAFGIINNPR FRANGIPANI
AAFGLLNRTY FLAGRANTLY
AAFGLNRRTY FRAGRANTLY
AAFHIINNOS IN A FASHION
AAFIIILRSS FILARIASIS
AAFIILLMRY FAMILIARLY
AAFIILMNRU UNFAMILIAR
AAFILNOOTT FLOATATION
AAFMNORSTW MAN OF
    STRAW
AAGGHINNRU HARANGUING
AAGGIILNTT TAILGATING
AAGGIINNRR ARRAIGNING
AAGGIINNSY GAINSAYING
AAGGIINNTV NAVIGATING
AAGGINNSTT STAGNATING
AAGGINORRT ARROGATING
AAGGINRSTZ STARGAZING
AAGGKLNNPS GANGPLANKS
AAGGLLLOSS GALLOGLASS
AAGGLLNNYY
    YLANG-YLANG
AAGGNNORTU
    ORANGUTANG
AAGHHIMNWY
    HIGHWAYMAN
AAGHHINORT HOGARTHIAN
AAGHIILMNP MALPIGHIAN
AAGHILMNRS MARSHALING
AAGHILNPST ASPHALTING
AAGHILOPPY POLYPHAGIA
AAGHILORTY HAGIOLATRY
AAGHINPRSS SPRINGHAAS
AAGHNOPPRT PANTOGRAPH
AAGHOPRSTU AUTOGRAPHS
AAGHOPRSTY PYTHAGORAS
AAGHOPRTUY
    AUTOGRAPHY
AAGIIKMNNR RAINMAKING
AAGIILNPT PALLIATING
AAGIILMNNT LAMINATING
AAGIILMPRS PLAGIARISM
AAGIILNNPS SALPINGIAN
AAGIILNNUV UNAVAILING
AAGIILNRTV TRAVAILING
AAGIILNSTV SALIVATING
AAGIILPRST PLAGIARIST
AAGIIMNNRT MARINATING
AAGIINNOPT PAGINATION
AAGIINNOTV NAVIGATION
AAGIINOSTT AGITATIONS

AAGIINPPRS APPRAISING
AAGIINPRST ASPIRATING
AAGIJKLNWY JAYWALKING
AAGILLMNRY ALARMINGLY,
    MARGINALLY
AAGILLORSS GLOSSARIAL
AAGILLORST ALLIGATORS
AAGILMNORS ORGANISMAL
AAGILMOPRS PARALOGISM
AAGILNNOQU ALGONQUIAN
AAGILNNOTU ANGULATION
AAGILNOORT GORNO-ALTAI
AAGILNOPRS SPORANGIAL
AAGILNPRSY PARALYSING
AAGILNRRTU TRIANGULAR
AAGILNRTUY ANGULARITY
AAGILNSSTU ASSAULTING
AAGILOPRST PARALOGIST
AAGILOSUVY YUGOSLAVIA
AAGIMMPRST PRAGMATISM
AAGIMNNOST ANTAGONISM
AAGIMNNPRW WARMING
    PAN
AAGIMNOTTU AUTOMATING
AAGIMNPTTU AMPUTATING
AAGIMNSSTY GYMNASIAST
AAGIMPRSTT PRAGMATIST
AAGINNNOTT ANNOTATING
AAGINNOSTT ANTAGONIST,
    STAGNATION
AAGINNRRTW WARRANTING
AAGINNRSUY SANGUINARY
AAGINOORRT ARROGATION
AAGINORSTV NAVIGATORS
AAGINOSSTT GAS STATION
AAGINRRTVY GRAVY TRAIN
AAGINRSTTU ANTITRAGUS,
    SATURATING
AAGLLMOOSU
    ALLOGAMOUS
AAGLLNOPTT TOPGALLANT
AAGLMOOPRR
    POLAROGRAM
AAGLNNOOSX
    ANGLO-SAXON
AAGLNNSTTY STAGNANTLY
AAGLNORRTU GRANULATOR
AAGLNORRTY ARROGANTLY
AAGMOOSTUU
    AUTOGAMOUS
AAGNNNOSTY NANNY
    GOATS
AAGNORRSTU
    GUARANTORS
AAGOOPPRRT PROPAGATOR
AAHHILMOPT OPHTHALMIA
AAHHIMRRTY ARRHYTHMIA
AAHHLORSTT THROATLASH
AAHIIKMNRS KASHMIRIAN

AAHIILNNOT INHALATION
AAHIILNNTU LITHUANIAN
AAHIILNOPS HISPANIOLA
AAHIIMPRSS PHARISAISM
AAHIINNSTY HINAYANIST
AAHILMNSTU MALTHUSIAN
AAHILMTTUZ ALTAZIMUTH
AAHILNNOPT ANTIPHONAL
AAHILOPPSY APOPHYSIAL
AAHILORSTU HAUSTORIAL
AAHIMMNOTY MYTHOMANIA
AAHIMMNSSS SHAMANISMS
AAHIMNSSST SHAMANISTS
AAHINNOTTX XANTHATION
AAHINOPRTW ON A PAR
    WITH
AAHINPSTXY ASPHYXIANT
AAHIPPRSSY PARAPHYSIS
AAHKKNNPYY
    HANKY-PANKY
AAHKLOORSY
    YOSHKAR-OLA
AAHLLMOPSY HYALOPLASM
AAHNOPRTTU NATUROPATH
AAHNORRSTU ANARTHROUS
AAIIILLMNW WILLIAMINA
AAIIILMMNT MILITIAMAN
AAIIILMMNX MAXIMILIAN
AAIIILMNRT LIMITARIAN
AAIIJLNORT JANITORIAL
AAIIKLLNTY ALKALINITY
AAIIKMNNST KANTIANISM
AAIIKNPSST PAKISTANIS
AAIILLNOPT PALLIATION
AAIILMMRST MARTIALISM
AAIILMMSTX MAXIMALIST
AAIILMNNOT ANTIMONIAL,
    LAMINATION
AAIILMRSTT MARTIALIST
AAIILNORRT IRRATIONAL
AAIILNOSTV SALIVATION
AAIILNRSTY SANITARILY
AAIILPRTTY PARTIALITY
AAIILPSTTY SPATIALITY
AAIIMMNRSX MARXIANISM
AAIIMNNOPT IMPANATION
AAIIMNNORT MARINATION
AAIIMNNRSTU SANITARIAN
AAIIMPRSST PARASITISM
AAIINNOSTT SANITATION
AAIINNRRTU RURITANIAN
AAIINNRSTU UNITARIANS
AAIINNRSTY INSANITARY
AAIINOPPRT APPARITION
AAIINOPRST ASPIRATION
AAIINOPRTT TRITANOPIA
AAIINORSTV VARIATIONS
AAIIRSSSTY SATYRIASIS
AAIKLLNOTY ALKYLATION

AAILLNNOTY NATIONALLY
AAILLNNOVV VILLANOVAN
AAILLNOPST SPALLATION
AAILLNORTY RATIONALLY
AAILLRSTUY SALUTARILY
AAILMNOTTU MUTATIONAL
AAILMNRRTU INTRAMURAL
AAILMNRSTU NATURALISM
AAILMOPPRX APPROXIMAL
AAILMPRSSU MARSUPIALS
AAILNNNOTU ANNULATION
AAILNNOOTT NOTATIONAL
AAILNNOPTT PLANTATION
AAILNNOTTU NUTATIONAL
AAILNNPQSU PALANQUINS
AAILNOORTT ROTATIONAL
AAILNOPPST PALPATIONS
AAILNOSTTU SALUTATION
AAILNOSTUV VALUATIONS
AAILNPPPTU AN APT PUPIL
AAILNPRSTU TARPAULINS
AAILNRSTTU NATURALIST
AAILNSSSTU STANISLAUS
AAIMMOSTTU AUTOMATISM
AAIMMRSTTU TRAUMATISM
AAIMNOOTTU AUTOMATION
AAIMNOPTTU AMPUTATION
AAIMNOQSTU SQUAMATION
AAIMNORSTU SANATORIUM
AAIMNORTTU MATURATION
AAIMNOSSTT ANATOMISTS
AAIMNPRSST SPARTANISM
AAIMOSTTTU AUTOMATIST
AAINNNOOST SAN ANTONIO
AAINNNOOTT ANNOTATION
AAINNORRST NARRATIONS
AAINNRSTUY UNSANITARY
AAINOOPPRT PROTANOPIA
AAINOPSTTY PAY STATION
AAINORSTTU SATURATION
AAINORSTTV STARVATION
AAINORSTTY STATIONARY
AAINSSSSTT ASSISTANTS
AAIOPRRSTY ASPIRATORY
AAKKMORRST KRAMATORSK
AAKLMOPRSY KARYOPLASM
AAKLNORSUY ANKYLOSAUR
AAKMMNORSW
   MARKSWOMAN
AALLLLOTWW
   WALL-TO-WALL
AALLMNTUUY AUTUMNALLY
AALLPRSTWY PARTY WALLS
AALLPSSWYY PALSY-WALSY
AALLRSTTWY STALWARTLY
AALMOOPPRS MALAPROPOS
AALMOOPRTY LAPAROTOMY
AALMOPRSXY PAROXYSMAL
AALNNOOPST PANTALOONS

AALNNPRSTT TRANSPLANT
AALNNRRSTU TRANSLUNAR
AALNOOPPRV ON APPROVAL
AALNOOPUZZ POZZUOLANA
AALNOPRRST TRANSPOLAR
AALNORRSTT TRANSLATOR
AALOPRRSTU AUSTRALORP
AALOPRRSTY PORTRAYALS
AALOPSTTUY AUTOPLASTY
AALORSTTUY SALUTATORY
AAMNNOTTTU TANTAMOUNT
AAMNOOSTTU
   AUTOMATONS
AAMOOSSTTU ASTOMATOUS
AAMOOSTTUU
   AUTOMATOUS
AANOOPRSTU ANATROPOUS
AANORSSTTU ASTRONAUTS
AAOOPPRRST PARATROOPS
ABBBDENRRU RUBBER
   BAND
ABBBEEILSU BLUE BABIES
ABBBEGILNR BLABBERING
ABBBEHISSU BUSHBABIES
ABBBELOPSU SOAP BUBBLE
ABBCCDEKMO
   BACKCOMBED
ABBCDEKLOU DOUBLE
   BACK
ABBCDEMRRU
   BREADCRUMB
ABBCDIKLRS BLACKBIRDS
ABBCDKORSU BUCKBOARDS
ABBCEGGHUY BEACH
   BUGGY
ABBCEGINRU BARBECUING
ABBCEIKRST BACKBITERS
ABBCEILMNO COMBINABLE
ABBCEILRSU SUBCALIBRE
ABBCEINSSS SCABBINESS
ABBCEKLLST BLACK BELTS
ABBCEKLOSX BLACK BOXES
ABBCEKLRRY BLACKBERRY
ABBCEKMNRU BACK
   NUMBER
ABBCENORSY ABSORBENCY
ABBCGIIKNT BACKBITING
ABBCGILNRS SCRABBLING
ABBCILPRSU PUBLIC BARS
ABBCKLOOST BOOTBLACKS
ABBDDEEILO ABLE-BODIED
ABBDEEGILR BRIDGEABLE
ABBDEEHLPS PEBBLEDASH
ABBDEEIRRW BARBED WIRE
ABBDEELNNU UNBENDABLE
ABBDEELORU BELABOURED
ABBDEELRSU BLUEBEARDS
ABBDEFIORR FIBREBOARD
ABBDEIMNRY BABY-MINDER

ABBDEIMORR BOMBARDIER
ABBDELLNRU LANDLUBBER
ABBDELMOOZ
   BAMBOOZLED
ABBDELORSY ABSORBEDLY
ABBDELOSSU DOUBLE BASS
ABBDGIMNOR BOMBARDING
ABBDHLOOST BLOODBATHS
ABBDILLORS BILLBOARDS
ABBDKLNOOS BLOOD
   BANKS
ABBDNORSSU BRASSBOUND
ABBEEEILLV BELIEVABLE
ABBEEILLVY BELIEVABLY
ABBEELORSV OBSERVABLE
ABBEELRTTU REBUTTABLE
ABBEENORST BREASTBONE
ABBEENORTW
   BROWBEATEN
ABBEENRTTU BUTTER BEAN
ABBEFILNSS FLABBINESS
ABBEFMORRU FOAM
   RUBBER
ABBEGJLSUU SUBJUGABLE
ABBEHHIKSS SHISH KEBAB
ABBEHINSSS SHABBINESS
ABBEILLMSU SUBLIMABLE
ABBEILMOPR IMPROBABLE
ABBEIRSTTY BABY-SITTER
ABBEKLNOTT BOTTLE BANK
ABBELMOORZ BAMBOOZLER
ABBELMSSUU SUBSUMABLE
ABBELORSVY OBSERVABLY
ABBELOSSTY STABLE BOYS
ABBENORSST ABSORBENTS
ABBFHIIRST RABBITFISH
ABBFHLLSSU FLASHBULBS
ABBFILORST FIBROBLAST
ABBGIINRTT RABBITTING
ABBGILNQSU SQUABBLING
ABBHILMSUU LUBUMBASHI
ABBILMOPRY IMPROBABLY
ABBILORSTU SUBORBITAL
ABBOOPRSTY BOOBY TRAPS
ABBOORRSWY BARROW
   BOYS
ABCCCEMNUY
   ACCUMBENCY
ABCCDEEIRT BRECCIATED
ABCCEEELNS ALBESCENCE
ABCCEEENST TABESCENCE
ABCCEEILMP IMPECCABLE
ABCCEEILSS ACCESSIBLE
ABCCEENRSU BUCCANEERS
ABCCEHILRU CHERUBICAL
ABCCEILMPY IMPECCABLY
ABCCEINOSU SUBOCEANIC
ABCCEJNSUY SUBJACENCY
ABCCELNRSU CARBUNCLES

ABCCGHLSTU CLUTCH BAGS
ABCCHHKNSU
HUNCHBACKS
ABCCHIIMOR CHORIAMBIC
ABCCHIIRRT TRIBRACHIC
ABCCHIKLPT PITCH-BLACK
ABCCHIKSTT BACKSTITCH
ABCCHIKSTW SWITCHBACK
ABCCHIOOPR ACROPHOBIC
ABCCHKLOST BACKCLOTHS
ABCCIMOORT MOBOCRATIC
ABCCINORTU BUCCINATOR
ABCCMOPSTU SUBCOMPACT
ABCCNOOPRY CARBON
COPY
ABCDDKORSU
DUCKBOARDS
ABCDEEEELR DECREEABLE
ABCDEEEELX EXCEEDABLE
ABCDEEEHSU DEBAUCHEES
ABCDEEEILV DECEIVABLE
ABCDEEELLT DELECTABLE
ABCDEEELRT CELEBRATED
ABCDEEELTT DETECTABLE
ABCDEEHLLY BELLYACHED
ABCDEEHRUY DEBAUCHERY
ABCDEEILLN DECLINABLE
ABCDEEILNU INEDUCABLE
ABCDEEILPR PREDICABLE
ABCDEEILPS DESPICABLE
ABCDEEILRT CREDITABLE
ABCDEELLNY BELLY DANCE
ABCDEELLTY DELECTABLY
ABCDEELLUX EXCLUDABLE
ABCDEELORR RECORDABLE
ABCDEFIRTU BIFURCATED
ABCDEFOSTU OBFUSCATED
ABCDEGHINU DEBAUCHING
ABCDEHIILR HERBICIDAL
ABCDEHKLOS BLOCKHEADS
ABCDEHKMPU
HUMPBACKED
ABCDEHLNUW
BUCHENWALD
ABCDEHORSS CHESSBOARD
ABCDEIILNT INDICTABLE
ABCDEIILNV VINDICABLE
ABCDEIIMRT IMBRICATED
ABCDEIIORT ABORTICIDE
ABCDEIIRSS SACRED IBIS
ABCDEIKLRS BACKSLIDER
ABCDEIKOUV BIVOUACKED
ABCDEIKRSS DISC BRAKES
ABCDEILLLU DULCIBELLA
ABCDEILLNU INCLUDABLE
ABCDEILLPU DUPLICABLE
ABCDEILNUY INEDUCABLY
ABCDEILPSY DESPICABLY

ABCDEILRTU LUBRICATED,
TRADUCIBLE
ABCDEILRTY CREDITABLY
ABCDEINORS CARBONISED
ABCDEINORZ CARBONIZED
ABCDELLORY LOCAL DERBY
ABCDELPRUW
PUB-CRAWLED
ABCDEOORRS
SCOREBOARD
ABCDERSTTU SUBTRACTED
ABCDGIKLNO BLOCKADING
ABCDGINNOS ABSCONDING
ABCDGKNORU
BACKGROUND
ABCDHIILNR BRAINCHILD
ABCDHINNRU NUDIBRANCH
ABCDHIOOPR BRACHIOPOD
ABCDHLOORT BROADCLOTH
ABCDHNOPRU
PUNCHBOARD
ABCDHNRSTU DUTCH
BARNS
ABCDIIISTY DIBASICITY
ABCDIILLSY DISYLLABIC
ABCDIIMNOY BIODYNAMIC
ABCDIISTUY SUBACIDITY
ABCDIKLOWW BLACK
WIDOW
ABCDIKOPRR DROP A BRICK
ABCDILLNOO BILL AND COO
ABCDILNOST CNIDOBLAST
ABCDILOPRS CLIPBOARDS
ABCDKLNOSU CLOUDBANKS
ABCDKLOORS ROADBLOCKS
ABCEEEHKRS SCHAERBEEK
ABCEEEIKRR ICEBREAKER
ABCEEEILRV RECEIVABLE
ABCEEEJLRT REJECTABLE
ABCEEELLRR CEREBELLAR
ABCEEELNRS SCREENABLE
ABCEEELPTX EXCEPTABLE,
EXPECTABLE
ABCEEELTUX EXECUTABLE
ABCEEENRUX EXUBERANCE
ABCEEFFORS COFFEE BARS
ABCEEFHNNR FRENCH BEAN
ABCEEFIILN BENEFICIAL
ABCEEFNORT BENEFACTOR
ABCEEGKNRS GREENBACKS
ABCEEHILNR HIBERNACLE
ABCEEHKLPS BLACK SHEEP
ABCEEHKLST SKETCHABLE
ABCEEHKRTU HACKBUTEER
ABCEEHLLSY BELLYACHES
ABCEEHLNQU QUENCHABLE
ABCEEHNORR
ABHORRENCE
ABCEEHORSU HERBACEOUS

ABCEEIILLT ELICITABLE
ABCEEIJLNT INJECTABLE
ABCEEILLNR RECLINABLE
ABCEEILLNS LICENSABLE
ABCEEILLOT BIOCELLATE
ABCEEILLPX EXPLICABLE
ABCEEILMMT EMBLEMATIC
ABCEEILNNU ENUNCIABLE
ABCEEILNOT NOTICEABLE
ABCEEILNTU BINUCLEATE
ABCEEILPTZ PECTIZABLE
ABCEEILRTX EXTRICABLE
ABCEEINNOZ BENZOCAINE
ABCEEINNST ABSTINENCE
ABCEEINOSS OBEISANCES
ABCEEKLOPT POCKETABLE
ABCEEKRSTT BACK STREET
ABCEEKSTTU BUCKET SEAT
ABCEELLNOS ENCLOSABLE
ABCEELLORT BROCATELLE
ABCEELLPUX EXCULPABLE
ABCEELLRRY CEREBRALLY
ABCEELNNOV CONVENABLE
ABCEELNORS CENSORABLE
ABCEELNOVY CONVEYABLE
ABCEELNRSU CENSURABLE
ABCEELOPRU RECOUPABLE
ABCEELOPRW PACE
BOWLER
ABCEELORRT CELEBRATOR
ABCEEMMRST
CAMEMBERTS
ABCEEMOOTY
AMOEBOCYTE
ABCEENORSV OBSERVANCE
ABCEENRRTY BARYCENTRE
ABCEEOPPRS SPACE PROBE
ABCEEPRRSU CUPBEARERS
ABCEFHLSSU FLASHCUBES
ABCEFHOSTW FOB
WATCHES
ABCEFLNOSU CONFUSABLE
ABCEGIKLNN BLACKENING
ABCEGIKNRT BRACKETING
ABCEGILMNR CLAMBERING
ABCEGILNOZ COGNIZABLE
ABCEGINNNY BENIGNANCY
ABCEGJLNOU CONJUGABLE
ABCEGLNOOT CONGLOBATE
ABCEHHJOTT HATCHET JOB
ABCEHIIRST HEBRAISTIC
ABCEHILPRT BIRTHPLACE
ABCEHILRST CHRISTABEL
ABCEHILSTW SWITCHABLE
ABCEHINRRY CHINABERRY
ABCEHIOOPR AEROPHOBIC
ABCEHKLLOS BLACK HOLES
ABCEHKMNRS BENCH
MARKS

ABCEHKORSY CHEBOKSARY
ABCEHLLOTT TABLECLOTH
ABCEHMMNRU MACH NUMBER
ABCEHMOPRT CHAMBER POT
ABCEHMOSTX MATCHBOXES
ABCEHORTTX CHATTERBOX
ABCEIILLMT BIMETALLIC
ABCEIILLNN INCLINABLE
ABCEIILLNR BRILLIANCE
ABCEIILMTU UMBILICATE
ABCEIILPST EPIBLASTIC
ABCEIINTUV INCUBATIVE
ABCEIIOORT AEROBIOTIC
ABCEIKLRRY BRICKLAYER
ABCEILLNOU INOCULABLE
ABCEILLNPU INCULPABLE
ABCEILLNRS CRANESBILL
ABCEILLPXY EXPLICABLY
ABCEILLSSU CASUS BELLI
ABCEILLTUV CULTIVABLE
ABCEILMOPT COMPATIBLE
ABCEILNOSU UNSOCIABLE
ABCEILNOTY NOTICEABLY
ABCEILNPRU REPUBLICAN
ABCEILNRRU INCURRABLE
ABCEILPRSU RES PUBLICA
ABCEIMOORT COIMBATORE
ABCEIMORRT BAROMETRIC
ABCEINRRST TRANSCRIBE
ABCEIORSUU RUBIACEOUS
ABCEJKLMRU LUMBERJACK
ABCEKKORST BACKSTROKE
ABCEKLLNOU UNLOCKABLE
ABCEKLNORU COALBUNKER
ABCEKLOPRW BLACK POWER
ABCEKLRTTU TURTLEBACK
ABCELLLORU BLUE-COLLAR
ABCELLNOOR COLLARBONE
ABCELLNOOS CONSOLABLE
ABCELLOORU COLOURABLE
ABCELLOOST BLASTOCOEL
ABCELLRSSW SCREWBALLS
ABCELMMNOO COMMONABLE
ABCELMMOTU COMMUTABLE
ABCELMNRSU UNSCRAMBLE
ABCELMOPTU COMPUTABLE
ABCELNORRY BARLEYCORN
ABCELNOSST CONSTABLES
ABCELRRTUU TUBERCULAR
ABCEMNOPRU PERNAMBUCO
ABCEMOOPRT AMBOCEPTOR
ABCENNSTUY SUBTENANCY

ABCENSSSTU SUBSTANCES
ABCERRSTTU SUBTRACTER
ABCFGIIKNR BACKFIRING
ABCFILMORU BACULIFORM
ABCGGIKPSY PIGGYBACKS
ABCGHIINOT COHABITING
ABCGHIIOPR BIOGRAPHIC
ABCGHLORYY BRACHYLOGY
ABCGIILLOO BIOLOGICAL
ABCGIINNTU INCUBATING
ABCGILMNRS SCRAMBLING
ABCGIMNOTT COMBATTING
ABCHHIOPRS ARCHBISHOP
ABCHIILLNS CHILBLAINS
ABCHIILMOP AMPHIBOLIC
ABCHIKLMST BLACKSMITH
ABCHIKLRST BLACKSHIRT
ABCHKLNORT BLACKTHORN
ABCHKMSTTU THUMBTACKS
ABCHKORSTW THROWBACKS
ABCHLLNPSU PUNCH BALLS
ABCIIINOTT ANTIBIOTIC
ABCIIJMOST JACOBITISM
ABCIILLNRY BRILLIANCY
ABCIILLSST BALLISTICS
ABCIILMOPS BIOPLASMIC
ABCIILRTUY CURABILITY
ABCIINNOTU INCUBATION
ABCIINOSSS ABSCISSION
ABCIIOSSTT BIOSTATICS
ABCIKLLSST BLACKLISTS
ABCILMOPTY COMPATIBLY
ABCILMOSUX MUSICAL BOX
ABCILMRUUV VIBRACULUM
ABCILMSSTY CYMBALISTS
ABCILNORSU BINOCULARS
ABCILNRSTU LUBRICANTS
ABCILORRTU LUBRICATOR
ABCILPSTUY SUBTYPICAL
ABCIMMOPRU PROCAMBIUM
ABCINORSTU INCUBATORS
ABCIORRRTU RUBRICATOR
ABCKKNOOTU KNOCKABOUT
ABCKLOPSST BLACK SPOTS
ABCKNPRTUY BANKRUPTCY
ABCKOOPRSS SCRAPBOOKS
ABCLOORRSU COLOUR BARS
ABCLORRTUU LUCUBRATOR
ABCLORRTUY ROTARY CLUB
ABCLOSSTTY BLASTOCYST
ABCNORSTTY BY CONTRAST
ABDDEEEFLN DEFENDABLE
ABDDEEEHNO BONEHEADED
ABDDEEEELNP DEPENDABLE
ABDDEEGGLR BEDRAGGLED
ABDDEEGHIR BRIDGEHEAD

ABDDEEHLLU BULLHEADED
ABDDEEKORY KEYBOARDED
ABDDEELNPY DEPENDABLY
ABDDEELOTU DOUBLE DATE
ABDDEEPRSS BEDSPREADS
ABDDEERSTY TEDDY BEARS
ABDDEGINRU UNABRIDGED
ABDDEGIRRW DRAWBRIDGE
ABDDEHHINN BEHINDHAND
ABDDEHILNR HILDEBRAND
ABDDEHILOR HARD-BOILED
ABDDEHINRS BRANDISHED
ABDDEHMOTU BAD-MOUTHED
ABDDEIIMRS BRIDESMAID
ABDDEILLLS SADDLEBILL
ABDDEILNST BLIND DATES
ABDDEIORSS BROADSIDES, SIDEBOARDS
ABDDELNORR BORDERLAND
ABDDELNRTU BLADDERNUT
ABDDGIINNS DISBANDING
ABDDGORSUY BODYGUARDS
ABDDLMOORU MOULDBOARD
ABDDOORRSW BROADSWORD
ABDEEEELMR REDEEMABLE
ABDEEEFHRT FEATHER BED
ABDEEEFILS DEFEASIBLE
ABDEEEFLRR DEFERRABLE
ABDEEEGGLR BARELEGGED
ABDEEEGGRW BEGGARWEED
ABDEEEHQTU BEQUEATHED
ABDEEEILMR REMEDIABLE
ABDEEEILRT DELIBERATE
ABDEEELLPT DEPLETABLE
ABDEEELMRY REDEEMABLY
ABDEEELNPX EXPENDABLE
ABDEEELNRR RENDERABLE
ABDEEELNRT TENDERABLE
ABDEEELSTT DETESTABLE
ABDEEEMNST DEBASEMENT
ABDEEENRTT BERNADETTE
ABDEEERSTW SWEETBREAD
ABDEEFFHLU BUFFLEHEAD
ABDEEFHLRS HALF-BREEDS
ABDEEFHNOR BEFOREHAND
ABDEEFIITU BEAUTIFIED
ABDEEFLMOR DEFORMABLE
ABDEEFLNRU REFUNDABLE
ABDEEFORRS FREEBOARDS
ABDEEGILNS DESIGNABLE
ABDEEGLORT GOLD-BEATER
ABDEEHIKNR BIRKENHEAD
ABDEEHILLS DÉSHABILLÉ
ABDEEHILRR HALBERDIER

ABDEEHIMRT TIMBERHEAD
ABDEEHIMSV MISBEHAVED
ABDEEHINRT HIBERNATED
ABDEEHLMPS BLASPHEMED
ABDEEHLOTT TABLE D'HÔTE
ABDEEHORST BROADSHEET
ABDEEIILTT DEBILITATE
ABDEEIINRT INEBRIATED
ABDEEIKNNY KIDNEY BEAN
ABDEEILMRY REMEDIABLY
ABDEEILMTT TIMETABLED
ABDEEILNNU UNDENIABLE
ABDEEILNRS BREADLINES
ABDEEILPRU REPUDIABLE
ABDEEILPRV DEPRIVABLE
ABDEEILRSV VERBALISED
ABDEEILRVZ VERBALIZED
ABDEEINNRR BERNARDINE
ABDEEIRRVW WEAVERBIRD
ABDEEISTTU BEATITUDES
ABDEEKLOTU DOUBLE TAKE
ABDEEKORRY KEYBOARDER
ABDEELLOPR DEPLORABLE
ABDEELLORS SOLDERABLE
ABDEELLSTY SELL-BY DATE
ABDEELMNOZ EMBLAZONED
ABDEELMRRU DEMURRABLE
ABDEELNOPR PONDERABLE
ABDEELNORS
   BANDOLEERS, ENDORSABLE
ABDEELNSST STEEL BANDS
ABDEELOPRT DEPORTABLE
ABDEELORTT BATTLEDORE
ABDEELSTTY DETESTABLY
ABDEEMRRSU
   EMBRASURED
ABDEENOPSU SUBPOENAED
ABDEENPRRY PREBENDARY
ABDEENRRST BARTENDERS
ABDEENSTTU DEBUTANTES
ABDEEOPSST SPEEDBOATS
ABDEERRSST REDBREASTS
ABDEFFGLSU DUFFEL BAGS
ABDEFFORSS BRASSED OFF
ABDEFIILMO MODIFIABLE
ABDEFILMOR FORMIDABLE
ABDEFINRRS FIREBRANDS
ABDEFIRRTU BREADFRUIT
ABDEGGIRRU BUDGERIGAR
ABDEGGNOOT
   TOBOGGANED
ABDEGHINSU SUBHEADING
ABDEGIMNRT ABRIDGMENT
ABDEGINNOR BROADENING
ABDEGJSTUU SUBJUGATED
ABDEGLNNRU
   BURGENLAND
ABDEGNNRUU
   GRAUBUNDEN

ABDEHIILLS DISHABILLE
ABDEHINRRS BRANDISHER
ABDEHINRTT HARD-BITTEN
ABDEHIORTW WHITEBOARD
ABDEHLOSTW DEATHBLOWS
ABDEHMNNSU
   HUSBANDMEN
ABDEHNORTU EARTHBOUND
ABDEHNRSTU SUBTRAHEND
ABDEHORRST SHORTBREAD
ABDEIIKLLS DISLIKABLE
ABDEIILMSS ADMISSIBLE
ABDEIILSST STABILISED
ABDEIILSTZ STABILIZED
ABDEIINOST ANTIBODIES
ABDEIKNRSW WINDBREAKS
ABDEILLLNY BLIND ALLEY
ABDEILMSTU SUBLIMATED
ABDEILNNUW UNWINDABLE
ABDEILNNUY UNDENIABLY
ABDEILOPSS DISPOSABLE
ABDEILPSTU DISPUTABLE
ABDEILRRSY EARLY BIRDS
ABDEILRSTU BRUTALISED
ABDEILRTTW WATTLEBIRD
ABDEILRTUZ BRUTALIZED
ABDEIMNRST DISBARMENT
ABDEIMNSTU SUBMEDIANT
ABDEIMRRTY TIMBERYARD
ABDEIMRTUW DUMBWAITER
ABDEINORSU BOUNDARIES
ABDEIRRSTW WATER BIRDS
ABDEIRTTTU ATTRIBUTED
ABDEJORSTT OBJETS D'ART
ABDEKLLNOR BANKROLLED
ABDEKLLOTU DOUBLE-TALK
ABDEKLOPRU DOUBLE-PARK
ABDEKNORSW
   BREAKDOWNS
ABDEKNPRTU BANKRUPTED
ABDELLNOSW SNOWBALLED
ABDELLOPRY DEPLORABLY
ABDELLORUY LABOUREDLY
ABDELMORST BLASTODERM
ABDELMRRUY LUMBERYARD
ABDELNORTU ROUND-TABLE
ABDELOOORT BOOTLOADER
ABDELORSUV BOULEVARDS
ABDELORTUY OBDURATELY
ABDENRRSST ST BERNARDS
ABDENRSSTY BYSTANDERS
ABDENSSTUY SUNDAY BEST
ABDERRTTYY DRY BATTERY
ABDFILMORY FORMIDABLY
ABDFILNORU FLORIBUNDA
ABDFINSSTU IFS AND BUTS
ABDFLOOORR FLOORBOARD
ABDFORRSSU SURFBOARDS
ABDGHINNSU HUSBANDING

ABDGIINPRU UPBRAIDING
ABDGIINRRS DISBARRING
ABDGIINSSU DISABUSING
ABDGINNRUU BURGUNDIAN
ABDGINORTU GROUND BAIT
ABDHILMOOR RHOMBOIDAL
ABDHIOPRSS SHIPBOARDS
ABDIIILSTY DISABILITY
ABDIIILTUY AUDIBILITY
ABDIIKNNRY BRADYKININ
ABDIILMNOU ALBUMINOID
ABDIILORRT TAILORBIRD
ABDIILPTUY DUPABILITY
ABDIILRTUY DURABILITY
ABDIINOTTU DUBITATION
ABDIIRSSUY SUBSIDIARY
ABDILNOOST BLOODSTAIN
ABDILNORSU SUBORDINAL
ABDILOORTY BOTRYOIDAL
ABDILPSTUY DISPUTABLY
ABDIMPQSSU DAMP SQUIBS
ABDINOSWWY BAY
   WINDOWS
ABDINRSSTW WRISTBANDS
ABDLMOORYY BLOODY
   MARY
ABDMOOORRS
   BOARDROOMS
ABDNOORTUU
   ROUNDABOUT
ABDOORRTUU
   TROUBADOUR
ABEEEEFRST BEEFEATERS
ABEEEERSSZ SEA BREEZES
ABEEEFLPRR PREFERABLE
ABEEEGGLRS SEGREGABLE
ABEEEGLSTV VEGETABLES
ABEEEGNNRS GREEN BEANS
ABEEEHITTV HEBETATIVE
ABEEEHLSSW WHEELBASES
ABEEEHQRTU BEQUEATHER
ABEEEHRSTT HARTEBEEST
ABEEEIKRRT TIEBREAKER
ABEEEIILRV RELIEVABLE
ABEEEILRVW REVIEWABLE
ABEEELLLPX EXPELLABLE
ABEEELLNVY ABNEY LEVEL
ABEEELLSTT SETTLEABLE
ABEEELMPRT TEMPERABLE
ABEEELMRSS REASSEMBLE
ABEEELNPRT PENETRABLE
ABEEELQSUZ SQUEEZABLE
ABEEELRRSV RESERVABLE
ABEEENNOZZ AZOBENZENE
ABEEENNRTT BANNERETTE
ABEEEORSTT STEREOBATE
ABEEERRTTV VERTEBRATE
ABEEFFLMNT BAFFLEMENT
ABEEFFLRSU SUFFERABLE

ABEEFGINRS FREE-BASING
ABEEFIILRV VERIFIABLE
ABEEFIKRRS FIREBREAKS
ABEEFILLLR REFILLABLE
ABEEFILLRT FILTERABLE
ABEEFILNTT FLEA-BITTEN
ABEEFILRSS BAS-RELIEFS
ABEEFIRRSU FEBRUARIES
ABEEFLOPRR PERFORABLE
ABEEFLPRRY PREFERABLY
ABEEFLSTTY SAFETY BELT
ABEEGHNORU
    HAUBERGEON
ABEEGHNTTU BEAT THE
    GUN
ABEEGIKNPS BESPEAKING
ABEEGILLNY EYEBALLING
ABEEGILMNR GERMINABLE
ABEEGILNOT NEGOTIABLE
ABEEGILNRT INTEGRABLE
ABEEGIMNRS BESMEARING
ABEEGINRSU AUBERGINES
ABEEGLNORV GOVERNABLE
ABEEGLOPRS BARGE POLES
ABEEGNRSTT ABSTERGENT
ABEEHHRRTY HEATHBERRY
ABEEHILLRS RELISHABLE
ABEEHILPRS PERISHABLE
ABEEHIMRSV MISBEHAVER
ABEEHINOTT HEBETATION
ABEEHKNORS BONESHAKER
ABEEHKORSS BRAKE SHOES
ABEEHLMPRS BLASPHEMER
ABEEHMORTT BATHOMETER
ABEEHNORSU OBERHAUSEN
ABEEHOORRS SEBORRHOEA
ABEEHORSTU HEREABOUTS
ABEEHPRRSY BARYSPHERE
ABEEIILLMN ELIMINABLE
ABEEIILLRS LIBERALISE
ABEEIILLRZ LIBERALIZE
ABEEIILNPX INEXPIABLE
ABEEIILNTV INEVITABLE
ABEEIILSST BESTIALISE
ABEEIILSTZ BESTIALIZE
ABEEIINRST INEBRIATES
ABEEIIRSST BESTIARIES
ABEEILLMNR BELLARMINE
ABEEILLMOR MELIORABLE
ABEEILLNNT TABLE LINEN
ABEEILLNRU UNRELIABLE
ABEEILLNST LISTENABLE
ABEEILLNTV VENTILABLE
ABEEILLRTT LITTLE BEAR
ABEEILMNRT TERMINABLE
ABEEILMNSU ALBUMENISE
ABEEILMNUZ ALBUMENIZE
ABEEILMOST METABOLISE
ABEEILMOTT METABOLITE

ABEEILMOTZ METABOLIZE
ABEEILMRTT REMITTABLE
ABEEILMSSS ASSEMBLIES
ABEEILMSTT TIMETABLES
ABEEILNNUV UNENVIABLE
ABEEILNOPR INOPERABLE
ABEEILNORX INEXORABLE
ABEEILNPSX EXPANSIBLE
ABEEILNRSS BLEARINESS
ABEEILNRST EAST BERLIN,
    INSERTABLE
ABEEILNRTU REUNITABLE
ABEEILNRWY BARLEY WINE
ABEEILNSTV INVESTABLE
ABEEILORTT OBLITERATE
ABEEILPPTZ PEPTIZABLE
ABEEILPRRS RESPIRABLE
ABEEILQRRU REQUIRABLE
ABEEILQRTU REQUITABLE
ABEEILRRSV VERBALISER
ABEEILRRVZ VERBALIZER
ABEEILRSST ASSERTIBLE
ABEEILRSSU REISSUABLE
ABEEILSSTT BEASTLIEST
ABEEIRRSSS BRASSERIES,
    BRASSIERES
ABEEJLLMSU JUMBLE SALE
ABEEJLLNSY JELLY BEANS
ABEEJMMNNT ENJAMBMENT
ABEEKLNRSV BLANK VERSE
ABEEKLNTTW WET BLANKET
ABEEKMMNNT
    EMBANKMENT
ABEEKMMNRT
    EMBARKMENT
ABEEKNOPST KEEP TABS ON
ABEELLMNTU ANTEBELLUM
ABEELLMOPY EMPLOYABLE
ABEELLNRUV VULNERABLE
ABEELLORSV RESOLVABLE
ABEELLORVV REVOLVABLE
ABEELLPRUV PULVERABLE
ABEELMMMNT
    EMBALMMENT
ABEELMNRST RESEMBLANT
ABEELMNRSU
    LEBENSRAUM, MENSURABLE
ABEELMNTTT BATTLEMENT
ABEELMORST BLASTOMERE
ABEELMPRSU PRESUMABLE
ABEELNOPRS PERSONABLE
ABEELNRRTU RETURNABLE
ABEELNSSST STABLENESS
ABEELOPRRT REPORTABLE
ABEELOPRRV REPROVABLE
ABEELOPRTX EXPORTABLE
ABEELORRST RESTORABLE
ABEELPSTTU UPSETTABLE
ABEELRSUVY SURVEYABLE

ABEEMORRST BAROMETERS
ABEEMRRSSU EMBRASURES
ABEENNNRRU RUNNER
    BEAN
ABEENNRRSS BARRENNESS
ABEENNRSSU URBANENESS
ABEENNRSSZ BRAZENNESS
ABEENORRTW
    WATERBORNE
ABEENORSSS BARONESSES
ABEEOPRRRT REPROBATER
ABEEOPRRST REPROBATES
ABEEOPRSSW POWER
    BASES
ABEFFGILRU FEBRIFUGAL
ABEFFILLOR BILL OF FARE
ABEFGIINTY BEATIFYING
ABEFGILORV FORGIVABLE
ABEFGILRSS FIBREGLASS,
    GLASS FIBRE
ABEFGINORR FORBEARING
ABEFHIRRTT AFTERBIRTH
ABEFIILLLN INFALLIBLE
ABEFIILNOT NOTIFIABLE
ABEFILLLOS BILL OF SALE
ABEFILMORR MORAL FIBRE
ABEFILOPRT PROFITABLE
ABEFKNORRT BREAKFRONT
ABEFLLLOOW FOLLOWABLE
ABEFLLLORW BALLFLOWER
ABEFLLOORT FOOTBALLER
ABEFLLOSTU FAT-SOLUBLE
ABEFNNORUZ BENZOFURAN
ABEGGIMNOR EMBARGOING
ABEGGNOORT
    TOBOGGANER
ABEGGNOPSS SPONGE
    BAGS
ABEGHILNRT BLATHERING
ABEGHINRRS HARBINGERS
ABEGHIOPRR BIOGRAPHER
ABEGHLLLUY BELLY LAUGH
ABEGHLNOOP ANGLOPHOBE
ABEGHMRRSU
    HAMBURGERS
ABEGHNRRSU BUSHRANGER
ABEGHQSUUU
    USQUEBAUGH
ABEGIILNNT INTANGIBLE
ABEGIILNOR OIL-BEARING
ABEGIILNRT LIBERATING
ABEGIILOTV OBLIGATIVE
ABEGIINNRT BRIGANTINE
ABEGIINORS ABORIGINES
ABEGIINOST ABIOGENIST
ABEGIKLNNT BLANKETING
ABEGILLNTY BLEATINGLY
ABEGILMNSS ASSEMBLING
ABEGILNSSU SUBLEASING

ABEGILRRSU BURGLARIES
ABEGINNOTY BAYONETING
ABEGINNQTU BANQUETING
ABEGINNRST STRING BEAN
ABEGINRSTU GAS TURBINE
ABEGKRSSTU GRUBSTAKES
ABEGLLNOOY BALNEOLOGY
ABEGLNORRY LOGANBERRY
ABEGLNORSU LOUNGE
   BARS
ABEGLOOSTZ GO TO BLAZES
ABEGLORRRV VORARLBERG
ABEGMNOORS
   BOOMERANGS
ABEGMORSUU
   UMBRAGEOUS
ABEGNNSTTU SUBTANGENT
ABEGNOORTU BATON
   ROUGE
ABEHHILLST SHEATHBILL
ABEHHIOOPT THEOPHOBIA
ABEHHMMRSU
   BUSHHAMMER
ABEHHORRTT HEARTTHROB
ABEHIILMNT HABILIMENT
ABEHIKLNRS SHRINKABLE
ABEHILNPSU PUNISHABLE
ABEHILOPST HOSPITABLE
ABEHILPSTT BATTLESHIP
ABEHILPSTU BISULPHATE
ABEHILRSST HERBALISTS
ABEHIMNNST BANISHMENT
ABEHINNORT ON THE BRAIN
ABEHINOOPX XENOPHOBIA
ABEHINOPRV VIBRAPHONE
ABEHINORRT HIBERNATOR
ABEHINRSSS BRASHINESS
ABEHIRRSTT BIRTH-RATES
ABEHKOOPRS PHRASEBOOK
ABEHLMOOST SMOOTHABLE
ABEHLNOORU
   HONOURABLE
ABEHLOPRSY HYPERBOLAS
ABEHLORRTY LAY BROTHER
ABEHLORSTT BETROTHALS
ABEHLORTTU BLUETHROAT
ABEHMORTTY BATHOMETRY
ABEHMRSSTU BUSHMASTER
ABEHMRTTYY BATHYMETRY
ABEHNRSSTU SUNBATHERS
ABEHOOSSTU
   BOATHOUSES, HOUSEBOATS
ABEIIILMNT INIMITABLE
ABEIIILNSS SENSIBILIA
ABEIIILLMRS LIBERALISM
ABEIIILLNNY BIENNIALLY
ABEIIILLNOV INVIOLABLE
ABEIIILLRST LIBERALIST
ABEIIILLRTY LIBERALITY

ABEIIILLTUZ UTILIZABLE
ABEIILMNSS LESBIANISM
ABEIILMPRT IMPARTIBLE
ABEIILMRST BIMESTRIAL
ABEIILNORT LIBERATION
ABEIILNPRS INSPIRABLE
ABEIILNTTU INTUITABLE
ABEIILNTTY TENABILITY
ABEIILNTVY INEVITABLY
ABEIILQTUY EQUABILITY
ABEIILRSST STABILISER
ABEIILRSTZ STABILIZER
ABEIILSTTY BESTIALITY
ABEIINNRRT INTERBRAIN
ABEIINNRSS BRAININESS
ABEIINRRSV RIVER BASIN
ABEIIOORSS AEROBIOSIS
ABEIIORSTU OBITUARIES
ABEIKNSTUZ UZBEKISTAN
ABEILLMSTU STIMULABLE
ABEILLNOSV INSOLVABLE
ABEILLPPSU SUPPLIABLE
ABEILLPSTU STIPULABLE
ABEILLSUXY BISEXUALLY
ABEILMMOST METABOLISM
ABEILMNNRU MELBURNIAN
ABEILMNQRU LAMBREQUIN
ABEILMOOTU AUTOMOBILE
ABEILMOPRV IMPROVABLE
ABEILMRSSU SURMISABLE
ABEILMSSTU SUBLIMATES
ABEILNNOOW ON A
   BOWLINE
ABEILNORXY INEXORABLY
ABEILNSTUU UNSUITABLE
ABEILOPRRV PROVERBIAL
ABEILOPSTU BIPETALOUS
ABEILOPSTY POLYBASITE
ABEILORRST LIBERATORS
ABEILORTVY ABORTIVELY
ABEILRRTTU TRITURABLE
ABEILRSTUV VESTIBULAR
ABEILRSUVV SURVIVABLE
ABEIMMOQUZ MOZAMBIQUE
ABEIMNNOTT OBTAINMENT
ABEIMNNORTU TAMBOURINE
ABEIMNRRSU SUBMARINER
ABEIMNRSSU SUBMARINES
ABEIMOSSTU ABSTEMIOUS
ABEINNORTU EBURNATION
ABEINNOSTT ABSTENTION
ABEINNRSSW BRAWNINESS
ABEINORTTX EXORBITANT
ABEINRSSSS BRASSINESS
ABEIOPPRSY PRESBYOPIA
ABEIOPRSTV ABSORPTIVE
ABEIOSSSST ASBESTOSIS
ABEIPRSTTY BAPTISTERY
ABEIRRRSST BARRISTERS

ABEIRRTTTU ATTRIBUTER
ABEIRSTTTU ATTRIBUTES
ABEKKMOORS
   BOOKMAKERS
ABEKKORSTW
   BASKETWORK, WORKBASKET
ABEKLLORWY YELLOWBARK
ABEKLNNOUW
   UNKNOWABLE
ABEKLNORUW
   UNWORKABLE
ABEKLOOPST BOOKPLATES
ABEKLOPRRR PORK BARREL
ABEKMNNOTU
   MOUNTEBANK
ABEKNOPRRW
   PAWNBROKER
ABEKORRSTW
   BREASTWORK
ABELLLLOVY VOLLEYBALL
ABELLNRUVY VULNERABLY
ABELLORVVY REVOLVABLY
ABELLOSTUY ABSOLUTELY
ABELLSSSUY SYLLABUSES
ABELMMNOSU
   SUMMONABLE
ABELMNORYZ EMBLAZONRY
ABELMOOPRT PROMOTABLE
ABELMPRSUY PRESUMABLY
ABELNNORUV VERBAL
   NOUN
ABELNOOPST TABLESPOON
ABELNOPRSY PERSONABLY
ABELNORSTU NEUROBLAST
ABELNRRTUU NURTURABLE
ABELNRSSTU SUBALTERNS
ABELNRSTTU TURNTABLES
ABELOOPPRS PROPOSABLE
ABELOOPRST BLASTOPORE
ABELOOSSTT OSTEOBLAST
ABELOPPSSU SUPPOSABLE
ABELPRRTUU RUPTURABLE
ABEMMNORSU
   MEMBRANOUS
ABEMNNOSTU
   SUBMONTANE
ABEMNOORRW BONE
   MARROW, MARROWBONE
ABENNSSTTU SUBTENANTS
ABENOPRRSS PRESS BARON
ABENOPRSTU BEANSPROUT
ABENORRRTW
   BARRENWORT
ABENPRSSTU ABRUPTNESS
ABEOOPRSTW
   POWERBOATS
ABEOPSTTUY BEAUTY SPOT
ABEOQSSUUU SUBAQUEOUS
ABERRRSTWY STRAWBERRY

ABERSTTTUW WATER BUTTS
ABFGILNOTY FLYING BOAT
ABFGILORVY FORGIVABLY
ABFGNOORRU GO FOR A
    BURN
ABFIIILRTY FRIABILITY
ABFIILLLNY INFALLIBLY
ABFIILNORV RIBOFLAVIN
ABFILOPRTY PROFITABLY
ABFLLOSTUY BOASTFULLY
ABFLLOSUUY FABULOUSLY
ABGGGILNRY BRAGGINGLY
ABGGIILNOT OBLIGATING
ABGGIKNPSY PIGGYBANKS
ABGHIIINNT INHABITING
ABGHIILNOS ABOLISHING
ABGHIJNORS JOBSHARING
ABGHINNSTU SUNBATHING
ABGHINORRU HARBOURING
ABGHIORTTU RIGHTABOUT
ABGHIRRRSU HARRISBURG
ABGHOORRUY
    YARBOROUGH
ABGIIILNNT NAIL-BITING
ABGIILLNSU BILINGUALS
ABGIILNNTY INTANGIBLY
ABGIILNOOT OBLIGATION
ABGIILNOPR PARBOILING
ABGIINNOTZ BOTANIZING
ABGILLNNOO BALLOONING
ABGILLNSUU SUBLINGUAL
ABGILLOSST GLOBALISTS
ABGILLOSTY BILLY GOATS
ABGILMOSUY BIGAMOUSLY
ABGILNOSTY BOASTINGLY
ABGILOORTY OBLIGATORY
ABGINNORRT BARRINGTON
ABGINOORTW ROWING
    BOAT
ABGINORTUV OUTBRAVING
ABGJOORRTU OBJURGATOR
ABGJORSTUU SUBJUGATOR
ABGLLORUUU LULUABOURG
ABGORRSSTU STRASBOURG
ABHHNORSSW HASH
    BROWNS
ABHIIMOPSU AMPHIBIOUS
ABHIKMRRST BIRTHMARKS
ABHILMNSTU THUMBNAILS
ABHILNRSTY LABYRINTHS
ABHILOPSTY HOSPITABLY
ABHILORTUW WHIRLABOUT
ABHIMNOOOP MONOPHOBIA
ABHINPRSTU PAINTBRUSH
ABHLLMSTTU THUMBSTALL
ABHLNOORUY
    HONOURABLY
ABHMNORRTU
    RHUMBATRON

ABIIILLPTY PLIABILITY
ABIIILLTVY LIVABILITY
ABIIILMNTY INIMITABLY
ABIIILMTXY MIXABILITY
ABIIILNOST SIBILATION
ABIIINOSST ANTIBIOSIS
ABIIJLNOTU JUBILATION
ABIILLMNSU SUBLIMINAL
ABIILLOTVY LOVABILITY
ABIILMOTVY MOVABILITY
ABIILMTTUY MUTABILITY
ABIILNOTTY NOTABILITY
ABIILOPTTY POTABILITY
ABIIMORSSV BRAVISSIMO
ABIINNOTTU INTUBATION
ABIINORSTV VIBRATIONS
ABIINOTTTU TITUBATION
ABIIORSTTU OBITUARIST
ABIJLLNTUY JUBILANTLY
ABIKKNSTUY AKTYUBINSK
ABIKLNNOPT POINT-BLANK
ABILLNOOST BALLOONIST
ABILLNOOTU LOBULATION
ABILLNOPST BALLPOINTS
ABILMNOSUU ALBUMINOUS
ABILMNOTUX TOXALBUMIN
ABILMOSSTU ABSOLUTISM
ABILNNOORU LABOR UNION
ABILNOOSTU ABSOLUTION
ABILNOTTUU TUBULATION
ABILORSSUU SALUBRIOUS
ABILOSSTUY SABULOSITY
ABILRSTTUU SUBTITULAR
ABILRTTUUY TUBULARITY
ABIMNORRST BRAINSTORM
ABIMRSSSTU STRABISMUS
ABINNOSTVV BON VIVANTS
ABINOOPRST ABSORPTION
ABINOOSSST BASSOONIST
ABINOSSTTU BUS STATION,
    SUBSTATION
ABKLLOOSST BOOKSTALLS
ABLOORSTUY ABSOLUTORY
ABMOOORSTT
    MOTORBOATS
ABMRSSTTUU SUBSTRATUM
ABNORSTTUU
    ABOUT-TURNS, TURNABOUTS
ABOOPRSSTT BOOTSTRAPS
ABOORSTTUU ROUSTABOUT
ACCCDIIIPR PICRIC ACID
ACCCDIIIRT CITRIC ACID
ACCCEENRST ACCRESCENT
ACCCEFHKOR COCKCHAFER
ACCCEGINOS CACOGENICS
ACCCEHILOT CHALCOCITE
ACCCEHORTW
    COWCATCHER
ACCCEIILRT CICATRICLE

ACCCEIIRST CICATRICES
ACCCEILLNY ENCYCLICAL
ACCCEILMOP ACCOMPLICE
ACCCGLNOOO
    GONOCOCCAL
ACCCHINOOP CACOPHONIC
ACCCHKOPST SPATCHCOCK
ACCCHLOORY
    OCHLOCRACY
ACCCHOOTUU
    CAOUTCHOUC
ACCCHOPRST CATCH CROPS
ACCCILLLYY CYCLICALLY
ACCCILMORY CYCLORAMIC
ACCCIMORTY MACROCYTIC
ACCCINOPPU CAPPUCCINO
ACCDDEEIRT ACCREDITED
ACCDDEEIST DESICCATED
ACCDDEIRRT CREDIT CARD
ACCDEEHIST CATECHISED
ACCDEEHITZ CATECHIZED
ACCDEEHKMT CHECKMATED
ACCDEEHNOR
    ENCROACHED
ACCDEEHQRU CHEQUE
    CARD
ACCDEEIILS DELICACIES
ACCDEEINNS INCANDESCE
ACCDEEIQSU ACQUIESCED
ACCDEELPTY ACCEPTEDLY
ACCDEFIIRS SACRIFICED
ACCDEGHORT DOGCATCHER
ACCDEHIKRS DECKCHAIRS
ACCDEHKOST COCKED HATS
ACCDEHLNOY CHALCEDONY
ACCDEIILNY INDELICACY
ACCDEIILST DIALECTICS
ACCDEIKLNW CANDLEWICK
ACCDEILLOP PECCADILLO
ACCDEILNOT OCCIDENTAL
ACCDEILNTU INCULCATED
ACCDEILRTU CIRCULATED
ACCDEIMNNY MENDICANCY
ACCDEIMORT DEMOCRATIC
ACCDEINNTU INDUCTANCE
ACCDEINOOS OCCASIONED
ACCDEINSST DESICCANTS
ACCDEIORST DESICCATOR
ACCDELLOOT COLLOCATED
ACCDEMOSTU
    ACCUSTOMED
ACCDENORTT CONTRACTED
ACCDENPSSU DUNCE'S
    CAPS
ACCDEOPRST CADET CORPS
ACCDEORRSS SCORECARDS
ACCDEORSSW SACRED
    COWS
ACCDEORSTU CORUSCATED

ACCDFIILTY FLACCIDITY
ACCDFIIMOR FORMIC ACID
ACCDGIIILT TIGLIC ACID
ACCDHHRRUY
   CHURCHYARD
ACCDHIINOR DIACHRONIC
ACCDHILORV CLAVICHORD
ACCDHORSTW
   CATCHWORDS
ACCDIIINRT NITRIC ACID
ACCDIIIRST DIACRITICS
ACCDIILLPY PICCADILLY
ACCDIILOTU TOLUIC ACID
ACCDINOORS ACCORDIONS
ACCDINORTT CONTRADICT
ACCDKNORSW
   CRACKDOWNS
ACCDLOORSV VOCAL
   CORDS
ACCDNNOORT
   CONCORDANT
ACCDNOORST CONCORDATS
ACCDORRSTU COURT
   CARDS
ACCEEEEHKS CHEESECAKE
ACCEEEHRTY EYE-CATCHER
ACCEEELPRT RECEPTACLE
ACCEEHILLR CHELICERAL
ACCEEHILNP ENCEPHALIC
ACCEEHINRS CHANCERIES
ACCEEHISST CATECHESIS
ACCEEHKMST CHECKMATES
ACCEEHNORR
   ENCROACHER
ACCEEILLRT ELECTRICAL
ACCEEILMNU ECUMENICAL
ACCEEILNTY ACETYLENIC
ACCEEILORV VARICOCELE
ACCEEIMSST ACCESS TIME
ACCEEIORSU ERICACEOUS
ACCEEIRTUX EXCRUCIATE
ACCEELNOST COALESCENT
ACCEELNOSV CONVALESCE
ACCEELNPRU CRAPULENCE
ACCEELNRTU RELUCTANCE
ACCEELNSTT LACTESCENT
ACCEELNSTU CAULESCENT
ACCEELPSST SPECTACLES
ACCEEMNRST
   MARCESCENT, SCARCEMENT
ACCEEMOSTY ASCOMYCETE
ACCEENNNOV
   CONVENANCE
ACCEENNOVY CONVEYANCE
ACCEENOPRR COPARCENER
ACCEENORST CONSECRATE
ACCEENPTXY EXPECTANCY
ACCEENRSSS SCARCENESS
ACCEEOPPRS PEACE CORPS

ACCEEORRSU RACECOURSE
ACCEEORSTU CRETACEOUS
ACCEFFIINY INEFFICACY
ACCEFHLOST FACECLOTHS
ACCEFHLRTY FLYCATCHER
ACCEFIIRRS SACRIFICER
ACCEFIIRSS SACRIFICES
ACCEFILLOR CALCIFEROL
ACCEFILMOR CALCEIFORM
ACCEFINOST CONFISCATE
ACCEFLLOTU FLOCCULATE
ACCEGILLNN CANCELLING
ACCEGILLNO COLLAGENIC
ACCEGILLOO ECOLOGICAL
ACCEGILNNO CONCEALING
ACCEGILNOS COALESCING
ACCEGILNOT LACTOGENIC
ACCEGINNOR CARCINOGEN
ACCEGINNOZ COGNIZANCE
ACCEHHIPRT HEPTARCHIC
ACCEHIILMR CHIMERICAL
ACCEHIINNT TECHNICIAN
ACCEHIKNRS RAIN CHECKS
ACCEHILLMY CHEMICALLY
ACCEHILLTY HECTICALLY
ACCEHILNOS COCHINEALS
ACCEHIMNSS MISCHANCES
ACCEHIMSST CATECHISMS
ACCEHINNRY IN CHANCERY
ACCEHINNSS CHANCINESS
ACCEHINOPT CENOTAPHIC
ACCEHINSST CATCHINESS
ACCEHIORRY HIEROCRACY
ACCEHIORST ESCHAROTIC
ACCEHIORTT RHEOTACTIC,
   THEOCRATIC
ACCEHIRRST SCRATCHIER
ACCEHIRRTT TETRARCHIC
ACCEHIRSTT ARCHITECTS
ACCEHISSTT CATECHISTS
ACCEHLLNOR CHANCELLOR
ACCEHLMOOR
   HOMOCERCAL
ACCEHLOOST CHOCOLATES
ACCEHLOSUY CHYLACEOUS
ACCEHNNPTY CATCHPENNY
ACCEHNNRTY TRENCHANCY
ACCEHNOOTY
   CHOANOCYTE
ACCEHNORTT
   TECHNOCRAT, TRENCH COAT
ACCEHOPSTT SCOTCH TAPE
ACCEIILNOT CONCILIATE
ACCEIILRTT TECTRICIAL
ACCEIIMSST ASCETICISM
ACCEIINPRT IN PRACTICE
ACCEIINRST CISTERCIAN
ACCEIIRRST CICATRISER
ACCEIIRRTZ CICATRIZER

ACCEIIRSST SCARCITIES
ACCEIKRSSW WISECRACKS
ACCEILLLPS SCALPELLIC
ACCEILLLRY CLERICALLY
ACCEILLNSY SCENICALLY
ACCEILMMOR COMMERCIAL
ACCEILMNOO ECONOMICAL
ACCEILMNOP COMPLIANCE
ACCEILMOPT COMPLICATE
ACCEILMOST CACOMISTLE
ACCEILNRST CALCSINTER
ACCEILOPPT APOPLECTIC
ACCEILOPRR RECIPROCAL
ACCEILOPRV PREVOCALIC
ACCEIMNORS SCIOMANCER
ACCEIMOOPR COMIC OPERA
ACCEIMORST MESOCRATIC
ACCEINNNOV CONNIVANCE
ACCEINNORT CONCERTINA
ACCEINNSSY INCESSANCY
ACCEINOOST CONSOCIATE
ACCEINORST ACCRETIONS
ACCEINOSSS ACCESSIONS
ACCEIOORSU CORIACEOUS
ACCEIOPPSY EPISCOPACY
ACCEIORSTX EXSICCATOR
ACCEIOSSTU CISTACEOUS
ACCEJNOSUU JUNCACEOUS
ACCEKKLMOR
   CLOCKMAKER
ACCEKNORRS CORNCRAKES
ACCEKNRRTU NUTCRACKER
ACCELLLOSS CLOSE CALLS
ACCELLSSUU CALCULUSES
ACCELMNOPT COMPLACENT
ACCELNOPTU CONCEPTUAL
ACCELOOPST LACTOSCOPE
ACCEMNNORY
   NECROMANCY
ACCENNNOOS
   CONSONANCE
ACCENOORSU
   CORNACEOUS
ACCENORTTU COUNTERACT
ACCEORRSSW
   SCARECROWS
ACCEORSUUV CURVACEOUS
ACCFFFFHHI CHIFFCHAFF
ACCFGIILNY CALCIFYING
ACCFHIRTTW WITCHCRAFT
ACCFIINNOT FANTOCCINI
ACCFILSSUU FASCICULUS
ACCFKOORST FROCK COATS
ACCFLLNOTU FLOCCULANT
ACCGHIILOR OLIGARCHIC
ACCGHINRST SCRATCHING
ACCGHIOPTY PHAGOCYTIC
ACCGHORSSU COUCH
   GRASS

ACCGIILORT GO CRITICAL
ACCGIIMORT TRAGICOMIC
ACCGILNSUY ACCUSINGLY
ACCGIMNOPT COMPACTING
ACCGINNOTT CONTACTING
ACCGINNOTU ACCOUNTING
ACCHHIILLN CHINCHILLA
ACCHHORSST CROSSHATCH
ACCHIIILST CHILIASTIC
ACCHIIMSST SCHISMATIC
ACCHIKMSTT MATCHSTICK
ACCHILLOOS ALCOHOLICS
ACCHILMOPS ACCOMPLISH
ACCHILNNPS SPLANCHNIC
ACCHILNOOT CATHOLICON
ACCHILOSST SCHOLASTIC
ACCHILRSTY SCRATCHILY
ACCHILTTYY TACHYLYTIC
ACCHIMNORY CHIROMANCY
ACCHIMORST CHROMATICS
ACCHIOPRSZ SCHIZOCARP
ACCHIOSSTT STOCHASTIC
ACCHNORRST CORNSTARCH
ACCHOPRSST CROSSPATCH
ACCIIILLLP PICCALILLI
ACCIIINNNT CINCINNATI
ACCIILLLNY CLINICALLY
ACCIILLOST LOCALISTIC
ACCIILLRTY CRITICALLY
ACCIILMSSS CLASSICISM
ACCIILNNOT CALCITONIN
ACCIILNRTU UNCRITICAL
ACCIILORTY CALORICITY
ACCIILSSST CLASSICIST
ACCIIMNNNO CINNAMONIC
ACCIIMNOOT ICONOMATIC
ACCIIMNOST SCIOMANTIC
ACCIINNNPY PICCANINNY
ACCIINNOTY CANONICITY
ACCIIOPRSU CAPRICIOUS
ACCIIOTTVY COACTIVITY
ACCIKKKKNN KNICK-KNACK
ACCILLMOSY COSMICALLY
ACCILMNNOU COUNCILMAN
ACCILMNOOS ICONOCLASM
ACCILNOOST ICONOCLAST
ACCILNORTU INCULCATOR
ACCILNOSTV CONCLAVIST
ACCILNSSTY SYNCLASTIC
ACCILOPPRY POLYCARPIC
ACCILORRTU CIRCULATOR
ACCILRRRUU CURRICULAR
ACCIMNOOPR MONOCARPIC
ACCIMNOORT MONOCRATIC
ACCIMORSSY COSMIC RAYS
ACCINNOOOS ON OCCASION
ACCINOOPRU CORNUCOPIA
ACCINOOPTU OCCUPATION
ACCINOPRRS CAPRICORNS

ACCINOPRSY CONSPIRACY
ACCINSSTTY SYNTACTICS
ACCIOPRSTT CATOPTRICS
ACCKKNOOOS COCK A
SNOOK
ACCKLMOORU
COCKALORUM
ACCLOPRTUY PLUTOCRACY
ACCMMOORSS
MACROCOSMS
ACCNNOOSTU
NO-ACCOUNTS
ACCNOOORTV
CONVOCATOR
ACCNOOPRRY
PORNOCRACY
ACCNOORRTT CONTRACTOR
ACDDEEENOS DODECANESE
ACDDEEENRT DEAD CENTRE
ACDDEEEPRT DEPRECATED
ACDDEEERST DESECRATED
ACDDEEERTU RE-EDUCATED
ACDDEEHLOO
COOL-HEADED
ACDDEEHNOR
DECAHEDRON
ACDDEEHPST DESPATCHED
ACDDEEIIPT DIAPEDETIC
ACDDEEILTU ELUCIDATED
ACDDEEIPRT PREDICATED
ACDDEELLSY CLYDESDALE
ACDDEELNRY DRY-CLEANED
ACDDEELNTY DECADENTLY
ACDDEENNST DESCENDANT
ACDDEENRTU UNDERACTED
ACDDEENTUU UNEDUCATED
ACDDEFFHNU HANDCUFFED
ACDDEFFIRT DIFFRACTED
ACDDEGHIRS DISCHARGED
ACDDEGIINT DEDICATING
ACDDEHIKNP HANDPICKED
ACDDEHINSW SANDWICHED
ACDDEHIPST DISPATCHED
ACDDEHIRRS HARD CIDERS
ACDDEHIRSV CRASH-DIVED
ACDDEHNNOS
SECOND-HAND
ACDDEIILMS DISCLAIMED
ACDDEIINOT DEDICATION
ACDDEIINTV VINDICATED
ACDDEILMOU DUODECIMAL
ACDDEILOST DISLOCATED
ACDDEILPTU DUPLICATED
ACDDEILTTW WILDCATTED
ACDDEINSTY SYNDICATED
ACDDEIORTY DEDICATORY
ACDDEIRSTT DISTRACTED
ACDDEKLLNO LANDLOCKED
ACDDEKLORS DREADLOCKS

ACDDELNNOO
COLONNADED
ACDDELNOOW
CANDLEWOOD
ACDDENNRUY
REDUNDANCY
ACDDENORSW SWORD
DANCE
ACDDFHIORU CHAUDFROID
ACDDGHILNR GRANDCHILD
ACDDGIINRS DISCARDING
ACDDHHNSSU
DACHSHUNDS
ACDDIINOST ADDICTIONS
ACDDINORST DISCORDANT
ACDEEEEHHS HEADCHEESE
ACDEEEELRT DECELERATE
ACDEEEEPRS PREDECEASE
ACDEEEFLNR
FER-DE-LANCE, FREELANCED
ACDEEEFMNT DEFACEMENT
ACDEEEGNRY DEGENERACY
ACDEEEHIPS HEADPIECES
ACDEEEHRRS RESEARCHED
ACDEEEIPRT DEPRECIATE
ACDEEEKNPP KNEECAPPED
ACDEEENNTT ANTECEDENT
ACDEEENRTV ADVERTENCE
ACDEEEORRT REDECORATE
ACDEEFFHRT FARFETCHED
ACDEEFFLTY AFFECTEDLY
ACDEEFFNTU UNAFFECTED
ACDEEFGINT DEFECATING
ACDEEFINOT DEFECATION
ACDEEFINRT INTERFACED
ACDEEFKOPR POKER-FACED
ACDEEFOPRW FACE
POWDER
ACDEEFORST FORECASTED
ACDEEFRRSU RESURFACED
ACDEEGHLLN CHALLENGED
ACDEEGHNNO
HENDECAGON
ACDEEGINRR ADRENERGIC
ACDEEGINRS DECREASING
ACDEEGINRT CENTIGRADE
ACDEEGNORU
ENCOURAGED
ACDEEHILNR CHANDELIER
ACDEEHIMNS MECHANISED
ACDEEHIMNZ MECHANIZED
ACDEEHIMRS ARCHIMEDES
ACDEEHLLNN CHANNELLED
ACDEEHLNRT ANDERLECHT
ACDEEHMNTT DETACHMENT
ACDEEHNOPR CHAPERONED
ACDEEHOPPR COPPERHEAD
ACDEEHOPRR REPROACHED

ACDEEHORRV
OVERARCHED
ACDEEHPRST DESPATCHER
ACDEEHPSST DESPATCHES
ACDEEHPSSY SPEECH DAYS
ACDEEIILMP EPIDEMICAL
ACDEEIILMS DECIMALISE
ACDEEIILMZ DECIMALIZE
ACDEEIILNT INDELICATE
ACDEEIIMRT ACIDIMETER
ACDEEIIMTV MEDICATIVE
ACDEEIJSTV ADJECTIVES
ACDEEIILLNR CINDERELLA
ACDEEIILLOS DELOCALISE
ACDEEIILLOZ DELOCALIZE
ACDEEIILLRS ESCADRILLE
ACDEEIILLTY DELICATELY
ACDEEILMPR PREMEDICAL
ACDEEILNPP APPENDICLE
ACDEEILNRT INTERLACED
ACDEEILOSV DEVOCALISE
ACDEEILOVZ DEVOCALIZE
ACDEEILPRT REPLICATED
ACDEEILPTU PEDICULATE
ACDEEILPTX EXPLICATED
ACDEEIMMNT MEDICAMENT
ACDEEIMNPS IMPEDANCES
ACDEEIMORT ACIDOMETER
ACDEEIMPRT MERCAPTIDE
ACDEEINNNT INTENDANCE
ACDEEINNTU DENUNCIATE,
ENUNCIATED
ACDEEINPPS APPENDICES
ACDEEINRTT INTERACTED
ACDEEINSST DESISTANCE
ACDEEIORTV DECORATIVE
ACDEEIORTX EXCORIATED
ACDEEIOTTX DETOXICATE
ACDEEIPRRT TRADE PRICE
ACDEEIPRST PEDERASTIC,
PREDICATES
ACDEEIRSTU CAUTERISED
ACDEEIRTTV DETRACTIVE
ACDEEIRTTX EXTRICATED
ACDEEIRTUZ CAUTERIZED
ACDEEITTUX EXACTITUDE
ACDEELMORT ECTODERMAL
ACDEELMORU
LEUCODERMA
ACDEELNOST ADOLESCENT
ACDEELNRRY DRY CLEANER
ACDEELOPRT PERCOLATED
ACDEELORRT CORRELATED
ACDEELORTU EDULCORATE
ACDEELPSTU SPECULATED
ACDEELPTUX EXCULPATED
ACDEEMMNOR
COMMANDEER

ACDEEMMNPT
DECAMPMENT
ACDEEMNOTY
ADENECTOMY
ACDEENNOST CONDENSATE
ACDEENNOTV COVENANTED
ACDEENORST SECOND-RATE
ACDEENRSSS SACREDNESS
ACDEENRTTU DETRUNCATE
ACDEEOOPRT COOPERATED
ACDEEOPRRT DEPRECATOR,
PROCREATED
ACDEEORRST DESECRATOR
ACDEEPRRTU RECAPTURED
ACDEFFIIOT OFFICIATED
ACDEFFIKRT TRAFFICKED
ACDEFFLORS SCAFFOLDER
ACDEFFLOTU DUFFEL COAT
ACDEFFMORS COFFERDAMS
ACDEFFOSTU SUFFOCATED
ACDEFHILNS CANDLEFISH
ACDEFHINRS FRANCHISED
ACDEFHOSUV VOUCHSAFED
ACDEFIILSS CLASSIFIED
ACDEFIINST SANCTIFIED
ACDEFIIRRT FRATRICIDE
ACDEFIJKKN JACK-KNIFED
ACDEFILLOS COALFIELDS
ACDEFILSSY DECLASSIFY
ACDEFINORT FORNICATED
ACDEFIORST FACTORISED
ACDEFIORTZ FACTORIZED
ACDEFKLNOR FOLK DANCER
ACDEFKLNOS FOLK DANCES
ACDEFLMORS COLD
FRAMES
ACDEFLNOOT FOOT-CANDLE
ACDEFLTTUU FLUCTUATED
ACDEFNORRU
UNCARED-FOR
ACDEFNORTU FECUNDATOR
ACDEFNRSSY FANCY DRESS
ACDEGHIRRS DISCHARGER
ACDEGHIRSS DISCHARGES
ACDEGHRRSU
SURCHARGED
ACDEGIILMN DECLAIMING
ACDEGIILMR GERMICIDAL
ACDEGIILNS ANGLICISED
ACDEGIILNZ ANGLICIZED
ACDEGIIMNT DECIMATING
ACDEGIINOR RADIOGENIC
ACDEGIINOU AUDIOGENIC
ACDEGIINST DIE-CASTING
ACDEGILNRW ARC WELDING
ACDEGILOOP LOGOPAEDIC
ACDEGILRTT CATTLE GRID
ACDEGIMMRS SCRIMMAGED
ACDEGIMNOY GEODYNAMIC

ACDEGINNOR ANDROGENIC
ACDEGINORR CORRIGENDA
ACDEGINORT DECORATING
ACDEGINRTT DETRACTING
ACDEGINRTY GARDEN CITY
ACDEGIORSU DISCOURAGE
ACDEGIRRST CARTRIDGES
ACDEGJNOTU CONJUGATED
ACDEGKNORR ROCK
GARDEN
ACDEGMMRSU
SCRUMMAGED
ACDEGORRTU
CORRUGATED
ACDEHIIMRT DIATHERMIC
ACDEHILMOT METHODICAL
ACDEHIMMST MISMATCHED
ACDEHIMNOP CHAMPIONED
ACDEHIMORT DICHROMATE
ACDEHINNRS HINDRANCES
ACDEHINNST DISENCHANT
ACDEHINOPS DEACONSHIP
ACDEHINOPT DICTAPHONE
ACDEHINORT ACHONDRITE
ACDEHINSSW SANDWICHES
ACDEHIPSST DISPATCHES
ACDEHIRSSV CRASH-DIVES
ACDEHKPSST SKETCHPADS
ACDEHLNOST DECATHLONS
ACDEHLOOPP CEPHALOPOD
ACDEHMPRSY PACHYDERMS
ACDEHNOORT
OCTAHEDRON
ACDEHNORST ON THE
CARDS
ACDEHNORSZ SCHERZANDO
ACDEHORRTT TETRACHORD
ACDEHRTTU DUTCH TREAT
ACDEIIILST IDEALISTIC,
ITALICISED
ACDEIIILTZ ITALICIZED
ACDEIIINST DIETICIANS
ACDEIIINTV INDICATIVE
ACDEIIJTUV JUDICATIVE
ACDEIIKNNR KINCARDINE
ACDEIIKNNS DICKENSIAN
ACDEIILLOT IDIOLECTAL
ACDEIILMMT DILEMMATIC
ACDEIILMPT IMPLICATED
ACDEIILMRS DISCLAIMER
ACDEIILMRV VERMICIDAL
ACDEIILNNT INCIDENTAL
ACDEIILNOS DECISIONAL
ACDEIILOPR PERIODICAL
ACDEIILOSS SOCIALISED
ACDEIILOSZ SOCIALIZED
ACDEIILPST PESTICIDAL,
SEPTICIDAL

ACDEIIMNOT DECIMATION,
MEDICATION
ACDEIIMPRU EPICARDIUM
ACDEIIMRRS MISCARRIED
ACDEIIMRST MATRICIDES
ACDEIINNRY INCENDIARY
ACDEIINOSY ISOCYANIDE
ACDEIIORSU IRIDACEOUS
ACDEIIOSST DISSOCIATE
ACDEIIPRRS PARRICIDES
ACDEIIPRST PATRICIDES,
PEDIATRICS
ACDEIIPRTY PERACIDITY
ACDEIJNTUV ADJUNCTIVE
ACDEIJRTUU JUDICATURE
ACDEIKRSST SIDETRACKS
ACDEILLORR CORDILLERA
ACDEILLOST OSCILLATED
ACDEILLTUV VICTUALLED
ACDEILMNNO NONMEDICAL
ACDEILMNOP COMPLAINED
ACDEILMOPR PROCLAIMED
ACDEILNNOR ENDOCRINAL
ACDEILNNPS CANDLEPINS
ACDEILNOTU INOCULATED
ACDEILNPTU INCULPATED
ACDEILNSUV VULCANISED
ACDEILNUVZ VULCANIZED
ACDEILORTU ELUCIDATOR
ACDEILOTTU COLATITUDE
ACDEILPSTU DUPLICATES
ACDEILTTUV CULTIVATED
ACDEIMMORT DERMATOMIC
ACDEIMMORY IMMODERACY
ACDEIMNNOT DEMICANTON
ACDEIMNNST MENDICANTS
ACDEIMNORU ANDROECIUM
ACDEIMNOSU MENDACIOUS
ACDEINNNTY INTENDANCY
ACDEINNORS ORDINANCES
ACDEINNOSS DISSONANCE
ACDEINNOST SANCTIONED
ACDEINNRSS RANCIDNESS
ACDEINOORT CAROTENOID,
COORDINATE, DECORATION
ACDEINOPRS SCORPAENID
ACDEINORTT DETRACTION
ACDEINOSTT ANECDOTIST
ACDEINOTTX DETOXICANT
ACDEINPRST DISCREPANT
ACDEINSSTY SYNDICATES
ACDEINSTTU SANCTITUDE
ACDEIOOPRS RADIOSCOPE
ACDEIOPRSU PREDACIOUS
ACDEIOPRTT TETRAPODIC
ACDEIOPSSU SPADICEOUS
ACDEIORSST OSTRACISED
ACDEIORSTZ OSTRACIZED
ACDEIPQRSU QUADRICEPS

ACDEIPRSTU CUSTARD PIE
ACDEIQRSTU QUADRISECT
ACDEIRRSTT DISTRACTER
ACDEIRSSTT DICTATRESS
ACDEIRSTTU RUSTICATED
ACDEJKSTTU DUST JACKET
ACDEKKMOPR
POCKMARKED
ACDELLOORT DECOLLATOR
ACDELNNOOS COLONNADES
ACDELNOORT DECOLORANT
ACDELNOOTY ACOTYLEDON
ACDELOPPTU CLAPPED-OUT
ACDELOPRRU PROCEDURAL
ACDELOSSTU OUTCLASSED
ACDEMMNORS
COMMANDERS
ACDEMMOSTU
CUSTOM-MADE
ACDEMOORST
MOTORCADES
ACDEMOOTVY DEMY
OCTAVO
ACDEMOPRSU DAMP
COURSE
ACDENNNOOR
ORDONNANCE
ACDENNNOOS
NANOSECOND
ACDENOPPSW
SNOW-CAPPED
ACDENOPSTY SYNCOPATED
ACDENORSTT CONTRASTED
ACDENORSTU UNDERCOATS
ACDENPTTUU PUNCTUATED
ACDENRRRTU REDCURRANT
ACDENRRSTU TRANSDUCER
ACDEOORRST DECORATORS
ACDEOORRVW
WOODCARVER
ACDEOORSTT DOCTORATES
ACDEOPPRSU PSEUDOCARP
ACDEOPRRTT PROTRACTED
ACDEOPRSUU DRUPACEOUS
ACDEOPSTTU COUPS D'ÉTAT
ACDEORRSTT DETRACTORS
ACDFGIIINY ACIDIFYING
ACDFGIILNU FUNGICIDAL
ACDFINNOST CONFIDANTS
ACDFLNOSSY CANDYFLOSS
ACDFORRSTW
SWORDCRAFT
ACDGGIINRS DISGRACING
ACDGHIOPRT DICTOGRAPH
ACDGHNOOTU
TOUCH-AND-GO
ACDGIIIMNR GRAMICIDIN
ACDGIIINNT INDICATING
ACDGIILNPS DISPLACING

ACDGIIMOOS MOGADISCIO
ACDGIINNRS DINING CARS
ACDGIINNST DISTANCING
ACDGIINOST DIAGNOSTIC
ACDGIKLNOP PADLOCKING
ACDGIKNOST STOCKADING
ACDGILLOSU GLUCOSIDAL
ACDGILNNOO CANOODLING
ACDGILNOOT ODONTALGIC
ACDGILOORY CARDIOLOGY
ACDGIMMNNO
COMMANDING
ACDGLLOORS DOG
COLLARS
ACDGLOTYYZ ZYGODACTYL
ACDGMNOPRU
CAMPGROUND
ACDHIIIOPT IDIOPATHIC
ACDHILLPSY CHILD'S PLAY
ACDHILMNOY MY OLD
CHINA
ACDHILRSUY HYDRAULICS
ACDHIORRSW DISC
HARROW
ACDHIORTTY TRACHYTOID
ACDHIRSSSW SWISS CHARD
ACDHLOORRU
UROCHORDAL
ACDHLOORRY
HYDROCORAL
ACDHLOOSSY DAY SCHOOLS
ACDHMNORYY
HYDROMANCY
ACDHNOOPRR DROP
ANCHOR
ACDHORSTWW
WATCHWORDS
ACDIIIMMRU MIRACIDIUM
ACDIIIMNST DIACTINISM
ACDIIINNOT INDICATION
ACDIIJLLUY JUDICIALLY
ACDIILLSUY SUICIDALLY
ACDIILMOPT DIPLOMATIC
ACDIILORTY CORDIALITY
ACDIILORUX UXORICIDAL
ACDIIMNNOS DOMINICANS
ACDIIMNORT ANTIDROMIC
ACDIIMNOST MONADISTIC
ACDIIMNOSY ISODYNAMIC
ACDIIMNSTY DYNAMISTIC
ACDIINNNOR INDIAN CORN
ACDIINNORY INORDINACY
ACDIINOORV ORDOVICIAN
ACDIINORST INDICATORS
ACDIINORTV VINDICATOR
ACDIINORTY DICTIONARY,
INDICATORY
ACDIINOSTT DICTATIONS
ACDIIOORTX RADIOTOXIC

ACDIJORTUY JUDICATORY	ACEEEELNPSW CLEAN SWEEP	ACEEGILRSS SACRILEGES
ACDIKNQSSU QUICKSANDS	ACEEELORTT ELECTORATE	ACEEGILSTU SLUICEGATE
ACDIKRRSTT DIRT TRACKS	ACEEELRSTT TELECASTER	ACEEGINNOS CASEINOGEN
ACDIKRSSTY YARDSTICKS	ACEEEMNNPR	ACEEGINNPT PANGENETIC
ACDILNOPRS SPINAL CORD	PERMANENCE	ACEEGINRRT RECREATING
ACDILOPRTU DUPLICATOR	ACEEEMNNST ENCASEMENT	ACEEGINRSV GRIEVANCES
ACDILPSSTY DYSPLASTIC	ACEEEMNPRT TEMPERANCE	ACEEGINRTX EXECRATING
ACDIMMORUY	ACEEEMNPST ESCAPEMENT	ACEEGIOPTT COTTAGE PIE
MYOCARDIUM	ACEEEMNRTT METACENTRE	ACEEGIORST CATEGORIES,
ACDIMOORSU MORDACIOUS	ACEEEMORTT ACETOMETER	CATEGORISE
ACDINOSSTU CUSTODIANS	ACEEENNOTV COVENANTEE	ACEEGIORTZ CATEGORIZE
ACDINSSSTU DISCUSSANT	ACEEENNPRT PENETRANCE,	ACEEGIOTTX EXCOGITATE
ACDIOOPRSY RADIOSCOPY	REPENTANCE	ACEEGIRSTT CIGARETTES
ACDJOORSTU COADJUTORS	ACEEENNRRT RE-ENTRANCE	ACEEGKNOPS SPONGE
ACDKLMOSSY	ACEEENNSTV EVANESCENT	CAKE
LADY'S-SMOCK	ACEEENRSSV SEVERANCES	ACEEGKORTT GET A
ACDKLORSTU TRUCKLOADS	ACEEEPPPRR CREPE PAPER	ROCKET
ACDKNORSTU	ACEEEPRRTU RECUPERATE	ACEEGLLOSU COLLEAGUES
SOUNDTRACK	ACEEFFIMNY EFFEMINACY	ACEEGLMNOR
ACDKORSSTY STOCKYARDS	ACEEFFLOTY FEET OF CLAY	CAMERLENGO
ACDLLOOPSW CODSWALLOP	ACEEFFNRSU SUFFERANCE	ACEEGLNRST RECTANGLES
ACDLLOPTYY POLYDACTYL	ACEEFHHTTW CHEW THE	ACEEGLNRTU GREAT-UNCLE
ACDLLORSSW	FAT	ACEEGMMOSU
WORLD-CLASS	ACEEFIILTT FELICITATE	GEMMACEOUS
ACDLLORSTU COLLAR STUD	ACEEFIJKLT LIFE JACKET	ACEEGMOTTY
ACDLMNOPSW	ACEEFILMNT MALEFICENT	GAMETOCYTE
CLAMPDOWNS	ACEEFILNRS CRANE FLIES	ACEEGNNORV
ACDMPRRSTU TRUMP	ACEEFILNSS FACILENESS	GOVERNANCE
CARDS	ACEEFILPRS FIREPLACES	ACEEGNNPRU REPUGNANCE
ACDOORRSSS CROSSROADS	ACEEFINRST INTERFACES	ACEEGNNSWY NEWS
ACDORRSTUY COURTYARDS	ACEEFIOPSS PIECE OF ASS	AGENCY
ACEEEFFKTT TAKE EFFECT	ACEEFIORTV VOCIFERATE	ACEEGNORRU
ACEEEFFMNT EFFACEMENT	ACEEFIRRTV REFRACTIVE	ENCOURAGER
ACEEEFFTTU EFFECTUATE	ACEEFIRSSS FRICASSEES	ACEEGNRSSV SCAVENGERS
ACEEEFIPRS FIRE ESCAPE	ACEEFLLNTU FLATULENCE	ACEEHHILRW WHEELCHAIR
ACEEEFIPRT AFTERPIECE	ACEEFLLORV CLOVERLEAF	ACEEHHIRRS HERESIARCH
ACEEEFIRSS CEASE-FIRES	ACEEFLLPUY PEACEFULLY	ACEEHHIRST HATCHERIES
ACEEEFLNRR FREELANCER	ACEEFLNSTV FLAVESCENT	ACEEHHLLRT HATCHELLER
ACEEEFLNRS FREELANCES	ACEEFLORST FORECASTLE	ACEEHHMNTT HATCHET
ACEEEFMNNT ENFACEMENT	ACEEFLOSTV VOLTE-FACES	MEN
ACEEEGILNN INELEGANCE	ACEEFORRST FORECASTER	ACEEHHPTTU HEPTATEUCH
ACEEEGINRT GREAT-NIECE	ACEEGGNORT CONGREGATE	ACEEHIIPRS HAIRPIECES
ACEEEGNNSV VENGEANCES	ACEEGHHRTW CHEW THE	ACEEHILMNN MANCHINEEL
ACEEEGNPRT PERCENTAGE	RAG	ACEEHILPTT TELEPATHIC
ACEEEGNRRY REGENERACY	ACEEGHINNP CHEAPENING	ACEEHILRSV CHEVALIERS
ACEEEHIMRX HEXAEMERIC	ACEEGHLLNR CHALLENGER	ACEEHILSTT ESTHETICAL
ACEEEHRRRS RESEARCHER	ACEEGHLLNS CHALLENGES	ACEEHIMNPZ CHIMPANZEE
ACEEEHRRSS RESEARCHES	ACEEGHLNSS CHANGELESS	ACEEHIMNRS MECHANISER
ACEEEIMRRS CREAMERIES	ACEEGHNNOP	ACEEHIMNRZ MECHANIZER
ACEEEIPPPS PEACE PIPES	COPENHAGEN	ACEEHIMRTX HEXAMETRIC
ACEEEIPPRV APPERCEIVE	ACEEGHNORV	ACEEHIMSST SCHEMATISE
ACEEEIRRST SECRETAIRE	CHANGEOVER	ACEEHIMSTZ SCHEMATIZE
ACEEEIRSTV EVISCERATE,	ACEEGHNSSU GAUCHENESS	ACEEHIMTTT METATHETIC
TEA SERVICE	ACEEGHORRV	ACEEHINNPT PHENACETIN
ACEEEIRTVX EXECRATIVE	OVERCHARGE	ACEEHINPSS PEACHINESS
ACEEEKRRST RACKETEERS	ACEEGIKTTW WICKET GATE	ACEEHINSTT ANESTHETIC
ACEEELLNRT CRENELLATE	ACEEGILLNR ALLERGENIC	ACEEHIORRT CHARIOTEER
ACEEELMNNT ENLACEMENT	ACEEGILLOT COLLEGIATE	ACEEHISSTT AESTHETICS
ACEEELNPRV PREVALENCE	ACEEGILNTU GENICULATE	ACEEHISTUW WHITE SAUCE

ACEEHKLNRT HALTERNECK
ACEEHLLNNR CHANNELLER
ACEEHLLNOP CELLOPHANE
ACEEHLMNOS CHAMELEONS
ACEEHLNNOP ENCEPHALON
ACEEHLNPRU LEPRECHAUN
ACEEHLNPTT PLANCHETTE
ACEEHLOPTY POLYCHAETE
ACEEHLOSSV CLOSE SHAVE
ACEEHLRSTW CARTWHEELS
ACEEHMMRSU
　MEERSCHAUM
ACEEHMNNST ENCASHMENT
ACEEHMNOOR
　ANEMOCHORE
ACEEHMNPRT PREACHMENT
ACEEHMORTT TACHOMETER
ACEEHMRTTY TACHYMETER
ACEEHMSSTT STEAM-CHEST
ACEEHNNRST ENCHANTERS
ACEEHNPTTU PENTATEUCH
ACEEHOPRRR REPROACHER
ACEEHOPRRS
　ARCHESPORE, REPROACHES
ACEEHORRSS RACEHORSES
ACEEHPRSTY ARCHETYPES
ACEEHPTTTX EXCEPT THAT
ACEEHRRSTT CHATTERERS
ACEEHRRSTU CHARTREUSE
ACEEIILMST ELEATICISM
ACEEIILNTT LICENTIATE
ACEEIILPSS SPECIALISE
ACEEIILPST TAILPIECES
ACEEIILPSZ SPECIALIZE
ACEEIILSST ELASTICISE
ACEEIILSTZ ELASTICIZE
ACEEIIMNPT IMPATIENCE
ACEEIINNRT CREATININE,
　INCINERATE
ACEEIIRTTV RECITATIVE
ACEEIITTVX EXCITATIVE
ACEEIJLNQU JACQUELINE
ACEEIJLRTT TRAJECTILE
ACEEIKLNRT TRANCELIKE
ACEEIKNOTT TAKE NOTICE
ACEEIKNRSS CREAKINESS
ACEEIKPRTT TICKERTAPE
ACEEIKRSST ICE-SKATERS
ACEEIILLMTY EMETICALLY
ACEEIILLPRX PRELEXICAL
ACEEIILLPSY ESPECIALLY
ACEEILMNNT CLEMENTINA
ACEEILMNOR CEREMONIAL
ACEEILMNOT COLEMANITE
ACEEILMNOU LEUCOMAINE
ACEEILMNRT MERCANTILE
ACEEILMNST CENTESIMAL,
　LEMNISCATE
ACEEILMOSU MELIACEOUS

ACEEILNNNT CENTENNIAL
ACEEILNOPU LEUCOPENIA
ACEEILNOTV EVECTIONAL
ACEEILNPRS PRASELENIC
ACEEILNPRT EPICENTRAL
ACEEILNRST CENTRALISE,
　LINECASTER
ACEEILNRTV CANTILEVER
ACEEILNRTZ CENTRALIZE
ACEEILRRTT RETRACTILE
ACEEILRSSU SECULARISE
ACEEILRSUZ SECULARIZE
ACEEILRTTU RETICULATE
ACEEILRTUV ULCERATIVE
ACEEILRTVY CREATIVELY,
　REACTIVELY
ACEEILSTUV VESICULATE
ACEEIMNORT ACTINOMERE
ACEEIMNRSS CREAMINESS
ACEEIMNRSV SERVICEMAN
ACEEIMNRTT REMITTANCE
ACEEIMORRT AEROMETRIC
ACEEIMORTT EROTEMATIC
ACEEIMPRST SPERMACETI
ACEEIMRSST MASSETERIC
ACEEINNRST TRANSIENCE
ACEEINORRT RECREATION
ACEEINORSU ERINACEOUS
ACEEINORTU AUCTIONEER
ACEEINORTX EXECRATION
ACEEINPPRT APPRENTICE
ACEEINPRST INTERSPACE
ACEEINPRSU EPICUREANS
ACEEINRSST ANCESTRIES,
　RESISTANCE
ACEEINRTVY INVETERACY
ACEEINSSTV ACTIVENESS
ACEEIOOPRS AECIOSPORE
ACEEIOPPST EPISCOPATE
ACEEIOPSST CAESPITOSE
ACEEIOQTUV EQUIVOCATE
ACEEIORTVV OVERACTIVE,
　REVOCATIVE
ACEEIPPRTY PARTY PIECE
ACEEIPQRSU PICARESQUE
ACEEIQRSTU REQUIESCAT
ACEEIRRSST CAREERISTS
ACEEIRRTTV RETRACTIVE
ACEEIRTTUV ERUCTATIVE
ACEEIRTTVX EXTRACTIVE
ACEEKLLRSS SALESCLERK
ACEEKNRRRT RACK-RENTER
ACEEKNRTTV TRACK EVENT
ACEEKORRSW
　CASEWORKER
ACEELLNRSW ALLEN SCREW
ACEELLRSSY CARELESSLY
ACEELLSTTU SCUTELLATE
ACEELMNOTY MELANOCYTE

ACEELMNPST PLACEMENTS
ACEELMORST LATECOMERS
ACEELMORTT LACTOMETER
ACEELNOPRV PROVENÇALE
ACEELNOPST OPALESCENT
ACEELNOPSY CLAP EYES ON
ACEELNORTU ENUCLEATOR
ACEELNPRSY SCREENPLAY
ACEELORRST CORRELATES
ACEELORSSS CASSEROLES
ACEELPPRTU PERCEPTUAL
ACEELQRRUU CRAQUELURE
ACEEMMNNPT
　ENCAMPMENT
ACEEMMNOTT
　COMMENTATE
ACEEMMORSU
　COMMEASURE
ACEEMMNNPRY
　PERMANENCY
ACEEMMNNSTT ENACTMENTS
ACEEMNOOPS
　ANEMOSCOPE
ACEEMNOPST COMPENSATE
ACEEMNPRST ESCARPMENT
ACEEMOSTUZ ECZEMATOUS
ACEENNOPRS CAN OPENERS
ACEENNOPRV PROVENANCE
ACEENNORSS RESONANCES
ACEENNORTV
　CONTRAVENE, COVENANTER
ACEENNRSSV CRAVENNESS
ACEENNSSTU SUSTENANCE
ACEENORSSS COARSENESS
ACEENPRRST CARPENTERS
ACEENPRUVY PURVEYANCE
ACEENRSSST ANCESTRESS
ACEENRSSTW NEWSCASTER
ACEENRSTTU UTTERANCES
ACEENSTTUX EXECUTANTS
ACEEOSSTTU TESTACEOUS
ACEEPRSTTY TYPECASTER
ACEERRSSTT STREETCARS
ACEERRSSTW WATERCRESS
ACEFFFILOT FACT OF LIFE
ACEFFHLNOR FRENCH LOAF
ACEFFHRSUU CHAUFFEURS
ACEFFIILTV AFFLICTIVE
ACEFFIKRRT TRAFFICKER
ACEFFINOST AFFECTIONS
ACEFFOSTUU TUFFACEOUS
ACEFGILNST SELF-ACTING
ACEFGINRRT REFRACTING
ACEFGLLRUY GRACEFULLY
ACEFHHIRRS ARCHERFISH
ACEFHIINST CHIEFTAINS
ACEFHILRTU ULTRAFICHE
ACEFHINRSS FRANCHISES
ACEFHIRSSY CRAYFISHES

ACEFHIRTTY CITY FATHER
ACEFHKMMOU MAKE MUCH OF
ACEFHKORST AFTERSHOCK
ACEFHORRTV HOVERCRAFT
ACEFHORSTU HOUSECRAFT
ACEFIIILST FACILITIES
ACEFIILMSS FACSIMILES
ACEFIILRSS CLASSIFIER
ACEFIINNRS FINANCIERS
ACEFIINRST SANCTIFIER
ACEFIIOPRS FAIR COPIES
ACEFIIRRST ARTIFICERS
ACEFIIRSTV FRICATIVES
ACEFIKLNPS CLASP KNIFE
ACEFIKRSTU FRUITCAKES
ACEFILLNOT FLECTIONAL
ACEFILNOST SELF-ACTION
ACEFILNTUU FUNICULATE
ACEFILOOSU FOLIACEOUS
ACEFINORRT FOR CERTAIN, REFRACTION
ACEFINORTV VOCIFERANT
ACEFINRSST CRAFTINESS
ACEFIRRTTU TRIFURCATE
ACEFKLNORS CORNFLAKES
ACEFKORSST TASK FORCES
ACEFLOOPTU OUT OF PLACE
ACEFMNNOWY FANCY WOMEN
ACEFORRRTY REFRACTORY
ACEFRRSSTU SURFCASTER
ACEGGHILNN CHANGELING
ACEGGHINNX EXCHANGING
ACEGGHINRR RECHARGING
ACEGGILLOO GEOLOGICAL
ACEGGILNNO CONGEALING
ACEGGINNOO OCEANGOING
ACEGGINNSV SCAVENGING
ACEGGIRSST SCRAGGIEST
ACEGHHIJKR HIGHJACKER
ACEGHHINOT HIGH-OCTANE
ACEGHHOPRT HECTOGRAPH
ACEGHIILMT MEGALITHIC
ACEGHIIMNP IMPEACHING
ACEGHIIMTW WHITE MAGIC
ACEGHIINNN ENCHAINING
ACEGHIINRS CASHIERING
ACEGHIIPPR EPIGRAPHIC
ACEGHILMPT PHLEGMATIC
ACEGHILNPR NEPHRALGIC
ACEGHIMNNU MACHINE GUN
ACEGHIMNOP MEGAPHONIC
ACEGHINNNT ENCHANTING
ACEGHINNST CHASTENING
ACEGHINOPT PATHOGENIC
ACEGHINRRT CHARTERING
ACEGHINRTT CHATTERING

ACEGHIOOPS HAGIOSCOPE
ACEGHIRSTW SWITCHGEAR
ACEGHOPRRY CEROGRAPHY
ACEGHOPSTY PHAGOCYTES
ACEGHRRRSU SURCHARGER
ACEGHRRSSU SURCHARGES
ACEGIIKNRY A GIN RICKEY
ACEGIIKNST ICE-SKATING
ACEGIILLRS GALLICISER
ACEGIILLRZ GALLICIZER
ACEGIILLST LEGALISTIC
ACEGIILMNR RECLAIMING
ACEGIILMNX EXCLAIMING
ACEGIILMTY LEGITIMACY
ACEGIILNNO LIGNOCAINE
ACEGIIMNTT MAGNETITIC
ACEGIIMOST ISOGAMETIC
ACEGIIMPTT PEGMATITIC
ACEGIINNRS INCREASING
ACEGIINORT IATROGENIC
ACEGIIOTTV COGITATIVE
ACEGIIPRST EPIGASTRIC
ACEGIIRRST GERIATRICS
ACEGIKLNNS SLACKENING
ACEGIKNPPR PREPACKING
ACEGILLNOO NEOLOGICAL
ACEGILLNPR PARCELLING
ACEGILLOOS OLIGOCLASE
ACEGILMNNY MENACINGLY
ACEGILNNOT CONGENITAL
ACEGILNOPY CLAY PIGEON
ACEGILNORT RELOCATING
ACEGILNOTU GLAUCONITE
ACEGILNPTU PECULATING
ACEGILNQRU LACQUERING
ACEGILNRTT CLATTERING
ACEGILNRTU ULCERATING
ACEGILNTXY EXACTINGLY
ACEGILOOPT APOLOGETIC
ACEGIMMRRS SCRIMMAGER
ACEGIMMRSS SCRIMMAGES
ACEGIMNPRS SCAMPERING
ACEGIMNRST CENTIGRAMS
ACEGIMOPRS MEGASPORIC
ACEGIMORST GASOMETRIC
ACEGINNNRT ENTRANCING
ACEGINNORS COARSENING
ACEGINOPRS SAPROGENIC
ACEGINORTV OVERACTING
ACEGINPRRS SCARPERING
ACEGINPRSY PANEGYRICS
ACEGINPSTT SPECTATING
ACEGINRRTT RETRACTING
ACEGINRSTT SCATTERING
ACEGINRTTX EXTRACTING
ACEGIOSSTT GEOSTATICS
ACEGIRSSTT STRATEGICS

ACEGLMOSUU GLUMACEOUS
ACEGLNOOOY OCEANOLOGY
ACEGLOOPSY ESCAPOLOGY
ACEGLOOTUY AUTECOLOGY
ACEGMMRRSU SCRUMMAGER
ACEGMMRSSU SCRUMMAGES
ACEGNNOSTT COTANGENTS
ACEGNRSTTU SCATTER-GUN
ACEGOORSUU COURAGEOUS
ACEGOPRRSU SUPERCARGO
ACEHHIKSTT HIT THE SACK
ACEHHILTWZ WITCH-HAZEL
ACEHHIPSTT HEPTASTICH
ACEHHNNORSU RANCH HOUSE
ACEHHOOSTT TOOTHACHES
ACEHIILLPT PHILATELIC
ACEHIILMOS ISOCHEIMAL
ACEHIIMRTT ARITHMETIC
ACEHIINNOP PHOENICIAN
ACEHIINOTV INCHOATIVE
ACEHIIPRRT PERITRICHA
ACEHIIRSTT TRACHEITIS
ACEHIKLNSS CHALKINESS
ACEHIKMNOS CHAIN-SMOKE
ACEHIKMNSY HACKNEYISM
ACEHIKORST ARTICHOKES
ACEHILLNTY ETHNICALLY
ACEHILLOOS ALCOHOLISE
ACEHILLOOZ ALCOHOLIZE
ACEHILLORY HEROICALLY
ACEHILLPRY CAERPHILLY
ACEHILLTTY THETICALLY
ACEHILMMOS CHAMOMILES
ACEHILMMST MISCH METAL
ACEHILMNOR CHLORAMINE
ACEHILMOOP PHOCOMELIA
ACEHILMOTY HAEMOLYTIC
ACEHILMSST ALCHEMISTS
ACEHILNNOT NONETHICAL
ACEHILNORT CHLORINATE
ACEHILOORZ COLEORHIZA
ACEHILOPST TELOPHASIC
ACEHILORRT RHETORICAL
ACEHILPSST SALES PITCH
ACEHILRSTU HERACLITUS
ACEHILRSTY HYSTERICAL
ACEHIMMNSS MECHANISMS
ACEHIMMSST MISMATCHES, SCHEMATISM
ACEHIMNNOR ENHARMONIC
ACEHIMNORS MONARCHIES
ACEHIMNORW CHAIRWOMEN

ACEHIMNRSV REVANCHISM	ACEIIKRSTT RICKETTSIA	ACEILLMRTY METRICALLY
ACEHIMNSTY MYASTHENIC	ACEIILLLPT ELLIPTICAL	ACEILLNNNO CANNELLONI
ACEHIMOPRS SEMAPHORIC	ACEIILLNPR PERICLINAL	ACEILLNOOT OCELLATION
ACEHIMOPRT AMPHOTERIC,	ACEIILLNRY IRENICALLY	ACEILLNORT CITRONELLA
METAPHORIC	ACEIILLOST LOCALITIES	ACEILLNRTU LENTICULAR
ACEHIMOPTU APOTHECIUM	ACEIILLOSU LILIACEOUS	ACEILLOPSW PILLOWCASE
ACEHIMOSTX CHEMOTAXIS	ACEIILLRTY ILLITERACY	ACEILLOPTY POETICALLY
ACEHIMPSTY METAPHYSIC	ACEIILLTXY LEXICALITY	ACEILLORTV VORTICELLA
ACEHIMRSTU RHEUMATICS	ACEIILMMST MELISMATIC	ACEILLORTY EROTICALLY
ACEHINOPST ASTHENOPIC	ACEIILMNST MELANISTIC	ACEILLOTXY EXOTICALLY
ACEHINORRT CHITARRONE	ACEIILMOPT ATOMIC PILE	ACEILLPRUY PECULIARLY
ACEHINORST ANCHORITES,	ACEIILMPSS SPECIALISM	ACEILLPSTY SEPTICALLY
CHAIN STORE	ACEIILMRST SALIMETRIC	ACEILLRSTY STERICALLY
ACEHINORTV CHEVROTAIN	ACEIILNOTT ACTINOLITE	ACEILLRTUV VICTUALLER
ACEHINPSST PATCHINESS	ACEIILNPST PLASTICINE	ACEILLRTVY VERTICALLY
ACEHINPSTT PENTASTICH	ACEIILNRST IN ARTICLES	ACEILMMNSS CLAMMINESS
ACEHINPSTU EPICANTHUS	ACEIILNTVY INACTIVELY	ACEILMNOPR COMPLAINER
ACEHINRRSU HURRICANES	ACEIILORSS SOCIALISER	ACEILMNORS SERMONICAL
ACEHINRSSU SEA URCHINS	ACEIILORSZ SOCIALIZER	ACEILMNRST CENTRALISM
ACEHINRSTU RAUNCHIEST	ACEIILOSST SOCIALITES	ACEILMNRUW LAWRENCIUM
ACEHINRSTV REVANCHIST	ACEIILOSTU TILIACEOUS	ACEILMRRUV VERMICULAR
ACEHIORSTT RHEOSTATIC	ACEIILPPRT PARTICIPLE	ACEILMRSSU SECULARISM
ACEHIPPSSS SPACESHIPS	ACEIILPRTT TRIPLICATE	ACEILMTUUV CUMULATIVE
ACEHIRSSTT STARCHIEST	ACEIILPSST PLASTICISE,	ACEILNNOOP NAPOLEONIC
ACEHIRSTTT TETRASTICH	SPECIALIST	ACEILNNORS CORNELIANS
ACEHLLMNOY MELANCHOLY	ACEIILPSTY SPECIALITY	ACEILNNOTU NUCLEATION
ACEHLLPRSU SEPULCHRAL	ACEIILPSTZ PLASTICIZE	ACEILNNUVY UNIVALENCY
ACEHLMOOST SCHOOLMATE	ACEIILSTTY ELASTICITY	ACEILNOORT ICONOLATER,
ACEHLMORSY LACHRYMOSE	ACEIIMNRRU CINERARIUM	RELOCATION
ACEHLNORST CHARLESTON	ACEIIMRRST ERRATICISM	ACEILNOPPS SCALOPPINE
ACEHLOORST ORTHOCLASE	ACEIIMRSST ARMISTICES	ACEILNOPRT PRATINCOLE
ACEHLOOSSU COALHOUSES	ACEIIMRSTT TASIMETRIC	ACEILNOPST NEOPLASTIC,
ACEHLOPXYY OXYCEPHALY	ACEIINNRTY ITINERANCY	PLEONASTIC
ACEHLORRST ORCHESTRAL	ACEIINOPST SPECIATION	ACEILNOPTU PECULATION
ACEHLPRTYY PHYLACTERY	ACEIINORTT RECITATION	ACEILNORTU ULCERATION
ACEHMMNOOR	ACEIINOSTV VESICATION	ACEILNORTY LECTIONARY
CHROMONEMA	ACEIINOTTX EXCITATION,	ACEILNOSSS SOCIALNESS
ACEHMNPRST PARCHMENTS	INTOXICATE	ACEILNOSST COASTLINES
ACEHMOORUX	ACEIINPSTT ANTISEPTIC,	ACEILNOSTU INOSCULATE
AUXOCHROME	PSITTACINE	ACEILNOTUV NOVACULITE
ACEHMORRTU ROUTE	ACEIINRTVY INVERACITY	ACEILNPPSU SUPPLIANCE
MARCH	ACEIINSTTU AUSTENITIC	ACEILNRSTU LACUSTRINE
ACEHMORTTY TACHOMETRY	ACEIIORRRT CERTIORARI	ACEILNRSUV VULCANISER
ACEHMOSSTU MOUSTACHES	ACEIIORSTT ATROCITIES	ACEILNRTTY CENTRALITY
ACEHMRTTYY TACHYMETRY	ACEIIPPSST EPISPASTIC	ACEILNRTVY TRIVALENCY
ACEHNORRTT TROCHANTER	ACEIIRSSST SACRISTIES	ACEILNRUUX LUXURIANCE
ACEHNSSTTU STAUNCHEST	ACEIIRTTVY CREATIVITY,	ACEILNRUVZ VULCANIZER
ACEHOOPPRR CARPOPHORE	REACTIVITY	ACEILOOSUV OLIVACEOUS,
ACEHOOSSTU HOUSECOATS	ACEIJKKNSV JACK KNIVES	VIOLACEOUS
ACEHOPPRTU TOUCHPAPER	ACEIJNORTT TRAJECTION	ACEILOPPRS SAPROPELIC
ACEHORRSST CARTHORSES,	ACEIKKNNTU KENTUCKIAN	ACEILOPRTX EXPLICATOR
ORCHESTRAS	ACEIKLRSTV TRAVELSICK	ACEILOPTUV COPULATIVE
ACEHORTTWW	ACEIKMPRST STRIKE CAMP	ACEILOQTUY COEQUALITY
WATCHTOWER	ACEIKNORSS CROAKINESS	ACEILPPPRS PAPER CLIPS
ACEHPRRSSU PURCHASERS	ACEIKNPSTT SEPTIC TANK	ACEILPPSTU SUPPLICATE
ACEIIIMNST INTIMACIES	ACEIKOPRST AIRPOCKETS	ACEILPRTUU APICULTURE
ACEIIISTTV ACTIVITIES	ACEILLLPRU PELLICULAR	ACEILRSSTU SECULARIST
ACEIIJLSTU JESUITICAL	ACEILLMNSY MISCELLANY	ACEILRSTTU TESTICULAR
ACEIIKMNST KINEMATICS	ACEILLMORT ALLOMETRIC	ACEILRSTUY SECULARITY

ACEILRTUUV AVICULTURE
ACEIMMNORT MANOMETRIC
ACEIMMRSTY ASYMMETRIC
ACEIMNNOST CISMONTANE
ACEIMNNRUY INNUMERACY
ACEIMNOPRT IMPORTANCE
ACEIMNOPSU MENOPAUSIC
ACEIMNORST CREMATIONS
ACEIMNORUY AUREOMYCIN
ACEIMNPSTU PNEUMATICS
ACEIMNRRTY TERRAMYCIN
ACEIMNRSST MISCREANTS
ACEIMORSVW MICROWAVES
ACEIMORTTT TETRATOMIC
ACEIMORTTU TAUTOMERIC
ACEIMSSTTY SYSTEMATIC
ACEINNNSTU UNCANNIEST
ACEINNORST CONTAINERS,
SANCTIONER
ACEINNORTU ENUNCIATOR
ACEINNRSSU INSURANCES
ACEINNRSTY TRANSIENCY
ACEINNRTUU NUNCIATURE
ACEINNSSST SCANTINESS
ACEINOORTV REVOCATION
ACEINOOSTV EVOCATIONS
ACEINOPRTU PRECAUTION
ACEINOPSTT CONSTIPATE
ACEINORRST CONTRARIES
ACEINORRSV CARNIVORES
ACEINORRTT RETRACTION
ACEINORSSY CESSIONARY
ACEINORTTU ERUCTATION
ACEINORTTW TONIC WATER
ACEINORTTX EXTRACTION
ACEINOSSST CESSATIONS
ACEINOSTTU UNICOSTATE
ACEINPSSSU PUISSANCES
ACEINQSTTU QUITTANCES
ACEINRSSTW SCRAWNIEST
ACEINSSSTT SCATTINESS
ACEIOOPRTZ AZEOTROPIC
ACEIOOPTTV COOPTATIVE
ACEIOOSTUU AUTOECIOUS
ACEIOPRRSU PRECARIOUS
ACEIOPSTTT PETTICOATS
ACEIOQSSUU SEQUACIOUS
ACEIORRSST OSTRACISER
ACEIORRSTZ OSTRACIZER
ACEIORSTTT TRICOSTATE
ACEIPPRSST SCRAPPIEST
ACEIPSSSTU SPACESUITS
ACEISSTTTY CITY-STATES
ACEJKKRSSY SKYJACKERS
ACEJKLPPSU SUPPLEJACK
ACEJKNOSST JACKSTONES
ACEJORRTTY TRAJECTORY
ACEKKMOSST SMOKESTACK

ACEKKMRRSU
MUCKRAKERS
ACEKLLRSTU LACKLUSTRE
ACEKLNOPST ALPENSTOCK
ACEKLOPRSW
WORKPLACES
ACEKMNORRW
CANKERWORM
ACEKPRRSSY SKYSCRAPER
ACELLLMORU COLUMELLAR
ACELLLORSS SOLAR CELLS
ACELLNOSSW CALLOWNESS
ACELLOPSTU LEUCOPLAST
ACELLOPTUY EUCALYPTOL
ACELLORSSW LOWER
CLASS
ACELLPRUUV VULPECULAR
ACELLSSTTY TACTLESSLY
ACELMMNOOW
COMMONWEAL
ACELMNNOTT MALCONTENT
ACELMNOORT MONTE
CARLO
ACELNNOSSU CONSENSUAL
ACELNNOTUV CONVENTUAL
ACELNOPRRU PRONUCLEAR
ACELNOPRSY NARCOLEPSY
ACELNORRTY NECROLATRY
ACELNOSSTU CONSULATES
ACELNOTTUX CONTEXTUAL
ACELOOPRRT PERCOLATOR
ACELOOSSTT OSTEOCLAST
ACELOPPRST PARCEL POST
ACELOPRSTU SPECULATOR
ACELOSSSTU LOST CAUSES
ACELPPRSSU UPPER CLASS
ACELPRSSSU SUPERCLASS
ACELPSTUUY EUCALYPTUS
ACELRSSTTY CRYSTAL SET
ACEMMNORTY
COMMENTARY
ACEMMNOSTU
CONSUMMATE
ACEMMOSTTY
MASTECTOMY
ACEMNNNOTT
CANTONMENT
ACEMNNORST
MONSTRANCE
ACEMNOOPSS
MOONSCAPES
ACEMNOOTYZ
MYCETOZOAN
ACEMNOPRRY
PYROMANCER
ACEMNOSTTY NEMATOCYST
ACEMOOPRRS
MACROSPORE

ACEMOORSTU
OCTAMEROUS
ACEMORSTUY MYRTACEOUS
ACENNNORSU
ANNOUNCERS
ACENNOORTV
COVENANTOR
ACENNORSTV CONVERSANT
ACENNOSTTT CONTESTANT
ACENNRSTTU ENCRUSTANT
ACENOPSSTW TOWNSCAPES
ACENORRSTU RACONTEURS
ACENORSSTU COURTESANS
ACENPRSSUU PURSUANCES
ACEOOOPRRT COOPERATOR
ACEOOPPRRS CARPOSPORE
ACEOOPRRRT PROCREATOR
ACEOOPSSTT STATOSCOPE
ACEOPRSSTT SPECTATORS
ACEORRRSVY
CARRY-OVERS
ACEORRSTTX EXTRACTORS
ACEORSTUXY EXCUSATORY
ACERRSTUUV CURVATURES
ACFFGIILNT AFFLICTING
ACFFIILLOY OFFICIALLY
ACFFIILNOT AFFLICTION
ACFFIILNOU UNOFFICIAL
ACFFIIOORT OFFICIATOR
ACFFILLNUY FANCIFULLY
ACFGHINRSS GRASSFINCH
ACFGIILNRY CLARIFYING
ACFGIINRSY SCARIFYING
ACFGILNNOT CONFLATING
ACFGILOPRY PROFLIGACY
ACFGINRRTU FRACTURING
ACFHIILRST CHAIR LIFTS
ACFHIOPRST FACTORSHIP
ACFHLLTUWY WATCHFULLY
ACFHLNORSW HALF
CROWNS
ACFHLORSTW FLOWCHARTS
ACFIILNOPT PONTIFICAL
ACFIILNORT FRICTIONAL
ACFIIMNORT ACTINIFORM
ACFIINNORS INFRASONIC
ACFIINNORT INFARCTION,
INFRACTION
ACFIIOSTTU FACTITIOUS
ACFILLLORU FOLLICULAR
ACFILNNOOT CONFLATION
ACFILNNOTU FUNCTIONAL
ACFILNOOPT FOCAL POINT
ACFILNOOST TONIC SOL-FA
ACFILNRSUU FUNICULARS
ACFILRSSST FIRST-CLASS
ACFINOORRT FORNICATOR
ACFKMRRSTU TRUCK
FARMS

ACFLLOOPRT PORT OF CALL
ACFLNOORTW
  CONTRAFLOW
ACFLNRRUUU FURUNCULAR
ACFLOORSTU COLOURFAST
ACGGHIILOO HAGIOLOGIC
ACGGHIINNR CHAGRINING
ACGGHINOTT CHITTAGONG
ACGGIILLOT GLAGOLITIC
ACGGIILNNO GANGLIONIC
ACGGIINOTT COGITATING
ACGGILLNNY GLANCINGLY
ACGGILLOOY GLACIOLOGY
ACGGIMOSTY MYSTAGOGIC
ACGHHHIIRS HIGH CHAIRS
ACGHIIJKNS HIJACKINGS
ACGHIIMOPR AMPHIGORIC
ACGHIINSST CHASTISING
ACGHIIPRRT TRIGRAPHIC
ACGHILLOOP HAPLOLOGIC
ACGHILLOTY GOTHICALLY
ACGHILMNRY CHARMINGLY
ACGHILNSTY SCATHINGLY
ACGHIMNNOP CHAMPIGNON
ACGHIMNOOR
  HOMORGANIC
ACGHIMNOST STOMACHING
ACGHIMOPRR MICROGRAPH
ACGHIMOPRY MYOGRAPHIC
ACGHINNSTU STAUNCHING
ACGHINOPRZ ZINCOGRAPH
ACGHINPRSU PURCHASING
ACGHIOOPRR OROGRAPHIC
ACGHIOOPRZ ZOOGRAPHIC
ACGHIOPPRT PICTOGRAPH
ACGHMNOORR
  CHRONOGRAM
ACGHOOPPRY
  COPROPHAGY
ACGIIILLRT ARGILLITIC
ACGIIKMNNN NICKNAMING
ACGIILLMNS MISCALLING
ACGIILLNOZ LOCALIZING
ACGIILLOST LOGISTICAL
ACGIILLOTY LOGICALITY
ACGIILLRTU LITURGICAL
ACGIILMNPS MISPLACING
ACGIILMNSS ANGLICISMS
ACGIILMORS ALGORISMIC
ACGIILNRTU CURTAILING,
  GRANULITIC
ACGIILNRTY LARYNGITIC
ACGIILNTUV VICTUALING
ACGIIMNNRU MANICURING
ACGIIMNORR MARCONI RIG
ACGIIMNORS ORGANICISM
ACGIIMNRST SCINTIGRAM
ACGIIMNSST MISCASTING
ACGIINNNOT CONTAINING

ACGIINNNOZ CANONIZING
ACGIINNNST INSTANCING
ACGIINNOTU AUCTIONING,
  CAUTIONING
ACGIINNRTU CURTAINING
ACGIINOOTT COGITATION
ACGIINORST ORGANICIST
ACGIINPRST PRACTISING
ACGIINQTTU ACQUITTING
ACGIJKKNSY SKYJACKING
ACGIKKMNRU MUCKRAKING
ACGILLNOPS COLLAPSING,
  SCALLOPING
ACGILLNORR CORRALLING
ACGILLOOOR OROLOGICAL
ACGILLOOOT OTOLOGICAL
ACGILLOOOZ ZOOLOGICAL
ACGILLOPRY PYROGALLIC
ACGILLRSUY SURGICALLY
ACGILMNORU CLAMOURING
ACGILNNPRY PRANCINGLY
ACGILNOORY CRANIOLOGY
ACGILNOPTU COPULATING
ACGILORSUY GLYCOSURIA,
  GRACIOUSLY
ACGIMNOORS AGRONOMICS
ACGIMNOOSU ASCOGONIUM
ACGIMNSSTY GYMNASTICS
ACGINNNNOU ANNOUNCING
ACGINNOOST CONTAGIONS
ACGINNORRY CARRYING-ON
ACGINNRTTU TRUNCATING
ACGINOOSTU CONTAGIOUS
ACGINOPRTY AGRYPNOTIC
ACGINOPSUU PUGNACIOUS
ACGINORRST CO-STARRING
ACGIOOPRTV VAGOTROPIC
ACGIORSTTY GYROSTATIC
ACGJNOORTU CONJUGATOR
ACGLMNOOOS
  COSMOGONAL
ACGLNOORSU
  CLANGOROUS
ACHHIILPST PHTHISICAL
ACHHILMOPT OPHTHALMIC
ACHHILMRTY RHYTHMICAL
ACHHILOPTY HALOPHYTIC
ACHHINSTUY HYACINTHUS
ACHHIOPPST PHOSPHATIC
ACHHIPPRSU HIPPARCHUS
ACHHIPRSSU PUSHCHAIRS
ACHHLOSSTU SLOUCH HATS
ACHHLOSSTW WASHCLOTHS
ACHHNOOTTU
  AUTOCHTHON
ACHHOPPSTY PSYCHOPATH
ACHIIIMNOY ICHINOMIYA
ACHIIIMNST HISTAMINIC
ACHIIIMRTY HIMYARITIC

ACHIIIRSST TRICHIASIS
ACHIILLMPS PHALLICISM
ACHIILLPST PHALLICIST
ACHIILORST HISTORICAL
ACHIILORTU THIOURACIL
ACHIIMNNOR INHARMONIC
ACHIIMNSST MACHINISTS
ACHIIMNSTU HUMANISTIC
ACHIIMNSUV CHAUVINISM
ACHIINNOOT INCHOATION
ACHIINNORT CORINTHIAN
ACHIINNPQU CHINQUAPIN
ACHIINORTT ANORTHITIC
ACHIINPSSY PHYSICIANS
ACHIINRSST CHRISTIANS
ACHIINRSTT ANTICHRIST
ACHIINSTUV CHAUVINIST
ACHIIOPRST APHORISTIC
ACHIIOPSST PISTACHIOS
ACHIIPRSTY PHYSIATRIC
ACHIIRRSTT ARTHRITICS
ACHIIRSSTV ARCHIVISTS
ACHIKLOORW WORKAHOLIC
ACHIKMNOST MACKINTOSH
ACHILLMOOS ALCOHOLISM
ACHILLMSSU MUSIC HALLS
ACHILLNNSY CLANNISHLY
ACHILLNOOP ALLOPHONIC
ACHILLNOPY PHONICALLY
ACHILLOPRT PROTHALLIC
ACHILLPSYY PHYSICALLY
ACHILMOPTY POLYMATHIC
ACHILMPSTY ITCHY PALMS
ACHILNOORS ISOCHRONAL
ACHILNORUY HYALURONIC
ACHILORSUV CHIVALROUS
ACHIMMNORS MONARCHISM
ACHIMNOPTT MATCH POINT
ACHIMNOPTY AMPHICTYON
ACHIMNORST MONARCHIST
ACHIMORRTT TRICHROMAT
ACHIMORRYZ MYCORRHIZA
ACHIMORSTT CHROMATIST
ACHIMOSSST MASOCHISTS
ACHIMOSSTU MUSTACHIOS
ACHINNOSST STANCHIONS
ACHINNOSTW CHINATOWNS
ACHINOOPSX SAXOPHONIC
ACHINPRSST CHINSTRAPS
ACHIOOPPTT POTATO CHIP
ACHIOOPSTY SOCIOPATHY
ACHIOPRSTY PHYSIOCRAT
ACHIOPTTUY AUTOPHYTIC
ACHIPRSTYY PSYCHIATRY
ACHIRSTTWW WRISTWATCH
ACHKOPRSTW
  PATCHWORKS
ACHLLOOPSY PLAYSCHOOL

ACHLMMOORS
  SCHOOLMARM
ACHLMNORUU
  HOMUNCULAR
ACHLOOSSTU HOLOCAUSTS
ACHNOOPSYZ SCYPHOZOAN
ACHNOOPSSTY SYCOPHANTS
ACHORSTTTU CUTTHROATS
ACIIILNOPT POLITICIAN
ACIIILNPST SINCIPITAL
ACIIILORTV VARIOLITIC
ACIIILSTTV VITALISTIC
ACIIINNOTT INCITATION
ACIIINNRSTT INARTISTIC
ACIIINSTTV NATIVISTIC
ACIIINTTVY INACTIVITY
ACIIJRSTUY JUSTICIARY
ACIIKNRSST SANSKRITIC
ACIILLMNRY CRIMINALLY
ACIILLNNOS SCILLONIAN
ACIILLNORY IRONICALLY
ACIILMORST MORALISTIC
ACIILNOOST COALITIONS
ACIILNOPRV PROVINCIAL
ACIILNORTT TINCTORIAL
ACIILNPPRS PRINCIPALS
ACIILNSSTV CALVINISTS
ACIILOPRST SAPROLITIC
ACIILOPTTY TOPICALITY
ACIILORSTY ROYALISTIC
ACIILOSSST SOCIALISTS
ACIILOSSUV LASCIVIOUS
ACIILPSTTY PLASTICITY
ACIILRSTTU ALTRUISTIC,
  ULTRAISTIC
ACIILRTTTY TRACTILITY
ACIIMMNOPT PANTOMIMIC
ACIIMMNSTU NUMISMATIC
ACIIMMNOSS INSOMNIACS
ACIIMNORST MORTICIANS
ACIIMNPTTY TYMPANITIC
ACIIMNRSSS NARCISSISM
ACIIMNRSTU MANICURIST
ACIIMOSTTT STOMATITIC
ACIINNOOTV INVOCATION
ACIINNOSTU INSOUCIANT
ACIINNOTTX INTOXICANT
ACIINOPRST ASCRIPTION,
  CRISPATION
ACIINOPRTT TRITANOPIC
ACIINORSTV VICTORIANS
ACIINORTTU URTICATION
ACIINOSTUU INCAUTIOUS
ACIINRSSST NARCISSIST
ACIIOPSSUU AUSPICIOUS
ACIIORSTVY VARICOSITY
ACIISSSTTT STATISTICS
ACIJLNNOTU JUNCTIONAL
ACIJLORTUY JOCULARITY

ACIKKLMNOR KILMARNOCK
ACIKLNNOPT PLANKTONIC
ACIKLOORSW SOCIAL WORK
ACIKLORTYY KARYOLYTIC
ACIKOPRTYY KARYOTYPIC
ACIKRSSTTU TRACKSUITS
ACILLLOOQU COLLOQUIAL
ACILLMNNOO MONOCLINAL
ACILLMOORT COLLIMATOR
ACILLMOPYY MYOPICALLY
ACILLMSTYY MYSTICALLY
ACILLNOOPT CALL OPTION
ACILLNOOST COLLATIONS
ACILLNOOTU ALLOCUTION,
  LOCULATION
ACILLNORUU UNILOCULAR
ACILLNORUV INVOLUCRAL
ACILLOOPRT ALLOTROPIC
ACILLOORST OSCILLATOR
ACILLOPRTY TROPICALLY
ACILLORRTU TRILOCULAR
ACILMMOORS MICROSOMAL
ACILMMOSTT COMMITTALS
ACILMMRSUU SIMULACRUM
ACILMNOORT MICROTONAL
ACILMNOPST COMPLAINTS
ACILMNOSUU CALUMNIOUS
ACILMNOTUU CUMULATION
ACILMNRSUU MINUSCULAR
ACILMOOPTY POLYATOMIC
ACILMOPRRY MICROPYLAR
ACILMORSUU MIRACULOUS
ACILNNOPTY NONTYPICAL
ACILNOOORT COLORATION
ACILNOOPTU COPULATION
ACILNOORST CONSORTIAL
ACILNOORTU INOCULATOR
ACILNOORTY ICONOLATRY
ACILNOOSTU OSCULATION
ACILNOOTTT COTTONTAIL
ACILNORRTU TRINOCULAR
ACILNORRTY CONTRARILY
ACILNORSTU ULTRASONIC
ACILNOSTUY LACUNOSITY
ACILNPPSTU SUPPLICANT
ACILNRTTUY TACITURNLY
ACILOOPRRT PROCTORIAL
ACILOOPSTZ ZOOPLASTIC
ACILOOQSUU LOQUACIOUS
ACILOOSSUX SAXICOLOUS
ACILOPSSUY SPACIOUSLY
ACILOPSTUY CAPTIOUSLY
ACILORTTUV CULTIVATOR
ACILOSTUUY CAUTIOUSLY
ACILPRRSTU SCRIPTURAL
ACIMMORSSS COMMISSARS
ACIMMORSSY COMMISSARY
ACIMNNOOPS COMPANIONS
ACIMNNOSTY SANCTIMONY

ACIMNOOPRS COMPARISON
ACIMNOOPSS COMPASSION
ACIMNOORTY CRANIOTOMY
ACIMNOOSST ONOMASTICS
ACIMNOOSTY ACTOMYOSIN
ACIMNOPPRS PRISON CAMP
ACIMNOPRTY PATRONYMIC,
  PYROMANTIC
ACIMNOSTTY MYCOSTATIN
ACIMNOTTUY TAUTONYMIC
ACIMNPRSTU MANUSCRIPT
ACIMOOPRTT COMPATRIOT
ACIMOORTVY VARICOTOMY
ACIMOPSTTY ASYMPTOTIC
ACINNNOSTT INCONSTANT
ACINNNOTTU CONTINUANT
ACINNOOORT CORONATION
ACINNOPTTU PUNCTATION
ACINNORSTT CONSTRAINT
ACINNORTTU TRUNCATION
ACINNSTTYY NYCTINASTY
ACINOOOPTT COOPTATION
ACINOOPPRT PROTANOPIC
ACINOORSTT CARTOONIST
ACINOORTVY INVOCATORY
ACINORSSST CROISSANTS
ACINPRRSTT TRANSCRIPT
ACIOPRSTTY PYROSTATIC
ACIORRSTTU RUSTICATOR
ACJKOPRSST JOCKSTRAPS
ACKLLNRSTU TRUNK CALLS
ACKLMNOORS ROCK
  SALMON
ACKLMOOORS
  CLOAKROOMS
ACKLNOPRST ROCK PLANTS
ACKLORSSSW CROSSWALKS
ACLLLOOSSY COLOSSALLY
ACLLLRTUUY CULTURALLY
ACLLMRSUUY MUSCULARLY
ACLLNPTUUY PUNCTUALLY
ACLLPRSTUU SCULPTURAL
ACLMMNOOTY
  COMMONALTY
ACLMOORSSS CLASSROOMS
ACLNNOSTTU CONSULTANT
ACLNNOSTTY CONSTANTLY
ACLNNPTUUU UNPUNCTUAL
ACLNNRSUUU RANUNCULUS
ACLNOORSTT CONTRALTOS
ACLNOPSTUY POSTULANCY
ACLOOORSTU OSCULATORY
ACLOPRSTTU PLUTOCRATS
ACLRRSTTUU STRUCTURAL
ACMMOORTTU
  COMMUTATOR
ACMMPPUUUV VACUUM
  PUMP

ACMNNORTUY
COUNTRYMAN
ACMNOORRST
CORMORANTS
ACMNOOSSTU
COSMONAUTS
ACNNNOOSST CONSONANTS
ACNOOPRSTY SYNCOPATOR
ACNOPRSSUY SYNCARPOUS
ACNOPRTTUU PUNCTUATOR
ACOOOPRRRT CORPORATOR
ACOOOPSTTV POST OCTAVO
ACOOPRRRTT PROTRACTOR
ACOOPRRRTU PROCURATOR
ACOPRRSSST SPORTS CARS
ADDDDEEKLS SKEDADDLED
ADDDEEFHIL FIDDLEHEAD
ADDDEEGILM MIDDLE-AGED
ADDDEEHNRU
DUNDERHEAD
ADDDEEHRRU
RUDDERHEAD
ADDDEEHRTY DEHYDRATED
ADDDEEILSS SIDESADDLE
ADDDEGNORW
DOWNGRADED
ADDDELNOOW
DOWNLOADED
ADDEEEEPST DEEP-SEATED
ADDEEEFHNR
FREE-HANDED
ADDEEEFLOR FREELOADED
ADDEEEFNTU UNDEFEATED
ADDEEEGNNR
ENDANGERED
ADDEEEHLRT ETHELDREDA
ADDEEEHNNV
EVEN-HANDED
ADDEEEILNT DELINEATED
ADDEEEIRST DESIDERATE
ADDEEELNTT DEAD-NETTLE
ADDEEELRST SADDLETREE
ADDEEELRTT DEAD LETTER
ADDEEERSSS ADDRESSEES
ADDEEFHLNT LEFT-HANDED
ADDEEFHOST SOFT-HEADED
ADDEEFILOT DEFOLIATED
ADDEEFNNST DEFENDANTS
ADDEEGGINS DISENGAGED
ADDEEGHILR HILDEGARDE
ADDEEGHLNO
LONG-HEADED
ADDEEGILMS MIDDLE AGES
ADDEEGINRR DEAD RINGER
ADDEEGINRT DENIGRATED
ADDEEGINST DESIGNATED
ADDEEGLLNR GELDERLAND
ADDEEHHNTU HEADHUNTED
ADDEEHLNRU UNHERALDED

ADDEEHNNOP
OPEN-HANDED
ADDEEIIPSS DIAPEDESIS
ADDEEIKMNW
WEAK-MINDED
ADDEEILMMN MIDDLE NAME
ADDEEILMST MIDDLE EAST
ADDEEILNSS DEADLINESS
ADDEEILOTV DOVETAILED
ADDEEILPSS DISPLEASED
ADDEEILRSS SADDLERIES
ADDEEILRSV DAREDEVILS
ADDEEILRWY WIDELY READ
ADDEEIMNRR MIND READER
ADDEEIOPTV VIDEOTAPED
ADDEEIPRSW WIDESPREAD
ADDEEIPRTU REPUDIATED
ADDEEIRSTV ADVERTISED
ADDEEIRTTX EXTRADITED
ADDEEJRSTU READJUSTED
ADDEELLMTU MEDULLATED
ADDEELMNOR
ENDODERMAL
ADDEELMOTU DEMODULATE
ADDEELOORV OVERLOADED
ADDEELOPRR ROPE LADDER
ADDEELORSS SADDLE-SORE
ADDEELPRST STEPLADDER
ADDEEMNNRU
UNDERNAMED
ADDEEMNOPR
PROMENADED
ADDEENNPST DEPENDANTS
ADDEENNTTU UNATTENDED
ADDEENQRSU
SQUANDERED
ADDEENRRTU UNDERRATED
ADDEENSSWY
WEDNESDAYS
ADDEEOPRSS DESPERADOS
ADDEEORSTT ROAD-TESTED
ADDEFGINRU DEFRAUDING
ADDEFHILPS PADDLEFISH
ADDEFHNORU
FOUR-HANDED
ADDEFIIMNR FAIR-MINDED
ADDEFLLRUY DREADFULLY
ADDEGGILNN GLADDENING
ADDEGHHHIN HIGH-HANDED
ADDEGHLORT GOLDTHREAD
ADDEGILLNW WINDGALLED
ADDEGINRSS ADDRESSING
ADDEGIORRS DORSIGRADE
ADDEGLLMOS GOLD
MEDALS
ADDEGLLOPT GOLD-PLATED
ADDEHIIMRS DIE-HARDISM
ADDEHILMNS MISHANDLED
ADDEHIMNOO MAIDENHOOD

ADDEHIMNOS ADMONISHED
ADDEHMNNOW
HAND-ME-DOWN
ADDEHNORSU
ROUNDHEADS
ADDEHORRTY DEHYDRATOR
ADDEIILLSV ILL-ADVISED
ADDEIILMPY EPIDIDYMAL
ADDEIILQTU LIQUIDATED
ADDEIINNRS RED INDIANS
ADDEIINOTU AUDITIONED
ADDEIINRST DISTRAINED
ADDEIIPSST DISSIPATED
ADDEILLNSS LANDSLIDES
ADDEILLOSW DISALLOWED
ADDEILMNST DISMANTLED
ADDEILMTTY ADMITTEDLY
ADDEILNNOS DANDELIONS
ADDEILNSSY DEADLY SINS
ADDEINNOOT ENDODONTIA
ADDEINNOPT ODD-PINNATE
ADDEINNOTU DENUDATION
ADDEINNRRU UNDERDRAIN
ADDEINOORS RADIOSONDE
ADDEINRSTW TRADE WINDS
ADDELMORRW DREAM
WORLD
ADDELNNORW
WONDERLAND
ADDELNOORW
WOODLANDER
ADDELNOPWY
DOWNPLAYED
ADDELPQRUU QUADRUPLED
ADDENNPRUU
UP-AND-UNDER
ADDENNRSTU UNDERSTAND
ADDENOORST DEODORANTS
ADDEPQRSUU QUADRUPEDS
ADDFGIOORY GOOD FRIDAY
ADDFIILNSU DISDAINFUL
ADDGIIINNS DISDAINING
ADDGIINSSU DISSUADING
ADDGILLNWY WADDLINGLY
ADDGILNNSU UNSADDLING
ADDGILNRST STRADDLING
ADDHIILMOS OLD MAIDISH
ADDHILORSU SHROUD-LAID
ADDIIILNUV INDIVIDUAL
ADDIIINNOT IN ADDITION
ADDILLLLYY DILLYDALLY
ADDIMNOSUY DIDYNAMOUS
ADDIMOORSU DIADROMOUS
ADDNNOOTUW
DOWN-AND-OUT
ADEEEEGNRT DEGENERATE
ADEEEFILRS FEDERALISE
ADEEEFILRZ FEDERALIZE
ADEEEFIRTV FEDERATIVE

ADEEEFLORR FREELOADER
ADEEEFRRRT FREE-TRADER
ADEEEGGRST SEGREGATED
ADEEEGLRSV EVERGLADES
ADEEEGLRTU DEREGULATE
ADEEEHHPSS SHEEPSHEAD
ADEEEHLPSY SLEEPYHEAD
ADEEEHLRTT LETTERHEAD
ADEEEHNRTT THREATENED
ADEEEHNSST HEATEDNESS
ADEEEIPRRT PIED-À-TERRE
ADEEEIRRTT REITERATED
ADEEEIRSTT EASTERTIDE
ADEEELLMNP EMPANELLED
ADEEELLNRW
   WELL-EARNED
ADEEELLRVY REVEALEDLY
ADEEELNNUV UNLEAVENED
ADEEELNSST ELATEDNESS
ADEEELPRTY REPEATEDLY
ADEEEMNNRT
   ENDEARMENT
ADEEEMNRTU ENUMERATED
ADEEEMNRUV
   MANEUVERED
ADEEENORTX EXONERATED
ADEEENPRTT PENETRATED
ADEEENRRSW
   NEWSREADER
ADEEENRSST EAST ENDERS
ADEEENSSST SEDATENESS
ADEEENTTUX EXTENUATED
ADEEFFIMRR REAFFIRMED
ADEEFFORST AFFORESTED
ADEEFGHIRU FIGUREHEAD
ADEEFGINRT FEDERATING
ADEEFGLNNW
   NEWFANGLED
ADEEFGLRRS SELF-REGARD
ADEEFGMNRT FRAGMENTED
ADEEFHLNRT LEFT-HANDER
ADEEFHNRTU UNFATHERED
ADEEFILLNS SELF-DENIAL
ADEEFILMRS FEDERALISM
ADEEFILORR RELIEF ROAD
ADEEFILRST FEDERALIST
ADEEFIMNST MANIFESTED
ADEEFINORT FEDERATION
ADEEFIRSTU DISFEATURE
ADEEFISSTT DEFEATISTS
ADEEFLLLNN FLANNELLED
ADEEFLLORW FALLOW DEER
ADEEFLRSTU DEFAULTERS
ADEEFMNORW
   FREEDWOMAN
ADEEFNOPRR FREE PARDON
ADEEFNORRW
   FOREWARNED
ADEEFOPRRT PERFORATED

ADEEGGHLOR
   LOGGERHEAD
ADEEGGILNT DELEGATING
ADEEGGLNOS GOLDEN
   AGES
ADEEGGMOSU
   DEMAGOGUES
ADEEGGNRSS RAGGEDNESS
ADEEGGOPSU PEDAGOGUES
ADEEGGORUW OWE A
   GRUDGE
ADEEGIINSS DIAGENESIS
ADEEGIJLNR DARJEELING
ADEEGILLST LEGISLATED
ADEEGILMNR MALINGERED
ADEEGILNOT DELEGATION
ADEEGILNRR RINGLEADER
ADEEGIMNNR MEANDERING
ADEEGIMNRT GERMINATED
ADEEGIMNST MAGNETISED
ADEEGIMNTZ MAGNETIZED
ADEEGINNOT DENEGATION
ADEEGINNRS SERENADING
ADEEGINOTT NEGOTIATED
ADEEGINRRS GRENADIERS
ADEEGINRRT INTERGRADE,
   RETREADING
ADEEGINRTT INTEGRATED
ADEEGIORTV DEROGATIVE
ADEEGLLNOS GOLDENSEAL
ADEEGLLRUW
   WELL-ARGUED
ADEEGLMNNO GOLDEN
   MEAN
ADEEGLNRUZ UNDERGLAZE
ADEEGLOPUU GUADELOUPE
ADEEGLPPRY DAPPLE-GREY
ADEEGLRRSS REGARDLESS
ADEEGMNORT
   DERMATOGEN
ADEEGNOTXY OXYGENATED
ADEEGOORSV
   OVERDOSAGE
ADEEGOORSW
   GREASEWOOD
ADEEGORRRT RETROGRADE
ADEEGPRTUX EXPURGATED
ADEEHHILMR HEMIHEDRAL
ADEEHHILST HEAT SHIELD
ADEEHHLOSV SHOVELHEAD
ADEEHHMNOT
   HEATHENDOM
ADEEHHNOPS HEADPHONES
ADEEHHNORX
   HEXAHEDRON
ADEEHHNPTY HYPHENATED
ADEEHHNRTU HEADHUNTER
ADEEHIIRRW WIRE-HAIRED
ADEEHILNOT ETHANEDIOL

ADEEHILNTU HEULANDITE
ADEEHILPPR HARELIPPED
ADEEHILPRS DEALERSHIP,
   LEADERSHIP
ADEEHILSWY DAISY WHEEL
ADEEHIMNSU DEHUMANISE
ADEEHIMNUZ DEHUMANIZE
ADEEHIMPSS EMPHASISED
ADEEHIMPSZ EMPHASIZED
ADEEHINRST DISHEARTEN
ADEEHINRTT THENARDITE
ADEEHIPRRS READERSHIP
ADEEHIRRSS SHERARDISE
ADEEHIRRSZ SHERARDIZE
ADEEHIRRTY HEREDITARY
ADEEHKORRW
   HEADWORKER
ADEEHLLNRT ENTHRALLED
ADEEHLLNSS HANDLELESS
ADEEHLLNOTW
   DOWN-AT-HEEL
ADEEHLORUV OVERHAULED
ADEEHMNPRU
   UNHAMPERED
ADEEHMOSST HOMESTEADS
ADEEHNNRTU UNDERNEATH
ADEEHNOSST HEADSTONES
ADEEHOSSWY EYE
   SHADOWS
ADEEHRSSTW WATERSHEDS
ADEEIIJNRR JARDINIÈRE
ADEEIILMNT ELIMINATED
ADEEIILNTV EVIDENTIAL
ADEEIILRSS SERIALISED
ADEEIILRSZ SERIALIZED
ADEEIILSTV DEVITALISE
ADEEIILTVZ DEVITALIZE
ADEEIIMTTV MEDITATIVE
ADEEIINRST DISTRAINEE
ADEEIINSST DESSIATINE,
   EAST INDIES
ADEEIIRTVV DERIVATIVE
ADEEIJMNRS RED JASMINE
ADEEIJOPRS JEOPARDISE
ADEEIJOPRZ JEOPARDIZE
ADEEIKLLWW WEAK-WILLED
ADEEIKRSST ASTERISKED
ADEEILLMNP IMPANELLED
ADEEILLMRY REMEDIALLY
ADEEILLPRS ESPADRILLE
ADEEILLRRU DERAILLEUR
ADEEILLRTT ILL-TREATED
ADEEILLUVV VAUDEVILLE
ADEEILMNPT PEDIMENTAL
ADEEILMNRT DERAILMENT
ADEEILMORS DEMORALISE
ADEEILMORZ DEMORALIZE
ADEEILMPRR PERIDERMAL
ADEEILNORT DELINEATOR

ADEEILNPRT INTERPLEAD
ADEEILNRTU ADULTERINE
ADEEILNTTT DILETTANTE
ADEEILNTTV VENTILATED
ADEEILOPRS DEPOLARISE
ADEEILOPRZ DEPOLARIZE
ADEEILPRRV PEARL DIVER
ADEEIMMORT IMMODERATE
ADEEIMMUVW MEDIUM WAVE
ADEEIMNNOT DENOMINATE, EMENDATION
ADEEIMNNTT DETAINMENT
ADEEIMNRRS REMAINDERS
ADEEIMNRSS DREAMINESS
ADEEIMNRTT TERMINATED
ADEEIMORRT RADIOMETER
ADEEIMORTU AUDIOMETER
ADEEIMOTTV DEMOTIVATE
ADEEIMPPRS PIPE DREAMS
ADEEINORTT ORIENTATED
ADEEINOTTV DENOTATIVE, DETONATIVE
ADEEINPPSX APPENDIXES
ADEEINPRST PEDANTRIES, PEDESTRIAN
ADEEINRRSS DREARINESS
ADEEINRRST RESTRAINED
ADEEINRSSV VARIEDNESS
ADEEINRSTT REINSTATED, STRAITENED
ADEEINRTTT TRIDENTATE
ADEEISSSST STEADINESS
ADEEIOPRSX PEROXIDASE
ADEEIOSXYY OXEYE DAISY
ADEEIPRSTT TAPESTRIED
ADEEIPRTTX EXTIRPATED
ADEEIPRTUV DEPURATIVE
ADEEIRRSTV ADVERTISER
ADEEJRRSTU READJUSTER
ADEEKMNRSS MARKEDNESS
ADEEKMRRSS DRESSMAKER
ADEEKNNRTU UNDERTAKEN
ADEEKNRRTU UNDERTAKER
ADEELLNQUU UNEQUALLED
ADEELLNRUV UNRAVELLED
ADEELLOPRY ROLE-PLAYED
ADEELLOPST SELLOTAPED
ADEELLORSS LOSS LEADER
ADEELLOSTY DESOLATELY
ADEELLQRRU QUARRELLED
ADEELMMORS MESODERMAL
ADEELMNORT ENTODERMAL
ADEELMNPUX UNEXAMPLED
ADEELMORTY MODERATELY
ADEELMRSUY MEASUREDLY
ADEELNNQSU QUEENSLAND
ADEELNOSSY SEASONEDLY

ADEELNRRSS SLANDERERS
ADEELNRUUV UNDERVALUE
ADEELOPPRV OVERLAPPED
ADEELOPPTU DEPOPULATE
ADEELOPRSS LEOPARDESS
ADEELOPRVY OVERPLAYED
ADEELPPRRY PREPAREDLY
ADEELPRSTT SPLATTERED
ADEELRRSTU ADULTERERS
ADEELRSSTU ADULTERESS
ADEEMMNNRT REMANDMENT
ADEEMMNNST AMENDMENTS
ADEEMNNNRU UNMANNERED
ADEEMNNORT ORNAMENTED
ADEEMNNORV OVERMANNED
ADEEMNOPRR PROMENADER
ADEEMNOPRS PROMENADES
ADEEMNORSU DEMEANOURS
ADEEMNORTY EMENDATORY
ADEEMNORUV MANOEUVRED
ADEEMNORYY READY MONEY
ADEEMNPRTT DEPARTMENT
ADEEMNRSUU UNMEASURED
ADEEMOORRS AERODROMES
ADEEMOOSTU OEDEMATOUS
ADEENNOSSU UNSEASONED
ADEENNPTTU UNPATENTED
ADEENORSUV ENDEAVOURS
ADEENPPRRU UNPREPARED
ADEENPRRTU ENRAPTURED
ADEENPRSST DEPRESSANT
ADEENPRSTY PRESENT-DAY
ADEENQRRSU SQUANDERER
ADEENRRTUV ADVENTURER
ADEENRRTUW UNDERWATER
ADEENRSTTU UNDERSTATE
ADEENRSTUV ADVENTURES
ADEEOPPRRR ORDER PAPER
ADEEORRTTU TRADE ROUTE
ADEEORSTTV OVERSTATED
ADEEORSTVY OVERSTAYED
ADEEPPRSST SPEED TRAPS
ADEEPRRSTU DEPARTURES
ADEEPRSSST TRESPASSED

ADEERRSTYY STARRY-EYED
ADEERSSSTW STEWARDESS
ADEERSSTYY YESTERDAYS
ADEFFGGGIR GAFF-RIGGED
ADEFFLOOTT FLAT-FOOTED
ADEFGGINOR GOD-FEARING
ADEFGHIRST FARSIGHTED
ADEFGHORST GODFATHERS
ADEFGIILNN ENFILADING
ADEFGIINOR FOREIGN AID
ADEFGILNTU DEFAULTING
ADEFGILRSU LIFEGUARDS
ADEFGIRRSU FIREGUARDS
ADEFGLOOST FLOODGATES
ADEFGNOORR ROOF GARDEN
ADEFHHLOOT HEALTH FOOD
ADEFHHOORT FATHERHOOD
ADEFHILMSS DAMSELFISH
ADEFHILTTW HALF-WITTED
ADEFHINPRT PATHFINDER
ADEFHIRTWW WHITE DWARF
ADEFHLOOSS FALSEHOODS
ADEFHOORSW FORESHADOW
ADEFIILPSS FISSIPEDAL
ADEFIINQTU QUANTIFIED
ADEFIINRTU INFURIATED
ADEFIIRSTT STRATIFIED
ADEFILLLSU FULL-SAILED
ADEFILLNTY INFLATEDLY
ADEFILLSSU FUSILLADES
ADEFILMNOR MANIFOLDER
ADEFILMNTU FULMINATED
ADEFILMORS FORMALISED
ADEFILMORZ FORMALIZED
ADEFILNOST DEFOLIANTS
ADEFILOORT DEFOLIATOR
ADEFILORTU FLUORIDATE
ADEFIMRRRT DIRT FARMER
ADEFINOORR FOREORDAIN
ADEFINORSS SANFORISED
ADEFINORSZ SANFORIZED
ADEFINRSTX TRANSFIXED
ADEFIRSSTX FIXED STARS
ADEFKLNOTU OUTFLANKED
ADEFLMORTU FORMULATED
ADEFLNRTUU FRAUDULENT
ADEFNOORRW FOR A WONDER
ADEFOOPSST SOFT-SOAPED
ADEFORRSTV OVERDRAFTS
ADEFRRSTTU FRUSTRATED
ADEGGHOSTU SHAGGED OUT
ADEGGIMOPS PEDAGOGISM
ADEGGINORT DEROGATING
ADEGGINSUW WIND GAUGES

ADEGGNOPTU
　GET-UP-AND-GO
ADEGHHIKNT KNIGHTHEAD
ADEGHHILNR HIGHLANDER
ADEGHHILST HEADLIGHTS
ADEGHHINST NIGHTSHADE
ADEGHIILNN HEADLINING
ADEGHILLNO HELIGOLAND
ADEGHILNOO HALOGENOID
ADEGHILNOR LONGHAIRED
ADEGHILNSU LANGUISHED
ADEGHINPRS HEADSPRING,
　SPRINGHEAD
ADEGHIOPRY IDEOGRAPHY
ADEGHLORSS GASHOLDERS
ADEGHLRTUY DAUGHTERLY
ADEGHMOPRY
　DEMOGRAPHY
ADEGHMORSU HOME
　GUARDS
ADEGHNORST
　HEADSTRONG
ADEGHORSUU
　GUARDHOUSE
ADEGIIILNZ IDEALIZING
ADEGIIILST DIGITALISE
ADEGIIILTZ DIGITALIZE
ADEGIILMNS MISLEADING
ADEGIILNOT GADOLINITE,
　GELATINOID
ADEGIILNPR LIP-READING
ADEGIILNRT RING-TAILED
ADEGIILNSS SIGNALISED
ADEGIILNSZ SIGNALIZED
ADEGIIMMRT IMMIGRATED
ADEGIIMNRS MISREADING
ADEGIIMNTT MEDITATING
ADEGIINNRT DETRAINING
ADEGIINORT ORIGINATED
ADEGIINPRS DESPAIRING
ADEGIINSTT INSTIGATED
ADEGIIOPRR PRAIRIE DOG
ADEGILMNRY DREAMINGLY
ADEGILMORS GLAMORISED
ADEGILMORZ GLAMORIZED
ADEGILNNNO NONALIGNED
ADEGILNNNT LANDING NET
ADEGILNNRS SANDERLING,
　SLANDERING
ADEGILNNRU LAUNDERING
ADEGILNOST DESOLATING
ADEGILNOTT GLOTTIDEAN
ADEGILNRUV GERUNDIVAL
ADEGILOOPS APOLOGISED
ADEGILOOPZ APOLOGIZED
ADEGILRSUV VULGARISED
ADEGILRUVZ VULGARIZED
ADEGIMNNRU MAUNDERING
ADEGIMNOPU IMPOUNDAGE

ADEGIMNORS GORMANDISE
ADEGIMNORT MODERATING
ADEGIMNORZ GORMANDIZE
ADEGIMNPST STAMPEDING
ADEGIMNSTU MAGNITUDES
ADEGIMORST DOGMATISER
ADEGIMORTZ DOGMATIZER
ADEGINNOTT DETONATING
ADEGINNRSW WANDERINGS
ADEGINOORT DEROGATION
ADEGINORRS GARRISONED
ADEGINORRT DENIGRATOR
ADEGINORST DESIGNATOR
ADEGINPRSU PERSUADING
ADEGIPRRST PARTRIDGES
ADEGJLMNTU JUDGMENTAL
ADEGKNRRRU
　KRUGERRAND
ADEGLNORSU GLANDEROUS
ADEGMMOPRR
　PROGRAMMED
ADEGMNOOSU
　ENDOGAMOUS
ADEGNOOORW
　ORANGEWOOD
ADEGNOPRST GODPARENTS
ADEGNORSSU
　SANDGROUSE
ADEGOOORTY
　DEROGATORY
ADEGOORSST STAGE
　DOORS
ADEHHIIPRT DIPHTHERIA
ADEHHIRSSW DISHWASHER
ADEHHLLOOR HOLOHEDRAL
ADEHIILMTU HUMILIATED
ADEHIILNPR NEPHRIDIAL
ADEHIILRSS HAIR SLIDES
ADEHIINOPR HEPARINOID
ADEHIIPSUU EUPHAUSIID
ADEHILLORU LOUDHAILER
ADEHILNNRT HINTERLAND
ADEHILNOPS SPHENOIDAL
ADEHILNRRS HARD-LINERS
ADEHILNRST DISENTHRAL
ADEHILOPRS SPHEROIDAL
ADEHILPSTU DISULPHATE
ADEHIMNORS
　ADMONISHER, HARMONISED
ADEHIMNORZ HARMONIZED
ADEHIMORTU RHEUMATOID
ADEHIMOSSU HOUSEMAIDS
ADEHINOSST ASTONISHED
ADEHINQSUV VANQUISHED
ADEHINRSTY HYDRASTINE
ADEHIOPRSS RHAPSODIES,
　RHAPSODISE
ADEHIOPRSZ RHAPSODIZE
ADEHIORSTU AUTHORISED

ADEHIORTUZ AUTHORIZED
ADEHIOSSTW SHADOWIEST
ADEHIRRTTY TRIHYDRATE
ADEHIRRTWW
　WITHDRAWER
ADEHJMPRSU JAMSHEDPUR
ADEHKNORRW
　WORK-HARDEN
ADEHKNORST HANDSTROKE
ADEHKNOSSW
　SHAKEDOWNS
ADEHKORRSS DARK
　HORSES
ADEHLLNOUW
　UNHALLOWED
ADEHLLOPRY POLYHEDRAL
ADEHLLOSTT DEATH TOLLS
ADEHLMNOSY
　HANDSOMELY
ADEHLMOPTY METHYLDOPA
ADEHLRTTWY THWARTEDLY
ADEHMNNOSU
　UNHANDSOME
ADEHMOORST
　MASTERHOOD
ADEHMORRTW
　THREADWORM
ADEHMORSTY MOTHER'S
　DAY
ADEHNOOPRT
　PARENTHOOD, THEROPODAN
ADEHOORSSU
　ROADHOUSES
ADEHOORSVW
　OVERSHADOW
ADEHORRSSW
　SHOREWARDS
ADEIIIKNSS DIAKINESIS
ADEIIILLNT INITIALLED
ADEIIIMNTT INTIMIDATE
ADEIILLMPX MAXILLIPED
ADEIILLSTT DISTILLATE
ADEIILLTTT TITILLATED
ADEIILMMTU MULTIMEDIA
ADEIILMNOR MERIDIONAL
ADEIILMPPS MISAPPLIED
ADEIILNOPT DEPILATION
ADEIILNRTT INTERTIDAL
ADEIILNTTT DILETTANTI
ADEIILORST EDITORIALS,
　IDOLATRISE
ADEIILORTZ IDOLATRIZE
ADEIILSSUV VISUALISED
ADEIILSUVZ VISUALIZED
ADEIIMNOTT MEDITATION
ADEIIMNOTV DOMINATIVE
ADEIIMNRST ADMINISTER
ADEIIMPRSU PRAESIDIUM
ADEIIMRSTT DERMATITIS

ADEIINNNOS INDONESIAN
ADEIINNORT INORDINATE
ADEIINNOTW NATIONWIDE
ADEIINNOTX INDEXATION
ADEIINNPPT PINNATIPED
ADEIINNSST DAINTINESS
ADEIINNSTU INSINUATED
ADEIINNSTW WEST INDIAN
ADEIINORTV DERIVATION
ADEIINOSTV DEVIATIONS
ADEIINPPRS DRAINPIPES
ADEIINPTTU INAPTITUDE
ADEIIPRRSS DISPRAISER
ADEIIPRSST DISSIPATER
ADEIIPRSTV PRIVATISED
ADEIIPRTVZ PRIVATIZED
ADEIISSSUV DISSUASIVE
ADEIJMMNRW WINDJAMMER
ADEIKLLLRY LADY-KILLER
ADEIKLLMMT MALTED MILK
ADEIKNPPRS KIDNAPPERS
ADEILLMNOS MEDALLIONS
ADEILLMRST TREADMILLS
ADEILLMSST MEDALLISTS
ADEILLNOOS SOLENOIDAL
ADEILLNOPT POLLINATED
ADEILLNOSU DELUSIONAL
ADEILLNPSS PALLIDNESS
ADEILLNRRT TENDRILLAR
ADEILLNRTU ILL-NATURED
ADEILLNRUV UNRIVALLED
ADEILLQRSU QUADRILLES
ADEILLRRST ILL-STARRED
ADEILMNOPR PALINDROME
ADEILMNORS NORMALISED
ADEILMNORZ NORMALIZED
ADEILMNRST DISMANTLER
ADEILMNSSS DISMALNESS
ADEILMOTUV MODULATIVE
ADEILMSTTU STIMULATED
ADEILNNORT INTERNODAL
ADEILNOOST DESOLATION
ADEILNOOTV DEVOTIONAL
ADEILNPRTU PRUDENTIAL
ADEILNSSSW WINDLASSES
ADEILNSTTU TESTUDINAL
ADEILNSTUY UNSTEADILY
ADEILOORST OESTRADIOL
ADEILOPRTT TETRAPLOID
ADEILOPRTY DEPILATORY
ADEILOPSSU DISEPALOUS
ADEILOPSTU DIPETALOUS
ADEILOQSSU ODALISQUES
ADEILORTUV OUTRIVALED
ADEILOSSTT SOLID-STATE
ADEILPSTTU PLATITUDES,
     STIPULATED
ADEILRSTTU STRIDULATE
ADEILRTTXY DEXTRALITY

ADEILRTUUX LUXURIATED
ADEIMMNRST MASTERMIND
ADEIMMRSSU SUMMARISED
ADEIMMRSUZ SUMMARIZED
ADEIMNOORT MODERATION
ADEIMNPRRS REPRIMANDS
ADEIMNRSSU NURSEMAIDS
ADEIMORRTY RADIOMETRY
ADEIMORSST DERMATOSIS
ADEIMORTUY AUDIOMETRY
ADEIMRSTUX ADMIXTURES
ADEINNOOTT DENOTATION,
     DETONATION
ADEINNOPWW
     WINDOWPANE
ADEINNORSW RAWINSONDE
ADEINNORTU TRADE UNION
ADEINNRSTU UNSTRAINED
ADEINNRSTY TYRANNISED
ADEINNRTYZ TYRANNIZED
ADEINOPRST PATRONISED
ADEINOPRTU DEPURATION
ADEINOPRTZ PATRONIZED
ADEINOPTTU DEPUTATION
ADEINORSST ADROITNESS
ADEINORSUV ADENOVIRUS
ADEINOSTVY VIDEO NASTY
ADEINPPRSS SANDPIPERS
ADEINPPSST STANDPIPES
ADEINPRRST TRANSPIRED
ADEINPRSSY DISPENSARY
ADEINRSSTW TAWDRINESS
ADEINRSTTU UNSTRIATED
ADEINSSSTU UNASSISTED
ADEIOPPRSV DISAPPROVE
ADEIOPRRTU REPUDIATOR
ADEIOPRSTY DEPOSITARY
ADEIOPRSTZ TRAPEZOIDS
ADEIORSSTT SIDEROSTAT
ADEIPPRRTY DAY-TRIPPER
ADEJMNSTTU ADJUSTMENT
ADEJOPSTUX JUXTAPOSED
ADEKMNORTW
     DOWN-MARKET
ADEKMOPRST POSTMARKED
ADEKNOPRST POND-SKATER
ADEKNRRSSS DRESS RANKS
ADELLLPTUU PULLULATED
ADELLNORRU
     ALL-ROUNDER
ADELLNORSW
     LOWLANDERS
ADELLOORRR ROAD ROLLER
ADELLOORRU EURODOLLAR
ADELMOPSTU DEUTOPLASM
ADELMORSST OLD MASTERS
ADELNOOSST LOADSTONES
ADELNORRSV LAND ROVERS
ADELNORSSU SLANDEROUS

ADELNPPSTU SUPPLANTED
ADELNRSTUW WANDERLUST
ADELOOPRST DOORPLATES
ADELOPSTTU POSTULATED
ADELORRWWY
     WORLD-WEARY
ADELORSTUU ADULTEROUS
ADELPQRTUU QUADRUPLET
ADELPQRUUX QUADRUPLEX
ADEMMMNORU
     MEMORANDUM
ADEMMOOSTU
     STOMODAEUM
ADEMNNORSS
     RANDOMNESS
ADEMNNORST
     ADORNMENTS
ADEMNORSTW
     DOWNSTREAM
ADEMNRRSSU SNARE
     DRUMS
ADEMNRSTTU TRANSMUTED
ADEMOORRST
     MODERATORS
ADEMOQRTUY DEMY
     QUARTO
ADEMORSTTU OUTSMARTED
ADENNORRRU
     ROADRUNNER
ADENNPRSTU UNDERPANTS
ADENNRRRSU RUN
     ERRANDS
ADENNSSSTW NEWSSTANDS
ADENOORSTT DETONATORS
ADENOPRSST TRANSPOSED
ADENPRSSUW
     UPWARDNESS
ADENRRSSTW STERNWARDS
ADENRRSUYY DAY NURSERY
ADEOPRRSTT PROSTRATED
ADEORRSSWW
     SWEARWORDS
ADEPPRSTUU SUPPURATED
ADFFGILNOO OFF-LOADING
ADFGIILRRY GIRL FRIDAY
ADFGINORRU FAIRGROUND
ADFGINORRW FORWARDING
ADFHILLORS DOLLARFISH
ADFHINNORU FOUR-IN-HAND
ADFHNOORST AND SO
     FORTH
ADFIIINNPT PINNATIFID
ADFIIKMNRU FAIR DINKUM
ADFIILMRSU DISULFIRAM
ADFIILQSUY DISQUALIFY
ADFIIOSSTU FASTIDIOUS
ADFIISSSTY DISSATISFY
ADFINNOOTU FOUNDATION

ADFLMNTUUU MUTUAL
FUND
ADFMOOPSST FOOD STAMPS
ADFNOORTUY FOUDROYANT
ADFNOPRSTU STAND UP FOR
ADFNORRSTW
FRONTWARDS
ADGGIINNOS DIAGNOSING
ADGGINNOOR DRAGOONING
ADGGINNORU GAIN
GROUND
ADGHHOPRRY
HYDROGRAPH
ADGHIILNOY HOLIDAYING
ADGHILLLSU GUILDHALLS
ADGHIMNOPP HOPPING MAD
ADGHINNPRS HANDSPRING
ADGHIRRSTW RIGHTWARDS
ADGHIRSTTU DISTRAUGHT
ADGHLPRSUU SULPHA
DRUG
ADGIIILMST DIGITALISM
ADGIIILNNV INVALIDING
ADGIIIMNOR MIGRAINOID
ADGIIINOTT DIGITATION
ADGIIKNNPP KIDNAPPING
ADGIILMNOU GADOLINIUM
ADGIILMNRY ADMIRINGLY
ADGIILNPSY DISPLAYING
ADGIIMNNOT DOMINATING
ADGIIMNNTY DYNAMITING
ADGIIMNPRS RISING DAMP
ADGIIMNSST DISMASTING
ADGIINNNTU INUNDATING
ADGIINNPRW DRAWING PIN
ADGIINOSVW DISAVOWING
ADGIJNNORU ADJOURNING
ADGIKNORWY WORKING
DAY
ADGIKOORRV KIROVOGRAD
ADGILLNOPR POLLARDING
ADGILLOPRY PRODIGALLY
ADGILMNOTU MODULATING
ADGILNNTUU UNDULATING
ADGILNOOPW WADING POOL
ADGIMOSSTT DOGMATISTS
ADGINNOSTU ASTOUNDING
ADGINNPSTU UPSTANDING
ADGINOPSTT POSTDATING
ADGINPRRSX GRANDS PRIX
ADGINRRSTW DRAWSTRING
ADGIORSSWW GRASS
WIDOW
ADGLMNOOOY
MONADOLOGY
ADGLNNOPRU GROUND
PLAN
ADGLNOPRUY PLAYGROUND

ADGMNNORSU
GROUNDSMAN
ADGMNORSSU
GROUNDMASS
ADGMOORRSU
GUARDROOMS
ADGNNORSUY
GYNANDROUS
ADGNOOORRT
DRAGONROOT
ADHHNOSTTU THOUSANDTH
ADHIIKKNNT KITH AND KIN
ADHIILMNOT MIDLOTHIAN
ADHIIMMNPS MIDSHIPMAN
ADHIIMSTTU HUMIDISTAT
ADHIINNSTU HINDUSTANI
ADHIIPRTTY HIT PAY DIRT
ADHILLLOPY PHYLLODIAL
ADHILNOSTU OUTLANDISH
ADHILOOPRS DROSOPHILA
ADHILOQRRU HARD LIQUOR
ADHIMNORSY DISHARMONY
ADHINNOOOT NATIONHOOD
ADHINOOPRT ANTHROPOID
ADHINOOPRY RADIOPHONY
ADHINOOPRZ RHIZOPODAN
ADHINOSSWW SASH
WINDOW
ADHIOPRSST RHAPSODIST
ADHIPRRTTY THIRD PARTY
ADHLNOPSSW
SPLASHDOWN
ADHNORRSTW
NORTHWARDS
ADHOORRTWY
ROADWORTHY
ADHORSSTUW
SOUTHWARDS
ADIIILMNSV INVALIDISM
ADIIILMRSS DISSIMILAR
ADIIILNOSV DIVISIONAL
ADIIILNTVY INVALIDITY
ADIIINNOTV DIVINATION
ADIIINOOST IODISATION
ADIIINOOTZ IODIZATION
ADIILMMNSU MAUDLINISM
ADIILMNOXY MIXOLYDIAN
ADIILMOPRR PRIMORDIAL
ADIILMOPRS PRISMOIDAL
ADIILMSSSS DISMISSALS
ADIILNORRY ORDINARILY
ADIILNOSSU SINUSOIDAL
ADIILNRSTU INDUSTRIAL
ADIILOPPSY POLYDIPSIA
ADIILOQRTU LIQUIDATOR
ADIILORSSY RADIOLYSIS
ADIILORSTY SOLIDARITY
ADIILQSTUY SQUALIDITY
ADIIMMMOTU OMMATIDIUM

ADIIMNNNOO ANNO DOMINI
ADIIMNNOOT ADMONITION,
DOMINATION
ADIIMNNORV MORDVINIAN
ADIIMNOSSS ADMISSIONS
ADIIMOPRST DIATROPISM,
PRISMATOID
ADIIMORTUU AUDITORIUM
ADIINNNOTU INUNDATION
ADIINNOORT ORDINATION
ADIINOPPST DISAPPOINT
ADIINOPSSS DISPASSION
ADIINORRST DISTRAINOR
ADIINORSTT TRADITIONS
ADIINORTVY DIVINATORY
ADIINOSSSU DISSUASION
ADIIOPRSTT PODIATRIST
ADILLLOSYY DISLOYALLY
ADILLNSSTT STANDSTILL
ADILLOSTYY DISLOYALTY
ADILMMOPSU PLASMODIUM
ADILMNOOOP MONOPODIAL
ADILMNOOTU MODULATION
ADILMOPSST PSALMODIST
ADILNNOTUU UNDULATION
ADILOORSTU IDOLATROUS
ADIMNOORTY ADMONITORY
ADIMNRRTUV TRIVANDRUM
ADINNOPSTT STANDPOINT
ADINNOSSTU INS AND OUTS
ADINOOPRST ADSORPTION
ADINOOSSTW SATINWOODS
ADINORSSTW DOWNSTAIRS
ADIORSSSTU DISASTROUS
ADJLOPRTUU PLAT DU JOUR
ADJMMOOORS
MAJOR-DOMOS
ADJMMORRSU DRUM
MAJORS
ADKNORRSTU TRUNK
ROADS
ADLMOOORSU
MALODOROUS
ADLNORSTUU ULTRASOUND
ADLNORTUUY UNDULATORY
ADLNORTUWY
UNTOWARDLY
ADLOOOSSTT TOADSTOOLS
ADMNNOORSU
MONANDROUS
ADMNORSSST SANDSTORMS
ADMOOOPSTT
STOMATOPOD
ADNNORRTUU
TURNAROUND
AEEEEGKMPR GAMEKEEPER
AEEEEGKPRT GATEKEEPER
AEEEEGLNSS SENEGALESE
AEEEEGNRRT REGENERATE

AEEEEGRTTV REVEGETATE	AEEEHNORTY HONEY-EATER	AEEFHIKNST SNEAK THIEF
AEEEEELNOPT ELAEOPTENE	AEEEHNRRTT THREATENER	AEEFHINPRT PINFEATHER
AEEEEENRTTX EXENTERATE	AEEEHOPRRS AEROSPHERE	AEEFHLOPPR LEAF-HOPPER
AEEEESTTTT TÊTE-À-TÊTES	AEEEHRSTTW SWEETHEART	AEEFHLRSST FATHERLESS
AEEEFFIMNT EFFEMINATE	AEEEIIPPRT PERIPETEIA	AEEFHMORTT FATHOMETER
AEEEFGLNRU ENFLEURAGE	AEEEILNRST ETERNALISE	AEEFHOSSSU SAFE HOUSES
AEEEFGNRST FREE AGENTS	AEEEILNRTV INTERLEAVE	AEEFHPRSTT STEPFATHER
AEEEFHLSTT FALSE TEETH	AEEEILNRTZ ETERNALIZE	AEEFHRRSTW FRESHWATER
AEEEFHRRTT THEREAFTER	AEEEIMNRRX RE-EXAMINER	AEEFIIRRRS FIRE-RAISER
AEEEFINRTZ ANTIFREEZE	AEEEIMNSTV VIETNAMESE	AEEFIKNPPR PAPER KNIFE
AEEEFIRRST FIRE-EATERS	AEEEIMPRTV PERMEATIVE	AEEFIKNRSS FREAKINESS
AEEEFLLNST FENESTELLA	AEEEINRSTT ENTREATIES	AEEFILMPRS RELIEF MAPS
AEEEFLMNSS FEMALENESS	AEEEINRTTV INVETERATE	AEEFILMRTY FAMILY TREE
AEEEFNRRST TRANSFEREE	AEEEINRTVV ENERVATIVE	AEEFILOPRT PERFOLIATE
AEEEFPRSSS FREE PASSES	AEEEINRTVW INTERWEAVE	AEEFILRSTV AFTERLIVES
AEEEGGGNRS GREENGAGES	AEEEJKRRRT TEARJERKER	AEEFIMNRRT FREEMARTIN
AEEEGGMNNT	AEEEJNRTUV REJUVENATE	AEEFINRRST FRATERNISE
ENGAGEMENT	AEEEKKPPRR PARK KEEPER	AEEFINRRTZ FRATERNIZE
AEEEGGRSST EASTER EGGS	AEEEKMRRST MARKETEERS	AEEFLLNNOT FONTANELLE
AEEEGHLPRT TELPHERAGE	AEEEKNSSSW WEAKNESSES	AEEFLLNRUY FUNEREALLY
AEEEGHNRRT GREENHEART	AEEEKPSSTW SWEEPSTAKE	AEEFLLRSSY FEARLESSLY
AEEEGILNNV EVANGELINE	AEEELLRTVW WATER LEVEL	AEEFLMOPRX FOR EXAMPLE
AEEEGILNRS GENERALISE	AEEELLSSTT TESSELLATE	AEEFLRRSTT FLATTERERS
AEEEGILNRZ GENERALIZE	AEEELMMNPT EMPALEMENT	AEEFMNORSS FREEMASONS
AEEEGILNSV EVANGELISE	AEEELMMNRT EMMENTALER	AEEFNORRRW
AEEEGILNVZ EVANGELIZE	AEEELMNNTT LENTAMENTE,	FOREWARNER
AEEEGIMNRS MENAGERIES	TENEMENTAL	AEEFNSSSST FASTNESSES
AEEEGINNOR AERO-ENGINE	AEEELMNRTT MANTELTREE	AEEFNSSTTY SAFETY NETS
AEEEGINRTV GENERATIVE	AEEELMNRTV REVEALMENT	AEEFORRRSW
AEEEGITTVV VEGETATIVE	AEEELMNRTY ELEMENTARY	FORSWEARER
AEEEGKLOPR GOALKEEPER	AEEELNNUVZ VENEZUELAN	AEEGGHILRT LIGHTERAGE
AEEEGLMNRT REGALEMENT	AEEELNPRST PLANE TREES	AEEGGHOPRR
AEEEGLNNOR GREEN	AEEEMMNORT	GEOGRAPHER
ANOLE	ANEMOMETER	AEEGGILNRS GINGER ALES
AEEEGLNOST EAGLESTONE	AEEEMNOPSS OPEN SESAME	AEEGGILNRT RELEGATING
AEEEGLRRSV GEAR LEVERS	AEEEMNPRTT PENTAMETER	AEEGGINNRT GENERATING
AEEEGLSSSY EYEGLASSES	AEEEMNRRTU REMUNERATE	AEEGGINRRS GRANGERISE
AEEEGMNNRT	AEEEMSSTTW SWEETMEATS	AEEGGINRRZ GRANGERIZE
ENRAGEMENT	AEEENNNSST TENNESSEAN	AEEGGINTTV VEGETATING
AEEEGMNRSS MEAGRENESS	AEEENNRRSST EASTERNERS	AEEGGIRSSV AGGRESSIVE
AEEEGMNRST AGREEMENTS	AEEEPPRRTT PERPETRATE	AEEGGMORST
AEEEGNPPRR GREEN PAPER	AEEEPPRTTU PERPETUATE	MORTGAGEES
AEEEGPRSSX EXPRESSAGE	AEEERRSTYY YESTERYEAR	AEEGGNRSSU GREASE
AEEEGQSTUU SQUETEAGUE	AEEERSSTTY EASY STREET	GUNS
AEEEGRSTTZ GAZETTEERS	AEEFFHORRT FOREFATHER	AEEGGORRST SEGREGATOR
AEEEHHINST HEATHENISE	AEEFFLLORR FREE-FOR-ALL	AEEGGRRSSW
AEEEHHINTZ HEATHENIZE	AEEFFORRST REAFFOREST	SWAGGERERS
AEEEHHPRST THREE-PHASE	AEEFFSSTUY SAFETY FUSE	AEEGHHMORR
AEEEHLLRTY ETHEREALLY	AEEFGGHIRT FREIGHTAGE	HEMORRHAGE
AEEEHLRTWW	AEEFGHINRT FEATHERING	AEEGHIILMP HEMIPLEGIA
WATERWHEEL	AEEFGHORRT FOREGATHER	AEEGHIKMTW MAKEWEIGHT
AEEEHMNORX	AEEFGIINRT FIRE-EATING	AEEGHIKNNR HEARKENING
HEXAEMERON	AEEFGILLNT LEAFLETING	AEEGHILNSS SINGHALESE
AEEEHMNRTW	AEEFGILNRR RIFLE RANGE	AEEGHILPST LEGATESHIP
WEATHERMEN	AEEFGILPRS PERSIFLAGE	AEEGHIMRST HERMITAGES
AEEEHMPRTT HEPTAMETER	AEEFGLPRSU PRESAGEFUL	AEEGHINNRT HEARTENING
AEEEHMRSTX HEXAMETERS	AEEFGORRRU FOURRAGÈRE	AEEGHINPRT PREHEATING
AEEEHNNNPT NEPENTHEAN	AEEFHHINRT FAHRENHEIT	AEEGHINRRS REHEARSING
AEEEHNNSTV HEAVEN-SENT	AEEFHIKLRT FATHER-LIKE	AEEGHINRTW WEATHERING

AEEGHIPPRR EPIGRAPHER	AEEGINNRTT ENTREATING	AEEHIKLLRT HALTER-LIKE
AEEGHKNNRS GREENSHANK	AEEGINNRTV ENERVATING,	AEEHIKLMMR HAMMER-LIKE
AEEGHLMORT	VENERATING	AEEHILLORT HELIOLATER
GEOTHERMAL	AEEGINNSUX EXSANGUINE	AEEHILMRST THERMALISE
AEEGHLNTVW WAVELENGTH	AEEGINORRS REORGANISE	AEEHILMRTZ THERMALIZE
AEEGHLORTT ALTOGETHER	AEEGINORRZ REORGANIZE	AEEHILMTTW WHITE METAL
AEEGHLPRST TELEGRAPHS	AEEGINORVY A ROVING EYE	AEEHILPPRR PERIPHERAL
AEEGHLPRTY TELEGRAPHY	AEEGINOTTV VEGETATION	AEEHILPPSY EPIPHYSEAL
AEEGHMNOOT	AEEGINPRSV GRAPEVINES	AEEHILPRST SPHALERITE
HOMOGENATE	AEEGINPRSY PANEGYRISE	AEEHILPSST SHAPELIEST
AEEGHMNOPS	AEEGINPRYZ PANEGYRIZE	AEEHILRSTT EARTHLIEST,
MEGAPHONES	AEEGINRRTT RETREATING	STEALTHIER
AEEGHMORTY	AEEGINRRTX GENERATRIX	AEEHILSTTW WEALTHIEST
HETEROGAMY	AEEGINRSSS GREASINESS	AEEHIMMRSX HEXAMERISM
AEEGHOSSTU GATEHOUSES	AEEGINRSSV VERNISSAGE	AEEHIMNOPP EPIPHONEMA
AEEGIILLLS ILLEGALISE	AEEGIPPRRT PAPER TIGER	AEEHIMNPRT HEMIPTERAN
AEEGIILLLZ ILLEGALIZE	AEEGIRSSTT STRATEGIES	AEEHIMSSTT METATHESIS
AEEGIILMTT LEGITIMATE	AEEGLLNOSS LOS ANGELES	AEEHINORST ANTIHEROES
AEEGIILNST GELATINISE	AEEGLLORTT ALLEGRETTO	AEEHINPRST HEN PARTIES,
AEEGIILNTZ GELATINIZE	AEEGLMNNTT TANGLEMENT	INTERPHASE
AEEGIIMRTV EMIGRATIVE	AEEGLMRRSW	AEEHINRSST EARTHINESS,
AEEGIINRRT GARNIERITE	LEG-WARMERS	HEARTINESS
AEEGILLMNN ENAMELLING	AEEGLNORTU OUTGENERAL	AEEHIPPRTW WHITE PAPER
AEEGILLORS ALLEGORIES,	AEEGLORTUV TRAVELOGUE	AEEHIRTTWW WHITEWATER
ALLEGORISE	AEEGMNNOST	AEEHISTUVX EXHAUSTIVE
AEEGILLORZ ALLEGORIZE	MANGOSTEEN	AEEHKLNPRS PLANK-SHEER
AEEGILMNNP EMPANELING	AEEGMNOQSU	AEEHKMMORS
AEEGILMNRR MALINGERER	MONEGASQUE	HOMEMAKERS
AEEGILMNRT REGIMENTAL	AEEGMNRSTY SEGMENTARY	AEEHKMPRST THEME PARKS
AEEGILMNSV EVANGELISM	AEEGMORRST	AEEHKOPSSV SPOKESHAVE
AEEGILNNSV LEAVENINGS	STEREOGRAM	AEEHKORSTT HEATSTROKE
AEEGILNORT REGELATION,	AEEGMORSST GASOMETERS	AEEHKOSSTU STEAKHOUSE
RELEGATION	AEEGMPRTUU UP A	AEEHLLMRTY HEMELYTRAL
AEEGILNOTV ELONGATIVE	GUMTREE	AEEHLLNRRT ENTHRALLER
AEEGILNRST GENERALIST	AEEGMPSTTU GET UP	AEEHLLORSW WHOLESALER
AEEGILNRTU ARGENTEUIL	STEAM	AEEHLMMRSS
AEEGILNRTY GENERALITY	AEEGMRRTTY GREY	HAMMERLESS
AEEGILNSTV EVANGELIST	MATTER	AEEHLMNNOP
AEEGILNTVY NEGATIVELY	AEEGMRSSTU GAUSSMETER	PHENOMENAL
AEEGILOSTY LAY SIEGE TO	AEEGNNORSS SENSE	AEEHLMPRSW SPERM
AEEGILPSTT TITLE PAGES	ORGAN	WHALE
AEEGILRRSU REGULARISE	AEEGNNSSTW	AEEHLNOSTT ON THE SLATE
AEEGILRRUZ REGULARIZE	NEWSAGENTS	AEEHLNRSTT NETTLE RASH
AEEGILRTUV REGULATIVE	AEEGNOPRSS PERSONAGES	AEEHLORSTW WATERHOLES
AEEGIMNNSV GIVEN NAMES	AEEGNORRST GENERATORS	AEEHLRSTTX TAX SHELTER
AEEGIMNPRT IMPREGNATE,	AEEGNORSTU ENTOURAGES	AEEHMNNSSU
PERMEATING	AEEGNORSTV GRAVESTONE	HUMANENESS
AEEGIMNRRS GERMANISER	AEEGNPRSSS PASSENGERS	AEEHMOPRRU
AEEGIMNRRZ GERMANIZER	AEEGNPRSST PRESS AGENT	AMPERE-HOUR
AEEGIMNRST MAGNETISER	AEEHHHINST HEATHENISH	AEEHMOPRSS SEMAPHORES
AEEGIMNRTZ MAGNETIZER	AEEHHILMOP HAEMOPHILE	AEEHMOPRST ATMOSPHERE
AEEGIMPRRR GRIM REAPER	AEEHHILSTT HEALTHIEST	AEEHMORRRT
AEEGIMRRTU MARGUERITE	AEEHHIMNST HEATHENISM	ARTHROMERE
AEEGIMRRTV GRAVIMETER	AEEHHINRST EARTHSHINE	AEEHMORSUX
AEEGINNNSU ENSANGUINE	AEEHHKNPSS SHEEPSHANK	HEXAMEROUS
AEEGINNORT GENERATION	AEEHHLMSTU METHUSELAH	AEEHMORTTY METATHEORY
AEEGINNPSS PANGENESIS	AEEHHPSSTU HEPHAESTUS	AEEHNNOORT ONE
AEEGINNRRT INTERREGNA	AEEHIILLPT EPITHELIAL	ANOTHER
AEEGINNRST TANGERINES	AEEHIISTTV HESITATIVE	AEEHNORSSS HOARSENESS

AEEHNPPTVY HAPPY EVENT
AEEHNPRRSS SHARPENERS
AEEHOOPRRS HORSE
  OPERA
AEEHOOPRST PEASHOOTER
AEEHOOPSST APOTHEOSES
AEEHORSSUW
  WAREHOUSES
AEEHORSTVW
  WHATSOEVER
AEEHRRSSTV HARVESTERS
AEEIIKNRST KERATINISE
AEEIIKNRTZ KERATINIZE
AEEIILLRTT ILLITERATE
AEEIILMNRS MINERALISE
AEEIILMNRZ MINERALIZE
AEEIILNPRU EPINEURIAL
AEEIILRRTV IRRELATIVE
AEEIILRSST ISRAELITES
AEEIILRSTV REVITALISE
AEEIILRTVZ REVITALIZE
AEEIIMNNST INSEMINATE
AEEIIMNNTT TIEMANNITE
AEEIIMNRSS SEMINARIES
AEEIIMNSTT ANTI-SEMITE
AEEIIMPRTV IMPERATIVE
AEEIIMRSSS EMISSARIES
AEEIIMSTTV ESTIMATIVE
AEEIINPPRZ PIPERAZINE
AEEIIPRSST ASPERITIES,
  PATISSERIE
AEEIJLOSSU JEALOUSIES
AEEIJOPRTV PEJORATIVE
AEEIKLNNRT INTERLAKEN
AEEIKLNSSW WEAKLINESS
AEEIKNNSSS SNEAKINESS
AEEIKQSSTU SQUEAKIEST
AEEIKRRSTW WATER SKIER
AEEIKRSSTT STREAKIEST
AEEILLLLNV VILLANELLE
AEEILLMNST ENAMELLIST
AEEILLNSVV EVANSVILLE
AEEILLPSTT STIPELLATE
AEEILLRSSV VERSAILLES
AEEILLRTTY LITERATELY
AEEILLRTVY RELATIVELY
AEEILLSSTT SATELLITES
AEEILMMNPT IMPALEMENT
AEEILMNNST LINEAMENTS
AEEILMNNTT ENTAILMENT
AEEILMNPRT PLANIMETER
AEEILMNRST STREAMLINE
AEEILMNSSS MEASLINESS
AEEILMRSTT ALTIMETERS
AEEILNNPRS PERENNIALS
AEEILNNPST SEPTENNIAL
AEEILNNSTT SENTENTIAL
AEEILNNSTV VALENTINES
AEEILNNTTU LIEUTENANT

AEEILNOPRT PERITONEAL
AEEILNORTV REVELATION
AEEILNOSTV ELEVATIONS
AEEILNPPPS PINEAPPLES
AEEILNPRSS PEARLINESS
AEEILNPRST ALPESTRINE
AEEILNQSTU SEQUENTIAL
AEEILNQTUV EQUIVALENT
AEEILNRRTV IRRELEVANT
AEEILNRSTU NEUTRALISE
AEEILNRSTW IN A SWELTER
AEEILNRTTY ETERNALITY
AEEILNRTUZ NEUTRALIZE
AEEILNSSST ESSENTIALS
AEEILNSSSZ SLEAZINESS
AEEILNSTVX SEXIVALENT
AEEILORTTV TOLERATIVE
AEEILPPRRT PERIPTERAL
AEEILPRSST PSALTERIES
AEEILPRSSY ERYSIPELAS
AEEILPSTTU ESTIPULATE
AEEILQRSSU EQUALISERS
AEEILQRSUZ EQUALIZERS
AEEILRRSTT AIR-LETTERS
AEEILRRSVW SILVERWARE
AEEILRRTTU LITERATURE
AEEIMMMRST METAMERISM
AEEIMMOPRT EMMETROPIA
AEEIMNNPRT PINE MARTEN
AEEIMNNRTT RETAINMENT
AEEIMNNRTU INNUMERATE
AEEIMNNSZZ MEZZANINES
AEEIMNOPRT PERMEATION
AEEIMNORTT MARIONETTE
AEEIMNOSTT MAISONETTE
AEEIMNRSSS NEAR MISSES,
  SMEARINESS
AEEIMNRSTT MARTENSITE
AEEIMNRTUV NUMERATIVE
AEEIMNSSST STEAMINESS
AEEIMORRTV VARIOMETER
AEEIMPRRST PRIME RATES
AEEIMQRSUV SEMIQUAVER
AEEIMRSTTX TAXIMETERS
AEEINNNTVY IN ANY EVENT
AEEINNORTV ENERVATION,
  VENERATION
AEEINNOTTT ANTOINETTE
AEEINNPQTU PENTAQUINE
AEEINNRTUV AVENTURINE
AEEINNSSSU UNEASINESS
AEEINOPPST APPOINTEES
AEEINOPRST PROTEINASE
AEEINOPTTT POTENTIATE
AEEINORTVV RENOVATIVE
AEEINPPRSS PAPERINESS
AEEINPRSTU RESUPINATE
AEEINPRTVY EVEN PARITY
AEEINPSTTU UNISEPTATE

AEEINQRSTU EQUESTRIAN
AEEINQSSSU QUEASINESS
AEEINQSTTU TITANESQUE
AEEINRRRST RESTRAINER
AEEINRRTTV TRAVERTINE
AEEINRRTVY VETERINARY
AEEINRSSTW WATERINESS
AEEINRSTTT INTERSTATE
AEEINSSSTW SWEATINESS
AEEINSSSTY YEASTINESS
AEEIOPRSTV OPERATIVES
AEEIPPRSST APPETISERS
AEEIPPRSTW WATER PIPES
AEEIPPRSTZ APPETIZERS
AEEIPRRSTV PRIVATEERS
AEEIPRSSTT STRIPTEASE,
  TAPESTRIES
AEEIPRSSTU PASTEURISE
AEEIPRSSUV PERSUASIVE
AEEIPRSTTX SEXPARTITE
AEEIPRSTUZ PASTEURIZE
AEEIPRTTUV VITUPERATE
AEEIRRSSTU TREASURIES
AEEIRSSTTV TRAVESTIES
AEEIRSTUVY EASY VIRTUE
AEEJLNORSU JOURNALESE
AEEJMORSTT MAJORETTES
AEEKLMNORW
  ENAMELWORK
AEEKMMNORY
  MONEYMAKER
AEEKMMRRRY
  MERRYMAKER
AEEKMORRTU
  EUROMARKET
AEEKMPRRTV VERKRAMPTE
AEEKMRSSTY MASTER KEYS
AEELLMNOTV MALEVOLENT
AEELLMNRTU ALLUREMENT
AEELLNOPRT PETRONELLA
AEELLNRRUV UNRAVELLER
AEELLNRTVY RELEVANTLY
AEELLNRTXY EXTERNALLY
AEELLNTUVY EVENTUALLY
AEELLORSTT ROSTELLATE
AEELLORTTY TEA TROLLEY
AEELLQRRRU QUARRELLER
AEELLRRSTV TRAVELLERS
AEELLRSTTW WALL STREET
AEELMMNORU
  NEUROLEMMA
AEELMMNRTV
  MARVELMENT
AEELMNNOTT MENTAL NOTE
AEELMNOPRT PLANOMETER
AEELMNORTW
  WATERMELON
AEELMNOSSW
  SALESWOMEN

AEELMNSTTV VESTMENTAL
AEELMOPRTV VOLT-AMPERE
AEELMOPSTT PALMETTOES
AEELNNPTTU ANTEPENULT
AEELNPRTTW WENTLETRAP
AEELORSTTU LOTUS-EATER
AEELORSTVW WATER VOLES
AEELPRRSST PLASTERERS
AEELQRSSTU SEQUESTRAL
AEELRRSTUW LUSTREWARE
AEEMMNORST
   MANOMETERS
AEEMMNORTT
   ANTE-MORTEM
AEEMMNORTY
   ANEMOMETRY
AEEMMNSSTU
   AMUSEMENTS
AEEMMRRSST STAMMERERS
AEEMNNPRST PERMANENTS
AEEMNNPRTT ENTRAPMENT
AEEMNOPPRY PAPER
   MONEY
AEEMNOQRSU
   ROMANESQUE
AEEMNORRTU
   ENUMERATOR
AEEMNORRUV
   MANOEUVRER
AEEMNORSST SARMENTOSE
AEEMNORSUV
   MANOEUVRES
AEEMNPPRTY PREPAYMENT
AEEMNPRRTU
   AMPERE-TURN
AEEMNPRSTY REPAYMENTS
AEEMNRSSST MARE'S
   NESTS
AEEMNRSTTT TREATMENTS
AEEMNRSTTU MENSTRUATE
AEEMNSSSST ASSESSMENT
AEEMNSSSTT MEANS TESTS
AEEMNSSTTT STATEMENTS,
   TESTAMENTS
AEEMORRSTV OVERMASTER
AEEMORRTTV OVERMATTER
AEEMORSSSY MAYORESSES
AEEMPRRTTU EAR TRUMPET
AEEMRSSSST SEAMSTRESS
AEEMRSSSTT MATTRESSES,
   SMEAR TESTS
AEENNOOPSS OPEN SEASON
AEENNORSST ORNATENESS
AEENNPPRRT TREPPANNER
AEENOORRTX EXONERATOR
AEENOPQSSU OPAQUENESS
AEENOPRRTT PENETRATOR
AEENOPSTTT POTENTATES
AEENORSTUX EXTRANEOUS

AEENORTTUX EXTENUATOR
AEENPPRSSW NEWSPAPERS
AEENPPRSTT STEPPARENT
AEENPRSSSS SPARSENESS
AEENQRSSSU SQUARENESS
AEENRRSSTV TRANSVERSE
AEENSSSSTV VASTNESSES
AEENSSSTTU ASTUTENESS
AEEOPPRSSU PEA SOUPERS
AEEOPRRSTT TETRASPORE
AEEOPRRTWW
   WATERPOWER
AEEOPRSSSV OVERPASSES
AEEOPRSSTT POETASTERS
AEEPRRSSST TRESPASSER
AEEPRRSSTY SPARE TYRES
AEEPRSSSST TRESPASSES
AEEPRSSWXY EXPRESSWAY
AEEQRSSSTU SETSQUARES
AEEQSSTTUU STATUESQUE
AEERRRSSTU TREASURERS
AEERRSTTVX EXTRAVERTS
AEESSTTTTU STATUETTES
AEFFHILSST FLATFISHES
AEFFHLLOTW
   OFF-THE-WALL
AEFFIIINST AFFINITIES
AEFFIIINTV AFFINITIVE
AEFFIKLLOW WALK OF LIFE
AEFFIKPSST PIKESTAFFS
AEFFILNSTU INSUFFLATE
AEFFLMOOPR FLAMEPROOF
AEFFLMOORW
   FOAMFLOWER
AEFFNRSSTU STAFF NURSE
AEFFOOSTTU AFFETTUOSO
AEFGHHLLNT HALF-LENGTH
AEFGHILSTW WHITE FLAGS
AEFGHINRRW WHARFINGER
AEFGHKNOUU HUA
   KUO-FENG
AEFGHNORTU FEARNOUGHT
AEFGIILNNR FINGERNAIL
AEFGIILNSV LIFE-SAVING
AEFGIIMNRS MAGNIFIERS
AEFGIINNRR REFRAINING
AEFGIINSTU IGNES FATUI
AEFGIIRTUV FIGURATIVE
AEFGILLNNN FLANNELING
AEFGILMNNU MEANINGFUL
AEFGILMNOS FLAMINGOES
AEFGILNNTT FLATTENING
AEFGILNOUW GUINEA FOWL
AEFGILNRTT FLATTERING
AEFGILOPRT PROFLIGATE
AEFGILRSUY LAY FIGURES
AEFGIMNORR FOREARMING
AEFGINNSST FASTENINGS
AEFGIPRRTU GRAPEFRUIT

AEFGIRSSTT GAS FITTERS
AEFGLLLOWY YELLOW FLAG
AEFGLLRTUY GRATEFULLY
AEFGLMRSTU GULF STREAM
AEFGLNOSST FLAGSTONES
AEFGLNRTUU UNGRATEFUL
AEFGLORSTW AFTERGLOWS
AEFHIKLRSY FREAKISHLY
AEFHIKMSST MAKESHIFTS
AEFHILNSSS FLASHINESS
AEFHILRSST HALF-SISTER
AEFHIMMNST FAMISHMENT
AEFHINOPTY IN THE PAY OF
AEFHINOSSS OAFISHNESS
AEFHIRSSST STARFISHES
AEFHLLLOVY HALF VOLLEY
AEFHLLMSUY SHAMEFULLY
AEFHLLSTUY HASTEFULLY
AEFHLMOSST FATHOMLESS
AEFHMORSSU FARMHOUSES
AEFHOOPSTU OUT OF
   PHASE, OUT OF SHAPE
AEFIILLNSS FILIALNESS
AEFIILMNSS SEMIFINALS
AEFIILMPRS AMPLIFIERS
AEFIILNOTU UNIFOLIATE
AEFIILNRTT INFILTRATE
AEFIILORTT TRIFOLIATE
AEFIILQRSU QUALIFIERS
AEFIINOPRS SAPONIFIER
AEFIINQRTU QUANTIFIER
AEFIKNOPRS FAIR-SPOKEN
AEFILLNNRY INFERNALLY
AEFILLNNUZ INFLUENZAL
AEFILLRTVY RIFT VALLEY
AEFILMNSTY MANIFESTLY
AEFILMORRS FORMALISER
AEFILMORRZ FORMALIZER
AEFILMORTW WOLFRAMITE
AEFILNORSU LANIFEROUS
AEFILNORTU FLUORINATE
AEFILNSSTU FAULTINESS
AEFILOQRTU QUATREFOIL
AEFILORSSU SALIFEROUS
AEFIMNOSST MANIFESTOS
AEFIMNRSST FIRST NAMES
AEFINNRSSU UNFAIRNESS
AEFINOOPRT FORTE-PIANO,
   PIANOFORTE
AEFINORRST RAIN FOREST
AEFINORTTU REFUTATION
AEFINPSSTY SAFETY PINS
AEFINRRTTY FRATERNITY
AEFIOPRSTU FETIPAROUS
AEFIORRSSU AURIFEROUS
AEFIORSTUV FAVOURITES
AEFKLNOSSW SNOWFLAKES
AEFKMORRSW
   FRAMEWORKS

AEFLLLOPWY PLAYFELLOW
AEFLLLORWW
  WALLFLOWER
AEFLLLPTTU AT FULL PELT
AEFLLLSSWY FLAWLESSLY
AEFLLNOSSW FALLOWNESS
AEFLLNSSUW LAWFULNESS
AEFLLSTTUY TASTEFULLY
AEFLLSTUWY WASTEFULLY
AEFLMNNSSU MANFULNESS
AEFLMORRSV SALVERFORM
AEFLNOPRRT PREFRONTAL
AEFLNRSSTU ARTFULNESS
AEFLOOPSTT FOOTPLATES
AEFLORRSTW STARFLOWER
AEFLORSTWW
  WATERFOWLS
AEFLRSTTWY FLYSWATTER
AEFMNORSTW MEN OF
  STRAW
AEFMNOSSSU FAMOUSNESS
AEFMOPRRST PERMAFROST
AEFNNOORST AFTERNOONS
AEFNOPPRRU
  RUN-OF-PAPER
AEFNORRRST TRANSFEROR
AEFNORRTTW WATERFRONT
AEFOOPRRRT PERFORATOR
AEFOOPRRTW WATERPROOF
AEFOORRSTT TORT-FEASOR
AEFOQRRSUU FOURSQUARE
AEFRRRSTTU FRUSTRATER
AEGGGILNNY ENGAGINGLY
AEGGGINRST STAGGERING
AEGGGINRSW SWAGGERING
AEGGHILNRT RIGHT ANGLE
AEGGHINRST GATHERINGS
AEGGHINSSS SHAGGINESS
AEGGHIOPST GEOPHAGIST
AEGGHOOPSU
  GEOPHAGOUS
AEGGIILLNZ LEGALIZING
AEGGIILMPR PILGRIMAGE
AEGGIILNNR REALIGNING
AEGGIILNVW LIVING WAGE
AEGGIIMNRT EMIGRATING
AEGGIINNSV ENVISAGING
AEGGIINNTV NEGATIVING
AEGGIINPSU GUINEA PIGS
AEGGIJMRST JIGGERMAST
AEGGILLMNY GLEAMINGLY
AEGGILLNRV GRAVELLING
AEGGILNNNT ENTANGLING
AEGGILNNOT ELONGATING
AEGGILNRTU REGULATING
AEGGILRRST STRAGGLIER
AEGGIMNNTU AUGMENTING
AEGGIMNRRS GRANGERISM
AEGGINNRST ESTRANGING

AEGGINNRSV ENGRAVINGS
AEGGINORSS AGGRESSION
AEGGIORRSU GREGARIOUS
AEGGJNRTUU JUGGERNAUT
AEGGLLNOOY ANGELOLOGY
AEGGLOORTY GERATOLOGY
AEGGLRRSST STRAGGLERS
AEGGMOSTUY
  MYSTAGOGUE
AEGGNNORSU
  GANGRENOUS
AEGGNOSSUY
  SYNAGOGUES
AEGGNPRSSS PRESSGANGS
AEGGORRSSS AGGRESSORS
AEGHHILLLS SHILLELAGH
AEGHHILOPR HELIOGRAPH
AEGHHILRTT EARTHLIGHT
AEGHHIMNWY
  HIGHWAYMEN
AEGHHIMSSS HIGH MASSES
AEGHHINOSS HIGH SEASON
AEGHHINSST SHEATHINGS
AEGHHISTTU HAUGHTIEST
AEGHHLORSU HORSELAUGH
AEGHHMOPPT
  APOPHTHEGM
AEGHHNOPPR
  NEPHOGRAPH
AEGHHRRSTU HEARTHRUGS
AEGHIILMRT ALMIGHTIER
AEGHIIMNRS MISHEARING
AEGHIINSTT HESITATING
AEGHIIPRST GRAPHITISE
AEGHIIPRTZ GRAPHITIZE
AEGHIKMMNO
  HOMEMAKING
AEGHIKMNOS SHOEMAKING
AEGHIKNNRS HANKERINGS
AEGHILLNOP ANGLOPHILE
AEGHILMNNS ENGLISHMAN
AEGHILMORT LITHOMARGE
AEGHILNNSU UNLEASHING
AEGHILNOOT THEOLOGIAN
AEGHILNRST EARTHLINGS
AEGHILNRSU LANGUISHER
AEGHILRSTY LIGHT YEARS
AEGHILSSTT GHASTLIEST
AEGHIMMOPR MIMEOGRAPH
AEGHIMNRST NIGHTMARES
AEGHIMSTTT STEAMTIGHT
AEGHINNPPS HAPPENINGS
AEGHINNPRS SHARPENING
AEGHINNRSS HARNESSING
AEGHINNRST NEAR THINGS
AEGHINNRTU UNEARTHING
AEGHINPRRS REPHRASING
AEGHINRSSS GARISHNESS

AEGHINRSTT SHATTERING,
  STRAIGHTEN
AEGHINRSTV HARVESTING
AEGHINSTTU NAUGHTIEST
AEGHINSTUX EXHAUSTING
AEGHIPRRSY SERIGRAPHY
AEGHIRRSTT STRAIGHTER
AEGHIRTTTW WATERTIGHT
AEGHLMOOOT
  HOMOLOGATE
AEGHLNNOOP
  ANGLOPHONE
AEGHLNOORS
  ALONGSHORE
AEGHLNOOSU
  HALOGENOUS
AEGHLNSTWY LENGTHWAYS
AEGHLOOORR
  LOGORRHOEA
AEGHLOOPRY OLEOGRAPHY
AEGHLOSSSU GLASSHOUSE
AEGHMMORRT
  THERMOGRAM
AEGHMNOOPR
  GRAMOPHONE
AEGHNOOORR
  GONORRHOEA
AEGHNOPRRY
  GRANOPHYRE
AEGHNOPRST STENOGRAPH
AEGHNORRST
  SHORT-RANGE
AEGHOOPRRR
  OROGRAPHER
AEGHOOPRRZ
  ZOOGRAPHER
AEGHOOPSSU OESOPHAGUS
AEGHOPPRRU ROUGH
  PAPER
AEGHOPRRXY
  XEROGRAPHY
AEGIIILNTV INVIGILATE
AEGIIIMTTV MITIGATIVE
AEGIIIRRTV IRRIGATIVE
AEGIIKNOPP PIG IN A POKE
AEGIILLLTY ILLEGALITY
AEGIILMNRT TRIGEMINAL
AEGIILMNST TIME SIGNAL
AEGIILMNSX MAXISINGLE
AEGIILNNPX EXPLAINING
AEGIILNNPZ PENALIZING
AEGIILNNSS GAINLINESS
AEGIILNOTV LEVIGATION
AEGIILNPRV PREVAILING
AEGIILNQUZ EQUALIZING
AEGIILNRSS GLAIRINESS
AEGIILNSTV VIGILANTES
AEGIILNTTV LEVITATING
AEGIILRTTT GLITTERATI

AEGIIMNNOT GEMINATION
AEGIIMNORT EMIGRATION
AEGIIMNSTT ESTIMATING
AEGIIMNSTV NEGATIVISM,
   TIMESAVING
AEGIIMSSTT STIGMATISE
AEGIIMSTTZ STIGMATIZE
AEGIINNNRT ENTRAINING
AEGIINNOST ISOANTIGEN
AEGIINNPRT PERTAINING
AEGIINNRSS GRAININESS
AEGIINORTV INVIGORATE
AEGIINPPTZ APPETIZING
AEGIINSTTV NEGATIVIST
AEGIIRSTTU GRATUITIES
AEGIKKMNRS KINGMAKERS
AEGIKLMNOV LOVEMAKING
AEGIKLNNSY SNEAKINGLY
AEGIKNNSST TAKINGNESS
AEGILLMNRV MARVELLING
AEGILLNORY REGIONALLY
AEGILLNPSY PLEASINGLY
AEGILLNRTV TRAVELLING
AEGILLOPTT EPIGLOTTAL
AEGILLORST ALLEGORIST,
   LEGISLATOR
AEGILLPSSX PLEXIGLASS
AEGILLRRSU GUERRILLAS
AEGILLRSSS SALESGIRLS
AEGILMNNST ALIGNMENTS
AEGILMNOOP MONOPLEGIA
AEGILMNORS ROSEMALING
AEGILMNORY MINERALOGY
AEGILMORRS GLAMORISER,
   RIGMAROLES
AEGILMORRZ GLAMORIZER
AEGILMSTTU MULTISTAGE
AEGILNNNRU UNLEARNING
AEGILNNOOT ELONGATION
AEGILNNPSS GLANS PENIS
AEGILNNRUV UNRAVELING
AEGILNNSSS SLANGINESS
AEGILNNSUY SANGUINELY
AEGILNOOSU OLEAGINOUS
AEGILNORTT TOLERATING
AEGILNORTU REGULATION,
   UROGENITAL
AEGILNORVY OVERLAYING
AEGILNOSTU GELATINOUS
AEGILNPRST PLASTERING
AEGILNPRTY TAPERINGLY
AEGILNQRRU QUARRELING
AEGILNRSTV STARVELING
AEGILNRSWY SWEARINGLY
AEGILNRVWY WAVERINGLY
AEGILNRWYY WEARYINGLY
AEGILNSSSS GLASSINESS
AEGILOOPRS APOLOGISER
AEGILOOPRZ APOLOGIZER

AEGILOORST AEROLOGiST
AEGILOPRTT GRAPTOLITE
AEGILORRSS GRESSORIAL
AEGILORSSS GLOSSARIES
AEGILRRRSU IRREGULARS
AEGILRRSUV VULGARISER
AEGILRRTUY REGULARITY
AEGILRRUVZ VULGARIZER
AEGILRSTTZ SALZGITTER
AEGIMMNRST STAMMERING
AEGIMNNRST SMARTENING
AEGIMNNSST ASSIGNMENT
AEGIMNOPRS ANGIOSPERM
AEGIMNORRT GERMINATOR
AEGIMNORSU GRAMINEOUS
AEGIMNPRTY PIGMENTARY
AEGIMNPTTT ATTEMPTING
AEGIMNRRRY REMARRYING
AEGIMNRRST RINGMASTER
AEGIMNRSTT SMATTERING
AEGIMRRTVY GRAVIMETRY
AEGINNNPRT TREPANNING
AEGINNORST RESONATING
AEGINNORTV RENOVATING
AEGINNOSSS SEASONINGS
AEGINNPPRT ENTRAPPING
AEGINNPRRT PARTNERING
AEGINNPRTT PATTERNING
AEGINNRSTT ASTRINGENT
AEGINNRSTU SAUNTERING
AEGINOORTT NEGOTIATOR
AEGINORRSS ORGANISERS
AEGINORRSZ ORGANIZERS
AEGINORRTT INTEGRATOR
AEGINORRTV OVERRATING
AEGINORTVX OVERTAXING
AEGINOSSTT GESTATIONS
AEGINPRSTT SPATTERING
AEGINPRSTU SUPERGIANT
AEGINPRSTY PANEGYRIST
AEGINQRRTU QUARTERING
AEGINRRSSU REASSURING
AEGINRRSTT REGISTRANT
AEGINRRSTU TREASURING
AEGINRRSTV TRAVERSING
AEGINRSSSS GRASSINESS
AEGINRSSTU SUGARINESS
AEGINRSSTU SIGNATURES
AEGINRSTWW WATERWINGS
AEGIPRSTUV PURGATIVES
AEGIRRRSST REGISTRARS
AEGIRSSTTT STRATEGIST
AEGKMNOSXY OXYGEN
   MASK
AEGLLMORRU
   GLOMERULAR
AEGLLMRTUY METALLURGY
AEGLLNNPTY PLANGENTLY
AEGLLNOSST GALLSTONES

AEGLLOPRSU PELLAGROUS
AEGLMOOSTY SEMATOLOGY
AEGLMOPRTU PROMULGATE
AEGLNNPRTY PREGNANTLY
AEGLNRRSST STRANGLERS
AEGLNRSSUV VULGARNESS
AEGLNSSSSU SUNGLASSES
AEGLOORRST ASTROLOGER
AEGLOORTTY TERATOLOGY
AEGLORRSTU REGULATORS
AEGLORRTUY REGULATORY
AEGLORSSUV GROSS VALUE
AEGLPRSSUU SURPLUSAGE
AEGLPSSSSY SPYGLASSES
AEGMMNOPRU
   PNEUMOGRAM
AEGMMNRTUU
   ARGUMENTUM
AEGMMOPRRR
   PROGRAMMER
AEGMMOPRRS
   PROGRAMMES
AEGMNOORST
   GASTRONOME
AEGMNOOSUX
   XENOGAMOUS
AEGMNORRSW
   WARMONGERS
AEGMOPRRRS
   PROGRAMERS
AEGNNRTUUY UNGUENTARY
AEGNOOSTUU
   AUTOGENOUS
AEGNRRSSST TRANSGRESS
AEGOORSTUU
   OUTRAGEOUS
AEGOPRRSSU SOUR GRAPES
AEGOPRRTUX EXPURGATOR
AEGORRSSTU SURROGATES
AEGPRRRSUY PRAYER RUGS
AEGPRRSSSU SUPERGRASS
AEHHIILMOP HEMOPHILIA
AEHHILNSTU HELIANTHUS
AEHHILPSSW WHIPLASHES
AEHHINOPRT HIEROPHANT
AEHHINPSST THE SPANISH
AEHHIOPSST HEPHAISTOS
AEHHMOOOPT
   HOMOEOPATH
AEHHMOOPST HOMEOPATHS
AEHHMOOPTY
   HOMEOPATHY
AEHHNOOPRT ANTHOPHORE
AEHHOPPSST PHOSPHATES
AEHHPSSTTU HATSHEPSUT
AEHIIILNNS SINHAILIEN
AEHIIKLRTW WRAITHLIKE
AEHIILLMNW WILHELMINA
AEHIILOSTX HELIOTAXIS

AEHIIMNSTU HUMANITIES
AEHIINORTT THORIANITE
AEHIINOSTT HESITATION
AEHIINPPRS SAPPHIRINE
AEHIINSSTT ANTITHESIS
AEHIIPPSTT EPITAPHIST
AEHIKKLMSS MILK SHAKES
AEHIKNRSSS RAKISHNESS
AEHILLOPSV SLAVOPHILE
AEHILLORTY HELIOLATRY
AEHILLSTTY STEALTHILY
AEHILMNNUY INHUMANELY
AEHILMNOPY ANEMOPHILY
AEHILMNOSY HAEMOLYSIN
AEHILMORST ISOTHERMAL,
THIMEROSAL
AEHILMOSSY HAEMOLYSIS
AEHILNNOPS ALPHONSINE
AEHILNOSSS SHOALINESS
AEHILNOSST HAILSTONES
AEHILNOTTY ETHYLATION
AEHILNQRSU HARLEQUINS
AEHILNSSSV LAVISHNESS
AEHILNSTTY HESITANTLY
AEHILOPTVY TOP-HEAVILY
AEHILPSSST SPLASHIEST
AEHILRSSTY HAIRSTYLES
AEHILRSTVY SHRIEVALTY
AEHIMMPRRT TRIPHAMMER
AEHIMMRSTU RHEUMATISM
AEHIMNNPPS PENMANSHIP
AEHIMNNSTV VANISHMENT
AEHIMNORRS HARMONISER
AEHIMNORRZ HARMONIZER
AEHIMNOTUX EXHUMATION
AEHIMNRSSS MARSHINESS
AEHIMNRSTV RAVISHMENT
AEHIMNSSTU ENTHUSIASM
AEHIMOOPTY MYTHOPOEIA
AEHIMPRSST MASTERSHIP,
SHIPMASTER
AEHIMPSSST STEAMSHIPS
AEHIMPSSTY SYMPATHIES,
SYMPATHISE
AEHIMPSTYZ SYMPATHIZE
AEHINOPRTU EUPHORIANT
AEHINOPSTT ON THE TAPIS,
TIP ONE'S HAT
AEHINORRTV HOVERTRAIN
AEHINOSTUX EXHAUSTION
AEHINPSSTT PANTHEISTS
AEHINQRSUV VANQUISHER
AEHINRSSST TRASHINESS
AEHINSSTTU ENTHUSIAST
AEHIOOPSST APOTHEOSIS
AEHIORRSTU AUTHORISER
AEHIORRTUZ AUTHORIZER
AEHIORSSST AIR-HOSTESS
AEHIORSTTT THROATIEST

AEHIPRSSTT THERAPISTS
AEHIQSSSTU SQUASHIEST
AEHIRSSTTW SWARTHIEST,
SWEATSHIRT
AEHKLOPRSW SHOPWALKER
AEHKMNOSTU
SNAKEMOUTH
AEHKORRSTW
EARTHWORKS
AEHLLMRSSY HARMLESSLY
AEHLLMSTUU HAUSTELLUM
AEHLLOOPRT HARTLEPOOL
AEHLLOPRXY PHYLLOXERA
AEHLLOSSTW SHALLOWEST
AEHLMOOSUX
HOMOSEXUAL
AEHLMORTTY METHYLATOR
AEHLMOSSSU
ALMS-HOUSES
AEHLNNOPTT PENTATHLON
AEHLNOPSTU HOUSEPLANT,
SULPHONATE
AEHLOOPRRY PYORRHOEAL
AEHLOPSSUY PLAYHOUSES
AEHLPRSTUU SULPHURATE
AEHLRTTUUV TRUTH-VALUE
AEHMNOORSU MANOR
HOUSE
AEHMNOORSW
HORSEWOMAN
AEHMNORRTT
MATTERHORN
AEHMNORRTW
HARROWMENT
AEHMNPRSUU
SUPERHUMAN
AEHMOORSTX
MESOTHORAX
AEHMORRSTW
EARTHWORMS
AEHMORSTTT THERMOSTAT
AEHNNNOOTY
HOOTENANNY
AEHNOOPSSU SOUSAPHONE
AEHNOOPSSX SAXOPHONES
AEHNOPRSWY PHONEY
WARS
AEHNOPRTUY NEUROPATHY
AEHOOPPRST APOSTROPHE
AEHOOPRYZZ ZAPOROZHYE
AEHOOPSSTT OSTEOPATHS
AEHOOPSTTT TOOTHPASTE
AEHOOPSTTY OSTEOPATHY
AEHOORSSTY SOOTHSAYER
AEHOOSSSTU OAST HOUSES
AEHOPPRSTY SAPROPHYTE
AEHOPRSTUY HOUSE PARTY
AEHOPSSSTW SWEATSHOPS

AEHORRRSTW
RESTHARROW
AEIIIILNST INITIALISE
AEIIIILNTZ INITIALIZE
AEIIIINTTV INITIATIVE
AEIIILMRST MILITARISE
AEIIILMRTZ MILITARIZE
AEIIILRSTV TRIVIALISE
AEIIILRTVZ TRIVIALIZE
AEIIINSTTV NATIVITIES
AEIIIRRTTV IRRITATIVE
AEIIJMORST MAJORITIES
AEIIKKSTTW KITTIWAKES
AEIIKLLNPR PAINKILLER
AEIIILLLMMS MILLESIMAL
AEIIILLLMNN MILLENNIAL
AEIIILLMNOR MINERAL OIL
AEIIILLMNTU ILLUMINATE
AEIIILLMPRY IMPERIALLY
AEIIILLMRST LITERALISM
AEIIILLOSTV VOLATILISE
AEIIILLOTVZ VOLATILIZE
AEIIILLPRTT TRIPLETAIL
AEIIILLPSTT PISTILLATE
AEIIILLRRTT TRILITERAL
AEIIILLRRTY LITERARILY
AEIIILLRSTT LITERALIST
AEIIILMMMOR IMMEMORIAL
AEIIILMNORT ELIMINATOR
AEIIILMNRSU LUMINARIES
AEIIILMNSTY SEMINALITY
AEIIILMNTTY INTIMATELY
AEIIILMORST MORALITIES
AEIIILMOSSS ISOSEISMAL
AEIIILMRSTV RELATIVISM
AEIIILMRSVV REVIVALISM
AEIIILMSTUV SIMULATIVE
AEIIILMTTUV MUTILATIVE
AEIIILNNORS ROSANILINE
AEIIILNNSTT INTESTINAL
AEIIILNOOTT ETIOLATION
AEIIILNORST INTER ALIOS
AEIIILNORSV REVISIONAL
AEIIILNORTT LITERATION
AEIIILNOSTT TONALITIES
AEIIILNOTTV LEVITATION
AEIIILNOTUV ELUVIATION
AEIIILNPRST REPTILIANS
AEIIILNQTUY INEQUALITY
AEIIILNSSTW WAISTLINES
AEIIILOPRST POLARITIES
AEIIILORSST SOLITAIRES,
SOLITARIES
AEIIILRSSUV VISUALISER
AEIIILRSTTV RELATIVIST
AEIIILRSTTZ STRELITZIA
AEIIILRSTVV REVIVALIST
AEIIILRSUVZ VISUALIZER
AEIIILRTTVY RELATIVITY

AEIIMMMNOR	IN MEMORIAM
AEIIMMNPRT	IMPAIRMENT
AEIIMMNRST	ANTIMERISM
AEIIMNNNOT	INNOMINATE
AEIIMNNOTV	NOMINATIVE
AEIIMNOSTT	ESTIMATION
AEIIMNPQRU	PRIMAQUINE
AEIIMNQRTU	MARTINIQUE
AEIIMNQTUY	EQUANIMITY
AEIIMNRSTU	MINIATURES
AEIIMNRTUV	RUMINATIVE
AEIIMOPRRS	IMPRESARIO
AEIIMOTTVV	MOTIVATIVE
AEIIMPTTUV	IMPUTATIVE
AEIINNOTVV	INNOVATIVE
AEIINNPRTT	TRIPINNATE
AEIINNPRTY	ANTIPYRINE
AEIINNPSTT	IN-PATIENTS
AEIINOPPST	INAPPOSITE
AEIINOPRTX	EXPIRATION
AEIINOPSTT	POINSETTIA
AEIINOQTTU	EQUITATION
AEIINOSTTV	NOVITIATES
AEIINOTUVX	EXUVIATION
AEIINPSSST	ANTISEPSIS
AEIINQSTTU	QUANTITIES
AEIINRSTTV	TRANSITIVE
AEIINRTTTW	IN A TWITTER
AEIIOPPRTT	PROPITIATE
AEIIOPPSTV	APPOSITIVE
AEIIPPSSSW	PIPSISSEWA
AEIIPRRTTT	TRIPARTITE
AEIIPRSTTV	PARTITIVES
AEIJLNORSU	JOURNALISE
AEIJLNORUZ	JOURNALIZE
AEIJMNOSSS	JAM SESSION
AEIJNNSSTU	JAUNTINESS
AEIJNOOPRT	PEJORATION
AEIKKLLOOS	LOOK-ALIKES
AEIKLMNSTY	MISTAKENLY
AEIKLNORST	OIL TANKERS
AEIKLNSSST	STALKINESS
AEIKLNSSTU	ESKILSTUNA
AEIKMNPRRT	PRINTMAKER
AEIKNNPRSS	SPINNAKERS
AEIKNNSSSW	SWANKINESS
AEIKPPQSSU	PIPSQUEAKS
AEILLLMSTT	LITTLE SLAM
AEILLLOTWY	YELLOWTAIL
AEILLLSUVY	ALLUSIVELY
AEILLMMORS	ALLOMERISM
AEILLMMRST	MILLSTREAM,
	SMALL-TIMER
AEILLMNPTU	MULTIPLANE
AEILLMNRTY	TERMINALLY
AEILLMRSTW	WATERMILLS
AEILLMTTUY	ULTIMATELY
AEILLNNRTY	INTERNALLY
AEILLNOPRT	PETRONILLA

AEILLNOPTT	POTENTILLA
AEILLNPSST	PANELLISTS
AEILLNPSSY	PAINLESSLY
AEILLPRRSU	PLURALISER
AEILLPRRUZ	PLURALIZER
AEILLPSSSS	SALES SLIPS
AEILLPSSTT	PASTELLIST
AEILLQSSTU	SQUALLIEST
AEILLRSSTW	STAIRWELLS
AEILLRSTTU	ILLUSTRATE
AEILMMRTUY	IMMATURELY
AEILMNNOPR	PRENOMINAL
AEILMNNSTT	INSTALMENT
AEILMNOPRS	IMPERSONAL
AEILMNOPRT	TRAMPOLINE
AEILMNORTU	TOURMALINE
AEILMNOSTY	MELANOSITY
AEILMNPRTY	PLANIMETRY
AEILMNRSTU	NEUTRALISM
AEILMNSSSU	SENSUALISM
AEILMNSTTU	LAST MINUTE
AEILMOORRT	MELIORATOR
AEILMOPPSS	AMPELOPSIS
AEILMOPRST	PERISTOMAL
AEILMOPSTT	PTOLEMAIST
AEILMORRSS	MORALISERS
AEILMORRSZ	MORALIZERS
AEILMPPSST	PALIMPSEST
AEILMPRSST	SLIPSTREAM
AEILMPRSTU	PSALTERIUM
AEILMPRTUU	PARI-MUTUEL
AEILMRRSSU	SURREALISM
AEILMRRSTT	TRIMESTRAL
AEILMSTTUX	TEXTUALISM
AEILNNNSTW	LAWN TENNIS
AEILNNOPRS	NONPAREILS
AEILNNOPSY	POLYNESIAN
AEILNNOPTT	ANTILEPTON
AEILNNORTT	INTOLERANT
AEILNNPRSU	PENINSULAR
AEILNNPSSU	PENINSULAS
AEILNNRRTU	INTERLUNAR
AEILNOOPRT	TROPAEOLIN
AEILNOOPSS	POLONAISES
AEILNOORTT	TOLERATION
AEILNOPRST	INTERPOSAL
AEILNOPRTU	ERUPTIONAL
AEILNORRTT	TORRENTIAL
AEILNORTTV	VENTILATOR
AEILNOTTUX	EXULTATION
AEILNPRSST	PALTRINESS
AEILNPRSTY	PARTY LINES
AEILNRSTTU	NEUTRALIST
AEILNRTTUY	NEUTRALITY
AEILNSSSTU	SENSUALIST
AEILNSSTUY	SENSUALITY
AEILOOPTTZ	TOPAZOLITE
AEILOPPRSU	POPULARISE
AEILOPPRUZ	POPULARIZE

AEILOPRSSU	PLESIOSAUR
AEILOPRSTY	EPISTOLARY
AEILORRTTU	ELUTRIATOR
AEILORSTTU	STAUROLITE
AEILPRRSTY	PERISTYLAR
AEILRRSSTU	SURREALIST
AEILRSSSTY	LAY SISTERS
AEILRSTTUV	LUSTRATIVE
AEILSTTTUX	TEXTUALIST
AEIMMNNRSS	MANNERISMS
AEIMMNOPST	PANTOMIMES
AEIMMNORST	MONETARISM
AEIMMNSTZZ	MIZZENMAST
AEIMMPRSTU	SPERMATIUM
AEIMMRRSSU	SUMMARISER
AEIMMRRSUZ	SUMMARIZER
AEIMNNNOST	MINNESOTAN
AEIMNNNOTT	ANOINTMENT
AEIMNNNQSU	MANNEQUINS
AEIMNNORTU	NUMERATION
AEIMNOPRTT	ARMIPOTENT
AEIMNOPTTT	TEMPTATION
AEIMNOQSUU	EQUANIMOUS
AEIMNORRTT	TERMINATOR
AEIMNORSST	STEAM IRONS
AEIMNORSSW	WOMANISERS
AEIMNORSTT	MONETARIST
AEIMNORSWZ	WOMANIZERS
AEIMNPSTTY	TYMPANITES
AEIMNRRRTY	INTERMARRY
AEIMOOSTTU	AUTOTOMISE
AEIMOOTTUV	AUTOMOTIVE
AEIMOOTTUZ	AUTOTOMIZE
AEIMOPRRTT	IMPETRATOR
AEIMOPRTUU	EUPATORIUM
AEIMORRSTU	MORTUARIES
AEIMORSSTT	ESTIMATORS
AEIMORSSTV	MOVIE STARS
AEIMPRSSTU	PASTEURISM
AEIMPRSTUZ	TRAPEZIUMS
AEIMPSSTUV	ASSUMPTIVE
AEIMQRSTUZ	QUIZMASTER
AEINNNOQSU	SINE QUA NON
AEINNOORST	RESONATION
AEINNOORTV	RENOVATION
AEINNOPRSY	PENSIONARY
AEINNOPSSX	EXPANSIONS
AEINNOQRTU	QUATERNION
AEINNORSTT	STENTORIAN
AEINNOSSST	SENSATIONS
AEINNOSTTT	ATTENTIONS
AEINNOSTTV	NONSTATIVE
AEINNPPSSS	SNAPPINESS
AEINNQSSTU	QUAINTNESS
AEINNRRSTY	TYRANNISER
AEINNRRTYZ	TYRANNIZER
AEINNSSSZZ	SNAZZINESS
AEINOOPPRT	PROPIONATE
AEINOOPRRT	PERORATION

AEINOOPRST OPERATIONS
AEINOPRRST PATRONISER
AEINOPRRTZ PATRONIZER
AEINOPRSSS ASPERSIONS
AEINOPRSSU PERSUASION
AEINOPRTTU REPUTATION
AEINOPTTTU OUTPATIENT
AEINORRSTT REINSTATOR
AEINORSSST ASSERTIONS
AEINORSSTT STATIONERS
AEINORSSTY TYROSINASE
AEINORSTTY STATIONERY
AEINPRRTTU PARTURIENT
AEINPRTTTW PATENT WRIT
AEINRRSSST STARRINESS
AEINRRSSTT RESTRAINTS
AEINRSSSTT STRAITNESS
AEINRSTUYZ SUZERAINTY
AEIOPRRRST RESPIRATOR
AEIOPRRTTX EXTIRPATOR
AEIOPRRTXY EXPIRATORY
AEIPRSTUUV USURPATIVE
AEJMNNORUY
   JOURNEYMAN
AEJMPRSTUW WATER JUMPS
AEKKLRTTUY TALK TURKEY
AEKMNORTTW MARKET
   TOWN
AEKMORRSTW
   MASTERWORK
AEKMRRSSST STRESS MARK
AEKNOPRRSY NOSY PARKER
AEKNOQRSTU SQUARE
   KNOT
AEKNPRRSST PRANKSTERS
AEKORRSTWW
   WATERWORKS
AELLMNOSTT ALLOTMENTS
AELLMOORSU ALLOMEROUS
AELLMOPSSY PLASMOLYSE
AELLMORSUV MARVELLOUS
AELLNOPPRT PROPELLANT
AELLNOPRSY PERSONALLY
AELLNOPTVY POLYVALENT
AELLNORTTY TOLERANTLY
AELLNOSSSW SALLOWNESS
AELLNPTTUY PETULANTLY
AELLNRSTTY SLATTERNLY
AELLNTTUXY EXULTANTLY
AELLOPPRSU ALL-PURPOSE
AELLOPSTUV POLE VAULTS
AELLRSSTVY SYLVESTRAL
AELLRTTUXY TEXTURALLY
AELMMNNOTU
   MONUMENTAL
AELMMOOPSS
   PLASMOSOME
AELMMORSST MAELSTROMS

AELMMOSSUU
   MAUSOLEUMS
AELMNNNRUY
   UNMANNERLY
AELMNNNSTU ANNULMENTS
AELMNNOOPS
   MONOPLANES
AELMNNOOTV
   MONOVALENT
AELMNOOPRT PROTONEMAL
AELMNOOPRY
   LAMPOONERY
AELMNOPRTY PLANOMETRY
AELMNORSWW
   LAWNMOWERS
AELMOOPRTU TROPAEOLUM
AELMOPPRUY PROPYLAEUM
AELMOPRTTU PETROLATUM
AELMOPSSST EPSOM SALTS
AELMOQSSUU
   SQUAMULOSE
AELMORSSTU SOMERSAULT
AELMORSTTT LATTERMOST
AELNNOPRYY PENNYROYAL
AELNNORSTY RESONANTLY
AELNNOSTWW NEWTON'S
   LAW
AELNOPPRTW POWER
   PLANT
AELNOPRSSY LAYPERSONS
AELNOPRSTY PERSONALTY
AELNORSUVY RAVENOUSLY
AELNOSSUUY NAUSEOUSLY
AELNOSTUVV
   VOL-AU-VENTS
AELNPPRSTU SUPPLANTER
AELNPRRSUU SUPERLUNAR
AELOOPSSTV SEVASTOPOL
AELOPPRRRU POURPARLER
AELOPPRTUV UPPER VOLTA
AELOPSSTTU POSTULATES
AELORRSSTT LAST RESORT
AELPPSSTUY PLATYPUSES
AEMMNORRTT
   MONTMARTRE
AEMNNNOPTY
   NONPAYMENT
AEMNNOORSS ROMAN
   NOSES
AEMNNOOSST
   STONEMASON
AEMNNORTTT ATTORNMENT
AEMNNORTTU
   TOURNAMENT
AEMNNRRSUY
   NURSERYMAN
AEMNOOPRTT PORTAMENTO
AEMNOORRST
   ASTRONOMER

AEMNORRSTU
   NUMERATORS
AEMNORSSTT ASSORTMENT
AEMNRRSTTU TRANSMUTER
AEMOOPSTTY SOMATOTYPE
AEMOORSSTT STATEROOMS
AEMOPRSSTT POSTMASTER
AEMOPRSSTU MOUSETRAPS
AEMORRSTTY ASTROMETRY
AENNNOSSTW
   WANTONNESS
AENNORRSSW
   NARROWNESS
AENNORRSTT NONSTARTER
AENOOPRRST PERSONATOR
AENOORRSST RESONATORS
AENOPRRSST TRANSPOSER
AENOPRSSUV SUPERNOVAS
AENOPRSTTT PROTESTANT
AENPRRSTTU TRANSPUTER
AEOOPPRSTU TROPOPAUSE
AEOOQRRSTU SQUARE
   ROOT
AEOPPRRRTU RAPPORTEUR
AEOPRRSSTW SPORTSWEAR
AEOPRSTTUW WATERSPOUT
AEORSSSTUU TROUSSEAUS
AEORSSTUUX TROUSSEAUX
AEPRRSSSTU SUPERSTARS
AFFGIILNSY FALSIFYING
AFFGIMRSSU SUFFRAGISM
AFFGINNORT AFFRONTING
AFFGIRSSTU SUFFRAGIST
AFFHILLTUY FAITHFULLY
AFFHILNTUU UNFAITHFUL
AFFIILNPST PLAINTIFFS
AFFIIMNRSU RUFFIANISM
AFFLLORUUV FLAVOURFUL
AFFLOOSTTU FOOT FAULTS
AFFMNNRSUY FUNNY
   FARMS
AFGGGILNNU UNFLAGGING
AFGGIIMNNY MAGNIFYING
AFGGIIMNTU FUMIGATING
AFGGIINRTY GRATIFYING
AFGHHILLST FLASHLIGHT
AFGHHILPTT FLIGHT PATH
AFGHIILRTY FAIRY LIGHT
AFGHIINNOS FASHIONING
AFGHIIRSTU GUITARFISH
AFGHIORTWY RIGHT OF WAY
AFGIIILNNZ FINALIZING
AFGIIILNRT AIR-LIFTING
AFGIILMNPY AMPLIFYING
AFGIILNNTY FAINTINGLY
AFGIILNQUY QUALIFYING
AFGIILOSTU FLAGITIOUS
AFGIIMNOTU FUMIGATION
AFGIINORTU FIGURATION

AFGIINSSTY SATISFYING
AFGIKMNORS
  KING-OF-ARMS
AFGIKNRSST SKIN GRAFTS
AFGILNORUV FLAVOURING
AFGIMNORSU AUSFORMING
AFGIMNORTT FORMATTING
AFGINNPRSY FRYING PANS
AFHHLRSTTU HALF-TRUTHS
AFHILNOPST FLASH POINT
AFHIOPRRST PARROTFISH
AFHKLLNTUY THANKFULLY
AFHKLNNTUU UNTHANKFUL
AFHLLORSST SHORTFALLS
AFHLLORSUY ROYAL FLUSH
AFHLLRTUWY WRATHFULLY
AFIILLRRTY FRITILLARY
AFIILNORSU INFUSORIAL
AFIILNORTT FILTRATION,
  FLIRTATION
AFIKLLMOST MILK FLOATS
AFILLMNORY INFORMALLY
AFILLNOPRU PLAIN FLOUR
AFILLNPPTY FLIPPANTLY
AFILLOOPRS APRIL FOOLS
AFILMNORTU FULMINATOR
AFILMORSST FORMALISTS
AFILNOOSTT FLOTATIONS
AFILNORTTY FRONTALITY
AFIMMORTUU FUMATORIUM
AFIMNNORST INFORMANTS
AFIMNOORST FORMATIONS
AFIMORRSTT STRATIFORM
AFLLLNUUWY UNLAWFULLY
AFLLNOORSU ON ALL FOURS
AFLMOORRTU FORMULATOR
AFNORSTTUU FORTUNATUS
AGGGGIINZZ ZIGZAGGING
AGGGILLNWY WAGGLINGLY
AGGGILNRST STRAGGLING
AGGGIMNORT MORTGAGING
AGGHIINNRS GARNISHING
AGGHILLNUY LAUGHINGLY
AGGHILMNPU GALUMPHING
AGGHILNNSY GNASHINGLY
AGGHLOOPRY
  GRAPHOLOGY, LOGOGRAPHY
AGGIIILNTT LITIGATING
AGGIIIMNTT MITIGATING
AGGIIINRRT IRRIGATING
AGGIIILLNNS SIGNALLING
AGGIILNNST TINGALINGS
AGGIILNNTU AGGLUTININ
AGGIINNORZ ORGANIZING
AGGILLNOTY GLOATINGLY
AGGILNNNTU UNTANGLING
AGGILNNORY GROANINGLY
AGGILNNRST STRANGLING
AGGIMNOPRR PROGRAMING

AGGINOORRT RARING TO
  GO
AGGINORRTT GARROTTING
AGGLNOOOORY
  ORGANOLOGY
AGGLNOOOORZ
  GORGONZOLA
AGGMOORRST
  MORTGAGORS
AGHHILOPRT LITHOGRAPH
AGHHLOOPRY
  HOLOGRAPHY
AGHHMOOPRS
  HOMOGRAPHS
AGHHNOOPPR
  PHONOGRAPH
AGHHOOPPRT PHOTOGRAPH
AGHHOPPTYY PHYTOPHAGY
AGHHORTUWY
  THROUGHWAY
AGHIIINNSU NINGSIA HUI
AGHIILLMTY ALMIGHTILY
AGHIILLSTT TAILLIGHTS
AGHIIMNNUZ HUMANIZING
AGHIINNRST TARNISHING
AGHIINNRSV VARNISHING
AGHIINNRTU THURINGIAN
AGHIINPRRS HAIRSPRING
AGHIINRTWW WAINWRIGHT
AGHILLNOSW SHALLOWING
AGHILLNSSY SLASHINGLY
AGHILMORST ALGORITHMS,
  LOGARITHMS
AGHILNNTUY HAUNTINGLY
AGHILNPSTY PLAYTHINGS
AGHILNRSTT STRINGHALT
AGHILNSSWY SWASHINGLY
AGHILOPPSY GYPSOPHILA
AGHILORSTT GASTROLITH
AGHILPRTWY PLAYWRIGHT
AGHIMNNOTT NOTTINGHAM
AGHIMNOOPS SHAMPOOING
AGHIMNRSST HAMSTRINGS
AGHIMORSST HISTOGRAMS
AGHINNOOPR HARPOONING
AGHINNOSTW WASHINGTON
AGHINOPRTY ATROPHYING
AGHIOPPRRS SPIROGRAPH
AGHLMOOSTU
  GOALMOUTHS
AGHLNOOOORT
  ORTHOGONAL
AGHLNOSSTU ONSLAUGHTS
AGHLOPPRSY POLYGRAPHS
AGHLOPRSTY STYLOGRAPH
AGHLOPRXYY XYLOGRAPHY
AGHMMOOOSU
  HOMOGAMOUS

AGHMNOOPRS
  MONOGRAPHS
AGHMNOOPRY
  NOMOGRAPHY
AGHMNOORTU MOUTH
  ORGAN
AGHMOOPRTY
  TOMOGRAPHY
AGHNOOPRSY
  NOSOGRAPHY
AGHOOOPSUZ
  ZOOPHAGOUS
AGHOOPPRTY TOPOGRAPHY
AGHOPPRRYY PYROGRAPHY
AGHOPPRTYY TYPOGRAPHY
AGIIIILNNT INITIALING
AGIIIINNTT INITIATING
AGIIILMNNN MAINLINING
AGIIILMNTT MILITATING
AGIIILNOTT LITIGATION
AGIIMMNNXZ MAXIMIZING
AGIIIMNNTT INTIMATING
AGIIIMNOTT MITIGATION
AGIIINNSTZ SANITIZING
AGIIINORRT IRRIGATION
AGIIINRRTT IRRITATING
AGIIINRSTZ SATIRIZING
AGIIINTTTV TITIVATING
AGIIKNNNPR NAPKIN RING
AGIILLMMRS MILLIGRAMS
AGIILLNNST INSTALLING
AGIILLNORY ORIGINALLY
AGIILLNPRS SPIRALLING
AGIILLNRTU TRILINGUAL
AGIILLNRTY TRAILINGLY
AGIILLNTVY VIGILANTLY
AGIILMMNOT IMMOLATING
AGIILMNNPT IMPLANTING
AGIILMNORZ MORALIZING
AGIILMNOST ANTILOGISM
AGIILMNSTU SIMULATING
AGIILMNTTU MUTILATING
AGIILNNORU UNORIGINAL
AGIILNNSTU INSULATING
AGIILNOPRZ POLARIZING
AGIILNPRST SPRINGTAIL
AGIILNRSTY LARYNGITIS
AGIILNSSTV VITAL SIGNS
AGIILOOPST APIOLOGIST
AGIILOOSTX AXIOLOGIST
AGIIMMNRST IMMIGRANTS
AGIIMMORRT IMMIGRATOR
AGIIMMOSST MISOGAMIST
AGIIMMSSTT STIGMATISM
AGIIMNNNOT NOMINATING
AGIIMNNOWZ WOMANIZING
AGIIMNNPRS MAINSPRING
AGIIMNNRTU RUMINATING
AGIIMNORST MIGRATIONS

AGIIMNORTZ AMORTIZING
AGIIMNOTTV MOTIVATING
AGIIMNSSTT MISSTATING
AGIIMNSSUV VAGINISMUS
AGIIMSSTTT STIGMATIST
AGIINNNOTV INNOVATING
AGIINNOPPT APPOINTING
AGIINNORSS SIGNORINAS
AGIINNORTZ NOTARIZING
AGIINNOSTT STATIONING
AGIINNSSTU SUSTAINING
AGIINOORRT ORIGINATOR
AGIINOPRRR RIP-ROARING
AGIINOPRVZ VAPORIZING
AGIINORSTT INSTIGATOR
AGIINORSUV VIRAGINOUS
AGIIRSSTTU GUITARISTS
AGIKKLNRSY SKYLARKING
AGIKLMNOOT TOOL-MAKING
AGIKLNOPRT PARKING LOT
AGIKLNOSTT TALKING-TOS
AGIKLNOTTU OUTTALKING
AGIKMNNORW
    WORKINGMAN
AGIKMNNOTU KUOMINTANG
AGIKNNORTU OUTRANKING
AGILLNNRSY SNARLINGLY
AGILLNNSTY SLANTINGLY
AGILLNOPRT PATROLLING
AGILLNOSWW SWALLOWING
AGILLNRSUY SINGULARLY
AGILLNTTTY TATTLINGLY
AGILLOOSSS ISOGLOSSAL
AGILMNNOOP LAMPOONING
AGILMNNRSTY SMARTINGLY
AGILMOOSTU GLIOMATOUS
AGILMOPSTY POLYGAMIST
AGILNNOPTY POIGNANTLY
AGILNNPPSY SNAPPINGLY
AGILNNTTUY TAUNTINGLY
AGILNNTUVY VAUNTINGLY
AGILNOPPRS PROLAPSING
AGILNOPPTU POPULATING
AGILNOPTUY OUTPLAYING
AGILNOSSTW WAGONS-LITS
AGILNOSTTU OUTLASTING
AGILOOPSST APOLOGISTS
AGILORSSST GLOSSARIST
AGIMMNOOST MONOGAMIST
AGIMMNSSUY GYMNASIUMS
AGIMNNOSVV MOVING VANS
AGIMNNSSUU UNASSUMING
AGIMNOORST AGRONOMIST
AGIMNOPRSU SPORANGIUM
AGINNOPTTU AT GUNPOINT
AGINNPPSUW SWAN-UPPING
AGINOPRRTY PORTRAYING
AGINORSTTU OUTSTARING
AGINOSTTUY OUTSTAYING

AGINPRSSSU SURPASSING
AGIORSTTUU GRATUITOUS
AGKLORSSSW
    GLASSWORKS
AGKLPPRSSU SPARK PLUGS
AGKNNNORTY GRANNY
    KNOT
AGLLLLOPPU GALLUP POLL
AGLLLOOPRY PYROGALLOL
AGLLNOOPYY PALYNOLOGY
AGLMOOOSTY
    SOMATOLOGY
AGLMOOPSUY
    POLYGAMOUS
AGLNOORSUU
    LANGUOROUS
AGLOPPRSUY PLAYGROUPS
AGMMNOOOSU
    MONOGAMOUS
AGMMNOPSUU MAGNUM
    OPUS
AGMNOORSTY
    GASTRONOMY
AGMOOORSST MATO
    GROSSO
AGMOORSTTY
    GASTROTOMY
AGOOORRSSST GRASS ROOTS
AHHIIILNTW WITHIN HAIL
AHHIIRRSST HAIR SHIRTS
AHHIOPRSTU AUTHORSHIP
AHHISSWWYY
    WISHY-WASHY
AHHMORRSTW
    HARMSWORTH
AHHOPPRSUY HAPPY
    HOURS
AHIIIMMPSX AMPHIMIXIS
AHIIKMNRSS KRISHNAISM
AHIILMORTU HUMILIATOR
AHIILRSSTT SHIRTTAILS
AHIIMNNOTU INHUMATION
AHIIMNNTUY INHUMANITY
AHIIMNORSW IRISHWOMAN
AHIINORSST HISTORIANS
AHIKKNNSTT THINK TANKS
AHIKKSTUUY KITAKYUSHU
AHIKNPRRSW SHRINK-WRAP
AHILMORSST HAILSTORMS
AHILMPSSYY SYMPHYSIAL
AHILNOORTZ HORIZONTAL
AHILNOPPTY HIPPOLYTAN
AHILNOPSTU SULPHATION
AHILNPPSSY SNAPPISHLY
AHILORSSTW SHOW TRIALS
AHIMMNORSU
    HARMONIUMS
AHIMNOOOSU HOMOOUSIAN
AHIMNOORRU HONORARIUM

AHIMNOORSU HARMONIOUS
AHIMNPRTTU TRIUMPHANT
AHIMORSTUU HAUSTORIUM
AHIMPPPRSU PARISH-PUMP
AHINOPRSUX XIPHOSURAN
AHIOOPSTTX PHOTOTAXIS
AHKLMOPRYY KARYOLYMPH
AHLLMORSSU SMALL
    HOURS
AHLLOPRSTU PROTHALLUS
AHLMNNORTU LUNAR
    MONTH
AHLMNOORST SOLAR
    MONTH
AHLMOOPRTU
    PHOTOMURAL
AHLMOOPSTY HOMOPLASTY
AHLMPRSUWY MURPHY'S
    LAW
AHLNOPSTUY POLYANTHUS
AHLORRSTTU ULTRASHORT
AHMNNOOSTU
    MONANTHOUS
AHMNOOPRTU
    PROTOHUMAN
AHNNOSTTWY
    SHANTYTOWN
AHNOOPSTTY PHOTONASTY
AHNOPPRTTY TRYPTOPHAN
AHOOPPRTTY PROTOPATHY
AHOOPSSTTT PHOTOSTATS
AIIIINNOTT INITIATION
AIIILLMNTU ILLUMINATI
AIIILLMRTY MILITARILY
AIIILMMNST MINIMALIST
AIIILMMRST MILITARISM
AIIILMNOTT LIMITATION,
    MILITATION
AIIILMRSTT MILITARIST
AIIILMRSTY SIMILARITY
AIIILORSTV VISITORIAL
AIIILRTTVY TRIVIALITY
AIIIMNNOTT INTIMATION
AIIIMNOPSS PIANISSIMO
AIIIMNOSTT IMITATIONS
AIIINNOOST IONISATION
AIIINNOOTZ IONIZATION
AIIINNOTTV INVITATION
AIIINORRTT IRRITATION
AIIINORTTY INITIATORY
AIIINOSTTV VISITATION
AIIINOTTTV TITIVATION
AIIIPRSSTY PITYRIASIS
AIIIPRTVVY VIVIPARITY
AIILLMNNTU ILLUMINANT
AIILLMNTTY MILITANTLY
AIILLNOOTV VOLITIONAL
AIILLNOSUV VILLAINOUS
AIILLORSTY SOLITARILY

AIILLOSSTT SOLSTITIAL
AIILLOTTVY VOLATILITY
AIILLSTUVV VALVULITIS
AIILMMNNOS NOMINALISM
AIILMMNOOT IMMOLATION
AIILMMORST IMMORALIST
AIILMMORTY IMMORALITY
AIILMNNOST NOMINALIST
AIILMNOORT MONITORIAL
AIILMNORTY MINATORILY
AIILMNOSTU SIMULATION
AIILMNOTTU MUTILATION
AIILMNRSSU INSULARISM
AIILNNOOST INSOLATION
AIILNNOSTU INSULATION
AIILNOOPPT OPPILATION
AIILNOOPST POSITIONAL,
  SPOLIATION
AIILNOOSTV VIOLATIONS
AIILNOSSTU SAINT LOUIS
AIILNRSSUY URINALYSIS
AIILNRSTUY INSULARITY
AIILORSSTU SAILOR SUIT
AIILPRSSTU SPIRITUALS
AIILRTTUVY VIRTUALITY
AIIMMNNOTU AMMUNITION
AIIMMPRRTU IMPRIMATUR
AIIMMRTTUY IMMATURITY
AIIMNNNOOT NOMINATION
AIIMNNORTU RUMINATION
AIIMNNRSTT MINISTRANT
AIIMNOOTTV MOTIVATION
AIIMNOPRTV PROVITAMIN
AIIMNOPSTU UTOPIANISM
AIIMNOPTTU IMPUTATION
AIIMNORSSU MISSOURIAN
AIIMNORSSY MISSIONARY
AIIMNPRSTU PURITANISM
AIIMNPSSTT TIMPANISTS
AIIMNPSSTU IMPUISSANT
AIIMNPSTTY TYMPANITIS
AIIMOPRSTT PATRIOTISM
AIIMOSSTTT STOMATITIS
AIINNNOOTT INTONATION
AIINNNOOTV INNOVATION
AIINNORSTT TRANSITION
AIINNORSTU INSINUATOR
AIINOOPPST APPOSITION
AIINOPRSTT PARTITIONS
AIINOPRSTV PRIVATIONS
AIINORSSTT STRIATIONS
AIINORTTVY INVITATORY
AIINOSSTTU SITUATIONS
AIIOPRSUVV VIVIPAROUS
AIIPRSTTVY VARITYPIST
AIJLMNORSU JOURNALISM
AIJLNORSTU JOURNALIST
AIJMORSSTU MAJOR SUITS
AIKLLLOPTW PILLOW TALK

AIKLOPSTUV VOLAPUKIST
AIKLORSSYY KARYOLYSIS
•AILLMNOOPY POLYNOMIAL
AILLMNPRST SMALL PRINT
AILLMOSSYY AMYLOLYSIS
AILLNOOPRT POLLINATOR
AILLNOOPTY OPTIONALLY
AILLNQRTUY TRANQUILLY
AILLPRSSTU PLURALISTS
AILMMSTTUU ULTIMATUMS
AILMNNOOPR PRONOMINAL
AILMNORSST MORTAL SINS
AILMNORTUY UNMORALITY
AILMNSSTTU STIMULANTS
AILMOOPSTU LIPOMATOUS
AILMORSSTU SIMULATORS
AILMORSTTU STIMULATOR
AILNOOPPTU POPULATION
AILNOOPRSS SPONSORIAL
AILNOOSTUV OVULATIONS
AILNOPSSTU PULSATIONS
AILNORSSTU INSULATORS
AILNORSTTU LUSTRATION
AILNOSTTUU USTULATION
AILNPPSSTU SUPPLIANTS
AILOPPRTUY POPULARITY
AILOPRSTTU STIPULATOR
AILRRSTUUV ULTRAVIRUS
AIMMNORSTU STRAMONIUM
AIMMNOSSTU SUMMATIONS
AIMMOORRTU MORATORIUM
AIMNNOOSTU ANTIMONOUS
AIMNOOSTTU AUTONOMIST
AIMNOOSTTX TAXONOMIST
AIMNOPSSTU ASSUMPTION
AIMNORRSST RAINSTORMS
AIMNRSTTUU NASTURTIUM
AIMOOORTVY OVARIOTOMY
AINNOOPRTT ANTIPROTON
AINNOORSTV INNOVATORS
AINOOPRSTY ANISOTROPY
AINOOQSTTU QUOTATIONS
AINOOSTTTU OUTSTATION
AINOPRSTUU USURPATION
AINORRSSTT TRANSISTOR
AINORRSTTY TRANSITORY
AINPRSTUUV PURSUIVANT
AIOOPRRSUU UPROARIOUS
AIOORRSTTU TRAITOROUS
AIOOSSTTTT TATTOOISTS
AIOPPPRSUU PUPIPAROUS
AIORRRTTTU TRITURATOR
AKKKLLNUUX KU KLUX
  KLAN
AKKMMNORSU
  KOMMUNARSK
AKLOPRRRSY LORRY PARKS
ALLNOPSTTU POLLUTANTS
ALLOPRSSTW STRAW POLLS

ALMNOPRTUY POULTRYMAN
ALMOOPPRST PROTOPLASM
ALMOPPSSUY PLAY POSSUM
ALNOPSSTTU POSTULANTS
ALOOORSTUZ ZOOLATROUS
ALOOPPRSTT PROTOPLAST
ALOOPPRTTY PROTOTYPAL
ALOOPRSTTU POSTULATOR
ALOPRTUUVY VOLUPTUARY
AMMOOSTUXY
  MYXOMATOUS
AMNNOOSTWW
  TOWNSWOMAN
AMNOOOSTUU
  AUTONOMOUS
AMNOOPRSUY
  PARONYMOUS
AMOPPRSTTU POSTPARTUM
ANOOOPRSTZ PROTOZOANS
ANOPRRSSTT TRANSPORTS
AOOORRSTTV ROTOVATORS
AOOPQRSTTU POST QUARTO
AORRRSTWWY
  WORRYWARTS
BBBCKOOSSY BOBBY
  SOCKS,
BBBEEELMSU BUMBLEBEES
BBBEEIINRW WINEBIBBER
BBBEGILNRU BLUBBERING
BBBGHINNOO HOBNOBBING
BBBHIINRSU RUBBISH BIN
BBBLLOOWWY
  BLOW-BY-BLOW
BBCDEIRSSU SUBSCRIBED
BBCEEKNRRU RUBBERNECK
BBCEELNOOU BUBONOCELE
BBCEGILNOR CLOBBERING
BBCEHINSSU CHUBBINESS
BBCEHLOSUY CUBBYHOLES
BBCEILRRSS SCRIBBLERS
BBCEIRRSSU SUBSCRIBER
BBCEIRSSTU SCRUBBIEST
BBCGIILNRS SCRIBBLING
BBCIIILOST BIBLIOTICS
BBDDEEIMOV DIVE-BOMBED
BBDDEELOSU DOUBLE BEDS
BBDDEILNOU DOUBLE BIND
BBDEEIMORV DIVE-BOMBER
BBDEIKNOOR BOOKBINDER
BBDEIOSSUY BUSYBODIES
BBDHIIOPRS BISHOPBIRD
BBEEERRRTU RUBBER TREE
BBEEIILRRS BILBERRIES
BBEEIRRRSU BURBERRIES
BBEELLOTTU BLUEBOTTLE
BBEELMORTT LETTER BOMB
BBEGHILOSS BOBSLEIGHS
BBEGHIORRT BIG BROTHER
BBEGILNORS SLOBBERING

BBEGINRSSU GRUBBINESS
BBEHHILOST SHIBBOLETH
BBEHHOORSY HOBBYHORSE
BBEHLLMOSS BOMBSHELLS
BBEIILLOOP BIBLIOPOLE
BBEIKLMOOO BOOKMOBILE
BBEIKLNOST KNOBBLIEST
BBEILNOSSW WOBBLINESS
BBEINSSSTU STUBBINESS
BBEIOOPRSY BOOBY PRISE
BBEIOOPRYZ BOOBY PRIZE
BBEKLORRUW
    RUBBLEWORK
BBEMNORSUX BOX
    NUMBERS
BBENORRSTU STUBBORNER
BBFHIINORS RIBBONFISH
BBGHIINRSU RUBBISHING
BBGHILLSTU LIGHT BULBS
BBGHILNOOS HOBGOBLINS
BBGILNNSUY SNUBBINGLY
BBHILNOSSY SNOBBISHLY
BBIIIIMMNOT IMBIBITION
BBIIILOSTT BIBLIOTIST
BBIKMNOSST STINK-BOMBS
BBJMMMOOUU MUMBO
    JUMBO
BBLMOORSUY
    BLOOMSBURY
BBLNORSTUY STUBBORNLY
BCCCKMOOSS
    COCKSCOMBS
BCCDEEEMNU
    DECUMBENCE
BCCDEILNOU CONDUCIBLE
BCCEEEMNRU
    RECUMBENCE
BCCEEEENPSU PUBESCENCE
BCCEEEENRSU RUBESCENCE
BCCEEINRTY CYBERNETIC
BCCEIMNNUY INCUMBENCY
BCCEINNOSU CONCUBINES
BCCEKOSSTU STOCK CUBES
BCCGIMNSUU SUCCUMBING
BCCHHIINNY INCH BY INCH
BCCHIINORT BRONCHITIC
BCCIILSSTY BICYCLISTS
BCDDEEILTU DEDUCTIBLE
BCDDIIKRSY DICKYBIRDS
BCDEEEFNOR CORNED BEEF
BCDEEEIINT BENEDICITE
BCDEEEMNRU
    ENCUMBERED
BCDEEHIMRS BESMIRCHED
BCDEEHLOST BEDCLOTHES
BCDEEIILNR INCREDIBLE
BCDEEINSSU SUBSIDENCE
BCDEEIPRRS PRESCRIBED
BCDEEKLLNU BULLNECKED

BCDEENOSST SECOND BEST
BCDEEORRSS CROSSBREED
BCDEFLOOTU CLUBFOOTED
BCDEGHINOU DEBOUCHING
BCDEGIINRS DESCRIBING
BCDEHIILOR BICHLORIDE
BCDEHILNOU DOUBLE CHIN
BCDEIILNRY INCREDIBLY
BCDEIILPSU PUBLICISED
BCDEIILPUZ PUBLICIZED
BCDEILOORR CORRODIBLE
BCDEILOPRU PRODUCIBLE
BCDEILORTT BITTER COLD
BCDEIOPRRS PROSCRIBED
BCDEKLOOOS CLOSED
    BOOK
BCDELNOORU CORDON
    BLEU
BCDELORRUY CLOUDBERRY
BCDEMMNRUU
    CUMMERBUND
BCDEORSTTU OBSTRUCTED
BCDGIIOSTU DOG BISCUIT
BCDHHIILRT CHILDBIRTH
BCDHLNOOTU
    CLOTHBOUND
BCDIILMORU LUMBRICOID
BCDIIOPRRT TROPICBIRD
BCDINOSTUU SUBDUCTION
BCDKLOOOST BLOODSTOCK
BCDKLOOOSW
    WOODBLOCKS
BCDKMRSTUU
    DUMBSTRUCK
BCDLNOOOTU BLOOD
    COUNT
BCDLORSTUU CLOUDBURST
BCDOPRSTUY BY-PRODUCTS
BCEEEEHLSU BLUE CHEESE
BCEEEFFILT EFFECTIBLE
BCEEEFINNT BENEFICENT
BCEEEFLLRT TREBLE CLEF
BCEEEGHINS BESEECHING
BCEEEHKNOS CHEEKBONES
BCEEEIILNU EBULLIENCE
BCEEEELLMRU CEREBELLUM
BCEEEELQRSU BECQUERELS
BCEEENRSTU ERUBESCENT
BCEEFORRTU BRUTE FORCE
BCEEGIINOT BIOGENETIC
BCEEGINRSU SUBGENERIC
BCEEHKLNOU HUCKLEBONE
BCEEHKOOQU
    CHEQUEBOOK
BCEEHKORRY CHOKEBERRY
BCEEHMORUU
    EMBOUCHURE
BCEEHNOOPR NECROPHOBE

BCEEHNORRX BRONX
    CHEER
BCEEIILPST PLEBISCITE
BCEEIJOSTV OBJECTIVES
BCEEIJSTUV SUBJECTIVE
BCEEIILNPU BLUE-PENCIL
BCEEILLOOS CELLOBIOSE
BCEEILMOST COMESTIBLE
BCEEILNOTY BY-ELECTION
BCEEIOOSVX VOICE BOXES
BCEEIPRRRS PRESCRIBER
BCEEIPRRSY SPICEBERRY
BCEEIPSSSU SUBSPECIES
BCEEJNORST JOB CENTRES
BCEEJOSSTX SEX OBJECTS
BCEEKLNOTT BOTTLENECK
BCEELNOTTU CUTTLEBONE
BCEELNRTUU TURBULENCE
BCEEMMORSU
    CUMBERSOME
BCEEMMORTY
    EMBRECTOMY
BCEFFIOOSX BOX OFFICES
BCEFFIOOSY OFFICE BOYS
BCEFHNNORT FRONTBENCH
BCEFIIKRRS FIREBRICKS
BCEFIJSTUY SUBJECTIFY
BCEGHIINTW BEWITCHING
BCEGHIKNNS KING'S BENCH
BCEGHINRTU BUTCHERING
BCEGIILORR CORRIGIBLE
BCEGIJNSTU SUBJECTING
BCEGILMNOY BECOMINGLY
BCEGILOOOY BIOECOLOGY
BCEGIMNNOU UNBECOMING
BCEHHNNOUY
    HONEYBUNCH
BCEHIINSST BITCHINESS
BCEHIISSSU HIBISCUSES
BCEHILNOOR BRONCHIOLE
BCEHILOPRY HYPERBOLIC
BCEHILOSTT BLOTCHIEST
BCEHILRRUV BUR CHERVIL
BCEHINNSSU BUNCHINESS
BCEHINOOPX XENOPHOBIC
BCEHINOSST BOTCHINESS
BCEHKKOOST SKETCHBOOK
BCEHKLOOSU BLOCKHOUSE
BCEHKOPSTU BUCKET SHOP
BCEHLOSSUU CLUBHOUSES
BCEHMNOOSY
    HONEYCOMBS
BCEHMRSTUW
    THUMBSCREW
BCEIIILMMS IMMISCIBLE
BCEIIILMTY IMBECILITY
BCEIIILNNV INVINCIBLE
BCEIIKLLLS SICKLEBILL
BCEIILMMOS EMBOLISMIC

BCEIJNOOST OBJECTIONS
BCEIJNOSTU SUBJECTION
BCEILMNOSU COLUMBINES
BCEILMOORT BOLOMETRIC
BCEILMRSTU CRUMBLIEST
BCEILNRTUU TUBERCULIN
BCEIMNNSTU INCUMBENTS
BCEINNOSSU BOUNCINESS
BCEINORTTU CONTRIBUTE
BCEINOSSTU SUBSECTION
BCEIOPPRSY PRESBYOPIC
BCEIORSSTT OBSTETRICS
BCEKKOOOPT POCKETBOOK
BCEKLNRTUU TURNBUCKLE
BCEKLOORTW TOWER
  BLOCK
BCEKLOOSTV BLOCK VOTES
BCELRSTUUU SUBCULTURE
BCEMNOPRTU
  PROCUMBENT
BCENOORSSS CROSSBONES
BCEORRSTTU OBSTRUCTER
BCEPRSTTUU BUTTERCUPS
BCFIIMORRR CRIBRIFORM
BCGHILNSTU NIGHTCLUBS
BCGIIINNRS INSCRIBING
BCGIKLNNUU UNBUCKLING
BCGINOOTTY BOYCOTTING
BCHIINORST BRONCHITIS
BCHIIOPRSS BISHOPRICS
BCHIIOPSSY BIOPHYSICS
BCHIMNOOOP MONOPHOBIC
BCHIMOORTT THROMBOTIC
BCHIOPRTYY BRYOPHYTIC
BCHLNOPSUW PUNCH
  BOWLS
BCHMOOOSTT
  TOOTHCOMBS
BCIIILNNVY INVINCIBLY
BCIILNOPSY PSILOCYBIN
BCIILORSUU LUBRICIOUS
BCIILPSSTU PUBLICISTS
BCIIMNOSTY SYMBIONTIC
BCIKMOORST BROOMSTICK
BCILPRSSTU STRIP CLUBS
BCIMNOOOSS SONIC BOOMS
BCIMNOOSTU COMBUSTION
BCIOPRSSTU SUBTROPICS
BCKLLOOPSU BOLLOCKS-UP
BCKMOOOORTT ROCK
  BOTTOM
BDDDEEINTW TWIN-BEDDED
BDDDEELOOR
  RED-BLOODED
BDDDEIISUV SUBDIVIDED
BDDEEEFINR BEFRIENDED
BDDEEEILLV BEDEVILLED
BDDEEEILRW BEWILDERED

BDDEEEELMNO
  EMBOLDENED
BDDEEELORU
  DOUBLE-REED
BDDEEGLNOU
  BLUDGEONED
BDDEEILMSS DISSEMBLED
BDDEEINRST BESTRIDDEN
BDDEENNRUU
  UNBURDENED
BDDEFILLOU FULL-BODIED
BDDEFLOOSU BLOOD FEUDS
BDDEGIILOS DISOBLIGED
BDDEGIOOSS DOGSBODIES
BDDEHLNOOR
  BONDHOLDER
BDDEHLOOOT
  HOT-BLOODED
BDDEIIRSUV SUBDIVIDER
BDDEIISSSU SUBSIDISED
BDDEIISSUZ SUBSIDIZED
BDDEILMORW MIDDLEBROW
BDDFGIINOR FORBIDDING
BDDFILLNOS BLINDFOLDS
BDDGIINOTU OUTBIDDING
BDDHLNOOOU
  BLOODHOUND
BDDIKLNNRU BLIND DRUNK
BDDILLORSY DOLLY BIRDS
BDEEEEMMRR
  REMEMBERED
BDEEEFILNS DEFENSIBLE
BDEEEFLOTT BOTTLE-FEED
BDEEEGHILR HEIDELBERG
BDEEEHLLNR HELLBENDER
BDEEEHLSST THE BLESSED
BDEEEHMORW
  HOME-BREWED
BDEEEIILSV DISBELIEVE
BDEEEEILNTX EXTENDIBLE
BDEEEILSTW WILDEBEEST
BDEEEIMRTT EMBITTERED
BDEEEINRRT INTERBREED
BDEEEIRTTW BITTERWEED
BDEEEELMTUW
  TUMBLEWEED
BDEEELNOSS NOSEBLEEDS
BDEEEELORTU DOUBLETREE
BDEEELRRRY ELDERBERRY
BDEEENRSTU DEBENTURES
BDEEFGIINR DEBRIEFING
BDEEFILNSY DEFENSIBLY
BDEEFLLOSW BEDFELLOWS
BDEEFLORSW FLOWERBEDS
BDEEFOORSS BED OF ROSES
BDEEGGLOOT BOOTLEGGED
BDEEGIILNV BEDEVILING
BDEEGIILST DIGESTIBLE
BDEEGIINNR INBREEDING

BDEEGIMOSU DISEMBOGUE
BDEEGLNORU BLUDGEONER
BDEEHIMOOS HOMEBODIES
BDEEHIMRSU HUMBERSIDE
BDEEHLNNOR HORNBLENDE
BDEEIILMOS DEMOBILISE
BDEEIILMOZ DEMOBILIZE
BDEEIILRTV DIVERTIBLE
BDEEIILSTV DIVESTIBLE
BDEEIILLNNR DINNER BELL
BDEEIILLOPT POTBELLIED
BDEEILMOSW DISEMBOWEL
BDEEILMOTU DOUBLE TIME
BDEEILMRSS DISSEMBLER
BDEEILNORR BORDERLINE
BDEEILNOTY OBEDIENTLY
BDEEILORSW BOWDLERISE
BDEEILORWZ BOWDLERIZE
BDEEIMMNOT EMBODIMENT
BDEEIMORRY EMBROIDERY
BDEEIMRRSU REIMBURSED
BDEEINNORZ BENZODRINE
BDEEIPRSSW SPIDERWEBS
BDEEIRSSTT BED-SITTERS
BDEEKOOOORV
  OVERBOOKED
BDEELLNRUY UNDERBELLY
BDEELMRRUU BLUE
  MURDER
BDEELNNOSS BLONDENESS
BDEELNRRSU BLUNDERERS
BDEELQRSUU BURLESQUED
BDEEMNNRUU
  UNNUMBERED
BDEEMNORSU
  BURDENSOME
BDEENORRUV
  OVERBURDEN
BDEEORSSTY OYSTER BEDS
BDEERSSTTU BUTTRESSED
BDEFFIILSU DIFFUSIBLE
BDEFFNOORW
  BROWNED-OFF
BDEFGINOOR FOREBODING
BDEFGIOORT FOOTBRIDGE
BDEFILOOST SOFT-BOILED
BDEFINORSY BOYFRIENDS
BDEFIOPRRY BIRD OF PREY
BDEGGGINRU BEGRUDGING
BDEGHHIINR HIGHBINDER
BDEGHINNRU HINDENBURG
BDEGHLNOUU
  DOUBLE-HUNG
BDEGIIILRS DIRIGIBLES
BDEGIILLNV DIVING BELL
BDEGIILNRU REBUILDING
BDEGIINNRR RING BINDER
BDEGIINOSY DISOBEYING
BDEGIINRST BESTRIDING

BDEGIINSTU SUBEDITING
BDEGIIPPRS BIG DIPPERS
BDEGIKORRW BRIDGEWORK
BDEGILNNRU BLUNDERING
BDEGILNORU REDOUBLING
BDEGIMOORR BRIDEGROOM
BDEGINNORU REBOUNDING
BDEGINNSTU SUBTENDING
BDEGIOPRRT BRIDGEPORT
BDEHIILPSU BISULPHIDE
BDEHIIOPRT PROHIBITED
BDEHIIRRSY HYBRIDISER
BDEHIIRRYZ HYBRIDIZER
BDEHNOOSUU
  HOUSEBOUND
BDEHNRRSUU
  UNDERBRUSH
BDEIIILNRV BILIVERDIN
BDEIIJNOSS INSIDE JOBS
BDEIIKLOOS OBELISKOID
BDEIILMORS DISEMBROIL
BDEIIRSSSU SUBSIDISER
BDEIIRSSUZ SUBSIDIZER
BDEIIRSTTU DISTRIBUTE
BDEIJLRRUY JERRY-BUILD
BDEIKNNORW
  WIND-BROKEN
BDEILLORWY YELLOWBIRD
BDEILLOSSU DISSOLUBLE
BDEILLOTUX BILLET-DOUX
BDEILMORSW BOWDLERISM
BDEILMOSSY SYMBOLISED
BDEILMOSYZ SYMBOLIZED
BDEILNNOST STONE-BLIND
BDEILNOOSS BLOODINESS
BDEIMNORSS MORBIDNESS
BDEINOORSS BROODINESS
BDEINOSSSU DO BUSINESS
BDEIOORTTW BITTERWOOD
BDEIORSSTU SUBEDITORS
BDEKNNOORW
  BROKEN-DOWN
BDELLNOPSU SPELLBOUND
BDELLORSUZ BULLDOZERS
BDELLORTUY TROUBLEDLY
BDELMMNOUY
  MOLYBDENUM
BDELMNOOOY BLOOD
  MONEY
BDELMNOTUW
  TUMBLEDOWN
BDELNOOOST BLOODSTONE
BDELOOPSTU DOUBLE-STOP
BDELOOPSTY BLOOD TYPES
BDENOPTTUU BUTTONED UP
BDFLLOTUUY DOUBTFULLY
BDFNOORSTU FROSTBOUND
BDGIINRSSU DISBURSING
BDGIINRSTU DISTURBING

BDGIKMNOSU SUBKINGDOM
BDGILLNOUZ BULLDOZING
BDGILNORWY BLOW-DRYING
BDGLOOOPRU BLOOD
  GROUP
BDHIILRRWY WHIRLYBIRD
BDHIMNOORY MONOHYBRID
BDHMNOSTUW THUMBS
  DOWN
BDHNNOORTU
  NORTHBOUND
BDHNOOSTUU
  SOUTHBOUND
BDIIILNOSU LIBIDINOUS
BDILNOPSST BLIND SPOTS
BDINNOORRU ROUND ROBIN
BDINOOSWWW BOW
  WINDOWS
BDKNNOOORY
  DONNYBROOK
BDLLOOSSTU BLOOD LUSTS
BDLOOOPRST BLOOD SPORT
BDMNOORSTU
  STORMBOUND
BDNNOOTTUW
  BUTTON-DOWN
BDNOOOTTUW
  BUTTONWOOD
BEEEEFLNSS FEEBLENESS
BEEEEGLSTU BETELGEUSE
BEEEEMMRRR
  REMEMBERER
BEEEFGILNN ENFEEBLING
BEEEFOORRT FREEBOOTER
BEEEGGINRR GINGER BEER
BEEEGHINRS HEISENBERG
BEEEGINRRR GREENBRIER
BEEEGLNRST GREEN BELTS
BEEEGNOSTW
  GO-BETWEENS
BEEEHLLRTW BELLWETHER
BEEEILMPTX EXEMPTIBLE
BEEEILNRUV UNBELIEVER
BEEEILNSTX EXTENSIBLE
BEEEILRRSV REVERSIBLE
BEEEILRRTV REVERTIBLE
BEEEIMRRTT EMBITTERER
BEEEIMRSSV SEMIBREVES
BEEEINRSSZ BREEZINESS
BEEEIRRSTW SWEETBRIER
BEEEKKOOPR BOOKKEEPER
BEEELLRSST BEST-SELLER
BEEELMMNST EMBLEMENTS
BEEELMRSZZ EMBEZZLERS
BEEELNNOTV BENEVOLENT
BEEEMNRTTT BETTERMENT
BEEEOQSUXZ SQUEEZEBOX
BEEFFNORUZ BUFFER ZONE
BEEFGIINNT BENEFITING

BEEFGRSTUU SUBTERFUGE
BEEFIILLNX INFLEXIBLE
BEEFIORSSU SEBIFEROUS
BEEFLMNOTU BEFOULMENT
BEEGGIILLN NEGLIGIBLE
BEEGGLOORT BOOTLEGGER
BEEGGNRRSU REGENSBURG
BEEGHILNRT BLETHERING
BEEGHINRRT BRIGHTENER
BEEGHMNRTU GREEN
  THUMB
BEEGIIILLN INELIGIBLE
BEEGIILNRT GILBERTINE
BEEGIILNST INGESTIBLE
BEEGIINOSS BIOGENESIS
BEEGIKNNOT BETOKENING
BEEGILLNRR BELL-RINGER
BEEGILMNRS RESEMBLING
BEEGILMNZZ EMBEZZLING
BEEGINRSTW BESTREWING
BEEGMNORYY
  EMBRYOGENY
BEEGNOORRS
  GREENSBORO
BEEGOORRSY GOOSEBERRY
BEEHIIITVX EXHIBITIVE
BEEHILLMOR LIMBER HOLE
BEEHILMMOO MOBILE HOME
BEEHILMOST BLITHESOME
BEEHILNSST BLITHENESS
BEEHIMMPRS MEMBERSHIP
BEEHIORRSV HERBIVORES
BEEHKMNOOR BROKEN
  HOME
BEEHLMNSSU HUMBLENESS
BEEHLOPRSY HYPERBOLES
BEEHMOORST
  BOTHERSOME
BEEHMOORTT
  MOTHER-TO-BE
BEEHNOOPSX PHONE BOXES
BEEHOORSSX HORSEBOXES
BEEIIJORTU BIJOUTERIE
BEEIIKLMRT KIMBERLITE
BEEIILLLRV LIBREVILLE
BEEIILMMRS IMMERSIBLE
BEEIILMNRT TIMBERLINE
BEEIILMRSS REMISSIBLE
BEEIILNNSS INSENSIBLE
BEEIILNNTV INVENTIBLE
BEEIILNRST LIBERTINES
BEEIILNRTV INVERTIBLE
BEEIILSSTX BISSEXTILE
BEEILLLNTU LUTINE BELL
BEEILLLOVW BOLL WEEVIL
BEEILLLOWY YELLOW BILE
BEEILLNORS REBELLIONS
BEEILLOPST POTBELLIES
BEEILLORSU REBELLIOUS

BEEILLRSTT BELLETRIST
BEEILMNNSS NIMBLENESS
BEEILMRRSU MULBERRIES
BEEILNOPRS NOBEL PRISE
BEEILNOPRZ NOBEL PRIZE
BEEILNOSST OSTENSIBLE
BEEILOSTTU OUBLIETTES
BEEILSSTTU SUBTLETIES
BEEILSSTUV VESTIBULES
BEEIMRRRSU REIMBURSER
BEEINNRSTU INNER TUBES
BEEINORRTT TORBERNITE
BEEINRSSTT BITTERNESS
BEEINSSSSU BUSINESSES
BEEIOSSSSV OBSESSIVES
BEEIQRSTTU BRIQUETTES
BEEIRSSUVV SUBVERSIVE
BEEKLLOORS BOOKSELLER
BEEKNNORSS BROKENNESS
BEELMNRSSU NUMBERLESS
BEELMRRSSU SLUMBERERS
BEELNPRTUU PUBERULENT
BEELNSSSTU SUBTLENESS
BEELQRRSUU BURLESQUER
BEELQRSSUU BURLESQUES
BEELRRSSTU BLUSTERERS
BEEMMNNOTT
　ENTOMBMENT
BEEMMNOSST
　EMBOSSMENT
BEEMNOOSXY
　MONEYBOXES
BEEMNORSSS SOMBRENESS
BEENOSSSTU OBTUSENESS
BEENPRSSSU SUPERBNESS
BEENQSSTUU SUBSEQUENT
BEEOPRSSSX PRESS BOXES
BEEPRRSTYY PRESBYTERY
BEERSSSTTU BUTTRESSES
BEFFHILOOT OFF THE BOIL
BEFFNOORUY BUFFOONERY
BEFGIINNOR FIBRINOGEN
BEFGILNORW FINGER BOWL
BEFGKOOORR GO FOR
　BROKE
BEFHILLMTU THIMBLEFUL
BEFHIRSTTU BUTTERFISH
BEFIILLNXY INFLEXIBLY
BEFIILRSTU FILIBUSTER
BEFLLLOPSY BELLY FLOPS
BEFNNNOSUY FUNNY
　BONES
BEGGHMRUUY
　HUMBUGGERY
BEGGIILLNY NEGLIGIBLY
BEGGIINNNS BEGINNINGS
BEGGILNNOS BELONGINGS
BEGGIMNRSU SUBMERGING
BEGGINNORU BURGEONING

BEGHIIINTX EXHIBITING
BEGHIIKNNT BETHINKING
BEGHIILMNS BLEMISHING
BEGHIILNRT BLITHERING
BEGHILMNOO HEMOGLOBIN
BEGHINNRTU BURTHENING
BEGHINORSU NEIGHBOURS
BEGHINORTT BETROTHING
BEGHINRSST BRIGHTNESS
BEGHMNOORT
　THROMBOGEN
BEGIIILLTY LEGIBILITY
BEGIILLNTT BELITTLING
BEGIILMNOR EMBROILING
BEGIILNRST BLISTERING
BEGIILNRTT BITTERLING
BEGIINRRST BESTIRRING
BEGIJRSTTU JITTERBUGS
BEGIKLNRUY REBUKINGLY
BEGILMNRSU SLUMBERING
BEGILNORST BOLSTERING
BEGILNORSY SOBERINGLY
BEGILNRSTU BLUSTERING
BEGILNSTTU SUBLETTING
BEGILOOOXY EXOBIOLOGY
BEGINPRRTU PERTURBING
BEGINRSTUV SUBVERTING
BEGLMOORYY
　EMBRYOLOGY
BEGLMORUUX
　LUXEMBOURG
BEGNORRUYY
　YOUNGBERRY
BEHHIIRSTT THE BRITISH
BEHIIIINTV INHIBITIVE
BEHIIINOTX EXHIBITION
BEHIILPSTU BISULPHITE
BEHIIOPRRT PROHIBITER
BEHIIORSTX EXHIBITORS
BEHIIORTXY EXHIBITORY
BEHIIRRSST BRITISHERS
BEHIKLOSSV BOLSHEVIKS
BEHILLORWW WILLOWHERB
BEHILMOSSV BOLSHEVISM
BEHILPRSSU PUBLISHERS
BEHIMSSSTU MISS THE BUS
BEHINORSTT BIRTHSTONE
BEHINOSSSY BOYISHNESS
BEHKNOOOPS PHONE
　BOOKS
BEHKNOSSUU BUNKHOUSES
BEHLMOOPTY PHLEBOTOMY
BEHLNOOTTU BUTTONHOLE
BEHMOOORST
　SMOOTHBORE
BEHMOORSST
　THROMBOSES
BEHMOORSTY MOTHER'S
　BOY

BEHMPRTTUU
　TUB-THUMPER
BEHNOOOORTU ON THE
　BUROO
BEHOOPRSSU RUSSOPHOBE
BEHRRSSUWY
　SHREWSBURY
BEIIILMMOS IMMOBILISE
BEIIILMMOZ IMMOBILIZE
BEIIILNOST NOBILITIES
BEIIIMNSTU BITUMINISE
BEIIIMNTUZ BITUMINIZE
BEIIIOOPSS BIOPOIESIS
BEIILLNOTU EBULLITION
BEIILLOSSU SOLUBILISE
BEIILLOSUZ SOLUBILIZE
BEIILMOPSS IMPOSSIBLE
BEIILMRTUY MULIEBRITY
BEIILNNSSY INSENSIBLY
BEIILNRSTT LITTERBINS
BEIILORSTT TRILOBITES
BEIILORSTU BOILER SUIT
BEIILRSSTU SUBTILISER
BEIILRSSTY RESISTIBLY
BEIILRSTTT LIBRETTIST
BEIILRSTUZ SUBTILIZER
BEIIMSSSUV SUBMISSIVE
BEIINORSTY INSOBRIETY
BEIJLRRTUY JERRY-BUILT
BEIKLMRTTU BUTTERMILK
BEIKMOORST MOTORBIKES
BEIKMORRTW TIMBERWORK
BEIKNOORUY ON YOUR BIKE
BEILLMNPSU PLUMB LINES
BEILMNOOSW SNOWMOBILE
BEILMNOOTT BOTTOM LINE
BEILMOOOST LOBOTOMIES
BEILNOSSTY OSTENSIBLY
BEILNOSSWZ BLOWZINESS
BEILNOSTUY NEBULOSITY
BEILNPRSTU BLUEPRINTS
BEILOOPRST POTBOILERS
BEILOOTUVV OBVOLUTIVE
BEIMMRSTYY BISYMMETRY
BEIMNNOOPT EMBONPOINT
BEIMNORSSU SUBMERSION
BEINNOSTUV SUBVENTION
BEINOOSSSS OBSESSIONS
BEINOPRSTU SUBREPTION
BEINORSSUV SUBVERSION
BEINORSTUU SUBROUTINE
BEINOSSTWX WITNESS BOX
BEINSSSTTU SUBSISTENT
BEIOOQSSUU OBSEQUIOUS
BEIOORSSST SOB STORIES
BEIOORSSTU BOISTEROUS
BEIOPSTTTU PITOT TUBES
BEIOQRSSTU SOBRIQUETS
BEIOQRSTUU SOUBRIQUET

BEIORSTTUY TUBEROSITY
BEISSTTTUU SUBSTITUTE
BEKKNOOOST BOOK
TOKENS
BEKNOORSTY STONY BROKE
BELLMOPSTU POST-BELLUM
BELLNOSUUY NEBULOUSLY
BELLORSTUY TROLLEYBUS
BELMMOORRU
LUMBER-ROOM
BELMOOSSTT BOTTOMLESS
BELMORSSUU SLUMBEROUS
BELOOPRSTT LOBSTERPOT
BEMNOOSSTT TOMBSTONES
BENNOORSTW
BROWNSTONE
BENORSSSTU ROBUSTNESS
BEORRTTTUW BUTTERWORT
BFFFFILOTU BIT OF FLUFF
BFFFIOSTTU BIT OF STUFF
BFGHIINRSU FURBISHING
BFGHILLSTU BULLFIGHTS
BFGHILNTYY FLY-BY-NIGHT
BFGILLMNUY FUMBLINGLY
BFIIILSTUY FUSIBILITY
BFIIIORSST FIBROSITIS
BFIIKORSTT BIT OF SKIRT
BFIILMMORU UMBILIFORM
BFILLNOUUW IN FULL BLOW
BFILLLSSUY BLISSFULLY
BFLMOOPTUU OUT OF
PLUMB
BGGIILLNOY OBLIGINGLY
BGGIINNPRU UPBRINGING
BGHHIIRRTT BIRTHRIGHT
BGHIIIINNT INHIBITING
BGHIILNPSU PUBLISHING
BGHIINNRSU BURNISHING
BGHIKNOORU KINBOROUGH
BGHIKORRTW BRIGHTWORK
BGHILLMNUY HUMBLINGLY
BGHILLNSUY BLUSHINGLY
BGHILLOUWY WILLOUGHBY
BGHILMOORU MILBOROUGH
BGHILNNSUU UNBLUSHING
BGHIPRSTTU PITTSBURGH
BGHLOOPSUY PLOUGHBOYS
BGIIILMNOZ MOBILIZING
BGIIILNOTY IGNOBILITY
BGIIJNNOSU SUBJOINING
BGIIKLNNNU UNBLINKING
BGIILMOORS IMBROGLIOS
BGIILOOSST BIOLOGISTS
BGIIMNSTTU SUBMITTING
BGIINORSUU RUBIGINOUS
BGIINSSSTU SUBSISTING
BGIJLLMNUY JUMBLINGLY
BGIKNOPRSS SPRINGBOKS
BGILLMMNUY MUMBLINGLY

BGILLMNRUY RUMBLINGLY
BGILMNOOSS BLOSSOMING
BGILOORSTY BRYOLOGIST
BGILORSUUU LUGUBRIOUS
BGIMNNOOSU UNBOSOMING
BGINNOOORU BUON
GIORNO
BGINOORRSW BORROWINGS
BHHIMORSTY BIORHYTHMS
BHHOORSTTU TOOTHBRUSH
BHIIINNOT INHIBITION
BHIILLNOST BILLIONTHS
BHIILLRSTT STILLBIRTH
BHIILMRTTU MULTIBIRTH
BHIMOORSST THROMBOSIS
BHIMOSSTUU BISMUTHOUS
BHKNOOOTTU
BUTTONHOOK
BHLLOOOSTT TOLLBOOTHS
BHLLOOSSUU HOLUS-BOLUS
BHLLRRUUYY HURLY-BURLY
BHNOPSTTUU PUSH-BUTTON
BHOOOOPSUZ
ZOOPHOBOUS
BIIIILRSTY RISIBILITY
BIIIILSTVY VISIBILITY
BIIILMMOTY IMMOBILITY
BIILLOSTUY SOLUBILITY
BIILLOTUVY VOLUBILITY
BIILMOPSSY IMPOSSIBLY
BIIMNOSSSU SUBMISSION
BIIMNOSTUU BITUMINOUS
BIIOQSTUUU UBIQUITOUS
BIKLLORSST STORKSBILL
BILMOORSWW
LOWBROWISM
BILNOOOTUV OBVOLUTION
BILOOPRSTU POLITBUROS
BIMNOORSTT TROMBONIST
BIMOOPPRRU OPPROBRIUM
BKLLMNSSUU NUMBSKULLS
BKMOOOPPRT
PROMPTBOOK
BMMOOOSTTT
BOTTOMMOST
BOOPPRRSTU TURBOPROPS
CCCEEINNOS CONSCIENCE
CCCEEINRST CRESCENTIC,
ECCENTRICS
CCCEELNSUU SUCCULENCE
CCCEENORRU
OCCURRENCE
CCCEHIILMY HEMICYCLIC
CCCEHIILNO COLCHICINE
CCCEHKORSS CROSSCHECK
CCCEIILPRY PERICYCLIC
CCCEIIMRSU CIRCUMCISE
CCCEILOTUY LEUCOCYTIC
CCCEINNOOP CONCEPCIÓN

CCCEINNORT CONCENTRIC
CCCEINOOTV CONCOCTIVE
CCCEINOOTY COENOCYTIC
CCCEKLNOOR
CORNCOCKLE
CCCGINNOOT CONCOCTING
CCCGNOOOSU
GONOCOCCUS
CCCHILMOOY HOMOCYCLIC
CCCIIMORTY MICROCYTIC
CCCILLOPYY POLYCYCLIC
CCCILMNOOY MONOCYCLIC
CCCILNSTUY SUCCINCTLY
CCCILOPSTY POST-CYCLIC
CCCINNOOOT CONCOCTION
CCCIOOPRSY CRYOSCOPIC
CCDDEELNOY CONCEDEDLY
CCDDEENNOS
CONDESCEND
CCDEEEENPR PRECEDENCE
CCDEEEHINS DEHISCENCE
CCDEEENRST DECRESCENT
CCDEEERRSU RECRUDESCE
CCDEEFIINY DEFICIENCY
CCDEEFINNO CONFIDENCE
CCDEEGINSU SUCCEEDING
CCDEEHHTUW CHEW THE
CUD
CCDEEHIORT RICOCHETED
CCDEEHNOSY SYNECDOCHE
CCDEEIIIPT EPIDEICTIC
CCDEEIILRT DIELECTRIC
CCDEEIIPPR PRECIPICED
CCDEEIKLRV CLEVER DICK
CCDEEILNOR RECONCILED
CCDEELNNOO
CONDOLENCE
CCDEENORSS CRESCENDOS
CCDEFILNOT CONFLICTED
CCDEHILLOS COLD CHISEL
CCDEHILNOR CHRONICLED
CCDEHLNTUU DUTCH
UNCLE
CCDEIIIRST CRITICISED
CCDEIIIRTZ CRITICIZED
CCDEIILOPY EPICYCLOID
CCDEIINNOR ENDOCRINIC
CCDEIINNOT COINCIDENT
CCDEIJKOSY DISC JOCKEY
CCDEILOORS CROCODILES
CCDEIMOOOT OCTODECIMO
CCDEINNOST DISCONNECT
CCDEINOOPS ENDOSCOPIC
CCDEINOOST DECOCTIONS
CCDEINOPUU UNOCCUPIED
CCDEINORST DISCONCERT
CCDEINOTUV CONDUCTIVE
CCDENOOPRU RED
PUCCOON

CCDGIIINNO COINCIDING
CCDGIILOSY GLYCOSIDIC
CCDGIKLNOU CUCKOLDING
CCDGILNNOU CONCLUDING
CCDGINNOTU CONDUCTING
CCDHIINORT CHONDRITIC
CCDIMNOSTU MISCONDUCT
CCDINNOOTU CONDUCTION
CCDNOORSTU
    CONDUCTORS
CCEEEEHIKP CHEEKPIECE
CCEEEELLNX EXCELLENCE
CCEEEENNSS SENESCENCE
CCEEEFNNOR CONFERENCE
CCEEEFNRSU RUFESCENCE
CCEEEGINOS GEOSCIENCE
CCEEEIINPR RECIPIENCE
CCEEEINPRS PRESCIENCE
CCEEEINQSU QUIESCENCE
CCEEEINRSV VIRESCENCE
CCEEEIOPSS ECOSPECIES
CCEEEELLNXY EXCELLENCY
CCEEEMMNOR
    RECOMMENCE
CCEEEMNOPT COMPETENCE
CCEEEMNSTU TUMESCENCE
CCEEENRRRU RECURRENCE
CCEEENRSTX EXCRESCENT
CCEEFFIINY EFFICIENCY
CCEEFFILNO OFF-LICENCE
CCEEFHHRRU FREE
    CHURCH
CCEEFILLSY LIFE CYCLES
CCEEFLNNOU CONFLUENCE
CCEEGHINRS SCREECHING
CCEEGINNOR CONGENERIC
CCEEGINORS CONCIERGES
CCEEGINORT EGOCENTRIC,
    GEOCENTRIC
CCEEGNNORU
    CONGRUENCE
CCEEHINOSS CHOICENESS
CCEEHNOSTU ESCUTCHEON
CCEEHOSTTU COUCHETTES
CCEEIIINNP INCIPIENCE
CCEEIILMRS SEMICIRCLE
CCEEIIPPRS PRECIPICES
CCEEIKRRST CRICKETERS
CCEEILLOTV COLLECTIVE
CCEEILMNNY INCLEMENCY
CCEEILNOPU LEUCOPENIC
CCEEILNORR RECONCILER
CCEEILNORT ELECTRONIC
CCEEILOPST TELESCOPIC
CCEEILORVY COERCIVELY
CCEEINNNOT CONTINENCE
CCEEINNOTV CONNECTIVE
CCEEINNRRU INCURRENCE
CCEEINNRST INCRESCENT

CCEEINOPRW CROWNPIECE
CCEEINOPTV CONCEPTIVE
CCEEINORST CONCRETISE
CCEEINORTV CONCRETIVE
CCEEINORTX EXOCENTRIC
CCEEINORTZ CONCRETIZE
CCEEINOSSV CONCESSIVE
CCEEINOTVV CONVECTIVE
CCEEINRRSU CURRENCIES
CCEEIOPRSS CROSSPIECE
CCEEIORRTV CORRECTIVE
CCEEISSSUV SUCCESSIVE
CCEEJNORTU CONJECTURE
CCEELMORTY CYCLOMETER
CCEELNOPRU CORPULENCE
CCEELNORTY CONCRETELY
CCEELNRTUU TRUCULENCE
CCEELOSTTU COS LETTUCE
CCEELOSTUY LEUCOCYTES
CCEEMNOPTY
    COMPETENCY
CCEENOPRRT PRECONCERT
CCEFHIIMOR MICROFICHE
CCEFIIINST SCIENTIFIC
CCEFIINPSU UNSPECIFIC
CCEFIIRSUX CRUCIFIXES
CCEFIKLSTT CLEFT STICK
CCEFILMRUX CIRCUMFLEX
CCEFIMRSUU CIRCUMFUSE
CCEFINNOOT CONFECTION
CCEFLLNOTU FLOCCULENT
CCEFLSSSUU SUCCESSFUL
CCEGGHOSST SCOTCH
    EGGS
CCEGGILNOY GLYCOGENIC
CCEGHHORRU
    CHURCHGOER
CCEGHIIIOP PICHICIEGO
CCEGHINORT CROCHETING
CCEGIILNNR ENCIRCLING
CCEGIINNOV CONCEIVING
CCEGILLNOT COLLECTING
CCEGIMMNNO
    COMMENCING
CCEGINNNOR CONCERNING
CCEGINNNOS ENSCONCING
CCEGINNNOT CONNECTING
CCEGINNORT CONCRETING
CCEGINNORT CORRECTING
CCEGINORSY CRYOGENICS
CCEHHILOTV CLOVE HITCH
CCEHIINNNO CINCHONINE
CCEHIINNOS CINCHONISE
CCEHIINNOZ CINCHONIZE
CCEHIKLSST CHECKLISTS
CCEHIKMOOR
    MOCK-HEROIC
CCEHIKNOPT CHECKPOINT
CCEHIKNOPX CHICKEN POX

CCEHILNORR CHRONICLER
CCEHILNORS CHRONICLES
CCEHIMOSSY ECCHYMOSIS
CCEHINRSTU CRUNCHIEST
CCEHKMOORS
    CHECKROOMS
CCEHKOORSS COCKHORSES
CCEHKOPSST SPOT CHECKS
CCEHKORTUU
    CHUCKER-OUT
CCEHMOORTY
    CYTOCHROME
CCEIIINNPY INCIPIENCY
CCEIIIRRST CRITICISER
CCEIIIRRTZ CRITICIZER
CCEIIIRSTV CERVICITIS
CCEIIKNPRS PICNICKERS
CCEIILMNOR MICROCLINE
CCEIILOSST SOLECISTIC
CCEIIMOORS SERIOCOMIC
CCEIIMPSST SCEPTICISM
CCEIINOTVV CONVICTIVE
CCEIINRTTY CENTRICITY
CCEIIOPPRS PERISCOPIC
CCEIIORTVY COERCIVITY
CCEIKKOPPT PICKPOCKET
CCEIKMNOSY COCKNEYISM
CCEILLLOSU CELLULOSIC
CCEILLNOOT COLLECTION
CCEILMNNOU COUNCILMEN
CCEILNNOSU NUCLEONICS
CCEILNOSUV CONCLUSIVE
CCEILOOQTU COQUELICOT
CCEIMNNOOU UNECONOMIC
CCEIMNRTUV CIRCUMVENT
CCEIMOOPRS MICROSCOPE
CCEINNNOOT CONNECTION
CCEINNOOPT CONCEPTION
CCEINNOORT CONCERTINO,
    CONCRETION
CCEINNOOSS CONCESSION
CCEINNOOTV CONVECTION
CCEINOOOPS ICONOSCOPE
CCEINOORRT CORRECTION
CCEINOSSSU SUCCESSION
CCEINOSSUV CONCUSSIVE
CCEIOOPRSU PRECOCIOUS
CCEIOPRSST COST PRICES
CCEISSSUUV SUCCUSSIVE
CCEKLOORTW CLOCK
    TOWER
CCEKORRSSW
    CORKSCREWS
CCELLOORST COLLECTORS
CCELLOSTYY CYCLOSTYLE
CCELMOORTY
    MOTORCYCLE
CCELMOOSTY CYCLOSTOME
CCELMORTYY CYCLOMETRY

CCELNSSTUU SUCCULENTS
CCELOPRSSU CORPUSCLES
CCEMOSTTYY CYSTECTOMY
CCENNORRTU
CONCURRENT
CCENOORSSU CONCOURSES
CCENOORSTV CONVECTORS
CCENOPSSTU CONSPECTUS
CCEOOPSSTY CYSTOSCOPE
CCEORSSSSU SUCCESSORS
CCFGHIKOST COCKFIGHTS
CCFGIINRUY CRUCIFYING
CCFILMORUU CUCULIFORM
CCGHHHHIRU HIGH CHURCH
CCGHINNRSU SCRUNCHING
CCGHLNOOOY
CONCHOLOGY
CCGIIIKNNP PICNICKING
CCGIINNNOV CONVINCING
CCGIINNOTV CONVICTING
CCGILORSUY GLYCOSURIC
CCGIMNOOOS COSMOGONIC
CCGINNORRU CONCURRING
CCGINNOSSU CONCUSSING
CCGINORSUU SUCCOURING
CCGIOOPRSY GYROSCOPIC
CCHHHOOPTT HOTCHPOTCH
CCHHIIOTTY ICHTHYOTIC
CCHIIIRSTT TRISTICHIC
CCHIILNNOO CONCHIOLIN
CCHIILOPRY CRYOPHILIC
CCHIIMNNOS CINCHONISM
CCHIIMOPRS MICROCHIPS
CCHIINORTY CHRONICITY
CCHIKLOSTT LOCKSTITCH
CCHIKOPSST CHOPSTICKS
CCHIMOSSTT SCOTCH MIST
CCHINNORSY SYNCHRONIC
CCHIOOOPRS HOROSCOPIC
CCHIOPSSTY PSYCHOTICS
CCHIORSTTY TRICHOCYST
CCHKLNOSUU NO SUCH
LUCK
CCHNOOSTUY COCONUT
SHY
CCHOOPSSUU
HOCUS-POCUS
CCIIIMRSST CRITICISMS
CCIILLNOPY POLYCLINIC
CCIILMNNOO MONOCLINIC
CCIILMOPTY COMPLICITY
CCIILNSTUY UNICYCLIST
CCIILOOPRT COPROLITIC
CCIIMMOORT MICROTOMIC
CCIIMOPRST COMIC STRIP
CCIIMOSSTT SCOTTICISM
CCIINNNOTY CONCINNITY
CCIINNOOTV CONVICTION
CCIINOOPRS SCORPIONIC

CCIIOOPRTX PICROTOXIC
CCIIORSTUU CIRCUITOUS
CCIKNOOPTU CUCKOOPINT
CCILLNOORU COUNCILLOR
CCILLOOPTY COLLOTYPIC
CCILMRRUUU CURRICULUM
CCILNNOOSU CONCLUSION
CCIMMOORSS MICROCOSMS
CCIMOOPRSY MICROSCOPY
CCINNNOOSU CONCINNOUS
CCINNOOSSU CONCUSSION
CCINOPRSST CONSCRIPTS
CCINOSSSUU SUCCUSSION
CCINOSTUVY VISCOUNTCY
CCIOOPRTYZ CRYPTOZOIC
CCIOPPRRTY PROCRYPTIC
CCIORRSSSS CRISSCROSS
CCNOORRTUW CROWN
COURT
CCNORSSTTU CONSTRUCTS
CCOOPSSTYY CYSTOSCOPY
CDDEEEENNP DEPENDENCE
CDDEEEHIPR DECIPHERED
CDDEEEINRT INTERCEDED
CDDEEEINUV UNDECEIVED
CDDEEEIRRT REDIRECTED
CDDEEEJLTY DEJECTEDLY
CDDEEEENNPY DEPENDENCY
CDDEEEENNST DESCENDENT
CDDEEFFIIN DIFFIDENCE
CDDEEGINNS DESCENDING
CDDEEIINSS DISSIDENCE
CDDEEIJPRU PREJUDICED
CDDEEIMNOR ENDODERMIC
CDDEEINORS CONSIDERED
CDDEEINRTU UNDIRECTED
CDDEEIORSV DISCOVERED
CDDEELMOSU
CUDDLESOME
CDDEEMNOTU
DOCUMENTED
CDDEEMOOPS
DECOMPOSED
CDDEEOPRRU REPRODUCED
CDDEFNNOOU
CONFOUNDED
CDDEHIILOR DICHLORIDE
CDDEIIOSSV VIDEODISCS
CDDEIMMNOO
INCOMMODED
CDDEIMMOOS DISCOMMODE
CDDEINNOOT ENDODONTIC
CDDEINNOSW SECOND
WIND
CDDEINORTU INTRODUCED
CDDEINOSTU DEDUCTIONS,
DISCOUNTED
CDDEIORSSU DISCOURSED

CDDEMNOOPU
COMPOUNDED,
DECOMPOUND
CDDENOPRTU END
PRODUCT
CDDEOORTUW CROWDED
OUT
CDDHILLOSY CLODDISHLY
CDDIILNORY CYLINDROID
CDDILOOPSU DIPLODOCUS
CDDINNOOTY DICYNODONT
CDEEEEINPX EXPEDIENCE
CDEEEENRRT DETERRENCE
CDEEEENRRV REVERENCED
CDEEEFFHOS CHEESED OFF
CDEEEFFINR DIFFERENCE
CDEEEFFIST SIDE EFFECT
CDEEEFHIKR KERCHIEFED
CDEEEFILTV DEFLECTIVE
CDEEEFMNNS MEND
FENCES
CDEEEGINRV DIVERGENCE
CDEEEGNRTY DETERGENCY
CDEEEHIPRR DECIPHERER
CDEEEHLRSU RESCHEDULE
CDEEEHNNRT ENTRENCHED
CDEEEHNRRT RETRENCHED
CDEEEIINNV IN EVIDENCE
CDEEEIINRS DECREE NISI
CDEEEILOPV VELOCIPEDE
CDEEEILQSU DELIQUESCE
CDEEEIMNNO COMEDIENNE
CDEEEIMNNP IMPENDENCE
CDEEEINNST TENDENCIES
CDEEEINPST CENTIPEDES
CDEEEINPXY EXPEDIENCY
CDEEEINRRT INTERCEDER
CDEEEINRSS RESIDENCES
CDEEEINRSW WIDE-SCREEN
CDEEEINRUV UNDECEIVER
CDEEEISTTV DETECTIVES
CDEEELOPST TELESCOPED
CDEEELORST ELECTRODES
CDEEEMNNOT
ENCODEMENT
CDEEENNRSU UNSCREENED
CDEEENPRST PRECEDENTS
CDEEENPTUX UNEXPECTED
CDEEEPRSTU PERSECUTED
CDEEFGILNT DEFLECTING
CDEEFIINRT DENTIFRICE
CDEEFILNNU INFLUENCED
CDEEFILNOT DEFLECTION
CDEEFINORR REINFORCED
CDEEFINOST DEFECTIONS
CDEEFINTUV DEFUNCTIVE
CDEEFKLPSY FLYSPECKED
CDEEFLNORT CENTRE-FOLD
CDEEFLNORY ENFORCEDLY

CDEEFLOORS FORECLOSED
CDEEFNORSS FORCEDNESS
CDEEGHHITT GET HITCHED
CDEEGIIMRS GERMICIDES
CDEEGIKNNR RING-NECKED
CDEEGILNNU INDULGENCE
CDEEGILNUV DIVULGENCE
CDEEGINOPR PROCEEDING
CDEEGINORS RECOGNISED
CDEEGINORZ RECOGNIZED
CDEEGINRVY DIVERGENCY
CDEEHIILOP OPHICLEIDE
CDEEHIMNOR ECHINODERM
CDEEHINNRT INTRENCHED
CDEEHINRST CHRISTENED
CDEEHKNPUY KEYPUNCHED
CDEEHLRTWY WRETCHEDLY
CDEEHMNOPR
　COMPREHEND
CDEEIIINSV INDECISIVE
CDEEIILSVY DECISIVELY
CDEEIIMNRS REMINISCED
CDEEIIMPRS SPERMICIDE
CDEEIIMRST METRICISED
CDEEIIMRTZ METRICIZED
CDEEIINRST INDISCREET,
　INDISCRETE, IRIDESCENT
CDEEIIORRT CORDIERITE,
　DIRECTOIRE
CDEEIIPRTV PREDICTIVE
CDEEIIPSST PESTICIDES
CDEEIIRSSV DISSERVICE
CDEEIIRSTV DIRECTIVES
CDEEIJPRSU PREJUDICES
CDEEIKNSSW WICKEDNESS
CDEEILLNST STENCILLED
CDEEILNNOS DECLENSION
CDEEILNNSU UNLICENSED
CDEEILNNTY INDECENTLY
CDEEILNOOS DECOLONISE
CDEEILNOOZ DECOLONIZE
CDEEILNOSU NUCLEOSIDE
CDEEILNOTU NUCLEOTIDE
CDEEILOORS DECOLORISE
CDEEILOORZ DECOLORIZE
CDEEILORST CLOISTERED
CDEEILRSTY DISCREETLY,
　DISCRETELY
CDEEIMMOXY MYXOEDEMIC
CDEEIMNNTU INDUCEMENT
CDEEIMNOOS ECONOMISED
CDEEIMNOOZ ECONOMIZED
CDEEIMNOSU EUDEMONICS
CDEEIMNPRU IMPRUDENCE
CDEEINNRSW WINDSCREEN
CDEEINNSSU SECUNDINES
CDEEINOPRV PROVIDENCE
CDEEINOPST DECEPTIONS

CDEEINORRS CONSIDERER,
　RECONSIDER
CDEEINORTT CREDIT NOTE
CDEEINPRRU UNDERPRICE
CDEEINPRSY PRESIDENCY
CDEEINRSST DIRECTNESS
CDEEINRSTY DYSENTERIC
CDEEIORRSV DISCOVERER
CDEEIPRSST DISRESPECT
CDEEIRRSST DIRECTRESS
CDEEIRRSTT RESTRICTED
CDEEKKKNNO
　KNOCK-KNEED
CDEEKOOPRW
　WOODPECKER
CDEELLNOSU COUNSELLED
CDEELLNRSU CULLENDERS
CDEELNOSSY CLOYEDNESS
CDEEMNNOST
　SECONDMENT
CDEEMOOPRS
　DECOMPOSER
CDEEMOPRSS
　COMPRESSED, DECOMPRESS
CDEENNORSS CONDENSERS
CDEENNORST CONTENDERS
CDEENOORRS ROOD
　SCREEN
CDEENOOSTT COTTONSEED
CDEENORRSU UNDERSCORE
CDEENORRUV
　UNDERCOVER
CDEENOSTUU CONSUETUDE
CDEENSSSSU CUSSEDNESS
CDEEOPPRST PROSPECTED
CDEEOPRRRU REPRODUCER
CDEEOPRRSU PROCEDURES
CDEEOPRSTU PROSECUTED
CDEERSSSTU SEDUCTRESS
CDEFFIIRTU FRUCTIFIED
CDEFGHIKLT FLIGHT DECK
CDEFGIINSU FUNGICIDES
CDEFGIKNOR DEFROCKING
CDEFHILOSS COLD FISHES
CDEFILNOUU FLUID OUNCE
CDEFINNNOU UNCONFINED
CDEFINNOTU FUNCTIONED
CDEFINOORV CONFERVOID
CDEFLNOSUY CONFUSEDLY
CDEFNNOORT CONFRONTED
CDEFNNOORU
　CONFOUNDER
CDEFNORRTU UNDERCROFT
CDEGGILLNU CUDGELLING
CDEGHILNSU SCHEDULING
CDEGIINNRS DISCERNING,
　RESCINDING
CDEGIINPRT PREDICTING
CDEGIINSST DISSECTING

CDEGILNOPU DECOUPLING
CDEGILNPRU PRECLUDING
CDEGILNSUY SEDUCINGLY
CDEGIMMNNO
　COMMENDING
CDEGIMNNNO CONDEMNING
CDEGINNNOS CONDENSING
CDEGINNNOT CONTENDING
CDEGINNNOU DENOUNCING
CDEGINORRS RECORDINGS
CDEGMNORUU
　CURMUDGEON
CDEGNORRUW GROUND
　CREW
CDEHHHIIKT HITCHHIKED
CDEHHIIRRT THIRD REICH
CDEHIIISTT DITHEISTIC
CDEHIILOPS DISCOPHILE
CDEHIILORU HIERODULIC
CDEHIILPTY DIPHYLETIC
CDEHIINOST HEDONISTIC
CDEHILOPTW LOW-PITCHED
CDEHIMOPRY HYPODERMIC
CDEHINOPST DOCENTSHIP
CDEHINOPTY ENDOPHYTIC
CDEHINOSTW SWITCHED-ON
CDEHLNOOSU
　UNSCHOOLED
CDEHLOOPPR CLODHOPPER
CDEHLOOPRY COPYHOLDER
CDEHLOOPSS CLOSED SHOP
CDEHNOSTUV DUTCH
　OVENS
CDEHOPTTUY
　TOUCH-TYPED
CDEIIILNNS DISINCLINE
CDEIIILNPS DISCIPLINE
CDEIIIMRSV RECIDIVISM
CDEIIIMSTV VICTIMISED
CDEIIIMTVZ VICTIMIZED
CDEIIINNOS INDECISION
CDEIIINTVV VINDICTIVE
CDEIIIRSTV RECIDIVIST
CDEIILNPPR PRINCIPLED
CDEIILNRTY INDIRECTLY
CDEIILOSTU SOLICITUDE
CDEIIMNNTT INDICTMENT
CDEIIMNOST MIDSECTION
CDEIIMOORT IODOMETRIC
CDEIIMORRS MISERICORD
CDEIIMORST DOSIMETRIC
CDEIIMORTY IRIDECTOMY,
　MEDIOCRITY
CDEIIMPPSU PIPED MUSIC
CDEIINOPRT PREDICTION
CDEIINOPST DEPICTIONS
CDEIINORST DIRECTIONS,
　DISCRETION
CDEIINORTY TYROCIDINE

CDEIINOSST DISSECTION
CDEIINRSTT INTERDICTS
CDEIIOORRS SORORICIDE
CDEIIPRSTU PEDICURIST
CDEIIRSSUV DISCURSIVE
CDEIKLOPST STOCKPILED
CDEIKNRRTU UNDERTRICK
CDEIKNRSUW WINDSUCKER
CDEIKNSSTY STICKY ENDS
CDEILLLPUY PELLUCIDLY
CDEILNOSSU CLOUDINESS
CDEILOPSUU PEDICULOUS
CDEILORSSS CROSS-SLIDE
CDEILORSSU DISCLOSURE
CDEIMMNOPU COMPENDIUM
CDEIMNNOST CONDIMENTS
CDEIMNOOST ENDOSMOTIC
CDEIMNOPRS PRINCEDOMS
CDEIMNOSTU MISCOUNTED
CDEIMOOPSS DISCOMPOSE
CDEIMOSSTU CUSTOMISED
CDEIMOSTUZ CUSTOMIZED
CDEINNOSTT DISCONTENT
CDEINOORSU INDECOROUS
CDEINORRTU INTRODUCER
CDEINORSSX CROSS-INDEX
CDEINORSTU DISCOUNTER,
　REDISCOUNT, REDUCTIONS
CDEINPRSTU UNSCRIPTED
CDEINRSTTU INSTRUCTED
CDEIOPRTUV PRODUCTIVE
CDEIORRSSU DISCOURSER
CDEIORSSSU DISCOURSES
CDEKLORTUY COLD TURKEY
CDEKNORSTU UNDERSTOCK
CDELLNOORT CONTROLLED
CDELNOORUY
　EUROCLYDON
CDELNOOSSW
　CLOSEDOWNS
CDELNOOTUV CONVOLUTED
CDELNORSSU SCOUNDRELS
CDELOORSUY DECOROUSLY
CDELPRSTUU SCULPTURED
CDEMMOOORS
　COMMODORES,
　COSMODROME
CDEMNOOPRU
　COMPOUNDER
CDENNOOPRU
　PRONOUNCED
CDENOOPRRS CORRESPOND
CDEOORTTUW
　WOODCUTTER
CDEORRSTTU DESTRUCTOR
CDERRSTTUU STRUCTURED
CDFFIILTUY DIFFICULTY
CDFIMOORST DISCOMFORT
CDFLNOORST COLD FRONTS

CDGHIILMOU GLOCHIDIUM
CDGHILOORY HYDROLOGIC
CDGIIILNRU RIDICULING
CDGIIKNNOO IN GOOD NICK
CDGIILNOSS DISCLOSING
CDGIINSSSU DISCUSSING
CDGIKLLOOS GOLDILOCKS
CDGILLNOSY SCOLDINGLY
CDHHIILLSY CHILDISHLY
CDHHILOSST DISHCLOTHS
CDHIIINOOP IDIOPHONIC
CDHIINPSSY SYNDICSHIP
CDHIIOSSTU DISTICHOUS
CDHILORTYY HYDROLYTIC
CDHINOOPRY HYDROPONIC
CDHIOPRSTY DYSTROPHIC
CDHKNNPRUU
　PUNCH-DRUNK
CDHLLOOOSS OLD SCHOOLS
CDHNOOSTUW
　TOUCHDOWNS
CDIIILNOTY INDOCILITY
CDIIINNSTT INDISTINCT
CDIIKRRTTY DIRTY TRICK
CDIILNOOSU NIDICOLOUS
CDIILNSTTY DISTINCTLY
CDIILOPPSY POLYDIPSIC
CDIILORSUU RIDICULOUS
CDIIMNNORST DOCTRINISM
CDIINNOOST CONDITIONS
CDIINNOSTU INDUCTIONS
CDIINOSSSU DISCUSSION
CDIKLLORST DRILLSTOCK
CDIKMRSSTU DRUMSTICKS
CDIKORSSTW SWORDSTICK
CDILLMOOSU MOLLUSCOID
CDILMOOORX LOXODROMIC
CDILMOOPUY LYCOPODIUM
CDIMMOOOSU
　COMMODIOUS
CDIMNOOOTY MONOCYTOID
CDINOOPRTU PRODUCTION
CDINORSSSW CROSSWINDS
CDLMOORSTU STORM
　CLOUD
CDMNNORSUU
　CONUNDRUMS
CDNNOOSTUW
　COUNTDOWNS
CDNOOOOTTW
　COTTONWOOD
CDOOORRSSSW
　CROSSWORDS
CEEEEFFRSV EFFERVESCE
CEEEEFNPRR PREFERENCE
CEEEEFNRRR REFERENCER
CEEEEFNRRS REFERENCES
CEEEEGIPTX EPEXEGETIC
CEEEEHIPRT THREE-PIECE

CEEEEHNPRT THREEPENCE
CEEEEIMRST CEMETERIES
CEEEEINPRX EXPERIENCE
CEEEELLNPR REPELLENCE
CEEEENRRRV REVERENCER
CEEEENRRSV REVERENCES
CEEEFFGLNU EFFULGENCE
CEEEFFLORS EFFLORESCE
CEEEFGLNRU REFULGENCE
CEEEFILNSS FLEECINESS
CEEEFILRTV REFLECTIVE
CEEEFINNRS INFERENCES
CEEEFINRRT CENTRE-FIRE
CEEEFINRSS FIERCENESS
CEEEFIPRTV PERFECTIVE
CEEEFNORRR RE-ENFORCER
CEEEFPRRTU PREFECTURE
CEEEGGILNN NEGLIGENCE
CEEEGIINPT EPIGENETIC
CEEEGIINSX EXIGENCIES
CEEEGILNRT RE-ELECTING
CEEEGINORS RECOGNISEE
CEEEGINORZ RECOGNIZEE
CEEEGINRST ENERGETICS
CEEEGINRTV VICEGERENT
CEEEGLNORS CONGER EELS
CEEEGNRRSU RESURGENCE
CEEEHHLORS HORSELEECH
CEEEHIKNSS CHEEKINESS
CEEEHIMSTT CHEMISETTE
CEEEHINPRR ENCIPHERER
CEEEHINPTT EPENTHETIC
CEEEHINRSS CHEERINESS
CEEEHINSSS CHEESINESS
CEEEHKPRTU UP THE CREEK
CEEEHLLSSY SEYCHELLES
CEEEHLPSSS SPEECHLESS
CEEEHMMNSY
　MESENCHYME
CEEEHNNRRT ENTRENCHER
CEEEHOQRUU
　EUROCHEQUE
CEEEIILNRS RESILIENCE
CEEEIIMPST TIMEPIECES
CEEEIINRSV VICEREINES
CEEEILLMNO EMOLLIENCE
CEEEILLNST CLIENTELES
CEEEILMNNT CLEMENTINE
CEEEILMORT CEILOMETER
CEEEILMRTT TELEMETRIC
CEEEILNORT RE-ELECTION
CEEEILNPRT PERCENTILE
CEEEILNPST PESTILENCE
CEEEIMNNTT ENTICEMENT
CEEEIMNORS CEREMONIES
CEEEIMNRST MESENTERIC
CEEEIMNRSV SERVICEMEN
CEEEIMNRTT CENTIMETRE,
　REMITTENCE

441

CEEEIMNTTX EXCITEMENT
CEEEINNPRT PERTINENCE
CEEEINPRSS CREEPINESS
CEEEINPRST EPICENTRES
CEEEINSSTX EXISTENCES
CEEEINTTWY WINCEYETTE
CEEEIORRST CORSETIÈRE
CEEEIORRSV RECOVERIES
CEEEIPPRTV PERCEPTIVE,
    PRECEPTIVE
CEEEIPRSTV RESPECTIVE
CEEEISTUVX EXECUTIVES
CEEEJLORTT ELECTROJET
CEEEKKLOPR LOCK KEEPER
CEEEKRRSSU SEERSUCKER
CEEELNOORU NEUROCOELE
CEEELNRSSV CLEVERNESS
CEEELNSSST SELECTNESS
CEEELOPSST TELESCOPES
CEEEMNOPRS RECOMPENSE
CEEEMNOORT
    CENTROMERE
CEEEMNOTYZ ECTOENZYME
CEEEMNRSTU SECUREMENT
CEEENNRSST RECENTNESS
CEEENOPRST OPEN SECRET
CEEENRSSSU SECURENESS
CEEENRSSTT SCREEN TEST
CEEEPRRSST RESPECTERS
CEEFFHIMOO HOME OFFICE
CEEFFHOOPS COFFEE SHOP
CEEFFOOPST COFFEEPOTS
CEEFGHINNR GREENFINCH
CEEFGILNRT REFLECTING
CEEFGINPRT PERFECTING
CEEFGINRTU CENTRIFUGE
CEEFGLLNTU NEGLECTFUL
CEEFHHNORT HENCEFORTH
CEEFHLLRUY CHEERFULLY
CEEFHORTTU FOURCHETTE
CEEFIIILST FELICITIES
CEEFIILNTV INFLECTIVE
CEEFIIORST FEROCITIES
CEEFIIRRST RECTIFIERS
CEEFIKLNSS FICKLENESS
CEEFILNNRU INFLUENCER
CEEFILNNSU INFLUENCES
CEEFILNORT REFLECTION
CEEFINOPRT PERFECTION
CEEFKLLSSY FECKLESSLY
CEEFLNOORW
    CONEFLOWER
CEEFLORRST REFLECTORS
CEEFLPPRTU PLUPERFECT
CEEFLPRSTU RESPECTFUL
CEEFMNNORT CONFERMENT
CEEFNRSTTU FRUTESCENT
CEEFOORRSU FORECOURSE
CEEFORRRSS CROSS-REFER

CEEGGILNNT NEGLECTING
CEEGHIILMP HEMIPLEGIC
CEEGHIMOST GEOCHEMIST
CEEGHINNOT ETHNOGENIC
CEEGHKMNRU
    KREMENCHUG
CEEGHLOPST CLOTHES PEG
CEEGIINOPR EPIROGENIC
CEEGIINOTV GIVE NOTICE
CEEGIINPRV PERCEIVING
CEEGIINRSX EXERCISING
CEEGIINSTT GENETICIST
CEEGIINSTU EUGENICIST
CEEGINNNST SENTENCING
CEEGINNORU NEUROGENIC
CEEGINNOSS CONSIGNEES
CEEGINNQSU SEQUENCING
CEEGINNRSS SCREENINGS
CEEGINNRST NIGRESCENT
CEEGINNRSU INSURGENCE
CEEGINOORT EROTOGENIC
CEEGINORRS RECOGNISER
CEEGINORRV RE-COVERING
CEEGINORRZ RECOGNIZER
CEEGINOSTV CONGESTIVE
CEEGINPRST RESPECTING
CEEGINRSTY SYNERGETIC
CEEGNNORTV
    CONVERGENT
CEEGNOOSTU ECTOGENOUS
CEEGNORSSS CONGRESSES
CEEGNRSTTU TURGESCENT
CEEGORSTTU COURGETTES
CEEHHHIMOR HOCHHEIMER
CEEHHIMORT COME HITHER
CEEHHOPSST HOPE CHESTS
CEEHIIMRST ERETHISMIC
CEEHIKNRST THICKENERS
CEEHIKPPRS SCHIPPERKE
CEEHIKSSTT SKETCHIEST
CEEHILLRSS CHISELLERS
CEEHILNORU EUCHLORINE
CEEHILOPRT HELICOPTER
CEEHILORRT LOIR-ET-CHER
CEEHILOSVY COHESIVELY
CEEHILQRSU SQUELCHIER
CEEHIMNNRT ENRICHMENT
CEEHIMNTTU TECHNETIUM
CEEHIMOPTU MOUTHPIECE
CEEHIMORRT RHEOMETRIC
CEEHIMORTX EXOTHERMIC
CEEHIMSSTU SHEET MUSIC
CEEHINNORT INCOHERENT
CEEHINOPPR HIPPOCRENE
CEEHINQSTU TECHNIQUES
CEEHINRRST CHRISTENER,
    RECHRISTEN
CEEHINRSTW WINCHESTER
CEEHINSSST CHESTINESS

CEEHINSSTT TETCHINESS
CEEHIOPPRS PROPHECIES
CEEHIOPSSW SHOWPIECES
CEEHIORSTT THEORETICS
CEEHIRRSTT STRETCHIER
CEEHKKOOYY HOKEY
    COKEY
CEEHKNPRUY KEYPUNCHER
CEEHKNPSUY KEYPUNCHES
CEEHLLNOSW
    WELL-CHOSEN
CEEHLNORTY COHERENTLY
CEEHLPRSSU SEPULCHRES
CEEHMMMOORR
    CHROMOMERE
CEEHNNOSSU NONESUCHES
CEEHNOOPPS NEPHOSCOPE
CEEHNOOPRT CTENOPHORE
CEEHRRSSTT STRETCHERS
CEEIIKLNPR PINCERLIKE
CEEIILLLOS ICE LOLLIES
CEEIILLMRV VERMICELLI
CEEIILLORS COLLIERIES
CEEIILNOSU ISOLEUCINE
CEEIILNRSY RESILIENCY
CEEIILNRTT CENTILITRE
CEEIILOSTV VELOCITIES
CEEIILPPST EPILEPTICS
CEEIILPRSV LIP SERVICE
CEEIILRTTY ERECTILITY
CEEIILTTVY ELECTIVITY
CEEIIMNNTT INCITEMENT
CEEIIMORTT METEORITIC
CEEIIMPRRT PERIMETRIC
CEEIINNSST INSISTENCE
CEEIINNSTV INCENTIVES
CEEIINOPST CENTIPOISE
CEEIINPPRT PERCIPIENT
CEEIINPRST RECIPIENTS
CEEIINPSTV INSPECTIVE
CEEIINRSTT INTERSTICE
CEEIINTTVX EXTINCTIVE
CEEIIORRST ESCRITOIRE
CEEIIRSSTU SECURITIES
CEEIJLOPRT PROJECTILE
CEEIJNORST REJECTIONS
CEEIJOPRTV PROJECTIVE
CEEIJRSTUV SURJECTIVE
CEEIKLNRSS SILK SCREEN
CEEIKNPRTY PERNICKETY
CEEIKNSSSS SICKNESSES
CEEILLNRST STENCILLER
CEEILLNSTT INTELLECTS
CEEILLOOPT COLEOPTILE
CEEILLORSS RECOILLESS
CEEILLRSSU SCULLERIES
CEEILMNOPT INCOMPLETE
CEEILMNORT CLINOMETER
CEEILMNOSS COMELINESS

CEEILMOPTV COMPLETIVE
CEEILNOSST SELECTIONS
CEEILNQSTU LIQUESCENT
CEEILNRSTV VENTRICLES
CEEILNRSUY INSECURELY
CEEILNRTTY RETICENTLY
CEEILPRSTT TELESCRIPT
CEEILPRSUV PRECLUSIVE
CEEILSSUVX EXCLUSIVES
CEEIMMOPRT EMMETROPIC
CEEIMMORRT MICROMETER
CEEIMMOSTT COMMITTEES
CEEIMNNOPR PROMINENCE
CEEIMNNRST INCREMENTS
CEEIMNOORS ECONOMISER
CEEIMNOORZ ECONOMIZER
CEEIMORSTV VISCOMETER
CEEIMOSSTV VICOMTESSE
CEEINNNOTV CONVENIENT
CEEINNPSST SPINESCENT
CEEINOPPRT PERCEPTION
CEEINOPRSS PRECESSION
CEEINOPRST RECEPTIONS
CEEINOPSTX EXCEPTIONS
CEEINORRST CORRIENTES
CEEINORSSS RECESSIONS
CEEINORSST SECRETIONS
CEEINORSTV VENTRICOSE
CEEINORSTX EXCRETIONS
CEEINOSSTX EXOTICNESS
CEEINOSTTX COEXISTENT
CEEINOSTUX EXECUTIONS
CEEINPRSSS PRINCESSES
CEEINPRSTU PUTRESCINE
CEEINRRSTU SCRUTINEER
CEEINRSSTY SYNCRETISE
CEEINRSTTV VITRESCENT
CEEINRSTYZ SYNCRETIZE
CEEIOORSVV VOICE-OVERS
CEEIOPPRSS PERISCOPES
CEEIOPRTTV PROTECTIVE
CEEIOQRSTU COQUETRIES
CEEIORSSTU COURTESIES
CEEIPRSSUV PERCUSSIVE
CEEIPSSTUV SUSCEPTIVE
CEEKLLRSSY RECKLESSLY
CEEKLNRTTU TURTLENECK
CEEKLORRWW
  CREWELWORK
CEELLMOPTY COMPLETELY
CEELMMNOPT
  COMPLEMENT
CEELMNNOOS
  SOMNOLENCE
CEELMOORTU
  COULOMETER
CEELNORSSU ENCLOSURES
CEELNORSVY CONVERSELY
CEELORRSTY CLERESTORY

CEEMMOTXYY
  MYXOMYCETE
CEEMNNSTTY ENCYSTMENT
CEEMNOORST
  CENTROSOME
CEEMNOPRTU
  RECOUPMENT
CEEMNOPRTY PYCNOMETER
CEEMNORTUY
  NEURECTOMY
CEEMNPSSTU SPUMESCENT
CEEMOPRSSS COMPRESSES
CEEMOSSSTY ECOSYSTEMS
CEENNOQSTU CONSEQUENT
CEENNORSTU ENCOUNTERS
CEENNPRSSY PENNYCRESS
CEENOORSTV COVER
  NOTES
CEENOPPPRR PEPPERCORN
CEENOPPRTY PREPOTENCY
CEENOPRRST PRECENTORS
CEENORRSTV CONVERTERS
CEENORTTUX CONTEXTURE
CEENOSSSTU COUNTESSES
CEENPRSSSU SPRUCENESS
CEENPRSTTU PUTRESCENT
CEEOPRRSTT RETROSPECT
CEEOPRRSTU PERSECUTOR
CEEOQRSTTU CROQUETTES
CEEORRSSST CROSSTREES
CEFFFFHOTU OFF THE CUFF
CEFFHIINOR CHIFFONIER
CEFFIIKKLN FLICK KNIFE
CEFFIINSTU SUFFICIENT
CEFFIIRRTU FRUCTIFIER
CEFFIOOPST POST OFFICE
CEFFIRSSTU SCRUFFIEST
CEFFLLORUY FORCEFULLY
CEFGHILNST FLETCHINGS
CEFGHILNTY FETCHINGLY
CEFGIIKLNR FLICKERING
CEFGIILNNT INFLECTING
CEFGIINPSY SPECIFYING
CEFGIINRTY CERTIFYING,
  RECTIFYING
CEFGINNORR CONFERRING
CEFGINNOSS CONFESSING
CEFGLOORSU GOLF COURSE
CEFHHNNORR FRENCH
  HORN
CEFHIILSSS FISH SLICES
CEFHIIRRST FIRST REICH
CEFHIKNRSS FRENCH KISS
CEFHIKRSSU SUCKERFISH
CEFHILSTTU CUTTLEFISH
CEFIIILNTV INFLICTIVE
CEFIIILNTY INFELICITY
CEFIILNNOT INFLECTION
CEFIILNOQU CINQUEFOIL

CEFIILOSTU FELICITOUS
CEFIIMNNTU MUNIFICENT
CEFIINNOST INFECTIONS
CEFIINOPRT PROFICIENT
CEFIINOSTU INFECTIOUS
CEFILLMRUY MERCIFULLY
CEFILMNRUU UNMERCIFUL
CEFILMOORS FROLICSOME
CEFIMORSUY CYMIFEROUS
CEFINNOOSS CONFESSION
CEFINOORSU CONIFEROUS
CEFIOORSUV VOCIFEROUS
CEFKLOPSTU POCKETFULS
CEFLNOORRW
  CORNFLOWER
CEFMNOORRS
  CONFORMERS
CEFMOORRST COMFORTERS
CEFNNOORRT CONFRONTER
CEFNOORSSS CONFESSORS
CEFOORRSTU FORECOURTS
CEGGHIMNUW CHEWING
  GUM
CEGGILNOSS CLOGGINESS
CEGGINNORV CONVERGING
CEGGINOOST GEOGNOSTIC
CEGHHIINRS CHERISHING
CEGHIIKNNT THICKENING
CEGHIIKNRW WHICKERING
CEGHIILLNS CHISELLING
CEGHIILOOR HIEROLOGIC
CEGHIINNUY UNHYGIENIC
CEGHIINORZ RHIZOGENIC
CEGHILMNSY SCHEMINGLY
CEGHILNOOT ETHNOLOGIC
CEGHILNOPY PHYLOGENIC
CEGHILNOST CLOSE THING
CEGHILNPPS SCHLEPPING
CEGHILNQSU SQUELCHING
CEGHIMMNOO
  HOMECOMING
CEGHIMOOPR GEOMORPHIC
CEGHINOOPT PHOTOGENIC
CEGHINOORT ORTHOGENIC
CEGHINOPTY PHYTOGENIC,
  TYPHOGENIC
CEGHINORTU RETOUCHING
CEGHINORTY TRICHOGYNE
CEGHINOTUU HUGUENOTIC
CEGHINRSTT STRETCHING
CEGHIOPSSY GEOPHYSICS
CEGHIORSTU GROUCHIEST
CEGHKNORSU
  ROUGHNECKS
CEGHLNOOTY TECHNOLOGY
CEGIIIMNNT MENINGITIC
CEGIIKLLNN NICKELLING
CEGIIKNNQU QUICKENING
CEGIIKNNRS SNICKERING

CEGIIKPRST PIGSTICKER	CEGOOPRSSY GYROSCOPES	CEHINOPSTT PITCHSTONE
CEGIIILLNNP PENCILLING	CEHHHIIKRT HITCHHIKER	CEHINOPTTY ENPHYTOTIC,
CEGIILNNPR PRINCELING	CEHHIILMNT HELMINTHIC	ENTOPHYTIC
CEGIILNNSS CLINGINESS	CEHHILNRTU IN THE LURCH	CEHINOSSTU TOUCHINESS
CEGIILNNST STENCILING	CEHHIMRTUY EURHYTHMIC	CEHINPRSST SPHINCTERS
CEGIILNNTY ENTICINGLY	CEHHIOOPST THEOSOPHIC	CEHIOOPRRT RHEOTROPIC
CEGIILNOSU GENIUS LOCI	CEHHKLLOSS SHELLSHOCK	CEHIOORRRT RETROCHOIR
CEGIILNPRY PIERCINGLY	CEHHOOPSSU CHOPHOUSES	CEHIOPRSTT PROSTHETIC
CEGIILNTXY EXCITINGLY	CEHIIINRST TRICHINISE	CEHIOPRSTY HYPOCRITES
CEGIILORTU OLIGURETIC	CEHIIINRTZ TRICHINIZE	CEHIOPRTXY XEROPHYTIC
CEGIILOSTU EULOGISTIC	CEHIILLNSS CHILLINESS	CEHIOQSTTU COQUETTISH
CEGIINNOST SECTIONING	CEHIILMOST HOMILETICS,	CEHIORRSST CHORISTERS
CEGIINNPST INSPECTING	MESOLITHIC	CEHKOOOSSU
CEGIINORXZ EXORCIZING	CEHIILNOTX XENOLITHIC	COOKHOUSES
CEGIINOSTX COEXISTING	CEHIILOPTY HELIOTYPIC	CEHLMOOPRY
CEGIINRRTU RECRUITING	CEHIIMNORT THERMIONIC	POLYCHROME
CEGIINRSTT TRISECTING	CEHIIMNORY HIERONYMIC	CEHLMOPTYY LYMPHOCYTE
CEGIJNOPRT PROJECTING	CEHIIMOPPR EPIMORPHIC	CEHLOOOPRT TOCOPHEROL
CEGIKNNORS RECKONINGS	CEHIIMOPRT HEMITROPIC	CEHLOOPPRS PREP SCHOOL
CEGIKNOOPR PRECOOKING	CEHIIMRSTY MYTHICISER	CEHLOOPRSS PRESCHOOLS
CEGIKNORST RESTOCKING	CEHIIMRTYZ MYTHICIZER	CEHLORRTTY TERRYCLOTH
CEGILLMNOP COMPELLING	CEHIIMSTTW TIME SWITCH	CEHMMNOOOR
CEGILLOOXY LEXICOLOGY	CEHIINPRSS CHIRPINESS	MONOCHROME
CEGILMNOOP MONOPLEGIC	CEHIINPSST PITCHINESS	CEHMMOOORS
CEGILMNOPT COMPLETING	CEHIINSSTT IN STITCHES	CHROMOSOME
CEGILNNOST CLINGSTONE	CEHIINSTTZ CHINTZIEST	CEHMOOPRTY
CEGILNRSTU CLUSTERING	CEHIIOSTTY HISTIOCYTE	CORMOPHYTE, ECTOMORPHY
CEGILNRTTU CLUTTERING	CEHIIPPSST PSESPHITIC	CEHNNORSTU TRUNCHEONS
CEGILOOSST ECOLOGISTS	CEHIIPRSTY SPHERICITY	CEHNOOOPPS PHONOSCOPE
CEGILOOSTT CETOLOGIST	CEHIIPSTUU EUPHUISTIC	CEHNOOSTTU TOUCHSTONE
CEGIMMNNOT COMMENTING	CEHIIRRTTU URETHRITIC	CEHNOPRSTY PHENOCRYST
CEGIMNOORS ERGONOMICS	CEHIIRSSTU HEURISTICS	CEHNORSTVY CHERNOVTSY
CEGIMNOORV OVERCOMING	CEHIKNNSSU CHUNKINESS	CEHOOOOPRSS HOROSCOPES
CEGINNNORU RENOUNCING	CEHIKOPPST HIP POCKETS	CEHOORSTUU COURTHOUSE
CEGINNNOST CONSENTING	CEHIKPRSSW SHIPWRECKS	CEHORSTTTU OUTSTRETCH
CEGINNNOTT CONTENTING,	CEHILNNPSU PUNCH LINES	CEIIILSTV CIVILITIES
CONTINGENT	CEHILNOSTU TOUCHLINES	CEIIIINSTV VICINITIES
CEGINNOOST CONGESTION	CEHILNSSTZ SCHNITZELS	CEIIILLMNO LIMICOLINE
CEGINNOQRU CONQUERING	CEHILOPRST LECTORSHIP	CEIIILLNNP PENICILLIN
CEGINNORSV CONSERVING,	CEHILORSTY CHRYSOLITE,	CEIIILNPTX INEXPLICIT
CONVERSING	CHRYSOTILE	CEIIILNSVY INCISIVELY
CEGINNORTU COUNTERING,	CEHIMMNSSU CHUMMINESS	CEIIILOPST POLITICISE
RECOUNTING	CEHIMNOOPR MICROPHONE	CEIIILOPTZ POLITICIZE
CEGINNORTV CONVERTING	CEHIMNOOTT NOMOTHETIC	CEIIIMMPRS EMPIRICISM
CEGINNORUV UNCOVERING	CEHIMNOPTY CHIMNEYPOT	CEIIIMPRST EMPIRICIST
CEGINNOSTT CONTESTING	CEHIMOOORT HOMOEROTIC	CEIIIMRSTV VICTIMISER
CEGINNRSTY STRINGENCY	CEHIMOOPTY HOMEOTYPIC,	CEIIIMRTVZ VICTIMIZER
CEGINNRSUW UNSCREWING	MYTHOPOEIC	CEIIINPPRT PRECIPITIN
CEGINNRSUY INSURGENCY	CEHIMOPRTY MICROPHYTE	CEIIIOPSST ISOPIESTIC
CEGINOORRZ RECOGNIZOR	CEHIMOPSTY MESOPHYTIC	CEIIJNNOST INJECTIONS
CEGINOORST CREOSOTING	CEHIMRSTUY EURYTHMICS	CEIIJNNTUV INJUNCTIVE
CEGINOPRSS PROCESSING	CEHINNNPPY PINCHPENNY	CEIIJNSSTU INJUSTICES
CEGINOPRTT PROTECTING	CEHINNPSSU PUNCHINESS	CEIIKKLNPT TICKLE PINK
CEGINOSSTT COSSETTING	CEHINNRSTY STRYCHNINE	CEIIKLMORT KILOMETRIC
CEGINPPRSU SCUPPERING	CEHINOORRS RHINOCEROS	CEIIKLNRST CRINKLIEST
CEGINPSSTU SUSPECTING	CEHINOPPRR PRONEPHRIC	CEIIKLNSSS SICKLINESS
CEGLNOOSYY SYNECOLOGY	CEHINOPPSS CHOPPINESS	CEIIKLPRST PRICKLIEST
CEGNORRSSU	CEHINOPPTY PHENOTYPIC	CEIIKNPRST NITPICKERS
SCROUNGERS	CEHINOPRSS CENSORSHIP	CEIIKNRSST TRICKINESS

CEIIKNSSST STICKINESS
CEIILLLSTU CELLULITIS
CEIILLNNOT CENTILLION
CEIILLNRTU CITRULLINE
CEIILLOSSU SILICULOSE
CEIILLPTXY EXPLICITLY
CEIILMOPST POLEMICIST
CEIILNNORS CRINOLINES
CEIILNOSTU LICENTIOUS
CEIILNOSTV NOVELISTIC
CEIILNPPRS PRINCIPLES
CEIILOQRSU LIQUORICES
CEIILPRSST LIST PRICES
CEIIMMORSS MICROSEISM
CEIIMNNOST OMNISCIENT
CEIIMNRSSU SINECURISM
CEIIMORSST ISOMETRICS
CEIIMOSTTT TOTEMISTIC
CEIINNOPST INCEPTIONS,
  INSPECTION
CEIINNOTTX EXTINCTION
CEIINOPRSS PRECISIONS
CEIINOPRST ISENTROPIC
CEIINOPRSU PERNICIOUS
CEIINOPRTV VOICEPRINT
CEIINOPSTT NEPOTISTIC
CEIINORRST CRITERIONS
CEIINORSSS RESCISSION
CEIINPRSSS CRISPINESS
CEIINRSSTU SCRUTINIES,
  SCRUTINISE, SINECURIST
CEIINRSTUY INSECURITY
CEIINRSTUZ SCRUTINIZE
CEIINSSSTT SCIENTISTS
CEIIOORSTU TRIOECIOUS
CEIIOPRSTY PRECIOSITY
CEIIOPSSTY SPECIOSITY
CEIIORSTVV VIVISECTOR
CEIJNOOPRT PROJECTION
CEIJNORSTU SURJECTION
CEIKKORRWW
  WICKERWORK
CEIKLNNOST CLINKSTONE
CEIKLNPSSU PLUCKINESS
CEIKLOPRST STOCKPILER
CEIKLOPSST STOCKPILES
CEIKNOSSST STOCKINESS
CEIKPQSSTU QUICKSTEPS
CEIKRRSSTT TRICKSTERS
CEIILLNOORS COLOR LINES
CEILLOOQSU COLLOQUIES
CEILMMNOPT COMPLIMENT
CEILMNOOPT COMPLETION
CEILMNOOPX COMPLEXION
CEILMNOOSS SEMICOLONS
CEILMNORTY CLINOMETRY
CEILMNSSSU CLUMSINESS
CEILMOOOTV LOCOMOTIVE
CEILMOOPST LEPTOSOMIC

CEILMOPSUV COMPULSIVE
CEILMOPTXY COMPLEXITY
CEILMORSTU SCLEROTIUM
CEILMORTUV VOLUMETRIC
CEILMOSTUU METICULOUS
CEILNNNOTY INNOCENTLY
CEILNNOSVY INSOLVENCY
CEILNOOPRS NECROPOLIS
CEILNOORRS RESORCINOL
CEILNOORSS COLONISERS
CEILNOORSZ COLONIZERS
CEILNOPRSU PRECLUSION
CEILNORSSU INCLOSURES
CEILNORTTY CONTRITELY
CEILNOSSST COSTLINESS
CEILNOSUVV CONVULSIVE
CEILOPRSTY PROSELYTIC
CEILOPRSUY PRECIOUSLY
CEILOPSSUY SPECIOUSLY
CEILORSTTU COURTLIEST
CEIMMMNOTT COMMITMENT
CEIMMNOORT METRONOMIC
CEIMMNOQUU
  COMMUNIQUÉ
CEIMMNORTY METRONYMIC
CEIMMOOPRS COMPROMISE
CEIMMOORST OSMOMETRIC
CEIMMORRTY MICROMETRY
CEIMMORSSU COMMISSURE
CEIMNOOOSU MONOECIOUS
CEIMNOORTT TONOMETRIC
CEIMNOOSST ECONOMISTS
CEIMNOPRSU PROSCENIUM
CEIMNORSTT METRIC TONS
CEIMNORSUU CERUMINOUS
CEIMNRSSTY SYNCRETISM
CEIMOOPRRS MICROSPORE
CEIMOOPRTT COMPETITOR,
  OPTOMETRIC
CEIMOOPSST COMPOSITES
CEIMOORSTY SOCIOMETRY
CEIMOPRRTY PYROMETRIC
CEIMORSSTU COSTUMIERS
CEIMORSTVY VISCOMETRY
CEIMOSSTUV MUSCOVITES
CEINNNOOTT CONTENTION
CEINNNOOTV CONVENTION
CEINNNOSTT CONTINENTS
CEINNOORSV CONVERSION
CEINNOPTUX EXPUNCTION
CEINNORSTU CENTURIONS
CEINNOSSTT CONSISTENT
CEINOOPRSS PROCESSION
CEINOOPRTT PROTECTION
CEINOORSSU CENSORIOUS
CEINOOSSUY SYNOECIOUS
CEINOPPRSU PORCUPINES
CEINOPRSST INSPECTORS

CEINOPRSSU PERCUSSION,
  SUPERSONIC
CEINOPRSTT INTROSPECT
CEINOPRSTU SUPERTONIC
CEINOPSTTY STENOTYPIC
CEINOQTUYZ QUEZON CITY
CEINORRSTW TOWN CRIERS
CEINORSSUX EXCURSIONS
CEINOSSTUU INCESTUOUS
CEINOSTTTU CONSTITUTE
CEINRSSSTT STRICTNESS
CEINRSSSTU CRUSTINESS
CEINRSSSUV SCURVINESS
CEINRSSTTY SYNCRETIST
CEIOOPRRTU PUERTO RICO
CEIOOPRRTY CORPOREITY
CEIOOPRRTUV CORRUPTIVE
CEIOPRRTUY EURYTROPIC
CEIOPRRTWY COPYWRITER
CEIORRSSSY RESCISSORY
CEIORRSTUU COUTURIERS
CEIPPRRSST PRESCRIPTS
CEIPPRSTTY TYPESCRIPT
CEIRRSSTTU STRICTURES
CEJOOPRRST PROJECTORS
CEKKORSSTY SKYROCKETS
CEKLMOOORR LOCKER
  ROOM
CEKLNORSTW TOWN
  CLERKS
CELLNOORRT CONTROLLER
CELLNOORSU COUNSELLOR
CELLOORSSU COLOURLESS
CELMOORSSU LOOSE
  SCRUM
CELMOORSTY SCLEROTOMY
CELNOPRSUU PRONUCLEUS
CELOOSSSSU COLOSSUSES
CELOOSTUVY COVETOUSLY
CELPRSSSTU SCULPTRESS
CELPRSSTUU SCULPTURES
CEMMNNOOSS
  COMMONNESS
CEMMNNOOTW COMMON
  NEWT
CEMMNOOPST
  COMPONENTS
CEMMNORTUY
  COUNTRYMEN
CEMOOPRRSS
  COMPRESSOR
CENNOOPRRU
  PRONOUNCER
CENOOQRRSU
  CONQUERORS
CENOORRTTV CONTROVERT
CENOPRSTUY COUNTERSPY
CENORSSSTW CROW'S
  NESTS

445

CEOOPPRRST PROSPECTOR
CEOOPRRSSS PROCESSORS
CEOOPRRSTT PROTECTORS
CEOOPRRSTU PROSECUTOR
CEOOPRRTTY PROTECTORY
CEOPPRSSTU PROSPECTUS
CEOPRRRSSU PRECURSORS
CEOPRRRSUY PRECURSORY
CEPPRRSTUU UPPER CRUST
CERRSSTTUU STRUCTURES
CFFFIISSTU FISTICUFFS
CFFGIIKNOT TICKING OFF
CFFGILNOSY SCOFFINGLY
CFGIIILNNT INFLICTING
CFGIIKLNOR FROLICKING
CFGIIMNNOR CONFIRMING
CFGIINNORU FINNO-UGRIC
CFGIKNNORU UNFROCKING
CFGIMNNOOR CONFORMING
CFGIMNOORT COMFORTING
CFHIIKSSST FISH STICKS
CFHIIKSSTT SHIFT STICK,
   STICK SHIFT
CFHIINOORS HONORIFICS
CFHIKOPRST PITCHFORKS
CFHIMOPRSY SCYPHIFORM
CFHKOOOPRS SHOCKPROOF
CFHLLOOOORT FLOOR CLOTH
CFHLMOOORR
   CHLOROFORM
CFIIILNNOT INFLICTION
CFIIINOSTT FICTIONIST
CFIIIOSTTU FICTITIOUS
CFIIKKLNSS SKIN FLICKS
CFIILLLNOU FOLLICULIN
CFIILMMORS MICROFILMS
CFIILORSST FLORISTICS
CFIINNNOOT NONFICTION
CFIIRSTTUU FUTURISTIC
CFIKLLNOST FLINTLOCKS
CFILMMORUU CUMULIFORM
CFIMNOORST CONFORMIST
CFIMNOORTY CONFORMITY
CFLLNORSUY SCORNFULLY
CFLOOOORRUU
   FOUR-COLOUR
CFLOORSSUU SCROFULOUS
CGGIIKNPSU SUCKING PIG
CGGIINNNOS CONSIGNING
CGGINNORSU SCROUNGING
CGHHHILOOS HIGH SCHOOL
CGHHILORTT TORCHLIGHT
CGHHIORSTU HIGH COURTS
CGHIIKNSTT NIGHTSTICK
CGHIIKSTTT STICKTIGHT
CGHIILLOOT LITHOLOGIC
CGHIILOPST PHLOGISTIC
CGHIILPRTY TRIGLYPHIC
CGHIINNOSU CUSHIONING

CGHIKLNOSY SHOCKINGLY
CGHILLNRUY LURCHINGLY
CGHILLOORS SCHOOLGIRL
CGHILNOTUY TOUCHINGLY
CGHILOORTY TRICHOLOGY
CGHINOOOPR GONOPHORIC
CGHINOOPRY GYNOPHORIC
CGHINOOSYZ SCHIZOGONY
CGHIOPRSTY COPYRIGHTS
CGHLNOOORY
   CHRONOLOGY
CGHLOOPSYY PSYCHOLOGY
CGHOPRTUUU CUT UP
   ROUGH
CGIIIILNVZ CIVILIZING
CGIIIJNOST JINGOISTIC
CGIIIKNNPT NITPICKING
CGIIILNNTY INCITINGLY
CGIIILNOST SOLICITING
CGIIILNSTU LINGUISTIC
CGIIILPSTU PUGILISTIC
CGIIIORRST RIGORISTIC
CGIIJNNNOO CONJOINING
CGIIKLLNOR ROLLICKING
CGIIKLNRTY TRICKINGLY
CGIILNNOOZ COLONIZING
CGIILOOSTT ISOGLOTTIC
CGIIMMNOTT COMMITTING
CGIIMNNORS CRIMSONING
CGIIMNNOPRS COMPRISING
CGIINNNOTU CONTINUING
CGIINNOPRS CONSPIRING
CGIINNORTV CONTRIVING
CGIINNOSST CONSISTING
CGIINOTTUY CONTIGUITY
CGIKOOPSST POGO STICKS
CGILLNOOPS SCOLLOPING
CGILLNOSWY SCOWLINGLY
CGILLOSSYY GLYCOLYSIS
CGILMOOSTY MYCOLOGIST
CGILMOOSUY MUSICOLOGY
CGILNNOPUU UNCOUPLING
CGILNNORSY SCORNINGLY
CGILNNOSTU CONSULTING
CGILNNOSUV CONVULSING
CGILNOOOST NOSTOLOGIC,
   ONCOLOGIST
CGILNOORSU COLOURINGS
CGILNOPSUV LOVING CUPS
CGILOOOPRT TROPOLOGIC
CGILOOOTXY TOXICOLOGY
CGILOOSTTY CYTOLOGIST
CGIMNOOPRT COMPORTING
CGIMNOOPST COMPOSTING
CGINNOORSS CONSIGNORS
CGINNOORST CONSORTING
CGINNOORTT CONTORTING
CGINNOORTU CONTOURING
CGINNOOSTT COTTON GINS

CGINNORSTU CONSTRUING
CGINNPRTUU PUNCTURING
CGINOOPRST PROGNOSTIC
CGINOOSTUU CONTIGUOUS
CGINOPRRTU CORRUPTING
CGIOOPRSYZ ZYGOSPORIC
CGLOOOPRTY PROCTOLOGY
CHHIIOSSTY ICHTHYOSIS
CHHIIPSTTW WHIPSTITCH
CHHILLRSUY CHURLISHLY
CHHILOOPTY HOLOPHYTIC
CHHIMNOOOP HOMOPHONIC
CHHINSTTUW WITCH-HUNTS
CHHIOOPPRS PHOSPHORIC
CHHKLLOOSY HOLLYHOCKS
CHIIIILNST NIHILISTIC
CHIIILLOPP LIPOPHILIC
CHIIILPPPS PHILIPPICS
CHIIILPSTY SYPHILITIC
CHIIINORST HISTRIONIC
CHIIKLLSTY TICKLISHLY
CHIILMNOOT MONOLITHIC
CHIILMOOTT LITHOTOMIC
CHIILNOOPT PHONOLITIC
CHIILOSTTY HISTOLYTIC
CHIIMOOPRS ISOMORPHIC
CHIIMOPRRT TRIMORPHIC
CHIIMORRST TRICHROISM
CHIIMORSTU HUMORISTIC
CHIINNOPSU PINCUSHION
CHIINORSTU TRICHINOUS
CHIIOOOPRT OOPHORITIC
CHIIPSSSTY PHYSICISTS
CHIKLMOSST LOCKSMITHS
CHIKOOPSTT TOOTHPICKS
CHILLNOOST LOINCLOTHS
CHILLNOSWY CLOWNISHLY
CHILNOOPPY POLYPHONIC
CHILNOOPXY XYLOPHONIC
CHILNOPSSU CONSULSHIP
CHILOOPTTY PHOTOLYTIC
CHIMNNOOOP MONOPHONIC
CHIMOOOPRZ ZOOMORPHIC
CHIMOORTTY TRICHOTOMY
CHIMPSSTYY SYMPHYSTIC
CHINOOOPTT PHOTOTONIC
CHINOOPPTY PHONOTYPIC
CHINOOPRSY RHINOSCOPY
CHIOOORSSU ISOCHROOUS
CHIOOPPRRY PYROPHORIC
CHIOOPPTTY PHOTOTYPIC
CHIOPRSSTU COURTSHIPS
CHIORSTTTW STITCHWORT
CHKLOOOORSW
   SCHOOLWORK
CHLMNOSUUU
   HOMUNCULUS
CHLMOOPRYY
   POLYCHROMY

CIIIILNTVY INCIVILITY
CIIIILLMPTY IMPLICITLY
CIIILMPSST SIMPLISTIC
CIIILMPSTY SIMPLICITY
CIIILNTUVY UNCIVILITY
CIIILPRTTY TRIPLICITY
CIIIMNNOST NICOTINISM
CIIIMNPPRU PRINCIPIUM
CIIIMOPSTT OPTIMISTIC
CIIIMSSTTW WITTICISMS
CIIINNNOTT INTINCTION
CIIINNOSTU UNIONISTIC
CIIJLNOPST CLIP JOINTS
CIIJNNNOTU INJUNCTION
CIIKOSTTTU STICK IT OUT
CIILLMOOSU LIMICOLOUS
CIILLNOOSS COLLISIONS
CIILLNOOST COTILLIONS
CIILLNOOTU ILLOCUTION
CIILLOSTTY STYLOLITIC
CIILMMNTUU NUMMULITIC
CIILNNOSSU INCLUSIONS
CIILNOPSTU PUNCTILIOS
CIILOORSST SOLICITORS
CIILOOSSTU SOLICITOUS
CIILOPRTVY PROCLIVITY
CIILRRSTUY SCURRILITY
CIILSSSTTY STYLISTICS
CIIMMNNOOSS COMMISSION
CIIMMNNOOTZ MONZONITIC
CIIMMNOPRRT MICROPRINT
CIIMORRSTT TRICROTISM
CIINNOORTT CONTRITION
CIINNORSSU INCURSIONS
CIINNOTTUY CONTINUITY
CIINOOPRTX PICROTOXIN
CIINOPSSSU SUSPICIONS
CIIOORSTUV VICTORIOUS
CIIOPSSSUU SUSPICIOUS
CIIPSTTTYY STYPTICITY
CIJKOSSSST JOSS STICKS
CIJLNNOOTY CONJOINTLY
CIJNNOSTTU T-JUNCTIONS
CIKLLOSSTT STOCK-STILL
CIKLNOOSTT SILK COTTON
CILLMOOQUU COLLOQUIUM
CILLOPRSTU PORTCULLIS
CILLOSSUUY LUSCIOUSLY
CILMNOOOOT LOCOMOTION
CILMNOOPSU COMPULSION
CILMNOSSTU COLUMNISTS
CILNNOOSUV CONVULSION
CILOORRSTU TRICOLOURS
CILORRSSUU SCURRILOUS
CIMMNNOOSU
  COMMUNIONS
CIMMNOOOST COMMOTIONS
CIMMNOSSTU COMMUNISTS
CIMNNOOOPP NINCOMPOOP

CIMNNOSTUU CONTINUUMS
CIMNOORSTU CONSORTIUM
CIMOOOPRST COMPOSITOR
CIMOPSTTUU PUT TO MUSIC
CINNOOORTT CONTORTION
CINNOOSSTU CONTUSIONS
CINNOOSTUU CONTINUOUS
CINOOPRRTU CORRUPTION
CINOORSSTY CONSISTORY
CINORRSTTU INSTRUCTOR
CINOSTTUUY UNCTUOSITY
CIOOPRSSTU UROSCOPIST
CIOPPRSSTT POSTSCRIPT
CIPPRRSTUU STIRRUP CUP
CKLLOORRSW
  SCROLLWORK
CKMNOORSTU
  MOONSTRUCK
CKMOOORSST
  STOCKROOMS
CKOPRSSTTU TRUCK STOPS
CLMMNNOOUY
  UNCOMMONLY
CLMOOOORTU
  OCULOMOTOR
CLMOOPRSUY
  COMPULSORY
CLNOOOOTTW COTTON
  WOOL
CLNOOPRSSU PROCONSULS
CLNOSTUUUY UNCTUOUSLY
CLOOOPRRTU PROLOCUTOR
CLOPRSSUUU SCRUPULOUS
CMMMNOOOOR COMMON
  ROOM
CMMNNNOOOU COMMON
  NOUN
CNNNOOSTUU COUNT
  NOUNS
CNNOOTTUWY COUNTY
  TOWN
DDDDDFUUYY
  FUDDY-DUDDY
DDDEEEFNNU UNDEFENDED
DDDEEFIOST EISTEDDFOD
DDDEEIOORS DEODORISED
DDDEEIOORZ DEODORIZED
DDDEEIORRS DISORDERED
DDDEFILOOW FIDDLEWOOD
DDEEEEGNNR ENGENDERED
DDEEEFLORW DEFLOWERED
DDEEEFORST DEFORESTED
DDEEEHHPRS SHEPHERDED
DDEEEHNOWY
  HONEYDEWED
DDEEEILSTT TITLE DEEDS
DDEEEIMNOR DOMINEERED
DDEEEIMNRT DETERMINED
DDEEEINRST TENDERISED

DDEEEINRTZ TENDERIZED
DDEEEELLMOR REMODELLED
DDEEEELMMOS
  MEDDLESOME
DDEEEELMNTY DEMENTEDLY
DDEEEELOPRY REDEPLOYED
DDEEEELRSVY DESERVEDLY
DDEEEENRRTU UNDETERRED
DDEEEENRSUX UNDERSEXED
DDEEEOOPRT DEEP-ROOTED
DDEEEPRSSU SUPERSEDED
DDEEFIIINT IDENTIFIED
DDEEFIINTU DEFINITUDE
DDEEFLNORU FLOUNDERED
DDEEFMOOOR
  FOREDOOMED
DDEEGGHOOP
  HODGEPODGE
DDEEGGNOSS
  DOGGEDNESS
DDEEGILNSY DESIGNEDLY
DDEEGJLLUW WELL-JUDGED
DDEEHIISSS SIDE DISHES
DDEEHILMOS DEMOLISHED
DDEEHINNSS HIDDENNESS
DDEEHLORSU SHOULDERED
DDEEHNORSU
  ENSHROUDED
DDEEHOORTU
  OUT-HERODED
DDEEIIKLMN LIKE-MINDED
DDEEIILMNV EVIL-MINDED
DDEEIINRSW SIDEWINDER
DDEEIIORSX DEOXIDISER
DDEEIIORXZ DEOXIDIZER
DDEEIIPSSW SIDESWIPED
DDEEIIQSTU DISQUIETED
DDEEILMSTW MIDDLE WEST
DDEEILNNRU UNDERLINED
DDEEILNOSY ONE-SIDEDLY
DDEEILNOTT DOTTED LINE
DDEEILRTVY DIVERTEDLY
DDEEIMNNOP OPEN-MINDED
DDEEIMNNRU UNDERMINED
DDEEIMNORS ENDODERMIS,
  MODERNISED
DDEEIMNORZ MODERNIZED
DDEEINNNTU UNINTENDED
DDEEINNRTU INDENTURED
DDEEINNSSW WINDEDNESS
DDEEINORRV OVERRIDDEN
DDEEINORSW
  DISENDOWER, EIDERDOWNS
DDEEINRSSU UNDERSISED
DDEEINRSUZ UNDERSIZED
DDEEIOORRS DEODORISER
DDEEIOORRZ DEODORIZER
DDEEIORRSS SIDE ORDERS
DDEEIRSSST DISTRESSED

DDEELLOORW OLDE
WORLDE
DDEELLORWW
WELL-WORDED
DDEELMORSU
SMOULDERED
DDEELRRSSU RUDDERLESS
DDEENNOPST DESPONDENT
DDEENNOSSS SODDENNESS
DDEENNPRSU UNDERSPEND
DDEENNSSSU SUDDENNESS
DDEFGIIRSU DISFIGURED
DDEFGILLOS GOLDFIELDS
DDEFHIIIMU HUMIDIFIED
DDEFHIIMUY DEHUMIDIFY
DDEFIIILOS SOLIDIFIED
DDEFILOOST FLOOD TIDES
DDEFIMNORR DENDRIFORM
DDEFLORSSU DUSSELDORF
DDEGGGILOR GOLD DIGGER
DDEGHHIIMN HIGH-MINDED
DDEGHINRSU SHUDDERING
DDEGIINNST DISTENDING
DDEGILLMNY MEDDLINGLY
DDEGILNNOW LONGWINDED
DDEGINNORU REDOUNDING
DDEGIOOPRR DO PORRIDGE
DDEGLLLOOR ROLLED GOLD
DDEGLNOORY
DENDROLOGY
DDEHHNRSTU HUNDREDTHS
DDEHIIIMNS DIMINISHED
DDEHIILNSW WINDSHIELD
DDEHIILPSU DISULPHIDE
DDEHIKNOOW
HOODWINKED
DDEHINOSSS SHODDINESS
DDEHLNOSTU HUDDLESTON
DDEIIILQSU LIQUIDISED
DDEIIILQUZ LIQUIDIZED
DDEIIIMPSY EPIDIDYMIS
DDEIIIPRST DISPIRITED
DDEIIJNOST DISJOINTED
DDEIIKRSSV DISK DRIVES
DDEIIMNNOU DIMINUENDO
DDEIINOPSS INDISPOSED
DDEIINOSTU DUODENITIS
DDEIINSSST DISSIDENTS
DDEIIOPRSS DISPERSOID
DDEIKNNRUW WUNDERKIND
DDEILLNPSY SPLENDIDLY
DDEILORRSY DISORDERLY
DDEIMNOSTU DISMOUNTED
DDEINOPRUV UNPROVIDED
DDEINOPSUW UPSIDE DOWN
DDEINORSSS SORDIDNESS
DDEINPSTUU UNDISPUTED
DDEIRSSTTU DISTRUSTED

DDELNORRUW
UNDERWORLD
DDENOOPPRU
PROPOUNDED
DDENOORSTU
UNDERSTOOD
DDENORRSUU
SURROUNDED
DDENRSTUUY UNDERSTUDY
DDEOPRRSTU RUDDERPOST
DDGGIILNOS DISLODGING
DDGGOOOOYY
GOODY-GOODY
DDGHRRUUYY
HURDY-GURDY
DDGIINPRRY DRIP-DRYING
DDGILLMNUY MUDDLINGLY
DDGILLNOPY PLODDINGLY
DDHILORRTW THIRD WORLD
DDHINOOPTY DIPHYODONT
DDHOOOOUWY HOW DO
YOU DO
DEEEEEFPRZ DEEP FREEZE
DEEEEFFLRS SELF-FEEDER
DEEEEFNRTT TENDERFEET
DEEEEGINNR ENGINEERED
DEEEEGNNRR ENGENDERER
DEEEEHLLLW WELL-HEELED
DEEEEKNRSW
WEEKENDERS
DEEEEPRRSV PERSEVERED
DEEEFGIKNS KNIFE-EDGES
DEEEFHILNS NEEDLEFISH
DEEEFHLORR FREEHOLDER
DEEEFILMNT DEFILEMENT
DEEEFILNTV FIELD EVENT
DEEEFINRRT INTERFERED
DEEEFINRTW WINTERFEED
DEEEFINSSV DEFENSIVES
DEEEFLORRW DEFLOWERER
DEEEFMNRRU
REFERENDUM
DEEEFMNRST DEFERMENTS
DEEEFNQRTU FREQUENTED
DEEEFNRTTU UNFETTERED
DEEEFORRST DEFORESTER,
REFORESTED
DEEEGGGLOY
GOGGLE-EYED
DEEEGHHINT HEIGHTENED
DEEEGHLNNT LENGTHENED
DEEEGHOOWZ GOOD
WHEEZE
DEEEGIIMRV DEMIVIERGE
DEEEGIKNNW WEEKENDING
DEEEGILMTY GIMLET-EYED
DEEEGIMNRT REGIMENTED
DEEEGINRSS GREEDINESS
DEEEGIRRST REGISTERED

DEEEGNRSTT DETERGENTS
DEEEHIPRSS HESPERIDES
DEEEHLLSSY HEEDLESSLY
DEEEHLNOPT TELEPHONED
DEEEHNORTY HETERODYNE
DEEEHNRRTU THEREUNDER
DEEEIILRSV DELIVERIES
DEEEIKLLRW WEEDKILLER
DEEEILLMOS DEMOISELLE
DEEEILLMPS MILLEPEDES
DEEEILMRSS REMEDILESS
DEEEILNRSS SLENDERISE
DEEEILNRSZ SLENDERIZE
DEEEILNRUV UNRELIEVED
DEEEILRRVY REDELIVERY
DEEEILRSVW SILVERWEED
DEEEIMMRSS MESMERISED
DEEEIMMRSZ MESMERIZED
DEEEIMNOST DEMONETISE
DEEEIMNOTZ DEMONETIZE
DEEEIMNRRT DETERMINER
DEEEIMNRST DENSIMETER
DEEEIMORTU EUDIOMETER
DEEEIMRSSY MERSEYSIDE
DEEEINNPTV PENDENTIVE
DEEEINNRTV INTERVENED
DEEEINPRST PREDESTINE
DEEEINPSSS SPEEDINESS
DEEEINPSTX EXPEDIENTS
DEEEINRRST TENDERISER
DEEEINRRTZ TENDERIZER
DEEEINRSTT INTERESTED
DEEEIPRSSV DEPRESSIVE
DEEEIPRSTX PREEXISTED
DEEEIRSSTT SIDE STREET
DEEEKLNORW
NEEDLEWORK
DEEEKOOPRR DOORKEEPER
DEEELLMORR REMODELLER
DEEELLNORW
NE'ER-DO-WELL
DEEELLNSSY NEEDLESSLY
DEEELLOWWY
YELLOWWEED
DEEELNRTTU UNLETTERED
DEEELOPRSV DEVELOPERS
DEEELRRSVY RESERVEDLY
DEEEMNNOTT
DENOTEMENT
DEEEMNNOTU
DENOUEMENT
DEEEMNNOYZ
ENDOENZYME
DEEEMNOTTV DEVOTEMENT
DEEEMNRSSU DEMURENESS
DEEEMNSTTV VESTMENTED
DEEENNRSST TENDERNESS
DEEENPRRST PRETENDERS
DEEENPRSUV SUPERVENED

DEEENRRSTT DETERRENTS
DEEENRRSUV UNRESERVED
DEEEOPPRRY EYEDROPPER
DEEEORSSTV STEVEDORES
DEEEPPPRRS RED PEPPERS
DEEEPRRSSU SUPERSEDER
DEEERSSUVX DEUX-SÈVRES
DEEFFHLRSU RESHUFFLED
DEEFGHINRT FRIGHTENED
DEEFGINPRY DEEP FRYING
DEEFGINRTY GENTRIFYED
DEEFGINSST GIFTEDNESS
DEEFGIPRRU PREFIGURED
DEEFIIINNT INDEFINITE
DEEFIIINRT IDENTIFIER
DEEFIIINTV DEFINITVE
DEEFIIIRVV REVIVIFIED
DEEFIILMNS MINEFIELDS
DEEFIILMSU EMULSIFIED
DEEFIILNRR FRIENDLIER
DEEFIILNRS FRIENDLIES,
INFIELDERS
DEEFIILNTY DEFINITELY
DEEFIILRST FERTILISED
DEEFIILRTZ FERTILIZED
DEEFIINRVW VIEWFINDER
DEEFIIPRTT PRETTIFIED
DEEFILLLSW SELF-WILLED
DEEFILLRSU FLEUR-DE-LIS
DEEFILMOSU FIELDMOUSE
DEEFILNOST FIELDSTONE
DEEFILNRSS FRIENDLESS
DEEFILNRYZ FRENZIEDLY
DEEFILORTU OUTFIELDER
DEEFILSSTT FIELD-TESTS
DEEFINNPRS PEN FRIENDS
DEEFIORRRT FERRITE-ROD
DEEFKNORSS FORKEDNESS
DEEFLLSSTY SELF-STYLED
DEEFLMNNOT ENFOLDMENT
DEEFLOORVW
OVERFLOWED
DEEFNOORTT TENDERFOOT
DEEFOORSTU SUREFOOTED
DEEFORRSST DEFROSTERS
DEEGGNRSSU RUGGEDNESS
DEEGGRSTUY
GREEDY-GUTS
DEEGHINOPS DIPHOSGENE
DEEGHINRRR RED HERRING
DEEGHINSTU GESUNDHEIT
DEEGHIOTUW OUTWEIGHED
DEEGIILNRV DELIVERING
DEEGIILNSU GUIDELINES
DEEGIILOOS IDEOLOGIES
DEEGIILPRV PRIVILEGED
DEEGIINNRT INGREDIENT
DEEGIINPTX EXPEDITING
DEEGIIRSSV DIGRESSIVE

DEEGIISSTV DIGESTIVES
DEEGILMNOR REMODELING
DEEGILNNOW GWENDOLINE
DEEGILNOPV DEVELOPING
DEEGILNRSY RESIGNEDLY
DEEGILOOSU IDEOLOGUES
DEEGILOPRS RIDGEPOLES
DEEGINNPRT PRETENDING
DEEGINNRRS RENDERINGS
DEEGINOOPT PIGEON-TOED
DEEGINORSS DEGRESSION
DEEGINOTTU TONGUE-TIED
DEEGINPRSS DEPRESSING
DEEGINRRSS REDRESSING
DEEGKNOTTT GET
KNOTTED!
DEEGKOPRSW POWDER
KEGS
DEEGLLNORU GOLDEN RULE
DEEGNNOOSU
ENDOGENOUS
DEEGOPRRSS PROGRESSED
DEEHHISSTW THE SWEDISH
DEEHIINPRS HESPERIDIN
DEEHIIRSTT HEREDITIST
DEEHILLRSV SHRIVELLED
DEEHILMORS DEMOLISHER
DEEHILOOTT THEODOLITE
DEEHIMORST METHODISER
DEEHIMORTZ METHODIZER
DEEHINOOPV VIDEOPHONE
DEEHINORST THRENODIES
DEEHINRSSW SWINEHERDS
DEEHIOPPRS PROPHESIED
DEEHIORSTV SHROVETIDE
DEEHIOSSTU TIED HOUSES
DEEHKNOOSS HOOKEDNESS
DEEHLLMOPR PHELLODERM
DEEHNNORSS HORNEDNESS
DEEHNOORTT HETERODONT
DEEHNRRSTU THUNDERERS
DEEHNRSSSW
SHREWDNESS
DEEHOORTXY HETERODOXY
DEEHSSSTTU DUSTSHEETS
DEEIIINPPR PIPERIDINE
DEEIIINSTT IDENTITIES
DEEIILLMPR IMPERILLED
DEEIILLMPS MILLIPEDES
DEEIILLNOS LINSEED OIL
DEEIILLOPT LEPIDOLITE
DEEIILMPST SPEED LIMIT
DEEIILNNVY VINYLIDENE
DEEIILNSTT DISENTITLE
DEEIILOPPT EPILEPTOID
DEEIILORST SIDEROLITE
DEEIILPRRV PILE DRIVER
DEEIILRSST STERILISED
DEEIILRSTZ STERILIZED

DEEIILRSVY DERISIVELY
DEEIIMMNPT IMPEDIMENT
DEEIIMNRST MINISTERED
DEEIIMOPST EPITOMISED
DEEIIMOPTZ EPITOMIZED
DEEIINNRTT TRIDENTINE
DEEIINNSTW DISENTWINE
DEEIINOPTT PETITIONED
DEEIINOPTX EXPEDITION
DEEIINPTTU INEPTITUDE
DEEIINQTUU INQUIETUDE
DEEIINSSST SENSITISED
DEEIINSSTZ SENSITIZED
DEEIIOPRTT PERIDOTITE
DEEIIPRSSV DISPERSIVE
DEEIIPRSSW SIDESWIPER
DEEIIPSSSW SIDESWIPES
DEEIISSSSU SIDE ISSUES
DEEIJNORRS REJOINDERS
DEEIJNOSTT JETTISONED
DEEIKNNSSS KINDNESSES
DEEIKORSST SIDESTROKE
DEEILLMPSS MISSPELLED
DEEILLORRS DROLLERIES
DEEILLRRSV DRIVELLERS
DEEILLRSSU SLIDE RULES
DEEILLSUVY DELUSIVELY
DEEILMNOSS SOLEMNISED
DEEILMNOSU EMULSIONED
DEEILMNOSZ SOLEMNIZED
DEEILNNORT TENDERLOIN
DEEILNNQTU DELINQUENT
DEEILNPRST SPLINTERED
DEEILNRSSW WILDERNESS
DEEILNRSTU INTERLUDES
DEEILPRSUV PULVERISED
DEEILPRUVZ PULVERIZED
DEEIMMNOSU EUDEMONISM
DEEIMNNNTT INTENDMENT
DEEIMNNRRU UNDERMINER
DEEIMNOOTV MONTEVIDEO
DEEIMNOPRT REDEMPTION
DEEIMNOPTT IDEMPOTENT
DEEIMNORRS MODERNISER
DEEIMNORRZ MODERNIZER
DEEIMNORSS SERMONISED
DEEIMNORSZ SERMONIZED
DEEIMNRRTU ERMINTRUDE
DEEIMNRSTT DETRIMENTS
DEEIMNRSTW
MIDWESTERN, STEM-WINDER
DEEIMNRSTY DENSIMETRY
DEEIMNSTTV DIVESTMENT
DEEIMOPRST TEMPORISED
DEEIMOPRTZ TEMPORIZED
DEEIMORTUY EUDIOMETRY
DEEINNNOSU INNUENDOES
DEEINNRSST TRENDINESS
DEEINNRSSU INUREDNESS

DEEINNRSTU INDENTURES
DEEINNSSTU UNITEDNESS
DEEINOPRSS DEPRESSION
DEEINOPRST INTERPOSED
DEEINOQSTU QUESTIONED
DEEINORSST DESERTIONS
DEEINPRRST RINDERPEST
DEEINPRSSS DISPENSERS
DEEINPRSST PRESIDENTS
DEEINQRTUU UNREQUITED
DEEINRRTUW UNDERWRITE
DEEINRSSSS DRESSINESS
DEEINRSSST DISSENTERS
DEEINSTTTV VENDETTIST
DEEIOPPRRT PROPERTIED
DEEIOPPRSS PREDISPOSE
DEEIOPRSUX SUPEROXIDE
DEEIOPRSVW POWER DIVES
DEEIOPRTTU PIROUETTED
DEEIORRRST TERRORISED
DEEIORRRTZ TERRORIZED
DEEIPRRTUY EURYPTERID
DEEIPRSSUV SUPERVISED
DEEKLLNORS SNORKELLED
DEEKLMRTTU KETTLEDRUM
DEEKLOOORV OVERLOOKED
DEEKLRSSUU LESSER KUDU
DEEKOORRVW
  OVERWORKED
DEELLMOORS ROLE
  MODELS
DEELLNRTUW
  WELL-TURNED
DEELMMNOPU NOM DE
  PLUME
DEELMNOPTY DEPLOYMENT
DEELMNOPUY
  UNEMPLOYED
DEELMPRSUY PRESUMEDLY
DEELNNOOSU UNLOOSENED
DEELNNORWY
  RENOWNEDLY
DEELNOOSST LODESTONES
DEELNORSUV UNRESOLVED
DEELNOSTUU EDENTULOUS
DEELNPRRSU PLUNDERERS
DEELOPRRTY REPORTEDLY
DEELORTTUV TURTLEDOVE
DEELPRSTTU SPLUTTERED
DEEMNNORSS
  MODERNNESS
DEEMNNORTW
  WONDERMENT
DEEMNNOSTW
  ENDOWMENTS
DEEMNOORRY MONEY
  ORDER
DEEMNOPRTT DEPORTMENT

DEEMNORSTU
  TREMENDOUS
DEEMNRRTUY
  ERMYNTRUDE
DEENNOOSSW
  WOODENNESS
DEENNOPRST RESPONDENT
DEENNORSTU UNDERTONES
DEENNORSVW
  NEWSVENDOR
DEENOQRTUU
  UNDERQUOTE
DEENORRTUV OVERTURNED
DEENORRTUW
  UNDERWROTE
DEENORSSSU ROUSEDNESS
DEENORSUVZ RENDEZVOUS
DEENOSSTUV DEVOUTNESS
DEENPRSSSU SUSPENDERS
DEENRRRSSU SURRENDERS
DEENRSSSTU UNSTRESSED
DEEOOPPRTV OVERTOPPED
DEEOOPRRSU UREDOSPORE
DEEOOPRRSU SUPERORDER
DEEORRSSTY DESTROYERS
DEEPPRRSUU SUPERDUPER
DEEPPRSSSU SUPPRESSED
DEFFGINOOR FINGER FOOD
DEFFINNOST SOFT-FINNED
DEFFOPPRUW POWDER
  PUFF
DEFGGILLNS FLEDGLINGS
DEFGGILLRU FULL-RIGGED
DEFGHILLTU DELIGHTFUL
DEFGHOOOSU HOUSE OF
  GOD
DEFGIILNRR GIRLFRIEND
DEFGIILNYY EDIFYINGLY
DEFGIINNUY UNEDIFYING
DEFGIIRRSU DISFIGURER
DEFGINNORU FOUNDERING
DEFGINORST DEFROSTING
DEFGNOORRU
  FOREGROUND
DEFHIIMRU HUMIDIFIER
DEFHIILNSY FIENDISHLY
DEFHIINNSU UNFINISHED
DEFHIINPRS FRIENDSHIP
DEFHILOPST SHOPLIFTED
DEFHILORSU FLOURISHED
DEFHLNOSUW FLESH
  WOUND
DEFHLOOOSW
  WHOLEFOODS
DEFHNOOPRU
  UNHOPED-FOR
DEFHORRRTU RUTHERFORD
DEFIIILMPS SIMPLIFIED
DEFIIILNTY INFIDELITY

DEFIIILORS SOLIDIFIER
DEFIIINNOT DEFINITION
DEFIIINNTU INFINITUDE
DEFIILLNRY FRIENDLILY
DEFIILLRRS FIRE DRILLS
DEFIILOSSS FOSSILISED
DEFIILOSSZ FOSSILIZED
DEFIILPRST FIELD TRIPS
DEFIILSTTU STULTIFIED
DEFIINOPTX FIXED-POINT
DEFIIOPRSU PERFIDIOUS
DEFILLORWW WILDFOWLER
DEFILMNORY INFORMEDLY
DEFILNNRUY UNFRIENDLY
DEFILNORWW WINDFLOWER
DEFILNOSSW SNOWFIELDS
DEFILPRSUU SUPERFLUID
DEFIMNNORU UNINFORMED
DEFINRRSUW WIND-SURFER
DEFLNOORRU UNDERFLOOR
DEFNOOPRRU UNDERPROOF
DEGGHIILNT DELIGHTING
DEGGHIIPRS SHIP-RIGGED
DEGGIILRSU GIRL GUIDES
DEGGIINRSS DIGRESSING
DEGGIJNPRU PREJUDGING
DEGGIJRRUY JURY-RIGGED
DEGGINNORU UNDERGOING
DEGGINORUV GIVE GROUND
DEGHIILSST SIDELIGHTS
DEGHIMNRSU HUMDINGERS
DEGHINNORT DETHRONING
DEGHINNRTU THUNDERING
DEGHINRSST NIGHTDRESS
DEGHIORRRU ROUGHRIDER
DEGHIOSTTU DOUGHTIEST
DEGHLORSSU GOLD
  RUSHES
DEGHMOORST
  GODMOTHERS
DEGHNORSUY
  GREYHOUNDS
DEGIIILMNT DELIMITING
DEGIIILNNS SIDELINING
DEGIIIRSST DIGITISERS
DEGIIIRSTZ DIGITIZERS
DEGIIKLNNR REKINDLING
DEGIILLMRX MIXED GRILL
DEGIILLNPS DISPELLING
DEGIILLNRV DRIVELLING
DEGIILLNTY DILIGENTLY
DEGIILLNYY YIELDINGLY
DEGIILMNPY IMPEDINGLY
DEGIILNNUY UNYIELDING
DEGIILNOPS DESPOILING
DEGIILNORS SOLDIERING
DEGIILOOST IDEOLOGIST
DEGIINNOSU INDIGENOUS
DEGIINNOSV NOSEDIVING

DEGIINNPSS DISPENSING
DEGIINNSST DISSENTING
DEGIINOPST DEPOSITING
DEGIINORRV OVERRIDING
DEGIINORSS DIGRESSION
DEGIINOSST DIGESTIONS
DEGIINPRSS DISPERSING
DEGIINPRST SPRING TIDE
DEGIINPTUZ DEPUTIZING
DEGIIQSSTU SQUIDGIEST
DEGILLOOTY DELTIOLOGY
DEGILMNORS SMOLDERING
DEGILMNORU
　MOULDERING, REMOULDING
DEGILMNRSU MUDSLINGER
DEGILNNPRU PLUNDERING
DEGILNNRSU UNDERLINGS
DEGILNNRUY ENDURINGLY,
　UNDERLYING
DEGILNOORS GONDOLIERS
DEGILNOOSS GOODLINESS
DEGILNOSTU LONGITUDES
DEGILNRSTU DISGRUNTLE
DEGILOOPST PEDOLOGIST
DEGIMNSSSU SMUDGINESS
DEGINNOPRS RESPONDING
DEGINNOPRT PORTENDING
DEGINNOPUX EXPOUNDING
DEGINNORST GRINDSTONE,
　STRINGENDO
DEGINNORSU RESOUNDING
DEGINNPSSU SUSPENDING
DEGINNRSSU UNDRESSING
DEGINOOPRT TORPEDOING
DEGINOORSV OVERDOSING
DEGINOPSST SIGNPOSTED
DEGINORSTY DESTROYING
DEGINOSSST STODGINESS
DEGKLOOOOR GOOD
　LOOKER
DEGLMNOOOY
　DEMONOLOGY
DEGLMOOORT MOTOR
　LODGE
DEGLNNRSUU UNDERSLUNG
DEGLNOOOTY
　DEONTOLOGY
DEGLNOORSU LOSE
　GROUND
DEGLNORRUU GROUND
　RULE
DEGLNORSSU GROUNDLESS
DEGLOORTTY TROGLODYTE
DEGMNNORSU
　GROUNDSMEN
DEGNNORRTU GROUND
　RENT
DEGNNORRUW
　UNDERGROWN

DEGNOORRSW
　WRONGDOERS
DEGORRSSTU DRUGSTORES
DEHHIKMOSS SHEIKHDOMS
DEHHILOPRS HOLDERSHIP
DEHHILORTW WITHHOLDER
DEHHIMOORR HEMORRHOID
DEHHLOOSSU HOUSEHOLDS
DEHHLORSST THRESHOLDS
DEHHMOOORT
　MOTHERHOOD
DEHHOOOOPP
　POOH-POOHED
DEHIIINOTT DITHIONITE
DEHIIINRST DISINHERIT
DEHIIKLLOO LIKELIHOOD
DEHIIKMRSS SKIRMISHED
DEHIILLOOV LIVELIHOOD
DEHIILLSVY DEVILISHLY
DEHIILMNPU DELPHINIUM
DEHIILNPSY SYLPHIDINE
DEHIIMMNPS MIDSHIPMEN
DEHIIMNOPR PREHOMINID
DEHIIMNPRU NEPHRIDIUM
DEHIIOPRST EDITORSHIP
DEHIIRSTVW WHIST DRIVE
DEHIKNOORW
　HOODWINKER
DEHIKNRSZZ DZERZHINSK
DEHILNNOOP INDOPHENOL
DEHILOOPSS SHOPSOILED
DEHILORSTV SHORT-LIVED
DEHILOSSTW DISH TOWELS
DEHIMMNORR
　HORN-RIMMED
DEHIMNORST HINDERMOST
DEHIMNOSSS MODISHNESS
DEHIMOOPPR HIPPODROME
DEHIMOSSTT METHODISTS
DEHINNPSUU UNPUNISHED
DEHINOPSTY HYPNOTISED
DEHINOPTYZ HYPNOTIZED
DEHINORRSS HORRIDNESS
DEHINOSSTY DISHONESTY
DEHINRRSTU UNDERSHIRT
DEHIOOPRST PRIESTHOOD
DEHIOORSST SISTERHOOD
DEHIOPPRSW WORSHIPPED
DEHKLOOSST STOKEHOLDS
DEHLLOOSSU DOLL'S HOUSE
DEHLNOOPRY POLYHEDRON
DEHLORRSYY HYDROLYSER
DEHMMOORSU
　MUSHROOMED
DEHMNOOPRY
　ENDOMORPHY
DEHNNOSSUW
　NEWSHOUNDS

DEHNOORRSU
　HORRENDOUS
DEHNOORSTU
　UNDERSHOOT
DEHNOORSUU
　ROUNDHOUSE
DEHNORSTUU
　THUNDEROUS
DEHOOPRSUU
　HOUSE-PROUD
DEHOOSSSSU DOSSHOUSES
DEIIIINSTV DIVINITIES
DEIIIKNSTT IDENTIKITS
DEIIILMSTU SIMILITUDE
DEIIILQRSU LIQUIDISER
DEIIILQRUZ LIQUIDIZER
DEIIILSVVY DIVISIVELY
DEIIIMNPRY PYRIMIDINE
DEIIIMNTUV DIMINUTIVE
DEIIIMSSSV DISMISSIVE
DEIIJMNORS MISJOINDER
DEIIKLNNSS KINDLINESS
DEIIKNRSSV SKIN DIVERS
DEIILLMPTU MULTIPLIED
DEIILLNOTU TOLLUIDINE
DEIILLNUWY UNWIELDILY
DEIILLRSST DISTILLERS
DEIILLRSTY DISTILLERY
DEIILMNOOT DEMOLITION
DEIILNPRTY INTREPIDLY
DEIILNPSST SPINDLIEST
DEIILORRSY DERISORILY
DEIILPRSTY SPIRITEDLY
DEIIMNNOSS DIMENSIONS
DEIIMNOPRS IMPRISONED
DEIIMNPRST MISPRINTED
DEIIMOPRSV IMPROVISED
DEIIMORTXY OXIDIMETRY
DEIIMPRSSU PRESIDIUMS
DEIINNOPPT PINPOINTED
DEIINNORST RENDITIONS
DEIINNOSSS DISSENSION
DEIINNOSST DISTENSION
DEIINNPRSU UNINSPIRED
DEIINNSSTU UNTIDINESS
DEIINOOPST DEPOSITION,
　POSITIONED
DEIINOPRSS DISPERSION
DEIINOPRXY PYRIDOXINE
DEIINORSSV DIVERSIONS
DEIINPPRST PINSTRIPED
DEIINRSSTU INDUSTRIES
DEIINSTTTU INSTITUTED
DEIIORSTTV DISTORTIVE
DEIIPRSTUV DISRUPTIVE
DEIJNNNOOR NONJOINDER
DEIKMPPRSU MUDSKIPPER
DEIKNNNORR NONDRINKER
DEIKNNNSSU UNKINDNESS

DEIKNRRSTU UNDERSKIRT
DEILLMNSSY MINDLESSLY
DEILLNNOTY INDOLENTLY
DEILLNORSS LORDLINESS
DEILLORSTW WORLDLIEST
DEILMMOSTY IMMODESTLY
DEILMNOSSU MOULDINESS
DEILMNPTUY IMPUDENTLY
DEILMRSSUY SURMISEDLY
DEILMSTTUU MULTITUDES
DEILNNNTUW WIND TUNNEL
DEILNOOTUV DEVOLUTION
DEILNRSTTY STRIDENTLY
DEILOORRTV LORD IT OVER
DEILOSTTWW SLOW-WITTED
DEIMMNORSS MODERNISMS
DEIMNNOSTW DISOWNMENT
DEIMNOOSSS ENDOSMOSIS
DEIMNOPRTU IMPORTUNED
DEIMNOPRUV UNIMPROVED
DEIMNORSST MODERNISTS
DEIMOPRSSU DISPERMOUS
DEIMRSSTTU MISTRUSTED
DEINOOPRSS DROOPINESS
DEINOOPTTU OUTPOINTED
DEINOORSWW ROSE
   WINDOW
DEINOOSSST ENDOSTOSIS
DEINOOSSSU ODIOUSNESS
DEINOOSTTX EXODONTIST
DEINOPSSSU SUSPENSOID
DEINORSSSS DROSSINESS
DEINORSSSW DROWSINESS
DEINPSSSTU STUPIDNESS
DEINRSSSTU STURDINESS
DEIOOPRSST DEPOSITORS
DEIOOPRSTY DEPOSITORY
DEIOPRRSTW SPIDERWORT
DEIOPSSSSS DISPOSSESS
DEIRRSSTTU DISTRUSTER
DEKKNOORWY
   DONKEYWORK
DEKLORSSVV SVERDLOVSK
DEKNOOPRUV
   UNPROVOKED
DEKNOORRWW
   WONDERWORK
DEKOOORRWW
   WOODWORKER
DELLOOOWWY
   YELLOWWOOD
DELLORSSWY WORDLESSLY
DELLOSSUUY SEDULOUSLY
DELNNOPSSU NONPLUSSED
DELNOOPRTU PLEURODONT
DELNOPRSUU PLUNDEROUS
DELOOPRRWW WORLD
   POWER
DELOPPSSUY SUPPOSEDLY

DELORRTTUY TORTUREDLY
DEMMOORSUW
   SUMMERWOOD
DEMNOPPRTU
   UNPROMPTED
DEMNOPSSUY
   PSEUDONYMS
DEMNORSTUU
   SURMOUNTED
DEMNPRRTUU
   UNDERTRUMP
DEMOOOPRRW POWDER
   ROOM
DENNORSSUW
   SUNDOWNERS
DENOOPPRRU
   PROPOUNDER
DENOPRRTTU PROTRUDENT
DENOPSSTUU STUPENDOUS
DEOORRSSUU
   UREDOSORUS
DEPRSSSSTU PRESS-STUDS
DFFFOOSSTU FOODSTUFFS
DFGGIIINNY DIGNIFYING
DFGHILLOOT FLOODLIGHT
DFGIIIMORT DIGITIFORM
DFGIINOSUU NIDIFUGOUS
DFGILLNNOY FONDLINGLY
DFGILLNNOSU FOUNDLINGS
DFHILOORSY HYDROFOILS
DFHLNOOSUW
   WOLFHOUNDS
DFHLNSSSUU SLUSH FUNDS
DFHLOOOOPT PHOTOFLOOD
DFHLOOORTU HOLD OUT
   FOR
DFIKLOPPSY FLOPPY DISK
DFINOPRTUY PROFUNDITY
DFINORSSTW SNOWDRIFTS
DFLNOOPRUY PROFOUNDLY
DFNOOOPRSU
   SOUNDPROOF
DFNOOOORST FRONT
   DOORS
DFNRSSTTUU TRUST FUNDS
DFOOOORSTU OUT OF
   DOORS
DGGGIINORS DISGORGING
DGGGILNRUY GRUDGINGLY
DGGGINNRUU UNGRUDGING
DGGIIIINTZ DIGITIZING
DGGIIINSSU DISGUISING
DGGIIJMNSU MISJUDGING
DGGIILMNNO GOLD-MINING
DGGIINSSTU DISGUSTING
DGGILNNORU GROUNDLING
DGGINNOORW
   WRONGDOING
DGHHIKNOOT KNIGHTHOOD

DGHHINOPST DIPHTHONGS
DGHIILLNNO HILLINGDON
DGHILMOSST GOLDSMITHS
DGHINNNOTU HUNTINGDON
DGHLNOORST
   STRONGHOLD
DGIIIKNNSV SKIN DIVING
DGIIILLNST DISTILLING
DGIIIMNSSS DISMISSING
DGIIINNSTU DISUNITING
DGIIINPTUY PINGUIDITY
DGIILNOOST INDOLOGIST
DGIILNOSSV DISSOLVING
DGIIMNNOOR DINING ROOM
DGIIMNNOPU IMPOUNDING
DGIINNPRSY SPIN-DRYING
DGIINOPRST DISPORTING
DGIINOPRSV DISPROVING
DGIINORSTT DISTORTING
DGIINPRSTU DISRUPTING
DGIIOOPRSU PRODIGIOUS
DGILNNOUWY WOUNDINGLY
DGINOOPRSW SPRINGWOOD
DGINOPRRTU PROTRUDING
DGKNOORRUW
   GROUNDWORK
DGLNOOOOTY
   ODONTOLOGY
DGNNORSTUU
   GROUNDNUTS
DHIILNRSWW WHIRLWINDS
DHIIMMOPRS DIMORPHISM
DHILLOPSUY DIPHYLLOUS
DHILMMOOSU HOODLUMISM
DHILORSSYY HYDROLYSIS
DHIMOOPRSU DIMORPHOUS
DHINOOOPRT ORNITHOPOD
DHINOOPSWW
   WINDOW-SHOP
DHINOPRSUW
   WHIP-ROUNDS
DHIOOPPRRY PORPHYROID
DHLMOOSTUU
   LOUDMOUTHS
DHNNOSTUUW
   SHUNT-WOUND
DHNOOORTUX
   UNORTHODOX
DIIIINPSTY INSIPIDITY
DIIILSTTUY DISUTILITY
DIIIMMORSU OSMIRIDIUM
DIIIMNNOTU DIMINUTION
DIILLNOSWW WINDOWSILL
DIIMMOPRRU PRIMORDIUM
DIINOORSTT DISTORTION
DIINOPRSTU DISRUPTION
DILLLOSSTY LLOYD'S LIST
DILLOOPPYY POLYPLOIDY
DILORSSTUU STRIDULOUS

DILOSSTUUY STUDIOUSLY
DIMMNOOOPU
MONOPODIUM
DIMNORSSTW WINDSTORMS
DIMOPRSSUY DYSPROSIUM
DINOPRRSTU ROUND TRIPS
DIOOPQQRUU QUID PRO
QUO
DLLOOORSUY DOLOROUSLY
DLOOOPPSUY POLYPODOUS
DMORSSSTTU DUST STORMS
DNNORRSTUU
TURNROUNDS
DNOOPSSTUW
DOWNSPOUTS
DNOOSSTTUY NOT SO
DUSTY
EEEEEHMTTY MEET THE EYE
EEEEFFNSST EFFETENESS
EEEEFGINRR REFEREEING
EEEEFKLRSS SELF-SEEKER
EEEEFLMSST SELF-ESTEEM
EEEEGHHLTT GET THE HEEL
EEEEGIPSSX EPEXEGESIS
EEEEGNRRSV EVERGREENS
EEEEHIMRSU EUHEMERISE
EEEEHIMRUZ EUHEMERIZE
EEEEHPSSSY SHEEP'S EYES
EEEEHRRVWY
EVERYWHERE
EEEEIKMPRT TIMEKEEPER
EEEEKMRRSY KERSEYMERE
EEEEELLSSSV SLEEVELESS
EEEEENNRRVV NEVER-NEVER
EEEEENNRSSS SERENENESS
EEEEENNTWYY TEENY
WEENY
EEEEENOPRSY EYE-OPENERS
EEEEENRSSSV SEVERENESS
EEEEENRSSTW SWEETENERS
EEEEERRRTTV TERRE-VERTE
EEEFGIINNR FIRE ENGINE
EEEFGILNRS GREENFLIES
EEEFGIMRSU REFUGEEISM
EEEFGINORS FORESEEING
EEEFGLNRUV REVENGEFUL
EEEFHOORRT HERETOFORE
EEEFHORRSW
WHEREFORES
EEEFHORSSU FREE HOUSES
EEEFIINRRS REFINERIES
EEEFILRSVX REFLEXIVES
EEEFIMNNRT REFINEMENT
EEEFINRRRT INTERFERER
EEEFKNOPRS FREE-SPOKEN
EEEFLLORRT FORETELLER
EEEFMNPRRT PREFERMENT
EEEFNNORSU UNFORESEEN
EEEFNQRRTU FREQUENTER

EEEGHHINRT HEIGHTENER
EEEGHHINTT EIGHTEENTH
EEEGHIMNOT EIGHTEENMO
EEEGHKLNNT KNEE-LENGTH
EEEGHLNNRT LENGTHENER
EEEGHNNOST STONEHENGE
EEEGHNORSU GREENHOUSE
EEEGHNORTW GET
NOWHERE
EEEGIINPSS EPIGENESIS
EEEGIJNNST JET ENGINES
EEEGIMORST GEOMETRISE
EEEGIMORTZ GEOMETRIZE
EEEGINNPST STEEPENING
EEEGINNSTW SWEETENING
EEEGINOPRY EPEIROGENY
EEEGINORSV OVERSEEING
EEEGINORTY EROGENEITY
EEEGIRRRST REGISTERER
EEEGIRRSSV REGRESSIVE
EEEGLNNSST GENTLENESS
EEEGMNRSSS MESSENGERS
EEEGNNORST GREENSTONE
EEEHHIMPRS HEMISPHERE
EEEHHLOSUW
WHEELHOUSE
EEEHHOTTTT TO THE TEETH
EEEHIKLLMT HELMET-LIKE
EEEHILLNRS HELLENISER
EEEHILLNRZ HELLENIZER
EEEHILMORT HELIOMETER
EEEHILNPRS PREHENSILE
EEEHILPSSS LESSEESHIP
EEEHIMMRSU EUHEMERISM
EEEHIMPRSU EUPHEMISER
EEEHIMPRUZ EUPHEMIZER
EEEHIMRSTU EUHEMERIST
EEEHIMSSTT TIME SHEETS
EEEHINNNTT NINETEENTH
EEEHINNTTV IN THE EVENT
EEEHINPSST EPENTHESIS
EEEHINSSWZ WHEEZINESS
EEEHINSTTV SEVENTIETH
EEEHJNOSST THE JONESES
EEEHKLOPTT KEEL THE POT
EEEHKOPPRS SHOPKEEPER
EEEHLMNTVY VEHEMENTLY
EEEHLMSSTV THEMSELVES
EEEHLNOPRT TELEPHONER
EEEHLNOPST TELEPHONES
EEEHMOPRSS MESOSPHERE
EEEHMORSST THREESOMES
EEEHNORSSS HORSE SENSE
EEEHNORSVW
WHENSOEVER
EEEHNPRSTT THE PRESENT
EEEHNSSSTW NEWSSHEETS
EEEHOPPRRT TREEHOPPER
EEEHORRTVY EVERY OTHER

EEEHRSSTTU USHERETTES
EEEIINRSTT ETERNITIES
EEEIIPRTTV REPETITIVE
EEEIIRSSTV SEVERITIES
EEEIJLMRSS IJSSELMEER
EEEIKLMSWY SEMIWEEKLY
EEEIKLNSSS LIKENESSES
EEEIKNNPRS INNKEEPERS
EEEILMMORT MILEOMETER
EEEILMNRST RESILEMENT
EEEILMNRTV REVILEMENT
EEEILMNSSS SEEMLINESS
EEEILMNSTY MESITYLENE
EEEILNPRRT TERREPLEIN
EEEILNPSSS SLEEPINESS
EEEILNSSST STEELINESS
EEEILORRTU EURE-ET-LOIR
EEEILPSTVX EXPLETIVES
EEEILRRTTW TELEWRITER
EEEILRSSSW WIRELESSES
EEEILRSSTW WESTERLIES
EEEIMMRRSS MESMERISER
EEEIMMRRSZ MESMERIZER
EEEIMNNPRT PRE-EMINENT
EEEIMNORST REMONETISE
EEEIMNORTZ REMONETIZE
EEEIMNPRTX EXPERIMENT
EEEIMNRRTT RETIREMENT
EEEIMNRSTT TENSIMETER
EEEIMORSTT METEORITES
EEEIMPPRTV PRE-EMPTIVE
EEEIMPRRST PERIMETERS
EEEIMRRSTV TIMESERVER
EEEINNPRSS PERSIENNES
EEEINNPRST SERPENTINE
EEEINNPRTV PREVENIENT
EEEINNRRTV INTERVENER
EEEINNRSST ENTIRENESS
EEEINPRRST ENTERPRISE
EEEINPRSTV VESPERTINE
EEEINPRTVV PREVENTIVE
EEEINRRRTV IRREVERENT
EEEINRSSTW WESTERNISE
EEEINRSTWZ WESTERNIZE
EEEINSSTWY EYEWITNESS
EEEIOPRRRT REPERTOIRE
EEEIPRRSSV REPRESSIVE
EEEIPRSSVX EXPRESSIVE
EEEIRRRSTV RETRIEVERS
EEEIRSSTTV SERVIETTES
EEEIRSSTTW STREETWISE
EEEJRSSTTT JET-SETTERS
EEEKLNRSUV LEVERKUSEN
EEEKMRSSTU MUSKETEERS
EEELLNPRST REPELLENTS
EEELLNPSUV ELEVEN-PLUS
EEELLNRSST RELENTLESS
EEELMMOSTT METTLESOME
EEELMNOPST ELOPEMENTS

EEELMNOSTT NETTLESOME
EEELMNOTVV EVOLVEMENT
EEELMNSTTT SETTLEMENT
EEELNOPRTT OPEN LETTER
EEELNOSTTV NOVELETTES
EEELNOTTVW

TWELVE-TONE

EEELNRRTVY REVERENTLY
EEELNRSTTW NEWSLETTER
EEELORSVWW

WEREWOLVES

EEELPRRSVY PERVERSELY
EEEMNNORST MESENTERON
EEEMNNRSTT RESENTMENT
EEEMNORSST REMOTENESS
EEEMNRSTTV REVETMENTS
EEEENNSSUV UNEVENNESS
EEENORSTWZ SNEEZEWORT
EEENPRRSST PRESENTERS
EEENPRSSTX EXPERTNESS
EEENRRSSTW WESTERNERS
EEEOOPRSVX OVEREXPOSE
EEEOPRRRTX RE-EXPORTER
EEEOPRSTTY STEREOTYPE
EEEORRRSTV RETROVERSE
EEEPPPRSTU PUPPETEERS
EEEPRRRSSV PRESERVERS
EEEPRSTTTY TYPESETTER
EEFFFKLRSU KERFUFFLES
EEFFGIINRV FIVE-FINGER
EEFFGINORR FOREFINGER
EEFFHINSTT FIFTEENTHS
EEFFHLRRSU REFRESHFUL
EEFFHLRSSU RESHUFFLES
EEFFILSUVY EFFUSIVELY
EEFFINOSSV OFFENSIVES
EEFFINRSST STIFFENERS
EEFFIORRST FORFEITERS
EEFFIORRTU FORFEITURE
EEFFLORSST EFFORTLESS
EEFFNORRTY EFFRONTERY
EEFGHHIILR HIGH RELIEF
EEFGHINNRS FRESHENING
EEFGHINRRS REFRESHING
EEFGHINRRT FRIGHTENER
EEFGHIRRST FREIGHTERS
EEFGHLOOSS GOOSEFLESH
EEFGIILLNS SINGLE FILE
EEFGIILNRV FREE-LIVING
EEFGILLNRU REFUELLING
EEFGILLNTY FLEETINGLY
EEFGILNRTW LEFT-WINGER
EEFGIMNNRT FERMENTING
EEFGINNRRT REFRINGENT
EEFGINORRS FOREIGNERS
EEFGINPRRR PREFERRING
EEFGKLLNOT GENTLEFOLK
EEFGLLMNOR FELLMONGER
EEFGLLNUVY VENGEFULLY

EEFGLMNNTU ENGULFMENT
EEFHHLORSS HORSEFLESH
EEFHIINRRS REFINISHER
EEFHILLSSV SHELF LIVES
EEFHILNSSS FLESHINESS
EEFHILORSS HORSEFLIES
EEFHILOSSU HOUSEFLIES
EEFHILRSVY FEVERISHLY
EEFHLNOORS HOLOFERNES
EEFHNORTTU FOURTEENTH
EEFIILLMPS SIMPLE LIFE
EEFIILMRSU EMULSIFIER
EEFIILNSSW WIFELINESS
EEFIILRRST FERTILISER
EEFIILRRTZ FERTILIZER
EEFIIMNNNU UNFEMININE
EEFIINNNRS SINN FEINER
EEFIINRRST FINISTERRE
EEFIKLLORW FLOWER-LIKE
EEFIKLORST FOREST-LIKE
EEFILLLSSY LIFELESSLY
EEFILLNOTU FEUILLETON
EEFILLSSTY LIFESTYLES
EEFILMRSTT FILMSETTER
EEFILNNORT FLORENTINE
EEFILNPPTT FELT-TIP PEN
EEFILNRTUV INTERFLUVE
EEFINNORRT INTERFERON
EEFINNQRTU INFREQUENT
EEFIOPRRST PROFITEERS
EEFIORRRTX FOX TERRIER
EEFIORRSTT FORSTERITE
EEFIRRRSTU FRUITERERS
EEFKLNOOST FOLKESTONE
EEFLLLSSSY SELFLESSLY
EEFLLNTUVY EVENTFULLY
EEFLLORSSW FLOWERLESS
EEFLMORRSU REMORSEFUL
EEFLNNTUUV UNEVENTFUL
EEFLNOSSUW WOEFULNESS
EEFLNQRTUY FREQUENTLY
EEFLNRSSUU RUEFULNESS
EEFLNSSSUU USEFULNESS
EEFMOPRRRS PERFORMERS
EEFNNORRRU FORERUNNER
EEFNNORSSZ FROZENNESS
EEFNOOPRRS FOR OPENERS
EEFNOORSTY FESTOONERY
EEFORRSSST FORTRESSES
EEGGHILNRT GREEN LIGHT
EEGGIINNRZ ENERGIZING
EEGGIMNNST SEGMENTING
EEGGINOTUV GIVE TONGUE
EEGGINRRSS REGRESSING
EEGGINRRTT REGRETTING
EEGGISSTUV SUGGESTIVE
EEGHHIISTT EIGHTIETHS
EEGHHILNST THE ENGLISH
EEGHHINOTT EIGHTH NOTE

EEGHHINSSS HIGHNESSES
EEGHHIRSTT HIGH STREET
EEGHHORSTU

SEE-THROUGH

EEGHIKLRSU KIESELGUHR
EEGHIKNSTW WEEKNIGHTS
EEGHILMNNS ENGLISHMEN
EEGHILNOOP PIGEONHOLE
EEGHILNRST SHELTERING
EEGHILNSTT LENGTHIEST
EEGHILNSTY SEETHINGLY
EEGHILNWYZ WHEEZINGLY
EEGHILOOST THEOLOGIES,

THEOLOGISE

EEGHILOOTZ THEOLOGIZE
EEGHILSSTW WEIGHTLESS
EEGHIMNOOS HOMOGENISE
EEGHIMNOOZ HOMOGENIZE
EEGHINOPST PHOSGENITE
EEGHINPRST REGENTSHIP
EEGHINRTVY EVERYTHING
EEGHIORTVW OVERWEIGHT
EEGHIRSSST SIGHTSEERS
EEGHLOORTY HETEROLOGY
EEGHMNOSST THEME

SONGS

EEGHNNORRS

GREENHORNS

EEGHNNRSTT STRENGTHEN
EEGHNOORTY

HETEROGONY

EEGHOSSTUU GUESTHOUSE
EEGIIILMST LEGITIMISE
EEGIIILMTZ LEGITIMIZE
EEGIIKLPRS KRIEGSPIEL
EEGIILNNNV ENLIVENING
EEGIILNSTV TELEVISING
EEGIILPRSV PRIVILEGES
EEGIINNOPR PIONEERING
EEGIINNQTU QUIETENING
EEGIINPRRV REPRIEVING
EEGIINPRVW PREVIEWING
EEGIINRRTV RETRIEVING
EEGIINRSSV INGRESSIVE
EEGIIRRSST REGISTRIES
EEGIKLLNNN KENNELLING
EEGILMNORS MONGRELISE
EEGILMNORZ MONGRELIZE
EEGILNNOPV ENVELOPING
EEGILNNRSY SNEERINGLY
EEGILNNSSS SINGLENESS
EEGILNNSUY UNSEEINGLY
EEGILNOSST TELEGNOSIS
EEGILNPPRX PERPLEXING
EEGILNPSWY SWEEPINGLY
EEGILNRSTT RESETTLING
EEGILNRSTW SWELTERING
EEGIMNNOTT MIGNONETTE
EEGIMNNTTU INTEGUMENT

EEGIMNOORT GONIOMETER
EEGIMNOPPT PEEPING TOM
EEGIMNOPRW EMPOWERING
EEGIMNPPRT PRE-EMPTING
EEGINNOOTT OTTO ENGINE
EEGINNOPPS PEPSINOGEN
EEGINNPRST PRESENTING
EEGINNPRTV PREVENTING
EEGINOPSSY PYOGENESIS
EEGINORRSS REGRESSION
EEGINORSSV SOVEREIGNS
EEGINORSTY GENEROSITY
EEGINORSXY OXYGENISER
EEGINORXYZ OXYGENIZER
EEGINPRRSS REPRESSING
EEGINPRRSV PRESERVING
EEGINPRRTV PERVERTING
EEGINPRSSX EXPRESSING
EEGINPRSTT PRESETTING
EEGINQRSTU REQUESTING
EEGLLLOSWY YELLOWLEGS
EEGLLNOOSY SELENOLOGY
EEGLLOOPSY SPELEOLOGY
EEGLLORRSV GROVELLERS
EEGLMORSUY GRUESOMELY
EEGLNORSTT LORGNETTES
EEGLNORSUY GENEROUSLY
EEGLOOORRST ERGOSTEROL
EEGMNNOORT
MONTENEGRO
EEGMNNORTV
GOVERNMENT
EEGNNORSUU
UNGENEROUS
EEGNNOTTXY OXYGEN
TENT
EEGOOPSSST GOOSESTEPS
EEGOPRRSSS PROGRESSES
EEGOPRSTUU PORTUGUESE
EEGOQRSSTU GROTESQUES
EEGORRRSST RETROGRESS
EEHHILMPTT PITH HELMET
EEHHILPSSY SHEEPISHLY
EEHHIMNOST HENOTHEISM
EEHHINOSSS SHOESHINES
EEHHINOSTT HENOTHEIST
EEHHINRTTT THIRTEENTH
EEHHIOPSTW WHITE HOPES
EEHHIORRSS SHIRE HORSE
EEHHIORSTW WHITE HORSE
EEHHIOSTUW WHITE HOUSE
EEHHOORSSS HORSESHOES
EEHHOORSUW
WHOREHOUSE
EEHHOPSSTY HYPOTHESES
EEHIILMPTU EPITHELIUM
EEHIILNOPR PERIHELION
EEHIIMNNOT METHIONINE
EEHIINNSTT NINETIETHS

EEHIJRSTTT THE JITTERS
EEHIKNPSSS SHEEPSKINS
EEHIKOSSTT TO THE SKIES
EEHIKPPTUW KEEP UP WITH
EEHILLLMSW MILLWHEELS
EEHILLRSWW WELL-WISHER
EEHILMNOSS HOMELINESS
EEHILMOPRT THERMOPILE
EEHILMORTY HELIOMETRY
EEHILNNOOS HOLES IN ONE
EEHILNNRTY INHERENTLY
EEHILNOSSS HOLINESSES
EEHILOOPRT HELIOTROPE
EEHILOPRST PRIEST-HOLE
EEHILORSST HOSTELRIES
EEHILOSTTU SILHOUETTE
EEHILPRSTU SPHERULITE
EEHIMMOOSV HOME
MOVIES
EEHIMMPSSU EUPHEMISMS
EEHIMNNOTY IN THE MONEY
EEHIMNOPPS HIPPOMENES
EEHIMNOPRT HEMIPTERON
EEHIMNPRST RESHIPMENT
EEHINNOPRS PREHENSION
EEHINNOPRT INTERPHONE
EEHINNORST RHINESTONE
EEHINOOPRS IONOSPHERE
EEHINSSSTX SIXTH SENSE
EEHINSSSTY SYNTHESISE
EEHINSSTTX SIXTEENTHS
EEHINSSTYZ SYNTHESIZE
EEHINSTTTW TWENTIETHS
EEHIOPPRRS PROPHESIER
EEHIOPPRSS PROPHESIES
EEHIOSSUVW HOUSEWIVES
EEHIPRRSSW WHISPERERS
EEHKKOOPYY
HOKEY-POKEY
EEHKMOOSSU
SMOKEHOUSE
EEHKNOORTT TENTERHOOK
EEHLLLPSSY HELPLESSLY
EEHLLMNOOP MELLOPHONE
EEHLLNOOPS HENLE'S LOOP
EEHLLNOPST HELLESPONT
EEHLLOPSSY HOPELESSLY
EEHLLORSST HOSTELLERS
EEHLMNOOYZ
HOLOENZYME
EEHLMNORTY HEMELYTRON
EEHLMORSST MOTHERLESS
EEHLNOOSSV SHOVELNOSE
EEHLNOOSTW WHOLE
NOTES
EEHLOORSUW LOWER
HOUSE
EEHMNNNOOP
PHENOMENON

EEHMNOOPRT
PHONOMETER
EEHMNOORSW
HORSEWOMEN
EEHMNOORTY
HETERONOMY
EEHMNORSTT NETHERMOST
EEHMNPSTTU UMPTEENTHS
EEHMOOPRTT PHOTOMETER
EEHMOPRSSU MORPHEUSES
EEHMOPRSTT STEPMOTHER
EEHMOQRSUU
HUMORESQUE
EEHMRRSSTY RHYMESTERS
EEHNNOPSSY PHONEYNESS
EEHNNORRRT NORTHERNER
EEHNNOSSST HONESTNESS
EEHNOORTTU ON THE
OUTER
EEHNOPSSTU PENTHOUSES
EEHNOPSTUY HYPOTENUSE
EEHNORRSTU SOUTHERNER
EEHNOSSTTW WHETSTONES
EEHNPPRSSU PEN PUSHERS
EEHNRSSSTU HUNTRESSES
EEHOOPRRSW
HORSEPOWER
EEHOOPRSUW
POWERHOUSE
EEHOOPRTTY HETEROTOPY
EEHOOPSTTY OSTEOPHYTE
EEHOORSSTU STOREHOUSE
EEHOOSTTTW SWEET
TOOTH
EEHOPPRSUU UPPER HOUSE
EEHOPRRSTV SHREVEPORT
EEIIINQSTU INEQUITIES
EEIIKLNPRW PERIWINKLE
EEIILLMMRT MILLIMETRE
EEIILLNSSV LIVELINESS
EEIILMNSST TIMELINESS
EEIILNNRRT INTERLINER
EEIILNOSTV TELEVISION
EEIILORSTT TOILETRIES
EEIILPRRST PRIESTLIER
EEIILRRSST STERILISER
EEIILRRSTZ STERILIZER
EEIIMNNPTT IMPENITENT
EEIIMNORST ENORMITIES
EEIIMNPRUU EPINEURIUM
EEIIMNRSTX IN EXTREMIS
EEIIMNRTTW WINTERTIME
EEIIMNRTZZ INTERMEZZI
EEIIMOPRST EPITOMISER
EEIIMOPRTZ EPITOMIZER
EEIIMPRSSV IMPRESSIVE,
PERMISSIVE
EEIINNNNTY NINETY-NINE
EEIINNNSTT INSENTIENT

EEIINNRTTW INTERTWINE
EEIINNSSSW SINEWINESS
EEIINNSSTT INTESTINES
EEIINNSTTX INEXISTENT
EEIINOPRTT PETITIONER,
   REPETITION
EEIINRSSST SENSITISER
EEIINRSSTZ SENSITIZER
EEIINRSTVW INTERVIEWS
EEIIORRSST ROTISSERIE
EEIIPQRSTU PERQUISITE
EEIIQRSSTU REQUISITES
EEIJLORSSV OVERIJSSEL
EEIJMNNNOT ENJOINMENT
EEIKLMORST KILOMETRES
EEIKMORRTW TIMEWORKER
EEIKMRSSTU MUSKETRIES
EEIKNRRSTT RENT STRIKE
EEIKORRRWW
   WIREWORKER
EEILLLPSTV SPLIT-LEVEL
EEILLMMORT IMMORTELLE
EEILLMNOST EMOLLIENTS
EEILLMNSSS SMELLINESS
EEILLMPPPR PEPPER MILL
EEILLMSSTY TIMELESSLY
EEILLNNOSS LONELINESS
EEILLNOSSV LOVELINESS
EEILLNRSSV SNIVELLERS
EEILLORSTT TITLE ROLES
EEILLRSSTY TIRELESSLY
EEILMMNPST IMPLEMENTS
EEILMMORST MILOMETERS
EEILMNNSTT ENLISTMENT
EEILMNORSS SOLEMNISER
EEILMNORSZ SOLEMNIZER
EEILMNOSST MILESTONES
EEILMNOSSU MOUSSELINE
EEILMNPPRS PIMPERNELS
EEILMNPSSS SIMPLENESS
EEILMOPRSY POLYMERISE
EEILMOPRYZ POLYMERIZE
EEILMORSTY TIRESOMELY
EEILMOSSTV MOTIVELESS
EEILMOSSVW SEMIVOWELS
EEILMPRSTU PULSIMETER
EEILNNOQTU INELOQUENT
EEILNNPTTY PENITENTLY
EEILNNSSST SILENTNESS
EEILNOPRRT INTERLOPER
EEILNOPSST POLITENESS
EEILNPRTXY INEXPERTLY
EEILOOPRST TELIOSPORE
EEILOPRSTX EXPLOITERS
EEILOPSSVX EXPLOSIVES
EEILORRSTU IRRESOLUTE
EEILORRTTW ROTTWEILER
EEILPPRTXY PERPLEXITY
EEILPPSTUV SUPPLETIVE

EEILPRRSTY SPERRYLITE
EEILPRRSUV PULVERISER
EEILPRRUVZ PULVERIZER
EEILPRSSTY PERISTYLES
EEILRSSSST RESISTLESS
EEIMMMRSTU SUMMERTIME
EEIMMOPRRV PRIME MOVER
EEIMMRSSST MESMERISTS
EEIMMRSSTY SYMMETRISE
EEIMMRSTYZ SYMMETRIZE
EEIMNNNRTT INTERNMENT
EEIMNNOPTT PENTIMENTO
EEIMNNORST MINESTRONE
EEIMNNRSTT INTERMENTS
EEIMNNSSST SENTIMENTS
EEIMNNSSTU MINUTENESS
EEIMNNSTTV INVESTMENT
EEIMNOPPRT PRE-EMPTION
EEIMNOPRTU PERITONEUM
EEIMNOPSTX EXEMPTIONS
EEIMNORRSS SERMONISER
EEIMNORRSZ SERMONIZER
EEIMNORRTT NITROMETER
EEIMNORTZZ INTERMEZZO
EEIMNPPPRT PEPPERMINT
EEIMNPRSTU EPISTERNUM
EEIMNRSSSS REMISSNESS
EEIMNRSSTU TERMINUSES
EEIMNRSSTW WESTERNISM
EEIMOPRRST SPIROMETER,
   TEMPORISER
EEIMOPRRTZ TEMPORIZER
EEIMOPRSTU PERIOSTEUM
EEIMPPRRUU PUERPERIUM
EEIMPRSTUV RESUMPTIVE
EEIMRRSSTT TRIMESTERS
EEIMRSSSST MISTRESSES
EEIMRSSSTY SYSTEMISER
EEIMRSSTYZ SYSTEMIZER
EEINNNSSTT INTENTNESS
EEINNOPRSS PENSIONERS
EEINNOPRST PRETENSION,
   TIN OPENERS
EEINNOPRTV PREVENTION
EEINNORTVW INTERWOVEN
EEINNOSSTX EXTENSIONS
EEINNPRTTU TURPENTINE
EEINNPSSSU SUPINENESS
EEINNQSSUU UNIQUENESS
EEINOPPRST PEPTONISER
EEINOPPRTZ PEPTONIZER
EEINOPQTTU EQUIPOTENT
EEINOPRRSS REPRESSION
EEINOPRRST INTERPOSER
EEINOPRRSV PERVERSION
EEINOPRSSV RESPONSIVE
EEINOPRSSX EXPRESSION
EEINOPRSXY EPOXY RESIN
EEINOPRTXY PYROXENITE

EEINOQRSTU QUESTIONER
EEINOSSTVV VOTIVENESS
EEINPRSSTT PERSISTENT,
   PRETTINESS
EEINPSSSUV SUSPENSIVE
EEIOPPRRST PROPERTIES
EEIOPPRSSV OPPRESSIVE
EEIOPPRRSTV RESORPTIVE
EEIOPRSSST STEREOPSIS
EEIOPRSTTT OPERETTIST
EEIOPRSTTU PIROUETTES
EEIOPSSSSV POSSESSIVE
EEIORRRRST TERRORISER
EEIORRRRTZ TERRORIZER
EEIORRRSST ROISTERERS
EEIORRRSSV RESERVOIRS
EEIPPRTTUY PERPETUITY
EEIPRRSSSU PRESSURISE
EEIPRRSSUZ PRESSURIZE
EEIPRRSTVY PERVERSITY
EEIPRRTTWY TYPEWRITER
EEIPRSSSTT STEPSISTER
EEIRRSSSTV RESERVISTS
EEJMNNORUY JOURNEYMEN
EEJMNNOSTY ENJOYMENTS
EEKLLNOPSW
   WELL-SPOKEN
EEKLOOPPRW
   WORKPEOPLE
EEKLORSSTW STEELWORKS
EELLMNOOSS LEMON SOLES
EELLMNOSSW
   MELLOWNESS
EELLNNSSSU SULLENNESS
EELLNOPPRT PROPELLENT
EELLNOQTUY ELOQUENTLY
EELLNOSSTY TONELESSLY
EELLNSSTUY TUNELESSLY
EELLOPPRRS PROPELLERS
EELLORSTUY RESOLUTELY
EELLRSSSTY RESTLESSLY
EELMMNOPTY
   EMPLOYMENT
EELMMNNOSTU
   EMOLUMENTS
EELMNNORST ENROLMENTS
EELMNNOSSS SOLEMNNESS
EELMNOOSSZ ZOOM LENSES
EELMNPPSTU SUPPLEMENT
EELMNPTUZZ PUZZLEMENT
EELMOOPSTT TOTEM POLES
EELNOPRSTW SPLEENWORT
EELNORSTUV VOLUNTEERS
EELNPPRSSU PURPLENESS
EELNPPSSSU SUPPLENESS
EELOOPRSTT PROTOSTELE
EELOPRRSTU POULTERERS
EELOPRSSTY PROSELYTES
EELORSSUVY YOURSELVES

456

EELPRRSTTU SPLUTTERER
EELPSSTTUX SEXTUPLETS
EEMMNOORST
METRONOMES
EEMNNOPSTT PENTSTEMON
EEMNNRRSUY
NURSERYMEN
EEMNOORSSS MOROSENESS
EEMNOORTTY
ENTEROTOMY
EEMOOPPRRT PRO
TEMPORE
EEMOORSTTY STEREOTOMY
EEMOPPRRTY
PEREMPTORY, PRE-EMPTORY
EEMORSSTTU METOESTRUS
EEMPRRSTTU TRUMPETERS
EEMQRSSTUU SEQUESTRUM
EENNNNOOSS
NO-NONSENSE
EENNOOOSST ON ONE'S
TOES
EENNOPSSTT POTENTNESS
EENNORSSTT ROTTENNESS
EENNOSSSUV VENOUSNESS
EENOOPPSSS POPE'S NOSES
EENOPPRRSS PROPERNESS
EEOPPPPRST PEPPER POTS
EEOPPPRRTW PEPPERWORT
EEOPPPRRSU PRESUPPOSE
EEOPPRRSUW
SUPERPOWER
EEOPPRRSSS PREPOSSESS
EEOPRRSSTT PROTESTERS
EEOPRSTTYY STEREOTYPY
EEOORRSTVX EXTROVERTS
EEORSSSTUW
SOU'WESTERS
EERRSSTTTU STUTTERERS
EFFFILNSSU FLUFFINESS
EFFGHIINRS FISH FINGER
EFFGIINNST STIFFENING
EFFGIINORT FORFEITING
EFFGILLNOT TELLING-OFF
EFFGINOPRR PROFFERING
EFFGINOSTT OFFSETTING
EFFGINRSSU SUFFERINGS
EFFIIKLOSS KISS OF LIFE
EFFIILRSTU FRUIT FLIES
EFFIIORRST FORTIFIERS
EFFIIQSSTU SQUIFFIEST
EFFILLMNTU FULFILMENT
EFFINNSSSU SNUFFINESS
EFFINSSSTU STUFFINESS
EFFNNOOSTU OFF ONE'S
NUT
EFGGHIINRT FREIGHTING
EFGGIILNNR FINGERLING
EFGGIILNNY FEIGNINGLY

EFGGIINNRR RING FINGER
EFGGINOORS FOREGOINGS
EFGGINORTT FORGETTING
EFGHHIILRS HIGH-FLIERS
EFGHIIKNRS KINGFISHER
EFGHIILSTT FLIGHTIEST
EFGHIIPRST PRISEFIGHT
EFGHIIPRTZ PRIZEFIGHT
EFGHILLSST FLIGHTLESS
EFGHILORTV OVERFLIGHT
EFGHILSTWY FLYWEIGHTS
EFGHIMNORS FISHMONGER
EFGHINRRTU FURTHERING
EFGHIORSST GIFT HORSES
EFGHLLLNTU FULL-LENGTH
EFGHLLNORU FLUGELHORN
EFGHOOPPRR FROGHOPPER
EFGIIILNNR FIRING LINE
EFGIILNQUY LIQUEFYING
EFGIIMNORS FOREIGNISM
EFGIINNNTU FINE-TUNING
EFGIINPRST FINGERTIPS
EFGIINPRSY PRESIGNIFY
EFGIINPRTY PETRIFYING
EFGIINRRTT FRITTERING
EFGIINRRTY TERRIFYING
EFGIINRSTU SURFEITING
EFGIINSTTY TESTIFYING
EFGILLLUUY GUILEFULLY
EFGILLNNNU FUNNELLING
EFGILLORRW FLOWER GIRL
EFGILNORST FOSTERLING
EFGILNORVY OVERFLYING
EFGILNRSTU FLUSTERING
EFGILNRTTU FLUTTERING
EFGIMNOPRR PERFORMING
EFGINNOOST FESTOONING
EFGINNORUV UNFORGIVEN
EFGINOPRSS PROFESSING
EFGINPRTUY PUTREFYING
EFGINPSTUY STUPEFYING
EFGLOOSTUV
TUGS-OF-LOVE
EFHHIOORTT HIT THE ROOF
EFHHLOSSTU HOT FLUSHES
EFHIIKNSSV FISH KNIVES
EFHIILNSST FILTHINESS
EFHIILRSSV SILVERFISH
EFHIINSSST SHIFTINESS
EFHIIRSTTT THRIFTIEST
EFHIISSSTT FETISHISTS
EFHILLOPSW FELLOWSHIP
EFHILOPRST SHOPLIFTER
EFHILORRSU FLOURISHER
EFHILORSSU FLOURISHES
EFHILRSSTT THRIFTLESS
EFHIMNNOPR PHENFORMIN
EFHINORSST FROTHINESS
EFHLLOOPRS SHELLPROOF

EFHLLOSSUU FULL HOUSES
EFHLOOPSSU FLOPHOUSES
EFHNORSTUX FOXHUNTERS
EFIIIINNTV INFINITIVE
EFIIILMPRS SIMPLIFIER
EFIIILNNTY INFINITELY
EFIIIMNNTY FEMININITY
EFIIKNRSSS FRISKINESS
EFIILLLSST STILL LIFES
EFIILLNRSS FRILLINESS
EFIILMNSSS FLIMSINESS
EFIILNNSST FLINTINESS
EFIILOPRSU PILIFEROUS
EFIILPRSTT FILTER TIPS
EFIILRSTTU STULTIFIER
EFIIMORRSU FOURIERISM
EFIINORSUV VINIFEROUS
EFIINRSSTU FRUITINESS
EFIINRSSZZ FRIZZINESS
EFIIORRSTU FOURIERIST
EFIKLNOSSS FOLKSINESS
EFILLMORST STELLIFORM
EFILLNSSUW WILFULNESS
EFILLOOPRW LOW PROFILE
EFILLPSTUY SPITEFULLY
EFILMNPTTU UPLIFTMENT
EFILMOOPRS SIMFEROPOL
EFILNNSSSU SINFULNESS
EFILNOPPSS FLOPPINESS
EFILNORTWW TWINFLOWER
EFILOPRSST PROFITLESS
EFIMNORSTU MISFORTUNE
EFIMOOPRSU POMIFEROUS
EFIMORRSST FIRESTORMS
EFINNORRTY FORTY-NINER
EFINOOPRSS PROFESSION
EFINOORSSU SONIFEROUS
EFINORSSST FROSTINESS
EFINORSSWZ FROWZINESS
EFINORSTTU STONE FRUIT
EFIOOPRRSU PORIFEROUS
EFIOORSSSU OSSIFEROUS
EFIOORSSTX SIX-FOOTERS
EFIOPRSTTU PETIT FOURS
EFIORSTTTU OUTFITTERS
EFJLNOSSUY JOYFULNESS
EFKNOOPSST SOFT-SPOKEN
EFKOORRSTU FOUR-STROKE
EFLLMORSSY FORMLESSLY
EFLLOPRUWY POWERFULLY
EFLMNOOORW
MOONFLOWER
EFLMOOOORTY TOMFOOLERY
EFLNORSSUW SUNFLOWERS
EFLOOPRSTW FLOWERPOTS
EFLOPPRSUU PURPOSEFUL
EFNNOORRSU NONFERROUS
EFOOPRRSSS PROFESSORS
EFOOPRRSTU FOUR-POSTER

EGGGIINNRS SNIGGERING
EGGGIINRRT TRIGGERING
EGGGINORSS GROGGINESS
EGGGINSSTU SUGGESTING
EGGHHIPRSU HIPHUGGERS
EGGHIILNNV INVEIGHING
EGGHIILNNT LIGHTENING
EGGHIINNTT TIGHTENING
EGGHINNORU ROUGHENING
EGGHINNOTU TOUGHENING
EGGIIILNNV INVEIGLING
EGGIIILMMNR GLIMMERING
EGGIILNNST GLISTENING
EGGIILNOUZ EULOGIZING
EGGIILNRTT GLITTERING
EGGIILNRVY GRIEVINGLY
EGGIINNTTV VIGNETTING
EGGILLNORV GROVELLING
EGGILMOOST GEMOLOGIST
EGGILNSSUY GUESSINGLY
EGGILOOSST GEOLOGISTS
EGGINNORSS ENGROSSING
EGGINNPSTU TUNING PEGS
EGGINNRSTU GINGER NUTS
EGGINOORSV GOINGS-OVER
EGGINOPRRU REGROUPING
EGGINOSSTU SUGGESTION
EGGIOPRSTT GET TO GRIPS
EGGIORRSTU OUTRIGGERS
EGGLLOOOPX GOOGOLPLEX
EGGLOOPTYY EGYPTOLOGY
EGGLOORSUY GORGEOUSLY
EGHHHIORSS HIGH HORSES
EGHHIINRTT IN THE RIGHT
EGHHIIPRST HIGH PRIEST
EGHHIJMPRU HIGH JUMPER
EGHHILOPRY HIEROGLYPH
EGHHILOSTU LIGHTHOUSE
EGHHINORTU IN THE ROUGH
EGHHOORSUU
   ROUGHHOUSE
EGHIIINNRT INHERITING
EGHIIKNNRT RETHINKING
EGHIILNRST SLITHERING
EGHIILNRSV SHRIVELING
EGHIILNTVY THIEVINGLY
EGHIIMMNRS SHIMMERING
EGHIIMNPRW WHIMPERING
EGHIIMNSST MIGHTINESS
EGHIINNNRS ENSHRINING
EGHIINNPRT TREPHINING
EGHIINNPSS ENSIGNSHIP
EGHIINORTZ THEORIZING
EGHIINPRSW WHISPERING
EGHIINSSTY HYGIENISTS
EGHIINSTUX EXTINGUISH
EGHILLNOST HOSTELLING
EGHILLNOSV SHOVELLING
EGHILMOOOS HOMOLOGISE

EGHILMOOOZ HOMOLOGIZE
EGHILNNOST NEON LIGHTS
EGHILNORVY HOVERINGLY
EGHILNSSST SLIGHTNESS
EGHILOOPPT PHLOGOPITE
EGHILOORST RHEOLOGIST
EGHILOOSTT ETHOLOGIST
EGHILOSSTT GHOSTLIEST
EGHILRSTVY VERY LIGHTS
EGHIMNORST SMOTHERING
EGHINNNORT ENTHRONING
EGHINNORST SHORTENING
EGHINNRSSU HUNGRINESS
EGHINORSST SHOESTRING
EGHINRSTTU SHUTTERING
EGHIOPRSTT TIGHTROPES
EGHIORSSTV OVERSIGHTS
EGHIORSTTW GHOSTWRITE
EGHIORTTWY TROY WEIGHT
EGHJMNPTUU JUMP THE
   GUN
EGHLLOORSY GLORY HOLES
EGHLNOOPRY PHRENOLOGY
EGHLOOPPSY PSEPHOLOGY
EGHLOPPRTY PETROGLYPH
EGHMNOOOSU
   HOMOGENOUS
EGHMOOOTYZ
   HOMOZYGOTE
EGIIILMMST LEGITIMISM
EGIIILMSTT LEGITIMIST
EGIIILNORR IRRELIGION
EGIIIMNNOS IGNOMINIES
EGIIIMNNST MENINGITIS
EGIIKLNNSS KINGLINESS
EGIIKNPPRS SKIPPERING
EGIIKNRSTT SKITTERING
EGIILLNNSV SNIVELLING
EGIILLNOTU GUILLOTINE
EGIILLNRVY REVILINGLY
EGIILLNSVW SWIVELLING
EGIILNOPTX EXPLOITING
EGIILNRSSS GRISLINESS
EGIILNRVVY REVIVINGLY
EGIILNSSTU GUILTINESS
EGIILOPSTT EPIGLOTTIS
EGIILRSSTT GRISTLIEST
EGIIMMNORZ MEMORIZING
EGIIMNNNOT MENTIONING
EGIIMNNOST MOISTENING
EGIIMNPRSS IMPRESSING
EGIIMNPRST SPRINGTIME
EGIIMNPRTT PERMITTING
EGIINNNOPS PENSIONING
EGIINNORSS INGRESSION
EGIINNPRRT REPRINTING
EGIINNRRSU REINSURING
EGIINNSSST STINGINESS
EGIINNSSTW WITNESSING

EGIINPPRRS PERSPIRING
EGIINPRSST PERSISTING,
   SPRINGIEST
EGIINRSSTT GRITTINESS,
   STRINGIEST
EGIINRTTTW TWITTERING
EGIINSTTTV VIGNETTIST
EGIJKNNSTU JUNKETINGS
EGIJNNORUY JOURNEYING
EGIKLNNOOS INGLENOOKS
EGIKLNNPSU SPELUNKING
EGIKLNORVY REVOKINGLY
EGIKNNOORS SNOOKERING
EGIKNNORTW NETWORKING
EGILLMMNPU PUMMELLING
EGILLMOSTU GUILLEMOTS
EGILLNNNTU TUNNELLING
EGILLNNOTW WELLINGTON
EGILLNOPPR PROPELLING
EGILLNORWY LOWERINGLY
EGILLNOSTU OUTSELLING
EGILLNPRSW WELLSPRING
EGILLNTUXY EXULTINGLY
EGILLORSSY SYLLOGISER
EGILLORSYZ SYLLOGIZER
EGILMMNORS MONGRELISM
EGILMMNPTU PLUMMETING
EGILMNOOSS GLOOMINESS,
   NEOLOGISMS
EGILMNOPTT MELTING POT
EGILMNOSUU LEGUMINOUS
EGILMNPTTY TEMPTINGLY
EGILMOOSSY SEISMOLOGY
EGILNNOSST SINGLETONS
EGILNNRRUY UNERRINGLY
EGILNNRSSU NURSELINGS
EGILNNSTTU UNSETTLING
EGILNOOOST OENOLOGIST
EGILNOOPST PENOLOGIST
EGILNORRUV OVERRULING
EGILNOSSSS GLOSSINESS
EGILNOSTUU LOUNGE SUIT
EGILNPRSSY PRESSINGLY
EGILNQSTUY QUESTINGLY
EGILNRSVWY SWERVINGLY
EGILOORSST SEROLOGIST
EGILOOSSTX SEXOLOGIST
EGILORSUVY GRIEVOUSLY
EGILOSUUXY EXIGUOUSLY
EGIMNNOORR IRONMONGER
EGIMNNORTT TORMENTING
EGIMNNORTU REMOUNTING
EGIMNOORTY GONIOMETRY
EGIMNPRSSU GRUMPINESS
EGIMNPRTTU TRUMPETING
EGIMOOPRST GEOTROPISM
EGINNOPSSS SPONGINESS
EGINNRSSTU INSURGENTS
EGINNRSSTY TRYINGNESS

EGINNRSTTU ENTRUSTING
EGINNRSTUW WET-NURSING
EGINNRSUVW UNSWERVING
EGINOOPRRT PROGENITOR
EGINOPPRRS PROSPERING
EGINOPPRSS OPPRESSING
EGINOPPRST STOPPERING
EGINOPRRTU INTERGROUP
EGINOPRSUY PERIGYNOUS
EGINOPSSSS POSSESSING
EGINORRSTW SONGWRITER
EGINORSSTT GROTTINESS
EGINORSTUW OUTSWINGER
EGINPRRSSU PRESSURING
EGINPRSTTU SPUTTERING
EGINRSTTTU STUTTERING
EGJLLOORRY JOLLY ROGER
EGJLMNOPRU
   LONG-JUMPER
EGLLMORSSY GORMLESSLY
EGLLMORSUU GLOMERULUS
EGLMNOOOSU
   MONOLOGUES
EGLMNOOOTY
   ENTOMOLOGY
EGLMNOORUY
   NUMEROLOGY
EGLMNOOYYZ
   ENZYMOLOGY
EGLNNOSSUU SUN
   LOUNGES
EGLOOOORRWW
   WOOLGROWER
EGMMNOORTY
   MONTGOMERY
EGMMNOPRSY
   GYMNOSPERM
EGMNNOOOSU
   MONOGENOUS
EGMOORSSTU
   GUESTROOMS
EGNNNRRSUU
   GUNRUNNERS
EGNNORSSST STRONGNESS
EGNORRSTUV OVERSTRUNG
EGNORSSSST SONGSTRESS
EGNORSSTUY YOUNGSTERS
EHHIILSTVY THIEVISHLY
EHHIIMSTTW WHITESMITH
EHHIIRSTTT THIRTIETHS
EHHILOPRSU HEROPHILUS
EHHILOPSTU THEOPHILUS
EHHILOPTTY LITHOPHYTE
EHHILORTWW WORTHWHILE
EHHILRSSWY SHREWISHLY
EHHIMORSTT HITHERMOST
EHHIOPSSTY HYPOTHESIS
EHHLOOOOPPR LOPHOPHORE

EHHMNOOOPS
   HOMOPHONES
EHHMORSTTU HOME
   TRUTHS
EHHOOOPPRT PHOTOPHORE
EHIIILNPPP PHILIPPINE
EHIIILNPST PHILISTINE
EHIIKMRRSS SKIRMISHER
EHIIKMRSSS SKIRMISHES
EHIILLOOPS HELIOPOLIS
EHIILLOPSY LYOPHILISE
EHIILLOPYZ LYOPHILIZE
EHIILNOOPS EOSINOPHIL
EHIILNQRSU RELINQUISH
EHIILPRTTY TRIPHYLITE
EHIIMNPSSS IMPISHNESS
EHIIMOPRSV IMPOVERISH
EHIIMPPRSU UMPIRESHIP
EHIINNPRST INTERNSHIP
EHIIQSSSTU SQUISHIEST
EHIIRRSTTU URETHRITIS
EHIIRSSSTW IRISH STEWS
EHIIRSSTTT THIRSTIEST
EHIKNORSTW IN THE WORKS
EHILLNRSSS SHRILLNESS
EHILLNSTUV HUNTSVILLE
EHILMNOOOS HOMOLOSINE
EHILMNSSSU MULISHNESS
EHILMOPSTY POLYTHEISM
EHILNNOSSU UNHOLINESS
EHILNOPRTU NEUTROPHIL
EHILNSSSSU SLUSHINESS
EHILOPRSSU RUSSOPHILE
EHILOPSTTY POLYTHEIST
EHILORRTTY ERYTHRITOL
EHILPRSSUU SULPHURISE
EHILPRSUUZ SULPHURIZE
EHIMMNOOST MONOTHEISM
EHIMMOPRTU PROMETHIUM
EHIMNNPSTU PUNISHMENT
EHIMNOOSTT MONOTHEIST
EHIMNOPSSY SYMPHONIES
EHIMNOPSUU EUPHONIUMS
EHIMNORSUY HIERONYMUS
EHIMNSSTTY SYNTHETISM
EHIMORRSTT THERMISTOR
EHINNORSST THORNINESS
EHINNSSSTU NISSEN HUTS
EHINOOPSSU EUPHONIOUS
EHINOOSSTT TOOTHINESS
EHINOPPRTY PERIPHYTON
EHINOPPSSS POPISHNESS
EHINORSSTW WORTHINESS
EHINORSTUU RUTHENIOUS
EHINPPSSSU UPPISHNESS
EHINSSSTTY SYNTHESIST
EHINSSTTTY SYNTHETIST
EHIOQPRSTW POOR WHITES
EHIOORSSTX SIX-SHOOTER

EHIOPPRRSW WORSHIPPER
EHIOPRRSTY PREHISTORY
EHIOPRRTTY PYRRHOTITE
EHIOPRSSST PROSTHESIS
EHJMOPRSUW SHOW
   JUMPER
EHKOORRSSW
   WORKHORSES
EHLLNOOSSW
   HOLLOWNESS
EHLLRSSTUY RUTHLESSLY
EHLMNOPPTY NYMPHOLEPT
EHLMORSSUU
   HUMOURLESS
EHLNOOPRST NORTH POLES
EHLNOOPSXY XYLOPHONES
EHLNOORSSU HONOURLESS
EHLOORRRTY HOLY TERROR
EHLOPRSTUY UPHOLSTERY
EHMMOOPRSY
   MESOMORPHY
EHMMOORSUU
   HUMOURSOME
EHMNNOOOSY
   HONEYMOONS
EHMNOOPRTY
   NEPHROTOMY
EHMNOOSSST SMOOTHNESS
EHMNOPSTTU ON THE
   STUMP
EHMOOOPRSS
   SOPHOMORES
EHMOOPRTTY PHOTOMETRY
EHMOORRTTW
   MOTHERWORT
EHNNOPRTWY
   PENNYWORTH
EHNOOPPRRS PRONEPHROS
EHNOORRTVW
   OVERTHROWN
EHNOORTTWY
   NOTEWORTHY
EHNOOSSTUW TOWN
   HOUSES
EHNOPRSTTU POTHUNTERS
EHNOQSTTUU QUONSET
   HUT
EHNORSTWWY
   NEWSWORTHY
EHOOOPPRRS SPOROPHORE
EHOOOPRSSU POORHOUSES
EHOOPPRSTY SPOROPHYTE
EHOOPPRTTY TROPOPHYTE
EHOORRSTVW
   OVERTHROWS
EHOPPSTTUU UP THE SPOUT
EHORRSTTUV OVERTHRUST
EIIIINQSTU INIQUITIES
EIIILLLMRT MILLILITRE

EIIILMMSTT TIME LIMITS
EIIILORSTV VITRIOLISE
EIIILORTVZ VITRIOLIZE
EIIIMNORST MINORITIES
EIIIMNPSTU IMPUNITIES
EIIIMNRSST MINISTRIES
EIIIMPRSTU IMPURITIES
EIIIMPRSTV PRIMITIVES
EIIIMSSTVY EMISSIVITY
EIIINPRRST INSPIRITER
EIIIOPRRST PRIORITIES,
   PRIORITISE
EIIIOPRRTZ PRIORITIZE
EIIJLNTUVY JUVENILITY
EIIJMNRTUY INJURY TIME
EIIKLLORST KILOLITRES
EIIKLNNSSS SLINKINESS
EIIKLNORST TRISKELION
EIIKMNPSSS SKIMPINESS
EIIKNNNSSS SKINNINESS
EIIKNQRSSU QUIRKINESS
EIIILLLOSUV LOUISVILLE
EIIILMMNNU MILLENNIUM
EIIILMOPTY IMPOLITELY
EIIILMPRTU MULTIPLIER
EIIILLNOPST SEPTILLION
EIIILLNOSTX SEXTILLION
EIIILLPSSTY PITILESSLY
EIIILMMNNTY IMMINENTLY
EIIILMNNSTT INSTILMENT
EIIILMNOSST LENTISSIMO
EIIILMNOSSU LIMOUSINES
EIIILMNPPSS PIMPLINESS
EIIILMOSTTV LEITMOTIVS
EIIILNPPSSS SLIPPINESS
EIIILNPTUVY PUNITIVELY
EIIILOPSTVY POSITIVELY
EIIILPRSSST SPIRITLESS
EIIIMMPRSUY PERIMYSIUM
EIIMNNORSU REUNIONISM
EIIMNOPRRS IMPRISONER
EIIMNOPRSS IMPRESSION,
   PERMISSION
EIIMNORSSS REMISSIONS
EIIMOOPSTY EPISIOTOMY
EIIMOPRRSV IMPROVISER
EIIMOPRSUV IMPERVIOUS
EIIMORSSTU MOISTURISE
EIIMORSTUZ MOISTURIZE
EIIMPSSSST PESSIMISTS
EIINNNOSTT INTENTIONS
EIINNNOSTV INVENTIONS
EIINNORSST INSERTIONS
EIINNORSSV INVERSIONS
EIINNORSTU REUNIONIST
EIINNPPSSS SNIPPINESS
EIINNRSSTW WINTRINESS
EIINOOPRST REPOSITION
EIINOOPSTX EXPOSITION

EIINOPPTTT PETIT POINT
EIINOPRSSV PREVISIONS
EIINOPSTVW VIEWPOINTS
EIINORTTWZ ZWITTERION
EIINPPRSST PINSTRIPES
EIINPRSSSS PRISSINESS
EIINRSTUVY UNIVERSITY
EIINSSTTTU INSTITUTES
EIIOORRSST SORORITIES
EIIOPPSSTT PETITS POIS
EIIPRTTUVY ERUPTIVITY
EIJLMNPSTU MINT JULEPS
EIJLMPPRTU TRIPLE JUMP
EIKLNPRRSS SPRINKLERS
EIKNNORRST NON-STRIKER
EIKNNOSSTT STINKSTONE
EIKNNPSSSU SPUNKINESS
EIKNOOPSSS SPOOKINESS
EIKORSTTTY TROTSKYITE
EILLLOORTT TOILET ROLL
EILLLSSSTY LISTLESSLY
EILLMNOSST MILLSTONES
EILLMORSTU LUMISTEROL
EILLNNOSTY INSOLENTLY
EILLNOORRT RITORNELLO
EILLNOOSSW WOOLLINESS
EILLNRTUVY VIRULENTLY
EILLOOPRSY ROLY-POLIES
EILLOPRSSV OVERSPILLS
EILLOPRSUY PERILOUSLY
EILLORTTTU LITTERLOUT
EILMMOPRSY POLYMERISM
EILMNOOOPS MONOPOLIES,
   MONOPOLISE
EILMNOOOPZ MONOPOLIZE
EILMNOOSST MOTIONLESS
EILMNOPSST SIMPLETONS
EILMNOPTTY IMPOTENTLY
EILMNOSSSS LISSOMNESS
EILMNRSSTY MINSTRELSY
EILMOOPRST METROPOLIS
EILMOPPRRY IMPROPERLY
EILNNNOOTV NONVIOLENT
EILNNOOSTW LOW-TENSION
EILNNOSSTV INSOLVENTS
EILNNRSSUU UNRULINESS
EILNOOPSSX EXPLOSIONS
EILNOORSTU RESOLUTION
EILNOORTUV REVOLUTION
EILNOPPRTW NIPPLEWORT
EILNOPPSSS SLOPPINESS
EILNOPPSTU SUPPLETION
EILNOPRSST PORTLINESS
EILNOPRSSU REPULSIONS
EILNOPSSUX EXPULSIONS
EILNORSSTY STORY LINES
EILNOSTUUV VELUTINOUS
EILNPQTTUU QUINTUPLET
EILNPRRTUY PRURIENTLY

EILNRSSSTU SULTRINESS
EILNRSSTTU TURNSTILES
EILOOPPRST PETROPOLIS
EILOORSSTT SITOSTEROL
EILOPPRSUV PROPULSIVE
EILOPRRSTU PROTRUSILE
EILOPRSTUY PYROLUSITE
EILOPRSTVY SPORTIVELY,
   VERY PISTOL
EILOPRSUVY PREVIOUSLY
EILOPSSTTT TEST PILOTS
EIMMNOPRSS PERSIMMONS
EIMNNOOPTT OMNIPOTENT
EIMNNOSSYY SYNONYMISE
EIMNNOSYYZ SYNONYMIZE
EIMNNRSTTU INSTRUMENT
EIMNOOPRSS SPOONERISM
EIMNOOSTTT TENOTOMIST
EIMNOPRRTU IMPORTUNER
EIMNOPRSTU RESUMPTION
EIMNORSSST STORMINESS
EIMNOSTTZZ MEZZOTINTS
EIMNPSSSTU STUMPINESS
EIMNSSSTTU SMUTTINESS
EIMOOQSSTU MOSQUITOES
EIMOPPSSSU MISSUPPOSE
EIMOPRRSTY SPIROMETRY
EIMOPRSSTU IMPOSTURES
EIMORSSTUY MYSTERIOUS
EIMRRSSTTU MISTRUSTER
EINNOOSSST SNOOTINESS
EINNOPSSSU SUSPENSION
EINNOSSSTT SNOTTINESS
EINNOSSTTU SUSTENTION
EINOOPPRSS OPPRESSION
EINOOPPRTW POWER POINT
EINOOPRRST RESORPTION
EINOOPSSSS POSSESSION
EINOOPTTTT TOTIPOTENT
EINOORSTTX EXTORTIONS
EINOPPRSTY PROPENSITY
EINOPRSSST SPORTINESS
EINOPSSSTT SPOTTINESS
EINOQRTTUU TOURNIQUET
EINORRSTTV INTROVERTS
EINORSSTUX EXTRUSIONS
EINRSSSTTU TRUSTINESS
EIOOOPRSTZ SPOROZOITE
EIOOPPRRRT PROPRIETOR
EIOOPRRSST POSTERIORS
EIOOPRRSTY REPOSITORY
EIOOPRSTXY EXPOSITORY
EIOORRSSTU ROISTEROUS
EIOORRTVWY IVORY TOWER
EIOPPRRSTY PROSPERITY
EIOPPRSSTT STROPPIEST
EIOPPRSTUV SUPPORTIVE
EIOPRRSSUV SUPERVISOR
EIOPRRSTTU TRIPTEROUS

EIOPRRSTUV PROTRUSIVE
EIOPRSTTTU PROSTITUTE
EIOQRSSTUU TURQUOISES
EIORRRSSTT TERRORISTS
EIPPRRSUVY PRIVY PURSE
EJLLLLORSY JELLY ROLLS
EJMOSSSTTU MOTS JUSTES
EJNNSSSTUU UNJUSTNESS
EJNOORRSSU SOJOURNERS
EJNOOSSSUY JOYOUSNESS
EKLOOPRRSW
    SLOPWORKER
EKLOORRTUW
    WORK-TO-RULE
EKMNNOORSS
    NONSMOKERS
EKMNNOSTUY MONKEY
    NUTS
EKNORRTTUU TRUNK
    ROUTE
EKOOORRSTUW
    OUTWORKERS
ELLLOSSSUY SOULLESSLY
ELLOPSSSTY SPOTLESSLY
ELMNOORSUY
    ENORMOUSLY
ELMNOOSUVY
    VENOMOUSLY
ELMNORSUUY
    NUMEROUSLY
ELMOOPRSUY POLYMEROUS
ELMOOPRTUY PLEUROTOMY
ELMOOPRTXY PROTOXYLEM
ELMOOPSSUY POLYSEMOUS
ELNOSSSUUY SENSUOUSLY
ELOPPRSTUY SUPPLETORY
EMMNOOOORSU
    MONOMEROUS
EMMOOPRSTT
    POSTMORTEM
EMNNOOORTU
    MOTONEURON
EMNNOOOSST
    MOONSTONES
EMNOOOPRST
    MONOPTEROS
EMNOORRSTT
    TORMENTORS
EMNOPPRSST PROMPTNESS
EMNORRSTUU
    SURMOUNTER
EMNORSSTUU
    MENSTRUOUS
EMOOOORRSST
    STOREROOMS
EMOOORRSTV
    SERVOMOTOR
ENNOOPPRRU PROPER
    NOUN

ENNOOPPRST PROPONENTS
ENOOPRRSSY RESPONSORY
ENOOPRSSSU POROUSNESS
ENOOPRSTTU PORTENTOUS
ENOPRSSSUY SUSPENSORY
EOOOOPRSSUX EXOSPOROUS
EOOPPRRSSS OPPRESSORS
EOOPPRRSSU PROSPEROUS
EOOPPRSTTY PROTOTYPES
EOOPRRSSTU PRO-OESTRUS
EOOPRSSSSS POSSESSORS
EOOPRSSSSY POSSESSORY
EOOORRSSTTU STERTOROUS
EOPPRRSSSU SUPPRESSOR
EOPPRRSSTU SUPPORTERS
EOPRSSSSUU SOURPUSSES
FFFFIITTYY FIFTY-FIFTY
FFGHHIOSTY FIGHT SHY OF
FFGHIILNSY FLYING FISH,
    FLY-FISHING
FFGHIIOPPR HIPPOGRIFF
FFGHORSTUU ROUGH STUFF
FFGIILLLNU FULFILLING
FFGIILNNSY SNIFFINGLY
FFGIINORTY FORTIFYING
FFGILNNSUY SNUFFINGLY
FFGINOPTTU OFF-PUTTING
FFILLRTUUY FRUITFULLY
FFILNRTUUU UNFRUITFUL
FFILOORRST FIRST FLOOR
FFIORSSTTU SOFT FRUITS
FGGHHIILNY HIGH-FLYING
FGGHIIINNT INFIGHTING
FGGIIINNNR INFRINGING
FGGIIINNSY SIGNIFYING
FGGIILNORY GLORIFYING
FGHHIIINSTT NIGHT SHIFT
FGHHIORRTT FORTHRIGHT
FGHHLOTTUU THOUGHTFUL
FGHIILNSTU INSIGHTFUL
FGHIILNSTY SHIFTINGLY
FGHIINNRSU FURNISHING
FGHIINORRY HORRIFYING
FGHIINRSTT FIRST NIGHT
FGHIIOTTTU FIGHT IT OUT
FGHILLRTUY RIGHTFULLY
FGHILOOSTT FOOTLIGHTS
FGHINNOTUX FOXHUNTING
FGHINOOOTT HOTFOOTING
FGHINORSTT FORTNIGHTS
FGIIINRTVY VITRIFYING
FGIIJNSTUY JUSTIFYING
FGIILLMNOY MOLLIFYING
FGIILLNNUY NULLIFYING
FGIILLNRTY FLIRTINGLY,
    TRIFLINGLY
FGIILLNSTY STIFLINGLY
FGIILMNORU LINGUIFORM
FGIILNOSUU FULIGINOUS

FGIIMMMNUY MUMMIFYING
FGIIMNORTY MORTIFYING
FGIIMNSTYY MYSTIFYING
FGIIMORRST STRIGIFORM
FGIINOTTTU OUTFITTING
FGIINRRSTY STIR-FRYING
FGIKNNORTU TUNING FORK
FGILLNOOSW FOLLOWINGS
FGILLNOTUY FLOUTINGLY
FGILMMNOUX FLUMMOXING
FGILNNORWY FROWNINGLY
FGLLNORUWY
    FULLY-GROWN, WRONGFULLY
FGLOORTUUY FUTUROLOGY
FGNNOOSSSU
    SONS-OF-GUNS
FHILLMRTUY MIRTHFULLY
FHILMOORRR HORROR FILM
FHILOPRSUW WORSHIPFUL
FHIMORSSTX SIXTH FORMS
FHINORRSTT SHIRTFRONT
FHLLLOSTUY SLOTHFULLY
FHLLOTUUYY YOUTHFULLY
FHLLRTTUUY TRUTHFULLY
FHLNRTTUUU UNTRUTHFUL
FHLOOORSSW FLOOR
    SHOWS
FIIKLNNSST SKINFLINTS
FIILMMNOOR MONILIFORM
FIILMPRSST FILMSTRIPS
FIIMNORTUY UNIFORMITY
FIIMOORSST FORTISSIMO
FIIMORSTTU FORTUITISM
FIIORSTTTU FORTUITIST
FIKLLOORST FOLKLORIST
FIKNORSTWY FORTY WINKS
FILLLMORSU FLOURMILLS
FILLOOSTUW FOLLOW SUIT
FILOOOPRST PORTFOLIOS
FINOOOPSTT SOFT OPTION
FINOOPRSTT FOOTPRINTS
FIOORSTTUU FORTUITOUS
FLLMNORUUY MOURNFULLY
FLLRSTTUUY TRUSTFULLY
FLOOOOSSTT FOOTSTOOLS
FMNOOOORRST FRONT
    ROOMS
FMOOOPRRST STORMPROOF
FOOORSSTTU OUT OF SORTS
GGGILLNRUY GURGLINGLY
GGGILNRSTU STRUGGLING
GGHHHIILST HIGHLIGHTS
GGHHIILNTT NIGHTLIGHT
GGHHINRSTU HIGH-STRUNG
GGHIIILRSW WHIRLIGIGS
GGHIILNNST LIGHTNINGS
GGHIILPRSY PRIGGISHLY
GGHILLSSUY SLUGGISHLY
GGIIIINSTV GINGIVITIS

GGIIIMNSSV MISGIVINGS
GGIIINNRTU INTRIGUING
GGIIILLNNTY TINGLINGLY
GGIILNNSTY STINGINGLY
GGIILNNSWY SWINGINGLY
GGIILNPPRY GRIPPINGLY
GGILLLNOOR LOGROLLING
GGILLNTTUY GLUTTINGLY
GGILNNOOPR PROLONGING
GGILNNRTUY GRUNTINGLY
GGINNNNRUU GUNRUNNING
GGINOOPRRU PROROGUING
GGINOORTUW
    OUTGROWING
GGLLNNOOOW
    WOLLONGONG
GHHIILPSST LIGHTSHIPS
GHHIINOPST HIGH POINTS
GHHIINRSTT NIGHTSHIRT
GHHIIPRSTW SHIPWRIGHT
GHHILRSSTU RUSHLIGHTS
GHHINOPRTT TRIPHTHONG
GHHLOORTUY
    THOROUGHLY
GHHNORRTUU
    RUN-THROUGH
GHHOORTTUU
    THROUGHOUT
GHHOOTTTUU
    THOUGHT-OUT
GHHOPRTTUU
    THROUGHPUT
GHIIKNNNTU UNTHINKING
GHIILLMRTW MILLWRIGHT
GHIILLNRWY WHIRLINGLY
GHIILLOPTT PILOT LIGHT
GHIILNRTWY WRITHINGLY
GHIILNSSWY SWISHINGLY
GHIILNSTTW WHITTLINGS
GHIIMNPRTU TRIUMPHING
GHIINNORSU NOURISHING
GHIINNOSTU OUTSHINING
GHIINOPRSW WORSHIPING
GHILMNPTUY THUMPINGLY
GHILMOOORU HOROLOGIUM
GHILNOOPST PHLOGISTON
GHILNOOSTY SOOTHINGLY
GHILNORTTT THROTTLING
GHILNOSSST SLINGSHOTS
GHILNRRUYY HURRYINGLY
GHILOOORST HOROLOGIST
GHILOOPSYY PHYSIOLOGY
GHILOPSSTT SPOTLIGHTS
GHLLOOPTYY TYPHLOLOGY
GHLMOOOOSU
    HOMOLOGOUS
GHLMOOOOPRY
    MORPHOLOGY

GHLNOOPSUW
    SNOWPLOUGH
GHMNOOOOSU
    HOMOGONOUS
GHMOOOSUYZ
    HOMOZYGOUS
GHNOOSSTTW GHOST
    TOWNS
GHOORSTTUW
    OUTGROWTHS
GIIIIMMNNNZ MINIMIZING
GIIILLNNST INSTILLING
GIIILNNTVY INVITINGLY
GIIIMMNNUZ IMMUNIZING
GIIIMNNPRT IMPRINTING
GIIIMNOPTZ OPTIMIZING
GIIINNNOUZ UNIONIZING
GIIKLLNNSY SLINKINGLY
GIIKLMNRSY SMIRKINGLY
GIIKLNNPRS SPRINKLING
GIIKLNNSTW TWINKLINGS
GIIKLNNSTY STINKINGLY
GIIKLNRSTY STRIKINGLY
GIIKNRSTWY SKYWRITING
GIILLNNOPR ROLLING PIN
GIILLNOPRY PILLORYING
GIILLNPPRY RIPPLINGLY
GIILLNPPSY SLIPPINGLY
GIILLNRSWY SWIRLINGLY
GIILMMNSWY SWIMMINGLY
GIILMNOORV LIVING ROOM
GIILMNOPSY IMPOSINGLY
GIILMOOSST MISOLOGIST
GIILNNOPRU PURLOINING
GIILNNRTUY UNTIRINGLY
GIILNOORSU INGLORIOUS
GIILNOOSST SINOLOGIST
GIILNPPRTY TRIPPINGLY
GIILNPRSST SPLIT RINGS,
    STRIPLINGS
GIILNRRSTY STIRRINGLY
GIILNSTTWY TWISTINGLY
GIILOORSTV VIROLOGIST
GIIMNNNORU IN MOURNING
GIIMNNOORT MONITORING
GIIMNNOPSU UNIMPOSING
GIIMNOORTZ MOTORIZING
GIIMNOQSTU MISQUOTING
GIIMNOSSTY MISOGYNIST
GIINNNSTTU UNSTINTING
GIINNOOPRT PORTIONING
GIINNOPRST PISTON RING
GIINNRSTTU INTRUSTING
GIINOTTTUW OUTWITTING
GIINPRRSSU SURPRISING
GIJNNOORSU SOJOURNING
GIKMNNNOOS NONSMOKING
GIKNNOOPRR NORRKOPING
GILLMOSSSY SYLLOGISMS

GILLNOPRRS SPRING ROLL
GILLNPUYZZ PUZZLINGLY
GILLNRSTUY RUSTLINGLY
GILLOORSUY GLORIOUSLY
GILMMNOOUY
    IMMUNOLOGY
GILMNOOOST MONOLOGIST,
    NOMOLOGIST
GILMOOOPST POMOLOGIST
GILMOOSTYZ ZYMOLOGIST
GILNNNSTUY STUNNINGLY
GILNNOOSWY SWOONINGLY
GILNNORSTY SNORTINGLY
GILNOOOPSY OLIGOPSONY
GILNOOOSST NOSOLOGIST
GILNOOPPSY OPPOSINGLY
GILNOOPPTY TYPING POOL
GILNOOPSTY STOOPINGLY
GILNOPRSTY SPORTINGLY
GILNOPSTYY POLYGYNIST
GILNORRWYY WORRYINGLY
GILNPRSUUY USURPINGLY
GILOOOPSTT TOPOLOGIST
GILOOOSSTZ ZOOLOGISTS
GILOOPRSTT PROGLOTTIS
GILOOPSTTY TYPOLOGIST
GILOORRSUY RIGOROUSLY
GILOORSUVY VIGOROUSLY
GIMMNNOSSU
    SUMMONSING
GIMMNPSSUU
    SUMMINGS-UP
GIMMPPTUYY GIPPY TUMMY
GIMNNOORSS MONSIGNORS
GIMNNOOSTY MONOGYNIST
GIMNOOSSUY MISOGYNOUS
GINNNORTUU OUTRUNNING
GINNOOPPST POSTPONING
GINNOOPRSS SPONSORING
GINNOPPSTU UNSTOPPING
GINOOPRTUU OUTPOURING
GINOPPRRTU PURPORTING
GINOPPRSTU SUPPORTING
GINTTTTTUU TUT-TUTTING
GLNOOPSUYY POLYGYNOUS
GLNOOSTTUU GLUTTONOUS
GMNNOOOSUY
    MONOGYNOUS
GMNOOORRST STRONG
    ROOM
GNNOOSTUWY
    YOUNGSTOWN
HHILOOPPSY PHILOSOPHY
HHILOOPPTY PHOTOPHILY
HHIMOOPRRZ RHIZOMORPH
HHLMOPRTYY POLYRHYTHM
HHOOPPRSSU PHOSPHORUS
HIIKLSSTTY SKITTISHLY
HIILLMNOST MILLIONTHS

HIILLNORTT TRILLIONTH
HIILMOOPSZ ZOOPHILISM
HIILOPRSTY HOLY SPIRIT
HIILORTTTY LITHOTRITY
HIILOSSSTY HISTOLYSIS
HIIMMNOPRS MORPHINISM
HIINOORSST ORNITHOSIS
HIIOOOPRST OOPHORITIS
HIIOOTTTYY HOITY-TOITY
HIKLMOOSTT MILK TOOTHS
HILLOOPRSW WHIRLPOOLS
HILMNORTTY TRIMONTHLY
HILNORTUWY UNWORTHILY
HILOOOPSUZ ZOOPHILOUS
HILOOPSSTY PHOTOLYSIS
HILOPPSTUY HIPPOLYTUS
HILORSSSTT SHORT LISTS
HIMMNOOTYY
　　HOMONYMITY
HIMNOPSSTY SYMPHONIST
HINOOPTTXY PHYTOTOXIN
HINOPSSTTY HYPNOTISTS
HIOOOSTTTU SHOOT IT OUT
HIOOPPRSST TROOPSHIPS
HIOOPRTTXY THIXOTROPY
HIORSSTTUU STRUTHIOUS
HLLOOPPRSY SPOROPHYLL
HLMOORSUUY
　　HUMOROUSLY
HLOPRSSUUU SULPHUROUS
HMOOPSSTUU
　　POSTHUMOUS
HNOOOPSTTU PHOTOTONUS
HOORRSSTTY SHORT STORY
IIILLMMNSU ILLUMINISM
IIILLMNSTU ILLUMINIST
IIILMMOTTY IMMOTILITY
IIILNOSSTV VIOLINISTS
IIIMNOOPST IMPOSITION
IIIMNOPRSS MISPRISION
IIIMOPSSTV POSITIVISM

IIINNOSTTU INTUITIONS
IIINOQRSTU INQUISITOR
IIINOQSTUU INIQUITOUS
IIIOPSSTTV POSITIVIST
IILLLLNWYY WILLY-NILLY
IILLLORSUY ILLUSORILY
IILLNOOPSS POLLINOSIS
IILMNOOPSS IMPLOSIONS
IILMNOPSSU IMPULSIONS
IILMNOPSTY POSTLIMINY
IILMNOSTUY LUMINOSITY
IILNNOOSTU IN SOLUTION
IILNNOOTUV INVOLUTION
IILNOOPSST POSTILIONS
IIMNNOOOUX OXONIUM ION
IIMNNOOSSU INSOMNIOUS
IIMNORSSTU MINOR SUITS
IINNORSSTU INTRUSIONS
IINOOOPPST OPPOSITION
IINOOPRSSV PROVISIONS
IINOPRRSTU IRRUPTIONS
IINORSSSTU SINISTROUS
IINORSTTTU INSTITUTOR
IINORSTTUU NUTRITIOUS
IIOOOPRSTV OVIPOSITOR
IIOOPPRSTU PROPITIOUS
IIOPRSSTUU SPIRITUOUS
IIORSTTUVY VIRTUOSITY
IKLOOPPRSU PRUSIK LOOP
IKMORSSTTY TROTSKYISM
IKORSSTTTY TROTSKYIST
ILLMNOSUUY LUMINOUSLY
ILLNOORSSU ROUSSILLON
ILLOOSSSVY SOLVOLYSIS
ILMMNOOOPS MONOPOLISM
ILMNOOOPST MONOPOLIST
ILMNOOOSTW SLOW
　　MOTION
ILMNOOSUUV VOLUMINOUS
ILMNOSTUUY MUTINOUSLY
ILMOORSTUY TIMOROUSLY

ILMOOSTTXY XYLOTOMIST
ILMOSTTUUY TUMULOSITY
ILNOOOSSYZ OZONOLYSIS
ILNOOPPRSU PROPULSION
ILOOPPRSST SPOILSPORT
ILOPRSSUUY SPURIOUSLY
ILORSTUUVY VIRTUOUSLY
IMMOOPRSTU PROSTOMIUM
IMMOPSSSUY SYMPOSIUMS
IMNNOSTYYY SYNONYMITY
IMNOOOOPRST PROMOTIONS
IMNOOOPSTT MOOT POINTS
IMNOOORSUV OMNIVOROUS
IMOOPRRSSY PROMISSORY
IMOOPRSSTU IMPOSTROUS
INOOOPPRRT PROPORTION
INOOPRRSTU PROTRUSION
INRSSTTTUU UNIT TRUSTS
IOOOPRSSTU ISOTROPOUS
IOOPPRRSTU POTPOURRIS
IOOPPRRSTU PROPOSITUS
IOORSTTTUY TORTUOSITY
LLORSSTUUY LUSTROUSLY
LMOOOSTUXY
　　XYLOTOMOUS
LMOSTTUUUU TUMULTUOUS
LNOOOORSSUY SONOROUSLY
LOOPSTUUUV VOLUPTUOUS
LOORSTTUUY TORTUOUSLY
MMOOPRRSUU RUMPUS
　　ROOM
MNNOOOOSTU
　　MONOTONOUS
MNNOOSSUYY
　　SYNONYMOUS
MNOOOPRRTY
　　PROMONTORY
MNOORSSSTW
　　SNOWSTORMS
NOOOPPSSSU SOUP SPOONS
OPRSTTUVYY TOPSY-TURVY

AAAAABBCDRR ABRACADABRA
AAAAABBCHILN BAHIA BLANCA
AAAAABBCORSS CABORA BASSA
AAAAABBINRST SABBATARIAN
AAAAABCCHILN BACCHANALIA
AAAAABDIIRSU SAUDI ARABIA
AAAAABEKMSTT MAKE A STAB AT
AAAAACHHKKLM MAKHACHKALA
AAAAADEGLMMT AMALGAMATED
AAAAADELMRSS DAR ES SALAAM
AAAAAFGNOSTT ANTOFAGASTA
AAAAAFINRRST RASTAFARIAN
AAAAAGHIPPRR PARAGRAPHIA
AAAAAGJNNNRY NARAYANGANJ
AAAAAGORRSTZ STARA ZAGORA
AAAAAHHMRRST MAHARASHTRA
AAAAAILRSSTU AUSTRALASIA
AAAABBCEELLN BALANCEABLE
AAAABBCILSST SABBATICALS
AAAABCDDIRRY BRADYCARDIA
AAAABCDEIORS SCARABAEOID
AAAABCEEIMRT BACTERAEMIA
AAAABCEGGGRS BAGGAGE CARS
AAAABCEGGNRS GARBAGE CANS
AAAABCEGILLR ALGEBRAICAL
AAAABCEGKPSS BACK PASSAGE
AAAABCEHINRT ABRANCHIATE
AAAABCELRTTT ATTRACTABLE
AAAABCIKLMRS BLACK MARIAS
AAAABDDENORW DRAW A BEAD ON
AAAABDEGGNOV VAGABONDAGE
AAAABDMORSSS AMBASSADORS
AAAABEEGLLSV SALVAGEABLE
AAAABEHIMNPS AMPHISBAENA
AAAABEIILNRS RABELAISIAN
AAAABEIKLLLZ ALKALIZABLE
AAAABEILLNUV UNAVAILABLE
AAAABELLNPTU UNPALATABLE
AAAABELNRRTW WARRANTABLE
AAAABGHIOOPR AGORAPHOBIA
AAAABHIOPRST ASTRAPHOBIA
AAAABHMPRRTU BRAHMAPUTRA
AAAABIKNNNSS BANANA SKINS
AAAACCCEINPT CAPACITANCE
AAAACCCILSTT CATACLASTIC
AAAACCCISTTU CATACAUSTIC
AAAACCDEIIMN ACADEMICIAN
AAAACCDEILMS ACADEMICALS
AAAACCDHIRTY TACHYCARDIA
AAAACCEEHSTT ATTACHÉ CASE
AAAACCEILLOR CALCEOLARIA
AAAACCEILPRT PALAEARCTIC
AAAACCHILLRY ARCHAICALLY
AAAACCIILNRU CANALICULAR
AAAACCILLPRT PARALLACTIC
AAAACCILMNOT ACCLAMATION
AAAACCILPSTT CATAPLASTIC
AAAACCLMORTY ACCLAMATORY
AAAACDEEGKLP PACKAGE DEAL

AAACDEEIKMR MADEIRA CAKE
AAACDEEIMRR CAMARADERIE
AAACDEEMRRY CAMERA-READY
AAACDEERSWY CARAWAY SEED
AAACDEILMPR PARAMEDICAL
AAACDEILNRT CARDINALATE
AAACDEILPSS PAS-DE-CALAIS
AAACDEIMMRS MACADAMISER
AAACDEIMMRZ MACADAMIZER
AAACDIINNSV SCANDINAVIA
AAACDILNOPS PIÑA COLADAS
AAACDILOPRX PARADOXICAL
AAACEEFLMNS MALFEASANCE
AAACEENPPRS APPEARANCES
AAACEFLQSTU CATAFALQUES
AAACEGILLNN GALLINACEAN
AAACEGILMNO EGOMANIACAL
AAACEGIRRWY CARRIAGEWAY
AAACEHKRTTT HEART ATTACK
AAACEHLMNNP PANCHEN LAMA
AAACEHLMRST STEAL A MARCH
AAACEILLMNR ALL-AMERICAN
AAACEIMNNPR PAN-AMERICAN
AAACEINPSST SEA CAPTAINS
AAACELMNPTU CAMPANULATE
AAACELMNRST SACRAMENTAL
AAACELMOPRT PARACETAMOL
AAACENOPRRT NOT CARE A RAP
AAACERRSTTU TARTAR SAUCE
AAACFIIORST AFRO-ASIATIC
AAACFILLNTY FANATICALLY
AAACFIMNRRT AIRCRAFTMAN
AAACGHIMNOP PHAGOMANIAC
AAACGHIMNSU AS MUCH AGAIN
AAACGHIPPRR PARAGRAPHIC
AAACGHNOOTT CHATTANOOGA
AAACGIINNRU AURIGNACIAN
AAACGILMMRT GRAMMATICAL
AAACGINNNRV CARAVANNING
AAACHIKPPRT APPARATCHIK
AAACHILMRRT MATRIARCHAL
AAACHILNOTU ANACOLUTHIA
AAACHILPRRT PATRIARCHAL
AAACIKLMNPS PACK ANIMALS
AAACILLMNRU ANIMALCULAR
AAACILLMORT CLAMATORIAL
AAACILLNOTT LACTATIONAL
AAACILLNRST SCARLATINAL
AAACILLNSTY SATANICALLY
AAACILLQTUY AQUATICALLY
AAACILNNRST LANCASTRIAN
AAACILPPRST PARAPLASTIC
AAADDFHNRST HARD-AND-FAST
AAADEELQRSU A SQUARE DEAL
AAADEENRRTW WEAR AND TEAR
AAADEGILMNN MAGDALENIAN
AAADEGMNORR ROAD MANAGER
AAADEGMNPRR RAMP AND RAGE
AAADEGNOTTV TO ADVANTAGE

464

AAADEHLPRST   HARD PALATES
AAADEHPPRRS   PARAPHRASED
AAADEILMRRR   REAR ADMIRAL
AAADEILNNRX   ALEXANDRINA
AAADEILNRSS   ALESSANDRIA
AAADEILRRSV   ADVERSARIAL
AAADELLMPRT   MAR DEL PLATA
AAADELLOSTV   VALLE D'AOSTA
AAADELMNRSS   SALAMANDERS
AAADELMPPSS   ADAM'S APPLES
AAADENNPRST   TRANSPADANE
AAADGGINORT   AGGRADATION
AAADGIILMNR   MADRIGALIAN
AAADGILNORT   GRADATIONAL
AAADGINNPST   GIANT PANDAS
AAADHHLPRYZ   HAPHAZARDLY
AAADHILNRSS   HARD AS NAILS
AAADHMMMNSU   MUHAMMADANS
AAADIILNORR   RADIOLARIAN
AAADIILNORT   RADIATIONAL
AAADILLLNOT   ALLANTOIDAL
AAADILMORRS   RADIO ALARMS
AAADILNORSV   SALVADORIAN
AAADINOPSTT   ADAPTATIONS
AAADLLNRSTW   WARTS AND ALL
AAADLNORSSV   SAN SALVADOR
AAAEEGGLRSS   GARAGE SALES
AAAEEGGMNST   STAGE-MANAGE
AAAEEGMSSTU   SAUSAGE MEAT
AAAEEGRTTVX   EXTRAVAGATE
AAAEEHINSST   ANAESTHESIA
AAAEELNPRTY   PENALTY AREA
AAAEERSTTVX   EXTRAVASATE
AAAEFHHKMOS   MAKE A HASH OF
AAAEFLLMRSS   FALSE ALARMS
AAAEGGILMNT   GAMETANGIAL
AAAEGIILNRT   EGALITARIAN
AAAEGILMMNO   MEGALOMANIA
AAAEGILNNST   EAST ANGLIAN
AAAEGKLPTTU   TAKE A PLUG AT
AAAEGNRTTVX   EXTRAVAGANT
AAAEHILNOPR   AEOLIAN HARP
AAAEHIMNNRT   AMARANTHINE
AAAEHIMOSST   HAEMOSTASIA
AAAEHKLMPSS   MAKE A SPLASH
AAAEHPPRRSS   PARAPHRASES
AAAEIKLLNNT   ANTALKALINE
AAAEILMNNOT   EMANATIONAL
AAAEILNPSTT   PALATINATES
AAAEILPPRRS   REAPPRAISAL
AAAEIMNQRSU   AQUAMARINES
AAAEIMOPRRT   AMOR PATRIAE
AAAEINSSSST   ASSASSINATE
AAAEKNPTTTU   TAKE A PUNT AT
AAAELLNRSTT   TARANTELLAS
AAAELNRRSTV   TRANSVAALER
AAAEPPRSSTU   APPARATUSES
AAAFGHINNST   AFGHANISTAN
AAAFIKPRRSS   SAFARI PARKS

AAAGGGINRTV   AGGRAVATING
AAAGGHHIOPR   HAGIOGRAPHA
AAAGGINORTV   AGGRAVATION
AAAGIIMNRRS   AGRARIANISM
AAAGIINRSTT   SAGITTARIAN
AAAGILNNPQU   AQUAPLANING
AAAGIMMNRRS   GRAMMARIANS
AAAGMMRRRSS   MARRAM GRASS
AAAGMPPRSSS   PAMPAS GRASS
AAAHILNPSXY   ANAPHYLAXIS
AAAIILNORTV   VARIATIONAL
AAAIIMNNRTU   MAURITANIAN
AAAIINNQRTU   ANTIQUARIAN
AAAILLNOSTV   SALVATIONAL
AAAILLNOTUV   VALUATIONAL
AAAILLORSTT   SALTATORIAL
AAAILMNOPPR   MALAPROPIAN
AAAILMRRSTT   MARTIAL ARTS
AAAILNNOSTY   ANALYSATION
AAAILNRSSTU   AUSTRALIANS, SATURNALIAS
AAAINNNNOST   SAN ANTONIAN
AAAINNOOPST   PIANO SONATA
AABBBEHRSTY   BABY'S-BREATH
AABBCDEINRT   BRACE AND BIT
AABBCDEKLLL   BLACKBALLED
AABBCDKLORS   BLACKBOARDS
AABBCEEELMR   EMBRACEABLE
AABBCEINORT   BICARBONATE
AABBCIJKRST   JACKRABBITS
AABBDDDENOR   BED AND BOARD
AABBDDEORRS   BREADBOARDS
AABBDEEIRTV   ABBREVIATED
AABBDEEKRST   BREADBASKET
AABBDEEORRV   BEAVERBOARD
AABBEEIRRTV   REBARBATIVE
AABBEEKLNRU   UNBREAKABLE
AABBEFGLRST   FLABBERGAST
AABBEGILLNR   BALL BEARING
AABBEHIILNT   INHABITABLE
AABBEHNRSUW   BHUBANESWAR
AABBEIILLNV   ABBEVILLIAN
AABBEIIRRST   BARBARITIES
AABBEIORRTV   ABBREVIATOR
AABBEIRRTTU   BARBITURATE
AABBGIINRRZ   BARBARIZING
AABBIIILMNO   BIBLIOMANIA
AABBLORRSUY   BARBAROUSLY
AABCCDDIRRY   BRADYCARDIC
AABCCDEIIIT   ABIETIC ACID
AABCCDEKKRT   BACKTRACKED
AABCCEHHIRS   BEACHCHAIRS
AABCCEILPRT   PRACTICABLE
AABCCEKKPRS   BACKPACKERS
AABCCELLMUU   ACCUMULABLE
AABCCELNOTU   ACCOUNTABLE
AABCCERRUUY   BUREAUCRACY
AABCCGIKKNP   BACKPACKING
AABCCILPRTY   PRACTICABLY
AABCCKNNOTU   BANK ACCOUNT

AABCCLNRRUU CARBUNCULAR
AABCDDEEKLP BACKPEDALED
AABCDDIKMNO DIAMONDBACK
AABCDEEERTX EXACERBATED
AABCDEEFLRY BAREFACEDLY
AABCDEFIIIL ACIDIFIABLE
AABCDEHIMMR CHAMBERMAID
AABCDEHKNRS BACKHANDERS
AABCDEIILNT INDICATABLE
AABCDEIKLLM BLACKMAILED
AABCDEILNST ELASTIC BAND
AABCDEINOOR RADIO BEACON
AABCDEKNRRS BANKER'S CARD
AABCDELMNRU CANDELABRUM
AABCDELNOTU OUTBALANCED
AABCDEORRST BROADCASTER
AABCDGGIOOR BRAGGADOCIO
AABCDGIINRR BARRICADING
AABCDGKLRSU BLACKGUARDS
AABCDHKLORS CHALKBOARDS
AABCDHMNORY RHABDOMANCY
AABCDIINOST ABDICATIONS
AABCDIIQRTU BIQUADRATIC
AABCDINOORR RADIOCARBON
AABCEEELLPR REPLACEABLE
AABCEEELRRT RETRACEABLE
AABCEEFLRRT REFRACTABLE
AABCEEFNORR FORBEARANCE
AABCEEHILMP IMPEACHABLE
AABCEEHKLRT LEATHERBACK
AABCEEHLMPS PEACH MELBAS
AABCEEHMNRT ANTECHAMBER
AABCEEILLMR RECLAIMABLE
AABCEEILMNV AMBIVALENCE
AABCEEILNPS INESCAPABLE
AABCEEILNRS INCREASABLE
AABCEEILPPR APPRECIABLE
AABCEELNORV OVERBALANCE
AABCEELNRST TABERNACLES
AABCEELORTT BRACTEOLATE
AABCEELRRTT RETRACTABLE
AABCEELRSTT SCATTERABLE
AABCEELRTTX EXTRACTABLE
AABCEFIIRTV FABRICATIVE
AABCEFLMNOY FLAMBOYANCE
AABCEFLNOTU CONFABULATE
AABCEFLRRTU FRACTURABLE
AABCEGIRRRS CARRIER BAGS
AABCEGLMNNS BLANCMANGES
AABCEHILLRY HEBRAICALLY
AABCEHILMNR CHAMBERLAIN
AABCEHILSST CHASTISABLE
AABCEHLNPUX BLUE PANCHAX
AABCEHLNSTU STAUNCHABLE
AABCEHLPRSU PURCHASABLE
AABCEHMRRST STAR CHAMBER
AABCEHNOOTV A NOTCH ABOVE
AABCEIILNNS CANNIBALISE
AABCEIILNNZ CANNIBALIZE

AABCEIINSTU BEAUTICIANS
AABCEIKLLMR BLACKMAILER
AABCEILLLOZ LOCALIZABLE
AABCEILMNRY CARBYLAMINE
AABCEILNPSY INESCAPABLY
AABCEILNRTT INTRACTABLE
AABCEILPPRY APPRECIABLY
AABCEIMNPRR PRECAMBRIAN
AABCEIRSTTV ABSTRACTIVE
AABCEKKLMRT BLACK MARKET
AABCEKLMSSS BLACK MASSES
AABCEKLPPRS BACKSLAPPER
AABCEKNRRSU SAARBRUCKEN
AABCELLOORT COLLABORATE
AABCELLQRTU RACQUETBALL
AABCELMOPSS COMPASSABLE
AABCELORSXY CARBOXYLASE
AABCELORTXY CARBOXYLATE
AABCENOPPRR CARBON PAPER
AABCENOPRST ABSORPTANCE
AABCEOORTTZ AZOTOBACTER
AABCERRSTUU BUREAUCRATS
AABCFGIINRT FABRICATING
AABCFIINORT FABRICATION
AABCGHIOOPR AGORAPHOBIC
AABCGHIOPRR BAROGRAPHIC
AABCGIILNRT CALIBRATING
AABCGILNNNU UNBALANCING
AABCGINRSTT ABSTRACTING
AABCGLRRSTU CAT BURGLARS
AABCHIINNTY INHABITANCY
AABCHIINORT BRACHIATION
AABCHILNSTU BALUCHISTAN
AABCHIOPRST ASTRAPHOBIC
AABCIIILMTY AMICABILITY
AABCIILLPTY PLACABILITY
AABCIILMNNS CANNIBALISM
AABCIILNORT CALIBRATION
AABCIILSTUY CAUSABILITY
AABCILLMNTU LACTALBUMIN
AABCILLNOTY BOTANICALLY
AABCILNNRUU INCUNABULAR
AABCILNRTTY INTRACTABLY
AABCILOSTTY BIOCATALYST
AABCINNOORT CARBONATION
AABCINORSTT ABSTRACTION
AABCKLMOORS BLACKAMOORS
AABCLLLRSTY CRYSTAL BALL
AABCLLNNOSS CANNONBALLS
AABCLPRSSUU SUBSCAPULAR
AABDDDEFMNU DEAF-AND-DUMB
AABDDEGGORR DAGGERBOARD
AABDDEGLLLR GALL BLADDER
AABDDEHHNRT HANDBREADTH
AABDDEHMORY HEBDOMADARY
AABDDEILSSU DISSUADABLE
AABDDEINOST BASTINADOED
AABDDEIRSST BASTARDISED
AABDDEIRSTZ BASTARDIZED

AABDDELNNOY ABANDONEDLY
AABDDELNSST SANDBLASTED
AABDDNRSSTU SUBSTANDARD
AABDEEFKRST BREAKFASTED
AABDEEHHRRS HABERDASHER
AABDEEHINRR HAREBRAINED
AABDEEILLMP IMPLEADABLE
AABDEELNSST DATABLENESS
AABDEELPRSU PERSUADABLE
AABDEEMRRSS EMBARRASSED
AABDEGGORSU BROAD GAUGES
AABDEGHILNS BANGLADESHI
AABDEGILNOS DIAGNOSABLE
AABDEHHIRRT HAIRBREADTH
AABDEHINRSW BRAINWASHED
AABDEHRSTWY BREADTHWAYS
AABDEIILLNT DENTILABIAL
AABDEIILNSV INADVISABLE
AABDEIILRTY READABILITY
AABDEIKNORT DEBARKATION
AABDEILLNOT LABIODENTAL
AABDEILLRVY ADVERBIALLY
AABDEILNOUV UNAVOIDABLE
AABDEILORRT LABRADORITE
AABDEIMRTUV ADUMBRATIVE
AABDEINOSST BASTINADOES
AABDEKORSST SKATEBOARDS
AABDELLNSTU UNBALLASTED
AABDELNORST BAROTSELAND
AABDELNRSST SANDBLASTER
AABDELNRSTU SALAD BURNET
AABDELRSSTU BALUSTRADES
AABDEMNNNOS ONE-MAN BANDS
AABDEMNNNOT ABANDONMENT
AABDEMNRSST BANDMASTERS
AABDEMRSTTU MASTURBATED
AABDEOPRSST PASTEBOARDS
AABDFIIINPS SPINA BIFIDA
AABDGGGINNS SANDBAGGING
AABDGIILRTY GRADABILITY
AABDGIMNOSV VAGABONDISM
AABDGIMNRTU ADUMBRATING
AABDHIILNTU HABITUDINAL
AABDHIKLNOY BANK HOLIDAY
AABDHINNOPS ABANDON SHIP
AABDHIOSTTV BODHISATTVA
AABDHLOPRSS SPLASHBOARD
AABDHMMOORY RHABDOMYOMA
AABDIILLTUY LAUDABILITY
AABDIILMNTY DAMNABILITY
AABDIILMQRU LIQUIDAMBAR
AABDIINNRRS BRAIN DRAINS
AABDIJOORSU OUIJA BOARDS
AABDIMNORTU ADUMBRATION
AABDLLMOOPS BLOOD PLASMA
AABDMOORRRT MORTARBOARD
AABDNOOPRSX PANDORA'S BOX
AABEEEEGRRV EAGER BEAVER
AABEEEFKRRS SAFEBREAKER

AABEEEGLLNR ENLARGEABLE
AABEEEELRRST TALEBEARERS
AABEEFHORST FEATHER BOAS
AABEEFLLRTT FLATTERABLE
AABEEGINNRT ANNABERGITE
AABEEGLMNTU AUGMENTABLE
AABEEGLMSSS ASSEMBLAGES
AABEEHILNTZ ELIZABETHAN
AABEEHILPST ALPHABETISE
AABEEHILPTZ ALPHABETIZE
AABEEHKLNSU UNSHAKEABLE
AABEEHLRSTY BREATHALYSE
AABEEIILLNN INALIENABLE
AABEEIILNPX EXPLAINABLE
AABEEIILLNRT INALTERABLE
AABEEILNPRS INSEPARABLE
AABEEILORTV ELABORATIVE
AABEEILPRRR IRREPARABLE
AABEEINRRRT TRAINBEARER
AABEEINRRST BRAINTEASER
AABEEINSSTT BASTNAESITE
AABEEJKRRSW JAWBREAKERS
AABEEKLNPSU UNSPEAKABLE
AABEEKLRRSW LAW-BREAKERS
AABEELLMNOT BALLETOMANE
AABEELLNRTU UNALTERABLE
AABEELLORTY ELABORATELY
AABEELLPRRS PALLBEARERS
AABEELLPRSU PLEASURABLE
AABEELMNSST TAMABLENESS
AABEELMPRTU PERAMBULATE
AABEELMPTTT ATTEMPTABLE
AABEELNORST TREASONABLE
AABEELNRTTU ENTABLATURE
AABEELNSSSV SAVABLENESS
AABEELPRSTT BREASTPLATE
AABEELRRSTU TREASURABLE
AABEELRRSTV TRAVERSABLE
AABEELRRTWY BARLEY WATER
AABEELRSTTW WATER TABLES
AABEEMMOPRT MEPROBAMATE
AABEFFIILLS FALSIFIABLE
AABEFGIILMN MAGNIFIABLE
AABEFHILNOS FASHIONABLE
AABEFIILLMP AMPLIFIABLE
AABEFIILLQU QUALIFIABLE
AABEFIILSST SATISFIABLE
AABEFILLMMN INFLAMMABLE
AABEFILLRTT FILTRATABLE
AABEFLLNPPU UNFLAPPABLE
AABEGGGMOOR BAGGAGE ROOM
AABEGIILNNV INVAGINABLE
AABEGIKLNRW LAWBREAKING
AABEGILNORT ELABORATING
AABEGIRRRTU ARBITRAGEUR
AABEGLLMOST MEGALOBLAST
AABEGLNORRR BARREL ORGAN
AABEGLRRSUY BARLEY SUGAR
AABEHIILLNN ANNIHILABLE

AABEHILNRST TARNISHABLE
AABEHILORUV BEHAVIOURAL
AABEHINRRSW BRAINWASHER
AABEHLPRRSV PHRASAL VERB
AABEIILLMSS ASSIMILABLE
AABEIILLSTY SALEABILITY
AABEIILMMOR MEMORABILIA
AABEIILMNTY AMENABILITY
AABEIILNRRT LIBERTARIAN
AABEIILRTWY WEARABILITY
AABEIKMNORT EMBARKATION
AABEILLLRTY BILATERALLY
AABEILLOPRZ POLARIZABLE
AABEILLRRST LIBERAL ARTS
AABEILLRRTZ TRAILBLAZER
AABEILLRVZZ BRAZZAVILLE
AABEILMMRSU BARIUM MEALS
AABEILMORTZ AMORTIZABLE
AABEILNOORT ELABORATION
AABEILNPRSY INSEPARABLY
AABEILNRSTT TRANSITABLE
AABEILNSSTU SUSTAINABLE
AABEILOPRVZ VAPORIZABLE
AABEILPRRRY IRREPARABLY
AABEILPRTUU BUILT-UP AREA
AABEIMNRRTT ARBITRAMENT
AABEIMPRSTV VAMPIRE BATS
AABEINOPSTT BE AT PAINS TO
AABEINORRST ABERRATIONS
AABEIOPPRTV APPROBATIVE
AABEKLNPSUY UNSPEAKABLY
AABELLLOSWW SWALLOWABLE
AABELLORSUV SLAVE LABOUR
AABELLORTTY BATTLE ROYAL
AABELLPRSUY PLEASURABLY
AABELMMNSSY ASSEMBLYMAN
AABELNORSTY TREASONABLY
AABELOPRRTY PORTRAYABLE
AABELORSSST ALBATROSSES
AABELPRSSSU SURPASSABLE
AABFLLNPPUY UNFLAPPABLY
AABGGGGINNN GANG-BANGING
AABGHHIOOPP PHAGOPHOBIA
AABGHIINTTU HABITUATING
AABGHILNOOP ANGLOPHOBIA
AABGIILNORS ABORIGINALS
AABGIILNOST SAILING BOAT
AABGIIMNNOT ABOMINATING
AABGIINRRTT ARBITRATING
AABGIKNNSSV SAVINGS BANK
AABGILMNRSU SUBMARGINAL
AABGINOORST ABROGATIONS
AABGIRSSSTU BASS GUITARS
AABGKLOOTUW GO WALKABOUT
AABGLLMORSY SYLLABOGRAM
AABHIILORTT HABILITATOR
AABHIILSTWY WASHABILITY
AABHIINNSTT INHABITANTS
AABHIINOSTT HABITATIONS

AABHIINOTTU HABITUATION
AABHIMNPSST BATSMANSHIP
AABHIMRSTVZ BAR MITZVAHS
AABHLLLOOSU HULLABALOOS
AABIIILRTVY VARIABILITY
AABIIILSTTY SATIABILITY
AABIIKLLTTY TALKABILITY
AABIILLNORT LIBRATIONAL
AABIILLPPTY PALPABILITY
AABIILLSTVY SALVABILITY
AABIILMNRUU ALBUMINURIA
AABIILNORTV VIBRATIONAL
AABIILRRRTY ARBITRARILY
AABIIMNNOOT ABOMINATION
AABIINORRTT ARBITRATION
AABILLRSUXY SUBAXILLARY
AABILMNORTY ABNORMALITY
AABILNOOPRT PROBATIONAL
AABILNORTUY ABLUTIONARY
AABILNOSTTU TABULATIONS
AABILNSSTTU SUBSTANTIAL
AABINOOPPRT APPROBATION
AABIORRRSTT ARBITRATORS
AABKKOORRSU KOOKABURRAS
AABLOPRRTUY LABOUR PARTY
AABNOORRSTW NARROW BOATS
AABNOORSTTY ASTROBOTANY
AACCCDENORS ACCORDANCES
AACCCDEOSUY CYCADACEOUS
AACCCEENPST ACCEPTANCES
AACCCEJKKRR CRACKERJACK
AACCCGHIOPR CACOGRAPHIC
AACCCIIILRT CICATRICIAL
AACCCILMSTY CATACLYSMIC
AACCCNNOTUY ACCOUNTANCY
AACCDDEIINS CANDIDACIES
AACCDEEELRT ACCELERATED
AACCDEELNOR ACCELERANDO
AACCDEENTTU ACCENTUATED
AACCDEGHRRS CHARGE CARDS
AACCDEHNORS ARCHDEACONS
AACCDEIILLT DIALECTICAL
AACCDEIIMMS ACADEMICISM
AACCDEIMNOP ACCOMPANIED
AACCDEIRRTU CARICATURED
AACCDELMTUU ACCUMULATED
AACCDEMMOOT ACCOMMODATE
AACCDEORSUU CARDUACEOUS
AACCDERSSTY SCAREDY CATS
AACCDGIIILN ALGINIC ACID
AACCDHILNOR CHANCROIDAL
AACCDHPRSST SCRATCHPADS
AACCDIIILRT DIACRITICAL
AACCDIILMNO MALONIC ACID
AACCDIOSSTU CAUSTIC SODA
AACCEEFILNT CALEFACIENT
AACCEEINRRT INCARCERATE
AACCEELLNOT COLLECTANEA
AACCEELNSTU ACAULESCENT

AACCEELORRT ACCELERATOR
AACCEENNOTT CONCATENATE
AACCEFHSTTY SAFETY CATCH
AACCEFILNOT CALEFACTION
AACCEFLORTY CALEFACTORY
AACCEGHILNR ARCHANGELIC
AACCEGHNRTT GNATCATCHER
AACCEGIKNPS PACKING CASE
AACCEGILMOR ACROMEGALIC
AACCEGILORT CATEGORICAL
AACCEGORRTY ERGATOCRACY
AACCEHHMOST STOMACHACHE
AACCEHHPRST CATCHPHRASE
AACCEHIIMNN MECHANICIAN
AACCEHILLNT CHALCANLITE
AACCEHILMOT MACHICOLATE
AACCEHILMST CATECHISMAL
AACCEHIOORZ ARCHAEOZOIC
AACCEHIRSST CATACHRESIS
AACCEHLNNNO NONCHALANCE
AACCEIILMST ACCLIMATISE
AACCEIILMTZ ACCLIMATIZE
AACCEILLSTY ASCETICALLY
AACCEILMPRT MALPRACTICE
AACCEILNOSS ACCESSIONAL
AACCEILORSS ACCESSORIAL
AACCEILOSSU SALICACEOUS
AACCEIMNOPR ACCOMPANIER
AACCEINOPTT ACCEPTATION
AACCEINQTTU ACQUITTANCE
AACCEIORSTU AUTOCRACIES
AACCEIRRSTU CARICATURES
AACCEISSTUV ACCUSATIVES
AACCEKLLNOY CYCLOALKANE
AACCEKMNOTT MAKE CONTACT
AACCELNRTUU CARUNCULATE
AACCELPRSTU SPECTACULAR
AACCELRTTUU ACCULTURATE
AACCENOPRRY COPARCENARY
AACCENRSSTU CRUSTACEANS
AACCFIIILRS SACRIFICIAL
AACCFIILLPY PACIFICALLY
AACCFIILRTY FARCICALITY
AACCFIIMNOR ACINACIFORM
AACCFINNRSS FRANCISCANS
AACCGHIMOPR MACROPHAGIC
AACCGIINNTV VACCINATING
AACCGILLNTU CALCULATING
AACCHIIMRST CHARISMATIC
AACCHIINRST ANARCHISTIC
AACCHIINRTT ANTHRACITIC
AACCHILLOTY CHAOTICALLY
AACCHILMNOR MONARCHICAL
AACCHILMOST STOMACHICAL
AACCHILNOTU ANACOLUTHIC
AACCHLNOOTY CHOANOCYTAL
AACCIILLNTY ACTINICALLY
AACCIILMPRT IMPRACTICAL
AACCIILNNOT CALCINATION

AACCIILNSTT ANTICLASTIC
AACCIILORSS SACROILIACS
AACCIILSTTT STALACTITIC
AACCIINNOTV VACCINATION
AACCIINOSTU ACOUSTICIAN
AACCIINRTTZ CICATRIZANT
AACCILLLNOY LACONICALLY
AACCILLNOTU CALCULATION
AACCILLNRTU CURTAIN CALL
AACCILLNSUU CANALICULUS
AACCILLPRTY PRACTICALLY
AACCILLSTUY CAUSTICALLY
AACCILNOSST CLASS ACTION
AACCILNOSTU SACCULATION
AACCILNPRTU UNPRACTICAL
AACCILOPPTY APOCALYPTIC
AACCILOPSUY CAPACIOUSLY
AACCILRRSUW CIRCULAR SAW
AACCIMNOPST ACCOMPANIST
AACCINOORTT COARCTATION
AACCINOSSTU ACCUSATIONS
AACCIORRSTY ARISTOCRACY
AACCKLLMORS ALARM CLOCKS
AACCLLORSTU CALCULATORS
AACCLMORTUU ACCUMULATOR
AACCLNORTTU CONTRACTUAL
AACCNNOSTTU ACCOUNTANTS
AACCOOPRRSU ACROCARPOUS
AACCORRSTTY STRATOCRACY
AACDDDEIJTU ADJUDICATED
AACDDEEEHLR CLEAR-HEADED
AACDDEEELST DE-ESCALATED
AACDDEEHMRS DEAD MARCHES
AACDDEEIMPS AIDES-DE-CAMP
AACDDEEIPTT DECAPITATED
AACDDEGLNOO DODECAGONAL
AACDDEHINPP HANDICAPPED
AACDDEHLNRS CRASH-LANDED
AACDDEILNOR ENDOCARDIAL
AACDDEILNSS SCANDALISED
AACDDEILNSZ SCANDALIZED
AACDDIJORTU ADJUDICATOR
AACDEEGHRST GATECRASHED
AACDEEHILMX HEXADECIMAL
AACDEEHNRTU HARDECANUTE
AACDEEIILNT ACETANILIDE
AACDEEIIRTV ERADICATIVE
AACDEEILRTV DECLARATIVE
AACDEEIMNPT EMANCIPATED
AACDEEINRST ASCERTAINED
AACDEEIPPRT APPRECIATED
AACDEEIRTTV REACTIVATED
AACDEELLSTT CASTELLATED
AACDEELMSTU EMASCULATED
AACDEELRTUW CATERWAULED
AACDEEMNNTV ADVANCEMENT
AACDEENNSTT ATTENDANCES
AACDEENQRSU SQUARE DANCE
AACDEFGLMOU CAMOUFLAGED

AACDEFIILTT FACILITATED
AACDEFILNOT DEFALCATION
AACDEGHHNNS CHANGE HANDS
AACDEGHHNRS CHARGE HANDS
AACDEGIIMNT DIAMAGNETIC
AACDEGIINRT ERADICATING
AACDEGIMNRT DEMARCATING
AACDEHILLPY EDAPHICALLY
AACDEHILORS ICOSAHEDRAL
AACDEHINOTT ANTICATHODE
AACDEHINPPR HANDICAPPER
AACDEHINRSS SEDAN CHAIRS
AACDEHINRST CANTHARIDES
AACDEHINRTU HARDICANUTE
AACDEHMOORR CHOREODRAMA
AACDEIILPST CAPITALISED
AACDEIILPTZ CAPITALIZED
AACDEIINNRT INCARDINATE
AACDEIINORT ERADICATION
AACDEIINPTT ANTICIPATED
AACDEIIORTV RADIOACTIVE
AACDEIIPRST PAEDIATRICS
AACDEILMNOT DECLAMATION
AACDEILMNTU CALUMNIATED
AACDEILNORT DECLARATION, REDACTIONAL
AACDEILNOTU EDUCATIONAL
AACDEILNRSS RADICALNESS, SCANDALISER
AACDEILNRSZ SCANDALIZER
AACDEILPTTU CAPITULATED
AACDEILRSTT STRAITLACED
AACDEILRTTU ARTICULATED
AACDEILRTTY DAIRY CATTLE
AACDEIMNNOP PANDEMONIAC
AACDEIMNORT DEMARCATION
AACDEIMNORY AERODYNAMIC
AACDEINOTUV COADUNATIVE
AACDEIOPRTT DECAPITATOR
AACDEIORRST ERADICATORS
AACDEIORTTV DEACTIVATOR
AACDELMNNOR ROMAN CANDLE
AACDELMORTY DECLAMATORY
AACDELNPTTY PENTADACTYL
AACDELNSSST SANDCASTLES
AACDELORRTY DECLARATORY
AACDEMORRRU ARMOURED CAR
AACDEMRRSST MASTER CARDS
AACDFHINRST HANDICRAFTS
AACDFIILRRT FRATRICIDAL
AACDFIINOOS AFICIONADOS
AACDGGHIIST HAGGADISTIC
AACDGHIOPRR CARDIOGRAPH
AACDGILNNPS LANDSCAPING
AACDGILNNVY ADVANCINGLY
AACDGILNPRY PLAYING CARD
AACDGIMRRTU DRAMATURGIC
AACDGINNSST SAND-CASTING
AACDGORSSTU COASTGUARDS
AACDHIIOPRS APHRODISIAC
AACDHLNOSYY HALCYON DAYS

AACDHMOPRSY PSYCHODRAMA
AACDIILNOTT DICTATIONAL
AACDIILNOTU ACIDULATION
AACDIILNSTV VANDALISTIC
AACDIILORTT DICTATORIAL
AACDIIMNOPS DIPSOMANIAC
AACDIINNOTY CYANIDATION
AACDIIOPRTY RADIOPACITY
AACDIIORRTV DIVARICATOR
AACDILLMNOY NOMADICALLY
AACDILLMNYY DYNAMICALLY
AACDILLRSTY DRASTICALLY
AACDILNOSTY ANISODACTYL
AACDILNPSST LANDSCAPIST
AACDILORTTY ARTIODACTYL
AACDILOSUUY AUDACIOUSLY
AACDIMOORST SARCOMATOID
AACDINNOOTU COADUNATION
AACDMMNNOST COMMANDANTS
AACDMOORSTU CATADROMOUS
AACEEEHLMOT HAEMATOCELE
AACEEEHPRST SPACE HEATER
AACEEFFMNRT RAMAN EFFECT
AACEEFIMNSS MISFEASANCE
AACEEFLLPTT CLEFT PALATE
AACEEFNNNOS NONFEASANCE
AACEEGHLMPY MEGACEPHALY
AACEEGHNOPR CHAPERONAGE
AACEEGHRRST GATECRASHER
AACEEGILLLY ELEGIACALLY
AACEEGILLNS ALLEGIANCES
AACEEGILLNV EVANGELICAL
AACEEGINPRT PARAGENETIC
AACEEGMMORT MACROGAMETE
AACEEHHLTUX HEXATEUCHAL
AACEEHHMMOR HAEMACHROME
AACEEHILNST CHATELAINES
AACEEHIMPPR PAPIER-MACHÉ
AACEEHINSTT ANAESTHETIC
AACEEHKPSST CHEAPSKATES
AACEEHLMNOP ENCEPHALOMA
AACEEHLNNSV CLEAN-SHAVEN
AACEEHMPRST SPERMATHECA
AACEEHPPRSS PAPER CHASES
AACEEHRRTTT TETRARCHATE
AACEEIIMNRS AMERICANISE
AACEEIIMNRZ AMERICANIZE
AACEEIIMPST SEPTICAEMIA
AACEEIJLTUV EJACULATIVE
AACEEIKLMNR AMERICAN ELK
AACEEILLMNS MESALLIANCE, MISCELLANEA
AACEEILLRTV VARICELLATE
AACEEILNRTT INTERCALATE
AACEEILPRST ALTARPIECES
AACEEILRRST SECRETARIAL
AACEEILSSTT ATELECTASIS
AACEEIMNNNT MAINTENANCE
AACEEIMSSST SIAMESE CATS
AACEEINNNRT CENTENARIAN

AACEEINNRRT REINCARNATE	AACEHILLMNO MELANCHOLIA
AACEEINNRSS RENAISSANCE	AACEHILLNTU HALLUCINATE
AACEEIPRRTV PREVARICATE	AACEHILLPTY APHETICALLY
AACEEIRRSTT SECRETARIAT	AACEHILRSTT THEATRICALS
AACEEKLMPRT MARKETPLACE	AACEHIMMSTT MATHEMATICS
AACEELNPSTU ENCAPSULATE	AACEHIMNNOY HAEMOCYANIN
AACEENRRSSU REASSURANCE	AACEHIMORST ACHROMATISE ·
AACEFFHINRS AFFRANCHISE	AACEHIMORTT HAEMATOCRIT
AACEFFIIRTV AFFRICATIVE	AACEHIMORTZ ACHROMATIZE
AACEFFILNOT AFFECTIONAL	AACEHIMOSTT HAEMOSTATIC
AACEFFINOTT AFFECTATION	AACEHINOTTY THIOCYANATE
AACEFGHINRR FAR-REACHING	AACEHJKMMRS JACKHAMMERS
AACEFGLMOSU CAMOUFLAGES	AACEHKMMRST MATCHMAKERS
AACEFGLOOTT COTTAGE LOAF	AACEHKMRSTW WATCHMAKERS
AACEFHMSTTY SAFETY MATCH	AACEHMMNNRT MERCHANTMAN
AACEFIILNRV ACRIFLAVINE	AACEHMNORSU RHAMNACEOUS
AACEFIINSTV FASCINATIVE	AACEHMNSTTT ATTACHMENTS
AACEFILMNOT MALEFACTION	AACEHMSSSTU MASSACHUSET
AACEFILTTUV FACULTATIVE	AACEHNNORST ANTHRACNOSE
AACEFIMNRRT AIRCRAFTMEN	AACEHOPRSTT CATASTROPHE
AACEFINORRT RAREFACTION	AACEHOPSSTU SPATHACEOUS
AACEFINORSU FARINACEOUS	AACEHPRRSTY SEARCH PARTY
AACEFINORTT FRACTIONATE	AACEHPRSTUX PURCHASE TAX
AACEFLMORST MALEFACTORS	AACEIILLMNS MISALLIANCE
AACEFLNSSTU FACTUALNESS	AACEIILLNRS ANCILLARIES
AACEFMNRTUU MANUFACTURE	AACEIILLNRT LACERTILIAN
AACEGGGKLRU LUGGAGE RACK	AACEIILLPRS CAPILLARIES
AACEGGILPTU TEGUCIGALPA	AACEIILMRSV CAVALIERISM
AACEGGINRRU GUN CARRIAGE	AACEIILNPRR PERICRANIAL
AACEGGINRSV SAVING GRACE	AACEIILNRRT INTERRACIAL
AACEGHHNOTT CHAETOGNATH	AACEIILPPRR PERICARPIAL
AACEGHILOPR ARCHIPELAGO	AACEIILPPTV APPLICATIVE
AACEGHLLMNS SMALL CHANGE	AACEIILSTTU ACTUALITIES
AACEGHLLSSV CHEVAL GLASS	AACEIIMMNRS AMERICANISM
AACEGHLOORY ARCHAEOLOGY	AACEIIMNRTV CARMINATIVE
AACEGHNORST COAT HANGERS	AACEIIMQSTU SEMIAQUATIC
AACEGHNORTU AUTOCHANGER	AACEIINORTT RATIOCINATE
AACEGHPRTTU GUTTA-PERCHA	AACEIIOSSTV ASSOCIATIVE
AACEGIIMRRS MISCARRIAGE	AACEIIPPRTT PARTICIPATE
AACEGIJLNTU EJACULATING	AACEIJLNOTU EJACULATION
AACEGILLLNY ANGELICALLY	AACEILLLSTY ELASTICALLY
AACEGILLLOR ALLEGORICAL	AACEILLMPRY MIRACLE PLAY
AACEGILLOPS PLAGIOCLASE	AACEILLMPUX AMPLEXICAUL
AACEGILMNPS PLASMAGENIC	AACEILLNTTY TETANICALLY
AACEGILNPRY PANEGYRICAL	AACEILLPRRT CATERPILLAR
AACEGILOTUV COAGULATIVE	AACEILLPTVY CAPITAL LEVY
AACEGILPPRS PARAPLEGICS	AACEILLRRTY ERRATICALLY
AACEGIMNPRS CAMPAIGNERS	AACEILMMPST METAPLASMIC
AACEGINNRTW WATERING CAN	AACEILMNORT RECLAMATION
AACEGINPPRT RATE-CAPPING	AACEILMNOTX EXCLAMATION
AACEGKOPRTU PACKAGE TOUR	AACEILMNSSU MAIN CLAUSES
AACEGLNRRTU RECTANGULAR	AACEILMRTTU MATRICULATE
AACEGMNOORR GRAECO-ROMAN	AACEILNNOSS ASCENSIONAL
AACEGNOORSU ONAGRACEOUS	AACEILNNRTU ANTINUCLEAR
AACEGRRSSTU CASTER SUGAR	AACEILNORST LACERATIONS
AACEHHIKNNV NAKHICHEVAN	AACEILNORTT ALTERCATION
AACEHIILMPT EPITHALAMIC	AACEILNOTTY ACETYLATION
AACEHIILSTT ATHEISTICAL	AACEILNPSTU INCAPSULATE
AACEHIIMMNS MANICHAEISM	AACEILNRRTU RETINACULAR

AACEILNRRTY INTERCALARY
AACEILPRSTU SPIRACULATE
AACEILPRTTU PARTICULATE
AACEILSSTTT STALACTITES
AACEILSTUVY CAUSATIVELY
AACEIMMNOST SCAMMONIATE
AACEIMNNOTT CONTAMINATE
AACEIMNOORT EROTOMANIAC
AACEIMNOPRT EMANCIPATOR
AACEIMOPRTV COMPARATIVE
AACEINNORTT RECANTATION
AACEINORRTY REACTIONARY
AACEINORSTU AERONAUTICS
AACEINORSTV VACATIONERS
AACEINOSTUV EVACUATIONS
AACEINOSTVX EXCAVATIONS
AACEINPRSST PERSIAN CATS
AACEINRSSTU SANCTUARIES
AACEIORSSTT AEROSTATICS
AACEJLORTUY EJACULATORY
AACEKLLNOPR PANCAKE ROLL
AACEKLMRSST SMART ALECKS
AACEKLMRSTY SMART ALECKY
AACEKLRRSTY TRACKLAYERS
AACELLLRSST SALTCELLARS
AACELLNOOST CELLO SONATA
AACELLOPRSU ACARPELLOUS
AACELMMRSUU MARE CLAUSUM
AACELMORSTU EMASCULATOR
AACELMORTXY EXCLAMATORY
AACELNOOSSU SOLANACEOUS
AACELNORSTT TRANSLOCATE
AACELNRRSUV VERNACULARS
AACELOPPSSY APOCALYPSES
AACELPRSSTT PLASTER CAST
AACELQRTUUU AQUACULTURE
AACENNNORTW WATER CANNON
AACENOOPSSU SAPONACEOUS
AACENORRTVY CONTRAYERVA
AACEOOPSSTU SAPOTACEOUS
AACEOPPRSUY PAPYRACEOUS
AACFFIJMRST TRAFFIC JAMS
AACFFIORRTT TRAFFICATOR
AACFFMORRTY FACTORY FARM
AACFGIINNST FASCINATING
AACFHKNRSST CRANKSHAFTS
AACFHMORSSU FORASMUCH AS
AACFIILLNNY FINANCIALLY
AACFIILORTT FACILITATOR
AACFIINNOST FASCINATION
AACFILLNRTY FRANTICALLY
AACFILMORRS SCALARIFORM
AACFILNORST INFRACOSTAL
AACFINORRTY FRACTIONARY
AACFKLMSUUV VACUUM FLASK
AACFMNORTUY MANUFACTORY
AACFMOORSST COATS OF ARMS
AACFNORSTUU ANFRACTUOUS
AACGGIIMNNP CAMPAIGNING

AACGGIINSTT CASTIGATING
AACGGILLOOR AGROLOGICAL
AACGGILNOSY SYNAGOGICAL
AACGGILNOTU CATALOGUING, COAGULATING
AACGHHOPRST TACHOGRAPHS
AACGHIKMMNT MATCHMAKING
AACGHIKMNTW WATCHMAKING
AACGHILLOPR ALLOGRAPHIC
AACGHILLPRY CALLIGRAPHY, GRAPHICALLY
AACGHINOPPR APPROACHING
AACGHINPRTU PARACHUTING
AACGHIOPRTU AUTOGRAPHIC
AACGHKNNOWW KWANGCHOWAN
AACGHLMOORU CHAULMOOGRA
AACGHNOOPRR CORONAGRAPH
AACGHOPRRTY CARTOGRAPHY
AACGHOPRSSU SARCOPHAGUS
AACGIILLNPY CALLIPYGIAN
AACGIILLNTV VACILLATING
AACGIILLOOX AXIOLOGICAL
AACGIILMNNS ANGLICANISM
AACGIILMSTT STALAGMITIC, STIGMATICAL
AACGIILNNOR CAROLINGIAN
AACGIIMNSTT MASTICATING
AACGIINNNRT INCARNATING
AACGIINNOTV VACATIONING
AACGIINNQTU ACQUAINTING
AACGIINOSST ASSOCIATING
AACGIINOSTT CASTIGATION
AACGIINPTTV CAPTIVATING
AACGILLNORY ORGANICALLY
AACGILLOPST POSTGLACIAL
AACGILNOOPR CARPOGONIAL
AACGILNOOTU COAGULATION
AACGILNORSS CORS ANGLAIS
AACGILNPTTU CATAPULTING
AACGILOSSUY SAGACIOUSLY
AACGINNRSTT TRANSACTING
AACGINPRVYZ CRAZY PAVING
AACGLMNOOPY CAMPANOLOGY
AACGORRSSTU CASTOR SUGAR
AACHHIIMPRT AMPHITRICHA
AACHHILMOPT OPHTHALMIAC
AACHIIINRST CHRISTIANIA
AACHIIMNNOT MACHINATION
AACHIIMNSST SHAMANISTIC
AACHIINRSSU SAURISCHIAN
AACHIKMNORV MARKOV CHAIN
AACHIKMNPRU KANCHIPURAM
AACHILLOPRY PAROCHIALLY
AACHILMNOOS MONOCHASIAL
AACHILMOPPP HIPPOCAMPAL
AACHIMMNOTY MYTHOMANIAC
AACHIMMORST ACHROMATISM
AACHIMNNORS ANACHRONISM
AACHIMNORSS MARASCHINOS
AACHIMOPPRR PARAMORPHIC
AACHIMPRSST PHARMACISTS
AACHINNNOTY ANTHOCYANIN

AACHIPRSTTU PARACHUTIST
AACHLLOOSTU HOLOCAUSTAL
AACHLNNOOTU ANACOLUTHON
AACHMMRRSUU HARUM-SCARUM
AACHMNOSTWY YACHTSWOMAN
AACHMOORSTU ACHROMATOUS
AACHPRSSTTW WATCHSTRAPS
AACIIILNNOT LACINIATION
AACIIILNOST LAICISATION
AACIIILNOTZ LAICIZATION
AACIIILPPRT PARTICIPIAL
AACIIJNOTTT JACTITATION
AACIILLMRTU MULTIRACIAL
AACIILLNOOT COALITIONAL
AACIILLNOTV VACILLATION
AACIILLNTTY TITANICALLY
AACIILLPRTY CAPILLARITY, PIRATICALLY
AACIILLRSTY SATIRICALLY
AACIILMNORT LACRIMATION
AACIILMNOST ANOMALISTIC
AACIILNNNOOST LANCINATION
AACIILNOPPT APPLICATION
AACIILNPRTU PURITANICAL
AACIILOPRST PISCATORIAL
AACIILPSSTT CAPITALISTS
AACIILSSTTT STATISTICAL
AACIIMNNNOTU ACUMINATION
AACIIMNNORTT INTRA-ATOMIC
AACIIMNNOSTT MASTICATION
AACIIMORTTY AROMATICITY
AACIINNNORT INCARNATION
AACIINNNOTT INCANTATION
AACIINOOSST ASSOCIATION
AACIINOPRTT ANTICIPATOR
AACIINOPSTT CAPITATIONS
AACIINOPTTV CAPTIVATION
AACIINPPRTT PARTICIPANT
AACILLLMOPS ALLOPLASMIC
AACILLLPSTY PLASTICALLY
AACILLMNOSY MASONICALLY
AACILLMOSTY SOMATICALLY
AACILLNOOST ALLOCATIONS
AACILLNOPRS RAPSCALLION
AACILLOPRSY PROSAICALLY
AACILLOSSUY SALACIOUSLY
AACILLPRTUU APICULTURAL
AACILLPSSTY SPASTICALLY
AACILLSTVWY CAVITY WALLS
AACILMNNOPT COMPLAINANT
AACILMNOPST COMPLAISANT
AACILMNRTTU MATRICULANT
AACILMORRTY LACRIMATORY
AACILNOOTUV VACUOLATION
AACILNOPRTY COPLANARITY
AACILNOPSTU CAPSULATION
AACILNORSTT INTRACOSTAL
AACILNORTVY CLAIRVOYANT
AACILOPPRTY APPLICATORY
AACILOPRSUY RAPACIOUSLY

AACILOPRTTU CAPITULATOR
AACILOPSTTU AUTOPLASTIC
AACILORRTTU ARTICULATOR
AACILPRRSTU PARTICULARS
AACILPRSSTT PLASTIC ARTS
AACILRSTUVY VASCULARITY
AACIMMNNOOS MONOMANIACS
AACIMNNNOTT CONTAMINANT
AACIMNOORST ARONOMASTIC
AACIMNOOSTT ANASTOMOTIC
AACIMNOPRSY PYROMANIACS
AACIMORSTTY MASTICATORY
AACINNNORTU ANNUNCIATOR
AACINNORSTT TRANSACTION
AACINNRRSTU TRANSURANIC
AACINOOOPPT APOCOPATION
AACINORSTTT ATTRACTIONS
AACINORSTTU ASTRONAUTIC
AACIORRSSTT ARISTOCRATS
AACLLNRUUVY AVUNCULARLY
AACLNNNOOST CONSONANTAL
AACLOOORTVY ROYAL OCTAVO
AACLOOPPRSY LAPAROSCOPY
AACLOORRSTU COLORATURAS
AACLORSTTUU AUSCULTATOR
AACMNOPRTUY PARAMOUNTCY
AADDDEGINRS GRANDADDIES
AADDDEIILPT DILAPIDATED
AADDDEILRRT TARRADIDDLE
AADDEEEHPRS SPEARHEADED
AADDEEFGRSU SAFEGUARDED
AADDEEHHNVY HEAVY-HANDED
AADDEEHHRRT HARD-HEARTED
AADDEEHHSST DEATH'S-HEADS
AADDEEHIMNS MAIDENHEADS
AADDEEHLPRY PARALDEHYDE
AADDEEILNST DESALINATED
AADDEEIPPRS DISAPPEARED
AADDEELLNRS DARDANELLES
AADDEELLPTW WELL-ADAPTED
AADDEELRTTU ADULTERATED
AADDEEMQRSU MASQUERADED
AADDEEMRRSY DAYDREAMERS
AADDEENPPRS SANDPAPERED
AADDEGILLNY LEADING LADY
AADDEGIMNRY DAYDREAMING
AADDEGINORT DEGRADATION
AADDEGINRRS DISARRANGED
AADDEHIMNNS HANDMAIDENS
AADDEHNORTY READY TO HAND
AADDEHQSSTU DEATH SQUADS
AADDEIILNTV INVALIDATED
AADDEILMRRS RED ADMIRALS
AADDEINRSST STANDARDISE
AADDEINRSTZ STANDARDIZE
AADDEJLMSTU MALADJUSTED
AADDELPQRUU QUADRUPEDAL
AADDGNNRSST GRANDSTANDS
AADDIIINNRT TRINIDADIAN

AADDIILOPRT DILAPIDATOR
AADDNNNORST NONSTANDARD
AADEEEGGRTX EXAGGERATED
AADEEEGLPRS SPREAD-EAGLE
AADEEEHLNNR ENNEAHEDRAL
AADEEEPRSTX EXASPERATED
AADEEERSSTV ASSEVERATED
AADEEFGLLLT FLAGELLATED
AADEEFHHLRT HALF-HEARTED
AADEEGIKNTV GIVE-AND-TAKE
AADEEGILOPR A RIPE OLD AGE
AADEEGNORVW AVERAGE DOWN
AADEEGNPRRR PREARRANGED
AADEEHHLPRT HEPTAHEDRAL
AADEEHHRTXY HEXAHYDRATE
AADEEHILRTX EXHILARATED
AADEEHINRRV RAVEN-HAIRED
AADEEHLNNRT NEANDERTHAL
AADEEHLRRTT TETRAHEDRAL
AADEEHLRTTT DEATH RATTLE
AADEEHMRRTW WARM-HEARTED
AADEEHMRSST HEADMASTERS
AADEEHNRSVW HEAVENWARDS
AADEEIILNNR DAIL EIREANN
AADEEIILMORT AMELIORATED
AADEEIMMNNS MAIDEN NAMES
AADEEIMRRRS SIERRA MADRE
AADEEINPPRT APPERTAINED
AADEEIPPRRS REAPPRAISED
AADEEIPRRTT REPATRIATED
AADEEIPRTTX EXPATRIATED
AADEEIRRSSV ADVERSARIES
AADEEIRRTTV RETARDATIVE
AADEEIRSTVV ADVERSATIVE
AADEEISTTVV DEVASTATIVE
AADEEKOPRTW TAKE A POWDER
AADEELLLLPR PARALLELLED
AADEELLNPTT DENTAL PLATE
AADEELLPPRW WALLPAPERED
AADEEMORTWW WATER MEADOW
AADEEMQRRSU MASQUERADER
AADEEMQRSSU MASQUERADES
AADEEMRRSTU ESTREMADURA
AADEENRSTVY VETERANS DAY
AADEENRSWYY NEW YEAR'S DAY
AADEEORRTWY READY-TO-WEAR
AADEFGHNRRT GRANDFATHER
AADEFGMNNSU FUN AND GAMES
AADEFHLNRST FATHERLANDS
AADEFIKLNNR RANK AND FILE
AADEFIMRRRY DAIRY FARMER
AADEFLMNNTU FUNDAMENTAL
AADEFLSSTTY STEADFASTLY
AADEGGGHLNU HAND LUGGAGE
AADEGGHNRSS HAGGARDNESS
AADEGGILNNR LANDING GEAR
AADEGGINRRS AGGRANDISER
AADEGGINRRZ AGGRANDIZER
AADEGGOSSSU SAUSAGE DOGS

AADEGHIINRS HEARING AIDS
AADEGHINRRW HARDWEARING
AADEGHOPRTU AUTOGRAPHED
AADEGIILNTT INTAGLIATED
AADEGIILPRS PLAGIARISED
AADEGIILPRZ PLAGIARIZED
AADEGIINRTT INGRATIATED
AADEGILLNNP PINEAL GLAND
AADEGILLNTV GALLIVANTED
AADEGILNNRS GARDEN SNAIL
AADEGILNPRT PLANTIGRADE
AADEGINNOST ANTAGONISED
AADEGINNOTZ ANTAGONIZED
AADEGINRTUU INAUGURATED
AADEGINSTTV DEVASTATING
AADEGLNQRSU QUADRANGLES
AADEGLNRSSU GRADUALNESS
AADEGLNSSTW SWEAT GLANDS
AADEGMNRRST GRAND MASTER
AADEGNNPRRT GRANDPARENT
AADEGNOPRRS GRAND OPERAS
AADEGNPRRTY GARDEN PARTY
AADEHIILNNT ANNIHILATED
AADEHIILNRT ANTHERIDIAL
AADEHILLNOS HOLLANDAISE
AADEHILMNNT THE MAINLAND
AADEHIPSTXY ASPHYXIATED
AADEHLNNPRS PANHANDLERS
AADEHMMMNOS MOHAMMEDANS
AADEIIIRRTV IRRADIATIVE
AADEIILMNST MEDIASTINAL
AADEIILMSST ASSIMILATED
AADEIILNRRT INTERRADIAL
AADEIILPRTY PRAEDIALITY
AADEIIMNNOT DEAMINATION
AADEIINORRT RERADIATION
AADEILLLMOT METALLOIDAL
AADEILLNOPT PLANETOIDAL
AADEILMNPTU MANIPULATED
AADEILMNRRT INTRADERMAL
AADEILNNQRU QUADRENNIAL
AADEILNORTY ARYTENOIDAL
AADEILNOTUV DEVALUATION
AADEILNRSTU NATURALISED
AADEILNRTUZ NATURALIZED
AADEILPRSTY DISPARATELY
AADEIMMNRST DISARMAMENT
AADEIMNRSTV MAIDSERVANT
AADEIMRSTTU TRAUMATISED
AADEIMRTTUZ TRAUMATIZED
AADEINNQRTU QUARANTINED
AADEINOPRTV DEPRAVATION
AADEINORRTT RETARDATION
AADEINORSST DIATESSARON
AADEINOSTTV DEVASTATION
AADEINPQRSU PASQUINADER
AADEKNRSSWW AWKWARDNESS
AADELLNNORT RALLENTANDO
AADELMMOPSS PLASMODESMA

AADELORRTTU ADULTERATOR
AADEMNORSTW TRADESWOMAN
AADENNRRTUW UNWARRANTED
AADENRSSWWY WAYWARDNESS
AADENRSTTUU UNSATURATED
AADEQRRSTUY QUARTER DAYS
AADFFORRSTW FAST-FORWARD
AADFGHINNST HANDFASTING
AADFHHILLOY HALF-HOLIDAY
AADFILRSSTU FRUIT SALADS
AADFLLLOOSY ALL FOOLS' DAY
AADGGIINPRS DISPARAGING
AADGGOOOUUU OUAGADOUGOU
AADGHHOPRSW SHADOWGRAPH
AADGHILMNNN MANHANDLING
AADGHILNNNP PANHANDLING
AADGHINOSSW WASHING SODA
AADGHINRSWW WASH DRAWING
AADGHINSSWY WASHING DAYS
AADGHIOPRRY RADIOGRAPHY
AADGHLPRSSU SPLASH GUARD
AADGHMNRSTU DRAUGHTSMAN
AADGIIINRRT IRRADIATING
AADGIIKLNNR KALININGRAD
AADGIILMRST MADRIGALIST
AADGIILNNNO ANGLO-INDIAN
AADGIILNNVZ VANDALIZING
AADGIILNORR RAILROADING
AADGIIMNRTZ DRAMATIZING
AADGINNOPRS GRAND PIANOS
AADGINORSTU GRADUATIONS
AADGNNOPRSS SNAPDRAGONS
AADGNOOPRST GASTROPODAN
AADHHINSTTT THIS AND THAT
AADHIIMOPRS ADIAPHORISM
AADHIIOPRST ADIAPHORIST
AADHILRSTWW WITHDRAWALS
AADHIOOPRSU ADIAPHOROUS
AADHIOPPRTY PARATYPHOID
AADHIOPRRTY PARATHYROID
AADHLORSUYZ HAZARDOUSLY
AADHORRSSUU HADROSAURUS
AADIIINNNOR INDO-IRANIAN
AADIIINORRT IRRADIATION
AADIIJNOSTU JUDAISATION
AADIIJNOTUZ JUDAIZATION
AADIILLNTTU ALTITUDINAL, LATITUDINAL
AADIILNOOTX OXIDATIONAL
AADIILNOPSS ANADIPLOSIS
AADIILNORTT TRADITIONAL
AADIILNORTV INVALIDATOR
AADIILNOSTV VALIDATIONS
AADIILNOSTY DIALYSATION
AADIILNTTTU ATTITUDINAL
AADIILOSUUV AUDIO-VISUAL
AADIIMNORST ADMIRATIONS
AADIINNORSU DINOSAURIAN
AADIINNOTTX ANTIOXIDANT
AADIIPRSSST ASPIDISTRAS

AADILLMNOOT AMONTILLADO
AADILLMORTY MALADROITLY
AADILMNORTY MANDATORILY
AADILOORSTV VASODILATOR
AADILOPPRSV DISAPPROVAL
AADIMNNOPRS PRIMA DONNAS
AADJMNNPRSU PANJANDRUMS
AADJNNORRST TRANS-JORDAN
AADLMNNNOSS NO-MAN'S-LANDS
AAEEEFFLMMT FEMME FATALE
AAEEEGNSTTT ESTATE AGENT
AAEEEGRSTWY STEERAGEWAY
AAEEEHNRRTW EARTHENWARE
AAEEEHNRTVW WEATHER VANE
AAEEEIKPSSS SPEAKEASIES
AAEEEMNNOSS SEA ANEMONES
AAEEEMNPPST APPEASEMENT
AAEEEMPRSTU TAPE MEASURE
AAEEENNRRST NEAR EASTERN
AAEEEPRRSTX EXASPERATER
AAEEFGMRRRW GERM WARFARE
AAEEFHHILRT FAITH HEALER
AAEEFHIRRTW FAIR-WEATHER
AAEEFHLMTWY MEET HALFWAY
AAEEFHRSSTV AFTERSHAVES
AAEEFKLMRST FLEA MARKETS
AAEEFLSTVVY SAFETY VALVE
AAEEFNRRSST TRANSFERASE
AAEEFRSSTTT AFTERTASTES
AAEEGGLMORT AGGLOMERATE
AAEEGGORRTX EXAGGERATOR
AAEEGHHMORR HAEMORRHAGE
AAEEGHLOOPS OESOPHAGEAL
AAEEGHNPPRR PAPERHANGER
AAEEGIKLNTV LEAVE TAKING
AAEEGILLLNS SELAGINELLA
AAEEGILLLTT TAGLIATELLE
AAEEGILLNNT GENTIANELLA
AAEEGILMSSX SEXAGESIMAL
AAEEGILNPPT EATING APPLE
AAEEGILPRTT TETRAPLEGIA
AAEEGINNNRT ARGENTINEAN
AAEEGINPPRR REAPPEARING
AAEEGINPRSS PARAGENESIS
AAEEGINPRST GREASEPAINT
AAEEGINRRTW GRANITEWARE
AAEEGINRSTV VEGETARIANS
AAEEGLMMRSU RUMMAGE SALE
AAEEGLMNOPT PLANOGAMETE
AAEEGLNNPTT PLANTAGENET
AAEEGLNRTTV TRAVEL AGENT
AAEEGLORTVY LAEVOGYRATE
AAEEGLPRSTY PEARLY GATES
AAEEGMMNNST MANAGEMENTS
AAEEGMMORRS AEROGRAMMES
AAEEGMNNRRT ARRANGEMENT
AAEEGMNOPRT POMEGRANATE
AAEEGMNRSTY EAST GERMANY
AAEEGMNSSTU ASSUAGEMENT

AAEEGNPRRRR PREARRANGER
AAEEHHLNNPT NAPHTHALENE
AAEEHILMOPR HEMERALOPIA
AAEEHIMMNPT AMPHETAMINE
AAEEHIMNRTT METATHERIAN
AAEEHIPRSST PARESTHESIA
AAEEHKMOPTY TAKE-HOME PAY
AAEEHKQRSTU EARTHQUAKES
AAEEHLLOSTW AT WHOLESALE
AAEEHLLSTTU HAUSTELLATE
AAEEHLNPTTV HEPTAVALENT
AAEEHMNOORR AMENORRHOEA
AAEEIILLTVV ALLEVIATIVE
AAEEIILMRST MATERIALISE
AAEEIILMRTZ MATERIALIZE
AAEEIILRRST ARTERIALISE
AAEEIILRRTZ ARTERIALIZE
AAEEIILRTTV RETALIATIVE
AAEEIINRSSV SANSEVIERIA
AAEEIKLLMRT ALKALIMETER
AAEEILLMNNT LINEAMENTAL
AAEEILLPPTV APPELLATIVE
AAEEILLQRTU EQUILATERAL
AAEEILMMPST SEMIPALMATE
AAEEILNNPRT PENETRALIAN
AAEEILNRTTV ALTERNATIVE
AAEEIMNNRSS SAN MARINESE
AAEEIMSSSTT METASTASISE
AAEEIMSSTTZ METASTASIZE
AAEEIOPRTVV EVAPORATIVE
AAEEIPPRRTV PREPARATIVE
AAEEIPRSTTX EXPATRIATES
AAEEKLNRSTT RATTLESNAKE
AAEELLNRTTY ALTERNATELY
AAEELLNSTTV AT ALL EVENTS
AAEELLOOSST A SLATE LOOSE
AAEELLPRSTY PLATELAYERS
AAEELMNSTTT TESTAMENTAL
AAEELMQRSSU SQUARE MEALS
AAEELNNPTTV PENTAVALENT
AAEELNPSSTT PLEASANTEST
AAEELNPSTTV SEPTAVALENT
AAEELNRTTTV TETRAVALENT
AAEELOPRTTX EXTRAPOLATE
AAEEMNORTUX AUXANOMETER
AAEEMQRSSTU MARQUESSATE
AAEENNRSSUW UNAWARENESS
AAEFFIIMRTV AFFIRMATIVE
AAEFFILORSV LOVE AFFAIRS
AAEFGHILNRT FARTHINGALE
AAEFGILPRST SEPTIFRAGAL
AAEFGLLLNST FLAGELLANTS
AAEFGLSSSTY SAFETY GLASS
AAEFGMNRRTY FRAGMENTARY
AAEFHILNRTW FATHER-IN-LAW
AAEFIIILMRS FAMILIARISE
AAEFIIILMRZ FAMILIARIZE
AAEFIIORRSV SAVOIR-FAIRE
AAEFILMMNRT FIRMAMENTAL

AAEFILMMNSY FAMILY NAMES
AAEFILMNRTY FILAMENTARY
AAEFLLNRRTY FRATERNALLY
AAEFLMPSSTY SAFETY LAMPS
AAEFLOPSSTT SOFT PALATES
AAEFLRSSSTT FALSE STARTS
AAEFORRSTYZ SAFETY RAZOR
AAEGGGGINRT AGGREGATING
AAEGGGINORT AGGREGATION
AAEGGGLNSUV LUGGAGE VANS
AAEGGIIMNTW WAITING GAME
AAEGGILNTTU AGGLUTINATE
AAEGGIMMNTU GAMETANGIUM
AAEGGINNRRR REARRANGING
AAEGGLRRUUY A REGULAR GUY
AAEGGNORRUW NARROW GAUGE
AAEGHHIIKST HIGH AS A KITE
AAEGHIINRVW HAIRWEAVING
AAEGHIMNORR MENORRHAGIA
AAEGHINNNSS SHENANIGANS
AAEGHLLNOXY HEXAGONALLY
AAEGHLMOOTY HAEMATOLOGY
AAEGHLNPRTU HEPTANGULAR
AAEGHLOPPRY PALEOGRAPHY
AAEGHMNOPRY ANEMOGRAPHY
AAEGHMOPRRS PHRASEOGRAM
AAEGHNOPRTY PYTHAGOREAN
AAEGHNPRRST STRAPHANGER
AAEGHNSTTTU SET AT NAUGHT
AAEGIIIMNTV IMAGINATIVE
AAEGIILLNTV ALLEVIATING
AAEGIILMRST MAGISTERIAL
AAEGIILNRTT RETALIATING
AAEGIILPRRS PLAGIARISER
AAEGIILPRRZ PLAGIARIZER
AAEGIIMNNRT REANIMATING
AAEGIIMNRSS MINAS GERAIS
AAEGIINNOTV EVAGINATION
AAEGIINORTV VARIEGATION
AAEGIINPTTX EXPATIATING
AAEGIIRTTVV GRAVITATIVE
AAEGIKMNPST MASKING TAPE
AAEGILLLNPR PARALLELING
AAEGILLNNST SAINT GALLEN
AAEGILLNOST ALLEGATIONS
AAEGILLNPPR APPARELLING
AAEGILLNPPY APPEALINGLY
AAEGILLNRST GALLANTRIES
AAEGILMMNOS MAGLEMOSIAN
AAEGILMNRTT MALTREATING
AAEGILMNSTT STALEMATING
AAEGILMSSTT STALAGMITES
AAEGILNNRTT ALTERNATING
AAEGILNORTY LEGATIONARY
AAEGILNOSTT GESTATIONAL
AAEGILNQRUU EQUIANGULAR
AAEGILNRTTU TRIANGULATE
AAEGILNRTUV GRANULATIVE
AAEGIMNNRRT ARRAIGNMENT

AAEGIMRSSTT	MAGISTRATES
AAEGINNOPRS	SINGAPOREAN
AAEGINNTTTU	ATTENUATING
AAEGINOPRTV	EVAPORATING
AAEGIOPPRTV	PROPAGATIVE
AAEGIOPSTTY	STEATOPYGIA
AAEGIPRSSTT	STAG PARTIES
AAEGLLNNSST	GALLANTNESS
AAEGLLOPRTY	PYROGALLATE
AAEGLLORSSU	SAUSAGE ROLL
AAEGLMOPRRU	PARLOUR GAME
AAEGLNNPRTU	PENTANGULAR
AAEGLNRSTTU	STRANGULATE
AAEGNNRSSTV	VAGRANTNESS
AAEHHIILMOP	HAEMOPHILIA
AAEHHOPPSST	PHOSPHATASE
AAEHHOTUVWY	WHAT HAVE YOU
AAEHIIMNOPS	HEMIANOPSIA
AAEHIIMNSST	HISTAMINASE
AAEHIINPSTT	ANTIPATHIES
AAEHILLMTTY	I'LL EAT MY HAT
AAEHILNPSTW	WESTPHALIAN
AAEHILORRTX	EXHILARATOR
AAEHIMOSSST	HAEMOSTASIS
AAEHKLORSTT	HOLKAR STATE
AAEHKLRSSST	SALT SHAKERS
AAEHLNOPPRY	ALPHA PYRONE
AAEHLNPRSTY	PHALANSTERY
AAEHMNOOOTZ	HAEMATOZOON
AAEHMNORSTU	ATHERMANOUS
AAEHMNORSWW	WASHERWOMAN
AAEHMOPRTTU	THAUMATROPE
AAEHMOSSTTY	STAY-AT-HOMES
AAEIIIKNNOS	ANISEIKONIA
AAEIIILRSUX	AUXILIARIES
AAEIIJNRSSS	JANISSARIES
AAEIILLMNNR	MILLENARIAN
AAEIILLMNRT	MATRILINEAL
AAEIILLNOTV	ALLEVIATION
AAEIILLNPRT	PATRILINEAL
AAEIILLPSTV	PALLIATIVES
AAEIILMMRST	MATERIALISM
AAEIILMNRRT	AIR TERMINAL
AAEIILMRSTT	MATERIALIST
AAEIILMRTTY	MATERIALITY
AAEIILNNOST	NATIONALISE
AAEIILNNOTZ	NATIONALIZE
AAEIILNNPST	PALESTINIAN
AAEIILNORST	RATIONALISE, REALISATION
AAEIILNORTT	RETALIATION
AAEIILNORTZ	RATIONALIZE, REALIZATION
AAEIILPPRSS	PARALEIPSIS
AAEIILQTTUV	QUALITATIVE
AAEIIMNNORT	REANIMATION
AAEIIMNNOTX	EXAMINATION, EXANIMATION
AAEIINPRSST	ERASTIANISM
AAEIINNPPRT	PARIPINNATE
AAEIINOPTTX	EXPATIATION
AAEIINOSTTV	AESTIVATION

AAEIKLLMRTY	ALKALIMETRY
AAEIKLMNOPT	KLEPTOMANIA
AAEILLLMNOT	LAMELLATION
AAEILLLMPRS	PARALLELISM
AAEILLLOSTV	SAL VOLATILE
AAEILLLPRST	PARALLELIST
AAEILLNNPTY	TIN PAN ALLEY
AAEILLNOOTV	ALVEOLATION
AAEILLNOPPT	APPELLATION
AAEILLQRSTU	AQUARELLIST
AAEILMMNRST	MATERNALISM
AAEILMNNOTT	LAMENTATION
AAEILMNORST	MONASTERIAL
AAEILMNPRST	PARLIAMENTS, PATERNALISM
AAEILMNPRTU	PLANETARIUM
AAEILMNRRTU	ULTRAMARINE
AAEILMOORRT	AMELIORATOR
AAEILMOPTTT	TOTIPALMATE
AAEILNNOPTX	EXPLANATION
AAEILNNORTT	ALTERNATION
AAEILNNOSST	SENSATIONAL
AAEILNNPRST	TRANSALPINE
AAEILNOOPRT	OPERATIONAL
AAEILNOPPRY	PLAYER PIANO
AAEILNOPRRT	PROLETARIAN
AAEILNORSTT	ALTERATIONS
AAEILNORSTX	RELAXATIONS
AAEILNORTUV	REVALUATION
AAEILNOSTUV	EVALUATIONS
AAEILNPRSST	PARTIALNESS
AAEILNPRSTT	PATERNALIST
AAEILNPRSTW	LAWN PARTIES
AAEILNRRSTU	SERTULARIAN
AAEILNRSTTV	AT INTERVALS
AAEILOPRRTT	PROLETARIAT
AAEILORRTTY	RETALIATORY
AAEILORSSSS	ASSESSORIAL
AAEIMMOOPST	MESOPOTAMIA
AAEIMNNOSSY	MAYONNAISES
AAEIMNNSTTT	ATTAINMENTS
AAEIMOPPRTX	APPROXIMATE
AAEINNNOSTX	ANNEXATIONS
AAEINNOSSTT	ASSENTATION
AAEINNOSTTT	NATION STATE
AAEINNOTTTU	ATTENUATION
AAEINNRRSVY	ANNIVERSARY
AAEINOOPRTV	EVAPORATION
AAEINOORSTT	AEROSTATION
AAEINOPPRRT	PREPARATION
AAEINOPRRST	REPARATIONS
AAEINOPRSST	SEPARATIONS
AAEINORSSTU	AUSTRONESIA
AAEINOSTTTT	ATTESTATION
AAEIOPPPRRT	APPROPRIATE
AAEIORSSTTV	ASSORTATIVE
AAEIPRSSSTT	SEPARATISTS
AAEKMRSSSTT	TASKMASTERS
AAELLNOPRSS	SOLAR PANELS
AAELLOPSSTT	ELASTOPLAST

AAELLORRSTT STELLARATOR
AAELMNORSVV REMOVAL VANS
AAELMNPQTUU QUANTUM LEAP
AAELMOPRRTU ARMOUR PLATE
AAELNNRSSTU NATURALNESS
AAELNOPRTXY EXPLANATORY
AAELNORRSTT ALTERNATORS
AAELNRRSSTV TRANSVERSAL
AAELNRRSTUV TRANSVALUER
AAELPRRSTTT RATTLETRAPS
AAEMNNRSSTV MANSERVANTS
AAEMNOPRTTU PORTMANTEAU
AAEMNOSSTTW STATESWOMAN
AAEMOOPRSTZ SPERMATOZOA
AAEMORSSTTT TOASTMASTER
AAEMPRSSSTT PAST MASTERS
AAENNPPRTTU APPURTENANT
AAENNPRRSTT TRANSPARENT
AAENNPRSTTU SUPERNATANT
AAENRRSSTTU RESTAURANTS
AAEOOPPRRRT PARATROOPER
AAEOPPRRRTY PREPARATORY
AAEOPRRTUVW WATER VAPOUR
AAEOPRSSTTU STRATOPAUSE
AAEPPRSSTTY A PRETTY PASS
AAFFGIIILNT AFFILIATING
AAFFGILOPST GAFF-TOPSAIL
AAFFGIMNRSU RAGAMUFFINS
AAFFIIILNOT AFFILIATION
AAFFIIMNORT AFFIRMATION
AAFGHILNNOU FIONNGHUALA
AAFGHIMNOSV SHAVING FOAM
AAFGIINNSTZ FANTASIZING
AAFGILLNRST FALLING STAR
AAFGINORRSU FARRAGINOUS
AAFIIILMRTY FAMILIARITY
AAFIINNOTTU INFATUATION
AAFILLMNORW LAMINAR FLOW
AAFILMNOORT FORMATIONAL
AAFILNOOSTT FLOATATIONS
AAFIMNNNRTY INFANTRYMAN
AAFINNOOPRT PROFANATION
AAFLNNOORST NASOFRONTAL
AAFNOOPRRTY PROFANATORY
AAGGGHILNSU LAUGHING GAS
AAGGHHIINNS SHANGHAIING
AAGGHHIOPRY HAGIOGRAPHY
AAGGHIIJMNT THINGAMAJIG
AAGGIILNNVZ GALVANIZING
AAGGIIMMNNS MISMANAGING
AAGGIINRTTV GRAVITATING
AAGGIKLMNSS GLASS-MAKING
AAGGILLNOST ALGOLAGNIST
AAGGILNNTTU AGGLUTINANT
AAGGINOPPRT PROPAGATING
AAGGHHLOPPRY HAPLOGRAPHY
AAGHIIINRRS HAIR-RAISING
AAGHIILLNOP ANGLOPHILIA

AAGHIKLLMNR HALLMARKING
AAGHILLMNPY LYMPHANGIAL
AAGHILLMNRS MARSHALLING
AAGHILNRSSY HARASSINGLY
AAGHIRSTTWY STRAIGHTWAY
AAGHLNOPPRY PLANOGRAPHY
AAGHLOOPPRR POLAROGRAPH
AAGHNOPPRST PANTOGRAPHS
AAGHNOPPRTY PANTOGRAPHY
AAGHNOPRRUY URANOGRAPHY
AAGIIILMNRY IMAGINARILY
AAGIIIMNNNT MAINTAINING
AAGIIIMNNOT IMAGINATION
AAGIIKNNPST PAINSTAKING
AAGIILMNORT MIGRATIONAL
AAGIILMNRTY MARGINALITY
AAGIILMPRSS PLAGIARISMS
AAGIILNNTTZ TANTALIZING
AAGIILNPPTT PALPITATING
AAGIILOPRRT GLORIA PATRI
AAGIILPRSST PLAGIARISTS
AAGIIMMNNTY MAGNANIMITY
AAGIIMMSSTT ASTIGMATISM
AAGIIMNNORT MARGINATION
AAGIIMSSSSU MISSISSAUGA
AAGIINNOSST ASSIGNATION
AAGIINORTTV GRAVITATION
AAGIIRSSTTU SAGITTARIUS
AAGIJKNOPRT JOKING APART
AAGILLLNPPY APPALLINGLY
AAGILLLOOSS GLOSSOLALIA
AAGILLMNNTY MALIGNANTLY
AAGILLMRSTY MAGISTRALLY
AAGILLNRTUV VULGAR LATIN
AAGILMMMOST MAMMALOGIST
AAGILNNORTU GRANULATION
AAGILNNRSTT TRANSLATING
AAGILNOSUVY YUGOSLAVIAN
AAGILNRRTUY GRANULARITY
AAGILOPRRTU PURGATORIAL
AAGIMMNNOSU MAGNANIMOUS
AAGIMNNOSST ANTAGONISMS
AAGIMNNPRSW WARMING PANS
AAGIMNOOSSU ANISOGAMOUS
AAGIMNOOSTU ANGIOMATOUS
AAGIMPRSSTT PRAGMATISTS
AAGINNOSSTT ANTAGONISTS
AAGINOOPPRT PROPAGATION
AAGINORRTUU INAUGURATOR
AAGINOSSSTT GAS STATIONS
AAGLLMNRTUU MULTANGULAR
AAGLNNOOSSX ANGLO-SAXONS
AAGLNOOPRTW PATROL WAGON
AAGOOPPRRST PROPAGATORS
AAHIILMNNOT HAMILTONIAN
AAHIILNNORT ANNIHILATOR
AAHIILNNOST INHALATIONS
AAHIILNNRSV NAIL VARNISH
AAHIINPRSST ANTIPHRASIS

AAHILMPRSTY AMPHISTYLAR
AAHIMMNNOPY NYMPHOMANIA
AAHIMMNNOPRS ANAMORPHISM
AAHIMNOPRSS OARSMANSHIP
AAHINNOPRTY ANTIPHONARY
AAHIOPRSTXY ASPHYXIATOR
AAHKOPRRSWW SPARROWHAWK
AAHLLMMORSW MARSHMALLOW
AAHMNNRSTTU TRANSHUMANT
AAHNNOPRSXY NASOPHARYNX
AAHNNRRSTUY THYRSANURAN
AAHNOPRSTTU NATUROPATHS
AAHNOPRTTUY NATUROPATHY
AAIIILMNOTT IMITATIONAL
AAIIILNRTTU UTILITARIAN
AAIIJKLMNOR KILIMANJARO
AAIIKNNOSTY KYANISATION
AAIIKNNOTYZ KYANIZATION
AAIILLLPSUZ LAPIS LAZULI
AAIILLMPRTY IMPARTIALLY
AAIILMMNORT MATRIMONIAL
AAIILMNNOST NATIONALISM
AAIILMNOPRT PATRIMONIAL
AAIILMNOPST MAINTOPSAIL
AAIILMNORST RATIONALISM
AAIILNNOSTT NATIONALIST
AAIILNNOTTY NATIONALITY
AAIILNOORTV VARIOLATION
AAIILNOPPTT PALPITATION
AAIILNORSTT RATIONALIST
AAIILNORTTT ATTRITIONAL
AAIILNORTTY RATIONALITY
AAIILNOSTTU SITUATIONAL
AAIIMMNNOOT AMMONIATION
AAIIMMNORSV MORAVIANISM
AAIIMNOOSTT ATOMISATION
AAIIMNOOTTZ ATOMIZATION
AAIIMNOPRTT IMPARTATION
AAIIMNOPSTT IMPASTATION
AAIIMNORRST ROTARIANISM
AAIIMNRSSTU SANITARIUMS
AAIINOPPRST APPARITIONS
AAIINOPRSST ASPIRATIONS
AAILLLOSTWW SWALLOWTAIL
AAILLORRSTY SARTORIALLY
AAILMMNOSTU SUMMATIONAL
AAILMMOPPRS MALAPROPISM
AAILMNOPRTU MANIPULATOR
AAILMNRSTTT TRANSMITTAL
AAILNNOPSTT PLANTATIONS
AAILNNORSTT TRANSLATION
AAILNOPPSSY PASSION PLAY
AAILNOSSTTU SALUTATIONS
AAILNRSSTTU NATURALISTS
AAILOORTTTZ TOTALIZATOR
AAILOPRRTUV VAPOUR TRAIL
AAIMMNOPSTT MAIN-TOPMAST
AAIMMNOSSUY IMMUNOASSAY
AAIMNOOSSST ANASTOMOSIS

AAIMNOPSTTU AMPUTATIONS
AAIMNORSSTU SANATORIUMS
AAINNNOOSTT ANNOTATIONS
AAINNNOPRST NONPARTISAN
AAINNOPRSTT PATRON SAINT
AAINOPSSTTY PAY STATIONS
AAKKNORRSSY KRASNOYARSK
AAKLLMPRUUU KUALA LUMPUR
AALLMNOOSUY ANOMALOUSLY
AALLNNRTUUY UNNATURALLY
AALMMOOPSST SOMATOPLASM
AALNNPRSSTT TRANSPLANTS
AALNORRSSTT TRANSLATORS
AALOOQRRTUY ROYAL QUARTO
AALORSSTTTU ALTOSTRATUS
AAMNPRSSTTY SMARTY-PANTS
ABBBDENRRSU RUBBER BANDS
ABBBELOPSSU SOAP BUBBLES
ABBCCEEHKNR BACKBENCHER
ABBCCEEHKNS BACKBENCHES
ABBCCEEHMOR BEACHCOMBER
ABBCCGIKMNO BACKCOMBING
ABBCDEEFIKO BIOFEEDBACK
ABBCDEEILRS DESCRIBABLE
ABBCDEENRSS CRABBEDNESS
ABBCDEMRRSU BREADCRUMBS
ABBCEEEHRRS BEAR'S-BREECH
ABBCEEJLSTU SUBJECTABLE
ABBCEHIILOT BIBLIOTHECA
ABBCEIILNRS INSCRIBABLE
ABBCEKMNRSU BACK NUMBERS
ABBCHHIRTTU RABBIT HUTCH
ABBCHINPRTU RABBIT PUNCH
ABBCIILMNOY BIBLIOMANCY
ABBCKMOOORY BACKROOM BOY
ABBDDEGIORR BRIDGEBOARD
ABBDDEIINRR BIRD-BRAINED
ABBDEELORTU REDOUBTABLE
ABBDEGNNRRU BRANDENBURG
ABBDEIILNTU INDUBITABLE
ABBDEIINRRU INDIA RUBBER
ABBDEILRSSU DISBURSABLE
ABBDEIMNRSY BABY-MINDERS
ABBDEIMORRS BOMBARDIERS
ABBDELLNRSU LANDLUBBERS
ABBDELORTUY REDOUBTABLY
ABBDEMMNORT BOMBARDMENT
ABBDGIIINNS BIAS BINDING
ABBDHIINORZ BIROBIDZHAN
ABBDIILNTUY INDUBITABLY
ABBEELPRRTU PERTURBABLE
ABBEEMNSSTU SUBBASEMENT
ABBEENRSTTU BUTTER BEANS
ABBEGIKLMOO GO LIKE A BOMB
ABBEGILNORU BELABOURING
ABBEGINORTW BROWBEATING
ABBEHHIKSSS SHISH KEBABS
ABBEHIIILNT INHIBITABLE
ABBEHILLPSU PUBLISHABLE

ABBEHILNRSU BURNISHABLE
ABBEIILLMOZ MOBILIZABLE
ABBEILMSTTU SUBMITTABLE
ABBEINRSTUU SUBURBANITE
ABBEIRSSTTY BABY-SITTERS
ABBEKLNOSTT BOTTLE BANKS
ABBELMSSSUY SUBASSEMBLY
ABBELNPRRTU RUBBER PLANT
ABBELPRRTUY PERTURBABLY
ABBEMPRRSTU RUBBER STAMP
ABBGIINSTTY BABY-SITTING
ABBGILMNOOZ BAMBOOZLING
ABBGILNORSY ABSORBINGLY
ABBIILLORTY BIBLIOLATRY
ABBIILMOPRS PROBABILISM
ABBIILOPRST PROBABILIST
ABBIILOPRTY PROBABILITY
ABCCCHKKLOO CHOCK-A-BLOCK
ABCCDEEELSU SUCCEEDABLE
ABCCDEEIIRT BACTERICIDE, TEREBIC ACID
ABCCDEHHKNU HUNCHBACKED
ABCCDEKLMOY BLACK COMEDY
ABCCDENNORT CONCERT BAND
ABCCEEILNOV CONCEIVABLE
ABCCEEKLOPU PEACOCK BLUE
ABCCEELLLOT COLLECTABLE
ABCCEELORRT CORRECTABLE
ABCCEEMNNRU ENCUMBRANCE
ABCCEFILNOS CONFISCABLE
ABCCEFIORSU BACCIFEROUS
ABCCEGINNOU CONCUBINAGE
ABCCEIILPTY PECCABILITY
ABCCEIKKLST STICKLEBACK
ABCCEILNOTV CONVICTABLE
ABCCEILNOVY CONCEIVABLY
ABCCEILOSTT ECTOBLASTIC
ABCCEINORRT CENTROBARIC
ABCCELMOOST CLOSE COMBAT
ABCCELORSUU SUCCOURABLE
ABCCHIKSSTW SWITCHBACKS
ABCCIIMOORT MACROBIOTIC
ABCCIINOTVY BICONCAVITY
ABCCILLLOUY BUCOLICALLY
ABCCILORSTU SUBCORTICAL
ABCCINOOSTT TOBACCONIST
ABCCIOORSUV BACCIVOROUS
ABCCKNORTUY BACK COUNTRY
ABCCMOPSSTU SUBCOMPACTS
ABCCNORSTTU SUBCONTRACT
ABCDDEEELNS DESCENDABLE
ABCDDEEFIIN BID DEFIANCE
ABCDDEEFLOU DOUBLE-FACED
ABCDDEEILRS SLICED BREAD
ABCDDEFINOR FORBIDDANCE
ABCDDEKLORS BADDERLOCKS
ABCDEEEERRT DECEREBRATE
ABCDEEEILPR DEPRECIABLE
ABCDEEFHNRR FRENCH BREAD
ABCDEEGGKLL BLACKLEGGED

ABCDEEIILMM IMMEDICABLE
ABCDEEILLMN CLEAN-LIMBED
ABCDEEILNRS RESCINDABLE
ABCDEEILORV DIVORCEABLE
ABCDEEILPRT PREDICTABLE
ABCDEEINORS DECARBONISE
ABCDEEINORZ DECARBONIZE
ABCDEELLNRY BELLY DANCER
ABCDEELLNSY BELLY DANCES
ABCDEELLPRU PRECLUDABLE
ABCDEELMMNO COMMENDABLE
ABCDEELMNNO CONDEMNABLE
ABCDEELMORU DOUBLE CREAM
ABCDEELNNOS CONDENSABLE
ABCDEELNRRY CANDLEBERRY
ABCDEELOPSU DOUBLE-SPACE
ABCDEENORRT CENTREBOARD
ABCDEHILSTW SWITCHBLADE
ABCDEHIRRTW BIRD-WATCHER
ABCDEHORSSS CHESSBOARDS
ABCDEIILOSS DISSOCIABLE
ABCDEIILTUY EDUCABILITY
ABCDEIIORTT OBITER DICTA
ABCDEIKLLST BLACKLISTED
ABCDEIKLRSS BACKSLIDERS
ABCDEILNOST ENDOBLASTIC
ABCDEILPRTY PREDICTABLY
ABCDEINOORT NOTICE BOARD
ABCDEINRRST TRANSCRIBED
ABCDEINRSTU DISTURBANCE
ABCDELMMNOY COMMENDABLY
ABCDELMNRSU UNSCRAMBLED
ABCDEOORRSS SCOREBOARDS
ABCDGIIKLNS BACKSLIDING
ABCDGKNORSU BACKGROUNDS
ABCDHIIMRTY DITHYRAMBIC
ABCDHIIRSTU HUDIBRASTIC
ABCDHINOOPR BRANCHIOPOD
ABCDHIOPSTX DISPATCH BOX
ABCDHIORSTW SWITCHBOARD
ABCDHNOORRY HYDROCARBON
ABCDIIILOST IDIOBLASTIC
ABCDIILLSSY DISSYLLABIC
ABCDIILORUV VIBRACULOID
ABCDIIMNOSY BIODYNAMICS
ABCDIKLOSWW BLACK WIDOWS
ABCDMNORRUU CARBORUNDUM
ABCEEEFFKOR COFFEE BREAK
ABCEEEFFLOT COFFEE TABLE
ABCEEEFLNOR ENFORCEABLE
ABCEEEHIKRT BREAK THE ICE
ABCEEEIKRRS ICEBREAKERS
ABCEEEILPRV PERCEIVABLE
ABCEEEILRSV RECEIVABLES, SERVICEABLE
ABCEEEILRSX EXERCISABLE
ABCEEEILRTV CELEBRATIVE
ABCEEELMNRS RESEMBLANCE
ABCEEELORRV RECOVERABLE
ABCEEELPRST RESPECTABLE

ABCEEEMMNRR REMEMBRANCE
ABCEEEMMNRT EMBRACEMENT
ABCEEFHNNRS FRENCH BEANS
ABCEEFIILPS SPECIFIABLE
ABCEEFIILRT CERTIFIABLE, RECTIFIABLE
ABCEEFIINRY BENEFICIARY
ABCEEFILLMR LEAF-CLIMBER
ABCEEFINNOT BENEFACTION
ABCEEFINRTU RUBEFACIENT
ABCEEFNORST BENEFACTORS
ABCEEGIINOT ABIOGENETIC
ABCEEGILNRT CELEBRATING
ABCEEHHILRS CHERISHABLE
ABCEEHKLNQU BLANK CHEQUE
ABCEEHLORTU RETOUCHABLE
ABCEEHLRSTT STRETCHABLE
ABCEEHORRRT TORCHBEARER
ABCEEIILLNTU INELUCTABLE
ABCEEILNORT CELEBRATION
ABCEEILNPST INSPECTABLE
ABCEEILNSUX INEXCUSABLE
ABCEEILORRV IRREVOCABLE
ABCEEILRRSU IRRECUSABLE
ABCEEILRRTU RECRUITABLE
ABCEEILRSTT BATTLE CRIES
ABCEEILRSVY SERVICEABLY
ABCEEINNRTY BICENTENARY
ABCEEINORRT CEREBRATION
ABCEEINORST BARONETCIES
ABCEEINORTX EXORBITANCE
ABCEEINRRRS CRANBERRIES
ABCEEKLPPPR BLACK PEPPER
ABCEEKLRRRW KERB CRAWLER
ABCEEKRSSTT BACK STREETS
ABCEEKSSTTU BUCKET SEATS
ABCEELNORSV CONSERVABLE,
  CONVERSABLE
ABCEELOPRSW PACE BOWLERS
ABCEELOSTUU BETULACEOUS
ABCEELPRSTY RESPECTABLY
ABCEELRTTUU TUBERCULATE
ABCEENORRST ARBORESCENT
ABCEENORSSV OBSERVANCES
ABCEEOPPRSS SPACE PROBES
ABCEFHNOOPR FRANCOPHOBE
ABCEFIMNORY BY MAIN FORCE
ABCEFINORTU RUBEFACTION
ABCEFLMNOOR CONFORMABLE
ABCEFLMOORT COMFORTABLE
ABCEGHILLNY BELLYACHING
ABCEGHORRTU TURBOCHARGE
ABCEGILNNOS CONSIGNABLE
ABCEGILNOST BLASTOGENIC
ABCEHHIOOPT THEOPHOBIAC
ABCEHHJOSTT HATCHET JOBS
ABCEHHKRSUW BUSHWHACKER
ABCEHIILPRT BLEPHARITIC
ABCEHIKLNSY CHELYABINSK
ABCEHILNORV OLIVE BRANCH

ABCEHILOPSU BICEPHALOUS
ABCEHILPRST BIRTHPLACES
ABCEHIMORTT BATHOMETRIC
ABCEHIMRTTY BATHYMETRIC
ABCEHINOOPR NECROPHOBIA
ABCEHKNOORS ON HORSEBACK
ABCEHKPSSTU PASS THE BUCK
ABCEHLLOSTT TABLECLOTHS
ABCEHLNOTUU UNTOUCHABLE
ABCEHLNRSUU UNCRUSHABLE
ABCEHMOPRST CHAMBER POTS
ABCEIIJLSTU JUSTICIABLE
ABCEIILNOTX INTOXICABLE
ABCEIILRTUV LUBRICATIVE
ABCEIIMNOTV COMBINATIVE
ABCEIKNORTW CABINETWORK
ABCEILLLOPS COLLAPSIBLE
ABCEILLMORU BIMOLECULAR
ABCEILLNOOZ COLONIZABLE
ABCEILLNTUY INELUCTABLY
ABCEILLRTUV CARVEL-BUILT
ABCEILMOPRS COMPRISABLE
ABCEILMOPRT PROBLEMATIC
ABCEILMORST BLASTOMERIC, MEROBLASTIC
ABCEILMOTVY COMBATIVELY
ABCEILNOSTT ENTOBLASTIC
ABCEILNPRSU REPUBLICANS
ABCEILNRSTU INSCRUTABLE
ABCEILNSUXY INEXCUSABLY
ABCEILORRVY IRREVOCABLY
ABCEIMNOORT EMBROCATION
ABCEINNORTY CYBERNATION
ABCEINRRRST TRANSCRIBER
ABCEIRSTTUV SUBTRACTIVE
ABCEJKLMRSU LUMBERJACKS
ABCEKKORSST BACKSTROKES
ABCEKLNORSU COALBUNKERS
ABCELLLMNOO COLLEMBOLAN
ABCELLNOORS COLLARBONES
ABCELMNRRSU UNSCRAMBLER
ABCELNNOTUU UNCOUNTABLE
ABCELNPRTUU PUNCTURABLE
ABCEOOOORRRT CORROBORATE
ABCEORRRTTU CARBURETTOR
ABCEORSTUUY BUTYRACEOUS
ABCFGIINRTU BIFURCATING
ABCFGINOSTU OBFUSCATING
ABCFHINOOST SON-OF-A-BITCH
ABCFIILLMOR BACILLIFORM
ABCFIINORTU BIFURCATION
ABCFINOOSTU OBFUSCATION
ABCFLMNOORY CONFORMABLY
ABCFLMOORTY COMFORTABLY
ABCGHHIOOPP PHAGOPHOBIC
ABCGIIKNOUV BIVOUACKING
ABCGIILNRTU LUBRICATING
ABCGIINNORZ CARBONIZING
ABCGILLOORY BRYOLOGICAL
ABCGILNPRUW PUB-CRAWLING

ABCGINRSTTU SUBTRACTING	ABDEEEHLLVW WELLBEHAVED
ABCHHIILOTT BATHOLITHIC	ABDEEEILLRV DELIVERABLE
ABCHHILOOOP OCHLOPHOBIA	ABDEEEELLOPV DEVELOPABLE
ABCHHIOPRSS ARCHBISHOPS	ABDEEEELMNRU DENUMERABLE
ABCHHLNOOPR LOPHOBRANCH	ABDEEEELNSST BELATEDNESS
ABCHIIIMOPT AMPHIBIOTIC	ABDEEEELRRSS REDRESSABLE
ABCHIILOPSY BIOPHYSICAL	ABDEEEMNSST DEBASEMENTS
ABCHIKLMSST BLACKSMITHS	ABDEEEPRSTT BESPATTERED
ABCHIKLRSST BLACKSHIRTS	ABDEEERSSTW SWEETBREADS
ABCHILLOOST HOLOBLASTIC	ABDEEFGIIRR FIRE BRIGADE
ABCHILNOORR BRONCHIOLAR	ABDEEFIILNN INDEFINABLE
ABCHINOOPTY NYCTOPHOBIA	ABDEEFILLTT BATTLEFIELD
ABCHINORRSY CHRYSAROBIN	ABDEEGGINRR GINGERBREAD
ABCHKLMORUU BLACK HUMOUR	ABDEEGLLOUZ DOUBLE-GLAZE
ABCHKOOSSUY YAH BOO SUCKS	ABDEEGLNOTU DOUBLE AGENT
ABCIIILOSTY SOCIABILITY	ABDEEGMNOOR BOOMERANGED
ABCIIIMNORT IMBRICATION	ABDEEHILRTY HEREDITABLY
ABCIIINOSTT ANTIBIOTICS	ABDEEHILSST ESTABLISHED
ABCIILLMRSU LUMBRICALIS	ABDEEHORSST BROADSHEETS
ABCIILLPTUY CULPABILITY	ABDEEIILLRS LIBERALISED
ABCIILNOPTU PUBLICATION	ABDEEIILLRZ LIBERALIZED
ABCIILNORTU LUBRICATION	ABDEEIILRST DETRIBALISE
ABCIIMNNOOT COMBINATION	ABDEEIILRTZ DETRIBALIZE
ABCIINORRTU RUBRICATION	ABDEEIILSST DESTABILISE
ABCIINORSTT ABSTRICTION	ABDEEIILSTZ DESTABILIZE
ABCIKLLMMSU BLACK MUSLIM	ABDEEIKNNSY KIDNEY BEANS
ABCILMMORUU COLUMBARIUM	ABDEEILMNNO DENOMINABLE
ABCILNORTUU LUCUBRATION	ABDEEILMNST DISABLEMENT
ABCILNRSTUY INSCRUTABLY	ABDEEILMSSS DISASSEMBLE
ABCILOOPRST BLASTOPORIC	ABDEEILNNRT DINNER TABLE
ABCILOPRSTU SUBTROPICAL	ABDEEILNPSS DISPENSABLE
ABCILORRSTU LUBRICATORS	ABDEEILNRSU UNDESIRABLE
ABCINNOORTU CONURBATION	ABDEEILORRT DELIBERATOR
ABCINOORSTU OBSCURATION	ABDEEILORTT OBLITERATED
ABCINORSTTU SUBTRACTION	ABDEEINNRRW BREADWINNER
ABCLLRSTUUU SUBCULTURAL	ABDEEKLOSTU DOUBLE TAKES
ABCNORRSTUY SUBCONTRARY	ABDEEKNORSZ BAKER'S DOZEN
ABDDDEELOTU DOUBLE DATED	ABDEEKORRSY KEYBOARDERS
ABDDDEIMNOR BROADMINDED	ABDEELLNPRU PLUNDERABLE
ABDDEEEILRT DELIBERATED	ABDEELLSSTY SELL-BY DATES
ABDDEEENSSS DEBASEDNESS	ABDEELMNORZ BRONZE MEDAL
ABDDEEIILTT DEBILITATED	ABDEELMNOTU DEMOUNTABLE
ABDDEEIKMRS DISEMBARKED	ABDEELORRTW WORLD-BEATER
ABDDEELOSTU DOUBLE DATES	ABDEELORSTY DESTROYABLE
ABDDEFFILNN EFF AND BLIND	ABDEFGINORR FINGERBOARD
ABDDEGIRRSW DRAWBRIDGES	ABDEFGIRSSU FIGURED BASS
ABDDEHKLNNU BUNDELKHAND	ABDEFIILNNY INDEFINABLY
ABDDEHLLNOO LO AND BEHOLD	ABDEFIRRSTU BREADFRUITS
ABDDEHOOSWX SHADOW-BOXED	ABDEFLLOTUU DOUBLE FAULT
ABDDEIMNNST DISBANDMENT	ABDEGGILNOT GOLD-BEATING
ABDDELMOORW WARM-BLOODED	ABDEGGIRRSU BUDGERIGARS
ABDDELNORRS BORDERLANDS	ABDEGHINSSU SUBHEADINGS
ABDDELORRTW BLADDERWORT	ABDEGIILNNT DINING TABLE
ABDDGIINORV DIVINGBOARD	ABDEGIILSSU DISGUISABLE
ABDDOORRSSW BROADSWORDS	ABDEGIKNORY KEYBOARDING
ABDEEEEGLRU BELEAGUERED	ABDEGIMNRST ABRIDGMENTS
ABDEEEFHRST FEATHER BEDS	ABDEGLNNOOU GO A BUNDLE ON
ABDEEEFRRST FAST-BREEDER	ABDEGOOOORRV GO OVERBOARD
ABDEEEHILRT HEREDITABLE	ABDEHIINNPR HAIRPIN BEND

ABDEHIINNTU UNINHABITED
ABDEHIORSTW WHITEBOARDS
ABDEHLNSSSU HUSBANDLESS
ABDEIIJLNOS DISJOINABLE
ABDEIILLLST DISTILLABLE
ABDEIILLTWY WELDABILITY
ABDEIILMNOT INDOMITABLE
ABDEIIRSSTU ABSURDITIES
ABDEIKLNNRU UNDRINKABLE
ABDEIILLNSY BLIND ALLEYS
ABDEILLLSSY DISSYLLABLE
ABDEILLOSSV DISSOLVABLE
ABDEILMOTTU TOLBUTAMIDE
ABDEILMSSSY DISASSEMBLY
ABDEILNRSUY UNDESIRABLY
ABDEILOPRSV DISPROVABLE
ABDEIMRSTUW DUMBWAITERS
ABDEINORSTU SUBORDINATE
ABDELMOORST BLOODSTREAM
ABDELMRRSUY LUMBERYARDS
ABDELOPRRTU PROTRUDABLE
ABDEMNORRST BARNSTORMED
ABDENOPRSUU SUPERABOUND
ABDFILMOORR DOLABRIFORM
ABDFLOOORRS FLOORBOARDS
ABDGHIINNRS BRANDISHING
ABDGHIMNOTU BAD-MOUTHING
ABDGINOPRRS SPRINGBOARD
ABDGINORRST STRINGBOARD
ABDGMOORRSS SMORGASBORD
ABDHHIOOPRY HYDROPHOBIA
ABDHINOOPRS ON SHIPBOARD
ABDIIILTTUY DUTIABILITY
ABDIILMNOTY INDOMITABLY
ABDIINOSTUU SUBAUDITION
ABDILNOOSST BLOODSTAINS
ABDIMNNOSTU SUBDOMINANT
ABDINORRSUY SUBORDINARY
ABDLNOOOSTT ODONTOBLAST
ABDNOORSTUU ROUNDABOUTS
ABDOOORRSTUU TROUBADOURS
ABEEEEFLORS FORESEEABLE
ABEEEEGLNRR REGENERABLE
ABEEEEIKLMV MAKE-BELIEVE
ABEEEEMNRTV BEREAVEMENT
ABEEEERRRTV REVERBERATE
ABEEEFLMNRT FERMENTABLE
ABEEEGLORSW ELBOW GREASE
ABEEEGLRRTT REGRETTABLE
ABEEEHHINPR HEBEPHRENIA
ABEEEHMNRRV BREMERHAVEN
ABEEEHRSSTT HARTEBEESTS
ABEEEIKRRST TIEBREAKERS
ABEEEIILLPRV REPLEVIABLE
ABEEEILMMPR IMPERMEABLE
ABEEEILMMST EMBLEMATISE
ABEEEILMMTZ EMBLEMATIZE
ABEEEILPRRV REPRIEVABLE
ABEEEILRRTV RETRIEVABLE

ABEEEIMNSST ABSENTEEISM
ABEEELMNNTT ENTABLEMENT
ABEEELMNRRU REMUNERABLE
ABEEELNPRST PRESENTABLE
ABEEELNPRTV PREVENTABLE
ABEEELPRRSV PRESERVABLE
ABEEELPSTUY BEAUTY SLEEP
ABEEENQTUUY BEAUTY QUEEN
ABEEENRRRTV REVERBERANT
ABEEERRSTTV VERTEBRATES
ABEEFFILORT FORFEITABLE
ABEEFFRSTTU BUFFER STATE
ABEEFGILNRR REFRANGIBLE
ABEEFGLORTT FORGETTABLE
ABEEFIILLQU LIQUEFIABLE
ABEEFIILNRT ANTIFEBRILE
ABEEFILPRTU PUTREFIABLE
ABEEFILRRTU IRREFUTABLE
ABEEFLLNSSU BALEFULNESS
ABEEFLMOPRR PERFORMABLE
ABEEFLSSTTY SAFETY BELTS
ABEEFNRRRTU AFTERBURNER
ABEEGGILNPS SLEEPING BAG
ABEEGHINQTU BEQUEATHING
ABEEGIINOSS ABIOGENESIS
ABEEGILMNPR IMPREGNABLE
ABEEGILRRST REGISTRABLE
ABEEGINORRV OVERBEARING
ABEEGINRRTU TRUE BEARING
ABEEGLLLNSU ANGELUS BELL
ABEEGLRRTTY REGRETTABLY
ABEEHHPRSTY BATHYSPHERE
ABEEHIILNRT INHERITABLE
ABEEHILMPSS BLASPHEMIES
ABEEHILPRSS PERISHABLES
ABEEHILRSST ESTABLISHER
ABEEHILSTUX EXHAUSTIBLE
ABEEHINRSSS BEARISHNESS
ABEEHINRSST BREATHINESS
ABEEHKNORRT HEARTBROKEN
ABEEHKNORSS BONESHAKERS
ABEEHLMPRSS BLASPHEMERS
ABEEHLOORRS SEBORRHOEAL
ABEEHLORRWW WHEELBARROW
ABEEHORSTTU THEREABOUTS
ABEEHORSTUW WHEREABOUTS
ABEEIILLRRS LIBERALISER
ABEEIILLRRZ LIBERALIZER
ABEEIILMNPS PLEBEIANISM
ABEEIILMNST INESTIMABLE
ABEEIILNQTU INEQUITABLE
ABEEIILQRTU EQUILIBRATE
ABEEIKLLNSS LIKABLENESS
ABEEIKLLRSV BASKERVILLE
ABEEIKLMORR BOILERMAKER
ABEEIKLNNST LINEN BASKET
ABEEILLNORT INTOLERABLE
ABEEILLNRSS LIBERALNESS
ABEEILLNSSV LIVABLENESS

ABEEILLOPRT   BOILERPLATE
ABEEILLOPTX   EXPLOITABLE
ABEEILLRUVZ   ULVERIZABLE
ABEEILMMORZ   MEMORIZABLE
ABEEILMMRRU   MARE LIBERUM
ABEEILMNNOT   MENTIONABLE
ABEEILMNNRU   INNUMERABLE
ABEEILMORRV   IRREMOVABLE
ABEEILMORST   STEAM-BOILER
ABEEILNNOPS   PENSIONABLE
ABEEILNNSTT   TABLE TENNIS
ABEEILNPRSU   INSUPERABLE
ABEEILNRRTV   INVERTEBRAL
ABEEILNRSST   TRIABLENESS
ABEEILNSSST   BEASTLINESS
ABEEILNSSSZ   SIZABLENESS
ABEEILNSSTW   WITNESSABLE
ABEEILORSTT   BITTER ALOES
ABEEILRRSST   LIBERATRESS
ABEEILRRTVY   RETRIEVABLY
ABEEINNQRTU   BARQUENTINE
ABEEINORSSU   BUENOS AIRES
ABEEINRSSTW   BEAR WITNESS
ABEEINRSTUX   EXURBANITES
ABEEINSSSUV   ABUSIVENESS
ABEEIOPRRTV   REPROBATIVE
ABEEIPRRRSS   RASPBERRIES
ABEEJLLMSSU   JUMBLE SALES
ABEEKLNSTTW   WET BLANKETS
ABEEKMMNNST   EMBANKMENTS
ABEELLLMSSY   BLAMELESSLY
ABEELLLMTUU   UMBELLULATE
ABEELMMNSSY   ASSEMBLYMEN
ABEELMNPRTU   NUMBERPLATE
ABEELMNSTTT   BATTLEMENTS
ABEELNNOOPR   NONOPERABLE
ABEELNNOSST   NOTABLENESS
ABEELNPRSTY   PRESENTABLY
ABEELNPRTVY   PREVENTABLY
ABEELNRTTUU   UNUTTERABLE
ABEELNRTUXY   EXUBERANTLY
ABEELOSTUUY   BEAUTEOUSLY
ABEELPRRSTY   PRESBYTERAL
ABEELQQRUUU   ALBUQUERQUE
ABEEMNRSSTU   SURBASEMENT
ABEENNNRRSU   RUNNER BEANS
ABEFFIILORT   FORTIFIABLE
ABEFFILLORS   BILLS OF FARE
ABEFFLNORRU   BARREL OF FUN
ABEFGIIILNS   SIGNIFIABLE
ABEFGIILLOR   GLORIFIABLE
ABEFGIILNNR   INFRANGIBLE
ABEFGIINTUY   BEAUTIFYING
ABEFHHLORRT   HALF-BROTHER
ABEFHIRRSTT   AFTERBIRTHS
ABEFHLNSSSU   BASHFULNESS
ABEFIIILNRT   NITRIFIABLE
ABEFIIILRTV   VITRIFIABLE
ABEFIIILSTY   FEASIBILITY

ABEFIIJLSTU   JUSTIFIABLE
ABEFIILLLMO   MOLLIFIABLE
ABEFIILLOOT   BIFOLIOLATE
ABEFIILNOSS   FISSIONABLE
ABEFILLLOSS   BILLS OF SALE
ABEFILLTUUY   BEAUTIFULLY
ABEFILRRTUY   IRREFUTABLY
ABEFLLOORST   FOOTBALLERS
ABEFLMOORTT   FOOT-LAMBERT
ABEFLMOOSTT   FALSE BOTTOM
ABEGGHRSSTU   STAGGERBUSH
ABEGGIILNOR   GLOBIGERINA
ABEGHIIMNSV   MISBEHAVING
ABEGHIINNRT   HIBERNATING
ABEGHIIOPRS   BIOGRAPHIES
ABEGHILMNOO   HAEMOGLOBIN
ABEGHILMNPS   BLASPHEMING
ABEGHIOPRRS   BIOGRAPHERS
ABEGHLLLSUY   BELLY LAUGHS
ABEGHLNOOPS   ANGLOPHOBES
ABEGIIINNRT   INEBRIATING
ABEGIILMNTT   TIMETABLING
ABEGIILNRVZ   VERBALIZING
ABEGIILRTUV   GIVE IT A BURL
ABEGIIRRSTU   SUBIRRIGATE
ABEGILMNNOZ   EMBLAZONING
ABEGILMNOTY   AMBLYGONITE
ABEGILMNPRY   IMPREGNABLY
ABEGILNNRTY   BANTERINGLY
ABEGILNORSU   SUBREGIONAL
ABEGILNOSSX   SIGNAL BOXES
ABEGILRRYZZ   GRIZZLY BEAR
ABEGINNOPSU   SUBPOENAING
ABEGINNORRT   INTERROBANG
ABEGINNRSST   STRING BEANS
ABEGINRSSTU   GAS TURBINES
ABEGLLORSSW   GLASSBLOWER
ABEGMORRSTU   BURGOMASTER
ABEHHIRRSSU   HAIRBRUSHES
ABEHHORRSTT   HEARTTHROBS
ABEHIILMOPT   AMPHIBOLITE
ABEHIILPSTT   BLEPHATITIS
ABEHIINNORT   HIBERNATION
ABEHIKLNNTU   UNTHINKABLE
ABEHILMNOST   ABOLISHMENT
ABEHILNRSSU   NAILBRUSHES
ABEHILOOPRU   AILUROPHOBE
ABEHILOPRSW   WORSHIPABLE
ABEHILPSSTT   BATTLESHIPS
ABEHINOORTT   BOTHERATION
ABEHINOPRSV   VIBRAPHONES
ABEHKOOPRSS   PHRASEBOOKS
ABEHLMOORTW   BARTHOLOMEW
ABEHLMOPSSU   BLASPHEMOUS
ABEHLMORTWY   BLAMEWORTHY
ABEHLORRSSU   HARBOURLESS
ABEHLORRSTY   LAY BROTHERS
ABEHNNOOTTY   ETHNOBOTANY
ABEIIIILLST   LIABILITIES

ABEIIILLLMT   ILLIMITABLE
ABEIIILLNOR   BILLIONAIRE
ABEIIILLRTY   RELIABILITY
ABEIIINNORT   INEBRIATION
ABEIILLLLRY   ILLIBERALLY
ABEIILLMMST   BIMETALLISM
ABEIILLMPSU   IMPLAUSIBLE
ABEIILLMTTY   MELTABILITY
ABEIILLRSTT   BRISTLETAIL
ABEIILMNSTY   INESTIMABLY
ABEIILMSSUX   BISEXUALISM
ABEIILNQRTU   EQUILIBRANT
ABEIILNQTUY   INEQUITABLY
ABEIILNRRTT   INTERTRIBAL
ABEIILNRTTY   RENTABILITY
ABEIILOPPRT   PROPITIABLE
ABEIILOPRTY   OPERABILITY
ABEIILORTXY   EXORABILITY
ABEIILRSSST   STABILISERS
ABEIILRSSTZ   STABILIZERS
ABEIILRSTTU   BRUTALITIES
ABEIILRSTUY   REUSABILITY
ABEIILSTTTY   TESTABILITY
ABEIILSTUXY   BISEXUALITY
ABEIILTTTWY   WETTABILITY
ABEIINNOSTT   SINO-TIBETAN
ABEIINRRSSV   RIVER BASINS
ABEIIRRSTTU   TRIBUTARIES
ABEIIRTTTUV   ATTRIBUTIVE
ABEILLMORTU   RAMBOUILLET
ABEILLNORTY   INTOLERABLY
ABEILLNRSSY   BRAINLESSLY
ABEILLOPRSX   PILLAR BOXES
ABEILMMOSST   METABOLISMS
ABEILMOOSTU   AUTOMOBILES
ABEILNNPRTU   UNPRINTABLE
ABEILNOOSSS   OBSESSIONAL
ABEILNOSTTY   OBSTINATELY
ABEILNPRSUY   INSUPERABLY
ABEILOORRTT   OBLITERATOR
ABEILORSSTW   BELOW STAIRS
ABEILQRRTUY   BIQUARTERLY
ABEILRRSTTT   BRITTLE-STAR
ABEIMNNSSSU   BUSINESSMAN
ABEIMNORSTU   TAMBOURINES
ABEIMNRRSSU   SUBMARINERS
ABEINNNRSTU   BURNT SIENNA
ABEINNORSTV   INOBSERVANT
ABEINNOSSTT   ABSTENTIONS
ABEINOOPRRT   PROBATIONER, REPROBATION
ABEINOORSTV   OBSERVATION
ABEINORSTUV   SUBORNATIVE
ABEINOSSTTU   ABSTENTIOUS
ABEINSSTTUV   SUBSTANTIVE
ABEIRSSTTUV   SUBSTRATIVE
ABEKKORSSTW   WORKBASKETS
ABEKLOPRRRS   PORK BARRELS
ABEKMNNOSTU   MOUNTEBANKS
ABEKNOPRRSW   PAWNBROKERS

ABEKOOSTTTU   STATUTE BOOK
ABELLNNORVY   NONVERBALLY
ABELMNORRSY   SALMONBERRY
ABELNNORSUV   VERBAL NOUNS
ABELNOOPPST   POSTPONABLE
ABELNOOPSST   TABLESPOONS
ABELNOPPSTU   UNSTOPPABLE
ABELNRTTUUY   UNUTTERABLY
ABELOPPRSTU   SUPPORTABLE
ABELRRSTTUU   SURREBUTTAL
ABEMNOORRSW   BONE MARROWS,
     MARROWBONES
ABEMNORRRST   BARNSTORMER
ABENOPRRSSS   PRESS BARONS
ABENOPRRTTU   PROTUBERANT
ABENOPRSSTU   BEANSPROUTS
ABEOORRSTVY   OBSERVATORY
ABEOPSSTTUY   BEAUTY SPOTS
ABFGHNOORRU   FARNBOROUGH
ABFGILNOSTY   FLYING BOATS
ABFIIILLLTY   FALLIBILITY
ABFIIIMNORT   FIMBRIATION
ABFIIJLSTUY   JUSTIFIABLY
ABFILMNSTUU   FUNAMBULIST
ABFIMOORSTU   FIBROMATOUS
ABGGGINNOOT   TOBOGGANING
ABGGIIMTUUY   AMBIGUGUITY
ABGGIJNSTUU   SUBJUGATING
ABGGILOOORY   AGROBIOLOGY
ABGHIINRSTT   BRATTISHING
ABGHIINSTTU   BATHING SUIT
ABGHIKPRRST   BRIGHT SPARK
ABGHILMOOPY   AMPHIBOLOGY
ABGHINNTTUY   ANYTHING BUT
ABGHLMOORRU   MARLBOROUGH
ABGIIILNSTZ   STABILIZING
ABGIIILNTTY   TANGIBILITY
ABGIILMNSTU   SUBLIMATING
ABGIILNOOST   OBLIGATIONS
ABGIILNRTUZ   BRUTALIZING
ABGIILNRTVY   VIBRATINGLY
ABGIINRTTTU   ATTRIBUTING
ABGIJNOORTU   OBJURGATION
ABGIJNOSTUU   SUBJUGATION
ABGIKLLNNOR   BANKROLLING
ABGIKNNOPRW   PAWNBROKING
ABGIKNNPRTU   BANKRUPTING
ABGILLNNOSW   SNOWBALLING
ABGILLNORUY   LABOURINGLY
ABGILMOSUUY   AMBIGUOUSLY
ABGIMNOSUUU   UNAMBIGUOUS
ABGINOORSTU   SUBROGATION
ABGINOORSTW   ROWING BOATS
ABGJOORRTUY   OBJURGATORY
ABHHIKRSTTU   TURKISH BATH
ABHHIOOOPPT   PHOTOPHOBIA
ABHILMMNOPT   PHANTOM LIMB
ABHIMNORRTU   NORTHUMBRIA
ABHIOOPRSSU   RUSSOPHOBIA

ABHLLMOPSTY LYMPHOBLAST	ACCCEHORSTW COWCATCHERS
ABHLOOPRSTT TROPHOBLAST	ACCCEIILMRT CLIMACTERIC
ABIIIILMTTY IMITABILITY	ACCCEIILLNSY ENCYCLICALS
ABIIIILNTVY INVIABILITY	ACCCEILMOPS ACCOMPLICES
ABIIILLOSTY ISOLABILITY	ACCCEILORTU LEUCOCRATIC
ABIIILLOTVY VIOLABILITY	ACCCELMNOPY COMPLACENCY
ABIIILNRSTY RINSABILITY	ACCCHIILLOT LACCOLITHIC
ABIIILNSTTY INSTABILITY	ACCCHILOOORT OCHLOCRATIC
ABIIILPSSTY PASSIBILITY	ACCCHOOPRTY PTOCHOCRACY
ABIIILRTTVY VIBRATILITY	ACCCIIOOPRS CAPRICCIOSO
ABIIILSTTUY SUITABILITY	ACCCILLOOSU CALCICOLOUS
ABIIINOPRTT BIPARTITION	ACCCIMMOORS MACROCOSMIC
ABIIKLORTWY WORKABILITY	ACCCIMOOPRS MACROSCOPIC
ABIIILLMPSUY IMPLAUSIBLY	ACCCIOOPRSTY CYSTOCARPIC
ABIIILLOSTVY SOLVABILITY	ACCDDEEIINO DECANEDIOIC
ABIILMNOSTU SUBLIMATION	ACCDDEHNPRU PUNCHED CARD
ABIILMOSTUY AMBITIOUSLY	ACCDDEIIRST DISACCREDIT
ABIILNORTTU TRIBULATION	ACCDDEINORS DISCORDANCE
ABIILNRSTUY INSALUBRITY	ACCDDEIRRST CREDIT CARDS
ABIILOPRTTY PORTABILITY	ACCDDELLMOU MALOCCLUDED
ABIILOPRTVY PROVABILITY	ACCDDELOPPU CLOUD-CAPPED
ABIILOQTTUY QUOTABILITY	ACCDDIIIMST DIDACTICISM
ABIILRRTTUY TRIBUTARILY	ACCDEEEENNT ANTECEDENCE
ABIIMNNOORT BROMINATION	ACCDEEEFNRT FACE-CENTRED
ABIIMNOSTUU UNAMBITIOUS	ACCDEEELNOS ADOLESCENCE
ABIINNORTTU TURBINATION	ACCDEEELNST DECALESCENT
ABIINOOPSTT OBSTIPATION	ACCDEEFIILR DECALCIFIER
ABIINOORSTT ABORTIONIST	ACCDEEFNORY CONFEDERACY
ABIINORTTTU ATTRIBUTION	ACCDEEGOPRU COUP DE GRACE
ABILLNOOSST BALLOONISTS	ACCDEEHIMNO MACHINE CODE
ABILLOORSUY LABORIOUSLY	ACCDEEHIORS ARCHDIOCESE
ABILLORSTTU SUBLITTORAL	ACCDEEHQRSU CHEQUE CARDS
ABILNNOORSU LABOR UNIONS	ACCDEEIISTV DESICCATIVE
ABIMNORRSST BRAINSTORMS	ACCDEEIKRSW WISECRACKED
ABINNOOOPRT ON PROBATION	ACCDEEIMORS DEMOCRACIES
ABINNOORSTU SUBORNATION	ACCDEEIORTT DECORTICATE
ABINOORRSTU BRONTOSAURI	ACCDEELNOSV CONVALESCED
ABINOOSSSST BASSOONISTS	ACCDEEMNSUU SUCCEDANEUM
ABINOSSSTTU BUS STATIONS, SUBSTATIONS	ACCDEENORST CONSECRATED
ABINRRSSTTU BRAINS TRUST	ACCDEFINOST CONFISCATED
ABOORSSTTUU ROUSTABOUTS	ACCDEFNOSTU SAFE-CONDUCT
ACCCDEHILNO CHALCEDONIC	ACCDEGHORST DOGCATCHERS
ACCCDEIILNU NUCLEIC ACID	ACCDEGIINST DESICCATING
ACCCDENNOOR CONCORDANCE	ACCDEHHITTT CHITCHATTED
ACCCDENNOTU CONDUCTANCE	ACCDEHHRSSU ARCHDUCHESS
ACCCDILLOOP DIPLOCOCCAL	ACCDEHILPRY DIPHYCERCAL
ACCCDIMOPST COMPACT DISC	ACCDEHNPRSU CARDPUNCHES
ACCCEEELNOS COALESCENCE	ACCDEHNRSTU UNSCRATCHED
ACCCEEELNST LACTESCENCE	ACCDEHOPSTT SCOTCH TAPED
ACCCEEEMNRS MARCESCENCE	ACCDEIIIMRT ACIDIMETRIC
ACCCEEHILRS ECCLESIARCH	ACCDEIILLTY DEICTICALLY
ACCCEELMNOP COMPLACENCE	ACCDEIILNOT CONCILIATED
ACCCEELNOPT CONCEPTACLE	ACCDEIINOST DESICCATION
ACCCEFHKORS COCKCHAFERS	ACCDEIKLNST CANDLESTICK
ACCCEHIISTT CATECHISTIC	ACCDEIKLNSW CANDLEWICKS
ACCCEHIMOTT CHEMOTACTIC	ACCDEILLOPS PECCADILLOS
ACCCEHIOPRT ECHOPRACTIC	ACCDEILMOPT COMPLICATED
ACCCEHKOORS COCKROACHES	ACCDEILNOST OCCIDENTALS
ACCCEHNORTY TECHNOCRACY	ACCDEINOOTU COEDUCATION

ACCDEINPRSY DISCREPANCY
ACCDEIPRRTU PICTURE CARD
ACCDEKORRRT TRACK RECORD
ACCDELMOPTY COMPACTEDLY
ACCDELNOSSS SECOND-CLASS
ACCDENNOTUU UNACCOUNTED
ACCDFIIINOP INDO-PACIFIC
ACCDGILNORY ACCORDINGLY
ACCDHHNSSUU SUCH AND SUCH
ACCDHHRRSUY CHURCHYARDS
ACCDHIIILOP ACIDOPHILIC
ACCDHIIMORT DICHROMATIC
ACCDHIINORT ACHONDRITIC
ACCDHILORSV CLAVICHORDS
ACCDHINOPRY HYDNOCARPIC
ACCDHINORYY HYDROCYANIC
ACCDIILLNRY CYLINDRICAL
ACCDIILLORY CODICILLARY
ACCDIILNOOR CROCODILIAN
ACCDIIOOPRS RADIOSCOPIC
ACCDIIPRSSU PRUSSIC ACID
ACCDIMOSSTU DISACCUSTOM
ACCDNNOOTTY COTTON CANDY
ACCEEEEHKSS CHEESECAKES
ACCEEEEHMRS CREAM CHEESE
ACCEEEENNSV EVANESCENCE
ACCEEEFIKOP PIECE OF CAKE
ACCEEEFILMN MALEFICENCE
ACCEEEFLNRT REFLECTANCE
ACCEEEHILRT CHELICERATE
ACCEEEIKKLO COCK-A-LEEKIE
ACCEEELNOPS OPALESCENCE
ACCEEELNRST RECALESCENT
ACCEEELPRST RECEPTACLES
ACCEEFIIRTT CERTIFICATE
ACCEEFIKRRR FIRECRACKER
ACCEEFINORV VOCIFERANCE
ACCEEGHILMO GEOCHEMICAL
ACCEEGHINTY EYE-CATCHING
ACCEEGHORRV COVER CHARGE
ACCEEGILRRT GREAT CIRCLE
ACCEEHHIRST CHESHIRE CAT
ACCEEHIINRS CHICANERIES
ACCEEHILMNO CHAMELEONIC
ACCEEHILNRT CHANTICLEER
ACCEEHINRRT ARCHENTERIC
ACCEEHKORTW WEATHERCOCK
ACCEEHLLNRY CHANCELLERY
ACCEEHLNOXY CYCLOHEXANE
ACCEEIILNRT ELECTRICIAN
ACCEEIIMPST SEPTICAEMIC
ACCEEIISTVX EXSICCATIVE
ACCEEIKNPRS SCIENCE PARK
ACCEEIKRRSW WISECRACKER
ACCEEILNNST INCALESCENT
ACCEEIMNOPS CINEMASCOPE
ACCEEIMNRTT METACENTRIC
ACCEEINQSTU ACQUIESCENT
ACCEEIOPRRT RECIPROCATE

ACCEEIORSSS ACCESSORIES
ACCEELMNNOT CONCEALMENT
ACCEEMNNORR NECROMANCER
ACCEEMNOPPU COME-UPPANCE
ACCEENNNOTU COUNTENANCE
ACCEENNORSV CONVERSANCE
ACCEENNORTT CONCENTRATE,
   CONCERTANTE
ACCEENNORVY CONVEYANCER
ACCEENNOSVY CONVEYANCES
ACCEENPSSTU SUSCEPTANCE
ACCEEOPRSUY CYPERACEOUS
ACCEEORRSSU RACECOURSES
ACCEFFHHINS CHAFFINCHES
ACCEFFIIOSU EFFICACIOUS
ACCEFHLRSTY FLYCATCHERS
ACCEFIINRRY FERRICYANIC
ACCEFILORSU CALCIFEROUS
ACCEFINORRY FERROCYANIC
ACCEFMNNOOR CONFORMANCE
ACCEGGIKNRT GET CRACKING
ACCEGHHITTW CATCHWEIGHT
ACCEGHIINTZ CATECHIZING
ACCEGHIKMNT CHECKMATING
ACCEGHIKNQU QUICK-CHANGE
ACCEGHINNOR ENCROACHING
ACCEGHIOPRR CEROGRAPHIC
ACCEGIINQSU ACQUIESCING
ACCEGILLOOT CETOLOGICAL
ACCEGILLOPY CYCLOPLEGIA
ACCEGINNORS CARCINOGENS
ACCEGINNOSZ COGNIZANCES
ACCEHHHHIIR CHICHIHAERH
ACCEHHIISTX HEXASTICHIC
ACCEHHISSTY HESYCHASTIC
ACCEHIILOST CATHOLICISE
ACCEHIILOTT HELIOTACTIC
ACCEHIILOTZ CATHOLICIZE
ACCEHIIMNST MECHANISTIC
ACCEHIINNST TECHNICIANS
ACCEHIIORRT HIEROCRATIC
ACCEHIIRSTU EUCHARISTIC
ACCEHILLMNO MELANCHOLIC
ACCEHILLNTY TECHNICALLY
ACCEHILMOOZ ZOOCHEMICAL
ACCEHILOPPR PROCEPHALIC
ACCEHILOPXY OXYCEPHALIC
ACCEHIMNNOR CHROMINANCE
ACCEHIMORTT TACHOMETRIC
ACCEHIMORTU EUCHROMATIC
ACCEHIMRTTY TACHYMETRIC
ACCEHIRSSTT SCRATCHIEST
ACCEHKOPPTT PATCH POCKET
ACCEHLLMNOY COLLENCHYMA
ACCEHLLNORS CHANCELLORS
ACCEHLOOSSW SLOWCOACHES
ACCEHNORSTT TECHNOCRATS, TRENCH
   COATS
ACCEHOOSTWZ CZESTOCHOWA

ACCEIIILLNN ACLINIC LINE
ACCEIIILSTV ACCLIVITIES
ACCEIIINPRT ACCIPITRINE
ACCEIIINRST INTRICACIES
ACCEIILLNPR PRECLINICAL
ACCEIILMOSV SEMIVOCALIC
ACCEIILPRRT PRECRITICAL
ACCEIILPRST PERICLASTIC
ACCEIILRRSU CIRCULARISE
ACCEIILRRUZ CIRCULARIZE
ACCEIILRTUV CIRCULATIVE
ACCEIIMNOST COSMETICIAN, ENCOMIASTIC
ACCEIINNOSU INSOUCIANCE
ACCEIINOSTV CONCAVITIES
ACCEIINOSTX EXSICCATION
ACCEIKKOTTT TICK-TACK-TOE
ACCEIKNRSSS CARSICKNESS
ACCEILLPSTY SCEPTICALLY
ACCEILMMORS COMMERCIALS
ACCEILMOPST ECTOPLASMIC
ACCEILNNOTY ANTICYCLONE
ACCEILNOPRT NARCOLEPTIC
ACCEILNORTT CONTRACTILE
ACCEILNORTU CORNICULATE
ACCEILOPRST CEROPLASTIC
ACCEILORSSY ACCESSORILY
ACCEIMMNOTU COMMUNICATE
ACCEIMNNORT NECROMANTIC
ACCEIMOOPRS COMIC OPERAS
ACCEIMORRTY MERITOCRACY
ACCEINNNOTU CONTINUANCE
ACCEINNORST CONCERTINAS
ACCEINNORSU COINSURANCE
ACCEINNORTV CONTRIVANCE
ACCEINOORRY COERCIONARY
ACCEINOOTVV CONVOCATIVE
ACCEINORTTV CONTRACTIVE
ACCEINSSSTU CAUSTICNESS
ACCEIOORSSU SCORIACEOUS
ACCEIORSTUU URTICACEOUS
ACCEJLNOSTU CONJECTURAL
ACCEKNRRSTU NUTCRACKERS
ACCELLOSTTU COALSCUTTLE
ACCELMMNOOP COMMONPLACE
ACCELNNOSTT CONTACT LENS
ACCELORSSSU SUCCESSORAL
ACCELPRRSUU CREPUSCULAR
ACCEMNOPSST COMPACTNESS
ACCENNNOOSS CONSONANCES
ACCENNORSVY CONSERVANCY
ACCENOOPRTU POCOCURANTE
ACCENOORRST CONSECRATOR
ACCENOPRRTT PRECONTRACT
ACCENORRTTU CONTRACTURE
ACCENPRTUUU ACUPUNCTURE
ACCEOORSSTU ECTOSARCOUS
ACCEORSSTUU CRUSTACEOUS
ACCFGIIINRS SACRIFICING
ACCFGILOSUU CALCIFUGOUS

ACCFIIMOORR CORACIIFORM
ACCFINOORST CONFISCATOR
ACCGHIIOOPS HAGIOSCOPIC
ACCGIILNNTU INCULCATING
ACCGIILNOTU GLAUCONITIC
ACCGIILNRTU CIRCULATING
ACCGIINNOOS OCCASIONING
ACCGILLMOOY MYCOLOGICAL
ACCGILLNOOO ONCOLOGICAL
ACCGILLNOOT COLLOCATING
ACCGILLOOTY CYTOLOGICAL
ACCGIMNOSTU ACCUSTOMING
ACCGIMOPRTY CRYPTOGAMIC
ACCGINNORTT CONTRACTING
ACCGINORSTU CORUSCATING
ACCHHIILLNS CHINCHILLAS
ACCHHIIMOPR AMPHICHROIC
ACCHHIINSTT CHAIN STITCH
ACCHHMNORUW CHURCHWOMAN
ACCHIILLSTY STICHICALLY
ACCHIILMOST CATHOLICISM
ACCHIILOSST SCHOLIASTIC
ACCHIILOTTY CATHOLICITY
ACCHIIMNORT CHROMATINIC
ACCHIIMOSST MASOCHISTIC
ACCHIIMSSST SCHISMATICS
ACCHIIOOPST SOCIOPATHIC
ACCHIIOPPRT HIPPOCRATIC
ACCHIIORSTT RHOTACISTIC
ACCHIIPRSTY PSYCHIATRIC
ACCHIKMSSTT MATCHSTICKS
ACCHILLNORY CHRONICALLY
ACCHILLPSYY PSYCHICALLY
ACCHILMOTYY CYCLOTHYMIA
ACCHILOPTTY PHYLOTACTIC
ACCHINOPSTY SYCOPHANTIC
ACCHIOOPTTT PHOTOTACTIC
ACCHIOORRSU CHIAROSCURO
ACCHNOOOPSU CACOPHONOUS
ACCIIIKKNPW PICKWICKIAN
ACCIIILNSTV CALVINISTIC
ACCIIILOSST SOCIALISTIC
ACCIILNNOTU INCULCATION
ACCIILNNQUU QUINCUNCIAL
ACCIILNOORT CONCILIATOR
ACCIILNORTU CIRCULATION
ACCIILNOTVY VOLCANICITY
ACCIILOSTUV ACCLIVITOUS
ACCIILRRTUY CIRCULARITY
ACCIILSSSST CLASSICISTS
ACCIIMNNOTY ACTINOMYCIN
ACCIINNSTTY NYCTINASTIC
ACCIINOORTT CORTICATION
ACCIJNNOTUV CONJUNCTIVA
ACCIKKKKNNS KNICK-KNACKS
ACCILLNOOOT COLLOCATION
ACCILLPRTYY CRYPTICALLY
ACCILMNRRUU CIRCUMLUNAR
ACCILMOPRRU CIRCUMPOLAR

ACCILMOPSTY CYTOPLASMIC
ACCILNOOSST ICONOCLASTS
ACCILNOOTTU OCCULTATION
ACCILOPRSTY PYROCLASTIC
ACCILOPRTTU PLUTOCRATIC
ACCILORRTUY CIRCULATORY
ACCIMMNNOTU COMMUNICANT
ACCIMNNOOTT CONCOMITANT
ACCINNNOSTY INCONSTANCY
ACCINNOOOTV CONVOCATION
ACCINNOORTT CONTRACTION
ACCINOOPRSU CORNUCOPIAS
ACCINOOPSTU OCCUPATIONS
ACCINOORRRW CARRION CROW
ACCINOORSTU CORUSCATION
ACCINOPRRSU CAPRICORNUS
ACCIORSSSTY SYSSARCOTIC
ACCLLLOOORU LOCAL COLOUR
ACCLNNOSTUY CONSULTANCY
ACCLOPRRSUU CORPUSCULAR
ACCNOORRSTT CONTRACTORS
ACDDDEEILTY DEDICATEDLY
ACDDEEINRTU CUT-AND-DRIED
ACDDEEEELRT DECELERATED
ACDDEEEEPRS PREDECEASED
ACDDEEEIPRT DEPRECIATED
ACDDEEEORRT REDECORATED
ACDDEEFFIST DISAFFECTED
ACDDEEGIKLR GRIDDLECAKE
ACDDEEHHIKT THICKHEADED
ACDDEEHHKOS SHOCKHEADED
ACDDEEHLORT COLD-HEARTED
ACDDEEHNORW CROWNED HEAD
ACDDEEHNRSU DUDE RANCHES
ACDDEEIILMS DECIMALISED
ACDDEEIILMZ DECIMALIZED
ACDDEEIIPRS RICE PADDIES
ACDDEEIKRST SIDETRACKED
ACDDEEINRSX CARD INDEXES
ACDDEENNRST TRANSCENDED
ACDDEENNSST DESCENDANTS
ACDDEGIORSU DISCOURAGED
ACDDEHLLOST SADDLECLOTH
ACDDEHNNOSS SECOND HANDS
ACDDEHNOOPY DODECAPHONY
ACDDEIINOST DEDICATIONS
ACDDEIIOSST DISSOCIATED
ACDDEILLMSS MIDDLE CLASS
ACDDEIMNORU ENDOCARDIUM
ACDDEINOORT COORDINATED
ACDDENORRSW SWORD DANCER
ACDDENORSSW SWORD DANCES
ACDEEEEHLRR CHEERLEADER
ACDEEEFFTTU EFFECTUATED
ACDEEEFILNR ILE-DE-FRANCE
ACDEEEFNORT CONFEDERATE
ACDEEEGLLOT DÉCOLLETAGE
ACDEEEHLRTW CARTWHEELED
ACDEEEHORRV OVERREACHED

ACDEEEILNRV DELIVERANCE
ACDEEEIPRTT DECREPITATE
ACDEEEIPRTV DEPRECATIVE
ACDEEEIRSTV EVISCERATED
ACDEEELLNRT CRENELLATED
ACDEEELORRT DECELERATOR
ACDEEENNSTT ANTECEDENTS
ACDEEEOORRTV OVERREACTED
ACDEEEPRRTU RECUPERATED
ACDEEFFHRUU CHAUFFEURED
ACDEEFHLSTT FLAT-CHESTED
ACDEEFIILTT FELICITATED
ACDEEFIORTV VOCIFERATED
ACDEEFLNRUU FRAUDULENCE
ACDEEFMORRS ARMED FORCES
ACDEEGGNORT CONGREGATED
ACDEEGHNRRU UNDERCHARGE
ACDEEGHORRV OVERCHARGED
ACDEEGINPRT DEPRECATING
ACDEEGINRST DESECRATING
ACDEEGINRTU RE-EDUCATING
ACDEEGIORST CATEGORISED
ACDEEGIORST CATEGORIZED
ACDEEGIOTTT TIED COTTAGE
ACDEEGKLNOW ACKNOWLEDGE
ACDEEHIINOT ETHANEDIOIC
ACDEEHILNOT ENDOTHECIAL
ACDEEHILNPP CHIPPENDALE
ACDEEHILNRS CHANDELIERS
ACDEEHILPSY PSYCHEDELIA
ACDEEHIMNRS MERCHANDISE
ACDEEHIMSST SCHEMATISED
ACDEEHIMSTZ SCHEMATIZED
ACDEEHINRTW WINDCHEATER
ACDEEHIORTT OCTAHEDRITE
ACDEEHLLOSU CLOSE-HAULED
ACDEEHMNORW REACH-ME-DOWN
ACDEEHMNSTT DETACHMENTS
ACDEEHNRRTU UNCHARTERED
ACDEEIILLTY EIDETICALLY
ACDEEIILMTV MALEDICTIVE
ACDEEIILPSS SPECIALISED
ACDEEIILPSZ SPECIALIZED
ACDEEIILTUV ELUCIDATIVE
ACDEEIIMMNN MEDICINE MAN
ACDEEIINNRT INCINERATED
ACDEEIIOPPS EPIDIASCOPE
ACDEEIIPRTV PREDICATIVE
ACDEEILLMNY ENDEMICALLY
ACDEEILLNRS CINDERELLAS
ACDEEILNNST CLANDESTINE
ACDEEILNOTT DELECTATION
ACDEEILNRST CENTRALISED, CREDENTIALS
ACDEEILNRSY INCREASEDLY
ACDEEILNRTZ CENTRALIZED
ACDEEILNTTU DENTICULATE
ACDEEILPRTU REDUPLICATE
ACDEEILRSSU SECULARISED
ACDEEILRSTT DECRETALIST

ACDEEILRSUZ SECULARIZED
ACDEEILRTTU RETICULATED
ACDEEIMMNST MEDICAMENTS
ACDEEIMNPRT PREDICAMENT
ACDEEIMORRR MICROREADER
ACDEEIMORST DEMOCRATISE
ACDEEIMORTZ DEMOCRATIZE
ACDEEIMOSTT DOMESTICATE
ACDEEINOPRT DEPRECATION
ACDEEINORST CONSIDERATE, DESECRATION
ACDEEINORTU RE-EDUCATION
ACDEEINPPRT APPRENTICED
ACDEEIOPRRT DEPRECIATOR
ACDEEIOQTUV EQUIVOCATED
ACDEEIORRSV SERVICE ROAD
ACDEEIORRTT DIRECTORATE
ACDEEIPRRST TRADE PRICES
ACDEEIRSTTX DIRECT TAXES
ACDEEISSSTU CASE STUDIES
ACDEEKQRRTU QUARTERDECK
ACDEELLMORU LEUCODERMAL
ACDEELMORRS SCLERODERMA
ACDEELNOPRW CANDLEPOWER
ACDEELNOSST ADOLESCENTS
ACDEELNPTUU PEDUNCULATE
ACDEELNRRSY DRY CLEANERS
ACDEEMMNOTT COMMENTATED
ACDEEMNOPSS ENCOMPASSED
ACDEEMNOPST COMPENSATED
ACDEEMNRTTU TRADUCEMENT
ACDEENNORTV CONTRAVENED
ACDEENORRST SECOND-RATER
ACDEEOPRRTY DEPRECATORY
ACDEFFIIRTV DIFFRACTIVE
ACDEFFLOSTTU DUFFEL COATS
ACDEFGHMORR FROGMARCHED
ACDEFGILRSU DISGRACEFUL
ACDEFHILPST FELDSPATHIC
ACDEFHLORTW FLOWCHARTED
ACDEFHMOOST SMOOTH-FACED
ACDEFIIINNT INFANTICIDE
ACDEFIIINOT DEIFICATION, EDIFICATION
ACDEFIILSTU FEUDALISTIC
ACDEFIIORTY EDIFICATORY
ACDEFIIRRST FRATRICIDES
ACDEFINNOTU FECUNDATION
ACDEFKLNORS FOLK DANCERS
ACDEFLLNORU UNCALLED-FOR
ACDEFLMMNOS SELF-COMMAND
ACDEFNORTUY FECUNDATORY
ACDEGHHIOWY HIGHWAY CODE
ACDEGHIILOT GLOCHIDIATE
ACDEGHIIMNR MICHIGANDER
ACDEGHILLNT CANDLELIGHT
ACDEGHIMOPR DEMOGRAPHIC
ACDEGHINPST DESPATCHING
ACDEGHLOORS GRADE SCHOOL
ACDEGIILLOO IDEOLOGICAL
ACDEGIILNTU ELUCIDATING

ACDEGIIMNSU MISGUIDANCE
ACDEGIINPRT PREDICATING
ACDEGIINSST DIE-CASTINGS
ACDEGILLOOP PEDOLOGICAL
ACDEGILNNRY DRY-CLEANING
ACDEGILOOPS LOGOPAEDICS
ACDEGILRSTT CATTLE GRIDS
ACDEGIMNOSY GEODYNAMICS
ACDEGIMORTY TRAGICOMEDY
ACDEGINNOQU QUINDECAGON
ACDEGINNRTU UNDERACTING
ACDEGIORRSU DISCOURAGER
ACDEGKNORRS ROCK GARDENS
ACDEGLOORST COLD STORAGE
ACDEHIILMPS DICEPHALISM
ACDEHIIOPRT DIAPHORETIC
ACDEHIKMNOS CHAIN-SMOKED
ACDEHILNORT CHLORINATED
ACDEHILOPSU DICEPHALOUS
ACDEHIMOPRS COMRADESHIP
ACDEHIMOSTU MUSTACHIOED
ACDEHINOORS ICOSAHEDRON
ACDEHINOPST DICTAPHONES
ACDEHIOOPRT ORTHOPAEDIC
ACDEHKMRSTU DEUTSCHMARK
ACDEHLLLOPY PHYLLOCLADE
ACDEHLMOSUY CHLAMYDEOUS
ACDEHLNPRTU THUNDERCLAP
ACDEHLRSTTY STRATHCLYDE
ACDEHMNNOOR ENCHONDROMA
ACDEHMNORRY HYDROMANCER
ACDEHOORRTU UROCHORDATE
ACDEHORRTWW DRAW THE CROW
ACDEHORRTYY CRYOHYDRATE
ACDEHRSTTTU DUTCH TREATS
ACDEIIILMOT DOMICILIATE
ACDEIIINSTV INDICATIVES
ACDEIIJLPRU PREJUDICIAL
ACDEIIKNRST INSIDE TRACK
ACDEIILLMNY MEDICINALLY
ACDEIILLNTY IDENTICALLY
ACDEIILLORV VARICELLOID
ACDEIILMNOT MALEDICTION
ACDEIILMRSS DISCLAIMERS
ACDEIILNNOT DECLINATION
ACDEIILNNST INCIDENTALS
ACDEIILNORT DIRECTIONAL
ACDEIILNOST SLIDE-ACTION
ACDEIILNOTU ELUCIDATION
ACDEIILNOTV VALEDICTION
ACDEIILNPTU INDUPLICATE
ACDEIILOPRS PERIODICALS
ACDEIILORRT DIRECTORIAL
ACDEIILPTUV DUPLICATIVE
ACDEIIMNOST MEDICATIONS
ACDEIIMORRT RADIOMETRIC
ACDEIIMORTU AUDIOMETRIC
ACDEIIMPRRU PERICARDIUM
ACDEIINNRTY TYRANNICIDE

ACDEIINOPRT   PREDICATION
ACDEIINORRT   DOCTRINAIRE
ACDEIINOTTX   INTOXICATED
ACDEIIRSTTV   DISTRACTIVE
ACDEIJRSTUU   JUDICATURES
ACDEIKRSTTU   TRACKSUITED
ACDEILLLMOY   MELODICALLY
ACDEILLMNOY   DEMONICALLY
ACDEILLNOOT   DECOLLATION
ACDEILLORRS   CORDILLERAS
ACDEILMNOPS   ENDOPLASMIC
ACDEILMOPRR   DIMERCAPROL
ACDEILNOOST   CONSOLIDATE
ACDEILNORSY   SECONDARILY
ACDEILNORTU   RADIOLUCENT, REDUCTIONAL
ACDEILNORTY   DECLINATORY
ACDEILORTUY   ELUCIDATORY
ACDEILORTVY   VALEDICTORY
ACDEILPPSTU   SUPPLICATED
ACDEIMNNORU   ENDOCRANIUM
ACDEIMNORRS   MORRIS DANCE
ACDEINNORST   CONSTRAINED
ACDEINNORTU   DENUNCIATOR
ACDEINNOSSS   DISSONANCES
ACDEINOOPRS   SCORPAENOID
ACDEINOORST   COORDINATES, DECORATIONS
ACDEINOPSTT   CONSTIPATED
ACDEINOSSTU   DECUSSATION
ACDEINOSTTU   OUTDISTANCE
ACDEINOSTTW   WAINSCOTTED
ACDEINPRSTU   UNPRACTISED
ACDEIOOPRSU   ADIPOCEROUS
ACDEIOPRRTY   PREDICATORY
ACDEIPRSSTU   CUSTARD PIES
ACDEJKSSTTU   DUST JACKETS
ACDELLNOOTY   COTYLEDONAL
ACDELOPRTTY   PTERODACTYL
ACDEMMMNNOT   COMMANDMENT
ACDEMMNOSTU   CONSUMMATED
ACDEMNNORTU   COUNTERMAND
ACDEMNORTUY   DOCUMENTARY
ACDEMOORRST   OSTRACODERM
ACDEMOPRSSU   DAMP COURSES,
    MASS-PRODUCE
ACDENNNNOUU   UNANNOUNCED
ACDENRRRSTU   REDCURRANTS
ACDEORRSSST   STAR-CROSSED
ACDFFGHINNU   HANDCUFFING
ACDFFGIINNT   FACT-FINDING
ACDFFGIINRT   DIFFRACTING
ACDFFGILNOS   SCAFFOLDING
ACDFFIILMOO   OFFICIALDOM
ACDFFIINORT   DIFFRACTION
ACDFGHHIINS   CHAFING DISH
ACDFGIIMNOR   ACID-FORMING
ACDGGHIINRS   DISCHARGING
ACDGHIIIOPR   IDIOGRAPHIC
ACDGHIINNSW   SANDWICHING
ACDGHIINPST   DISPATCHING

ACDGHIINRSV   CRASH-DIVING
ACDGHIMOOSU   DICHOGAMOUS
ACDGHIOPRSY   DISCOGRAPHY
ACDGHIRRRYY   HYDRARGYRIC
ACDGIIILMNS   DISCLAIMING
ACDGIIILOST   DIALOGISTIC
ACDGIIINNTV   VINDICATING
ACDGIILNOST   DISLOCATING
ACDGIILNPTU   DUPLICATING
ACDGIINNSTY   SYNDICATING
ACDGIINOSST   DIAGNOSTICS
ACDGIINRSTT   DISTRACTING
ACDGILLOOOX   DOXOLOGICAL
ACDGILNRTUY   TRADUCINGLY
ACDGIMNNOPU   UP AND COMING
ACDGINOORVW   WOODCARVING
ACDGLLOOTYY   DACTYLOLOGY
ACDGMNOPRSU   CAMPGROUNDS
ACDHHIMOTUW   WITH MUCH ADO
ACDHHIOPRRS   HARPSICHORD
ACDHIIIMRTT   MITHRIDATIC
ACDHIILLMOY   HOMICIDALLY
ACDHIILOPSU   ACIDOPHILUS
ACDHIINOOPR   RADIOPHONIC
ACDHIIOPRST   DIASTROPHIC
ACDHIMNOORT   TRICHOMONAD
ACDHIMNORTY   HYDROMANTIC
ACDHINNORYY   CYANOHYDRIN
ACDHIORRSSW   DISC HARROWS
ACDHIRSSSSW   SWISS CHARDS
ACDHLLOOOOW   WOOD ALCOHOL
ACDHLNOOORT   NOTOCHORDAL
ACDIIILLNPS   DISCIPLINAL
ACDIIILLOTY   IDIOTICALLY
ACDIIILMORY   DOMICILIARY
ACDIIIMNOST   DIATONICISM
ACDIIIMOTTY   DIATOMICITY
ACDIIINNOST   INDICATIONS
ACDIIINNOTV   VINDICATION
ACDIILLLLYY   IDYLLICALLY
ACDIILLORST   CLOSTRIDIAL
ACDIILMNNRU   CLINANDRIUM
ACDIILMNOPR   PALINDROMIC
ACDIILMNSSY   SYNDICALISM
ACDIILNNOOT   CONDITIONAL
ACDIILNNOTU   INDUCTIONAL
ACDIILNOOST   DISLOCATION
ACDIILNOPTU   DUPLICATION
ACDIILNSSTY   SYNDICALIST
ACDIILOORRS   SORORICIDAL
ACDIILPRSTU   TRICUSPIDAL
ACDIIMNORSS   SARDONICISM
ACDIIMORSTY   MYOCARDITIS
ACDIINNOSTY   SYNDICATION
ACDIINOPSTU   CUSPIDATION
ACDIINORSTT   DISTRACTION
ACDIINORTVY   VINDICATORY
ACDIKKPSTUU   KICK UP A DUST
ACDILLORSTY   CRYSTALLOID

ACDILNOPRSS SPINAL CORDS
ACDILOPRSTU DUPLICATORS
ACDINNNOOOT CONDONATION
ACDINOOORRT COORDINATOR
ACDKLLNOORR ROCK-AND-ROLL
ACDKNORSSTU SOUNDTRACKS
ACDLLORSSTU COLLAR STUDS
ACDLNOOOORTY CONDOLATORY
ACDNNOOPRSS PROS AND CONS
ACDOOORSSTU OSTRACODOUS
ACEEEFFFRTT AFTEREFFECT
ACEEEFFKNOT TAKE OFFENCE
ACEEEFHLNRV FRENCH LEAVE
ACEEEFIOPPP PIPE OF PEACE
ACEEEFIPRSS FIRE ESCAPES
ACEEEFLNRRU NUCLEAR-FREE
ACEEEGHHRST CHARGE SHEET
ACEEEGIMNRT RACE MEETING
ACEEEGIMNTT METAGENETIC
ACEEEGNPRST PERCENTAGES
ACEEEGNRSTT SECRET AGENT
ACEEEHIMNRS ARCHENEMIES
ACEEEHIMNTV ACHIEVEMENT
ACEEEHINNTT CANINE TEETH
ACEEEHIORVV OVERACHIEVE
ACEEEHIRRST TREACHERIES
ACEEEHIRSTT CATHETERISE
ACEEEHIRTTZ CATHETERIZE
ACEEEHLLNRT CHANTERELLE
ACEEEHLLRSV SACHEVERELL
ACEEEHMNNNT ENHANCEMENT
ACEEEHMORTT TACHEOMETER
ACEEEHRRRSS RESEARCHERS
ACEEEILMNPT MANTELPIECE
ACEEEILNPPR PIPE CLEANER
ACEEEILNQUV EQUIVALENCE
ACEEEILNRRV IRRELEVANCE
ACEEEIMNRRS MERCENARIES
ACEEEIMPRST MASTERPIECE
ACEEEINNRST CENTENARIES
ACEEEINRSSS NECESSARIES
ACEEEINSSTT NECESSITATE
ACEEEIPTTVX EXPECTATIVE
ACEEEIRRSST SECRETARIES
ACEEEIRSSTV TEA SERVICES
ACEEEJKLPST STEEPLEJACK
ACEEEJORSTT EJECTOR SEAT
ACEEELLMNOT METALLOCENE
ACEEELLMNOV MALEVOLENCE
ACEEELLSSSY CEASELESSLY
ACEEELMMNPT EMPLACEMENT
ACEEELMNPRT REPLACEMENT
ACEEELMNRRT RECREMENTAL
ACEEELMNRTX EXCREMENTAL
ACEEELNPSSW CLEAN SWEEPS
ACEEELORSTT ELECTORATES
ACEEEMNPSST ESCAPEMENTS
ACEEEMNRRTT RETRACEMENT
ACEEEOPRTTX EXPECTORATE

ACEEFFIILOS OFFICIALESE
ACEEFFILNTU INEFFECTUAL
ACEEFFLLTUY EFFECTUALLY
ACEEFGILNNR FREELANCING
ACEEFHINNRS ENFRANCHISE
ACEEFHNRRTU FURTHERANCE
ACEEFIILOPT PIECE OF TAIL
ACEEFIJKLST LIFE JACKETS
ACEEFILRSTV SERVICE FLAT
ACEEFIMNORS FREEMASONIC
ACEEFIMNTTU TUMEFACIENT
ACEEFINOPTT TEPEFACTION
ACEEFLLNRST CRESTFALLEN
ACEEFLNRSSU CAREFULNESS
ACEEFLORSUU FERULACEOUS
ACEEFLPRRTU PREFECTURAL
ACEEFMNOPRR PERFORMANCE
ACEEFORRSST FORECASTERS
ACEEFPPRSTT PAST PERFECT
ACEEGGIMMNO EMMENAGOGIC
ACEEGGIMNOT GAMETOGENIC,
    GAMOGENETIC, GEOMAGNETIC
ACEEGHILOOT OLIGOCHAETE
ACEEGHILPRT TELEGRAPHIC
ACEEGHINNRT INTERCHANGE
ACEEGHINRRS RESEARCHING
ACEEGHLLNRS CHALLENGERS
ACEEGHLNOOS LOOSE CHANGE
ACEEGHNORSV CHANGEOVERS
ACEEGHNRRSU CHARGE NURSE
ACEEGHORRSV OVERCHARGES
ACEEGHPRRSU SUPERCHARGE
ACEEGIILNNT GEANTICLINE
ACEEGIKNNPP KNEECAPPING
ACEEGIKSTTW WICKET GATES
ACEEGILLNRY GENERICALLY
ACEEGILLNTY GENETICALLY
ACEEGILLNUY EUGENICALLY
ACEEGILNPRS SLEEPING CAR
ACEEGILNPSS SINGLE-SPACE
ACEEGILSTTU GESTICULATE
ACEEGIMMORT MICROGAMETE
ACEEGINNPRS PREGNANCIES
ACEEGINORTT TERATOGENIC
ACEEGINOTTU AUTOGENETIC
ACEEGIRRRTY CERARGYRITE
ACEEGKNOPSS SPONGE CAKES
ACEEGLLRSSY GRACELESSLY
ACEEGLMNNOT CONGEALMENT
ACEEGMNORRS SCAREMONGER
ACEEGNPRSSY PRESS AGENCY
ACEEHHIIRRS HIERARCHIES
ACEEHHIKLTT HATCHET-LIKE
ACEEHHILRSW WHEELCHAIRS
ACEEHHLMRST CRASH HELMET
ACEEHHMMOOR HAEMOCHROME
ACEEHHMMSTU MUCH THE SAME
ACEEHHNORST SHEET ANCHOR
ACEEHIILNST LECITHINASE

ACEEHIINNRT INHERITANCE
ACEEHIIRSTT HETAERISTIC
ACEEHIKNRTW KITCHENWARE
ACEEHILLNNP PANHELLENIC
ACEEHILLRTY HERETICALLY
ACEEHILMOPR HEMERALOPIC
ACEEHILMPRT HALTEMPRICE
ACEEHILNRTT CHAIN LETTER
ACEEHILNSST ETHICALNESS
ACEEHILORTT THEORETICAL
ACEEHIMMNPT IMPEACHMENT
ACEEHIMNNNT ENCHAINMENT
ACEEHIMNPSZ CHIMPANZEES
ACEEHIMORTT THEOREMATIC
ACEEHIMRTTY ERYTHEMATIC
ACEEHINNSTZ NIETZSCHEAN
ACEEHINPRTT PARENTHETIC
ACEEHINSSTT ANESTHETICS
ACEEHIOPRST SPIROCHAETE
ACEEHIORRST CHARIOTEERS
ACEEHIPRSTT PARESTHETIC
ACEEHIPRTTU THERAPEUTIC
ACEEHIPRTVY HYPERACTIVE
ACEEHKLNRST HALTERNECKS
ACEEHLLNTTU CALL THE TUNE
ACEEHLMMNSY MESENCHYMAL
ACEEHLMNRUU HERCULANEUM
ACEEHLMOPSY MESOCEPHALY
ACEEHLNOPSU ENCEPHALOUS
ACEEHLNPRSU LEPRECHAUNS
ACEEHLOORRU LEUCORRHOEA
ACEEHLOPRRT PERCHLORATE
ACEEHLOSSSV CLOSE SHAVES
ACEEHMMNNRT MERCHANTMEN
ACEEHMMRSSU MEERSCHAUMS
ACEEHMNNNTT ENCHANTMENT
ACEEHMNNRRT TRENCHERMAN
ACEEHMNOSTU MENTHACEOUS
ACEEHMORSTT TACHOMETERS
ACEEHMSSTTT TEST MATCHES
ACEEHNNORRT ARCHENTERON
ACEEHNNRSST ENCHANTRESS
ACEEHNOPRTT ON THE CARPET
ACEEHORRSTT ORCHESTRATE
ACEEHORRSTU TREACHEROUS
ACEEIILLNPT PENICILLATE
ACEEIILNRRT RECTILINEAR
ACEEIILNSTT LICENTIATES
ACEEIILPRTV REPLICATIVE
ACEEIILPTVX EXPLICATIVE
ACEEIIMNRRT RECRIMINATE
ACEEIINNTUV ENUNCIATIVE
ACEEIINRSST RESISTENCIA
ACEEIINRSTT CERTAINTIES
ACEEIINRTTV INTERACTIVE
ACEEIIPPRTT PERIPATETIC, PRECIPITATE
ACEEIIRSSTT CASSITERITE
ACEEIIRSTTV RECITATIVES
ACEEIKMPRRT MARKET PRICE

ACEEIKNSSSS SEASICKNESS
ACEEILLNNSS CLEANLINESS
ACEEILLNPST SPLENETICAL
ACEEILMNNRT INCREMENTAL
ACEEILMNORS CEREMONIALS
ACEEILMNRRY MERCENARILY
ACEEILMORRT CALORIMETER
ACEEILMORST ELASTOMERIC
ACEEILMPSST ESEMPLASTIC
ACEEILMPSTU TIME CAPSULE
ACEEILMRTUV VERMICULATE
ACEEILNNNST CENTENNIALS
ACEEILNNORT INTOLERANCE
ACEEILNNOTU ENUCLEATION
ACEEILNNTUY LIEUTENANCY
ACEEILNOPTX EXCEPTIONAL
ACEEILNORSS RECESSIONAL
ACEEILNORST RESECTIONAL
ACEEILNOSSS SECESSIONAL
ACEEILNOSST COESSENTIAL
ACEEILNPRTT CENTRIPETAL
ACEEILNPSSS SPECIALNESS
ACEEILNPSST PLICATENESS
ACEEILNQUVY EQUIVALENCY
ACEEILNRSST TREACLINESS
ACEEILNRSSY NECESSARILY
ACEEILNRSTV CANTILEVERS
ACEEILNSTTT CLIENT STATE
ACEEILOORVV CAVO-RELIEVO
ACEEILOPRTV PERCOLATIVE
ACEEILOPSTT POLICE STATE
ACEEILORRTV CORRELATIVE
ACEEILORTUX EXECUTORIAL
ACEEILPRRTY PRELITERACY
ACEEILPSTUV SPECULATIVE
ACEEILRRSSU SECULARISER
ACEEILRRSUZ SECULARIZER
ACEEILSTTTU TESTICULATE
ACEEIMMNORT ANEMOMETRIC
ACEEIMMORST COMMISERATE
ACEEIMNNOTT CEMENTATION
ACEEIMNOPRT ARMIPOTENCE
ACEEIMNORRT CRANIOMETER
ACEEIMNORTT ACTINOMETER
ACEEIMNOSTX INCOME TAXES
ACEEIMNQRTU ACQUIREMENT
ACEEIMNRSTT REMITTANCES
ACEEIMOSSTV VASECTOMIES
ACEEINNNSST ANCIENTNESS
ACEEINNORTV NONCREATIVE
ACEEINNRRSU REINSURANCE
ACEEINNSSTX INEXACTNESS
ACEEINOPTTX EXPECTATION
ACEEINORRST RECREATIONS
ACEEINORSTU AUCTIONEERS
ACEEINORSTX EXECRATIONS
ACEEINPPRST APPRENTICES
ACEEINPRRST TRANSPIERCE
ACEEINRRSTV TRANSCEIVER

ACEEINRSSST RESISTANCES	ACEFIIINORT REIFICATION
ACEEIOOPRTV COOPERATIVE	ACEFIILORTT FELICITATOR
ACEEIOPPRSU PIPERACEOUS	ACEFIILPRSU SUPERFICIAL
ACEEIORRSTV EVISCERATOR	ACEFIINOPTT PONTIFICATE
ACEEIORRTTV RETROACTIVE	ACEFIINORST FRACTIONISE
ACEEIPPRSTY PARTY PIECES	ACEFIINORTZ FRACTIONIZE
ACEEIRSSTTU RESUSCITATE	ACEFILLLOTU FOLLICULATE
ACEEJNPRSTU SUPERJACENT	ACEFILLORUW CAULIFLOWER
ACEEKLLRSSS SALESCLERKS	ACEFILMMOTU COMME IL FAUT
ACEEKNRSTTV TRACK EVENTS	ACEFILORSTU LACTIFEROUS
ACEEKORRSSW CASEWORKERS	ACEFILOSTUY FACETIOUSLY
ACEELLMNRSS SMALL SCREEN	ACEFIMNOTTU TUMEFACTION
ACEELLNOSTT CONSTELLATE	ACEFINNORST FOR INSTANCE
ACEELMNNOOV MONOVALENCE	ACEFINOTTUV CONFUTATIVE
ACEELMNOPTT CONTEMPLATE	ACEFIOORRTV VOCIFERATOR
ACEELMOPRRU COME A PURLER	ACEFIPRRSTT PRIESTCRAFT
ACEELNNNSSU UNCLEANNESS	ACEFLNSSTTU TACTFULNESS
ACEELNOOPRT COLEOPTERAN	ACEFOOPSTTX EX POST FACTO
ACEELNOOSSS CLOSE SEASON	ACEGGHILLNN CHALLENGING
ACEELNOPSTT PENTECOSTAL	ACEGGHILNNS CHANGELINGS
ACEELNORRTX RENAL CORTEX	ACEGGILLMOO GEMOLOGICAL
ACEELNPRSSY SCREENPLAYS	ACEGGILOORT GERATOLOGIC
ACEELNPTTXY EXPECTANTLY	ACEGGINNORU ENCOURAGING
ACEELOPPPRT COPPERPLATE	ACEGGINRSSS SCRAGGINESS
ACEELORSTTW WATER CLOSET	ACEGGLNOOYY GYNAECOLOGY
ACEEMMMOORT COMMEMORATE	ACEGGNOORRT CONGREGATOR
ACEEMMNNPST ENCAMPMENTS	ACEGHILOPRR HELICOGRAPH
ACEEMNOOSWY COME ONE'S WAY	ACEGHHILRST SEARCHLIGHT
ACEEMNPRSST ESCARPMENTS	ACEGHHINORW WEIGH ANCHOR
ACEENNOPRTU COUNTERPANE	ACEGHHMNRRU HUNGER MARCH
ACEENNORRTV CONTRAVENER	ACEGHHNORST SHORT-CHANGE
ACEENNORSTT CONSTERNATE	ACEGHHOOPRR CHOREOGRAPH
ACEENNRSSUY UNNECESSARY	ACEGHHOPRTY HECTOGRAPHY
ACEENOORSTT COTONEASTER	ACEGHIIIMNT MICHIGANITE
ACEENOPRSTV VAPORESCENT	ACEGHIILORS OLIGARCHIES
ACEENOPRTTX EXPECTORANT	ACEGHIIMNNZ MECHANIZING
ACEENRSSSTW NEWSCASTERS	ACEGHIKLLNS SHELLACKING
ACEEOPRRRTU RECUPERATOR	ACEGHIKMNOP EPOCH-MAKING
ACEEORRSTUW WATERCOURSE	ACEGHILLNNN CHANNELLING
ACEEPPRRTTU PAPER-CUTTER	ACEGHILLOOR RHEOLOGICAL
ACEFFFILOST FACTS OF LIFE	ACEGHILLOOT THEOLOGICAL
ACEFFGHILNR CLIFFHANGER	ACEGHILNRSY SEARCHINGLY
ACEFFGILNTY AFFECTINGLY	ACEGHILOOPR OLEOGRAPHIC
ACEFFIITTVY AFFECTIVITY	ACEGHILOPSY GEOPHYSICAL
ACEFFIKRRST TRAFFICKERS	ACEGHIMNNSU MACHINEGUNS
ACEFFIOSTUV SUFFOCATIVE	ACEGHIMNORR MENORRHAGIC
ACEFGHLLNOT FOCAL LENGTH	ACEGHIMNORU ARCHEGONIUM
ACEFGIIMNNT MAGNIFICENT	ACEGHIMNRSY CRYING SHAME
ACEFGIINNRT INTERFACING	ACEGHINNOPR CHAPERONING
ACEFGILNRTU CENTRIFUGAL	ACEGHINOPRR REPROACHING
ACEFGINORST FORECASTING	ACEGHINORRV OVERARCHING
ACEFGINRRSU RESURFACING	ACEGHIOPRRX XEROGRAPHIC
ACEFHILNOPR FRANCOPHILE	ACEGHLNOPTT PLECTOGNATH
ACEFHIRSTTY CITY FATHERS	ACEGHLOOSTY ESCHATOLOGY
ACEFHLOPRRU REPROACHFUL	ACEGHNOPRSY SCENOGRAPHY
ACEFHMNNORW FRENCHWOMAN	ACEGHOOPRSU CREOPHAGOUS
ACEFHNNOOPR FRANCOPHONE	ACEGHORRSTU ROUGHCASTER
ACEFHNORSTT FRENCH TOAST	ACEGIIKNPRS ASKING PRICE
ACEFHORRSTV HOVERCRAFTS	ACEGIILLOOT ETIOLOGICAL

ACEGIILLOTV COLLIGATIVE
ACEGIILNNRT INTERLACING
ACEGIILNPRT REPLICATING
ACEGIILNPTX EXPLICATING
ACEGIILOSTT EGOTISTICAL
ACEGIILRSST SACRILEGIST
ACEGIIMNOST ISOMAGNETIC
ACEGIIMRRTV GRAVIMETRIC
ACEGIINNNTU ENUNCIATING
ACEGIINNRTT INTERACTING
ACEGIINORTX EXCORIATING
ACEGIINRTTX EXTRICATING
ACEGIINRTUZ CAUTERIZING
ACEGIJNOTUV CONJUGATIVE
ACEGIKLNRST SINGLE-TRACK
ACEGILLMRTU METALLURGIC
ACEGILLNNOY CONGENIALLY
ACEGILLNOOO OENOLOGICAL
ACEGILLNOOP PENOLOGICAL
ACEGILMNRSY SCREAMINGLY
ACEGILMOSTY CLEISTOGAMY
ACEGILNNOOT CONGELATION
ACEGILNNPRS SPRING-CLEAN
ACEGILNOPRT PERCOLATING
ACEGILNOPSY CLAY PIGEONS
ACEGILNORRT CORRELATING
ACEGILNPSTU SPECULATING
ACEGILNPTUX EXCULPATING
ACEGILNRSSY CARESSINGLY
ACEGILNTUUU UNGUICULATE
ACEGILOOPST APOLOGETICS
ACEGILOORTT TERATOLOGIC
ACEGILRRTUU AGRICULTURE
ACEGIMNOTVY VAGINECTOMY
ACEGIMORSST MESOGASTRIC
ACEGINNNOTV COVENANTING
ACEGINNRSTY ASTRINGENCY
ACEGINOOPRT COOPERATING
ACEGINOPRRT PROCREATING
ACEGINOSTTV CASTING VOTE
ACEGINPRRTU RECAPTURING
ACEGINPSTTY TYPECASTING
ACEGIOORTTX EXCOGITATOR
ACEGIOPSTTY STEATOPYGIC
ACEGKRSSTTU STAGESTRUCK
ACEGLNOPRTY CALYPTROGEN
ACEGLNORTUY GRANULOCYTE
ACEGLRSSTTU GLASSCUTTER
ACEGMNNORSS CONGRESSMAN
ACEGMOPRRST SPECTROGRAM
ACEGMORSTTY GASTRECTOMY
ACEGNORRSST CROSS-GARNET
ACEGOOPRSST GASTROSCOPE
ACEHHIILMOP HAEMOPHILIC, HEMOPHILIAC
ACEHHIIMRRS HIERARCHISM
ACEHHIINNTY HYACINTHINE
ACEHHIMOOPT HOMEOPATHIC
ACEHHINOSTX HEXASTICHON
ACEHHNORSSU RANCH HOUSES

ACEHIIINPSS HISPANICISE
ACEHIIINPSZ HISPANICIZE
ACEHIILLOPT PALEOLITHIC
ACEHIILLOST ISOLECITHAL
ACEHIILMSTT ATHLETICISM
ACEHIILNOPR NECROPHILIA
ACEHIILOSTT CHIASTOLITE, HELIOSTATIC
ACEHIILSTWW WELWITSCHIA
ACEHIINNOPT PHONETICIAN
ACEHIINORRT RHETORICIAN
ACEHIINPSTT PANTHEISTIC
ACEHIKKLMMO HAMMOCK-LIKE
ACEHIKLPRRS PARISH CLERK
ACEHIKLPRTY PRICKLY HEAT
ACEHIKMNORS CHAIN-SMOKER
ACEHIKMRTUY RHEUMATICKY
ACEHILLMORY HOMERICALLY
ACEHILLORTW WHITE-COLLAR
ACEHILMNOOT MACHINE TOOL
ACEHILMNOST SLOT MACHINE
ACEHILNPRST SPHINCTERAL
ACEHILNSTTY SYNTHETICAL
ACEHILRSSSY CHRYSALISES
ACEHIMMOPRT METAMORPHIC
ACEHIMNORSS MARCHIONESS
ACEHIMNORTU EUCHROMATIN
ACEHIMOOSTT HOMEOSTATIC
ACEHIMOPRST ATMOSPHERIC
ACEHIMORRRT ARTHROMERIC
ACEHIMORRST CHOIRMASTER
ACEHIMORTTX THERMOTAXIC
ACEHIMPSSTY METAPHYSICS
ACEHIMPSTTY SYMPATHETIC
ACEHIMRSSST CHRISTMASES
ACEHINNOOTT CANINE TOOTH
ACEHINNPSSU PAUNCHINESS
ACEHINNRSSU RAUNCHINESS
ACEHINOOPRZ PHANEROZOIC
ACEHINOPRRS CHAIRPERSON
ACEHINOPRRT CHIROPTERAN
ACEHINOPRTU NEUROPATHIC
ACEHINORSST CHAIN STORES
ACEHINRSSST STARCHINESS
ACEHIOOPSTT OSTEOPATHIC
ACEHIOOPTTV PHOTOACTIVE
ACEHIOPPRST HIPPOCRATES
ACEHIORSSTY CASE HISTORY
ACEHIQRRSUY SQUIREARCHY
ACEHKMRRSTT STRETCHMARK
ACEHLLMSSTY MATCHLESSLY
ACEHLMMNOOR CHROMONEMAL
ACEHLMOOSST SCHOOLMATES
ACEHLMRSSUV SCRUMHALVES
ACEHLNNRTTY TRENCHANTLY
ACEHLORSTUY LYTHRACEOUS
ACEHMNOPRSY PROSENCHYMA
ACEHMOORTTY TRACHEOTOMY
ACEHMOPRSTU CHAMPERTOUS
ACEHNNOOPRT CTENOPHORAN

ACEHNNSSSTU STAUNCHNESS
ACEHOPPRSTU TOUCHPAPERS
ACEHOPRRSSY CHRYSOPRASE
ACEHOPRRTYY CRYOTHERAPY
ACEHOPSSTTW STOPWATCHES
ACEHORSTTWW WATCHTOWERS
ACEIIIKNNOS ANISEIKONIC
ACEIIILMPTV IMPLICATIVE
ACEIIILNOTT ELICITATION
ACEIIIMNNRT INCRIMINATE
ACEIIIMNOST SEMIOTICIAN
ACEIIIMNSTT ANTI-SEMITIC
ACEIIIQSTUV ACQUISITIVE
ACEIIKLLNTY KINETICALLY
ACEIIKLRSTT RICKETTSIAL
ACEIIKNOTTU AUTOKINETIC
ACEIIKNRSSS AIRSICKNESS
ACEIILLMMTY MIMETICALLY
ACEIILLMNNU ILLUMINANCE
ACEIILLMOTY MEIOTICALLY
ACEIILLMPRY EMPIRICALLY
ACEIILLMSSY SEISMICALLY
ACEIILLNSTT SCINTILLATE
ACEIILMNPRT PLANIMETRIC
ACEIILMNSTT MENTALISTIC
ACEIILMOPST ATOMIC PILES
ACEIILMORST ISOMETRICAL
ACEIILMOTTU ITACOLUMITE
ACEIILMPSSS SPECIALISMS
ACEIILNNORT RECLINATION
ACEIILNOPPR PILOCARPINE
ACEIILNOPRT REPLICATION
ACEIILNOPTX EXPLICATION
ACEIILNOQTU EQUINOCTIAL
ACEIILNOTUV INOCULATIVE
ACEIILNPRUY PECUNIARILY
ACEIILNRRUV CURVILINEAR
ACEIILNRSTT CLARINETIST
ACEIILNRSTU UNREALISTIC
ACEIILNRTTY INTRICATELY
ACEIILOPRST TROPICALISE
ACEIILOPRTZ TROPICALIZE
ACEIILPPRST PARTICIPLES
ACEIILPRSST PLASTICISER
ACEIILPRSTT PERISTALTIC, TRIPLICATES
ACEIILPRSTZ PLASTICIZER
ACEIILPRTUY PECULIARITY
ACEIILPSSST SPECIALISTS
ACEIILRTTVY VERTICALITY
ACEIIMNNRST MANNERISTIC
ACEIIMNOPRT IMPRECATION
ACEIIMNORST ANISOMETRIC, MISCREATION,
    REACTIONISM, ROMANTICISE
ACEIIMNORTT INTERATOMIC, METRICATION
ACEIIMNORTZ ROMANTICIZE
ACEIIMNPRRU PERICRANIUM
ACEIIMNPSSU IMPUISSANCE
ACEIIMNRSTT MARTENSITIC
ACEIIMNRSTU INSECTARIUM

ACEIIMNSSTT SEMANTICIST
ACEIINNNOTU ENUNCIATION
ACEIINNOPTT PECTINATION
ACEIINNORRT INCINERATOR
ACEIINNORTT INTERACTION
ACEIINNPSTT PINNATISECT
ACEIINOORTX EXCORIATION
ACEIINOPRTT CREPITATION
ACEIINOPSTT PECTISATION
ACEIINOPTTZ PECTIZATION
ACEIINORSTT RECITATIONS
ACEIINORTTX EXTRICATION
ACEIINPPRTT PRECIPITANT
ACEIINPRTTY ANTIPYRETIC, PERTINACITY
ACEIINPSSTT ANTISEPTICS
ACEIIOOPPST APOSIOPETIC
ACEIKKLNPTY PENALTY KICK
ACEIKLLPSTY SKEPTICALLY
ACEIKLNPSSV CLASP KNIVES
ACEIKLPPRRY PRICKLY PEAR
ACEIKNPSSTT SEPTIC TANKS
ACEILLLMNOR LAMELLICORN
ACEILLLMOPY POLEMICALLY
ACEILLLNORT CITRONELLAL
ACEILLLNRUU UNICELLULAR
ACEILLMNNOT NONMETALLIC
ACEILLMNRUY NUMERICALLY
ACEILLMOTTY TOTEMICALLY
ACEILLMRRUY MERCURIALLY
ACEILLNNOOO NEOCOLONIAL
ACEILLNOPTU CUPELLATION
ACEILLNRSTY CRYSTALLINE
ACEILLOORRS COROLLARIES
ACEILLOPSSW PILLOWCASES
ACEILLOQUVY EQUIVOCALLY
ACEILLRSSTY CRYSTALLISE
ACEILLRSTTY CRYSTALLITE
ACEILLRSTYZ CRYSTALLIZE
ACEILLRTUVY LUCRATIVELY
ACEILMMNOSU COMMUNALISE
ACEILMMNOTY METONYMICAL
ACEILMMNOUZ COMMUNALIZE
ACEILMMRSTY SYMMETRICAL
ACEILMNOOPS SCOPOLAMINE
ACEILMNOOPW POLICEWOMAN
ACEILMNOPRS COMPLAINERS
ACEILMNOPRT PLANOMETRIC
ACEILMNOPTY AMYLOPECTIN
ACEILMNRTTU CURTAILMENT
ACEILMNRTUU RETINACULUM
ACEILMNSSSU MUSICALNESS
ACEILMORRTY CALORIMETRY
ACEILMRRTUU MARICULTURE
ACEILNNNOSS NONSENSICAL
ACEILNNNOTT CONTINENTAL
ACEILNNNOTU ANTINUCLEON
ACEILNNORTU CRENULATION
ACEILNNRTUY UNCERTAINLY
ACEILNNSSTY INCESSANTLY

ACEILNOOPRR INCORPOREAL
ACEILNOOPRT PERCOLATION
ACEILNOORRT CORRELATION
ACEILNOORSU ARENICOLOUS
ACEILNOPRST INSPECTORAL
ACEILNOPSTU PECULATIONS, SPECULATION
ACEILNOPTUX EXCULPATION
ACEILNOQUUV UNEQUIVOCAL
ACEILNORSTT INTERCOSTAL
ACEILNORTUV COUNTERVAIL, INVOLUCRATE
ACEILNOSSST STOICALNESS
ACEILNOSTUY TENACIOUSLY
ACEILNPSSTY TYPICALNESS
ACEILNRRTUV VENTRICULAR
ACEILOOPPRS POLARISCOPE
ACEILOOSSST OSTEOCLASIS
ACEILOPRRTT PROTRACTILE
ACEILORSUVY VERACIOUSLY
ACEILORTVYY VICEROYALTY
ACEILPRSTTY SPECTRALITY
ACEILQRTUUU AQUICULTURE
ACEILRRTTUU TURRICULATE
ACEIMMOOSSU MIMOSACEOUS
ACEIMMORRTU CREMATORIUM
ACEIMMOTTUV COMMUTATIVE
ACEIMNNNOTT CONTAINMENT
ACEIMNOPRRS MARINE CORPS
ACEIMNORRTU MERCURATION
ACEIMNORRTY CRANIOMETRY
ACEIMNORTTY ACTINOMETRY
ACEIMOPRRTY IMPRECATORY
ACEIMORRSTT ASTROMETRIC
ACEIMPRSSTU SUPREMACIST
ACEIMSSSTTY SYSTEMATICS
ACEINNNOSTT CONSTANTINE
ACEINNOOTTV CONNOTATIVE
ACEINNORRST CONSTRAINER
ACEINNORSTT TRANSECTION
ACEINNPTUUV NUNCUPATIVE
ACEINNRSSSW SCRAWNINESS
ACEINNRTTUY UNCERTAINTY
ACEINOOOPRT COOPERATION
ACEINOOPRRT INCORPORATE, PROCREATION
ACEINOOPRTU APONEUROTIC
ACEINOORRTT RETROACTION
ACEINOORSTV REVOCATIONS
ACEINOPRRTU PUERTO RICAN
ACEINOPRSSS PROSAICNESS
ACEINOPRSTU PRECAUTIONS
ACEINORRSTT RETRACTIONS
ACEINORRTTY CONTRARIETY
ACEINORSTTU ERUCTATIONS
ACEINORSTTV CONTRASTIVE
ACEINORSTTX EXTRACTIONS
ACEINPPRSSS SCRAPPINESS
ACEINPRRTUY PARTURIENCY
ACEINRRTUUV INCURVATURE
ACEINRSSSSU NARCISSUSES
ACEIOOPRRTV CORPORATIVE

ACEIOOPRTVV PROVOCATIVE
ACEIOPRRSTT TETRASPORIC, TRICERATOPS
ACEIOPRRTTV PROTRACTIVE
ACEIOPRSTUU PRECAUTIOUS
ACEKKLOPTTU TAKE POTLUCK
ACEKKMORSTT STOCK MARKET
ACEKKMOSSST SMOKESTACKS
ACEKNNORSTU COUNTERSANK
ACEKNOPPRRS COPPER'S NARK
ACEKPRRSSSY SKYSCRAPERS
ACELLMNOPSU NUCLEOPLASM
ACELLNOPRUY POLYNUCLEAR
ACELLNOPVYY POLYVALENCY
ACELLNOSSSU CALLOUSNESS
ACELLNRTTUY RELUCTANTLY
ACELLOOPRRY CORPOREALLY
ACELMNNOORT NOMENCLATOR
ACELMNNOORU MONONUCLEAR
ACELMNNOSTT MALCONTENTS
ACELMRSTUUU MUSCULATURE
ACELNNOOPVX PLANO-CONVEX
ACELNNRSTTU TRANSLUCENT
ACELNORSUVY CAVERNOUSLY
ACELNORTTUX CONTEXTURAL
ACELNOSTTTU TALENT SCOUT
ACELOOPRRST PERCOLATORS
ACELOOPRRTT PROTECTORAL
ACELOOPRRTY CORPORATELY
ACELOORRTUW WATERCOLOUR
ACELOPRSSTU SPECULATORS
ACELOPRTUXY EXCULPATORY
ACELRSSSTTY CRYSTAL SETS
ACEMMNOORTT COMMENTATOR
ACEMMNOPRTT COMPARTMENT
ACEMNNORSST MONSTRANCES
ACEMNOOPRST COMPENSATOR
ACEMORSSTTU SCOUTMASTER
ACENNOSSTTT CONTESTANTS
ACENOORRSTV CONSERVATOR
ACENOPRRSTU PROCRUSTEAN
ACENOPRRTTU COUNTERPART
ACENORSSSUU RAUCOUSNESS
ACENORSTTUY COUNTRY SEAT
ACENOSSSUUV VACUOUSNESS
ACEOOOPRRST COOPERATORS
ACEOOPRSSTU STAUROSCOPE
ACFFGIIINOT OFFICIATING
ACFFGIIKNRT TRAFFICKING
ACFFGINOSTU SUFFOCATING
ACFFIIINOOT OFFICIATION
ACFFIILNOST AFFLICTIONS
ACFFILMNOOR FALCONIFORM
ACFFINOOSTU SUFFOCATION
ACFGHIINNRS FRANCHISING
ACFGHINOSUV VOUCHSAFING
ACFGIIINNST SIGNIFICANT
ACFGIIJKKNN JACK-KNIFING
ACFGIILNSSY CLASSIFYING
ACFGIINNORT FORNICATING

ACFGIINNSTY SANCTIFYING
ACFGIINORTZ FACTORIZING
ACFGIINSTTU FUNGISTATIC
ACFGIKNORRV CARVING FORK
ACFGILNTTUU FLUCTUATING
ACFGINRSSTU SURFCASTING
ACFIIINNOTU UNIFICATION
ACFIIINORTV VINIFICATOR
ACFIILLNOTY FICTIONALLY
ACFIILMNORU CALIFORNIUM
ACFIILMORST FORMALISTIC
ACFIILNOPST PONTIFICALS
ACFIIMNOORT FORMICATION
ACFIINNOORT FORNICATION
ACFIINNORST INFRACTIONS
ACFIIOPRRTU PURIFICATOR
ACFILLMORUY FORMULAICLY
ACFILMNNOTU MALFUNCTION
ACFILNNOOST CONFLATIONS
ACFILNOTTUU FLUCTUATION
ACFILORSTUY FRACTIOUSLY
ACFINNOOTTU CONFUTATION
ACFINNORTUY FUNCTIONARY
ACFLLOOPRST PORT OF CALLS
ACFLNOORSTW CONTRAFLOWS
ACFORRRUUVY CURRY FAVOUR
ACGGHILOOPR GRAPHOLOGIC
ACGGHINRRSU SURCHARGING
ACGGIIILNNZ ANGLICIZING
ACGGIILMNRY GRIMACINGLY
ACGGIIMMNRS SCRIMMAGING
ACGGIJNNOTU CONJUGATING
ACGGIMMNRSU SCRUMMAGING
ACGHHILOOPR HOLOGRAPHIC
ACGHHIMOOPR HOMOGRAPHIC
ACGHHINOPRY ICHNOGRAPHY
ACGHHIOPRRY CHIROGRAPHY
ACGHHNOOPRR CHRONOGRAPH
ACGHHOOPRRY CHOROGRAPHY
ACGHHOPPRSY PSYCHOGRAPH
ACGHIILMNPT ITCHING PALM
ACGHIILMORT ALGORITHMIC, LOGARITHMIC
ACGHIILNORT GRANOLITHIC
ACGHIIMMNST MISMATCHING
ACGHIIMNNOP CHAMPIONING
ACGHIIPRSST SPHRAGISTIC
ACGHIKMOPRY KYMOGRAPHIC
ACGHILLMOOO HOMOLOGICAL
ACGHILMOOPR LAGOMORPHIC
ACGHILMOORT COLOGARITHM
ACGHILMOOST LOGOMACHIST
ACGHILOPPRY POLYGRAPHIC
ACGHILOPRXY XYLOGRAPHIC
ACGHIMNOOPR MONOGRAPHIC,
　NOMOGRAPHIC, PHONOGRAMIC
ACGHIMOPRRY MICROGRAPHY
ACGHINOOPRS NOSOGRAPHIC
ACGHINOOPRY ICONOGRAPHY
ACGHINOPRRY GRANOPHYRIC

ACGHINOPRYZ ZINCOGRAPHY
ACGHIOOPPRT TOPOGRAPHIC
ACGHIOPPRRY PYROGRAPHIC
ACGHIOPPRTY TYPOGRAPHIC
ACGHIORRSTT GASTROTRICH
ACGHOPPRRTY CRYPTOGRAPH
ACGIIIILNTZ ITALICIZING
ACGIIILMNPT IMPLICATING
ACGIIILNOST LOGISTICIAN
ACGIIILNOSZ SOCIALIZING
ACGIIILNPST SALPINGITIC
ACGIILLLLOY ILLOGICALLY
ACGIILLNOOS SINOLOGICAL
ACGIILLNOOT COLLIGATION
ACGIILLNOST OSCILLATING
ACGIILLNTUV VICTUALLING
ACGIILLOORV VIROLOGICAL
ACGIILMNNOP COMPLAINING
ACGIILMNOPR PROCLAIMING
ACGIILNNOTU INOCULATING
ACGIILNNPTU INCULPATING
ACGIILNNUVZ VULCANIZING
ACGIILNTTUV CULTIVATING
ACGIIMNOSST AGNOSTICISM
ACGIIMNRRSY MISCARRYING
ACGIINNNOST SANCTIONING
ACGIINNNOTZ INCOGNIZANT
ACGIINNOSTW WAINSCOTING
ACGIINOOSTT COGITATIONS
ACGIINORSTZ OSTRACIZING
ACGIINRSTTU RUSTICATING
ACGIJKKNSSY SKYJACKINGS
ACGIJLNOTUY CONJUGALITY
ACGIJNNOOTU CONJUGATION
ACGIKKNOSTT STOCKTAKING
ACGILLMNOOO NOMOLOGICAL
ACGILLMOOOP POMOLOGICAL
ACGILLMOORS OSCILLOGRAM
ACGILLMOOTY CLIMATOLOGY
ACGILLNOOOS NOSOLOGICAL
ACGILLNOOOT ONTOLOGICAL
ACGILLOOPTY TYPOLOGICAL
ACGILLOTYYZ ZYGOTICALLY
ACGILMOOOST SOMATOLOGIC
ACGILNOSSTU OUTCLASSING
ACGILOOPRST CARPOLOGIST
ACGILOOSSTT SCATOLOGIST
ACGIMNNOORT MORNING COAT
ACGIMNOOPRU CARPOGONIUM
ACGIMNOORST GASTRONOMIC
ACGINNOPSTY SYNCOPATING
ACGINNORSTT CONTRASTING
ACGINNPTTUU PUNCTUATING
ACGINOORRTU CORRUGATION
ACGINOORSTY COSIGNATORY
ACGINOPRRTT PROTRACTING
ACGIORSSTTY GYROSTATICS
ACGLLNOOOVY VOLCANOLOGY
ACGLMNNOOUY AGONY COLUMN

ACGMOOPRSSY GYROCOMPASS
ACGOOPRSSTY GASTROSCOPY
ACHHIILLPTY ITHYPHALLIC
ACHHILLMOOT HOMOTHALLIC
ACHHILOPRSS SCHOLARSHIP
ACHHOPPSSTY PSYCHOPATHS
ACHHOPPSTYY PSYCHOPATHY
ACHIIIMNPSS HISPANICISM
ACHIIINPSST HISPANICIST
ACHIILLMSWY WHIMSICALLY
ACHIILMPSSY PHYSICALISM
ACHIILOOPPR COPROPHILIA
ACHIILOSTTT STATOLITHIC
ACHIILPSSTY PHYSICALIST
ACHIIMNORST HARMONISTIC
ACHIINNRSTU UNCHRISTIAN
ACHIINSSTUV CHAUVINISTS
ACHIIPRSSTY PHYSIATRICS
ACHIKLOORSW WORKAHOLICS
ACHILLMOOPR ALLOMORPHIC
ACHILLOPRTY TROPHICALLY
ACHILMOOPST HOMOPLASTIC
ACHILMOPSUY POLYCHASIUM
ACHILMORRYZ MYCORRHIZAL
ACHILNOORRT CHLORINATOR
ACHIMMNOOSU MONOCHASIUM
ACHIMNNNOOR NONHARMONIC
ACHIMNOPSTT MATCH POINTS
ACHIMNOPTYY AMPHICTYONY
ACHIMNORSST MONARCHISTS
ACHIMOPPPSU HIPPOCAMPUS
ACHIMOPSSTY SCYPHISTOMA
ACHIMORRSTY CHRISMATORY
ACHINNOOPTY APOCYNTHION
ACHINOOPSTT PHOTONASTIC
ACHIOOPPRTT PROTOPATHIC
ACHIOOPPSTT POTATO CHIPS
ACHIOOPRTTU AUTOTROPHIC
ACHIOOPSTTT PHOTOSTATIC
ACHIOPPRSTY SAPROPHYTIC
ACHIOPRRSTU CURATORSHIP
ACHLLOOPRST CHLOROPLAST
ACHLLOOPSSY PLAYSCHOOLS
ACHLMMOOORS CHROMOSOMAL
ACHLMMOOPRS CHROMOPLASM
ACHLMMOORSS SCHOOLMARMS
ACHLMOOPRST CHROMOPLAST
ACHMMNOOOORT MONOCHROMAT
ACHMMOPPSTU STOMACH PUMP
ACHMOOOORTTY THORACOTOMY
ACIIILMNOPT IMPLICATION
ACIIILMNRTY CRIMINALITY
ACIIILNNNOT INCLINATION
ACIIILNOPST POLITICIANS
ACIIILRSTTU RITUALISTIC
ACIIINNOTTT NICTITATION
ACIIINOQSTU ACQUISITION
ACIILLLOPTY POLITICALLY
ACIILLMNOOS COLONIALISM

ACIILLMNOOT COLLIMATION
ACIILLMNPUY MUNICIPALLY
ACIILLMOSUY MALICIOUSLY
ACIILLMOTTY MITOTICALLY
ACIILLNOOST COLONIALIST, OSCILLATION
ACIILLNOPTU UNPOLITICAL
ACIILLNOVVY CONVIVIALLY
ACIILLNPPRY PRINCIPALLY
ACIILLOPRTY PICTORIALLY
ACIILLPRSTU PLURALISTIC
ACIILLQUYZZ QUIZZICALLY
ACIILMNNOPT INCOMPLIANT
ACIILMNNOTU CULMINATION
ACIILMNOOPT COMPILATION
ACIILMNORTU TOURMALINIC
ACIILMNSTUY MASCULINITY
ACIILNNOOTU INOCULATION
ACIILNNOPTU INCULPATION
ACIILNOPRSV PROVINCIALS
ACIILNOPSSU SUSPICIONAL
ACIILNOTTUV CULTIVATION
ACIILOPRTTY TROPICALITY
ACIILORSTTU STAUROLITIC
ACIILORSUVY VICARIOUSLY
ACIILOSUVVY VIVACIOUSLY
ACIIMMMNOST MAMMONISTIC
ACIIMMNNOOT COMMINATION
ACIIMMNORST ROMANTICISM
ACIIMMNOSST MONASTICISM
ACIIMMNSSTU NUMISMATICS
ACIIMNOORSU ACRIMONIOUS
ACIIMNORSTT ROMANTICIST
ACIIMNRSSTU MANICURISTS
ACIIMOPRSTT TROPISMATIC
ACIINNOOSTV INVOCATIONS
ACIINNORRTU IRON CURTAIN
ACIINNORTUV INCURVATION
ACIINNOSTTX INTOXICANTS
ACIINOOPRST ANISOTROPIC
ACIINOORTTX INTOXICATOR
ACIINOPRTTU UNPATRIOTIC
ACIINORSTTU RUSTICATION
ACIINRSSSST NARCISSISTS
ACIINRTTTUY TACITURNITY
ACIIOPSSSTT PSITTACOSIS
ACIJNNOORTU CONJURATION
ACIKNNORSYY SYNKARYONIC
ACILLMNOORY MORONICALLY
ACILLMNOPTY COMPLIANTLY
ACILLMOOSTY OSMOTICALLY
ACILLMOPSTY PLASMOLYTIC
ACILLMOTYYZ ZYMOTICALLY
ACILLNNOTUY CONTINUALLY
ACILLNOOOPT LOCAL OPTION
ACILLOORRTT TORTICOLLAR
ACILLOORSST OSCILLATORS
ACILLOORSTY OSCILLATORY
ACILMMMNOSU COMMUNALISM
ACILMMNNOOU COMMUNIONAL

ACILMMNOOOT COMMOTIONAL
ACILMMNOSTU COMMUNALIST
ACILMMNOTUY COMMUNALITY
ACILMMORSSU COMMISSURAL
ACILMMRSSUU SIMULACRUMS
ACILMOOPSTX TOXOPLASMIC
ACILMORSTUY CUSTOMARILY
ACILMRSTUUY MUSCULARITY
ACILNNOOOST CONSOLATION
ACILNOOSTTT COTTONTAILS
ACILNORSSTU ULTRASONICS
ACILNPPSSTU SUPPLICANTS
ACILNPTTUUY PUNCTUALITY
ACILOOPRRTY CORPORALITY
ACILOORSTUY ATROCIOUSLY
ACILOORSUVY VORACIOUSLY
ACILORSTTUV CULTIVATORS
ACIMMNOORTY COMMINATORY
ACIMMNOOTTU COMMUTATION
ACIMMOPSTTY SYMPTOMATIC
ACIMNNOORTU MUCRONATION
ACIMNOOPRSS COMPARISONS
ACIMNOOPTTU COMPUTATION
ACIMNOPPRSS PRISON CAMPS
ACIMNOPRSTY PATRONYMICS
ACIMNPRSSTU MANUSCRIPTS
ACIMOOPRSTT COMPATRIOTS
ACINNNNOOST INCONSONANT
ACINNNOOOTT CONNOTATION
ACINNOOOORST CORONATIONS
ACINNOOPRTT CONTRAPTION
ACINNOOPSTY SYNCOPATION
ACINNOORTTU CONTINUATOR
ACINNOPTTUU PUNCTUATION
ACINNORSSTT CONSTRAINTS
ACINOOOPRRT CORPORATION
ACINOOOPRTV PROVOCATION
ACINOOPRRST CONSPIRATOR
ACINOOPRRTT PROTRACTION
ACINOOPRRTU PROCURATION
ACINOORRSUV CARNIVOROUS
ACINOORSSTT CARTOONISTS
ACINPRRSSTT TRANSCRIPTS
ACIOOPPRSTT POTATO CRISP
ACIORSSSSSY SYSSARCOSIS
ACLLMOSTUUU ALTOCUMULUS
ACLLNNORTUY NOCTURNALLY
ACLNNOSSTTU CONSULTANTS
ACLNCOOORSTY CONSOLATORY
ACLNOOPRRSU PROCONSULAR
ACLNOORRSUY RANCOROUSLY
ACLOOPRSUXY XYLOCARPOUS
ACMMNOORSTU CONSUMMATOR
ACMMOORSTTU COMMUTATORS
ACMMPPSUUUV VACUUM PUMPS
ACMOOOSSTTU SCOTOMATOUS
ACOOPRRRSTT PROTRACTORS
ADDDDENNOSS ODDS AND ENDS
ADDDEEERRSS READDRESSED

ADDDEEGIRRS DISREGARDED
ADDDEEHNRSU DUNDERHEADS
ADDDEEILSSS SIDESADDLES
ADDDEGIKLNS SKEDADDLING
ADDDERSSTTU STAR-STUDDED
ADDEEEEGNRT DEGENERATED
ADDEEEEHLLV LEVEL-HEADED
ADDEEEGLRTU DEREGULATED
ADDEEEHIKNS HIDE-AND-SEEK
ADDEEEHMPTY EMPTY-HEADED
ADDEEEHNPPR APPREHENDED
ADDEEEHRSSS HEADDRESSES
ADDEEEIMNRR REMAINDERED
ADDEEELRSTT DEAD LETTERS
ADDEEENORUV ENDEAVOURED
ADDEEEOPRSS DESPERADOES
ADDEEFHLRUY FURALDEHYDE
ADDEEFLOPST SOFT-PEDALED
ADDEEFMNORU UNDREAMED-OF
ADDEEFMNRTU DEFRAUDMENT
ADDEEGHHILT LIGHT-HEADED
ADDEEGHILPY PIGHEADEDLY
ADDEEGHNORW WRONGHEADED
ADDEEGILMNR LARGE-MINDED
ADDEEGINRRS DEAD RINGERS
ADDEEGIRRRS DISREGARDER
ADDEEGNRSSU GUARDEDNESS
ADDEEHHLOTY HOTHEADEDLY
ADDEEHIKNRT KIND-HEARTED
ADDEEHIMNSU DEHUMANISED
ADDEEHIMNUZ DEHUMANIZED
ADDEEHISTTU DEATH DUTIES
ADDEEHMNPTY EMPTY-HANDED
ADDEEHNORTW DOWNHEARTED
ADDEEHPRRSS HARD-PRESSED
ADDEEIILSTV DEVITALISED
ADDEEIILTVZ DEVITALIZED
ADDEEIINNNW WINE AND DINE
ADDEEIJOPRS JEOPARDISED
ADDEEIJOPRZ JEOPARDIZED
ADDEEILLSVW WELL-ADVISED
ADDEEILMMNS MIDDLE NAMES
ADDEEILNRRT INTERLARDED
ADDEEILRRVY DAREDEVILRY
ADDEEIMNNOT DENOMINATED
ADDEEIMNPRR REPRIMANDED
ADDEEIMNRRS MIND READERS
ADDEEIMORRS DROMEDARIES
ADDEEIMOTTV DEMOTIVATED
ADDEEIMRSTU DESIDERATUM
ADDEEINOPRR PREORDAINED
ADDEEINOPRT DEPREDATION
ADDEEIRTTWY READY-WITTED
ADDEELNNSTU SUDETENLAND
ADDEELNPRUY UNDERPLAYED
ADDEELNRUUV UNDERVALUED
ADDEELOPPTU DEPOPULATED
ADDEELOPRRS ROPE LADDERS
ADDEELPRSST STEPLADDERS

ADDEEMNNNRU UNDERMANNED
ADDEEMNOPPR NAMEDROPPED
ADDEENORTWW WATERED-DOWN
ADDEENRSTTU UNDERSTATED
ADDEFFHLNOY OFFHANDEDLY
ADDEFILORTU FLUORIDATED
ADDEGGHORTU GODDAUGHTER
ADDEGGIIIRT DIGITIGRADE
ADDEGHHINRT RIGHT-HANDED
ADDEGHINRTY DEHYDRATING
ADDEGHNORTU DREADNOUGHT
ADDEGIIMNNR MIND READING
ADDEGIKNRRS KIND REGARDS
ADDEGILLNRW GRINDELWALD
ADDEGILMNNY MADDENINGLY
ADDEGILNNSY SADDENINGLY
ADDEGIMNNNU UNDEMANDING
ADDEGIMNORS GORMANDISED
ADDEGIMNORZ GORMANDIZED
ADDEGJMNTUY JUDGMENT DAY
ADDEGNOORTU GOOD-NATURED
ADDEHHNORST SHORTHANDED
ADDEHIILMOT THALIDOMIDE
ADDEHILNORS RHODE ISLAND
ADDEHILOPSU DIADELPHOUS
ADDEHINORTY DEHYDRATION
ADDEHINOSWW WINDOW SHADE
ADDEHIOPRSS RHAPSODISED
ADDEHIOPRSZ RHAPSODIZED
ADDEHMNNOSW HAND-ME-DOWNS
ADDEHMORSUY HYDROMEDUSA
ADDEIIIMNTT INTIMIDATED
ADDEIIINOOR RADIOIODINE
ADDEIIINTUV INDIVIDUATE
ADDEILLMMNS SMALL-MINDED
ADDEILNSUVY UNADVISEDLY
ADDEILOSVWY DISAVOWEDLY
ADDEILRSTTU STRIDULATED
ADDEIOPPRSV DISAPPROVED
ADDELMOORTU DEMODULATOR
ADDELMORRSW DREAM WORLDS
ADDELNNORSW WONDERLANDS
ADDELNNRTUY REDUNDANTLY
ADDEMNOOOORT RODOMONTADE
ADDGGINNORW DOWNGRADING
ADDGHILNOOR ROADHOLDING
ADDGILNNOOW DOWNLOADING
ADDIIIIMNOT DIMIDIATION
ADDIIILNSUV INDIVIDUALS
ADDILLNNOUV NULL AND VOID
ADDILMNORTY DIRTY OLD MAN
ADDNNOOSTUW DOWN-AND-OUTS
ADDNNOPSSUW UPS AND DOWNS
ADEEEEFGHRT FEATHEREDGE
ADEEEEFHRRT FREE-HEARTED
ADEEEEGGRST DESEGREGATE
ADEEEEGNRRT REGENERATED
ADEEEEGNRST DEGENERATES
ADEEEEHKNTY THE NAKED EYE

ADEEEFILNRT DEFERENTIAL
ADEEEFLORRS FREELOADERS
ADEEEFNRSTT FENESTRATED
ADEEEGGLLNO GOLDEN EAGLE
ADEEEGHLPRT TELEGRAPHED
ADEEEGILMNR LEGERDEMAIN
ADEEEGILNRS GENERALISED
ADEEEGILNRZ GENERALIZED
ADEEEGILNSV EVANGELISED
ADEEEGILNVZ EVANGELIZED
ADEEEGIMNRR GENDARMERIE
ADEEEGIMNST DEMAGNETISE
ADEEEGIMNTZ DEMAGNETIZE
ADEEEGINNRT TRAGEDIENNE
ADEEEGLLNRT LEGAL TENDER
ADEEEGLNNRR GREENLANDER
ADEEEGMNNRT DERANGEMENT
ADEEEGNOTXY DEOXYGENATE
ADEEEHLLORS LEASEHOLDER
ADEEEHLPSSY SLEEPYHEADS
ADEEEHLRSTT LETTERHEADS
ADEEEHMORST HOMESTEADER
ADEEEHNNNOR ENNEAHEDRON
ADEEEHNOPRT OPENHEARTED
ADEEEHNRRSU UNREHEARSED
ADEEEHPRSST SPREADSHEET
ADEEEHRRTTU TRUEHEARTED
ADEEEIILNTV DELINEATIVE
ADEEEIIMMOR AIDE-MEMOIRE
ADEEEILSSUX DESEXUALISE
ADEEEILSUXZ DESEXUALIZE
ADEEEIMNRTT DETERMINATE
ADEEEIMPRTT PREMEDITATE
ADEEEINNRTT ENTERTAINED
ADEEEIORRTT DETERIORATE
ADEEEIPRRST PIEDS-À-TERRE
ADEEEJNRTUV REJUVENATED
ADEEEKLLPSW SLEEPWALKED
ADEEEKLRRST DEERSTALKER
ADEEEKLSTTW SWEET-TALKED
ADEEELLNSWY WENSLEYDALE
ADEEELLSSTT TESSELLATED
ADEEELMNNOW NEEDLEWOMAN
ADEEELNNRSS LEARNEDNESS
ADEEELNRSST RELATEDNESS
ADEEELNRTTU LAUNDERETTE
ADEEELNSSTX EXALTEDNESS
ADEEELPRSTY DESPERATELY
ADEEEMNNRST ENDEARMENTS
ADEEEMNRRTU REMUNERATED
ADEEEMOSTWW MEADOWSWEET
ADEEENOPRTU DEUTERANOPE
ADEEENORRUV ENDEAVOURER
ADEEENRRSSW NEWSREADERS
ADEEEPPRRTT PERPETRATED
ADEEEPPRTTU PERPETUATED
ADEEEPRSSSU SUPERSEDEAS
ADEEFFIINRT DIFFERENTIA
ADEEFFORSTV OVERSTAFFED

ADEEFGGLOPR LEAPFROGGED
ADEEFGHIRSU FIGUREHEADS
ADEEFGHORRT FORGATHERED
ADEEFGIINNR FINE-GRAINED
ADEEFGILNOR FREELOADING
ADEEFGINNRR RANGE FINDER
ADEEFHLNRST LEFT-HANDERS
ADEEFHORSTT SOFTHEARTED
ADEEFILORRS RELIEF ROADS
ADEEFILRSST FEDERALISTS
ADEEFINORST FEDERATIONS
ADEEFINRRST FRATERNISED
ADEEFINRRTZ FRATERNIZED
ADEEFIOPSST SAFE-DEPOSIT
ADEEFLLORST FORESTALLED
ADEEFLRSSSU SELF-ASSURED
ADEEFNOPRRS FREE PARDONS
ADEEFNRRRST TRANSFERRED
ADEEFOOPRRR PROOFREADER
ADEEGGHLORS LOGGERHEADS
ADEEGGIINRS DISAGREEING
ADEEGGILRVY AGGRIEVEDLY
ADEEGGINNNR ENDANGERING
ADEEGGLORTW WATERLOGGED
ADEEGGMORUY DEMAGOGUERY
ADEEGGNPRSS PRESSGANGED
ADEEGHINRST NEARSIGHTED
ADEEGHIRRST SIGHT-READER
ADEEGHLRSTU SLAUGHTERED
ADEEGHMOPRR DEMOGRAPHER
ADEEGHNORTY HYDROGENATE
ADEEGIILNNT DELINEATING
ADEEGIINSTV DESIGNATIVE
ADEEGIIRSST GREAT DIESIS
ADEEGILNNRY ENDEARINGLY
ADEEGILNNST DISENTANGLE
ADEEGILNOST DELEGATIONS
ADEEGILNRRS RINGLEADERS
ADEEGILNTTU DEGLUTINATE
ADEEGILRRSU REGULARISED
ADEEGILRRUZ REGULARIZED
ADEEGIMNNRS MEANDERINGS
ADEEGIMNPRT IMPREGNATED
ADEEGINORRS REORGANISED
ADEEGINORRZ REORGANIZED
ADEEGKRRTUU GREATER KUDU
ADEEGLPPRSY DAPPLE-GREYS
ADEEGMNNORY DANGER MONEY
ADEEGMNRRRY GERRYMANDER
ADEEGMORTUY DEUTEROGAMY
ADEEHHILSST HEAT SHIELDS
ADEEHHIMRTY HEMIHYDRATE
ADEEHHISTWW WHITEWASHED
ADEEHHLORRS SHAREHOLDER
ADEEHHNOPRT HEPTAHEDRON
ADEEHHNRSTU HEADHUNTERS
ADEEHIINPRS HESPERIDIAN
ADEEHIIOPRS ISODIAPHERE
ADEEHILLNOT ENDOTHELIAL

ADEEHILNOPT ELEPHANTOID
ADEEHILNORT LION-HEARTED
ADEEHILNPRR PHILANDERER
ADEEHILNSST DEATHLINESS
ADEEHILPRSS DEALERSHIPS
ADEEHILSSWY DAISY WHEELS
ADEEHINRSST THREADINESS
ADEEHIPRRSS READERSHIPS
ADEEHIRRRSS HAIRDRESSER
ADEEHIRRSTW HARRIS TWEED
ADEEHKLORST STAKEHOLDER
ADEEHLLNOSW SWOLLEN HEAD
ADEEHLLSSTY DEATHLESSLY
ADEEHLMNOTT MENTHOLATED
ADEEHLNNRST NETHERLANDS
ADEEHLOORTW LEATHERWOOD
ADEEHNNOPRT PENTAHEDRON
ADEEHNORRTT TETRAHEDRON
ADEEIILMMSV MEDIEVALISM
ADEEIILMMTY IMMEDIATELY
ADEEIILMNOT MATINÉE IDOL
ADEEIILMSTV MEDIEVALIST
ADEEIILNNOT DELINEATION
ADEEIILNRST RESIDENTIAL
ADEEIILRSTV REVITALISED
ADEEIILRTVZ REVITALIZED
ADEEIIMMNPT IMPEDIMENTA
ADEEIIMNNST INSEMINATED
ADEEIIMNSST DISSEMINATE
ADEEIINRRTV VERATRIDINE
ADEEIIPRSTV DEPRAVITIES
ADEEIIPRTUV REPUDIATIVE
ADEEIIRSSTV ADVERSITIES
ADEEIIRSTVV DERIVATIVES
ADEEILLMNNR ILL-MANNERED
ADEEILLMRSV SILVER MEDAL
ADEEILMNNST ENLISTED MAN
ADEEILMNORT ENDOMETRIAL
ADEEILMNRST DERAILMENTS, STREAMLINED
ADEEILMNRTT DETRIMENTAL
ADEEILMNRVY DELIVERYMAN
ADEEILMORRS DEMORALISER
ADEEILMORRZ DEMORALIZER
ADEEILMORTT DILATOMETER
ADEEILNNPTT PENTLANDITE
ADEEILNNPUX UNEXPLAINED
ADEEILNNRTT INTERDENTAL
ADEEILNRSTU NEUTRALISED
ADEEILNRSTY SEDENTARILY
ADEEILNRTUZ NEUTRALIZED
ADEEILNSTTT DILETTANTES
ADEEILOPRRS DEPOLARISER
ADEEILOPRRZ DEPOLARIZER
ADEEILPRRSV PEARL DIVERS
ADEEILPRSSU DISPLEASURE
ADEEILRRSVV SLAVE DRIVER
ADEEIMNNOST EMENDATIONS
ADEEIMNNPTU ANTEPENDIUM
ADEEIMNNRTT DETERMINANT, DETRAINMENT

ADEEIMNOPRT PREDOMINATE	ADEFHIRSTWW WHITE DWARFS
ADEEIMNPRRR REPRIMANDER	ADEFIILNNRS LINDISFARNE
ADEEIMNRSTY SEDIMENTARY	ADEFIILNOOT DEFOLIATION
ADEEIMORSTT STADIOMETER	ADEFIILNQUU UNQUALIFIED
ADEEIMRTTTY TETRADYMITE	ADEFIILNRTT INFILTRATED
ADEEINNRTTV INADVERTENT	ADEFIIMNRSU FREUDIANISM
ADEEINOPRST DESPERATION	ADEFIINSSTU UNSATISFIED
ADEEINORRST RAISON D'ETRE	ADEFILLORUV ILL-FAVOURED
ADEEINOSTTT DETESTATION	ADEFILNOORT DEFLORATION
ADEEINPRSST PEDESTRIANS	ADEFILSSTTU DISTASTEFUL
ADEEIPRSSTU PASTEURISED	ADEFIMNOORT DEFORMATION
ADEEIPRSTUZ PASTEURIZED	ADEFIMRRRST DIRT FARMERS
ADEEIRRSSTV ADVERTISERS	ADEFLLNOSST DENTAL FLOSS
ADEEKLOPRSU LOUDSPEAKER	ADEFLNOORRS FOOL'S ERRAND
ADEEKMRRSSS DRESSMAKERS	ADEFLOOPSTY SPLAYFOOTED
ADEEKNRRSTU UNDERTAKERS	ADEFMNORRST TRANSFORMED
ADEELLMNSSW MENDEL'S LAWS	ADEFNORRSSW FORWARDNESS
ADEELLMRSSY DREAMLESSLY	ADEGGGIINNS DISENGAGING
ADEELLNOSTW STONEWALLED	ADEGGHILNRT RIGHT-ANGLED
ADEELLNRTUV UNTRAVELLED	ADEGGIINNRT DENIGRATING
ADEELLOPTUV POLE VAULTED	ADEGGIINNST DESIGNATING
ADEELLORSSS LOSS LEADERS	ADEGGILNRUU UNGULIGRADE
ADEELMNOORT DEMONOLATER	ADEGHHILNNP HELPING HAND
ADEELNNRTUW UNTERWALDEN	ADEGHHILNRS HIGHLANDERS
ADEELNOORST ALDOSTERONE	ADEGHHINNTU HEADHUNTING
ADEELNRRUUV UNDERVALUER	ADEGHHINRRT RIGHT-HANDER
ADEELNRTTVY ADVERTENTLY	ADEGHHINSST NIGHTSHADES
ADEELRRSSUY REASSUREDLY	ADEGHHORRTU READ-THROUGH
ADEEMMNORTY DYNAMOMETER	ADEGHINOORT IN GOOD HEART
ADEEMNNNSSU MUNDANENESS	ADEGHMNORRT GRANDMOTHER
ADEEMNNOOOW WOOD ANEMONE	ADEGHMNRSTU DRAUGHTSMEN
ADEEMNOPPRR NAMEDROPPER	ADEGHORRTUV OVERDRAUGHT
ADEEMNORSTT DEMONSTRATE	ADEGHORSSUU GUARDHOUSES
ADEEMNPRSTT DEPARTMENTS	ADEGIILNTV INVIGILATED
ADEEMNRSTTU MENSTRUATED	ADEGIIINRST DIGNITARIES
ADEENNNPPSY SPEND A PENNY	ADEGIILNNRW LINE DRAWING
ADEENPRSSSU UNDERPASSES	ADEGIILNNRY INGRAINEDLY
ADEENQRRSSU SQUANDERERS	ADEGIILNOST DIGESTIONAL
ADEENRRSTUV ADVENTURERS	ADEGIILNOTV DOVETAILING
ADEENRSSSSU ASSUREDNESS	ADEGIILNPSS DISPLEASING
ADEENRSSTUV ADVENTURESS	ADEGIIMNTTU UNMITIGATED
ADEEOPPRRRS ORDER PAPERS	ADEGIIMSSTT STIGMATISED
ADEEORRSTTU TRADE ROUTES	ADEGIIMSTTZ STIGMATIZED
ADEFFILNRTU FAULT-FINDER	ADEGIINNORT DENIGRATION
ADEFFIMMNOR FRAME OF MIND	ADEGIINNOST DESIGNATION
ADEFFINRSST FAST FRIENDS	ADEGIINOPRR PERIGORDIAN
ADEFFIORSST DISAFFOREST	ADEGIINOPTV VIDEOTAPING
ADEFFLOOTTU FOOT FAULTED	ADEGIINORSS DISORGANISE
ADEFGHLOORT HEART OF GOLD	ADEGIINORSZ DISORGANIZE
ADEFGIILNOT DEFOLIATING	ADEGIINORTV INVIGORATED
ADEFGILLNOS SELF-LOADING	ADEGIINPRTU REPUDIATING
ADEFGILNORS DRAGONFLIES	ADEGIINRSTV ADVERTISING
ADEFGIPPRTW GIFT-WRAPPED	ADEGIINRTTU INGRATITUDE
ADEFGKNOORS GODFORSAKEN	ADEGIINRTTX EXTRADITING
ADEFGNOOPRS ROOF GARDENS	ADEGIIOPRRS PRAIRIE DOGS
ADEFHHLOOST HEALTH FOODS	ADEGIJNRRSU GRAND JURIES
ADEFHIKOSST KISS OF DEATH	ADEGIJNRSTU READJUSTING
ADEFHINPRST PATHFINDERS	ADEGIKMNRSS DRESSMAKING
ADEFHINRRTY FIRE HYDRANT	ADEGIKNNRTU UNDERTAKING

ADEGILLOSSU GLADIOLUSES
ADEGILLPTUY PLEAD GUILTY
ADEGILNNNST LANDING NETS
ADEGILNNRWY WANDERINGLY
ADEGILNOORV OVERLOADING
ADEGILNORST TSELINOGRAD
ADEGILNRRTY RETARDINGLY
ADEGILOOPST PAEDOLOGIST
ADEGIMNNOPR PROMENADING
ADEGIMNORRS GORMANDISER
ADEGIMNORRZ GORMANDIZER
ADEGIMNORSU GOURMANDISE
ADEGINNNOPS UNORGANISED
ADEGINNORUZ UNORGANIZED
ADEGINNPRUY UNDERPAYING
ADEGINNQRSU SQUANDERING
ADEGINNRRTU UNDERRATING
ADEGINORRVW OVERDRAWING
ADEGINORSTT ROAD TESTING
ADEGKNRRRSU KRUGERRANDS
ADEGLMOORTY DERMATOLOGY
ADEGLMOPRTU PROMULGATED
ADEGLNORSUY DANGEROUSLY
ADEGMMMNOOR MONOGRAMMED
ADEGNNOORSU ANDROGENOUS
ADEHHIORRSS HORSERADISH
ADEHHIRSSSW DISHWASHERS
ADEHIIMNRTU ANTHERIDIUM
ADEHIIOPRSS DIAPHORESIS
ADEHIIORSTT HISTORIATED
ADEHILLNRST DISENTHRALL
ADEHILLORSU LOUDHAILERS
ADEHIMMPPUY HAPPY MEDIUM
ADEHIMORRTY RADIOTHERMY
ADEHIMPSSTY SYMPATHISED
ADEHIMPSTYZ SYMPATHIZED
ADEHINNRSUV UNVARNISHED
ADEHINNRTTW HANDWRITTEN
ADEHINOORTZ ANTHEROZOID
ADEHINOSSSW SHADOWINESS
ADEHINQRRTU HINDQUARTER
ADEHINRSTTW WITHSTANDER
ADEHIPRSSTW STEWARDSHIP
ADEHIPRSTTW SHARP-WITTED
ADEHLLLMORS SMALLHOLDER
ADEHLLLORST STALLHOLDER
ADEHLORSTYY HYDROLYSATE
ADEHMNOORTY MONOHYDRATE
ADEHNNOPSTU OPEN-AND-SHUT
ADEHNOORTTW DOWN-TO-EARTH
ADEHOPRSSTW SHOP STEWARD
ADEIIILMRST MILITARISED
ADEIIILMRTZ MILITARIZED
ADEIIILMSST DISSIMILATE
ADEIIILRSTV TRIVIALISED
ADEIIILRTVZ TRIVIALIZED
ADEIIIMOSTT OTITIS MEDIA
ADEIIIMRSTY SEMIARIDITY
ADEIIINNTTU UNINITIATED

ADEIIIPRSST DISPARITIES
ADEIIIPSSTV DISSIPATIVE
ADEIILLLOPS ELLIPSOIDAL
ADEIILLMNTU ILLUMINATED
ADEIILLORTY EDITORIALLY
ADEIILMNNOS DIMENSIONAL
ADEIILMNRSU SEMIDIURNAL
ADEIILMSSTU DISSIMULATE
ADEIILNORSV DIVERSIONAL
ADEIILORRST IDOLATRISER
ADEIILORRTZ IDOLATRIZER
ADEIIMMNSTU MEDIASTINUM
ADEIIMNOPSS IMPASSIONED
ADEIIMNOSTT MEDITATIONS
ADEIIMPRSSU PRAESIDIUMS
ADEIIMRSTTX TAXIDERMIST
ADEIINNNOTT INDENTATION
ADEIINNOOPT OPINIONATED
ADEIINNORTT DENITRATION
ADEIINNOSTT DESTINATION
ADEIINOPRTT PARTITIONED, TREPIDATION
ADEIINOPRTU REPUDIATION
ADEIINOPRTV DEPRIVATION
ADEIINOPSST PASSIONTIDE
ADEIINORSTV DERIVATIONS
ADEIINORSTY SEDITIONARY
ADEIINORTTX EXTRADITION
ADEIINPRSTY STIPENDIARY
ADEIINQSTTU EQUIDISTANT
ADEIINRSTVY VINEYARDIST
ADEIIOPPRTT PROPITIATED
ADEIJMMNRSW WINDJAMMERS
ADEIKLLLRSY LADY-KILLERS
ADEIKLLMMST MALTED MILKS
ADEILLMRRST DRILLMASTER
ADEILLORSST ILL-ASSORTED
ADEILLORTUV OUTRIVALLED
ADEILLOSVWW SWALLOW DIVE
ADEILLRSTTU ILLUSTRATED
ADEILMMOOTY MYELOMATOID
ADEILMNNSSU MAUDLINNESS
ADEILMNOPRS PALINDROMES
ADEILMNOPTU DEPLUMATION
ADEILMORTTY DILATOMETRY
ADEILNOOPRT PERIODONTAL
ADEILNRSTWZ SWITZERLAND
ADEILNSSTUY SUSTAINEDLY
ADEILOPPRSS PREDISPOSAL
ADEILOPPRSU POPULARISED
ADEILOPPRUZ POPULARIZED
ADEILOPRRTY PREDATORILY
ADEIMMNNOPU PANDEMONIUM
ADEIMMNRSST MASTERMINDS
ADEIMMNSSTT DISMASTMENT
ADEIMNNOORT DENOMINATOR
ADEIMNNOPRT PREDOMINANT
ADEIMNNQRUU QUADRENNIUM
ADEIMNOPSTU DESPUMATION
ADEIMNRRTUY RUDIMENTARY

ADEIMNRSTTT TRANSMITTED
ADEIMNRSTUV ADVENTURISM
ADEINNOOSTT DENOTATIONS, DETONATIONS
ADEINNOPSWW WINDOWPANES
ADEINNORSTU TRADE UNIONS
ADEINOOPPRT APPORTIONED
ADEINOOPRTT DEPORTATION
ADEINOPSTTU DEPUTATIONS
ADEINRSTTUV ADVENTURIST
ADEIOPPRRSV DISAPPROVER
ADEIOPRRTUY REPUDIATORY
ADEJMNNORTU ADJOURNMENT
ADEJMNSSTTU ADJUSTMENTS
ADELLMNORSW SMALL WONDER
ADELLNNNOOP LONDON PLANE
ADELLNORRSU ALL-ROUNDERS
ADELLNSSTUY DAUNTLESSLY
ADELLOOPPRT PETRODOLLAR
ADELLOORRRS ROAD ROLLERS
ADELLOORRSU EURODOLLARS
ADELMNOORTY DEMONOLATRY
ADELMNORRTU ULTRAMODERN
ADELOOPPRST POSTAL ORDER
ADELOPPRSUU DUAL-PURPOSE
ADELOPRRRSY LORD'S PRAYER
ADELPQRSTUU QUADRUPLETS
ADEMMMNORSU MEMORANDUMS
ADEMMNNOUYY MAUNDY MONEY
ADEMMNORTYY DYNAMOMETRY
ADEMNNOPTWY DOWN PAYMENT
ADENNOPRRST TRANSPONDER
ADENOPRRSTT TRANSPORTED
ADENORSSSUU ARDUOUSNESS
ADENORSTUUV ADVENTUROUS
ADENPRSSSUU UNSURPASSED
ADFFFFHNPUU HUFF AND PUFF
ADFFGNORSTU GROUND STAFF
ADFFHINOSST STANDOFFISH
ADFGHIINNPT PATHFINDING
ADFGHIINOOT IN GOOD FAITH
ADFGIILRRSY GIRL FRIDAYS
ADFGIINQRSU FIRING SQUAD
ADFGILNNOST SOFT LANDING
ADFGILNQSUY FLYING SQUAD
ADFGINORRSU FAIRGROUNDS
ADFHHNOOSSW SHOW OF HANDS
ADFIIILLNNU NULLIFIDIAN
ADFIIIMNNTU AD INFINITUM
ADFINNOOSTU FOUNDATIONS
ADFLMNSTUUU MUTUAL FUNDS
ADFLNOOOPTU FOOT-POUNDAL
ADGGGHIILNN HANG GLIDING
ADGGLNORSSU GROUND GLASS
ADGHHIINRTT HARD-HITTING
ADGHHILNOPT DIPHTHONGAL
ADGHHOPRRYY HYDROGRAPHY
ADGHIILMNNS MISHANDLING
ADGHIIMNNOS ADMONISHING
ADGHIINNRTW HANDWRITING

ADGHIINRTWW WITHDRAWING
ADGHIOPRTTY DITTOGRAPHY
ADGHLPRSSUU SULPHA DRUGS
ADGHMRRRUYY HYDRARGYRUM
ADGHNOOOPRT ODONTOGRAPH
ADGIIILNQTU LIQUIDATING
ADGIIINNNOT INDIGNATION
ADGIIINNOTU AUDITIONING
ADGIIINNRST DISTRAINING
ADGIIINPSST DISSIPATING
ADGIILLNOSW DISALLOWING
ADGIILMNNST DISMANTLING
ADGIILNNNTY INDIGNANTLY
ADGIILOORST RADIOLOGIST
ADGIILOOSTU AUDIOLOGIST
ADGIILOPRTY PRODIGALITY
ADGIINNPRSW DRAWING PINS
ADGIINOPTUY AUDIOTYPING
ADGIINORSTY GRANDIOSITY
ADGIKNNOORT GORDIAN KNOT
ADGIKNORSWY WORKING DAYS
ADGILNNOPWY DOWNPLAYING
ADGILNOOPSW WADING POOLS
ADGILNPQRUU QUADRUPLING
ADGIMMNORSU GOURMANDISM
ADGIMNOORRW DRAWING ROOM
ADGINNOSTTU OUTSTANDING
ADGINOPRSTT TRADING POST
ADGINRRSSTW DRAWSTRINGS
ADGIORSSSWW GRASS WIDOWS
ADGLNNOPRSU GROUND PLANS
ADGLNOPRSUY PLAYGROUNDS
ADGNNOORSUY ANDROGYNOUS
ADHHNOSSTTU THOUSANDTHS
ADHIIOPPSSY DIAPOPHYSIS
ADHIIORRSST DIARTHROSIS
ADHILMNOOSW OLD-WOMANISH
ADHINNOPRSX ANDROSPHINX
ADHINOSSSWW SASH WINDOWS
ADHLNOPSSSW SPLASHDOWNS
ADIIILNOOST IDOLISATION
ADIIILNOOTZ IDOLIZATION
ADIIILNOQTU LIQUIDATION
ADIIIMNORTT INTIMIDATOR
ADIIIMOSSTT MASTOIDITIS
ADIIINNOSTV DIVINATIONS
ADIIINOOSTX OXIDISATION
ADIIINOOTXZ OXIDIZATION
ADIIINOPSST DISSIPATION
ADIILLMNOOT TOIL AND MOIL
ADIILLNOQRU QUADRILLION
ADIILMNNOST MANDOLINIST
ADIILMOPSTT DIPLOMATIST
ADIILOQRSTU LIQUIDATORS
ADIIMNNOOST ADMONITIONS
ADIIMNOOPST ADOPTIONISM
ADIIMORSTUU AUDITORIUMS
ADIINNNOSTU INUNDATIONS
ADIINNOORST ORDINATIONS

ADIINOOPSTT ADOPTIONIST
ADIINOPSTTU DISPUTATION
ADIIOOPRSUV AVOIRDUPOIS
ADIIOPRSSTT PODIATRISTS
ADIIOPSTTUY AUDIOTYPIST
ADIKLOOSTVV VLADIVOSTOK
ADILLLOOPPY POLYPLOIDAL
ADILMNOOSTU MODULATIONS
ADILNNOSTUU UNDULATIONS
ADILOOSSTWW SOW WILD OATS
ADILORRSTTU STRIDULATOR
ADILOSSSUUY ASSIDUOUSLY
ADIMOOPRSUY MYRIAPODOUS
ADINNOPSSTT STANDPOINTS
ADJLOPRSTUU PLATS DU JOUR
ADLNOOPRSUY POLYANDROUS
ADLNOOPRSWY PLAY ON WORDS
ADNNORRSTUU TURNAROUNDS
ADNOOPRRSTU PROTANDROUS
ADOOOPRSSUU SAUROPODOUS
AEEEEGKMPRS GAMEKEEPERS
AEEEEGKPRST GATEKEEPERS
AEEEEHILRST ETHEREALISE
AEEEEHILRTZ ETHEREALIZE
AEEEEHLRTTT LEATHERETTE
AEEEENRSVWY NEW YEAR'S EVE
AEEEFFLOPPT TOFFEE APPLE
AEEEFFLORRT FREE-FLOATER
AEEEFGIKNPS SAFEKEEPING
AEEEFGIRRRT REFRIGERATE
AEEEFHINRRT HEREINAFTER
AEEEFILNRRT REFERENTIAL
AEEEFLLNNTT FLANNELETTE
AEEEFLNSSSU EASEFULNESS
AEEEFLRSSTU FEATURELESS
AEEEFPRSTTU SUPERFETATE
AEEEGGHIMTV GIVE THE GAME
AEEEGGIKMNP GAMEKEEPING
AEEEGGILNOS GENEALOGIES
AEEEGGIRSTV SEGREGATIVE
AEEEGGMMNOU EMMENAGOGUE
AEEEGGMMNST ENGAGEMENTS
AEEEGHLPRRT TELEGRAPHER
AEEEGHNPRTW GREAT-NEPHEW
AEEEGHNRTWY GET ANYWHERE
AEEEGHORRTT THEATREGOER
AEEEGILNRRS GENERALISER
AEEEGILNRRZ GENERALIZER
AEEEGILNRSV EVANGELISER
AEEEGILNRVZ EVANGELIZER
AEEEGIMNNST STEAM-ENGINE
AEEEGIMNSST METAGENESIS
AEEEGINORTT RENEGOTIATE
AEEEGINPRRT PEREGRINATE
AEEEGKLOPRS GOALKEEPERS
AEEEGKLPRRU KEEP REGULAR
AEEEGLMNNRT ENLARGEMENT
AEEEGLNNRSS GENERALNESS
AEEEGLNSSSS AGELESSNESS

AEEEGMNNRSS GERMANENESS
AEEEGNPPRRS GREEN PAPERS
AEEEHHNNSST HEATHENNESS
AEEEHILNNPT ELEPHANTINE
AEEEHILRTTY ETHEREALITY
AEEEHIMSSTT METATHESISE
AEEEHIMSTTZ METATHESIZE
AEEEHINSSTT ANESTHETISE
AEEEHINSTTZ ANESTHETIZE
AEEEHIRSTWW WEATHER-WISE
AEEEHKMOOPW MAKE WHOOPEE
AEEEHLLMPRY EPHEMERALLY
AEEEHLMPPRT PAMPHLETEER
AEEEHLPRRWY PRAYER WHEEL
AEEEHLRSTWW WATERWHEELS
AEEEHNNORRW NOWHERE NEAR
AEEEHNPRSST PARENTHESES
AEEEHRSSTTW SWEETHEARTS
AEEEIILNRRT INERTIA REEL
AEEEIINPPRT PERIPETEIAN
AEEEIIRRTTV REITERATIVE
AEEEILNORRS SIERRA LEONE
AEEEILNRRTT INTERRELATE
AEEEILNRRTV REVERENTIAL
AEEEILNRSTX EXTERNALISE
AEEEILNRTXZ EXTERNALIZE
AEEEILPRRTT PRELITERATE
AEEEIMNPRTT INTEMPERATE
AEEEIMNRTTX EXTERMINATE
AEEEIMNRTUV ENUMERATIVE
AEEEINNRRTT ENTERTAINER
AEEEINOPRSU EUROPEANISE
AEEEINOPRUZ EUROPEANIZE
AEEEINORTVX EXONERATIVE
AEEEINPRTTV PENETRATIVE
AEEEINRRTVW INTERWEAVER
AEEEINSSSVV EVASIVENESS
AEEEJKRRRST TEARJERKERS
AEEEJLMSSTY LESE-MAJESTY
AEEEKKPPRRS PARK KEEPERS
AEEEKLLOSTX EXOSKELETAL
AEEEKLLPRSW SLEEPWALKER
AEEEKPSSSTW SWEEPSTAKES
AEEELLOPPSS SALESPEOPLE
AEEELLORTTT TEETOTALLER
AEEELLRSTVW WATER LEVELS
AEEELMMNNPT EMPANELMENT
AEEELMNNSTV ENSLAVEMENT
AEEELMRSSSU MEASURELESS
AEEELNOPPVY PAY ENVELOPE
AEEELRSTTUV STREET VALUE
AEEEMMNORST ANEMOMETERS
AEEEMMNPRTT TEMPERAMENT
AEEEMMNRSTU MEASUREMENT
AEEEMNNNRST ENSNAREMENT
AEEEMNNRTTT ENTREATMENT
AEEEMNOPSSS OPEN SESAMES
AEEEMNOSSSW AWESOMENESS
AEEEMNPRSTT PENTAMETERS

AEEEMNRSTTT RESTATEMENT
AEEEMPRRTTU TEMPERATURE
AEEENNRSSST EARNESTNESS
AEEENOPRSTT STEAROPTENE
AEEENPRRSTV PERSEVERANT
AEEENRSSSTU AUSTERENESS
AEEEQRSSTTU SEQUESTRATE
AEEFFGRSTTU SUFFRAGETTE
AEEFFHORRST FOREFATHERS
AEEFFILMRTU FEATURE FILM
AEEFFLLORRS FREE-FOR-ALLS
AEEFFLNRSSU FEARFULNESS
AEEFFLNSSTU FATEFULNESS
AEEFGHORRTT HETEROGRAFT
AEEFGILLNSS SELF-SEALING
AEEFGILNPRT FINGERPLATE
AEEFGILNRRS RIFLE RANGES
AEEFGINRRRT REFRIGERANT
AEEFHHIKNST SHEATH KNIFE
AEEFHHORSTU HOUSEFATHER
AEEFHILNNPS HALFPENNIES
AEEFHLLMNST MANTELSHELF
AEEFHLNSSTU HATEFULNESS
AEEFIILNNRT INFERENTIAL
AEEFIILOTVX EXFOLIATIVE
AEEFIIRRRSS FIRE-RAISERS
AEEFILLNRST SELF-RELIANT
AEEFILMRSTY FAMILY TREES
AEEFILOPRRT PROLIFERATE
AEEFIMNNRRT REFRAINMENT
AEEFIMNOSST MANIFESTOES
AEEFIMOPRRT IMPERFORATE
AEEFIMORRTV REFORMATIVE
AEEFINRRRST FRATERNISER
AEEFINRRRTZ FRATERNIZER
AEEFIOPRRTV PERFORATIVE
AEEFKLNSSUW WAKEFULNESS
AEEFLLORRST FORESTALLER
AEEFLLPRSUU PLEASUREFUL
AEEFLNRSSTU TEARFULNESS
AEEFLRRSSTT SELF-STARTER
AEEFMNORRSY FREEMASONRY
AEEFNNOPRSS PROFANENESS
AEEFNORRSVW WAR OF NERVES
AEEFOQRRRTU FOREQUARTER
AEEGGGINRST SEGREGATING
AEEGGHIOPRS GEOGRAPHIES
AEEGGHOPRRS GEOGRAPHERS
AEEGGIINORS SEIGNIORAGE
AEEGGIKLNOP GOALKEEPING
AEEGGILNOST GENEALOGIST
AEEGGIMNOSS GAMOGENESIS
AEEGGINORST SEGREGATION
AEEGGINQSTU GIGANTESQUE
AEEGGINRRRS GRANGERISER
AEEGGINRRRZ GRANGERIZER
AEEGGIRRTTU REGURGITATE
AEEGGORSTTY GEOSTRATEGY
AEEGHHITVWY HEAVYWEIGHT

AEEGHHMORRS HEMORRHAGES
AEEGHIILMNS HEGELIANISM
AEEGHILNPRS GENERALSHIP
AEEGHILNPSS SINGLE-PHASE
AEEGHINNRTT THREATENING
AEEGHINORRV OVERHEARING
AEEGHINORVZ HERZEGOVINA
AEEGHIPPRTW PAPERWEIGHT
AEEGHLNOPRS SELENOGRAPH
AEEGHLNSTVW WAVELENGTHS
AEEGHLORSTT ALTOGETHERS
AEEGHLRRSTU SLAUGHTERER
AEEGHMOOPRT GAMETOPHORE
AEEGHMOPTTY GAMETOPHYTE
AEEGHOPRRRX XEROGRAPHER
AEEGHOPRRST STEREOGRAPH
AEEGHOPSSSU ESOPHAGUSES
AEEGIILLSTV LEGISLATIVE
AEEGIILNNOR LEGIONNAIRE
AEEGIILNORS LEGIONARIES
AEEGIILNRST GELATINISER
AEEGIILNRTZ GELATINIZER
AEEGIINRRTT REITERATING
AEEGIINRTTV INTEGRATIVE, VINAIGRETTE
AEEGIINSTTV INVESTIGATE
AEEGILLMNNP EMPANELLING
AEEGILLMNNW WELL-MEANING
AEEGILLNNTY INELEGANTLY
AEEGILLNRVY REVEALINGLY
AEEGILLRSTU LEGISLATURE
AEEGILMNNRT ENGRAILMENT, REALIGNMENT
AEEGILMNNSS MEANINGLESS
AEEGILMNRRS MALINGERERS
AEEGILMNRST REGIMENTALS
AEEGILNNNRT INTERREGNAL
AEEGILNRSTV EVERLASTING
AEEGILNSSTV EVANGELISTS
AEEGIMNNRTU ENUMERATING
AEEGIMNNRUV MANEUVERING
AEEGIMSSTTU GUESSTIMATE
AEEGINNORST GENERATIONS
AEEGINNORTX EXONERATING
AEEGINNPRTT PENETRATING
AEEGINNRSTV EVENING STAR
AEEGINNTTUX EXTENUATING
AEEGINORRRS REORGANISER
AEEGINORRRZ REORGANIZER
AEEGINORRTT INTERROGATE
AEEGINOSSTU AUTOGENESIS
AEEGIOPRRTV PREROGATIVE
AEEGIPPRRST PAPER TIGERS
AEEGLLMNNTY GENTLEMANLY
AEEGLLMORTU GLOMERULATE
AEEGLLOPSWY YELLOW PAGES
AEEGLMNNOTW GENTLEWOMAN
AEEGLMNOOPR PROLEGOMENA
AEEGLOOPRRT PORTO ALEGRE
AEEGLORSTUV TRAVELOGUES
AEEGMNNNORT MONTENEGRAN

AEEGMNORRTV OVERGARMENT
AEEGNNORSSS SENSE ORGANS
AEEGNNRSSST STRANGENESS
AEEGNORSSTV GRAVESTONES
AEEGNOSSSSU GASEOUSNESS
AEEGNPRSSST PRESS AGENTS
AEEHHHOSTTV HAVE THE HOTS
AEEHHILNSST HEALTHINESS
AEEHHILRTWW WHEREWITHAL
AEEHHIPRSTW WEATHER SHIP
AEEHHIRSTWW WHITEWASHER
AEEHHISSTWW WHITEWASHES
AEEHHMORSTV HARVEST HOME
AEEHHNORSTT HEARTHSTONE
AEEHIILMOPT EPITHELIOMA
AEEHIKLLLRW KILLER WHALE
AEEHIKLNRSS HARNESS-LIKE
AEEHIKNSTTV HAVE KITTENS
AEEHIKPPRSS SPEAKERSHIP
AEEHIKPSSTT TAKE THE PISS
AEEHILLMOST MESOTHELIAL
AEEHILLMRTY HEMIELYTRAL
AEEHILMMNTY METHYLAMINE
AEEHILMSTTW WHITE METALS
AEEHILNNOST STENOHALINE
AEEHILNPPRS PLANISPHERE
AEEHILNPSSS SHAPELINESS
AEEHILNRSST EARTHLINESS
AEEHILNSSTW WEALTHINESS
AEEHILPPRRS PERIPHERALS
AEEHILPSTTT TELEPATHIST
AEEHILRSTVW WHITE-SLAVER
AEEHILSSTTT STEALTHIEST
AEEHIMMNRST HAMMERSTEIN
AEEHIMNSTTY AMETHYSTINE
AEEHINPRSST PARENTHESIS
AEEHINSSTTT ANESTHETIST
AEEHIOOPRTT HETEROTOPIA
AEEHIOOPSST APOTHEOSISE
AEEHIOOPSTZ APOTHEOSIZE
AEEHIORSTTX HETEROTAXIS
AEEHIORTTVX EXHORTATIVE
AEEHIPPRRSS PERIPHRASES
AEEHIPPRSTW WHITE PAPERS
AEEHKMPRRTY HYPERMARKET
AEEHLLMSSSY SHAMELESSLY
AEEHLLORSSW WHOLESALERS
AEEHLLPSSSY SHAPELESSLY
AEEHLLRSSTY HEARTLESSLY
AEEHLMNNRTT ENTHRALMENT
AEEHLMORSTY HEARTSOMELY
AEEHLMOSSTV STEAM SHOVEL
AEEHLMOSTTY STATELY HOME
AEEHLMPRSSW SPERM WHALES
AEEHLMRRTUY EURYTHERMAL
AEEHLNPSSSS HAPLESSNESS
AEEHLNRSSSS HARNESSLESS
AEEHLOOPRRT HETEROPOLAR
AEEHLPPRRTU PURPLE HEART

AEEHLRSSSTV HARVESTLESS
AEEHLRSSTTX TAX SHELTERS
AEEHMNOPRST METANEPHROS
AEEHMNORSWW WASHERWOMEN
AEEHMOPRSST ATMOSPHERES
AEEHMOPRSTU HEPTAMEROUS
AEEHMORSSTU HOUSEMASTER
AEEHNOPRSTU HOUSEPARENT
AEEHNORRSTT NORTHEASTER
AEEHNPPSTVY HAPPY EVENTS
AEEHOOPRRSS HORSE OPERAS
AEEHOOPRRST PEASHOOTERS
AEEHOPRRSST ASTROSPHERE
AEEHORRSSTU HOUSE ARREST
AEEHORSSTTU SOUTHEASTER
AEEHRSSSTUU THESAURUSES
AEEIIILMNTV ELIMINATIVE
AEEIIINNNST EINSTEINIAN
AEEIIINRRST ITINERARIES
AEEIILLRRST ARTILLERIES
AEEIILLRSTW WATER LILIES
AEEIILMMORS MEMORIALISE
AEEIILMMORZ MEMORIALIZE
AEEIILMNRRS MINERALISER
AEEIILMNRRZ MINERALIZER
AEEIILMNSTT MENTALITIES
AEEIILMORTV MELIORATIVE
AEEIILMRRST SEMITRAILER
AEEIILNNPTT PENITENTIAL
AEEIILNNRRT INTERLINEAR
AEEIILNNRST INTERNALISE
AEEIILNNRTZ INTERNALIZE
AEEIILNNSST INESSENTIAL
AEEIILNORST ORIENTALISE
AEEIILNORTZ ORIENTALIZE
AEEIILNSTTX EXISTENTIAL
AEEIILNTTVV VENTILATIVE
AEEIILQRRSU RELIQUARIES
AEEIIMNRTTV TERMINATIVE
AEEIIMNSSTT ANTI-SEMITES
AEEIIMNSSTW SIAMESE TWIN
AEEIIMPRSTV IMPERATIVES
AEEIIMPRTTV IMPETRATIVE
AEEIINNTTTV INATTENTIVE
AEEIINOPRTV INOPERATIVE
AEEIINORRTT REITERATION
AEEIIPRSSST PATISSERIES
AEEIIPRTTVX EXTIRPATIVE
AEEIIRSSTTU AUSTERITIES
AEEIKMNSTTU MINUTE STEAK
AEEIKNPPRSV PAPER KNIVES
AEEIKNRSSST STREAKINESS
AEEIKRRSSTW WATER SKIERS
AEEILLMMNPT IMPLEMENTAL
AEEILLMNOPS PSILOMELANE
AEEILLMPRXY EXEMPLARILY
AEEILLNNPRY PERENNIALLY
AEEILLNOPPT EN PAPILLOTE
AEEILLNRSST LITERALNESS

AEEILLNSSTY ESSENTIALLY
AEEILLPRSTV SILVER PLATE
AEEILMNNSTT SENTIMENTAL
AEEILMNORST SALINOMETER
AEEILMNPRST SEMPITERNAL
AEEILMNPTTU PENULTIMATE
AEEILMNRSTX EXTERNALISM
AEEILMNSSSS AIMLESSNESS
AEEILMNSSWY WESLEYANISM
AEEILMOPRRT POLARIMETER
AEEILMORRST SOLARIMETER
AEEILMOSTTT TEETOTALISM
AEEILMPPRRS PERISPERMAL
AEEILNNOPTX EXPONENTIAL
AEEILNNOSTX EXTENSIONAL
AEEILNNSSST SALIENTNESS
AEEILNNSSTU UNESSENTIAL
AEEILNNSTTU LIEUTENANTS
AEEILNOPRSS PERSONALISE
AEEILNOPRSZ PERSONALIZE
AEEILNOPRTT INTERPOLATE
AEEILNORSTV REVELATIONS
AEEILNPSTTV SEPTIVALENT
AEEILNPSVXY EXPANSIVELY
AEEILNQSTUV EQUIVALENTS
AEEILNRRSTU NEUTRALISER
AEEILNRRTUZ NEUTRALIZER
AEEILNRSSSS AIRLESSNESS
AEEILNRSTTX EXTERNALIST
AEEILNRSTUX INTERSEXUAL
AEEILNRTTXY EXTERNALITY
AEEILNSSSTT STATELINESS
AEEILNTTTVY ATTENTIVELY, TENTATIVELY
AEEILNTTUVY EVENTUALITY
AEEILOPPRTT TOILET PAPER
AEEILOPRRRT REPERTORIAL
AEEILORTTTW TOILET WATER
AEEILPPRRSV SILVER PAPER
AEEILPRSTUV SUPERLATIVE
AEEILPRSVVY PERVASIVELY
AEEILPSTTUX EXSTIPULATE
AEEILQRRSTU QUARTERLIES
AEEILRRRSTT TERRESTRIAL
AEEILRRSTTU LITERATURES
AEEILRRTTTU LITTERATEUR
AEEILRSSTVY ASSERTIVELY
AEEIMMNNPRT IMPERMANENT
AEEIMMRRSTT TETRAMERISM
AEEIMNNNOQU MENAQUINONE
AEEIMNNNRTT ENTRAINMENT
AEEIMNNORTU ENUMERATION,
  MOUNTAINEER
AEEIMNNPRST PINE MARTENS
AEEIMNNSTTT INSTATEMENT
AEEIMNNOPRST IMPERSONATE
AEEIMNOPRSU EUROPEANISM
AEEIMNORSST MONASTERIES
AEEIMNORSTT MARIONETTES
AEEIMNOSSTT MAISONETTES

AEEIMNRSTUV MENSURATIVE
AEEIMNSSSSV MASSIVENESS
AEEIMOPRRTV VAPORIMETER
AEEIMORRSTU TEMERARIOUS
AEEIMQRSSUV SEMIQUAVERS
AEEIMQRSTTU MARQUISETTE
AEEIMSSSTTY SYSTEMATISE
AEEIMSSTTYZ SYSTEMATIZE
AEEINNOORTX EXONERATION
AEEINNOPRTT PENETRATION
AEEINNORSTV ANTEVERSION
AEEINNOTTUV EVENTUATION
AEEINNOTTUX EXTENUATION
AEEINOPRSTV PERSONATIVE
AEEINORRSTV RESERVATION
AEEINPSSSSV PASSIVENESS
AEEIOPPRRTX EXPROPRIATE
AEEIORRSTTV RESTORATIVE
AEEIORSSTTX STEREOTAXIS
AEEIPRRSSTU PASTEURISER
AEEIPRRSTUZ PASTEURIZER
AEEIPRSSSTT SPESSARTITE, STRIPTEASES
AEEJNORRTUV REJUVENATOR
AEEKLLORRST ROLLER SKATE
AEEKLMORRTW METALWORKER
AEEKMMNORSY MONEYMAKERS
AEEKMMRRRSY MERRYMAKERS
AEEKMPRRSTU SUPERMARKET
AEEKNPRRSTU SUPERTANKER
AEELLMNRSTU ALLUREMENTS
AEELLMORRST STEAMROLLER
AEELLNORRTT RETROLENTAL
AEELLNORSTW STONEWALLER
AEELLNPRTVY PREVALENTLY
AEELLNSSSSW LAWLESSNESS
AEELLOPRTUV POLE VAULTER
AEELLORSTTY TEA TROLLEYS
AEELLPPRTUY PERPETUALLY
AEELLSSSTTY TASTELESSLY
AEELMMORTTV VOLTAMMETER
AEELMNNOSTT MENTAL NOTES
AEELMNNPRTY PERMANENTLY
AEELMNNRTUV UNRAVELMENT
AEELMNORSTW WATERMELONS
AEELMOPRSTT PLASTOMETER
AEELMOQRRSU QUARRELSOME
AEELMPRRTUY PREMATURELY
AEELNNPRTTY REPENTANTLY
AEELNNQSSUU UNEQUALNESS
AEELNNSSSSU SENSUALNESS
AEELNOPRSSS SALESPERSON
AEELNOPRSST PROLATENESS
AEELNOSSSUZ ZEALOUSNESS
AEELNRSSSST ARTLESSNESS
AEELOPSTTUX EXPOSTULATE
AEELORSSTTU LOTUS-EATERS
AEEMNOPRRTY PYRANOMETER
AEEMNOPRSTU PENTAMEROUS
AEEMNORRRTU REMUNERATOR

AEEMNORRSTT REMONSTRATE
AEEMNORRSSTT EASTERNMOST
AEEMNSSSSST ASSESSMENTS
AEEMORRSTTU TETRAMEROUS
AEEMPRRSTTU EAR TRUMPETS
AEENNOOPSSS OPEN SEASONS
AEENNOPRRTU NEUROPTERAN
AEENOPRRSTT PATERNOSTER
AEENOQRRTTU QUARTER NOTE
AEENORTTUXY EXTENUATORY
AEENPPRSSTT STEPPARENTS
AEENQRSSTTU SEQUESTRANT
AEEOOPSTTTW SWEET POTATO
AEEOPPRRRTT PERPETRATOR
AEEPRSSSWXY EXPRESSWAYS
AEFFGIIMNRR REAFFIRMING
AEFFGIMSTUU SUFFUMIGATE
AEFFGINORST AFFORESTING
AEFFHHILTTU THE FAITHFUL
AEFFHIKMOTW MAKE OFF WITH
AEFFHINRSSS RAFFISHNESS
AEFFIIMNORR FORAMINIFER
AEFFIKLLOSW WALKS OF LIFE
AEFFIRSSTTY SAFETY-FIRST
AEFFKNRRRTU FRANKFURTER
AEFFNRSSSTU STAFF NURSES
AEFGGHIRSTT STAGE FRIGHT
AEFGGIMNNRT FRAGMENTING
AEFGHORSTTU SOUGHT-AFTER
AEFGIIINRRS FIRE-RAISING
AEFGIILNNRS FINGERNAILS
AEFGIIMNNST MANIFESTING
AEFGILLLNNN FLANNELLING
AEFGILLNRST FINGERSTALL
AEFGILLNRTY FALTERINGLY
AEFGILNNRTU UNFALTERING
AEFGILNNSSU GAINFULNESS
AEFGILOPRST PROFLIGATES
AEFGINNNSSW FAWNINGNESS
AEFGINNORRW FOREWARNING
AEFGINOPRRT PERFORATING
AEFGINORRSW FORSWEARING
AEFGINRRSTU TRANSFIGURE
AEFGIPRRSTU GRAPEFRUITS
AEFHHLLLTUY HEALTHFULLY
AEFHILLSSTY FAITHLESSLY
AEFHILRSSST HALF-SISTERS
AEFHIMNOPRS FOREMANSHIP
AEFHKOORTTU OUT OF THE ARK
AEFHLLLOSVY HALF VOLLEYS
AEFHLMNRSSU HARMFULNESS
AEFHMORRSTT FARTHERMOST
AEFHOOTTUWY OUT-OF-THE-WAY
AEFIIIMNRRS INFIRMARIES
AEFIIKLNNRT FRANKLINITE
AEFIILLNNTU INFLUENTIAL
AEFIILMORST FORMALITIES
AEFIILNNRTY INFERNALITY
AEFIILNOOTX EXFOLIATION

AEFIILOPRRW PRAIRIE WOLF
AEFIIMNORTV INFORMATIVE
AEFIINNOSTT FESTINATION, INFESTATION,
    SINFONIETTA
AEFIINNRSTT TRANSFINITE
AEFIINOPRST PROFANITIES
AEFIINORSTT FIRE STATION
AEFIINQRSTU QUANTIFIERS
AEFILLLMMOR LAMELLIFORM
AEFILLMOPRT PATELLIFORM
AEFILLRRTTU ULTRAFILTER
AEFILLRSTVY RIFT VALLEYS
AEFILMORRSU FORMULARISE
AEFILMORRUZ FORMULARIZE
AEFILMORTVY FORMATIVELY
AEFILMPRSUY SUPERFAMILY
AEFILNNPSSU PAINFULNESS
AEFILNORSUY NEFARIOUSLY
AEFILOOPRST FORE-TOPSAIL
AEFILOOPSTY PLAY FOOTSIE
AEFILOPRRTY PREFATORILY
AEFIMMMORSU MAMMIFEROUS
AEFIMNNNRTY INFANTRYMEN
AEFIMNNOOTT FOMENTATION
AEFIMNOORRT REFORMATION
AEFINNNOPTU FOUNTAIN PEN
AEFINNRRRST TRANSFERRIN
AEFINOOPRRT PERFORATION
AEFINOORSTT FORESTATION
AEFINORRSST RAIN FORESTS
AEFINORSTTU REFUTATIONS
AEFINRSSTUV TRANSFUSIVE
AEFKLLOORRW FLOORWALKER
AEFLLLOPRUW ALL-POWERFUL
AEFLLLOPSWY PLAYFELLOWS
AEFLLLORSWW WALLFLOWERS
AEFLLLSSTUY FAULTLESSLY
AEFLLMRSTUY MASTERFULLY
AEFLLNPSSUY PLAYFULNESS
AEFLLORSSUV FLAVOURLESS
AEFLMOORSUV FLAVOURSOME
AEFLNORTTUY FORTUNATELY
AEFLORRSTWW STRAWFLOWER
AEFLRSSTTWY FLYSWATTERS
AEFMNORRRST TRANSFORMER
AEFMOOPRSTT FORE-TOPMAST
AEFMOORRRTY REFORMATORY
AEFNNORTTUU UNFORTUNATE
AEFNORRSTTW WATERFRONTS
AEFNOSSSTUU FATUOUSNESS
AEFOOPRRSTW WATERPROOFS
AEGGGNORSTU GO GREAT GUNS
AEGGHHINSSS HAGGISHNESS
AEGGHIILNNT NIGHTINGALE
AEGGHIIRRRT HAIR TRIGGER
AEGGHILNRST RIGHT ANGLES
AEGGHINSSSW WAGGISHNESS
AEGGHLOOPRR LOGOGRAPHER
AEGGIILLNST LEGISLATING

AEGGIILMNNR MALINGERING
AEGGIILMPRS PILGRIMAGES
AEGGIIMNNRT GERMINATING
AEGGIIMNNTZ MAGNETIZING
AEGGIINNOTT NEGOTIATING
AEGGIINNRTT INTEGRATING
AEGGIINRTTU INGURGITATE
AEGGILNNORW LONGWEARING
AEGGILNNRSS GLARINGNESS
AEGGILRSSTT STRAGGLIEST
AEGGIMNOSST MAGGOTINESS
AEGGINNOTXY OXYGENATING
AEGGINPRTUX EXPURGATING
AEGGINRRTTU REGURGITANT
AEGGJNRSTUU JUGGERNAUTS
AEGHHILOPRS HELIOGRAPHS
AEGHHILOPRY HELIOGRAPHY
AEGHHINNPTY HYPHENATING
AEGHHINORST HIGH TREASON
AEGHHINSSTU HAUGHTINESS
AEGHHLOPRSU PLOUGHSHARE
AEGHHLORSSU HORSELAUGHS
AEGHHMOPRRT THERMOGRAPH
AEGHHNOPRTY ETHNOGRAPHY
AEGHHNOSTTU THAT'S ENOUGH!
AEGHIIKMNNT IN THE MAKING
AEGHIILMSTT ALMIGHTIEST
AEGHIIMNPSZ EMPHASIZING
AEGHIIMNRST TIME-SHARING
AEGHIIPPRST EPIGRAPHIST
AEGHILLNNRT ENTHRALLING
AEGHILLNOPS ANGLOPHILES
AEGHILNNSST HALTINGNESS
AEGHILNOOST ANTHOLOGIES,
ANTHOLOGISE, THEOLOGIANS
AEGHILNOOTZ ANTHOLOGIZE
AEGHILNORUV OVERHAULING
AEGHILNOTTU GLUTATHIONE
AEGHILNSSST GHASTLINESS
AEGHIMMOPRS MIMEOGRAPHS
AEGHIMNNRST GARNISHMENT
AEGHIMOPRSS SEISMOGRAPH
AEGHINNSSTU NAUGHTINESS
AEGHIRSSTTT STRAIGHTEST
AEGHLNOOORR GONORRHOEAL
AEGHLOOPRSY PHRASEOLOGY
AEGHLOPPRYY PYELOGRAPHY
AEGHLOPRRXY XYLOGRAPHER
AEGHLORSSSU HOURGLASSES
AEGHLOSSSSU GLASSHOUSES
AEGHMNOOPRR MONOGRAPHER,
NOMOGRAPHER
AEGHMNOOPRS GRAMOPHONES
AEGHMNOPPRU PNEUMOGRAPH
AEGHNOOPRRS NOSOGRAPHER
AEGHNOPRSTY STENOGRAPHY
AEGHNOPSSTU STENOPHAGUS
AEGHOOPPRRT TOPOGRAPHER

AEGHOPPRRRY PYROGRAPHER,
REPROGRAPHY
AEGHOPPRRSS GRASSHOPPER
AEGHOPPRRTY PETROGRAPHY,
TYPOGRAPHER
AEGIIILMNNT ELIMINATING
AEGIIILNRSZ SERIALIZING
AEGIIINSTTV INSTIGATIVE
AEGIIKLLNRT GIANT KILLER
AEGIIKNRSST ASTERISKING
AEGIIKNRSTW WATER SKIING
AEGIILLMNNP IMPANELLING
AEGIILLNOST LEGISLATION
AEGIILLNRTT ILL-TREATING
AEGIILLSTVY VESTIGIALLY
AEGIILMNORS REGIONALISM
AEGIILMNSST TIME SIGNALS
AEGIILNNRTU INTERLINGUA
AEGIILNNTTV VENTILATING
AEGIILNORST REGIONALIST
AEGIILNRSSU SINGULARISE
AEGIILNRSUZ SINGULARIZE
AEGIILOOSTT AETIOLOGIST
AEGIILRSTUV VULGARITIES
AEGIIMMMNUW MINIMUM WAGE
AEGIIMMORRR MIRROR IMAGE
AEGIIMNNORT GERMINATION
AEGIIMNNRTT TERMINATING
AEGIIMNORST EMIGRATIONS
AEGIIMPRSTU EPIGASTRIUM
AEGIIMRSSTT STIGMATISER
AEGIIMRSTTZ STIGMATIZER
AEGIINNOOTT NEGOTIATION
AEGIINNORST RESIGNATION
AEGIINNORTT INTEGRATION, ORIENTATING
AEGIINNRRST RESTRAINING
AEGIINNRSTT REINSTATING
AEGIINORSST SIGNATORIES
AEGIINPPRTW WIRE-TAPPING
AEGIINPRTTX EXTIRPATING
AEGIJLNRUUV JUGULAR VEIN
AEGIKMMNNOY MONEYMAKING
AEGIKMMNRRY MERRYMAKING
AEGILLMNNTY LAMENTINGLY
AEGILLMOOPS MEGALOPOLIS
AEGILLNNRUV UNRAVELLING
AEGILLNOPRY ROLE PLAYING
AEGILLNOPST SELLOTAPING
AEGILLNQRRU QUARRELLING
AEGILLORSST LEGISLATORS
AEGILLPRSSU ASPERGILLUS
AEGILLRRRUY IRREGULARLY
AEGILMMNOTU GEMMULATION
AEGILMNOORT GLOMERATION
AEGILMNOPRU PELARGONIUM
AEGILMNOSTU LIGAMENTOUS
AEGILMOOSSY SEMASIOLOGY
AEGILNNOOST ELONGATIONS
AEGILNOOSSX XENOGLOSSIA

AEGILNOPPRV OVERLAPPING
AEGILNOPRVY OVERPLAYING
AEGILNORSTU REGULATIONS
AEGILNPRSTT SPLATTERING
AEGILNQRUVY QUAVERINGLY
AEGILNRRSTY ARRESTINGLY
AEGILNRSSTV STARVELINGS
AEGILOOSTTU TAUTOLOGIES, TAUTOLOGISE
AEGILOOTTUZ TAUTOLOGIZE
AEGILRSTTUU GUTTURALISE
AEGILRTTUUZ GUTTURALIZE
AEGIMMOPRSU GEMMIPAROUS
AEGIMNNNORT ORNAMENTING
AEGIMNNNORV OVERMANNING
AEGIMNNNRTU RUNNING MATE
AEGIMNNORUV MANOEUVRING
AEGIMNNSSST ASSIGNMENTS
AEGIMNOPRRT IMPREGNATOR
AEGIMNORSSU IGNORAMUSES
AEGIMNRRSST RINGMASTERS
AEGIMNRSSTT SMATTERINGS
AEGINNNORSU UNREASONING
AEGINNOORRV VINEGARROON
AEGINNOOTXY OXYGENATION
AEGINNOPSTV PAVING STONE
AEGINNOSSUU SANGUINEOUS
AEGINNPRRTU ENRAPTURING
AEGINNPRSSS SPARINGNESS
AEGINNRSSTT ASTRINGENTS
AEGINOORSTT NEGOTIATORS
AEGINOPRTUX EXPURGATION
AEGINOQSTTU QUESTION TAG
AEGINORSTTV OVERSTATING
AEGINORSTVY OVERSTAYING
AEGINPRSSST TRESPASSING
AEGIPRRRTYY PYRARGYRITE
AEGIRSSSTTT STRATEGISTS
AEGKLORRSSW GLASS-WORKER
AEGKMNOSSXY OXYGEN MASKS
AEGLOORRSST ASTROLOGERS
AEGMMOPRRRS PROGRAMMERS
AEGMNOORSST GASTRONOMES
AEGNOOPRSSY GREASY SPOON
AEGOORRRTUV ROTOGRAVURE
AEGOPRRTUXY EXPURGATORY
AEHHIIILNNS HSIN-HAI-LIEN
AEHHIKNSSSW HAWKISHNESS
AEHHILLNTUY UNHEALTHILY
AEHHIMMMRST HAMMERSMITH
AEHHIMOPRTY HYPOTHERMIA
AEHHINNOPTY HYPHENATION
AEHHIOPPSST PHOSPHATISE
AEHHIOPPSTZ PHOSPHATIZE
AEHHIORTTTW WHITETHROAT
AEHHLLOPTTY THALLOPHYTE
AEHHLMMOORT HOMOTHERMAL
AEHHMOOOPST HOMOEOPATHS
AEHHMOOOPTY HOMOEOPATHY
AEHHMOSSTUW MOUTHWASHES

AEHHNOPRRTY TENORRHAPHY
AEHHOOPPRST PHOSPHORATE
AEHIIILMTUV HUMILIATIVE
AEHIILLOPRU AILUROPHILE
AEHIILLPSTT PHILATELIST
AEHIILOPSST HOSPITALISE
AEHIILOPSTZ HOSPITALIZE
AEHIIMNRSTT MARTINETISH
AEHIINOPRRS PARISHIONER
AEHIINOSSTT HESITATIONS
AEHIIORSTTU AUTHORITIES
AEHIIPPRRSS PERIPHRASIS
AEHIKLNOOPR HARPOON-LIKE
AEHIKLNRSSS LARKISHNESS
AEHIKMNSSSW MAWKISHNESS
AEHILLOPPTY APOPHYLLITE
AEHILLOPRST HOSPITALLER
AEHILMNNOOP AMINOPHENOL
AEHILMNORTW MOTHER-IN-LAW
AEHILMNOTTY METHYLATION
AEHILMNRSTU LUTHERANISM
AEHILMQSSUY SQUEAMISHLY
AEHILMRRSTY ERYTHRISMAL
AEHILNPRRTY PLATYRRHINE
AEHILNPSSSS SPLASHINESS
AEHILNSSSSV SLAVISHNESS
AEHIMNNNSSS MANNISHNESS
AEHIMNOOPPR APOMORPHINE
AEHIMNOOPSS HOMO SAPIENS
AEHIMNOPRST MISANTHROPE
AEHIMNOSTUX EXHUMATIONS
AEHIMNSSSTU ENTHUSIASMS
AEHIMOOSSST HOMEOSTASIS
AEHIMOPSSTY HAEMOPTYSIS
AEHIMORSTTX THERMOTAXIS
AEHIMPPRSTU HIPPEASTRUM
AEHIMPRSSTY SYMPATHISER
AEHIMPRSTYZ SYMPATHIZER
AEHINNPPSSU UNHAPPINESS
AEHINOORSTT ANORTHOSITE
AEHINOORTTX EXHORTATION
AEHINOPSSTT STEPHANOTIS
AEHINORRSST ENARTHROSIS
AEHINORSSTT THROATINESS
AEHINPPRRST PARTNERSHIP
AEHINPSSSSW WASPISHNESS
AEHINQSSSSU SQUASHINESS
AEHINRSSSTW SWARTHINESS
AEHINSSSTTU ENTHUSIASTS
AEHIRSSSTTW SWEATSHIRTS
AEHJNOORRST TROJAN HORSE
AEHKLLNSSTY THANKLESSLY
AEHKLOPRSSW SHOPWALKERS
AEHLLMOOSTY LOATHSOMELY
AEHLLNOSSSW SHALLOWNESS
AEHLMNOQSSU LEMON SQUASH
AEHLMOOSSUX HOMOSEXUALS
AEHLMOPPRRY LAMPROPHYRE
AEHLNNOPSTT PENTATHLONS

AEHLNOPSSTU HOUSEPLANTS
AEHLOPPRSXY PROPHYLAXES
AEHMMOOOPRT OMMATOPHORE
AEHMNOORSSU MANOR HOUSES
AEHMNOORSTV HARVEST MOON
AEHMORSSTTT THERMOSTATS
AEHNOOPRRTT ORTHOPTERAN
AEHNOOPSSSU SOUSAPHONES
AEHOOOPSTTT HOT POTATOES
AEHOOPPRSST APOSTROPHES
AEHOOPRRRST ARTHROSPORE
AEHOOPRRSTT TRAPSHOOTER
AEHOORSSSTY SOOTHSAYERS
AEHOQRRRTUU QUARTER-HOUR
AEIIIINSTTV INITIATIVES
AEIIIILLMNOR MILLIONAIRE
AEIIIILLMNST SILLIMANITE
AEIIIILLTTTV TITILLATIVE
AEIIIILMMPRS IMPERIALISM
AEIIILMNNOT ELIMINATION
AEIIILMNRST MINISTERIAL
AEIIILMNSST ANTIMISSILE
AEIIILMPRST IMPERIALIST
AEIIILMRRSV VERISIMILAR
AEIIILMTTVY IMITATIVELY
AEIIIMNOSST ANIMOSITIES
AEIIIMNOSTT ITEMISATION
AEIIIMNOTTZ ITEMIZATION
AEIIIMNRSTU MINIATURISE
AEIIIMNRTUZ MINIATURIZE
AEIIINNORTT ITINERATION
AEIIINNSTUV INSINUATIVE
AEIIINORSSV VISIONARIES
AEIIINPRSTV INSPIRATIVE
AEIIINQSTTU ANTIQUITIES
AEIIINRSSTT INITIATRESS
AEIIIPRSTTU PITUITARIES
AEIIKLLNPRS PAINKILLERS
AEIIKLLOPRT REALPOLITIK
AEIIILLMNORS MINERAL OILS
AEIIILLMSTTU SATELLITIUM
AEIIILLNPTVY PLAINTIVELY
AEIIILLNTUUX LUXULIANITE
AEIIILLPRSTU PLURALITIES
AEIIILMMORST IMMORTALISE, MEMORIALIST
AEIIILMMORTZ IMMORTALIZE
AEIIILMNNOPS MINNEAPOLIS
AEIIILMNOORT MELIORATION
AEIIILMNORST ORIENTALISM
AEIIILMNOSTT TESTIMONIAL
AEIIILMNPRRY PRELIMINARY
AEIIILMNPTTY IMPATIENTLY
AEIIILMORSTT MORTALITIES
AEIIILMPSSVY IMPASSIVELY
AEIIILMSTTUV STIMULATIVE
AEIIILNNNOST INTENSIONAL
AEIIILNNNOTT INTENTIONAL
AEIIILNNNOTV INVENTIONAL
AEIIILNNORST INSERTIONAL

AEIILNNORTV INVENTORIAL
AEIILNNOTTV VENTILATION
AEIILNNRRST LINERTRAINS
AEIILNNRTTY INTERNALITY
AEIILNNSSST SAINTLINESS
AEIILNORSSS INSESSORIAL
AEIILNORSTT ORIENTALIST
AEIILNORTTU ELUTRIATION
AEIILNRSSTW SISTER-IN-LAW
AEIILORRRTT TERRITORIAL
AEIILPRSSST PERISTALSIS
AEIILPRTTVY PARTITIVELY
AEIILRSSTTV REVIVALISTS
AEIILRSTTVY VERSATILITY
AEIIMMNRSTT MARTINETISM
AEIIMNNOPRY AMINOPYRINE
AEIIMNNORST INSEMINATOR, NITROSAMINE
AEIIMNNORTT TERMINATION
AEIIMNNORTV VERMINATION
AEIIMNNOSTV NOMINATIVES
AEIIMNOPRTT IMPETRATION
AEIIMOOPRST ISOMETROPIA
AEIIMOPPRRT IMPROPRIATE
AEIIMOPRRSS IMPRESARIOS
AEIIMRRTTUV TRIUMVIRATE
AEIINNNORTV INNERVATION
AEIINNNOTTT INATTENTION
AEIINNOORTT ORIENTATION
AEIINOPPSTT PEPTISATION
AEIINOPPTTZ PEPTIZATION
AEIINOPRRST RESPIRATION
AEIINOPRRTT PARTITIONER, REPARTITION
AEIINOPRTTX EXTIRPATION
AEIINOPRTTY PETITIONARY
AEIINOPSSTT POINSETTIAS
AEIINPRSSTY ANTIPYRESIS
AEIINRSSTTV TRANSITIVES
AEIINSSTTUV ANTITUSSIVE
AEIIOOPPSSS APOSIOPESIS
AEIIOOPRRST A POSTERIORI
AEIJLNORRSU JOURNALISER
AEIJLNORRUZ JOURNALIZER
AEIJMNOSSSS JAM SESSIONS
AEIKKLMNORW WORKMANLIKE
AEIKLNNOPPS PLAINSPOKEN
AEIKLNOPSTT KINETOPLAST
AEILLLMOSTY LAMELLOSITY
AEILLMMRSST SMALL-TIMERS
AEILLMNOOTY EMOTIONALLY
AEILLMNOSTY SEMITONALLY
AEILLMNOTTW LITTLE WOMAN
AEILLMNTTUV MULTIVALENT
AEILLNOPTTY POTENTIALLY
AEILLNOSSSY SILLY SEASON
AEILLNRSTUV SURVEILLANT
AEILLNRSUVY UNIVERSALLY
AEILLORSSTT TALL STORIES
AEILLORTTUV ULTRAVIOLET
AEILMMNORTY MOMENTARILY

AEILMNNNNSSU UNMANLINESS	AEINOOPRRST PERORATIONS
AEILMNNOPRT MINOR PLANET	AEINOOPRSSU APONEUROSIS
AEILMNNOSSW WOMANLINESS	AEINOOPRTTX EXPORTATION
AEILMNNSSTT INSTALMENTS	AEINOORRSTT RESTORATION
AEILMNOOSTT MOLESTATION	AEINOORSUVX OVERANXIOUS
AEILMNOPRRT TRAMPOLINER	AEINOPPRSTT POSTER PAINT
AEILMNOPRSS PERSONALISM	AEINOPRSSSU PERSUASIONS
AEILMNOPRST TRAMPOLINES	AEINOPRSSSV VASOPRESSIN
AEILMNORSTY SALINOMETRY	AEINOPRSTTU REPUTATIONS
AEILMOPRRSU LEPROSARIUM	AEINOPSTTTU OUTPATIENTS
AEILMOPRRTY POLARIMETRY, TEMPORARILY	AEINOQRSTUY QUESTIONARY
AEILMOPRTTY TEMPORALITY	AEINORSSSUV VARIOUSNESS
AEILMOPRTXY PROXIMATELY	AEIOPPRRRTY PROPRIETARY
AEILMPPSSST PALIMPSESTS	AEIOPRRRSST RESPIRATORS
AEILMPRSSST SLIPSTREAMS	AEIOPRRRSTY RESPIRATORY
AEILMPRSTUU PARI-MUTUELS	AEIOPRRRTTU PORTRAITURE
AEILNNOPRSU UNIPERSONAL	AEIOPRRTTUV VITUPERATOR
AEILNOOPRTX EXPLORATION	AEIPPRSTUUV SUPPURATIVE
AEILNOPPTTY PLATINOTYPE	AEKMNOOPSSW SPOKESWOMAN
AEILNOPRSST PERSONALIST	AEKMNORSTTW MARKET TOWNS
AEILNOPRSTY PERSONALITY	AEKMORRSSTW MASTERWORKS
AEILNOPSSSS PASSIONLESS	AEKMRRSSSST STRESS MARKS
AEILNORRSTU SERRULATION	AEKNOPRRSSY NOSY PARKERS
AEILNORSTTV VENTILATORS	AEKNOQRSSTU SQUARE KNOTS
AEILNORSTUV VOLUNTARIES	AELLNOPPRST PROPELLANTS
AEILNORTTVY VENTILATORY	AELLNPRSTUU NE PLUS ULTRA
AEILNSSSSTU SENSUALISTS	AELLOPRSSUX SOLAR PLEXUS
AEILOPPRRSU POPULARISER	AELMNOPRRSU SUPERNORMAL
AEILOPPRRUZ POPULARIZER	AELMOPRSTTY PLASTOMETRY
AEILOSSSTTY STEATOLYSIS	AELMOPSSTUY SYMPETALOUS
AEILOSTUVXY VEXATIOUSLY	AELMORSSSTU SOMERSAULTS
AEILRRSSSTU SURREALISTS	AELMORSSSTY SOLAR SYSTEM
AEIMMNRSSSU SUMMARINESS	AELMPRSTYYY MYSTERY PLAY
AEIMMORSTTU TAUTOMERISM	AELNNNOPRTW TOWN PLANNER
AEIMMPRSSTU SUPREMATISM	AELNOPPRSTW POWER PLANTS
AEIMMSSSTTY SYSTEMATISM	AELNOPPSTTY PENALTY SPOT
AEIMNNNOSTT ANOINTMENTS	AELNPRRSUUY SUPERLUNARY
AEIMNNOPPTT APPOINTMENT	AELOOPRRTXY EXPLORATORY
AEIMNNORSTU MENSURATION,	AELOOPSSTTY OSTEOPLASTY
NUMERATIONS	AELPPRSTUWY WATER SUPPLY
AEIMNNSSTTU SUSTAINMENT	AEMNNOOSSST STONEMASONS
AEIMNOORSSU ANISOMEROUS	AEMNNORRSTT REMONSTRANT
AEIMNOPRTTU IMPORTUNATE, PERMUTATION	AEMNNORSTTU TOURNAMENTS
AEIMNOPSTTT TEMPTATIONS	AEMNOOPRSTY TRYPANOSOME
AEIMNORRTTY TERMINATORY	AEMNOOORRSST ASTRONOMERS
AEIMNORSSTT MONETARISTS	AEMNOORSSSU AMOROUSNESS
AEIMNRRSTTT TRANSMITTER	AEMNOORSTUU NEUROMATOUS
AEIMPRSSTTU SUPREMATIST	AEMNORSSSTT ASSORTMENTS
AEIMQRSSTUZ QUIZMASTERS	AEMNOSTTTUX MANTOUX TEST
AEIMSSSTTTY SYSTEMATIST	AEMOOPPRRRU AMOUR-PROPRE
AEINNNOQSSU SINE QUA NONS	AEMOPRSSSTT POSTMASTERS
AEINNNORTTU ANTINEUTRON	AENNOOPRSSS PARSON'S NOSE
AEINNOOPRST PERSONATION	AENNOOPSSTU SPONTANEOUS
AEINNOORSTV RENOVATIONS	AENNORRSSTT NONSTARTERS
AEINNOOSTTT OSTENTATION	AENOPRRRSTT TRANSPORTER
AEINNOPSTTY SPONTANEITY	AENOPRSSTTT PROTESTANTS
AEINNORSTUV INTRAVENOUS	AENORRSTTTU STERNUTATOR
AEINNOSSSUX ANXIOUSNESS	AENPRRSSTTU TRANSPUTERS
AEINOOPPRRT APPORTIONER, REAPPORTION	AEOOPPPRRTY PARTY POOPER

AEOOQRRSSTU SQUARE ROOTS
AEOPPRRTTVY POVERTY TRAP
AEOPRSSTTUW WATERSPOUTS
AFFGHIIMNRS FISH FARMING
AFFGHLOPSTU PLOUGHSTAFF
AFFILNORSTU INSUFFLATOR
AFFOOORTUUV OUT OF FAVOUR
AFGGILNRTUU FULGURATING
AFGHHIILNTU HIGHFALUTIN
AFGHHILLSST FLASHLIGHTS
AFGHHILPSTT FLIGHT PATHS
AFGHIILRSTY FAIRY LIGHTS
AFGHILMOPRY FILMOGRAPHY
AFGHIORSTWY RIGHTS OF WAY
AFGHIPPTTUU PUT UP A FIGHT
AFGIIINNRTU INFURIATING
AFGIILLMNNY INFLAMINGLY
AFGIILLNNUY UNFAILINGLY
AFGIILMNNTU FULMINATING
AFGIILMNORZ FORMALIZING
AFGIILNNOTU ANTIFOULING
AFGIINNQTUY QUANTIFYING
AFGIINNRSTX TRANSFIXING
AFGIINRSTTY STRATIFYING
AFGIINSSTUU IGNIS FATUUS
AFGIKLNNOTU OUTFLANKING
AFGILLNNTUY FLAUNTINGLY
AFGILMNORTU FORMULATING
AFGILNORSUV FLAVOURINGS
AFGILNORTUU FULGURATION
AFGILNORUVY FAVOURINGLY
AFGILNRSTTY FLYING START
AFGINOOPSST SOFT-SOAPING
AFGINRRSTTU FRUSTRATING
AFHILNOPSST FLASH POINTS
AFIIIILNNTV INFINITIVAL
AFIIILMNNST INFANTILISM
AFIIILNNTTY INFANTILITY
AFIIINNORTU INFURIATION
AFIILMNNOTU FULMINATION
AFIILMNORTY INFORMALITY
AFIILNORRTT INFILTRATOR
AFIILNORSTT FLIRTATIONS
AFIILORSTTU FLIRTATIOUS
AFIIMNNOORT INFORMATION
AFIIMNOORSU OMNIFARIOUS
AFIIMORSTUV FAVOURITISM
AFIINNORSTX TRANSFIXION
AFIIOPRSSSU FISSIPAROUS
AFILMNOORTU FORMULATION
AFILMNORTUY FULMINATORY
AFINNORSSTU TRANSFUSION
AFINORRSTTU FRUSTRATION
AGGHHIIKNNR HIGH-RANKING
AGGHHLOPPRY GLYPHOGRAPH
AGGHIILNNSU LANGUISHING
AGGHIILOOST HAGIOLOGIST
AGGHINORRTW RIGHT A WRONG
AGGHMMOPRSY SPHYGMOGRAM

AGGIIILNNSZ SIGNALIZING
AGGIIIMMNRT IMMIGRATING
AGGIIINNORT ORIGINATING
AGGIIINNSTT INSTIGATING
AGGIILMNORZ GLAMORIZING
AGGIILNNOYZ AGONIZINGLY
AGGIILNOOPZ APOLOGIZING
AGGIILNRUVZ VULGARIZING
AGGIINNORRS GARRISONING
AGGIINORTTU GURGITATION
AGGIMMNOPRR PROGRAMMING
AGGINOPSSTT STAGING POST
AGGLLNOORYY LARYNGOLOGY
AGGLOOORSTY AGROSTOLOGY
AGHHIIMNRST NIGHTMARISH
AGHHILOPRST LITHOGRAPHS
AGHHILOPRTY LITHOGRAPHY
AGHHIMNRSTU HUMAN RIGHTS
AGHHNOOPPRS PHONOGRAPHS
AGHHNOOPPRY PHONOGRAPHY
AGHHOOPPRST PHOTOGRAPHS
AGHHOOPPRTY PHOTOGRAPHY
AGHHOOPRRTY ORTHOGRAPHY
AGHHOPPRTYY PHYTOGRAPHY
AGHHORSTUWY THROUGHWAYS
AGHIIILMNTU HUMILIATING
AGHIILMNOOS HOOLIGANISM
AGHIILNNSVY VANISHINGLY
AGHIILNRSVY RAVISHINGLY
AGHIIMNNORZ HARMONIZING
AGHIIMOSTTX THIGMOTAXIS
AGHIINNOSST ASTONISHING
AGHIINNQSUV VANQUISHING
AGHIINORTUZ AUTHORIZING
AGHIINPRRSS HAIRSPRINGS
AGHIINPRSTY PHARYNGITIS
AGHILNOOSTT ANTHOLOGIST
AGHILNORRWY HARROWINGLY
AGHILOOPSTT PATHOLOGIST
AGHILPRSTWY PLAYWRIGHTS
AGHIMNOPRST PROGNATHISM
AGHINOPRSTT PARTING SHOT
AGHIORSTTTU STRAIGHT-OUT
AGHLOOPSUXY XYLOPHAGOUS
AGHLOPRSTYY STYLOGRAPHY
AGHMNOOOPSU MONOPHAGOUS
AGHMNOORSTU MOUTHORGANS
AGHMOOOPRRT GRAPHOMOTOR
AGHNOOPPRRY PORNOGRAPHY
AGHNOOPRSTU PROGNATHOUS
AGIIIILLNNT INITIALLING
AGIIILLMNST MAILING LIST
AGIIILLNTTT TITILLATING
AGIIILNNOPT OIL PAINTING
AGIIILNNORS ORIGINAL SIN
AGIIILNORTV INVIGILATOR
AGIIILNORTY ORIGINALITY
AGIIILNPSST SALPINGITIS
AGIIILNSTTW WAITING LIST

AGIIILNSUVZ VISUALIZING
AGIIIMMNORT IMMIGRATION
AGIIINNNSTU INSINUATING
AGIIINNOORT ORIGINATION
AGIIINNOSTT INSTIGATION
AGIIINPRTVZ PRIVATIZING
AGIIKNNNPRS NAPKIN RINGS
AGIILLNNOPT POLLINATING
AGIILMNNORZ NORMALIZING
AGIILMNPPSY MISAPPLYING
AGIILMNSTTU STIMULATING
AGIILNNRSTY STRAININGLY
AGIILNORTUV OUTRIVALING
AGIILNPSTTU STIPULATING
AGIILNRSTUY SINGULARITY
AGIILNRTUUX LUXURIATING
AGIIMMNRSUZ SUMMARIZING
AGIIMNNOPTU IMPUGNATION
AGIIMNNPRSS MAINSPRINGS
AGIIMNOORTW WAITING ROOM
AGIINNNRTYZ TYRANNIZING
AGIINNOPRTZ PATRONIZING
AGIINNPRRST TRANSPIRING
AGIINOOORRST ORIGINATORS
AGIINOORRTV INVIGORATOR
AGIINORSSTT INSTIGATORS
AGIJNOPSTUX JUXTAPOSING
AGIKLNOPRST PARKING LOTS
AGIKMNOPRST POSTMARKING
AGILLLNPTUU PULLULATING
AGILLMNNOOU MONOLINGUAL
AGILLNPRTTY PRATTLINGLY
AGILLNRSTTY STARTLINGLY
AGILMOOPRTY PRIMATOLOGY
AGILMOPSSTY POLYGAMISTS
AGILNNPPSTU SUPPLANTING
AGILNNPRSUY UNSPARINGLY
AGILNOOOPRS SPOROGONIAL
AGILNOPPRVY APPROVINGLY
AGILNOPSTTU POSTULATING
AGILNORSUVY SAVOURINGLY
AGILOORSSYY ASSYRIOLOGY
AGIMNNORRST MORNING STAR
AGIMNNRSTTU TRANSMUTING
AGIMNOOPRST PROTAGONISM
AGIMNORSTTU OUTSMARTING
AGINNOPRSST TRANSPOSING
AGINOOOPRRT PROROGATION
AGINOOPRSTT PROTAGONIST
AGINOORRSTU SURROGATION
AGINOORRSUV GRANIVOROUS
AGINOPRRSTT PROSTRATING
AGINPPRSTUU SUPPURATING
AGKNNNORSTY GRANNY KNOTS
AGLLLLOPPSU GALLUP POLLS
AGLLMOORSUY GLAMOROUSLY
AGLLOOPSTTT GLOTTAL STOP
AGLLORRSUUY GARRULOUSLY
AGLMNOORTYY LARYNGOTOMY

AGLMOOOSTTY STOMATOLOGY
AGLMOOPRRTU PROMULGATOR
AGLMOORRTYY MARTYROLOGY
AGMOORSSTTY GASTROSTOMY
AHHIIIPRSST PHTHIRIASIS
AHHILMOPSTY HALOPHYTISM
AHHILNOORTU HOLOTHURIAN
AHHIMNOPSSW SHOWMANSHIP
AHHLLNOPTXY XANTHOPHYLL
AHIIILMNOTU HUMILIATION
AHIIIMNNOSY NISHINOMIYA
AHIILLORSUY HILARIOUSLY
AHIILMORTUY HUMILIATORY
AHIILOPSTTY HOSPITALITY
AHIILRSSTTY HAIRSTYLIST
AHIIMNNRRTU ANTIRRHINUM
AHIIMNOOOSU HOMOIOUSIAN
AHIIMOOPPPT HIPPOPOTAMI
AHIKKOORRSW KWASHIORKOR
AHIKLMOORSW WORKAHOLISM
AHIKLOTTUWW WALK OUT WITH
AHIKMNOPRSW WORKMANSHIP
AHILLOPSTXY PHYLLOTAXIS
AHILLOTUWWY WHAT YOU WILL
AHILNOORSTZ HORIZONTALS
AHILNOPRSTY RHINOPLASTY
AHILOORRTTY HORTATORILY
AHILOPPRSXY PROPHYLAXIS
AHILOPRRUXY PYRRHULOXIA
AHIMNOORRSU HONORARIUMS
AHIMNOPRSTY MISANTHROPY
AHIMOORSTUZ RHIZOMATOUS
AHINOOPSSTX SAXOPHONIST
AHINORSTTTT THAT'S TORN IT
AHKNNOPSSSY SHANKS'S PONY
AHLMNNORSTU LUNAR MONTHS
AHLMNOTUXYZ ZANTHOXYLUM
AHLMOOPRSUY AMORPHOUSLY
AHMNNOOPRTT NORTHAMPTON
AHMNOOPSTTU SOUTHAMPTON
AHNNOSSTTWY SHANTYTOWNS
AIIIINNOSTT INITIATIONS
AIIILLLNPTU LILLIPUTIAN
AIIILLNOTTT TITILLATION
AIIILLNOTUV ILLUVIATION
AIIILMNOSST IN ALTISSIMO
AIIILMNOSTT LIMITATIONS
AIIILMNPRTT TRIPALMITIN
AIIILMRSSTT MILITARISTS
AIIILNNOOST LIONISATION
AIIILNNOOTZ LIONIZATION
AIIILNNOTTU INTUITIONAL
AIIILNOSTTU UTILISATION
AIIILNOTTUZ UTILIZATION
AIIIMNNOSTT INTIMATIONS
AIIIMNRSTTU MINIATURIST
AIIIMPPRRTY PRIMIPARITY
AIIIMPSSTVY IMPASSIVITY
AIIINNNOSTU INSINUATION

AIIINNOPRST INSPIRATION
AIIINNOSTTV INVITATIONS
AIIINORRSTT IRRITATIONS
AIIINOSSTTV VISITATIONS
AIIKLRSTUVV SURVIVAL KIT
AIIKNRSSSTT SANSKRITIST
AIILLMMNOTU MULTINOMIAL
AIILLMNORTU ILLUMINATOR
AIILLNNOOPT POLLINATION
AIILLNORSUY ILLUSIONARY
AIILLPRSTUY SPIRITUALLY
AIILLPSTTUY PULSATILITY
AIILMMORTTY IMMORTALITY
AIILMNOOPRT IMPLORATION
AIILMNOOPST MALPOSITION
AIILMNOOSST SOLMISATION
AIILMNOOSTZ SOLMIZATION
AIILMNOSSTU SIMULATIONS
AIILMNOSTTU MUTILATIONS, STIMULATION
AIILMNOSTUY ALUMINOSITY
AIILMPRTTUY MULTIPARITY
AIILNNORSTU INTRUSIONAL
AIILNNORTTU NUTRITIONAL
AIILNOOPRSV PROVISIONAL
AIILNOPRTUY UNIPOLARITY
AIILNOPSTTU STIPULATION
AIILNORTUUX LUXURIATION
AIILNOSSTTY STYLISATION
AIILNOSTTYZ STYLIZATION
AIILNQRTTUY TRANQUILITY
AIILORSSSTU SAILOR SUITS
AIIMMNOPSTT PANTOMIMIST
AIIMMNSSTTU NUMISMATIST
AIIMMPRRSTU IMPRIMATURS
AIIMNNNOOST NOMINATIONS
AIIMNNORSTU RUMINATIONS
AIIMNNRSSTT MINISTRANTS
AIIMNOOPRTT IMPORTATION
AIIMNOOPRTX PROXIMATION
AIIMNOPSTTU IMPUTATIONS
AIIMOPPRRSU PRIMIPAROUS
AIINNNOOSTT INTONATIONS
AIINNNOOSTV INNOVATIONS
AIINNNORRTT NONIRRITANT
AIINNOOOSTZ OZONISATION
AIINNOOOTZZ OZONIZATION
AIINNOORRST IRON RATIONS
AIINNORSSTT TRANSITIONS
AIINOPRRSTY INSPIRATORY
AIINOPRRTTU PARTURITION
AIINORRTTTU TRITURATION
AIIOOPPRRTT PROPITIATOR
AIIOPRRSTTT PORTRAITIST
AIIOPRSSTTT PROSTATITIS
AIJLNORSSTU JOURNALISTS
AIKNOORSTTW WORKSTATION
AILLLMNOOPP LOLLIPOP MAN
AILLLNOOPRU ALLOPURINOL
AILLLNOPTUU PULLULATION

AILLMOPSSSY PLASMOLYSIS
AILLNOPRSUU NULLIPAROUS
AILLNORTUVY VOLUNTARILY
AILLNRTUUXY LUXURIANTLY
AILLORRSTTU ILLUSTRATOR
AILMNNOSUUY UNANIMOUSLY
AILMNOOOPRT PROMOTIONAL
AILMNOPPSSS SIMPLON PASS
AILMNOPRTTY IMPORTANTLY
AILMNORSTUV VOLUNTARISM
AILMOOPRRTY IMPLORATORY
AILMOOPRUYZ POLYZOARIUM
AILMOPRSTUU MULTIPAROUS
AILNNORTUVY INVOLUNTARY
AILNOOPPSTU POPULATIONS
AILNOOPRSTU SPORULATION
AILNOOPSTTU POSTULATION
AILNOPPSTTU POSTNUPTIAL
AILNOPSTTUU PUSTULATION
AILNORSTTUV VOLUNTARIST
AILNORSUUVY UNSAVOURILY
AILNRSSTUUU LAURUSTINUS
AILOPRSTTUY STIPULATORY
AILORSTTTUY STATUTORILY
AIMMOOSSTXY MYXOMATOSIS
AIMNNOOPTTU MOUNTAINTOP
AIMNNOOSTUU MOUNTAINOUS
AIMNOPSSSTU ASSUMPTIONS
AIMNRSSTTUU NASTURTIUMS
AINNNOOOORTT TORONTONIAN
AINOOPRRSTT PROSTRATION
AINOPPRSTUU SUPPURATION
AINORRSSSTT TRANSISTORS
AINORRSSTUU SUSURRATION
AKLNNOOOPTZ ZOOPLANKTON
ALLNOOOPPRR PROPRANOLOL
ALLOORSTWWW SWALLOWWORT
ALMNNOOSUYY ANONYMOUSLY
ALMNOOORSTU MONOLATROUS
ALMNOORSTTU SALMON TROUT
ALOPRRSTUUY RAPTUROUSLY
AMNOOPRSSTW SPORTSWOMAN
BBBEGIIINNW WINEBIBBING
BBBHIINRSSU RUBBISH BINS
BBCCEEHKLOR BREECHBLOCK
BBCDEHIRRTU BUTCHERBIRD
BBCEELNOOST COBBLESTONE
BBCEILMOSTU COMBUSTIBLE
BBCEINRSSSU SCRUBBINESS
BBCEIRRSSSU SUBSCRIBERS
BBCEJKOORST STOCKJOBBER
BBCEKLORSTU BLOCKBUSTER
BBCELMORSTU CLUSTER BOMB
BBCGIINRSSU SUBSCRIBING
BBDDEELLOOU BLUE-BLOODED
BBDDEILLNOU DOUBLE-BLIND
BBDDEILNOSU DOUBLE BINDS
BBDEEELOUYY BLUE-EYED BOY
BBDEEGHILOS BOBSLEIGHED

BBDEEHHLOOY HOBBLEDEHOY
BBDEEILLLOW I'LL BE BLOWED
BBDEEIMORSV DIVE-BOMBERS
BBDEFFLLOUU DOUBLE BLUFF
BBDEGIIMNOV DIVE-BOMBING
BBDEIKNOORS BOOKBINDERS
BBDEIKNOORY BOOKBINDERY
BBDELNRSSUU BLUNDERBUSS
BBDGIIKNNOO BOOKBINDING
BBEEEILRRSU BLUEBERRIES
BBEEERRRSTU RUBBER TREES
BBEEGIILLNR GIBBERELLIN
BBEEHIRRSSU SHRUBBERIES
BBEEILMRSSU SUBMERSIBLE
BBEELLOSTTU BLUEBOTTLES
BBEELMORSTT LETTER BOMBS
BBEENORRSYY BOYSENBERRY
BBEFILORSUU BULBIFEROUS
BBEGIINSSSU BIG BUSINESS
BBEGINOSSSU GIBBOUSNESS
BBEHHILOSST SHIBBOLETHS
BBEHHOORSSY HOBBYHORSES
BBEHIIILLOP BIBLIOPHILE
BBEHINRSSSU SHRUBBINESS
BBEIKLMOOOS BOOKMOBILES
BBEIOOPRSSY BOOBY PRISES
BBEIOOPRSYZ BOOBY PRIZES
BBELLMOOSTT BELL-BOTTOMS
BBELLNOTTUY BELLY BUTTON
BBEMNNOORTU NEUTRON BOMB
BBENORSSTTU STUBBORNEST
BBGHILNORTY THROBBINGLY
BBGIILLNQUY QUIBBLINGLY
BBHIIILMOPS BIBLIOPHISM
BCCDEEHKLOU DOUBLE-CHECK
BCCDEILNOTU CONDUCTIBLE
BCCEEEEFINN BENEFICENCE
BCCEEEENRSU ERUBESCENCE
BCCEEIILNOR INCOERCIBLE
BCCEEILNNOT CONNECTIBLE
BCCEEILNOSS CONCESSIBLE
BCCEEINRSTY CYBERNETICS
BCCEFFIKLOO OFFICE BLOCK
BCCEFIIPSSU SUBSPECIFIC
BCCEHINOOPR NECROPHOBIC
BCCEIILNNOV CONVINCIBLE
BCCEIINOORT NECROBIOTIC
BCCHHOORSTT SCOTCH BROTH
BCCHINOOPTY NYCTOPHOBIC
BCCLNORTUUY COUNTRY CLUB
BCDDDELLOOO COLD-BLOODED
BCDDEEEILNS DESCENDIBLE
BCDDEEIIRTT DIRECT DEBIT
BCDDEENORTY BODY-CENTRED
BCDDEHLOTUU DOUBLE-DUTCH
BCDEEEIINNT BENEDICTINE
BCDEEEIORRS CEREBROSIDE
BCDEEHILNPT PITCHBLENDE
BCDEEHMNOOY HONEYCOMBED

BCDEEHMNOTU DEBOUCHMENT
BCDEEIIILRT LIBERTICIDE
BCDEEIILNRS DISCERNIBLE
BCDEEIILRRU IRREDUCIBLE
BCDEEIILSST DISSECTIBLE
BCDEEIINNOT BENEDICTION
BCDEEIMNRSU DISENCUMBER
BCDEEINORTY BENEDICTORY
BCDEEINSSSU SUBSIDENCES
BCDEEORRSSS CROSSBREEDS
BCDEGHNRRSU BERGSCHRUND
BCDEHILNNOR HORNBLENDIC
BCDEHILNOSU DOUBLE CHINS
BCDEHILORSU SUBCHLORIDE
BCDEIIILRTY CREDIBILITY
BCDEIILNRSY DISCERNIBLY
BCDEIILRRUY IRREDUCIBLY
BCDEIILSSSU DISCUSSIBLE
BCDEIKLOQUU DOUBLE-QUICK
BCDEINORTTU CONTRIBUTED
BCDEIOOPRSS PROBOSCIDES
BCDEKLOORSU BLOODSUCKER
BCDELMNOSUU MUSCLE-BOUND
BCDELOORSSU DOUBLE-CROSS
BCDEMMNRSUU CUMMERBUNDS
BCDGIIKMNOR MOCKINGBIRD
BCDGIIOSSTU DOG BISCUITS
BCDGILLLOPU BULLDOG CLIP
BCDIILOOPTY BODY POLITIC
BCDIINRTUUY RUBICUNDITY
BCDILLNOORU COLOUR-BLIND
BCDLNOOOSTU BLOOD COUNTS
BCDLORSSTUU CLOUDBURSTS
BCEEEEHLSSU BLUE CHEESES
BCEEEELNNOV BENEVOLENCE
BCEEEFILPRT PERFECTIBLE
BCEEEFLLRST TREBLE CLEFS
BCEEEHHINPR HEBEPHRENIC
BCEEEHNNQSU QUEEN'S BENCH
BCEEEIILRST CELEBRITIES
BCEEEILPPRT PERCEPTIBLE
BCEEEILPRTX EXCERPTIBLE
BCEEENQSSUU SUBSEQUENCE
BCEEFKLNRRU BUCKLER-FERN
BCEEGILNOST CONGESTIBLE
BCEEGIMNNRU ENCUMBERING
BCEEGIMNORY EMBRYOGENIC
BCEEGKLMNRU MECKLENBURG
BCEEHJKLOWY CHEEK BY JOWL
BCEEHKLRRUY HUCKLEBERRY
BCEEHKNORSW WORKBENCHES
BCEEHNORRSX BRONX CHEERS
BCEEIILPSST PLEBISCITES
BCEEIILRSSS RESCISSIBLE
BCEEIINOSST OBSCENITIES
BCEEIIJLOTVY OBJECTIVELY
BCEEILMNNOT CONTEMNIBLE
BCEEILMOSST COMESTIBLES
BCEEILNORTV CONVERTIBLE

BCEEILNOSTY BY-ELECTIONS	BCIILMOSSTY SYMBOLISTIC
BCEEIILPPRTY PERCEPTIBLY	BCIJNNOSTUU SUBJUNCTION
BCEEIILPSSTU SUSCEPTIBLE	BCIKLOPRSUW PUBLIC WORKS
BCEEINSSSTU SUBSISTENCE	BCIKMOORSST BROOMSTICKS
BCEEIPRRSSU SUPERSCRIBE	BCILMOSTTUU CUSTOM-BUILT
BCEEKKLNNOU KNUCKLEBONE	BCINOORRTTU CONTRIBUTOR
BCEEKLNOSTT BOTTLENECKS	BCINOORSTTU OBSTRUCTION
BCEELMMOOTY EMBOLECTOMY	BCKLLOOPSSU BOLLOCKS-UPS
BCEELNOOSST OBSOLESCENT	BDDDEEEGLOU DOUBLE-EDGED
BCEEMMORTYY EMBRYECTOMY	BDDDEEEINRT INTERBEDDED
BCEFFKORSTU BUFFER STOCK	BDDDEEIIMOS DISEMBODIED
BCEFHILLNSU BULLFINCHES	BDDDEEINRRU UNDERBIDDER
BCEFIIOPRST FIBRE OPTICS	BDDDEFILLNO BLINDFOLDED
BCEGHHIMOWY HIGH WYCOMBE	BDDDEFMNOUU DUMBFOUNDED
BCEGHIIMNRS BESMIRCHING	BDDEEEIILSV DISBELIEVED
BCEGHILLNNY BLENCHINGLY	BDDEEEIMMRS DISMEMBERED
BCEGIINPRRS PRESCRIBING	BDDEEEIMNRT DEBRIDEMENT
BCEGILNOOOY BIOCENOLOGY	BDDEEEIMORR EMBROIDERED
BCEHIIIMNRS HIBERNICISM	BDDEEIINOST DISOBEDIENT
BCEHIILRRSV SILVER BIRCH	BDDEEILMRTU TUMBLE-DRIED
BCEHILMOOPT PHLEBOTOMIC	BDDEEILORSW BOWDLERISED
BCEHILNOSST BLOTCHINESS	BDDEEILORWZ BOWDLERIZED
BCEHILOPSUU PUBLIC HOUSE	BDDEELOOPRU PUREBLOODED
BCEHKLOOSSU BLOCKHOUSES	BDDEENSSSUU SUBDUEDNESS
BCEHKOPSSTU BUCKET SHOPS	BDDEFLLLOOU FULL-BLOODED
BCEHLORRSYY CHRYSOBERYL	BDDEFMNORUU DUMBFOUNDER
BCEHMOORTTY THROMBOCYTE	BDDEGIIMNNN MIND-BENDING
BCEHMRSSTUW THUMBSCREWS	BDDEGIINORV OVERBIDDING
BCEIIJMOSTV OBJECTIVISM	BDDEHINRRTU THUNDERBIRD
BCEIIJOSTTV OBJECTIVIST	BDDEHLNOORS BONDHOLDERS
BCEIIJOTTVY OBJECTIVITY	BDDEIIRSTTU DISTRIBUTED
BCEIILLOSTY BELLICOSITY	BDDEILMORSW MIDDLEBROWS
BCEIIMMRSTY BISYMMETRIC	BDDELNOTUUY UNDOUBTEDLY
BCEIINOORSS NECROBIOSIS	BDDGIIINSUV SUBDIVIDING
BCEIIORSSTU OBSCURITIES	BDDHIIIMRSY DIHYBRIDISM
BCEIJNSTUUV SUBJUNCTIVE	BDDHLNOOOSU BLOODHOUNDS
BCEIKOOPRTU PICTURE BOOK	BDEEEEIIMRR BIEDERMEIER
BCEILLORSSU BRUCELLOSIS	BDEEEHILLMS EMBELLISHED
BCEILOPRRTU CORRUPTIBLE	BDEEEHILMTW THIMBLEWEED
BCEINOSSSTU SUBSECTIONS	BDEEEIILRSV DISBELIEVER
BCEIOOPRSSS PROBOSCISES	BDEEEILMNTV BEDEVILMENT
BCEIORSTTUV OBSTRUCTIVE	BDEEEILPRSS DEPRESSIBLE
BCEKKOOOORY COOKERY BOOK	BDEEEILSSTW WILDEBEESTS
BCEKKOOOPST POCKETBOOKS	BDEEEIMMRRS DISMEMBERER
BCEKKOORRST STOCKBROKER	BDEEEIMORRR EMBROIDERER
BCEKLOORSTW TOWER BLOCKS	BDEEELNSSSS BLESSEDNESS
BCELORSTUUU TUBERCULOUS	BDEEFGIINNR BEFRIENDING
BCELRSSTUUU SUBCULTURES	BDEEFHIRRSU REFURBISHED
BCEOOOPRSST STROBOSCOPE	BDEEGGHIIRW WEIGHBRIDGE
BCGIIILNPUZ PUBLICIZING	BDEEGGINSUU DUNE BUGGIES
BCGIINOPRRS PROSCRIBING	BDEEGHILNTY BENIGHTEDLY
BCGILOOORYY CRYOBIOLOGY	BDEEGIILLNV BEDEVILLING
BCGINORSTTU OBSTRUCTING	BDEEGIILNRW BEWILDERING
BCHHIOOOPPT PHOTOPHOBIC	BDEEGILMNNO EMBOLDENING
BCHIIIPSSTU SHIP BISCUIT	BDEEHILMNSU UNBLEMISHED
BCHIOOPRSSU RUSSOPHOBIC	BDEEIILNSST DISTENSIBLE
BCHMOOOTTTU TOUCH BOTTOM	BDEEILLNNRS DINNER BELLS
BCHNOORSSTU HOT-CROSS BUN	BDEEILLNPRS SPELLBINDER
BCIIIILMSTY MISCIBILITY	BDEEILMNOTY MOLYBDENITE

BDEEILMRSSS DISSEMBLERS
BDEEILNORRS BORDERLINES
BDEEILNPSSU SUSPENDIBLE
BDEEIMNORST DISROBEMENT
BDEEINNSSSU BUSINESS END
BDEEINORSTX TINDERBOXES
BDEEIOORSXY DEOXYRIBOSE
BDEELLOOSSV BLOOD VESSEL
BDEELMRRSUU BLUE MURDERS
BDEELMRRTUY TUMBLE-DRYER
BDEELNRRSSU BLURREDNESS
BDEEMNORTUU OUTNUMBERED
BDEENPRRTUU UNPERTURBED
BDEFGINOORS FOREBODINGS
BDEFGIOORST FOOTBRIDGES
BDEFIOPRRSY BIRDS OF PREY
BDEGGILNNOU BLUDGEONING
BDEGIILLNNS SINGLE-BLIND
BDEGIILLNSV DIVING BELLS
BDEGIILMNSS DISSEMBLING
BDEGIINNRRS RING BINDERS
BDEGIMORRSY DOGBERRYISM
BDEGINNNRUU UNBURDENING
BDEHHOOORRT BROTHERHOOD
BDEHIIILNTY INHIBITEDLY
BDEHIIINNTU UNINHIBITED
BDEHIILPRSU SHIPBUILDER
BDEHIINNPTU NIP IN THE BUD
BDEHIKLNOTU DOUBLETHINK
BDEHILLSTTU BULLSHITTED
BDEHILNPSUU UNPUBLISHED
BDEHLNOOTTU BUTTONHOLED
BDEHLNORTTU THUNDERBOLT
BDEIIIILNSV INDIVISIBLE
BDEIIIILNTY INEDIBILITY
BDEIIILMMOS IMMOBILISED
BDEIIILMMOZ IMMOBILIZED
BDEIIILMSSS DISMISSIBLE
BDEIIILNTVY VENDIBILITY
BDEIILMRSUU SUBDELIRIUM
BDEIINNRTUW WIND TURBINE
BDEIIRSSSSU SUBSIDISERS
BDEIIRSSSUZ SUBSIDIZERS
BDEIKNORSTU STRIKEBOUND
BDEILLLNORR ROLLER BLIND
BDEILLOSTUX BILLETS-DOUX
BDEILNNOOOS IN ONE'S BLOOD
BDEILNORSTY BLINDSTOREY
BDEIMMNOPRU PREMIUM BOND
BDEINOOSWWX WINDOW BOXES
BDEINOSSSUU DUBIOUSNESS
BDEISSTTTUU SUBSTITUTED
BDELLLOOSSY BLOODLESSLY
BDELLNOSSUY BOUNDLESSLY
BDELMNOOSUY MOLYBDENOUS
BDGGIIILNOS DISOBLIGING
BDGHIIMMNRU HUMMINGBIRD
BDGIIINSSUZ SUBSIDIZING
BDGIILMNNOW MIND-BLOWING

BDGIILNOTUU OUTBUILDING
BDGLOOOPRSU BLOOD GROUPS
BDHIILRRSWY WHIRLYBIRDS
BDIIIILNSVY INDIVISIBLY
BDIIINOSSUV SUBDIVISION
BDIIMNORTUY MORIBUNDITY
BDIIORRSTTU DISTRIBUTOR
BDINNOORRSU ROUND ROBINS
BDLMNOOTTUU BUTTONMOULD
BDLOOOPRSST BLOOD SPORTS
BEEEFHINRSS FINES HERBES
BEEEFOORRST FREEBOOTERS
BEEEGGINRRS GINGER BEERS
BEEEGIINNOR BIOENGINEER
BEEEGILLNRT BELLIGERENT
BEEEGILMNTU BEGUILEMENT
BEEEGIMMNRR REMEMBERING
BEEEGLNORTT BOTTLE GREEN,
    GREENBOTTLE
BEEEHILLMRS EMBELLISHER
BEEEHILLNOR HELLEBORINE
BEEEILNRSUV UNBELIEVERS
BEEEILPRRSS REPRESSIBLE
BEEEILPRRTV PERVERTIBLE
BEEEILPRSSX EXPRESSIBLE
BEEEIMMMRRS MISREMEMBER
BEEEINORSST BÊTES-NOIRES
BEEEIRSTTTW BITTERSWEET
BEEEKKOOPRS BOOKKEEPERS
BEEELLRSSST BEST-SELLERS
BEEELMNNNOT ENNOBLEMENT
BEEELORSTTX LETTERBOXES
BEEENOPPRTY TEENYBOPPER
BEEFFNORSUZ BUFFER ZONES
BEEFGLLOORW GLOBEFLOWER
BEEFGRSSTUU SUBTERFUGES
BEEFILRSTTU BUTTERFLIES
BEEGGILSSTU SUGGESTIBLE
BEEGGLOORST BOOTLEGGERS
BEEGHINNORR HERRINGBONE
BEEGIIMNRTT EMBITTERING
BEEGIIOORSU BOURGEOISIE
BEEGIKKNOOP BOOKKEEPING
BEEGILLNSST BEST-SELLING
BEEGIMNOSTT MISBEGOTTEN
BEEGKLNTTUU TELUKBETUNG
BEEHILMMOOS MOBILE HOMES
BEEHILPRRSU REPUBLISHER
BEEHIMMPRSS MEMBERSHIPS
BEEHIMNOORT THEOBROMINE
BEEHKNOORSU HOUSEBROKEN
BEEHLMNORUW WHOLE NUMBER
BEEHMNOOSST MESOBENTHOS
BEEHMOORSTT MOTHERS-TO-BE
BEEHOPRRSTT STEPBROTHER
BEEIILMPRSS IMPRESSIBLE, PERMISSIBLE
BEEIILNSSSV VISIBLENESS
BEEIIRRTTUV RETRIBUTIVE
BEEILLLNTUY EBULLIENTLY

BEEILLLOSVW BOLL WEEVILS
BEEILLORRSU IRRESOLUBLE
BEEILLRRRTU BULL TERRIER
BEEILMMNORT EMBROILMENT
BEEILNNOSTW TENNIS ELBOW
BEEILNOPRSS NOBEL PRISES, RESPONSIBLE
BEEILNOPRSZ NOBEL PRIZES
BEEILNRSSTT BRITTLENESS
BEEIMMNPRRU PRIME NUMBER
BEEIMNNSSSU BUSINESSMEN
BEEINORSTTY TENEBROSITY
BEEINRSSTUV SUBSERVIENT
BEEIRSSSUVV SUBVERSIVES
BEEJOORTTUV OBJET TROUVE
BEEKLLOORSS BOOKSELLERS
BEEKOOPRRRW POWER BROKER
BEELLNOSSSU SOLUBLENESS
BEELMOORSTU TROUBLESOME
BEEMMNNOSTT ENTOMBMENTS
BEENORSSTXY SENTRY BOXES
BEENQRSSSUU BRUSQUENESS
BEERRRSTTUU SURREBUTTER
BEFGHILLRTU BULLFIGHTER
BEFGIILNTTY BEFITTINGLY
BEFGILNORSW FINGER BOWLS
BEFHIILLLLT FILL THE BILL
BEFHILLMSTU THIMBLEFULS
BEFHILLOOTT FOOT THE BILL
BEFHLMORTUU RULE OF THUMB
BEFIIILLTXY FLEXIBILITY
BEFIILNORRU NEUROFIBRIL
BEFIILRSSTU FILIBUSTERS
BEFINORSSSU FIBROUSNESS
BEFINORSTTT FROSTBITTEN
BEFLLOOPRTU BULLETPROOF
BEGGGGILNOOT BOOTLEGGING
BEGGIILLNNR BELL-RINGING
BEGGIILLNUY BEGUILINGLY
BEGHILNORUY NEIGHBOURLY
BEGHILORSTT STROBE LIGHT
BEGIIIILLTY ELIGIBILITY
BEGIIMNRRSU REIMBURSING
BEGIKNOOORV OVERBOOKING
BEGILLMNRTY TREMBLINGLY
BEGILLMNRUY LUMBERINGLY
BEGILLNNNOY ENNOBLINGLY
BEGILNQRSUU BURLESQUING
BEGINRSSTTU BUTTRESSING
BEGNOORSSTX STRONGBOXES
BEHIIILLLLS HILLBILLIES
BEHIIINOSTX EXHIBITIONS
BEHIIIOPRTV PROHIBITIVE
BEHIKNOOSSS BOOKISHNESS
BEHILLNSSSU BULLISHNESS
BEHINOOPRSS BOORISHNESS
BEHINRSSSTU BRUTISHNESS
BEHIOORRSUV HERBIVOROUS
BEHLNOOSTTU BUTTONHOLES
BEHLOOORRSTU SOUL BROTHER

BEHMNOORTUU BOURNEMOUTH
BEHMOORSSTY MOTHER'S BOYS
BEHMPRSTTUU TUB-THUMPERS
BEIIILMMORS IMMOBILISER
BEIIILMMORZ IMMOBILIZER
BEIIILMNRST LIBERTINISM
BEIIILMQRUU EQUILIBRIUM
BEIIILNSSTY SENSIBILITY
BEIIILNSTTY TENSIBILITY
BEIIILQRSTU EQUILIBRIST
BEIILLNOSSW BILLOWINESS
BEIILLORTUV BLUE VITRIOL
BEIILMPRSSY PERMISSIBLY
BEIILNOSSSU BILIOUSNESS
BEIILORSSTU BOILER SUITS
BEIILRSSTTT LIBRETTISTS
BEIINORRTTU RETRIBUTION
BEILLLLOSUY LIBELLOUSLY
BEILLMPSTUU SUBMULTIPLE
BEILLNOSTTU BLUE STILTON
BEILMNOOSSW SNOWMOBILES
BEILNOPRSSY RESPONSIBLY
BEILORSTUVY OBTRUSIVELY
BEIMPSSTUUV SUBSUMPTIVE
BEINNOSSTUV SUBVENTIONS
BEINOOSSSUV OBVIOUSNESS
BEINORSSTUU SUBROUTINES
BEINORSTUUV UNOBTRUSIVE
BEINSSTTTUU SUBSTITUENT
BEIOQRSSTUU SOUBRIQUETS
BEISSSTTTUU SUBSTITUTES
BELLNRTTUUY TURBULENTLY
BELMMOORRSU LUMBER-ROOMS
BELNOOSTUUY BOUNTEOUSLY
BELOOPRSSTT LOBSTERPOTS
BELOOPRSTTU TROUBLE SPOT
BENNOORSSTW BROWNSTONES
BFFFFILOSTU BIT OF FLUFFS
BFGIIILNTUY FUNGIBILITY
BFILLLMNOOU IN FULL BLOOM
BGGILLMNRUY GRUMBLINGLY
BGHHIIRRSTT BIRTHRIGHTS
BGHIIINOPRT PROHIBITING
BGHIIINRRTV VIRGIN BIRTH
BGHIINOPPWY WHIPPING BOY
BGHIMNPTTUU TUB-THUMPING
BGIIILLLTUY GULLIBILITY
BGIILMNOSYZ SYMBOLIZING
BGILLMNSTUY STUMBLINGLY
BGILLNORTUY TROUBLINGLY
BGILMOOSSTY SYMBOLOGIST
BHIIIINNOST INHIBITIONS
BHIIINOOPRT PROHIBITION
BHIILLRSSTT STILLBIRTHS
BHIIOOPRRTY PROHIBITORY
BHILMOOSTYY TOMBOYISHLY
BHIMNOOPRRT PROTHROMBIN
BIIILOPSSTY POSSIBILITY
BIIILORSTTY TORSIBILITY

BIIKNOORSSV NOVOSIBIRSK
BIILLOOSUVY OBLIVIOUSLY
BIILOOQSTUU OBLIQUITOUS
BIIMNOSSSSU SUBMISSIONS
BILMOPSTUUY BUMPTIOUSLY
BILNOOOSUXY OBNOXIOUSLY
BIMNOORSSTT TROMBONISTS
BIMNOPSSTUU SUBSUMPTION
BIMORSSTUUU RUMBUSTIOUS
BIOOOPPRRSU OPPROBRIOUS
CCCCIMOORSU MICROCOCCUS
CCCCKKLOOOU CUCKOO CLOCK
CCCDEEEENRS DECRESCENCE
CCCDEEIINNO COINCIDENCE
CCCDEHINOSY SYNECDOCHIC
CCCDEIIMRSU CIRCUMCISED
CCCDGINOOOO GONOCOCCOID
CCCDIIIOOSS COCCIDIOSIS
CCCDILOOPSU DIPLOCOCCUS
CCCEEEENRSX EXCRESCENCE
CCCEEENRSXY EXCRESCENCY
CCCEEFIIOPS ECOSPECIFIC
CCCEEFLLNOU FLOCCULENCE
CCCEEFOORSS FRESCO SECCO
CCCEEIILMST ECLECTICISM
CCCEEINNOSS CONSCIENCES
CCCEENNORRU CONCURRENCE
CCCEENORRSU OCCURRENCES
CCCEFIINOPS CONSPECIFIC
CCCEFIOORSU COCCIFEROUS
CCCEIMPRSTU CIRCUMSPECT
CCCEINNOTTU CONNECTICUT
CCCEIRSSTUY CYSTICERCUS
CCCHILMOTYY CYCLOTHYMIC
CCCIIMMOORS MICROCOSMIC
CCCIIMOOPRS MICROSCOPIC
CCCINNOOOST CONCOCTIONS
CCCIOOOPPST POCTOSCOPIC
CCCIOOPSSTY CYSTOSCOPIC
CCDDELNNOUU UNCONCLUDED
CCDEEEEINNR NICENE CREED
CCDEEEFHIKN CHICKENFEED
CCDEEEGINOT GENETIC CODE
CCDEEEIINRS IRIDESCENCE
CCDEEEELLORT RECOLLECTED
CCDEEEENRRST RED CRESCENT
CCDEEFINNOS CONFIDENCES
CCDEEHHMOSY ECHCHYMOSED
CCDEEHILPSY PSYCHEDELIC
CCDEEHINORS SECOND REICH
CCDEEHIORTT RICOCHETTED
CCDEEHKOPST SPOT CHECKED
CCDEEIIINST INSECTICIDE
CCDEEIKLRSV CLEVER DICKS
CCDEEILNOTY CONCEITEDLY
CCDEEILRRSS DRESS CIRCLE
CCDEEINNORT ENDOCENTRIC
CCDEEIOPPRU PREOCCUPIED
CCDEEJNORTU CONJECTURED

CCDEELLLOTY COLLECTEDLY
CCDEELNNOOS CONDOLENCES
CCDEELNNORY CONCERNEDLY
CCDEELNORTY CONCERTEDLY
CCDEENNNORU UNCONCERNED
CCDEENNNOTU UNCONNECTED
CCDEHILLOSS COLD CHISELS
CCDEHIOOPRS DICHROSCOPE
CCDEHLNSTUU DUTCH UNCLES
CCDEIILOORT CROCIDOLITE
CCDEIJKOSSY DISC JOCKEYS
CCDEIMNOORS MICROSECOND
CCDEINNNOUV UNCONVINCED
CCDEINOPRST CONSCRIPTED
CCDEINORSTT CONSTRICTED
CCDELLOSTYY CYCLOSTYLED
CCDENORSSTU CONDUCTRESS
CCDENORSTTU CONSTRUCTED
CCDFLMOOORT COLD COMFORT
CCDHHILLOOS SCHOOLCHILD
CCDHIOORTTW WITCHDOCTOR
CCDHIOOSTUU STUDIO COUCH
CCDKMOSUUVY MUSCOVY DUCK
CCEEEEILRTY ELECTRIC EYE
CCEEEEINPRT CENTREPIECE
CCEEEFHIKNR NECKERCHIEF
CCEEEFHIRTV HECTIC FEVER
CCEEEFLNORS FLORESCENCE
CCEEEFNNORS CONFERENCES
CCEEEFNRSTU FRUTESCENCE
CCEEEGINNRS NIGRESCENCE
CCEEEGINRVY VICEGERENCY
CCEEEGNNORV CONVERGENCE
CCEEEGNRSTU TURGESCENCE
CCEEEHHLOST CHEESECLOTH
CCEEEHINNOR INCOHERENCE
CCEEEIINPPR PERCIPIENCE
CCEEEILNORT COELENTERIC
CCEEEILNQSU LIQUESCENCE
CCEEEINNNOV CONVENIENCE
CCEEEINNPSS SPINESCENCE
CCEEEINOPRV PRECONCEIVE
CCEEEINOPSS CENOSPECIES
CCEEEINOSTX COEXISTENCE
CCEEEINRRST CIRENCESTER
CCEEEINRSTV VITRESCENCE
CCEEELORTTU ELECTROCUTE
CCEEEMNPSSU SPUMESCENCE
CCEEENNOQSU CONSEQUENCE
CCEEENPRSTU PUTRESCENCE
CCEEENRRRSU RECURRENCES
CCEEFFIINOT COEFFICIENT
CCEEFFILNOS OFF-LICENCES
CCEEFIIMNNU MUNIFICENCE
CCEEFLNNOSU CONFLUENCES
CCEEFLNOPST SELF-CONCEPT
CCEEGINNNOT CONTINGENCE
CCEEGINOOTT GEOTECTONIC
CCEEGNNORVY CONVERGENCY

CCEEGNOORRT CONCERTGOER
CCEEHHKORRY CHOKECHERRY
CCEEHINORTT THEOCENTRIC
CCEEHKLLLOS COCKLESHELL
CCEEHMOPTYY PHYCOMYCETE
CCEEHNOSSTU ESCUTCHEONS
CCEEIILMRSS SEMICIRCLES
CCEEIILORST ISOELECTRIC
CCEEIILRTTY ELECTRICITY
CCEEIIMNNOS OMNISCIENCE
CCEEIIMNOSV MISCONCEIVE
CCEEIINOPTV NOCICEPTIVE
CCEEILLOSTV COLLECTIVES
CCEEILNNOTV CONVENTICLE
CCEEILNORST ELECTRONICS
CCEEILPPRTU PEPTIC ULCER
CCEEIMNOORT ECONOMETRIC
CCEEIMNORRT CENTROMERIC
CCEEIMNRSTU MUSIC CENTRE
CCEEINOSTUV CONSECUTIVE
CCEEIOPRSSS CROSSPIECES
CCEEIORRSTV CORRECTIVES
CCEEJNORRTU CONJECTURER
CCEEJNORSTU CONJECTURES
CCEELOSSTTU COS LETTUCES
CCEENORRSST CORRECTNESS
CCEFFIINSUY SUFFICIENCY
CCEFHHILSTU HECTIC FLUSH
CCEFHIIMORS MICROFICHES
CCEFIIIPSTY SPECIFICITY
CCEFIILNOTV CONFLICTIVE
CCEFIINOPRY PROFICIENCY
CCEFIKLSSTT CLEFT STICKS
CCEFINNOOST CONFECTIONS
CCEFIORRSUU CRUCIFEROUS
CCEGHHORRSU CHURCHGOERS
CCEGHIILNOR CHOLINERGIC
CCEGHIINORT RICOCHETING
CCEGHIMNOOR CHROMOGENIC
CCEGHINOPSY PSYCHOGENIC
CCEGIILNNOR RECONCILING
CCEGIINOOTX TOXICOGENIC
CCEGILNOORY ECCRINOLOGY
CCEGILNOOSY SYNECOLOGIC
CCEGINNNOTY CONTINGENCY
CCEGINNOOST COGNOSCENTI
CCEGINOPRTY CRYPTOGENIC
CCEHHKOOORT CROCHET HOOK
CCEHIILNOPR NECROPHILIC
CCEHIKNOPST CHECKPOINTS
CCEHILNOORT TECHNICOLOR
CCEHILNOPTY POLYTECHNIC
CCEHILNORRS CHRONICLERS
CCEHIMMOOST CHEMOSMOTIC
CCEHIMNOORT HOMOCENTRIC
CCEHIMOOPRT CHEMOTROPIC,
   ECTOMORPHIC
CCEHINNRSSU CRUNCHINESS
CCEHINOOSTZ ZOOTECHNICS

CCEHINOPRTY PYROTECHNIC
CCEHKLOSTTU SHUTTLECOCK
CCEHNOOOPRS CHRONOSCOPE
CCEIIINSSTT SCIENTISTIC
CCEIIKLRSTY CITY SLICKER
CCEIIKNSSTT STICK INSECT
CCEIILMNORT CLINOMETRIC
CCEIIMMORRT MICROMETRIC
CCEIIMOORST SOCIOMETRIC
CCEIIMORSTV VISCOMETRIC
CCEIINOORST COERCIONIST
CCEIIOPRRTY RECIPROCITY
CCEIJNNOTUV CONJUNCTIVE
CCEIKKOPPST PICKPOCKETS
CCEIKLNOPRU CUPRONICKEL
CCEILLNOOST COLLECTIONS
CCEILLNOTTU NOCTILUCENT
CCEILNORRTY INCORRECTLY
CCEIMNOORST CENTROSOMIC
CCEIMNOPRTY PYCNOMETRIC
CCEIMOOPRSS MICROSCOPES
CCEINNNOOST CONNECTIONS
CCEINNOOPST CONCEPTIONS
CCEINNOOSSS CONCESSIONS
CCEINNOOSTU CONSECUTION
CCEINNOPRRW CROWN PRINCE
CCEINNOSSTY CONSISTENCY
CCEINOORRST CORRECTIONS
CCEINOSSSSU SUCCESSIONS
CCEJNNORTUU CONJUNCTURE
CCEKLOORSTW CLOCK TOWERS
CCEKMNOSTUU COME UNSTUCK
CCELMOORSTY MOTORCYCLES
CCENORRSTTU RECONSTRUCT
CCEOOOPPRST PROCTOSCOPE
CCFGIILNNOT CONFLICTING
CCFIIINORUX CRUCIFIXION
CCFIILNNOOT CONFLICTION
CCGGHHINORU CHURCHGOING
CCGHIILNNOR CHRONICLING
CCGIIIINRTZ CRITICIZING
CCGIOOPRSSY GYROSCOPICS
CCHHILOOORS CHOIR SCHOOL
CCHIIILNOPS SILICON CHIP
CCHIIIOSTTY HISTIOCYTIC
CCHIILORSTY CHRYSOLITIC
CCHIIMNOOPR MICROPHONIC
CCHIIMNOOST MONOSTICHIC
CCHIIMOORTT TRICHOTOMIC
CCHIIMOPRTY MICROPHYTIC
CCHIINOOPRS RHINOSCOPIC
CCHILMOPTYY LYMPHOCYTIC
CCHIMMNOOOR MONOCHROMIC
CCHIMOOPRTY CORMOPHYTIC
CCHIMOSSSTT SCOTCH MISTS
CCHIOOOPRST ORTHOSCOPIC
CCHIORSSSTT CROSS-STITCH
CCIILOORSTU COLOURISTIC
CCIIMMNOSTU COMMUNISTIC

CCIIMOOPRRS MICROSPORIC
CCIIMOPRSST COMIC STRIPS
CCIINNOOSTV CONVICTIONS
CCIINOPRTTY NYCTITROPIC
CCIJNNNOOTU CONJUNCTION
CCIKLMNOOTU COCONUT MILK
CCILLNOORSU COUNCILLORS
CCILMRRSUUU CURRICULUMS
CCILNNOOSSU CONCLUSIONS
CCILNOOSSUY CONSCIOUSLY
CCIMNNOOPTU COMPUNCTION
CCINNOOSSUU UNCONSCIOUS
CCINOOPSSUU CONSPICUOUS
CCINOORRSTT CONSTRICTOR
CCLNNOOORWY CROWN COLONY
CCNOORRSTTU CONSTRUCTOR
CCNOORRSTUW CROWN COURTS
CCNOORTTUUY COUNTY COURT
CCOOOOPPRSTY PROCTOSCOPY
CDDDEEEEGKL DECKLE-EDGED
CDDDEEIIRST DISCREDITED
CDDDEEIILNUY UNDECIDEDLY
CDDDEIMMOOS DISCOMMODED
CDDEEEHLRSU RESCHEDULED
CDDEEEIPRTU DECREPITUDE
CDDEEEMMNOR RECOMMENDED
CDDEEEOPRRR PRERECORDED
CDDEEFIINST DISINFECTED
CDDEEFILNSU SELF-INDUCED
CDDEEHLNSUU UNSCHEDULED
CDDEEHNNRSU SUNDRENCHED
CDDEEIIMRST MISDIRECTED
CDDEEIINORT RODENTICIDE
CDDEEILNOOS DECOLONISED
CDDEEILNOOZ DECOLONIZED
CDDEEILTUVY DEDUCTIVELY
CDDEELOORUV OVERCLOUDED
CDDEENNOPSY DESPONDENCY
CDDEENORRSU UNDERSCORED
CDDEENORSSW CROWDEDNESS
CDDEEOORRVW OVERCROWDED
CDDEFIIMOST DISCOMFITED
CDDEGHILNOR GODCHILDREN
CDDEHIILMNR CHILDMINDER
CDDEIIILNNS DISINCLINED
CDDEIIILNPS DISCIPLINED
CDDEIILPPSS SLIPPED DISC
CDDEIINNOOT CONDITIONED
CDDEIINOSUU INDECIDUOUS
CDDEIKOPSTT SPOTTED DICK
CDDEILNOOTY DICOTYLEDON
CDDEILNOSSU UNDISCLOSED
CDDEILOORSU DISCOLOURED
CDDEIMOOPSS DISCOMPOSED
CDDEINNOOST ENDODONTICS
CDDELLLMOOY MOLLYCODDLE
CDDENOORSTU COTES-DU-NORD
CDDENOPRSTU END PRODUCTS
CDEEEEFFLNS SELF-DEFENCE

CDEEEEFFRSV EFFERVESCED
CDEEEEFLNSS DEFENCELESS
CDEEEEINPRX EXPERIENCED
CDEEEFFFILT FIELD-EFFECT
CDEEEFFINRS DIFFERENCES
CDEEEFFISST SIDE EFFECTS
CDEEEFGLNTU GENUFLECTED
CDEEEFHIIPS SPEECHIFIED
CDEEEFHORUV CHEF D'OEUVRE
CDEEEFIILNS FIN DE SIÈCLE
CDEEEFIILRT ELECTRIFIED
CDEEEFILTVY DEFECTIVELY
CDEEEFLNRST SELF-CENTRED
CDEEEFLNRTU UNREFLECTED
CDEEEFMNORT DEFORCEMENT
CDEEEGILNXY EXCEEDINGLY
CDEEEGINRSV DIVERGENCES
CDEEEIIMMNN MEDICINE MEN
CDEEEIINNRS IN-RESIDENCE
CDEEEIIOPPR PERIOD PIECE
CDEEEIJNRTT INTERJECTED
CDEEEIILNSTT DELITESCENT
CDEEEIILOPSV VELOCIPEDES
CDEEEIILORTT LIE DETECTOR
CDEEEILPTVY DECEPTIVELY
CDEEEINPRTT INTERCEPTED
CDEEEINRSTT INTERSECTED
CDEEEINSSTX EXCITEDNESS
CDEEEMMNORR RECOMMENDER
CDEEEMNOPRS RECOMPENSED
CDEEENNOPRS RESPONDENCE
CDEEENNORTU ENCOUNTERED
CDEEEOPRRSS PREDECESSOR, REPROCESSED
CDEEERRRSTU RESURRECTED
CDEEFFIKNST STIFF-NECKED
CDEEFHIKLOY FIELD HOCKEY
CDEEFIILNTY DEFICIENTLY
CDEEFIINPSU UNSPECIFIED
CDEEFILLTUY DECEITFULLY
CDEEFILNOST DEFLECTIONS
CDEEFILOSST CLOSEFISTED
CDEEFLNORST CENTRE-FOLDS
CDEEFLNOSSY CONFESSEDLY
CDEEFNNORST FRONDESCENT
CDEEFOORRTU TOUR DE FORCE
CDEEFOPRRTW WORD-PERFECT
CDEEGGINTTU CUTTING EDGE
CDEEGGLORSS CROSS-LEGGED
CDEEGHIINPR DECIPHERING
CDEEGIINNRT INTERCEDING
CDEEGIINNUV UNDECEIVING
CDEEGIINRRT REDIRECTING
CDEEGILNNSU INDULGENCES
CDEEGINOPRS PROCEEDINGS
CDEEGNOSSSU SECOND-GUESS
CDEEHIINNOS INDOCHINESE
CDEEHIINNST INDEHISCENT
CDEEHIKPRSW SHIPWRECKED
CDEEHILOPRR PERCHLORIDE

CDEEHIMNORT ENDOTHERMIC
CDEEHIMNOTU ENDOTHECIUM
CDEEHIOQSTU DISCOTHEQUE
CDEEHPRSTTU UPSTRETCHED
CDEEIIILSTV DECLIVITIES
CDEEIIKLNSS SLICKENSIDE
CDEEIILNORT DERELICTION
CDEEIIMNRST DENSIMETRIC
CDEEIIMORTU EUDIOMETRIC
CDEEIIMPRSS SPERMICIDES
CDEEIINORRT REDIRECTION
CDEEIINRSTV VIRIDESCENT
CDEEIINRTTU INCERTITUDE
CDEEIIORRST DIRECTORIES
CDEEIIORSSV DISCOVERIES
CDEEIIPRSTV DESCRIPTIVE
CDEEIKLNNOO NICKELODEON
CDEEIKLNORT INTERLOCKED
CDEEILMOOSW LOW COMEDIES
CDEEILNNOSS DECLENSIONS
CDEEILNNQUY DELINQUENCY
CDEEILSTUVY SEDUCTIVELY
CDEEIMNNRST DISCERNMENT, RESCINDMENT
CDEEIMNNSTU INDUCEMENTS
CDEEIMNOPRS ENDOSPERMIC
CDEEIMNORTV DIVORCEMENT
CDEEIMOOSTX SEXTODECIMO
CDEEINNRSSW WINDSCREENS
CDEEINOPRSV PROVIDENCES
CDEEINOPRTV OPEN VERDICT
CDEEINORRTU REINTRODUCE
CDEEINORSTT CREDIT NOTES
CDEEINPRSUU SUPERINDUCE
CDEEIORRSSV DISCOVERERS
CDEEIORRTXY EX-DIRECTORY
CDEEIRRRSVW SCREWDRIVER
CDEEIRSTTUV DESTRUCTIVE
CDEEKKORSTY SKYROCKETED
CDEEKNOORSS CROOKEDNESS
CDEEKOOPRSW WOODPECKERS
CDEEKOORSTV OVERSTOCKED
CDEELNNOTTY CONTENTEDLY
CDEEMNNOSST SECONDMENTS
CDEENNORTUV UNCONVERTED
CDEENNOSTTU UNCONTESTED
CDEENOORRRT TROCORNERED
CDEENOORRSS ROOD SCREENS
CDEENPSSTUU UNSUSPECTED
CDEEOOPPRRV OVERCROPPED
CDEEOOPRRUV OVERPRODUCE
CDEEOPRRRSU REPRODUCERS
CDEFFGIOOOS GOOD OFFICES
CDEFGHIKLST FLIGHT DECKS
CDEFGHILNOS GOLDFINCHES
CDEFHIKOPRT PITCHFORKED
CDEFHNOORRS FRENCH DOORS
CDEFIIILMSU SEMIFLUIDIC
CDEFIILMMOR MICROFILMED
CDEFIIMORST DISCOMFITER

CDEFIINORST DISINFECTOR
CDEFIINORTU COUNTRIFIED
CDEFILNNOTY CONFIDENTLY
CDEFILNOSUU FLUID OUNCES
CDEGHHHIIPT HIGH-PITCHED
CDEGHINOSST SECOND SIGHT
CDEGIIJNPRU PREJUDICING
CDEGIINNORS CONSIDERING
CDEGIINORSV DISCOVERING
CDEGIMNNOTU DOCUMENTING
CDEGIMNOOPS DECOMPOSING
CDEGIMNORRU CORRIGENDUM
CDEGINOPRRU REPRODUCING
CDEGMNORSUU CURMUDGEONS
CDEGNORRSUW GROUND CREWS
CDEHHNOOOPR CHORDOPHONE
CDEHIIKTTTW THICK-WITTED
CDEHIILLNOT DECILLIONTH
CDEHIILOOTT THEODOLITIC
CDEHIILORRT TRICHLORIDE
CDEHIIMOOST DICHOTOMIES, DICHOTOMISE
CDEHIIMOOTZ DICHOTOMIZE
CDEHIINOOPV VIDEOPHONIC
CDEHIIPSSTW DIPSWITCHES
CDEHILPRTUU PULCHRITUDE
CDEHIMNOOPR ENDOMORPHIC
CDEHIMNORST CHRISTENDOM
CDEHIMOPRSY HYPODERMICS
CDEHINOPRRY PONDICHERRY
CDEHIOOOPPT PHOTOCOPIED
CDEHKLOORST STOCKHOLDER
CDEHLOOPPRS CLODHOPPERS
CDEHLOOPSSS CLOSED SHOPS
CDEIIILNPRS DISCIPLINER
CDEIIILNPSS DISCIPLINES
CDEIIILNSUV UNCIVILISED
CDEIIILNUVZ UNCIVILIZED
CDEIIILOPST POLITICISED
CDEIIILOPTZ POLITICIZED
CDEIIIMORTX OXIDIMETRIC
CDEIIINNORT INDIRECTION
CDEIIINSTTV DISTINCTIVE
CDEIIIOPRTT PERIDOTITIC
CDEIIIOPRTY PERIODICITY
CDEIIIRSSTV RECIDIVISTS
CDEIIISSTUV VICISSITUDE
CDEIIJNSTUV DISJUNCTIVE
CDEIIKQTTUW QUICK-WITTED
CDEIILLMNOS MILLISECOND
CDEIILLOORV COD-LIVER OIL
CDEIILLOSUY DELICIOUSLY
CDEIILLPTUY PELLUCIDITY
CDEIILNRTUY INCREDULITY
CDEIILNTUVY INDUCTIVELY
CDEIILOORST SCLEROTIOID
CDEIILOPSSU PEDICULOSIS
CDEIILOSTUV DECLIVITOUS
CDEIIMMOOST COMMODITIES
CDEIIMNNSTT INDICTMENTS

CDEIIMNORST MODERNISTIC
CDEIIMOSTTY DOMESTICITY
CDEIIMPPRUY CYPRIPEDIUM
CDEIINNOORT CONDITIONER, RECONDITION
CDEIINNOSTU DISCONTINUE
CDEIINOOPRT PERIODONTIC
CDEIINOPRST DESCRIPTION, PREDICTIONS
CDEIINORRTT INTERDICTOR
CDEIINOSSST DISSECTIONS
CDEIINRSSTU SCRUTINISED
CDEIINRSTUZ SCRUTINIZED
CDEIIPRSSTU PEDICURISTS
CDEIJLNNOOY CONJOINEDLY
CDEIJNRSTUU DISJUNCTURE
CDEIJOOSTTU DO JUSTICE TO
CDEILNNNOOU ON CLOUD NINE
CDEILNOPSST SPLIT SECOND
CDEILNORSUU INCREDULOUS
CDEILORSSSU DISCLOSURES
CDEIMMNOPSU COMPENDIUMS
CDEIMMNOTTU UNCOMMITTED
CDEIMMOOPRS COMPROMISED
CDEIMNOOPSU COMPENDIOUS
CDEIMNOSSTY SYNDESMOTIC
CDEINNOORSU ENDOCRINOUS
CDEINNOOSTU CONTUSIONED
CDEINNOPRST NONDESCRIPT
CDEINNORSTU DSCONTINUER
CDEINOOPSST ENDOSCOPIST
CDEINORSTTU DESTRUCTION
CDEINORSTUY COUNTRYSIDE
CDEINOSTTTU CONSTITUTED
CDEIORSSTUY DISCOURTESY
CDEKKNOOORR DOORKNOCKER
CDELLORSUUY CREDULOUSLY
CDENOORRTUW COUNTERWORD
CDEOOORSTTUW WOODCUTTERS
CDEOPRRRUWY CURRY POWDER
CDFGIILNNOY CONFIDINGLY
CDFGINNNOOU CONFOUNDING
CDFIMOORSST DISCOMFORTS
CDFINNOSTUY DYSFUNCTION
CDGIIKNNSUW WIND-SUCKING
CDGIIKNSTTU SITTING DUCK
CDGIIMMNNOO INCOMMODING
CDGIINNORTU INTRODUCING
CDGIINNOSTU DISCOUNTING
CDGIINORSSU DISCOURSING
CDGILOORTTY TROGLODYTIC
CDGIMNNOOPU COMPOUNDING
CDGINOOTTUW WOODCUTTING
CDGINOPRSTU CROP-DUSTING
CDHIIIMOOPR IDIOMORPHIC
CDHIILPRSUU DISULPHURIC
CDHIIMOOSTT DICHOTOMIST
CDHIIOOPRST CHIROPODIST
CDHIMOOOSTU DICHOTOMOUS
CDHINOOOORTT ORTHODONTIC
CDHINOOPRSY HYDROPONICS

CDIIIJNOSUU INJUDICIOUS
CDIIILNTTUY INDUCTILITY
CDIIINNNOOT IN CONDITION
CDIIINNOSTT DISTINCTION
CDIIJLOSUUY JUDICIOUSLY
CDIIJNNOSTU DISJUNCTION
CDIIKRRSTTY DIRTY TRICKS
CDIILMORSTU CLOSTRIDIUM
CDIIMMNNOOU CONDOMINIUM
CDIINOSSSSU DISCUSSIONS
CDIIOOOOSTV VOODOOISTIC
CDILLORSUUY LUDICROUSLY
CDILMOOORSX LOXODROMICS
CDILOOORUUU DOUROUCOULI
CDINNOOPRTY CYPRINODONT
CDINOOPRSTU PRODUCTIONS
CDLMOORSSTU STORM CLOUDS
CDOORRSSSSW CROSS SWORDS
CEEEEFNPRRS PREFERENCES
CEEEEGIMNRS EMERGENCIES
CEEEEHHRRST THREE CHEERS
CEEEEHNPRST THREEPENCES
CEEEEILNORT ELECTIONEER
CEEEEIMNNPR PRE-EMINENCE
CEEEEIMNNSS MISE-EN-SCÈNE
CEEEEINPRSX EXPERIENCES
CEEEEINRRRV IRREVERENCE
CEEEENNRRTV NERVE CENTRE
CEEEFFGINOV GIVE OFFENCE
CEEEFFHOOSU COFFEE HOUSE
CEEEFFIINTV INEFFECTIVE
CEEEFFILTVY EFFECTIVELY
CEEEFHIIPRS SPEECHIFIER
CEEEFIILRRT ELECTRIFIER
CEEEFIKQRUZ QUICK-FREEZE
CEEEFILRSSV SELF-SERVICE
CEEEFINQRSU FREQUENCIES
CEEEFIORRST REFECTORIES
CEEEFLPRSST SELF-RESPECT
CEEEFMNNORT ENFORCEMENT
CEEEFPRRSTU PREFECTURES
CEEEGGHINNS GEGENSCHEIN
CEEEGGNORRR GREENGROCER
CEEEGIKNORT GREENOCKITE
CEEEGINNOTX XENOGENETIC
CEEEGINNRRV REVERENCING
CEEEGINOSST ECTOGENESIS
CEEEHHKLNOP HECKELPHONE
CEEEHHMOPRS CHEMOSPHERE
CEEEHHNRSTT THE TRENCHES
CEEEHIKNTTT KITCHENETTE
CEEEHILORTT HETEROCLITE
CEEEHIMNRTU HERMENEUTIC
CEEEHIMORST HETEROECISM
CEEEHISSSSW SWISS CHEESE
CEEEHLLRSSY CHEERLESSLY
CEEEHMNNRRT TRENCHERMEN
CEEEHOQRSUU EUROCHEQUES
CEEEHRRSTWY SWEET CHERRY

CEEEIIKLNTT TELEKINETIC
CEEEIIMNNPT IMPENITENCE
CEEEIINNNRT INTERNECINE
CEEEIINNNST INSENTIENCE
CEEEIINNSTX INEXISTENCE
CEEEIINSSST NECESSITIES
CEEEILLSTVY SELECTIVELY
CEEEILNNOQU INELOQUENCE
CEEEILNOPST PLEISTOCENE
CEEEILNORST RE-ELECTIONS
CEEEILNPSST PESTILENCES
CEEEILPRTVY RECEPTIVELY
CEEEILRSTVY SECRETIVELY
CEEEILSSVXY EXCESSIVELY
CEEEIMMNRTX CEMENT MIXER
CEEEIMMPSUU MUSEUM PIECE
CEEEIMNNSTT ENTICEMENTS
CEEEIMNRSTT CENTIMETRES
CEEEIMNSTTX EXCITEMENTS
CEEEINNOSTV VENESECTION
CEEEINORTUX EXECUTIONER
CEEEINOSTVX COEXTENSIVE
CEEEINPRSSS PRECISENESS
CEEEINPRSST PERSISTENCE
CEEEIPPRSTV PERSPECTIVE
CEEEIPRSTUV PERSECUTIVE
CEEEJNNSTUV JUVENESCENT
CEEEKKLOPRS LOCK KEEPERS
CEEEKMNORSS SMOKESCREEN
CEEELLLNTXY EXCELLENTLY
CEEELLORSTY ELECTROLYSE
CEEELLORTTY ELECTROLYTE
CEEELMNOSSW WELCOMENESS
CEEELMORRST ELECTROMERS,
   SCLEROMETER
CEEELNNOORT COELENTERON
CEEELOPRTTY ELECTROTYPE
CEEELORSTVW SWEET CLOVER
CEEEMNOPRRS RECOMPENSER
CEEENNORRTU ENCOUNTERER
CEEENOPRSST OPEN SECRETS
CEEENRSSSTT SCREEN TESTS
CEEEOOPRSST STEREOSCOPE
CEEFFHIIORS IRISH COFFEE
CEEFFHINRRS FRENCH FRIES
CEEFFHOOPSS COFFEE SHOPS
CEEFFIIINNT INEFFICIENT
CEEFFIILLOS SLICE OF LIFE
CEEFFIILNTY EFFICIENTLY
CEEFGIMOORT COME TO GRIEF
CEEFGINNRRY REFRINGENCY
CEEFGINRSTU CENTRIFUGES
CEEFGLNORTU GENUFLECTOR
CEEFHHNORTT THENCEFORTH
CEEFHILMRST FLETCHERISM
CEEFHILORSU CHELIFEROUS
CEEFIKKNOPT POCKETKNIFE
CEEFIKOOPRW PIECE OF WORK
CEEFILMPRTY IMPERFECTLY

CEEFILNORST REFLECTIONS
CEEFILNORSU FLUORESCEIN
CEEFIMNNNOT CONFINEMENT
CEEFIMOPRSS FORM SPECIES
CEEFINNQRUY INFREQUENCY
CEEFINOPRST IN RESPECT OF
CEEFINORTTU COUNTERFEIT
CEEFINOSSTY OF NECESSITY
CEEFLMOORRT ELECTROFORM
CEEFLNORSTU FLUORESCENT
CEEFLOORRSU FORECLOSURE
CEEFLORRSUU RESOURCEFUL
CEEFMNNORST CONFERMENTS
CEEGHILLNOP PHELLOGENIC
CEEGHINNNRT ENTRENCHING
CEEGHINNRRT RETRENCHING
CEEGHINRSST SIGHTSCREEN
CEEGHLOPSST CLOTHES PEGS
CEEGIINPRST STRINGPIECE
CEEGIINSSTT GENETICISTS
CEEGIIOOTVV GIVE VOICE TO
CEEGILNNOSY GEOSYNCLINE
CEEGILNOPST TELESCOPING
CEEGILNOPTY POLYGENETIC
CEEGILNOSTT TELEGNOSTIC
CEEGIMNNOOT MONOGENETIC
CEEGIMNORST EGOCENTRISM
CEEGINOORST OESTROGENIC
CEEGINOSSTY CYTOGENESIS
CEEGINPRSTU PERSECUTING
CEEGMNNORSS CONGRESSMEN
CEEHHIIMPRS HEMISPHERIC
CEEHHILMOOR HELIOCHROME
CEEHHIMRSTT HEMSTITCHER
CEEHHKMOORV CHEREMKHOVO
CEEHHMORSTT HOME STRETCH
CEEHIIINORS CHINOISERIE
CEEHIILLNST HELLENISTIC
CEEHIILMORT HELIOMETRIC
CEEHIIMPRTU PERITHECIUM
CEEHIIMPSTU EUPHEMISTIC
CEEHIKNSSST SKETCHINESS, THICKNESSES
CEEHILLNOPU NUCLEOPHILE
CEEHILLNOST CLOTHESLINE
CEEHILMNORT THERMOCLINE
CEEHILOPRST ELECTORSHIP, HELICOPTERS
CEEHILORTTY HETEROLYTIC
CEEHILPRSTU LECTURESHIP
CEEHILQSSTU SQUELCHIEST
CEEHIMNOPRS MESONEPHRIC
CEEHIMOPRSS MESOSPHERIC
CEEHIMOPRTT PITCHOMETER
CEEHIMOPSTU MOUTHPIECES
CEEHIOOPRTT HETEROTOPIC
CEEHIOPRTTY HETEROTYPIC
CEEHIRSSTTT STRETCHIEST
CEEHKLNOSUY HONEYSUCKLE
CEEHKNORSUY HONEYSUCKER
CEEHKNPRSUY KEYPUNCHERS

CEEHLLOORST CHOLESTEROL
CEEHLLORSUY LECHEROUSLY
CEEHLNOOPRR CHLOROPRENE
CEEHMNOORRT CHRONOMETER
CEEHMNOPRTY NEPHRECTOMY
CEEHMOOPRST THERMOSCOPE
CEEHNOORRTT ORTHOCENTRE
CEEHOOPSSTT STETHOSCOPE
CEEHORRTTYY ERYTHROCYTE
CEEIIINNRST INNER CITIES
CEEIIKNRSST RICKETINESS
CEEIILMRTUV VERMICULITE
CEEIILNNRSY INSINCERELY
CEEIILSTTVY SELECTIVITY
CEEIIMMPRST METEMPIRICS
CEEIIMNNRST REMINISCENT
CEEIIMOPRTZ PIEZOMETRIC
CEEIIMOPTTV COMPETITIVE
CEEIIMORSST ESOTERICISM
CEEIIMORSTX EXOTERICISM
CEEIINORSTV INSECTIVORE
CEEIINOSTVX CONVEXITIES
CEEIINRSSTT INTERSTICES
CEEIIPRTTVY RECEPTIVITY
CEEIIRRSTTV RESTRICTIVE
CEEIJLOPRST PROJECTILES
CEEIJNORRTT INTERJECTOR
CEEIKLNORRT INTERLOCKER
CEEIKMMOSUY MICKEY MOUSE
CEEIKNPRSTY PERSNICKETY
CEEILLMRSSY MERCILESSLY
CEEILLSUVXY EXCLUSIVELY
CEEILMNNSTU LUMINESCENT
CEEILMNOOPW POLICEWOMEN
CEEILMNOSTU CONTUMELIES
CEEILMNRSTU MULTISCREEN
CEEILMOORRT COLORIMETER
CEEILMOOSTU LEUCOTOMIES
CEEILNNOOV NONVIOLENCE
CEEILNQSTUY QUIESCENTLY
CEEILRRSTUU SERICULTURE
CEEIMMORRST MICROMETERS
CEEIMNNOOPT OMNIPOTENCE
CEEIMNNOPRS PROMINENCES
CEEIMNNOPTT INCOMPETENT
CEEIMNNORTU COUNTERMINE
CEEIMNNSTTU INTUMESCENT
CEEIMNOORSU CEREMONIOUS
CEEIMNRRTTU RECRUITMENT
CEEIMOOPSSS SEISMOSCOPE
CEEIMOORRSV ROOM SERVICE
CEEIMOPRSSV COMPRESSIVE
CEEIMOPRSTU COMPUTERISE
CEEIMOPRTUZ COMPUTERIZE
CEEINNNOSTT CONSENTIENT
CEEINNOORRT RECONNOITRE
CEEINNOOSTX COEXTENSION
CEEINOOPRST RETINOSCOPE
CEEINOPPRSS SNIPERSCOPE

CEEINOPRRTT INTERCEPTOR
CEEINOPRSSS PRECESSIONS
CEEINOPRSTU PERSECUTION
CEEINOPRTTX EXCERPTTION
CEEINORRSST INTERCESSOR
CEEINORRSTU INTERCOURSE
CEEINOSSSTU NECESSITOUS
CEEINRRSSTU SCRUTINEERS
CEEIOPPRSTV PROSPECTIVE
CEEIOPRSTTY STEREOTYPIC
CEEIPQRSTUU PICTURESQUE
CEEIRSTTVVY CIVVY STREET
CEEJLNORSWW CROWN JEWELS
CEEKLNRSTTU TURTLENECKS
CEEKMNOOPTY POCKET MONEY
CEEKOORRRTT RETRO-ROCKET
CEELMMNOPST COMPLEMENTS
CEELMNNOSTU LOCUM TENENS
CEELMNOPSTY SPLENECTOMY
CEELMNOPTTY COMPETENTLY
CEELNRRRTUY RECURRENTLY
CEEMMNNOOSS COMMON SENSE
CEEMMNOPTUY PNEUMECTOMY
CEEMMOOPRTT COMPTOMETER
CEEMMOORSTT COME TO TERMS
CEEMNNNOTTT CONTENTMENT
CEEMNOORTUV COUNTERMOVE
CEEMNOPRRTU PROCUREMENT
CEEMNOPRSTT CONTRETEMPS
CEENNOORRST CORNERSTONE
CEENNOSSSSU CONSENSUSES
CEENOPPPRRS PEPPERCORNS
CEENOPRTTUY COUNTERTYPE
CEENORSTTTU STONECUTTER
CEEOOPRRTTV OVERPROTECT
CEEOOPRSSTY STEREOSCOPY
CEEOPRRSSTT PROTECTRESS
CEEOPRRSSTU PERSECUTORS
CEERRRSTTUU RESTRUCTURE
CEFFHIINORS CHIFFONIERS
CEFFHIRSSTT FESTSCHRIFT
CEFFIOOPSST POST OFFICES
CEFGIILNNNU INFLUENCING
CEFGIINNORR REINFORCING
CEFGIKLLNOS SELF-LOCKING
CEFGILNOORS FORECLOSING
CEFGLOORSSU GOLF COURSES
CEFHHNNORRS FRENCH HORNS
CEFHIIISSTT FETISHISTIC
CEFHILLRTUY FILTHY LUCRE
CEFHOOSSTTU SOFT TOUCHES
CEFIIKKLNSV FLICK KNIVES
CEFIILNNOST INFLECTIONS
CEFIINORSUZ ZINCIFEROUS
CEFILMORSUU CULMIFEROUS
CEFILNOORTU COUNTERFOIL
CEFILOORSUY FEROCIOUSLY
CEFINNOOSSS CONFESSIONS
CEFIOPRRSUU CUPRIFEROUS

CEFLLNOORST SELF-CONTROL
CEFLMOORSST COMFORTLESS
CEFLNOORRSW CORNFLOWERS
CEFLOOOPRSU FLUOROSCOPE
CEFNOPRRTUY PERFUNCTORY
CEGGIINNORZ RECOGNIZING
CEGHIINNNRT INTRENCHING
CEGHIINNRST CHRISTENING
CEGHIMMNOOS HOMECOMINGS
CEGHINORSSU GROUCHINESS
CEGHIOOPRST GEOSTROPHIC
CEGIIIMNNRS REMINISCING
CEGIIIMNRTZ METRICIZING
CEGIIKLNNSY SICKENINGLY
CEGIILLNNST STENCILLING
CEGIILLNORY RECOILINGLY
CEGIILMNOST CLOSING TIME
CEGIILMOOSS SEISMOLOGIC
CEGIILNOOST NEOLOGISTIC
CEGIILNORST CLOISTERING
CEGIILNOTVY COGNITIVELY
CEGIILOOPST GEOPOLITICS
CEGIIMMNNOU IMMUNOGENIC
CEGIIMNNOOZ ECONOMIZING
CEGIIMNOORT GONIOMETRIC
CEGIINNOORT RECOGNITION
CEGIINORSTU CONGRUITIES
CEGIINRRSTT RESTRICTING
CEGILLNNOSU COUNSELLING
CEGILNNOSSY CLOYINGNESS
CEGILNOORST NECROLOGIST
CEGILNOOSTY SCIENTOLOGY
CEGILNORSSS SINGLE-CROSS
CEGILNRRRUY RECURRINGLY
CEGIMNNNOST CONSIGNMENT
CEGIMNOOOSS COSMOGONIES
CEGIMNOPRSS COMPRESSING
CEGIMOOORRV MICROGROOVE
CEGIMOOPRST COME TO GRIPS
CEGINNNOSTT CONTINGENTS
CEGINNORSTU COUNTERSIGN
CEGINOPPRST PROSPECTING
CEGINOPRSTU PROSECUTING
CEGLMMOORYY MYRMECOLOGY
CEGLMOOSSTY GLOSSECTOMY
CEGLNNORTUY CONGRUENTLY
CEGORRRSUYY CRYOSURGERY
CEHHHIIKRST HITCHHIKERS
CEHHIIILLOT HELIOLITHIC
CEHHIIMMOPR HEMIMORPHIC
CEHHILMRSUY HELICHRYSUM
CEHHIMRSTUY EURHYTHMICS
CEHHINRTTUW WITCH-HUNTER
CEHHIOPRRST CHRISTOPHER
CEHHIOPSTYZ SCHIZOPHYTE
CEHHLOOOSSU SCHOOLHOUSE
CEHHMNORSSY SYNCHROMESH
CEHHMOOOPRR CHROMOPHORE
CEHHOOOPRRT TROCHOPHORE

CEHIIINPSST CITISENSHIP
CEHIIINPSTZ CITIZENSHIP
CEHIIJPSSTU JUSTICESHIP
CEHIIJSTTUW WITH JUSTICE
CEHIIKLNOPS PICK HOLES IN
CEHIIKNSSTT IN THE STICKS
CEHIILOOPRT HELIOTROPIC
CEHIILPRSTU SPHERULITIC
CEHIIMNORST THERMIONICS
CEHIIMOPPRR PERIMORPHIC
CEHIIMOSSUV MISCHIEVOUS
CEHIINOOPRS IONOSPHERIC
CEHIINOORSS ISOCHRONISE
CEHIINOORSZ ISOCHRONIZE
CEHIIOPPTTY EPIPHYTOTIC
CEHIIOPRRST PREHISTORIC
CEHIIOPRSVY VICEROYSHIP
CEHIIOSSSVY VICHYSSOISE
CEHIKMRSSTU HUCKSTERISM
CEHIKNOPSTU SOUP KITCHEN
CEHIKNPSSSU PUCKISHNESS
CEHILLMOPSY MESOPHYLLIC
CEHILMOOPPR PLEOMORPHIC
CEHILMOOPRS PLEOCHROISM
CEHILMORTTY THERMOLYTIC
CEHILNOOQRU CHLOROQUINE
CEHILNOSSST COLTISHNESS
CEHILNOSSSU SLOUCHINESS
CEHIMMOOPRS MESOMORPHIC
CEHIMMOOSSS CHEMOSMOSIS
CEHIMNOOPRS MICROPHONES
CEHIMNOOPRT PHONOMETRIC
CEHIMNOOPRX XENOMORPHIC
CEHIMNOPSTY CHIMNEYPOTS
CEHIMOOPRRX XEROMORPHIC
CEHIMOOPRTT PHOTOMETRIC
CEHIMOOSSST SCHISTOSOME
CEHIMOPPRST COPPERSMITH
CEHIMORSTTY STICHOMETRY
CEHINNORSSY SYNCHRONISE
CEHINNORSYZ SYNCHRONIZE
CEHINOOPRRS CORONERSHIP
CEHIOOOPPRT PHOTOCOPIER
CEHIOOOPPST PHOTOCOPIES
CEHIOOPSTTY OSTEOPHYTIC
CEHIOPRSSTT PROSTHETICS
CEHKNOOSSTT ON THE STOCKS
CEHLOOPPRSS PREP SCHOOLS
CEHMMNOORSW COMMON SHREW
CEHMMOOORSS CHROMOSOMES
CEHMMOOORSX X CHROMOSOME
CEHMMOOORSY Y CHROMOSOME
CEHMNOORRTY CHRONOMETRY
CEHMOPRSTYY PSYCHOMETRY
CEHNNOSSTUU UNCOUTHNESS
CEHNOOSSTTU TOUCHSTONES
CEHOOPSSTTY STETHOSCOPY
CEHOORSSTUU COURTHOUSES
CEIIILLMNPU PENICILLIUM

CEIIILLPTTY ELLIPTICITY
CEIIILNNPTY INCIPIENTLY
CEIIIMNOPRS IMPRECISION
CEIIIMNOSST MISONEISTIC
CEIIIMPSSST PESSIMISTIC
CEIIINNRSTY INSINCERITY
CEIIINNSTTV INSTINCTIVE
CEIIINOPRTT PERITONITIC
CEIIINOSTVV VIVISECTION
CEIIINPRSTV INSCRIPTIVE
CEIIIOPRSTT PERIOSTITIC
CEIIIORSSTU CURIOSITIES
CEIIIOSSTTV SOVIETISTIC
CEIIKLLPSTT LICKSPITTLE
CEIIKLNNRSS CRINKLINESS
CEIIKLNPRSS PRICKLINESS
CEIIKLQRSUV QUICKSILVER
CEIIKNOSSTY CYTOKINESIS
CEIIKNRSSST TRICKSINESS
CEIIKPRSSTT SPITSTICKER
CEIILLNSUVY INCLUSIVELY
CEIILNRTUUV VINICULTURE
CEIILRTTUUV VITICULTURE
CEIILRTTUVY RELUCTIVITY
CEIIMMNOSTU COMMUNITIES
CEIIMNOOPTT COMPETITION
CEIIMNOPSUU IMPECUNIOUS
CEIIMNORRTT NITROMETRIC
CEIIMNORSTU NEUROTICISM
CEIIMNPRSSS SCRIMPINESS
CEIIMOPRRST SPIROMETRIC
CEIIMOPRSST SEMITROPICS
CEIINNNNOTT INCONTINENT
CEIINNNORTU INTERNUNCIO
CEIINNOPSST INSPECTIONS
CEIINORRSTT RESTRICTION
CEIINOSSSUV VICIOUSNESS
CEIINRRSSTU SCRUTINISER
CEIINRRSTUZ SCRUTINIZER
CEIINRSTTUV INSTRUCTIVE
CEIIOPPRSTU PRECIPITOUS
CEIIORRRSTT TERRORISTIC
CEIIORSTUVY VOYEURISTIC
CEIIPPRSTUY PERSPICUITY
CEIJNOOPRST PROJECTIONS
CEIKLLMOORS ROLLICKSOME
CEIKLMOORST MORTISE LOCK
CEIKLNNSSUU UNLUCKINESS
CEIKLNOORRT CRINKLEROOT
CEIKNNORSTU COUNTERSINK
CEILLLNOOOV VIOLONCELLO
CEILLNOPRSU CURL ONE'S LIP
CEILMMNOPST COMPLIMENTS
CEILMMOPRUY PROMYCELIUM
CEILMNOOPSX COMPLEXIONS
CEILMNOTYYZ ENZYMOLYTIC
CEILMOOOOPST COSMOPOLITE
CEILMOOOSTV LOCOMOTIVES
CEILMOPRTUU POMICULTURE

CEILNOOPRTU PERLOCUTION
CEILNORSSTU COURTLINESS
CEILNRSTUUV VENTRICULUS
CEILOOPRSTT PROTOSTELIC
CEILOOPRTTY PROTEOLYTIC
CEILOORRSTU TERRICOLOUS
CEILOORRSUV VERSICOLOUR
CEILOORRSVY CORROSIVELY
CEIMMMNOSTT COMMITMENTS
CEIMMNOQSUU COMMUNIQUÉS
CEIMMNORSSU CONSUMERISM
CEIMMOOPRRS COMPROMISER
CEIMMOOPRSS COMPROMISES
CEIMNOOPRSS COMPRESSION
CEIMNOOPRTU MUCOPROTEIN
CEIMNOORSTU COTERMINOUS
CEIMNOPRSSU PROSCENIUMS
CEIMNOPSTUV CONSUMPTIVE
CEIMNORSSTU MISCONSTRUE
CEIMOOPRSTT COMPETITORS
CEINNNOOSTT CONTENTIONS
CEINNNOOSTV CONVENTIONS
CEINNOORSSU CONNOISSEUR
CEINNOORSSV CONVERSIONS
CEINNOOSTTU CONTENTIOUS
CEINNOSTTTU CONSTITUENT
CEINOOPRSSS PROCESSIONS
CEINOOPRSTT PROTECTIONS, STENOTROPIC
CEINOOPRSTU PROSECUTION
CEINOOPRSTY RETINOSCOPY
CEINOOPTTTY TOTIPOTENCY
CEINOPRSSSU SUPERSONICS
CEINORSSSUU CURIOUSNESS
CEINORSTTTU CONSTITUTER
CEINOSSSSUV VISCOUSNESS
CEINOSSSTUV VISCOUNTESS
CEIOOOOPRRTZ PROTEROZOIC
CEIOOPRTTYZ CRYPTOZOITE
CEIOPPRSSUU PERSPICUOUS
CEIOPRRSTWY COPYWRITERS
CEIORRRSTUVY VERRUCOSITY
CEIPPRRSSTU SUPERSCRIPT
CEIPPRSSTTY TYPESCRIPTS
CEKLMOOOORRS LOCKER ROOMS
CEKNNORSTUU COUNTERSUNK
CEKNOORRTUW COUNTERWORK
CELLMOOPRRT COMPTROLLER
CELLNNOOPTU POLLEN COUNT
CELLNOORRST CONTROLLERS
CELLNOORSSU COUNSELLORS
CELLNRTTUUY TRUCULENTLY
CELMNOORTUU MONOCULTURE
CELMOOPRTYY PYLORECTOMY
CELNOOPRTTU COUNTERPLOT
CELOORSTUUY COURTEOUSLY
CEMMNOOPRTT COMPORTMENT
CEMOOPRRSSS COMPRESSORS
CENOORRSTVY CONTROVERSY
CENOPRRSSTU CORRUPTNESS

CENORSTTUWY WEST COUNTRY
CEOOPPRRSST PROSPECTORS
CEOOPRRSSTU PROSECUTORS
CEPRRSSTTUU SUPERSTRUCT
CFFGIIKNOST TICKINGS OFF
CFFGIINRTUY FRUCTIFYING
CFFHILMNOTU FIFTH COLUMN
CFFIIINOOSU INOFFICIOUS
CFFIILOOSUY OFFICIOUSLY
CFGHIILLNNY FLINCHINGLY
CFGHIILNNNU UNFLINCHING
CFGHIMNOORT FORTHCOMING
CFGIINNNOTU FUNCTIONING
CFGILNNOSUY CONFUSINGLY
CFGINNNOORT CONFRONTING
CFGINOSTUUY YOUNG FUSTIC
CFHHIKMNOTU THINK MUCH OF
CFHIIKSSSTT SHIFT STICKS, STICK SHIFTS
CFHLLOOORST FLOOR CLOTHS
CFIIILNNOST INFLICTIONS
CFIILMORSTU FORMULISTIC
CFIINORSSTU FIRST COUSIN
CFIMNOORSST CONFORMISTS
CFINNOORSTU INNS OF COURT
CFLOOOPRSUY FLUOROSCOPY
CGGHIILOOPR LOGOGRIPHIC
CGGIIIKNPST PIGSTICKING
CGGIIKNPSSU SUCKING PIGS
CGGILNORSUY SCOURGINGLY
CGHHHIIIKNT HITCHHIKING
CGHHHILOOSS HIGH SCHOOLS
CGHHILNOOST NIGHT SCHOOL
CGHHILOOTYY ICHTHYOLOGY
CGHIIILRSTV CIVIL RIGHTS
CGHIIKNSSTT NIGHTSTICKS
CGHIILNTTWY TWITCHINGLY
CGHILLNOSUY SLOUCHINGLY
CGHILMOOOPR MORPHOLOGIC
CGHILOOPSTY PHYCOLOGIST
CGHILOORSTY CHRISTOLOGY
CGHIMNOORST SHORTCOMING
CGHIMOOOTYZ HOMOZYGOTIC
CGHIMOOPRYZ ZYGOMORPHIC
CGHINOPTTUY TOUCH-TYPING
CGIIIIMNTVZ VICTIMIZING
CGIIIKLNOPT POLITICKING
CGIIILNSSTU LINGUISTICS
CGIIILRSTTU LITURGISTIC
CGIIKLLNORS ROLLICKINGS
CGIIKLLNRTY TRICKLINGLY
CGIIKLNOPST STOCKPILING
CGIIILLOSSTY SYLLOGISTIC
CGIILMMNOOU IMMUNOLOGIC
CGIILMNOORY CRIMINOLOGY
CGIILNNNSUU CUNNILINGUS
CGIILNOOOST ICONOLOGIST
CGIILOOOSST SOCIOLOGIST
CGIIMNNOSTU MISCOUNTING
CGIIMNOSTUZ CUSTOMIZING

CGIINNORTUY INCONGRUITY
CGIINNRSTTU INSTRUCTING
CGILLNNOORT CONTROLLING
CGILMOOOSST COSMOLOGIST
CGILNPRSTUU SCULPTURING
CGILOOSSTTY CYTOLOGISTS
CGIMNOOOSST COSMOGONIST
CGINNNOOPRU PRONOUNCING
CGINNOORSUU INCONGRUOUS
CGINRRSTTUU STRUCTURING
CHHIILOPTTY LITHOPHYTIC
CHHIIMORSTY ISORHYTHMIC
CHHIIMRTTYY RHYTHMICITY
CHHILLMOOPY HOMOPHYLLIC
CHHILMOOOPR HOLOMORPHIC
CHHIMMOOOPR HOMOMORPHIC
CHHIOORSTTY ORTHOSTICHY
CHHLLLOOPRY CHLOROPHYLL
CHIILLPSSTY SYPHILITICS
CHIIIMORSST HISTORICISM
CHIIINORSST HISTRIONICS, TRICHINOSIS
CHIIIORSSTT HISTORICIST
CHIIIORSTTY HISTORICITY
CHIILLNOOTT OCTILLIONTH
CHIILOOPRTT PROTOLITHIC
CHIINNOPSSU PINCUSHIONS
CHIINORRTTY TYROTHRICIN
CHIIOOPRTTX THIXOTROPIC
CHIIOPPRRTY PORPHYRITIC
CHIIORRSSTY SCIRRHOSITY
CHIIORSSTTU TRISTICHOUS
CHIIOSSSTTY SCHISTOSITY
CHILNOPSSSU CONSULSHIPS
CHILOOPPRTY POLYTROPHIC
CHILOORSTUU ULOTRICHOUS
CHIMMNOOOPR MONOMORPHIC
CHIMNNORSSY SYNCHRONISM
CHIMNOOPRRS PROCHRONISM
CHIOOOPPRTT PHOTOTROPIC
CHIOOOPRRTT ORTHOTROPIC
CHIOOPPRSTY SPOROPHYTIC
CHIOOPPRTTY TROPOPHYTIC
CHIOPSTTTUY TOUCH-TYPIST
CHKOOOPRSST SHOCK TROOPS
CHMNOOPSTTU MUTTONCHOPS
CHMNOOPTTUU NOT UP TO MUCH
CHMOOOOPRSTY PSYCHOMOTOR
CHNNOORRSTY SYNCHROTRON
CHNNOORSSUY SYNCHRONOUS
CIIILLMMNOR MILLIMICRON
CIIILOPSSST SOLIPSISTIC
CIIILRSTTUU UTRICULITIS
CIIINNOPRST INSCRIPTION
CIIINOOSTTY ISOTONICITY
CIIINORSTUY INCURIOSITY
CIIJNNNOSTU INJUNCTIONS
CIILLOORSTT TORTICOLLIS
CIILMMNNOOS MONOCLINISM
CIILNOPSTUU PUNCTILIOUS

CIIMMNNOOTU COMMINUTION
CIIMMNOOSSS COMMISSIONS
CIIMMOORSTT MICROTOMIST
CIIMNOOOPST COMPOSITION
CIIMOPRRSTU SCRIPTORIUM
CIIMOPRSTUY PROMISCUITY
CIINNORSTTU INSTRUCTION
CIIOOPRSSUV PISCIVOROUS
CILMNNOOOSU MONOCLINOUS
CILMNOOPSSU COMPULSIONS
CILNNOOOTUV CONVOLUTION
CILNNOOSSUV CONVULSIONS
CILNNOOSUUY INNOCUOUSLY
CIMNNOOOPPS NINCOMPOOPS
CIMNNOOPSTU CONSUMPTION
CIMNOORSSTU CONSORTIUMS
CIMNOPPSTUU SUCTION PUMP
CIMOOOPRSST COMPOSITORS
CIMOOPRSSUU PROMISCUOUS
CIMOPRSSTUU SCRUMPTIOUS
CINNOOORSTT CONTORTIONS
CINOOPRRSTU CORRUPTIONS
CINORRSSTTU INSTRUCTORS
CIOPPRSSSTT POSTSCRIPTS
CIPPRRSSTUU STIRRUP CUPS
CIRRSSTTTUU STRUCTURIST
CLLNOOSUUVV CONVOLVULUS
CMMMNOOOORS COMMON ROOMS
CMMNNNOOOSU COMMON NOUNS
CNNOOSTTUWY COUNTY TOWNS
DDDEEFIOSST EISTEDDFODS
DDDEEIILMSS MIDDLE-SISED
DDDEEIILMSZ MIDDLE-SIZED
DDDEELMNSSU MUDDLEDNESS
DDDEGILNORY DODDERINGLY
DDDENNOORTW DOWNTRODDEN
DDEEEEFIRRZ FREEZE-DRIED
DDEEEEHNPRR REPREHENDED
DDEEEELOPRV REDEVELOPED
DDEEEFILLNW WELL-DEFINED
DDEEEFILSTT FIELD-TESTED
DDEEEGHIRRT THIRD-DEGREE
DDEEEGIPRST PREDIGESTED
DDEEEHILLSV DISHEVELLED
DDEEEILNRSS SLENDERISED
DDEEEILNRSZ SLENDERIZED
DDEEEIMNOST DEMONETISED
DDEEEIMNOTZ DEMONETIZED
DDEEEIMPRST DISTEMPERED
DDEEEINNNPT INDEPENDENT
DDEEEINPRST PREDESTINED
DDEEEIPPSST SIDESTEPPED
DDEEELLNOWW WELL-ENDOWED
DDEEELNOPUV UNDEVELOPED
DDEEELNPRTY PRETENDEDLY
DDEEENOSSTV DEVOTEDNESS
DDEEENRRRSU SURRENDERED
DDEEEORRSSV OVERDRESSED
DDEEFFGLLLU FULL-FLEDGED

DDEEFHILNOT ON THE FIDDLE
DDEEFIIIMNN INDEMNIFIED
DDEEFIIIRSV DIVERSIFIED
DDEEFIIMNNU DEFINIENDUM
DDEEFIIMSTY DEMYSTIFIED
DDEEFIORSST DISFORESTED
DDEEFLLNOUW WELL-FOUNDED
DDEEGINNRSU UNDERSIGNED
DDEEGNOPRSU GROUNDSPEED
DDEEHIILRSS DISRELISHED
DDEEHNNORSW SEND HER DOWN
DDEEIILPPSS SIDESLIPPED
DDEEIINRRST DISINTERRED
DDEEIIQSTUU DISQUIETUDE
DDEEIKNNRSS KINDREDNESS
DDEEILNOSTT DOTTED LINES
DDEEINNNPRU UNDERPINNED
DDEEINSSSTU STUDIEDNESS
DDEEIOPPRSS PREDISPOSED
DDEELLNORUW WELL-ROUNDED
DDEENNORSSU ROUNDEDNESS
DDEFFIILNTY DIFFIDENTLY
DDEGGGILORS GOLD DIGGERS
DDEGGIINNRW WEDDING RING
DDEGHIIMNRT RIGHT-MINDED
DDEGIILMSUY MISGUIDEDLY
DDEGIINOORZ DEODORIZING
DDEGIINORRS DISORDERING
DDEGILMNOST DISLODGMENT
DDEGILNRSTU DISGRUNTLED
DDEGILSSTUY DISGUSTEDLY
DDEGNNORRUU UNDERGROUND
DDEHHIIOPRT DIPHTHEROID
DDEHIILNSSW WINDSHIELDS
DDEHINOORSU DISHONOURED
DDEHINORSTW SHORT-WINDED
DDEHLMOOTUU LOUDMOUTHED
DDEIIMNNOSU DIMINUENDOS
DDEILMNORTY DIRTY OLD MEN
DDEINNOOSTT ENDODONTIST
DDELNNOORRY LONDONDERRY
DDGGGGIILNO GOLD-DIGGING
DDGIILNOORS SLIDING DOOR
DDGILMNPPUU PLUM PUDDING
DDHOOOOSUWY HOW DO YOU DOS
DDIIKLNSTWY TIDDLYWINKS
DDINOOOPRTT DIPROTODONT
DEEEEEFHLRW FREEWHEELED
DEEEEEFPRSZ DEEP FREEZES
DEEEEHILRSW SIDE-WHEELER
DEEEEHNPRRR REPREHENDER
DEEEELMNNOW NEEDLEWOMEN
DEEEELOPRRV REDEVELOPER
DEEEEMOPRST SPEEDOMETER
DEEEENPRRST REPRESENTED
DEEEEQRSSTU SEQUESTERED
DEEEFFGHIRT FIFTH-DEGREE
DEEEFFNOOST TOFFEE-NOSED
DEEEFGIRRST FIRST-DEGREE

DEEEFHLNSSU HEEDFULNESS
DEEEFHLORRS FREEHOLDERS
DEEEFIILMPX EXEMPLIFIED
DEEEFILNSTV FIELD EVENTS, SELF-EVIDENT
DEEEFILNSVY DEFENSIVELY
DEEEFIOPRRT PROFITEERED
DEEEFLNNSSU NEEDFULNESS
DEEEFMNRRSU REFERENDUMS
DEEEGGINNNR ENGENDERING
DEEEGHHOPPR HEDGEHOPPER
DEEEGHILNNT ENLIGHTENED
DEEEGLORRSU GUELDER-ROSE
DEEEHHPRSSS SHEPHERDESS
DEEEHIINNPT PHENETIDINE
DEEEHILNPRS REPLENISHED
DEEEHIMRRSU RUDESHEIMER
DEEEHLMORVW OVERWHELMED
DEEEHMOPRTT HOT-TEMPERED
DEEEIIJORVV JOIE DE VIVRE
DEEEIIMPRSS EPIDERMISES
DEEEIINNPTX INEXPEDIENT
DEEEIINRTVW INTERVIEWED
DEEEIINSSST DESENSITISE
DEEEIINSSTZ DESENSITIZE
DEEEILLMPRT ILL-TEMPERED
DEEEILMMNPT IMPLEMENTED
DEEEILMMNUV MENDELEVIUM
DEEEILMNNST ENLISTED MEN
DEEEILMNRVY DELIVERYMEN
DEEEILNNOPT NEEDLEPOINT
DEEEILNPTXY EXPEDIENTLY
DEEEILORSTU DELETERIOUS
DEEEIMNRRST DETERMINERS
DEEEINPRRTT INTERPRETED
DEEEINPRTUX EXPENDITURE
DEEEINRRSSV VINEDRESSER
DEEEINRSSTW DESSERT WINE, WESTERNISED
DEEEINRSTWZ WESTERNIZED
DEEEIPPRSST SIDESTEPPER
DEEEIRSSSTT SIDE STREETS
DEEEJMPQUUU QUEUE-JUMPED
DEEEKOOPRRS DOORKEEPERS
DEEELLNORSW NE'ER-DO-WELLS
DEEELLNRRSU UNDERSELLER
DEEELLPPRXY PERPLEXEDLY
DEEELMNNORY MONEYLENDER
DEEELMNOPTV DEVELOPMENT
DEEELMNOTVV DEVOLVEMENT
DEEELNNPRST RESPLENDENT
DEEELNNRSSS SLENDERNESS
DEEELNNSSSS ENDLESSNESS
DEEELNORTUV VOLUNTEERED
DEEELNRRTTU UNDERLETTER
DEEELOOPRVV OVERDEVELOP
DEEELPRRTVY PERVERTEDLY
DEEEMNNORST ENDORSEMENT
DEEEMNNOSTU DENOUEMENTS
DEEEMPRTTUW TRUMPETWEED
DEEEMRRSSSU MURDERESSES

DEEENOPRSUX UNDEREXPOSE
DEEENOPSSSX EXPOSEDNESS
DEEENPRSSUX UNEXPRESSED
DEEENRRRRSU SURRENDERER
DEEENRRSTTT TRENDSETTER
DEEEOOPRRVW OVERPOWERED
DEEEOOPRSVX OVEREXPOSED
DEEEOPPRSTV OVERSTEPPED
DEEEOPRSSSS REPOSSESSED
DEEEOPRSTTY STEREOTYPED
DEEEORRRTTV RETROVERTED
DEEEORRTTVX EXTROVERTED
DEEEPRRSSST PRESTRESSED
DEEEPRRSSUU SUPERSEDURE
DEEFFIINNRT INDIFFERENT
DEEFFILNRTY DIFFERENTLY
DEEFFINSSSU DIFFUSENESS
DEEFFIOOPRR FIREPROOFED
DEEFFORSTUV OVERSTUFFED
DEEFGHIORST FORESIGHTED
DEEFGIINNRX INDEX FINGER
DEEFGILNNSY SELF-DENYING
DEEFGILNORW DEFLOWERING
DEEFGINORST DEFORESTING
DEEFHILLLOR FIELD-HOLLER
DEEFIIIMMNR INDEMNIFIER
DEEFIIINNST INTENSIFIED
DEEFIIIRRSV DIVERSIFIER
DEEFIILMRSU DEMULSIFIER
DEEFIILNRST FRIENDLIEST
DEEFIIMORST DEFORMITIES
DEEFIINOPRS PERSONIFIED
DEEFIINRSVW VIEWFINDERS
DEEFIKLORRW FIELDWORKER
DEEFILLRSSU FLEURS-DE-LIS
DEEFILMOPSS SELF-IMPOSED
DEEFILORSTU OUTFIELDERS
DEEFLLNOSSU DOLEFULNESS
DEEFLOPRSSY PROFESSEDLY
DEEFNOORSTT TENDERFOOTS
DEEFNOPRSSU UNPROFESSED
DEEGGINNOOV GOOD EVENING
DEEGHHINPRS SHEPHERDING
DEEGHHINRST RING THE SHED
DEEGHHIOPRW HIGH-POWERED
DEEGHILLNWY WHEEDLINGLY
DEEGHILNOOP PIGEONHOLED
DEEGHIMNOOS HOMOGENISED
DEEGHIMNOOZ HOMOGENIZED
DEEGHINORSY HYDROGENISE
DEEGHINORYZ HYDROGENIZE
DEEGHINRRRS RED HERRINGS
DEEGHINRTUW UNDERWEIGHT
DEEGHNORSTU GROUNDSHEET
DEEGIIILMST LEGITIMISED
DEEGIIILMTZ LEGITIMIZED
DEEGIIINSTV INDIGESTIVE
DEEGIIMNNOR DOMINEERING
DEEGIIMNNRT DETERMINING

DEEGIINNRST INGREDIENTS
DEEGIINNRTZ TENDERIZING
DEEGILLMNOR REMODELLING
DEEGILNOPRY REDEPLOYING
DEEGILNORUV OVERINDULGE
DEEGILNRSVY DESERVINGLY
DEEGILNRTVY DIVERGENTLY
DEEGINPRSSU SUPERSEDING
DEEGJMNPRTU PREJUDGMENT
DEEGLLMOORW WELL-GROOMED
DEEGLNORSSY ENGROSSEDLY
DEEGLNOSSSS GODLESSNESS
DEEHHLOORSU HOUSEHOLDER
DEEHIIMPRSU HESPERIDIUM
DEEHILLORTT TITLEHOLDER
DEEHILMNOTU ENDOTHELIUM
DEEHILOOSTT THEODOLITES
DEEHILOSTTU SILHOUETTED
DEEHIMOSTTW WISDOM TEETH
DEEHINOSSSU HIDEOUSNESS
DEEHINRRSSU HURRIEDNESS
DEEHINSSSTY SYNTHESISED
DEEHINSSTYZ SYNTHESIZED
DEEHLOPRSTU UPHOLSTERED
DEEHMNNOOOY HONEYMOONED
DEEHMNOOPTU OPEN-MOUTHED
DEEHMOORRTY HYDROMETEOR
DEEHOORRSUV HORS D'OEUVRE
DEEIIIMNNST INDEMNITIES
DEEIIKLLMSS SEMISKILLED
DEEIIKLNNRT INTERLINKED
DEEIIILLRVY LILY-LIVERED
DEEIILMNSSU DISSEMINULE
DEEIILMPSST SPEED LIMITS
DEEIILNOPRS LEPIDOSIREN
DEEIILOPRSY ERYSIPELOID
DEEIILPRRSV PILE DRIVERS
DEEIIMMNPST IMPEDIMENTS
DEEIIMMNRST DETERMINISM
DEEIIMNOPTT PIEDMONTITE
DEEIIMNPSST DISSEPIMENT
DEEIIMNRRST IRREDENTISM
DEEIIMNRSTT DETERMINIST
DEEIINNRTTW INTERTWINED
DEEIINNSSTT DISSENTIENT
DEEIINOPSTX EXPEDITIONS
DEEIINPRSTY SERENDIPITY
DEEIINRRSTT IRREDENTIST
DEEIINRSSTT DISINTEREST
DEEIIOPSTUX EXPEDITIOUS
DEEIIOQSSUX SESQUIOXIDE
DEEIIRSTTUV DIVESTITURE
DEEIKMNPPSU PUMPKINSEED
DEEILMNOPST DESPOILMENT
DEEILNNQSTU DELINQUENTS
DEEILNORRSS ORDERLINESS
DEEILNSSSTT STILTEDNESS
DEEILOPPPTY POLYPEPTIDE
DEEILORRSSW WORLD SERIES

DEEILQRRRSU RED SQUIRREL
DEEIMMNORTU ENDOMETRIUM
DEEIMNNORUU ENDONEURIUM
DEEIMNOSSTU SEDIMENTOUS
DEEIMOOPRTT DIOPTOMETER
DEEIMOPRRST MISREPORTED
DEEINNNORST NONRESIDENT
DEEINNOPSST POINTEDNESS
DEEINNOSTTU TENDENTIOUS
DEEINNPRSTU SUPERINTEND
DEEINNSSTUW UNWITNESSED
DEEINOPRSSS DEPRESSIONS
DEEINORRRVW OWNER-DRIVER
DEEINORRTTV INTROVERTED
DEEINORSSUW SERIES-WOUND
DEEINOSSSTU TEDIOUSNESS
DEEINOSSSUV DEVIOUSNESS
DEEINPRRTTU INTERRUPTED
DEEINRRRTUW UNDERWRITER
DEEIPRRSSSU PRESSURISED
DEEIPRRSSUZ PRESSURIZED
DEEKLMRSTTU KETTLEDRUMS
DEEKNNNRSSU DRUNKENNESS
DEELMMNOPSU NOMS DE PLUME
DEELMNOOTTU TOUT LE MONDE
DEELMNORTTY TORMENTEDLY
DEELORSTTUV TURTLEDOVES
DEELORSTUXY DEXTEROUSLY
DEEMNOORRSY MONEY ORDERS
DEENNOPRSST RESPONDENTS
DEENNORSSVW NEWSVENDORS
DEENNPRSSTU PRUDENTNESS
DEENNSSSTTU STUNTEDNESS
DEEOPPPRSSU PRESUPPOSED
DEFFIINORSU REDIFFUSION
DEFFILLLNUU UNFULFILLED
DEFFOPPRSUW POWDER PUFFS
DEFGGIILNTY FIDGETINGLY
DEFGGLOOOST FOOTSLOGGED
DEFGHIISTTT TIGHTFISTED
DEFGHILOOTT LIGHT-FOOTED
DEFGIIINNTY IDENTIFYING
DEFGIILNNSW SELF-WINDING
DEFGIILNPRS SPRINGFIELD
DEFGIILNRRS GIRLFRIENDS
DEFGILNNORU FLOUNDERING
DEFGJMNORTU FORJUDGMENT
DEFGNOORRSU FOREGROUNDS
DEFHHLOORTT HOLD THE FORT
DEFHIIIMRSU HUMIDIFIERS
DEFHIINPRSS FRIENDSHIPS
DEFHINPRSTT SPENDTHRIFT
DEFHIORSSSW SWORDFISHES
DEFHLLMOTUU FULL-MOUTHED
DEFHLMOOTUU FOUL-MOUTHED
DEFHLNOSSUW FLESH WOUNDS
DEFHMOOOPRT MOTHPROOFED
DEFIIINNOST DEFINITIONS
DEFIIJNSTUU UNJUSTIFIED

DEFIILMSTYY MYSTIFIEDLY
DEFIIMMNORS MISINFORMED
DEFIIMORRSV DIVERSIFORM
DEFIINNNPSY SPINY-FINNED
DEFIINORRRU FOURDRINIER
DEFILMNNSSU MINDFULNESS
DEFILNSSTUU DUTIFULNESS
DEFILRSSSTU DISTRESSFUL
DEFINRRSSUW WIND-SURFERS
DEFIOOORRSU ODORIFEROUS
DEFKLNOOORU UNLOOKED-FOR
DEFLLNORUWY WONDERFULLY
DEFOOPRRSTU RUSTPROOFED
DEFOOPSSTUY PUSSYFOOTED
DEGGHHHIILT HIGHLIGHTED
DEGGHILNOST LONGSIGHTED
DEGGIINNNSU UNDESIGNING
DEGGILOOPRS SLOOP-RIGGED
DEGGKLRSUUY SKULDUGGERY
DEGHIIINRTV DIVINE RIGHT
DEGHIILMNOS DEMOLISHING
DEGHIILNNRY HINDERINGLY
DEGHIILPPTT TIGHT-LIPPED
DEGHILNORSU SHOULDERING
DEGHINNORSU ENSHROUDING
DEGHINOORTU OUT-HERODING
DEGHINOPSTT POTTING SHED
DEGHLMOOOTY METHODOLOGY
DEGHNOORSUY HYDROGENOUS
DEGHNOORXYY OXYHYDROGEN
DEGHNORRTUW UNDERGROWTH
DEGIIIINNST INDIGNITIES
DEGIIINNOST INDIGESTION
DEGIIINPSSW SIDESWIPING
DEGIIINQSTU DISQUIETING
DEGIIKNRSTW WRITING DESK
DEGIILLMRSX MIXED GRILLS
DEGIILLNOTU GUILLOTINED
DEGIILNNNRU UNDERLINING
DEGIILNOTTU DEGLUTITION
DEGIILNRTVY DIVERTINGLY
DEGIIMNNNRU UNDERMINING
DEGIIMNNORZ MODERNIZING
DEGIIMNNPSS MISSPENDING
DEGIINNNRTU INDENTURING
DEGIINORSSS DIGRESSIONS
DEGIINPRSST SPRING TIDES
DEGIINRSSST DISTRESSING
DEGIJMMNSTU MISJUDGMENT
DEGILLNNTUY INDULGENTLY
DEGILLNOPRY DEPLORINGLY
DEGILMNORSU SMOULDERING
DEGILNNORWY WONDERINGLY
DEGILNNOSSU UNGODLINESS
DEGILNORUVY DEVOURINGLY
DEGILOOPRTY PTERIDOLOGY
DEGINNNORSST GRINDSTONES
DEGINOPRSST TOPDRESSING
DEGKLOOOORS GOOD LOOKERS

DEGLLNORSUW GROUNDSWELL
DEGLMOOORST MOTOR LODGES
DEGLNOOOPTT GOLDEN POTTO
DEGLNOPRSUY GOLDEN SYRUP
DEGLNORRSUU GROUND RULES
DEGLOORSTTY TROGLODYTES
DEGNNOORSTU STONE-GROUND
DEGNNORRSTU GROUND RENTS
DEHHIILMNOT HELMINTHOID
DEHHILMOORS HOLOHEDRISM
DEHHILNOOSW HINSHELWOOD
DEHHIMOORRS HEMORRHOIDS
DEHHLNOSTUU SLEUTHHOUND
DEHIIINOTTT INDO-HITTITE
DEHIIKNNNST THIN-SKINNED
DEHIILLOOSV LIVELIHOODS
DEHIILMNPSU DELPHINIUMS
DEHIILPRSTU TRISULPHIDE
DEHIINSTTUW WHITSUNTIDE
DEHIIRSSTVW WHIST DRIVES
DEHILNOSSTY DISHONESTLY
DEHILNOSTTW THISTLEDOWN
DEHILOPSUXY OXYSULPHIDE
DEHILORSSTT SHORT-LISTED
DEHINOORRSU DISHONOURER
DEHINOPRRST THIRD PERSON
DEHINPRSSSU PRUDISHNESS
DEHINPSSTTU STUDENTSHIP
DEHINRRSSTU UNDERSHIRTS
DEHIOOOPPRT PHOTOPERIOD
DEHIOORSSST SISTERHOODS
DEHLLOOSSSU DOLL'S HOUSES
DEHLNNOOOSW HOLD ONE'S OWN
DEHMMNRSSUU HUMDRUMNESS
DEHMMORSTUW MUM'S THE WORD
DEHMOOPPRSU PSEUDOMORPH
DEHNOOOOPRT ODONTOPHORE
DEHNRRSTTUU UNDERTHRUST
DEHOOOPRTTW TOOTH POWDER
DEIIILLSSUV DISILLUSIVE
DEIIILQRSSU LIQUIDISERS
DEIIILQRSUZ LIQUIDIZERS
DEIIIMNORSS MINOR DIESIS
DEIIIMNSTUV DIMINUTIVES
DEIIINPRTTY INTREPIDITY
DEIIIOPRRST PRIORITISED
DEIIIOPRRTZ PRIORITIZED
DEIIIPSSTTU STUPIDITIES
DEIIKKLMMMS SKIMMED MILK
DEIILLORSUY DELIRIOUSLY
DEIILMNOOST DEMOLITIONS
DEIILMPRSTW LIMP-WRISTED
DEIILNOORWW ORIEL WINDOW
DEIILNOPRRY PYRROLIDINE
DEIILOPRSTW LOW-SPIRITED
DEIILOSSTUV DISSOLUTIVE
DEIILOSSTUY SEDITIOUSLY
DEIIMNOPRTV IMPROVIDENT
DEIIMOORRST DORMITORIES

DEIIMORSSTU MOISTURISED
DEIIMORSTUZ MOISTURIZED
DEIIMQRTTUU TERTIUM QUID
DEIINNNOOTW DOWN IT IN ONE
DEIINNOSSSS DISSENSIONS
DEIINOOPRSV PROVISIONED
DEIINOOPSST DEPOSITIONS
DEIINORSTTU ROTUNDITIES
DEIINOSSSTU DISSENTIOUS
DEIINOSTTTU DESTITUTION
DEILLMOOSUY MELODIOUSLY
DEILLNORSSW WORLDLINESS
DEILLORSTUY DESULTORILY
DEILLORSWWY WORLDLY-WISE
DEILLOSSTUY DISSOLUTELY
DEILMNOOOPS MONOPOLISED
DEILMNOOOPZ MONOPOLIZED
DEILMNPRTUY IMPRUDENTLY
DEILMOORRTY DOLORIMETRY
DEILNNNSTUW WIND TUNNELS
DEILNOPRTVY PROVIDENTLY
DEILPRRSSUY SURPRISEDLY
DEIMMRSSTYY DISSYMMETRY
DEIMNOSSSSY SYNDESMOSIS
DEIMOOPRTTY DIOPTOMETRY
DEIMOPPRTTU PROMPTITUDE
DEINNPSSUUY SUNNY-SIDE UP
DEINOORSSWW ROSE WINDOWS
DEIOPPRSTTU OUTSTRIPPED
DEIOPRSTTTU PROSTITUTED
DEKLLOOPRST ROLLTOP DESK
DEKNOORRSWW WORK WONDERS
DELLNOPSUUY PENDULOUSLY
DELLNOSSSUY SOUNDLESSLY
DELMORRSUUY MURDEROUSLY
DELNOOPRSSU SPLENDOROUS
DELNOOPRSUY PONDEROUSLY
DELOOPRRSWW WORLD POWERS
DEMOOOPRRSW POWDER ROOMS
DENNOOOOPSW WOODEN SPOON
DENOOOPRSSU ENDOSPOROUS
DENOOORSSSU ODOROUSNESS
DEOOOPPRRST DOORSTOPPER
DFFIIISTUVY DIFFUSIVITY
DFGGIIINRSU DISFIGURING
DFGHIIIMNUY HUMIDIFYING
DFGHILLOOST FLOODLIGHTS
DFGIIILNOSY SOLIDIFYING
DFGIIKNNNSU SINKING FUND
DFGIILLNOWW WILDFOWLING
DFGIINNRSUW WIND-SURFING
DFGLNOOOORU GROUND FLOOR
DFIKLOPPSSY FLOPPY DISKS
DFILRSSTTUU DISTRUSTFUL
DGGIIILLNRR DRILLING RIG
DGGIILLNNUY INDULGINGLY
DGGIILMNNSU MUDSLINGING
DGGIKLNOOOO GOOD-LOOKING
DGGILNNORSU GROUNDLINGS

DGGIMNNOOOR GOOD MORNING
DGGINNOORSW WRONGDOINGS
DGHHHIIOOPTU UP TO HIGH DOH
DGHHIILNOTW WITHHOLDING
DGHHIKNOOST KNIGHTHOODS
DGHIIIIMNNS DIMINISHING
DGHIIINSSTU DISTINGUISH
DGHIIKNNOOW HOODWINKING
DGHIIMNNSTU MIDNIGHT SUN
DGHILOORSTY HYDROLOGIST
DGHLNOORSST STRONGHOLDS
DGHLNOORUUY UNGODLY HOUR
DGIIIILNQUZ LIQUIDIZING
DGIIIINPRST DISPIRITING
DGIILLNNSWY SWINDLINGLY
DGIILNNRTUY INTRUDINGLY
DGIIMNNOORS DINING ROOMS
DGIIMNNOSTU DISMOUNTING
DGIINRSSTTU DISTRUSTING
DGIKNOOORWW WOODWORKING
DGINNOOPPRU PROPOUNDING
DGINNORRSUU SURROUNDING
DHHMNOOOSTU SMOOTH HOUND
DHIIIORSTTY THYROIDITIS
DHILLNOOPPY PODOPHYLLIN
DHIMOOOSTTW WISDOM TOOTH
DHIOOOPRSUZ RHIZOPODOUS
DHLOOPRXYYY POLYHYDROXY
DHMNOOOORXYY MONOHYDROXY
DIIIIMNOSSV DIVISIONISM
DIIIINOSSTV DIVISIONIST
DIIILLNOSSU DISILLUSION
DIIILNOSSUY INSIDIOUSLY
DIIILNOSUVY INVIDIOUSLY
DIIIMNNOSTU DIMINUTIONS
DIIINOOPSST DISPOSITION
DIILLNOSSWW WINDOWSILLS
DIILNOOSSTU DISSOLUTION
DIILNOPSSTY SPONDYLITIS
DIINOORSSTT DISTORTIONS
DIINOPRSSTU DISRUPTIONS
DIINORSSTUU INDUSTRIOUS
DILMOOPSTUY STYLOPODIUM
DIOOPQQRSUU QUID PRO QUOS
EEEEFKLRSSS SELF-SEEKERS
EEEEFLRSTTT FLEET STREET
EEEEGLNNSST GENTEELNESS
EEEEGNPPPRR GREEN PEPPER
EEEEHIMNPRT HEMITERPENE
EEEEHKOPRSU HOUSEKEEPER
EEEEHNNSTTV SEVENTEENTH
EEEEHORRSVW WHERESOEVER
EEEEIINRTVW INTERVIEWEE
EEEEIKMPRST TIMEKEEPERS
EEEEIMNPRSW MINESWEEPER
EEEEKOPRRST STOREKEEPER
EEEELNPRSST REPLETENESS
EEEELRRSTTT TRESTLETREE
EEEEMNRSSTX EXTREMENESS

EEEENNRRSVV NEVER-NEVERS
EEEEPPPRSTW SWEET PEPPER
EEEFFHILRTW WHIFFLETREE
EEEFFILORTW EIFFEL TOWER
EEEFGIINNRS FIRE ENGINES
EEEFGIKLNSS SELF-SEEKING
EEEFGLLNSSU GLEEFULNESS
EEEFHIKNRRT FREETHINKER
EEEFHILNSSY FISH-EYE LENS
EEEFHILRRSW FERRIS WHEEL
EEEFHMNRRST REFRESHMENT
EEEFHOORRTT THERETOFORE
EEEFIILMPRX EXEMPLIFIER
EEEFILSSSTT TSETSE FLIES
EEEFILSTTZZ TZETZE FLIES
EEEFIMMRRSW FREE-SWIMMER
EEEFIMNNRST REFINEMENTS
EEEFLLORVWY YELLOW FEVER
EEEFNNRSSTV FERVENTNESS
EEEGGHORTTT GET-TOGETHER
EEEGGIINNNR ENGINEERING
EEEGGIINNRV VEREENIGING
EEEGGMNNORT ENGORGEMENT
EEEGHHINSTT EIGHTEENTHS
EEEGHILNNRT ENLIGHTENER
EEEGHNORSSU GREENHOUSES
EEEGIINPSST EPIGENESIST
EEEGILLLNST TELESELLING
EEEGINNNSSU GENUINENESS
EEEGINNORVW OVERWEENING
EEEGINNOSSX XENOGENESIS
EEEGINNRRTW WINTERGREEN
EEEGINPRRSV PERSEVERING
EEEGLMNNOTW GENTLEWOMEN
EEEGLNOORVY VENEREOLOGY
EEEGLNOPRRV GREEN PLOVER
EEEGNORSSSV GOVERNESSES
EEEHHILLLNP PHILHELLENE
EEEHHILPPTW HEPPLEWHITE
EEEHHIMPRSS HEMISPHERES
EEEHHLOSSUW WHEELHOUSES
EEEHHOPRTTY HETEROPHYTE
EEEHIILNNPT NEPHELINITE
EEEHIIPPRRS PERIPHERIES
EEEHILNPRRS REPLENISHER
EEEHILRSSTV SHIRTSLEEVE
EEEHIMNRSST SMITHEREENS
EEEHINNNSTT NINETEENTHS
EEEHINPSSSV PEEVISHNESS
EEEHINSSTTV SEVENTIETHS
EEEHIPPPRTW WHITE PEPPER
EEEHKOPPRSS SHOPKEEPERS
EEEHLNNOSST NONETHELESS
EEEHMMORRTT THERMOMETER
EEEHMNOQRTU QUEEN MOTHER
EEEHMOPRRST SPHEROMETER
EEEIIKLNSST TELEKINESIS
EEEIIMRSTTX EXTREMITIES
EEEIINNPSVX INEXPENSIVE

EEEIINRRTTV IRRETENTIVE
EEEIINRRTVW INTERVIEWER
EEEIIORRSTX EXTERIORISE
EEEIIORRTXZ EXTERIORIZE
EEEIIPRRTTV PRETERITIVE
EEEIKLNOSST SKELETONISE
EEEIKLNOSTZ SKELETONIZE
EEEILMMNPRT IMPLEMENTER
EEEILMNNNTV ENLIVENMENT
EEEILMNNTTT ENTITLEMENT
EEEILNNQSSU QUEENLINESS
EEEILNPRRTT TELEPRINTER
EEEILNPSVXY EXPENSIVELY
EEEILNRTTVY RETENTIVELY
EEEILNSSSUV ELUSIVENESS
EEEILNSTVXY EXTENSIVELY
EEEIMNNNTTW ENTWINEMENT
EEEIMNORSTT TENSIOMETER
EEEIMNOSSTV EMOTIVENESS
EEEIMNPRSTX EXPERIMENTS
EEEIMNQRRTU REQUIREMENT
EEEIMNQRTTU REQUITEMENT
EEEIMNRRSTT RETIREMENTS
EEEIMOPRSTX EXTEMPORISE
EEEIMOPRTXZ EXTEMPORIZE
EEEIMRRSSTV TIMESERVERS
EEEINNPRSTT PRESENTIENT
EEEINNPSSSV PENSIVENESS
EEEINORRRSV REVERSIONER
EEEINORSSSV EROSIVENESS
EEEINPRRRST ENTERPRISER
EEEINPRRRTT INTERPRETER
EEEINPRRSST ENTERPRISES, INTERSPERSE
EEEINPRSTTX PRE-EXISTENT
EEEINPRSTVV PREVENTIVES
EEEINRSSSTV RESTIVENESS
EEEIOPRRRST REPERTOIRES, REPERTORIES
EEEJMPQRUUU QUEUE-JUMPER
EEEKKLNOSTY SKELETON KEY
EEEKLNOOSTX EXOSKELETON
EEEKLORRSTW STEELWORKER
EEELLLPSSSY SLEEPLESSLY
EEELLNRSSVY NERVELESSLY
EEELLNSSSSY SENSELESSLY
EEELMNNOPTV ENVELOPMENT
EEELMNSSTTT SETTLEMENTS
EEELMORRSSS REMORSELESS
EEELNNOOPPS PELOPONNESE
EEELNOPRSTT OPEN LETTERS
EEELNRSSTTW NEWSLETTERS
EEELNSSSSSU USELESSNESS
EEELNSSSSSX SEXLESSNESS
EEELPRRSSTT LETTERPRESS
EEEMMNOPRTW EMPOWERMENT
EEEMNNPRSTT PRESENTMENT
EEEMNORSTUV VENTURESOME
EEEMNPRSSSU SUPREMENESS
EEEMORRSTTY STEREOMETRY
EEEMPRSSSTT TEMPTRESSES

EEEOPRRSTTY STEREOTYPER
EEEOPRSSTTY STEREOTYPES
EEEPRSSTTTY TYPESETTERS
EEFFGHIIRRT FIRE FIGHTER
EEFFGILNRSU GLUE-SNIFFER
EEFFGINORRS FOREFINGERS
EEFFHLNSSTU THE SNUFFLES
EEFFIILLORY LIFE OF RILEY
EEFFIILMOPR PRIME OF LIFE
EEFFIINNOSV INOFFENSIVE
EEFFILNOSVY OFFENSIVELY
EEFFIOORRST OFFERTORIES
EEFFIORRRSU FERRIFEROUS
EEFFLNRSSTU FRETFULNESS
EEFGGIOPRTT PETTIFOGGER
EEFGHIILRRT FIRELIGHTER
EEFGIINNRRT INTERFERING
EEFGILLNORT FORETELLING
EEFGILNRSTW LEFT-WINGERS
EEFGINNQRTU FREQUENTING
EEFGINORRST REFORESTING
EEFGINORSSV FORGIVENESS
EEFGLLRRTUY REGRETFULLY
EEFGMNOORTT FORGET-ME-NOT
EEFHIJLLSSY JELLYFISHES
EEFHILLNSSS FLESHLINESS
EEFHILNSSSS SELFISHNESS
EEFHILOSUWY HOUSEWIFELY
EEFHIORSUWY HOUSEWIFERY
EEFHLLNPSSU HELPFULNESS
EEFHLNOPSSU HOPEFULNESS
EEFHMORRRTU FURTHERMORE
EEFHNOORRST FORESHORTEN
EEFHNORSTTU FOURTEENTHS
EEFHOORRSTW FOR THE WORSE
EEFIIINNRST INTENSIFIER
EEFIILORSST LIFE STORIES
EEFIILRRSST FERTILISERS
EEFIILRRSTZ FERTILIZERS
EEFILLLMRSU MILLEFLEURS
EEFILLMORSU MELLIFEROUS
EEFILNORSSW FLOWERINESS
EEFILNPPSTT FELT-TIP PENS
EEFILOOPRRT PROFITEROLE
EEFILOORSST LOOSESTRIFE
EEFINRSSTUV FURTIVENESS
EEFIOPRSSTU PESTIFEROUS
EEFIORRRSTX FOX TERRIERS
EEFLLNRSTUY RESENTFULLY
EEFLMNOSSSU FULSOMENESS
EEFLMOORRTU FLUOROMETER
EEFLNNSSTUU TUNEFULNESS
EEFLNPSSSUU SUSPENSEFUL
EEFLNRSSSTU RESTFULNESS
EEFLNSSSTUZ ZESTFULNESS
EEFMOOPRTTU OUT OF TEMPER
EEFNNORRRSU FORERUNNERS
EEFNOPRSSSU PROFUSENESS
EEGGHHIINNT HEIGHTENING

EEGGHIINSST SIGHTSEEING
EEGGHILNNNT LENGTHENING
EEGGIIMNNRT REGIMENTING
EEGGIINNPRW WINNIPEGGER
EEGGIINRRST REGISTERING
EEGGILLNNTY NEGLIGENTLY
EEGGILNNRVY REVENGINGLY
EEGGILORSUY EGREGIOUSLY
EEGHHHLOOTW THE WHOLE HOG
EEGHHILRTWW WHEELWRIGHT
EEGHIINSSTW WEIGHTINESS
EEGHILNNOPT TELEPHONING
EEGHILNNSST LENGTHINESS
EEGHILNOOPS PIGEONHOLES
EEGHILOORST THEOLOGISER
EEGHILOORTZ THEOLOGIZER
EEGHILRSTTT STREETLIGHT
EEGHIMNOORS HOMOGENISER
EEGHIMNOORZ HOMOGENIZER
EEGHIMNOOTY HOMOGENEITY
EEGHIMOORST ISOGEOTHERM
EEGHINNOSTT ETHNOGENIST
EEGHINNPTWY PENNYWEIGHT
EEGHINOORTV IN THE GROOVE
EEGHLOOPRTY HERPETOLOGY
EEGHMNOOOSU HOMOGENEOUS
EEGHOSSSTUU GUESTHOUSES
EEGIILLNNTT INTELLIGENT
EEGIILMNNRT INTERMINGLE
EEGIIMMNNPT IMPINGEMENT
EEGIIMMNRSZ MESMERIZING
EEGIIMNNOPT OPENING TIME
EEGIIMNRSTV TIMESERVING
EEGIINNNRTV INTERVENING
EEGIINNORST NITROGENISE
EEGIINNORTZ NITROGENIZE
EEGIINNRSTT INTERESTING
EEGIINNRTTW WIRE NETTING
EEGIINOPRTV PROGENITIVE
EEGIINPRSTX PRE-EXISTING
EEGIKKNORWW WORKING WEEK
EEGILLLNPRY REPELLINGLY
EEGILLLSSUY GUILELESSLY
EEGILLMOOST TELEOLOGISM
EEGILLNORSV OVERSELLING
EEGILLOOSTT TELEOLOGIST
EEGILMOOSTY ETYMOLOGIES
EEGILNNNRTU UNRELENTING
EEGILNOPSSY POLYGENESIS
EEGILNPRSTY PESTERINGLY
EEGILOPRSTT POLTERGEIST
EEGIMNNOOSS MONOGENESIS
EEGIMNNORSU MONSEIGNEUR
EEGIMNNRRTU INTERREGNUM
EEGIMNNSTTU INTEGUMENTS
EEGIMNOPPST PEEPING TOMS
EEGIMNOSSYZ ZYMOGENESIS
EEGINNPRSUV SUPERVENING
EEGINORRSTU TERRIGENOUS

EEGINORSTVY	SOVEREIGNTY	
EEGINPRSTTU	GUTTERSNIPE	
EEGIOPRRSSV	PROGRESSIVE	
EEGKLLMNSUU	MUSKELLUNGE	
EEGKORRSTUW	GUEST WORKER	
EEGLMOOORTY	METEOROLOGY	
EEGLNSSSSTU	GUTLESSNESS	
EEGLOPPPTUV	GLOVE PUPPET	
EEGLOQRSTUY	GROTESQUELY	
EEGMNNORSST	ENGROSSMENT	
EEGMNNORSTV	GOVERNMENTS	
EEGNNOSTTXY	OXYGEN TENTS	
EEGOQRRSTUY	GROTESQUERY	
EEGPRRSSTTU	GUTTER PRESS	
EEHHIKLOTTW	THE WHOLE KIT	
EEHHILLNSSS	HELLISHNESS	
EEHHILMPSTT	PITH HELMETS	
EEHHILOPRST	LITHOSPHERE	
EEHHINRSTTT	THIRTEENTHS	
EEHHIOPRRSZ	RHIZOSPHERE	
EEHHIORRSSS	SHIRE HORSES	
EEHHIORSSTW	WHITE HORSES	
EEHHMOORSTU	HOUSEMOTHER	
EEHHMOPRTUV	OVER THE HUMP	
EEHHNOOPRTY	HETEROPHONY	
EEHHNOORRTW	WHETHER OR NO	
EEHHOOPPRST	PHOTOSPHERE	
EEHHOORSSUW	WHOREHOUSES	
EEHIIKNPSTY	PIE IN THE SKY	
EEHIILNOPRS	PERIHELIONS	
EEHIIMNRSTT	THEREMINIST	
EEHIIMPPRRS	PREMIERSHIP	
EEHILLRSSWW	WELL-WISHERS	
EEHILMMOSTU	MESOTHELIUM	
EEHILMNORTY	HEMIELYTRON	
EEHILMOORTT	LITHOMETEOR	
EEHILMOPPRS	SPERMOPHILE	
EEHILNOPRRT	LEPTORRHINE	
EEHILNOPSTT	TELEPHONIST	
EEHILOOPRST	HELIOTROPES	
EEHILORSSTY	HETEROLYSIS	
EEHILOSSTTU	SILHOUETTES	
EEHIMOPPRRS	EMPERORSHIP	
EEHIMOPRSTU	HEMIPTEROUS	
EEHINNORSST	RHINESTONES	
EEHINNOSSSU	HEINOUSNESS	
EEHINPSSSTT	PETTISHNESS	
EEHINRSSSTU	HIRSUTENESS	
EEHINRSSSTY	SYNTHESISER	
EEHINRSSTYZ	SYNTHESIZER	
EEHIPRSSTTU	TRUSTEESHIP	
EEHKNOORSTT	TENTERHOOKS	
EEHKOORRSUW	HOUSEWORKER	
EEHLMNOOSUW	UNWHOLESOME	
EEHLMNOTTVW	TWELVEMONTH	
EEHLOPRRSTU	REUPHOLSTER, UPHOLSTERER	
EEHLORSTTYY	HETEROSTYLY	
EEHMMORRTTY	THERMOMETRY	

EEHMMORSSUU	SUMMERHOUSE
EEHMNNOOORY	HONEYMOONER
EEHMNOOORTV	OVER THE MOON
EEHMNOOPRSS	MESONEPHROS
EEHNNORRRST	NORTHERNERS
EEHNNORSSTT	HORNET'S NEST
EEHNOOOPRSZ	OZONOSPHERE
EEHNORRSSTU	SOUTHERNERS
EEHNORRSTTW	NORTHWESTER
EEHOOPPRRST	TROPOSPHERE
EEHOOPRRSTU	PORTERHOUSE
EEHOOPRRSTY	HETEROSPORY
EEHOOPRSSUW	POWERHOUSES
EEHOOPRSTTT	PHOTOSETTER
EEHOORSSSTU	STOREHOUSES
EEHORSSTTUW	SOUTHWESTER
EEIIIMNNSTU	EINSTEINIUM
EEIIINNSSTV	INSENSITIVE
EEIIINSTTVV	INVESTITIVE
EEIIKLLNNNS	ENNISKILLEN
EEIIKLNPRSW	PERIWINKLES
EEIILLMMRST	MILLIMETRES
EEIILLNRSTY	RESILIENTLY
EEIILLPPRST	PIPISTRELLE
EEIILLPRSTV	SPIRIT LEVEL
EEIILMNOSST	SOLEMNITIES
EEIILMNRSSS	MISERLINESS
EEIILNNPRRT	LINE PRINTER
EEIILNNSTVY	INTENSIVELY
EEIILNNTVVY	INVENTIVELY
EEIILNOSSTV	TELEVISIONS
EEIILNRSSSV	SILVERINESS
EEIILNSSTVY	SENSITIVELY
EEIILPRSSTT	PRIESTLIEST
EEIILQSTUXY	EXQUISITELY
EEIILRRSSST	STERILISERS
EEIILRRSSTZ	STERILIZERS
EEIIMNNPRTT	IMPERTINENT
EEIIMNOSSTT	TESTIMONIES
EEIIMNPRRUU	PERINEURIUM
EEIINNNNSTY	NINETY-NINES
EEIINNNOSTT	NONENTITIES
EEIINNOOPRT	POINTE-NOIRE
EEIINNORSTV	INVENTORIES
EEIINOPRRTT	PRETERITION
EEIINOPRSTT	PETITIONERS, REPETITIONS
EEIINRSTTUV	INVESTITURE
EEIINRTTTVY	RETENTIVITY
EEIIOPPRRST	PROPRIETIES
EEIIOPPRSTV	PREPOSITIVE
EEIIOPRSSTT	POSTERITIES
EEIIOPRSTTU	REPETITIOUS
EEIIORRRSTT	TERRITORIES
EEIIORRSSST	ROTISSERIES
EEIIPQRSSTU	PERQUISITES
EEIIRSTTTUV	RESTITUTIVE
EEIKNRRSSTT	RENT STRIKES
EEILLMNOPRT	MONTPELLIER
EEILLMOOPRT	TROMPE L'OEIL

EEILLMPPPRS	PEPPER MILLS
EEILLMPRTUX	MULTIPLEXER
EEILLNOPQTU	EQUIPOLLENT
EEILLNOSSSY	NOISELESSLY
EEILLNPSSSY	SPINELESSLY
EEILLOPSVXY	EXPLOSIVELY
EEILLPRSUVY	REPULSIVELY
EEILMNNOTVV	INVOLVEMENT
EEILMNNSSTT	ENLISTMENTS
EEILMNOOSST	EMOTIONLESS
EEILMOPRTUV	PLUVIOMETER
EEILNNPRTTY	PERTINENTLY
EEILNNSSSSS	SINLESSNESS
EEILNOPRRST	INTERLOPERS
EEILNSSSSTW	WITLESSNESS
EEILOPRSSTY	PROSELYTISE
EEILOPRSTYZ	PROSELYTIZE
EEIMMNOPRTV	IMPROVEMENT
EEIMMNPRSST	IMPRESSMENT
EEIMMNRSSSU	SUMMERINESS
EEIMMOPRRSV	PRIME MOVERS
EEIMNNNORTV	ENVIRONMENT
EEIMNNNRSTT	INTERNMENTS
EEIMNNOOSSS	NOISOMENESS
EEIMNNOPRST	OMNIPRESENT
EEIMNNORSSV	MONS VENERIS
EEIMNNOSSSW	WINSOMENESS
EEIMNNSSTTV	INVESTMENTS
EEIMNOPRSTU	PERITONEUMS
EEIMNORSTZZ	INTERMEZZOS
EEIMNPPPRST	PEPPERMINTS
EEIMNRSSTTW	WESTMINSTER
EEIMOPPRSSU	SUPERIMPOSE
EEIMPPRSTUV	PRESUMPTIVE
EEINNNORRTU	INTERNEURON
EEINNNOSTTX	NONEXISTENT
EEINNOPRSST	PRETENSIONS
EEINNOSSSUV	ENVIOUSNESS
EEINNOSSTTU	SENTENTIOUS
EEINOPRRSSS	REPRESSIONS
EEINOPRRSSV	PERVERSIONS
EEINOPRSSSX	EXPRESSIONS
EEINOPRSTTU	PRETENTIOUS
EEINOPSSSTU	PITEOUSNESS
EEINOQRSSTU	QUESTIONERS
EEINORRSTUV	ENTEROVIRUS
EEINORSSSSU	SERIOUSNESS
EEINPRRRTTU	INTERRUPTER
EEINPRTTTWY	TYPEWRITTEN
EEIOPSSSSSV	POSSESSIVES
EEIPPRSSSUV	SUPPRESSIVE
EEIPRRRSSSU	PRESSURISER
EEIPRRRSSUZ	PRESSURIZER
EEIPRRSTTWY	TYPEWRITERS
EEIPRSSSSTT	STEPSISTERS
EEJLNOSSSSY	JOYLESSNESS
EEKKOORRRTV	VOORTREKKER
EEKLORRSTTW	TRESTLEWORK
EEKMNNPSSTU	UNKEMPTNESS
EEKNOORRSTW	STONEWORKER
EELLLLOPSTU	LULL TO SLEEP
EELLLOORRTW	ROLLER TOWEL
EELLNNOSSSW	SWOLLENNESS
EELLNOOSTWY	YELLOWSTONE
EELLNOPSTUY	PLENTEOUSLY
EELLNPRTUUV	PULVERULENT
EELLOPRSSWY	POWERLESSLY
EELLORRSTTY	STORYTELLER
EELMMNOPSTY	EMPLOYMENTS
EELMNOSSSUU	EMULOUSNESS
EELMNPPSSTU	SUPPLEMENTS
EELNNSSSSSU	SUNLESSNESS
EELNOOPPSTW	TOWNSPEOPLE
EELNOORRSUY	ERRONEOUSLY
EELNOPRSTYY	POLYSTYRENE
EELOPPRSSSU	PURPOSELESS
EELOPRRSSUW	LOW-PRESSURE
EEMNNRSTTTU	ENTRUSTMENT
EEMNOORSTTY	ENTEROSTOMY
EEMNORSSTTW	WESTERNMOST
EEMOORRSTTU	TORTURESOME
EEMOPSSTTUU	TEMPESTUOUS
EENNOORSSSU	ONEROUSNESS
EENNOORSTTT	ROTTENSTONE
EENNORSSSUV	NERVOUSNESS
EENNOSSSTUU	TENUOUSNESS
EENNPPRTTYY	PRETTY PENNY
EEOOPRRSSSS	REPOSSESSOR
EEOPQRSSTTU	REQUEST STOP
EFFGHHHIIRS	HIGH SHERIFF
EFFGHIINNOT	IN THE OFFING
EFFGHIINOTT	IN THE GIFT OF
EFFGHIINRSS	FISH FINGERS
EFFGHILNRSU	RESHUFFLING
EFFGILLNOST	TELLING-OFFS
EFFGILNOSXY	FLYING FOXES
EFFGILNRSUY	SUFFERINGLY
EFFGLLORTUY	FORGETFULLY
EFFHOOOPSTT	PHOTO-OFFSET
EFFIOORRSTT	FIRST-FOOTER
EFGGHIINNRT	FRIGHTENING
EFGGHIIRRST	TRIGGERFISH
EFGGIINNRRS	RING FINGERS
EFGGIINNRTY	GENTRIFYING
EFGGIINPRRU	PREFIGURING
EFGHHIILOPR	HIGH PROFILE
EFGHHOORTTU	FORETHOUGHT
EFGHIIKNRSS	KINGFISHERS
EFGHIILNOST	LINE OF SIGHT
EFGHIILNSST	FLIGHTINESS
EFGHIIPRSST	PRISEFIGHTS
EFGHIIPRSTZ	PRIZEFIGHTS
EFGHILOOSST	LOSE SIGHT OF
EFGHIMNORSS	FISHMONGERS
EFGHINORSSU	SURGEONFISH
EFGIIILLNNR	FRINGILLINE
EFGIIILNRTZ	FERTILIZING
EFGIIINRVVY	REVIVIFYING

EFGIILLMORU FLORILEGIUM	EFLLNSSSTUU LUSTFULNESS
EFGIILMNSTT FILMSETTING	EFLMOORRTUY FLUOROMETRY
EFGIILMNSUY EMULSIFYING	EFLNNOORRSS FORLORNNESS
EFGIILNPSTY SELF-PITYING	EFLNNORTUUX NEUTRON FLUX
EFGIINNPRRT FINGERPRINT	EFLOPRSSUUU SUPERFLUOUS
EFGIINPRTTY PRETTIFYING	EFNNNORRRTU FRONT-RUNNER
EFGILLLORWY GILLYFLOWER	EFNOOPRRTTY PORT OF ENTRY
EFGILLORRSW FLOWER GIRLS	EFOOPRRSSTU FOUR-POSTERS
EFGILNOORVW OVERFLOWING	EGGGINOPRRU GINGER GROUP
EFGILNORSTY FOSTERINGLY	EGGHHIILTTW LIGHTWEIGHT
EFGINORRSUU FERRUGINOUS	EGGHHINOSSS HOGGISHNESS
EFGIOPRSSUY GYPSIFEROUS	EGGHIINOTUW OUTWEIGHING
EFGLNNOSSSU SONGFULNESS	EGGHIINPSSS PIGGISHNESS
EFHIINRSSTT THRIFTINESS	EGGHIINRRTW RIGHT-WINGER
EFHILLOPSSW FELLOWSHIPS	EGGHLNOORSW HORNSWOGGLE
EFHILLOSTWW WOLF WHISTLE	EGGIILLNNRY LINGERINGLY
EFHILLSSSTY SHIFTLESSLY	EGGIILQSSTU SQUIGGLIEST
EFHILNOOSSS FOOLISHNESS	EGGIINNRTWW WRINGING WET
EFHILNOSSSW WOLFISHNESS	EGGILLLNRUY GRUELLINGLY
EFHILNSSSUW WISHFULNESS	EGGILLNORWY GLOWERINGLY
EFHILOPRSST SHOPLIFTERS	EGGINOPRRSS PROGRESSING
EFHIMORRSTX SIXTH-FORMER	EGGINOSSSTU SUGGESTIONS
EFHINOPPSSS FOPPISHNESS	EGGLNOOOORTY GERONTOLOGY
EFHLNOOOPRR FORLORN HOPE	EGHHIIKNTTW WHITE KNIGHT
EFHLNRSSTUU HURTFULNESS	EGHHIINNOST HIGH-TENSION
EFHMORRSTTU FURTHERMOST	EGHHIIPRSST HIGH PRIESTS
EFHOOOPRRSW SHOWERPROOF	EGHHIJMPRSU HIGH JUMPERS
EFIIIIMNRST INFIRMITIES	EGHHILNNORS ENGLISH HORN
EFIIIINNSTV INFINITIVES	EGHHILOPRSY HIEROGLYPHS
EFIIILNRTTY INFERTILITY	EGHHILOSSTU HOUSE LIGHTS, LIGHTHOUSES
EFIIILORSTV FRIVOLITIES	EGHHLOSSTTU THOUGHTLESS
EFIIIMNNNSS SINN FEINISM	EGHIILLNRSV SHRIVELLING
EFIIINORRTY INFERIORITY	EGHIILLNRSY RELISHINGLY
EFIIKRRSSTT FIRST STRIKE	EGHIILLNSWW WELL-WISHING
EFIILNPSSTU PITIFULNESS	EGHIILNPRSY PERISHINGLY
EFIINNORSTU INTERFUSION	EGHIILNRSSS GIRLISHNESS
EFIINOOPTVW POINT OF VIEW	EGHIILNRSVY SHIVERINGLY
EFIINOPRSSU SPINIFEROUS	EGHIILNSSST SIGHTLINESS
EFIINORRSUU URINIFEROUS	EGHIILOORST HIEROLOGIST
EFIIOPRRSSU SPIRIFEROUS	EGHIINNOPSS SPHINGOSINE
EFIKLLNSSSU SKILFULNESS	EGHIIOPPRSU HIPPO REGIUS
EFIKLOORTTU OUT OF KILTER	EGHIIRSSSTU RIGHTS ISSUE
EFILLLMOSUU MELLIFLUOUS	EGHILMNOORT MOONLIGHTER
EFILLLNPTUY PLENTIFULLY	EGHILMOOORS HOMOLOGISER
EFILLOOPRSW LOW PROFILES	EGHILMOOORZ HOMOLOGIZER
EFILLRSSTUY FRUITLESSLY	EGHILMOOSTY MYTHOLOGIES,
EFILNSSSTUW WISTFULNESS	MYTHOLOGISE
EFILOOPRRSU PROLIFEROUS	EGHILMOOTYZ MYTHOLOGIZE
EFILPRSTUUY SUPERFLUITY	EGHILNOOPST NEPHOLOGIST, PHENOLOGIST
EFIMNNORSSU UNIFORMNESS	EGHILNOOSTT ETHNOLOGIST
EFIMNORSSTU MISFORTUNES	EGHILNOSSST GHOSTLINESS
EFINNORRRTU IN RETURN FOR	EGHILORSTUY RIGHTEOUSLY
EFINOOORSUZ OZONIFEROUS	EGHIMNNORSU NURSING HOME
EFINOOPRSSS PROFESSIONS	EGHIMNOSTUU HUGUENOTISM
EFINOPRRSST FIRST PERSON	EGHIMOOTTUV GIVE MOUTH TO
EFINORSSSUU FURIOUSNESS	EGHINNNOSST NOTHINGNESS
EFINORSSTTU STONE FRUITS	EGHINNPSSSU PUSHINGNESS
EFIORRSTTUY YTTRIFEROUS	EGHINOPPRSY PROPHESYING
EFLLNOSSSUU SOULFULNESS	EGHINORSSST SHOESTRINGS

EGHINORSSSU ROGUISHNESS
EGHINORSTUU UNRIGHTEOUS
EGHINPRSSTU UPRIGHTNESS
EGHIORRSTTW GHOSTWRITER
EGHKNOOPRSU ROUGH-SPOKEN
EGHLLLPPTUU PULL THE PLUG
EGHOORRTUVW OVERWROUGHT
EGIIILLMNPR IMPERILLING
EGIIILMNORS RELIGIONISM
EGIIILNNNRT INTERLINING
EGIIILNRSTZ STERILIZING
EGIIILORRSU IRRELIGIOUS
EGIIILORSTY RELIGIOSITY
EGIIIMNNRST MINISTERING
EGIIIMNOPTZ EPITOMIZING
EGIIINNOPRT PRE-IGNITION
EGIIINNOPTT PETITIONING
EGIIINNSSTZ SENSITIZING
EGIIJNNOSTT JETTISONING
EGIIKNPRSTT SPIRKETTING
EGIIILLMNPSS MISSPELLING
EGIIILLNNSSW WILLINGNESS
EGIIILLNORTU GUILLOTINER
EGIIILLNORTY LOITERINGLY
EGIIILLNOSTU GUILLOTINES
EGIIILLORSUY RELIGIOUSLY
EGIIILMMNRSY SIMMERINGLY
EGIIILMNNOSU EMULSIONING
EGIIILMNNOSZ SOLEMNIZING
EGIIILMNNSSS SMILINGNESS
EGIIILMNPRSY SIMPERINGLY
EGIIILNNOSTU LENTIGINOUS
EGIIILNNOSUY INGENIOUSLY
EGIIILNNPRST SPLINTERING
EGIIILNPRUVZ PULVERIZING
EGIIILNQRUVY QUIVERINGLY
EGIIILNRSSST GRISTLINESS
EGIIILNRSSTY RESISTINGLY
EGIIILNRTTTY TITTERINGLY
EGIIIMNNORSZ SERMONIZING
EGIIIMNNRTTU UNREMITTING
EGIIIMNOPRTZ TEMPORIZING
EGIIINNNNSSW WINNINGNESS
EGIIINNOPRST INTERPOSING
EGIIINNOQSTU QUESTIONING
EGIIINNPRSSS SPRINGINESS
EGIIINNRSSST STRINGINESS
EGIIINOPRSSU SERPIGINOUS
EGIIINOPRTTU PIROUETTING
EGIIINORRRTZ TERRORIZING
EGIIINORSTUV VERTIGINOUS
EGIIINPRSSUV SUPERVISING
EGIIINPRTTWY TYPEWRITING
EGIIIOPRSSTU PRESTIGIOUS
EGIKLLNNORS SNORKELLING
EGIKLNOOOORV OVERLOOKING
EGIKNOORRVW OVERWORKING
EGILLLNOTXY EXTOLLINGLY
EGILLLOOVXY VEXILLOLOGY

EGILLLSSTUY GUILTLESSLY
EGILLNNOSTW WELLINGTONS
EGILLNORTVY REVOLTINGLY
EGILLNORVVY REVOLVINGLY
EGILLNPRSSW WELLSPRINGS
EGILMNOORTY TERMINOLOGY
EGILMNOPSTT MELTING POTS
EGILMNPRSUY PRESUMINGLY
EGILMNRTTUY MUTTERINGLY
EGILMOORSTT METROLOGIST
EGILMOOSTTY ETYMOLOGIST
EGILNNNOOSU UNLOOSENING
EGILNNOPSSS SLOPINGNESS
EGILNNOSUUY INGENUOUSLY
EGILNNRSTTY STRINGENTLY
EGILNOOOPST STOOLPIGEON
EGILNOORSTU NEUROLOGIST
EGILNOPRRVY REPROVINGLY
EGILNOSSTUU LOUNGE SUITS
EGILNPRSTTU SPLUTTERING
EGILOOOSSTT OSTEOLOGIST
EGILOOPRSTT PETROLOGIST
EGILOOSSSTX SEXOLOGISTS
EGIMNNOORRS IRONMONGERS
EGIMNNOORRY IRONMONGERY
EGIMNOORRSV MISGOVERNOR
EGIMNOORRTT TRIMETROGON
EGINNNORRUV OVERRUNNING
EGINNOORSTU NITROGENOUS
EGINNOPRSTY TRYPSINOGEN
EGINNORRTUV OVERTURNING
EGINOOPPRTV OVERTOPPING
EGINOOPRRSS PROGRESSION
EGINOOPRRST PROGENITORS
EGINPPRSSSU SUPPRESSING
EGJLMNOPRSU LONG JUMPERS
EGLMNNOOOPRT PROLONGMENT
EGNOOOOPRSSU SPOROGENOUS
EHHILOOPPRS PHILOSOPHER
EHHIMOOPRRT THERIOMORPH
EHHIMOOPSST THEOSOPHISM
EHHINNNSSSU HUNNISHNESS
EHHIOOPPRST PHOSPHORITE
EHHIOOPRRSW HERO WORSHIP
EHHIOOPSSTT THEOSOPHIST
EHHLOOSTTUY YOUTH HOSTEL
EHIIILNPPPS PHILIPPINES
EHIIILNPSST PHILISTINES
EHIIILOSSTT HOSTILITIES
EHIIIPRSTTW WHITE SPIRIT
EHIIKLNSTTY KITTENISHLY
EHIIKMNOOSS SHIMONOSEKI
EHIIKMRRSSS SKIRMISHERS
EHIILMRSSTV SILVERSMITH
EHIILNOOPRT HELIOTROPIN
EHIILOOPTTX TOXOPHILITE
EHIIMMOPRST HEMITROPISM
EHIIMNOSSTT SMITHSONITE
EHIINNPRSST INTERNSHIPS

EHIINNSSSSW SWINISHNESS
EHIINPRSSST SPINSTERISH
EHIINRSSSTT THIRSTINESS
EHIIOPRSSST SOPHISTRIES
EHILLMRSSTY MIRTHLESSLY
EHILMMNOSTY SEMIMONTHLY
EHILMNOOPTY ENTOMOPHILY
EHILMOOPRSU HERMOUPOLIS
EHILMORSSTY THERMOLYSIS
EHILNOORSSZ HORIZONLESS
EHILNOSSSTU LOUTISHNESS
EHILNSSSSTY STYLISHNESS
EHILOOPRSUX XEROPHILOUS
EHILOPSSTTY POLYTHEISTS
EHIMMOOORST HOMOEROTISM
EHIMMOOPSTY MYTHOPOEISM
EHIMMOORSTU MESOTHORIUM
EHIMNNORSTU NOURISHMENT
EHIMNNPSSTU PUNISHMENTS
EHIMNOORTTU NOTOTHERIUM
EHIMNOOSSTT MONOTHEISTS
EHIMNORRSTU MOTHER'S RUIN
EHIMOOPRRST RHEOTROPISM
EHIMOOPSTTY MYTHOPOEIST
EHIMOPRSTXY XEROPHYTISM
EHINNRSSSTU RUNTISHNESS
EHINOOPRRTT ORNITHOPTER
EHINOSSSSTT SOTTISHNESS
EHINRSSSTTU RUTTISHNESS
EHIOOOPRTTZ TROPHOZOITE
EHIOORSSSTX SIX-SHOOTERS
EHIOPPRRSSW WORSHIPPERS
EHJMOPRSSUW SHOW JUMPERS
EHKNOOPRSST SHORT-SPOKEN
EHLLORSSTWY WORTHLESSLY
EHLMNOPPSYY NYMPHOLEPSY
EHLOPRSSUUU SULPHUREOUS
EHMNOOOPRST MONOSTROPHE
EHMOOOOPRSTU HOMOPTEROUS
EHNNOPRSTWY PENNYWORTHS
EHNOORSSTTW STONE'S THROW
EHNOQSSTTUU QUONSET HUTS
EHOOPPRSSTW SHOWSTOPPER
EIIIINQSTUV INQUISITIVE
EIIILLLMRST MILLILITRES
EIIILMPRTVY PRIMITIVELY
EIIILNTTUVY INTUITIVELY
EIIIMMNRSTU MINISTERIUM
EIIIMNORSSV REVISIONISM
EIIINOPRSTT PERITONITIS
EIIINOQRSTU REQUISITION
EIIINORSSTV REVISIONIST
EIIINOSSSTU SINUOSITIES
EIIINSSTTVY SENSITIVITY
EIIINSTTTUV INSTITUTIVE
EIIIOPRSSTT PERIOSTITIS
EIIIRSSTTVY RESISTIVITY
EIILLLMSSTY LIMITLESSLY
EIILLMPSUVY IMPULSIVELY

EIILLOOQSSU SOLILOQUIES, SOLILOQUISE
EIILLOOQSUZ SOLILOQUIZE
EIILMOPRSUY IMPERIOUSLY
EIILNNSSTTY INSISTENTLY
EIILNOOPPRT LIPOPROTEIN
EIILNOPRSTV SILVERPOINT
EIIMNNOOPRT PREMONITION
EIIMNNOPRTU PREMUNITION
EIIMNOPRSSS IMPRESSIONS
EIIMNOPSSSU IMPIOUSNESS
EIIMNORRTTT INTERMITTOR
EIIMOORRSTU MERITORIOUS
EIIMOPPRRTY IMPROPRIETY
EIIMOPRSSST PRESTISSIMO
EIIMOPSTTUY IMPETUOSITY
EIIMORRSSTU MOISTURISER
EIIMORRSTUZ MOISTURIZER
EIINOOPPRST PREPOSITION
EIINOOPRRSV PROVISIONER
EIINOOPSSTX EXPOSITIONS
EIINOPRSSUV SUPERVISION
EIINORRSSST SINISTRORSE
EIINORSTTTU RESTITUTION
EIIOPPSSTUV SUPPOSITIVE
EIIOPRRSTUY SUPERIORITY
EIKLLORRSTW TRELLISWORK
EILLLMNOOPP LOLLIPOP MEN
EILLLOORSTT TOILET ROLLS
EILLNOPSSTY POINTLESSLY
EILLORSTTTU LITTERLOUTS
EILMNNOPRTY PROMINENTLY
EILMNOOOPRS MONOPOLISER
EILMNOOOPRZ MONOPOLIZER
EILMNOSSYYZ ENZYMOLYSIS
EILMOPRSSTY PROSELYTISM
EILMOPRTUVY PLUVIOMETRY
EILMOPSTUUY IMPETUOUSLY
EILMORSTTUY MULTISTOREY
EILNOORSSTU RESOLUTIONS
EILNOORSTUV REVOLUTIONS
EILNOPRSUUY PENURIOUSLY
EILNPQSTTUU QUINTUPLETS
EILOOPRSSTY PROTEOLYSIS
EIMNNOOSSSU OMINOUSNESS
EIMNNRSSTTU INSTRUMENTS
EIMNOOPRRTY PREMONITORY
EIMNOOPRSSS SPOONERISMS
EIMNOOQSTTU MOSQUITO NET
EIMNOORSTTU NEUROTOMIST
EIMNOPPRSTU PRESUMPTION
EIMOOPRSTTT OPTOMETRIST
EIMOORRSUVV VERMIVOROUS
EINNOOPPRTU INOPPORTUNE
EINNOOPRSSS RESPONSIONS
EINNOOSSSUX NOXIOUSNESS
EINNOPSSSSU SUSPENSIONS
EINNOQRSTUU NON SEQUITUR
EINNOSSSSUU SINUOUSNESS
EINOOPPRSTW POWER POINTS

543

EINOOPSSSSS POSSESSIONS
EINOORSSSTU RIOTOUSNESS
EINOPPRSSSU SUPPRESSION
EINOPSSTTTY STENOTYPIST
EINOQRSTTUU TOURNIQUETS
EINORSSTTUY STRENUOSITY
EIOOPPRRRST PROPRIETORS
EIOORRSTVWY IVORY TOWERS
EIOPRRSSSUV SUPERVISORS
EIOPRRSSUVY SUPERVISORY
EIOPRSSTTTU PROSTITUTES
EIOQRRSTTUU TRIQUETROUS
EKKOOPPRSVY PROKOPYEVSK
EKLNOOPSTUY OUTSPOKENLY
EKNNNNOSSUW UNKNOWNNESS
EKNORRSTTUU TRUNK ROUTES
ELLMNNOOSTY SOMNOLENTLY
ELLMORSTUUY TREMULOUSLY
ELLOQRSUUUY QUERULOUSLY
ELMNOPPSUYY MONEY SUPPLY
ELNOOORTTUY ONLY TOO TRUE
ELNOQPPRTUY OPPORTUNELY
ELNORSSTUUY STRENUOUSLY
EMMOOPRSSTT POSTMORTEMS
EMNOOPPSSSU POMPOUSNESS
EMOOORRSSTV SERVOMOTORS
EMORRSTTUYY MYSTERY TOUR
ENNOOPPRRSU PROPER NOUNS
EOPPRRSSSSU SUPPRESSORS
FFGHILLRTUY FRIGHTFULLY
FGGHIINOTTU OUTFIGHTING
FGGIILNORVY FORGIVINGLY
FGHHIINSSTT NIGHT SHIFTS
FGHIILNOPST SHOPLIFTING
FGHIILNORSU FLOURISHING
FGHIINNRSSU FURNISHINGS
FGHIINRSSTT FIRST NIGHTS
FGHILNORTTY FORTNIGHTLY
FGHILOPTTTU PUT TO FLIGHT
FGIIILMNPSY SIMPLIFYING
FGIIILNOSSZ FOSSILIZING
FGIIILLNOORT ROOT FILLING
FGIIILMNNORY INFORMINGLY
FGIILNSTTUY STULTIFYING
FGIINRRSSTT FIRST-STRING
FGIKNNORSTU TUNING FORKS
FGIOORRSUUV FRUGIVOROUS
FHHIINOOPST PHOTO FINISH
FHHIORRSSTT SHORT SHRIFT
FHILMOORRRS HORROR FILMS
FHINORRSSTT SHIRTFRONTS
FHMOOORTUUU OUT OF HUMOUR
FIIIMNNOSSU INFUSIONISM
FIIINNOSSTU INFUSIONIST
FIIOOPPRRST PROOF SPIRIT
FIIRTTTTTUU TUTTI FRUTTI
FILLOORSUVY FRIVOLOUSLY
FILMRSSTTUU MISTRUSTFUL
FILNOORSSTY FRONTOLYSIS

FINOOOPSSTT SOFT OPTIONS
FLLOORRSUWY SORROWFULLY
GGGIILLNRWY WRIGGLINGLY
GGHHIILNSTT NIGHTLIGHTS
GGHIILLNSTY SLIGHTINGLY
GGHIIMNNSTU GUNSMITHING
GGIILNOPSSY GOSSIPINGLY
GGIINNOPSST SIGNPOSTING
GGILNOOORWW WOOLGROWING
GHHHIORTTUW THROUGH WITH
GHHIINRSSTT NIGHTSHIRTS
GHHIIPRSSTW SHIPWRIGHTS
GHHINOOOOPP POOH-POOHING
GHHINOOPRTU THOROUGHPIN
GHHMNNOOOPT MONOPHTHONG
GHHNORRSTUU RUN-THROUGHS
GHHOPRSTTUU THROUGHPUTS
GHIIIKMNRSS SKIRMISHING
GHIIKLNNRSY SHRINKINGLY
GHIILLLNRTY THRILLINGLY
GHIILLOOPST PHILOLOGIST
GHIILLOOSTT LITHOLOGIST
GHIILLOPSTT PILOT LIGHTS
GHIILNNPSUY PUNISHINGLY
GHIILNOORST RHINOLOGIST
GHIILOOOPST OPHIOLOGIST
GHIILOOSSTT HISTOLOGIST
GHIINNOPTYZ HYPNOTIZING
GHIINOPPRSW WORSHIPPING
GHIINOPTTUW WHITING POUT
GHIJMNOPSUW SHOW JUMPING
GHILLOOOPST HOPLOLOGIST
GHILLOOPSYY SYPHILOLOGY
GHILMOOSTTY MYTHOLOGIST
GHILNOOOPST PHONOLOGIST
GHILNOOORTY ORNITHOLOGY
GHILOOOPRTY OLIGOTROPHY
GHIMMNOORSU MUSHROOMING
GHIMNOOPSYY PHYSIOGNOMY
GHIMOOOSSYZ HOMOZYGOSIS
GHINOORRTUW WROUGHT IRON
GHLNOOPSSUW SNOWPLOUGHS
GIIIKLMNNSS MISSING LINK
GIIIKNNNPRT PRINTING INK
GIIILLNNORT ROLLING IN IT
GIIILNNPRSY INSPIRINGLY
GIIILNNQRUY INQUIRINGLY
GIIIMNNOOSU IGNOMINIOUS
GIIIMNNOPRS IMPRISONING
GIIIMNNPRST MISPRINTING, STRIP MINING
GIIIMNOPRSV IMPROVISING
GIIINNNOPPT PINPOINTING
GIIINNNPRSU UNINSPIRING
GIIINNOOPST POSITIONING
GIIINNSTTTU INSTITUTING
GIIKLNNPRSS SPRINKLINGS
GIILLLLMNOR ROLLING MILL
GIILLLNNUWY UNWILLINGLY
GIILLMNOOST LIMNOLOGIST

GIILLMNOPRY IMPLORINGLY
GIILLMNPTUY MULTIPLYING
GIILLNNOPRS ROLLING PINS
GIILMNOORSV LIVING ROOMS
GIILMNOPRSY PROMISINGLY
GIILMNOPRVY IMPROVINGLY
GIILMNQRSUY SQUIRMINGLY
GIILNNTTUWY UNWITTINGLY
GIILNOOSSST SINOLOGISTS
GIIMNNOPRSU UNPROMISING
GIIMNNOPRTU IMPORTUNING
GIIMNOORSTT SITTING ROOM
GIIMNOSSSTY MISOGYNISTS
GIIMNRSSTTU MISTRUSTING
GIIMOORRRST RIGOR MORTIS
GIINNNOOPRS SPRING ONION
GIINNNOPSTW WINNING POST
GIINNOOPTTU OUTPOINTING
GIINNOPRSST PISTON RINGS
GIINOORSTUV VORTIGINOUS
GIINRTTTTYY NITTY-GRITTY
GIJMNNNPRUU RUNNING JUMP
GIKLNNNOUWY UNKNOWINGLY
GIKLNOOPRVY PROVOKINGLY
GILLMOOPSTY POLYGLOTISM
GILLNOPRRSS SPRING ROLLS
GILMMNRRUUY MURMURINGLY
GILNNNOPSSU NONPLUSSING
GILNOOPPSTY TYPING POOLS
GILNORRTTUY TORTURINGLY
GILNRSTTTUY STRUTTINGLY
GIMNNORSTUU SURMOUNTING
GIMNOOOPRSU SPOROGONIUM
GINNOOPRSTT STRONG POINT
GINOOPRSTUU OUTPOURINGS
GMNOOORRSST STRONG ROOMS
GNOOOPRSTUY PROTOGYNOUS
HHIMOOPPRSS PHOSPHORISM
HHMNOOOOPSU HOMOPHONOUS
HHOOOPPRSSU PHOSPHOROUS
HIILLNNNOOT NONILLIONTH
HIILLNORSTT TRILLIONTHS
HIILMOOSTTT LITHOTOMIST
HIILNORTTYY HOLY TRINITY
HIIMMOOPRSS ISOMORPHISM
HIIMMOPRRST TRIMORPHISM
HIIMNOOPRST MONITORSHIP
HILNOOPSTXY XYLOPHONIST
HILNOORSSTU HONOURS LIST
HIMMOOOOPRSZ ZOOMORPHISM
HIMNOOPSSUY SYMPHONIOUS
HINOOPPRSSS SPONSORSHIP
HINOOPPSTTY PHONOTYPIST
HINOOPRRTTY THYROTROPIN
HLNOOOPPSUY POLYPHONOUS
HMOOOOPRSSU HOMOSPOROUS
HORRSTTTUWY TRUSTWORTHY

IIIILMNNQSU INQUILINISM
IIIIMMPRSTV PRIMITIVISM
IIIIMNSTTUV INTUITIVISM
IIIIMPPSSSS MISSISSIPPI
IIIIMPRSTTV PRIMITIVIST
IIIINNOQSTU INQUISITION
IIIINSTTTUV INTUITIVIST
IIIILLMNOPST POINTILLISM
IIIILLMNOSSU ILLUSIONISM
IIIILLNNOQTU QUINTILLION
IIIILLNOPSTT POINTILLIST
IIIILLNOSSTT TONSILLITIS
IIIILLNOSSTU ILLUSIONIST
IIIILNNOQSUU INQUILINOUS
IIIMNOOPSST IMPOSITIONS
IIINNNORTTU INNUTRITION
IIINNOSTTTU INSTITUTION
IIINOOOPSTV OVIPOSITION
IIINOQRSSTU INQUISITORS
IIIOPSSSTTV POSITIVISTS
IIJLNORSUUY INJURIOUSLY
IILLNNOOOPP OPINION POLL
IILLOOQSSTU SOLILOQUIST
IILLORSSTUU ILLUSTRIOUS
IILMOORTTUY UTILITY ROOM
IILOOPRRSVY PROVISORILY
IILOSSSTTXY STYLOSTIXIS
IIMNOOPRSTU POSITRONIUM
IIMNOPRTTUY IMPORTUNITY
IINOOOOPPRST PROPOSITION
IINOOOPPSST OPPOSITIONS
IINOOPPSSTU SUPPOSITION
IINOPPQRTUY PROPINQUITY
IKORSSSTTTY TROTSKYISTS
ILLOPSSUWWY PUSSY WILLOW
ILLORSUUUXY LUXURIOUSLY
ILMNOOOPSST MONOPOLISTS
ILNOOOPSSUY POISONOUSLY
ILNOOORSTUY NOTORIOUSLY
ILOOPPRSSST SPOILSPORTS
IMNOOPPRSTU OPPORTUNISM
IMNOORSSTTY MONSTROSITY
IMPPPRRSTUU STIRRUP PUMP
INOOOOPPRRST PROPORTIONS
INOOPPRSTTU OPPORTUNIST
INOOPRTTTUY OPPORTUNITY
INOOPRRSSTU PROTRUSIONS
IOOPPRSSTUY SUPPOSITORY
IOOPRRSTTTU PROSTITUTOR
LMNOOOSSTUY MONOSTYLOUS
LMNOORSSTUY MONSTROUSLY
LMOPSSTUUUY SUMPTUOUSLY
LOORRSTTUUY TORTUROUSLY
MMOOPRRSSUU RUMPUS ROOMS

545

AAAAAALMRSTT TARAMASALATA
AAAAABBCDRRS ABRACADABRAS
AAAAABBINRSST SABBATARIANS
AAAABCCHILNN BACCHANALIAN
AAAABDIINRSU SAUDI ARABIAN
AAAACCCCIRTU ACCIACCATURA
AAAACDIILPRS PARADISIACAL
AAAACDIMMNTU MACADAMIA NUT
AAAACEHHKTVW HAVE A WHACK AT
AAAACEHKMSTV HAVE A SMACK AT
AAAACEINRRSV CARAVANSERAI
AAAACGIMMNRT ANAGRAMMATIC
AAAACHILNPPS APPALACHIANS
AAAACIMNRSST ANTIMACASSAR
AAAADEHMRSTT MAD AS A HATTER
AAAAEGGLNPRU PARALANGUAGE
AAAAEGNRTVXZ EXTRAVAGANZA
AAAAFINRRSST RASTAFARIANS
AAAAGGILMMNT AMALGAMATING
AAAAGILMMNOT AMALGAMATION
AAAAILLPRRSS SARSAPARILLA
AAAAILMNPRTY MALAYAN TAPIR
AAAAILNNRSTV TRANSVAALIAN
AAAAILNRSSTU AUSTRALASIAN
AAABBCEGIRRY BABY CARRIAGE
AAABBCILLRRY BARBARICALLY
AAABBIIMNRRS BARBARIANISM
AAABCCDERRSS SACRED SCARAB
AAABCDEHLNNU BECHUANALAND
AAABCEGKPSSS BACK PASSAGES
AAABCEHILLPT ALPHABETICAL
AAABCEHILNPT ANALPHABETIC
AAABCEHLOPPR APPROACHABLE
AAABCEILLRWY CABLE RAILWAY
AAABCELNRRTU TABERNACULAR
AAABCGIINNRT CANTABRIGIAN
AAABDDJNNORY DARBY AND JOAN
AAABDEELLMNT MATABELELAND
AAABDEILMRTZ DRAMATIZABLE
AAABDEMRSSSS AMBASSADRESS
AAABDGHMNRSS SMASH-AND-GRAB
AAABDIILPTTY ADAPTABILITY
AAABDIJMNNRS BANDJARMASIN
AAABDILLOOPR PARABOLOIDAL
AAABEEGILMRR MARRIAGEABLE
AAABEEGLMNNU UNMANAGEABLE
AAABEELLNPPU UNAPPEALABLE
AAABEHIKPPPT PHI BETA KAPPA
AAABEHLMOSTT HAEMATOBLAST
AAABEIILMNNT MAINTAINABLE
AAABEILLNSSU UNASSAILABLE
AAABEILNNTTU UNATTAINABLE
AAABEINNSSST SAN SEBASTIAN
AAABELLLPRRS PARALLEL BARS
AAABELLNRSTT TRANSLATABLE
AAABELNOOPTY PALAEOBOTANY
AAABGIILNRRT GIBRALTARIAN
AAABGLLMRRRU BURGLAR ALARM
AAABHIILNOTT HABITATIONAL

AAABIIILLTVY AVAILABILITY
AAABIILLPTTY PALATABILITY
AAABILLNQRRU BARRANQUILLA
AAACCCDHIRTY TACHYCARDIAC
AAACCCEHKPTT CATCH A PACKET
AAACCDEIIMNS ACADEMICIANS
AAACCDEILLMY ACADEMICALLY
AAACCDEILMNO DECALCOMANIA
AAACCDHNRRSY CASH AND CARRY
AAACCDIINRRT INTRACARDIAC
AAACCDIIRRTT TARTARIC ACID
AAACCEEHSSTT ATTACHÉ CASES
AAACCEGILMTT METAGALACTIC
AAACCEGIORSU AGARICACEOUS
AAACCEHNOSTU ACANTHACEOUS
AAACCEIINPTT INCAPACITATE
AAACCEINNQTU ACQUAINTANCE
AAACCHILLNRY ANARCHICALLY
AAACCHILNPTY ANAPHYLACTIC
AAACCIILMRST MARCASITICAL
AAACCIINOPTT CAPACITATION
AAACCILMNOST ACCLAMATIONS
AAACCILORSTU ACCUSATORIAL
AAACDEEGKLPS PACKAGE DEALS
AAACDEELNRRY CALENDAR YEAR
AAACDEGILMOR MEGALOCARDIA
AAACDEGIMPRS PARADIGM CASE
AAACDEINRSTT TRADESCANTIA
AAACDENNOPSU PANDANACEOUS
AAACDGIIMMRT DIAGRAMMATIC
AAACDGIIMPRT PARADIGMATIC
AAACDIINNNSV SCANDINAVIAN
AAACDILLMRTY DRAMATICALLY
AAACEEEENPPRR REAPPEARANCE
AAACEEFLMNSS MALFEASANCES
AAACEEGNRTVX EXTRAVAGANCE
AAACEESSSTVW SWEET CASSAVA
AAACEFIMNORR AFRO-AMERICAN
AAACEGGGLOTU GALACTAGOGUE
AAACEGILMMNO MEGALOMANIAC
AAACEGIMNPRT PARAMAGNETIC
AAACEGIRRSWY CARRIAGEWAYS
AAACEHHNRTTU HARTHACANUTE
AAACEHILMMTT MATHEMATICAL
AAACEHIPRRTT PATRIARCHATE
AAACEHKNSSTW SASKATCHEWAN
AAACEHKRSTTT HEART ATTACKS
AAACEHLMORTY HAEMATOCRYAL
AAACEILMOOST OSTEOMALACIA
AAACEILNORTU AERONAUTICAL
AAACELNOSSTU SANTALACEOUS
AAACFGILNNRU LINGUA FRANCA
AAACFIINRRTT ANTI-AIR-CRAFT
AAACFLMNRTUU MANUFACTURAL
AAACGGILLNOY ANAGOGICALLY
AAACGGILLOPY APAGOGICALLY
AAACGIILNPST CAPITAL GAINS
AAACGIIMNSTT ANASTIGMATIC
AAACGILLLNVY GALVANICALLY

AAACGILLMMMO MAMMALOGICAL
AAACHIKPPRST APPARATCHIKS
AAACHILLLMTY THALAMICALLY
AAACHILMNRST CHARLATANISM
AAACHIMNORTU TAUROMACHIAN
AAACHIPPRRST PARAPHRASTIC
AAACIILNNOST CANALISATION
AAACIILNNOTZ CANALIZATION
AAACIILNNRRT INTRACRANIAL
AAACILLLNTYY ANALYTICALLY
AAACILLMNOTY ANATOMICALLY
AAACILLMORTY AROMATICALLY
AAACILMMNNOO MONOMANIACAL
AAACILMNOPRY PYROMANIACAL
AAACILNSTTTY ANTICATALYST
AAADDEGINSTV DISADVANTAGE
AAADDFHLLOOO ALL OF A DOODAH
AAADDGILLMOY AMYGDALOIDAL
AAADDLMNPRST STANDARD LAMP
AAADEEGGMNST STAGE-MANAGED
AAADEEGINNRV EVER AND AGAIN
AAADEEINRRSV SIERRA NEVADA
AAADEGIMQRSU QUADRAGESIMA
AAADEGMNORRS ROAD MANAGERS
AAADEGNOSTUV ADVANTAGEOUS
AAADEHNRRTTW DEATH WARRANT
AAADEILMNNRS SALAMANDRINE
AAADEILMRRRS REAR ADMIRALS
AAADEINSSSST ASSASSINATED
AAADEMNNSSWY WAYS AND MEANS
AAADFIINORST FARADISATION
AAADFIINORTZ FARADIZATION
AAADGIILLORT GLADIATORIAL
AAADGLNQRRUU QUADRANGULAR
AAADGLOORSVW AVOGADRO'S LAW
AAADGMNNNOOR MOAN AND GROAN
AAADHIINOPRS ANAPHRODISIA
AAADIILLNOTT DILATATIONAL
AAAEEGGLMNTU METALANGUAGE
AAAEEGGMNRST STAGE MANAGER
AAAEEGINNRSX SEXAGENARIAN
AAAEEGMNNPRT PERMANGANATE
AAAEEHIMNSTT ANATHEMATISE
AAAEEHIMNTTZ ANATHEMATIZE
AAAEEHIPRSST PARAESTHESIA
AAAEEKRRSTTT STEAK TARTARE
AAAEELNPRSTY PENALTY AREAS
AAAEGHLOPPRY PALAEOGRAPHY
AAAEGILLMNRY MANAGERIALLY
AAAEGINNNNOR NONAGENARIAN
AAAEGNOPRRST PERSONA GRATA
AAAEIILNQRTU EQUALITARIAN
AAAEILLLNPRT ANTIPARALLEL
AAAEILLNPSST PALATIALNESS
AAAEILMRRTTX EXTRAMARITAL
AAAEILNNNOTX ANNEXATIONAL
AAAEILPPRRSS REAPPRAISALS
AAAELQQRSUUV QUAQUAVERSAL
AAAEMMRRSSTT MASTER-AT-ARMS

AAAGGINORSTV AGGRAVATIONS
AAAGGIOPPRTU APPOGGIATURA
AAAGHINPPRRS PARAPHRASING
AAAGHIRSTTWY STRAIGHTAWAY
AAAGIILNNOTV NAVIGATIONAL
AAAGIINNOPST PAGANISATION
AAAGIINNOPTZ PAGANIZATION
AAAGIINNOSTV GAVANISATION
AAAGIINNOTVZ GAVANIZATION
AAAGILLLORRT GRALLATORIAL
AAAHHHJNPRSU SHAHJAHANPUR
AAAHIILNNOTT ANTIHALATION
AAAHIIMNNRTU HUMANITARIAN
AAAHIKLTWWWY WALK AWAY WITH
AAAHILLNSTTT HALLSTATTIAN
AAAHLLLMNPRS MARSHALL PLAN
AAAIILMNPRSU MARSUPIALIAN
AAAIILMPRRTY PARAMILITARY
AAAIILNNOSST NASALISATION
AAAIILNNOSTZ NASALIZATION
AAAIILNORTTT TOTALITARIAN
AAAIIMMNRSST SAMARITANISM
AAAIINNQRSTU ANTIQUARIANS
AAAIKLNNOPRT NATIONAL PARK
AAAILMNORTTU MATURATIONAL
AAAILNNRSTVY TRANSYLVANIA
AAAILNOPRSTY PARALYSATION
AAAINOOPPSST APPASSIONATO
AABBCCEMOOSU BOMBACACEOUS
AABBCDEKLLNU BLACK AND BLUE
AABBCEGIKKNR BACKBREAKING
AABBCGIKLLLN BLACKBALLING
AABBCIILMNO BIBLIOMANIAC
AABBDEEFLOTU FEEL BAD ABOUT
AABBEGIINRTV ABBREVIATING
AABBEGILLNRS BALL BEARINGS
AABBEIIKLLOS BIELSKO-BIALA
AABBEIINORTV ABBREVIATION
AABBEILRTTTU ATTRIBUTABLE
AABBEIMMNPSY NAMBY-PAMBIES
AABBEINRRRTW RABBIT WARREN
AABBEIRRSTTU BARBITURATES
AABBHIIILTTY HABITABILITY
AABCCDEIILRT BACTERICIDAL
AABCCDEIKNRR CRACKBRAINED
AABCCDEILLSY DECASYLLABIC
AABCCEEHLNRT CARTE BLANCHE
AABCCEELNPTU UNACCEPTABLE
AABCCEILLLNU INCALCULABLE
AABCCEILMNOR MICROBALANCE
AABCCEIRRTUU BUREAUCRATIC
AABCCENOORSU CARBONACEOUS
AABCCGIKKNRT BACKTRACKING
AABCCHHIIMPR AMPHIBRACHIC
AABCCIILOTTY BIOCATALYTIC
AABCCILLLNUY INCALCULABLY
AABCCINRSTTU SUBANTARCTIC
AABCCKLNRRTU BLACKCURRANT
AABCCKNNOSTU BANK ACCOUNTS

AABCDDEEILNT BALANCED DIET
AABCDDEEKLLP BACKPEDALLED
AABCDDEHKLNY BACKHANDEDLY
AABCDDEKLRRW BLADDERWRACK
AABCDDGINORR BOARDING CARD
AABCDEEHKLRT BLACK-HEARTED
AABCDEEIILNR INERADICABLE
AABCDEEIILLPS DISPLACEABLE
AABCDEELLLNW WELL-BALANCED
AABCDEELLLSY DECASYLLABLE
AABCDEELNORV OVERBALANCED
AABCDEENOSTU SUBDEACONATE
AABCDEFLNOTU CONFABULATED
AABCDEGIKLNP BACKPEDALING
AABCDEHIINRT DIBRANCHIATE
AABCDEHIMMRS CHAMBERMAIDS
AABCDEHORRTY CARBOHYDRATE
AABCDEIILNNS CANNIBALISED
AABCDEIILNNZ CANNIBALIZED
AABCDEIILNRY INERADICABLY
AABCDEILNSST ELASTIC BANDS
AABCDEINOORS RADIO BEACONS
AABCDEINOSTU SUBDIACONATE
AABCDEKNRRSS BANKER'S CARDS
AABCDEKNRSSW BACKWARDNESS
AABCDELLOORT COLLABORATED
AABCDELMNRSU CANDELABRUMS
AABCDELOPPRR CLAPPERBOARD
AABCDELRSTTY ABSTRACTEDLY
AABCDENOPRSW BOW AND SCRAPE
AABCDEORRSST BROADCASTERS
AABCDGINNORT CARBON DATING
AABCDGINORST BROADCASTING
AABCDGKLLRUY BLACKGUARDLY
AABCDIILLLOY DIABOLICALLY
AABCDKMNOOSW BACKWOODSMAN
AABCEEEFFILN INEFFACEABLE
AABCEEEGHLNX EXCHANGEABLE
AABCEEEHLNST BALANCE SHEET
AABCEEEHLRRS RESEARCHABLE
AABCEEFIPRRT PREFABRICATE
AABCEEGGPRRT CARPETBAGGER
AABCEEGINRTX EXACERBATING
AABCEEHLMNRT MERCHANTABLE
AABCEEHLNRSU UNSEARCHABLE
AABCEEHLOPRR REPROACHABLE
AABCEEHMNRST ANTECHAMBERS
AABCEEIKMNRT CABINET-MAKER
AABCEEINORTX EXACERBATION
AABCEELLNOOT OBLANCEOLATE
AABCEELLNSSS SCALABLENESS
AABCEFHKMOOT MAKE A BOTCH OF
AABCEFIILLSS CLASSIFIABLE
AABCEFIILLTY BEATIFICALLY
AABCEFIILNST SANCTIFIABLE
AABCEFLNRSTU BLAST FURNACE
AABCEGGKRRTU GARBAGE TRUCK
AABCEHIIMNPS AMPHISBAENIC
AABCEHILMNRS CHAMBERLAINS

AABCEHILNRTU UNCHARITABLE
AABCEHIRRRRS CRASH BARRIER
AABCEHKLNPRT BLACK PANTHER
AABCEHKMNNRT MERCHANT BANK
AABCEHLLORTT CALL TO THE BAR
AABCEHLMNORS ELASMOBRANCH
AABCEHLOPRRY REPROACHABLY
AABCEHMRRSST STAR CHAMBERS
AABCEHOPRSSU HABEAS CORPUS
AABCEIIILPST CAPABILITIES
AABCEIILLNPP INAPPLICABLE
AABCEIILLLOSZ SOCIALIZABLE
AABCEIILLRTY LACERABILITY
AABCEIILRTTY TRACEABILITY
AABCEIILRTUU BIAURICULATE
AABCEIKLLMRS BLACKMAILERS
AABCEILLLORT BICOLLATERAL
AABCEILLNUVZ VULCANIZABLE
AABCEILMNOPR INCOMPARABLE
AABCEILNNOST SANCTIONABLE
AABCEILORSTZ OSTRACIZABLE
AABCEILORSUV VOCABULARIES
AABCEINRRSTT SCATTERBRAIN
AABCEKLPPRSS BACKSLAPPERS
AABCENOPPRRS CARBON PAPERS
AABCENORSSST CONTRABASSES
AABCFIINORST FABRICATIONS
AABCFLNOORTU CONFABULATOR
AABCGHIILOPR BIOGRAPHICAL
AABCGHIOOPRS AGORAPHOBICS
AABCGHKLLNOY BY A LONG CHALK
AABCGIIKLLMN BLACKMAILING
AABCGIKLNPPS BACKSLAPPING
AABCGILNNOTU OUTBALANCING
AABCHIIMORTT MICROHABITAT
AABCHIINOOTT COHABITATION
AABCHILNRTUY UNCHARITABLY
AABCIIILNPTY INCAPABILITY
AABCIILLNPPY INAPPLICABLY
AABCIILLPRSY PARISYLLABIC
AABCIILNNOTU INCUBATIONAL
AABCIILNORST CALIBRATIONS
AABCIILRTTTY TRACTABILITY
AABCILLLLSYY SYLLABICALLY
AABCILMNOPRY INCOMPARABLY
AABCILRRSUUU SUBAURICULAR
AABCINORSSTT ABSTRACTIONS
AABCLLLRSSTY CRYSTAL BALLS
AABCLLOOORRT COLLABORATOR
AABCLNORSTUY CONSTABULARY
AABCMNNNOOTT NONCOMBATANT
AABDDEEELMNR REDEMANDABLE
AABDDEGLLLRS GALL BLADDERS
AABDDEHLLMOY HEBDOMADALLY
AABDDGHORRTU DRAUGHTBOARD
AABDDGINORRW DRAWING BOARD
AABDEEEGILRS DISAGREEABLE
AABDEEGILRSY DISAGREEABLY
AABDEEHHRRSS HABERDASHERS

AABDEEHHRRSY HABERDASHERY
AABDEEHORRTW WEATHERBOARD
AABDEEILRTTX EXTRADITABLE
AABDEEJLRSTU READJUSTABLE
AABDEELMPRTU PERAMBULATED
AABDEELNOPRS LEOPARD'S-BANE
AABDEGGLNOUY BODY LANGUAGE
AABDEGIIMSTU DISAMBIGUATE
AABDEHHIRRST HAIR'S BREADTH
AABDEHILRTWW WITHDRAWABLE
AABDEIILNRST DISTRAINABLE
AABDEIKNORST DEBARKATIONS
AABDEILLLOSW DISALLOWABLE
AABDEILNNOTT NATIONAL DEBT
AABDEIMRRSSS DISEMBARRASS
AABDELOPRRST PLASTERBOARD
AABDGIINNOST BASTINADOING
AABDGIINRSTZ BASTARDIZING
AABDGILNNSST SANDBLASTING
AABDHIKLNOSY BANK HOLIDAYS
AABDIIILLTTY DILATABILITY
AABDIIILSTVY ADVISABILITY
AABDIILMNRTY MILITARY BAND
AABDIMNORSTU ADUMBRATIONS
AABDINOOTTUY AUTOANTIBODY
AABDMOORRRST MORTARBOARDS
AABEEEEGRRSV EAGER BEAVERS
AABEEEEFKRRSS SAFEBREAKERS
AABEEEEHKRRRT HEARTBREAKER
AABEEEILMNRX RE-EXAMINABLE
AABEEEELMNRUV MANEUVERABLE
AABEEFGILLLT BIFLAGELLATE
AABEEFGILRRR IRREFRAGABLE
AABEEFHINRRT FEATHERBRAIN
AABEEFILMNST MANIFESTABLE
AABEEFLMOSTV MOVABLE FEAST
AABEEFLNRRST TRANSFERABLE
AABEEGGLMORT MORTGAGEABLE
AABEEGILMNTZ MAGNETIZABLE
AABEEGMMORRU OBERAMMERGAU
AABEEHIILRTT REHABILITATE
AABEEHILNSTZ ELIZABETHANS
AABEEHILPRST ALPHABETISER
AABEEHILPRTZ ALPHABETIZER
AABEEHLMQRSU ALHAMBRESQUE
AABEEHLRRTYZ BREATHALYZER
AABEEILMMRSU IMMEASURABLE
AABEEILNRRST RESTRAINABLE
AABEEINRRRST TRAINBEARERS
AABEEINRRSST BRAINTEASERS
AABEELLNSSUV VALUABLENESS
AABEELMNNRST TABLE MANNERS
AABEELMNORUV MANOEUVRABLE
AABEELMNRSUU UNMEASURABLE
AABEELNNORSU UNREASONABLE
AABEELNNOSSU UNSEASONABLE
AABEELNNRSUW UNANSWERABLE
AABEELNRSTTU SUBALTERNATE
AABEELORUVYY A BY-YOUR-LEAVE

AABEENNRRSTU SUBTERRANEAN
AABEENNRTUUV BUENAVENTURA
AABEFFLORTUW WATER BUFFALO
AABEFGIKNRST BREAKFASTING
AABEFHLMNOTU UNFATHOMABLE
AABEFIILNOPS SAPONIFIABLE
AABEFIILNQTU QUANTIFIABLE
AABEFLLMMNNO NONFLAMMABLE
AABEFLNORUUV UNFAVOURABLE
AABEGGGMOORS BAGGAGE ROOMS
AABEGGILLNTU AGGLUTINABLE
AABEGHIKNRTT BREATHTAKING
AABEGHILLOSU HELIOGABALUS
AABEGHIMNTTW BANTAMWEIGHT
AABEGIILMNNU UNIMAGINABLE
AABEGILNOPRU ABELIAN GROUP
AABEGIMNRRSS EMBARRASSING
AABEGIMNRRTT BATTERING RAM
AABEGIRRRSTU ARBITRAGEURS
AABEGLLRSSTU GLAUBER'S SALT
AABEGLMMOPRR PROGRAMMABLE
AABEGLNORRRS BARREL ORGANS
AABEGLRRSSUY BARLEY SUGARS
AABEHIINORST HEBRAISATION
AABEHIINORTZ HEBRAIZATION
AABEHILMNNOT HAMBLETONIAN
AABEHILMNORZ HARMONIZABLE
AABEHILNQSUV VANQUISHABLE
AABEHILNSSTU HABITUALNESS
AABEHLPRRSSV PHRASAL VERBS
AABEIIILLNTY ALIENABILITY
AABEIILLLMTY MALLEABILITY
AABEIILLRTTY ALTERABILITY
AABEIILNRRST LIBERTARIANS
AABEIILPRRTY REPARABILITY
AABEIILPRSTY SEPARABILITY
AABEIILQTTUY EQUATABILITY
AABEIKLMNSTU UNMISTAKABLE
AABEIKMNORST EMBARKATIONS
AABEIKNORSTT STATION BREAK
AABEILLMNTVY AMBIVALENTLY
AABEILLNRRTU TURBELLARIAN
AABEILLPRRTY LIBERAL PARTY
AABEILMMRSUY IMMEASURABLY
AABEILMMRSUZ SUMMARIZABLE
AABEILNOORST ELABORATIONS
AABEILNPRRST TRANSPIRABLE
AABEILOORRST LABORATORIES
AABEILOPPPRR APPROPRIABLE
AABEINSSTTTU SUBSTANTIATE
AABEKLMORRTU LABOUR MARKET
AABELLORSTTY BATTLE ROYALS
AABELMMNOSTU SOMNAMBULATE
AABELMNRSTTU TRANSMUTABLE
AABELMOPRRTU PERAMBULATOR
AABELNNORSUY UNREASONABLY
AABELNNOSSUY UNSEASONABLY
AABELNOPRSST TRANSPOSABLE
AABFGIIILTTY FATIGABILITY

AABFHLMNOTUY UNFATHOMABLY	AACCEEEILRTV ACCELERATIVE
AABFIILLMMTY FLAMMABILITY	AACCEEGHILMP MEGACEPHALIC
AABFIILLOTTY FLOATABILITY	AACCEEGHOSST STAGECOACHES
AABFLLMNOTYY FLAMBOYANTLY	AACCEEGILNRT ACCELERATING
AABFLNORUUVY UNFAVOURABLY	AACCEEHIMNOR AEROMECHANIC
AABGHIINNRSW BRAINWASHING	AACCEEHIRRST CHARACTERISE
AABGIIILNTVY NAVIGABILITY	AACCEEHIRRTZ CHARACTERIZE
AABGIILLNOOT OBLIGATIONAL	AACCEEIILLPR CAPERCAILLIE
AABGIILLNRTZ TRAILBLAZING	AACCEEILNORT ACCELERATION
AABGIILNOSST SAILING BOATS	AACCEELORRST ACCELERATORS
AABGIKNNSSSV SAVINGS BANKS	AACCEFHLRRTU CHARACTERFUL
AABGILNORSUV LABOURSAVING	AACCEGHIILPR ARCHIPELAGIC
AABGIMNRSTTU MASTURBATING	AACCEGIKNPSS PACKING CASES
AABHIIILNOTT HABILITATION	AACCEGINNTTU ACCENTUATING
AABHIIILRSSZ BILHARZIASIS	AACCEHHIILRR HIERARCHICAL
AABHIIINNOTT INHABITATION	AACCEHHMOSST STOMACHACHES
AABHIILOOPRU AILUROPHOBIA	AACCEHHPRSST CATCHPHRASES
AABIIILNOSST ASSIBILATION	AACCEHIILNPS CHAPLAINCIES
AABIIILNSTTY STAINABILITY	AACCEHIIMNRV VICE-CHAIRMAN
AABIILNOORTY ABOLITIONARY	AACCEHILLMNO MELANCHOLIAC
AABIILRSTTUY SATURABILITY	AACCEHILLMNY MECHANICALLY
AABIIMNNOOST ABOMINATIONS	AACCEHILNPRT PENTARCHICAL
AABIINNORSTU URBANISATION	AACCEHILPRTY ARCHETYPICAL
AABIINNORTUZ URBANIZATION	AACCEHIMORTT METATHORACIC
AABIINOORRST ARBORISATION	AACCEHINOOSX HEXACOSANOIC
AABIINOORRTZ ARBORIZATION	AACCEHPPRRST SCRATCH PAPER
AABIKLMNSTUY UNMISTAKABLY	AACCEIILLNRT ANTICLERICAL
AABILLMRSUXY SUBMAXILLARY	AACCEIILMRST ACCLIMATISER
AABILNSSTTUV SUBSTANTIVAL	AACCEIILMRTZ ACCLIMATIZER
AABILOPRRSTU SUPRAORBITAL	AACCEILLMSTU MISCALCULATE
AABIMNORSTTU MASTURBATION	AACCEILLNNOT CANCELLATION
AABINOOPRRTY PROBATIONARY	AACCEILLNOSS NEOCLASSICAL
AABLMMNNOSTU SOMNAMBULANT	AACCEILLOPSU CAPILLACEOUS
AABMNNOOTTUW MAN-ABOUT-TOWN	AACCEILLSTTY ECSTATICALLY
AACCCEEHILTT CATECHETICAL	AACCEILMMORT MACROCLIMATE
AACCCEGNORYY GYNAECOCRACY	AACCEILMNOPS COMPLAISANCE
AACCCEHIRSTT CATACHRESTIC	AACCEILMOSSU SMILACACEOUS
AACCCEIINRSU INACCURACIES	AACCEILMPRST MALPRACTICES
AACCDDEHIIRS DISACCHARIDE	AACCEILMTUUV ACCUMULATIVE
AACCDDEMMOOT ACCOMMODATED	AACCEILNORVY CLAIRVOYANCE
AACCDDIILLTY DIDACTICALLY	AACCEILNRRTT RECALCITRANT
AACCDDIILOPR DIPLOCARDIAC	AACCEILNRTUY INACCURATELY
AACCDEEFHHTT HATCHET-FACED	AACCEINNORST TRANSOCEANIC
AACCDEEHHIKS SICK HEADACHE	AACCEINNOTTU ACCENTUATION
AACCDEEIMORS ICE-CREAM SODA	AACCEINOORTV COACERVATION
AACCDEEINRRT INCARCERATED	AACCEINORRRT INCARCERATOR
AACCDEENNOTT CONCATENATED	AACCEIOPRTVY OVERCAPACITY
AACCDEHINORS ARCHDIOCESAN	AACCELLRRSTY CRYSTAL CLEAR
AACCDEHNORRY ARCHDEACONRY	AACCELNNOOPV PLANO-CONCAVE
AACCDEIIILNT DIALECTICIAN	AACCELPRSSTU SPECTACULARS
AACCDEIILMST ACCLIMATISED	AACCENOOPSUY APOCYNACEOUS
AACCDEIILMTZ ACCLIMATIZED	AACCEORSSTUY STYRACACEOUS
AACCDEIILLNTY ACCIDENTALLY	AACCFIIINOPT PACIFICATION
AACCDEKMPUUV VACUUM-PACKED	AACCFIILMOPT FAIT ACCOMPLI
AACCDGINRRRY CARD-CARRYING	AACCFIILSTTU FACTUALISTIC
AACCDIIILRST RADICALISTIC	AACCFIIORRST SCARIFICATOR
AACCDIILNOTU CLAUDICATION	AACCFINNORSS SAN FRANCISCO
AACCDILLLTYY DACTYLICALLY	AACCGHHIKNOW CHANGCHIAKOW
AACCDILLNORY DRACONICALLY	AACCGHHLOPRY CHALCOGRAPHY

AACCGHIILLPR CALLIGRAPHIC
AACCGHIMOPRR MACROGRAPHIC
AACCGHIOPRRT CARTOGRAPHIC
AACCGIINRRTU CARICATURING
AACCGILLOOPR CARPOLOGICAL
AACCGILLOOST SCATOLOGICAL
AACCGILMNTUU ACCUMULATING
AACCGIMNNOPY ACCOMPANYING
AACCHIIINRTT ANTIRACHITIC
AACCHIINNNOT CACHINNATION
AACCHIINRSTY SACCHARINITY
AACCHILLORTY TROCHAICALLY
AACCHILLOSST SCHOLASTICAL
AACCHILMOPRS ARCHOPLASMIC
AACCHIMNOPRT PANCHROMATIC
AACCHIMOOPRT APOCHROMATIC
AACCHINOOSTT COACH STATION
AACCHIOPRSTT CATASTROPHIC
AACCIILLLLMTY CLIMATICALLY
AACCIILLSSTY CLASSICALITY
AACCIILPRTTY PRACTICALITY
AACCIINNOSTV VACCINATIONS
AACCIINRSTTU TRACUCIANIST
AACCIIORRSTT ARISTOCRATIC
AACCIIRRSTTU CARICATURIST
AACCILLLNOVY VOLCANICALLY
AACCILLNOOSY OCCASIONALLY
AACCILLNORTY NARCOTICALLY
AACCILLNOSTU CALCULATIONS
AACCILLNRSTU CURTAIN CALLS
AACCILLORSTY ACROSTICALLY
AACCILLOSTUY ACOUSTICALLY
AACCILMNOTUU ACCUMULATION
AACCILNOOPTU OCCUPATIONAL
AACCILNOSSST CLASS ACTIONS
AACCILRRSSUW CIRCULAR SAWS
AACCIMNOPSST ACCOMPANISTS
AACCINOPRSTY PANTISOCRACY
AACCIORRSTTT STRATOCRATIC
AACCLMORSTUU ACCUMULATORS
AACDDDEEHLOR DODECAHEDRAL
AACDDEEEHLTY ACETALDEHYDE
AACDDEFIILSS CLASSIFIED AD
AACDDEGNNNOS SONG AND DANCE
AACDDGIIJNTU ADJUDICATING
AACDDIIJNOTU ADJUDICATION
AACDDIJORSTU ADJUDICATORS
AACDDIKMNNRU MANDARIN DUCK
AACDDLNORSTY SCOTLAND YARD
AACDEEFHLMSY SHAMEFACEDLY
AACDEEGHIMNT MAGNETIC HEAD
AACDEEGHLNNO HENDECAGONAL
AACDEEGILNST DE-ESCALATING
AACDEEIIMNRS AMERICANISED
AACDEEIIMNRZ AMERICANIZED
AACDEEIINQSU INADEQUACIES
AACDEEILMMNT MEDICAMENTAL
AACDEEILMRVY DEVIL-MAY-CARE
AACDEEILNOST DE-ESCALATION

AACDEEINNRRT REINCARNATED
AACDEEIPRRTV PREVARICATED
AACDEENQRSSU SQUARE DANCES
AACDEFILNSTY FASCINATEDLY
AACDEFMNRTUU MANUFACTURED
AACDEGIINPTT DECAPITATING
AACDEGILLOOP PAEDOLOGICAL
AACDEGILMORY CARDIOMEGALY
AACDEGLNOPRR DROP A CLANGER
AACDEHILLLRY HERALDICALLY
AACDEHILLNTU HALLUCINATED
AACDEHIMNRTY DIATHERMANCY
AACDEHINORRT RIDE AT ANCHOR
AACDEHLMOSUY ACHLAMYDEOUS
AACDEHLNOOPP CEPHALOPODAN
AACDEHLOPRRT PROCATHEDRAL
AACDEHLORRTT TETRACHORDAL
AACDEHNOPRTY HYDNOCARPATE
AACDEIIINPRT PEDIATRICIAN
AACDEIIIPRST PARASITICIDE
AACDEIINNORT DERACINATION
AACDEIINOPTT DECAPITATION
AACDEIINOTTV DEACTIVATION
AACDEIIOSSST DISASSOCIATE
AACDEIIPPRTT PARTICIPATED
AACDEIJLLTVY ADJECTIVALLY
AACDEILLMNOY DAEMONICALLY,
   DEMONIACALLY
AACDEILLNOSW DISALLOWANCE
AACDEILLNPTY PEDANTICALLY
AACDEILMMORT MELODRAMATIC
AACDEILMNOST DECLAMATIONS
AACDEILMRTTU MATRICULATED
AACDEILNORST DECLARATIONS
AACDEILNPPRU APPENDICULAR
AACDEIMNNOTT CONTAMINATED
AACDEIMNORSY AERODYNAMICS
AACDEIMOOSTU DIATOMACEOUS
AACDEINNOPRS CAPARISONNED
AACDEINNOSSY ASCENSION DAY
AACDEINNQTUU UNACQUAINTED
AACDEINOPSSU SAPINDACEOUS
AACDEKKNRRSY KNACKER'S YARD
AACDELMNNORS ROMAN CANDLES
AACDELMOPRSU CAMELOPARDUS
AACDEMORRRSU ARMOURED CARS
AACDFGILNNRT LANDING CRAFT
AACDFHIKNSTT THICK AND FAST
AACDFIIILNNT INFANTICIDAL
AACDGHIINNPP HANDICAPPING
AACDGHIIOPRR RADIOGRAPHIC
AACDGHILNNRS CRASH LANDING
AACDGHIOPRRY CARDIOGRAPHY
AACDGIILLOOR RADIOLOGICAL
AACDGIILLOOU AUDIOLOGICAL
AACDGIILNNSZ SCANDALIZING
AACDGIILRSTU GRADUALISTIC
AACDGILLMOTY DOGMATICALLY
AACDGILNPRSY PLAYING CARDS

AACDHHILORRY ACHLORHYDRIA
AACDHIIOPRSS APHRODISIACS
AACDHINOPQRU QUADRAPHONIC
AACDIIINORTV DIVARICATION
AACDIIJLORTU JUDICATORIAL
AACDIILLLTYY DIALYTICALLY
AACDIILLNOTY DIATONICALLY
AACDIILLSSTY SADISTICALLY
AACDIILMNOST DISCLAMATION
AACDIILNNRTY TYRANNICIDAL
AACDIIMNNORS DRACONIANISM
AACDIIMNOPSS DIPSOMANIACS
AACDIIMNRSTU TRADUCIANISM
AACDIINNORRT DOCTRINARIAN
AACDIKNNPPSS SPICK-AND-SPAN
AACDILLNORSY SARDONICALLY
AACDILLOPRSY SPORADICALLY
AACDIMMNOORT MONODRAMATIC
AACDLLNOSSUY SCANDALOUSLY
AACEEEGHNRTX EXCHANGE RATE
AACEEEGNSTTY ESTATE AGENCY
AACEEEHPRSST SPACE HEATERS
AACEEEENPRSVY SEVERANCE PAY
AACEEFFIMNRR REAFFIRMANCE
AACEEFFINOTT AFFECTIONATE
AACEEFLLPSTT CLEFT PALATES
AACEEFLMRSST MALEFACTRESS
AACEEGGILLNO GENEALOGICAL
AACEEGGIMNOT AGAMOGENETIC
AACEEGHIMNOT HAEMATOGENIC
AACEEGHNPRTX PART EXCHANGE
AACEEGHRRSST GATECRASHERS
AACEEGIMNPTT MAGNETIC TAPE
AACEEGIMNRST EAST GERMANIC
AACEEGINORSU GERANIACEOUS
AACEEGLMORTT GALACTOMETER
AACEEGLNRTVY TRAVEL AGENCY
AACEEHHIKRTT TAKE THE CHAIR
AACEEHIINSTT AESTHETICIAN
AACEEHINSSTT ANAESTHETICS
AACEEHINTTTU AUTHENTICATE
AACEEHIOPRST APOTHECARIES
AACEEHIPRSTT PARAESTHETIC
AACEEHKMNRRS SNAKE CHARMER
AACEEHLMPRST SPERMATHECAL
AACEEHLMRTTY METHACRYLATE
AACEEHNNPPST HAPPENSTANCE
AACEEIILPRST RECAPITALISE
AACEEIILPRTZ RECAPITALIZE
AACEEIIMNPTV EMANCIPATIVE
AACEEIIMNRRS AMERICANISER
AACEEIIMNRRZ AMERICANIZER
AACEEIIPPRTV APPRECIATIVE
AACEEIKLNNRS RANKINE SCALE
AACEEILMMMNY MECAMYLAMINE
AACEEILMPPRS PRE-ECLAMPSIA
AACEEILMSTUV EMASCULATIVE
AACEEILNORRT RECREATIONAL
AACEEILPRTTU RECAPITULATE

AACEEINNNRST CENTENARIANS
AACEEINNRSSS RENAISSANCES
AACEEIOPRSTT ECTOPARASITE
AACEEIRRSSTT SECRETARIATS
AACEEKLMPRST MARKETPLACES
AACEELMRRSUU RÉAUMUR SCALE
AACEELNRRTUX EXTRANUCLEAR
AACEELNRTTVY TETRAVALENCY
AACEEMNORSTU RAMENTACEOUS
AACEEMOPRTTV CAVEAT EMPTOR
AACEENNPPRTU APPURTENANCE
AACEENRRSSSU REASSURANCES
AACEFFHHNSSU SCHAFFHAUSEN
AACEFFINOSTT AFFECTATIONS
AACEFFMORTTT MATTER-OF-FACT
AACEFIIILTTV FACILITATIVE
AACEFIIINORT AERIFICATION
AACEFILNORRT REFRACTIONAL
AACEFIORRSTU SURFACE-TO-AIR
AACEFLLNORTU CALL OF NATURE
AACEFLNNORRT CONFRATERNAL
AACEFMNRRTUU MANUFACTURER
AACEGGGKLRSU LUGGAGE RACKS
AACEGGHILOPR GEOGRAPHICAL
AACEGGHINRST GATECRASHING
AACEGGINRRSU GUN CARRIAGES
AACEGGINRSSV SAVING GRACES
AACEGHHIMORR HAEMORRHAGIC
AACEGHILLPRR CALLIGRAPHER
AACEGHILMOOT HAEMATOLOGIC
AACEGHILOPRS ARCHIPELAGOS
AACEGHIMNOPR ANEMOGRAPHIC,
   PHANEROGAMIC
AACEGHIMNRSV SHAVING CREAM
AACEGHNOOPRY OCEANOGRAPHY
AACEGHOPRRRT CARTOGRAPHER
AACEGIIINRRT GERIATRICIAN
AACEGIILLNNT GEANTICLINAL
AACEGIILLNRT INTERGLACIAL
AACEGIILLOOT AETIOLOGICAL
AACEGIILMNNS MALIGNANCIES
AACEGIIMMPRT EPIGRAMMATIC
AACEGIIMNNPT EMANCIPATING
AACEGIIMNNTT ANTIMAGNETIC
AACEGIIMRRSS MISCARRIAGES
AACEGIIMRSST MAGISTRACIES
AACEGIINNRST ASCERTAINING
AACEGIINNPPRT APPRECIATING
AACEGIINRTTV REACTIVATING
AACEGILLMNTY MAGNETICALLY
AACEGILLNOSU GALLINACEOUS
AACEGILLORSU ARGILLACEOUS
AACEGILLPRSU SUPERGLACIAL
AACEGILMNNRT MAGIC LANTERN
AACEGILMNSTU EMASCULATING
AACEGILNOOSU LOGANIACEOUS
AACEGILNRTUW CATERWAULING
AACEGINNOORT OCTOGENARIAN
AACEGINNRSTW WATERING CANS

AACEGINPPRRT   TRACING PAPER
AACEGKOPRSTU   PACKAGE TOURS
AACEGLMORTTY   GALACTOMETRY
AACEGLNOOPSV   GALVANOSCOPE
AACEGLNORTTU   CONGRATULATE
AACEGLRRSTYZ   CRYSTAL GAZER
AACEHHIILMOP   HAEMOPHILIAC
AACEHIILLOPT   PALAEOLITHIC
AACEHIILLRTY   HIERATICALLY
AACEHIILNTTT   ANTITHETICAL
AACEHIIMRRST   MATRIARCHIES
AACEHIINPTTT   ANTIPATHETIC
AACEHIINRRST   CHRISTIAN ERA
AACEHIIPRRST   PATRIARCHIES
AACEHILLLTTY   ATHLETICALLY
AACEHILLMPTY   EMPATHICALLY,
    EMPHATICALLY
AACEHILLMTTY   THEMATICALLY
AACEHILLPTTY   PATHETICALLY
AACEHILLRTTY   THEATRICALLY
AACEHILMNPRU   ALPHANUMERIC
AACEHILMOPRT   METAPHORICAL
AACEHILMOTXY   HAEMATOXYLIC
AACEHILMPSTY   METAPHYSICAL
AACEHILOPRRS   ARCHESPORIAL
AACEHIMPRSTT   METAPHRASTIC
AACEHMNNRSTU   TRANSHUMANCE
AACEHMNNRTVY   MERCHANT NAVY
AACEHOPRSSTT   CATASTROPHES
AACEIIINPTTV   ANTICIPATIVE
AACEIIKLLMRT   ALKALIMETRIC
AACEIILLMNSS   MISALLIANCES
AACEIILLMNTU   NAUTICAL MILE
AACEIILLMRTT   ALTIMETRICAL
AACEIILMNSTX   ANTICLIMAXES
AACEIILNOPPS   EPISCOPALIAN
AACEIILNOSTT   ELASTICATION
AACEIILNPRTT   ANTIPARTICLE
AACEIILNRTTU   INARTICULATE
AACEIIMMNRSS   AMERICANISMS
AACEIIMNNOPT   EMANCIPATION
AACEIIMNORST   RACEMISATION
AACEIIMNORTZ   RACEMIZATION
AACEIIMNRSST   SECTARIANISM
AACEIINNNTUV   ANNUNCIATIVE
AACEIINOPPRT   APPRECIATION
AACEIINORTTV   REACTIVATION
AACEIIPRSSTT   SEPARATISTIC
AACEIJKRSTTT   STRAITJACKET
AACEIJLLMSTY   MAJESTICALLY
AACEIJLNOSTU   EJACULATIONS
AACEIKLMNOPT   KLEPTOMANIAC
AACEILLLLMTY   METALLICALLY
AACEILLMMTUY   IMMACULATELY
AACEILLMNSTY   SEMANTICALLY
AACEILLMPRSY   MIRACLE PLAYS
AACEILLNOORT   REALLOCATION
AACEILLNOSTT   CASTELLATION
AACEILLOPRTY   OPERATICALLY

AACEILLPRRST   CATERPILLARS
AACEILLRTTUY   ARTICULATELY
AACEILLSTTUY   EUSTATICALLY
AACEILMMNORT   COMMENTARIAL
AACEILMNOSTU   EMASCULATION
AACEILMNOSTX   EXCLAMATIONS
AACEILNNOPTT   PLACENTATION
AACEILNNRRTU   INTRANUCLEAR
AACEILNORSTT   ALTERCATIONS
AACEILRSTTTU   STRATICULATE
AACEILRTTTVY   ATTRACTIVELY
AACEIMNNOOPT   COMPANIONATE
AACEIMNOPRTY   EMANCIPATORY
AACEINNNORST   NONSECTARIAN
AACEINNORSTT   RECANTATIONS
AACEINOPSSTT   SPACE STATION
AACEINRTTTUV   UNATTRACTIVE
AACEIOPRRRTV   PREVARICATOR
AACEJKLNNORT   JACK-O'-LANTERN
AACEKLLNOPRS   PANCAKE ROLLS
AACEKNNORSTU   CANTANKEROUS
AACELLMOPSUU   AMPULLACEOUS
AACELMNORSTW   SCARLET WOMAN
AACELPRSSSTT   PLASTER CASTS
AACENNNORSTW   WATER CANNONS
AACENNPRRSTY   TRANSPARENCY
AACFFIORRSTT   TRAFFICATORS
AACFFMORRSTY   FACTORY FARMS
AACFGGILMNOU   CAMOUFLAGING
AACFGIIILNTT   FACILITATING
AACFGIIINOST   GASIFICATION
AACFIIILLRTY   ARTIFICIALLY
AACFIIILNOST   SALIFICATION
AACFIIILNOTT   FACILITATION
AACFIIIMNORT   RAMIFICATION
AACFIIINORTT   RATIFICATION
AACFIILMNOST   FACTIONALISM
AACFIILNOOST   FOCALISATION
AACFIILNOOTZ   FOCALIZATION
AACFIILNOSTT   FACTIONALIST
AACFIINOSSTT   SATISFACTION
AACFILLLOSUY   FALLACIOUSLY
AACFILLNORTY   FRACTIONALLY
AACFILMORSTT   STALACTIFORM
AACFINOORRTT   FRACTIONATOR
AACFIORSSTTY   SATISFACTORY
AACFKLMSSUUV   VACUUM FLASKS
AACGGHHIIOPR   HAGIOGRAPHIC
AACGGIILLNTY   GIGANTICALLY
AACGHIILLNOP   ANGLOPHILIAC
AACGHILLNOOT   ANTHOLOGICAL
AACGHILLOOPT   PATHOLOGICAL
AACGHILNOPPR   PLANOGRAPHIC
AACGHINOPPRT   PANTOGRAPHIC
AACGHINOPRRU   URANOGRAPHIC
AACGHLMOOPRY   PHARMACOLOGY
AACGHMMOORRT   CHROMATOGRAM
AACGHOOPPRSU   CARPOPHAGOUS
AACGIIILNPTZ   CAPITALIZING

AACGIIILPRST PLAGIARISTIC
AACGIIINNPTT ANTICIPATING
AACGIILLMOPX PLAGIOCLIMAX
AACGIILMNNTU CALUMNIATING
AACGIILNPTTU CAPITULATING
AACGIILNRTTU ARTICULATING
AACGIILOPRST PARALOGISTIC
AACGIIMPRSTT PRAGMATISTIC
AACGIINNOSTT ANTAGONISTIC
AACGILLMOOST MALACOLOGIST
AACGILLOORST ASTROLOGICAL
AACGILLOOTTU TAUTOLOGICAL
AACGILLRRTUU AGRICULTURAL
AACGILNNOOTV LONG VACATION
AACGIMMNNOOU COMMON IGUANA
AACGIMMOPRRT PROGRAMMATIC
AACGINOPPRTU GROUP CAPTAIN
AACGLMOOSTUU GLAUCOMATOUS
AACGLNOOPSVY GALVANOSCOPY
AACHHIIMNPRS CHAIRMANSHIP
AACHIIINNSTY HINAYANISTIC
AACHIILMOPRS PAROCHIALISM
AACHIIMNNOST MACHINATIONS
AACHILLMNNORY HARMONICALLY
AACHILLMOPSY HYALOPLASMIC
AACHILLNORTU HALLUCINATOR
AACHILMNNOSU NO SUCH ANIMAL
AACHIMMNNOPY NYMPHOMANIAC
AACHIMNNORSS ANACHRONISMS
AACHIMNOPRRS PARACHRONISM
AACHINOPRTTU NATUROPATHIC
AACHIPRSSTTU PARACHUTISTS
AACHLLNNNOTY NONCHALANTLY
AACHMOORSTTU TRACHOMATOUS
AACIIINNOPTT ANTICIPATION
AACIIINNOTTV INACTIVATION
AACIIINNRSSU UNCINARIASIS
AACIIINSSTTT STATISTICIAN
AACIILLMOTTY AMITOTICALLY
AACIILLNOOST LOCALISATION
AACIILLNOOTZ LOCALIZATION
AACIILLNOSTV VACILLATIONS
AACIILLORSTY AORISTICALLY
AACIILLRSTTY ARTISTICALLY
AACIILLSTTUY AUTISTICALLY
AACIILMMORSS COMMISSARIAL
AACIILMNNOTU CALUMNIATION
AACIILNNOOTV INVOCATIONAL
AACIILNOOSTV VOCALISATION
AACIILNOOTVZ VOCALIZATION
AACIILNOPPST APPLICATIONS
AACIILNOPTTU CAPITULATION
AACIILNORTTU ARTICULATION
AACIILNRSTTU NATURALISTIC
AACIILORSUVY AVARICIOUSLY
AACIIMMORSST COMMISSARIAT
AACIINNNNOTU ANNUNCIATION
AACIINNNOOST CANONISATION
AACIINNNOOTZ CANONIZATION

AACIINNNORST INCARNATIONS
AACIINNNOSTT INCANTATIONS
AACIINNORSST INCRASSATION
AACIINOORRTT RATIOCINATOR
AACIINOOSSST ASSOCIATIONS
AACIINOPRTTY ANTICIPATORY
AACIINORRSTU CURARISATION
AACIINORRTUZ CURARIZATION
AACIINPPRSTT PARTICIPANTS
AACIIOPPRRTT PARTICIPATOR
AACIKLMOPRSY KARYOPLASMIC
AACILLLNOPTY PLATONICALLY
AACILLLNOSVY SLAVONICALLY
AACILLMNORTY ROMANTICALLY
AACILLMNOSTY MONASTICALLY
AACILLMOSTUY CALAMITOUSLY
AACILLNNRTYY TYRANNICALLY
AACILLNOPPTY PANOPTICALLY
AACILLNOPRSS RAPSCALLIONS
AACILLNPSTYY SYNAPTICALLY
AACILLOORRTY ORATORICALLY
AACILLPRRTUY PARTICULARLY
AACILLQRTUUU AQUICULTURAL
AACILMNNOPST COMPLAINANTS
AACILMNOOPRT PROCLAMATION
AACILMNOORST ASTRONOMICAL
AACILMNORSTY MICROANALYST
AACILMORRTTU COURT-MARTIAL,
   MATRICULATOR
AACILNORSTVY CLAIRVOYANTS
AACILNOSTTUU AUSCULTATION
AACILORRTTUY ARTICULATORY
AACIMMOPSTTY ASYMPTOMATIC
AACIMNNNOSTT CONTAMINANTS
AACIMNNOOPWY COMPANIONWAY
AACIMNNOORTT CONTAMINATOR
AACIMNNOOSTT ANTONOMASTIC
AACIMOORSSST SARCOMATOSIS
AACINNORSSTT TRANSACTIONS
AACINORSSTTU ASTRONAUTICS
AACLNNOPRTTU CONTRAPUNTAL
AACLNPRSTTYY CRYPTANALYST
AACMOOPRSSST ASTROCOMPASS
AADDDEGIRSSU SUGAR DADDIES
AADDDEINRSST STANDARDISED
AADDDEINRSTZ STANDARDIZED
AADDDGLNORST GOLD STANDARD
AADDEEEGLPRS SPREAD-EAGLED
AADDEEEHHMMR HAMMERHEADED
AADDEEHHRTXY HEXAHYDRATED
AADDEEHNSSWY ASH WEDNESDAY
AADDEEIMNRTV ANIMADVERTED
AADDEFFIILST FIT AS A FIDDLE
AADDEFINORTU DEFRAUDATION
AADDEFLLNOSU ALL OF A SUDDEN
AADDEGINORST DEGRADATIONS
AADDEGNOPRRU PARADE GROUND
AADDEIMNRSTT STANDARD TIME
AADDEINRRSST STANDARDISER

AADDEINRRSTZ STANDARDIZER
AADDELNOORTV VOLTA REDONDA
AADDHIILORRT DIARTHRODIAL
AADDIIILNOPT DILAPIDATION
AADDIIILLNOTY ADDITIONALLY
AADDLLNNRSUY ALL AND SUNDRY
AADEEEGMMNNT ENDAMAGEMENT
AADEEEHHRTVY HEAVYHEARTED
AADEEEHIRSST HEART DISEASE
AADEEELNNRWZ NEW ZEALANDER
AADEEFFNORRT FORE-AND-AFTER
AADEEFHINRTT FAINT-HEARTED
AADEEFILLMRT FLEET ADMIRAL
AADEEGGLMORT AGGLOMERATED
AADEEGHINPRS SPEARHEADING
AADEEGKMNRRT MARKET GARDEN
AADEEGKNOPTW TAKE DOWN A PEG
AADEEHILNQRU HARLEQUINADE
AADEEHIMNOTZ DIAZOMETHANE
AADEEHLNNRST NEANDERTHALS
AADEEHLRSTTT DEATH RATTLES
AADEEHQRRSTU HEADQUARTERS
AADEEIIKMTVW TAKE A DIM VIEW
AADEEIILMRST MATERIALISED
AADEEIILMRTZ MATERIALIZED
AADEEIIMNNRT ANTEMERIDIAN
AADEEILNQTUY INADEQUATELY
AADEEILNRSTU DENATURALISE
AADEEILNRTUZ DENATURALIZE
AADEEIMMNNRR REMAINDERMAN
AADEEIMMNNST MISDEMEANANT
AADEEINOPRST ENDOPARASITE
AADEEINOPRTU DEUTERANOPIA
AADEEJLNNRTW LANTERN-JAWED
AADEELLLNPRU UNPARALLELED
AADEELLNPSTT DENTAL PLATES
AADEELLRZZZZ RAZZLE-DAZZLE
AADEELMNPRTT DEPARTMENTAL
AADEELOPRTTX EXTRAPOLATED
AADEEMNNRTUX EXTRAMUNDANE
AADEEMORSTWW WATER MEADOWS
AADEEMQRRSSU MASQUERADERS
AADEFFHLNOTT FAT OF THE LAND
AADEFFIIILST DISAFFILIATE
AADEFGGINRSU SAFEGUARDING
AADEFGHNRRST GRANDFATHERS
AADEFGILNORT DEFLAGRATION
AADEFHILLMRS FIELD MARSHAL
AADEFHINNOTU FOUNTAINHEAD
AADEFIIILMRS FAMILIARISED
AADEFIIILMRZ FAMILIARIZED
AADEFIKMNORR AFRIKANERDOM
AADEFILMORTY DEFAMATORILY
AADEFILNORTY DEFLATIONARY
AADEFILNSSTY SAFETY ISLAND
AADEFILNTTUY INFATUATEDLY
AADEFIMRRRSY DAIRY FARMERS
AADEFLMNNSTU FUNDAMENTALS
AADEFLOOSSST A DOSE OF SALTS

AADEGGILNNST LANDING STAGE
AADEGHIMMORX HEXAGRAMMOID
AADEGHIOPRRR RADIOGRAPHER
AADEGHNOPRRY PARAHYDROGEN
AADEGIILNNST DESALINATING
AADEGIILPQRU QUADRIPLEGIA
AADEGIIMMNST DIAMAGNETISM
AADEGIINPPRS DISAPPEARING
AADEGILLNNPS PINEAL GLANDS
AADEGILNRTTU ADULTERATING
AADEGILNSSST STAINED GLASS
AADEGIMNQRSU MASQUERADING
AADEGINNPPRS SANDPAPERING
AADEGINOPPRS PROPAGANDISE
AADEGINOPPRZ PROPAGANDIZE
AADEGLLNNSUY AULD LANG SYNE
AADEGLNPRSST STAR-SPANGLED
AADEGLNRSTTU STRANGULATED
AADEGMNRRSST GRAND MASTERS
AADEGNNPRRST GRANDPARENTS
AADEGOPRSTTU POSTGRADUATE
AADEHHIILLPP PHILADELPHIA
AADEHIKLMORY HOLIDAYMAKER
AADEHILNORRT ENARTHRODIAL
AADEHINOPRST HEROD ANTIPAS
AADEHIOPRRTY RADIOTHERAPY
AADEHMMNNRSTT HERMANNSTADT
AADEHPRRSTTU UTTAR PRADESH
AADEIIILNOST IDEALISATION
AADEIIILNOTZ IDEALIZATION
AADEIIILLNUVV VAUDEVILLIAN
AADEIILMNNOT DELAMINATION
AADEIILNNOST DESALINATION,
   NATIONALISED
AADEIILNNOTZ NATIONALIZED
AADEIILNNTUV ANTEDILUVIAN
AADEIILNORST RATIONALISED
AADEIILNORTV DERIVATIONAL
AADEIILNORTZ RATIONALIZED
AADEIILNRSTT INTERSTADIAL
AADEIIMNRSTT ADMINISTRATE
AADEIINNORST TARDENOISIAN
AADEILNNSSTT STATEN ISLAND
AADEILNORTTU ADULTERATION
AADEILNOSTUV DEVALUATIONS
AADEILNQRTUV QUADRIVALENT
AADEIMNOQSTU DESQUAMATION
AADEIMNRSSTV MAIDSERVANTS
AADEIMOPPRTX APPROXIMATED
AADEIMPRRSTY TRYPARSAMIDE
AADEINNORTTU DENATURATION
AADEIOPPPRRT APPROPRIATED
AADELLNNORST RALLENTANDOS
AADELMNNRTUU ULTRAMUNDANE
AADELMOPRRTU ARMOUR-PLATED
AADELNNPRSTT TRANSPLANTED
AADEMNNNRSTU TRANSMUNDANE
AADEMNOPPRTU PUT A DAMPER ON
AADFFFHLNOST STANDOFF HALF

AADFHHILLOSY HALF-HOLIDAYS
AADFILNNOOTU FOUNDATIONAL
AADFINNOOSTU SODA FOUNTAIN
AADGGIINNRRS DISARRANGING
AADGHHIMNNRT RIGHT-HAND MAN
AADGHIINPRSU GUARDIANSHIP
AADGHILNORSZ LOSING HAZARD
AADGHINRSSWW WASH DRAWINGS
AADGHLPRSSSU SPLASH GUARDS
AADGIIILNNTV INVALIDATING
AADGIILMRTUV MULTIGRAVIDA
AADGIILNNNOS ANGLO-INDIANS
AADGIILQRUUV GUADALQUIVIR
AADGILLNPPUY APPLAUDINGLY
AADGIMNOPPRS PROPAGANDISM
AADGIMNPRSTT TRADING STAMP
AADGINOPPRST PROPAGANDIST
AADHIIKNSTTZ TADZHIKISTAN
AADHIILOPPSY DIAPOPHYSIAL
AADHILNOOPRT ANTHROPOIDAL
AADHINPRSSTY DANISH PASTRY
AADHIOPRRSTY PARATHYROIDS
AADHJKLMMORS HAMMARSKJOLD
AADIIILNNOPS INDIANAPOLIS
AADIIILNNOTV INVALIDATION
AADIIINORRST IRRADIATIONS
AADIIKNNRSST KRISTIANSAND
AADIILMNOQRU QUADRINOMIAL
AADIILMOPRST PRISMATOIDAL
AADIILNOOSTV VASODILATION
AADIINOOTTUX AUTOXIDATION
AADIIRRSSTUV STRADIVARIUS
AADILNOPPRST POSTPRANDIAL
AADLMNNORUWY LAUNDRYWOMAN
AADMNOQRSUUU QUADRUMANOUS
AADNORRSTTUY TRANSUDATORY
AAEEEFLRSTTW WELFARE STATE
AAEEEGGHRTUW WEATHER GAUGE
AAEEEGGIRTVX EXAGGERATIVE
AAEEEGMNRSSS MANAGERESSES
AAEEEGNSSTTT ESTATE AGENTS
AAEEEHILRTTY AETHEREALITY
AAEEEHILSSTT TELAESTHESIA
AAEEEHIMMSST HAEMATEMESIS
AAEEEHINSSTT ANAESTHETISE
AAEEEHINSTTZ ANAESTHETIZE
AAEEEHLNPRST ELEPHANT'S-EAR
AAEEEHLPQRSU RAPHAELESQUE
AAEEEHNRSTVW WEATHER VANES
AAEEELMNPSTX SET AN EXAMPLE
AAEEELOPRTTU POET LAUREATE
AAEEEMNPPSST APPEASEMENTS
AAEEEMPRSSTU TAPE MEASURES
AAEEENPRSSST SEPARATENESS
AAEEFFGLNRST GENERAL STAFF
AAEEFHHILRST FAITH HEALERS
AAEEFHILRRTU HEART FAILURE
AAEEFHLMRSSU HALF MEASURES
AAEEFIILRSSZ LAISSEZ-FAIRE

AAEEFLSSTVVY SAFETY VALVES
AAEEFMNNRRTT TENANT FARMER
AAEEFNNPRSST SNAP FASTENER
AAEEGGGINRTX EXAGGERATING
AAEEGGIMNOSS AGAMOGENESIS
AAEEGGIMNRTV GRAM-NEGATIVE
AAEEGGINNRTU GUARANTEEING
AAEEGGINORTX EXAGGERATION
AAEEGGLNNOTU TONE LANGUAGE
AAEEGHLOPPRR PALEOGRAPHER
AAEEGHLRSSTW WEATHERGLASS
AAEEGHNPPRRS PAPERHANGERS
AAEEGIKLNSTV LEAVE TAKINGS
AAEEGILNOTTV VEGETATIONAL
AAEEGILNPPST EATING APPLES
AAEEGILRSSUV LIVER SAUSAGE
AAEEGIMNORST MÉNAGE À TROIS
AAEEGIMNTTUV AUGMENTATIVE
AAEEGIMPSSTU SEPTUAGESIMA
AAEEGINPRSTX EXASPERATING
AAEEGINRSSTV ASSEVERATING
AAEEGJLMNORR MAJOR GENERAL
AAEEGLMMRSSU RUMMAGE SALES
AAEEGLMNORTV GALVANOMETER
AAEEGLNRSTTV TRAVEL AGENTS
AAEEGLOPRSSS OPERA GLASSES
AAEEGMNNRRST ARRANGEMENTS
AAEEGMNOPRST POMEGRANATES
AAEEHHIMPRTT AMPHITHEATRE
AAEEHHORRTTT HEART-TO-HEART
AAEEHIIKNSST KINAESTHESIA
AAEEHIILRTVX EXHILARATIVE
AAEEHIIMPRST HEMIPARASITE
AAEEHIKNOSTT TAKE A SHINE TO
AAEEHILPRSTU LAUREATESHIP
AAEEHIMMNPST AMPHETAMINES
AAEEHINNRSTU NEURASTHENIA
AAEEHINPPRRT HEIR APPARENT
AAEEHINSSSTY SYNAESTHESIA
AAEEHINSSTTT ANAESTHETIST
AAEEHLNOPPRS APLANOSPHERE
AAEEHMNNORSUW WAREHOUSEMAN
AAEEHOORRSTT STEATORRHOEA
AAEEIIKKLLTW WALKIE-TALKIE
AAEEIILLMRSS MARSEILLAISE
AAEEIILLRTTV ALLITERATIVE
AAEEIILMNTTV ALIMENTATIVE
AAEEIILMORTV AMELIORATIVE
AAEEIILMRRST MATERIALISER
AAEEIILMRRTZ MATERIALIZER
AAEEIILNQSTU ITALIANESQUE
AAEEIILLMNPST PLANETESIMAL
AAEEIILLNORTV REVELATIONAL
AAEEIILLNRSTW ARTESIAN WELL
AAEEIILLPRSTT SEPTILATERAL
AAEEIILMNRRTW MINERAL WATER
AAEEIILNNORTV VENERATIONAL
AAEEIILNPRSST PLEASANTRIES
AAEEIILNRSTTV ALTERNATIVES

AAEEILQRSSTU SESQUIALTERA
AAEEINOPRSTX EXASPERATION
AAEEINORSSTV ASSEVERATION
AAEEKLNRSSTT RATTLESNAKES
AAEELMMNRTTT MALTREATMENT
AAEELNNOSSSS SEASONALNESS
AAEELNNPSSST PLEASANTNESS
AAEEMNNPPRSW NEWSPAPERMAN
AAEEMNNPRTWY PERMANENT WAY
AAEEMNRSTTTY TESTAMENTARY
AAEENNPPRSST APPARENTNESS
AAEENNPRSTUU SUPERANNUATE
AAEERRRSTTUU RESTAURATEUR
AAEFFIIMRSTV AFFIRMATIVES
AAEFFQRRSTTU QUARTERSTAFF
AAEFGGILLLNT FLAGELLATING
AAEFGHHIILNT FAITH HEALING
AAEFGILLLNOT FLAGELLATION
AAEFGINNORTT ENGRAFTATION
AAEFHHLOSUWY HALFWAY HOUSE
AAEFHIKLNSUV HAVE A SKINFUL
AAEFHILNRSTW FATHERS-IN-LAW
AAEFIIILMRRS FAMILIARISER
AAEFIIILMRRZ FAMILIARIZER
AAEFIILMNRSS FAMILIARNESS
AAEFIILMPSST FISSIPALMATE
AAEFILLNSSSY SELF-ANALYSIS
AAEFILMNRRST FRATERNALISM
AAEFILNORRTY REFLATIONARY
AAEFILNQRRTU QUARTERFINAL
AAEFILORSSTY FORESTAYSAIL
AAEFLLNOPSTU PULL A FAST ONE
AAEFMORRSSTT MASTER OF ARTS
AAEFORRSSTYZ SAFETY RAZORS
AAEGGGILNNSU SIGN LANGUAGE
AAEGGGINORST AGGREGATIONS
AAEGGHHIOPRR HAGIOGRAPHER
AAEGGHINNPPR PAPERHANGING
AAEGGHMNOPRT MAGNETOGRAPH
AAEGGINNPRRR PREARRANGING
AAEGGINRSTTT STARTING GATE
AAEGGNORRSUW NARROW GAUGES
AAEGHHIKNRST EARTHSHAKING
AAEGHHOPPRRS PHRASEOGRAPH
AAEGHIILNRTX EXHILARATING
AAEGHILNNOOT HALOGENATION
AAEGHIMMNPSS GAMESMANSHIP
AAEGHIMMNSTT METAGNATHISM
AAEGHIMNRRTW HEARTWARMING
AAEGHIMORRRT METRORRHAGIA
AAEGHLLNNOTT TEN-GALLON HAT
AAEGHLMNRSTU MANSLAUGHTER
AAEGHLOPRTTU TELAUTOGRAPH
AAEGHMNOSTTU METAGNATHOUS
AAEGHNOPPRRT PANTOGRAPHER
AAEGHNOPRRRU URANOGRAPHER
AAEGHNPRRSST STRAPHANGERS
AAEGIIKKLLMN MAKE A KILLING
AAEGIIILLNOST LEGALISATION

AAEGIILLNOTZ LEGALIZATION
AAEGIILMNORT AMELIORATING,
    EMIGRATIONAL
AAEGIILNRSTU ANGULARITIES
AAEGIIMNNORT EMARGINATION
AAEGIINNPPRT APPERTAINING
AAEGIINOQSTU GIANT SEQUOIA
AAEGIINPPRRS REAPPRAISING
AAEGIINPRRTT REPATRIATING
AAEGIINPRTTX EXPATRIATING
AAEGILLLLNPR PARALLELLING
AAEGILLNNTTY TANGENTIALLY
AAEGILLNPPRW WALLPAPERING
AAEGILNNSTUY NAUSEATINGLY
AAEGIMNNOTTU AUGMENTATION
AAEGIMNNRRST ARRAIGNMENTS
AAEGIMNRRSTT TRANSMIGRATE
AAEGIMRRSTTU MAGISTRATURE
AAEGINNOPTTV VANTAGEPOINT
AAEGLLORSSSU SAUSAGE ROLLS
AAEGLMNORTVY GALVANOMETRY
AAEGLMOOPSSU GAMOSEPALOUS
AAEGLMOOPSTU GAMOPETALOUS
AAEGLMOPRRSU PARLOUR GAMES
AAEGLMOPRSST ERGASTOPLASM
AAEGMOPPSSTT POSTAGE STAMP
AAEHHNOPRTTW ON THE WARPATH
AAEHIIILNNTV ANNIHILATIVE
AAEHIILMMPTU EPITHALAMIUM
AAEHIILNORTX EXHILARATION
AAEHIINOPRTZ AZATHIOPRINE
AAEHILLMORSV VILLAHERMOSA
AAEHILMNOTXY HAEMATOXYLIN
AAEHILMNPSSS SALESMANSHIP
AAEHILMOSSTY HAEMATOLYSIS
AAEHILMRSTUY AMATEURISHLY
AAEHILNNOPTY PAY ON THE NAIL
AAEHIMMRSSTU SHAMATEURISM
AAEHIMNPRSTW WATERMANSHIP
AAEHKKLLNPTW WALK THE PLANK
AAEHLMNOOTXY HAEMATOXYLON
AAEHLRSSTTTW THE LAST STRAW
AAEHMOORSTTU ATHEROMATOUS
AAEHMOPRSSTY MASSOTHERAPY
AAEIIILMSSTV ASSIMILATIVE
AAEIIILPRSTT PARTIALITIES
AAEIILLLNOSV LEVALLOISIAN
AAEIILLMNNRS MILLENARIANS
AAEIILLNORTT ALLITERATION
AAEIILMMPRST MARITIME ALPS
AAEIILMNNOTT ALIMENTATION
AAEIILMNNRRT INTERLAMINAR
AAEIILMNOORT AMELIORATION
AAEIILMNPTUV MANIPULATIVE
AAEIILMNRRST AIR TERMINALS
AAEIILMNRSST INERTIAL MASS
AAEIILMRSSTT MATERIALISTS
AAEIILNNOPST PENALISATION
AAEIILNNOPTZ PENALIZATION

AAEIILNOQSTU EQUALISATION
AAEIILNOQTUZ EQUALIZATION
AAEIILNORRST RATIONALISER
AAEIILNORRTZ RATIONALIZER
AAEIILNORSST REALISATIONS
AAEIILNORSTV VELARISATION
AAEIILNORSTZ REALIZATIONS
AAEIILNORTVZ VELARIZATION
AAEIILNPRSTT INTERSPATIAL
AAEIIMNNOSTX EXAMINATIONS
AAEIINNOSTTT TETANISATION
AAEIINNOTTTZ TETANIZATION
AAEIINNRSSST SANITARINESS
AAEIINOPRRTT REPATRIATION
AAEIINOPRTTX EXPATRIATION
AAEIINQTTTUV QUANTITATIVE
AAEIKMNPPSTY MAKE IT SNAPPY
AAEILLLMPRSS PARALLELISMS
AAEILLLMRTTU MULTILATERAL
AAEILLLNRTUY UNILATERALLY
AAEILLMNRRTY ARTILLERYMAN
AAEILLMPRRTY PREMARITALLY
AAEILLMPRRXY PREMAXILLARY
AAEILLNOPPST APPELLATIONS
AAEILMNNOSTT LAMENTATIONS
AAEILMNPRSTU PLANETARIUMS
AAEILNNNPSVY PENNSYLVANIA
AAEILNNOPSTX EXPLANATIONS
AAEILNNOPTTX EXPLANTATION
AAEILNNORSTT ALTERNATIONS
AAEILNOPPRSY PLAYER PIANOS
AAEILNOPRRST PROLETARIANS
AAEILNOPSSTY PASSIONATELY
AAEILNORSTUV REVALUATIONS
AAEILNPRSSTT PATERNALISTS
AAEILNRSSSTU SALUTARINESS
AAEIMMMOSSTT METASOMATISM
AAEIMMNOOPST MESOPOTAMIAN
AAEIMNOOOOPT ONOMATOPOEIA
AAEINNOPRSXY EXPANSIONARY
AAEINNORSSTU AUSTRONESIAN
AAEINNOSSTTT NATION STATES
AAEINOPPRRST PREPARATIONS
AAEINOSSTTTT ATTESTATIONS
AAEIPPRRSTTV PRIVATE PARTS
AAEKLMORRTWW LOW-WATER MARK
AAEKLOPRSTTY KERATOPLASTY
AAEKNOQRRSUW NARROW SQUEAK
AAELLMNNORTY ORNAMENTALLY
AAELLNNPSTUY UNPLEASANTLY
AAELMMNNORRU ROMAN NUMERAL
AAELMNNORTTU ULTRAMONTANE
AAELMNPQSTUU QUANTUM LEAPS
AAELMOOPRSTZ SPERMATOZOAL
AAELNNPRRSTT TRANSPLANTER
AAELNPRRSTUU SUPERNATURAL
AAELNRSSSTTW STALWARTNESS
AAELOOPRRTTX EXTRAPOLATOR
AAEMNNOPRSST MONTPARNASSE

AAEMNOPRSTTU PORTMANTEAUS
AAEMNOPRTTUX PORTMANTEAUX
AAEMORSSSTTT TOASTMASTERS
AAEOOPPRRRST PARATROOPERS
AAEOPPRSSTTU PASSE-PARTOUT
AAFFIIILNOST AFFILIATIONS
AAFFIIMNORST AFFIRMATIONS
AAFGILLNRSST FALLING STARS
AAFHLMOSTUUY SAY A MOUTHFUL
AAFIIILNNOST FINALISATION
AAFIIILNNOTZ FINALIZATION
AAFIIILNRTTU FUTILITARIAN
AAFIILMMNNOT INFLAMMATION
AAFIILNNORTY INFLATIONARY
AAFIINNOSTTU INFATUATIONS
AAFILMMNOORT MALFORMATION
AAFILMMNORTY INFLAMMATORY
AAFINNOOPRST PROFANATIONS
AAGGHIIJMNST THINGAMAJIGS
AAGGHINNPRST STRAPHANGING
AAGGHINOPRTU AUTOGRAPHING
AAGGHNOOPRRY ORGANOGRAPHY
AAGGIIILNPRZ PLAGIARIZING
AAGGIIINNRTT INGRATIATING
AAGGIILLNNTV GALLIVANTING
AAGGIINNNOTZ ANTAGONIZING
AAGGIINNRTUU INAUGURATING
AAGGLMMOORTY GRAMMATOLOGY
AAGHIIILNNNT ANNIHILATING
AAGHIINPSTXY ASPHYXIATING
AAGHILOORSTU HAGIOLATROUS
AAGHIPRRSTTY STRATIGRAPHY
AAGHLMOOTTUY THAUMATOLOGY
AAGHLOOPPRRY POLAROGRAPHY
AAGHOOPPRSSU SAPROPHAGOUS
AAGIIILLNNPS PLAIN SAILING
AAGIIILMNSST ASSIMILATING
AAGIIILNORRT IRRIGATIONAL
AAGIIIMNNOST IMAGINATIONS
AAGIIINNNOTV INVAGINATION
AAGIIINNORTT INGRATIATION
AAGIILLNNPTW WALL PAINTING
AAGIILMNNPTU MANIPULATING
AAGIILNNRSUY SANGUINARILY
AAGIILNNRTUZ NATURALIZING
AAGIILNPPRSY APPRAISINGLY
AAGIIMNRTTUZ TRAUMATIZING
AAGIINNNQRTU QUARANTINING
AAGIINNOORST ORGANISATION
AAGIINNOORTZ ORGANIZATION
AAGIINNORTUU INAUGURATION
AAGIINNOSSST ASSIGNATIONS
AAGILLMNTUWY MULLIGATAWNY
AAGILLNOUVVV VULVOVAGINAL, APPALLING
AAGILMNNNNOT NONMALIGNANT
AAGILNORSTTU GASTRULATION
AAGILOOPRSTY PARASITOLOGY
AAGIMNNRRSTT TRANSMIGRANT
AAGINNOOSTTW STATION WAGON

AAGLLOPRSTTU SUPRAGLOTTAL
AAGLNOOPRSTW PATROL WAGONS
AAHHIOPPRSTU PHOSPHATURIA
AAHHIPRSSTTW ATHWARTSHIPS
AAHIIILLLOPRU AILUROPHILIA
AAHIIILNNNOT ANNIHILATION
AAHIIMNNOSTU HUMANISATION
AAHIIMNNOTUZ HUMANIZATION
AAHIINOPSTXY ASPHYXIATION
AAHIINPPRSST PARTISANSHIP
AAHIKMMNPRSS MARKSMANSHIP
AAHILLMOOTXY HOMOTAXIALLY
AAHILLMOPRSX MORPHALLAXIS
AAHILLOPRSTX TROPHALLAXIS
AAHILMNOOPRT PROTHALAMION
AAHIMMOPPRRS PARAMORPHISM
AAHIMNOOPRSS ANAMORPHOSIS
AAHLLMMORSSW MARSHMALLOWS
AAIIILMNOSST ASSIMILATION
AAIIILMPRTTY IMPARTIALITY
AAIIILNNOSTT LATINISATION
AAIIILNNOSTV INSALIVATION
AAIIILNNOTTZ LATINIZATION
AAIIILNOPRTT TRIPOLITANIA
AAIIILNOSTTV VISITATIONAL, VITALISATION
AAIIILNOTTVZ VITALIZATION
AAIIILORSTTV VISITATORIAL
AAIIIMMNOSTX MAXIMISATION
AAIIIMMNOTXZ MAXIMIZATION
AAIIIMNNRSTU UNITARIANISM
AAIIIMNOSSTV AVITAMINOSIS
AAIIINORSSTT SATIRISATION
AAIIINORSTTZ SATIRIZATION
AAIILLLPSSUZ LAPIS LAZULI
AAIILLMMNRTU MULTILAMINAR
AAIILLMNPRSU SUPRALIMINAL
AAIILLNNOSTT INSTALLATION
AAIILLNORRTY IRRATIONALLY
AAIILMNNOPTT IMPLANTATION
AAIILMNNOPTU MANIPULATION
AAIILMNOORST MORALISATION
AAIILMNOORTZ MORALIZATION
AAIILMNOOTTV MOTIVATIONAL
AAIILMNOSSTV SALVATIONISM
AAIILNNNOOTT INTONATIONAL
AAIILNNNOOTV INNOVATIONAL
AAIILNNOOSTV VIOLIN SONATA
AAIILNNORSTT TRANSITIONAL
AAIILNNOSSTT NATIONALISTS
AAIILNOOPRST POLARISATION
AAIILNOOPRTZ POLARIZATION
AAIILNOORSST SOLARISATION
AAIILNOORSTV VALORISATION
AAIILNOORSTZ SOLARIZATION
AAIILNOORTVZ VALORIZATION
AAIILNOPPSTT PALPITATIONS
AAIILNORRSTU RURALISATION
AAIILNORRTUZ RURALIZATION
AAIILNORSSTT RATIONALISTS

AAIILNORSTTY STATIONARILY
AAIILNOSSTTV SALVATIONIST
AAIILNPTTVYY NATIVITY PLAY
AAIIMNOORSTT AMORTISATION
AAIIMNOORTTZ AMORTIZATION
AAIINNOQSTTU QUANTISATION
AAIINNOQTTUZ QUANTIZATION
AAIINOOPRSTV VAPORISATION
AAIINOOPRTVZ VAPORIZATION
AAILLMNOPRTT ALL-IMPORTANT
AAILLMOPRTYY MORALITY PLAY
AAILLORSTTUY SALUTATORILY
AAILMMOPPRSS MALAPROPISMS
AAILMNOPRTUY MANIPULATORY
AAILNNORSSTT TRANSLATIONS
AAILNOPPSSSY PASSION PLAYS
AAILOORSTTTZ TOTALIZATORS
AAILOPRRSTUV VAPOUR TRAILS
AAINNOPRSSTT PATRON SAINTS
AAINNORSTTUU UNSATURATION
AAINOOORTTTU AUTOROTATION
AAKLNNNNOOPT NANOPLANKTON
AALMNOOPRSTY TRYPANOSOMAL
ABBBCEHLOPSY PSYCHOBABBLE
ABBBCGINNOUY BOUNCING BABY
ABBBDEEIILSS SIDI-BEL-ABBES
ABBBEESTTTUY TEST-TUBE BABY
ABBBEHLMORTU BLABBERMOUTH
ABBCCEEHKNRS BACKBENCHERS
ABBCCEEHMORS BEACHCOMBERS
ABBCDEFKNOOY BACK OF BEYOND
ABBCEEGGHISU BEACH BUGGIES
ABBCEEIKLRRS BLACKBERRIES
ABBCFIILORST FIBROBLASTIC
ABBCKMOOORSY BACKROOM BOYS
ABBDEEFLORSS SELF-ABSORBED
ABBDEELOSSSU DOUBLE BASSES
ABBDEHIILRYZ HYBRIDIZABLE
ABBDEIILSSUZ SUBSIDIZABLE
ABBDEILOPSYY PLAY BOBSY-DIE
ABBDELLLNRUY LANDLUBBERLY
ABBDEMMNORST BOMBARDMENTS
ABBDEOOPPRTY BOOBY-TRAPPED
ABBEEEHNORST THE BARE BONES
ABBEEEILLNUV UNBELIEVABLE
ABBEEILLNUVY UNBELIEVABLY
ABBEEILMRRSU REIMBURSABLE
ABBEELORRRSU RABBLE-ROUSER
ABBEHIJMNNSU BENJAMIN BUSH
ABBEINRSSTUU SUBURBANITES
ABBELNPRRSTU RUBBER PLANTS
ABBEMPRRSSTU RUBBER STAMPS
ABBGHIILOPRY BIBLIOGRAPHY
ABBHLOORTWWY THROW A WOBBLY
ABBHMOOOOSST BAMBOO SHOOTS
ABCCCIILMSTU SUBCLIMACTIC
ABCCDEEEELPST BESPECTACLED
ABCCDEHILORU COACHBUILDER
ABCCDHILNSUW CLUB SANDWICH

ABCCDIILORXY DICARBOXYLIC
ABCCEEEEELRSU CAUSE CÉLÈBRE
ABCCEEEHLNRT TREBLE CHANCE
ABCCEEEELNORT CONCELEBRATE
ABCCEEEENORRS ARBORESCENCE
ABCCEEIILNSS INACCESSIBLE
ABCCEEIILLNOR RECONCILABLE
ABCCEEIILOSST ACCESSIBLE TO
ABCCEEMNNRRU ENCUMBRANCER
ABCCEEMNNRSU ENCUMBRANCES
ABCCEHILLRUY CHERUBICALLY
ABCCEHIMMRSU CHAMBER MUSIC
ABCCEHOPRSST BATCH PROCESS
ABCCEIILNSSY INACCESSIBLY
ABCCEIINRRSU CABIN CRUISER
ABCCEIKKLSST STICKLEBACKS
ABCCEILLNORY RECONCILABLY
ABCCEILMMNOU COMMUNICABLE
ABCCEILNNOOS CONSCIONABLE
ABCCEILNORTT CONTRACTIBLE
ABCCEILORSTU SCROBICULATE
ABCCEINOOPRS CARBON COPIES
ABCCEKLMNOOY BLACK ECONOMY
ABCCHILLMORU CHLORAMBUCIL
ABCCILLOOSTY OCTOSYLLABIC
ABCCILMMNOUY COMMUNICABLY
ABCCINOOSSTT TOBACCONISTS
ABCCKLNORTUY BLACK COUNTRY
ABCDDGIKLNPU BLACK PUDDING
ABCDEEEEHILPR DECIPHERABLE
ABCDEEEHIRSU DEBAUCHERIES
ABCDEEEHLORR BREECHLOADER
ABCDEEEILNUV UNDECEIVABLE
ABCDEEHOQRRU CHEQUERBOARD
ABCDEEIILLNN INDECLINABLE
ABCDEEIILLORS LOCAL DERBIES
ABCDEEIILMNSS DISSEMBLANCE
ABCDEEIILMOST DOMESTICABLE
ABCDEEIILNORS CONSIDERABLE
ABCDEEIILORSV DISCOVERABLE
ABCDEEIMNNTY AMBITENDENCY
ABCDEEINORRS DECARBONISER
ABCDEEINORRZ DECARBONIZER
ABCDEEILLNRSY BELLY DANCERS
ABCDEEELMOOPS DECOMPOSABLE
ABCDEGHIILNR CHILDBEARING
ABCDEGHORRTU TURBOCHARGED
ABCDEGILNOTU DOUBLE-ACTING
ABCDEHILSSTW SWITCHBLADES
ABCDEHIRRSTW BIRD-WATCHERS
ABCDEHMOORST HORS DE COMBAT
ABCDEHNORSTY BODY SNATCHER
ABCDEIIILLRT LIBERTICIDAL
ABCDEIILRSTT DISTRACTIBLE
ABCDEIINNSST CITISENS' BAND
ABCDEIINNSTZ CITIZENS' BAND
ABCDEILMORST BLASTODERMIC
ABCDEILNORSY CONSIDERABLY
ABCDEILNOSTU DISCOUNTABLE

ABCDEINOOPRS PROBOSCIDEAN
ABCDEINOORST NOTICE BOARDS
ABCDEINRSSTU DISTURBANCES
ABCDEKMNOOSW BACKWOODSMEN
ABCDEKNORRTU ROUND BRACKET
ABCDELOOPRUV CUPBOARD LOVE
ABCDEOOOORRRT CORROBORATED
ABCDHIORSSTW SWITCHBOARDS
ABCDHHNOORRSY HYDROCARBONS
ABCDIILLOPST DIPLOBLASTIC
ABCEEEFFKORS COFFEE BREAKS
ABCEEEFFLOST COFFEE TABLES
ABCEEEFNRSST BENEFACTRESS
ABCEEEHLNRRT RETRENCHABLE
ABCEEELMNRSS RESEMBLANCES
ABCEEEMMNRRR REMEMBRANCER
ABCEEEMMNRRS REMEMBRANCES
ABCEEENORSUV VERBENACEOUS
ABCEEFFIINRT FEBRIFACIENT
ABCEEFIILLNY BENEFICIALLY
ABCEEFINNOST BENEFACTIONS
ABCEEFLLOQRS FORECLOSABLE
ABCEEGILNORZ RECOGNIZABLE
ABCEEHKLNQSU BLANK CHEQUES
ABCEEHLORSUY HERBACEOUSLY
ABCEEHMMNNRT EMBRANCHMENT
ABCEEHORSTTX CHATTERBOXES
ABCEEIILLNPX INEXPLICABLE
ABCEEIILNRTX INEXTRICABLE
ABCEEILLSSTU SUBCELESTIAL
ABCEEILNORST CELEBRATIONS
ABCEEILNORSU RIBONUCLEASE
ABCEEILRSSTU RESUSCITABLE
ABCEEINNORSV INOBSERVANCE
ABCEEINRRTVY INVERTEBRACY
ABCEEJKLMRTU LUMBERJACKET
ABCEEKLNNORU UNRECKONABLE
ABCEEKLRRRSW KERB CRAWLERS
ABCEELOPRSTU PROSECUTABLE
ABCEENOPRRTU PROTUBERANCE
ABCEEORRSSUU BURSERACEOUS
ABCEGGGIKLLN BLACKLEGGING
ABCEGHIKLLNS BLACK ENGLISH
ABCEGHORRRTU TURBOCHARGER
ABCEGIKLNRRW KERB CRAWLING
ABCEGILMNOST SINGLE COMBAT
ABCEGILNORYZ RECOGNIZABLY
ABCEGILOORTY BACTERIOLOGY
ABCEHIJKNOTX JACK-IN-THE-BOX
ABCEHIKNRSSS BRACKISHNESS
ABCEHILMNRUU HIBERNACULUM
ABCEHILSTTTY CHASTITY BELT
ABCEHIRRRRSU CRUSH BARRIER
ABCEHKLRSSUW SWASHBUCKLER
ABCEHLNOSTUU UNTOUCHABLES
ABCEIIILLRST LIBERALISTIC
ABCEIIILTTXY EXCITABILITY
ABCEIILLNPXY INEXPLICABLY
ABCEIILMNOPT INCOMPATIBLE

ABCEIILNRTXY INEXTRICABLY
ABCEIILOORST BOROSILICATE
ABCEIILORTVY REVOCABILITY
ABCEIINORSTT OBSTETRICIAN
ABCEIIRSTTUW WATER BISCUIT
ABCEIKNPRSTU BANKRUPTCIES
ABCEILLNNOOS INCONSOLABLE
ABCEILMMNOTU INCOMMUTABLE
ABCEILMNNOSU INCONSUMABLE
ABCEILMNOPTU INCOMPUTABLE
ABCEILMOSSUX MUSICAL BOXES
ABCEILNOOPRR INCORPORABLE
ABCEILOOSSTT OSTEOBLASTIC
ABCEIMNOORST EMBROCATIONS
ABCELLLNOORT CONTROLLABLE
ABCELLLOOSTY OCTOSYLLABLE
ABCELMNOSTTU MESCAL BUTTON
ABCELNORSTTU COUNTERBLAST
ABCENOSSTUUU SUBCUTANEOUS
ABCEORRRSTTU CARBURETTORS
ABCFIILLMORY MORBIFICALLY
ABCFIINORSTU BIFURCATIONS
ABCFLNOOORRU FLUOROCARBON
ABCGHLOORSUY BRACHYLOGOUS
ABCGIIKLLNST BLACKLISTING
ABCGIILLLOOY BIOLOGICALLY
ABCGIINNRRST TRANSCRIBING
ABCGILLMOOSY SYMBOLOGICAL
ABCGILMNNRSU UNSCRAMBLING
ABCGILNNOOOT CONGLOBATION
ABCHIIKLOSTY SHOCKABILITY
ABCHIMORSSTX CHRISTMAS BOX
ABCIIIILRSTY IRASCIBILITY
ABCIIILMNOTU UMBILICATION
ABCIIILNRTUY INCURABILITY
ABCIILLMNOOY BIONOMICALLY
ABCIILMNOPTY INCOMPATIBLY
ABCIILNNOTUY CONNUBIALITY
ABCIILNOPPRY PRINCIPAL BOY
ABCIILNOPSTU PUBLICATIONS
ABCIILNPPRSU SUBPRINCIPAL
ABCIILORRTUY ORBICULARITY
ABCIIMNNOOST COMBINATIONS
ABCIJKNNOORS JACK ROBINSON
ABCIKLLMMSSU BLACK MUSLIMS
ABCILLLMOSYY SYMBOLICALLY
ABCILLLOPSYY POLYSYLLABIC
ABCILLMNOOSY MONOSYLLABIC
ABCILLNNOOSY INCONSOLABLY
ABCILMMNOSTU NOCTAMBULISM
ABCILMNNOOSU NO-CLAIM BONUS
ABCILMNOSTTU NOCTAMBULIST
ABCIMNORSSTU OBSCURANTISM
ABCIMNORSTUU RAMBUNCTIOUS
ABCINNOORSTU CONURBATIONS
ABCINORSSTTU OBSCURANTIST,
   SUBTRACTIONS
ABCOOOORRRRT CORROBORATOR
ABDDEEEHLLTU BULLET-HEADED

ABDDEEEHLNYZ BENZALDEHYDE
ABDDEEEHLORU DOUBLE-HEADER
ABDDEEELLORU DOUBLE-DEALER
ABDDEEGLLOUZ DOUBLE-GLAZED
ABDDEEHLLLUY BULLHEADEDLY
ABDDEEIILSST DESTABILISED
ABDDEEIILSTZ DESTABILIZED
ABDDEEIMNNST ABSENT-MINDED
ABDDEEKLLOTU DOUBLE-TALKED
ABDDEEKLOPRU DOUBLE-PARKED
ABDDEGILNOTU DOUBLE-DATING
ABDDEILNOOST BLOODSTAINED
ABDDEINORSTU SUBORDINATED
ABDDEKMOOOSY DOMESDAY BOOK
ABDDGIINORSV DIVINGBOARDS
ABDDGIMNNPRU BUMP AND GRIND
ABDEEEEILMRR IRREDEEMABLE
ABDEEEERRRTV REVERBERATED
ABDEEEFIILNS INDEFEASIBLE
ABDEEEIILMRR IRREMEDIABLE
ABDEEEIILRTV DELIBERATIVE
ABDEEEIILRTY DELIBERATELY
ABDEEEILMNRT DETERMINABLE
ABDEEEILMRRY IRREDEEMABLY
ABDEEEINPRRS PREBENDARIES
ABDEEELMNTZZ BEDAZZLEMENT
ABDEEELPRSSU SUPERSEDABLE
ABDEEFGIIRRS FIRE BRIGADES
ABDEEFHILMRT HALF-TIMBERED
ABDEEFIIILNT IDENTIFIABLE
ABDEEFILLSTT BATTLEFIELDS
ABDEEFINSTUU SUBINFEUDATE
ABDEEGIILNRT DELIBERATING
ABDEEGLNOSTU DOUBLE AGENTS
ABDEEHNORTUW WEATHER-BOUND
ABDEEIIILTTV DEBILITATIVE
ABDEEIILMRRY IRREMEDIABLY
ABDEEIILNORT DELIBERATION
ABDEEILLNORR BANDERILLERO
ABDEEILMNOPR IMPONDERABLE
ABDEEILMNSST DISABLEMENTS
ABDEEILNOSSV VOIDABLENESS
ABDEEILNRSSU UNDESIRABLES
ABDEEILPRSTU DISREPUTABLE
ABDEEINNRRSW BREADWINNERS
ABDEEINNRSTU NUBIAN DESERT
ABDEEINNSSSU UNBIASEDNESS
ABDEEIRRSTTY DRY BATTERIES
ABDEEKNORRRS BANKER'S ORDER
ABDEELMNORST DEMONSTRABLE
ABDEELMNORSZ BRONZE MEDALS
ABDEELORRSTW WORLD-BEATERS
ABDEEOORRSTT BORED TO TEARS
ABDEFFHLORSU SHUFFLEBOARD
ABDEFGINORRS FINGERBOARDS
ABDEFIIILLOS SOLIDIFIABLE
ABDEFLLOSTUU DOUBLE FAULTS
ABDEGIIILNTT DEBILITATING
ABDEGIIKMNRS DISEMBARKING

ABDEGIILNNST DINING TABLES
ABDEGIKNOPRW BAKING POWDER
ABDEGILLLNNY BELLY-LANDING
ABDEGILNORTW WORLD-BEATING
ABDEGINNPSTU BE UPSTANDING
ABDEHHLMOORR RHOMBOHEDRAL
ABDEHHNOSSUU HOUSE HUSBAND
ABDEHIIILMNS DIMINISHABLE
ABDEHIILSSST DISESTABLISH
ABDEHIINNPRS HAIRPIN BENDS
ABDEHLLORSYY HYDROLYSABLE
ABDEHNNORSSU RUB ONE'S HANDS
ABDEIIIILSST DISABILITIES
ABDEIIILMNSS INADMISSIBLE
ABDEIIILMTXY MIXED-ABILITY
ABDEIIILNOTT DEBILITATION
ABDEIIILRSTY DESIRABILITY
ABDEIIIRSSSU SUBSIDIARIES
ABDEIILNPSTU INDISPUTABLE
ABDEIILNRTUY ENDURABILITY
ABDEIIOOPRSS BASIDIOSPORE
ABDEILMNOSTU DISMOUNTABLE
ABDEILPRSTUY DISREPUTABLY
ABDEIMORSTUX AMBIDEXTROUS
ABDEINORRRSU SOUND BARRIER
ABDEINORSSTU SUBORDINATES
ABDELMNORSTY DEMONSTRABLY
ABDELMOORSST BLOODSTREAMS
ABDEMOORRTTW BOTTOM DRAWER
ABDENOQRRTUU QUARTER-BOUND
ABDFGIILLLNO BILL OF LADING
ABDFIILNNRUU INFUNDIBULAR
ABDFIILNOOOV BIOFLAVONOID
ABDGHINOOSWX SHADOW-BOXING
ABDGIILOOORY RADIOBIOLOGY
ABDGIINNOORR IRONING BOARD
ABDGINOPRRSS SPRINGBOARDS
ABDGMOORRSSS SMORGASBORDS
ABDIIIILNTUY INAUDIBILITY
ABDIIILMNSSY INADMISSIBLY
ABDIIILRSSUY SUBSIDIARILY
ABDIIIMORSST TROMBIDIASIS
ABDIILLMOTUY MODULABILITY,
   MOULDABILITY
ABDIILNPSTUY INDISPUTABLY
ABDIIRRSTTUY DISTRIBUTARY
ABDLNNOSSTTU NUTS AND BOLTS
ABEEEEMNRSTV BEREAVEMENTS
ABEEEFLNQRTU FREQUENTABLE
ABEEEGGILNRU BELEAGUERING
ABEEEGILNORT RENEGOTIABLE
ABEEEHILMPTU EAT HUMBLE PIE
ABEEEHKORRSU HOUSEBREAKER
ABEEEHLOPRST OBLATE SPHERE
ABEEEIIILLRRV IRRELIEVABLE
ABEEEILMNPRT IMPENETRABLE
ABEEEILMNRTX EXTERMINABLE
ABEEEILNNSSV ENVIABLENESS
ABEEEILNRRST EAST BERLINER

ABEEEIMNQSTU MESQUITE BEAN
ABEEEINRRTTV INVERTEBRATE
ABEEELOOPTTT POTATO BEETLE
ABEEELQRSSTU SEQUESTRABLE
ABEEEMPRSTTU SUBTEMPERATE
ABEEENQSTUUY BEAUTY QUEENS
ABEEEORRRRTV REVERBERATOR
ABEEEPRRSTTY PRESBYTERATE
ABEEFFILNRSU INSUFFERABLE
ABEEFFRSSTTU BUFFER STATES
ABEEFGHILNRT FRIGHTENABLE
ABEEFIILLMSU EMULSIFIABLE
ABEEFIILLRTZ FERTILIZABLE
ABEEFKLNOORW FOREKNOWABLE
ABEEFLLMNSSU BLAMEFULNESS
ABEEFLLMSSSY SELF-ASSEMBLY
ABEEGGILNPSS SLEEPING BAGS
ABEEGGILNRSS BEGGARLINESS
ABEEGHMNOOPR GERMANOPHOBE
ABEEGIILNSTV INVESTIGABLE
ABEEGIKNPSTU SPEAKING TUBE
ABEEGILNORRS LOGANBERRIES
ABEEGILNOXYZ OXYGENIZABLE
ABEEGLNNORUV UNGOVERNABLE
ABEEHHPRSSTY BATHYSPHERES
ABEEHIILMPRS IMPERISHABLE
ABEEHILLMORT THERMOLABILE
ABEEHILOPPRS PROPHESIABLE
ABEEHILRRSTW WELSH RAREBIT
ABEEHIQRRSUU HARQUEBUSIER
ABEEHKLNNOTT ON THE BLANKET
ABEEHLMORSTT THERMOSTABLE
ABEEHLOPRSST BLASTOSPHERE
ABEEHLORRSWW WHEELBARROWS
ABEEIIILLRST LIBERALITIES
ABEEIIILLRSTZ STERILIZABLE
ABEEIILMMMOR IMMEMORIABLE
ABEEIILMNNRT INTERMINABLE
ABEEIILMNRTX INTERMIXABLE
ABEEIILMPRTY PERMEABILITY
ABEEIILNPRTX INEXTIRPABLE
ABEEIILNPSST PITIABLENESS
ABEEIILNRTVY VENERABILITY
ABEEIILNRTWY RENEWABILITY
ABEEIILORTTV OBLITERATIVE
ABEEIILPRRRS IRRESPIRABLE
ABEEIKLNNSST LINEN BASKETS
ABEEIILLMNSSY ASSEMBLY LINE
ABEEIILNNRUV INVULNERABLE,
   VILLEURBANNE
ABEEIILLORRSV IRRESOLVABLE
ABEEIILLRSTVY LIVERY STABLE
ABEEIILMMOORS AEROEMBOLISM
ABEEIILMNRRSU SERIAL NUMBER
ABEEIILNOPRST INTERPOSABLE
ABEEIILNOQSTU QUESTIONABLE
ABEEIILNSSSTU SUITABLENESS
ABEEIILOPPRRX EXPROPRIABLE
ABEEIILPRRSTY PRESBYTERIAL

ABEEINORRTTV VERTEBRATION
ABEEINPRRSTY PRESBYTERIAN
ABEEIRRRSSTW STRAWBERRIES
ABEEKLMORRTU TROUBLEMAKER
ABEEKMRRSTUY BUYER'S MARKET
ABEEKORRSSTT BREASTSTROKE
ABEELLMNOPUY UNEMPLOYABLE
ABEELLMNOTTT BALLOTTEMENT
ABEELMMNNOTZ EMBLAZONMENT
ABEELMNPRSTU NUMBERPLATES
ABEELNNNOSTT NANSEN BOTTLE
ABEELNOSSSTU ABSOLUTENESS
ABEELNOSSTUV SOLVENT ABUSE
ABEELOORSTUZ ABSOLUTE ZERO
ABEELOPPRSSU SUPERPOSABLE
ABEENPRTTTUU PEANUT BUTTER
ABEENRSSSSTU ABSTRUSENESS
ABEFFIIILNTY INEFFABILITY
ABEFFILNRSUY INSUFFERABLY
ABEFGILNORRY FORBEARINGLY
ABEFGILNORUV UNFORGIVABLE
ABEFGINNRRTU AFTERBURNING
ABEFHHILLLOT BILL OF HEALTH
ABEFHHLORRST HALF-BROTHERS
ABEFIILLOSSZ FOSSILIZABLE
ABEFIILRTTUY REFUTABILITY
ABEFILNOPRTU UNPROFITABLE
ABEFILNRSSTU TRANSFUSIBLE
ABEFLLOOORUV LABOUR OF LOVE
ABEFLMOOSSTT FALSE BOTTOMS
ABEFLNOSSSTU BOASTFULNESS
ABEFLNOSSSUU FABULOUSNESS
ABEGGHIOOPRY BIOGEOGRAPHY
ABEGGIMNNOOR BOOMERANGING
ABEGHIILNSST ESTABLISHING
ABEGHJNNORSU JOHANNESBURG
ABEGIIILLNRZ LIBERALIZING
ABEGIILNORTT OBLITERATING
ABEGIILNPRTY PREGNABILITY
ABEGIKLNNOOR BOOK-LEARNING
ABEGILLLNOWY BOWLING ALLEY
ABEGILLNOOST BALNEOLOGIST
ABEGILNNRTTU TABLE-TURNING
ABEGILRRSSST BRISTLE-GRASS
ABEGILRRSYZZ GRIZZLY BEARS
ABEGLLORSSSW GLASSBLOWERS
ABEGLNORSSSU GLABROUSNESS
ABEHIILNNSU HUSEIN IBN-ALI
ABEHIIILRTTY HERITABILITY
ABEHIIIMNNRS HIBERNIANISM
ABEHIILNNRTY LABYRINTHINE
ABEHIILNOPST INHOSPITABLE
ABEHIIMORSUV BEHAVIOURISM,
　MISBEHAVIOUR
ABEHIIORSTUV BEHAVIOURIST
ABEHILNORRTW BROTHER-IN-LAW
ABEHINPRSSTU PAINTBRUSHES
ABEHLORRSTTY ERYTHROBLAST
ABEIIILLLRTY ILLIBERALITY

ABEIIIILLNNRT BRILLIANTINE
ABEIIIILLNSTY ENSILABILITY
ABEIIIILRSTVY REVISABILITY
ABEIIIILRTVVY REVIVABILITY
ABEIIIKLORTVY REVOKABILITY
ABEIIILLLMPTU MULTIPLIABLE
ABEIILMMORTY MEMORABILITY
ABEIILMNNRTY INTERMINABLY
ABEIILMORTVY REMOVABILITY
ABEIILNNOSTU NEBULISATION
ABEIILNNOTUZ NEBULIZATION
ABEIILNNTTUY UNTENABILITY
ABEIILNOORTT OBLITERATION
ABEIILOQRRTU EQUILIBRATOR
ABEIILPRSTUY SUPERABILITY
ABEIILPRTTUY REPUTABILITY
ABEIIMOQRSTU BARQUISIMETO
ABEIINORSSTU SUBERISATION
ABEIINORSTUZ SUBERIZATION
ABEIILNNRUVY INVULNERABLY
ABEILLNOPPRT BIPROPELLANT
ABEILLOPRRVY PROVERBIALLY
ABEILMOSSTUY ABSTEMIOUSLY
ABEILNOQSTUY QUESTIONABLY
ABEILNORSSUY BYELORUSSIAN
ABEILNORTTXY EXORBITANTLY
ABEILNPRSSUU PRUSSIAN BLUE
ABEINOOPRRST PROBATIONERS
ABEINOORSSTV OBSERVATIONS
ABEINOPRRTTU PERTURBATION
ABEINSSSTTUV SUBSTANTIVES
ABELLLLOPSYY POLYSYLLABLE
ABELLLMNOOSY MONOSYLLABLE
ABELMNORSTUU SURMOUNTABLE
ABEMNNOOTTUW MEN-ABOUT-TOWN
ABEMNORRRSST BARNSTORMERS
ABFGIIILNRTY FRANGIBILITY
ABFIIILLNORT FIBRILLATION
ABGGILLNOSSW GLASS-BLOWING
ABGHIIMMNSTW SWIMMING BATH
ABGHIINSSTTU BATHING SUITS
ABGIIIILNTTY IGNITABILITY
ABGIIILLMNSU BILINGUALISM
ABGIILLOORTY OBLIGATORILY
ABGILNOOPSST SPONGIOBLAST
ABGILOOORSTY ASTROBIOLOGY
ABGIMNNORRST BARNSTORMING
ABHHIKRSSTTU TURKISH BATHS
ABHIIKMNNPRS BRINKMANSHIP
ABHIILNOPSTY INHOSPITABLY
ABHIINOPRSTV VIBRAPHONIST
ABHIMNNORRTU NORTHUMBRIAN
ABIIIILRRTTY IRRITABILITY
ABIIIILLPSTUY PLAUSIBILITY
ABIIILMMOVTY IMMOVABILITY
ABIIILMMTTUY IMMUTABILITY
ABIIILMNOOST ABOLITIONISM, MOBILISATION
ABIIILMNOOTZ MOBILIZATION
ABIIILMPTTUY IMPUTABILITY

ABIIILNOOSTT ABOLITIONIST
ABIIILNPRTTY PRINTABILITY
ABIIILNRSTUY INSURABILITY
ABIIILSTTTWY TWISTABILITY
ABIILMOOSTTU AUTOMOBILIST
ABIILNOORSTT STROBILATION
ABIILNORSSUU INSALUBRIOUS
ABIILNORSTTU TRIBULATIONS
ABIILOOPPSTY OPPOSABILITY
ABIILRSTTTUY TRUSTABILITY
ABIIMNORSTTU TAMBOURINIST
ABIINOORSSTT ABORTIONISTS
ABIIOPRSTTVY ABSORPTIVITY
ABILMMMNOSSU SOMNAMBULISM
ABILMMNOSSTU SOMNAMBULIST
ABILMNORSTUY SUBNORMALITY
ABIMNORSSTTU NIMBOSTRATUS
ABINRRSSSTTU BRAINS TRUSTS
ABNOORRSSTUU BRONTOSAURUS
ACCCCEIILRRT ARCTIC CIRCLE
ACCCDEEEELNS DECALESCENCE
ACCCDENNOORS CONCORDANCES
ACCCDIMOPSST COMPACT DISCS
ACCCEEEELNRS RECALESCENCE
ACCCEEEILNNS INCALESCENCE
ACCCEEEINQSU ACQUIESCENCE
ACCCEEIILSST ECCLESIASTIC
ACCCEEILLLTY ECLECTICALLY
ACCCEGIINNOR CARCINOGENIC
ACCCEHILMOTY CYTOCHEMICAL
ACCCEIILMRST CLIMACTERICS
ACCCEIMNNOOT CONCOMITANCE
ACCCEIMNRSTU CIRCUMSTANCE
ACCCHIIOPRRT CHIROPRACTIC
ACCCIIILLOSS LOCI CLASSICI
ACCCIIILSSST CLASSICISTIC
ACCCIILNNOTY ANTICYCLONIC
ACCCIILNOOST ICONOCLASTIC
ACCDDEHINOOP DODECAPHONIC
ACCDDEHNPRSU PUNCHED CARDS
ACCDDEIINORT ENDOCARDITIC
ACCDDEINORTT CONTRADICTED
ACCDEEFIIRTT CERTIFICATED
ACCDEEFLLOTU DEFLOCCULATE
ACCDEEGOPRSU COUPS DE GRACE
ACCDEEHIILNP DIENCEPHALIC
ACCDEEHIMNOS MACHINE CODES
ACCDEEHIORSS ARCHDIOCESES
ACCDEEIILNOT INDOLEACETIC
ACCDEEILLOPS PECCADILLOES
ACCDEEILNOPY ENCYCLOPEDIA
ACCDEEINNNST INCANDESCENT
ACCDEEINNORT CONCERTINAED
ACCDEEIOPRRT RECIPROCATED
ACCDEELMORTT CLOTTED CREAM
ACCDEELOOPRU CAPE COLOURED
ACCDEENNNOTU COUNTENANCED
ACCDEENNORTT CONCENTRATED
ACCDEENORTTU COUNTERACTED

ACCDEEENOSSU SUCCEDANEOUS
ACCDEGHORTUU DUTCH COURAGE
ACCDEGIILRSY LYSERGIC ACID
ACCDEGNNORRT CONCERT GRAND
ACCDEHHNRRUW CHURCHWARDEN
ACCDEHILMOPS ACCOMPLISHED
ACCDEHILOOPP CEPHALOPODIC
ACCDEHIOORSU ORCHIDACEOUS
ACCDEHNRRRUY HARD CURRENCY
ACCDEIIILNST INSECTICIDAL
ACCDEIIIPRRT PERICARDITIC
ACCDEIILLOPY EPICYCLOIDAL
ACCDEIILNNOT COINCIDENTAL
ACCDEIILRRSU CIRCULARISED
ACCDEIILRRUZ CIRCULARIZED
ACCDEIKLNSST CANDLESTICKS
ACCDEILNOPTU CONDUPLICATE
ACCDEIMMNOTU COMMUNICATED
ACCDEIMNORTU UNDEMOCRATIC
ACCDEINORRTT CONTRADICTER
ACCDEIOORRTT DECORTICATOR
ACCDEIPRRSTU PICTURE CARDS
ACCDEKORRRST TRACK RECORDS
ACCDEMNOSTUU UNACCUSTOMED
ACCDENNORTUY COUNTRY DANCE
ACCDFIIINOOT CODIFICATION
ACCDHIINORTW IN ACCORD WITH
ACCDHINOTTUU DUTCH AUCTION
ACCDIINOORST ACCORDIONIST
ACCDIINOSTTY SYNDIOTACTIC
ACCEEEGINNOT CAENOGENETIC
ACCEEEHILNPP EPENCEPHALIC
ACCEEEHLORRT HETEROCERCAL
ACCEEEENOPRSV VAPORESCENCE
ACCEEFFHKLOT COFFEE KLATCH
ACCEEFGIIMNN MAGNIFICENCE
ACCEEFHIMSTU FACE THE MUSIC
ACCEEFHMNORT FRANCHE-COMTÉ
ACCEEFIIRSTT CERTIFICATES
ACCEEFIKRRRS FIRECRACKERS
ACCEEGHIMNOS GEOMECHANICS
ACCEEGHNNORX CORN EXCHANGE
ACCEEGHORRSV COVER CHARGES
ACCEEGILRRST GREAT CIRCLES
ACCEEGINNORZ RECOGNIZANCE
ACCEEHHIRSST CHESHIRE CATS
ACCEEHIILNPT ENCEPHALITIC
ACCEEHILMOPS MESOCEPHALIC
ACCEEHILRRST RICHTER SCALE
ACCEEHIMORTT TACHEOMETRIC
ACCEEHIORTTT HETEROTACTIC
ACCEEHIRRTTU ARCHITECTURE
ACCEEHKORSTW WEATHERCOCKS
ACCEEHLMNRSY SCLERENCHYMA
ACCEEHLMORTY THE REAL MCCOY
ACCEEHMNNORT ENCROACHMENT
ACCEEIILNRST ELECTRICIANS
ACCEEIINPPRT PRECIPITANCE
ACCEEIKNPRSS SCIENCE PARKS

ACCEEILLLRTY ELECTRICALLY
ACCEEILLMNUY ECUMENICALLY
ACCEEILNPTTU CENTUPLICATE
ACCEEILNRTTY TETRACYCLINE
ACCEEIMNOTTY ACTINOMYCETE
ACCEEIORSTTT STEREOTACTIC
ACCEELLOORTT COLLECTORATE
ACCEELMNOPTU ACCOUPLEMENT
ACCEELNNOPTY CYCLOPENTANE
ACCEELNNOSTV CONVALESCENT
ACCEELNNRSTU TRANSLUCENCE
ACCEELPRRWYY CREEPY-CRAWLY
ACCEEMNNORRS NECROMANCERS
ACCEEMNOPPSU COME-UPPANCES
ACCEEMNORTTU ACCOUTREMENT
ACCEEMOOPPRR COME A CROPPER
ACCEENNNOSTU COUNTENANCES
ACCEENNORSTT CONCENTRATES
ACCEFGIIINNS SIGNIFICANCE
ACCEFIILLMRY FAMILY CIRCLE
ACCEFIILLPSY SPECIFICALLY
ACCEGHHIOPRT HECTOGRAPHIC
ACCEGHINOPRS SCENOGRAPHIC
ACCEGIIKNRSW WISECRACKING
ACCEGIINNNOZ INCOGNIZANCE
ACCEGIINRTUX EXCRUCIATING
ACCEGILLLOOY ECOLOGICALLY
ACCEGILLNOOR NECROLOGICAL
ACCEGILNNOSV CONVALESCING
ACCEGINNNOVY CONVEYANCING
ACCEGINNNORST CONSECRATING
ACCEGNOORRTY GERONTOCRACY
ACCEHHLMNORY CHLORENCHYMA
ACCEHIILLNST CALLISTHENIC
ACCEHIILMNOPR NECROPHILIAC
ACCEHIILNSST CALISTHENICS
ACCEHIILNTTY TECHNICALITY
ACCEHIIRSTTT TETRASTICHIC
ACCEHIKMNSTY CHIMNEYSTACK
ACCEHILLLORY CHOLERICALLY
ACCEHILMOPRS ACCOMPLISHER
ACCEHILMOPRY MICROCEPHALY,
  PYROCHEMICAL
ACCEHILNNNOT NONTECHNICAL
ACCEHILNOOOT ECHOLOCATION
ACCEHILOPRTY CHALCOPYRITE
ACCEHIMOORST MESOTHORACIC
ACCEHINNNOPT PANTECHNICON
ACCEHINRSSST SCRATCHINESS
ACCEHIOPSTVY PSYCHOACTIVE
ACCEHKLOOSVZ CZECHOSLOVAK
ACCEHKOPPSTT PATCH POCKETS
ACCEHLOOPRTY PYROCATECHOL
ACCEHLOORSSU SCHORLACEOUS
ACCEHMNOOORT COME TO ANCHOR
ACCEHOPRSSST CROSSPATCHES
ACCEIIILPSST SPECIALISTIC
ACCEIIINNNPS PICCANINNIES
ACCEIIKKMNRS CAMI-KNICKERS

ACCEIILLLNTY ENCLITICALLY
ACCEIILLLPTY ECLIPTICALLY
ACCEIILMMORT MICROCLIMATE
ACCEIILMNNOP INCOMPLIANCE
ACCEIILMORRT CALORIMETRIC
ACCEIILMRRSU SEMICIRCULAR
ACCEIILNORTV INTERVOCALIC
ACCEIILORRTV OVERCRITICAL
ACCEIILRRRSU CIRCULARISER
ACCEIILRRRUZ CIRCULARIZER
ACCEIILRSSTU SECULARISTIC
ACCEIIMNORRT CRANIOMETRIC
ACCEIIMNORTT ACTINOMETRIC
ACCEIIMNOSST COSMETICIANS
ACCEIINOPRSS CONSPIRACIES
ACCEIINORTUX EXCRUCIATION
ACCEIIPPRSTY PERSPICACITY
ACCEILLMMORY COMMERCIALLY
ACCEILLMNOOY ECONOMICALLY
ACCEILLMOSTY COSMETICALLY
ACCEILLNNORT CENTROCLINAL
ACCEILLNOTTY TECTONICALLY
ACCEILLOPRRY RECIPROCALLY
ACCEILLOPTYY ECOTYPICALLY
ACCEILMMNORU UNCOMMERCIAL
ACCEILMNNOOU UNECONOMICAL
ACCEILMNORTU COUNTERCLAIM
ACCEILNNNOOT CONNECTIONAL
ACCEILNNOOPT CONCEPTIONAL
ACCEILNNOOTV CONVECTIONAL
ACCEILNNOSTY ANTICYCLONES
ACCEILNOSSSU SUCCESSIONAL
ACCEILOOSSTT OSTEOCLASTIC
ACCEILOPRSTU PLUTOCRACIES
ACCEIMNOSTTY NEMATOCYSTIC
ACCEIMNRTTUU CIRCUMNUTATE
ACCEINNNNOOS INCONSONANCE
ACCEINNOORST CONSECRATION
ACCEINNORSTV CONTRIVANCES
ACCEIOOPRRRT RECIPROCATOR
ACCELLMNOPTY COMPLACENTLY
ACCELLNOPTUY CONCEPTUALLY
ACCELLOOORSU COROLLACEOUS
ACCELLOSSTTU COALSCUTTLES
ACCELMMNOOPS COMMONPLACES
ACCELMNORSUU MACRONUCLEUS
ACCELMOOSTTY CYCLOSTOMATE
ACCELNNRSTUY TRANSLUCENCY
ACCELORSUUVY CURVACEOUSLY
ACCEMOOSSTUY ASCOMYCETOUS
ACCENNOORRTT CONCENTRATOR
ACCENOORRSTY CONSECRATORY
ACCFGHHIOSTT CATCH SIGHT OF
ACCFGIINNOST CONFISCATING
ACCFIIMNNOSU CONFUCIANISM
ACCFIINNOOST CONFISCATION
ACCFIINNOSTU CONFUCIANIST
ACCFILLNOOTU FLOCCULATION
ACCFINOORSTY CONFISCATORY

ACCGGHHIKNOU HACKING COUGH
ACCGHHIINOPR ICHNOGRAPHIC
ACCGHHIINTTT CHITCHATTING
ACCGHHIIOPRR CHIROGRAPHIC
ACCGHHIOOPRR CHOROGRAPHIC
ACCGHIIKNORR ROCKING CHAIR
ACCGHIILLNOO ICHNOLOGICAL
ACCGHIIMOPRR MICROGRAPHIC
ACCGHIIMOTTT THIGMOTACTIC
ACCGHIINOOPR ICONOGRAPHIC
ACCGHIINOPRZ ZINCOGRAPHIC
ACCGHILLOOPY PHYCOLOGICAL
ACCGHINOPSTT SCOTCH TAPING
ACCGIIILNNOT CONCILIATING
ACCGIIINORST ORGANICISTIC
ACCGIILLMOOT CLIMATOLOGIC
ACCGIILLNOOO ICONOLOGICAL
ACCGIILLOOOS SOCIOLOGICAL
ACCGIILMNOPT COMPLICATING
ACCGILLMOOOS COSMOLOGICAL
ACCGILNORTUY GRANULOCYTIC
ACCGIOOPRSST GASTROSCOPIC
ACCHHIOPPSTY PSYCHOPATHIC
ACCHIIINSTUV CHAUVINISTIC
ACCHIILLOOTY ALCOHOLICITY
ACCHIILOPRTY HYPOCRITICAL
ACCHIIMMORST CHROMATICISM
ACCHIIMNOPTY AMPHICTYONIC
ACCHIIMNORST MONARCHISTIC
ACCHIIMOORST ISOCHROMATIC
ACCHIIMORRTT TRICHROMATIC
ACCHIIMORTTY CHROMATICITY
ACCHIINOOPTT PHOTOACTINIC
ACCHIIOPRSTY PHYSIOCRATIC
ACCHILOOPSSY PSYCHOSOCIAL
ACCHILOPPRTY PROPHYLACTIC
ACCHIMOPRSSY MACROPHYSICS
ACCHINOOPSTT PHONOTACTICS
ACCHIOOPRRRT CHIROPRACTOR
ACCHIOORRSSU CHIAROSCUROS
ACCIIILNNOOT CONCILIATION
ACCIIINRSSST NARCISSISTIC
ACCIILLNRTUY UNCRITICALLY
ACCIILLRSTTY CRYSTALLITIC
ACCIILMNOOPT COMPLICATION
ACCIILNOORST CONCILIATORS
ACCIILNOORTY CONCILIATORY
ACCIILOPRSUY CAPRICIOUSLY
ACCIIMOOPRTT COMPATRIOTIC
ACCIINNOOOST CONSOCIATION
ACCIJLNNOTUV CONJUNCTIVAL
ACCILLMNOOSU MALOCCLUSION
ACCILLNOOOST COLLOCATIONS
ACCIMMNNOSTU COMMUNICANTS
ACCIMMNOORTU COMMUNICATOR
ACCIMNNOOSTT CONCOMITANTS
ACCIMNOOSTUU CONTUMACIOUS
ACCIMOORSSTY MACROCYTOSIS
ACCINNOOOSTV CONVOCATIONS

ACCINNOORSTT CONTRACTIONS
ACCJLNNORTUU CONJUNCTURAL
ACDDDEEHNOOR DODECAHEDRON
ACDDDEGINOOR GOOD RIDDANCE
ACDDEEEFLSTU SELF-EDUCATED
ACDDEEEFNORT CONFEDERATED
ACDDEEEHIMST SEMIDETACHED
ACDDEEELLTUW WELL-EDUCATED
ACDDEEEMMNOR COMMANDEERED
ACDDEEFIILSS DECLASSIFIED
ACDDEEGHNRRU UNDERCHARGED
ACDDEEGKLNOW ACKNOWLEDGED
ACDDEEHIMNRS MERCHANDISED
ACDDEEHINNST DISENCHANTED
ACDDEEHNORSW CROWNED HEADS
ACDDEEILPRTU REDUPLICATED
ACDDEEIMORST DEMOCRATISED
ACDDEEIMORTZ DEMOCRATIZED
ACDDEEIMOSTT DOMESTICATED
ACDDEEINNRSU REDUNDANCIES
ACDDEFIRSTUV FIVE-CARD STUD
ACDDEFNNNOOR CANNON FODDER
ACDDEGHINRSU UNDISCHARGED
ACDDEGIILLNO DIALLING CODE
ACDDEIILNORU RADIONUCLIDE
ACDDEIINORST ENDOCARDITIS
ACDDEIINRTTY IDENTITY CARD
ACDDEILNOOST CONSOLIDATED
ACDDEILRSTTY DISTRACTEDLY
ACDDEINOSTTU OUTDISTANCED
ACDDEINPRSTY CANDY-STRIPED
ACDDEMOPRSSU MASS-PRODUCED
ACDDENORRSSW SWORD DANCERS
ACDDHIMNORYY HYDRODYNAMIC
ACDDILNORSTY DISCORDANTLY
ACDDOOOORRUY CORDUROY ROAD
ACDEEEEHLRRS CHEERLEADERS
ACDEEEFFNSST AFFECTEDNESS
ACDEEEFNORST CONFEDERATES
ACDEEEGILNRT DECELERATING
ACDEEEGINOPT PAEDOGENETIC
ACDEEEGINPRS PREDECEASING
ACDEEEGLLOST DÉCOLLETAGES
ACDEEEGLNOOU EAU DE COLOGNE
ACDEEEHINRUV UNDERACHIEVE
ACDEEEILNORT DECELERATION
ACDEEEILNPRT PRECEDENTIAL
ACDEEEILNRST DECENTRALISE
ACDEEEILNRTZ DECENTRALIZE
ACDEEEILNSST DELICATESSEN
ACDEEEINNRTV INADVERTENCE
ACDEEEINRSSV DISSEVERANCE
ACDEEEINSSTT NECESSITATED
ACDEEEOPRRRT TAPE RECORDER
ACDEEEOPRTTX EXPECTORATED
ACDEEFFLNTUY UNAFFECTEDLY
ACDEEFFNORRT FORT-DE-FRANCE
ACDEEFHHIKNR HANDKERCHIEF
ACDEEFHINNRS ENFRANCHISED

ACDEEFIILRST FEDERALISTIC
ACDEEFIINRRY FERRICYANIDE
ACDEEFILMTTU MULTIFACETED
ACDEEFILOPPR PRIDE OF PLACE
ACDEEFINORRY FERROCYANIDE
ACDEEFNOSSTW TWO-FACEDNESS
ACDEEFNRRSUU UNDERSURFACE
ACDEEGHILRST CLEAR-SIGHTED
ACDEEGHINNRT INTERCHANGED
ACDEEGHLLNNU UNCHALLENGED
ACDEEGHPRRSU SUPERCHARGED
ACDEEGIINPRT DEPRECIATING
ACDEEGIINRST GARDEN CITIES
ACDEEGILNORS CLOSE-GRAINED
ACDEEGILSTTU GESTICULATED
ACDEEGINORRT REDECORATING
ACDEEGIOSTTT TIED COTTAGES
ACDEEGKLNORW ACKNOWLEDGER
ACDEEGNNOSTT DECONGESTANT
ACDEEGNOORVW COVERED WAGON
ACDEEHHIMORT HEMICHORDATE
ACDEEHILMNOR ECHINODERMAL
ACDEEHILNNOP DIENCEPHALON
ACDEEHIMNRRS MERCHANDISER
ACDEEHINNRST DISENCHANTER
ACDEEHINRSTW WINDCHEATERS
ACDEEHKMRSTU DEUTSCHE MARK
ACDEEHLORTTY HETERODACTYL
ACDEEHMNORSW REACH-ME-DOWNS
ACDEEHORRSTT ORCHESTRATED
ACDEEIILLNTY INDELICATELY
ACDEEIILLTTY DIETETICALLY
ACDEEIIMNRRT RECRIMINATED
ACDEEIIMNRTY INTERMEDIACY
ACDEEIINOPRT DEPRECIATION
ACDEEIINQSTU EQUIDISTANCE
ACDEEIINTTUX INEXACTITUDE
ACDEEIIPPRTT PRECIPITATED
ACDEEIJKNNRT DINNER JACKET
ACDEEIKLOOPS KALEIDOSCOPE
ACDEEILLNNOS DECLENSIONAL
ACDEEILLNRTY INTERLACEDLY
ACDEEILMNPST DISPLACEMENT
ACDEEILNPQTU QUINDECAPLET
ACDEEILNRSTT DECENTRALIST
ACDEEILORTVY DECORATIVELY
ACDEEIMMORST COMMISERATED
ACDEEIMNNOPR PREDOMINANCE
ACDEEIMNPRST PREDICAMENTS
ACDEEIMORRTX XERODERMATIC
ACDEEINOORST AERODONETICS
ACDEEINOPRTU DEUTERANOPIC
ACDEEINOSSSU EDACIOUSNESS
ACDEEIOPPRTU PROPAEDEUTIC
ACDEEIOPRRTY DEPRECIATORY
ACDEEIORRSSV SERVICE ROADS
ACDEEIORRSTT DIRECTORATES
ACDEEIRSSTTU RESUSCITATED
ACDEEJKKNOTY DONKEY JACKET

ACDEELMNOPTT CONTEMPLATED
ACDEELNOOSSS CLOSED SEASON
ACDEELOPRRRY RECORD PLAYER
ACDEEMMMOORT COMMEMORATED
ACDEEMNOPPTY APPENDECTOMY
ACDEENNNOTUV UNCOVENANTED
ACDEENNNRSTT TRANSCENDENT
ACDEENNORSTU SECOND NATURE
ACDEFFIINOST DISAFFECTION
ACDEFHIINRSS DISFRANCHISE
ACDEFHOORSSU HOUSE OF CARDS
ACDEFIIINNST INFANTICIDES
ACDEFIILNNOT CONFIDENTIAL
ACDEFIILNSSU UNCLASSIFIED
ACDEFIINNSTT DISINFECTANT
ACDEFIINOPTT PONTIFICATED
ACDEFILRTTUX FLUIDEXTRACT
ACDEGHHNORST SHORT-CHANGED
ACDEGHIILRSY RAYLEIGH DISC
ACDEGHIOPRRS DISCOGRAPHER
ACDEGHLOORSS GRADE SCHOOLS
ACDEGIIILMNZ DECIMALIZING
ACDEGIIKNRST SIDETRACKING
ACDEGIILLNSS SLIDING SCALE
ACDEGIILLOOO IDEOLOOGICAL
ACDEGIILPQRU QUADRIPLEGIC
ACDEGIIOOPRT DIAGEOTROPIC
ACDEGILLOOTY DIALECTOLOGY
ACDEGILNNOST LONG-DISTANCE
ACDEGINNNRST TRANSCENDING
ACDEGINORRSS CROSS-GRAINED
ACDEHHHNOTTW DOWN THE HATCH
ACDEHHLOPRYY HYDROCEPHALY
ACDEHHOOOPTT PHOTOCATHODE
ACDEHIILLLOY HELICOIDALLY
ACDEHIILMMOT IMMETHODICAL
ACDEHIIMNNOT INDOMETHACIN
ACDEHIIMORST RADIOCHEMIST
ACDEHILLMOTY METHODICALLY
ACDEHINNOPSW OPEN SANDWICH
ACDEHINOPTTU PUT THE ACID ON
ACDEHIOOPRST ORTHOPAEDICS
ACDEHKMRSSTU DEUTSCHMARKS
ACDEHLNPRSTU THUNDERCLAPS
ACDEIIILNTVY INDICATIVELY
ACDEIIILRTVY VERIDICALITY
ACDEIIMNNNOT NICOTINAMIDE
ACDEIIIMNNRS INCENDIARISM
ACDEIIIMNNRT INCRIMINATED
ACDEIIIMNRST DISCRIMINATE
ACDEIIIMORST ISODIAMETRIC
ACDEIIINOPRT ANTIPERIODIC
ACDEIIINORST DICTIONARIES
ACDEIIINPPST APPENDICITIS
ACDEIIIOPRTY APERIODICITY
ACDEIIIOSSTV DISSOCIATIVE
ACDEIIIPRRST PERICARDITIS
ACDEIILLNNTY INCIDENTALLY
ACDEIILLNSTT SCINTILLATED

ACDEIILLOPRY PERIODICALLY
ACDEIILLOPSY EPISODICALLY
ACDEIILLRTUY DIURETICALLY
ACDEIILMNOST MALEDICTIONS
ACDEIILMORTT DILATOMETRIC
ACDEIILNNNOT NONIDENTICAL
ACDEIILNNOST DECLINATIONS
ACDEIILNOSTV VALEDICTIONS
ACDEIILRRTUV DIVERTICULAR
ACDEIIMNORST ROMANTICISED
ACDEIIMNORTZ ROMANTICIZED
ACDEIINNNOTU DENUNCIATION
ACDEIINNOORT INCOORDINATE
ACDEIINNORTT INDOCTRINATE
ACDEIINOOTTX DETOXICATION
ACDEIIORSSTT SIDEROSTATIC
ACDEIKMNNORT ONE-TRACK MIND
ACDEIKNORSTT STOCK-IN-TRADE
ACDEILLMOSTY DOMESTICALLY
ACDEILLNSTYY SYNDETICALLY
ACDEILLOPSTY DESPOTICALLY
ACDEILLRSSTY CRYSTALLISED
ACDEILLRSTYZ CRYSTALLIZED
ACDEILMNOSUY MENDACIOUSLY
ACDEILMOPSTU DEUTOPLASMIC
ACDEILNOOORT DECOLORATION
ACDEILNOORTU EDULCORATION
ACDEILNOORTY COORDINATELY
ACDEILNOOSST DISCONSOLATE
ACDEILNORSSW COWARDLINESS
ACDEILOORRUV VARICOLOURED
ACDEIMMNNOOT COMMENDATION
ACDEIMMNNORTY DYNAMOMETRIC
ACDEIMMOOORR AIR COMMODORE
ACDEIMNNNOOT CONDEMNATION
ACDEIMNORRRS MORRIS DANCER
ACDEIMNORRSS MORRIS DANCES
ACDEIMOORSTT DOMESTICATOR
ACDEINNNOOST CONDENSATION
ACDEINNNOSTU UNSANCTIONED
ACDEINNORTTU DETRUNCATION
ACDEINNORTUY DENUNCIATORY
ACDEINOOPRRT INCORPORATED
ACDELMOPRTUW TALCUM POWDER
ACDELNOORTYY COTYLEDONARY
ACDELOPRRTTY PROTRACTEDLY
ACDELOPRSTTY PTERODACTYLS
ACDEMMMNNOST COMMANDMENTS
ACDEMMNOORTY COMMENDATORY
ACDEMNNOORTY CONDEMNATORY
ACDEMOPRRSSU MASS-PRODUCER
ACDEOPRSTTUW WASTE PRODUCT
ACDFIIIINNOT NIDIFICATION
ACDFIIIMNOOT MODIFICATION
ACDFIIMOORTY MODIFICATORY
ACDFILMOORTY FAMILY DOCTOR
ACDGGIINORSU DISCOURAGING
ACDGHHIOPRRY HYDROGRAPHIC
ACDGHIIOPRTT DITTOGRAPHIC

ACDGIIINOSST DISSOCIATING
ACDGIIINRSTV VISITING CARD
ACDGIILOORST CARDIOLOGIST
ACDGIINNOORT COORDINATING
ACDHHINOOPRY HYPOCHONDRIA
ACDHHIOPRRSS HARPSICHORDS
ACDHIIMMORST DICHROMATISM
ACDHIIOPRSST RHAPSODISTIC
ACDHIIOPRSTT DICTATORSHIP
ACDHILLOORTY TROCHOIDALLY
ACDHIMNOOPTY PHOTODYNAMIC
ACDHLNOOSSUY SUNDAY SCHOOL
ACDHNRSTTTUU CUT AND THRUST
ACDIIILNPRSY DISCIPLINARY
ACDIIIMNNOOT NONIDIOMATIC
ACDIIIMNNRST DISCRIMINANT
ACDIIINNOORT AIR-CONDITION
ACDIIINOOSST DISSOCIATION
ACDIIIOSSTTU ADSCITITIOUS
ACDIILLLOOTY COLLOIDALLY
ACDIILLMNPTU MULTIPLICAND
ACDIILLOPRTY DIOPTRICALLY
ACDIILNOOSST DISLOCATIONS
ACDIILNORTTY DOCTRINALITY
ACDIILNOSSSU DISCUSSIONAL
ACDIILNSSSTY SYNDICALISTS
ACDIINNOOORT COORDINATION
ACDIINORSSTT DISTRACTIONS
ACDIINORSSYY IDIOSYNCRASY
ACDILMNSSTYY SYNDACTYLISM
ACDILNOOORST CONSOLIDATOR
ACDILNOOPRTU PRODUCTIONAL
ACDINNORSTTU TRANSDUCTION
ACDINOOQRSTU CONQUISTADOR
ACDLOOOPRSTT POSTDOCTORAL
ACEEEEFJKRRT REEFER JACKET
ACEEEEHLPSST STEEPLECHASE
ACEEEELMNRTT TRACE ELEMENT
ACEEEELNORTT COELENTERATE
ACEEEENPRRSV PERSEVERANCE
ACEEEFFFRSTT AFTEREFFECTS
ACEEEFILLNRS SELF-RELIANCE
ACEEEFIOPPPS PIPES OF PEACE
ACEEEFLNPSSU PEACEFULNESS
ACEEEFLNSSSS FACELESSNESS
ACEEEFLORRST STEER CLEAR OF
ACEEEFLRRSTV SCARLET FEVER
ACEEEFNNRRST TRANSFERENCE
ACEEEGHHRSST CHARGE SHEETS
ACEEEGHINPRS CHEESEPARING
ACEEEGIIMNNR ANCIEN RÉGIME
ACEEEGILLTXY EXEGETICALLY
ACEEEGIMNRST RACE MEETINGS
ACEEEGINNOSS CAENOGENESIS
ACEEEGINNSSW NEWS AGENCIES
ACEEEGNNRRUY UNREGENERACY
ACEEEGNRSSTT SECRET AGENTS
ACEEEHHILLLS ACHILLES' HEEL
ACEEEHHILNOT ACE IN THE HOLE

ACEEEHILSTTT TELAESTHETIC
ACEEEHIMNQTU CINEMATHEQUE
ACEEEHIMNSTV ACHIEVEMENTS
ACEEEHINOSST COENESTHESIA
ACEEEHLMOPRT CEPHALOMETER
ACEEEHLNNOPP EPENCEPHALON
ACEEEHMNNNST ENHANCEMENTS
ACEEEILLLNTT LENTICELLATE
ACEEEILLNPST LICENSE PLATE
ACEEEILMNPST MANTELPIECES
ACEEEILNNNSV VALENCIENNES
ACEEEILNPPRS PIPE CLEANERS
ACEEEILNRRSV IRRELEVANCES
ACEEEIMMNNPR IMPERMANENCE
ACEEEIMNNPRT INTEMPERANCE
ACEEEIMNRSVX EX-SERVICEMAN
ACEEEIMPRSST MASTERPIECES
ACEEEINRSSTV REACTIVENESS
ACEEEIPPPRTV APPERCEPTIVE
ACEEEIPRRTUV RECUPERATIVE
ACEEEJKLPSST STEEPLEJACKS
ACEEEJORSSTT EJECTOR SEATS
ACEEELLOPRTT ELECTROPLATE
ACEEELLORSVV CLOVERLEAVES
ACEEELMMNPST EMPLACEMENTS
ACEEELMNPRST REPLACEMENTS
ACEEELNOTXYY OXYACETYLENE
ACEEELNRSSSS CARELESSNESS
ACEEEMNNNRTT ENTRANCEMENT
ACEEENNRRTTY TERCENTENARY
ACEEENNRSTXY SEXCENTENARY
ACEEEOPPRRTT PRECEPTORATE
ACEEFFFGILNS SELF-EFFACING
ACEEFFGHILNO CHANGE OF LIFE
ACEEFFGINTTU EFFECTUATING
ACEEFFHOTTTT TO THAT EFFECT
ACEEFFILTTUY EFFECTUALITY
ACEEFFINOTTU EFFECTUATION
ACEEFFNNORSU ON SUFFERANCE
ACEEFGILNRST SELF-CATERING
ACEEFGLNRSSU GRACEFULNESS
ACEEFGNNOOST AGE OF CONSENT
ACEEFHINNRRS ENFRANCHISER
ACEEFHLNORSV FRENCH LOAVES
ACEEFHLOPRRS SELF-REPROACH
ACEEFHMORTTY AT THE MERCY OF
ACEEFHNOPRTU PUT HER FACE ON
ACEEFHNORSTU ON THE SURFACE
ACEEFHOPPRST PART OF SPEECH
ACEEFIIIRTVV VERIFICATIVE
ACEEFIILNQTU LIQUEFACIENT
ACEEFIILQTUV LIQUEFACTIVE
ACEEFIKNNNRS FRANKINCENSE
ACEEFILLNORT REFLECTIONAL
ACEEFILLNRTY FRENETICALLY
ACEEFILNNORT CONFERENTIAL
ACEEFILNNOST LINE OF ASCENT
ACEEFILOPRRT PREFECTORIAL
ACEEFILRSSTV SERVICE FLATS

ACEEFINPSTTU STUPEFACIENT
ACEEFIPRTTUV PUTREFACTIVE
ACEEFKMORRST MARKET FORCES
ACEEFMNOPRRS PERFORMANCES
ACEEFPPRSSTT PAST PERFECTS
ACEEGGINORTV CONGREGATIVE
ACEEGHILNOSU CHAISE LONGUE
ACEEGHILNRTW CARTWHEELING
ACEEGHILOORS ARCHEOLOGIES
ACEEGHINNRST INTERCHANGES
ACEEGHINOPTT PATHOGENETIC
ACEEGHINORRV OVERREACHING
ACEEGHIRRSST CASH REGISTER
ACEEGHLLNSSY CHANGELESSLY
ACEEGHLOPRRT ELECTROGRAPH
ACEEGHMNNORY MONEYCHANGER
ACEEGHNOPRRS SCENOGRAPHER
ACEEGHNRRSSU CHARGE NURSES
ACEEGHPRRRSU SUPERCHARGER
ACEEGIILNNPT PALINGENETIC
ACEEGIILNSTV EVANGELISTIC
ACEEGIINRSTV EVISCERATING
ACEEGIIOTTVX EXCOGITATIVE
ACEEGIKNNRRV NERVE-RACKING
ACEEGILLLNTY TELGENICALLY
ACEEGILLLOOT TELEOLOGICAL
ACEEGILMNOPT MAGNETIC POLE
ACEEGILNPRSS SLEEPING CARS
ACEEGILNPSTT PLACE SETTING
ACEEGIMNORTY ATOMIC ENERGY
ACEEGINNSSTX EXACTINGNESS
ACEEGINORRTV OVERREACTING
ACEEGINPRRTU RECUPERATING
ACEEGLMNOORT CONGLOMERATE
ACEEGMNORRSS SCAREMONGERS
ACEEHHIPRRSU HIRE PURCHASE
ACEEHHKNPPRU KERENHAPPUCH
ACEEHHLMRSST CRASH HELMETS
ACEEHHLNORSU CHARNEL HOUSE
ACEEHHMOPRTY CHEMOTHERAPY
ACEEHHNORSST SHEET ANCHORS
ACEEHHOPRSTU CHAPTERHOUSE
ACEEHHOPRTTY TRACHEOPHYTE
ACEEHIIKNSTT KINAESTHETIC
ACEEHIILNPST ENCEPHALITIS
ACEEHIIMOOPT HAEMOPOIETIC
ACEEHIIMSSTT AESTHETICISM
ACEEHIINNRST INHERITANCES
ACEEHIINORTT THEORETICIAN
ACEEHIINSTUU HAUTE CUISINE
ACEEHILLLLNY HELLENICALLY
ACEEHILLMRTY HERMETICALLY
ACEEHILLSTTY ESTHETICALLY
ACEEHILNORSS HEROICALNESS
ACEEHILNRSTT CHAIN LETTERS
ACEEHILPSSST SALES PITCHES
ACEEHIMMNTTY ENTHYMEMATIC
ACEEHIMNSSTT CHASTISEMENT
ACEEHIMOPRTV OVEREMPHATIC

ACEEHIMRSSTV CHRISTMAS EVE
ACEEHINNRSTU NEURASTHENIC
ACEEHINORUUV NOUVEAU RICHE
ACEEHINSSTTY SYNAESTHETIC
ACEEHIOSTTUW WITHOUT CEASE
ACEEHIPRSTTU THERAPEUTICS
ACEEHLLOORRU LEUCORRHOEAL
ACEEHLLOORSV SCHOOL-LEAVER
ACEEHLMOPRTY CEPHALOMETRY
ACEEHLPSSTTU SPACE SHUTTLE
ACEEHMNNNSTT ENCHANTMENTS
ACEEHMORRSSTU ROUTE MARCHES
ACEEHNNSSSTU UNCHASTENESS
ACEEHOPPRRRS SHARECROPPER
ACEEHORTTUUU HAUTE COUTURE
ACEEIIILPSST SPECIALITIES
ACEEIILLMNSS MISCELLANIES
ACEEIILLRTTV VERTICILLATE
ACEEIILMMPRT METEMPIRICAL
ACEEIILMRRSU MERCURIALISE
ACEEIILMRRUZ MERCURIALIZE
ACEEIILNOSST SECTIONALISE
ACEEIILNOSTZ SECTIONALIZE
ACEEIIMMRSTT MERISTEMATIC
ACEEIIMNPRSU EPICUREANISM
ACEEIINNORST CONTAINERISE
ACEEIINNORTZ CONTAINERIZE
ACEEIINNRTUV RENUNCIATIVE
ACEEIINORSTV EVISCERATION
ACEEIIPPRSTT PRECIPITATES
ACEEIJORRSTT TRAJECTORIES
ACEEIKKNOPST TAKE ONE'S PICK
ACEEIKMPRRST MARKET PRICES
ACEEIKNOSSTT SEASON TICKET
ACEEILLLNTTU INTELLECTUAL
ACEEILLMMRSY MESMERICALLY
ACEEILLMNORY CEREMONIALLY
ACEEILLMORTY METEORICALLY
ACEEILLNNORT CRENELLATION
ACEEILLNORTY NEOTERICALLY
ACEEILLNOTUV INVOLUCELATE
ACEEILLNRSUV SURVEILLANCE
ACEEILLORSTY ESOTERICALLY
ACEEILLORTXY EXOTERICALLY
ACEEILMMNPST MISPLACEMENT
ACEEILMPSSTU TIME CAPSULES
ACEEILNOPPRT PERCEPTIONAL
ACEEILNOPRRT PRECENTORIAL
ACEEILNOPRSS PRECESSIONAL
ACEEILNORSSS RECESSIONALS
ACEEILNPRTTY PETIT LARCENY
ACEEILNSSTTT CLIENT STATES
ACEEILOPPRRT PRECEPTORIAL
ACEEILOPSSTT POLICE STATES
ACEEILORRSTV CORRELATIVES
ACEEILPPSSTTU SEPTUPLICATE
ACEEILPSTTUX SEXTUPLICATE
ACEEIMMMNNOTT COMMITTEEMAN
ACEEIMMNORST COMMENTARIES

ACEEIMMMOSSTT MASTECTOMIES
ACEEIMNOPSTV COMPENSATIVE
ACEEIMNORSSX CROSS-EXAMINE
ACEEINOORRTV OVERREACTION
ACEEINOPPPRT APPERCEPTION
ACEEINOPRRTU RECUPERATION
ACEEINOPRSTT INSPECTORATE
ACEEINOPSTTX EXPECTATIONS
ACEEINORRSTY SECRETIONARY
ACEEINORSTVV CONSERVATIVE
ACEEIOOPRSTV COOPERATIVES
ACEELLORSSSW LOWER CLASSES
ACEELMNNORTU NOMENCLATURE
ACEELMNOOSTU LOMENTACEOUS
ACEELMNORSTW SCARLET WOMEN
ACEELMORSSST MALTESE CROSS
ACEELNOOSSSS CLOSE SEASONS
ACEELNPRTTYY PETTY LARCENY
ACEELNSSSSTT TACTLESSNESS
ACEELOOPPPTT POPOCATEPETL
ACEELORSSTTW WATER CLOSETS
ACEELPSSTUUY EUCALYPTUSES
ACEEMMNORSTU COMMENSURATE
ACEEMNNNNOTU ANNOUNCEMENT
ACEEMNNORRST REMONSTRANCE
ACEEMOPRSTTY SPERMATOCYTE
ACEENNOPRSTU COUNTERPANES
ACEENOPRSTUU PERCUTANEOUS
ACEEOOPRRTTT PROTECTORATE
ACEEOOPRRTTX EXPECTORATOR
ACEEORRSSTUW WATERCOURSES
ACEFFFFHIOST CHIEF OF STAFF
ACEFFFIORST STAFF OFFICER
ACEFFGHILNRS CLIFFHANGERS
ACEFFGHINRUU CHAUFFEURING
ACEFFILNNSSU FANCIFULNESS
ACEFFILOSSUU USUAL OFFICES
ACEFFORRSUUU FURFURACEOUS
ACEFGIIILNTT FELICITATING
ACEFGIIKNNRV CARVING KNIFE
ACEFGIINORTV VOCIFERATING
ACEFGILNRSUY FLYING SAUCER
ACEFHIIMNRTU FRUIT MACHINE
ACEFHLNSSTUW WATCHFULNESS
ACEFHNORSTTU COUNTERSHAFT
ACEFHORRSSTU RHESUS FACTOR
ACEFIIILNOST FICTIONALISE
ACEFIIILNOTT FELICITATION
ACEFIIILNOTZ FICTIONALIZE
ACEFIIINORTV VERIFICATION
ACEFIILLNNOT INFLECTIONAL
ACEFIILLRRTY TERRIFICALLY
ACEFIILNOQTU LIQUEFACTION
ACEFIILORSTU LATICIFEROUS
ACEFIINOORTV VOCIFERATION
ACEFIINOPRTT PETRIFACTION
ACEFIINOPSTT PONTIFICATES
ACEFIIPRRSUY SUPERFICIARY
ACEFILLNORSY FORENSICALLY

ACEFILLORSUW CAULIFLOWERS
ACEFILNNOOSS CONFESSIONAL
ACEFILORRRTY REFRACTORILY
ACEFINOORRTT TORREFACTION
ACEFINOPRTTU PUTREFACTION
ACEFINOPSTTU STUPEFACTION
ACEFINOSSSTU FACTIOUSNESS
ACEFLLMOOPRW CAMP FOLLOWER
ACEGGGINNORT CONGREGATING
ACEGGHINORRV OVERCHARGING
ACEGGIILNNST SINGLE-ACTING
ACEGGIINNSST GIGANTICNESS
ACEGGIINORTZ CATEGORIZING
ACEGGILLLOOY GEOLOGICALLY
ACEGGIMNORTY GYROMAGNETIC
ACEGGINNOORT CONGREGATION
ACEGHHIILOPR HELIOGRAPHIC
ACEGHHILRSST SEARCHLIGHTS
ACEGHHINOPRT ETHNOGRAPHIC
ACEGHHIOPRRR CHIROGRAPHER
ACEGHHNOPRTY TECHNOGRAPHY
ACEGHHNORRST SHORT-CHANGER
ACEGHHOOPRRR CHOROGRAPHER
ACEGHHOOPRRS CHOREOGRAPHS
ACEGHHOOPRRY CHOREOGRAPHY
ACEGHIILLNYY HYGIENICALLY
ACEGHIIMNSTZ SCHEMATIZING
ACEGHIKLLNSS SHELLACKINGS
ACEGHILLNNOU HALLUCINOGEN
ACEGHILLNOOP NEPHOLOGICAL,
    PHENOLOGICAL
ACEGHILLNOOT ETHNOLOGICAL
ACEGHILLRTUY THEURGICALLY
ACEGHILOPPRY PYELOGRAPHIC
ACEGHILOPRXY LEXICOGRAPHY
ACEGHIMOOPRT GAMETOPHORIC
ACEGHIMOPRRR MICROGRAPHER
ACEGHIMOPTTY GAMETOPHYTIC
ACEGHINOOPRR ICONOGRAPHER
ACEGHINOPRRZ ZINCOGRAPHER
ACEGHINOPRST STENOGRAPHIC
ACEGHINORRSU HARE COURSING
ACEGHIOPPRRR REPROGRAPHIC
ACEGHIOPPRRT PETROGRAPHIC
ACEGHIOPRRST CEROGRAPHIST
ACEGHLMNOOUY HUMAN ECOLOGY
ACEGHOPPRRST SPECTROGRAPH
ACEGIIILLMTY ILLEGITIMACY
ACEGIIILNPSZ SPECIALIZING
ACEGIIINNNRT INCINERATING
ACEGIIINSTTV NEGATIVISTIC
ACEGIIKNPRSS ASKING PRICES
ACEGIILLOOPT GEOPOLITICAL
ACEGIILLOSTY EGOISTICALLY
ACEGIILNNOST SINGLE-ACTION
ACEGIILNNOTU GENICULATION
ACEGIILNNOTY CONGENIALITY
ACEGIILNNRSY INCREASINGLY
ACEGIILNNRTZ CENTRALIZING

ACEGIILNRSUZ SECULARIZING
ACEGIILORSSU SACRILEGIOUS
ACEGIINNPPRT APPRENTICING
ACEGIINOOTTX EXCOGITATION
ACEGIINOQTUV EQUIVOCATING
ACEGIKLNOOPP COOKING APPLE
ACEGILLLNOOY NEOLOGICALLY
ACEGILLMOORT METROLOGICAL
ACEGILLMOOTY ETYMOLOGICAL
ACEGILLNNOSY GEOSYNCLINAL
ACEGILLNNOTY CONGENITALLY
ACEGILLNOORU NEUROLOGICAL
ACEGILLNOORY OROGENICALLY
ACEGILLOOOST OSTEOLOGICAL
ACEGILLOOPRT PETROLOGICAL
ACEGILMMOPSY OLYMPIC GAMES
ACEGILNNNRTY ENTRANCINGLY
ACEGILNNOTTU CONGLUTINATE
ACEGILNOOPRT ORGANOLEPTIC
ACEGILOOPSST ESCAPOLOGIST
ACEGILORSTTU GESTICULATOR
ACEGIMMNNOTT COMMENTATING
ACEGIMNNOPSS ENCOMPASSING
ACEGIMNNOPST COMPENSATING
ACEGINNNORTV CONTRAVENING
ACEGINNORSTT NONSTRATEGIC
ACEGINORSSSU GRACIOUSNESS
ACEGINOSSTTV CASTING VOTES
ACEGIOOOPPRT APOGEOTROPIC
ACEGLNOOPRSY LARYNGOSCOPE
ACEGLOOORSUY COURAGEOUSLY
ACEGLRSSSTTU GLASSCUTTERS
ACEHHIILMOPS HEMOPHILIACS
ACEHHIIMMPTU AMPHITHECIUM
ACEHHIINOPRT HIEROPHANTIC
ACEHHILMOPTX EXOPHTHALMIC
ACEHHILOPTTY HYPOTHETICAL
ACEHHINOPRTT THEANTHROPIC
ACEHHLLLOOTY ETHYL ALCOHOL
ACEHHLOOPRTY ORTHOCEPHALY
ACEHIIINNRST CHRISTIANISE
ACEHIIINRSTZ CHRISTIANIZE
ACEHIILLMPTY MEPHITICALLY
ACEHIILLMRTY HERMITICALLY
ACEHIILLSTTY THEISTICALLY
ACEHIILNPPRS PLANISPHERIC
ACEHIINNOPPR HIPPOCRENIAN
ACEHIINNOPST PHONETICIANS
ACEHIINORRST RHETORICIANS
ACEHIINSSTTU ENTHUSIASTIC
ACEHIINTTTUY AUTHENTICITY
ACEHIIOPSSTT SOPHISTICATE
ACEHIIPPRRST PERIPHRASTIC
ACEHIKLPRRSS PARISH CLERKS
ACEHIKMNORSS CHAIN-SMOKERS
ACEHIKMNOSST MACKINTOSHES
ACEHILLLMNOY MELANCHOLILY
ACEHILLLPTYY PHYLETICALLY
ACEHILLMNNTU MULTICHANNEL

ACEHILLMNOPY PHONEMICALLY
ACEHILLNOPST PLAIN-CLOTHES
ACEHILLNOPTY PHONETICALLY
ACEHILLNOPUY EUPHONICALLY
ACEHILLOPRUY EUPHORICALLY
ACEHILLORRTY RHETORICALLY
ACEHILLRSTYY HYSTERICALLY
ACEHILMNOOST MACHINE TOOLS
ACEHILMNOSST SLOT MACHINES
ACEHILMOOPSU AMPHICOELOUS
ACEHILMOPTYY POLYCYTHEMIA
ACEHILNNNSSS CLANNISHNESS
ACEHILNPSSSY PHYSICALNESS
ACEHIMOPRSST ATMOSPHERICS
ACEHIMORRSST CHOIRMASTERS
ACEHIMORSTTT THERMOSTATIC
ACEHINNOOPRT NEOANTHROPIC
ACEHINOPRRSS CHAIRPERSONS
ACEHINOPRRTT TRICHOPTERAN
ACEHIOPRRSTT ORCHESTRA PIT
ACEHIRSSTTWW WRISTWATCHES
ACEHKMRRSSTT STRETCHMARKS
ACEHLMMNOOTW COMMONWEALTH
ACEHLMOORSST SCHOOLMASTER
ACEHLNOOPRTU PHOTONUCLEAR
ACEHLOOPSTUY POLYCHAETOUS
ACEHLOPSSUXY PSYCHOSEXUAL
ACEHMOORSTTY TRACHEOSTOMY
ACEHNNOOPRRS ANCHORPERSON
ACEIIILLRSTT LITERALISTIC
ACEIIILMNNSS INIMICALNESS
ACEIIILMNPSU MUNICIPALISE
ACEIIILMNPUZ MUNICIPALIZE
ACEIIILNNOTT LICENTIATION
ACEIIILNSTTY INELASTICITY
ACEIIILRSTTV RELATIVISTIC
ACEIIILRSTVV REVIVALISTIC
ACEIIIMNOSST SEMIOTICIANS
ACEIIIMNPRSS PRECISIANISM
ACEIIINNNORT INCINERATION
ACEIIINOTTVX INTOXICATIVE
ACEIIKKNORTY KARYOKINETIC
ACEIILLLLPTY ELLIPTICALLY
ACEIILLLNSUV ALL-INCLUSIVE
ACEIILLMNSST MISCELLANIST
ACEIILLMPTTU MULTIPLICATE
ACEIILMMNRST MERCANTILISM
ACEIILMNORST SALINOMETRIC
ACEIILMNOSST SECTIONALISM
ACEIILMNRSTT MERCANTILIST
ACEIILMOPPSS EPISCOPALISM
ACEIILMOPRRT POLARIMETRIC
ACEIILMOPRST SEMITROPICAL
ACEIILNNNRTU INTERNUNCIAL
ACEIILNNOPST INSPECTIONAL
ACEIILNOPRST REPLICATIONS
ACEIILNORTTU RETICULATION
ACEIILNOSSTT SECTIONALIST
ACEIILNOSTUV VESICULATION

ACEIILNRSTTT CLARINETTIST
ACEIILNRSTVV CIVIL SERVANT
ACEIILOQSSUU SILIQUACEOUS
ACEIILOQTUVY EQUIVOCALITY
ACEIILPRRSUY SUPERCILIARY
ACEIILRRSSTU SURREALISTIC
ACEIILRRTTTY RETRACTILITY
ACEIIMMNORST CREMATIONISM
ACEIIMMORSSS COMMISSARIES
ACEIIMNOPRST IMPRECATIONS
ACEIIMNORRRT RECRIMINATOR
ACEIIMNORSTT CREMATIONIST
ACEIINNNORTU RENUNCIATION
ACEIINNORRST INCINERATORS
ACEIINNORRTY INCRETIONARY
ACEIINNORSTT INTERACTIONS
ACEIINNOTTUV CONTINUATIVE
ACEIINOOQTUV EQUIVOCATION
ACEIINOORSTX EXCORIATIONS
ACEIINOPRRTT PRACTITIONER
ACEIINOPRSTU PERTINACIOUS
ACEIINORRSTW CONTRARIWISE
ACEIIOPPRRTT PRECIPITATOR
ACEIJKLLNOSV JACKSONVILLE
ACEIJLNOOPRT PROJECTIONAL
ACEIKKNORRST NOT A SKERRICK
ACEIKLOORRSW SOCIAL WORKER
ACEIKLPPRRSY PRICKLY PEARS
ACEIKNNORSST IN ONE'S TRACKS
ACEIKORRRTTT TRICK OR TREAT
ACEILLMMNNOY MNEMONICALLY
ACEILLMMNOOT MONOMETALLIC
ACEILLMNRTUU MULTINUCLEAR
ACEILLMNTUVY MULTIVALENCY
ACEILLMORRTU TRIMOLECULAR
ACEILLMSSTYY SYSTEMICALLY
ACEILLMTUUVY CUMULATIVELY
ACEILLNNORRU CARILLONNEUR
ACEILLNOOTYZ ENZOOTICALLY
ACEILLNORTUY NEUROTICALLY
ACEILLNOSTTU SCUTELLATION
ACEILLNOTTUY TEUTONICALLY
ACEILLRRSTUU SERICULTURAL
ACEILMMMNOSS COMMENSALISM
ACEILMMNOORT MONOMETRICAL
ACEILMNNOOPT COMPONENTIAL
ACEILMNOORTU NEUROTOMICAL
ACEILMNRSTTU CURTAILMENTS
ACEILMOPRSTT PLASTOMETRIC
ACEILMOPRSUU PRIMULACEOUS
ACEILNNNOOTT CONTENTIONAL
ACEILNNNOOTV CONVENTIONAL
ACEILNNNOSTT CONTINENTALS
ACEILNNOORSV CONVERSIONAL
ACEILNNOOPRSS PROCESSIONAL
ACEILNOOPRST PERCOLATIONS
ACEILNOOPRTT LACTOPROTEIN
ACEILNOORRST CORRELATIONS
ACEILNOORTUY ELOCUTIONARY

ACEILNOPSSTU SPECULATIONS
ACEILNORSUXY EXCLUSIONARY
ACEILNOSTTUV CONSULTATIVE
ACEILOOPRRTY CORPOREALITY
ACEILOOPSSTT OSTEOPLASTIC
ACEILOPRRSUY PRECARIOUSLY
ACEIMMNOSTUV CONSUMMATIVE
ACEIMMOORRST COMMISERATOR
ACEIMMORRSTU CREMATORIUMS
ACEIMNNOOPST COMPENSATION
ACEIMNOOOOPT ONOMATOPOEIC
ACEIMNORSSTV CONSERVATISM
ACEIMOOPRSTZ ZOOSPERMATIC
ACEIMPRRRSTW WRITER'S CRAMP
ACEIMPRSSSTU SUPREMACISTS
ACEINNOORSTV CONSERVATION,
  CONVERSATION
ACEINNOOSTTT CONTESTATION
ACEINNORRSST CONTRARINESS
ACEINNORSTTU ENCRUSTATION
ACEINOPPRRTU PORT-AU-PRINCE
ACEINOPSSSSU SPACIOUSNESS
ACEINOPSSSTU CAPTIOUSNESS
ACEINOSSSTUU CAUTIOUSNESS
ACEIOOPRRRRT TROOP CARRIER
ACEIOOQRTUVY EQUIVOCATORY
ACEIOORSTUUV OVERCAUTIOUS
ACEIORRSSTTU RESUSCITATOR
ACEKKMORSSTT STOCK MARKETS
ACEKMMMNOORT COMMON MARKET
ACELLNOTTUXY CONTEXTUALLY
ACELMMNOSTUY CONSUMMATELY
ACELMNOOPRTT CONTEMPLATOR
ACELNOOPRSTU PROCONSULATE
ACELNOSSTTTU TALENT SCOUTS
ACELOORRSTUW WATERCOLOURS
ACEMMMOOORRT COMMEMORATOR
ACEMMNOORSTT COMMENTATORS
ACEMMNOPRSTT COMPARTMENTS
ACEMMPRSSSTU MASS SPECTRUM
ACEMNOOPRRTY CONTEMPORARY
ACEMNOOPRSTY COMPENSATORY
ACEMOOPRRSTU MACROPTEROUS
ACEMORSSSTTU SCOUTMASTERS
ACENNRRRSTTU TRANSCURRENT
ACENOORRSTVY CONSERVATORY
ACENOPRRSTTU COUNTERPARTS
ACENORSSTTUY COUNTRY SEATS
ACFFGGHIILNN CLIFFHANGING
ACFFGHIILRTT TRAFFIC LIGHT
ACFFIILLNOUY UNOFFICIALLY
ACFGGHIMNORR FROGMARCHING
ACFGHILNORTW FLOWCHARTING
ACFGIIILNOTU UGLIFICATION
ACFGIKNORRSV CARVING FORKS
ACFHHLNORSSY SYNCHROFLASH
ACFHIILLORRY HORRIFICALLY
ACFHKMOOOSTU ASK TOO MUCH OF
ACFIIIILNOTV VILIFICATION

ACFIIIIMNNOT MINIFICATION
ACFIIIINOTVV VIVIFICATION
ACFIIINNOOTT NOTIFICATION
ACFIIINOOSST OSSIFICATION
ACFIIINOPRTU PURIFICATION
ACFIIINOPTTY TYPIFICATION
ACFIILLLOPRY PROLIFICALLY
ACFIILNNNOOT NONFICTIONAL
ACFIIMNNOORT CONFIRMATION
ACFIINORRTTU TRIFURCATION
ACFIIOPRRTUY PURIFICATORY
ACFILLNNOTUY FUNCTIONALLY
ACFILMNNOSTU MALFUNCTIONS
ACFILNOSTTUU FLUCTUATIONS
ACFIMNNOOORT CONFORMATION
ACFIMNOORRTY CONFIRMATORY
ACFINNOOSTTU CONFUTATIONS
ACFRRSTUUUUY USUFRUCTUARY
ACGGHIMNNOOR CHANGING ROOM
ACGGIILLOOST GLACIOLOGIST
ACGHHHIOPTYY ICHTHYOPHAGY
ACGHHIILOPRT LITHOGRAPHIC
ACGHHIOOPPRT PHOTOGRAPHIC
ACGHHIOOPRRT ORTHOGRAPHIC
ACGHHNOOPRRS CHRONOGRAPHS
ACGHHOPPRSYY PSYCHOGRAPHY
ACGHIIKMNNOS CHAIN-SMOKING
ACGHIILLLOOP PHILOLOGICAL
ACGHIILLNOOR RHINOLOGICAL
ACGHIILLOOOP OPHIOLOGICAL
ACGHIILLOOST HISTOLOGICAL
ACGHIILMNPTY LYMPHANGITIC
ACGHIILNNORT CHLORINATING
ACGHIILNORTY TRICHOGYNIAL
ACGHIIOPPRRS SPIROGRAPHIC
ACGHIIPRSSST SPHRAGISTICS
ACGHIKNOOSTW WHAT'S COOKING?
ACGHILLMOOTY MYTHOLOGICAL
ACGHILLNOOOP PHONOLOGICAL
ACGHILLOOPRS OSCILLOGRAPH
ACGHILOPRSTY STYLOGRAPHIC
ACGHINOOPPRR PORNOGRAPHIC
ACGHIOOPSSTY PHAGOCYTOSIS
ACGHKLOPPUYY HAPPY-GO-LUCKY
ACGHOOOPPRSU COPROPHAGOUS
ACGHOPPRRTYY CRYPTOGRAPHY
ACGIIILLLOTY ILLOGICALITY
ACGIIINNOTTX INTOXICATING
ACGIIKKLNSTW WALKING STICK
ACGIILLLMNOO LIMNOLOGICAL
ACGIILLLOSTY LOGISTICALLY
ACGIILLLRTUY LITURGICALLY
ACGIILMNOSUU MUCILAGINOUS
ACGIILNOORST CRANIOLOGIST
ACGIILNPPSTU SUPPLICATING
ACGIIMMNOOST MONOGAMISTIC
ACGIINNNOOST CONSIGNATION
ACGIINNNORST CONSTRAINING
ACGIJNNOOSTU CONJUGATIONS

ACGIKLNORSSW WORKING CLASS
ACGILLLOOORY OROLOGICALLY
ACGILLMNNOOY GNOMONICALLY
ACGILNNNOTTU CONGLUTINANT
ACGILNOOQSTUY CONTAGIOUSLY
ACGILNOPSUUY PUGNACIOUSLY
ACGIMMNNOSTU CONSUMMATING
ACGIMNNOORST MORNING COATS
ACGINOOORRSTU CORRUGATIONS
ACGINOPPRRSY CROP-SPRAYING
ACGLLNOORSUY CLANGOROUSLY
ACGLMNNOOSUY AGONY COLUMNS
ACGLNOOPRSYY LARYNGOSCOPY
ACHHIILMNOPR PHILHARMONIC
ACHHIIMNOPPS CHAMPIONSHIP
ACHHIIMOSTYZ SCHIZOTHYMIA
ACHHILLMRTYY RHYTHMICALLY
ACHHILLOPTTY THALLOPHYTIC
ACHHILOOPRST HOLOPHRASTIC
ACHHILOPRSSS SCHOLARSHIPS
ACHHIOPPRSTU PHOSPHATURIC
ACHHNNOOOOPRY ONYCHOPHORAN
ACHIIIINRSST TRICHINIASIS
ACHIIILMSTWY WHIMSICALITY
ACHIIIMNPSSU MUSICIANSHIP
ACHIIINRSTTY CHRISTIANITY
ACHIILLLOSTY HOLISTICALLY
ACHIILLNOSSU HALLUCINOSIS
ACHIILLORSTY HISTORICALLY
ACHIILNNOORT CHLORINATION
ACHIILNOPRST RHINOPLASTIC
ACHIIMNOPRST MISANTHROPIC
ACHIIPRSSTTY PSYCHIATRIST
ACHILLNOPTYY HYPNOTICALLY
ACHILLORSUVY CHIVALROUSLY
ACHILMORSTYY LACHRYMOSITY
ACHILOOPPRRS CORPORALSHIP
ACHIMNNORSSY ASYNCHRONISM
ACHINOOPTTUY AUTOHYPNOTIC
ACHINOPRSSTY CORNISH PASTY
ACHIOOPRRRST ARTHROSPORIC
ACHIOOPRRSUZ RHIZOCARPOUS
ACHIOPRRSSTU CURATORSHIPS
ACHIOPRSSSTY ASTROPHYSICS
ACHMMOPPSSTU STOMACH PUMPS
ACHNNOORSSUY ASYNCHRONOUS
ACHOOPRRRTTU PORT HARCOURT
ACIIIILMRSTT MILITARISTIC
ACIIIILNOSTV CIVILISATION
ACIIIILNOTVZ CIVILIZATION
ACIIILMNNOST NOMINALISTIC
ACIIILMNOPST IMPLICATIONS
ACIIILMNPTUY MUNICIPALITY
ACIIILNNNOST INCLINATIONS
ACIIILNOOSTT COALITIONIST, SOLICITATION
ACIIILNOPRTT TRIPLICATION
ACIIILNOTVVY CONVIVIALITY
ACIIILNPPRTY PRINCIPALITY
ACIIILQTUYZZ QUIZZICALITY

ACIIIMNNNORRT INCRIMINATOR
ACIIIMNORSTV VICTORIANISM
ACIIINNOOTTX INTOXICATION
ACIIINOPSSUU INAUSPICIOUS
ACIIINOQSSTU ACQUISITIONS
ACIIJLNORSTU JOURNALISTIC
ACIIKKPRSSTU KICK UPSTAIRS
ACIILLMNOSTY MONISTICALLY
ACIILLNNOOPT NONPOLITICAL
ACIILLNOOSST COLONIALISTS, OSCILLATIONS
ACIILLNOPRVY PROVINCIALLY
ACIILLNORSTT SCINTILLATOR
ACIILLNRTUUV VINICULTURAL
ACIILLOOPSTY ISOTOPICALLY
ACIILLOQTUXY QUIXOTICALLY
ACIILLOSSUVY LASCIVIOUSLY
ACIILLPRSTUY PURISTICALLY
ACIILLRTTUUV VITICULTURAL
ACIILMMNOOSS COMMISSIONAL
ACIILMNNOOTU COLUMNIATION
ACIILMNOOPST COMPILATIONS
ACIILMNORSTU MATRICLINOUS
ACIILMOPRTUV VICTORIA PLUM
ACIILNNOOOST COLONISATION
ACIILNNOOOTZ COLONIZATION
ACIILNNOOSTU INOCULATIONS, INOSCULATION
ACIILNNOTTUY CONTINUALITY
ACIILNOORSST CONSISTORIAL
ACIILNOPPSTU SUPPLICATION
ACIILNOPRSTU PATRICLINOUS
ACIILNORSSSS NAIL SCISSORS
ACIILNOSTUUY INCAUTIOUSLY
ACIILOPSSUUY AUSPICIOUSLY
ACIILPRSTTUU APICULTURIST
ACIILRSTTUUV AVICULTURIST
ACIIMNOPRTTU PROTACTINIUM
ACIIMNORSSTT ROMANTICISTS
ACIINNNOOTTU CONTINUATION
ACIINNOOPSTT CONSTIPATION
ACIINNORSTTU INCRUSTATION
ACILLLLOOQUY COLLOQUIALLY
ACILLMOOOTYZ ZOOTOMICALLY
ACILLNNOSTYY SYNTONICALLY
ACILLNOOOPST LOCAL OPTIONS
ACILLNOPSTYY SYNOPTICALLY
ACILLOOQSUUY LOQUACIOUSLY
ACILMNNOOTT NONCOMMITTAL
ACILMNOOOPST COSMOPOLITAN
ACILMOOPPRST PROTOPLASMIC
ACILNNOOORTT CONTORTIONAL
ACILNNOOOSST CONSOLATIONS
ACILNNOOSTTU CONSULTATION
ACILNNORTTUY NOCTURNALITY
ACILNNOOORSTU ICONOLATROUS
ACILOOPPRSTT PROTOPLASTIC
ACILOPPRSTUY SUPPLICATORY
ACILORSSSTTU TOURIST CLASS
ACIMMNNOOSTU CONSUMMATION

ACIMMNOOSTTU COMMUTATIONS
ACIMNOOPPSST COMPASS POINT
ACIMNOOPSTTU COMPUTATIONS
ACINNNOOOSTT CONNOTATIONS
ACINNOOPRSTT CONTRAPTIONS
ACINNOORSTTT IN CONTRAST TO
ACINOOOOPRRRT INCORPORATOR
ACINOOOPRRST CORPORATIONS
ACINOOOPRSTV PROVOCATIONS
ACINOOPRRSST CONSPIRATORS
ACINOOPRRSTT STRIP CARTOON
ACIOOPPRSSTT POTATO CRISPS
ACIORRRSSTTU CIRROSTRATUS
ACKLNNOOPRTY CRYOPLANKTON
ACLLRRSTTUUY STRUCTURALLY
ACMNOOOOTTXYY CYTOTAXONOMY
ADDDDEEEHLMU MUDDLE-HEADED
ADDDDEEFFILL FIDDLE-FADDLE
ADDDEEEHNOOW WOODENHEADED
ADDDEIILLLLY DILLYDALLIED
ADDEEEEGGRST DESEGREGATED
ADDEEEGIMNST DEMAGNETISED
ADDEEEGIMNTZ DEMAGNETIZED
ADDEEEIIRSTV DESIDERATIVE
ADDEEEIMPRTT PREMEDITATED
ADDEEEIORRTT DETERIORATED
ADDEEELLNTTW WELL-ATTENDED
ADDEEELRRTTY RED-LETTER DAY
ADDEEENPRSSV DEPRAVEDNESS
ADDEEEOPPRSV EAVESDROPPED
ADDEEFFNRSTU UNDERSTAFFED
ADDEEFHLMORY FORMALDEHYDE
ADDEEFHOORSW FORESHADOWED
ADDEEFINOORR FOREORDAINED
ADDEEFLLOPST SOFT-PEDALLED
ADDEEFLNRSSU DREADFULNESS
ADDEEGHILNNS SINGLE-HANDED
ADDEEGILNNST DISENTANGLED
ADDEEGINPPSU PEASE PUDDING
ADDEEGINRRSS READDRESSING
ADDEEHHIMRTY HEMIHYDRATED
ADDEEHLLOOWY WOOLLY-HEADED
ADDEEHLNNOPY OPEN-HANDEDLY
ADDEEHOORSVW OVERSHADOWED
ADDEEIIMMNNO DEMIMONDAINE
ADDEEIIMNRST ADMINISTERED
ADDEEIIMNSST DISSEMINATED
ADDEEIINORST DESIDERATION
ADDEEIMMNRST MASTERMINDED
ADDEEIMNOPRT PREDOMINATED
ADDEEINOPRST DEPREDATIONS
ADDEEJLLSTUW WELL-ADJUSTED
ADDEELNOSSTT STADDLESTONE
ADDEEMNORSTT DEMONSTRATED
ADDEFGIILLNN LANDING FIELD
ADDEFGILRRSU DISREGARDFUL
ADDEFHILNOOS OLD-FASHIONED
ADDEFIIILQSU DISQUALIFIED
ADDEFIIISSST DISSATISFIED

ADDEFLNNNOUW NEWFOUNDLAND
ADDEGGIINRRS DISREGARDING
ADDEGHHHILNY HIGH-HANDEDLY
ADDEGHNORSTU DREADNOUGHTS
ADDEGIINORSS DISORGANISED
ADDEGIINORSZ DISORGANIZED
ADDEHHLORRSU HARD SHOULDER
ADDEHINOSSWW WINDOW SHADES
ADDEHMNORSUY HYDROMEDUSAN
ADDEIILMSSTU DISSIMULATED
ADDEIINOPPST DISAPPOINTED
ADDEILMNOOTU DEMODULATION
ADDEILMNOPRS PROMISED LAND
ADDEIMMMRSUY MIDSUMMER DAY
ADDEIMNNORRW NARROW-MINDED
ADDFIILLNSUY DISDAINFULLY
ADDGHIMNOORU ROUGH DIAMOND
ADDGIILNSSTU STUDDINGSAIL
ADDGILLNOOPP PADDLING POOL
ADDHIILLMOPP AMPHIDIPLOID
ADDIIILLNUVY INDIVIDUALLY
ADDIIINORTUV INDIVIDUATOR
ADEEEEGINRTV DEGENERATIVE
ADEEEEGLRSST EASTER-LEDGES
ADEEEEHHNRRT HERE AND THERE
ADEEEFFORRST REAFFORESTED
ADEEEFGIRRRT REFRIGERATED
ADEEEFIMTUUX FAUTE DE MIEUX
ADEEEFMNSSTU DEAF-MUTENESS
ADEEEGGILNRT LATEENRIGGED
ADEEEGGINNRT DEGENERATING
ADEEEGGLLNOS GOLDEN EAGLES
ADEEEGGNRSTU UNSEGREGATED
ADEEEGHLMMRS SLEDGEHAMMER
ADEEEGIMNRST DEMAGNETISER,
    DISAGREEMENT
ADEEEGIMNRTZ DEMAGNETIZER
ADEEEGINNORT DEGENERATION
ADEEEGINNRST TRAGEDIENNES
ADEEEGINOPSS PAEDOGENESIS
ADEEEGINRRTT REDINTEGRATE
ADEEEGLNORTU OUTGENERALED
ADEEEGMNNNRT ENDANGERMENT
ADEEEGMNNRST DERANGEMENTS
ADEEEHHLORTW WHOLE-HEARTED
ADEEEHIMNRTT HEREDITAMENT
ADEEEHINSSSV ADHESIVENESS
ADEEEHINSSTT ANESTHETISED
ADEEEHINSTTZ ANESTHETIZED
ADEEEHIRRTTT TETRAHEDRITE
ADEEEHLLORSS LEASEHOLDERS
ADEEEHLNNRRT NETHERLANDER
ADEEEHMNPRSS HAMPEREDNESS
ADEEEHMORSTV MOHAVE DESERT
ADEEEHPRSSST SPREADSHEETS
ADEEEIILNPTX EXPEDIENTIAL
ADEEEIIMMNRT ANTE MERIDIEM
ADEEEIIMMRST SEMIDIAMETER
ADEEEIIMNRTT INTERMEDIATE

ADEEEILLMMOS MADEMOISELLE
ADEEEILMNORT RADIOELEMENT
ADEEEILNPRRT INTERPLEADER
ADEEEILNRSTX EXTERNALISED
ADEEEILNRTXZ EXTERNALIZED
ADEEEIMNRTTX EXTERMINATED
ADEEEINPRSTT PREDESTINATE
ADEEEIOPPSTX EXOPEPTIDASE
ADEEEKLLNOST ENDOSKELETAL
ADEEEKLRRSST DEERSTALKERS
ADEEEILLMNNRW WELL-MANNERED
ADEEELLNSSWY WENSLEYDALES
ADEEELNRSTTU LAUNDERETTES
ADEEELOPPRST TRADESPEOPLE
ADEEEMNORSST MODERATENESS
ADEEEMORRSTV OVERMASTERED
ADEEENOPPRRT PREPONDERATE
ADEEENPPRRSS PREPAREDNESS
ADEEENPRRTUV PERADVENTURE
ADEEEOPPRRSV EAVESDROPPER
ADEEEQRSSTTU SEQUESTRATED
ADEEFFIILNRT DIFFERENTIAL
ADEEFGHILNRS HARD FEELINGS
ADEEFGILLSSS FIELD GLASSES
ADEEFGINNRRS RANGE FINDERS
ADEEFGINNRST FREESTANDING
ADEEFHLOPSST FELDSPATHOSE
ADEEFHOORRSW FORESHADOWER
ADEEFILOPRRT PROLIFERATED
ADEEFLLORUVW WELL-FAVOURED
ADEEFNOPRRTU UNPERFORATED
ADEEFOOPRRRS PROOFREADERS
ADEEFOOPRRTW WATERPROOFED
ADEEGGHIRSTT STRAIGHTEDGE
ADEEGGILNRTU DEREGULATING
ADEEGGIQRRSU SQUARE-RIGGED
ADEEGGIRRTTU REGURGITATED
ADEEGGHHILRTT LIGHT-HEARTED
ADEEGHIMMOPR MIMEOGRAPHED
ADEEGHINNPPR APPREHENDING
ADEEGHINNRRT HEARTRENDING
ADEEGHINRSTT STRAIGHTENED
ADEEGHIRRSST SIGHT-READERS
ADEEGHMOPRRS DEMOGRAPHERS
ADEEGHOPRRSW HEDGE SPARROW
ADEEGHPRSTTU STEPDAUGHTER
ADEEGIIMNNRR REMAINDERING
ADEEGIINRSTT DISINTEGRATE
ADEEGIINSTTV INVESTIGATED
ADEEGIKNNRRT KINDERGARTEN
ADEEGIKNRRST RING-STREAKED
ADEEGILMNNRY MEANDERINGLY
ADEEGILNORTU DEREGULATION
ADEEGINNORUV ENDEAVOURING
ADEEGINORRTT INTERROGATED
ADEEGMNNRRTU UNDERGARMENT
ADEEGNPRTUUX UNEXPURGATED
ADEEGNRRSSST TRANSGRESSED
ADEEGORRTTXY DEXTROGYRATE

ADEEHHIKNRRS HEADSHRINKER
ADEEHHLORRSS SHAREHOLDERS
ADEEHHNNPTUY UNHYPHENATED
ADEEHIILRRTY HEREDITARILY
ADEEHILMNOOT ENDOTHELIOMA
ADEEHILMORTT MAITRE D'HOTEL
ADEEHILNPRRS PHILANDERERS
ADEEHIMNPPRS MISAPPREHEND
ADEEHINORSTU HOUSE-TRAINED
ADEEHIRRRSSS HAIRDRESSERS
ADEEHKLORSST STAKEHOLDERS
ADEEHLLLMOPR PHELLODERMAL
ADEEHLLNOSSW HALLOWEDNESS
ADEEHLMMOTUY MEALY-MOUTHED
ADEEHMNNOSSS HANDSOMENESS
ADEEHMOPRTTY DERMATOPHYTE
ADEEHNOPSTTY SPOTTED HYENA
ADEEHNORSTTY STONY-HEARTED
ADEEHOPRRTTW THE TOP DRAWER
ADEEHORSTTTU STOUTHEARTED
ADEEIIILMRST DEMILITARISE
ADEEIIILMRTZ DEMILITARIZE
ADEEIIILMTTV DELIMITATIVE
ADEEIIILORST EDITORIALISE
ADEEIIILORTZ EDITORIALIZE
ADEEIIJNOORR RIO DE JANEIRO
ADEEIILMMNPT IMPEDIMENTAL
ADEEIILMNNSS MAIDENLINESS
ADEEIILMNOST MATINÉE IDOLS
ADEEIILMTTVY MEDITATIVELY
ADEEIILNNRST INTERNALISED
ADEEIILNNRTZ INTERNALIZED
ADEEIILNPRST PRESIDENTIAL
ADEEIILOPRST DEPILATORIES
ADEEIILRTVVY DERIVATIVELY
ADEEIIMNNOTV DENOMINATIVE
ADEEIIMNRRRT INTERMARRIED
ADEEIIMNRRTY INTERMEDIARY
ADEEIINORSTT DISORIENTATE
ADEEIINOSSTV VIDEO NASTIES
ADEEIINPRSSS DISPENSARIES
ADEEIINRRSTY RESIDENTIARY
ADEEIKLMSTTT ATTESTED MILK
ADEEILLMRSSV SILVER MEDALS
ADEEILLNNRST LANTERNSLIDE
ADEEILLOSTVW OLD WIVES' TALE
ADEEILLSTTUW WELL-SITUATED
ADEEILMMORTY IMMODERATELY
ADEEILMNOPRT REDEMPTIONAL
ADEEILMPRSST SLIPSTREAMED
ADEEILNOPPRT LEPIDOPTERAN
ADEEILNOPRSS PERSONALISED
ADEEILNOPRSZ PERSONALIZED
ADEEILNOPRTT INTERPOLATED
ADEEILNRRSTY RESTRAINEDLY
ADEEILRRSSVV SLAVE DRIVERS
ADEEIMMNORSU MISDEMEANOUR
ADEEIMNNRSTT DETERMINANTS
ADEEIMNOPRST IMPERSONATED

ADEEIMNRSTUV MISADVENTURE
ADEEIMOPRRTT PREMEDITATOR
ADEEIMSSSTTY SYSTEMATISED
ADEEIMSSTTYZ SYSTEMATIZED
ADEEINNOOPRU INDO-EUROPEAN
ADEEINNRRSTU UNRESTRAINED
ADEEINNRSSST STRAINEDNESS
ADEEINNSSSTU UNSTEADINESS
ADEEINORRSST RAISON D'ETRES
ADEEINRRSSUY DAY NURSERIES
ADEEIOPPRRTX EXPROPRIATED
ADEEJMNRSTTU READJUSTMENT
ADEEKLLORRST ROLLER SKATED
ADEEKLOPRSSU LOUDSPEAKERS
ADEEKNORSSYY DONKEY'S YEARS
ADEELLMMNRTU UNTRAMMELLED
ADEELLORSSTW WELL-ASSORTED
ADEELMNOSTTT OLD TESTAMENT
ADEELMORSSTU SOMERSAULTED
ADEELOPSTTUX EXPOSTULATED
ADEEMNNPRTUY UNDERPAYMENT
ADEEMNOPPRRS NAMEDROPPERS
ADEEMNORRSTT REMONSTRATED
ADEENNOORRST ANDROSTERONE
ADEENNOPPRRT PREPONDERANT
ADEENOPSSTTU UP-TO-DATENESS
ADEENORSSTUW SWEET-AND-SOUR
ADEFFIMMNORS FRAMES OF MIND
ADEFGHHIOORT HAIR OF THE DOG
ADEFGHILNSUW LUDWIGSHAFEN
ADEFGHILRSTY FARSIGHTEDLY
ADEFGIILLNPY PLAYING FIELD
ADEFGIIMMNRX MIXED FARMING
ADEFGILNOPST SOFT-PEDALING
ADEFGILNRSSY LADY'S FINGERS
ADEFGINOOPRR PROOFREADING
ADEFGINRRSTU TRANSFIGURED
ADEFHILLTTWY HALF-WITTEDLY
ADEFHINRRSTY FIRE HYDRANTS
ADEFHINRSSSW DWARFISHNESS
ADEFIIILNNOT DEFINITIONAL
ADEFIIILQRSU DISQUALIFIER
ADEFIILNOSTT DEFLATIONIST
ADEFIILNPRSU FREUDIAN SLIP
ADEFIINRSTTU UNSTRATIFIED
ADEFILORRSST FIRST SEA LORD
ADEFILOSSSTV FAST DISSOLVE
ADEFIMNOORST DEFORMATIONS
ADEFLLNRTUUY FRAUDULENTLY
ADEGGHIILLNT LEADING LIGHT
ADEGGHIINRST SIGHT-READING
ADEGGINNORRR ORGAN GRINDER
ADEGGLNRSSSU SLUGGARDNESS
ADEGHHILNNPS HELPING HANDS
ADEGHHILOPRT LITHOGRAPHED
ADEGHHIMNNRT RIGHT-HAND MEN
ADEGHHINRRST RIGHT-HANDERS
ADEGHHIPRSST SHARP-SIGHTED
ADEGHHOOPPRT PHOTOGRAPHED

ADEGHHOPRRRY HYDROGRAPHER
ADEGHIILNNPR PHILANDERING
ADEGHIIMNNUZ DEHUMANIZING
ADEGHIINRRSS HAIRDRESSING
ADEGHINORRST HORSE-TRADING
ADEGHIORRTTW WITH REGARD TO
ADEGHLLNORST STRANGLEHOLD
ADEGHLNORSTY HEADSTRONGLY
ADEGHMNORRST GRANDMOTHERS
ADEGHNOORRTY HYDROGENATOR
ADEGHNOPRSTU SHARP-TONGUED
ADEGIIILNTVZ DEVITALIZING
ADEGIIJNOPRZ JEOPARDIZING
ADEGIILLMNSY MISLEADINGLY
ADEGIILLNNOT DIALLING TONE
ADEGIILLNNTU DENTILINGUAL
ADEGIILMNTTY MEDITATINGLY
ADEGIILNNRRT INTERLARDING
ADEGIILNNRSW LINE DRAWINGS
ADEGIILNORSS DIGRESSIONAL
ADEGIILNPRSY DESPAIRINGLY
ADEGIIMNNNOT DENOMINATING
ADEGIIMNNPRR REPRIMANDING
ADEGIIMNOTTV DEMOTIVATING
ADEGIINNOPRR PREORDAINING
ADEGIINNOSST DESIGNATIONS
ADEGIINOORRT GRANODIORITE
ADEGIINORRSS DISORGANISER
ADEGIINORRSZ DISORGANIZER
ADEGIKNNRSTU UNDERTAKINGS
ADEGILNNPRUY UNDERPLAYING
ADEGILNNRUUV UNDERVALUING
ADEGILNOPPTU DEPOPULATING
ADEGILOORRTY DEROGATORILY
ADEGIMNNOPPR NAMEDROPPING
ADEGINNRSTTU UNDERSTATING
ADEGJLMNSTTU LAST JUDGMENT
ADEHHILLPPSU PHILADELPHUS
ADEHHIMOORRS HAEMORRHOIDS
ADEHHOPRRTYY HYDROTHERAPY
ADEHIILNSTTT DILETTANTISH
ADEHIILOPSST HOSPITALISED
ADEHIILOPSTZ HOSPITALIZED
ADEHIINNRSTY HYDRASTININE
ADEHIIPRRSTT THIRD PARTIES
ADEHILMNOPSU SULPHONAMIDE
ADEHILMNORSU MALNOURISHED
ADEHIMMPPSUY HAPPY MEDIUMS
ADEHINQRRSTU HINDQUARTERS
ADEHIOOPRSTT ORTHOPAEDIST
ADEHIORSSTTW SHORT-WAISTED
ADEHLLLMORSS SMALLHOLDERS
ADEHLLLORSST STALLHOLDERS
ADEHLMNOOPSU MONADELPHOUS
ADEHLNNOPSTY SHETLAND PONY
ADEHOOPSTTTT PHOTOSTATTED
ADEHOPRSSSTW SHOP STEWARDS
ADEIIILMNOTT DELIMITATION
ADEIIILORSTT EDITORIALIST

ADEIIIMNOSTV DEVIATIONISM
ADEIIINNORRV VIN ORDINAIRE
ADEIIINOSTTV DEVIATIONIST
ADEIIINSTTTU ATTITUDINISE
ADEIIINTTTUZ ATTITUDINIZE
ADEIILLMNOST MEDALLIONIST
ADEIILLNPRUV LIVERPUDLIAN
ADEIILLOSSTY DISLOYALTIES
ADEIILLSTUVV VAUDEVILLIST
ADEIILMMNPRT MALIMPRINTED
ADEIILMMORST IMMORTALISED
ADEIILMMORTZ IMMORTALIZED
ADEIILMNSTTT DILETTANTISM
ADEIILNNORTY INORDINATELY
ADEIILNOOPST DESPOLIATION
ADEIILNOPRTV PROVIDENTIAL
ADEIILNORSST DILATORINESS
ADEIIMMNNRSU INDIAN SUMMER
ADEIIMMNOORT IMMODERATION
ADEIIMMNNNOOT DENOMINATION
ADEIIMNNOSTU MOUNTAINSIDE
ADEIIMNNRSTT DISTRAINMENT
ADEIIMNOOTTV DEMOTIVATION
ADEIIMNOPRST POSTMERIDIAN
ADEIIMNOPRXY PYRIDOXAMINE
ADEIIMNORSST DISSEMINATOR
ADEIIMORSTTU AUDIOMETRIST
ADEIIMRSSTTX TAXIDERMISTS
ADEIINNNOSTT INDENTATIONS
ADEIINNOPSST DISPENSATION
ADEIINNORRSS ORDINARINESS
ADEIINNOSSTT DESTINATIONS
ADEIINOOPRST DISOPERATION
ADEIINOPPRST DISAPPOINTER
ADEIINOPRSTV DEPRIVATIONS
ADEIINORRSVY DIVERSIONARY
ADEIINORSSTT DISSERTATION
ADEIINORSTTX EXTRADITIONS
ADEIINOSTTUV ADVENTITIOUS
ADEIIOOOPRST RADIOISOTOPE
ADEIILLNOPPRT DIPROPELLANT
ADEIILLNPRTUY PRUDENTIALLY
ADEILLOSSVWW SWALLOW DIVES
ADEILLPPRSSY LADY'S-SLIPPER
ADEILMNNNSTU DISANNULMENT
ADEILNOOPPTU DEPOPULATION
ADEILNORRSTV DORSIVENTRAL
ADEIMMNNOPSU PANDEMONIUMS
ADEIMMOPRSUY PRASEODYMIUM
ADEIMNNOORST DENOMINATORS
ADEIMNOOPRRT PREDOMINATOR
ADEIMOOPRSTZ SPERMATOZOID
ADEINOOPRSTT DEPORTATIONS
ADEINOPRSSTY DISPENSATORY
ADEINOPRTTTY POTTY-TRAINED
ADEJLORSSSTU LOSS ADJUSTER
ADEJMNNORSTU ADJOURNMENTS
ADEKOOPRSTVZ PETROZAVODSK
ADELLNORSSUY SLANDEROUSLY

ADELLOOPRRST PETRODOLLARS
ADELNOORRSTV DORSOVENTRAL
ADELOOPRRSST POSTAL ORDERS
ADEMNNOPSTWY DOWN PAYMENTS
ADEMNOORRSTT DEMONSTRATOR
ADENNOPRRSST TRANSPONDERS
ADENNORSSTUW UNTOWARDNESS
ADFFGIILNNTU FAULT-FINDING
ADFFGNORSSTU GROUND STAFFS
ADFGIILNORTU FLUORIDATING
ADFGIINQRSSU FIRING SQUADS
ADFGILNNOSST SOFT LANDINGS
ADFGILNQSSUY FLYING SQUADS
ADFHIMNOOORU MAID OF HONOUR
ADFHMNOOOTTU FOOT-AND-MOUTH
ADFIIILNNOST DISINFLATION
ADFIIILNOSTU FLUIDISATION
ADFIIILNOTUZ FLUIDIZATION
ADFIILNOORTU FLUORIDATION
ADFIILOSSTUY FASTIDIOUSLY
ADGGIIMNNORZ GORMANDIZING
ADGGILNNNOST LONG-STANDING
ADGHIINNSTTW WITHSTANDING
ADGHIINOPRSZ RHAPSODIZING
ADGHIKLNORSW WORLDSHAKING
ADGHILLLMNOS SMALLHOLDING
ADGHNOOOOPRTY ODONTOGRAPHY
ADGIIIIMNNTT INTIMIDATING
ADGIIIINOSTT DIGITISATION
ADGIIIINOTTZ DIGITIZATION
ADGIILLNNOTU LONGITUDINAL
ADGIILNNPRST LANDING STRIP
ADGIILNRSTTU STRIDULATING
ADGIILOORSST RADIOLOGISTS
ADGIINOPPRSV DISAPPROVING
ADGIKNNORRRU ROARING DRUNK
ADGILNNOSTUY ASTOUNDINGLY
ADGIMNNOOOST SANTO DOMINGO
ADGIMNNOORST STANDING ROOM
ADGIMNOORRSW DRAWING ROOMS
ADGINNOOOPRT GONADOTROPIN
ADGINOPRSSTT TRADING POSTS
ADGLNNOORTUW LONG-DRAWN-OUT
ADGOOOPRSSTU GASTROPODOUS
ADHIIIMMRSTT MITHRIDATISM
ADHIIMOPRSST DIASTROPHISM
ADHILLNOSTUY OUTLANDISHLY
ADHILMMOOPTY LYMPHOMATOID
ADHLNOOOOPRT ODONTOPHORAL
ADHOOOOPRRSTU ARTHROPODOUS
ADIIIIMNNOTT INTIMIDATION
ADIIIINNOSTV DIVINISATION
ADIIIINNOTVZ DIVINIZATION
ADIIIILLMRSSY DISSIMILARLY
ADIIILLNOSTT DISTILLATION
ADIIINORSTTT TRADITIONIST
ADIILLMOPRRY PRIMORDIALLY
ADIILLNOQRSU QUADRILLIONS
ADIILLNRSTUY INDUSTRIALLY

ADIILLOPSTUV POSTDILUVIAL
ADIILLORSTTY DISTILLATORY
ADIILMOPSSTT DIPLOMATISTS
ADIILMORSSTU DISSIMULATOR
ADIILNOORSTT DISTORTIONAL
ADIILNOPSTUV POSTDILUVIAN
ADIILNORSTTU STRIDULATION
ADIINOPSSTTU DISPUTATIONS
ADIIOPSSTTUU DISPUTATIOUS
ADILLOORSTUY IDOLATROUSLY
ADILORRSTTUY STRIDULATORY
ADILORSSSTUY DISASTROUSLY
ADLNOOPRSSWY PLAYS ON WORDS
AEEEEGHLPRST TELEGRAPHESE
AEEEEGHMORTT HETEROGAMETE
AEEEEGINRRTV REGENERATIVE
AEEEEGNNRRTU UNREGENERATE
AEEEEHHPRRSS SHEEPSHEARER
AEEEEIMNNRST SEINE-ET-MARNE
AEEEEKLNNNOV ON AN EVEN KEEL
AEEEEELPRRSSS PRESS RELEASE
AEEEEFFILMNTY EFFEMINATELY
AEEEEFFLOPPST TOFFEE APPLES
AEEEEFHINRRTT THEREINAFTER
AEEEEFIKLNPTT PALETTE KNIFE
AEEEEFILNPRRT PREFERENTIAL
AEEEEFIMNRTTV FERMENTATIVE
AEEEEFLNRSSSS FEARLESSNESS
AEEEEFMNORSSS FEARSOMENESS
AEEEEGGINNRRT REGENERATING
AEEEEGHLPRRST TELEGRAPHERS
AEEEEGHORRSTT THEATREGOERS
AEEEEGIILNRST GENERALITIES
AEEEEGIKLNNNW WANKEL ENGINE
AEEEEGILNNRRV LINE-ENGRAVER
AEEEEGILNOPTV NEGATIVE POLE
AEEEEGIMNNSTV ENVISAGEMENT
AEEEEGINNORRT REGENERATION
AEEEEGINNSSTV NEGATIVENESS
AEEEEGINORTTV REVEGETATION
AEEEEGIRRSTTV TERGIVERSATE
AEEEEGLMNNNTT ENTANGLEMENT
AEEEEGLMNNRST ENLARGEMENTS
AEEEEGMMNORTT MAGNETOMETER
AEEEEGMNNRSTT ESTRANGEMENT
AEEEEHHNNNPRT PHENANTHRENE
AEEEEHHNOTTXY ETHOXYETHANE
AEEEEHIKNSSTV SNEAK THIEVES
AEEEEHILMPRTY EPHEMERALITY
AEEEEHILNNSSV HEAVENLINESS
AEEEEHILNRSST LEATHERINESS
AEEEEHINPPRSV APPREHENSIVE
AEEEEHINPRSST PARENTHESISE
AEEEEHINPRSTZ PARENTHESIZE
AEEEEHLMPPRST PAMPHLETEERS
AEEEEHLNRSSTT NETTLE RASHES
AEEEEHLORSTUX HETEROSEXUAL
AEEEEHLPRRSWY PRAYER WHEELS
AEEEEHLRRSTTY HARLEY STREET

AEEEEHMORTTTX METHOTREXATE
AEEEEHQRRRTTU THREE-QUARTER
AEEEEIILMNORT MAINE-ET-LOIRE
AEEEEIILNPRTX EXPERIENTIAL
AEEEEIILNRRST INERTIA REELS
AEEEEIINNNSTT SAINT-ÉTIENNE
AEEEEIKNNORST ENTEROKINASE
AEEEEIKNPRSVW SNEAK PREVIEW
AEEEEIILLNPRTT INTERPELLATE
AEEEEILMNPRTX EXPERIMENTAL
AEEEEILNOORST SAONE-ET-LOIRE
AEEEEILNRSSTT LITERATENESS
AEEEEIMNRRTUV REMUNERATIVE
AEEEEIMOPRRTV EVAPORIMETER
AEEEEIMORSTTV OVERESTIMATE
AEEEEINNORTTX EXENTERATION
AEEEEINNRRSTT ENTERTAINERS
AEEEEINPRSTTV PRESENTATIVE
AEEEEINRRTTUX EXTRAUTERINE
AEEEEIPRRSTVV PRESERVATIVE
AEEEEKLLPRSSW SLEEPWALKERS
AEEEEKLRRSTTW STREETWALKER
AEEEELLORSTTT TEETOTALLERS
AEEEELMNORSYY ELEEMOSYNARY
AEEEELNOPPSVY PAY ENVELOPES
AEEEELRSSTTUV STREET VALUES
AEEEEMMNPRSTT TEMPERAMENTS
AEEEEMMNRSSTU MEASUREMENTS
AEEEEMMNNSTTTW NEW TESTAMENT
AEEEEMNRSSTTT RESTATEMENTS
AEEEEMPRRSTTU TEMPERATURES
AEEEEMRSSSSST SEAMSTRESSES
AEEEFFGHIRRTU FATHER FIGURE
AEEEFFGILNORT FREE-FLOATING
AEEEFFGRSSTTU SUFFRAGETTES
AEEEFFHKOORST FOR THE SAKE OF
AEEEFFILMRSTU FEATURE FILMS
AEEEFGIKRRSTU FIGURE SKATER
AEEEFGILNORRT FORETRIANGLE
AEEEFGILNPRST FINGERPLATES
AEEEFGINRRRST REFRIGERANTS
AEEEFGIORRRRT REFRIGERATOR
AEEEFGLNRSSTU GRATEFULNESS
AEEEFHHORSSTU HOUSEFATHERS
AEEEFHIKNRSSS FREAKISHNESS
AEEEFHILNRSST FATHERLINESS
AEEEFHIOOORRST RAISE THE ROOF
AEEEFHLLOOSTW FOLLOW THE SEA
AEEEFHLLRRSTU FULLER'S EARTH
AEEEFHLMNSSSU SHAMEFULNESS
AEEEFHLMORRTW FLAME-THROWER
AEEEFHLOOSTTT ATHLETE'S FOOT
AEEEFHMNORRWY ANYWHERE FROM
AEEEFHOOPRRTW WEATHERPROOF
AEEEFHORSTTTU FOURTH ESTATE
AEEEFIILMPPRR PREAMPLIFIER
AEEEFIINRRSTT FRATERNITIES
AEEEFIKLLMOTT MAKE LITTLE OF
AEEEFILOPRSTU PETALIFEROUS

AEEFIMNNORTT FERMENTATION
AEEFIMOPRRTV PERFORMATIVE
AEEFINNORSTT FENESTRATION
AEEFLMNORSTT FORESTALMENT, MAN OF
    LETTERS
AEEFLNSSSTTU TASTEFULNESS
AEEFLNSSSTUW WASTEFULNESS
AEEFLOPQRSUW PASQUEFLOWER
AEEFLRRSSSTT SELF-STARTERS
AEEFNORRSSVW WARS OF NERVES
AEEGGGINNNSS ENGAGINGNESS
AEEGGHILNPRT TELEGRAPHING
AEEGGIILNNRZ GENERALIZING
AEEGGIILNNVZ EVANGELIZING
AEEGGILNOSST GENEALOGISTS
AEEGGILRSSVY AGGRESSIVELY
AEEGGIMMNOST GEOMAGNETISM
AEEGGINNTTTW WETTING AGENT
AEEGGIQRRRSU SQUARE-RIGGER
AEEGHHILOPRR HELIOGRAPHER
AEEGHHISTVWY HEAVYWEIGHTS
AEEGHHNOPRRT ETHNOGRAPHER
AEEGHHOPRRTY HETEROGRAPHY
AEEGHILLMMRT HELLGRAMMITE
AEEGHILMNOPR GERMANOPHILE
AEEGHILNNRTY HEARTENINGLY
AEEGHILNORTW WATERING HOLE
AEEGHILORRUV HELIOGRAVURE
AEEGHINOPSST PATHOGENESIS
AEEGHINPTTVY HEAVY PETTING
AEEGHINRRSTT STRAIGHTENER
AEEGHIPPRSTW PAPERWEIGHTS
AEEGHIPRSSTW STAGE WHISPER
AEEGHLNOPRSY SELENOGRAPHY
AEEGHLOORRTW WOOLGATHERER
AEEGHMOOPRRT METEOROGRAPH
AEEGHMOORSTU HETEROGAMOUS
AEEGHNOOPRTV PHOTOENGRAVE
AEEGHNOPRRST STENOGRAPHER
AEEGHOOPSSSU OESOPHAGUSES
AEEGHOPPRRRT PETROGRAPHER
AEEGHOPRRSTY STEREOGRAPHY
AEEGIIILLLST ILLEGALITIES
AEEGIIILLMTT ILLEGITIMATE
AEEGIIILMSTT LEGITIMATISE
AEEGIIILMTTZ LEGITIMATIZE
AEEGIIILLMTTY LEGITIMATELY
AEEGIIILNNORS LEGIONNAIRES
AEEGIILNNPSS PALINGENESIS
AEEGIINNNRTT ENTERTAINING
AEEGIINNRTVW INTERWEAVING
AEEGIJNNRTUV REJUVENATING
AEEGIKLLNPSW SLEEPWALKING
AEEGIKLNSTTW SWEET-TALKING
AEEGIKMNPRRT PARKING METER
AEEGIKNNNSSS SNEAKINGNESS
AEEGIKNRSTUY KEY SIGNATURE
AEEGILLRSSST LEGISLATRESS
AEEGILLRSSTU LEGISLATURES

AEEGILMNNRST REALIGNMENTS
AEEGILNNPSSS PLEASINGNESS
AEEGILNNRTTY ENTREATINGLY
AEEGIMNNNOSTT SEGMENTATION
AEEGIMNNRRTU REMUNERATING
AEEGIMSSSTTU GUESSTIMATES
AEEGINNNSSSU SANGUINENESS
AEEGINOPRRRT PEREGRINATOR
AEEGINPPRRTT PERPETRATING
AEEGINPPRTTU PERPETUATING
AEEGIOPRRSTV PREROGATIVES
AEEGKNOORSTU KERATOGENOUS
AEEGLLMNOOPR PROLEGOMENAL
AEEGLLMNOPSY SPLENOMEGALY
AEEGLLMNRUWZ MANGEL-WURZEL
AEEGLLPRRSSY PRESS GALLERY
AEEGLMNNORTV GOVERNMENTAL
AEEGLNNOORTT LOT-ET-GARONNE
AEEGMMNORTTY MAGNETOMETRY
AEEGPRRSSSSU SUPERGRASSES
AEEHHHILNSTY HEATHENISHLY
AEEHHIKNSSTV SHEATH KNIVES
AEEHHILMNSTY MYELIN SHEATH
AEEHHILOPRTY HELIOTHERAPY
AEEHHILRSTWW WHEREWITHALS
AEEHHIPRSSTW WEATHER SHIPS
AEEHHLOSSTTW STEAL THE SHOW
AEEHHMORSSTV HARVEST HOMES
AEEHHNOPPRTY PHANEROPHYTE
AEEHIIMOOPSS HAEMOPOIESIS
AEEHIINORSTT ETHERISATION
AEEHIINORTTZ ETHERIZATION
AEEHIKLLLRSW KILLER WHALES
AEEHIKLNNPPT PINK ELEPHANT
AEEHILLMNNPS PANHELLENISM
AEEHILLNNPST PANHELLENIST
AEEHILLPPRRY PERIPHERALLY
AEEHILNSSSTT STEALTHINESS
AEEHILORRSTU TRAILER HOUSE
AEEHILRSTVWY WHITE SLAVERY
AEEHILSTUVXY EXHAUSTIVELY
AEEHIMNNORTT NITROMETHANE
AEEHINNOPPRS APPREHENSION
AEEHINOORSTU HETEROOUSIAN
AEEHINOPSSTV TOP-HEAVINESS
AEEHINSSSTTT ANESTHETISTS
AEEHIOPPSTTV STOVEPIPE HAT
AEEHIOPRSSTU HOUSE PARTIES
AEEHIORRRRST HAIR-RESTORER
AEEHIORSSSST AIRHOSTESSES
AEEHKMPRRSTY HYPERMARKETS
AEEHLLMMORWY YELLOWHAMMER
AEEHLLMNNOPY PHENOMENALLY
AEEHLLNORSTY LONELY HEARTS
AEEHLMNORSTT STENOTHERMAL
AEEHLMNRSSSS HARMLESSNESS
AEEHLMOSSSTV STEAM SHOVELS
AEEHLMOSSTTY STATELY HOMES
AEEHLNOPRTUY POLYURETHANE

AEEHLOPRSTTY HETEROPLASTY
AEEHLPPRRSTU PURPLE HEARTS
AEEHMMOOPRST METAMORPHOSE
AEEHMNORRTTU MOTHER NATURE
AEEHMORSSSTU HOUSEMASTERS
AEEHNNORRSTT NORTHEASTERN
AEEHNOPRSSTU HOUSEPARENTS
AEEHNORRSSTT NORTHEASTERS
AEEHNORSSTTU SOUTHEASTERN
AEEHOPRRSSTT STRATOSPHERE
AEEHORRSSSTU HOUSE ARRESTS
AEEIIILNQSTU INEQUALITIES
AEEIIJNOQSSU JE NE SAIS QUOI
AEEIIKLMNPRS MARLINESPIKE
AEEIIKMNNSSY KEYNESIANISM
AEEIIILLLRTTY ILLITERATELY
AEEIIILLNOSTV TELEVISIONAL
AEEIIILLNPSTT PESTILENTIAL
AEEIIILMMORRS MEMORIALISER
AEEIIILMMORRZ MEMORIALIZER
AEEIIILMNOOST EMOTIONALISE
AEEIIILMNOOTZ EMOTIONALIZE
AEEIIILMNSSST ESSENTIALISM
AEEIIILMPRTVY IMPERATIVELY
AEEIIILNNSSST INESSENTIALS
AEEIIILNRRSST LITERARINESS
AEEIIILNRSSUV UNIVERSALISE
AEEIIILNRSUVZ UNIVERSALIZE
AEEIIILNSSSTT ESSENTIALIST
AEEIIILNSSTTY ESSENTIALITY
AEEIIILOPTTVX EXPLOITATIVE
AEEIIMNSSSTW SIAMESE TWINS
AEEIINNORSTT ETERNISATION
AEEIINNORTTZ ETERNIZATION
AEEIINNPRTTY PENITENTIARY
AEEIINNRRTTU INTRAUTERINE
AEEIINORRSTT REITERATIONS
AEEIIPRTTUVV VITUPERATIVE
AEEIJLOPRTVY PEJORATIVELY
AEEIJNNORTUV REJUVENATION
AEEIKMNSSTTU MINUTE STEAKS
AEEILLMNRTTT ILL-TREATMENT
AEEILLNNPRTT INTERPELLANT
AEEILLNOSSTT TESSELLATION
AEEILLNQSTUY SEQUENTIALLY
AEEILLNQTUVY EQUIVALENTLY
AEEILLNRRSTT INTERSTELLAR
AEEILLNRRTVY IRRELEVANTLY
AEEILLNSSSUV ALLUSIVENESS
AEEILLTTTTTT TITTLE-TATTLE
AEEILMNNNRSS MANNERLINESS
AEEILMNNPTTU PENNULTIMATE
AEEILMNRSSST MASTERLINESS
AEEILNNNOSST NONESSENTIAL
AEEILNNOPRTV OPEN INTERVAL
AEEILNOPRRTT INTERPOLATER
AEEILNOPRSSX EXPRESSIONAL
AEEILNPRRRST LASER PRINTER
AEEILPRSSTUV SUPERLATIVES

AEEILPRSSUVY PERSUASIVELY
AEEILRRSTTTU LITTERATEURS
AEEIMMNNORSTT AMORTISEMENT
AEEIMMNNORTTZ AMORTIZEMENT
AEEIMMNRSTTT MISTREATMENT
AEEIMMNRSTTT MISSTATEMENT
AEEIMNNORRTU REMUNERATION
AEEIMNNNORSTT SENARMONTITE
AEEIMNNNORSTU ENUMERATIONS,
   MOUNTAINEERS
AEEIMNORRTTX EXTERMINATOR
AEEIMRSSSTTY SYSTEMATISER
AEEIMRSSTTYZ SYSTEMATIZER
AEEINNOOPRTV NONOPERATIVE
AEEINNOPRSTT PRESENTATION
AEEINOORRSSU AERONEUROSIS
AEEINOORTTTX EXTORTIONATE
AEEINOPPRRTT PERPETRATION
AEEINOPPRTTU PERPETUATION
AEEINOPRRSTV PRESERVATION
AEEINOPRRSTY ARSENOPYRITE
AEEINORRRSVY REVERSIONARY
AEEINORRSSTV RESERVATIONS
AEEINRSSTTTV TRANSVESTITE
AEEINRSTTTUV STERNUTATIVE
AEEIORRSSTTV RESTORATIVES
AEEIPPRRTTTT PITTER-PATTER
AEEKLLORRRST ROLLER-SKATER
AEEKLLORRSST ROLLER SKATES
AEEKLMORRSTW METALWORKERS
AEEKMORRSSTT MASTERSTROKE
AEEKMPRRSSTU SUPERMARKETS
AEEKNPRRSSTU SUPERTANKERS
AEELLLMNOTVY MALEVOLENTLY
AEELLLORTTWY YELLOW RATTLE
AEELLMNPPSTU SUPPLEMENTAL
AEELLMORRSST STEAMROLLERS
AEELLNORSSTW STONEWALLERS
AEELLOPRSTUV POLE VAULTERS
AEELMNPRRSTU PREMENSTRUAL
AEELMOOPRSTU SOMATOPLEURE
AEELNORSTUXY EXTRANEOUSLY
AEELNRRSSTVY TRANSVERSELY
AEELOOPPRTUV OVERPOPULATE
AEELOPPRRRTY REAL PROPERTY
AEEMNOORTUUV OUTMANOEUVRE
AEENNORSSSUV RAVENOUSNESS
AEENNOSSSSUU NAUSEOUSNESS
AEENOPRRSSTT PATERNOSTERS
AEENOQRRSTTU QUARTER NOTES
AEENORRSSTXY EXTRASENSORY
AEEOOPSSTTTW SWEET POTATOS
AEEOPPRRRSTT PERPETRATORS
AEEOPRRSTTTU TETRAPTEROUS
AEEOQRRSSTTU SEQUESTRATOR
AEFFGILLLMOR FLAGELLIFORM
AEFFHILNSSTU FAITHFULNESS
AEFFILRRSSTU FIRST REFUSAL
AEFFKNRRRSTU FRANKFURTERS

AEFGGGILNOPR LEAPFROGGING
AEFGGHINORRT FORGATHERING
AEFGHHOORRTU THOROUGHFARE
AEFGHHOORTTU AFORETHOUGHT
AEFGHHORTTTU AFTERTHOUGHT
AEFGIILRTUVY FIGURATIVELY
AEFGIINNRRTZ FRATERNIZING
AEFGIINPPSWW WIFE SWAPPING
AEFGILLMNNUY MEANINGFULLY
AEFGILLNORST FORESTALLING
AEFGILLNRSST FINGERSTALLS
AEFGILLNRTTY FLATTERINGLY
AEFGILLNSSUW WINEGLASSFUL
AEFGILNNRTTU UNFLATTERING
AEFGINNRRRST TRANSFERRING
AEFGLLNRTUUY UNGRATEFULLY
AEFHKLMORSST THERMOS FLASK
AEFHKLNNSSTU THANKFULNESS
AEFHKNOOSTTV VOTE OF THANKS
AEFHLLORSSUY ROYAL FLUSHES
AEFHLNRSSTUW WRATHFULNESS
AEFHOOPRRSTT SHATTERPROOF
AEFIIILMNSST SEMIFINALIST
AEFIIILNRTTV INFILTRATIVE
AEFIIIMNNOST FEMINISATION
AEFIIIMNNOTZ FEMINIZATION
AEFIILLMOTTU MULTIFOLIATE
AEFIILLNOOTU UNIFOLIOLATE
AEFIILLNRTUV INTERFLUVIAL
AEFIILMNORUV FLUVIOMARINE
AEFIILNOOPRT PERFOLIATION
AEFIINNOSSTT INFESTATIONS
AEFIINORSSTT FIRE STATIONS
AEFIINORSTTU TITANIFEROUS
AEFILMMNNOOT MONOFILAMENT
AEFILMORRRSU FORMULARISER
AEFILMORRRUZ FORMULARIZER
AEFILNOOPRSS PROFESSIONAL
AEFILNOOPRTV FLAVOPROTEIN
AEFILOOPRRSS PROFESSORIAL
AEFILOPPRSUU PAPULIFEROUS
AEFILOPRRSTT SELF-PORTRAIT
AEFIMNNORRST FRONTIERSMAN
AEFIMNOOPRRT PREFORMATION
AEFIMNOORRST REFORMATIONS
AEFINNNOPSTU FOUNTAIN PENS
AEFINNORSSTU STANNIFEROUS
AEFINOOPRRST PERFORATIONS
AEFKLLOORRSW FLOORWALKERS
AEFLLMNORSTU SMALL FORTUNE
AEFLLNNSSUUW UNLAWFULNESS
AEFLLOOPRSSY FOOL'S-PARSLEY
AEFMNORRRSST TRANSFORMERS
AEFNNORSTTUU UNFORTUNATES
AEGGGILNNOTU AGGLUTINOGEN
AEGGGILNRSTY STAGGERINGLY
AEGGGILNRSWY SWAGGERINGLY
AEGGGINNPRSS PRESSGANGING
AEGGHIIKLNNU HEILUNGKIANG

AEGGHIILNNST NIGHTINGALES
AEGGHIIRRRST HAIR TRIGGERS
AEGGHILNRSTU SLAUGHTERING
AEGGHINSSSTT GASTIGHTNESS
AEGGHIPPRRTY TRIGGER-HAPPY
AEGGHLNOOSTT SNAGGLETOOTH
AEGGHOOOPRYZ ZOOGEOGRAPHY
AEGGIILNRRUZ REGULARIZING
AEGGIIMNNPRT IMPREGNATING
AEGGIINNORRZ REORGANIZING
AEGGILORRSUY GREGARIOUSLY
AEGGIMNNORRW WARMONGERING
AEGGLOOORSTY ASTROGEOLOGY
AEGHHIINSTWW WHITEWASHING
AEGHHILOPRRT LITHOGRAPHER
AEGHHLOPRSSU PLOUGHSHARES
AEGHHMOPRRTY THERMOGRAPHY
AEGHHNOOPPRR PHONOGRAPHER
AEGHHOOPPRRT PHOTOGRAPHER
AEGHHOOPRRRT ORTHOGRAPHER
AEGHIIKLNNTY LIKE ANYTHING
AEGHIILMNSST ALMIGHTINESS
AEGHIILNSTTY HESITATINGLY
AEGHIINNSTTU UNHESITATING
AEGHIKNNRRTT KNIGHT-ERRANT
AEGHILLPRSTU SUGAR THE PILL
AEGHILMNNOSW ENGLISHWOMAN
AEGHILMNNSTU LANGUISHMENT
AEGHILNRSTTY SHATTERINGLY
AEGHILQRRTTU QUARTERLIGHT
AEGHIMMNOSST MESOGNATHISM
AEGHIMNORSUW HOUSEWARMING
AEGHIMOOPRST MASTIGOPHORE
AEGHIMOOPRSS SEISMOGRAPHS
AEGHIMOPRSSY SEISMOGRAPHY
AEGHINNOPPPT PHONE-TAPPING
AEGHINOOOTTV NOT GIVE A HOOT
AEGHINRRRTUY TEARING HURRY
AEGHINRRSSTT HEARTSTRINGS
AEGHINRSSSTT STRAIGHTNESS
AEGHLMNNOORS LONGSHOREMAN
AEGHLORSSTUU SLAUGHTEROUS
AEGHMNOOOPTT PHOTOMONTAGE
AEGHMNOOSSTU MESOGNATHOUS
AEGHMNOPSSUW HUMP ONE'S SWAG
AEGHNOOPPRRR PORNOGRAPHER
AEGHOOPPRRST TOPOGRAPHERS
AEGHOOPRRTUV PHOTOGRAVURE
AEGHOPPRRSSS GRASSHOPPERS
AEGHOPPRRSTY TYPOGRAPHERS
AEGHOPPRRTUY GROUP THERAPY
AEGIIILMNOTT LEGITIMATION
AEGIIILNRTVZ REVITALIZING
AEGIIIMNNNST INSEMINATING
AEGIIINNPRSW AWE-INSPIRING
AEGIIINORTVV INVIGORATING
AEGIIKLLNRST GIANT KILLERS
AEGIILLMRRSU GUERRILLAISM
AEGIILLNPRVY PREVAILINGLY

AEGIILMMNNST MISALIGNMENT	AEHHLOOOPPRT LOPHOPHORATE
AEGIILMNNRST STREAMLINING	AEHHOOPPRTTY PHOTOTHERAPY
AEGIILMNORST MINERALOGIST	AEHHOOPRRSST SHARPSHOOTER
AEGIILNNNSSU UNGAINLINESS	AEHIIIMNNOST THIOSINAMINE
AEGIILNNORTU URINOGENITAL	AEHIIIMNNSTU INHUMANITIES
AEGIILNNRTUZ NEUTRALIZING	AEHIIILPSSTT PHILATELISTS
AEGIILNPPTYZ APPETIZINGLY	AEHIILNOPRST RELATIONSHIP
AEGIILNPRSTT EARSPLITTING	AEHIILPRRSTT HAIRSPLITTER
AEGIILNRSTVV VESTAL VIRGIN	AEHIINNOPRTT TREPHINATION
AEGIILRRRTUY IRREGULARITY	AEHIINOORSTT THEORISATION
AEGIIMMMMNSUW MINIMUM WAGES	AEHIINOORTTZ THEORIZATION
AEGIIMMORRRS MIRROR IMAGES	AEHIINOPRRSS PARISHIONERS
AEGIIMNNOPRT IMPREGNATION	AEHIIRRSSTTW SHIRTWAISTER
AEGIIMNNOPTT PIGMENTATION	AEHILLOORSTU HELIOLATROUS
AEGIIMOPRSTV GRAM-POSITIVE	AEHILMNOOPSU ANEMOPHILOUS
AEGIINNNRSTT INTRANSIGENT	AEHILMNORSTW MOTHERS-IN-LAW
AEGIINNOOSTT NEGOTIATIONS	AEHIMMMOPRST METAMORPHISM
AEGIINNORSST RESIGNATIONS	AEHIMNNOOPRT ENANTIOMORPH
AEGIINNSTUXY EXSANGUINITY	AEHIMNNOPPSU ONE-UPMANSHIP
AEGIINORRSTT REGISTRATION	AEHIMNNOSSSW WOMANISHNESS
AEGIINORSTTV INVESTIGATOR	AEHIMNNOSSTT ASTONISHMENT
AEGIINPPRRTW WRITING PAPER	AEHIMNNQSTUV VANQUISHMENT
AEGIINPRSTUZ PASTEURIZING	AEHIMNOPRSST MISANTHROPES
AEGIJLNRSUUV JUGULAR VEINS	AEHIMNOPRSTW WITH OPEN ARMS
AEGIJLPSUWZZ JIGSAW PUZZLE	AEHIMNPRSSST TRAMPISHNESS
AEGIKLMNORTW METALWORKING	AEHIMPRSSSTY SYMPATHISERS
AEGIKMMNOPRT TEMPO MARKING	AEHIMPRSSTYZ SYMPATHIZERS
AEGILLMRSTTU METALLURGIST	AEHINNNOSTTT ON THE INSTANT
AEGILLNNOSTW STONEWALLING	AEHINNPPSSSS SNAPPISHNESS
AEGILLNOPTUV POLE VAULTING	AEHINOOPRRTT PROTOTHERIAN
AEGILMMNRSTY STAMMERINGLY	AEHINOORSTTX EXHORTATIONS
AEGILMNNNNOT NONALIGNMENT	AEHINOOSSTTU STATION HOUSE
AEGILMNNOQTU MAGNILOQUENT	AEHINPNPRRSST PARTNERSHIPS
AEGILMORSSTT STIGMASTEROL	AEHIOOPPRSST APOSTROPHISE
AEGILNNNOSTU SANGUINOLENT	AEHIOOPPRSTZ APOSTROPHIZE
AEGILNNRSSSU SINGULARNESS	AEHIOPRRSTWY PRAISEWORTHY
AEGILNNRSTTY ASTRINGENTLY	AEHJNOORRSST TROJAN HORSES
AEGILNRRSSUY REASSURINGLY	AEHLMPRSTTTU THE LAST TRUMP
AEGILOORSTTT TERATOLOGIST	AEHLNOPSSTUY POLYANTHUSES
AEGILORRSSTU GROSSULARITE	AEHLOPPRSTUY PYROSULPHATE
AEGIMMORSSTU MESOGASTRIUM	AEHMNOOPRTUX PNEUMOTHORAX
AEGIMMNNNRSTU RUNNING MATES	AEHMNOORSSTV HARVEST MOONS
AEGIMNNRSTTU MENSTRUATING	AEHOOPRRSSUW HOUSE SPARROW
AEGINNOPSSTV PAVING STONES	AEIIIILMRSST SIMILARITIES
AEGINOORRRTT INTERROGATOR	AEIIIILRSTTV TRIVIALITIES
AEGINOPRSTUX EXPURGATIONS	AEIIILLMNORS MILLIONAIRES
AEGINOPRSTWY STAYING POWER	AEIIILLMNTUV ILLUMINATIVE
AEGINOQSSTTU QUESTION TAGS	AEIIILMMORST IMMORALITIES
AEGLLNOOOPTY PALEONTOLOGY	AEIIILMPRSST IMPERIALISTS
AEGLNRSSTTUU GUTTURALNESS	AEIIILNRSTTT INTERSTITIAL
AEGLOORSTUUY OUTRAGEOUSLY	AEIIILPRSSTU SPIRITUALISE
AEGMMNOPSSUU MAGNUM OPUSES	AEIIILPRSTUZ SPIRITUALIZE
AEGNOOPRSSSY GREASY SPOONS	AEIIIMMNSSTT ANTI-SEMITISM
AEGNORRRSSST TRANSGRESSOR	AEIIIMNNNOST INSEMINATION
AEGOOPSSTTUY STEATOPYGOUS	AEIIIMNORSSS MISSIONARIES
AEHHILOPSTTU THIOSULPHATE	AEIIIMNRSTTV MINISTRATIVE
AEHHIMNOPRSS HORSEMANSHIP	AEIIINNRSTTV INTRANSITIVE
AEHHIMOOPSTT HOMEOPATHIST	AEIIIOPPRTTV PROPITIATIVE
AEHHLMOOPSTX EXOPHTHALMOS	AEIIKKNORSSY KARYOKINESIS

AEIILLNQRSTU   TRANQUILLISE
AEIIILLNQRTUZ   TRANQUILLIZE
AEIIILLRSTTUV   ILLUSTRATIVE
AEIILMMNOOST   EMOTIONALISM
AEIILMMORRST   IMMORTALISER
AEIILMMORRTZ   IMMORTALIZER
AEIILMNOOSTT   EMOTIONALIST
AEIILMNOOTTY   EMOTIONALITY
AEIILMNOPRSS   IMPRESSIONAL
AEIILMNOSSTT   TESTIMONIALS
AEIILMNRSSUV   UNIVERSALISM
AEIILMNRTUVY   RUMINATIVELY
AEIILMNSTTUY   SIMULTANEITY
AEIILMPRTTTU   MULTIPARTITE
AEIILNNNQQUU   QUINQUENNIAL
AEIILNOOPSTX   EXPOSITIONAL
AEIILNOOPTTX   EXPLOITATION
AEIILNOOSTVW   VOWELISATION
AEIILNOOTVWZ   VOWELIZATION
AEIILNOPTTTY   POTENTIALITY
AEIILNORSSST   SOLITARINESS
AEIILNORSSTT   ORIENTALISTS
AEIILNRSSSTW   SISTERS-IN-LAW
AEIILNRSSTUV   UNIVERSALIST
AEIILNRSTUVY   UNIVERSALITY
AEIILNSTUUXY   UNISEXUALITY
AEIILORRRSTT   TERRITORIALS
AEIIMMNOORST   MEMORISATION
AEIIMMNOORTZ   MEMORIZATION
AEIIMNNOOSTT   MONETISATION
AEIIMNNOOTTZ   MONETIZATION
AEIIMNNOPSSX   EXPANSIONISM
AEIIMNNORSTT   TERMINATIONS
AEIIMNRSSSTV   TRANSMISSIVE
AEIIMRRSTTUV   TRIUMVIRATES
AEIINNNORTTU   ANTINEUTRINO
AEIINNOORSTT   ORIENTATIONS
AEIINNOPRSTU   RESUPINATION
AEIINNOPSSTX   EXPANSIONIST
AEIINNORSTTT   STRONTIANITE
AEIINOPPRRST   PERSPIRATION
AEIINOPRTTUV   VITUPERATION
AEIKMNOQRSTU   QUESTION MARK
AEILLMMMSSTY   SYMMETALLISM
AEILLMNOPRSY   IMPERSONALLY
AEILLNNORTTY   INTOLERANTLY
AEILLNOOSTTW   WOLLASTONITE
AEILLORRRTTY   ROTARY TILLER
AEILMNNOPRST   MINOR PLANETS
AEILMNNORSST   MATRONLINESS
AEILMNNOSSTW   WINSTON-SALEM
AEILMNNRSTTU   INSTRUMENTAL
AEILMNOOPRTT   METROPOLITAN
AEILMNOOSSTU   SIMULTANEOUS
AEILMOORSTTT   STROMATOLITE
AEILNNRTTUWW   UNWRITTEN LAW
AEILNOOOPRRT   POOR RELATION
AEILNOOPRSTX   EXPLORATIONS
AEILNOOORTUVY   EVOLUTIONARY

AEILNORRSUVY   REVULSIONARY
AEILOPRSTUUV   VOLUPTUARIES
AEIMNNOPPSTT   APPOINTMENTS
AEIMNNORSTTU   MENSTRUATION
AEIMNOOPRRST   IMPERSONATOR
AEIMNOPRSTTU   PERMUTATIONS
AEIMNRRSSTTT   TRANSMITTERS
AEIMNRSSSTTV   TRANSVESTISM
AEINNNORSSTT   NONRESISTANT
AEINNOOPRSTU   PUT ONE'S OAR IN
AEINNORSTTTU   STERNUTATION
AEINOOPRSTTT   PROTESTATION
AEINOOPRSTTW   POWER STATION
AEINOORRSSTT   RESTORATIONS
AEINOORRTTXY   EXTORTIONARY
AEINOOSSTTTU   OSTENTATIOUS
AEINOPPRSSTT   POSTER PAINTS
AEINOPRRSTTV   TRANSPORTIVE
AEINORRSTVWY   WINTER SAVORY
AEIOOOOPPPRS   PROSOPOPOEIA
AEIOOPPRRRTX   EXPROPRIATOR
AEIOPPRRRSTY   PERSPIRATORY
AEKLLPPSSTUU   PULL UP STAKES
AEKLMNNOOPRT   MEROPLANKTON
AELLLMORSUVY   MARVELLOUSLY
AELLMMNNOTUY   MONUMENTALLY
AELLOOPPSSUY   POLYSEPALOUS
AELLOOPPSTUY   POLYPETALOUS
AELMNOOOPSSU   MONOSEPALOUS
AELMNOOOPSTU   MONOPETALOUS
AELMORSSSSTY   SOLAR SYSTEMS
AELMPRSSTYYY   MYSTERY PLAYS
AELNNNOPRSTW   TOWN PLANNERS
AELOOPRSTTUX   EXPOSTULATOR
AEMMORRSSUVY   SUMMER SAVORY
AEMNNOORSSTY   STONEMASONRY
AEMNOOOPRSTZ   SPERMATOZOON
AEMNOOOPRSZZ   MEZZO-SOPRANO
AEMNOORRRSTT   REMONSTRATOR
AEMNOQSSSSUU   SQUAMOUSNESS
AEMPRRSSTTUU   SUPERSTRATUM
AENNOOPRSSSS   PARSON'S NOSES
AENOOPRSSSUV   VAPOROUSNESS
AENOPRRRSSTT   TRANSPORTERS
AENORRSTTTUY   STERNUTATORY
AEOOPPPRRSTY   PARTY POOPERS
AEOPPRRSSTTU   SUPRAPROTEST
AEOPPRRSTTVY   POVERTY TRAPS
AFFGILNOOTTU   FOOT FAULTING
AFFHILLNTUUY   UNFAITHFULLY
AFFIILNNOSTU   INSUFFLATION
AFGGGILLNNUY   UNFLAGGINGLY
AFGGIILNRTYY   GRATIFYINGLY
AFGGIINPPRTW   GIFT-WRAPPING
AFGIIILNNRTT   INFILTRATING
AFGIIILLMNORU   ANGUILLIFORM
AFGIILLNQUYY   QUALIFYINGLY
AFGIILNSSTYY   SATISFYINGLY
AFGIIMNOPRRT   PROFIT MARGIN

AFGIKNOORSTT TOASTING FORK	AGIIILNORSTV INVIGILATORS
AFGIMNNORRST TRANSFORMING	AGIIILNSSTTW WAITING LISTS
AFGIMNORRSTY TRANSMOGRIFY	AGIIINNOORTV INVIGORATION
AFIIILMNNOST INFLATIONISM	AGIIINNOPRTT PARTITIONING
AFIIILNNORTT INFILTRATION	AGIIINOPPRTT PROPITIATING
AFIIILNNOSTT INFLATIONIST	AGIIKLNNOPTT TALKING POINT
AFIILMNNOSTU FULMINATIONS	AGIILLLMNTUU MULTILINGUAL
AFIILMORSTUU MULTIFARIOUS	AGIILLLNRTUY TRILINGUALLY
AFIILNNOORTU FLUORINATION	AGIILLMNORYZ MORALIZINGLY
AFIILNORRSTT INFILTRATORS	AGIILLNORTUV OUTRIVALLING
AFIILORRSSST FISSIROSTRAL	AGIILLNRSTTU ILLUSTRATING
AFIIMMNNORST MISINFORMANT	AGIILLOPSSSS SALPIGLOSSIS
AFILMNOORSTU FORMULATIONS	AGIILMNNRTUY RUMINATINGLY
AFIMMNORRSST TRANSFORMISM	AGIILNNSSTUY SUSTAININGLY
AFIMNORRSSTT TRANSFORMIST	AGIILNOORSUV VAINGLORIOUS
AFINNORSSSTU TRANSFUSIONS	AGIILNOPPRUZ POPULARIZING
AFINORRSSTTU FRUSTRATIONS	AGIIMNNRSTTT TRANSMITTING
AGGGILLNRSTY STRAGGLINGLY	AGIIMNOORSTW WAITING ROOMS
AGGHHLOPPRYY GLYPHOGRAPHY	AGIINNOOPPRT APPORTIONING
AGGHHMOPPRSY SPHYGMOGRAPH	AGIKMNNOORWW WORKINGWOMAN
AGGHIIKLNPRT PARKING LIGHT	AGIKNOPRRTWY WORKING PARTY
AGGHIIKNNSTV THANKSGIVING	AGILLNOOPSTY PALYNOLOGIST
AGGHIIMNNRST HAMSTRINGING	AGILMNNSSUUY UNASSUMINGLY
AGGHILMNNRSY RHYMING SLANG	AGILMNOOOOSY ONOMASIOLOGY
AGGHILOOPRST GRAPHOLOGIST	AGILMNOOPRTU PROMULGATION
AGGHLNOOPRYY PHARYNGOLOGY	AGILMOOOSSTT SOMATOLOGIST
AGGHLOOPRSSY GLOSSOGRAPHY	AGILNNNNOPTW TOWN PLANNING
AGGHLOPPRTYY GLYPTOGRAPHY	AGILNNOOOPRT PROLONGATION
AGGIIIILNNTV INVIGILATING	AGILNPRSSSUY SURPASSINGLY
AGGIIIMNSTTZ STIGMATIZING	AGILORSTTUUY GRATUITOUSLY
AGGIIINNORTV INVIGORATING	AGIMNOORSSTT GASTRONOMIST
AGGIINNOPRSW GROWING PAINS	AGINNOPRRSST APRON STRINGS
AGGIKLLNOOSS LOOKING GLASS	AGINNOPRRSTT TRANSPORTING
AGGIKMNOORST MAGNITOGORSK	AGINNRRSSSTU SATURN'S RINGS
AGGILMNOPRTU PROMULGATING	AGINOOOPRRST PROROGATIONS
AGGILNOOORST ORGANOLOGIST	AGINOOPRSSTT PROTAGONISTS
AGGINOPSSSTT STAGING POSTS	AGINOPRSSTTT STARTING POST
AGHHILNOPRTT TRIPHTHONGAL	AGLLNOORSUUY LANGUOROUSLY
AGHHIOPPRSYY PHYSIOGRAPHY	AGLLOOPSSTTT GLOTTAL STOPS
AGHHOOPPSTUY PHYTOPHAGOUS	AGLMMNOOOSUY MONOGAMOUSLY
AGHIILMNPSTY LYMPHANGITIS	AGLMOOPRRSTU PROMULGATORS
AGHIIMNPSTYZ SYMPATHIZING	AHHIILMOPSTT OPHTHALMITIS
AGHIINOPPRTU UPRIGHT PIANO	AHHILLLLSSYY SHILLY-SHALLY
AGHILMNOOOOT HOMOLOGATION	AHHILLMMOOST HOMOTHALLISM
AGHILNOOSSTT ANTHOLOGISTS	AHHILNOPPRTY PHILANTHROPY
AGHILOOPSSTT PATHOLOGISTS	AHHINNOPRSTT STROPHANTHIN
AGHINOOPRSTT TRAPSHOOTING	AHHNOPRSSTTU STROPHANTHUS
AGHINOORSSTT SHOOTING STAR	AHIIILMNOSTU HUMILIATIONS
AGHINOPRSSTT PARTING SHOTS	AHIIMNNOORSU INHARMONIOUS
AGHIOPPSSYYZ ZYGAPOPHYSIS	AHIKLOORTTUW KILOWATT-HOUR
AGHLLMOOPSUY GAMOPHYLLOUS	AHILLMMOOPRS ALLOMORPHISM
AGHLNOOOPRTY ANTHROPOLOGY	AHILLNOORTYZ HORIZONTALLY
AGHMNOOPRTYY PHARYNGOTOMY	AHILMNOORSUY HARMONIOUSLY
AGIIIILMNRTZ MILITARIZING	AHILMNPRTTUY TRIUMPHANTLY
AGIIILNNOTV INVIGILATION	AHILMOOOPRTY HOMOPOLARITY
AGIIIILNRTVZ TRIVIALIZING	AHILNOPRSTUU SULPHURATION
AGIIILLMNNTU ILLUMINATING	AHIMOOPPPSTU HIPPOPOTAMUS
AGIIILLMNSST MAILING LISTS	AHIMOOPPRSTT HAPTOTROPISM
AGIIILNNOPST OIL PAINTINGS	AHIMOOPPRSTU AMPHITROPOUS

AHINNOPRSSTU SINANTHROPUS
AHINOOPSSSTU SOUSAPHONIST
AHINOOPSSSTX SAXOPHONISTS
AHINOOPSSTUY AUTOHYPNOSIS
AHINORRSSSTY SYNARTHROSIS
AHKLLNNOOOPT HOLOPLANKTON
AHNOOOPRRTTY PROTHONOTARY
AIIIIMMNNOST MINIMISATION
AIIIIMMNNOTZ MINIMIZATION
AIIILLMNNOTU ILLUMINATION
AIIILLNNOSTT INSTILLATION
AIIILMNOOSST ISOLATIONISM
AIIILMPRSSTU SPIRITUALISM
AIIILNOOSSTT ISOLATIONIST
AIIILPRSSTTU SPIRITUALIST
AIIILPRSTTUY SPIRITUALITY
AIIIMMNNOSTU IMMUNISATION
AIIIMMNNOTUZ IMMUNIZATION
AIIIMMNNORSTT MINISTRATION
AIIIMNOOPSTT OPTIMISATION
AIIIMNOOPTTZ OPTIMIZATION
AIIIMNRSSTTU MINIATURISTS
AIIINNNOOSTU UNIONISATION
AIIINNNOOTUZ UNIONIZATION
AIIINNNOSSTU INSINUATIONS
AIIINNOPRSST INSPIRATIONS
AIIINOOPPRTT PROPITIATION
AIIINOPRRTTT TRIPARTITION
AIIKLRSSTUVV SURVIVAL KITS
AIIILLNNOOTUV INVOLUTIONAL
AIIILLNORSTTU ILLUSTRATION
AIIILLNQRTTUY TRANQUILLITY
AIIILMNNNOOTU MOUNTAIN LION
AIIILMNNORTTU MALNUTRITION
AIIILNNOTTUUV INVULTUATION
AIIILNOOOOPPST OPPOSITIONAL
AIIILNOPSSTTU STIPULATIONS
AIIILNORRSSST SINISTRORSAL
AIIILNORRSTTY TRANSITORILY
AIIIMMNSSSTTU NUMISMATISTS
AIIMNNORSSST TRANSMISSION
AIIMNOOOORSTT MOTORISATION
AIIMNOOOORTTZ MOTORIZATION
AIIMNOOPRSSU PARSIMONIOUS
AIIMNOOPRSTT IMPORTATIONS
AIIMNOOQSTTU MISQUOTATION
AIIMOOPPRRRT IMPROPRIATOR
AIIINNOOOPSST OPSONISATION
AIIINNOOOPSTZ OPSONIZATION
AIIOOPPRRTTY PROPITIATORY
AIKNOORSSTTW WORKSTATIONS
AILLMNNOOPRY PRONOMINALLY
AILLNOOPSTTY POLYTONALIST
AILLNOOPTTYY POLYTONALITY
AILLORRSSTTU ILLUSTRATORS
AILMNORSTUVY VOLUNTARYISM
AILNOOOPPRRT PROPORTIONAL
AILNOPPRTUUY UNPOPULARITY
AILNORSTTUVY VOLUNTARYIST

AILOOPRRSUUY UPROARIOUSLY
AILOORRSTTUY TRAITOROUSLY
AIMNNOOPRSSU PONS ASINORUM
AIMNNOOPSTTU MOUNTAINTOPS
AIMOORRRTWWY TWO-WAY MIRROR
AINOOPRRSSTT PROSTRATIONS
ALMNOOOSTUUY AUTONOMOUSLY
ALMNOORSSTTU SALMON TROUTS
BBBBBEEHLLUU HUBBLE-BUBBLE
BBCDEEEKNRRU RUBBERNECKED
BBCEELNOOSST COBBLESTONES
BBCEILMOSSTU COMBUSTIBLES
BBCEJKOORSST STOCKJOBBERS
BBCEJKOORSTY STOCKJOBBERY
BBCEKLORSSTU BLOCKBUSTERS
BBCELLLOOSWY COLLYWOBBLES
BBCELMORSSTU CLUSTER BOMBS
BBCENOORRSTU BRONCOBUSTER
BBDDDDEEELOU DOUBLE-BEDDED
BBDEEELOSUYY BLUE-EYED BOYS
BBDEEGGKLOOO GOBBLEDEGOOK
BBDEEHHLOOSY HOBBLEDEHOYS
BBDEFFLLOSUU DOUBLE BLUFFS
BBDEGGKLOOOY GOBBLEDYGOOK
BBDEGHINRRUY RUBBER DINGHY
BBDEGHMNOORY HYDROGEN BOMB
BBDEHLOOORRT BLOOD BROTHER
BBEEEHLLOTTW BELOW THE BELT
BBEEGMNORRUY MONEY-GRUBBER
BBEEILMRSSSU SUBMERSIBLES
BBEENNNRRSUU BUNSEN BURNER
BBEGGHIILNOS BOBSLEIGHING
BBEHIIILLOPS BIBLIOPHILES
BBEHIILLLOTY BOIL THE BILLY
BBEHINNOSSSS SNOBBISHNESS
BBELLNOSTTUY BELLY BUTTONS
BBEMNNOORSTU NEUTRON BOMBS
BBENNORSSSTU STUBBORNNESS
BBHJNNOOOOSS HOBSON-JOBSON
BCCCEIIMRRSU CIRCUMSCRIBE
BCCDEEIJORTT DIRECT OBJECT
BCCEEEHKRRRY CHECKERBERRY
BCCEEELNOOSS OBSOLESCENCE
BCCEEHKLMOOR CHECKERBLOOM
BCCEEHNORRSS CROSSBENCHER
BCCEEHNORSSS CROSSBENCHES
BCCEEIIMNNSU INCUMBENCIES
BCCEFFIKLOOS OFFICE BLOCKS
BCCEHNOOOPRS BRONCHOSCOPE
BCCEHORSTTTU BUTTERSCOTCH
BCCEILOPRSTU PUBLIC SECTOR
BCCHILLOOPSU PUBLIC SCHOOL
BCCHIMOORTTY THROMBOCYTIC
BCCHNOOOPRSY BRONCHOSCOPY
BCCINOOSSSUU SUBCONSCIOUS
BCCIOOOPRSST STROBOSCOPIC
BCCLNORSTUUY COUNTRY CLUBS
BCDDEEEIINOS DISOBEDIENCE
BCDDEEEKLORU DOUBLE-DECKER

BCDDEEIIRSTT DIRECT DEBITS
BCDDEELLLOOR RED BLOOD CELL
BCDDEIIILTUY DEDUCIBILITY
BCDEEEIINNST BENEDICTINES
BCDEEEKORRST STOCKBREEDER
BCDEEFHIILNT CHILD BENEFIT
BCDEEIINNOST BENEDICTIONS
BCDEEILOPRRU REPRODUCIBLE
BCDEEILRSTTU DESTRUCTIBLE
BCDEIIILRTUY REDUCIBILITY
BCDEIILNORTU INTRODUCIBLE
BCDEIIMORTTU OBITER DICTUM
BCDEKLOORSSU BLOODSUCKERS
BCDGHHIIILTW BIG WITH CHILD
BCDGIIKMNORS MOCKINGBIRDS
BCDGIKNOOSTY BODY STOCKING
BCDGILLLOPSU BULLDOG CLIPS
BCEEEEEHKNRS KNEE BREECHES
BCEEEEGHRRSU CHEESEBURGER
BCEEEEGILLNR BELLIGERENCE
BCEEEFILNNTY BENEFICENTLY
BCEEEGILLNRY BELLIGERENCY
BCEEEINRSSUV SUBSERVIENCE
BCEEEIRRRSVY SERVICEBERRY
BCEEEELNORTVY CONVEYER BELT
BCEEFHNNORRT FRONTBENCHER
BCEEFHNNORST FRONTBENCHES
BCEEFILNORSS FORCIBLENESS
BCEEIIIILMST IMBECILITIES
BCEEIILLRSTT BELLETRISTIC
BCEEIJLSTUVY SUBJECTIVELY
BCEEILMNOPTT CONTEMPTIBLE
BCEEILMOPRSS COMPRESSIBLE
BCEEILNORSTV CONVERTIBLES
BCEEIMMOSTTU SUBCOMMITTEE
BCEEJLNOOSST OBJECT LESSON
BCEEKLLORSTT BLOCK LETTERS
BCEFFKORSSTU BUFFER STOCKS
BCEFGIIINNOR FIBRINOGENIC
BCEFIMNNOORU UNCIFORM BONE
BCEFIMOPRTTU BIT OF CRUMPET
BCEFOORSTUYY BY COURTESY OF
BCEGHIILNTWY BEWITCHINGLY
BCEGIIILNORR INCORRIGIBLE
BCEGIILOOOST BIOECOLOGIST
BCEGIKLNOSTU BLUESTOCKING
BCEHIIMORSTY BIOCHEMISTRY
BCEHIINOSTTY BIOSYNTHETIC
BCEHILOPSSUU PUBLIC HOUSES
BCEIIILLRTVY CIVIL LIBERTY
BCEIIJMSSTUV SUBJECTIVISM
BCEIIJSSTTUV SUBJECTIVIST
BCEIIJSTTUVY SUBJECTIVITY
BCEIIKLLNRTU CLINKER-BUILT
BCEIILNRSTTU INSTRUCTIBLE
BCEIINORTTUV CONTRIBUTIVE
BCEIIPRSSTUV SUBSCRIPTIVE
BCEIJNSSTUUV SUBJUNCTIVES
BCEIKNNRSUWW NEW BRUNSWICK

BCEIKOOPRSTU PICTURE BOOKS
BCEILLOOPSUY EBULLIOSCOPY
BCEILMNOPTTY CONTEMPTIBLY
BCEILORSSTUU TUBERCULOSIS
BCEINNNOSTTU SUBCONTINENT
BCEKKOOOORSY COOKERY BOOKS
BCEKKOORRSST STOCKBROKERS
BCEOOOOPRSST STROBOSCOPES
BCERRSSTTUUU SUBSTRUCTURE
BCFIIILNORTY FIBRINOLYTIC
BCGIIILMNNOR CLIMBING IRON
BCGIIILNORRY INCORRIGIBLY
BCGIILMOOORY MICROBIOLOGY
BCGIINNORTTU CONTRIBUTING
BCGIINOOOSTT GNOTOBIOTICS
BCHHIMOOORRT ORTHORHOMBIC
BCHIIIOPSSTY BIOPHYSICIST
BCHILNOORRTT BIRTH CONTROL
BCHNOORSSSTU HOT-CROSS BUNS
BCIIILPPRSTU PUBLIC SPIRIT
BCIINNOORTTU CONTRIBUTION
BCIINOPRSSTU SUBSCRIPTION
BCILMMNOSUUU CUMULONIMBUS
BCINOORRSTTU CONTRIBUTORS
BCINOORRTTUY CONTRIBUTORY
BCINOORSSTTU OBSTRUCTIONS
BDDDEEFIILNR BLIND FREDDIE
BDDDEELOOTTU DOUBLE-DOTTED
BDDDEILMNOOY BLOODY-MINDED
BDDEEEEFILMN FEEBLEMINDED
BDDEEEEGNNRR GENDER-BENDER
BDDEEEILMOSW DISEMBOWELED
BDDEEEINNSST INDEBTEDNESS
BDDEEENORRUV OVERBURDENED
BDDEEILMOSUX MIXED DOUBLES
BDDFGIILLNNO BLINDFOLDING
BDDFGIILNORY FORBIDDINGLY
BDDFGIMNNOUU DUMBFOUNDING
BDEEEFIILNNS INDEFENSIBLE
BDEEEIILRSSV DISBELIEVERS
BDEEEIIMNOST BIDE ONE'S TIME
BDEEEIIMORRS EMBROIDERIES
BDEEEIIRSVWY BIRD'S-EYE VIEW
BDEEEIILLNRSU UNDERBELLIES
BDEEEILMNRTW BEWILDERMENT
BDEEFIILNNSY INDEFENSIBLY
BDEEFIILRSTU FILIBUSTERED
BDEEGGHIIRSW WEIGHBRIDGES
BDEEGHHIINRS DENBIGHSHIRE
BDEEGIIILNST INDIGESTIBLE
BDEEGIIILNSV DISBELIEVING
BDEEGIIMMNRS DISMEMBERING
BDEEGIIMNORR EMBROIDERING
BDEEGLNOOTUU DOUBLE-TONGUE
BDEEHINOSTUU HEBETUDINOUS
BDEEIIMRRTTU TURBIDIMETER
BDEEIIRRSTTU REDISTRIBUTE
BDEEILLNPRSS SPELLBINDERS
BDEEIMNRSSTU DISBURSEMENT

BDEEINNORSTV INVERTED SNOB
BDEELLOOSSSV BLOOD VESSELS
BDEELMRRSTUY TUMBLE-DRYERS
BDEFHNOOORTU DEBT OF HONOUR
BDEGGGILNRUY BEGRUDGINGLY
BDEGHHOOORRTU THOROUGHBRED
BDEGIIILNSTY INDIGESTIBLY
BDEGIIILLNNPS SPELLBINDING
BDEGIILNORWZ BOWDLERIZING
BDEGILLNNRUY BLUNDERINGLY
BDEGILLNOOTT BLOODLETTING
BDEGILMNRTUY TUMBLE-DRYING
BDEHHMNOOORR RHOMBOHEDRON
BDEHHOOOORRST BROTHERHOODS
BDEHIILPRSSU SHIPBUILDERS
BDEHLNORSTTU THUNDERBOLTS
BDEHMOOOORRTU MOUTHBROODER
BDEIIIILLNTY INDELIBILITY
BDEIIIRSTTUV DISTRIBUTIVE
BDEIIILLNOSSU INDISSOLUBLE
BDEIINNRSTUW WIND TURBINES
BDEILLLNORRS ROLLER BLINDS
BDEIMMNOPRSU PREMIUM BONDS
BDFGHILLOOSW GOLDFISH BOWL
BDFIILMNNUUU INFUNDIBULUM
BDGGGIILMNNO MIND-BOGGLING
BDGHIIILNPSU SHIPBUILDING
BDGHIIMMNRSU HUMMINGBIRDS
BDGIIIILRTY DIRIGIBILITY
BDGIIINRSTTU DISTRIBUTING
BDGIILNOSTUU OUTBUILDINGS
BDHILOORSTTY BLOODTHIRSTY
BDIIIIILSTVY DIVISIBILITY
BDIIILLNOSUY LIBIDINOUSLY
BDIIINORSTTU DISTRIBUTION
BDIIINOSSSUV SUBDIVISIONS
BDIIILLNOSSUY INDISSOLUBLY
BDIIIORRSSTTU DISTRIBUTORS
BDKNNNOOOSUW KNOW NO BOUNDS
BEEEEEFLMNNT ENFEEBLEMENT
BEEEEEFHINORR HEREINBEFORE
BEEEEELMMNTZZ EMBEZZLEMENT
BEEEEEOQSSUXZ SQUEEZEBOXES
BEEEGILLNRST BELLIGERENTS
BEEEGIMNPRSU SUPREME BEING
BEEEGIOORRSS GOOSEBERRIES
BEEEHHRRSTTU THERE'S THE RUB
BEEEHIINNRTT TEREBINTHINE
BEEEEHLNOOPTX TELEPHONE BOX
BEEEHNNNOOPZ BENZOPHENONE
BEEEIILNNSTX INEXTENSIBLE
BEEEIILRRRSV IRREVERSIBLE
BEEEILLMNTTT BELITTLEMENT
BEEEILNNSSSS SENSIBLENESS
BEEEILNRRSST TERRIBLENESS
BEEEIMMNRTTT EMBITTERMENT
BEEEINNNORTZ NITROBENZENE
BEEEIPRRSSTY PRESBYTERIES
BEEEELLNNOTVY BENEVOLENTLY

BEEELMNOSTTU TOUT ENSEMBLE
BEEELNOOSSST OBSOLETENESS
BEEENOPPRSTY TEENYBOPPERS
BEEFGIINNRRT BIREFRINGENT
BEEFIILRRSTU FILIBUSTERER
BEEFILMNNOOT BLOEMFONTEIN
BEEGGILNNORW BOWLING GREEN
BEEGHHILLRST SHE'LL BE RIGHT
BEEGHIILLMNS EMBELLISHING
BEEGHINNORRS HERRINGBONES
BEEGHOOPRRTU PETERBOROUGH
BEEGIIILLLNT INTELLIGIBLE
BEEGIINNSSTT BESETTING SIN
BEEGLOORRTTT GLOBETROTTER
BEEHIIINORTX EXHIBITIONER
BEEHILNORRSS HORRIBLENESS
BEEHLMNORSUW WHOLE NUMBERS
BEEHLORRRTWY WHORTLEBERRY
BEEHOPRRSSTT STEPBROTHERS
BEEIILMRRSS IRREMISSIBLE
BEEIIILRRSST IRRESISTIBLE
BEEIIKLNSSSU BUSINESSLIKE
BEEIILRRRSVY IRREVERSIBLY
BEEILLLORSUY REBELLIOUSLY
BEEILLRRRSTU BULL TERRIERS
BEEILPPRSSSU SUPPRESSIBLE
BEEILRSSUVVY SUBVERSIVELY
BEEIMMNPRRSU PRIME NUMBERS
BEEINNNOOQUZ BENZOQUINONE
BEEINNORRTUW WINTERBOURNE
BEEINOSSSTWX WITNESS BOXES
BEEKOOPRRRSW POWER BROKERS
BEELLORSSTUY TROLLEYBUSES
BEELNNOSSSUU NEBULOUSNESS
BEELNQSSTUUY SUBSEQUENTLY
BEEOOPRRSSTU OBSTREPEROUS
BEFGHIINRRSU REFURBISHING
BEFGHILLRSTU BULLFIGHTERS
BEFHINNOOORS ONE FOR HIS NOB
BEFHLMORSTUU RULES OF THUMB
BEFILLNSSSSU BLISSFULNESS
BEFILMOPRSUU PLUMBIFEROUS
BEGGHIINNORU NEIGHBOURING
BEGHILORSSTT STROBE LIGHTS
BEGIIIILLLTY ILLEGIBILITY
BEGIIILLLNTY INTELLIGIBLY
BEGIIILLLNTY BELITTLINGLY
BEGIIILNNRTT BLISTERINGLY
BEGIILOOOSTX EXOBIOLOGIST
BEGIINORRSVW VIRGIN'S-BOWER
BEGILLMNRSUY SLUMBERINGLY
BEGILLNORSTY BOLSTERINGLY
BEGILLNRSTUY BLUSTERINGLY
BEGILMOORSTY EMBRYOLOGIST
BEGILNPRRTUY PERTURBINGLY
BEGIMNNORTUU OUTNUMBERING
BEGIMNORRSTT BRING TO TERMS
BEHHOOORSSTTU TOOTHBRUSHES
BEHIIIMNSTTU BISMUTHINITE

BEHIINOSSSTY BIOSYNTHESIS
BEHILMOOPSTT PHLEBOTOMIST
BEHINOSSSSUW SHOW BUSINESS
BEHLOORRSSTU SOUL BROTHERS
BEIIILRRSSTY IRRESISTIBLY
BEIILLORSTUY RESOLUBILITY
BEIILMMMOPRU PRIMUM MOBILE
BEIILMSSSUVY SUBMISSIVELY
BEIINNOOPRTW BROWNIE POINT
BEIINSSSSTUU BUSINESS SUIT
BEIISSTTTUUV SUBSTITUTIVE
BEILLOORSSTT STILBOESTROL
BEILOOQSSUUY OBSEQUIOUSLY
BEILOORSSTUY BOISTEROUSLY
BEILOPPRSTUU PURPOSE-BUILT
BELMNOOPRYYY POLYEMBRYONY
BELOOPRSSTTU TROUBLE SPOTS
BFFIIILLMORR FIBRILLIFORM
BFGGHIILLNTU BULLFIGHTING
BFGHIILLORST BILL OF RIGHTS
BFIIIILNSTUY INFUSIBILITY
BFIIIILNNORSY FIBRINOLYSIN
BFIIILNORSSY FIBRINOLYSIS
BGGHHLOOORUU LOUGHBOROUGH
BGHIILLNSTTU BULLSHITTING
BGHIINOPPSWY WHIPPING BOYS
BGHILLNOOOPT POLLING BOOTH
BGHILNNOOTTU BUTTONHOLING
BGIIIILMMNOZ IMMOBILIZING
BGIIILNNOOPT BOILING POINT
BGIILMNSTTUY SUBMITTINGLY
BGIILNSSSTUY SUBSISTINGLY
BGIINSSTTTUU SUBSTITUTING
BGILLORSUUUY LUGUBRIOUSLY
BHIIINOOPRST PROHIBITIONS
BIIIIILNSTVY INVISIBILITY
BIIIILLNOSTUY INSOLUBILITY
BIIKOOORSSTV VISITORS' BOOK
BIILOQSTUUUY UBIQUITOUSLY
BIINOSSTTTUU SUBSTITUTION
CCCCEEEENNORS CONCRESCENCE
CCCCEHINOOSU ECHINOCOCCUS
CCCCHHIOPRTU COPTIC CHURCH
CCCCKKLOOOSU CUCKOO CLOCKS
CCCDEEHKORSS CROSSCHECKED
CCCDEEIINNOS COINCIDENCES
CCCDEEIILNOPY ENCYCLOPEDIC
CCCDEIIORSTY CYSTICERCOID
CCCDHIIOOPRS DICHROSCOPIC
CCCEEEEENRSSX EXCRESCENCES
CCCEEHILORTY HETEROCYCLIC
CCCEEHKNORTU COUNTERCHECK
CCCEEIINRTTY ECCENTRICITY
CCCEEILMNOTY METONIC CYCLE
CCCEEILNNOTU NOCTILUCENCE
CCCEEENNORRSU CONCURRENCES
CCCEHINOPRTT CONCERT PITCH
CCCEILOOTTUY LEUCOCYTOTIC
CCCEINNOPSTU CONCUPISCENT

CCCEINNSSSTU SUCCINCTNESS
CCCEIOOPRSTT STREPTOCOCCI
CCCEMNOOPSUU PNEUMOCOCCUS
CCCGIIIMNRSU CIRCUMCISING
CCCHHHIRRSTU CHRISTCHURCH
CCCHIIORSTTY TRICHOCYSTIC
CCCHINOOOPRS CHRONOSCOPIC
CCCIIIMNORSU CIRCUMCISION
CCCIIIMORRTU MICROCIRCUIT
CCDDDEEEENNOS CONDESCENDED
CCDDEEIINNOST DISCONNECTED
CCDDEEIINORST DISCONCERTED
CCDDEIMNOSTU MISCONDUCTED
CCDEEEEIILNST DELITESCENCE
CCDEEEEMNSTU DETUMESCENCE
CCDEEEFIIINS DEFICIENCIES
CCDEEEFIILNV CIVIL DEFENCE
CCDEEEFNNORS FRONDESCENCE
CCDEEEHIINNS INDEHISCENCE
CCDEEEHIPRST DIRECT SPEECH
CCDEEEHNOSTU ESCUTCHEONED
CCDEEEIINRSV VIRIDESCENCE
CCDEEEINOPRV PRECONCEIVED
CCDEEEELORTTU ELECTROCUTED
CCDEEFIINNNO IN CONFIDENCE
CCDEEGILNSUY SUCCEEDINGLY
CCDEEIIINNSST INSECTICIDES
CCDEEIIMNOSV MISCONCEIVED
CCDEEILRRSSS DRESS CIRCLES
CCDEEIMNRTUV CIRCUMVENTED
CCDEEINNORST DISCONNECTER
CCDEEIORRTTU CORRECTITUDE
CCDEELOOPPRS CLOSE-CROPPED
CCDEGIMNNOOS SECOND COMING
CCDEHIIINNNO CINCHONIDINE
CCDEIIIIRSTV RECIDIVISTIC
CCDEIMNOORSS MICROSECONDS
CCDEINNOOSSU SECOND COUSIN
CCDEIORRSSSS CRISSCROSSED
CCDHHILOORRY HYDROCHLORIC
CCDHIOORSTTW WITCHDOCTORS
CCDIINOTTUVY CONDUCTIVITY
CCDNNNOOORTU NONCONDUCTOR
CCEEEEIILLNSX EXCELLENCIES
CCEEEEIILRSTY ELECTRIC EYES
CCEEEEINPRST CENTREPIECES
CCEEEEJNNSUV JUVENESCENCE
CCEEEFHHRRSU FREE CHURCHES
CCEEEFHIKNRS NECKERCHIEFS
CCEEEFLNORSU FLUORESCENCE
CCEEEGIIMNST MISCEGENETIC
CCEEEGNNORSV CONVERGENCES
CCEEEHIIMNPY CHIMNEYPIECE
CCEEEHINOSTT COENESTHETIC
CCEEEHOOPRRT PORTE-COCHERE
CCEEEIIMNNRS REMINISCENCE
CCEEEIILLORTV RECOLLECTIVE
CCEEEILMNNRT ENCIRCLEMENT
CCEEEILMNNSU LUMINESCENCE

CCEEEILOPRST SECRET POLICE
CCEEEIMNNOPT INCOMPETENCE
CCEEEIMNNSTU INTUMESCENCE
CCEEEINNNOST CONSENTIENCE
CCEEEINNNOSV CONVENIENCES
CCEEEINORSSV COERCIVENESS
CCEEEELOOPRST ELECTROSCOPE
CCEEEMMMNNOT COMMENCEMENT
CCEEEENNOQSSU CONSEQUENCES
CCEEFFIIINNY INEFFICIENCY
CCEEFFIINOST COEFFICIENTS
CCEEFHIIJSTU CHIEF JUSTICE
CCEEFINNOORT CONFECTIONER
CCEEGGILNOTU GLUCOGENETIC
CCEEGGILNOTY GLYCOGENETIC
CCEEGILLNORT RECOLLECTING
CCEEGILLOOSY ECCLESIOLOGY
CCEEGINOSTTY CYTOGENETICS
CCEEGNOORRST CONCERTGOERS
CCEEHHILOSTV CLOVE HITCHES
CCEEHHIMOPRS CHEMOSPHERIC
CCEEHIILNORT HELIOCENTRIC
CCEEHIMOSTYZ SCHIZOMYCETE
CCEEHINNORTT ETHNOCENTRIC
CCEEHINNOSTU INESCUTCHEON
CCEEHKLLLOSS COCKLESHELLS
CCEEHKLOORST ELECTROSHOCK
CCEEHLMOORSU COLOUR SCHEME
CCEEIIILRSVV CIVIL SERVICE
CCEEIIILLOSTV COLLECTIVISE
CCEEIIILLOTVZ COLLECTIVIZE
CCEEIILOOPTU LEUCOPOIETIC
CCEEIIMNORSV MISCONCEIVER
CCEEIINNNNOT INCONTINENCE
CCEEIILLLOTVY COLLECTIVELY
CCEEIILNOORT RECOLLECTION
CCEEIILLORTTY ELECTROLYTIC
CCEEIILMORRST SCLEROMETRIC
CCEEIILNNOSTV CONVENTICLES
CCEEIILNOORTT ELECTROTONIC
CCEEIILOPRRTY PYROELECTRIC
CCEEIILORRTVY CORRECTIVELY
CCEEIILPPRSTU PEPTIC ULCERS
CCEEIILSSSUVY SUCCESSIVELY
CCEEIMNOORST ECONOMETRICS
CCEEIMNRRTUV CIRCUMVENTER
CCEEIMNRSSTU MUSIC CENTRES
CCEEINNNORTT INTERCONNECT
CCEEIOOPRSST STEREOSCOPIC
CCEENOPSSSTU CONSPECTUSES
CCEEOOPPRSST SPECTROSCOPE
CCEFHINOORSU CONCHIFEROUS
CCEFIIINNSTU UNSCIENTIFIC
CCEFLLSSSUUY SUCCESSFULLY
CCEFLNSSSUUU UNSUCCESSFUL
CCEGGINNNOOR GOING CONCERN
CCEGHIINORTT RICOCHETTING
CCEGHIKNOPST SPOT-CHECKING
CCEGIILNOPRS CLOSING PRICE

CCEGIJNNORTU CONJECTURING
CCEGINOPPRUY PREOCCUPYING
CCEHHIILMOOR HELIOCHROMIC
CCEHIILLNOPU NUCLEOPHILIC
CCEHIIMORSTT STICHOMETRIC
CCEHIINOORRT RHINOCEROTIC
CCEHIKLOSSTT LOCKSTITCHES
CCEHILNOPSTY POLYTECHNICS
CCEHIMNOORRT CHRONOMETRIC
CCEHIMOOPRST THERMOSCOPIC
CCEHIMOPRSTY PSYCHOMETRIC
CCEHINOOSSTU COCONUT SHIES
CCEHINOPRSTY PYROTECHNICS
CCEHIOOPSSTT STETHOSCOPIC
CCEHIORRTTYY ERYTHROCYTIC
CCEHKLOSSTTU SHUTTLECOCKS
CCEHLOOSTTUY HECTOCOTYLUS
CCEHNOOPRSSY SYNCHROSCOPE
CCEIIIMMORSS MICROSEISMIC
CCEIIINOORRT ONEIROCRITIC
CCEIIKKSTTWY STICKY WICKET
CCEIIKNSSSTT STICK INSECTS
CCEIIILLMOSTV COLLECTIVISM
CCEIIILLOSTTV COLLECTIVIST
CCEIIILLOTTVY COLLECTIVITY
CCEIILMOORRT COLORIMETRIC
CCEIILNNOSUV INCONCLUSIVE
CCEIILPRSTUU PISCICULTURE
CCEIILRRTTUU CITRICULTURE
CCEIIMOOPSSS SEISMOSCOPIC
CCEIINNOSSSU IN SUCCESSION
CCEIINOOPRST RETINOSCOPIC
CCEIINORSTTV CONSTRICTIVE
CCEIINOSSTUV VISCOUNTCIES
CCEIJNNOSTUV CONJUNCTIVES
CCEILLNOSUVY CONCLUSIVELY
CCEILLOOOPSS OSCILLOSCOPE
CCEILMNORSUU MICRONUCLEUS
CCEILOOPRSUY PRECOCIOUSLY
CCEILOOSSTUY LEUCOCYTOSIS
CCEINNOPRRSW CROWN PRINCES
CCEINNOSTTUY CONSTITUENCY
CCEINOOPRSSU PRECONSCIOUS
CCEINOORSSST CROSS-SECTION
CCEINORSTTUV CONSTRUCTIVE
CCEIORRSSSSS CRISSCROSSES
CCEJNNORSTUU CONJUNCTURES
CCELNNORRTUY CONCURRENTLY
CCENORRRSSTU CROSSCURRENT
CCEOOPPRSSTY SPECTROSCOPY
CCFGGHIIKNOT COCKFIGHTING
CCFIIMNORSUU CIRCUMFUSION
CCFILMORSUUU CIRCUMFLUOUS
CCFILOOOPRSU FLUOROSCOPIC
CCGHHIILOOTY ICHTHYOLOGIC
CCGHILNOOOST CONCHOLOGIST
CCGIILNNNOVY CONVINCINGLY
CCGIINNNNOUV UNCONVINCING
CCGIINNOPRST CONSCRIPTING

CCGIINNORSTT CONSTRICTING
CCGILLNOSTYY CYCLOSTYLING
CCGINNORSTTU CONSTRUCTING
CCHHIIMOSTYZ SCHIZOTHYMIC
CCHHIIOPSTYZ SCHIZOPHYTIC
CCHHIKOSSTWY SCOTCH WHISKY
CCHHILOOORSS CHOIR SCHOOLS
CCHHIMOOOPRR CHROMOPHORIC
CCHIIILNOPSS SILICON CHIPS
CCHIIILNOOPRR CHLOROPICRIN
CCHIIMOPRSSY MICROPHYSICS
CCHIIORRSTTU SHORT CIRCUIT
CCHIORSSSTUU HORTUS SICCUS
CCIILNNNOOSU IN CONCLUSION
CCIILNOPRUVY PRIVY COUNCIL
CCIILORSTUUY CIRCUITOUSLY
CCIIMOOPRSST MICROSCOPIST
CCIINNOOPRST CONSCRIPTION
CCIINNOORSTT CONSTRICTION
CCIJNNNOOSTU CONJUNCTIONS
CCILMOORSTTY MOTORCYCLIST
CCILMORRSUUU CIRROCUMULUS
CCIMNOOPSTUU COMPUNCTIOUS
CCINNOORSTTU CONSTRUCTION
CCINOORRSSTT CONSTRICTORS
CCNOORRSSTTU CONSTRUCTORS
CCNOORRSSTUY CROSS-COUNTRY
CCNOORSTTUUY COUNTY COURTS
CDDDEEFIIOST EISTEDDFODIC
CDDDELLLMOOY MOLLYCODDLED
CDDEEEEGNORS SECOND-DEGREE
CDDEEEEINNNP INDEPENDENCE
CDDEEEEINNPS DEPENDENCIES
CDDEEEEJNSST DEJECTEDNESS
CDDEEEHMNOPR COMPREHENDED
CDDEEEINNNPY INDEPENDENCY
CDDEEEINORRS RECONSIDERED
CDDEEEIRRSTT DERESTRICTED
CDDEEELNSSSU SECLUDEDNESS
CDDEEEMOPRSS DECOMPRESSED
CDDEEHLNNOSU NONSCHEDULED
CDDEEIJNPRUU UNPREJUDICED
CDDEEILMORSU MIDDLE COURSE
CDDEEINNORSU UNCONSIDERED
CDDEEINNOSTT DISCONTENTED
CDDEELLNOORT DECONTROLLED
CDDEENOOPRRS CORRESPONDED
CDDEFIIKLSST FIDDLESTICKS
CDDEFLNNOOUY CONFOUNDEDLY
CDDEGIIINRST DISCREDITING
CDDEHIILMNRS CHILDMINDERS
CDDEHILLMOOS MIDDLE SCHOOL
CDDEHILNOSSS CLODDISHNESS
CDDEHLLOORSU COLD SHOULDER
CDDEHLNORTUU THUNDERCLOUD
CDDEIINNOSTU DISCONTINUED
CDDEIKOPSSTT SPOTTED DICKS
CDDEILNOOPRS SCOLOPENDRID
CDDGHIIILMNN CHILDMINDING

CDDGHIILOPRY CHILD PRODIGY
CDDGIIMMNOOS DISCOMMODING
CDDIIMMOOSTY DISCOMMODITY
CDEEEEIINNPX INEXPEDIENCE
CDEEEEIKLPRW PICKERELWEED
CDEEEEILLRVW WELL-RECEIVED
CDEEEELNNPRS RESPLENDENCE
CDEEEEFFGINOR FORCE-FEEDING
CDEEEFFIINNR INDIFFERENCE
CDEEEFHILRST CHESTERFIELD
CDEEEFHORSUV CHEFS D'OEUVRE
CDEEEGIKLNRS SINGLE-DECKER
CDEEEHIMNPRT DECIPHERMENT
CDEEEHNRSSTW WRETCHEDNESS
CDEEEIINNSST DISSENTIENCE
CDEEEIINPRSS PRESIDENCIES
CDEEEIINSSSV DECISIVENESS
CDEEEIIOPPRS PERIOD PIECES
CDEEEILMNORT DECLINOMETER
CDEEEILNQSTU DELIQUESCENT
CDEEEILORRST CLERESTORIED
CDEEEILORSTT LIE DETECTORS
CDEEEIMNORTT MINE DETECTOR
CDEEEINNNORS NONRESIDENCE
CDEEEINRSSST DISCREETNESS,
    DISCRETENESS
CDEEELMMNOPT COMPLEMENTED
CDEEEMNNNOTU DENOUNCEMENT
CDEEEOPRRSSS PREDECESSORS
CDEEFFHILOOR OFFICEHOLDER
CDEEFFHOORRT OFF-THE-RECORD
CDEEFFIMNOOT DOMINO EFFECT
CDEEFFNOSSTU SOUND EFFECTS
CDEEFILNNNUU UNINFLUENCED
CDEEFLLOORSU SELF-COLOURED
CDEEFLRSSTTU SELF-DESTRUCT
CDEEGHILNRSU RESCHEDULING
CDEEGIILRRTY TRIGLYCERIDE
CDEEGIKNOPRR PECKING ORDER
CDEEGIMMNNOR RECOMMENDING
CDEEGINNORSU UNRECOGNISED
CDEEGINNORUZ UNRECOGNIZED
CDEEGINOPRRR PRERECORDING
CDEEHHKLLOSS SHELLSHOCKED
CDEEHILLNORV LOVECHILDREN
CDEEHILNPRST STEPCHILDREN
CDEEHIOQSSTU DISCOTHEQUES
CDEEHKLNOSUY HONEYSUCKLED
CDEEHLNORSTU UNDERCLOTHES
CDEEHORSTTTU OUTSTRETCHED
CDEEIIILNSVY INDECISIVELY
CDEEIIILOPST DEPOLITICISE
CDEEIIILOPTZ DEPOLITICIZE
CDEEIIIMORST MEDIOCRITIES
CDEEIIINNOST DENICOTINISE
CDEEIIINNOTZ DENICOTINIZE
CDEEIIINNSTV DISINCENTIVE
CDEEIIINRTTV INTERDICTIVE
CDEEIILNOPRT PREDILECTION

CDEEIILNOORST DERELICTIONS
CDEEIILNRSTY INDISCREETLY
CDEEIILPRTVY PREDICTIVELY
CDEEIIMNOPRV IMPROVIDENCE
CDEEIINNRSST INDIRECTNESS
CDEEILMMNOPT COMPLIMENTED
CDEEILNOOOTV DO VIOLENCE TO
CDEEILRRSTTY RESTRICTEDLY
CDEEIMMNOOXY MIXED ECONOMY
CDEEIMOPRSTU COMPUTERISED
CDEEIMOPRTUZ COMPUTERIZED
CDEEINNOORRT RECONNOITRED
CDEEINOPRSTV OPEN VERDICTS
CDEEINRRSTTU UNRESTRICTED
CDEEIOPRRTUV REPRODUCTIVE
CDEEIORRSTUV DISCOVERTURE
CDEEIRRRSSVW SCREWDRIVERS
CDEELOOORRSU ROSE-COLOURED
CDEENNOOPRSS SECOND PERSON
CDEENNOOPRST CORESPONDENT
CDEENNRRRTUU UNDERCURRENT
CDEEORRRSSSS CROSS-DRESSER
CDEERRRSTTUU RESTRUCTURED
CDEFFIIILSTU DIFFICULTIES
CDEFGIIINNST DISINFECTING
CDEFIIINNOST DISINFECTION
CDEFIIMORSTU DISCOMFITURE
CDEFKLOOOTUW OUT OF WEDLOCK
CDEGIIIMNRST MISDIRECTING
CDEGIILNNOOZ DECOLONIZING
CDEGILNOORUV OVERCLOUDING
CDEGINNORRSU UNDERSCORING
CDEGINNORSST SECOND-STRING
CDEGINNRTTUU UNDERCUTTING
CDEGINOORRVW OVERCROWDING
CDEGLMNORUUY CURMUDGEONLY
CDEHHIIIPRTT DIPHTHERITIC
CDEHHIILNSSS CHILDISHNESS
CDEHIIILPPSS DISCIPLESHIP
CDEHIIKKNNST THICK-SKINNED
CDEHIIKNORTY HYDROKINETIC
CDEHIINOOOPR CONIDIOPHORE
CDEHIIOPRRST DIRECTORSHIP
CDEHILLOOOST OLD SCHOOL TIE
CDEHILLOOPRY POLICYHOLDER
CDEHILMNOOOR MONOCHLORIDE
CDEHIMNOOORS CHONDRIOSOME
CDEHINNORSSY SYNCHRONISED
CDEHINNORSYZ SYNCHRONIZED
CDEHKLOORSST STOCKHOLDERS
CDEIIIILNNPS INDISCIPLINE
CDEIIIJRSTUV JURISDICTIVE
CDEIIILNTVVY VINDICTIVELY
CDEIIIMNORST MISDIRECTION
CDEIIINNORST INDISCRETION
CDEIIINNORTT INTERDICTION
CDEIIISSSTUV VICISSITUDES
CDEIILMRTUUV DIVERTICULUM

CDEIILNNPPRU UNPRINCIPLED
CDEIILRSSUVY DISCURSIVELY
CDEIIMMNOOSS COMMISSIONED
CDEIIMMRSSTY DISSYMMETRIC
CDEIINNOOPRT PRECONDITION
CDEIINNOORST CONDITIONERS
CDEIINNSSSTT DISTINCTNESS
CDEIINOOPRST PERIODONTICS
CDEIINOPRSST DESCRIPTIONS
CDEILNOORSUY INDECOROUSLY
CDEILNOPSSST SPLIT SECONDS
CDEILOPRTUVY PRODUCTIVELY
CDEIMNNORSSTU MISCONSTRUED
CDEIMOOPRSSU DISCOMPOSURE
CDEINOOPRRTU REPRODUCTION
CDEINOPRTUUV UNPRODUCTIVE
CDEIOORSSTUU DISCOURTEOUS
CDEKKNOOORRS DOORKNOCKERS
CDEKLNNOOORT LONDON ROCKET
CDELLNOOTUVY CONVOLUTEDLY
CDELNNOOPRUY PRONOUNCEDLY
CDELNOOOSTUY COTYLEDONOUS
CDENRRSTTUUU UNSTRUCTURED
CDFGIIIMNOST DISCOMFITING
CDFGILNOORTY FLYING DOCTOR
CDFHILOORRUY HYDROFLUORIC
CDGGIKLLNUUY UGLY DUCKLING
CDGIIIILNNPS DISCIPLINING
CDGIIINNNOOT CONDITIONING
CDGIIKNSSTTU SITTING DUCKS
CDGIILNOORSU DISCOLOURING
CDGIIMNOOPSS DISCOMPOSING
CDGIKLNOOSTU DUCKING STOOL
CDGINNNOOORR NONCORRODING
CDHHILNOORRY CHLOROHYDRIN
CDHIIOOPRSST CHIROPODISTS
CDHIMNNOOSTY SYNODIC MONTH
CDHINOOORSTT ORTHODONTICS
CDIIIJNORSTU JURISDICTION
CDIIILNNSTTY INDISTINCTLY
CDIINNOSSTT DISTINCTIONS
CDIILLORSUUY RIDICULOUSLY
CDIIMMNNOOSU CONDOMINIUMS
CDIIMMNOOOSU INCOMMODIOUS
CDIINNOORTTU INTRODUCTION
CDIIOPRTTUVY PRODUCTIVITY
CDILMMOOOSUY COMMODIOUSLY
CDINOOORRTTUY INTRODUCTORY
CEEEEFFNRSTV EFFERVESCENT
CEEEEFHNORTV OVER THE FENCE
CEEEEFINNRRT INTERFERENCE
CEEEEHNORSVW WHENCESOEVER
CEEEEIINNPRX INEXPERIENCE
CEEEEIKKPRTW WICKET KEEPER
CEEEEIMNNSSS MISE-EN-SCÈNES
CEEEEIMNRSVX EX-SERVICEMEN
CEEEEINPRSTX PRE-EXISTENCE
CEEEELMORRTT ELECTROMETER
CEEEENNRRSTV NERVE CENTRES

CEEEFFGINRSV EFFERVESCING
CEEEFFHOOSSU COFFEE HOUSES
CEEEFFLNORST EFFLORESCENT
CEEEFGHIIOPT PIECE OF EIGHT
CEEEFHINRSST SCENESHIFTER
CEEEFHLNRSSU CHEERFULNESS
CEEEFIIMPRTV IMPERFECTIVE
CEEEFILNRTUV UNREFLECTIVE
CEEEFKLNSSSS FECKLESSNESS
CEEEGGNORRRS GREENGROCERS
CEEEGGNORRRY GREENGROCERY
CEEEGIILLNNT INTELLIGENCE
CEEEGIINNPRX EXPERIENCING
CEEEGIINRSTT ENERGETICIST
CEEEHHIINSTW CHINESE WHITE
CEEEHIIMRSTU EUHEMERISTIC
CEEEHIIPRRSV RECEIVERSHIP
CEEEHIKNSTTT KITCHENETTES
CEEEHIMNNPRT ENCIPHERMENT
CEEEHIMNPSWY CHIMNEYSWEEP
CEEEHIMNRSTU HERMENEUTICS
CEEEHINOSSST COENESTHESIS
CEEEHINOSSSV COHESIVENESS
CEEEHIOORSTU HETEROECIOUS
CEEEHLLPSSSY SPEECHLESSLY
CEEEHLNNOTTU LUNCHEONETTE
CEEEHLNOOPRT ELECTROPHONE
CEEEHLOQQSUU QUELQUE CHOSE
CEEEHMNNNRTT ENTRENCHMENT
CEEEHMNNRRTT RETRENCHMENT
CEEEHMOORRST STEREOCHROME
CEEEHNOPRRST CENTROSPHERE
CEEEIILLNTTV INTELLECTIVE
CEEEIIMNNPRT IMPERTINENCE
CEEEIIMPPRTV IMPERCEPTIVE
CEEEIINPRTTV INTERCEPTIVE
CEEEIIPRRSTV IRRESPECTIVE
CEEEILLNOPQU EQUIPOLLENCE
CEEEILORRSST CLERESTORIES
CEEEILPPRTVY PERCEPTIVELY
CEEEILPRSTVY RESPECTIVELY
CEEEIMMMNOTT COMMITTEEMEN
CEEEIMMNRSTX CEMENT MIXERS
CEEEIMMPSSUU MUSEUM PIECES
CEEEIMNNOPRS OMNIPRESENCE
CEEEIMNNORST MESENTERONIC
CEEEIMORRSTT STEREOMETRIC
CEEEINNNOSTX NONEXISTENCE
CEEEINNQSSTU QUINTESSENCE
CEEEINORSTUX EXECUTIONERS
CEEEIORRSSTV RETROCESSIVE
CEEEIPPRSSTV PERSPECTIVES
CEEEIPRRSSUV REPERCUSSIVE
CEEEKLNRSSSS RECKLESSNESS
CEEEKMNORSSS SMOKESCREENS
CEEELLNPRUUV PULVERULENCE
CEEELLORRSTY ELECTROLYSER
CEEELLORSTTY ELECTROLYTES
CEEELMNOPSST COMPLETENESS

CEEELMORRTTY ELECTROMETRY
CEEELOPRRTTY ELECTROTYPER
CEEELORRSSSU RESOURCELESS
CEEEMNNNORTU RENOUNCEMENT
CEEEMOPRRSTT SPECTROMETER
CEEEOOPRRTTX EXTEROCEPTOR
CEEFFHIIORSS IRISH COFFEES
CEEFFIOPRTTY PETTY OFFICER
CEEFFLNORSSU FORCEFULNESS
CEEFGGILNNTU GENUFLECTING
CEEFGHIINPSY SPEECHIFYING
CEEFGIILNRTY ELECTRIFYING
CEEFGILLNRTY REFLECTINGLY
CEEFGILNNOTU GENUFLECTION
CEEFGLLLNTUY NEGLECTFULLY
CEEFHIKNRSSS FRENCH KISSES
CEEFHILSSTTU CUTTLEFISHES
CEEFIIMNOPRT IMPERFECTION
CEEFIINOPRST FRONTISPIECE
CEEFIKOOPRSW PIECES OF WORK
CEEFILMNRSSU MERCIFULNESS
CEEFILNNORST INFLORESCENT
CEEFIMNNNOST CONFINEMENTS
CEEFLLPRSTUY RESPECTFULLY
CEEFLOORRSSU FORECLOSURES
CEEGGILNOSSU GLUCOGENESIS
CEEGGILNOSSY GLYCOGENESIS
CEEGHIINOSTT HISTOGENETIC
CEEGHILNOOST TECHNOLOGIES
CEEGHILOOPRT HERPETOLOGIC
CEEGHIMORSTY GEOCHEMISTRY
CEEGHINOORTT ORTHOGENETIC
CEEGHINOPTTY PHYTOGENETIC
CEEGIIJNNRTT INTERJECTING
CEEGIINNNSST ENTICINGNESS
CEEGIINNPRTT INTERCEPTING
CEEGIINNRSSU INSURGENCIES
CEEGIINNRSTT INTERSECTING
CEEGIINOPRTV PRECOGNITIVE
CEEGIKLLNOPS GLOCKENSPIEL
CEEGIKNNOSTV EVENING STOCK
CEEGIMNNOPRS RECOMPENSING
CEEGINNNORTU ENCOUNTERING
CEEGINNOPTTX NOT EXCEPTING
CEEGINOPRRSS REPROCESSING
CEEGINRRRSTU RESURRECTING
CEEGMNOORRST COSTERMONGER
CEEHHIINOSTT HENOTHEISTIC
CEEHHLOORSST CLOTHESHORSE
CEEHHMOOPRRS CHROMOSPHERE
CEEHHOOPPRSS PHOSPHORESCE
CEEHIIMNSSTZ NIETZSCHEISM
CEEHIIMSSTTW TIME SWITCHES
CEEHIINNPPPS PINCH PENNIES
CEEHIKMNOSSS HOMESICKNESS
CEEHILLNOSST CLOTHESLINES
CEEHILMMOPRY MYRMECOPHILE
CEEHILNNORTY INCOHERENTLY
CEEHILPRSSTU LECTURESHIPS

593

CEEHIMMORRTT THERMOMETRIC
CEEHIMNOOSTU HOME COUNTIES
CEEHIMNORSTT THEOCENTRISM
CEEHINNNPPRY PENNY PINCHER
CEEHINOOPRST STEREOPHONIC
CEEHINOORRSS RHINOCEROSES
CEEHINRSSSTT STRETCHINESS
CEEHIOPRSTUX EXECUTORSHIP
CEEHKLNOSSUY HONEYSUCKLES
CEEHKMNNORWY MONKEY WRENCH
CEEHLLMOORWY CHROME YELLOW
CEEHLMOOPRTU THERMOCOUPLE
CEEHLOPRSSST CLOTHES-PRESS
CEEHMNOORRST CHRONOMETERS
CEEHMNORSTUX HERSTMONCEUX
CEEHMOORRSTY STEREOCHROMY
CEEHMOPRRSTY PSYCHROMETER
CEEHMORSTTYY HYSTERECTOMY
CEEHOOPRRSTU URETHROSCOPE
CEEHOOPSSSTT STETHOSCOPES
CEEIIINNSSSV INCISIVENESS
CEEIIINPRRTU PERINEURITIC
CEEIIJNNORTT INTERJECTION
CEEIIJNORTTV INTROJECTIVE
CEEIILLNNOTT INTELLECTION
CEEIILMNNORT INCLINOMETER
CEEIILMOPSTX COMPLEXITIES
CEEIILNNPRSS PRINCELINESS
CEEIILNPSSTX EXPLICITNESS
CEEIILOOPSSU LEUCOPOIESIS
CEEIIMNOPPRT IMPERCEPTION
CEEIIMNOSSSS SECESSIONISM
CEEIIMOPRSSU SEMIPRECIOUS
CEEIIMORRSTU MERETRICIOUS
CEEIINNNNOTV INCONVENIENT
CEEIINNOPRTT INTERCEPTION
CEEIINNORSST INTERCESSION
CEEIINNORSTT INTERSECTION
CEEIINOPRSTT RECEPTIONIST
CEEIINORSSTV INSECTIVORES
CEEIINOSSSST SECESSIONIST
CEEIIPPRRSTV PRESCRIPTIVE
CEEIIPPRTTVY PERCEPTIVITY
CEEIJNORRTTY INTERJECTORY
CEEIKLMNPPRU PUMPERNICKEL
CEEIKNNOOPST IN ONE'S POCKET
CEEILLMNOPTY INCOMPLETELY
CEEILLORSSTY ELECTROLYSIS
CEEILMOOPRSY COPOLYMERISE
CEEILMOOPRYZ COPOLYMERIZE
CEEILNNNOTVY CONVENIENTLY
CEEILNOOPRSS NECROPOLISES
CEEILOPRTTVY PROTECTIVELY
CEEIMMMNORTT RECOMMITMENT
CEEIMNNOPSTT INCOMPETENTS
CEEIMNOOPRST CONTEMPORISE
CEEIMNOOPRTZ CONTEMPORIZE
CEEINNNOQSTU INCONSEQUENT
CEEINNOORRRT RECONNOITRER

CEEINNOORRSV RECONVERSION
CEEINNPRTUUV VENIPUNCTURE
CEEINNRRRTTU INTERCURRENT
CEEINOOPRRTT INTEROCEPTOR
CEEINOOPRSTT STEREOPTICON
CEEINOOPRSTU COUNTERPOISE
CEEINOORRSST RETROCESSION
CEEINOPRRSSU REPERCUSSION
CEEINOPRRSTT INTERCEPTORS
CEEINOPRSSSU PRECIOUSNESS
CEEINOPRSSTU PERSECUTIONS
CEEINOPSSSSU SPECIOUSNESS
CEEINORRRSTU RESURRECTION
CEEINORRSSTY INTERCESSORY
CEEINORSTTTU RECONSTITUTE
CEEIOOPRRSTT STEREOTROPIC
CEEKOORRRSTT RETRO-ROCKETS
CEELLNOORTTV ELECTRONVOLT
CEELNNOQSTUY CONSEQUENTLY
CEELNOORSTTU ELECTROTONUS
CEELOOOPRSTU COLEOPTEROUS
CEEMOPRRSTTY SPECTROMETRY
CEEMOPRRSTUU SUPREME COURT
CEENNOOQRSTU QUEEN CONSORT
CEENNOORRSST CORNERSTONES
CEENNOORRTTU COUNTERTENOR
CEENOOOPPRSS SNOOPERSCOPE
CEENOORRRTTV CONTROVERTER
CEENOOSSSTUV COVETOUSNESS
CEEOPPRSSSTU PROSPECTUSES
CEFFHMNOOPSU OFF ONE'S CHUMP
CEFFIIINNSTU INSUFFICIENT
CEFFIILOOPRT PILOT OFFICER
CEFFIORRSTUU FRUCTIFEROUS
CEFFIORSSTUU SUFFRUTICOSE
CEFGIIKLLNRY FLICKERINGLY
CEFGIIKLNPTY FLYING PICKET
CEFHHILNOPRS FRENCH POLISH
CEFHILMNNOUY ICHNEUMON FLY
CEFHLLLOOOSW SCHOOLFELLOW
CEFIIILNOSTU INFELICITOUS
CEFIIILORSSU SILICIFEROUS
CEFIIIORRSTU FOURIERISTIC
CEFIILLOSTUY FELICITOUSLY
CEFIILMNNTUY MUNIFICENTLY
CEFIILNOORRS FERROSILICON
CEFIILNOPRSS PROLIFICNESS
CEFIILNOPRTY PROFICIENTLY
CEFIILNOSTUY INFECTIOUSLY
CEFILLORRTUU FLORICULTURE
CEFILMOORRTU FLUOROMETRIC
CEFILNOORSTU COUNTERFOILS
CEFILOORSUVY VOCIFEROUSLY
CEFKKLOORRSW CLERK OF WORKS
CEFLNNORSSSU SCORNFULNESS
CEFNOOOPRRTU COUNTERPROOF
CEGHHIILOPRY HIEROGLYPHIC
CEGHIIKNPRSW SHIPWRECKING
CEGHIILNRSTT CHITTERLINGS

CEGHIINNRSST CHRISTENINGS
CEGHIIOPSSTY GEOPHYSICIST
CEGHIKNNOSSS SHOCKINGNESS
CEGHIKNOORRS ROCKING HORSE
CEGHILLNQSUY SQUELCHINGLY
CEGHILNOOORS CHRONOLOGIES
CEGHILNOOSTT TECHNOLOGIST
CEGHILOOPSSY PSYCHOLOGIES,
  PSYCHOLOGISE
CEGHILOOPSYZ PSYCHOLOGIZE
CEGIIIILMSTT LEGITIMISTIC
CEGIIKLLMNRY MERCY KILLING
CEGIIKLNNORT INTERLOCKING
CEGIIKLNNRSY SNICKERINGLY
CEGIILLOOSTX LEXICOLOGIST
CEGIILMNOSST CLOSING TIMES
CEGIILNNPSTY INSPECTINGLY
CEGIINNOOPRT PRECOGNITION
CEGIINNOORST RECOGNITIONS
CEGIINOPTTYY GENOTYPICITY
CEGIKKNORSTY SKYROCKETING
CEGIKLNNOSSU KING'S COUNSEL
CEGIKNOORSTV OVERSTOCKING
CEGILLLMNOPY COMPELLINGLY
CEGILNNNOTTY CONTINGENTLY
CEGILNNORSTU CURLING STONE
CEGILNOOPRTY GLYCOPROTEIN
CEGIMNNNOSST CONSIGNMENTS
CEGINNNNOSTU UNCONSENTING
CEGINNNOORTW CONNING TOWER
CEGINNORSSTU COUNTERSIGNS
CEGINNOSTTTU STONECUTTING
CEGINNPSSTUU UNSUSPECTING
CEGINOOPPRRV OVERCROPPING
CEGINPRSSTTU PRESS CUTTING
CEHHILNRSSSU CHURLISHNESS
CEHHIMMOOOPR HOMEOMORPHIC
CEHHIMOOPRTT PHOTOTHERMIC
CEHHIMOOPSTT PHOTOCHEMIST
CEHHIOOPPRST PHOTOSPHERIC
CEHHLOOOSSSU SCHOOLHOUSES
CEHIIILNOOPS EOSINOPHILIC
CEHIIKLNSSST TICKLISHNESS
CEHIIKNOOPTT PHOTOKINETIC
CEHIILMNOPRS NECROPHILISM
CEHIILNQSSSU CLIQUISHNESS
CEHIILOPSTTY POLYTHEISTIC
CEHIIMNOOSTT MONOTHEISTIC
CEHIIMNOPRUY PERIONYCHIUM
CEHIINNOPRTY PERICYNTHION
CEHIIOPRRSTU PERITRICHOUS
CEHIKLMORSTY LOCKSMITHERY
CEHIKNOPSSTU SOUP KITCHENS
CEHILLOPPTYY POLYPHYLETIC
CEHILMNOOPTY MONOPHYLETIC
CEHILMNOPPTY NYMPHOLEPTIC
CEHILNNOSSSW CLOWNISHNESS
CEHILOQSTTUY COQUETTISHLY
CEHILORRTTUU HORTICULTURE

CEHIMMOOPRST CHEMOTROPISM
CEHIMNORRTYY ERYTHROMYCIN
CEHIMOOPRRTT THERMOTROPIC
CEHIMOORSTYZ ZOOCHEMISTRY
CEHINNORRSSY SYNCHRONISER
CEHINNORRSYZ SYNCHRONIZER
CEHIOOOPPRST PHOTOCOPIERS
CEHLMMOORSSU SUMMER SCHOOL
CEHMMOOORSSX X CHROMOSOMES
CEHMMOOORSSY Y CHROMOSOMES
CEHMNORSTUUX HURSTMONCEUX
CEHMOOOOPPST PHOTOCOMPOSE
CEHMOOOOPRTY OOPHORECTOMY
CEHNOOPRRTTU PHOTOCURRENT
CEHOOPRRSTUY URETHROSCOPY
CEIIIIILNSTV INCIVILITIES
CEIIILMNPSST IMPLICITNESS
CEIIILOPRSTV PROCLIVITIES
CEIIIMNOPRSS PRECISIONISM
CEIIINNORSTU REUNIONISTIC
CEIIINNOSSTW WISCONSINITE
CEIIINOPRSST PRECISIONIST
CEIIINORTTWZ ZWITTERIONIC
CEIIINOSSTVV VIVISECTIONS
CEIIJNNOORTT INTROJECTION
CEIIKLSSTWZZ SWIZZLE STICK
CEIIKRRSSTUY SECURITY RISK
CEIILLNOSTUY LICENTIOUSLY
CEIILLRSTUUV SILVICULTURE
CEIILMOPRTUV PLUVIOMETRIC
CEIILNOOSTTU ELOCUTIONIST
CEIILNOPRSUY PERNICIOUSLY
CEIILOPRSSUU SUPERCILIOUS
CEIILRRTTUUV VITICULTURER
CEIIMMNOORSS COMMISSIONER
CEIIMMNOPRTU MINICOMPUTER
CEIIMNOOPSTT COMPETITIONS
CEIIMOOPRSTT PROTOSEMITIC
CEIIMOORSSTT SOCIOMETRIST
CEIINNNOSSTT INCONSISTENT
CEIINNORRSTU INSURRECTION
CEIINOOPRRTY INCORPOREITY
CEIINOPPRRST PRESCRIPTION
CEIINORRSSTT RESTRICTIONS
CEIINORSSTUX EXCURSIONIST
CEIINORSTTVY VENTRICOSITY
CEIINOSTTTUV CONSTITUTIVE
CEIIOPPRRSTV PROSCRIPTIVE
CEIIPRRRSTTW SCRIPTWRITER
CEIIPSSTTUVY SUSCEPTIVITY
CEIKLMOORSST MORTISE LOCKS
CEILLLNOOOSV VIOLONCELLOS
CEILLMOPSUVY COMPULSIVELY
CEILLMOSTUUY METICULOUSLY
CEILLNOSUVVY CONVULSIVELY
CEILLOPRSSTU PORTCULLISES
CEILMNOOSTUU CONTUMELIOUS
CEILMNOPRSTY POLYCENTRISM
CEILNNOSSTTY CONSISTENTLY

CEILNOORRTTU INTERLOCUTOR
CEILNOORSSUY CENSORIOUSLY
CEILNOSSSSUU LUSCIOUSNESS
CEILNOSSTUUY INCESTUOUSLY
CEIMMNOOPSST COMPOS MENTIS
CEIMNNOOPRSU MISPRONOUNCE
CEIMNNOORSTU CONTERMINOUS
CEIMNOPRSTTY STREPTOMYCIN
CEIMNOPSSTUV CONSUMPTIVES
CEIMOOORRSTV VISCEROMOTOR
CEINNOOPRTTU COUNTERPOINT
CEINNOORSSSU CONNOISSEURS
CEINNOSSTTTU CONSTITUENTS
CEINOOPRSSTU PROSECUTIONS
CEINPSSSTTUU INTUSSUSCEPT
CEJNOORRRSUY CORONER'S JURY
CELLLOORSSUY COLOURLESSLY
CELLMOOPRRST COMPTROLLERS
CELLNNOOPSTU POLLEN COUNTS
CELMNOPRTUUU MUCOPURULENT
CELOOOPRRSTU POSTER COLOUR
CEMMNNNOOSSU UNCOMMONNESS
CEMMOOSTUXYY MYXOMYCETOUS
CEMNOOPSTTUU CONTEMPTUOUS
CEMOOOOORRSTT MOTOR SCOOTER
CENNOSSSTUUU UNCTUOUSNESS
CFFHILMNOSTU FIFTH COLUMNS
CFGHIIKNOPRT PITCHFORKING
CFGIIILMMNOR MICROFILMING
CFGIILNOOSTV COST OF LIVING
CFGILMNOORTY COMFORTINGLY
CFIIILOSTTUY FICTITIOUSLY
CFIIKLLOORST FOLKLORISTIC
CFIILLNOOSTU SOLIFLUCTION
CFIIMNNOORTY INCONFORMITY
CFIINORSSSTU FIRST COUSINS
CFILNORSSUUU FURUNCULOSIS
CFIMNNOORTUY UNCONFORMITY
CGHHIINNTTUW WITCH-HUNTING
CGHHIINORTUW WITCHING HOUR
CGHIIKKNNOPS SHOCKING PINK
CGHIILOOOPRT OLIGOTROPHIC
CGHIILOOOSTY STOICHIOLOGY
CGHIILOORSTT TRICHOLOGIST
CGHIIMNOOPSY PHYSIOGNOMIC
CGHIIMOOPRTT THIGMOTROPIC
CGHILMOOPSSY PSYCHOLOGISM
CGHILNOOORST CHRONOLOGIST
CGHILOOPSSTY PSYCHOLOGIST
CGHIMNOORSST SHORTCOMINGS
CGHINOOOPPTY PHOTOCOPYING
CGHINOOPSSSY PSYCHOGNOSIS
CGIIIILNOPTZ POLITICIZING
CGIIINNRSTUZ SCRUTINIZING
CGIIKLLLNORY ROLLICKINGLY
CGIILMOOSSTU MUSICOLOGIST
CGIILNNNOTUY CONTINUINGLY
CGIILOOOSSST SOCIOLOGISTS
CGIILOOOSTTX TOXICOLOGIST

CGIIMMNOOPRS COMPROMISING
CGIINNOSTTTU CONSTITUTING
CGIKLLNOORST ROLLING STOCK
CGILNOOSTUUY CONTIGUOUSLY
CGILOOOPRSTT PROCTOLOGIST
CGILOOPRSTTY CRYPTOLOGIST
CGINOOPRSSTY PYROGNOSTICS
CHHIIOOPPRST PHOSPHORITIC
CHHILMOPRTYY POLYRHYTHMIC
CHHIMOOOOPRRT ORTHOMORPHIC
CHHINORRSSTT CHRIST'S-THORN
CHHMMOOOOORSU HOMOCHROMOUS
CHIIILOOPTTX TOXOPHILITIC
CHIIMNNRSSTY STRYCHNINISM
CHIJLNOOORSU JUNIOR SCHOOL
CHILOOOPPRSU COPROPHILOUS
CHIMMNOOOORST MONOCHROMIST
CHIMNOOOOPRST MONOSTROPHIC
CHIMNOOORSTU MONOTRICHOUS
CHIMNOPRSTYY CHYMOTRYPSIN
CHIMOOOPPRRT PROTOMORPHIC
CHIOOOPPRRTT PROTOTROPHIC
CHMMNOOOORSST SHORT COMMONS
CIIIIOPSSTTV POSITIVISTIC
CIIILLMPTTUY MULTIPLICITY
CIIINNOPRSST INSCRIPTIONS
CIILLOOSSTUY SOLICITOUSLY
CIILMNNORSUY SYNCLINORIUM
CIILMNOOOPST MONOPOLISTIC
CIILOOORSTUVY VICTORIOUSLY
CIILOPSSSUUY SUSPICIOUSLY
CIIMMNNOOSTU COMMUNIONIST
CIIMNOOOPSST COMPOSITIONS
CIIMNOPRSTTY NYCTITROPISM
CIINNOOSTTTU CONSTITUTION
CIINNORSSTTU INSTRUCTIONS
CIINOOPPRRST PROSCRIPTION
CIJLNORSSTUU JURISCONSULT
CILLMOOPRSUY COMPULSORILY
CILLORRSSUUY SCURRILOUSLY
CILNNOOOSTUV CONVOLUTIONS
CILNNOOSTUUY CONTINUOUSLY
CIMMOOORSSTU MICROSTOMOUS
CIMNNOOPSSTU CONSUMPTIONS
CIMNOPPSSTUU SUCTION PUMPS
CLLOPRSSUUYY SCRUPULOUSLY
CLNOPRSSUUUU UNSCRUPULOUS
DDDDDEFISUUY FUDDY-DUDDIES
DDDEEEGINNOP PODDED ENGINE
DDDEEEENRRSSU UNDERDRESSED
DDDEEFHILRSU HUDDERSFIELD
DDDEEINRSTUU UNDERSTUDIED
DDDEHNNOOORR RHODODENDRON
DDEEEELLRSVW WELL-DESERVED
DDEEEEMNNSST DEMENTEDNESS
DDEEEENNSSTX EXTENDEDNESS
DDEEEENRSSSV DESERVEDNESS
DDEEEFHLNOTU DO THE NEEDFUL
DDEEEFMNORSS DEFORMEDNESS

DDEEEIINSSST DESENSITISED
DDEEEIINSSTZ DESENSITIZED
DDEEEIMNNRTU UNDETERMINED
DDEEEINNNPST INDEPENDENTS
DDEEEINNOSSS ONE-SIDEDNESS
DDEEELNOPRUV UNDERDEVELOP
DDEEEENOPRSUX UNDEREXPOSED
DDEEFFGLLLUY FULLY-FLEDGED
DDEEFGIILMNR MIDDLE FINGER
DDEEFHIIIMRU DEHUMIDIFIER
DDEEFIIINNTU UNIDENTIFIED
DDEEGHIILMTW MIDDLEWEIGHT
DDEEGHIINTWW WHITE WEDDING
DDEEGIILMNNS SINGLE-MINDED
DDEEGILMNOST DISLODGEMENT
DDEEGILNORUV OVERINDULGED
DDEEGLLNORUW WELL-GROUNDED
DDEEHIIINRST DISINHERITED
DDEEHIILNOOT ENDOTHELIOID
DDEEIILMMNPS SIMPLE-MINDED
DDEEIILQSTUY DISQUIETEDLY
DDEEIINPRRST PRIEST-RIDDEN
DDEEILLOPRVW WELL-PROVIDED
DDEEILLOPSSW WELL-DISPOSED
DDEEILMNNOPY OPEN-MINDEDLY
DDEEILNNORUW LIE DOWN UNDER
DDEEILNNPSSS SPLENDIDNESS
DDEEIMNNOSTW DISENDOWMENT
DDEEINRSSTUU UNDERSTUDIES
DDEEIOPSSSSS DISPOSSESSED
DDEELNNOPSTY DESPONDENTLY
DDEFNOOOPRSU SOUNDPROOFED
DDEGGIINNRSW WEDDING RINGS
DDEGGIOOOOSY GOODY-GOODIES
DDEGHHIILMNY HIGH-MINDEDLY
DDEGHILNRSUY SHUDDERINGLY
DDEGHIRRSUUY HURDY-GURDIES
DDEGHMOOORUU GOOD-HUMOURED
DDEGILLNNOWY LONGWINDEDLY
DDEGILNNOPSS PLODDINGNESS
DDEGILNOORST DENDROLOGIST
DDEGIMNNORST STRONG-MINDED
DDEGINNORSSW DRESSING-DOWN
DDEGNNORRSUU UNDERGROUNDS
DDEHILNNOOPR PHILODENDRON
DDEHINOORSTU RIDE TO HOUNDS
DDEIIILPRSTY DISPIRITEDLY
DDEIIJLNOSTY DISJOINTEDLY
DDEIILNNOORR LIRIODENDRON
DDEIIMNOSUVV MODUS VIVENDI
DDEIMOOPPSUU PSEUDOPODIUM
DDELNORRSUUY SURROUNDEDLY
DDGIILNOORSS SLIDING DOORS
DDGILMNPPSUU PLUM PUDDINGS
DEEEEMNPRTV EVEN-TEMPERED
DEEEEGIILNNS DIESEL ENGINE
DEEEEGMNNNRT ENGENDERMENT
DEEEEHILRSSW SIDE-WHEELERS
DEEEEHLNSSSS HEEDLESSNESS

DEEEEILNNPTT PENDENTE LITE
DEEEEIMNPRRT PREDETERMINE
DEEEEIMNPRTX EXPERIMENTED
DEEEELLMPRTW WELL-TEMPERED
DEEEELNNSSSS NEEDLESSNESS
DEEEEMOPRSST SPEEDOMETERS
DEEEENRRSSSV RESERVEDNESS
DEEEFGHORRTU FOURTH-DEGREE
DEEEFGINRRYZ FREEZE-DRYING
DEEEFIINNSST DEFINITENESS
DEEEFLLMOPSY SELF-EMPLOYED
DEEEFNNQRTUU UNFREQUENTED
DEEEGHINNPRR REPREHENDING
DEEEGHNNRSTT STRENGTHENED
DEEEGIINNRRV ENGINE DRIVER
DEEEGILNOPRV REDEVELOPING
DEEEGINNRSSS RESIGNEDNESS
DEEEGINNRSSV EVENING DRESS
DEEEGJMNPRTU PREJUDGEMENT
DEEEGOOPPSST GOOSESTEPPED
DEEEGORRRSST RETROGRESSED
DEEEHHIPPRSS SHEPHERD'S PIE
DEEEHIILRTVW WHITE-LIVERED
DEEEHILMNSTV DISHEVELMENT
DEEEHINPRRSV REVERENDSHIP
DEEEHINRSSTW WITHEREDNESS
DEEEHMNNORTT DETHRONEMENT
DEEEIILNORRT INDRE-ET-LOIRE
DEEEIINRSSST DESENSITISER
DEEEIINRSSSV DERISIVENESS
DEEEIINRSSTZ DESENSITIZER
DEEEIILLPPQUW WELL-EQUIPPED
DEEEILNRSSSW WILDERNESSES
DEEEILNRSTTY INTERESTEDLY
DEEEIMNNORST DENSITOMETER
DEEEIMNRRSTW MIDWESTERNER
DEEEIMOPRSTX EXTEMPORISED
DEEEIMOPRTXZ EXTEMPORIZED
DEEEINNRSTTU UNINTERESTED
DEEEINPRRSST INTERSPERSED
DEEEINRSSSTW DESSERT WINES
DEEEJLLOPPRT JET-PROPELLED
DEEEKLNNOOST ENDOSKELETON
DEEELMNNORSY MONEYLENDERS
DEEELMNOPRTY REDEPLOYMENT
DEEELMNOPSTV DEVELOPMENTS
DEEELMNPPSTU SUPPLEMENTED
DEEELNORSSSV RESOLVEDNESS
DEEELNRRSUVY UNRESERVEDLY
DEEEMNNORSST ENDORSEMENTS
DEEENRRSSTTT TRENDSETTERS
DEEEOPPRSSSS PREPOSSESSED
DEEFFHINRRSU UNDERSHERIFF
DEEFGIILNSTT FIELD-TESTING
DEEFGIINNRSX INDEX FINGERS
DEEFGINNOOPS SPOON-FEEDING
DEEFGKNOORTU FORKED TONGUE
DEEFHIINNSSS FIENDISHNESS
DEEFIIIILNST INFIDELITIES

DEEFIIILNNTY INDEFINITELY
DEEFIIILNTVY DEFINITIVELY
DEEFIILNNRSS FRIENDLINESS
DEEFIILPPRTT FILTER-TIPPED
DEEFIKLORRSW FIELDWORKERS
DEEFILLMNORW WELL-INFORMED
DEEFILNRRSUY USER-FRIENDLY
DEEFLOORSTUY SUREFOOTEDLY
DEEGGHHINOPP HEDGEHOPPING
DEEGGIINPRST PREDIGESTING
DEEGGIMNORST DISGORGEMENT
DEEGHIINNSTW WINDING SHEET
DEEGHIINSTUX EXTINGUISHED
DEEGHINRSSST NIGHTDRESSES
DEEGHNORSSTU GROUNDSHEETS
DEEGIILMNNRT INTERMINGLED
DEEGIILMOOPY EPIDEMIOLOGY
DEEGIILNNRSZ SLENDERIZING
DEEGIILNNSSY YIELDINGNESS
DEEGIILOPSTT EPIGLOTTIDES
DEEGIIMNNOTZ DEMONETIZING
DEEGIIMNPRST DISTEMPERING
DEEGIINNPRST PREDESTINING
DEEGIINOPRST PREDIGESTION
DEEGIINPPSST SIDESTEPPING
DEEGIINPRSTW SPEEDWRITING
DEEGIJMMNSTU MISJUDGEMENT
DEEGILLNNRSU UNDERSELLING
DEEGILLNOOOR GOLDEN ORIOLE
DEEGILMNNNOY MONEYLENDING
DEEGILNPRSSY DEPRESSINGLY
DEEGINNRRRSU SURRENDERING
DEEGINNRSTTT TRENDSETTING
DEEGINORRSSV OVERDRESSING
DEEGJMNPRSTU PREJUDGMENTS
DEEGLLOOSTYY DYSTELEOLOGY
DEEGLNOOOSTU LOOSE-TONGUED
DEEHHIIMOPRS HEMISPHEROID
DEEHHIOPPRSW HORSEWHIPPED
DEEHHLOORSSU HOUSEHOLDERS
DEEHIILNQRSU RELINQUISHED
DEEHIILNSSSV DEVILISHNESS
DEEHIIMOPRSV IMPOVERISHED
DEEHIINPRSST RESIDENTSHIP
DEEHILLORSTT TITLEHOLDERS
DEEHILMMNOST DEMOLISHMENT
DEEHIMMNORST ENDOTHERMISM
DEEHIMNOORTU TIME-HONOURED
DEEHINNSSTUY THE SUNNY SIDE
DEEHIOPPRTTY PTERIDOPHYTE
DEEHNNORSTTU THUNDERSTONE
DEEHOORRSSUV HORS D'OEUVRES
DEEIIIILLRSST DISTILLERIES
DEEIIINSSSVV DIVISIVENESS
DEEIILNNSSUW UNWIELDINESS
DEEIIMMOPRST POST MERIDIEM
DEEIIMNNRSTT DISINTERMENT
DEEIIMNORTTV DIVERTIMENTO
DEEIIMORRTTU DUMORTIERITE

DEEIINPRSSST SPIRITEDNESS
DEEIIOOPRSST DEPOSITORIES
DEEIJLNOOOST LOOSE-JOINTED
DEEIJNORRRSU SURREJOINDER
DEEILLNORRSS SLENDER LORIS
DEEILMNNSSSS MINDLESSNESS
DEEILNOOPPRT LEPIDOPTERON
DEEILOPRSSTY PROSELYTISED
DEEILOPRSTYZ PROSELYTIZED
DEEIMMNNOOSS SOMEONE'S MIND
DEEIMNORSTTY DENSITOMETRY
DEEIMOPPRRST PTERIDOSPERM
DEEIMOPPRSSU SUPERIMPOSED
DEEINNNORSST NONRESIDENTS
DEEINNOQSTUU UNQUESTIONED
DEEINNRRTTUW UNDERWRITTEN
DEEINORRRSVW OWNER-DRIVERS
DEEINRRRSTUW UNDERWRITERS
DEEKNOORRRWW WONDER-WORKER
DEELMNORSTUY TREMENDOUSLY
DEELNORSSSSW WORDLESSNESS
DEELNOSSSSUU SEDULOUSNESS
DEENOOPRSSST DESSERTSPOON
DEENOPRRSTTU UNDER PROTEST
DEFFHIRSSTTU STUFFED SHIRT
DEFFHLNOOPSU POUND OF FLESH
DEFGGINORRUU FIGURE-GROUND
DEFGHHIIILTY HIGH FIDELITY
DEFGHILLLTUY DELIGHTFULLY
DEFGIIIMNNNY INDEMNIFYING
DEFGIIINRSVY DIVERSIFYING
DEFGIIMNSTYY DEMYSTIFYING
DEFGIINORSST DISFORESTING
DEFHINPRSSTT SPENDTHRIFTS
DEFHLOOORSSU HOUSE OF LORDS
DEFIIILMSTUY SEMIFLUIDITY
DEFIILOPRSUY PERFIDIOUSLY
DEFIINOPRSTU PROFUNDITIES
DEFILOORSTUY DO-IT-YOURSELF
DEFINOOOPRRT POINT OF ORDER
DEFIOORRSSUU SUDORIFEROUS
DEFNNOOPRSSU PROFOUNDNESS
DEGGHILNOOSU LODGING HOUSE
DEGGINNORSSW DRESSING GOWN
DEGHHIIIPRST HIGH-SPIRITED
DEGHHIINOPST DIPHTHONGISE
DEGHHIINOPTZ DIPHTHONGIZE
DEGHHIORRSTT SHORTSIGHTED
DEGHIIILNRSS DISRELISHING
DEGHILNNRTUY THUNDERINGLY
DEGHINOORSTV OVERDO THINGS
DEGHINOPSSTT POTTING SHEDS
DEGIIILNPPSS SIDESLIPPING
DEGIIINNRRST DISINTERRING
DEGIIKNRSSTW WRITING DESKS
DEGIILLOOSTT DELTIOLOGIST
DEGIILNNOSUY INDIGENOUSLY
DEGIINNNNPRU UNDERPINNING
DEGIINNOSSUU DISINGENUOUS

DEGIIINNRRTUW UNDERWRITING
DEGIIINOPPRSS PREDISPOSING
DEGIJMMNSSTU MISJUDGMENTS
DEGIKNOORRRW WORKING ORDER
DEGILLNORSTW STRONG-WILLED
DEGILMNOOOST DEMONOLOGIST
DEGILNNORSUY RESOUNDINGLY
DEGILNOOOSTT DEONTOLOGIST
DEGIMNNORRSS MORNING DRESS
DEGIMNOORRSS DRESSING ROOM
DEGINOOPPRST DOORSTEPPING
DEGINOPRSSST TOPDRESSINGS
DEGKNOORRSTU GROUND STROKE
DEGLLNORSSUW GROUNDSWELLS
DEGLLNORSSUY GROUNDLESSLY
DEGMNOORRRUY MERRY-GO-ROUND
DEHHHMMORTTY RHYTHM METHOD
DEHIIIMMNNST DIMINISHMENT
DEHIIKLLNOOU UNLIKELIHOOD
DEHILLOPPSUY POLYSULPHIDE
DEHIMMNOOPRS ENDOMORPHISM
DEHINNORRSUU UNDERNOURISH
DEHINOOPRSST SPINSTERHOOD
DEHLLOORRTWY OTHERWORLDLY
DEHLNOORRSUY HORRENDOUSLY
DEHLNORSTUUY THUNDEROUSLY
DEHLOOOSTTTW TWO-TOED SLOTH
DEHMNORRSTTU THUNDERSTORM
DEHNOOOORSTUW SOUTHERNWOOD
DEIIKLNNNSSU UNKINDLINESS
DEIILLOOQSSU SOLILOQUISED
DEIILLOOQSUZ SOLILOQUIZED
DEIILNOORSWW ORIEL WINDOWS
DEIILPRSTUVY DISRUPTIVELY
DEIIOOPPRRST POOR-SPIRITED
DEIJNPRRSTUU JURISPRUDENT
DEILLOOSSSVW SLOW DISSOLVE
DEIMNOPSTUYY PSEUDONYMITY
DEINOOOPPRRT PROPORTIONED
DEINOSSSSTUU STUDIOUSNESS
DEIOOPRSSSSS DISPOSSESSOR
DEKLLOOPRSST ROLLTOP DESKS
DELNNOOPSTYY POLYSYNDETON
DELNOPSSTUUY STUPENDOUSLY
DEMNOOPSSUUY PSEUDONYMOUS
DENNOORSSSUW WONDROUSNESS
DEOOOOPPRRSST DOORSTOPPERS
DFGHIINOPSSY SPINY DOGFISH
DFGIIKNNNSSU SINKING FUNDS
DFGLNOOOORRSU GROUND FLOORS
DFHILNOOOPSU POUND-FOOLISH
DGGHHIINNOSU HIGH-SOUNDING
DGGHIINNNOOT NOTHING DOING
DGGIILNSSTUY DISGUSTINGLY
DGHIINNOORSU DISHONOURING
DGIIILNNOOSV LONG DIVISION
DGIILOOPRSUY PRODIGIOUSLY
DGILNOOOOSTT ODONTOLOGIST
DGINNORRSSUU SURROUNDINGS

DHHIILOOPPPS PHOSPHOLIPID
DHIIIMMOOPRS IDIOMORPHISM
DHLNOOOOPPTYY POLYPHYODONT
DHMMPPTTUUYY HUMPTY DUMPTY
DIIIINOQSSTU DISQUISITION
DIIINOOPSSST DISPOSITIONS
DIILNOOSSSTU DISSOLUTIONS
DIILNOOSSTUU SOLITUDINOUS
EEEEEHHLRRTW THREE-WHEELER
EEEEFGHILNRW FREEWHEELING
EEEEGHMORSTW GET SOMEWHERE
EEEEGIÍLNPSS SPIEGELEISEN
EEEEGNPPPRRS GREEN PEPPERS
EEEEHINPRRSV REPREHENSIVE
EEEEHKOPRSSU HOUSEKEEPERS
EEEEHLMNOPRT NEPHELOMETER
EEEEHLNRSSTV NEVERTHELESS
EEEEHNNSSTTV SEVENTEENTHS
EEEEIINRSTVW INTERVIEWEES
EEEEIMNPRRTX EXPERIMENTER
EEEEIMNPRSSW MINESWEEPERS
EEEEINNQRSTU EQUESTRIENNE
EEEEINSSSTWY EYEWITNESSES
EEEEKOPRRSST STOREKEEPERS
EEEELMNRSTTT RESETTLEMENT
EEEELNOPRRTT LETTER OPENER
EEEELNRSSSST TREELESSNESS
EEEEMNORSTTX EXTENSOMETER
EEEENNPRRRTU ENTREPRENEUR
EEEENNRRSSTV REVERENTNESS
EEEENPRRSSSV PERVERSENESS
EEEEORRTTTTT TEETER-TOTTER
EEEEPPPRSSTW SWEET PEPPERS
EEEFFIILNNTT IN FINE FETTLE
EEEFFIMORSTU EFFUSIOMETER
EEEFFINSSSUV EFFUSIVENESS
EEEFFLLNNORW FENNELFLOWER
EEEFGGINNRRS GREEN FINGERS
EEEFGLNNSSUV VENGEFULNESS
EEEFGNNOORSS FOREGONENESS
EEEFHHINOTTT IN THE TEETH OF
EEEFHIKNRRST FREETHINKERS
EEEFHILRRSSW FERRIS WHEELS
EEEFHINNOTTV IN THE EVENT OF
EEEFHINRSSSV FEVERISHNESS
EEEFHMNRRSST REFRESHMENTS
EEEFIILLLLMU MILLEFEUILLE
EEEFIILMMPRR FILM PREMIÈRE
EEEFIILNRRTT INTERFERTILE
EEEFILLNSSSS LIFELESSNESS
EEEFILNRSSTT SELF-INTEREST
EEEFJLNNOOSY ENJOY ONESELF
EEEFLLNSSSSS SELFLESSNESS
EEEFLMNORSTT MEN OF LETTERS
EEEFLNNSSTUV EVENTFULNESS
EEEGGHORSTTT GET-TOGETHERS
EEEGHIKNOPSU HOUSEKEEPING
EEEGHILRTTWW WELTERWEIGHT
EEEGHIMNOSTU MEETINGHOUSE

EEEGHINSTTVY SEVENTY-EIGHT
EEEGHNNRRSTT STRENGTHENER
EEEGHNOORSTU HETEROGENOUS
EEEGHNORSSTT TOGETHERNESS
EEEGHOORTTYZ HETEROZYGOTE
EEEGIIMNNPSW MINESWEEPING
EEEGIINNORRT ORIENTEERING
EEEGIINORSST GENEROSITIES
EEEGIKMNNNOY MONKEY ENGINE
EEEGIKNOPRST STOREKEEPING
EEEGILNOPRSV OVERSLEEPING
EEEGINNPRRST REPRESENTING
EEEGINNPSSSW SWEEPINGNESS
EEEGMNORSSSU GRUESOMENESS
EEEGNNORSSSU GENEROUSNESS
EEEGNOOPRRST PROGESTERONE
EEEGNOOORRSUV OVERGENEROUS
EEEHHINPSSSS SHEEPISHNESS
EEEHHLNORTUV ELEVENTH HOUR
EEEHHMOPRRST THERMOSPHERE
EEEHILLOSTTT STILETTO HEEL
EEEHILMNORST HERMOTENSILE
EEEHILRSSSTV SHIRTSLEEVES
EEEHIMNNNRST ENSHRINEMENT
EEEHIMNRSTTU HERMENEUTIST
EEEHINNPRSSS REPREHENSION
EEEHINNORSTW NONE THE WISER
EEEHJMPQTUUU JUMP THE QUEUE
EEEHLLNOPTYY POLYETHYLENE
EEEHLLNPSSSS HELPLESSNESS
EEEHLMNOSSSS HOMELESSNESS
EEEHLNOPSSSS HOPELESSNESS
EEEHLOPRSTTW POTTER'S WHEEL
EEEHMMORRSTT THERMOMETERS
EEEHMNNNORTT ENTHRONEMENT
EEEHMNOQRSTU QUEEN MOTHERS
EEEHMOORRSTU HETEROMEROUS
EEEHNOPRRRSY REPREHENSORY
EEEHNORSSTTT ON THE STREETS
EEEHNOSSSTUY SHUT ONE'S EYES
EEEHOPRRSSTZ HERPES ZOSTER
EEEIILPPRSTX PERPLEXITIES
EEEIIMNRSSTT MESENTERITIS
EEEIINPRRTTV INTERPRETIVE
EEEIINPRSSVX INEXPRESSIVE
EEEIINRRSTVW INTERVIEWERS
EEEIIPPRSTTU PERPETUITIES
EEEIIPQRRSTU PREREQUISITE
EEEIIPRRSSTV PERVERSITIES
EEEIILLOPPTT LITTLE PEOPLE
EEEILMNNPRTY PRE-EMINENTLY
EEEILMNNSSSU UNSEEMLINESS
EEEILMNORSTU SON ET LUMIERE
EEEILMNSSSST TIMELESSNESS
EEEILMOORVZZ MEZZO-RELIEVO
EEEILMPPRTVY PRE-EMPTIVELY
EEEILNPRRSTT TELEPRINTERS
EEEILNPRTVVY PREVENTIVELY
EEEILNRRRTVY IRREVERENTLY

EEEILNRSSSST TIRELESSNESS
EEEILNRSSSTW WESTERLINESS
EEEILPRRSSVY REPRESSIVELY
EEEILPRSSVXY EXPRESSIVELY
EEEIMNNPRSTT PRESENTIMENT
EEEIMNNPRSTU SUPEREMINENT
EEEIMNNRSTTV REINVESTMENT
EEEIMNORSSST TIRESOMENESS
EEEIMNORSSTT SENSITOMETER
EEEIMNPRRSST MISREPRESENT
EEEIMNQRRSTU REQUIREMENTS
EEEIMOORRSST STEREOISOMER
EEEIMOPRRSTX EXTEMPORISER
EEEIMOPRRTXZ EXTEMPORIZER
EEEIMOPRSTUX TIME EXPOSURE
EEEIINNPRSSTX INEXPERTNESS
EEEIINNPRSTUV SUPERVENIENT
EEEINPRRRSTT INTERPRETERS
EEEINPRSSUVX UNEXPRESSIVE
EEEINRRTTTUX INTERTEXTURE
EEEIORRSTVVX EXTROVERSIVE
EEEJMPQRSUUU QUEUE-JUMPERS
EEEKKLNOSSTY SKELETON KEYS
EEEKLOOPPPSS SPOKESPEOPLE
EEELLLNRSSTY RELENTLESSLY
EEELLMORRTTU TELLUROMETER
EEELLOPPPRWY YELLOW PEPPER
EEELMMNOPRTY RE-EMPLOYMENT
EEELMNNOOSSS LONESOMENESS
EEELMNNOOSTT ON ONE'S METTLE
EEELMNNSTTTU UNSETTLEMENT
EEELMNPPRSTU SUPPLEMENTER
EEELMOPPRRTT TELEPROMPTER
EEELNNOQSSTU ELOQUENTNESS
EEELNNOSSSST TONELESSNESS
EEELNNSSSSTU TUNELESSNESS
EEELNORSSSTU RESOLUTENESS
EEELNRSSSSST RESTLESSNESS
EEELOOPRSTTU TELEUTOSPORE
EEEMPRSSTTXY EXPERT SYSTEM
EEENOORSSTTT TESTOSTERONE
EEEOPRRTTTVY REVERT TO TYPE
EEFFGHIIRRST FIRE FIGHTERS
EEFFGILNRSSU GLUE-SNIFFERS
EEFFIIILLORX ELIXIR OF LIFE
EEFFLLORSSTY EFFORTLESSLY
EEFGHIIKNNRT FREETHINKING
EEFGHIILNRRT FREIGHTLINER
EEFGHIILRRST FIRELIGHTERS
EEFGHIILRTTW WEIGHT LIFTER
EEFGHIIPRRST PRISEFIGHTER
EEFGHIIPRRTZ PRIZEFIGHTER
EEFGHILNRRSY REFRESHINGLY
EEFGIILLNRTT LITTLE FINGER
EEFGIILMNPXY EXEMPLIFYING
EEFGIIMMNRSW FREE-SWIMMING
EEFGIIMNNNRT INFRINGEMENT
EEFGIINOPRRT PROFITEERING
EEFGMNOORSTT FORGET-ME-NOTS

EEFHHMMMOOOR   HOME FROM HOME
EEFHIILRSSSV   SILVERFISHES
EEFIIINNRSST   INTENSIFIERS
EEFIIMNORSSU   SEMINIFEROUS
EEFIINORRSSU   RESINIFEROUS
EEFILLORSSTU   STELLIFEROUS
EEFILMOOORST   TOMFOOLERIES
EEFILMORSTTU   FLITTERMOUSE
EEFILNNQRTUY   INFREQUENTLY
EEFILNOORRTX   RETROFLEXION
EEFILNPSSSTU   SPITEFULNESS
EEFIMNNORRST   FRONTIERSMEN
EEFLLMORRSUY   REMORSEFULLY
EEFLLNNTUUVY   UNEVENTFULLY
EEFLLNOOOPSW   ONE FELL SWOOP
EEFLMNORSSSS   FORMLESSNESS
EEFLNOPRSSUW   POWERFULNESS
EEGGGGHMRRUU   HUGGER-MUGGER
EEGGHIILNNNT   ENLIGHTENING
EEGGHIINTTUV   GIVE IT THE GUN
EEGGIILNNRSS   GINGERLINESS
EEGGILSSTUVY   SUGGESTIVELY
EEGGNOORSSSU   GORGEOUSNESS
EEGHHILRSTWW   WHEELWRIGHTS
EEGHHIPRRSSU   HIGH-PRESSURE
EEGHIILNNPRS   REPLENISHING
EEGHIINOSSST   HISTOGENESIS
EEGHIINPRRTZ   THE PRIZE RING
EEGHIINRSTUX   EXTINGUISHER
EEGHIKNRRSTU   HUNGER STRIKE
EEGHILLSSTWY   WEIGHTLESSLY
EEGHILMNORVW   OVERWHELMING
EEGHINOORSST   ORTHOGENESIS
EEGHINOPSSTY   PHYTOGENESIS
EEGHLLOOPRST   HOT-GOSPELLER
EEGHLMNNOORS   LONGSHOREMEN
EEGHLOOORSTU   HETEROLOGOUS
EEGHMNOORSTU   THERMOGENOUS
EEGHMNOORTTU   MOTHER TONGUE
EEGHNOOORSTU   HETEROGONOUS
EEGHNOORSTUY   HETEROGYNOUS
EEGHOOORSTUYZ   HETEROZYGOUS
EEGIIIINNRTVW   INTERVIEWING
EEGIILLLNPPS   SLEEPING PILL
EEGIILLNNNVY   ENLIVENINGLY
EEGIILMMNNPT   IMPLEMENTING
EEGIILNORRTV   GREEN VITRIOL
EEGIILOPSSTT   EPIGLOTTISES
EEGIIMNNOPST   OPENING TIMES
EEGIINNPRRST   ENTERPRISING
EEGIINNPRRTT   INTERPRETING
EEGIINNRSTWZ   WESTERNIZING
EEGIJMNPQUUU   QUEUE-JUMPING
EEGIKKNORSWW   WORKING WEEKS
EEGILLNOOSST   SELENOLOGIST
EEGILLNRSTWY   SWELTERINGLY
EEGILLOOPSST   SPELEOLOGIST
EEGILLOOSSTT   TELEOLOGISTS
EEGILMNOOOST   ENTOMOLOGISE

EEGILMNOOOTZ   ENTOMOLOGIZE
EEGILMOOPPSS   GOOSE PIMPLES
EEGILMOOPSTY   EPISTEMOLOGY
EEGILNNORTUV   VOLUNTEERING
EEGILNNSSSSW   WINGLESSNESS
EEGILNOPRTTU   TRIPLE-TONGUE
EEGILOPRSSTT   POLTERGEISTS
EEGILQRRRSUY   GREY SQUIRREL
EEGIMNNRRSTU   INTERREGNUMS
EEGINNPRSSSS   PRESSINGNESS
EEGINOOPRRVW   OVERPOWERING
EEGINOOPRSSS   SPOROGENESIS
EEGINOOPRSVX   OVEREXPOSING
EEGINOPPRSTV   OVERSTEPPING
EEGINOPRSSSS   REPOSSESSING
EEGINOPRSTTY   STEREOTYPING
EEGINORSSSUV   GRIEVOUSNESS
EEGINOSSSUUX   EXIGUOUSNESS
EEGINPRSSTTU   GUTTERSNIPES
EEGIOPRRSSSV   PROGRESSIVES
EEGKORRSSTUW   GUEST WORKERS
EEGLMNNOOOPR   PROLEGOMENON
EEGLOPPPSTUV   GLOVE PUPPETS
EEGNNOORRSUU   NEUROSURGEON
EEGNORRRSUUY   NEUROSURGERY
EEHHIIMMOPRT   HEMIMORPHITE
EEHHIINSSSTV   THIEVISHNESS
EEHHILLNOPTY   THEOPHYLLINE
EEHHINRSSSSW   SHREWISHNESS
EEHHIOPPRRSW   HORSEWHIPPER
EEHHLLNNOORZ   HOHENZOLLERN
EEHHLLOPRTYY   HETEROPHYLLY
EEHHMOORSSTU   HOUSEMOTHERS
EEHHOOOSSTUU   HOUSE-TO-HOUSE
EEHHOOSSUUYY   HOUSEY-HOUSEY
EEHIIIMNNRTT   IN THE INTERIM
EEHIILNQRRSU   RELINQUISHER
EEHIIMNPPRRU   PERINEPHRIUM
EEHIIMOPRRSV   IMPOVERISHER
EEHIIMPPRRSS   PREMIERSHIPS
EEHIINNSSSVX   VIXENISHNESS
EEHILMNORSST   MOTHERLINESS
EEHILNNPSTWY   PENNY WHISTLE
EEHILNOOPSST   SIPHONOSTELE
EEHILNOPSSTT   TELEPHONISTS
EEHIMOPRSTTY   MORE'S THE PITY
EEHINRSSSSTY   SYNTHESISERS
EEHINRSSSTYZ   SYNTHESIZERS
EEHIPRSSSTTU   TRUSTEESHIPS
EEHLNRSSSSTU   RUTHLESSNESS
EEHLOORRSTTU   RULE THE ROOST
EEHLOPRRSSTU   UPHOLSTERERS
EEHMMORSSSUU   SUMMERHOUSES
EEHMNNOOORSY   HONEYMOONERS
EEHMNOOORSTU   HETERONOMOUS
EEHMNOORSTUY   HETERONYMOUS
EEHMNRRRSUYY   NURSERY RHYME
EEHNNORRSTTW   NORTHWESTERN
EEHNNORSSSTT   HORNET'S NESTS

EEHNORSSTTUW SOUTHWESTERN
EEHOOPRRSSTU PORTERHOUSES
EEIIIMNRSSTV INTERMISSIVE
EEIIINPRRSTU PERINEURITIS
EEIIINRSSTUV UNIVERSITIES
EEIIKLLNNSSU UNLIKELINESS
EEIILLPRSSTV SPIRIT LEVELS
EEIILMNNPTTY IMPENITENTLY
EEIILMNNSSTU UNTIMELINESS
EEIILMNOPSST IMPOLITENESS
EEIILMPRSSVY IMPRESSIVELY, PERMISSIVELY
EEIILNNPRRST LINE PRINTERS
EEIILNPPRSSS SLIPPERINESS
EEIILNPRSSST PRIESTLINESS
EEIILNPSSSST PITILESSNESS
EEIILNRSSSST SISTERLINESS
EEIILOOPPSTV POSITIVE POLE
EEIIMNNRTTTT INTERMITTENT
EEIIMNOPRRSS REIMPRESSION
EEIIMNOQSTTU QUESTION TIME
EEIIMNPRRSTT MISINTERPRET
EEIIMNPRSSUV UNIMPRESSIVE
EEIIMNPRSTTY SEMPITERNITY
EEIIMNRRTTUX INTERMIXTURE
EEIIMORSSTUV SEMIVITREOUS
EEIINNNORTTV INTERVENTION
EEIINNPSSTUV PUNITIVENESS
EEIINNRSSSST SINISTERNESS
EEIINOORSSTV STEREOVISION
EEIINOPPRSST PROPENSITIES
EEIINOPRRSSV IRRESPONSIVE
EEIINOPSSSTV POSITIVENESS
EEIINORRSTVV INTROVERSIVE
EEIINPRRTTUV INTERRUPTIVE
EEIINRSSTTUV INVESTITURES
EEIIOOPRRSST REPOSITORIES
EEIIPRSSTVXY EXPRESSIVITY
EEIKLMNNOSTY MILTON KEYNES
EEIKOPRRRSTW WORKER-PRIEST
EEILLNNOSSSV SLOVENLINESS
EEILLNSSSSST LISTLESSNESS
EEILLORRSTUY IRRESOLUTELY
EEILMMNNOPTY IN EMPLOYMENT
EEILMOOPRSST METROPOLISES
EEILMOPPRRTY PEREMPTORILY
EEILNNOOPSVX NONEXPLOSIVE
EEILNOOORSSU OLEORESINOUS
EEILNOOPPRSY POLYISOPRENE
EEILNOORRSTU RESOLUTIONER
EEILNOPRSSSU PERILOUSNESS
EEILNOPRSSVY RESPONSIVELY
EEILNPRSSTTY PERSISTENTLY
EEILOPPRSSVY OPPRESSIVELY
EEILOPRRSSTY PROSELYTISER
EEILOPRRSTYZ PROSELYTIZER
EEILOPSSSSVY POSSESSIVELY
EEIMMMNSSTUY IMMUNE SYSTEM
EEIMMNOPRSTV IMPROVEMENTS
EEIMNNNOPRSY MONEY-SPINNER

EEIMNNNORSTV ENVIRONMENTS
EEIMNORSSTTY SENSITOMETRY
EEINNOPRSSUV UNRESPONSIVE
EEINNORSSSSU RESINOUSNESS
EEINOOPPSSST OPPOSITENESS
EEINOOPRSSSS REPOSSESSION
EEINOORRRSTV RETROVERSION
EEINOORRSTVX EXTROVERSION
EEINOPRSSSSU SUPERSESSION
EEINOPRSSSTV SPORTIVENESS
EEINOPRSSSUV PERVIOUSNESS,
  PREVIOUSNESS
EEINORSSSTUV VITREOUSNESS
EEKLMNOPUYZZ MONKEY-PUZZLE
EEKNOOPPRSSS SPOKESPERSON
EELLLOORRSTW ROLLER TOWELS
EELLNNNOOSSV NOLENS VOLENS
EELLNOSSSSSU SOULLESSNESS
EELLORRSSTTY STORYTELLERS
EELMMNNOPTUY UNEMPLOYMENT
EELMOPRRSTTY STORMY PETREL
EELNOORSSSST ROOTLESSNESS
EELNOPSSSSST SPOTLESSNESS
EEMNNOOPPSTT POSTPONEMENT
EEMNNOORSSSU ENORMOUSNESS
EEMNNORSSSUU NUMEROUSNESS
EENNOOPPRSSU ON ONE'S UPPERS
EENNOSSSSSUU SENSUOUSNESS
EENOOPRRSTUU NEUROPTEROUS
EEOOOPPRRSSTU PREPOSTEROUS
EEOPQRSSSTTU REQUEST STOPS
EEOPRRRSSSTU TROUSER PRESS
EEPPRRTTTTYY PRETTY-PRETTY
EFFGGHIIINRT FIRE FIGHTING
EFFGGIILNNSU GLUE-SNIFFING
EFFGHHHIIRSS HIGH SHERIFFS
EFFGIINOOPRR FIREPROOFING
EFFILNRSSTUU FRUITFULNESS
EFGGGIINOPTT PETTIFOGGING
EFGHHIILOPRS HIGH PROFILES
EFGHIILNOSST LINES OF SIGHT
EFGHIINNSSST SHIFTINGNESS
EFGHIINRRSTT FIRST-NIGHTER
EFGHILNRSSTU RIGHTFULNESS
EFGHLNOOPUUY YOUNG HOPEFUL
EFGIIINNNSTY INTENSIFYING
EFGIILNRRTYY TERRIFYINGLY
EFGIINNOPRSY PERSONIFYING
EFGIINNPRRST FINGERPRINTS
EFGILLNRTTUY FLUTTERINGLY
EFGILNPSTUYY STUPEFYINGLY
EFGLNNORSSUW WRONGFULNESS
EFHHILLOOOSY HOLY OF HOLIES
EFHIILQRRSSU SQUIRRELFISH
EFHILLMNORTU RUN-OF-THE-MILL
EFHILLOSSTWW WOLF WHISTLES
EFHILMNRSSTU MIRTHFULNESS
EFHIMNPRSSSU FRUMPISHNESS
EFHLLNOSSSTU SLOTHFULNESS

EFHLNNOOPRTY HORN OF PLENTY
EFHLNOSSTUUY YOUTHFULNESS
EFHLNRSSTTUU TRUTHFULNESS
EFIILMOPRSVY OVERSIMPLIFY
EFIINOOPSTVW POINTS OF VIEW
EFILLOPRSSTY PROFITLESSLY
EFIOOOPRRSSU SOPORIFEROUS
EFLLOPPRSUUY PURPOSEFULLY
EFLMNNORSSUU MOURNFULNESS
EFLNOPRSSSTU SPORTFULNESS
EFLNRSSSTTUU TRUSTFULNESS
EFNNNORRRSTU FRONT-RUNNERS
EFNOOPRRSTTY PORTS OF ENTRY
EGGGIILNNRSY SNIGGERINGLY
EGGGILNSSTUY SUGGESTINGLY
EGGGINOPRRSU GINGER GROUPS
EGGHHIILSTTW LIGHTWEIGHTS
EGGHHIINSSSW WHIGGISHNESS
EGGHIIKLNNSS KING'S ENGLISH
EGGHIILNNOOP PIGEONHOLING
EGGHIIMNNOOZ HOMOGENIZING
EGGHIINPRSSS PRIGGISHNESS
EGGHIINRRSTW RIGHT-WINGERS
EGGHILNSSSSU SLUGGISHNESS
EGGHLOOOOPTY PHOTOGEOLOGY
EGGIIIILMNTZ LEGITIMIZING
EGGIILLMMNRY GLIMMERINGLY
EGGIIILLNNSTY GLISTENINGLY
EGGIIILLNRTTY GLITTERINGLY
EGGILLLNORVY GROVELLINGLY
EGGILNNORSSY ENGROSSINGLY
EGGILOOPSTTY EGYPTOLOGIST
EGGIMNOOPRSS GOSSIPMONGER
EGHHIIKNSTTW WHITE KNIGHTS
EGHHILNNORSS ENGLISH HORNS
EGHHILNOSSSU GHOULISHNESS
EGHHNOORSSTU THOROUGHNESS
EGHIILMMNRSY SHIMMERINGLY
EGHIILMNPRWY WHIMPERINGLY
EGHIILNOSTTU SILHOUETTING
EGHIILOOPSSY PHYSIOLOGIES
EGHIINNSSTYZ SYNTHESIZING
EGHIIRSSSSTU RIGHTS ISSUES
EGHILMNOORST MOONLIGHTERS
EGHILMOOOPRS MORPHOLOGIES
EGHILMOORSTY MYTHOLOGISER
EGHILMOORTYZ MYTHOLOGIZER
EGHILNOOPRST PHRENOLOGIST
EGHILNOOSSTT ETHNOLOGISTS
EGHILNOPRSTU UPHOLSTERING
EGHILOOPPSST PSEPHOLOGIST
EGHIMNNNOOOY HONEYMOONING
EGHIMNNORSSU NURSING HOMES
EGHIMNOOORSU ROOMING HOUSE
EGHINNOOSSST SOOTHINGNESS
EGHINOOOORSTV OVERSHOOTING
EGHINOOPRRSV GOVERNORSHIP
EGHINOORRTVW OVERTHROWING
EGIIIKLNNNRT INTERLINKING

EGIIILNNNPRT LINE PRINTING
EGIIIMNOPSTU IMPETIGINOUS
EGIIINNNRTTW INTERTWINING
EGIIKLNPPRRS KLIPSPRINGER
EGIIKNNNSSST STINKINGNESS
EGIIKNNRSSST STRIKINGNESS
EGIIKNOPPPRS SKIPPING-ROPE
EGIIILLMNPSSS MISSPELLINGS
EGIIILLNNOPST SELLING POINT
EGIILMMNORVY LIVING MEMORY
EGIILMNNOPTT MELTING POINT
EGIILMOOSSST SEISMOLOGIST
EGIILNNPPSSS SLIPPINGNESS
EGIILNPPRRSY PERSPIRINGLY
EGIIMNOOPRRT PRIMOGENITOR
EGIIMNOPRRST MISREPORTING
EGIINNPRRTTU INTERRUPTING
EGIINPRRSSUZ PRESSURIZING
EGIKKNNOPRTY PONY-TREKKING
EGIILLNOORST ROLLING STONE
EGIILLNORSTY STORYTELLING
EGILMNNORTTY TORMENTINGLY
EGILMNOOOSTT ENTOMOLOGIST
EGILMNOOSTYZ ENZYMOLOGIST
EGILMOOSSTTY ETYMOLOGISTS
EGILNOOOPSST STOOLPIGEONS
EGILNOOPRSUY PYROLIGNEOUS
EGILNOORSSSU GLORIOUSNESS
EGILNOORSSTU NEUROLOGISTS
EGILNOPPRSSY OPPRESSINGLY
EGILNOPRSTTY PROTESTINGLY
EGILNRSTTTUY STUTTERINGLY
EGILOOPRSSTT PETROLOGISTS
EGIMMNOOPRSU SPERMOGONIUM
EGIMNOORRTTY TRIGONOMETRY
EGINOOPRRSSS PROGRESSIONS
EGINOORRSSSU RIGOROUSNESS
EGINOORSSSUV VIGOROUSNESS
EGINOPPPRSSU PRESUPPOSING
EGINPRRSSSTU PURSE STRINGS
EGMMNOORRRUU RUMOURMONGER
EHHIILOOPPSS PHILOSOPHIES, PHILOSOPHISE
EHHIILOOPPSZ PHILOSOPHIZE
EHHIIMMMOPRS HEMIMORPHISM
EHHILOOPPRSS PHILOSOPHERS
EHHIMNOOPRST THERMOSIPHON
EHHINOOOPPRS SIPHONOPHORE
EHHLOOSSTTUY YOUTH HOSTELS
EHHMNOOOPRTY PHYTOHORMONE
EHIIILNNOPTW WHIP INTO LINE
EHIIILORTTVW WHITE VITRIOL
EHIIKNOOPSST PHOTOKINESIS
EHIIKNSSSSTT SKITTISHNESS
EHIILLNOPSTT SEPTILLIONTH
EHIILLNOSTTX SEXTILLIONTH
EHIILLOPSTWW WILL-O'-THE-WISP
EHIILMOOPRST HELIOTROPISM
EHIILMRSSSTV SILVERSMITHS
EHIILNOSTTTW WHITE STILTON

EHIIMMOPPRRS PERIMORPHISM
EHIIMNPRSTUX XIPHISTERNUM
EHIIMOOPPRSS EPIMORPHOSIS
EHILLOPPRTYY PYROPHYLLITE
EHILMMOOPPRS PLEOMORPHISM
EHILNOORTTWY NOTEWORTHILY
EHILNSSSSTTU SLUTTISHNESS
EHIMMMOOPRSS MESOMORPHISM
EHIMOOPPRRTY PYROMORPHITE
EHIMOOPRSTTT PHOTOMETRIST
EHINNORSSTUW UNWORTHINESS
EHIOORRSSSTT SHORT STORIES
EHIOPRRSSUVY SURVEYORSHIP
EHKMNOOOOPSST SMOOTH-SPOKEN
EHLMOOOOPPRTY PHOTOPOLYMER
EHMMOOOOPRSSU MESOMORPHOUS
EHMNNOORRSTT NORTHERNMOST
EHMNOORSSSUU HUMOROUSNESS
EHMNOORSSTTU SOUTHERNMOST
EHNNOOOPRTTU PHOTONEUTRON
EHOOOOPRRSTTU ORTHOPTEROUS
EHOOPPRSSSTW SHOWSTOPPERS
EIIIMMMMNORSS IMMERSIONISM
EIIIMMNORSST IMMERSIONIST
EIIIMNNORSST INTERMISSION
EIIIMNNPRSTT INSPIRITMENT
EIIIMNOOPRST REIMPOSITION
EIIIMPRTTTVY PERMITTIVITY
EIIINOQRSSTU REQUISITIONS
EIIINORSSSTV REVISIONISTS
EIILLLLMNOPS PLIMSOLL LINE
EIILLNORSSSU ILLUSORINESS
EIILMNOOSTUV EVOLUTIONISM
EIILMOOPPRST PLEIOTROPISM
EIILNNNOSTUV TUNNEL VISION
EIILNOOOOPPST POLE POSITION
EIILNOORRSTU IRRESOLUTION
EIILNOOSTTUV EVOLUTIONIST
EIILOOPRSTXY EXPOSITORILY
EIIMMNNOPRST IMPRISONMENT
EIIMNNNQQUUU QUINQUENNIUM
EIIMNNOOPRST PREMONITIONS
EIINNOORRSTV INTROVERSION
EIINNOPRRTTU INTERRUPTION
EIINOOPPRSST PREPOSITIONS
EIINOORSTTTX EXTORTIONIST
EIINOPRSSTTU SUPERSTITION
EIIOOPPSSTTV POSTPOSITIVE
EILLMNOOSSTY MOTIONLESSLY
EILLNNNOOTVY NONVIOLENTLY
EILLOPPRSTUY SUPPLETORILY
EILMOPPRSTUU MULTIPURPOSE
EILMORSSTUYY MYSTERIOUSLY
EIMNNNOOOTTT NOT TO MENTION
EIMNNNOSSSUU NUMINOUSNESS
EIMNOOOOPRRST PROMONTORIES
EIMNOOOORRSST SENSORIMOTOR
EIMNOOQSSTTU MOSQUITO NETS
EIMNOORSSSTU TIMOROUSNESS

EIMNOPPRSSTU PRESUMPTIONS
EINNOPRSSSUW WIN ONE'S SPURS
EINNOQRSSTUU NON SEQUITURS
EINOORSSSUUX UXORIOUSNESS
EINOPRRSSTTW WINTER SPORTS
EINOPRSSSSUU SPURIOUSNESS
EINORSSSSUUU USURIOUSNESS
EINORSSSTUUV VIRTUOUSNESS
EKKNNOOSTUVZ NOVOKUZNETSK
ELNOOPPSSSUU POPULOUSNESS
ELNOOPRSTTUY PORTENTOUSLY
ELOOPPRRSSUY PROSPEROUSLY
ELOOPPRRSTTY LOST PROPERTY
ELOORRSSTTUY STERTOROUSLY
EMMNOOOOPRSSU MONOSPERMOUS
EMOOOOPRRRSTT STORM TROOPER
EMOPPRSSTUUU PRESUMPTUOUS
EMORRSSTTUYY MYSTERY TOURS
ENNOOOORSSSSU SONOROUSNESS
ENOORSSSTTUU TORTUOUSNESS
FFGIINOORSTT FIRST-FOOTING
FFHJLOORTUUY FOURTH OF JULY
FGGGILNOOOST FOOTSLOGGING
FGHHLLOTTUUY THOUGHTFULLY
FGHIILNORRYY HORRIFYINGLY
FGHIMNOOOOPRT MOTHPROOFING
FGIIILLNOSSV LIVING FOSSIL
FGIIIMMNNORS MISINFORMING
FGIIJLNSTUYY JUSTIFYINGLY
FGIILLLMNOYY MOLLIFYINGLY
FGIILMNORTYY MORTIFYINGLY
FGIILMNSTYYY MYSTIFYINGLY
FGILOORSTTUU FUTUROLOGIST
FGINOOPRRSTU RUSTPROOFING
FGINOOPSSTUY PUSSYFOOTING
FHLLNOOOOORRU ROLL OF HONOUR
FIILMMORTTUY MULTIFORMITY
FILLMNOSUUUX LUMINOUS FLUX
FILOORSTTUUY FORTUITOUSLY
FMNNOORSSTUU FROM SUN TO SUN
GGGHHHIIILNT HIGHLIGHTING
GGGILLNRSTUY STRUGGLINGLY
GGHHILNRSTUY HIGHLY STRUNG
GGHIILMNNOOT MOONLIGHTING
GGHIILNOPSTT SPOTLIGHTING
GGIIILLNNOTU GUILLOTINING
GGIIILNNRTUY INTRIGUINGLY
GGIILMMNNOSWY GO SWIMMINGLY
GGILMNNOORRY MORNING GLORY
GHHMNNOOOOPST MONOPHTHONGS
GHIIKLNNNTUY UNTHINKINGLY
GHIILLOOPSST PHILOLOGISTS
GHIILNNORSUY NOURISHINGLY
GHIILNORSSTT SHORT-LISTING
GHIILOOPSSTY PHYSIOLOGIST
GHILMOOOOPRST MORPHOLOGIST
GHILMOOSSTTY MYTHOLOGISTS
GHILNOOOOPSST PHONOLOGISTS
GHIMMOOPRSYZ ZYGOMORPHISM

GHINOOPPSSTW SHOWSTOPPING
GHLMNOOOOSUY HOMOGONOUSLY
GHLMOOOSUYYZ HOMOZYGOUSLY
GIIIINOPRRTZ PRIORITIZING
GIIIKLMNNSSS MISSING LINKS
GIIIMNNPRSST STRIP MININGS
GIIIMNORSTUZ MOISTURIZING
GIIINNOOPRSV PROVISIONING
GIIILLLLMNORS ROLLING MILLS
GIIILLNOORSUY INGLORIOUSLY
GIIILMMNOOPSW SWIMMING POOL
GIILMMNOOSTU IMMUNOLOGIST
GIILMNNOOOPZ MONOPOLIZING
GIILNPRRSSUY SURPRISINGLY
GIIMNOORSSTT SITTING ROOMS
GIINNNOOPRSS SPRING ONIONS
GIINNNOPRTTU TURNING POINT
GIINOPPRSTTU OUTSTRIPPING
GIINOPRSTTTU PROSTITUTING
GIJMNNNPRSUU RUNNING JUMPS
GINNOOPRSSTT STRONG POINTS
GLLNOOSTTUUY GLUTTONOUSLY
GLOOOOOPRTYZ PROTOZOOLOGY
HHILOOOPPSTU PHOTOPHILOUS
HHIMMMOOOPRS HOMOMORPHISM
HHIOOTTTUUWW TU-WHIT TU-WHOO
HHMMOOOTTTUU MOUTH-TO-MOUTH
HIIIILMNPSST PHILISTINISM
HIILLOOPPRWW WHIPPOORWILL
HIKLMMOORSTW SILKWORM MOTH
HILMMOOPPRSY POLYMORPHISM
HILOOOPPRSTU TROPOPHILOUS
HIMMMNOOOPRS MONOMORPHISM
HIMOOOPPRSTT PHOTOTROPISM
HIMOOOPRRSTT ORTHOTROPISM
HINOOPPPRRSY PORPHYROPSIN
HIOOOOPRRSTTY PROTOHISTORY
HLLMNOOOOPSUY MONOPHYLLOUS
HLMOOOPPRSUY POLYMORPHOUS

HLMOOPSSTUUY POSTHUMOUSLY
HMOOOPSSSTUY PHYSOSTOMOUS
HOOOOPRRSTTU ORTHOTROPOUS
IIIIMNNOSTTU INTUITIONISM
IIIINNOQSSTU INQUISITIONS
IIIINNOSTTTU INTUITIONIST
IIIILLNOPSSTT POINTILLISTS
IIIILLNOSSSTU ILLUSIONISTS
IIIILNOQSTUUY INIQUITOUSLY
IIIMNOORTTUV VOMITURITION
IIINNORSTTTU NUTRITIONIST
IIINNORSTTUU INNUTRITIOUS
IIINNNOSTTTU INSTITUTIONS
IIIOPRSSTTUY SPIRITUOSITY
IILLNNOOOOPPS OPINION POLLS
IILMNOOSTUVY VOLUMINOSITY
IILMOORSTTUY UTILITY ROOMS
IILNORSTTUUY NUTRITIOUSLY
IILOOPPRSTUY PROPITIOUSLY
IINNOOOOPPTTT POINT-TO-POINT
IINOOOOPPRSST PROPOSITIONS
IINOOOOPPSSTT POSTPOSITION
IINOOPPSSSTU SUPPOSITIONS
IINOOPRSTTTU PROSTITUTION
IIOOPPSSSTUU SUPPOSITIOUS
ILLMNOOOSTTY TONSILLOTOMY
ILLMNOOSUUVY VOLUMINOUSLY
ILLOPSSSUWWY PUSSY WILLOWS
IMPPPRRSSTUU STIRRUP PUMPS
INNNOOOOPSSU NONPOISONOUS
INOOPPRSSTTU OPPORTUNISTS
LLMOSTTUUUUY TUMULTUOUSLY
LLOOPSTUUUVY VOLUPTUOUSLY
LMNNOOOOOSTUY MONOTONOUSLY
LMNNOOSSUYYY SYNONYMOUSLY
MNPPRRSTTUUU TURN UP TRUMPS

AAAAACINNRSTT SANTA CATARINA
AAAAADGGIINNN AGAIN AND AGAIN
AAAAABCCEELRTU BACCALAUREATE
AAAAABCCHILMRR HAMILCAR BARCA
AAAABCCEEKKSTT TAKE A BACK SEAT
AAAAABDILMORSS AMBASSADORIAL
AAAAACCDIIKLLS LACKADAISICAL
AAAAACCINRSSTU TRANSCAUCASIA
AAAAACCLMNORST MALACOSTRACAN
AAAAACEINRRSSV CARAVANSERAIS
AAAAACILLLNPTY APLANATICALLY
AAAAACILLNOPRY PARANOIACALLY
AAAAACIMNRSSST ANTIMACASSARS
AAAAADEGHLMNOP ALPHA AND OMEGA
AAAAEGIMMNRST ANAGRAMMATISE
AAAAAEGIMMNRTZ ANAGRAMMATIZE
AAAAAEGNRSTVXZ EXTRAVAGANZAS
AAAAAEHILNPPRR PARAPHERNALIA
AAAAAGILMMNOST AMALGAMATIONS
AAAAAGIMMMNRST ANAGRAMMATISM
AAAAAGIMMNRSTT ANAGRAMMATIST
AAAAAILNRSSSTU AUSTRALASIANS
AAAABBCEGIRRSY BABY CARRIAGES
AAAABCCILLORTY ACROBATICALLY
AAAABCCILMNOTY BY ACCLAMATION
AAAABCDEHINRTU CHATEAUBRIAND
AAAABCDIKNORTW BACKWARDATION
AAAABCEEILNRST ASCERTAINABLE
AAAABCEGILLLRY ALGEBRAICALLY
AAAABCEILLNORY ANAEROBICALLY
AAAABCEILLRSWY CABLE RAILWAYS
AAAABCEILMNRRU ARABIC NUMERAL
AAAABCEIRSSTTV BITTER CASSAVA
AAAABCILLLOPRY PARABOLICALLY
AAAABDDELNTTUW WATTLE AND DAUB
AAAABDEGIILMTY DAMAGEABILITY
AAAABDEGMNNNOR RAG-AND-BONE MAN
AAAABEEELLRTUV RATEABLE VALUE
AAAABEGIILMNTY MANAGEABILITY
AAAABEGILNNOTZ ANTAGONIZABLE
AAAABEHIKPPPST PHI BETA KAPPAS
AAAABEILLMNPTU MANIPULATABLE
AAAABELNNRRTUW UNWARRANTABLE
AAAABGLLMRRRSU BURGLAR ALARMS
AAAABHILLMPSTU AMPHIBLASTULA
AAAABIIILLNOST LABIALISATION
AAAABIIILLNOTZ LABIALIZATION
AAAABIIILNTTTY ATTAINABILITY
AAAABIIKLNNOST BALKANISATION
AAAABIIKLNNOTZ BALKANIZATION
AAAACCCEGIKNPR A CRACKING PACE
AAAACCDEIINPTT INCAPACITATED
AAAACCDHIILNOR ARCHIDIACONAL
AAAACCEEELLNRS CLEARANCE SALE
AAAACCEEHMNRTT CATCHMENT AREA
AAAACCEGILRTTX EXTRAGALACTIC
AAAACCEINNQSTU ACQUAINTANCES
AAAACCFINNNRSS SAN FRANCISCAN
AAAACCGILLLMOO MALACOLOGICAL

AAAACCHILLRTTY CATHARTICALLY
AAAACCHLORSSTY THALASSOCRACY
AAAACCILLMNORY MACARONICALLY
AAAACCILLRSSTY SARCASTICALLY
AAAACDDIILLSTY DADAISTICALLY
AAAACDEEINPPRS DISAPPEARANCE
AAAACDEEELNRRSY CALENDAR YEARS
AAAACDEGINRRSS AIRS AND GRACES
AAAACDEIIINPRT PAEDIATRICIAN
AAAACDEIIORTTV RADIOACTIVATE
AAAACDELNPPRRT PART AND PARCEL
AAAACDFNRRSSTT ARTS AND CRAFTS
AAAACDGHIIMPRT DIAPHRAGMATIC
AAAACDHIINOPRS ANAPHRODISIAC
AAAACDIIILPRST PARASITICIDAL
AAAACDIILMNOPS DIPSOMANIACAL
AAAACDILLOPRXY PARADOXICALLY
AAAACEEGNRSTVX EXTRAVAGANCES
AAAACEEELNRSTTY SCALY ANTEATER
AAAACEEENNNOPPR NONAPPEARANCE
AAAACEEENOPRRSW A NARROW ESCAPE
AAAACEEOPPRSUV PAPAVERACEOUS
AAAACEFIILNNRY FINANCIAL YEAR
AAAACEFILNORRT RAREFACTIONAL
AAAACEFMORRRTT CREAM OF TARTAR
AAAACEGHILOPPR PALAEOGRAPHIC
AAAACEGIINNRSS CASSEGRAINIAN
AAAACEGILMMNOS MEGALOMANIACS
AAAACEGILMNNOR ANGLO-AMERICAN
AAAACEHIILLMNV MACHIAVELLIAN
AAAACEHIIMMNTT MATHEMATICIAN
AAAACEHILLPTTY APATHETICALLY
AAAACEHIMOOPPR PHARMACOPOEIA
AAAACEHNRRRSTW SEARCH WARRANT
AAAACEIILMNNRT LATIN AMERICAN
AAAACEIKLMOSTT STAKE A CLAIM TO
AAAACEILLMNOTX EXCLAMATIONAL
AAAACEILLMOOST OSTEOMALACIAL
AAAACEILNNSSST SATANICALNESS
AAAACELRRSTUVX EXTRAVASCULAR
AAAACENRRRSTTU RESTAURANT CAR
AAAACENRSTTTTX SEX ATTRACTANT
AAAACFGILNNRSU LINGUA FRANCAS
AAAACFILLNSTTY FANTASTICALLY
AAAACFIMNORRTW AIRCRAFTWOMAN
AAAACGGILLOPRY PARAGOGICALLY
AAAACGIIMNPRTT ANTIPRAGMATIC
AAAACGILLMMRTY GRAMMATICALLY
AAAACGILLMPRTY PRAGMATICALLY
AAAACHILLMSTTY ASTHMATICALLY
AAAACHILLNOPRY ANAPHORICALLY
AAAACHILNRSSSU HALICARNASSUS
AAAACIILLMOTXY AXIOMATICALLY
AAAACIILLPRSTY PARASITICALLY
AAAACIILLSTTVY ATAVISTICALLY
AAAACIILNNNOTT INCANTATIONAL
AAAACIILNOSTTU ACTUALISATION
AAAACIILNOTTUZ ACTUALIZATION
AAAACIIORSSTTU AUSTRO-ASIATIC

AAACIKOPRRSST SICK AS A PARROT
AAACILLLPRTYY PARALYTICALLY
AAACILLMNOPRY PANORAMICALLY
AAACILLMOTTUY AUTOMATICALLY
AAACILLMRTTUY TRAUMATICALLY
AAACILNNORSSY NARCOANALYSIS
AAACILNNORSTT TRANSACTIONAL
AAACILNNRSTTT TRANSATLANTIC
AAACILOSSTTUY AUTOCATALYSIS
AAADDDEELTUVX VALUE-ADDED TAX
AAADDDEGINSTV DISADVANTAGED
AAADDEGINSSTV DISADVANTAGES
AAADDEHHNPRRS ANDHRA PRADESH
AAADDLMNPRSST STANDARD LAMPS
AAADEEEINNNRS SEANAD EIREANN
AAADEEFHNRRTT TAR AND FEATHER
AAADEEGMRRRSU DEMERARA SUGAR
AAADEEHHLNRTY HALE AND HEARTY
AAADEEHIMNSTT ANATHEMATISED
AAADEEHIMNTTZ ANATHEMATIZED
AAADEGGILNNRU GUARDIAN ANGEL
AAADEGINORRRT A ROARING TRADE
AAADEHHNPRSSZ HAPHAZARDNESS
AAADEHNRRSTTW DEATH WARRANTS
AAADEILLQRRTU QUADRILATERAL
AAADEINOPPRTT PREADAPTATION
AAADGIMNOORST GOOD SAMARITAN
AAADHHILNRRSU HARUN AL-RASHID
AAADHIMMMMNSU MUHAMMADANISM
AAADIIMNORSTT DRAMATISATION
AAADIIMNORTTZ DRAMATIZATION
AAADKLMRRSTTX KARL-MARX-STADT
AAAEEEHKNPRSS SHAKESPEAREAN
AAAEEGGLMNSTU METALANGUAGES
AAAEEGGMNRSST STAGE MANAGERS
AAAEEGINNRSSX SEXAGENARIANS
AAAEEGINNRTTT GIANT ANTEATER
AAAEEJLNRSTTW SERJEANT AT LAW
AAAEFFHINORST AFTER A FASHION
AAAEFGMOPRSSS PASSAGE OF ARMS
AAAEFGNPRRSSU ASPARAGUS FERN
AAAEFIILMMRST MATERFAMILIAS
AAAEFIILMPRST PATERFAMILIAS
AAAEGGGIKNPRR PARKING GARAGE
AAAEGGGIMNNST STAGE-MANAGING
AAAEGIILMMNOR EMILIA-ROMAGNA
AAAEGILNNPRTT GREAT PLANTAIN
AAAEGIMMNPRST PARAMAGNETISM
AAAEGINNNNORS NONAGENARIANS
AAAEGINORTTVX EXTRAVAGATION
AAAEGLLLMOPRR PARALLELOGRAM
AAAEGLNRTTVXY EXTRAVAGANTLY
AAAEHIMNRSSTT THE SAMARITANS
AAAEIILMNNOTX EXAMINATIONAL
AAAEILMNPRRTY PARLIAMENTARY
AAAEINORSTTVX EXTRAVASATION
AAAEMMRRSSSTT MASTERS-AT-ARMS
AAAFILMNNOSTW TASMANIAN WOLF
AAAGGGILNRTVY AGGRAVATINGLY

AAAGIILNORTTV GRAVITATIONAL
AAAGIINNSSSST ASSASSINATING
AAAGILNOOPPRT PROPAGATIONAL
AAAHIIMNNRSTU HUMANITARIANS
AAAHIINORRTTU AUTHORITARIAN
AAAIIILMNNOST ANIMALISATION
AAAIIILMNNOTZ ANIMALIZATION
AAAIILNNOSTTT TANTALISATION
AAAIILNNOTTTZ TANTALIZATION
AAAIIMNNOOSTT ANATOMISATION
AAAIIMNNOOTTZ ANATOMIZATION
AAAIIMNOORSTT AROMATISATION
AAAIIMNOORTTZ AROMATIZATION
AAAIINNORSTTV INTRAVASATION
AAAIINNOSSSST ASSASSINATION
AAAIINORRSTTT TARTARISATION
AAAIINORRTTTZ TARTARIZATION
AAAIKLNNOPRST NATIONAL PARKS
AAAILLNNORSTT TRANSLATIONAL
AAAILLNNORRTTU ULTRANATIONAL
AAAILLNNORRST TRANSLATORIAL
AAAILMNORSTVY SALVATION ARMY
AAAILNNNRSTVY TRANSYLVANIAN
AAAILNNOPRSTU SUPRANATIONAL
AABBBIILORSTY ABSORBABILITY
AABBCEEHILNOS BELISHA BEACON
AABBCEGINPRTU TURNIP CABBAGE
AABBCEHIKNSTT STAB IN THE BACK
AABBCEILNRRST TRANSCRIBABLE
AABBCILLMOSTY BOMBASTICALLY
AABBDDEEGILOR BIODEGRADABLE
AABBDEEFGLRST FLABBERGASTED
AABBDIILORSTY ADSORBABILITY
AABBEEILLMOTZ METABOLIZABLE
AABBEHIILNNTU UNINHABITABLE
AABBEIILLOSSU BOUILLABAISSE
AABBEIINORSTV ABBREVIATIONS
AABBEINRRRSTW RABBIT WARRENS
AABBENORRSSSU BARBAROUSNESS
AABBIIILNOTTY OBTAINABILITY
AABCCEEFIILRS SACRIFICEABLE
AABCCEEIRRSUU BUREAUCRACIES
AABCCEHHLPRYY BRACHYCEPHALY
AABCCEHILNPRS SPECIAL BRANCH
AABCCEIILMPRT IMPRACTICABLE
AABCCEIILPTTY ACCEPTABILITY
AABCCEIORSSSU BRASSICACEOUS
AABCCELNNOTUU UNACCOUNTABLE
AABCCIIILNNST CANNIBALISTIC
AABCCIILLLTUY CALCULABILITY
AABCCIILMPRTY IMPRACTICABLY
AABCCILLLOSTU LACTOBACILLUS
AABCCKLNRRSTU BLACKCURRANTS
AABCCLNNOTUUY UNACCOUNTABLY
AABCDDEEILNST BALANCED DIETS
AABCDDGINORRS BOARDING CARDS
AABCDDHINORSW SANDWICH BOARD
AABCDEEEFNRSS BAREFACEDNESS
AABCDEEFIPRRT PREFABRICATED

AABCDEEGHILRS DISCHARGEABLE
AABCDEELRRSTT BATTLE-SCARRED
AABCDEENNORUV OVERABUNDANCE
AABCDEGIKLLNP BACKPEDALLING
AABCDEHIILTTY DETACHABILITY
AABCDEHIKLNTW BLACK AND WHITE
AABCDEHORRSTY CARBOHYDRATES
AABCDELLMNOOR BALLROOM DANCE
AABCDELOPPRRS CLAPPERBOARDS
AABCDGIKLMRSU BLACKGUARDISM
AABCDINNORSTT CONTRABANDIST
AABCEEEELNPSS PEACEABLENESS
AABCEEEGHLLLN CHALLENGEABLE
AABCEEEHLNSST BALANCE SHEETS
AABCEEEILLPRR IRREPLACEABLE
AABCEEGGPRRST CARPETBAGGERS
AABCEEGHIOPRT BACTERIOPHAGE
AABCEEHILMNPU UNIMPEACHABLE
AABCEEIILLMRR IRRECLAIMABLE
AABCEEIKMNRST CABINET-MAKERS
AABCEEILMNRSV VRAISEMBLANCE
AABCEEKQRRSTU SQUARE BRACKET
AABCEFGIMOTTU COMBAT FATIGUE
AABCEFIIINOTT BEATIFICATION
AABCEFIINORTT ABORTIFACIENT
AABCEFIOPRRRT PREFABRICATOR
AABCEFLNRSSTU BLAST FURNACES
AABCEGGKRRSTU GARBAGE TRUCKS
AABCEGHIILNTY CHANGEABILITY
AABCEGHIILRTY CHARGEABILITY
AABCEGHINORRS A CRASHING BORE
AABCEGILLLNOO BALNEOLOGICAL
AABCEGILLMOST MEGALOBLASTIC
AABCEGILNNORV OVERBALANCING
AABCEGINOORSU BORAGINACEOUS
AABCEHILLLMNR LAMELLIBRANCH
AABCEHILMNPUY UNIMPEACHABLY
AABCEHIRRRRSS CRASH BARRIERS
AABCEHKMNNRST MERCHANT BANKS
AABCEIINORRTT NITROBACTERIA
AABCEIIRSTTTY TETRABASICITY
AABCEILLLMOTY METABOLICALLY
AABCEILLOORTV COLLABORATIVE
AABCEILLRSTTY TETRASYLLABIC
AABCEILMNNOOP COMPANIONABLE
AABCEIMRRSTUU BUREAUCRATISM
AABCEINOORRST SERBO-CROATIAN
AABCEINRRSSTT SCATTERBRAINS
AABCELMMNNOSU SOMNAMBULANCE
AABCFGILNNOTU CONFABULATING
AABCFIILORTTY FACTORABILITY
AABCFIKMNOORT BACK FORMATION
AABCFILNNOOTU CONFABULATION
AABCFILORRSUV FIBROVASCULAR
AABCFLNOORTUY CONFABULATORY
AABCGIIILNNNZ CANNIBALIZING
AABCGILLNOORT COLLABORATING
AABCHIIILMNTY MACHINABILITY
AABCIIILLMPTY IMPLACABILITY

AABCIIILLPPTY APPLICABILITY
AABCIILLLLSTY BALLISTICALLY
AABCIILLNORTU LUBRICATIONAL
AABCIILLOSTTY BIOSTATICALLY
AABCIILLRSTYY SYBARITICALLY
AABCIILMOPRTY COMPARABILITY
AABCIINNOORST CARBONISATION
AABCIINNOORTZ CARBONIZATION
AABCIINORRSTU CARBURISATION
AABCIINORRTUZ CARBURIZATION
AABCILLNOOOORT COLLABORATION
AABCILMNNOOPY COMPANIONABLY
AABCINORSSSTT CONTRABASSIST
AABCLLOOORRST COLLABORATORS
AABCMNNNOOSTT NONCOMBATANTS
AABCNNOOORSST CONTRABASSOON
AABDDEGINNPRS BANDSPREADING
AABDDEHIILNNR HILDEBRANDIAN
AABDDGHILORTY BROAD DAYLIGHT
AABDDGIINNORR DRAINING BOARD
AABDDGINORRSW DRAWING BOARDS
AABDEEFGIILNT INDEFATIGABLE
AABDEEHIILRTT REHABILITATED
AABDEEHORRSTW WEATHERBOARDS
AABDEFGIILNTY INDEFATIGABLY
AABDEFGIOPRSS BIRD OF PASSAGE
AABDEFGKORSST DOG'S BREAKFAST
AABDEGIINNRRT GRIN AND BEAR IT
AABDEIILNRTUY UNREADABILITY
AABDEILNNOSTT NATIONAL DEBTS
AABDEINNNORRS SAN BERNARDINO
AABDEINSSTTTU SUBSTANTIATED
AABDEKLNRSTUY LAUNDRY BASKET
AABDENNPRSTUU SUPERABUNDANT
AABDENOOPRSSX PANDORA'S BOXES
AABDHIMNORSTT RHABDOMANTIST
AABDIIILLSTYY DIALYSABILITY
AABEEEEGLNRSS AGREEABLENESS
AABEEEEHNRTTW WEATHER-BEATEN
AABEEEFLMNSST SELF-ABASEMENT
AABEEEELNORSST ELABORATENESS
AABEEEELOORRTV OVERELABORATE
AABEEFILNNOTU FONTAINEBLEAU
AABEEFLMOSSTV MOVABLE FEASTS
AABEEGHIKNRRT HEARTBREAKING
AABEEIILLRTVY REVEALABILITY
AABEEIILPRTTY REPEATABILITY
AABEELLLRSTTY TETRASYLLABLE
AABEEMMNNRRSST EMBARRASSMENT
AABEFFLORSTUW WATER BUFFALOS
AABEFHILNNOSU UNFASHIONABLE
AABEFIILLNQUU UNQUALIFIABLE
AABEFILLNOPTU FALLOPIAN TUBE
AABEFILMORSSU BALSAMIFEROUS
AABEFLMNORRST TRANSFORMABLE
AABEGHIMNOOPR GERMANOPHOBIA
AABEGHIMNSTTW BANTAMWEIGHTS
AABEGHINQRSSU SQUARE-BASHING
AABEGIILLNOUV BOUGAINVILLEA

AABEGILMNPRTU PERAMBULATING
AABEGILNORRTU GUBERNATORIAL
AABEGILNRRSTT SABRE-RATTLING
AABEGIMNRRSTT BATTERING RAMS
AABEHILLORUVY BEHAVIOURALLY
AABEIIILNRTTY RETAINABILITY
AABEIIKLMRTTY MARKETABILITY
AABEIILLLOTVZ VOLATILIZABLE
AABEIILMNORST ABNORMALITIES
AABEIILMRSTUY MEASURABILITY
AABEIILMSTTTY METASTABILITY
AABEIILNORSTV VERBALISATION
AABEIILNORTVZ VERBALIZATION
AABEIILNRSTWY ANSWERABILITY
AABEIILOPRTVY EVAPORABILITY
AABEIILRRUVXY AUXILIARY VERB
AABEIIMNNRSTU ANTISUBMARINE
AABEIINRRRSST ARBITRARINESS
AABEIKNORSSTT STATION BREAKS
AABEILMNOPRTU PERAMBULATION
AABEILNOOPPRT APPORTIONABLE
AABEILNOORSTV OBSERVATIONAL
AABEILOQRSTUU SUBEQUATORIAL
AABELMOPRRSTU PERAMBULATORS
AABELMOPRRTUY PERAMBULATORY
AABELNOPRRSTT TRANSPORTABLE
AABELOPRRTUUY BEAUTY PARLOUR
AABGGILLMMNOU GAMMA GLOBULIN
AABGHIOOPRTUY AUTOBIOGRAPHY
AABGHLLOPRSYY SYLLABOGRAPHY
AABGIIILNSSTY ASSIGNABILITY
AABGIILOPPRTY PROPAGABILITY
AABHIIILNPRRS LIBRARIANSHIP
AABIIIILNRTVY INVARIABILITY
AABIIIILNSTTY INSATIABILITY
AABIIILLMPPTY IMPALPABILITY
AABIIILMPSSTY IMPASSABILITY
AABIIILNOSSTT STABILISATION
AABIIILNOSTTZ STABILIZATION
AABIILNNNRTTU TINTINNABULAR
AABIILNNSSTTU INSUBSTANTIAL
AABIILNORSTTU BRUTALISATION
AABIILNORTTUZ BRUTALIZATION
AABIILOPRTUVY VAPOURABILITY
AABIILOSTTTUY AUTOSTABILITY
AABILLNSSTTUY SUBSTANTIALLY
AABILNNSSTTUU UNSUBSTANTIAL
AABINORSSTTTU SUBSTANTIATOR
AABLMMNOORSTU SOMNAMBULATOR
AACCCEEILNRRT RECALCITRANCE
AACCCEGHNORTU CHARGE ACCOUNT
AACCCEGINORTY GYNAECOCRATIC
AACCCEIILLMRT CLIMACTERICAL
AACCCFIIILNOT CALCIFICATION
AACCCGHHILOPR CHALCOGRAPHIC
AACCCIIILMNTT ANTICLIMACTIC
AACCCIILMMORT MACROCLIMATIC
AACCDEEHHIKSS SICK HEADACHES
AACCDEEHINOPT HEPTADECANOIC

AACCDEEHIRRST CHARACTERISED
AACCDEEHIRRTZ CHARACTERIZED
AACCDEEIILNRU CLAIRAUDIENCE
AACCDEEIMORSS ICE-CREAM SODAS
AACCDEGHHNNOP CHOP AND CHANGE
AACCDEHIILMOR RADIOCHEMICAL
AACCDEHIIRRST TRISACCHARIDE
AACCDEIIILNST DIALECTICIANS
AACCDEIILNOST DIATONIC SCALE
AACCDEIINNOPT PENTANOIC ACID
AACCDEIINORTT ACCREDITATION
AACCDEILLMSTU MISCALCULATED
AACCDEILNOOTU COEDUCATIONAL
AACCDEIMMOOTV ACCOMMODATIVE
AACCDEIMNNOPU UNACCOMPANIED
AACCDFIIIINOT ACIDIFICATION
AACCDGHIIOPRR CARDIOGRAPHIC
AACCDGIILLOOR CARDIOLOGICAL
AACCDGIMMNOOT ACCOMMODATING
AACCDHIMRRSST CHRISTMAS CARD
AACCDIILLOPTY APODICTICALLY
AACCDIIMNOORT CARCINOMATOID
AACCDIMMNOOOT ACCOMMODATION
AACCEEFHSSTTY SAFETY CATCHES
AACCEEFIRSTUV SURFACE-ACTIVE
AACCEEHHIMNNT THE MAIN CHANCE
AACCEEHILMNOT CATECHOLAMINE
AACCEEHIMNORS AEROMECHANICS
AACCEEHIMRRST SACCHARIMETER
AACCEEHLMNPRY MACRENCEPHALY
AACCEEHLRRSST CHARACTERLESS
AACCEEHMORRST SACCHAROMETER
AACCEELMNRUUV VACUUM CLEANER
AACCEFIIINOTT ACETIFICATION
AACCEFILORRSU CALCARIFEROUS
AACCEGHHLOPRR CHALCOGRAPHER
AACCEGHINOOPR OCEANOGRAPHIC
AACCEGIILNRTT INTERGALACTIC
AACCEGIINNRRT INCARCERATING
AACCEGILLOOTU AUTECOLOGICAL
AACCEGILLORTY CATEGORICALLY
AACCEGILLOTTY GEOTACTICALLY
AACCEGINNNOTT CONCATENATING
AACCEHHLNPRTY CHANTRY CHAPEL
AACCEHIINNORT CHAIN REACTION
AACCEHIINOSTT CATECHISATION
AACCEHIINOTTZ CATECHIZATION
AACCEHIKMRSST CHRISTMAS CAKE
AACCEHILLMSTY SCHEMATICALLY
AACCEHILOSSTT SCHOLASTICATE
AACCEHILRRTTU ARCHITECTURAL
AACCEHIMMORTT METACHROMATIC
AACCEHIMPRSTU PHARMACEUTICS
AACCEHIPPRRST SHARP PRACTICE
AACCEIILLMNTY CINEMATICALLY
AACCEIINNORRT INCARCERATION
AACCEIIOPRSTT ECTOPARASITIC
AACCEIIORRSST ARISTOCRACIES
AACCEIJKLOPRT PRACTICAL JOKE

AACCEILLMRTUV CIRCUMVALLATE
AACCEILLNNOST CANCELLATIONS
AACCEILLNSTUY ENCAUSTICALLY
AACCEIMMNNOPT ACCOMPANIMENT
AACCEINNNOOTT CONCATENATION
AACCEINNOSTTU ACCENTUATIONS
AACCEINOPSSSU CAPACIOUSNESS
AACCEKNORTTTU COUNTERATTACK
AACCELLNOOPRR LANCE CORPORAL
AACCELLPRSTUY SPECTACULARLY
AACCELORSSSUU CRASSULACEOUS
AACCFIIILLRSY SACRIFICIALLY
AACCFIIILNORT CLARIFICATION
AACCFIIINNORT CARNIFICATION
AACCFIIINOPRT CAPRIFICATION
AACCFIIINORST SCARIFICATION
AACCFIILLLORY CALORIFICALLY
AACCFIILLSSTY FASCISTICALLY
AACCFIILNOSTU FASCICULATION
AACCGGIILLLOO GLACIOLOGICAL
AACCGHILLNOOT ANGLO-CATHOLIC
AACCGIIILMNTZ ACCLIMATIZING
AACCGIILLNOOR CRANIOLOGICAL
AACCGILNOOPSV GALVANOSCOPIC
AACCHIILMNOOT MACHICOLATION
AACCHIILMRSSU MUSICAL CHAIRS
AACCHIIMNNORT ANTIMONARCHIC
AACCHIINNORST ANACHRONISTIC
AACCHILLLLOOY ALCOHOLICALLY
AACCHILLMORTY CHROMATICALLY
AACCHILLOPRTT TROPHALLACTIC
AACCHILMNOORT ROMAN CATHOLIC
AACCHINOOSSTT COACH STATIONS
AACCIIINNOOST COCAINISATION
AACCIIINNOOTZ COCAINIZATION
AACCIIINORSTT CICATRISATION
AACCIIINORTTZ CICATRIZATION
AACCIILLMPRTY IMPRACTICALLY
AACCIILLSSTUY CASUISTICALLY
AACCIILMNOOSS OCCASIONALISM
AACCIILMNORTY MICROANALYTIC
AACCIIRRSSTTU CARICATURISTS
AACCILLNSTTYY SYNTACTICALLY
AACCILMNOSTUU ACCUMULATIONS
AACCILNNOOOTV CONVOCATIONAL
AACCILNNOORTT CONTRACTIONAL
AACCILNORTTUU ACCULTURATION
AACCILNPRTTYY CRYPTANALYTIC
AACCINORSSTTY SACROSANCTITY
AACCLLNORTTUY CONTRACTUALLY
AACDDEEEHLLRY CLEAR-HEADEDLY
AACDDEEELLNVV ADVANCED LEVEL
AACDDEFIILSSS CLASSIFIED ADS
AACDDEIIOSSST DISASSOCIATED
AACDDFIIINNOT DANDIFICATION
AACDDIKMNNRSU MANDARIN DUCKS
AACDEEGHIMNST MAGNETIC HEADS
AACDEEGINRRRU UNDERCARRIAGE
AACDEEHINTTTU AUTHENTICATED

AACDEEILPRTTU RECAPITULATED
AACDEEIMNNOTT DECONTAMINATE
AACDEEIQRSTTU ACQUIRED TASTE
AACDEENNNNOTT NONATTENDANCE
AACDEFFIIMNRS DISAFFIRMANCE
AACDEFFINRRTW TRAFFIC WARDEN
AACDEFGHIRSTT STRAIGHT-FACED
AACDEFLLNNOOR ONCE AND FOR ALL
AACDEGGILLMOY DEMAGOGICALLY
AACDEGGILLOPY PEDAGOGICALLY
AACDEGHIOPRRR CARDIOGRAPHER
AACDEGJLNOSUU JUGLANDACEOUS
AACDEGLMNNORS SCANDALMONGER
AACDEGLNORTTU CONGRATULATED
AACDEHIIMNRRT ARCHIMANDRITE
AACDEHLMNNORT CALENDAR MONTH
AACDEIIINPRST PEDIATRICIANS
AACDEIIJLRTUX EXTRAJUDICIAL
AACDEIILLMRTY DIAMETRICALLY
AACDEIILLOPRY APERIODICALLY
AACDEIILOPPRR PERICARPOIDAL
AACDEIILRSTTU DISARTICULATE
AACDEIINNRSTT TRANSACTINIDE
AACDEIINOPRST ENDOPARASITIC
AACDEIINOPSTT DECAPITATIONS
AACDEIKLLNPST SLAP AND TICKLE
AACDEILLMORTY DECLAMATORILY
AACDEILLNSTYY ASYNDETICALLY
AACDEILLORRTY DECLARATORILY
AACDEILNQRUVY QUADRIVALENCY
AACDEILPQRTUU QUADRUPLICATE
AACDEIMNNNOTT DECONTAMINANT
AACDEINNORSUU ARUNDINACEOUS
AACDEINOSSSUU AUDACIOUSNESS
AACDELNOPRSSY PLAY ONE'S CARDS
AACDFFIILNRST TRAFFIC ISLAND
AACDFIIIMNNOT DAMNIFICATION
AACDFMNOORSTW WOODCRAFTSMAN
AACDGHILNNRSS CRASH LANDINGS
AACDGIIINNOST DIAGNOSTICIAN
AACDHIIIOPRST ADIAPHORISTIC
AACDHILLLRUYY HYDRAULICALLY
AACDHILLOPRSY RHAPSODICALLY
AACDHILMNOORT TRICHOMONADAL
AACDHIMMOOSSS SADOMASOCHISM
AACDHIMOOSSST SADOMASOCHIST
AACDIIILLMOTY IDIOMATICALLY
AACDIIILPQRTU QUADRICIPITAL
AACDIIINNNORT INCARDINATION
AACDIIIORTTVY RADIOACTIVITY
AACDIIKNNNOPR RACK-AND-PINION
AACDIILLLSTUY DUALISTICALLY
AACDIILLORTTY DICTATORIALLY
AACDIILNNOPRT CARDINAL POINT
AACDIIMNOPSST ANTISPASMODIC
AACDIIMNNORRTY DRAMATIC IRONY
AACDILLMOPSSY SPASMODICALLY
AACDIMNORSSTY ASTRODYNAMICS
AACEEEGHNRSTX EXCHANGE RATES

AACEEEHJKLRTT LEATHERJACKET
AACEEFHMSSTTY SAFETY MATCHES
AACEEFLNRSSSU SELF-ASSURANCE
AACEEGHILOPRS ARCHIPELAGOES
AACEEGHLLSSSV CHEVAL GLASSES
AACEEGHLMNOPR ENCEPHALOGRAM
AACEEGHLMOPSU MEGACEPHALOUS
AACEEGHNOOPRR OCEANOGRAPHER
AACEEGHNPRSTX PART EXCHANGES
AACEEGIILLNPR ALPINE GLACIER
AACEEGILNPRTW WATERING PLACE
AACEEGIMNPSTT MAGNETIC TAPES
AACEEGINNOSTU GENTIANACEOUS
AACEEGLOOSTTV COTTAGE LOAVES
AACEEHIILNPST ELEPHANTIASIC
AACEEHILLSTTY AESTHETICALLY
AACEEHILMPRTT HEPTAMETRICAL
AACEEHILNPRTT PARENTHETICAL
AACEEHIPRRSST SEARCH PARTIES
AACEEHKMNRRSS SNAKE CHARMERS
AACEEHMNOPSUY NYMPHAEACEOUS
AACEEIILLPSTV CAPITAL LEVIES
AACEEIILNRTTV INTERCALATIVE
AACEEIINNRSST NECESSITARIAN
AACEEIINORRST REACTIONARIES
AACEEIILLMMRTY METAMERICALLY
AACEEILMMNORT ANEMOMETRICAL
AACEEILNNRSTW SAINT LAWRENCE
AACEEILNNSUUV NUISANCE VALUE
AACEEIMNNRSTT ASCERTAINMENT
AACEELLLRRTUX EXTRACELLULAR
AACEENNPPRSTU APPURTENANCES
AACEFGILNORTV CONFLAGRATIVE
AACEFIILLNRTY INTERFACIALLY
AACEFILLMNRUY NUCLEAR FAMILY
AACEFILMNRSST MASSIF CENTRAL
AACEFINRSTTUY SAFETY CURTAIN
AACEFMNRRSTUU MANUFACTURERS
AACEFNOPRRSTT TRANSPORT CAFE
AACEGGHJKNNNU KANGCHENJUNGA
AACEGHILLLRTY LETHARGICALLY
AACEGHILLMPRY GRAPHEMICALLY
AACEGHILNPRSS GRAPHICALNESS
AACEGHILOORST ARCHAEOLOGIST
AACEGHIMNOPRT CINEMATOGRAPH
AACEGHOPRRRST CARTOGRAPHERS
AACEGHOPRSSSU SARCOPHAGUSES
AACEGIIIMMNNRZ AMERICANIZING
AACEGIIINNRRST GERIATRICIANS
AACEGIILLMNOR MINERALOGICAL
AACEGIILLMNTY ENIGMATICALLY
AACEGIILLNNTY ANTIGENICALLY
AACEGIINNNRRT REINCARNATING
AACEGIINPRRTV PREVARICATING
AACEGILLLLORY ALLEGORICALLY
AACEGILLLMRTU METALLURGICAL
AACEGILLMTUYZ ZEUGMATICALLY
AACEGILLRSTTY STRATEGICALLY
AACEGILMNNRST MAGIC LANTERNS

AACEGILMNOOSU MAGNOLIACEOUS
AACEGILMNORTV GALVANOMETRIC
AACEGIMNOPSTU COME UP AGAINST
AACEGINNOORST OCTOGENARIANS
AACEGINOSSSSU SAGACIOUSNESS
AACEGLLMMORRU GRAM-MOLECULAR
AACEGLLOOPSUY POLYGALACEOUS
AACEGLMNORRSS MARRONS GLACÉS
AACEGLRRSSTYZ CRYSTAL GAZERS
AACEHHILNOPRZ RHIZOCEPHALAN
AACEHHLOOPRTX CEPHALOTHORAX
AACEHIIMNRTT ARITHMETICIAN
AACEHIILLSTTY ATHEISTICALLY
AACEHIILNOPST CEPHALISATION
AACEHIILNOPTZ CEPHALIZATION
AACEHIILRTTTY THEATRICALITY
AACEHIIMNNOST MECHANISATION
AACEHIIMNNOTZ MECHANIZATION
AACEHIIMNNRST CHRISTIAN NAME
AACEHIIMNPSTY METAPHYSICIAN
AACEHILLNTTUY AUTHENTICALLY
AACEHILMNPRRU HURRICANE LAMP
AACEHINOPRTTY ACTINOTHERAPY
AACEHINORTTTU AUTHENTICATOR
AACEHLNOPSSYY PSYCHOANALYSE
AACEHLNOPSYYZ PSYCHOANALYZE
AACEHMSSSSTTU MASSACHUSETTS
AACEHNOPPRRTY PARTHENOCARPY
AACEIIILMRSTT MATERIALISTIC
AACEIIIMPRSST SEMIPARASITIC
AACEIIKLLMNTY KINEMATICALLY
AACEIILLLRSTY REALISTICALLY
AACEIILLMNSSY MESSIANICALLY
AACEIILMNSTU NAUTICAL MILES
AACEIILLNRRTY INTERCALARILY,
     INTERRACIALLY
AACEIILMMNRSU UNICAMERALISM
AACEIILMNRSTT MATERNALISTIC
AACEIILMNRSTU UNICAMERALIST
AACEIILNNORTT INTERACTIONAL,
     INTERCALATION
AACEIILNNOSTT CAT-O'-NINE-TAILS
AACEIILNOPPSS EPISCOPALIANS
AACEIILNPRSTT PATERNALISTIC
AACEIILNRSSST SATIRICALNESS
AACEIILPRRSTU PARTICULARISE
AACEIILPRRTUZ PARTICULARIZE
AACEIIMMNOSTTU SEMIAUTOMATIC
AACEIIMOPRRST MICROPARASITE
AACEIINNNORRT REINCARNATION
AACEIINOPPRST APPRECIATIONS
AACEIINOPRRTV PREVARICATION
AACEIINORSTTU CAUTERISATION
AACEIINORTTUZ CAUTERIZATION
AACEIINRRRSTU CURTAIN RAISER
AACEIJKRSSTTT STRAITJACKETS
AACEIKLMNOPST KLEPTOMANIACS
AACEIKLOPRSTT KERATOPLASTIC
AACEILLLNRRTU INTRACELLULAR

AACEILLMNPTUY PNEUMATICALLY
AACEILLMORTXY EXCLAMATORILY
AACEILLMPRSTY SPERMATICALLY
AACEILMNRRSUV VERNACULARISM
AACEILMOPRTVY COMPARATIVELY
AACEILNNOPSTU ENCAPSULATION
AACEILNOSSSSU SALACIOUSNESS
AACEILNRRSTUU CRANIAL SUTURE
AACEILOOPPRSS LAPAROSCOPIES
AACEILRSSTTTU TRUCIAL STATES
AACEIMNNRSTTT TRANSMITTANCE
AACEIMNNOOPSST COMPASSIONATE
AACEINNOOTTTV CONNOTATATIVE
AACEINOPRRSTT PROCRASTINATE
AACEINOPRRTUY PRECAUTIONARY
AACEINOPSSSTT SPACE STATIONS
AACEIOPRRRSTV PREVARICATORS
AACEJKLNNORST JACK-O'-LANTERNS
AACELMMNOPRTT COMPARTMENTAL
AACELNORRSUUV NEUROVASCULAR
AACELNRSSTTUU SUSTENTACULAR
AACELORSSSTUU ASSAULT COURSE
AACEMNNOORSTT ENTOMOSTRACAN
AACEMNNOPPRTY PARENT COMPANY
AACFFIIILNOST FALSIFICATION
AACFGHIILRRTT LIGHT AIRCRAFT
AACFGIIIMNNOT MAGNIFICATION
AACFGIIINORTT GRATIFICATION
AACFGIILNNSTY FASCINATINGLY
AACFGILNNOORT CONFLAGRATION
AACFGIMNNRTUU MANUFACTURING
AACFHIMNPRSST CRAFTSMANSHIP
AACFIIIILRTTY ARTIFICIALITY
AACFIIILMNOPT AMPLIFICATION
AACFIIILNOQTU QUALIFICATION
AACFIIIMNORST RAMIFICATIONS
AACFIILOQRTUY QUALIFICATORY
AACFIINNOORTT FRACTIONATION
AACFIINOORSTT FACTORISATION
AACFIINOORTTZ FACTORIZATION
AACFIINOSSSTT SATISFACTIONS
AACFINORSTTUY ANFRACTUOSITY
AACFORRSSTTTU FRACTOSTRATUS
AACGGHIKNNSUW KWANGSI-CHUANG
AACGGHINOOPRR ORGANOGRAPHIC
AACGGILLNOOOR ORGANOLOGICAL
AACGGILMMOORT LOGOGRAMMATIC
AACGGILNRSTYZ CRYSTAL GAZING
AACGHHIMNNTTW NIGHT WATCHMAN
AACGHIILLNNTU HALLUCINATING
AACGHIILLPRST CALLIGRAPHIST
AACGHIIPRRSTT STRATIGRAPHIC
AACGHILMNOOPR NOMOGRAPHICAL
AACGHILOOPPRT TOPOGRAPHICAL
AACGHILOPPRTY TYPOGRAPHICAL
AACGHLMMOORRS GRAMMAR SCHOOL
AACGHMNOOPRSY PHARMACOGNOSY
AACGIIILLMSTY IMAGISTICALLY
AACGIIILLNOST GALLICISATION

AACGIIILLNOTZ GALLICIZATION
AACGIIILNNOST ANGLICISATION
AACGIIILNNOTZ ANGLICIZATION
AACGIIIMSSTTT ASTIGMATISTIC
AACGIIINPPRTT PARTICIPATING
AACGIILLLNTVY VACILLATINGLY
AACGIILLNNORY INORGANICALLY
AACGIILMNRTTU MATRICULATING
AACGIILNORSTU CARTILAGINOUS
AACGIIMNNNOTT CONTAMINATING
AACGIINNNOPRS CAPARISONNING
AACGIJLNNOOTU CONJUGATIONAL
AACGILLLNOOPY PALYNOLOGICAL
AACGILLLNOSTY NOSTALGICALLY
AACGILMNOOPST CAMPANOLOGIST
AACGILNNOOSTV LONG VACATIONS
AACGILNOOPRTV GALVANOTROPIC
AACGIMMMNOORT MONOGRAMMATIC
AACGINOPPRSTU GROUP CAPTAINS
AACGKNOOORRTU KANGAROO COURT
AACGLNOORRTTU CONGRATULATOR
AACHHIIMNPRSS CHAIRMANSHIPS
AACHHILPSTXYY TACHYPHYLAXIS
AACHHIMNPSSTY YACHTSMANSHIP
AACHIILLNNOTU HALLUCINATION
AACHILLLMPTYY LYMPHATICALLY
AACHILLNOPPSY PANSOPHICALLY
AACHILLNORTUY HALLUCINATORY
AACHILOPRSSTY ASTROPHYSICAL
AACHIMMNNOPSY NYMPHOMANIACS
AACHIMMNOPRST PANCHROMATISM
AACHIMMOOPRST APOCHROMATISM
AACHIMOPRSSTT CATASTROPHISM
AACHIOPRSSTTT CATASTROPHIST
AACHLNOPSSTYY PSYCHOANALYST
AACHLOOPRSTTY THORACOPLASTY
AACIIIILNOSTT ITALICISATION
AACIIIILNOTTZ ITALICIZATION
AACIIILLNNNOT INCLINATIONAL
AACIIILLPPRTY PARTICIPIALLY
AACIIILNNOSTT NATIONALISTIC
AACIIILNOOSST SOCIALISATION
AACIIILNOOSTZ SOCIALIZATION
AACIIILNORSTT RATIONALISTIC
AACIIINNOORTT RATIOCINATION
AACIIINOPPRTT PARTICIPATION
AACIIINNSSSTTT STATISTICIANS
AACIILLMNNOTY ANTINOMICALLY
AACIILLMORTTY MATRILOCALITY,
    TRIATOMICALLY
AACIILLMOSTTY ATOMISTICALLY
AACIILLNPRTUY PURITANICALLY
AACIILLOPRTTY PATRIOTICALLY
AACIILLPRSTTY PATRISTICALLY
AACIILLSSTTTY STATISTICALLY
AACIILMNORSSY MICROANALYSIS
AACIILMNORTTU MATRICULATION
AACIILMPRRSTU PARTICULARISM
AACIILNNOOSTV VOLCANISATION

AACIILNNOOOTVZ VOLCANIZATION
AACIILNNOPSTU INCAPSULATION
AACIILNNOSTUV VULCANISATION
AACIILNNOTUVZ VULCANIZATION
AACIILNOPSTTU CAPITULATIONS
AACIILNORSTTU ARTICULATIONS
AACIILPRRSTTU PARTICULARIST
AACIILPRRTTUY PARTICULARITY
AACIIMMNNORTU COMMUNITARIAN
AACIIMMORSSST COMMISSARIATS
AACIIMNNNOOTT CONTAMINATION
AACIIMNNORTUU ACTINOURANIUM
AACIINNNOOSST CANONISATIONS
AACIINNNOOSTZ CANONIZATIONS
AACIINNOORSTT NARCOTISATION
AACIINNOORTTZ NARCOTIZATION
AACIINNOPSSTT PANIC STATIONS
AACILLMNOOTUY AUTONOMICALLY
AACILLMNOOTXY TAXONOMICALLY
AACILLMNOPSTY COMPLAISANTLY
AACILLMPRSTYY SYMPATRICALLY
AACILMNOOPRST PROCLAMATIONS
AACILMNOOPTTU COMPUTATIONAL
AACILMNRRSTUU INTRAMUSCULAR
AACILMOOPSSTT SOMATOPLASTIC
AACILMORRSTTU COURT MARTIALS,
   COURTS-MARTIAL
AACILNNOORSTT TRANSLOCATION
AACILNPRSSTYY CRYPTANALYSIS
AACIMNNOOPSWY COMPANIONWAYS
AACIMNNOORSTT CONTAMINATORS
AACIMNNRSTTTY TRANSMITTANCY
AADDDELNOORSW RED SANDALWOOD
AADDEEEFHNSST FATHEADEDNESS
AADDEEEHIRRTW READ-WRITE HEAD
AADDEEEELMPRST PADDLE STEAMER
AADDEEGIILLNS LEADING LADIES
AADDEEGINNRRU UNDERDRAINAGE
AADDEEGNRRTUU UNDERGRADUATE
AADDEEHHINNST HEAD IN THE SAND
AADDEEHHLRRTY HARD-HEARTEDLY
AADDEELNRTTUU UNADULTERATED
AADDEFFIIILST DISAFFILIATED
AADDEGGHNRRTU GRANDDAUGHTER
AADDEGHNORRUY ROUGH-AND-READY
AADDEGHOPRRSS ADDRESSOGRAPH
AADDEGILNRSSS SALAD DRESSING
AADDEGINOPPRS PROPAGANDISED
AADDEGINOPPRZ PROPAGANDIZED
AADDEGNOPRRSU PARADE GROUNDS
AADDEILNRSSST DASTARDLINESS
AADDGIINNRSTZ STANDARDIZING
AADDIIILNOPST DILAPIDATIONS
AADEEEGGLRTXY EXAGGERATEDLY
AADEEEHINSSTT ANAESTHETISED
AADEEEHINSTTZ ANAESTHETIZED
AADEEEHIRSSST HEART DISEASES
AADEEEIKNSSWW WIDE-AWAKENESS
AADEEEIMNNRRT MEDITERRANEAN

AADEEEELPRSTXY EXASPERATEDLY
AADEEEMMNRSTU ADMEASUREMENT
AADEEEMMORSTU MADE-TO-MEASURE
AADEEFHHLLRTY HALF-HEARTEDLY
AADEEFILLMRST FLEET ADMIRALS
AADEEFNSSSSTT STEADFASTNESS
AADEEGGILNPRS SPREAD-EAGLING
AADEEGILMORRT RADIOTELEGRAM
AADEEGILMQRSU MADRIGALESQUE
AADEEGIMNPRST DISPARAGEMENT
AADEEGINPRRST GARDEN PARTIES
AADEEGINRSTTT TRADING ESTATE
AADEEGKMNRRST MARKET GARDENS
AADEEGLLMNRRW WALL GERMANDER
AADEEHLMRRTWY WARM-HEARTEDLY
AADEEHLOPRRTZ TRAPEZOHEDRAL
AADEEHLORRTTT TETARTOHEDRAL
AADEEHMNNSSSU UNASHAMEDNESS
AADEEIILNNOST DENATIONALISE
AADEEIILNNOTZ DENATIONALIZE
AADEEIILNNNORR NORADRENALINE
AADEEELNPPPRST PEPPER-AND-SALT
AADEEENNPRSTUU SUPERANNUATED
AADEFFMNOORSW MEADOW SAFFRON
AADEFGHHINORR HARD OF HEARING
AADEFHILLMRSS FIELD MARSHALS
AADEFIILNOSTU FEUDALISATION
AADEFIILNOTUZ FEUDALIZATION
AADEFILNSSSTY SAFETY ISLANDS
AADEFILOOPRSS FOOL'S PARADISE
AADEFLLMNNTUY FUNDAMENTALLY
AADEGGILNNSST LANDING STAGES
AADEGHILNRTUW DAUGHTER-IN-LAW
AADEGHIOPRRRS RADIOGRAPHERS
AADEGIIMNNRTV ANIMADVERTING
AADEGILNSTTVY DEVASTATINGLY
AADEGOPRSSTTU POSTGRADUATES
AADEHHILMOORR HAEMORRHOIDAL
AADEHIILMOSSY HAEMODIALYSIS
AADEHIILNPSUZ SULPHADIAZINE
AADEHIKLMORSY HOLIDAYMAKERS
AADEHILNORSUY HYALURONIDASE
AADEHIMMMMNOS MOHAMMEDANISM
AADEHIMNORSTU DIATHERMANOUS
AADEHNORRSTTW NORTHEASTWARD
AADEHNORSSSUZ HAZARDOUSNESS
AADEHORSSTTUW SOUTHEASTWARD
AADEIIILNOSST IDEALISATIONS
AADEIIILNOSTZ IDEALIZATIONS
AADEIIIMNOSTT MEDIATISATION
AADEIIIMNOTTZ MEDIATIZATION
AADEIIILLMORTY MEDIATORIALLY
AADEIIILLMPRXY MAXILLIPEDARY
AADEIILMMNRST MALADMINISTER
AADEIIMNNORSV ANIMADVERSION
AADEIINOPSSST DISPASSIONATE
AADEIIPQRRTTU QUADRIPARTITE
AADEILMMORSTT MELODRAMATIST
AADEILMNORSST MALADROITNESS

AADEIMNNRSSSU RUSSIAN DESMAN
AADEINORRRTXY EXTRAORDINARY
AADEINRRSTTWW WITWATERSRAND
AADEJLMMNSTTU MALADJUSTMENT
AADELMOPRSTTY DERMATOPLASTY
AADEMNORSTTUY TETRADYNAMOUS
AADFFIKNRSSTT STIFF AND STARK
AADFILLOOPRSY APRIL FOOLS' DAY
AADFINNOORTUY FOUNDATIONARY
AADFINNOOSSTU SODA FOUNTAINS
AADGGIILNPRSY DISPARAGINGLY
AADGHIIKLMNOY HOLIDAYMAKING
AADGHIINNNRWZ WINNING HAZARD
AADGIIILNNTWY LADY-IN-WAITING
AADGIIMNOOSTT DOGMATISATION
AADGIIMNOOTTZ DOGMATIZATION
AADGILNNOPRST PROSTAGLANDIN
AADGIMNPRSSTT TRADING STAMPS
AADGINOPPRSST PROPAGANDISTS
AADHILNORRSTY SYNARTHRODIAL
AADHMNNOORTTW NOT WORTH A DAMN
AADIIIINOOSTTZ DIAZOTISATION
AADIIIINOOTTZZ DIAZOTIZATION
AADIILLNORTTY TRADITIONALLY
AADIIMNNOORST RANDOMISATION
AADIIMNNOORTZ RANDOMIZATION
AADIIMNNORRSTT ADMINISTRATOR
AAEEEEFFLMMSST FEMMES FATALES
AAEEEEFGHMMNOT NAME OF THE GAME
AAEEEEFLRSSTTW WELFARE STATES
AAEEEEGHLMPRST GREASE THE PALM
AAEEEEGLMMNRSS GERMAN MEASLES
AAEEEEGMNNRRRT REARRANGEMENT
AAEEEEHIILLSSS HAILE SELASSIE
AAEEEEHILPPRRT PRE-RAPHAELITE
AAEEEEHLNPRTTT PATENT LEATHER
AAEEEEILNNORRS SIERRA LEONEAN
AAEEEELMMNPRTT TEMPERAMENTAL
AAEEEELOPRSTTU POETS LAUREATE
AAEEEMNNNPRTVW PERMANENT WAVE
AAEEFFGNRSSTT STAFF SERGEANT
AAEEFGILLNNNS SELF-ANNEALING
AAEEFHORSTTTT STATE-OF-THE-ART
AAEEFKKMMNOOY MAKE A MONKEY OF
AAEEFMNNRRSTT TENANT FARMERS
AAEEFNNPRSSST SNAP FASTENERS
AAEEGGILMNRST MARAGING STEEL
AAEEGGILMORTV AGGLOMERATIVE
AAEEGGILNORST SEGREGATIONAL
AAEEGGINNOPRT GENERATION GAP
AAEEGGINORSTX EXAGGERATIONS
AAEEGGLNNOSTU TONE LANGUAGES
AAEEGHLOPPRRS PALEOGRAPHERS
AAEEGHMNOOSTU HAEMATOGENOUS
AAEEGIILMNRRS MARRIAGE LINES
AAEEGIILMPRTX EXEMPLI GRATIA
AAEEGIIMMPRST EPIGRAMMATISE
AAEEGIIMMPRTZ EPIGRAMMATIZE
AAEEGIIMNRRRT INTERMARRIAGE

AAEEGIIMNRSTV VEGETARIANISM
AAEEGIMMMNNST MISMANAGEMENT
AAEEGIMNRTTUV ARGUMENTATIVE
AAEEGINOPRSTU EUSPORANGIATE
AAEEGJLMNORRS MAJOR GENERALS
AAEEGJMNORRST SERGEANT MAJOR
AAEEGLPPPRSSU PURPLE PASSAGE
AAEEGNNNOORTT TARN-ET-GARONNE
AAEEHHIMPRSTT AMPHITHEATRES
AAEEHHMOPPSTT METAPHOSPHATE
AAEEHHORRSTTT HEART-TO-HEARTS
AAEEHIILNPSST ELEPHANTIASIS
AAEEHILLNNNPY PHENYLALANINE
AAEEHINPPRRST HEIRS APPARENT
AAEEHINSSSTTT ANAESTHETISTS
AAEEHLLLLOSVW ALLHALLOWS EVE
AAEEHMNOSTTUX EXANTHEMATOUS
AAEEHNORSSTTT EAST-NORTHEAST
AAEEHOSSSTTTU EAST-SOUTHEAST
AAEEIIILMMRST IMMATERIALISE
AAEEIIILMMRTZ IMMATERIALIZE
AAEEIIKKLLSTW WALKIE-TALKIES
AAEEIILMNNRTT INTERLAMINATE
AAEEIIMNNORTX RE-EXAMINATION
AAEEIINNRRSSV ANNIVERSARIES
AAEEIKLMNSSTT STATESMANLIKE
AAEEIKLNSSTTV TALKATIVENESS
AAEEILLNRSSTW ARTESIAN WELLS
AAEEILLNRTTVY ALTERNATIVELY
AAEEILMNRRSTW MINERAL WATERS
AAEEILNNNOPPT PENEPLANATION
AAEEILNOPRSTX EXPLANATORIES
AAEEILNRRSTTT TRANSLITERATE
AAEEILOPRTTVX EXTRAPOLATIVE
AAEEINNPRSTTY SPINY ANTEATER
AAEEINORRSTTU EURASIAN OTTER
AAEEINORSSSTV ASSEVERATIONS
AAEEKMMNPRSTU AMUSEMENT PARK
AAEELNPRRRTTU PRETERNATURAL
AAEEMNNPRSTWY PERMANENT WAYS
AAEEMPPRRSSTU SEMPER PARATUS
AAEEMQRRRSTTU QUARTERMASTER
AAEEQRRSSTTUV QUARTERSTAVES
AAEERRRSSTTUU RESTAURATEURS
AAEFFIILMNORR FORAMINIFERAL
AAEFFIILMRTVY AFFIRMATIVELY
AAEFFIIMNORRT REAFFIRMATION
AAEFFINOORSTT AFFORESTATION
AAEFFQRRSSTTU QUARTERSTAFFS
AAEFGILLLMNST FLAGELLANTISM
AAEFGIMNNORTT FRAGMENTATION
AAEFHHLOSSUWY HALFWAY HOUSES
AAEFIIIILMRST FAMILIARITIES
AAEFIIMNNOSTT MANIFESTATION
AAEFILMNOORRT REFORMATIONAL
AAEFILNQRRSTU QUARTERFINALS
AAEFMORRSSSTT MASTERS OF ARTS
AAEGGGILMNORT AGGLOMERATING
AAEGGHHIIOPRS HAGIOGRAPHIES

AAEGGHHILNNUY LAUGHING HYENA
AAEGGIILNTTUV AGGLUTINATIVE
AAEGGILMNOORT AGGLOMERATION
AAEGGIMNNOORT AGGIORNAMENTO
AAEGGINRSSTTT STARTING GATES
AAEGGLNOOPRTU PROTOLANGUAGE
AAEGHHIKMRRTW HIGH-WATER MARK
AAEGHHOPPRRSY PHRASEOGRAPHY
AAEGHIILMNOPR GERMANOPHILIA
AAEGHILMOOSTT HAEMATOLOGIST
AAEGHIPRRRSTT STRATIGRAPHER
AAEGHLLMOPRTY METALLOGRAPHY
AAEGHLLNNOSTT TEN-GALLON HATS
AAEGHLOPPSYYZ ZYGAPOPHYSEAL
AAEGHLOPRTTUY TELAUTOGRAPHY
AAEGHNOOPRRTY ORGANOTHERAPY
AAEGIIILMNRTZ MATERIALIZING
AAEGIIILMNTVY IMAGINATIVELY
AAEGIILLLORST LEGISLATORIAL
AAEGIILLMRSTY MAGISTERIALLY
AAEGIILNNTTTY TANGENTIALITY
AAEGIIMMMPRST EPIGRAMMATISM
AAEGIIMMPRSTT EPIGRAMMATIST
AAEGIIMNNORST GERMANISATION
AAEGIIMNNORTZ GERMANIZATION
AAEGIIMNNOSTT MAGNETISATION
AAEGIINNNOTTZ MAGNETIZATION
AAEGIIMNNQQSUU QUINQUAGESIMA
AAEGIKLNPPRSW WALKING PAPERS
AAEGILLMNOOPT MEGALOPOLITAN
AAEGILNOPRTTX EXTRAPOLATING
AAEGIMNNORTTU ARGUMENTATION
AAEGIMNNOSTTU AUGMENTATIONS
AAEGINNOPSTTV VANTAGE POINTS
AAEGINOORSTTY GEOSTATIONARY
AAEGLLNOOOPTY PALAEONTOLOGY
AAEGLLOOOOPYZ PALAEOZOOLOGY
AAEGMOPPSSSTT POSTAGE STAMPS
AAEHHILLNORTY A ROLL IN THE HAY
AAEHHILMOPRTX XEROPHTHALMIA
AAEHIIILMNSSS LEISHMANIASIS
AAEHIIIMNNSTT ANTIHISTAMINE
AAEHIIORTTTUV AUTHORITATIVE
AAEHIMNPSSSTT STATESMANSHIP
AAEHINNNOQRTU ANTHRAQUINONE
AAEHINPRSSSTY PARASYNTHESIS
AAEHNNOPRSTTY PARASYNTHETON
AAEIIILMMMRST IMMATERIALISM
AAEIIILMMRSTT IMMATERIALIST
AAEIIILMMRTTY IMMATERIALITY
AAEIIILNNOSTT NATIONALITIES
AAEIIILNORSST SERIALISATION
AAEIIILNORSTZ SERIALIZATION
AAEIIIMNNPPRT IMPARIPINNATE
AAEIIKLMNPSST SEMIPALATINSK
AAEIILLMNOSTT METALLISATION
AAEIILLMNOTTZ METALLIZATION
AAEIILLMNRSTU UNILATERALISM
AAEIILLQTTUVY QUALITATIVELY

AAEIILMNNORTT TERMINATIONAL
AAEIILNNNORTT INTERNATIONAL
AAEIILNNOORTT ORIENTATIONAL
AAEIILNNORSTV VERNALISATION
AAEIILNNORTVZ VERNALIZATION
AAEIILNOPRRST RESPIRATIONAL
AAEIILNORRTTT TRILATERATION
AAEIIMNNNOSTX ANNEXATIONISM
AAEIIMNOOPRST ANISOMETROPIA
AAEIINNNOSTTX ANNEXATIONIST
AAEIINOPPPRRT INAPPROPRIATE
AAEILLNNOSSTY SENSATIONALLY
AAEILLNOOPRTY OPERATIONALLY
AAEILLNOPRTXY EXPLANATORILY
AAEILMNNORSTU MENSURATIONAL
AAEILMNOPRTTU PERMUTATIONAL
AAEILMOPPRTXY APPROXIMATELY
AAEILNNNNPSVY PENNSYLVANIAN
AAEILNNOPRRST INTRAPERSONAL
AAEILNOOORTTV LAEVOROTATION
AAEILNOOPRTTX EXTRAPOLATION
AAEILNORSTTWY SANITARY TOWEL
AAEILOPPPRRTY APPROPRIATELY
AAEILOPPRRRTY PREPARATORILY
AAEIMNNNOORTT ORNAMENTATION
AAEIMNORSSTTT STATIONMASTER
AAEINNNOSSTTU INSTANTANEOUS
AAEINNOPRSTTU SUPERNATATION
AAEKLMORRSTWW LOW-WATER MARKS
AAEKNOQRRSSUW NARROW SQUEAKS
AAELLMOOPRSTU SOMATOPLEURAL
AAELMMNNORRSU ROMAN NUMERALS
AAELNNNRSSTUU UNNATURALNESS
AAELNNPRRSTTY TRANSPARENTLY
AAELOOOORRTTVY LAEVOROTATORY
AAFFGHINPRSSU SUFFRAGANSHIP
AAFFIINNOPRRT NITROPARAFFIN
AAFGIIIILMNRZ FAMILIARIZING
AAFHINOOPRRST PARROT-FASHION
AAFIIILMNRTUY UNFAMILIARITY
AAFIILMNNNOST INFLAMMATIONS
AAFIILMNNOORT INFORMATIONAL
AAFIILMNOORST FORMALISATION
AAFIILMNOORTZ FORMALIZATION
AAFILMMNOORST MALFORMATIONS
AAGGIILNNOTTU AGGLUTINATION
AAGGILNNRSTTU STRANGULATING
AAGHHINOOPPRT ANTHROPOPHAGI
AAGHIILMNORTT ANTILOGARITHM
AAGHIINNNOSTW WASHINGTONIAN
AAGHIMNOOPRST MASTIGOPHORAN
AAGIIILMMNORT IMMIGRATIONAL
AAGIIILNNNOTZ NATIONALIZING
AAGIIILNNORTZ RATIONALIZING
AAGIIJNNOORST JARGONISATION
AAGIIJNNOORTZ JARGONIZATION
AAGIIKLNNPSTY PAINSTAKINGLY
AAGIILLNNPSTW WALL PAINTINGS
AAGIILLNNTTYZ TANTALIZINGLY

AAGIILMNOORST GLAMORISATION
AAGIILMNOORTZ GLAMORIZATION
AAGIILNNORTTU TRIANGULATION
AAGIILNORSTUV VULGARISATION
AAGIILNORTUVZ VULGARIZATION
AAGIILNRRTTUY TRIANGULARITY
AAGIIMNNPRSTY PRAYING MANTIS
AAGIIMNOPPRTX APPROXIMATING
AAGIINNOORSST ORGANISATIONS
AAGIINNOORSTZ ORGANIZATIONS
AAGIINNORSTUU INAUGURATIONS
AAGIINOPPPRRT APPROPRIATING
AAGILMMNNOSUY MAGNANIMOUSLY
AAGILNNNPRSTT TRANSPLANTING
AAGILNNORSTTU STRANGULATION
AAGILNOOOPRSZ ZOOSPORANGIAL
AAGIMNORRRSTT TRANSMIGRATOR
AAGINNOOSSTTW STATION WAGONS
AAGLMNOORSTUU GRANULOMATOUS
AAHHNOOPPRTTY ANTHROPOPATHY
AAHIILMMNSSTU MALTHUSIANISM
AAHIIMNNOORST HARMONISATION
AAHIIMNNOORTZ HARMONIZATION
AAHIINOORSTTU AUTHORISATION
AAHIINOORTTUZ AUTHORIZATION
AAHINOPSSSSTT SHOP ASSISTANT
AAIIILNNOPRST INSPIRATIONAL
AAIIILNNOPRTT TRIPOLITANIAN
AAIIILNNOPSTT PLATINISATION
AAIIILNNOPTTZ PLATINIZATION
AAIIILNOORSTV VARIOLISATION
AAIIILNOORTVZ VARIOLIZATION
AAIIILNORRTTY IRRATIONALITY
AAIIILNOSSTUV VISUALISATION
AAIIILNOSTUVZ VISUALIZATION
AAIIINOPRSTTV PRIVATISATION
AAIIINOPRTTVZ PRIVATIZATION
AAIIINOPSSSTV PASSIVISATION
AAIIINOPSSTVZ PASSIVIZATION
AAIILLMNNOTTU MULTINATIONAL
AAIILLNNOSSTT INSTALLATIONS
AAIILLNOPRSTU PLURALISATION
AAIILLNOPRTUZ PLURALIZATION
AAIILMNNOORST NORMALISATION
AAIILMNNOORTZ NORMALIZATION
AAIILMNNOPSTU MANIPULATIONS
AAIILMNOOPTTT TOTIPALMATION
AAIILNOSSSTTV SALVATIONISTS
AAIILNPSTTVYY NATIVITY PLAYS
AAIIMMNNORSSTU SUMMARISATION
AAIIMMNORSTUZ SUMMARIZATION
AAIIMNOOPPRTX APPROXIMATION
AAIIMNORRSTTY MARTYRISATION
AAIIMNORRTTYZ MARTYRIZATION
AAIINNOPRRSTT TRANSPIRATION
AAIINOOPPPRRT APPROPRIATION
AAIJLMMOORRTY MORAL MAJORITY
AAIKLNNOPRSSW PARKINSON'S LAW
AAIKMNOOQRTTU QUOTATION MARK

AAILLMOOPPSTU PAPILLOMATOUS
AAILLMOPRSTYY MORALITY PLAYS
AAILNNOPPSTTU SUPPLANTATION
AAILNNORSTTTU NATIONAL TRUST
AAIMNNORSTTTU TRANSMUTATION
AAINOPRRRSTTY TRANSPIRATORY
AALMOOPSSTTTY STOMATOPLASTY
AANNORRSSTUUY TYRANNOSAURUS
ABBBEHLMORSTU BLABBERMOUTHS
ABBCDEEIILNRS INDESCRIBABLE
ABBCDEIILNRSY INDESCRIBABLY
ABBCEEIJLNOOT OBJECTIONABLE
ABBCEGIKLNRRY BLACKBERRYING
ABBCEGILNOPUU BUBONIC PLAGUE
ABBCEHHIRSTTU RABBIT HUTCHES
ABBCEHILNORTU BRONCHIAL TUBE
ABBCEHINPRSTU RABBIT PUNCHES
ABBCEHKOORRSS SHOCK ABSORBER
ABBCEIJLNOOTY OBJECTIONABLY
ABBCGHIIILOPR BIBLIOGRAPHIC
ABBCIIILOPRST PROBABILISTIC
ABBDEEFNORSTU BEAST OF BURDEN
ABBDEEMPRRSTU RUBBER-STAMPED
ABBDEIILRSTTU DISTRIBUTABLE
ABBDEILLNORTU BULLETIN BOARD
ABBDFFILMNNSU BLIND MAN'S BUFF
ABBEEHILLPRSU REPUBLISHABLE
ABBEEILLMNRTY BLANTYRE-LIMBE
ABBEEILMPRRTU IMPERTURBABLE
ABBEELMMNOOTZ BAMBOOZLEMENT
ABBEGGHINORTY BIG BANG THEORY
ABBEGHIILOPRR BIBLIOGRAPHER
ABBEGILNORRSU RABBLE-ROUSING
ABBEIIILOPRST PROBABILITIES
ABBEIILLMORRY MOBILE LIBRARY
ABBEILMPRRTUY IMPERTURBABLY
ABBEILSSTTTUU SUBSTITUTABLE
ABBGINOOPPRTY BOOBY TRAPPING
ABBIIILMOPRTY IMPROBABILITY
ABCCDEEIKLMOS BLACK COMEDIES
ABCCDEHILORSU COACHBUILDERS
ABCCDENORSTTU SUBCONTRACTED
ABCCDIILLMORU UMBILICAL CORD
ABCCEEIILNNOV INCONCEIVABLE
ABCCEGIILLOOO BIOECOLOGICAL
ABCCEIIILMPTY IMPECCABILITY
ABCCEIIILSSTY ACCESSIBILITY
ABCCEIILLMORS SOCIAL CLIMBER
ABCCEIILNNOVY INCONCEIVABLY
ABCCEIILORTTY BACTERIOLYTIC
ABCCEIIMMNRTU CIRCUMAMBIENT
ABCCEIINRRSSU CABIN CRUISERS
ABCCEIMMORTUY MYCOBACTERIUM
ABCCHHIIOPRRS ARCHBISHOPRIC
ABCCILMNOPPUY PUBLIC COMPANY
ABCCNOORRSTTU SUBCONTRACTOR
ABCDDEEIILRST DISCREDITABLE
ABCDDEEILTTUX TAX-DEDUCTIBLE
ABCDDEIILRSTY DISCREDITABLY

ABCDDEIINOORX CARBON DIOXIDE
ABCDDGIKLNPSU BLACK PUDDINGS
ABCDEEEGHNRST BERCHTESGADEN
ABCDEEEINORRT DECEREBRATION
ABCDEEELMMNOR RECOMMENDABLE
ABCDEEHILPTTT PITCHED BATTLE
ABCDEEIILOPRT PERIODIC TABLE
ABCDEEIIMOSTY BASIDIOMYCETE
ABCDEEILNNNOS INCONDENSABLE
ABCDEEILNPRTU UNPREDICTABLE
ABCDEELLOPRST CORPS DE BALLET
ABCDEEMNOOPRY BEYOND COMPARE
ABCDEHIOPSSTX DISPATCH BOXES
ABCDEHNORSSTY BODY SNATCHERS
ABCDEIIILLNPS DISCIPLINABLE
ABCDEIIILMRTU MIRABILE DICTU
ABCDEIIILNTUY INEDUCABILITY
ABCDEIIILPRTY PREDICABILITY
ABCDEIIILPSTY DESPICABILITY
ABCDEIILLOQTU QUODLIBETICAL
ABCDEIIILLTUXY EXCLUDABILITY
ABCDEILORRRRY RECORD LIBRARY
ABCDEKNORRSTU ROUND BRACKETS
ABCDIIIILNTVY VINDICABILITY
ABCDIIIILLPTUY DUPLICABILITY
ABCDILNOOOSTT ODONTOBLASTIC
ABCEEEELNRSSX EXECRABLENESS
ABCEEEFIIINRS BENEFICIARIES
ABCEEEFIILLRT ELECTRIFIABLE
ABCEEEFILLNNU INFLUENCEABLE
ABCEEEHMMRRRT CHARTER MEMBER
ABCEEEIINNRST BICENTENARIES
ABCEEEIILNOPTX EXCEPTIONABLE
ABCEEEILNRSUV UNSERVICEABLE
ABCEEEILORRRV IRRECOVERABLE
ABCEEEELMNOPRS RECOMPENSABLE
ABCEEELNSSSUX EXCUSABLENESS
ABCEEHILLPTUW THE PUBLIC WEAL
ABCEEHILNORSV OLIVE BRANCHES
ABCEEHIMNRSTY CHIMNEYBREAST
ABCEEIILNPRSU REPUBLICANISE
ABCEEIILNPRUZ REPUBLICANIZE
ABCEEILMOORSU BROMELIACEOUS
ABCEEILNNOSTT INCONTESTABLE
ABCEEILNOPRRS CEREBROSPINAL
ABCEEILORRRVY IRRECOVERABLY
ABCEEILRRSTTU BATTLE CRUISER
ABCEEJMRSTTUU SUBJECT MATTER
ABCEELMMNORSU COMMENSURABLE
ABCEELNNOOPRU PRONOUNCEABLE
ABCEENOORRSSS BEAR ONE'S CROSS
ABCEENOPRRSTU PROTUBERANCES
ABCEFGIIILNNT FILING CABINET
ABCEFGIILMMNR CLIMBING FRAME
ABCEFHIILLMRU LIEBFRAUMILCH
ABCEFIIINORTV VERBIFICATION
ABCEFINOORRSU CARBONIFEROUS
ABCEFLMNNOORU UNCONFORMABLE
ABCEFLMNOORTU UNCOMFORTABLE

ABCEGHIMNNSUU SUBMACHINE GUN
ABCEGHORRRSTU TURBOCHARGERS
ABCEGIINNOOSU BIGNONIACEOUS
ABCEGILLMOORY EMBRYOLOGICAL
ABCEGINORRSSZ ZEBRA CROSSING
ABCEHILSSTTTY CHASTITY BELTS
ABCEHIRRRRSSU CRUSH BARRIERS
ABCEHLOOPRSTU CLAUSTROPHOBE
ABCEHOPRRSTUY BRACHYPTEROUS
ABCEIIILNNTUY ENUNCIABILITY
ABCEIIILNOTTY NOTICEABILITY
ABCEIILLMORTY BIOMETRICALLY
ABCEIILMNPRSU REPUBLICANISM
ABCEIILNOPRTU REPUBLICATION
ABCEIILORSSTY BACTERIOLYSIS
ABCEIIMNNOORT RECOMBINATION
ABCEIINORSSTT OBSTETRICIANS
ABCEIIRSSTTUW WATER BISCUITS
ABCEILLLPSTTU PLASTIC BULLET
ABCEILLMNORYY EMBRYONICALLY
ABCEILLORSTTY OBSTETRICALLY
ABCEILNNOSTTY INCONTESTABLY
ABCEILNORTTUU TUBERCULATION
ABCEILNSSSSSU BUSINESS CLASS
ABCEILOORSSTU STROBILACEOUS
ABCEILORRRTUU ARBORICULTURE
ABCEIOOOORRRTV CORROBORATIVE
ABCEKKLNRSSSU BRASS KNUCKLES
ABCELNORSSTTU COUNTERBLASTS
ABCFLMNOORTUY UNCOMFORTABLY
ABCGGHINORRTU TURBOCHARGING
ABCGHIKLNSSUW SWASHBUCKLING
ABCGIKLNORSTT STARTING BLOCK
ABCGINOOORRRT CORROBORATING
ABCHHINOOPRST OPISTHOBRANCH
ABCHILLMOPSTY LYMPHOBLASTIC
ABCHILOOPRSTT TROPHOBLASTIC
ABCIIIILLNOTUY INOCULABILITY
ABCIIIILLNPTUY INCULPABILITY
ABCIIIILMOPTTY COMPATIBILITY
ABCIIIILNOSTUY UNSOCIABILITY
ABCIIILLOPRSTT TRIPLOBLASTIC
ABCIILMOPTTUY COMPUTABILITY
ABCIILNOPPRSY PRINCIPAL BOYS
ABCILNOORSTTU OBSTRUCTIONAL
ABCIMNNNOOOOP BOON COMPANION
ABCINOOOORRRT CORROBORATION
ABCLRRSSSTUUU SUBSTRUCTURAL
ABCOOOOORRRRST CORROBORATORS
ABDDDEEEEFHRT FEATHERBEDDED
ABDDDEILMNORY BROADMINDEDLY
ABDDEEEGHINSS BIGHEADEDNESS
ABDDEEELLORSU DOUBLE-DEALERS
ABDDEEFILNNOY BADLY IN NEED OF
ABDDEEGILLNOU DOUBLE-DEALING
ABDDEEHIILNNR HILDEBRANDINE
ABDDEEHLLORSU SHOULDER BLADE
ABDDEEHLRTUYY BUTYRALDEHYDE
ABDDEEIILNPTY DEPENDABILITY

ABDDEFHLLNOOS FLESH AND BLOOD
ABDDEILNNNSSS SAND-BLINDNESS
ABDDGINNOORSU SOUNDING BOARD
ABDEEEEHLNPRR REPREHENDABLE
ABDEEEFLORTUU DOUBLE FEATURE
ABDEEEGKLLNOW KNOWLEDGEABLE
ABDEEEHKNORRT BROKEN-HEARTED
ABDEEEHLNOPTY BEYOND THE PALE
ABDEEEIILMRTY REDEEMABILITY
ABDEEEILMNNST DISENABLEMENT
ABDEEFGIRSSSU FIGURED BASSES
ABDEEFGLMOORR GAMBREL-ROOFED
ABDEEFIIILRSV DIVERSIFIABLE
ABDEEGIILNRST DISINTEGRABLE
ABDEEGILNRSST DRESSING TABLE
ABDEEGKLLNOWY KNOWLEDGEABLY
ABDEEIILNNNTV VENETIAN BLIND
ABDEEIILNNPSS INDISPENSABLE
ABDEEIILNORST DELIBERATIONS
ABDEEIILNPTXY EXPENDABILITY
ABDEEIILSTTTY DETESTABILITY
ABDEEIIMRTTXY AMBIDEXTERITY
ABDEEILMNOPRS IMPONDERABLES
ABDEEKNORRRSS BANKER'S ORDERS
ABDEFIILLORRT DEFIBRILLATOR
ABDEGGILLNOUZ DOUBLE-GLAZING
ABDEGHINOORSU BOARDINGHOUSE
ABDEGIIILNSTZ DESTABILIZING
ABDEGIKLLNOTU DOUBLE-TALKING
ABDEGIKLNOPRU DOUBLE-PARKING
ABDEGILLLNNSY BELLY-LANDINGS
ABDEHHNOSSSUU HOUSE HUSBANDS ·
ABDEHILMNNSST BLANDISHMENTS
ABDEHILNOORSU DISHONOURABLE
ABDEIILNNPSSY INDISPENSABLY
ABDEIILNOPRTY PONDERABILITY
ABDEIINNORSTU INSUBORDINATE
ABDEIINORSTUV SUBORDINATIVE
ABDEILLNOOOORT BLOOD RELATION
ABDEMOORRSTTW BOTTOM DRAWERS
ABDFGIIILLNOS BILLS OF LADING
ABDFIIIILMOTY MODIFIABILITY
ABDFIIILMORTY FORMIDABILITY
ABDGIIKNORRST SKIRTING BOARD
ABDGIINNOORRS IRONING BOARDS
ABDGIINNORSTU SUBORDINATING
ABDHIIINORSTY HYBRIDISATION
ABDHIIINORTYZ HYBRIDIZATION
ABDHILNOORSUY DISHONOURABLY
ABDIIIILMSSTY ADMISSIBILITY
ABDIIIILNOSSUV SUBDIVISIONAL
ABDIIIILOPSSTY DISPOSABILITY
ABDIIIILPSTTUY DISPUTABILITY
ABDIIINOSSSTU SUBSIDISATION
ABDIIINOSSTUZ SUBSIDIZATION
ABDIINNOORSTU SUBORDINATION
ABDILLMNNOPTU PLATINUM-BLOND
ABDMOOOORRTTU OUTBOARD MOTOR
ABEEEEFLNORSU UNFORESEEABLE

ABEEEEILMMPRS SEMIPERMEABLE
ABEEEEIRRRTVV REVERBERATIVE
ABEEEEELNPRRST REPRESENTABLE
ABEEEFIILLMPX EXEMPLIFIABLE
ABEEEGINRRRTV REVERBERATING
ABEEEHILNPPRS APPREHENSIBLE
ABEEEHKORRSSU HOUSEBREAKERS
ABEEEHLOPRSST OBLATE SPHERES
ABEEEIILLPRRV IRREPLEVIABLE
ABEEEIILRRRTV IRRETRIEVABLE
ABEEEIKKRRRST STRIKEBREAKER
ABEEEILMNRSSS MISERABLENESS
ABEEEILMNSSST ESTIMABLENESS
ABEEEILNPRRTT INTERPRETABLE
ABEEEILNQSSTU EQUITABLENESS
ABEEEILNRSSTV VERITABLENESS
ABEEEIMMPRRTV PRIVATE MEMBER
ABEEEINORRRTV REVERBERATION
ABEEEINRRSTTV INVERTEBRATES
ABEEELLMNSSSS BLAMELESSNESS
ABEEELLNORSST TOLERABLENESS
ABEEELNRSSTTU UTTERABLENESS
ABEEELOOPSTTT POTATO BEETLES
ABEEEORRRRTVY REVERBERATORY
ABEEFFIMMORRT FAR BE IT FROM ME
ABEEFGIILNRRR IRREFRANGIBLE
ABEEFGLNORTTU UNFORGETTABLE
ABEEFHOPRSTTT THE BEST PART OF
ABEEFIILNOPRS PERSONIFIABLE
ABEEFIILPRRTY PREFERABILITY
ABEEGHHLPRSTU BUSH TELEGRAPH
ABEEGHIKNORSU HOUSEBREAKING
ABEEGHLORSTTT GHETTO BLASTER
ABEEGILMNNRS NEGRI SEMBILAN
ABEEGIKNPSSTU SPEAKING TUBES
ABEEGILNORRVY OVERBEARINGLY
ABEEGILNOSSST BLASTOGENESIS
ABEEHIILNSTUX INEXHAUSTIBLE
ABEEHILMNSSTT ESTABLISHMENT
ABEEHILRRSSTW WELSH RAREBITS
ABEEHKLNORRTY HEARTBROKENLY
ABEEIIILLRRSUV AUBERVILLIERS
ABEEIILMPRTTY TEMPERABILITY
ABEEIILNNORTV INVENTORIABLE
ABEEIILNPRTTY PENETRABILITY
ABEEIILRRRTVY IRRETRIEVABLY
ABEEIIOOPRRRT RIBEIRAO PRETO
ABEEILLMNSSSY ASSEMBLY LINES
ABEEILLRSSTVY LIVERY STABLES
ABEEILMNNNOTU UNMENTIONABLE
ABEEILMNRRSSU SERIAL NUMBERS
ABEEILNNRSSSS BRAINLESSNESS
ABEEILNNSTTUU SUBLIEUTENANT
ABEEILNOORTTX EXTORTIONABLE
ABEEINPRRSSTY PRESBYTERIANS
ABEEIOORRSSTV OBSERVATORIES
ABEEKLMORRSTU TROUBLEMAKERS
ABEEKMNNORTUY MOUNTEBANKERY
ABEELNNNORRTU NONRETURNABLE

ABEFGLNORTTUY   UNFORGETTABLY
ABEFHHILLLOST   BILLS OF HEALTH
ABEFHOOOPRSTT   A SPOT OF BOTHER
ABEFIIILLRTTY   FILTERABILITY
ABEFIILNORRRU   NEUROFIBRILAR
ABEFLLOOORSUV   LABOURS OF LOVE
ABEGGIIIMSTUU   AMBIGUGUITIES
ABEGIIILNOTTY   NEGOTIABILITY
ABEGIIILNRTTY   INTEGRABILITY
ABEGIILNORTVY   GOVERNABILITY
ABEGILLLNOSWY   BOWLING ALLEYS
ABEGILNOPPRTT   BLOTTING PAPER
ABEGIMNOSSSUU   AMBIGUOUSNESS
ABEHHINNOORST   HEATH ROBINSON
ABEHIIILPRSTY   PERISHABILITY
ABEHIILNSTUXY   INEXHAUSTIBLY
ABEHIIORSSTUV   BEHAVIOURISTS
ABEHILNORRSTW   BROTHERS-IN-LAW
ABEHLLMOPSSUY   BLASPHEMOUSLY
ABEIIILNSSTT   INSTABILITIES
ABEIIIILNTTVY   INEVITABILITY
ABEIIIILNRTUY   UNRELIABILITY
ABEIIILMNRTTY   TERMINABILITY
ABEIIILNOPRTY   INOPERABILITY
ABEIIILNOQRTU   EQUILIBRATION
ABEIIILNORTXY   INEXORABILITY
ABEIIILNPSTXY   EXPANSIBILITY
ABEIIILPRRSTY   RESPIRABILITY
ABEIIILMOPTYY   EMPLOYABILITY
ABEIIILNRTUVY   VULNERABILITY
ABEIIILLORSTVY   RESOLVABILITY
ABEIIILMNRSSST   TRANSMISSIBLE
ABEIIILNRRTTUY   RETURNABILITY
ABEIIILOPRTTXY   EXPORTABILITY
ABEIIILRTTTUVY   ATTRIBUTIVELY
ABEIIMNOSSSTU   AMBITIOUSNESS
ABEIIMOORSTUV   OVERAMBITIOUS
ABEIINSSSTTUV   SUBSTANTIVISE
ABEIINSSTTUVZ   SUBSTANTIVIZE
ABEILNOORSSSU   LABORIOUSNESS
ABEILNOPPRSTU   INSUPPORTABLE
ABEILNSSTTUVY   SUBSTANTIVELY
ABEIMNNOSSSUW   BUSINESSWOMAN
ABEINNORSTUVY   SUBVENTIONARY
ABELLLLOPSSYY   POLYSYLLABLES
ABELLLMNOOSSY   MONOSYLLABLES
ABELNOPRRTTUY   PROTUBERANTLY
ABFGHIILLORTT   BIT OF ALL RIGHT
ABFIIIILLLNTY   INFALLIBILITY
ABFIIILOPRTTY   PROFITABILITY
ABFLLLOOOOPST   FOOTBALL POOLS
ABGGIILOOORST   AGROBIOLOGIST
ABGHIIMMNSSTW   SWIMMING BATHS
ABGIIIILNNTTY   INTANGIBILITY
ABGIIINORRSTU   SUBIRRIGATION
ABGIIMNNORRST   BRAINSTORMING
ABHIIILNPSTUY   PUNISHABILITY
ABHIIINOORSTV   VASOINHIBITOR
ABIIIILMNTTY   INIMITABILITY

ABIIIILLNOTVY   INVIOLABILITY
ABIIIILMPRTTY   IMPARTIBILITY
ABIIIILLNOSTVY   INSOLVABILITY
ABIIIILMNOOSST   MOBILISATIONS
ABIIIILMNOOSTZ   MOBILIZATIONS
ABIIILMOPRTVY   IMPROVABILITY
ABIIILNOOSSTT   ABOLITIONISTS
ABIIILNOSSTTU   SUBTILISATION
ABIIILNOSTTUZ   SUBTILIZATION
ABIIILNSTTUUY   UNSUITABILITY
ABIIILRSTUVVY   SURVIVABILITY
ABIILMNNNTTUU   TINTINNABULUM
ABIILMNOOSSTY   SYMBOLISATION
ABIILMNOOSTYZ   SYMBOLIZATION
ABIILMORRTTUV   MULTIVIBRATOR
ABILLMMNOOSSY   MONOSYLLABISM
ABILMMNOSSSTU   SOMNAMBULISTS
ABILNOOPPSTUU   SUBPOPULATION
ACCCDEEEINNNS   INCANDESCENCE
ACCCDEINORTTU   CREDIT ACCOUNT
ACCCEEEELNNOSV   CONVALESCENCE
ACCCEEHIILRRT   ELECTRIC CHAIR
ACCCEEIILNOSS   SOCIAL SCIENCE
ACCCEEIILSSST   ECCLESIASTICS
ACCCEEILLNRTY   ECCENTRICALLY
ACCCEFFIILRRT   TRAFFIC CIRCLE
ACCCEHILMMMOR   MICROCHEMICAL
ACCCEHIILMOPR   MICROCEPHALIC
ACCCEHIINORTT   ARCHITECTONIC
ACCCEIMMNOOOR   MACROECONOMIC
ACCCEIMNRSSTU   CIRCUMSTANCES
ACCCELOOPRSTT   STREPTOCOCCAL
ACCCENNOOOVVX   CONCAVO-CONVEX
ACCCGHILLNOOO   CONCHOLOGICAL
ACCCHILOOPSTY   STAPHYLOCOCCI
ACCCIIILMMORT   MICROCLIMATIC
ACCCIIKKLOSTT   COCKTAIL STICK
ACCCIIMNOOTTY   ACTINOMYCOTIC
ACCCILOPRSTTY   CRYPTOCLASTIC
ACCDDEEHRRSTU   STARCH-REDUCED
ACCDEEEFINORS   CONFEDERACIES
ACCDEEENNNRST   TRANSCENDENCE
ACCDEEGHNORRR   RECORD-CHANGER
ACCDEEHHORRST   SCORCHED EARTH
ACCDEEIILNOST   OCCIDENTALISE
ACCDEEIILNOTZ   OCCIDENTALIZE
ACCDEEIINPRSS   DISCREPANCIES
ACCDEEILNOPSY   ENCYCLOPEDIAS
ACCDEEINNOPRT   ACCIDENT-PRONE
ACCDEELOOPRSU   CAPE COLOUREDS
ACCDEENNNRSTY   TRANSCENDENCY
ACCDEGNNORRST   CONCERT GRANDS
ACCDEHHIKLLTY   LATCHKEY CHILD
ACCDEHHILOPRY   HYDROCEPHALIC
ACCDEHHNRRSUW   CHURCHWARDENS
ACCDEHINOORTW   WITH ONE ACCORD
ACCDEIIKLOOPS   KALEIDOSCOPIC
ACCDEIILMNOST   OCCIDENTALISM
ACCDEIILNNOOT   CODECLINATION

ACCDEIILNOSTT OCCIDENTALIST
ACCDEIINOORTT DECORTICATION
ACCDEIINORTTV CONTRADICTIVE
ACCDEILLMOPTY COMPLICATEDLY
ACCDEILMNOPTU UNCOMPLICATED
ACCDENNORSTUY COUNTRY DANCES
ACCDFIIINOOST CODIFICATIONS
ACCDGIINNORTT CONTRADICTING
ACCDHHINOOPRY HYPOCHONDRIAC
ACCDHIILORSTV CLAVICHORDIST
ACCDHIILPRSUU SULPHURIC ACID
ACCDHIMNOPSYY PSYCHODYNAMIC
ACCDHINOSTTUU DUTCH AUCTIONS
ACCDIIILNSSTY SYNDICALISTIC
ACCDIIINORSTY IDIOSYNCRATIC
ACCDIILLLNRYY CYLINDRICALLY
ACCDIIMMNNOOU INCOMMUNICADO
ACCDIINNOORTT CONTRADICTION
ACCDILNOORRTU CONDUCTOR RAIL
ACCDINOOORRTY CONTRADICTORY
ACCEEEEGHOSTT COTTAGE CHEESE
ACCEEEELLNPRX PAR EXCELLENCE
ACCEEEELMORRT ACCELEROMETER
ACCEEEGHIRRSV SERVICE CHARGE
ACCEEEHILLNPT TELENCEPHALIC
ACCEEEHILLNRS CHANCELLERIES
ACCEEEHILMNPS MESENCEPHALIC
ACCEEEHILMNPT METENCEPHALIC
ACCEEEILLORST ECCLESIOLATER
ACCEEFFIILRSS SELF-SACRIFICE
ACCEEFIIIPSTV SPECIFICATIVE
ACCEEGHILNTYY EYE-CATCHINGLY
ACCEEGHKNOSTX STOCK EXCHANGE
ACCEEGHNNORSX CORN EXCHANGES
ACCEEGHNORRTU COUNTERCHARGE
ACCEEHHLOORST SCHOOLTEACHER
ACCEEHILLNOTY ACETYLCHOLINE
ACCEEHILMOPRT CEPHALOMETRIC,
    PETROCHEMICAL
ACCEEHMNNORST ENCROACHMENTS
ACCEEHORRSTTY OYSTERCATCHER
ACCEEIILLNRTV INTERCLAVICLE
ACCEEIILMMNSU ECUMENICALISM
ACCEEIILMMORS COMMERCIALISE
ACCEEIILMMORZ COMMERCIALIZE
ACCEEIILORSSV SOCIAL SERVICE
ACCEEIIMORRST MERITOCRACIES
ACCEEIIOPRRTV RECIPROCATIVE
ACCEEIKLNOPRS COCKER SPANIEL
ACCEEIILLORSTY ECCLESIOLATRY
ACCEEILNOPSTU CONCEPTUALISE
ACCEEILNOPTUZ CONCEPTUALIZE
ACCEEILNPSSST SCEPTICALNESS
ACCEEILNQSTUY ACQUIESCENTLY
ACCEEILORSTTT ELECTROSTATIC
ACCEEIMMNOTUX EXCOMMUNICATE
ACCEEINNORSSV CONSERVANCIES
ACCEEINNORTTV CONCENTRATIVE
ACCEEINOPRTTV CONTRACEPTIVE

ACCEEINORSSSS ACCESSORINESS
ACCEEINORTTUV COUNTERACTIVE
ACCEELLMMOORU MACROMOLECULE
ACCEELNNOSSTT CONTACT LENSES
ACCEELNNOSSTV CONVALESCENTS
ACCEEMNORSTTU ACCOUTREMENTS
ACCEEOOORRSSTU STERCORACEOUS
ACCEFFIIINOSU INEFFICACIOUS
ACCEFFIILOSUY EFFICACIOUSLY
ACCEFIIINOPST SPECIFICATION
ACCEFIIINORTT CERTIFICATION,
    RECTIFICATION
ACCEFIIORRTTY CERTIFICATORY
ACCEFINNOORTY CONFECTIONARY
ACCEFIOOPRTTU OUT OF PRACTICE
ACCEGHHIOOPRR CHOREOGRAPHIC
ACCEGHIILOPRX LEXICOGRAPHIC
ACCEGHILLNOOT TECHNOLOGICAL
ACCEGHILNNORY ENCROACHINGLY
ACCEGIILLLOOX LEXICOLOGICAL
ACCEGIINNNORT CONCERTINAING
ACCEGIINOPRRT RECIPROCATING
ACCEGILMNOORT CONGLOMERATIC
ACCEGINNNNOTU COUNTENANCING
ACCEGINNNORTT CONCENTRATING
ACCEGINNORTTU COUNTERACTING
ACCEGINOOORRTT GERONTOCRATIC
ACCEGIOPPRRTU GROUP PRACTICE
ACCEHHIILMOST HISTOCHEMICAL
ACCEHHIINSSTT CHAIN STITCHES
ACCEHHILMOOPT PHOTOCHEMICAL
ACCEHHILOOPRT ORTHOCEPHALIC
ACCEHHORRSSTT RORSCHACH TEST
ACCEHIILLNSST CALLISTHENICS
ACCEHIILNOPRS NECROPHILIACS
ACCEHIILPRRTY HYPERCRITICAL
ACCEHIKLLMOOT MILK CHOCOLATE
ACCEHIKMNSSTY CHIMNEYSTACKS
ACCEHILLOOPSS SPECIAL SCHOOL
ACCEHIMNORSST CHROMATICNESS
ACCEHINNNOPST PANTECHNICONS
ACCEHIOOPSSTT TACHISTOSCOPE
ACCEIIKLNOSTW ANTICLOCKWISE
ACCEIIKNNPRST PANIC-STRICKEN
ACCEIILMMMORS COMMERCIALISM
ACCEIILMMORST COMMERCIALIST
ACCEIILMMORTY COMMERCIALITY
ACCEIILMNOSSS NEOCLASSICISM
ACCEIILNOSSST NEOCLASSICIST
ACCEIILOPRRTY RECIPROCALITY
ACCEIIMMNOTUV COMMUNICATIVE
ACCEIINNNOSST INCONSTANCIES
ACCEIINOOPRRT RECIPROCATION
ACCEIIOPPRSSU PERSPICACIOUS
ACCEIILLNNOUY NUCLEONICALLY
ACCEILLMNOPSU NUCLEOPLASMIC
ACCEILMNNNOOP NONCOMPLIANCE
ACCEILMNOPSTU CONCEPTUALISM
ACCEILMNORSTU COUNTERCLAIMS

ACCEILNNOSSTU CONSULTANCIES
ACCEILNOPSTTU CONCEPTUALIST
ACCEINNNOORTT CONCENTRATION
ACCEINNOOPRTT CONTRACEPTION
ACCEINNOORRTY CONCRETIONARY
ACCEINNOORSSY CONCESSIONARY
ACCEINNOORTTU COUNTERACTION
ACCEINOOPPRTU PREOCCUPATION
ACCEINOPPRSSU PERCUSSION CAP
ACCELOOPRRSST PECTORAL CROSS
ACCFGIIILNRSY SACRIFICINGLY
ACCFIIINOORST SCORIFICATION
ACCFIINNOOSST CONFISCATIONS
ACCFLMORSTUUU FRACTOCUMULUS
ACCGGHHIKNOSU HACKING COUGHS
ACCGHHHHIMNRU HIGH CHURCHMAN
ACCGHHINOOPRR CHRONOGRAPHIC
ACCGHHINORSST CROSS-HATCHING
ACCGHHIOPPRSY PSYCHOGRAPHIC
ACCGHIIKNORRS ROCKING CHAIRS
ACCGHIILMNOPS ACCOMPLISHING
ACCGHILLNOOOR CHRONOLOGICAL
ACCGHILLOOPSY PSYCHOLOGICAL
ACCGHIOPPRRTY CRYPTOGRAPHIC
ACCGIIILNRRUZ CIRCULARIZING
ACCGIILLMOOSU MUSICOLOGICAL
ACCGIILLOOOTX TOXICOLOGICAL
ACCGIIMMNNOTU COMMUNICATING
ACCGILLOOOPRT PROCTOLOGICAL
ACCGILNOOPRSY LARYNGOSCOPIC
ACCHHIMMOOORT HOMOCHROMATIC
ACCHIIILPSSTY PHYSICALISTIC
ACCHIILMOPRSY MICROPHYSICAL
ACCHIILMOSSST SCHOLASTICISM
ACCHIIMNOOPRT ACTINOMORPHIC
ACCHIIMORRSSU CHIAROSCURISM
ACCHIIORRSSTU CHIAROSCURIST
ACCHILLOOPRST CHLOROPLASTIC
ACCHILLOPSTYY PSYCHOTICALLY
ACCHILMMOOPRS CHROMOPLASMIC
ACCHILMOOPRTY POLYCHROMATIC
ACCHILOPPRSTY PROPHYLACTICS
ACCHIMMNOOORT MONOCHROMATIC
ACCHIMOOPSSTY PSYCHOSOMATIC
ACCHIOOPRRRST CHIROPRACTORS
ACCHIOOPRSSUZ SCHIZOCARPOUS
ACCIIILNNORTU IN CIRCULATION
ACCIIIMMNOOST ICONOMATICISM
ACCIIINNOPSTW IT WAS NO PICNIC
ACCIILLPRSTUU PISCICULTURAL
ACCIILMMNOSTU COMMUNALISTIC
ACCIILMNOOPST COMPLICATIONS
ACCIILNORTTTY CONTRACTILITY
ACCIIMMNNOOTU COMMUNICATION
ACCIIMNOOSSTY ACTINOMYCOSIS
ACCIIOORRSSTV VICTORIA CROSS
ACCIJLNNNOOTU CONJUNCTIONAL
ACCILMNNOOTTY CONCOMITANTLY
ACCIMMNOOORTUY COMMUNICATORY

ACCIMNOOOTTXY CYTOTAXONOMIC
ACDDEEEGSSTUU EDUCATED GUESS
ACDDEEEHHNNOR HENDECAHEDRON
ACDDEEEHIMSST SEMIDETACHEDS
ACDDEEEHINRUV UNDERACHIEVED
ACDDEEEILNRST DECENTRALISED
ACDDEEEILNRTZ DECENTRALIZED
ACDDEEEKMNOPR PROMENADE DECK
ACDDEEENOPRTT TOP DEAD CENTRE
ACDDEEFFILSTY DISAFFECTEDLY
ACDDEEGIKNNOR DEAD RECKONING
ACDDEEHHIITTW DICE WITH DEATH
ACDDEEHLLORTY COLD-HEARTEDLY
ACDDEEIMNOOTY ADENOIDECTOMY
ACDDEELNOORSS SECOND SEA LORD
ACDDEEMNNORTU COUNTERMANDED
ACDDEENRSSTUV SEVEN-CARD STUD
ACDDEFHIINRSS DISFRANCHISED
ACDDEGHILNNRR GRANDCHILDREN
ACDDEGIILLNOS DIALLING CODES
ACDDEGILLNOOR DENDROLOGICAL
ACDDEGLLNSSTU DUCTLESS GLAND
ACDDEHIILMOSU DICHLAMIDEOUS
ACDDEHIMNOOPS DODECAPHONISM
ACDDEHINOOPST DODECAPHONIST
ACDDEIIIMNRST DISCRIMINATED
ACDDEIILLNRTY DENDRITICALLY
ACDDEIINNORTT INDOCTRINATED
ACDDEIINRSTTY IDENTITY CARDS
ACDDEINNOORTU UNCOORDINATED
ACDDELMMMNOOU COMMAND MODULE
ACDDHIMNORSYY HYDRODYNAMICS
ACDDOOOORRRSUY CORDUROY ROADS
ACDEEEHINNSTT INDECENT HASTE
ACDEEEHINRRUV UNDERACHIEVER
ACDEEEHLNOOPS HOLD ONE'S PEACE
ACDEEEHORRSTU TERRACED HOUSE
ACDEEEILNSSST DELICATESSENS
ACDEEELNOPRST PREADOLESCENT
ACDEEELNPRRSU SUPERCALENDER
ACDEEENNOPPRR PREPONDERANCE
ACDEEEOPRRRST TAPE RECORDERS
ACDEEFGIILMNT MAGNETIC FIELD
ACDEEFGINNORT CONFEDERATING
ACDEEFHHIKNRS HANDKERCHIEFS
ACDEEFHNORRTW THENCEFORWARD
ACDEEFIIILMRT CERTIFIED MAIL
ACDEEFILNNOST SELF-CONTAINED
ACDEEFINNOORT CONFEDERATION
ACDEEFNORRRTW CENTRE FORWARD
ACDEEGHHOOPRR CHOREOGRAPHED
ACDEEGHIKNNRT KITCHEN GARDEN
ACDEEGHIMNNNU MACHINEGUNNED
ACDEEGIIMORST TRAGICOMEDIES
ACDEEGILNNPRS SPRING-CLEANED
ACDEEGILNPRTY DEPRECATINGLY
ACDEEGIMMNNOR COMMANDEERING
ACDEEGNNOSSTT DECONGESTANTS
ACDEEGNOORSVW COVERED WAGONS

ACDEEHIIKMNNY   KIDNEY MACHINE
ACDEEHIKLOTTT   TICKLE TO DEATH
ACDEEHILORRTT   TETRACHLORIDE
ACDEEHINPRSSS   CASH DISPENSER
ACDEEHLNNOOORR   HOLE-AND-CORNER
ACDEEIIILMSTV   MEDIEVALISTIC
ACDEEIILNNNQU   QUINDECENNIAL
ACDEEIIILPRTUV   REDUPLICATIVE
ACDEEIIILPRTVY   PREDICATIVELY
ACDEEIIMNNRTY   INDETERMINACY
ACDEEIIMNOPRT   PREMEDICATION
ACDEEIIMOSTTV   DOMESTICATIVE
ACDEEIINNORST   CONTAINERISED,
    INCONSIDERATE
ACDEEIINNORTZ   CONTAINERIZED
ACDEEIINOPRTT   DECREPITATION
ACDEEIJKNNRST   DINNER JACKETS
ACDEEIKLOOPSS   KALEIDOSCOPES
ACDEEILLNNSTY   CLANDESTINELY
ACDEEILMNPSST   DISPLACEMENTS
ACDEEILNORSTY   CONSIDERATELY
ACDEEILNPPRRU   PERPENDICULAR
ACDEEILOPRRTY   DEPRECATORILY
ACDEEIMMNORTV   INVERTED COMMA
ACDEEIMNORSSX   CROSS-EXAMINED
ACDEEIMNORSTU   DOCUMENTARIES
ACDEEINNORSSS   SECONDARINESS
ACDEEJKKNOSTY   DONKEY JACKETS
ACDEELNOOSSSS   CLOSED SEASONS
ACDEELOPRRRSY   RECORD PLAYERS
ACDEEMNNOPSTU   UNCOMPENSATED
ACDEFGHHIINSS   CHAFING DISHES
ACDEFGIILNSSY   DECLASSIFYING
ACDEFGILLRSUY   DISGRACEFULLY
ACDEFHLLOTTUY   THE CALL OF DUTY
ACDEFHOORSSSU   HOUSES OF CARDS
ACDEFIIILNOST   FICTIONALISED
ACDEFIIILNOTZ   FICTIONALIZED
ACDEFIINNSSTT   DISINFECTANTS
ACDEFILMNNOTU   MALFUNCTIONED
ACDEGGHIINPRS   GRAPHIC DESIGN
ACDEGGHINNRRU   UNDERCHARGING
ACDEGGIKLNNOW   ACKNOWLEDGING
ACDEGGINORRSS   GRADE CROSSING
ACDEGHHOOPRTU   THOROUGHPACED
ACDEGHIIMNNRS   MERCHANDISING
ACDEGIIILLLOOY   IDEOLOGICALLY
ACDEGIILLNSSS   SLIDING SCALES
ACDEGIILNPRTU   REDUPLICATING
ACDEGIIMNORTZ   DEMOCRATIZING
ACDEGIIMNOSTT   DOMESTICATING
ACDEGIIMNOSTY   GEODYNAMICIST
ACDEGILLMNOOO   DEMONOLOGICAL
ACDEGILLNOOOT   DEONTOLOGICAL
ACDEGIMMNNORW   WING COMMANDER
ACDEHHILNPRSS   SHIP'S CHANDLER
ACDEHHLOPRSUY   HYDROCEPHALUS
ACDEHIIMRSSTT   CHRISTMASTIDE
ACDEHIIOPSSTT   SOPHISTICATED

ACDEHILMNOPTY   ENDOLYMPHATIC
ACDEHIMMNOPRS   COMMANDERSHIP
ACDEHIMMNORTY   THERMODYNAMIC
ACDEHIMOPRTTY   DERMATOPHYTIC
ACDEHLMOOPRSY   CHLAMYDOSPORE
ACDEHMRSTTTUU   CUT THE MUSTARD
ACDEHOOOOPRRTT   PROTOCHORDATE
ACDEIIILNNTTW   IDENTICAL TWIN
ACDEIIIMNORST   DOSIMETRICIAN
ACDEIIKLRSTTW   WILDCAT STRIKE
ACDEIILNNOTTU   DENTICULATION
ACDEIILNOPRTU   REDUPLICATION
ACDEIIMNOOSTT   DOMESTICATION
ACDEIIINNNOSTU   DENUNCIATIONS
ACDEIIINNOORST   CONSIDERATION
ACDEIIINNOQRSTU   QUADRISECTION
ACDEIINORRSTY   DISCRETIONARY
ACDEIKMNNORST   ONE-TRACK MINDS
ACDEIKNNNORTT   DARK CONTINENT
ACDEILLMMOUWY   CADMIUM YELLOW
ACDEILMNORTUY   DOCUMENTARILY
ACDEILNNOPTUU   PEDUNCULATION
ACDEILNNORSTY   CONSTRAINEDLY
ACDEILOOPRRTU   PARTI-COLOURED
ACDEILOPRSSTY   PERISSODACTYL
ACDEIMMNNOOST   COMMENDATIONS
ACDEIMMOOORRS   AIR COMMODORES
ACDEIMMOOSTTY   MASTOIDECTOMY
ACDEIMNNNOOST   CONDEMNATIONS
ACDEIMNNOOTTU   DOCUMENTATION
ACDEIMNORRRSS   MORRIS DANCERS
ACDEINNNORSTU   UNCONSTRAINED
ACDEKLLNOORRR   ROCK-AND-ROLLER
ACDELNOOOSTUY   ACOTYLEDONOUS
ACDELOOORRSTUW   STRAW-COLOURED
ACDEMMNNOSTUU   UNCONSUMMATED
ACDEOPRSSTTUW   WASTE PRODUCTS
ACDFIIIMNOOST   MODIFICATIONS
ACDFILMOORSTY   FAMILY DOCTORS
ACDGHINOOOPRT   ODONTOGRAPHIC
ACDGIIINNRSSTV   VISITING CARDS
ACDGIILNNOOST   CONSOLIDATING
ACDGIINNOSTTU   OUTDISTANCING
ACDGILLNOOOOT   ODONTOLOGICAL
ACDGILMOSTYYZ   ZYGODACTYLISM
ACDGIMNOPRSSU   MASS-PRODUCING
ACDGLOOSTUYYZ   ZYGODACTYLOUS
ACDHIIKKNPSUY   KICK UP A SHINDY
ACDHIILMNOORT   MITOCHONDRIAL
ACDHIINOPSSTU   CUSTODIANSHIP
ACDHIIOPRSSTT   DICTATORSHIPS
ACDHILMNOOORS   CHONDRIOSOMAL
ACDHIMNOOPSTY   PHOTODYNAMICS
ACDHKLORRSTUY   HARD-LUCK STORY
ACDHLNOOSSSUY   SUNDAY SCHOOLS
ACDHMNOOOORSTU   CHONDROMATOUS
ACDIIIILNNOPTU   INDUPLICATION
ACDIIIMNORRST   DISCRIMINATOR,
    DOCTRINAIRISM

ACDIIIOOOPRST RADIOISOTOPIC
ACDIIILLLNSSSY SCILLY ISLANDS
ACDIILLNNOOTY CONDITIONALLY
ACDIILNNNOOTU UNCONDITIONAL
ACDIILNNOOOST CONSOLIDATION
ACDIILNOOORST DISCOLORATION
ACDIIILPQRTUUY QUADRUPLICITY
ACDIIINNOORRTT INDOCTRINATOR
ACDINOOQRSSTU CONQUISTADORS
ACDLLOOPSTUYY POLYDACTYLOUS
ACDLMNOOOSTUY CONDYLOMATOUS
ACEEEEEKNOPPS KEEP ONE'S PEACE
ACEEEEEFJKRRST REEFER JACKETS
ACEEEEEHLPRSST STEEPLECHASER
ACEEEEEHLPSSST STEEPLECHASES
ACEEEEELMNRSTT TRACE ELEMENTS
ACEEEEENNPPPRY CAYENNE PEPPER
ACEEEEEPPRRSTW CARPET SWEEPER
ACEEEFFGINOPR PEACE OFFERING
ACEEEFGGNNOOS EGG ON ONE'S FACE
ACEEEFHHITTVY HAVE ITCHY FEET
ACEEEFMORRRTT REFRACTOMETER
ACEEEGILLNRTY ENERGETICALLY
ACEEEGINPRSSS PRESS AGENCIES
ACEEEGLMNORTT ELECTROMAGNET
ACEEEGLNNRRUY NUCLEAR ENERGY
ACEEEGLNRSSSS GRACELESSNESS
ACEEEGMNNORTU ENCOURAGEMENT
ACEEEHHILLLSS ACHILLES' HEELS
ACEEEHHPPRSTY SPEECH THERAPY
ACEEEHIKMNSTY SMACK IN THE EYE
ACEEEHINRSTVY SEVEN-YEAR ITCH
ACEEEHLLNNOPT TELENCEPHALON
ACEEEHLMNNOPS MESENCEPHALON
ACEEEHLMNNOPT METENCEPHALON
ACEEEHNNRSSST ENCHANTRESSES
ACEEEIINNRSTV INTENSIVE CARE
ACEEEIINSSTTV NECESSITATIVE
ACEEEIKNOPTTX TAKE EXCEPTION
ACEEEILLNPSST LICENSE PLATES
ACEEEILMNNRTT INTERLACEMENT
ACEEEILNRSSVY NECESSARY EVIL
ACEEEIMNNRRSS MERCENARINESS
ACEEEIMNORSVY YEOMAN SERVICE
ACEEEINNOPRVX AIX-EN-PROVENCE
ACEEEINOSSTVV EVOCATIVENESS
ACEEEELLNORTTV ELECTROVALENT
ACEEEELLOPRRTT ELECTROPLATER
ACEEFFHINNPRS AFFENPINSCHER
ACEEFFILLNTUY INEFFECTUALLY
ACEEFGIIMNRRT FERRIMAGNETIC
ACEEFGIMNORRT FERROMAGNETIC
ACEEFHHIRSTTT FEATHERSTITCH
ACEEFHIMNNRST FRANCHISEMENT
ACEEFHMNOSTUV VOUCHSAFEMENT
ACEEFHOPPRSST PARTS OF SPEECH
ACEEFINOSSSTU FACETIOUSNESS
ACEEFMNORSTUU FRUMENTACEOUS
ACEEFMORRRTTY REFRACTOMETRY

ACEEGGINNOORT ORGANOGENETIC
ACEEGHHIOPRRT HETEROGRAPHIC
ACEEGHHLNORST CLOTHES HANGER
ACEEGHHMNRRRU HUNGER MARCHER
ACEEGHHMNRRSU HUNGER MARCHES
ACEEGHHOOPRRR CHOREOGRAPHER
ACEEGHIIMNNSW SEWING MACHINE
ACEEGHILNOPRS SELENOGRAPHIC
ACEEGHILNORSU CLEARINGHOUSE
ACEEGHILNOSSU CHAISE LONGUES
ACEEGHILOPRRX LEXICOGRAPHER
ACEEGHIOPRRST STEREOGRAPHIC
ACEEGHIRRSSST CASH REGISTERS
ACEEGHLOPRRTY ELECTROGRAPHY
ACEEGHMNNORSY MONEYCHANGERS
ACEEGHPRRRSSU SUPERCHARGERS
ACEEGIILSTTUV GESTICULATIVE
ACEEGIIMNNOST MISCEGENATION
ACEEGIINNNRST INTRANSIGENCE
ACEEGIINNSSTT NECESSITATING
ACEEGIINOPRRR CARRIER PIGEON
ACEEGILLLOOPS SPELEOLOGICAL
ACEEGILLMORTY GEOMETRICALLY
ACEEGILMNNOQU MAGNILOQUENCE
ACEEGILMNOPST MAGNETIC POLES
ACEEGILNPSSTT PLACE SETTINGS
ACEEGIMMNORTT MAGNETOMETRIC
ACEEGINNNSSSU UNCEASINGNESS
ACEEGINOPRTTX EXPECTORATING
ACEEGLMNOORST CONGLOMERATES
ACEEHHILLORTT HETEROTHALLIC
ACEEHHIRVWWYY EVERY WHICH WAY
ACEEHHLNORSSU CHARNEL HOUSES
ACEEHIILMMNPS SIMPLE MACHINE
ACEEHIIORSSST CASE HISTORIES
ACEEHIIQRRSSU SQUIREARCHIES
ACEEHIKNRSSST HEARTSICKNESS
ACEEHILLORTTY THEORETICALLY
ACEEHILNPRSSS SPHERICALNESS
ACEEHILOPRSTT HETEROPLASTIC
ACEEHIMNORSSS MARCHIONESSES
ACEEHIMNRSSST CHASTISEMENTS
ACEEHIMRRSSTT CHRISTMAS TREE
ACEEHINOPRRST TERPSICHOREAN
ACEEHIPRRSSTY SECRETARYSHIP
ACEEHLLMOOORT ALCOHOLOMETER
ACEEHLLOORSSV SCHOOL-LEAVERS
ACEEHLLOPPSTU LEPTOCEPHALUS
ACEEHLMMNOOTW THE COMMON WEAL
ACEEHLMNORRTU THERMONUCLEAR
ACEEHLMNSSSST MATCHLESSNESS
ACEEHLORRSTUY TREACHEROUSLY
ACEEHLPPRSTUY SUPPLY TEACHER
ACEEHLPSSSTTU SPACE SHUTTLES
ACEEHMNOPPRRT RAPPROCHEMENT
ACEEIIILPRSTU PECULIARITIES
ACEEIIIMNRRTV RECRIMINATIVE
ACEEIIIPPRRTTV PRECIPITATIVE
ACEEIILLLPPTY EPILEPTICALLY

ACEEIILMMNORS CEREMONIALISM
ACEEIILMNOPRS SEMIPORCELAIN
ACEEIILMNORST CEREMONIALIST
ACEEIILMNPRSS EMPIRICALNESS
ACEEIILNNNRTT TRICENTENNIAL
ACEEIILNRTTVY INTERACTIVELY
ACEEIILPPRTTY PRECIPITATELY
ACEEIIMMORSTV COMMISERATIVE
ACEEIIMNNOSST AMNIOCENTESIS
ACEEIIMNORRST MERCERISATION
ACEEIIMNORRTZ MERCERIZATION
ACEEIINNOSSTT NECESSITATION
ACEEIINORSSVV VARICOSE VEINS
ACEEIIRSSTTUV RESUSCITATIVE
ACEEIKNOSSSTT SEASON TICKETS
ACEEILLLNRRTU INTERCELLULAR
ACEEILLLNSTTU INTELLECTUALS
ACEEILLMNNRTY INCREMENTALLY
ACEEILLMNOSSU MISCELLANEOUS
ACEEILLMOQRUU EQUIMOLECULAR
ACEEILLNNNSSU UNCLEANLINESS
ACEEILLNOPTXY EXCEPTIONALLY
ACEEILLPSTUVY SPECULATIVELY
ACEEILLRRSSTY RECRYSTALLISE
ACEEILLRRSTYZ RECRYSTALLIZE
ACEEILMNOPTTV CONTEMPLATIVE
ACEEILMNRRSSU MERCURIALNESS
ACEEILMOPRSTU PRECIOUS METAL
ACEEILNNOPRTV CONVERTIPLANE
ACEEILNNOPTUX UNEXCEPTIONAL
ACEEILNNOQSTU CONSEQUENTIAL
ACEEILNNRRTUW NUCLEAR WINTER
ACEEILNNRSSUY UNNECESSARILY
ACEEILNORSTTU INTEROSCULATE
ACEEILNOSTTUX CONTEXTUALISE
ACEEILNOTTUXZ CONTEXTUALIZE
ACEEILNRTTUUV ENCULTURATIVE
ACEEILOOPRTVY COOPERATIVELY
ACEEILOPPRSSW SPECIAL POWERS
ACEEILOPRSTTY STEREOTYPICAL
ACEEILORRTTVY RETROACTIVELY
ACEEILORTTUVV OVERCULTIVATE
ACEEIMMMOORTV COMMEMORATIVE
ACEEIMNORRSSX CROSS-EXAMINER
ACEEIMNPRTTUY PNEUMATIC TYRE
ACEEINNNRSSTU UNCERTAINNESS
ACEEINNOORSVZ CONVERSAZIONE
ACEEINNOSSSTU TENACIOUSNESS
ACEEINOOPRSTU PROTEINACEOUS
ACEEINOOPRTTX EXPECTORATION
ACEEINOORRSTV CONSERVATOIRE,
  OVERREACTIONS
ACEEINOPRSSTT INSPECTORATES
ACEEINORSSSUV VERACIOUSNESS
ACEEINORSSTVV CONSERVATIVES
ACEEIOPRRSTTV PRIVATE SECTOR
ACEELLNOOPRSU PORCELLANEOUS
ACEELLNSSSSSS CLASSLESSNESS
ACEELLOORRRST ROLLER COASTER

ACEELMMNOPRTY COMPLEMENTARY
ACEELMNNORSTU NOMENCLATURES
ACEEMMNNOPSST ENCOMPASSMENT
ACEEMNNNNOSTU ANNOUNCEMENTS
ACEEMNNORRSST REMONSTRANCES
ACEEOOPRRSTTT PROTECTORATES
ACEFFFFHIOSST CHIEFS OF STAFF
ACEFFFFIORSST STAFF OFFICERS
ACEFGHIINNNRS ENFRANCHISING
ACEFGIIIINSTV SIGNIFICATIVE
ACEFGIILMNNTY MAGNIFICENTLY
ACEFGIILNNRTU LUNATIC FRINGE
ACEFGIKKOOTTU GET A KICK OUT OF
ACEFGILNRSSUY FLYING SAUCERS
ACEFHHIIINPST CHIEFTAINSHIP
ACEFHIIMNRSTU FRUIT MACHINES
ACEFHLLOPRRUY REPROACHFULLY
ACEFIIIJLLNOT JELLIFICATION
ACEFIIILNOSTT FELICITATIONS
ACEFIIINNORTU REUNIFICATION
ACEFIIINORSTV VERSIFICATION
ACEFIIINOSTTT TESTIFICATION
ACEFIILLPRSUY SUPERFICIALLY
ACEFIILNORSTY FORENSICALITY
ACEFIINNORSTU FUNCTIONARIES
ACEFIINOORSTV VOCIFERATIONS
ACEFILNNOOSSS CONFESSIONALS
ACEFILNOOPRSS FALSE SCORPION
ACEFINNOORSSY CONFESSIONARY
ACEFINNORRTTY CONFRATERNITY
ACEFINORSSSTU FRACTIOUSNESS
ACEFJKKLNOORT NORFOLK JACKET
ACEFLLMOOPRSW CAMP FOLLOWERS
ACEFOOOORRTTWW WATER CROWFOOT
ACEGGGHIINNNR CHANGE RINGING
ACEGGHIINNNRT INTERCHANGING
ACEGGHINPRRSU SUPERCHARGING
ACEGGHIOOOPRZ ZOOGEOGRAPHIC
ACEGGIILNSTTU GESTICULATING
ACEGGILLOOPTY EGYPTOLOGICAL
ACEGGILNNORUY ENCOURAGINGLY
ACEGGILNOOSTY GYNAECOLOGIST
ACEGGINNOORST CONGREGATIONS
ACEGGLLRSSSTU CLASS STRUGGLE
ACEGHHIMOPRRT THERMOGRAPHIC
ACEGHHNOOPRRR CHRONOGRAPHER
ACEGHIIMNNRTU TURING MACHINE
ACEGHIIMOPRSS SEISMOGRAPHIC
ACEGHILLLOOTY ETHOLOGICALLY,
  THEOLOGICALLY
ACEGHILLNOOPR PHRENOLOGICAL
ACEGHILLOOPPS PSEPHOLOGICAL
ACEGHILNOPRRY REPROACHINGLY
ACEGHILNORSSU SOUL-SEARCHING
ACEGHILOOSSTT ESCHATOLOGIST
ACEGHIMNNORTT MAGNETIC NORTH
ACEGHINORRSTT ORCHESTRATING
ACEGHNOOPPRSY PHARYNGOSCOPE
ACEGHOPPRRRTY CRYPTOGRAPHER

ACEGHOPPRRSTY SPECTROGRAPHY
ACEGIIILNOOPT GEOPOLITICIAN
ACEGIIIMNNRRT RECRIMINATING
ACEGIIINORTTY IATROGENICITY
ACEGIIINPPRTT PRECIPITATING
ACEGIIKNNRSVV CARVING KNIVES
ACEGIILLLOOTY ETIOLOGICALLY
ACEGIILLNNSSW LICENSING LAWS
ACEGIILLOSTTY EGOTISTICALLY
ACEGIILNNOORT RECOGNITIONAL
ACEGIILNOSTTU GESTICULATION
ACEGIIMMNORST COMMISERATING
ACEGIINOORSST COSIGNATORIES
ACEGIINOPRSTY SAPROGENICITY
ACEGIINPRRSTT STARTING PRICE
ACEGIINRSSTTU RESUSCITATING
ACEGIKLNOOPPS COOKING APPLES
ACEGILLMNOOOT ENTOMOLOGICAL
ACEGILLMNOORU NUMEROLOGICAL
ACEGILLMNOORY ERGONOMICALLY
ACEGILLMNOOYZ ENZYMOLOGICAL
ACEGILLNNOOTY ONTOGENICALLY
ACEGILLOOPRTY GEOTROPICALLY
ACEGILLSTYYYZ SYZYGETICALLY
ACEGILMNNOPTT CONTEMPLATING
ACEGILMNOPSTY SALPINGECTOMY
ACEGILMOOSSTU CLEISTOGAMOUS
ACEGILNNNOSUY SANGUINOLENCY
ACEGILNNOORSS CONGRESSIONAL
ACEGILNORRSUU NEUROSURGICAL
ACEGILOOPSSST ESCAPOLOGISTS
ACEGIMMMNOORT COMMEMORATING
ACEGIMNOPRSTU PNEUMOGASTRIC
ACEGINOOPRSTT PROGNOSTICATE
ACEGLNOOOPSUU POLYGONACEOUS
ACEGMNNOORSSW CONGRESSWOMAN
ACEHHIINOPRSX HIERACOSPHINX
ACEHHIINOPRSZ SCHIZOPHRENIA
ACEHHILMOPRTX XEROPHTHALMIC
ACEHHLLLMOOTY METHYL ALCOHOL
ACEHHMMNRSTUY CHRYSANTHEMUM
ACEHHMOOOPRRT CHROMATOPHORE
ACEHHOPPRSTYY PSYCHOTHERAPY
ACEHIIINRRSST CHRISTIANISER
ACEHIIINRRSTZ CHRISTIANIZER
ACEHIILLLMOTY HOMILETICALLY
ACEHIILLPPTYY EPIPHYTICALLY
ACEHIILLRSTUY HEURISTICALLY
ACEHIILMNSSSTW WHIMSICALNESS
ACEHIILOOPPRT APHELIOTROPIC
ACEHIIMMRSSTT CHRISTMASTIME
ACEHIIOPSSSTT SOPHISTICATES
ACEHIJKLPRSSY PHYSICAL JERKS
ACEHILLMMOPRY MORPHEMICALLY
ACEHILLNORSSS SCHOLARLINESS
ACEHILLNSTTYY SYNTHETICALLY
ACEHILLOOPRTY ORTHOEPICALLY
ACEHILLOPPRTY PROPHETICALLY
ACEHILLOPRTTY PROTHETICALLY

ACEHILMOPRSTT THERMOPLASTIC
ACEHILOOPRSTV PRIVATE SCHOOL
ACEHILPPRSSUY SUPERPHYSICAL
ACEHIMOORSTTT TRACHEOTOMIST
ACEHIMORSSTTT THERMOSTATICS
ACEHINNOORRSTT ORCHESTRATION
ACEHIOPRRSSTT ORCHESTRA PITS,
   STRATOSPHERIC
ACEHIORSSTTTU TETRASTICHOUS
ACEHLMOORSSST SCHOOLMASTERS
ACEHMMOPSTTYY SYMPATHECTOMY
ACEHNNOOPRRSS ANCHORPERSONS
ACEHNNOORRTTY ON THE CONTRARY
ACEHNOORRTTTY TO THE CONTRARY
ACEIIIILMPRST IMPERIALISTIC
ACEIIILLNNOPT PENICILLATION
ACEIIILNORSTT ORIENTALISTIC
ACEIIILNOSTVV VIVISECTIONAL
ACEIIILQSTUVY ACQUISITIVELY
ACEIIIMNNORRT RECRIMINATION
ACEIIINOPPRTT PRECIPITATION
ACEIIINRTTTVY INTERACTIVITY
ACEIIKLMOSTTU STICK OUT A MILE
ACEIILLNORRTY ACRYLONITRILE
ACEIILLNRRTTU INTRATELLURIC
ACEIILLNRSTXY EXTRINSICALLY
ACEIILLOOPTYZ EPIZOOTICALLY
ACEIILMNOPSST NEOPLASTICISM
ACEIILMNORTUV VERMICULATION
ACEIILMNOSSSU MALICIOUSNESS
ACEIILNOOPSTT POLICE STATION
ACEIILNOPRRTT INTERTROPICAL
ACEIILNOPRSST PERSONALISTIC
ACEIILNORSTTU RETICULATIONS
ACEIILNPQTTUU QUINTUPLICATE
ACEIILNRSSTTT CLARINETTISTS
ACEIILNRSSTVV CIVIL SERVANTS
ACEIIMMNOORST COMMISERATION
ACEIIMNNOOOST ECONOMISATION
ACEIIMNNOOOTZ ECONOMIZATION
ACEIIMNORRRTY RECRIMINATORY
ACEIINNNORSTU RENUNCIATIONS
ACEIINNOOPRST PRECONISATION
ACEIINNOOPRTZ PRECONIZATION
ACEIINOOPRRTV INCORPORATIVE
ACEIINOOQSTUV EQUIVOCATIONS
ACEIINOPRRSTT PRACTITIONERS
ACEIINORSSSUV VICARIOUSNESS
ACEIINORSSTTU RESUSCITATION
ACEIINOSSSUVV VIVACIOUSNESS
ACEIIORRTTTVY RETROACTIVITY
ACEIKLOORRSSW SOCIAL WORKERS
ACEILLLLMRTUU MULTICELLULAR
ACEILLLLPSTYY SYLLEPTICALLY
ACEILLLOPPRTY PROLEPTICALLY
ACEILLMMRSTYY SYMMETRICALLY
ACEILLNNNOSSY NONSENSICALLY
ACEILLNNOOSTT CONSTELLATION
ACEILLNOOPRRY INCORPOREALLY

ACEILLNOQUUVY UNEQUIVOCALLY
ACEILLOPSTUUY EUCALYPTUS OIL
ACEILMMNOPRTY COMPLIMENTARY
ACEILMNNOOPTT CONTEMPLATION
ACEILMNNORRTU INTERCOLUMNAR
ACEILMNNSSSUU UNMUSICALNESS
ACEILMNOOPRSS COMPRESSIONAL
ACEILMNOPRVYY LIVERY COMPANY
ACEILNNORTTUU ENCULTURATION
ACEILNOORRSTV CONTROVERSIAL
ACEILOOPRTVVY PROVOCATIVELY
ACEIMMMNOOOORT COMMEMORATION
ACEIMNNORRTTU MACRONUTRIENT
ACEINNNOORSTT CONSTERNATION
ACEINNNOORTTV CONTRAVENTION
ACEINNOORSSTV CONVERSATIONS
ACEINOORSSSTU ATROCIOUSNESS
ACEINOPRRSSST CONSPIRATRESS
ACEIOOPRRRRST TROOP CARRIERS
ACELLMMNOOOORU MONOMOLECULAR
ACELLNOORSTTY CONSTELLATORY
ACELMNOPRRSUU SUPERCOLUMNAR
ACELMNORRSUUU NEUROMUSCULAR
ACELNOOPRSSTU PROCONSULATES
ACELOOPRSSSVY SOLVAY PROCESS
ACEMOOPRSTTTY PROSTATECTOMY
ACENNOOOOPRRT NONCOOPERATOR
ACENNOORRSSSU RANCOROUSNESS
ACFFGHIILRSTT TRAFFIC LIGHTS
ACFFGILNOSTUY SUFFOCATINGLY
ACFFIIINOORTT FORTIFICATION
ACFFIINNOOPTT IN POINT OF FACT
ACFGIIIILNNOT LIGNIFICATION
ACFGIIIINNNST INSIGNIFICANT
ACFGIIIINNOST SIGNIFICATION
ACFGIIIILNNSTY SIGNIFICANTLY
ACFGIIIILNOORT GLORIFICATION
ACFGIIINNOPTT PONTIFICATING
ACFGIINNOORTU CONFIGURATION
ACFHIIINOORRT HORRIFICATION
ACFHIIILLNOORY HONORIFICALLY
ACFIIIILNOSTV VILIFICATIONS
ACFIIIINNORTT NITRIFICATION
ACFIIIINORTTV VITRIFICATION
ACFIIIJLLNOOT JOLLIFICATION
ACFIIIJNOSTTU JUSTIFICATION
ACFIIILLMNOOT MOLLIFICATION
ACFIIILLNNOTU NULLIFICATION
ACFIIIMMMNOTU MUMMIFICATION
ACFIIIMNOORTT MORTIFICATION
ACFIIIMNOSTTY MYSTIFICATION
ACFIIINNOOSTT NOTIFICATIONS
ACFIIJORSTTUY JUSTIFICATORY
ACFIILLLORSTY FLORISTICALLY
ACFIILLOOPRSY SOPORIFICALLY
ACFIILMNNOSTU FUNCTIONALISM
ACFIILNNOSTTU FUNCTIONALIST
ACFIIMNNOORST CONFIRMATIONS
ACFILLLORRTUU FLORICULTURAL

ACFIMNNOOOORST CONFORMATIONS
ACFINNNOOOORTT CONFRONTATION
ACGGHHILOPPRY GLYPHOGRAPHIC
ACGGHHINNORST SHORT-CHANGING
ACGGHIKLNOSTU LAUGHINGSTOCK
ACGGHILOPPRTY GLYPTOGRAPHIC
ACGGHIMNNOORS CHANGING ROOMS
ACGHHIIOPPRSY PHYSIOGRAPHIC
ACGHHILMOOOPR HOMOLOGRAPHIC
ACGHHIMNOOSTT SHOOTING MATCH
ACGHIILLOOPSY PHYSIOLOGICAL
ACGHILLLMOOOY HOMOLOGICALLY
ACGHILLMOOOPR MORPHOLOGICAL
ACGHILLOOPRSY OSCILLOGRAPHY
ACGHIMNNOOOPT PATHOGNOMONIC
ACGHNOOPPRSYY PHARYNGOSCOPY
ACGIIIIMNNNRT INCRIMINATING
ACGIIILLNNSTT SCINTILLATING
ACGIIIMNNORTZ ROMANTICIZING
ACGIIKKLNSSTW WALKING STICKS
ACGIILLLOSSTY SYLLOGISTICAL
ACGIILLMNNOPY COMPLAININGLY
ACGIILLMOOSTT CLIMATOLOGIST
ACGIILLNRSTYZ CRYSTALLIZING
ACGIILMNNNOPU UNCOMPLAINING
ACGIILRRSTTUU AGRICULTURIST
ACGIIMMNNOORRS MICROORGANISM
ACGIINNNOSTUY CONSANGUINITY
ACGIINNOOPRRT INCORPORATING
ACGILLLMNOOOY NOMOLOGICALLY
ACGILLLNOOOSY NOSOLOGICALLY
ACGILLLNOOOTY ONTOLOGICALLY
ACGILLLOOOPTY TOPOLOGICALLY
ACGILLNOOOSTV VOLCANOLOGIST
ACGINNNOOOSTU NONCONTAGIOUS
ACGIOOPRSSSTT GASTROSCOPIST
ACHHIIINNORST ORNITHISCHIAN
ACHHIILLOOPPS PHILOSOPHICAL
ACHHIILNOPPRT PHILANTHROPIC
ACHHIIMNOPPSS CHAMPIONSHIPS
ACHHIIMOPRSTU AMPHITRICHOUS
ACHHIINOOSTTW IN CAHOOTS WITH
ACHHILMMOORSS SCHOOLMARMISH
ACHHIMNOORSTX XANTHOCHROISM
ACHHIMNOOSTTU AUTOCHTHONISM
ACHHLLNOOOSTU ALLOCHTHONOUS
ACHHNOOOSTTUU AUTOCHTHONOUS
ACHIIIJPRSSTU JUSTICIARSHIP
ACHIIIMNOSTTY MYTHICISATION
ACHIIIMNOTTYZ MYTHICIZATION
ACHIILLOPSSTY SOPHISTICALLY
ACHIIMMORRSTT TRICHROMATISM
ACHIIMNNOOPPS COMPANIONSHIP
ACHIIOOPRSSTT SOPHISTICATOR
ACHIIPRSSSTTY PSYCHIATRISTS
ACHILLMNOPSYY SYMPHONICALLY
ACHILLMPSSYYY SYMPHYSICALLY
ACHILLORRTTUU HORTICULTURAL
ACHILMOOPRRSY PRIMARY SCHOOL

ACHILMOORSSTY CHROMATOLYSIS
ACHILMOPSTTYY SYMPATHOLYTIC
ACIIIILNOSSTV CIVILISATIONS
ACIIIILNOSTVZ CIVILIZATIONS
ACIIIIMNNNORT INCRIMINATION
ACIIIIMNOSTTV VICTIMISATION
ACIIIIMNOTTVZ VICTIMIZATION
ACIIILLLORTVY VITRIOLICALLY
ACIIILLNNOSTT SCINTILLATION
ACIIILLNNRSTY INTRINSICALLY
ACIIILMNNORTU ANTICLINORIUM
ACIIILMNOPRSV PROVINCIALISM
ACIIILNNOPRST INSCRIPTIONAL
ACIIILNOOSSTT SOLICITATIONS
ACIIILNOPRTVY PROVINCIALITY
ACIIIMNNORRTY INCRIMINATORY
ACIILLLMOOQSU COLLOQUIALISM
ACIILLLRSTUUV SILVICULTURAL
ACIILLLSSTTYY STYLISTICALLY
ACIILLNOORTUY ILLOCUTIONARY
ACIILLNRSTTYY CRYSTALLINITY
ACIILMNOOOOPST COMPOSITIONAL
ACIILMNOORSUY ACRIMONIOUSLY
ACIILMNOORTTY MICROTONALITY
ACIILMOORSTTT STROMATOLITIC
ACIILMOPRSTUV VICTORIA PLUMS
ACIILNNORSTTU INSTRUCTIONAL
ACIILNOPPSSTU SUPPLICATIONS
ACIILNORSTTUV VOLUNTARISTIC
ACIILQRSTTUUU AQUICULTURIST
ACIIMMNNOOSTU COMMUNISATION
ACIIMMNNOOTUZ COMMUNIZATION
ACIIMMOOPRSTT COMPATRIOTISM
ACIIMNNOOSSTU SANCTIMONIOUS
ACIINNNOOPRTU PRONUNCIATION
ACIINNNOOSTTU CONTINUATIONS
ACIINNOOOPRRT INCORPORATION
ACIINNOPRRSTT TRANSCRIPTION
ACIINNORSSTTU INCRUSTATIONS
ACILMMOOPSSSY MYCOPLASMOSIS
ACILMNOOOOPSST COSMOPOLITANS
ACILMNOOPRRRUY PRIMARY COLOUR
ACILMRRSSTTUU STRUCTURALISM
ACILNNOOSSTTU CONSULTATIONS
ACILRRSSTTTUU STRUCTURALIST
ACIMMNNOOSSTU CONSUMMATIONS
ACIMNOOPPSSST COMPASS POINTS
ACINNOPRSTTTU CONTRAPUNTIST
ACINOOPRRSSTT STRIP CARTOONS
ACKKMNNOOPSST POSTMAN'S KNOCK
ACLMORSSTTUUU CUMULOSTRATUS,
  STRATOCUMULUS
ADDDEEEFLRSSS SELF-ADDRESSED
ADDDEEHLNNRUY UNDERHANDEDLY
ADDDEGGLLNOSY DADDY LONGLEGS
ADDEEEEHNRRTT TENDERHEARTED
ADDEEEGHINPSS PIGHEADEDNESS
ADDEEEGHNORSY DEHYDROGENASE
ADDEEEGHNORTY DEHYDROGENATE

ADDEEEEGMNRRRY GERRYMANDERED
ADDEEEHHNOSST HOT-HEADEDNESS
ADDEEEHLLNOSW SWOLLEN HEADED
ADDEEEILMNRST MIDDLE EASTERN
ADDEEEINOPPST ENDOPEPTIDASE
ADDEEELRRSTTY RED-LETTER DAYS
ADDEEENOPPRRT PREPONDERATED
ADDEEFFHNNOSS OFFHANDEDNESS
ADDEEFFIORSST DISAFFORESTED
ADDEEFLNNPRUY PENNY-DREADFUL
ADDEEGHHILLTY LIGHT-HEADEDLY
ADDEEGHLNORWY WRONGHEADEDLY
ADDEEGIINRSTT DISINTEGRATED
ADDEEGNNRSSUU UNGUARDEDNESS
ADDEEHIKLNRTY KIND-HEARTEDLY
ADDEEHLNORTWY DOWNHEARTEDLY
ADDEEIIILMRST DEMILITARISED
ADDEEIIILMRTZ DEMILITARIZED
ADDEEIINORSTT DISORIENTATED
ADDEEIMNNSSSY MANY-SIDEDNESS
ADDEEINNSSSUV UNADVISEDNESS
ADDEFGIILLNNS LANDING FIELDS
ADDEGHILNOOTU GO INTO A HUDDLE
ADDEGINNNRSTU UNDERSTANDING
ADDEGINNORRST STANDING ORDER
ADDEGLNOORTUY GOOD-NATUREDLY
ADDEHHLORRSSU HARD SHOULDERS
ADDEHILNORTUY THE DAILY ROUND
ADDEIIIILNSUV INDIVIDUALISE
ADDEIIIILNUVZ INDIVIDUALIZE
ADDEIIINOOSTX DEOXIDISATION
ADDEIIINOOTXZ DEOXIDIZATION
ADDEIILNNOTTY AN OLD IDENTITY
ADDEIINOOOORST DEODORISATION
ADDEIINOOOORTZ DEODORIZATION
ADDEIINOPRSTU SUPERADDITION
ADDEIKMNOOSST IT MAKES NO ODDS
ADDEILMNOPRSS PROMISED LANDS
ADDEIMNNRSSTU MISUNDERSTAND
ADDEIMNOOPRSU MODUS OPERANDI
ADDGHIMNOORSU ROUGH DIAMONDS
ADDGIILLLLNYY DILLYDALLYING
ADDGILLNOOPPS PADDLING POOLS
ADDIIIILMNSUV INDIVIDUALISM
ADDIIIILNSTUV INDIVIDUALIST
ADDIIIILNTUVY INDIVIDUALITY
ADDIIIINNOTUV INDIVIDUATION
ADEEEEEHLLRRW WHEELER-DEALER
ADEEEEFHINRTV FEATHER-VEINED
ADEEEEGHHNOTV HAVE THE EDGE ON
ADEEEEGHKLPTT TAKE THE PLEDGE
ADEEEEHHLORSV HEAD OVER HEELS
ADEEEEHNRTTVY THREE-DAY EVENT
ADEEEFFGILNST SELF-DEFEATING
ADEEEFFIINRTT DIFFERENTIATE
ADEEEFILLNRTY DEFERENTIALLY
ADEEEGGGINRST DESEGREGATING
ADEEEGGIMNNST DISENGAGEMENT
ADEEEGGINORST DESEGREGATION

ADEEEGHLMMRSS SLEDGEHAMMERS
ADEEEGIMNRSST DISAGREEMENTS
ADEEEGLLNORTU OUTGENERALLED
ADEEEGOPRRTUY DAGUERREOTYPE
ADEEEHIMNRSTT HEREDITAMENTS
ADEEEHLNOPRTY OPENHEARTEDLY
ADEEEIIMNNRTT INDETERMINATE
ADEEEIIMNRTTV DETERMINATIVE
ADEEEIIMPRTTV PREMEDITATIVE
ADEEEIINPRSST PEDESTRIANISE
ADEEEIINPRSTZ PEDESTRIANIZE
ADEEEIIORRTTV DETERIORATIVE
ADEEEILNNNRUV INLAND REVENUE
ADEEEILNOPRSS DEPERSONALISE
ADEEEILNOPRSZ DEPERSONALIZE
ADEEEILOPRTTY RADIOTELETYPE
ADEEEILORSSTW LOWER EAST SIDE
ADEEEIMNRSTTU UNDERESTIMATE
ADEEEIMNRSTTV ADVERTISEMENT
ADEEEIMORSTTV OVERESTIMATED
ADEEEINNRSSST SEDENTARINESS
ADEEEINOPQRTU EQUIPONDERATE
ADEEELLMNOPTV DEVELOPMENTAL
ADEEELLMORRST STEAMROLLERED
ADEEENRSSSTUV ADVENTURESSES
ADEEEOPPRRSSV EAVESDROPPERS
ADEEFFIILNRST DIFFERENTIALS
ADEEFFIILSSST SELF-SATISFIED
ADEEFGLNRRSSU REGARDFULNESS
ADEEFIILLLQUW WELL-QUALIFIED
ADEEFILLNOORV OIL OF LAVENDER
ADEEFILNOPPST SELF-APPOINTED
ADEEFINOORSTT DEFORESTATION
ADEEGGGINSSZZ ZIGZAGGEDNESS
ADEEGGHIRSSTT STRAIGHTEDGES
ADEEGGIIMNNTZ DEMAGNETIZING
ADEEGGLNNPRSU GELANDESPRUNG
ADEEGHHNORVYY HEAVY HYDROGEN
ADEEGHILNRSTY NEARSIGHTEDLY
ADEEGHLMNORST GOLDEN HAMSTER
ADEEGHOPRRSSW HEDGE SPARROWS
ADEEGIINNNRSS INGRAINEDNESS
ADEEGIINNRRTT INTERGRADIENT
ADEEGIINORRTT DETERIORATING
ADEEGIKNNRRST KINDERGARTENS
ADEEGILNNOOPS OLD AGE PENSION
ADEEGIMORSTTU DEUTEROGAMIST
ADEEGINNNOOTXY DEOXYGENATION
ADEEGINOPPRSV EAVESDROPPING
ADEEGJLMNTUUV VALUE JUDGMENT
ADEEGLNNORSTU DENTAL SURGEON
ADEEGMNNRRSTU UNDERGARMENTS
ADEEGOPRRTUYY DAGUERREOTYPY
ADEEHHIKNRRSS HEADSHRINKERS
ADEEHHILNOOTT TOAD-IN-THE-HOLE
ADEEHHIMOPRRT HERMAPHRODITE
ADEEHHLMNOOSU HOUSEHOLD NAME
ADEEHIILMNNPY DIPHENYLAMINE
ADEEHIIMNORTT TRIMETHADIONE

ADEEHILMNORST SIDEREAL MONTH
ADEEHIMMOPRTX MIXED METAPHOR
ADEEHIMNSSTUU HUMANE STUDIES
ADEEHMMOOPRST METAMORPHOSED
ADEEHMNOORRSY DYSMENORRHOEA
ADEEHNOOPRRTZ TRAPEZOHEDRON
ADEEHORSSTUVY SHROVE TUESDAY
ADEEIIILORRST EDITORIALISER
ADEEIIILORRTZ EDITORIALIZER
ADEEIIIMMNPRR PRIME MERIDIAN
ADEEIIIMNSSTV DISSEMINATIVE
ADEEIIINPRSST STIPENDIARIES
ADEEIIILMNNSTT DISENTAILMENT
ADEEIIILMNPSST DISSEPIMENTAL
ADEEIIILMNRSTY SEDIMENTARILY
ADEEIIILNORTTT TOILET-TRAINED
ADEEIIIMNNORTT DETERMINATION
ADEEIIIMNNOSTT SEDIMENTATION
ADEEIIMNOPRTT PREMEDITATION
ADEEIIMNORRTT INTERMEDIATOR
ADEEIINNORSTT TENDERISATION
ADEEIINNORTTZ TENDERIZATION
ADEEIINOORRTT DETERIORATION
ADEEIINOPRTXY EXPEDITIONARY
ADEEIILMNRTTY DETRIMENTALLY
ADEEIILLNNRSST LANTERNSLIDES
ADEEIILLNOPPTW WELL-APPOINTED
ADEEIILLNORRVY ORDINARY LEVEL
ADEEIILLOSSTVW OLD WIVES' TALES
ADEEIILLTTTTTT TITTLE-TATTLED
ADEEIILMMNNSTT DISMANTLEMENT
ADEEIILMNOORTZ METRONIDAZOLE
ADEEIILNNRTTVY INADVERTENTLY
ADEEIIMMNORSSU MISDEMEANOURS
ADEEIIMNORSTTV DEMONSTRATIVE
ADEEIIMNPRRTTT PRINTED MATTER
ADEEIIMNRSSTUV MISADVENTURES
ADEEIINNOPQRTU EQUIPONDERANT
ADEEIINNOSSTTW AT ONE'S WITS' END
ADEEIINOPRRSST PREDATORINESS
ADEEIINOPRRSTU SUPERORDINATE
ADEEIJMMORRTTU DRUM MAJORETTE
ADEEJMNRSSTTU READJUSTMENTS
ADEELOOPPRTUV OVERPOPULATED
ADEEMNOORTUUV OUTMANOEUVRED
ADEEMNRSTTTUU MATURE STUDENT
ADEFFHILLNOSU FULL-FASHIONED
ADEFGHHILNOST SLEIGHT OF HAND
ADEFGHINOORSW FORESHADOWING
ADEFGIILLNPSY PLAYING FIELDS
ADEFGIINNOORR FOREORDAINING
ADEFGILLNOPST SOFT-PEDALLING
ADEFGNNOOOORT GOOD AFTERNOON
ADEFHILNOORSS FOOLHARDINESS
ADEFIILNPRSSU FREUDIAN SLIPS
ADEFILLSSTTUY DISTASTEFULLY
ADEFLLOOPSTYY SPLAYFOOTEDLY
ADEGGHIILLNST LEADING LIGHTS
ADEGGIILNNNST DISENTANGLING

628

ADEGGIILNNRSS NIGGARDLINESS
ADEGGINNORRRS ORGAN GRINDERS
ADEGHIKNNORRW WORK-HARDENING
ADEGHINNNOSTT ONE-NIGHT STAND
ADEGHINNOORTY HYDROGENATION
ADEGHINOORSVW OVERSHADOWING
ADEGHLLNORSST STRANGLEHOLDS
ADEGIIIMNNRST ADMINISTERING
ADEGIIIMNNSST DISSEMINATING
ADEGIIKNNRRTW DRINKING WATER
ADEGIIILLNNOST DIALLING TONES
ADEGIILNNOTTU DEGLUTINATION
ADEGIIMMNNRST MASTERMINDING
ADEGIIMNNOPRT PREDOMINATING
ADEGIIMOOPRST DIAGEOTROPISM
ADEGIINNNPRTU UNDERPAINTING
ADEGIINORRSTT DISINTEGRATOR
ADEGIKLNNOTWY TAKE LYING DOWN
ADEGILMOORSTT DERMATOLOGIST
ADEGILNNOQRTU GRANDILOQUENT
ADEGILNNQRSUY SQUANDERINGLY
ADEGIMNNORSTT DEMONSTRATING
ADEGIMNORRSUY YOUNG MARRIEDS
ADEHHIIILMOOP HAEMOPHILIOID
ADEHIILMNPSTY LYMPHADENITIS
ADEHIIMNOOSTT METHODISATION
ADEHIIMNOOTTZ METHODIZATION
ADEHILNNOPRSW LANDOWNERSHIP
ADEHINNRSSTWW WITHDRAWNNESS
ADEHINRSTUVYY HEAVY INDUSTRY
ADEHIOOPPRSST APOSTROPHISED
ADEHIOOPPRSTZ APOSTROPHIZED
ADEHLLOOPPSUY POLYADELPHOUS
ADEHLOPRRSSTU SHOULDER STRAP
ADEHNORRSTTWY NORTHWESTWARD
ADEHORSSTTUWW SOUTHWESTWARD
ADEIIIILMSSTV DISSIMILATIVE
ADEIIIILMSSTUV DISSIMULATIVE
ADEIIILNPSTTU PLATITUDINISE
ADEIIILNPTTUZ PLATITUDINIZE
ADEIIILNRSSTU INDUSTRIALISE
ADEIIILNRSTUZ INDUSTRIALIZE
ADEIIIMNNOSST DISSEMINATION
ADEIIINOSSTTV DEVIATIONISTS
ADEIIINRSSTTV DITRANSITIVES
ADEIIINRSTTTU ATTITUDINISER
ADEIIINRTTTUZ ATTITUDINIZER
ADEIIKPRRSTTY STRIKE PAY DIRT
ADEIIILLNQRSTU TRANQUILLISED
ADEIIILLNQRTUZ TRANQUILLIZED
ADEIIILMNOPSSY IMPASSIONEDLY
ADEIIILNOOTTVY DEVOTIONALITY
ADEIIMMNNOOTT TIME-AND-MOTION
ADEIIMMNNRSSU INDIAN SUMMERS
ADEIIMNNNOOST DENOMINATIONS
ADEIIMNNOOPRT PREDOMINATION
ADEIIMNNOORST MODERNISATION
ADEIIMNNOORTZ MODERNIZATION
ADEIIMNNORSTU TRADE UNIONISM

ADEIIMNNOSSTU MOUNTAINSIDES
ADEIINNNOSTTU UNITED NATIONS
ADEIINNOOPRRT PREORDINATION
ADEIINNOPSSST DISPENSATIONS
ADEIINNORSTTU TRADE UNIONIST
ADEIINORSSSTT DISSERTATIONS
ADEILLNRSTTUU UNILLUSTRATED
ADEILMNNOPRTY PREDOMINANTLY
ADEILNOORTUVY DEVOLUTIONARY
ADEIMNNOORSTT DEMONSTRATION
ADEINOSSSSSUU ASSIDUOUSNESS
ADEJLORSSSSTU LOSS ADJUSTERS
ADELNOPRRSTTY TRANSPORTEDLY
ADELNORSTUUVY ADVENTUROUSLY
ADEMNOORRSSTT DEMONSTRATORS
ADENNORSTUUUV UNADVENTUROUS
ADFFHILNOSSTY STANDOFFISHLY
ADFGGHHIILLNN HIGHLAND FLING
ADFGIIILNQSUY DISQUALIFYING
ADFGIIINSSSTY DISSATISFYING
ADFGIINNOPRTY INFANT PRODIGY
ADFHIMNOOORSU MAIDS OF HONOUR
ADGGHHHIIMNTY HIGH-AND-MIGHTY
ADGHIILMNNOSY ADMONISHINGLY
ADGHILLLMNOSS SMALLHOLDINGS
ADGHMNNOOPRRY GYNANDROMORPH
ADGIIILMNNSSTU DISSIMULATING
ADGIIIMNNOPPST DISAPPOINTING
ADGIILNNPRSST LANDING STRIPS
ADGIIMNNOSTUU MAGNITUDINOUS
ADGILNNOSTTUY OUTSTANDINGLY
ADHIILLNOQRTU QUADRILLIONTH
ADHIILNOPPSST SPIT AND POLISH
ADHIIMNOORSSU DISHARMONIOUS
ADHILNOORSTYY HYDROLYSATION
ADHIMNOPRSSSW SWORDSMANSHIP
ADIIIILMNOSST DISSIMILATION
ADIIIILMNPRTU PLATINIRIDIUM
ADIIIILMRSSTY DISSIMILARITY
ADIIIILLNOSSTT DISTILLATIONS
ADIIILMNOSSTU DISSIMULATION
ADIIILMNRSSTU INDUSTRIALISM
ADIIILMORSSTY DISSIMILATORY
ADIIILNOOPSST DISPOSITIONAL
ADIIILNRSSTTU INDUSTRIALIST
ADIILNNNORSTU NONINDUSTRIAL
ADIILNOPSTTUU PLATITUDINOUS
ADIMNNOORSSWY IN SO MANY WORDS
AEEEEEINPRRRS ARRIÈRE-PENSÉE
AEEEEFHNRTTTV AFTER THE EVENT
AEEEEHHNNSTVV SEVENTH HEAVEN
AEEEEILNRRSST RENSSELAERITE
AEEEEIMNPRSST PASSEMENTERIE
AEEEELPRRSSSS PRESS RELEASES
AEEEEMNPRSSTT TEMPERATENESS
AEEEFGHHIRTTW FEATHERWEIGHT
AEEEFGHLNRTTU FEATURE-LENGTH
AEEEFGIIRRRTV REFRIGERATIVE
AEEEFILRSSSTV SELF-ASSERTIVE

AEEEFINQRTTUV FREQUENTATIVE
AEEEFNORRSTTW WATER SOFTENER
AEEEGGIMNOSST GAMETOGENESIS
AEEEGHHINPRSS SHEEPSHEARING
AEEEGHLLOPPRT TELEGRAPH POLE
AEEEGHLNOPRRS SELENOGRAPHER
AEEEGHMNOPRST MAGNETOSPHERE
AEEEGIKLMNRTT TELEMARKETING
AEEEGIKLNRRST GENERAL STRIKE
AEEEGILMNNORT NOLI-ME-TANGERE
AEEEGILNOPSTV NEGATIVE POLES
AEEEGIMNPRRTY PRAYER MEETING
AEEEGLMNNNSTT ENTANGLEMENTS
AEEEGMNNRSSTT ESTRANGEMENTS
AEEEGNOOPRRST OPERATOR GENES
AEEEHHILNPTTW WHITE ELEPHANT
AEEEHHNOPRSST ASTHENOSPHERE
AEEEHHOPPRSTU PAPER THE HOUSE
AEEEHIIMMNNTT IN THE MEANTIME
AEEEHILMNNOPP EPIPHENOMENAL
AEEEHIMOPRSSV OVEREMPHASIS
AEEEHIMOPRSVZ OVEREMPHASIZE
AEEEHLLMNSSTV MANTELSHELVES
AEEEHLMNSSSSS SHAMELESSNESS
AEEEHLNPSSSSS SHAPELESSNESS
AEEEHLNRSSSST HEARTLESSNESS
AEEEHLORSSTUX HETEROSEXUALS
AEEEHMNORSSST HEARTSOMENESS
AEEEIIILLLNTV ILLE-ET-VILAINE
AEEEIIIMMNRST SEINE-MARITIME
AEEEIILNSTTUV EVENTUALITIES
AEEEIIMNRTTVX EXTERMINATIVE
AEEEIKLLOPPST SLEEP LIKE A TOP
AEEEIKLNPSTTV PALETTE KNIVES
AEEEIKNPRSSVW SNEAK PREVIEWS
AEEEILLNRRTVY REVERENTIALLY
AEEEILMNPRSSX EXEMPLARINESS
AEEEILMNPRTTY INTEMPERATELY
AEEEILNPRTTVY PENETRATIVELY
AEEEIMNNNRTTT ENTERTAINMENT
AEEEIMNNRSTTT REINSTATEMENT
AEEEIMNORSSSW WEARISOMENESS
AEEEIMORSSTTV OVERESTIMATES
AEEEINNPSSSVX EXPANSIVENESS
AEEEINNSSTTTV ATTENTIVENESS,
    TENTATIVENESS
AEEEINOPRRSTV PERSEVERATION
AEEEINOPRSSTV OPERATIVENESS
AEEEINPRSSSVV PERVASIVENESS
AEEEINRSSSSTV ASSERTIVENESS
AEEEIPRRSSTVV PRESERVATIVES
AEEEKLLMRRSST SELLER'S MARKET
AEEEKLRRSSTTW STREETWALKERS
AEEELLNSSSSUV VALUELESSNESS
AEEELNPRSTTTT LETTERS PATENT
AEEELNSSSSSTT STATELESSNESS,
    TASTELESSNESS
AEEEMMNOPRTTU PNEUMATOMETER
AEEEMNORSTTTV OVERSTATEMENT

AEEEMNPRRSSTU PREMATURENESS
AEEENOPRSSTTT POSTE RESTANTE
AEEEORRRSTTUV TREASURE TROVE
AEEFFGHIRRSTU FATHER FIGURES
AEEFFGINORRST REAFFORESTING
AEEFFHIMOPPTW WIPE OFF THE MAP
AEEFGGIINRRRT REFRIGERATING
AEEFGIINORRRT REFRIGERATION
AEEFGIIPRRTUV PREFIGURATIVE
AEEFGIKRRSSTU FIGURE SKATERS
AEEFGINORRSTU ARGENTIFEROUS
AEEFGIORRRRST REFRIGERATORS
AEEFHHLLNSSTU HEALTHFULNESS
AEEFHILNSSSST FAITHLESSNESS
AEEFHKMMOOSTT MAKE THE MOST OF
AEEFHLMOOPRRT MOTHER-OF-PEARL
AEEFHLMORRSTW FLAME-THROWERS
AEEFHLNOOPSTT ELEPHANT'S-FOOT
AEEFIILLNNRTY INFERENTIALLY
AEEFIILOPRRTV PROLIFERATIVE
AEEFILLMORSTU METALLIFEROUS
AEEFILNORSSST SELF-ASSERTION
AEEFILNRRSSTT SELF-RESTRAINT
AEEFIMNORSSTV FORMATIVENESS
AEEFIMOORRRST REFORMATORIES
AEEFINNOQRTTU FREQUENTATION
AEEFINNORSSSU NEFARIOUSNESS
AEEFINOORRSTT REFORESTATION
AEEFINOPRSTTU SUPERFETATION
AEEFIOOPRRSST PROFESSORIATE
AEEFLLNSSSSTU FAULTLESSNESS
AEEFLMNRSSSTU MASTERFULNESS
AEEGGHHOOOPRRZ ZOOGEOGRAPHER
AEEGGIILNNNRV LINE-ENGRAVING
AEEGGIILNNORTU OUTGENERALING
AEEGGINNOORSS ORGANOGENESIS
AEEGGINNSTTTW WETTING AGENTS
AEEGGLLORRSUY ROGUES' GALLERY
AEEGHHMOPRRRT THERMOGRAPHER
AEEGHHMPRSTUV HAVE THE GRUMPS
AEEGHHNOPRRST ETHNOGRAPHERS
AEEGHIINNSTTZ ANESTHETIZING
AEEGHILMOORST ISOGEOTHERMAL
AEEGHILNNRTTY THREATENINGLY
AEEGHILNORSTW WATERING HOLES
AEEGHIMOPRRSS SEISMOGRAPHER
AEEGHIPRSSSTW STAGE WHISPERS
AEEGHNOOPRRTV PHOTOENGRAVER
AEEGHNOPRRSST STENOGRAPHERS
AEEGIIINSTTVV INVESTIGATIVE
AEEGIILMNORSS GENERALISSIMO
AEEGIILNNRTXZ EXTERNALIZING
AEEGIIMNNORTT REGIMENTATION
AEEGIIMNNRTTX EXTERMINATING
AEEGIIMNRSTTU TIME SIGNATURE
AEEGIINNOORTT RENEGOTIATION
AEEGIINNOPRRT PEREGRINATION
AEEGIINORRTTV INTERROGATIVE
AEEGIKMNPRRST PARKING METERS

AEEGIKNRSSTUY KEY SIGNATURES	AEEIIMNPSSSSV IMPASSIVENESS
AEEGILLLNPRST SELLING-PLATER	AEEIIMNQRSSTU EQUESTRIANISM
AEEGILLMNNSSY MEANINGLESSLY	AEEIINNOQRSTU QUESTIONNAIRE
AEEGILLNRSTVY EVERLASTINGLY	AEEIKNOPRSSTT STREPTOKINASE
AEEGILNNPRTTY PENETRATINGLY	AEEILLMNNSTTY SENTIMENTALLY
AEEGILNNTTUXY EXTENUATINGLY	AEEILLNNOPTXY EXPONENTIALLY
AEEGIMMNOOTTV MAGNETOMOTIVE	AEEILLNOPRRTT INTERPELLATOR
AEEGIMNNRTTUY INTEGUMENTARY	AEEILLPRSTUVY SUPERLATIVELY
AEEGIMNORRSTV OVERMASTERING	AEEILLRRRSTTY TERRESTRIALLY
AEEGINNRSTTUU SIGNATURE TUNE	AEEILLRTTTTTT TITTLE-TATTLER
AEEGINQRSSTTU SEQUESTRATING	AEEILMNNNORTV ENVIRONMENTAL
AEEGINRRSSSTV TRANSGRESSIVE	AEEILMOPRRTXY EXTEMPORARILY
AEEGIORRRSTTV TERGIVERSATOR	AEEILNNNOOPPS PELOPONNESIAN
AEEGLLMNRSUWZ MANGEL-WURZELS	AEEILNNNOPRST ANTIPERSONNEL
AEEHHIINNOPTZ PHENOTHIAZINE	AEEILNNOPRRST INTERPERSONAL
AEEHHILLMNSVW WILHELMSHAVEN	AEEILNNPRRSTT SILENT PARTNER
AEEHHILMMNNTT NEMATHELMINTH	AEEILNNQQTUUV QUINQUEVALENT
AEEHHILNNSSTU UNHEALTHINESS	AEEILNNRSSSUV UNIVERSALNESS
AEEHHMOPRRTTY THERMOTHERAPY	AEEILNOORRSTV LATEROVERSION
AEEHIILLNNOST HELLENISATION	AEEILNPRRRSST LASER PRINTERS
AEEHIILLNNOTZ HELLENIZATION	AEEILOPRSSTUY ERYSIPELATOUS
AEEHIKLNNPPST PINK ELEPHANTS	AEEILPPRSSTUW WATER SUPPLIES
AEEHILMMNNOPS PHENOMENALISM	AEEIMMNSSSTTT MISSTATEMENTS
AEEHILMNNOPST PHENOMENALIST	AEEIMNNOPPRTT REAPPOINTMENT
AEEHILNNRSSTU UNEARTHLINESS	AEEIMNOPRRSST TEMPORARINESS
AEEHILORRSSTU TRAILER HOUSES	AEEIMNOPRSSTX PROXIMATENESS
AEEHIMNQSSSSU SQUEAMISHNESS	AEEIMNORRSTTV REMONSTRATIVE
AEEHINNOPPRSS APPREHENSIONS	AEEIMNORRSTTX EXTERMINATORS
AEEHINORSSSTW SEAWORTHINESS	AEEINNNRSSSTU SATURNINENESS
AEEHIOPPSSTTV STOVEPIPE HATS	AEEINNOPRSSTT PRESENTATIONS
AEEHIORRRRSST HAIR-RESTORERS	AEEINOOPRRTTX RE-EXPORTATION
AEEHIPRRRSSTU TREASURERSHIP	AEEINOORRSTUV ARTERIOVENOUS
AEEHKLNNSSSST THANKLESSNESS	AEEINOQRSSTTU SEQUESTRATION
AEEHLMNOOSSST LOATHSOMENESS	AEEINOSSSTUVX VEXATIOUSNESS
AEEHLNORRSTTY NORTHEASTERLY	AEEINRSSSTTTV TRANSVESTITES
AEEHLORSSTTUY SOUTHEASTERLY	AEEIOOPPRSTTV POSTOPERATIVE
AEEHMMOOPRSST METAMORPHOSES	AEEIPPRRSSSTT ASSET-STRIPPER
AEEHMMOPSSTUY EMPHYSEMATOUS	AEEKLLORRRSST ROLLER-SKATERS
AEEHMNOOPPRTU PNEUMATOPHORE	AEEKMORRSSSTT MASTERSTROKES
AEEHMOOPPRRST SPERMATOPHORE	AEELMNPPRSTUY SUPPLEMENTARY
AEEHMOOPPRSTTY SPERMATOPHYTE	AEELNOOPSSTTU STENOPETALOUS
AEEIIILMNPRRS PRELIMINARIES	AEEMMNOPRTTUY PNEUMATOMETRY
AEEIIIMNSSTTV IMITATIVENESS	AEEMNOOPRSTTU TREPONEMATOUS
AEEIIILLNNPTTY PENITENTIALLY	AEEMNPRRRSUUY SUPERNUMERARY
AEEIILMNOPRSS IMPERSONALISE	AEFFGIMRSSTTM SUFFRAGETTISM
AEEIILMNOPRSZ IMPERSONALIZE	AEFGGIIKNRSTU FIGURE-SKATING
AEEIILNNORRTT INTERRELATION	AEFGHHOORRSTU THOROUGHFARES
AEEIILNNPSSTV PLAINTIVENESS	AEFGHHORSTTTU AFTERTHOUGHTS
AEEIILNNTTTVY INATTENTIVELY	AEFGHIKMNNOOT MAKE NOTHING OF
AEEIILNOPQTTU EQUIPOTENTIAL	AEFGHINNNPRTY PENNY-FARTHING
AEEIILNOPRSST PERSONALITIES	AEFGIILLORRSU ARGILLIFEROUS
AEEIILNOPRTTV INTERPOLATIVE	AEFGIILNOPRRT PROLIFERATING
AEEIILNORSTTV REVELATIONIST	AEFGIINOPRRTU PREFIGURATION
AEEIILNORSTVY TELEVISIONARY	AEFGILLNNRTUY UNFALTERINGLY
AEEIILNQSTTUY SEQUENTIALITY	AEFGILNNORRWY FOREWARNINGLY
AEEIILORRRTTX EXTERRITORIAL	AEFGILNOORTTV FLOATING VOTER
AEEIIMMNORSST MESMERISATION	AEFGINOOPRRTW WATERPROOFING
AEEIIMMNORSTZ MESMERIZATION	AEFHKLMORSSST THERMOS FLASKS
AEEIIMNNORTTX EXTERMINATION	AEFHKNOOSSTTV VOTES OF THANKS

AEFHLOOSTTUUU OUT OF THE USUAL
AEFIIIILMNNST INFINITESIMAL
AEFIIIILMNSSST SEMIFINALISTS
AEFIIIILNORSTT FERTILISATION
AEFIIIILNORTTZ FERTILIZATION
AEFIIILLLNNTUY INFLUENTIALLY
AEFIILMNORSUU ALUMINIFEROUS
AEFIILMNORTVY INFORMATIVELY
AEFIILNOOPRRT PROLIFERATION
AEFIILNOOPRSTU PLATINIFEROUS
AEFIIMNOOPRRT IMPERFORATION
AEFIIMNORSSTU STAMINIFEROUS
AEFIINRRSTTTY INTERSTRATIFY
AEFILLOPRSSTW LOW-PASS FILTER
AEFILMNOPRSTT SELF-IMPORTANT
AEFILNOOPRSSS PROFESSIONALS
AEFILNOOPRSSW PASSIONFLOWER
AEFILNOOQSTUW QUESTION OF LAW
AEFINOOPRRRSW PRISONER OF WAR
AEFIOQRRSTUUZ QUARTZIFEROUS
AEFLLMNORSSTU SMALL FORTUNES
AEFLNNORTTUUY UNFORTUNATELY
AEGGGIINRRTTU REGURGITATING
AEGGHHLOPPRRY GLYPHOGRAPHER
AEGGHIILNRRTT RIGHT TRIANGLE
AEGGHIIMMNOPR MIMEOGRAPHING
AEGGHIINNRSTT STRAIGHTENING
AEGGHILNOORTW WOOLGATHERING
AEGGHLOOPRRSS GLOSSOGRAPHER
AEGGHLOPPRRTY GLYPTOGRAPHER
AEGGIIIMNPSTT SPITTING IMAGE
AEGGIIINNSTTV INVESTIGATING
AEGGIINNORRTT INTERROGATING
AEGGIINORRTTU REGURGITATION
AEGGIINRSTTTT SITTING TARGET
AEGGINNNOORSS NONAGGRESSION
AEGGINNRRSSST TRANSGRESSING
AEGHHILNORSSY ROYAL HIGHNESS
AEGHHIOPPRRSY PHYSIOGRAPHER
AEGHHOOPPRRST PHOTOGRAPHERS
AEGHIIKNNPRSS PINKING SHEARS
AEGHIINNSTTUX EXTINGUISHANT
AEGHIIPRRRSST REGISTRARSHIP
AEGHIKNNRRSTT KNIGHTS-ERRANT
AEGHILLLNNRTY ENTHRALLINGLY
AEGHILNORSTUV VAULTING HORSE
AEGHILOOPRSST PHRASEOLOGIST
AEGHIMNORSSUW HOUSEWARMINGS
AEGHIMNORTTUW MOUTH-WATERING
AEGHINNOORSST ON A SHOESTRING
AEGHIOPRRSSTU SURROGATESHIP
AEGHLMMOORTTY THREMMATOLOGY
AEGHMNOOOPSTU ENTOMOPHAGOUS
AEGHNNOOPTTUY PUT ON THE AGONY
AEGHNOOPPRRRS PORNOGRAPHERS
AEGIIILNNNRTZ INTERNALIZING
AEGIIILNRSSTU SINGULARITIES
AEGIIINNOSTTV INVESTIGATION
AEGIIILLOPRSSS ASPERGILLOSIS

AEGIILMNORSST MINERALOGISTS
AEGIILMNORSYY SYRINGOMYELIA
AEGIILMNPRSST SLIPSTREAMING
AEGIILMOOSSST SEMASIOLOGIST
AEGIILNNOPRSZ PERSONALIZING
AEGIILNNOPRTT INTERPOLATING
AEGIILNNRRSTY RESTRAININGLY
AEGIILNRSSTVV VESTAL VIRGINS
AEGIIMNNOPRST IMPERSONATING
AEGIIMNNRRRTY INTERMARRYING
AEGIIMNSSTTYZ SYSTEMATIZING
AEGIINNOORRTT INTERROGATION
AEGIINOPPRRTX EXPROPRIATING
AEGIINORRSSTT REGISTRATIONS
AEGIINORSSTTV INVESTIGATORS
AEGIJLPSSUWZZ JIGSAW PUZZLES
AEGIKLLNORRST ROLLER SKATING
AEGILLLMNSSST SMELLING SALTS
AEGILLMNOORSS LEMON GRASS OIL
AEGILLMRSSTTU METALLURGISTS
AEGILMNORSSTU SOMERSAULTING
AEGILNOOPRRSS PROGRESSIONAL
AEGILNOPSTTUX EXPOSTULATING
AEGIMNNOPRRRY MORNING PRAYER
AEGIMNNORRSTT REMONSTRATING
AEGIMNOOPRSSU ANGIOSPERMOUS
AEGIMOOOPPRST APOGEOTROPISM
AEGINNORRSSST TRANSGRESSION
AEGINOORRRSTT INTERROGATORS
AEGINOORRRTTY INTERROGATORY
AEGLMNOORSSSU GLAMOROUSNESS
AEGLMOOSSTTYY SYSTEMATOLOGY
AEGLNORRSSSUU GARRULOUSNESS
AEGNORRRSSSST TRANSGRESSORS
AEHHHINOPRRRY HERNIORRHAPHY
AEHHIIILMNSST HELMINTHIASIS
AEHHIINORSTTW WITHIN EARSHOT
AEHHILLMNPTTY PLATYHELMINTH
AEHHIMNOPRSTT THEANTHROPISM
AEHHINOPRSTTT THEANTHROPIST
AEHHIOPPRSTYY PHYSIOTHERAPY
AEHHLLMORSSTU THE SMALL HOURS
AEHHLNORRTUUY UNEARTHLY HOUR
AEHHLOOPPRSSY PHOSPHORYLASE
AEHHOOPPPRSTY PYROPHOSPHATE
AEHHOOPRRSSST SHARPSHOOTERS
AEHIILNOPRSST RELATIONSHIPS
AEHIILNORSSSU HILARIOUSNESS
AEHIINORRSSTW AIRWORTHINESS
AEHIIRRSSSTTW SHIRTWAISTERS
AEHILMMNORTUY ALUMINOTHERMY
AEHILMOOSTUXY HOMOSEXUALITY
AEHILMOPPRSTY AMPHIPROSTYLE
AEHIMMNOPRTUY IMMUNOTHERAPY
AEHIMMOOPRSST METAMORPHOSIS
AEHIMNNPRSSTT TRANSSHIPMENT
AEHIMNPRSTUUY SUPERHUMANITY
AEHINNOORSSTT NORTH OSSETIAN
AEHINOOSSSTTU STATION HOUSES

AEHINOPRSSSUV	VAPOURISHNESS
AEHLMNOOPRTVW	WOLVERHAMPTON
AEHMNOOPRRTTY	ANTHROPOMETRY
AEHMNOOPRSSSU	AMORPHOUSNESS
AEHMNOQRTTUUY	QUANTUM THEORY
AEHOOPRRSSSUW	HOUSE SPARROWS
AEIIILLLMNNST	MILLENNIALIST
AEIIILLMNORSS	MILLIONAIRESS
AEIIILLMNPRRY	PRELIMINARILY
AEIIILLMNRSTY	MINISTERIALLY
AEIIILNORSSTT	STERILISATION
AEIIILNORSTTU	REUTILISATION
AEIIILNORSTTZ	STERILIZATION
AFIIILNORTTUZ	REUTILIZATION
AEIIILPRRSSTU	SPIRITUALISER
AEIIILPRRSTUZ	SPIRITUALIZER
AEIIIMNOOPSTT	EPITOMISATION
AEIIIMNOOPTTZ	EPITOMIZATION
AEIIIMNOORSST	ISOMERISATION
AEIIIMNOORSTZ	ISOMERIZATION
AEIIINNORSSSV	VISIONARINESS
AEIIINNOSSSTT	SENSITISATION
AEIIINNOSSTTZ	SENSITIZATION
AEIIINOOSSTTV	SOVIETISATION
AEIIINOOSTTVZ	SOVIETIZATION
AEIIILLNNNOTTY	INTENTIONALLY
AEIIILLNOQRTUV	VENTRILOQUIAL
AEIIILLNQRRSTU	TRANQUILLISER
AEIIILLNQRRTUZ	TRANQUILLIZER
AEIILMNNOOPRS	PRONOMINALISE
AEIILMNNOOPRZ	PRONOMINALIZE
AEIILMNNOOSST	SOLEMNISATION
AEIILMNNOOSTZ	SOLEMNIZATION
AEIILMNNOPSTU	EMULSION PAINT
AEIILMNOORSTT	TOLERATIONISM
AEIILMNOPRSTY	IMPERSONALITY
AEIILNNNNOTTU	UNINTENTIONAL
AEIILNNNORTTU	INTERLUNATION
AEIILNNOOPRTT	INTERPOLATION
AEIILNOOPPRST	PREPOSITIONAL
AEIILNOOPSTTX	SEXPLOITATION
AEIILNOORSTTT	TOLERATIONIST
AEIILNOPRSTUV	PULVERISATION
AEIILNOPRTUVZ	PULVERIZATION
AEIILOOPPRRRT	PROPRIETORIAL
AEIILOPPRRRTY	PROPRIETARILY
AEIIMNNOOPRST	IMPERSONATION
AEIIMNOOPRRTT	REIMPORTATION
AEIIMNOOPRSTT	TEMPORISATION
AEIIMNOOPRTTZ	TEMPORIZATION
AEIIMNOSSSTTY	SYSTEMISATION
AEIIMNOSSTTYZ	SYSTEMIZATION
AEIINNOOPPSTT	PEPTONISATION
AEIINNOOPPTTZ	PEPTONIZATION
AEIINNOPSSSTX	EXPANSIONISTS
AEIINOOPPRRTX	EXPROPRIATION
AEIINOOPRSSTT	ESPIRITO SANTO
AEIINOOPRSTTX	EXTRAPOSITION
AEIINOORRRSTT	TERRORISATION
AEIINOORRRTTZ	TERRORIZATION
AEIINORRSSSTT	TRANSISTORISE
AEIINORRSSTTZ	TRANSISTORIZE
AEIKLMNOPRSST	SPORTSMANLIKE
AEIKMNOQRSSTU	QUESTION MARKS
AEILLLMNOOSSS	SALMONELLOSIS
AEILLMMMNOOST	MONOMETALLISM
AEILLMMNOOSTT	MONOMETALLIST
AEILLNOPRTTWW	WILLOW PATTERN
AEILLNOPSSSSY	PASSIONLESSLY
AEILLORRRSTTY	ROTARY TILLERS
AEILMMNNOTTUY	MONUMENTALITY
AEILMNOOPRSTT	METROPOLITANS
AEILMNOPRTTUY	IMPORTUNATELY
AEILMNOPSSTUY	PNEUMATOLYSIS
AEILNNORSSTUV	VOLUNTARINESS
AEILNNORSTUVY	INTRAVENOUSLY
AEILNNRSTTUWW	UNWRITTEN LAWS
AEILNOOOOPRRST	POOR RELATIONS
AEILNOOPRSTTT	PETROL STATION
AEILNOOPSTTUX	EXPOSTULATION
AEILNOORRTUVY	REVOLUTIONARY
AEILOOOOPPPRS	PROSOPOPOEIAL
AEIMNNOOPPRTT	APPORTIONMENT
AEIMNNOORRSTT	REMONSTRATION
AEIMNNORSSTTU	MENSTRUATIONS
AEIMNOOPRRSST	IMPERSONATORS
AEIMNOPRSSTTT	PROTESTANTISM
AEIMPRRRSSSTY	PRIMARY STRESS
AEINNORSSSUUV	UNSAVOURINESS
AEINOOOOPPRRTT	PROPORTIONATE
AEINOOPRSSTTT	PROTESTATIONS
AEINOOPRSSTTW	POWER STATIONS
AEIOOOPPRRRSTX	EXPROPRIATORS
AEKLOOOPPRSTVV	PETROPAVLOVSK
AELNNOOPSSTUY	SPONTANEOUSLY
AELOOPRSTTUXY	EXPOSTULATORY
AEMMNOOOORSTTU	MONOTREMATOUS
AEMNOOOPRSSZZ	MEZZO-SOPRANOS
AENNNORSSSTUY	TYRANNOUSNESS
AENOOOOPPRRTXY	PROPAROXYTONE
AENOPRRSSSTUU	RAPTUROUSNESS
AFFGIIMNOSTUU	SUFFUMIGATION
AFGGHHIIRSTTT	STRAIGHT FIGHT
AFGGIINNRRSTU	TRANSFIGURING
AFGHIINOPRRST	PROFIT SHARING
AFGHIKNOORTUW	FOR AUGHT I KNOW
AFGIIILNNRTUY	INFURIATINGLY
AFGIILNNOOPTT	FLOATING-POINT
AFGIIMNOPRRST	PROFIT MARGINS
AFGIKNOORSSTT	TOASTING FORKS
AFIIILNNORSTT	INFILTRATIONS
AFIIILNOOSSST	FOSSILISATION
AFIIILNOOSSTZ	FOSSILIZATION
AFIIILNOOOPRS	FLORIANOPOLIS
AFIILLORSTTUY	FLIRTATIOUSLY
AFILNOPPRRUUV	FLAVOPURPURIN
AGGHHIILNOPRT	LITHOGRAPHING
AGGHHINOOPPRT	PHOTOGRAPHING

AGGHHMOPPRSYY   SPHYGMOGRAPHY
AGGHIIKLNPRST   PARKING LIGHTS
AGGHIIKNNSSTV   THANKSGIVINGS
AGGHILOOPRSST   GRAPHOLOGISTS
AGGIIILNNOSTU   ISOAGGLUTININ
AGGIIILNNSTTY   INSTIGATINGLY
AGGIIINNORTTU   INGURGITATION
AGGIILNNOPPRR   GRAPPLING IRON
AGGILLNOORSTY   LARYNGOLOGIST
AGHHIILMNRSTY   NIGHTMARISHLY
AGHHILMNOPPSU   PLOUGHMANSHIP
AGHHIMNOORSTT   ORTHOGNATHISM
AGHHLLMOOOPTY   OPHTHALMOLOGY
AGHHLMNNOOOPT   MONOPHTHONGAL
AGHHNOOORSTTU   ORTHOGNATHOUS
AGHIIILLMNTUY   HUMILIATINGLY
AGHIIILNOPSTZ   HOSPITALIZING
AGHIIILNPRSTT   HAIR-SPLITTING
AGHIILNNOSSTY   ASTONISHINGLY
AGHIINOPPRSTU   UPRIGHT PIANOS
AGHINOOPSTTTT   PHOTOSTATTING
AGHINOORSSSTT   SHOOTING STARS
AGHLLMOORSUUW   GALLOWS HUMOUR
AGIIILLLNTTTY   TITILLATINGLY
AGIIILLMNRSTU   TRILINGUALISM
AGIIILMMNNPRT   MALIMPRINTING
AGIIILMMNORTZ   IMMORTALIZING
AGIIILNNNOOPT   NO OIL PAINTING
AGIIKLNNOPSTT   TALKING POINTS
AGIILLMNSTTUY   STIMULATINGLY
AGIILLNOOSSTY   SYLLOGISATION
AGIILLNOOSTYZ   SYLLOGIZATION
AGIILMOOPPRST   PLAGIOTROPISM
AGIILNNNRTYYZ   TYRANNIZINGLY
AGIILNNOPRTYZ   PATRONIZINGLY
AGIILOORSSSTY   ASSYRIOLOGIST
AGIIMNOORRSUV   GRAMINIVOROUS
AGIINNOPRTTTY   POTTY-TRAINING
AGILMMNOOSTUY   NUMISMATOLOGY
AGILMOORRSTTY   MARTYROLOGIST
AGILNNOOOOPRST   PROLONGATIONS
AGIMNOOOPRSUZ   ZOOSPORANGIUM
AHHNOOOPPRSTY   ANTHROPOSOPHY
AHIIILNOOPRRT   HORRIPILATION
AHIIILNOPSTTY   INHOSPITALITY
AHIIMMNOOOSSU   HOMOOUSIANISM
AHIJNNOPRSTUZ   ZINJANTHROPUS
AHIMNOPPRSSST   SPORTSMANSHIP
AHKLNNOOPPTTY   PHYTOPLANKTON
AHLLMMMOOOTWY   WOOLLY MAMMOTH
AHMMOOOOOPRSTU   OMMATOPHOROUS
AIIIILNNOQSTU   INQUISITIONAL
AIIIILNOQRSTU   INQUISITORIAL
AIIIIMNPPSSSS   MISSISSIPPIAN
AIIILLMNNOSTU   ILLUMINATIONS
AIIILLMNPSTUY   PUSILLANIMITY
AIIILNNOSTTTU   INSTITUTIONAL
AIIILNOOSSSTT   ISOLATIONISTS
AIIILPRSSSTTU   SPIRITUALISTS

AIIIMMNNOSSTU   IMMUNISATIONS
AIIIMMNNOSTUZ   IMMUNIZATIONS
AIIIMNOOPPRRT   IMPROPRIATION
AIIIMNOOPRSTV   IMPROVISATION
AIIINNNOOSTTV   INNOVATIONIST
AIIIOOPPRSTTU   PROPITIATIOUS
AIIJNOOPSTTUX   JUXTAPOSITION
AIILLMNOPSSUU   PUSILLANIMOUS
AIILLNNORTUVY   INVOLUNTARILY
AIILLNOOPRSVY   PROVISIONALLY
AIILLNORSSTTU   ILLUSTRATIONS
AIILMNNNOOSTU   MOUNTAIN LIONS
AIILNOOOPPRST   PROPOSITIONAL
AIILNOOPPSSTU   SUPPOSITIONAL
AIILNOOPSSSTU   SAN LUIS POTOSI
AIIMNNORSSSST   TRANSMISSIONS
AIIMNOOQSSTTU   MISQUOTATIONS
AIINNOOPRSSTT   TRANSPOSITION
AIIOOOPRSUVVV   OVOVIVIPAROUS
AILMOOOPSSSTX   TOXOPLASMOSIS
AIMOORRRSTWWY   TWO-WAY MIRRORS
BBCDEELMORSTU   CLUSTER-BOMBED
BBCDGIIKLLNOU   BUILDING BLOCK
BBCEEGIKNNRRU   RUBBERNECKING
BBCEEIORRSSUV   OVERSUBSCRIBE
BBCEHMOORRSTU   BUTCHER'S-BROOM
BBCEIILMNOSTU   INCOMBUSTIBLE
BBCGGHIILNNTU   NIGHTCLUBBING
BBDEELNRSSSUU   BLUNDERBUSSES
BBDEGHMNOORSY   HYDROGEN BOMBS
BBDEHLOOOORRST   BLOOD BROTHERS
BBDIIILNOOSVY   DIVISION LOBBY
BBEEEEEEHIIJS   HEEBIE-JEEBIES
BBEEFGHIMORRT   FIGHTER-BOMBER
BBEEGMNORRSUY   MONEY-GRUBBERS
BBEENNNRRSSUU   BUNSEN BURNERS
BBEGGIMNNORUY   MONEY-GRUBBING
BBINNOOOORRSTT   TORN TO RIBBONS
BCCCDEIIMRRSU   CIRCUMSCRIBED
BCCCHINOOOPRS   BRONCHOSCOPIC
BCCDDEEEHKLOU   DOUBLE-CHECKED
BCCDEEIJORSTT   DIRECT OBJECTS
BCCEEHIKKKTTU   KICK THE BUCKET
BCCEEHNORRSSS   CROSSBENCHERS
BCCEEIILORRTT   TRIBOELECTRIC
BCCEEIINRSTTY   CYBERNETICIST
BCCEEILORRTTU   TURBO-ELECTRIC
BCCEEHHINOOOSS   HOBSON'S CHOICE
BCCEIIIJOSTTV   OBJECTIVISTIC
BCCEIIILNNNOV   INCONVINCIBLE
BCCEILNORSTTU   CONSTRUCTIBLE
BCCHILLOOPSSU   PUBLIC SCHOOLS
BCDDDELLLOOOY   COLD-BLOODEDLY
BCDDEEEEKLORSU   DOUBLE-DECKERS
BCDDEELLLOORS   RED BLOOD CELLS
BCDDEELOORSSU   DOUBLE-CROSSED
BCDDEIIILTTUY   DEDUCTIBILITY
BCDDGILLNOORU   BLOODCURDLING
BCDEEEILLLNPU   BLUE-PENCILLED

BCDEEEKORRSST STOCKBREEDERS
BCDEEEGIKNORST STOCKBREEDING
BCDEEEGINORRSS CROSSBREEDING
BCDEEIIILNNRS INDISCERNIBLE
BCDEELOORRSSU DOUBLE-CROSSER
BCDEELOORSSSU DOUBLE-CROSSES
BCDEIIILNRTY INCREDIBILITY
BCDEIILNORTUY INDOLEBUTYRIC
BCDGHIIKKRRTU KIRKCUDBRIGHT
BCDGIKNOOSSTY BODY STOCKINGS
BCDIIILOORRTY CORRODIBILITY
BCDIIILOPRTUY PRODUCIBILITY
BCEEEEFFILRSV EFFERVESCIBLE
BCEEEEFKNOORR REFERENCE BOOK
BCEEEFGIINNHH BIREFRINGENCE
BCEEEGIINORST BIOENERGETICS
BCEEEGILLNORT COBELLIGERENT
BCEEEHIKLRRSU HUCKLEBERRIES
BCEEEHLNNOORZ CHLOROBENZENE
BCEEEIILMPPRT IMPERCEPTIBLE
BCEEEIJNOSSTV OBJECTIVENESS
BCEEEIILNOPRWY EYEBROW PENCIL
BCEEEELNORSTVY CONVEYER BELTS
BCEEFHNNORRST FRONTBENCHERS
BCEEGILMNNRUY ENCUMBERINGLY
BCEEHIILRRSSV SILVER BIRCHES
BCEEIILMPPRTY IMPERCEPTIBLY
BCEEIILNNORTV INCONVERTIBLE
BCEEIILNPSSTU INSUSCEPTIBLE
BCEEIILPPRRST PRESCRIPTIBLE
BCEEIMMOSSTTU SUBCOMMITTEES
BCEEJLNOOSSST OBJECT LESSONS
BCEFFIOOOPSTX POST OFFICE BOX
BCEFHIMNOOOTT FINE-TOOTH COMB
BCEFHINOOSSST SONS-OF-BITCHES
BCEFJMOOORRST JOB'S COMFORTER
BCEGHILNOOOTY BIOTECHNOLOGY
BCEGIKLNOSSTU BLUESTOCKINGS
BCEIIIILQRSTU EQUILIBRISTIC
BCEIILNOPRRTU INCORRUPTIBLE
BCEILMNOOPRYY POLYEMBRYONIC
BCEILORSTTUVY OBSTRUCTIVELY
BCEINNNOSSTTU SUBCONTINENTS
BCERRSSSTTUUU SUBSTRUCTURES
BCFGIIMMNNOOR COMBINING FORM
BCGHILNOOOORY CHRONOBIOLOGY
BCGHILOOOPSYY PSYCHOBIOLOGY
BCGIIIILORRTY CORRIGIBILITY
BCGIILMNNORS CLIMBING IRONS
BCGIILOOORSTY CRYOBIOLOGIST
BCIIIIILMMSTY IMMISCIBILITY
BCIIIIILNNTVY INVINCIBILITY
BCIILNOPRRTUY INCORRUPTIBLY
BCIINNOORSTTU CONTRIBUTIONS
BCIINOPRSSSTU SUBSCRIPTIONS
BDDEEEEGNNRRS GENDER-BENDERS
BDDEEEGINNRRU UNDERBREEDING
BDDEEEILLMOSW DISEMBOWELLED
BDDEEIILNOSTY DISOBEDIENTLY

BDDEEIIMMNOST DISEMBODIMENT
BDDEEIIRRSTTU REDISTRIBUTED
BDDEEIJLNOOTU DOUBLE-JOINTED
BDDEEIMNNRSTU DISBURDENMENT
BDDEGHILMORSU MIDDLESBROUGH
BDDEIILMMORSW MIDDLEBROWISM
BDDEIINRSTTUU UNDISTRIBUTED
BDDEILNNORSSW WORD BLINDNESS
BDEEEEFILNOSS BESIDE ONESELF
BDEEEEFGIKRRRS FREDERIKSBERG
BDEEEEFGILNOTT BOTTLE-FEEDING, FEEDING BOTTLE
BDEEEGIINNRRT INTERBREEDING
BDEEEGIJLLNOU GOLDEN JUBILEE
BDEEEIIRSSVWY BIRD'S-EYE VIEWS
BDEEEIMMMNRST DISMEMBERMENT
BDEEEELNNSSSSU UNBLESSEDNESS
BDEEFGILORSUU DOUBLE FIGURES
BDEEFIIILNSTY DEFENSIBILITY
BDEEGIILLNRWY BEWILDERINGLY
BDEEGIILMNOSW DISEMBOWELING
BDEEGIILMNSSX MIXED BLESSING
BDEEGIINORSUW BROWNIE GUIDES
BDEEGINNNNSSU UNBENDINGNESS
BDEEGINNORRUV OVERBURDENING
BDEEIIILNTTXY EXTENDIBILITY
BDEEIMNRSSSTU DISBURSEMENTS
BDEEINNORSSTV INVERTED SNOBS
BDEELLNOOSSSS BLOODLESSNESS
BDEELNNOSSSSU BOUNDLESSNESS
BDEELOOPRRSSU BLOOD PRESSURE
BDEFFNOOOOPRRU BURDEN OF PROOF
BDEFHNOOOORSTU DEBTS OF HONOUR
BDEGHHINOOORU NEIGHBOURHOOD
BDEGHHOORRSTU THOROUGHBREDS
BDEGIIIILSTTY DIGESTIBILITY
BDEHIIILNNTUY UNINHIBITEDLY
BDEHNOOOPRSTU BOUSTROPHEDON
BDEILNNNOSSSW SNOW BLINDNESS
BDEKLNOOOORTWY OLD-BOY NETWORK
BDFFIIIILSTUY DIFFUSIBILITY
BDFGHILLOOSSW GOLDFISH BOWLS
BDGGIIILLNOSY DISOBLIGINGLY
BDIIILLOSSTUY DISSOLUBILITY
BDIIINORSSTTU DISTRIBUTIONS
BEEEEHILNPRRS REPREHENSIBLE
BEEEELLLRSSTT BELLES-LETTRES
BEEEFFGIINNRT FRINGE BENEFIT
BEEEHILLMMNST EMBELLISHMENT
BEEEHILNPRRSY REPREHENSIBLY
BEEEIIJLLRSUV SILVER JUBILEE
BEEEIILNPRSSX INEXPRESSIBLE
BEEEIILPRRRSS IRREPRESSIBLE
BEEEILNPRSSSU SUPERSENSIBLE
BEEEIMMNRRSTU REIMBURSEMENT
BEEEINOSSSSSV OBSESSIVENESS
BEEFGINRRSTTU BUTTERFINGERS
BEEFHIMNRRSTU REFURBISHMENT
BEEFILLMORSUU UMBELLIFEROUS

BEEGGILNNORSW BOWLING GREENS
BEEGHNRRSTTTU BRUTE STRENGTH
BEEGIIILLNNUVY UNBELIEVINGLY
BEEGLOORRSTTT GLOBETROTTERS
BEEHILMRRTUWY WHITE MULBERRY
BEEHILNOOORTZ BELO HORIZONTE
BEEHILNORRSST BROTHERLINESS
BEEIIILMMPRSS IMPERMISSIBLE
BEEIIILNSTTXY EXTENSIBILITY
BEEIIILRRSTVY REVERSIBILITY
BEEIILNOPRRSS IRRESPONSIBLE
BEEIILNPRRTTU INTERRUPTIBLE
BEEIILNPRSSXY INEXPRESSIBLY
BEEIILPRRRSSY IRREPRESSIBLY
BEEILNRSSTUVY SUBSERVIENTLY
BEEINORSSSTUV OBTRUSIVENESS
BEENNOOSSSTUU BOUNTEOUSNESS
BEFFGINNORRTU BURNT OFFERING
BEFGIIILNRSTU FILIBUSTERING
BEFGIILNOOPRS BE SPOILING FOR
BEFGILLOORSUU GLOBULIFEROUS
BEFIIIILLNTXY INFLEXIBILITY
BEFILNNOSSTUU BOUNTIFULNESS
BEFINNNSSSUUY FUNNY BUSINESS
BEGGIIIILLNTY NEGLIGIBILITY
BEGGILNOORTTT GLOBETROTTING
BEGHNOOORRTTU ROTTEN BOROUGH
BEGIIIIILLNTY INELIGIBILITY
BEGIILNNNOPTW TENPIN BOWLING
BEHIIIIMNOSTX EXHIBITIONISM
BEHIIIINOSTTX EXHIBITIONIST
BEHIIILOPRTVY PROHIBITIVELY
BEHILOORRSUVY HERBIVOROUSLY
BEIIILMRSSTY REMISSIBILITY
BEIIILNNSSTY INSENSIBILITY
BEIIIILNRTTVY INVERTIBILITY
BEIIIILOPSSST POSSIBILITIES
BEIIIILRSSTTY RESISTIBILITY
BEIIILNOSSTTY OSTENSIBILITY
BEIILNOOSSSUV OBLIVIOUSNESS
BEIILNOPRRSSY IRRESPONSIBLY
BEIINNOOPRSTW BROWNIE POINTS
BEIINSSSSSTUU BUSINESS SUITS
BEIIOPRSSTTUU SUBREPTITIOUS
BEILNORSTUUVY UNOBTRUSIVELY
BEIMNOPSSSTUU BUMPTIOUSNESS
BEINNOOOSSSUX OBNOXIOUSNESS
BFGHIILLORSST BILLS OF RIGHTS
BFILLLMNOOSSU IN FULL BLOSSOM
BFILLOORSTUUU TUBULIFLOROUS
BGHILLNOOOPST POLLING BOOTHS
BGIIILNNOOPST BOILING POINTS
BIIIILMOPSSTY IMPOSSIBILITY
BIIKOOORSSSTV VISITORS' BOOKS
BIINOSSSTTTUU SUBSTITUTIONS
BILOOOPPRRSUY OPPROBRIOUSLY
CCCCEEINNOPSU CONCUPISCENCE
CCCDEEEEENRRSU RECRUDESCENCE
CCCDEIILORSTU CLOSED-CIRCUIT

CCCDEIIMNRSUU UNCIRCUMCISED
CCCEEEEFIMNRRU CIRCUMFERENCE
CCCEEEEIILNOPT POETIC LICENCE
CCCEEEILOOPRST ELECTROSCOPIC
CCCEEGHIKNORSS CROSSCHECKING
CCCEEHIIMOSTYZ SCHIZOMYCETIC
CCCEEIIILORSUV VICIOUS CIRCLE
CCCEEIIMNOOOOS SOCIOECONOMIC
CCCEEIINNORTTY CONCENTRICITY
CCCEEILMPRSTUY CIRCUMSPECTLY
CCCEEIOOPPRSST SPECTROSCOPIC
CCCEEOOPRSSTTU STREPTOCOCCUS
CCCIIIMNORSSU CIRCUMCISIONS
CCCILNNOOTUUY COUNTY COUNCIL
CCDDEEEELLMNNO CONDEMNED CELL
CCDDEEGINNNOS CONDESCENDING
CCDDENOORTTUU CONDUCTED TOUR
CCDEEEEIILNQSU DELIQUESCENCE
CCDEEEELLNNOTW WELL-CONNECTED
CCDEEHILORRTY HYDROELECTRIC
CCDEEIINNOSTV DISCONNECTIVE
CCDEEILMNOPSY ENCYCLOPEDISM
CCDEEILNOPSTY ENCYCLOPEDIST
CCDEEIMOORRTT MICRODETECTOR
CCDEEIINNOOSS CONDESCENSION
CCDEEIINNOSSUV CONDUCIVENESS
CCDEEINOOPRUW OWNER-OCCUPIED
CCDEEINRRRTTU DIRECT CURRENT
CCDEELNNNORUY UNCONCERNEDLY
CCDEENNOOPRSY CO-RESPONDENCY
CCDEENORRSTTU RECONSTRUCTED
CCDEGIINNNOST DISCONNECTING
CCDEGIINNORST DISCONCERTING
CCDEGINNNOORT CONNECTING ROD
CCDEHIOOSSTUU STUDIO COUCHES
CCDEHKLNOORTU ROUND THE CLOCK
CCDEIINNNOOST DISCONNECTION
CCDEIINNOORST DISCONCERTION
CCDEIMNOORSTU SEMICONDUCTOR
CCDEINNOOSSSU SECOND COUSINS
CCDGIIMNNOSTU MISCONDUCTING
CCDNNNOOORSTU NONCONDUCTORS
CCEEEEEFFNRSV EFFERVESCENCE
CCEEEEFFLNORS EFFLORESCENCE
CCEEEEHIKNRSV NECKERCHIEVES
CCEEEEIRRSSTV SECRET SERVICE
CCEEEFFIOSTTV COST-EFFECTIVE
CCEEEFILNNORS INFLORESCENCE
CCEEEFILORRRT FERROELECTRIC
CCEEEFNOORRRT FERROCONCRETE
CCEEEHIIMNPSY CHIMNEYPIECES
CCEEEHMOOPRRT CHEMORECEPTOR
CCEEEIILOPRTZ PIEZOELECTRIC
CCEEEIIMNNRSS REMINISCENCES
CCEEEIINNNNOV INCONVENIENCE
CCEEEILMNNORT RECONCILEMENT
CCEEEILMORRTT ELECTROMETRIC
CCEEEIMNORRTX CONCRETE MIXER
CCEEEINNNOQSU INCONSEQUENCE

CCEEEINNRRRTU INTERCURRENCE
CCEEEMMMNNOST COMMENCEMENTS
CCEEFFIIINSSU SUFFICIENCIES
CCEEFFIILOOPR POLICE OFFICER
CCEEFHIIJSSTU CHIEF JUSTICES
CCEEFINNOORST CONFECTIONERS
CCEEFINNOORTY CONFECTIONERY
CCEEGHIINOSTZ SCHIZOGENETIC
CCEEGHINOPSTY PSYCHOGENETIC
CCEEGIINNNOST CONTINGENCIES
CCEEGIINORTTY EGOCENTRICITY
CCEEGILNORTTU ELECTROCUTING
CCEEHIILLOPRT ELECTROPHILIC
CCEEHILNOOPRT ELECTROPHONIC
CCEEHILOOPRTT PHOTOELECTRIC
CCEEHILOOPRTU HEROIC COUPLET
CCEEHIMMNOOOS HOME ECONOMICS
CCEEHIMNNORRY CHIMNEY CORNER
CCEEHLMOORSSU COLOUR SCHEMES
CCEEHMMOORRRU MERCUROCHROME
CCEEIIIORRSTV OVERCRITICISE
CCEEIIIORRTVZ OVERCRITICIZE
CCEEIIJOPSTTU POETIC JUSTICE
CCEEIILNOORST ISOELECTRONIC
CCEEIINNOSSST CONSISTENCIES
CCEEILLNOORST RECOLLECTIONS
CCEEILNOORTTU ELECTROCUTION
CCEEILNOSSSUV OCCLUSIVENESS
CCEEILNOSTUVY CONSECUTIVELY
CCEEIMOPRRSTT SPECTROMETRIC
CCEEINNOOPPRT PRECONCEPTION
CCEEINNORRSST INCORRECTNESS
CCEEINOOPRRUW OWNER-OCCUPIER
CCEENNOOOVVXX CONVEXO-CONVEX
CCEEOOPPRSSST SPECTROSCOPES
CCEFFIIINNSUY INSUFFICIENCY
CCEFIILMNORUX CIRCUMFLEXION
CCEFILNOOSSSU SELF-CONSCIOUS
CCEGHIIKNNPRS SPRING CHICKEN
CCEGIIIMMNNOSV MISCONCEIVING
CCEGIILLNNORY RECONCILINGLY
CCEGIILNNRRTU TURNING CIRCLE
CCEGIILNOPRSS CLOSING PRICES
CCEGIIMNNRTUV CIRCUMVENTING
CCEHHIINOPRSZ SCHIZOPHRENIC
CCEHHIMOOPRRS CHROMOSPHERIC
CCEHIIKNOPSTY PSYCHOKINETIC
CCEHILMNOORTY CHLOROMYCETIN
CCEHIMOPRSSTY PSYCHOMETRICS
CCEHIMORSTTYY CYTOCHEMISTRY
CCEHIOOPRRSTU URETHROSCOPIC
CCEHIORSSSSTT CROSS-STITCHES
CCEHMOOPSTUYY PHYCOMYCETOUS
CCEIIILLOSTTV COLLETIVISTIC
CCEIIMNNOOPST MISCONCEPTION
CCEIIMNNORTUV CIRCUMVENTION
CCEIIMNOOSSSU SEMICONSCIOUS
CCEIIINNNOSSTY INCONSISTENCY
CCEIINNOOSSTU CONSCIENTIOUS

CCEIKKKLLOORW LIKE CLOCKWORK
CCEILNNOOORSW CROWN COLONIES
CCEIMMOOPRRTU MICROCOMPUTER
CCEINNOOPRRST PRINCE CONSORT
CCEINNOOSSSSU CONSCIOUSNESS
CCEINNOPRRSSW CROWN PRINCESS
CCEINOORSSSST CROSS-SECTIONS
CCENNNNOORRTU NONCONCURRENT
CCENOORRRSTTU RECONSTRUCTOR
CCENORRRSSSTU CROSSCURRENTS
CCGHILNOOOSST CONCHOLOGISTS
CCGHINOOPSSTY PSYCHOGNOSTIC
CCGIIKNNOOPTT COTTON-PICKING
CCGIINORRSSSS CRISSCROSSING
CCHHIILOPPRSY PSYCHROPHILIC
CCHHIOPPSSSYY PSYCHOPHYSICS
CCHIINNORSSTY SYNCHRONISTIC
CCHIIORRSSTTU SHORT CIRCUITS
CCHILMOOPTTYY LYMPHOCYTOTIC
CCIINNOOPSSUU INCONSPICUOUS
CCIINNOORSSTT CONSTRICTIONS
CCILMOORSSTTY MOTORCYCLISTS
CCILNNOOSSUUY UNCONSCIOUSLY
CCILNOOPSSUUY CONSPICUOUSLY
CCINNOORSSTTU CONSTRUCTIONS
CCINNOORSTUUY COUNTRY COUSIN
CDDDEEEINNSSU UNDECIDEDNESS
CDDEEEENNPRTU UNPRECEDENTED
CDDEEEGNOSSSU SECOND-GUESSED
CDDEEEHIORRTT OTHER-DIRECTED
CDDEEIILLNORS ILL-CONSIDERED
CDDEEIINNOORT RECONDITIONED
CDDEEIKLMNNOS CONDENSED MILK
CDDEHHILOORRY HYDROCHLORIDE
CDDEHILLMOOSS MIDDLE SCHOOLS
CDDEHLNORSTUU THUNDERCLOUDS
CDDEIIILNNPSU UNDISCIPLINED
CDDEIINNNOOTU UNCONDITIONED
CDDEILMOOPSSY DISCOMPOSEDLY
CDDGILLLMNOOY MOLLYCODDLING
CDDIIMMOOOSSU DISCOMMODIOUS
CDEEEEEHMMNRT CRÈME DE MENTHE
CDEEEEFILPSTV SELF-DECEPTIVE
CDEEEEFINSSTV DEFECTIVENESS
CDEEEEHNORRRT THREE-CORNERED
CDEEEEIINNPRX INEXPERIENCED
CDEEEEINNPRUX UNEXPERIENCED
CDEEEEINPSSTV DECEPTIVENESS
CDEEEEIQRSTUZ CREDIT SQUEEZE
CDEEEFFLNOSSS SELF-CONFESSED
CDEEEFHILRSST CHESTERFIELDS
CDEEEFILNNSST INFLECTEDNESS
CDEEEFILNOPST SELF-DECEPTION
CDEEEFILNSSTU DECEITFULNESS
CDEEEFINORTTU COUNTERFEITED
CDEEEFORRRRSS CROSS-REFERRED
CDEEEGHINOPST PIGEON-CHESTED
CDEEEGIIKNNSV KING'S EVIDENCE
CDEEEGIKLNRSS SINGLE-DECKERS

CDEEEIILNNQSU DELINQUENCIES
CDEEEIINNRRSV DINNER SERVICE
CDEEEIINPRSTV VICE PRESIDENT
CDEEEIKMPQRTU QUICK-TEMPERED
CDEEEIMNORSTT MINE DETECTORS
CDEEEIMOPRSSV DECOMPRESSIVE
CDEEEINNORSST RECONDITENESS
CDEEEINSSSTUV SEDUCTIVENESS
CDEEFFHILOORS OFFICEHOLDERS
CDEEFFIILLNST SELF-INFLICTED
CDEEFFILNNOST SELF-CONFIDENT
CDEEFIIIKLMRT CERTIFIED MILK
CDEEFIIILMRSS MID-LIFE CRISES
CDEEFIILNSTUV SELF-INDUCTIVE
CDEEFILPRSSTU DISRESPECTFUL
CDEEFINNOORTV OVERCONFIDENT
CDEEGGHIINPTW PITCHING WEDGE
CDEEGHIMNNOPR COMPREHENDING
CDEEGIINNORRS RECONSIDERING
CDEEGIKNOPRRS PECKING ORDERS
CDEEGIMNOPRSS DECOMPRESSING
CDEEGINNORSTU COUNTERSIGNED
CDEEGLOORSTUX DEXTROGLUCOSE
CDEEHIINOPRTY DRYOPITHECINE
CDEEHILLNSSSS CHILDLESSNESS
CDEEIIIMNRSTT DETERMINISTIC
CDEEIIIMOSSTT DOMESTICITIES
CDEEIIINNSSTV DISINCENTIVES
CDEEIIILNOPRST PREDILECTIONS
CDEEIIILNOSSSU DELICIOUSNESS
CDEEIIILPRSTVY DESCRIPTIVELY
CDEEIIMNORSTT DENSITOMETRIC
CDEEIINNOORRT RECONDITIONER
CDEEIIORSSSTU DISCOURTESIES
CDEEIJNPRRSUU JURISPRUDENCE
CDEEILNNOOPRS SCOLOPENDRINE
CDEEILRSTTUVY DESTRUCTIVELY
CDEEIMNOOPRSS DECOMPRESSION
CDEEINOOPRSTU COUNTERPOISED
CDEEINORSTTTU RECONSTITUTED
CDEEIOPPRRSST ESPRIT DE CORPS
CDEEKKLNRSTUU KNUCKLE-DUSTER
CDEENNOOPRRST CORRESPONDENT
CDEENNOOPRSST CO-RESPONDENTS
CDEENNRRRSTUU UNDERCURRENTS
CDEEORRRSSSSS CROSS-DRESSERS
CDEFHINNORSWW FRENCH WINDOWS
CDEFIIIILMRSS MID-LIFE CRISIS
CDEFIILNNOSTU SELF-INDUCTION
CDEFOOOOPRRSS FOOD PROCESSOR
CDEGHHNOOSTTU SECOND THOUGHT
CDEGIIMOOOPSS SIGMOIDOSCOPE
CDEGIIINNNOSTT DISCONTENTING
CDEGIKNNNORUW UNCROWNED KING
CDEGILLNNOOORT DECONTROLLING
CDEGILNNOOORY ENDOCRINOLOGY
CDEGINNOOPRRS CORRESPONDING
CDEGINORRSSSS CROSS-DRESSING
CDEHHIOOOORRST RHODOCHROSITE

CDEHIIIOPRSTY SPHEROIDICITY
CDEHIIKMNSTTU STICK-IN-THE-MUD
CDEHIIKNORSTY HYDROKINETICS
CDEHIIMNOPRRU PERICHONDRIUM
CDEHIIOOOPPRT PHOTOPERIODIC
CDEHIIOPPRTTY PTERIDOPHYTIC
CDEHIIOPRRSST DIRECTORSHIPS
CDEHILLOOOSST OLD SCHOOL TIES
CDEHIMOOPPRSU PSEUDOMORPHIC
CDEHIMOORTTYY THYROIDECTOMY
CDEHKNRRSTTUU THUNDERSTRUCK
CDEIIIINNSTTV INDISTINCTIVE
CDEIIILNSTTVY DISTINCTIVELY
CDEIIIMPRSSTV DESCRIPTIVISM
CDEIIINNORSST INDISCRETIONS
CDEIIJNOSSSUU JUDICIOUSNESS
CDEIIMNOOOPST DECOMPOSITION
CDEIINNOOPRST PRECONDITIONS
CDEIINOPRTUWW PICTURE WINDOW
CDEILLMOORTUU MULTICOLOURED
CDEILLNORSUUY INCREDULOUSLY
CDEILMNOOPSUY COMPENDIOUSLY
CDEILNORSSSUU LUDICROUSNESS
CDEINNOOPRTUV NONPRODUCTIVE
CDEINOOPRRSTU REPRODUCTIONS
CDEINOORSSTTU DISCOUNT STORE
CDELLNOOOPTYY POLYCOTYLEDON
CDELMNNOOOOTY MONOCOTYLEDON
CDEOOOPRRRSSW WORD PROCESSOR
CDFGILNOORSTY FLYING DOCTORS
CDFIIMNOORSTY DISCONFORMITY
CDGGIKLLNSUUY UGLY DUCKLINGS
CDGIIINNNOSTU DISCONTINUING
CDGIIMOOOPSSY SIGMOIDOSCOPY
CDGIKLNOOSSTU DUCKING STOOLS
CDHIIMNNOOORT MITOCHONDRION
CDIIIJLNOSUUY INJUDICIOUSLY
CDIIINNOSTTUY DISCONTINUITY
CDIINNOORSTTU INTRODUCTIONS
CDIINNOOSSTUU DISCONTINUOUS
CEEEEEIILNORRT ELECTIONEERER
CEEEEFFILPRTT PELTIER EFFECT
CEEEEFFINSSTV EFFECTIVENESS
CEEEEFLPRRTTT LETTER-PERFECT
CEEEEFMNNORRT RE-ENFORCEMENT
CEEEEGHINORTT HETEROGENETIC
CEEEEGIIMNNRS ÉMINENCE GRISE
CEEEEHLNRSSSS CHEERLESSNESS
CEEEEIKKPRSTW WICKET KEEPERS
CEEEEIILNSSSTV SELECTIVENESS
CEEEEIMNNPRSU SUPEREMINENCE
CEEEEINNPRSUV SUPERVENIENCE
CEEEEINRSSSSV RECESSIVENESS
CEEEEINRSSSTV SECRETIVENESS
CEEEEINRSSSVX EXCESSIVENESS
CEEEEIOPRTTVX EXTEROCEPTIVE
CEEEEJNNRSTUV REJUVENESCENT
CEEEFFIILNTVY INEFFECTIVELY
CEEEFFPRRTTUU FUTURE PERFECT

CEEEFGHIIOPST PIECES OF EIGHT
CEEEFHINRSSST SCENESHIFTERS
CEEEFIINNSSTV INFECTIVENESS
CEEEFIMNNORRT REINFORCEMENT
CEEEFINORRTTU COUNTERFEITER
CEEEFNOORSTUV VOTE OF CENSURE
CEEEGGINORRTU GEIGER COUNTER
CEEEGHIKLNNRS GELSENKIRCHEN
CEEEGHILLNOPT PHELLOGENETIC
CEEEGIIILNNRV CIVIL ENGINEER
CEEEGIIKNNRTY KINETIC ENERGY
CEEEHIILNNSTT LIECHTENSTEIN
CEEEHILLLMOSU HEMICELLULOSE
CEEEHILLOPRST ELECTROPHILES
CEEEHIMNOPRSV COMPREHENSIVE
CEEEHIMNPSSWY CHIMNEYSWEEPS
CEEEHLNNOSTTU LUNCHEONETTES
CEEEHLNORSSSU LECHEROUSNESS
CEEEHNSSTTTUW SWEET CHESTNUT
CEEEIIMNNRTTT INTERMITTENCE
CEEEIINOPRTTV INTEROCEPTIVE
CEEEILMMORRST ELECTROMERISM
CEEEILMNRSSSS MERCILESSNESS
CEEEILMOORTTV ELECTROMOTIVE
CEEEILNOSSSSV VOICELESSNESS
CEEEILNPRSSSS PRICELESSNESS
CEEEILNSSSSUV SECLUSIVENESS
CEEEILNSSSUVX EXCLUSIVENESS
CEEEINRSSSUVX EXCURSIVENESS
CEEEIOPRRSTTV RETROSPECTIVE
CEEELNNOQSSUU QUEEN'S COUNSEL
CEEEOPRRRSSSV PROCESS-SERVER
CEEFFFGIINOOR FOREIGN OFFICE
CEEFFIIILNNTY INEFFICIENTLY
CEEFFIOPRSTTY PETTY OFFICERS
CEEFGILNNOSTU GENUFLECTIONS
CEEFIIKLNORSU NICKELIFEROUS
CEEFIIMNOPRST IMPERFECTIONS,
  PERFECTIONISM
CEEFIINOPRSST FRONTISPIECES
CEEFIINOPRSTT PERFECTIONIST
CEEFINOORSSSU FEROCIOUSNESS
CEEFLLORRSUUY RESOURCEFULLY
CEEGHIINOSSSZ SCHIZOGENESIS
CEEGHIIRRSTUW CRUISERWEIGHT
CEEGHIMNOOPRT MORPHOGENETIC
CEEGHINOPSSSY PSYCHOGENESIS
CEEGHINORTTUW COUNTERWEIGHT
CEEGHLNNOOTWY NEW TECHNOLOGY
CEEGIIMMNNOTU IMMUNOGENETIC
CEEGIKLLNOPSS GLOCKENSPIELS
CEEGILLNORSSV LEVEL CROSSING
CEEGILMMNNOPT COMPLEMENTING
CEEGMNOORRSST COSTERMONGERS
CEEHHIMMORSTT THERMOCHEMIST
CEEHHIMOOPRRT HETEROMORPHIC
CEEHHIOOPRRTT HETEROTROPHIC
CEEHHLOORSSST CLOTHESHORSES
CEEHHNORSSTTU HORSE CHESTNUT

CEEHIMNNOOPRS COMPREHENSION
CEEHIMNNORSTT ETHNOCENTRISM
CEEHINNNPPRSY PENNY-PINCHERS
CEEHIOPPPRRST PRECEPTORSHIP
CEEHIOPRSTTTW WITH RESPECT TO
CEEHLNOOOPRTT PHOTOELECTRON
CEEHLOOPRRSTU ELECTROPHORUS
CEEHNOORSSTTW STONE THE CROWS
CEEHOOOPPRRTT PHOTORECEPTOR
CEEIIILMRSSSU CRUISE MISSILE
CEEIIIMMPRSTT METEMPIRICIST
CEEIIINNORSST SENIOR CITISEN
CEEIIINNORSTZ SENIOR CITIZEN
CEEIIJNNORSTT INTERJECTIONS
CEEIIILMOPTTVY COMPETITIVELY
CEEIILRRSTTVY RESTRICTIVELY
CEEIIMNOPTTUV UNCOMPETITIVE
CEEIIMPPRSSTV PERSPECTIVISM
CEEIINNOPRSTT INTERCEPTIONS
CEEIINNORSSST INTERCESSIONS
CEEIINNORSSTT INTERSECTIONS
CEEIINOPRSSTT RECEPTIONISTS
CEEIINOPRSTTV INTROSPECTIVE
CEEIINOSSSSST SECESSIONISTS
CEEIKLNNOSTUU KINETONUCLEUS
CEEILMNNOPTTY INCOMPETENTLY
CEEILMNOORSUY CEREMONIOUSLY
CEEILNNOOPRTU NUCLEOPROTEIN
CEEILNOOPRRST SCLEROPROTEIN
CEEILNOSSSTUY NECESSITOUSLY
CEEILOOPRSTTU TELEUTOSPORIC
CEEILPQRSTUUY PICTURESQUELY
CEEIMNNOORSUU UNCEREMONIOUS
CEEIMNOOOPRRT RECEPTION ROOM
CEEINNNORSTTU RECONSTITUENT
CEEINOOPRRSTT RETROSPECTION
CEEINOOPRSSTU COUNTERPOISES,
  PRECIOUS STONE
CEEINOORRSSSV CORROSIVENESS
CEEINOORRSSTV CONTROVERSIES
CEEINOPRRSSSU REPERCUSSIONS
CEEINORRRSSTU RESURRECTIONS
CEEINOSSSSTUV VISCOUNTESSES
CEEIOOPRSSSTT STEREOSCOPIST
CEELMNOOOORRTT REMOTE CONTROL
CEELPQRSSTUUU SCULPTURESQUE
CEEMMNNOOPTUY PNEUMONECTOMY
CEEMNNNOOPRTU PRONOUNCEMENT
CEENNOOQRSSTU QUEENS CONSORT
CEENNOORRSTTU COUNTERTENORS
CEENOORSSSTUU COURTEOUSNESS
CEFFFGIILNORY FLYING OFFICER
CEFFIILOOPRST PILOT OFFICERS
CEFFIINOOSSSU OFFICIOUSNESS
CEFGIIKLNPSTY FLYING PICKETS
CEFHIMMOORRRU FERROCHROMIUM
CEFHLLLOOOSSW SCHOOLFELLOWS
CEFIINNNOOSTU NONINFECTIOUS
CEFILNOPRRTUY PERFUNCTORILY

CEFKKLOORRSSW CLERKS OF WORKS
CEGGHLNOOOORY GEOCHRONOLOGY
CEGHHIILOPRSY HIEROGLYPHICS
CEGHIIILLNNPS SPINE-CHILLING
CEGHIINNNNPPY PENNY-PINCHING
CEGHIKNOORRSS ROCKING HORSES
CEGHILNOOSSTT TECHNOLOGISTS
CEGHINNOOSTUU COUNTINGHOUSE
CEGHOPRRSSUYY PSYCHOSURGERY
CEGIIILNOORST CORELIGIONIST
CEGIIINNORSTU INCONGRUITIES
CEGIIKLLMNRSY MERCY KILLINGS
CEGIILMMNNOPT COMPLIMENTING
CEGIILMNNORSYY SYRINGOMYELIC
CEGIILNNORRTY NITROGLYCERIN
CEGIILNOOSSTT SCIENTOLOGIST
CEGIIMMNNNOSTU TIME-CONSUMING
CEGIIMNNOORRTT TRIGONOMETRIC
CEGIIMNNOPRTUV MOVING PICTURE
CEGIIMNOPRTUZ COMPUTERIZING
CEGIINNNOOORRT RECONNOITRING
CEGIKLNNOSSSU KING'S COUNSELS
CEGILMMOORSTY MYRMECOLOGIST
CEGIMNNNNOOST ON CONSIGNMENT
CEGINNNOORSTW CONNING TOWERS
CEGINPRSSSTTU PRESS CUTTINGS
CEGINRRRSTTUU RESTRUCTURING
CEHHIIMMOOORT HOMOIOTHERMIC
CEHHIIMOOPRRT THERIOMORPHIC
CEHHOOPRTTTTU PUT TO THE TORCH
CEHHOOPTTTTUU PUT TO THE TOUCH
CEHIIKNOPSSSY PSYCHOKINESIS
CEHIILMOOPPTY LYMPHOPOIETIC
CEHIILMOSSUVY MISCHIEVOUSLY
CEHIILNOOPSST SIPHONOSTELIC
CEHIIMMOOORST HOMOEROTICISM
CEHIIMNOOPRST CHEMISORPTION
CEHIIMOORSTTY STOICHIOMETRY
CEHIINOPPRSST INSPECTORSHIP
CEHIMMMNNOOTUY COMMUNITY HOME
CEHIMNOOOOPRRT CHROMOPROTEIN
CEHLMMOORSSSU SUMMER SCHOOLS
CEHLNOORRSSUY NURSERY SCHOOL
CEHMNOORRTTUY MOTHER COUNTRY
CEHMOOOOOPPRST PHOTOCOMPOSER
CEIIILNNSTTVY INSTINCTIVELY
CEIIJNOOPRSTT PROJECTIONIST
CEIIKLSSSTWZZ SWIZZLE STICKS
CEIIKRRSSSTUY SECURITY RISKS
CEIIILLNOOSTV VIOLONCELLIST
CEIILMNOPSUUY IMPECUNIOUSLY
CEIILNNOORTTU INTERLOCUTION
CEIILNRSTTUVY INSTRUCTIVELY
CEIILOOPPRSTW POWER POLITICS
CEIILOPPRSTUY PRECIPITOUSLY
CEIILRRSSTTUU SERICULTURIST
CEIIMMNOORSSS COMMISSIONERS
CEIIMMNOPRSTU MINICOMPUTERS
CEIIMNNORRTTU MICRONUTRIENT

CEIIMNOOOPRST RECOMPOSITION
CEIIMNOOPRSTT PROTECTIONISM
CEIIMNOOPRTTU MOTION PICTURE
CEIINNOOPRSTT INTROSPECTION
CEIINNORRSSTU INSURRECTIONS
CEIINOOPRSSTT RETINOSCOPIST
CEIINOOPRSSTT PROTECTIONIST
CEIINOORSSTUV INSECTIVOROUS
CEIINOPPRRSST PRESCRIPTIONS
CEIINOPRSSSTU PERCUSSIONIST
CEIIPRRRSSTTW SCRIPTWRITERS
CEILLMNOOSTTY TONSILLECTOMY
CEILMNNOOOSSU MONONUCLEOSIS
CEILMNOORSTUY COTERMINOUSLY
CEILNNOOSTTUY CONTENTIOUSLY
CEILNOORRSTTU INTERLOCUTORS
CEILNOORRTTUY INTERLOCUTORY
CEINNNOOSSSUU INNOCUOUSNESS
CEINNOOPRSTTU COUNTERPOINTS
CEINOOOQRSSSTU CROSS-QUESTION
CEIOOOPPPRRRT PROPRIOCEPTOR
CELLNOOSSUUVV CONVOLVULUSES
CELOOOPRRSSTU POSTER COLOURS
CEMOOOORRSSTT MOTOR SCOOTERS
CEOOPPRRSSSSU CROSS-PURPOSES
CFFIKKLORRTTU FORKLIFT TRUCK
CFGHIILLNNNUY UNFLINCHINGLY
CFGHILMNOOORR CHLOROFORMING
CFGILLNOORSUY FLYING COLOURS
CFHINNORTTTUU TRUTH-FUNCTION
CFIMMNNNOOORS NONCONFORMISM
CFIMNNNOOORST NONCONFORMIST
CFIMNNNOOORTY NONCONFORMITY
CGGHHINOOOPUW WHOOPING COUGH
CGGILNNOORRWY CROWNING GLORY
CGHHIILOOSTTY ICHTHYOLOGIST
CGHIIKNOOSSTT SHOOTING STICK
CGHIILOORSSTT CHRISTOLOGIST,
    TRICHOLOGISTS
CGHIINNNORSYZ SYNCHRONIZING
CGHILOOPSSSTY PSYCHOLOGISTS
CGIIIKNNOPSTT STICKING POINT
CGIIILLOOOPST OLIGOPOLISTIC
CGIIILMNOORST CRIMINOLOGIST
CGIIILNOOSSTU SOCIOLINGUIST
CGIIIMMNNOOSS COMMISSIONING
CGIIINPRRSTTW SCRIPTWRITING
CGIILOOOSSTTX TOXICOLOGISTS
CGIIMMNNOSSTU MISCONSTRUING
CGILNNOORSUUY INCONGRUOUSLY
CHHIOOORSSTTU ORTHOSTICHOUS
CHHIOOPRSSTYY PSYCHOHISTORY
CHIIILOOPRSST SOLICITORSHIP
CHIIOOOPRRSTT PROTOHISTORIC
CHIJLNOOOORSSU JUNIOR SCHOOLS
CHILMMNNOOOUY HOLY COMMUNION
CHILMOOPSSTYY LYMPHOCYTOSIS
CHILOOPSSSTUY PHYSOCLISTOUS
CIIIIIMPRSTTV PRIMITIVISTIC

CIIIILLNOSSTU ILLUSIONISTIC
CIIILNRSTTUUV VINICULTURIST
CIIILLNOPSTUUY PUNCTILIOUSLY
CIILMMOOOPSST COSMOPOLITISM
CIIMNNOOOPSST MONOPSONISTIC
CIINNOOOORSTTT CONTORTIONIST
CIINNOOSSTTTU CONSTITUTIONS
CIINOOPPRRSST PROSCRIPTIONS
CIINOOPPRSTTU OPPORTUNISTIC
CIINOOPRRSTTU CORRUPTIONIST
CILMOOPRSSUUY PROMISCUOUSLY
DDDEEGGILNNOW GOLDEN WEDDING
DDDEHNNOOORRS RHODODENDRONS
DDEEEEIMNPRRT PREDETERMINED
DDEEEELLLOPVW WELL-DEVELOPED
DDEEEELOOPRVV OVERDEVELOPED
DDEEEGHINORSY DEHYDROGENISE
DDEEEGHINORYZ DEHYDROGENIZE
DDEEEIIMPRRST RED SPIDER MITE
DDEEEIINRSSTT DISINTERESTED
DDEEEILMNRSTW MIDDLE WESTERN
DDEEEILNNNPTY INDEPENDENTLY
DDEEEINNPRSTU SUPERINTENDED
DDEEEELMNOPRUY UNDEREMPLOYED
DDEEFGIILMNRS MIDDLE FINGERS
DDEEFNNNOSSUU UNFOUNDEDNESS
DDEEGHHINRTUW HUNDREDWEIGHT
DDEEGHIILMSTW MIDDLEWEIGHTS
DDEEGHIINSTWW WHITE WEDDINGS
DDEEGIIILMSSU GUIDED MISSILE
DDEEGIILNRSVW SILVER WEDDING
DDEEHILNOOTWY DYED-IN-THE-WOOL
DDEEIIKMNRRST KIDDERMINSTER
DDEEIIMNSSTTW DIM-WITTEDNESS
DDEEINORRSSWW WINDOW-DRESSER
DDEFINOOPRRUV UNPROVIDED FOR
DDEGHHIOORRSU RIDE ROUGHSHOD
DDEGHIIINSSTU DISTINGUISHED
DDEGINNRSTUUY UNDERSTUDYING
DDEGLNNOOOOTY ENDODONTOLOGY
DDEHIIKNOORZZ ORDZHONIKIDZE
DDEHINOOPPSWW WINDOW-SHOPPED
DDEIIIILMSSTU DISSIMILITUDE
DDEIIIILLNOSSU DISILLUSIONED
DDEIMNOORSSTU MISUNDERSTOOD
DDEMNNOORSSWY DOWN'S SYNDROME
DEEEEEFFGIRRRZ FRIDGE-FREEZER
DEEEEFGGINNRR GREEN-FINGERED
DEEEEFINNSSSV DEFENSIVENESS
DEEEEGIILNNSS DIESEL ENGINES
DEEEEHHPRSSSS SHEPHERDESSES
DEEEEIMNPRRRT PREDETERMINER
DEEEELLPRRSVW WELL-PRESERVED
DEEEELMNOPRTV REDEVELOPMENT
DEEEENNPRRSTU UNREPRESENTED
DEEEENPRRSSTV PERVERTEDNESS
DEEEFGJMNORTU FOREJUDGEMENT
DEEEFGKLLNOSW SELF-KNOWLEDGE
DEEEFGKLNOORW FOREKNOWLEDGE

DEEEFHHIORRRS HEREFORDSHIRE
DEEEEFHNOORRST FORESHORTENED
DEEEFIILMPRSS SEMPER FIDELIS
DEEEFIILLNSTVY SELF-EVIDENTLY
DEEEFLLLOPPRS SELF-PROPELLED
DEEEFLNORSSUW SUNFLOWER SEED
DEEEFLOPSSSSS SELF-POSSESSED
DEEEGGHILNPST SIGN THE PLEDGE
DEEEGHILNNNTU UNENLIGHTENED
DEEEGIINNRRSV ENGINE DRIVERS
DEEEGJMNPRSTU PREJUDGEMENTS
DEEEHLMNNOOWY HONEYDEW MELON
DEEEHMOPRRSTT SHORT-TEMPERED
DEEEIILLORSTUY DELETERIOUSLY
DEEEINOQSTUVX VEXED QUESTION
DEEEKLMMRRTTU KETTLEDRUMMER
DEEEELLNNORRSU ENROLLED NURSE
DEEEELLNNPRSTY RESPLENDENTLY
DEEENOPRRSUUX UNDEREXPOSURE
DEEENORSSSTUX DEXTEROUSNESS
DEEFFFINORRST FIRST OFFENDER
DEEFFIILNNRTY INDIFFERENTLY
DEEFFLNNRSSUU UNRUFFLEDNESS
DEEFFOORSTUWW SWEET WOODRUFF
DEEFGGHIILNRT LIGHT-FINGERED
DEEFGIIMNRSTU DISFIGUREMENT
DEEFGIINNPRRT FINGERPRINTED
DEEFGIILLNTU SELF-INDULGENT
DEEFHHIORRRST HERTFORDSHIRE
DEEFILNOPRSSU SPLENDIFEROUS
DEEFLNNORSSUW WONDERFULNESS
DEEGGHHIPRRSSU HIGH-PRESSURED
DEEGHIINNSSTW WINDING SHEETS
DEEGHILLNOSUW DWELLING HOUSE
DEEGHILMOOOST METHODOLOGIES
DEEGIIINNSSTZ DESENSITIZING
DEEGIJMMNSSTU MISJUDGEMENTS
DEEGILMNOOSTY SEDIMENTOLOGY
DEEGILNORSTUV SILVER-TONGUED
DEEGIMNNNOPSY SPENDING MONEY
DEEGINNOPRSUX UNDEREXPOSING
DEEGINNORSTTW DOWNING STREET
DEEHHIINNOSSS HOIDENISHNESS
DEEHHINNOSSSY HOYDENISHNESS
DEEHHNORRSTUW THUNDERSHOWER
DEEHIINNPRSTU INDENTURESHIP
DEEIIIMMNNRST INDETERMINISM
DEEIIIMNNRSTT INDETERMINIST
DEEIIINOQRSTU REQUISITIONED
DEEIIILLNORSSS SOLDIERLINESS
DEEIIILMNNOSSS DIMENSIONLESS
DEEIIILNORSSSU DELIRIOUSNESS
DEEIIILOPPRSTT LEPIDOPTERIST
DEEIIILOPSTUXY EXPEDITIOUSLY
DEEIIMNNRSSTT DISINTERMENTS
DEEIIIMNNSTTV DISINVESTMENT
DEEIIMNOORSST ENDOMETRIOSIS
DEEIIMOORRSTU DEMERITORIOUS
DEEIINOSSSSTU SEDITIOUSNESS

DEEILMNOOSSSU MELODIOUSNESS
DEEILNNOSTTUY TENDENTIOUSLY
DEEILNORSSSTU DESULTORINESS
DEEILNOSSSSTU DISSOLUTENESS
DEEILOOPPRSTU LEPIDOPTEROUS
DEEIMNOSSSTUW WOMEN'S STUDIES
DEEINNPRRTTUU UNINTERRUPTED
DEELLOPPRSTUW WELL-SUPPORTED
DEELNNOSSSSSU SOUNDLESSNESS
DEEMNORRSSSUU MURDEROUSNESS
DEEMOOOOPRRSST DEPRESSOMOTOR
DEENNOOPRSSSU PONDEROUSNESS
DEENOOPRSSSST DESSERTSPOONS
DEFFHIRSSSTTU STUFFED SHIRTS
DEFFIIILNOOSV FIELD OF VISION
DEFHILMRRTTYY MERTHYR TYDFIL
DEFIILPRSTUUY SUPERFLUIDITY
DEFIMNNOOOSTU OUT OF ONE'S MIND
DEFINOOOOPRRST POINTS OF ORDER
DEGGHILNOOSSU LODGING HOUSES
DEGGIILNNORUV OVERINDULGING
DEGGINNORSSSW DRESSING GOWNS
DEGHHNOOORRTY ORTHOHYDROGEN
DEGHIIIINNRST DISINHERITING
DEGHIIINRSSTU DISTINGUISHER
DEGHILMOOOSTT METHODOLOGIST
DEGHIMNOOOSTT DO SOMETHING TO
DEGHMNOOOSTTU SMOOTH-TONGUED
DEGIIILNPSSTT SIDESPLITTING
DEGIILMNNNRUY UNDERMININGLY
DEGIILNNOORRS SOLDERING IRON
DEGIILNRSSSTY DISTRESSINGLY
DEGIILOOPRSTT PTERIDOLOGIST
DEGIINNNNPRSU UNDERPINNINGS
DEGIINOPSSSSS DISPOSSESSING
DEGIKNNOORRWW WONDER-WORKING
DEGIMNOORRSSS DRESSING ROOMS
DEGKNOORRSSTU GROUND STROKES
DEGMNOORRRSUY MERRY-GO-ROUNDS
DEHHIILOOPPSS PHILOSOPHISED
DEHHIILOOPPSZ PHILOSOPHIZED
DEHINOOPPRSWW WINDOW-SHOPPER
DEHMNORRSSTTU THUNDERSTORMS
DEIIILMNOOSTT DEMOLITIONIST
DEIIINNOSSSSU INSIDIOUSNESS
DEIIINNOSSSUV INVIDIOUSNESS
DEIIIOPSSSTTU UTI POSSIDETIS
DEIILMNOPRTVY IMPROVIDENTLY
DEIINOOOPPRST PROPOSITIONED
DEIINOOPSSSSS DISPOSSESSION
DEINNNOSSTTUU STUDENTS' UNION
DEIOOPRSSSSSY DISPOSSESSORY
DFGGHIILLNOOT FLOODLIGHTING
DFGHHIMOOOSST SMOOTH DOGFISH
DFGIINNOOOOPS FOOD POISONING
DFGINNOOOPRSU SOUNDPROOFING
DFIINOORSTTUU FORTITUDINOUS
DFILLRSSTTUUY DISTRUSTFULLY
DGGHINNNORTUU HUNTING GROUND

DGGINNOOPRRUV PROVING GROUND
DGLMNOOOOSSTU ODONTOGLOSSUM
DHIIIMMOOPRSS ISODIMORPHISM
DHIIMOOOPRSSU ISODIMORPHOUS
DIIIINNOOPSST INDISPOSITION
DIIIINOQSSSTU DISQUISITIONS
DIILMNOSTTUUU MULTITUDINOUS
DIILNORSSTUUY INDUSTRIOUSLY
DIINOOOOPPRRST DISPROPORTION
DILNOOOPSSSUY ISOSPONDYLOUS
DLNOOOOPPRTTY POLYPROTODONT
EEEEFHILNSSSY FISH-EYE LENSES
EEEEFILNRSSVX REFLEXIVENESS
EEEEFILPRRRSV LIFE PRESERVER
EEEEFKLNOOPST KEEP TO ONESELF
EEEEFLNOOPSSX EXPOSE ONESELF
EEEEGHILNRSTW STEERING WHEEL
EEEEGHINORSST HETEROGENESIS
EEEEGHINORTTY HETEROGENEITY
EEEEGHNOORSTU HETEROGENEOUS
EEEEGNOPRRRSS REPRESSOR GENE
EEEEHKLLRRSTT HELTER-SKELTER
EEEEINNPSSSVX EXPENSIVENESS
EEEEINNRSSTTV RETENTIVENESS
EEEEINNSSSTVX EXTENSIVENESS
EEEELLNPSSSSS SLEEPLESSNESS
EEEELNNRSSSSV NERVELESSNESS
EEEELNNSSSSSS SENSELESSNESS
EEEELNOPRRSTT LETTER OPENERS
EEEELPRRSSSTT LETTERPRESSES
EEEENNPRRRSTU ENTREPRENEURS
EEEEORRSTTTTT TEETER-TOTTERS
EEEFFGILLLNOW FELLOW FEELING
EEEFFINNOSSSV OFFENSIVENESS
EEEFGILNNNSSU UNFEELINGNESS
EEEFGIMNPRRTU PREFIGUREMENT
EEEFGLNRRSSTU REGRETFULNESS
EEEFIILMMPRRS FILM PREMIÈRES
EEEFLLNORRTTU FORTUNE-TELLER
EEEFLNNRSSSTU RESENTFULNESS
EEEFLNOPRSSSU REPOSEFULNESS
EEEGGINORSSSU EGREGIOUSNESS
EEEGHILMNNNTT ENLIGHTENMENT
EEEGHILNNQSSU QUEEN'S ENGLISH
EEEGHILRSTTWW WELTERWEIGHTS
EEEGHIMNORSST THERMOGENESIS
EEEGHIMNOSSTU MEETINGHOUSES
EEEGIIMNNPRTX EXPERIMENTING
EEEGILLNNPRSS REPELLINGNESS
EEEGILLNSSSSU GUILELESSNESS
EEEGILNNORVWY OVERWEENINGLY
EEEGILNOORSTV VENEREOLOGIST
EEEGINOPRRSTW POWER STEERING
EEEGIORRRSSTV RETROGRESSIVE
EEEGNOQRSSSTU GROTESQUENESS
EEEHHIILNPRTW THREE-LINE WHIP
EEEHHNOOSSTTW SHOW ONE'S TEETH
EEEHIIILNNPPT IN THE PIPELINE
EEEHILLOSSTTT STILETTO HEELS

EEEHILMNNPRST REPLENISHMENT	EEGGINORRRSST RETROGRESSING
EEEHILMOPRRTY PYRHELIOMETER	EEGHHIILOPSVX HIGH EXPLOSIVE
EEEHILMPPRSSX HERPES SIMPLEX	EEGHIILNNNPSW SPINNING WHEEL
EEEHIMNNNOOPP EPIPHENOMENON	EEGHIINNRSSTW WITHERINGNESS
EEEHINNOSTTTX SIXTEENTH NOTE	EEGHIINRSSTUX EXTINGUISHERS
EEEHLLNOOPSTT TELEPHOTO LENS	EEGHIKNOOSSTT SKEET SHOOTING
EEEHLMNOOSSSW WHOLESOMENESS	EEGHIKNRRRSTU HUNGER STRIKER
EEEHLOPRSSTTW POTTER'S WHEELS	EEGHIKNRRSSTU HUNGER STRIKES
EEEHMNNNORSTT ENTHRONEMENTS	EEGHILNSSSSST SIGHTLESSNESS
EEEHOOPRRSTTU HETEROPTEROUS	EEGHILOOPRSTT HERPETOLOGIST
EEEIILLNRSSSU LEISURELINESS	EEGHIMNOOPRSS MORPHOGENESIS
EEEIILNNPSVXY INEXPENSIVELY	EEGHIMNORSTTT THERMOSETTING
EEEIINNNSSTVV INVENTIVENESS	EEGHINNOSSTTW SWEET NOTHINGS
EEEIINNSSSSTV SENSITIVENESS	EEGHINORSSSTU RIGHTEOUSNESS
EEEIINQSSSTUX EXQUISITENESS	EEGHIOORSSTYZ HETEROZYGOSIS
EEEIINRSSSSTV RESISTIVENESS	EEGHLLOOPRSST HOT-GOSPELLERS
EEEIIPQRRSSTU PREREQUISITES	EEGHLMNNOOOPY PHENOMENOLOGY
EEEILNNNPSSSS PENNILESSNESS	EEGHLMNOOOSUY HOMOGENEOUSLY
EEEILNNOSSSSS NOISELESSNESS	EEGHMNOORSTTU MOTHER TONGUES
EEEILNNPSSSSS SPINELESSNESS	EEGIILLLNNTTY INTELLIGENTLY
EEEILNOPSSSVX EXPLOSIVENESS	EEGIILLLNPPSS SLEEPING PILLS
EEEILNPRSSSUV REPULSIVENESS	EEGIILLNNNTTU UNINTELLIGENT
EEEIMNNORSSSV MONS VENERISES	EEGIILMNOORST TERMINOLOGIES
EEEIMNNPRSSTT PRESENTIMENTS	EEGIILNNRSTTY INTERESTINGLY
EEEIMNOOPRTTT POTENTIOMETER	EEGIILNORSSSU RELIGIOUSNESS
EEEIMOPRSSTUX TIME EXPOSURES	EEGIIMNOPRRTU PRIMOGENITURE
EEELLMORRSSSY REMORSELESSLY	EEGIIMNOPRTXZ EXTEMPORIZING
EEELMOPPRRSTT TELEPROMPTERS	EEGIINNPRRSST INTERSPERSING
EEELNNOPSSSTU PLENTEOUSNESS	EEGILLNNNRTUY UNRELENTINGLY
EEELNOPRSSSSW POWERLESSNESS	EEGILLNSSSSTU GUILTLESSNESS
EEEMPRSSSTTXY EXPERT SYSTEMS	EEGILLOOPSSST SPELEOLOGISTS
EEENNOORRSSSU ERRONEOUSNESS	EEGILMNNPPSTU SUPPLEMENTING
EEEFFGGHIIORTU FIGURE OF EIGHT	EEGILMOOORSTT METEOROLOGIST
EEFFGLNORSSTU FORGETFULNESS	EEGILOPRRSSVY PROGRESSIVELY
EEFFIILNNOSVY INOFFENSIVELY	EEGIMMNNORSTV MISGOVERNMENT
EEFGHIILNRRST FREIGHTLINERS	EEGINNNOSSSUU INGENUOUSNESS
EEFGHIILRSTTW WEIGHT LIFTERS	EEGINNOPPSSTT STEPPING-STONE
EEFGHIIPRRSST PRISEFIGHTERS	EEGINOORRRSST RETROGRESSION
EEFGHIIPRRSTZ PRIZEFIGHTERS	EEGINOPPRSSSS PREPOSSESSING
EEFGHILORSSTU SELF-RIGHTEOUS	EEGINOPRRSTTU INTEREST GROUP
EEFGIILLNRSTT LITTLE FINGERS	EEGINORSTTTUW TONGUE TWISTER
EEFGIILNNRRTY INTERFERINGLY	EEGOPPRRRSSUU PRESSURE GROUP
EEFGIIMNNNRST INFRINGEMENTS	EEHHIILLLMNPS PHILHELLENISM
EEFGIINNOPRTZ FREEZING POINT	EEHHIMNNNOOPP PHI-PHENOMENON
EEFGINNOORSST FRONTOGENESIS	EEHHMMNOOOPPR MORPHOPHONEME
EEFGINOORRRRT REIGN OF TERROR	EEHIIMOOPSSTV PHOTOEMISSIVE
EEFHHINOORSTT IN THE THROES OF	EEHILLOORSSTT TORTOISESHELL
EEFHILNNSSSSU UNSELFISHNESS	EEHILMNRSSSST MIRTHLESSNESS
EEFHILNSSSSST SHIFTLESSNESS	EEHILNNPSSTWY PENNY WHISTLES
EEFHNNORRTTUU FORTUNE HUNTER	EEHILNORSSSTU SOUTHERLINESS
EEFIILLMNOSTU FEUILLETONISM	EEHIMNOPTTTUU UP-TO-THE-MINUTE
EEFIILLNOSTTU FEUILLETONIST	EEHIMORSSSSTU HOUSEMISTRESS
EEFILLNNPSSTU PLENTIFULNESS	EEHKNNOOORSTT ON TENTERHOOKS
EEFILNNOOSSSU FELONIOUSNESS	EEHLNORRSTTWY NORTHWESTERLY
EEFILNRSSSSTU FRUITLESSNESS	EEHLNORSSSSTW WORTHLESSNESS
EEGGHHHLOOOTW GO THE WHOLE HOG	EEHLOORSSTTUY HETEROSTYLOUS
EEGGHINNNRSTT STRENGTHENING	EEHLORSSTTUWY SOUTHWESTERLY
EEGGIJKOPRRYY JIGGERY-POKERY	EEHMNOOOSSSTT TOOTHSOMENESS
EEGGINOOPPSST GOOSESTEPPING	EEHMNRRRSSUYY NURSERY RHYMES

EEHNORSSTTTWW WEST-NORTHWEST
EEHOOOOPRRSSTU HETEROSPOROUS
EEHOSSSTTTUWW WEST-SOUTHWEST
EEIIILNNSSTVY INSENSITIVELY
EEIIIMMNPRRST PRIME MINISTER
EEIIIMMNPRSSTV PRIMITIVENESS
EEIIIMOPPRRST IMPROPRIETIES
EEIIINNSSTTUV INTUITIVENESS
EEIIINOQRRSTU REQUISITIONER
EEIIILLMNSSSST LIMITLESSNESS
EEIIILMNNPRTTY IMPERTINENTLY
EEIIILMNPSSSUV IMPULSIVENESS
EEIILMOOSSTTY OSTEOMYELITIS
EEIILNOORSTUV REVOLUTIONISE
EEIILNOORTUVZ REVOLUTIONIZE
EEIILNOQRSTUV VENTRILOQUISE
EEIILNOQRTUVZ VENTRILOQUIZE
EEIILOOPPSSTV POSITIVE POLES
EEIIMNOPRSSSU IMPERIOUSNESS
EEIIMNOPRSSSX EXPRESSIONISM
EEIINNNORSTTV INTERVENTIONS
EEIINNOPRRSST INTERSPERSION
EEIINOPRSSSTX EXPRESSIONIST
EEIILLMNOOSSTY EMOTIONLESSLY
EEILLMOPRSTTU MULTIPLE STORE
EEILLNOOPQRSU NOLLE PROSEQUI
EEILMPPRSTUVY PRESUMPTIVELY
EEILNNOPSSSST POINTLESSNESS
EEILNNOSSTTUY SENTENTIOUSLY
EEILNOPRSTTUY PRETENTIOUSLY
EEILOPRRSSSTY PROSELYTISERS
EEILOPRRSSTYZ PROSELYTIZERS
EEIMNNNOPRSST PROMINENTNESS
EEIMNNNOPRSSY MONEY-SPINNERS
EEIMNNORSSSUV VERMINOUSNESS
EEIMNOOPRSSTV PROMOTIVENESS
EEIMNOPSSSTUU IMPETUOUSNESS
EEIMOOPRRSSTT STEREOTROPISM
EEINNOPRSTTUU UNPRETENTIOUS
EEINOOPPRSSSS PREPOSSESSION
EEINOPPRRSSTU PRESSURE POINT
EEINOPPRSSSUV PURPOSIVENESS
EEKLMNOPSUYZZ MONKEY-PUZZLES
EEKNNOOPSSSTU OUTSPOKENNESS
EELLNOOPPPRYY POLYPROPYLENE
EELLOPPRSSSUY PURPOSELESSLY
EELMNORSSSTUU TREMULOUSNESS
EELMOPRRSSTTY STORMY PETRELS
EELMOPSSTTUUY TEMPESTUOUSLY
EELNOQRSSSUUU QUERULOUSNESS
EEMNNOOPPSSTT POSTPONEMENTS
EEMNORSSSTUVY NERVOUS SYSTEM
EENNOOPPRSSTU OPPORTUNENESS
EENNORSSSSTUU STRENUOUSNESS
EFFGGILNNORSU LONGSUFFERING
EFFGHILNRSSTU FRIGHTFULNESS
EFFIILOORSSSU FOSSILIFEROUS
EFFIILPPPRSTU STIFF UPPER LIP
EFGGHIIILNTTW WEIGHT LIFTING

EFGGHIIINPRST PRISEFIGHTING
EFGGHIIINPRTZ PRIZEFIGHTING
EFGGHIILNNRTY FRIGHTENINGLY
EFGGIINNORSSV FORGIVINGNESS
EFGHHLLOOTTUW WELL-THOUGHT-OF
EFGIILLNPSTYY SELF-PITYINGLY
EFGIKLNNOORWY FOREKNOWINGLY
EFHHIINOOPSST PHOTO FINISHES
EFHIOOPPRRSSS PROFESSORSHIP
EFHLNNOOPRSTY HORNS OF PLENTY
EFHMMNOORTTTU MOMENT OF TRUTH
EFHOOOPPRTTTU PUT TO THE PROOF
EFIILLNOOPRSU POLLINIFEROUS
EFILNOOORSSTU STOLONIFEROUS
EFILNOORSSSUV FRIVOLOUSNESS
EFLLOPRSSUUUY SUPERFLUOUSLY
EFLNOORRSSSUW SORROWFULNESS
EGGHIIINNSTUX EXTINGUISHING
EGGHILLNOOPST HOT-GOSPELLING
EGGHLMOOOOPRY GEOMORPHOLOGY
EGGIIILMNNNRT INTERMINGLING
EGGILNOOORSTT GERONTOLOGIST
EGHHIILOPRSTY HIEROGLYPHIST
EGHHIINOPPRSW HORSEWHIPPING
EGHHILLMNOOTY HELMINTHOLOGY
EGHHLLOSSTTUY THOUGHTLESSLY
EGHIIILNNQRSU RELINQUISHING
EGHIIIMNOPRSV IMPOVERISHING
EGHIILMNNOPSY SPHINGOMYELIN
EGHIILNNSSSTU UNSIGHTLINESS
EGHIILNPRSSST SPRIGHTLINESS
EGHIIMNOOPSSY PHYSIOGNOMIES
EGHIIMNOPSSTY PHYSOSTIGMINE
EGHILOOPPSSST PSEPHOLOGISTS
EGHIMNOOORSSU ROOMING HOUSES
EGIIIILNORRST IRRELIGIONIST
EGIIILNOSSSTU LITIGIOUSNESS
EGIIJNNNNNPSY SPINNING JENNY
EGIILLLOOSTVX VEXILLOLOGIST
EGIILLNNNSSUW UNWILLINGNESS
EGIILLNNOPSST SELLING POINTS
EGIILMNNOPSTT MELTING POINTS
EGIILMNNRTTUY UNREMITTINGLY
EGIILMNOORSTT TERMINOLOGIST
EGIILMNOPRTYZ TEMPORIZINGLY
EGIILMOOSSSST SEISMOLOGISTS
EGIILNNOPRSTY INTERPOSINGLY
EGIILNNOQSTUY QUESTIONINGLY
EGIILNOPRSTYZ PROSELYTIZING
EGIIMNNOPRSSS PROMISINGNESS
EGIIMNOPPRSSU SUPERIMPOSING
EGIIMOPRRSSSV PROGRESSIVISM
EGIIINNNOQSTUU UNQUESTIONING
EGIINNOORRSST INTROGRESSION
EGIINNPPRRSST PRINTING PRESS
EGIINPRSTTTTY SITTING PRETTY
EGIIOPRRSSSTV PROGRESSIVIST
EGILLNNOORSST ROLLING STONES
EGILMNOOOSSTT ENTOMOLOGISTS

EGILNNOSSSTUU GLUTINOUSNESS
EGILNOPPRRSTU SPLINTER GROUP
EGIMMMNOPRSSY GYMNOSPERMISM
EGMMNOOPRSSUY GYMNOSPERMOUS
EGMMNOORRRSUU RUMOURMONGERS
EHHIILOOPPRSS PHILOSOPHISER
EHHIILOOPPRSZ PHILOSOPHIZER
EHHIMMMOOOPRS HOMEOMORPHISM
EHILLOPSSTWW WILL-O'-THE-WISPS
EHIILMOOPPSSY LYMPHOPOIESIS
EHIIMNOOOPSST PHOTOEMISSION
EHILLNNOOPQUY PHYLLOQUINONE
EHILMNOOOPSTU ENTOMOPHILOUS
EHILNOPSSSTYY POLYSYNTHESIS
EHIMMOOPRRSTT THERMOTROPISM
EHLLLOOPPSTUY LEPTOPHYLLOUS
EHLLNOOPSSTUY STENOPHYLLOUS
EIIIILNQSTUVY INQUISITIVELY
EIIIINNSSTTVY INSENSITIVITY
EIIILLMOOPSTY POLIOMYELITIS
EIIIMMNOPRSSS IMPRESSIONISM
EIIIMNNORSSST INTERMISSIONS
EIIIMNOPRSSST IMPRESSIONIST
EIIINNOOPRSTT INTERPOSITION
EIILLLLMNOPSS PLIMSOLL LINES
EIILMNOQRSTUV VENTRILOQUISM
EIILMOORRSSTUY MERITORIOUSLY
EIILNOOOOPPSST POLE POSITIONS
EIILNOORSTTUV REVOLUTIONIST
EIILNOQRSTTUV VENTRILOQUIST
EIIMNOORSSSTT MONSTROSITIES
EIINNOPRRSTTU INTERRUPTIONS
EIINOOPPRSSTU SUPERPOSITION
EIINOOPPRSTTU OPPORTUNITIES
EIINOORSSTTTX EXTORTIONISTS
EIINOPRSSSTTU SUPERSTITIONS
EIIOOPPRSSSTU SUPPOSITORIES
EIIOPRRSSTTUU SURREPTITIOUS
EIIOPRSSSTTUU SUPERSTITIOUS

EIJLNOOPPRSTU JET PROPULSION
EILNNOOPPRTUY INOPPORTUNELY
EINNOOOPSSSSU POISONOUSNESS
EINNOOORSSSTU NOTORIOUSNESS
EMNOPSSSSTUUU SUMPTUOUSNESS
EMOOOPRRRSSTT STORM TROOPERS
FFIIINNOOSSSU FISSION-FUSION
FFLLLLNOOOORR ROLL-ON ROLL-OFF
FGHHLLOOORTUW FOLLOW-THROUGH
FGHIILLMNOOTT MOONLIGHT FLIT
FGHIILLNORSUY FLOURISHINGLY
FGIIIILLNOSSSV LIVING FOSSILS
FHLLNOOOORRSU ROLL OF HONOURS
FILLMRSSTTUUY MISTRUSTFULLY
GGGHHINOOORTU THOROUGHGOING
GGHIIILNPRSTT STRIP LIGHTING
GHIILLOOPSSTY SYPHILOLOGIST
GHIILNOOORSTT ORNITHOLOGIST
GHIILNOPPRSWY WORSHIPPINGLY
GHIILOOPSSSTY PHYSIOLOGISTS
GHIIMMOOPRSTT THIGMOTROPISM
GHIIMNOOPSSTY PHYSIOGNOMIST
GIIIILNNPRSTY INSPIRITINGLY
GIIILLNOOQSUZ SOLILOQUIZING
GIIILMNNOOSUY IGNOMINIOUSLY
GIILMNNOOPSSW SWIMMING POOLS
GIILMNRSSTTUY MISTRUSTINGLY
GIINNNOPRSTTU TURNING POINTS
GIINNOOOPPRRT PROPORTIONING
GILLLMOOPSSYY POLYSYLLOGISM
HHIMOOOPRRSUZ RHIZOMORPHOUS
HIIILLNNOQTTU QUINTILLIONTH
HIILLOOPPRSWW WHIPPOORWILLS
HILORRSTTTUWY TRUSTWORTHILY
IIINOOOPPSSTT OPPOSITIONIST
IIINOOPRRSSTV PRISON VISITOR
IILLLORSSTUUY ILLUSTRIOUSLY
IIMNOOOPPRRST MISPROPORTION
IINNOOOPPSTTT POINT-TO-POINTS

AAAABCCEELRSTU BACCALAUREATES
AAAABEHKLLLMRU MAHALLA EL KUBRA
AAAACCDEINORSU ANACARDIACEOUS
AAAACCILLPRTTY PARATACTICALLY
AAAACCINNRSSTU TRANSCAUCASIAN
AAAACDIIMMNOST MACADAMISATION
AAAACDIIMMNOTZ MACADAMIZATION
AAAACEGILLMMNO MEGALOMANIACAL
AAAACEHMNORSTU AMARANTHACEOUS
AAAACEIMNNRRST SACRAMENTARIAN
AAAACHIILNNRSS HALICARNASSIAN
AAAADEGINNQRRU QUADRAGENARIAN
AAAADELLLNORRV ANDORRA LA VELLA
AAAAEGLNRSTTUW NATURAL WASTAGE
AAAAEHILNPPRRS PARAPHERNALIAS
AAAAFIILNNPRRS INFRALAPSARIAN
AAAAFIIMNRRSST RASTAFARIANISM
AAAAGHIMNOPRST PHANTASMAGORIA
AAAAHHIKMNPSTV VISHAKHAPATNAM
AAAAIILLNOPSTT PALATALISATION
AAAAIILLNOPTTZ PALATALIZATION
AAAABBCEILNNPRU BANANA REPUBLIC
AAAABCCDHILRTYY BRACHYDACTYLIA
AAAABCCEIILLMTZ ACCLIMATIZABLE
AAAABCCILMNNOOY CYANOCOBALAMIN
AAAABCDEEFLNORT BALANCE OF TRADE
AAAABCDEGINOSTU SANTIAGO DE CUBA
AAAABCEFLMNRTUU MANUFACTURABLE
AAAABCEHILLLPTY ALPHABETICALLY
AAAABCEHILMOSTT HAEMATOBLASTIC
AAAABCEHILNOPPR INAPPROACHABLE
AAAABCEHLNOPPRU UNAPPROACHABLE
AAAABCEILMNOSSU BALSAMINACEOUS
AAAABCEILMNRRSU ARABIC NUMERALS
AAAABDDEEEHORST BEAT A DEAD HORSE
AAAABDDEELLLLNN BE-ALL AND END-ALL
AAAABDDEENRRRST STANDARD-BEARER
AAAABDEEELMPSTX SET A BAD EXAMPLE
AAAABDEEMRSSSSS AMBASSADRESSES
AAAABDHIMOPRSSS AMBASSADORSHIP
AAAABDIINORSSTT BASTARDISATION
AAAABDIINORSTTZ BASTARDIZATION
AAAABEEEELLRSTUV RATEABLE VALUES
AAAABEGGIILNNPR PLEA BARGAINING
AAAABEIILLMNPRR PRIMA BALLERINA
AAAABEILNOOPSTT PALAEOBOTANIST
AAAABELLNNPRSTT TRANSPLANTABLE
AAAABIILNOOPRST PARABOLISATION
AAAABIILNOOPRTZ PARABOLIZATION
AAAABIILNRRTTWY WARRANTABILITY
AAAACCDEHIINORT ARCHIDIACONATE
AAAACCDEHINRRSS CASH AND CARRIES
AAAACCDEIMNNOOR ADENOCARCINOMA
AAAACCDEIOPPRSU CAPPARIDACEOUS
AAAACCDILORRSUV CARDIOVASCULAR
AAAACCEEELLNRSS CLEARANCE SALES
AAAACCEEFHHKLTT AT THE CHALKFACE
AAAACCEEHILMNOR AEROMECHANICAL
AAAACCEEHMNRSTT CATCHMENT AREAS

AAAACCEGHILLOOR ARCHAEOLOGICAL
AAAACCEHILMPRTU PHARMACEUTICAL
AAAACCEILNNORTX EXTRACANONICAL
AAAACCELMNOPSUU CAMPANULACEOUS
AAAACCGHILOPRRT CARTOGRAPHICAL
AAAACCGIIINNPTT INCAPACITATING
AAAACCHIILNRSTT CHARLATANISTIC
AAAACCHILLMORTY ACHROMATICALLY
AAAACCIIINNOPTT INCAPACITATION
AAAACCILLOPRTTUY AUTOCRATICALLY
AAAACCLMOORSSTU MALACOSTRACOUS
AAAACDDEGGKLNOR CLOAK-AND-DAGGER
AAAACDEEGHILNRR HEGIRA CALENDAR
AAAACDEEINPPRSS DISAPPEARANCES
AAAACDEFGNORRUV GRACE-AND-FAVOUR
AAAACDEGIKLNNNP PANCAKE LANDING
AAAACDEIIIMNNNR AMERICAN INDIAN
AAAACDEIIINPRST PAEDIATRICIANS
AAAACDFHIMNNRST HANDICRAFTSMAN
AAAACDHILNOOPRS ACHONDROPLASIA
AAAACDHINNRSTTU TRISTAN DA CUNHA
AAAACDIILNNOSST SCANDALISATION
AAAACDIILNNOSTZ SCANDALIZATION
AAAACEEGILNSSTU AGUASCALIENTES
AAAACEEILLNORRS ALSACE-LORRAINE
AAAACEEILNORSUV VALERIANACEOUS
AAAACEFGIORSSUX SAXIFRAGACEOUS
AAAACEFIILNNRSY FINANCIAL YEARS
AAAACEFILLLNSTY SELF-ANALYTICAL
AAAACEGILMNNORS ANGLO-AMERICANS
AAAACEHIILMRRSV AIR VICE-MARSHAL
AAAACEHIIMMNSTT MATHEMATICIANS
AAAACEHILLMMTTY MATHEMATICALLY
AAAACEHILMOOPPR PHARMACOPOEIAL
AAAACEHILNOPPRT PALAEANTHROPIC
AAAACEHIMOOPPRS PHARMACOPOEIAS
AAAACEHNRRRSSTW SEARCH WARRANTS
AAAACEIIMMNNPRS PAN-AMERICANISM
AAAACEILLMNNSTY ANAMNESTICALLY
AAAACEILLMSTTTY METASTATICALLY
AAAACEILMMNRSST SACRAMENTALISM
AAAACEILMNRSSTT SACRAMENTALIST
AAAACEILMNRSTTY SACRAMENTALITY
AAAACENRRRSSTTU RESTAURANT CARS
AAAACFIILLLSTTY FATALISTICALLY
AAAACFIILNOSSTT SATISFACTIONAL
AAAACGHIKLNSSTT SLASHING ATTACK
AAAACGHIMNOPRST PHANTASMAGORIC
AAAACGIILLMSTTY ASTIGMATICALLY
AAAACGIILLNPSTY PAGANISTICALLY
AAAACGIILMMRTTY GRAMMATICALITY
AAAACGILLMNORTY MORGANATICALLY
AAAACGLORRSSTUV GASTROVASCULAR
AAAACHILLLLOPTY ALLOPATHICALLY
AAAACHILMMNNOPY NYMPHOMANIACAL
AAAACHILMOPRTTU THAUMATROPICAL
AAAACIIILNOPSTT CAPITALISATION
AAAACIIILNOPTTZ CAPITALIZATION
AAAACILLLLOPRTY ALLOPATRICALLY

AAADEEGHHMSTTW WHAT'S THE DAMAGE?
AAADEEHLLORTTT LEAD TO THE ALTAR
AAADEEHLMNNNRT NEANDERTHAL MAN
AAADEGGILNNRSU GUARDIAN ANGELS
AAADEGLNOSTUVY ADVANTAGEOUSLY
AAADEHMNPSTTYY TEA AND SYMPATHY
AAADEIILNNRTUV VALETUDINARIAN
AAADEILLQRRSTU QUADRILATERALS
AAADEIMNNORRSY ORDINARY SEAMAN
AAADFIILLMORRY FAIRY ARMADILLO
AAADGHIOOPRRTU AUTORADIOGRAPH
AAADGIILLMNORT GIANT ARMADILLO
AAADGIMNOORSST GOOD SAMARITANS
AAADIIILNNRTTU LATITUDINARIAN
AAADIIMNORSSTT DRAMATISATIONS
AAADIIMNORSTTZ DRAMATIZATIONS
AAADIJNNNORRST TRANS-JORDANIAN
AAAEEFGIKMOPRS MAKE A PIG'S EAR OF
AAAEEGINNPRSTU SEPTUAGENARIAN
AAAEEGMNRRSSTT SERGEANT-AT-ARMS
AAAEEHHLMMORTT HAEMATOTHERMAL
AAAEEHIIMNRRTT HENRIETTA MARIA
AAAEEHMNRRSTWX MANX SHEARWATER
AAAEEIILLPRTXY EPITAXIAL LAYER
AAAEEJMNRRSSTT SERJEANT-AT-ARMS
AAAEGGGIKNPRRS PARKING GARAGES
AAAEGHIIMNNTTZ ANATHEMATIZING
AAAEGHLNNOPRSY NASOPHARYNGEAL
AAAEGIIILMNRST EGALITARIANISM
AAAEGLLLMOPRRS PARALLELOGRAMS
AAAEGLMOPRRSSU MASSAGE PARLOUR
AAAEHILMNNNOTT NATIONAL ANTHEM
AAAGIILNNOORST ORGANISATIONAL
AAAGIILNNOORTZ ORGANIZATIONAL
AAAGIIMMNPRSTT ANTIPRAGMATISM
AAAGIINNNOOSTT ANTAGONISATION
AAAGIINNNOOTTZ ANTAGONIZATION
AAAGINOORRSTTV ASTRONAVIGATOR
AAAHIINORRSTTU AUTHORITARIANS
AAAIILNNORSTTU NATURALISATION
AAAIILNNORTTUZ NATURALIZATION
AAAIILNORSTTWY RAILWAY STATION
AAAIIMNORSTTTU TRAUMATISATION
AAAIIMNORTTTUZ TRAUMATIZATION
AAAIINNOSSSSST ASSASSINATIONS
AAAILNNORSTTUV TRANSVALUATION
AABBCEEFINORST ABSORBEFACIENT
AABBCEEHILNOSS BELISHA BEACONS
AABBDDEEGILORS BIODEGRADABLES
AABBDDEENRRTTU BREAD-AND-BUTTER
AABBDEEHIMNORT BROAD IN THE BEAM
AABBEEEELNNRSSU UNBEARABLENESS
AABBEEFGGILNRST FLABBERGASTING
AABBEIILLOSSSU BOUILLABAISSES
AABBELOPRRRSWY BLOW A RASPBERRY
AABBHIIIILNTTY INHABITABILITY
AABCCCDHILRTYY BRACHYDACTYLIC
AABCCCEHHILPRY BRACHYCEPHALIC
AABCCCDEKKLLNOT BLOCK AND TACKLE

AABCCEELNNORTU COUNTERBALANCE
AABCCEGHIIOPRT BACTERIOPHAGIC
AABCCEHILLMOPS ACCOMPLISHABLE
AABCCEHNOOORSU OROBANCHACEOUS
AABCCEIIORSTTT BACTERIOSTATIC
AABCCEILMMRTUU CIRCUMAMBULATE
AABCCIIILPRTTY PRACTICABILITY
AABCCIILNOTTUY ACCOUNTABILITY
AABCDDEEHKNNSS BACKHANDEDNESS
AABCDDHINORSSW SANDWICH BOARDS
AABCDEEEGHNRUU BUREAU DE CHANGE
AABCDEEEMMNRRY REMEMBRANCE DAY
AABCDEEFIILLSS DECLASSIFIABLE
AABCDEEHLOTTTU CHATEAU BOTTLED
AABCDEEHNNRUZZ NEBUCHADNEZZAR
AABCDEEHORTTUY CATHODE RAY TUBE
AABCDEEIKRRSTV BACK-SEAT DRIVER
AABCDEEINRRSTT SCATTERBRAINED
AABCDEEKMNOPPY KEEP BAD COMPANY
AABCDEENNPRSUU SUPERABUNDANCE
AABCDEENRSSSTT ABSTRACTEDNESS
AABCDEGIILLNNV ADVANCE BILLING
AABCDEGIKLNRRT BLANK CARTRIDGE
AABCDEHOORRSST ACROSS-THE-BOARD
AABCDEIILLNOSS DIABOLICALNESS
AABCEEEEFLNOSV LEAVE OF ABSENCE
AABCEEEGHLNNSS CHANGEABLENESS
AABCEEEEHKNRTTT THE BEATEN TRACK
AABCEEEKKLMRRT BLACK MARKETEER
AABCEEFLNOOPRW BALANCE OF POWER
AABCEEGHLNORUX LABOUR EXCHANGE
AABCEEGILNRTXY EXACERBATINGLY
AABCEEHIKLMNNS BLACKEN HIS NAME
AABCEEHILNRSST CHARITABLENESS
AABCEEHILOPRRR IRREPROACHABLE
AABCEEHINSTTUU EUSTACHIAN TUBE
AABCEEIILLPRTY REPLACEABILITY
AABCEEILLLMMTY EMBLEMATICALLY
AABCEEKQRRSSTU SQUARE BRACKETS
AABCEFGIINPRRT PREFABRICATING
AABCEFIIINOSTT BEATIFICATIONS
AABCEFIIINOTTU BEAUTIFICATION
AABCEFIINOPRRT PREFABRICATION
AABCEGHHIIMNNT BATHING MACHINE
AABCEHIIILMPTY IMPEACHABILITY
AABCEHIILLRSTY HEBRAISTICALLY
AABCEHILOPRRRY IRREPROACHABLY
AABCEIILLORSST AEROBALLISTICS
AABCEIILNNPRTU ANTIREPUBLICAN
AABCEIILRRTTTY RETRACTABILITY
AABCEIILRTTTXY EXTRACTABILITY
AABCEIIORSSSTT BACTERIOSTASIS
AABCEILLMORRTY BAROMETRICALLY
AABCEILNORSSTU CONSTABULARIES
AABCEIMOORSSUU SIMAROUBACEOUS
AABCFIKMNOORST BACK FORMATIONS
AABCFILNNOOSTU CONFABULATIONS
AABCGGIILLOOOR AGROBIOLOGICAL
AABCGHIILLMOOP AMPHIBOLOGICAL

AABCGHIILLOPRY BIOGRAPHICALLY
AABCGHIIOOPRTU AUTOBIOGRAPHIC
AABCGHIMOOPRRR MICROBAROGRAPH
AABCHIILPRSTUY PURCHASABILITY
AABCHILOOPRSTU CLAUSTROPHOBIA
AABCIIILLMPRSY IMPARISYLLABIC
AABCIIILNRTTTY INTRACTABILITY
AABCIIMNORSSTT ABSTRACTIONISM
AABDDEEIMNNORT ONE-ARMED BANDIT
AABDDEELNNRSTU UNDERSTANDABLE
AABDDEFIIOPRRS BIRD OF PARADISE
AABDDELNNRSTUY UNDERSTANDABLY
AABDDGIINNORRS DRAINING BOARDS
AABDEEEFHINRRT FEATHERBRAINED
AABDEEEHHIRRSS HABERDASHERIES
AABDEEEHILNNNR BANNER HEADLINE
AABDEFGIOPRSSS BIRDS OF PASSAGE
AABDEFIIILLQSU DISQUALIFIABLE
AABDEIIKMNORST DISEMBARKATION
AABDEIILPRSTUY PERSUADABILITY
AABDEKLNRSSTUY LAUNDRY BASKETS
AABDHHNPRSSUUW WASH AND BRUSH-UP
AABDHILMNOSSUY BUSMAN'S HOLIDAY
AABDIIIILNSTVY INADVISABILITY
AABDIIIILNOTUVY UNAVOIDABILITY
AABDIINOOPPRST DISAPPROBATION
AABEEEFMNNOOST BEMOAN ONE'S FATE
AABEEEINORRSWY RAISE AN EYEBROW
AABEEEKLMNRRSS REMARKABLENESS
AABEEEELNNORSSS REASONABLENESS
AABEEEELNNOSSSS SEASONABLENESS
AABEEFGILNNOST SELF-ABNEGATION
AABEEFLNORSSUV FAVOURABLENESS
AABEEGIKMNORRR BROKEN MARRIAGE
AABEEHIIILRTTV REHABILITATIVE
AABEEHIIILPRSS HERPES LABIALIS
AABEEHIILRTTWY WEATHERABILITY
AABEEHJKMNORST JAM ON THE BRAKES
AABEEIMNNORTUV MOUNTAIN BEAVER
AABEEMMNRRSSST EMBARRASSMENTS
AABEFGHLLORRSU BARREL OF LAUGHS
AABEFILLMMNNNO NONINFLAMMABLE
AABEFILLNOPSTU FALLOPIAN TUBES
AABEGHIIILNRTT REHABILITATING
AABEGHIOOPRRTU AUTOBIOGRAPHER
AABEGIILLNOSUV BOUGAINVILLEAS
AABEGILMNRRSSY EMBARRASSINGLY
AABEHIIILNORTT REHABILITATION
AABEIIIILLNNTY INALIENABILITY
AABEIIIILLNORST LIBERALISATION
AABEIIIILLNORTZ LIBERALIZATION
AABEIIIILLNRTTY INALTERABILITY
AABEIIIILMNRRST LIBERTARIANISM
AABEIIILNPRSTY INSEPARABILITY
AABEIIILPRRRTY IRREPARABILITY
AABEIILRRSUVXY AUXILIARY VERBS
AABEIINSSTTTUV SUBSTANTIATIVE
AABEILMNOPRSTU PERAMBULATIONS
AABEILNNORSTTU SUBALTERNATION

AABEKMRRRRSTWY STRAWBERRY MARK
AABELOPRRSTUUY BEAUTY PARLOURS
AABENORRRRSTWY STRAWBERRY ROAN
AABFIIILLMMNTY INFLAMMABILITY
AABFIIILLNPPTUY UNFLAPPABILITY
AABGIINNSSTTTU SUBSTANTIATING
AABHIIINPPRSST BIPARTISANSHIP
AABIIIILLMNPTUY MANIPULABILITY
AABIILMNSSSTTU SUBSTANTIALISM
AABIILNSSSTTTU SUBSTANTIALIST
AABIILNSSTTTUY SUBSTANTIALITY
AABIINNOSSTTTU SUBSTANTIATION
AABILMMNNOOSTU SOMNAMBULATION
AACCCCENNOOOVV CONCAVO-CONCAVE
AACCCDHIIINOTY THIOCYANIC ACID
AACCCEEHILLTTY CATECHETICALLY
AACCCEEIIILLSST ECCLESIASTICAL
AACCCEGHNORSTU CHARGE ACCOUNTS
AACCCEHIIRRSTT CHARACTERISTIC
AACCCHLLOOPSTY STAPHYLOCOCCAL
AACCDDDEEHHNRT CATCH RED-HANDED
AACCDDEMMNOOTU UNACCOMMODATED
AACCDEHILOPRSY POLYSACCHARIDE
AACCDEHIMNOORS MONOSACCHARIDE
AACCDEIINNORTT CONTRAINDICATE
AACCDEILLMORTY DEMOCRATICALLY
AACCDHIMOOPRSTY PSYCHODRAMATIC
AACCDHIMRRSSST CHRISTMAS CARDS
AACCDIIINRSTTU TRADUCIANISTIC
AACCDIINNNORTT CONTRAINDICANT
AACCDIMMNOOOST ACCOMMODATIONS
AACCEEGHILLMOP MEGALOCEPHALIC
AACCEEGIILNTTT TELANGIECTATIC
AACCEEILMNNRSTU NATURAL SCIENCE
AACCEEINNNORSS RECONNAISSANCE
AACCEELMNRSUUV VACUUM CLEANERS
AACCEELNORRRTU NUCLEAR REACTOR
AACCEGGHINRRRY CARRYING CHARGE
AACCEGGILLNOOY GYNAECOLOGICAL
AACCEGHIINRRTZ CHARACTERIZING
AACCEGHILLOOST ESCHATOLOGICAL
AACCEGIILOOPTT GALACTOPOIETIC
AACCEGIIMNRTUV CIRCUMNAVIGATE
AACCEGINNOSTUY NYCTAGINACEOUS
AACCEHHIILLRRY HIERARCHICALLY
AACCEHHLNPRSTY CHANTRY CHAPELS
AACCEHIILOPPRS ARCHIEPISCOPAL
AACCEHIINNORST CHAIN REACTIONS
AACCEHIKLOOSSV CSECHOSLOVAKIA
AACCEHIKMRSSST CHRISTMAS CAKES
AACCEHILLNOOPT PLAIN CHOCOLATE
AACCEHILLORTTY THEOCRATICALLY
AACCEHILLPRTYY ARCHETYPICALLY
AACCEHINOPPRRT PARTHENOCARPIC
AACCEIILLPRSTT PRACTICALITIES
AACCEIILRRTUUV CURRICULA VITAE
AACCEIJKLOPRST PRACTICAL JOKES
AACCEILLLOPPTY APOPLECTICALLY
AACCEILLMTUUVY ACCUMULATIVELY

AACCEIMMNNOPST ACCOMPANIMENTS
AACCEINNNOOSTT CONCATENATIONS
AACCEKNORSTTTU COUNTERATTACKS
AACCELLMMOORRU MACROMOLECULAR
AACCELLNOOPRRS LANCE CORPORALS
AACCELNNORSUUU RANUNCULACEOUS
AACCELOOPRSTUU PORTULACACEOUS
AACCFHOORRRRTY CARRY A TORCH FOR
AACCFIIILNORST CLARIFICATIONS
AACCFIIILNOSST CLASSIFICATION
AACCFIIINNOSTT SANCTIFICATION
AACCFIILMOPSST FAITS ACCOMPLIS
AACCFIILORSSTY CLASSIFICATORY
AACCFLOOOOPSTV FOOLSCAP OCTAVO
AACCFNNORTTTUU TURF ACCOUNTANT
AACCGHHHHIINSU SHIHCHIACHUANG
AACCGHIILLLORY OLIGARCHICALLY
AACCGHILLNOOST ANGLO-CATHOLICS
AACCGIILLMNSTU MISCALCULATING
AACCGIILLMORTY TRAGICOMICALLY
AACCGILLLNOOOV VOLCANOLOGICAL
AACCGINNOSSTUV SAVINGS ACCOUNT
AACCHIILLMSSTY SCHISMATICALLY
AACCHILLOSSTTY STOCHASTICALLY
AACCHILMNOORST ROMAN CATHOLICS
AACCHILNOPSTYY PSYCHOANALYTIC
AACCIIILMPRTTY IMPRACTICALITY
AACCIIIMOPRRST MICROPARASITIC
AACCIILLMNOSTU MISCALCULATION
AACCIILLNNOORR CONRAIL, CONRAIL
AACCIILMNRSTTU CIRCUMSTANTIAL
AACCIILNPRTTUY UNPRACTICALITY
AACCIIMNOORSST CARCINOMATOSIS
AACCILLNOOPTUY OCCUPATIONALLY
AACCKLNNNOPSTT PLANCK CONSTANT
AACDDDEKKNRSSU DUCKS AND DRAKES
AACDDEEELLNSVV ADVANCED LEVELS
AACDDEEILOSTVV DEVIL'S ADVOCATE
AACDDEEIMNNOTT DECONTAMINATED
AACDDEILNOTTUU ADULT EDUCATION
AACDEEEFHMNSSS SHAMEFACEDNESS
AACDEEGHHNORST CHASE THE DRAGON
AACDEEGIILLNRT LEADING ARTICLE
AACDEEGINRRRSU UNDERCARRIAGES
AACDEEGIPPRRRT CARTRIDGE PAPER
AACDEEILLNQTUW WELL-ACQUAINTED
AACDEEILOPPRTU PROPAEDEUTICAL
AACDEEIQRSSTTU ACQUIRED TASTES
AACDEELNNNRSTT TRANSCENDENTAL
AACDEENORSSSUV CADAVEROUSNESS
AACDEFFINRRSTW TRAFFIC WARDENS
AACDEGILLMOORT DERMATOLOGICAL
AACDEGINOPRSST DATA PROCESSING
AACDEGLMNNORSS SCANDALMONGERS
AACDEHIIMNRRST ARCHIMANDRITES
AACDEHILORRSTT TRISOCTAHEDRAL
AACDEHLMNNORST CALENDAR MONTHS
AACDEHLNOPSSYY PSYCHOANALYSED
AACDEHMOPRSTUY PACHYDERMATOUS

AACDEIIILLLSTY IDEALISTICALLY
AACDEIIILMNOST DECIMALISATION
AACDEIIILMNOTZ DECIMALIZATION
AACDEIILLNOOST DELOCALISATION
AACDEIILLNOOTZ DELOCALIZATION
AACDEIILMMNOST DOMESTIC ANIMAL
AACDEIILNNOPTY PLATINOCYANIDE
AACDEIILNOSTTU EDUCATIONALIST
AACDEIILPRRSTU PARTICULARISED
AACDEIILPRRTUZ PARTICULARIZED
AACDEIINORTTTX DIRECT TAXATION
AACDEILMOPRSTT DERMATOPLASTIC
AACDEILMORRTTU COURT-MARTIALED
AACDEILNOPRSSS SPORADICALNESS
AACDEIMNNNOTTU UNCONTAMINATED
AACDEIMNNOORTT DECONTAMINATOR
AACDEINOPRRSTT PROCRASTINATED
AACDELNNOSSSSU SCANDALOUSNESS
AACDFFIILNRSST TRAFFIC ISLANDS
AACDGHIMOOPRRY MYOCARDIOGRAPH
AACDGIIINOSSST DISASSOCIATING
AACDGIILLNOSTY DIAGNOSTICALLY
AACDHIMOOSSSST SADOMASOCHISTS
AACDIIIILNNPRS DISCIPLINARIAN
AACDIIINOOSSST DISASSOCIATION
AACDIILLLMOPTY DIPLOMATICALLY
AACDIILNNOPRST CARDINAL POINTS
AACDIILORRSTTU DISARTICULATOR
AACDIKNNPQRSSU QUIPS AND CRANKS
AACDILNOOSSTUY ANISODACTYLOUS
AACDILOORSTTUY ARTIODACTYLOUS
AACEEEEGINSSTT ESTATE AGENCIES
AACEEEFGHNORTX RATE OF EXCHANGE
AACEEEFHINRSTT STARE IN THE FACE
AACEEEGILNRSTV TRAVEL AGENCIES
AACEEEGIPPRRTT CIGARETTE PAPER
AACEEEHIMNNOST IN THE SAME CANOE
AACEEEHKMRRRST MARKET RESEARCH
AACEEEHLMOSTUY THYMELAEACEOUS
AACEEEHMMORTTY HAEMACYTOMETER
AACEEEIILLRSTUV RELATIVE CLAUSE
AACEEFFILNOTTY AFFECTIONATELY
AACEEGGILLLNOY GENEALOGICALLY
AACEEGHHLNOPPR ENCEPHALOGRAPH
AACEEGHILNNRTT CENTRAL HEATING
AACEEGHNOOPRRS OCEANOGRAPHERS
AACEEGIILLMNSV EVANGELICALISM
AACEEGIILNSSTT TELANGIECTASIS
AACEEGIIPRSVWY GIVEAWAY PRICES
AACEEGILLNNPTY PANGENETICALLY
AACEEGILNPRSTW WATERING PLACES
AACEEHHMNOPRTY MECHANOTHERAPY
AACEEHHNOPPRST ON THE SCRAPHEAP
AACEEHIIMOOPTT HAEMATOPOIETIC
AACEEHILLLPTTY TELEPATHICALLY
AACEEHILMNPSST EMPHATICALNESS
AACEEHILRRTUVX EXTRAVEHICULAR
AACEEHIMNNRSTV MERCHANT NAVIES
AACEEHIPRSSTTY CRYPTAESTHESIA

AACEEIIINPPRTV INAPPRECIATIVE
AACEEIILOPRSTV OVERCAPITALISE
AACEEIILOPRTVZ OVERCAPITALIZE
AACEEIILPPRTVY APPRECIATIVELY
AACEEIILPRTTUV RECAPITULATIVE
AACEEIINPPRTUV UNAPPRECIATIVE
AACEEILNPPPRRT RICE-PAPER PLANT
AACEEILNPRTTUV VENTURE CAPITAL
AACEEILNRSSTTU ARTICULATENESS
AACEEINNPRRSST TRANSPARENCIES
AACEEINRSSTTTV ATTRACTIVENESS
AACEFFINORRRTW WARRANT OFFICER
AACEFFLMORTTTY MATTER-OF-FACTLY
AACEFIINPRRTTU PARTURIFACIENT
AACEFILLNOSSSU FALLACIOUSNESS
AACEFINRSSTTUY SAFETY CURTAINS
AACEFNOPRRSSTT TRANSPORT CAFES
AACEGGHILLOPRY GEOGRAPHICALLY
AACEGGHINNORRT GREGORIAN CHANT
AACEGGILNNOORT CONGREGATIONAL
AACEGHHIIMNNSW WASHING MACHINE
AACEGHHIOPPRRS PHRASEOGRAPHIC
AACEGHIILLPPRY EPIGRAPHICALLY
AACEGHIILMOPSU MALPIGHIACEOUS
AACEGHIINNTTTU AUTHENTICATING
AACEGHIJKRSTTT STRAIGHTJACKET
AACEGHILLLMPTY PHLEGMATICALLY
AACEGHILLMNOPY MEGAPHONICALLY
AACEGHILLMOPRT METALLOGRAPHIC
AACEGHILLOOPRS PHRASEOLOGICAL
AACEGHILOORSST ARCHAEOLOGISTS
AACEGHILOPRTTU TELAUTOGRAPHIC
AACEGHIMNOPRTY CINEMATOGRAPHY
AACEGIILLLLSTY LEGALISTICALLY
AACEGIILLMOOSS SEMASIOLOGICAL
AACEGIILNPRTTU RECAPITULATING
AACEGIILOOPSST GALACTOPOIESIS
AACEGIINNOPRST ANGINA PECTORIS
AACEGIINOORSTT CATEGORISATION
AACEGIINOORTTZ CATEGORIZATION
AACEGILLLOOPTY APOLOGETICALLY
AACEGILLMNOORT ORGANOMETALLIC
AACEGILNRRTTUY RECTANGULARITY
AACEHHILNNOPTY PHTHALOCYANINE
AACEHIIIMNRSTT ARITHMETICIANS
AACEHIILLLLPTY PHILATELICALLY
AACEHIILLMRTTY ARITHMETICALLY
AACEHIILLNTTTY ANTITHETICALLY
AACEHIILMNSTUV MALE CHAUVINIST
AACEHIIMNNRSST CHRISTIAN NAMES
AACEHIIMNOSSTT SCHEMATISATION
AACEHIIMNOSTTZ SCHEMATIZATION
AACEHIINNOTTTU AUTHENTICATION
AACEHILLLNNOUY UNHOLY ALLIANCE
AACEHILLMNNORY ENHARMONICALLY
AACEHILLMOOPRSY SEMAPHORICALLY
AACEHILLMOPRTY METAPHORICALLY
AACEHILLMPSTYY METAPHYSICALLY
AACEHILMNPRRSU HURRICANE LAMPS

AACEHIMMMORSTT METACHROMATISM
AACEHIMOOPPRST PHARMACOPOEIST
AACEHLNOPRSYYZ PSYCHOANALYZER
AACEHMNOOOPPRS ANAMORPHOSCOPE
AACEHMNOPRSTUY PARENCHYMATOUS
AACEIIILNOPSST SPECIALISATION
AACEIIILNOPSTZ SPECIALIZATION
AACEIILLMNNOOT CALAMINE LOTION
AACEIILLNPSTTY ANTISEPTICALLY
AACEIILLNRTTUY INARTICULATELY
AACEIILMOOPRTV IMPERIAL OCTAVO
AACEIILNNORSTT CENTRALISATION
AACEIILNNORTTZ CENTRALIZATION
AACEIILNOPRTTU RECAPITULATION
AACEIILNORSSTU SECULARISATION
AACEIILNORSTUZ SECULARIZATION
AACEIILPPPRSTT PAST PARTICIPLE
AACEIILPRRRSTU PARTICULARISER
AACEIILPRRRTUZ PARTICULARIZER
AACEIINNNORRST REINCARNATIONS
AACEIINOPRRSTV PREVARICATIONS
AACEIINRRRSSTU CURTAIN RAISERS
AACEILLLNOPSTY PLEONASTICALLY
AACEILLMMNORTY MANOMETRICALLY
AACEILLMMRSTYY ASYMMETRICALLY
AACEILLMNORRTU INTRAMOLECULAR
AACEILLMSSTTYY SYSTEMATICALLY
AACEILNNNRSSTY TYRANNICALNESS
AACEILNNOORSTV CONSERVATIONAL,
    CONVERSATIONAL
AACEILNNOPSSTU ENCAPSULATIONS
AACEILNORSTTUX EXCLAUSTRATION
AACEIMNOPRSTTU STORM IN A TEACUP
AACEINNORSTTUU INTRACUTANEOUS
AACEINOPRSSSST CAST ASPERSIONS
AACEKLNNORSTUY CANTANKEROUSLY
AACELLLOPPRRYY POLYCARPELLARY
AACELLMNOOPRRY MONOCARPELLARY
AACELLMOPRRSUU SUPRAMOLECULAR
AACELORSSSSTUU ASSAULT COURSES
AACFFGIMNORRTY FACTORY FARMING
AACFFIIILNOSST FALSIFICATIONS
AACFGHIILRRSTT LIGHT AIRCRAFTS
AACFGIIIMNNOST MAGNIFICATIONS
AACFGIIINORSTT GRATIFICATIONS
AACFGILNNOORST CONFLAGRATIONS
AACFGILNORRTUV VULGAR FRACTION
AACFIIILNOQSTU QUALIFICATIONS
AACFIIIMMNNOOT AMMONIFICATION
AACFIIINNOOPST SAPONIFICATION
AACFIIINNOQTTU QUANTIFICATION
AACFIIINORSTTT STRATIFICATION
AACFIILLMORTTU MULTIFACTORIAL
AACFIILORSSTTY SATISFACTORILY
AACFINORSSTTUY UNSATISFACTORY
AACFLOOOPQRSTU FOOLSCAP QUARTO
AACGGIILLLNOORY LARYNGOLOGICAL
AACGGIILLMOSTYY MYSTAGOGICALLY
AACGGIILNNORTTU CONGRATULATING

AACGHHILOOPRRT ORTHOGRAPHICAL
AACGHHIMNNSTTW NIGHT WATCHMANS
AACGHHMOOPRRTY CHROMATOGRAPHY
AACGHIILLPRSST CALLIGRAPHISTS
AACGHILLLOOPTY PATHOLOGICALLY
AACGHILLMOPRYY MYOGRAPHICALLY
AACGHILLOOPRRY OROGRAPHICALLY
AACGHILMOOPRST PHARMACOLOGIST
AACGHLMMOORRSS GRAMMAR SCHOOLS
AACGHLOOPPRSYY PARAPSYCHOLOGY
AACGILLLOORSTY ASTROLOGICALLY
AACGILLLOOTTUY TAUTOLOGICALLY
AACGILLMOORRTY MARTYROLOGICAL
AACGILMNOOPSST CAMPANOLOGISTS
AACGILNNOORTTU CONGRATULATION
AACGKNOOORRSTU KANGAROO COURTS
AACGLNOORRTTUY CONGRATULATORY
AACHHINOOPPRTT ANTHROPOPATHIC
AACHIILLNNOSTU HALLUCINATIONS
AACHIILLNOOOST ALCOHOLISATION
AACHIILLNOOOTZ ALCOHOLIZATION
AACHIIMNNORSTT ANTIMONARCHIST
AACHILLOORTTUY LOCAL AUTHORITY
AACHILLOPTTUYY AUTOPHYTICALLY
AACHILNOPSSSYY PSYCHOANALYSIS
AACHLLLMOOPSUY MALACOPHYLLOUS
AACHLNOPSSSTYY PSYCHOANALYSTS
AACIIILLNRSTTY INARTISTICALLY
AACIIILMNOPPST MISAPPLICATION
AACIIILNOPRTTY ANTICIPATORILY
AACIIILNOPSSTT PLASTICISATION
AACIIILNOPSTTZ PLASTICIZATION
AACIIIMNOOSSST ASSOCIATIONISM
AACIILLLMORSTY MORALISTICALLY
AACIILLLRSTTUY ALTRUISTICALLY
AACIILMOOPTTTU AUTOMATIC PILOT
AACIILNOOPRRST CONSPIRATORIAL
AACIILNORSTTTU STRATICULATION
AACIILNPPPRRST PRINCIPAL PARTS
AACIILOPRSSTTY SOCIALIST PARTY
AACIINNOOSSTTT ACTION STATIONS
AACILLLLOOPRTY ALLOTROPICALLY
AACILLLNORSTUY ULTRASONICALLY
AACILLMNOORSTY ASTRONOMICALLY
AACILLMOPSTTYY ASYMPTOTICALLY
AACINOOOPRRTTX CORPORATION TAX
AACINOOPRRRSTT PROCRASTINATOR
AACLLNNOPRTTUY CONTRAPUNTALLY
AADDDEEEHHNRSS HARD-HEADEDNESS
AADDEEEELMPRSST PADDLE STEAMERS
AADDEEFGHLOORS FLOG A DEAD HORSE
AADDEEGNRRSTUU UNDERGRADUATES
AADDEEIILNNOST DENATIONALISED
AADDEEIILNNOTZ DENATIONALIZED
AADDEELNOQRRSU SQUADRON LEADER
AADDEGGHNRRSTU GRANDDAUGHTERS
AADDEGILNRSSSS SALAD DRESSINGS
AADDEGINNRSTVW GRANDSTAND VIEW
AADDHMNRSTUUYY MAUNDY THURSDAY

AADEEEFGIOPRST PÂTÉ DE FOIE GRAS
AADEEEGKMNRRRT MARKET GARDENER
AADEEEHLLRTTTY TETRAETHYL LEAD
AADEEEHLRRRSSS DRESS REHEARSAL
AADEEEILLLPPPR PARALLELEPIPED
AADEEEELMNRSSTT ELDER STATESMAN
AADEEEMNNNPRSY PYRENEAN DESMAN
AADEEFGHILMNRY FLYING HEAD MARE
AADEEFGILLLNOT DINOFLAGELLATE
AADEEFGLLNRRUV GLANDULAR FEVER
AADEEFHILNRTTY FAINT-HEARTEDLY
AADEEFIILNORST FEDERALISATION
AADEEFIILNORTZ FEDERALIZATION
AADEEGGIMNNRST AGGRANDISEMENT
AADEEGGIMNNRTZ AGGRANDIZEMENT
AADEEGHILOPRRT RADIOTELEGRAPH
AADEEGIMNNRRST DISARRANGEMENT
AADEEGIMNPRSST DISPARAGEMENTS
AADEEGINRSSTTT TRADING ESTATES
AADEEHHIMPRSST HEADMASTERSHIP
AADEEIILNPQSSU SESQUIPEDALIAN
AADEEIINNPRRST PREDESTINARIAN
AADEEIKLMOPRTV EVAPORATED MILK
AADEEILNRRSTTT TRANSLITERATED
AADEEINNPRSSTT ANTIDEPRESSANT
AADEEINNQSSTTU ANTIQUATEDNESS
AADEEPRRSSTTUU SUPERSATURATED
AADEFFHLNOSSTV STANDOFF HALVES
AADEFFIILNSTUV DIVINE AFFLATUS
AADEFILMMNNSTU FUNDAMENTALISM
AADEFILMNNSTTU FUNDAMENTALIST
AADEFILMNNTTUY FUNDAMENTALITY
AADEGHILNRSTUW DAUGHTERS-IN-LAW
AADEGIINNORRTT INTERGRADATION
AADEGINOORRRTT RETROGRADATION
AADEGOORRRRTTY RETROGRADATORY
AADEHHKLLNNOOV HOEK VAN HOLLAND
AADEHIILLMNPSU SULPHANILAMIDE
AADEHIIMNNOSTU DEHUMANISATION
AADEHIIMNNOTUZ DEHUMANIZATION
AADEHIINORRSST SHERARDISATION
AADEHIINORRSTZ SHERARDIZATION
AADEHIINPRSSST DANISH PASTRIES
AADEHIIOPRRSTT RADIOTHERAPIST
AADEHINNOPSSSU DIAPHANOUSNESS
AADEHORSSSTTUW SOUTHEASTWARDS
AADEIIILNOSTTV DEVITALISATION
AADEIIILNOTTVZ DEVITALIZATION
AADEIIIMNRSTTV ADMINISTRATIVE
AADEIIKLRSSTTW SIDEWALK ARTIST
AADEIILMNNNOOT DENOMINATIONAL
AADEIILMNOORST DEMORALISATION
AADEIILMNOORTZ DEMORALIZATION
AADEIILNNOPSST DISPENSATIONAL
AADEIILNOOPRST DEPOLARISATION
AADEIILNOOPRTZ DEPOLARIZATION
AADEIILNORSSTT DISSERTATIONAL
AADEIIMNNORSSV ANIMADVERSIONS
AADEILNNORTUUV UNDERVALUATION

651

AADEILNOOPSSST AT ONE'S DISPOSAL
AADEINOPPPRRTU UNAPPROPRIATED
AADELLOPSSTTTU SLOTTED SPATULA
AADELMPRRSSTTU MUSTARD PLASTER
AADFFGIIIILNST DISAFFILIATING
AADFFIIIILNOST DISAFFILIATION
AADGGIINNOPPRZ PROPAGANDIZING
AADGIIIILNOSTT DIGITALISATION
AADGIIIILNOTTZ DIGITALIZATION
AADIIILMNORSTT TRADITIONALISM
AADIIILNORSTTT TRADITIONALIST
AADIIIMNNORSTT ADMINISTRATION
AADIIIMNRRSTTX ADMINISTRATRIX
AADIIMNORRSSTT ADMINISTRATORS
AAEEEFGMNNORRS FERROMANGANESE
AAEEEGGGHINRTT IN THE AGGREGATE
AAEEEGHIMNOSST HAEMATOGENESIS
AAEEEGMNNPRRRT PREARRANGEMENT
AAEEEGMNNRRRST REARRANGEMENTS
AAEEEHHIMRSSTT THERMAESTHESIA
AAEEEHILPPRRST PRE-RAPHAELITES
AAEEEEINPRSSSTV SEPARATIVENESS
AAEEEELNOPRSSTT PERSONAL ESTATE
AAEEEMNNPRSTVW PERMANENT WAVES
AAEEFFGNRSSSTT STAFF SERGEANTS
AAEEFFHIIMRTTV THE AFFIRMATIVE
AAEEFFILLNOOSV AVAIL ONESELF OF
AAEEFGIMNNORRS FERROMAGNESIAN
AAEEFHHLORSTTT SALT OF THE EARTH
AAEEFILNNRRSTT TRANSFERENTIAL
AAEEGGGILNRTXY EXAGGERATINGLY
AAEEGHIINNSTTZ ANAESTHETIZING
AAEEGHLLMOPRRT METALLOGRAPHER
AAEEGHLLNOOPTY PALAEETHNOLOGY
AAEEGHLMNNOOPX HAPAX LEGOMENON
AAEEGIILNNORST GENERALISATION
AAEEGIILNNORTZ GENERALIZATION
AAEEGIILNNOSTV EVANGELISATION
AAEEGIILNNOTVZ EVANGELIZATION
AAEEGILNPRSTXY EXASPERATINGLY
AAEEGJMNORRSST SERGEANT MAJORS
AAEEGLMNPRSSTU SUPRASEGMENTAL
AAEEGLPPPRSSSU PURPLE PASSAGES
AAEEGMNOPRSSSU RAMPAGEOUSNESS
AAEEGOPRRRSTTW GREAT SPEARWORT
AAEEHIIMOOPSST HAEMATOPOIESIS
AAEEHIMNRSSSTU AMATEURISHNESS
AAEEHINORSTTTW WEATHER STATION
AAEEHMNNOPRSTTU APARTMENT HOUSE
AAEEHMOOPRRRST SPERMATORRHOEA
AAEEIILLLRTTVY ALLITERATIVELY
AAEEIILMMPRSST ALPES MARITIMES
AAEEIILNNNORTT INTERNATIONALE
AAEEIILNNORSTT ETERNALISATION
AAEEIILNNORTTZ ETERNALIZATION
AAEEIKLNRRSSTU KAISERSLAUTERN
AAEEILNNOPRSTT PRESENTATIONAL
AAEEILNNPRRTTY INTERPLANETARY
AAEEIMNPRSTTTV PAVEMENT ARTIST

AAEEINNOPSSSST PASSIONATENESS
AAEEINRRSSTTTW WATER-RESISTANT
AAEEKMMNPRSSTU AMUSEMENT PARKS
AAEELNNNPSSSTU UNPLEASANTNESS
AAEEMQRRRSSTTU QUARTERMASTERS
AAEFFFGIINORRS FOREIGN AFFAIRS
AAEFFIIMNORRST REAFFIRMATIONS
AAEFGLLNOOPRTT FORE-TOPGALLANT
AAEFHHMMOOTTTU FOAM AT THE MOUTH
AAEFHINNORRRST FINSTERAARHORN
AAEFIIMNNOSSTT MANIFESTATIONS
AAEFIINNORRSTT FRATERNISATION
AAEFIINNORRTTZ FRATERNIZATION
AAEFILOPPRRSST PLASTER OF PARIS
AAEFIMNORRSTTV TRANSFORMATIVE
AAEFLLNOPRRRUU FUNERAL PARLOUR
AAEGGGGLNNORSTU STRONG LANGUAGE
AAEGGHIILMNNTU HAEMAGGLUTININ
AAEGGIINNORRST GRANGERISATION
AAEGGIINNORRTZ GRANGERIZATION
AAEGGILMNOORST AGGLOMERATIONS
AAEGGILMNOSSYZ GLOSSY MAGAZINE
AAEGHHIKMRRSTW HIGH WATER MARKS
AAEGHIILLNRTXY EXHILARATINGLY
AAEGHILMNRRTWY HEARTWARMINGLY
AAEGIIILLLNOST ILLEGALISATION
AAEGIIILLLNOTZ ILLEGALIZATION
AAEGIIILNNOSTT GELATINISATION
AAEGIIILNNOTTZ GELATINIZATION
AAEGIILLNOORST ALLEGORISATION
AAEGIILLNOORTZ ALLEGORIZATION
AAEGIILNORRSTT REGISTRATIONAL
AAEGIILNORRSTU REGULARISATION
AAEGIILNORRTUZ REGULARIZATION
AAEGIIMNRRSTTV TRANSMIGRATIVE
AAEGIINNNRSSSU SANGUINARINESS
AAEGIINNOORRST REORGANISATION
AAEGIINNOORRTZ REORGANIZATION
AAEGILMNOOPRST SPERMATOGONIAL
AAEGILNOOPRSTT PROGESTATIONAL
AAEGIMNNRRTTTY MATERNITY GRANT
AAEHHILLOPSTUZ SULPHATHIAZOLE
AAEHIIIMNNSSTT ANTIHISTAMINES
AAEHILLMNOPSTT MENTAL HOSPITAL
AAEHIMOPRSSSTT MASSOTHERAPIST
AAEHLMOOPPRRST SPERMATOPHORAL
AAEIIIKNNORSTT KERATINISATION
AAEIIIKNNORTTZ KERATINIZATION
AAEIIILLMMNNRS MILLENARIANISM
AAEIIILMNNORST MINERALISATION
AAEIIILMNNORTZ MINERALIZATION
AAEIIILNORSSST SERIALISATIONS
AAEIIILNORSSTZ SERIALIZATIONS
AAEIIILNORSTTV REVITALISATION
AAEIIILNORTTVZ REVITALIZATION
AAEIIIMMPRSSST SEMIPARASITISM
AAEIIINNNRSSST INSANITARINESS
AAEIIINNPPRTTT PINNATIPARTITE
AAEIIILLNNORSTT REINSTALLATION

AAEIILMNNOSSST SENSATIONALISM
AAEIILMNOOPRST OPERATIONALISM
AAEIILMNOPRRST PROLETARIANISM
AAEIILMNSSTYZZ MIZZEN STAYSAIL
AAEIILMOPQRRTU IMPERIAL QUARTO
AAEIILNNNORSTT INTERNATIONALS
AAEIILNNORSTTU NEUTRALISATION
AAEIILNNORTTUZ NEUTRALIZATION
AAEIILNNOSSSTT SENSATIONALIST
AAEIILNQTTTUVY QUANTITATIVELY
AAEIIMOPPPRRST MISAPPROPRIATE
AAEIINNORSSSTT STATIONARINESS
AAEIINNPPRRSTT ANTIPERSPIRANT
AAEIINOPRSSTTU PASTEURISATION
AAEIINOPRSTTUZ PASTEURIZATION
AAEIKKKLMNRSSU KAMENSK-URALSKI
AAEILLLLMORRST LAMELLIROSTRAL
AAEILLLLMRTTUY MULTILATERALLY
AAEILMOOPPRSTT SPATIOTEMPORAL
AAEILNORRRSTTT TRANSLITERATOR
AAEILNORSSTTWY SANITARY TOWELS
AAEIMNORSSSTTT STATIONMASTERS
AAEINNNOPRSTUU SUPERANNUATION
AAELLNPRRSTUUY SUPERNATURALLY
AAELMNSSSSTTYY SYSTEMS ANALYST
AAENNNOPPRSSST NANSEN PASSPORT
AAFGIILLMNNNPY FAMILY PLANNING
AAFIIIMNNORRTU UNIFORMITARIAN
AAFIILLMMNORTY INFLAMMATORILY
AAFIMNNOORRSTT TRANSFORMATION
AAGGHINOOPRRST ORGANOGRAPHIST
AAGGIIILNNRTTY INGRATIATINGLY
AAGGILMMOORSTT GRAMMATOLOGIST
AAGHIIINOPRSTT GRAPHITISATION
AAGHIIINOPRTTZ GRAPHITIZATION
AAGHIILMNORSTT ANTILOGARITHMS
AAGIIIMNOSSTTT STIGMATISATION
AAGIIIMNOSTTTZ STIGMATIZATION
AAGIILNORSSTUV VULGARISATIONS
AAGIILNORSTUVZ VULGARIZATIONS
AAGIILOOPRSSTT PARASITOLOGIST
AAGIIMNNORRSTT TRANSMIGRATION
AAGILMNOOPRSTV GALVANOTROPISM
AAGIMNORRRSTTY TRANSMIGRATORY
AAHHIIMOPRRSST AMPHIARTHROSIS
AAHIINOORSSTTU AUTHORISATIONS
AAHIINOORSTTUZ AUTHORIZATIONS
AAHILMOPPRRSTY AMPHIPROSTYLAR
AAHILNOOOPRRTT PROTHONOTARIAL
AAHILNORRSTTUY NATURAL HISTORY
AAHINOPSSSSSTT SHOP ASSISTANTS
AAHLLOPPSSTTYY STAPHYLOPLASTY
AAIIIIILNNOSTT INITIALISATION
AAIIIIILNNOTTZ INITIALIZATION
AAIIIILMNORSTT MILITARISATION
AAIIIILMNORTTZ MILITARIZATION
AAIIIILMNRSTTU UTILITARIANISM
AAIIIILNORSTTV TRIVIALISATION
AAIIIILNORTTVZ TRIVIALIZATION

AAIIIILLNOOSTTV VOLATILISATION
AAIIIILLNOOTTVZ VOLATILIZATION
AAIIIINNOOOSTTU AUTOIONISATION
AAIIIINNOOOTTUZ AUTOIONIZATION
AAIIJLNNOORSTU JOURNALISATION
AAIIJLNNOORTUZ JOURNALIZATION
AAIILLLLNORSTTU ILLUSTRATIONAL
AAIILLMNNOSTTU MULTINATIONALS
AAIILLMOOPPSST PAPILLOMATOSIS
AAIILLNNORSTTY TRANSITIONALLY
AAIILNOOPPRSTU POPULARISATION
AAIILNOOPPRTUZ POPULARIZATION
AAIIMNOOPPRSTX APPROXIMATIONS
AAIINOOPPPRRST APPROPRIATIONS
AAIKMNOOQRSTTU QUOTATION MARKS
AAILMMNNORSTTU ULTRAMONTANISM
AAILMNNORSTTTU ULTRAMONTANIST
AAIMNNORSSTTTU TRANSMUTATIONS
AAINNOOPRRSTTT TRANSPORTATION
ABBBEEEISSTTTU TEST-TUBE BABIES
ABBCDEEEIORRSU BERBERIDACEOUS
ABBCEHILNORSTU BRONCHIAL TUBES
ABBCEHKOORRSSS SHOCK ABSORBERS
ABBCEIIJLSTTUY SUBJECTABILITY
ABBCEIKLLLRRYY BLACKBERRY LILY
ABBCGHILLNOORU RUBBING ALCOHOL
ABBDDEEEELORSTU DOUBLE-BREASTED
ABBDEEFNORSSTU BEASTS OF BURDEN
ABBDEILLNORSTU BULLETIN BOARDS
ABBDIIIILNTTUY INDUBITABILITY
ABBEEEFHLLLLOT BELLE OF THE BALL
ABBEEEELNORSSSV OBSERVABLENESS
ABBEEEFHNORRTTU BEAR THE BRUNT OF
ABBEEHINNOOPRT PHENOBARBITONE
ABBEGHIIILOPRS BIBLIOGRAPHIES
ABBEGHIILOPRRS BIBLIOGRAPHERS
ABBEGIMNPRRSTU RUBBER-STAMPING
ABCCCEEIIMMNRU CIRCUMAMBIENCE
ABCCCEIORSTUUU CUCURBITACEOUS
ABCCDEEHOPRSST BATCH PROCESSED
ABCCDEHILNSSUW CLUB SANDWICHES
ABCCDIILLMORSU UMBILICAL CORDS
ABCCEEEEELRSSSU CAUSES CÉLÈBRES
ABCCEEEELORRRTX CEREBRAL CORTEX
ABCCEEFHILNOST CHIEF CONSTABLE
ABCCEEIIKRRRTU CIRCUIT BREAKER
ABCCEEIILLNORR IRRECONCILABLE
ABCCEEILLNRRTYY CYBERNETICALLY
ABCCEEILMMNOUX EXCOMMUNICABLE
ABCCEEILNNOORT CONCELEBRATION
ABCCEHIINORSST BRONCHIECTASIS
ABCCEHIKLNPSST PITCH-BLACKNESS
ABCCEIILLMORSS SOCIAL CLIMBERS
ABCCEIILLNORRY IRRECONCILABLY
ABCCEIILMMNNOU INCOMMUNICABLE
ABCCEIILNNPSUU PUBLIC NUISANCE
ABCCEILNNNOOSU UNCONSCIONABLE
ABCCGINNORSTTU SUBCONTRACTING
ABCCHHIIOPRRSS ARCHBISHOPRICS

ABCCHILOOPRSTU CLAUSTROPHOBIC
ABCCILNNNOOSUY UNCONSCIONABLY
ABCCNOORRSSTTU SUBCONTRACTORS
ABCDEEEEFHMMMR FEMME DE CHAMBRE
ABCDEEEEILNSSV DECEIVABLENESS
ABCDEEEELLNSST DELECTABLENESS
ABCDEEEHIILNPR INDECIPHERABLE
ABCDEEEIILRSSV DISSERVICEABLE
ABCDEEEILNRSST CREDITABLENESS
ABCDEEEILPRSST DISRESPECTABLE
ABCDEEELLOOORT COLORADO BEETLE
ABCDEEGIKNORRR RECORD-BREAKING
ABCDEEHIILNPRY INDECIPHERABLY
ABCDEEHILPSTTT PITCHED BATTLES
ABCDEEIILNNORS INCONSIDERABLE
ABCDEGIIILPRTY CREDIBILITY GAP
ABCDEIIILPRTTY PREDICTABILITY
ABCDEIILNNOSTY CONDENSABILITY
ABCDEIMNNOOOORX CARBON MONOXIDE
ABCDENOOOORRRTU UNCORROBORATED
ABCDGHILNOOORS BOARDING SCHOOL
ABCDIIIILOSSTY DISSOCIABILITY
ABCEEEHMMRRRST CHARTER MEMBERS
ABCEEFIILNORTY ENFORCEABILITY
ABCEEEGHIKLOORT GLOBE ARTICHOKE
ABCEEGIILLNOTY BIOGENETICALLY
ABCEEGIINORSUZ ZINGIBERACEOUS
ABCEEGILNNORUZ UNRECOGNIZABLE
ABCEEGKKOORRST STOCKBROKERAGE
ABCEEGKNNOOSTW GET ONE'S OWN BACK
ABCEEHHHRTTTUY BURY THE HATCHET
ABCEEHIIKSTTTU TAKE THE BISCUIT
ABCEEHIJKNOSTX JACK-IN-THE-BOXES
ABCEEHIMNNRSSTY CHIMNEYBREASTS
ABCEEHIOOPRSUU EUPHORBIACEOUS
ABCEEIIILPRTVY PERCEIVABILITY
ABCEEIIILRSTVY SERVICEABILITY
ABCEEIILORRTVY RECOVERABILITY
ABCEEIILPRSTTY RESPECTABILITY
ABCEEILNNSTUUY SUBLIEUTENANCY
ABCEEILRRSSTTU BATTLE CRUISERS
ABCEEMMMNORSUU MUCOUS MEMBRANE
ABCEFGIIILNNST FILING CABINETS
ABCEFGIILMMNRS CLIMBING FRAMES
ABCEGHIMNNSSUU SUBMACHINE GUNS
ABCEGIIJNRSSTU SUBJECT-RAISING
ABCEGIILOORSTT BACTERIOLOGIST
ABCEGILNNORSWW BROWN LACEWINGS
ABCEGINORRSSSZ ZEBRA CROSSINGS
ABCEHIILRSTTTY STRETCHABILITY
ABCEHILLLOPRYY HYPERBOLICALLY
ABCEHILORRSTTY ERYTHROBLASTIC
ABCEHIMORSSSTX CHRISTMAS BOXES
ABCEIIILLNTTUY INELUCTABILITY
ABCEIIILNSTUXY INEXCUSABILITY
ABCEIIILORRTVY IRREVOCABILITY
ABCEIINOOPSSUV ABOVE SUSPICION
ABCEILLLMOORTY BOLOMETRICALLY
ABCEILLLPSSTTU PLASTIC BULLETS

ABCEILLMNOPSUU PNEUMOBACILLUS
ABCEILLMNOSSSY SYMBOLICALNESS
ABCEILMNNOOSSU NO-CLAIM BONUSES
ABCEILNNNOSTTU SUBCONTINENTAL
ABCELLLNNOORTU UNCONTROLLABLE
ABCELNOSSTUUUY SUBCUTANEOUSLY
ABCEMMMNOORSUU MUCOMEMBRANOUS
ABCFFFLMOOORTY COMFORTABLY OFF
ABCFIILMNOORTY CONFORMABILITY
ABCGIILLMOOOTY BIOCLIMATOLOGY
ABCGIILNOOPSST SPONGIOBLASTIC
ABCGIKLNORSSTT STARTING BLOCKS
ABCHIILNOTTUUY UNTOUCHABILITY
ABCHILMOOPRSTT THROMBOPLASTIC
ABCIIIIJLSTTUY JUSTICIABILITY
ABCIIILLLOPSTY COLLAPSIBILITY
ABCIIILNRSTTUY INSCRUTABILITY
ABCIILLMNOSTYY SYMBIONTICALLY
ABCIILMMNOSSTU SOMNAMBULISTIC
ABCIILNOOORRTU CONTRIBUTORIAL
ABCILMNORSTUUY RAMBUNCTIOUSLY
ABCIMNNNOOOOPS BOON COMPANIONS
ABDDEEEFGHINRT FEATHERBEDDING
ABDDEEEHLLNSSU BULLHEADEDNESS
ABDDEEHIILSSST DISESTABLISHED
ABDDEEHLLORSSU SHOULDER BLADES
ABDDEEHLNOOSTU DOUBLET AND HOSE
ABDDEEIIJLMNOU DIAMOND JUBILEE
ABDDEEILMNNSTY ABSENT-MINDEDLY
ABDDEEMNNOSSTU METES AND BOUNDS
ABDDGINNOORSSU SOUNDING BOARDS
ABDEEEEILNRSST DELIBERATENESS
ABDEEEFFIILNRT DIFFERENTIABLE
ABDEEEFLORSTUU DOUBLE FEATURES
ABDEEEGHIIRTVW GIVE A WIDE BERTH
ABDEEEGILNRSST SINGLE-BREASTED
ABDEEEIILMNNRT INDETERMINABLE
ABDEEEIMNNOOTV ABOVE-MENTIONED
ABDEEELLNOPRSS DEPLORABLENESS
ABDEEFIIILNNTU UNIDENTIFIABLE
ABDEEFIOOPSSTX SAFE-DEPOSIT BOX
ABDEEGHIOSTWYY GO BY THE WAYSIDE
ABDEEGILNRSSST DRESSING TABLES
ABDEEHIIILRTTY HEREDITABILITY
ABDEEIILLRSSTU LIBERAL STUDIES
ABDEEIILMNNRTY INDETERMINABLY
ABDEEIILNNNSTV VENETIAN BLINDS
ABDEFIINNOSTUU SUBINFEUDATION
ABDEFINORSTUUY SUBINFEUDATORY
ABDEFMOOOORRSTW FROM BAD TO WORSE
ABDEGHINOORSSU BOARDINGHOUSES
ABDEGHLMNORTUU ROUGH-AND-TUMBLE
ABDEGIILLNNRRY LENDING LIBRARY
ABDEHHLMNRSTUY RHYTHM AND BLUES
ABDEHLMNNORRTU NORTHUMBERLAND
ABDEIIILMNOOST DEMOBILISATION
ABDEIIILMNOOTZ DEMOBILIZATION
ABDEIIILNPSSTY DISPENSABILITY
ABDEIIILNRSTUY UNDESIRABILITY

ABDEIIINRSSSSU SUBSIDIARINESS
ABDEIILNOORSTW BOWDLERISATION
ABDEIILNOORTWZ BOWDLERIZATION
ABDEILLMNNOPTU PLATINUM BLONDE
ABDEILLMOPRUWY UPWARDLY-MOBILE
ABDEILLNOOORST BLOOD RELATIONS
ABDEILMORSTUXY AMBIDEXTROUSLY
ABDEILRRRSTWWY WILD STRAWBERRY
ABDGHIMNOOSTTU DOUBTING THOMAS
ABDGIIILOOORST RADIOBIOLOGIST
ABDGIIKNORRSST SKIRTING BOARDS
ABDIIIILMNOTTY INDOMITABILITY
ABDIIIILLOSSTVY DISSOLVABILITY
ABDIIILNORSTTU DISTRIBUTIONAL
ABDIIOOOPRSSSU BASIDIOSPOROUS
ABDMOOOORRSTTU OUTBOARD MOTORS
ABEEEEEFGIKLNTV VEGETABLE KNIFE
ABEEEEFFILNNOOS BANE OF ONE'S LIFE
ABEEEEFILNNRRTT ENFANT TERRIBLE
ABEEEGHHIMNSTV MIGHT-HAVE-BEENS
ABEEEEHLNRSSSST BREATHLESSNESS
ABEEEEIKKRRRSST STRIKEBREAKERS
ABEEEEIMMPRRSTV PRIVATE MEMBERS
ABEEEEINORRRSTV REVERBERATIONS
ABEEEELNNOPRSSS PERSONABLENESS
ABEEFIILMNRTTY FERMENTABILITY
ABEEGHIILNSTUX EXTINGUISHABLE
ABEEGHILMMNOOT METHAEMOGLOBIN
ABEEGHLORSSTTT GHETTO BLASTERS
ABEEGIIKKNRRST STRIKEBREAKING
ABEEGILNRRSSST TRANSGRESSIBLE
ABEEGNOORRRTTU TURBOGENERATOR
ABEEHILMNSSSTT ESTABLISHMENTS
ABEEHILNOPSSST HOSPITABLENESS
ABEEHLNNOORSSU HONOURABLENESS
ABEEHLOORTTTTW HOT-WATER BOTTLE
ABEEIIILMMPRTY IMPERMEABILITY
ABEEIIILRRTTVY RETRIEVABILITY
ABEEIILMNNOSSU EMISSION NEBULA
ABEEIILMNOPRSS IMPRESSIONABLE
ABEEIILMNRRTUY REMUNERABILITY
ABEEIILPRRSTVY PRESERVABILITY
ABEEILMNNNOSTU UNMENTIONABLES
ABEEILNNOQSTUU UNQUESTIONABLE
ABEEILNNSSTTUU SUBLIEUTENANTS
ABEEILRRRSSTTU SUBTERRESTRIAL
ABEEIMNOSSSSTU ABSTEMIOUSNESS
ABEEKLNNNOSSUW UNKNOWABLENESS
ABEFGIIILNRRTY REFRANGIBILITY
ABEFIIILRRTTUY IRREFUTABILITY
ABEFILNOOPRSST SELF-ABSORPTION
ABEGGHHINORRTU ROUGH BREATHING
ABEGHILMNOOOXY OXYHAEMOGLOBIN
ABEGHLMNRRSSTU BREMSSTRAHLUNG
ABEGIIILMNPRTY IMPREGNABILITY
ABEGIILORRSSTY GYROSTABILISER
ABEGIILORRSTYZ GYROSTABILIZER
ABEHIIIILNRTTY INHERITABILITY
ABEHIIIILSTTUXY EXHAUSTIBILITY

ABEIIIILMNSTTY INESTIMABILITY
ABEIIIILLNORTTY INTOLERABILITY
ABEIIIILMNNRTUY INNUMERABILITY
ABEIIIILMORRTVY IRREMOVABILITY
ABEIIILNPRSTUY INSUPERABILITY
ABEIILMNOPRSSY IMPRESSIONABLY
ABEIIMNOPRRTTU IMPERTURBATION
ABEIINNORTTTUV NONATTRIBUTIVE
ABEILMNNORSTUU INSURMOUNTABLE
ABEILNNOQSTUUY UNQUESTIONABLY
ABEILNORSSSSUU SALUBRIOUSNESS
ABFGIIIILNNRTY INFRANGIBILITY
ABFIIIIILRTTVY VITRIFIABILITY
ABFIIIIJLSTTUY JUSTIFIABILITY
ABFIIIILNOSSTY FISSIONABILITY
ABHIIIKLNNTTUY UNTHINKABILITY
ABHIIINOOPRRTY PROHIBITIONARY
ABHIIINOORSTVY VASOINHIBITORY
ABHILLMNOPSTTU PUT IN MOTHBALLS
ABHILMNOOPRSTT THROMBOPLASTIN
ABIIIIILLLMTTY ILLIMITABILITY
ABIIIILLMPSTUY IMPLAUSIBILITY
ABIIIILMMNOOST IMMOBILISATION
ABIIIILMMNOOTZ IMMOBILIZATION
ABIIIIMNNOSTTU BITUMINISATION
ABIIIIMNNOTTUZ BITUMINIZATION
ABIILOPPRSTTUY SUPPORTABILITY
ACCCDEIIIILNOR RICINOLEIC ACID
ACCCDEINORSTTU CREDIT ACCOUNTS
ACCCEEEIILLNPS SPECIAL LICENCE
ACCCEEHILLNORV VICE-CHANCELLOR
ACCCEEIILNOSSS SOCIAL SCIENCES
ACCCEEENNOOOVVX CONVEXO-CONCAVE
ACCCEFFIILRRST TRAFFIC CIRCLES
ACCCEFINOOPRRT TROPIC OF CANCER
ACCCEHHILMOPSY PSYCHOCHEMICAL
ACCCEHIINORSTT ARCHITECTONICS
ACCCEIMMNOOORS MACROECONOMICS
ACCCENNORRTTUU CURRENT ACCOUNT
ACCCHIIOOPSSTT TACHISTOSCOPIC
ACCCHLOOPSSTUY STAPHYLOCOCCUS
ACCCIIKKLOSSTT COCKTAIL STICKS
ACCCILLOSSSSUU LOCUS CLASSICUS
ACCCILNOOSSSSU CLASS-CONSCIOUS
ACCDDDEKLOOOOO COCK-A-DOODLE-DOO
ACCDEEEELNOPRS PREADOLESCENCE
ACCDEEEHHIKNRT CHICKENHEARTED
ACCDEEFILNNSTU SELF-INDUCTANCE
ACCDEEHINRRRSU HARD CURRENCIES
ACCDEEIILLLRTY DIELECTRICALLY
ACCDEEIILMMORS COMMERCIALISED
ACCDEEIILMMORZ COMMERCIALIZED
ACCDEEILMNORTY DYNAMOELECTRIC,
    ELECTRODYNAMIC
ACCDEEILNNNSTY INCANDESCENTLY
ACCDEEILNOPSTU CONCEPTUALISED
ACCDEEILNOPTUZ CONCEPTUALIZED
ACCDEEILOOORRST CROCODILE TEARS
ACCDEEIMMNOTUX EXCOMMUNICATED

ACCDEEIMNOPPTY APPENDICECTOMY
ACCDEEINNNOSTU DISCOUNTENANCE
ACCDEELLMOSTUW WELL-ACCUSTOMED
ACCDEFILLNOOTU DEFLOCCULATION
ACCDEFNNOORTUU UNACCOUNTED-FOR
ACCDEHHIMNORSY HYDROMECHANICS
ACCDEHILMNOPSU UNACCOMPLISHED
ACCDEHINORSSUW SANDWICH COURSE
ACCDEHKLNOORTU AROUND THE CLOCK
ACCDEIIILLNNOTY COINCIDENTALLY
ACCDEIINNNOSTU DISCONTINUANCE
ACCDEINOOPSTTU DEPOSIT ACCOUNT
ACCDHHINOOPRSY HYPOCHONDRIACS
ACCDHIIIMMORST DICHROMATICISM
ACCDHIMNOPSSYY PSYCHODYNAMICS
ACCDIILNNOOPTU CONDUPLICATION
ACCDIINNOORSTT CONTRADICTIONS
ACCDILNOORRSTU CONDUCTOR RAILS
ACCEEEFFHKLOST COFFEE KLATCHES
ACCEEEFILNPTXY LIFE EXPECTANCY
ACCEEEGHIRRSSV SERVICE CHARGES
ACCEEEHILLMNPY MYELENCEPHALIC
ACCEEEILOPSTVY ESCAPE VELOCITY
ACCEEEILPRRSWY CREEPY-CRAWLIES
ACCEEELLMOPRTX ELECTRA COMPLEX
ACCEEELLNORTVY ELECTROVALENCY
ACCEEENNOPSTUX EXPENSE ACCOUNT
ACCEEEOORRSSTUW WORCESTER SAUCE
ACCEEFFHHNNOOT ON THE OFF CHANCE
ACCEEFILLMORTV COLLECTIVE FARM
ACCEEFIMORRRTT REFRACTOMETRIC
ACCEEGHILOPRRT ELECTROGRAPHIC
ACCEEGHKNOSSTX STOCK EXCHANGES
ACCEEGILLNORTY EGOCENTRICALLY,
   GEOCENTRICALLY
ACCEEHHIILNNPR RHINENCEPHALIC
ACCEEHHILMMORT THERMOCHEMICAL
ACCEEHHLOORSST SCHOOLTEACHERS
ACCEEHIIILNSTT TECHNICALITIES
ACCEEHILMOPRST PETROCHEMICALS
ACCEEHKLNORRTU ROCKET-LAUNCHER
ACCEEHORRSSTTY OYSTERCATCHERS
ACCEEIILORSSSV SOCIAL SERVICES
ACCEEIIMNNOORT ECONOMETRICIAN
ACCEEIINNOORSS CONCESSIONAIRE
ACCEEIKLNOPRSS COCKER SPANIELS
ACCEEILLLNORTY ELECTRONICALLY
ACCEEILLLOPSTY TELESCOPICALLY
ACCEEILORSSTTT ELECTROSTATICS
ACCEEILORSSTUU STERCULIACEOUS
ACCEEINOPRSTTV CONTRACEPTIVES
ACCEFGGHHIINNT FIGHTING CHANCE
ACCEFGIIIINNNS INSIGNIFICANCE
ACCEFIIIILLNSTY SCIENTIFICALLY
ACCEFIIINOPSST SPECIFICATIONS
ACCEFIIINORSTT RECTIFICATIONS
ACCEGHIILLNNOU HALLUCINOGENIC
ACCEGHIIMNNPRR PRINCE CHARMING
ACCEGHIOPPRRST SPECTROGRAPHIC

ACCEGIILNRTUXY EXCRUCIATINGLY
ACCEGIKLLNOOTU COCKTAIL LOUNGE
ACCEGILLMMOORY MYRMECOLOGICAL
ACCEGIOPPRRSTU GROUP PRACTICES
ACCEHHORRSSSTT RORSCHACH TESTS
ACCEHIKLLMOORY MOCK-HEROICALLY
ACCEHILLOOPSSS SPECIAL SCHOOLS
ACCEHILMMNOPST ACCOMPLISHMENT
ACCEHILMOOPRSU MICROCEPHALOUS
ACCEHILOORSSTU HORATIUS COCLES
ACCEIIILNNOORT RECONCILIATION
ACCEIIILNOORRT ONEIROCRITICAL
ACCEIILLMOORSY SERIOCOMICALLY
ACCEIILLOPPRSY PERISCOPICALLY
ACCEIILNOORRTY RECONCILIATORY
ACCEIILORSSTUY SOCIAL SECURITY
ACCEIINNOORSTT CONCRETISATION
ACCEIINNOORTTZ CONCRETIZATION
ACCEIINOPRSSSU CAPRICIOUSNESS
ACCEILLMNNOOUY UNECONOMICALLY
ACCEILNOORSSST CROSS-SECTIONAL
ACCEIMMNOORTUX EXCOMMUNICATOR
ACCEINNNOORSTT CONCENTRATIONS
ACCEINNOORSTTU COUNTERACTIONS
ACCEINOOPPRSTU PREOCCUPATIONS
ACCEINOPPRSSSU PERCUSSION CAPS
ACCFFIIINORTTU FRUCTIFICATION
ACCFIIIILLNOST SILICIFICATION
ACCFIMMNNOOORT COMMON FRACTION
ACCGHIILLOOPRS OSCILLOGRAPHIC
ACCGHIILLOORST CHRISTOLOGICAL
ACCGHILOPRSSUY PSYCHOSURGICAL
ACCGHINOOPPRSY PHARYNGOSCOPIC
ACCGIIILLMNOOR CRIMINOLOGICAL
ACCGILLLOOOSY SOCIOLOGICALLY
ACCHHILOPPSSYY PSYCHOPHYSICAL
ACCHHIMOOOPRRT CHROMATOPHORIC
ACCHHIMOOORRTT ORTHOCHROMATIC
ACCHIIILNORSTT ANTICHLORISTIC
ACCHIIINNNOOST CINCHONISATION
ACCHIIINNNOOTZ CINCHONIZATION
ACCHIILLOPRTYY HYPOCRITICALLY
ACCHILLNNORSYY SYNCHRONICALLY
ACCHIMOOPSSSTY PSYCHOSOMATICS
ACCIIILLOOOPST SOCIOPOLITICAL
ACCIILNNOOPRST CONSCRIPTIONAL
ACCIIMMNNOOSTU COMMUNICATIONS
ACCIIMNNORTTUU CIRCUMNUTATION
ACCILLLOPPRTYY PROCRYPTICALLY
ACCILMNOOSTUUY CONTUMACIOUSLY
ACCILNNOORSTTU CONSTRUCTIONAL
ACDDDEEIILMNST MIDDLE-DISTANCE
ACDDEEEKMNOPRS PROMENADE DECKS
ACDDEEGILNNNOR ENDOCRINE GLAND
ACDDEGLLNSSSTU DUCTLESS GLANDS
ACDDEIIINNOORT AIR-CONDITIONED
ACDDELMMMNOOSU COMMAND MODULES
ACDEEEEINSSTTV STATE'S EVIDENCE
ACDEEEHINRRSUV UNDERACHIEVERS

ACDEEEEHNORSSTY   DO THE NECESSARY
ACDEEEEHORRSSTU   TERRACED HOUSES
ACDEEEEIIMNNPTT   PATENT MEDICINE
ACDEEEEILOOPRST   RADIO TELESCOPE
ACDEEEEIMNOPPST   APPENDECTOMIES
ACDEEEEINNOPQRU   EQUIPONDERANCE
ACDEEEENRRRSTUY   UNDERSECRETARY
ACDEEFFIMORRTT   DIFFRACTOMETER
ACDEEFGIILMNST   MAGNETIC FIELDS
ACDEEFHIINNRSS   DISENFRANCHISE
ACDEEFHORRSSTW   CHEST OF DRAWERS
ACDEEFINNOORST   CONFEDERATIONS
ACDEEFINOQRRUY   RADIO FREQUENCY
ACDEEFNORRRSTW   CENTRE FORWARDS
ACDEEGHIIMNNNV   VENDING MACHINE
ACDEEGHIINNRUV   UNDERACHIEVING
ACDEEGHIKNNRST   KITCHEN GARDENS
ACDEEGHILLRSTY   CLEAR-SIGHTEDLY
ACDEEGHILOOSSW   WILD-GOOSE CHASE
ACDEEGIILNNRTZ   DECENTRALIZING
ACDEEGIIMNORRS   ORGANISED CRIME
ACDEEGIIMNORRZ   ORGANIZED CRIME
ACDEEGIINORSTT   STAGE DIRECTION
ACDEEGILNNOQRU   GRANDILOQUENCE
ACDEEGIMNORSTU   DISCOURAGEMENT
ACDEEGKLMNNOTW   ACKNOWLEDGMENT
ACDEEHIIINNRST   DISINHERITANCE
ACDEEHIIKMNNSY   KIDNEY MACHINES
ACDEEHILMNOSST   METHODICALNESS
ACDEEHIMNNNSTT   DISENCHANTMENT
ACDEEHINNOPSSW   OPEN SANDWICHES
ACDEEHINPRSSSS   CASH DISPENSERS
ACDEEIILNRSSTU   DIURETICALNESS
ACDEEIKORRRTTT   TRICK OR TREATED
ACDEEILLLNNOSY   DECLENSIONALLY
ACDEEILLNORSTV   CLOSED INTERVAL
ACDEEILNPPRRSU   PERPENDICULARS
ACDEEIMMNNOORT   RECOMMENDATION
ACDEEIMMNORSTV   INVERTED COMMAS
ACDEEIMNNOSSSU   MENDACIOUSNESS
ACDEEIMNNOSTWW   CASEMENT WINDOW
ACDEEINOPRSSSU   PREDACIOUSNESS
ACDEELNNNRSTTY   TRANSCENDENTLY
ACDEEMMNOORRTY   RECOMMENDATORY
ACDEENNORRSUVY   ORDNANCE SURVEY
ACDEENOPRRSSTT   PROTRACTEDNESS
ACDEFGHILMNORR   FRENCH MARIGOLD
ACDEFGIKNNOORY   DAY OF RECKONING
ACDEFIIIINNOTT   IDENTIFICATION
ACDEFIILLNNOTY   CONFIDENTIALLY
ACDEGGINORRSSS   GRADE CROSSINGS
ACDEGHILLMOOOT   METHODOLOGICAL
ACDEGHIMNORRRS   MARCHING ORDERS
ACDEGHIMNORSTY   HYDROMAGNETICS
ACDEGHINNORSTU   COUNTERSHADING
ACDEGIILLLOOOY   IDEOLOOGICALLY
ACDEGIILLOOPRT   PTERIDOLOGICAL
ACDEGIILLOOSTT   DIALECTOLOGIST
ACDEGILNNNRSTY   TRANSCENDINGLY

ACDEGIMMNNORSW   WING COMMANDERS
ACDEGIMNNNORTU   COUNTERMANDING
ACDEGINOOPRSTT   PROGNOSTICATED
ACDEGMMNNOOORR
    COMMON-OR-GARDEN
ACDEHHIILOORTZ   CHLOROTHIAZIDE
ACDEHHIIMOPRRT   HERMAPHRODITIC
ACDEHHILNPRSSS   SHIP'S CHANDLERS
ACDEHIILLMMOTY   IMMETHODICALLY
ACDEHIILLOPRSY   SPHEROIDICALLY
ACDEHIIMORRSTY   RADIOCHEMISTRY
ACDEHILLMOPRYY   HYPODERMICALLY
ACDEHILLNOPTYY   ENDOPHYTICALLY
ACDEHILMOOPPRR   CHLORPROPAMIDE
ACDEHIMMNORSTY   THERMODYNAMICS
ACDEHINOORRSTT   TRISOCTAHEDRON
ACDEHLOOOOPPRSV   APPROVED SCHOOL
ACDEIIIIMNNRST   INDISCRIMINATE
ACDEIIILNNORTU   UNIDIRECTIONAL
ACDEIIILNNSTTW   IDENTICAL TWINS
ACDEIIILNORTTY   DIRECTIONALITY
ACDEIIINORSSSY   IDIOSYNCRASIES
ACDEIIKLRSSTTW   WILDCAT STRIKES
ACDEIILLMNPRTU   PNEUMATIC DRILL
ACDEIILLMOORTY   IODOMETRICALLY
ACDEIILNNOOOST   DECOLONISATION
ACDEIILNNOOOTZ   DECOLONIZATION
ACDEIILNOOORST   DECOLORISATION
ACDEIILNOOORTZ   DECOLORIZATION
ACDEIINNOORSST   CONSIDERATIONS
ACDEILLMNOOSTY   ENDOSMOTICALLY
ACDEILLNOOSSTY   DISCONSOLATELY
ACDEIMMNNOPSUY   PNEUMODYNAMICS
ACDEINNOOPRRTU   UNINCORPORATED
ACDEINNORSTUUY   CONSUETUDINARY
ACDEINOOQRSSTU   CONQUISTADORES
ACDFGHIIINNRSS   DISFRANCHISING
ACDFHIIIIMNOTU   HUMIDIFICATION
ACDFIIIILNOOST   SOLIDIFICATION
ACDGGIILNORSUY   DISCOURAGINGLY
ACDGHILLLOORYY   HYDROLOGICALLY
ACDGHILMNNOOPY   HOLDING COMPANY
ACDGIIIIMNNRST   DISCRIMINATING
ACDGIIINNNORTT   INDOCTRINATING
ACDHHIIOPRRSST   HARPSICHORDIST
ACDHIIOOOPPRTT   DIAPHOTOTROPIC
ACDIIIILNNNOST   DISINCLINATION
ACDIIIIMMNNORST   DISCRIMINATION
ACDIIIJLNORSTU   JURISDICTIONAL
ACDIIILNNOOTTY   CONDITIONALITY
ACDIIIMNORRSTY   DISCRIMINATORY
ACDIIINNNOOORT   INCOORDINATION
ACDIIINNNOORTT   INDOCTRINATION
ACDIILNNOOOSST   CONSOLIDATIONS,
    DISCONSOLATION
ACDIILNOOOORSST   DISCOLORATIONS
ACDILLLMOOOORXY   LOXODROMICALLY
ACDIMNOOPRSSTU   MASS PRODUCTION
ACEEEEFFFLMNST   SELF-EFFACEMENT

ACEEEEFHHLNPRT THREE-HALFPENCE
ACEEEEFLNPRSST FALSE PRETENCES
ACEEEEGILLPTXY EPEXEGETICALLY
ACEEEEHHILNRTW CATHERINE WHEEL
ACEEEEILMNPPRS MALICE PREPENSE
ACEEEEINNRRSTT TERCENTENARIES
ACEEEEPPRRSSTW CARPET SWEEPERS
ACEEEFFGINOPRS PEACE OFFERINGS
ACEEEFHIMRRTUV RHEUMATIC FEVER
ACEEEFINRRSSTV REFRACTIVENESS
ACEEEGGILNNRSW GREEN LACEWINGS
ACEEEGHNNNOSTU CHANGE ONE'S TUNE
ACEEEGIILLNPTY EPIGENETICALLY
ACEEEGIMMOSTTT COMMITTEE STAGE
ACEEEGMNNORSTU ENCOURAGEMENTS
ACEEEHHILLORTT HETEROLECITHAL
ACEEEHILNNNRST CHINESE LANTERN
ACEEEHILNORSST CHOLINESTERASE
ACEEEHLLMNNOPY MYELENCEPHALON
ACEEEHLLMORRTT ELECTROTHERMAL
ACEEEHMMOORTTY HAEMOCYTOMETER
ACEEEHNORTTTTU TO THE UTTERANCE
ACEEEHOORRSTUV HAVE RECOURSE TO
ACEEEIILMNNNST SEMICENTENNIAL
ACEEEILLLMRTTY TELEMETRICALLY
ACEEEILMNORTTU ROMAINE LETTUCE
ACEEEILMORRSTT STEREOMETRICAL
ACEEEILNNNOQUV NONEQUIVALENCE
ACEEEILNPRSTTY PETTY LARCENIES
ACEEEELMORSSSST MALTESE CROSSES
ACEEEMNOOPRSTV OVERCOMPENSATE
ACEEEMNORRSTUU COUNTERMEASURE
ACEEFFGLNNORSU LONG-SUFFERANCE
ACEEFFIILNTTUY INEFFECTUALITY
ACEEFHIIINORTT ETHERIFICATION
ACEEFHILORSSTW AS THE CROW FLIES
ACEEFIIINORSTT ESTERIFICATION
ACEEFILMNOPRST SELF-IMPORTANCE
ACEEFILMPRRSTU SIMPLE FRACTURE
ACEEFINORRRSST REFRACTORINESS
ACEEGHHLNORSST CLOTHES HANGERS
ACEEGHHMNRRRSU HUNGER MARCHERS
ACEEGHHOOPRRRS CHOREOGRAPHERS
ACEEGHIIMNNSSW SEWING MACHINES
ACEEGHIKLNNRSU RECKLINGHAUSEN
ACEEGHILNORSSU CLEARINGHOUSES
ACEEGHILNOSSSU CHAISES LONGUES
ACEEGHILOPRRSX LEXICOGRAPHERS
ACEEGHIMMNORTT THERMOMAGNETIC
ACEEGHIMOOPRRT METEOROGRAPHIC
ACEEGIINNNORTT TRACTION ENGINE
ACEEGIINOPRRRS CARRIER PIGEONS
ACEEGILLLLOOTY TELEOLOGICALLY
ACEEGILLMOOORT METEOROLOGICAL
ACEEGIILLNRSTYY SYNERGETICALLY
ACEEGLNRRSTTUU STRUCTURAL GENE
ACEEGNOORSSSUU COURAGEOUSNESS
ACEEHHIIKSSTTV THICK AS THIEVES
ACEEHHHILNNNOPR RHINENCEPHALON

ACEEHHIMOPRSTT CHEMOTHERAPIST
ACEEHIIILNPSTT LICENTIATESHIP
ACEEHIIINSTTTU AUTHENTICITIES
ACEEHIILLNNPST PANHELLENISTIC
ACEEHIILMMNPSS SIMPLE MACHINES
ACEEHIINPPPRST APPRENTICESHIP
ACEEHILLMNNOSS MELANCHOLINESS
ACEEHILLMORTXY EXOTHERMICALLY
ACEEHILNNOPSSU EUPHONICALNESS
ACEEHIMMNORSSV SERVOMECHANISM
ACEEHIMRRSSSTT CHRISTMAS TREES
ACEEHINORSUUVX NOUVEAUX RICHES
ACEEHKMNORSTTT SHOCK TREATMENT
ACEEHLNNOOPPRS PROSENCEPHALON
ACEEHLPPRSSTUY SUPPLY TEACHERS
ACEEHMNOPPRRST RAPPROCHEMENTS
ACEEHPRRRSTTTY STRETCHER PARTY
ACEEIIILLLMPST SEMIELLIPTICAL
ACEEIIJLNNORTT INTERJECTIONAL
ACEEIIILLNPSST ELLIPTICALNESS
ACEEIIILLMPRRTY PERIMETRICALLY
ACEEIIILLRRSTTV VERTICILLASTER
ACEEIILNNNOPTT EPICONTINENTAL
ACEEIILNNNORSST INTERCESSIONAL
ACEEIILNNORSTT INTERSECTIONAL
ACEEIILNOPTTXY EXCEPTIONALITY
ACEEIILNOSSTTY COESSENTIALITY
ACEEIILNPRSTTT PETIT LARCENIST
ACEEIINORSSTTV SERVICE STATION
ACEEIKLNRSSSTV TRAVELSICKNESS
ACEEIILLLLNTTUY INTELLECTUALLY
ACEEILLMNORRTU INTERMOLECULAR
ACEEILMNOOOPSU POLEMONIACEOUS
ACEEILMOPRSSTU PRECIOUS METALS
ACEEILNNQQUUVY QUINQUEVALENCY
ACEEILNNRRSTUW NUCLEAR WINTERS
ACEEILNORRRSTU RESURRECTIONAL
ACEEILNORSTVVY CONSERVATIVELY
ACEEIMMNNORSTU INCOMMENSURATE
ACEEIMNOOOORRRT RECREATION ROOM
ACEEIMNOOPRRST CONTEMPORARIES
ACEEIMNOPPRRTU MERCAPTOPURINE
ACEEIMNORRSSSX CROSS-EXAMINERS
ACEEINNOOOPRTV NONCOOPERATIVE
ACEEINOORRSSTV CONSERVATOIRES,
    CONSERVATORIES
ACEEINOPRRSSSU PRECARIOUSNESS
ACEELLOORRRSST ROLLER COASTERS
ACEFFIIOSSTTUY SUFFICE IT TO SAY
ACEFFINOOQSTTU QUESTION OF FACT
ACEFGIIINNORTT GENTRIFICATION
ACEFGIINNORTTU CENTRIFUGATION
ACEFHHIIINPSST CHIEFTAINSHIPS
ACEFHIIIOTTVVY HIVE OF ACTIVITY
ACEFIIILLMPSTY SIMPLIFICATIVE
ACEFIIIINORTVV REVIVIFICATION
ACEFIIIILMNOSTU EMULSIFICATION
ACEFIIILPRSTUY SUPERFICIALITY
ACEFIINOSSSTTU FACTITIOUSNESS

ACEFINOOPPRRRT PROPER FRACTION
ACEFINRRRSTTUU INFRASTRUCTURE
ACEFJKKLNOORST NORFOLK JACKETS
ACEFLNOORSSSTU COLOURFASTNESS
ACEGGHHINOOPRR CHOREOGRAPHING
ACEGGHIIMNNNNU MACHINEGUNNING
ACEGGIILNNNPRS SPRING-CLEANING
ACEGGILLNOOOORT GERONTOLOGICAL
ACEGGILNOOSSTY GYNAECOLOGISTS
ACEGHILLLNOOTY ETHNOLOGICALLY
ACEGHILLNOOPTY PHOTOGENICALLY
ACEGHILLNOORTY ORTHOGENICALLY
ACEGHLMOOPSTYY METAPSYCHOLOGY
ACEGHMMOOPRSUY MYRMECOPHAGOUS
ACEGHOPPRRRSTY CRYPTOGRAPHERS
ACEGIIINNNORTZ CONTAINERIZING
ACEGIILLLOSTUY EULOGISTICALLY
ACEGIILLMNOORT TERMINOLOGICAL
ACEGIILLORSSUY SACRILEGIOUSLY
ACEGIILNNORTUV COUNTERVAILING
ACEGIILNNOTTUV CONGLUTINATIVE
ACEGIILNOQTUVY EQUIVOCATINGLY
ACEGIILNOSSTTU GESTICULATIONS
ACEGIIMNNORSSX CROSS-EXAMINING
ACEGIINPRRSSTT STARTING PRICES
ACEGILLLMOOTYY ETYMOLOGICALLY
ACEGILLLOOOSTY OSTEOLOGICALLY
ACEGILMNNOOOORT CONGLOMERATION
ACEGILNOPRSSTU PLASTIC SURGEON
ACEGILPRRSSTUY PLASTIC SURGERY
ACEGIMMMOPRRSU PROGRAMME MUSIC
ACEGINNNOOSSUU CONSANGUINEOUS
ACEGINNOOSSSTU CONTAGIOUSNESS
ACEGINNOPSSSUU PUGNACIOUSNESS
ACEHHIINOPRRTT THERIANTHROPIC
ACEHHILLOOPSTY THEOSOPHICALLY
ACEHHILLOPTTYY HYPOTHETICALLY
ACEHHILOOPRSUZ RHIZOCEPHALOUS
ACEHHLMOOOOPPST OPHTHALMOSCOPE
ACEHHMMNRSSTUY CHRYSANTHEMUMS
ACEHIIIILMSSTW WHIMSICALITIES
ACEHIIILLPSTUUY EUPHUISTICALLY
ACEHIILNORSSST HISTORICALNESS
ACEHIIMNNOOPRT ENANTIOMORPHIC
ACEHIINNSSTTUU UNENTHUSIASTIC
ACEHIINOOPRTTU EUTROPHICATION
ACEHIINOPPRSST SPINTHARISCOPE
ACEHIINOPRSSST CORNISH PASTIES
ACEHIIOOPRSSST SPIROCHAETOSIS
ACEHIIOORRSTTT OSTEOARTHRITIC
ACEHILLNOPPTYY PHENOTYPICALLY
ACEHILLOPRSTTY PROSTHETICALLY
ACEHILLOPRTXYY XEROPHYTICALLY
ACEHILMNOOPRRZ CHLORPROMAZINE
ACEHILMNOPRSST THERMOPLASTICS
ACEHILOOPRSSTV PRIVATE SCHOOLS
ACEHIMNOOPRRTT ANTHROPOMETRIC
ACEHIMOPPRSTTY SPERMATOPHYTIC
ACEHINNORSSSTY NARCOSYNTHESIS

ACEHINOOORRSSTT ORCHESTRATIONS
ACEIIIILMNPSTU MUNICIPALITIES
ACEIIIILNPPRST PRINCIPALITIES
ACEIIIILLMOPRTY MILITARY POLICE
ACEIIIILLMPTTUV MULTIPLICATIVE
ACEIIILLNORTTV VERTICILLATION
ACEIIILLOPSSTY ISOPIESTICALLY
ACEIIIILMNOOSTT EMOTIONALISTIC
ACEIIILNRRTUVY CURVILINEARITY
ACEIIILNRSSTUV UNIVERSALISTIC
ACEIIIMMNOORSS COMMISSIONAIRE
ACEIIIMNNORRST RECRIMINATIONS
ACEIIINNOPSSTX EXPANSIONISTIC
ACEIIINOPPRSTT PRECIPITATIONS
ACEIILLLNRTUUY UNICELLULARITY
ACEIILLMNNOOOS NEOCOLONIALISM
ACEIILLNNOOOST NEOCOLONIALIST
ACEIILMNNNOSTT CONTINENTALISM
ACEIILNNNOSTTT CONTINENTALIST
ACEIILNNNOTTTY CONTINENTALITY
ACEIILNNOOPRST IN LOCO PARENTIS
ACEIILNNORRSTU INSURRECTIONAL
ACEIILNOOPSSTT POLICE STATIONS
ACEIILNOPRSTUY PERTINACIOUSLY
ACEIILNOSSSSUV LASCIVIOUSNESS
ACEIIMMNNOORTU IMMUNOREACTION
ACEIIMMNOORSST COMMISERATIONS
ACEIINNOOORSVZ CONVERSAZIOONI
ACEIINNORSSTTY SYNCRETISATION
ACEIINNORSTTYZ SYNCRETIZATION
ACEIINNOSSSTUU INCAUTIOUSNESS
ACEIINOPSSSSUU AUSPICIOUSNESS
ACEILLLMORTUVY VOLUMETRICALLY
ACEILLMMOORSTY OSMOMETRICALLY
ACEILLMNOORRSS CRIMSON ROSELLA
ACEILLMOPRRTYY PYROMETRICALLY
ACEILLNNNOOTVY CONVENTIONALLY
ACEILLNNOOSSTT CONSTELLATIONS
ACEILLNOOPRSST CROSS-POLLINATE
ACEILLNOPRSSUY SUPERSONICALLY
ACEILMNNOOORTUV MACROEVOLUTION
ACEILMNNOOPRRTY CONTEMPORARILY
ACEILNNNNOOTUV UNCONVENTIONAL
ACEILNNNOOPSTT CONSTANTINOPLE
ACEILNNOOOPRST SPIRONOLACTONE
ACEILNOOPRRTUY PERLOCUTIONARY
ACEILNOPRRRTUV PROVENTRICULAR
ACEILOORRSTTUW WATERCOLOURIST
ACEIMMNNOORSTU COMMENSURATION
ACEINNNOOOOPRT NONCOOPERATION
ACEINNNOORSTTV CONTRAVENTIONS
ACELLMNNOOPRSU PERSONAL COLUMN
ACELNOPRSSSSWY LAWSON'S CYPRESS
ACELRRRSTTTUUU ULTRASTRUCTURE
ACEMNNOOORSSTTU ENTOMOSTRACOUS
ACFFIIINOORSTT FORTIFICATIONS
ACFGIIILLNNOTZ FICTIONALIZING
ACFGIIIINNOSST SIGNIFICATIONS
ACFGIIILNOORST GLORIFICATIONS

ACFGIILMNNNOTU MALFUNCTIONING
ACFGIINNNOORSTU CONFIGURATIONS
ACFIIIILMNOPST SIMPLIFICATION
ACFIIIJLLNOOST JOLLIFICATIONS
ACFIIILNOSTTTU STULTIFICATION
ACFIILLRSTTUUY FUTURISTICALLY
ACFIILNNOSSTTU FUNCTIONALISTS
ACFIMNOOORSTTT COMFORT STATION
ACFINNNOOOORSTT CONFRONTATIONS
ACGGHHIMOPPRSY SPHYGMOGRAPHIC
ACGGHIKLNOSSTU LAUGHINGSTOCKS
ACGHHHIOOPSTUY ICHTHYOPHAGOUS
ACGHIIILNOPSTT ANTIPHLOGISTIC
ACGHIIKNNOSTTT STICK AT NOTHING
ACGHIILLLLOOPY PHILOLOGICALLY
ACGHIILLLLOOTY LITHOLOGICALLY
ACGHIILLLOOSTY HISTOLOGICALLY
ACGHIILLNOOOORT ORNITHOLOGICAL
ACGHILLNOOOPY PHONOLOGICALLY
ACGIIILLLNSTUY LINGUISTICALLY
ACGIIILLLPSTUY PUGILISTICALLY
ACGIIILNNOTTXY INTOXICATINGLY
ACGIIILPRRSSTU SURGICAL SPIRIT
ACGIILRRSSTTUU AGRICULTURISTS
ACGIIMMNOORRSS MICROORGANISMS
ACGILNOOPRSSTY LARYNGOSCOPIST
ACGINOOOOPRRSTT PROGNOSTICATOR
ACHHILLMNOOOPY HOMOPHONICALLY
ACHHIMMMOOOORST HOMOCHROMATISM
ACHHINOOOOPPRST ANTHROPOSOPHIC
ACHHLMOOOOPPSTY OPHTHALMOSCOPY
ACHIIIINNORSTT TRICHINISATION
ACHIIIINNORTTZ TRICHINIZATION
ACHIIILLLPSTYY SYPHILITICALLY
ACHIIILLNORSTY HISTRIONICALLY
ACHIIIMNOORSST TRICHOMONIASIS
ACHIIINOOPSSTT SOPHISTICATION
ACHIILLLMNOOTY MONOLITHICALLY
ACHIILLLOSTTYY HISTOLYTICALLY
ACHIIOPRSSSTTY ASTROPHYSICIST
ACHILLLNOOPPYY POLYPHONICALLY
ACHILLOOPPTTYY PHOTOTYPICALLY
ACHILMMOOPRSTY POLYCHROMATISM
ACHILMOOPRRSSY PRIMARY SCHOOLS
ACHIMMMNOOOORST MONOCHROMATISM
ACIIIILNOOPSTT POLITICISATION
ACIIIILNOOPTTZ POLITICIZATION
ACIIIILPRSSTTU SPIRITUALISTIC
ACIIILLLMPSSTY SIMPLISTICALLY
ACIIILLMNOPTTU MULTIPLICATION
ACIIILLMOPSTTY OPTIMISTICALLY
ACIIILMNOPRSSV PROVINCIALISMS
ACIIILNOPSSUUY INAUSPICIOUSLY
ACIILLLMOOQSSU COLLOQUIALISMS
ACIILNNOOSTTTU CONSTITUTIONAL
ACIINNNOOPRSTU PRONUNCIATIONS
ACIINNOOOPRSTT CONTRAPOSITION
ACIINNOPRRSSTT TRANSCRIPTIONS
ACIKMNNOORSTUY ROCKY MOUNTAINS

ACILLMMNNOOTTY NONCOMMITTALLY
ACILMOOPRRRSUY PRIMARY COLOURS
ACIMMOOOORSSTTU MICROSTOMATOUS
ACIMNOOOSTTTXY CYTOTAXONOMIST
ADDDDEGIIMNNOW DIAMOND WEDDING
ADDDEIIIILNSUV INDIVIDUALISED
ADDDEIIIILNUVZ INDIVIDUALIZED
ADDEEEEHNNNSSV EVEN-HANDEDNESS
ADDEEEFFIINRTT DIFFERENTIATED
ADDEEEFHLNNSST LEFT-HANDEDNESS
ADDEEEFILMNTXY EXTENDED FAMILY
ADDEEEHIMNPPRS MISAPPREHEND
ADDEEEHNNNOPSS OPEN-HANDEDNESS
ADDEEEIKMNNSSW WEAK-MINDEDNESS
ADDEEEILMPRTTY PREMEDITATEDLY
ADDEEEILNNNPSS PINS AND NEEDLES
ADDEEEIMNPRTTU UNPREMEDITATED
ADDEEEIMNRSTTU UNDERESTIMATED
ADDEEFFHLRRUUY FURFURALDEHYDE
ADDEEFIIMNNRSS FAIR-MINDEDNESS
ADDEEFLNNNORUW NEWFOUNDLANDER
ADDEEFLNNPRSUY PENNY DREADFULS
ADDEEGHHHINNSS HIGH-HANDEDNESS
ADDEEHIIMNNRTY DIMENHYDRINATE
ADDEEILMNNPRSU NIL DESPERANDUM
ADDEEINNNRSSWY NINE DAYS' WONDER
ADDEGILNOORRSU RIO GRANDE DO SUL
ADDEGINNNRSSTU UNDERSTANDINGS
ADDEGINNORRSST STANDING ORDERS
ADDEIIIILNRSUV INDIVIDUALISER
ADDEIIIILNRUVZ INDIVIDUALIZER
ADDEIIILNRSSTU INDUSTRIALISED
ADDEIIILNRSTUZ INDUSTRIALIZED
ADDEIILLNNOPTW WIND-POLLINATED
ADDEIILNOPPSTY DISAPPOINTEDLY
ADDIIIILNSSTUV INDIVIDUALISTS
ADEEEEEGNNRSST DEGENERATENESS
ADEEEEEHLLRRSW WHEELER-DEALERS
ADEEEEFHINRSUW AUF WIEDERSEHEN
ADEEEEGHILLNRW WHEELER-DEALING
ADEEEEHHLMMPST HEMEL HEMPSTEAD
ADEEEEHNRSTTVY THREE-DAY EVENTS
ADEEEEIMNPRRTT PREDETERMINATE
ADEEEELMNRSSTT ELDER STATESMEN
ADEEEELNNNRRVV NEVER-NEVER LAND
ADEEEFGILORRTU TIERRA DEL FUEGO
ADEEEFHOOPRRTW WEATHERPROOFED
ADEEEFIMNNOORT AFOREMENTIONED
ADEEEFIMNRSTTU DISFEATUREMENT
ADEEEFINNORSTT DEFENESTRATION
ADEEEGHHMNPRRS GERMAN SHEPHERD
ADEEEGHNOORRRY HONORARY DEGREE
ADEEEGIILMNRST LEGERDEMAINIST
ADEEEGIINRRTTV REDINTEGRATIVE
ADEEEGIKNNRRRT KINDERGARTENER
ADEEEGLNRRSSSS REGARDLESSNESS
ADEEEGOPRRRTUY DAGUERREOTYPER
ADEEEGOPRRSTUY DAGUERREOTYPES
ADEEEHHLLORTWY WHOLE-HEARTEDLY

ADEEEHIINRRSST HEREDITARINESS
ADEEEHIKMNOSSU HOUSEMAID'S KNEE
ADEEEHILNOOPRT RADIOTELEPHONE
ADEEEHIMNNRSTT DISHEARTENMENT
ADEEEHIRRSSTTV THE DRIVER'S SEAT
ADEEEIIMNRRST INTERMEDIARIES
ADEEEIIMMQRSUV DEMISEMIQUAVER
ADEEEIIMNSSTTV MEDITATIVENESS
ADEEEILMORRTTY RADIOTELEMETRY
ADEEEIMNRSSTTU UNDERESTIMATES
ADEEEMNNRSTTTU UNDERSTATEMENT
ADEEENNPPRRSSU UNPREPAREDNESS
ADEEFFIINORRTT DIFFERENTIATOR
ADEEFGHINRSSST FARSIGHTEDNESS
ADEEFGINNOSTTU DETONATING FUSE
ADEEFGLLOOPRSU GOLD-OF-PLEASURE
ADEEFHILLNOSTU THE LIFE AND
   SOUL
ADEEFHILNSSTTW HALFWITTEDNESS
ADEEFIMNNOORRT FOREORDAINMENT
ADEEFLLLMOORWY FOLLOW-MY-LEADER
ADEEGGIMNNRRRY GERRYMANDERING
ADEEGHHNOOOSTV HAVE THE GOODS ON
ADEEGHILNNRRTY HEARTRENDINGLY
ADEEGHILNRSSTU DAUGHTERLINESS
ADEEGHNNORSSST HEADSTRONGNESS
ADEEGIIINRSTTV DISINTEGRATIVE
ADEEGIINNORRTT REDINTEGRATION
ADEEGINNOPPRRT PREPONDERATING
ADEEGINOOORRSST DEROGATORINESS
ADEEGJLMNSTUUV VALUE JUDGMENTS
ADEEGLNNORSSTU DENTAL SURGEONS
ADEEHHIILMOPRS HEMISPHEROIDAL
ADEEHHIMOPRRST HERMAPHRODITES
ADEEHHLMNOOSSU HOUSEHOLD NAMES
ADEEHILMNNRSTT DISENTHRALMENT
ADEEHILNNOPSST SHETLAND PONIES
ADEEHILNOOPRTY RADIOTELEPHONY
ADEEHIMMOPRSTX MIXED METAPHORS
ADEEHLMNOORRSY DYSMENORRHOEAL
ADEEHMNNNOSSSU UNHANDSOMENESS
ADEEIIINORSSTV RADIOSENSITIVE
ADEEIILNNNORST NONRESIDENTIAL
ADEEIILOPRRSTV PRIVATE SOLDIER
ADEEIIMNNOOSTT DEMONETISATION
ADEEIIMNNOOTTZ DEMONETIZATION
ADEEIINNOPRSTT PREDESTINATION
ADEEIINSSSSSUV DISSUASIVENESS
ADEEILLNORRSVY ORDINARY LEVELS
ADEEILNNRRSTUY UNRESTRAINEDLY
ADEEILNORRSSWW WORLD-WEARINESS
ADEEIMNNORRSST ARRONDISSEMENT
ADEEINNOOPPRRT PREPONDERATION
ADEEJMMORRSTTU DRUM MAJORETTES
ADEELNNOPPRRTY PREPONDERANTLY
ADEELNNORSSSSU SLANDEROUSNESS
ADEEMNRSSTTTUU MATURE STUDENTS
ADEFFGHINNORTU FOUNDING FATHER
ADEFFGIINORSST DISAFFORESTING

ADEFFHILLNOSUY FULLY-FASHIONED
ADEFGHIMOORRTY FAIRY GODMOTHER
ADEFGIIMNORRST TRANSMOGRIFIED
ADEFIIINNOSSTT DISINFESTATION
ADEFIINOORSSTT DISFORESTATION
ADEFIINOSSSSTU FASTIDIOUSNESS
ADEGGIIINNRSTT DISINTEGRATING
ADEGGILLNRSSSU SLUGGARDLINESS
ADEGHIKNNOORTT THE GORDIAN KNOT
ADEGHINNNOSSTT ONE-NIGHT STANDS
ADEGIIIILMNRTZ DEMILITARIZING
ADEGIIINNORSTT DISINTEGRATION,
   DISORIENTATING
ADEGIIILLMNPRSY PYRAMID SELLING
ADEGIILMNNPRRY REPRIMANDINGLY
ADEGILMOORSSTT DERMATOLOGISTS
ADEGINNNPSSSTU UPSTANDINGNESS
ADEHHIILLLLSSY SHILLY-SHALLIED
ADEHHIMOPRRSTU HERMAPHRODITUS
ADEHILNNOSSSTU OUTLANDISHNESS
ADEHIMOOOPPRSS PAEDOMORPHOSIS
ADEHIMOOOORTTUW WITHOUT MORE
   ADO
ADEHINOORRSSTW ROADWORTHINESS
ADEHLOPRRSSSTU SHOULDER STRAPS
ADEHORSSSTTUWW SOUTHWESTWARDS
ADEIIILMNNORST TRIDIMENSIONAL
ADEIIILMNNOSTY DIMENSIONALITY
ADEIIILNPRSTTU PLATITUDINISER
ADEIIILNPRTTUZ PLATITUDINIZER
ADEIIINNOORSTT DISORIENTATION
ADEIIILLMNRRTUY RUDIMENTARILLY
ADEIIILLNOPRTVY PROVIDENTIALLY
ADEIILMNNNOOSX MASON-DIXON LINE
ADEIILMNNOOSTW TWO-DIMENSIONAL
ADEIIMNNOORSST MODERNISATIONS
ADEIIMNNOORSTZ MODERNIZATIONS
ADEIIMNNOPPSTT DISAPPOINTMENT
ADEIINNOOPRRST PREORDINATIONS
ADEIINNORSSTTU TRADE UNIONISTS
ADEIINORRSSSTT TRANSISTORISED
ADEIINORRSSTTZ TRANSISTORIZED
ADEILMMNORRSTU ULTRAMODERNISM
ADEILMNORRSTTU ULTRAMODERNIST
ADEIMNNOORSSTT DEMONSTRATIONS
ADEINOOOORRTTTX DEXTROROTATION
ADEOOOORRRTTTXY DEXTROROTATORY
ADFGGHHIILLNNS HIGHLAND FLINGS
ADFGGIINNNOORT TO-ING AND FRO-ING
ADFGIKLNOOORRW FORWARD-LOOKING
ADFHNNOOOOORRST AND SO ON *OR* FORTH
ADGGGHOORSSTYY SHAGGY-DOG STORY
ADGGIMNNOPRSTU STAMPING GROUND
ADGHILOOORRSVV VOROSHILOVGRAD
ADGIILLLNNOTUY LONGITUDINALLY
ADGIILNOPPRSVY DISAPPROVINGLY
ADIIILMNOSSSTU DISSIMULATIONS
ADIIILNRSSSTTU INDUSTRIALISTS
ADIILOPSSTTUUY DISPUTATIOUSLY

AEEEEFHNOPSTTX   AT THE EXPENSE OF
AEEEEFLNOOPPSY   APPLE OF ONE'S EYE
AEEEEGINSSTTVV   VEGETATIVENESS
AEEEEILMNNRSST   ELEMENTARINESS
AEEEEINNPRRTTT   INTERPENETRATE
AEEEEINPRRSTTV   REPRESENTATIVE
AEEEEELLNPRRTTW   WATER-REPELLENT
AEEEFGHHIRSTTW   FEATHERWEIGHTS
AEEEFHOQRSTTTU   AT THE REQUEST OF
AEEEFIILNNRRTT   INTERFERENTIAL
AEEEFILLNPRRTY   PREFERENTIALLY
AEEEFNORRSSTTW   WATER SOFTENERS
AEEEGGGIMNNNRT   ENGAGEMENT RING
AEEEGGINRSSSSV   AGGRESSIVENESS
AEEEGHLLOPPRST   TELEGRAPH POLES
AEEEGHLNPRSTTT   GRASP THE NETTLE
AEEEGIILNNRSTT   LARGE INTESTINE
AEEEGIKLNRRSST   GENERAL STRIKES
AEEEGILLPRRSSS   PRESS GALLERIES
AEEEGIMNPRRSTY   PRAYER MEETINGS
AEEEGNNOOPQRTU   ROENTGENOPAQUE
AEEEGNNOORRSTT   ENTEROGASTRONE
AEEEHHHILRTTWW   THE WHEREWITHAL
AEEEHHHINNSSST   HEATHENISHNESS
AEEEHHILNPSTTW   WHITE ELEPHANTS
AEEEHIINNPPRSV   INAPPREHENSIVE
AEEEHILNPPRSVY   APPREHENSIVELY
AEEEHIMNNRSTTT   MAN IN THE STREET
AEEEHINSSSTUVX   EXHAUSTIVENESS
AEEEHLLORSTUXY   HETEROSEXUALLY
AEEEIIINNPRSTT   PENITENTIARIES
AEEEIILMNNSSTT   SENTIMENTALISE
AEEEIILMNNSTTZ   SENTIMENTALIZE
AEEEIINPRRTTTV   INTERPRETATIVE
AEEEILLMNPRTXY   EXPERIMENTALLY
AEEEILMMRSSTTY   REAL-TIME SYSTEM
AEEEILMNRRTUVY   REMUNERATIVELY
AEEEILNOPRSTUV   SUPERELEVATION
AEEEIMNNNRSTTT   ENTERTAINMENTS
AEEEIMNNRSSTTT   REINSTATEMENTS
AEEEINNPRRTTTT   INTERPENETRANT
AEEEINNOPRRSTT   REPRESENTATION
AEEEINPRSSSSUV   PERSUASIVENESS
AEEEIOOPRRRTTV   RETRO-OPERATIVE
AEEEELLNOOPRRRU   EUROPEAN ROLLER
AEEEELMNNNRSSSS   MANNERLESSNESS
AEEEELNOOPRRSST   PERSONAL STEREO
AEEEMNNOOPRSTUX   EXTEMPORANEOUS
AEEEMNORSSTTTV   OVERSTATEMENTS
AEEEENNORSSSTUX   EXTRANEOUSNESS
AEEEENNRRSSSSTV   TRANSVERSENESS
AEEEENQSSSSTTUU   STATUESQUENESS
AEEEEORRRSSTTUV   TREASURE TROVES
AEEFGGHILNRSTT   FLIGHT SERGEANT
AEEFGHJLLNOTUW   LAW OF THE JUNGLE
AEEFGIIMMNRRST   FERRIMAGNETISM
AEEFGIINRSSTUV   FIGURATIVENESS
AEEFGILMNNNSSU   MEANINGFULNESS
AEEFGIMMNORRST   FERROMAGNETISM

AEEFGLNNRSSTUU   UNGRATEFULNESS
AEEFHINNOSTTTT   NOT THE FAINTEST
AEEFHLNNNNPPYY   PENNY-HALFPENNY
AEEFIILNOQQTUU   QUINQUEFOLIATE
AEEFNOOPRRSSTW   WATERPROOFNESS
AEEGGHLNORSTTT   TO GREAT LENGTHS
AEEGGIINORSSTT   SEGREGATIONIST
AEEGGILLNNORTU   OUTGENERALLING
AEEGGINORRSSSU   GREGARIOUSNESS
AEEGGIOSSTTUUV   AUTOSUGGESTIVE
AEEGHHLORSSTUU   SLAUGHTERHOUSE
AEEGHILNNOOPTY   PILE ON THE AGONY
AEEGHIMNSSSTTT   STEAMTIGHTNESS
AEEGHINRSSTTTW   WATERTIGHTNESS
AEEGIIILLLMTTY   ILLEGITIMATELY
AEEGIIIILLNNRST   INERTIA SELLING
AEEGIIILLNNSTT   INTELLIGENTSIA
AEEGIIILRRRSTU   IRREGULARITIES
AEEGIILMNORSSS   GENERALISSIMOS
AEEGIILMNNPRRTY   ENTERTAININGLY
AEEGIIMNNNNORTU   MOUNTAINEERING
AEEGIIMNORSTTV   OVERESTIMATING
AEEGIIMNRSSTTU   TIME SIGNATURES
AEEGIINNOPRRST   PEREGRINATIONS
AEEGIINORRSTTV   INTERROGATIVES,
    TERGIVERSATION
AEEGILLMNORRST   STEAMROLLERING
AEEGINNRSSTTUU   SIGNATURE TUNES
AEEGIORRRSTTVY   TERGIVERSATORY
AEEGNOORSSSTUU   OUTRAGEOUSNESS
AEEHHLMNNOPSTU   SULPHONMETHANE
AEEHHOPPPRSSTU   SUPERPHOSPHATE
AEEHIKNOOPRRUY   KEEP YOUR HAIR ON!
AEEHILLMNOTTTW   THE LITTLE WOMAN
AEEHILLNOPRVXY   VINE PHYLLOXERA
AEEHILOOPRRTTY   HETEROPOLARITY
AEEHIMNORSSTUV   OVERENTHUSIASM
AEEHINPPPPRRSW   WHIPPERSNAPPER
AEEIIILMMMMORT   TIME IMMEMORIAL
AEEIIILMNSSTTX   EXISTENTIALISM
AEEIIILNNSSTTY   INESSENTIALITY
AEEIIILNOPSTTT   POTENTIALITIES
AEEIIILNSSTTTX   EXISTENTIALIST
AEEIIILORRRSTT   TERRITORIALISE
AEEIIILORRRTTZ   TERRITORIALIZE
AEEIIILLMNNSSTT   SMALL INTESTINE
AEEIIILLNNOPRTT   INTERPELLATION
AEEIILMMNNOPTT   IMPLEMENTATION
AEEIILMMNNSSTT   SENTIMENTALISM
AEEIILMNNSSTTT   SENTIMENTALIST
AEEIILMNNSTTTY   SENTIMENTALITY
AEEIIILNNNORTTV   INTERVENTIONAL
AEEIIILNNORRSTT   INTERRELATIONS
AEEIILNNOSTTXY   EXTENSIONALITY
AEEIILNNQSSTTU   QUINTESSENTIAL
AEEIILNRSTTUXY   INTERSEXUALITY
AEEIILPRTTUVVY   VITUPERATIVELY
AEEIIMNNOORSTT   REMONETISATION
AEEIIMNNOORTTZ   REMONETIZATION

AEEIIMNOORSTTV OVERESTIMATION	AEGIILMNNOORST MONGRELISATION
AEEIINNOPRRTTT INTERPRETATION	AEGIILMNNOORTZ MONGRELIZATION
AEEIINNOQRSSTU QUESTIONNAIRES	AEGIILNNNRSTTY INTRANSIGENTLY
AEEIINNORSSTTW WESTERNISATION	AEGIINNOORRSTT INTERROGATIONS
AEEIINNORSTTWZ WESTERNIZATION	AEGIINPPRSSSTT ASSET-STRIPPING
AEEIINNRSSSTTV TRANSITIVENESS	AEGILLNOOOPSTT PALEONTOLOGIST
AEEIINPQQRTTUU QUINQUEPARTITE	AEGIMMNOOPRSTU SPERMATOGONIUM
AEEIILLNNRSSSTT SLATTERNLINESS	AEGIMNNOORTUUV OUTMANOEUVRING
AEEIILNNPRRSSTT SILENT PARTNERS	AEGINNORRSSSST TRANSGRESSIONS
AEEIILNOORTTTXY EXTORTIONATELY	AEGINNPRSSSSSU SURPASSINGNESS
AEEIMNOQRSSTTU QUESTION MASTER	AEGINORSSSTTUU GRATUITOUSNESS
AEEINOQRSSSTTU SEQUESTRATIONS	AEGKKMNOORSSTU UST-KAMENOGORSK
AEFFHILNNSSTUU UNFAITHFULNESS	AEGLLMOPRRTUYY PYROMETALLURGY
AEFFHLNOOOORRUW FLOWER-OF-AN-HOUR	AEHHHILNOORTTU HOLIER-THAN-THOU
AEFGGHIKNSTUWY GUY FAWKES NIGHT	AEHHHOOOPPRSTT ORTHOPHOSPHATE
AEFGHIILMPRRST PILGRIM FATHERS	AEHHIILLLLRSSY SHILLYSHALLIER
AEFGHINNNPRSTY PENNY-FARTHINGS	AEHHNNNOORRSTTT NORTH-NORTHEAST
AEFGIINOORRRST ROARING FORTIES	AEHHOOSSSTTTUU SOUTH-SOUTHEAST
AEFGIINOPRRSTU PREFIGURATIONS	AEHIIKLLMOOPRT POIKILOTHERMAL
AEFGILNOORSTTV FLOATING VOTERS	AEHIILOPRRSTWY PRAISEWORTHILY
AEFHHLNNOPRTWY HALFPENNYWORTH	AEHIINNOSSSTTY SYNTHESISATION
AEFHKLNNNSSTUU UNTHANKFULNESS	AEHIINNOSSTTTY SYNTHETISATION
AEFIILNOOPRRST PROLIFERATIONS	AEHIINNOSSTTYZ SYNTHESIZATION
AEFILLNOOPRSSY PROFESSIONALLY	AEHIINNOSTTTYZ SYNTHETIZATION
AEFILLOOPRRSSY PROFESSORIALLY	AEHIIOORRSSTTT OSTEOARTHRITIS
AEFILNNOOPRSSU UNPROFESSIONAL	AEHIJKMOOOOSTV KOSOVO-METOHIJA
AEFILNOOPSSSSW PASSIONFLOWERS	AEHILLOOPSSUXZ SULPHISOXAZOLE
AEFINOOPRRRSSW PRISONERS OF WAR	AEHILNNOORSSTZ HORIZONTALNESS
AEGGHHOOPPRTYY PHYTOGEOGRAPHY	AEHIMNNOORSSSU HARMONIOUSNESS
AEGGHIILNRRSTT RIGHT TRIANGLES	AEHIMOOPPPSSTU HIPPOPOTAMUSES
AEGGHINNOOPRTV PHOTOENGRAVING	AEIIILMORRRSTT TERRITORIALISM
AEGGIIIMNPSSTT SPITTING IMAGES	AEIIILNNNOTTTY INTENTIONALITY
AEGGIILLNNOSTT ILL-GOTTEN GAINS	AEIIILNNNRSTTVY INTRANSITIVELY
AEGGIINRSSTTTT SITTING TARGETS	AEIIILORRRSTTT TERRITORIALIST
AEGGIKLLNOOSSS LOOKING GLASSES	AEIIILORRRTTTY TERRITORIALITY
AEGGINOOSSTTUU AUTOSUGGESTION	AEIIINOQRRSTUY REQUISITIONARY
AEGHHLMOPPRSTY PLETHYSMOGRAPH	AEIIJLNNORSTUV UNIVERSAL JOINT
AEGHIILNOOOSTT THEOLOGISATION	AEIILLLMNNOPST POSTMILLENNIAL
AEGHIILNOOOTTZ THEOLOGIZATION	AEIILLLRSTTUVY ILLUSTRATIVELY
AEGHIIMNNOOOST HOMOGENISATION	AEIILLMNOPRSSY IMPRESSIONALLY
AEGHIIMNNOOOTZ HOMOGENIZATION	AEIILLNNOSSSUV VILLAINOUSNESS
AEGHIKNNRRRTTY KNIGHT-ERRANTRY	AEIILLNQRRSSTU TRANQUILLISERS
AEGHILNORSSTUV VAULTING HORSES	AEIILLNQRRSTUZ TRANQUILLIZERS
AEGHIMMNOOPRST METAMORPHOSING	AEIILMNNOPSSTU EMULSION PAINTS
AEGHLLMOOPPRSY MEGASPOROPHYLL	AEIILMNOOPRSTY POLYMERISATION
AEGHLNOOOOPRTUY NEUROPATHOLOGY	AEIILMNOOPRTYZ POLYMERIZATION
AEGHMMOOPRRTTY PHOTOGRAMMETRY	AEIILNNOOPRSTT INTERPOLATIONS
AEGHNNNOOORTTUY TURN ON THE AGONY	AEIILNNOPRSTUY UNIPERSONALITY
AEGIIIILMNOSTT LEGITIMISATION	AEIIMMNORSSTTY SYMMETRISATION
AEGIIIILMNOTTZ LEGITIMIZATION	AEIIMMNORSTTYZ SYMMETRIZATION
AEGIIIILNNORTTT TOILET TRAINING	AEIIMNNOOPRSST IMPERSONATIONS
AEGIIIILNNPRSWY AWE-INSPIRINGLY	AEIINNORRSSSTT TRANSITORINESS
AEGIIIIMNNORRTT INTERMIGRATION	AEIINOOPPRRSTX EXPROPRIATIONS
AEGIIINNNORSTTT INTEGRATIONIST	AEIINOPRRSSSTU PRESSURISATION
AEGIIINNOSSTTV INVESTIGATIONS	AEIINOPRRSSTUZ PRESSURIZATION
AEGIIKMNOPSSSV PASSIVE SMOKING	AEILLMNOSSTUUY SIMULTANEOUSLY
AEGIIKNOPRRSTW WORKING PARTIES	AEILLOOPPRRRTY PROPRIETORALLY
AEGIILLLNNRSTW ALL-IN WRESTLING	AEILMNOPRRSTUY SUPERNORMALITY
AEGIILLNTTTTTT TITTLE-TATTLING	AEILNOOOPPRTUV OVERPOPULATION

AEILNOOPRSSTTT PETROL STATIONS
AEILNOOPSSTTUX EXPOSTULATIONS
AEILNOOSSTTTUY OSTENTATIOUSLY
AEIMNNOOPPRSTT APPORTIONMENTS
AEINOORRSSSTTU TRAITOROUSNESS
AELLMNNOOOPPRT MONOPROPELLANT
AFFGHNNOOSSTUW SAWN-OFF SHOTGUN
AFGGHHIIRSSTTT STRAIGHT FIGHTS
AFGIIILLNNOSTT FILLING STATION
AFIIIMMNNOORST MISINFORMATION
AFIILLMORSTUUY MULTIFARIOUSLY
AGGHIIIKNNRSUU SINKIANG-UIGHUR
AGGHILNOOPRSTY PHARYNGOLOGIST
AGGIIILNNORTVY INVIGORATINGLY
AGGIILNNOPPRRS GRAPPLING IRONS
AGGLLNOOOORTYY OTOLARYNGOLOGY
AGHHIIOOPRRSTY HISTORIOGRAPHY
AGHHILOOOPSTTY HISTOPATHOLOGY
AGHHLOOOPPTTYY PHYTOPATHOLOGY
AGHIILMNPSTYYZ SYMPATHIZINGLY
AGHIINOOPPRSTZ APOSTROPHIZING
AGHILNOOOOPRSTT ANTHROPOLOGIST
AGIIILLNNQRTUZ TRANQUILLIZING
AGIIILNOSTUVVV VULVOVAGINITIS
AGIILLNNOOPSTT POLLING STATION
AGIILMNNNOSTTU NONSTIMULATING
AGINOPPPRRSTTU SUPPORTING PART
AGLMMOOOOPSTTYY SYMPTOMATOLOGY
AHHIILNOPPRSTT PHILANTHROPIST
AHHLLNOOPSTUXY XANTHOPHYLLOUS
AHIIIMMNOOOSSU HOMOIOUSIANISM
AHIILMNNOORSUY INHARMONIOUSLY
AHIILMOOPSSSST HISTOPLASMOSIS
AHIILNOPRSSTUU SULPHURISATION
AHIILNOPRSTUUZ SULPHURIZATION
AIIIILNOORSTTV VITRIOLISATION
AIIIILNOORTTVZ VITRIOLIZATION
AIIIMNOOPRSSTV IMPROVISATIONS
AIIIMNRSSSTTVY TRANSMISSIVITY
AIIINNNOOSTTUW NO-WIN SITUATION
AIIINNORSTTTUY INSTITUTIONARY
AIILMNNOOOOPST MONOPOLISATION
AIILMNNOOOOPTZ MONOPOLIZATION
AIILMNOOPRSSUY PARSIMONIOUSLY
AIILNOOOOPPSSTT POSTPOSITIONAL
AIINNOOPRSSSTT TRANSPOSITIONS
AILLNOOOOPPRRTY PROPORTIONALLY
BBBCGHINRRSSUU SCRUBBING BRUSH
BBCDEEIORRSSUV OVERSUBSCRIBED
BBCDGIIKLLNOSU BUILDING BLOCKS
BBCEGILMNORSTU CLUSTER BOMBING
BBCGIKLLMNOSTU STUMBLING BLOCK
BBCIIILMOSTTUY COMBUSTIBILITY
BBCILNOOOOPPRU PRO BONO PUBLICO
BBDEEGHIINRRSU RUBBER DINGHIES
BBDEEGILNOOOSU BOIS DE BOULOGNE
BBEEEGILLNOOSS NOBLESSE OBLIGE
BBEIIILMRSSTUY SUBMERSIBILITY
BCCCGIIIMNRRSU CIRCUMSCRIBING

BCCCIIMOOPRSSU SUBMICROSCOPIC
BCCDEEGHIKLNOU DOUBLE-CHECKING
BCCDEEIIJNORTT INDIRECT OBJECT
BCCEEEEGILRTTU ICEBERG LETTUCE
BCCEEIKKKNORRS KNICKERBOCKERS
BCCEIIIJSSTTUV SUBJECTIVISTIC
BCCHINOOOOPRSST BRONCHOSCOPIST
BCCILNOOSSSUUY SUBCONSCIOUSLY
BCDEEEEILRRSTT STREET-CREDIBLE
BCDEEHHNOORSUU BOUCHES-DU-RHONE
BCDEEHILLLOOTW WHITE BLOOD CELL
BCDEEIILNRSTTU INDESTRUCTIBLE
BCDEELOORRSSSU DOUBLE-CROSSERS
BCDEEMOOOOPPRTT COPPER-BOTTOMED
BCDEGILNOORSSU DOUBLE-CROSSING
BCDEIIIILRRTUY IRREDUCIBILITY
BCDEIIIILPPRSTU PUBLIC-SPIRITED
BCDEIILNRSTTUY INDESTRUCTIBLY
BCEEEEFKNOORRS REFERENCE BOOKS
BCEEEHILMNOPRS COMPREHENSIBLE
BCEEEILNOPRSWY EYEBROW PENCILS
BCEEFIIILPRTTY PERFECTIBILITY
BCEEGIILLLNNPU BLUE-PENCILLING
BCEEGIMNNNOSSU UNBECOMINGNESS
BCEEHIILNOPRSY HYPERBOLIC SINE
BCEEHILMNOPRSY COMPREHENSIBLY
BCEEIILPPRTTY PERCEPTIBILITY
BCEEIILMNNOSTU BIOLUMINESCENT
BCEEIILMNOPRSS INCOMPRESSIBLE
BCEEILNOORRTTV CONTROVERTIBLE
BCEEIMNNPRSTUU SUPERINCUMBENT
BCEFHIKLOOOSTT LICK THE BOOTS OF
BCEFHIMNOOOSTT FINE-TOOTH COMBS
BCEFJMOOOORRSST JOB'S COMFORTERS
BCEIIILNORTTVY CONVERTIBILITY
BCEIIILPSSTTUY SUSCEPTIBILITY
BCFGIIMMNNOORS COMBINING FORMS
BCGIIILMOOOORST MICROBIOLOGIST
BCIIILOPRRTTUY CORRUPTIBILITY
BCIIMNOORSSTTU OBSTRUCTIONISM
BCIINOORSSTTTU OBSTRUCTIONIST
BCIKMNNOPRTUUY COUNTRY BUMPKIN
BDDEEEELNNORTU DOUBLE ENTENDRE
BDDEEEILNOOPRX PEROXIDE BLONDE
BDDEFFIINORRTU FORBIDDEN FRUIT
BDDEFGIINNORSS FORBIDDINGNESS
BDEEEFGILNOSTT FEEDING BOTTLES
BDEEEGIJLLNOSU GOLDEN JUBILEES
BDEEEGIMMNOSTU DISEMBOGUEMENT
BDEEEHHIIMNSTT BEHIND THE TIMES
BDEEEHINORTTTT TO THE BITTER END
BDEEEIINNNORTZ DINITROBENZENE
BDEEEILMMNOSTW DISEMBOWELMENT
BDEEFILMNPRRSU PLUMBER'S FRIEND
BDEEGGHILMNOST THE MIND BOGGLES
BDEEGIIILLNSVY DISBELIEVINGLY
BDEEGIILLMNOSW DISEMBOWELLING
BDEEGILLNRSTUW TUNBRIDGE WELLS
BDEEIMNOOOORRTW ON BORROWED TIME

BDEELOOPRRSSSU BLOOD PRESSURES
BDEGHHINOOORSU NEIGHBOURHOODS
BDEGHIILNNNSST NIGHT BLINDNESS
BDEGIIINRRSTTU REDISTRIBUTING
BDEIIIILMQRSUU DISEQUILIBRIUM
BDEIIIILNSSTTY DISTENSIBILITY
BDEIIILNNOSSSU LIBIDINOUSNESS
BDEIIILNPSSTUY SUSPENDIBILITY
BDEIIILRSTTUVY DISTRIBUTIVELY
BDEIIINORRSTTU REDISTRIBUTION
BDGIILNNOOOOPS BLOOD POISONING
BDHIILLOORSTTY BLOODTHIRSTILY
BDIIIIILNSTVY INDIVISIBILITY
BEEEEEHLNOOPSTX TELEPHONE BOXES
BEEEELMNORSTUV BOULEVERSEMENT
BEEEFFGIINNRST FRINGE BENEFITS
BEEEFFGIKNOOST GET OFF ONE'S BIKE
BEEEGGIIINNNOR BIOENGINEERING
BEEEHHLNOOOOPTT TELEPHONE BOOTH
BEEEHILLMMNSST EMBELLISHMENTS
BEEEHILORRRSTW WHORTLEBERRIES
BEEEIIJLLRSSUV SILVER JUBILEES
BEEEIILNORSSSU REBELLIOUSNESS
BEEEIMMNRRSSTU REIMBURSEMENTS
BEEEINRSSSSUVV SUBVERSIVENESS
BEEEELLNOOOSSTT LOSE ONE'S BOTTLE
BEEGIIILLLNNTU UNINTELLIGIBLE
BEEGIIOOPRSTTU PETIT BOURGEOIS
BEEGIOOPRSTTUY PETTY BOURGEOIS
BEEHHHILMNTTTU HUNT THE THIMBLE
BEEHLOOOORRSTTU TROUBLESHOOTER
BEEIILNOSSTVWY LIVE BY ONE'S WITS
BEEIILNPPRSSSU INSUPPRESSIBLE
BEEIILOPRSSTVX VISIBLE EXPORTS
BEEIIMNSSSSSUV SUBMISSIVENESS
BEEIKMNNOSSSUY MONKEY BUSINESS
BEEIMNOOPPRSTU OPPOSITE NUMBER
BEEINOOQSSSSUU OBSEQUIOUSNESS
BEEINOORSSSSTU BOISTEROUSNESS
BEELMNORSSSSUU SLUMBEROUSNESS
BEELOOPPRSSTUY OBSTREPEROUSLY
BEFFGINNORRSTU BURNT OFFERINGS
BEFGILNRSSTTUY FLYING BUTTRESS
BEGGIIILSSTTUY SUGGESTIBILITY
BEGGILNOORSTTT GLOBETROTTINGS
BEGHNOOOORRSTTU ROTTEN BOROUGHS
BEGILNORSSSUUU LUGUBRIOUSNESS
BEHHIKNOOPSTTU PUT THE KIBOSH ON
BEHIIIINOSSTTX EXHIBITIONISTS
BEIIIILMPRSSTY PERMISSIBILITY
BEIIIILLORRSTUY IRRESOLUBILITY
BEIIIILMOPRSSTV VISIBLE IMPORTS
BEIIIILNOPRSSTY RESPONSIBILITY
BEIINOQSSSTUUU UBIQUITOUSNESS
BELOPRRSSSSTUU BRUSSELS SPROUT
BGIILLMMNNOOUU IMMUNOGLOBULIN
BHIIIIMNOOPRST PROHIBITIONISM
BHIIIINOOPRSTT PROHIBITIONIST
CCCDEEEENRRSSU RECRUDESCENCES

CCCDEEHIIOOPRT CERCOPITHECOID
CCCDGILOOOORRTU GLUCOCORTICORD
CCCEEEFIMNRRSU CIRCUMFERENCES
CCCEEEHHHIINNR CHINCHERINCHEE
CCCEEEIIINRSTT ECCENTRICITIES
CCCEEFIIINNOST SCIENCE FICTION
CCCEHHINOPSSTY PSYCHOTECHNICS
CCCEIIILMRSSSU CIRCUMSCISSILE
CCCEIIILORSSUV VICIOUS CIRCLES
CCCEEIIMMNOOORS MICROECONOMICS
CCCEEIIMNOPRSTU CIRCUMSPECTION
CCCIIIMORRRTUY MICROCIRCUITRY
CCCIILMNOORTUU CIRCUMLOCUTION
CCCILMOORRTUUY CIRCUMLOCUTORY
CCCILNNOOSTUUY COUNTY COUNCILS
CCDDEEEELLMNNOS CONDEMNED CELLS
CCDDEEILNNOSTY DISCONNECTEDLY
CCDEEEEIIILLRST DIESEL-ELECTRIC
CCDEEEEFFILNNOS SELF-CONFIDENCE
CCDEEEHIINPRST INDIRECT SPEECH
CCDEEEIINNNNOV INCONVENIENCED
CCDEEEIINPRSVY VICE-PRESIDENCY
CCDEEEENNOOPRRS CORRESPONDENCE
CCDEEGIIILNNRV DRIVING LICENCE
CCDEGIILNNOOOR ENDOCRINOLOGIC
CCDEGINNNOORST CONNECTING RODS
CCDEHHILLNOORS SCHOOLCHILDREN
CCDEHIIORRSTTU SHORT-CIRCUITED
CCDEIIINPRRTTU PRINTED CIRCUIT
CCDEIIMNNOOSTU SEMICONDUCTION
CCDEIINNNOOSST DISCONNECTIONS
CCDEIIOOOORRSTT CORTICOSTEROID
CCDEIMNOORSSTU SEMICONDUCTORS
CCDENOOPRRSTUU SUPERCONDUCTOR
CCDGIIIMOOOPSS SIGMOIDOSCOPIC
CCDHHHOOOORRTUX ORTHODOX CHURCH
CCDHNOOOOPRTTU PHOTOCONDUCTOR
CCEEEEEJNNRSUV REJUVENESCENCE
CCEEEEFHIITUVX CHIEF EXECUTIVE
CCEEEEFNNNORSW NEWS CONFERENCE
CCEEEEFNORRRSS CROSS-REFERENCE
CCEEEEMMMNNORT RECOMMENCEMENT
CCEEEFIIOPRSST STEREOSPECIFIC
CCEEEGJLNNORTU CONCRETE JUNGLE
CCEEEHILMORRTT THERMOELECTRIC
CCEEEHILMORSTT ELECTROCHEMIST
CCEEEIIKLNORTT ELECTROKINETIC
CCEEEIINNNNOSV INCONVENIENCES
CCEEEIMNORRSTX CONCRETE MIXERS
CCEEEINSSSSSUV SUCCESSIVENESS
CCEEFFIILOOPRS POLICE OFFICERS
CCEEFFIILOORST CORIOLIS EFFECT
CCEEFHIINOPRST CHIEF INSPECTOR
CCEEFLÑSSSSSUU SUCCESSFULNESS
CCEEGHHHINNOSU CHECHENO-INGUSH
CCEEGIILLOOSST ECCLESIOLOGIST
CCEEHHIMNOSTTY CHEMOSYNTHETIC
CCEEHIINORTTTY THEOCENTRICITY
CCEEHILOOPRSTU HEROIC COUPLETS

CCEEHIMNNORRSY CHIMNEY CORNERS
CCEEHINOPRSSTY PYROTECHNICSES
CCEEIINNOSSTTU CONSTITUENCIES
CCEEIILLMOORSTT COLLECTOR'S ITEM
CCEEIILLNNOOTUV COLLECTIVE NOUN
CCEEILNOORSTTU ELECTROCUTIONS
CCEEINNOOPPRST PRECONCEPTIONS
CCEEINOOOORRSTT CORTICOSTERONE
CCEEINOOPRRSUW OWNER-OCCUPIERS
CCEEINOOPRSSSU PRECOCIOUSNESS
CCEEINORRSTTUV RECONSTRUCTIVE
CCEGHIIKNNPRSS SPRING CHICKENS
CCEGIILNNRRSTU TURNING CIRCLES
CCEGINNORRSTTU RECONSTRUCTING
CCEHHIIKOSSSTW SCOTCH WHISKIES
CCEHHIINOPRSSZ SCHIZOPHRENICS
CCEHHIOOPSSUYZ SCHIZOPHYCEOUS
CCEHIIIMOORSTT STOICHIOMETRIC
CCEHIIMMORRSTY MICROCHEMISTRY
CCEHIMMNOSTTUY COMMUNITY CHEST
CCEHIMOOSSTUYZ SCHIZOMYCETOUS
CCEHINOOPRSTUY PSYCHONEUROTIC
CCEIILLNNOSUVY INCONCLUSIVELY
CCEIIMNNOOPSST MISCONCEPTIONS
CCEILNORSTTUVY CONSTRUCTIVELY
CCEILOOOORRSSTU STERCORICOLOUS
CCEIMMOOPRRSTU MICROCOMPUTERS
CCEIMOOOPRRRSS MICROPROCESSOR
CCEIMORRRSTTUU MICROSTRUCTURE
CCEINNOOPRRSST PRINCES CONSORT
CCEINNOORRSTTU RECONSTRUCTION
CCEINOORRSSSTU CROSS-COUNTRIES
CCEIOOPPRSSSTT SPECTROSCOPIST
CCGHIILOOPSSTY PSYCHOLOGISTIC
CCGIILNNNNOUVY UNCONVINCINGLY
CCHIINOOOPRRTT CORTICOTROPHIN
CCHIIOPRRRTVYY PYRRHIC VICTORY
CCIIIJNNOSTTUV CONJUNCTIVITIS
CCIIIILPRSSTTUU PISCICULTURIST
CCIILMNOORTUUV CIRCUMVOLUTION
CCIIMNORSSTTUV CONSTRUCTIVISM
CCIINORSSTTTUV CONSTRUCTIVIST
CCILMOORRTUUVY CIRCUMVOLUTORY
CCINNOORSSTUUY COUNTRY COUSINS
CDDDEEHLLOORSU COLD SHOULDERED
CDDEEEFLRSSTTU SELF-DESTRUCTED
CDDEEEELLMNOTUW WELL-DOCUMENTED
CDDEEILNNOSTTY DISCONTENTEDLY
CDDEGHIIILOPRS CHILD PRODIGIES
CDDEHIILMOORSU SODIUM CHLORIDE
CDDEILNOOOSTUY DICOTYLEDONOUS
CDEEEEEINNQSUV QUEEN'S EVIDENCE
CDEEEEEHOPPRRST REPORTED SPEECH
CDEEEEEILNPRSTT PRESIDENT-ELECT
CDEEEEIORSTTTV STORE DETECTIVE
CDEEEEEIQRSSTUZ CREDIT SQUEEZES
CDEEEENNPSSTUX UNEXPECTEDNESS
CDEEEFGILLNNSU SELF-INDULGENCE
CDEEEFILORRTTT LETTER OF CREDIT

CDEEEFIMNNOPRS PRESENCE OF MIND
CDEEEGILNNORUV OVERINDULGENCE
CDEEEIIMMNOOSX MIXED ECONOMIES
CDEEEIINNRRSSV DINNER SERVICES
CDEEEILOOPRSTT ELECTRODEPOSIT
CDEEEINRRSSSTT RESTRICTEDNESS
CDEEEELNNNOOORT NOLO CONTENDERE
CDEEEENNNOQRUUW UNCROWNED QUEEN
CDEEEFGHINNRRSS FRENCH DRESSING
CDEEEFHHILNOPRS FRENCH POLISHED
CDEEEFIIILLNPSS SELF-DISCIPLINE
CDEEEFLLLNOORST SELF-CONTROLLED
CDEEEGGINNOSSSU SECOND-GUESSING
CDEEEHILNNORSSW CHINLESS WONDER
CDEEEHLLLOORSUY HYDROCELLULOSE
CDEEEIIINNSSTVV VINDICTIVENESS
CDEEEIIINOPPRST EDITIO PRINCEPS
CDEEEIINRSSSSUV DISCURSIVENESS
CDEEEILLNOOPTUY POLYNUCLEOTIDE
CDEEEILMOOPPSUX OEDIPUS COMPLEX
CDEEEIMNNNOSTTT DISCONTENTMENT
CDEEEINNOORSSSU INDECOROUSNESS
CDEEEINOPRSSTUV PRODUCTIVENESS
CDEEEKKLNRSSTUU KNUCKLE-DUSTERS
CDEEENNOOPRRSST CORRESPONDENTS
CDEEFIIIMMMOSSU FIDEICOMMISSUM
CDEEFOOOOPRRSSS FOOD PROCESSORS
CDEEGHHIIILNPPR HIGH-PRINCIPLED
CDEEGHHILLOORUY HIGHLY COLOURED
CDEEGHHNOOSSTTU SECOND THOUGHTS
CDEEGIIINNNOORT RECONDITIONING
CDEEGINOOPRRSSW WORD PROCESSING
CDEEHILMNNOOPTT HOLD IN CONTEMPT
CDEEHINOOOORRSTY HYDROCORTISONE
CDEEIIIILRSTTUV DIVERTICULITIS
CDEEIIILORSSTUV DIVERTICULOSIS
CDEEIIINNNSSSTT INDISTINCTNESS
CDEEIILNNOOPRTU PRODUCTION LINE
CDEEIILNORSSSUU RIDICULOUSNESS
CDEEIINNOORRTTU REINTRODUCTION
CDEEIINNOPRSSUU UNDER SUSPICION
CDEEIINNOPRSTUU SUPERINDUCTION
CDEEIINOPRSTUWW PICTURE WINDOWS
CDEEIINORSSTTTU DESTRUCTIONIST
CDEEILOORSSTUUY DISCOURTEOUSLY
CDEEINOOOPRRTUV OVERPRODUCTION
CDEEINOORSSSTTU DISCOUNT STORES
CDEEOOOPRRRSSSW WORD PROCESSORS
CDFIINNOOOOTTU OUT OF CONDITION
CDGIILMNOOPSSY DISCOMPOSINGLY
CDHHILLLOOOPRY CHLOROPHYLLOID
CDHINOOOOPRSSTT PROSTHODONTICS
CDIIJNNNNOOSTU NONDISJUNCTION
CDIILMMNOOOSUY INCOMMODIOUSLY
CDIILNOORRTTUY INTRODUCTORILY
CEEEEFFLNRSTVY EFFERVESCENTLY
CEEEEFILNRSSTV REFLECTIVENESS
CEEEEFNPPRRSTT PRESENT PERFECT
CEEEEGIILNNORT ELECTIONEERING

CEEEEHLNPSSSSS SPEECHLESSNESS
CEEEEFFGHIOPRSU FIGURE OF SPEECH
CEEEEFFGIIORRST REGISTER OFFICE
CEEEEFFGILNRSVY EFFERVESCINGLY
CEEEEFFLLPRSSTU SELF-RESPECTFUL
CEEEEFGILNPRSST SELF-RESPECTING
CEEEEFGLLNNSSTU NEGLECTFULNESS
CEEEEFIIOPRRSTV IRRESPECTIVE OF
CEEEEFIMNNORRST REINFORCEMENTS
CEEEEFINORRSTTU COUNTERFEITERS
CEEEEFLNPRSSSTU RESPECTFULNESS
CEEEEFNOORSSTUV VOTES OF CENSURE
CEEEEGGINORRSTU GEIGER COUNTERS
CEEEEGIIILNNRSV CIVIL ENGINEERS
CEEEEGIIILLNNNTU UNINTELLIGENCE
CEEEEGIIMNOPRST SPERMIOGENETIC
CEEEEGILNORRTTV COVERING LETTER
CEEEEGLORRRSTUY ELECTROSURGERY
CEEEEHIKNNOPPSU KEEP ONE'S CHIN UP
CEEEEHIMNOPRSSV COMPREHENSIVES
CEEEEHIMORSSTTY HYSTERECTOMIES
CEEEEHKMNNORSWY MONKEY WRENCHES
CEEEEHLMNOORRTT THERMOELECTRON
CEEEEHNOORRTTUV OVER THE COUNTER
CEEEEIIKNNPRSST PERNICKETINESS
CEEEEIIMMOORRTT MICROMETEORITE
CEEEEILMMNOPRST COMPLEMENTISER
CEEEEILMMNOPRTZ COMPLEMENTIZER
CEEEEILMNNOPSST INCOMPLETENESS
CEEEEIMMNNOPRTV PINCER MOVEMENT
CEEEEINOPRSSTTV PROTECTIVENESS
CEEEEIOPRRSSTTV RETROSPECTIVES
CEEEEKOOPRRRSSU PRESSURE COOKER
CEEELNNOQSSSUU QUEEN'S COUNSELS
CEEEEMNNORRSTUU COUNTERMENSURE
CEEEENNOPPPRRRT PEPPERCORN RENT
CEEFFFIILNSSTU SELF-SUFFICIENT
CEEFFGIIORRSTY REGISTRY OFFICE
CEEFGIIINNORTTU COUNTERFEITING
CEEFGINORRRRSS CROSS-REFERRING
CEEFHIILMNNOSU ICHNEUMON FLIES
CEEFIILNOSSSTU FELICITOUSNESS
CEEFIILORRSSST CROSS-FERTILISE
CEEFIILORRSSTZ CROSS-FERTILIZE
CEEFIINNOSSSTU INFECTIOUSNESS
CEEFIINOPRSSTT PERFECTIONISTS
CEEFILNOOPRSTT SELF-PROTECTION
CEEFINOOOOPSTV TOP OF ONE'S VOICE
CEEFINOORSSSUV VOCIFEROUSNESS
CEEGHINNOPPRST SHOPPING CENTRE
CEEGIILNNORRTY NITROGLYCERINE
CEEGIIMMNNOSTU IMMUNOGENETICS
CEEGIINNNPRRST SCREEN PRINTING
CEEGILLLLNOOSU LIGNOCELLULOSE
CEEGILLNORSSS LEVEL CROSSINGS
CEEHHIMNOSSSTY CHEMOSYNTHESIS
CEEHHMOOORRSTU HETEROCHROMOUS
CEEHHNOOPPRSST PHOSPHORESCENT
CEEHHNORSSSTTU HORSE CHESTNUTS

CEEHIILMOPRRTY PYRHELIOMETRIC
CEEHIIMOPRSTYZ PIEZOCHEMISTRY
CEEHIIOOPRRTTY ERYTHROPOIETIC
CEEHIMMOPSSSTY METEMPSYCHOSIS
CEEHIMNNOOPRSS COMPREHENSIONS
CEEHIMNNORSSTT ETHNOCENTRISMS
CEEHIMOPRRSTTY PETROCHEMISTRY
CEEHNOPRSSTTUW PUT THE SCREWS ON
CEEIIILMRSSSSU CRUISE MISSILES
CEEIIIMPPRTTVY IMPERCEPTIVITY
CEEIIINNORSSST SENIOR CITISENS
CEEIIINNORSSTZ SENIOR CITIZENS
CEEIILLMNORSTT SCINTILLOMETER
CEEIILMORRSTUY MERETRICIOUSLY
CEEIILNNNNOTVY INCONVENIENTLY
CEEIILNNOSSSTU LICENTIOUSNESS
CEEIILNORSSTTW WINTER SOLSTICE
CEEIILPPRRSTVY PRESCRIPTIVELY
CEEIINNOPRSSSU PERNICIOUSNESS
CEEIIMNNORRSTV NONRESTRICTIVE
CEEIIOOPPPRRTV PROPRIOCEPTIVE
CEEIKLNOORSTTT SILK-COTTON TREE
CEEIKNORRRRSTT TERROR-STRICKEN
CEEILLLNOORSTU NITROCELLULOSE
CEEILMMORSSSTU SUMMER SOLSTICE
CEEILMNOPSSSUV COMPULSIVENESS
CEEILMNOSSSTUU METICULOUSNESS
CEEILNORRSSTTU INTERLOCUTRESS
CEEILNORRSSUYY YOURS SINCERELY
CEEIMMOOPRRRTY MICROPYROMETER
CEEIMNOOOOPRRST RECEPTION ROOMS
CEEINNOORSSSSU CENSORIOUSNESS
CEEINNOSSSSTUU INCESTUOUSNESS
CEEINOOOPRRTTV OVERPROTECTION
CEEINOOPRSSSTU PRECIOUS STONES
CEELLNOORSSSSU COLOURLESSNESS
CEEMNNNOOPRSTU PRONOUNCEMENTS
CEEPRRRSSTTUUU SUPERSTRUCTURE
CEFFFGIILNORSY FLYING OFFICERS
CEFFIIILLNNOST SELF-INFLICTION
CEFFIIILNNSTUY INSUFFICIENTLY
CEFGHIMNOORSUZ GNOMES OF ZÜRICH
CEFGIIKLLNORST STOCKING-FILLER
CEFHMMNOOOOSSU HOUSE OF COMMONS
CEFIIINOSSSTTU FICTITIOUSNESS
CEGGHHHILNOOTY HIGH TECHNOLOGY
CEGGIINNNORSTU COUNTERSIGNING
CEGHIJNOOPRSTU HOUSING PROJECT
CEGHIMMNPRSSTU SPRECHSTIMMUNG
CEGHINNOOSSTUU COUNTINGHOUSES
CEGIIILNOORSST CORELIGIONISTS
CEGIIKNNNORSTU COUNTERSINKING
CEGIIMNOPRSTUV MOVING PICTURES
CEGIINNOOPRSTU COUNTERPOISING
CEGIINNORSTTTU RECONSTITUTING
CEHHIIMORSSTTY HISTOCHEMISTRY
CEHHIMMNOOOPPR MORPHOPHONEMIC
CEHHIMOOPRSTTY PHOTOCHEMISTRY
CEHHINOOPSTTTY PHOTOSYNTHETIC

CEHHOOOOPPPRSS PHOSPHOROSCOPE
CEHIINOPRRSTTT STREPTOTHRICIN
CEHIJMNNOORTTU THERMOJUNCTION
CEHIKNOORRRRST HORROR-STRICKEN
CEHILMMOOPRSUY MYRMECOPHILOUS
CEHILMOORSSSST SCHOOLMISTRESS
CEHIMMMNOOSTUY COMMUNITY HOMES
CEHINOOPRSSSUY PSYCHONEUROSIS
CEHLNOORRSSSUY NURSERY SCHOOLS
CEIIIINOSSTTVV VIVISECTIONIST
CEIIILNOOSTTUV EVOLUTIONISTIC
CEIIIMPPRRSSTV PRESCRIPTIVISM
CEIIINORRSSTTT RESTRICTIONIST
CEIIIPPRRSSTTV PRESCRIPTIVIST
CEIIJNOOPRSSTT PROJECTIONISTS
CEIILLOPRSSUUY SUPERCILIOUSLY
CEIILNNNOSSTTY INCONSISTENTLY
CEIILNOORRRSTT TRINITROCRESOL
CEIILNOOSSSSTU SOLICITOUSNESS
CEIIMMNNNOORTU INTERCOMMUNION
CEIIMNNOOOPSSU PNEUMOCONIOSIS
CEIIMNOOPRSTTU MOTION PICTURES
CEIINNOORSTTTU RECONSTITUTION
CEIINOOPRSSTTT PROTECTIONISTS
CEIINOORSSSTUV VICTORIOUSNESS
CEIINOPPRRSSTU SUPERSCRIPTION
CEIINOPRSSSSTU PERCUSSIONISTS
CEIINOPSSSSSUU SUSPICIOUSNESS
CEILLMNOOSTUUY CONTUMELIOUSLY
CEILNOPRRSTUUV PROVENTRICULUS
CEILNORRSSSSUU SCURRILOUSNESS
CEIMMMMOOORTTY COMMIT TO MEMORY
CEKLMOOPRSTTUU MOCK TURTLE SOUP
CELMNOOPSTTUUY CONTEMPTUOUSLY
CELNOPRSSSSUUU SCRUPULOUSNESS
CFFHIILMNOSTTU FIFTH COLUMNIST
CFFIKKLORRSTTU FORKLIFT TRUCKS
CFIILLORRSTTUU FLORICULTURIST
CFIINOOQRRTUUY COURT OF INQUIRY
CFIMNNNOOORSST NONCONFORMISTS
CGHHIIIMMNOOSS HIGH COMMISSION
CGHIIKNOOSSSTT SHOOTING STICKS
CGHIILNOPSSTUY PSYCHOLINGUIST
CGHILOOOOPSTYY PHYTOSOCIOLOGY
CGIIIKNNOPSSTT STICKING POINTS
CGIIILMNOORSST CRIMINOLOGISTS
CGIIILNNRSTUYZ SCRUTINIZINGLY
CGIILNOOOPSST OLIGOPSONISTIC
CGIIMMNNOOPRSU UNCOMPROMISING
CHHKNOORSSTTUW NOT WORTH SHUCKS
CHHLLLOOOOPRSUY CHLOROPHYLLOUS
CHIILORRSTTTUU HORTICULTURIST
CHIINOPRRSSTTU INSTRUCTORSHIP
CHIIOOOORSSTTXY THYROTOXICOSIS
CHILMOOORSTTUY TRICHOTOMOUSLY
CIIILLRSSTTUUV SILVICULTURIST
CIINNOOORSSTTT CONTORTIONISTS
CLLNOPRSSUUUUY UNSCRUPULOUSLY
DDDEEGGILNNOSW GOLDEN WEDDINGS

DDEEEEEGNRRSWY DYER'S-GREENWEED
DDEEEEIMNNRSST DETERMINEDNESS
DDEEEEINNNPRTT INTERDEPENDENT
DDEEEELMMNOSSS MEDDLESOMENESS
DDEEEIIKLMNNSS LIKE-MINDEDNESS
DDEEEIILMNNSSV EVIL-MINDEDNESS
DDEEEIINQSSSTU DISQUIETEDNESS
DDEEEIMNNNOPSS OPEN-MINDEDNESS
DDEEEIMNNNORTU UNDERMENTIONED
DDEEGHHIIMNNSS HIGH-MINDEDNESS
DDEEGIIILMSSSU GUIDED MISSILES
DDEEGIILLMNNSY SINGLE-MINDEDLY
DDEEGIILNRSSVW SILVER WEDDINGS
DDEEGILNNNOSSW LONGWINDEDNESS
DDEEHINNORRSUU UNDERNOURISHED
DDEEIIJNNOSSST DISJOINTEDNESS
DDEEIILNORRSSS DISORDERLINESS
DDEEINNOPSSSUW UPSIDE-DOWNNESS
DDEGGHINNOSTUW SHOTGUN WEDDING
DDEGHLMOOORUUY GOOD-HUMOUREDLY
DDEGIINNORSSWW WINDOW DRESSING
DDEGILMNNORSTY STRONG-MINDEDLY
DDEHIILNOPSSSS SLIPSHODDINESS
DDEHIMNNOPSTUW DOWN IN THE DUMPS
DEEEEFFGIRRRSZ FRIDGE-FREEZERS
DEEEEFILNRSSTT SELF-INTERESTED
DEEEEGHHNORTTT TO THE NTH DEGREE
DEEEEGINNRSSSV EVENING DRESSES
DEEEEHMNORRRTV REVEREND MOTHER
DEEEEILLMMOSSS MESDEMOISELLES
DEEEEIMNPRRRST PREDETERMINERS
DEEEEIMNPRRSST MISREPRESENTED
DEEEEINRSSTTTV VESTED INTEREST
DEEEELMNOPRSTV REDEVELOPMENTS
DEEEENNRRSSSUV UNRESERVEDNESS
DEEEEFFGOORRSST DEGREES OF FROST
DEEEFIIINNNSST INDEFINITENESS
DEEEFILNNRSSSS FRIENDLESSNESS
DEEEFNOORSSSTU SUREFOOTEDNESS
DEEEGIIKLNNNTT KNITTING NEEDLE
DEEEGIIMNNPRRT PREDETERMINING
DEEEGILNOOPRVV OVERDEVELOPING
DEEEGIOPRRSSTT REGISTERED POST
DEEEHHLOORSTTT THREE-TOED SLOTH
DEEEHHPPRRSSSU SHEPHERD'S-PURSE
DEEEHLLMOOOPPS OLD PEOPLE'S HOME
DEEEHLMNNOOSWY HONEYDEW MELONS
DEEEIIMNPRRSTT MISINTERPRETED
DEEEIIMNRSSTTV DIVERTISSEMENT
DEEEIINORRSSVV REVISED VERSION
DEEEILNPRRSSTY INTERSPERSEDLY
DEEEINNNPRSTTU SUPERINTENDENT
DEEEINOQSSTUVX VEXED QUESTIONS
DEEELLNNORRSSU ENROLLED NURSES
DEEEMNNORSSSTU TREMENDOUSNESS
DEEFFFINORRSST FIRST OFFENDERS
DEEFFIIIMMNNRST INDIFFERENTISM
DEEFFIIINNRSTT INDIFFERENTIST
DEEFGHILLNSSTU DELIGHTFULNESS

DEEFGHINOORSTW THE WRONG SIDE OF
DEEFGIIMNRSSTU DISFIGUREMENTS
DEEFIIILMOPRSV OVERSIMPLIFIED
DEEFIILNNNRSSU UNFRIENDLINESS
DEEFIINOPRSSSU PERFIDIOUSNESS
DEEFILOORRSTUY DO-IT-YOURSELFER
DEEFLOORRRTTUW FOUR-LETTER WORD
DEEGHILLNOSSUW DWELLING HOUSES
DEEGIIILMOOPST EPIDEMIOLOGIST
DEEGIINNNOSSSU INDIGENOUSNESS
DEEGIINNNPRSTU SUPERINTENDING
DEEGILMNNRSTTU DISGRUNTLEMENT
DEEGLNNORSSSSU GROUNDLESSNESS
DEEHHIOOPPRRSW HERO WORSHIPPED
DEEHNNOORRSSSU HORRENDOUSNESS
DEEIIIILMRSTUV VERISIMILITUDE
DEEIIILNOPRSTV VESPERTILIONID
DEEIILNOORSTUV REVOLUTIONISED
DEEIILNOORTUVZ REVOLUTIONIZED
DEEKNOOPPRRSTV DNEPROPETROVSK
DEENNOOOOPRSST ON ONE'S DOORSTEP
DEENNOPSSSSTUU STUPENDOUSNESS
DEFFIIILNOOSSV FIELDS OF VISION
DEFHILLNOQTTUU NOT THE FULL QUID
DEGHHIIILMNOTT THE MIDNIGHT OIL
DEGHHIIKLRSTTU TURKISH DELIGHT
DEGHHILORSSTTY SHORTSIGHTEDLY
DEGHILNOORSSYY HYDROGENOLYSIS
DEGIIKLNNNOSSV LOVING KINDNESS
DEGIILNNOORRSS SOLDERING IRONS
DEGIILNNOSSUUY DISINGENUOUSLY
DEGIINOOPRSSSU PRODIGIOUSNESS
DEGILNOORSSTUY SOUL-DESTROYING
DEHIIMOOOPPRST PHOTOPERIODISM
DEHIMMOOPPRSSU PSEUDOMORPHISM
DEHINOOPPRSSWW WINDOW-SHOPPERS
DEIIINOOPPRSST PREDISPOSITION
DEIILOOPPRRSTY POOR-SPIRITEDLY
DEIIMNNNRSTTUW WIND INSTRUMENT
DEILMNOOOPSSTU DIPLOSTEMONOUS
DEILNNOPRSSUU SUN IN SPLENDOUR
DEILNORSSSSTUU STRIDULOUSNESS
DEINNNOSSSTTUU STUDENTS' UNIONS
DFGGHINNOOOORT GOOD-FOR-NOTHING
DGGHIIIINNSSTU DISTINGUISHING
DGGHINNNORSTUU HUNTING GROUNDS
DGGINNOOPRRSUV PROVING GROUNDS
DGHIINNOOPPSWW WINDOW-SHOPPING
DGIIIILLNNOSSU DISILLUSIONING
DHINOOOPRSSTTT PROSTHODONTIST
DIIIINNOOPSSST INDISPOSITIONS
EEEEEFINPRRRST FREE ENTERPRISE
EEEEEKMNOPPRST KEEP ONE'S TEMPER
EEEEELPRSTTTTY TELETYPESETTER
EEEEFHINNOORTY ONE IN THE EYE FOR
EEEEFILPRRRSSV LIFE PRESERVERS
EEEEFIMNORRRTT INTERFEROMETER
EEEEGHILNRSSTW STEERING WHEELS
EEEEGINRRSSSSV REGRESSIVENESS

EEEEGJLLORRSUW JEWELLER'S ROUGE
EEEEHKLLRRSSTT HELTER-SKELTERS
EEEEIINPRSSTTV REPETITIVENESS
EEEEIMNPRRRSST MISREPRESENTER
EEEEINNPRSSTVV PREVENTIVENESS
EEEEINPRRSSSSV REPRESSIVENESS
EEEEINPRSSSSVX EXPRESSIVENESS
EEEELLNNRSSSST RELENTLESSNESS
EEEELMNOOPRSST LOSE ONE'S TEMPER
EEEFFLNORSSSST EFFORTLESSNESS
EEEFGLMNNORSTV SELF-GOVERNMENT
EEEFIMNORRRTTY INTERFEROMETRY
EEEFLLMMNOPSTY SELF-EMPLOYMENT
EEEFLLNORRSTTU FORTUNE-TELLERS
EEEFLMNORRSSSU REMORSEFULNESS
EEEFLNNNSSTUUV UNEVENTFULNESS
EEEGGINSSSSTUV SUGGESTIVENESS
EEEGHILNSSSSTW WEIGHTLESSNESS
EEEGIIMNOPRSSS SPERMIOGENESIS
EEEHHIILNPRSTW THREE-LINE WHIPS
EEEHHILMOPPSST MEPHISTOPHELES
EEEHIINPRSSTVY HYPERSENSITIVE
EEEHINNOSSTTTX SIXTEENTH NOTES
EEEIILMNOPSSST IMPOLITENESSES
EEEIILMNPRSSTT SIMPLE INTEREST
EEEIIMNPRRRSTT MISINTERPRETER
EEEIIMNPRSSSSV IMPRESSIVENESS,
  PERMISSIVENESS
EEEILMNOSSSSTV MOTIVELESSNESS
EEEILNOPRSSSSX EXPRESSIONLESS
EEEIMNOPPRRSST PEREMPTORINESS
EEEINNOPRSSSSV RESPONSIVENESS
EEEINNPSSSSSUV SUSPENSIVENESS
EEEINOPPRSSSSV OPPRESSIVENESS
EEEINOPSSSSSSV POSSESSIVENESS
EEEJLLLMOPRTUY PETROLEUM JELLY
EEEMMMNNOOSTVW WOMEN'S
  MOVEMENT
EEEOPRRRSSSSTU TROUSER PRESSES
EEFFGGHIIORSTU FIGURES OF EIGHT
EEFGGHINOOSTTT NOT THE FOGGIEST
EEFGGIIIKLNNNS SINKING FEELING
EEFGHINNOORRST FORESHORTENING
EEFGIINNOPRSTZ FREEZING POINTS
EEFGINOOORRRST REIGNS OF TERROR
EEFHIIINNORRST IRONS IN THE FIRE
EEFHILNRSSSSTT THRIFTLESSNESS
EEFHNNORRSTTUU FORTUNE HUNTERS
EEFIIILNRRTTTY INTERFERTILITY
EEFILNOOPSSSSS SELF-POSSESSION
EEFLNOPPRSSSUU PURPOSEFULNESS
EEGGHHIILNNSTT SHEET LIGHTNING
EEGGHIILLNNNTY ENLIGHTENINGLY
EEGGIILNNNSTTT STINGING NETTLE
EEGHHIIILLMNTT IN THE LIMELIGHT
EEGHHIILOPSSVX HIGH EXPLOSIVES
EEGHIILNNNPSSW SPINNING WHEELS
EEGHIIMNNSTTUX EXTINGUISHMENT
EEGHIKNRRRSSTU HUNGER STRIKERS

EEGHILLMNORVWY OVERWHELMINGLY
EEGHINOOPPRRTY PORPHYROGENITE
EEGHLNOOOORSTUY HETEROGONOUSLY
EEGIILMNORTTUU ULTIMOGENITURE
EEGIILMOOPSSTT EPISTEMOLOGIST
EEGIILNNPRRSTY ENTERPRISINGLY
EEGILMOOOORSSTT METEOROLOGISTS
EEGILNOOPRRVWY OVERPOWERINGLY
EEGINNOOPRRSSV NONPROGRESSIVE
EEGINNOPPSSSTT STEPPING-STONES
EEGINOPRRSSSTTU INTEREST GROUPS
EEGINORSSTTTUW TONGUE TWISTERS
EEGINPRRSSSSTU PURSE STRINGES
EEGOPPRRRSSSSUU PRESSURE GROUPS
EEHHILNOORSTWW WORTH ONE'S WHILE
EEHHILNORSSTWW WORTHWHILENESS
EEHHIMMOOPPRRST HETEROMORPHISM
EEHHLLOOPRSTUY HETEROPHYLLOUS
EEHHLLOORSTTUY YOUTH HOSTELLER
EEHIILMNNQRSTU RELINQUISHMENT
EEHIILNOPPRSTY PYELONEPHRITIS
EEHIINOOPSSSTT PHOTOSENSITISE
EEHIINOOPSSTTV PHOTOSENSITIVE
EEHIINOOPSSTTZ PHOTOSENSITIZE
EEHIIOOPRRSSTY ERYTHROPOIESIS
EEHILLOORSSSTT TORTOISESHELLS
EEHIMOOPRRRSTU MOTHER SUPERIOR
EEHINNOORSSTTW NOTEWORTHINESS
EEHINNOPRRTTTU THREE-POINT TURN
EEHINNORSSSTWW NEWSWORTHINESS
EEHINOOPPQSTTU POP THE QUESTION
EEHINOPQSTTTUU PUT THE QUESTION
EEHLMNOOOORSTUY HETERONOMOUSLY
EEHLMNOORSTUYY HETERONYMOUSLY
EEHLMNORSSSSUU HUMOURLESSNESS
EEHMOOOPPRRTTY PYROPHOTOMETER
EEIIIMMNPRRSST PRIME MINISTERS
EEIIILMNNRTTTTY INTERMITTENTLY
EEIILNOORRSTUV REVOLUTIONISER
EEIILNOORRTUVZ REVOLUTIONIZER
EEIILNPRSSSSST SPIRITLESSNESS
EEIINNOPRSTUVY OPEN UNIVERSITY
EEIINOPRSSSSTX EXPRESSIONISTS
EEILLMOPRSSTTU MULTIPLE STORES
EEILMNNOOSSSST MOTIONLESSNESS
EEIMNORSSSSTUY MYSTERIOUSNESS
EEINOOPPRSSSSS PREPOSSESSIONS
EEINOPPRRSSSTU PRESSURE POINTS
EEINOPRRSSSTUV PROTRUSIVENESS
EELOOPPRRSSTUY PREPOSTEROUSLY
EEMNORSSSSTUVY NERVOUS SYSTEMS
EENNOOOOPPRRSST PERSON-TO-PERSON
EENNOOPRSSSTTU PORTENTOUSNESS
EENOOPPRRSSSSU PROSPEROUSNESS
EENOORRSSSSTTU STERTOROUSNESS
EFFGHHLOORTTUU FORETHOUGHTFUL
EFFGIIJLNSSTUY SELF-JUSTIFYING

EFFILNNRSSTUUU UNFRUITFULNESS
EFGGIIINNNPRRT FINGERPRINTING
EFGHHINORRSSTT FORTHRIGHTNESS
EFGHHLNOSSTTUU THOUGHTFULNESS
EFGHLNOOOORSTWY GLORY-OF-THE-SNOW
EFGILNOPPRSSTU SELF-SUPPORTING
EFHILNOPRSSSUW WORSHIPFULNESS
EFHIOOPPRRSSSS PROFESSORSHIPS
EFHMMNOORSTTTU MOMENTS OF TRUTH
EFINOORSSSTTUU FORTUITOUSNESS
EGGHHIINPRRSSU HIGH-PRESSURING
EGGIILMNNOORRS MORNING GLORIES
EGHHILNNOOOTTT LONG IN THE TOOTH
EGHHILNNORRSTT NORTHERN LIGHTS
EGHHILNORSSTTU SOUTHERN LIGHTS
EGIIIINNOQRSTU REQUISITIONING
EGIIILMNNRTTTY INTERMITTINGLY
EGIIILNNNRTTWY INTERTWININGLY
EGIINNPRRSSSSU SURPRISINGNESS
EGILNOPPRRSSTU SPLINTER GROUPS
EHHINOOOOPPPRST PHOSPHOPROTEIN
EHHINOOPSSSTTY PHOTOSYNTHESIS
EHHNNOORRSTTTW NORTH-NORTHWEST
EHHOOSSSTTTUUW SOUTH-SOUTHWEST
EHIILNNOOPRRTT TRINITROPHENOL
EHILMNOPSSSTYY POLYSYNTHESISM
EHINNOOPRSSTTU PUT ONE'S SHIRT ON
EHLNOPRSSSSUUU SULPHUROUSNESS
EHMOOOOPPRRTTYY PYROPHOTOMETRY
EIIIMNOPRSSSST IMPRESSIONISTS
EIIINNOOPRSSTT INTERPOSITIONS
EIILNOQRSSTTUV VENTRILOQUISTS
EIINNORSSSTTUU NUTRITIOUSNESS
EIINOOPPPRSSTU PRESUPPOSITION
EIINOOPPRSSSTU PROPITIOUSNESS
EIKNNNNOOOOSSW KNOW ONE'S ONIONS
EILMNNOOSSSUUV VOLUMINOUSNESS
EIMNNOOOOPPRRTT PROPORTIONMENT
EIMNOPRSSSSTTU STIR ONE'S STUMPS
EINNOOPQRRSTUU NON PROSEQUITUR
ELMNOSSSTTUUUU TUMULTUOUSNESS
ELMOPPRSSTUUUY PRESUMPTUOUSLY
ELNOOPSSSTUUUV VOLUPTUOUSNESS
EMNNNOOSSSSUYY SYNONYMOUSNESS
FGHHLLOOOORSTUW FOLLOW-THROUGHS
FGHIILLMNOOSTT MOONLIGHT FLITS
GHHIIILNOOPPSZ PHILOSOPHIZING
GHIILNOOOORSSTT ORNITHOLOGISTS
GIIINNOOOOPPRST PROPOSITIONING
GIIKMMNNRSSTUW SWIMMING TRUNKS
GILOOOOOOPRSTTZ PROTOZOOLOGIST
HHINOOOOOPPRSSU SIPHONOPHOROUS
IIIIINNOQSSTTU INQUISITIONIST
IIINOOPRRSSSTV PRISON VISITORS

AAAAACDEHHMMRRS MAD AS A MARCH
  HARE
AAAAAADDEGINSTTV AT A DISADVANTAGE
AAAAABBDIKKLNORR KABARDINO-BALKAR
AAAAABCEILLNOOPT PALAEOBOTANICAL
AAAAABGHKKNNOORR
  NAGORNO-KARABAKH
AAAACCDIIKLLLSY LACKADAISICALLY
AAAACCEHHLNNOPT ACANTHOCEPHALAN
AAAACCILLLLPRTY PARALLACTICALLY
AAAACDEGILRRUWY DUAL CARRIAGEWAY
AAAACEFFMORSTTT AS A MATTER OF FACT
AAAACEGHILLOPPR PALAEOGRAPHICAL
AAAACEILLMNNRTY ALIMENTARY CANAL
AAAACFGHHILMNSU HALF AS MUCH AGAIN
AAAACGHILLPPRRY PARAGRAPHICALLY
AAAAEIILMNNPRRT PARLIAMENTARIAN
AAAAFIIMNRRSSST RASTAFARIANISMS
AAAABBCEILNNPRSU BANANA REPUBLICS
AAAABBDDIIILNNQZ INQILAB ZINDABAD
AAAABCEEHINRRTTT TETRABRANCHIATE
AAAABCHIILOPPRTY APPROACHABILITY
AAAABCIIILNNNOTZ CANNIBALIZATION
AAAABDGHHKNNOORS
  GORNO-BADAKHSHAN
AAAABDHIMOPRSSSS AMBASSADORSHIPS
AAAABEGHHINOTTUV HAVE A THING ABOUT
AAAABEGIIILMRRTY MARRIAGEABILITY
AAAABEHIILNOPSTT ALPHABETISATION
AAAABEHIILNOPTTZ ALPHABETIZATION
AAAABEIILLMNPRRS PRIMA BALLERINAS
AAAABIILLNRSTTTY TRANSLATABILITY
AAAABILNNRSSTTTU TRANSUBSTANTIAL
AAAACCDEEILOPSSU ASCLEPIADACEOUS
AAAACCDHIMMNOPRY PHARMACODYNAMIC
AAAACCEEFHILMRRW CHEMICAL WARFARE
AAAACCEEGHIKNRRY HACKNEY CARRIAGE
AAAACCEEINORRSSU SARRACENIACEOUS
AAAACCEFHILLPTTY PATHETIC FALLACY
AAAACCEFIIRRRRRT AIRCRAFT CARRIER
AAAACCEMOPPRRSTU CARPOMETACARPUS
AAAACCGHILLMOOPR PHARMACOLOGICAL
AAAACCHIILLNRSTY ANARCHISTICALLY
AAAACCIIILMNOSTT ACCLIMATISATION
AAAACCIIILMNOTTZ ACCLIMATIZATION
AAAACCILLLLOPPTYY APOCALYPTICALLY
AAAACDEEEMMNRSTU AMUSEMENT
  ARCADE
AAAACDEEFFGHIRRS CHARGÉ D'AFFAIRES
AAAACDEFGIORRRRW CARRIAGE FORWARD
AAAACDEFJKLLORST JACK-OF-ALL-TRADES
AAAACDEGIILLMNTY DIAMAGNETICALLY
AAAACDEILLMNORYY AERODYNAMICALLY
AAAACDEILLMORSUY AMARYLLIDACEOUS
AAAACDEIMNNOORTT ANIMATED CARTOON
AAAACDFGIILMNORR AFRICAN MARIGOLD
AAAACDIIINOORTTV RADIOACTIVATION
AAAACDIILLNOOORT RADIOLOCATIONAL
AAAACEEGILLNPRTY PARAGENETICALLY

AAAACEEHIMMMSTTT METAMATHEMATICS
AAAACEFHHIILMRRS AIR CHIEF MARSHAL
AAAACEFILLLMNOWY FAMILY ALLOWANCE
AAAACEGILMNOPRTY MALACOPTERYGIAN
AAAACEHIILMRRSSV AIR VICE-MARSHALS
AAAACEHIIMNNPRSS SPANISH-AMERICAN
AAAACEHIMPPRSTTY PARASYMPATHETIC
AAAACEIIIMNNORST AMERICANISATION
AAAACEIIIMNNORTZ AMERICANIZATION
AAAACEIKLMMNORTX EXCLAMATION MARK
AAAACGGHIJKLNSSU LAUGHING JACKASS
AAAACHIIMNOORTTZ ACHROMATIZATION
AAAACIILLLMNOSTY ANOMALISTICALLY
AAAACIILNORSSTUV VASCULARISATION
AAAACIILNORSTUVZ VASCULARIZATION
AAAACILLNORSTTUY ASTRONAUTICALLY
AAAADDDEEEELSTUVX VALUE-ADDED TAXES
AAAADDEGINOSSTUV DISADVANTAGEOUS
AAAADDIINNORSSTT STANDARDISATION
AAAADDIINNORSTTZ STANDARDIZATION
AAAADEEEEHIIKLSV A HEAD LIKE A SIEVE
AAAADEEEILLRTVWY ELEVATED RAILWAY
AAAADEEGNNOOSTTV TO ONE'S
  ADVANTAGE
AAAADEFHHOOPRTTT AT THE DROP OF A HAT
AAAADEIILNNRSTUV VALETUDINARIANS
AAAADGHILLMNRRSY MARSHALLING YARD
AAAADGHIOOPRRTUY AUTORADIOGRAPHY
AAAAEEFHMMMNNNORV MANNA FROM
  HEAVEN
AAAAEEGGHILMNTTU HAEMAGGLUTINATE
AAAAEEGINNPRSSTU SEPTUAGENARIANS
AAAAEEGLMMNNRSTT
  GENTLEMAN-AT-ARMS
AAAAEEGMNRRSSSTT SERGEANTS-AT-ARMS
AAAAEFIILMNNOSTT MANIFESTATIONAL
AAAAEGGHIINNRSTT AGAINST THE GRAIN
AAAAEGHLNOOPPRTY PALAEONTOGRAPHY
AAAAEGIINNNQQRUU QUINQUAGENARIAN
AAAAEGINORSSTTVW STARVATION WAGES
AAAAEGLMOPRRSSSU MASSAGE PARLOURS
AAAAEGNNNOOPRRST PERSONA NON GRATA
AAAAEHILMNNNOSTT NATIONAL ANTHEMS
AAAAEIIILMNQRSTU EQUALITARIANISM
AAAAEIIILNORRSTT ARTERIALISATION
AAAAEIIILNORRTTZ ARTERIALIZATION
AAAAEILMNNPRRTUY UNPARLIAMENTARY
AAAAEMORRSSSTTTU TARSOMETATARSUS
AAAAFFIKMMMNNRRTU FRANKFURT AM MAIN
AAAAFIIIILMNORST FAMILIARISATION
AAAAFIIIILMNORTZ FAMILIARIZATION
AAAAGIINNOORSTTV ASTRONAVIGATION
AAAAHIIIMMNNRSTU HUMANITARIANISM
AAAAHIIIMNNRSTTU HUMANITARIANIST
AAAAIIILLMMNOSST MALASSIMILATION
AAAAIIILMNORSTTT TOTALITARIANISM
AAAAIIILNNNOOSTT NATIONALISATION
AAAAIIILNNNOOTTZ NATIONALIZATION
AABBCGHIIILLOPR BIBLIOGRAPHICAL

AABCCCELMOORSUU COOL AS A CUCUMBER
AABCCDEEHILLNSY HENDECASYLLABIC
AABCCDEELNNORTU COUNTERBALANCED
AABCCDEGHHLMNNO MONCHEN-GLADBACH
AABCCDEKKLLNOST BLOCK AND TACKLES
AABCCEELNNORSTU COUNTERBALANCES
AABCCEELORRRSUV CEREBROVASCULAR
AABCCEEMNOORSST CRAB SOMEONE'S ACT
AABCCEGIILLOORT BACTERIOLOGICAL
AABCCEGIILMNRUV CIRCUMNAVIGABLE
AABCDEEEHLLLNSY HENDECASYLLABLE
AABCDEEHORSTTUY CATHODE RAY TUBES
AABCDEEIKRRSSTV BACK-SEAT DRIVERS
AABCDEGIKLNRRST BLANK CARTRIDGES
AABCDEIILNOORST ANABOLIC STEROID
AABCDEIINNOORST DECARBONISATION
AABCDEIINNOORTZ DECARBONIZATION
AABCDEILNOORTXY DECARBOXYLATION
AABCDGIIILLOOOR RADIOBIOLOGICAL
AABCDGILLMNNOOR BALLROOM DANCING
AABCDHIILLMRTYY DITHYRAMBICALLY
AABCEEEFKLRRTVW BLACKWATER FEVER
AABCEEEKKLMRRST BLACK MARKETEERS
AABCEEFFIIILNTY INEFFACEABILITY
AABCEEGGIIMNNRT MAGNETIC BEARING
AABCEEGHIILNTXY EXCHANGEABILITY
AABCEEGHILNNRTY INTERCHANGEABLY
AABCEEGHLNORSUX LABOUR EXCHANGES
AABCEEHINSSTTUU EUSTACHIAN TUBES
AABCEEINOQRSSTU SESQUICARBONATE
AABCEFHKLOORRTY THE BACK OF A LORRY
AABCEGGHIILOOPR BIOGEOGRAPHICAL
AABCEGHHIIMNNST BATHING MACHINES
AABCEGHIOOPRSTU BACTERIOPHAGOUS
AABCEGILMNOPSUU PLUMBAGINACEOUS
AABCEILLLMOPRTY PROBLEMATICALLY
AABCEILLLMORSTY MEROBLASTICALLY
AABCFIIILLNOSTY SYLLABIFICATION
AABCGHKLLNNOOTY NOT BY A LONG CHALK
AABCHIILLLNRTYY LABYRINTHICALLY
AABCHILLLLOOSTY HOLOBLASTICALLY
AABCIIIILLNPPTY INAPPLICABILITY
AABCIIIILMNOPRTY INCOMPARABILITY
AABCIINOORSSTTU BIOASTRONAUTICS
AABDDDGGILNNOOR BOARD AND LODGING
AABDDEEIMNNORST ONE-ARMED BANDITS
AABDDEFIIOPRRSS BIRDS OF PARADISE
AABDEEEHILNNNRS BANNER HEADLINES
AABDEEFFHIORRST BIRDS OF A FEATHER
AABDEEGHINORRTW WEATHERBOARDING
AABDEIIILNORSTT DETRIBALISATION
AABDEIIILNORTTZ DETRIBALIZATION
AABDEIIILNOSSTT DESTABILISATION
AABDEIIILNOSTTZ DESTABILIZATION
AABDHILMNOSSSUY BUSMAN'S HOLIDAYS

AABEEEEFIKLMNOR MAKE A BEELINE FOR
AABEEELNNORSSST TREASONABLENESS
AABEEFHILNNOSSS FASHIONABLENESS
AABEEGHIILRTTTY A TIGER BY THE TAIL
AABEEGHIKLNRRTY HEARTBREAKINGLY
AABEFGIIILRRRTY IRREFRAGABILITY
AABEFIILNRRSTTY TRANSFERABILITY
AABEFLNORRTTUZZ BURNT TO A FRAZZLE
AABEGHHMOOPRRRT THERMOBAROGRAPH
AABEGHIILMNOORU HAEMOGLOBINURIA
AABEGHIIOOPRSTU AUTOBIOGRAPHIES
AABEIIILMMRSTUY IMMEASURABILITY
AABEIILMNORTUVY MANOEUVRABILITY
AABEKMRRRRSSTWY STRAWBERRY MARKS
AABGGIIILLNTTUY AGGLUTINABILITY
AABIILNOPRSSTTY TRANSPOSABILITY
AACCCCEIILNRRTT ANTARCTIC CIRCLE
AACCDEEHHLOOPRT CEPHALOCHORDATE
AACCDEEKNORTTTU COUNTERATTACKED
AACCDEGHIILOORS OLIGOSACCHARIDE
AACCDEGIILLLOOT DIALECTOLOGICAL
AACCDEGIIMNRTUV CIRCUMNAVIGATED
AACCDEHHILMNORY HYDROMECHANICAL
AACCDEIIIILLMRTY ACIDIMETRICALLY
AACCDEILMOORSST SOCIAL DEMOCRATS
AACCDEIMNPPRRSS SCRIMP AND SCRAPE
AACCDGILMMNOOTY ACCOMMODATINGLY
AACCDHIIMOOSSST SADOMASOCHISTIC
AACCDHILNOOPRST ACHONDROPLASTIC
AACCDIILLOOPRSY RADIOSCOPICALLY
AACCEEEGILNPRRT GENERAL PRACTICE
AACCEEGHILMMNOT MAGNETOCHEMICAL
AACCEEHIIOPPRST ARCHIEPISCOPATE
AACCEEHILMNORSV SERVOMECHANICAL
AACCEEHILORSSTT THE COAST IS CLEAR
AACCEEILLNNOPRT PRECANCELLATION
AACCEEILLNORTTY ELECTROANALYTIC
AACCEEILNNOPSTT PENTATONIC SCALE
AACCEEILNNRSSTU NATURAL SCIENCES
AACCEEINNNORSSS RECONNAISSANCES
AACCEEKNORRTTTU COUNTERATTACKER
AACCEEELNORRRSTU NUCLEAR REACTORS
AACCEFIILOOPRSU CAPRIFOLIACEOUS
AACCEGGHINRRRSY CARRYING CHARGES
AACCEGHIIMNOPRT CINEMATOGRAPHIC
AACCEHHILMNOOPT PHOTOMECHANICAL
AACCEHIIILLMNSTY MECHANISTICALLY
AACCEHIILLRSTUY EUCHARISTICALLY
AACCEHILLLLMNOY MELANCHOLICALLY
AACCEHILLMORTTY TACHOMETRICALLY
AACCEHILLMRTTYY TACHYMETRICALLY
AACCEHILLRRTTUY ARCHITECTURALLY
AACCEIIILLMNRST ANTICLERICALISM
AACCEIILLMNOSTY ENCOMIASTICALLY
AACCEIILLNNRTUV INTERCLAVICULAR
AACCEILRRRRTUUX EXTRACURRICULAR
AACCFFFGHKLOOOT GO OFF AT HALF-COCK
AACCFIIILNOSSST CLASSIFICATIONS

AACCFNNORSTTTUU TURF ACCOUNTANTS
AACCGHHIMOOPRRT CHROMATOGRAPHIC
AACCGHIMMNOORRT CHRONOGRAMMATIC
AACCGHIMNOOPRST PHARMACOGNOSTIC
AACCGIIMNORRTUV CIRCUMNAVIGATOR
AACCGINNOSSSTUV SAVINGS ACCOUNTS
AACCHHIINNRRTUU UNITARIAN CHURCH
AACCHHIIOOPPRTT HIPPOCRATIC OATH
AACCHIIILNOOSTT CATHOLICISATION
AACCHILLNOPSTYY SYCOPHANTICALLY
AACCIIILLLOSSTY SOCIALISTICALLY
AACCIIILNORRSTU CIRCULARISATION
AACCIIILNORRTUZ CIRCULARIZATION
AACCIIILPRRSTTU PARTICULARISTIC
AACCIILLMNORTUV CIRCUMVALLATION
AACCIILLMNOSSTU MISCALCULATIONS
AACCILLLOPRTTUY PLUTOCRATICALLY
AACDDEEEEHLNRSS CLEAR-HEADEDNESS
AACDDEEEGNSSTUU AN EDUCATED GUESS
AACDDEEILOSSTVV DEVIL'S ADVOCATES
AACDDHIKMNORRTY TOM, DICK, AND HARRY
AACDEEEEGIORSST ASSOCIATE DEGREE
AACDEEEHNPRRSTV CHAPTER AND VERSE
AACDEEGIILLNPPS SPECIAL PLEADING
AACDEEGIILLNRST LEADING ARTICLES
AACDEEHIKLMMNRS HAMMER AND SICKLE
AACDEEHIMNNOTUU HUMANE EDUCATION
AACDEEHKKNRRSTY THE KNACKER'S YARD
AACDEEIILNPRSTU UNDERCAPITALISE
AACDEEIILNPRTUZ UNDERCAPITALIZE
AACDEEIILOPRSTV OVERCAPITALISED
AACDEEIILOPRTVZ OVERCAPITALIZED
AACDEEIIMNNOTTV DECONTAMINATIVE
AACDEEILNNSSTTU INDECENT ASSAULT
AACDEGIIIKKLNNV ALIVE AND KICKING
AACDEGIIMNNNOTT DECONTAMINATING
AACDEHOORRSSSTT AT THE CROSSROADS
AACDEIILLMORTUY AUDIOMETRICALLY
AACDEIILMMNOSST DOMESTIC ANIMALS
AACDEIILNOSSTTU EDUCATIONALISTS
AACDEIIMNOORSTT DEMOCRATISATION
AACDEIIMNOORTTZ DEMOCRATIZATION
AACDEILLMORRTTU COURT-MARTIALLED
AACDEILNNOOSSTT SEA ISLAND COTTON
AACDFIIINOSSSTT DISSATISFACTION
AACDFIIORSSSTTY DISSATISFACTORY
AACDHIILLNOOPRY RADIOPHONICALLY
AACDIIIILNNPRSS DISCIPLINARIANS
AACDIIIILNORSTTU DISARTICULATION
AACDIILNOPQRTUU QUADRUPLICATION
AACEEEFGHNORSTX RATE OF EXCHANGES
AACEEEFHORRSTTW WEATHER FORECAST
AACEEEGIPPRRSTT CIGARETTE PAPERS
AACEEEEILLRSSTUV RELATIVE CLAUSES
AACEEEILNRSSSST SALES RESISTANCE
AACEEEENNQRRTTUY QUATERCENTENARY
AACEEFFHIMNNRST AFFRANCHISEMENT

AACEEFGHLMNORRT FARM THE LONG ACRE
AACEEFHINNOSTTT AT THE INSTANCE OF
AACEEFIILLMNRSU NUCLEAR FAMILIES
AACEEFIINOORSST FREE ASSOCIATION
AACEEGHHLNOPPRY ENCEPHALOGRAPHY
AACEEGHILLLPRTY TELEGRAPHICALLY
AACEEGHIMNOPRRT CINEMATOGRAPHER
AACEEGHLLLNORWY YELLOW ARCHANGEL
AACEEHIINORTTTZ CATHETERIZATION
AACEEHILLMORTTY THEOREMATICALLY
AACEEHILLNPRTTY PARENTHETICALLY
AACEEHILLPRTTUY THERAPEUTICALLY
AACEEHMNOPRRTWW COME THE RAW PRAWN
AACEEIILLPPRTTY PERIPATETICALLY
AACEEIILNNORSTV NATIONAL SERVICE
AACEEILLNNPRSTU INTERNAL CAPSULE
AACEEFFINORRRSTW WARRANT OFFICERS
AACEEFHHIMRRSSTT FATHER CHRISTMAS
AACEEFILOOPRSSSU PASSIFLORACEOUS
AACEEGGHINNORRST GREGORIAN CHANTS
AACEEGHHIIMNNSSW WASHING MACHINES
AACEEGHHMOOPRRRT CHROMATOGRAPHER
AACEEGHIJKRSSTTT STRAIGHTJACKETS
AACEEGHILLOPRRXY XEROGRAPHICALLY
AACEEGHILOOPSTTT COTTAGE HOSPITAL
AACEEGIIMNORSSTV MOVING STAIRCASE
AACEEHILLNOPRTUY NEUROPATHICALLY
AACEEHILLOOPSTTY OSTEOPATHICALLY
AACEEHLMORSSTUUW WALRUS MOUSTACHE
AACEIIILMNOPPSS EPISCOPALIANISM
AACEIIILNOPSSST SPECIALISATIONS
AACEIIILNOPSSTZ SPECIALIZATIONS
AACEIIILPRRSTTU PARTICULARITIES
AACEIIIMNNOPSTT EMANCIPATIONIST
AACEIILLLMNSTTY MENTALISTICALLY
AACEIILLLPRSTTY PERISTALTICALLY
AACEIILLMNNRSTY MANNERISTICALLY
AACEIILMNOPRRTT MALPRACTITIONER
AACEIILNNPRSSTU PURITANICALNESS
AACEIILNOPRSTTU RECAPITULATIONS
AACEIILPPPRSSTT PAST PARTICIPLES
AACFGILNORRSTUV VULGAR FRACTIONS
AACFIIINNOORSTT FRACTIONISATION
AACFIIINNOORTTZ FRACTIONIZATION
AACFIIINORSSTTT STRATIFICATIONS
AACGGHILLNOOPRY PHARYNGOLOGICAL
AACGHHILLLOOPRY HOLOGRAPHICALLY
AACGHIIILMNORTT ANTILOGARITHMIC
AACGHIILLLMORTY ALGORITHMICALLY, LOGARITHMICALLY
AACGHIILLOPPRYY POLYGRAPHICALLY
AACGHILLMNOOPRY MONOGRAPHICALLY, NOMOGRAPHICALLY
AACGHILLNOOOPRT ANTHROPOLOGICAL
AACGHILLOOPPRTY TOPOGRAPHICALLY
AACGHILLOPPRTYY TYPOGRAPHICALLY

AACGHILMOOPRSST PHARMACOLOGISTS
AACGIIILNPRRTUZ PARTICULARIZING
AACGIILMNORRTTU COURT-MARTIALING
AACGIINNOPRRSTT PROCRASTINATING
AACGILLMNOORSTY GASTRONOMICALLY
AACGILNNOORSTTU CONGRATULATIONS
AACGILNOORSSTUY AGRANULOCYTOSIS
AACGIMMNOOPRRSU MACROSPORANGIUM
AACHIIIINNOPSST HISPANICISATION
AACHIIIINNOPSTZ HISPANICIZATION
AACHIILLMNORSTY HARMONISTICALLY
AACHILLLMOOPSTY HOMOPLASTICALLY
AACHILLOPPRSTYY SAPROPHYTICALLY
AACHILLOPPSSTTY STAPHYLOPLASTIC
AACIIILLLRSTTUY RITUALISTICALLY
AACIIMMNNOORSTT ROMANTICISATION
AACIIMMNNOORTTZ ROMANTICIZATION
AACIILLLMOPSTUY POLITICAL ASYLUM
AACIILLNORSSTTY CRYSTALLISATION
AACIILLNORSTTYZ CRYSTALLIZATION
AACIILMMNNOOSTU COMMUNALISATION
AACIILMMNNOOTUZ COMMUNALIZATION
AACIILMNOOSSSTY ANCYLOSTOMIASIS
AACIILMOOPSTTTU AUTOMATIC PILOTS
AACIILNNOPRRSTT TRANSCRIPTIONAL
AACIINNOOPRRSTT PROCRASTINATION
AACIKMNNOPRTTUU PUNCTUATION MARK
AACILLLLMOPSTYY PLASMOLYTICALLY
AACILLMMOPSTTYY SYMPTOMATICALLY
AACLLRRRSTTTUUU ULTRASTRUCTURAL
AADDDEINNNORSST NONSTANDARDISED
AADDDEINNNORSTZ NONSTANDARDIZED
AADDDELMNNPPSUY SUPPLY AND DEMAND
AADDEHILNOOSTWW WHITE SANDALWOOD
AADDEIILNOPRSTU SUPERADDITIONAL
AADEEEEEILNRSSV VENEREAL DISEASE
AADEEEELMNOPRTV DEVELOPMENT AREA
AADEEEFHHLNRSST HALF-HEARTEDNESS
AADEEEFHIMNOOST AHEAD OF ONE'S TIME
AADEEEGKMNRRRST MARKET GARDENERS
AADEEEGLMOOPSTX SET A GOOD EXAMPLE
AADEEEHLRRRSSSS DRESS REHEARSALS
AADEEEHMNRRSSTW
    WARM-HEARTEDNESS
AADEEEILMNPRSTT DEPARTMENTALISE
AADEEEILMNPRTTZ DEPARTMENTALIZE
AADEEEMNPRSTTTT STATE DEPARTMENT
AADEEGGIKMNNRRT MARKET GARDENING
AADEEGHILOPRRTY RADIOTELEGRAPHY
AADEEGIIMNNOSTT DEMAGNETISATION
AADEEGIIMNNOTTZ DEMAGNETIZATION
AADEEHIIIMNRRST HEREDITARIANISM
AADEEIILNOSSTUX DESEXUALISATION
AADEHIIOPRRSSTT RADIOTHERAPISTS
AADEIIKLRSSSTTW SIDEWALK ARTISTS
AADEIILNOPSSSTY DISPASSIONATELY
AADEIILNORRRTXY EXTRAORDINARILY
AADEIIMOPPPRRST MISAPPROPRIATED
AADEILMNNOORSTT DEMONSTRATIONAL

AADEINPRRSSSSTT STARS AND STRIPES
AADELLOPSSSTTTU SLOTTED SPATULAS
AADELMPRRSSSTTU MUSTARD PLASTERS
AADELNOPRSTTUUY POLYUNSATURATED
AADEMNNOOPRRTTUW PORTMANTEAU
    WORD
AADFGHIORRRSTTW STRAIGHTFORWARD
AADFHMNNOOSSTUY A MONTH OF
    SUNDAYS
AADFIIILNNORSTY DISINFLATIONARY
AADGHHIMNPRSSTU DRAUGHTSMANSHIP
AADGIIINNOORSST DISORGANISATION
AADGIIINNOORSTZ DISORGANIZATION
AADIIILNORSSTTT TRADITIONALISTS
AADIIIMNNORSSTT ADMINISTRATIONS
AADIIMMNSSTTTUU MUTATIS MUTANDIS
AAEEEEEEHNOPRTWY A WEATHER EYE
    OPEN
AAEEEFGLMMNNRRT GENTLEMAN FARMER
AAEEEGILLNNRRTT ETERNAL TRIANGLE
AAEEEGLMMNNRSTT GENTLEMEN-AT-ARMS
AAEEEILMNNPTTTU ANTEPENULTIMATE
AAEEELLMMNPRTTY TEMPERAMENTALLY
AAEEFFINOORRSTT REAFFORESTATION
AAEEFGIMNNRRSST FRAGMENTARINESS
AAEEFHILRSSTTVV HARVEST FESTIVAL
AAEEFIIILMRSSSZ LAISSEZ-FAIREISM
AAEEFIILMNNOSTX SELF-EXAMINATION
AAEEFLLNOPRSTXY SELF-EXPLANATORY
AAEEGGIIINNRSTV NEGATIVE-RAISING
AAEEGHHINRRSTTT EARTHSHATTERING
AAEEGIILNNORSST GENERALISATIONS
AAEEGIILNNORSTZ GENERALIZATIONS
AAEEGILMNRTTUVY ARGUMENTATIVELY
AAEEHINOPRRSTVY AVERSION THERAPY
AAEEHINORSSTTTW WEATHER STATIONS
AAEEHMNOPRSSTTU APARTMENT HOUSES
AAEEIILNNORSTTX EXTERNALISATION
AAEEIILNNORTTXZ EXTERNALIZATION
AAEEIINNOOPRSTU EUROPEANISATION
AAEEIINNOOPRTUZ EUROPEANIZATION
AAEEILNNOPRRSST PROLETARIANNESS
AAEEIMNPRSSTTTV PAVEMENT ARTISTS
AAEEINOPPPRRSST APPROPRIATENESS
AAEEELLNPRRRTTUY PRETERNATURALLY
AAEENNNPRRSSSTT TRANSPARENTNESS
AAEFLLNOPRRRSUU FUNERAL PARLOURS
AAEGHILLLNOTTTU LET IT ALL HANG OUT
AAEGIIILNNOSTTV INVESTIGATIONAL
AAEGIIKNNNPSSST PAINSTAKINGNESS
AAEGIILNNOORRTT INTERROGATIONAL
AAEGIILNNRRSTTT TRANSLITERATING
AAEGIIMNNPRSSTY PRAYING MANTISES
AAEGILLNOOOPSTT PALAEONTOLOGIST
AAEGILLOOOOPSTZ PALAEOZOOLOGIST
AAEGIMMNNNOSSSU MAGNANIMOUSNESS
AAEHIILORTTTUVY AUTHORITATIVELY
AAEHILLMNOPSSTT MENTAL HOSPITALS
AAEIIIILMMNPRST ANTI-IMPERIALISM

AAEIIIILMNPRSTT ANTI-IMPERIALIST
AAEIIILMMNOORST MEMORIALISATION
AAEIIILMMNOORTZ MEMORIALIZATION
AAEIIILMNNNORTT INTERLAMINATION
AAEIIILNNNORSTT INTERNALISATION
AAEIIILNNOORTTZ ORIENTALIZATION
AAEIIILNPRSSSTT ANTIPERISTALSIS
AAEIIILLMNNNRSTTU TRANSILLUMINATE
AAEIILLNNNORTTY INTERNATIONALLY
AAEIILMORRRRTTY TERRITORIAL ARMY
AAEIILNNOOPRSST PERSONALISATION
AAEIILNNOOPRSTZ PERSONALIZATION
AAEIILNNORRSTTT TRANSLITERATION
AAEIILNNOSSSSTT SENSATIONALISTS
AAEIILNOPPPRRTY INAPPROPRIATELY
AAEIIMNOSSSTTTY SYSTEMATISATION
AAEIIMNOSSTTTYZ SYSTEMATIZATION
AAEIINNPPRRSSTT ANTIPERSPIRANTS
AAEILLLMNNNPSTT INSTALLMENT PLAN
AAEILMNPRRSSTUU SUPERNATURALISM
AAEILNNNOSSTTUY INSTANTANEOUSLY
AAEILNPRRSSTTUU SUPERNATURALIST
AAEINNNNOPSSSTT ANTS IN ONE'S PANTS
AAELMNSSSSSTTYY SYSTEMS ANALYSTS
AAENNORRSSSTUUY TYRANNOSAURUSES
AAFGGGIILMNNSSY MAGNIFYING GLASS
AAFGIINNORRSTTU TRANSFIGURATION
AAFIIIILMNRSTTU FUTILITARIANISM
AAFIILNORRTTTU ULTRAFILTRATION
AAFIILMNOORRSTU FORMULARISATION
AAFIILMNOORRTUZ FORMULARIZATION
AAFIMNNOORRSSTT TRANSFORMATIONS
AAGIIILNNORSSTU SINGULARISATION
AAGIIILNNORSTUZ SINGULARIZATION
AAGIILNORSTTTUU GUTTURALISATION
AAGIILNORTTTUUZ GUTTURALIZATION
AAHHHLOPPRRSTYY STAPHYLORRHAPHY
AAHHIINOOPPSSTT PHOSPHATISATION
AAHHIINOOPPSTTZ PHOSPHATIZATION
AAHIIILNOOPSSTT HOSPITALISATION
AAHIIILNOOPSTTZ HOSPITALIZATION
AAIIIIMNNORSTTU MINIATURISATION
AAIIIIMNNORTTUZ MINIATURIZATION
AAIIILMMNOORSTT IMMORTALISATION
AAIIILMMNOORTTZ IMMORTALIZATION
AAIIILMNOOPRSTV IMPROVISATIONAL
AAIIJLNOOPSTTUX JUXTAPOSITIONAL
AAIILLNNORRTTUVY INVOLUNTATARILY
AAIILNNOOPRSSTT TRANSPOSITIONAL
AAIIMNNOOPRSSSTY TRYPANOSOMIASIS
AAIINNOOPRSTTTU SATURATION POINT
ABBCCEFIIMNNORU FIBONACCI NUMBER
ABBCEEEFFKLOOOT COFFEE-TABLE BOOK
ABBDDEEEELLLORRU DOUBLE-BARRELLED
ABBDEEELNORSSTU REDOUBTABLENESS
ABBDEGHILORRTYY DAYLIGHT ROBBERY
ABBEEIIILLMORRS MOBILE LIBRARIES
ABBEEIIILLNTUVY UNBELIEVABILITY
ABBEIIIILMOPRST IMPROBABILITIES

ABCCCDEIIILNORU RIBONUCLEIC ACID
ABCCEEFHILNOSST CHIEF CONSTABLES
ABCCEEIIKRRRSTU CIRCUIT BREAKERS
ABCCEEILLNOOPST POLICE CONSTABLE
ABCCEFIIIJNOOTT OBJECTIFICATION
ABCCEFIIILLPSSUY SUBSPECIFICALLY
ABCCEGHINOPRSST BATCH PROCESSING
ABCCEIIIILNSSTY INACCESSIBILITY
ABCCEIIIILLNORTY RECONCILABILITY
ABCCEIILMNOPPSU PUBLIC COMPANIES
ABCCEIILNNPSSUU PUBLIC NUISANCES
ABCCIIILNORTTTY CONTRACTIBILITY
ABCCIIKLMNNOOOT COMBINATION LOCK
ABCDEEEEGHLORRS BACHELOR'S DEGREE
ABCDEEEELLOOORST COLORADO BEETLES
ABCDEEHIIILPRTY DECIPHERABILITY
ABCDEEIILORRRRS RECORD LIBRARIES
ABCDEELMNORRSUU CONSUMER
    DURABLE
ABCDEGHIKNNORTU IN THE BACKGROUND
ABCDEGIIILPRSTY CREDIBILITY GAPS
ABCDEIILLLOQTUY QUODLIBETICALLY
ABCDEIILMOOPSTY DECOMPOSABILITY
ABCDEIIMOOSSTUY BASIDIOMYCETOUS
ABCEEEIIILLNOSTV CABLE TELEVISION
ABCEEEILNNOPTUX UNEXCEPTIONABLE
ABCEEGHIKLOORST GLOBE ARTICHOKES
ABCEEGHINORSSTT TOSSING THE CABER
ABCEEHHLMNNOOPR RHOMBENCEPHALON
ABCEEILMMNNORSU INCOMMENSURABLE
ABCEEILMNNNOOOU ONCE IN A BLUE
    MOON
ABCEEILNNOPTUXY UNEXCEPTIONABLY
ABCEELNNNOOPRUU UNPRONOUNCEABLE
ABCEGIIILNORTYZ RECOGNIZABILITY
ABCEGIILOORSSTT BACTERIOLOGISTS
ABCEIIIILLNPTXY INEXPLICABILITY
ABCEIIIILNRTTXY INEXTRICABILITY
ABCEIILLMMRSTYY BISYMMETRICALLY
ABCEIILLNOPRSTU PUBLIC RELATIONS
ABCGIILLNOOOTTY GNOTOBIOTICALLY
ABCIIIILMNOPTTY INCOMPATIBILITY
ABCIIILLNNOOSTY INCONSOLABILITY
ABCIIILMMNOTTUY INCOMMUTABILITY
ABCIIILMNOPTTUY INCOMPUTABILITY
ABCIIILNNOORSUV BINOCULAR VISION
ABCIILLLMOSSTYY SYMBOLISTICALLY
ABDDDEEIMNNORSS BROADMINDEDNESS
ABDDDEHLNNOORTU
    BLOOD-AND-THUNDER
ABDDEEEEHNOORSUW BONDED
    WAREHOUSE
ABDDEEIIJLMNOSU DIAMOND JUBILEES
ABDDEELMNOORSSW
    WARM-BLOODEDNESS
ABDEEEHILLLSSTW WELL-ESTABLISHED
ABDEEEHKLNORRTY BROKEN-HEARTEDLY
ABDEEEIIILMRRTY IRREDEEMABILITY
ABDEEEILNORRTVY BEYOND RETRIEVAL

ABDEIIILMNOPRTY IMPONDERABILITY
ABDEIIILPRSTTUY DISREPUTABILITY
ABDEIILMNORSTTY DEMONSTRABILITY
ABDEIILNNORSTUY INSUBORDINATELY
ABDEILLMNNOPSTU PLATINUM BLONDES
ABDIIIILMNSSTY INADMISSIBILITY
ABDIIIILNPSTTUY INDISPUTABILITY
ABDIIINNNOORSTU INSUBORDINATION
ABEEEEGIKLNSTVV VEGETABLE KNIVES
ABEEEEILNNPRRTT INTERPENETRABLE
ABEEEELNNPRSSST PRESENTABLENESS
ABEEEFHHLMORSTT STAR-OF-BETHLEHEM
ABEEEFHOPRRTTTT THE BETTER PART OF
ABEEEGHHHLNOSTW THE WHOLE
  SHEBANG
ABEEEHKNNORRSST HEARTBROKENNESS
ABEEHILMNORSSTW BLAMEWORTHINESS
ABEEIILNNORSTUV LABOUR-INTENSIVE
ABEEIIMNPRRSSTY PRESBYTERIANISM
ABEEINNSSSSTTUV SUBSTANTIVENESS
ABEGHHIMNOORSTT SMOOTH BREATHING
ABEHIIIILMPRSTY IMPERISHABILITY
ABEHIILMORSTTTY THERMOSTABILITY
ABEHILMNOOORRTT TRIBROMOETHANOL
ABEIIIILLNNRTUVY INVULNERABILITY
ABEIIIILLORRSTVY IRRESOLVABILITY
ABEIILLMNOPTUYY UNEMPLOYABILITY
ABEINOOOPRSSTTV OBSERVATION POST
ABFIILNOPRTTUY UNPROFITABILITY
ABFILMMNOOOORSTY SYMBOL-FORMATION
ABHNNOOOORTTTTUW NOT WORTH A
  BUTTON
ACCCCEGHIKNNOTU CHECKING ACCOUNT
ACCCDDKLLNOOOUU
    CLOUD-CUCKOO-LAND
ACCCEEGIILLLOOS ECCLESIOLOGICAL
ACCCEEHILLNORSV VICE-CHANCELLORS
ACCCEEIIILMSSST ECCLESIASTICISM
ACCCEEILOORSTTU ELECTROACOUSTIC
ACCCEFIIKNNOOTY COCKNEYFICATION
ACCCEHHIILMOPSY PHYSICOCHEMICAL
ACCCEHHILNOPSTY PSYCHOTECHNICAL
ACCCEIIILMMORST COMMERCIALISTIC
ACCCEIILNOPSTTU CONCEPTUALISTIC
ACCCEILOOPRSTUU ACOUSTIC COUPLER
ACCCENNORRSTTUU CURRENT ACCOUNTS
ACCCHIOOPSSSTUY PSYCHOACOUSTICS
ACCCIILLMOOPRSY MICROSCOPICALLY
ACCDDDEKLOOOOOS
    COCK-A-DOODLE-DOOS
ACCDDEEINNNOSTU DISCOUNTENANCED
ACCDDEIMMNNNOOS
    SECOND-IN-COMMAND
ACCDEEEEEHQRRRU CHEQUERED CAREER
ACCDEEHILLLPSYY PSYCHEDELICALLY
ACCDEEHINOOOPSU CHENOPODIACEOUS
ACCDEEILMNOPSST COMPLICATEDNESS
ACCDEEILMNORSTY ELECTRODYNAMICS

ACCDEFFFGHKLOOO GO OFF
  HALF-COCKED
ACCDEFGHHLNNORU CHURCH OF
  ENGLAND
ACCDEHINORSSSUW SANDWICH COURSES
ACCDEIIILMNNSTU INCIDENTAL MUSIC
ACCDEINOOPSSTTU DEPOSIT ACCOUNTS
ACCDEIOPPRRSTTU PICTURE POSTCARD
ACCDFHIIINNOORT CHONDRIFICATION
ACCEEEFIMNORSST MASTER OF SCIENCE
ACCEEEGILMNORTT ELECTROMAGNETIC,
  MAGNETOELECTRIC
ACCEEEIINORSTVV ON ACTIVE SERVICE
ACCEEEENNOPSSTUX EXPENSE ACCOUNTS
ACCEEFHIIINOPST SPEECHIFICATION
ACCEEFIIILNORTT ELECTRIFICATION
ACCEEFIILMNRRTU CIRCUMFERENTIAL
ACCEEFILLMORSTV COLLECTIVE FARMS
ACCEEFINNOOOSSS SENSE OF OCCASION
ACCEEGILLORRSTU ELECTROSURGICAL
ACCEEHHIMOORRTT HETEROCHROMATIC
ACCEEHILOORRSTT ATHEROSCLEROTIC
ACCEEIIMMNOTUVX EXCOMMUNICATIVE
ACCEEIINNOORSSS CONCESSIONAIRES
ACCEEILNORTTXYY OXYTETRACYCLINE
ACCEFFGIIILNRSS SELF-SACRIFICING
ACCEFGIIIPRSTVY SPECIFIC GRAVITY
ACCEFHHMMNOSSUU MUCH OF A
  MUCHNESS
ACCEGHIIILNNORT ANTICHOLINERGIC
ACCEGHIIMNNPRRS PRINCE CHARMINGS
ACCEGHILLLNOOTY TECHNOLOGICALLY
ACCEGHILLNOPSYY PSYCHOGENICALLY
ACCEGIIILMMNORZ COMMERCIALIZING
ACCEGIIILNNOPRSS PELICAN CROSSING
ACCEGIIILNNOPTUZ CONCEPTUALIZING
ACCEGIIMMNNOTUX EXCOMMUNICATING
ACCEGIKLLNOOSTU COCKTAIL LOUNGES
ACCEGILLLNOOSYY SYNECOLOGICALLY
ACCEHHILLMNOOPR CHLORAMPHENICOL
ACCEHIIILLPRRTYY HYPERCRITICALLY
ACCEHIILNORSSTT INTERSCHOLASTIC
ACCEHIIMNOPRSTY PSYCHOMETRICIAN
ACCEHILLMNOORTY HOMOCENTRICALLY
ACCEHILLMOOPRTY CHEMOTROPICALLY
ACCEHILMMNOPSST ACCOMPLISHMENTS
ACCEHINNOOPRRTT ANTHROPOCENTRIC
ACCEIIKNNORSSTW STICK IN ONE'S CRAW
ACCEIILMRRTUUUV CURRICULUM VITAE
ACCEIILNNOPRSUY INSURANCE POLICY
ACCEIILOPPRSSUY PERSPICACIOUSLY
ACCEIIMMNNOOTUX EXCOMMUNICATION
ACCEIIMMNNOTUUV UNCOMMUNICATIVE
ACCEIIOORRSSSTV VICTORIA CROSSES
ACCEILMOOPRRSTU ULTRAMICROSCOPE
ACCELLNOOOSUUVV CONVOLVULACEOUS
ACCFIMMNNOOOORST COMMON FRACTIONS
ACCGHIIILLOOOST STOICHIOLOGICAL
ACCGHILLLNOOORY CHRONOLOGICALLY

ACCGHILLLOOPSYY PSYCHOLOGICALLY
ACCHHILMOOOOPPST OPHTHALMOSCOPIC
ACCHIILNNOORTTY THYROCALCITONIN
ACCIKLLMOOOOTTV MOLOTOV COCKTAIL
ACDDEEEELNNPSTU DEPENDENT CLAUSE
ACDDEEEEHHIKNSST THICKHEADEDNESS
ACDDEEEHILMSSTU DUTCH ELM DISEASE
ACDDEEEHLNORSST COLD-HEARTEDNESS
ACDDEEGILNNNORS ENDOCRINE GLANDS
ACDDEEHIILLRSUY DIESEL-HYDRAULIC
ACDDEEMNNOORRSY SECONDARY
   MODERN
ACDDEFLMOOOORSSW SWORD OF
   DAMOCLES
ACDDIIIILNSTUV INDIVIDUALISTIC
ACDEEEEEGGHLRRT THREE-LEGGED RACE
ACDEEEEFILMNTTV MENTAL DEFECTIVE
ACDEEEEILNNORTT ENTENTE CORDIALE
ACDEEEFHILLNORS HALL OF RESIDENCE
ACDEEEFIIILNRTT DEFINITE ARTICLE
ACDEEEGHILORRTT CIGARETTE HOLDER
ACDEEEIIMNNPSTT PATENT MEDICINES
ACDEEEINNORSSST CONSIDERATENESS
ACDEEEEMNOOPRSTV OVERCOMPENSATED
ACDEEFHORRSSSTW CHESTS OF DRAWERS
ACDEEFILNORRRTU FUNERAL DIRECTOR
ACDEEFLMNNORRRT CLERMONT-FERRAND
ACDEEFMMNNOORSY COMEDY OF
   MANNERS
ACDEEGGHIINPRRS GRAPHIC DESIGNER
ACDEEGHHIINORTU HIGHER EDUCATION
ACDEEGHIIMNNNSV VENDING MACHINES
ACDEEGHILOOSSSW WILD-GOOSE CHASES
ACDEEGIIILLMOOP EPIDEMIOLOGICAL
ACDEEGIINORSSTT STAGE DIRECTIONS
ACDEEGIMNORSSTU DISCOURAGEMENTS
ACDEEGKLMNNOSTW
   ACKNOWLEDGMENTS
ACDEEHIILNOOPRT RADIOTELEPHONIC
ACDEEHILLMNORTY ENDOTHERMICALLY
ACDEEIILNNORSTY INCONSIDERATELY
ACDEEIIMMOORRRT RADIOMICROMETER
ACDEEIINNOORRST RECONSIDERATION
ACDEEILLNPPRRUY PERPENDICULARLY
ACDEEIMMNNOORST RECOMMENDATIONS
ACDEEIMNNOSSTWW CASEMENT
   WINDOWS
ACDEELMOORRSSTU SCLERODERMATOUS
ACDEEMNNNOORSTY STAND ON
   CEREMONY
ACDEENORRSSSSTY SECONDARY STRESS
ACDEFGIKNNOORSY DAYS OF RECKONING
ACDEFIIIIMNNNOT INDEMNIFICATION
ACDEFIIIINNORTT DENITRIFICATION
ACDEFIIIINORSTV DIVERSIFICATION
ACDEFIIIINORTTV DEVITRIFICATION
ACDEFIIILMNOSTU DEMULSIFICATION
ACDEFIIILNNOTTY CONFIDENTIALITY
ACDEGIKNOOPSSTT SPIGOT AND SOCKET

ACDEGILNNNOSTTU CONSENTING ADULT
ACDEGINORSTTTUY COTTAGE INDUSTRY
ACDEHIIILNPSSTU DUAL CITISENSHIP
ACDEHIIILNPSTUZ DUAL CITIZENSHIP
ACDEHIILLMOSTTY METHODISTICALLY
ACDEHIINOPSSTTU UNSOPHISTICATED
ACDEHIKLORRSSTU HARD LUCK STORIES
ACDEHLOOOPPRSSV APPROVED SCHOOLS
ACDEHMNNOOORSTU
   ENCHONDROMATOUS
ACDEIIILMNNOORT OMNIDIRECTIONAL
ACDEIIILNORRSTY DISCRETIONARILY
ACDEIIINNNOORST INCONSIDERATION
ACDEIIINNORRSTY INDISCRETIONARY
ACDEIIILLMNORSTY MODERNISTICALLY
ACDEIILLMNPRSTU PNEUMATIC DRILLS
ACDGHIMNNOOPRRY GYNANDROMORPHIC
ACDGIIIINNNOORT AIR-CONDITIONING
ACDHIIILLMOOPRY IDIOMORPHICALLY
ACDHIIIMNOOOSTT DICHOTOMISATION
ACDHIIIMNOOOTTZ DICHOTOMIZATION
ACDIIIILNNNOSST DISINCLINATIONS
ACDIIIINRSSTUVY VICISSITUDINARY
ACDIIIINNNOOSTTU DISCONTINUATION
ACDIILLNNNOOTUY UNCONDITIONALLY
ACEEEEELNOPSSUV ACE UP ONE'S SLEEVE
ACEEEEGILLNNORT GENERAL ELECTION
ACEEEEGILNORTTV ELECTRONEGATIVE
ACEEEEHHILNRSTW CATHERINE WHEELS
ACEEEFGGHINNORX FOREIGN EXCHANGE
ACEEEFGILNNOPRR PEREGRINE FALCON
ACEEEFHIMNNNRST ENFRANCHISEMENT
ACEEEGIILLNORTT INTERCOLLEGIATE
ACEEEGIMMOSSTTT COMMITTEE STAGES
ACEEEGIMNOPRSTT SPERMATOGENETIC
ACEEEHHHLNOOPRX HEXACHLOROPHENE
ACEEEHHIPPRSSTT SPEECH THERAPIST
ACEEEHILLMNRTUY HERMENEUTICALLY
ACEEEHILNNNRSST CHINESE LANTERNS
ACEEEHNORRSSSTU TREACHEROUSNESS
ACEEEIILLLNSTTU INTELLECTUALISE
ACEEEIILLLNTTUZ INTELLECTUALIZE
ACEEEILNNOPSSTX EXCEPTIONALNESS
ACEEEILNORRSSTV CORRELATIVENESS
ACEEEILNPSSSTUV SPECULATIVENESS
ACEEEIMMNOPRSSU MENISPERMACEOUS
ACEEEMNORRSSTUU COUNTERMEASURES
ACEEENOPPRSSSTY PAY ONE'S RESPECTS
ACEEFHHMNOOORRT REACH FOR THE
   MOON
ACEEFHLNOPRRSSU REPROACHFULNESS
ACEEFIIILMNOPTX EXEMPLIFICATION
ACEEFIINNORRSTT CONFRATERNITIES
ACEEFILMPRRSSTU SIMPLE FRACTURES
ACEEGGIILLNNORT TRAINING COLLEGE
ACEEGHINNOOPRTT ANTHROPOGENETIC
ACEEGIILLMOOPST EPISTEMOLOGICAL
ACEEGIINNNORSTT TRACTION ENGINES
ACEEGIINORRSTTT GASTROENTERITIC

ACEEGILLLNOPTYY POLYGENETICALLY
ACEEGILLNOORSTY OESTROGENICALLY
ACEEHHIIKNNOTTT TAKE IT ON THE CHIN
ACEEHHIMNOORRTT HETEROCHROMATIN
ACEEHHINOOPPRST PHOSPHOCREATINE
ACEEHIILLLLNSTY HELLENISTICALLY
ACEEHIINPPPRSST APPRENTICESHIPS
ACEEHILOORRSSST ATHEROSCLEROSIS
ACEEHIMMNORSSSV SERVOMECHANISMS
ACEEIIINQSSSTUV ACQUISITIVENESS
ACEEIILLLMNSTTU INTELLECTUALISM
ACEEIILLLNSTTTU INTELLECTUALIST
ACEEIILLLNTTTUY INTELLECTUALITY
ACEEIILLMOPRTYZ PIEZOMETRICALLY
ACEEIILMNOPRSVY LIVERY COMPANIES
ACEEIILNNNOOSTV CONVENTIONALISE
ACEEIILNNNOOTVZ CONVENTIONALIZE
ACEEIILNNNOQSTU INCONSEQUENTIAL
ACEEIINORSSSTTV SERVICE STATIONS
ACEEILLLMNOSSUY MISCELLANEOUSLY
ACEEILLNOORSTTY ELECTROLYSATION
ACEEILMMNRSSSTY SYMMETRICALNESS
ACEEINOOPRSSTVV PROVOCATIVENESS
ACEEINORRRRSTUY RESURRECTIONARY
ACEELMNOOQRRSUU LOURENÇO
  MARQUES
ACEEMNNOOOOPRSTU CONTEMPORANEOUS
ACEFFGIJLMNOPPU JUMPING-OFF PLACE
ACEFIIINNNOSTT INTENSIFICATION
ACEFIIILMNNOOST SOLEMNIFICATION
ACEFIIINNOOPRST PERSONIFICATION
ACEFIILORRSTTUV ARTICLES OF VIRTU
ACEFINOOPPRRRST PROPER FRACTIONS
ACEFINRRRSSTTUU INFRASTRUCTURES
ACEGHHIMNOOSSTT SHOOTING MATCHES
ACEGHIIIKMNNNTT KNITTING MACHINE
ACEGHILLLOOPPSY PSEPHOLOGICALLY
ACEGHIMMOOPRRTT PHOTOGRAMMETRIC
ACEGHLLOOPSUYYZ ZYGOPHYLLACEOUS
ACEGIILLMMNNOUY IMMUNOGENICALLY
ACEGIILLMNOOOORT TERMINOLOOGICAL
ACEGIINOOPRSTTV PROGNOSTICATIVE
ACEGILLNORRSUUY NEUROSURGICALLY
ACEGILMNNOOOORST CONGLOMERATIONS
ACEGILNOPRSSSTU PLASTIC SURGEONS
ACEHHIILLMNPTTY PLATYHELMINTHIC
ACEHHIKNORTTUVW HAVE NO TRUCK WITH
ACEHHINNPSSSTTU SPANISH CHESTNUT
ACEHHINOPPRSTTU PITHECANTHROPUS
ACEHHIOPPRSSTTY PSYCHOTHERAPIST
ACEHIILLLOOPRTY HELIOTROPICALLY
ACEHIILLOPRRSTY PREHISTORICALLY
ACEHIILOOPSTTTY PHOTOELASTICITY
ACEHIIMMMOPSTTY SYMPATHOMIMETIC
ACEHILLMNNOOPRXY XENOMORPHICALLY
ACEHILLMOOPRTTY PHOTOMETRICALLY
ACEHILOPSSTUXYY PSYCHOSEXUALITY
ACEHINOPRRSTUYY NEUROPSYCHIATRY
ACEHMNOOPRSSTUY PROSENCHYMATOUS

ACEIIILLMPSSSTY PESSIMISTICALLY
ACEIIIMMNOORSSS COMMISSIONAIRES
ACEIILLORSTUVYY VOYEURISTICALLY
ACEIILMNNNOOSTV CONVENTIONALISM
ACEIILNNNOOSTTV CONVENTIONALIST
ACEIILNNNOOTTVY CONVENTIONALITY
ACEIILNNOOPRSTT INTROSPECTIONAL
ACEIILNNOORSTTU INTEROSCULATION
ACEIIMNNOORSSTV CONSERVATIONISM
ACEIIMNOOPRSTTU COMPUTERISATION
ACEIIMNOOPRTTUZ COMPUTERIZATION
ACEIINNOORSSTTV CONSERVATIONIST
ACELNOOOOPPRRSTU COUNTERPROPOSAL
ACELPRRRSSTTUUU SUPERSTRUCTURAL
ACEOOPPRRSSSSTU AT CROSS-PURPOSES
ACFGIIIILNNNSTY INSIGNIFICANTLY
ACFIIIILMNOPSST SIMPLIFICATIONS
ACFIIMNNOOOSTTY COMITY OF NATIONS
ACFIMNOOORSSTTT COMFORT STATIONS
ACGGIINNOOPRSTT PROGNOSTICATING
ACGHHIIIOOPRRST HISTORIOGRAPHIC
ACGHHIMOOOOPPRRT MICROPHOTOGRAPH,
  PHOTOMICROGRAPH
ACGHHINOOOOPPRTZ PHOTOZINCOGRAPH
ACGHHLLMNNOPSUU PLOUGHMAN'S
  LUNCH
ACGHHLOOOPPSTYY PSYCHOPATHOLOGY
ACGHILLLMOOOOPRY MORPHOLOGICALLY
ACGIIILLLNNSTTY SCINTILLATINGLY
ACGIIINNNNOOTTX NONINTOXICATING
ACHHMOOOOPRRSTU
  CHROMATOPHOROUS
ACHIIIMOOSSSSST SCHISTOSOMIASIS
ACHIINNNOORSSTY SYNCHRONISATION
ACHIINNNOORSTYZ SYNCHRONIZATION
ACHIIOPRSSSSTTY ASTROPHYSICISTS
ACHIKLNNOOPPTTY PHYTOPLANKTONIC
ACHILLLORRTTUUY HORTICULTURALLY
ACIIILNNOPQTTUU QUINTUPLICATION
ACIILMMNOOOPSST COSMOPOLITANISM
ACIILMNNOOSSTUY SANCTIMONIOUSLY
ACIILNNOOSSTTTU CONSTITUTIONALS
ADDDDEGIIMNNOSW DIAMOND WEDDINGS
ADDDEEEHNNNRSSU UNDERHANDEDNESS
ADDDEEFHILMOORT MIDDLE-OF-THE-ROAD
ADDEEEEEHLLNSSV LEVEL-HEADEDNESS
ADDEEEEHLNRRTTY TENDERHEARTEDLY
ADDEEEGHHILNSST LIGHT-HEADEDNESS
ADDEEEGHNNORSSW
  WRONGHEADEDNESS
ADDEEEHIKNNRSST KIND-HEARTEDNESS
ADDEEGHHINNRSST RIGHT-HANDEDNESS
ADDEEGHINNOORTY DEHYDROGENATION
ADDEEGNNOORSSTU GOOD-NATUREDNESS
ADDEEHHNNORSSST SHORT-HANDEDNESS
ADDEEILLMMNNSSS SMALL-MINDEDNESS
ADDEEINNNORSSWY NINE DAYS' WONDERS
ADDEGHIIKNRRSTW WITH KIND REGARDS

ADDEIMNNNOPQSSS MIND ONE'S P'S AND Q'S
ADDGIIIILNNUVZ INDIVIDUALIZING
ADEEEEEGGHHORTVV HAVE THE EDGE OVER
ADEEEEEGILLNRRVY GENERAL DELIVERY
ADEEEEEHHNRRTTUW UNDER THE WEATHER
ADEEEEHNNOPRSST OPENHEARTEDNESS
ADEEEEFGHINORSTU UNDER THE AEGIS OF
ADEEEEFHNORSSSTT SOFTHEARTEDNESS
ADEEEGHHMNPRRSS GERMAN SHEPHERDS
ADEEEGHINNRSSST NEARSIGHTEDNESS
ADEEEGILMNNNSTT DISENTANGLEMENT
ADEEEGILNNOOPRS OLD AGE PENSIONER
ADEEEHIMNNRSSTT DISHEARTENMENTS
ADEEEIIINNNSSST SEINE-SAINT-DENIS
ADEEEIILMNNSSTT SENTIMENTALISED
ADEEEIILMNNSTTZ SENTIMENTALIZED
ADEEEEMNNRSSTTTU UNDERSTATEMENTS
ADEEEEMNOPRRSTTT DEPARTMENT STORE
ADEEFFFHHLLNOTY FLY OFF THE HANDLE
ADEEFFGIIINNRTT DIFFERENTIATING
ADEEFFIIINNORTT DIFFERENTIATION
ADEEFILNSSSSTTU DISTASTEFULNESS
ADEEGIIMNNRSTTU UNDERESTIMATING
ADEEHILNNOORSTW LET ONE'S HAIR DOWN
ADEEHINPRSSSTTW SHARP-WITTEDNESS
ADEEIIINNOSSSTT DESENSITISATION
ADEEIIINNOSSTTZ DESENSITIZATION
ADEEIIILOPRRSSTV PRIVATE SOLDIERS
ADEEIIMNNOPRTTU UNPREMEDITATION
ADEEIIMNNORSTTU UNDERESTIMATION
ADEEIINNNOOPSST OPINIONATEDNESS
ADEEILMNOPRRSTU MENSTRUAL PERIOD
ADEEILMNORSTTVY DEMONSTRATIVELY
ADEEIMNNORSTTUV UNDEMONSTRATIVE
ADEFFGHINNORSTU FOUNDING FATHERS
ADEFFHINNOSSSST STANDOFFISHNESS
ADEFGHIMOORRSTY FAIRY GODMOTHERS
ADEFGIIIILLNQSTU SELF-LIQUIDATING
ADEGHLLMORRTUYY HYDROMETALLURGY
ADEGIIIOPRRSTTT PRESTIDIGITATOR
ADEHHIIMMOPRRST HERMAPHRODITISM
ADEHILMNOOPSTTU PENTOTHAL SODIUM
ADEHIMOOPRSSTTY DERMATOPHYTOSIS
ADEIIIIILMRSSST DISSIMILARITIES
ADEIIINORSSSTTT DISSERTATIONIST
ADEIIJLNPRRSTUU JURISPRUDENTIAL
ADEIILNORRSSTTX SINISTRODEXTRAL
ADEIILNORRSTTVY DORSIVENTRALITY
ADEIIMNNOPPSSTT DISAPPOINTMENTS
ADEILMOPSTTUUUY PSEUDOMUTUALITY
ADGGIMNNOPRSSTU STAMPING GROUNDS
ADGHIINNNOSTTTW NOTWITHSTANDING
ADGIIIILNNRSTUZ INDUSTRIALIZING
ADGIIIILNNOPPSTY DISAPPOINTINGLY
AEEEFHIIKNNNOSV HAVE ONE'S KNIFE IN

AEEEFHOORRRSTWW THE WORSE FOR WEAR
AEEEFIILNPRRTTY PREFERENTIALITY
AEEEFLLLLORRTVW FELLOW TRAVELLER
AEEEGGGIMNNNRST ENGAGEMENT RINGS
AEEEGGILLORRSSU ROGUES' GALLERIES
AEEEGGLNNOORRRV GOVERNOR-GENERAL
AEEEGHHILNORTTT IN THE ALTOGETHER
AEEEGHINNOPRSST PARTHENOGENESIS
AEEEGIILNNRSSTT LARGE INTESTINES
AEEEGILLMNNNSST GENTLEMANLINESS
AEEEGILMNNNSSSS MEANINGLESSNESS
AEEEGILNNPPRRST SLEEPING PARTNER
AEEEGILNNRSSSTV EVERLASTINGNESS
AEEEGIMNOPRSSST SPERMATOGENESIS
AEEEHHILMNOPPST MEPHISTOPHELEAN
AEEEHIIMMNORRST IMMERSION HEATER
AEEEHIIMNPPRSSV MISAPPREHENSIVE
AEEEHILORSTTUXY HETEROSEXUALITY
AEEEHORRRSSTTUW WEAR THE TROUSERS
AEEEIILMMNPRSTX EXPERIMENTALISM
AEEEIILMNPRSTTX EXPERIMENTALIST
AEEEIIMNNOPRTTX EXPERIMENTATION
AEEEIINNNSSTTTV INATTENTIVENESS
AEEEIILNPRSSSTUV SUPERLATIVENESS
AEEEIMNOPRRSSTX EXTEMPORARINESS
AEEEIMNPRRRSSUU SUPERNUMERARIES
AEEEINNOPRRSSTT REPRESENTATIONS
AEEEELMNOQRRSSSU QUARRELSOMENESS
AEEELNOOPRRSSST PERSONAL STEREOS
AEEELOPRRRSSSTW LESSER SPEARWORT
AEEFGGHILNRSSTT FLIGHT SERGEANTS
AEEFGHIMNNORRTT THE MORNING AFTER
AEEFGHINOOPRRTW WEATHERPROOFING
AEEFGIMNNRRSTTU TRANSFIGURATION
AEEFHILLLLOTVYY LILY OF THE VALLEY
AEEFIILNNRSTTTU FIRST LIEUTENANT
AEEFNNNORSSTTUU UNFORTUNATENESS
AEEFNOOOPRRTTWY POWER OF ATTORNEY
AEEGGHHOOPPRRTY PHYTOGEOGRAPHER
AEEGGHLORRSSTTW LET THE GRASS GROW
AEEGHHILNORSSSY ROYAL HIGHNESSES
AEEGHHLOOPPRTTY PHOTOTELEGRAPHY, TELEPHOTOGRAPHY
AEEGHHLORSSSTUU SLAUGHTERHOUSES
AEEGHIKLOPRRTTW TIGHTROPE WALKER
AEEGHINNOOPRSST ANTHROPOGENESIS
AEEGHLLMNOOSSTZ THOMSON'S GAZELLE
AEEGIILNORRTTVY INTERROGATIVELY
AEEGIINOORRRSTT INTERROGATORIES
AEEGIINORRSSTTT GASTROENTERITIS
AEEGIMNOPRSSTTY OPERATING SYSTEM
AEEHHHILLNNOPPT PHENOLPHTHALEIN
AEEHHIJNOSSSTVW JEHOVAH'S WITNESS
AEEHIILMOOPSTTU EPITHELIOMATOUS
AEEHIIMNNOPPRSS MISAPPREHENSION
AEEHIKLNNOPRTUY PHENYLKETONURIA

AEEHILMMNOOPRRY HOLY ROMAN EMPIRE
AEEHINPPPPRRSSW WHIPPERSNAPPERS
AEEIIILMMMMORST TIMES IMMEMORIAL
AEEIIINOORRSTTX EXTERIORISATION
AEEIIINOORRTTXZ EXTERIORIZATION
AEEIILLMNNSSSTT SMALL INTESTINES
AEEIILMNNSSSTTT SENTIMENTALISTS
AEEIILNNOPPRTTY PLENIPOTENTIARY
AEEIILNOORRSTUV REVOLUTIONARIES
AEEIIMNNOPRSSTT PRESENTATIONISM
AEEIIMNOOPRSTTX EXTEMPORISATION
AEEIIMNOOPRTTXZ EXTEMPORIZATION
AEEIINNOPRRSTTT INTERPRETATIONS
AEEIINNOPRSSTTT PRESENTATIONIST
AEEIILLMMNOOOPSS OIL SOMEONE'S PALM
AEEIILLMNNNORTVY ENVIRONMENTALLY
AEEIILLMNPPRSTUY SUPPLEMENTARILY
AEEIILMNNOOPPRUU PLEUROPNEUMONIA
AEEILMNNOPPSTTU SUPPLEMENTATION
AEEILNNOOPRRTUV RELATIVE PRONOUN
AEEILNNOPSSSSSS PASSIONLESSNESS
AEEILNORRSSTTUU RUSSIAN ROULETTE
AEEIMNOQRSSSTTU QUESTION MASTERS
AEEIMPRRRSSSSTY PRIMARY STRESSES
AEEINOQRRSSSSTU QUARTER SESSIONS
AEENNNOOPSSSSTU SPONTANEOUSNESS
AEFGGHJLOORRTUU GO FOR THE JUGULAR
AEFIIIILLMNNSTY INFINITESIMALLY
AEFIILLLNNOOPST SELF-POLLINATION
AEFIILMNOOPRSSS PROFESSIONALISM
AEFIILNOOPRSSST PROFESSIONALIST
AEFIILNORSSSTTU FLIRTATIOUSNESS
AEFILLMNOPRSTTY SELF-IMPORTANTLY
AEGGHILLNOORSTY SHOOTING GALLERY
AEGGIILNNORRTTY INTERROGATINGLY
AEGGILNNRRSSSTY TRANSGRESSINGLY
AEGHHIIMNNRSSST NIGHTMARISHNESS
AEGHHIIOOPRRRST HISTORIOGRAPHER
AEGHIINNOPRSSTW WITHIN ONE'S GRASP
AEGIIINNNNOORSTT NITROGENISATION
AEGIIINNNOORTTZ NITROGENIZATION
AEGIIINNNRSSTTT INTRANSIGENTIST
AEGIILNOORRRTTY INTERROGATORILY
AEGILLNOOOPSSTT PALEONTOLOGISTS
AEGILLNOPSTTUXY EXPOSTULATINGLY
AEHHIIMNOPRRSTT THERIANTHROPISM
AEHHIIOPPRSSTTY PHYSIOTHERAPIST
AEHIIJJMNOORTTY JOIN THE MAJORITY
AEHIIMMNNOOPRST ENANTIOMORPHISM
AEHIMNOOPRRSTTT ANTHROPOMETRIST
AEIIILMMMNNRSSX MARXISM-LENINISM
AEIIILMNNRSSTTX MARXIST-LENINIST
AEIIJLNNORSSTUV UNIVERSAL JOINTS
AEIIILLNOOPPRSTY PREPOSITIONALLY
AEIIILNOORRTUVY REVOLUTIONARILY
AEIILMMNNRSSTTU INSTRUMENTALISM
AEIILMMNOOPRSTT METROPOLITANISM
AEIILMNNRSSTTTU INSTRUMENTALIST
AEIILMNNRSTTTUY INSTRUMENTALITY

AEIILNNNORSSTUV INVOLUNTARINESS
AEIILNOOPRSSTTY PROSELYTISATION
AEIILNOOPRSTTYZ PROSELYTIZATION
AEIIMNNNORSTTTU INSTRUMENTATION
AEILNOOOPPRRTTY PROPORTIONATELY
AELNNNOOOPPRRSU PERSONAL PRONOUN
AFFGHNNOOSSSTUW SAWN-OFF
   SHOTGUNS
AFFHILLORSTUUYY YOURS FAITHFULLY
AFGGIIMNNORRSTY TRANSMOGRIFYING
AFGHLMOOOOPRRTU
   PHOTOFLUOROGRAM
AFGIIILLNNOSSTT FILLING STATIONS
AFGIIKMNNNOOPRT NON-PROFIT-MAKING
AGHHHILOOOPPRTT PHOTOLITHOGRAPH
AGHHIILLLLNSSYY SHILLY-SHALLYING
AGHHIIMNOOPSSTT OPISTHOGNATHISM
AGHHILLMOOOPSTT OPHTHALMOLOGIST
AGHHINOOOPSSTTU OPISTHOGNATHOUS
AGHHOOOOPPPRTTY PHOTOTOPOGRAPHY
AGHHOOOPPPRTTYY PHOTOTYPOGRAPHY
AGHIILMNOOOSTTY MYTHOLOGISATION
AGHIILMNOOOTTYZ MYTHOLOGIZATION
AGHILNOOOOPRSTT ANTHROPOLOGISTS
AGIIINNORRSSTTZ TRANSISTORIZING
AGIILLNNOOPSSTT POLLING STATIONS
AGINOPPPRRSSTTU SUPPORTING PARTS
AHHIILNOPPRSSTT PHILANTHROPISTS
AHIJLMNOOOPRSTU PHOTOJOURNALISM
AHIJLNOOOPRSTTU PHOTOJOURNALIST
AHINOOOPRRSSTTT PHOTOTRANSISTOR
AIIIILLNOQRSTUY INQUISITORIALLY
AIIINNNOOSSTTUW NO-WIN SITUATIONS
AIILLLMNOPSSUUY PUSILLANIMOUSLY
AIILNOOOPPRRTTY PROPORTIONALITY
AIKNNNNOQTTUUWY UNKNOWN QUANTITY
BBBBEEFGIIILRTT FLIBBERTIGIBBET
BBBDEEHLLLMNOOS BLONDE BOMBSHELL
BBCEEKKLOORRSTT STOCKBROKER BELT
BBCGIKLLMNOSSTU STUMBLING BLOCKS
BBCHIIIIILLOPST BIBLIOPHILISTIC
BBDEIIIILNOOSSV DIVISION LOBBIES
BBDIMOORRRSTUUY DORMITORY SUBURB
BBEHILMMMOOORST THROMBOEMBOLISM
BCCDEEIIJNORSTT INDIRECT OBJECTS
BCCEEEEGILRSTTU ICEBERG LETTUCES
BCCEEEIILMNNOSU BIOLUMINESCENCE
BCCEEEIMNNPRSUU SUPERINCUMBENCE
BCCEEILNORRSTTU RECONSTRUCTIBLE
BCCEEINOPRSSSTU SUBSISTENCE CROP
BCCEGHIMNNNRRUU NUMBER-CRUNCHING
BCDDDEELLNOOOSS COLD-BLOODEDNESS
BCDEEEIMMNNRSTU DISENCUMBERMENT
BCDEEHILLLOOSTW WHITE BLOOD CELLS
BCDEGIILNOSTUY BUILDING SOCIETY
BCDEIIILOPRRTUY REPRODUCIBILITY
BCDEIIILRSTTTUY DESTRUCTIBILITY
BCDEILLNNOORSSU COLOUR BLINDNESS
BCEEEFFGILNORTY BENEFIT OF CLERGY

BCEEEFGHIIOPRTT TIP OF THE ICEBERG
BCEEEFIIKNNSSST SICKNESS BENEFIT
BCEEEILNPSSSSTU SUSCEPTIBLENESS
BCEEFFIOOOPSSTX POST OFFICE BOXES
BCEEHILLOOPRSSS PHLEBOSCLEROSIS
BCEEIIILMPPRRST IMPRESCRIPTIBLE
BCEEINORSSSTTUV OBSTRUCTIVENESS
BCEGHIILNOOOSTT BIOTECHNOLOGIST
BCEHIIIIINOSTTX EXHIBITIONISTIC
BCEHIILNOPPRSUW PUBLIC OWNERSHIP
BCEIIILMNOPTTTY CONTEMPTIBILITY
BCEIIILMOPRSSTY COMPRESSIBILITY
BCGHIILOOOPSSTY PSYCHOBIOLOGIST
BCGIIIIILNORRTY INCORRIGIBILITY
BCGIIILMOOORSST MICROBIOLOGISTS
BCGIINNNNOORTTU NONCONTRIBUTING
BCIINOORSSSTTTU OBSTRUCTIONISTS
BCINNNOOORRTTUY NONCONTRIBUTORY
BDDEEEELNNORSTU DOUBLE ENTENDRES
BDDEEEILNOOPRSX PEROXIDE BLONDES
BDDEEFLLLNOOSSU FULL-BLOODEDNESS
BDEEFIIIILNNSTY INDEFENSIBILITY
BDEEFILMNPRRSSU PLUMBER'S FRIENDS
BDEGIIIIILNSTTY INDIGESTIBILITY
BDFFIIILMNNORUU INFUNDIBULIFORM
BDIIIIILNOSSTUY INDISSOLUBILITY
BEEEEFILNNNOOSS FEEL IN ONE'S BONES
BEEEGGILNSSSSTU SUGGESTIBLENESS
BEEEIINNNORRTTZ TRINITROBENZENE
BEEEILNNOPRSSSS RESPONSIBLENESS
BEEELMNOORSSSTU TROUBLESOMENESS
BEEGHHIILLNOOTW THE WHOLE BOILING
BEEGHIILNNORSSU NEIGHBOURLINESS
BEEHIIINOPRSSTV PROHIBITIVENESS
BEEHILNOOPSTTUW UP TO THE ELBOWS IN
BEEHINOORRSSSUV HERBIVOROUSNESS
BEEHLOOOORRSSTTU TROUBLESHOOTERS
BEEIIIIILNNSSST INSENSIBILITIES
BEEIIIILNNSTTXY INEXTENSIBILITY
BEEIIIILRRRSTVY IRREVERSIBILITY
BEEIMNOOPPRSSTU OPPOSITE NUMBERS
BEEINNORSSSTUUV UNOBTRUSIVENESS
BEFHHLMOOOOTTUY THE BLOOM OF
　　YOUTH
BEGIIIIILLLNTTY INTELLIGIBILITY
BEIIIIILMRRSSTY IRREMISSIBILITY
BEIIIIILRRSSTTY IRRESISTIBILITY
BEIMNORSSSSTUUU RUMBUSTIOUSNESS
BELLLORSSTUUWYY SLOWLY BUT SURELY
BELOPRRSSSSSTUU BRUSSELS SPROUTS
BFILLNOPPSTUUUY BOUNTIFUL SUPPLY
BHIIIINOOPRSSTT PROHIBITIONISTS
CCCDEEEIIMNOSST DOMESTIC SCIENCE
CCCDEEFIIKNNORT CONFIDENCE TRICK
CCCEEEIMNNNOOSY CONSCIENCE MONEY
CCCEEHLMOOSTTYY CHOLECYSTECTOMY
CCCEEIILMNOORRT MICROELECTRONIC
CCCEIILNORSTUUY SECURITY COUNCIL
CCCIIMNOPRRSTU CIRCUMSCRIPTION

CCCIILMNOORSTUU CIRCUMLOCUTIONS
CCDDDEHHILNOOOS SECOND CHILDHOOD
CCDEEEFFNOORRTT CONCERTED EFFORT
CCDEEEFINNNOOOV CONVENIENCE FOOD
CCDEEEIIMORSSTV DOMESTIC SERVICE
CCDEEENNNNORSSU UNCONCERNEDNESS
CCDEEENNNNOSSTU UNCONNECTEDNESS
CCDEEGIIILNNRSV DRIVING LICENCES
CCDEEINOPRSTUUV SUPERCONDUCTIVE
CCDEELLNORSTTUW WELL-CONSTRUCTED
CCDEGIIILNNORSTY DISCONCERTINGLY
CCDEIIINPRRSTTU PRINTED CIRCUITS
CCDEINNOOPRSTUU SUPERCONDUCTION
CCDENOOPRRSSTUU SUPERCONDUCTORS
CCDHIIKLLOSUWWW
　　CHUCK-WILL'S-WIDOW
CCDHINNOOOOPTTU PHOTOCONDUCTION
CCEEEEFNNNORSSW NEWS CONFERENCES
CCEEEEFNNOPRRSS PRESS CONFERENCE
CCEEEEFNORRRSSS CROSS-REFERENCES
CCEEEEHHINQRSSU CHINESE CHEQUERS
CCEEEEILMMOSTTT SELECT COMMITTEE
CCEEEFFILOSTTVY COST-EFFECTIVELY
CCEEEFIINNOORST CONFECTIONERIES
CCEEEGJLNNORSTU CONCRETE JUNGLES
CCEEEHHNOOPPRSS PHOSPHORESCENCE
CCEEEHILOOPRRTT ELECTROPHORETIC
CCEEEIIKLNORSTT ELECTROKINETICS
CCEEFFFIILNSSUY SELF-SUFFICIENCY
CCEEFHIINOPRSST CHIEF INSPECTORS
CCEEGIIINNNNNOV INCONVENIENCING
CCEEHIIILNORTTY HELIOCENTRICITY
CCEEHIINNORTTTY ETHNOCENTRICITY
CCEEHNORRSTTTUU TECHNOSTRUCTURE
CCEEIIINNNOSSST INCONSISTENCIES
CCEEIILOPRRTTYY PYROELECTRICITY
CCEEIINNNNOORTT INTERCONNECTION
CCEEIILLMOORSSTT COLLECTOR'S ITEMS
CCEEIILLNNOOSTUV COLLECTIVE NOUNS
CCEEIMMNNORTTUY COMMUNITY CENTRE
CCEEINNOPRRSSSW CROWN PRINCESSES
CCEFILLNOOSSSUY SELF-CONSCIOUSLY
CCEHIIMMOOPSTTY PSYCHOTOMIMETIC
CCEHIMMNOSSTTUY COMMUNITY CHESTS
CCEIIILLNOOOORSSU COLLISION COURSE
CCEIILNNOOSSTUY CONSCIENTIOUSLY
CCEIMOOOPRRRSSS MICROPROCESSORS
CCEINNNOOSSSSUU UNCONSCIOUSNESS
CCEINNOOPSSSSUU CONSPICUOUSNESS
CCEINNOORRSSTTU RECONSTRUCTIONS
CCGHIIINORRSTTU SHORT-CIRCUITING
CCGIIIILNOOSSTU SOCIOLINGUISTIC
CCIIINNOOORSTTT CONTORTIONISTIC
CCIIINNOOPRSSTT CONSCRIPTIONIST
CCIILLNOOPRRUVY PRIVY COUNCILLOR
CCIILNNOOPSSUUY INCONSPICUOUSLY
CCIIMNNOORSSTTU MISCONSTRUCTION
CDDEEEEEINNNPRT INTERDEPENDENCE
CDDEEEELNNPRTUY UNPRECEDENTEDLY

CDDEEFIIILLNPSS SELF-DISCIPLINED
CDDEEFIIINNORRT DIRECTION FINDER
CDDEFNNOOOOPSTU
    FOOT-POUND-SECOND
CDDEGHILLNOORSU COLD-SHOULDERING
CDDEINNOOPRRTUU UNDERPRODUCTION
CDEEEEEINNQSSUV QUEEN'S EVIDENCES
CDEEEEFLNNRSSST SELF-CENTREDNESS
CDEEEEINNNPRSTU SUPERINTENDENCE
CDEEEEIORSSTTTV STORE DETECTIVES
CDEEEFILORRSTTT LETTERS OF CREDIT
CDEEEHHILPRSTUW WHITED SEPULCHRE
CDEEEHNNORRTTUU
    UNDER-THE-COUNTER
CDEEEIINNPRRSWW WINDSCREEN WIPER
CDEEEIINPRSSSTV DESCRIPTIVENESS
CDEEEIMNNPRSTUU SUPERINDUCEMENT
CDEEEINNNPRSTUY SUPERINTENDENCY
CDEEEINRSSSTTUV DESTRUCTIVENESS
CDEEELLMMNOOPSW COMMON
    SPEEDWELL
CDEEFFILLNNOSTY SELF-CONFIDENTLY
CDEEFGILNRSSTTU SELF-DESTRUCTING
CDEEFIILNORSTYY FRIENDLY SOCIETY
CDEEFIILORRSSST CROSS-FERTILISED
CDEEFIILORRSSTZ CROSS-FERTILIZED
CDEEFILLPRSSTUY DISRESPECTFULLY
CDEEFILNORSSTTU SELF-DESTRUCTION
CDEEHIIKNSSTTTW THICK-WITTEDNESS
CDEEHILNNORSSSW CHINLESS WONDERS
CDEEIIIIMNNRSTT INDETERMINISTIC
CDEEIIINNSSSTTV DISTINCTIVENESS
CDEEIIKNQSSTTUW QUICK-WITTEDNESS
CDEEILMNNOOPTWY ENDOWMENT POLICY
CDEEILNNORSSSUU INCREDULOUSNESS
CDEEEINOOQRSSSTU CROSS-QUESTIONED
CDEGIILNNOOORST ENDOCRINOLOGIST
CDEGILNNOOPRRSY CORRESPONDINGLY
CDEIIIINNOSSTTU DISCONTINUITIES
CDEIIIJNNOSSSUU INJUDICIOUSNESS
CDEIILNNOOPRSTU PRODUCTION LINES
CDHIILNOPRSTUUU PULCHRITUDINOUS
CDIILNNOOSSTUUY DISCONTINUOUSLY
CDIINNOOPRTTUVY NONPRODUCTIVITY
CEEEEELOOPRSSTT TELESTEREOSCOPE
CEEEEFFIINNSSTV INEFFECTIVENESS
CEEEEFHORRRRSSU REFRESHER COURSE
CEEEEGIIMNNRSSS ÉMINENCES GRISES
CEEEEKLNNOOPSSU KEEP ONE'S COUNSEL
CEEEFFGHIOPRSSU FIGURES OF SPEECH
CEEEFFGIIORRSST REGISTER OFFICES
CEEEFIIMNORRRTT INTERFEROMETRIC
CEEEFLNORRSSSUU RESOURCEFULNESS
CEEEGGILNNOOSSU GLUCONEOGENESIS
CEEEGHILORRSSTU GLOUCESTERSHIRE
CEEEGILNORRSTTV COVERING LETTERS
CEEEHIIMNNOPRSV INCOMPREHENSIVE
CEEEHILMNOPRSVY COMPREHENSIVELY
CEEEHILOOPRRSST ELECTROPHORESIS

CEEEHIMORRSSTTY STEREOCHEMISTRY
CEEEIILLNNOSUUV NOUVELLE CUISINE
CEEEIILOOPRSTTV ELECTROPOSITIVE
CEEEIIMNOPSSTTV COMPETITIVENESS
CEEEIIMOORRSSTT STEREOISOMETRIC
CEEEIINRRSSSTTV RESTRICTIVENESS
CEEEILOPRRSTTVY RETROSPECTIVELY
CEEEIMMNNOPRSTV PINCER MOVEMENTS
CEEEIMNNOORSSSU CEREMONIOUSNESS
CEEEINPQRSSSTUU PICTURESQUENESS
CEEEKOOPRRRSSSU PRESSURE COOKERS
CEEENNOPPPRRRST PEPPERCORN RENTS
CEEFFGIIORRSSTY REGISTRY OFFICES
CEEFHIIIKMNNOTT IN THE NICK OF TIME
CEEFIIIILLNOSTTU FEUILLETONISTIC
CEEFINNOPRRSSTU PERFUNCTORINESS
CEEGHIILNNORSST CROSSING THE LINE
CEEGHINNOPPRSST SHOPPING CENTRES
CEEGIIIKMOSSTTV GIVE IT SOME STICK
CEEGLLLNOOPPRYY PROPYLENE GLYCOL
CEEHHIMMORRSTTY THERMOCHEMISTRY
CEEHIIMNNNOOPRS INCOMPREHENSION
CEEHIIMNOSSSSUV MISCHIEVOUSNESS
CEEHIINOPRRSSTT HISTORIC PRESENT
CEEHILLNOOORRSXY HEXYLRESORCINOL
CEEHIMNOORRSTTU MOTHER COUNTRIES
CEEIIINOPRSSSTX EXPRESSIONISTIC
CEEIILNOPRSTTVY INTROSPECTIVELY
CEEIIMNNOPSSSUU IMPECUNIOUSNESS
CEEIIMNORRRSSTU RESURRECTIONISM
CEEIINOPPRSSSTU PRECIPITOUSNESS
CEEIINORRRSSTTU RESURRECTIONIST
CEEIINPSSSTTUUV INTUSSUSCEPTIVE
CEEIKNOPRRSTTVY POVERTY-STRICKEN
CEEILMNNOORSUUY UNCEREMONIOUSLY
CEEIMNNNOOOOSTW COME INTO ONE'S
    OWN
CEEINNNOOSSSTTU CONTENTIOUSNESS
CEEINNOOQRRSSTU CORONER'S INQUEST
CEEINOOQRRSSSTU CROSS-QUESTIONER
CEEINOPPRSSSSUU PERSPICUOUSNESS
CEEPRRRSSSTTUUU SUPERSTRUCTURES
CEFGHHIILNNOPRS FRENCH POLISHING
CEFGHIILNNNNSSU UNFLINCHINGNESS
CEFGIIKLLNORSST STOCKING-FILLERS
CEGHIJNOOPRSSTU HOUSING PROJECTS
CEGIIKMNNNORSSS MORNING SICKNESS
CEGIIMMMNOSSTUW SWIMMING COSTUME
CEGILNOOPPSSSTY SYNOPTIC GOSPELS
CEGINNNNOORSSSUU INCONGRUOUSNESS
CEGINOOOPRRSSTY CROSSOPTERYGION
CEHHIMMNOOOOPPRS MORPHOPHONEMICS
CEHIIMMMNORSTUY IMMUNOCHEMISTRY
CEHLNOOOORSSSUW SHOW ONE'S
    COLOURS
CEHNNNOORSSSSUY SYNCHRONOUSNESS
CEIIIIMNOPRSSST IMPRESSIONISTIC
CEIIIINOSSSTTVV VIVISECTIONISTS
CEIILNNOPSSSTUU PUNCTILIOUSNESS

CEIINNOPSSSTTUU INTUSSUSCEPTION
CEIMMNNNOOOPSST NON COMPOS MENTIS
CEIMNOOPRSSSSUU PROMISCUOUSNESS
CEIMNOPRSSSSTTUU SCRUMPTIOUSNESS
CEKLLNOOPPSSSUU PULL ONE'S SOCKS UP
CFFHIILMNOSSTTU FIFTH COLUMNISTS
CFGHHHLOOOOSTTU SCHOOL OF
   THOUGHT
CFGHHIIILNNOOSS FINISHING SCHOOL
CFHILMNOOOORRRT NITROCHLOROFORM
CFIINOOQRRSTUUY COURTS OF INQUIRY
CGHHIIIMMNOOSSS HIGH COMMISSIONS
CHHHINNOORRSTUY ORNITHORHYNCHUS
CHILLMOOOPPRRSY MICROSPOROPHYLL
DDDEEHLNOORRSUU
   ROUND-SHOULDERED
DDEEEFHILMNOORW MIDDLE OF NOWHERE
DDEFGHLNOOOPSSU SLOUGH OF DESPOND
DDEGGHINNOSSTUW SHOTGUN WEDDINGS
DDEGHIIINNSSTUU UNDISTINGUISHED
DEEEEGINRRRSSTU REGISTERED NURSE
DEEEEHMNORRRSTV REVEREND MOTHERS
DEEEEINRSSSTTTV VESTED INTERESTS
DEEEELMNOOPRTVV OVERDEVELOPMENT
DEEEFGHINORSSST FORESIGHTEDNESS
DEEEFLLOPSSSSSY SELF-POSSESSEDLY
DEEEHLLMOOOPPSS OLD PEOPLE'S HOMES
DEEEIILLNNNOTTW WELL-INTENTIONED
DEEEIILMMNRRSTU DELIRIUM TREMENS
DEEEIINOPSSSTUX EXPEDITIOUSNESS
DEEEINNNOSSSTTU TENDENTIOUSNESS
DEEEINNNPRSSTTU SUPERINTENDENTS
DEEELMMNNOPRTUY UNDEREMPLOYMENT
DEEHIINOOPSSSTT PHOTOSENSITISED
DEEHIINOOPSSTTZ PHOTOSENSITIZED
DEEHIMOORRSTTTU RIDE OUT THE STORM
DEEILNNPRRTTUUY UNINTERRUPTEDLY
DEFFIILLNNORSTY FLY INTO FLINDERS
DEFGGHIIKLNNORT FORKED LIGHTNING
DEFHHLLNOOOSTUW FOLLOW THE
   HOUNDS
DEFHIIMNNOORSTU FOURTH DIMENSION
DEFILNRSSSSTTUU DISTRUSTFULNESS
DEGHHIIILNRRSVW WHIRLING DERVISH
DEGHHIINNNORSTU HUNTINGDONSHIRE
DEIIILLMNNOSSTU DISILLUSIONMENT
DEIIINOOPPRSSST PREDISPOSITIONS
DEIIMNNNRSSTTUW WIND INSTRUMENTS
DEIINNORSSSSTUU INDUSTRIOUSNESS
DEIINNRRSSSTUUY SUNRISE INDUSTRY
EEEEGILNPSTTTTY TELETYPESETTING
EEEEGNNNOORSSTV GET ON ONE'S
   NERVES
EEEEHLLNOOPSSTT TELEPHOTO LENSES
EEEEHNOPQSTTUUZ PUT THE SQUEEZE ON
EEEEIINNNPSSSVX INEXPENSIVENESS
EEEELMNORRSSSSS REMORSELESSNESS
EEEEMNNORSSSTUV VENTURESOMENESS
EEEFFIINNNOSSSV INOFFENSIVENESS

EEEEFHIILNOSSSUW HOUSEWIFELINESS
EEEEFHNNOOOORRSTW NONE THE WORSE
   FOR
EEEFILMMNOPRSTV SELF-IMPROVEMENT
EEEEGHMNNOOOSSSU
   HOMOGENEOUSNESS
EEEGIILLMOSTVWY GIVE IT SOME WELLY
EEEGIIMNNPRRSST MISREPRESENTING
EEEGIINNOPRSSTV PROGENITIVENESS
EEEGILORRRSSTVY RETROGRESSIVELY
EEEIIILNNOPRSTV VESPERTILIONINE
EEEIIMMOORRSSST STEREOISOMERISM
EEEIINOPRSSSTTU REPETITIOUSNESS
EEEEILLLMNOPPRWY YELLOW PIMPERNEL
EEEEILNNOOPPRSTT POISON-PEN LETTER
EEEIMNPPRSSSTUV PRESUMPTIVENESS
EEEINNNOSSSSTTU SENTENTIOUSNESS
EEEINNNOPRSSTTU PRETENTIOUSNESS
EEELNOPPRSSSSSU PURPOSELESSNESS
EEEMNOPSSSSTTUU TEMPESTUOUSNESS
EEFFFHILNOORSST SHIFT FOR ONESELF
EEFGHILLORSSTUY SELF-RIGHTEOUSLY
EEFGHNOORRSTTTW TOWER OF
   STRENGTH
EEFGIOOPRRRSSSU REGIUS PROFESSOR
EEFHMMNOOPRSTTU
   SPUR-OF-THE-MOMENT
EEFILLLMNOSSSUU MELLIFLUOUSNESS
EEFLNOPRSSSSUUU SUPERFLUOUSNESS
EEFMMNOORRSSTTT FROM STEM TO
   STERN
EEGGIILNNNSSTTT STINGING NETTLES
EEGHHLNOSSSSTTU THOUGHTLESSNESS
EEGHIMNOORSSSTY MOOG SYNTHESISER
EEGHIMNOORSSTYZ MOOG SYNTHESIZER
EEGIIIJNNNNNPSS SPINNING JENNIES
EEGIIIMNNPRRSTT MISINTERPRETING
EEGIINNORSSSTUV VERTIGINOUSNESS
EEGIINNPPRRSSST PRINTING PRESSES
EEGIINOPRSSSSTU PRESTIGIOUSNESS
EEHHILNOORTTTWW THROW IN THE
   TOWEL
EEHHLLOORSSTTUY YOUTH HOSTELLERS
EEHIKNOOPRRSTUY KEEP YOUR SHIRT ON
EEHILNNOOORSSST LOSE ONE'S SHIRT ON
EEHIMOOPRRSSSTU MOTHER SUPERIORS
EEHINNOPRRSTTTU THREE-POINT TURNS
EEHLNOPRSSSSUUU SULPHUREOUSNESS
EEIIIINNQSSSTUV INQUISITIVENESS
EEIIIMNNNORSTTV INTERVENTIONISM
EEIIINNNORSTTTV INTERVENTIONIST
EEIILNNOORRTTTU TRINITROTOLUENE
EEIINNNNNOORTTV NONINTERVENTION
EEILNNOPRSTTUUY UNPRETENTIOUSLY
EEINNNOOPPRSSTU INOPPORTUNENESS
EFGIIILMNOPRSVY OVERSIMPLIFYING
EFIIIILNNPSTTV SPLIT INFINITIVE
EFILMNRSSSSTTUU MISTRUSTFULNESS
EGGHIIIKLNNRSTT LIGHTNING STRIKE

EGHHIILLMNOOSTT HELMINTHOLOGIST
EGHHIINOOPPRRSW HERO-WORSHIPPING
EGHHILLNOOSTTUY YOUTH HOSTELLING
EGHHILNOOPRSTTT PLIGHT ONE'S TROTH
EGHIIIKLNNORSTV SHRINKING VIOLET
EGHILNOOOPRSUYY NEUROPHYSIOLOGY
EGIIILNNOORTUVZ REVOLUTIONIZING
EHHINOOPPRSSUYY NEUROHYPOPHYSIS
EHIIIKLMMOOPRST POIKILOTHERMISM
EHIILLMOOPPRTTU PHOTOMULTIPLIER
EHILOOPRSSTTTUW WHISTLE-STOP TOUR
EHINORRSSSTTTUW TRUSTWORTHINESS
EIIIMNOOPPRSSTU SUPERIMPOSITION
EIILOPRRSSTTUUY SURREPTITIOUSLY
EIILOPRSSSTTUUY SUPERSTITIOUSLY
EIINOOPPPRSSSTU PRESUPPOSITIONS
FFGHIIINNORSSSTU SOFT FURNISHINGS
FGHHIIIKLNNSTUW WISHFUL THINKING
FGHIINNNNNOOOSWW NO SHOW OF
WINNING
AAAAACDDEELLPPSS CALL A SPADE A
SPADE
AAAAACEEEKMNNPPR MAKE AN
APPEARANCE
AAAAAACGILLMMNRTY
ANAGRAMMATICALLY
AAAAABBDGGILNORTT RAGTAG AND
BOBTAIL
AAAAABCEHILLLNPTY ANALPHABETICALLY
AAAAACCHILLLNPTYY ANAPHYLACTICALLY
AAAAACDEGILRRSUWY DUAL
CARRIAGEWAYS
AAAAACDEHHLNPRRSU ARUNACHAL
PRADESH
AAAAACDGIILLMMRTY DIAGRAMMATICALLY
AAAAACDGIILLMPRTY PARADIGMATICALLY
AAAAACEEHILMMMTTT
METAMATHEMATICAL
AAAAACEELLNOPPRST TO ALL
APPEARANCES
AAAAACEILLMNNRSTY ALIMENTARY CANALS
AAAAADEGHIIRSSSTT AS STRAIGHT AS A DIE
AAAAEHIIMNNOSTTT ANATHEMATISATION
AAAAEHIIMNNOTTTZ ANATHEMATIZATION
AAAAEIILMNNPRRST PARLIAMENTARIANS
AAABBDDEEFKNRSST BED AND
BREAKFASTS
AAABCCEILLRRTUUY BUREAUCRATICALLY
AAABCDDHHMNNOOTT HAND-TO-HAND
COMBAT
AAABCDEGGIIILORR REGGIO DI CALABRIA
AAABCEEGHHILNNNT HANG IN THE
BALANCE
AAABCEEKKLLNRSTT BLACK
RATTLESNAKE
AAABCEFILLMNOORT AMERICAN
FOOTBALL
AAABCGHIILOOPRTU AUTOBIOGRAPHICAL

AAAABEEEKPPRSSTTW WASTEPAPER
BASKET
AAAABEEGGLLMNSSUY ASSEMBLY
LANGUAGE
AAAABEINNRSSTTTTU TRANSUBSTANTIATE
AAACCCFHIIINORST SACCHARIFICATION
AAACCDHIMMNOPRSY
PHARMACODYNAMICS
AAACCDIIILLLRSTY RADICALISTICALLY
AAACCEEGHIKNRRSY HACKNEY
CARRIAGES
AAACCEEHHIKKRRSS
KARACHAI-CHERKESS
AAACCEEHHILLMNPT THALAMENCEPHALIC
AAACCEEIILNOPSSU CAESALPINIACEOUS
AAACCEFIIRRRRRST AIRCRAFT CARRIERS
AAACCEGHILLLOORY ARCHAEOLOGICALLY
AAACCEHIINNPQSTU ACQUAINTANCESHIP
AAACCEHIINORRSTT CHARACTERISATION
AAACCEHIINORRTTZ CHARACTERIZATION
AAACCEHILLMPRTUY PHARMACEUTICALLY
AAACCFIIILLNOSST CLASSIFICATIONAL
AAACCGHIILLLLPRY CALLIGRAPHICALLY
AAACCHILLOPRSTTY CATASTROPHICALLY
AAACCIILLORRSTTY ARISTOCRATICALLY
AAACDEEEMMNRSSTU AMUSEMENT
ARCADES
AAACDEEFFGHIRRSS CHARGÉS
D'AFFAIRES
AAACDEGINORRRSTU REARGUARD
ACTIONS
AAACDEILLLMMORTY MELODRAMATICALLY
AAACDEIMNNOORSTT ANIMATED
CARTOONS
AAACEEEILMNNOPRT AMERICAN
ANTELOPE
AAACEEGGILLMNOTY
AGAMOGENETICALLY
AAACEEGHIMMNORST
ARCHAEOMAGNETISM
AAACEEHHLLMNNOPT
THALAMENCEPHALON
AAACEEKLLNOORRTW LOCAL AREA
NETWORK
AAACEFHHIILMRRSS AIR CHIEF MARSHALS
AAACEGHILLMNOPRY
ANEMOGRAPHICALLY
AAACEGHILNOOPPRT PALAEONTOGRAPHIC
AAACEGHINNOPRTTY
ACANTHOPTERYGIAN
AAACEGIILLMMPRTY EPIGRAMMATICALLY
AAACEGILLLNOOOPT PALAEONTOLOGICAL
AAACEGILLLOOOOPZ PALAEOZOOLOGICAL
AAACEHIILLNPTTTY ANTIPATHETICALLY
AAACEHILLLMNPRUY ALPHANUMERICALLY
AAACEHILLMPRSTTY METAPHRASTICALLY
AAACEIIILNOPRSTT RECAPITALISATION
AAACEIIILNOPRTTZ RECAPITALIZATION

AAACEIKLMMNORSTX EXCLAMATION
MARKS
AAACEINNORTTTTTT ATTRACT ATTENTION
AAACFHIIILLNSSTT ATLANTIC SAILFISH
AAACGHILLLNOPPRY PLANOGRAPHICALLY
AAACGHILLNOPPRTY PANTOGRAPHICALLY
AAACGIILLNNOSTTY ANTAGONISTICALLY
AAACIILLLNRSTTUY NATURALISTICALLY
AAACILLMMOPSTTYY ASYMPTOMATICALLY
AAACILLMNNOOSTTY ANTONOMASTICALLY
AAACILLMNOOPRSTY PARONOMASTICALLY
AAADDDEEKLNNRSSS SNAKES AND
LADDERS
AAADDEEFHLMOPRRY
PARAFORMALDEHYDE
AAADEEEILLRSTVWY ELEVATED RAILWAYS
AAADEEGNNOSSSTUV
ADVANTAGEOUSNESS
AAADEEIMNOPRRSST DRAMATIS
PERSONAE
AAADEFJLMMNOSSTT FLOTSAM AND
JETSAM
AAADEGHIMPPRRSSY DIAPHRAGM
PESSARY
AAADEGIILNNORRTT INTERGRADATIONAL
AAADEIILNNORSTTU DENATURALISATION
AAADEIILNNORTTUZ DENATURALIZATION
AAADGHILLMNRRSSY MARSHALLING
YARDS
AAADIILMMNORRSTT MALADMINISTRATOR
AAAEEEEGLNRSSTTT REAL ESTATE
AGENTS
AAAEEEEHHKMRTVWY MAKE HEAVY
WEATHER
AAAEEEGLMNPRRSTY PAYMASTER
GENERAL
AAAEEEJLNNNPRSST JAPANESE LANTERNS
AAAEEFLLMMNNNORS ALL MANNER OF
MEANS
AAAEEGIILNOQRTUU EQUATORIAL GUINEA
AAAEEHIINNOSSTTT ANAESTHETISATION
AAAEEHIINNOSTTTZ ANAESTHETIZATION
AAAEEIIMNNOPPRTX EXAMINATION PAPER
AAAEILLMNNOOPSYY
MALAYO-POLYNESIAN
AAAFILMNNOORRSTT TRANSFORMATIONAL
AAAGIILLNNOORSTY ORGANISATIONALLY
AAAGIILLNNOORTYZ ORGANIZATIONALLY
AAAGIILMNNORRSTT TRANSMIGRATIONAL
AAAHIIIMNORRSTTU AUTHORITARIANISM
AAAIIIILNNOORSSTT RATIONALISATIONS
AAAIIIILNNOORSTTZ RATIONALIZATIONS
AAAIIILLMNNORSTTU ULTRANATIONALISM
AAAIIILLNNORSTTTU ULTRANATIONALIST
AAAIIILMNNOPRSSTU SUPRANATIONALISM
AABBDDELNNOPSSUY BY LEAPS AND
BOUNDS
AABBEIIILLMOTTYZ METABOLIZABILITY
AABCCDEIIIMNNOOZ AMINOBENZOIC ACID

AABCCEEGGLLOORRT GARBAGE
COLLECTOR
AABCCEEHHMORRRST CHAMBER
ORCHESTRA
AABCCEGILNNNORTU
COUNTERBALANCING
AABCCIIIILMPRTTY IMPRACTICABILITY
AABCCIILMMNNORTUU CIRCUMAMBULATION
AABCCILMMORRTUUY
CIRCUMAMBULATORY
AABCDEEIIMNNOORW AMERICAN
WOODBINE
AABCDEIILNOORSST ANABOLIC STEROIDS
AABCDGILMNOOPTUY GUNBOAT
DIPLOMACY
AABCEEEILLMMNSST EMBLEMATICALNESS
AABCEEHILNNRSSTU UNCHARITABLENESS
AABCEFGILLMNORRU AMERICAN
BULLFROG
AABCEHIIILMNPTUY UNIMPEACHABILITY
AABCEIIIILLMRRTY IRRECLAIMABILITY
AABCGIILNORSSTUU SUBCARTILAGINOUS
AABCIILLMNOOORST COLLABORATIONISM
AABCIILLNOOORSTT COLLABORATIONIST
AABCILLLLLOPSYYY POLYSYLLABICALLY
AABCILLLLMNOOSYY MONOSYLLABICALLY
AABCINNOOORSSSTT CONTRABASSOONIST
AABDDEEFGIKNRSTW WEDDING
BREAKFAST
AABDEEEEFFNNRTWW FEW AND FAR
BETWEEN
AABDEEEEGILNRSSS DISAGREEABLENESS
AABDEEEIMNOORRRT ANEROID
BAROMETER
AABDEEFHILLSTWYY FALL BY THE WAYSIDE
AABDEEIMMNRRSSST
DISEMBARRASSMENT
AABDEFGIIIILNTTY INDEFATIGABILITY
AABEEEGHLLLMNOWW WHOLE NEW BALL
GAME
AABEEEGLMORRSTVW VEGETABLE
MARROWS
AABEEELNNNORSSSU
UNREASONABLENESS
AABEEEELNNNOSSSSU
UNSEASONABLENESS
AABEEFGHIKLNRSST ENGLISH BREAKFAST
AABEEFLNNORSSUUV
UNFAVOURABLENESS
AABIIILNNNNOTTTU TINTINNABULATION
AABIIILNNSSTTTUY INSUBSTANTIALITY
AABIILNNSSTTTUUY UNSUBSTANTIALITY
AABIILNOPRRSTTTY TRANSPORTABILITY
AACCCDEFIILNOORR AFRICAN CROCODILE
AACCCDEHIINNORTW IN ACCORDANCE
WITH
AACCCDIIINORRSTY IDIOSYNCRACRATIC
AACCCEEIILLLSSTY ECCLESIASTICALLY

AACCCEHIKMRRRSST CHRISTMAS
CRACKER
AACCCIILLLNOOSTY ICONOCLASTICALLY
AACCDEEHHIILPRTT TEREPHTHALIC ACID
AACCDEEILNNOORTU
DEUTEROCANONICAL
AACCDEFGHKLNORRT GRANDFATHER
CLOCK
AACCDEFIIILNOSST DECLASSIFICATION
AACCDEFIILLOPTTY FILLED TO CAPACITY
AACCDEGILLLNNOST LONG-DISTANCE CALL
AACCDIIINNNOORTT CONTRAINDICATION
AACCEEFGIKNNOOTZ TAKE COGNIZANCE
OF
AACCEEHILLMORTTY TACHEOMETRICALLY
AACCEEILLORSTTTY STEREOTACTICALLY
AACCEEKNORRSTTTU
COUNTERATTACKERS
AACCEELLNOOSSTTW COALS TO
NEWCASTLE
AACCEEMNOPRRSTYY COMPANY
SECRETARY
AACCEGHHILLOPRTY HECTOGRAPHICALLY
AACCEGHIIMMPSTTY SYMPATHETIC MAGIC
AACCEGHILLNOPRSY SCENOGRAPHICALLY
AACCEGIKNNORTTTU COUNTERATTACKING
AACCEGILLLNRSTUU INTEGRAL CALCULUS
AACCEHHHILNNOPRY
RHYNCHOCEPHALIAN
AACCEHHIIIMNPRSV VICE-CHAIRMANSHIP
AACCEHIILMNSSSST SCHISMATICALNESS
AACCEHLLOOPRSUYY
CARYOPHYLLACEOUS
AACCEIILLLNORTVY INTERVOCALICALLY
AACCFILOOPRRRSTU PROCURATOR FISCAL
AACCGGIIIMNNRTUV CIRCUMNAVIGATING
AACCGHIILLMNOOST ANGLO-CATHOLICISM
AACCGHIILLMOPRRY MICROGRAPHICALLY
AACCGHILLOPRRSTY CRYSTALLOGRAPHIC
AACCGIIIMNNORTUV CIRCUMNAVIGATION
AACCHHILLOPPSTYY PSYCHOPATHICALLY
AACCHIIILLNSTUVY CHAUVINISTICALLY
AACCHIIINNNORSST ANACHRONISNISTIC
AACCHIILMMNOORST ROMAN
CATHOLICISM
AACCHILLLOPPRTYY PROPHYLACTICALLY
AACCIILLMNRSTTUY CIRCUMSTANTIALLY
AACCILLOOPRSSTUY STAUROSCOPICALLY
AACDDEEIILNPRSTU UNDERCAPITALISED
AACDDEEIILNPRTUZ UNDERCAPITALIZED
AACDDEGHLNOOSSTT GOODS AND
CHATTELS
AACDDEHLLNNOOOTT NOT HOLD A
CANDLE TO
AACDDHILLMNORYYY
HYDRODYNAMICALLY
AACDEEEEGIORSSST ASSOCIATE DEGREES
AACDEEEELORRSSUY DAY RELEASE
COURSE

AACDEEEIMNNNORRT MAINTENANCE
ORDER
AACDEEFGILLNORTT FLAGRANTE DELICTO
AACDEEGHIILOPRRT RADIOTELEGRAPHIC
AACDEEGIILMRRRST MEDICAL REGISTRAR
AACDEEHIIOPRRTTU RADIOTHERAPEUTIC
AACDEEIILNNNQRTU QUADRICENTENNIAL
AACDEEIILNNORSTT DECENTRALISATION
AACDEEIILNNORTTZ DECENTRALIZATION
AACDEEILNNSSSTTU INDECENT ASSAULTS
AACDEELLNNNRSTTY
TRANSCENDENTALLY
AACDEFIILMNNSTTU FUNDAMENTALISTIC
AACDEHHIILNPRSST CHRISTADELPHIANS
AACDEHIIKKMNNRST KITCHEN-SINK
DRAMA
AACDEIILLLMORTTY DILATOMETRICALLY
AACDEINOPRSSSSST SCISSORS-AND-PASTE
AACDFIIIILNOQSTU DISQUALIFICATION
AACDGHHILLOPRRYY
HYDROGRAPHICALLY
AACDIIIILMNNORST DISCRIMINATIONAL
AACDIIIILNORSTTT TRADITIONALISTIC
AACDIIILNNORSTTU INDUSTRIAL ACTION
AACEEEEGLNRRRSTY
SECRETARY-GENERAL
AACEEEFHORRSSTTW WEATHER
FORECASTS
AACEEEHHHLNOORTX
HEXACHLOROETHANE
AACEEEIINPPRSSTV APPRECIATIVENESS
AACEEFFMNORSSTTT
MATTER-OF-FACTNESS
AACEEFHKNNOORTTV ARK OF THE
COVENANT
AACEEGHILLMNPSST PHLEGMATICALNESS
AACEEGIILLLNNPTY PALINGENETICALLY
AACEEGIILLLNSTVY EVANGELISTICALLY
AACEEGILLNPRSSTT LAST RESTING PLACE
AACEEGLMNOOPRTUU ANALOGUE
COMPUTER
AACEEGNOOPRRTTUV AGENT
PROVOCATEUR
AACEEHILLNNRSTUY NEURASTHENICALLY
AACEEHILMNOPRSST METAPHORICALNESS
AACEEHIMOPRSSTTU MASSOTHERAPEUTIC
AACEEIIILNNPSTTV CAPITAL-INTENSIVE
AACEEIIIMNNRSSST NECESSITARIANISM
AACEEIIILLRRSTTTV VERTICILLASTRATE
AACEEIIILMNRRSSSU MACLAURIN'S SERIES
AACEEIILNNRSSTTU INARTICULATENESS
AACEEIKMNNOORSTV MAKE
CONVERSATION
AACEEILLNNORSTTU NATURAL SELECTION
AACEEILLNOOPRTUV PALACE REVOLUTION
AACEEILMMNOPRSTT COMPARTMENTALISE
AACEEILMMNOPRTTZ COMPARTMENTALIZE
AACEEILMNSSSSTTY SYSTEMATICALNESS

AACEEKNNNORSSSTU
  CANTANKEROUSNESS
AACEFFIILNOSSSTT SELF-SATISFACTION
AACEFGILLNRRTTUU ULTRACENTRIFUGAL
AACEFIINORSSSSTT SATISFACTORINESS
AACEGHHIILNOPSTT TEACHING HOSPITAL
AACEGHHILLNOPRTY ETHNOGRAPHICALLY
AACEGHILLOPPRRTY PETROGRAPHICALLY
AACEGHILOOPSSTTT COTTAGE HOSPITALS
AACEGHLLOPRRRSTY
  CRYSTALLOGRAPHER
AACEGIIILNOPRTVZ OVERCAPITALIZING
AACEGIIMNORSSSTV MOVING STAIRCASES
AACEHHIILLNOPRTY HIEROPHANTICALLY
AACEHIILLNSSTTUY ENTHUSIASTICALLY
AACEHIILLOORSTTU LOCAL AUTHORITIES
AACEHIILLPPRRSTY PERIPHRASTICALLY
AACEHIILMNNORRTV HARMONIC INTERVAL
AACEHILLMORSTTTY THERMOSTATICALLY
AACEHLMORSSSTUUW WALRUS
  MOUSTACHES
AACEIIILLLLRSTTY LITERALISTICALLY
AACEIIILLLRSTTVY RELATIVISTICALLY
AACEIIILMNORRSTU MERCURIALISATION
AACEIIILMNORRTUZ MERCURIALIZATION
AACEIILNNOOSSTT SECTIONALISATION
AACEIIILNNOOSTTZ SECTIONALIZATION
AACEIIILNNOSSSTT SENSATIONALISTIC
AACEIIILNOOPRSTT OPERATIONALISTIC
AACEIIINNNOORSTT CONTAINERISATION
AACEIIINNNOORTTZ CONTAINERIZATION
AACEIIINNNORRSTT REINCARNATIONIST
AACEIIILLLRRSSTUY SURREALISTICALLY
AACEIILNORRRTTUV ATRIOVENTRICULAR
AACEIIMNNOORSSTX CROSS-EXAMINATION
AACEILLLMNNOPRTY PLANNOMETRICALLY
AACEILLMNOOOOPTY
  ONOMATOPOEICALLY
AACEILLNNOORSTVY CONVERSATIONALLY
AACEILNNNNORSTTT TRANSCONTINENTAL
AACELOOOPRRSTUVY SUPER ROYAL
  OCTAVO
AACFIIIILNNOOSTT FICTIONALISATION
AACFIIIILNNOOTTZ FICTIONALIZATION
AACGHHIILLLOPRTY LITHOGRAPHICALLY
AACGHHILLLMOOOPT
  OPHTHALMOLOGICAL
AACGHHILLOOPPRTY PHOTOGRAPHICALLY
AACGHHILLOOPRRTY ORTHOGRAPHICALLY
AACGHIIILNNPRSTY PHYSICAL TRAINING
AACGHILLLOPRSTYY STYLOGRAPHICALLY
AACGHILLNOOPPRRY PORNOGRAPHICALLY
AACGIIINNNOPPRTT NONPARTICIPATING
AACGIILLMNORRTTU COURT-MARTIALLING
AACHHHILOPPRRSTY STAPHYLORRHAPHIC
AACHIIIINNORSSTT CHRISTIANISATION
AACHIIIINNORSTTZ CHRISTIANIZATION
AACHIILLMNOPRSTY MISANTHROPICALLY
AACHILLNOOPTTUYY AUTOHYPNOTICALLY

AACIIIILLLMRSTTY MILITARISTICALLY
AACIIIILMNNOPSTU MUNICIPALISATION
AACIIIILMNNOPTUZ MUNICIPALIZATION
AACIIILLLMNOPTTU MULTIPLICATIONAL
AACIILLNOOOPRRSTY CONSPIRATORIALLY
AACIKMNNOPRSTTUU PUNCTUATION
  MARKS
AACILNNORRSTTTUU TRANSCULTURATION
AADDDDEEEGILMPRS MIDDLE AGED
  SPREAD
AADDEEEGILMMMNNT MIDDLE
  MANAGEMENT
AADDEEGHHKLNNOSS GOLDEN
  HANDSHAKES
AADDEEIIKMPRRSST MAKE RAPID STRIDES
AADDFGIILNNORSTV STANDARD OF LIVING
AADEEEEEILNRSSSV VENEREAL DISEASES
AADEEEEELMNOPRSTV DEVELOPMENT
  AREAS
AADEEEEFFGIILNRRT DIFFERENTIAL GEAR
AADEEEFHINNRSSTT FAINT-HEARTEDNESS
AADEEEGHHNRSTTUW THE GREAT
  UNWASHED
AADEEHILMORRRSTT TETARROHEDRALISM
AADEEHLNNOOPRSVY OVERPLAY ONE'S
  HAND
AADEEIIKNRSTTTTU STRIKE AN ATTITUDE
AADEEIILNRSSTTTU INDUSTRIAL ESTATE
AADEFFIIILNOORRT AFFILIATION ORDER
AADEFFIINOORSSTT DISAFFORESTATION
AADEIIIILMNORSTT DEMILITARISATION
AADEIIIILMNORTTZ DEMILITARIZATION
AADEIIIILNOORSTT EDITORIALISATION
AADEIIIILNOORTTZ EDITORIALIZATION
AADEIIILMNRSTTVY ADMINISTRATIVELY
AADEMNOOPRRSTTUW PORTMANTEAU
  WORDS
AAEEEFGOOPPPRRRS GREASEPROOF
  PAPER
AAEEEGLNNORRSTTY ATTORNEY
  GENERALS
AAEEEILNNOPRRSTT REPRESENTATIONAL
AAEEEILRRRRSTTTX EXTRATERRESTRIAL
AAEEFFHIIIMNRTTV IN THE AFFIRMATIVE
AAEEFHILRSSSTTVV HARVEST FESTIVALS
AAEEFHLMNOOPRTUY POLYURETHANE
  FOAM
AAEEGHHIILMNSTVY TIME HANGS HEAVILY
AAEEGHIJNNOPRRTU EUROPEAN NIGHTJAR
AAEEGHILLNOOPSTT PALAEETHNOLOGIST
AAEEGILOOPRRRTVY ROYAL PREROGATIVE
AAEEGPPRRRRSSTUY SPARE-PART
  SURGERY
AAEEIIILNNNORSTT INTERNATIONALISE
AAEEIIILNNNORTTZ INTERNATIONALIZE
AAEEIILNNOPRRTTT INTERPRETATIONAL
AAEEIILNNORSSTTX EXTERNALISATIONS
AAEEIILNNORSTTXZ EXTERNALIZATIONS
AAEEIILORRRRTTTX EXTRATERRITORIAL

AAEEILMNPRRRSTTU PRETERNATURALISM
AAEEILMNPRRTTUWY MANUAL TYPEWRITER
AAEELNNPRRSSSTUU SUPERNATURALNESS
AAEFFHOOOPRSSTTV HAVE A SOFT SPOT FOR
AAEFHIIILLNNNOST SELF-ANNIHILATION
AAEGGIIILNOSTTUV ISOAGGLUTINATIVE
AAEGIIIILMNOSTTT LEGITIMATISATION
AAEGIIIILMNOTTTZ LEGITIMATIZATION
AAEGIILNNORSSTTT GASTROINTESTINAL
AAEIIILMNNNORSTT INTERNATIONALISM
AAEIIILMNNOOOSTT EMOTIONALISATION
AAEIIILMNNOOOTTZ EMOTIONALIZATION
AAEIIILNNNORSTTT INTERNATIONALIST
AAEIIILNNNORTTTY INTERNATIONALITY
AAEIIILNNORSSTUV UNIVERSALISATION
AAEIIILNNORSTUVZ UNIVERSALIZATION
AAEIIKNNOORRSTTW SANITATION WORKER
AAEIILNNORRSSTTT TRANSLITERATIONS
AAEILNOPRRSSSSYY SENSORY PARALYSIS
AAELOOPQRRRSTUUY SUPER ROYAL QUARTO
AAFGIINNORRSSTTU TRANSFIGURATIONS
AAGGIIILNNOOSTTU ISOAGGLUTINATION
AAGHHOOOPPRRSTTY ASTROPHOTOGRAPHY
AAGIIIMNOPPPRRST MISAPPROPRIATING
AAIIIILNOPRSSTTU SPIRITUALISATION
AAIIIILNOPRSTTUZ SPIRITUALIZATION
AAIIILLNNOQRSTTU TRANQUILLISATION
AAIIILLNNOQRTTUZ TRANQUILLIZATION
AAIIIMNOOPPPRRST MISAPPROPRIATION
AAIIILLMNNORRSTTU TRANSILLUMINATOR
AAIIMNNORSSTTTTU TRANSMUTATIONIST
ABBBCDEEIKNRSTTU BEST BIB AND TUCKER
ABBCDDEEGHIKMPRU HUMPBACKED BRIDGE
ABBCDEIIIILNRSTY INDESCRIBABILITY
ABBCEEEFFKLOOOST COFFEE-TABLE BOOKS
ABBCEHLNOORSSTTU BACHELOR'S-BUTTONS
ABBCEIIIJLNOOTTY OBJECTIONABILITY
ABBDEEEGMNRRTTUW BADEN-WURTTEMBERG
ABBDEELNORRRSTWY STRAWBERRY BLONDE
ABBEEEEINNNNOOST A BEE IN ONE'S BONNET
ABBEIIILMPRRTTUY IMPERTURBABILITY
ABBIIILSSTTTTUUY SUBSTITUTABILITY
ABCCDKLLNOORSTUY COCK-AND-BULL STORY
ABCCEEEIKLLNRSTT ELECTRIC BLANKETS
ABCCEEHILNOPRSTY HYPERBOLIC SECANT
ABCCEEILLNOOPSST POLICE CONSTABLES

ABCCEFIIIJNOSTTU SUBJECTIFICATION
ABCCEGHIILLNOOOT BIOTECHNOLOGICAL
ABCCEIIIILNNOTVY INCONCEIVABILITY
ABCCGHIILLOOOPSY PSYCHOBIOLOGICAL
ABCCIIKLMNNOOOST COMBINATION LOCKS
ABCCILLOOOPRSSTY STROBOSCOPICALLY
ABCDDEEEMNOORTTT BOTTOM DEAD CENTRE
ABCDEEEEGHLORRSS BACHELOR'S DEGREES
ABCDEEEHHLLOOOTW THE WHOLE CABOODLE
ABCDEEGILNNORSSU CUDGEL ONE'S BRAINS
ABCDEEHIMNNOPRRS DOBERMAN PINSCHER
ABCDEELMNORRSSUU CONSUMER DURABLES
ABCDEGIILLNOSSTT DISCLOSING TABLET
ABCDEGKNNOOOORSW GO BACK ON ONE'S WORD
ABCDEIIILNNNOSTY INCONDENSABILITY
ABCDEIIILNPRTTUY UNPREDICTABILITY
ABCEEEEFILNRRRRY REFERENCE LIBRARY
ABCEEEEHRRRRSSTT STRETCHER-BEARERS
ABCEFFIINOOOOPRRT PROBATION OFFICER
ABCEFGIIILLNNORY FIBRINOGENICALLY
ABCEHIILLNOSTTYY BIOSYNTHETICALLY
ABCEHIMNNNOOOPRU BRONCHOPNEUMONIA
ABCEIIIILLLMSSST BALLISTIC MISSILE
ABCEIILNNOSTTTY INCONTESTABILITY
ABCEIMNNORSSSTUU RAMBUNCTIOUSNESS
ABCFIILMNNOORTUY UNCONFORMABILITY
ABDDEEEHNOORSSUW BONDED WAREHOUSES
ABDDEEEIMNNNSSST ABSENT-MINDEDNESS
ABDDEHLNNNOOOOSS BLOOD ON ONE'S HANDS
ABDEEEFIIILNNSST IDENTIFIABLENESS
ABDEEEFIOOPSSSTX SAFE-DEPOSIT BOXES
ABDEEEILNPRSSSTU DISREPUTABLENESS
ABDEEFIIMNNORRST FIRE-AND-BRIMSTONE
ABDEEFIOOPSSTTXY SAFETY-DEPOSIT BOX
ABDEEGGILMNPRRSU GINGERBREAD PLUMS
ABDEEGIIILLNNRRS LENDING LIBRARIES
ABDEEHIILMNSSSTT DISESTABLISHMENT
ABDEEKNNOORRSUVW NERVOUS BREAKDOWN
ABDEFIIIILLRSTVY DIVERSIFIABILITY
ABDEGHIMNOOSSTTU DOUBTING THOMASES
ABDEIIIIILLLMTTY LIMITED LIABILITY
ABDEIIIILNNPSSTY INDISPENSABILITY
ABDFIIILNOOORSUV DIVISION OF LABOUR

ABDFILNNOOORSSTU BLOOD
TRANSFUSION
ABEEEFILNNRRSSTT ENFANTS TERRIBLES
ABEEEGLNNNORSSUV
UNGOVERNABLENESS
ABEEEIIILMMPRSTY SEMIPERMEABILITY
ABEEEIILMNNNRSST INTERMINABLENESS
ABEEEIILNPRRSTTY REPRESENTABILITY
ABEEEILNNOQSSSTU QUESTIONABLENESS
ABEEGHIIILNNSTUX INEXTINGUISHABLE
ABEEGIIMPRRRTTUZ PIETERMARITZBURG
ABEEIIIILRRRTTVY IRRETRIEVABILITY
ABEEIIILNPRRTTTY INTERPRETABILITY
ABEELMNNORSSSTUU
SURMOUNTABLENESS
ABEFGIIIILNRRRTY IRREFRANGIBILITY
ABEHIIIILNSTTUXY INEXHAUSTIBILITY
ABEHILOORRSSSTTY ERYTHROBLASTOSIS
ABEINOOOPRSSSTTV OBSERVATION POSTS
ABIIIILMNRSSSTTY TRANSMISSIBILITY
ACCCCEEEILNNOSSU CONSCIENCE
CLAUSE
ACCCCEGHIKNNOSTU CHECKING
ACCOUNTS
ACCCDDHHIILOORRY HYDROCHLORIC ACID
ACCCDEEILLLNOPYY ENCYCLOPEDICALLY
ACCCDFHHLNOORSTU CHURCH OF
SCOTLAND
ACCCEEEGHILLLNOT TECHNICAL COLLEGE
ACCCEEEILNOSSSUV CONCESSIVE CLAUSE
ACCCEEGHHILLORTU COLLEGIATE
CHURCH
ACCCEEHIIINNRSST CHRISTIAN SCIENCE
ACCCEEIIIILLNOPST POLITICAL SCIENCE
ACCCEEILOORSSTTU ELECTROACOUSTICS
ACCCEEHHIINNOPSTY PSYCHOTECHNICIAN
ACCCEILOOPRSSTUU ACOUSTIC COUPLERS
ACCCIILMOOPRRSTU ULTRAMICROSCOPIC
ACCDDEIMMNNNOOSS
SECONDS-IN-COMMAND
ACCDEEEMNNOOPRRT PROMENADE
CONCERT
ACCDEEFHIIMMNNOR COMMANDER IN
CHIEF
ACCDEEHHIKLLNRTY LATCHKEY CHILDREN
ACCDEFHIKLOOOSVW FIVE O'CLOCK
SHADOW
ACCDEFMNOOPRRTUU COMPOUND
FRACTURE
ACCDEGIINNNNOSTU DISCOUNTENANCING
ACCDEHHIILLMOOPS DOLICHOCEPHALISM
ACCDEHIIMOOSSTTY HOMOSCEDASTICITY
ACCDEIOPPRRSSTTU PICTURE POSTCARDS
ACCEEEEFIILNPSTX LIFE EXPECTANCIES
ACCEEEEGLLLLOORT ELECTORAL
COLLEGE
ACCEEEELLMOPRSTX ELECTRA
COMPLEXES
ACCEEEFFIIILORRV OFFICIAL RECEIVER

ACCEEEFHIINOOPTT PIECE OF THE ACTION
ACCEEEFIMNORSSST MASTERS OF
SCIENCE
ACCEEFMOORRRSTTU CREATURE
COMFORTS
ACCEEHIILLLNORTY HELIOCENTRICALLY
ACCEEHILLNNORTTY ETHNOCENTRICALLY
ACCEEHLMNORSSTUY
SCLERENCHYMATOUS
ACCEEIILOORRRSTT ARTERIOSCLEROTIC
ACCEEIIMMNNORTTU INTERCOMMUNICATE
ACCEEIKNOOPRRTTT PROTECTION RACKET
ACCEEILLOOPRSSTY STEREOSCOPICALLY
ACCEEIMNNOPRSSTY COPERNICAN
SYSTEM
ACCEFIIILLNNSTUY UNSCIENTIFICALLY
ACCEGIILNNOPRSSS PELICAN CROSSINGS
ACCEHIINOPRRSTUY NEUROPSYCHIATRIC
ACCEHILLMOOPRSTY THERMOSCOPICALLY
ACCEHILMOPRSTYY PSYCHOMETRICALLY
ACCEIIIILLNOOSTTV COLLECTIVISATION
ACCEIIIILLNOOTTVZ COLLECTIVIZATION
ACCEIIILOSSSTTTX LEXICOSTATISTICS
ACCEIILLMNORRSTY MICROCRYSTALLINE
ACCEIILLNOOPRSTY RETINOSCOPICALLY
ACCEIIMMNNOOSTUX
EXCOMMUNICATIONS
ACCEIINOORSSTTVV VASOCONSTRICTIVE
ACCFILLLOOOPRSUY FLUOROSCOPICALLY
ACCGHHIILLLOOTYY ICHTHYOLOGICALLY
ACCGIILLMMOOOORTY MICROCLIMATOLOGY
ACCHHIIOOPRRSTTY ORTHOPSYCHIATRIC
ACCIINNOOORSSTTV VASOCONSTRICTION
ACCIKLLMOOOOSTTV MOLOTOV
COCKTAILS
ACDDDEFILNNOOSTU CONSOLIDATED
FUND
ACDDEEEELNNPSSTU DEPENDENT
CLAUSES
ACDDEEMNNOORRSSY SECONDARY
MODERNS
ACDDEFHIIIIMNOTU DEHUMIDIFICATION
ACDDEGHILLNOSSTW SWADDLING
CLOTHES
ACDDGHIIMNPRSSTU CHRISTMAS PUDDING
ACDDHHJNNOPSUUWY PUNCH-AND-JUDY
SHOW
ACDEEEEEGGHLRRST THREE-LEGGED
RACES
ACDEEEEFILMNSTTV MENTAL DEFECTIVES
ACDEEEEHIMNNRTUV
UNDERACHEIVEMENT
ACDEEEEIIKMNNOST TAKE ONE'S
MEDICINE
ACDEEEEIIPRTTTVV PRIVATE DETECTIVE
ACDEEEEINRRRSSTU UNDERSECRETARIES
ACDEEEFHILLNORSS HALLS OF RESIDENCE
ACDEEEFIIILNRSTT DEFINITE ARTICLES
ACDEEEFIINOQRRSU RADIO FREQUENCIES

ACDEEEFLLOORRUVV FOUR-LEAVED
 CLOVER
ACDEEEEGHILNRSSST CLEAR-SIGHTEDNESS
ACDEEEGHILORRSTT CIGARETTE HOLDERS
ACDEEEGHKLPSTTUU TAKE UP THE
 CUDGELS
ACDEEEIIILNPRSTV VICE-PRESIDENTIAL
ACDEEEIILLLNSTTU INTELLECTUALISED
ACDEEEIIMNPRSSSV MANIC-DEPRESSIVES
ACDEEEILNNNOSTTU SECOND LIEUTENANT
ACDEEENNNNRSSSTT
 TRANSCENDENTNESS
ACDEEFHIIMNNRSST DISFRANCHISEMENT
ACDEEFHINORRTTUU FURTHER
 EDUCATION
ACDEEFIIMNNOORST CONFEDERATIONISM
ACDEEFIINNOORSTT CONFEDERATIONIST
ACDEEFILNORRRSTU FUNERAL DIRECTORS
ACDEEFINNOPRSTUU SUPERFECUNDATION
ACDEEGGHIINPRRSS GRAPHIC DESIGNERS
ACDEEGINNOORRRTU RECREATION
 GROUND
ACDEEGMMOOPRRRSU PROGRAMMED
 COURSE
ACDEEHIILMNOPRTY DIACETYLMORPHINE
ACDEEIIILLMNOSTUY EUDEMONISTICALLY
ACDEEIILMNNORSTU RADIOLUMINESCENT
ACDEEIILNPPRRTUY PERPENDICULARITY
ACDEEJKLNOORSSVY DAVY JONES'S
 LOCKER
ACDEFIIIIMNNNOST INDEMNIFICATIONS
ACDEFIILNNNORTTT CONTINENTAL DRIFT
ACDEFINNOOORSTUU FOUNDATION
 COURSE
ACDEGHIILMNNOOPS HOLDING COMPANIES
ACDEGHILLLMOOOTY
 METHODOLOGICALLY
ACDEGIIIKNNRSSTT STRIKING DISTANCE
ACDEGIILMOPRSTTU DIGITAL COMPUTERS
ACDEGILNNNOSSTTU CONSENTING
 ADULTS
ACDEGMNOOPRRSSTU SOUND
 SPECTROGRAM
ACDEHILLMOPSTTUY SHUTTLE DIPLOMACY
ACDEIIIILMNNRSTY INDISCRIMINATELY
ACDEIIIILLMNORTTU MULTIDIRECTIONAL
ACDEIILMNORRSTTU ULTRAMODERNISTIC
ACDEIINORRSTTTTY DISTRICT ATTORNEY
ACDEILOOPRSSSTUY PERISSODACTYLOUS
ACDIIIIIMNNNORST INDISCRIMINATION
ACDIIIILMNORRSTY DISCRIMINATORILY
ACEEEEEFFFMNORRR FRAME OF
 REFERENCE
ACEEEEGILLNNORST GENERAL ELECTIONS
ACEEEEHLLQRRSTUV TRAVELLER'S
 CHEQUE
ACEEEFGILNNOPRRS PEREGRINE FALCONS
ACEEEGGHIILRRTTT CIGARETTE LIGHTER

ACEEEGHKLNOPSSTU GET ONE'S
 HACKLES UP
ACEEEGIIINPRRRSV VIRGINIA CREEPERS
ACEEEGILMMNORSTT
 ELECTROMAGNETISM
ACEEEGINNOOPRSTU
 COUNTERESPIONAGE
ACEEEHHIILNNPRSTY CHRYSELEPHANTINE
ACEEEHHIPPRSSSTT SPEECH THERAPISTS
ACEEEHIILLMRSTUY EUHEMERISTICALLY
ACEEEHIPRRRSSTTT STRETCHER PARTIES
ACEEEHLLMNOORSTY ELEMENTARY
 SCHOOL
ACEEEIILLLNRSTTU INTELLECTUALISER
ACEEEIILLLNRTTUZ INTELLECTUALIZER
ACEEEIILNNNQSSTU SESQUICENTENNIAL
ACEEEILLMNPPRRST SCARLET PIMPERNEL
ACEEFGINORRSTTVY CENTRES OF
 GRAVITY
ACEEFHILLNNNOSTT CONTINENTAL SHELF
ACEEFIIILMNOPSTX EXEMPLIFICATIONS
ACEEFIKNOOPRSTWY NASTY PIECE OF
 WORK
ACEEGGIILLNNORST TRAINING COLLEGES
ACEEGHHILOOPPRTT
 PHOTOTELEGRAPHIC, TELEPHOTOGRAPHIC
ACEEGHIILLNOSTTY HISTOGENETICALLY
ACEEGHILLLOOPRTY HERPETOLOGICALLY
ACEEGHILLMNNOOOP
 PHENOMENOLOGICAL
ACEEGHILLNOORTTY ORTHOGENETICALLY
ACEEGHILLNOPTTYY PHYTOGENETICALLY
ACEEGHIMMNORSTTY
 MAGNETOCHEMISTRY
ACEEGIILLNOORRST SOLICITOR GENERAL
ACEEGIILNORSSSSU SACRILEGIOUSNESS
ACEEGIIMNORSTTTV MAGNETOSTRICTIVE
ACEEGIMNNOOPRSTV
 OVERCOMPENSATING
ACEEGLMMNOOPRTTV GLOVE
 COMPARTMENT
ACEEHHIINNOPPRTT PITHECANTHROPINE
ACEEHHIMMOORRSTT
 HETEROCHROMATISM
ACEEHHIOOPPRTTTU PHOTOTHERAPEUTIC
ACEEHIILMNNORSTVV THERMIONIC VALVES
ACEEHIINORSSTTUV OVERENTHUSIASTIC
ACEEHILLMMORRTTY
 THERMOMETRICALLY
ACEEHILLNOOPRSTY STEREOPHONICALLY
ACEEIILLLOPPSSTVX PLASTIC EXPLOSIVE
ACEEIILNNNNORTTT INTERCONTINENTAL
ACEEIILNNOQSTTUY CONSEQUENTIALITY
ACEEIILOORRRSSST ARTERIOSCLEROSIS
ACEEIMNNOOOPRSTV
 OVERCOMPENSATION
ACEEINNOOPPRSTTY PRESENTATION COPY
ACEELMNOOPPRRSTU PERSONAL
 COMPUTER

ACEEMNOOOPRRSTVY
OVERCOMPENSATORY
ACEFFGIJLMNOPPSU JUMPING-OFF PLACES
ACEFIIINNOOPRSST PERSONIFICATIONS
ACEFIIMNOOPPRRRT IMPROPER FRACTION
ACEFLLMNNOORTUWY FELLOW
COUNTRYMAN
ACEGGHILLMOOOOPR
GEOMORPHOLOGICAL
ACEGHHIILLLMNOOT HELMINTHOLOGICAL
ACEGHHIILLLOPRYY HIEROGLYPHICALLY
ACEGIIKLNPRSSSTT STICKING PLASTERS
ACEGIILNNOORSSST CONGRESSIONALIST
ACEGIIMNNOORSTTT MAGNETOSTRICTION
ACEGILNNNOOSSUUY
CONSANGUINEOUSLY
ACEHHILLMOOPRTTY PHOTOTHERMICALLY
ACEHHILMOOPPRSXY
CHEMOPROPHYLAXIS
ACEHHILMOOPRSSST SCHOOLMASTERSHIP
ACEHHIOPPRSSSTTY PSYCHOTHERAPISTS
ACEHIIKLLNOOPTTY PHOTOKINETICALLY
ACEHIILLLOPSTTYY POLYTHEISTICALLY
ACEHIILLMNOOSTTY MONOTHEISTICALLY
ACEHIILMOPRSTTTY THERMOPLASTICITY
ACEHILLLLOPPTYYY POLYPHYLETICALLY
ACEHIMNNOOPRRSTT
ANTHROPOCENTRISM
ACEIIIKKNNRSSTTW KNICKERS IN A TWIST
ACEIIINNOPSSSSUU INAUSPICIOUSNESS
ACEIILLLMOPRTUVY PLUVIOMETRICALLY
ACEIILLNNNOQTTTU CONTINENTAL QUILT
ACEIILMNOOOOPRSTY COPOLYMERISATION
ACEIILMNOOOOPRTYZ COPOLYMERIZATION
ACEIILMNOORRSSTV CONTROVERSIALISM
ACEIILNNOOOOPRSST CONSOLATION PRISE
ACEIILNNOOOOPRSTZ CONSOLATION PRIZE
ACEIILNOORRSSTTV CONTROVERSIALIST
ACEIINNOORSSSTTV CONSERVATIONISTS
ACEIKNNOOPRSSSTT STOP IN ONE'S
TRACKS
ACEILLNOPRSSTTUY PERSONALITY CULTS
ACFGIIIMNNOORSTU CONFIGURATIONISM
ACFGIIINNOORSTTU CONFIGURATIONIST
ACFIIIILLNNOSTTU NULLIFICATIONIST
ACGHHHILMOOOPRRT
CHROMOLITHOGRAPH
ACGHHIMOOOOPPRRTY
MICROPHOTOGRAPHY, PHOTOMICROGRAPHY
ACGHHINOOOOPPRTYZ
PHOTOZINCOGRAPHY
ACGHIILLLNOOOORTY ORNITHOLOGICALLY
ACGHIILLMNOOPSYY PHYSIOGNOMICALLY
ACGIINNOOOPRSSTT PROGNOSTICATIONS
ACHHIOOOOPPRTTTU
PHOTOAUTOTROPHIC
ACHIILLORRSTTTUU HORTICULTURALIST
ACIIIILLOPSSTTVY POSITIVISTICALLY
ACIIIMNNNOOPRSTU MISPRONUNCIATION

ACIILLLMNOOOPSTY MONOPOLISTICALLY
ACIILLNNOOOOPRSST CROSS-POLLINATION
ACIILLNNOOSTTTUY CONSTITUTIONALLY
ACIILNNNOOSTTTUU UNCONSTITUTIONAL
ADDDDEEEEEHLMNSSU
MUDDLE-HEADEDNESS
ADDEEEEFIILMNSTX EXTENDED FAMILIES
ADDEEEEIMNNNNPST INDEPENDENT
MEANS
ADDEEGINNOOORRRT RIO GRANDE DO
NORTE
ADDEEIIIKKLLNSSS LIKES AND DISLIKES
ADDEEIMMMMNRSSSU MIDSUMMER
MADNESS
ADDEEIMNNNORRSSW
NARROW-MINDEDNESS
ADDEGIIMNNNRSSTU MISUNDERSTANDING
ADEEEEFHHLOORSTU LEADER OF THE
HOUSE
ADEEEEHHLNORSSTW
WHOLEHEARTEDNESS
ADEEEEIIMNPRRTTV PREDETERMINATIVE
ADEEEFGHMNOORTUY YEOMEN OF THE
GUARD
ADEEEFGIIILNNRTT DEFINITE INTEGRAL
ADEEEGGIINORSSTT DESEGREGATIONIST
ADEEEGHILNOOPRRT GARDEN
HELIOTROPE
ADEEEGILNNOOPRSS OLD AGE
PENSIONERS
ADEEEHIILMNNORST THREE-DIMENSIONAL
ADEEEHNNORSSSTTY
STONY-HEARTEDNESS
ADEEEHNORSSSTTTU
STOUTHEARTEDNESS
ADEEEIIMNNOPRRTT PREDETERMINATION
ADEEEINNNRRSSSTU UNRESTRAINEDNESS
ADEEEMNOPRRSSTTT DEPARTMENT
STORES
ADEEFFIIINNORSTT DIFFERENTIATIONS
ADEEGGGHIILNNRST GREASED LIGHTNING
ADEEGHHINPRSSSST SHARP-SIGHTEDNESS
ADEEGIILNNOQSSTU LEADING QUESTIONS
ADEEGILNNOPPRRTY PREPONDERATINGLY
ADEEHHHHIINRRTTT HITHER AND THITHER
ADEEHHILMMNRRRUU MULHEIM AN DER
RUHR
ADEEHIINNNOORSST A THORN IN ONE'S
SIDE
ADEEILMNOPRRSSTU MENSTRUAL
PERIODS
ADEFHINOOOORRTTUY OUT OF THE
ORDINARY
ADEFINNNOOOSSTTU FOUNDATION
STONES
ADEGGGHIOORSSSTY SHAGGY-DOG
STORIES
ADEGIIIINOPRSTTT PRESTIDIGITATION

ADEHHHINOOPPSSYY
ADENOHYPHOPHYSIS

ADEIIIINORSSTTVY RADIOSENSITIVITY

ADEIIMNOPRRRTTTX DOT-MATRIX PRINTER

ADEIINOOOPPRRSTT DISPROPORTIONATE

ADELLNOOORSSSWWW SWALLOW ONE'S
WORDS

ADFGIIIKNNNNORTU DRINKING FOUNTAIN

ADGHHIIINNOOPSTT DIPHTHONGISATION

ADGHHIIINNOOPTTZ DIPHTHONGIZATION

ADGHIMMNNOOPRRSY
GYNANDROMORPHISM

ADHHINOPRSSSTTTY SHORTHAND TYPISTS

AEEEEFGLMMNNRRST GENTLEMEN
FARMERS

AEEEEFIMNNRSSTTV FERMENTATIVENESS

AEEEEHHIKLNOPSTW A SPOKE IN THE
WHEEL

AEEEEHINNPPRSSSV APPREHENSIVENESS

AEEEEIINNPRRTTTV INTERPENETRATIVE

AEEEEIINNPRSSSTTV PRESENTATIVENESS

AEEEEFFFHLMOORSTT
FLAME-OF-THE-FOREST

AEEEEFHILNNNNPPSY PENNY-HALFPENNIES

AEEEEFILNOPRRSSTV SELF-PRESERVATION

AEEEEFLLLLORRSTVW FELLOW
TRAVELLERS

AEEEGGIIILLLLMNOR REGGIO NELL'EMILIA

AEEEGGINNORSSSST SEASON'S
GREETINGS

AEEEGGGLNNOORRRSV
GOVERNORS-GENERAL, GOVERNOR-GENERALS

AEEEGHIINNNRRTWY RING IN THE NEW
YEAR

AEEEGHIMNOOOSSVW GIVE SOMEONE A
SHOW

AEEEGHNOPRRRSTUY OPEN-HEART
SURGERY

AEEEGILNNPPRRSST SLEEPING PARTNERS

AEEEHHILMNNPRTTY TRIPHENYLMETHANE

AEEEHIILMMNNOPPS EPIPHENOMENALISM

AEEEHIILMNNOPPST EPIPHENOMENALIST

AEEEHIIMMNORRSST IMMERSION HEATERS

AEEEIINNNOPRRTTT INTERPENETRATION

AEEELMNOOPRSTUXY
EXTEMPORANEOUSLY

AEEFGHIILLNNTTTU FLIGHT LIEUTENANT

AEEFIILMNOOPRSSS SEMIPROFESSIONAL

AEEFIILNNRSSTTTU FIRST LIEUTENANTS

AEEFNOOOPRRSTTWY POWERS OF
ATTORNEY

AEEGGHHHIILTTVWY LIGHT HEAVYWEIGHT

AEEGGIIILMNNNRST MINISTERING ANGEL

AEEGGLNOOORRSTTY
GASTROENTEROLOGY

AEEGHIKLOPRRSTTW TIGHTROPE
WALKERS

AEEGHMMMNOOPRSTY
SPHYGMOMANOMETER

AEEGIIILMNNNSTTZ SENTIMENTALIZING

AEEGIIJKMNNORSSV KING JAMES VERSION

AEEGIMNOPRSSSTTY OPERATING SYSTEMS

AEEHIIMMNOPPRSSS MISAPPREHENSIONS

AEEHIINOPRRSSSTW PRAISEWORTHINESS

AEEHMNOORSSSTTTU
SOUTHEASTERNMOST

AEEIIIILNSSSTTTX EXISTENTIALISIST

AEEIIIILNOPQTTTUY EQUIPOTENTIALITY

AEEIIILORRRTTTXY EXTERRITORIALITY

AEEIILLNNQSSTTUY QUINTESSENTIALLY

AEEIILMMNNNORSTV ENVIRONMENTALISM

AEEIILMNNNORSTTV ENVIRONMENTALIST

AEEIIMNNRSSSSSTV TRANSMISSIVENESS

AEEIIMNOOPRSSTTX EXTEMPORISATIONS

AEEIIMNOOPRSTTXZ EXTEMPORIZATIONS

AEEILMNNOSSSSTUU SIMULTANEOUSNESS

AEEILNNOOPRRSTUV RELATIVE PRONOUNS

AEELNOOPPPRRRSTY PERSONAL
PROPERTY

AEFFGIIILLNORRSSU SELF-RAISING FLOUR

AEFGIIILLMNNOPRRT MORNING-AFTER PILL

AEFHIOPPRSSSTTTT FIRST PAST THE POST

AEFIIKMNOOOPRRSV MAKE PROVISION
FOR

AEFIILLNOOPPRSTY PELLITORY OF SPAIN

AEFIILMNORSSSTUU MULTIFARIOUSNESS

AEFIILNNNOOOPRRT NONPROLIFERATION

AEFILLNNOOPRSSUY UNPROFESSIONALLY

AEGHIIILLNNORTTWW WRITING ON THE
WALL

AEGHILNOOOPRSTTU NEUROPATHOLOGIST

AEGHIMMOOPRRSTTT
PHOTOGRAMMETRIST

AEHHIIOPPRSSSTTY PHYSIOTHERAPISTS

AEHHIMNOOOPPRRST
ANTHROPOMORPHISE

AEHHIMNOOOPPRRTZ
ANTHROPOMORPHIZE

AEHIIMNNNOORSSSU INHARMONIOUSNESS

AEIIIILLLMMNORTU MULTIMILLIONAIRE

AEIIIILNNOSSTTTU INSTITUTIONALISE

AEIIIILNNOSTTTUZ INSTITUTIONALIZE

AEIIILMNNRSSSTTX MARXIST-LENINISTS

AEIILLNOPPRSSTTY SPLIT PERSONALITY

AEIILMNNRSSSTTTU INSTRUMENTALISTS

AEIIMNNOOPRSSSSU PARSIMONIOUSNESS

AEINOQRRSTTUUVYY QUANTITY
SURVEYOR

AELNNNOOOPPRRSSU PERSONAL
PRONOUNS

AFILLMOOOPPRRSTT FROM PILLAR TO
POST

AGGIILMMMNOPRRTU
MULTIPROGRAMMING

AGGILLNOOOOORSTTY
OTOLARYNGOLOGIST

AGHHHILOOOOPPRTTY
PHOTOLITHOGRAPHY

AGHHILLMOOOPSSTT OPHTHALMOLOGISTS
AGHHILOOOPPSTTTY PHYTOPATHOLOGIST
AHHIIILNOOOOPPSST PHILOSOPHISATION
AHHIIILNOOOOPPSTZ PHILOSOPHIZATION
AHHIMMNOOOOPPRRST
   ANTHROPOMORPHISM
AHHIMNOOOOPPRRSTT
   ANTHROPOMORPHIST
AHHMNOOOOPPRRSTU
   ANTHROPOMORPHOUS
AIIIILMNNOSSTTTU INSTITUTIONALISM
AIIIILNNOSSTTTTU INSTITUTIONALIST
AKKLMMMNOOOORSSU
   KOMSOMOLSK-ON-AMUR
BBBBEEFGIIILRSTT FLIBBERTIGIBBETS
BBBCEGHINRRSSSUU SCRUBBING
   BRUSHES
BBCEEKKLOORRSSTT STOCKBROKER
   BELTS
BBCEKLNOOOOOOPSTY BLOT ONE'S
   COPYBOOK
BBCIIIILMNOSTTUY INCOMBUSTIBILITY
BBDEEEINNORRSTVY INVERTED SNOBBERY
BBEEHHNNOOOORSSY ON ONE'S
   HOBBYHORSE
BBEHHIILMOOPRSTT THROMBOPHLEBITIS
BCCDEEIILNOORUXY DEOXYRIBONUCLEIC
BCCEEHIILNOOPRSY HYPERBOLIC COSINE
BCCEEIIILORRTTTY TRIBOELECTRICITY
BCCEEINOPRSSSSTU SUBSISTENCE CROPS
BCCEILOOPPRRSTUU PUBLIC PROSECUTOR
BCCEINNOOSSSSSUU SUBCONSCIOUSNESS
BCCIIIIILNNNOTVY INCONVINCIBILITY
BCDDEEGKNOOORTTW GET DOWN TO
   BEDROCK
BCDDEGHIILNNPTUU IN THE PUDDING
   CLUB
BCEEEHIILMNNOPRS INCOMPREHENSIBLE
BCEEEELMOOOPRRST
   SPECTROBOLOMETER
BCEEFINNNNOOOOTT BONE OF
   CONTENTION
BCEEHIILMNNOPRSY INCOMPREHENSIBLY
BCEEIIIILMPPRTTY IMPERCEPTIBILITY
BCEEIILMNNORSTTU TRIBOLUMINESCENT
BCEEIILNNOORRTTV INCONTROVERTIBLE
BCEIIIILNNORTTVY INCONVERTIBILITY
BCEIIIILNPSSTTUY INSUSCEPTIBILITY
BCEIIIILPPRRSTTY PRESCRIPTIBILITY
BCEIILNNOORRTTVY INCONTROVERTIBLY
BCIIIILNOPRRTTUY INCORRUPTIBILITY
BDDDEEILMNNOOSSY
   BLOODY-MINDEDNESS
BDDEEEEEFILMNNSS FEEBLEMINDEDNESS
BDEEGIINNOPRSSSU SUSPENSION BRIDGE
BDEHIILNOORSSSTT BLOODTHIRSTINESS
BEEEEELNQRRRSSUUY QUEENSBERRY
   RULES
BEEEGHILNORSTTTU TEETHING TROUBLES

BEEEGIIOOPRSSTTU PETIT BOURGEOISES
BEEEGIOOPRSSTTUY PETTY BOURGEOISES
BEEEHIIILNPRRSTY REPREHENSIBILITY
BEEENOOPRRSSSSTU
   OBSTREPEROUSNESS
BEEFGILNRSSSTTUY FLYING BUTTRESSES
BEEIIIILNOPRSSST RESPONSIBILITIES
BEEIIIILNPRSSTXY INEXPRESSIBILITY
BEEIIIILPRRRSSTY IRREPRESSIBILITY
BEEIIILNOPRSSTVX INVISIBLE EXPORTS
BEIIIIILMMPRSSTY IMPERMISSIBILITY
BEIIIILMNOPRSSTV INVISIBLE IMPORTS
BEIIIILNOPRRSSTY IRRESPONSIBILITY
CCCDEEFIIKNNORST CONFIDENCE TRICKS
CCCEEEINNNNOOOSS ON ONE'S
   CONSCIENCE
CCCEEIILMNNOORRST MICROELECTRONICS
CCCEEIKLNOORSTUW
   COUNTERCLOCKWISE
CCCHLNNOOOORRSTYY
   SYNCHROCYCLOTRON
CCDEEEFFINNOOOTV VOTE OF
   CONFIDENCE
CCDEEEFINNNOOOSV CONVENIENCE
   FOODS
CCDEEHIILORRTTYY HYDROELECTRICITY
CCDIINOOPRTTUVYY PYROCONDUCTIVITY
CCEEEEFNNOPRRSSS PRESS
   CONFERENCES
CCEEEEILMMOSSTTT SELECT COMMITTEES
CCEEEELOOPPRSSTT TELESPECTROSCOPE
CCEEEFIILORRRTTY FERROELECTRICITY
CCEEEHIILMMNNSTU CHEMILUMINESCENT
CCEEEHILMORRSTTY ELECTROCHEMISTRY
CCEEEIIILOPRTTYZ PIEZOELECTRICITY
CCEEHIILOOPRTTTY PHOTOELECTRICITY
CCEEIILNNNOSSSUV INCONCLUSIVENESS
CCEEIILNOORRSTTT ELECTROSTRICTION
CCEEIMMNNORSTTUY COMMUNITY
   CENTRES
CCEEINNOOPRSSSSU PRECONSCIOUSNESS
CCEEINNORSSSTTUV CONSTRUCTIVENESS
CCEHIIIOPRRRSTVY PYRRHIC VICTORIES
CCEIILLNOOORSSSU COLLISION COURSES
CCGHIIILNOPSSTUY PSYCHOLINGUISTIC
CCGIIIILNOOSSSTU SOCIOLINGUISTICS
CCIILLNOOPRRSUVY PRIVY COUNCILLORS
CCIIMNNOORSSSTTU MISCONSTRUCTIONS
CDDDEEEEILORRRVY RECORDED
   DELIVERY
CDDEEEEHILMNOPRY HYPODERMIC
   NEEDLE
CDDEEEINNNOSSSTT DISCONTENTEDNESS
CDDEEFIIINNORRST DIRECTION FINDERS
CDDEGHIIILRRSTTT RED-LIGHT DISTRICT
CDDEGHLNNOOOOORRY
   DENDROCHRONOLOGY
CDEEEEINNOPRSTUX INDECENT
   EXPOSURE

CDEEEFHIMNOORSTW DEMISE OF THE CROWN
CDEEEHHILPRSSTUW WHITED SEPULCHRES
CDEEEIINNPRRSSWW WINDSCREEN WIPERS
CDEEEILMOOPPSSUX OEDIPUS COMPLEXES
CDEEEINOPRRSSTUV REPRODUCTIVENESS
CDEEEELLMNOOOORRTT REMOTE-CONTROLLED
CDEEHIIJOPRTTUUW WITHOUT PREJUDICE
CDEEIMNNOOPRSTTU COMPOUND INTEREST
CDEEINOORSSSSTUU DISCOURTEOUSNESS
CDEFFGIILNOOOOPR COOLING-OFF PERIOD
CDEGIIKLMMNNOOTU UNTIL KINGDOM COME
CDELLNOOOOOPSTUYY POLYCOTYLEDONOUS
CDELMNNOOOOOSTUY MONOCOTYLEDONOUS
CEEEEEFFGHNORSTU GREENHOUSE EFFECT
CEEEEEFFMNORRRST TERMS OF REFERENCE
CEEEEEKKNOPPPRSU KEEP ONE'S PECKER UP
CEEEEFHORRRRSSSU REFRESHER COURSES
CEEEEHHLNOPPRSTU THE UPPER ECHELONS
CEEEEJLLMORSTUWY COSTUME JEWELLERY
CEEEFFINNOORSTUV COUNTEROFFENSIVE
CEEEGGIIIILNÑNRV CIVIL ENGINEERING
CEEEGIIKLNNPSSSS SLEEPING SICKNESS
CEEEHHMMOOOOORRST HETEROCHROMOSOME
CEEEHLOOOOPPRTTTY PHOTOELECTROTYPE
CEEEHMOORRRTTTYY ERYTHROCYTOMETER
CEEEIIMNORRSSSTU MERETRICIOUSNESS
CEEEIINOPRRSSSTV PRESS INTO SERVICE
CEEFFGIINNORRRTU RETURNING OFFICER
CEEFLOOORSTTTTUU SETTLE OUT OF COURT
CEEGIILLLNNOPPPR PROPELLING PENCIL
CEEGILMMOOOOORRTY MICROMETEOROLOGY
CEEHHLNOOPPRSSTY PHOSPHORESCENTLY
CEEHILMNNOOPSTTU PHOTOLUMINESCENT
CEEHMOORRRTTTYYY ERYTHROCYTOMETRY
CEEIILNOPRSSSSUU SUPERCILIOUSNESS
CEEIINOPPRRSSSTV PROSCRIPTIVENESS

CEEINOOQRRSSSSTU CROSS-QUESTIONERS
CEELLMNOOPPRSTUU COLOUR SUPPLEMENT
CEFGIIILNORRSSTZ CROSS-FERTILIZING
CEGHHIIIMMNOORSS HIGH COMMISSIONER
CEGHIMNNOOPRSTYY CHYMOTRYPSINOGEN
CEGIIILNNORRRTTY TRINITROGLYCERIN
CEGIIMMMNOSSSTUW SWIMMING COSTUMES
CEGIINNOOQRSSSTU CROSS-QUESTIONING
CEIIINNOOPRSSTTT INTROSPECTIONIST
CEIIINNORRSSSTTU INSURRECTIONISTS
CELNNOPRSSSSUUUU UNSCRUPULOUSNESS
CFGHHHLOOOOSSTTU SCHOOLS OF THOUGHT
CFGHHIIILNNOOSSS FINISHING SCHOOLS
CGGHLLNOOOOORRTY GLOTTOCHRONOLOGY
CGHHILOOOPPSSYYY PSYCHOPHYSIOLOGY
CGHIILOOOOPSSTTY PHYTOSOCIOLOGIST
CGIIIMMNNOOORSSV ROVING COMMISSION
CGIILMMNNOOPRSUY UNCOMPROMISINGLY
CHIIMNOOOOOPPSTT PHOTOCOMPOSITION
DDEEEEILNNNPRTTY INTERDEPENDENTLY
DDEEEEELMNNOPRTUV UNDERDEVELOPMENT
DDEEEGHINOOPRRXY HYDROGEN PEROXIDE
DDEEEGIILMNNNSSS SINGLE-MINDEDNESS
DDEEEIILMMNNPSSS SIMPLE-MINDEDNESS
DDEEGGGGHIILLPYY HIGGLEDY-PIGGLEDY
DDEEGIMNNNORSSST STRONG-MINDEDNESS
DDEEHIKNNOPRRSZZ DNEPRODZERZHINSK
DDEEHILOORRSSSUY DISORDERLY HOUSES
DDEGHIIKNOPRRSUY YORKSHIRE PUDDING
DEEEEEGMNNORRSTY GREEN-EYED MONSTER
DEEEEGINRRRSSSTU REGISTERED NURSES
DEEEEINNNRSSSTTU UNINTERESTEDNESS
DEEEHILLNORRSTVW SELL DOWN THE RIVER
DEEEHIMMNOSSSTVW SWEDISH MOVEMENTS
DEEFFILNOOOORRSTU SOLDIER OF FORTUNE
DEEGGIKKLNNOORWW WORKING KNOWLEDGE
DEEGHHIIINPRSSST HIGH-SPIRITEDNESS
DEEGHHILNOPRSTUY HYDROGEN SULPHITE
DEEGHHINORSSSSTT SHORTSIGHTEDNESS

DEEGHLMOOOORRTYY
HYDROMETEOROLOGY
DEEGHNNOOOOSSSTT
HONEST-TO-GOODNESS
DEEGIINNNOSSSSUU DISINGENUOUSNESS
DEEEHILLNOORRSSTW
OTHERWORLDLINESS
DEEEHIMMNOOORSSTT MONTESSORI
METHOD
DEEEHIMNNNORRSTUU
UNDERNOURISHMENT
DEEEILLNOOOPPRRTW
WELL-PROPORTIONED
DEFFFIIIIMMNSTUUVX DIMINUTIVE SUFFIX
DEHIIIINNOOOORRTTY TRIIODOTHYRONINE
EEEEEEGHINOSTTVY GIVE ONE'S
EYETEETH
EEEEEHHILNNRTTVW REINVENT THE
WHEEL
EEEEEHLLMMORSTTU
MEURTHE-ET-MOSELLE
EEEEGHINNOOSTTTT GET ONE'S TEETH
INTO
EEEEHINNPPRRRSTU ENTREPRENEURSHIP
EEEEINNPRSSSSSUVX UNEXPRESSIVENESS
EEEFGHIIINRRSTUX FIRE EXTINGUISHER
EEEFGIILNNOORRTW OIL OF
WINTERGREEN
EEEGHHIIMMPSTTUV IT GIVES ME THE
HUMP
EEEGHHMMOOOORRSTY MOTHER GOOSE
RHYME
EEEEHIIMPPRRSSTUV HEIRS PRESUMPTIVE
EEEEILLNOPRSSSSXY EXPRESSIONLESSLY
EEEEILNNOOPPRSSTT POISON-PEN LETTERS
EEEENOOPPRRSSSSTU
PREPOSTEROUSNESS
EEFGHNOORRSSTTTW TOWERS OF
STRENGTH
EEFHHIILOOPRTTWW WIPE THE FLOOR
WITH
EEFHIILMNNNOTTTY FLY IN THE OINTMENT
EEFIIIILMMNNOPRST LIFE IMPRISONMENT
EEGHHHHIOPRSTTTU PERISH THE
THOUGHT!
EEEGHINOOPPSTTTTY PHOTOTYPESETTING
EEGHLLMNOOOOPRSY
SELENOMORPHOLOGY
EEHMNNOORRSSTTTW
NORTHWESTERNMOST
EEHMNOORSSSTTTUW
SOUTHWESTERNMOST
EEMNOPPRSSSSTUUU
PRESUMPTUOUSNESS
EFFGIILLNORRSSSU SELF-RISING FLOURS
EFIIIIILNNPSSTTV SPLIT INFINITIVES
EGGHHILNNOOPRSTU
HOUGHTON-LE-SPRING
EGGHIIIKLNNRSSTT LIGHTNING STRIKES

EGHIIIKLNNNORSSTV SHRINKING VIOLETS
EGHIIINNOOPSSTTZ PHOTOSENSITIZING
EHIIINOOPSSTTTVY PHOTOSENSITIVITY
EHILOOPRSSSTTTUW. WHISTLE-STOP
TOURS
EIINOOPPSSSSSTUU SUPPOSITIOUSNESS
AAAAAABDEGLMORRSST
AMBASSADOR-AT-LARGE
AAAAABDDEGHIINRRRV DRIVE A HARD
BARGAIN
AAAAABDELNRSSTTTUY ASSAULT AND
BATTERY
AAAACCDEIIKLLNSSS
LACKADAISICALNESS
AAAACDGHIILLMPRTY
DIAPHRAGMATICALLY
AAAACEEHIIMMMNTTT
METAMATHEMATICIAN
AAAACEEINNNPPPRTU PUT IN AN
APPEARANCE
AAAAFIIILMNNPRRSS INFRALAPSARIANISM
AAAAGIILMNORSSTTV GRAVITATIONAL
MASS
AAABCEEFLMNNOPSTY BALANCE OF
PAYMENTS
AAABCEEHIILLLMNRT
LAMELLIBRANCHIATE
AAAABCEFGIILLOORRW BIOLOGICAL
WARFARE
AAAABCHIIILNOPPRTY INAPPROACHABILITY
AAAABEEEKPPRSSSTTW WASTEPAPER
BASKETS
AAAABEEGGLLMNSSSUY ASSEMBLY
LANGUAGES
AAAABEEHLNNOOOPTTY
PALAEOETHNOBOTANY
AAAACCCIIILLLMNTTY ANTICLIMACTICALLY
AAAACCCIILLLMMORTY
MACROCLIMATICALLY
AAAACCDEHHKLNOSSST SACKCLOTH AND
ASHES
AAAACCEEEIIKLLLMNS SICKLE-CELL
ANAEMIA
AAAACCEGHILLNOOPRY
OCEANOGRAPHICALLY
AAAACCEHIINORRSSTT
CHARACTERISATIONS
AAAACCEHIINORRSTTZ
CHARACTERIZATIONS
AAAACCHIILLNNORSTY
ANACHRONISTICALLY
AAACDEEGGILNNORRR GREGORIAN
CALENDAR
AAAACDEIINOQQRTTUU QUADRATIC
EQUATION
AAAACEEEEKNPPPPRSU KEEP UP
APPEARANCES
AAAACEEGHILLLNOOPT
PALAEETHNOLOGICAL

AAACEEIIIMNNOPRSU PERNICIOUS ANAEMIA
AAACEEKLLNOORRSTW LOCAL AREA NETWORKS
AAACEFFIIIMNORTTV AFFIRMATIVE ACTION
AAACEFIILLNOSSTTU SELF-ACTUALISATION
AAACEFIILLNOSTTUZ SELF-ACTUALIZATION
AAACEGGHIJKLNSSSU LAUGHING JACKASSES
AAACEGILLLMOOOPTY PALAEOCLIMATOLOGY
AAACEIIILLLMRSTTY MATERIALISTICALLY
AAACEIILLLNPRSTTY PATERNALISTICALLY
AAACEIILNNNNORSTU NATIONAL INSURANCE
AAACGGILLLMMOORTY LOGOGRAMMATICALLY
AAACIIIILNNNNOSTTT ANTINATIONALISTIC
AAACIIILLLNNOSTTY NATIONALISTICALLY
AAACIIILLLNORSTTY RATIONALISTICALLY
AAACIIILNOPRRSTTU PARTICULARISATION
AAACIIILNOPRRTTUZ PARTICULARIZATION
AAADDEGILNOSSTUVY DISADVANTAGEOUSLY
AAADEFJLMMNOSSSTT FLOTSAM AND JETSAMS
AAADEIIILMNNRSTUV VALETUDINARIANISM
AAADEIIILNNNOOSTT DENATIONALISATION
AAADEIIILNNNOOTTZ DENATIONALIZATION
AAADGHINNORRRSTTW STRAIGHT AND NARROW
AAADIIIILMNNRSTTU LATITUDINARIANISM
AAADIIILMMNNORSTT MALADMINISTRATION
AAAEEEGLMNPRRSSTY PAYMASTER GENERALS
AAAEEIIMNNOPPRSTX EXAMINATION PAPERS
AAAEHIILLNNSSSTTY IN THE LAST ANALYSIS
AAAEIIKLNNPRSSSSTY SPINNAKER STAYSAIL
AAAEILNNOPRSSSSTT PERSONAL ASSISTANT
AABBCDDEEKNORRSVW BEND OVER BACKWARDS
AABCCEEGGLLOORRST GARBAGE COLLECTORS
AABCCEEHHMORRRSST CHAMBER ORCHESTRAS
AABCCEELNNNOSSTUU UNACCOUNTABLENESS
AABCDDEHIKNORSSST SHORT BACK AND SIDES
AABCDEEEEHLNRRSST REDRESS THE BALANCE
AABCDEEILNORSSTUU SUBORDINATE CLAUSE
AABCDEIMNNNSSSTUU IN SUM AND SUBSTANCE

AABCEEEGHHIILNNTW WEIGH IN THE BALANCE
AABCEHIIILOPRRRTY IRREPROACHABILITY
AABCEIIILNNOPRSTU REPUBLICANISATION
AABCEIIILNNOPRTUZ REPUBLICANIZATION
AABCIILLNOOOORSSTT COLLABORATIONISTS
AABCIINNNOOSSTTTU CONSUBSTANTIATION
AABDDEEFGIKNRSSTW WEDDING BREAKFASTS
AABDEEEIMNOORRRST ANEROID BAROMETERS
AABEEEIKLMNRRSTTT TIMBER RATTLESNAKE
AABEEFGHIKLNRSSST ENGLISH BREAKFASTS
AABIIILNNNNOSTTTU TINTINNABULATIONS
AACCCDEIMNOPRSTTU CUSTOM AND PRACTICE
AACCCEEEHILLMNORT ELECTROMECHANICAL
AACCCEEEILNRRSTUY SECURITY CLEARANCE
AACCCEHIILLNORTTY ARCHITECTONICALLY
AACCCEHIKLNOOOORRT ORIENTAL COCKROACH
AACCCEHIKMRRRSSST CHRISTMAS CRACKERS
AACCCEIMNNNOOPRTT CONCENTRATION CAMP
AACCCIIILLLMMORTY MICROCLIMATICALLY
AACCDEEGILMOORRRT ELECTROCARDIOGRAM
AACCDEEIOOPPRRSTU DIPTEROCARPACEOUS
AACCDEFGHKLNORRST GRANDFATHER CLOCKS
AACCDEGILLLNNOSST LONGDISTANCE CALLS
AACCDEIIILNNOOSTT OCCIDENTALISATION
AACCDEIIILNNOOTTZ OCCIDENTALIZATION
AACCDEIIKLLLOOPSY KALEIDOSCOPICALLY
AACCDHILLMNOPSYYY PSYCHODYNAMICALLY
AACCDIIIILLNORSTYY IDIOSYNCRATICALLY
AACCDIIINNNOORSTT CONTRAINDICATIONS
AACCEEILLLORSTTTY ELECTROSTATICALLY
AACCEGHHILLOOPRRY CHOREOGRAPHICALLY
AACCEGHIILLLOPRXY LEXICOGRAPHICALLY
AACCEGHILLMOOPSTY METAPSYCHOLOGICAL

AACCEHILOOPRRSSUU
SCROPHULARIACEOUS

AACCEIIILMMNOORST
COMMERCIALISATION

AACCEIIILMMNOORTZ
COMMERCIALIZATION

AACCEIILNNOOPSTTU
CONCEPTUALISATION

AACCEIILNNOOPTTUZ
CONCEPTUALIZATION

AACCEINNOORRTTTTU
COUNTERATTRACTION

AACCFILOOPRRRSSTU PROCURATOR
FISCALS

AACCGHHILLOPPRSYY
PSYCHOGRAPHICALLY

AACCGHILLOPPRRTYY
CRYPTOGRAPHICALLY

AACCHILLMMNOOOORTY
MONOCHROMATICALLY

AACCHILLMOOPSSTYY
PSYCHOSOMATICALLY

AACCIIILMNRSTTTUY CIRCUMSTANTIALITY

AACCIIIMNNORSTTTU CIRCUMSTANTIATION

AACDEEEELNOPRSSUV A CARD UP ONE'S
SLEEVE

AACDEEEELORRSSSUY DAY RELEASE
COURSES

AACDEEEIMNNNORRST MAINTENANCE
ORDERS

AACDEEHIMMNOORRTY
AEROTHERMODYNAMIC

AACDEEIINORRTTTUY TERTIARY
EDUCATION

AACDEEILMMNOPRSTT
COMPARTMENTALISED

AACDEEILMMNOPRTTZ
COMPARTMENTALIZED

AACDEEILMNNNRSSTT
TRANSCENDENTALISM

AACDEEILNNNRSSTTT
TRANSCENDENTALIST

AACDEEILNNNRSTTTY
TRANSCENDENTALITY

AACDEGHINNORSSTTT NO STRINGS
ATTACHED

AACDEGIIILNNPRTUZ UNDERCAPITALIZING

AACDEHIIKKMMNNRSST KITCHEN-SINK
DRAMAS

AACDEHILLMMNORTYY
THERMODYNAMICALLY

AACDEHILNNNPSTUVY PENNSYLVANIA
DUTCH

AACDFIIIILNOQSSTU DISQUALIFICATIONS

AACEEEEFHORRRSTTW WEATHER
FORECASTER

AACEEEEEGLNRRRSSTY
SECRETARY-GENERALS

AACEEEEINNQRRSTTU
QUATERCENTENARIES

AACEEEEHLPPPRSTTTU UPSET THE
APPLECART

AACEEFHHIMRRSSSTT FATHER
CHRISTMASES

AACEEGGILLNNOORTY
ORGANOGENETICALLY

AACEEEGHILLLNOPRSY
SELENOGRAPHICALLY

AACEEEGHINOOPRRTTU
ORGANOTHERAPEUTIC

AACEEEGLMNOOPRSTUU ANALOGUE
COMPUTERS

AACEEEHIILNOPPRTTV HEPATIC PORTAL
VEIN

AACEEEHIILNOPRSTTU
AUSTRALOPITHECINE

AACEEEILLNOOPRSTUV PALACE
REVOLUTIONS

AACEEEILNNOORSTTTT EASTERN
COTTONTAIL

AACEEEILNORRSTTUVV
ULTRACONSERVATIVE

AACEEEINOPRRSTTVVY CONSERVATIVE
PARTY

AACEEFFIIILNNNNOOS A NAIL IN ONE'S
COFFIN

AACEEGGHILLOOOPRYZ
ZOOGEOGRAPHICALLY

AACEEGGIILMNNOORST
CONGREGATIONALISM

AACEEGGIILNNOORSTT
CONGREGATIONALIST

AACEEGGIILRRRRSSTU SURGICAL
REGISTRAR

AACEEGHHIILNOPSSTT TEACHING
HOSPITALS

AACEEHIILMNNPPSTTU CAPITAL
PUNISHMENT

AACEEHLOOOPPRRRSTY PREPARATORY
SCHOOL

AACEIIIILLLMPRSTY IMPERIALISTICALLY

AACEIIILNORRSSTTY RECRYSTALLISATION

AACEIIILNORRSTTYZ RECRYSTALLIZATION

AACEIILNNOORSSTTV
CONVERSATIONALIST

AACEIILNPRRSSTTUU SUPERNATURALISTIC

AACEIIMNNOORSSSTX
CROSS-EXAMINATIONS

AACEILMNOOORRTUVY
MACROEVOLUTIONARY

AACGGILLLNOOOORTY
OTOLARYNGOLOGICAL

AACGHHIILLOOOPSTT
HISTOPATHOLOGICAL

AACGHHILLOOOPPTTY
PHYTOPATHOLOGICAL

AACGHHIOOOPPRRSTT
ASTROPHOTOGRAPHIC

AACGHIIILNNPRSSTY PHYSICAL TRAININGS

AACGHILLLNOOOPRTY
ANTHROPOLOGICALLY

AACGHILLMNNOOOPTY
PATHOGNOMONICALLY

AACHHIILLLNOPPRTY
PHILANTHROPICALLY, PHILANTRHOPICALLY

AADDDEHILLLNNOPUW UP HILL AND
DOWN DALE

AADDEEGHINNORRSSU
ROUGH-AND-READINESS

AADDEEGHINPRRSTUU
UNDERGRADUATESHIP

AADDFGIILNNORSSTV STANDARDS OF
LIVING

AADDIIIIILNNOSTUV INDIVIDUALISATION

AADDIIIIILNNOTUVZ INDIVIDUALIZATION

AADEEEFFGIILNRRST DIFFERENTIAL
GEARS

AADEEEFFHIINRRRTW FAIR-WEATHER
FRIEND

AADEEEEGILNOORSSTT SANTIAGO DEL
ESTERO

AADEEEEHIMMNOPRTTX
DEXTROAMPHETAMINE

AADEEEEHLLNORTZZZZ ON THE
RAZZLE-DAZZLE

AADEEEEHORSSTTTTYY STEADY STATE
THEORY

AADEEEEILMNNPRRTTT
INTERDEPARTMENTAL

AADEEGHILLLLNOTVY ALL THE LIVELONG
DAY

AADEEGHIMRRTTUWWY GET AWAY WITH
MURDER

AADEEGIILNNOORTTT TRENTINO-ALTO
ADIGE

AADEEIIILMNPQSSSU SESQUIPEDALIANISM

AADEEIIILNNNORSTT INTERNATIONALISED

AADEEIIILNNNORTTZ INTERNATIONALIZED

AADEEIIIMNNPRRSST PREDESTINARIANISM

AADEEIINNOPRSSTT PEDESTRIANISATION

AADEEIINNOPRSTTZ PEDESTRIANIZATION

AADEEIIKNNOPRSSSS PARKINSON'S
DISEASE

AADEEIILNNOOPRSST
DEPERSONALISATION

AADEEIILNNOOPRSTZ
DEPERSONALIZATION

AADEEIILNRSSSTTTU INDUSTRIAL ESTATES

AADEEIINNOPSSSSST DISPASSIONATENESS

AADEEIINNORRRSSTX
EXTRAORDINARINESS

AADEFFIIILNOORRST AFFILIATION ORDERS

AADEFGIMNNNOORTTU FOUNDATION
GARMENT

AADEIIILMMNNNOOST
DENOMINATIONALISM

AADEIIILMNNNOOSTT
DENOMINATIONALIST

AADFGHILORRRSTTWY
STRAIGHTFORWARDLY

AADIIIILNNORSSTTU INDUSTRIALISATION

AADIIIILNNORSTTUZ INDUSTRIALIZATION

AADIIIILNPSSTUUVY VISUAL DISPLAY UNIT

AAEEEEIIKLMMORSVY A MEMORY LIKE A
SIEVE

AAEEEGIMNNRSSTTUV
ARGUMENTATIVENESS

AAEEEGLMNOPRRSSTT POSTMASTER
GENERAL

AAEEEHHHLLMNNPTTY
METHYLNAPHTHALENE

AAEEEELNNPRRRSSTTU
PRETERNATURALNESS

AAEEGHHILNRRSTTY
EARTHSHATTERINGLY

AAEEEHIINORSSTTTUV
AUTHORITATIVENESS

AAEEEIILORRRRSTTTW TERRITORIAL
WATERS

AAEEEIINNOPPPRRSST INAPPROPRIATENESS

AAEEEILLMNNOPPRRTTU
LUMPENPROLETARIAT

AAEEEINNNNOSSSSTTU
INSTANTANEOUSNESS

AAEFGGGIILMNNSSSY MAGNIFYING
GLASSES

AAEFGHINNOOORRSTT A FROG IN ONE'S
THROAT

AAEGHHMMMMOOPRRTY
MAMMOTHERMOGRAPHY

AAEGIIIKNNOOORRSTV VIRGINIA
SNAKEROOT

AAEGIIKMNNOORRRTT INTERROGATION
MARK

AAEIIILMNNOOPRSST IMPERSONALISATION

AAEIIILMNNOOPRSTZ IMPERSONALIZATION

AAEIIILNNNORSSTTT INTERNATIONALISTS

AAEIIKNNOORRSSTTW SANITATION
WORKERS

AAEIILNNOORRTTUVY
ANTIREVOLUTIONARY

AAFIIIIMMNNNORRSTU UNIFORMITARIANISM

AAHHILLNOOPPRSTUY NATURAL
PHILOSOPHY

AAIIILLMNNNORSTTU TRANSILLUMINATION

AAIIILMNNNOOOPRST
PRONOMINALISATION

AAIIILMNNNOOOPRTZ
PRONOMINALIZATION

AAIIIMNOOPPPRRSST MISAPPROPRIATIONS

ABBCDDEEGHIKMPRSU HUMPBACKED
BRIDGES

ABBDEEIKLLMNOOOOS MAKE ONE'S
BLOOD BOIL
ABBDEEELNORRRSSTWY STRAWBERRY
BLONDES
ABCCCEEEFHMMMOORR CHAMBER OF
COMMERCE
ABCCEEIILMMNNORTU
INTERCOMMUNICABLE
ABCCEIIIILLNORRTY IRRECONCILABILITY
ABCCEIIIJLLOSTTVY OBJECTIVISTICALLY
ABCCIIIILMMNNOTUY INCOMMUNICABILITY
ABCDEEEEEGGRRRSTT GREAT CRESTED
GREBE
ABCDEEHIIIILNPRTY INDECIPHERABILITY
ABCDEEIIILPRSSTTY DISRESPECTABILITY
ABCEEEEFGMNOORSST ESSENCE OF
BERGAMOT
ABCEEEEEILNNOPSSTX
EXCEPTIONABLENESS
ABCEEEFLNOQRSTUUY ABSOLUTE
FREQUENCY
ABCEEEGIKMMNNRRRS KING'S
REMEMBRANCER
ABCEEGHILNNOPRTTY HYPERBOLIC
TANGENT
ABCEEGHOPRRRRSTUU
TURBOSUPERCHARGER
ABCEEGKKLNRSSTUUY KENTUCKY
BLUEGRASS
ABCEEIIINPRRSSTTY PRESBYTERIANISTIC
ABCEFFIINOOOPRRST PROBATION
OFFICERS
ABCEIIIILLLMSSSST BALLISTIC MISSILES
ABCIILLLNNOORTTUY
UNCONTROLLABILITY
ABDDEFFGGIIILNNNN EFFING AND
BLINDING
ABDEEEGHIOORRSTTT SABRE-TOOTHED
TIGER
ABDEEFFIIIILNRTTY DIFFERENTIABILITY
ABDEEGHHILLNRSTUU LIGHT UNDER A
BUSHEL
ABDEEKNNOORRSSUVW NERVOUS
BREAKDOWNS
ABDEGHIIIILNNSSTU INDISTINGUISHABLE
ABDEIILNOOOPPRRST
DISPROPORTIONABLE
ABDFILNNOOORSSSTU BLOOD
TRANSFUSIONS
ABDGHIIIILNNSSTUY INDISTINGUISHABLY
ABEEEEHHNRRSSTTTU HUNTER'S
HARTEBEEST
ABEEEFGGILNNNOOSS A SENSE OF
BELONGING
ABEEHILMNNNOOORTU HONOURABLE
MENTION
ABEIIIILMNOPRSSTY IMPRESSIONABILITY
ABEIIILNNOQSTTUUY UNQUESTIONABILITY
ABIIILMNNORSTTUUY INSURMOUNTABILITY

ABIIILNOOOPPRRTTY PROPORTIONABILITY
ACCCCEEEILNNOSSSU CONSCIENCE
CLAUSES
ACCCDIIMMNNOOORTU COMMUNICATION
CORD
ACCCEEEGHILLLNOST TECHNICAL
COLLEGES
ACCCEEEEILNOSSSSUV CONCESSIVE
CLAUSES
ACCCEHHILMOOPPRTY
CHEMOPROPHYLACTIC
ACCCEHIKKLNNOOTTU TECHNICAL
KNOCKOUT
ACCCEIILLMNOOOOSY
SOCIOECONOMICALLY
ACCCEILLOOPPRSSTY
SPECTROSCOPICALLY
ACCCEILMNNOOOOSTU COME TO A
CONCLUSION
ACCCFIINOOOPPRRRT TROPIC OF
CAPRICORN
ACCCGIIILLMMOOORT
MICROCLIMATOLOGIC
ACCDDEEEEFIIINSSY DEFICIENCY DISEASE
ACCDEEEEEIINPRSST PIÈCE DE
RÉSISTANCE
ACCDEEEIILMNNORSU
RADIOLUMINESCENCE
ACCDEEEMNNOOPRRST PROMENADE
CONCERTS
ACCDEEFHIIMMNNORS COMMANDERS IN
CHIEF
ACCDEEGIIINRRTTTU INTEGRATED CIRCUIT
ACCDEEHILLLORRTYY
HYDROELECTRICALLY
ACCDEEIIMMNNORTTU
INTERCOMMUNICATED
ACCDEFIILNNOORSTT
SELF-CONTRADICTION
ACCDEFILNOORRSTTY
SELF-CONTRADICTORY
ACCDEFMNOOPRRSTUU COMPOUND
FRACTURES
ACCDEIIILMNOOOORRT
MINERALOCORTICOID
ACCDEIIINNORSTTTV CONTRADISTINCTIVE
ACCDHHIIIILOPRSTUU THIOSULPHURIC
ACID
ACCDIIINNNOORSTTT CONTRADISTINCTION
ACCEEEEFHIJOPSTTU JUSTICE OF THE
PEACE
ACCEEEEGLLLLOORST ELECTORAL
COLLEGES
ACCEEEFFGILNNNOOV FLAG OF
CONVENIENCE
ACCEEEFFIIILORRSV OFFICIAL RECEIVERS
ACCEEEFIILPPPRRTT PERFECT PARTICIPLE
ACCEEEFILLLORRRTY
FERROELECTRICALLY

ACCEEEHIILLMNOPTY
ENCEPHALOMYELITIC

ACCEEEHIKKORRSTTV KICK OVER THE
TRACES

ACCEEEIILLLOPRTYZ PIEZOELECTRICALLY

ACCEEEIINNOOPRSTV CONVERSATION
PIECE

ACCEEFGIIIIPRSSTV SPECIFIC GRAVITIES

ACCEEGHILLNOPSTYY
PSYCHOGENETICALLY

ACCEEGHILLNRRTTUU THE CULTURAL
CRINGE

ACCEEHHIOPPRSTTUY
PSYCHOTHERAPEUTIC

ACCEEHIINOOOORSSTT RISE TO THE
OCCASION

ACCEEHILLLOOPRTTY
PHOTOELECTRICALLY

ACCEEIIILLLNSTTTU INTELLECTUALISTIC

ACCEEIIILNNOPRSSU INSURANCE POLICIES

ACCEEIILMMNNOOTTU
TELECOMMUNICATION

ACCEEIINOPPRSSSSU
PERSPICACIOUSNESS

ACCEEIKNOOPRRSTTT PROTECTION
RACKETS

ACCEHHIILLNOPRSYZ
SCHIZOPHRENICALLY

ACCEHIIKLLNOPSTYY
PSYCHOKINETICALLY

ACCEEIIKMMNNOOTTTTU COMMUTATION
TICKET

ACCEIIMMNNOORRTTU
INTERCOMMUNICATOR

ACCEILLNOPRRSTTYY
CRYPTOCRYSTALLINE

ACCGHHIIMOOOOPPRRT
MICROPHOTOGRAPHIC, PHOTOMICROGRAPHIC

ACCGHIIKMNORSSSTT CHRISTMAS
STOCKING

ACCGHIILLOOOOPSTY
PHYTOSOCIOLOGICAL

ACCHIILLNNORSSTYY
SYNCHRONISTICALLY

ACCIJKMNNOOOPSTTY JOINT-STOCK
COMPANY

ACDDEEEEEHNNNTTTY DENY THE
ANTECEDENT

ACDDEEEEILNNNPSTU INDEPENDENT
CLAUSE

ACDDGHIIMNPRSSSTU CHRISTMAS
PUDDINGS

ACDDHHJNNOPSSUUWY
PUNCH-AND-JUDY SHOWS

ACDEEEEIIPRSTTTVV PRIVATE DETECTIVES

ACDEEEFIIIILNNRTT INDEFINITE ARTICLE

ACDEEEFIMMNNOORSS COMEDIES OF
MANNERS

ACDEEEFLLOORRSUVV FOUR-LEAVED
CLOVERS

ACDEEEHJOOOOPRRRTV OVERHEAD
PROJECTOR

ACDEEEIINNNORSSST
INCONSIDERATENESS

ACDEEEILNNNOSSTTU SECOND
LIEUTENANTS

ACDEEENORRSSSSSTY SECONDARY
STRESSES

ACDEEFHIINOORSTTT AT THE DISCRETION
OF

ACDEEGIINORSSTTTU COTTAGE
INDUSTRIES

ACDEEGINNOORRRSTU RECREATION
GROUNDS

ACDEEGMMOOPRRRSSU PROGRAMMED
COURSES

ACDEEHHIMMOOOORRTY
HAEMORRHOIDECTOMY

ACDEEHHLNNOORTTTW NOT WORTH THE
CANDLE

ACDEEIIIMNOOSSTTU SITUATION
COMEDIES

ACDEEIINOOOORRRRTT INTERIOR
DECORATOR

ACDEEENNNORRSTTUWY COUNTRY AND
WESTERN

ACDEFINNOOOORSSTUU FOUNDATION
COURSES

ACDEGGILLNNOOPRRY LONG-PLAYING
RECORD

ACDEGHNNOORSSSSTU NOUGHTS AND
CROSSES

ACDEGIIIKNNRSSSTT STRIKING DISTANCES

ACDEHIILLOOOOPPRTY
PHOTOPERIODICALLY

ACDEIIIILNNPPRRSTY INTERDISCIPLINARY

ACDEIILNNNNOOSSTU
UNCONDITIONALNESS

ACDEIINNNNOOOORST ON NO
CONSIDERATION

ACDEIINORRSSTTTTY DISTRICT
ATTORNEYS

ACDEIMMMMNNNOOOORT COMMON
DENOMINATOR

ACDGHIIINNORSSTTU
CONTRADISTINGUISH

ACDHLMOPRRSSTUUYY MUSCULAR
DYSTROPHY

ACDIIIILLMMNPRSTUY MULTIDISCIPLINARY

ACEEEEEFFFMNORRRS FRAMES OF
REFERENCE

ACEEEEEGHHLNNOPTX TELEPHONE
EXCHANGE

ACEEEEFILNQRRTUVY RELATIVE
FREQUENCY

ACEEEEGHIIMMNNRTW GREENWICH
MEAN TIME

ACEEEEGHILLNORTTY
HETEROGENETICALLY

ACEEEEHLLQRRSSTUV TRAVELLER'S
CHEQUES

ACEEEFFFGGGILLOTU LEFT LUGGAGE
OFFICE

ACEEEFFIILNOOPTTX EXPECTATION OF
LIFE

ACEEEGGHIILRRSTTT CIGARETTE
LIGHTERS

ACEEEGIILLMNNOPPS SLEEPING
POLICEMAN

ACEEEGIILNORTTTVY
ELECTRONEGATIVITY

ACEEEGLLLMORRTTUY
ELECTROMETALLURGY

ACEEEGLMNNNORRTTV CENTRAL
GOVERNMENT

ACEEEHIILLMNOPSTY
ENCEPHALOMYELITIS

ACEEEHLLMNOORSSTY ELEMENTARY
SCHOOLS

ACEEEIILNPPPRRSTT PRESENT PARTICIPLE

ACEEEILLMNNOSSSSU
MISCELLANEOUSNESS

ACEEEILLMNPPRRSST SCARLET
PIMPERNELS

ACEEEILNORRSSTUUX SEXUAL
INTERCOURSE

ACEEELNNNOPSTTUWY
NEWCASTLE-UPON-TYNE

ACEEFGIIIINNSSSTV SIGNIFICATIVENESS

ACEEGHHILOOPPRRST
SPECTROHELIOGRAPH

ACEEGIIILLLNNSTTU INTELLECTUALISING

ACEEGIILLNOORRSST SOLICITORS
GENERAL

ACEEGLMMNOOPRSTTV GLOVE
COMPARTMENTS

ACEEHHLLNNOOOPPRT
PENTACHLOROPHENOL

ACEEHIJMNNOORTTUW NAME TO
CONJURE WITH

ACEEIIILNNNOOSTTV CONVENTIONALITIES

ACEEIILLNNNOQSTUY
INCONSEQUENTIALLY

ACEEIIILLOPPSSSTVX PLASTIC EXPLOSIVES

ACEEIILNNNOPRRSTTT TELETRANSCRIPTION

ACEELMNOOPPRRSSTU PERSONAL
COMPUTERS

ACEFFFHIINNOOOSST CONFESSION OF
FAITH

ACEFFIIIJLNOSSTTU SELF-JUSTIFICATION

ACEFIIMNOOPPRRRST IMPROPER
FRACTIONS

ACEGHHIMOOOPPRRRT
PHOTOMICROGRAPHER

ACEGHHLLMNNOPSSUU PLOUGHMAN'S
LUNCHES

ACEGIILLLMNOOORTY
TERMINOLOOGICALLY

ACEGIILLMNOORRTTY
TRIGONOMETRICALLY

ACEHHIILLNOOPPSSS
PHILOSOPHICALNESS

ACEHIIKMNNNOORRSU CHINK IN ONE'S
ARMOUR

ACEHIIKNNOORSSTTT STICK IN ONE'S
THROAT

ACEHIINOPRRSSTTUY
NEUROPSYCHIATRIST

ACEHLLMNOOOPPRRUY
POLYMORPHONUCLEAR

ACEIIIILLLMNORTTUY MULTICOLLINEARITY

ACEIIILMNNNOORTTU
INTERCOLUMNIATION

ACEIIINNOORRRTTTU COUNTERIRRITATION

ACEIIILLNNNOQSTTTU CONTINENTAL
QUILTS

ACEIILMMNNRSSTTUU MUSICAL
INSTRUMENT

ACEIILNNNNOOTTUVY
UNCONVENTIONALITY

ACEIILNNOOOOPRSSST CONSOLATION
PRISES

ACEIILNNOOOPRSSTZ CONSOLATION
PRIZES

ACEIIMNNNOOSSSSTU
SANCTIMONIOUSNESS

ACGHHHILMOOOOPRRTY
CHROMOLITHOGRAPHY

ACGHHILOOOPPSSTTY
PSYCHOPATHOLOGIST

ACHHIIOOPRRSSTTTY
ORTHOPSYCHIATRIST

ACHIIJLNOOOOPRSTTU
PHOTOJOURNALISTIC

ACHIILLORRSSTTTUU HORTICULTURALISTS

ACIIILMNNOOSSTTTU CONSTITUTIONALISM

ACIIILNNOOSSTTTTU CONSTITUTIONALIST

ACIIILNNOOSTTTTUY CONSTITUTIONALITY

ACIILNNNNOOOSTTTU
NONCONSTITUTIONAL

ADDEEEEEHNNRRSSTT
TENDERHEARTEDNESS

ADDEEEFFIIINNORTT DEDIFFERENTIATION

ADDEEGHIINNOORSTY
DEHYDROGENISATION

ADDEEGHIINNOORTYZ
DEHYDROGENIZATION

ADDEGHHIIMNNOORTU DIAMOND IN THE
ROUGH

ADDEGIIMNNNRSSSTU
MISUNDERSTANDINGS

ADEEEFIILMNNORSTT
SELF-DETERMINATION

ADEEEGGMMNNOORTTW ENDOWMENT
MORTGAGE

ADEEEHHINNORRTTTU THEATRE IN THE ROUND

ADEEEINOOPRRRRSTV PRESERVATION ORDER

ADEEFIIMMNOOPPRRVX VERMIFORM APPENDIX

ADEEGHIILMNNPPRSY MISAPPREHENDINGLY

ADEEGHILNOORRTTUY RING OUT THE OLD YEAR

ADEEHIILMPRSSTTTY METHYLATED SPIRITS

ADEEHIINOORRSSTUV AUTHORISED VERSION

ADEEHIINOORRSTUVZ AUTHORIZED VERSION

ADEEIINOPPRRRSSTU DRAINPIPE TROUSERS

ADEIIIILMNNORSTTY TRIDIMENSIONALITY

ADEIIIILNNOSSTTTU INSTITUTIONALISED

ADEIIIILNNOSTTTUZ INSTITUTIONALIZED

ADEIIIILMNNOOSTTWY TWO-DIMENSIONALITY

ADEIIMNOPRRRSTTTX DOT-MATRIX PRINTERS

ADFGIIIKNNNNORSTU DRINKING FOUNTAINS

ADGIIIILNNOOOQTTU GO INTO LIQUIDATION

AEEEEEFHHLLORTTTTW THE LETTER OF THE LAW

AEEEEIIMNPRRSSTTV MISREPRESENTATIVE

AEEEEIINPPRRRSTTV PRIVATE ENTERPRISE

AEEEEELLNNOPRTTTYZ PENTYLENETETRAZOL

AEEEFGHINNOOOORTTV ONE FOOT IN THE GRAVE

AEEEFGIINPRRSSTUV PREFIGURATIVENESS

AEEEFHIILLLLOSTVY LILIES OF THE VALLEY

AEEEFHILLLLLMOTWW HAIL-FELLOW-WELL-MET

AEEEGHIIMNNOORSST GET IN SOMEONE'S HAIR

AEEEGILMNNNORRTTV INTERGOVERNMENTAL

AEEEHHIJNOSSSSTVW JEHOVAH'S WITNESSES

AEEEIIILNNOPPRSTT PLENIPOTENTIARIES

AEEEIIMNNOPRRSSTT MISREPRESENTATION

AEEFFIIILLNORSSTT SELF-FERTILISATION

AEEFFIIILLNORSTTZ SELF-FERTILIZATION

AEEFGHIILLNNSTTTU FLIGHT LIEUTENANTS

AEEFGHLLLNOSTTUUW FULL TO THE GUNWALES

AEEFHHHIIKLNNOPTT IN THE PINK OF HEALTH

AEEGGHHHIILSTTVWY LIGHT HEAVYWEIGHTS

AEEGGHIILLNOORSST SHOOTING GALLERIES

AEEGGIIILMNNNRSST MINISTERING ANGELS

AEEGMNOOOORRSSTTTY GASTROENTEROSTOMY

AEEHIIILNNOPRRSTT INTERRELATIONSHIP

AEEHIKNNNOPRRSSTW SPANNER IN THE WORKS

AEEIIIILNSSSSTTTX EXISTENTIALISISTS

AEEIIIMNNOPRRSTTT MISINTERPRETATION

AEEIILMNNNORSSTTV ENVIRONMENTALISTS

AEEIILNNNNNOORTTV NONINTERVENTIONAL

AEEINNOOOPPRRSSTT PROPORTIONATENESS

AEFGIILLMNNOPRRST MORNING-AFTER PILLS

AEFILLNOPPRRRSSTU FIRST PERSON PLURAL

AEGGHHHIILNNRSTTU THRUSH NIGHTINGALE

AEGHHHILOOOPPRRTT PHOTOLITHOGRAPHER

AEIIIILLLMMNORSTU MULTIMILLIONAIRES

AEIIKNNNNOQSTTUUW UNKNOWN QUANTITIES

AEINOQRRSSTTUUVYY QUANTITY SURVEYORS

AFGHHLOOOOPPRRTUY PHOTOFLUOROGRAPHY

AHHIMNOOOOPPRRSST ANTHROPOMORPHOSIS

BBDEEEILMNNOOPRTV RIBBON DEVELOPMENT

BCCCEEEIILNNNOPUV PUBLIC CONVENIENCE

BCCDDEEEIIIILNOSV CIVIL DISOBEDIENCE

BCCEEEIILMNNORSTU TRIBOLUMINESCENCE

BCCEEILMOOOPRRSTT SPECTROBOLOMETRIC

BCCEILOOPPRRSSTUU PUBLIC PROSECUTORS

BCDEEEIIILRRSTTTY STREET-CREDIBILITY

BCDEEGIIIILNOSSTU BUILDING SOCIETIES

BCDEIIIILNRSTTTUY INDESTRUCTIBILITY

BCEEHIIILMNOPRSTY COMPREHENSIBILITY

BCEIIIILMNOPRSSTY INCOMPRESSIBILITY

BDDEEEEEILLPRSSWY BIRD'S-EYE SPEEDWELL

BDDEEHILMNOSSTTUW TWIDDLE ONE'S THUMBS

BDEEGIINNOPRSSSSU SUSPENSION BRIDGES

BDEEGINNOOSSSTTUW GET DOWN TO BUSINESS

BEEHHILOOPSTTTUWW UP TO THE
ELBOWS WITH
BEEHIIIMMMRRSSTTU BRITISH SUMMER
TIME
CCCEEEEHIILMMNNSU
CHEMILUMINESCENCE
CCCEEEHILLLOOPRTT PHOTOELECTRIC
CELL
CCDEEEEEFLNORRSTT LETTERS OF
CREDENCE
CCDEEEFFINNOOOSTV VOTES OF
CONFIDENCE
CCDEEEEILLLNOORTVY COLLECT ON
DELIVERY
CCDEEEGHIKNNOSSTTT NIGHT-SCENTED
STOCK
CCDEEINOOOPRRTTUUV
COUNTERPRODUCTIVE
CCDEEEIOOPRSTTTUVY PROTECTIVE
CUSTODY
CCDEIINOPRSTTUUVY
SUPERCONDUCTIVITY
CCDHIINOOOOPTTTUVY
PHOTOCONDUCTIVITY
CCEEEEFFINOSSSTTV
COST-EFFECTIVENESS
CCEEEHIILMORRTTTY
THERMOELECTRICITY
CCEEEHILMNNOOPSTU
PHOTOLUMINESCENCE
CCEEEHILOOOPPRSST
SPECTROHELIOSCOPE
CCEEEEILLNOORSTUVV
ELECTROCONVULSIVE
CCEEFILNNOOSSSSSU
SELF-CONSCIOUSNESS
CCEEGINNNORRSTUUY
COUNTERINSURGENCY
CCEEIIMNNOOSSSSSU
SEMICONSCIOUSNESS
CCEEIINNNOOSSSSTU
CONSCIENTIOUSNESS
CCEIINNNOOPSSSSUU
INCONSPICUOUSNESS
CCGHIIILNOPSSSTUY PSYCHOLINGUISTICS
CCIJLMNNOOOPSSTUU JUMP TO
CONCLUSIONS
CDDEEEEIIMNNNNOPT INDEPENDENT
INCOME
CDDEEEFIILNNOORTX CONDITIONED
REFLEX
CDDEEFIILNOORTTUY DERELICTION OF
DUTY
CDDEGHIIILRRSSTTT RED-LIGHT DISTRICTS
CDEEEEFHILNNNRTUU UNDER THE
INFLUENCE
CDEEEFIIILNORSSTY FRIENDLY SOCIETIES
CDEEEGIIKNNNRSTUV TURN KING'S
EVIDENCE

CDEEEIILMNNOOPSTW ENDOWMENT
POLICIES
CDEEEIILNOOOPRSTT
ELECTRODEPOSITION
CDEEGHIIIMNNPSSST DISPENSING
CHEMIST
CDEEGILNNOOPRTUVY DEVELOPING
COUNTRY
CDEEINNNOOPRSSTUV
NONPRODUCTIVENESS
CDEFFGIILNOOOOPRS COOLING-OFF
PERIODS
CEEEEGIILLMNNOPPS SLEEPING
POLICEMEN
CEEEEGIIMMNORSTTT STEERING
COMMITTEE
CEEEEHHHKNORRTTTU TURN THE OTHER
CHEEK
CEEEEHHINPRSSSSTY SPEECH
SYNTHESISER
CEEEEHHINPRSSSTYZ SPEECH
SYNTHESIZER
CEEEEINOPRRSSSTTV
RETROSPECTIVENESS
CEEEFFINNOORSSTUV
COUNTEROFFENSIVES
CEEEFGHHINQRRUVYY VERY HIGH
FREQUENCY
CEEEEHHILLNOORRTTY
TRICHLOROETHYLENE
CEEEHILMMNNORSTTU
THERMOLUMINESCENT
CEEEHMOOOPPRRSTTT
SPECTROPHOTOMETER
CEEEIMNNNOORSSSUU
UNCEREMONIOUSNESS
CEEFFGIINNORRRSTU RETURNING
OFFICERS
CEEGHHIILLNOSSSTW
SCHLESWIG-HOLSTEIN
CEEGHIIIPPRRRSTTV PRESCRIPTIVE RIGHT
CEEGHILLOOOPRSTYY
ELECTROPHYSIOLOGY
CEEGIILLLNNOPPPRS PROPELLING
PENCILS
CEEHMOOOPPRRSTTTY
SPECTROPHOTOMETRY
CEEIIILLLMOPRSSSTU MULTIPLE SCLEROSIS
CEEILNNOOOORRTTUUV
COUNTER-REVOLUTION
CEELLMNOOPPRSSTUU COLOUR
SUPPLEMENTS
CEFIIJKNOOOOPRSTY JOCKEY FOR
POSITION
CEGHHIIIMMNOORSSS HIGH
COMMISSIONERS
CEIINOPRRSSTTTUUU COITUS
INTERRUPTUS

CGIIIMMNNOOORSSSV ROVING
COMMISSIONS
DDEEEEIINNRSSSSTT DISINTERESTEDNESS
DDEGHIIKNOPRRSSUY YORKSHIRE
PUDDINGS
DEEEEHIMNORRSUUYY HERE'S MUD IN
YOUR EYE
DEEFFILNOOORRSSTU SOLDIERS OF
FORTUNE
DEEHIIMNNOOOPSTTU THIOPENTONE
SODIUM
DEEIIINNRRSSSSSTUU SUNRISE INDUSTRIES
DEHHIIIMOOOOSTTYY HIDEYOSHI
TOYOTOMI
DEIILMNNOSSSTTUUU
MULTITUDINOUSNESS
EEEEIIMNNNNOPRRSTT RETIREMENT
PENSION
EEEELLLNOOOPRSSSUV ROLL UP ONE'S
SLEEVES
EEEFGHIIINNRRSSTUX FIRE EXTINGUISHERS
EEEFGHILNORSSSSTU
SELF-RIGHTEOUSNESS
EEEGHHMMOOOORRSSTY MOTHER GOOSE
RHYMES
EEEGINNOPPRSSSSSS
PREPOSSESSINGNESS
EEEINNNOPRSSSTTUU
UNPRETENTIOUSNESS
EEFIIILMMNNOPRSST LIFE IMPRISONMENTS
EEHHILNOOOOPPRSSST PHILOSOPHER'S
STONE
EEHIIIIMMNPPRRSST PRIME MINISTERSHIP
EEIINOPRRSSSSSTTUU SURREPTITIOUSNESS
EEIINOPRSSSSSTTUU SUPERSTITIOUSNESS
EGHHIIKNOOPRSSTWY WORKING
HYPOTHESIS
EGHIILNOOOPRSSTUY
NEUROPHYSIOLOGIST
EIIIMMNOOOPPRSSSST POSTIMPRESSIONISM
EIIIMNOOPPRSSSSTT POSTIMPRESSIONIST
AAAACDEEIIILMNNOSST ESSENTIAL AMINO
ACID
AAACEEILLMNNORTTWY MATERNITY
ALLOWANCE
AAADEEEEHHMNNORTVV MOVE HEAVEN
AND EARTH
AAAEFHIIILLNNNSSTY IN THE FINAL
ANALYSIS
AABCCEEEHIILMNPRST SPLICE THE
MAINBRACE
AACCCDEEFHINOPRSTT CHAPTER OF
ACCIDENTS
AACCEEEEFIKMNNNNOOV MAKE A
CONVENIENCE OF
AACCEEGIILLNNNORTT CONTINENTAL
GLACIER
AACDDDEEEHHIKNQTTU THE QUICK AND
THE DEAD

AACDDEEHILNOOPRSTT DENTAL
ORTHOPAEDICS
AACDEEKNNNNOORRVYY EVERY NOOK
AND CRANNY
AACDEGHILNOPRRSSTY PLAY ONE'S
CARDS RIGHT
AACEEEFFHHMORTTTTT THE FACT OF
THE MATTER
AACEEEFIMOOPRRRSTV FARMERS'
COOPERATIVE
AACEEELNOPPPRSSTTU UPSET ONE'S
APPLECART
AACEEFGHHILMOORTTU MALICE
AFORETHOUGHT
AACEGIIIKNNNOPSSSU A SNEAKING
SUSPICION
AADDEEEGGINORSTWWY GET A WORD IN
EDGEWAYS
AADHILMMOPRSSTTWWY WITHDRAWAL
SYMPTOMS
AAEEEHKMMNOORSTTUW MAKE ONE'S
MOUTH WATER
AAEEHIKNNNOPRRSSTW A SPANNER IN
THE WORKS
ABBEEEHLNOPRRRTUUY POLYURETHANE
RUBBER
ABCCCEEHILNOOPRSTY HYPERBOLIC
COSECANT
ABCCDEGHIKNOOOORTT ACCORDING TO
THE BOOK
ABCEEEEEMMNNQRRRSU QUEEN'S
REMEMBRANCER
ABCEEIIKMNNOOPRSSS PICK SOMEONE'S
BRAINS
ABEEFHHMMOOOORTTTTY THE BOTTOM
OF MY HEART
ACCEEEFHKLNOOOORSST COCKLES OF
ONE'S HEART
ACDDEEIINNNOORRSTU UNDER
CONSIDERATION
ACDEEEEINNRSSTTTUV TURN STATE'S
EVIDENCE
ACDEEEFHINOPRSSTUU UNDER THE
AUSPICES OF
ACEEELMNOOOSSTTUWY OUTSTAY
ONE'S WELCOME
ADDEEEEEGLLMNPRRSW GERMANDER
SPEEDWELL
ADDEEEFIIIKLLPRRSW SPREAD LIKE
WILDFIRE
ADEEEHIMNOORSTTTT NOT THE
REMOTEST IDEA
ADEEEFGIIIILNNNRTT INDEFINITE
INTEGRAL
ADGGHHIIINNNNOOOTT ON A HIDING TO
NOTHING
AEEEHIILLMNORSTTTT TELL IT TO THE
MARINES

BBDDEFHIIMMNNOOOSTU BOMBED OUT OF HIS MIND

BBEFGINOOOOOOORSSTT TOO BIG FOR ONE'S BOOTS

BDEEEHMMNNOORSSTUU UNDER SOMEONE'S THUMB

BEELMNNOOOPRSTTUWW BLOW ONE'S OWN TRUMPET

CCEEEEIILPRRRTTTWY ELECTRIC TYPEWRITER

CCEEEHIJKLORSSTTTU CLERK TO THE JUSTICES

CCEEFGILNNNOOOORSU FOREGONE CONCLUSION

CDDEEHILMNNOOORTWW COME DOWN IN THE WORLD

CDEEEEEINNNQRSTUUV TURN QUEEN'S EVIDENCE

CDEEGIILMNOOOPRRSS MELODIC PROGRESSION

CEEEEHIMNOOPQRSSTU QUEER SOMEONE'S PITCH

CEEEIIJNNNOOSSTUWW STEW IN ONE'S OWN JUICE

CEFIINNNNOOOOPSSSU CONSENSUS OF OPINION

DEEEEEEEEKLNOPPSSY KEEP ONE'S EYES PEELED

EEEEHHHIILLNSSTWWW WHEELS WITHIN WHEELS

AAAAEIIILLNQSSTTUVY QUALITATIVE ANALYSIS

AAABCEEEEGHHLMORRRR CEREBRAL HAEMORRHAGE

AAACCEIIILLLNOORTTV VOCALIC ALLITERATION

AAACEGHHMOOPPPRRRTY PAPER CHROMATOGRAPHY

AAADDDGHHHIILNOSSYY HIGH DAYS AND HOLIDAYS

AAAAEEIILMNNNOPRRTT INTERNATIONAL AMPERE

AABCDEGKNOORSSSTTTW GET DOWN TO BRASS TACKS

AACCEEGHIMNNNOOPPST CATCH SOMEONE NAPPING

AACEEEEHIKKLMNORSSS MAKE ONE'S HACKLES RISE

AADEEGIIKMNNNORSTTV NOT GIVE A TINKER'S DAMN

AAEEEEGGLLMMNNNNSTT GENTLEMAN'S GENTLEMAN

AAEEGGHLLMNNNOPSTTU TUNGSTEN-HALOGEN LAMP

ABCCEEGHILNNOOPRTTY HYPERBOLIC COTANGENT

ABCDEEGGIINOOPRRSTT TO BEGGAR DESCRIPTION

ABEEEEFHHHLOORSTTTW THE BOWELS OF THE EARTH

ABEIILLLLOOPRSTTTWW BITTER PILL TO SWALLOW

ACCEEEEEEHKNNOQSSTTU TAKE THE CONSEQUENCES

ACCEEEEFGILNOPRRSTT REFRACTING TELESCOPE

ACCEEEEGGHIIILMNNNR CHEMICAL ENGINEERING

ACDEEEEEFLNNPRRSSTU UNDER FALSE PRETENCES

ACDEEEGLLOOORRSSSSU ROSE-COLOURED GLASSES

ACDIIIJMMNORRSSTUUY SUMMARY JURISDICTION

ACEEEELMNOOORSSTVWY OVERSTAY ONE'S WELCOME

ACEEEFFHIMNNOQRSTTU AFFIRM THE CONSEQUENT

ACEGHIIMNNOOOOPRRRSS HARMONIC PROGRESSION

ADDEEEELNNOPPRSTXYY EXPANDED POLYSTYRENE

AEFGIILNNOPRRRSSSTU FIRST PERSON SINGULAR

BBBEEEEGGLNNOOSSTYY LET BYGONES BE BYGONES

BCDDEEEELLMNOOOORSSU CURDLE SOMEONE'S BLOOD

BDEEEIILLNNNOOSTTWW NEW WINE IN OLD BOTTLES

BDEEILLLNOOOORSSTUV BLOODLESS REVOLUTION

CCEEEEEFGILLNOPRSTT REFLECTING TELESCOPE

CDEEHIIILLPPRRRSSVW PHILLIPS SCREWDRIVER

DEEEEEEIKKNNNOPSSSY KEEP ONE'S EYES SKINNED

DEEEGGHIIILNNOOPRTW NIGGER IN THE WOODPILE

DEEEGHINNNOOORSSTTT NOSE TO THE GRINDSTONE

DEEEHILLNNOOPSTTWYY LOW-DENSITY POLYTHENE

EEEEFGHLLLNOOPRSTTU PULL ONESELF TOGETHER

EEEHILLLOORRSSTTTTU TORTOISESHELL TURTLE

AAAAABCEIKKLLNNRSSTU AUSTRALIAN BLACKSNAKE

AAAAEIIILNNQSSTTTUVY QUANTITATIVE ANALYSIS

AAACDEILMNNORRSSSUUX ALARUMS AND EXCURSIONS

AAADEEILLLMNNSSTTTTW LAST WILL AND TESTAMENT

AABBDDEEEELNRRRTTTTU
BREAD-AND-BUTTER LETTER

AACCGHHLMMNOOOPRRTUY COLUMN
CHROMATOGRAPHY

AACDDEEIILLMOOPPRSTY
DIAMETRICALLY OPPOSED

AACEEEHIKKMMNOOSSTTW WHAT
MAKES SOMEONE TICK

ABCCDEEEIIKKLNNPSSTT TEN-SPINED
STICKLEBACK

ABEEHIILNNNNOOORSTTU HONOURABLE
INTENTIONS

ACCEEEEHHINNRSSTTTUW CHINESE
WATER CHESTNUT

ACCEHIIKNNNOORSSSSSU KRISHNA
CONSCIOUSNESS

ACDEEFGHIKNOORRSSTTW WRONG
SIDE OF THE TRACKS

ACEEGHHHILNOOPPRRSTY SCHLIEREN
PHOTOGRAPHY

ADEEEEFHHHNORRSSTWWY THE WHYS
AND WHEREFORES

ADEEEEHLMNNOORSSSTTU STEAL
SOMEONE'S THUNDER

ADEEGHNOOOPRTTTTTUWW PUT TWO
AND TWO TOGETHER

BCCEEEFFFHHKNORSTTUY BY THE
SCRUFF OF THE NECK

DDEEEFGHILOOPRSSSSTT LESSER
SPOTTED DOGFISH

DEEEGHHHIILNNOPSTTYY HIGH-DENSITY
POLYTHENE

AAAAACCDFHIIILNORRSSTV HARVARD
CLASSIFICATION

AAAAACCEEEFHIKMNNOQTTU MAKE THE
ACQUAINTANCE OF

AAACDEEIIILMNNNNOOSST
NONESSENTIAL AMINO ACID

AAAEEHIIILLMNNSSTTTUY IN THE
ULTIMATE ANALYSIS

AACCEEEEGGHIIILMNNNNR
MECHANICAL ENGINEERING

AACDEEIIKNNNOOORSTTT TAKE INTO
CONSIDERATION

AADEEFGGHHINOORRRTTUW GO
THROUGH FIRE AND WATER

ABCCEEMOOOPPRRSSSSTUY
MÖSSBAUER SPECTROSCOPY

ABCDEEEHIKLNNOOPRSTTU SKELETON
IN THE CUPBOARD

ABCEILLMNOOPRRSSTUUUY
PULMONARY TUBERCULOSIS

ACCEEEEEGGIIILLNNNRRT ELECTRICAL
ENGINEERING

ACCEEEEFHHKLNOOORSSTT THE
COCKLES OF ONE'S HEART

ACDEEEGIIMNOPRRTTTUVY
PRODUCTIVITY AGREEMENT

ACDEEHHIILNNOORRTTTUW WITHOUT
LET OR HINDRANCE

ADEEEGHMNOOOOORRRTTWY HERE
TODAY, GONE TOMORROW

BBCEEEEFGHINOOOORRSST TOO BIG
FOR ONE'S BREECHES

BCCEEFFKKKLMNNOOOOOSS KNOCK
SOMEONE'S BLOCK OFF

CCCDEEEENNOOOPRRRSSSU
CORRESPONDENCE COURSES

DEEFHIILNNNOOOPPSSUWY
PENNY-WISE, POUND-FOOLISH

AABCDDEEEHHIKLLNOOOTTW THE
WHOLE KIT AND CABOODLE

AABEEEEGGIKLLNNNOOSSST ALL
ONE'S EGGS IN ONE BASKET

AACDEEEFFIKLNNOOOORRTTU TAKE ON
A DIFFERENT COLOUR

AADEEEGHIILLNNNOORTVVV IRON
HAND IN A VELVET GLOVE

ABCCDEEEEHIIKKLNPRSSTT
THREE-SPINED STICKLEBACK

ABCDEEGINNNOOOORSSSTTW A
SECOND STRING TO ONE'S BOW

ABCEEHIIKKLMOORSSTTTUU STICK OUT
LIKE A SORE THUMB

ACCCCDDEEEIIMNNNRRSSTUU IN
REDUCED CIRCUMSTANCES

ACCCDEEEELLOOOPRRSSSTU
ROSE-COLOURED SPECTACLES

ACDEEHIILNNOOPRSSSSTUY
HYDROELASTIC SUSPENSION

ACEEEFHILMMNNOOOPSSSTT
COMPLIMENTS OF THE SEASON

AAAAABDDEIMNOORRRRSSTXY
AMBASSADOR EXTRAORDINARY

AAAACEIILLLNNNNOOORSTTT
CONSONANTAL ALLITERATION

AAACEEEEGGIIILNNNNORRTU
AERONAUTICAL ENGINEERING

AABBCDDEEEHHLNNNORSTTTU BURN
THE CANDLE AT BOTH ENDS

AADEEILLNNNOOPPRSSSTTTU TO ALL
INTENTS AND PURPOSES

ABCDEEEEEEFFFHLLNNOORSTT THE
NOBLE ART OF SELF-DEFENCE

ABCEEEEEFHHHOOPRRRSTTTTU PUT
THE CART BEFORE THE HORSE

ACCCEEFGIINNNOOOOORSSTUV
COURAGE OF ONE'S CONVICTIONS

ACCEEEEHILLNOOPRRSTTUVVY
ELECTROCONVULSIVE THERAPY

AAAAABDEEIILMNNOOPPRRSSTTY
AMBASSADOR PLENIPOTENTIARY

AEEEGHHHHHIKMOOORSTTTTUW
TAKE THE ROUGH WITH THE SMOOTH